May 18–22, 2015
Florence, Italy

Association for
Computing Machinery

Advancing Computing as a Science & Profession

WWW
2015
FLORENCE, ITALY

WWW'15

Proceedings of the 24th International Conference on World Wide Web

Sponsored by:

IW3C2

In co-operation with:

ACM SIGWEB

ISBN: 978-1-4503-3469-3 (Digital)

ISBN: 978-1-4503-3859-2 (Print)

Printed in the USA

WWW'15 General Chairs' Welcome

It is our great pleasure to welcome you to the 24th International World Wide Web Conference (WWW 2015) which will be held on May 18-22, 2015 in Florence, Italy. The annual World Wide Web Conference is the premier international forum to present and discuss progress in research, development, standards, and applications of the topics related to the Web. WWW is organized by the International World Wide Web Conference Steering Committee (IW3C2) in collaboration with local conference organizers of the host country. WWW 2015 offers a unique opportunity for sharing the latest insights of academic and industrial research, as well as to experience the unique environment of Florence, a city at the heart of artistic, cultural, and scientific developments since many centuries.

WWW 2015 will offer high quality technical activities, including research sessions, poster sessions, workshops, tutorials, demonstrations, an industry track, a Web Science track, a W3C track, panels, and a Ph.D. symposium. Co-located events include the 2nd edition of the Bigdata Innovators Gathering (BIG 2015), a novel Entrepreneurs Track (ET), the Digital Disease Detection Conference (DDD), the Digital Health Conference (DH), Digital Marketing 2015 -- Made in Italy on the Web (DM 2015), and the Web for All conference (W4A). WWW 2015 will also be collocated with the International Conference on Mobile Systems, Services and Applications (MobiSys 2015).

We hope you will be pleased with the quality of this year's program, featuring three keynote speeches by world-class experts. The Research track presents 131 high quality papers; 72 posters of the Poster track report short summaries of research; the Demo track shows 28 appealing demos; the Ph.D. Symposium track reports 9 presentations of doctoral students; the Industry track consists of 8 speeches from prominent industrial researchers; the Web Science track presents 12 papers and 14 posters on novel interdisciplinary research; W3C track is composed of sessions on the latest Web standards and emerging technologies; the Panel consists of a plenary panel discussing several relevant issues related to the impact of Web technologies on society. In addition to the tracks and special programs, workshops and tutorials are organized to report on-going work and to provide in-depth knowledge on important subjects; 26 workshops are organized to present contributed papers and several invited speeches; 14 tutorials are organized as lectures by experts. The detailed program is spelled out in the conference proceedings and in the companion proceedings for your future reference.

This conference is the result of the support and dedicated efforts of many individuals and institutions, all of whom are acknowledged in the subsequent pages of these proceedings. We would especially like to thank the authors, speakers, and panelists for providing the excellent technical content of the conference. In shaping the 2015 program, the chairs of the tracks and special programs worked with a large network of program committee members and external reviewers, and their collaboration with the members of the local organizing committee has been invaluable. We would also like to thank our sponsors for their generous financial contributions, and IW3C2, whose guidelines served as a valuable resource in preparing the conference. Special thanks to Wendy Hall, Chair of IW3C2, for her continued support and to Prabhakar Raghavan for his invaluable advice on all aspects of the organization of WWW 2015 that he generously provided as IW3C2 liason; research track co-chairs Chengxiang Zhai, and Krishna Gummadi for handling the large volume of submissions and assembling an excellent research paper program. We also thank the W3C Consortium and its Italian office, and the Institute of Cognitive Sciences and

Technologies of the Italian Research Council. Last but not least, we acknowledge the contribution of Sandra Celoni and Viviana Vitali from Professional Conference Organizer O.I.C. Florence for the highly professional work done on all aspects of the local organization of WWW 2015, as well as the Florence Convention Bureau that bootstrapped the plans for the first Italian WWW in Florence. We hope that this conference will contribute novel insights, valuable experiences, and opportunities to connect with colleagues and collaborators, and that you will have a pleasant time during your stay in Florence.

The WWW 2015 General Chairs

Aldo Gangemi
National Research Council, Italy

Stefano Leonardi
Sapienza University of Rome

Alessandro Panconesi
Sapienza University of Rome

WWW2015 FLORENCE, ITALY

WWW'15 Program Chairs' Welcome

We are delighted to present the technical program of the 24th International World Wide Web Conference (WWW 2015), held from May 18 to 22, 2015 in Florence, Italy. Since its inception in 1994, the International World Wide Web Conference has been the premier venue for researchers, academics, businesses, and standards organizations to convene and discuss the latest Web research and technologies.

This year, we have received a record number of 929 submissions for the research program, distributed over the following 11 Web-related technical areas: (1) Behavior Analysis and Personalization, (2) Crowdsourcing Systems and Social Media, (3) Content Analysis, (4) Internet Economics and Monetization, (5) Pervasive Web and Mobility, (6) Security and Privacy, (7) Semantic Web, (8) Social Networks and Graph Analysis, Web Infrastructure -- Data Centers, (9) Content Delivery Networks, (10) Web Mining, and (11) Web Search Systems and Applications. All submissions underwent a rigorous reviewing process, where at least three expert Program Committee (PC) members reviewed each submission and a fourth expert lead the discussion of the reviews. In total, a highly skilled and diverse team of 554 PC members were involved in the reviewing process and they collectively produced over 3000 reviews. The PC members were recruited by area chairs, who also oversaw the reviewing of the submissions in their area, made initial recommendations to accept or reject the submissions in their area, and participated in a two-day area chair meeting held in Kaiserslautern, Germany. The final acceptance decisions were made at the meeting, where the recommendations of the area chairs were discussed and voted on by all area chairs and the PC chairs. Submissions, where area chairs were conflicted, were handled separately PC chairs. The outcome of the meeting was to accept a total of 131 (14.1%) papers for the research program. We believe that these 131 accepted papers represent some of the best Web-related research conducted over the last year and we are confident that they would lead to fruitful discussions and new ideas at the conference.

It would not have been possible to put together this research program without the tireless efforts of a number of volunteers. We wish to thank everybody who contributed to the technical program, including the authors who submitted papers to WWW 2015, and the area chairs, PC members, and external reviewers who contributed their time and expertise. We extend special thanks to the general chairs Aldo Gangemi, Stefano Leonardi, and Alessandro Panconesi for their constant support and for assembling an excellent organizing team that put together an exciting conference program. We are grateful to the PC Chairs of WWW 2014, particularly Andrei Broder, for sharing their experiences and providing very helpful advice. We hope that both conference attendees and the readers of the proceedings would find the resulting program interesting and rewarding.

Krishna P. Gummadi

WWW 2015 Program Co-Chair
Max Planck Institute for Software Systems
Germany

ChengXiang Zhai

WWW 2015 Program Co-Chair
University of Illinois at Urbana-Champaign
U.S.A.

Table of Contents

WWW 2015 Organization & Committees

GENERAL CHAIRS
Aldo Gangemi, National Research Council, Italy & Paris 13 University-CNRS, France
Stefano Leonardi, Sapienza University of Rome, Italy
Alessandro Panconesi, Sapienza University of Rome, Italy

LOCAL ORGANIZING COMMITTEE

W3C TRACK CHAIR
Marie-Claire Forgue, W3C, France

PUBLICITY & SOCIAL MEDIA CHAIRS
Flavio Chierichetti, Sapienza University of Rome, Italy
Gabriella Pasi, University of Milano-Bicocca, Italy
Daniele Quercia, Yahoo Labs, Barcelona, Spain

WEB PRESENCE CHAIR
Aris Anagnostopoulos, Sapienza University of Rome, Italy

PRESS CHAIR
Marco Magrini, Florence, Italy

FINANCE CHAIRS
Stefano Leonardi, Sapienza University of Rome, Italy
Viviana Vitali, OIC-International Congress Organization, Florence, Italy

REGISTRATION CHAIR
Luca Becchetti, Sapienza University of Rome, Italy

SPONSORSHIP CHAIRS
Alessandro Panconesi, Sapienza University of Rome, Italy
Paola Velardi, Sapienza University of Rome, Italy

EXHIBITION CHAIRS
Aldo Gangemi, National Research Council, Italy & Paris 13 University-CNRS, France
Gioacchino La Vecchia, W3C, Italy

LOCAL ARRANGEMENTS CHAIR
Sandra Celoni, OIC-International Congress Organization, Florence, Italy

EVENT MOBILE APPLICATIONS CHAIR
Emanuele Panizzi, Sapienza University of Rome, Italy

MARKETING CHAIRS
Carlotta Ferrari, Florence Conference Bureau, Florence, Italy
Viviana Vitali, OIC-International Congress Organization, Florence, Italy
Gerry Turano, Rome, Italy

GRAPHICS CHAIR

COLOCATED EVENTS CHAIRS
Andrei Broder, Google Inc., USA
Ciro Cattuto, ISI Foundation, Turin, Italy
Stefano Leonardi, Sapienza University of Rome, Italy

PROCEEDINGS AND METADATA CHAIRS	Eva Blomqvist, University of Linköping, Sweden Paolo Boldi, University of Milano, Italy Valentina Presutti, National Research Council, Italy Li Ding, Memect LLC, USA
PANEL CHAIRS	Aris Anagnostopoulos, Sapienza University of Rome, Italy Fabrizio Silvestri, Yahoo Labs, Barcelona, Spain
VOLUNTEERS CHAIRS	Sebastien Forget, TD Bank, Canada Nicola Tonellotto, National Research Council, Italy
STUDENT TRAVEL GRANT CHAIRS	Filippo Geraci, National Research Council, Italy Marco Pellegrini, National Research Council, Italy

Program Committee Members

BEHAVIORAL ANALYSIS AND PERSONALIZATION

Mikhail Ageev, Moscow State University, Russia
Eugene Agichtein, Emory University, USA
Amr Ahmed, Google, USA
Omar Alonso, Microsoft Bing, USA
Jaime Arguello, University of North Carolina at Chapel Hill, USA
Peter Bailey, Microsoft Bing, Australia
Linas Baltrunas, Telefonica Research, Spain
Nicholas Belkin, Rutgers University, USA
Ralf Bierig, Vienna University of Technology, Austria
Peter Brusilovsky, University of Pittsburgh, USA
Pablo Castells, Universidad Autonoma de Madrid, Spain
Ed Chi, Google, USA
Wei Chu, Microsoft Bing, USA
Michael Cole, Rutgers University, USA
Nick Craswell, Microsoft Bing, USA
Paolo Cremonesi, Politecnico di Milano, Italy
Alex Deng, Microsoft Bing, USA
Chabane Djeraba, LIFL, University of Sciences and Technologies of Lille, France
Debora Donato, StumbleUpon, USA
Doug Downey, Northwestern University, USA
Georges Dupret, Yahoo!, USA
Andy Edmonds, Ebay, USA
Carsten Eickhoff, ETHZ, Switzerland
Hui Fang, Nayang Technological University, Singapore
Henry Feild, Endicott College, USA
Qi Guo, Microsoft Bing, USA
Ido Guy, Yahoo!, Israel
Jiawei Han, University of Illinois at Urbana Champaign, USA
Ahmed Hassan Awadallah, Microsoft Research, USA
Victor Hu, Microsoft Bing, USA
Jeff Huang, Brown University, USA
Pan Hui, Hong Kong University of Science and Technology, Hong Kong
Alejandro Jaimes, Yahoo!, Spain
Dieter Jannach, TU Dortmund, Germany
Robert Jäschke, L3S Research Center, Germany
Jiepu Jiang, University of Massachusetts, USA
Rosie Jones, Microsoft, USA
Joemon Jose, University of Glasgow, UK
Bhargav Kanagal, Google, USA
Diane Kelly, University of North Carolina at Chapel Hill, USA
Youngho Kim, University of Massachusetts, USA
Alex Kotov, Wayne State University, USA
Dmitry Lagun, Emory University, USA
Mounia Lalmas, Yahoo!, Spain

CROWDSOURCING SYSTEMS AND SOCIAL MEDIA (Continued)

Patty Kostkova, City ehealth Research Centre (CeRC), City University, London
Ee-Peng Lim, Singapore Management University
Yu-Ru Lin, University of Pittsburgh
Peter Marbach
Winter Mason, Facebook
Michael Mathioudakis
Julian Mcauley, UC San Diego
Panagiotis Metaxas, Wellesley College
Tanushree Mitra, Georgia Institute of Technology
Andres Monroy-Hernandez
Sue Moon, KAIST
Michael Muller, IBM Research
Aditya Pal, IBM
Stelios Paparizos, Microsoft Research
Walter Quattrociocchi, Labss,Institute of Cognitive Sciences and Technologies
Daniele Quercia, Yahoo Labs
Bruno Ribeiro, Carnegie Mellon University
Daniel Romero, University of Michigan
Derek Ruths, McGill University
Antonio Scala
Anna Squicciarini, The Pennsylvania State University
Markus Strohmaier, University of Koblenz-Landau
Arun Sundararajan, New York University
Siddhart Suri
Maja Vukovic, IBM Research
Claudia Wagner, GESIS-Leibniz Institute for the Social Sciences
Ingmar Weber, Qatar Computing Research Institute
Cong Yu, Google Research
Haiyi Zhu, Carnegie Mellon University

CONTENT ANALYSIS

Steven Bethard, University of Alabama at Birmingham
Yunbo Cao, Microsoft Research Asia
Taylor Cassidy, US Army Research Lab/IBM/CUNY
Wanxiang Che, Harbin Institute of Technology
Zhiyuan Chen, University of Illinois at Chicago
Hsin-Hsi Chen, National Taiwan University
Gao Cong, Nanyang Technological University
Eduard Dragut, Temple University
Koji Eguchi, Kobe University
Anthony Fader, University of Washington
Boi Faltings, EPFL
Radu Florian, IBM TJ Watson Research Center
Ralph Grishman, New York University
Ben Hachey, University of Sydney
Sanda Harabagiu, University of Texas at Dallas
Hongzhao Huang, Rensselaer Polytechnic Institute
Minlie Huang, Tsinghua University
Seung-Won Hwang, POSTECH

CONTENT ANALYSIS (Continued)

Jing Jiang, Singapore Management University
Dan Jurafsky, Stanford University
Wai Lam, The Chinese University of Hong Kong
Hang Li, Huawei Technologies
Fangtao Li, Google Research
Juanzi Li, Tsinghua University
Qi Li, Queens College and Graduate Center, CUNY
Sujian Li, Peking university
Hao Li, Rensselaer Polytechnic Institute
Ee-Peng Lim, Singapore Management University
Chin-Yew Lin, Microsoft Research Asia
Wei Liu, IBM Thomas J. Watson Research Center
Zhiyuan Liu, Tsinghua University
Kang Liu, Institute of Automation, Chinese Academy of Sciences
Ting Liu, Harbin Institute of Technology
David McClosky, IBM Research
Samaneh Moghaddam, Simon Fraser University
Alessandro Moschitti, University of Trento
Vincent Ng, University of Texas at Dallas
Sinno Jialin Pan, i2r, a*star, Singapore
Emily Pitler, Google
Tieyun Qian, Wuhan University
Delip Rao, Johns Hopkins University
Alan Ritter, University of Washington
Hinrich Schütze, University of Munich
Satoshi Sekine, New York University
Benoit Favre, Laboratoire d'Informatique Fondamentale de Marseille
Shuming Shi, Microsoft Research Asia
Kyuseok Shim, Seoul National University
Partha Talukdar, Indian Institute of Science
Yoshimasa Tsuruoka, The University of Tokyo
Benjamin Van Durme, Johns Hopkins University
V.G.Vinod Vydiswaran, University of Michigan
Xiaojun Wan, Peking University
Houfeng Wang, Peking University
Chi Wang, University of Illinois at Urbana-Champaign
Michael Wiegand, Saarland University
Kam-Fai Wong, The Chinese University of Hong Kong
Wei Xu, New York University
Nianwen Xue, Brandeis University
Xin Zhao, Peking University and Singapore Management University
Dongyan Zhao, Peking University
Jun Zhao, Institute of Automation, Chinese Academy of Sciences
Guodong Zhou, Soochow University
Xiaoyan Zhu, Tsinghua University
Imed Zitouni, Microsoft
Chengqing Zong, Institute of Automation, Chinese Academy of Sciences

INTERNET ECONOMICS AND MONETIZATION

Shipra Agrawal, Microsoft Research
Eytan Bakshy, Facebook
Liad Blumrosen, Hebrew University
Pranav Dandekar, Stanford
Xiaotie Deng, Shanghai Jiaotong University
Arpita Ghosh, Cornell
Gagan Goel, Google Research
Paul Goldberg, Oxford
Ralf Herbrich, Amazon
Nicole Immorlica, Microsoft Research
Krishnamurthy Iyer, Cornell
Kamal Jain, eBay Research
Radu Jurca, Google
Peter Key, Microsoft Research
Scott Kominers, Harvard
Vahab Mirrokni, Google
Markus Mobius, Microsoft Research
Hamid Nazerzadeh, USC
David Pennock, Microsoft Research
R. Preston McAfee, Microsoft
Tao Qin, Microsoft Research
Dou Shen, Baidu
Richard Steinberg, London School of Economics
Mukund Sundararajan, Stanford University
Neel Sundaresan, eBay Research
Steve Tadelis, Berkeley
Sergei Vassilvitskii, Google Research
Gabriel Weintraub, Columbia Business Schoo

PERVASIVE WEB AND MOBILITY

Aruna Balasubramian, University of Washington
Maria Ebling, IBM
Romit Roy Choudhury, University of Illinois at Urbana Champaign
Urs Hengartner, University of Waterloo
Wenjun Hu, Yale University
Eyal de Lara, University of Toronto
Cecilia Mascolo, University of Cambridge
Archan Misra, Singapore Management University (SMU)
Rama Ramasubramanian
Lenin Ravindranath Sivalingam, Microsoft Research
Stefan Saroiu, Microsoft Research
Souvik Sen, HP Labs
Matt Welsh, Google
Guoliang Xing, Michigan State University
Lin Zhong, Rice University

SECURITY AND PRIVACY

Davide Balzarotti, Eurecom
Rainer Boehme, University of Münster
Joseph Bonneau, Princeton University
Delphine Christin, University of Bonn
Sergej Dechand, University of Bonn
Tamara Denning, University of Utah
Adam Doupe
Dirk Dr. Wetter, OWASP German Chapter
Serge Egelman, UC Berkeley
Sascha Fahl, Leibniz University Hannover
Bernd Freisleben, University of Marburg
Thorsten Holz, Ruhr-Universität Bochum
Markus Jakobsson, Fatskunk
Suman Jana, University of Texas at Austin
Mike Just, Glasgow Caledonian University
Patrick Gage Kelley, University of New Mexico
Engin Kirda, Northeastern University
Katharina Krombholz, SBA Research
Christopher Kruegel, University of California, Santa Barbara
Zhenkai Liang, National University of Singapore
Heather Lipford, UNC Charlotte
Benjamin Livshits, Microsoft Research
Long Lu, Stony Brook University
Prateek Mittal, Princeton University
Esfandiar Mohammadi, Saarland University
Tyler Moore, Southern Methodist University
Nick Nikiforakis, Stony Brook University
Adrian Perrig, ETH Zurich
Konrad Rieck, University of Göttingen
Elaine Shi, PARC
Kapil Singh, IBM T.J. Watson Research Center
Robin Sommer, ICSI/LBNL
Xiaofeng Wang, Indiana University, USA
Christo Wilson, Northeastern University
Haifeng Yu, National University of Singapore
Mary Ellen Zurko, Cisco Systems

SEMANTIC WEB

Harith Alani, KMi, The Open University
Pramod Anantharam, Kno.e.sis Center
Kemafor Anyanwu, North Carolina State University
Marcelo Arenas, PUC Chile
Lora Aroyo, VU University Amsterdam
Sören Auer, University of Bonn & Fraunhofer IAIS
Isabelle Augenstein, Dept of Computer Science, The University of Sheffield
Sean Bechhofer, University of Manchester
Abraham Bernstein, University of Zurich
Roi Blanco, Yahoo! Research
Pierre-Antoine Champin, LIRIS
Key-Sun Choi, KAIST
Philipp Cimiano, University of Bielefeld
Oscar Corcho, Universidad Politécnica de Madrid
Philippe Cudré-Mauroux, U. of Fribourg
Claudia D'Amato, University of Bari
Mathieu D'Aquin, Knowledge Media Institute, the Open University
Brian Davis, DERI NUIG
Miriam Fernandez, Knowledge Media Institute
Lorenz Fischer, University of Zurich
Fabien Gandon, Inria
Paul Groth, VU University Amsterdam
Tudor Groza, School of ITEE, The University of Queensland
Andreas Harth, AIFB, Karlsruhe Institute of Technology
Tom Heath, Open Data Institute
Aidan Hogan, DCC, Universidad de Chile
Matthew Horridge, Stanford University
Lalana Kagal, MIT
Pavel Klinov, University of Ulm
Jacek Kopecky, University of Portsmouth
Spyros Kotoulas, IBM Research
Freddy Lecue, IBM Research
David Martin, SRI International
Diana Maynard, University of Sheffield
Robert Meusel, University of Mannheim
Dunja Mladenic, Jozef Stefan Institute
Axel-Cyrille Ngonga Ngomo, University of Leipzig
Nadeschda Nikitina, Oxford University
Josiane Parreira, Siemens
Peter Patel-Schneider, Nuance
Terry Payne, University of Liverpool
Dimitris Plexousakis, Institute of Computer Science, FORTH
Axel Polleres, Vienna University of Economics and Business – WU Wien
Valentina Presutti, STLab (ISTC-CNR)
Guilin Qi, Southeast University
Riccardo Rosati, DIS, Sapienza Universita' di Roma

SEMANTIC WEB (Continuied)

Manuel Salvadores, Stanford University
Cristina Sarasua, Universität Koblenz – Landau
Uli Sattler, University of Manchester
Ansgar Scherp, Kiel University and Leibniz Information Center for Economics, Kiel, Germany
Stefan Schlobach, Vrije Universiteit Amsterdam
Daniel Schwabe, Dept. of Informatics, PUC-Rio
Oshani Seneviratne, Massachusetts Institute of Technology
Juan F. Sequeda, Dept of Computer Science, The University of Texas at Austin
Amit Sheth, Wright State
Elena Simperl, University of Southampton
Kavitha Srinivas, IBM Research
Steffen Staab, University of Koblenz-Landau
Gerd Stumme,
Hideaki Takeda, National Institute of Informatics
Kerry Taylor, CSIRO & Australian National University
Raphaël Troncy, EURECOM
Tania Tudorache, Stanford University
Giovanni Tummarello, DERI, National University of Ireland galway
Jacopo Urbani, Vrije Universiteit Amsterdam
Victoria Uren, Aston University
Jacco van Ossenbruggen, CWI & VU University Amsterdam
Ruben Verborgh, Ghent University – iMinds
Johanna Völker, University of Mannheim
Chris Welty, IBM Research
Amapali Zaveri, AKSW Group, University of Leipzig
Antoine Zimmermann, École des Mines de Saint-Étienne

SOCIAL NETWORKS AND GRAPH ANALYSIS

Bruno Abrahao, Cornell University
Yong-Yeol Ahn, Indiana University Bloomington
Luca Maria Aiello, Yahoo Labs
Leman Akoglu, Stony Brook University
Aris Anagnostopoulos, Sapienza University of Rome
Luca Becchetti, University of Rome “La Sapienza”
Fabricio Benevenuto, Federal University of Minas Gerais
Paolo Boldi, Università degli Studi di Milano
Francesco Bonchi, Yahoo! Research
Ceren Budak, UCSB
James Caverlee, Texas A&M University
Yang Chen, Duke University
Wei Chen, Microsoft Research Asia
Hong Cheng, The Chinese University of Hong Kong
Aaron Clauset, University of Colorado Boulder
Gao Cong, Nanyang Technological University
Yafei Dai, Peking University
Atish Das Sarma, eBay Research Labs

SOCIAL NETWORKS AND GRAPH ANALYSIS (Continued)

Anirban Dasgupta, Purdue University
Emilio Ferrara, Indiana University Bloomington
Pierre Fraigniaud, CNRS and University of Paris 7
Sabrina Gaito, Università degli Studi di Milano
Aristides Gionis, Aalto University
Bruno Gonçalves, Aix-Marseille Université
Amit Goyal, University of Maryland
Stephan Günnemann, Carnegie Mellon University
Jake Hofman, Microsoft Research
Panos Kalnis, King Abdullah University of Science and Technology
Ioannis Koutis, University of Puerto Rico-Rio Piedras
Ponnurangam Kumaraguru, IIITD
Haewoon Kwak, QCRI
Theodoros Lappas, Stevens Institute of Technology
Matthieu Latapy, CNRS
Silvio Lattanzi, Google
Kristina Lerman, University of Southern California
David Liben-Nowell, Carleton College
Yu-Ru Lin, University of Pittsburgh
Nelly Litvak, University of Twente
Mohammad Mahdian, Google
Michael Mahoney, Stanford University
Madhav Marathe, Virginia Tech
Vahab Mirrokni, Google Research
Alan Mislove, Northeastern University
Sebastian Moreno, Purdue University
Mirco Musolesi, University of Birmingham
Alice Oh, KAIST
Ali Pinar, Sandia National Laboratories
Derek Ruths, McGill University
Alessandra Sala, Alcatel-Lucent Bell Labs
Grant Schoenebeck, University of Michigan
Aneesh Sharma, Twitter
Mauro Sozio, Télécom ParisTech
Nikolaj Tatti, Aalto University
Evimaria Terzi, Boston University
Panayiotis Tsaparas, University of Ioannina
Charalampos Tsourakakis, Carnegie Mellon University
Johan Ugander, Cornell University
Antti Ukkonen, Helsinki Institute for Information Technology
Sebastiano Vigna, University of Milan
Sarita Yardi Schoenebeck, University of Michigan
Georgios Zervas, Boston University School of Management
Ben Zhao, UC Santa Barbara
Heather Zheng, UC Santa Barbara

WEB MINING (Continued)

Srinivasan Parthasarathy
Jian Pei, Simon Fraser University
Simone Paolo Ponzetto, University of Mannheim
Naren Ramakrishnan, Virginia Tech
Rajeev Rastogi, Yahoo!
Tamas Sarlos, Google
H. Andrew Schwartz, University of Pennsylvania
Myra Spiliopoulou, U. Magdeburg
Yizhou Sun, Northeastern University
Neel Sundaresan, eBay Research Labs
Chenhao Tan, Cornell University
Jian Tang, Peking University
Cindi Thompson
Masashi Toyoda, University of Tokyo
Jianyong Wang, Tsinghua University
Ke Wang, Simon Fraser University
Jian Wang, LinkedIn Corporation
Hongning Wang, Dept of Computer Science at University of Virginia
Shuang-Hong Yang, Twitter Inc.
Philip Yu, University of Illinois at Chicago
Jeffery Xu Yu, Dept of Systems Engineering & Engineering Management, Chinese University of Hong Kong
Zhe Zhao, University of Michigan, Ann Arbor
Feida Zhu, Singapore Management University

WEB SEARCH SYSTEMS AND APPLICATIONS

James Allan, UMass Amherst, USA
Omar Alonso, Microsoft, USA
Ziv Bar-Yossef, Google, Israel
Behshad Behzadi, Google, Swizerland
Edward Bortnikov, Yahoo Labs, Israel
B. Barla Cambazoglu, Yahoo Labs, Spain
Kevin Chang, University of Illinois at Urbana-Champaign, USA
Xueqi Cheng, Chinese Academy of Sciences, China
Arjen de Vries, CWI, Netherlands
Fernando Diaz, Microsoft Research, USA
Marcus Fontoura, Google, USA
C. Lee Giles, Pennsylvania State University, USA
Nadav Golbandi, Yahoo Labs, USA
Luis Gravano, Columbia University, USA
Maxim Gurevich, RelateIQ, USA
Xu Hongbo, Chinese Academy of Sciences, China
Xuanjing Huang, Fudan University, China
Amruta Joshi, UCLA, USA
Jaap Kamps, University of Amsterdam, Netherlands
Oren Kurland, Technion – Israel Institute of Technology, Israel
Rui Li, University of Illinois at Urbana-Champaign, USA

WEB SEARCH SYSTEMS AND APPLICATIONS (Comtinued)

Ee-Peng Lim, Singapore Management University, Singapore
Hongfei Lin, Dalian University of Technology, China
Wei-Ying Ma, Microsoft Research, China
Ilya Markov, University of Lugano, Switzerland
Wolfgang Nejdl, Leibniz Universität Hannover, Germany
Hua Ouyang, Yahoo Labs, USA
Uri Schonfeld, Yahoo Labs, USA
Torsten Suel New York University, USA
Neel Sundaresan, eBay Research Labs, USA
Stratis Viglas, University of Edinburgh, UK
Wouter Weerkamp, 904Labs, Netherlands
Michael Welch, UCLA, USA
Ran Wolff, Yahoo Labs, Israel
Makoto Yamada, Yahoo Labs, USA
Hengshuai Yao, University of Alberta, Canada
Emine Yilmaz, Microsoft Research, UK
Min Zhang, Tsinghua University, China

Optimizing Display Advertising in Online Social Networks

Zeinab Abbassi
Dept. of Computer Science
Columbia University
zeinab@cs.columbia.edu

Aditya Bhaskara
Google Research
New York
bhaskaraaditya@google.com

Vishal Misra
Dept. of Computer Science
Columbia University
misra@cs.columbia.edu

ABSTRACT

Advertising is a significant source of revenue for most online social networks. Conventional online advertising methods need to be customized for online social networks in order to address their distinct characteristics. Recent experimental studies have shown that providing *social cues* along with ads, e.g. information about friends liking the ad or clicking on an ad, leads to higher click rates. In other words, the probability of a user clicking an ad is a function of the set of friends that have clicked the ad. In this work, we propose formal probabilistic models to capture this phenomenon, and study the algorithmic problem that then arises. Our work is in the context of *display advertising* where a contract is signed to show an ad to a pre-determined number of users. The problem we study is the following: given a certain number of impressions, what is the optimal *display strategy*, i.e. the optimal order and the subset of users to show the ad to, so as to maximize the expected number of clicks?

Unlike previous models of influence maximization, we show that this optimization problem is hard to approximate in general, and that it is related to finding dense subgraphs of a given size. In light of the hardness result, we propose several heuristic algorithms including a two-stage algorithm inspired by influence-and-exploit strategies in viral marketing. We evaluate the performance of these heuristics on real data sets, and observe that our two-stage heuristic significantly outperforms the natural baselines.

1. INTRODUCTION

Advertising is one of the main sources – if not the main source – of revenue for most online social networks; e.g., online advertising comprised about 91% of Facebook's revenue in 2013 [1]. A significant portion of this revenue comes from display ads where certain business rules from traditional advertising apply. Conventional display ads (and more generally traditional online advertising methods) have not been as successful in generating revenue in social networks compared to other types of online advertising such as sponsored search advertising. To increase their revenue, online social networks have utilized a new paradigm called *social advertising*, which aims to leverage the social influence of a user on their friends. In this paper, we develop a formal model to study social advertising in display ads, and formalize the algorithmic problem faced by a social network platform. We then present new theoretical and empirical results for this problem.

Let us start with a brief review of display advertising: An online social network has multiple pages where it displays ads in the form of images, video or text. Once a user visits a page, she views an ad. Her exposure to the ad is called an "impression." Advertisers buy blocks of impressions ahead of time via contracts, choosing blocks carefully to target a particular market segment. Once the contract is agreed upon, the advertiser expects a specified number of impressions to be delivered by the social network platform over an agreed-upon time period. In addition to delivering a predetermined number of impressions, the advertiser may choose to optimize other objectives like clicks or conversions [5, 4, 3].

It has been observed, however, that conventional methods of ad allocation are not very successful in the context of online social networks [7, 25], and the paradigm of *social advertising* was developed to address this shortcoming. The goal of social advertising is to leverage social influence among users. The impact of social influence among users has been confirmed in sociological studies, statistical models, and in online randomized experiments (see [7] and references therein). A social ad has been defined as "an ad that incorporates user interactions that the consumer has agreed to display and be shared. The resulting ad displays these interactions along with the user's persona (picture and/or name along with the ad content)" [21]. In other words, an ad being shown to a person can incorporate information about others who have clicked the ad in the past (assuming their consent).

The goal of our work is to understand how social ads can affect click-through rates in social networks. Recent field studies [25, 7] show that advertising using social cues are more effective than conventional demographic and behavioral targeting methods.

Our Contributions and Techniques. The main contributions of our paper are as follows:

- We propose a formal model for social ads in the context of display advertising. In our model, ads are shown to users one after the other. The probability of a user u clicking an ad depends on the users who have clicked (or taken a certain action on) this ad so far. This information is presented to u as a *social cue* (which could be of different kinds, as we see later), thus the click probability is a function of this cue.

- We introduce the *social display optimization* problem: suppose an advertiser has a contract with a publisher for showing some number (say B) impressions of an ad. What *strategy* should the publisher use to show these ads so as to maximize the expected number of clicks?[1]

[1]We will discuss publishers' motivations for this in Section 2.1.

WWW 2015, May 18–22, 2015, Florence, Italy.
ACM 978-1-4503-3469-3/15/05.
http://dx.doi.org/10.1145/2736277.2741648.

- We show that this optimization problem is APX hard.[2] In fact, under a complexity assumption known as the *planted dense subgraph* conjecture (widely believed to be true, see [11]), we prove that it is impossible to find a strategy that approximates the best one to a factor better than $n^{1/8-\epsilon}$, where n is the total number of users, and $\epsilon > 0$ is any constant.

- In light of the general hardness results, we develop heuristic algorithms and compare them to natural *baseline* ones. Inspired by influence-and-exploit strategies studied in [22, 19], we propose a two-stage algorithm: we first show the ad to αB users of highest influence, and then show it to users most likely to click (given the ones that clicked so far).

- Finally, we evaluate the performance of this as well as other heuristics on two real datasets with influence probabilities from Flixster.com and GoodReads.com.

Our model shares some common elements with previous work on influence maximization and viral marketing, but our aim is quite different: we care only about the users we show the ad to (which we are allowed to pick), and the *strategy* used for doing so (as opposed to creating a cascade over the *entire* graph). The strong inapproximability results mentioned above are also in contrast to constant-factor approximations known for influence maximization models.

Formally, a display *strategy* will consist of a set of users and a specificied order of showing ads, both of which are adaptive, in the sense they depend on which users have clicked the ad so far (thus it can be viewed as a decision tree). Indeed the number of such *strategy trees* can be doubly exponential in the size of the graph. Proving hardness results thus involves reasoning about arbitrary adaptive strategies. This is our main theoretical contribution that might find other applications.

This is also the reason proving worst approximation guarantees is difficult – because any approximation algorithm must (implicitly) certify that there is no strategy that could obtain a value much larger than that output by the algorithm. While this may suggest that the problem is hopeless, we will see in the experiments that our two-stage algorithm (outlined above) outperforms the baseline heuristics by a large margin – typically by about 11% to 100%.

1.1 Related Work

There is a rich and diverse body of work in the intersection of display advertising, social networks, marketing and influence maximization. For purposes of exposition, we will discuss these results in three categories. The most relevant to us is work on social network advertising, which is what we intend to formalize in the context of display advertising.

Social Network Advertising: Works on social advertising have looked at the impact of displaying social signals (cues) to users. In other words, they measure the increase in the likelihood of a user clicking an ad, given she knows that her friends have already taken an action on that ad. In particular, in [7], the authors run an experiment on Facebook to measure this impact. They find that showing social cues increases the probability of clicks on fan pages. Tucker [25] studies the same problem on a different network and makes similar observations. In a recent paper [8], the authors argue that viral marketing would be more effective if a large number of ordinary users are picked as influencers. None of the above work, however, looks at how one could optimize the number of clicks, likes or conversions in display ads by leveraging these social cues.

Recently, a social ad model considering user influence, called AdHeat, has been explored [9]. In this model, the advertising platform diffuses hint words of influential users to others and then matches ads for each user with aggregated hints. They perform experiments on a real-world data set, and show that AdHeat outperforms the traditional relevance models by a large factor. Although this study shows the effectiveness of using social network information in online advertising, they do not consider active propagation of ads by the users of the social network.

Viral Marketing and Influence Maximization: The problem of influence maximization in social networks has received a lot of attention in the past decade or so, with applications to viral marketing, studying the spread of diseases, and a variety of other settings. Introduced in the seminal work of Kempe, Kleinberg and Tardos [22], the goal is to pick a small set of vertices to *influence*, with the goal of maximizing the expected number of nodes that this influence *cascades* to. We do not get into the formal definitions, but note that these works [13, 22, 19, 24] give formal ways to model the probability of a user buying a product based on her friends buying the product.

This is very similar to the way in which our work models the click probability, and our model is indeed inspired by this literature. However, as we stated earlier, our goal is to find good display strategies, which is quite different from finding good nodes from which to start a cascade. Thus it seems the algorithmic tools developed there do not apply to our setting (indeed our hardness results imply that we *cannot* obtain constant factor approximations, as in the case of influence maximization).

Another related work is the revenue maximization model [19, 23], in which a person's decision to buy a product is influenced by the set of other people who own the product, as well as the price at which the item is offered. The results in this line of work have a more economic focus, and thus have a very different flavor compared to ours.

Online display ad allocation: The problem of optimal allocation for display ads has been recently studied as an online optimization problem [17, 16, 26]. The display ad optimization model considered in these papers is similar to our model in that there is a goal of delivering the ad to a predetermined number of impressions while trying to maximize the expected number of clicks or conversions. Incorporating social influence into these settings is partly the motivation for our work.

2. MODEL

We will first give a brief background on display advertising, and thus motivate our main question of study. This will help set up the notation for describing the model formally.

2.1 Display Advertising

There are three major pricing models for online ads on the Internet: Cost-per-mille/impression (CPM), Cost-per-click (CPC), and Cost-per-action (CPA). In these models, the advertisers pay the platform (publisher) for the number of impressions, clicks, or actions[3] respectively. Even though a majority (in terms of revenue) of search advertising operates on the CPC and CPA models, a significant portion (roughly 33 percent, as of 2013 [2]) of display ads are sold based on the CPM model.

The CPM model is simple to describe: an advertiser enters in a contract with a web publisher for its ads to be shown to a fixed number of site's visitors. The advertiser may specify a segment of the market or some demographic criteria to target the ads to. The

[2]Hard to approximate to some constant factor unless $P = NP$.

[3]Actions, or conversions correspond to a specific action by the online user, e.g., purchases of a product or signs up for newsletters on a website.

contract requires the publisher to show this number of impressions. Thus the publisher can choose which users to show the ad to (and on which pages). How should he make this choice?

Note that the more clicks an ad gets, the higher the chances that the advertiser would come back for another advertising campaign. Thus it is in the publisher's interest to show the ads to users more likely to click. This is a well-recognized objective – in fact, most of the advanced display-ad platforms offer tools to optimize metrics like clicks, conversions, or even return-on-investment (ROI) while delivering a predetermined number of ads [5, 4, 3]. This motivates the question of optimizing the expected number of clicks (or conversions) subject to displaying a specified number of ads. We study this question formally in the setting of social networks.

2.2 Display ads in Social Networks

Let us consider the situation in which the publisher is a social network. The contracts now require the publisher to show an ad (from an advertiser) to a fixed number (say B) users of the social network. As we saw above, the publisher wishes to maximize the number of clicks or 'likes' the ad would receive. This, in turn, could be used for pricing the contract, or improving the customer-loyalty.

We will develop a way to model how users react to *social cues*, and use the model to optimize the number of *clicks* an ad is expected to get. Social cues can be of different kinds. In its most general form, the publisher could display to a user the entire set of friends who have clicked the ad so far. This has many problems – the first is the privacy of the users who have clicked the ad. A fix for this is (as in the experiments of [7]) is to only show users who have given consent. Even so, displaying a list is cumbersome; a realistic way is to show a small subset (say, ones with closest ties) of friends, or the fraction of friends, who clicked the ad (and consented to spreading the information). Additional information, such as the number or demographics of other people (non-friends) who clicked the ad may also be provided. We would like to have a model that is general enough to capture the probability of a user's click probability in all of these settings.

We now formally describe such a model. Let B denote the *budget*, i.e. the number of ads that are to be displayed. We show ads one by one to users. At some point of time, suppose S is the set of users who have clicked the ad. Then the probability that a user u clicks the ad is given by an *influence* function $p_u(S)$. We assume that $p_u(S)$ is increasing with S, i.e., the probability that a user clicks an ad only increases if more people click the ad (e.g. $p_u(S)$ may be a linear function or a submodular function). Given this setting, the objective of the publisher (the social network) is to find the optimal set of users and the optimal *display strategy* (described below) in order to maximize the number of clicks the ad receives.

What kind of functions $p_u(S)$ are possible? From our discussion above, the user u does not see all of S, but only a *social cue*, which is something derived from S. Thus $p_u(S)$ is only a function of the social cue that u receives. In Section 2.2.1, we will see a list of reasonable candidates for $p_u(S)$ and the corresponding social cues.

Display strategy.

Formally a display strategy is a binary decision tree of depth B, the total number of impressions. The vertex at the root is the first user to be shown the ad. If the user clicks the ad, we follow the display strategy in the left subtree, else the right subtree, and so on. Note that even if the same user appears in the tree at the same depth, the probability of him/her clicking the ad will depend on the set of users who clicked so far (which is captured by the path from the root). Given a strategy, we can define the *expected clicks*, which is the expected number of users who click the ad if the publisher follows this strategy. This can be computed by a bottom-up computation in the tree.

The caveat here is that a strategy tree typically has exponential size (since it is a binary tree of depth B), thus computing the expected clicks is non-trivial. All the algorithms we consider will have a 'succinct description' of the tree (at each step, it will be a simple computation to pick the next root), however it is still not clear how to compute the expected clicks. We will compute this quantity using Monte-Carlo simulation. This can be done efficiently, because the variance is at most k^2 (in practice it is much smaller), and thus we get a good estimate of the expectation with only a few samples. The vast number of strategies is one reason it is difficult to reason about the optimal strategy (one with the largest expected clicks).

Adaptivity vs. non-adaptivity.

We have allowed our display strategy to be adaptive (the publisher can decide who to show the ad to based on which users clicked it so far). This is reasonable in most realistic cases. There are instances in which adaptivity gives a huge advantage (B vs. B^{ε}, for small ε). We do not get into them due to space constraints.

2.2.1 Influence Functions

In social advertising, the probability of a user u clicking or liking an ad could increase depending on the knowledge that certain other users have clicked the ad in the past, due to an inherent trust in the taste or judgement of those users. This is what we capture using *influence* functions, as we defined earlier. Below we will list out some influence functions $p_u(S)$ we consider.

- *Linear influence*: Here for each pair (u, v) of users, we have a weight $w(u, v)$ (not necessarily symmetric), and $p_u(S) = c_u + \sum_{v \in S} w(v, u)$.[4] The constant term c_u could be zero for certain vertices. An interesting special case is one in which the weights $w(u, v)$ are all in $\{0, p\}$, i.e., given a graph $G(V, E)$ over users, $w(u, v) = p$ if $(u, v) \in E(G)$ and 0 otherwise. In this case, $p_u(S) = c_u + p \cdot |S \cap N_u|$. This special case is particularly interesting because it is very easy to communicate $p_u(S)$ via social cues – we can simply tell a user the number of friends who clicked the ad so far.

- *Independent Cascade Model*: This is discussed and motivated in [22]. Here as above, we have influences $p(u, v)$ for pairs of users, and $p_u(S) = 1 - \Pi_S(1 - p(u, v))$. In our context, we need to allow certain vertices u to have $p_u(S) = c_u$ for constants c_u (otherwise no one would click the ad to start with). We note that when $p(u, v)$ are all small, $\Pi_S(1 - p(u, v))$ is roughly $1 - \sum_S p(u, v)$, in which case this is a special case of linear influence.

- *Concave influence*: We have weights $w(u, v)$ as before, and have a concave function $g : R \to R$ such that $p_u(S) = g(\sum_{v \in S} w(v, u))$. Interesting examples of such functions are $g(x) = x^d$ for $d < 1$, and $g(x) = \log x$.

The linear and concave functions for influence are inspired by similar models considered in [19]. We could also have another *threshold based* functions $p_u(S)$, again inspired by [22].

- *Deterministic threshold function*: We have weights $w(u, v)$, and thresholds T_u. We have $p_u(S) = 1$ if $\sum_{v \in S} w(v, u) \geq T_u$, and 0 otherwise. We also need to have some vertices with $p_u(S) = c_u$ as explained earlier.

[4] We cap probabilities at 1, though we do not explicitly write this.

Allowing thresholds makes the problem extremely hard to approximate (and possibly unrealistic), thus we do not study algorithmic results for it.

Let us now formally define our problem.

DEFINITION 1 ((SOCIAL DISPLAY OPTIMIZATION)). *Given a tuple (U, B, p) of a set of users U, a bound B on the number of users to show an ad to, and influence functions $p_u(\cdot)$, the goal is to find a (possibly adaptive) strategy for showing the ad to B users so as to maximize the expected clicks. Sometimes we will simply refer to the problem as* display optimization.

3. HARDNESS RESULTS

In this section, we will examine the complexity of the Display-Optimization problem (in terms of approximating the objective, which is the maximum expected clicks). We show that the problem is NP-hard to approximate up to a factor $(1 + \varepsilon)$ for some small constant $\varepsilon > 0$.[5] Such a result is also called APX-hardness. Then, under a stronger hardness assumption, called the planted dense subgraph conjecture, we will show that we cannot approximate the optimal display strategy problem to a factor roughly $n^{1/8}$, where n is the number of users.

We first present the latter result — strong inapproximability under planted dense subgraph assumption — because it seems to highlight the crux of the problem, which is the following: if we wish to influence k users in a network, and we wish to take advantage of the graph structure, we should be able to find a set of k users who are well connected to each other, and this is hard in general. The reasoning below will make this rough intuition formal, and also illustrate how to argue about adaptive algorithms.

3.1 Strong inapproximability

We prove that for any $\varepsilon > 0$, the Display-Optimization problem cannot be approximated to a factor better than $n^{1/8-\varepsilon}$, unless we can approximate the random-planted version of the densest k-subgraph (DkS) problem to a factor better than $n^{1/4-\varepsilon}$ (conjectured to be hard [11]).

Let B be the budget, and suppose the probability that u clicks given S is the set of vertices that have clicked before, is given by

$$p_u(S) = \min\{1,\ p_0 + c \cdot |S \cap N(u)|\},$$

where p_0 and c will be picked appropriately. So a user has an 'independent' probability p_0 of clicking,[6] and there is an increase depending on the number of friends who clicked the ad. The aim, of course, is to maximize the expected number of clicks.

The planted DkS problem is the following: let $\varepsilon > 0$ be any constant; define two distributions over graphs as follows

> $\mathcal{D}_1$: pick a graph from $G(n, n^{-1/2})$ (thus the expected degree is $n^{1/2}$).
>
> $\mathcal{D}_2$: pick a graph from $G(n, n^{-1/2})$, and a random subset P of size $n^{1/2}$. Replace the induced subgraph on P by a graph from $G(n^{1/2}, n^{-(1/4+\varepsilon)})$.

To see that $\mathcal{D}_1$ and $\mathcal{D}_2$ are statistically different, we note that:

1. For a graph in $\mathcal{D}_1$, every induced subgraph on $n^{1/2}$ vertices has average degree $\le O(\log n)$ with probability $1 - \exp(-n^{1/2})$. (Proof follows from Lemma 3.)
2. For a graph in $\mathcal{D}_2$, there exists an induced subgraph on $n^{1/2}$ vertices and average degree $\Omega(n^{1/4-\varepsilon})$ with probability $1 - \exp(-n^{1/2})$.

CONJECTURE 1 (PLANTED DENSE SUBGRAPH CONJECTURE). *Given a graph G, it is not possible in polynomial time to tell (with probability $> 2/3$) if $G \sim \mathcal{D}_1$ or $G \sim \mathcal{D}_2$. [11]*

Our theorem is now the following

THEOREM 2. *Assuming Conjecture 1 (for some $\varepsilon \in (0, 1/16)$), it is not possible to approximate the Display-Optimization problem to a factor better than $n^{1/8-\varepsilon}$ in polynomial time.*

PROOF. The reduction uses the same graph G (drawn from either $\mathcal{D}_1$ or $\mathcal{D}_2$), with parameters as follows:

$$B = n^{1/2}\ ;\ p_0 = \frac{1}{n^{1/8-\varepsilon/2}}\ ;\ c = \frac{1}{n^{1/8-\varepsilon/2}}.$$

We show that $\max \mathbb{E}[\#\text{clicks}]$ is (a) $O(\log^2 n) \cdot n^{3/8+\varepsilon/2}$ if $G \sim \mathcal{D}_1$, and is (b) $\Omega(n^{1/2})$ if $G \sim \mathcal{D}_2$, with high probability. These two claims easily imply the theorem.

It is easier to see (b). Suppose we are given a graph $G \sim \mathcal{D}_2$. Suppose P is the planted set of vertices, and suppose we show ads to the vertices in P (in a random order). Consider the situation after we show the ads to half the vertices in P. Of these vertices, $(B/2)p_0 = (1/2) \cdot n^{3/8+\varepsilon/2}$ vertices will have clicked the ad in expectation (and with very high probability, at least half this number). This means that for every remaining vertex in P, at least $\Omega(n^{1/8-\varepsilon/2})$ of its *neighbors* will have clicked the ad w.h.p. (Here we are using the fact that the planted subgraph is random and has degree $n^{1/4-\varepsilon}$). Thus by the choice of c, each subsequent vertex will click the ad with probability $\Omega(1)$, thus the expected number is $\Omega(n^{1/2})$ with high probability.

Now consider $G \sim \mathcal{D}_1$, and let $v_1, v_2, \dots, v_B$ be any sequence of B users. Now suppose a display strategy shows the ad to these users in this order. Let S_i be the subset of $\{v_1, v_2, \dots, v_{i-1}\}$ that clicked. We can upper bound $p_{v_i}(S_i)$ as:

$$p_{v_i}(S_i) = p_0 + c \cdot |S_i \cap N(v_i)| \le p_0 + c \cdot |\{v_1, \dots, v_{i-1}\} \cap N(v_i)|.$$

Now for $j \ge 1$, define vertex v_i to be in *level* j if $|\{v_1, \dots, v_{i-1}\} \cap N(v_i)|$ lies in the interval $[2^{j-1}, 2^j)$.[7] Then, Lemma 3 (proved below) shows that with high probability ($\ge 1 - 1/n^2$, say), for *every* sequence $v_1, v_2, \dots, v_B$, the number of v_i in level j is at most $\frac{O(\log n) n^{1/2}}{2^j}$.

Thus consider any (adaptive) display strategy. Suppose it shows the ad to users $v_1, v_2, \dots, v_B$. Now divide these users into levels as above, and consider some level j. By the above, there are at most $O(\log n) n^{1/2}/2^j$ users in level j. Thus the expected number of these who click on the ad is

$$\frac{O(\log n) n^{1/2}}{2^j} \cdot \left(p_0 + \frac{2^j}{n^{1/8-\varepsilon/2}}\right) \le O(\log n) \cdot n^{3/8+\varepsilon/2}.$$

By Chernoff bounds, the probability that the number who click is twice the expectation is $< 1/n^4$ in this case. Thus the total number of clicks is at most $O(\log^2 n) n^{3/8+\varepsilon/2}$ with probability at least $1 - 1/n^4$. This then implies that the expected number of clicks is at most $O(\log^2 n) n^{3/8+\varepsilon/2}$.

Note that the proof holds for every display strategy, thus concluding the proof. □

[5] Formally, it means that unless $P = NP$, it is impossible to tell if the optimal display strategy has expected clicks equal to M or expected clicks $\le M/(1 + \varepsilon)$ for some parameter M.

[6] This is necessary for the clicking to *kick off*. We can simulate this by adding a new user who clicks with probability 1, and is connected to everyone with an edge of weight p_0.

[7] Include vertices with no edges to their predecessors into level 1.

It only remains to show Lemma 3.

LEMMA 3. *Let $G = (V, E) \sim \mathcal{G}(n, n^{-1/2})$, and define $M = n^{1/2}$. Then with probability $(1 - 1/n^2)$, we have that for every $v_1, v_2, \dots, v_M$, the number of edges in the induced subgraph is at most $(2 \log n)M$. Consequently, the number of v_i with $> t$ neighbors among $\{v_1, \dots, v_M\}$ is at most $(4 \log n)M/t$.*

PROOF. Consider some $v_1, \dots, v_M$. The probability that there are $\geq k$ edges is essentially

$$\binom{M^2/2}{k} p^k < \left(\frac{M^2 pe}{2k}\right)^k.$$

Now for $k = 2M \log n$, since $Mp = 1$, we have the probability above to be less than $e^{-2M \log n}$. Thus we can take a union bound over all choices of $v_1, \dots, v_M$ (there are only $n^M = e^{M \log n}$ of them), completing the proof. □

3.2 APX hardness

The theorem here is the following. Though the factor is much weaker, it is based on a much more standard assumption (NP hardness). This is the reason we include the result.

THEOREM 4. *There is an absolute constant $\epsilon > 0$ such that it is NP-hard to approximate the Display Optimization problem to a factor $(1 + \epsilon)$.*

We apply a result about the complexity of the k-uniform set cover problem (set cover in which all sets have size precisely k) and present a reduction from this. Formally, an instance of this problem consists of a family $\mathcal{S}$ of m subsets $S_1, \dots, S_m$, each of size k, over a ground set of elements $[n] := \{1, 2, \dots, n\}$. The goal is to find a subfamily of $\mathcal{S}$ of minimum size that covers all of $[n]$. The following hardness result is known:

PROPOSITION 5. *[15] For every choice of constants $s_0 > 0$ and $\varepsilon > 0$, there exists a k (depending on ε) and instances of $k-$uniform regular set cover with n elements on which it is NP-hard to distinguish between the case in which all elements can be covered by $t = \frac{n}{k}$ disjoint sets (called YES instances), and the case in which every $s \leq s_0 t$ sets cover at most a fraction of $1 - (1 - \frac{1}{t})^s + \varepsilon$ of the elements (called NO instances).*

Reduction. We now give a reduction from k-uniform set cover to Display Optimization. Let V be the set of elements and $\mathcal{S} = \{S_1, S_2, \dots, S_m\}$ be a family of sets over V each of size k. The instance of Display-Optimization we construct is as follows: for each element $v \in V$, we have one user. For each $S_i \in \mathcal{S}$, we have a set U_i of $4 \log n/p$ users, where $p = 1/n^{1/4}$. The edges are as follows. We place an edge between $v \in V$ and $u \in U_i$ iff $u \in S_i$ (thus such a v has an edge to all the users in the 'group' U_i). Now the influence functions $p_u()$ are defined as follows. For users $u \in U_i$, $p_u(S) = p$ (i.e., these users click the ad with probability p independent of the rest). For users $v \in V$, we have

$$p_v(S) = \begin{cases} 1 \text{ if } |S \cap \Gamma(v)| \geq 1, \\ 0 \text{ otherwise.} \end{cases}$$

The number of users to show the ad to, i.e., the parameter B, is picked to be $(4t/p) + n$. (Recall $t = n/k$, defined above.)

We now show that if we started with a YES instance for set cover, there is a strategy which has expected clicks $\geq (1 - \delta)n + 4t$, and if we started with a NO instance, then *any* strategy has an expected clicks at most $(1 - \delta')n + 4t$, for some constants $\delta' > \delta > 0$. Recall that $t = n/k$ (k constant), so this will establish APX-hardness.

YES case. In this case there exists a sub-family of t sets – say $S_1, S_2, \dots, S_t$ which cover all the elements V. Now consider the following display strategy:

1. Show the ad to precisely $4t/p$ users, according to the following algorithm: first show the ad to users in U_1 until either one of them clicks the ad, or we have exhausted all of U_1, then do the same with U_2, and so on, until the ad is either shown to $4t/p$ users, or we have one click in each each U_i for $i = 1, \dots, t$. In the latter case, if we have not shown the ad to $4t/p$ users in total, show it to arbitrary (other) users in $\cup_j U_j$ so that the total is $4t/p$.

2. Then show the item to all the n users in V in any order.

LEMMA 6. *With probability $1 - 1/n^2$, step 1 of the algorithm ends up with at least one click in each of $U_1, \dots, U_t$.*

PROOF. The full proof is technical, so we only give an outline in this version. The intuition is that in each of the U_i, by showing the ad to $1/p$ users, there is a probability roughly $1/2$ of some user clicking. Thus in roughly $t/2$ of the groups U_i, the algorithm will show the ad only to $1/p$ users in the group. Now a similar argument will show that in roughly $1/2$ of the rest, we require showing the ad to $2/p$ users, and in general, roughly $t/2^j$ of the groups will require showing the ad to j/p users, for $j = 1, 2, \dots, \log n$. Thus the total number of users to show the ad to, will be

$$\sum_{j=1}^{\log n} \frac{j}{p} \cdot \frac{t}{2^j} < 2t/p.$$

By allowing some slack in each bound, we can get high-concentration versions of these, which completes the proof. □

Note that if we have one click in each U_i, $i \leq t$, then in step 2, we get n clicks. Further, the expected number of clicks in step 1 will be precisely $p \cdot (4t/p) = 4t$, and by Chernoff bounds, it will be $\geq 4t - \sqrt{40t \log n}$ with probability at least $(1 - 1/n^2)$. Thus with probability $\geq 1 - 2/n^2$, we have that in the YES case, the algorithm above gets $n + 4t - \sqrt{40t \log n}$ clicks. Thus the expectation is $\geq (1 - \delta)n + 4t$, for any constant $\delta > 0$ (for large enough n, since $t = n/k < n$). This completes the analysis.
NO case. Here we need to show that no display strategy can have expected clicks $> (1 - \delta')n + 4t$, for some absolute constant δ'. The key is to observe that an optimal strategy will (w.l.o.g.) first show the ad to users in U and then to users in V (this is because of the structure of our instance), and among the users in U, the order does not matter – the only thing that matters is the number of users in each U_i that are shown the ad.

LEMMA 7. *In any strategy, the number of users in U who click the ad is at most $Bp + \sqrt{10Bp \log n}$ with probability $\geq 1 - 1/n^2$.*

PROOF. Any strategy shows the ad to at most B users in U (B is in fact the total number of users it shows the ad to). For this lemma, it does not matter which users are shown the ad, because each user likes with probability p independent of all others. Thus the lemma follows by standard Chernoff bounds. □

Note that the bound above is $Bp = 4t + np + O(\sqrt{t \log n})$, for our choice of p. We introduce a bit of notation: we will call a group U_i "good" if at least one of the users in U_i clicks the ad.

LEMMA 8. *In any strategy, at most $40t$ of the groups are good with probability at least $1 - 1/n^2$.*

PROOF. From the way n, t, p are related, we have $B < 5t/p$, thus any strategy shows the ad only to $5t/p$ users in U. This means that the number of groups in which the ad was shown to $> 1/(2p)$ users is at most $10t$ (else we would get a contradiction).

Thus if $40t$ groups are good in total, it means that in at least $30t$ groups, the strategy shows the ad to at most $1/(2p)$ users, and it manages to have one of the users like the ad. We show that this is very unlikely – can happen with probability at most $1/n^2$. Let us now perform a finer division. For each j, let n_j be the number of groups in which the ad is shown to $1/jp$ users, for $j = 2, \ldots, (1/p)$.[8] Define these groups to be in *level* j. By a calculation similar to the above, we have that

$$\sum_{j=2}^{1/p} n_j \cdot \frac{1}{jp} < \frac{5t}{p}.$$

For convenience, denote the quantity n_j/j by C_j. Then the above inequality becomes $\sum_j C_j < 5t$. We claim that for each j, the probability that there are $> 4(C_j + \log n)$ good groups in level j, is at most $1/n^2$.

The probability that some group in level j is good, is at most $1 - (1-p)^{1/jp} \approx 1 - \exp(-1/j) < 2/j$, for $j \geq 2$. Thus the expected number of good groups in level j is at most $2n_j/j = 2C_j$. Simple concentration bounds then give the claim above (because groups being good are independent events).

This then implies that with prob. $1 - 1/n^2$, the total number of good groups is at most $\sum_j 4(C_j + \log n) < 20t + t\log^2 n/p < 30t$. This completes the proof. □

Once we have Lemmas 7, 8, it is easy to see that with probability $\geq 1 - 1/n^2$, the number of users who clicked the ad in total is at most (because we are in the NO instance of set cover)

$$4t + np + O(\sqrt{t \log n}) + \{(1-1/t)^{40t} + \varepsilon\} \cdot n < (1-\delta')n + 4t,$$

for some absolute constant δ' (since ε can be picked small enough). This completes the proof of APX hardness.

Deterministic thresolds.

The proof above can be modified to show that if the influence function is allowed to be hard threshold, then there is no hope of approximating. More precisely we can show:

THEOREM 9. *The Display-Optimization problem when some users are allowed to have a deterministic threshold function is NP-hard to approximate up to any polynomial (n^c) approximation factor.*

PROOF. (Sketch) We modify the reduction above, noting that in the YES case, all n vertices of V would click the ad (in our algorithm, w.h.p.), while in the NO case, at most $(1-\delta')$ fraction of V could click the ad w.h.p. (the same argument gives $1/n^{2c}$ instead of $1/n^2$ with minor changes). Now connect $M = n^{c+1}$ new users to all the users of V, and suppose these new users click the ad only if all n of V click the ad (threshold). Then in the YES case we get $M + O(n)$ clicks, while in the NO case we only get $O(n)$ clicks w.h.p. This shows inapproximability to an n^c factor. □

4. ALGORITHMS

In light of the above hardness results, we cannot hope to obtain algorithms with provably good approximation ratios. However, we will describe heuristics which perform much better than the natural baseline algorithms on real life data sets. The baseline algorithms are similar to those used in the context of influence maximization (and are known to give good algorithms for special cases).

[8]Formally, we need to have the interval $(1/(j+1)p, 1/jp]$.

Most Influential Greedy Heuristic

Input: (U, B, p_u).

Output: A sequence $(a_1, a_2, \ldots, a_B)$, and set S.

Goal: Maximize $E[|S|]$.

1. **Initialize:** $S = \emptyset$, $A = \emptyset$
2. **For** $i := 1$ **to** B **do**
3. **Let** $a_i \in U \backslash A$ be the user maximizing top-infl(u)
4. **Let** $A := A \cup \{a_i\}$.
5. With probability $p_{a_i}(S)$, **let** $S = S \cup \{a_i\}$.

Figure 1: Most Influential Greedy Heuristic

4.1 Baseline algorithms

We present two natural heuristics for the problem, which we then use to compare the performance of our algorithms.

4.1.1 Largest probability greedy

One simple algorithm is to pick users that are most likely to click on the ad at each time step, i.e., given an input (U, B, p_u), pick users $\{a_1, a_2, \ldots, a_B\}$ as follows: at the i'th step, let $a_i \in U \backslash \{a_1, a_2, \ldots, a_{i-1}\}$ be the user maximizing $p_{a_i}(S_{i-1})$ where $S_{i-1} \subset \{a_1, a_2, \ldots, a_{i-1}\}$ is the set of users who have clicked on the ad so far. Ties are broken arbitrarily.

The problem with this heuristic is, intuitively, that it ignores the *future*. While picking users most likely to click, we may have picked ones that do not influence others (we will see examples).

4.1.2 Most influential greedy

The heuristic above ignores the influence of the chosen users on others. We can consider the other extreme: algorithms that pick the most influential users at each step (and ignore the click probability).

Given an input (U, B, p_u) for an instance of social display optimization, we define a total influence infl(u) for each user u as $\sum_{v \in U} p_v(\{u\})$. The algorithm simply picks the top B users in the non-increasing order of infl(u). One issue with the above is that it considers the total influence of a vertex on all other nodes as opposed to the influence on at most B nodes. To deal with this, we define the *total top influence* top-infl(u) for each user u as $\sum_{v \in J(u)} p_v(\{u\})$, where $J(u) \subset U$ is a subset of users v with the B largest values of $p_v(\{u\})$. The greedy algorithm is to pick the top B users in the non-increasing order of top-infl(u).

This algorithm performs poorly in instances where the click probability and the influence are negatively correlated, but is reasonable on instances in which such correlations do not occur. We thus view the algorithm as a relevant baseline for evaluating better heuristics. The algorithm is formally stated in Figure 1.

4.1.3 Worst-case examples greedy heuristics

Let us describe concrete instances in which the baseline heuristics perform badly. These will inspire the more sophisticated algorithms.

For completeness, we also note that picking B vertices at random will perform very poorly. A simple example is a path with B vertices, in which the first vertex has a click probability 1 (always clicks), and each vertex has a click probability 1 if at least one neighbor has clicked, and 0 otherwise. It is easy to see that a random order does very badly, while the linear order obtains a value B. (The largest-probability greedy recovers this.)

Next we see that even in simple linear influence models with $B = n$, there are bad examples for the two greedy algorithms

Adaptive Hybrid Heuristic

Input: (U, B, p_u).
Output: A sequence $(a_1, a_2, \ldots, a_B)$, and set S.
Goal: Maximize $E[|S|]$.
1. **Initialize:** $S = \emptyset, A = \emptyset$
2. **For** $i := 1$ **to** B **do**
3. **Let** $a_i \in U \backslash A$ be the user maximizing $p_{a_i}(S) \times$ top-infl(a_i)
4. **Let** $A := A \cup \{a_i\}$.
5. With probability $p_{a_i}(S)$, **let** $S = S \cup \{a_i\}$.

Figure 2: Adaptive Hybrid Heuristic.

above. For the largest-probability greedy algorithm, consider a path as above, but with asymmetric weights: $w(i, i+1) = 1$ whereas $w(i+1, i) = 0$ (i influences the neighbor to the right, but not the one on the left). Suppose the probability $p_u(S) = \min\{1, \alpha + i\varepsilon + |S \cap N_i|\}$, where $\alpha = n^{\delta - 1}$ for small δ, and $\varepsilon = 1/n^2$. The greedy algorithm picks vertices in the order $n, n-1, \ldots$ (because of the $i\varepsilon$ terms), and the expected number of clicks is only n^δ. However if shown in the order $1, \ldots, n$, then in roughly $1/\alpha$ steps, we see at least one click, and all vertices following that will definitely click, thus the expected value is $\Omega(n)$ for this strategy.

It is not hard to construct counter examples for most-influential greedy heuristic, with two sets of vertices, one with slightly higher influence but low click probabilities, which fool the greedy strategy.

4.2 Better heuristics

4.2.1 *Adaptive Hybrid Heuristic*

This heuristic is based on the simplest way to take into account both the influence and the click probability – the product of the two. More specifically, given an input (U, B, p_u) for an instance of the social display optimization, the algorithm greedily picks users $\{a_1, \ldots, a_B\}$ as follows: in the i'th step, let $a_i \in U \backslash \{a_1, \ldots, a_{i-1}\}$ be the user maximizing $p_{a_i}(S_{i-1}) \times$ top-infl(a_i) where S is the set of users who clicked so far, and top-infl$(a_i) = \sum_{v \in J(u)} p_v(\{u\})$, where $J(u)$ consists of users v who have not yet been shown the ad, and who have the $(B - i)$ highest values of $p_v(\{a_i\})$. The algorithm is shown in Fig. 2.

4.2.2 *Two-stage heuristic*

Inspired by the idea of the the influence-and-exploit strategies in viral marketing [22, 19], and the greedy algorithm for Densest k-subgraph [11], we propose the following two-stage heuristic: follow the most-influential greedy heuristics for the first stage of the algorithm, and then switch to the largest-probability greedy algorithm in the second stage. More specifically, we can run the adaptive most-influential algorithm for the first αB steps, and then follow the naive greedy largest-probability heuristic in the last $(1 - \alpha)B$ steps. Our motivation for this greedy algorithm is to follow the intuition behind the greedy algorithm for influence maximization [22]. Although this algorithm does not provide a guaranteed approximation algorithm for this problem, we hope that this technique works well in practice, since the greedy heuristic has been very effective for influence maximization [22]. In fact, for the independent cascade model, the first part of the two-stage algorithm is the same as the maximum marginal greedy algorithm for influence maximization under cardinality constraint in this model. This algorithm achieves a $1 - 1/e$-approximation for the influence maximization problem with cardinality constraints. The optimal value

Two-stage Heuristic

Input: (U, B, p_u).
Output: A sequence $(a_1, a_2, \ldots, a_B)$, and set S.
Goal: Maximize $E[|S|]$.
1. **Initialize:** $S = \emptyset, A = \emptyset$
2. **For** $i := 1$ **to** αB **do**
3. **Let** $a_i \in U \backslash A$ be the user maximizing top-infl(u)
4. **Let** $A := A \cup \{a_i\}$.
5. With probability $p_{a_i}(S)$, **let** $S = S \cup \{a_i\}$.
6. **For** $i := \alpha B + 1$ **to** B do **do**
7. **Let** $a_i \in U \backslash A$ be the user maximizing $p_{a_i}(S)$
8. **Let** $A := A \cup \{a_i\}$.
9. With probability $p_{a_i}(S)$, **let** $S = S \cup \{a_i\}$.

Figure 3: The two-stage heuristic for specific α; the overall algorithm tries different α and picks the best

of α certainly depends on the influence functions and the structure of the influence among users. Such an optimal value of α can be computed by trying a range of values for α and estimating the expected number of clicks via simulations. As part of our empirical study, we report a number of insights for the optimal choice of α for various settings.

Bad examples. Note that our bad example for largest-probability greedy (path with asymmetric influence) can be modified easily to give an $n^{1-\delta}$ gap for both the heuristics above. Influence of every vertex in that example is precisely 1 – so the adaptive hybrid works exactly like largest-probability; if ties are broken badly (which is possible), this example is also bad for the two stage heuristic. However, the example is based on a *chain* of highly asymmetric influence, which is unlikely in real instances. We believe that this why our algorithms seem to perform quite well in real instances.

5. EMPIRICAL EVALUATION

In this section, we evaluate variants of four heuristics discussed in the previous section on two families of instances taken from real-world datasets. After elaborating on our datasets, we report the improvement of the two-stage and adaptive hybrid algorithms over the two baseline algorithms.

5.1 Datasets

It is important to explain how we obtain the instances of Display-Optimization (in particular the influences $w(u, v)$) from real data. There is no a priori "correct" way.

Flixster[9]: Flixster is a social network for rating movies. We obtained the Flixster dataset from Goyal et al's work [18, 10]. This dataset contains 13,000 users with 192,400 directed edges between them. There are 1.84 million ratings done by these users. These statistics are presented in Table 1. The influence probabilities are learned by looking at the log of user ratings with time: $< u, i, t, r >$ (meaning user u rated item i at time t with rating r). We estimate the influence probability of user u on user v as the fraction of times user v rated an item after user u had rated that item. This fraction is then normalized over all neighbors of user v to make the sum of influence probabilities equal to 1.[10]

[9] www.flixster.com

[10] This typically overestimates causality; for the next dataset we consider a different way to estimate influences.

# Users	13,000
# Friendship links	192,400
# Ratings	1.84M

Table 1: Summary of Flixster Data Statistics

Goodreads[11]**:** Goodreads is a social book cataloging website where users can register books to create personal bookshelves and also form friendships with each other. The dataset contains 4,654 users with 445,947 edges between them [6] (statistics in Table 2). This time, we produce the influence probabilities according to the so-called *voter model*. This was introduced by [12] and [20] to model probabilistic influence. The model explains the diffusion of opinions in a social network as follows: in each step, each node changes her opinion by choosing one of her neighbors at random and adopting that neighbor's opinion. In [14], the authors show that degree is a good predictor of influence probabilities.

# Users	592,081
# Friendship links	2,045,177
# Books	248,252

Table 2: Summary of Goodreads: owner-book information data

The voter model was introduced by [12] and [20] as a natural probabilistic influence model. The voter model explains the diffusion of opinions in a social network as follows: in each step, each node changes her opinion by choosing one of her neighbors at random and adopting that neighbor's opinion. In [14], the authors show that degree is a good predictor of influence probabilities.

5.2 Experimental Setup

Here, we report the performance of our algorithms on the Flixster and GoodReads data sets. For each data set, we study the performance of these algorithms with $B = \beta n$ for four different values β, $0.02, 0.05, 0.1$ and 0.15. I.e., we set the the goal of showing the ad to 2%, 5%, 10% or 15% of the whole population, and report the results for each value of B. The way we compute the edge weights (probabilities) is described in Secton 5.1. As for the choice of the influence function, we examine the independent cascade model, and linear and concave influences. The concave functions we examined are $g(x) = \sqrt{x}$ and $g(x) = \log x$.

Finally, for each node u, the individual click probability $p_u(\emptyset)$ is drawn from a log-normal distribution with a large mean (between 0.1 and 0.45). We chose a large mean for these distributions to make sure that in the final click probability, the individual click probability is not dominated by the incremental probability due to influence.[12] The performance of the algorithms under the independent cascade model were almost the same as linear influence (as we noted, this is not surprising), thus we report the plots for the independent cascade model, and concave influences with $\sqrt{x}$ and $\log x$. The reason we report the results for both of these is to illustrate that our empirical observations are similar for seemingly very different influence functions.

[11] www.GoodReads.com

[12] This probability could be much smaller for certain ad types. The goal of our empirical study is mainly to compare different heuristic methods. We observe that the magnitude of the click-through-rate numbers is not important for this comparison, and we expect to get similar relative performance if we scale all click-through-rates by the same factor. It is, however, important to choose the individual probability factors in such a way that their magnitude dominates that of the probabilities due to influence.

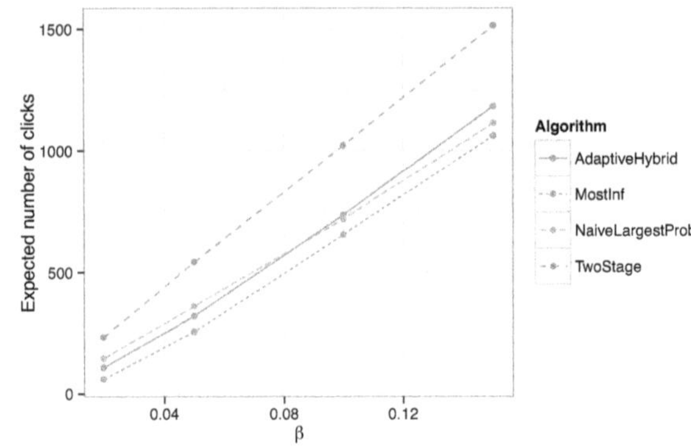

Figure 4: Performance of the heuristics on the Flixster dataset for the independent cascade model. The X axis shows β, where $B = \beta n$

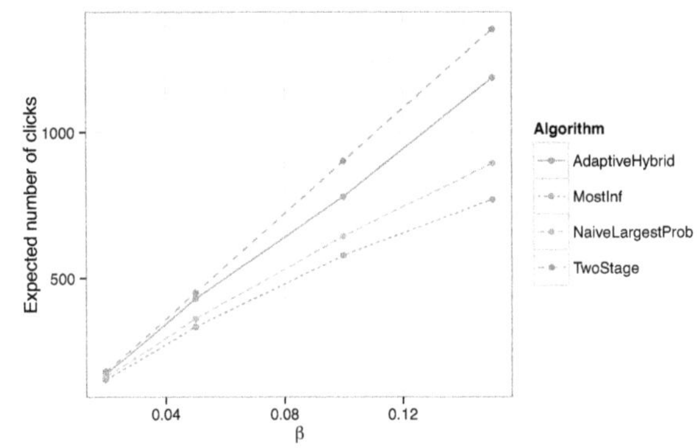

Figure 5: Performance of the heuristics on the Flixster dataset with a concave influence function, specifically $\log(x)$

As we discussed, we compare four algorithms (including two baseline heuristics). For the two-stage algorithm, we try different values of α and choose the α with maximum expected value.

5.3 Observations

The empirical results for both data sets and for all propagation cases that we ran can be found in Figures 4, 5, 6, 7, 8, and 9. In these plots, the X axis changes β where $B = \beta n$. The Y axis is the expected number of clicks during the simulation. Here we summarize our main observations in these plots:

- Most notably, we observe that the two-stage heuristic algorithm consistently outperforms all the other heuristics. Across all instances, the gap between the performance of the two-stage heuristic and other algorithms increases as the the budget B increases. For example, for $\beta = 0.15$, for the Flixster dataset, the percentage increases for the two-stage heuristic from the best of other algorithms (i.e., adaptive hybrid) is around 25%, 14%, and 6% for the three different influence propagation models. For the GoodReads dataset, the percentage increases are around 7%, 5%, and 12%. The percentage increases from the output of the largest-probability heuristic (that ignores the influence function) to the output of the two-stage are 26%, 62%, and 23%. The same percentage increases for the GoodReads dataset are 11%, 100%, and 12%. The interesting parameter in two-stage algorithms is the α at

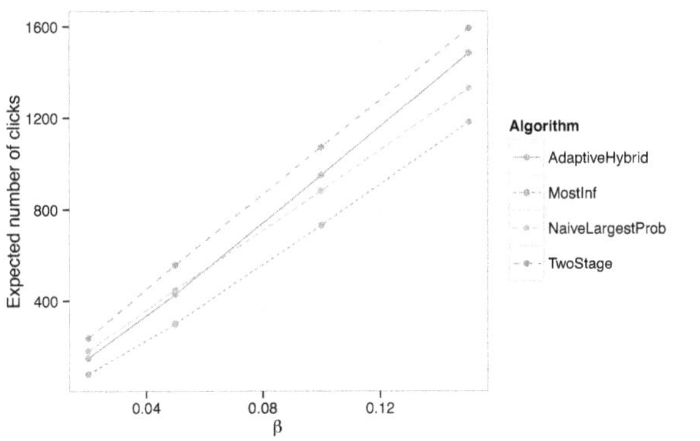

Figure 6: Performance of the heuristics on the Flixster dataset with a concave influence function, specifically $\sqrt{x}$

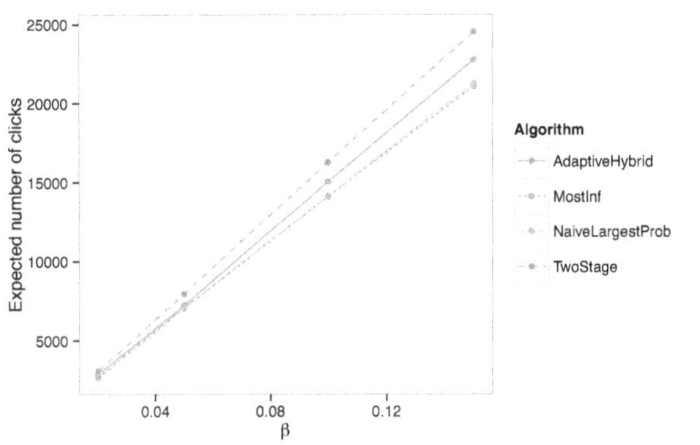

Figure 7: Performance of the heuristics on the GoodReads dataset for the independent cascade model

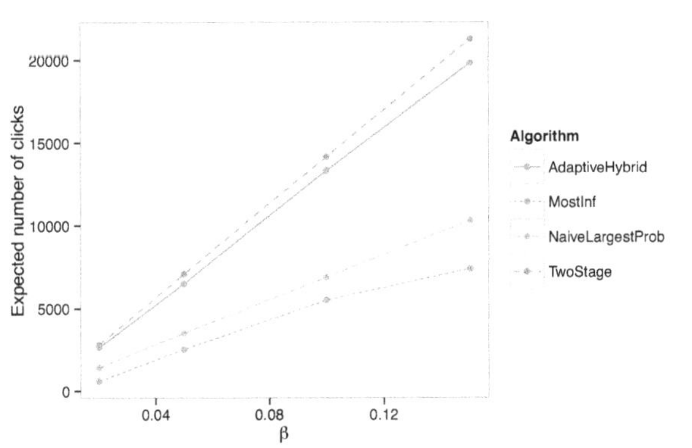

Figure 8: Performance of the heuristics on the GoodReads dataset with a concave influence function, specifically $\log(x)$

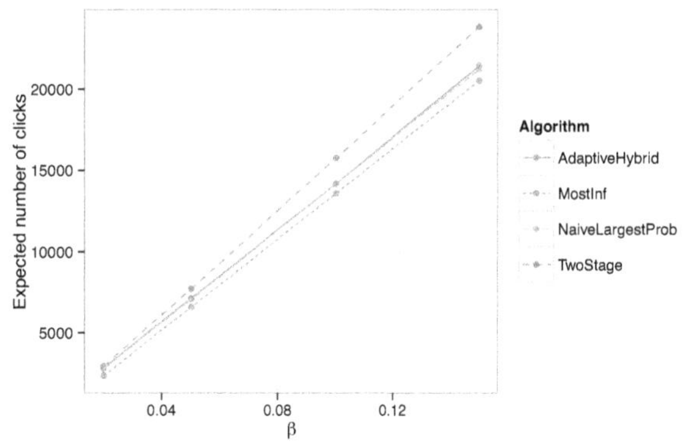

Figure 9: Performance of the heuristics on the GoodReads dataset with a concave influence function, specifically $\sqrt{x}$

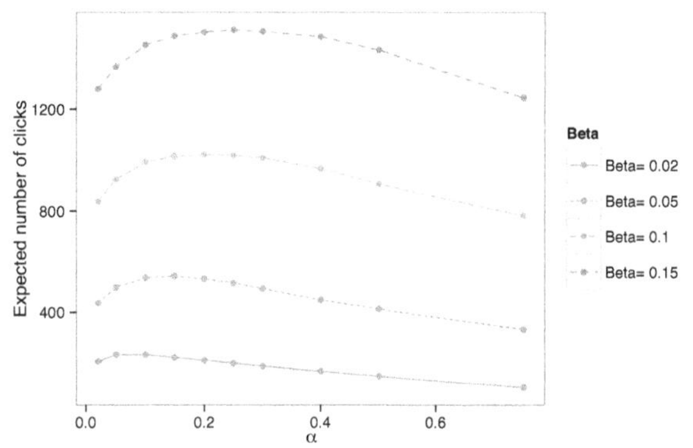

Figure 10: Two-stage heuristic for different values of α. Plot is for the independent cascade model on the Flixster dataset.

which the best performance is achieved. See below for a discussion on how this behaves.

- Even our first heuristic, the adaptive hybrid greedy algorithm, outperforms the baselines for all values of β except $\beta = 0.02$ where the largest-probability heuristic is slightly better for two instances, and $\beta = 0.05$ where the largest-probability heuristic is slightly better for one instance. Again the performance increase from largest-probability heuristic to the adaptive hybrid heuristic increases as the budget increases.

- Finally, the most-influential greedy algorithm performs the worst. This was expected since it only focuses on picking the most influential users and not on their click probability.

Optimal α for the two-stage heuristic: As we discussed, in order to find the optimal α for the two-stage algorithm, we tried several values and chose the best one. The expected number of clicks for each value of α and for different budgets is plotted in Figure 11. The optimal choice of α for each instance may be related to the optimal way of influencing the network through ads. We observe that the optimal α for different instances vary from 0.05 to 0.2. It is worth noting the following points in these plots:

- The optimal choice of α increases as β increase from 2% to 15%. This suggests that with a higher budget, we can afford to spend a bit more fraction of time on 'exploration' (influencing) and attain higher expected clicks.

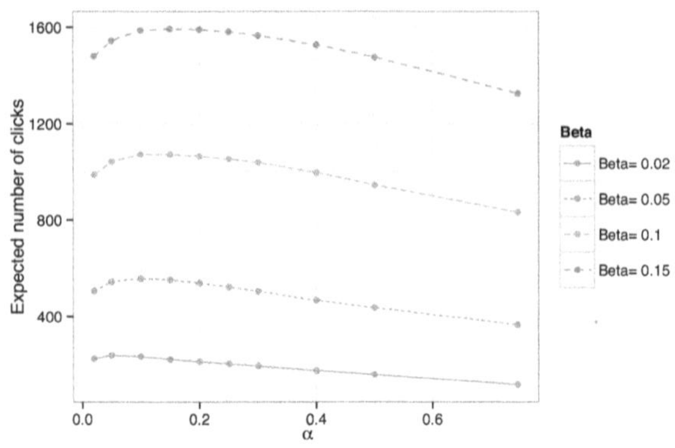

Figure 11: Two-stage heuristic for different values of α. Plot is for $\sqrt{x}$ influence function on the Flixter dataset.

- The optimal choice of α decrease as the exponent of the concave influence function decreases. This is reasonable, because the lesser the influence among users, the lesser the importance of the influencing steps.
- Fixing an instance (i.e., fixing β and an influence propagation model), we observe that as α increases, the expected number of clicks from the two-stage heuristic is first monotonically increasing, and then it decreases monotonically (i.e., it is unimodal). This is a curious fact which would be nice to prove in restricted models. Of course, it also implies that the optimal α can be found by trying only a logarithmic number of values of α (by essentially binary search).

6. CONCLUSION

Social advertising has emerged as a promising alternative to conventional online advertising methods. In the setting of display advertising, relying on the notion that leveraging social cues can increase clicks in online social networks, we proposed a formal model for social display ad optimization, and initiated the study of the problem of optimally allocating display ads by modeling the impact of social influence on users' decisions. We showed that the social display ad optimization problem is APX-hard and is unlikely to be approximable within a factor much better than $n^{1/8}$. On the algorithms side, we proposed new algorithms which seem to perform significantly better than the baseline heuristics on datasets from real social networks. E.g., our two-stage algorithm achieved a 11% to 100% improvement over the output of baseline greedy algorithms. We also examined the question of the optimal "influence/exploit trade-off" for the two-stage heuristic under different choices of influence functions.

As a first step towards better display advertising in social networks, our work raises many interesting questions: can we develop algorithms with provable guarantees for synthetic graphs, such as the well-studied models for social networks? What other restricted influence models can we study for which we can prove provable approximation algorithms? What are good ways to learn influence weights from real data? Can we extend the model to incorporate multiple advertisers (each having a certain number of impressions)?

Our work suggests that the structure of the (induced) graph between the target users is a crucial parameter in this model of 'social display advertising'. It suggests that the graph structure, used well, could significantly increase the expected click rate. Running experiments to test this on real advertising platforms is an interesting direction for future research.

7. ACKNOWLEDGEMENTS

We would like to thank Xi Chen, MohammdHossein Bateni and Vahab Mirrokni for valuable discussions.

8. REFERENCES

[1] *sec.gov/Archives/edgar/data/1326801/000132680114000007/fb-12312013x10k.htm* (2013).

[2] IABinternet advertising revenue report. `http://www.iab.net/media/file/IABInternetAdvertisingRevenueReportHY2013FINAL.pdf` (2013).

[3] Facebook doubleclick for publishers (dfp) optimization website. `https://www.facebook.com/business/a/online-sales/ad-optimization-measurement` (2014).

[4] Google doubleclick bid manager website. `http://www.thinkwithgoogle.com/products/doubleclick-bid-manager.html` (2014).

[5] Google doubleclick for publishers (dfp) optimization website. `http://static.googleusercontent.com/media/www.google.com/en/us/doubleclick/pdfs/optimization.pdf` (2014).

[6] ABBASSI, Z., ASSADI, S., AND TAHMASBI, M. Predicting ratings in online social networks: Friends or the crowd? *Working paper*.

[7] BAKSHY, E., ECKLES, D., YAN, R., AND ROSENN, I. Social influence in social advertising: evidence from field experiments. In *ACM Conference on Electronic Commerce* (2012), pp. 146–161.

[8] BAKSHY, E., HOFMAN, J. M., MASON, W. A., AND WATTS, D. J. Everyone's an influencer: quantifying influence on twitter. In *Proceedings of the fourth ACM international conference on Web search and data mining* (2011), ACM, pp. 65–74.

[9] BAO, H., AND CHANG, E. Y. Adheat: an influence-based diffusion model for propagating hints to match ads. In *Proceedings of the 19th international conference on World wide web* (2010), ACM, pp. 71–80.

[10] BHAGAT, S., GOYAL, A., AND LAKSHMANAN, L. V. Maximizing product adoption in social networks. In *Proceedings of the fifth ACM international conference on Web search and data mining* (2012), ACM, pp. 603–612.

[11] BHASKARA, A., CHARIKAR, M., CHLAMTAC, E., FEIGE, U., AND VIJAYARAGHAVAN, A. Detecting high log-densities: An o($n^{1/4}$) approximation for densest k-subgraph. In *Proceedings of the Forty-second ACM Symposium on Theory of Computing* (New York, NY, USA, 2010), STOC '10, ACM, pp. 201–210.

[12] CLIFFORD, P., AND SUDBURY, A. A model for spatial conflict. *Biometrika 60*, 3 (1973), 581–588.

[13] DOMINGOS, P., AND RICHARDSON, M. Mining the network value of customers. In *Proceedings of the seventh ACM SIGKDD international conference on Knowledge discovery and data mining* (2001), ACM, pp. 57–66.

[14] EVEN-DAR, E., AND SHAPIRA, A. A note on maximizing the spread of influence in social networks. *Internet and Network Economics* (2007), 281–286.

[15] Feige, U., Lovász, L., and Tetali, P. Approximating min sum set cover. *Algorithmica 40*, 4 (2004), 219–234.

[16] Feldman, J., Henzinger, M., Korula, N., Mirrokni, V., and Stein, C. Online stochastic packing applied to display ad allocation. In *ESA* (2010).

[17] Feldman, J., Korula, N., Mirrokni, V., Muthukrishnan, S., and Pal, M. Online ad assignment with free disposal. In *WINE* (2009).

[18] Goyal, A., Bonchi, F., and Lakshmanan, L. V. A data-based approach to social influence maximization. *Proceedings of the VLDB Endowment 5*, 1 (2011), 73–84.

[19] Hartline, J., Mirrokni, V., and Sundararajan, M. Optimal marketing strategies over social networks. In *Proceedings of the 17th international conference on World Wide Web* (2008), ACM, pp. 189–198.

[20] Holley, R. A., and Liggett, T. M. Ergodic theorems for weakly interacting infinite systems and the voter model. *The annals of probability* (1975), 643–663.

[21] Interactive-Advertising-Bureau:. social advertising best practices. *http://www.iab.net/media/file/Social-Advertising-Best-Practices-0509.pdf* (2009).

[22] Kempe, D., Kleinberg, J., and Tardos, É. Maximizing the spread of influence through a social network. In *Proceedings of the ninth ACM SIGKDD international conference on Knowledge discovery and data mining* (2003), ACM, pp. 137–146.

[23] Mirrokni, V. S., Roch, S., and Sundararajan, M. On fixed-price marketing for goods with positive network externalities. In *WINE* (2012), pp. 532–538.

[24] Mossel, E., and Roch, S. Submodularity of influence in social networks: From local to global. *SIAM J. Comput. 39*, 6 (2010), 2176–2188.

[25] Tucker, C. Social advertising. *Available at SSRN: http://ssrn.com/abstract=1975897 or http://dx.doi.org/10.2139/ssrn.1975897* (2012).

[26] Vee, E., Vassilvitskii, S., and Shanmugasundaram, J. Optimal online assignment with forecasts. In *ACM EC* (2010).

Frankenplace: Interactive Thematic Mapping for Ad Hoc Exploratory Search

Benjamin Adams
Centre for eResearch
Dept. of Computer Science
The University of Auckland
Auckland, New Zealand
b.adams@auckland.ac.nz

Grant McKenzie
Department of Geography
University of California, Santa Barbara
Santa Barbara, CA, USA
grant.mckenzie@geog.ucsb.edu

Mark Gahegan
Centre for eResearch
Dept. of Computer Science
The University of Auckland
Auckland, New Zealand
m.gahegan@auckland.ac.nz

ABSTRACT

Ad hoc keyword search engines built using modern information retrieval methods do a good job of handling fine-grained queries. However, they perform poorly at facilitating spatial and spatially-embedded thematic exploration of the results, despite the fact that many queries, e.g. *civil war*, refer to different documents and topics in different places. This is not for lack of data: geographic information, such as place names, events, and coordinates are common in unstructured document collections on the web. The associations between geographic and thematic contents in these documents can provide a rich groundwork to organize information for exploratory research. In this paper we describe the architecture of an interactive thematic map search engine, Frankenplace, designed to facilitate document exploration at the intersection of theme and place. The map interface enables a user to zoom the geographic context of their query in and out, and quickly explore through thousands of search results in a meaningful way. And by combining topic models with geographically contextualized search results, users can discover related topics based on geographic context. Frankenplace utilizes a novel indexing method called geoboost for boosting terms associated with cells on a discrete global grid. The resulting index factors in the geographic scale of the place or feature mentioned in related text, the relative textual scope of the place reference, and the overall importance of the containing document in the document network. The system is currently indexed with over 5 million documents from the web, including the English Wikipedia and online travel blog entries. We demonstrate that Frankenplace can support four distinct types of exploratory search tasks while being adaptive to scale and location of interest.

Categories and Subject Descriptors

H.3.3 [**Information Storage and Retrieval**]: General; H.2.8 [**Database Management**]: Database Applications—*Spatial Databases and GIS*

WWW 2015, May 18–22, 2015, Florence, Italy.
ACM 978-1-4503-3469-3/15/05.
http://dx.doi.org/10.1145/2736277.2741137.

General Terms

Measurement, Theory

Keywords

Geographic search; interactive search; information retrieval; information visualization; visual analytics; exploratory search

1. INTRODUCTION

Geographic location is playing an increasingly important role in information retrieval: to find places of interest that match a user's query and for personalizing search based on user location [44, 10]. Most of this work focuses on how to improve localized search results for a standard presentation like the top-N search page [16, 8, 4]. In this paper we propose that geographic references in text also provide a powerful way to organize and explore ad hoc information via an interactive thematic map interface. Ad hoc information retrieval is the task of finding relevant documents from a corpus given an unconstrained keyword query. Ad hoc retrieval implies that users will perform many different kinds of searches and for many different purposes, not only to find a specific document but for more exploratory reasons as well. Faceted browsing for ad hoc web search faces certain challenges not least due to the difficulty in coming up with a categorization scheme that is broadly useful [7]. This in part is why the non-faceted keyword search model exemplified by Google and other modern search engines supplanted the hierarchical category-based faceted browsing that companies like Yahoo! developed in the late 90's. We argue that there is a case to make again for spatial and temporal faceting for ad hoc search, because 1) geographic space is a common ordering principle in human discourse that is broadly applicable to a number of different kinds of searches, and 2) a massive number of online documents have spatial and temporal semantics that allow us to interpret their content along these dimensions and the technical capability to model these semantics from unstructured content has by now been developed.

Cartographers have known for centuries the power of organizing thematic information by geographic context and visualizing it on a map. This allows one to understand the spatial dynamics of a topic within a structure that has strong reference points in human experience (i.e., the places represented on the map). At the same time it tells us important information about the places, which can be used for their comparison (similarity, groupings, etc.). Recently, we have begun to see examples of thematic mapping interfaces for posts from social media applications like Twitter.[1] However, in these cases the georeferencing is based on simple point data provided by the service and there is very little work on using these interfaces for anything beyond simple visualization. Partly, this is because of the limited value in the retrieval of individual tweets that match the query versus the information gained from viewing the aggregate visualization from millions of tweets. The visualization alone is a useful product for understanding the query as it relates to place, but when coupled with ad hoc retrieval it becomes a way to geographically contextualize the documents for the user. For many corpora, such as web documents, there is real value in using the geographic context as a means to discover, organize, and interactively visualize the documents related to a search query. One obvious benefit of such a method is that instead of merely returning a list of the top-N matching documents, a thematic map enables geographic exploration of thousands of results.

In this paper we discuss the implementation of a system for geographic exploratory search of Wikipedia articles and online travel blog entries, called Frankenplace[2] (see Figure 1). In the design of such a system we are presented with the question of how to rank the relative importance of documents in a way that is sensitive to the geographic scale the user is interested in. That is, given that we know a place is associated with a document, how should the scale of that place reference inform how the document content is reflected in a thematic map at a given zoom level? For example, if a corpus contains articles about California (but without references to more localized places), but the user is zoomed into the local San Francisco area, should those California-related articles still be rendered in some form on the resulting map because they spatially intersect with the map window, or should only locally-referenced content be displayed? Utilizing a hierarchical discrete global grid, we introduce a text indexing method that adjusts the importance of documents based on the geographies of referenced places, so that search results are attuned to zoom level. In addition, apart from administrative regions, most popular map-based search tools (e.g., Google Maps and Bing Maps) focus on retrieving point-based geographic features (i.e., points of interest), even though visually representing *regions* or *areas of interest* is of significant value to the spatial search community. Our global grid approach combined with kernel density estimation provides a mechanism to visualize search results in a variety of ways, including as regions and surfaces.

It is helpful to consider a use case at this point. An economic historian is interested in exploring the evolution and history of ghost towns in the United States as they relate to economic changes, geographic environment, and cultural events such as the gold rush. At a preliminary stage of research this historian will first want to gather information about ghost towns in geographic context. A simple approach is to start using a search engine, such as Google, to explore for information by searching for *ghost town*. However, this search, as shown in Figure 1, returns 14.9 million results; it is unclear how to explore the results geographically. The historian can refine the search by adding geographic terms but this requires knowing in advance which locations to search for. In addition, the Google map interface is designed to emphasize commercial points of interest, and thus the results are not particularly useful for this task. In contrast, by organizing document information spatially and enabling interaction via a map interface, several more useful documents can be uncovered. Furthermore, geographically related topics such as *gold rush* become clear as the user navigates through the system. The quality of the results will, of course, depend on the underlying corpora used to build the index. Continued development to include additional sources, such as primary historical documents, will only improve the ability to perform these kinds of searches.

In this paper we detail the creation of a thematic map exploratory search engine designed to enable this kind of research. Our main novel contributions are as follows:

1. The use of a hierarchical discrete global grid to organize the geographic indexing of text to enable easy integration from multiple sources at multiple zoom levels.

2. A method for boosting terms associated with cells on the discrete global grid that factors in the geographic scale of the place or feature mentioned in related text, the relative textual scope of the place reference, and the overall importance of the term's document in the document network.

3. An interactive thematic map search interface that enables users to quickly browse to refine or expand the scope of their query geographically in an integrated system.

4. A technique to suggest new searches based on the current search results, filtered by a selected grid cell. Topic modeling is used to calculate a topic vector associated with each document when the index is created. Topic vectors are aggregated on the fly at query time providing suggestions that are query and geography specific.

The remainder of the paper is organized as follows. After a brief overview of the system architecture, Section 3 describes our methodology for geographic indexing of documents. Section 4 details the exploratory search interface design and implementation. In Section 5 we discuss some of the novel search tasks that Frankenplace enables with evaluation. Related work and finally our conclusion and directions of future work close out the paper.

2. SYSTEM OVERVIEW

The Frankenplace system architecture is shown in Figure 2. In the backend of the system, geographic data from multiple sources is combined to create a gazetteer that is used to match place names in documents to grid cells on a discrete global grid. Several sources of information are organized into two types of indices that are built to support geo-thematic search (details in Section 3). The first type is an inverted index of terms associated with grid cells, and the second is an index of individual documents and related topics. An exploratory search web client interactively renders search results from these indices to map out prominent places and highlight matching documents based on user selected locations (details in Section 4).

[1]See e.g., `http://mapd.csail.mit.edu/tweetmap-desktop`
[2]`http://frankenplace.com`. Note, a very early version of Frankenplace with substantially different architecture and functionality was previously described in [2].

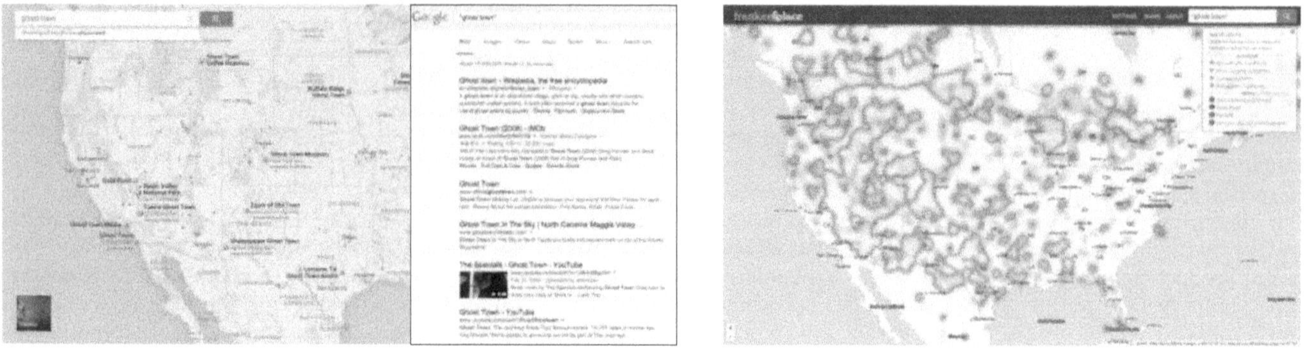

(a) (b)

Figure 1: Comparison of search results for the query *"ghost town"* from (a) a popular search engine, (b) Frankenplace system.

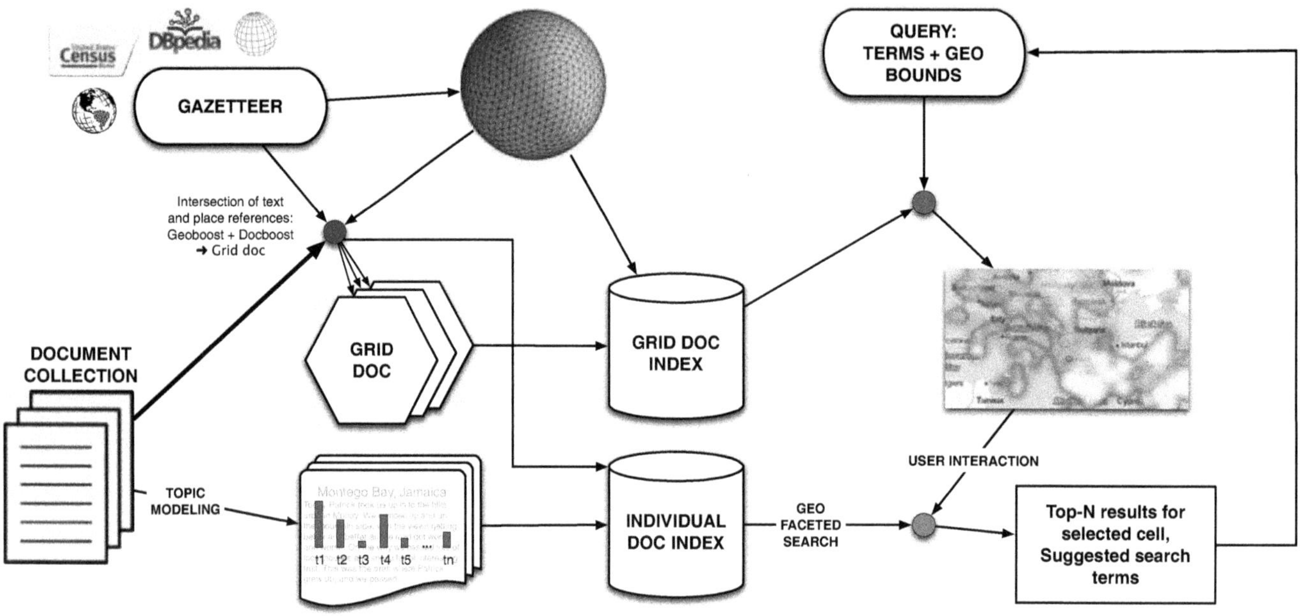

Figure 2: Overview of the Frankenplace system architecture from indexing to interactive search.

3. INDEXING

For a thematic keyword search that identifies relevant places based on the content of documents, one must create an inverted index from terms to places and regions on the Earth. In this section we describe the design of such an index (and related ranking algorithms) when the input data consists of millions of documents that intersect with these places in differing capacities. In a hyperlinked database, statistical network measures such as HITS are very effective at uncovering "important" documents [23]. But here we supplement this with an importance score for document sections based on their relationships to places. These scores are derived from both *overall* and *partial* references to places within a document. An overall reference means the entire document is about a place, and thus all the text contained within is relevant to index that place. An example of this would be a travel blog entry about the city of Tokyo. A partial reference, in contrast, is located within a text but only some subset of the content is related.

3.1 Mapping place names to global grid

Some work has been done on matching geographic information in text to geodesic grids, but without much care over geographic projection and consequent areal distortions [43, 1]. In contrast, in this work we create an information retrieval index that flexibly customizes results for multiple geographic scales (map zoom levels). Thus, it is important to design a system that organizes the information such that it facilitates scale dependency. Digital Earth systems that are designed to operate on multi-thematic, global geographic data sets (such as climate data) use discrete global grids (DGGs) to organize their information in this way [12]. The use of a DGG has the added advantage that search results can potentially be integrated with geographic information from a number of other geophysical and social science data sets, including land use, climate, and demographic data.

A DGG is a partitioning of the entire Earth's surface into equal area (or approximately equal area) grid cells at multiple, interrelated levels of resolution that can be indexed and searched quickly by geographic coordinates [32]. There are several approaches to building DGGs, but one common approach is to start with a polyhedron simplification of the spherical globe (usually an icosahedron) and then hierarchically partition the faces of the polyhedron into triangles, diamonds, or hexagon shaped cells. Depending on the orientation of the initial polyhedron, the transformation function between the polyhedral surfaces and the spherical globe, and the spatial partitioning technique used, several types of DGGs can be generated [36, 17]. In addition, alternative methods exist that do not use a polyhedral simplification, such as HEALPix, which was developed by the astronomical community for mapping star densities [13]. For web mapping (our purposes), a hierarchical triangular discrete global grid has the advantage that at every successive level the number of cells increases by a factor of four–the same as web tiles. As a result, the size of the grid cells can remain constant relative to the map features at all zoom levels.

Several online gazetteers exist that map place names to locations on the Earth, including geonames.org, NGA GEOnet Names Server, Getty Thesaurus of Geographic Names, and quattroshapes, as well as other sources containing this information, such as DBpedia structured data sourced from Wikipedia. In addition, coming out of the digital humanities community there is an increasing number of specialized gazetteers that focus on historical place names [37]. Despite movement toward the use of semantic technologies in gazetteers [22], these gazetteers vary widely in terms of their quality of representation, especially with respect to interoperability, classification, toponyms in multiple languages, and the geometric representation of spatial footprints. Most entries in available gazetteers use point geometry or occasionally simple bounding box representations for the spatial footprint of a place. As a result, in our work we found it was best to align identifiers across gazetteers and then improve the geometry when possible by linking in polygon data from national and regional authorities. For that task we included country, first order administrative region, and natural park polygon data from the North American Cartographic Information Society,[3] and TIGER data from the United States Census Bureau.[4] This gazetteer enrichment remains an ongoing process. The next step is to map each of these gazetteer entries to sets of cells in the discrete global grid. This is done by calculating the spatial intersection between the polygon or point representation of the place and grid cells at each level. The result of this process is a set of mappings from places in the gazetteer to sets of grid cells at multiple levels of the DGG.

3.2 Assigning weighted words to grid cells

We start with a collection of documents and place name entries in our gazetteer and from that we need to assign weight values of words for cells in the discrete global grids. We define two types of scopes for place references in a document: 1) *overall* place references, which are relationships between a place and the entire document; and 2) *partial* place references, which are places that are only related to a local scope of text, such as a sentence, paragraph, or section.

Identifying places in Wikipedia. Wikipedia has a great deal of structured geographic information associated with articles, often in the form of geographic coordinates, which have been extracted from Wikipedia into the DBpedia knowledge graph [25]. Since we want better-than-point representations when possible, it is not sufficient to simply match overall place references to latitude-longitude references on Wikipedia pages, however. Instead multiple sources of evidence are brought together to match articles to the identifiers in our integrated gazetteer. This gives us an excellent start to match places within the text as well. Links within a page that are instantiated in DBpedia as the `dbpedia:place` type are identified as partial place references. In addition, links to `dbpedia:event` pages that also have a georeference are matched. Since it is customary for Wikipedia pages only to link to the first occurrence of a related page, it is necessary to match for additional occurrences and assign links there as well, otherwise we will miss many paragraphs with place references.

Identifying places in travel blog entries. Travel blog entries come in a variety of formats on the web, so matching overall and partial place references in travel blog entries is more difficult. For this task we leveraged both the CLAVIN geoparser[5] and geonames.org web services to match place names to geonames ids that we could then match to points or areas in our integrated gazetteer. Improving geoparsing methods was not the main subject of this research; existing solutions work fairly well, though there is much room for improvement since false positives and missed place name matches occur often.

Computational sensemaking of how places relate to the discursive and narrative structure of a document remains at the frontier of natural language processing research and is beyond the scope of this research. However, assuming a linear narrative structure in most documents, we make the simplifying assumption that the scope of a partial place reference can be set to a fixed syntactic structure that the place reference falls within. In some sources, such as Wikipedia, the syntactic structure of paragraphs are clearly delineated and work as a useful proxy for text related to a place [20]. Crowdsourced information that has less quality control (such as travel blog entries) will need a more flexible scoping such as a sliding window of words.

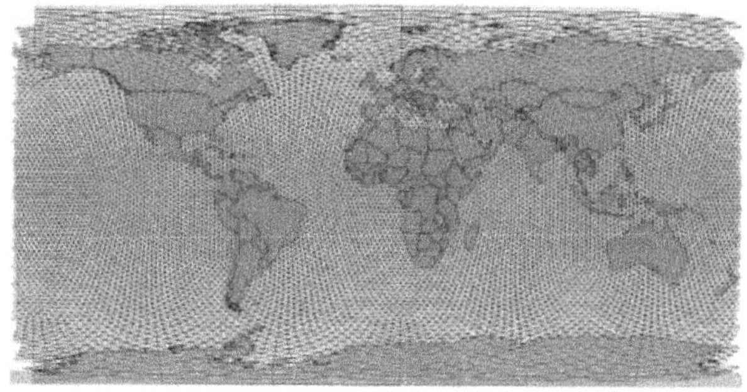

Figure 3: Triangular discrete global grid with approximately equal area cells.

3.2.1 Geoboost

Once we have relationships between words (in sections) and place names, it is possible to calculate a *geoboost* value in the range (0,...,1] associated with each word for each grid cell. In this way the same word from a given document can

[3] `http://www.naturalearthdata.com/`

[4] `https://www.census.gov/geo/maps-data/data/tiger.html`

[5] `https://github.com/Berico-Technologies/CLAVIN`

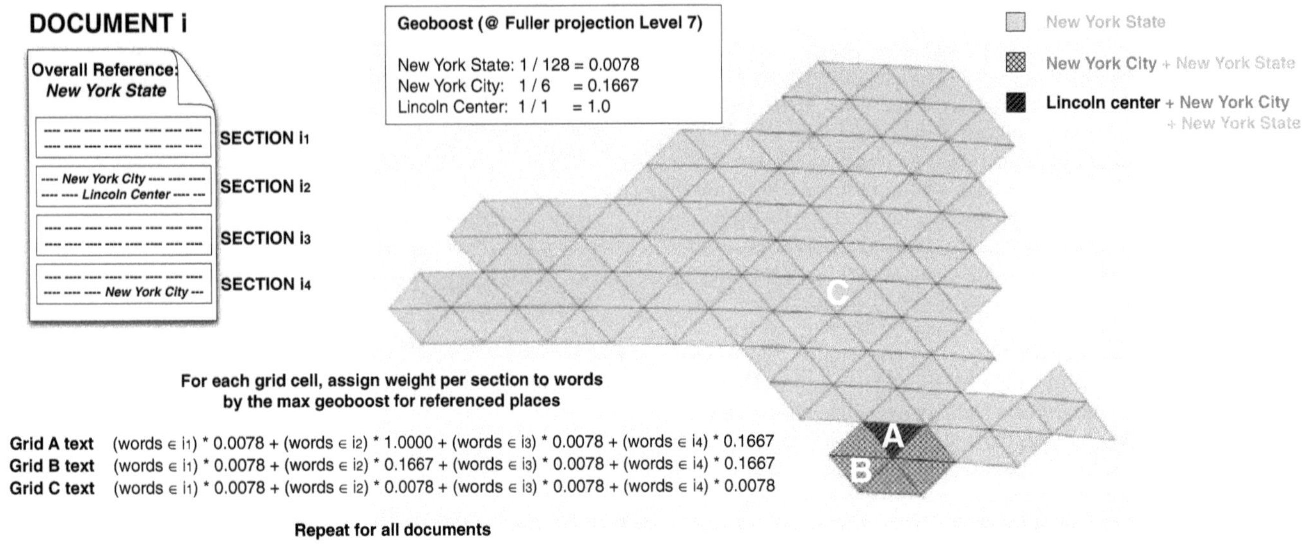

Figure 4: Example of how words are assigned with geoboosts from a sample document containing references to New York State, New York City, and Lincoln Center.

contribute with different weights to different grid cells. The *geoboost* (Equation 1) is a function of the number of grid cells covered by the place references associated with the word at a given resolution. Let $w_{i,j,k}$ be defined as word k from section j of document i. Let $\sigma(w_{i,j,k})$ be the section of word $w_{i,j,k}$, $pp(\sigma(w_{i,j,k}))$ be equal to the set of partial place references in the section, and $c(l, pp(\sigma(w_{i,j,k}))$ be the number of grid cells covered by the partial place at grid level l.

$$geoboost(g_{l/id}, w_{i,j,k}) = \frac{1}{min(c(pp(\sigma(w_{i,j,k}))))} \quad (1)$$

The rationale for geoboost is that more fine-grained place references should override coarse-grained place references when it comes to assigning importance of text to a grid cell. If a place reference only falls within one grid cell at a given scale, then the surrounding text should be weighted highly for that grid cell and less so for other grid cells that are covered by other larger area references in the same section. Figure 4 illustrates how the assignment of geoboosts is made with a simple example using three place references: New York State, New York City, and Lincoln Center. By tying the geoboost value to the number of grid cells matching the area of the place at a specific level, we automatically take into account the geographic scale at which the user is conducting the information retrieval task. For example, when using a coarse-grained grid (i.e., searching a zoomed out map) then text which references administrative regions, cities, and other areal spatial units will be as important as references to individual points of interest. When zoomed in and using a finer-grained grid, text associated with point of interest features will contribute more to a grid cell.

As is common for information retrieval in networked document collections, a relative importance weight for the entire document can also be calculated using HITS, PageRank, or similar algorithms [23, 30, 26]. In order to differentiate from the geoboost, we refer to the document weight in the network as the *docboost*. Combining these two values gives us an *composite boost value* for an individual word that has been mapped to a grid cell, equal to $docboost^m * geoboost^n$ where m and n are exponential scaling factors used to increase or decrease the relative weight of docboost versus geoboost. Finally, we can create a *grid document* that aggregates all the words with their boost values in all the sections that have place references intersecting with the cell. The *grid document* is a summary of all the content written about that grid area in such a way that text is considered to matter more or less depending on the scale of place references and importance of the document. The advantage of this approach is that the resulting *grid document* has the same form as a single document, and thus can serve as input into a number of compatible information retrieval indexing algorithms [26].

3.2.2 Probabilistic index

We can anticipate spatial heterogeneity in terms of the distribution of source material. That is, certain places (such as London, UK in the English Wikipedia) will have orders of magnitude more words indexed against them than other places that are represented in the source material. In our experiments, the distribution of word counts for grid documents tends to follow a log normal distribution (see Figure 5). For ranking this creates a problem similar to the case of matching a query against a corpus with documents of widely differing lengths, so it is necessary that document length normalization take this into account.

Although the grid document can serve as input into any indexing algorithm, because the grid documents are themselves aggregate documents, we need a model of information retrieval that captures the informative content of terms with respect to the structure of the documents and overall corpus. This is better handled by probabilistic models of information retrieval than by standard TF/IDF related measures [31, 3, 26]. Divergence-from-randomness (DFR) is one such model incorporated in the Terrier IR platform that uses the Bose-Einstein distribution as the model to test the divergence of word mentions from that expected from a random document [3]. In Frankenplace we use the slightly simpler information model derivative of DFR as described in

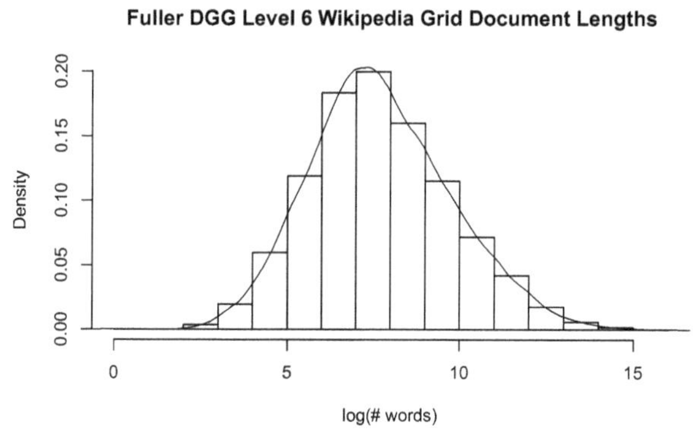

Figure 5: Log plot of word counts for the English Wikipedia grid documents for the Fuller level 6 discrete global grid.

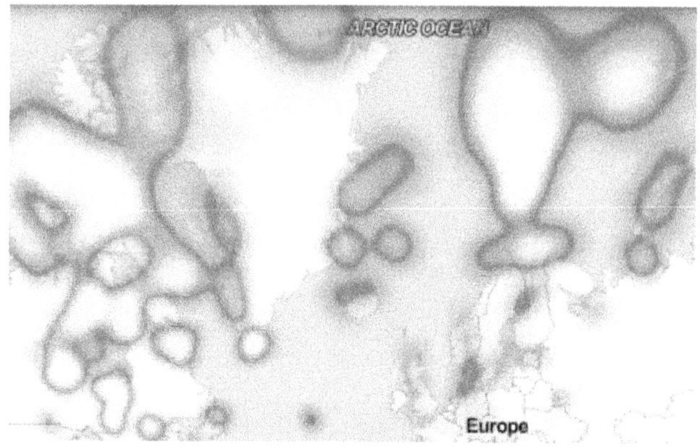

Figure 6: Heatmap that demonstrates the increasing bandwidth of the kernel density approaching latitudes farther north. (*polar bear* search)

[9], with word counts adjusted in incorporate the *composite boost values*.

3.3 Indexing individual documents

We are interested not only in searching for grid cells that match a query but also want to find the top documents that both match a grid cell and the query terms. This is necessary in order to make a fully ad hoc document search engine, otherwise we are left with matching the query only at the aggregate level. The solution is to build a parallel index for all the documents, faceted by grid cell, so that queries can be filtered to match a single or set of grid cells. As for the grid cell index, we boost the terms in the individual document by geoboost and docboost. However, we also want an additional damping effect to take into account cases where not all words in the document are associated with the grid cell (as will be the case in most partial place references). This damping factor, d, is the ratio shown in Equation 2.

$$d = \frac{\#\ words\ in\ the\ matching\ sections}{total\ number\ of\ words\ in\ the\ document} \tag{2}$$

4. BUILDING A THEMATIC MAP EXPLORATORY SEARCH ENGINE

In this section we describe the design of an interactive map search interface once indices have been created for grid cell documents (at multiple zoom levels) as well as for individual documents. A thematic map can be viewed as a specific type of information visualization, and from a user interface design and engineering perspective, building a thematic map keyword-based web search is more challenging than a traditional top-N search result page. The design choices are complex, because the manner in which ranking scores are visually rendered on the interactive map will have a bearing on user interpretation.

When a user submits a query, there are two related types of search results that need to be rendered. The first is a global view of the results that shows what grid cells on the Earth best match the query. This global view is a map of the search results over geographic space. The second result provides a localized view of the results by showing the top documents for the query faceted by the grid cell that is currently selected by the user. These two related results should be consistent with one another, but they have different purposes. The first search (the global map) is a ranking of *places* that match the query, and the second search is a ranking of *documents*.

A highly ranked grid cell should correspond in some way to a good match for the query based on an aggregation of documents for that cell, but it is not necessary that a highly scored grid cell (i.e., place) means there should necessarily be many document results. For example, a single document with high *geoboost* and *docboost* that ranks very highly for a given query (e.g., many instances of the query term in the document) should be reflected in a higher ranking score for the grid cell that the document falls within, whereas a grid cell that has many documents that match the query but which are all very low on *geoboost* and *docboost* might correspond to a grid cell with very low score. The overall boosts that have been attached to terms in the index are designed to handle these cases.

4.1 Map visualization

One option is to render the search scores for the grid cells using a choropleth map[6], so that scores are mapped to an ordinal range of colors. Care must be taken to use a color scheme that accurately renders the relative scores of cells in a manner that is cognitively valid [6]. One solution is to use relatively small number of color classes (7 or fewer) that cluster the scores via a method such as Jenks natural breaks [21]. However, one drawback of the choropleth map is that the grid cells are arbitrarily discrete and convey a degree of certainty in the result that may be unmerited, and changing the grid can create very different results (because of the modifiable areal unit problem) [11].

With this in mind, we instead use a two-dimensional kernel density function with a bandwidth based on zoom level to generate a smooth surface of the search results over the map (i.e., a heat map) [38]. The input to the kernel density function is a set of points corresponding to the centroids of the grid cells, with count values set to the respective search score. In order to calculate the kernel density efficiently on the client-side of the application, a simple radial-symmetric triangular kernel is used [34]. An additional challenge is

[6]A map with regions that are colored or shaded to represent an associated attribute value.

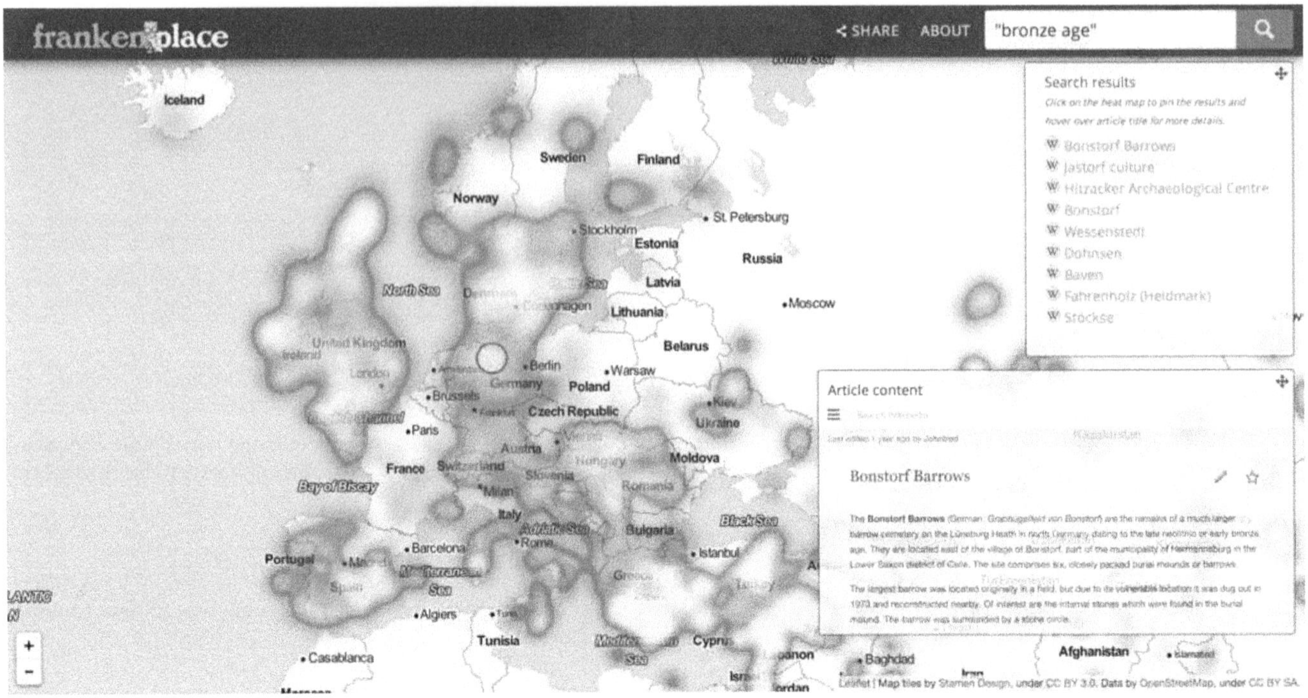

Figure 7: Search result for *bronze age* using Frankenplace. This screenshot shows the global result as a heat map over Europe, and the local result pinned to an area of northern Germany (red circle). The top documents for the local result are shown in a window on the right side of the screen, and a preview of one selected document is shown at the bottom.

presented when generating a heat map in the standard web Mercator projection from data that is based on an equal area grid, because the centroids of the grid cells are farther apart in the projected space as one gets closer to the poles.

Our solution is to vary the bandwidth, h, in the kernel density function based on a bandwidth scale factor equal to the secant of the latitude (Equation 3).

$$h' = h \cdot \sec(\phi) \tag{3}$$

This creates an *approximation* of a heat map generated in an equal area space and then projected to web mercator. Figure 6 shows an example of a heat map that significantly increases in bandwidth as it approaches the north polar region.

The visualization and user interface shown in Figure 7 is built on open source mapping software (`http://leafletjs.com/`) and uses HTML5 SVG. The heat map creates a visual overlay on the map but the interaction events are handled by creating a transparent SVG div of the original grid cell polygons overlaying the map. This way, click and mouseover events can be quickly mapped to grid cell identifiers that are used to facet search on the individual document index.

4.2 Exploring by geography and theme

We have established a means to geographically explore the results of a query, but to better enable exploratory search we also need a means to move through the thematic space as well. Probabilistic topic modeling provides a data-driven way to discover the topics in a large corpus of documents, where topics are multinomial distributions over words in the corpus. Latent Dirichlet allocation (LDA) is the simplest and most commonly used generative Bayesian probabilistic topic model [5]. As a pre-processing step during the index building, we run a variant of LDA with β hyper parameter estimation on the Wikipedia corpus to get a fixed number of topics [41]. In addition, this gives us a distribution over topics (i.e., a topic vector) for each document in the corpus. This topic vector is stored in the index as an array associated with each document identifier, so that it can be retrieved at query time.

When a search is made to match documents for a grid cell, the topic vectors are returned along with the ranking score. An aggregate topic vector is calculated at query time equal to the weighted sum of all the vectors from the top n matching documents, where the weight is set to the score from the search algorithm. Let $\mathbf{t}_i$ be the topic vector for document i and s_i be the search score. The aggregate topic vector $\mathbf{a}$ is calculated in Equation 4.

$$\mathbf{a} = \sum_{i}^{n} s_i \mathbf{t}_i \tag{4}$$

By selecting the topics with highest probabilities in $\mathbf{a}$, we can identify important related topics as defined by the original search query and the geography of the grid cell. The most common words from these contextually-related topics are then used as suggestions for new searches in the application. Figure 8 demonstrates this with two different results for the query *civil war* for locations in the United States and England, with very different suggested searches. The grid cell in the United States has related searches *confederate army* and *union troops*, whereas the grid cell in England has *anglo saxon* and *oliver cromwell*. Because data-driven topic models are used, rather than a hierarchical category structure that is pre-built from a global perspective, the se-

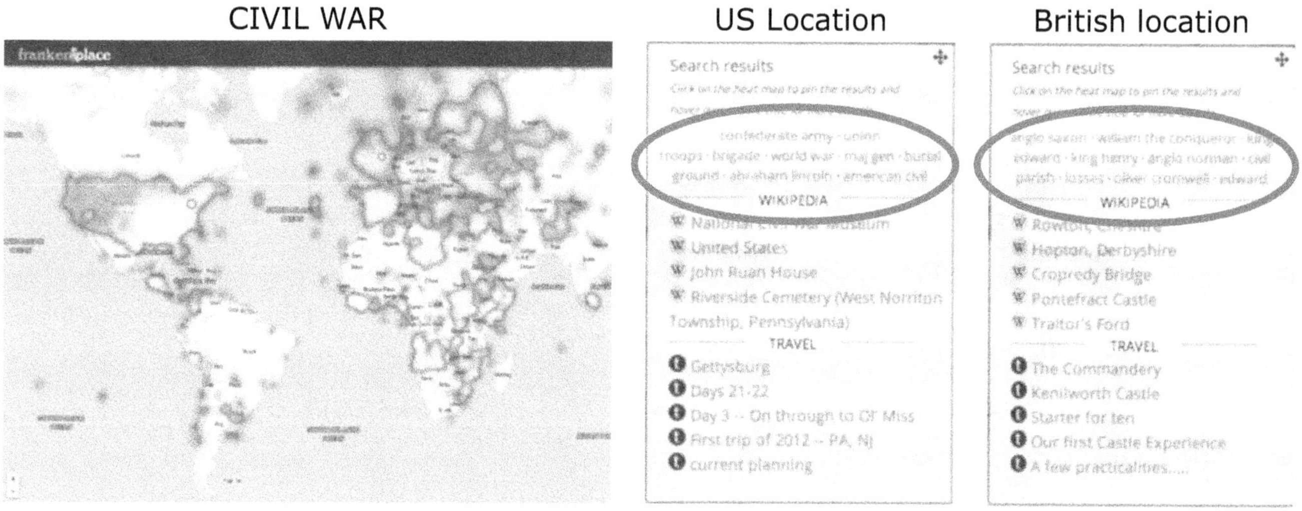

Figure 8: This figure shows how related documents and suggested searches reflect the intersection of geography and the user provided query. The search results, including suggestions for new searches, for the query *"civil war"* are shown for two locations in Pennsylvania, USA and England.

mantic heterogeneity of search terms based on geography is better captured.

With the addition of the related topics into the index the user now has the ability to do exploratory search, zooming in and out in scope both geographically and thematically. This completes the loop in Figure 2, enabling the system to not only work for user-prompted information retrieval but also providing a recommender system to further explore the corpus through the orthogonal lenses of geography and thematic topics.

5. EVALUATION

A live version of the Frankenplace system is available online, which has allowed us to do preliminary observation of exploratory search behavior with the system in the wild. Server logs from 1,697 users give us insight into the kinds of queries that users are performing and how they interact with the system. On average individual users made requests for multiple query plus geographic bounding box combinations per session (mean: 11.4, median: 7). These users searched 4,982 unique terms covering a broad range of topics. Figure 9 shows a sample of the range of query topics, including people, geographic feature types, historical eras and trends. A non-exhaustive taxonomy of search tasks that users perform with the system are listed below.

1. Geographic search of a topic. The interactive thematic map can be used to explore search results via hierarchical geographic facets: by interpreting the overall heat map, zooming in and out, panning from one location to another, and moving the mouse over grid cells to examine the search results at different locations. The search logs indicate that users are performing all of these actions with the system. The number of grid cells the user examines to view search results is mean 26.7, median 13, which indicates that on average users are examining search results over a range of geographic areas. Figure 10 shows the trajectory of mouse movements made by a sample user who is geographically-refining a query for *ski*. Examining users' geographic foci of attention for different queries is potentially a rich source of data for user modeling and predictive analytics.

2. Thematic zooming and panning based on geography. In this case a user begins with a broad topic such as *history* or *civil war* and uses the interactive map to suggest related searches that are geographically contextualized. This allows the user to zoom in the query thematically. In addition, associations based on the intersection of a narrow topic and geography enables thematic zooming out (or horizontal thematic stepping) as well.

3. Comparing corpora. By comparing the maps from different corpora for the same search, it is possible to uncover interesting differences in how a topic is covered by a community. Frankenplace enables this in the current version with a slider that adjusts the weighting of the 2 corpora in the heat map visualization. For example, in Figure 11 it shows how *archaeology* in the context of tourism is most dominant in travel blog entries about Greece, but in Wikipedia there are entries all over the world, including many places where people do not travel and visit archaeological sites.

4. Searching for related places When a user does a search for a place name, as expected from the first law of geography, nearby places are also highlighted on the map [40]. However, connections to other places far away in physical space can also be discovered, reflecting the important relational and networked aspects of places [15]. As an example, Figure 12 demonstrates references to London in articles georeferenced in Italy.

6. RELATED WORK

Although the top-N search result page is the most prevalent way of presenting document-based information retrieval results, there have been a number of research studies looking at alternative approaches to visualizing search results. An early system called Envision visualized various characteristics of the results, including the categories that the document falls within [29]. Schneiderman et al. [33] highlighted the limitations of presenting search results in a top-N list and proposed a system of hierarchical axes, called hieraxes,

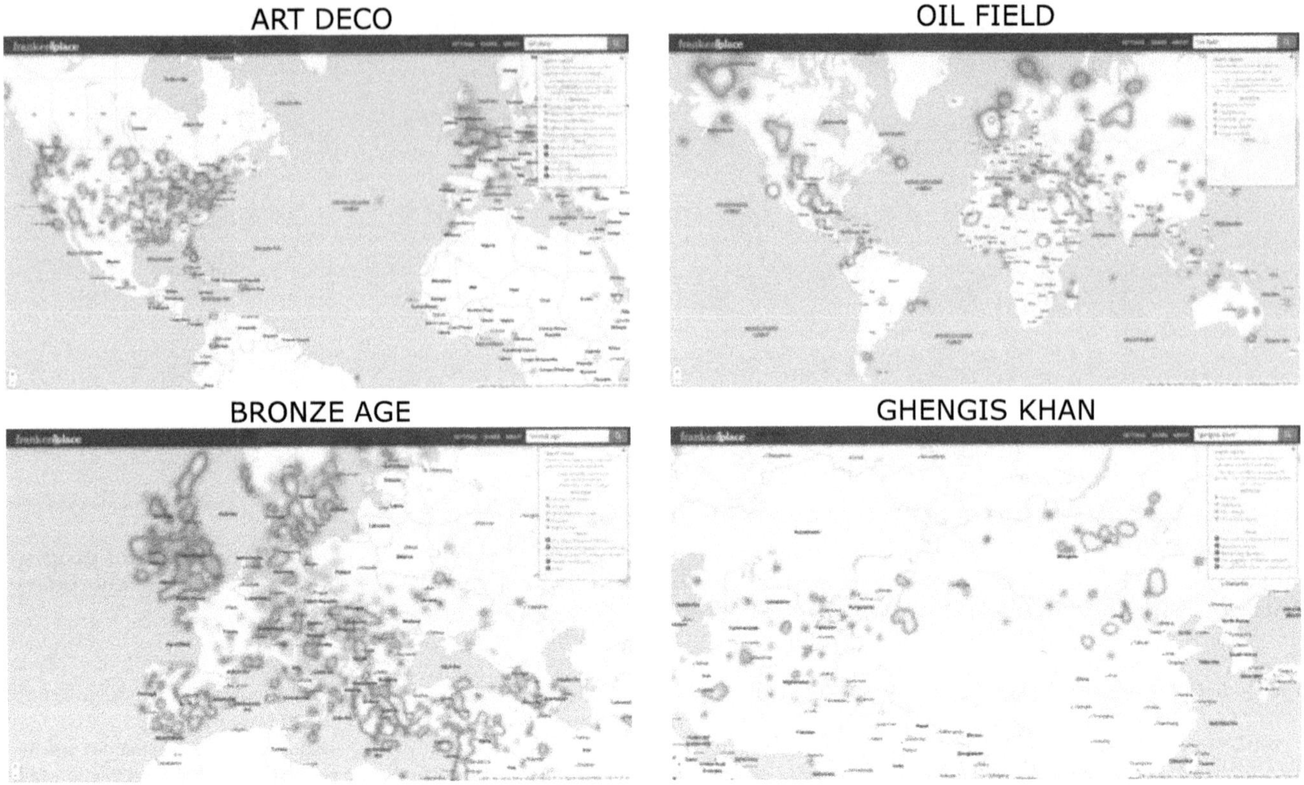

Figure 9: Example searches that users have made.

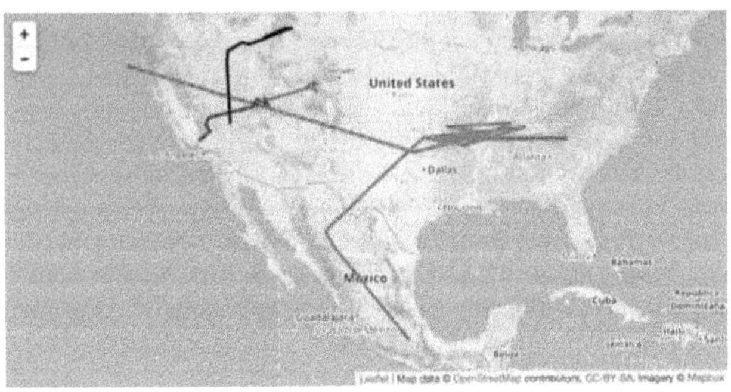

Figure 10: Trajectory of grid cells that the user's mouse passed over while searching for the query *ski*. The red line is map zoom level 3 and shows the user exploring from Mexico with detailed interest in the Ozarks in the southern US (an area not generally well known for skiing) and then the west. The blue, green, and black lines show successive zooming to levels 4, 5, and 6 respectively, as the user focuses the search on the Rocky Mountains.

to organize information along two-dimensional axes based on user-defined variables while also letting users zoom in and out based on hierarchical categories. Chen and Dumais [7] suggested the use of support vector machines to automatically hierarchically categorize search results for better presentation. More recently, data driven visualizations of search results based on topic modeling have become popular [28, 18].

Exploratory search differs from the standard lookup model in information retrieval [42]. Whereas the lookup task is concerned with one-time retrieval of facts or information objects such as web pages, the goal of exploratory search is to learn and investigate using systems that support the tasks of knowledge acquisition, synthesis, and discovery [27]. In other words, the goal of exploratory search is to assist human learning, and search tasks are more integrated with browsing activities in an iterative manner, because the results of the information retrieval task lead to new queries [42]. An empirical user study of people doing exploratory search tasks using faceted search interfaces showed that the facets are important informational cues to users [24].

The notion of using space and time dimensions to organize document collections has been advanced in previous work. An early map-based interface for exploring document collections based on historical events was proposed as part of the Perseus Digital Library project [35]. Tezuka, et al. [39] argued that better integration of web search systems with the data models and analytical methods from geographic information systems will enable new search result presentation methods and facilitate knowledge discovery through geographic aggregation. The use of spatialization to enhance exploratory search is the basis for the Atlasify system, which uses a number of spatial layouts (including periodic tables and congressional seating charts) to contextualize search results [19].

7. CONCLUSIONS AND FUTURE WORK

In this paper we presented an innovative system for exploratory search at the intersection geography and theme.

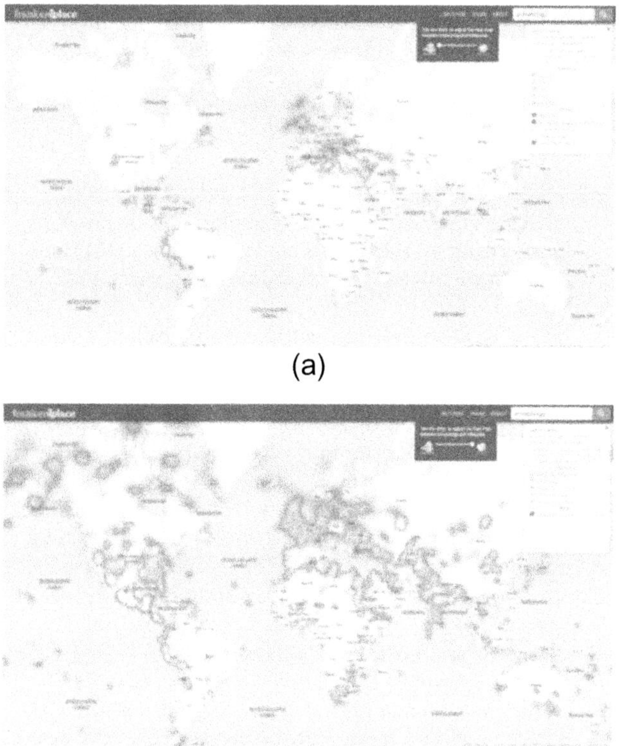

Figure 11: Maps for *archaeology* for (a) travel blog entries and (b) Wikipedia.

We described a novel approach to indexing using a discrete global grid and term boosting that is geographic scale-dependent. We introduced Frankenplace, a prototype thematic map ad hoc search engine for exploratory search, that utilizes this indexing method on two corpora, and demonstrated how, using topic modeling, it can be used to explore information by zooming in and out both geographically and thematically. As the system continues to be developed, adding new content and features (such as temporal faceting) while adding new users, we anticipate being able to investigate a host of research related to exploratory search with thematic maps. With Frankenplace, we demonstrated we can support four distinct types of exploratory search tasks while being adaptive to both scale and location of interest, and since the index is emergent rather than using formally defined semantics it can easily be extended to new corpora. Our next steps in system development will be to add temporal faceting and an API that will enable users to index and search their own data sets.

Moving forward, combining map-based visualization with ad hoc information retrieval creates many interesting research questions at the intersection of spatial cognition and information seeking behavior. Can we develop appropriate cognitive models of information retrieval tasks given a thematic map interface? What roles do background geographic knowledge and visual interpretation of search results play in how people interpret search results and interact with the system for exploratory search? Extensive research on the cognitive modeling of map understanding can inform the visualizations and interaction paradigms of future iterations. Any

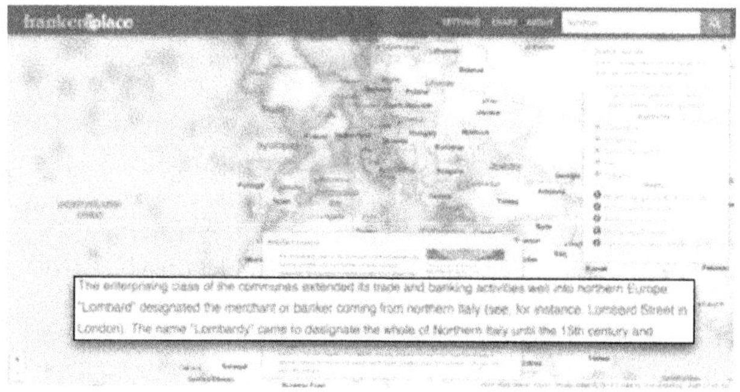

Figure 12: This figure shows places with connections with *London*. In this case demonstrating the globalization of northern Italy during the Renaissance.

map-based visualization of search results will undoubtedly lead to interpretations about the places themselves, but as has been well established for decades, comparisons of places based on aggregate measures are prone to problems such as the ecological fallacy [14]. Thus, there is the question of how to reconcile the opaqueness (to the user) of the indexing process in a modern information retrieval system–including the design choices for spatial and temporal organization–with the common tendency to view thematic maps as some kind of "truth" about the places represented.

8. REFERENCES

[1] B. Adams and K. Janowicz. On the geo-indicativeness of non-georeferenced text. In *ICWSM*, pages 375–378. The AAAI Press, 2012.

[2] B. Adams and G. McKenzie. Frankenplace: An application for similarity-based place search. In *ICWSM*, pages 616–617. The AAAI Press, 2012.

[3] G. Amati and C. J. Van Rijsbergen. Probabilistic models of information retrieval based on measuring the divergence from randomness. *ACM Transactions on Information Systems (TOIS)*, 20(4):357–389, 2002.

[4] L. Backstrom, J. Kleinberg, R. Kumar, and J. Novak. Spatial variation in search engine queries. In *WWW*, pages 357–366. ACM, 2008.

[5] D. M. Blei, A. Y. Ng, and M. I. Jordan. Latent dirichlet allocation. *Journal of Machine Learning Research*, 3(4/5):993–1022, 2003.

[6] C. A. Brewer and L. Pickle. Evaluation of methods for classifying epidemiological data on choropleth maps in series. *Annals of the Association of American Geographers*, 92(4):662–681, 2002.

[7] H. Chen and S. Dumais. Bringing order to the web: Automatically categorizing search results. In *SIGCHI*, pages 145–152. ACM, 2000.

[8] Y.-Y. Chen, T. Suel, and A. Markowetz. Efficient query processing in geographic web search engines. In *SIGMOD*, pages 277–288. ACM, 2006.

[9] S. Clinchant and E. Gaussier. Information-based models for ad hoc IR. In *SIGIR*, pages 234–241. ACM, 2010.

[10] G. Cong, C. S. Jensen, and D. Wu. Efficient retrieval of the top-k most relevant spatial web objects. *Proceedings of the VLDB Endowment*, 2(1):337–348, 2009.

[11] A. S. Fotheringham and D. W. Wong. The modifiable areal unit problem in multivariate statistical analysis. *Environment and planning A*, 23(7):1025–1044, 1991.

[12] M. F. Goodchild, H. Guo, A. Annoni, L. Bian, K. de Bie, F. Campbell, M. Craglia, M. Ehlers, J. van Genderen, D. Jackson, A. J. Lewis, M. Pesaresi, G. Remetey-Fülöpp, R. Simpson, A. Skidmore, C. Wang, and P. Woodgate. Next-generation digital earth. *PNAS*, 109(28):11088–11094, 2012.

[13] K. M. Gorski, E. Hivon, A. Banday, B. D. Wandelt, F. K. Hansen, M. Reinecke, and M. Bartelmann. HEALPix: A framework for high-resolution discretization and fast analysis of data distributed on the sphere. *The Astrophysical Journal*, 622(2):759, 2005.

[14] C. A. Gotway and L. J. Young. Combining incompatible spatial data. *Journal of the American Statistical Association*, 97(458):632–648, 2002.

[15] S. Graham and P. Healey. Relational concepts of space and place: Issues for planning theory and practice. *European Planning Studies*, 7(5):623–646, 1999.

[16] L. Gravano, V. Hatzivassiloglou, and R. Lichtenstein. Categorizing web queries according to geographical locality. In *CIKM*, pages 325–333. ACM, 2003.

[17] R. W. Gray. Exact transformation equations for Fuller's world map. *Cartographica*, 32(3):17–25, 1995.

[18] B. Gretarsson, J. O'Donovan, S. Bostandjiev, T. Höllerer, A. Asuncion, D. Newman, and P. Smyth. Topicnets: Visual analysis of large text corpora with topic modeling. *ACM Transactions on Intelligent Systems and Technology (TIST)*, 3(2):23, 2012.

[19] B. Hecht, S. H. Carton, M. Quaderi, J. Schöning, M. Raubal, D. Gergle, and D. Downey. Explanatory semantic relatedness and explicit spatialization for exploratory search. In *SIGIR*, pages 415–424. ACM, 2012.

[20] B. Hecht and M. Raubal. GeoSR: Geographically explore semantic relations in world knowledge. In L. Bernard, A. Friis-Christensen, and H. Pundt, editors, *The European Information Society*, pages 95–113. Springer Berlin Heidelberg, 2008.

[21] G. F. Jenks. The data model concept in statistical mapping. *International Yearbook of Cartography*, 7(1):186–190, 1967.

[22] C. Keßler, K. Janowicz, and M. Bishr. An agenda for the next generation gazetteer: Geographic information contribution and retrieval. In *SIGSPATIAL*, pages 91–100. ACM, 2009.

[23] J. M. Kleinberg. Authoritative sources in a hyperlinked environment. *Journal of the ACM*, 46(5):604–632, 1999.

[24] B. Kules, R. Capra, M. Banta, and T. Sierra. What do exploratory searchers look at in a faceted search interface? In *JCDL*, pages 313–322, New York, NY, USA, 2009. ACM.

[25] J. Lehmann, R. Isele, M. Jakob, A. Jentzsch, D. Kontokostas, P. N. Mendes, S. Hellmann, M. Morsey, P. van Kleef, S. Auer, and C. Bizer. DBpedia - A large-scale, multilingual knowledge base extracted from wikipedia. *Semantic Web Journal*, 2014.

[26] C. D. Manning, H. Schütze, and P. Raghavan. *Introduction to Information Retrieval.* Cambridge University Press, Cambridge, UK, 2008.

[27] G. Marchionini. Exploratory search: from finding to understanding. *Communications of the ACM*, 49(4):41–46, 2006.

[28] D. Newman, T. Baldwin, L. Cavedon, E. Huang, S. Karimi, D. Martinez, F. Scholer, and J. Zobel. Visualizing search results and document collections using topic maps. *Web Semantics*, 8(2):169–175, 2010.

[29] L. T. Nowell, R. K. France, D. Hix, L. S. Heath, and E. A. Fox. Visualizing search results: Some alternatives to query-document similarity. In *SIGIR*, pages 67–75. ACM, 1996.

[30] L. Page, S. Brin, R. Motwani, and T. Winograd. The pagerank citation ranking: Bringing order to the web. Technical Report 1999-66, Stanford InfoLab, 1999.

[31] J. M. Ponte and W. B. Croft. A language modeling approach to information retrieval. In *SIGIR*, pages 275–281. ACM, 1998.

[32] K. Sahr, D. White, and A. J. Kimerling. Geodesic discrete global grid systems. *Cartography and Geographic Information Science*, 30(2):121–134, 2003.

[33] B. Shneiderman, D. Feldman, A. Rose, and X. F. Grau. Visualizing digital library search results with categorical and hierarchical axes. In *ACM DL*, pages 57–66. ACM, 2000.

[34] B. W. Silverman. *Density estimation: for statistics and data analysis. Monographs on Statistics and Applied Probability 26.* Chapman and Hall/CRC, 1986.

[35] D. A. Smith. Detecting and browsing events in unstructured text. In *SIGIR*, pages 73–80. ACM, 2002.

[36] J. P. Snyder. An equal-area map projection for polyhedral globes. *Cartographica*, 29(1):10–21, 1992.

[37] H. Southall, R. Mostern, and M. L. Berman. On historical gazetteers. *International Journal of Humanities and Arts Computing*, 5(2):127–145, 2011.

[38] G. R. Terrell and D. W. Scott. Variable kernel density estimation. *The Annals of Statistics*, 20(3):1236–1265, 1992.

[39] T. Tezuka, T. Kurashima, and K. Tanaka. Toward tighter integration of web search with a geographic information system. In *WWW*, pages 277–286. ACM, 2006.

[40] W. Tobler. A computer movie simulating urban growth in the Detroit region. *Economic Geography*, 46(Supplement):234–240, Jun 1970.

[41] H. Wallach, D. Mimno, and A. McCallum. Rethinking LDA: Why priors matter. In *NIPS*, pages 1973–1981, 2009.

[42] R. W. White and R. A. Roth. Exploratory search: Beyond the query-response paradigm. *Synthesis Lectures on Information Concepts, Retrieval, and Services*, 1(1):1–98, 2009.

[43] B. Wing and J. Baldridge. Simple supervised document geolocation with geodesic grids. In *ACL*, pages 955–964. ACL, 2011.

[44] Y. Zhou, X. Xie, C. Wang, Y. Gong, and W.-Y. Ma. Hybrid index structures for location-based web search. In *CIKM*, pages 155–162, New York, NY, USA, 2005. ACM.

Towards Reconciling SPARQL and Certain Answers

Shqiponja Ahmetaj
TU Vienna
ahmetaj@dbai.tuwien.ac.at

Wolfgang Fischl
TU Vienna
wfischl@dbai.tuwien.ac.at

Reinhard Pichler
TU Vienna
pichler@dbai.tuwien.ac.at

Mantas Šimkus
TU Vienna
simkus@dbai.tuwien.ac.at

Sebastian Skritek
TU Vienna
skritek@dbai.tuwien.ac.at

ABSTRACT

SPARQL entailment regimes are strongly influenced by the big body of works on ontology-based query answering, notably in the area of Description Logics (DLs). However, the semantics of query answering under SPARQL entailment regimes is defined in a more naive and much less expressive way than the certain answer semantics usually adopted in DLs. The goal of this work is to introduce an intuitive certain answer semantics also for SPARQL and to show the feasibility of this approach. For OWL 2 QL entailment, we present algorithms for the evaluation of an interesting fragment of SPARQL (the so-called well-designed SPARQL). Moreover, we show that the complexity of the most fundamental query analysis tasks (such as query containment and equivalence testing) is not negatively affected by the presence of OWL 2 QL entailment under the proposed semantics.

Categories and Subject Descriptors

H.2.3 [**Database Management**]: Languages—*Query Languages*; H.2.5 [**Database Management**]: Heterogeneous Databases

General Terms

Theory, Algorithms

Keywords

SPARQL; Certain Answers; DL-Lite; Query Answering; Query Rewriting; Complexity

1. INTRODUCTION

In the recently released recommendation [12], the W3C has defined various SPARQL entailment regimes to allow users to specify implicit knowledge about the vocabulary in an RDF graph (see [10] for a tutorial). The theoretical underpinning to the systems for query answering under rich entailment regimes (see e.g.[16, 6, 30]) is provided by the big body of work on ontology-based query answering, notably in the area of Description Logics (DLs) [3]. Superficially, query answering of basic graph patterns (BGPs) under an entailment regime looks exactly like answering conjunctive queries (CQs) under the corresponding DL. However, there is a huge difference between the two in that SPARQL entailment regimes do not consider non-distinguished variables:

Example 1. Consider an RDF graph G containing a single triple $(b, \mathsf{a}, \mathsf{Prof})$ – stating that b is a professor – and an ontology $\mathcal{O}$ containing a single concept inclusion stating that every professor teaches somebody. In our notation introduced in Section 2, this inclusion will be denoted as $(\mathsf{Prof}, \texttt{rdfs:sc}, \exists\mathsf{teaches})$.
Now consider the following simple SPARQL query:

$\text{SELECT } ?x \text{ WHERE } (?x, \mathsf{teaches}, ?y)$.[1]

According to the SPARQL entailment regimes standard [12], this query yields as result the empty set.

Clearly, the empty set as the result in the above example is rather unintuitive: by the inclusion $(\mathsf{Prof}, \texttt{rdfs:sc}, \exists\mathsf{teaches})$, we know for certain that b teaches somebody. However, the SPARQL entailment standard requires that all values assigned to any variable in the BGP must come from the RDF graph – thus treating distinguished variables (which are ultimately output) and non-distinguished variables (which are eventually projected out) in the same way. In contrast, query answering in the DL world is based on the *certain answer semantics*. We thus consider the models of the database (i.e., the RDF graph) and the ontology and we accept all those mappings as solutions that make the query true in every possible model. In the above example, every such model contains a triple $(b, \mathsf{teaches}, u)$ for some value u. Hence, even though there are distinct values u in different models, the projection onto the first component always yields the mapping $\mu = \{?x \to b\}$ as an answer to the query.

Depending on the expressive power of a particular DL, query answering under the certain answer semantics may be computationally very expensive. E.g. the problem is often 2EXPTIME-complete for the so-called *very expressive DLs* [21, 11]. However, there exists a family of DLs with reasonable expressive power and very nice computational properties, namely the DL-Lite family [7]. A member of this family is DL-Lite$_\mathcal{R}$, which provides the theoretical underpinning of the OWL 2 QL entailment regime. Recall that – even without taking any DLs into account – answering CQs as well as basic query analysis tasks like testing containment or equivalence are NP-complete [8]. Somehow surprisingly, this complexity does not increase if we consider CQ answering and CQ containment/equivalence under DL-Lite [7]. In other words, the significant increase of expressive power has no serious effect on the complexity. The **goal of this work** is to introduce an intuitive certain answer semantics also for SPARQL under OWL 2 QL entailment with similarly favourable results as for CQ answering under DL-Lite.

[1]Following [25], we use a more algebraic style notation, denoting triples in parentheses with comma-separated components rather than the blank-separated turtle notation.

WWW 2015, May 18–22, 2015, Florence, Italy.
ACM 978-1-4503-3469-3/15/05.
http://dx.doi.org/10.1145/2736277.2741636.

If we were contented with evaluating BGPs under OWL 2 QL according to the certain answer semantics, we could literally take over all results on CQ answering under DL-Lite. But of course, there are more facets to SPARQL than just BGPs. A crucial extension of BGPs is given by the OPTIONAL operator (henceforth referred to as OPT operator, for short). It allows one to express that a mapping should mandatorily bind some of the variables in the query and, if possible, it should be extended to further variables. If the extension is impossible, we simply keep the unextended mapping – but we do not dismiss it.

The OPT operator has an enormous impact on the complexity of query evaluation: indeed, even if SPARQL is restricted to the use of conjunction and the OPT operator, query evaluation is PSPACE-complete [29]. In [25], the authors therefore introduced *well-designed SPARQL* as an interesting fragment where certain restrictions on the occurrence of variables are imposed. It is shown in [25] that for well-designed SPARQL, the complexity of query evaluation drops from PSPACE-completeness to coNP-completeness. Moreover, as shown in [19], well-designed SPARQL queries have a very nice and intuitive representation by so-called *pattern trees*, i.e.: rooted, unordered trees where the nodes are labelled with BGPs and the tree structure reflects the nesting of OPTs (for details on well-designed SPARQL and pattern trees, see Section 2).

Recall that the natural definition of certain answers to a query is to collect all those mappings that are a solution in all possible models of the data and the ontology. As long as we restrict ourselves to answering conjunctive queries, this notion of certain answers is intuitive and constitutes the generally agreed semantics. In contrast, as soon as we extend CQs by the OPT operator, this approach turns out to be highly unsatisfactory, as the following example illustrates.

Example 2. Consider the SPARQL query:

$$\text{SELECT } ?x, ?z \text{ WHERE } (?x, \mathsf{teaches}, ?y) \\ \text{OPT } (?y, \mathsf{knows}, ?z)$$

over the graph $G = \{(b, \mathsf{teaches}, c)\}$ and empty ontology $\mathcal{O}$. The query yields as only solution the mapping $\mu = \{?x \rightarrow b\}$. Clearly, also the graph $G' = G \cup \{(c, \mathsf{knows}, d)\}$ is a model of $(G, \mathcal{O})$. But in G', μ is no longer a solution since μ can be extended to solution $\mu' = \{?x \rightarrow b, ?z \rightarrow d\}$. Hence, there exists no mapping which is a solution in every possible model of $(G, \mathcal{O})$.

The reason for the unintuitive behaviour in the above example is the non-monotonicity of the OPT operator. However, as observed in [2], even if well-designed SPARQL is non-monotone, at least it is *weakly monotone* in the following sense: if a model M' extends a model M by introducing additional facts, then every solution of a well-designed SPARQL query Q in M *can be extended* to a solution of Q in M'. Hence, the key idea for an appropriate definition of certain answers of well-designed SPARQL under OWL 2 QL entailment will be to consider those mappings as certain which can be extended to a solution in all possible models of the RDF graph and the ontology. Actually, yet a further modification of the semantics definition will be required in order to arrive at a uniquely defined, intuitive semantics without resorting to bag semantics. The details are worked out in Section 3.

The special behaviour of the OPT operator and the modification of the certain answer semantics require an adaptation and extension of the CQ answering algorithms for DL-Lite. Moreover, also the complexity of query evaluation and of containment/equivalence testing for well-designed SPARQL requires a new analysis in the presence of OWL 2 QL entailment. We shall show that, analogously to CQ answering under DL-Lite, the additional expressive power due to OWL 2 QL entailment can be obtained without paying a price in terms of complexity.

Organization and main results. In Section 2, we recall some basic notions and results. A conclusion and outlook to future work are given in Section 8. Our main results are detailed in Sections 3 – 7:

- In Section 3, we discuss the difficulties with a literal adoption of certain answer semantics in the presence of the non-monotone OPT operator. To overcome these difficulties, we propose a modified definition of certain answers for well-designed SPARQL queries. By relating the resulting semantics to SPARQL evaluation without entailment regimes we illustrate the naturalness of our definition.
- Several adaptations and extensions of the rewriting-based CQ evaluation under DL-Lite [7] are needed in order to incorporate the OPT operator. In Sections 4 and 5, we present two different approaches to answering well-designed SPARQL queries under OWL 2 QL entailment: the first one proceeds in a modular way by rewriting each BGP individually. A new data structure – so-called guides – has to be introduced to ensure the consistency of local solutions for each BGP when combining them to a solution of the overall SPARQL query. Our second algorithm takes a holistic approach by rewriting the entire well-designed SPARQL query at once. The CQ-rewriting under DL-Lite has to be significantly extended to take the peculiarities of the OPT operator into account. The two algorithms are discussed in Section 6.
- In Section 7, we analyse the complexity of well-designed SPARQL evaluation under OWL 2 QL entailment as well as the complexity of basic query analysis tasks such as query containment and query equivalence. We show that – analogously to CQs under DL-Lite – the complexity remains essentially the same no matter whether we consider well-designed SPARQL with or without OWL 2 QL entailment.

Due to space limitations, we only give proof ideas of our results. All details will be provided in the full version of the paper.

2. PRELIMINARIES

RDF graphs and OWL 2 QL. We let $\mathbf{U}$ denote a countably infinite set of *URIs*. An *RDF triple* t is any tuple $t \in \mathbf{U} \times \mathbf{U} \times \mathbf{U}$. An *RDF graph* G is any (possibly infinite) set $G \subseteq \mathbf{U} \times \mathbf{U} \times \mathbf{U}$ of triples. Note that we do not allow blank nodes, i.e. all RDF triples and graphs are *ground*. The *active domain* of an RDF graph G, denoted $\mathsf{dom}(G)$, is the set of all URIs that appear in G.

We next define *membership and inclusion triples*, which are special triples to enrich RDF graphs with OWL 2 QL or RDFS semantic information. Let $\mathbf{C}$, $\mathbf{A}$ and $\mathbf{R}$ be countably infinite and mutually disjoint subsets of $\mathbf{U}$ that denote *constants*, *atomic concepts* (a.k.a. *classes*) and *atomic roles* (a.k.a. *properties*), respectively. A *basic role* Q is either an atomic role from $\mathbf{R}$ or an expression R^-, where $R \in \mathbf{R}$. A *basic concept* B is either an atomic concept $A \in \mathbf{A}$ or an expression $\exists Q$, where Q is a basic role.

We further assume the dedicated URIs [2]

- "a" to assert membership of a constant in a concept,
- "`rdfs:sc`" to assert the inclusion relation between concepts,
- "`rdfs:sp`" to assert the inclusion relation between roles,
- "`owl:disjointWith`" to assert *concept disjointness*, and
- "`owl:propertyDisjointWith`" to assert *role disjointness*.

[2]For the special RDF property `rdf:type` we use the common abbreviation "a". For the RDFS properties `rdfs:subClassOf` and `rdfs:subPropertyOf` we use the abbreviations "`rdfs:sc`" and "`rdfs:sp`", resp.

A *membership assertion* (*MA*) is any triple of the form (c, a, B) or (c, Q, c'), where c, c' are constants from $\mathbf{C}$, B is a basic concept and Q is a basic role. For a role R, we simplify $(R^-)^-$ to R. Given an RDF graph G, we write

- $G \models (c, Q, c')$ if $(c, Q, c') \in G$ or $(c', Q^-, c) \in G$,
- $G \models (c, \mathsf{a}, A)$ if $(c, \mathsf{a}, A) \in G$, and
- $G \models (c, \mathsf{a}, \exists Q)$ if $G \models (c, Q, c')$ for some c'.

We define the notion of *inclusions*. An *RDFS inclusion* is any triple having the form $(B, \texttt{rdfs:sc}, A)$ or $(Q_1, \texttt{rdfs:sp}, Q_2)$, where B is a basic concept, A is an atomic concept, and Q_1, Q_2 are basic roles. An *OWL 2 QL inclusion* is any RDFS inclusion or a triple of the form (i) $(B_1, \texttt{rdfs:sc}, B_2)$, (ii) $(B_1, \texttt{owl:disjointWith}, B_2)$ or (iii) $(Q_1, \texttt{owl:propertyDisjointWith}, Q_2)$, where B_1, B_2 are basic concepts and Q_1, Q_2 are basic roles. Given an RDF graph G, we write

- $G \models (B_1, \texttt{rdfs:sc}, B_2)$ if $G \models (a, \mathsf{a}, B_1)$ implies $G \models (a, \mathsf{a}, B_2)$ for any URI a,
- $G \models (Q_1, \texttt{rdfs:sp}, Q_2)$ if $G \models (a, Q_1, b)$ implies $G \models (a, Q_2, b)$ for any pair a, b of URIs,
- $G \models (B_1, \texttt{owl:disjointWith}, B_2)$ if $G \models (a, \mathsf{a}, B_1)$ implies $G \not\models (a, \mathsf{a}, B_2)$ for any URI a, and
- $G \models (Q_1, \texttt{owl:propertyDisjointWith}, Q_2)$ if $G \models (a, Q_1, b)$ implies $G \not\models (a, Q_2, b)$ for any pair a, b of URIs.

Concepts $\exists Q$ in triples $(B, \texttt{rdfs:sc}, \exists Q)$ are to simplify presentation; we can write $(\exists Q, \texttt{rdfs:sc}, A)$, $(\exists Q^-, \texttt{rdfs:sc}, A)$ instead of $(Q, \texttt{rdfs:domain}, A)$, $(Q, \texttt{rdfs:range}, A)$, respectively. The role R^- is a convenient representation of the role r_1, where $(r_1, \texttt{owl:inverseOf}, R)$. Similar, triples of the form $(B, \texttt{rdfs:sc}, \exists Q)$ represent the following OWL 2 triples:

$$(B, \texttt{rdfs:sc}, c_1), (c_1, \mathsf{a}, \texttt{owl:Restriction}),$$
$$(c_1, \texttt{owl:onProperty}, Q),$$
$$(c_1, \texttt{owl:someValuesFrom}, \texttt{owl:Thing}).$$

An *OWL 2 QL ontology* (resp., *RDFS ontology*) $\mathcal{O}$ is any set of OWL 2 QL (resp., RDFS) inclusions. W.l.o.g. we assume $(Q_1^-, \texttt{rdfs:sp}, Q_2^-) \in \mathcal{O}$ for each $(Q_1, \texttt{rdfs:sp}, Q_2) \in \mathcal{O}$. Given a graph G and an ontology $\mathcal{O}$, we write $G \models \mathcal{O}$ if $G \models \sigma$ for all $\sigma \in \mathcal{O}$. A *knowledge base* (KB) is any pair $\mathcal{G} = (G, \mathcal{O})$, where G is a graph and $\mathcal{O}$ is an ontology. Let $\mathcal{G} = (G, \mathcal{O})$ be a KB. Given a graph G', we say G' is a *model* of $\mathcal{G}$, denoted by $G' \models \mathcal{G}$ if $G \subseteq G'$ and $G' \models \mathcal{O}$. We say $\mathcal{G}$ is *consistent* if there exists a model G', s.t. $G' \models \mathcal{G}$. Finally, for an RDF triple t, we say $\mathcal{G} \models t$ if $G' \models t$ for every $G' \models \mathcal{G}$. Analogously, $\mathcal{O} \models t$ if $G' \models t$ for every $G' \models \mathcal{O}$.

SPARQL. Let $\mathbf{V}$ be an infinite set of variables, s.t. $\mathbf{U} \cap \mathbf{V} = \emptyset$. We denote variables with a leading question mark, e.g. $?x$. A SPARQL triple pattern t is a tuple in $(\mathbf{U} \cup \mathbf{V}) \times (\mathbf{U} \cup \mathbf{V}) \times (\mathbf{U} \cup \mathbf{V})$. Throughout this paper we will consider only triple patterns of the form $(?x, \mathsf{a}, B)$ or $(?x, Q, ?y)$, where B is a basic concept and Q a basic role.[3]

The set of SPARQL graph patterns is defined recursively as follows: (1) a triple pattern t is a graph pattern ; (2) if P_1 and P_2 are graph patterns, then $(P_1 \text{ UNION } P_2)$, $(P_1 \text{ AND } P_2)$, $(P_1 \text{ OPT } P_2)$ are graph patterns. Note that we follow the algebraic style notation from [25], where an explicit AND operator is used. For a graph pattern P, we write $\mathsf{vars}(P)$, to denote the set of variables occurring in P.

In order to define the semantics of SPARQL graph patterns, we first introduce some additional terminology. A *substitution* is any partial function σ from $\mathbf{V}$ to $\mathbf{U} \cup \mathbf{V}$. We use $\mathsf{dom}(\sigma)$ and $\mathsf{rng}(\sigma)$ to denote the domain and the range of σ, respectively. Given a triple pattern t and a substitution σ, we use $\sigma(t)$ to denote the triple obtained from t by replacing every variable $?x \in \mathsf{vars}(t) \cap \mathsf{dom}(\sigma)$ by $\sigma(?x)$. A *(SPARQL) mapping* is any partial function μ from $\mathbf{V}$ to $\mathbf{U}$. Note that mappings are substitutions. Two mappings μ_1 and μ_2 are *compatible* (written $\mu_1 \sim \mu_2$) if $\mu_1(?x) = \mu_2(?x)$ for all $?x \in \mathsf{dom}(\mu_1) \cap \mathsf{dom}(\mu_2)$. A mapping μ_1 is *subsumed* by μ_2 (written $\mu_1 \sqsubseteq \mu_2$) if $\mu_1 \sim \mu_2$ and $\mathsf{dom}(\mu_1) \subseteq \mathsf{dom}(\mu_2)$. We write $\mu_1 \sqsubset \mu_2$ if $\mu_1 \sqsubseteq \mu_2$ and $\mu_2 \not\sqsubseteq \mu_1$. For a mapping μ and sets M, M' of mappings, we say $\mu \sqsubseteq M$ if $\mu \sqsubseteq \mu'$ for some $\mu' \in M$, and $M' \sqsubseteq M$ if $\mu \sqsubseteq M$ for every $\mu \in M'$.

We formalize the evaluation of graph patterns over an RDF graph G as a function $[\![\cdot]\!]_G$ that, given a graph pattern, returns a set of mappings. For a graph pattern P, it is defined as follows [25]:

1. $[\![t]\!]_G = \{\mu \mid \mathsf{dom}(\mu) = \mathsf{vars}(t) \text{ and } \mu(t) \in G\}$ for a triple pattern t.
2. $[\![P_1 \text{ AND } P_2]\!]_G = \{\mu_1 \cup \mu_2 \mid \mu_1 \in [\![P_1]\!]_G, \mu_2 \in [\![P_2]\!]_G, \text{ and } \mu_1 \sim \mu_2\}$.
3. $[\![P_1 \text{ OPT } P_2]\!]_G = [\![P_1 \text{ AND } P_2]\!]_G \cup \{\mu_1 \in [\![P_1]\!]_G \mid \forall \mu_2 \in [\![P_2]\!]_G : \mu_1 \nsim \mu_2\}$.
4. $[\![P_1 \text{ UNION } P_2]\!]_G = [\![P_1]\!]_G \cup [\![P_2]\!]_G$.

A *basic graph pattern (BGP)* is a set of triple patterns $P = \{t_1, \ldots, t_n\}$ – equivalently written as t_1 AND ... AND t_n. Hence, we have $[\![P]\!]_G = \{\mu \mid \mathsf{dom}(\mu) = \mathsf{vars}(P), \text{ and } \mu(t) \in G \text{ for all } t \in P\}$. Note that, as in [25] and in the vast majority of works on query answering in DLs, we assume set semantics. In this paper we focus on *well-designed* SPARQL graph patterns. A graph pattern P, built only from AND and OPT is well-designed if there does not exist a subpattern $P' = (P_1 \text{ OPT } P_2)$ of P and a variable $?x \in \mathsf{vars}(P_2)$ that occurs in P outside of P', but not in P_1. A graph pattern $P = P_1 \text{ UNION } \ldots \text{ UNION } P_n$ is well-designed if each subpattern P_i is UNION free and well-designed.

Pattern trees. Another class of graph patterns defined in [25] are graph patterns in OPT *normal form*. A pattern containing only the operators AND and OPT is in OPT normal form if the OPT operator never occurs in the scope of an AND operator. It was shown that every well-designed graph pattern can be transformed into OPT normal form in polynomial time. Moreover, such graph patterns allow for a natural tree representation, formalized by so-called *pattern trees* in [19]. A *pattern tree (PT)* $\mathcal{T}$ is a pair $(T, \mathcal{P})$, where $T = (V, E, r)$ is a rooted, unordered, tree and $\mathcal{P} = \{P_n \mid n \in V\}$ is a labelling of the nodes in V, s.t. P_n is a non-empty set of triple patterns for every $n \in V$. Given $\mathcal{T}$, we write $V(\mathcal{T})$ to denote the set V of vertices. The next example illustrates this idea.

Example 3. The following SPARQL graph pattern asks for all professors $?x$ and, if available, their email address $?w$. Independently of the available information on the email address $?w$, the pattern also tries to retrieve all professors $?y$ that $?x$ knows.

$$((?x, \mathsf{a}, \mathsf{Prof}) \text{ OPT } (?x, \mathsf{email}, ?w))$$
$$\text{OPT } ((?x, \mathsf{knows}, ?y) \text{ AND } (?y, \mathsf{a}, \mathsf{Prof}))$$

The corresponding pattern tree looks as follows:

[3]Constants in place of $?x$ and $?y$ can be simulated by using fresh variables and auxiliary triples in queries and input RDF graphs.

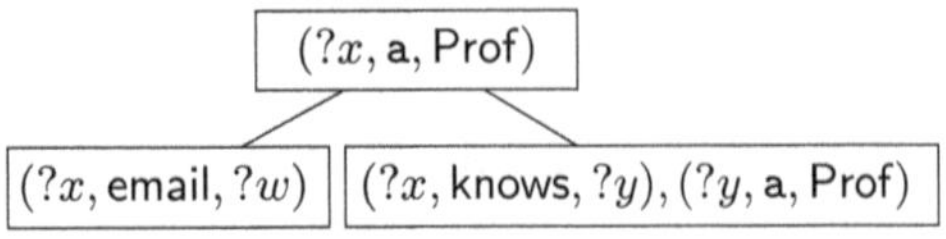

Let $\mathcal{T} = ((V, E, r), \mathcal{P})$ be a pattern tree. We call a PT $\mathcal{T}' = ((V', E', r'), \{P_n \mid n \in V'(\mathcal{T}')\})$ a *subtree of* $\mathcal{T}$ if (V', E', r') is a subtree of (V, E, r). Throughout this article we only consider subtrees containing the root (i.e. $r = r'$), and will thus refer to them simply as "subtrees", omitting the phrase "containing the root". For a PT $\mathcal{T} = (T, \mathcal{P})$, we denote with $\mathsf{pat}(\mathcal{T})$ the set $\bigcup_{n \in V(\mathcal{T})} P_n$ of triple patterns occurring in $\mathcal{T}$. We write $\mathsf{vars}(\mathcal{T})$ (resp. $\mathsf{vars}(n)$ for $n \in V(\mathcal{T})$) as an abbreviation for $\mathsf{vars}(\mathsf{pat}(\mathcal{T}))$ (resp. $\mathsf{vars}(\mathsf{pat}(n))$).

A *well-designed pattern tree (wdPT)* is a pattern tree $\mathcal{T} = (T, \mathcal{P})$ where for every variable $?x \in \mathsf{vars}(\mathcal{T})$, the nodes $\{n \in V(\mathcal{T}) \mid ?x \in \mathsf{vars}(n)\}$ induce a connected subgraph of T.

Recall that wdPTs are a *representation* of well-designed SPARQL graph patterns. Also, for every wdPT $\mathcal{T}$, there exists a straight forward translation into a well-designed graph pattern $P_{\mathcal{T}}$ in OPT normal form. Moreover, all well-designed graph patterns represented by $\mathcal{T}$ are equivalent to $P_{\mathcal{T}}$ (see [19] for details). For some RDF graph G, we thus define $[\![\mathcal{T}]\!]_G = [\![P_{\mathcal{T}}]\!]_G$.

Projection. Projection in SPARQL is realized via the SELECT result modifier on top of graph patterns (or equivalently of pattern trees). For a mapping μ and a set $\mathcal{X}$ of variables, let $\mu|_{\mathcal{X}}$ denote the projection of μ to the variables in $\mathcal{X}$, that is, the mapping μ' defined as $\mathsf{dom}(\mu') := \mathcal{X} \cap \mathsf{dom}(\mu)$ and $\mu'(?x) := \mu(?x)$ for all $?x \in \mathsf{dom}(\mu')$. We extend projection to a set M of mappings as $M|_{\mathcal{X}} = \{\mu|_{\mathcal{X}} \mid \mu \in M\}$. The result of projecting a graph pattern P to $\mathcal{X}$ is defined as $[\![(P, \mathcal{X})]\!]_G = \{\mu|_{\mathcal{X}} \mid \mu \in [\![P]\!]_G\}$. Analogously, we define $[\![(\mathcal{T}, \mathcal{X})]\!]_G = \{\mu|_{\mathcal{X}} \mid \mu \in [\![\mathcal{T}]\!]_G\}$ for a wdPT $\mathcal{T}$. We refer to the pair $(\mathcal{T}, \mathcal{X})$ as a *projected wdPT (pwdPT)*.

3. CERTAIN ANSWER SEMANTICS

In this section, we propose an intuitive definition of certain answers for well-designed SPARQL queries or, more precisely, for pwdPTs. Moreover, we shall establish the relationship of these certain answers with the canonical model – an important tool in the DL world. A natural first idea (inspired by investigations in [2] on the relationship between the official SPARQL semantics and the open world assumption for RDF data) was already mentioned in Section 1, namely: rather than requesting that certain answers must be a solution in every possible model, at least one should be able to extend certain answers to a solution in every possible model. However, this idea alone still does not yield a satisfactory result as the following example shows.

Example 4. Consider the following query

SELECT $?x, ?z$ WHERE $(?x, \mathsf{teaches}, ?y)$
OPT $(?y, \mathsf{knows}, ?z)$

over the graph $G = \{(a, \mathsf{teaches}, b), (b, \mathsf{knows}, c), (a, \mathsf{teaches}, d)\}$ and empty ontology $\mathcal{O}$. As possible models of $(G, \mathcal{O})$ we have all supergraphs of G. Hence, $\mu = \{?x \rightarrow a, ?z \rightarrow c\}$ is a certain answer and so is $\mu' = \{?x \rightarrow a\}$ ($?y$ is bound to d).

Now let $G' = \{(a, \mathsf{teaches}, b), (b, \mathsf{knows}, c)\}$. If we take as certain answers all mappings that can be extended to some solution in every possible model, then μ' is still a certain answer.

The problem in the above example is that SPARQL queries with projection and/or the UNION operator may have "subsumed" solutions, i.e., solutions such that also a proper extension is a solution. But then – with set semantics – we cannot recognize the reason why some subsumed solution (such as μ' in the above example) is possibly not a solution in some possible model: Note that in the above example, there are models for G in which μ' is not a solution, e.g., in the model $G'' = G \cup \{(d, \mathsf{knows}, c)\}$. In this model, μ is the only solution – with multiplicity 2 though.

In our first step towards reconciling SPARQL and certain answers, we decide to stick to *set semantics* in order to be able to build upon the broad DL-literature. Indeed, apart from very few exceptions (such as [18]), there hardly exist any works on query answering in DLs under *bag semantics*.

A key idea in our definition of certain answers is to only allow "maximal" solutions. For a mapping μ and some property A, we shall say that μ is *$\sqsubseteq$-maximal w.r.t. A* if μ satisfies A, and there is no μ' such that $\mu \sqsubset \mu'$ and μ' satisfies A.

Definition 1. Let $\mathcal{G} = (G, \mathcal{O})$ be a KB and $(\mathcal{T}, \mathcal{X})$ a pwdPT. A mapping μ is a *certain answer* to $(\mathcal{T}, \mathcal{X})$ over $\mathcal{G}$ if it is a $\sqsubseteq$-maximal mapping such that (1) $\mu \sqsubseteq [\![(\mathcal{T}, \mathcal{X})]\!]_{G'}$ for every model G' of $\mathcal{G}$, and (2) $\mathsf{vars}(\mathcal{T}') \cap \mathcal{X} = \mathsf{dom}(\mu)$ for some subtree $\mathcal{T}'$ of $\mathcal{T}$. We denote by $\mathsf{cert}(\mathcal{T}, \mathcal{X}, \mathcal{G})$ the set of all certain answers to $(\mathcal{T}, \mathcal{X})$ over $\mathcal{G}$.

Hence, in Example 2, only μ is a certain answer over graph G, while the subsumed solution μ' is dismissed.

The above definition ensures an important property of solutions to pwdPTs, namely: the domain of every solution must correspond to the free variables of some subtree in the pwdPT. However, for the design of algorithms to actually compute the certain answers for some entailment regime, it will turn out convenient if, in the first place, we do not need to check this condition. This leads to the following definition of *certain pre-answers* for pwdPT.

Definition 2. Let $\mathcal{G} = (G, \mathcal{O})$ be a KB and $(\mathcal{T}, \mathcal{X})$ a pwdPT. A mapping μ is a *certain pre-answer* to $(\mathcal{T}, \mathcal{X})$ over $\mathcal{G}$ if μ is a $\sqsubseteq$-maximal mapping such that $\mu \sqsubseteq [\![(\mathcal{T}, \mathcal{X})]\!]_{G'}$ for every model G' of $\mathcal{G}$. We denote by $\mathsf{certp}(\mathcal{T}, \mathcal{X}, \mathcal{G})$ the set of all certain pre-answers to $(\mathcal{T}, \mathcal{X})$ over $\mathcal{G}$.

We note that models of a KB $\mathcal{G} = (G, \mathcal{O})$ are invariant under renaming of URIs that do not occur in G. Hence, certain pre-answers and certain answers have mappings only to constants in $\mathsf{dom}(G)$. The following example shows the difference between them. In Theorem 1 below, we shall then establish their precise relationship.

Example 5. Consider the following query

SELECT $?x, ?y, ?z$ WHERE $(?x, \mathsf{a}, \mathsf{Prof})$
OPT $((?x, \mathsf{teaches}, ?y)$ AND $(?x, \mathsf{knows}, ?z))$

and the following KB: $G = \{(a, \mathsf{a}, \mathsf{Prof}), (a, \mathsf{knows}, c)\}$ and $\mathcal{O} = \{(\mathsf{Prof}, \texttt{rdfs:sc}, \exists\mathsf{teaches})\}$. The mapping $\mu = \{?x \rightarrow a, ?z \rightarrow c\}$ is the certain pre-answer, whereas $\mu' = \{?x \rightarrow a\}$ is the certain answer.

THEOREM 1. *Let $\mathcal{G}$ be a KB and $(\mathcal{T}, \mathcal{X})$ a pwdPT. Then $\mu \in \mathsf{cert}(\mathcal{T}, \mathcal{X}, \mathcal{G})$ iff μ is a $\sqsubseteq$-maximal mapping such that:*

(1) $\mu \sqsubseteq \mathsf{certp}(\mathcal{T}, \mathcal{X}, \mathcal{G})$, and

(2) $\mathsf{vars}(\mathcal{T}') \cap \mathcal{X} = \mathsf{dom}(\mu)$ for some subtree $\mathcal{T}'$ of $\mathcal{T}$.

PROOF SKETCH. '$\Rightarrow$' Let $\mu \in \mathsf{cert}(\mathcal{T}, \mathcal{X}, \mathcal{G})$. Since, $\mu \sqsubseteq [\![(\mathcal{T}, \mathcal{X})]\!]_{G'}$ for every graph $G' \models \mathcal{G}$, $\mu \sqsubseteq \mathsf{certp}(\mathcal{T}, \mathcal{X}, \mathcal{G})$. The mapping μ is $\sqsubseteq$-maximal trivially from Definition 1. '$\Leftarrow$' Let μ be $\sqsubseteq$-maximal and satisfying (1) and (2) We prove Definition 1 condition (1): Since $\mu \sqsubseteq \mathsf{certp}(\mathcal{T}, \mathcal{X}, \mathcal{G})$, $\mu \sqsubseteq [\![(\mathcal{T}, \mathcal{X})]\!]_{G'}$ for every $G' \models \mathcal{G}$; condition (2): Follows from the $\sqsubseteq$-maximality of μ w.r.t. to (1) and (2). $\square$

By the above theorem, the set of certain answers of some pwdPT can be easily computed from the set of certain pre-answers by retaining only those mappings that bind all free variables of some subtree. Hence, in the rest of the paper, we shall focus on certain pre-answers. The computation of the certain answers is then a simple post-processing step.

As a further simplification in our algorithms, we shall also ignore for a while the distinction between distinguished and non-distinguished variables. Indeed, it is easy to see that to compute the certain pre-answers of a pwdPT $(\mathcal{T}, \mathcal{X})$, it suffices to first compute the certain pre-answers of $\mathcal{T}$ (without projection, i.e. $\mathcal{X} = \mathsf{vars}(\mathcal{T})$) and then to project over $\mathcal{X}$ as shown in the following proposition.

PROPOSITION 1. *Let $\mathcal{G}$ be a KB and $(\mathcal{T}, \mathcal{X})$ a pwdPT. Then $\mu \in \mathsf{certp}(\mathcal{T}, \mathcal{X}, \mathcal{G})$ iff μ is a $\sqsubseteq$-maximal mapping s.t. (1) $\mu \sqsubseteq \mathsf{certp}(\mathcal{T}, \mathcal{G})$, and (2) $\mathsf{dom}(\mu) \subseteq \mathcal{X}$.*

Thus, from now on, we consider only certain *pre-answers* for well-designed pattern trees *without projection*.

In many Description Logics, the *canonical model* provides the basis for actually computing the certain answers for CQs or unions of CQs. Since our ontology is a variant of the DL *DL-Lite*$_\mathcal{R}$, we will also employ canonical models, which we define similarly to [5]. The canonical model of a consistent KB $\mathcal{G} = (G, \mathcal{O})$ is a graph G' that can be homomorphically mapped (preserving the constants occurring G) into any other model G'' of $\mathcal{G}$. From now on, we assume $\mathcal{G}$ is consistent.

In addition to the URIs in $\mathbf{C}$, we introduce a new set of URIs $\mathbf{A}_\mathcal{G} \subseteq \mathbf{U}$ with $\mathbf{A}_\mathcal{G} \cap \mathbf{C} = \emptyset$. The URIs in $\mathbf{A}_\mathcal{G}$ have the following form: $aQ_1Q_2 \dots Q_n$, where $n \geq 1$, $a \in \mathsf{dom}(G)$ and $Q_1, \dots, Q_n$ are basic roles. The set $\mathbf{A}_\mathcal{G}$ consists of those URIs which satisfy (1) $\mathcal{G} \models (a, \mathsf{a}, \exists Q_1)$; (2) for every $i \in \{1, \dots, n-1\}$, $\mathcal{O} \models (\exists Q_i^-, \mathtt{rdfs:sc}, \exists Q_{i+1})$ and $Q_i^- \neq Q_{i+1}$. We denote by $\mathsf{tail}(u)$ the last role in a URI $u \in \mathbf{A}_\mathcal{G}$, and define $\mathsf{can}_\mathcal{O}(G)$ for basic roles Q, Q' and a basic concept B:

$$G \cup \tag{1}$$

$$\{(a, \mathsf{a}, B) \mid \mathcal{G} \models (a, \mathsf{a}, B)\} \cup \tag{2}$$

$$\{(a, Q, b) \mid \mathcal{G} \models (a, Q, b)\} \cup \tag{3}$$

$$\{(u, \mathsf{a}, B) \mid u \in \mathbf{A}_\mathcal{G}, \mathcal{O} \models (\exists \mathsf{tail}(u)^-, \mathtt{rdfs:sc}, B)\} \cup \tag{4}$$

$$\{(u_1, Q, u_2) \mid u_2 \in \mathbf{A}_\mathcal{G}, u_2 = u_1Q', \mathcal{O} \models (Q', \mathtt{rdfs:sp}, Q)\} \cup \tag{5}$$

$$\{(u_2, Q, u_1) \mid u_2 \in \mathbf{A}_\mathcal{G}, u_2 = u_1Q', \mathcal{O} \models (Q', \mathtt{rdfs:sp}, Q^-)\} \tag{6}$$

We denote by $\mathsf{comp}_\mathcal{O}(G)$ the triples obtained from the union of Equations (1)-(3). Notice that $\mathsf{comp}_\mathcal{O}(G) = \mathsf{can}_{\mathcal{O}_{RDFS}}(G)$, where $\mathcal{O}_{RDFS}$ is the set of all RDFS inclusions σ, s.t. $\mathcal{O} \models \sigma$ (for a similar result see [9] or [27]). We will write $\mathsf{can}(G)$ (resp., $\mathsf{comp}(G)$) instead of $\mathsf{can}_\mathcal{O}(G)$ (resp., $\mathsf{comp}_\mathcal{O}(G)$) if $\mathcal{O}$ is clear from the context. Note that $\mathsf{can}(G)$ can be infinite in size. The following well-known result from databases and DLs can be shown for $\mathsf{can}(G)$ (see e.g. the proof of Theorem 2 in [24]).

PROPOSITION 2. *Let $\mathcal{G} = (G, \mathcal{O})$ be a KB. Then*

(a) $\mathsf{can}(G) \models \mathcal{G}$, and

(b) for any G', s.t. $G' \models \mathcal{G}$, there is a homomorphism h from $\mathsf{can}(G)$ to G' s.t. for every $a \in \mathsf{dom}(G)$, $\mathsf{h}(a) = a$.

In Theorem 2, we shall establish the relationship between certain pre-answers to wdPTs and the canonical model. To this end, we first introduce the following useful definition.

Definition 3. For a mapping μ, we let $\mu\!\downarrow = \mu|_{\{?x \mid \mu(?x) \in \mathbf{C}\}}$, i.e. $\mu\!\downarrow$ is the restriction of μ to mappings into constants. Assume a set M of mappings. Then $M\!\downarrow = \{\mu\!\downarrow \mid \mu \in M\}$.

Moreover, $\mathrm{MAX}(M) = \{\mu \in M \mid \nexists \mu' \in M \text{ s.t. } \mu \sqsubset \mu'\}$, i.e. $\mathrm{MAX}(M)$ is the set of $\sqsubseteq$-maximal mappings in M.

THEOREM 2. *Let $\mathcal{G} = (G, \mathcal{O})$ be a KB and $\mathcal{T}$ a wdPT. Then, $\mathsf{certp}(\mathcal{T}, \mathcal{G}) = \mathrm{MAX}([\![\mathcal{T}]\!]_{\mathsf{can}(G)}\!\downarrow)$.*

PROOF SKETCH. It suffices to prove $\mathsf{certp}(\mathcal{T}, \mathcal{G}) \sqsubseteq [\![\mathcal{T}]\!]_{\mathsf{can}(G)}\!\downarrow$, and $\mathsf{certp}(\mathcal{T}, \mathcal{G}) \sqsupseteq [\![\mathcal{T}]\!]_{\mathsf{can}(G)}\!\downarrow$. For '$\sqsubseteq$' let μ be a mapping in $\mathsf{certp}(\mathcal{T}, \mathcal{G})$. Then, μ is subsumed by an answer of $\mathcal{T}$ in every model. Hence, also by an answer μ' in $\mathsf{can}(G)$. Since, μ only maps variables to constants in $\mathsf{dom}(G)$, μ is still subsumed by $\mu'\!\downarrow$. For '$\sqsupseteq$' let μ be a mapping in $[\![\mathcal{T}]\!]_{\mathsf{can}(G)}\!\downarrow$. By Proposition 2, μ can be homomorphically mapped into every model of $\mathcal{G}$, hence μ is part of a solution in every model, i.e. also maximal solutions. □

4. MODULAR QUERY REWRITING

In this section we provide our first method to compute certain answers to well-designed pattern trees under OWL 2 QL entailment. In particular, we present a *query rewriting* procedure to compute $\mathsf{certp}(\mathcal{T}, \mathcal{G})$ for a given wdPT $\mathcal{T}$ and a KB $\mathcal{G} = (G, \mathcal{O})$. To this end, we extend the well-known query reformulation algorithm of Calvanese et al. for answering *conjunctive queries (CQs)* over DL knowledge bases $K = (T, A)$, where T is a DL-Lite TBox and A is an ABox [7]. The algorithm of Calvanese et al. transforms a CQ q and a TBox T into a union Q of CQs such that, given any ABox A, computing the certain answers to q over $K = (T, A)$ is equivalent to evaluating Q over A, where A is seen as a plain relational database.

In the presented approach, given a wdPT $\mathcal{T}$ and an ontology $\mathcal{O}$ we apply a rewriting at each node of $\mathcal{T}$, obtaining a tree $\mathcal{T}'$ of sets of BGPs. Roughly speaking, given any RDF graph G, computing $\mathsf{certp}(\mathcal{T}, \mathcal{G})$ then corresponds to evaluating $\mathcal{T}'$ in a bottom-up fashion over G. Since nodes of $\mathcal{T}$ are rewritten in isolation but may share variables, the rewriting involves some bookkeeping, which we describe next. In particular, $\mathcal{T}'$ will be expressed as an *enriched query*.

Definition 4. Let Paths be the set of all words of the form $?xQ_1 \dots Q_n$, where $Q_1, \dots, Q_n$ are basic roles with $n \geq 0$. Given a set of variables $L \subseteq \mathbf{V}$, an *L-guide* is a partial function γ from variables to words in Paths such that (a) $\mathsf{dom}(\gamma) \cap L = \emptyset$, and (b) for any $?x \in \mathsf{dom}(\gamma)$ with $\gamma(?x) = ?zQ_1 \dots Q_n$ we have that $?z \in L$. An *enriched BGP* is any tuple $\langle P, \gamma \rangle$, where P is a BGP and γ is a $\mathsf{vars}(P)$-guide. Expressions constructed from enriched BGPs by applying the AND, OPT and UNION connectives are called *enriched queries*. We use $E, E_1, E_2, \dots$ to denote enriched queries.

We are ready to define the standard semantics of enriched queries. Intuitively, the answer to an enriched BGP $\langle P, \gamma \rangle$ over a graph G is obtained by first evaluating P using the standard semantics and then extending the obtained mappings with additional assignments prescribed by γ, potentially introducing assignments to elements from $\mathbf{A}_\mathcal{G}$. The semantics is then generalized to full enriched queries using the standard operations on mappings.

Definition 5. Assume a mapping μ and a $\mathsf{dom}(\mu)$-guide γ. We let $\mathsf{expand}(\mu, \gamma) = \mu \cup \{?x \to \mu(?y)Q_1 \dots Q_n \mid \gamma(?x) = ?yQ_1 \dots Q_n\}$. Assume an RDF graph G. Then the evaluation of enriched queries is defined inductively as follows:

no	Triple t	Inclusion α	$\mathsf{gr}(t,\alpha)$
r1	$(?x, \mathtt{a}, A)$	$(A_1, \mathtt{rdfs:sc}, A)$	$\langle(?x, \mathtt{a}, A_1), \emptyset\rangle$
r2	$(?x, \mathtt{a}, A)$	$(\exists Q, \mathtt{rdfs:sc}, A)$	$\langle(?x, Q, ?x'), \emptyset\rangle$
r3	$(?x, Q, ?y)$	$(A, \mathtt{rdfs:sc}, \exists Q)$	$\langle(?x, \mathtt{a}, A), ?y \to ?xQ\rangle$
r4	$(?x, Q, ?y)$	$(\exists Q_1, \mathtt{rdfs:sc}, \exists Q)$	$\langle(?x, Q_1, ?x'), ?y \to ?xQ\rangle$
r5	$(?x, Q, ?y)$	$(Q', \mathtt{rdfs:sp}, Q)$	$\langle(?x, Q', ?y), \emptyset\rangle$

Table 1: The result $\mathsf{gr}(t,\alpha)$ of applying an inclusion α to a triple t. Here $?x'$ denotes a fresh variable.

- $[\![E]\!]_G = \{\mathsf{expand}(\mu,\gamma) \mid \mu \in [\![P]\!]_G\}$ in case $E = (P,\gamma)$ is an enriched BGP.
- $[\![E_1 \text{ AND } E_2]\!]_G = \{\mu_1 \cup \mu_2 \mid \mu_1 \in [\![E_1]\!]_G, \mu_2 \in [\![E_2]\!]_G$, and $\mu_1 \sim \mu_2\}$.
- $[\![E_1 \text{ OPT } E_2]\!]_G = [\![E_1 \text{ AND } E_2]\!]_G \cup \{\mu_1 \in [\![E_1]\!]_G \mid \forall \mu_2 \in [\![E_2]\!]_G : \mu_1 \nsim \mu_2\}$.
- $[\![E_1 \text{ UNION } E_2]\!]_G = [\![E_1]\!]_G \cup [\![E_2]\!]_G$.

Our rewriting procedure relies on the following "lifting" property of OWL 2 QL. For a guide γ, let $||\gamma||$ denote the maximum $|w|$ over all $w \in \mathsf{rng}(\gamma)$. Given a wdPT $\mathcal{T}$ and an ontology $\mathcal{O}$, we let $\mathsf{d}(\mathcal{T},\mathcal{O}) = 2k_1 + k_2$, where k_1 is the number of atomic roles occurring in $\mathcal{T}$ and $\mathcal{O}$, and k_2 is the number of triples in $\mathcal{T}$.

PROPOSITION 3. *Assume a wdPT $\mathcal{T}$, a KB $\mathcal{G} = (G,\mathcal{O})$, and a mapping $\mu \in [\![\mathcal{T}]\!]_{\mathsf{can}(G)}$. Then there exists a mapping $\mu' \in [\![\mathcal{T}]\!]_{\mathsf{can}(G)}$ such that (a) $\mu\!\downarrow = \mu'\!\downarrow$, and (b) $|w| \leq \mathsf{d}(\mathcal{T},\mathcal{O})$ for every $w \in \mathsf{rng}(\mu')$.*

Intuitively, the above says that any mapping μ for a wdPT $\mathcal{T}$ in the canonical model of $\mathcal{G}$ can be transformed into a mapping μ' that is confined to the first $\mathsf{d}(\mathcal{T},\mathcal{O})$ levels of the canonical model yet agrees with μ on the assignments to constants. The property follows from the well known fact that in each branch of the canonical model of $\mathcal{G}$ one finds only a small number of *types* (see e.g. [4]). We note that the above property does not hold in the presence of full OWL 2.

With the semantics and the desired properties of enriched queries established, we can describe the rewriting algorithm. The procedure exhaustively rewrites triples of an enriched BGP by applying inclusions "backwards". Assume a BGP P. We say an inclusion α is *applicable* to a triple t w.r.t. P if t and α have the following forms:

(i) $t = (?x, \mathtt{a}, A)$ and $\alpha = (B, \mathtt{rdfs:sc}, A)$;

(ii) $t = (?x, Q, ?y)$, where $?y$ does not appear in any other triple of P, and α has $\exists Q$ in the third position;

(iii) $t = (?x, Q, ?y)$, $?x$ does not appear in any other triple of P, and α has $\exists Q^-$ in the third position;

(iv) $t = (?x, Q, ?y)$ and $\alpha = (Q', \mathtt{rdfs:sp}, Q)$.

Let $\mathsf{App}(P)$ denote the binary relation such that $(t,\alpha) \in \mathsf{App}(P)$ iff an inclusion α is applicable to a triple t w.r.t. P.

In Algorithm 1 we present the rewriting routine RefBGP, which reformulates an input BGP P_0 by taking into account the inclusions of $\mathcal{O}$. It returns *pr*, which is a union of enriched BGPs. The procedure is parametrized by an integer k, which restricts the length of guide ranges and thus guarantees termination. As we shall see, Proposition 3 ensures that we do not lose completeness. The procedure employs the function $\mathsf{gr}(t,\alpha)$, which returns a tuple $\langle t',\gamma\rangle$, where t' is a triple and γ is a singleton guide, both obtained from t by applying α as described by Table 1. $P[t/t']$ denotes the BGP obtained from P by replacing the triple t with t'. Given a BGP P and a substitution σ, we let $\sigma(P) = \{\sigma(t) \mid t \in P\}$. A *unifier* of a pair t_1, t_2 of triples is a substitution σ such that $\sigma(t_1) = \sigma(t_2)$. We call σ a *most general unifier (MGU)* of t_1, t_2 if for any unifier σ' of t_1, t_2 there exists a unifier σ'' of t_1, t_2 such that $\sigma' = \sigma \circ \sigma''$.

Algorithm 1: RefBGP

input : a BGP P_0, an inclusion set $\mathcal{O}$, and an integer k
output : a set *pr* of enriched BGPs

$pr \leftarrow \{\langle P_0, \emptyset\rangle\}$
repeat
  $pr' \leftarrow pr$
  foreach $\langle P,\gamma\rangle \in pr'$ *s.t.* $||\gamma|| \leq k$ **do**
    foreach $t \in P$ *and* $\alpha \in \mathcal{O}$ *s.t.* $(t,\alpha) \in \mathsf{App}(P)$ **do**
      $\langle t',\gamma'\rangle \leftarrow \mathsf{gr}(t,\alpha)$
      $pr \leftarrow pr \cup \{\langle P[t/t'], \mathsf{expand}(\gamma',\gamma)\rangle\}$
    foreach *pair* t_1, t_2 *in* P *with a MGU* σ **do**
      $pr \leftarrow pr \cup \{\langle \sigma(P), \mathsf{expand}(\sigma,\gamma)\rangle\}$
until $pr' = pr$
return *pr*

Using an adaptation of the proof in [7], we can show that evaluating the output of RefBGP over a plain RDF graph corresponds to evaluating the original query over an initial segment of the canonical model. More formally:

PROPOSITION 4. *Let P be a BGP, $\mathcal{G} = (G,\mathcal{O})$ a KB, k an integer and pr the union of enriched BGPs returned by $\mathsf{RefBGP}(P,\mathcal{O},k)$. Then $([\![pr]\!]_G)|_{\mathsf{vars}(\mathcal{T})} = [\![P]\!]_{G'}$, where G' is the restriction of $\mathsf{can}(G)$ to URIs $a \in \mathbf{U}$ such that $|a| \leq k$.*

We can now generalize the rewriting from BGPs to full wdPTs. Given a wdPT $\mathcal{T}$ and an ontology $\mathcal{O}$, we simply apply RefBGP to the BGP of every node in $\mathcal{T}$.

Definition 6. Let $\mathcal{T}$ be a wdPT and $\mathcal{O}$ an ontology. Let $\mathsf{RefPT}(\mathcal{T},\mathcal{O})$ denote the enriched query obtained by replacing in $\mathcal{T}$ every BGP P by $\mathsf{RefBGP}(P,\mathcal{O},\mathsf{d}(\mathcal{T},\mathcal{O}))$.

We arrive at the main technical result of this section.

THEOREM 3. *Let $\mathcal{T}$ be a wdPT and $\mathcal{G} = (G,\mathcal{O})$ be a KB. Let $M = ([\![\mathsf{RefPT}(\mathcal{T},\mathcal{O})]\!]_G)|_{\mathsf{vars}(\mathcal{T})}$. Then*

$$\mathsf{certp}(\mathcal{T},(G,\mathcal{O})) = \mathrm{MAX}(M\!\downarrow).$$

PROOF (SKETCH). First note that by using Proposition 4 and induction on the structure of $\mathcal{T}$, one can show ($\star$) $M = [\![\mathcal{T}]\!]_{G'}$, where G' is the restriction of $\mathsf{can}(G)$ to URIs $a \in \mathbf{U}$ such that $|a| \leq \mathsf{d}(\mathcal{T},\mathcal{O})$.

Due to Theorem 2, to prove the present theorem it suffices to show that $([\![\mathcal{T}]\!]_{\mathsf{can}(G)})\!\downarrow = M\!\downarrow$.

Take an arbitrary mapping $\mu^* \in ([\![\mathcal{T}]\!]_{\mathsf{can}(G)})\!\downarrow$. Then there exists a mapping $\mu \in ([\![\mathcal{T}]\!]_{\mathsf{can}(G)})$ such that $\mu\!\downarrow = \mu^*\!\downarrow$. Moreover, due to Proposition 3 we can w.l.o.g. assume that $|w| \leq \mathsf{d}(\mathcal{T},\mathcal{O})$ for every $w \in \mathsf{rng}(\mu)$. Then due to ($\star$), $\mu' \in M$. Thus also $\mu^* \in M\!\downarrow$.

Take an arbitrary mapping $\mu^* \in M\!\downarrow$. Then there exists $\mu \in M$ such that $\mu\!\downarrow = \mu^*\!\downarrow$. Then due to ($\star$), $\mu \in [\![\mathcal{T}]\!]_{G'}$. Thus trivially $\mu \in [\![\mathcal{T}]\!]_{\mathsf{can}(G)}$ and $\mu^* \in ([\![\mathcal{T}]\!]_{\mathsf{can}(G)})\!\downarrow$. □

We put our algorithm to work in the following example.

Example 6. Let $\mathcal{O}$ be the following set of inclusions:

$$(\mathsf{Person}, \mathtt{rdfs:sc}, \exists \mathsf{knows}), \quad (7)$$
$$(\mathsf{Prof}, \mathtt{rdfs:sc}, \exists \mathsf{teaches}), \quad (8)$$

which states that every Person object knows somebody and that every Prof object teaches somebody. Let G be an RDF graph containing the following triples: $(a, \mathsf{a}, \mathsf{Person}), (b, \mathsf{a}, \mathsf{Prof})$. We want to derive answers for the following query $\mathcal{T}$ over the above knowledge base:

$$(?x, \mathsf{teaches}, ?y) \text{ OPT } \big((?z, \mathsf{teaches}, ?y) \text{ OPT } (?u, \mathsf{knows}, ?y)\big)$$

This query asks for all $?x, ?z, ?u$ s.t. $?x$ teaches some $?y$ and optionally all $?z$, s.t. $?z$ teach the same $?y$ as $?x$ and optionally all $?u$ that know $?y$. We derive new queries by rewriting each node of the pattern tree corresponding to the above query separately.

1. *We start with the first BGP* $(?x, \mathsf{teaches}, ?y)$*:* We use $t = (?x, \mathsf{teaches}, ?y)$. Equation 8 is applicable to t, hence in Line 6 $\langle t', \gamma' \rangle = \langle (?x, \mathsf{a}, \mathsf{Prof}), ?y \rightarrow ?x \cdot \mathsf{teaches} \rangle$, which will be the enriched query that we add to *pr* in Line 7. Since our BGP consists of a single triple pattern, we will not unify any pairs of triple patterns in Line 8 and 9. No further application of inclusions leads to a new query. Hence, $\mathsf{RefBGP}((?x, \mathsf{teaches}, ?y), \mathcal{O}, \mathsf{d}(\mathcal{T}, \mathcal{O}))$ outputs:

$$\langle (?x, \mathsf{teaches}, ?y), \emptyset \rangle \quad (9)$$
$$\langle (?x, \mathsf{a}, \mathsf{Prof}), ?y \rightarrow ?x \cdot \mathsf{teaches} \rangle \quad (10)$$

2. *Similar as above for the second BGP:* $\mathsf{RefBGP}((?z, \mathsf{teaches}, ?y), \mathcal{O}, \mathsf{d}(\mathcal{T}, \mathcal{O}))$ outputs:

$$\langle (?z, \mathsf{teaches}, ?y), \emptyset \rangle \quad (11)$$
$$\langle (?z, \mathsf{a}, \mathsf{Prof}), ?y \rightarrow ?z \cdot \mathsf{teaches} \rangle \quad (12)$$

3. *And similar as above for the third BGP:* $\mathsf{RefBGP}((?u, \mathsf{knows}, ?y), \mathcal{O}, \mathsf{d}(\mathcal{T}, \mathcal{O}))$ outputs:

$$\langle (?u, \mathsf{knows}, ?y), \emptyset \rangle \quad (13)$$
$$\langle (?u, \mathsf{a}, \mathsf{Person}), ?y \rightarrow ?u \cdot \mathsf{knows} \rangle \quad (14)$$

Evaluating each of the enriched queries (9)-(14) over G gives the following mappings: Query (10) evaluated over G outputs $\{?x \rightarrow b, ?y \rightarrow b \cdot \mathsf{teaches}\}$, Query (12) $\{?z \rightarrow b, ?y \rightarrow b \cdot \mathsf{teaches}\}$ and Query (14) $\{?u \rightarrow a, ?y \rightarrow a \cdot \mathsf{knows}\}$. Combining the answers via Definition 5 gives the mapping: $\{?x \rightarrow b, ?z \rightarrow b\}$.

5. HOLISTIC QUERY REWRITING

The modular approach from the previous section follows the general philosophy of SPARQL entailment regimes from [12] which also proceeds by first treating each BGP individually. However, a possible disadvantage of our modular approach is that we need to maintain additional data structures (in particular, the "guides") to ensure consistency when combining the partial solutions from different nodes in the pattern tree to an overall solution. As a consequence, our whole algorithm has to be implemented from scratch because standard tools cannot handle these additional data structure. In this section, we therefore present a second approach to SPARQL evaluation under OWL 2 QL entailment. Its main goal is to make use of standard technology as far as possible. We thus aim at a transformation of OWL 2 QL entailment under our novel certain answer semantics into SPARQL evaluation with respect to RDFS Entailment. For the latter task, strong tools (e.g. [13, 22]) are available. For the actual rewriting, we shall follow the rewriting from [9] (see also [28] for a similar approach) which incorporates several improvements compared with the original algorithm from [7] used in the previous section. The most important conceptual difference between our two algorithms, however, is that the algorithm presented below proceeds in a holistic way, i.e., our query rewriting always takes the entire pattern tree into account. Further differences between our modular and holistic algorithm will be discussed in Section 6.

As the modular rewriting, the holistic rewriting may unify and thus eliminate original variables; this needs to be memorized in order to construct correct answers in the end. Thus the rewriting operates on pairs $\langle \mathcal{T}, \beta \rangle$, where $\mathcal{T}$ is a wdPT and β a partial function from variables to sets of variables. Intuitively, $?x \in \beta(?u)$ says that $?x$ was substituted by the variable $?u$ during the rewriting. The evaluation of a pair $\langle \mathcal{T}, \beta \rangle$ over an RDF graph is defined as follows:

$$[\![\langle \mathcal{T}, \beta \rangle]\!]_G = \{\mathsf{expand}(\mu, \beta) \mid \mu \in [\![\mathcal{T}]\!]_G\}, \text{ where}$$
$$\mathsf{expand}(\mu, \beta) = \{?z \rightarrow \mu(?u) \mid ?z \in \beta(?u), ?u \in \mathsf{dom}(\mu)\}$$

The rewriting of $\langle \mathcal{T}, \beta \rangle$ is obtained by applying exhaustively the following procedure.

Definition 7. For a wdPT $\mathcal{T}$ together with a function β and an ontology $\mathcal{O}$, we write $\langle \mathcal{T}, \beta \rangle \rightarrow_{\mathcal{O}} \langle \mathcal{T}', \beta' \rangle$ if $\mathcal{T}'$ and β' can be obtained from $\mathcal{T}$ and β by the following steps:

(S1) non-deterministically pick a variable $?x \in \mathsf{vars}(\mathcal{T})$ and a role Q.

(S2) pick a concept B_Q, s.t. $\mathcal{O} \models (B_Q, \mathtt{rdfs:sc}, \exists Q)$ and Q is a basic role. If no such concept B_Q exists, continue with (S1).

(S3) Set $\langle \mathcal{T}', \beta' \rangle = \langle \mathcal{T}, \beta \rangle$. Drop from $\mathcal{T}'$ every subtree whose root has an triple of the form

(a) $(?z, Q_1, ?x)$ such that $\mathcal{O} \not\models (Q, \mathtt{rdfs:sp}, Q_1)$, or
(b) $(?x, Q_1, ?z)$ such that $\mathcal{O} \not\models (Q, \mathtt{rdfs:sp}, Q_1^-)$, or
(c) $(?x, \mathsf{a}, A)$ such that $\mathcal{O} \not\models (\exists Q^-, \mathtt{rdfs:sc}, A)$.

Note that $?z$ is an arbitrary variable.

(S4) Let $\mathsf{neighbours}_{\mathcal{T}'}(?x) = \{?z \mid (?x, P, ?z) \in \mathsf{pat}(\mathcal{T}') \text{ or } (?z, P, ?x) \in \mathsf{pat}(\mathcal{T}')\}$. Take a fresh variable $?u$ and replace in $\mathcal{T}'$ all $?z \in \mathsf{neighbours}_{\mathcal{T}'}(?x)$ with $?u$. In other words, collapse all neighbours of $?x$ into $?u$. Moreover, let $\beta'(?u) = \bigcup_{?z \in \mathsf{neighbours}_{\mathcal{T}'}(?x)} \beta(?z)$.

(S5) In all nodes n of $\mathcal{T}'$ where $?x \in \mathsf{vars}(n)$:

- if B_Q is an atomic concept: add $(?u, \mathsf{a}, B_Q)$.
- if B_Q is of the form $\exists Q'$: add $(?u, Q', ?y)$, where $?y$ is a new variable, i.e. not yet occurring in $\mathcal{T}'$.

(S6) In $\mathcal{T}'$, drop every triple t where $?x \in \mathsf{vars}(t)$.

We write $\langle \mathcal{T}, \beta \rangle \rightarrow^*_{\mathcal{O}} \langle \mathcal{T}', \beta' \rangle$ if $\langle \mathcal{T}', \beta' \rangle$ can be obtained from $\langle \mathcal{T}, \beta \rangle$ by finitely many rewrite iterations. We let $\mathsf{rew}_{\mathcal{O}}(\mathcal{T}, \beta) = \{\langle \mathcal{T}', \beta' \rangle \mid \langle \mathcal{T}, \beta \rangle \rightarrow^*_{\mathcal{O}} \langle \mathcal{T}', \beta' \rangle\}$.

Example 7. Let us revisit the KB and the query of Example 6. Let $\mathcal{T}$ denote the wdPT corresponding to this, and let $\beta_{\mathcal{T}}$ be defined as in Theorem 4. Then, the set $\mathsf{rew}_{\mathcal{O}}(\mathcal{T}, \beta_{\mathcal{T}})$ is obtained as follows. We start with the query $\langle \mathcal{T}, \beta_{\mathcal{T}} \rangle$ and proceed as in Definition 7. The steps that change the PT are depicted in Figure 1.

(S1) Let us pick variable $?y$ and the role teaches.

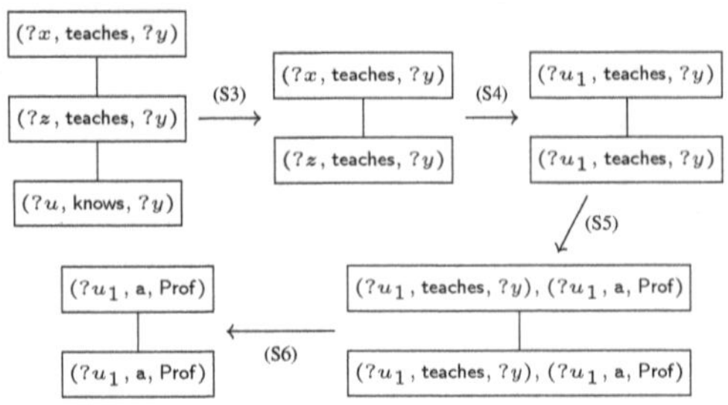

Figure 1: Holistic rewriting given in Example 7.

(S2) Since $\mathcal{O} \models (\mathsf{Prof}, \mathtt{rdfs:sc}, \exists\mathsf{teaches})$, we pick the concept Prof.

(S3) $\mathcal{T}'$ contains a node with $(?u, \mathsf{knows}, ?y)$, since $\mathcal{O} \not\models (\mathsf{teaches}, \mathtt{rdfs:sp}, \mathsf{knows}^-)$, we drop from $\mathcal{T}'$ the subtree rooted at the node containing $(?u, \mathsf{knows}, ?y)$.

(S4) Now, $\mathsf{neighbours}_{\mathcal{T}'}(?y) = \{?x, ?z\}$. We introduce a fresh variable $?u_1$ and replace all occurrences of $?x$ and $?z$ in $\mathcal{T}'$ with $?u_1$. In addition, we set $\beta'(?u_1) = \beta(?x) \cup \beta(?z) = \{?x, ?z\}$.

(S5) In all nodes of $\mathcal{T}'$ with an occurrence of $?y$ we add $(?u_1, \mathsf{a}, \mathsf{Prof})$.

(S6) We now drop all triples where $?y$ occurs.

After this step, we will have the pattern tree depicted in the lower left of Figure 1 together with the function β', where $\beta'(?u_1) = \{?x, ?z\}$. Due to lack of space, we omit further rewriting steps. The evaluation of the query depicted in Figure 1 over the Graph G given in Example 6 outputs the mapping $\{?u_1 \to b\}$. Then, $\mathsf{expand}(\{?u_1 \to b\}, \beta') = \{?x \to b, ?z \to b\}$, which is the answer also obtained in Example 6.

In order to compute the certain pre-answers $\mathsf{certp}(\mathcal{T}, \mathcal{G})$, it just remains to eliminate all non-maximal mappings:

THEOREM 4. *Let $\mathcal{G} = (G, \mathcal{O})$ be a KB and $\mathcal{T}$ a wdPT. Let $\beta_{\mathcal{T}}$ be the function s.t. for every $?x \in \mathsf{vars}(\mathcal{T}) : \beta_{\mathcal{T}}(?x) = \{?x\}$. Let $M = (\llbracket \mathsf{rew}_{\mathcal{O}}(\mathcal{T}, \beta_{\mathcal{T}}) \rrbracket_{\mathsf{comp}(G)})|_{\mathsf{vars}(\mathcal{T})}$. Then,*

$$\mathsf{certp}(\mathcal{T}, (G, \mathcal{O})) = \mathrm{MAX}(M).$$

PROOF IDEA. For soundness, one shows the correctness of every rewriting step $\langle \mathcal{T}, \beta \rangle \to_{\mathcal{O}} \langle \mathcal{T}', \beta' \rangle$. For this, one shows if $\mu \in \llbracket \langle \mathcal{T}', \beta' \rangle \rrbracket_{\mathsf{can}(G)}$, then there is a $\mu' \in \llbracket \langle \mathcal{T}, \beta \rangle \rrbracket_{\mathsf{can}(G)}$, s.t. $\mu \sqsubseteq \mu'$. For completeness, one shows for a mapping $\mu \in \mathsf{certp}(\mathcal{T}, \mathcal{G})$ that a sequence of rewriting steps to a query $\langle \mathcal{T}', \beta' \rangle$, s.t. $\mu \in \llbracket \langle \mathcal{T}', \beta' \rangle \rrbracket_{\mathsf{comp}(G)}$, can be found. □

6. DISCUSSION

In the previous sections, we have presented two algorithms for obtaining certain answers of well-designed SPARQL queries over OWL 2 QL ontologies. The obvious difference between the two algorithms is that the first one proceeds by rewriting each node of the pattern tree individually while the second one targets the complete pattern tree at once. We now aim at a more detailed analysis of the characteristics of each of the two algorithms. In particular, we want to identify typical settings which favour one or the other. To this end, we look at a simple ontology consisting of a single inclusion triple: $(A, \mathtt{rdfs:sc}, \exists R)$.

First, consider the following pattern tree with 2 nodes:

$$(?x, P, ?y_1), \ldots, (?x, P, ?y_n)$$
$$|$$
$$(?z_1, R, ?y_1), \ldots, (?z_n, R, ?y_n)$$

- *Modular rewriting* gives a total number of queries whose order of magnitude is $O(2^n)$, since:
  a) In the *root node* we cannot apply any inclusion triple to the BGP. Hence, the algorithm just outputs one query.
  b) In the *child node* we can immediately apply the inclusion $(A, \mathtt{rdfs:sc}, \exists R)$ to any of the n triples. This can be done in any order, i.e. the total number of queries obtained is $O(2^n)$.
- *Holistic rewriting* outputs only the original query. Whatever variable $?y_i$ we pick in Step (S1), we will drop the complete query in Step (S3), since $\mathcal{O} \not\models (R, \mathtt{rdfs:sp}, P)$. Picking any other variable $?x$ or $?z_i$ does not lead to further queries either.

For this query, the holistic approach by far outperforms the modular rewriting. Observe that all $?y_i$ variables are shared by the two nodes in the wdPT. Hence, if some $?y_i$ is mapped into the anonymous part of the canonical model, we would need to infer that the R edge is also a P edge, which is of course not true. Consequently, there exists no rewriting of the entire wdPT. However, in the modular approach, each node of the wdPT is processed individually. Hence, we do not detect that it is impossible to map the variable $?y_i$ in the root node to the same anonymous element as $?y_i$ in the child node.

Second, we consider the following wdPT with n nodes:

$$(?x_1, P, ?z), (?x_1, R, ?y_1)$$
$$\vdots$$
$$(?x_n, P, ?z), (?x_n, R, ?y_n)$$

- *Modular rewriting* gives a total number of $2 * n$ queries since, in each of the n nodes, we apply $(A, \mathtt{rdfs:sc}, \exists R)$ independently.
- *Holistic rewriting* will do the same as the modular rewriting, but it copies with each rewriting also all other nodes, which then in turn must again be rewritten. Therefore, the holistic rewriting outputs a total number of queries whose order of magnitude is $O(2^n)$.

For the second query, clearly, the modular rewriting by far outperforms the holistic rewriting. We observe that now, the $?y_i$ variables which have to be picked, only appear once in the tree. Hence, the nodes are independent of each other. This is in sharp contrast to the first query, where the two nodes shared all of the $?y_i$ variables.

These two examples show that neither of the two algorithms is uniformly better than the other: depending on the setting, each of the two algorithms may produce exponentially fewer rewritings than the other. The way in which the same variables occur in multiple nodes looks like the key feature to distinguish situations where one or the other algorithm is preferable. The main strength of the holistic approach is to recognize incompatible occurrences of the same variable in different nodes, which allows the pruning of subtrees in the wdPT. The main strength of the modular approach is to avoid the same rewriting of subtrees in the wdPT for different rewritings in a parent node by treating each node individually. At any rate, it seems advantageous to have both algorithms in one's portfolio.

7. COMPUTATIONAL COMPLEXITY

Having proposed two concrete algorithms for computing the certain answers to well-designed SPARQL queries according to our new semantics, we will next study the computational complexity of the *evaluation problem*. We show that the certain answer semantics does not increase its complexity compared to the setting without ontologies. Formally, we thus study the following problem.

OWL 2 QL-EVALUATION	
Input:	pwdPT $(\mathcal{T}, \mathcal{X})$, KB $\mathcal{G}$, mapping μ.
Question:	$\mu \in \mathsf{cert}(\mathcal{T}, \mathcal{X}, \mathcal{G})$?

For establishing several of the complexity results presented in this section, including the one on OWL 2 QL-EVALUATION, it is convenient to first consider the following problem.

PARTIAL OWL 2 QL-EVALUATION	
Input:	pwdPT $(\mathcal{T}, \mathcal{X})$, KB $\mathcal{G}$, mapping μ.
Question:	$\mu \sqsubseteq \mathsf{cert}(\mathcal{T}, \mathcal{X}, \mathcal{G})$?

THEOREM 5. *The problem* PARTIAL OWL 2 QL-EVALUATION *is* NP*-complete.*

PROOF SKETCH. The *membership* can be shown using Theorem 4: First, compute $\mathsf{comp}(G)$ in polynomial time. Next, guess a subtree $\langle \mathcal{T}', \beta' \rangle$ of a rewriting $\langle \mathcal{T}'', \beta'' \rangle \in \mathsf{rew}_{\mathcal{O}}(\mathcal{T}, \beta_{\mathcal{T}})$ (with $\mathsf{dom}(\mu) \subseteq \mathsf{vars}(\langle \mathcal{T}', \beta' \rangle)$) and an extension λ of μ s.t. $\lambda(\mathsf{pat}(\mathcal{T}')) \subseteq \mathsf{comp}(G)$.

Hardness follows immediately from the NP-completeness of the query evaluation problem for CQs. □

Deciding OWL 2 QL-EVALUATION can now be reduced to several calls of PARTIAL OWL 2 QL-EVALUATION.

THEOREM 6. *The problem* OWL 2 QL-EVALUATION *is* DP*-complete. Hardness holds even if the ontology is empty.*

PROOF IDEA. For *membership*, note that OWL 2 QL-EVALUATION $((\mathcal{T}, \mathcal{X}), (G, \mathcal{O}), \mu)$ can be solved by deciding:

1. $\mu \sqsubseteq \mathsf{cert}(\mathcal{T}, \mathcal{X}, (G, \mathcal{O}))$, and
2. for all $\mu' : \bar{\mathcal{X}} \to \mathsf{dom}(G)$ with $\bar{\mathcal{X}} \subseteq \mathcal{X}$ and $\mu \sqsubset \mu'$: $\mu' \not\sqsubseteq \mathsf{cert}(\mathcal{T}, \mathcal{X}, (G, \mathcal{O}))$?

Step (1) is in NP as shown in Theorem 5. For step (2), the co-problem is in NP: It can be solved by first guessing a mapping μ' (of polynomial size) and then checking if $\mu' \sqsubseteq \mathsf{cert}(\mathcal{T}, \mathcal{X}, (G, \mathcal{O}))$. Guessing μ' and the witness for $\mu' \sqsubseteq \mathsf{cert}(\mathcal{T}, \mathcal{X}, (G, \mathcal{O}))$ can be done in one step. Thus step (2) is in coNP.

The *hardness* is shown in the full version. □

We continue by studying typical query analysis tasks, i.e., subsumption ($\sqsubseteq$), containment ($\subseteq$), and equivalence ($\equiv$) between pwdPTs. First of all, we have to adapt these notions to our setting including ontologies. That is, let $(\mathcal{T}_1, \mathcal{X}_1)$ and $(\mathcal{T}_2, \mathcal{X}_2)$ be pwdPTs, and $\mathcal{O}$ be an ontology. We say that $(\mathcal{T}_1, \mathcal{X}_1) \circ (\mathcal{T}_2 \mathcal{X}_2)$ (for $\circ \in \langle \sqsubseteq_{\mathcal{O}}, \subseteq_{\mathcal{O}}, \equiv_{\mathcal{O}} \rangle$) if $\mathsf{cert}(\mathcal{T}_1, \mathcal{X}_1, (G, \mathcal{O})) \circ' \mathsf{cert}(\mathcal{T}_2, \mathcal{X}_2, (G, \mathcal{O}))$ (for $\circ' \in \langle \sqsubseteq, \subseteq, = \rangle$, respectively). This allows us to define the query analysis problems studied in this section.

OWL 2 QL-SUBSUMPTION/OWL 2 QL-CONTAINMENT/ OWL 2 QL-EQUIVALENCE	
Input:	pwdPTs $(\mathcal{T}_1, \mathcal{X}_1)$, $(\mathcal{T}_2, \mathcal{X}_2)$, ontology $\mathcal{O}$.
Question:	$(\mathcal{T}_1, \mathcal{X}_1) \sqsubseteq_{\mathcal{O}} / \subseteq_{\mathcal{O}} / \equiv_{\mathcal{O}} (\mathcal{T}_2, \mathcal{X}_2)$?

These problems can be decided by using (PARTIAL) OWL 2 QL-EVALUATION. For characterizing the relationships between these problems, we have to introduce some additional notation first. Let $(\mathcal{T}, \mathcal{X})$ be a pwdPT. We use $\mathsf{fvars}(\mathcal{T}) = \mathsf{vars}(\mathcal{T}) \cap \mathcal{X}$ to denote the set of free variables in $\mathcal{T}$. Moreover, let $\mathsf{db}(.)$ be a bijective function that assigns to each variable $?x \in \mathsf{vars}(\mathcal{T})$ a unique, new URI $\mathsf{db}(?x)$, and that maps constants onto themselves. Then the *frozen RDF graph* G for $\mathcal{T}$ is the set of triples $G = \{\mathsf{db}(t) \mid t \in \mathsf{pat}(\mathcal{T})\}$. Finally, for a subtree $\mathcal{T}'$ of $\mathcal{T}$, let $\mu_{\mathcal{T}'}$ be defined as $\mathsf{dom}(\mu_{\mathcal{T}'}) := \mathsf{fvars}(\mathcal{T}')$ and $\mu_{\mathcal{T}'}(?x) := \mathsf{db}(?x)$ for each $?x \in \mathsf{dom}(\mu)$.

This allows us to characterize the *subsumption* problem in terms of PARTIAL OWL 2 QL-EVALUATION.

THEOREM 7. *Given pwdPTs $(\mathcal{T}_1, \mathcal{X}_1)$, $(\mathcal{T}_2, \mathcal{X}_2)$, and an ontology $\mathcal{O}$, we have $(\mathcal{T}_1, \mathcal{X}_1) \sqsubseteq_{\mathcal{O}} (\mathcal{T}_2, \mathcal{X}_2)$ iff for every subtree $\mathcal{T}_1'$ of $\mathcal{T}_1$ we have $\mu_{\mathcal{T}_1'} \sqsubseteq \mathsf{cert}(\mathcal{T}_2, \mathcal{X}_2, (\mathsf{db}(\mathcal{T}_1'), \mathcal{O}))$.*

Intuitively, the idea is that given some G and $\mu \in \mathsf{cert}(\mathcal{T}_1, \mathcal{X}_1, (G, \mathcal{O}))$, an extension $\mu' \sqsubseteq \mathsf{cert}(\mathcal{T}_2, \mathcal{X}_2, (G, \mathcal{O}))$ can be obtained by a combination of μ and the mapping witnessing $\mu_{\mathcal{T}_1'} \sqsubseteq \mathsf{cert}(\mathcal{T}_2, \mathcal{X}_2, (\mathsf{db}(\mathcal{T}_1'), \mathcal{O}))$.

The *containment* problem on the other hand can be characterized in terms of OWL 2 QL-SUBSUMPTION and OWL 2 QL-EVALUATION. In fact, the following result presents a characterization of $\not\subseteq_{\mathcal{O}}$, i.e. a characterization of the co-problem, since we think it is more intuitive.

THEOREM 8. *Given pwdPTs $(\mathcal{T}_1, \mathcal{X}_1)$, $(\mathcal{T}_2, \mathcal{X}_2)$, and an ontology $\mathcal{O}$. Then $(\mathcal{T}_1, \mathcal{X}_1) \not\subseteq_{\mathcal{O}} (\mathcal{T}_2, \mathcal{X}_2)$ iff*

1. *$\mathcal{X}_1 \neq \mathcal{X}_2$, or*
2. *$(\mathcal{T}_1, \mathcal{X}_1) \not\sqsubseteq_{\mathcal{O}} (\mathcal{T}_2, \mathcal{X}_2)$, or*
3. *there exist subtrees $\mathcal{T}_1'$ of $\mathcal{T}_1$ and $\mathcal{T}_2'$ of $\mathcal{T}_2$ with $\mathsf{fvars}(\mathcal{T}_1') \subsetneq \mathsf{fvars}(\mathcal{T}_2')$ s.t. $\mu_{\mathcal{T}_1'} \in \mathsf{cert}(\mathcal{T}_1, \mathcal{X}_1, (\mathsf{db}(\mathcal{T}_1') \cup \mathsf{db}(\mathcal{T}_2'), \mathcal{O}))$.*

We briefly discuss the idea of this characterization: By properties 1 and 2, containment cannot hold. Now assume $(\mathcal{T}_1, \mathcal{X}_1) \sqsubseteq_{\mathcal{O}} (\mathcal{T}_2, \mathcal{X}_2)$. Then clearly the only reason for some certain answer μ of $\mathcal{T}_1$ not being a certain answer of $\mathcal{T}_2$ is that some proper extension μ' of μ is actually a certain answer of $\mathcal{T}_2$. This situation is covered by the third property: $\mathcal{T}_1'$ represents μ, $\mathcal{T}_2'$ represents μ'. Finally $\mu_{\mathcal{T}_1'} \in \mathsf{cert}(\mathcal{T}_1, \mathcal{X}_1, (\mathsf{db}(\mathcal{T}_1') \cup \mathsf{db}(\mathcal{T}_2'), \mathcal{O}))$ ensures that while μ can be extended to μ' on $\mathcal{T}_2$, this is not possible on $\mathcal{T}_1$.

The *equivalence* problem can of course be solved by checking mutual containment. Moreover, it is easy to see that $(\mathcal{T}_1, \mathcal{X}_1) \equiv_{\mathcal{O}} (\mathcal{T}_2, \mathcal{X}_2)$ iff $(\mathcal{T}_1, \mathcal{X}_1) \sqsubseteq_{\mathcal{O}} (\mathcal{T}_2, \mathcal{X}_2)$ and $(\mathcal{T}_2, \mathcal{X}_2) \sqsubseteq_{\mathcal{O}} (\mathcal{T}_1, \mathcal{X}_1)$. Just consider the case that for some RDF graph G, assuming mutual subsumption, there is some $\mu \in \mathsf{cert}(\mathcal{T}_1, \mathcal{X}_1, (G, \mathcal{O}))$, s.t. $\mu \notin \mathsf{cert}(\mathcal{T}_2, \mathcal{X}_2, (G, \mathcal{O}))$. Then there must be $\mu' \in \mathsf{cert}(\mathcal{T}_2, \mathcal{X}_2, (G, \mathcal{O}))$ with $\mu \sqsubset \mu'$. Thus either μ' or some extension of it must be contained in $\mathsf{cert}(\mathcal{T}_1, \mathcal{X}_1, (G, \mathcal{O}))$, which contradicts $\mu \in \mathsf{cert}(\mathcal{T}_1, \mathcal{X}_1, (G, \mathcal{O}))$.

Observe that Theorems 7 and 5 give an immediate Π_2^P upper bound on the complexity of OWL 2 QL-SUBSUMPTION. Also, this result combined with Theorem 6 provides a Π_2^P upper bound for OWL 2 QL-CONTAINMENT (via a Σ_2^P bound for the co-problem). Finally, these results imply the same upper bound for OWL 2 QL-EQUIVALENCE. By proving matching lower bounds, we show that this is in fact the exact complexity of all three problems.

THEOREM 9. *The problems* OWL 2 QL-SUBSUMPTION, OWL 2 QL-CONTAINMENT, *and* OWL 2 QL-EQUIVALENCE *are* Π_2^P*-complete. Hardness holds even for empty ontologies.*

PROOF IDEA. *Membership* results follow from the above discussion. *Hardness* for OWL 2 QL-SUBSUMPTION follows from the hardness of subsumption without ontologies [19]. The hardness for OWL 2 QL-CONTAINMENT and OWL 2 QL-EQUIVALENCE is shown in the full version. □

Of course, we cannot compare these results directly with the known results for well-designed SPARQL queries in settings without ontologies. In fact, over plain RDF graphs, most of the problems have even a higher complexity: The evaluation problem is Σ_2^P-complete [19] while the containment and equivalence problem are even undecidable [26]. Only the subsumption problem was shown to have the same complexity [26]. The reason for the higher complexity, or even undecidability, respectively, is the existence of subsumed mappings in query answers. Recall that, for any RDF graph G, pwdPT $(\mathcal{T}, \mathcal{X})$ and ontology $\mathcal{O}$, the set $[\![(\mathcal{T}, \mathcal{X})]\!]_G$ may contain subsumed mappings. This is not the case for $\text{cert}(\mathcal{T}, \mathcal{X}, (G, \mathcal{O}))$, due to the restriction to maximal mappings in our definition of certain answers.

For the subsumption problem, this of course does not make a difference, since for two sets of mappings M, M' we clearly have $M \sqsubseteq M'$ if and only if $\text{MAX}(M) \sqsubseteq \text{MAX}(M')$ (observe however, that in the presence of subsumed answers, pairwise subsumption does not guarantee equivalence [19]). However, for a reasonable comparison of the other problems under our new certain answer semantics with the settings without ontologies, we need to study suitable variants of these problems first. We thus investigate the following problem.

MAXEVALUATION	
Input:	pwdPT $(\mathcal{T}, \mathcal{X})$, RDF graph G, mapping μ.
Question:	$\mu \in \text{MAX}([\![(\mathcal{T}, \mathcal{X})]\!]_G)$?

For containment and equivalence, we consider the relations $\subseteq^{MAX}$ and $\equiv^{MAX}$ where, for pwdPTs $(\mathcal{T}_1, \mathcal{X}_1)$, $(\mathcal{T}_2, \mathcal{X}_2)$, we have $(\mathcal{T}_1, \mathcal{X}_1) \circ (\mathcal{T}_2, \mathcal{X}_2)$ (for $\circ \in \langle \subseteq^{MAX}, \equiv^{MAX} \rangle$) if $\text{MAX}([\![(\mathcal{T}_1, \mathcal{X}_1)]\!]_G) \circ \text{MAX}([\![(\mathcal{T}_2, \mathcal{X}_2)]\!]_G)$ (for $\circ \in \langle \subseteq, = \rangle$, resp.) for all RDF graphs G. This gives the following problems.

MAXCONTAINMENT/MAXEQUIVALENCE	
Input:	pwdPTs $(\mathcal{T}_1, \mathcal{X}_1)$, $(\mathcal{T}_2, \mathcal{X}_2)$.
Question:	$(\mathcal{T}_1, \mathcal{X}_1) \subseteq^{MAX} / \equiv^{MAX} (\mathcal{T}_2, \mathcal{X}_2)$?

THEOREM 10. *The problem* MAXEVALUATION *is* DP-*complete. The problems* MAXCONTAINMENT *and* MAXEQUIVALENCE *are* Π_2^P*-complete*

PROOF IDEA. The corresponding problems in the presence of an ontology of course provide an upper bound. *Hardness* results are provided in the full version. □

We have thus pinpointed the complexity of the most relevant reasoning problems related to query evaluation and query analysis: Starting from the problems respecting our new certain answer semantics, we also reconsidered the corresponding problems for settings without ontologies where we remove subsumed mappings from the query answers.

Our results show that for all the problems analysed in this section, applying the certain answer semantics does not increase their computational complexity compared to the case without ontologies.

8. CONCLUSION AND FUTURE WORK

Summary. In this work, we have provided an intuitive definition of certain answers for well-designed SPARQL queries under entailment regimes. As a basis for the design of evaluation algorithms, we have established the relationship between certain answers and canonical models. It should be noted that this part of our work is completely generic in the sense that it applies to any entailment regime. We have then turned our attention to a concrete entailment regime – OWL 2 QL – for which we have presented novel evaluation algorithms together with a detailed complexity analysis. We have thus shown that – analogously to CQ-answering under DL-Lite [7] – one can extend SPARQL evaluation to OWL 2 QL entailment without significantly increasing the complexity.

Related Work. Work related to our findings first and foremost includes the work our approaches are based upon [7, 9, 12, 2] as discussed throughout this paper. There is a huge body of results on query answering under different Description Logics (cf. [7, 27, 9, 23]). However, the queries considered there are typically CQs. So far, query languages comparable to well-designed SPARQL have not yet been studied in the context of Description Logics. The problem of answering SPARQL queries under OWL 2 QL via rewriting has been recently studied in [16], where a translation of the problem into SQL is provided. Unlike our work, the authors do not modify the semantics defined by the entailment regime [12]. Investigating aggregate functions, similar to our observation in the presence of weak monotonicity, the authors of [18] notice that defining certain answers as the intersection over all possible worlds does not provide satisfactory answers. For the counting operator, they solve this problem by defining the certain answer to be the minimum over all possible worlds. In [1], the authors describe a rewriting of SPARQL query answering under OWL 2 QL into Datalog$^\pm$. A modification of this translation allows them to remove the restriction to map all variables to actual values from the RDF graph. However, this relaxation applies only to variables occurring in a single BGP, while we allow this for all non-distinguished variables. Also, a discussion of the resulting semantics is missing. Libkin [20] also criticizes the standard notion of certain answers in case of non-monotone queries. Similar to his suggestion to use the greatest lower bounds in terms of informativeness, our approach chooses the most informative solutions as certain answers.

Future Work. Above all, we want to investigate further entailment regimes under our certain answer semantics. The implementation of the rewriting algorithms, the development of suitable benchmarks and alternative methods, e.g. employing materialization [15], is a challenging task as well. It also remains to be seen whether the optimization in [14] can be adopted by the proposed semantics. Moreover, we want to study combinations of our semantics with other approaches: our definition of certain answers is a *relaxation* of the current semantics; it allows to infer additional mappings that logically follow from the knowledge base. Recently, a *stronger* semantics was presented in [17], which discards entire mappings whose possible extensions to optional subqueries would imply inconsistencies in the knowledge base. A semantics that would integrate both principles is also an exciting research problem. Another extension envisaged refers to the restrictions imposed on the fragment of SPARQL considered here: so far, we have only considered *well-designed SPARQL*, which was *further restricted* to queries of the form $(?x, \mathsf{a}, B)$ or $(?x, Q, ?y)$. However, since SPARQL allows for variables in all positions, i.e. also $(?x, ?y, ?z)$ is a valid triple pattern, we will extend our work to allow these triple patterns as well. Even though we obtain nice complexity results, by investigating well-designed SPARQL, for the certain answer semantics this restriction should not be of big importance. Hence, we want to further investigate the certain answer semantics in the presence of standard SPARQL queries over OWL 2 QL ontologies.

Acknowledgements

This work was supported by the Vienna Science and Technology Fund (WWTF), project ICT12-15 and by the Austrian Science Fund (FWF): P25207-N23 and P25518-N23.

9. REFERENCES

[1] M. Arenas, G. Gottlob, and A. Pieris. Expressive languages for querying the semantic web. In *Proc. of PODS 2014*, pages 14–26. ACM, 2014.

[2] M. Arenas and J. Pérez. Querying semantic web data with SPARQL. In *Proc. of PODS 2011*, pages 305–316. ACM, 2011.

[3] F. Baader, D. Calvanese, D. L. McGuinness, D. Nardi, and P. F. Patel-Schneider, editors. *The Description Logic Handbook: Theory, Implementation, and Applications*. Cambridge University Press, 2003.

[4] M. Bienvenu, T. Eiter, C. Lutz, M. Ortiz, and M. Šimkus. Query answering in the description logic $\mathcal{S}$. In *Proc. of DL 2010*. CEUR-WS.org, 2010.

[5] M. Bienvenu, M. Ortiz, M. Šimkus, and G. Xiao. Tractable queries for lightweight description logics. In *Proc. of IJCAI 2013*. IJCAI/AAAI, 2013.

[6] S. Bischof, M. Krötzsch, A. Polleres, and S. Rudolph. Schema-agnostic query rewriting in SPARQL 1.1. In *Proc. of ISWC 2014*, pages 584–600. Springer, 2014.

[7] D. Calvanese, G. De Giacomo, D. Lembo, M. Lenzerini, and R. Rosati. Tractable reasoning and efficient query answering in description logics: The DL-Lite family. *J. Autom. Reasoning*, 39(3):385–429, 2007.

[8] A. K. Chandra and P. M. Merlin. Optimal implementation of conjunctive queries in relational data bases. In *Proc. of STOC 1977*, pages 77–90. ACM, 1977.

[9] T. Eiter, M. Ortiz, M. Šimkus, T. Tran, and G. Xiao. Query rewriting for Horn-$\mathcal{SHIQ}$ plus rules. In *Proc. of AAAI 2012*. AAAI Press, 2012.

[10] B. Glimm. Using SPARQL with RDFS and OWL entailment. In *Reasoning Web 2011, Tutorial Lectures*, pages 137–201. Springer, 2011.

[11] B. Glimm, C. Lutz, I. Horrocks, and U. Sattler. Conjunctive query answering for the description logic SHIQ. *J. Artif. Intell. Res. (JAIR)*, 31:157–204, 2008.

[12] B. Glimm and C. Ogbuji. SPARQL 1.1 Entailment Regimes. W3C Recommendation, W3C, Mar. 2013. `http://www.w3.org/TR/sparql11-entailment.`

[13] F. Goasdoué, I. Manolescu, and A. Roatis. Efficient query answering against dynamic RDF databases. In *In Proc. of EDBT 2013*, pages 299–310. ACM, 2013.

[14] I. Kollia and B. Glimm. Optimizing SPARQL query answering over OWL ontologies. *J. Artif. Intell. Res. (JAIR)*, 48:253–303, 2013.

[15] R. Kontchakov, C. Lutz, D. Toman, F. Wolter, and M. Zakharyaschev. The combined approach to query answering in DL-Lite. In *Proc. of KR 2010*. AAAI Press, 2010.

[16] R. Kontchakov, M. Rezk, M. Rodriguez-Muro, G. Xiao, and M. Zakharyaschev. Answering SPARQL queries over databases under OWL 2 QL entailment regime. In *Proc. of ISWC 2014*, pages 552–567. Springer, 2014.

[17] E. V. Kostylev and B. C. Grau. On the semantics of SPARQL queries with optional matching under entailment regimes. In *Proc. of ISWC 2014*, pages 374–389. Springer, 2014.

[18] E. V. Kostylev and J. L. Reutter. Answering counting aggregate queries over ontologies of the DL-Lite family. In *Proc. of AAAI 2013*. AAAI Press, 2013.

[19] A. Letelier, J. Pérez, R. Pichler, and S. Skritek. Static analysis and optimization of semantic web queries. *ACM Trans. Database Syst.*, 38(4):25, 2013.

[20] L. Libkin. Incomplete data: what went wrong, and how to fix it. In *Proc. PODS 2014*, pages 1–13. ACM, 2014.

[21] C. Lutz. The complexity of conjunctive query answering in expressive description logics. In *Proc. of IJCAR 2008*, pages 179–193. Springer, 2008.

[22] B. Motik, Y. Nenov, R. Piro, I. Horrocks, and D. Olteanu. Parallel materialisation of datalog programs in centralised, main-memory RDF systems. In *Proc. AAAI 2014*, pages 129–137. AAAI Press, 2014.

[23] M. Ortiz, D. Calvanese, and T. Eiter. Data complexity of query answering in expressive description logics via tableaux. *Journal of Automated Reasoning*, 41(1):61–98, 2008.

[24] M. Ortiz, S. Rudolph, and M. Šimkus. Query answering in the horn fragments of the description logics SHOIQ and SROIQ. In *Proc. of IJCAI 2011*, pages 1039–1044. IJCAI/AAAI, 2011.

[25] J. Pérez, M. Arenas, and C. Gutierrez. Semantics and complexity of SPARQL. *ACM Trans. Database Syst.*, 34(3), 2009.

[26] R. Pichler and S. Skritek. Containment and equivalence of well-designed SPARQL. In *Proc. of PODS 2014*, pages 39–50. ACM, 2014.

[27] R. Rosati. On conjunctive query answering in EL. In *Proc. DL 2007*. CEUR-WS.org, 2007.

[28] R. Rosati and A. Almatelli. Improving query answering over DL-Lite ontologies. In *Proc. of KR 2010*. AAAI Press, 2010.

[29] M. Schmidt, M. Meier, and G. Lausen. Foundations of SPARQL query optimization. In *Proc. of ICDT 2010*, pages 4–33. ACM, 2010.

[30] J. F. Sequeda, M. Arenas, and D. P. Miranker. OBDA: query rewriting or materialization? In practice, both! In *Proc. of ISWC 2014*, pages 535–551. Springer, 2014.

Donor Retention in Online Crowdfunding Communities: A Case Study of DonorsChoose.org

Tim Althoff
Stanford University
althoff@cs.stanford.edu

Jure Leskovec
Stanford University
jure@cs.stanford.edu

ABSTRACT

Online crowdfunding platforms like DonorsChoose.org and Kickstarter allow specific projects to get funded by targeted contributions from a large number of people. Critical for the success of crowdfunding communities is recruitment and continued engagement of donors. With donor attrition rates above 70%, a significant challenge for online crowdfunding platforms as well as traditional offline non-profit organizations is the problem of donor retention.

We present a large-scale study of millions of donors and donations on DonorsChoose.org, a crowdfunding platform for education projects. Studying an online crowdfunding platform allows for an unprecedented detailed view of how people direct their donations. We explore various factors impacting donor retention which allows us to identify different groups of donors and quantify their propensity to return for subsequent donations. We find that donors are more likely to return if they had a positive interaction with the receiver of the donation. We also show that this includes appropriate and timely recognition of their support as well as detailed communication of their impact. Finally, we discuss how our findings could inform steps to improve donor retention in crowdfunding communities and non-profit organizations.

Categories and Subject Descriptors: H.2.8 [**Database Management**]: Database applications—*Data mining*

Keywords: Donor Retention; User Retention; Crowdfunding.

1. INTRODUCTION

Crowd-sourced fundraising, or *crowdfunding*, for short, provides a revolutionary way for organizations and projects to collect funding. Online crowdfunding platforms such as Kickstarter.com or DonorsChoose.org allow individuals to post project requests in order to raise funds for the development of new products, to support artistic and scientific endeavors, and to contribute to public education [27, 38]. Anyone can become a donor and direct small contributions to specific projects and this way, the "crowd" collectively contributes to the funding of the project. Even though, projects solely rely on contributions from a large number of individuals, crowdfunding projects have raised over $2.7 billion in 2012 alone [24].

WWW 2015, May 18–22, 2015, Florence, Italy.
ACM 978-1-4503-3469-3/15/05.
http://dx.doi.org/10.1145/2736277.2741120.

A critical component for the success of fundraising campaigns is the recruitment of new and engagement of existing donors. *Donor retention* refers to the problem of keeping donors that continue to make donations year after year.

Present donor retention rates are only around 25% for first time donors [3, 35] and increasing donor retention would have significant impact on the effectiveness of online as well as offline fundraising campaigns. First, it can be much more cost-effective to maintain relationships with existing donors than to recruit new donors. And second, even small improvements in donor retention can have a significant impact on the amount of collected funds. For example, a 10% improvement in donor retention could yield up to a 200% increase in obtained donations [35].

Despite the importance of donor retention for fundraising campaigns, many of its basic aspects are still not well understood. Current knowledge about donor retention largely consists of anecdotal evidence from fundraising professionals and small lab experiments in artificial environments (for a survey, see [35]). There are many questions about donor retention that remain open. For instance, are different donor subgroups affected differently by timely acknowledgments? What does timely even mean and what can we infer about the donor's expectations from their behavior?

Present work: Donor retention in online crowdfunding communities. In this paper, we study the *intersection* of crowdfunding communities and charitable organizations by studying an online charity that allows donors to donate to very specific small projects of their choosing (*i.e.*, operating exactly like a crowdfunding platform): DonorsChoose.org (DC.org).

We focus on the problem of donor retention as it is a fundamental problem both for online crowdfunding platforms as well as to a large and rapidly growing sector of non-profit organizations and charities [3, 4, 35].

We analyze a complete trace of donor and project activity from DonorsChoose.org, a U.S. nonprofit organization that allows teachers to easily post requests for donations to purchase materials in support of their classroom. Through DC.org, teachers compose a short essay on their students and project plans and itemize needed materials. An example project is shown in Figure 1 in which an elementary school teacher in a high-poverty district of New York City asks for "$305 to purchase colorful permanent markers and books to create beautiful paisley art inspired by one of their favorite fruits from India — mangoes!"

Our data contains complete project activity from the inception of DC.org in March 2000 to October 2014. In this time, DC.org attracted over 1.5M donors, 638k projects, and 3.9M donations for a total of $282M. More than 60% of all public schools in the U.S. have raised money for their classrooms through DC.org to date [9].

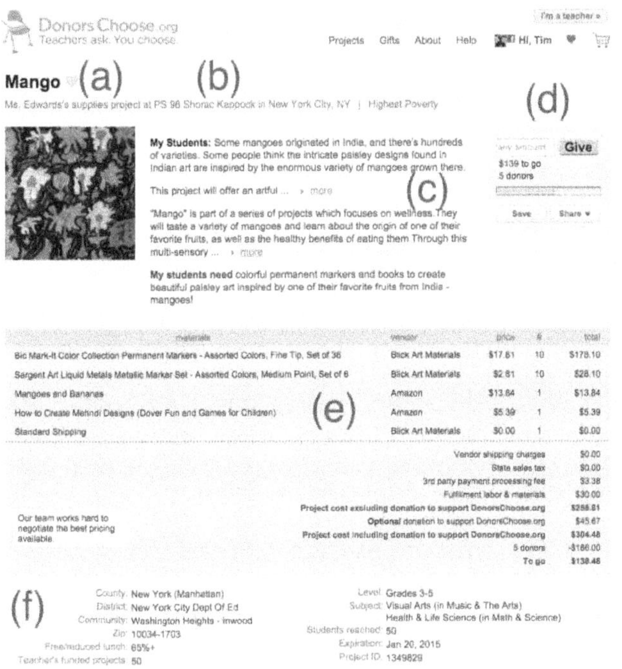

Figure 1: Example project request from DonorsChoose.org. Every project page contains the project title (a); the teacher and school (b); an essay by the teacher about their students, their project, and their specific need (c); the remaining amount to fund the project and the number of donors who have given already (d); needed materials in itemized form (e); and more information about the school and its students (f). This project asks for art supplies for a primary school in New York City.

To the best of our knowledge the present work is the first study of donor retention in online crowdfunding platforms.

Summary of results. Online crowdfunding platforms face the same problem of donor retention as traditional non-profit organizations. We show that only 26% of first-time donors ever return and donate a second time. Thus, increasing donor retention on DC.org would have huge impact that tens of thousands of public schools could benefit from. We start addressing this issue by analyzing the donation behavior of first-time donors, for which the attrition rate is largest. We identify a set of factors related to donor retention in the context of DC.org. We study these factors empirically and quantify their effect on donor retention. We find that factors such as entering the community through different means, geographical patterns of donations, the donation amount, and disclosure of optional personal information all shine light on the donor's initial motivations and signal commitment to the crowdfunding community. Furthermore, factors including project cost, project success, and timely responses by the teacher (highlighting the impact the donor has made) can affect the donor's sense of personal impact and trust in the organization (which are known to positively influence retention in offline charities [35]). In addition, we show that the teacher's ability to retain donors is correlated with their experience, timely writing thank you notes, and the use of Facebook for solicitation.

We also show that whether a donor will return for a second donation can be predicted just based on the properties of the donor's first donation. We build a machine learning model to predict donor return on an individual level with promising accuracy. Finally, we discuss how these results could be translated into actionable suggestions for online crowdfunding communities as well as traditional offline non-profits and charitable organizations.

Outline. The rest of the paper is structured as follows. Section 2 introduces DonorChoose.org, the dataset, and donor retention within the community. The analysis of retention factors is split into three perspectives: project (Section 3), donor (Section 4), and teacher (Section 5). We provide a brief summary (Section 6) before demonstrating that donor retention can be predicted on an individual level (Section 7). We describe related work in Section 8 and conclude with a discussion and future work in Section 9.

2. DATASET DESCRIPTION

This section gives details on the mechanics of the DC.org crowdfunding platform, the dataset used in this paper, and a first look at the state of donor retention on DC.org.

2.1 The Mechanics of DonorsChoose.org

DC.org enables *teachers* to request materials and resources for their classrooms and makes these project requests available to individual *donors* through its website (teachers can act as donors, too). In contrast to most offline non-profit organizations (NPOs), *projects* on DC.org are very concrete and provide an itemized list of the materials they ask for. In this regard, DC.org is more similar to other crowdfunding platforms. *Project pages* contain an essay by the teacher and further information about the concrete need, the school, location, poverty level, subject, grade level, how many students are reached by this project, and how many projects by the teacher have been successfully funded in the past (see Figure 1). If a partially funded project expires (*i.e.*, fails to attract full funding within a four month period), donors get their donations returned as account credits, which they can use towards other projects. When a project does get fully funded, DC.org purchases the materials and ships them to the school directly. At this point the teacher will send a so-called *confirmation note* to all donors thanking them for their donations. After the materials arrive in the teacher's classroom, the teacher will compose an *impact letter* giving insights on how the donor's support has made an impact in their classrooms. Often, these impact letters will come with photos of students using the donated materials. Donors who contribute $50 or more to a project can also request hand-written *thank you notes* from the students.

Donors can enter the site through different means. Some enter through the DC.org front page and use the search interface to find projects they feel passionate about (allowing them to filter or sort by many attributes including school name, teacher name, location, school subject, school material requested, keywords, cost, *etc.*). By default, the interface sorts projects by urgency (high poverty and close to finish line) and displays those projects at the top of the page. There is no further personalization, i.e. all visitors to the site see the same projects. We will refer to these donors as *site donors* for the rest of this paper. Other donors are referred by the teacher to make a donation to their own project on DC.org. For example, teachers often share the project URL with friends, family, parents of their students, or through posts on social media. DC.org tracks how donors enter the site and attributes any resulting donations to the teacher's fundraising efforts. We will refer to this group of donors as *teacher-referred*. Donors give about $55 dollars on average per donation (minimum $1, median $25).

2.2 The Dataset

We use a complete dataset of all projects and donations to DC.org from their inception in March 2000 to October 2014. Our dataset contains 3.9M donations by 1.5M donors to 638k projects over a total amount of $282M. We restrict our analysis to donations after Jan 1, 2009. Before then DC.org was relatively small and only started operating nationwide in 2008; also, the website interface has

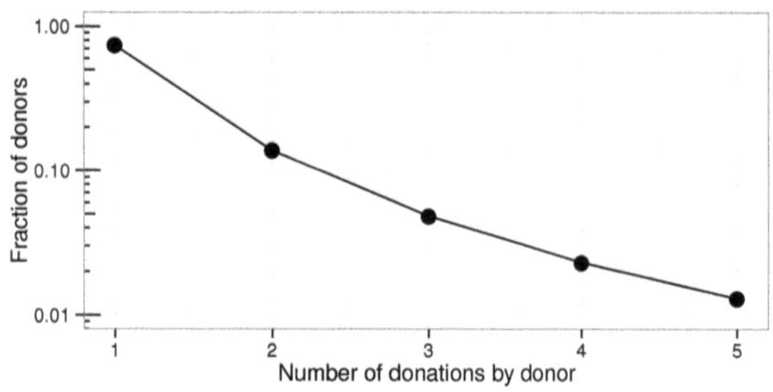

Figure 2: Fraction of donors by number of total donations by the donor. Note the log scale of the Y axis. 74% of donors donate exactly once and do not return. 26% return for a second donation and 14% do not return afterwards. Only 1% of donors make five donations. Online crowdfunding is facing the same attrition problem as offline NPOs.

changed over time. In all our analyses we filter out grant accounts held by special partners, promotions, gift card purchases that do not go towards a specific project, all donations by teachers, and all donations that are fully paid by account credit (*i.e.*, we require the donor to spend actual money).

2.3 Donor Retention on DonorsChoose.org

In this paper, we focus on donors and ask the question which donors return to make another donation. We identify that of all donors that do return over the course of our observation period, most do so within one year. Therefore we give every donor at least one year to return (*i.e.*, we only look at donations until September 2013 and use the following year to determine whether the donor returned or not). The presented results are robust to slight variations of this definition.

Figure 2 shows what fraction of donors makes how many donations within the entire observation period: 74% of donors make exactly one donation and never return, 14% return for a second donation, and only 1% of all donors make five donations (over a five year period). Attrition is highest and most potential is lost after the first donation and this is where we focus our attention in this paper (the importance of obtaining a second donation for donor retention has also been recognized recently in [22]).

Thus we focus our analyses on a set of 470k first-time donors of which 26% returned for a second donation. We also analyze return to the same teacher (as opposed to the overall site) for which we additionally require that the second donation went to the same teacher as the first donation (more in Section 5). Our dataset is representative of the issues the field is facing with very low retention rates. We observe a negative trend over time similar to what has been reported for offline NPOs [4]. In particular, in DC.org the donor retention for first-time donors fell from about 35% in 2009 to under 25% in 2013.

We structure our following analysis of donor retention factors into three parts focusing on projects (Section 3), donors (Section 4), and teachers (Section 5).

3. PROJECT PERSPECTIVE

Many factors around the donor's first interaction with DC.org are related to donor retention. This section focuses on the subset of factors around the project that the donor supported with their first donation. In particular, we study the effect of project success and project cost on donor retention.

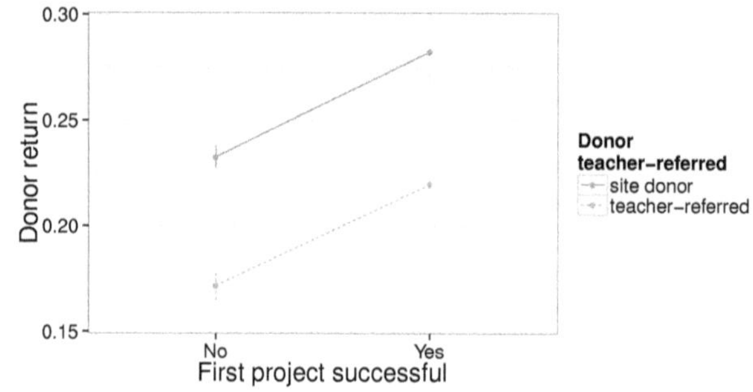

Figure 3: Whether or not the first project is successful is strongly correlated with retention for both teacher-referred and site donors. Donors whose first project succeeded are 5% more likely to return and donate again. Note: The error bars in all plots represent 95% confidence intervals on the corresponding mean estimate.

3.1 Trusting the System – Project Success

Trust between donor and organization has been identified as a key driver of loyalty [35]. Arguably, project failure indicates inability (of the site or teacher) to use the donated funds successfully towards the shared goal of improving public education. Therefore, we might expect to see higher return rates among donors whose first project was successfully funded compared to return rates of donors that were unsuccessful initially. The results are shown in Figure 3. We find that first-time donors are about 5% more likely to return if their first project is successfully funded. This means that when a person donates to a project that fails to attract enough funds, that person is less likely to make another donation. The effect is substantial if one considers the low baseline rates (a relative increase of 29%) and the fact that even small retention increases can have a high impact on total donations [35].

However, the finding could be confounded by the fact that successful projects are likely to ask for a smaller total amount and receive higher than average donations (and we find they do). To control for the effect of these confounders we use an almost-exact matching strategy [33] in which we pair donations that are identical in donation size (less than one cent difference on average), project cost (less than one dollar difference on average), and a variety of other factors (donation included optional support, grade level, poverty level of school district, being teacher-referred). Performing the analysis on 20k matched pairs of donations we find the same effect, albeit slighty reduced (3.2% increase).

To sum up, we conclude that donors who donate to a successful project are substantially more likely to return. The observation could be explained by several factors: donors trust the site more as their donation actually gets used, and also by donating to the successful project donors might get a greater sense of impact. It is exactly the impact that we examine next.

3.2 A Personal Sense of Impact – Project Cost

Most projects on DC.org ask for amounts between \$200 and \$600. Even though DC.org instructs teachers that smaller projects are more likely to be successful, some teachers ask for more than \$1500 (*e.g.*, for expensive computer equipment). Such projects usually require more donors (often several dozen) to get funded. In this context, an individual donor might have less of a sense of personal impact. If they are, say, one of a small number of donors that fully funded the project they might have a greater sense of accomplishment and impact than if they are one of many donors to a project [35].

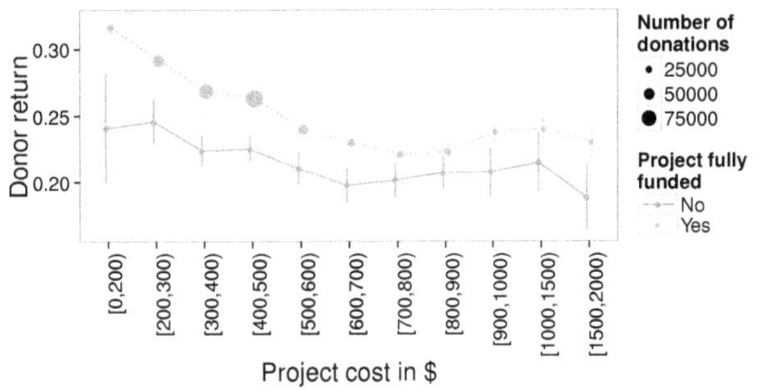

Figure 4: First-time donors to small projects are much more likely to return than donors to large projects. This effect could be explained through having a greater sense of personal impact when fewer people make the project succeed.

We show a graph of return rates as a function of project cost in Figure 4. The graph shows two curves: donor return for fully funded projects (blue) and donor return for non-funded projects (red). To give a sense for the donation distribution, the area of the circles is proportional to the number of donations to a project of a given amount.

We make several observations. First, the blue curve (successful projects) is always above the red curve (unsuccessful projects), which is consistent with the previous finding (Section 3.1) that donor return rate is positively correlated with the project success across all project sizes. Second, we observe that donors to small successful projects are much more likely to return (32%) than donors to large projects (23%).[1] For projects larger than $600 we observe no difference. And third, we find find the same effect for donors that make small donations as well as donors that make large donations (not shown in figure; more about donation sizes in Section 4.4).

4. DONOR PERSPECTIVE

Next, we explore retention factors around the donors themselves and the first donation they make.

4.1 Tracking How Donors Joined DC.org – Teacher-referred Donors

Considering how a particular donor found out about DC.org can shine light on their personal motivations and even whether they might know the teacher who started the project personally.

We split first-time donors into two groups *teacher-referred* donors and *site* donors (see Section 2.1). These two groups of donors are arguably quite different. While donors of the first group presumably entered the community to support a specific teacher, the donors of the second one could have joined the community because they wanted to support the cause of improving public education and/or the community as a whole.

We show retention rates for both groups in Figure 5. The plot shows the propensity to return as a function of the number of future projects by the same teacher (of the first project donated to). The distinction is relevant as it controls for the amount of future solicitation by the teacher who is likely to reach out to previous donors again when he or she starts a new project. Overall teacher-referred donors are less likely to return than site donors (blue vs. red curve).

We notice that for teachers that only create very few additional projects, the return rates are very different between the two groups.

[1]Note that most differences in mean return rate for successful projects are statistically significant as the 95% confidence intervals (error bars) are disjoint.

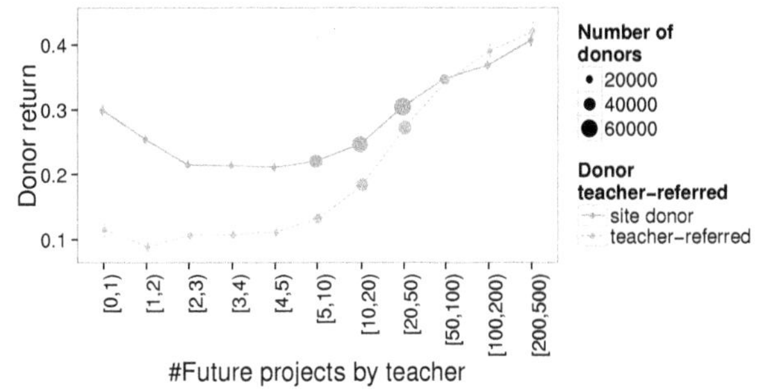

Figure 5: The propensity to return as a function of the number of projects by the same teacher in the future. Teacher-referred donors (blue) are less likely to return than site donors (red). Both types of donors are much more likely to return if they donate to (future) "high-profile" teachers.

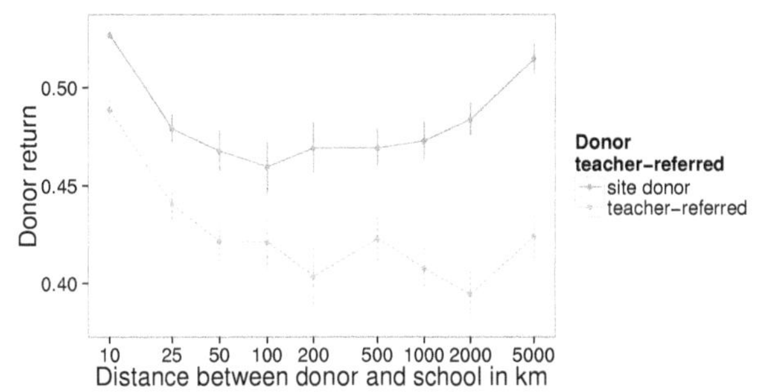

Figure 6: Retention rate across donors located at varying distances from the projects they funded with their first donation. Local donors are generally more likely to return and distant *site* donors are particularly loyal to DC.org as well.

The non-teacher-referred donors (site donors; red) arguably have higher intrinsic motivation to continue donating whereas teacher-referred donors (blue) lost their main reason to be part of the crowdfunding community and thus rarely return. However, the more projects the teacher will start in the future (*i.e.*, the more often the teacher returns) the more likely are teacher-referred donors to return. Likely this is due to increased solicitation efforts by that teacher. Interestingly, the return rate also increases for non-teacher referred donors. This could be explained by the fact that teachers are likely to reach out to these donors for future projects. In addition, DC.org might notify both kinds of users of future projects as part of their recommender system.

4.2 Distance as a Proxy for Involvement

On DC.org donors can specify their location and zip code in their user profile. In addition, all projects are highly geo-specific as they are funding a particular classroom within a particular school at a particular location. Having location information on both donors and projects allows us to put these in relation and measure how far donors live from the project and then explore how this is correlated with donor retention.

We form groups of donors based on the distance between them and the school they funded with their first donation (using the center point of their zip code and latitude/longitude coordinates for the school). The return rates within those groups are shown in Figure 6, separately for teacher-referred and site donors. The x-axis labels correspond to the upper bound on the distance interval of that group, for example "25" corresponds to all donors of the (10km, 25km] range. Again, we observe that teacher-referred donors are less likely to return across all distance groups. We find that local donors within 25km are most likely to return for both groups. As discussed before, these are the donors that could be more likely to be personally involved with the school or particularly care about impacting their local community. Interestingly, the retention rate increases again for distant site donors, forming a "U-shape". Site donors that live across the country (DC.org is a solely USA-based community) are almost as likely to return as their local counterparts. This subpopulation represents donors that are very passionate about the community and overall cause that they will even fund projects across the country when they (most likely) do not know the teacher. This effect is not as present for teacher-referred donors where the retention rate seems to plateau for distant donors.

Note that the above analysis is constrained to donors that share their location. Also note that the average return rate in Figure 6 is significantly higher than the overall average (26%). Whether or not a donor gives away their location is a signal in itself that we analyze in Section 4.5. We will also see in Section 4.3 that local giving is a large driver of donation volume.

4.3 The Donor's Role within the Project – Donation Position

Next, we investigate what we can learn about the donor based on the role they are assuming in the project they fund through their first donation. This is connected to the concepts of self-definition and identificiation of the donor that the fundraising literature has identified als influencers of donor loyalty [35].

We hypothesize that donors might fall into three categories: *starters* that like to start off new projects with an initial donation, *closers* that like to finish off projects that are close to completion, and a third group that does not particularly follow any of the previous two behaviors. How likely are these three groups to return?

Figure 7 (top) shows donor retention across donation position for successful projects that received between one and eight total donations. We observe a remarkably consistent "U-shape" trend across all project sizes in which donors in the middle of the project's lifetime are less likely to return than the starters. Moreover, closers, by far, display the highest propensity to return for another donation.

It seems unlikely that donation position by itself would have such a strong effect on the return rate (although it is conceivable that starters or closers feel a greater sense of impact when the project succeeds). More likely, these are actually different groups of users that interact with the project at different points of its lifetime.

Let us attempt to understand how these groups of donors might be different. Consider Figure 7 (bottom) that shows the distance distribution (cumulative distribution function; CDF) for first-time donors that make the first donation to their project (starters in red) and and for first-time donors that make the last donation to their project (closers in blue). We find that starters are more likely to be local and that closers are more likely to be distant (consistent with findings in [1]). From Section 4.2, we know that local as well as very distant donors are more likely to return, which leads to the U-shape in Figure 6. Early donors are also more likely to be teacher-referred, this group is also generally less likely to return (Figure omitted due to space constraints). This partially explains the large effect and U-shape in Figure 7 (top). Figure 7 (bottom) also shows that local giving is very important on DC.org as donations from within a 10km neighborhood around the school make up to 28% of first donations to projects and donations from within 100km make up about 50% of all donations (of donors that specified their location). Note that this effect is not due to the user interface or personalization as projects are not sorted by distance (which could favor local projects; see Section 2.1).

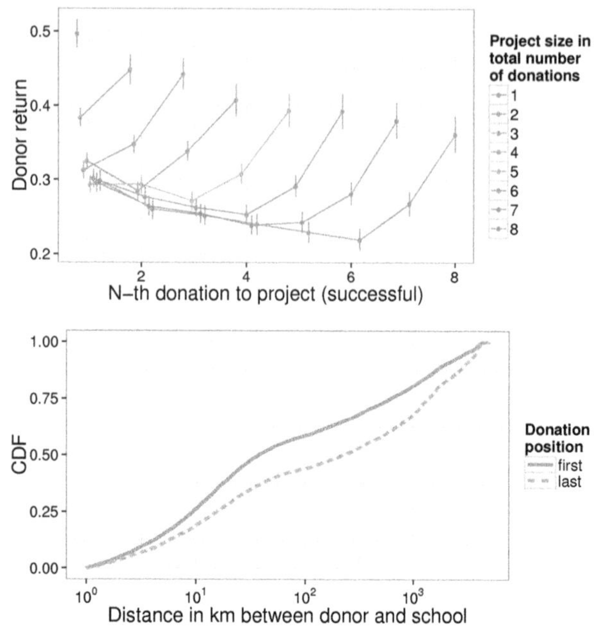

Figure 7: Top: Donors that donate last to projects are much more likely to return than other donors (for successful projects). Early donors are more likely to return than middle ones. Across all project sizes we observe a consistent "U-shape". Bottom: Early donors tend to be local and late donors tend to be distant.

4.4 Are You Committed to DonorsChoose.org? – Donation Amount

This section analyzes the relationship between donor return and the donation amount of the donor's first donation. Arguably, giving large amounts of money is one way to display high levels of commitment (though we recognize that less affluent donors can be committed as well). In the absence of a direct measure of commitment, we are therefore using donation amounts as a proxy. The fundraising literature defines commitment to an organization as the donor's desire to maintain a relationship or, alternatively, a genuine passion for the future of the organization and the work it is trying to achieve. Since commitment is positively correlated with loyalty [35] we would expect that first-time donors giving larger amounts are more likely to return in the future.

DC.org raises money to support their organization by asking for an optional support with each donation. By default, 15% of each donation goes towards DC.org and most people (85%) include this optional support for the site/organization. This gives us another signal of how committed donors are to the organization—if they explicitly opt out of supporting DC.org we would expect that they care more about the particular project or teacher they are supporting than they care about DC.org more generally.

We show retention rates across different donation amounts in Figure 8. The first donation amount is highly indicative of donor return. This effect is particularly strong for extreme donation amounts ($100+) that are less common. It shows that we can use initial donation amounts to predict whether a donor will return in the future. Note that these high donations amounts often occur to complete a project (see Section 4.3).

Interestingly, opting out of supporting DC.org is not an indicator of donors with low propensity to return. In fact, donors that opt out are at least as likely to return as their opt-in counterparts across all donation sizes. For very small donations ($1-$5) that do not include

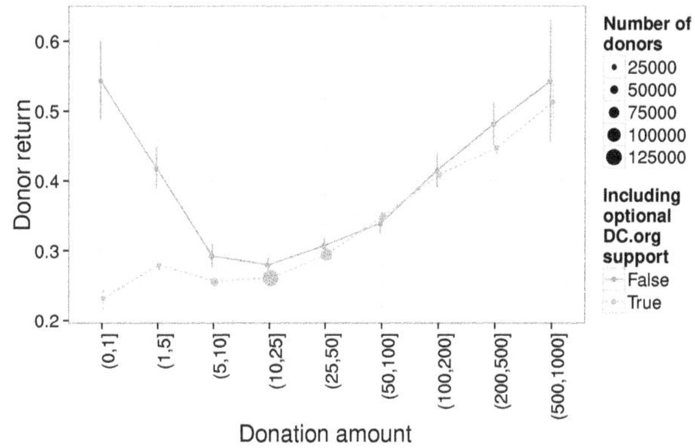

Figure 8: **Donors expressing commitment to DC.org through generous donation amounts are more likely to return. Donors opting out of supporting DC.org and making small donations are surprisingly loyal to the site (see the text for details).**

Donor TR	Donor DPI	#Donors	Donation Amount	Return Rate
Site donor	no PI	154965	$43.70	16.4%
Site donor	DPI	133543	**$67.01**	**41.1%**
TR donor	no PI	87248	$40.80	10.4%
TR donor	DPI	95033	**$53.24**	**31.8%**

Table 1: Return rate and average donation amount across donors that are (not) teacher-referred (TR) and do (not) disclose personal information (DPI; location or photo). Disclosure of personal information is strongly correlated with higher donation amounts and return rates (gains of 20% and more).

DC.org support we further observe very high return rates (though this is a relatively small group of donors). This counterintuitive finding — donors with small donations that do not include support for DC.org are actually very loyal — demands further investigation. Note that we do exclude all donations by teachers who are known to regularly support each other with very small donations as well as all donations affected by promotions. We observe the same behavior across teacher-referred and site donors as well.

4.5 Disclosure of Personal Information

Last, we explore how donor retention is correlated with increased disclosure of personal information. Sharing more personal information arguably expresses a certain level of trust towards the organization [25].

We define "discloses personal information" (DPI) as disclosing location or uploading picture (or both) and measure retention rates across the group of donors that does disclose information and the group that does not. The results are listed in Table 1. For both teacher-referred (TR) and site donors, those that disclose additional personal information (DPI) are much more likely to return. This effect is very large with differences of over 20% in both cases (which more than doubles the return rate). Furthermore, donors that disclose personal information make much larger donations on average.

Overall, these results show that disclosing personal information is correlated with higher levels of loyalty which allows us to exploit this correlation to understand and predict which groups are more likely to return.

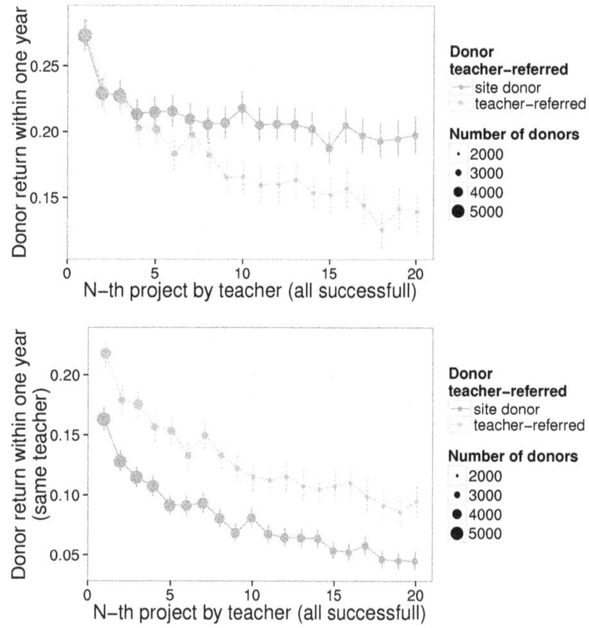

Figure 9: (Top) Teacher-referred donors are less likely to return to the site as the teacher posts new projects over time. For site donors, the effect levels off after an initial decrease in retention rate. (Bottom) Both teacher-referred and site donors are less and less likely to return to the same teacher over the "teacher lifetime".

5. TEACHER PERSPECTIVE

This section explores donor retention factors around the teachers involvement such as the repeated project efforts by the teacher, teacher-donor communication, and the teacher's use of Facebook for soliciting donations.

5.1 Expertise – Do Teachers Become More Successful Over Time?

We seek to empirically answer the question whether experienced teachers become more successful in retaining donors—both for the site and for their own projects—by measuring return rates for the teacher's first project, second project, and so on. To avoid bias of failed projects we restrict ourselves to only successful projects for this analysis and only consider teachers that posted at least 20 projects. As donors to earlier projects have more time to return compared to donors to later projects, we also require donors to return within one year.

The results are shown in Figure 9 (top: return to site; bottom: return to teacher). We observe the opposite from what one might expect. Experienced teachers do not become more effective at retaining donors. Instead, they are most successful in retaining donors (to DC.org; top plot) in their first projects. After those, the return rates are monotonically decreasing over time. However, we see that the effect levels off for site donors whereas the retention continues to decrease for teacher-referred donors. This could be explained by viewing teacher-referred donors as a limited resource available to the teacher. Teachers are only able to receive a certain amount of donors from their personal support network. This support is limited and asking over and over again for new projects is less and less likely to be successful as the teacher "drained" most of the resources available to them already. On the other hand, site donors are a much larger group which could explain why the red curve for site donors is leveling off instead of decreasing.

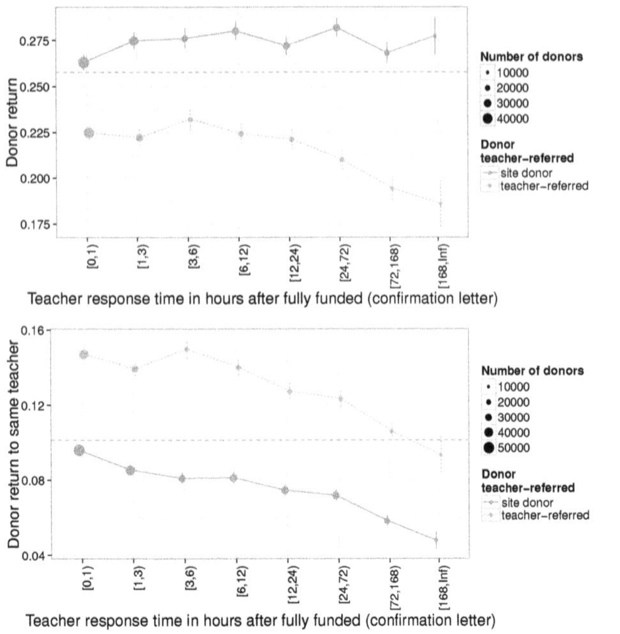

Figure 10: Effect of giving thanks through a confirmation note right after project becomes fully funded. Top: Donor return to site. Bottom: Donor return to same teacher. The dashed lines represent the respective average return rates.

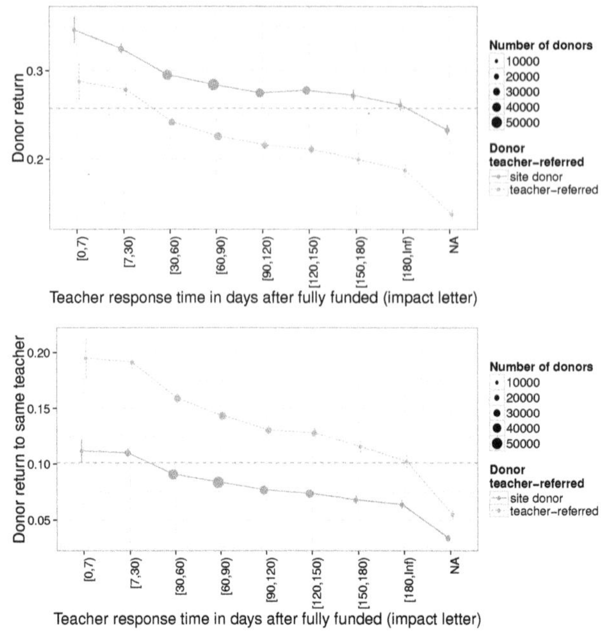

Figure 11: Effect of communicating impact through an impact letter. Top: Donor return to site. Bottom: Donor return to same teacher. In all cases, timely communication is very strongly correlated with donor return. The dashed lines represent the respective average return rates.

The bottom plot in Figure 9 shows return rates to the same teacher. Here, we observe decreasing retention rates for both teacher-referred and site donors. Note, however, that teacher-referred donors are now more likely to return, which is to be expected as they were referred by the teacher themselves. This picture seems somewhat discouraging for teachers looking for continued support for their classrooms. As donor retention becomes more and more challenging for the teacher, they are likely to be less successful over time (and in fact, that is what we observe in the data).

What are possible explanations for this negative trend? DC.org wants teachers to be successful, in particularly new teachers, and has implemented several features to support this. The main search interface for projects contains a filter option "never before funded teachers" (introduced in 2008, so before the start of our observation period). Furthermore, each project page lists the teacher's number of previous successful projects, making it easy for donors which are passionate about funding new teachers to direct their support. This suggests that donors are somewhat "fair" in distributing their support as they seem to favor supporting a new teacher instead of funding the 20th project by another.

5.2 Giving Thanks – Appropriate Recognition of Donors

Next, we quantify the effect of timely thank you messages on donor retention. As described in Section 2, teachers send out a "confirmation note" after the project becomes fully funded thanking their donors. We find that practically every teacher writes such a note eventually. Fundraising literature as well as anecdotal evidence from practitioners highlight the importance of providing appropriate recognition to the donor [35]. Failure to do so might lead to a lowering of future support or its complete termination [6].

We measure retention rates to the site and the same teacher across confirmation note response time in hours as shown in Figure 10. For site return (top) we only observe an effect for teacher-referred donors where slower response times show lower retention rates. In particular, response times within the first 24 hours are correlated with significantly higher return rates.

To sum up, donor retention on teacher level shows larger effects of response time for both teacher-referred and site donors. The effect is more pronounced for teacher-referred donors which suggests that they have higher expectations to be thanked or are more sensitive to hearing back promptly.

5.3 Communicating Impact – Let Donors Know The Difference

Similarly to thanking donors for their support (see Section 5.2), communicating impact has been identified as an important driver of donor loyalty [35]. As introduced in Section 2, DC.org asks teachers to write an "impact letter" to their donors for exactly these reasons after they have received the donated material. These impact letters usually include photos of students using the recently donated materials.

Similar to the previous section, we analyze the effect of timely response rates (in days) as well as failing to submit an impact letter on the teacher's part. The results are shown in Figure 11. In short, communicating impact to donors is very important for both retention to site (top) and to the same teacher (bottom) and for both teacher-referred donors as well as site donors. We observe strictly decreasing retention rates for longer response times with failure to submit an impact letter (NA) being the lowest. All differences in return rates are very large with return to the same teacher for teacher-referred donors again being the most pronounced.

5.4 Growing Your Support Network Through Social Media

DC.org offers teachers to automatically post key events about their project (first posted, first donation, *etc.*) on Facebook on their behalf. While we cannot know for sure the degree to which teachers make use of social media to raise support for their projects, surely

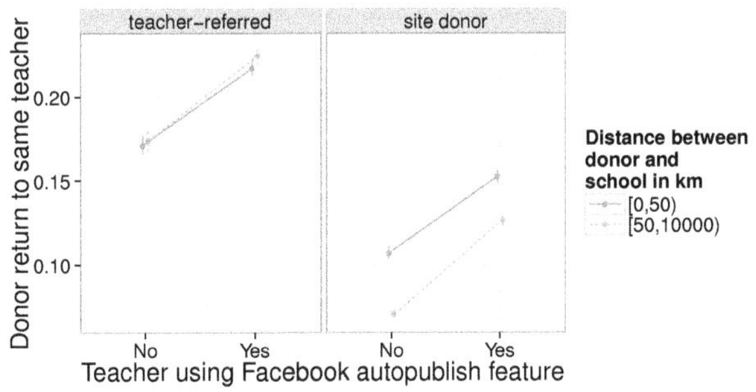

Figure 12: Donors that donate to teachers who allow DC.org to publish posts on their behalf are significantly more likely to return. However, the effect persists for both local and distant as well as teacher-referred and site donors suggesting that this is not a causal effect (see text for details).

the ones that opt in to use this autopublishing feature will regularly present friends and followers with updates on the teacher's fundraising efforts. Do teachers that opt in have higher return rates?

We show return rates in Figure 12. Donors that donate to "opt-in teachers" are more likely to return. However, this effect is identical for local and distant donors, and even more importantly exists for both teacher-referred and site donors (though we would expect that site donors are not connected to the teacher on Facebook). This strongly suggests that the observed effect is not causal (*i.e.*, due to the use of the Facebook feature) but that these might be a more fundamentally different group of teachers that is better at retaining donors for different reasons. Perhaps, teachers that opt in are generally more involved in soliciting donations from their peers.

This analysis cannot replace experiments specifically designed to measure the effect of social media use on support network within the crowdfunding community. However, since opting in is yet another signal that distinguishes returning donors from those that do not return it can still be helpful in predicting donor return.

6. SUMMARY OF RESULTS

In this Section we briefly summarize our findings on donor retention factors around the project (Section 3), donor (Section 4), and teacher (Section 5).

- **Project**: Donors experiencing a successful first project, small projects in particular, are more likely to return.
- **Donor**: Teacher-referred donors tend to be local and start off projects with early donations. Site donors fund projects much farther away and are more likely to finish off projects in which case they are very likely to return. Donors who give extraordinary amounts or disclose optional personal information about themselves are particularly loyal to DC.org.
- **Teacher**: Teachers are less successful over time in retaining donors. Timely recognition of donations as well as communicating the donor's impact is crucial, particularly for return to the same teacher and teacher-referred donors.

7. PREDICTING DONOR RETURN

Next, we build on insights from previous sections to predict donor retention on an individual level using standard machine learning techniques.

Features used for learning. We define a series of models that use different sets of features based on the factors explored in previous sections. We focus on four types of features:

Feature Set	Features
Time (1)	month of donation
Project (2)	eventual project success, project cost
Donor (10)	donation amount, donation includes optional support, distance to school, donation position (first, middle, last), donor photo published, donor teacher-referred, donor asked for student thank you notes
Teacher (8)	n-th project by teacher, completion and response time for confirmation note, impact letter, and student thank you notes, use of Facebook autopublish feature

Table 2: We consider four different categories of features as well as their combinations. The number in parenthesis denotes the number of features in the group.

- **Time:** We simply include the time of donation to control for temporal effects, like the state of the U.S. economy and changes in donor population.
- **Project:** Based on our analysis in Section 3 we describe the project with its cost and whether it succeeded eventually.
- **Donor:** In Section 4 we found features of the donor, like the geographic distance from the school and the donation position within the project to be important.
- **Teacher:** Insights gained in Section 5 demonstrate that properties of the teacher and communication with the donor to be important as well.

Table 2 gives a complete list of features. We include binned variants of donation amount and project cost and standardize all features to have zero mean and unit variance.

Experimental setup. We report performance of Logistic Regression models though Random Forest and SVM models gave very similar results. Because of the unbalanced dataset (74.6% of donors did not return for a second donation) and the trade-off between true and false positive rate associated with prediction we choose to compare models using the area under the receiver operating characteristic (ROC) curve (AUC) which is equal to the probability that a classifier will rank a randomly chosen positive instance higher than a randomly chosen negative one. Thus, a random baseline will score 50% on ROC AUC. We estimate ROC AUC through 10-fold cross-validation across the full dataset of 470,789 first-time donors. We experimented with weighting samples inversely proportional to class frequencies in the training set to address the class imbalance in the dataset and observed slight boosts in predictive accuracy at the expense of worse model calibration.

Summary of results. The results are given in Table 3. As reported in Section 2.3, donor retention has been decreasing over time. The Time model exploits this correlation and performs at 0.53 ROC AUC. Project features (success and cost) perform slightly better at 0.54 ROC AUC. The model based on donor features already performs quite well at 0.72 ROC AUC (note it is also the largest group of features). Teacher features perform slightly better than the Time or Project model at 0.55 ROC AUC.

Overall, we learn that the donor features are the most predictive of the return outcome. With about 0.72 AUC they help in distinguishing between returning and non-returning donors correctly. We further explore different feature set combinations and see performance improvements of 0.56 for Time + Project, 0.73 when adding Donor features, and finally up to 0.74 for the "full" model combining all features. This means that given two first-time donors, one

Model	ROC AUC
Random Baseline	0.50
Time (t)	0.53
Project (P)	0.54
Donor (D)	0.72
Teacher (T)	0.55
t + P	0.56
t + P + D	0.73
t + P + D + T	**0.74**

Table 3: Performance results for predicting donor return after observing the first donation only. Reported numbers are based on a Logistic Regression model on the full dataset (25.4% donor return probability) through 10-fold crossvalidation.

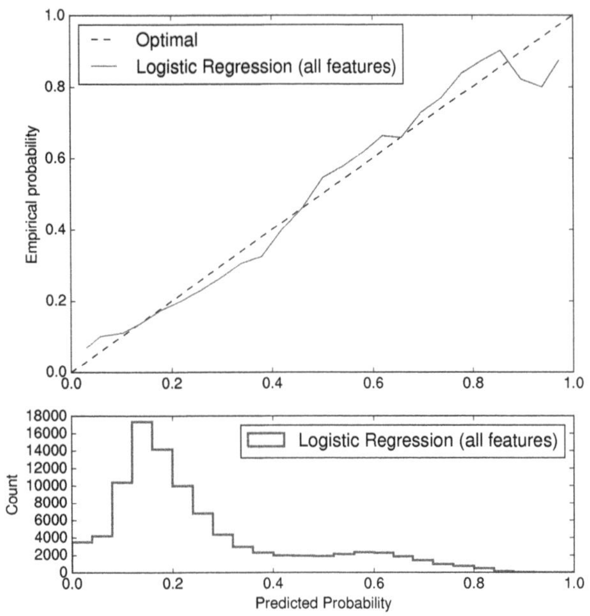

Figure 13: Model calibration plot of predicted probabilities of donor return against empirical probabilities showing that the Logistic Regression model using all features predicts well-calibrated probabilities.

returning and one non-returning, the model is able to pick the donor that is more likely to return in about 74% of all cases.

Exploring the model structure. Inspecting the full model for the largest absolute feature weights (though we caution about any absolute interpretation of importance) reveals that the model strongly relies on the following features: The model uses extraordinary donation amounts to infer higher donor return rates. As expected, smaller projects further increase the predicted donor return rate (see Section 3.2). In particular, the model relies more strongly on distance; that is, whether the donor is local (under 25km) or distant (1000km or more), or whether donor location was not disclosed. The predicted return probability is also strongly influenced by whether the donor was teacher-referred, whether the donor uploaded a photo, and whether the donor made the completing donation to the project. The model further puts particular emphasis on whether the teacher failed to upload thank you photos and how many projects the teacher has had before the current one. Lastly, the model exploits the temporal trend to downweight recent donors.

Model calibration. We plot return probabilities as predicted by our full model against empirical probabilities found in the test data in Figure 13. The Logistic Regression model using all features is well-calibrated (*i.e.*, predicts sensible donor return probabilities) and only diverges at the extremes for which we only have very few examples. Interestingly, the histogram of predicted probabilities reveals that there is a large population that is unlikely to come back (left) as well as a smaller population with high probability of return (right). It might be much harder and more costly to convince unlikely-to-return donors to make another donation compared to donors that are likely to return. To be more cost-effective, we therefore propose to concentrate marketing efforts on the latter group.

Discussion. Almost certainly, there is much room for improvement in predicting donor return on an individual level for example through additional features (*e.g.*, donor log-in history, content analysis of project essays, donor, and thank you messages) or through more powerful models. We see these results as an encouraging proof-of-concept that we can learn so much about donors, using information limited to only their first donation, that we can predict with reasonably high accuracy which donor is going to return for a second donation. Such models could prove to be very useful in informing fundraising campaigns and providing a basis for modeling effects on donor retention through targeted interventions. Perhaps, campaigns should focus more on the subpopulation that is more likely to return (cf. Figure 13).

8. RELATED WORK

We discuss related work in two parts. First, we mention the work that focuses on online crowdfunding platforms, which mostly deals with predicting success of funding campaigns. Second, we discuss survey-based research on donor retention in offline charities and non-profits.

Online crowdfunding platforms. Emergence of crowdfunding platforms, like Kickstarter, Kiva, and Prosper, has lead to a rich line of work on quantifying dynamics of funding campaigns [7, 8, 11, 13, 16, 21]. For example, studies have examined intrinsic dynamics of projects [27], how entrepreneurs use crowdfunding platforms [16], and how these platforms compare among themselves [13]. Research has also sought to develop tools that would help crowdfunding project creators [14] by predicting the probability of the project being successfully funded [14, 19, 31] and by predicting the number of contributions the project will eventually receive [23]. Other works have investigated the impact of factors like distance, promotional activities, project updates, and the use of social media on the success of projects [1, 23, 28, 39]. Common to all these works is that they investigate the dynamics of crowdfunding platforms from the viewpoint of the project and the project creator. The central question around these works is how to identify best practices and help project creators to get their projects eventually funded.

In contrast, our work does not focus on the dynamics of projects. Rather, we investigate the dynamics of donors. We examine the dynamics of crowdfunding platforms from the viewpoint of the donor and quantify donor behaviors that are indicative of donor's return and continued involvement with the crowdfunding platform. Another difference is that majority of works have investigated crowdfunding in the context of raising money for commercial projects. There, investors expect some return either by charging interest rate for the money they lend (as in the case of microlending platform Prosper) or by pre-ordering the product (as in the case of Kickstarter). In contrast, our work here examines charitable contributions where investors (*i.e.*, donors) do not expect any tangible return beyond the successful completion of the project (except perhaps the acknowledgement of their support or tax deductions).

Donor retention in charities. A rich line of research on traditional offline charities has emphasized high rates of donor attrition as well as the importance of donor retention for charities to achieve their goals [4, 35]. Using survey-based methodology, researchers have studied various factors related to donor retention [5]. For example, importance of acknowledging the donor by saying "thank you" has been recognized as an important factor [26, 37]. Furthermore, content analysis of arguments used in fundraising letters revealed that fundraisers tend to use emotional arguments more than logical ones [32]. Other important factors for donor retention include relationship building, communicating impact, trust, commitment, satisfaction, and involvement [29, 34, 35, 36].

Perhaps the most related to our work here is the research that investigates the roles that computational technology plays in support of non-profit fundraising [12]. In particular, recent work used the DC.org dataset in order to examine the value of completing crowdfunding projects and found that completing a project leads to larger donations and increased likelihood of returning to donate again [38]. Our work builds on this line of work and examines complete DC.org data in order to better understand donor attrition and identify means for increasing donor retention.

Our work further relates to the broader area of contributor retention in various online settings including newsgroups [2, 17], forums [20], Q&A sites [10, 30, 40], Wikipedia [15], and social networks [18]. We envision that our study could generalize to these settings as well by contributing proxies for the user's initial motivation and commitment as well as the dynamics around the recognition of their support.

9. DISCUSSION & CONCLUSION

Summary. Online crowdfunding platforms face the same challenge of maintaining a relationship with their donors as traditional non-profit organizations do. The present paper takes a first step towards addressing this challenge by analyzing donor behavior within a large crowdfunding platform DonorsChoose.org. In particular, we focus on first-time donors, the group for which the attrition is by far the largest. We identify a set of factors related to donor retention from project, donor, and teacher (project starter) perspectives and quantify the effects of these factors on donor retention, both to the site and to the individual teacher.

Using just the first donation interaction we show that we can learn a lot about the donor behavior to successfully predict the donor's propensity to return and make further donations. In particular, we learn about the donor's initial commitment through the means with which she enters the site (teacher-referred or not), their proximity to the project they are supporting, the amount they are giving, and whether they disclose personal information. We have proxies for the donor's sense of impact and trust in the organization through the project cost and size, whether the project is successful, and whether the donor receives a personal letter communicating the impact they have had on the project. Lastly, factors such as timely writing "thank you" notes to the donors, teacher experience on the site, or use of social media for solicitation are also correlated with the teacher's ability to retain donors.

Ideally, these factors would represent causal effects to help us understand how to improve donor retention. However, this is not a necessary requirement for such factors to be useful in machine learning models that predict whether or not donor is likely to return. We show that even simple models can predict donor return with reasonably high accuracy. Such models could prove to be very useful for crowdfunding platforms as well as non-profit organizations to efficiently target fundraising campaign efforts.

Implications. Our findings also inform steps to improve donor retention in crowdfunding communities and non-profit organizations. For example, our research suggests what factors are important in devising interventions and campaigns targeted at specific donor subpopulations. We showed that site donors and teacher-referred donors are very different in their behavior and campaign efforts and recommender systems should treat these two groups differently and expect different outcomes. Similarly, some donors prefer to support their local neighborhood whereas other donors are happy to help just about anywhere. This is valuable information for charitable organizations that should direct the flow of donations in a way that maximizes success for their organization and their users. Surely, this will involve many trade-offs (*e.g.*, focusing on first-time vs. high-profile donors or teachers) and this requires future work informing such decisions.

Furthermore, we hope that this work could serve crowdfunding communities and non-profit organizations as an encouragement to start collecting similarly valuable information about their donors and interactions in order to increase their fundraising efficiency. Even small increases in donor retention can have significant financial impact as donors keep donating for longer periods, very often increase their donation amount, help recruit new donors, and because of the potential savings in marketing to acquire new donors. We estimate that increasing donor retention by 10% in the case of DC.org would lead to an over 60% increase[2] in obtained donations (or an additional $15M assuming 100k donors).

Future work. Future work involves research on how prediction models could inform fundraising strategies (*e.g.*, through field experiments). We believe that a content analysis of project essays, donation messages, and thank you letters could further inform our understanding of the donor-teacher relationship. This paper could also be complemented by qualitative evidence from donors and teachers as well as online field experiments to examine which subgroups of donors to target and how to target them in order to increase donor retention rate. In designing such experiments, one should be mindful of ethical issues as interventions in this space could have negative impact on often already disadvantaged public school classrooms. Future work should further investigate how this work fits into the broad area of crowdsourcing and what retention factors prove to be valuable across a variety of platforms.

It is our hope that the present work will be able to serve as a basis for more research on maintaining donor relationships in online crowdfunding platforms as well as offline non-profit organizations that aim to improve their ability to retain donors for good causes.

Acknowledgments. We thank Vlad Dubovskiy and Thomas Vo at DonorsChoose.org for facilitating the research, Rok Sosič for many helpful discussions, and the anonymous reviewers for their valuable feedback. This research has been supported in part by NSF IIS-1016909, CNS-1010921, IIS-1149837, IIS-1159679, ARO MURI, DARPA SMISC, Boeing, Facebook, Volkswagen, Yahoo, and Stanford Data Science Initiative.

[2]Increasing donor retention 30% to 40% for new donors and 55% to 65% for existing donors and using increasing average donation amounts as estimated from the DC.org data.

10. REFERENCES

[1] A. K. Agrawal, C. Catalini, and A. Goldfarb. The geography of crowdfunding. Technical report, National Bureau of Economic Research, 2011.

[2] J. Arguello, B. S. Butler, E. Joyce, R. Kraut, K. S. Ling, C. Rosé, and X. Wang. Talk to me: foundations for successful individual-group interactions in online communities. In *SIGCHI*, 2006.

[3] Association of Fundraising Professionals and the Urban Institute. Fundraising Effectiveness Project: 2013 Fundraising Effectiveness Survey Report. `http://www.afpnet.org/files/ContentDocuments/FEP2013FinalReport.pdf`, 2013.

[4] P. Barber and B. Levis. Donor retention matters. *Urban Institute: Center on Nonprofits and Philantrophy*, 2013.

[5] R. Bennett. Predicting the lifetime durations of donors to charities. *Journal of Nonprofit & Public Sector Marketing*, 15(1-2):45–67, 2006.

[6] K. E. Boulding. *The economy of love and fear: A preface to grants economics*. Wadsworth Publishing Company Belmont, CA, 1973.

[7] S. Ceyhan, X. Shi, and J. Leskovec. Dynamics of bidding in a P2P lending service: Effects of herding and predicting loan success. In *WWW*, 2011.

[8] B. C. Collier and R. Hampshire. Sending mixed signals: Multilevel reputation effects in peer-to-peer lending markets. In *CSCW*, 2010.

[9] DonorsChoose.org. Impact. `http://www.donorschoose.org/about/impact.html`, 2014. Last retrieved on Nov 9, 2014.

[10] G. Dror, D. Pelleg, O. Rokhlenko, and I. Szpektor. Churn prediction in new users of Yahoo! answers. In *WWW*, 2012.

[11] M. Flannery. Kiva and the birth of person-to-person microfinance. *Innovations*, 2(1-2):31–56, 2007.

[12] J. Goecks, A. Voida, S. Voida, and E. D. Mynatt. Charitable technologies: Opportunities for collaborative computing in nonprofit fundraising. In *CSCW*, 2008.

[13] M. D. Greenberg, J. Hui, and E. Gerber. Crowdfunding: A resource exchange perspective. In *CHI EA*, 2013.

[14] M. D. Greenberg, B. Pardo, K. Hariharan, and E. Gerber. Crowdfunding support tools: Predicting success & failure. In *CHI EA*, 2013.

[15] A. Halfaker, R. S. Geiger, J. T. Morgan, and J. Riedl. The rise and decline of an open collaboration system: How wikipedia's reaction to popularity is causing its decline. *American Behavioral Scientist*, 2012.

[16] J. S. Hui, M. D. Greenberg, and E. M. Gerber. Understanding the role of community in crowdfunding work. In *CSCW*, 2014.

[17] E. Joyce and R. E. Kraut. Predicting continued participation in newsgroups. *Journal of Computer-Mediated Communication*, 11(3):723–747, 2006.

[18] M. Karnstedt, M. Rowe, J. Chan, H. Alani, and C. Hayes. The effect of user features on churn in social networks. In *WebSci*, 2011.

[19] V. Kuppuswamy and B. Bayus. Crowdfunding creative ideas: The dynamics of project backers in kickstarter. *SSRN Electronic Journal*, 2013.

[20] C. Lampe and E. Johnston. Follow the (slash) dot: effects of feedback on new members in an online community. In *SIGGROUP*, 2005.

[21] Y. Liu, R. Chen, Y. Chen, Q. Mei, and S. Salib. I loan because...: Understanding motivations for pro-social lending. In *WSDM*, 2012.

[22] J. Love. Low Donor Retention Takes More Than A Board Meeting To Solve. GuideStar Blog:`http://trust.guidestar.org/2014/08/18/low-donor-retention-takes-more-than-a-board-meeting-to-solve/`, 2014. Last retrieved on Nov 9, 2014.

[23] C.-T. Lu, S. Xie, X. Kong, and P. S. Yu. Inferring the impacts of social media on crowdfunding. In *WSDM*, 2014.

[24] K. MacLellan. Global Crowdfunding Volumes Rise 81% In 2012. *Huffington Post*, Aug 2013. Last retr. on Nov 9, 2014.

[25] D. H. McKnight, V. Choudhury, and C. Kacmar. The impact of initial consumer trust on intentions to transact with a web site: a trust building model. *The Journal of Strategic Information Systems*, 11(3-4):297–323, 2002.

[26] A. Merchant, J. B. Ford, and A. Sargeant. Don't forget to say thank you: The effect of an acknowledgement on donor relationships. *Journal of Marketing Management*, 26(7-8):593–611, 2010.

[27] E. Mollick. The dynamics of crowdfunding: An exploratory study. *Journal of Business Venturing*, 29(1):1 – 16, 2014.

[28] M. Muller, W. Geyer, T. Soule, and J. Wafer. Geographical and organizational distances in enterprise crowdfunding. In *CSCW*, 2014.

[29] J. Naskrent and P. Siebelt. The influence of commitment, trust, satisfaction, and involvement on donor retention. *Voluntas: International Journal of Voluntary and Nonprofit Organizations*, 22(4):757–778, 2011.

[30] J. S. Pudipeddi, L. Akoglu, and H. Tong. User churn in focused question answering sites: characterizations and prediction. In *WWW Companion*, 2014.

[31] H. Rao, A. Xu, X. Yang, and W.-T. Fu. Emerging dynamics in crowdfunding campaigns. In *Social Computing, Behavioral-Cultural Modeling and Prediction*, volume 8393 of *Lecture Notes in Computer Science*, pages 333–340. 2014.

[32] D. N. Ritzenhein. Content analysis of fundraising letters. *New Directions for Philanthropic Fundraising*, 1998(22):23–36, 1998.

[33] P. R. Rosenbaum. *Design of Observational Studies*. Springer, 2010.

[34] A. Sargeant. Relationship fundraising: How to keep donors loyal. *Nonprofit Management and Leadership*, 12(2):177–192, 2001.

[35] A. Sargeant. Donor retention: What do we know and what can we do about it? *A Report for the Association of Fundraising Professionals, Washington DC*, 2008.

[36] A. Sargeant, J. B. Ford, and D. C. West. Perceptual determinants of nonprofit giving behavior. *Journal of Business Research*, 59(2):155–165, 2006.

[37] I. Veldhuizen. Thank you! please visit us again. reflecting on the donor retention literature–implications for retention practices. *ISBT Science Series*, 5(n1):196–200, 2010.

[38] R. Wash. The value of completing crowdfunding projects. In *Proc. ICWSM*, 2013.

[39] A. Xu, X. Yang, H. Rao, W.-T. Fu, S.-W. Huang, and B. P. Bailey. Show me the money!: An analysis of project updates during crowdfunding campaigns. In *SIGCHI*, 2014.

[40] J. Yang, X. Wei, M. S. Ackerman, and L. A. Adamic. Activity lifespan: An analysis of user survival patterns in online knowledge sharing communities. In *ICWSM*, 2010.

Budget-Constrained Item Cold-Start Handling in Collaborative Filtering Recommenders via Optimal Design

Oren Anava*
Technion, Haifa, Israel
oanava@tx.technion.ac.il

Shahar Golan
Yahoo Labs, Haifa, Israel
shaharg@yahoo-inc.com

Nadav Golbandi
Yahoo Labs, Haifa, Israel
nadavg@yahoo-inc.com

Zohar Karnin
Yahoo Labs, Haifa, Israel
zkarnin@yahoo-inc.com

Ronny Lempel*
Outbrain Inc., Netanya, Israel
rlempel@outbrain.com

Oleg Rokhlenko
Yahoo Labs, Haifa, Israel
olegro@yahoo-inc.com

Oren Somekh
Yahoo Labs, Haifa, Israel
orens@yahoo-inc.com

ABSTRACT

It is well known that collaborative filtering (CF) based recommender systems provide better modeling of users and items associated with considerable rating history. The lack of historical ratings results in the user and the item cold-start problems. The latter is the main focus of this work. Most of the current literature addresses this problem by integrating content-based recommendation techniques to model the new item. However, in many cases such content is not available, and the question arises is whether this problem can be mitigated using CF techniques only. We formalize this problem as an optimization problem: given a new item, a pool of available users, and a budget constraint, select which users to assign with the task of rating the new item in order to minimize the prediction error of our model. We show that the objective function is monotone-supermodular, and propose efficient optimal design based algorithms that attain an approximation to its optimum. Our findings are verified by an empirical study using the Netflix dataset, where the proposed algorithms outperform several baselines for the problem at hand.

Categories and Subject Descriptors

H.2.8 [**Database Management**]: Database Applications—*Data Mining*

General Terms

Algorithms, Experimentation

Keywords

collaborative filtering, item cold-start, optimal design

*This work was done while the authors were at Yahoo Labs.

WWW 2015, May 18–22, 2015, Florence, Italy.
ACM 978-1-4503-3469-3/15/05.
http://dx.doi.org/10.1145/2736277.2741109.

1. INTRODUCTION

Recommendation technologies are increasingly being used to route relevant and enjoyable information to users. Whether they try to navigate through overwhelming Web content, choose a restaurant, or simply find a book to read, users find themselves being guided by modern online services that use recommendation systems. Usually, such services are based on users' feedback and stated preferences, and use editors, content analysis or wisdom of the crowds to tag their database items.

One of the most common and effective recommendation techniques is Collaborative filtering (CF). This technique relies only on past user behavior (e.g., previous transactions or feedback), and does not require the creation of explicit profiles. Moreover, it requires no domain knowledge or content analysis, and excels at exploiting popularity trends, which drive much of the observed user interaction. One of the fundamental problems arising when employing CF techniques is the *cold-start* problem. Roughly speaking, the cold-start problem is caused by the system's incapability of dealing with new items or new users due to the lack of relevant transaction history.

This work focuses on the item cold-start problem, *without* assuming any availability of context nor content-based information. In particular, we consider the following setting: a publisher has a set of users, and is aware of those users' historical ratings of items (movies, books, etc.). Now the publisher is interested in evaluating a new item, on which she has no prior knowledge. At her disposal is a pool of available users, from which she can assign B users to the task of rating the new item. After receiving their ratings, the publisher estimates, to the best extent possible, how the remaining users will rate the new item.

In order to mitigate the reviewing period, the B users are all selected at once - the publisher does not have the luxury to receive some ratings, and then to adaptively select additional users based on that signal. An important aspect of this problem setting is that the satisfaction of the assigned users does not factor into the equation - there is no cost associated with selecting a user who will dislike the item. The sole purpose is to select users who will provide best characterization of the new item.

The rest of this paper is organized as follows: the remaining of this section presents informal statement of our results, and surveys the related work. Section 2 introduces notations and concretely defines the problem. Section 3 then presents our optimal design based algorithms and analysis. Experimental results are reported in Section 4. We conclude and discuss future work in Section 5.

1.1 Informal Statement of Results

We adopt a common assumption in *Matrix Factorization* (MF)-based CF [16]: ratings of items by users can be well approximated by the product of two low-dimensional matrices, one representing low-dimensional latent vectors of users, and the other holding latent representations of items. The problem at hand then translates to the following mathematical abstraction: given latent vectors representing each of the users, and a new item whose latent vector is unknown, choose which B ratings to reveal so that the item's latent vector could be estimated most accurately.

The main contributions of this work are as follows: (1) We cast this budget-constrained user selection problem as an optimization problem, in which the objective function stands for the expected prediction error of our model. (2) We devise two novel optimal design based algorithms for the problem, each attains approximation to the optimum under certain assumptions. (3) We validate the theoretical results with an empirical study, by simulating the setting of the problem using the Netflix dataset and comparing the effectiveness of our algorithms to that of several baselines.

1.2 Related Work

The two major fields of CF are *neighborhood methods* and *Latent Factor Models* (LFM). LFM characterizes both items and users as vectors in a space automatically inferred from observed data patterns. The latent space representation strives to capture the semantics of items and users, which drive most of their observed interactions. One of the most successful realizations of LFM, which combines good scalability with predictive accuracy, is based on low-rank MF (e.g., see [16]). In particular, low-rank MF provides a substantial expressive power that allows modeling specific data characteristics such as temporal effects [15], item taxonomy [6], and attributes [1].

One of the inherent limitations of MF is the need for historical user-item interactions. When such history is limited, MF-based recommenders cannot reliably model new entities, leading to the item and user cold-start problems. Despite the fact that users and items are usually represented similarly in the latent space, these two problems are essentially different due to the ability to interview new users when joining the service in order to bootstrap their modeling. Moreover, each of these problems has a different line of previous works, as surveyed below.

User cold-start problem. Modeling the preferences of new users can be done most effectively by asking them to rate several carefully selected items of a seed set during a short interview [13, 21, 22, 8]. Item seed sets were constructed according to various criteria such as *popularity* (items should be known to the users), *contention* (items should be indicative of users' tendencies), and *coverage* (items should possess predictive power on other items).

The importance of adaptive interviewing process using adaptive seed sets was already recognized in [21]. Adaptive interviewing is commonly implemented by decision trees algorithms [22, 18, 9]. A method for solving the problem of initial interview construction within the context of learning user and item profiles is presented in [26].

Item cold-start problem. To mitigate the item-cold problem of CF, a common practice involves utilizing external content on top of users' feedback. The basic approach is to leverage items' attributes and combine them with the CF model in a way that allows treating new items [1, 10, 11, 19]. In [1] the authors proposed a regression-based latent factor model for cold-start recommendation. In their model a dyadic response matrix Y is estimated by a latent factor model $Y \approx U^{\top}V$, where the latent factor matrices, U and V, are estimated by regression $U \approx FX$ and $V \approx MZ$. The matrices X and Z are the user attribute and item feature matrices, and F and M are weight matrices learnt by regression. In a later work [19], the authors improve the performance achieved in [1] by solving a convex optimization problem that estimates the weight matrices, instead of computing the low-rank matrix decomposition of [1]. Another approach to tackle the item cold-start issue by combining content information with CF, based on *Boltzmann machines*, is studied in [10, 11].

The works described above require content or context data for new items. However, such data may not be available. In such cases, ratings for new items are arriving and one wishes to predict the missing ratings, with increasing accuracy, as more feedback is provided. Due to the incremental nature of the problem, one cannot afford to retrain the CF model with each arriving rating. A common heuristic approach is to estimate a new item's latent vector by a linear combination of the latent vectors of its raters and their respective ratings. It is based on the fact that users and items coexist as vectors in the same latent space and that ratings are usually estimated by user-item vector similarities. This principle was successfully practiced in various MF techniques [20, 14, 2, 3]. We note that this approach will serve us as baseline, as it does not require any content-based information and is thus suitable for our setting.

The optimal design approach. In the statistical field called *optimal design of experiments*, or just *optimal design* [4, 24], a statistician is faced with the task of choosing a limited amount of experiments to perform from a given pool, with the goal of gaining the most informative results. There are various measurements for the gain obtained from a subset of experiments. The measure of interest in our setting is referred to as the A-optimality criterion. According to this criterion, the experiments correspond to noisy outputs of a (usually linear) regression function and the goal is to minimize the Mean Squared Error (MSE) over all the possible inputs of the regressor.

An early attempt to tackle the user cold-start problem using optimal design techniques and an interviewing process appears in [25]. In this work, an adaptation of A-optimality, also referred to as *transductive optimal design*, aims to minimize the MSE over some arbitrary (yet known in advance) set of points (or users, in our context). Despite the original presentation in the setting of the user cold-start problem, the generality of the employed techniques allows handling the item cold-start problem in a similar manner. However, their work differs from ours due to the absence of performance guarantee for the proposed algorithms, and the use of an inferior prediction model.

2. PRELIMINARIES AND MODEL

2.1 The Latent Factor Model

We denote by $\mathcal{I}$ the set of all items, and by $\mathcal{U}$ the set of all users. The cardinality of these sets is denoted by $|\mathcal{I}| = m$, and $|\mathcal{U}| = n$. We use $\mathcal{R}$ to denote the rating matrix, which is of size $n \times m$. A rating r_{ui} indicates the preference of item i by user u, where high values mean stronger preference. The matrix $\mathcal{R}$ is typically sparse, since most users rate just a small portion of the items.

Using the notation above, the LFM (with k denoting its dimension) seeks to estimate each rating r_{ui} as follows:

$$r_{ui} \approx \mu + b_i + b_u + Q_i^\top P_u \ , \tag{1}$$

where $b_i \in \mathbb{R}$ and $Q_i \in \mathbb{R}^k$ are the bias and the latent factor vector of item i, respectively; $b_u \in \mathbb{R}$ and $P_u \in \mathbb{R}^k$ are the bias and the latent factor vector of user u, respectively; and $\mu \in \mathbb{R}$ denotes the overall average rating in $\mathcal{R}$. We use ε_{ui} to denote the residual error of our model with respect to user u and item i.

Intuitively, the term $Q_i^\top P_u$ captures the interaction (or affinity) between user u and item i, where high values implies stronger preference and vice versa. We denote by Q the $k \times m$ matrix, whose columns correspond to the vectors Q_i for $i = 1, \ldots, m$, and by P the $k \times n$ matrix, whose columns correspond to the vectors P_u for $u = 1, \ldots, n$.

An important aspect of our work is the following: as training the LFM is a completely orthogonal task to ours, we assume that we are given an already trained model and refer to it as ground truth. Practically, we assume that each rating r_{ui} complies with the following noisy model:

$$r_{ui} = \mu + b_i + b_u + Q_i^\top P_u + \varepsilon_{ui} \ , \tag{2}$$

where ε_{ui} is assumed to be a zero-mean noise term. This assumption is very common and can be found in several previous works (see [25] for instance). Moreover, a simple sanity check can verify that the assumption complies with the employed LFM: test the significance of the residuals as generated from a Gaussian distribution.

2.2 Problem Definition

We proceed to formally define our problem. Let i be a new item ($i \notin \mathcal{I}$), and denote by $\mathcal{U}^i \subset \mathcal{U}$ the pool of available users to rate it. Also, we denote the budget constraint by B (i.e., B is the number of users we are allowed to assign with the task of rating item i), and use the notation $\mathcal{U}_B^i$ for subsets of $\mathcal{U}^i$, which are of size B.

Now, given a budget constraint B, our goal is to select B users to rate item i in order to minimize the expected MSE on the set of the remaining users $\mathcal{U} \setminus \mathcal{U}_B^i$. More formally, we wish to solve the following optimization problem:

$$\min_{\mathcal{U}_B^i \subset \mathcal{U}^i} \left\{ \mathbb{E}\left[\frac{1}{|\mathcal{U} \setminus \mathcal{U}_B^i|} \sum_{u \in \mathcal{U} \setminus \mathcal{U}_B^i} (\tilde{r}_{ui} - r_{ui})^2 \right] \right\},$$

where $\tilde{r}_{ui}$ denotes our prediction of r_{ui}, and the expectation is taken over the noise terms consisting the ratings $\{r_{ui}\}$ (as defined in Equation (2)).

To simplify the notations, in the sequel we refer to the set of the remaining users as $\mathcal{U}$ (instead of $\mathcal{U} \setminus \mathcal{U}_B^i$). Essentially, this means that the sets $\mathcal{U}$ and $\mathcal{U}_B^i$ are disjoint, and the problem of interest is thus translated to:

$$\min_{\mathcal{U}_B^i \subset \mathcal{U}^i} \left\{ \mathbb{E}\left[\frac{1}{|\mathcal{U}|} \sum_{u \in \mathcal{U}} (\tilde{r}_{ui} - r_{ui})^2 \right] \right\}. \tag{3}$$

Clearly, the objective function inherently depends on how we generate the predictions $\{\tilde{r}_{ui}\}$ given the set of B users $\mathcal{U}_B^i$, and their ratings of item i. Thus we can divide the problem in Equation (3) into two distinct problems:

Rating Prediction (Problem A): given a subset of users $\mathcal{U}_B^i \subset \mathcal{U}^i$ and their ratings of item i, generate predictions $\{\tilde{r}_{ui}\}$ for all $u \in \mathcal{U}$.

User Selection (Problem B): given a pool of available users $\mathcal{U}^i$, select a subset of users $\mathcal{U}_B^i \subset \mathcal{U}^i$ to reveal their ranking of item i.

We shall point out that viewing the latent factor model as ground truth gives rise to an optimal solution for **Problem A**: least squares estimation (detailed in Section 3). However, in the CF literature there exist other approaches that can potentially function better in practice (especially if the data is not well represented by the LFM). These approaches are presented in Section 4.3, and will serve us as baselines for evaluating the merit of our approach.

3. ALGORITHMS AND ANALYSIS

In this section we tie together the two problems described in Section 2, and present a holistic approach that tackles the unified problem as a whole - the optimal design approach. *Optimal design* is a statistic paradigm [4, 24] that is aimed at selecting which experiments to conduct out of a given pool in order to maximize the result accuracy. In our setting, we wish to select a subset of users such that the prediction error of our model is minimized. Roughly speaking, the optimal design approach seeks to estimate the MSE (over the entire user set) for each selection of B users, *without* exposing their actual ratings. This way, we can evaluate the merit of any given subset of users (in terms of MSE), and make the selection accordingly.

Basically, the optimal design approach relies on the assumption that the ratings are generated via Equation (2), and consequently on the optimal solution for **Problem A**: least squares estimation. To make this point clearer we first introduce this estimator.

3.1 Least Squares Estimation

Assume we are given a new item $i \notin \mathcal{I}$, and a subset of users $\mathcal{U}_B^i \subset \mathcal{U}^i$ who provided their ratings for this item. Our task is to predict $\tilde{r}_{ui}$ for all $u \in \mathcal{U}$. Recall our modeling assumption regarding each of ratings r_{ui} from Equation (2). In particular, we assume that the ratings of the new item i by the users within $\mathcal{U}_B^i$ follow this model as well, where μ, b_u and P_u are given by our prediction model (Section 2), whereas b_i and Q_i are unknown to us (since the new item was not considered while training the model). Therefore, the least squares estimator seeks to estimate b_i and Q_i, and consequently to generate a prediction

$$\tilde{r}_{ui} = \mu + \tilde{b}_i + b_u + \tilde{Q}_i P_u.$$

From now on, we denote by (b_i, Q_i) the $(k+1)$-dimensional concatenation of b_i and the vector Q_i; the notation $(\tilde{b}_i, \tilde{Q}_i)$ shall stand for the corresponding estimator.

Using the notation above, the least squares estimator aims to estimate (b_i, Q_i) by minimizing the MSE over the set $\mathcal{U}_B^i$, that is, to solve the following problem:

$$\min_{\substack{b\in\mathbb{R}\\ q\in\mathbb{R}^k}} \left\{ \frac{1}{|\mathcal{U}_B^i|} \sum_{v\in\mathcal{U}_B^i} \left(r_{vi} - q^\top P_v - b - b_v - \mu \right)^2 \right\}.$$

This minimization problem is in fact analytically solvable, and yields the following solution:

$$(\tilde{b}_i, \tilde{Q}_i) = \left(\sum_{v\in\mathcal{U}_B^i} P'_v P'^\top_v \right)^{-1} \left(\sum_{v\in\mathcal{U}_B^i} (r_{vi} - b_v - \mu) P'_v \right),$$

where P'_v is the concatenated column vector $(1, P_v)$.

The above might not be well-defined since $\sum_{v\in\mathcal{U}_B^i} P'_v P'^\top_v$ need not be invertible in general. In practice, a regularization term of the form $\lambda\left(\|q\|_2^2 + b^2\right)$ is usually added to the objective function to avoid this problem. The estimator $(\tilde{b}_i, \tilde{Q}_i)$ then takes the following form:

$$\left(\lambda I + \sum_{v\in\mathcal{U}_B^i} P'_v P'^\top_v \right)^{-1} \left(\sum_{v\in\mathcal{U}_B^i} (r_{vi} - b_v - \mu) P'_v \right).$$

In the sequel, we will assume that $\sum_{v\in\mathcal{U}_B^i} P'_v P'^\top_v$ is invertible to ease the readability of the paper. We emphasize that all the results presented in this paper would still hold for the regularized estimator.

3.2 The Optimal Design Approach

We proceed to formally define necessary notations that will help us adapting the optimal design approach to our setting. We somewhat abuse notations and denote by P the matrix whose columns correspond to the latent factor vectors P'_u for $u \in \mathcal{U}$, and by P_B the matrix whose columns correspond to the latent factor vectors P'_v for $v \in \mathcal{U}_B^i$. Similarly, we use the notations $\varepsilon_{\mathcal{U}}$ and ε_B for vectors whose elements correspond to ε_{ui} for $u \in \mathcal{U}$ and ε_{vi} for $v \in \mathcal{U}_B^i$, respectively. Finally, we use r_B to denote the vector whose elements correspond to $(r_{vi} - b_v - \mu)$ for $v \in \mathcal{U}_B^i$.

We divide the analysis into two cases: (1) the noise terms $\{\varepsilon_{ui}\}$ are assumed to be zero-mean and i.i.d.; and (2) the noise terms $\{\varepsilon_{ui}\}$ are only assumed to be zero-mean and independent (but not necessarily identically distributed).

3.2.1 Identically Distributed Noise Terms

The following is our key observation: the optimization problem considered in Equation (3) can be reduced to a simpler problem, if the noise terms are assumed to be i.i.d. and the least squares estimator is used for estimating (b_i, Q_i). This observation is stated and proven below in Lemma 1.

Before we continue, we will assume without loss of generality that $PP^\top = |\mathcal{U}|\, I_{(k+1)\times(k+1)}$, meaning that the user vectors are in isotropic position. Otherwise , we can simply apply an invertible linear transformation to the LFM space of the users and its inverse to the space of the items; this does not affect our results as $(F^\top x)^\top (F^{-1} y) = x^\top y$ for all vectors x, y and invertible linear transformation F. This assumption is here merely to simplify the statements and proofs; the statements hold without it as well, and in particular, one is not required to compute the inverse of $PP^\top$ when implementing the algorithm.

Algorithm 1 Backward Greedy Selection (BGS1)

```
Input: users set U^i, and corresponding matrix P_{U^i}.
Output: users subset U_B^{ALG}.
Initialize P_B = P_{U^i} and U_B^{ALG} = U^i.
for j = 1 to |U^i| - B do
    v_j ← arg min_{v ∈ U_B^{ALG}} { tr( (P_{B\v} P_{B\v}^T)^{-1} ) }
    Update P_B ← P_{B\v_j}.
    Update U_B^{ALG} ← U_B^{ALG} \ v_j.
end for
```

Lemma 1 *Assume there exist b_i and Q_i, such that for every $u \in \mathcal{U}$ it holds that $r_{ui} = \mu + b_u + b_i + Q_i^\top P_u + \varepsilon_{ui}$, where $\mathbb{E}[\varepsilon_{ui}] = 0$ and $\mathbb{E}\left[\varepsilon_{ui}^2\right] = \sigma^2$. Then, the following is equivalent[1] to the problem presented in Equation (3):*

$$\min_{\mathcal{U}_B^i \subset \mathcal{U}^i} \left\{ \sigma^2 tr\left(\left(P_B P_B^\top \right)^{-1} \right) + \sigma^2 \right\},$$

if the least squares estimator is considered.

The expression in the lemma above has the following interpretation: the additive σ^2 term is the inherent model error. I.e., this is the term that cannot be avoided as long as we assume a latent factor model of dimension k. The second term of $\sigma^2 \mathrm{tr}\left((P_B P_B^\top)^{-1}\right)$ represents the error originating from a sub-optimal choice of the item's parameters, i.e., from the distance between $(\tilde{b}_i, \tilde{Q}_i)$ and (b_i, Q_i). The proof of the lemma appears in Appendix A.1.

After establishing a new (and equivalent) optimization problem, we turn now to present a simple greedy algorithm for finding an approximation to its optimum. Here, $P_{B\setminus v_j}$ refers to the matrix P_B, where the column that corresponds to the user v_j is removed. Before stating our main theorem, we introduce some necessary definitions:

Definition 1 *let $f : \mathbb{R}_+ \to \mathbb{R}$. For a positive definite matrix $A \in R^{k\times k}$ with the decomposition $A = U^\top diag(\lambda_1, \ldots, \lambda_k) U$, we extend the definition of f as follows:*

$$f(A) = U^\top diag(f(\lambda_1), \ldots, f(\lambda_k)) U.$$

Definition 2 *We say that f is* operator monotone *if for any positive definite matrices A and B:*

$$A \preceq B \Rightarrow f(A) \preceq f(B).$$

Definition 3 *We say that f is* operator antitone *if $-f$ is operator monotone.*

Definition 4 *We say that $f : 2^E \to \mathbb{R}$ is* supermodular *if*

$$f(A \cup \{x\}) - f(A) \geq f(B \cup \{x\}) - f(B),$$

for any $A \subset B \subset E$ and $x \in E \setminus B$.

[1]The equivalence here between the two problems is in the following sense: the value of both objective functions is the same for any subset $\mathcal{U}_B^i \subset \mathcal{U}^i$.

Definition 5 *The steepness of a decreasing supermodular function f is denoted by s and defined as follows:*

$$s = \max_{x \in E} \frac{[f(\phi) - f(x)] - [f(E \setminus \{x\}) - f(E)]}{[f(\phi) - f(x)]}.$$

In the last definition, if $f(\phi)$ is not defined we can simply extend it as follows:

$$f(\phi) = \max_{\substack{A,B \subset E \\ A \cap B = \phi}} \{f(A) + f(B) - f(A \cup B)\} \quad (4)$$

The following is our main theorem:

Theorem 2 *Let i be a new item, and $\mathcal{U}^i$ its corresponding set of available users, and assume that $\mathbb{E}[\varepsilon_{ui}] = 0$ and $\mathbb{E}[\varepsilon_{ui}^2] = \sigma^2$ for all $u \in \mathcal{U}$. Then, Algorithm 1 generates a subset $\mathcal{U}_B^{ALG} \subset \mathcal{U}^i$ for which:*

$$\mathbb{E}\left[MSE(\mathcal{U}_B^{ALG})\right] \leq \sigma^2 + \frac{e^t - 1}{t}\left(\mathbb{E}\left[MSE(\mathcal{U}_B^*)\right] - \sigma^2\right).$$

where $t = \frac{s}{1-s}$ and $\mathcal{U}_B^*$ is the optimal subset of B users, minimizing the expected MSE.

The above statement can be interpreted as follows. Both Algorithm 1 and the optimal solution have an additive term of σ^2, corresponding to the inherent LFM error. The additional term, corresponding to the sub-optimality of the choice of $(\tilde{b}_i, \tilde{Q}_i)$, is multiplicatively approximated by a factor of $(e^t - 1)/t$ compared to the optimal selection. Notice that the stated guarantee strictly dominates the following one:

$$\mathbb{E}\left[\text{MSE}(\mathcal{U}_B^{ALG})\right] \leq \frac{e^t - 1}{t}\mathbb{E}\left[\text{MSE}(\mathcal{U}_B^*)\right],$$

since $\sigma^2 > 0$ (trivially holds). We shall proceed to prove the main theorem.

PROOF. We first define an auxiliary function $\Phi : 2^{\mathcal{U}^i} \to \mathbb{R}$ as follows:

$$\Phi(\mathcal{U}_D^i) = \text{tr}\left(\left(P_D P_D^\top\right)^{-1}\right) - \varphi_i,$$

where $\varphi_i = \text{tr}\left(\left(P_{\mathcal{U}^i} P_{\mathcal{U}^i}^\top\right)^{-1}\right)$, and $\Phi(\varnothing)$ is defined as in Equation (4). Notice that Φ is well-defined for any subset $\mathcal{U}_D^i \subset \mathcal{U}^i$ (of size $0 \leq D \leq |\mathcal{U}^i|$), and not only for subsets of size B. The matrix P_D is then defined as the matrix whose columns correspond to the latent factor vectors P_v' for $v \in \mathcal{U}_D^i$.

Next, we show that Φ has the following three properties: it is supermodular, monotonically decreasing, and equal to 0 at $\mathcal{U}^i$. For such functions, [12] proved that the backward greedy algorithm, eliminating elements one by one, attains an $(\frac{e^t-1}{t})$-approximation to the optimum. The third property follows immediately from the definitions of Φ and φ_i, and thus we are left to prove the other two properties.

Before proving these properties, we provide a simple intuition. Notice first that $\mathbb{E}\left[\text{MSE}(\mathcal{U}_D^i)\right]$ can be written as a linear function of $\Phi(\mathcal{U}_D^i)$:

$$\mathbb{E}\left[\text{MSE}(\mathcal{U}_D^i)\right] = \sigma^2\left(\Phi(\mathcal{U}_D^i) + \varphi_i + 1\right).$$

Thus, minimizing Φ is equivalent to minimizing the MSE. Now, the monotonicity of Φ gives rise to the following insight: the MSE decreases as the number of users increases. The supermodularity then translates into the following rational: the marginal return of a user diminishes as the set of selected users expands.

We shall proceed to formally prove these properties. For the monotonicity, we take two subsets $\mathcal{U}_D^i, \mathcal{U}_E^i \subset \mathcal{U}^i$, such that $\mathcal{U}_D^i \subset \mathcal{U}_E^i$, and prove that $\Phi(\mathcal{U}_D^i) \geq \Phi(\mathcal{U}_E^i)$. Thus, denote by P_D and P_E the matrices that correspond to $\mathcal{U}_D^i$ and $\mathcal{U}_E^i$, respectively. Then, it holds that $P_E P_E^\top \succeq P_D P_D^\top$, which also implies that

$$\left(P_E P_E^\top\right)^{-1} \preceq \left(P_D P_D^\top\right)^{-1}.$$

Now, since the trace of a positive semidefinite (PSD) matrix is the sum of its eigenvalues, the above also implies that

$$\text{tr}\left(\left(P_E P_E^\top\right)^{-1}\right) \leq \text{tr}\left(\left(P_D P_D^\top\right)^{-1}\right),$$

which proves that Φ is monotonically decreasing.

For the supermodularity, we use recent techniques presented in [23], and specifically the following proposition:

Proposition 3 *Let $\mathcal{U}_D^i \subset \mathcal{U}^i$, and P_D be the matrix whose columns correspond to P_v' for $v \in \mathcal{U}_D^i$. Then, for $f : \mathbb{R}_+ \to \mathbb{R}$ such that f' is operator monotone, it holds that*

$$\Phi(\mathcal{U}_D^i) = tr\left(f(P_D P_D^\top)\right)$$

is supermodular.

In our case $f(x) = \frac{1}{x}$, and its derivative $f'(x) = -\frac{1}{x^2}$ is operator monotone, which implies that Φ is supermodular. The proof resembles the proof of Corollary 2.4 of [23], albeit plugging operator monotone derivative instead of operator antitone one.

Finally, as mentioned before, these three properties yield an $(\frac{e^t-1}{t})$-approximation to the problem of minimizing Φ. That is, Algorithm 1 generates a subset $\mathcal{U}_B^{ALG}$ for which:

$$\begin{aligned}
\Phi(\mathcal{U}_B^{ALG}) &\leq \left(\frac{e^t - 1}{t}\right) \min_{\mathcal{U}_B^i \subset \mathcal{U}^i} \Phi(\mathcal{U}_B^i) \\
&= \left(\frac{e^t - 1}{t}\right) \min_{\mathcal{U}_B^i \subset \mathcal{U}^i} \left\{\frac{\mathbb{E}\left[\text{MSE}(\mathcal{U}_B^i)\right]}{\sigma^2} - 1 - \varphi_i\right\} \\
&\leq \left(\frac{e^t - 1}{t}\right) \min_{\mathcal{U}_B^i \subset \mathcal{U}^i} \left\{\frac{\mathbb{E}\left[\text{MSE}(\mathcal{U}_B^i)\right]}{\sigma^2} - 1\right\} - \varphi_i \\
&= \left(\frac{e^t - 1}{t}\right)\left(\frac{\mathbb{E}\left[\text{MSE}(\mathcal{U}_B^*)\right]}{\sigma^2} - 1\right) - \varphi_i.
\end{aligned}$$

By substituting $\Phi(\mathcal{U}_B^{ALG}) = \frac{\mathbb{E}\left[\text{MSE}(\mathcal{U}_B^{ALG})\right]}{\sigma^2} - \varphi_i - 1$ in the inequality above, we get the stated result. □

3.2.2 Non-Identically Distributed Noise Terms

The analysis in Section 3.2.1 relies heavily on the assumption that $\{\varepsilon_{ui}\}$ are identically distributed. However, it is sometimes reasonable to assume that each user has a different noise distribution with respect to the employed model. In such cases, the identical distribution assumption only weakens our model. In this section we extend our analysis to the case where each of the users has a different (yet known in advance) noise distribution.

Thus, let i be a new item, and $\mathcal{U}_B^i \subset \mathcal{U}^i$ a subset of users assigned for the task of rating it. We start by introducing a new estimator for (b_i, Q_i), which generalizes the least

Algorithm 2 Backward Greedy Selection (BGS2)

1: Input: users set $\mathcal{U}^i$, and corresponding matrix $P_{\mathcal{U}^i}$.
2: Output: users subset $\mathcal{U}_B^{ALG}$.
3: Initialize $P_B = P_{\mathcal{U}^i}$, $C_B = C_{\mathcal{U}^i}$, and $\mathcal{U}_B^{ALG} = \mathcal{U}^i$.
4: **for** $j = 1$ to $|\mathcal{U}^i| - B$ **do**
5: $\quad v_j \leftarrow \arg\min_{v \in \mathcal{U}_B^{ALG}} \left\{ \mathrm{tr}\left(\left(P_{B\setminus v} C_{B\setminus v}^{-2} P_{B\setminus v}^\top \right)^{-1} \right) \right\}$
6: $\quad$ Update $P_B \leftarrow P_{B\setminus v_j}$ and $C_B \leftarrow C_{B\setminus v_j}$.
7: $\quad$ Update $\mathcal{U}_B^{ALG} \leftarrow \mathcal{U}_B^{ALG} \setminus v_j$.
8: **end for**

squares estimator:

$$\left(\tilde{b}_i, \tilde{Q}_i\right) = \left(P_B C_B^{-2} P_B^\top\right)^{-1} P_B C_B^{-2} r_B,$$

where again, C_B is the square root of the covariance matrix that corresponds to ε_{vi} for $v \in \mathcal{U}_B^i$. Intuitively, this estimator is a least squares estimator that considers variance-scaled users. In the sequel, we refer to this estimator as *generalized least squares estimator.* The following lemma states that this is indeed an unbiased estimator for (b_i, Q_i). The proof is technical and appears in Appendix A.2.

Lemma 4 *Assume there exist b_i and Q_i, such that for every $u \in \mathcal{U}$ it holds that $r_{ui} = \mu + b_u + b_i + Q_i^\top P_u + \varepsilon_{ui}$, where $\mathbb{E}[\varepsilon_{ui}] = 0$ and $\mathbb{E}\left[\varepsilon_{ui}^2\right] = \sigma_u^2$. Then,*

$$\left(\tilde{b}_i, \tilde{Q}_i\right) = \left(P_B C_B^{-2} P_B^\top\right)^{-1} P_B C_B^{-2} r_B \qquad (5)$$

is an unbiased estimator for $(b_i, Q_i^\top)$.

We proceed to state the lemma that encapsulates our parallel key observation for the case of non-identically distributed noise terms; its proof appears in Appendix A.3.

Lemma 5 *Assume there exist b_i and Q_i, such that for every $u \in \mathcal{U}$ it holds that $r_{ui} = \mu + b_u + b_i + Q_i^\top P_u + \varepsilon_{ui}$, where $\mathbb{E}[\varepsilon_{ui}] = 0$ and $\mathbb{E}\left[\varepsilon_{ui}^2\right] = \sigma_u^2$. Then, the following is equivalent to the problem presented in Equation (3):*

$$\min_{\mathcal{U}_B^i \subset \mathcal{U}^i} \left\{ tr\left(\left(P_B C_B^{-2} P_B^\top \right)^{-1} \right) + \frac{1}{|\mathcal{U}|} \sum_{u \in \mathcal{U}} \sigma_u^2 \right\},$$

if the generalized least squares estimator is considered.

After establishing here also an equivalent optimization problem, we turn to present a simple adaptation of Algorithm 1 to this problem. Here, the notation $C_{\mathcal{U}^i}$ refers to the square root of the covariance matrix of all available users, and the notations $P_{B\setminus v_j}$ and $C_{B\setminus v_j}$ are as defined in Section 3.2.1. For Algorithm 2 we can prove the following:

Theorem 6 *Let i be a new item, and $\mathcal{U}^i$ its corresponding set of available users, and assume that $\mathbb{E}[\varepsilon_{ui}] = 0$ and $\mathbb{E}\left[\varepsilon_{ui}^2\right] = \sigma_u^2$ for all $u \in \mathcal{U}$. Then, Algorithm 2 generates a subset $\mathcal{U}_B^{ALG} \subset \mathcal{U}^i$, for which the following holds:*

$$\mathbb{E}\left[MSE(\mathcal{U}_B^{ALG})\right] \leq \frac{1}{|\mathcal{U}|} \sum_{u \in \mathcal{U}} \sigma_u^2 + \frac{e^t - 1}{t} \left(\mathbb{E}\left[MSE(\mathcal{U}_B^*)\right] - \frac{1}{|\mathcal{U}|} \sum_{u \in \mathcal{U}} \sigma_u^2 \right).$$

The proof relies on the same techniques of Theorem 2, albeit plugging the variance-scaled matrix $P_B C_B^{-1}$ instead of the matrix P_B, and is thus omitted here.

Reduction to unknown variances. Until now, we assumed that each user has its own noise variance with respect to the model. Our analysis relied on the fact that these variances are known to us in advance. Clearly, this is never the case in real life. However, in the setting of CF-based recommender systems, we can utilize the past ratings of a given user to estimate this variance. Formally, let $\mathcal{R}(u)$ be the set of items that user u has rated. Then, σ_u^2 can be estimated as follows:

$$\tilde{\sigma}_u^2 = \frac{1}{|\mathcal{R}(u)|} \sum_{i \in \mathcal{R}(u)} (\tilde{r}_{ui} - r_{ui})^2,$$

where $\tilde{r}_{ui}$ is as predicted by the LFM (Equation (1)). In the experimental section, we show that despite the fact that the variances are estimated and not known, Algorithm 2 outperforms all the baselines (including Algorithm 1).

4. EXPERIMENTAL RESULTS

4.1 Dataset and Model

We consider a large movie ratings dataset released by Netflix as the basis of a well publicized competition [5]. The original dataset contains more than 100 million date-stamped ratings (integers between 1 and 5) collected between Nov. 11, 1999 and Dec. 31, 2005, from about 480,000 anonymous Netflix customers on 17,770 movies.

The dataset is processed as follows: a new ratings matrix (denoted henceforth by $\mathcal{R}$) is constructed from 17,000 arbitrarily chosen movies. The matrix $\mathcal{R}$ contains about 96 million ratings from the same number of users as in the original dataset. The other 770 movies are used as "new items" in the various experiments we conduct[2]. Note that since most users have not rated most of the movies, the ratings matrix $\mathcal{R}$ is very sparse (only 1% of all ratings exist).

We factorize $\mathcal{R}$ using the LFM (Equation (1)), with its dimension set to be $k = 20$. We use the common Root Mean Squared Error (RMSE) metric to measure the prediction accuracy of the resulted model. For the task of minimizing this metric, we apply the Stochastic Gradient Descent (SGD) algorithm, where the learning rate is inspired by the AdaGrad algorithm of [7].

4.2 Experimental Setup

We now describe how we test algorithms for user selection in an offline manner on the Netflix dataset. As mentioned before, a set of 770 movies is withheld from our model. We henceforth denote this set by $\mathcal{N}$, and think of it as a set of movies that are new to our recommender system. For each movie $i \in \mathcal{N}$, we denote by $\mathcal{R}(i)$ the set of Netflix users who have actually rated this movie. We then adapt the dataset to our setting as follows:

The pool of available users: we consider the set $\mathcal{R}(i)$ as the pool of available users to rate movie i, i.e., we set $\mathcal{U}_i = \mathcal{R}(i)$. Note that indeed, $\mathcal{U}^i$ changes for every movie i, as the actual available ratings differ from one

[2]Note we cannot use one of the official Netflix test sets, as none of them captures the notion of new items.

movie to another in the Netflix dataset. This coincides with the pool of available users changing in time.

Selecting a subset of users: the conceptual step of assigning a subset of users $\mathcal{U}_B^i \subset \mathcal{U}^i$ to rate movie i corresponds to the action of revealing their actual ratings in the dataset.

The set of all users: due to the small portion of actual ratings in the dataset, we cannot measure the prediction error on all users. Thus, after revealing the actual ratings of the subset $\mathcal{U}_B^i$, we use the remaining unrevealed ratings for this task, i.e., we set $\mathcal{U} = \mathcal{U}_i \setminus \mathcal{U}_B^i$. Note that we *essentially use the non-selected users for the evaluation task* in this step.

Despite the fact that our analysis was carried out using the MSE metric, we measure the prediction error of the different approaches using the RMSE metric:

$$\text{RMSE}(\mathcal{U}_B^i) = \sqrt{\frac{1}{|\mathcal{U}|}\sum_{u\in\mathcal{U}}(r_{ui} - \tilde{r}_{ui})^2}.$$

Since the root square is a monotone function, minimizing the MSE is equivalent to minimizing the RMSE (in the sense that both problems has the same minimizer). Thus, to be consistent with previous works, our experimental results are presented using the RMSE metric.

An important aspect of our experimental setup is the preselection of users who watched the "new" movie. This might seem unrealistic, since generally there is no guarantee that users will rate the new item (as we implicitly assume). We justify our setup as follows: each user we select to rate the new item is given some reward, which is (in most cases) sufficient to convince the user to provide rating. This mitigates the need to select "frequent raters", and highlights the rather interesting geometric aspect of the problem: selected users should be scattered (in a sense) in the LFM space.

4.3 Baselines

We turn to present several common and less common baselines from the recent literature. Recall that our problem (as defined in Equation (3)) was divided into two separate problems, and thus we consider two types of baselines. We begin with baselines for **Problem A**: rating prediction.

Similarity based estimator. Just like the least squares estimator, this baseline seeks to estimate (b_i, Q_i) and consequently generate a prediction $\tilde{r}_{ui} = \mu + \tilde{b}_i + b_u + \tilde{Q}_i P_u$. The estimation uses the assigned users who liked the item, and relies on the following underlying assumption: "good" user-item interaction is expressed by the closeness of the corresponding representative vectors in the LFM space. Thus, yielding the estimator:

$$\tilde{b}_i = \frac{1}{|\mathcal{U}_B^i|}\sum_{v\in\mathcal{U}_B^i}(r_{vi} - b_v) - \mu\ ,$$

$$\tilde{Q}_i = \frac{1}{|\{v \in \mathcal{U}_B^i | r_{vi} \geq \gamma\}|}\sum_{v\in\mathcal{U}_B^i | r_{vi}\geq\gamma} P_v\ ,$$

where γ is a predefined threshold (e.g., 4 or 5 for the Netflix dataset). We note that integrating negative feedback (low ratings) yields an empirically inferior similarity based estimator that is thus omitted here. This approach was successfully practiced in [20, 14, 2, 3].

We continue with presenting baselines for **Problem B**: user selection.

Forward greedy selection (B1). This baseline relies as well on the optimal design approach, and specifically on the A-optimality criterion. Basically, it aims to minimize the trace of the inverse of the information matrix $P_B P_B^\top$, similarly to our first algorithm. However, the selection is done in a forward manner: starting with an empty set, and greedily adding the user whose contribution is the highest. This approach was successfully practiced in many fields of active learning, rather than only for the item cold-start problem of CF-based recommenders (see [17] for a more comprehensive survey). However, we are not aware of any performance guarantee for this algorithm.

Clustering (B2). Intuitively, having a heterogeneous set of users will result in a more objective ratings of the item. To this end, we suggest to cluster the users with respect to their representation in the Euclidean LFM space and subsequently sample from the resulting clusters. For the clustering task, we use the standard k-means algorithm with cosine similarity as its similarity measure.

We propose two clustering-based baselines for the selection problem, each differs in the number of clusters and the sampling procedure: (1) split the pool of available users into B clusters, and select the users that are closest to the cluster center of mass (one user per cluster); and (2) split the pool of available users into c clusters (where $c < B$), and from each cluster select number of users at random and proportionally to the cluster size. For this baseline, the value of c is determined empirically.

Random selection (B3). In this baseline, the B users are selected randomly from the pool of available users. At first glance, this baseline seems rather weak. However, if B is sufficiently large, then $\mathcal{U}_B^i$ is a statistically good representative of $\mathcal{U}^i$, and this baseline cannot be easily beaten. Moreover, this baseline has many practical appeals and is thus very popular with state-of-the-art recommenders.

Frequent raters (B4). Here we select users who tend to provide many ratings. This baseline utilizes the following conjecture: users with extensive rating history have better modeling in CF-based recommender systems. Therefore, preferring these users over users that have limited rating history seems reasonable in our setting.

Edgy raters (B5). This baseline selects users that provide diverse ratings, or more accurately, ratings with large variance. Intuitively, these users provide more information regarding an item they like or dislike, than users that tend to rate all items in a similar manner.

Early birds raters (B6). This baseline slightly differs from the previous baselines: instead of actively selecting users to rate the new item, we conceptually invite all users to opine on the new item at their convenience, and consider the (chronologically) first B returned ratings as our selection. The intention here is not to offer another active selection baseline, but rather to study the utility of early reviews, coming from people who are enthusiastic about trying out the new item, for modeling the rest of the population.

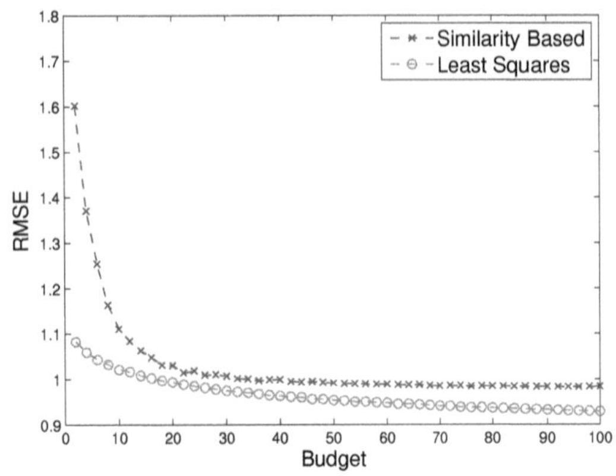

Figure 1: Rating prediction comparison.

4.4 Results

We separately report the results for each of the considered problems, starting with the rating prediction problem and moving on to the user selection problem.

4.4.1 Rating Prediction Comparison

We compare the performance of the least squares estimator and the similarity based estimator. To this end, we select 300 movies from the set $\mathcal{N}$, arbitrarily. For each of these movies, we randomly select B users ($B = 2, 4, \ldots, 100$), and apply both estimators to generate predictions for the remaining users. The prediction accuracy is measured using the RMSE metric over all predictions (and not separately for each movie). This routine is averaged over 50 runs to ensure stability.

As evident in Figure 1, the least squares estimator outperforms the considered baseline. Qualitatively, similar results were obtained when applying the other (non-random) selection schemes of B users, and are thus omitted here.

4.4.2 User Selection Comparison

Here the performance of our approach is compared with the baselines (presented in Section 4.3) for **Problem B**. To carry out the experiment, we select 300 movies from the set $\mathcal{N}$, arbitrarily. For each of these movies, we apply all six baselines (B1-B6) and our two algorithms (denoted by BGS1 and BGS2) to select a subset of B users. We then generate $(\tilde{b}_i, \tilde{Q}_i)$ using the least squares estimator (or the generalized least squares estimator for BGS2), regardless of how the selection was made. Since this estimator outperforms the similarity based estimator for any selection of B users (as demonstrated in Figure 1), we do not lose information by omitting them. Here again, we measure the prediction accuracy using the RMSE metric over all predictions. For the non-deterministic baselines: Clustering (B2) and Random (B3), we average the results over 50 runs to ensure stability.

As can be seen in Figure 2, the optimal design based algorithms outperform the other baselines for almost any budget. In particular, BGS2 (which accounts for independent yet not identically distributed noises) significantly [3] surpasses BGS1 and B1 (which are practically indistinguishable) for any budget. The second best performing baseline is B5, which utilizes the ratings of the "edgy" users. We conjecture that such users provide more information regarding a new item, in addition to being well-scattered in the LFM space. Baselines B2 and B3 (Random and Clustering[4]) seem to perform similarly in our setting, yet a closer look discovers that by clustering the users in the LFM space we get more stable results (in the sense of lower variance of the resulted RMSE). We remind the reader that our basic CF model was trained using state-of-the-art algorithms, where every percent of improvement is not easily achieved.

[3]The results are significant at any significance level, since we average them over $|\mathcal{N}| = 300$ movies.

5. CONCLUSIONS AND FUTURE WORK

In this work we started with a mature LFM model and tried to tackle the item cold-start problem by answering two questions: (a) given ratings of B users, how can we estimate other users' ratings of an arbitrary new item without retraining the model? and (b) how to choose the set of B users? We showed that in order to get approximately optimal results in terms of mean squared error, the above questions should be tackled jointly. In particular, we applied optimal design techniques and devised two greedy algorithms that achieve that goal under certain assumptions. We used the Netflix dataset to demonstrate the superiority of the proposed algorithms over a set of previously considered and non-considered baselines.

Our work can be seen as a "one-shot", non-adaptive active learning scheme that selects the B users at once. This leaves three interesting variants for future work. The first variant we consider is an *adaptive active learning* scheme, in which users are chosen sequentially, with each selection done only after receiving the ratings of the previously chosen user. The second variant tackles an *online* version of the problem, where potential users arrive one by one and the publisher must decide whether to assign them the item or not. In several recommendation settings, e.g. news recommendations, new items constantly arrive and have very short lifetimes, thereby requiring that the publisher identifies quickly which users to recommend them to. The tradeoff between (a) selecting a good set of users, and (b) quickly completing the reviewing process of the item, presents a challenging optimization problem. The third variant discusses a *multi-item* setting, where the publisher must concurrently explore several new items while users can review only one or a small fixed number of items. Note that the multi-item setting can be investigated in both the offline and the online settings.

In addition to the above variants, an interesting direction would be to study the user cold-start problem using the techniques we presented in this work. As discussed in the related work section, the user and the item cold-start problem are essentially different, mainly due to the ability to adaptively interview new users in order to bootstrap their modeling. Whereas this enables decision tree type solutions for user cold-start handling (which are currently the state-of-the-art), such solutions cannot be implemented in the setting considered in this paper. However, applying the optimal design approach to the user cold-start problem is possible and may potentially lead to better theoretical and empirical guarantees.

[4]We present here only the better performing clustering technique, which is the second one discussed in Section 4.3.

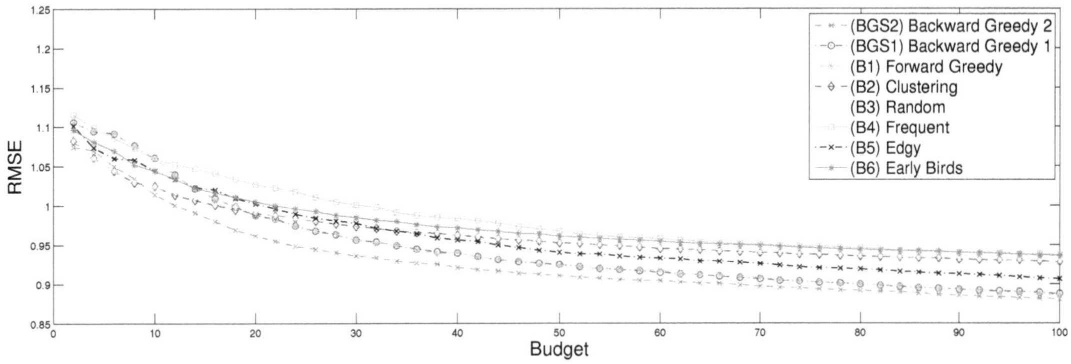

Figure 2: User selection comparison.

6. REFERENCES

[1] Deepak Agarwal and Bee-Chung Chen. Regression-based latent factor models. In *Proc. KDD*, 2009.

[2] Michal Aharon, Amit Kagian, Yehuda Koren, and Ronny Lempel. Dynamic personalized recommendation of comment-eliciting stories. In *Proc. RecSys*, 2012.

[3] Natalie Aizenberg, Yehuda Koren, and Oren Somekh. Build your own music recommender by modeling internet radio streams. In *Proc. WWW*, 2012.

[4] A. C. Atkinson and A. N. Donev. *Optimum Experimental Designs*. Oxford Univ. Press, 1992.

[5] J. Bennett and S. Lanning. The netflix prize. In *Proc. KDD Cup and Workshop*, 2007.

[6] Gideon Dror, Noam Koenigstein, and Yehuda Koren. Yahoo! music recommendations: Modeling music ratings with temporal dynamics and item. In *Proc. RecSys*, 2011.

[7] John Duchi, Elad Hazan, and Yoram Singer. Adaptive subgradient methods for online learning and stochastic optimization. *Journal of Machine Learning Research (JMLR)*, 12:2121–2159, 2011.

[8] Nadav Golbandi, Yehuda Koren, and Ronny Lempel. On bootstrapping recommender systems. In *Proc. CIKM*, 2010.

[9] Nadav Golbandi, Yehuda Koren, and Ronny Lempel. Adaptive bootstrapping of recommender systems using decision trees. In *Proc. WSDM*, 2011.

[10] Asela Gunawardana and Christopher Meek. Tied boltzmann machines for cold start recommendations. In *Proc. RecSys*, 2008.

[11] Asela Gunawardana and Christopher Meek. A unified approach to building hybrid recommender systems. In *Proc. RecSys*, 2009.

[12] Victor P. Il'ev. An approximation guarantee of the greedy descent algorithm for minimizing a supermodular set function. *Discrete Applied Mathematics*, 114(1):131–146, 2001.

[13] Arnd Kohrs and Bernard Merialdo. Improving collaborative filtering for new users by smart object selection. In *Proc. International Conference on Media Features (ICMF)*, 2001.

[14] Yehuda Koren. Factorization meets the neighborhood: a multifaceted collaborative filtering model. In *Proc. KDD*, 2008.

[15] Yehuda Koren. Collaborative filtering with temporal dynamics. *Commun. of the ACM*, 53(4):89–97, 2010.

[16] Yehuda Koren, Robert M. Bell, and Chris Volinsky. Matrix factorization techniques for recommender systems. *Computer, IEEE*, 42(8):30–37, 2009.

[17] Andreas Krause and Carlos Guestrin. Near-optimal observation selection using submodular functions. In *AAAI*, volume 7, pages 1650–1654, 2007.

[18] Shao-Lun Lee. Commodity recommendations of retail business based on decision tree induction. *Expert Systems with Applications*, 37(5):3685–3694, 2010.

[19] Seung-Taek Park and Wei Chu. Pairwise preference regression for cold-start recommendation. In *Proc. RecSys*, 2009.

[20] Arkadiusz Paterek. Improving regularized singular value decomposition for collaborative filtering. In *Proc. KDD cup and workshop*, 2007.

[21] Al Mamunur Rashid, Istvan Albert, Dan Cosley, Shyong K Lam, Sean M McNee, Joseph A Konstan, and John Riedl. Getting to know you: learning new user preferences in recommender systems. In *Proc. International Conference on Intelligent User Interfaces*, 2002.

[22] Al Mamunur Rashid, George Karypis, and John Riedl. Learning preferences of new users in recommender systems: an information theoretic approach. *ACM SIGKDD Explorations Newsletter*, 10(2):90–100, 2008.

[23] Guillaume Sagnol. Approximation of a maximum-submodular-coverage problem involving spectral functions, with application to experimental designs. *Discrete Applied Mathematics*, 161(1):258–276, 2013.

[24] Chien-Fu Wu. Some algorithmic aspects of the theory of optimal designs. *Annals of Statistics*, 6(6):1286–1301, 1978.

[25] Kai Yu, Jinbo Bi, and Volker Tresp. Active learning via transductive experimental design. In *Proc. ICML*, 2006.

[26] Ke Zhou, Shuang-Hong Yang, and Hongyuan Zha. Functional matrix factorizations for cold-start recommendation. In *Proc. SIGIR*, 2011.

APPENDIX

A. PROOFS

A.1 Proof of Lemma 1

Let i be a new item, and $\mathcal{U}^i$ its corresponding set of available users. Now, given a set of B users $\mathcal{U}_B^i \subset \mathcal{U}^i$, we can estimate (b_i, Q_i) using the least squares estimator:

$$\begin{aligned}(\tilde{b}_i, \tilde{Q}_i) &= \left(\sum_{v \in \mathcal{U}_B^i} P'_v P'^{\top}_v\right)^{-1} \left(\sum_{v \in \mathcal{U}_B^i} (r_{vi} - b_v - \mu) P'_v\right) \\ &= \left(P_B P_B^\top\right)^{-1} P_B r_B. \end{aligned} \tag{6}$$

Notice that according to Equation (2) we can also express the vector r_B as follows:

$$r_B = P_B^\top (b_i, Q_i) + \varepsilon_B,$$

and by substituting the above in Equation (6) and shifting sides we get that

$$(\tilde{b}_i, \tilde{Q}_i) - (b_i, Q_i) = \left(P_B P_B^\top\right)^{-1} P_B \varepsilon_B. \tag{7}$$

We denote by $\mathrm{MSE}(\mathcal{U}_B^i)$ the resulted MSE value by using the ratings of the users within $\mathcal{U}_B^i$ in our prediction model, that is, $\mathrm{MSE}(\mathcal{U}_B^i) = \frac{1}{|\mathcal{U}|}\sum_{u\in\mathcal{U}} (\tilde{r}_{ui} - r_{ui})^2$.

Then, we can derive:

$$\begin{aligned}\mathbb{E}\left[\mathrm{MSE}(\mathcal{U}_B^i)\right] &= \frac{1}{|\mathcal{U}|}\mathbb{E}\left[\sum_{u\in\mathcal{U}} (\tilde{r}_{ui} - r_{ui})^2\right] \\ &= \frac{1}{|\mathcal{U}|}\mathbb{E}\left[\left\|P^\top \left((\tilde{b}_i, \tilde{Q}_i) - (b_i, Q_i)\right) + \varepsilon_{\mathcal{U}}\right\|_2^2\right] \\ &\overset{(1)}{=} \frac{1}{|\mathcal{U}|}\mathbb{E}\left[\left\|P^\top \left(P_B P_B^\top\right)^{-1} P_B \varepsilon_B + \varepsilon_{\mathcal{U}}\right\|_2^2\right] \\ &\overset{(2)}{=} \frac{1}{|\mathcal{U}|}\mathbb{E}\left[\left\|P^\top \left(P_B P_B^\top\right)^{-1} P_B \varepsilon_B\right\|_2^2 + \|\varepsilon_{\mathcal{U}}\|_2^2\right],\end{aligned}$$

where the expectation is taken over the noise ε_{vi} and ε_{ui}. Equality (1) follows by substituting Equation (7); equality (2) holds since $\mathbb{E}[\varepsilon_{ui}] = 0$ for all $u \in \mathcal{U}$, and also since ε_B and $\varepsilon_{\mathcal{U}}$ are independent.

Next, we use the assumption $\mathbb{E}\left[\varepsilon_{ui}^2\right] = \sigma^2$ to get:

$$\begin{aligned}\mathbb{E}\left[\mathrm{MSE}(\mathcal{U}_B^i)\right] &= \frac{1}{|\mathcal{U}|}\mathbb{E}\left[\left\|P^\top \left(P_B P_B^\top\right)^{-1} P_B \varepsilon_B\right\|_2^2\right] + \sigma^2 \\ &\overset{(3)}{=} \frac{1}{|\mathcal{U}|}\left\|P^\top \left(P_B P_B^\top\right)^{-1} P_B C_B\right\|_F^2 + \sigma^2 \\ &\overset{(4)}{=} \sigma^2 \mathrm{tr}\left(\left(P_B P_B^\top\right)^{-1}\right) + \sigma^2,\end{aligned}$$

where C_B denotes the square root of the covariance matrix of ε_B; equality (3) follows from the definition of the Frobenius norm $\|\|_F$, and equality (4) holds since $C_B = \sigma^2 I_{B\times B}$, and since we assume that $PP^\top = |\mathcal{U}|\, I_{(k+1)\times(k+1)}$.

Thus, the lemma is obtained.

A.2 Proof of Lemma 4

By taking expectation we have that:

$$\begin{aligned}\mathbb{E}\left[(\tilde{b}_i, \tilde{Q}_i)\right] &= \mathbb{E}\left[\left(P_B C_B^{-2} P_B^\top\right)^{-1} P_B C_B^{-2} r_B\right] \\ &= \mathbb{E}\left[\left(P_B C_B^{-2} P_B^\top\right)^{-1} P_B C_B^{-2} P_B^\top (b_i, Q_i)\right] \\ &\quad + \mathbb{E}\left[\left(P_B C_B^{-2} P_B^\top\right)^{-1} P_B C_B^{-2} \varepsilon_B\right] \\ &= (b_i, Q_i) + \left(P_B C_B^{-2} P_B^\top\right)^{-1} P_B C_B^{-2} \mathbb{E}[\varepsilon_B] \\ &= (b_i, Q_i),\end{aligned}$$

where in the second equality we used the assumption that $r_B = P_B^\top (b_i, Q_i) + \varepsilon_B$.

A.3 Proof of Lemma 5

Recall that as before we assume that

$$PP^\top = |\mathcal{U}|\, I_{(k+1)\times(k+1)}\ .$$

Now, let i be a new item, and $\mathcal{U}_B^i \subset \mathcal{U}^i$ a subset of users assigned for the task of rating it. Then, we can substitute r_B in the generalized least squares estimator (Equation (5)) to get the following result:

$$(\tilde{b}_i, \tilde{Q}_i) - (b_i, Q_i) = \left(P_B C_B^{-2} P_B^\top\right)^{-1} P_B C_B^{-2} \varepsilon_B.$$

We substitute the above in the MSE equation, and rewrite our motivation problem:

$$\begin{aligned}&\mathbb{E}\left[\mathrm{MSE}(\mathcal{U}_B^i)\right] \\ &= \frac{1}{|\mathcal{U}|}\mathbb{E}\left[\sum_{u\in\mathcal{U}} (\tilde{r}_{ui} - r_{ui})^2\right] \\ &= \frac{1}{|\mathcal{U}|}\mathbb{E}\left[\left\|P^\top \left((\tilde{b}_i, \tilde{Q}_i) - (b_i, Q_i)\right) + \varepsilon_{\mathcal{U}}\right\|_2^2\right] \\ &= \frac{1}{|\mathcal{U}|}\mathbb{E}\left[\left\|P^\top \left(P_B C_B^{-2} P_B^\top\right)^{-1} P_B C_B^{-2} \varepsilon_B + \varepsilon_{\mathcal{U}}\right\|_2^2\right] \\ &= \frac{1}{|\mathcal{U}|}\mathbb{E}\left[\left\|P^\top \left(P_B C_B^{-2} P_B^\top\right)^{-1} P_B C_B^{-2} \varepsilon_B\right\|_2^2\right] + \frac{\mathbb{E}\left[\|\varepsilon_{\mathcal{U}}\|_2^2\right]}{|\mathcal{U}|} \\ &= \frac{1}{|\mathcal{U}|}\mathbb{E}\left[\left\|P^\top \left(P_B C_B^{-2} P_B^\top\right)^{-1} P_B C_B^{-2} \varepsilon_B\right\|_2^2\right] + \frac{1}{|\mathcal{U}|}\sum_{u\in\mathcal{U}} \sigma_u^2 \\ &= \frac{1}{|\mathcal{U}|}\left\|P^\top \left(P_B C_B^{-2} P_B^\top\right)^{-1} P_B C_B^{-1}\right\|_F^2 + \frac{1}{|\mathcal{U}|}\sum_{u\in\mathcal{U}} \sigma_u^2 \\ &= \mathrm{tr}\left(\left(P_B C_B^{-2} P_B^\top\right)^{-1}\right) + \frac{1}{|\mathcal{U}|}\sum_{u\in\mathcal{U}} \sigma_u^2,\end{aligned}$$

where the equalities follow similarly to Lemma 1.

Improved Theoretical and Practical Guarantees for Chromatic Correlation Clustering

Yael Anava*
Technion, Haifa, Israel
yaelan@tx.technion.ac.il

Noa Avigdor-Elgrabli
Yahoo Labs, Haifa, Israel
noaa@yahoo-inc.com

Iftah Gamzu
Yahoo Labs, Haifa, Israel
iftah.gamzu@yahoo.com

ABSTRACT

We study a natural generalization of the correlation clustering problem to graphs in which the pairwise relations between objects are categorical instead of binary. This problem was recently introduced by Bonchi et al. under the name of chromatic correlation clustering, and is motivated by many real-world applications in data-mining and social networks, including community detection, link classification, and entity de-duplication.

Our main contribution is a fast and easy-to-implement constant approximation framework for the problem, which builds on a novel reduction of the problem to that of correlation clustering. This result significantly progresses the current state of knowledge for the problem, improving on a previous result that only guaranteed linear approximation in the input size. We complement the above result by developing a linear programming-based algorithm that achieves an improved approximation ratio of 4. Although this algorithm cannot be considered to be practical, it further extends our theoretical understanding of chromatic correlation clustering. We also present a fast heuristic algorithm that is motivated by real-life scenarios in which there is a ground-truth clustering that is obscured by noisy observations. We test our algorithms on both synthetic and real datasets, like social networks data. Our experiments reinforce the theoretical findings by demonstrating that our algorithms generally outperform previous approaches, both in terms of solution cost and reconstruction of an underlying ground-truth clustering.

Categories and Subject Descriptors

F.2 [**Theory of Computation**]: Analysis of Algorithms and Problem Complexity; H.2.8 [**Information Systems**]: Database Applications – Data mining

*This work was done when the author was an intern at Yahoo Labs, Haifa, Israel.

WWW 2015, May 18–22, 2015, Florence, Italy.
ACM 978-1-4503-3469-3/15/05.
http://dx.doi.org/10.1145/2736277.2741629.

Keywords

Approximation algorithms; Categorical similarity; Clustering; Edge-labeled graphs

1. INTRODUCTION

Clustering is a fundamental research area in the field of data mining. The goal in clustering is to partition a collection of objects into groups, using data about the objects and their relationships, so that the objects in each group are more similar to one another than objects in other groups. The *correlation clustering* problem [6] received a great deal of attention in recent years due to its natural formulation and its applicability in a wide range of scenarios. Indeed, correlation clustering is regarded to be a basic primitive in the data mining practitioner's toolkit [15]. An instance of correlation clustering consists of an undirected graph where each edge (relation between objects) is labeled as either positive (similar) or negative (dissimilar). The goal is to partition the nodes (objects) into clusters in a way that minimizes the total number of disagreements. A disagreement happens if a positive edge becomes inter-cluster or a negative edge becomes intra-cluster.

In this paper, we study the *chromatic correlation clustering* problem which was recently introduced by Bonchi et al. [9]. This problem is a natural generalization of correlation clustering in which the pairwise similarity relations between objects are *categorical* instead of binary. The chromatic correlation clustering problem is motivated by many real-world applications in data-mining and social networks. Some of these applications extend natural applications of correlation clustering, like community detection, link classification, entity de-duplication, and more. To provide more intuition, a generic scenario in social networks follows. A social network can be modeled by a graph whose nodes represent individuals and its edges stand for the relationships between those individuals. Clearly, individuals in the social network have relationships of various types, e.g., familial, professional, social, and more. The chromatic correlation clustering paradigm can be utilized to classify those individuals into disjoint communities consisting of entities that are most similar under some relationship type. Intuitively, each such community is a cohesive group of individuals that share similar characteristics, and as such, one can leverage holistic knowledge about the community to characterize its individuals. It seems important to note that characterizing an individual based on her direct relationships of maximal occurring type may not be sufficient as the affiliated entities may only have sparse relationships between them, and hence, they do not carry meaningful joint information.

The categorical community discovery scenario described above underlies many applications of interest whose goal is to better understand the structure of networks. One example of such application is the link classification problem (see, e.g., [28, 26, 11]). The objective in this problem is to predict the category between two entities using the information provided in the rest of the network. For instance, a link classification method can be employed to infer an unknown relationship between two individuals in a social network. This classification can be later utilized by recommendation or prediction systems for various tasks, like viral marketing [31] and personalization [5]. Another application is the entity de-duplication problem (see, e.g., [17, 4, 20]). The goal in this case is to identify and potentially remove entities that are duplicates of one another according to some measure or category. Note that duplicates in the data occur in practice when the entities are obtained through independent sources. An entity de-duplication method can be used, for instance, to support a person search on next generation search engines [22]. In this case, a search query for a person should produce a cluster consisting of the most representative webpages associated with that person. There are many other relevant applications for categorical community discovery such as query refinements in web search [32] and webpage segmentation [12].

1.1 Problem definition

An instance of the chromatic correlation clustering problem consists of a finite set L of (positive) colors, a special (negative) color $\lambda \notin L$, and a colored graph, that is, a undirected graph $G = (V, E)$ with a coloring function $\chi : E \to L \cup \{\lambda\}$ on its edges. The objective is to find a colored clustering of the graph's nodes that minimizes the overall number of disagreements. More formally, we are interested in a partition $\mathcal{C} : V \to \{C_1, C_2, \ldots\}$ of the nodes into a collection of disjoint sets and an assignment of a color to each cluster $\psi : \{C_1, C_2, \ldots\} \to L$ that minimizes

$$|\{uv \in E : \mathcal{C}(u) \neq \mathcal{C}(v) \text{ and } \chi(uv) \neq \lambda\}| + \\ |\{uv \in E : C = \mathcal{C}(u) = \mathcal{C}(v) \text{ and } \psi(C) \neq \chi(uv)\}| \ .$$

Note that the first term counts the inter-cluster disagreements, while the latter term counts the intra-cluster disagreements. Also remark that no cluster can be assigned to the special color λ, and therefore, any λ-colored edge within a cluster implies a disagreement. Intuitively, a c-colored edge for some $c \in L$ indicates similarity of type c between two objects, and a λ-colored edge indicates a dissimilarity between two objects with respect to all types.

Chromatic correlation clustering was introduced by Bonchi et al. [9]. One can easily notice that the correlation clustering problem is the special case of this problem when $|L| = 1$, and thus, it immediately follows that the chromatic correlation clustering problem is NP-hard [6]. The study of correlation clustering under complete graphs has been given a considerable attention in the past (see, e.g., [6, 13, 2, 30, 15, 8]). Indeed, in many applications, the underlying graph is assumed to be complete as missing edges can be interpreted as negative. In the remainder of this paper, we assume that the input graph is complete, unless we specify otherwise. Bonchi et al. developed a randomized algorithm for complete graphs whose approximation guarantee is proportional to the maximum degree of the graph induced by the L-edges. This can be as bad as $O(|V|)$. They also suggested several additional heuristic algorithms for the problem.

1.2 Our results

We establish improved theoretical and practical guarantees for the chromatic correlation clustering problem. Our contributions can be summarized as follows:

- We develop three algorithmic approaches: (1) A fast and easy-to-implement constant approximation framework, which builds on a novel reduction of the problem to that of correlation clustering. In particular, this framework implies a linear-time randomized 11-approximation algorithm by utilizing the pivot-based algorithm of [2]. This is the first constant approximation result for the problem, significantly improving over a previous $O(|V|)$-approximation [9]; (2) A deterministic linear programming-based algorithm that achieves an improved approximation ratio of 4. Even though this algorithm cannot be considered to be practical, it extends our theoretical understanding of chromatic correlation clustering, and enables us to present additional insights and observations related to the problem; (3) A linear-time heuristic algorithm that is motivated by practical scenarios in which there is a ground-truth clustering that is obscured by noisy observations.
- We present an empirical evaluation of our new algorithms and previously leading algorithms on both synthetic and real datasets. Our experiments reinforce the theoretical findings by demonstrating that our algorithms generally outperform previous approaches, both in terms of solution cost and reconstruction of an underlying ground-truth clustering.

1.3 Related work

The task of clustering multi-dimensional networks has received some attention recently [37, 24]. This setting models multiple relationships between entities in a network by maintaining a collection of networks, each of which captures one type of relationships. Although this setting is conceptually close to ours, its objective is semantically far. Specifically, the common goal in this setting is to find a partition of the entities that is good with respect to *all* relationship dimensions at the same time. As it turns out, this reduces the problem to effectively integrating solutions for single-dimensional networks. Finding a single (multi-dimensional) clustering that agrees as much as possible with multiple (single-dimensional) clusterings has been studied under the name of clustering aggregation [18]. Note that our chromatic correlation clustering setting requires finding a partition of the entities that takes into account all the relationships together. In particular, it is not require to have guarantees with respect to each single-dimension network.

Bansal, Blum and Chawla [6] formalized the correlation clustering problem. They developed a constant factor approximation algorithm for complete graphs, and proved that this problem is NP-hard problem. Charikar, Guruswami and Wirth [13] improved the approximation guarantee to 4, and established that the problem is APX-hard. Subsequently, Ailon, Charikar and Newman [2] presented a randomized linear-time algorithm that attains an approximation ratio of 3, and a randomized LP-based approach that guarantees 2.5-approximation. These algorithms were derandomized by van Zuylen and Williamson [38]. Giotis and Guruswami [19], and later Karpinski and Schudy [23], developed a PTAS for the case that the number of clusters is fixed. Charikar et al. [13] and Demaine et al. [16] independently showed that the more general setting of arbitrary graphs admits an $O(\log |V|)$-approximation algorithm. The maximization variant of correlation clustering has also received considerable attention. Currently, the best known result for complete graphs is a polynomial-time approximation scheme [6], while the best result for general graphs is a 0.766-approximation [35]. Note that the latter setting is APX-hard [13]. Other papers studying correlation clustering and its variants are [3, 29, 10, 1]. The correlation clustering problem has also been studied in the context of computational biology [7, 14, 33].

2. ALGORITHMS

In this section, we present several efficient approximation algorithms for the chromatic correlation clustering problem. We first develop a fast and easy-to-implement constant approximation framework. This framework builds on a novel observation that reduces an underlying instance of the problem to that of correlation clustering, while losing only a small constant factor in the approximation. One can then employ any of the constant factor approximation algorithms developed for correlation clustering and attain a constant factor approximation. For example, one can utilize the fast randomized pivot-based algorithm of Ailon, Charikar and Newman [2] to obtain a linear-time randomized 11-approximation algorithm. We emphasize that this is the first constant approximation result for the chromatic correlation clustering problem, and it significantly improves over the algorithm of Bonchi et al. [9] whose approximation guarantee is $O(|V|)$.

We complement the above results by developing a linear programming-based algorithm, which applies deterministic rounding, and achieves an improved approximation ratio of 4. This algorithm builds on the approach of Charikar, Guruswami and Wirth [13] for the correlation clustering problem, augmented with additional insights and observations that enable its generalization to our chromatic setting. Although this algorithm cannot be considered to be practical, it extends our theoretical understanding of the chromatic correlation clustering problem. In fact, this approach can be adjusted to the arbitrary graph setting, attaining $O(\log |V|)$-approximation. This matches the best known approximation for the special case of correlation clustering [13, 16].

We then develop a fast heuristic algorithm that is motivated by realistic scenarios in which the input instance admits a ground-truth clustering. Indeed, in many practical settings of chromatic correlation clustering, there is an unknown but correct way to partition the objects into clusters. Note that although this underling true clustering exists, it may not be readily identifiable from the data due to noisy similarity observations. Our algorithm is specifically designed to take these into consideration. We remark that similar assumptions have been suggested and utilized in the past with respect to the correlation clustering problem (see, e.g., [21, 34, 3, 30]). Notably, noisy model assumptions led to algorithms that successfully clustered real gene expression data [7].

2.1 A fast constant-factor approximation

We develop a fast and easy-to-implement randomized algorithm that attains an 11-approximation ratio. This result is achieved through a generic algorithmic framework that reduces an instance of chromatic correlation clustering to that of correlation clustering. The algorithmic framework consists of two main steps:

1. The algorithm initially modifies the input graph G. Specifically, the algorithm goes over the nodes of the graph one after the other, and associates a positive color with each one of them. The color $c_v \in L$ that is associated with a node v is the positive color that appears the most among the edges that are incident to v in G, breaking ties arbitrarily. Then, the algorithm modifies the color of all the edges incident to each node v that are different than c_v to the special negative color λ. We emphasize that at the end of this step, each edge of positive color $c \in L$ in the modified graph G' must be incident to two nodes whose associated color was c. This implies that if we only focus on positive edges and neglect all the negative λ-edges from G' then each connected component have exactly the same color, henceforth referred to as the color of the connected component.

2. The algorithm continues by executing any fast algorithm for the correlation clustering problem on each of the previously-mentioned connected components of the modified graph G'. All the clusters in each resulting clustering are given the positive color of the underlying connected component. Note that the ground sets of nodes of the resulting clusterings are pairwise disjoint, and therefore, the algorithm proceeds by uniting all those clustering to one clustering, which is then returned as the output of the algorithm.

In what follows, we focus on the above algorithm when the algorithm utilized in its second step is the randomized pivot-based algorithm of Ailon, Charikar and Newman [2]. This latter algorithm is fast and attains a 3-approximation for correlation clustering. It is also very simple: pick a pivot node uniformly at random, create a cluster that consists of this pivot and all the adjacent nodes that are connected to it using a positive edge, remove those nodes from the graph, and repeat as long as there are still nodes that are not clustered. We like to emphasize that the properties of the pivot-based algorithm enable us to directly employ it to the entire modified graph, while treating all positive color edges identically, without the need to identify each of its connected components first. This clearly simplifies our approach. However, note that even if we were required to identify the connected components as part of the framework, the asymptotic time complexity of the algorithm would not have changed since identification of connected components in a graph can be done in linear-time. A formal description of our algorithm, Reduce-and-Cluster, appears below.

2.1.1 Analysis

We begin by analyzing the approximation guarantee of our algorithmic framework. We emphasize that our analysis is generic in the sense that it is independent of the concrete correlation clustering algorithm employed in the second step. Let ALG_χ and OPT_χ be the cost of the solution generated by our algorithm and the optimal algorithm

Algorithm 1 Reduce-and-Cluster

Input: An undirected graph $G = (V, E)$ with an edge coloring $\chi : E \to L \cup \{\lambda\}$
Output: A clustering $\mathcal{C} : V \to \{C_1, C_2, \ldots\}$ with a coloring $\psi : \{C_1, C_2, \ldots\} \to L$

```
   ▷ Step 1: edges color modification
1: for v ∈ V do c_v ← argmax_{c∈L} |{u ∈ V : χ(uv) = c}|
2: for uv ∈ E do
3:     if (χ(uv) ≠ c_u or χ(uv) ≠ c_v) do χ(uv) ← λ
   ▷ Step 2: pivot-based correlation clustering
4: i ← 1
5: while V ≠ ∅ do
6:     v ← uniformly random node in V
7:     Γ(v) ← {u ∈ V : χ(uv) ≠ λ}
8:     C_i ← {v} ∪ Γ(v); ψ(C_i) ← c_v
9:     V ← V \ C_i; E ← E \ {uw : u ∈ C_i}; i ← i + 1
```

with respect to the input graph G, respectively. Similarly, let ALG_1 and OPT_1 be the cost of the solution generated in the second step of the algorithm and the optimal correlation clustering algorithm for the graph G' obtained after the edges color modification, respectively. Note that ALG_χ and ALG_1 correspond to the same clustering, but ALG_χ also assigns a color to each cluster. Finally, let $d_c(v)$ be the number of edges of color $c \in L$ adjacent to node v in G, and let $d_{\min}(v) = \sum_{c \neq c_v} d_c(v)$ be the total number of edges that are incident to v but have a different (positive) color than the leading color of the edges of v, as defined in line 1 of the algorithm.

LEMMA 2.1. $\text{ALG}_\chi \le \text{ALG}_1 + \sum_{v \in V} d_{\min}(v)$.

PROOF. Consider our output clustering when applied to the color modified graph G'. Notice that the cost of our colored clustering on G' is identical to the cost of the correlation clustering solution on G' when neglecting the colors of the edges (namely, ALG_1). This follows as the color assignment to each cluster is the same as the color of all positive edges incident to this cluster's nodes. This latter claim results as any cluster that the correlation clustering algorithm (and in particular, the pivot-based algorithm) creates is confined within a connected component of positive edges in G', and all the positive edges forming a connected component have the same color which the algorithm later assigns as the color of that cluster. Thus, the clusters coloring does not incur additional cost.

The proof of the lemma is completed by noticing that ALG_χ is not greater than the cost of that colored clustering with respect to G' by more than $D = \sum_{v \in V} d_{\min}(v)$. This is straight-forward since the color modification step changes the color of at most D edges, and those edges may imply an additional cost of at most D. □

LEMMA 2.2. $\text{OPT}_1 \le \text{OPT}_\chi + \sum_{v \in V} d_{\min}(v)$.

PROOF. Let OPT_1^G be the cost of the optimal correlation clustering for the graph G when all positive colored edges are simply treated as positive. Notice that OPT_1^G is at most OPT_χ. In particular, one can upper bound OPT_1^G by utilizing the clustering underling OPT_χ (without the color assignment), while observing that the cost may only improve as some colored intra-cluster edges may not contribute to the cost in the regular corelation clustering setting.

Recall that OPT_1 is the cost that the optimal correlation clustering for the modified graph G'. The proof of the lemma is completed by observing that OPT_1 can be larger than OPT_1^G by no more than $D = \sum_{v \in V} d_{\min}(v)$. This is straight-forward since the color modification step changes the color of at most D edges, and each of those edges may imply an additional cost. □

LEMMA 2.3. $\text{OPT}_\chi \ge \sum_{v \in V} d_{\min}(v)/2$.

PROOF. Let us concentrate on some node v, and suppose that the optimal solution assigns it to a cluster with a color c^*. This implies that all the edges that are incident on v and have a positive color $c \in L$ different than c^* contribute to the cost of the solution, whether they are inter-cluster or intra-cluster. Clearly, the cost of those edges is lower bounded by $d_{\min}(v)$. The lemma now follows by summing the costs implied by those incident edges across all nodes, while noticing that the cost implied by any such edge may be counted twice; once for each of its incident nodes. □

We are now ready to prove the main result of this subsection.

THEOREM 2.4. *Given an α-approximation algorithm for the correlation clustering problem, our algorithmic framework guarantees a $(3\alpha+2)$-approximation for chromatic correlation clustering.*

PROOF. Notice that

$$\begin{aligned}
\text{ALG}_\chi &\le \text{ALG}_1 + \sum_{v \in V} d_{\min}(v) \\
&\le \alpha \cdot \text{OPT}_1 + \sum_{v \in V} d_{\min}(v) \\
&\le \alpha \cdot \text{OPT}_\chi + (\alpha + 1) \sum_{v \in V} d_{\min}(v) \\
&\le (3\alpha + 2) \cdot \text{OPT}_\chi ,
\end{aligned}$$

where the first inequity is due to Lemma 2.1, the second inequality results by the approximation guarantee of the correlation clustering algorithm, the third inequality is by Lemma 2.2, and the last inequality follows from Lemma 2.3.

We like to emphasize that the fact that the correlation clustering algorithm is applied sequentially to the connected components of the modified graph G', and not to the entire graph, does not change its approximation ratio. This results from the way we constructed G', which guarantees that the optimal solution does not create clusters that consist of nodes residing in different connected components. Specifically, assume for the sake of contradiction that there is a cluster in the optimal clustering that consists of nodes from different components. One can split that cluster into several clusters, each consisting of the originating cluster nodes residing in different components, and reduce the overall cost. It is easy to validate that the reduction in the cost is equal to the number of (negative) edges between the underlying nodes in different components. □

We can now use this result for the analysis of algorithm Reduce-and-Cluster. Recall that this algorithm is a special case of our framework when the randomized pivot-based algorithm is employed as its second step.

COROLLARY 2.5. *Algorithm Reduce-and-Cluster is a linear-time algorithm that achieves an approximation ratio of 11 for the chromatic correlation clustering problem.*

PROOF. We start with analyzing the time complexity of the algorithm. The edges color modification step of the algorithm can be easily implemented in $O(|V|+|E|)$-time since each node and each edge is accessed at most a constant number of times. The second step of the algorithm can also be implemented in $O(|V|+|E|)$-time using a simple but careful design. Specifically, generating a random order of the nodes of the graph can be done once in $O(|V|)$-time using the Fisher-Yates shuffle (see, e.g., [25]), and building the clusters, including updating the random order to reflect the removal of the nodes assigned to each cluster, can be done in $O(|V|+|E|)$-time as each node and each edge is only accessed constant number of times. In particular, once a cluster is formed, the underlying nodes and edges are not considered again in the remainder of the algorithm. In conclusion, the time complexity of the algorithm is linear. The proof is now completed by recalling that the pivot-based algorithm of Ailon, Charikar and Newman [2] achieves 3-approximation. □

2.2 An improved approximation via LP-based approach

We design a deterministic linear programming-based algorithm that attains a 4-approximation ratio. Our algorithm and analysis extends and refines the approach of Charikar, Guruswami and Wirth [13] for the correlation clustering problem. Note that this algorithm improves over the approximation guarantee suggested by Theorem 2.4. In particular, the current best algorithm for correlation clustering has an approximation ratio of 2.5, and thus, plugging it into our framework results in a 9.5-approximation for the chromatic setting. This 2.5-approximation algorithm employs LP-based techniques, but randomly rounds the fractional solution using the pivot-based algorithm [2]. We emphasize that our algorithm applies a deterministic rounding for the linear program, which makes our entire approach deterministic. We also like to note that it is not clear if the former LP-based approach [2] can be extended to the chromatic setting.

The algorithm. We begin by describing a linear program (LP) that captures the chromatic correlation clustering problem:

$$
\begin{array}{llll}
\text{minimize} & \displaystyle\sum_{\substack{uv\in E:\\ c=\chi(uv)\in L}} x^c_{uv} + \sum_{\substack{uv\in E:\\ \chi(uv)=\lambda}} \sum_{c\in L} (1-x^c_{uv}) & & \\
\text{subject to} & (1) \ \displaystyle\sum_{c\in L} x^c_v = |L|-1 & \forall v\in V & \\
& (2) \ x^c_{uv} \geq x^c_u, x^c_v & \forall u,v\in V, \forall c\in L & \\
& (3) \ x^c_{uv} + x^c_{vw} \geq x^c_{uw} & \forall u,v,w\in V, \forall c\in L & \\
& (4) \ x^c_{uv}, x^c_v \in [0,1] & \forall u,v\in V, \forall c\in L &
\end{array}
$$

In an integral solution, the variable x^c_v indicates if node v is (not) in a cluster of color c, that is, if $x^c_v = 0$ then the v is part of a cluster of color $c \in L$. Similarly, the variable x^c_{uv} indicates whether an edge uv is (not) in a cluster of color c, namely, if $x^c_{uv} = 0$ then uv is part of a cluster of color $c \in L$. Note that we regard each pair ot nodes uv to be unordered, so there is no difference between x^c_{uv} and x^c_{vu}, and we use them interchangeably. Constraint (1) guarantees that each node is assigned to one colored cluster, i.e., it is far from exactly $|L|-1$ colors. Constraint (2) ensures that the edge uv is in cluster of color c only if both u and v are in a cluster of that color. Note that constraint (1) and (2) together imply that each edge is assigned to one color. Constraint (3) is the triangle inequality, guaranteeing that if edges uv and vw are in the same colored cluster then the edge uw must also be in the same cluster. The objective function consists of two summations: the first one captures the cost implied by positive color edges, while the latter one captures the cost of implied by negative color edges. More specifically, a negative edge does not contribute a cost only if its incident nodes are far from each other with respect to any color, that is, $x^c_{uv} = 1$ for any color $c \in L$. Similarly, a positive edge does not contribute a cost only if its incident nodes are close to each other under the edge color.

We turn to describe our rounding procedure. For ease of presentation, we first identify an important property of the fractional solution.

OBSERVATION 2.6. *Given distinct nodes $u, v \in V$ and a color $c_1 \in L$ such that $x^{c_1}_{uv} < 1/2$ then $x^{c_2}_{uw} > 1/2$ for every node $w \in V \setminus \{u\}$ and a color $c_2 \in L \setminus \{c_1\}$.*

PROOF. Notice that constraint (2) ensures that $x^{c_1}_u \leq x^{c_1}_{uv} < 1/2$. In consequence, constraint (1) implies that

$$\sum_{c_2\in L\setminus\{c_1\}} x^{c_2}_u > |L| - \frac{3}{2}\,,$$

A simple counting argument suggests that $x^{c_2}_u > 1/2$ for every $c_2 \in L \setminus \{c_1\}$. By using constraint (2) again, we get that $x^{c_2}_{uw} \geq x^{c_2}_u > 1/2$, for every node $w \in V \setminus \{u\}$. □

Our rounding procedure works in steps. At each step, the algorithms picks an arbitrary (pivot) node v that is still not clustered. It considers all the unclustered nodes that are close to v with respect to some positive color. A node $u \in V$ is regraded as *close* to v under some color $c \in L$ if $x^c_{uv} < 1/2$. Notice that Observation 2.6 ensures that all the nodes close to v must be close under the same color. Denote this color by c_v. Now, if the average distance between v and the nodes under consideration with respect to c_v is at most 1/4, the algorithm creates a new cluster of color c_v that consists of v and the underlying nodes; otherwise, the algorithm creates a new singleton cluster that only consist of v (with an arbitrary color). A formal description of this rounding procedure appears below.

Algorithm 2 LP-Rounding

Input: An undirected graph $G = (V, E)$ with an edge coloring $\chi : E \rightarrow L \cup \{\lambda\}$, an optimal fraction solution x for the linear program (LP)
Output: A clustering $\mathcal{C} : V \rightarrow \{C_1, C_2, \ldots\}$ with a coloring $\psi : \{C_1, C_2, \ldots\} \rightarrow L$

$i \leftarrow 1$
while $V \neq \emptyset$ **do**
  $v \leftarrow$ arbitrary node in V
  $c_v \leftarrow \text{argmin}_{c\in L}\{x^c_{vu} : u \in V\}$
  $\Gamma(v) \leftarrow \{u \in V : x^{c_v}_{vu} < 1/2\}$
  if $\sum_{u\in\Gamma(v)} x^{c_v}_{vu} \leq |\Gamma(v)|/4$ **do**
    $C_i \leftarrow \{v\} \cup \Gamma(v)$; $\psi(C_i) \leftarrow c_v$
  else
    $C_i \leftarrow \{v\}$; $\psi(C_i) \leftarrow c_v$
  $V \leftarrow V \setminus C_i$; $E \leftarrow E \setminus \{uw : u \in C_i\}$; $i \leftarrow i + 1$

2.2.1 Analysis

We present a charging scheme that associates between the cost implied by our output clustering and the cost of the fractional LP solution. We make this calculation separately for each cluster. Consider a cluster C of color $c = \psi(C)$ that was created by our algorithm for a pivot node v when the set of remaining unclustered nodes were V_C.

Case I: $C = \{v\}$ is a singleton cluster. Notice that all costs in this case are due to inter-cluster disagreements of positive color edges. Let $U_L = \{u \in V_C : \chi(vu) \in L\}$ be the endpoints corresponding to those edges and let $|U_L|$ denote their cost. In case $x_{vu}^{\chi(vu)} \geq 1/2$ for every $u \in U_L$ then we are done since the LP cost of the positive color edges is at least $|U_L|/2$. Hence, in what follows, we may assume that there is at least one such variable whose value is less than $1/2$. Recall that Observation 2.6 implies that all the variables of edges incident on v which have a value smaller than $1/2$ must have the color c. Let $\Gamma(v) = \{u \in V_C : x_{vu}^c < 1/2\}$ be that endpoints corresponding to those edges. Let $L_c = L \setminus \{c\}$, and observe that the LP cost of the of the edges corresponding to $\Gamma(v)$ is

$$\begin{aligned}\Lambda_1 &\triangleq \sum_{\substack{u\in\Gamma(v):\\ \chi(vu)=c}} x_{vu}^c + \sum_{\substack{u\in\Gamma(v):\\ \chi(vu)\in L_c}} x_{vu}^{\chi(vu)} + \sum_{\substack{u\in\Gamma(v):\\ \chi(vu)=\lambda}} \sum_{\ell\in L}(1-x_{vu}^\ell)\\ &\geq \sum_{\substack{u\in\Gamma(v):\\ \chi(vu)=c}} x_{vu}^c + \sum_{\substack{u\in\Gamma(v):\\ \chi(vu)\in L_c}} x_{vu}^c + \sum_{\substack{u\in\Gamma(v):\\ \chi(vu)=\lambda}} x_{vu}^c\\ &= \sum_{u\in\Gamma(v)} x_{vu}^c > \frac{1}{4}|\Gamma(v)|,\end{aligned}$$

where the first inequality holds since $x_{vu}^{\chi(vu)} > x_{vu}^c$ for every edge vu with $\chi(vu) \in L_c$ by Observation 2.6, and since $\sum_{\ell\in L}(1 - x_{vu}^\ell) \geq 1 - x_{vu}^c > x_{vu}^c$ for every edge vu with $x_{vu}^c < 1/2$. The last inequality follows as the singleton cluster was created since the condition on line 6 of the rounding procedure failed. Now, notice that the LP cost over all the edges incident on v is at least

$$\sum_{u\in U_L\setminus\Gamma(v)} x_{vu}^{\chi(vu)} + \Lambda_1 > \frac{1}{2}|U_L \setminus \Gamma(v)| + \frac{1}{4}|\Gamma(v)| \geq \frac{1}{4}|U_L|\,,$$

where the first inequality follows by recalling that $x_{vu}^{\chi(vu)} \geq 1/2$ for every $u \in U_L \setminus \Gamma(v)$.

Case II: $C = \{v\} \cup \Gamma(v)$ is a non-singleton cluster. We analyze the cost contribution of each edge that is incident to the cluster based on its type:

(a) Edges with color $\ell \in L\setminus\{c\}$. Consider an edge $uw \in E$ such that $u \in C$ and $\ell = \chi(uv) \in L \setminus \{c\}$. This edge implies either an intra-cluster or an inter-cluster disagreement, and hence, its cost is 1. Note that the contribution of this edge to the LP cost is x_{uw}^ℓ. We next argue that the value of this variable is at least $1/2$. We consider two cases: if u or w is the pivot node v then the argument follows by Observation 2.6, while recalling that $\ell \neq c$; otherwise, the argument follows since $x_{vu}^c < 1/2$, and thus, $x_{uw}^\ell \geq 1/2$, again by Observation 2.6. Note that above proof implies that our algorithm did not pay more than twice the cost that the LP solution paid for that edge. We like to emphasize that this gives us some room for flexibility since we only need this variable to have a value of at least $1/4$ to guarantee 4-approximation. Consequently, we can use up to half of the value of each such variable in later cases.

(b) Intra-cluster λ-edges. Consider an edge $uw \in E$ such that $u, w \in C$ and $\chi(uw) = \lambda$. Note that this edge contributes a cost of 1 to our solution, while its LP cost is $\sum_{\ell\in L}(1 - x_{uw}^\ell)$. We analyze the cost according to the following cases:

- If u or w is the pivot node v, we get that $x_{uw}^c < 1/2$. Therefore, the LP cost of that edge is at least $1-x_{uw}^c > 1/2$.
- If $x_{vu}^c \leq 3/8$ and $x_{vw}^c \leq 3/8$ then $x_{uw}^c \leq 3/4$ by the triangle inequality in constraint (3) of the linear program. Therefore, the LP cost of that edge is $1 - x_{uw}^c > 1/4$.
- We are left to deal with the case that at least one of $x_{vw}^c, x_{vu}^c \in (3/8, 1/2)$. Let us assume without loss of generality that $x_{vw}^c \geq x_{vu}^c$. We associate the cost of the edge uw to node w. We next demonstrate that (at least $1/4$ of) the cost assigned to each node $w \in \Gamma(v)$ having $x_{vw}^c \in (3/8, 1/2)$ can be associated with the LP cost of its neighboring edges. Formally, given a node w and a set $A \subseteq L \cup \{\lambda\}$, we define $U_w^A = \{u \in \Gamma(v) : \chi(uw) \in A \text{ and } x_{vw}^c \geq x_{vu}^c\}$. Note that the solution cost associated with w can be identified by $|U_w^{\{\lambda\}}|$. Let $L_c = L \setminus \{c\}$, we concentrate on the edges xw such that $x \in U_w^{\{\lambda\}} \cup U_w^{\{c\}} \cup U_w^{L_c}$, and analyze their LP cost. Recall that we may have utilized at most half of the LP cost of the edges yw such that $y \in U_w^{L_c}$ in the analysis of case (a) above. Hence, we may use half of the LP cost of those edges in a charging argument related to the current case, and still maintain a 4-approximation. Accordingly, the (un-utilized) LP cost related to w is at least

$$\begin{aligned}\Lambda_2 &\triangleq \sum_{y\in U_w^{\{\lambda\}}} (1 - x_{yw}^c) + \sum_{y\in U_w^{\{c\}}} x_{yw}^c + \frac{1}{2}\sum_{y\in U_w^{L_c}} x_{yw}^{\chi(yw)}\\ &\geq \sum_{y\in U_w^{\{\lambda\}}} (1 - x_{vw}^c - x_{vy}^c) + \sum_{y\in U_w^{\{c\}}} (x_{vw}^c - x_{vy}^c)\\ &\quad + \frac{1}{2}\sum_{y\in U_w^{L_c}} x_{yw}^{\chi(yw)}\\ &\geq |U_w^{\{\lambda\}}| \cdot (1 - x_{vw}^c) + |U_w^{\{c\}}| \cdot x_{vw}^c\\ &\quad - \sum_{y\in U_w^{\{\lambda,c\}}} x_{vy}^c + \frac{1}{4}|U_w^{L_c}|\\ &\geq \frac{1}{2}|U_w^{\{\lambda\}}| + \frac{3}{8}|U_w^{\{c\}}| - \frac{1}{4}|U_w^{L\cup\{\lambda\}}| + \frac{1}{4}|U_w^{L_c}|\\ &\geq \frac{1}{4}|U_w^{\{\lambda\}}|\,.\end{aligned}$$

The first inequality follows from the triangle inequality in constraint (3) of the linear program. The second inequality results since $x_{yw}^{\chi(yw)} \geq 1/2$ for every $y \in U_w^{L_c}$. The third inequality holds since $x_{vw}^c \in (3/8, 1/2)$, and

$$\sum_{y\in U_w^{\{\lambda,c\}}} x_{vy}^c \leq \sum_{y\in U_w^{L\cup\{\lambda\}}} x_{vy}^c \leq \frac{1}{4}|U_w^{L\cup\{\lambda\}}|\,.$$

Here, the last inequality is due to the fact that the average value of all x_{vy}^c such that $y \in \Gamma(v)$ is at most

1/4 by the condition on line 6 of the rounding procedure. As the nodes $y \in U_w^{L\cup\{\lambda\}}$ correspond to a subset of those variables with the smallest values, it follows that their average value is also smaller than 1/4.

(c) Inter-cluster c-edges. Consider an edge $uw \in E$ such that $u \in C$, $w \notin C$ and $\chi(uw) = c$. Note that this edge contributes a cost of 1 to our solution, while its LP cost is x^c_{uw}. We analyze the cost according to the following cases:

- If u is the pivot node v, we get that $x^c_{uw} > 1/2$. Thus, the LP cost of that edge is 1/2.
- If $x^c_{vw} \geq 3/4$ then $x^c_{uw} > 1/4$ by the triangle inequality in constraint (3) and the fact that $x^c_{vw} < 1/2$. Hence, the LP cost of that edge is at least 1/4.
- We are left to deal with the case that $x^c_{vw} \in [1/2, 3/4)$. Again, we will associate the cost of the edge uw to node w. We next demonstrate that (at least 1/4 of) the cost assigned to each such node w can be associated with the LP cost of its neighboring edges. We use similar notation to that of case (b), and define the set $U_w^A = \{u \in C \setminus \{v\} : \chi(uw) \in A\}$ for a node w and a set $A \subseteq L \cup \{\lambda\}$. Note that the solution cost associated with w can be identified by $|U_w^{\{c\}}|$. Let $L_c = L \setminus \{c\}$, by the same arguments as in case (b), one can derive that the (un-utilized) LP cost related to w is at least

$$\begin{aligned}\Lambda_3 &\triangleq |U_w^{\{\lambda\}}| \cdot (1 - x^c_{vw}) + |U_w^{\{c\}}| \cdot x^c_{vw} \\ &\quad - \frac{1}{4}|U_w^{L\cup\{\lambda\}}| + \frac{1}{4}|U_w^{L_c}| \\ &\geq \frac{1}{4}|U_w^{\{\lambda\}}| + \frac{1}{2}|U_w^{\{c_i\}}| - \frac{1}{4}|U_w^{L\cup\{\lambda\}}| + \frac{1}{4}|U_w^{L_c}| \\ &= \frac{1}{4}|U_w^{\{c_i\}}|,\end{aligned}$$

where the inequality holds since $x^c_{vw} \in [1/2, 3/4)$.

We conclude by emphasizing that it is not hard to validate that our scheme never charges the cost of an LP variable more than once. In particular, the only set of edges whose LP cost may be used in two different cases (of the non-singleton setting) are edges that have a color in $L \setminus \{c\}$. We use at most half of the LP cost of those edges in case (a), and another half of their LP cost in cases (b) and (c). Note that the set of relevant edges in cases (b) and (c) are disjoint, and thus, we do not overcharge any edge.

THEOREM 2.7. *There is a polynomial-time LP-based algorithm that attains 4-approximation for the chromatic correlation clustering problem.*

We like to note that the LP-based approach can be extended to the weighted arbitrary graph setting in which there may be object relations that are not known, that is, neither positive nor negative. This generalization requires slight refinement of the ideas suggested in [13, 16], and hence, we defer the formalities to the final version of this paper. The approximation result in this case is $O(\log |V|)$, which matches the best known result for the special case of correlation clustering.

2.3 A deep clustering heuristic

We develop a fast heuristic algorithm that is motivated by real-life scenarios in which there is a ground-truth clustering that is obscured by noisy observations. Algorithm Deep-Cluster, formally described below, follows a similar outline to that of algorithm Reduce-and-Cluster from Section 2.1. Initially, the algorithm modifies the input graph by negating all positive edges incident on each node v whose color is different than the leading color of v. It continues by picking a pivot node uniformly at random, and creating a cluster that consists of this pivot and all the adjacent nodes connected to it using a positive edge (i.e., first-level nodes). The algorithm then considers each of the nodes that are connected to the first-level nodes by a positive edge (i.e., second-level nodes), and greedily adds it to the underlying cluster if it improves the post-assignment cost. Once this step is completed, all the cluster nodes are removed from the graph, and the algorithm begins a new iteration by randomly picking a new pivot node.

Algorithm 3 Deep-Cluster

Input: An undirected graph $G = (V, E)$ with an edge coloring $\chi : E \to L \cup \{\lambda\}$
Output: A clustering $\mathcal{C} : V \to \{C_1, C_2, \ldots\}$ with a coloring $\psi : \{C_1, C_2, \ldots\} \to L$

▷ Step 1: edges color modification
for $v \in V$ **do** $c_v \leftarrow \text{argmax}_{c\in L} |\{u \in V : \chi(uv) = c\}|$
for $uv \in E$ **do**
  if $(\chi(uv) \neq c_u$ or $\chi(uv) \neq c_v)$ **do** $\chi(uv) \leftarrow \lambda$
▷ Step 2: pivot-based deep clustering
$i \leftarrow 1$
while $V \neq \emptyset$ **do**
  $v \leftarrow$ uniformly random node in V
  $\Gamma_1(v) \leftarrow \{u \in V : \chi(uv) \neq \lambda\}$ ▷ 1st-level
  $C_i \leftarrow \{v\} \cup \Gamma_1(v)$; $\psi(C_i) \leftarrow c_v$
  for $u \in \Gamma_1(v)$ **do**
    $\Gamma_2(u) \leftarrow \{w \in V \setminus C_i : \chi(uw) \neq \lambda\}$ ▷ 2nd-level
    for $w \in \Gamma_2(u)$ **do**
      $\deg_w \leftarrow |\{x \in V : \chi(wx) \neq \lambda\}|$
      $\Delta_{\text{cur}} \leftarrow |\{x \in C_i : \chi(wx) \neq \lambda\}|$
      $\Delta_{\text{inter}} \leftarrow \deg_w - \Delta_{\text{cur}}$
      $\Delta_{\text{intra}} \leftarrow |C_i| - \Delta_{\text{cur}}$
      if $\Delta_{\text{cur}} > (\Delta_{\text{inter}} + \Delta_{\text{intra}})$ **do**
        $C_i \leftarrow C_i \cup \{w\}$
  $V \leftarrow V \setminus C_i$; $E \leftarrow E \setminus \{uw : u \in C_i\}$; $i \leftarrow i + 1$

The intuition behind the algorithm is straight-forward. Under the assumption that a chromatic correlation clustering scenario admits a ground-truth clustering, one main difficulty in identifying this clustering is that the noisy observations obscure the underlying cliques structure. Our algorithm targets this situation by adding an extra validation step to the basic pivot-based approach which mitigates the noise effects. Recall that the basic approach creates a cluster in each iteration that consists of all the nodes similar to some pivot node. Our algorithm augments this approach by finding additional nodes that, although appearing dissimilar to the pivot due to noise, have high similarity to the other cluster nodes.

We complete the description of the heuristic algorithm by pointing out that one can implement it in linear time in the input size. Specifically, it is easy to validate that the time complexity of the color modification step of the algorithm and the operations related to the first-level nodes is linear. This can be established along the same line of argumentations used in the analysis of algorithm Reduce-and-Cluster. Thus, we are left to bound the time complexity of the operations related to the second-level nodes. A naïve implementation in this case may take quadratic time in the input size. Indeed, it is possible that each node w will be considered E_w^L times as a second-level node, and in each such case, it may take $O(E_w)$-time to calculate Δ_{cur}, its intersection size with the cluster under consideration. Here, E_w and E_w^L are the number of edges and colored edges incident of w, respectively. Nevertheless, one can carefully design this step to run in linear time. This can be done by initially going over all first-level nodes, and identifying all its second-level nodes. During this step, we maintain a counter for each second-level node that is incremented every time that this node is explored by an adjacent first-level node. Notice that eventually, the counter associated with each second-level node holds its intersection size with the underlying cluster. Hence, the greedy decision whether to add that node to the cluster can be done in constant time. Note that in case that a second-level node is added to the cluster, we explore its edges and increment the counters of remaining second-level nodes in a similar manner. The crucial observation is that all edges that were explored during the above process are removed from the graph once the cluster is formed. Since they are not considered again in the remainder of the algorithm, we conclude that the overall number of operations related to second-level nodes during the algorithm is no more than $O(E)$.

3. EXPERIMENTAL EVALUATION

We present our empirical results for the algorithms Reduce-and-Cluster and Deep-Cluster, which we refer by RC and DC, respectively. We test our algorithms on both synthetically-generated graphs, and graphs that are derived from real datasets. We compare the results with the performance of the leading algorithms developed by Bonchi et al. [9]. Specifically, we focus on the Chromatic Balls algorithm and the Lazy Chromatic Balls heuristic, abbreviated CB and LCB, respectively. The code of those algorithms was obtained directly from the authors of [9]. Informally, CB is an algorithm that iteratively builds a cluster around a randomly chosen pivot *edge*, while LCB is a heuristic that is better suited for scenarios with small number of colors, and tries to minimize the risk of selecting bad pivots. Note that we decided not to present the results of the simple baseline approach and the Alternating Minimization heuristic from [9] since in all cases, at least one of the algorithms CB or LCB outperforms them. Our experiments reinforce the theoretical findings by demonstrating that our algorithms generally outperform previous approaches, both in terms of solution cost and reconstruction of an underlying ground-truth clustering.

3.1 Synthetic datasets

We evaluate the algorithms on several synthetic graphs, each of which is parameterized by the number of nodes n, number of clusters k, number of positive colors $|L|$, and a noise probability p. Each graph is generated by the following simple process: We first partition the n nodes of a complete graph into k clusters uniformly in random, and assign each cluster a random color $c \in L$. Specifically, for each intra-cluster edge, assign the color of the underlying cluster, and for each inter-cluster edge, we assign a color of λ. Then, we change the color of each edge independently at random with probability p to some different random color in $L \cup \{\lambda\}$. This latter step models the noisy observations that commonly happen in practice.

Notice that the first step in our generation process creates an instance that admits a chromatic correlation clustering of zero cost. This clustering is referred to as the *ground-truth clustering*. As part of our experiments, we evaluate the performance of the algorithm in retrieving this true clustering. For this purpose, we use the overall F-measure for clustering (see, e.g., [36]). Given a ground-truth clustering $\mathcal{C}^* = C_1^*, C_2^*, \dots C_{k^*}^*$, and a clustering solution $\mathcal{C} = C_1, C_2, \dots C_k$, their F-measure is defined as follows.

$$F(\mathcal{C}, \mathcal{C}^*) = \frac{1}{n} \sum_{i=1}^{k^*} |C_i^*| \max_{1 \le j \le k} F_{ij} \ ,$$

where F_{ij} is the similarity between the clusters C_i^* and C_j, calculated by the standard F-measure. Specifically, $F_{ij} = (2P_{ij}R_{ij})/(P_{ij} + R_{ij})$, where $P_{ij} = |C_i^* \cap C_j|/|C_j|$ is the precision, and $R_{ij} = |C_i^* \cap C_j|/|C_i^*|$ is the recall. Note that $F(\mathcal{C}, \mathcal{C}^*) \in [0, 1]$, and that greater overall F-measure values indicate higher similarity between clusterings.

Our experiments cover many datasets with varying parameters. For ease of presentation and due to space limitations, we only report the results attained for one set of base parameters. Specifically, we present the results obtained by exploring different values for each underlying parameter, while keeping the remaining parameters fixed at their base values. Our measurements indicate the average values attained for 10 runs. We like to emphasize that the trends that we identify for the setting under consideration are also evident in all other tested settings, although they vary in the intensity. In particular, we observe that our algorithms outperform previous approaches on all tested datasets, both in terms of solution cost and reconstruction of an underlying ground-truth clustering, except maybe in some extreme cases.

Most of the trends exhibited above are rather intuitive. For example, the performance of all algorithms becomes worse as the noise increases, and their performance improves as the number of colors increases. Focusing on the graphs of varying number of ground-truth clusters, one can see that the F-measure of all algorithms decrease as the number of clusters increase. However, the solution costs graph exhibits a more interesting phenomenon in which all the cost curves of the algorithms show a convex behavior, some even presenting a slightly increased cost for higher number of clusters. We believe that this convex behavior is related to the graph structure. Clearly, as the number of clusters increase, their average size decreases and the graph becomes sparser. As smaller clusters are easier to lose in the noise and since sparsity makes clustering problems noisier in general, the algorithms performance is expected to deteriorate at some point. The concrete point in which this happens depends on the exact properties of the algorithm. One additional observation that seems worth noting is that our new algorithms, and especially, algorithm DC, are much more robust to noise than previous algorithms, having high F-measure even with high levels of noise.

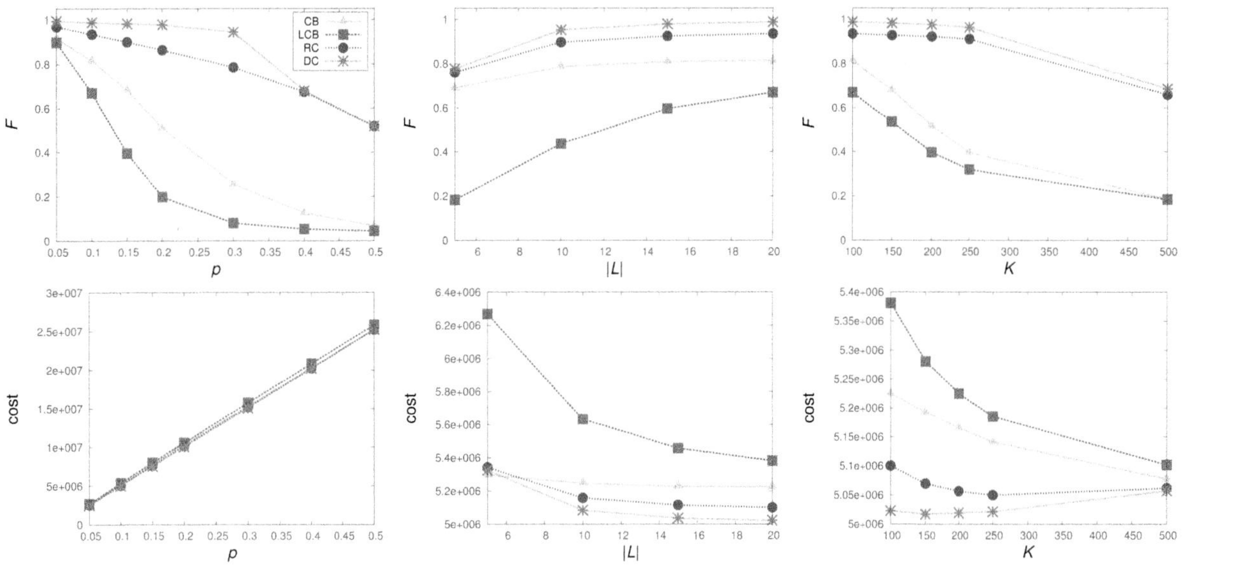

Figure 1: The results obtained for a base setting with parameters of $n = 10000$, $k = 100$, $|L| = 20$, and $p = 0.1$. The upper row shows the F-measure, while the lower row shows the solution cost. The results are presented with respect to varying level of noise (left most column), number of positive colors (middle column), and number of ground-truth clusters (right-most column).

3.2 Real datasets

We test our algorithms on four datasets that are publicly available. In particular, we experiment with two datasets (e.g., DBLP and STRING) that were identified and prepared by Bonchi et al. [9]. Note that all the datasets were processed so that the minimal node degree is at least 10. This was done to avoid sparse networks, which are of less interest. Indeed, the most interesting practical setting is when the graph is dense, and communities carry meaningful information.

dataset	nodes	edges	colors	avg deg	max deg
DBLP	73624	835414	100	22.69	502
Facebook	1072	42008	26	78.37	262
Twitter	4523	127068	35	56.18	623
STRING	18152	401582	4	44.25	264

DBLP. This dataset represents a co-authorship network of collaborations between researchers. It can be found at `http://dblp.uni-trier.de/xml/`. The dataset is an undirected graph in which nodes represent authors, the edges represent co-authorship of at least one paper, and there are 100 topic-based collaboration types. The topics were assigned by Bonchi et al. [9]. Specifically, they identified a collection of topics for all papers using a latent Dirichlet allocation topic-modeling, and then, assigned each edge the most prominent topic arising from the papers coauthored by the authors. A cluster of nodes in this case stands for a topic-coherent community of researchers.

Facebook and Twitter. These datasets are small snapshots from the social networks Facebook and Twitter. They are distributed by Stanford Network Analysis Project [27], and can be found at `http://snap.stanford.edu/data/`. Each dataset is an undirected graph in which nodes represent users, and edges represent friendship between users. There are 26 friendship types in Facebook and 35 friendship types in Twitter. We inferred those types from the users social circles. A circle is a social network feature that enable users to organize their internal networks by categorizing their friends. All users of a circle are assumed to share some mutual characteristics. A friendship edge between users is associated with some circle (category) only if both its incident nodes are identified within that circle. For edges with multiple associated categories, we picked one category arbitrarily. A cluster of nodes in this case represents a community of friends with dense relationships of specific type.

STRING. This dataset contains experimentally verified and computationally predicted protein-protein interactions (PPI) network. It is available at `http://string-db.org/`. The dataset is an undirected graph in which nodes represent proteins, edges represent interactions occurring between proteins, and there are 4 interaction types. A cluster of nodes in this case may designate a protein complex or a functional module. Although this dataset does not arise in the context of social networks, we decided to present it in order to highlight the applicability and effectiveness of our approach across diverse data domains.

The following table summarizes the performance of the algorithms on the real datasets. Our measurements represent average values attained for 50 runs. Similarly to the results on the synthetic data, our newly-developed algorithms, and especially, algorithm DC, generally outperform the previous algorithms. For example, algorithm DC achieves an improvement in the cost with respect to previously studied algorithms of at least 3.7% for the DBLP dataset, 11.1% for the Facebook dataset, 1.6% for the Twitter dataset, and 15.8% for the STRING dataset. Algorithm RC attains roughly the same costs as algorithm CB. As far as the runtime, we observe that all methods are very efficient, taking no more than few seconds on large graphs. Focusing on the different trends, we see that the our algorithms are slightly slower than algorithm CB, but are better than algorithm LCB as the number of colors and graph complexity increase. This

	cost				runtime (s)			
	CB	LCB	RC	DC	CB	LCB	RC	DC
DBLP	617200	651210	617447	594292	1.07	5.71	1.73	1.81
Facebook	29979	29818	29581	26509	0.022	0.026	0.046	0.092
Twitter	108102	128495	111334	106348	0.092	0.082	0.163	0.224
STRING	160572	159722	158292	134464	0.38	0.36	0.48	0.63

is rather expected as our algorithms, and especially algorithm DC, are more complex than algorithm CB. We like to emphasize that the running time of our algorithms is linear in the input size. Finally, we believe that the running time of our algorithms can be improved by utilizing better data structures and optimizing the code.

4. CONCLUSIONS

We revisit the chromatic correlation clustering problem. This problem has many interesting applications, including community detection, entity de-duplication, and link classification. Our contribution is both theoretical and practical. From a theoretical point of view, our main contribution is a linear-time constant factor approximation algorithm that significantly improves over previous results. From a practical point of view, our main contribution is by demonstrating that our algorithms generally perform better than previous algorithms on both synthetic and real datasets. We think that it will be interesting and valuable to study the maximization variant of correlation clustering, as well as other correlation clustering variants, within a chromatic setting.

Acknowledgments

We like to thank Francesco Bonchi, Aristides Gionis, Francesco Gullo, and Antti Ukkonen [9] for kindly sharing their algorithms code and datasets.

5. REFERENCES

[1] N. Ailon, N. Avigdor-Elgrabli, E. Liberty, and A. van Zuylen. Improved approximation algorithms for bipartite correlation clustering. *SIAM J. Comput.*, 41(5):1110–1121, 2012.

[2] N. Ailon, M. Charikar, and A. Newman. Aggregating inconsistent information: Ranking and clustering. *J. ACM*, 55(5), 2008.

[3] N. Ailon and E. Liberty. Correlation clustering revisited: The "true" cost of error minimization problems. In *36th ICALP*, pages 24–36, 2009.

[4] A. Arasu, C. Ré, and D. Suciu. Large-scale deduplication with constraints using dedupalog. In *25th ICDE*, pages 952–963, 2009.

[5] L. Backstrom and J. Leskovec. Supervised random walks: predicting and recommending links in social networks. In *4th WSDM*, pages 635–644, 2011.

[6] N. Bansal, A. Blum, and S. Chawla. Correlation clustering. *Machine Learning*, 56(1-3):89–113, 2004.

[7] A. Ben-Dor, R. Shamir, and Z. Yakhini. Clustering gene expression patterns. *Journal of Computational Biology*, 6(3/4):281–297, 1999.

[8] F. Bonchi, D. García-Soriano, and E. Liberty. Correlation clustering: from theory to practice. In *20th KDD*, page 1972, 2014.

[9] F. Bonchi, A. Gionis, F. Gullo, and A. Ukkonen. Chromatic correlation clustering. In *18th KDD*, pages 1321–1329, 2012.

[10] F. Bonchi, A. Gionis, and A. Ukkonen. Overlapping correlation clustering. In *11th ICDM*, pages 51–60, 2011.

[11] N. Cesa-Bianchi, C. Gentile, F. Vitale, and G. Zappella. A correlation clustering approach to link classification in signed networks. In *25th COLT*, pages 34.1–34.20, 2012.

[12] D. Chakrabarti, R. Kumar, and K. Punera. A graph-theoretic approach to webpage segmentation. In *17th WWW*, pages 377–386, 2008.

[13] M. Charikar, V. Guruswami, and A. Wirth. Clustering with qualitative information. *J. Comput. Syst. Sci.*, 71(3):360–383, 2005.

[14] Z. Chen, T. Jiang, and G. Lin. Computing phylogenetic roots with bounded degrees and errors. *SIAM J. Comput.*, 32(4):864–879, 2003.

[15] F. Chierichetti, N. N. Dalvi, and R. Kumar. Correlation clustering in mapreduce. In *20th KDD*, pages 641–650, 2014.

[16] E. D. Demaine, D. Emanuel, A. Fiat, and N. Immorlica. Correlation clustering in general weighted graphs. *Theor. Comput. Sci.*, 361(2-3):172–187, 2006.

[17] A. K. Elmagarmid, P. G. Ipeirotis, and V. S. Verykios. Duplicate record detection: A survey. *IEEE Trans. Knowl. Data Eng.*, 19(1):1–16, 2007.

[18] A. Gionis, H. Mannila, and P. Tsaparas. Clustering aggregation. *TKDD*, 1(1), 2007.

[19] I. Giotis and V. Guruswami. Correlation clustering with a fixed number of clusters. *Theory of Computing*, 2(1):249–266, 2006.

[20] O. Hassanzadeh, F. Chiang, R. J. Miller, and H. C. Lee. Framework for evaluating clustering algorithms in duplicate detection. *PVLDB*, 2(1):1282–1293, 2009.

[21] T. Joachims and J. E. Hopcroft. Error bounds for correlation clustering. In *22nd ICML*, pages 385–392, 2005.

[22] D. V. Kalashnikov, Z. Chen, S. Mehrotra, and R. Nuray-Turan. Web people search via connection analysis. *IEEE Trans. Knowl. Data Eng.*, 20(11):1550–1565, 2008.

[23] M. Karpinski and W. Schudy. Linear time approximation schemes for the gale-berlekamp game and related minimization problems. In *41st STOC*, pages 313–322, 2009.

[24] M. Kivelä, A. Arenas, M. Barthelemy, J. P. Gleeson, Y. Moreno, and M. A. Porter. Multilayer networks. *arXiv preprint arXiv:1309.7233*, 2013.

[25] D. E. Knuth. *The Art of Computer Programming, Volume 2 (3rd Ed.): Seminumerical Algorithms, 2nd*

Edition. Addison-Wesley Longman Publishing Co., Inc., 1997.

[26] J. Leskovec, D. P. Huttenlocher, and J. M. Kleinberg. Predicting positive and negative links in online social networks. In *19th WWW*, pages 641–650, 2010.

[27] J. Leskovec and A. Krevl. Snap datasets: Stanford large network dataset collection.

[28] D. Liben-Nowell and J. M. Kleinberg. The link-prediction problem for social networks. *JASIST*, 58(7):1019–1031, 2007.

[29] C. Mathieu, O. Sankur, and W. Schudy. Online correlation clustering. In *27th STACS*, pages 573–584, 2010.

[30] C. Mathieu and W. Schudy. Correlation clustering with noisy input. In *21st SODA*, pages 712–728, 2010.

[31] M. Richardson and P. Domingos. Mining knowledge-sharing sites for viral marketing. In *8th KDD*, pages 61–70, 2002.

[32] E. Sadikov, J. Madhavan, L. Wang, and A. Y. Halevy. Clustering query refinements by user intent. In *19th WWW*, pages 841–850, 2010.

[33] R. Shamir, R. Sharan, and D. Tsur. Cluster graph modification problems. *Discrete Applied Mathematics*, 144(1-2):173–182, 2004.

[34] R. Shamir and D. Tsur. Improved algorithms for the random cluster graph model. *Random Struct. Algorithms*, 31(4):418–449, 2007.

[35] C. Swamy. Correlation clustering: maximizing agreements via semidefinite programming. In *15th SODA*, pages 526–527, 2004.

[36] P. Tan, M. Steinbach, and V. Kumar. *Introduction to Data Mining*. Addison-Wesley, 2005.

[37] L. Tang, X. Wang, and H. Liu. Community detection via heterogeneous interaction analysis. *Data Min. Knowl. Discov.*, 25(1):1–33, 2012.

[38] A. van Zuylen and D. P. Williamson. Deterministic pivoting algorithms for constrained ranking and clustering problems. *Math. Oper. Res.*, 34(3):594–620, 2009.

Global Diffusion via Cascading Invitations: Structure, Growth, and Homophily

Ashton Anderson
Stanford University
ashton@cs.stanford.edu

Daniel Huttenlocher
Cornell University
dph@cs.cornell.edu

Jon Kleinberg
Cornell University
kleinber@cs.cornell.edu

Jure Leskovec
Stanford University
jure@cs.stanford.edu

Mitul Tiwari
LinkedIn Corporation
mtiwari@linkedin.com

ABSTRACT

Many of the world's most popular websites catalyze their growth through invitations from existing members. New members can then in turn issue invitations, and so on, creating cascades of member signups that can spread on a global scale. Although these diffusive invitation processes are critical to the popularity and growth of many websites, they have rarely been studied, and their properties remain elusive. For instance, it is not known how viral these cascades structures are, how cascades grow over time, or how diffusive growth affects the resulting distribution of member characteristics present on the site.

In this paper, we study the diffusion of LinkedIn, an online professional network comprising over 332 million members, a large fraction of whom joined the site as part of a signup cascade. First we analyze the structural patterns of these signup cascades, and find them to be qualitatively different from previously studied information diffusion cascades. We also examine how signup cascades grow over time, and observe that diffusion via invitations on LinkedIn occurs over much longer timescales than are typically associated with other types of online diffusion. Finally, we connect the cascade structures with rich individual-level attribute data to investigate the interplay between the two. Using novel techniques to study the role of homophily in diffusion, we find striking differences between the local, edge-wise homophily and the global, cascade-level homophily we observe in our data, suggesting that signup cascades form surprisingly coherent groups of members.

Categories and Subject Descriptors: H.2.8 [**Database management**]: Database applications—*Data mining*.
Keywords: cascades; product diffusion; social networks.

1. INTRODUCTION

One of the central dynamics on the Web is the tremendous growth of new sites and services that expand from small sets of early adopters to huge user populations. There are several mechanisms through which this can occur, and here we consider one that has been crucial for a number of the world's largest websites: attracting participants through a cascade of signups, where current users invite others to join the site. In this process, users have the option of issuing invitations to people not yet on the site. When these invitations are accepted, the resulting new users can issue further invitations, and the process continues, potentially diffusing through multiple levels. Several large sites (including Gmail) began with a period where this type of diffusive growth was the exclusive path for new signups; other sites (including LinkedIn and many others) have grown through a mix of cascading signups and direct signups at the site.

Since many of the most popular sites acquire their large audiences in part through invitations mechanisms like this, Web users experience the effects of these diffusive growth processes on a daily basis. Despite this, however, we have very little understanding of what these processes look like at a global level, nor what consequences they have for the makeup of a site's user population.

In this paper we address questions about cascading adoption processes using a dataset that represents the complete diffusion of LinkedIn, an online professional network that contains over 332 million users. To our knowledge, this is the largest structural analysis of a cascading adoption event ever undertaken. In addition its global scale, a significant fraction of LinkedIn's growth came through invitations, making it an ideal domain for addressing core questions about successful cascading processes. We note that while the particular numerical results presented here are of course specific to LinkedIn, they clearly illustrate certain patterns that are markedly different from what has been found in earlier diffusion studies, and they point to properties that may be characteristic of other large product diffusions as well.

The Present Work: Structure and Growth of Cascading Signups. We first analyze the underlying structure and growth dynamics of the LinkedIn cascades. The cascading signups can be naturally organized into a collection of trees: each time a user signs up directly, without an invitation, she forms the root of a new tree, and every user B who accepts an invitation from a user A joins the tree containing A, as the child of A.

We contrast these trees with the kinds of trees that arise in *information-sharing cascades*, in which users pass small information units (*e.g.*, links, photos, or other memes) to their friends. Like our cascading signups here, information-sharing cascades are also a form of online diffusion, but we discover that the properties of these two types of cascades are quite different. The work on information-sharing cascades has suggested that their temporal dynamics unfold

WWW 2015, May 18–22, 2015, Florence, Italy.
ACM 978-1-4503-3469-3/15/05.
http://dx.doi.org/10.1145/2736277.2741672.

very quickly, that most of their adoptions occur very close to the root, and that their size and their structural virality are essentially uncorrelated [8, 14, 13].

Our analysis of diffusion patterns in LinkedIn signups provides evidence that signup cascades, in contrast, are significantly more viral than previously-studied online diffusion datasets in a number of dimensions. Additionally, we find that size and structural virality are strongly correlated, suggesting that the largest signup cascades grow almost exclusively through viral, multi-step diffusion. Moreover, cascade growth plays out over much longer periods of time: users in a cascade remain active in spreading LinkedIn to new users months or even years after their own registration. The result is an approximately *linear* rate of tree growth for the large trees, and with a growth rate over time that is remarkably uniform across different trees. The commonality across trees suggests that there is a characteristic growth pattern for these signups that seems to be truly independent of the tree in which it occurs.

The Present Work: Homophily in Cascades. In addition to examining the architecture of the cascading adoption process itself, we also connect cascade structure with attributes of the users in the trees and investigate the interplay between the two. We find that attributes such as geography and industry play a substantial role in the cascades, exhibiting a pattern of homophily in which people share characteristics with those who invited them. But our investigations strongly suggest that this is a deeper process, arising from something more than just similarity between the inviter and invitee.

In particular, our fine-grained view of the invitation process suggests that we can think about the basic issue of homophily at two fundamental levels of scale: locally, in which users invite friends with similar characteristics, and globally, in which entire trees may or may not exhibit certain levels of homogeneity. One way to approach the connection between local and global patterns of similarity is through the following question: Is the direct similarity between inviters and invitees, when propagated through the structure of an entire tree, sufficient to account for the level of user homogeneity that we see in the full trees?

We find that, surprisingly, the local similarity between inviters and invitees is in fact *not* sufficient to produce the global levels of homophily we observe. This gap between the local and global properties of the trees raises the question of what other factors are playing a role in the global patterns of similarity that we observe.

To address this question, we ask what happens if the distribution of user attributes were based on a Markov process defined on the cascade trees, with the attributes of each node in the tree arising probabilistically from the attributes of its parent node. Such models have been considered in a very different context, in work that studies genetic inheritance with mutation on evolutionary trees [12, 31, 32, 35]. A way to summarize the disconnect between the local and global properties of our cascade trees is to say that this first-order Markov process gives rise to less homogeneity among a tree's nodes than we find in the real data. However, we find that higher-order Markov models, in which a node's attributes can depend not just on its parent but on its earlier ancestors as well, produce a level of homogeneity that more closely matches the data. This suggests that LinkedIn signup cascades are coherent, in that they are comprised of users who are more uniform than pairwise similarities can account for. The alignment with this higher-order Markov models suggests new ways of thinking about how user characteristics become correlated in these types of cascading processes.

The paper is outlined as follows: we discuss our structural analyses in Section 2, then investigate local and global homophily in Section 3 and cascade growth in Section 4, and finally we summarize related work in Section 5 and conclude in Section 6.

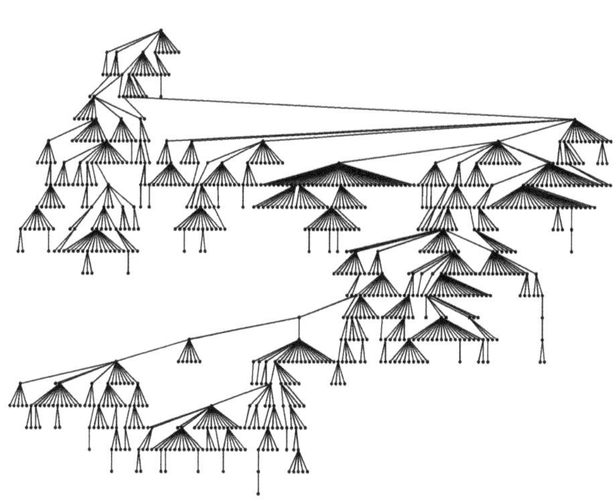

Figure 1: Example LinkedIn signup cascade.

2. STRUCTURAL CHARACTERISTICS

We begin with a structural analysis of the LinkedIn signup cascades. First we describe the invitation process and how sets of signups form cascades.

2.1 LinkedIn Signup Cascades

There are two ways in which a user B can join LinkedIn: she can either sign up directly at the site (a *cold signup*), or she can accept an invitation from an existing LinkedIn member (a *warm signup*). To count as a warm signup, it is not sufficient for B to simply have received an invitation from a member—she must also click on such an invitation and sign up through the resulting interface. The member A who sent the invitation that B used to register is then recorded, and we consider this an accepted invitation $A \to B$. At most one edge is created per signup.

We construct an accepted-invitation graph F where every member of LinkedIn is a node, and there is an edge between A and B if B joined LinkedIn by accepting an invitation from A. Note that F is a forest (a set of trees): every cold signup is the root of its own (potentially trivial) tree, every warm signup has exactly one parent, and cycles are impossible because edge sources always join earlier than their destinations. Studying the structural properties of this signup forest is the focus of this section (see Fig. 1 for an example cascade).

Before examining the data and discussing our results, we note that the LinkedIn signup forest is particularly well-suited to our goals. First, as is typical of data derived from an online platform, it is very fine-grained: every member signup is recorded and timestamped, and the identity of the inviter (if any) is known. This allows us to perfectly reconstruct the massive LinkedIn registration process as it unfolded over time. Second, the diffusion of LinkedIn from one member to another is unambiguous: every warm signup has a unique parent. People can receive multiple invitations to join LinkedIn, but they can only use one of them to sign up—therefore, there is no ambiguity in which member is the parent. It is certainly true that there will often be other factors in an individual's decision to join beyond just the accepted invitation, including receiving other invitations, but it is also the case that the edges in our graph correspond to precisely the invitations that were actually accepted. Third, with over 332 million users, LinkedIn is one of the most successful membership-based sites on the Web, and a large fraction of

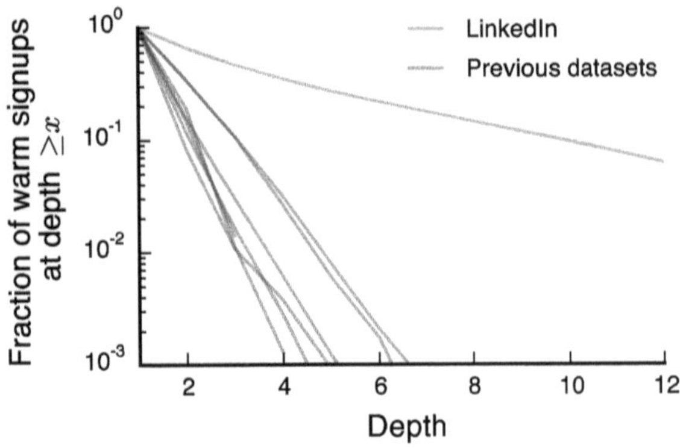

Figure 2: Distribution over adoption depth, excluding root nodes. LinkedIn adoptions occur much further from the root.

its members registered via invitations, which makes it an ideal subject for a case study investigating the structure of a massive online product diffusion event.

Our analyses demonstrate the contrast between the structural properties of the cascades studied in the past [14, 22, 26] and the structure of the signup cascades from a large popular website as we study here. We compare structural properties of the diffusion of LinkedIn with the diffusion of news stories, videos, online applications, and services reported in [14].

A recurring theme in our analysis is that the viral structure of LinkedIn's signup forest isn't necessarily due to its large size. In particular, many of the measures we consider can be relatively constant for cascades of widely varying sizes; the fact that the LinkedIn forest is so different for a number of these measures thus does not follow from pure scale, but instead is indicative of the nature of its propagation.

2.2 Quantifying Virality of LinkedIn Adoption

Adoptions as a function of depth. A natural way to measure the extent to which viral propagation accounts for adoption is to examine the distribution over tree depths (number of steps from the root) where adoptions occur. Since we are interested in quantifying person-to-person transmission, or warm signups, we restrict our attention to nodes at depth at least 1; the normalized distribution is shown in Fig. 2. We observe that a substantial fraction of warm signups occur far from the root: for example, 30% of warm signups on LinkedIn occur at depth 5 or greater. Comparing this distribution with those reported in the previous work of [14], the difference is quite striking; for instance, less than 1% of adoptions in the distributions from this earlier work are at depth 5 or greater. (Note that our results are qualitatively the same whether or not we include root nodes, as was done in the original analysis of [14].)

Adoptions by cascade type. Another way to gauge the virality of diffusion events is by measuring what fraction of adoptions reside in deep or large cascades.

In Fig. 3(top), we show the fraction of non-singleton members that reside in trees of increasing sizes. The differences between LinkedIn signup cascades and the previously studied cascades are again substantial. For example, 40% of non-singleton members are part of cascades with over 100 nodes, whereas the same ratio is at most around 20% in the previous datasets. Furthermore, 10% of non-singleton members reside in cascades with at least 10,000 members, whereas the largest cascades in many previous studies only have around few hundred nodes [14, 22, 26]. A similarly large

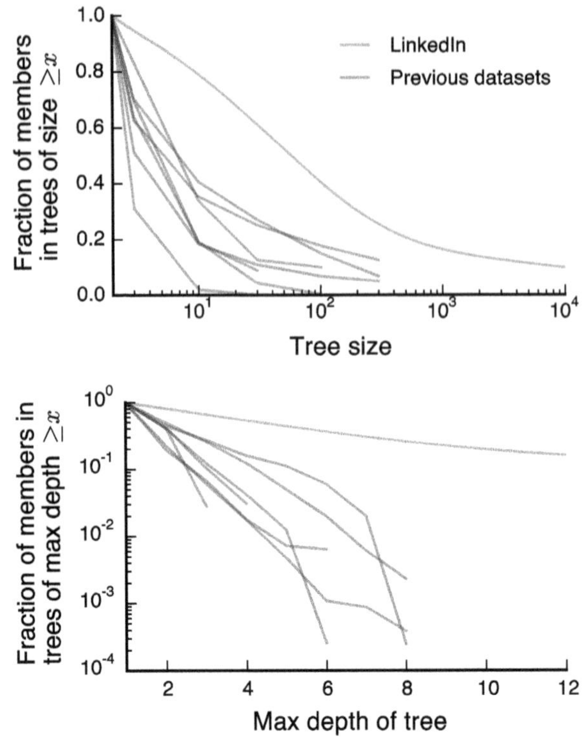

Figure 3: Fraction of non-singleton members in trees of specific size and depth. A greater portion of the LinkedIn signup forest is concentrated in large and deep cascades compared to previously studied diffusion datasets.

gap exists when we consider tree depth: on LinkedIn 36% of non-singleton members reside in trees with maximum depth 6 or greater, whereas the fraction in previous datasets varies between 0.1% and 6% (Fig. 3(bottom)). As before, the comparisons with the previous datasets are qualitatively unchanged if we instead consider all trees (including singletons).

It is important to note that there are two distinct ways in which the LinkedIn signup forest is more viral than previously studied adoption structures. First, the unnormalized versions of the measures we considered above—the proportions of nodes that adopt far from root nodes, and that reside in large and deep trees—are much higher on LinkedIn. Second, even when we restrict attention to nodes explicitly involved in diffusion (either non-root nodes or nodes in non-singleton trees, depending on the analysis), the proportions are *still* significantly higher, often by an order of magnitude or more. This second difference does not necessarily follow from the first. It would have been possible for LinkedIn to be "more viral" in the sense of a larger proportion of nodes being involved in member-to-member transmission, with the transmission itself being as it was in the previous datasets. Yet this is not the case, as the conditional distributions in Figs. 2 and 3 indicate.

2.3 Structural Virality of Signup Cascades

In addition to quantifying the virality of the signup forest as a whole, we also quantify the shape of signup cascades by measuring their *structural virality*. The goal of structural virality, introduced in [13], is to numerically disambiguate between shallow, broadcast-like diffusion and the deep branching structures called to mind by the biological "viral" metaphor. The structural virality

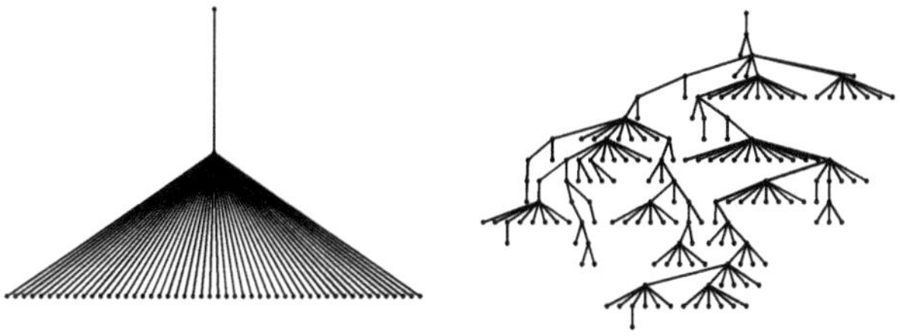

Figure 4: Two LinkedIn signup cascades, one with (left) low structural virality (Wiener index = 1.99), and one with (right) high structural virality (Wiener index = 9.5).

measure, called the Wiener index, is equal to the average path distance between two nodes in the tree. Pure broadcast diffusion (*i.e.*, a star-like cascade) results in very low scores on this measure (just under 2), while deep narrowly branching structures will have very high scores as the paths between nodes get very long (see Fig. 4 for examples of what real cascades with low and high Wiener indices look like). Low structural virality corresponds to broadcast-dominated diffusion, whereas high structural virality corresponds to multi-step transmission. In this section, we restrict our analysis to cascades with over 100 nodes, as was done in [13].

Interestingly, the distribution of structural virality over LinkedIn cascades with more than 100 nodes is qualitatively similar to the distributions reported for Twitter cascades with more than 100 nodes in [13]. Thus, although our analyses above show that the LinkedIn signup forest as a whole is significantly more viral than previously analyzed datasets, large LinkedIn signup cascades are roughly as viral as large Twitter information-sharing cascades. It's possible that LinkedIn's overall virality stems from the preponderance of large cascades, rather than the structural virality of the individual large cascades themselves, but more direct comparisons are needed to validate this hypothesis.

However, there remains an important sense in which the structural virality of LinkedIn trees follows different properties from the structural virality of the Twitter cascades in earlier work. A central finding in earlier analysis is that, for cascades across all major domains on Twitter, the correlation between structural virality and size is surprisingly low, ranging between 0 and 0.2 [13]. This implies that an information cascade's size does not reveal much about the structural mechanism by which it spread. In contrast, for LinkedIn signup cascades the correlation is a strikingly high 0.72, implying that the largest LinkedIn signup cascades truly spread through a viral process that is both deep and relatively narrow (Fig. 5 visualizes the structural virality of LinkedIn signup cascades as a function of their size). This high correlation appears to be related to the relative lack of broadcasts in LinkedIn: there are very few examples of a member "broadcasting" LinkedIn to hundreds or thousands of others, whereas on sites like Twitter this type of mass adoption from a single influential member is far more prevalent. As far fewer broadcast channels are available to drive adoption, sigup cascades on LinkedIn must therefore, by this definition, be more structurally viral if they are to spread to large populations. This departure from previously-studied cascades is a good example of how these differences do not follow purely from size.

Taken together, these analyses indicate that multi-step diffusion has played a much larger role in the adoption of LinkedIn than it did for the variety of domains considered in previous work. This result complements those found in previous work on information sharing cascades [13, 14, 22, 26]. Whereas they found a surprising general lack of viral propagation across a wide variety of domains,

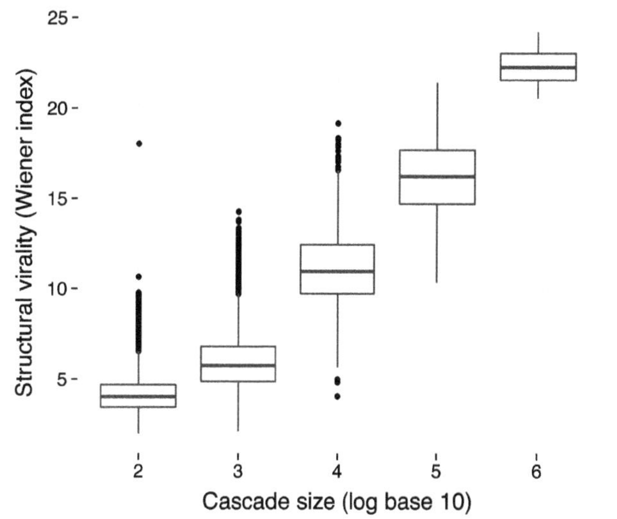

Figure 5: Structural virality as a function of cascade size (log base 10). The correlation is remarkably high, in contrast with previous findings on information-sharing cascades.

here we show that in the important case of a major global website, large-scale viral propagation does occur. We emphasize that this outcome was not preordained by size; merely because an adoption event was huge does not necessarily imply that it achieved its popularity through viral growth.

3. LOCAL AND GLOBAL HOMOPHILY

We have established that person-to-person transmission is an important mechanism through which LinkedIn has spread around the world. But what is the interplay between the diffusion structures we observe and the attributes of people involved in the diffusion process? Previous large-scale diffusion studies have largely treated users alike and concentrated on determining how—and whether—information, products, and services spread, just as we have in the previous section. As a consequence, our understanding of who is transmitting to whom (in terms of underlying user attributes) in large-scale diffusion events is very limited. Here, we connect our global signup cascades with the rich individual-level attribute data available on LinkedIn to investigate this question.

Since virtually all interpersonal networks display *homophily*, the tendency of people to associate with others like themselves, it is natural to expect that much of LinkedIn's diffusion is homophily-driven. What is less clear is how this homophily manifests itself in the composition of user attributes in the cascades, an effect that in principle can be substantial. By investigating this empirical composition, we seek to shed light on a fundamental question: are cascades more homogeneous—more *coherent*—than one would expect simply from the local level of homophily between inviters and invitees? Or is the level of homophily between inviters and invitees, when propagated over entire cascade trees, sufficient to account for the global level of homogeneity that we see in the trees as a whole?

LinkedIn is an ideal domain to study this question for two reasons: first, we have observed a high prevalence of multi-step diffusion; and second, there is a wealth of individual-level attribute data available, since most members fill in impressively detailed profiles. We have high coverage for a diversity of individual traits, such as country of residence, geographic sub-region, professional industry of employment, age, job type, job seniority level, and others.

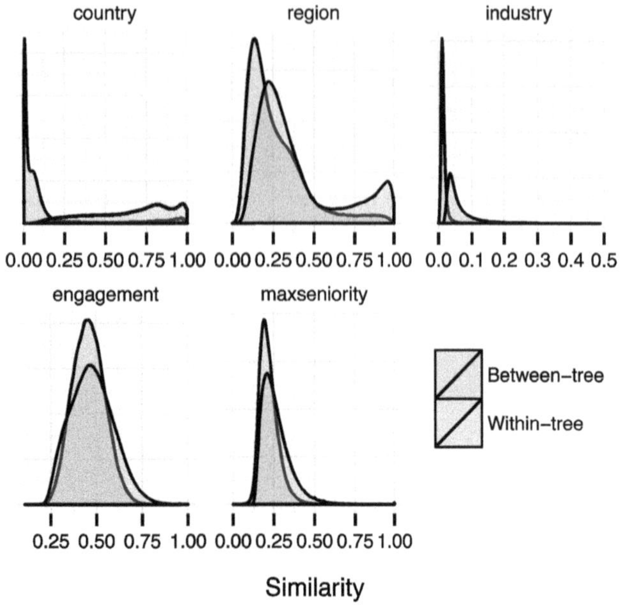

Figure 6: Within-tree and between-tree similarity on country, region, industry, engagement, and maximum job seniority.

3.1 Homophily in LinkedIn Signups

First we conduct an observational analysis of homophily in signups along various member attribute dimensions.

Edge homophily. Since homophily is such a pervasive phenomenon in interpersonal networks, we expect to see members inviting (and having their invitations accepted by) people like themselves. We can check this straightforwardly by computing, for every pair of attribute values A_1 and A_2, the conditional probability $P(A_2|A_1)$ that a warm signup has attribute value A_2 given that their inviter has attribute value A_1. This is simply equal to the empirical fraction $N(A_1 \rightarrow A_2)$ / $N(A_1)$, where $N(A_1)$ is the number of signup edges originating from members with attribute value A_1, and $N(A_1 \rightarrow A_2)$ is the number of signup edges where the source and destination have attribute values A_1 and A_2, respectively.

Examining these probabilities reveals that there is indeed a significant amount of edge homophily present in our data. The "self-loop" probabilities $P(A_1|A_1)$, where members accept invitations from others like themselves to join, are much higher than the transition probabilities $P(A_2|A_1)$ between different values $A_1 \neq A_2$. For example, for the country attribute, the conditional probabilities $P(\text{Brazil}, \text{Brazil})$ and $P(\text{India}, \text{India})$ are both greater than 0.80.

Comparing these probabilities to a randomized baseline where the attribute of each node is simply drawn from the overall distribution of the LinkedIn population confirms that the real self-loop probabilities are much higher than they would be if there were no edge homophily. Thus, members invite others like themselves, beyond what we would expect from the underlying group populations.

Cascade homophily. Now we investigate the extent to which the signup *cascades* display homophily along various dimensions.

Our main object of analysis in this section is the distribution over various attributes among members within the same cascade tree. To ensure the distributions are not skewed by small-sample effects, we restrict our attention to cascades comprising at least 100 members. There are over 100,000 such cascades in our dataset.

Given a distribution over member attributes, we would like a way to quantify how similar or diverse it is. We also wish to compare two distributions, and measure how similar they are. Ideally, these two quantities should be directly comparable. We fulfill these desiderata by adopting the *population diversity* measure used in sociology [28]. We define:

- The *within-similarity* $W_A(T)$ of a group T on a particular attribute A is the probability that two randomly selected members match on attribute A.
- The *between-similarity* $B_A(T_1, T_2)$ of two groups T_1 and T_2 is the probability that a randomly selected member from the first population and a randomly selected member from the second population match on attribute A.

These metrics have the advantages of being easily interpretable and directly comparable, and are not affected by the size of the populations being considered.

For every "large" tree T (over 100 members) and attribute A, we compute the within-tree similarity $W_A(T)$ of the members in the tree. Then we can examine the distribution over $W_A(T)$ for every attribute A. However, as was the case with edge homophily, a large amount of cascade *similarity* is insufficient to conclude that cascade *homophily* is present. Thus, we also take a random sample of pairs of trees and calculate the between-tree similarity $B_A(T_1, T_2)$ of the two member attribute distributions. The distribution over these between-tree similarities then provides a baseline to compare against. If there were no cascade homophily on A at all, then the within-tree and between-tree similarity distributions would be exactly the same. The extent to which they differ, then, is a direct measure of cascade homophily in our data.

In Fig. 6, we show the distributions W_A and B_A over all large trees for the following attributes: country, region, industry, engagement, and maximum seniority (top job level over one's career, as reflected by the job title). There are several important points to observe. First, there is a striking amount of homophily along some dimensions. The signup cascades are extremely homophilous on the geographical attributes, especially on country: many trees have within-tree similarity values close to 1, whereas the between-tree overlap is almost always below 0.25. Industry also displays significant homophily, in that W_{industry} and B_{industry} are almost non-overlapping. Second, the extent to which homophily is present varies widely across the attributes, since there is little to no homophily on engagement or maximum seniority. Finally, the geographic attributes display an intriguing pattern: their within-tree similarity distributions are bimodal. This suggests that there are two distinct ways in which signups cascade through countries and regions, with little interpolation between the two. We will return to this fact later in this Section.

Homophily by root country. Even in the absence of homophily, members with popular attributes are more likely to be associated with each other than members with rare attributes simply because there are more of them. Thus cascades that start in the United States are more likely to display high similarity than those that start in Belgium. Here we explore how similarity and homophily change with the specific value of the root attribute, focusing on country since it displays the highest within-tree similarity.

In Fig. 7, we plot the distribution of within-tree similarity W_A for large trees rooted in Brazil, Canada, France, India, and the United States. All five countries show a high degree of similarity, the exact magnitude of which correlates with the size of country's membership on LinkedIn. The fact that a single attribute value results in such high and homogeneous similarity distributions demonstrates the remarkably strong homophily we observe on country.

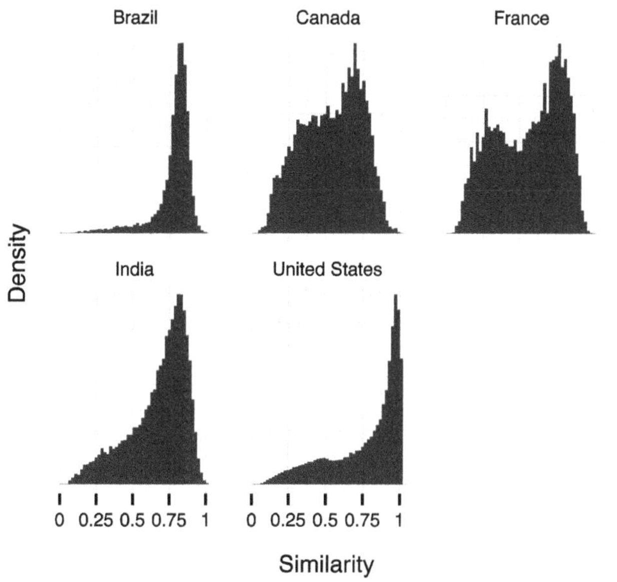

Figure 7: Within-tree similarity for trees rooted in Brazil, Canada, France, India, and the US.

Also, the similarity distribution is unimodal for almost every country in our dataset. A few countries, such as France in Fig. 7, have strong bimodality on their own, but most do not; the overall bimodality we observed in Fig. 6 is related to the diversity in country size, with the resulting cascade similarity depending on where the cascade is rooted.

3.2 Levels of Homophily

We have established that there are strong edge homophily effects present in LinkedIn signups, and there are also strong cascade-level homophily effects present in the signup cascades. Already, these empirical facts have important ramifications for how the site population will evolve: given that many new members are invited to join by existing ones, and that cascades display strong homophily effects, it follows that the warm signups of tomorrow will look like the inviters of today.

However, it is unclear whether the homophily effects present in the signup cascades are different from the homophily present at a local level. Do the distributions over country of residence in cascades simply follow from the basic level of edge homophily present?

Modeling edge homophily. To explore this, we simulate a warm signup process with the same cascade topologies we observe in the data, but where member countries are drawn according to a first-order Markov chain derived from empirical data. This first-order Markov chain M_1 is defined with the conditional probabilities $P(A_2|A_1)$ computed in the previous section as transition probabilities. In our synthetic model, the member country at a given node is determined by applying one step of the empirical Markov chain transition to the country of the parent. Hence the first-order Markov chain models edge homophily, and the question is whether such a model of local edge homophily is able to reproduce the observed global homophily patterns of cascades.

We proceed as follows. For each cascade, the country of the root node is kept the same as it is in the data. Then the countries of each of the root's children are drawn independently from the Markov chain. The same is done for their children, and so on down the cascade. This induces a distribution over countries in the tree, from which we compute within-tree similarity for each cascade as before. We can then compare the distribution over within-tree similarity induced by this simple first-order Markov process with the actual distribution observed in empirical data.

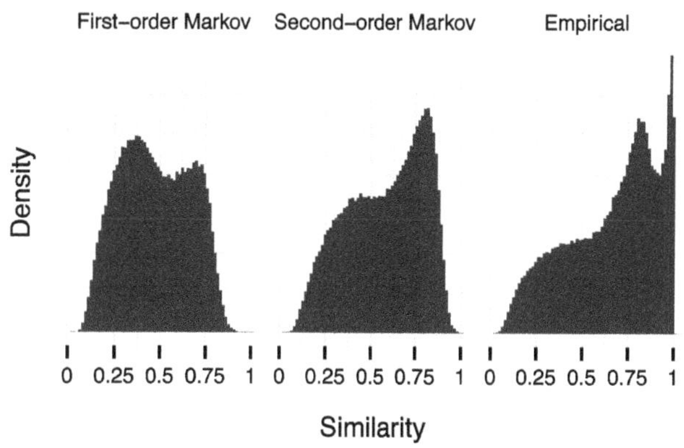

Figure 8: Within-tree similarity on real tree topologies with countries drawn from: (left) first-order Markov transitions M_1, and (middle) second-order Markov transitions M_2; (right) empirical within-tree similarity.

From edge to cascade homophily: First-order effects. The outcome of the above process for the country attribute is shown in Fig. 8(left), in which two important patterns are immediately apparent. First, the distribution of similarity across trees is bimodal, just as it is in the empirical data (shown in Fig. 8(right)). This implies that edge homophily is sufficient to explain the bimodality in within-cascade similarity. In fact, edge homophily on a star topology (instead of the real cascade topologies) recovers the bimodality as well—thus it results from the combination of edge homophily on country and insufficient tree-depth to allow mixing to the overall country distribution.

Second, the absolute level of within-tree similarity in the Markov simulation, while still high, is significantly lower than what we observe in empirical data. A direct consequence of this is that the type of member who joins a specific invitation cascade is, on average, not entirely determined by the type of member who invites him (were that the case, the similarity patterns produced by a first-order Markov simulation would reproduce those we find empirically). For example, if a particular cascade has been spreading among members based in India, and a new member from Kuwait joins the cascade, it is more likely that this member's invitees will be from India than we would expect on average from someone from Kuwait.

Therefore, despite the strong presence of country homophily at the local (edge) level, it is insufficient to explain the country homophily we observe at the cascade level. Member attributes in cascades, then, are determined by some process above and beyond local, homophilous interactions alone, which we already found to be powerful. A new member's attributes are not governed only by her parent, but by the rest of the cascade she is a part of as well. This result illuminates a crucial point about the user composition of cascades, and answers the central question posed at the beginning of this Section: *cascades are not simply arbitrary subsets of members following global demographic correlations*—they are more coherent than this simple characterization would suggest.

From edge to cascade homophily: Second-order effects. To investigate the higher-order effects between new members and the cascades they join, we repeat the simulation above using a second-order Markov chain M_2 to generate node countries. M_2 is defined by a process analogous to the first-order case: the conditional probability that a new member with attribute value A_3 joins, given that her inviter has value A_2 and her inviter's inviter has value A_1, is $P(A_3|A_1, A_2) = N(A_1 \to A_2 \to A_3)/N(A_1 \to A_2)$, where $N(\cdot)$ again refers to the number of signup paths connecting nodes with particular attributes. If $N(A_1 \to A_2)$ is too small, then we ignore the grandparent and use the first-order probability $P(A_3|A_2)$. Using a second-order Markov chain allows us to capture effects such as in the India and Kuwait example described above.

The resulting distribution of within-tree similarity, shown in Fig. 8(middle), is shifted remarkably far to the right compared to the outcome of the first-order simulation—in this case, the "second-order effects" are actually quite large. The magnitude of the discrepancy between the first-order and second-order models shows how much more homophily structure there is at the cascade level. Furthermore, note that there is still the mode of cascades with near-perfect country similarity in empirical data that remains unaccounted for by the second-order Markov simulation, which further reinforces the coherency of signup cascades beyond local edge homophily effects.

3.3 Guessing the Root of a Cascade

The fact that the observed cascade homophily effects are not explainable via local edge homophily effects alone suggests that cascades tend to retain some "memory" of their starting point. Here we ask: how quickly does a cascade "lose" the attribute of the root node (its country, say) as the cascade grows and relaxes to the background distribution?

The process by which this happens is the subject of a well-known probabilistic model originating in the study of evolutionary trees—we imagine an attribute at the root of a tree and then this attribute is passed on to the children with some probability of mutation [12, 31, 32, 35]. In the genetic application, this attribute would be an allele of a gene, while in our case it would be some homophilous property of users, such as their country. The question is then whether, deep enough into the tree, the node attributes have mixed to some background distribution for the full population, or whether arbitrarily deep in the tree we can still infer something about the value at the root. Notice that if the tree were simply a path (*i.e.*, if each node had exactly one child), then we would expect the process to mix to the background distribution. However, on a tree with non-trivial branching factor, there are competing forces: the process tends to mix on each path, but there are many overlapping paths on which to preserve information about the value at the root.

To address this issue, we consider the following concrete "root-guessing" question for the trees in our cascade, and for the values of a particular attribute: for each depth d, how often does the plurality attribute among members at depth d match the root's attribute? Asking how often this plurality guess correctly predicts the root's value allows us to further elucidate the extent to which global homophily is present in the trees, by seeing how often the root's characteristics can be detected deep into the tree. We will also compare the results of the root-guessing experiment on the real LinkedIn data to the results when attribute values are generated by the natural first-order or second-order Markov chains defined as above.

The results of this computation using the country attribute are shown in Fig. 9. There are a number of interesting conclusions from this experiment. First, it takes a surprisingly long time for the attributes to fully relax to the background distribution: the empirical curve only intersects the global prior at depth 18, which is far beyond the maximum depth that most cascades reach. Second, the first-order Markov simulation relaxes to the global prior much faster than the empirical data does. Finally, the second-order Markov chain fares significantly better, again showing the strong higher-order homophily interactions present in signup cascades.

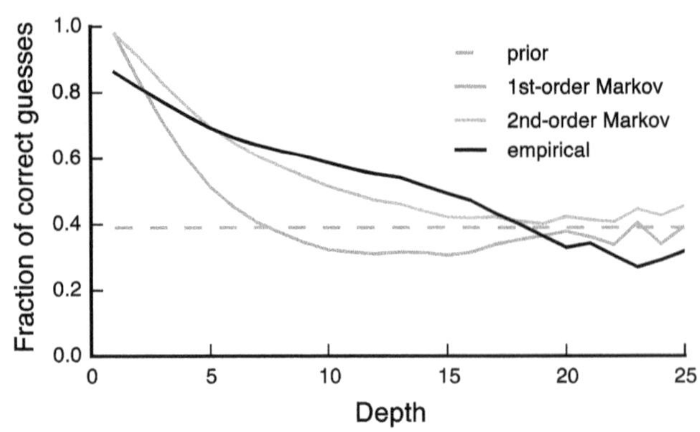

Figure 9: Fraction of time plurality attribute at depth d matches root attribute in root-guessing experiment. Empirical data retains "memory" of the root longer than baselines.

It is interesting to think about the role of the second-order Markov chain in light of the analogy to the genetic applications of the model. In genetic contexts, the process is a first-order Markov chain by the definition of genetic inheritance: conditional on knowing the true complete genotypes of an individuals' parents, there is in essence no additional information contained in the genotypes of the grandparents. But in our social setting, the country of a node's parent in the tree no longer serves as a sufficiently complete description—for example, if the parent is someone who moved from India to the US and simply lists the US as their country, then there may be information in the fact that the grandparent lists India as their country. In effect, a small amount of profile information may be serving more as a kind of "social phenotype" rather than a "social genotype," displaying only observable characteristics rather than deeper internal ones, and the use of the higher-order Markov chains may help fill in some of the missing information that results.

3.4 Status Gradients

Throughout this section, we've discussed how signup cascades show strong patterns of homophily along certain attributes like country and industry, whereas along other attributes signups aren't homophilous. However, some of these other attributes, such as age and job seniority, show other structure.

As in offline realms of professional life, *status* is an important part of one's identity on LinkedIn. Signup edges are inherently directed: one member issues an invitation and the other member joins a community through that person. Thus it is possible that on attributes with natural orderings, like age and job seniority, signups follow a *status gradient*, meaning people have a tendency to accept invitations from higher-status members.

We check the extent to which this effect occurs empirically. In Fig. 10(a), the color of the cell (x, y) shows how much more likely a member of type x is to send an accepted invitation to a member of type y than to receive and accept one (*i.e.*, it is equal to $P(y|x) - P(x|y)$, where $P(u|v)$ means the probability that a member of type u accepts an invitation, given that it originated from a member of type v). There is a clear effect on age: the grey below the $x = y$

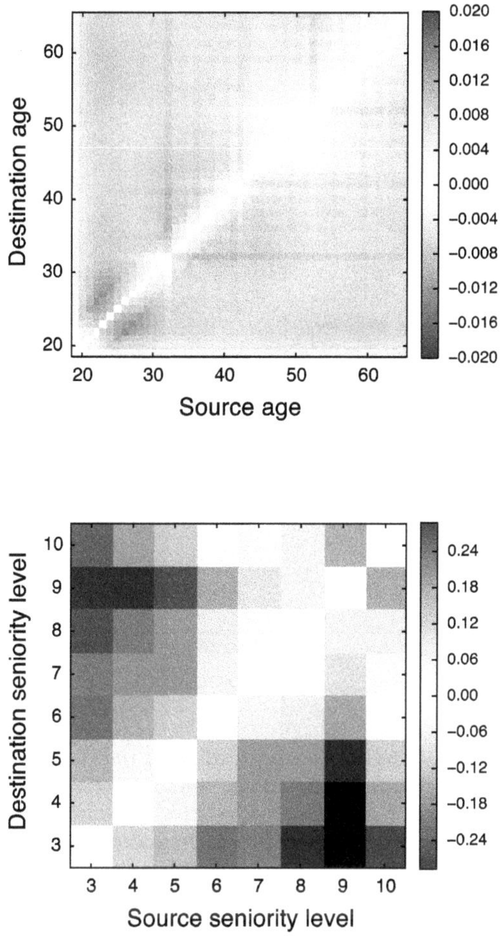

Figure 10: Status gradients on age and maximum seniority.

diagonal indicates that younger members are more likely to accept invitations from older members than vice versa, indicating there is a status effect on age governing who invites whom and who accepts whom's invitations. In Fig. 10(b), we show that an even stronger status gradient exists on job seniority (since members may have been employed in more than one job, and thus at more than one job seniority level, we define a member's seniority to be the highest level they've ever worked at).

Thus there are two fundamental ways signups flow through networks: along certain attributes, members tend to act homophilously and invite others like themselves, and along others, signups tend to progress down status gradients, flowing from higher-status users to lower-status users.

4. CASCADE GROWTH

Having considered the signup cascades as static objects, we now trace their development over time and investigate various aspects of their temporal evolution.

4.1 Timescales of transmission

A key characteristic of any diffusion process is how much time elapses between adjacent adoptions. In the biology-inspired terminology often employed in diffusion models, when does an "infected" node transmit the contagion (*i.e.*, the signup) to another?

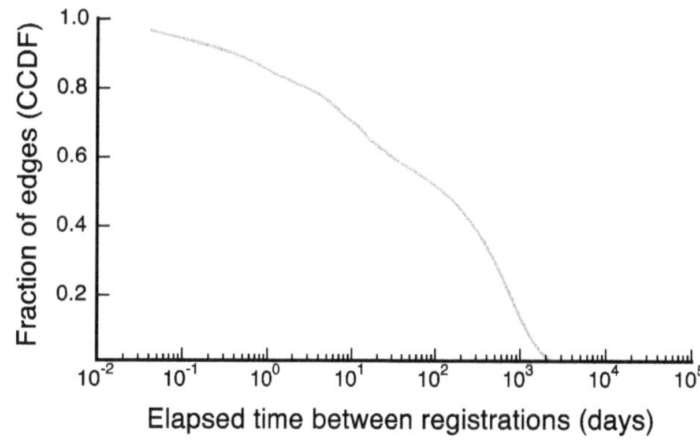

Figure 11: Complementary cumulative distribution function (CCDF) of elapsed times between inviter and invitee signup times. Adoptions are usually very separated in time.

To answer this question, we consider a cohort of members who joined LinkedIn at roughly the same time, and collect all signup edges (A, B) where A is a member of the cohort. Then we examine the distribution of elapsed times between when A joined and when B accepted the invitation from A. Fig. 12 shows this distribution for members who joined in 2006 (all time frames are qualitatively similar). It is immediately apparent that adjacent adoptions of LinkedIn are widely separated in time: around 40% of members who joined did so at least a year later than their inviters did. This is in contrast with other diffusion settings, such as information-sharing on Facebook or Twitter, where the majority of transmissions have been observed to occur within a few days of adoption [11, 39].

Long time spans between inviter and invitee signups could be caused by two different mechanisms: members could be sending out invitations long after they register, or invitees could be accepting invitations long after they receive them. We check this directly: Fig. 12 shows the fraction of invitations sent as a function of time for users who joined in March 2012 (other times were qualitatively similar). We find that the former explanation is the case: invitations are sent months or years after members join, and invitees accept them usually within a few days after they receive them (this latter fact is illustrated in Fig. 13).

Based on these results, we conclude that members of LinkedIn remain "infectious"—able to participate in member-to-member diffusion—over very long periods of time; it is not the case that the majority of transmissions occur in some narrow time frame relative to adoption. Extremely long infectious periods can clearly contribute to the success of a cascade, since members can invite others to the network during a wide range of times.

4.2 Cascade growth trajectories

This fact has a simple but important consequence: if individual edges often take months or years to form, then the cascades they make up must persist for long periods of time as well. In the faster-paced context of online social media, the adoption of popular pieces of online content is often concentrated within a narrow time frame [23, 39], and sharing cascades consequently achieve much of their growth during this small interval. But this is unlikely in our setting given how much longer signup cascades persist. Thus, we ask: How do LinkedIn cascades grow in size over time?

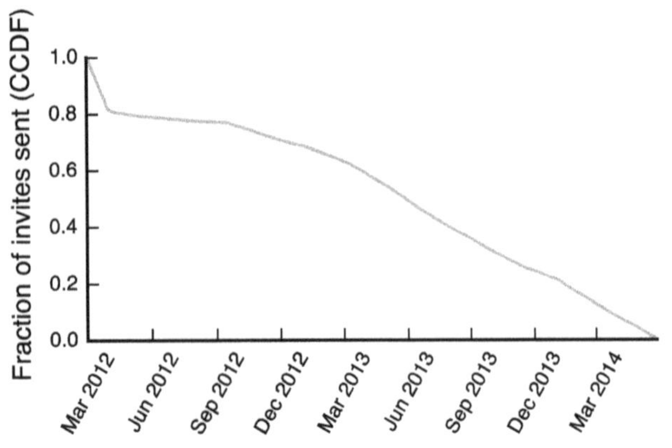

Figure 12: CCDF of the number of invites sent as a function of time for members who joined in March 2012. Most invitations are sent months after a member joins, meaning members remain "infectious" over very long periods of time.

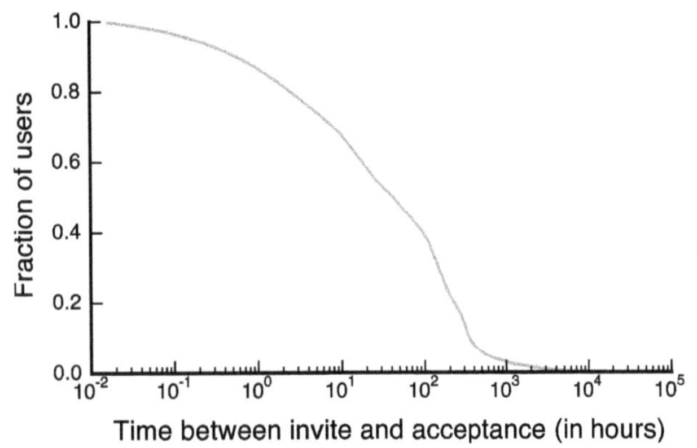

Figure 13: CCDF of the elapsed time between when an invitation was sent and when it was accepted. Invitations are accepted very quickly after they are sent.

To answer this question, we plot the growth trajectory of the 1,000 biggest cascades on LinkedIn in Fig. 14(a). For each cascade, we normalize both time and size to be between 0 and 1, and show the fraction of the cascade's eventual size at various points in time between the root's registration and the present day. A surprisingly robust linear growth pattern is apparent. Although in principle cascades could have reached their eventual size in very different ways, this doesn't happen in practice. There is very little variation in how big cascades became big on LinkedIn; virtually all of them gradually accumulated members at a constant rate over time. Thus, LinkedIn's rapid growth is not accounted for by individual cascades alone—it is the number of distinct cascades growing in parallel, each of which is growing relatively linearly, that increases so dramatically. In Fig. 14(b), the same type of plot is shown for 1,000 medium-sized cascades. Much more variation is present, but it is still around the same basic linear trend.

We conclude that, in contrast with the intuitive (and largely accurate) picture of viral videos, pictures, and news stories quickly spreading through online media and interpersonal networks before mostly burning out, the picture of diffusion that emerges from our study of LinkedIn is one of persistent, parallel accumulation of subpopulations at a much more deliberate pace.

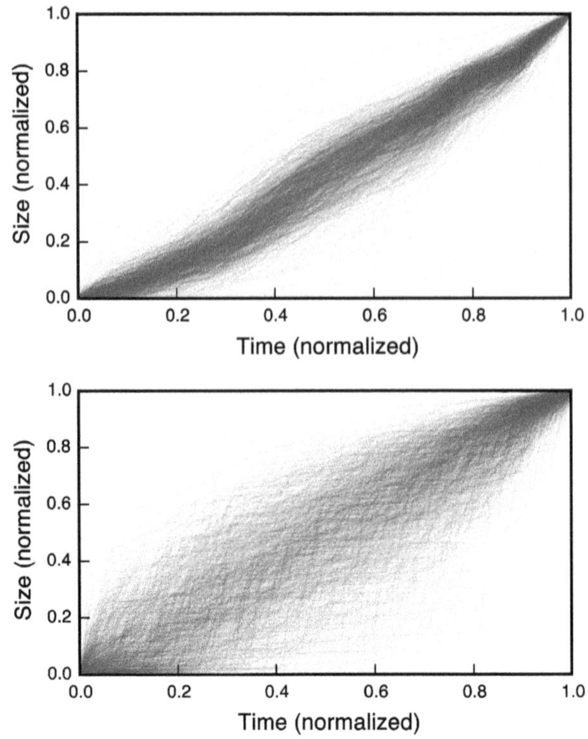

Figure 14: Patterns of cascade growth over time for (top) large cascades (over 4,000 members) and (bottom) medium cascades (500 members). Cascades grow relatively linearly over time, bigger cascades more consistently so than smaller ones.

Comparison with random baseline. The global picture of LinkedIn's growth involves many trees accumulating nodes in parallel at a notably linear rate. It's natural to ask whether a simple generative process of tree growth can reproduce the basic properties we've observed: the distribution over tree sizes, as well as the linear growth rate pattern.

Arguably the simplest such baseline model is to have nodes arrive sequentially, each identified as a cold or warm signup; a cold signup becomes the root of a new tree, while a warm signup attaches to a parent chosen uniformly at random from existing nodes. The choice of how nodes are assigned to be warm or cold is thus the only parameter in the process, and for this purpose we use the real exact ordering of warm and cold signups over the history of LinkedIn. The resulting distribution of cascade sizes is remarkably robust: 30 runs of this process are plotted in color in Fig. 15, and the empirical distribution of cascade sizes is shown in black (we only show non-trivial cascades, as in Section 2).

Relative to the real distribution, the slopes of the distribution for draws from the randomized baseline are roughly the same, but they are consistently shifted left: the individual trees are larger in the real distribution from LinkedIn.

To determine if this process gives linear growth trajectories for individual trees, we add timestamps to this model. We consider the same simple process as above, in which each node arrives with its true warm/cold status and now also its true arrival time, and randomly draws its parent uniformly at random from all existing nodes. We find that the rates of tree growth follow a linear trend very close to the real empirical distribution shown in Fig. 14, and with a variance across trees that is even smaller than in the real data.

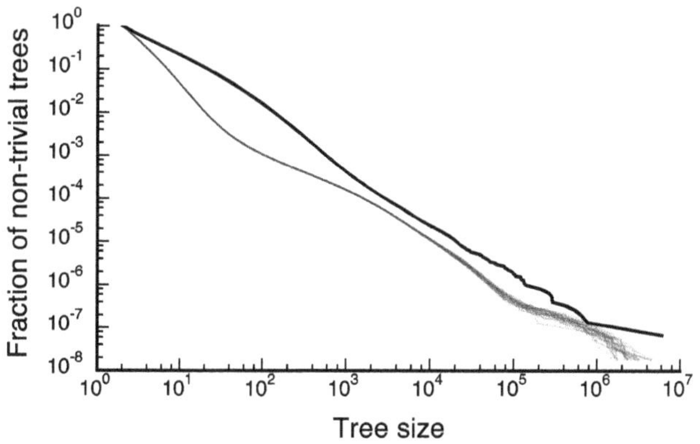

Figure 15: Distribution (CCDF) of cascade sizes on random baseline with real ordering of warm and cold signups (color) and empirical distribution of cascade sizes (black).

5. RELATED WORK

There are three lines of research related to our work here: the dynamics of cascades; the growth and evolution of online social networks; and analyses of homophily, the tendency of people to connect to others who are similar to them.

Cascades. Our work builds on the rich literature that studies diffusion and adoption of new ideas, products, and behaviors [33]. Early cascade research in the social science literature was based on focused empirical studies [9] as well as mathematical models [6, 16, 38]; only relatively recently have scientists have able to observe and measure large-scale diffusion events. Online cascades served as sources of detailed data about such events; studies drawing on this type of data have considered settings such as blogging [1, 17, 26], e-mail [15, 27], product recommendations [22], and the sharing of information in social sites such as Facebook, Flickr, and Twitter [7, 8, 11, 13, 14, 19, 21]. In work that aligns more closely with our focus on signup cascades, researchers have also studied cascades of group formation [4] and adoption of online services [3, 5, 34, 36]. Much of this previous work has the property that even the successful cascade events in the data were much smaller in scale [8, 22] than the signup cascades we consider here.

We compare the structure of LinkedIn's signup cascades with several datasets from [14]. In that work, Goel et al. characterized the structure of online diffusion networks in several domains, and observed that most cascades on the Web are shallow and small. In contrast, we find that LinkedIn signup cascades tend to be deeper and larger, and grow steadily over long periods of time. Our case study of the LinkedIn signups forest, an extreme example of online adoption, complements the general picture of online diffusion structures drawn in [14] by filling in what one of the largest online diffusion structures looks like. In addition, we apply the structural virality measure introduced in [13] and find that the correlation between size and structural virality is very high for LinkedIn signups, in contrast to the very low correlations found for information-sharing cascades in [13].

Growth and evolution of social networks. A second line of related work is on mechanisms for the evolution of online social networks, using data covering the growth of social networking services including Facebook [37], Flickr, [20, 30], LinkedIn [24], and others [25]. This line of work investigates the evolution of network structure assuming an underlying arrival process for new nodes. Our work, on the other hand, focuses on the mechanisms that underpins this arrival process, through the new members who join the network and the ways in which cascades of invitations spread.

Homophily in social networks. Homophily—the tendency of people to associate with others like themselves—is one of the most important forces shaping the structure of social networks [29]. Recent work using online data has considered the challenges in differentiating homophily from influence [2, 10, 34], and has established links between the evolution of social network structure and the emergence of homophily [18]. We focus here on a distinct issue that is particularly well-suited to analysis via our signup cascade data—the ways in which local patterns of homophily between pairs of individuals translate into more global forms of homophily at the level of an entire cascade, and how cascade-level homophily can transcend homophily observed at local levels.

As we discuss in Section ??, part of our analysis of this local-global link involves developing an intriguing connection with a body of mathematical work that has developed separately from the homophily literature—namely, research on phylogenetic tree reconstruction [12, 31]. That problem is formulated in terms of a process in which information (*e.g.*, a binary attribute) is recursively transmitted from a root node down a tree. At every step the attribute can mutate with some given probability, and the goal is to reconstruct the attribute of the root given the values of the attributes of all the children at depth d [32, 35]. The connection we develop begins with the observation that a homophilous attribute in a cascade can be thought of as analogous with a genetic trait that propagates down an evolutionary tree, changing to a new value with some probability. The extent to which genetic information can be reconstructed about ancestors then turns into the question of inferring properties of a cascade's initial starter from the properties of its eventual adopters. We show how this inference depends intimately on the structure of the cascade tree and the homophily of the attribute, and we argue that the type of Markov modeling assumption needed in the social context appears to differ from what is relevant in the genetic context.

6. CONCLUSION

By analyzing the global spread of LinkedIn, we have been able to formulate and address a broad set of questions about *signup cascades*—large diffusion events in which users become members of a Web site and invite friends to join as well. We found that the trees of signups arising from this process have characteristic structure and growth dynamics that look very different from the large information-sharing cascades that have been studied extensively in recent work. We also provide a new framework for analyzing homophily in these types of processes, identifying connections between the way homophily operates at multiple levels of scale.

Several points from our earlier discussions are worth drawing out in greater detail. First, while the cascading adoption of LinkedIn has reached a very large user population, it is important to emphasize that the structural properties of its spread are not due to scale alone. Indeed, recent work demonstrated that the virality of the cascade trees can be roughly independent of their size [13]. The massive signup cascades we study here show that very different kinds of diffusion are possible—in which virality increases with tree size, coupled with persistent linear tree growth over time.

Second, the interaction between local and global similarity in the cascade trees points to deeper issues about the nature of homophily. While we tend to think of homophily patterns as arising from the accumulation of local similarity along the links of a social network, our Markov-chain analysis shows that the cascade trees exhibit a higher level of global similarity than would follow from these purely local effects—members of signups cascades have a certain coherence to them that is not explainable via simple models of pairwise interaction. One possibility, suggested by the analogies to genetic models and the corresponding limitations we identify in these analogies, is that one needs a richer type of "social genome" to characterize each individual in the cascade—in essence, a profile detailed enough that knowing the profile of an individual's parent provides sufficient information to estimate properties of the individual. Identifying the bases for such profiles, and for the mechanisms by which these characteristics propagate through social networks, could provide a new way of reasoning about the processes by which large groups on the Web come together and adopt new products and innovations.

Acknowledgments. We thank Sam Shah and Myunghwan Kim of LinkedIn for their help. This research has been supported in part by a Google PhD Fellowship, a Simons Investigator Award, a Google Research Grant, a Facebook Faculty Research Grant, an ARO MURI grant, NSF grants IIS-1016909, IIS-1149837, IIS-1159679, CNS-1010921, IIS-0910664, Boeing, Facebook, Volkswagen, and Yahoo.

7. REFERENCES

[1] E. Adar, L. Zhang, L. A. Adamic, and R. M. Lukose. Implicit structure and the dynamics of blogspace. In *Workshop on the Weblogging Ecosystem*, 2004.

[2] A. Anagnostopoulos, R. Kumar, and M. Mahdian. Influence and correlation in social networks. In *Proc. KDD*, 2008.

[3] S. Aral and D. Walker. Creating social contagion through viral product design: A randomized trial of peer influence in networks. *Management Science*, 2011.

[4] L. Backstrom, D. Huttenlocher, J. Kleinberg, and X. Lan. Group formation in large social networks: Membership, growth, and evolution. In *Proc. KDD*, 2006.

[5] E. Bakshy, B. Karrer, and L. A. Adamic. Social influence and the diffusion of user-created content. In *Proc EC*, 2009.

[6] D. Centola and M. Macy. Complex contagions and the weakness of long ties. *American Journal of Sociology*, 2007.

[7] M. Cha, A. Mislove, B. Adams, and K. P. Gummadi. Characterizing social cascades in flickr. In *Proc. WOSN*, 2008.

[8] J. Cheng, L. Adamic, P. A. Dow, J. M. Kleinberg, and J. Leskovec. Can cascades be predicted? In *Proc. WWW*, 2014.

[9] J. Coleman, E. Katz, and H. Menzel. The diffusion of innovation among physicians. *Sociometry*, 1957.

[10] D. Crandall, D. Cosley, D. Huttenlocher, J. Kleinberg, and S. Suri. Feedback effects between similarity and social influence in online communities. In *Proc. KDD*, 2008.

[11] P. A. Dow, L. A. Adamic, and A. Friggeri. The anatomy of large facebook cascades. In *Proc. ICWSM*, 2013.

[12] W. Evans, C. Kenyon, Y. Peres, and L. J. Schulman. Broadcasting on trees and the ising model. *Annals of Applied Probability*, 2000.

[13] S. Goel, A. Anderson, J. Hofman, and D. Watts. The structural virality of online diffusion. *Under review*.

[14] S. Goel, D. J. Watts, and D. G. Goldstein. The structure of online diffusion networks. In *Proc. EC*, 2012.

[15] B. Golub and M. O. Jackson. Using selection bias to explain the observed structure of internet diffusions. *Proc. Natl. Acad. Sci.*, 2010.

[16] M. S. Granovetter. Threshold models of collective behavior. *American Journal of Sociology*, 1978.

[17] D. Gruhl, R. V. Guha, D. Liben-Nowell, and A. Tomkins. Information diffusion through blogspace. In *Proc. WWW*, 2004.

[18] G. Kossinets and D. J. Watts. Origins of homophily in an evolving social network. *American Journal of Sociology*, 2009.

[19] R. Kumar, M. Mahdian, and M. McGlohon. Dynamics of conversations. In *Proc. KDD*, 2010.

[20] R. Kumar, J. Novak, and A. Tomkins. Structure and evolution of online social networks. In *Proc. KDD*, 2006.

[21] H. Kwak, C. Lee, H. Park, and S. Moon. What is twitter, a social network or a news media? In *Proc. WWW*, 2010.

[22] J. Leskovec, L. Adamic, and B. Huberman. The dynamics of viral marketing. *ACM Transactions on the Web*, 2007.

[23] J. Leskovec, L. Backstrom, and J. Kleinberg. Meme-tracking and the dynamics of the news cycle. In *Proc. KDD*, 2009.

[24] J. Leskovec, L. Backstrom, R. Kumar, and A. Tomkins. Microscopic evolution of social networks. In *Proc. KDD*, 2008.

[25] J. Leskovec, J. M. Kleinberg, and C. Faloutsos. Graph evolution: Densification and shrinking diameters. *ACM Transactions on the KDD*, 2007.

[26] J. Leskovec, M. McGlohon, C. Faloutsos, N. Glance, and M. Hurst. Cascading behavior in large blog graphs. In *Proc SDM*, 2007.

[27] D. Liben-Nowell and J. Kleinberg. Tracing information flow on a global scale using Internet chain-letter data. *Proc. Natl. Acad. Sci.*, 2008.

[28] S. Lieberson. Measuring population diversity. *American Sociological Review*, 1969.

[29] M. McPherson, L. Smith-Lovin, and J. M. Cook. Birds of a feather: Homophily in social networks. *Annual review of sociology*, 2001.

[30] A. Mislove, H. S. Koppula, K. P. Gummadi, P. Druschel, and B. Bhattacharjee. Growth of the Flickr Social Network. In *Proc. WOSN*, 2008.

[31] E. Mossel. Phase transitions in phylogeny. *Transactions of the American Mathematical Society*, 2004.

[32] E. Mossel, S. Roch, and A. Sly. On the inference of large phylogenies with long branches: How long is too long? *Bulletin of mathematical biology*, 2011.

[33] E. M. Rogers. *Diffusion of Innovations*. Free Press, New York, fourth edition, 1995.

[34] A. S. Sinan Aral, Lev Muchnika. Distinguishing influence-based contagion from homophily-driven diffusion in dynamic networks. *Proc. Natl. Acad. Sci.*, 2009.

[35] A. Sly. Reconstruction for the potts model. In *Proc. STOC*, 2009.

[36] J. Ugander, L. Backstrom, C. Marlow, and J. Kleinberg. Structural diversity in social contagion. *Proc. Natl. Acad. Sci.*, 2012.

[37] B. Viswanath, A. Mislove, M. Cha, and K. P. Gummadi. On the Evolution of User Interaction in Facebook. In *Proc. WOSN*, 2009.

[38] D. J. Watts. A simple model of global cascades on random networks. *Proc. Natl. Acad. Sci.*, 2002.

[39] J. Yang and J. Leskovec. Patterns of temporal variation in online media. In *Proc. WSDM*, 2011.

Recommendation Subgraphs for Web Discovery*

Arda Antikacioglu †
Department of Mathematics
Carnegie Mellon University
aantikac@andrew.cmu.edu

R. Ravi ‡
Tepper School of Business
Carnegie Mellon University
ravi@cmu.edu

Srinath Sridhar
BloomReach Inc.
srinath@bloomreach.com

ABSTRACT

Recommendations are central to the utility of many popular e-commerce websites. Such sites typically contain a set of recommendations on every product page that enables visitors and crawlers to easily navigate the website. These recommendations are essentially universally present on all e-commerce websites. Choosing an appropriate set of recommendations at each page is a critical task performed by dedicated backend software systems.

We formalize the concept of recommendations used for discovery as a natural graph optimization problem on a bipartite graph and propose three methods for solving the problem in increasing order of sophistication: a local random sampling algorithm, a greedy algorithm and a more involved partitioning based algorithm. We first theoretically analyze the performance of these three methods on random graph models and characterize when each method will yield a solution of sufficient quality and the parameter ranges when more sophistication is needed. We complement this by providing an empirical analysis of these algorithms on simulated and real-world production data from a retail website. Our results confirm that it is not always necessary to implement complicated algorithms in the real-world, and demonstrate that very good practical results can be obtained by using simple heuristics that are backed by the confidence of concrete theoretical guarantees.

1. INTRODUCTION

1.1 Web Relevance Engines

The digital discovery divide [15] refers to the problem of companies not being able to present users with what they seek in the short time they spend looking for this information. The problem is prevalent not only in e-commerce websites but also in social networks and micro-blogging sites where surfacing relevant content quickly is important for user engagement.

BloomReach is a big-data marketing company that uses the client's content as well as web-wide data to optimize both customer acquisition and satisfaction for e-retailers. BloomReach's clients include top internet retail companies from around the country. In this paper, we describe the structure optimizer component of BloomReach's Web Relevance Engine. This component works on top of the recommendation engine so as to carefully add a set of links across pages that ensures that users can efficiently navigate the entire website.

1.2 Structure Optimization of Websites

An important concern of retail website owners is whether a significant fraction of the site is not recommended at all (or 'hardly' recommended) from other more popular pages within their site. One way to address this problem is to try to ensure that every page will obtain at least a baseline number of links from popular pages so that great content does not remain undiscovered, and thus bridge the discovery divide mentioned above. If the website remains connected, this also ensures a simple conductance for the underlying link graph.

We use this criterion of discoverability as the objective for the choice of the links to recommend. We start with a small set of already discovered or popular nodes available at a site, and want to use this set to make as many new nodes discoverable as possible. This objective leads to a new structural formulation of the recommendation selection problem. In particular, we think of commonly visited pages in a site as the already discovered pages, from which there are a large number of possible recommendations available (using more traditional information retrieval methods) to related but less visited peripheral pages. The problem of choosing a limited number of pages to recommend at each discovered page can be cast with the objective of maximizing the number of peripheral non-visited pages that are redundantly linked. We formulate this as a recommendation subgraph problem, and study practical algorithms for solving these problems at scale with real-life data.

1.3 Recommendation Systems as a Subgraph Selection Problem

Formally, we divide all pages in a site into two groups: the discovered pages and the undiscovered ones. Furthermore, we assume that traditional recommendation systems [1, 23, 25] provide us with a large set of related candidate undiscov-

*This work was supported in part by an internship at BloomReach Inc.
†Supported in part by NSF CCF-1347308
‡Supported in part by NSF CCF-1347308

WWW 2015, May 18–22, 2015, Florence, Italy.
ACM 978-1-4503-3469-3/15/05.
http://dx.doi.org/10.1145/2736277.2741680.

ered page recommendations for each discovered page using relevance metrics. In this work, we assume d such related candidates are available per page creating a candidate recommendation bipartite graph (with degree d at each discovered page node). Our goal is to analyze how to prune this set to $c < d$ recommendations such that globally we ensure that the number of undiscovered pages that have at least $a \geq 1$ recommendations to them in the chosen subgraph. This gives the (c, a)-recommendation subgraph introduced in Section 3.1. Even though the case of $a = 1$ reduces to a polynomially solvable version of a matching problem, the more usual cases of $a > 1$ are most likely NP-hard prohibiting exact solution methods at scale. Even the simple versions that reduce to matching are too computational expensive on memory and processing to run on real-life instances

1.4 Our Contributions

We introduce three simple heuristic methods that can be implemented in linear or near-linear time and thoroughly investigate their theoretical performance. In particular, we delineate when each method will work effectively on popular random graph models, and when a practitioner will need to employ a more sophisticated algorithm. We then evaluate how these simple methods perform on simulated data, both in terms of solution quality and running time. Finally, we show the deployment of these methods on BloomReach's real-world client link graph and measure their actual performance in terms of running-times, memory usage and accuracy. It is worthwhile to note that the simplest of the three methods that we propose (sampling) can be easily adapted to the incremental dynamic setting when the set of pages and candidate recommendations is changing rapidly.

To summarize, our contributions are as follows.

1. The development of a new structural model for recommendation systems as a subgraph selection problem for maximizing discoverability (Section 3).
2. The proposal of three methods (sampling, greedy and partition) with increasing sophistication to solve the problem at scale along with associated theoretical performance guarantee analyses (Section 4). In particular, we show very strong theoretical bounds on the size of the discoverable set for the sampling algorithm in the fixed degree random graph model (Theorem 1); in the Erdös-Renyi model for the greedy algorithm (Theorem 7) and for a partition-based algorithm (Theorem 10).
3. An empirical validation of our conclusions with simulated and real-life data (Section 5). Our simulations show that sampling is the least resource intensive and performs satisfactorily, while partition is the most resource intensive but performs better for small values of discoverability threshold a; Greedy is the overall best-performer using a single pass over the data and producing good results over a variety of parameters. In the tests with real retailer data, we see these trends broadly reflected in the results: Greedy performs well when c gets moderately large giving almost optimal starting from $a = 2$. The partition method is promising when the targeted a value is low. Sampling is typically worse than greedy, but unlike the partition algorithm, its performance improves dramatically as c becomes larger, and does not worsen as quickly when a gets larger.

2. RELATED WORK

Recommendation systems have been studied extensively in the literature, broadly separated into two different streams: collaborative filtering systems and content-based recommender systems [2]. Much attention has been focused on the former approach, where either users are clustered by considering the items they have consumed or items are clustered by considering the users that have bought them. Both item-to-item and user-to-user recommendation systems based on collaborative filtering have been adopted by many industry giants such as Twitter [12], Amazon [20] and Google [6] and Netflix [5].

Content based systems instead look at each item and its intrinsic properties. For example, Pandora has categorical information such as Artist, Genre, Year, Singer, Tempo etc. on each song it indexes. Similarly, Netflix has a lot of categorical data on movies and TV such as Cast, Director, Producers, Release Date, Budget, etc. This categorical data can then be used to recommend new songs that are similar to the songs that a user has liked before. Depending on user feedback, a recommender system can learn which of the categories are more or less important to a user and adjust its recommendations.

A drawback of the first type of system is that is that they require multiple visits by many users so that a taste profile for each user, or a user profile for each item can be built. Similarly, content-based systems also require significant user participation to train the underlying system. These conditions are possible to meet for large commerce or entertainment hubs, but not very likely for most online retailers that specialize in a just a few areas, but have a long-tail [3] of product offerings.

Because of this constraint, in this paper we focus on a recommender system that typically uses many different algorithms that extract categorical data from item descriptions and uses this data to establish weak links between items (candidate recommendations). In the absence of other data that would enable us to choose among these many links, we consider every potential recommendation to be of equal value and focus on the objective of discovery, which has not been studied before. Using heuristics for building this graph is not only practical, but is theoretically sound as well [24]. In this way, our work differs from all the previous work on recommendation systems that emphasize on finding recommendations of high relevance and quality rather than on structural navigability of the realized link structure. However, while it's not included in this paper for brevity, some of our approaches can be extended to the more general case where different recommendations have different weights (See Theorem 5).

On the graph algorithms side, our problem is related to the bipartite matching and more generally, the maximum b-matching problems. There has been considerable work done in this area. In particular, both the weighted matching and b-matching problems have exact polynomial time solutions [11]. Furthermore the matching problem admits a near linear time $(1 - \epsilon)$-approximation algorithm [9], while the weighted b-matching problem admits a 1/2-approximation algorithm [18]. However, all such algorithms are based on combinatorial properties of matchings and b-matchings, and do not carry over to the more important version of our problem when $a > 1$.

Finally, our problem bears resemblance to some covering problems. For example, the maximum coverage problem asks for the maximum number of elements that can be covered by a fixed number of sets and has a greedy $(1 - 1/e)$-approximation [22]. However, as mentioned earlier, our formulation requires multiple coverage of elements. Furthermore note that the collection of sets that can be used in the redundant coverage are all possible subsets of c out of the d candidate links, and is expressed implicitly in our problem. The currently known theoretical methods for maximum coverage heavily rely on the submodularity of the objective function, which our objective doesn't satisfy. Hence the line of recent work on approximation algorithms for submodular maximization does not apply to our problems.

3. OUR MODEL

We model the structure optimization of recommendations by using a bipartite digraph, where one partition L represents the set of discovered (i.e., often visited) items for which we are required to suggest recommendations and the other partition R representing the set of undiscovered (not visited) items that can be potentially recommended. If needed, the same item can be represented in both L and R.

3.1 The Recommendation Subgraph Problem

We introduce and study this as the **the (c, a)-recommendation subgraph problem** in this paper: *The input to the problem is the graph where each L-vertex has d recommendations. Given the space restrictions to display recommendations, the output is a subgraph where each vertex in L has $c < d$ recommendations. The goal is to maximize the number of vertices in R that have in-degree at least a target integer a.*

Note that if $a = c = 1$ this is simply the maximum bipartite matching problem [21]. If $a = 1$ and $c > 1$, we obtain a b-matching problem, that can be converted to a bipartite matching problem [11]. The typical and interesting cases when $a > 1$ is most likely NP-hard, ruling out the possibility of efficient exact algorithms.

We now describe typical web graph characteristics by discussing the sizes of L, R, c and a in practice. As noted before, in most websites, a small number of 'head' pages contribute to a significant amount of the traffic while a long tail of the remaining pages contribute to the rest [8, 14, 19]. This is supported by our own experience with the 80/20 rule, i.e. 80% of a site's traffic is captured by 20% of the pages. Therefore, the ratio $k = |L|/|R|$ is typically between 1/3 to 1/5, but may be even lower.

From our own work at BloomReach (and by observing recommendations of Quora, Amazon, and YouTube), typical values for c range from 3 to 20 recommendations per page. Values of a are harder to nail down but it typically ranges from 1 to 5.

3.2 Practical Requirements

There are two key requirements in making graph algorithms practical. The first is that the method used must be very simple to implement, debug, deploy and most importantly maintain long-term. The second is that the method must scale gracefully with larger sizes.

Graph matching algorithms require linear memory and super-linear run-time which does not scale well. For example, an e-commerce website of a client of BloomReach with 1M product pages and 100 recommendation candidates per product would require easily over 160GB in main memory to store the graph and run exact matching algorithms; this can be reduced by using graph compression techniques but that adds more technical difficulties in development and maintenance. Algorithms that are time intensive can sometimes be sped-up by using distributed computing techniques such as map-reduce [7]. However, efficient map-reduce algorithms for graph problems are notoriously difficult. Finally, all of these methods apply only to the special case of our problem when $a = 1$, leaving open the question of solving the more interesting and typical cases of redundant coverage when $a > 1$.

3.3 Simple Approximation Algorithms

To satisfy these practical requirements, we propose the study of three simple approximate solutions strategies that not only can be shown to scale well in practice but also have good theoretical properties that we demonstrate using approximation ratios.

- **Sampling:** The first solution is a simple random sampling solution that selects a random subset of c links out of the available d from every page. Note that this solution requires no memory overhead to store these results a-priori and the recommendations can be generated using a random number generator on the fly. While this might seem trivial at first, for sufficient (and often real-world) values of c and a we show that this can be optimal. Also, this method is very easy to adapt to the case when the underlying graph is dynamic with both nodes and edges changing over time. Furthermore, our approach can be extended to the case where the recommendation edges have weights representing varying strengths of association as is typically provided by the traditional methods that generate candidate recommendation links[1].

- **Greedy:** The second solution we propose is a greedy algorithm that chooses the recommendation links so as to maximize the number of nodes in R that can accumulate a in-links. In particular, we keep track of the number of in-links required for each node in R to reach the target of a and choose the links from each node in L giving preference to adding links to nodes in R that are closer to the target in-degree a. This method bears close resemblance in strategy with greedy methods used for maximum coverage and its more general submodular maximization variants.

- **Partition:** The third solution is inspired by a theoretically rigorous method to find optimal subgraphs in sufficiently dense graphs: it partitions the edges into a subsets by random sub-sampling, such that there is a good chance of finding a perfect matching from L to R in each of the subsets. The union of the matchings

[1]We omit a full description of this result for brevity.

so found will thus result in most nodes in R achieving the target degree a. We require the number of edges in the underlying graph to be significantly large for this method to work very well; moreover, we need to run a (near-)perfect matching algorithm in each of the edge-subsets which is also a computationally expensive subroutine. Hence, even though this method works very well in dense graphs, its resource requirements may not scale well in terms of running time and space.

As a summary, the table below shows the time and space complexity of our different algorithms.

	Sampling	Greedy	Partition
Time	$O(\|E\|)$	$O(\|E\|)$	$O(\|E\|\sqrt{\|V\|})$
Working Space	$O(1)$	$O(V)$	$O(\|E\|)$

Figure 1: Complexities of the different algorithms (assuming constant a and c)

In the next section, we elaborate on these methods, their running times, implementation details, and theoretical performance guarantees. In the section after that, we present our comprehensive empirical evaluations of all three methods, first the results on simulated data and then the results on real data from some clients of BloomReach.

4. ALGORITHMS FOR RECOMMENDATION SUBGRAPHS

4.1 The Sampling Algorithm

We present the sampling algorithm for the (c, a)-recommendation subgraph formally below.

```
Data: A bipartite graph G = (L, R, E)
Result: A (c, a)-recommendation subgraph H
for u in L do
    S ← a random sample of c vertices without
    replacement in N(u);
    for v in S do
        H ← H ∪ {(u, v)};
    end
end
return H;
```

Algorithm 1: The sampling algorithm

Given a bipartite graph G, the algorithm has runtime complexity of $O(|E|)$ since every edge is considered at most once. The space complexity can be taken to be $O(1)$, since the adjacency representation of G can be assumed to be pre-sorted by the endpoint of each edge in L.

We next introduce a simple random graph model for the supergraph from which we are allowed to choose recommendations and present a bound on its expected performance when the underlying supergraph $G = (L, R, E)$ is chosen probabilistically according to this model.

Fixed Degree Model: In this model for generating the candidate recommendation graph, each vertex $u \in L$ uniformly and independently samples d neighbors from R with replacement. While this allows each vertex in L to have the same vertex as a neighbor multiple times, in reality $r \gg d$ is so edge repetition is very unlikely. This model is similar to, but is distinct from the more commonly known Erdös-Renyi model of random graphs [16]. In particular, while the degree of each vertex in L is fixed under our model, concentration bounds can show that the degrees of the vertices in L would have similarly been concentrated around d for $p = d/r$ in the Erdös-Renyi model. We prove the following theorem about the performance of the Sampling Algorithm. We denote the ratio of the size of L and R by k, i.e., we define $k = \frac{l}{r}$.

Theorem 1. *Let S be the random variable denoting the number of vertices $v \in R$ such that $\deg_H(v) \geq a$ in the fixed-degree model. Then*

$$E[S] \geq r\left(1 - e^{-ck+\frac{a-1}{r}}\frac{(ck)^a - 1}{ck - 1}\right)$$

To get a quick sense of the very good performance bounds reflected in this theorem, please see Figure 2 that plots the approximation ratio as a function of ck for the $(c, 1)$-recommendation subgraph problem, as well as Figure 3 that shows how large c needs to be (in terms of k) for the solution to be 95% optimal for different values of a, both in the fixed degree model.

PROOF. We will analyze the sampling algorithm as if it picks the neighbors of each $u \in L$ with replacement, the same way the fixed-degree model generates G. This variant would obviously waste some edges, and perform worse than the variant which samples neighbors without replacement. This means that any performance guarantee we prove for this variant holds for our original statement of the algorithm as well.

To prove the claim let X_v be the random variable that represents the degree of the vertex $v \in R$ in our chosen subgraph H. Because our algorithm uniformly subsamples a uniformly random selection of edges, we can assume that H was generated the same way as G but sampled c instead of d edges for each vertex $u \in L$. Since there are cl edges in H that can be incident on v, and each of these edges has a $1/r$ probability of being incident on a given vertex in L, we can now calculate that

$$\Pr[X_v = i] = \binom{cl}{i}(1 - \frac{1}{r})^{cl-i}\left(\frac{1}{r}\right)^i$$
$$\leq (cl)^i(1 - \frac{1}{r})^{cl-i}\left(\frac{1}{r}\right)^i$$

Using a union bound, we can combine these inequalities to upper bound the probability that $\deg_H(v) < a$.

$$\Pr[X_v < a] = \sum_{i=0}^{a-1} \binom{cl}{i} \left(1 - \frac{1}{r}\right)^{cl-i} \left(\frac{1}{r}\right)^i$$
$$\leq \sum_{i=0}^{a-1} \left(\frac{cl}{r}\right)^i \left(1 - \frac{1}{r}\right)^{cl-i}$$
$$\leq \left(1 - \frac{1}{r}\right)^{cl-(a-1)} \sum_{i=0}^{a-1} (ck)^i$$
$$\leq \left(1 - \frac{1}{r}\right)^{cl-(a-1)} \frac{(ck)^a - 1}{ck - 1}$$
$$\leq e^{-ck + \frac{a-1}{r}} \frac{(ck)^a - 1}{ck - 1}$$

Letting $Y_v = [X_v \geq a]$, we now see that

$$\mathrm{E}[S] = \mathrm{E}\left[\sum_{v \in R} Y_v\right] \geq r\left(1 - e^{-ck + \frac{a-1}{r}} \frac{(ck)^a - 1}{ck - 1}\right)$$

□

We can combine this lower bound with a trivial upper bound to obtain an approximation ratio that holds in expectation.

Theorem 2. *The above sampling algorithm gives a $(1 - \frac{1}{e})$-factor approximation to the $(c, 1)$-graph recommendation problem in expectation.*

PROOF. The size of the optimal solution is bounded above by both the number of edges in the graph and the number of vertices in R. The former of these is $cl = ckr$ and the latter is r, which shows that the optimal solution size $OPT \leq r \min(ck, 1)$. Therefore, by simple case analysis the approximation ratio in expectation is at least $(1 - \exp(-ck))/\min(ck, 1) \geq 1 - \frac{1}{e}$ □

For the $(c, 1)$-recommendation subgraph problem the approximation obtained by this sampling approach can be much better for certain values of ck. In particular, if $ck > 1$, then the approximation ratio is $1 - \exp(-ck)$, which approaches 1 as $ck \to \infty$. When $ck = 3$, then the solution will be at least 95% as good as the optimal solution even with our trivial bounds. Similarly, when $ck < 1$, the approximation ratio is $(1 - \exp(-ck))/ck$ which also approaches 1 as $ck \to 0$. In particular, if $ck = 0.1$ then the solution will be at 95% as good as the optimal solution. The case when $ck = 1$ represents the worst case outcome for this model where we only guarantee 63% optimality. Figure 2 shows the approximation ratio as a function of ck for the $(c, 1)$-recommendation subgraph problem in the fixed degree model.

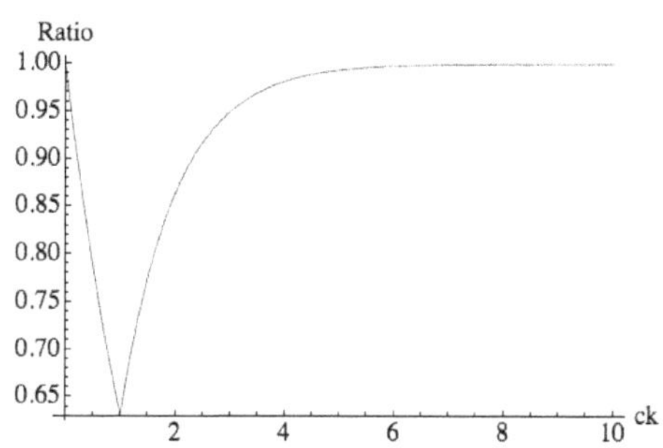

Figure 2: Approx ratio as a function of ck

For the general (c, a)-recommendation subgraph problem, if $ck > a$, then the problem is easy on average. This is in comparison to the trivial estimate of cl. For a fixed a, a random solution gets better as ck increases because the decrease in e^{-ck} more than compensates for the polynomial in ck next to it. However, in the more realistic case, the undiscovered pages in R too numerous to be all covered even if we used the full set of budgeted links allowed out of L, i.e. $cl < ra$ or rearranging, $ck < a$; in this case, we need to use the trivial estimate of ckr/a, and the analysis for $a = 1$ does not extend here. For practical purposes, the table in Figure 3 shows how large c needs to be (in terms of k) for the solution to be 95% optimal for different values of a, again in the fixed degree model.

a	1	2	3	4	5
c	$3.00k^{-1}$	$4.74k^{-1}$	$7.05k^{-1}$	$10.01k^{-1}$	$13.48k^{-1}$

Figure 3: The required ck to obtain 95% optimality for (c, a)-recommendation subgraph

We close out this section by showing that the main result that holds in expectation also hold with high probability for $a = 1$, using the following variant of Chernoff bounds.

Theorem 3. *[4] Let $X_1, \ldots, X_n$ be non-positively correlated variables. If $X = \sum_{i=1}^n X_i$, then for any $\delta \geq 0$*

$$\Pr[X \geq (1+\delta)\mathrm{E}[X]] \leq \left(\frac{e^\delta}{(1+\delta)^{1+\delta}}\right)^{E[X]}$$

Theorem 4. *Let S be the random variable denoting the number of vertices $v \in R$ such that $\deg_H(v) \geq 1$. Then $S \leq r(1 - 2\exp(-ck))$ with probability at most $(e/4)^{r(1-\exp(-ck))}$.*

For realistic scenarios where r is very large, the above theorem gives very tight bounds on the size of the solution, also explaining the effectiveness of the simple sampling algorithm in such instances.
The results presented in this section can be naturally extended to weighted models as shown by the theorem below. The proof is left out due to space constraints.

Theorem 5. *Let $G = K_{l,r}$ be a complete bipartite graph where the edges have i.i.d. weights and come from a distribution with mean μ that is supported on $[0, b]$; Assume that $ck\mu \gtrsim 1 + \epsilon$ for some $\epsilon > 0$. If the algorithm from Section 4.1 is used to sample a subgraph H from G and S is the set of vertices in R of incident weight at least one, then*

$$\mathrm{E}[S] = \sum_{v \in R} \mathrm{E}[X_v] = r\left(1 - \exp\left(-\frac{2l\epsilon^2}{b^2}\right)\right)$$

4.2 The Greedy Algorithm

We next analyze the natural greedy algorithm for constructing a (c, a)-recommendation subgraph H iteratively. In the following algorithm, we use $N(u)$ to refer to the neighbors of a vertex u.

The algorithm loops through each vertex in R, and considers each edge once. Therefore, the runtime is $\Theta(|E|)$. Furthermore, the only data structure we use is an array which keeps track of $\deg_H(u)$ for each $u \in L$, so the memory consumption is $\Theta(|L|)$. Finally, we prove the following tight approximation property of this algorithm.

```
Data: A bipartite graph G = (L, R, E)
Result: A (c, a)-recommendation subgraph H
for u in L do
  | d[u] ← 0
end
for v in R do
    F ← {u ∈ N(v)|d[u] < c};
    if |F| ≥ a then
        restrict F to a elements;
        for u in F do
            H ← H ∪ {(u, v)};
            d[u] ← d[u] + 1;
        end
    end
end
return H;
```

Algorithm 2: The greedy Algorithm

Theorem 6. *The greedy algorithm gives a $1/(a+1)$-approximation to the (c, a)-graph recommendation problem.*

PROOF. Let $R_{GREEDY}, R_{OPT} \subseteq R$ be the set of vertices that have degree $\geq a$ in the greedy and optimal solutions respectively. Note that any $v \in R_{OPT}$ along with neighbors $\{u_1, \ldots u_a\}$ forms a set of candidate edges that can be used by the greedy algorithm. Each selection of the greedy algorithm might result in some candidates becoming infeasible, but it can continue as long as the candidate pool is not depleted. Each time the greedy algorithm selects some vertex $v \in R$ with edges to $\{u_1, \ldots, u_a\}$, we remove v from the candidate pool. Furthermore each u_i could have degree c in the optimal solution and used each of its edges to make a neighbor attain degree a. The greedy choice of an edge to u_i requires us to remove such an edge to an arbitrary vertex $v_i \in R$ adjacent to u_i in the optimal solution, and thus remove v_i from further consideration in the candidate pool. Therefore, at each step of the greedy algorithm, we may remove at most $a+1$ vertices from the candidate pool as illustrated in Figure 4. Since our candidate pool has size OPT, the greedy algorithm can not stop before it has added $OPT/(a+1)$ vertices to the solution. □

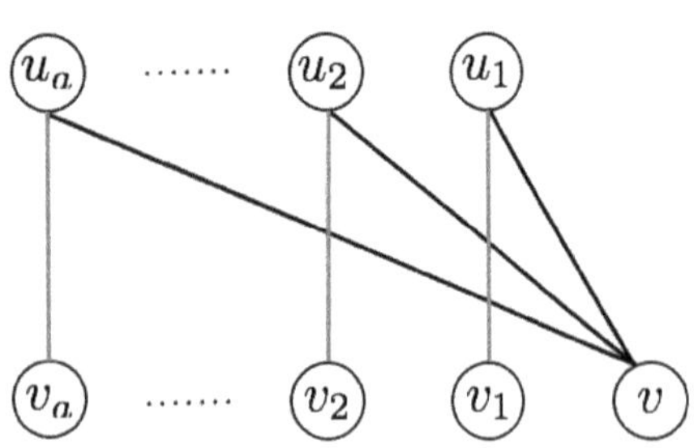

Figure 4: One step of the greedy algorithm. When v selects edges to $u_1, \ldots, u_a$, it can remove $v_1, \ldots, v_a$ from the pool of candidates that are available. The potentially invalidated edges are shown in red.

This approximation guarantee is as good as we can expect, since for $a = 1$ we recover the familiar 1/2-approximation of the greedy algorithm for matchings. Furthermore, even in the case of matchings ($a = 1$), randomizing the order in which the vertices are processed is still known to leave a constant factor gap in the quality of the solution [17]. Despite this result, the greedy algorithm fares much better when we analyze its expected performance. Switching to the **Erdös-Renyi model** [10] instead of the fixed degree model used in the previous section, we now prove the near optimality of the greedy algorithm for the (c, a)-recommendation subgraph problem. Recall that in this model (sometimes referred to as $G_{n,p}$), each possible edge is inserted with probability p independent of other edges. In our version $G_{l,r,p}$, we only add edges from L to R each with probability p independent of other edges in this complete bipartite candidate graph. For technical reasons, we need to assume that $lp \geq 1$ in the following theorem. However, this is a very weak assumption since lp is simply the expected degree of a vertex $v \in R$. Typical values for p for our applications will be $\Omega(\log(l)/l)$ making the expected degree $lp = \Omega(\log l)$.

Theorem 7. *Let $G = (L, R, E)$ be a graph drawn from the $G_{l,r,p}$ where $lp \geq 1$. If S is the size of the (c, a)-recommendation subgraph produced by the greedy algorithm, then:*

$$\mathrm{E}[S] \geq r - \frac{a(lp)^{a-1}}{(1-p)^a} \sum_{i=0}^{r-1} (1-p)^{l-\frac{ia}{c}}$$

When the underlying random graph is sufficiently dense, Theorem 8 shows that the above guarantee is asymptotically optimal.

PROOF. Note that if edges are generated uniformly, we can consider the graph as being revealed to us one vertex at a time as the greedy algorithm runs. In particular, consider the event X_{i+1} that the greedy algorithm matches the $(i+1)^{st}$ vertex it inspects. While, X_{i+1} is dependent on $X_1, \ldots, X_i$, the worst condition for X_{i+1} is when all the previous i vertices were from the same vertices in L, which are now not available for matching the $(i+1)^{st}$ vertex. The maximum number of such invalidated vertices is at most $\lceil ia/c \rceil$. Therefore, the bad event is that we have fewer than a of the at least $l - \lceil ia/c \rceil$ available vertices having an edge to this vertex. The probability of this bad event is at most $\Pr[Y \sim Bin(l - \frac{ia}{c}, p) : Y < a]$, the probability that a Binomial random variable with $l - \frac{ia}{c}$ trials of probability p of success for each trial has less than a successes. We can bound this probability by using a union bound and upper-bounding $\Pr[Y \sim Bin(l - \frac{ia}{c}, p) : Y = t]$ for each $0 \leq t \leq a-1$. By using the trivial estimate that $\binom{n}{i} \leq n^i$ for all n and i, we obtain:

$$\begin{aligned}\Pr[Y \sim Bin(l - \frac{ia}{c}, p) : Y = t] &= \binom{l - \frac{ia}{c}}{t} (1-p)^{l-\frac{ia}{c}-t} p^t \\ &\leq \left(l - \frac{ia}{c}\right)^t (1-p)^{l-\frac{ia}{c}-t} p^t \\ &\leq (lp)^t (1-p)^{l-\frac{ia}{c}-t}\end{aligned}$$

Notice that the largest exponent lp can take within the bounds of our sum is $a-1$. Similarly, the smallest exponent $(1-p)$ can take within the bounds of our sum is $l - \frac{ia}{c} - a + 1$. Now applying the union bound gives:

$$\begin{aligned}
&\Pr[Y \sim Bin(l - \frac{ia}{c}, p) : Y < a] \\
&\leq \sum_{t=0}^{a-1} \Pr[Y \sim Bin(l - \frac{ia}{c}, p) : Y = t] \\
&\leq \sum_{t=0}^{a-1} (lp)^t (1-p)^{l - \frac{ia}{c} - t} \\
&= a(lp)^{a-1}(1-p)^{l - \frac{ia}{c} - a + 1}
\end{aligned}$$

Finally, summing over all the X_i using the linearity of expectation and this upper bound, we obtain

$$\begin{aligned}
\mathrm{E}[S] &\geq r - \sum_{i=0}^{r-1} \mathrm{E}[\neg X_i] \\
&\geq r - \sum_{i=0}^{r-1} \Pr[Y \sim Bin(l - \frac{ia}{c}, p) : Y < a] \\
&\geq r - a(lp)^{a-1} \sum_{i=0}^{r-1} (1-p)^{l - \frac{ia}{c} - a + 1}
\end{aligned}$$

□

Asymptotically, this result explains why the greedy algorithm does much better in expectation than $1/(a+1)$ guarantee we can prove in the worst case. In particular, for a reasonable setting of the right parameters, we can prove that the error term of our greedy approximation will be sublinear.

Theorem 8. *Let $G = (L, R, E)$ be a graph drawn from the $G_{l,r,p}$ where $p = \frac{\gamma \log l}{l}$ for some $\gamma \geq 1$. Suppose that c, a and $\epsilon > 0$ are such that $lc = (1+\epsilon)ra$ and that l and r go to infinity while satisfying this relation. If S is the size of the (c, a)-recommendation subgraph produced by the greedy algorithm, then*

$$E[S] \geq r - o(r)$$

PROOF. We will prove this claim by applying Theorem 7. Note that it suffices to prove that $(lp)^{a-1} \sum_{i=0}^{r-1} (1-p)^{l - \frac{ia}{c}} = o(r)$ since the other terms are just constants. We first bound the elements of this summation. Using the facts that $p = \frac{\gamma \log l}{l}$, $lc/a = (1+\epsilon)r$ and that $i < r$ throughout the summation, we get the following bound on each term:

$$\begin{aligned}
(1-p)^{l - \frac{ia}{c}} &\leq \left(1 - \frac{\gamma \log l}{l}\right)^{l - \frac{ia}{c}} \\
&\leq \exp\left(-\frac{\gamma \log l}{l}\left(l - \frac{ia}{c}\right)\right) \\
&= \exp\left((-\log l)\left(\gamma - \frac{ia}{lc}\right)\right) \\
&= l^{-\gamma + \frac{ia}{lc}} = l^{-\gamma + \frac{i}{(1+\epsilon)r}} \\
&\leq l^{-1 + \frac{1}{1+\epsilon}} = l^{-\frac{\epsilon}{1+\epsilon}}
\end{aligned}$$

Finally, we can evaluate the whole sum:

$$\begin{aligned}
(lp)^{a-1} \sum_{i=0}^{r-1} (1-p)^{l - \frac{ia}{c}} &\leq \left(\log^{a-1} l\right) \sum_{i=0}^{r-1} l^{-\frac{\epsilon}{1+\epsilon}} \\
&\leq \left(\log^{a-1} l\right) r l^{-\frac{\epsilon}{1+\epsilon}} \\
&= \left(\log^{a-1} l\right) \frac{c}{(1+\epsilon)a} l^{1 - \frac{\epsilon}{1+\epsilon}} = o(l)
\end{aligned}$$

However, since r is a constant times l, any function that is $o(l)$ is also $o(r)$ and this proves the claim.

□

4.3 The Partition Algorithm

To motivate the partition algorithm, we first define optimal solutions for the recommendation subgraph problem.

Perfect Recommendation Subgraphs: We define a *perfect* (c, a)-recommendation subgraph on G to be a subgraph H such that $deg_H(u) \leq c$ for all $u \in L$ and $deg_H(v) = a$ for $\min(r, \lfloor cl/a \rfloor)$ of the vertices in R.

The reason we define perfect (c, a)-recommendation subgraphs is that when one exists, it's possible to recover it in polynomial time using a min-cost b-matching algorithm (matchings with a specified degree b on each vertex) for any setting of a and c. However, implementations of b-matching algorithms often incur significant overheads even over regular bipartite matchings. This motivates a solution that uses regular bipartite matching algorithms to find an approximately optimal solution given that a perfect one exists.

We do this by proving a sufficient condition for perfect (c, a)-recommendation subgraphs to exist with high probability in a bipartite graph G under the **Erdös-Renyi model** [10] where edges are sampled uniformly and independently with probability p. This argument then guides our formulation of a heuristic that overlays matchings carefully to obtain (c, a)-recommendation subgraphs.

Theorem 9. *[16] Let G be a bipartite graph drawn from $G_{n,n,p}$. If $p \geq \frac{\log n - \log\log n}{n}$, then as $n \to \infty$, the probability that G has a perfect matching approaches 1.*

We will prove that a perfect (c, a)-recommendation subgraph exists in random graphs with high probability by building it up from a matchings each of which must exist with high probability if p is sufficiently high. To find these matchings, we identify subsets of size l in R that we can perfectly match to L. These subsets overlap, and we choose them so that each vertex in R is in a subsets.

Theorem 10. *Let G be a random bipartite graph drawn from $G_{l,r,p}$ with $p \geq a\frac{\log l - \log\log l}{l}$ then the probability that G has a perfect (c, a)-recommendation subgraph tends to 1 as $l, r \to \infty$.*

This theorem guarantees the existence of an optimal recommendation subgraph in sufficiently dense subgraphs, and provides a constructive proof of this fact that is also the basis of our partition algorithm.

PROOF. We start by either padding or restricting R to a set of $\frac{lc}{a}$ before we start our analysis. If $r \geq \frac{lc}{a}$, then we restrict R to an arbitrary subset R' of size $\frac{lc}{a}$. Since induced subgraphs of Erdös-Renyi graphs are also Erdös-Renyi graphs, we can instead apply our analysis to the induced subgraph. Since the optimal solution has size bounded above by $\frac{lc}{a}$ a perfect (c, a)-recommendation subgraph in $G[L, R']$ will imply a perfect recommendation subgraph in $G[L, R]$.

On the other hand, if $r \leq \frac{lc}{a}$, then we can pad R with $\frac{lc}{a} - r$ dummy vertices and adding an edge from each such vertex to each vertex in L with probability p. We call the resulting right side of the graph R'. Note that $G[L, R']$ is still generated by the Erdős-Renyi process. Further, since the original graph $G[L, R]$ is a subgraph of this new graph, if we prove the existence of a perfect (c, a)-recommendation subgraph in this new graph, it will imply the existence of a perfect recommendation subgraph in $G[L, R]$.

Having picked an R' satisfying $|R'| = \frac{lc}{a}$, we pick an enumeration of the vertices in $R' = \{v_0, \ldots, v_{lc/a-1}\}$ and add each of these vertices into a subsets as follows. Define $R_i = \{v_{(i-1)l/a}, \ldots, v_{(i-1)l/a+l-1}\}$ for each $1 \leq i \leq c$ where the arithmetic in the indices is done modulo lc/a. Note both L and all of the R_i's have size l.

Using these new sets we define the graphs G_i on the bipartitions (L, R_i). Since the sets R_i are intersecting, we cannot define the graphs G_i to be induced subgraphs. However, note that each vertex $v \in R'$ falls into exactly a of these subsets.

Therefore, we can uniformly randomly assign each edge in G to one of a graphs among $\{G_1, \ldots, G_c\}$ it can fall into, and make each of those graphs a random graph. In fact, while the different G_i are coupled, taken in isolation we can consider any single G_i to be drawn from the distribution $G_{l,l,p/a}$ since G was drawn from $G_{l,r,p}$. Since $p/a \geq (\log l - \log\log l)/l$ by assumption, we conclude by Theorem 9, the probability that a particular G_i has no perfect matching is $o(1)$.

If we fix c, we can conclude by a union bound that except for a $o(1)$ probability, each one of the G_i's has a perfect matching. By superimposing all of these perfect matchings, we can see that every vertex in R' has degree a. Since each vertex in L is in exactly c matchings, each vertex in L has degree c. It follows that except for a $o(1)$ probability there exists a (c, a)-recommendation subgraph in G. □

Approximation Algorithm Using Perfect Matchings: The above result now enables us to design a near linear time algorithm with a $(1 - \epsilon)$ approximation guarantee to the (c, a)-recommendation subgraph problem by leveraging combinatorial properties of matchings. In particular, we use the fact a matching that does not have augmenting paths of length $> 2\alpha$ is a $1 - 1/\alpha$ approximation to the maximum matching problem. We call this method the Partition Algorithm, and we outline it below.

Theorem 11. *Let G be a bipartite random graph drawn from $G_{l,r,p}$ where $p \geq a\frac{\log l - \log\log l}{l}$. Then Algorithm 3 finds a $(1 - \epsilon)$-approximation in $O(\frac{|E|}{\epsilon})$ time with probability $1 - o(1)$.*

Proof. Using the previous theorem, we know that each of the graphs G_i has a perfect matching with high probability. These perfect matchings can be approximated to a $1 - \epsilon/c$ factor by finding matchings that do not have augmenting paths of length $\geq 2c/\epsilon$ [21]. This can be done for each G_i in $O(|E|c/\epsilon)$ time. Furthermore, the union of unmatched vertices makes up an at most $c(\epsilon/c)$ fraction of R', which proves the claim. □

Data: A bipartite graph $G = (L, R, E)$
Result: A (c,a)-recommendation subgraph H
$R' \leftarrow$ a random sample of $|L|c/a$ vertices from R;
Choose $G[L, R_1], \ldots, G[L, R_c]$ as in Theorem 10;
for *i in [1..c]* **do**
  $M_i \leftarrow$ A matching of $G[L, R_i]$ with no augmenting path of length $2c/\epsilon$;
end
$H \leftarrow M_1 \bigcup \ldots \bigcup M_c$;
return H;

Algorithm 3: The partition algorithm

Notice that if we were to run the augmenting paths algorithm to completeness for each matching M_i, then this algorithm would take $O(|E||L|)$ time. We could reduce this further to $O(|E|\sqrt{L})$ by using Hopcroft-Karp. [13]

Assuming a sparse graph where $|E| = \Theta(|L| \log |L|)$, the time complexity of this algorithm is $\Theta(|L|^{3/2} \log |L|)$. The space complexity is only $\Theta(|E|) = \Theta(|L| \log |L|)$, but a large constant is hidden by the big-Oh notation that makes this algorithm impractical in real test cases.

5. EXPERIMENTAL RESULTS

5.1 Simulated Data

We simulated performance of our algorithms on random graphs generated by the graph models we outlined. In the following figures, each data point is obtained by averaging the measurements over 100 random graphs. We first present the time and space usage of these algorithms when solving a $(10, 3)$-recommendation subgraph problem in different sized graphs. In all our charts, error bars are present, but too small to be noticeable. Note that varying the value of a and c would only change space and time usage by a constant, so these two graphs are indicative of time and space usage over all ranges of parameters. The code used conduct these experiments can be found at `https://github.com/srinathsridhar/graph-matching-source`

Recall that the partition algorithm split the graph into multiple graphs and found matchings (using an implementation of Hopcroft-Karp [13]) in these smaller graphs which were then combined into a recommendation subgraph. For this reason, a run of the partition algorithm takes much longer to solve a problem instance than either the sampling or greedy algorithms. It also takes significantly more memory as can be seen in Figures 5 and 6. Compare this to greedy and sampling which both require a single pass over the graph, and no advanced data structures. In fact, if the edges of G is pre-sorted by the edge's endpoint in L, then the sampling algorithm can be implemented as an online algorithm with constant space and in constant time per link selection. Similarly, if the edges of G is pre-sorted by the edge's endpoint in R, then the greedy algorithm can be implemented so that the entire graph does not have to be kept in memory. In this event, greedy uses only $O(|L|)$ memory.

Next, we analyze the relative qualities of the solutions each method produces. Figures 7 and 8 plot the average performance ratio of the three methods compared to the trivial upper bounds as the value of c, the number of recommendations allowed is varied, while keeping $a = 1$. They col-

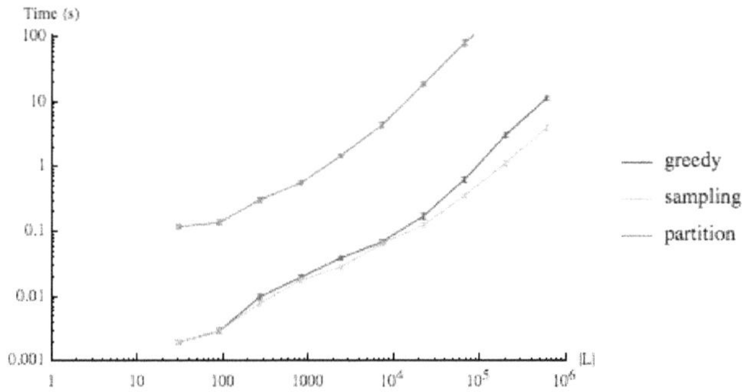

Figure 5: Time needed to solve a (10,3)-recommendation problem in random graphs where $|R|/|L| = 4$ (Notice the log-log scale.)

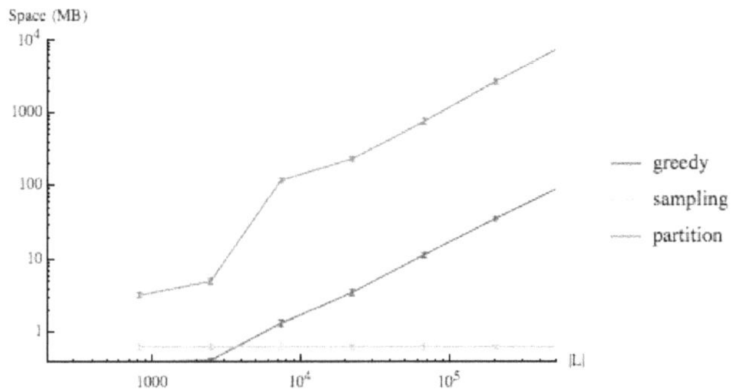

Figure 6: Space needed to solve a (10,3)-recommendation problem in random graphs where $|R|/|L| = 4$ (Notice the log-log scale.)

lectively show that the lower bound we calculated for the expected performance of the sampling algorithm accurately captures its behavior when $a = 1$. Indeed, the inequality we used is an accurate approximation of the expectation, up to lower order terms, as is demonstrated in these simulated runs. The random sampling algorithm does well, both when c is low and high, but falters when $ck = 1$. The greedy algorithm outperforms the sampling algorithm in all cases, but its advantage vanishes as c gets larger. Note that the dip in the graphs when $cl = ar$, at $c = 4$ in Figure 7 and $c = 2$ in Figure 8 is expected and was previously demonstrated in Figure 2. The partition algorithm is immune to this drop that affects both the greedy and the sampling algorithms, but comes with the cost of higher time and space utilization.

In contrast to the case when $a = 1$, the sampling algorithm performs worse when $a > 1$ but performs increasingly better with c as demonstrated by Figures 9 and 10. The greedy algorithm continues to produce solutions that are nearly optimal, regardless of the settings of c and a, even beating the partition algorithm with increasing values of a. Our simulations suggest that in most cases, one can simply use our sampling method for solving the (c, a)-recommendation subgraph problem. In cases where the sampling is not suitable as flagged by our analysis, we still find that the greedy performs adequately and is also simple to implement. These two algorithms thus confirm to our requirements we initially laid out for deployment in large-scale real systems in practice.

To summarize, our synthetic experiments show the following strengths of each algorithm:

Sampling Algorithm: Sampling uses little to no memory and can be implemented as an online algorithm. If keeping

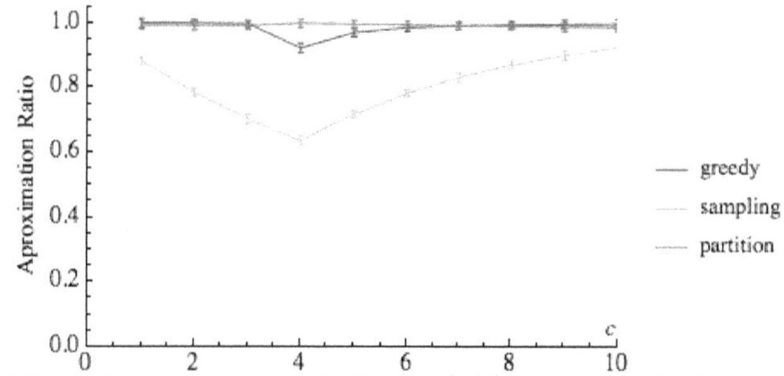

Figure 7: Solution quality for the $(c, 1)$-recommendation subgraph problem in graphs with $|L| = 25$k, $|R| = 100$k, $d = 20$

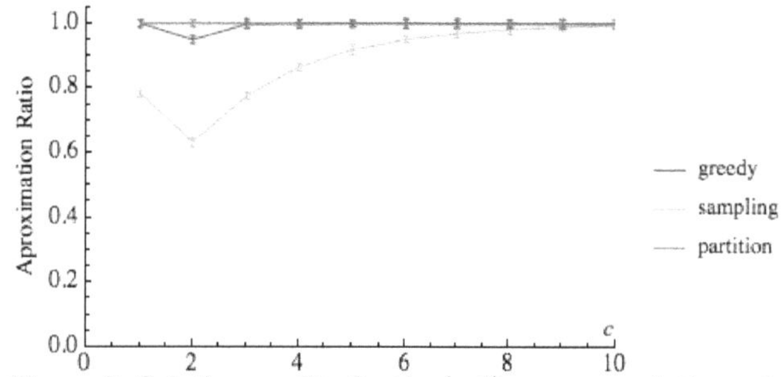

Figure 8: Solution quality for the $(c, 1)$-recommendation subgraph problem in graphs with $|L| = 50$k, $|R| = 100$k, $d = 20$

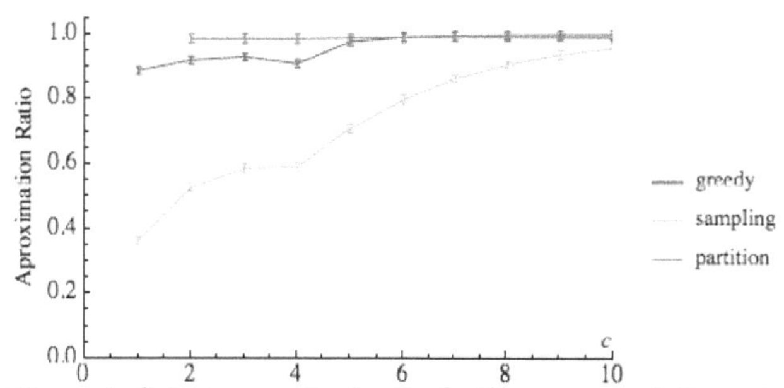

Figure 9: Solution quality for the $(c, 2)$-recommendation subgraph problem in graphs with $|L| = 50$k, $|R| = 100$k, $d = 20$

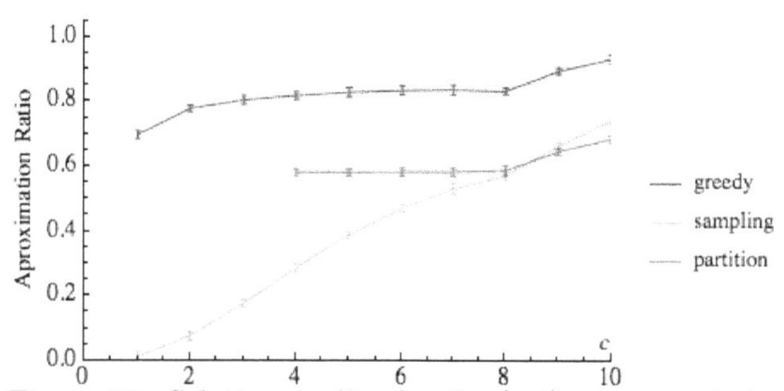

Figure 10: Solution quality for the $(c, 4)$-recommendation subgraph problem in graphs with $|L| = 50$k, $|R| = 100$k, $d = 20$

the underlying graph in memory is an issue, then chances are this algorithm will do well while only needing a fraction of the resources the other two algorithms would need.

Partition Algorithm: This algorithm does well, but only when a is small. In particular, when $a = 1$ or 2, partition seems to be the best algorithm, but the quality of the solutions degrade quickly after that point. However this performance comes at expense of significant runtime and space. Since greedy performs almost as well without requiring large amounts of space or time, partition is best suited for instances where a is low the quality of the solution is more important than anything else.

Greedy Algorithm: This algorithm is the all-round best performing algorithm we tested. It only requires a single pass over the data thus very quickly, and uses relatively little amounts of space enabling it run completely in memory for graphs with as many as tens of millions of edges. It is not as fast as sampling or accurate as partition when a is small, but it has very good performance over all parameter ranges.

5.2 Real Data

We now present the results of running our algorithms on several real datasets. In the graphs that we use, each node corresponds to a single product in the catalog of a merchant and the edges connect similar products. For each product up to 50 most similar products were selected by a proprietary algorithm of BloomReach that uses text-based features such as keywords, color, brand, gender (where applicable) as well as user browsing patterns to determine the similarity between pairs of products. Such algorithms are commonly used in e-commerce websites such as Amazon, Overstock, eBay etc to display the most related products to the user when they are browsing a specific product.

Two of the client merchants of BloomReach presented here had moderate-sized relation graphs with about 10^5 vertices and 10^6 input edges (candidate recommendations); the remaining merchants (3, 4 and 5) have on the order of 10^6 vertices and 10^7 input edges between them. We estimated an upper bound on the optimum solution by taking the minimum of $|L|c/a$ and the number of vertices in R of degree at least a. Figures 11, 12 and 13 plot the average of the optimality percentage of the sampling, greedy and partition algorithms across all the merchants respectively. Note that we could only run the partition algorithm for the first two merchants due to memory constraints.

From these results, we can see that that greedy performs exceptionally well when c gets even moderately large. For the realistic value of $c = 6$, the greedy algorithm produced a solution that was 85% optimal for all the merchants we tested. For several of the merchants, its results were almost optimal starting from $a = 2$.

The partition method is also promising, especially when the a value that is targeted is low. Indeed, when $a = 1$ or $a = 2$, its performance is comparable or better than greedy, though the difference is not as pronounced as it is in the simulations. However, for larger values of a the partition algorithm performs worse.

The sampling algorithm performs mostly well on real data, especially when c is large. It is typically worse than greedy, but unlike the partition algorithm, its performance improves dramatically as c becomes larger, and its performance does

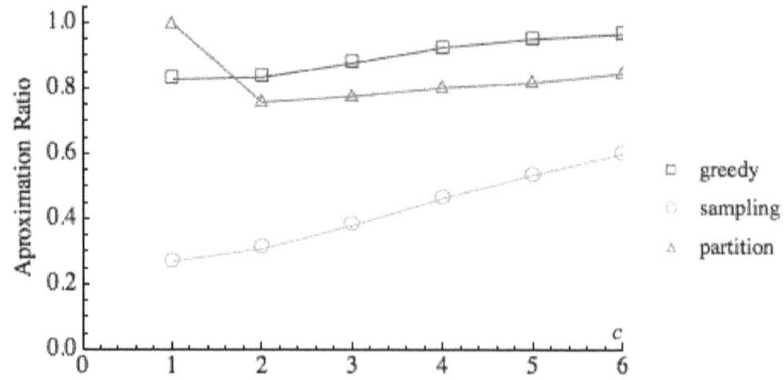

Figure 11: Solution quality for the $(c, 1)$-recommendation subgraph problem in retailer data

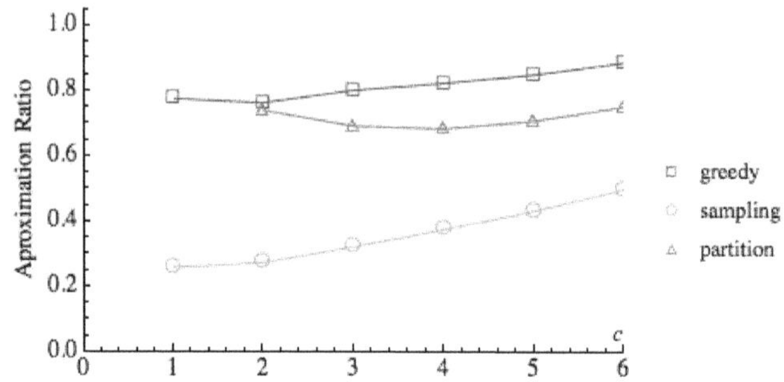

Figure 12: Solution quality for the $(c, 2)$-recommendation subgraph problem in retailer data

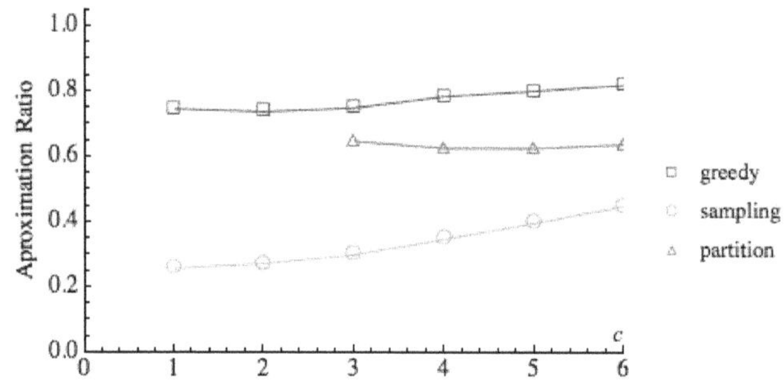

Figure 13: Solution quality for the $(c, 3)$-recommendation subgraph problem in retailer data

not worsen as quickly when a gets larger. Therefore, for large c sampling becomes a viable alternative to greedy mainly in cases where the linear memory cost of the greedy algorithm is too prohibitive.

6. SUMMARY AND FUTURE WORK

We have presented a new class of structural recommendation problems cast as computationally hard subgraph selection problems, and analyzed three algorithmic strategies to solve these problems. The sampling method is most efficient, the greedy approach trades off computational cost with quality, and the partition method is effective for smaller problem sizes. We have proved effective theoretical bounds on the quality of these methods, and also substantiated them with experimental validation both from simulated data and real data from retail web sites. Our findings have been very useful in the deployment of effective structural recommendations in web relevance engines that drive many of the leading websites of popular retailers.

We believe that our work lends itself to promising future work in two directions. The first is that through a better understanding of the underlying graph's topology, more precise or complex models can be used. This would require an empirical validation of the proposed graph model and the adaptation of our methods to different random graph models. We have made some initial progress on this front, which can be found in the full version of the paper.

The second is that most of our algorithms aren't particularly suited for the weighted setting. While our sampling result carries over to the weighted regime as seen in Theorem 5, our other algorithms don't, and even this result is weak compared to the unweighted result we presented in full. The problem presented by ignoring weights is that some really high value recommendations might be ignored by the algorithm by chance. In practice, it's possible to mitigate this issue by hardcoding in the really desirable edges, and using seeding either the greedy or sampling algorithm with these edges. While this can work well in practice, it would be nonetheless be valuable to prove strong approximation guarantees in the weighted regime as well.

Acknowledgments: We thank Alan Frieze and Ashutosh Garg for helpful discussions.

7. REFERENCES

[1] G. Adomavicius and A. Tuzhilin. Toward the next generation of recommender systems: A survey of the state-of-the-art and possible extensions. *IEEE Trans. on Knowl. and Data Eng.*, 17(6):734–749, June 2005.

[2] D. Almazro, G. Shahatah, L. Albdulkarim, M. Kherees, R. Martinez, and W. Nzoukou. A survey paper on recommender systems. *arXiv preprint arXiv:1006.5278*, 2010.

[3] C. Anderson. *The Long Tail: Why the Future of Business Is Selling Less of More.* Hyperion, 2006.

[4] A. Auger and B. Doerr. *Theory of Randomized Search Heuristics: Foundations and Recent Developments.* Series on Theoretical Computer Science. World Scientific Publishing Company, 2011.

[5] Robert M Bell, Yehuda Koren, and Chris Volinsky. The bellkor solution to the netflix prize.

[6] A. S. Das, M. Datar, A. Garg, and S. Rajaram. Google news personalization: scalable online collaborative filtering. In *Proceedings of the 16th international conference on World Wide Web*, pages 271–280. ACM, 2007.

[7] J. Dean and S. Ghemawat. Mapreduce: simplified data processing on large clusters. In *OSDI '04: Proceedings of the sixth conference on symposium on operating systems design and implementation.* USENIX Association, 2004.

[8] B. Du, M. Demmer, and E. Brewer. Analysis of www traffic in cambodia and ghana. In *Proceedings of the 15th international conference on World Wide Web*, WWW '06, pages 771–780. ACM, 2006.

[9] Ran Duan and Seth Pettie. Approximating maximum weight matching in near-linear time. In *Foundations of Computer Science (FOCS), 2010 51st Annual IEEE Symposium on*, pages 673–682. IEEE, 2010.

[10] P. Erdös and A. Rényi. On random graphs, I. *Publicationes Mathematicae*, 6:290–297, 1959.

[11] H. Gabow. An efficient reduction technique for degree-constrained subgraph and bidirected network flow problems. In *Proceedings of the fifteenth annual ACM symposium on Theory of computing*, STOC '83, pages 448–456. ACM, 1983.

[12] J. Hannon, M. Bennett, and B. Smyth. Recommending twitter users to follow using content and collaborative filtering approaches. In *Proceedings of the fourth ACM conference on Recommender systems*, pages 199–206. ACM, 2010.

[13] J. E. Hopcroft and R. M. Karp. An n^5/2 algorithm for maximum matchings in bipartite graphs. *SIAM Journal on computing*, 2(4):225–231, 1973.

[14] B. A. Huberman and L. A. Adamic. Internet: growth dynamics of the world-wide web. *Nature*, 401(6749):131–131, 1999.

[15] BloomReach Inc. Inside the technology: Web relevance engine.

[16] S. Janson, T. Luczak, and A. Rucinski. *Random Graphs.* Wiley Series in Discrete Mathematics and Optimization. Wiley, 2011.

[17] R. M. Karp, U. Vazirani, and V. Vazirani. An optimal algorithm for on-line bipartite matching. In *Proceedings of the twenty-second annual ACM symposium on Theory of computing.* ACM, 1990.

[18] Christos Koufogiannakis and Neal E Young. Distributed fractional packing and maximum weighted b-matching via tail-recursive duality. In *Distributed Computing*, pages 221–238. Springer, 2009.

[19] C. Kumar, J. B. Norris, and Y. Sun. Location and time do matter: A long tail study of website requests. *Decision Support Systems*, 47(4):500–507, 2009.

[20] G. Linden, B. Smith, and J. York. Amazon. com recommendations: Item-to-item collaborative filtering. *Internet Computing, IEEE*, 7(1):76–80, 2003.

[21] L Lovász and M. D. Plummer. *Matching theory.* North-Holland mathematics studies. Akadémiai Kiadó, 1986.

[22] George L Nemhauser, Laurence A Wolsey, and Marshall L Fisher. An analysis of approximations for maximizing submodular set functions. *Mathematical Programming*, 14(1):265–294, 1978.

[23] P. Resnick and H. R. Varian. Recommender systems. *Communications of the ACM*, 40(3):56–58, 1997.

[24] Purnamrita Sarkar, Deepayan Chakrabarti, and Andrew W Moore. Theoretical justification of popular link prediction heuristics. In *IJCAI Proceedings-International Joint Conference on Artificial Intelligence*, volume 22, page 2722, 2011.

[25] J. B. Schafer, J. Konstan, and J. Riedi. Recommender systems in e-commerce. In *Proceedings of the 1st ACM conference on Electronic commerce*, EC '99, pages 158–166. ACM, 1999.

Is Sniping A Problem For Online Auction Markets?

Matt Backus
Cornell University and eBay Research Labs
backus@cornell.edu

Thomas Blake
eBay Research Labs
thblake@ebay.com

Dimitriy V. Masterov
eBay Research Labs
dmasterov@ebay.com

Steven Tadelis
UC Berkeley, NBER, and eBay Research Labs
stadelis@haas.berkeley.edu

ABSTRACT

A common complaint about online auctions for consumer goods is the presence of "snipers," who place bids in the final seconds of sequential ascending auctions with predetermined ending times. The literature conjectures that snipers are best-responding to the existence of "incremental" bidders that bid up to their valuation only as they are outbid. Snipers aim to catch these incremental bidders at a price below their reserve, with no time to respond. As a consequence, these incremental bidders may experience regret when they are outbid at the last moment at a price below their reservation value. We measure the effect of this experience on a new buyer's propensity to participate in future auctions. We show the effect to be causal using a carefully selected subset of auctions from eBay.com and instrumental variables estimation strategy. Bidders respond to sniping quite strongly and are between 4 and 18 percent less likely to return to the platform.

General Terms

Online Auctions; Sniping

Keywords

Online Auctions; Sniping

1. INTRODUCTION

The rise of online marketplaces in general, and auction platforms such as eBay in particular, has offered researchers new sources of detailed data on the behavior of market participants. Over the past decade, there has been a growing literature focusing on auction ending rules and how these influence late-bidding behavior, often referred to as "sniping," where some bidders submit their bid at the very last possible moment.[1] In this paper we explore the effects of losing an auction to such a late bidder, in particular how such an experience affects the future participation of buyers in online auctions. We show that being sniped has a negative impact on the sniped new bidders' likelihood of bidding in a subsequent auction.

The pioneering papers in this literature, Roth and Ockenfels [13] and Bajari and Hortaçsu [1], document the prevalence of sniping on eBay and offer some explanations that rationalize this behavior. One explanation, suggested by Roth and Ockenfels [13] and is also explored in Gray and Reiley [9], suggests that if there are some naïve bidders who do not understand the "proxy bidding" nature of online auctions, and instead choose to raise their bid every time they are outbid by others like in an English auction, then sniping by rational bidders will be a best response.[2] The argument rests on the fact that if a rational bidder faces an "incremental" naïve bidder, then by bidding at the very last moment he will not offer the incremental bidder enough time to raise the bid further, and hence the rational player will win the auction at a lower price than he would if he bid earlier.[3]

We explore a natural prediction from this framework: if a naïve bidder does not anticipate being sniped, and as a result is upset by being sniped, that bidder should be discouraged from participating in future auctions. We develop a test for this prediction and quantify the long term effects on these incremental bidders which measures the magnitude of the externality imposed by snipers using a revealed preference approach.

Using data from eBay we indeed observe that there are many incremental bidders: as many as 30 percent of bidders have bid more than once in an auction. Over 30 percent of

[1]Sniping is a well known practice on eBay.com, and is discussed in detail in its buying guides (`http://www.ebay.com/gds/Sniping-The-Best-kept-secret-on-Ebay/10000000002571474/g.html`, April 7, 2014).

[2]Proxy bidding mechanisms are akin to second-price auctions and work as follows: a bidder submits his non-proxy bid which represents his maximum willingness to pay. As subsequent bids are submitted, the auction mechanism registers the current price as one increment above the second highest proxy bid and current winner as the highest proxy bidder.

[3]Another popular explanation is that snipers are informed bidders who wish to hide their information from less informed bidders in a common-values setting. While the identities of the bidders are masked on eBay, the feedback score and other data which can proxy for experience, are visible. The results in Bajari and Hortaçsu [1] are suggestive of this story playing a role.

WWW 2015, May 18–22, 2015, Florence, Italy.
ACM 978-1-4503-3469-3/15/05.
`http://dx.doi.org/10.1145/2736277.2741690.`

auctions have bids in the last 10 seconds of the auction, supporting the literature's prior evidence that sniping is prevalent. Prior studies, however, have been unable to explore long-term effects.

Figure 1 suggests that there may be negative impacts to the marketplace from sniping. The horizontal axis shows the time remaining from the end of the auction at which a bidder who was winning the auction got outbid by some other bidder. The vertical axis shows the probability that the bidder who was outbid will not return in the future to participate in another auction.[4] As the figure demonstrates, there is a rapid rise in the probability of not bidding ever again in a later auction as the time remaining from the end of the auction drops below a fraction of a minute (about 20 seconds). This means that being outbid in the last few seconds will cause the losing bidder to vote with his feet and be less likely to put in a bid on eBay again.

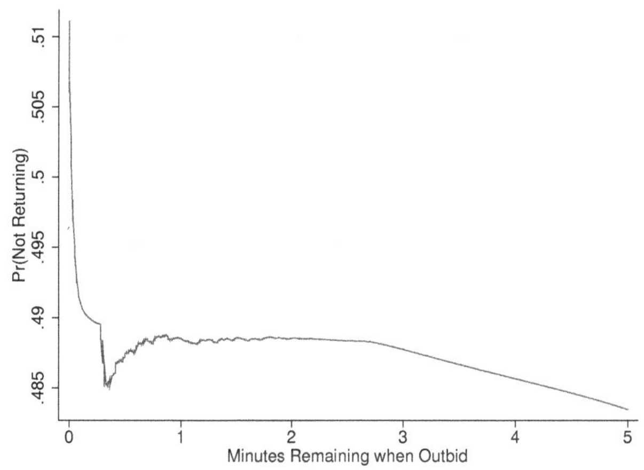

Figure 1: First-time Bidders Winning at 5 Minutes

To begin our analysis, we first define what it means to be sniped. We consider new eBay bidders who are all the high bidders with 5 minutes remaining until their auctions close. We then remove those bidders who ultimately win the auction. Hence, only new users who were winning at 5 minutes before the auction, but lost in the last five minutes, are considered. We define a bidder as sniped if he is outbid in the last 3 seconds. If he is outbid any earlier in the last 5 minutes, he will become part of the control group of losers who were not sniped. Therefore the empirical exercise compares how sniped bidders behave in the future compared to losers who were not sniped. Using a simple probit regression we first analyze the probability of leaving the site conditional on being sniped. The basic analysis shows that the likelihood that bidders who were sniped do not return to bid on eBay is about 3.5 percentage points higher than those who lose without being sniped, who fail to return 49 percent of the time.

Despite being suggestive, the simple plot in Figure 1, as well as regressions controlling for other variables such as price, category, etc., may suffer from endogeneity problems. In particular, sniping is more likely to occur in markets where there are few bidders.[5] It is these kind of markets for which a marketplace like eBay is most attractive to buyers, implying that bidders in these markets may be more likely to return to eBay. Hence, a positive correlation between sniping and auction thinness, and a positive correlation between auction thinness and the likelihood of returning to eBay, will bias downward any effect that sniping has on bidders ceasing to bid in auctions. We indeed demonstrate a positive correlation between sniping and market thinness, and develop another approach to measuring the true causal effect.

We use an instrumental variable (IV) strategy to address this concern. There are two ways that bidding occurs on eBay. First, bidders can manually insert their bid into the proxy bidding system. Second, bidders can use sniping software that does this automatically in the last seconds of the auction without their attentiveness. At night, there are fewer manual bidders active on the site, and consistent with this we observe that more auctions are won by snipers. However, 10pm in New York is only 7pm in San Francisco, while 10pm in San Francisco is 1am in New York. Therefore the 10pm San Francisco bidder is much more likely to be sniped than a 10pm New York bidder. If these bidders are otherwise comparable conditional on observables, then one can use their respective time zones as an instrument for variation in the likelihood of being sniped. This is the basis of our IV strategy.

To implement the IV approach outlined above, we use a bivariate probit regression model with local time of day and server time of day dummies as instruments to capture the exogenous variation in sniping that is due to more or less people from different time zones being awake and able to snipe. The estimates from the IV approach are much larger than the simple probit results: on average, the likelihood that bidders who were sniped do not return to bid on eBay is about 18 percentage points higher than those who lose without being sniped.

These results show that bidders respond quite strongly to being sniped.[6] It is quite clear that rational bidders, who bid their valuation and lose, should not be upset and then vote with their feet.[7] Hence, this behavior suggests that not only are there bidders who do not seem to understand the rules of proxy bidding, but a significant number of those are upset by the prospect of losing without being able to submit a counter-bid, and then chose not to bid in future auctions. As a result, sniping has a negative impact on the growth rate of the auction platform.

2. RELATED LITERATURE

There is an extensive literature on sniping in auction markets which seeks to answer two questions. The first is why bidders are willing to pay nonzero costs to snipe.[8] As Zei-

[4]The shape of Figure 1 is almost identical if the vertical axis shows the probability that the bidder who was outbid will not return in the future to eBay for fixed price purchases as well as auctions.

[5]See Figure 4.

[6]Users often voice their distaste for snipers on eBay on forums and blogs.

[7]Losing bidders may choose not to return to auctions if they believe that prices are not a good enough deal to justify the time spent on bidding. However, there is no reason that rational bidders will choose not to return disproportionately if they lost in the very last seconds of the auction.

[8]There are a variety of third-party websites which offer sniping services and software for eBay auctions. Bidders provide their account login credentials and may pay a small fee to

thammer and Adams [14] emphasize, this fact is inconsistent with the sealed-bid abstraction which renders auction markets so empirically tractable. They show that the salience of sniping is a challenge to the theoretical underpinnings of much empirical work on auctions. The second question is the economic significance of sniping. It remains an open question whether sniping significantly affects auction revenues or the health of an auction platform, and it is on this last point we contribute to the literature.

There are a number of papers which endeavor to explain the incentive to snipe. Bajari and Hortaçsu [1] demonstrated the prevalence of sniping and suggested that if there is a common-value component to bidders' valuations, they would have an incentive to conceal their bids until the end to avoid revealing information. Roth and Ockenfels [13] and Ockenfels and Roth [11; 12] compared the soft ending times of Amazon.com auctions (now defunct) to the hard ending times at eBay.com, and proposed that sniping is a rational response to the existence of a potentially small set of "incremental bidders." Barbaro and Bracht [2] highlight the argument that bidders may use sniping as a way to avoid being squeezed by sellers who use shill bids to narrow the gap between the second-highest and the latent, highest bid.

Evidence of the returns to sniping is limited. Ely and Hossain [7] and Gray and Reiley [9] both conduct field experiments. The former find an economically insignificant payoff to sniping (about 17 cents for a new DVD). They argue that the magnitude of these gains are roughly equal to the gains of bidding early to signal one's participation, in an attempt to deter entry by other bidders. The latter find that sniped auction final prices are 2.54% lower, but the difference is not statistically significant. Glover and Raviv [8] show that auctions with soft ending times on Yahoo! sell for substantially more than those with hard ending times, and conjecture that this is attributable to less sniping. In the public finance literature on charity auctions, Elfenbein and McManus [6; 5] and Carpenter et al. [3] show that sniping has a negative effect on auction revenues. The former go on to suggest that the "warm glow" of participating in charity auctions may deter bidders from adopting more aggressive bidding strategies such as late-bidding.

3. SNIPING

We define late bidding, or sniping, as bidding that happens in the final seconds of a time-limited auction, so that other bidders have little, if any, ability to respond with an incremental bid.

Figure 2 provides a vivid illustration, where we have shown the behavior of 4 participants in a 7 day auction that was won by a sniper. The y-axis shows the dollar value of the non-proxy bids, and the x-axis shows the hours remaining when each bid was made. Bidders are color-coded and bids of each person are connected by line segments if more than one was made. There was no reserve for this auction and the starting price was \$4.99 with a Buy It Now (BIN) option of \$9.99, and an increment of 0.50. The first bid of \$7 was placed by the lavender bidder with less than 18 hours left on the clock. He was the high bidder for most of the remaining time. Around the 7 hour mark, khaki buyer made a solitary bid of 6, which was sufficient to raise the price, but not to put him in the lead. An hour later, red user became the new

have their bid placed in the last seconds of an auction.

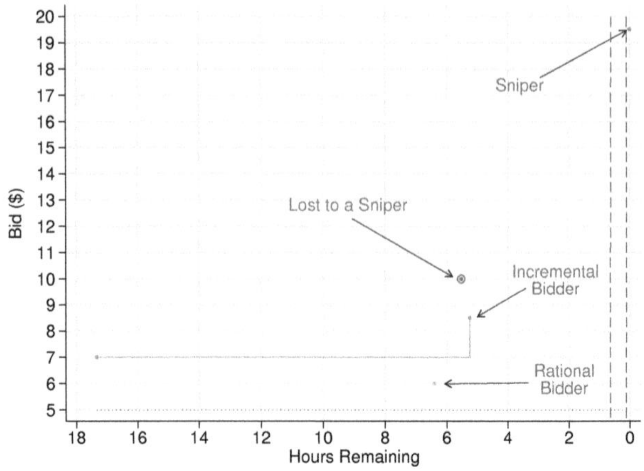

Figure 2: Bidding In An Auction

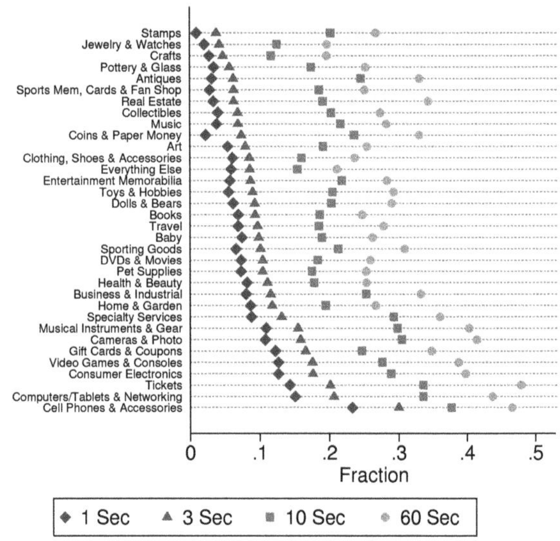

Figure 3: Sniping Rates By Meta Category

high bidder with a bid of \$10. In response, lavender bidder raised his bid to \$8.50, though that was not enough to put him back on top. Red looked to be winning for the next few hours, even with 5 minutes remaining (first dashed line).[9] With 3 seconds to go, a sniper placed a bid of \$19.52. He won and paid 10.50 for this item. We do not know whether the red bidder would have countered, but we do know that he had no time to respond.

Incremental bidding happens fairly frequently on eBay. We find that bidders place multiple bids 29 percent of the time. Moreover, 4.4 percent of bidders place five or more bids in a single auction. The prevalence of this behavior suggests that snipers may deny a substantial fraction of bidders the opportunity to counter bid.

Figure 3 shows that there is considerable variation in how prevalent sniping is in various product categories on eBay.[10]

[9]Dashed lines are not drawn to scale.

[10]Figure 3 shows data from the universe of auctions from Oc-

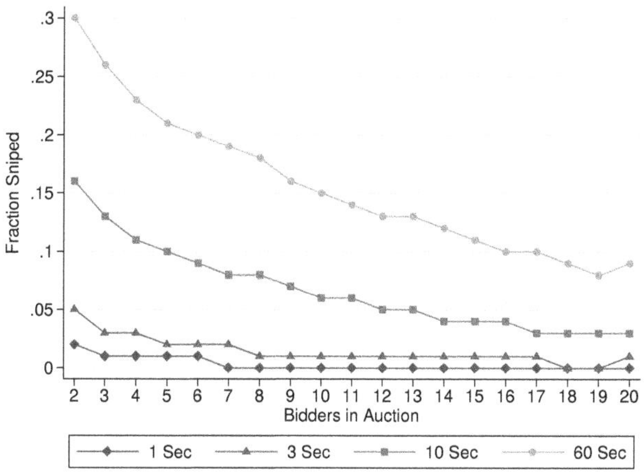

Figure 4: Sniping Rates By Number of Bidders

It plots the fraction of auctions in each meta category that were won through sniping. Mechanically, that fraction grows as we change the definition of sniping from bidding in the last one second to bidding in the last minute. For example, over a third of cell phone auctions were won in the last second, but over half were sniped in the last 60 seconds.

Using our preferred 3 second definition, sniped tickets are over twice as common as with crafts. We note that a rank order of the categories varies somewhat by definition, but not substantially. This confirms that sniping occurs at different rates for different products. In our sample, sniping is more prevalent in thinner markets, a fact that may confound analysis of its effects on follow-up behavior. Figure 4 plots the fraction of sniped auctions by the number of bidders in those auctions from our sample, which is described in Section 5.

We also see substantial variation in the sniping rate at different times of the day. Sniping, as a percentage of all bids, peaks in the middle of the night when many bidders are likely sleeping but automated sniping bots are still active.[11] By contrast, manual bids are more likely to happen in the evening hours when the site is busiest. We will use this variation in our IV estimation.

4. EMPIRICAL DESIGN

The ideal experiment to test our conjecture that sniping drives out buyers from the auction platform would have the following two features. First, we would want to focus on a cohort of *new* eBay users.[12] This group is still forming their expectations about how much surplus they can expect from the site, and so any effects should be readily apparent. Moreover, all users start out as new, and once buyers amass experience, it becomes considerably harder to adjust for that heterogeneity and to deal with the selection issues caused by attrition. For instance, if sniping-averse buyers leave eBay, the population of surviving seasoned users may consider sniping a feature since it allows them to purchase items at a lower price or because it has some ludic value for them, even if they are occasionally sniped themselves or suffer as sellers. On the other hand, this focus on new users somewhat circumscribes the external validity of the effects we estimate.

Once we have a population of auctions in which a new buyer becomes the current high bidder, we can flip a coin to select a random subset to be treated by being sniped in the last moment. New users in the *control* group would be outbid by us earlier on. Our winning bid for them would be set high enough that a control buyer who revises his bid upward would never regain his initial top position. For both groups, at the point of randomization, the auction would become "hidden" to restrict further entry by new bidders and "locked" to keep anyone other than the new buyer from revising his bid. This minimizes substitution bias from control units being treated, but also ensures that we have full control over the information that is revealed to the losers,[13] and over the time that they perceive to be in the lead. This is the second essential feature.

Once this hypothetical experiment starts, we can follow both groups for some period of time to track their activity. We can compare the average number of auction purchases, total revenue, or merely the proportion who bid in an auction again. The difference between the two groups in any of the those metrics would be the treatment effect of being sniped. Note that we are not comparing winners to losers. The treatment alters the manner in which a buyer lost, not whether he did.

The second aspect of this design renders the experiment infeasible since it is impossible to control the dynamics of auctions in the field. Instead we propose the following exercise. We take a large set of auctions and restrict attention to bidders who are winning with 5 minutes remaining until the auction closes. For each auction, there is a single bidder who meets this criterion. We proceed to exclude all but first-time bidders. We also exclude bidders who go on to win the auction, out of a concern that sniped bidders, who necessarily lose, have residual demand for the product being auctioned. We identify a bidder as sniped if he is outbid in the last 3 seconds. If he is outbid any earlier in the last 5 minutes, he is part of the control group. This allows us to compare outcomes for those losers who could have potentially responded by bringing their bid closer to their true reservation value, to those for whom this was impossible. Imagine that we could find another auction that had the exact same attributes and history of bids, but the final bid came in between the 2 vertical blue lines, the 5 minute and the 3 second marks in Figure 2. This would serve as a counterfactual auction for the sniped case, since the red bidder would have had enough time to respond to a bid that came in somewhat earlier.

We note that our arbitrary 3 second threshold may misclassify some bidders and cause attenuation bias in the estimated treatment effect. The bidders' ability to respond will depend on the quality of their internet connection and the mode of their connection, whether PC, mobile, or other.

tober 2009 to October 2011. Our chosen sample, discussed in Section 5, is a subset of these auctions.

[11]Figure 5 shows this pattern for each time zone.

[12]We consider an eBay user to be new if the observed auction is the first action, bid or purchase, made on the site. We allow users to have signed up as early as 6 months prior to our window.

[13]For example, if the observed standing price rises for the control group as more bids are made, the control group will learn more about by how much they lost than the treatment losers.

We have chosen 3 seconds because this both fits the visual presented in Figure 1 and because this is a logical threshold at which human response time limits the ability to counter bid. We choose a five minute counterfactual window because we want to limit the sample to auctions where the bidder was winning as the auction came to a close. We examine in the appendix how sensitive our results are to the 3 second definition of sniping and to the 5 minute window.

5. SAMPLE CONSTRUCTION

We want to measure the impact of sniping on consumer behavior, so we want to construct a sample of consumers that are similar in most respects but for the fact that some have been outbid in the last few seconds of the auction where there was no chance to respond. To do this we need to find i) a sample of users that are alike, in expectation, at the time of the auction and ii) are expected to have similar behavior after the auction but for the sniping. Therefore, we focus on i) first-time bidders and ii) bidders who lose their first auction. We identify *all* first-time bids between October 2009 and October of 2011 where the bidder did not win the auction. We chose this period so that we have a full year of data for all bidders after their first auction. This is over 2 million bidders. We then identify those bidders that were the winning bidder with exactly five minutes remaining in the auction. Some of these bidders were winning for only seconds and some where winning for days, but all were the winner at the 5 minute mark and eventually lost. Note that since each auction can have only one winner at a single moment in time, this eliminates any duplicate auctions so that each bidder-auction pair is unique. In our main specifications, we further limit the sample to bidders that were *still* winning with one minute remaining. Thus these bidders where winning for at least four minutes because they were winning at the five minute mark and the one minute mark.

Table 1: Sample Size

All first time losing bidders	2226307
Winning with 5 min remaining	705957
Outbid with less than 1 min remaining	458168
Covered by catalog	89168
Thick market (10 auctions of product)	32139

Finally, in some of our specifications we limit the analysis to the subsample of auctions that are in thicker markets. To do this, we first identify those auctions that are identified by eBay's product catalog, which are typically items with well defined manufacturer product codes. This further limits the sample because only a portion of eBay's inventory is covered by the catalog. We then find catalog products with more than 10 transactions over the two-year period. Table 1 shows the counts of each sample truncation.

In Table 2, we present summary statistics for our full sample of auctions with first-time bidders winning at 5 minutes. Although all the bidders in our sample were outbid, only 7 percent of these auctions were outbid in the last 3 seconds, 10 percent in the last 4 seconds, and so forth. In general, 49 percent of first-time bidders do not bid again in an eBay auction. We stress that this is specific to auction: many eBay users switch to fixed price listings. We still consider these users as not returning because we are interested in capturing an effect associated with a dis-utility of auctions, not the overall platform. Statistics for additional controls are shown as well.

Table 2: Sample Statistics

	Mean	SD	Min	Max	N
Sniped in 3 Seconds	0.0711	0.257	0	1	705957
Sniped in 4 Seconds	0.101	0.302	0	1	705957
Sniped in 6 Seconds	0.185	0.388	0	1	705957
Sniped in 8 Seconds	0.264	0.441	0	1	705957
Sniped in 10 Seconds	0.308	0.462	0	1	705957
Sniped (Power Seller Auction)	0.0260	0.159	0	1	705957
Bidder Does Not Return	0.488	0.500	0	1	705957
Minutes Remaining When Outbid	1.161	1.397	0	5	705957
Hours Left When Bid	10.01	23.37	0.1	399.5	705957
Own Bid as a Percentage of Highest Bid	0.749	0.219	0.0000	1.0	672049
Power seller auction	0.418	0.493	0	1	705957
Bid / Expected Highest Bid	0.739	0.343	0.0000	37	144647
Bid / Expected Category Highest	0.667	1.404	0.00000	375.9	705947
Bid / Best Expected Highest	0.684	1.357	0.00000	375.9	705947

6. ESTIMATION

The principal results are shown graphically in Figure 1, which shows a marked increase in the probability of not returning in the last few seconds of the auction. It plots a locally weighted smooth of not returning against minutes remaining when outbid conditional on winning with five minutes remaining in the auction.

To make the suggested results of Figure 1 concrete, we estimate probit regressions assessing the impact of being 'sniped', or outbid by late bidding, on future behavior. Figure 1 demonstrates a distinct jump in the probability of leaving the platform if outbid in the last few seconds of the auction. We then regress an indicator for whether the user does not participate in an eBay auction within 12 months of being outbid on an indicator for whether or not the time of outbid was within three seconds of the close of the auction.[14] We limit the regression to all auctions where the new bidder was still winning with one minute remaining.[15]

Table 3 presents the probit estimates of marginal effects of sniped on failure to return from several specifications. Column 1 presents the estimates without any controls and indicates a 3.3 percentage point increase in the probability of not returning. This confirms that the increase in not returning as outbid time approaches zero shown in Figure 1, which rises from 48 percent to 51 percent, is a statistically significant relationship. This estimate is unconditional, and since sniping is not a random occurrence, there are a variety of confounders we first try to address with controls.

In Column 2, we add controls for two important selection mechanisms. First, bidders who are outbid earlier in the auction are likely to have lower bids simply because lower bids are more likely to be outbid sooner as bidders arrive. Bidders that bid lower have different expectations of surplus from buying on the platform generally and may be more likely to leave the site once final prices are revealed. Lower bids could therefore be correlated with the timing of being outbid and not returning. We include the ratio of the bidder's (losing) bid to the highest (winning) bid as a control.

[14]A view of the data in Figure 1 suggests a kink in the return-time remaining relationship at three seconds.

[15]This limits the sample to all auctions where the new bidder was winning from five minutes to one minute before the auction. This improves the comparability among bidders: we are now only comparing losers in the last few seconds to the last minute.

Table 3: Probit Estimates, Dep Var = Pr(Not Returning)

	(1)	(2)	(3)	(4)	(5)	(6)
Sniped in 3 Seconds	0.0331***	0.0355***	0.0138***	0.0483***	0.01000	0.0380***
	(0.00236)	(0.00248)	(0.00253)	(0.00312)	(0.00705)	(0.00721)
Sniped (Power Seller Auction)				-0.0897***		
				(0.00468)		
Own Bid as a Percentage of Highest Bid		-0.159***	-0.0123	-0.00439		
		(0.0161)	(0.0164)	(0.0164)		
(Bid / Highest)^2		0.191***	0.0470***	0.0434***		
		(0.0128)	(0.0131)	(0.0131)		
Hours Left When Bid		0.00421***	0.00451***	0.00450***	0.00664***	
		(0.0000789)	(0.0000787)	(0.0000787)	(0.000459)	
(Hours Left When Bid)^2		-0.0000160***	-0.0000177***	-0.0000176***	-0.0000333***	
		(0.000000651)	(0.000000639)	(0.000000639)	(0.00000370)	
Bid / Expected Highest Bid					-0.0712**	-0.111***
					(0.0226)	(0.0236)
(Bid / Expected Highest)^2					0.0313*	0.0511***
					(0.0135)	(0.0139)
Category Dummies			Yes	Yes	Yes	
Window	1 min	1 min	1 min	1 min	1 min	1 min
Thick Markets					Yes	Yes
Product RE						Yes
N	458168	440670	440670	440670	32116	32116

Robust standard errors in parentheses
$^* p < 0.05$, $^{**} p < 0.01$, $^{***} p < 0.001$

We also include controls for the timing of the sniped bidders' bid. Since we condition on the bidder winning at 5 minutes remaining, auctions where bidders had been winning for longer are auctions with less activity and may be more likely to be sniped because potential bidders are lying in wait. Bidders that bid very early in the auction may have a different probability of returning. It is not a priori clear what direction these potential effects would bias the results, but the coefficient on sniping remains consistent at 3.5 percentage points.

From Figure 3 we see that there is some variation in sniping rates across categories so in Column 3 we include fixed effects for eBay's 35 top line product meta categories. As was shown in Figure 3, sniping rates vary across product types which naturally attract bidders with different propensities to return. The estimated effect decreases to 1.38 percentage points which hints that cross category effects may bias the results, but meta category is a very broad classification that masks important product level variation. So we explore several methods of controlling for more specific product attributes.

In Column 4, we add an interaction of the sniped indicator with an indicator for whether the item was listed by a power seller, eBay's designation for high volume, high quality sellers. These items are likely to attract bidders looking for very common items on eBay. It is perhaps not surprising that being sniped is much less burdensome for these buyers because there is a greater likelihood that they will try again.

In Columns 5 and 6, we limit the sample to auctions for items that are in 'thick' markets: the item is identified in eBay's product catalog and has more than 10 auctions in our full 2 year sample. These sets of auctions are likely to be very similar to one another and should reduce all selection effects related to product characteristics. We replace the own bid-to-highest-bid ratio with the ratio of the bid to the expected price for that product (average final price of the product), which is a better proxy for bid's seriousness. Column 5 shows that the estimate is not significantly different from the estimates in Column 3. The estimate loses significance only because we have a lower sample size. In Column 6, we estimate a probit model with product level random effects and notice that the coefficient rises to 3.8 percentage points.

We are concerned about the endogeneity of sniping selection and return rates, but the sign of the bias is not obvious. The returns from sniping would be higher in thinner markets, where incremental bidders are less likely to be bid up by non-sniping but rational bidders. And these thinner markets are more prevalent on eBay so bidders in these markets are more likely to return. Thus, the positive shock to sniping would be a negative shock to exit rates and would bias our estimates downward. Column 6 supports this view because removing much of that bias by focusing on within product variation in sniping increases the coefficient.

In order to more fully address the selection endogeneity, we leverage an instrumental variables strategy that relies on the fact that auctions on eBay are national events but that sniping is a function of the number of bidders on the site in the last few minutes of the auction. We want an instrument that shifts the probability of being outbid in the last few seconds, as opposed to being outbid in the last few minutes. Auctions that have more rational, non-sniping bidders watching the close are less likely be sniped because the first-time bidder will be outbid in a way that allows them to respond. We also need this instrument to be correlated with the probability of a bidder returning to the platform only through the probability of being sniping.

Auctions end on eBay simultaneously across the country and therefore at different *local* times of day depending on the time zone of the bidder. We found that the probability of being sniped varies dramatically by the closing time of the auction because the number of users browsing the site varies dramatically by time of day. When there are fewer users on the site, there are fewer non-incremental, non-sniping bidders to drive up the auction price earlier in the auction. This creates a cyclical relationship between the proportion of auctions that are sniped and the time of day. We show

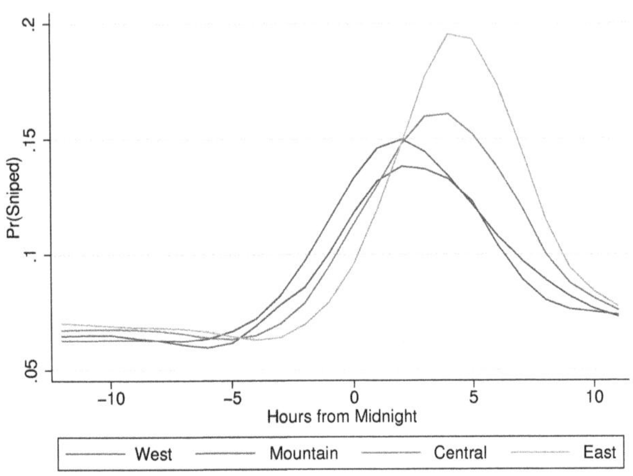

Figure 5: Probability of Sniping by Time Zone

in Figure 5 that this relationship actually varies by time zone. We plot a dummy for being sniped against the local auction end time of the first-time bidder for the auctions in our sample and then fit a local polynomial. As is evident, a bidder on the West Coast watching an auction at midnight has almost a 15 percent chance of being sniped but the same bidder on the east coast has only a roughly 8 percent chance of being sniped. This is because midnight on the east coast is still prime time on the west coast and there are more non-sniping rational bidders in the auction. Thus, two bidders bidding at midnight have a different chance of being sniped and their only difference is time zone. We assume that the probability of returning is otherwise uncorrelated with time zone, an assumption supported by eBay's national presence.

To implement this instrument, we utilize a bivariate probit regression with local time of day and server time of day dummies.[16] We use the server time dummies as the excluded instruments which are uncorrelated with churn, conditional on the local time of day.

Table 4 presents the marginal effects and average treatment effects estimates.[17] Columns 2 and 3 add category dummies and the hours remaining controls used before. Column 4 restricts the sample to power seller listings and first-time bidders still winning at one minute.

[16]Bivariate probit can serve as an instrumental variables estimator where both the dependent and independent variables are binary Greene [10].

[17]We use the approach of Chiburis et al. [4] to calculate the average treatment effect (ATE) and average treatment effect on the treated (ATT).

Table 4: Bivariate Probit Estimates

	(1)	(2)	(3)	(4)
β	1.105***	0.726***	0.397***	0.493***
	(0.13670)	(0.08794)	(0.06510)	(0.14566)
Marginal Effect	0.426***	0.280***	0.153***	0.186***
	(0.04999)	(0.03301)	(0.02483)	(0.05413)
Average Effects				
ATE	0.384***	0.269***	0.152***	0.189**
	(0.03353)	(0.02334)	(0.01929)	(0.06479)
ATT	0.403***	0.275***	0.152***	0.179**
	(0.03790)	(0.02516)	(0.01950)	(0.05878)
Category Dummies		Yes	Yes	Yes
Hours Remaining Controls			Yes	Yes
Perc of Highest Bid Controls			Yes	Yes
Power Seller				Yes
Window				1 min
N	320909	320909	305474	82819

The estimates are much larger than the probit results but are in line with the random effects estimate. In our most restrictive sample shown in Column 4, the ATE and ATT are about 18 percentage points. This demonstrates, at the very least, that the 3 percent estimates are biased downward and that the true effect is substantial. Taken together, the evidence bolsters the claim that being sniped has large effects on users' propensity to participate in future auctions.

7. CONCLUDING REMARKS

There is strong evidence that being sniped is an experience which discourages new bidders from returning to bid again. We find a sizeable effect in our probit specifications, which we believe to be biased downward, and a much larger effect when we use bidder time zones to instrument for the likelihood of being sniped. These findings are consistent with the story advanced in Roth and Ockenfels [13] that sniping is a rational response to the presence of incremental bidders.

The effect is economically significant from the perspective of an auction platform. Even small changes in the rate at which new participants join the platform can have a tremendous effect on long-term platform size.

The recent surge in availability of e-commerce data is a unique opportunity to re-examine hypotheses that had been formerly pursued using only scraped, field experiment, or lab experiment data. The advantage of using data directly from the e-commerce platform is that it is so extensive that we are able to narrow our empirical strategy to a subset of comparable auctions in order to identify the effects of interest, while still enjoying a wealth of data. We believe that this development offers researchers the opportunity to rigorously test theory where before we could have been little more than suggestive, and that this is an important direction for new work.

References

[1] Patrick Bajari and Ali Hortaçsu. The winner's curse, reserve prices, and endogenous entry: Empirical insights from eBay auctions. *RAND Journal of Economics*, 34: 329–355, 2003.

[2] Salvatore Barbaro and Bernd Bracht. Shilling, squeezing, sniping: Explaining late bidding in online second-price auctions. *Working article. University of Mainz, Mainz, Germany*, 2004.

[3] Jeffrey Carpenter, Jessica Holmes, and Peter Hans Matthews. Jumping and sniping at the silents: Does it matter for charities? *Journal of Public Economics*, 95(5):395–402, 2011.

[4] Richard Chiburis, Jishnu Das, and Michael Lokshin. A practical comparison of the bivariate probit and linear iv estimators. *World Bank Policy Research Working Paper 5601*, 2011.

[5] Daniel W Elfenbein and Brian McManus. A greater price for a greater good? Evidence that consumers pay more for charity-linked products. *American Economic Journal: Economic Policy*, 2(2):28–60, 2010.

[6] Daniel W Elfenbein and Brian McManus. Last-minute bidding in eBay charity auctions. *Economics Letters*, 107(1):42–45, 2010.

[7] Jeffrey C Ely and Tanjim Hossain. Sniping and squatting in auction markets. *American Economic Journal: Microeconomics*, 1(2):68–94, 2009.

[8] Brent Glover and Yaron Raviv. Revenue non-equivalence between auctions with soft and hard closing mechanisms: New evidence from Yahoo! *Journal of Economic Behavior & Organization*, 81(1):129–136, 2012.

[9] Sean Gray and David Reiley. Measuring the benefits to sniping on eBay: Evidence from a field experiment. *New York University working paper*, 2004.

[10] W.H. Greene. *Econometric Analysis*. Prentice Hall, 2003. ISBN 9780130661890. URL `http://books.google.com/books?id=JJkWAQAAMAAJ`.

[11] Axel Ockenfels and Alvin E Roth. The timing of bids in internet auctions: Market design, bidder behavior, and artificial agents. *AI magazine*, 23(3):79, 2002.

[12] Axel Ockenfels and Alvin E Roth. Late and multiple bidding in second price internet auctions: Theory and evidence concerning different rules for ending an auction. *Games and Economic Behavior*, 55(2):297–320, 2006.

[13] Alvin E Roth and Axel Ockenfels. Last-minute bidding and the rules for ending second-price auctions: Evidence from eBay and amazon auctions on the internet. *The American Economic Review*, 92(4):1093–1103, 2002.

[14] Robert Zeithammer and Christopher Adams. The sealed-bid abstraction in online auctions. *Marketing Science*, 29(6):964–987, 2010.

APPENDIX

A. ROBUSTNESS

A.1 Window

The probit results in Table 3 use a sample of auctions where the first-time bidder was winning at 5 minutes and still winning with 1 minute remaining. In Table 5 we present estimates from samples with different control windows. The estimates from Column 3 are those presented in Column 3 of Table 3. In Columns 1 and 2, we narrow the sample to auctions where the first-time bidder was outbid in 6 and 10 seconds. Column 1 shows that there is still a 1.1 percentage point increase in the probability of not returning for bidders who are outbid with less than 3 seconds left compared to those outbid between 3 and 6 seconds. This is slightly smaller than the other windows, which confirms the relationship shown in Figure 1. Conversely, Columns 4 and 5 show that there is actually very little effect of adding auctions where the outbidding occurs early in the auction.

A.2 Snipe Definition

Table 6 presents probit results for increasingly expansive definitions of sniping, from 6 seconds to almost 5 minutes (300 seconds). When we vary the sniping definition even a little, the estimates are negative suggesting that the up-tick in exit is only present for those auctions where the first-time bidder actually did not have time to respond. The fact that these probit results are negative is at first alarming, but actually consistent with the instrumental variable motivation.

A.3 Linear Probability Model

We use a probit model in our primary specifications but we can easily estimate a linear probability model for robustness. Table 7 presents the results from Table 3 with a linear model. The estimates are qualitatively similar. To check the robustness of the downward bias on exit from product selection, we leverage the time zone instrument with two stage least squares estimation of the linear model. Here the estimates are substantially larger, so large that we believe the linear model for the binary outcome is not well behaved. We interpret these results as consistent with the probit results because the negative bias persists and simple OLS estimates are similar to the base probit models. The bivariate probit is a more appropriate model given that both the dependent and independent variables are binary.

Table 8: Linear Probability Instrumental Variables

	(1)	(2)	(3)	(4)
Sniped	0.525***	0.411***	0.489***	0.141
	(0.0852)	(0.102)	(0.101)	(0.145)
Hours Remaining			0.00372***	0.00404***
			(0.000146)	(0.000175)
(Hours Remaining)^2			-0.0000127***	-0.0000156***
			(0.00000113)	(0.00000145)
Constant	0.406***	0.359***	0.309***	0.308***
	(0.0147)	(0.0133)	(0.0125)	(0.0183)
Category Dummies		Yes	Yes	Yes
Non-Power Sellers				Yes
Window		1 min	1 min	1 min
N	415285	415285	415285	172660

Standard errors in parentheses
* $p < 0.05$, ** $p < 0.01$, *** $p < 0.001$

Table 5: Varying the Control Windows

	(1) 6 Second Window	(2) 10 Second Window	(3) 60 Second Window	(4) 150 Second Window	(5) 300 Second Window
Sniped in 3 Seconds (d)	0.0106***	0.0120***	0.0135***	0.0135***	0.0131***
	(0.00312)	(0.00278)	(0.00254)	(0.00249)	(0.00246)
Own Bid as a Percentage of Highest Bid	0.00790	-0.00711	-0.0172	-0.0366*	-0.0652***
	(0.0262)	(0.0218)	(0.0164)	(0.0149)	(0.0136)
(Bid / Highest)^2	0.0204	0.0335	0.0510***	0.0722***	0.0991***
	(0.0217)	(0.0178)	(0.0131)	(0.0118)	(0.0108)
Hours Left When Bid	0.00461***	0.00447***	0.00451***	0.00449***	0.00451***
	(0.000140)	(0.000112)	(0.0000787)	(0.0000716)	(0.0000664)
(Hours Left When Bid)^2	-0.0000183***	-0.0000173***	-0.0000177***	-0.0000177***	-0.0000177***
	(0.00000113)	(0.000000919)	(0.000000640)	(0.000000582)	(0.000000542)
Category Dummies	Yes	Yes	Yes	Yes	Yes
N	125967	209920	440674	549116	672049

Robust standard errors in parentheses
(d) for discrete change of dummy variable from 0 to 1
* $p < 0.05$, ** $p < 0.01$, *** $p < 0.001$

Table 6: Varying the Sniping Definition

	(1) 6 Seconds Left	(2) 30 Seconds Left	(3) 60 Seconds Left	(4) 150 Seconds Left	(5) 250 Seconds Left
Sniped (d)	0.00144	-0.00170	-0.00257	-0.00278	-0.00226
	(0.00160)	(0.00125)	(0.00131)	(0.00160)	(0.00263)
Own Bid as a Percentage of Highest Bid	-0.0732***	-0.0750***	-0.0753***	-0.0751***	-0.0745***
	(0.0135)	(0.0135)	(0.0135)	(0.0135)	(0.0135)
(Bid / Highest)^2	0.104***	0.105***	0.105***	0.105***	0.105***
	(0.0107)	(0.0107)	(0.0107)	(0.0107)	(0.0107)
Hours Left When Bid	0.00452***	0.00453***	0.00453***	0.00453***	0.00453***
	(0.0000665)	(0.0000666)	(0.0000666)	(0.0000665)	(0.0000665)
(Hours Left When Bid)^2	-0.0000178***	-0.0000178***	-0.0000179***	-0.0000179***	-0.0000178***
	(0.000000542)	(0.000000543)	(0.000000543)	(0.000000542)	(0.000000542)
Category Dummies	Yes	Yes	Yes	Yes	Yes
Window	5 min	5 min	5 min	5 min	5 min
N	672049	672049	672049	672049	672049

Robust standard errors in parentheses
(d) for discrete change of dummy variable from 0 to 1
* $p < 0.05$, ** $p < 0.01$, *** $p < 0.001$

Table 7: Linear Probability Model

	(1)	(2)	(3)	(4)
Sniped in 3 Seconds	0.0331***	0.0350***	0.0132***	0.0461***
	(0.00236)	(0.00246)	(0.00245)	(0.00302)
Sniped (Power Seller Auction)				-0.0863***
				(0.00463)
Own Bid as a Percentage of Highest Bid		-0.162***	-0.0170	-0.00952
		(0.0159)	(0.0158)	(0.0158)
(Bid / Highest)^2		0.193***	0.0497***	0.0463***
		(0.0126)	(0.0126)	(0.0126)
Hours Left When Bid		0.00416***	0.00439***	0.00437***
		(0.0000745)	(0.0000739)	(0.0000739)
(Hours Left When Bid)^2		-0.0000162***	-0.0000175***	-0.0000174***
		(0.000000603)	(0.000000593)	(0.000000592)
Category Dummies			Yes	Yes
Window	1 min	1 min	1 min	1 min
N	458168	440674	440674	440674

Robust standard errors in parentheses
* $p < 0.05$, ** $p < 0.01$, *** $p < 0.001$

Essential Web Pages Are Easy to Find

Ricardo Baeza-Yates*
Yahoo Labs
Barcelona
Spain
rbaeza@acm.org

Paolo Boldi†
Dipartimento di Informatica
Università degli Studi di Milano
Italy
paolo.boldi@unimi.it

Flavio Chierichetti‡
Dipartimento di Informatica
Sapienza Università di Roma
Italy
flavio@di.uniroma1.it

ABSTRACT

In this paper we address the problem of estimating the index size needed by web search engines to answer as many queries as possible by exploiting the marked difference between query and click frequencies. We provide a possible formal definition for the notion of *essential web pages* as those that cover a large fraction of distinct queries — *i.e.*, we look at the problem as a version of MAXCOVER. Although in general MAXCOVER is approximable to within a factor of $1 - 1/e \approx 0.632$ from the optimum, we provide a condition under which the greedy algorithm does find the actual best cover (or remains at a known bounded factor from it). The extra check for optimality (or for bounding the ratio from the optimum) comes at a negligible algorithmic cost. Moreover, in most practical instances of this problem, the algorithm is able to provide solutions that are provably optimal, or close to optimal. We relate this observed phenomenon to some properties of the queries' click graph. Our experimental results confirm that a small number of web pages can respond to a large fraction of the queries (*e.g.*, 0.4% of the pages answers 20% of the queries). Our approach can be used in several related search applications, and has in fact an even more general appeal — as a first example, our preliminary experimental study confirms that our algorithm has extremely good performances on other (social network based) MAXCOVER instances.

Categories and Subject Descriptors

H.3.1 [**Content Analysis and Indexing**]: Information Storage and Retrieval; G.2.1 [**Combinatorics**]: Discrete Mathematics; G.1.6 [**Optimization**]: Numerical Analysis.

Keywords

Web search; query log analysis; layered indices; tiering; max cover; click graph; approximation algorithms; greedy algorithms.

*This research started when the second author was visiting Yahoo Labs Barcelona, and was performed using Yahoo's data and computation infrastructure.

WWW 2015, May 18–22, 2015, Florence, Italy.
ACM 978-1-4503-3469-3/15/05.
http://dx.doi.org/10.1145/2736277.2741100.

1. INTRODUCTION

Scalability is one of the main issues for web search engines, particularly with respect to query load and index size. In this paper we address the latter problem in a very general sense: it is obvious that having to deal with a smaller index implies the need of less resources and hence is less costly. Fortunately, query frequencies and the frequency of clicks on web pages that answer those queries follow very different power laws, and hence an index that contains a small fraction of all available web pages may answer well, as shown later, a large fraction of the query volume.

In fact, we can always view a search engine as logically composed by two indices. A small (main) index built from the essential web pages that answers the bulk of the queries, and another (secondary) larger index that is tailored to answer long tail queries (see [4, Section 11.4.4]). Here we consider the problem of selecting the web pages for the main index leaving the design of the secondary index for future work.

Formally, we address the following *essential web pages*[1] problem. Given a set Q of n queries and a set of m web pages P, that form a (bipartite) "relevance" graph (for some notion of relevance of a web page to a query, typically derived from user clicks), find a subset of pages $S \subseteq P$ of size K that maximizes the coverage of queries. We say that a query is *covered* if at least one of the pages that are relevant to it is in S, though, in general, one might consider different definitions of coverage as we will see later. In this work we aim to maximize the number of distinct covered queries, though it would also make sense to maximize their total volume (we discuss this case in the conclusions).

We use the following definition of *relevance*: we restrict P to the set of pages that users clicked on sufficiently enough (*i.e.*, at least a certain number of times) as a result of a search. That is, a page is relevant for a query if the ranking algorithm of the web search engine believes it is a relevant page and enough users agree. Our choice gives a very strong notion of relevance.

Notice that to solve the problem outlined above, in some sense all available pages need to be indexed. However, as this problem can be solved off-line, we do not need to construct the index to obtain a good estimation of the top ranked pages for every query. Moreover,

† Partially supported by the Yahoo Faculty Research and Engagement Program and by the MIUR-PRIN National Project "ARS TechnoMedia" (Algorithmics for Social Technological Networks).
‡ Partially supported by a Google Faculty Research Award and by the MIUR-PRIN National Project "ARS TechnoMedia" (Algorithmics for Social Technological Networks).
[1]We remark that our notion of "essential" has nothing to do with that described in [20], as better explained in the "Related work" section.

we discuss later that having the index allows to find solutions for specific instances that are interesting in their own right.

The essential web pages problem can be seen as a MAXCOVER [14] problem. Hence, it is in general NP-hard, although it is approximable to within a factor of $1 - 1/e$ from the optimum using a greedy approach [21]. In this paper, we show that, however, in many practical instances of our problem, the greedy algorithm in fact finds the *optimal* cover, or a cover which is close to optimal.

Our approach is based on the observation that the value of the optimal solution of MAXCOVER can be sandwiched from below by the greedy solution and from above by its relaxed LP formulation. It is known that the ratio of the two sides of the sandwich is always lower bounded by $1 - 1/e$. The gap is tight in some cases, in the sense that one can build instances that are as close as one wants to the above bound. By taking the dual of the relaxed MAXCOVER LP, one obtains a linear minimization program whose feasible solutions' values are upper bounds to the integral MAXCOVER problem. Therefore, the dual problem can be used to provide bounds on the approximation that the greedy algorithm produces: this is explained in Section 5. The computational cost of producing this bound is negligible, and the bound obtained is in many cases enough to prove that the greedy output is actually *optimal*, or very close to optimality. In the experiments on our largest click-graph dataset, for example, the bound produced was never worse than 98%; a simpler baseline depending on cardinality sum would yield much worse bounds (ranging from 87% to 93%). In fact, even our bound is too pessimistic: the real approximation ratio of the greedy algorithm for the click-graph datasets on which the exact ratio could be produced was never worse than 99.79%! From a practical standpoint, we observe that adding answer and inverted list caching would make these results even better.

We have also observed very good performances on a non web-index based dataset. We ran our same algorithm on a Twitter based dataset (having users as elements, and a set for each user u that contains u and all the users followed by u), obtaining slightly different, but still extremely good, guaranteed performances. Indeed, the bounds we obtained are not worse than 95% for each $K \geq 50$. It then appears that our algorithm can be used in a variety of settings, without decreasing its extremely good approximation guarantees.

More generally, it is striking to observe that our modified greedy algorithm on the instances of our problem (Section 7) guarantees an approximation that is (provably) extremely good, less than 2.5% away from the optimum when $K \leq 500$ (and less than 5% for $K \leq 140,000$). One might suspect that this extremely good approximation is due to the power-law distributions involved in our instances. However, we prove in Sections 3 and 4 that the $1 - 1/e$ bound cannot be improved on some of these instances.

While a satisfying explanation of this phenomenon is still missing, in Section 6 we provide a proof that the greedy algorithm produces with high probability an almost optimal solution provided that the following three conditions are satisfied:

1. the greedy algorithm is able to include at least $\Omega(\log n)$ queries at every step;
2. there are many queries only included in constantly many web pages; and
3. the instance is chosen uniformly at random, between those satisfying the given distributions.

Note that condition (2) is guaranteed if the queries' clicks follow a power-law distribution, as it happens in practice.

Our final coverage results are quite good. In fact, in our largest dataset, almost 25% of the queries are covered by just 0.7% of the web pages (Section 7). In the Conclusions we discuss our results and give other search related problems that can profit from this powerful imbalance.

2. RELATED WORK

Many recent papers focus their attention on various possible search scenarios that can lead to (variants of the) MAXCOVER problem, and analyze the issues they imply. Examples of applications include influence maximization in social networks [8, 16], whereas in the context of web search it was used to formalize the problem of discoverability of new content [13]. In the latter paper, they overcome the inherent difficulty of the problem using past observations. In fact, various query/documents covering problems have been studied in the literature (*i.e.*, index tiering [17, 5], stochastic query covering [1]).

All the cited scenarios deal with very large datasets, which raises the question of whether the greedy algorithm is amenable to being implemented in a MapReduce framework [9]. One interesting aspect of the algorithm we are presenting in this paper is that we can modify also the MapReduce-greedy algorithm given in [9] to obtain a behavior similar to the one that we describe here for the sequential case, at the expense of a reasonable increase in the number of the MapReduce iterations required.

Another stream of related research is the so-called pruned indices. Pruned indices are smaller indices where term and/or document related information is deleted to use less space. The most recent results show that caching is more effective than index pruning to improve answering time [19]. Nevertheless, the initial motivation of index pruning was to use less space [7], but the techniques used did not force that all references to a given document would need to disappear from the index.

A notion of "essential" page was introduced in a quite different context in [20], but with another meaning: they are not interested in covering queries but rather knowledge (terms), and they express this need as a form of coverage problem. Their problem is different from the vanilla (*i.e.*, unweighted) MAXCOVER problem. They do use a greedy approach to solve it, but do not provide bounds on the quality of the solution obtained. In fact, [11] considers a general problem that includes both MAXCOVER, and the problem in [20], as special cases. The authors of [11] provide an algorithm that returns a $1-1/e+\varepsilon$ approximation in time $O(poly(n) \cdot m^{1/poly(\varepsilon)})$; they also provide a variant of greedy for the same problem, but with larger approximation ratios.

3. MAX COVER

MAXCOVER is a well-known NP-hard problem [14] that consists in finding K sets in a given collection so as to maximize their union.

In our intended application items are queries, sets correspond to URLs,[2] and a query belongs to the set of a given URL if that URL is deemed "relevant" for the query. The actual definition of what relevant means is not really important here: in the experimental part of this paper (Section 7) we used a number of query logs of a search engine and extracted the click graph [12], to determine on which URLs people clicked after submitting a query. Other possible variants on the exact definition of the problem are discussed in the conclusions.

Formally, the MAXCOVER problem can be stated as follows:
Problem 1: MAXCOVER.
Input: An instance $\Pi = (\Omega, \mathcal{S}, K)$ is defined by a set Ω of n

[2]We use URL (or document) as a synonym of web page.

items, a family $\mathcal{S} = \{S_1, \dots, S_m\}$ of m subsets of Ω and an integer K.
Output: Find a subset $\mathcal{S}' \subseteq \mathcal{S}$ with $|\mathcal{S}'| \le K$ maximizing

$$\textsc{Opt}(\Pi) = \left| \bigcup_{S \in \mathcal{S}'} S \right| .$$

From time to time, we shall look at the pair $(\Omega, \mathcal{S})$ as a bipartite graph, with n vertices on the left-hand side (hereafter called *q-vertices*, where "q" stands for "queries", because items are queries) representing the items Ω (queries), and m vertices on the right-hand side (hereafter called *d-vertices*, where "d" stands for "documents") representing the sets $\mathcal{S}$ (web pages); edges represent membership of items to sets, as expressed by the notion of "relevance" adopted.

The degree sequence of q-vertices (*i.e.*, the list of their degrees sorted in non-decreasing order) will be called *q-sequence* ("q" stands for "query degree"), and similarly the degree sequence of d-vertices will be called *d-sequence* (for "document degree"). Since we observed (Section 7) that both sequences are power-law of exponents larger than 2, we are especially interested in dealing with this case.

The MaxCover problem can be formulated [21] as an integral linear programming problem with $n + m$ variables and $2n + 1$ constraints as follows: take one variable x_i (with $1 \le i \le n$) for every item and one variable y_j (with $1 \le j \le m$) for every set, where all variables are constrained to be non-negative (ideally, in $\{0, 1\}$) and $x_i = 1$ means that the i-th item is covered, whereas $y_j = 1$ means that the j-th set is output.

With this notation, we can formulate MaxCover as:

$$\begin{aligned} &\max \left(\sum_{i=1}^{n} x_i \right) \qquad \textbf{subject to} \\ &\sum_{j=1}^{m} y_j \le K \\ &x_i - \sum_{S_j \ni i} y_j \le 0 \quad \text{for } i = 1, \dots, n \\ &x_i, y_j \in [0, 1] \quad \text{for } i = 1, \dots, n \text{ and } j = 1, \dots, m. \end{aligned} \tag{1}$$

This LP model will be referred to as *MCLP* (for "MaxCover LP") if x_i and y_j are constrained to be integral. The first constraint simply means that we want to take at most K sets, the second i constraints impose that we can say that x_i is covered only if at least one of the sets containing it is taken, whereas the final set of constraints impose that x_i is zero or one.

If we relax the constraint that x_i and y_j be integral, we obtain a new LP model that we refer to as *relaxed MCLP*: an interpretation of this relaxed version is that a set can be "partially taken" (when y_j is strictly between 0 and 1), and hence an item can be "partially covered".

Integrality gap (general case).

We shall use LP(Π) to denote the value of the objective for the relaxed MCLP corresponding to the instance Π. Of course $\textsc{Opt}(\Pi) \le \text{LP}(\Pi)$. Actually the ratio between the two (called the "integrality gap") satisfies

$$1 - \frac{1}{e} \le \frac{\textsc{Opt}(\Pi)}{\text{LP}(\Pi)} \le 1.$$

The lower bound is tight, in the sense that for every $\varepsilon > 0$ there is an instance whose integrality gap is less than $1 - \frac{1}{e} + \varepsilon$. This is obtained with a classical [21] construction that we shall now describe, since we shall modify it later on.

We shall build an instance Π_M for every integer $M \ge 2$; the instance Π_M has M^2 sets $\mathcal{S} = \{S_1, \dots, S_{M^2}\}$ and Ω is made of $\binom{M^2}{M}$ items: for every choice of M sets out of the M^2 available there is one item that is put in exactly those sets. If you fix $K = M$, the optimal solution to MaxCover will have value

$$\textsc{Opt}(\Pi_M) = \binom{M^2}{M} - \binom{M^2 - M}{M},$$

because whichever class of $K = M$ sets you choose, all the items that were put in a disjoint class of M sets not overlapping them will not be covered. On the other hand, the optimal solution of the primal (1) for this instance is

$$\text{LP}(\Pi_M) = \binom{M^2}{M}.$$

The fact that $\binom{M^2}{M}$ is an upper bound follows trivially from $|\Omega| = \binom{M^2}{M}$. We give a feasible solution of (1) that achieves that value, thus proving our assertion. We set $y_j = M^{-1}$ for each set S_j. By definition, each item i is contained in exactly M sets, and we can therefore choose $x_i = 1$ without violating any constraint.

The integrality gap $\textsc{Opt}(\Pi_M)/\text{LP}(\Pi_M)$ is then bounded as follows:[3]

$$\begin{aligned} \frac{\textsc{Opt}(\Pi_M)}{\text{LP}(\Pi_M)} &= 1 - \frac{\binom{M^2-M}{M}}{\binom{M^2}{M}} \\ &= 1 - \frac{(M^2 - M) \cdots (M^2 - 2M + 1)}{M^2 \cdots (M^2 - M + 1)} \\ &\le 1 - \left(\frac{M^2 - 2M}{M^2 - M} \right)^M = 1 - \left(1 - \frac{1}{M-1}\right)^M \\ &\le 1 - \frac{1}{e} + O\left(\frac{1}{M}\right). \end{aligned}$$

Integrality gap (power-law case).

We want to show that the above construction can be modified so to prove that the lower bound is tight also for instances whose d-sequence is a power law distribution of exponent $\alpha > 2$.

Let us use Π_M to denote the instance described above. Observe that, by Stirling's approximation, the number of items $\binom{M^2}{M}$ in the instance Π_M is $\Theta\left(M^{M-\frac{1}{2}} e^M\right)$. Moreover, each set has cardinality $\binom{M^2-1}{M-1} = \Theta\left(M^{M-\frac{3}{2}} e^M\right)$.

Now suppose that we aim to create an instance Π' with a d-distribution (that is, a set-cardinality distribution) following a power law with some constant exponent $\alpha > 2$. Let $\zeta(\alpha) = \sum_{i=1}^{\infty} i^{-\alpha}$. For every integer M, the number of sets with cardinality $\binom{M^2-1}{M-1}$ needs to be at least

$$\frac{t}{\zeta(\alpha) \cdot \binom{M^2-1}{M-1}^{\alpha}} - O(1) \ge \Omega\left(t \cdot M^{\frac{3}{2}\alpha - M\alpha} e^{-M\alpha}\right),$$

where t is the number of sets in Π'.

For any given t, if we choose M to be an integer such that $t = \Theta\left(M^{M\alpha - \frac{3}{2}\alpha + 2} e^{M\alpha}\right)$ we are sure that in the instance Π' that we

[3]We are using the fact that $1 < a < b$ implies $\frac{a}{b} > \frac{a-1}{b-1}$, so $\frac{M^2-M-i}{M^2-i} > \frac{M^2-2M}{M^2-M}$.

construct, there will be at least M^2 sets of cardinality $\binom{M^2-1}{M-1}$. Let us use $\mathcal{S}$ to denote an arbitrary class of M^2 sets of cardinality $\binom{M^2-1}{M-1}$ in Π'.

Now, the largest set in Π' will have cardinality at most $O(t^{\frac{1}{\alpha}})$. We let all sets in $\Pi' - \mathcal{S}$ be subset of the largest set in Π'. Then, the total contribution of the sets not in $\mathcal{S}$ to a solution (whether integral or fractional) is at most

$$O\left(t^{\frac{1}{\alpha}}\right) = O\left(M^{M-\frac{3}{2}+\frac{2}{\alpha}}e^M\right).$$

As we already showed, if we choose $K = M$, then the solution composed of the sets in $\mathcal{S}$ has value $\Theta(n) = \Theta\left(M^{M-\frac{1}{2}}e^M\right)$. We have that $\Theta\left(\frac{t^{\frac{1}{\alpha}}}{n}\right) = O\left(M^{-1+\frac{2}{\alpha}}\right)$. Since $\alpha > 2$, the latter is $o(1)$. Therefore, the integrality gap of Π' can be upper bounded by the integrality gap of Π_M times at most $1 + o(1)$ — that is, it can be upper bounded by $1 - \frac{1}{e} + o(1)$.

4. THE DUAL PROBLEM AND ITS RELATION WITH THE GREEDY SOLUTION

In this section, we present a classical heuristic for MaxCover and discuss how good is the approximation ratio it provides. For this purpose, it is useful to see it in relation with the dual LP problem.

The dual of (1) is a new LP with $2n + 1$ variables T, z_i, w_i, and u_j (with $1 \le i \le n$ and $1 \le j \le m$) and $n + m$ constraints:

$$\min\left(K \cdot T + \sum_{i=1}^{n} z_i\right) \quad \textbf{subject to}$$

$$\begin{aligned} z_i + w_i &\ge 1 \quad \text{for } i = 1, \dots, n, \\ T - \sum_{x_i \in S_j} w_i &\ge 0 \quad \text{for } j = 1, \dots, m, \\ z_i, w_i &\ge 0 \quad \text{for } i = 1, \dots, n. \end{aligned} \tag{2}$$

Now, let us take an optimal solution of (2) and modify it as follows.

1. Observe that optimality guarantees that $z_i \le 1$ for each $i = 1, \dots, n$. Indeed, if $z_i > 1$, by assigning the value 1 to z_i, we decrease the value of the objective, and we keep every constraint satisfied.

2. For every index i, if $z_i + w_i > 1$, we assign to w_i the new value $w_i' = \max(0, 1 - z_i)$. We show that this substitution keeps intact the feasibility of the system. Observe that $w_i > 1 - z_i \ge \max(1 - z_i, 0) = w_i'$, so $w_i' < w_i$, and the substitution never breaks constraints from the second group; moreover, $z_i + w_i' = \max(1, z_i) \ge 1$, so the constraints from the first group will also be satisfied, and the solution will still be feasible.

In other words, under optimality we can assume that $w_i = 1 - z_i \in [0, 1]$, so the optimal solutions of (2) can be turned into optimal solutions of a simpler LP problem with $n + 1$ variables only:

$$\min\left(K \cdot T + \sum_{i=1}^{n} z_i\right) \quad \textbf{subject to}$$

$$\begin{aligned} T &\ge |S_j| - \sum_{x_i \in S_j} z_i \quad \text{for } j = 1, \dots, m, \\ z_i &\in [0, 1] \quad \text{for } i = 1, \dots, n. \end{aligned} \tag{3}$$

The optimal value of (3) on a given instance Π of the problem will be denoted by $\text{DLP}(\Pi)$; by the duality theorem

$$\text{DLP}(\Pi) \ge \text{LP}(\Pi) \ge \text{Opt}(\Pi).$$

In other words, solving either LP problems (either the primal or the dual) provides an upper bound to the value of the optimal solution, and as proved in Section 3 the gap between the optimum and the upper bound can be as large as $1 - 1/e$.

Sub-optimality of greedy algorithm (general case).

The *greedy solution* of the MaxCover problem is found by selecting iteratively the set (one of the sets) that cover the maximum number of yet-uncovered items, until K sets are selected. We write $\text{Greedy}(\Pi)$ for the number of items covered by the greedy solution on the instance Π.

Greedy solutions are sub-optimal, that is (looking at the overall picture) $\text{DLP}(\Pi) \ge \text{LP}(\Pi) \ge \text{Opt}(\Pi) \ge \text{Greedy}(\Pi)$ but it is known that [15]

$$1 - \frac{1}{e} \le \frac{\text{Greedy}(\Pi)}{\text{Opt}(\Pi)} \le 1,$$

with the lower bound being once more tight (*i.e.*, there are instances for which we can make the ratio as close to the lower bound as we want).

We now describe a classical construction that shows the tightness of the lower bound. Fix $K \ge 2$, and choose an integer $t \ge 1$. We create an instance $\Pi = \Pi(K, t)$. For each $i = 1, \dots, K$ and $j = 0, \dots, Kt - 1$, let us create a set Ω_i^j containing $K^{Kt-1} \cdot \left(\frac{K-1}{K}\right)^j$ unique elements. Let $\Omega = \bigcup_{i,j} \Omega_i^j$, $\Omega_i = \bigcup_j \Omega_i^j$ and $\Omega^j = \bigcup_i \Omega_i^j$.

We let the sets of the instance be Ω_i, for $i = 1, \dots, K$, and Ω^j, for $j = 0, \dots, Kt - 1$. Observe that picking the sets $\Omega_1, \dots, \Omega_K$ is an optimal solution, having value:

$$\begin{aligned} |\Omega| &= \sum_{i=1}^{K} |\Omega_i| = K \cdot K^{Kt-1} \cdot \sum_{j=0}^{Kt-1} \left(\frac{K-1}{K}\right)^j \\ &= K^{Kt+1} \cdot \left(1 - \left(1 - \frac{1}{K}\right)^{Kt}\right) \ge \left(1 - e^{-t}\right) K^{Kt+1}. \end{aligned}$$

On the other hand, each Ω^j is larger in cardinality than any Ω_i, so the greedy algorithm will pick the sets $\Omega^0, \dots, \Omega^{K-1}$ in this order, for a total value:

$$\begin{aligned} \left|\Omega^0 \cup \ldots \cup \Omega^{K-1}\right| &= K \cdot K^{Kt-1} \cdot \sum_{j=0}^{K-1} \left(\frac{K-1}{K}\right)^j \\ &= K^{Kt+1} \cdot \left(1 - \left(1 - \frac{1}{K}\right)^{K}\right). \end{aligned}$$

Therefore, the ratio between the value of the solutions produced by the greedy algorithm and the optimal solution is bounded by

$$\frac{\text{Greedy}(\Pi)}{\text{Opt}(\Pi)} \ge \frac{1 - \left(1 - \frac{1}{K}\right)^K}{1 - e^{-t}}.$$

By selecting $t = t(K) = \lceil \ln K \rceil$, we obtain that the ratio can be upper bounded by $1 - \frac{1}{e} + O\left(\frac{1}{K}\right)$. Hence, the ratio converges to $1 - \frac{1}{e}$ as $K \to \infty$.

Sub-optimality of greedy algorithm (power-law case).

We once again transform the above instance $\Pi\left(K, \lceil \ln K \rceil\right)$ into an instance having a power law d-distribution (*i.e.*, cardinality distribution) with exponent $\alpha > 1$. We will build the new instance

Π' so that it contains $m = \Theta\left(K^{\alpha K\lceil \ln K\rceil+1}\right)$ sets. An easy calculation shows that it will contain at least K sets of cardinality $|\Omega_1| = |\Omega_2| = \ldots = |\Omega_K|$, and at least 1 set for each of the cardinalities $|\Omega^0|, |\Omega^1|, \ldots, \left|\Omega^{K\lceil \ln K\rceil-1}\right|$. We will use these sets to recreate the instance Π within Π'.

The largest set in Π' will have size $\Theta\left(K^{K\lceil \ln K\rceil+\frac{1}{\alpha}}\right)$, and we build all the other sets of Π' so that they are subsets of this largest set.

Now, picking the sets $\Omega_1, \ldots, \Omega_K$ will still cover at least $(1-\frac{1}{K}) \cdot K^{K\lceil \ln K\rceil+1}$ elements. The greedy algorithm, on the other hand, will cover the set of maximum size – which will account for $\Theta\left(K^{K\lceil \ln K\rceil+\frac{1}{\alpha}}\right)$ elements – and, as in the instance Π, will necessarily cover at most $K^{K\lceil \ln K\rceil+1} \cdot \left(1-(1-\frac{1}{K})^K\right)$ other elements.

Therefore, $\text{GREEDY}(\Pi')/\text{OPT}(\Pi') \to 1-\frac{1}{e}$, as $K \to \infty$.

Sub-opt. of greedy algorithm (double power-law).

The previous proof still leaves some margin of hope: the tightness of the bound may fail to hold if we require both distributions to be power-law. A more complex construction, however, shows that even in this case the usual bound holds true:

Lemma 1 *Suppose that $\alpha > 2$ and $\beta > \alpha+1$.*[4] *Then, we can create instances Π' of increasing sizes $n = \Theta(m)$, having a q-degree α-power law distribution, and a d-degree β-power law distribution, such that*

$$\frac{\text{GREEDY}(\Pi')}{\text{OPT}(\Pi')} \xrightarrow{n\to\infty} 1-\frac{1}{e}.$$

PROOF. Let Π be any instance that has the given q-degree and d-degree distributions.

Observe that, since the sum of the degrees has to be equal to the sum of the cardinalities, and since $\alpha, \beta > 2$, Π satisfies $n = \Theta(m)$.

Let the largest cardinality be u; then $u = \Theta\left(n^{\frac{1}{\beta}}\right)$. Let $\mathcal{T} \subseteq \mathcal{S}$ be the subclass of sets having cardinality at least $\varepsilon \cdot u$, for an unspecified constant $\varepsilon = \varepsilon(\alpha, \beta) > 0$. We have $|\mathcal{T}| = \Theta\left(n^{\frac{1}{\beta}}\right)$. Also, let K be the largest integer such that there are at least K sets of cardinality at least $K^{K\lceil \ln K\rceil} \cdot \left(1-(1-\frac{1}{K})^{K\lceil \ln K\rceil}\right)$. Then, $K = \Theta\left(\frac{\ln n}{\ln^2 \ln n}\right)$.

Let $\mathcal{T}' \subseteq \mathcal{T}$ be the subclass of sets having the largest K cardinalities in $\mathcal{T}$ (breaking ties arbitrarily). We have $\max_{S\in\mathcal{T}'}|S| = u$, and $\min_{S\in\mathcal{T}'}|S| \leq u-K$.

We then create another subclass of sets $\mathcal{U}$: this class will contain $K\lceil \ln K\rceil$ sets, and will be disjoint from $\mathcal{T}$. Specifically, for each $j = 1, \ldots, K\lceil \ln K\rceil-1$, we put in $\mathcal{U}$ exactly one set S_j of cardinality $K^{K\lceil \ln K\rceil} \cdot \left(\frac{K-1}{K}\right)^j$. Moreover, $\mathcal{U}$ will contain one final set S_0 of cardinality $\sum_{S\in\mathcal{T}'}|S| - \sum_{j=1}^{K\lceil \ln K\rceil-1} K^{K\lceil \ln K\rceil} \cdot \left(\frac{K-1}{K}\right)^j$.

For each set $S \in \mathcal{T}\cup\mathcal{U}$, and for each element $e \in S$, (i) create a new set $S' = S'(S,e)$, (ii) remove e from S, and (iii) add e to S' (which will then have cardinality 1). Observe that, at the end of this process, no old item degree changes; all the sets that had cardinality at least εu are now empty, and we have introduced at most $\sum_{i=\varepsilon u}^{\infty}\left(i^{-\beta}\cdot i\cdot m\right) + u\cdot K = O\left(n^{\frac{2}{\beta}}\right)$ new sets of cardinality 1. Since the number of sets that had cardinality 1 was $\Theta(n)$, the d-degree power-law distribution is preserved at 1.

[4]Although in our data $\beta > \alpha+0.7$, this lemma seems to still hold.

As a second step, create a set X of $\sum_{S\in\mathcal{T}'}|S| = \Theta(u\cdot K)$ new elements — the elements in X will end up having degree 2 in our construction. That is: (i) assign each element $x \in X$ to exactly one set $S \in \mathcal{T}'$, so that each set gets a number of elements equal to its original cardinality; also (ii) assign each element $x \in X$ to exactly one set $S \in \mathcal{U}$, so that each set gets a number of elements equal to its original cardinality. In this step we also add $\Theta(u\cdot K) = o(n)$ new elements of degree 2 — again, since the number of degree 2 elements in the q-degree distribution was $\Theta(n)$, the distribution is preserved.

The third and final step of our construction fills up the sets in $\mathcal{T}-\mathcal{T}'$. Pick the largest such set S, and fill it with new elements. Make all the other sets in $\mathcal{T}-\mathcal{T}'$ subsets of S. Observe that there will be $|S| = O\left(n^{\frac{1}{\beta}}\right)$ new elements, and that their degree will be at most $|\mathcal{T}| = O\left(n^{\frac{1}{\beta}}\right)$.

The q-sequence guarantees that, for each $1 \leq d \leq O\left(n^{\frac{1}{\beta}}\right)$, the number of items having degree d is at least $\Omega\left(\frac{n}{d^\alpha}\right) \geq \Omega\left(n^{1-\frac{\alpha}{\beta}}\right)$. We add at most $O\left(n^{1/\beta}\right)$ new nodes with that degree; since $\beta-\alpha > 1$, we have that we add at most an $o(1)$ fraction of new nodes of degree d, for each possible d. The q-sequence is therefore preserved.

Finally, let Π' be the new instance. Observe that it follows the original q-degree power law, and d-degree power law, distributions. Observe also that greedy will pick the largest K sets in $\mathcal{U}$ (plus at most one set in $\mathcal{T}-\mathcal{T}'$), while the optimal solution would pick the sets in $\mathcal{T}'$. An easy calculation then shows the result. □

The instance showing the above bound is created by "embedding" the classical construction described in the previous subsection into an instance with degrees and cardinalities distributed like power laws. This has to be done in a very careful way: first we show that the largest sets in the power law instance are good enough to contain the elements in the largest sets of the classical instance. Then, we need to ensure that the other large sets in the power law instance will not change by more than a $(1+o(1))$ factor from the value of the greedy, and optimal, solutions. To do so, we include all those sets in one large set — this, of course, changes the degree distribution: the last part of our proof is then showing that the distribution does not change significantly and, in fact, still follows the same power law.

5. BOUNDING THE APPROXIMATION OF THE GREEDY SOLUTION

The previous section does not leave much room for hope: apparently even having an instance of MAXCOVER that has a power-law distribution of degrees on both sides may cause greedy to work as badly as it can. Also, on the other hand, the LP formulations do not help much, because they are themselves away from the optimum (in the other direction) for a large gap.

Nevertheless, we will be able to prove that greedy can exploit the dual problem to "certify" the quality of its own output, that is, to provide a bound on how far the solution is from the optimum. This property will allow us to modify the greedy algorithm so to make it produce this certificate along with the solution at a moderate computational cost (in many cases, asymptotically at no cost).

The basic property is stated in the following theorem; albeit seemingly unfathomable, we shall see how this result can be put at good use in a self-certifying version of the standard greedy algorithm.

Theorem 1 *For an integer $t \geq 1$, we say that a set is t-large if its cardinality is at least t, and that an item is t-certifying if it is contained in at most one t-large set.*
Consider an instance Π and let $S_1^*, \dots, S_K^*$ be a solution (that is, a sequence of sets) produced by greedy; define

$$\gamma = \left| S_K^* \setminus \bigcup_{j=1}^{K-1} S_j^* \right|,$$

that is, the "gain" produced by the last set. For all $j = 1, \dots, K-1$, let $\ell_j \geq 0$ be the smallest integer such that the number of γ-certifying items contained in S_j^* is at least $\gamma - \ell_j$. Then,

$$\mathrm{DLP}(\Pi) \leq \textsc{Greedy}(\Pi) + \sum_{j=1}^{K-1} \ell_j$$

and therefore $S_1^*, \dots, S_K^*$ is a solution of MaxCover *with an additive error of at most $\sum_{j=1}^{K-1} \ell_j$.*

Proof. Observe that, necessarily, for each $j = 1, \dots, K$, we have $|S_j^*| \geq \gamma$ — that is, all the S_j^*'s are γ-large. Therefore, if x is a γ-certifying item, then x can be in at most one set S_j^*, $1 \leq j \leq K$.

Now, for each $j = 1, \dots, K-1$, let T_j^* be equal to any subset of S_j^*, of cardinality $\gamma - \ell_j$, containing only γ-certifying items (observe that T_j^* is well-defined because of the assumption in the claim). By definition, the T_j^*'s are pairwise disjoint.

Consider the dual (2) and let

$$z_i = \begin{cases} 1 & \text{if } x_i \in \bigcup_{j=1}^{K-1} (S_j^* \setminus T_j^*) \\ 0 & \text{otherwise.} \end{cases}$$

Since $T_j^* \subseteq S_j^*$ and since the T_j^*'s are pairwise disjoint, we can write

$$\sum_{i=1}^{n} z_i = \left| \bigcup_{j=1}^{K-1} (S_j^* \setminus T_j^*) \right| = \left| \bigcup_{j=1}^{K-1} S_j^* \right| - \left| \bigcup_{j=1}^{K-1} T_j^* \right|$$
$$= \left| \bigcup_{j=1}^{K-1} S_j^* \right| - \gamma \cdot (K-1) + \sum_{i=1}^{K-1} \ell_j.$$

The value of the objective function of the dual is then $\left| \bigcup_{j=1}^{K-1} S_j^* \right| - \gamma \cdot (K-1) + K \cdot T + \sum_{j=1}^{K-1} \ell_j$.

By the definition of γ, we have $\left| \bigcup_{j=1}^{K-1} S_j^* \right| + \gamma = \left| \bigcup_{j=1}^{K} S_j^* \right|$. Therefore, the value of the objective function of the dual is

$$\left| \bigcup_{j=1}^{K} S_j^* \right| + K \cdot (T - \gamma) + \sum_{j=1}^{K-1} \ell_j.$$

We prove that setting $T = \gamma$ gives a feasible solution for the dual, *i.e.*, we show that it satisfies every constraint in the dual program: $\gamma = T \geq |S| - \sum_{x_i \in S} z_i$ for each set $S \in \mathcal{S}$ of the instance. We rewrite the constraint as:

$$\gamma \stackrel{?}{\geq} |S| - \left| S \cap \bigcup_{j=1}^{K-1} (S_j^* \setminus T_j^*) \right|.$$

If $S = S_j^*$, for some $j = 1, \dots, K-1$, then the constraint is trivially satisfied, since it simplifies to $\gamma \stackrel{?}{\geq} |T_j^*| = \gamma - \ell_j$. We therefore assume that S differs from each of the $S_1^*, \dots, S_{K-1}^*$ sets. Moreover, we can assume that $|S| > \gamma$, because otherwise once more the constraint will be trivially true.

Observe that $\cup_{j=1}^{K-1} T_j^*$ has empty intersection with S — indeed each node in the former set is part of exactly one γ-large set between $S_1^*, \dots, S_{K-1}^*$ and cannot therefore be part of a second γ-large set S. Thus, the constraint can be rewritten as:

$$\gamma \stackrel{?}{\geq} |S| - \left| S \cap \bigcup_{j=1}^{K-1} S_j^* \right| = \left| S - \bigcup_{j=1}^{K-1} S_j^* \right|.$$

The latter cannot be larger than γ, otherwise the greedy algorithm would have picked S instead of $S_K^* \neq S$.

Hence, we found a feasible solution of the dual whose objective is $\left| \bigcup_{j=1}^{K} S_j^* \right| + \sum_{j=1}^{K-1} \ell_j$. Since the solution of value $\left| \bigcup_{j=1}^{K} S_j^* \right|$ produced by the greedy algorithm is feasible in the primal, we obtain

$$\textsc{Greedy}(\Pi) + \sum_{j=1}^{K-1} \ell_j = \left| \bigcup_{j=1}^{K} S_j^* \right| + \sum_{j=1}^{K-1} \ell_j \geq \mathrm{DLP}(\Pi). \quad \square$$

A special case of Theorem 1 can in fact provide a guarantee of optimality: if for all $j = 1, \dots, K-1$, the number of γ-certifying items contained in S_j^* is at least γ, then all ℓ_j's are zero, and the solution produced by the greedy algorithm is optimal.

We can turn the additive bound of Theorem 1 into a multiplicative bound (or, if you prefer, into a bound on the approximation ratio):

Corollary 1 *If Π satisfies the hypothesis of Theorem 1 then*

$$\frac{1}{1 + \frac{\sum_{j=1}^{K-1} \ell_j}{\textsc{Greedy}(\Pi)}} \leq \frac{\textsc{Greedy}(\Pi)}{\textsc{Opt}(\Pi)} \leq 1.$$

Proof. Just recall that $\textsc{Greedy}(\Pi) + \sum_{j=1}^{K-1} \ell_j \geq \mathrm{DLP}(\Pi)$ and the latter is an upper bound for $\textsc{Opt}(\Pi)$. $\square$

Note that the actual ratio can be much better than the one obtained by Corollary 1 simply because the upper bound of Theorem 1 is not tight. If the instance is small enough, one can try to solve the dual LP to obtain a better bound (or even to show that greedy produces the optimum for the instance under test).

The claim of Theorem 1 could be seen as being too unwieldy to be useful. In the following, we will show that (i) the theorem can be directly turned into an efficient algorithm, and that (ii) the approximation ratio that Corollary 1 guarantees for this algorithm is, on our instances, *very* close to 1.

A certifying greedy algorithm.

Theorem 1 can be turned into an algorithm that is able to certify that the solution currently produced by the greedy algorithm satisfies the theorem and it is optimal, or more generally to provide a bound on its approximation ratio. This extra computation has a moderate extra cost in time, and only requires a $O(T \log T)$ preprocessing phase (and linear extra space), where T is the size of the instance.

Given a pair $(\Omega, \mathcal{S})$, for every item $x \in \Omega$ define ξ_x to be 1 plus the cardinality of the 2nd largest set $S_i \in \mathcal{S}$ containing x; of course, for every t, x is t-certifying if and only if $\xi_x \leq t$. Now, let us store, for every $S_i \in \mathcal{S}$, an array $xs_{S_i}[-]$ of $|S_i|$ entries, where $xs_{S_i}[1] \leq \cdots \leq xs_{S_i}[|S_i|]$ contain the values ξ_x (for all $x \in S_i$) in non-decreasing order.

By the observation above, for every t, S_i contains at least t items that are t-certifying iff $xs_{S_i}[t] \leq t$. More generally, for every t, let u be the largest index such that $xs_{S_i}[u] \leq t$ and let $\ell = \max(t-u, 0)$. Then, ℓ is the smallest non-negative integer such that S_i contains at

Algorithm 1 Certifying the greedy algorithm with the lower bound produced by Corollary 1. Here, c represents the number of items covered by the current solution $S_1^*, \ldots, S_K^*$, γ is the gain of the last set, and L is the sum $\sum_{j=1}^{K-1} \ell_j$ using the notation of Theorem 1.

Input: a pair $(\Omega, \mathcal{S} = \{S_1, \ldots, S_m\})$
  $K \leftarrow 1; c \leftarrow 0$
  while true **do**
    choose $i \in \{1, \ldots, m\}$ maximizing $\gamma = |S_i \setminus \cup_{j=1}^{K-1} S_j^*|$
    // check that all sets contain $\geq \gamma$ items that are γ-certifying
    $L \leftarrow 0$
    for j from 1 to $K-1$ **do**
      find the largest u such that $x_{S_j^*}[u] \leq \gamma$
      $L \leftarrow L + \max(0, \gamma - u)$
    $S_K^* \leftarrow S_i$
    $c \leftarrow c + \gamma$
    Solution $S_1^*, \ldots, S_K^*$ is not worse than a $\frac{1}{1+\frac{L}{c}}$ approximation
    $K \leftarrow K + 1$

least $t-\ell$ items that are t-certifying (because $t-\ell = t-t+u = u$). Index u can be found by binary search.

Armed with these observations, we can present Algorithm 1: it is a variant of the standard greedy algorithm, but at every step it provides a lower bound to the ratio between the greedy solution and the optimal one. The time required to produce the lower bound is $O(K \log n)$, where K is the size of the current solution. Since $K \leq m$, the cost per iteration is asymptotically $\log n$ larger than $O(m)$, the time required by the standard iteration of the greedy algorithm.[5] In particular, as long as $K \leq m/\log n$, Algorithm 1 is (asymptotically) not worse than the standard greedy algorithm.

6. CARDINALITY AND DEGREE-BOUND RANDOM INSTANCES

In this section we introduce a natural model to produce random instances, and we show that the greedy algorithm is going to be close to optimal on them, and that our certifying greedy algorithm will be able to certify this near-optimality.

Definition 1 *Let $1 \leq q_1 \leq \ldots \leq q_n \leq m$ and $d_1 \leq \ldots \leq d_m \leq n$ be two non-decreasing sequences such that*

$$\sum_{i=1}^{n} q_i = \sum_{j=1}^{m} d_j = M,$$

and such that $q_n \cdot d_m \leq M$. We build a bipartite graph with $n+m$ nodes, and for each $1 \leq i \leq n$ and $1 \leq j \leq m$, we add an edge between the nodes corresponding to q_i and d_j independently with probability $\frac{q_i \cdot d_j}{M}$. We denote this random bipartite graph by $B(\boldsymbol{q}, \mathbf{d})$ (here q_i correspond to queries and d_j to documents).

We interpret this bipartite graph $B(\boldsymbol{q}, \boldsymbol{d})$ as a set system: an item q will be part of the set S iff q has an edge to S. We observe that the expected degree[6] of the node corresponding to q_i (resp., d_j) is in fact q_i (resp., d_j).

[5]If only a test for optimality is needed, it can be done in time $O(K)$, by just checking at every step that $x_{S_i}[\gamma] \leq \gamma$ for every $i = 1, \ldots, K-1$, avoiding the binary search.

[6]This random construction does not guarantee that the degree sequences are exactly given by the q_i's and d_j's: this is true only in expectation. However, there is a trivial (albeit cumbersome) proof that the degree distributions will follow the original power laws.

We will consider power law distributed $\boldsymbol{q}$ and $\boldsymbol{d}$, so to match what we see in our datasets. We assume that $\boldsymbol{q}$ follows a power law with exponent $\alpha > 2$, and that $\boldsymbol{d}$ follows a power law with exponent $\beta > 2$. That is, we assume that the number of items with a value q_i equal to q will be $\Theta\left(M \cdot q^{-\alpha}\right)$, and the number of sets with a value d_j equal to d will be $\Theta\left(M \cdot d^{-\beta}\right)$. A simple calculation shows that $\alpha, \beta > 2$ imply that the condition $q_n \cdot d_m \leq M$ is satisfied.

We also point out that the power law distributions imply that the tails of $\boldsymbol{q}$ and $\boldsymbol{d}$ satisfy, for every integer $t \geq 1$:

$$\sum_{\substack{i \\ q_i \geq t}} q_i \geq \Theta\left(M \cdot t^{2-\alpha}\right), \text{ and } \sum_{\substack{j \\ d_j \geq t}} d_j \geq \Theta\left(M \cdot t^{2-\beta}\right).$$

Lemma 2 *Let Π be the instance corresponding to a sample of $B(\boldsymbol{q}, \mathbf{d})$, with $\mathbf{d}$ and $\mathbf{d}$ following, respectively, a power law with exponent $\alpha > 2$, and one with exponent $\beta > 2$.*

If Algorithm 1 is run on Π then, with high probability, for each K for which S_K^* produces a gain of at least $\frac{20 \ln n}{\varepsilon^2}$ new elements, then the algorithm returns, and certifies, a $(1 - O(\varepsilon))$-approximation for MAXCOVER.

PROOF. Let X_j be the number of elements having $q_i \leq Q = \varepsilon^{-\frac{1}{\alpha-2}}$ that end up inside S_j, and in no other set $S_{j'}$ such that $d_{j'} \geq L = \varepsilon^{-\frac{\alpha-1}{(\alpha-2)(\beta-2)}}$. Observe that X_j lower bounds the number of $(L+1)$-certifying elements of S_j. Then, a simple calculation shows that $E[X_j] \geq (1 - O(\varepsilon)) \cdot d_j$.

Let $G = \left\{j \mid d_j \geq \frac{10 \ln n}{\varepsilon^2}\right\}$. Since edges are inserted independently in the bipartite graph, the Chernoff bound guarantees that, with probability $1 - o(1)$, for each $j \in G$ it will hold that $X_j \geq (1 - O(\varepsilon)) \cdot d_j$.

Moreover, the Chernoff bound also guarantees that, with probability $1 - o(1)$, for each $j \in G$, it will hold that $|S_j| \leq (1 + O(\varepsilon)) \cdot d_j$. Analogously, with probability $1 - o(1)$, for each $j \in [m] - G$, we will have that $|S_j| \leq \frac{20 \ln n}{\varepsilon^2}$.

Now, let $G' = \left\{j \mid d_j \geq \frac{20 \ln n}{\varepsilon^2}\right\}$. We know that, for each $j \in G'$, it holds that $|S_j| = (1 \pm O(\varepsilon)) \cdot d_j$ and the number of $(L+1)$-certifying elements in S_j is at least $(1 - O(\varepsilon)) \cdot d_j$.

Now consider the generic iteration K of Algorithm 1 (or, of the classical greedy algorithm) . Suppose that it brings in the set S_k^*. Suppose furthermore, that it produces a gain γ satisfying $\gamma \geq \frac{20 \ln n}{\varepsilon^2}$. Then, since the gains are decreasing, we will have that $|S_1^*|, |S_2^*|, \ldots, |S_k^*| \geq \gamma$, and therefore each of them contains at least $(1 - O(\varepsilon)) \cdot \gamma$ many $(L+1)$-certifying elements. Since $L < \gamma$, this implies that we can choose $\ell_1, \ldots, \ell_{K-1} \leq \varepsilon\gamma$ in Theorem 1.

The decreasing property of the gains guarantees that the covering produced by greedy has cardinality at least $\gamma \cdot K$. Theorem 1 guarantees that the dual has value at most equal to the covering produced by greedy plus $(K-1) \cdot \varepsilon\gamma$. It follows that Algorithm 1 can return, and certify, a $(1 - O(\varepsilon))$-approximation. □

The interpretation of this result is essentially the following: under the conditions stated in the Lemma, the greedy algorithm will provide a very good approximation as long as sufficiently many items are brought in at every step — that is, as long as $\gamma = \Omega(\ln n)$. One of the key properties used in the proof is that, under the conditions in the lemma, every "large" set S contains *many items* that, excluding S, are only part of "small" sets — these elements will then be γ-certifying.

A fair point to make is that our instances are not "random". Nonetheless, we think that this result highlights some simple properties (which are sufficient for Theorem 1 to certify a good approx-

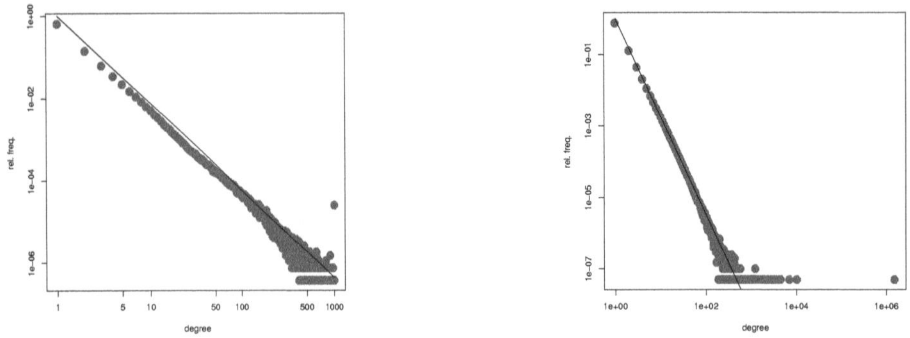

Figure 1: Plot in loglog-scale of the q-distribution (left) and d-distribution (right) of one of our largest datasets, and the corresponding power-law curve (with the exponent obtained by `plfit`). Note that in this example $k = 1\,000$, which caps the q-degrees (because a query cannot appear in more than $1\,000$ web pages).

imation) that are shared by real instances and random ones. This result is intended as a partial explanation of the surprisingly high quality of the greedy approximation.

7. EXPERIMENTAL RESULTS

Description of the datasets.

The bulk of our experiments involved four samples taken from the query logs of the Yahoo! search engine, covering different time periods, from few hours to many months. For each of the four query logs, we considered all (query,URL) pairs that corresponded to a click (the so-called click graph [12]). In order to reduce at the same time the size of the dataset and the level of noise, we performed the following cleaning operations: (i) we did not consider queries submitted less than c times, with $c \in \{5, 10, 20\}$; (ii) we did not consider (query, URL) pairs appearing less than f times, with $f \in \{5, 10, 20\}$; (iii) of the remaining pairs, for each query we only considered the (at most) top k URLs that were clicked most frequently for that query, with $k \in \{10, 50, 100, 1000\}$.

As a result, we worked on 144 click graphs, with a number of queries ranging from $10,935$ to $8,730,941$, and a number of URLs ranging from $15,393$ to $19,990,574$. The graphs were produced using Hadoop (from the distributed HFS containing the query logs) and were then compressed using WebGraph [6]: the largest of them (the one relative to a whole semester, with $c = f = 5$ and $k = 1\,000$) required 814 MB of storage.

To check the general applicability of our result we have also run our algorithm on a Twitter based instance (which we obtained from `http://an.kaist.ac.kr/traces/WWW2010.html`.) This Twitter social graph was translated into a MAXCOVER instance by creating one element, and one set, for each user account. The set S_u of user u contained u and all the users followed by u. Since the graph consists of more than 41M nodes and 2.5B edges, we obtained more than 41M elements and more than 41M sets. The sum of the cardinalities of these sets exceeded 2.5B.

Degree distributions.

For each of the click-graphs dataset, we computed the q- and d-distributions; recall that the d-distribution is the distribution on the sizes of the sets (*i.e.*, of the number of queries related to a specific clicked URL), whereas the q-distribution is the distribution of the number of sets in which an item appears (*i.e.*, of the number of URLs that were clicked for a specific query): because of the way data were filtered, the q-distribution is capped by k (no query will ever appear in more than k sets), whereas there is no upper bound on the largest possible value appearing in the d-distribution.

	min	1st q.	median	mean	3rd q.	max
q-degrees	1.991	2.090	2.124	2.141	2.180	2.398
d-degrees	2.571	2.837	2.892	2.937	2.982	3.258

Table 1: Statistics of the exponents of the power-law distributions for the graphs corresponding to our 144 datasets.

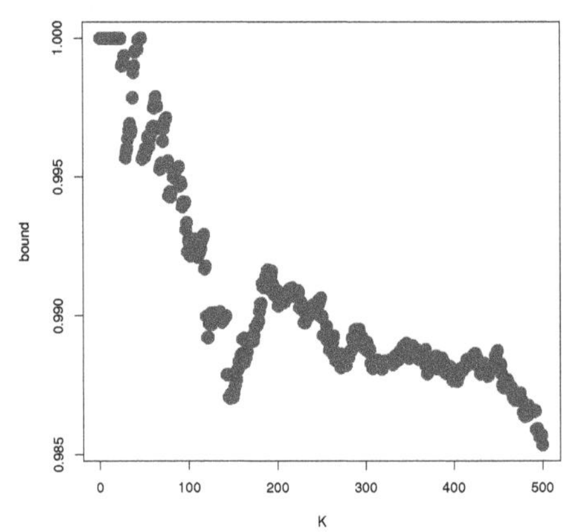

Figure 2: Bound output by Algorithm 1 for $K = 1, \ldots, 500$ on the largest of our click-graph datasets.

For every degree distribution, we used the techniques of [10] (as implemented in the `plfit` tool) to fit them to a power-law and to estimate the corresponding exponent. An example is given in Figure 1 and the statistics for all the exponents of the two distributions are reported in Table 1.

Running algorithm 1.

We ran the first 500 iterations of the certifying greedy algorithm (with $K = 1, \ldots, 500$) on each dataset, keeping track of the solution found and of the bound on its optimality, as produced by the algorithm. The running time was about 29 ms per iteration on an Intel Xeon CPU X5660 at 2.80GHz: this datum is averaged across 1000 iterations and includes the pre-processing time.

The overall behavior observed is the same across all the click-graph datasets, and it is drawn in Figure 2 for our largest dataset; the bound with $K = 500$ is still 0.9853, which means $< 2\%$ with respect to the optimum.

Independently on the choice of the parameters (c, f and k), the bound on the error for the largest dataset was never larger than 2%

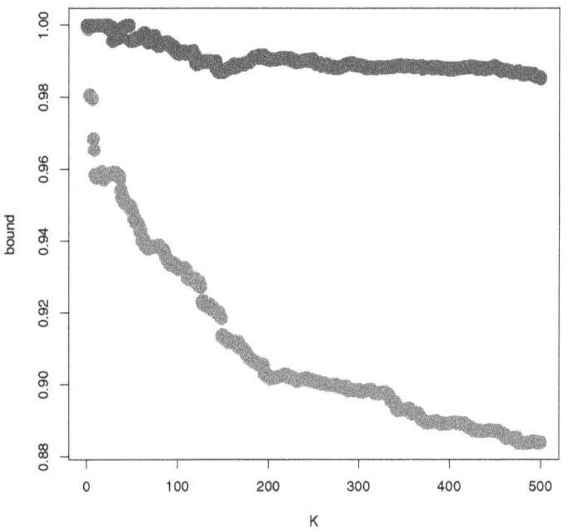

Figure 3: In blue, the bound output by Algorithm 1 for $K = 1, \dots, 500$ on the largest of our click-graph datasets; in red, the trivial bound.

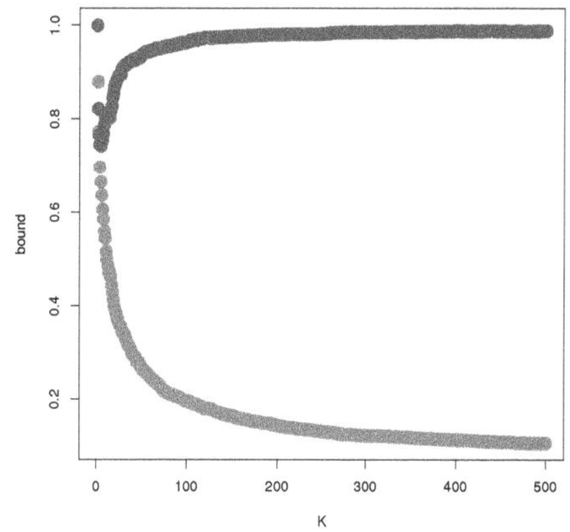

Figure 4: In blue, the bound output by Algorithm 1 on our Twitter dataset; in red, the trivial bound.

for all $K = 1, \dots, 500$. It is generally observed that increasing c and f or decreasing k leads to larger error bounds, simply because it makes the sets smaller: this is true across all datasets.

We compared our bound on the approximation ratio with a baseline (the ratio between the number of items covered by the greedy solution and the sum of the cardinalities of the sets selected). The baseline bound on the largest dataset is much weaker than our bound (the baseline gives ratios between 0.883 and 0.933): the comparison is shown in Figure 3.

It is worth noting that the impact of c introduces a different bias on the queries considered depending on the size of the time slot: on a one-hour log, disregarding queries appearing less than, say, 20 times means focussing on "hot topics", whereas the same value of c would produce many tail queries on a six-month log. The fact that there is no substantial difference in the results for the same value of c across different datasets means that our technique is not sensible to this bias. Moreover, we expect that considering even very infrequent queries (e.g., $c = 1$) might only further reduce the error bounds.

Interestingly our algorithm has a different behavior on the Twitter-based dataset (Figure 4): the guaranteed approximation ratio increases with K (and it converges quickly to $\approx 99\%$) — our click-graph datasets, instead, have a guaranteed approximation ratio that decreases with K. In both cases, though, our algorithm guarantees approximation ratios very close to 1. It would be extremely interesting to see if our algorithm still guarantees very good approximation ratios on other large-scale web, social or networking datasets.

The tightness of our bound.

The bound produced by the algorithm seems to witness that the greedy algorithm behaves much better than expected, especially on large datasets, which is the case for web search; in fact, the real approximation ratio may be even *better* than that!

We have tested this hypothesis by explicitly solving the linear program (using the IBM `cplex` optimizer[7]) on (each of) the smallest datasets for $K = 1, \dots, 500$. We could not run it on larger datasets for performance-related reasons (solving the LP would have taken too much time, and too much memory).

We were surprised to observe that, in each of these test cases, the LP value was *at most 8 additive units more than* the value of the solution produced by greedy; moreover, in each test case, the approximation ratio was at least 99.79%. In many cases the two values did coincide, showing that greedy was in fact producing the best solution. We find this observation extremely appealing. We are still lacking a completely satisfying explanation of this phenomenon — we see Theorem 1 and Section 6 as just a first step in this direction.

Rewiring the datasets.

Since we are interested in the way the degree distributions influence the behavior of our algorithm, for each of the 144 datasets we produced two rewired variants: (i) *q-scrambling* (the web page cardinalities were kept unchanged, but the queries contained in each web page were chosen u.a.r.); (ii) *d-scrambling* (the numbers of web pages where each query appears were kept unchanged, but the actual web pages to which each query belongs were chosen u.a.r.). In other words, the two variants are designed so that one of the two degree distributions matches the one summarized in Table 1 whereas the other becomes uniform.

We then ran Algorithm 1 on the scrambled datasets; the outcome was more or less the same for all cases: (i) On the q-scrambled datasets (same cardinalities but items chosen u.a.r.), the bound produced by the algorithm is extremely good for all $K = 1, \dots, 500$: essentially the greedy algorithm produces the *optimal solution* in all cases. Intuitively, the q-scrambled dataset resembles the *best possible world*: the largest sets are disjoint with high probability, and choosing the K largest ones provides a solution that is very close to the optimum. (ii) On the d-scrambled datasets (items have the same degrees but are assigned to sets u.a.r.), greedy performs much worse than in the original datasets. An intuitive reason is that sets are much smaller than in the original case, and therefore it is much harder for Algorithm 1 to find certifying elements.

Ratio of coverage.

One important aspect that we have not yet discussed is how many queries of the universe we are, in fact, covering. We observe that the number of queries covered at $K = 500$ is negligible (only 2.5% in our largest dataset). In Figure 5, we present Algorithm 1's results on our largest dataset for K up to $140,000$.

Recall that Algorithm 1 serves two complementary needs. First, it tries to select K web pages to maximize the number of queries covered. Second, it gives an upper bound on the maximum number of queries that can be covered with K web pages. Figure 5 shows the algorithm performance in these two tasks: the blue line repre-

[7] `http://www-01.ibm.com/software/commerce/optimization/cplex-optimizer/`

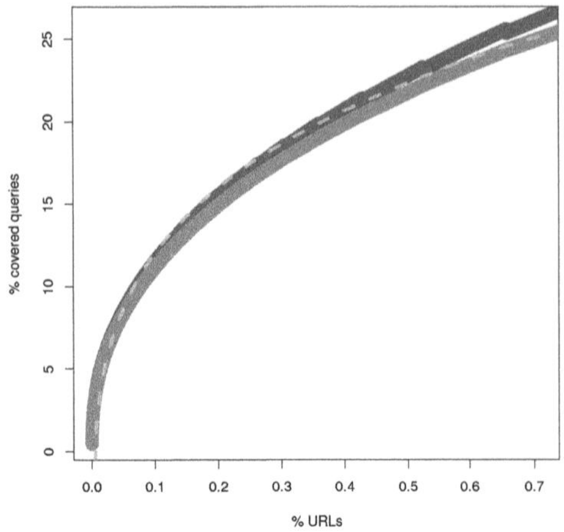

Figure 5: The fraction of queries (red) covered by Algorithm 1 with respect to the fraction of web pages on the largest of our datasets; for comparison, we show the upper bound on the fraction (blue) produced by Theorem 1, as well as the polynomial model (dashed).

sents the fraction of queries that Algorithm 1 could cover with a given K, while the red line represents the aforementioned upper bound.

For concreteness we mention that, for our largest dataset, 24.5% of the query universe can be covered with just less of 140,000 URLs (0.7% of the URLs!), and that it is impossible to cover the same percentage with fewer than 123,000 URLs. We also observe that the MaxCover approximation that Algorithm 1 can certify is quite good even at $K \approx 140,000$. At such a large K, the algorithm certifies an approximation of 0.95; the trivial sum-bound certificate at the same K would not be better than 0.74. In fact, up to $K \approx 360,000$ (1.8%) we can ensure that the solution is almost optimal.

If we fit a power law to the increments of unique queries covered by Algorithm 1 in Figure 5, we obtain an exponent of -0.76. This is not surprising, because usually the interaction of power laws gives another power law. In fact, this exponent is very close to the difference in the power law exponents of the q- and d-sequences. Hence, we fitted a model of the form $\alpha \cdot x^{0.24} - \beta$ to the coverage curve obtaining an error of just $5.7 \cdot 10^{-3}$ for $\alpha = 1.148$ and $\beta = 0.098$ (see dashed line in Figure 5). Notice that for $x = 1$ we obtain a coverage of 1.05! (a perfect model should have coverage 1). From this model we can estimate a coverage of 50% of the queries with just 6.6% of the URLs and a coverage of 87% when using 50% of the web pages (these estimations are pessimistic as the model grows slower than the real curve). This is quite remarkable considering that typically half of distinct queries are singletons (that is, they appear only once in the query log) and their overall volume is significant (say 25%).

8. CONCLUSIONS AND FUTURE WORK

We have shown that we can find an almost optimal small set of web pages that can cover a large subset of all possible unique queries — moreover, our algorithmic guarantee seems to hold even for other large-scale (non web page-related) data settings. We plan to extend our results to the weighted version (that is, to maximize the coverage of the query volume), and to other kinds of datasets. We believe that maximizing this case might be a harder task than our original one. However, the coverage results will be better. We expect the coverage to be at least 50% of the query volume with 5% of the web pages, because most important URLs are good answers for a large fraction of the query volume (*e.g.*, see [3]). We also plan to change the definition of relevance (*e.g.*, use all top answers and not only the clicked pages or weight the clicked pages by the dwell time to control for novelty and spam) and of coverage (*e.g.*, a query is covered only if the index contains at least t relevant pages).

Our results partly depend on a double power-law, one for queries and another for web pages. The power law of web pages do depend on the ranking function of the search engine. However, apart from simple ranking schemes such as PageRank that can be shown to be a power law, there is little on the study of score distributions for ranking functions (*e.g.*, see [18]). Nevertheless, in practice ranking score distributions should follow a power law, as it happens in typical features used for ranking functions, such as terms or clicks frequencies. Although in practice web indices contain hundreds of billions of pages, our findings show that our approach is invariant to scale (the results are similar from thousands to tens of millions), as expected given the power-law distributions involved. Hence, we believe that our results can be extrapolated to hundreds and billions of web pages if we have the right power law exponents of the distributions involved.

Another issue is that the query distribution of web search engines is not static. However, the changes in time are small. In fact, in [3] they find that the pairwise correlation among all possible 3-week periods of the query distribution for 15-weeks was always over 99.5%. This implies that daily or weekly updates to the set of essential web pages should be enough. These updates are not only necessary due to changes in the query stream, but also because in practice there will be changes in the set of web pages available for indexing. Hence, our approach can be another way to define periodical updates to the index of a web search engine.

Regarding the secondary index problem, we can design a crawling algorithm driven by the query distribution, as mentioned in [2]. This approach would gather relevant pages for the secondary index and should also improve the pool of pages available for selecting the essential web pages for the main index.

The problem we have solved not only can be used to reduce the size of the main index of a web search engine. Indeed, if we can predict the query intention, we could use the click knowledge of the overall web search engine to build optimized indices for vertical search engines tailored to a particular intention. The same idea applies to other query subsets such as queries coming from a given country or language. In these vertical search engines we can have tailored ranking functions as well as tailored user experiences.

Other problems where our results can be used include:

- Optimize the selection of the cache of web pages in web search engines, if there are limited memory resources.
- Optimizing the indexed web pages in each local server of a distributed web search architecture given finite memory resources [4, Section 10.6.2].
- Optimizing document caching in a distributed web search scheme [4, Section 11.4.5] where each local server caches a small set of documents (in principle, just the most frequently accessed) to reduce the query search time.
- Optimizing the indexed documents in any P2P distributed search scheme, given the local resources defined by every peer [4, Section 10.8].

9. REFERENCES

[1] A. Anagnostopoulos, L. Becchetti, S. Leonardi, I. Mele, and P. Sankowski. Stochastic Query Covering. In *Proc. of WSDM 2011*, pages 725–734, 2011. ACM.

[2] R. Baeza-Yates. Information retrieval in the web: beyond current search engines. *Int. J. Approx. Reasoning*, 34(2-3):97–104, 2003.

[3] R. Baeza-Yates, A. Gionis, F. Junqueira, V. Murdock, V. Plachouras, and F. Silvestri. Design trade-offs for search engine caching. *TWEB*, 2(4), 2008.

[4] R. Baeza-Yates and B. Ribeiro-Neto. *Modern Information Retrieval: The Concepts and Technology Behind Search.* Addison-Wesley, Harlow, UK, second edition, 2011.

[5] R. Baeza-Yates, V. Murdock, and C. Hauff. Efficiency trade-offs in two-tier web search systems. In *Proc. of SIGIR 2009*, pages 163–170, 2009.

[6] P. Boldi and S. Vigna. The WebGraph framework I: Compression techniques. In *Proc. of WWW 2004*, pages 595–601, Manhattan, USA, 2004. ACM Press.

[7] D. Carmel, D. Cohen, R. Fagin, E. Farchi, M. Herscovici, Y. S. Maarek, and A. Soffer. Static index pruning for information retrieval systems. In *Proc. of SIGIR 2001*, pages 43–50, 2001.

[8] W. Chen, Y. Wang, and S. Yang. Efficient influence maximization in social networks. In *Proc. of KDD 2009*, pages 199–208, New York, NY, USA, 2009. ACM.

[9] F. Chierichetti, R. Kumar, and A. Tomkins. Max-cover in map-reduce. In *Proc. of WWW 2010*, pages 231–240, New York, NY, USA, 2010. ACM.

[10] A. Clauset, C. R. Shalizi, and M. E. J. Newman. Power-law distributions in empirical data. *SIAM Rev.*, 51(4):661–703, Nov. 2009.

[11] R. Cohen and L. Katzir. The generalized maximum coverage problem. *Inf. Process. Lett.*, 108(1):15–22, 2008.

[12] N. Craswell and M. Szummer. Random walks on the click graph. In *Proc. of SIGIR 2007*, pages 239–246, New York, NY, USA, 2007. ACM.

[13] A. Dasgupta, A. Ghosh, R. Kumar, C. Olston, S. Pandey, and A. Tomkins. The discoverability of the web. In *Proc. of WWW 2007*, pages 421–430, New York, NY, USA, 2007. ACM.

[14] M. R. Garey and D. S. Johnson. *Computers and Intractability: A Guide to the Theory of NP-Completeness.* W. H. Freeman & Co., New York, NY, USA, 1979.

[15] D. S. Hochbaum. Approximating covering and packing problems: set cover, vertex cover, independent set, and related problems. In D. S. Hochbaum, editor, *Approximation algorithms for NP-hard problems*, pages 94–143. PWS Publishing Co., Boston, MA, USA, 1997.

[16] D. Kempe, J. Kleinberg, and E. Tardos. Maximizing the spread of influence through a social network. In *Proc. of KDD 2003*, pages 137–146, New York, NY, USA, 2003. ACM.

[17] K.M. Risvik, Y. Aasheim, and M. Lidal. Multi-Tier Architecture for Web Search Engines. In *Proc. of LA-WEB '03*, pages 132–, 2003. IEEE.

[18] S. Robertson. On score distributions and relevance. In *29th European Conference on IR Research*, LNCS, pages 40–51, Rome, Italy, April 2007. Springer.

[19] G. Skobeltsyn, F. Junqueira, V. Plachouras, and R. Baeza-Yates. Resin: a combination of results caching and index pruning for high-performance web search engines. In *SIGIR*, pages 131–138, 2008.

[20] A. Swaminathan, C. V. Mathew, and D. Kirovski. Essential pages. In *Proceedings of the 2009 IEEE/WIC/ACM International Joint Conference on Web Intelligence and Intelligent Agent Technology - Volume 01*, WI-IAT '09, pages 173–182, Washington, DC, USA, 2009. IEEE Computer Society.

[21] V. V. Vazirani. *Approximation algorithms.* Springer-Verlag New York, Inc., New York, NY, USA, 2001.

Design and Analysis of Benchmarking Experiments for Distributed Internet Services

Eytan Bakshy
Facebook
Menlo Park, CA
eytan@fb.com

Eitan Frachtenberg
Facebook
Menlo Park, CA
eitan@frachtenberg.org

ABSTRACT

The successful development and deployment of large-scale Internet services depends critically on performance. Even small regressions in processing time can translate directly into significant energy and user experience costs. Despite the widespread use of distributed server infrastructure (e.g., in cloud computing and Web services), there is little research on how to benchmark such systems to obtain valid and precise inferences with minimal data collection costs. Correctly A/B testing distributed Internet services can be surprisingly difficult because interdependencies between user requests (e.g., for search results, social media streams, photos) and host servers violate assumptions required by standard statistical tests.

We develop statistical models of distributed Internet service performance based on data from Perflab, a production system used at Facebook which vets thousands of changes to the company's codebase each day. We show how these models can be used to understand the tradeoffs between different benchmarking routines, and what factors must be taken into account when performing statistical tests. Using simulations and empirical data from Perflab, we validate our theoretical results, and provide easy-to-implement guidelines for designing and analyzing such benchmarks.

Keywords

A/B testing; benchmarking; cloud computing; crossed random effects; bootstrapping

Categories and Subject Descriptors

G.3 [**Probability and Statistics**]: Experimental Design

1. INTRODUCTION

Benchmarking experiments are used extensively at Facebook and other Internet companies to detect performance regressions and bugs, as well as to optimize the performance of existing infrastructure and backend services. They often involve testing various code paths with one or more users on multiple hosts. This introduces multiple sources of variability: each user request may involve different amounts of computation because results are dynamically customized to their own data. The amount of data varies from user to user and often follows heavy-tailed distributions for quantities such as friend count, feed stories, and search matches [2].

Furthermore, different users and requests engage different code paths based on their data, and can be affected differently by just-in-time (JIT) compilation and caching. User-based benchmarks therefore must take into account a good mix of both service endpoints and users making the requests, in order to capture the broad range of performance issues that may arise in production settings.

An additional source of variability comes from benchmarking on multiple hosts, as is common for cloud and Web-based services. Testing in a distributed environment is often necessary due to engineering or time constraints, and can even improve the representativeness of the overall performance data, because the production environment is also distributed. But each host has its own performance characteristics, which can also vary over time. The performance of computer architectures has grown increasingly nondeterministic over the years, and performance innovations often come at a cost of lower predictability. Examples include: dynamic frequency scaling and sleep states; adaptive caching, branch prediction, and memory prefetching; and modular, individual hardware components comprising the system with their own variance [5, 16].

Our research addresses challenges inherent to any benchmarking system which tests user traffic on a distributed set of hosts. Motivated by problems encountered in the development of Perflab [14], an automated system responsible for A/B testing hundreds of code changes every day at Facebook, we develop statistical models of user-based, distributed benchmarking experiments. These models help us address real-life challenges that arise in a production benchmarking system, including high variability in performance tests, and high rates of false positives in detecting performance regressions.

Our paper is organized as follows. Using data from our production benchmarking system, we motivate the use of statistical concepts, including two-stage sampling, dependence, and uncertainty (Section 3). With this framework, we develop a statistical model that allows us to formally evaluate the consequences of how known sources of variation — requests and hosts — on the precision of different experimental designs of distributed benchmarks (Section 4). These variance expressions for each design also informs how statistical tests should be computed. Finally, we propose and evaluate a bootstrapping procedure in Section 5 which shows good performance both in our simulations and production tests.

WWW 2015, May 18–22, 2015, Florence, Italy.
ACM 978-1-4503-3469-3/15/05
http://dx.doi.org/10.1145/2736277.2741082.

2. PROBLEM DESCRIPTION

We often want to make changes to software—a new user interface, a feature, a ranking model, a retrieval system, or virtual host—and need to know how each change affects performance metrics such as computation time or network load. This goal is typically accomplished by directing a subset of user traffic to different machines (hosts) running different versions of software and comparing their performance. This scheme poses a number of challenges that affect our ability to detect statistically significant differences, both with respect to Type I errors—a "false positive" where two versions are deemed to have different performance when in fact they don't, and Type II errors—an inability to detect significant differences where they do exist. These problems can result in financial loss, wasted engineering time, and misallocation of resources.

As mentioned earlier, A/B testing is challenging both from the perspective of reducing the variability in results, and from the perspective of statistical inference. Performance can vary significantly due to many factors, including characteristics of user requests, machines, and compilation. Experiments not designed to account for these sources of variation can obscure performance reversions. Furthermore, methods for computing confidence intervals for user-based benchmarking experiments which do not take into account these sources of variation can result in high false-positive rates.

2.1 Design goals

When designing an experiment to detect performance reversions, we strive to accomplish three main goals: (1) Representativeness: we wish to produce performance estimates that are valid (reflecting performance for the production use case), take samples from a representative subset of test cases, and generalize well to the test cases that weren't sampled; (2) Precision: performance estimates should be fine-grained enough to discern even small effects, per our tolerance limits; (3) Economy: estimates should be obtained with minimal cost (measured in wall time), subject to resource constraints.

In short, we wish to design a representative experiment that minimizes both the number of observations and the variance of the results. To simplify, we consider a single endpoint or service, and use the terms "request", "query", and "user" interchangeably.[1]

2.2 Testing environment

To motivate our model, as well as validate our results empirically, we discuss Facebook's in-house benchmarking system, Perflab [14]. Perflab can assess the performance impact of new code without actually installing it on the servers used by real users. This enables developers to use Perflab as part of their testing sequence even before they commit code. Moreover, Perflab is used to automatically check all code committed into the code repository, to uncover both logic and performance problems. Even small performance issues need to be monitored and corrected continuously, because if they are left to accumulate they can quickly lead to capacity problems and unnecessary expenditure on additional infrastructure. Problems uncovered by Perflab or other tests that cannot be resolved within a short time may cause the code revision to be removed from the push and delayed to a subsequent push, after the problems are resolved.

A Perflab experiment is started by defining two versions of the software/environment (which can be identical for an "A/A test"). Perflab reserves a set of hosts to run either version, and prepares them for a batch of requests by restarting them and flushing the caches of the backend services they rely on (which are copied and isolated from the production environment, to ensure Perflab has no side effects). The workload is selected as a representative subset of endpoints and users from a previous sample of live traffic. It is replayed repeatedly and concurrently at the systems under tests, which queue up the requests so that the system is under a relatively constant, near-saturation load, to represent a realistically high production load. This continues until we get the required number of observations, but we discard a number of initial observations ("warm-up" period) and final observations ("cool-down" period). This range was determined empirically by analyzing the autocorrelation function [13] for individual requests as a function of repetition number. Perflab then resets the hosts, swaps software versions so that hosts previously running version A now run version B and vice-versa, and reruns the experiment to collect more observations.

For each observation, we collect all the metrics of interest, which include: CPU time and instructions; database/key-value fetches and bandwidth; memory use; HTML size; and various others. These metrics detect not only performance changes, as in CPU time and instructions, but can also detect bugs. For example, a sharp drop in the number of database fetches (for a given user and endpoint) between two software versions is more often than not an undesired side effect and an indication of a faulty code path, rather than a miraculous performance improvement, since the underlying user data hasn't changed between versions.

[1]We discuss how our approach can be generalized to multiple endpoints in Section 7.

3. STATISTICS OF USER-BASED BENCHMARKS

In order to understand how best to design user-based benchmarks, we must first consider how to capture (sample) metrics over a population of requests. We begin by discussing the relationship between sampling theory and data collection for benchmarks. This leads us to confront sources of variability—first from requests, and then from hosts. We conclude this section with a very general model that brings these aspects together, and serves as the basis for the formal analysis of experimental designs for distributed benchmarks involving user traffic.

3.1 Sampling

3.1.1 Two-stage sampling of user requests

We wish to estimate the average performance of a given version of software, and do so by sending requests (e.g., loading a particular endpoint for various users) to a service, and measuring the sample average $\bar{y}$, for some outcome y_i for each observation. Our certainty about the true average value $\bar{Y}$ of the complete distribution Y increases with the number of observations. If each observations of Y is independent and identically distributed (iid), then the *standard error* of for our estimate of $\bar{Y}$ is $\text{SE}_{\text{iid}} = s/\sqrt{N}$, where N is the number of observations, and s is the sample standard deviation of our observed y_is. One can use the standard error to obtain the confidence interval for $\bar{Y}$ at significance level α by computing $\bar{y} \pm \Phi^{-1}(1-\alpha/2)\text{SE}$, where Φ^{-1} is the inverse cumulative distribution of the standard normal. For example, the 95% confidence interval for $\bar{Y}$ can be computed as $\bar{y} \pm 1.96\text{SE}$.

Often times data collected from benchmarks involving user traffic is not iid. For example, if we repeat requests for users multiple times, the observations may be clustered along certain values. Figure 1 shows how this kind of clustering occurs with respect to CPU time[2] for requests fulfilled to a heavily trafficked endpoint at Facebook. Here, we see 300 repetitions for 4, 16, and 256 different requests (recall that by different requests, we are referring to different users for a fixed endpoint). CPU time is distributed approximately

[2]Because relative performance is easier to reason about than absolute performance in this context, all outcomes in this paper are standardized, so that for any particular benchmark for an endpoint, the grand mean is subtracted from the outcome and then divided by the standard deviation.

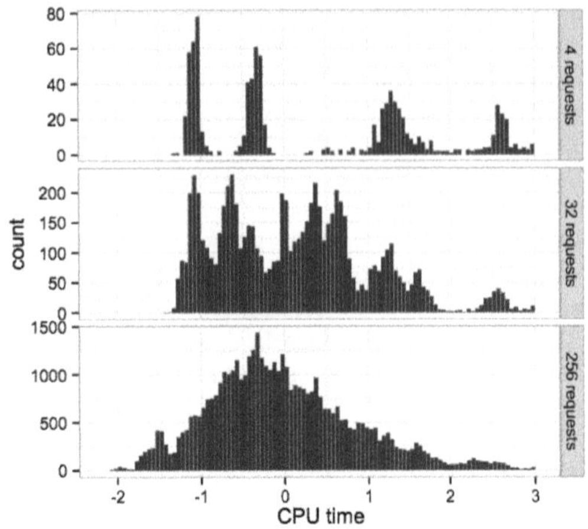

Figure 1: Clustering in the distribution of CPU times for requests. Panels correspond to different numbers of requests. Requests are repeated 300 times.

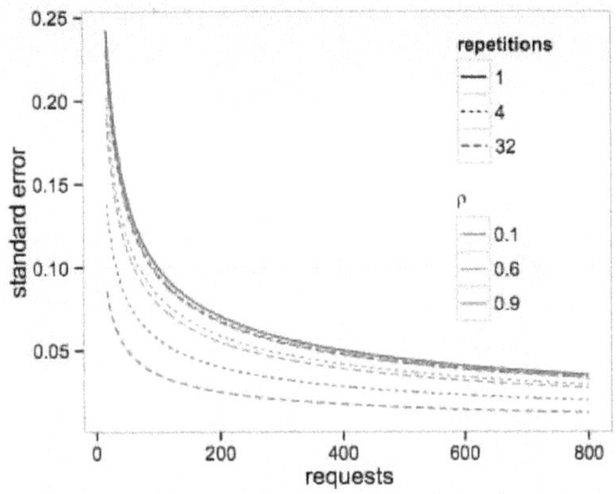

Figure 2: Standard error for clustered data (e.g., requests) as a function of the number of requests and repetitions for different intra-class correlation coefficients, ρ. Multiple repeated observations of the same request have little effect on the SE when ρ is large.

normally for any given request, but the amount of variability within a single request is much smaller than the overall variability between requests. When hundreds of different requests are mixed in, in fact, it's difficult to tell that this aggregate distribution is really the mixture of many, approximately normally distributed clusters.

If observations are clustered in some way (as in Figure 1), the effective sample size could be much smaller than the total number of observations. Measurements for the same request tend to be correlated, such that e.g., the execution time for requests for the same user are more similar to one another than requests related to different users. This is captured by the intra-class correlation coefficient (*ICC*) ρ, which is the ratio of between-cluster variation to total variation [28]:

$$\rho = \frac{\sigma_\alpha^2}{\sigma_\alpha^2 + \sigma_\varepsilon^2},$$

where σ_α is the standard deviation of the request effect and σ_ε is the standard deviation of the measurement noise. If ρ is close to 1, then repeated observations for the same request are nearly identical, and when it is close to 0, there is little relation between requests. It is easy to see that if most of the variability occurs between clusters, rather than within clusters (high ρ), additional repeated measurements for the same cluster do not help with obtaining a good estimate of the mean of Y, $\bar{Y}$. This idea is captured by the design effect [10], $d_{\text{eff}} = (1 + (T - 1)\rho)$, which is the ratio of the variance of the clustered sample (e.g., multiple samples from the same request) to the simple random sample (e.g., random samples of multiple independent requests), where T is the number of times each request is repeated.

Under sampling designs where we may choose both the number of requests R, and repetitions T, the standard error is instead:

$$\text{SE}_{\text{clust}} = \sigma / \sqrt{\frac{1}{RT}(1 + (T - 1)\rho)} \qquad (1)$$

such that additional repetitions only reduce the standard error of our estimate if ρ is small. Figure 2 shows the relationship between the standard error and R for small and large vales of ρ. For most of the top endpoints benchmarked at Facebook—including news feed loads and search queries—nearly all endpoints have values of ρ between 0.8 and 0.97. In other words, from our experience with user traffic, *mere repetition of requests is not an effective means of increasing precision when the intraclass correlation, ρ, is large.*

3.1.2 Sampling on a budget

Exploring the tradeoffs between collecting more requests vs. more repetitions needs to take into account not only the value of ρ but also the costs of switching requests. For example, it is often necessary to first "warm up" a virtual host or cache to reduce temporal effects (e.g., serial autocorrelation) [16] to get accurate estimates for an effect. That is, the fixed cost required to sample a request is often much greater than it is to gain additional repetitions. In situations in which ρ is small, it may be useful to consider larger numbers of repetitions per request. There is also an additional fixed cost S_f to set up an experiment (or a "batch"), which includes resetting the hardware and software as necessary and waiting for the runtime systems to warm up.

By considering the costs for each stage of a benchmarking routine, one can minimize the standard error. For example, if there is a fixed cost C_f for benchmarking a single request, a marginal cost for an additional repetition of a request, C_m, and an available budget, B, one could minimize Eq. 1 subject to the constraint that S_f + $R(C_f + TC_m) \leq B$.

3.2 Models of distributed benchmarks

While benchmarking on a single host is simple enough, we are often constrained to run benchmarks in a short period of time, which can be difficult to accomplish on only one host. Facebook, for example, runs automated performance tests on every single code commit to its main site, thousands of times a day [14]. It is therefore imperative to conduct benchmarks in parallel on multiple hosts. Using multiple hosts also has the benefit of surfacing performance issues that may affect one host and not another, for further investigation.[3] But multiple hosts also introduce new sources of variability, which we model statistically in the following sections.

To motivate and illustrate these models, let us look at an example of empirical data from a Perflab A/A benchmark (Figure 3). Two requests (corresponding to service queries for two distinct users under the same software version) are repeated across two different machines in two batches, running thirty times on each. For each batch, the software on the hosts was restarted, and caches and JIT environments were warmed up. The observations correspond to CPU time measured for an endpoint running under a PHP vir-

[3]Such investigation sometimes leads to identifying faulty systems in the benchmarking environment, but can also reveal unintended consequences of the software interacting with different subsystems.

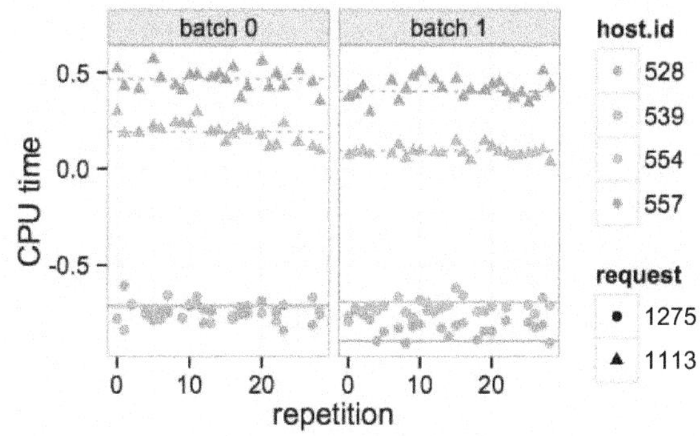

Figure 3: CPU time for two requests executed over 30 repetitions, executed on two hosts over two different batches. Each shape represents a different request, and each color represents a different host. Panels correspond to different batches. Lines represent a model fit based on Eq. 3.

tual machine. Note that each repetition of the same request on the same machine in the same batch is relatively similar and has few time trends. Furthermore, the between-request variability (circle vs. square shapes) tends to be greater than the per-machine variability (e.g., the green vs purple dots). Between-batch effects appear to be similar in size to the noise.

3.2.1 Random effects formulation

An observation from a benchmark can be thought of as being generated by several independent effects. In the simplest case, we could think of a single observation (e.g., CPU time) for some particular endpoint or service as having some average value (e.g., 500ms), plus some shift due to the user involved in the request (e.g., +500ms for a user with many friends), plus a shift due to the host executing the request (e.g., -200ms for a faster host), plus some random noise. This formulation is referred to as a crossed random effects model, and we refer to host and request-level shifts as a *random effects* [3, 26] or levels [28].

Formally, we can denote the request corresponding to an observation i as $r[i]$, and the host corresponding to i as $h[i]$. In the equation below, we denote the random effects (random variables) for requests, hosts, and noise for each observation i as $\alpha_{r[i]}$, $\beta_{h[i]}$, and ε_i, respectively. The mean value is given by μ. f denotes a transformation (a "link function"). For additive models, f is simply the identity function, but for multiplicative models (e.g., each effect induces a certain percent increase or decrease in performance), f may be the exponential function[4], $exp(\cdot)$:

$$Y_i = f(\mu + \alpha_{r[i]} + \beta_{h[i]} + \varepsilon_i)$$

Under the heterogeneous random effects model [26], each request and host can have its own variance. This model can be complex to manipulate analytically, and difficult to estimate in practice, so one common approach is to instead assume that random effects for requests or hosts are drawn from the same distribution.

Homogeneous random effects model for a single batch. Under this model, random effects for hosts and requests are respectively drawn from a common distribution.

$$Y_i = \mu + \alpha_{r[i]} + \beta_{h[i]} + \varepsilon_i$$
$$\alpha_r \sim \mathcal{N}(0, \sigma_\alpha^2), \quad \beta_h \sim \mathcal{N}(0, \sigma_\beta^2), \quad \varepsilon_i \sim \mathcal{N}(0, \sigma_\varepsilon^2). \quad (2)$$

In this homogenous random effects model each request has a constant effect, which is sampled from some common normal distribution, $\mathcal{N}(0, \sigma_\alpha^2)$. Any variability from the same request on the same host is independent of the request.

Homogeneous random effects model for multiple batches. Modern runtime environments are non-deterministic and for various reasons, restarting a service may cause the characteristic performance of hosts or requests to deviate slightly. For example, the dynamic request order and mix can vary and affect the code paths that the JIT compiles and keeps in cache. This can be specified by additional batch-level effects for hosts and requests. We model this behavior as follows: each time a service is initialized, we draw a batch effect for each request, $\gamma_{r[i],b[i]} \sim \mathcal{N}(0, \sigma_\gamma)$, and similarly for each host, $\eta_{h[i],b[i]} \sim \mathcal{N}(0, \sigma_\eta)$. That is, each time a host is restarted in some way (a new "batch"), there is some additional noise introduced that remains constant throughout the execution of the batch, either pertaining to the host or the request. Note that per-request and per-host batch effects are independent from batch to batch[5], similar to how ε is independent between observations:

$$Y_i = \mu + \alpha_{r[i]} + \beta_{h[i]} + \gamma_{r[i],b[i]} + \eta_{h[i],b[i]} + \varepsilon_i$$
$$\alpha_r \sim \mathcal{N}(0, \sigma_\alpha^2), \quad \beta_h \sim \mathcal{N}(0, \sigma_\beta^2),$$
$$\gamma_{r,b} \sim \mathcal{N}(0, \sigma_\gamma^2), \quad \eta_{h,b} \sim \mathcal{N}(0, \sigma_\eta^2), \quad \varepsilon_i \sim \mathcal{N}(0, \sigma_\varepsilon^2) \quad (3)$$

3.2.2 Estimation

How large are each of these effects in practice? We begin with some of observations from a real benchmark to illustrate the sources of variability, and then move on to estimating model parameters for several endpoints in production. Models such as Eq. 2 and Eq. 3 can be fit efficiently to benchmark data via restricted maximum likelihood estimation using off-the-shelf statistical packages, such as `lmer` in R. In Figure 3, the horizontal lines indicate the predicted values for each endpoint using the model from Eq. 3 fit to an A/A test (e.g., an experiment in which both versions have the same software) using `lmer`. In general, we find that the request-level random effects are much greater than the host level effects, which are similar in magnitude to the batch-level effects. We summarize estimates for top endpoints at Facebook in Table 1, and use them in subsequent sections to illustrate our analytical results.

endpoint	μ	σ_α	σ_β	σ_γ	σ_η	σ_ε
1	0.06	1.02	0.12	0.10	0.08	0.13
2	0.08	1.08	0.10	0.05	0.06	0.08
3	0.07	1.02	0.11	0.04	0.05	0.06
4	0.08	1.08	0.05	0.05	0.02	0.06
5	0.04	1.08	0.04	0.01	0.02	0.14

Table 1: Parameter estimates for the model in Eq. 3 for the five most trafficked endpoints benchmarked at Facebook.

4. EXPERIMENTAL DESIGN

Benchmarking experiments for Internet services are most commonly run to compare two different versions of software using a

[4]For the sake of simplicity we work with additive models, but it is often desirable to work with the multiplicative model, or equivalently $log(Y)$. The remaining results hold equally for the log-transformed outcomes.

[5]This formal assumption corresponds to no carryover effects from one batch to another [7]. As we describe in Section 2.2, the system we use in production is designed to eliminate carryover effects.

mix of requests and hosts (servers). How precisely we are able to measure differences can depend greatly on which requests are delivered to what machines, and what versions of the software those machines are running. In this section, we generalize the random effects model for multiple batches to include experimental comparisons, and derive expressions for how the standard error of experimental comparisons (i.e., the difference in means) depends on aspects of the experimental design. We then present four simple experimental designs that cover a range of benchmarking setups, including "live" benchmarks and carefully controlled experiments, and derive their standard errors. Finally, we will show how basic parameters, including the number of requests, hosts, and repetitions, affect the standard error of different designs.

4.1 Formulation

We treat the problem formally using the potential outcomes framework [24], in which we consider outcomes (e.g., CPU time) for an observation i (a request-host pair running within a particular batch), running under either version (the experimental condition), whose assignment is denoted by $D_i = 0$ or $D_i = 1$. We use $Y_i^{(1)}$ to denote the potential outcome of i under the treatment, and $Y_i^{(0)}$ for the control. Although we cannot simultaneously observe both potential outcomes for any particular i, we can compute the average treatment effect, $\delta = \mathbb{E}[Y_i^{(1)} - Y_i^{(0)}]$ because by linearity of expectation, it is equal to the difference in means $\mathbb{E}[Y_i^{(1)}] - \mathbb{E}[Y_i^{(0)}]$ across different populations when D_i is randomly assigned. In a benchmarking experiment, we identify δ by specifying a schedule of delivery of requests to hosts, along with hosts' assignments to conditions. The particulars of how this assignment procedure works is the experimental design, and it can substantially affect the precision with which we can estimate δ. We generalize the random effects model in Eq. 2 to include average treatment effects and treatment interactions:

$$\begin{gathered} Y_i^{(d)} = \mu^{(d)} + \alpha_{r[i]}^{(d)} + \beta_{h[i]}^{(d)} + \gamma_{r[i],b[i]} + \eta_{h[i],b[i]} + \varepsilon_i \\ \vec{\alpha}_r \sim \mathcal{N}(0, \Sigma_\alpha), \quad \vec{\beta}_h \sim \mathcal{N}(0, \Sigma_\beta), \\ \gamma_{r,b} \sim \mathcal{N}(0, \sigma_\gamma^2), \quad \eta_{h,b} \sim \mathcal{N}(0, \sigma_\eta^2), \quad \varepsilon_i \sim \mathcal{N}(0, \sigma_\varepsilon^2) \end{gathered} \tag{4}$$

Our goal therefore is to identify the true difference in means, $\delta = \mu^{(1)} - \mu^{(0)}$. Unfortunately, we can never observe δ directly, and instead must estimate it from data, with noise. Exactly how much noise there is depends on which hosts and requests are involved, the software versions, and how many batches are needed to run the experiment. More formally, we denote the number of observations for a particular request–host–batch tuple $\langle r, h, b\rangle$ running under the treatment condition d, by $n_{rhb}^{(d)}$. We express the total noise from requests, hosts, and residual error under each condition as:

$$\phi_R^{(d)} \equiv \sum_r \left[n_{r\bullet\bullet}^{(d)} \alpha_r^{(d)} + \sum_b n_{r\bullet b}^{(d)} \gamma_{r,b} \right]$$

$$\phi_H^{(d)} \equiv \sum_h \left[n_{\bullet h\bullet}^{(d)} \beta_h^{(d)} + \sum_b n_{\bullet hb}^{(d)} \eta_{h,b} \right]$$

$$\phi_E^{(d)} \equiv \sum_{i=1}^{2N} \varepsilon_i^{(d)} \mathbb{1}[D_i = d],$$

where, e.g., $n_{r\bullet b}^{(d)}$ represents the total number of observations involving a request r executed in batch b under condition d. We take the total number of observations per condition to be equal so that $n_{\bullet\bullet\bullet}^{(0)} = n_{\bullet\bullet\bullet}^{(1)} = N$.

We can then write down our estimate, $\hat{\delta}$, as

$$\hat{\delta} = \delta + \frac{1}{N}\left[(\phi_R^{(1)} - \phi_R^{(0)}) + (\phi_H^{(1)} - \phi_H^{(0)}) + (\phi_E^{(1)} - \phi_E^{(0)}) \right].$$

To obtain confidence intervals for $\hat{\delta}$, we also need to know its variance, $\mathrm{V}[\hat{\delta}]$. Following Bakshy & Eckles [4], we approach the problem by first describing how observations from each error component are repeated within each condition. We define the duplication coefficients [22, 23]:

$$\nu_R^{(d)} \equiv \frac{1}{N}\sum_r (n_{r\bullet\bullet}^{(d)})^2 \qquad \nu_H^{(d)} \equiv \frac{1}{N}\sum_h (n_{\bullet h\bullet}^{(d)})^2,$$

which are the average number of observations sharing the same request (ν_R) or host (ν_H). We then define the between-condition duplication coefficient [4], which gives a measure of how balanced hosts or requests are across conditions:

$$\omega_R \equiv \frac{1}{N}\sum_r n_{r\bullet\bullet}^{(0)} n_{r\bullet\bullet}^{(1)} \qquad \omega_H \equiv \frac{1}{N}\sum_h n_{\bullet h\bullet}^{(0)} n_{\bullet h\bullet}^{(1)}.$$

Furthermore, we only consider experimental designs in which the request-level and host-level duplication are the same in both conditions, so that $\nu_R^{(0)} = \nu_R^{(1)}$ and $\nu_H^{(0)} = \nu_H^{(1)}$, and omit the superscripts in subsequent expressions.[6]

Noting that because batch-level random effects are independent, the variance of their sums over batches can be expressed in terms of duplication coefficients, so that e.g.,

$$\mathrm{V}[\frac{1}{N}\sum_b n_{r\bullet b}^{(d)} \gamma_{r,b}] = \frac{1}{N^2}(n_{r\bullet\bullet}^{(d)})^2 \sigma_\gamma^2 = \frac{1}{N}\nu_R \sigma_\gamma^2,$$

and because all random effects are independent, it is straightforward to show that the variance of $\hat{\delta}$ can be written in terms of these duplication factors:

$$\begin{aligned} \mathrm{V}[\hat{\delta}] = \frac{1}{N}\Bigg[& \Big(\nu_R(\sigma_{\alpha^{(1)}}^2 + \sigma_{\alpha^{(0)}}^2 + 2\sigma_\gamma^2) - 2\omega_R \sigma_{\alpha^{(0)},\alpha^{(1)}} \Big) \\ & + \Big(\nu_H(\sigma_{\beta^{(1)}}^2 + \sigma_{\beta^{(0)}}^2 + 2\sigma_\eta^2) - 2\omega_H \sigma_{\beta^{(0)},\beta^{(1)}} \Big) \\ & + \Big(\sigma_{\varepsilon^{(0)}}^2 + \sigma_{\varepsilon^{(1)}}^2 \Big) \Bigg]. \end{aligned} \tag{5}$$

This expression illustrates how repeated observations of the same request or host affect the variance of our estimator for $\hat{\delta}$. Host-level variation is multiplied by how often hosts are repeated in the data, and similarly for requests. Variance is reduced when requests or hosts appear equally in both conditions, since, for example, ω_R is greatest when $n_{r\bullet\bullet}^{(0)} = n_{r\bullet\bullet}^{(1)}$ for all r. We use these facts to explore how different experimental designs—ways of delivering requests to hosts under different conditions—affect the precision with which we can estimate δ.

4.2 Four designs for distributed benchmarks

In this section, we describe four simple experimental designs that reflect basic engineering tradeoffs, and analyze their standard errors under a common set of conditions. In particular, we consider our certainty about experimental effects when:

[6] Note that the individual components, e.g., which requests appear in the treatment and control need not be the same for the duplication coefficients to be equal.

i	Host	Req.	Ver.	Batch
1	h_0	r_0	0	1
2	h_0	r_1	0	1
3	h_1	r_2	1	1
4	h_1	r_3	1	1

(a) Unbalanced

i	Host	Req.	Ver.	Batch
1	h_0	r_0	0	1
2	h_0	r_1	0	1
3	h_1	r_0	1	1
4	h_1	r_1	1	1

(b) Request balanced

i	Host	Req.	Ver.	Batch
1	h_0	r_0	0	1
2	h_1	r_1	0	1
3	h_0	r_2	1	2
4	h_1	r_3	1	2

(c) Host balanced

i	Host	Req.	Ver.	Batch
1	h_0	r_0	0	1
2	h_1	r_1	0	1
3	h_0	r_0	1	2
4	h_1	r_1	1	2

(d) Fully balanced

Table 2: Example schedules for the four experimental designs for experiments with two hosts ($H = 2$) in which two requests are executed per condition ($R = 2$). Each example shows four observations, each with a host ID, request ID (e.g., a request to an endpoint for a particular user), software version, and batch number.

1. The sharp null is true—that is, the experiment has no effects at all, so that δ is zero and all variance components are the same (e.g., $\sigma^2_{\alpha(0)} = \sigma^2_{\alpha(1)} = \sigma_{\alpha(0)\alpha(1)}$) [4], or
2. There are no treatment interactions, but there is a constant additive effect δ.[7]

Although these requirements are rather narrow, they correspond to a common scenario in which benchmarks are used for difference detection; by minimizing the standard error of the experiment, we are better able to detect situations in which there is a deviation from no change in performance.

In the four designs we discuss in the following sections, we constrain the design space to simplify presentation in a few ways. First, we assume symmetry with respect to the pattern of delivery of requests; we repeat each request the same number of times in each condition, so that $N = RT$. Second, because executing the same request on multiple hosts within the same condition would increase ν_R (and therefore inflate $V[\hat{\delta}]$), we only consider designs in which requests are executed on at most one machine per condition. And finally, since by (1) and (2), the variances of the error terms are equal, we drop the superscripts for each σ^2.

We consider two classes of designs: single-batch experiments, in which half of all hosts are assigned to the treatment, and the other half to the control, or two-batch experiments in which hosts run both versions of the software. Note that R requests are split among two batches in the latter case.[8]

In the single-batch design, each of the R requests is executed on either the first block of hosts or the second block, where each block is either assigned to the treatment or control. Therefore, when computing the host-level duplication coefficient, ν_H for a particular condition, we only sum across $H/2$ hosts:

$$\nu_H = \frac{1}{RT}\sum_{h=1}^{H/2}\left(\frac{RT}{H/2}\right)^2 = \frac{2RT}{H},$$

In the two-batch design, each of the R requests are executed in both the treatment and control across spread across all H hosts:

$$\nu_H = \frac{1}{RT}\sum_{h=1}^{H}\left(\frac{RT}{H}\right)^2 = \frac{RT}{H},$$

4.2.1 *Definitions*

Unbalanced design ("live benchmarking"). In the unbalanced design, each host only executes one version of the software, and each request is processed once. It can be carried out in one batch (see example layout in Table 2 (a)). This design is the simplest to implement since it does not require the ability to replay requests. It is often the design of choice when benchmarking live requests only, whether as a constraint or merely as a choice of convenience: it obviates the need for a possibly complex infrastructure to record and replay requests. The variance of the difference-in-means estimator for the unbalanced design is:

$$\mathrm{V}_{\mathrm{UB}}(\hat{\delta}) = 2T(\sigma_\alpha^2 + \sigma_\gamma^2) + 2\frac{2RT}{H}(\sigma_\beta^2 + \sigma_\eta^2) + 2\sigma_\epsilon^2$$

The standard error is $\sqrt{\frac{1}{RT}\mathrm{V}_{\mathrm{UB}}(\hat{\delta})}$. Expanding and simplifying this expression yields:

$$\mathrm{SE}_{\mathrm{UB}}(\hat{\delta}) = \sqrt{2(\frac{1}{R}(\sigma_\alpha^2 + \sigma_\gamma^2) + \frac{2}{H}(\sigma_\beta^2 + \sigma_\eta^2) + \frac{1}{RT}{\sigma_\epsilon}^2)}$$

The convenience of the unbalanced design comes at a price: the standard error term includes error components both from requests and hosts. We will show later that this design is the least powerful of the four: it achieves significantly lower accuracy (wider confidence intervals) for the same resource budget.

Request balanced design ("parallel benchmarking"). The request balanced design executes the same request in parallel on different hosts using different versions of the software. This requires that one has the ability to split or replay traffic, and can be done in one batch (see example layout in Table 2 (b)). Its standard error is defined as:

$$\mathrm{SE}_{\mathrm{RB}}(\hat{\delta}) = \sqrt{2(\frac{1}{R}\sigma_\gamma^2 + \frac{2}{H}(\sigma_\beta^2 + \sigma_\eta^2) + \frac{1}{RT}{\sigma_\epsilon}^2)}$$

The request balanced design cancels out the effect of the request, but noise due to each host is amplified by the average number of requests per host, $\frac{R}{H}$. Compared to live benchmarking, this design offers higher accuracy, with similar resources. Compared to sequential benchmarking, this design can be run in half the wall-clock time, but with twice as many hosts. It is therefore suitable for benchmarking when request replaying is available and time budget is more important than host budget.

Host balanced design ("sequential benchmarking"). The host balanced design executes requests using different versions of the software on the same host, and thus requires two batches. Each request is again only executed once, so a request replaying ability is not required (see Table 2 (c)).

Compared to live benchmarking, sequential benchmarking takes twice as long to run, but can use just half the number of hosts. It may therefore be useful in situations with no replay ability and a

[7] When the outcome variable is log-transformed, this δ corresponds to a multiplicative effect.

[8] Alternatively, one can think of the experiment as involving subjects and items [3] (which correspond to hosts and requests). The two-batch experiments correspond to within-subjects designs, and single-batch experiments correspond to between-subjects designs.

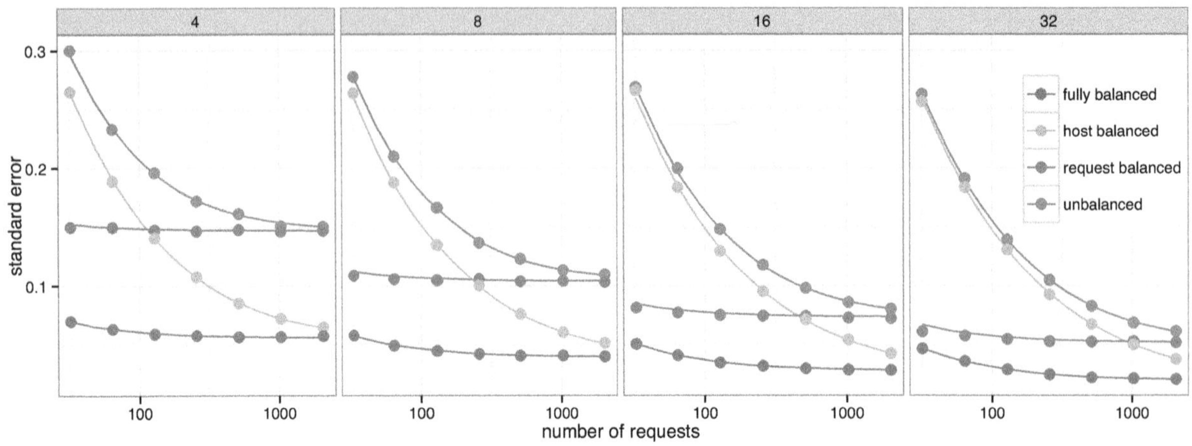

Figure 4: Standard errors for each of the four experimental designs as a function of the number of requests and hosts. Lines are theoretical standard errors from Section 4.2.1 and points are empirical standard errors from 10,000 simulations. Panels indicate the number of hosts used in the benchmark, and the number of requests are on a log scale.

limited number of hosts for benchmarking. It is also more accurate, for a given number of observations, as shown by its standard error:

$$\mathrm{SE}_{\mathrm{HB}}(\hat{\delta}) = \sqrt{2(\frac{1}{R}(\sigma_\alpha^2 + \sigma_\gamma^2) + \frac{1}{H}\sigma_\eta^2 + \frac{1}{RT}{\sigma_\epsilon}^2)}$$

The host balanced design cancels out the effect of the host, but one is left with noise due to the request. Note that the number of hosts does not affect the precision of the SEs in this design.

Fully balanced design ("controlled benchmarking"). The fully balanced design achieves the most accuracy with the most resources. It executes the same request on the same host using different versions of the software. This requires that one has the ability to split or replay traffic, and takes two batches to complete (see example layout in Table 2 (d)). This design has by far the least variance of the four designs, and is the best choice for benchmarking experiments in terms of accuracy, as shown by the standard error:

$$\mathrm{SE}_{\mathrm{FB}}(\hat{\delta}) = \sqrt{2(\frac{1}{R}\sigma_\gamma^2 + \frac{1}{H}\sigma_\eta^2 + \frac{1}{RT}{\sigma_\epsilon}^2)}$$

This design requires replay ability, as well as twice the machines of sequential benchmarking and twice the wall-clock time (batches) of live and parallel benchmarking. However, it is so much more accurate than the other designs that it requires far fewer observations (requests) to reach the same level of accuracy. Depending on the tradeoffs between request running time costs and batch setup cost, as well as the desired accuracy, this design may end up taking less computational resources than the other designs.

4.2.2 *Analysis*

We analyze each design via simulation and visualization. We obtained realistic simulation parameters from our model fits to the top endpoint (Table 1). Our simulation then simply draws random $\hat{y}$ values from normal distributions using these parameters. For any given design, the simulations differ in that host effects, request effects, and random noise are redrawn from a normal distribution with $\sigma_\alpha, \sigma_\beta$, and σ_ε, respectively.

We first consider simulations for each experimental design with a fixed number of hosts and requests and zero average effects. Figure 5 shows the distribution of $\hat{\delta}$s generated from 10,000 simulations. We can see that the fully balanced design has by far the least

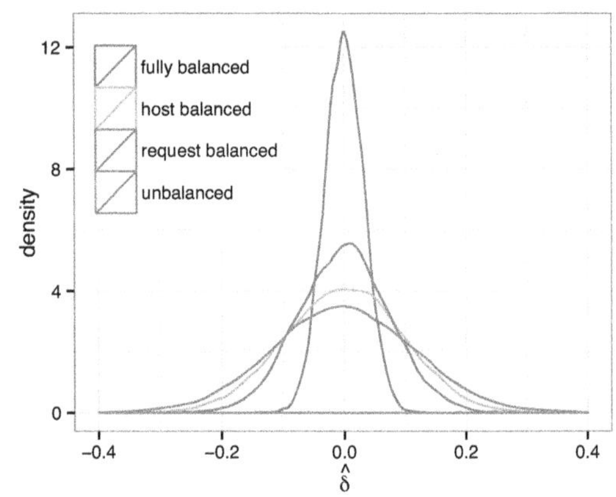

Figure 5: Distribution of $\hat{\delta}$s for each of the four experimental designs. The data was generated by simulating 10,000 hypothetical experiments from the random effects model in on Eq. 3 using parameter estimates from endpoint 1 in Table 1 with 16 hosts and 256 requests, for each design.

variance in $\hat{\delta}$, followed by the request balanced, host balanced, and unbalanced designs.

Next, we explore the parameter space of varying hosts and requests in Figure 4. In all cases, adding hosts or adding requests narrows the SE. For the unbalanced and host balanced designs, the effect of the number of requests on the SE is much more pronounced than that of the number of hosts: in the former because variability due to requests is much higher than that due to hosts, as shown in Figure 1; and in the latter because we control for the hosts. Similarly, the request balanced design controls for requests, and therefore shows little effect from varying the number of requests. And finally, the fully balanced design exhibits both the smallest SE in absolute terms, as well as the least sensitivity to the number of hosts.

5. BOOTSTRAPPING

So far we have discussed simple models that help us understand the main levers that can improve statistical precision in distributed, user-based benchmarks. Our theoretical results, however, assume that the model is correct, and that parameters are known or are easily estimated from data. This is generally not the case, and in fact, estimating models from the data may require many more observations than is necessary to estimate an average treatment effect.[9]

In this section we will review a simple non-parametric method for performing statistical inference—the bootstrap. We then evaluate how well it does at reconstructing known standard errors based on simulations from the random effects model. Finally, we demonstrate the performance of the bootstrap on real production benchmarks from Perflab.

5.1 Overview of the bootstrap

Often times we wish to generate confidence intervals for an average without making strong assumptions about how the data was generated. The bootstrap [12] is one such technique for doing this. The *bootstrap distribution* of a sample statistic (e.g., the difference in means between two experimental conditions) is the distribution of that statistic when observations are resampled [12] or reweighted [23, 25]. We describe the latter method because it is easiest to implement in a computationally efficient manner.

The most basic way of getting a confidence interval for an average treatment effect for iid data is to reweight observations independently, and repeat this process R times. We assign each observation i a weight $w_{r,i}$ from a mean-one random variable, (e.g., Uniform(0,2) or Pois(1)) [23, 25] and use them to average the data, using each replicate number r and observation number i as a random seed:

$$\hat{\delta}_r^* = \frac{1}{N_r^*}\sum_i w_{r,i} y_i I(D_i = 1) - \frac{1}{M_r^*}\sum_i w_{r,i} y_i I(D_i = 0)$$

Here, N_r^* and M_r^* denote the sum of the bootstrap weights (e.g., $\sum_i w_{r,i} I(D_i = 1)$) under the treatment and control, respectively. This process produces a distribution of our statistic, the sample difference in means, $\hat{\delta}^*_{r=1\ldots,R}$. One can then summarize this distribution to obtain confidence intervals. For example, to compute the 95% confidence interval for $\hat{\delta}$ by taking the 2.5th and 97.5th quantiles of the bootstrap distribution of $\hat{\delta}$. Another method is to use the central limit theorem (CLT). The distribution of our statistic is expected to be asymptotically normal, so that one can compute the 95% interval using the quantiles of the normal distribution with a mean and standard deviation set to the sample mean and standard deviation of the $\hat{\delta}_r^*$s. The CLT intervals are generally more stable than directly computing the quantiles of the bootstrap distribution, so we use this method for all bootstrap confidence intervals given in this paper.

Similar to how the iid standard errors in Section 3.1.1 underestimate the variability in $\bar{Y}$, we expect the iid bootstrap to underestimate the variance of $\hat{\delta}$ when observations are clustered, yielding overly narrow ("anti-conservative") confidence intervals and high false positive rates [21]. The solution to this problem is to use a *clustered bootstrap*. In the clustered bootstrap, weights are assigned for each factor level, rather than observation number. For example, if we wish to use a clustered bootstrap based on the request ID, as to capture variability due to the request, we can assign all observations for a particular host to a weight. In the case of requests, we would instead use host IDs and replicate numbers as our random number seed, and for each replicate, compute:

[9]For example, identifying host-level effects requires executing the same request on multiple machines, and identifying request-level effects requires multiple repetitions of the same request. Both increase request-level duplication, which reduces efficiency when request-level effects are large relative to the noise, σ_ε (Sec. 4.2).

$$\hat{\delta}_r^* = \frac{1}{N_r^*}\sum_i w_{r,h[i]} y_i I(D_i = 1) - \frac{1}{M_r^*}\sum_i w_{r,h[i]} y_i I(D_i = 0)$$

5.2 Bootstrapping experimental differences

Before examining the behavior of the bootstrap on production behavior, we validate its performance based on how well it approximates known standard errors, as generated by our idealized benchmark models from Section 3. To illustrate how this works, we can plot the true distribution of $\hat{\delta}$s drawn from the 10,000 simulations for the fully balanced design shown in Figure 6, along with the $\hat{\delta}^*$s under the host and request-clustered bootstrap for a single experiment. The host-clustered bootstrap, which accounts for the variation induced by repeated observations of the same host, tends to produce estimates of the standard errors that are similar to the true standard error, while the request-clustered bootstrap tends to be too narrow, in that it underestimates the variability of $\hat{\delta}$.

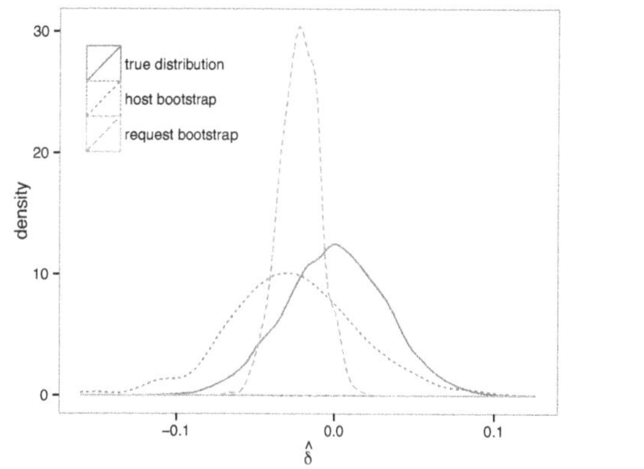

Figure 6: Comparison of the distribution of $\hat{\delta}$s generated by 10,000 simulations (solid line) with the distribution of bootstrapped $\hat{\delta}^*$s from a single experiment (dashed lines).

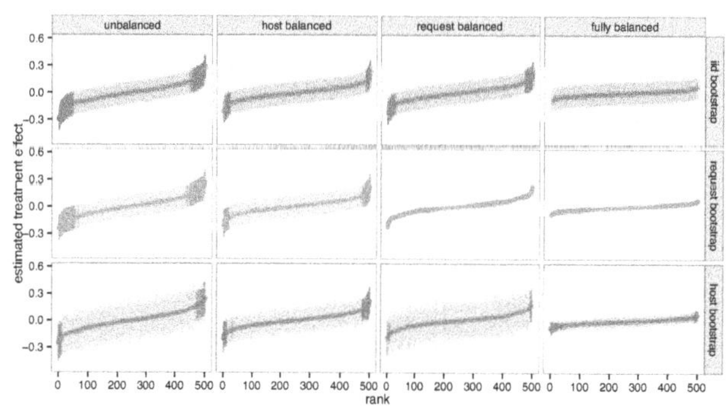

Figure 7: Visualization of bootstrap confidence intervals from 500 simulated A/A tests, run with different experimental designs and bootstrap methods. Experiments are ranked by estimated effect size. Shaded error bars indicate false positives. The request-level and iid bootstraps yield overly narrow confidence intervals.

Next, we evaluate three bootstrapping procedures—iid, host-clustered, and request-clustered—with each of the four designs for a single endpoint. To do this, we use the same model parameters from endpoint 1, as in previous plots. To get an intuitive picture for

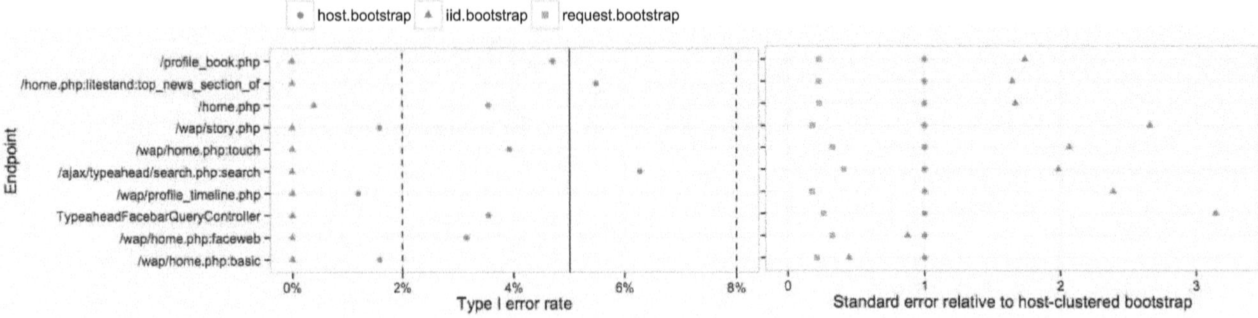

Figure 8: Empirical validation of bootstrap estimators for the top 10 endpoints using production data from Perflab. Left: Type I error rates for host-clustered and IID bootstrap (request-clustered bootstrap has a Type I error rate of $> 20\%$ for all endpoints and is not shown); Solid line indicates the desired 5% Type I error rate, and the dashed lines indicate the range of possible observed Type I error rates that would be consistent with a true error rate of 5%. Right: Standard error of host-clustered, request-clustered, and iid bootstrap relative to the host-clustered standard error.

how the confidence intervals are distributed, we run 500 simulated A/A tests, and for each configuration, we rank-order experiments by the point estimates of $\hat{\delta}$, and visualize their confidence intervals (Figure 7). Shaded regions represent false positives (i.e., their confidence intervals do not cross 0). The iid bootstrap consistently produces the widest CIs for all designs. This happens because the iid bootstrap doesn't preserve the balance across hosts or requests across conditions when resampling. There is also a clear relationship between the width of CIs and the Type I error rate, in that there are a higher proportion of type I error rates when the CIs are too narrow.

To more closely examine the precision of each bootstrap method with each design, we run 10,000 simulated A/A tests for each configuration and summarize their results in Table 3. For the request-balanced design, we also include an additional bootstrap strategy, which we call the host-block bootstrap, where pairs of hosts that execute the same requests are bootstrapped. This ensures that when whole hosts are bootstrapped, the balance of requests is not broken. This method turns out to produce standard errors with good coverage for the request-balanced design, and so we will henceforth refer to the host–block bootstrap strategy as the host-clustered bootstrap in further analyses. We can see that the host-clustered bootstrap appears to estimate the true SE most accurately for all designs.

Design	Bootstrap	Type I err.	$\widehat{\text{SE}}$	SE
unbalanced	request	21.4%	0.07	0.10
unbalanced	iid	17.8%	0.07	0.10
unbalanced	host	3.6%	0.11	0.10
request balanced	request	71.6%	0.01	0.07
request balanced	iid	10.8%	0.07	0.07
request balanced	host	0.8%	0.11	0.07
request balanced	host-block	5.7%	0.08	0.07
host balanced	request	8.4%	0.07	0.07
host balanced	iid	6.8%	0.07	0.07
host balanced	host	5.0%	0.08	0.07
fully balanced	request	46.8%	0.01	0.03
fully balanced	host	4.8%	0.03	0.03
fully balanced	iid	0.0%	0.07	0.03

Table 3: Comparison of Type I error rates and standard errors for each experimental design and bootstrap strategy. $\widehat{\text{SE}}$ indicates the average estimated standard error from the bootstrap, while SE indicates the true standard error from the analytical formulae. Anti-conservative bootstrap estimates of the standard errors produce high false positive rates (e.g., >5%).

5.3 Evaluation with production data

Finally, having verified that the bootstrap method provides a conservative estimate of the standard error when the true standard error is known (because it was generated by our statistical model), we turn toward testing the bootstrap on raw production data from Perflab, which uses the fully balanced design. To do this, we conduct 256 A/A tests using identical binaries of the Facebook WWW codebase. Figure 8 summarizes the results from these tests for the top 10 most visited endpoints that are benchmarked by Perflab.

Consistent with the results of our simulations, we find that the request-level bootstrap is massively anti-conservative, and produces confidence intervals that are far too narrow, resulting in a high false positive rate (i.e., $> 20\%$) across all endpoints. Similarly, we find that our empirical results echo that of the simulations: the iid bootstrap produces estimates of the standard error that are far wider than they should be. The host-clustered bootstrap, however, produces Type I error rates that are not significantly different from 5% for all but 3 of the endpoints; in these cases, the confidence intervals are slightly conservative, as is desired in our use case. For these reasons, all production benchmarks conducted at Facebook with Perflab use the host-clustered bootstrap.

6. RELATED WORK

Many researchers recognized the obstreperous nature of performance measurement tools, and addressed it piecemeal. Some focus on controlling architectural performance variability, which is still a very active research field. Statistical inference tools can be applied to reduce the effort of repeated experimentation [11, 19]. These studies focus primarily on managing host-level variability (and even intra-host-level variance), and do not spend much attention on the variability of software.

Variability in software performance has been examined in many other studies that attempt to quantify the efficacy of techniques such as: allowing for a warm-up period [8]; reducing random performance fluctuations using regression benchmarking [18]; randomizing multi-threaded simulations [1]; and application-specific benchmarking [27]. In addition, there is an increasing interest specifically in the performance of online systems and in the modeling of large-scale workloads and dynamic content [2, 6].

Several studies addressed the holistic performance evaluation of hardware, software, and users. Cheng et al. described a system called *Monkey* that captures and replays TCP workloads, allowing the repeated measuring of the system under test without generating synthetic workloads [9]. Gupta et al., in their *Diecast* system, addressed the challenge of scaling down massive-scale distributed systems into representative benchmarks [15]. In addition, representative characteristics of user-generated load is critical for benchmarking large-scale online systems, as discussed by Manley et al. [20]. Their system, *hbench:Web*, tries to capture user-level variation in terms of *user sessions* and user *equivalence classes*. Request-level variation is modeled statistically, as opposed to measuring it directly.

A few studies also proposed statistical models for benchmarking experiments. Kalibera et al. showed that simply averaged multiple repetitions of a benchmark without accounting for sources of variation can produce unrepresentative results [17, 18]. They developed models focusing on minimizing experimentation time under software/environment random effects, which can be generalized to other software-induced variability. These models are similar to the model developed here, but they do not take into account host-level or user-level effects, which are central to the experimental design and statistical inference problem we wish to address. To the best of our knowledge, this is the first work to rigorously address distributed benchmarking in the context of user data.

7. CONCLUSIONS AND FUTURE WORK

Benchmarking for performance differences in large Internet software systems poses many challenges. On top of the many well-studied requirements for accurate performance benchmarking, we have the additional dimension of user requests. Because of the potentially large performance variation from one user request to another, it is crucial to take the clustering of user requests into account. Yet another complicating dimension, which is nevertheless critical to scale large testing systems, is distributed benchmarking across multiple hosts. It too introduces non-trivial complications with respect to how hosts interact with request-level effects and experimental design to affect the standard error of the benchmark.

In this paper we developed a statistical model to understand and quantify these effects, and explored their practical impact on benchmarking. This model enables the analytical development of experimental designs with different engineering and efficiency tradeoffs. Our results from these models show that a fully balanced design—accounting for both request variability and host variability—is optimal in minimizing the benchmark's standard error given a fixed number of requests and machines. Although this design may require more computational resources than the other three, it is ideal for Facebook's rapid development and deployment mode because it minimizes developer resources.

Design effects due to repeated observations from the same host also show how residual error terms that cannot be canceled out via balancing, such as batch-level host effects due to JIT optimization and caching, can also be an important lever for further increasing precision, especially when there are few hosts relative to the number of requests.

From a practical point of view, estimating the model parameters to compute the standard errors for these experiments (especially in a live system) can be costly and complex. We showed how the clustered online bootstrap can be used to estimate the standard error for a variety of experimental designs. Using empirical data from Facebook's largest differential benchmarking system, Perflab, we confirm that this technique can reliably capture the true standard error with good accuracy. Consequently, all production Perflab experiments use a fully-balanced design, and the host-level bootstrap to evaluate changes in key metrics, including CPU time, instructions, memory usage, etc. Our hope is that this paper provides a simple and actionable understanding of the procedures involved in benchmarking for performance changes in other contexts as well. With a more quantitatively informed approach, practitioners can select the most suitable experimental design to minimize the benchmark's run time for any desired level of accuracy.

Our results focus on measuring the performance of a single endpoint or service. Often times one wishes to benchmark multiple such endpoints or services. Pooling across these endpoints to obtain a composite standard error is trivial if one could reasonably regard the performance of each endpoint as independent.[10] If there is a strong correlation between endpoints, however, the models here must be extended to take into account covariances between observations from different endpoints.

Finally, another area of development for future work is a more extensive evaluation of the costs associated with each of the four basic designs. For example, one might devise a cost model which takes as inputs the desired accuracy and parameters such as batch setup time, fixed and marginal costs per request, etc. These cost functions' formulae would depend on the particulars of the benchmarking platform. For example, in some systems the number of requests needed for stable measurements for may depend on some maximum load per host. How much "warm up" time different subsystems require is nonlinear in the number of different requests, and might also depend on how services are distributed across machines.

8. ACKNOWLEDGEMENTS

Perflab is developed by many engineers on the Site Efficiency Team at Facebook. We are especially thankful for all of the help from David Harrington and Eunchang Lee, who worked closely with us on implementing and deploying the testing routines discussed in this paper. This work would not be possible without their help and collaboration. We also thank Dean Eckles and Alex Deng for their suggestions and feedback on this work.

[10] If each endpoint i constitutes some fraction w_i of the traffic, and the outcomes for each endpoint are uncorrelated, the variance of δ pooled across all endpoints is simply $\text{Var}[\hat{\delta}_{\text{pool}}] = \sum_i w_i^2 \text{Var}[\hat{\delta}_i]$. This independence assumption can be made more plausible by loading endpoints with disjoint sets of users.

9. REFERENCES

[1] A. R. Alameldeen, C. J. Mauer, M. Xu, P. J. Harper, M. M. K. Martin, D. J. Sorin, M. D. Hill, and D. A. Wood. Evaluating non-deterministic multi-threaded commercial workloads. In *In Proceedings of the Fifth Workshop on Computer Architecture Evaluation Using Commercial Workloads*, pages 30–38, 2002.

[2] B. Atikoglu, Y. Xu, E. Frachtenberg, S. Jiang, and M. Paleczny. Workload analysis of a large-scale key-value store. In *Proceedings of the 12th Joint Conference On Measurement And Modeling of Computer Systems (SIGMETRICS/Performance'12)*, London, UK, June 2012.

[3] R. H. Baayen, D. J. Davidson, and D. M. Bates. Mixed-effects modeling with crossed random effects for subjects and items. *Journal of Memory and Language*, 59(4):390–412, 2008.

[4] E. Bakshy and D. Eckles. Uncertainty in online experiments with dependent data: An evaluation of bootstrap methods. In *Proceedings of the 19th ACM SIGKDD conference on knowledge discovery and data mining*. ACM, 2013.

[5] S. Balakrishnan, R. Rajwar, M. Upton, and K. Lai. The impact of performance asymmetry in emerging multicore architectures. In *Proceedings of the 32nd annual international symposium on Computer Architecture*, ISCA'05, pages 506–517, Washington, DC, USA, 2005. IEEE Computer Society.

[6] P. Barford and M. Crovella. Generating representative web workloads for network and server performance evaluation. In *Proceedings of the 1998 ACM SIGMETRICS joint International Conference on Measurement and modeling of Computer Systems*, SIGMETRICS '98/PERFORMANCE '98, pages 151–160, New York, NY, USA, 1998. ACM.

[7] G. E. Box, J. S. Hunter, and W. G. Hunter. *Statistics for Experimenters: Design, Innovation, and Discovery*, volume 13. Wiley Online Library, 2005.

[8] A. Buble, L. Bulej, and P. Tuma. Corba benchmarking: A course with hidden obstacles. In *Proceedings of the International Parallel and Distributed Processing Symposium (IPDPS'03)*, pages 6 pp.–, 2003.

[9] Y. chung Cheng, U. Hölzle, N. Cardwell, S. Savage, and G. M. Voelker. Monkey see, monkey do: A tool for tcp tracing and replaying. In *In USENIX Annual Technical Conference*, pages 87–98, 2004.

[10] W. G. Cochran. *Sampling techniques*. John Wiley & Sons, 2007.

[11] L. Eeckhout, H. Vandierendonck, and K. De Bosschere. Designing computer architecture research workloads. *Computer*, 36(2):65–71, 2003.

[12] B. Efron. Bootstrap methods: Another look at the jackknife. *The Annals of Statistics*, 7(1):1–26, 1979.

[13] D. G. Feitelson. Workload modeling for computer systems performance evaluation. Unpublished manuscript, v. 0.42. **www.cs.huji.ac.il/~feit/wlmod/wlmod.pdf**.

[14] D. G. Feitelson, E. Frachtenberg, and K. L. Beck. Development and Deployment at Facebook. *IEEE Internet Computing*, 17(4), July 2013.

[15] D. Gupta, K. V. Vishwanath, M. McNett, A. Vahdat, K. Yocum, A. Snoeren, and G. M. Voelker. Diecast: Testing distributed systems with an accurate scale model. *ACM Trans. Comput. Syst.*, 29(2):4:1–4:48, May 2011.

[16] R. Jain. *The Art of Computer Systems Performance Analysis: Techniques for experimental design, measurement, simulation, and modeling*. Wiley, 1991.

[17] T. Kalibera and R. Jones. Rigorous benchmarking in reasonable time. In *Proceedings of the 2013 International Symposium on International Symposium on Memory Management*, ISMM'13, pages 63–74, New York, NY, USA, 2013. ACM.

[18] T. Kalibera and P. Tuma. Precise regression benchmarking with random effects: Improving mono benchmark results. In *Formal Methods and Stochastic Models for Performance Evaluation*, volume 4054 of *Lecture Notes in Computer Science*, pages 63–77. Springer Berlin Heidelberg, 2006.

[19] B. C. Lee and D. M. Brooks. Accurate and efficient regression modeling for microarchitectural performance and power prediction. In *Proceedings of the 12th international conference on Architectural support for programming languages and operating systems*, ASPLOS XII, pages 185–194, New York, NY, USA, 2006. ACM.

[20] S. Manley, M. Seltzer, and M. Courage. A self-scaling and self-configuring benchmark for web servers (extended abstract). In *Proceedings of the 1998 ACM SIGMETRICS Joint International Conference on Measurement and Modeling of Computer Systems*, SIGMETRICS'98/PERFORMANCE'98, pages 270–291, New York, NY, USA, 1998. ACM.

[21] P. McCullagh. Resampling and exchangeable arrays. *Bernoulli*, 6(2):285–301, 2000.

[22] A. B. Owen. The pigeonhole bootstrap. *The Annals of Applied Statistics*, 1(2):386–411, 2007.

[23] A. B. Owen and D. Eckles. Bootstrapping data arrays of arbitrary order. *The Annals of Applied Statistics*, 6(3):895–927, 2012.

[24] D. B. Rubin. Estimating causal effects of treatments in randomized and nonrandomized studies. *Journal of Educational Psychology*, 66(5):688–701, 1974.

[25] D. B. Rubin. The Bayesian bootstrap. *The Annals of Statistics*, 9(1):130–134, 1981.

[26] S. R. Searle, G. Casella, C. E. McCulloch, et al. *Variance Components*. Wiley New York, 1992.

[27] M. Seltzer, D. Krinsky, K. Smith, and X. Zhang. The case for application-specific benchmarking. In *In Workshop on Hot Topics in Operating Systems (HOTOS'99)*, pages 102–107, 1999.

[28] T. A. Snijders. *Multilevel analysis*. Springer, 2011.

ACCAMS: Additive Co-Clustering to Approximate Matrices Succinctly

Alex Beutel
Computer Science, CMU
Pittsburgh, PA
abeutel@cs.cmu.edu

Amr Ahmed
Google ST
Mountain View, CA
amra@google.com

Alexander J. Smola
CMU MLD and Google ST
Pittsburgh, PA
alex@smola.org

ABSTRACT

Matrix completion and approximation are popular tools to capture a user's preferences for recommendation and to approximate missing data. Instead of using low-rank factorization we take a drastically different approach, based on the simple insight that an additive model of co-clusterings allows one to approximate matrices efficiently. This allows us to build a concise model that, per bit of model learned, significantly beats all factorization approaches in matrix completion. Even more surprisingly, we find that summing over small co-clusterings is more effective in modeling matrices than classic co-clustering, which uses just one large partitioning of the matrix.

Following Occam's razor principle, the fact that our model is more concise and yet just as accurate as more complex models suggests that it better captures the latent preferences and decision making processes present in the real world. We provide an iterative minimization algorithm, a collapsed Gibbs sampler, theoretical guarantees for matrix approximation, and excellent empirical evidence for the efficacy of our approach. We achieve state-of-the-art results for matrix completion on Netflix at a fraction of the model complexity.

Categories and Subject Descriptors

H.2.8 [**Database Management**]: Data mining; H.3.m [**Information Storage and Retrieval**]: Miscellaneous; I.5.3 [**Computing Methodologies**]: Clustering

Keywords

Recommender Systems; Collaborative Filtering; Clustering

1. INTRODUCTION

Given users' ratings of movies or products, how can we model a user's preferences for different types of items and recommend other items that the user will like? This problem, often referred to as the Netflix problem, has generated a flurry of research in collaborative filtering, with a variety of proposed matrix factorization models and inference methods. Top recommendation systems have used thousands of factors per item and per user, as was the case in the winning submissions in the Netflix prize [10]. Recent state-of-the-art methods have relied on learning even larger, more complex factorization models, often taking nontrivial combinations of multiple submodels [16, 13]. Such complex models are increasingly difficult to interpret, use large amounts of memory, and are often difficult integrate into larger systems.

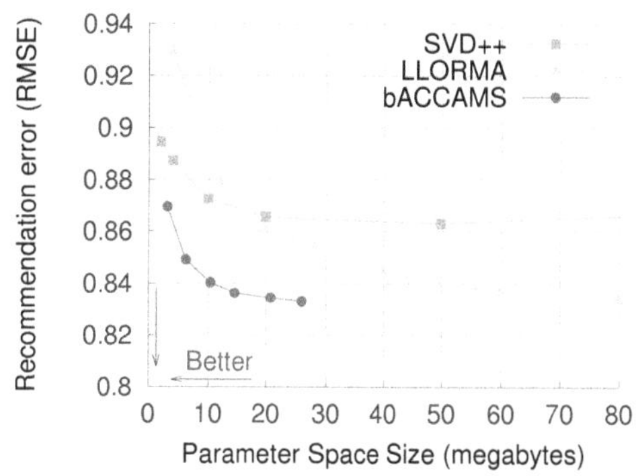

Figure 1: Accuracy of ACCAMS on Netflix, compared to [10] and [13]. Note that our model achieves state of the art accuracy at a fraction of the model size.

1.1 Linear combinations of attributes

Our approach is drastically different from previous collaborative filtering research. Rather than start with the assumptions of a matrix factorization model, we make *co-clustering* effective for high quality matrix completion and approximation. Co-clustering finds a clustering of the rows and columns of a matrix $\mathbf{R}$ so as to partition $\mathbf{R}$ into blocks that are highly similar. It has been well studied [2, 21] but was not previously competitive in large behavior modeling and matrix completion problems. To achieve state of the art results, we use an *additive model of simple co-clusterings* that we call stencils, rather than building a large single co-clustering. The result is a model that is conceptually simple, has a small parameter space, has interpretable structure, and still achieves the best published accuracy for matrix completion on Netflix, as seen in Figure 1.

Using a linear combination of co-clusterings corresponds to a rather different interpretation of user preferences and movie properties. Matrix factorization assumes that a movie preference is based on a weighted sum of preferences for

WWW 2015, May 18–22, 2015, Florence, Italy.
ACM 978-1-4503-3469-3/15/05.
http://dx.doi.org/10.1145/2736277.2741091.

different genres, with the movie properties being represented in vectorial form. Therefore, even if a movie is a comedy and the user likes comedies, the model still also offsets by how scary the movie is and does the user like scary movies.

Co-clustering on the other hand assumes there exists some "correct" partitioning of movies (and users). For instance, a user might be part of a group that likes all comedies but does not like romantic movies. Correspondingly, all romantic comedies might be split out into a separate cluster. If a group of users likes new movies but not old ones then each genre may be further partitioned by decade. This quickly leads to a combinatorial explosion.

By taking a linear combination of co-clusterings we benefit from both perspectives: by modeling the discrete nature of attributes we can avoid the cost of high-dimensional factorization models, and by adding the preferences for different attributes we can avoid the large models necessary to cover all combinations of attributes. Rather, through backfitting, we create a more powerful, hierarchical representation. For instance, a movie may be {funny, scary, sad}, it was made in some era, it has a certain age rating, it may contain a certain group of actors or be shot in a certain visual style. However, if a user likes comedies but doesn't like scary movies, it is generally unlikely that this preference will suddenly flip depending on the decade the movie was produced. Therefore, by taking linear combinations of co-clusterings we can efficiently take all of these attributes into account.

1.2 Succinct Stencils

The mathematical challenge that motivated this work is, how can we make a *succinct* model of user behavior that still provides high quality predictions? Designing a succinct model is difficult because it requires making assumptions and restrictions while not decreasing the model's accuracy. Factorization models are very flexible. In order to encode a rank-k matrix by a factorization, we need k numbers per row (and column) respectively. Rather, consider a stencil - a small $k \times k$ template of a matrix and its mapping to the row and column vectors respectively. We only need $\log_2 k$ bits per row (and column) plus $O(k^2)$ floating point numbers regardless of the size of the matrix.

Taking a linear combination of stencils we can model quite complex matrices. This is best understood by the example below: assume that we have two simple stencils containing 3×2 and 2×3 co-clusterings. Their linear combination yields a rather nontrivial 9×8 matrix of rank 5. Alternatively, classic co-clustering would require a $(3 \cdot 2) \times (2 \cdot 3)$ partitioning to match this structure. When we have S stencils of size $k \times k$, this would require a single co-clustering of size $k^S \times k^S$.

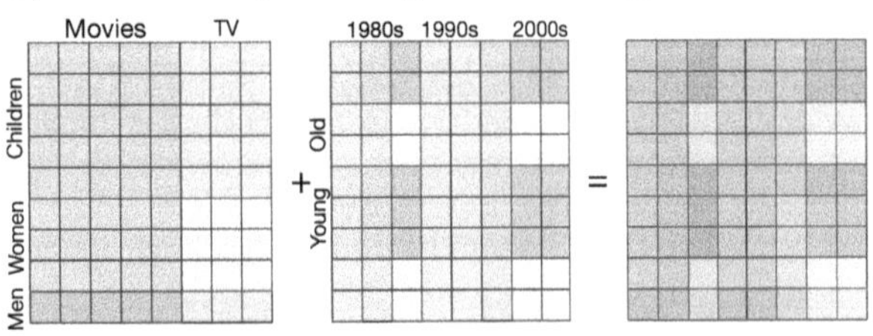

By design our model has a parameter space that is an order of magnitude smaller than competing methods, requiring only $S \log_2 k$ bits per user and per movie and Sk^2 floating point numbers, where k is generally quite small. While ACCAMS is more restrictive than classic factorization, we demonstrate that our assumptions do not increase the generalization error, achieving even better prediction accuracy than more complex models.

Finding succinct models for binary matrices, e.g. by minimizing the minimum description (MDL), has been the focus of significant research and valuable results in the data mining community [14, 11]. That said, these models are quite different. To the best of our knowledge, ours is the first work aimed at finding a parsimonious model for general (real-valued) matrix completion and approximation.

1.3 Contributions

Our paper makes a number of contributions to the problem of finding sparse representations of matrices.

- **Optimization algorithm:** We present ACCAMS, an iterative k-means style algorithm that minimizes the approximation error by backfitting the residuals of previous approximations.
- **Theoretical bounds:** We provide linear approximation rates exploiting the geometry of rows and columns of rating matrix.
- **Bayesian model:** We present a generative Bayesian non-parametric model and devise a collapsed Gibbs sampling algorithm, bACCAMS, for efficient inference.
- **State-of-the-art results:** Experiments confirm the efficacy of our approach, offering the best published results for matrix completion on Netflix, an interpretable hierarchy of content, and succinct matrix approximations for ratings, image, and network data.

We believe that these contributions offer a promising new direction for behavior modeling and matrix approximation.

Outline. We begin by discussing related work from recommendation systems, non-parametric Bayesian models, co-clustering, and minimum description length. We subsequently introduce the simple k-means style co-clustering and its approximation properties in Section 3. Subsequently, in Section 4.1 we define our Bayesian co-clustering model and collapsed Gibbs sampler for a single stencil. In Section 4.4 we extend our Bayesian model to multiple stencils. Section 5 reports our experimental results and we conclude with a discussion of future directions for the work.

2. RELATED WORK

Recommender Systems. Closest to our work is the research on behavior modeling and recommendation. Matrix factorization approaches, such as Koren's SVD++ [9], have enjoyed great success in recommender systems. Recent models such as DFC [16] and LLORMA [13] have focused on using ensembles of factorizations to exploit local structure.

More closely related to our model are Bayesian non-parametric approaches. For instance, [6, 5] use the Indian Buffet Process (IBP) for recommendation. In doing so they assume that each user (and movie) has certain preferential binary attributes. It can be seen as an extreme case of ACCAMS where the cluster size $k = 2$, while using a somewhat different strategy to handle cluster assignment and overall similarity within a cluster. Following a similar intuition as ACCAMS but different perspective and focus, [17] extended the IBP to handle $k > 2$ for link prediction tasks on binary graphs. Our work differs in its focus on general, real-valued matrices, its application of co-clustering, and its significantly simpler parameterization.

Co-clustering was incorporated into a factorization approach to recommendation in [3]. While the co-clustering improved modeling accuracy, it did not reduce the model complexity of the underlying factorization. Finally, [19] proposed a factorization model based on a Dirichlet process over users and columns. All these models are closely related to the mixed-membership stochastic blockmodels of [1].

Co-clustering. The technique was originally used for understanding the clustering of rows and columns of a matrix rather than for matrix approximation or completion [8]. This formulation was well suited for biological tasks but evolved to cover a wider variety of objectives [2]. [18] defined a soft co-clustering objective akin to a factorization model. Recent work has defined a Bayesian model for co-clustering focused on matrix modeling [21]. [24] focuses on exploiting co-clustering ensembles, but do so by finding a single consensus co-clustering. As far as we know, ours is the first work to use an additive combination of co-clusterings.

Matrix Approximation. There exists a large body of work on matrix approximation in the theoretical computer science community. They focus mainly on efficient low-rank approximations, e.g. by projection or by interpolation [7, 4]. Essentially one aims to find a general low-rank approximation of the matrix, similar to recommender models.

A more parsimonious strategy is to seek *interpolative* decompositions, approximating columns of a matrix by a linear combination of a subset of other columns [15]. Nonetheless this requires us to store at least one, possibly more scaling coefficients per column. Also note the focus on column interpolations — this can easily be extended to row and column interpolations. To the best of our knowledge, the problem of approximating matrices with piecewise constant block matrices as we propose here is not the focus of research in TCS.

Succinct modeling. The data mining community has focused on finding succinct models of data, often directly optimizing the model size described by the minimum description length (MDL) [20]. This approach has led to valuable results in pattern and item-set mining [23, 14] as well as graph summarization [11]. However, these approaches typically focus on modeling databases of discrete items rather than real-valued datasets with missing values.

3. MATRIX APPROXIMATION

We begin by defining our notation and the problem. We will denote matrices by bold capital letters, vectors by bold lowercase letters, and scalars by non-bold symbols. Unless otherwise specified, subscripts on matrices (or vectors) denote indices into the matrix (or vector), e.g. $\mathbf{R}_{u,m}$ is the scalar in the uth row and mth column of $\mathbf{R}$. Using : selects all indices, such that $\mathbf{R}_{u,:}$ represents the entire uth row of $\mathbf{R}$ and $\mathbf{R}_{:,m}$ is the entire mth column. Superscripts, as in $\mathbf{T}^{(\ell)}$, denote different matrices for different superscripts. A full list of the symbols used can be found in Table 1.

We consider now the problem of matrix approximation:

Problem Definition 1 ***(Matrix Approximation)***
Given: *a sparse matrix* $\mathbf{R} \in \mathbb{R}^{N \times M}$ *with indicator matrix* $\mathbf{I}$
Find: *a model* $\mathcal{M}$ *with parameters* θ*, such that the size of* θ *is small,* $|\theta| \ll \mathbf{R}$*, and* $\mathcal{M}(\theta)$ *approximates* $\mathbf{R}$ *well:*

$$\underset{\theta}{\text{minimize}} \sum_{u=1}^{N} \sum_{m=1}^{M} \mathbf{I}_{u,m}(\mathbf{R}_{u,m} - \mathcal{M}(\theta)_{u,m})^2 \qquad (1)$$

Symbol	Definition
N, M	Number of rows (users) and columns (movies)
$\mathbf{R}$	Data matrix $\in \mathbb{R}^{N \times M}$ (with missing values)
$\mathbf{I}$	Indicator matrix $\in \{0,1\}^{N \times M}$ for $\mathbf{R}$
S	Number of stencils
$k_n^{(\ell)}, k_m^{(\ell)}$	Number of user and movie clusters in stencil ℓ
$\mathbf{T}^{(\ell)}$	Matrix $\in \mathbb{R}^{k_n^{(\ell)} \times k_m^{(\ell)}}$ for stencil ℓ
$\mathbf{c}^{(\ell)}$	Vector of user assignments $\in \{1, \ldots, k_n^{(\ell)}\}^N$
$\mathbf{d}^{(\ell)}$	Vector of movie assignments $\in \{1, \ldots, k_m^{(\ell)}\}^M$
$\mathcal{S}(\mathbf{T}, \mathbf{c}, \mathbf{d})$	$\in \mathbb{R}^{N \times M}$ defined by $\mathcal{S}(\mathbf{T}, \mathbf{c}, \mathbf{d})_{u,m} = \mathbf{T}_{\mathbf{c}_u, \mathbf{d}_m}$
$\mathbf{n}_c$	Number of users in cluster c
$\mathbf{n}_c^{(-u)}$	Number of users in cluster c, ignoring user u
$\mathbf{N}_{c,d}$	Number of observations in block (c, d)
$\mathbf{r}_{c,d}$	Vector of observed ratings in block (c, d)

Table 1: Symbols used throughout this paper.

As stated above, we assume $\mathbf{R}$ is a sparse matrix where there is no data for many values in the matrix. The indicator matrix $\mathbf{I}$ denotes this information, where $\mathbf{I}_{i,j} = 1$ when there is an observed value for $\mathbf{R}_{i,j}$ and $\mathbf{I}_{i,j} = 0$ otherwise. Without loss of generality we assume that our data matrix, $\mathbf{R}$, has more rows than columns, i.e. $\mathbf{R} \in \mathbb{R}^{N \times M}$ with $N \geq M$.

The concept of a small model in the context of behavior modeling has typically been captured by the rank of a factorization. We generalize this concept and define a small model by the number of bits required to store it, more commonly known as the minimum description length (MDL).

3.1 Proposed Model

A stencil assigns each user u to a user cluster c, each movie to a movie cluster d, and for each (user cluster c, movie cluster d) combination there is a *block* of ratings which are predicted to have value $\mathbf{T}_{c,d}$. Formally:

Definition 1 (Stencil) *A stencil* $\mathcal{S}(\mathbf{T}, \mathbf{c}, \mathbf{d})$ *is a matrix* $\mathcal{S} \in \mathbb{R}^{N \times M}$ *with the property that* $\mathcal{S}(\mathbf{T}, \mathbf{c}, \mathbf{d})_{u,m} = \mathbf{T}_{\mathbf{c}_u, \mathbf{d}_m}$ *for a template* $\mathbf{T} \in \mathbb{R}^{k_n \times k_m}$ *and discrete index vectors* $\mathbf{c} \in \{1, \ldots, k_n\}^N$ *and* $\mathbf{d} \in \{1, \ldots, k_m\}^M$ *respectively.*

Therefore, our goal is to find a stencil $\mathcal{S}(\mathbf{T}, \mathbf{c}, \mathbf{d})$ with a small approximation error $\mathbf{R} - \mathcal{S}(\mathbf{T}, \mathbf{c}, \mathbf{d})$ and small cost for storing $\theta = \{\mathbf{T}, \mathbf{c}, \mathbf{d}\}$.

Lemma 2 (Compression) *Stencil* $\mathcal{S}(\mathbf{T}, \mathbf{c}, \mathbf{d})$ *can be stored with* $N \log_2 k_n$ *bits for row cluster assignments* $\mathbf{c}$*,* $M \log_2 k_m$ *bits for column cluster assignments* $\mathbf{d}$ *and* $32 k_n k_m$ *bits to store a 32-bit floating point number for each block in* $\mathbf{T}$*:*

$$\text{Bits}(\{\mathbf{T}, \mathbf{c}, \mathbf{d}\}) = N \log_2 k_n + M \log_2 k_m + 32 k_n k_m \qquad (2)$$

Note, it is trivial to get zero approximation error by setting $k_n = N$ and $k_m = M$, but this creates a very large model (the size of the original data) that is not useful.

As mentioned above, we can efficiently improve the approximation accuracy by using *multiple* stencils:

$$\underset{\{\mathbf{T}^{(\ell)}, \mathbf{c}^{(\ell)}, \mathbf{d}^{(\ell)}\}}{\text{minimize}} \sum_{u=1}^{N} \sum_{m=1}^{M} \mathbf{I}_{u,m} \left(\mathbf{R}_{u,m} - \sum_{\ell=1}^{S} \mathcal{S}\left(\mathbf{T}^{(\ell)}, \mathbf{c}^{(\ell)}, \mathbf{d}^{(\ell)}\right)_{u,m} \right)^2$$

That is, we would like to find an additive model of S stencils that minimizes the approximation error to $\mathbf{R}$.

Algorithm 1 Matrix Approximation

Require: matrix $\mathbf{R}$, indicator matrix $\mathbf{I}$, clusters k_n, k_m, max stencils S

1: $\hat{\mathbf{R}} \leftarrow \mathbf{R}$
2: **for** $\ell = 1$ **to** S **do**
3: $(\mathbf{c}^{(\ell)}, \mathbf{V}^{(\mathrm{row})}, \mathbf{L}) \leftarrow \textsc{Cluster}(\hat{\mathbf{R}}, k_n, \mathbf{I})$ {Rows}
4: $(\mathbf{d}^{(\ell)}, \cdot, \cdot) \leftarrow \textsc{Cluster}([\mathbf{V}^{(\mathrm{row})}]^\top, k_m, \mathbf{L}^\top)$ {Columns}
5: **for all** $a, b \in \{1, \dots k_n\} \times \{1, \dots k_m\}$ **do**
6: $\mathbf{T}^{(\ell)}_{a,b} \leftarrow \text{mean}\left\{\hat{\mathbf{R}}_{u,m} | \mathbf{c}^{(\ell)}_u = a \text{ and } \mathbf{d}^{(\ell)}_m = b\right\}$
7: **end for**
8: $\hat{\mathbf{R}} \leftarrow \hat{\mathbf{R}} - \mathcal{S}(\mathbf{T}^{(\ell)}, \mathbf{c}^{(\ell)}, \mathbf{d}^{(\ell)})$ {Backfit on residuals}
9: **end for**
10: **return** $\{\mathbf{T}^{(\ell)}, \mathbf{c}^{(\ell)}, \mathbf{d}^{(\ell)}\}_{\ell=1}^S$

Algorithm 2 $\textsc{Cluster}(\mathbf{M}, k, \mathbf{W})$

Require: matrix $\mathbf{M} \in \mathbb{R}^{N_1 \times N_2}$, weights $\mathbf{W} \in \mathbb{R}^{N_1 \times N_2}$, number of clusters k

1: Draw k rows from $\mathbf{M}$ at random without replacement and copy them to $\mathbf{V} = \{\mathbf{v}_1, \dots, \mathbf{v}_k\} \in \mathbb{R}^{k \times N_2}$.
2: **while** not converged **do**
3: $\mathbf{L} \leftarrow \mathbf{0} \in \mathbb{R}^{k \times N_2}$ and $\mathbf{Y} \leftarrow \mathbf{0} \in \mathbb{R}^{k \times N_2}$
4: **for** $i = 1$ **to** N_1 **do**
5: $\mathbf{c}_i \leftarrow \operatorname{argmin}_c \sum_j \mathbf{W}_{i,j}(\mathbf{M}_{i,j} - \mathbf{V}_{c,j})^2$
6: $\mathbf{Y}_{\mathbf{c}_i,:} \leftarrow \mathbf{Y}_{\mathbf{c}_i,:} + \mathbf{M}_{i,:}$ {Increment statistics}
7: $\mathbf{L}_{\mathbf{c}_i,:} \leftarrow \mathbf{L}_{\mathbf{c}_i,:} + \mathbf{I}_{i,:}$ {Increment counts}
8: **end for**
9: **for** $c = 1$ **to** k **do**
10: $\mathbf{V}_{c,:} \leftarrow \mathbf{Y}_{c,:} / \mathbf{L}_{c,:}$ {New cluster center}
11: **end for**
12: **end while**
13: **return** cluster assignments $\mathbf{c}$, clusters $\mathbf{V}$, counts $\mathbf{L}$

Given $\mathbf{R}$, it is our goal to *find* such stencils $\mathcal{S}(\mathbf{T}^{(\ell)}, \mathbf{c}^{(\ell)}, \mathbf{d}^{(\ell)})$ with good approximation properties. Unfortunately, finding linear combinations of co-clusterings is NP-hard. It is easy to see this by reducing co-clustering, which is NP-hard, to our problem by setting $S = 1$. We describe below two algorithms to learn our stencils that offer good approximation guarantees and work well in practice.

3.2 Algorithm

We consider a simple iterative procedure to learn stencils to approximate our data $\mathbf{R}$. Algorithm 1 gives the high level algorithm of learning each stencil one at a time. In learning each stencil we use the Cluster algorithm, similar to k-means, as given in Algorithm 2.

Row clustering. We first perform k-means clustering of the rows. That is, we aim to find an approximation of $\mathbf{R}$ that replaces all rows by a small subset thereof. Algorithm 2 is essentially a generalization of k-means clustering. By calling the algorithm with $\mathbf{M} = \mathbf{R}$, $k = k_n$, and $\mathbf{W} = \mathbf{1}^{N \times M}$, we find that the algorithm simplifies significantly to classic k-means. The cluster assignment in Line 5 is simply

$$\mathbf{c}_u \leftarrow \operatorname*{argmin}_c \|\mathbf{R}_{u,:} - \mathbf{v}_c\|_2^2 \tag{3}$$

and $\mathbf{L}$ stores the number of rows in each row cluster.

Column clustering. Once we have run the clustering algorithm on the rows, we now cluster the columns of previously learned row clusters, $\mathbf{V}^{(\mathrm{row})}$. In this case, we need to weight each row of $\mathbf{V}^{(\mathrm{row})}$ (corresponding to a row cluster) by the number of rows it represents (the number of rows in that cluster). As a result, rather than choose a column cluster assignment by the Euclidean distance, we use the Mahalanobis distance. Still, Algorithm 2 is a generalization of this concept. We use the assignment (for Line 5):

$$\mathbf{d}_m \leftarrow \operatorname*{argmin}_d \left(\mathbf{V}^{(\mathrm{row})}_{:,m} - \mathbf{V}_{:,d}\right)^\top \mathbf{D} \left(\mathbf{V}^{(\mathrm{row})}_{:,m} - \mathbf{V}_{:,d}\right) \tag{4}$$

where $\mathbf{V} \in \mathbb{R}^{k_n \times k_m}$ is the matrix obtained by stacking $\mathbf{V}_{:,d} = \mathbf{v}_d^\top$ and $\mathbf{D}$ would be the diagonal matrix of counts, i.e. $\mathbf{D}_{cc}$ is the number of rows of $\mathbf{R}$ in cluster c.

Missing entries. In many cases, however, $\mathbf{R}$ itself is incomplete. This is addressed quite easily by using the assignment shown in Line 5 of Algorithm 2. Therefore, in finding a good cluster for the row $\mathbf{R}_{u,:}$ we restrict ourselves to the coordinates in $\mathbf{V}_{c,:}$ where $\mathbf{R}_{u,m}$ exists (and also where $\mathbf{V}_{c,m}$ has been initialized).

For the purpose of obtaining the column clusters, we now need to weight each coordinate in $\mathbf{V}^{(\mathrm{row})}$ by how many elements in $\mathbf{R}$ contributed to it. Correspondingly denote by $\mathbf{L}_{c,m} := \sum_{(u,m) \in \mathbf{R}: \mathbf{c}_u = c} 1$ the number of entries mapped into coordinate $\mathbf{V}^{(\mathrm{row})}_{c,m}$. Then the assignment for column clusters is obtained via

$$\mathbf{d}_m \leftarrow \operatorname*{argmin}_d \sum_c \mathbf{L}_{c,m} \left(\mathbf{V}^{(\mathrm{row})}_{c,m} - \mathbf{V}_{c,d}\right)^2 \tag{5}$$

We observe that Algorithm 2 handles both row and column clustering correctly, by calling it appropriately as shown in Algorithm 1.

Backfitting. The outcome of running the row and column clustering described above on $\mathbf{R}$ is a single stencil $\mathcal{S}(\mathbf{T}, \mathbf{c}, \mathbf{d})$ consisting of the clusters obtained by first row and then column clustering. It may be desirable to alternate between row and column clustering for further refinement.

However, as noted above, additional stencils only reduce the objective function further - convergence to a local minimum is assured, with the same caveat on solution quality as in k-means clustering. Therefore, we take the residual $\hat{\mathbf{R}} = \mathbf{R} - \mathcal{S}(\mathbf{T}, \mathbf{c}, \mathbf{d})$ and use it as the starting point to learn a new stencil. By repeatedly learning new stencils on the residuals of the previous stencils, as shown in Algorithm 1, we obtain an additive model of co-clusterings that minimizes the approximation error to $\mathbf{R}$.

3.3 Approximation Guarantees

A key question is how well any given matrix $\mathbf{R}$ can be approximated by an appropriate stencil. For the sake of simplicity we limit ourselves to the case where all entries of the matrix are observed. Using covering numbers and the spectral properties of $\mathbf{R}$, we can obtain approximation guarantees for co-clustering. Denote by $\mathbf{\Sigma} = \operatorname{diag}(\sigma_1, \dots \sigma_n)$ the singular values of $\mathbf{R}$.

Theorem 3 (Approximation Guarantees) *Using k clusters for both rows and columns, the matrix $\mathbf{R}$ can be approximated with error at most*

$$\left\|\mathbf{R} - \mathbf{R}'\right\|_\infty \le 2 \left\|\mathbf{R}\right\|^{\frac{1}{2}} \epsilon_k \left(\mathbf{\Sigma}^{\frac{1}{2}}\right)$$

$$\left\|\mathbf{R} - \mathbf{R}'\right\|_2 \le (\sqrt{N} + \sqrt{M}) \left\|\mathbf{R}\right\|^{\frac{1}{2}} \epsilon_k \left(\mathbf{\Sigma}^{\frac{1}{2}}\right)$$

where

$$\epsilon_k(\mathbf{\Sigma}) \leq 6 \sup_{j \in \mathbb{N}} \left(\frac{1}{k} \prod_{i=1}^{j} \sigma_i \right)^{\frac{1}{j}} \leq 6\epsilon_k(\mathbf{\Sigma})$$

PROOF. We omit the proof of Theorem 3 due to space constraints. The complete proof can be found at http://arxiv.org/abs/1501.00199. □

Note that the above is a statement of *existence* rather than a constructive prescription. However, the main purpose of the above analysis is to obtain theoretical upper bounds on the rate of convergence. In practice, the results can be considerably better, as we show in Section 5.

4. GENERATIVE MODEL

As many frequentist algorithms have a Bayesian counterpart, we now devise a Bayesian counterpart to ACCAMS, which we will refer to as bACCAMS. We begin with the single stencil case, describing the model in Section 4.1 and a collapsed Gibbs sampler in Section 4.2. We then extend the model and sampler to many stencils in Section 4.4.

4.1 Co-Clustering with a Single Stencil

We begin with a simple Bayesian model of co-clustering. This is the basic template for single-stencil inference, and our model of additive co-clusters will use the same idea. Our model can be broken into two parts: (1) generating block values and (2) generating cluster assignments. We will go through each part of the model and then the model as a whole, as shown in Figure 2.

Block values. We begin by considering how we generate the prediction $\mathbf{T}_{c,d}$ for a particular block, corresponding to ratings from users in cluster c to movies in cluster d. Previously, as shown in Line 6 of Algorithm 1, each block merely took the average of the values that fell in that block. Subsequently, we would use that block mean directly as the prediction for all values in the block.

In our Bayesian model, we consider each $\mathbf{T}_{c,d}$ to come from a Gaussian distribution, centered at 0 and with variance τ^2. On top of this, each value in the matrix $\mathbf{R}_{u,m}$ is generated by a Gaussian with mean $\mathbf{T}_{\mathbf{c}_u,\mathbf{d}_m}$ and variance σ^2 (alternatively stated, with additive noise $\epsilon_{u,m} \sim \mathcal{N}(0, \sigma^2)$). As such we have

$$\mathbf{T}_{c,d} \sim \mathcal{N}(0, \tau^2) \qquad \mathbf{R}_{u,m} \sim \mathcal{N}\left(\mathbf{T}_{\mathbf{c}_u,\mathbf{d}_m}, \sigma^2\right) \quad (6)$$

Because τ^2 and σ^2 are not yet defined and are data dependent, they too are sampled from the conjugate prior distribution, specifically the Inverse Gamma distribution:

$$\tau^2 \sim \mathrm{IG}(\gamma) \qquad \sigma^2 \sim \mathrm{IG}(\eta) \quad (7)$$

Cluster assignments. In Algorithm 2, a user u (or movie m) is assigned to a particular cluster $\mathbf{c}_u$ ($\mathbf{d}_m$ for movies) based purely on the distance to the cluster center. As with most frequentist algorithms, there is no prior on the cluster assignments.

In our Bayesian model, we put a Dirichlet prior on the cluster assignments. More simply understood, we believe cluster assignments are generated by a Chinese Restaurant Process (CRP). One big advantage of using a CRP is that it allows for an unrestricted number of clusters, where new

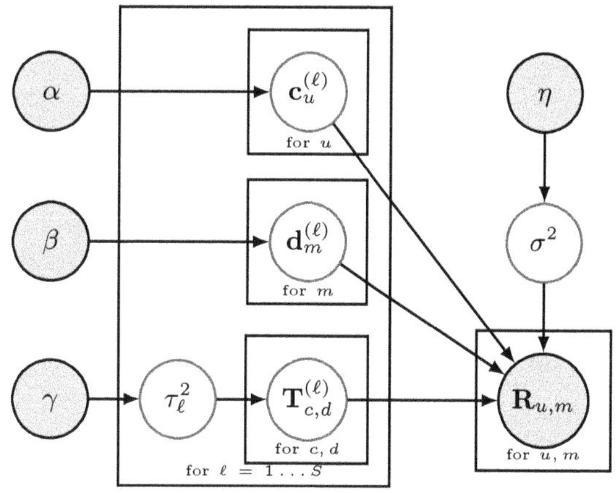

Figure 2: Generative model for recommdnation and matrix approximation (bACCAMS). For each stencil, as indexed by ℓ, row and cluster memberships $\mathbf{c}^{(\ell)}$ and $\mathbf{d}^{(\ell)}$ are drawn from a Chinese Restaurant Process. The values for the template $\mathbf{T}^{(\ell)}$ are drawn from a Normal Distribution. The observed ratings $\mathbf{R}_{u,m}$ are sums over the stencils $\mathcal{S}(\mathbf{T}^{(\ell)}, \mathbf{c}^{(\ell)}, \mathbf{d}^{(\ell)})$.

clusters can always be created with small probability. To understand the Chinese Restaurant Process, consider the following metaphor. A user u is at a Chinese restaurant and trying to pick a table (cluster) at which to sit. Each table is chosen with probability proportional to the number of users already at that table (in that cluster), and a new table is started with some small probability, proportional to α. To be concrete, we assume there are N users, and cluster c has $\mathbf{n}_c$ users in it; $\mathbf{n}_c^{(-u)}$ is the number of users in cluster c not including user u. The probability that user u will go to a particular cluster c is given by:

$$p(\mathbf{c}_u = c|\mathbf{c}^{(-u)}, \alpha) = \begin{cases} \frac{\mathbf{n}_c^{(-u)}}{\alpha+N-1} & \text{if } \mathbf{n}_c^{(-u)} > 0 \\ \frac{\alpha}{\alpha+N-1} & \text{new cluster } c \end{cases} \quad (8)$$

An analogous expression is available for movies: $p(\mathbf{d}_m = d|\mathbf{d}^{(-m)}, \beta)$. Under this model, large values of α and β encourage the formation of larger numbers of clusters.

Complete model. Putting these two elements together, we can now describe our complete Bayesian model for co-clustering:

$$\mathbf{c}_u \sim \mathrm{CRP}(\alpha) \qquad \mathbf{d}_m \sim \mathrm{CRP}(\beta) \quad (9a)$$
$$\mathbf{T}_{c,d} \sim \mathcal{N}(0, \tau^2) \qquad \mathbf{R}_{u,m} \sim \mathcal{N}\left(\mathbf{T}_{\mathbf{c}_u,\mathbf{d}_m}, \sigma^2\right) \quad (9b)$$
$$\tau^2 \sim \mathrm{IG}(\gamma) \qquad \sigma^2 \sim \mathrm{IG}(\eta) \quad (9c)$$

Consequently the joint probability distribution over all ratings, given the variances, is given by

$$p\left(\mathbf{R}, \mathcal{S}(\mathbf{T}, \mathbf{c}, \mathbf{d})|\alpha, \beta, \sigma^2, \tau^2\right) = \mathrm{CRP}(\mathbf{c}|\alpha)\mathrm{CRP}(\mathbf{d}|\beta) \times \quad (10)$$
$$\prod_{c,d} \frac{1}{\sqrt{2\pi\tau^2}} \exp\left(\frac{-\mathbf{T}_{c,d}^2}{2\tau^2}\right) \prod_{(u,m)} \frac{1}{\sqrt{2\pi\sigma^2}} \exp\left(-\frac{\left(\mathbf{R}_{u,m} - \mathbf{T}_{\mathbf{c}_u,\mathbf{d}_m}\right)^2}{2\sigma^2}\right)$$

This is an extremely simple model similar to [21], akin to a decision stump. The rationale for picking such a primitive model is that we will be taking linear combinations thereof to obtain a very flexible tool. We will now show that, by design, the model can be effeciently sampled.

4.2 Collapsed Gibbs Sampler

We now dive into the details of efficiently learning our model through a collapsed Gibbs sampler. There are three main parts of the model that need to be sampled: (1) the cluster assignments $\mathbf{c}$ and $\mathbf{d}$, (2) the block values $\mathbf{T}_{c,d}$, and (3) the variances τ^2 and σ^2. By design, in particular the use of conjugate priors, our model is efficient to sample. For sampling cluster assignments, we find that we can collapse out $\mathbf{T}_{c,d}$ so that sequential samples of cluster assignments are not based on stale values of $\mathbf{T}_{c,d}$ and we achieve a significantly faster sampler.

4.2.1 *Inferring Cluster Assignments*

We begin with the challenge of sampling the user cluster assignments $\mathbf{c}$ given only the data $\mathbf{R}$, the movie cluster assignments $\mathbf{d}$, and the priors α, σ^2, τ^2. To do this, we must collapse out the block values of $\mathbf{T}$.

In particular, at each step, we check how the likelihood of the data $\mathbf{R}$ changes by assigning a user (or movie) to a new cluster:

$$p(\mathbf{c}_u = c|\mathbf{R}, \mathbf{d}, \alpha, \sigma^2, \tau^2) \propto \mathrm{CRP}(c|\alpha)\frac{p(\mathbf{R}|\mathbf{c}^{(-u)}, \mathbf{c}_u = c, \mathbf{d}, \sigma^2, \tau^2)}{p(\mathbf{R}|\mathbf{c}^{(-u)}, \mathbf{d}, \sigma^2, \tau^2)}$$

We denote the observations for block (c, d), the ratings from users in cluster c to movies in cluster d, by the vector $\mathbf{r}_{c,d}$; the updated ratings in the block after the assignment is given by $\mathbf{r}'_{c,d}$. With this, the calculation above simplifies to:

$$p(\mathbf{c}_u = c|\mathbf{R}, \mathbf{d}, \alpha, \sigma^2, \tau^2) \propto \mathrm{CRP}(c|\alpha) \prod_d \frac{p(\mathbf{r}'_{c,d}|\sigma^2, \tau^2)}{p(\mathbf{r}_{c,d}|\sigma^2, \tau^2)}$$

As we shall see, this is easily calculated by keeping simple linear statistics of the ratings. Moreover, by integrating out $\mathbf{T}$ we avoid the problem of having to instantiate a new value whenever a new cluster is added.

For a given block (c, d) with associated $\mathbf{r}_{c,d}$, the distribution of ratings is Gaussian with mean 0 and with covariance matrix $\mathbf{\Sigma} = \sigma^2\mathbf{1} + \tau^2 1 1^\top$ (due to the independence of the variances and the additive nature of the normal distribution). Here we use $\mathbf{1}$ to denote the identity matrix and 1 to denote the vector of all 1. Denote by $\mathbf{N}_{c,d}$ the number of rating pairs (u, m) for which $\mathbf{c}_u = c$ and $\mathbf{d}_m = d$. Hence, the likelihood of the block (c, d), as observed in $\mathbf{r}_{c,d}$, is

$$p(\mathbf{r}_{c,d}|\sigma^2, \tau^2) = \frac{\exp\left[-\frac{1}{2}\mathbf{r}_{c,d}^\top \mathbf{\Sigma}^{-1}\mathbf{r}_{c,d}\right]}{(2\pi)^{\frac{\mathbf{N}_{c,d}}{2}} |\mathbf{\Sigma}|^{\frac{1}{2}}}$$

In computing the above expression we need to compute the determinant of $\mathbf{\Sigma}$, a diagonal matrix with rank-1 update, and the inverse of said matrix. For the former, we use the matrix-determinant lemma, and for the latter, the Sherman-Morrison-Woodbury formula:

$$\mathbf{r}_{c,d}^\top \mathbf{\Sigma}^{-1}\mathbf{r}_{c,d} = \frac{1}{\sigma^2}\|\mathbf{r}_{c,d}\|^2 - \frac{\tau^2}{\sigma^2} \cdot \frac{\left(1^\top \mathbf{r}_{c,d}\right)^2}{\sigma^2 + \mathbf{N}_{c,d}\tau^2}$$

$$\log|\mathbf{\Sigma}| = (\mathbf{N}_{c,d} - 1)\log\sigma^2 + \log\left[\sigma^2 + \mathbf{N}_{c,d}\tau^2\right]$$

This allows us to assess whether it is beneficial to assign a user u or a movie m to a different or a new cluster efficiently, since the only statistics involved in the operation are sums of ratings and of their squares, $1^\top \mathbf{r}_{c,d}$ and $\|\mathbf{r}_{c,d}\|^2$ respectively.

We denote by $\mathbf{N}'_{c,d}$ the new cluster count and by $\mathbf{r}'_{c,d}$ the new set of ratings, after having assigned user u to cluster c. Let

$$\Delta := \tfrac{\mathbf{N}'_{c,d} - \mathbf{N}_{c,d}}{2}\left[\log(2\pi) + \log\sigma^2\right] + \frac{1}{2\sigma^2}\left[\left\|\mathbf{r}'_{c,d}\right\|^2 - \|\mathbf{r}_{c,d}\|^2\right]$$

be a constant offset, in log-space, that only depends on the additional ratings that are added to a cluster. That is, Δ is *independent* of the cluster that the additional scores are assigned to and can be safely ignored. The result is:

$$p(\mathbf{c}_u = c|\mathbf{R}, \mathbf{d}, \alpha, \sigma^2, \tau^2) \propto \tfrac{\mathbf{n}_c^{(-u)}}{\alpha + N - 1} \prod_d \left[\frac{\sigma^2 + \mathbf{N}_{c,d}\tau^2}{\sigma^2 + \mathbf{N}'_{c,d}\tau^2}\right]^{\frac{1}{2}} \quad (11)$$

$$\times \exp\left[\frac{\tau^2}{2\sigma^2}\sum_d\left[\frac{\left(1^\top \mathbf{r}'_{c,d}\right)^2}{\sigma^2 + \mathbf{N}'_{c,d}\tau^2} - \frac{\left(1^\top \mathbf{r}_{c,d}\right)^2}{\sigma^2 + \mathbf{N}_{c,d}\tau^2}\right]\right]$$

For a new cluster this can be simplified since there is no data, hence $\mathbf{N}_{c,d} = 0$ and $\mathbf{r}_{c,d} = []$.

$$p(\mathbf{c}_u = c_{\text{new}}|\mathbf{R}, \mathbf{d}, \alpha, \sigma^2, \tau^2) \propto \tfrac{\alpha}{\alpha + N - 1} \prod_d \left[\tfrac{\sigma^2}{\sigma^2 + \mathbf{N}'_{c,d}\tau^2}\right]^{\frac{1}{2}} \quad (12)$$

$$\times \exp\left[\tfrac{\tau^2}{2\sigma^2}\sum_d \tfrac{\left(1^\top \mathbf{r}'_{c,d}\right)^2}{\sigma^2 + \mathbf{N}'_{c,d}\tau^2}\right]$$

The above expression is fairly straightforward to compute: we only need to track $\mathbf{N}_{c,d}$, i.e. the number of ratings assigned to a particular (user cluster, movie cluster) combination and $1^\top \mathbf{r}_{c,d}$, i.e. the sum of the ratings for this block.

4.2.2 *Inferring Block Values*

For the purpose of recommendation and for a subsequent combination of several matrices, we need to instantiate the block values $\mathbf{T}_{c,d}$. By checking (10) we see that $\mathbf{T}_{c,d}|\text{rest}$ is given by

$$\mathbf{T}_{c,d}|\text{rest} \sim \mathcal{N}\left(\tfrac{1^\top \mathbf{r}_{c,d}}{\rho \mathbf{N}_{c,d}}, \tfrac{\sigma^2}{\rho \mathbf{N}_{c,d}}\right) \text{ where } \rho = \left[1 + \tfrac{1}{\mathbf{N}_{c,d}}\tfrac{\sigma^2}{\tau^2}\right] \quad (13)$$

Here too sampling $\mathbf{T}_{c,d}$ only requires having the number of ratings $\mathbf{N}_{c,d}$ and sum of ratings in the block $1^\top \mathbf{r}_{c,d}$.

4.2.3 *Inferring Variances*

Last, we consider how to sample the variances for the priors, σ^2 and τ^2. Both σ^2 and τ^2 are generated by the Inverse Gamma distribution:

$$p(x|a, b) = b^a \Gamma^{-1}(a) x^{-a-1} e^{-\frac{b}{x}} \quad (14)$$

Denote by E the total number of observed values in $\mathbf{R}$. In this case, σ^2 is drawn from an Inverse Gamma prior with parameters (η'_a, η'_b):

$$\eta'_a \leftarrow \eta_a + \frac{E}{2} \text{ and } \eta'_b \leftarrow \eta_b + \sum_{(u,m)} \mathbf{I}_{u,m}(\mathbf{R}_{u,m} - \mathbf{T}_{\mathbf{c}_u,\mathbf{d}_m})^2 \quad (15)$$

Analogously, we draw τ^2 from an Inverse Gamma with parameters

$$\gamma'_a \leftarrow \gamma_a + \frac{k_n k_m}{2} \text{ and } \gamma'_b \leftarrow \gamma_b + \sum_{c,d} \mathbf{T}_{c,d}^2 \quad (16)$$

k_n and k_m denote the number of user and movie clusters.

4.3 Efficient Implementation

With these inference equations we can implement an efficient sampler, as seen in Algorithm 3. The key to efficient sampling is to cache the per-cluster sums of ratings $1^\top \mathbf{r}_{c,d}$. Then reassigning a user (or movie) to a different

Algorithm 3 StencilSampler($\mathbf{M}, \mathbf{T}, \mathbf{c}, \mathbf{d}$)

Initialize row-index and column-index of data in $\mathbf{M}$
Initialize statistics for each partition
    $\mathbf{N}_{c,d} := |\{(u,m) : \mathbf{c}_u = c, \mathbf{d}_m = d\}|$ and $\mathbf{Y}_{c,d} := \sum_{(u,m):\mathbf{c}_u=c,\mathbf{d}_m=d} \mathbf{M}_{u,m}$
while sampler not converged **do**
    for all users u **do**
        For all movie clusters $\mathbf{d}$ compute the incremental changes
        $\mathbf{l}_d^{(u)} := |\{(u,m) : \mathbf{d}_m = d\}|$ and $\mathbf{y}_d^{(u)} := \sum_{(u,m):\mathbf{d}_m=d} \mathbf{M}_{u,m}$
        Remove u from their cluster
            $\mathbf{N}_{\mathbf{c}_u,:} \leftarrow \mathbf{N}_{\mathbf{c}_u,:} - \mathbf{l}^{(u)}$ and $\mathbf{Y}_{\mathbf{c}_u,:} \leftarrow \mathbf{Y}_{\mathbf{c}_u,:} - \mathbf{y}^{(u)}$
        Sample new user cluster $\mathbf{c}_u$ using (11) and (12).
        Update statistics
            $\mathbf{N}_{\mathbf{c}_u,:} \leftarrow \mathbf{N}_{\mathbf{c}_u,:} + \mathbf{l}^{(u)}$ and $\mathbf{Y}_{\mathbf{c}_u,:} \leftarrow \mathbf{Y}_{\mathbf{c}_u,:} + \mathbf{y}^{(u)}$
    end for
    for all movies m **do**
        Sample movie cluster assignments analogously.
    end for
    for all (c,d) cluster partitions **do**
        Resample $\mathbf{T}_{c,d}$ using (13) and $\mathbf{N}_{c,d}, \mathbf{Y}_{c,d}$.
    end for
    Resample σ^2 and τ^2 using (15) and (16).
end while
return $\mathbf{T}, \mathbf{c}, \mathbf{d}$

(or new) cluster is just a matter of checking the amount of change that this would effect. Hence each sampling pass costs $O(k_n \cdot k_m \cdot (N + M) + E)$ operations. It is linear in the number of ratings and of partitions.

Note that once $\mathbf{y}^{(u)}$ and $\mathbf{l}^{(u)}$ are available for all users (or all movies), it is cheap to perform additional sampling sweeps at comparably low cost. It is therefore beneficial to iterate over all users (or all movies) more than once, in particular in the initial stages of the algorithm. Also note that the algorithm can be used on datasets that are being streamed from disk, provided that an index and an inverted index of $\mathbf{M}$ can be stored: we need to be able to traverse the data when ordered by users and when ordered by movies. It is thus compatible with solid state disks.

4.4 Additive Combinations of Stencils

As before, we find that using a linear combination of stencils is far more powerful than just a single stencil. Therefore, we enumerate the stencils by $\mathcal{S}(\mathbf{T}^{(\ell)}, \mathbf{c}^{(\ell)}, \mathbf{d}^{(\ell)})$, where stencil index ℓ ranges from 1 to S. Correspondingly we now need to sample from a set of $\mathcal{S}(\mathbf{T}^{(\ell)}, \mathbf{c}^{(\ell)}, \mathbf{d}^{(\ell)})$ and τ_ℓ^2 *per* stencil. However, we keep the additive noise term $\mathcal{N}(0, \sigma^2)$ unchanged. This is the model of Figure 2. The additivity of Gaussians makes inference easy:

$$\mathbf{R}_{u,m} \sim \mathcal{N}\left(\sum_\ell \mathcal{S}(\mathbf{T}^{(\ell)}, \mathbf{c}^{(\ell)}, \mathbf{d}^{(\ell)})_{u,m}, \sigma^2\right). \tag{17}$$

Note, though, that estimating $\mathcal{S}$ jointly *for all* indices ℓ is not tractable since various clusterings $(\mathbf{c}^{(\ell)}, \mathbf{d}^{(\ell)})$ overlap and intersect with each other, hence the joint normal distribution over all variables would be expensive to factorize.

Instead, we sample over one stencil at a time, as shown in Algorithm 4. This algorithm only requires repeated passes

Algorithm 4 bACCAMS

initialize residuals $\hat{\mathbf{R}} \leftarrow \mathbf{R}$ and $\mathbf{T}^{(\ell)} = 0\ \forall \ell$
while sampler not converged **do**
    for all stencils $\ell = 1 \ldots S$ **do**
        $\hat{\mathbf{R}} \leftarrow \hat{\mathbf{R}} + \mathcal{S}(\mathbf{T}^{(\ell)}, \mathbf{c}^{(\ell)}, \mathbf{d}^{(\ell)})$ {Without stencil ℓ}
        $(\mathbf{T}^{(\ell)}, \mathbf{c}^{(\ell)}, \mathbf{d}^{(\ell)}) \leftarrow$ StencilSampler($\hat{\mathbf{R}}, \mathbf{T}^{(\ell)}, \mathbf{c}^{(\ell)}, \mathbf{d}^{(\ell)}$)
        $\hat{\mathbf{R}} \leftarrow \hat{\mathbf{R}} - \mathcal{S}(\mathbf{T}^{(\ell)}, \mathbf{c}^{(\ell)}, \mathbf{d}^{(\ell)})$ {With stencil ℓ}
    end for
end while

through the dataset. Moreover, it can be modified into a backfitting procedure by fitting one matrix at a time and then fixing the outcome. Capacity control can be enforced by modifying α and β such that the probability of a new cluster decreases for larger ℓ, i.e. by decreasing α and β. As a result following the analysis in the single stencil case, each sampling pass costs $O(S \cdot (k_n \cdot k_m \cdot (N + M) + E))$ operations. It is linear in the number of ratings, in the number of partitions and in the number of stencils.

5. EXPERIMENTS

We evaluate our method based on its ability to perform matrix completion, matrix approximation and to give interpretable results. Here we describe our experimental setup and results on real world data, such as the Netflix ratings.

5.1 Implementation

We implemented both ACCAMS, the k-means-based algorithm, as well as bACCAMS, the Bayesian model. Unless specified otherwise, we run Algorithm 2 for up to $T = 50$ iterations. Our system can also iterate over the stencils multiple times, such that earlier stencils can be re-learned after we have learned later ones. In practice, we observe this only yields small gains in accuracy, hence we generally do not use it.

We implemented bACCAMS using Gibbs sampling (Section 4.4) and used the k-means algorithm ACCAMS for the initialization of each stencil. Following standard practice, we bound the range of σ by $\sigma_{\max}$ from above. This rejection sampler avoids pathological cases. For the sake of simplicity, we set $k = k_n = k_m$ to be the maximum number of clusters that can be generated in each stencil. When inferring the cluster assignments for a given stencil, we run three iterations of the sampler before proceeding to the next stencil. As common in MCMC algorithms, we use a burn-in period of at least 30 iterations (each with three sub-iterations of sampling cluster assignments) and then average the predictions over many draws. Code for both ACCAMS and bACCAMS is available at http://alexbeutel.com/accams.

5.2 Experimental Setup

Netflix. We run our algorithms on data from a variety of domains. Our primary testing dataset is the ratings dataset from the Netflix contest. The dataset contains 100 million ratings from 480,189 users and 17,770 movies. Following standard practice for testing recommendation accuracy, we average over three different random 90:10 splits for training and testing.

CMU Face Images. To test how well we can approximate arbitrary matrices, we use image data from the CMU Face

Images dataset[1]. It contains black and white images of 20 different people, each in 32 different positions, for a total of 640 images. Each image has 128×120 pixel resolution; we flatten this into a matrix of 640×15360, i.e. an image by pixel matrix.

AS Peering Graph. To assess our model's ability to deal with graph data we consider the AS graph[2]. It contains information on the peering information of 13,580 nodes. It thus creates a binary matrix of size $13,580 \times 13,580$ with 37k edges. Since our algorithm is not designed to learn binary matrices, we treat the entries $\{0, 1\}$ as real valued numbers.

Parameters. For all experiments, we set the hyperparameters in bACCAMS to $\alpha = \beta = 10$, $\eta_\alpha = 2$, $\eta_\beta = 0.3$, $\gamma_\alpha = 5$, and $\gamma_\alpha = 0.3$. Depending on the task, we compare ACCAMS against SVD++ using the GraphChi [12] implementation, SVD from Matlab for full matrices, and previously reported state-of-the-art results.

Model complexity. Since our model is structurally quite different from factorization models, we compare them based on the number of bits in the model and prediction accuracy. For factorization models, we consider each factor to be a 32 bit `float`. Hence the complexity of a rank r SVD++ model of N users and M movies is $32 \cdot r(N + M)$ bits.

For ACCAMS with S stencils and $k \times k$ co-clusters in each stencil, the cluster assignment for a given row or column is $\log_2 k$ bits and each value in the stencil is a `float`. As such, the complexity of a model is $S((N + M) \log_2 k + 32 \cdot k^2)$ bits.

In calculating the parameter space size for LLORMA, we make the very conservative estimate that each row and column is on average part of two factorizations, even though the model contains more than 30 factorizations that each row and column could be part of.

5.3 Matrix Completion

Since the primary motivation of our model is collaborative filtering we begin by discussing results on the classic Netflix problem; accuracy is measured in RMSE. To avoid divergence we set $\sigma_{\max} = 1$. We then vary both the number of clusters k and the number of stencils S.

A summary of recent results as well as results using our method can be found in Table 2. Using GraphChi we run SVD++ on our data. We use the reported values from LLORMA [13] and DFC [16], which were obtained using the same protocol as reported here.

As can be seen in Table 2, bACCAMS achieves the *best* published result. We achieve this while using a very different model that is significantly simpler both conceptually and in terms of parameter space size. We also did not use any of the temporal and contextual variants that many other models use to incorporate prior knowledge.

As shown in Figure 1, we observe that per bit our model achieves much better accuracy at a fraction of the model size. In Figure 3(a) we compare different configurations of our algorithm. As can be seen, classic co-clustering quickly overfits the training data and provides a less fine-grained ability to improve prediction accuracy than ACCAMS. Since ACCAMS has no regularization, it too overfits the training data. By using a Bayesian model with bACCAMS, we do not overfit the training data and thus can use more stencils for prediction, greatly improving the prediction accuracy.

[1]http://www.cs.cmu.edu/~tom/faces.html

[2]http://topology.eecs.umich.edu/data.html

Method	Parameters	Size	Test RMSE
SVD++ [12]	$R = 25$	49.8MB	0.8631
DFC-NYS [16]	Not reported		0.8486
DFC-PROJ [16]	Not reported		0.8411
LLORMA [13]	$R = 1$	3.98MB	0.9295
LLORMA [13]	$R = 5$, $a > 30$	19.9MB	0.8604
LLORMA [13]	$R = 10$, $a > 30$	39.8MB	0.8444
LLORMA [13]	$R = 20$, $a > 30$	79.7MB	0.8337
ACCAMS	$k = 10$, $s = 13$	2.69MB	0.8780
ACCAMS	$k = 100$, $s = 5$	2.27MB	0.8759
bACCAMS	$k = 10$, $s = 50$	10.4MB	0.8403
bACCAMS	$k = 10$, $s = 70$	14.5MB	0.8363
bACCAMS	$k = 10$, $s = 125$	**25.9MB**	**0.8331**

Table 2: bACCAMS achieves an accuracy for matrix completion on Netflix better than or on-par with the best published results, while having a parameter space a fraction of the size of other methods. a denotes the number of anchor points for LLORMA and sizes listed are the parameter space size.

5.4 Matrix Approximation

In addition to matrix completion, it is valuable to be able to approximate matrices well, especially for dimensionality reduction tasks. To test the ability of ACCAMS to model matrix data we analyze both how well our model fits the training data from the Netflix tests above as well as on image data from the CMU Faces dataset and a binary matrix from the AS peering graph. (Note, for Netflix we now use the training data from one split of the dataset.) For each of these of datasets we compare to the SVD (or SVD++ to handle missing values). We also use our algorithm to perform classic co-clustering by setting $S = 1$ and varying k.

As can be seen in Figure 3(b-d), ACCAMS models the matrices from all three domains much more compactly than SVD (or SVD++ in the case of the Netflix matrix, which contains missing values). In particular, we observe on the CMU Faces matrix that ACCAMS uses in some cases under $\frac{1}{4}$ of the bits as SVD for the same quality matrix approximation. Additionally, we observe that using a linear combination of stencils is more efficient to approximate the matrices than performing classic co-clustering where we have just one stencil. Ultimately, although the method was not designed specifically for image or network data, we observe that our method is effective for succinctly modeling the data.

5.5 Interpretability

In any model the structure of factors makes assumptions about the form of user preferences and decision making. The fact that our model uses a smaller parameter space while achieving an *improvement* in the generalization error suggests that our modeling assumptions better match the underlying data generation (how people make decisions). One advantage of our model being compact and conceptually simple is that we can understand our learned parameters.

To test the model's interpretability we use ACCAMS to model the Netflix data with $S = 20$ stencils and $k^2 = 100$ clusters (a model of similar size to a rank-3 matrix factorization). Here we look at two ways to interpret the results.

First we view the cluster assignments in stencils as inducing a hierarchy on the movies. That is, movies are split in the first level based on their cluster assignments in the first

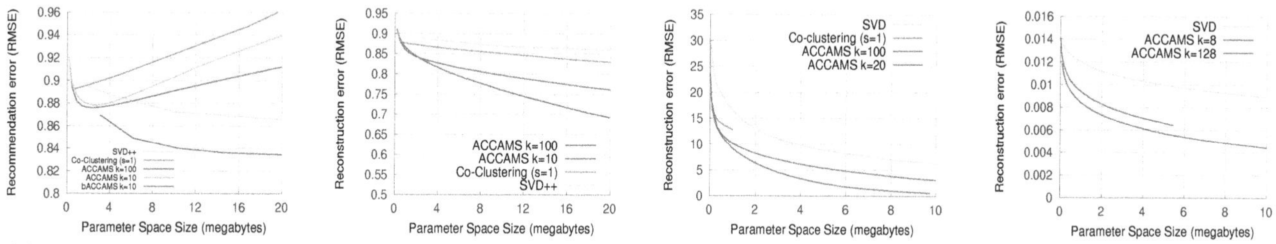

(a) Netflix Prediction Error (b) Netflix Training Error (c) Faces Approximation (d) AS Graph Approximation

Figure 3: On images, ratings, and binary graphs, ACCAMS approximates the matrix more efficiently than SVD, SVD++, or classic co-clustering.

stencil. At the second level, we split movies based on their cluster assignments in the second stencil, etc. In Figure 4 we observe the hierarchy of TV shows induced by the first three stencils learned by ACCAMS (we only include shows where there is more than one season of that show in the leaf and we pruned small partitions due to space restrictions).

As can be seen in the hierarchy, there are branches which clearly cluster together shows more focused on male audiences, female audiences, or children. However, beyond a first brush at the leaf nodes, we can notice some larger structural differences. For example, looking at the two large branches coming from the root, we observe that the left branch generally contains more recent TV shows from the late 1990s to the present, while the right branch generally contains older shows ranging from the 1960s to the mid 1990s. This can be most starkly noticed by "Friends," which shows up in both branches; Seasons 1 to 4 of "Friends" from 1994-1997 fall in the older branch, while Seasons 5 to 9 from 1998-2002 fall in the newer branch. Of course the algorithm does not know the dates the shows were released, but our model learns these general concepts just based on the ratings. From this it is clear the stencils can be useful for breaking down content in a meaningful structured way, something that is not possible under classic factorization approaches.

While the hierarchy demonstrates that our stencils are learning meaningful latent factors, it may be difficult to always understand individual clusters. Rather, to use knowledge from *all* of the stencils, we can look to the use case of "Users who watched X also liked Y," and ask given a movie or TV show to search, can we find other similar items? We do this by comparing the set of cluster assignments from the given movie to the set of cluster assignments of other items. We measure similarity between two movies using the Hamming distance between cluster assignments.

As can be seen in Table 5, we find the combination of clusters for different movies and TV shows can be used to easily find similar content. While we see some obvious cases where the method succeeds, e.g. "Sex and the City" returns six more seasons of "Sex and the City," we also notice the method takes into account more subtle similarities of movies beyond genre. For example, while the first season of "Seinfeld" returns the subsequent seasons of "Seinfeld," it is followed by three seasons of "Curb Your Enthusiasm," another comedy show by the same writer Larry David. Similarly, searching for Stanley Kubrick's "2001: A Space Odyssey" returns other Stanley Kubrick movies, as well as other critically acclaimed films from that era, particularly thematically similar science fiction movies. Searching for "Scooby-Doo" returns topically similar children's shows, specifically from

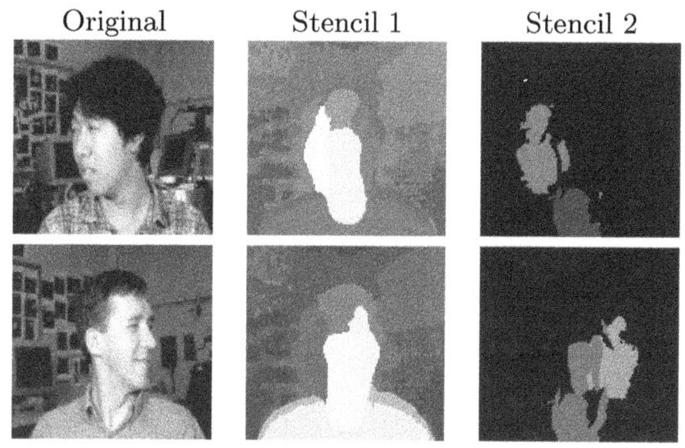

Figure 6: Examples of original images and the first two stencils. The decomposition is very similar to that of eigenfaces [22], albeit much more concise in its nature.

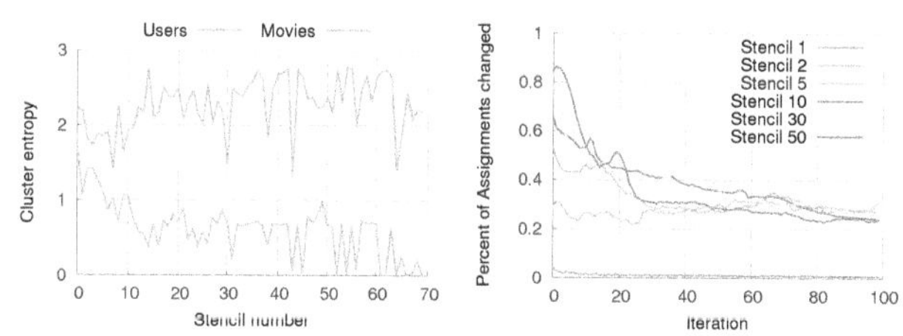

Figure 7: Left: Entropy in cluster assignments for users and movies. Right: Stability of the assignments in the sampler.

the mid to late 1900's. From this we get a sense that ACCAMS does not just find similarity in genre but also more subtle similarities.

5.6 Properties of ACCAMS

Aside from ACCAMS's success across matrix completion and approximation, it is valuable to understand how our method is working, particularly because of how different it is from previous models. First, because ACCAMS uses backfitting, we expect that the first stencil captures the largest features, the second captures secondary ones, etc. This idea is backed up by our theoretical results in Section 3.3, and we observe that this is working experimentally by the drop off in RMSE for our matrix approximation results in Figure 3. We can visually observe this in the image approximation of the CMU Faces. As can be seen in Figure 6, the first stencil captures general structures of the room and heads, and the second starts to fill in more fine grained details of the face.

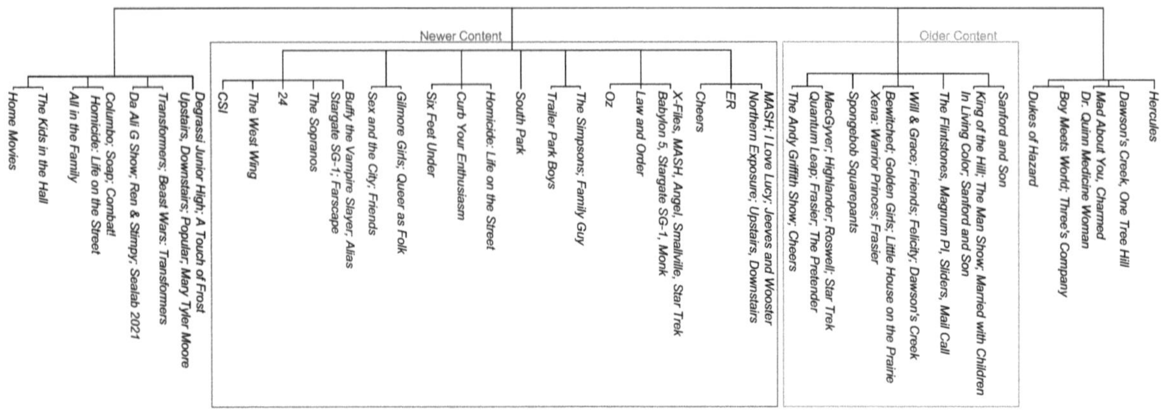

Figure 4: Hierarchy of TV Shows on Netflix based on the first three stencils generated by ACCAMS.

2001: A Space Odyssey	**Sex and the City: Season 1**	**Seinfeld: Seasons 1 & 2**	**Mean Girls**
Taxi Driver	Sex and the City: Season 2	Seinfeld: Season 3	Clueless
Chinatown	Sex and the City: Season 3	Seinfeld: Season 4	13 Going on 30
Citizen Kane	Sex and the City: Season 4	Curb Your Enthusiasm: Season 1	Best in Show
Dr. Strangelove	Sex and the City: Season 5	Curb Your Enthusiasm: Season 2	Particles of Truth
A Clockwork Orange	Sex and the City: Season 6.1	Curb Your Enthusiasm: Season 3	Charlie's Angels: Full Throttle
THX 1138: Special Edition	Sex and the City: Season 6.2	Arrested Development: Season 1	Amelie
Apocalypse Now Redux	Hercules: Season 3	Newsradio: Seasons 1 and 2	Me Myself I
The Graduate	Will & Grace: Season 1	The Kids in the Hall: Season 1	Bring it On
Blade Runner	Beverly Hills 90210: Pilot	The Simpsons: Treehouse of Horror	Chaos
The Deer Hunter	The O.C.: Season 1	Spin City: Michael J. Fox	Kissing Jessica Stein
Deliverance	Divine Madness	Curb Your Enthusiasm: Season 4	Nine Innings from Ground Zero

Star Wars: Episode V	**The Silence of the Lambs**	**Scooby-Doo Where Are You?**	**Law & Order: Season 1**
Star Wars: Episode IV	The Sixth Sense	The Flintstones: Season 2	Law & Order: Season 3
Star Wars: Episode VI	Alien: Collector's Edition	Classic Cartoon Favorites: Goofy	Law & Order: SVU (2)
Battlestar Galactica: Season 1	The Exorcist	Transformers: Season 1 (1984)	Law & Order: Criminal Intent (3)
Raiders of the Lost Ark	Schindler's List	Tom and Jerry: Whiskers Away!	Law & Order: Season 2
Star Wars: Clone Wars: Vol. 1	The Godfather	Boy Meets World: Season 1	MASH: Season 8
Gladiator: Extended Edition	Seven	The Flintstones: Season 3	ER: Season 1
Star Wars Trilogy: Bonus Material	Colors	Scooby-Doo's Greatest Mysteries	MASH: Season 7
LOTR: The Fellowship of the Ring	The Godfather, Part II	Care Bears: Kingdom of Caring	Rikki-Tikki-Tavi
LOTR: The Two Towers	GoodFellas: Special Edition	Aloha Scooby-Doo!	The X-Files: Season 6
Indiana Jones Trilogy: Bonus Material	Platoon	Scooby-Doo: Legend of the Vampire	The X-Files: Season 7
LOTR: The Return of the King	Full Metal Jacket	Rugrats: Decade in Diapers	ER: Season 3

Figure 5: For a given movie or TV show on Netflix, we can use the cluster assignments to find related content.

The Bayesian model, bACCAMS, backfits in the first iteration of the sampler but ultimately resamples each stencil many times thus loosening these properties. In Figure 7, we observe how the distribution of users and movies across clusters changes over iterations and number of stencils, based on our run of bACCAMS with $S = 70$ stencils and a maximum of $k = 10$ clusters per stencil. As we see in the plot of entropy, movies, across all 70 stencils, are well distributed across the 10 possible clusters. Users, however, are well distributed in the early stencils but then are only spread across a few clusters in later stencils. In addition, we notice that while the earlier clusters are stable, later stencils are much less stable with a high percentage of cluster assignments changing. Both of these properties follow from the fact that most users rate very few movies. For most users only a few clusters are necessary to capture their observed preferences. Movies, however, typically have more ratings and more latent information to infer. Thus through all 70 stencils we learn useful clusterings, and our prediction accuracy improves through $S = 125$ stencils.

6. DISCUSSION

Here we formulated a model of additive co-clustering. We presented both a k-means style algorithm, ACCAMS, as well as a generative Bayesian non-parametric model with a collapsed Gibbs sampler, bACCAMS; we obtained theoretical guarantees for matrix approximation through additive co-clustering; and we showed that our method is concise and accurate on a diverse range of datasets, including achieving the best published accuracy for matrix completion on Netflix.

Given the novelty and initial success of the method, we believe that domain-specific variants of ACCAMS, such as for community detection and topic modeling, can and will lead to new models and improved results. In addition, given the modularity of our framework, it is easy to incorporate side information, such as explicit genre and actor data, in modeling rating data that should lead to improved accuracy and interpretability.

Acknowledgements. We would like to thank Christos Faloutsos for his valuable feedback throughout the preparation of this paper. This research was supported by funds from Google, a Facebook Fellowship, a National Science Foundation Graduate Research Fellowship (Grant No. DGE-1252522), and the National Science Foundation under Grant No. CNS-1314632 and IIS-1408924. Any opinions, findings, and conclusions or recommendations expressed in this material are those of the author(s) and do not necessarily reflect the views of the National Science Foundation, or other funding parties.

References

[1] E. M. Airoldi, D. M. Blei, S. E. Fienberg, and E. P. Xing. Mixed-membership stochastic blockmodels. *Journal of Machine Learning Research*, 9:1981–2014, 2008.

[2] A. Banerjee, I. Dhillon, J. Ghosh, S. Merugu, and D. S. Modha. A generalized maximum entropy approach to bregman co-clustering and matrix approximation. In *Proceedings of the tenth ACM SIGKDD international conference on Knowledge discovery and data mining*, pages 509–514. ACM, 2004.

[3] A. Beutel, K. Murray, C. Faloutsos, and A. J. Smola. CoBaFi: Collaborative Bayesian Filtering. In *World Wide Web Conference*, pages 97–108, 2014.

[4] A. Gittens and M. W. Mahoney. Revisiting the nyström method for improved large-scale machine learning. In *ICML (3)*, pages 567–575, 2013.

[5] D. Görür, F. Jäkel, and C. E. Rasmussen. A choice model with infinitely many latent features. In *Proceedings of the 23rd international conference on Machine learning*, pages 361–368. ACM, 2006.

[6] T. Griffiths and Z. Ghahramani. The indian buffet process: An introduction and review. *Journal of Machine Learning Research*, 12:1185âĹŠ1224, 2011.

[7] N. Halko, P. Martinsson, and J. A. Tropp. Finding structure with randomness: Stochastic algorithms for constructing approximate matrix decompositions, 2009. oai:arXiv.org:0909.4061.

[8] J. A. Hartigan. Direct clustering of a data matrix. *Journal of the american statistical association*, 67(337):123–129, 1972.

[9] Y. Koren. Factorization meets the neighborhood: a multifaceted collaborative filtering model. In *Knowledge discovery and data mining KDD*, pages 426–434, 2008.

[10] Y. Koren, R. Bell, and C. Volinsky. Matrix factorization techniques for recommender systems. *IEEE Computer*, 42(8):30–37, 2009.

[11] D. Koutra, U. Kang, J. Vreeken, and C. Faloutsos. *VOG: Summarizing and Understanding Large Graphs*, chapter 11, pages 91–99. SIAM, 2014.

[12] A. Kyrola, G. Blelloch, and C. Guestrin. GraphChi: Large-scale graph computation on just a pc. In *OSDI*, Hollywood, CA, 2012.

[13] J. Lee, S. Kim, G. Lebanon, and Y. Singer. Local low-rank matrix approximation. In *Proceedings of The 30th International Conference on Machine Learning*, pages 82–90, 2013.

[14] M. Leeuwen, J. Vreeken, and A. Siebes. Identifying the components. *Data Mining and Knowledge Discovery*, 19(2):176–193, 2009.

[15] M. Li, G. L. Miller, and R. Peng. Iterative row sampling. In *FOCS 2013*, pages 127–136, 2013.

[16] L. W. Mackey, M. I. Jordan, and A. Talwalkar. Divide-and-conquer matrix factorization. In *Advances in Neural Information Processing Systems*, pages 1134–1142, 2011.

[17] K. Palla, D. Knowles, and Z. Ghahramani. An infinite latent attribute model for network data. In *International Conference on Machine Learning*, 2012.

[18] E. E. Papalexakis, N. D. Sidiropoulos, and R. Bro. From k-means to higher-way co-clustering: multilinear decomposition with sparse latent factors. *Signal Processing, IEEE Transactions on*, 61(2):493–506, 2013.

[19] I. Porteous, E. Bart, and M. Welling. Multi-HDP: A non parametric bayesian model for tensor factorization. In D. Fox and C. Gomes, editors, *Proceedings of the Twenty-Third AAAI Conference on Artificial Intelligence*, pages 1487–1490. AAAI Press, 2008.

[20] J. Rissanen. Modeling by shortest data description. *Automatica*, 14(5):465–471, 1978.

[21] H. Shan and A. Banerjee. Bayesian co-clustering. In *Data Mining, 2008. ICDM'08. Eighth IEEE International Conference on*, pages 530–539. IEEE, 2008.

[22] M. Turk and A. Pentland. Face recognition using eigenfaces. In *Proceedings CVPR*, pages 586–591, Hawaii, June 1991.

[23] J. Vreeken, M. Leeuwen, and A. Siebes. Krimp: mining itemsets that compress. *Data Mining and Knowledge Discovery*, 23(1):169–214, 2011.

[24] P. Wang, K. B. Laskey, C. Domeniconi, and M. I. Jordan. Nonparametric bayesian co-clustering ensembles. In *SDM*, pages 331–342. SIAM, 2011.

Who, What, When, and Where: Multi-Dimensional Collaborative Recommendations Using Tensor Factorization on Sparse User-Generated Data

Preeti Bhargava*[1], Thomas Phan[2], Jiayu Zhou[2], Juhan Lee[2]
[1]Department of Computer Science, University of Maryland, College Park
[2]Samsung Research America – Silicon Valley
prbharga@cs.umd.edu, {thomas.phan,jiayu.zhou,juhan.l}@samsung.com

ABSTRACT

Given the abundance of online information available to mobile users, particularly tourists and weekend travelers, recommender systems that effectively filter this information and suggest interesting participatory opportunities will become increasingly important. Previous work has explored recommending interesting locations; however, users would also benefit from recommendations for activities in which to participate at those locations along with suitable times and days. Thus, systems that provide collaborative recommendations involving multiple dimensions such as location, activities and time would enhance the overall experience of users.The relationship among these dimensions can be modeled by higher-order matrices called tensors which are then solved by tensor factorization. However, these tensors can be extremely sparse. In this paper, we present a system and an approach for performing multi-dimensional collaborative recommendations for Who (User), What (Activity), When (Time) and Where (Location), using tensor factorization on sparse user-generated data. We formulate an objective function which simultaneously factorizes coupled tensors and matrices constructed from heterogeneous data sources. We evaluate our system and approach on large-scale real world data sets consisting of 588,000 Flickr photos collected from three major metro regions in USA. We compare our approach with several state-of-the-art baselines and demonstrate that it outperforms all of them.

Categories and Subject Descriptors

H.3.3 [Information Search and Retrieval] : Information Filtering, Retrieval Models, Selection Process

General Terms

Algorithms; Design; Experimentation; Human Factors; Performance

Keywords

Recommender systems; Multi-dimensional recommendations; Collaborative recommendations; Tensor factorization

*This work was conducted while the first author was an intern at Samsung Research America – Silicon Valley.

WWW 2015, May 18–22, 2015, Florence, Italy.
ACM 978-1-4503-3469-3/15/05.
http://dx.doi.org/10.1145/2736277.2741077.

1. INTRODUCTION

Today's smartphones come equipped with a multitude of sensors such as GPS and increasingly-powerful computational, storage and communication capabilities. These features have enabled smartphone applications to emerge across a variety of tourism-related areas such as travel recommendations, location-based services, and social suggestions. However, because information overload can be a problem for mobile users, it is important that only relevant and personalized information is presented. As a result, recommender systems that suggest items of interest to mobile users based on context and preferences have become increasingly popular.

Since the GPS embedded in smartphones can be used to accurately localize a user, *location* has become the basis of many recommender systems. These systems recommend interesting places or landmarks for visit to mobile users, particularly tourists and weekend travelers. However, in location recommendations, contextual information such as *time* often plays an important role as certain places are open only between fixed hours or can host certain activities at fixed times of a day or on fixed days in a week. In addition, users who want suggestions or recommendations for places to visit would also benefit from recommendations for *activities* to participate in at the location along with a suitable time of participation. Here, activities refer to human lifestyle and recreational activities such as shopping, dining, surfing etc. Users may even have specific *preferences* for activities such as preferring outdoor rather than indoor activities. For instance, at Pier 39 in San Francisco, a list of all possible things that a tourist can do includes shopping, eating seafood at the various restaurants, riding the Venetian carousel, watching the sea lions at the nearby dock or getting a view of the Fourth of July fireworks display. However, all these activities happen at specific locations in Pier 39 and either in specific months, on specific days or at specific hours. Thus, recommender systems that generate collaborative recommendations involving multiple dimensions such as location, time, activities, and user preferences etc., would enhance the overall experience of users and provide them with the most helpful recommendations.

As a simplest formulation, recommender systems model preferences of *users* for *items* in the form of a *utility matrix* where rows represent users, columns represent items and the values represent the users' ratings or preferences for those items on a scale of say, 1 to 5. The goal of the recommender system is then to impute the missing values based on observed values in the matrix [26, 35] using a standard approach such as collaborative filtering. User-based collaborative filtering determines a subset of users most similar to the current user and predicts the missing ratings based on a weighted combination of the ratings provided by those other users [26]. Likewise, item-based collaborative filtering [23] focuses on predicting the missing ratings for items based on a weighted combination of the ratings given by the current user to similar items, where similarity between each pair of items is determined by the similarity of the ratings of those items provided by the users who have rated both items. Once the matrix has been completed (that is, all missing values have been imputed) by these neighborhood-based methods, a user can be given a recommendation list of ranked items ordered by descending predicted ratings.

An alternative powerful methodology that has been used with positive results in recommender systems is the latent factor model [21], an approach that emerged from research fueled by the Netflix prize[1]. Unlike neighborhood-based methods, latent factor models assume that similarity between users and items is simultaneously induced by some hidden lower-dimensional structure in the data. Some of the most successful realizations of latent factor models are based on matrix factorization, where users and items are simultaneously represented as unknown feature vectors (column vectors) along k latent dimensions. These methods have become prominent in recent years because they combine scalability with high predictive accuracy. In addition, they offer more flexibility for modeling practical scenarios where the data is very sparse.

In case of recommendations along a single dimension, the 2-dimensional user $\times$ item matrix factorization model can be applied successfully. For instance, location recommendations can be modeled as a user $\times$ location matrix and can be solved using standard approaches to matrix factorization. However, to model collaborative multi-dimensional recommendations involving location, activity, time and other contextual information, the relationship among the various dimensions is represented by higher-order matrices called *tensors*. To address them, standard matrix factorization approaches need to be generalized to tensor factorization.

Another major challenge in recommender systems is that, in practice, most users provide interest ratings for only a subset of the recommended items. For instance, a user will provide ratings for only a subset of all possible locations. Moreover, as the number of dimensions increases, data sparsity increases and becomes a major concern for systems that generate multi-dimensional recommendations from real-world datasets.

In this paper, we address these challenges and present a system and an approach for performing multi-dimensional collaborative recommendations for Who (User), What (Activity), When (Time) and Where (Location), using tensor factorization on sparse user-generated data. Our contributions in this paper are:

- We address n-dimensional collaborative recommendations (where $n \geq 4$ and includes user, location, activity, time and any other contextual information) by fusing data from multiple sources such as Flickr (a photo sharing website), Foursquare (a location based social network), Yelp (a crowd-sourced reviews based website) and Viator (a travel website). While our approach can be extended to any number of dimensions, we make the work in this paper concrete by focusing on 4 dimensions and provide detailed discussion on how additional dimensionality can be addressed.
- While most of the prior efforts in multi-dimensional recommendations have been attempted using a single tensor, they suffer from tensor sparsity. We present a novel solution to this sparsity problem by formulating an objective function that simultaneously factorizes coupled tensors and matrices constructed from heterogeneous data sources. We then minimize this function using gradient descent.
- We evaluate our system and approach on large-scale real world data sets consisting of 588,000 Flickr photos collected from three major metro regions in the USA — the San Francisco Bay Area, Las Vegas and Chicago. From this data, we extracted over 4900 users, 6100 locations, 120 activities, and 96 time slots. The tensors constructed from these datasets are 99.999% sparse.
- We compare our approach with several state-of-the-art baselines and demonstrate that it outperforms all of them.
- Our approach also demonstrates an improvement in runtime without the need for sacrificing performance.

The rest of the paper is organized as follows: Section 2 reviews related work in location and activity recommendations and tensor factorizations applications to recommender systems. In Sections 3 and 4, we describe our datasets and the information inferred from them. We explain our approach in Section 5 and present its evaluation and comparison with baselines in Section 6. Finally, we conclude and outline future work in Section 7.

2. RELATED WORK

Since our work involves multi-dimensional recommendations for location, activity and time using tensor factorization on extremely sparse user-generated data, we have categorized the related work into different sections. The first section covers existing literature in location and activity recommendations while the second covers existing work in recommender systems using tensor factorization. We differentiate our work from them and identify their shortcomings.

2.1 Location and Activity recommendations

Most of the existing literature has focused on recommendations along one dimension (for instance, location). A few researchers have explored collaborative location and activity recommendations. To the best of our knowledge, none of the works have attempted collaborative location, activity and time recommendations.

2.1.1 Photos as a data source

One of our main data sources for user locations are Flickr[2] photos. Many of the photos uploaded by users are geotagged, thereby providing a wealth of geospatial data. These photos have been used for many purposes, such as finding Point-of-Interest (POI) clusters [36], identifying the location of photos from visual, textual, and temporal features [9], determining when tourism is in season [12], and creating routes that are pleasing to the user [30].

2.1.2 Location/Landmark/Venue recommendations

Previous researchers have investigated the problem of making recommendations for geolocations that may be interesting to the user [7, 24, 32]. Such approaches use large bodies of collected geospatial data along with user preferences and then apply low-dimensional recommendation algorithms.

2.1.3 Activity Recommendations

Even though users seek recommendations on what activities they can engage in when they visit a place or at a given time, the area of activity recommendation has not been researched extensively. Recent research has focused on diurnal activity recognition from smartphone sensory data [25] or from location [22]. Belotti et al. [5] explored the idea of serendipitous activity based discovery of venues and activities via the Magitti Mobile Leisure Guide. Ducheneaut et al. [11] experiment with several models such as collaborative filtering, preference-based, distance-based, and a weighted combination of these to provide activity recommendations via Magitti.

2.1.4 Collaborative Location and Activity recommendations

Co-occurring location and activity collaborative recommendations were proposed by Zheng et al. in [38] where they addressed location recommendations given an activity, and activity recommendations given a location. They used Collective Matrix Factor-

[1] http://www.netflixprize.com/

[2] https://www.flickr.com/

Data Source	Type of Data	Dimensions extracted	Volume of raw data extracted
Flickr	Geotagged and Timestamped Photos	User, Location, Activity, Time	588,000 photos with 9 million words of text
Foursquare	Location and POI database	Location, Activity, Venue	274,000 locations with POI or venue information
Yelp	Business and service reviews	Activity	1060 service categories
Viator	Things to do in tourist spots	Activity	60 things to do categories

Table 1: Data fusion from heterogeneous data sources

ization (CMF) [33] to complete a sparsely populated 2-dimensional Location $\times$ Activity matrix and evaluated their approach on 162 users with recommendations for 5 activities. CMF takes advantage of correlations and sharing of information between data sets from multiple sources and simultaneously factorizes coupled matrices. It is shown to have achieved higher prediction accuracy than individual matrix factorization. Sattari et al. [31] used the same dataset as Zheng et al. in [38] but employed Singular Value Decomposition (SVD) in place of CMF to complete the Location $\times$ Activity matrix. Since SVD requires the matrix that needs to be decomposed to be fully populated, they padded it with zero values. They demonstrated an improvement in performance over [38].

Zheng et al. [37] modeled user, location and activity data as a 3-dimensional tensor and applied a regularized tensor and matrix factorization approach for location and activity recommendations. They formulated a CANDECOMP/PARAFAC (CP) [15, 8] decomposition style objective function and minimized it using gradient descent. This decomposition factorizes a tensor into a linear combination of component rank-one tensors. They evaluated their approach on a dataset of 164 users, 168 locations and 5 activities.

Our work stands out from the existing literature in several ways:

- We use large user-generated datasets which involves several thousand users and locations, and over a hundred popular lifestyle, recreational and tourist activities.
- We incorporate dimensions of user's context such as time in addition to location and activities.
- As opposed to the manual approach for activity inference from user comments that was employed in [38, 37], we propose an automated and unsupervised Natural Language Processing (NLP) based algorithm (Section 4.2) which is more robust and scalable to large real-world datasets.
- Moreover, a major limitation of using CP decomposition for tensors is that it is not suitable for very sparse tensors and demonstrates a sharp increase in error especially if more than 80% of the data is missing [2, 3]. Sparsity is a non trivial issue for us as our multi-dimensional data is 99.999% sparse. Hence, we propose our joint analysis and factorization based approach to solve the problem.

2.2 Other applications of Tensor Factorization to Recommender Systems

Symeonidis et al. [34] and Nanopoulos [28] applied Higher Order Singular Value Decomposition (HOSVD) [10] to a 3rd order tensor which represents users, items and tags in social tagging systems such as Last.fm and Bibsonomy. Karatzoglou et al. [18] address multi-dimensional recommendations by incorporating contextual information to model a User-Item-Context tensor. They utilize a sparse HOSVD style method that decomposes a D dimensional sparse tensor into D matrices and a D dimensional tensor. HOSVD is a generalization of the matrix SVD to a tensor. It assumes a dense tensor and is not suitable for very sparsely populated tensors. Moreover, unlike SVD, HOSVD may not provide the best low rank approximation of a tensor [20].

Hidasi and Tikk [17] apply an Alternating Least Squares (ALS) [19, 20] based tensor factorization approach for context-aware recommendations. ALS consists of three steps, each one being a conditional update of one of the factor matrices, given the others. However, it suffers from several drawbacks: It has poor convergence for sparse data [6] and is not scalable to large-scale data sets [2].

Region	Photos	Users	Land Area (km^2)
San Francisco Bay Area	280,045	7895	6053
Las Vegas	23,350	578	1818
Chicago	284,751	2423	1412

Table 2: Flickr.com raw dataset characteristics

To address these limitations and perform multi-dimensional recommendations on large-scale and sparse user-generated datasets, we formulate our recommendation model via the Coupled Matrix and Tensor Factorization (CMTF) framework [1, 3]. CMTF is an approach similar to CMF and proposes joint analysis of a matrix and an Nth-order tensor with a common mode or dimension, where the tensor is factorized using an R-component CP model and the matrix is factorized by extracting R factors using matrix factorization. CMTF is shown to have achieved better performance than standard CP decomposition especially if more than 80% of the data is missing [2, 3]. A variant of the CMTF approach [1, 2] performs the joint analysis of the tensor and matrix by ignoring the missing entries and fitting the tensor and/or the matrix model to the known data entries only. This approach has been shown to easily scale to handle very large data sets with up to 99% missing entries [2].

To this end, we model our multi-dimensional recommendation problem as a joint analysis of a sparsely populated tensor with several matrices which share one or more common modes with the tensor. These tensors and matrices are constructed by fusing data for the various dimensions (users, locations, activities and time) from multiple data sources. This is a challenging task since data sets are often incomplete and heterogeneous. We then factorize these tensors and matrices simultaneously using a gradient descent-based algorithm. As we show later in Section 6.5, our approach outperforms standard CP decomposition, HOSVD and ALS.

3. DATA

Table 1 summarizes the data sources, types of data, extracted dimensions and the volume of raw data from each source. Our primary dataset consists of 588,000 geotagged and timestamped publicly-available photos from Flickr.com, a popular photo-sharing website hosted in the USA. To obtain the data set, we searched specifically for photos taken with smartphones so that we could get the most accurate geospatial traces. Further, these photos spanned the time period of September 1, 2009, to September 1, 2013 and were taken from three major metro regions in the USA – the San Francisco Bay Area, Las Vegas and Chicago. Table 2 shows the characteristics of this dataset, while Figure 1 shows the geographical distribution of the photographs over the three regions. To improve legibility of the figure so that individual photo locations can be discerned, we sampled the number of photos down.

We extracted photos and their meta-content in JSON format using Flickr's public REST based API. Each photograph is marked with the user ID of the user who took it, geo-location in latitude and longitude format representing where it was taken, and an epoch timestamp representing when it was taken. We also extracted about 9 million words of user-generated text (including title, description, tags or comments) for these photos. Note that less than 50% of the photos are marked with any text. In addition, we also obtain POI or Venue information for 274,000 locations in the three geographical

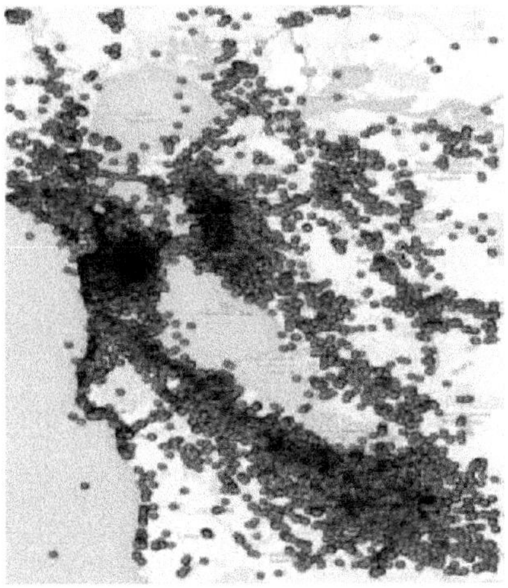

(a) San Francisco Bay Area

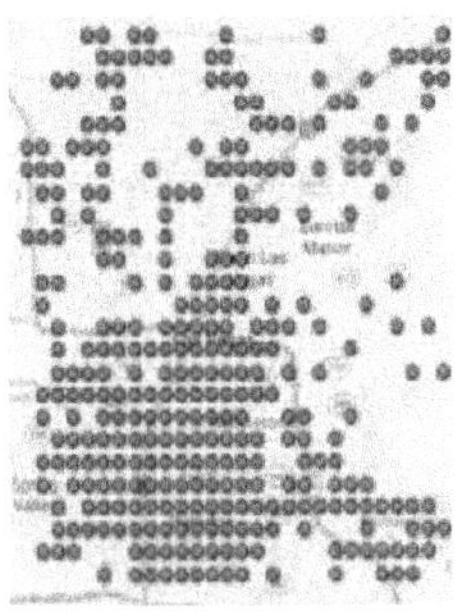

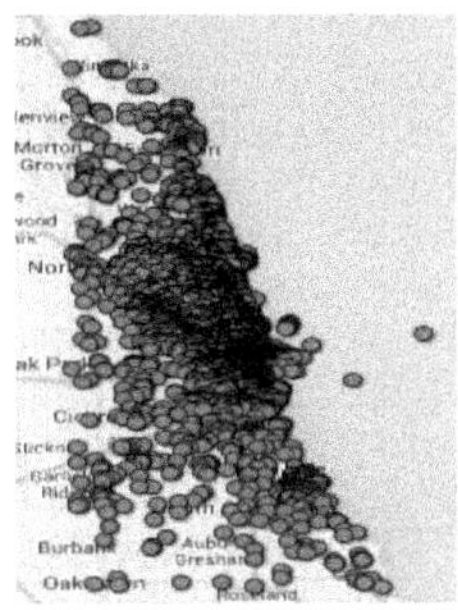

(b) Las Vegas (c) Chicago

Figure 1: Geographical distribution of photos from San Francisco Bay Area, Las Vegas and Chicago core regions. Map image tiles were provided by Google, and waypoint placement was performed using `http://www.gpsvisualizer.com/`.

regions from Foursquare[3]. Finally, we obtained information about popular activities from Yelp[4] and things to do in tourist spots from Viator[5]. We explain the inference and extraction of the various dimensions from the collected data in Sections 4 and 5.

4. INFERRING VARIOUS DIMENSIONS OF INFORMATION FROM FLICKR PHOTOS

As mentioned earlier, photos on Flickr have meta-data that includes a user ID, timestamp, location and text. We now infer the dimensions of user, location, activity and time from this meta-data.

4.1 Location Hashing

Our system relies on unique and discrete locations, but the Flickr geotags are stated as continuous floating-point latitude and longitude geocoordinate pairs. To discretize these values, we applied Cartographic Sparse Hashing, our O(1) algorithm (shown in Algorithm 1) that hashes a latitude and longitude pair into one of many virtual rectangular grid bins formed throughout the geocoordinate space. This algorithm takes as input (i) latitude and longitude as 64-bit floats and (ii) a bin resolution size r in meters as an integer. It then outputs a 64-bit integer key representing the final virtual bin. The algorithm leverages the fact that the latitude and longitude are expressed in decimal degrees, with the fifth decimal place corresponding roughly to 1 meter. Since this precision was acceptable to us, we truncated each value to five decimal places. The function then produces the resulting integer key with the longitude and latitude ending up in the high and low bits, respectively. This key

[3] `www.foursquare.com/` [4] `www.yelp.com/`
[5] `www.viator.com/`

Algorithm 1: Cartographic Sparse Hashing (CASH) algorithm

Input: $latitude$ as 64-bit float, $longitude$ as 64-bit float, grid resolution r in meters
Output: Hash value $hashResult$ as 64-bit integer
Trim $latitude$ digits past 5th decimal position;
$sigFig \leftarrow 10^5$;
$latitudeInt \leftarrow (int)(latitude \times sigFig)$;
Round down $latitudeInt$ to be divisible by r;
Repeat with $longitude$ to produce $longitudeInt$;
$hashResult \leftarrow shiftHigh(longitudeInt) + latitudeInt$;
return $hashResult$

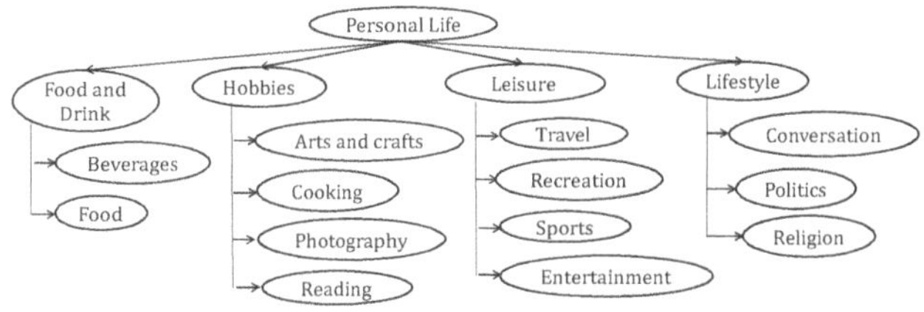

Figure 2: Partial view of the Activity Hierarchy showing all depth 1 nodes and a few depth 2 nodes

identifies a virtual bin approximately r meters per side, although the bin will be elongated north-to-south for regions further away from the equator due to the Earth's curvature.

We experimented with 4 different location grid sizes - 300m, 500m, 700m and 1000m. These were determined based on the venue density in each grid as well as human walking distance (as people may often prefer to walk or use public transport). If the grid size is too large, recommendations beyond a certain walking distance will not be helpful to the user. On the other hand, if the grid size is too small, there may not be any venue or place to recommend in the grid. We explain the selection of the appropriate size based on performance in Section 6.3.

4.2 Activity Inference

Previous research in activity recognition [22, 25] focused on recognizing daily activities such as 'walking', 'driving', 'biking' etc. from smartphone sensors such as the accelerometer and GPS. However, a real world recommender system should be capable of recommending a diverse set of activities to users in addition to such diurnal activities. To address this, we employ an activity hierarchy which consists of lifestyle, recreational and tourist activities for activity recommendations.

Figure 2 shows a partial view of our Activity Hierarchy. We generated it by manually combining popular activities from the Yelp category list, Viator things to do list, and the FourSquare venue category hierarchy. Our hierarchy has a tree structure of depth 4 and contains 120 activity nodes including the root node 'Personal Life'. There are 4 high-level (depth 1) activities which branch out into 15 coarse-grained activities (depth 2). All the high-level and some of the coarse-grained activities that they include are shown in Figure 2. Some of the coarse-grained activities at depth 2 are further categorized into 28 fine-grained activities (depth 3) which are further categorized into 128 leaf node activities. For instance, the root node 'Personal Life' branches out into coarse-grained activities including 'Leisure' which is further categorized into fine-grained activities such as 'Entertainment' and Recreation' etc. 'Entertainment' is further categorized into leaf node activities such as 'Music', 'Movies' and 'Dance'. It is possible that a user is engaged in an activity which is not present in our hierarchy. To address this, we have a generic category 'Other' at each depth.

Inferring users' activities from our data set is non-trivial and challenging. Unlike previous research, we do not have labeled sen-

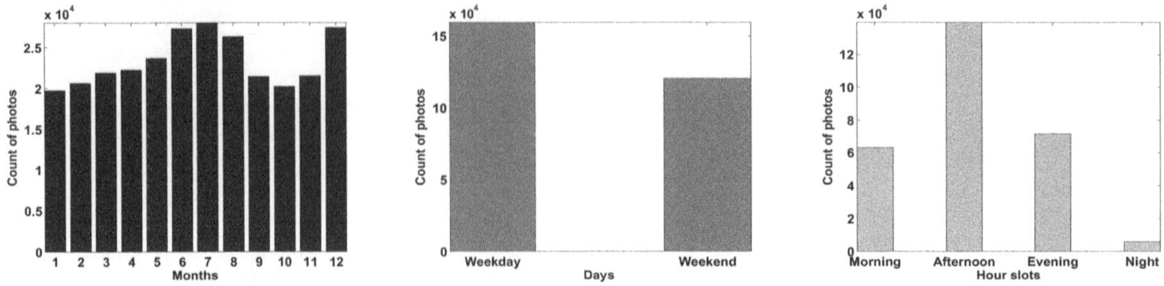

(a) Monthly distribution (b) Weekly distribution (c) Hourly distribution

Figure 3: Monthly, Weekly and Hourly distribution of photographs in the San Francisco Bay Area dataset

Algorithm 2: Activity inference from user-generated text

Input: Photo content items such as name, description, tag and comments and Activity Hierarchy
Output: Inferred Activities
Remove stop words from each photo content item;
Concatenate the content items to generate a search query;
Perform a web search using the search query and retrieve the text content of the top-most web search result;
Extract features such as named entities and types, document categories and social tags from the text content;
foreach *Activity in the Activity Hierarchy* **do**
  Compute SR scores between the features and the Activity;
  MaxSRScore for each activity ← arg max (SR Score between any of the features and the activity);
  if *MaxSRScore* < $SR_{threshold}$ **then**
    MaxSRScore ← 0.0;
end
MAXMaxSRScore ← arg max (MaxSRScore);
if *MAXMaxSRScore* ≠ *0* **then**
  MaxActivities ← Activities with MAXMaxSRScore;
if *MaxActivities* = ∅ **then**
  MaxActivities ← Propagated photo labels based on distance and time;
return *MaxActivities;*

sory data from users' phones. Though all the photos in our dataset are geotagged, a user could be engaged in several probable activities at a location. Also, less than 50% of the photographs are annotated with user-generated photo content such as a detailed name or a description, and even fewer photographs have tags or comments which can provide some indication of the activity occurring when the photograph was taken. In addition, crowd-sourcing the labeling of activities (as done in [38, 37]) is not feasible for 588,000 photos.

To address these challenges, we propose an automated and unsupervised NLP based algorithm (Algorithm 2) to infer a user's activity from user-generated text such as the photo content items. As shown, we first remove all stop words from each photo content item and concatenate the items. We then perform a web search query to elucidate the meaning of the concatenated items and retrieve the content of the top-most web search result. From this content, we extract features such as named entities, document categories and tags. These features are extracted using three NLP techniques:

- Named Entity Recognition - a subtask of information extraction that identifies names of persons, organizations etc. in a given text or sentence
- Document Categorization - a task that classifies the subject or topic of the text, and
- Social Tagging - the practice of generating tags or keywords by users rather than experts to describe online content.

For this feature extraction, we employ a tool called OpenCalais[6] which can recognize up to 39 entities from the text. It also categorizes the text into one or more 18 document categories such as Finance, Entertainment etc. In addition, it associates one or more social tags with it. The use of these techniques ensures that a large amount of world knowledge is exploited for feature extraction.

We then compute the Semantic Relatedness (SR) scores between each activity and each feature extracted from the web content. SR [14] is a metric for determining the similarity of two documents or phrases based on their semantic meaning. It is normalized to a value between 0 (little to no relatedness) and 1 (extremely high relatedness). While there are several techniques and systems available for computing SR, we employ the Semantic Textual Similarity (STS) system [13] for computing SR scores. STS is based on Latent Semantic Analysis (LSA) along with WordNet knowledge and is trained on the LDC Gigawords and Stanford Webbase corpora.

For each activity, we store the maximum SR score (MaxSRScore) between any of the features and the activity. If the MaxSRScore for an activity is less than a threshold, we set it to 0.0, thereby reducing noise and false positives. Since SR is a cosine similarity measure, a threshold of 0.293 (1 - cos 45 °) is generally considered an appropriate threshold, and we use that in our current implementation. Finally, we iterate over all the activities and select those with the highest MaxSR scores. If a photo has no labeled activities, we apply a simple label propagation technique to label it based on its nearest neighbors (with respect to location and time). This approach is intuitive because if two consecutive photos are close in time and location, it is highly probable that the user was performing the same activity in both.

To illustrate Algorithm 2 better, consider a photo which has been tagged as 'Brazen Wildcat Half' by the user. This phrase by itself does not convey any meaningful information about the user's activity, but a web search for it reveals content such as 'Brazen Wildcat Half Marathon Racing...'. From the web content text, we get features such as 'Trail Run', 'Athletics' and 'Recreation' etc. Algorithm 2 then maps these features to the activities: Sports, Running and Recreation. From this, we can infer that the user was engaged in these activities when the photo was taken.

4.3 Time hashing

Since each photo has a unique timestamp, the number of timestamps in our dataset is huge. To address this, we perform feature hashing to hash the value of each timestamp to a timeslot. In order to determine the granularity of timeslots, we analyzed the monthly, weekly, daily and hourly distribution of photographs.

Figure 3(a) shows the distribution of photographs in the San Francisco Bay Area dataset for months in a year (1= January until 12 = December). As evident, the number of photos varies with each month. Clearly, July and December have the highest photo counts as these months have the typical vacations of July 4th and Christmas. We also analyzed the differences in weekdays and weekends.

[6] `http://www.opencalais.com/`

Grid Size *r* (m)	# of unique hashed locations		
	San Francisco	Las Vegas	Chicago
300	7869	2747	5082
500	5565	1932	3665
700	4222	1475	2855
1000	2999	1058	2070

Table 3: Number of unique hashed locations in our 3 datasets

As shown in Figure 3(b), weekdays have a higher photo count.

We further considered the distribution of photographs at different hours in a day. To this end, we divided a day into 4 hourly slots:

- Morning - hours between 6 am and 12 pm
- Afternoon - hours between 12 pm and 6 pm
- Evening - hours between 6 pm and 12 am
- Night - hours between 12 am and 6 am

As seen in Figure 3(c), the highest count of photographs is taken in the afternoo.n Intuitively, the least number (5834) were taken at night. Based on this analysis, we generated buckets of hashed time slots. Since there are 12 months in a year, 2 types of days in a week - weekday and weekend, and each day has 4 hourly slots, the total number of hashed timeslots is 96. For each photo, we first convert its epoch timestamp to a standard date time format which is then hashed to a timeslot. For instance, a photo taken on August 19, 2013 at 2 pm will be hashed to 'WeekDay_8_Afternoon'.

5. OUR JOINT ANALYSIS AND FACTORIZATION BASED APPROACH

5.1 Data Modeling of various dimensions

After inferring the user, location, activity and time information from the Flickr photos, the data in each dataset needs to be modeled along the various dimensions of our multi-dimensional tensor. These dimensions are:

- Location dimension - We first apply data filtering to reduce noise. We retain only those unique hashed locations that have been visited by at least u_t users (where u_t = 5), Thus, for each unique hashed location present in our 3 datasets, we determine the number of unique users from that dataset who visited that location. We remove all locations that have ≤ 5 unique users. We perform this thresholding mainly to eliminate locations that can be residences of users or random spots such as roads. Table 3 shows the final count of locations in our datasets. The number of locations for each dataset varies with the hashed grid size, where we note that we discern at least 6127 locations in all with the largest grid size (1000m). These correspond to the Location dimension of our tensor.
- User dimension - Once the final set of locations for each dataset has been obtained, we use only those photographs which have been taken at these locations. The corresponding user IDs for these photographs represent the User dimension of our tensor. Our final set of users consists of 2498 unique users in the San Francisco Bay Area, 573 unique users in Las Vegas and 1850 unique users in Chicago.
- Activity dimension - The 120 activities in our activity hierarchy represent the Activity dimension of our tensor.
- Time dimension - The 96 hashed time slots represent the Time dimension of our tensor.

5.2 Constructing the tensors and matrices

We now construct a 4 dimensional tensor from these dimensions.

5.2.1 *User × Location × Activity × Time tensor*

The four dimensional (User, Location, Activity and Time) data modeled from each of the Flickr datasets can be represented as a sparse tensor $X \in \mathbb{R}^{u \times l \times a \times t}$ where u is # of users, l is # of locations, a is # of activities and t is # of time slots. The ratings placed into this tensor should represent the user's interest for performing a certain activity at a certain location at a certain time. However, in our data set, users do not provide any explicit ratings. Hence, we derive an implicit feedback [29] value normalized over [0.0, 1.0]. Each cell value of the tensor represents the frequency of the current user being at the current location performing the current activity at the current time. The counts are further normalized based on the total number of data points (photographs) for each user.

Moreover, each user typically visits a small subset of the possible locations at only a few of all the possible times and performs a fraction of all the activities possible. Hence, our tensor is very sparse and any given fiber will have only a few non-empty entries. After this construction, the tensors from the 3 datasets have a density of the order of $10^{-3}\%$. Thus, the tensors are 99.999% sparse.

To supplement the sparse 4 dimensional tensor, we further construct various 2-dimensional matrices which are *coupled* with the tensor i.e. they involve one or more of these dimensions and thus, share at least one mode in common with the tensor. We construct them using data obtained from various other data sources.

5.2.2 *Location × Activity Matrix*

Knowing what activities occur in a given location can enable inference of the activity a user is engaged in when he is at the location. As mentioned earlier, even though all the photographs have a geolocation, more than 50% of the photographs do not have any photo content to indicate what activity the user could be engaged in. Hence, this location-activity information can enable inference of the most likely activity a user could be engaged in at a location.

To obtain this relationship for each activity in our hierarchy, we query the Foursquare location database to find all the locations, in each of our datasets, where that particular activity can occur. Thus, for each location l_i in a dataset, we get an n-dimensional frequency vector $c_i = [c_1, c_2 \ldots c_n]$ for n activities (where n = 120). Each $c_{i,j}$ is normalized as $\frac{c_{i,j}}{\sum_{j=1}^{n} c_{i,j}}$. From this information, we construct a Location × Activity matrix $Y \in \mathbb{R}^{l \times a}$ which contains normalized counts for the activities that occur in each location.

5.2.3 *Location × Venue Matrix*

Activities typically occur at a venue or a POI such as a restaurant, shopping mall, etc. For instance, a user would 'Eat' at a 'Restaurant' or 'Shop' at a 'Shopping Mall' in a location. Hence, the knowledge of venues that are present in a location can be leveraged to enable the inference of the user's activity.

For each location in each of our datasets, we also obtain the counts of different venues (from the Foursquare location database) that are present in it. The venues belong to the Foursquare venue hierarchy that includes 470 different types of venues such as restaurants, movie theaters etc. Thus, for each location l_i in a dataset, we get an m-dimensional frequency vector $v_i = [v_1 \ldots v_m]$ for m venues (m = 470). Each $v_{i,j}$ is normalized as $\frac{v_{i,j}}{\sum_{j=1}^{m} v_{i,j}}$. From this information, we construct a Location × Venue matrix $J \in \mathbb{R}^{l \times v}$ which contains normalized counts for venues in each location.

5.2.4 *Location × Location Similarity Matrix*

The locations that have similar type and count of venues will host similar activities. Hence, we employ the Location × Venue matrix to compute the location similarity information. For each pair of locations l_i and l_j in each dataset, we calculate the cosine similarity between the venues vectors as $\text{sim}(l_i,l_j) = \frac{v_i \cdot v_j}{\|v_i\|\|v_j\|}$ where $0 \leq \text{sim}(l_i,l_j) \leq 1$. Using the location similarity information, we construct a symmetric Location × Location matrix $Z \in \mathbb{R}^{l \times l}$.

5.2.5 *Activity × Activity Correlation Matrix*

Users may often have preferences for activities that are similar and correlated. For instance, a user who likes sports might engage in several different types of outdoor sports such as basketball, tennis, etc. Hence, this knowledge of correlation between activities can be exploited easily to further boost the information about the kinds of activities a user could be interested in.

We use the SR metric (from Section 4.2) to compute correlation between all the activities present in our hierarchy. For each pair of activities a_i and a_j in our Activity hierarchy, we calculate the SR score between their descriptions to get sim(a_i,a_j). For instance, SR score between 'Sailing' and 'Surfing' is 0.63, indicating that they are correlated. This is intuitive as both are water sports. From this correlation information, we construct a symmetric Activity × Activity matrix $S \in \mathbb{R}^{a\times a}$.

5.3 Objective function formulation

We now perform joint analysis of the constructed tensor and matrices. We formulate an objective function that simultaneously factorizes the main 4-dimensional tensor and the four 2-dimensional coupled matrices that contain additional information. The tensor is factorized using a CP model while the matrices are factorized using matrix factorization. As discussed earlier, such an approach achieves better performance than standard CP decomposition for extremely sparse tensors. The objective function for our multi-dimensional recommendation problem is:

$$F = \frac{1}{2}\|W \times (X - U \circ L \circ A \circ T)\|^2 + \frac{\lambda_1}{2}\|Y - LA^\top\|^2 + \frac{\lambda_2}{2}\|S - AA^\top\|^2 + \frac{\lambda_3}{2}\|Z - LL^\top\|^2 + \frac{\lambda_4}{2}\|TR\|^2 + \frac{\lambda_5}{2}(\|U\|^2 + \|L\|^2 + \|A\|^2 + \|T\|^2)$$

Thus, the objective function comprises six summands and can be written in the form $F = F_1 + F_2 + F_3 + F_4 + F_5 + F_6$. The six summands and the terms and symbols that they include are:

- F_1 - The weighted least squares error term for the decomposition of the 4 dimensional tensor X into the factor matrices $U \in \mathbb{R}^{u\times k}$, $L \in \mathbb{R}^{l\times k}$, $A \in \mathbb{R}^{a\times k}$ and $T \in \mathbb{R}^{t\times k}$ where k is the number of factors. W is a weight tensor $\in \mathbb{R}^{u\times l\times a\times t}$ and indicates the missing entries in X such that:

  $$w_{u,l,a,t} = \begin{cases} 1 & \text{if } x_{u,l,a,t} \text{ is known} \\ 0 & \text{if } x_{u,l,a,t} \text{ is missing} \end{cases}$$

  This term tries to minimize the loss in only the known entries of the tensor.
- F_2 - The least squares error term for the decomposition of the 2-dimensional matrix Y (containing the Location - Activity information) into factor matrices $L \in \mathbb{R}^{l\times k}$ and $A \in \mathbb{R}^{a\times k}$.
- F_3 - The least squares error term for the decomposition of the 2-dimensional symmetric matrix S (containing the Activity - Activity correlation information) into the factor matrices A $\in \mathbb{R}^{a\times k}$ and its transpose $A^\top \in \mathbb{R}^{k\times a}$.
- F_4- The least squares error term for the decomposition of the 2-dimensional symmetric matrix Z (containing the Location - Location correlation information) into the factor matrices L $\in \mathbb{R}^{l\times k}$ and its transpose $L^\top \in \mathbb{R}^{k\times l}$.
- F_5 - Regularization term for temporal smoothing. It leverages the fact that human behavior in successive time periods will be similar and will have a gradual variation. Hence, it tries to reduce the error between consecutive time slots. R is a bi-diagonal matrix $\in \mathbb{R}^{k\times k}$ with 1 on the main diagonal and -1 on the diagonal above it.
- F_6 - Regularization term to avoid overfitting.
- λ_1 - λ_5 are model parameters.
- $\|\|^2$ denotes the Frobenius norm, $\circ$ denotes the outer product

In general, there is no closed form solution for F, so we use numerical methods, such as gradient descent, to solve this problem. By using the representations in [19], we take the first order derivatives of F with respect to each of the factors to get the following:

Algorithm 3: Gradient descent based algorithm

```
Input: Sparse tensor X∈ R^{u×l×a×t}, 2 D matrices Y ∈ R^{l×a},
       Z ∈ R^{l×l}, S ∈ R^{a×a}, k and convergence criteria
Output: Complete tensor M ∈ R^{u×l×a×t}
for n = 1:size(X) do
    Initialize U, L, A, T;
end
Initialize F, ∇_U F, ∇_L F, ∇_A F and ∇_T F;
Set i = 0;
while not converged do
    Compute step length α_i;
    Compute the gradients ∇_U F_i, ∇_L F_i, ∇_A F_i, ∇_T F_i;
    U_{i+1} = U_i - α_i ∇_U F_i, L_{i+1} = L_i - α∇_L F_i, A_{i+1} = A_i -
    α∇_A F_i, T_{i+1} = T_i - α∇_T F_i;
    Compute F_{i+1};
end
M ← U ∘ L ∘ A ∘ T;
return M;
```

$\nabla_U F = (W^{(1)} - X^{(1)})(T * A * L) + \lambda_5 U$

$\nabla_L F = (W^{(2)} - X^{(2)})(T * A * U) + \lambda_1(LA^\top - Y)A + \lambda_3(-Z - Z^\top + 2LL^\top)L + \lambda_5 L$

$\nabla_A F = (W^{(3)} - X^{(3)})(T * L * U) + \lambda_1(LA^\top - Y)^\top L + \lambda_2(-S - S^\top + 2AA^\top)A + \lambda_5 A$

$\nabla_T F = (W^{(4)} - X^{(4)})(A * L * U) + \lambda_4 TR + \lambda_5 T$

where $W^{(i)}$ and $X^{(i)}$ denotes the mode-i tensor unfolding or matricization [7] of W and X such that $W^{(1)}$ and $X^{(1)} \in \mathbb{R}^{u\times lat}$, $W^{(2)}$ and $X^{(2)} \in \mathbb{R}^{l\times uat}$, $W^{(3)}$ and $X^{(3)} \in \mathbb{R}^{a\times ult}$, and $W^{(4)}$ and $X^{(4)} \in \mathbb{R}^{t\times ula}$, and $*$ denotes the Khatri-Rao product.

5.4 Minimizing the objective function

We employ Algorithm 3, which uses gradient descent, to minimize F and its gradient G. We implemented it in MATLAB using the Tensor Toolbox [4]. As input, the algorithm takes the incomplete sparse tensor (X), the low dimensional matrices (Y, Z, and S), the number of factors (k) as well as the stopping or convergence criteria. The individual components (U, L, A, T) are initialized using the n-mode singular vectors of X which span the subspace of the mode-n fibers i.e. the left singular vectors of the n-mode matricization of X. In each iteration, we first compute the step length using the More-Thuente line-search method [27]. We then compute the values of the gradients for the objective function and the components, and update the objective function value by taking a step in the direction of the gradient. The convergence criteria are set as:

- Relative change in Function Value i.e. $\frac{F_{i+1}-F_i}{F_i} \leq 10^{-10}$
- Relative change in Gradient Value i.e. $\frac{G_{i+1}-G_i}{G_i} \leq 10^{-10}$
- Number of iterations $i \leq 10^5$

Finally, when the algorithm converges, we obtain the complete tensor $M \in \mathbb{R}^{u\times l\times a\times t}$ by taking the outer product of the individual components U, L, A and T.

5.5 Extending to N > 4 Dimensions

We note that while we have focused on N=4 dimensions for concreteness, we can extend the model to accommodate additional dimensions, without loss of generality, by performing data engineering and modifying the objective function. For instance, if we add another contextual dimension such as users' purchases, we can supplement the sparse tensors and matrices with User × Purchases or Location × Purchases matrix obtained from another data source.

[7] Matricization is generation of the matrix representation of a tensor in which all column or row matrices are stacked one after another.

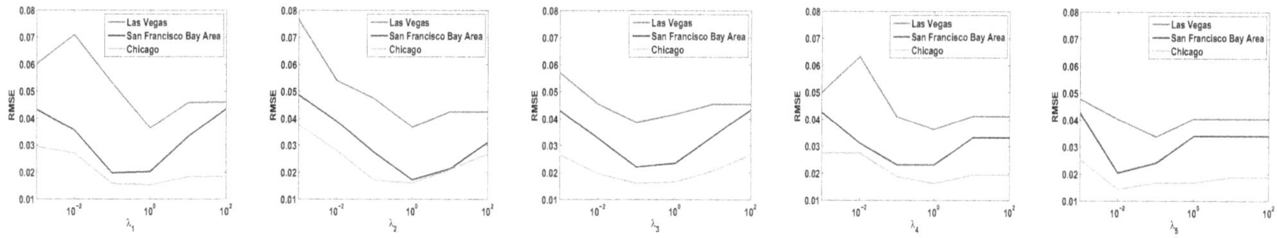

(a) RMSE variation for λ_1 (b) RMSE variation for λ_2 (c) RMSE variation for λ_3 (d) RMSE variation for λ_4 (e) RMSE variation for λ_5

Figure 4: Variation of RMSE for different values of λ_1 - λ_5 on the validation sets

We can then modify the objective function to include the purchases dimension and employ Algorithm 3 to minimize it.

6. EVALUATION

6.1 Methodology

To evaluate the recommendations produced by our system, we used the following methodology: we randomly split each of the three datasets (from San Francisco Bay Area, Las Vegas and Chicago) into training and testing sets with a 7:3 ratio, where we use the training set for training and tuning the model parameters. We use the held-out test set for computing the performance metrics over the predicted and ground truth values. More formally, we define P to be a test dataset containing n values. For each held out value $\in P$, y_i denotes ground truth value and $\hat{y_i}$ denotes predicted value.

6.2 Metrics

We use three standard performance metrics [16] for evaluating the performance of our approach on a test set P:

- Root Mean Squared Error (RMSE) - RMSE is computed as $\sqrt{\frac{\sum_{i=1}^{n}(\hat{y_i}-y_i)^2}{n}}$. However, RMSE can be susceptible to large errors and often places more emphasis on them. Hence, we compute Mean Absolute Error (MAE) as well to evaluate the performance of our approach.
- Mean Absolute Error (MAE) - MAE is computed as $\frac{\sum_{i=1}^{n}|\hat{y_i}-y_i|}{n}$. However, both RMSE and MAE may be less appropriate for tasks where a ranked result is returned to the user, who then only views items at the top of the ranking. For this, we compute Normalized Discounted Cumulative Gain (nDCG).
- Normalized Discounted Cumulative Gain (nDCG) - nDCG is commonly used in information retrieval to measure a search engine's performance. A higher nDCG value for a list of search results indicates that more relevant items were ranked higher in the list. In particular, nDCG@p measures the relevance of top p results and is defined as:

  $\text{nDCG@p} = \frac{\text{DCG@p}}{\text{iDCG@p}}$ where $\text{DCG@p} = rel_1 + \sum_{i=2}^{p}\frac{rel_i}{\log_2 rel_i}$, iDCG@p is the DCG@p value of ideal ranking list and rel_i is a relevance value. nDCG ranges from 0 to 1. The higher the nDCG value is, the better a ranking result list is.

6.3 Parameter Tuning

We performed parameter tuning via parameter-sweeping experiments on the different training sets. We randomly split each training set into training and validation sets with a 4:1 ratio. We held out the validation set and constructed the model using the training set with different values for the model parameters, λ_1 - λ_5, # of factors (k) and location grid size r. We computed RMSE on the held out validation sets and picked the parameter values that minimized it.

Grid Size r (m)	RMSE		
	San Francisco	Las Vegas	Chicago
300	0.0217	0.0378	0.0170
500	**0.0213**	**0.0376**	**0.0162**
700	0.0222	0.0392	0.0175
1000	0.0224	0.0437	0.0186

Table 4: RMSE on validation set for various location grid sizes

6.3.1 *Impact of model parameters*

For tuning each individual parameter, we set the remaining parameters as 0.00001 in order to reduce their impact on the model performance. We then ran the parameter-sweeping experiments 5 times for each parameter value and averaged the RMSE. Figure 4 shows the variation of RMSE for different values of the model parameters for the 3 validation sets. As evident, the RMSE first increases and later decreases as value of each parameter (λ_1 - λ_5) increases. This is because when a parameter value is too small, the model cannot fully utilize the information from the corresponding matrix. On the other hand, if it is too large, then the information from the matrix will dominate the objective function. After this tuning, we set $\lambda_1 = 1.0$, $\lambda_2 = 1.5$, $\lambda_3 = 0.5$, $\lambda_4 = 1.0$ and $\lambda_5 = 0.02$.

6.3.2 *Impact of number of factors*

We varied the number of latent factors (k) from 10 to 50. However, we observed that the RMSE did not exhibit significant variation which implies that changing the number of factors did not have a significant impact on performance, as also reported by Zheng et al. [37, 38]. For our experiments, we set $k = 30$.

6.3.3 *Impact of location grid size*

Table 4 shows the RMSE for the 3 validation datasets for different location grid sizes. The grid size of 500m has the lowest RMSE for all the validation sets and hence we use that for our experiments. This is also intuitive because recommended locations within a distance of 500m can be easily reached on foot.

Henceforth, all experiments will use the tuned parameter values.

6.4 Comparison with Baselines

We compare our approach with 7 state-of-the-art baselines.

6.4.1 *Collaborative Filtering baselines*

These baselines exploit similarity on each of the individual dimensions to complete the tensor. They take only the 4 dimensional tensor as input. We implemented 4 CF baselines:

- User-User Collaborative Filtering baseline (UCF) - This baseline exploits the user-user similarity information to fill in the missing entries of the sparse tensor X. In particular, for UCF, we consider CF on each user $\times$ location matrix with respect to each activity and each time slot, on each user $\times$ activity matrix with respect to each location and each time slot, and on each user $\times$ time matrix with respect to each location and each activity independently. To this end, we matricize X in Mode 1 to generate matrix $X^{(1)} \in \mathbb{R}^{u\times lat}$. We then use Pearson correlation coefficient between the vectors in the matrix to compute pairwise user similarity information. For each user, we compute the weighted average of the top N similar users to predict the missing values.

- Location-Location Collaborative Filtering baseline (LCF) - Similarly, the LCF baseline exploits the location-location similarity information to fill in the missing entries of X. We matricize X in Mode 2 to generate matrix $X^{(2)} \in \mathbb{R}^{l\times uat}$. We use Pearson correlation coefficient between the vectors in the matrix to compute pairwise location similarity information. For each location, we then compute the weighted average of the top N similar locations to predict the missing values.
- Activity-Activity Collaborative Filtering baseline (ACF) - The ACF baseline exploits the activity-activity similarity information to fill in the missing entries of X. We matricize X in Mode 3 to generate matrix $X^{(3)} \in \mathbb{R}^{a\times ult}$. We use Pearson correlation coefficient between the vectors in the matrix to compute pairwise activity similarity information. For each activity, we then compute the weighted average of the top N similar activities to predict the missing values.
- Time-Time Collaborative Filtering baseline (TCF) - Finally, the TCF baseline exploits the time- time similarity information to fill in the missing entries of X. We matricize X in Mode 4 to generate matrix $X^{(4)} \in \mathbb{R}^{t\times ula}$. We use Pearson correlation coefficient between the vectors in the matrix to compute pairwise time similarity information. For each time slot, we then compute the weighted average of the top N similar time slots to predict the missing values.

In these experiments, we set N = 10, since the prediction results do not depend on N significantly as suggested by Zheng et al. [37]

6.4.2 *Model based baselines*

We implemented the standard CP decomposition model which, when applied to our multi-dimensional recommendation problem, has an objective function of the form:

$$F = \frac{1}{2}\|X - U\circ L\circ A\circ T\|^2 + \frac{\lambda_5}{2}(\|U\|^2+\|L\|^2+\|A\|^2+\|T\|^2)$$

Thus, it takes only the 4 dimensional tensor as input and its objective function has only the tensor decomposition term along with the regularization term. This can be obtained by setting λ_1 - $\lambda_4 = 0$ in our objective function (see Section 5.3) and replacing the weighted least squares error term with the standard least squares error term in summand F_1. We then minimize this objective function using the gradient descent based Algorithm 3.

6.4.3 *Algorithmic baselines*

The 2 algorithmic baselines that we employ are:

- Higher Order Singular Value Decomposition (HOSVD) - We implement the HOSVD approach proposed by Lathauwer et al. [10]. This approach also takes only the 4 dimensional tensor as input. It first matricizes the 4 dimensional User × Location × Activity × Time tensor X along each of the 4 modes to get the matrices $X^{(1)}$, $X^{(2)}$, $X^{(3)}$ and $X^{(4)}$. On each matrix, SVD is applied to compute the low rank approximation: $X^{(i)} = U^{(i)} \cdot S^{(i)} \cdot {V^{(i)}}^{\top}$ where $1 \leq i \leq 4$.
  The core tensor S is then constructed as:
  $S = X \times_1 {U_{c_1}^{(1)}}^{\top} \times_2 {U_{c_2}^{(2)}}^{\top} \times_3 {U_{c_3}^{(3)}}^{\top} \times_4 {U_{c_4}^{(4)}}^{\top}$
  where ${U_{c_1}^{(1)}}^{\top}$, ${U_{c_2}^{(2)}}^{\top}$, ${U_{c_3}^{(3)}}^{\top}$, and ${U_{c_4}^{(4)}}^{\top}$ are the transpose of the c_1-dimensionally reduced $U^{(1)}$, c_2 - dimensionally reduced $U^{(2)}$, c_3-dimensionally reduced $U^{(3)}$, and c_4-dimensionally reduced $U^{(4)}$ matrices respectively.
  Finally, the completed matrix M is obtained as:
  $M = S \times_1 U_{c_1}^{(1)} \times_2 U_{c_2}^{(2)} \times_3 U_{c_3}^{(3)} \times_4 U_{c_4}^{(4)}$

Approach	RMSE		
	San Francisco	Las Vegas	Chicago
Our approach	**0.0197**	**0.0339**	**0.0153**
UCF	0.0324	0.0486	0.0293
LCF	0.0336	0.0430	0.0311
ACF	0.0333	0.0433	0.0317
TCF	0.0319	0.0484	0.0315
Standard CP	0.0224	0.0427	0.0178
HOSVD	0.0227	0.0405	0.0175
ALS	0.0222	0.0389	0.0173

Table 5: RMSE for our approach and baselines on the 3 test sets

Approach	MAE		
	San Francisco	Las Vegas	Chicago
Our approach	**0.0076**	**0.0179**	**0.0049**
UCF	0.0104	0.0314	0.0062
LCF	0.0102	0.0310	0.0066
ACF	0.0105	0.0323	0.0069
TCF	0.01	0.0354	0.0065
Standard CP	0.0095	0.0228	0.0058
HOSVD	0.0098	0.0239	0.0061
ALS	0.0093	0.0218	0.0054

Table 6: MAE for our approach and baselines on the 3 test sets

  where c_1, c_2, c_3 and c_4 are set empirically. Based on the experiments of Nanopoulos [28], we preserve 30% of the information in each matrix.
- Alternating Least Squares (ALS) - In ALS, the objective function is a standard CP formulation and the idea is to solve for each factor matrix, leaving all other factors fixed. We implement the ALS algorithm proposed by Kolda and Bader [19, 20] for the standard CP decomposition (see Section 6.4.2) of our multi-dimensional recommendation problem.

6.5 Results

For testing experiments, we held out the test dataset and generated the completed tensor using the training dataset with the tuned parameter values, number of factors *k* (30) and for the optimal grid size (500m). We then computed the RMSE and MAE between the predicted and the ground truth held out values of the test set.

Since we do not have human supplied relevance rankings, we compute nDCG on the held-out known values. We calculated nDCG with respect to each recommendation dimension by fixing the remaining dimensions and computing nDCG on the current dimension. Thus, for each of the held out values in the test set, we first fixed user, location and activity and ranked the time slots in the completed tensor. This ranking was used to calculate DCG (refer to Section 6.2) for time. To compute iDCG for time, we determined the ranking for the ground truth time values. We then calculated nDCG@p (with p = 5) for time. Finally, we averaged the values for all user, location and activity combinations to generate an averaged nDCG@5 for the time dimension. Similarly, we fixed user, location and time values and ranked activities to compute nDCG@5 for the activity dimension and fixed user, activity and time to compute nDCG@5 for the location dimension.

Tables 5, 6, and 7 show the results achieved by our approach as well as the baselines on the 3 test datasets for the 3 performance metrics: RMSE, MAE and nDCG@5. For RMSE and MAE, a lower value signifies superiors performance while for nDCG, a higher value signifies superior performance. For each metric, we ran all algorithms 5 times on each test dataset and averaged the result. Clearly, our approach outperforms these baselines.

Approach	nDCG@5 for location		
	San Francisco	Las Vegas	Chicago
Our approach	**0.898**	**0.835**	**0.821**
UCF	0.691	0.523	0.693
LCF	0.71	0.514	0.682
ACF	0.702	0.582	0.695
TCF	0.735	0.593	0.701
Standard CP	0.685	0.453	0.651
HOSVD	0.890	0.815	0.798
ALS	0.798	0.722	0.748
Approach	nDCG@5 for activity		
	San Francisco	Las Vegas	Chicago
Our approach	**0.869**	**0.827**	**0.798**
UCF	0.452	0.465	0.467
LCF	0.457	0.477	0.485
ACF	0.440	0.458	0.412
TCF	0.391	0.34	0.401
Standard CP	0.341	0.314	0.393
HOSVD	0.829	0.817	0.714
ALS	0.770	0.737	0.692
Approach	nDCG@5 for time		
	San Francisco	Las Vegas	Chicago
Our approach	**0.833**	**0.832**	**0.807**
UCF	0.581	0.612	0.605
LCF	0.563	0.605	0.567
ACF	0.541	0.609	0.575
TCF	0.593	0.632	0.582
Standard CP	0.578	0.605	0.563
HOSVD	0.812	0.82	0.798
ALS	0.732	0.725	0.656

Table 7: nDCG (for location, activity and time) for our approach and baselines on the 3 test sets

6.6 Discussion of Results

As evident from the results, the neighborhood-based Collaborative Filtering baselines exhibit poor performance with respect to all the 3 performance metrics. There are two possible reasons for this result. First, these approaches employ only the User $\times$ Location $\times$ Activity $\times$ Time tensor. Since the tensor is extremely sparse, computing similarity along any dimension will be error prone as most of the entries are missing. Hence, our approach which supplements the sparse tensor with additional information from external sources overcomes this hurdle. Second, each of these baselines predicts the missing values based on similarity along one dimension only, ignoring the other dimensions. Since our problem involves collaborative recommendations along multiple dimensions, it is important to employ all the dimensions for recommendations as we do.

The model based and algorithmic baselines such as Standard CP, HOSVD and ALS also utilize only the sparse tensor as input. As pointed out in Section 2, the standard CP approach demonstrates an increase in error if the data is extremely sparse. Similarly, ALS has poor convergence if the data is sparse and does not scale to large datasets. Moreover, HOSVD and ALS have high space complexity. On the other hand, our approach overcomes the sparsity of the data by supplementing the sparse tensor with coupled matrices and also scales to large datasets. Hence, it outperforms these baselines.

Also, we note that the nDCG values for location varies greatly for each dataset for each algorithm while the nDCG values for activity and time do not exhibit such a high variation. This is possibly because the number of locations in each of the dataset varies significantly while the number of activities and time slots are constant for each dataset. In addition, the nDCG values for location are higher

Approach	Time (in seconds)		
	San Francisco	Las Vegas	Chicago
Without weighting	12000	2465	10500
With weighting	9600	1180	8580

Table 8: Runtime comparison

in general for most of the algorithms and datasets, as compared to activity and time. This indicates that location is the most important dimension for recommendation, followed by time and activity. This is also intuitive because in our datasets, each photo has a location and timestamp but $< 50\%$ photos have meta data to enable activity inference. Hence, the activity data is sparser than for location and time. This would affect the performance of all the baselines since they use the sparse tensor as the only input. However, in our approach, we supplement this sparse tensor with additional matrices involving Location, Activity and Time. We also perform regularized temporal smoothing. Hence, the nDCG for Activity and Time are higher and comparable to that of Location for our approach.

6.7 Runtime Comparison

Since our data is very sparse, we performed a weighted decomposition of the tensor which minimizes the error in only the known entries of the tensor. We also experimented without the weighting imposed on the tensor i.e. minimize the error in all the entries of the tensor. In this case, our objective function is:

$$F = \frac{1}{2}\|X - U \circ L \circ A \circ T\|^2 + \frac{\lambda_1}{2}\|Y - LA^\top\|^2 + \frac{\lambda_2}{2}\|S - AA^\top\|^2 + \frac{\lambda_3}{2}\|Z - LL^\top\|^2 + \frac{\lambda_4}{2}\|TR\|^2 + \frac{\lambda_5}{2}(\|U\|^2 + \|L\|^2 + \|A\|^2 + \|T\|^2)$$

We minimized it using Algorithm 3. Both approaches have the same performance with respect to RMSE, MAE and nDCG@5. However, they differ in their runtime. As shown in Table 8, the weighted approach is faster as it minimizes the loss on only the known entries of the tensor. All experiments were run on a 64 bit Windows machine with core i7 processor and 16 GB RAM.

7. CONCLUSION AND FUTURE WORK

In this paper, we presented a system and an approach for performing multi-dimensional collaborative recommendations for Who (User), What (Activity), When (Time) and Where (Location), using tensor factorization on sparse user-generated data. To address the problem of sparsity for multi-dimensional recommendations, we modeled this problem as a joint analysis of a sparsely populated User $\times$ Location $\times$ Activity $\times$ Time tensor along with several matrices which share one or more common modes with the tensor. These tensors and matrices were constructed by fusing data for the various dimensions (users, locations, activities and time) from multiple heterogeneous data sources, namely Flickr, Foursquare, Yelp and Viator. We factorized these tensors and matrices simultaneously using a gradient descent-based algorithm. We evaluated our system and approach on our primary large-scale real-world data set consisting of 588,000 Flickr photos collected from three major metro regions in the USA — San Francisco Bay Area, Las Vegas and Chicago. We compared our approach with several state-of-the-art baselines and demonstrated that it outperforms all of them. Our approach also demonstrated an improvement in runtime without the need for sacrificing performance.

We now plan to create a Hadoop-based pipeline for performing multi-dimensional analytics. We will also work on scaling this approach to larger and more complex real-time datasets. In addition, we plan to analyze the space-time complexity of our algorithms and parallelize them to run on higher-dimensional data. We will also compare our approach more closely with other standards such as CMF and CMTF and evaluate our system's runtime performance against them.

8. REFERENCES

[1] E. Acar, D. M. Dunlavy, T. G. Kolda, and M. Mørup. Scalable tensor factorizations with missing data. In *Proceedings of the SIAM International Conference on Data Mining*, 2010.

[2] E. Acar, D. M. Dunlavy, T. G. Kolda, and M. Mørup. Scalable tensor factorizations for incomplete data. *Chemometrics and Intelligent Laboratory Systems*, 106(1):41–56, 2011.

[3] E. Acar, T. G. Kolda, and D. M. Dunlavy. All-at-once optimization for coupled matrix and tensor factorizations. In *Proceedings of Mining and Learning with Graphs*, 2011.

[4] B. W. Bader, T. G. Kolda, et al. Matlab tensor toolbox version 2.5. Available online, January 2012.

[5] V. Bellotti, B. Begole, E. H. Chi, N. Ducheneaut, J. Fang, E. Isaacs, T. King, M. W. Newman, K. Partridge, B. Price, et al. Activity-based serendipitous recommendations with the magitti mobile leisure guide. In *Proceedings of the ACM Conference on Human Factors in Computing Systems*, 2008.

[6] A. M. Buchanan and A. W. Fitzgibbon. Damped newton algorithms for matrix factorization with missing data. In *Proceedings of the IEEE Conference on Computer Vision and Pattern Recognition*, 2005.

[7] X. Cao, G. Cong, and C. Jensen. Mining significant semantic locations from gps data. In *Proceedings of VLDB*, 2010.

[8] A. Cichocki, R. Zdunek, A. H. Phan, and S.-i. Amari. *Nonnegative matrix and tensor factorizations: applications to exploratory multi-way data analysis and blind source separation*. John Wiley & Sons, 2009.

[9] D. Crandall, L. Backstrom, D. Huttenlocher, and J. Kleinberg. Mapping the world's photos. In *Proceedings of the 18th International Conference on World Wide Web*, 2009.

[10] L. De Lathauwer, B. De Moor, and J. Vandewalle. A multilinear singular value decomposition. *SIAM journal on Matrix Analysis and Applications*, 21(4):1253–1278, 2000.

[11] N. Ducheneaut, K. Partridge, Q. Huang, B. Price, M. Roberts, E. H. Chi, V. Bellotti, and B. Begole. Collaborative filtering is not enough? experiments with a mixed-model recommender for leisure activities. In *Proceedings of the 2009 International Conference on User Modeling, Adaptation, and Personalization*.

[12] F. Girardin, J. Blat, F. Calabrese, F. Dal Fiore, and C. Ratti. Digital footprinting: Uncovering tourists with user-generated content. *Pervasive Computing*, 7(4):36–43, 2008.

[13] L. Han, A. Kashyap, T. Finin, J. Mayfield, and J. Weese. Umbc ebiquity-core: Semantic textual similarity systems. In *Proceedings of the Second Joint Conference on Lexical and Computational Semantics*, 2012.

[14] S. Harispe, S. Ranwez, S. Janaqi, and J. Montmain. Semantic measures for the comparison of units of language, concepts or instances from text and knowledge representation analysis. *arXiv preprint arXiv:1310.1285*, 2013.

[15] R. A. Harshman. Foundations of the parafac procedure: models and conditions for an" explanatory" multimodal factor analysis. *UCLA Working Papers in Phonetics*, 16(1):1 – 84, 1970.

[16] J. L. Herlocker, J. A. Konstan, L. G. Terveen, and J. T. Riedl. Evaluating collaborative filtering recommender systems. *ACM Transactions on Information Systems (TOIS)*, 22(1):5–53.

[17] B. Hidasi and D. Tikk. Fast als-based tensor factorization for context-aware recommendation from implicit feedback. In *ECML PKDD 2012*, pages 67–82. Springer, 2012.

[18] A. Karatzoglou, X. Amatriain, L. Baltrunas, and N. Oliver. Multiverse recommendation: n-dimensional tensor factorization for context-aware collaborative filtering. In *Proceedings of the 4th ACM conference on Recommender systems*, 2010.

[19] T. G. Kolda. *Multilinear operators for higher-order decompositions*. United States. Department of Energy, 2006.

[20] T. G. Kolda and B. W. Bader. Tensor decompositions and applications. *SIAM Review*, 51(3):455–500, September 2009.

[21] Y. Koren, R. Bell, and C. Volinsky. Matrix factorization techniques for recommender systems. *Computer*, 42(8):30–37, 2009.

[22] L. Liao. *Location-based activity recognition*. PhD thesis, University of Washington, 2006.

[23] G. Linden, B. Smith, and J. York. Amazon. com recommendations: Item-to-item collaborative filtering. *Internet Computing, IEEE*, 7(1):76–80, 2003.

[24] B. Liu, Y. Fu, Z. Yao, and H. Xiong. Learning geographical preferences for point-of-interest recommendation. In *Proceedings of KDD*, pages 1043–1051. ACM, 2013.

[25] H. Lu, J. Yang, Z. Liu, N. D. Lane, T. Choudhury, and A. T. Campbell. The jigsaw continuous sensing engine for mobile phone applications. In *Proceedings of the 8th ACM Conference on Embedded Networked Sensor Systems*, 2010.

[26] P. Melville and V. Sindhwani. Recommender systems. In *Encyclopedia of machine learning*, pages 829–838. Springer, 2010.

[27] J. J. Moré and D. J. Thuente. Line search algorithms with guaranteed sufficient decrease. *ACM Transactions on Mathematical Software (TOMS)*, 20(3):286–307, 1994.

[28] A. Nanopoulos. Item recommendation in collaborative tagging systems. *Systems, Man and Cybernetics, Part A: Systems and Humans, IEEE Transactions on*, 41(4):760–771.

[29] D. W. Oard, J. Kim, et al. Implicit feedback for recommender systems. In *Proceedings of the AAAI workshop on recommender systems*, pages 81–83. Wollongong, 1998.

[30] D. Quercia, R. Schifanellai, and L. M. Aiello. The shortest path to happiness: Recommending beautiful, quiet, and happy routes in the city. In *Proceedings of ACM Hypertext 2014*.

[31] M. Sattari, M. Manguoglu, I. H. Toroslu, P. Symeonidis, P. Senkul, and Y. Manolopoulos. Geo-activity recommendations by using improved feature combination. In *Proceedings of the 2012 ACM Conference on Ubiquitous Computing*.

[32] Y. Shi, P. Serdyukov, A. Hanjalic, and M. Larson. Nontrivial landmark recommendation using geotagged photos. *ACM Transactions on Intelligent Systems and Technology*, 4(3):17–37, June 2013.

[33] A. P. Singh and G. J. Gordon. Relational learning via collective matrix factorization. In *Proceedings of the 14th ACM SIGKDD international conference on Knowledge discovery and data mining*, pages 650–658. ACM, 2008.

[34] P. Symeonidis, A. Nanopoulos, and Y. Manolopoulos. Tag recommendations based on tensor dimensionality reduction. In *Proceedings of the 2nd ACM conference on Recommender systems*, 2008.

[35] J. D. Ullman, J. Leskovec, and A. Rajaraman. *Mining of Massive Datasets*. Cambridge University Press, 2011.

[36] Y. Yang, Z. Gong, and L. Hou U. Identifying points of interest by self-tuning clustering. In *Proceedings of SIGIR*, pages 883–892. ACM, 2011.

[37] V. W. Zheng, B. Cao, Y. Zheng, X. Xie, and Q. Yang. Collaborative filtering meets mobile recommendation: A user-centered approach. In *AAAI*, 2010.

[38] V. W. Zheng, Y. Zheng, X. Xie, and Q. Yang. Collaborative location and activity recommendations with gps history data. In *Proceedings of the 19th international conference on World wide web*, 2010.

Secrets, Lies, and Account Recovery:
Lessons from the Use of Personal Knowledge Questions at Google

Joseph Bonneau*
Stanford University & EFF
jbonneau@cs.stanford.edu

Elie Bursztein
Google
elieb@google.com

Ilan Caron
Google
ilanc@google.com

Rob Jackson
Google
roj@google.com

Mike Williamson
Google
miwilliamson@google.com

ABSTRACT

We examine the first large real-world data set on personal knowledge question's security and memorability from their deployment at Google. Our analysis confirms that secret questions generally offer a security level that is far lower than user-chosen passwords. It turns out to be even lower than proxies such as the real distribution of surnames in the population would indicate. Surprisingly, we found that a significant cause of this insecurity is that users often don't answer truthfully. A user survey we conducted revealed that a significant fraction of users (37%) who admitted to providing fake answers did so in an attempt to make them "harder to guess" although on aggregate this behavior had the opposite effect as people "harden" their answers in a predictable way.

On the usability side, we show that secret answers have surprisingly poor memorability despite the assumption that reliability motivates their continued deployment. From millions of account recovery attempts we observed a significant fraction of users (e.g 40% of our English-speaking US users) were unable to recall their answers when needed. This is lower than the success rate of alternative recovery mechanisms such as SMS reset codes (over 80%).

Comparing question strength and memorability reveals that the questions that are potentially the most secure (e.g what is your first phone number) are also the ones with the worst memorability. We conclude that it appears next to impossible to find secret questions that are both secure and memorable. Secret questions continue have some use when combined with other signals, but they should not be used alone and best practice should favor more reliable alternatives.

Categories and Subject Descriptors

D.4.6 [**Software**]: Security and Protection—*authentication*

General Terms

Security, Privacy, Authentication

*Part of this research was conducted while Joseph Bonneau was at Google.

WWW 2015, May 18–22, 2015, Florence, Italy.
ACM 978-1-4503-3469-3/15/05.
http://dx.doi.org/10.1145/2736277.2741691.

Keywords

personal knowledge questions; account recovery

1. INTRODUCTION

Personal knowledge questions (also called "secret questions" or "challenge questions" among other names) have long been used as backup mechanism to reclaim lost accounts [20]. Many academic studies have argued in their favor on the ground that they should be more memorable than passwords [33, 10, 26] for two reasons: the presence of a question makes remembering the answer a *cued recall* task instead of a *free recall* task and the information being asked for is something users inherently remember rather than a secret stored explicitly for authentication. On the security side, previous work has highlighted the potential weakness of secret questions [28, 14] based on laboratory experiments and analysis.

In this work we provide the first large-scale empirical data analysis of secret questions based on their deployment at Google. We studied the distribution of hundreds of millions of secret answers and millions of account recovery claims, demonstrating that in practice secret questions have poor security and memorability. This poor level of security, their unreliability for successful account recovery, and the existence of alternative recovery options with significantly higher success rate motivated Google's decision to favor alternative options (SMS, Email) as a recovery mechanism. Secret questions are now only used as a last resort in conjunction with other signals.

Some of our key empirical findings are:

- Statistical attacks against secret questions are a real risk because there are commons answers shared among many users. For example using a single guess an attacker would have a 19.7% success rate at guessing English-speaking users' answers for the question "*Favorite food?*". Similarly, with a single guess the attacker would have a 3.8% success rate at guessing Spanish-speaking users' answers for the question "*Father's middle name?*". With 10 guesses an attacker would be able to guess 39% of Korean-speaking users' answers to "*City of birth?*" (Section 3.1).

- Questions that are supposedly more secure due to the expectation that each user will have a different answer (e.g phone number) in practice don't exhibit a flat distribution because people provide untruthful answers. As a result the security of these questions is significantly lower than hoped. For example with a single guess an ideal attacker would have a success rate of 4.2% at guessing English-speaking users' answers to the question "*Frequent flyer number?*". Similarly, they would be able to guess 2.4% of Russian-speaking users' phone number answers with a single try (Section 3.1).

- It is easy and cheap to create answer distributions that closely approximate real answer distributions using crowdsourcing services such as MTurk and CrowdFlower. Our experiment reveals that with as few as 1000 answers from crowdsourced users we are able to build approximate distributions which enable a guess rate that is between 75% and 80% as effective as the true distribution when making up to 100 guesses (Section 3.4).
- Users are no more likely to recover their accounts early or late in the lifetime of their account with the exception of the first 72 hours which see a surge with ≈10% of the recovery claims (Section 4.1).
- Questions that are potentially more secure have worse recall than unsafe questions: For the US English-speaking population the the question "*Father's middle name?*" had a success rate of 76% overall whereas the potentially safer question "*First phone number?*" had a 55% recall. The potentially safest questions have abysmal recall: "*Library card number?*" has a 22% recall and "*Frequent flyer number?*" only has a 9% recall rate (Section 4.2).
- Question memorability decreases significantly over time. For example the success rate for the question "*Favorite Food?*" is 74% after a month, 53% after 3 month and barely 47% after a year (Section 4.2).
- The decay of memorability over time is greater for questions about numbers assigned to people vs personal questions: for the question "*Frequent flyer card number?*" the recall rate decreased by 18% after a month whereas it only decreased by 6% for the question "*Father's middle name?*" (Section 4.3).
- Memorability is greatly impacted by people supplying untruthful answers. For the question "*First phone number?*" US users who supplied an answer with a plausible length of 7 digits have a 55% chance to recall their question while people who supplied an answer with a length of 6 characters only have an 18% chance to answer correctly (Section 4.4).
- The memorability of secret questions is influenced by cultural factors even when the language is the same. For instance the recall for English users from Great Britain is significantly lower than English users from the USA: 52% vs 61% (Section 4.5).
- Surveying the US population using Google Consumer Surveys reveals that people provide untruthful answers to secret questions because they try to make it harder to guess (37% of the 1500 respondents) or easier to remember (15%). Ironically of course, this behavior achieves exactly the opposite effect (Section 5).
- SMS and email-based account recovery have a significantly higher chance of success: 81% for SMS vs 75% for Email vs 61% (US/English) down to 44% (France/French) for secret questions (Section 6).

2. THREAT MODEL & GUESSING METRICS

In this section we discuss the threat model that is addressed by account recovery in general and secret questions in particular. Past research has highlighted many security weaknesses for personal knowledge questions:

- **Questions with common answers.** Many personal knowledge questions have common answers shared by many in the user population which an adversary might successfully guess. Schechter et al. were able to guess approximately 10% of user's answers by using a list of other answers provided by users in the same study [28]. Bonneau et al. [5] considered the difficulty of guessing common pieces of information used in personal knowledge questions using public statistics, for example using census records to estimate the difficulty of estimating of guessing a surname.
- **Questions with few plausible answers.** A number of potential questions, such as "*who is your favorite superhero?*" have very few possible answers. An empirical study by Rabkin of questions used in practice found that 40% had trivially small answer spaces [27]. User-chosen questions appear even worse: Just and Aspinall found that the majority of users choose questions with trivially few plausible answers [21].
- **Publicly available answers.** Rabkin found that 16% of questions had answers routinely listed publicly in online social-networking profiles [27]. Even if users keep data private on social networks, inference attacks enable approximating sensitive information from a user's friends [24]. Other questions can be found in publicly available records. For example, at least 30% of Texas residents' mothers' maiden names can be deduced from birth and marriage records [15].
- **Social engineering.** Users may not appreciate that the information in their security questions is of critical security importance. Karlof et al. were able to extract answers to personal knowledge questions from 92% of users via email phishing in a 2009 study [22].
- **Social guessing attacks.** Users' answers may be easily available to partners, friends, or even acquaintances. Schechter et al. found in a laboratory study that acquaintances could guess 17% of answers correctly in five tries or fewer [28], confirming similar results from earlier user studies [16, 26].

While all of these threats are important, in this work we focus solely on the problem of questions with common answers and the risk of online guessing. We consider the main threat against an account recovery system for an online service to be an adversary that aims to compromise accounts en masse by trying to guess common answers for a large number of accounts. This threat model is similar to that for passwords which are used to defend against account hijacking via mass guessing attacks [11].

Therefore the main security criteria for secret questions is their resistance to *statistical* guessing attacks by an attacker with no knowledge of the individual user. This attack model has not yet been rigorously evaluated. For example, Schechter et al. [28] and Bonneau et al. [5] attempted to estimate guessing difficulty but did not have access to actual answers chosen by real users. It remains unknown exactly how users answer these questions in practice and how different users' answers are from a theoretical distribution such as the population-distribution of surnames. Similarly there has been no published study of how effective distributions built via crowd-sourcing will be at approximating real distributions.

2.1 Evaluation metrics

Throughout this paper we use *statistical guessing metrics* to estimate the difficulty for our online adversary to guess secret answers. We start by using metrics which model an *ideal* attacker who knows the precise distribution of answers across the entire population of users, but has no per-user data. This ideal attacker provides a lower bound on security for any real attacker, hence we focus primarily on these metrics. We also use distribution comparison metrics to compare the difficulty of guessing secret answers with passwords and PIN codes. Finally we study how effective crowd-sourced distributions are at approximating the true distribution of answers.

Online guessing attacks: The simplest metric is "what percentage of users share the β most common answers?" An attacker able to make β guesses per account can expect to guess roughly this proportion of user's answers. Following the notation of Bonneau [3], we denote this proportion as λ_β for a given number of guesses β. This is the easiest metric to define and interpret when evaluating security against an online attacker who is limited to interacting with the genuine server and can only make a small fixed number of guesses before being locked out. In practice, Google limits users by default to three incorrect answers to prevent brute force attacks while accounting for typos and normal memory failures [8]. Other websites sometimes choose different guessing cutoffs, or require CAPTCHAs or other additional hurdles to increase the cost to attackers of making large numbers of guesses [1].

While Google rate-limits account recovery attempts and performs risk-analysis, to keep our analysis generic, we avoid making any particular assumption about an appropriate rate-limiting policy for personal knowledge questions as used in account recovery and instead present our data for various policies. In Table 1 we show λ_β for $\beta = 1, 3, 10, 100$, and 1000 as representative values.

Extended guessing attacks: We may also attempt to measure the difficulty of guessing a user's secret answer if the attacker is able to guess exhaustively up to their computational limits. Note that most websites have rate-limiting defenses to prevent such attacks. This scenario would only arise if no rate-limiting were in place, for example if a list of hashed answers was leaked from a compromised website, or if personal knowledge questions were used in offline application such as for encryption keys.

The simplest metric is the expected number of guesses before the correct answer is found for a randomly-chosen answer from the distribution. This is typically called *guessing entropy*. Unfortunately, this quantity can be deceivingly large in practice due to the presence of a small number of extremely difficult to guess answers, often due to users entering long random strings. For example, it was estimated that it actually takes over 2^{100} guesses to compromise an average password due to the presence of less than one in a million users choosing 128-bit random strings as passwords [3].

Instead, the best approach is to measure the expected number of guesses required for an adversary have a probability α of compromising a random user's account. This is denoted as G_α and called the α-guesswork. This quantity can also be converted into units of bits by comparing to a uniform distribution which would provide equivalent security (denoted $\tilde{G}_\alpha$) [3], which can be easier to interpret and compare.

A reasonable value for modeling the difficulty for an attacker of breaking a median user's account is $\tilde{G}_{0.5}$. Thus, we provide values of $\tilde{G}_\alpha$ for $\alpha = 0.1, 0.25$, and 0.5 in Table 1. We also list the min-entropy H_∞, which represents the limit of $\tilde{G}_\alpha$ as $\alpha \to 0$ and is thus a lower bound on any guessing attack. It is also more simply defined as simply $H_\infty = -\lg_2(p_0)$ where p_0 is the probability of the most commonly chosen answer in the distribution.

Sample size & significance: We use Bonneau's method to determine when estimates for both λ_β and $\tilde{G}_\alpha$ are accurate using bootstrap re-sampling [4]. This technique determines, given a desired confidence level and accuracy, a cutoff point α_* at which estimates for these metrics can be accepted. Generally, we are able to estimate metrics λ_β and $\tilde{G}_\alpha$ at a given sample size for values of $\alpha < \alpha_*$ and β such that $\lambda_\beta < \alpha_*$, as these metrics depend only on higher-probability answers which are most accurately estimated in the sample. Estimating the difficulty of more extended guessing attacks becomes inaccurate because rarer answers may only be observed a small number of times in the sample and hence their frequencies are poorly estimated.

We evaluate using a confidence level of $p = 0.98$ and an error of 0.1, meaning we are 98% confident the relative error of our estimate compared to the true value is less than 0.1. For most of the metrics we estimate the expected relative error is far lower than this. While we can't publish the exact size of our sample size, the data considered contains hundreds of millions of data points and each question analyzed had over 1 million answers. For most of the metrics we wish to compute the sample size we obtained was large enough to compute them to within our desired accuracy. For those which the error was higher than our cutoff, mostly estimates of $\tilde{G}_{0.5}$ for distributions of phone numbers, we simply show '–' in Table 1.

Bonneau also introduced techniques to estimate metrics beyond this bound for password distributions by fitting a parametric model to the observed data [4]. For example, distributions of human-chosen answers are often assumed to be approximately a Zipfian or other simple power-law distribution, although these have proven to be a poor fit to real password distributions. A more complicated distribution (specifically a zero-truncated generalized inverse-Gaussian/Poisson distribution) was used by Bonneau to successfully estimate metrics for passwords [4]. However, this model has not been validated for distributions of answers to personal knowledge questions, hence in this work for simplicity we only use non-parametric estimations in the well-approximated region of the distribution.

3. STRENGTH AGAINST GUESSING

In this section we evaluate the guessing difficulty of distributions of answers provided by Google users over the last 5 years. We use the guessing metrics discussed in Section 2.1.

3.1 Statistical evaluation

Table 1 lists statistics for distributions of answers to several commonly used questions in different languages. Several general trends emerge. First, nearly all questions have very low min-entropy (and hence high λ_β for low values of β) meaning there exist answers which are very common and therefore useful for an attacker to guess. Given the ability to make 10 guesses, for example, an attacker would have at least a 2% chance of answering correctly for any of the questions studied and often over 10%. This suggests that (without further abuse detection systems in place) nearly all questions are vulnerable to *trawling attacks* [5] where an attacker makes a few guesses of common answers for a large number of accounts in hopes of compromising a significant number of (random) accounts. Even a single guess can yield between 0.8% to 19.7% success rate.

As visible in the Table 1, questions about taste such as "*Favorite food?*" are the least secure questions. Questions about places and people are also very weak with a success rate well above 1% in most cases for a single guess. Cultural differences emerge as guessing difficulty varies significantly between countries and languages. For example the "*Place of birth?*" distribution is 10 times less secure given one guess for answers chosen by Korean-speaking users compared to English-speaking users due to the concentration of Korean-speaking users in a few major cities.

Most questions are further highly vulnerable to extended guessing attacks, with $\tilde{G}_{0.5} < 20$ bits for most questions studied. This confirms that personal knowledge questions are completely insecure

		online guessing (success %)					offline guessing (bits)			
question	lang.	λ_1	λ_3	λ_{10}	λ_{100}	λ_{1000}	H_∞	$\tilde{G}_{0.1}$	$\tilde{G}_{0.25}$	$\tilde{G}_{0.5}$
names										
best friend's name	Spanish	1.3%	3.5%	7.8%	27.8%	61.1%	6.3	7.2	8.3	9.6
	French	0.7%	1.7%	4.5%	23.6%	62.4%	7.2	8.2	8.7	9.7
childhood best friend's name	English	0.4%	1.0%	2.7%	13.3%	40.5%	8.1	9.3	10.2	11.7
	Portuguese	1.0%	2.7%	6.4%	27.6%	58.8%	6.7	7.5	8.3	9.7
	Russian	1.9%	4.2%	9.4%	35.8%	65.4%	5.7	6.8	7.5	8.8
	Spanish	1.0%	2.8%	7.2%	28.9%	63.0%	6.6	7.4	8.2	9.4
father's middle name	Chinese	2.2%	6.0%	15.0%	49.9%	85.7%	5.5	5.8	6.6	7.5
	English	2.7%	6.6%	14.6%	40.3%	64.9%	5.2	5.8	6.6	8.6
	Portuguese	2.7%	6.7%	15.4%	44.6%	73.8%	5.2	5.8	6.5	7.9
	Spanish	3.8%	8.9%	21.3%	58.1%	83.8%	4.7	5.1	5.7	6.8
first teacher's name	Arabic	7.7%	14.4%	23.7%	37.4%	61.4%	3.7	4.1	5.7	9.1
	English	0.4%	1.1%	2.8%	9.7%	26.7%	8.0	10.0	11.6	14.1
	Russian	1.5%	4.3%	11.3%	39.4%	61.4%	6.1	6.4	7.0	8.9
	Portuguese	6.0%	8.5%	13.0%	34.7%	65.2%	4.1	5.6	7.5	8.9
	Spanish	2.9%	5.3%	11.3%	37.6%	69.5%	5.1	6.4	7.4	8.5
first manager's name	English	0.9%	2.7%	5.9%	21.6%	46.8%	6.7	7.9	9.0	11.1
favorites										
favorite food	English	19.7%	26.0%	36.5%	59.4%	76.8%	2.3	2.3	3.4	5.9
	Korean	11.8%	30.5%	43.2%	70.0%	85.7%	3.1	3.1	3.3	5.0
	Spanish	7.3%	15.4%	28.1%	59.2%	80.1%	3.8	4.1	4.9	6.4
places										
place of birth	English	1.3%	3.0%	6.9%	24.6%	58.8%	6.2	7.5	8.6	9.9
	Korean	12.0%	25.0%	39.0%	70.1%	87.8%	3.1	3.1	3.7	5.4
high school	English	0.5%	0.9%	1.9%	7.6%	22.6%	7.7	10.7	12.2	13.6
numbers										
first telephone number	Arabic	2.9%	6.3%	13.0%	28.6%	38.5%	5.1	5.9	7.7	15.5
	Chinese	1.2%	2.4%	4.5%	7.9%	10.2%	6.3	12.9	–	–
	Korean	1.2%	2.8%	6.4%	13.0%	18.3%	6.3	8.4	13.8	–
	English	0.4%	1.0%	2.5%	5.5%	8.4%	7.9	14.9	21.5	–
	Portuguese	0.9%	2.2%	4.3%	10.8%	16.7%	6.8	9.5	15.6	–
	Russian	2.4%	4.2%	7.3%	14.6%	21.7%	5.4	7.8	13.5	–
	Spanish	0.6%	1.5%	4.4%	9.7%	14.1%	7.4	10.1	17.9	–
frequent flyer number	English	4.2%	7.8%	13.6%	26.8%	38.6%	4.6	5.5	8.1	13.5
	Portuguese	5.8%	11.8%	21.6%	43.2%	63.2%	4.1	4.6	5.8	8.4
vehicle registration number	English	0.8%	1.5%	2.6%	5.6%	11.2%	7.0	12.7	14.8	–
library card number	English	2.3%	6.4%	12.2%	22.5%	33.0%	5.4	5.9	9.3	15.5
user-chosen secrets (baseline)										
password (RockYou)	–	0.9%	1.4%	2.1%	4.6%	11.3%	6.8	12.8	15.9	19.8
password (Yahoo!) [3]	–	1.1%	1.4%	1.9%	3.6%	8.3%	6.5	14.0	17.6	–
4-digit PIN (iPhone) [6]	–	4.3%	9.2%	14.4%	29.3%	56.4%	4.5	5.2	7.7	10.1

Table 1: Guessing difficulty estimates for distributions of answers to various challenge questions. λ_β represents the success rate of an attacker limited to β guesses, while $\tilde{G}_\alpha$ represents the average amount of work (in bits) to compromise a proportion α of users in an offline attack. The min-entropy H_∞ is also included as a lower-bound on the difficulty of any offline attack. Values which could not be estimated accurately due to an insufficient sample size are represented by '–' (see Section 2.1).

against an attacker able to perform offline brute-force as 20 bits worth of brute force can typically be performed in less than one second and will be effective against over half of the population for most questions.

The impact of untruthful answers: The most surprising observation is that even on questions where answers are presumably unique (e.g. phone number, frequent flyer number) the distribution still contains answers that are shared by a significant fraction of users. For example 4.2% of English-speaking users have the "same" frequent flyer number and 0.4% have the same phone number. These untruthful answers significantly weaken the potentially most secure questions. The security of these questions against extended guessing attacks is considerably higher, as they are very difficult to guess for users who answer honestly. However for certain combinations of language and question this degradation makes those questions even less secure that the one based on name and places. For example, 2.9% of the Arabic-speaking users used the same phone number as their answer and 2.4% of the Russian-speaking users did. As we will discuss in Section 5 users often provide untruthful answers in an attempt to make the answer more secure. Perhaps they achieve this against targeted attackers (for example, a friend who knows their phone number) but this harms security against untargeted guessing.

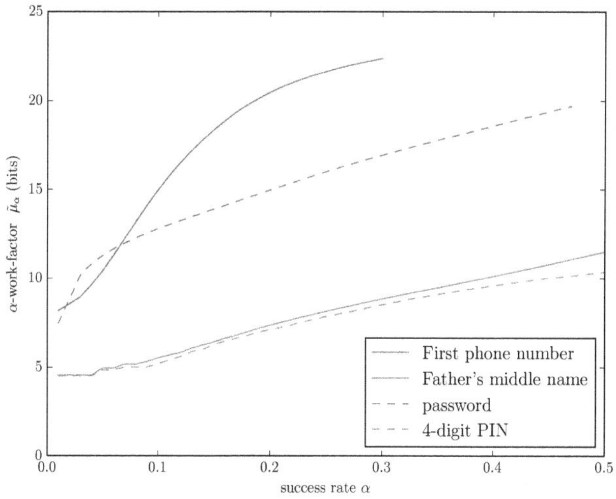

Figure 1: Guessing curve comparison for two representative personal knowledge questions and two user-chosen secrets (passwords from the leaked RockYou dataset and PINs from the leaked iPhone dataset [6].

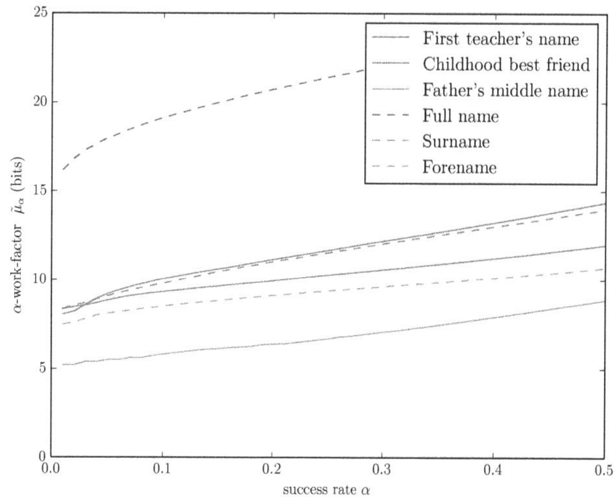

Figure 2: Guessing curve comparison for three personal knowledge questions asking for human names with population statistics on full human names, surnames and forenames collected from a 2009 crawl of Facebook's public directory [5]

3.2 Comparison to user-chosen secrets

We can compare the collected distributions of answers to personal knowledge questions with previously collected statistics on user choices of passwords and PINs. The bottom of Table 1 lists statistics from three datasets as baselines. First is the password distribution leaked from RockYou, a social gaming website, in 2009. This data set consisted of 32 million plaintext passwords and has been frequently used in password research. Second is the password distribution collected by Bonneau from Yahoo! in 2012 [3].[1] Finally there is a distribution of user-chosen 4-digit PINs leaked by an iPhone application developer in 2012 [6].

As a rule-of-thumb, most of the name-based personal knowledge questions produce a distribution with equivalent security to a user-chosen PIN and considerably less security than that of passwords. Numerical questions produce distributions with roughly equivalent security against guessing as user-chosen passwords. This arguably makes them effective for the purposes of account recovery as their use would be no more of a security risk than passwords which are the primary authentication mechanism.

This is shown graphically in Figure 1, showing the complete *guessing curve* for a representative high and low-security personal knowledge question alongside passwords and PINs. Note that "What is your father's middle name?" produces a statistically very similar distribution of answers to user-chosen PINs throughout. However, "What was your first phone number?" produces a very differently curve from a distribution of passwords. The weakest answers to the phone-number question are roughly similar to the weakest passwords, after which the phone numbers quickly become *more difficult* to guess than passwords.

3.3 Comparison to public distributions

We can also compare our figures to expected distributions based on published statistics, particularly for questions asking for human names for which population-wide statistics are readily available.[2] Bonneau et al. [5] evaluated many published distributions of human names; for this work we will take the largest distribution collected in that research, a crawl of over 100 million names in a public directory of Facebook users with separate distributions for complete names, surnames (last or family names) and forenames (first or given names). In Figure 2 we compare these name distributions to distributions of answers to three name-based questions: "*What is your father's middle name?*", "*What was your first teacher's name?*" and "*What was your childhood best friend's name?*"

Interestingly, the answer distribution for "*What was your first teacher's name?*" is statistically very similar to the population distribution of surnames, suggesting most users identify their first teacher by surname. By comparison, "*What was your childhood best friend's name?*" is somewhat between surnames and forenames (perhaps because there are multiple ways of naming this individual). Finally, "*What is your father's middle name?*" is significantly below the natural distribution of forenames, likely due to a significant number of users answering inaccurately.

None of the questions are close to the distribution of full names (first and last name combined), which is considerably stronger than any of the distributions we observed for personal knowledge questions. This suggests that if users could be asked to enter the full name of their childhood best friend, security might be significantly higher, though it appears users rarely do so.

3.4 Effectiveness of crowdsourcing attacks

So far all of the analysis in this section models an ideal attacker who knows the precise distribution of answers in the population; hence it can be considered a lower-bound on security since a real attacker may guess using an inaccurate approximation. To measure how easy it would be for an attacker to approximate the real distributions using crowd-sourcing services we asked 1000 users on CrowdFlower to answer the following two questions: "*Favorite food?*" and "*Father's middle name*". We then compared the effi-

[1]This password distribution was collected anonymously without observing user-chosen passwords; only the password frequencies were observed.

[2]We could attempt a similar exercise for telephone numbers or frequent flier numbers but this would not be interesting; the genuine distribution is nearly flat (with few users sharing an answer).

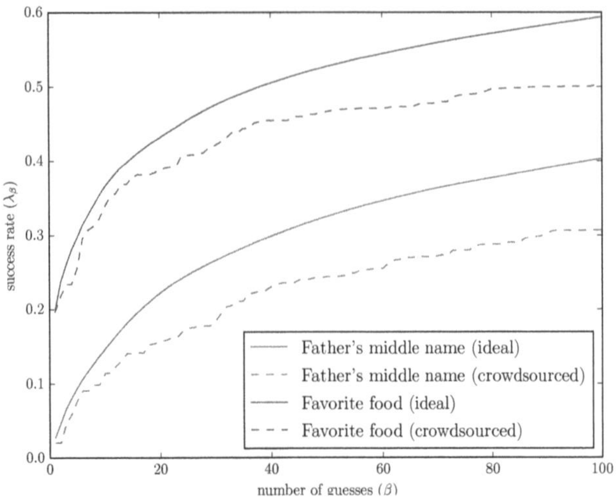

Figure 3: Effectiveness of a crowdsourcing attack. The solid lines demonstrate an attacker's success λ_β for up to $\beta = 100$ guesses. The dashed lines represent an attacker using an approximate distribution obtained by crowdsourcing.

ciency of those approximate distributions to an ideal attacker. As visible in Figure 3, in both cases, the attacker using a crowdsourced distribution does very well: with up to 100 guesses efficiency is at least 75% as high for the father's middle name distribution and at least 80% as high for the favorite food distribution. Thus, we conclude that it is not difficult for attackers to learn a reasonable approximation of the true answer distribution as our simple crowdsourcing attack cost only $100 and took less than a day.

4. QUESTION MEMORABILITY

In this section, we analyze the ability of users to remember their secret answers based on a random sample of 11 million account recovery claims that occurred in 2013, the year that Google started preferring alternative recovery methods and stopped collecting personal knowledge questions during web account signup. We chose this period to have meaningful temporal data: that is, claims that occurs shortly after setting the secret question and its answer. For every slice of data discussed in this section the number of claims by bucket is at least 500, and well in the ten of thousands in most cases. Note that the data presented in this section was filtered to remove blatantly fraudulent recovery attempts and restricted to one claim per user to prevent users that routinely use the account recovery process from skewing the data.

4.1 Time between enrollment and use

We start by looking at the time between users enrolling a secret question and using it in an account recovery claim. Figure 4 shows the distribution of time since enrolling a secret question for all of the claims in 2013 divided into ten deciles; the distribution is almost exactly linear. This demonstrates that people are no more likely to recover their accounts early or late in the lifetime of their secret question, for example because they are not used to their account password for old accounts and are more likely to have forgotten it.

There is one caveat to this linear relation: the first few hours after enrollment are much more likely to see the user attempt to use it for account recovery. This is visible in Figure 5 which shows an hour-by-hour breakdown of account claims in the first week after enrolling a new secret question This surge is related to questions being set during initial account creation and people not remembering the password they just set when logging in for the first time.

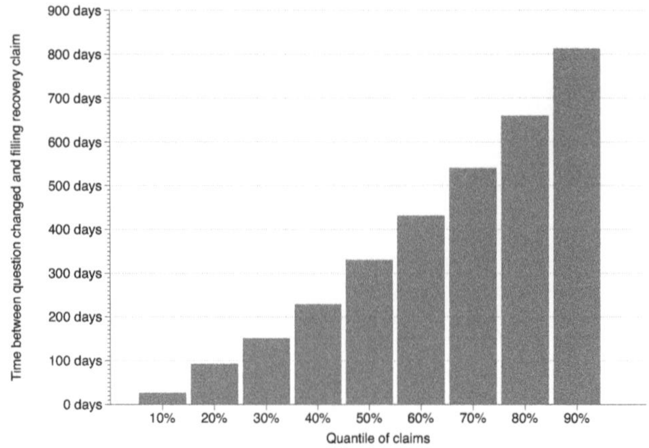

Figure 4: Quantile distribution of the time between the secret answer is set and the time of the claim in day.

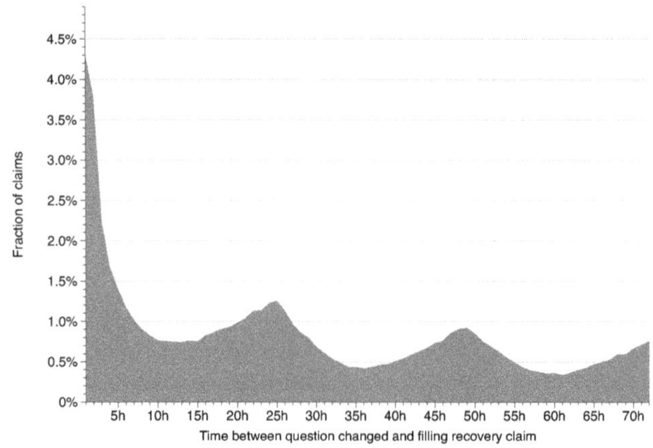

Figure 5: Overall frequency of account recovery claims for the first 72 hours after enrollment

question	overall success	success within n months 1	3	6	12
City of birth?	80.1%	83.9%	79.9%	79.2%	79.5%
Father's middle name?	75.6%	85.9%	75.7%	74.4%	74.3%
Childhood best friend?	68.5%	82.9%	65.0%	64.6%	63.7%
High school name?	67.3%	78.8%	62.8%	62.6%	61.4%
First phone number?	55.2%	70.0%	55.4%	53.3%	50.1%
Favorite food?	48.0%	73.6%	52.8%	50.1%	46.6%
First teacher's name?	47.1%	71.7%	45.9%	43.2%	39.8%
Library card number?	22.5%	49.6%	24.3%	19.9%	17.7%
Frequent flyer number?	9.0%	32.1%	8.5%	6.4%	6.4%

Table 2: Success rate for English questions broken-down by number of months since enrollment

4.2 Effects of question type on memorability

We chart the success rate of users attempting to answer their personal knowledge questions in Table 2 for various English-language questions. Success rates are broken down by the number of months since the question was enrolled; for all questions we observed that

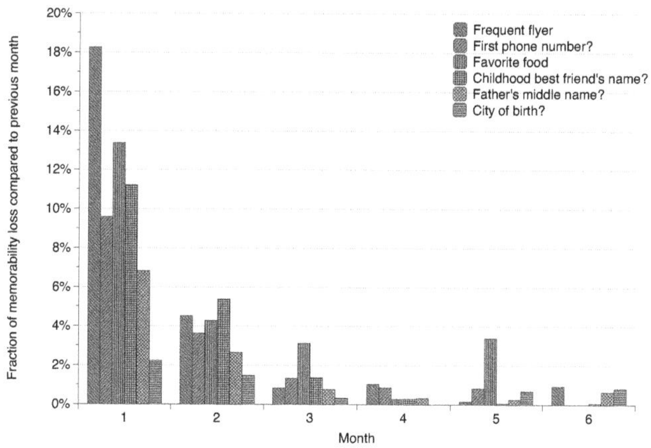

Figure 6: Loss of memorability compared to previous months for various English questions

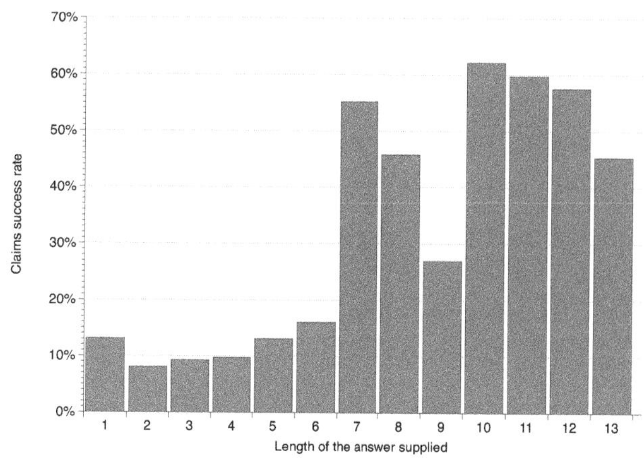

Figure 7: Success rate for the question "First phone number?" for US users broken down by secret answer length

language	country	months since registration 1	3	6	12
English	US	70.0%	55.4%	53.8%	49.8%
English	UK	68.4%	52.1%	49.7%	44.2%
German	Germany	69.2%	44.6%	42.3%	37.7%
Spanish	US	70.0%	59.2%	59.1%	57.6%
Spanish	Spain	68.6%	47.5%	41.5%	37.9%
French	France	75.6%	59.2%	58.5%	57.0%

Table 3: Recall for the questions "*First phone number?*" for various languages and countries

memorability monotonically declined with time since the question was enrolled.

Overall, we can note immediately that the success rate is below 80% for all questions, going against the common wisdom that personal knowledge questions provide a highly reliable means of authenticating users. Generally, questions involving names and places fared fairly well with success greater than 50%, with library card and frequent flyer number faring very poorly and being unreliable questions and suffering the steepest drop-off in memorability over time. Sadly the memorability order is inversely proportional to the security of these questions, as seen in Table 1. The mismatch between security and memorability highlights why personal knowledge questions are inherently difficult to use in practice.

This gap between security and memorability gets even wider when considering that what people remember the most are, unsurprisingly, the things closest to their heart: city of birth and father's middle name. As discussed in Section 2, such distribution are also the easiest to find from public records or online social networks.

Telephone numbers appear to offer the best balance, with memorability over 50% and security comparable to passwords (see Section 3.2). Of course, phone numbers are also liable to exist in public records and are likely known by many of a user's social contacts.

4.3 Impact of time

Table 2 showed a clear trend of decline in memorability over time. In Figure 4.3 we drill down further into this trend by plotting the loss of accuracy users suffer for 5 popular English language questions over the first 6 months of use. This graph suggests the decline in memorability is not gradual or linear but instead users suffer a very sharp decline within 1 month of enrollment for all questions. This is particularly true for "favorite food" and "childhood best friend," questions which are not necessarily factual and to which users may change their minds or have to choose from among several possibilities at the time of enrollment.

Curiously, this is also true for "frequent flyer number" even though this should be an unambiguous fact that is unlikely to change within one month. We speculate that this is due to the large number of inaccurate answers or "don't know" answers, either of which are susceptible to be forgotten quickly after being registered.

4.4 Impact of inaccurate answers

As discussed in Section 3, a key reason behind the insecurity of secret question is that people supply inaccurate answers. We hypothesize that this is in fact also a driver of users failing to remember their answers correctly in many cases, as inaccurate answers no longer represent a true memory the user holds.

To measure how this behavior also impairs users' ability to remember their answer, we looked at the success rate of users attempting to answer the question "*what was your first phone number?*" broken down by the length of the answer they initially enrolled. As shown in Figure 7 the set of answers that have plausible length for a phone number, namely 7 or 8 digits (a North American number without an area code, possibly with a space) or 10–13 characters (a North American number with an area code and possibly spaces, dashes or parentheses), exhibit a significantly higher memorability. Note that when verifying users' answers, spaces and punctuation characters are stripped out so the exact format used will not matter if the digits are all correct. Answers with a plausible length of 10 have an accuracy of 62% vs an accuracy of only 28% for answer which have a length of 9. Answers of fewer than 6 characters all had less than a 20% memorability.

This suggests that users who answer accurately are more successful at recovering their account. One possible explanation is that these users care more about security or have a better memory to begin with, but it seems far more likely to indicate that many users can't remember which inaccurate answer they may have provided. Thus, in addition to greatly harming security, inaccurate answers are also a significant problem for memorability.

language	country	months since registration 1	3	6	12
English	US	85.9%	75.7%	75.1%	74.4%
English	UK	81.2%	68.0%	64.6%	64.1%
German	Germany	81.9%	68.0%	64.4%	64.4%
Spanish	US	88.3%	81.3%	82.2%	80.8%
Spanish	Spain	85.3%	71.7%	70.2%	62.8%
French	France	56.8%	39.6%	37.6%	36.9%

Table 4: Recall for the questions "*Father's middle name?*" for various languages and countries

4.5 Impact of cultural differences

To understand the impact of cultural difference on secret questions we compared the success rate for various languages and countries for the same questions. Usually the question is semantically the same, but translated, with one exception: "*Father's middle name*" was replaced by "*Primer apellido del padre?*" which translate as "*Father's first surname?*" in Spanish as it is customary in many Spanish-speaking countries for individuals to use two surnames.

Overall as visible in Table 3 and Table 4, the same question in the same language can have a different recall for various countries. For example US English-speaking users have an easier time remember their first phone number than UK English speakers: 49.8% vs 44.2% after 12 months. The difference between the two is even wider for the question "*Father's middle name?*" where the recall gap reach 10% after 12 months: 74.43% vs 64.12%. The gap between various language/country groups can be very drastic. In particular after a few months the gap between the best performing country/language and the worst is as high as 44%: 36.9% for France/French users vs. 80.8% for US/English users for the question "*Father's middle name?*". Finally it is worth noting that depending on the question the top performing country/language groups are drastically different. France has the best recall for phone number and the worst for father's middle name. These shifts demonstrate that many cultural differences exist which are hard to predict or account for when designing a recovery system that needs to internationalize.

5. UNDERSTANDING USER PERCEPTIONS

In this section we discuss the result of a survey we ran on the US population to better understand users' perceptions of secret questions. The survey was using Google Consumer Surveys [30], a micro-survey platform for asking web users a small number of short questions as a replacement for advertisements.

5.1 Motivation for untruthful answers

As discussed in previous sections, one of the driving factors behind secret questions' poor security (Section 3.1) and usability (Section 4.4) is that a significant fraction of users provide untruthful answers. To better understand this behavior we ran a survey that asked as a filtering question "*When creating your primary email account, how did you answer the secret questions that are used to recover the password?*". For those that admitted to providing fake answers we asked why in a follow-up multi-choice question. As seen in Figure 8 two main reasons reported for providing a fake answer were to improve security (37% of respondents) and to make the answer easier to remember (15%), though the effect is the exact opposite. We also observed that a good fraction of the respondent (31.9%) didn't provide the real answers for privacy reasons. Addressing privacy concerns for various account recovery options is an open question.

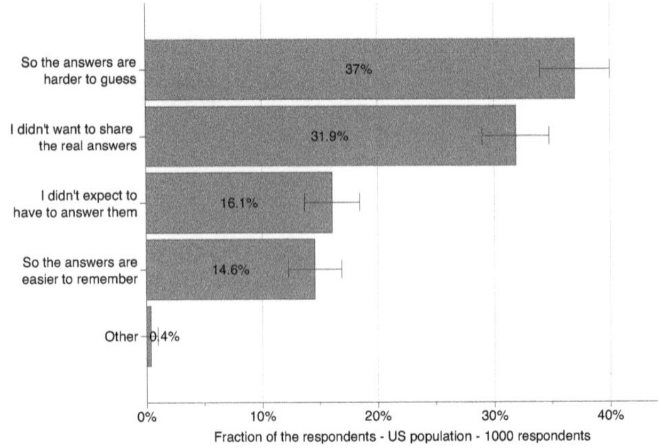

Figure 8: Survey answers for the question "*Why did you provide fake answers to your password recovery question?*"

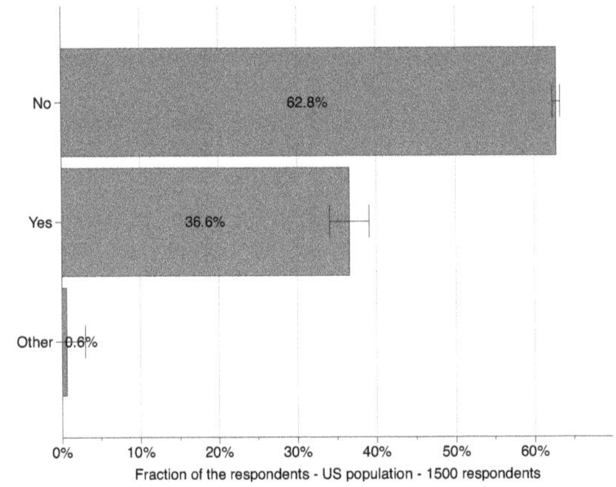

Figure 9: Survey responses for the questions "*Have you ever thought that someone might try to break into your primary personal email account by trying to reset your password?*"

5.2 Perceptions of security

Another hypothesis we had about why people provide very easy to guess answers was a false sense of security. To confirm this hypothesis we ran two additional independent surveys. In the first one we asked: *"Have you ever thought that someone might try to break into your primary personal email account by trying to reset your password?"*. As seen in Figure 9, the vast majority of the respondents (62.8%) never considered the possibility that their security question could be used against them. This lack of awareness potentially contribute to a false sense of security that leads users to not pay attention to secret questions.

In a second survey we asked respondents to answer Likert questions to compare how much trust they had in SMS recovery vs. personal questions. As seen in Figure 10, people have more trust in secret questions security than in SMS security which is opposed to reality. Overall this distorted perception of secret questions is yet one more reason to move away from security questions as people are not paying attention to them and are over-confident. Shifting their perception and habits would be very challenging and the energy seems better invested in convincing users to adopt two-factor authentication and switch to better recovery mechanisms.

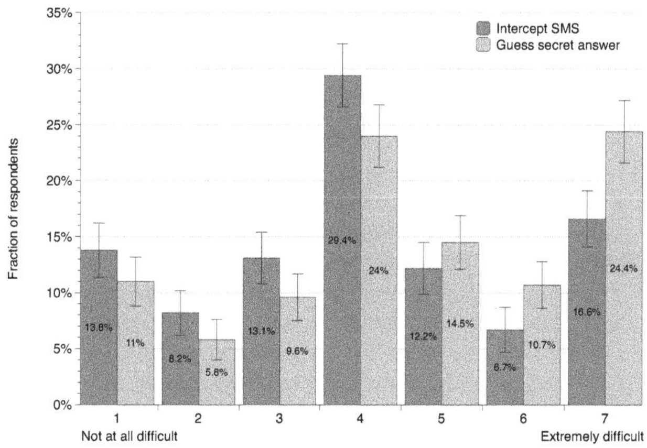

Figure 10: Survey responses for the question "*How difficult would it be for a hacker to _____ to break into your primary personal email account?*"

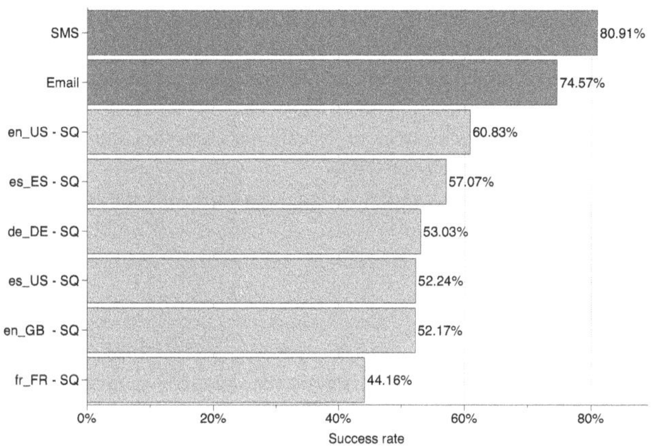

Figure 11: Success rate of various recovery options

6. CONCLUDING DISCUSSION

We analyzed the first large-scale empirical data on secret questions, based on their deployment at Google. Hundreds of millions of secret answers and millions of account recovery claims clearly demonstrate that secret questions have poor security and reliability. For reliability, we can directly compare to SMS and email-based recovery and find personal questions are inferior. The fact that secret questions are relatively less secure led Google to prefer those alternative options and only use secret questions in conjunction with other signals to compensate for their weaknesses.

6.1 Alternatives deployed at Google

Figure 6.1, summarizes the success rate of SMS and email-based recovery compared to secret questions. These statistics were computed based on a full month of account recovery claims. As visible in this figure, SMS recovery has a success rate which is 20% better than even the most successful secret answer language/population bucket (80.9% vs 60.8%). Similarly, email-based recovery increases the odd of a successful recovery by 14.5%.

Beside being more reliable, SMS recovery is also be preferred over email based recovery due to several additional security benefits. First, people might use the same password for their recovery email address as their Google account which they have forgotten. Second, some email providers, including Microsoft [31], expire email addresses after some period of inactivity and allows anyone to register them again, making email recovery sometimes unreliable. As of 2014, we estimate that 7% of the secondary emails our users provided for recovery have since been recycled.

6.2 Other potential alternatives

Beside SMS and email recovery, which are currently deployed, several potential alternatives have been proposed elsewhere. To counter statistical guessing, Jakobsson et al. developed "preference-based authentication" in 2008 [18, 19, 17]. In this scheme, users choose a number of items (16 is suggested) which they strongly like or dislike from a large set of items such as "rap music" or "vegetarian food." These preferences are claimed to not exist in online databases or public records, and a user study suggests a negligible false negative rate can be achieved while limiting statistical guessing to a 0.5% chance of success [19]. However, despite improvements [19] preference-based schemes require considerably more time to enroll users and authenticate them than individual questions making them less attractive to deploy in practice.

Graphical password schemes have also frequently been proposed as a potential alternative for backup authentication [2], particularly recognition-based schemes in which a user is asked to identify previously-seen images from a set of candidates [12]. Such schemes can be designed with firm security guarantees as the user's set of images is randomly chosen. However, while there is evidence that such schemes are more memorable than text passwords [9], they still require additional user training compare to personal knowledge questions and have not seen significant deployment.

Several other proposals have been made to automatically generate questions and answers based on data stored about users. Nosseir et al. suggested querying users' browsing history or location history to generate harder-to-guess questions [25], though such an approach appears to inevitably leak private data. A related proposal specifically for social networks is to require users to identify friends in tagged photographs [32]. While this has been effective in practice in the context of social networks, the risk of face recognition software and publicly-available photos may mean the security of this scheme is too weak for higher security applications [23].

Another proposal is requiring users to select a set of trusted friends to ask as delegates. In the event of a forgotten password, the user must contact a designated threshold of these delegates to receive one-time tokens from the server. Brainard et al. first proposed this idea in 2006 as "vouching-based" authentication [7]. A follow-up usability study by Schechter et al. found that only about 71% of participants could execute this scheme correctly and social-engineering attacks worked against about 10% of users [29]. It has been suggested that in place of an explicit user-conducted protocol, authentication could be performed automatically by communicating with the mobile devices of nearby users to establish a user's social context [13].

6.3 Secret questions' continued role

The ability to quickly confirm a user's identity when we suspect an account hijacking attempt has become an essential part of our login risk analysis system [11]. While Google prefers SMS and email recovery, no mechanism is perfect. For example, SMS will fail if the user doesn't have access to their phone while traveling abroad. In the context of a risk analysis system taking multiple signals into account, we have found personal knowledge questions can still be a useful lightweight signal when the risk level is considered low. Finding more identity confirmation questions that are both secure and easy to answer is an open question.

7. REFERENCES

[1] Mansour Alsaleh, Mohammad Mannan, and P.C. van Oorschot. Revisiting defenses against large-scale online password guessing attacks. *IEEE Transactions on Dependable and Secure Computing*, 2012.

[2] Robert Biddle, Sonia Chiasson, and P.C. van Oorschot. Graphical Passwords: Learning from the First Twelve Years. Technical Report TR-11-01, Carleton University, 2011.

[3] Joseph Bonneau. *The science of guessing: analyzing an anonymized corpus of 70 million passwords*, May 2012.

[4] Joseph Bonneau. *Guessing human-chosen secrets*. PhD thesis, University of Cambridge, May 2012.

[5] Joseph Bonneau, Mike Just, and Greg Matthews. What's in a name? Evaluating statistical attacks against personal knowledge questions. *Financial Cryptography*, 2010.

[6] Joseph Bonneau, Sören Preibusch, and Ross Anderson. A birthday present every eleven wallets? The security of customer-chosen banking PINs. *Financial Cryptography*, 2012.

[7] John Brainard, Ari Juels, Ronald L. Rivest, Michael Szydlo, and Moti Yung. Fourth-Factor Authentication: Somebody You Know. *CCS '06: The 13th ACM Conference on Computer and Communications Security*, 2006.

[8] Sacha Brostoff and Angela Sasse. "Ten strikes and you're out": Increasing the number of login attempts can improve password usability. *CHI Workshop on HCI and Security Systems*, 2003.

[9] Sacha Brostoff and M. Angela Sasse. Are Passfaces More Usable Than Passwords? A Field Trial Investigation. *People and Computers XIV: Usability or Else!: HCI 2000*, 2000.

[10] Julie Bunnell, John Podd, Ron Henderson, Renee Napier, and James Kennedy-Moffat. Cognitive, associative and conventional passwords: Recall and guessing rates. *Computers & Security*, 1997.

[11] Elie Bursztein, Borbala Benko, Daniel Margolis, Tadek Pietraszek, Andy Archer, Allan Aquino, Andreas Pitsillidis, and Stefan Savage. Handcrafted Fraud and Extortion: Manual Account Hijacking in the Wild. *Internet Measurement Conference*, 2014.

[12] Rachna Dhamija and Adrian Perrig. Déjà vu: A user study using images for authentication. *USENIX Security Symposium*, 2000.

[13] A.D. Frankel and M. Maheswaran. Feasibility of a Socially Aware Authentication Scheme. *CCNC '09: IEEE Consumer Communications and Networking Conference*, 2009.

[14] Simson L. Garfinkel. Email-Based Identification and Authentication: An Alternative to PKI? *IEEE Security & Privacy Magazine*, 1(6), 2003.

[15] Virgil Griffith and Markus Jakobsson. Messin' with Texas: Deriving Mother's Maiden Names Using Public Records. *Applied Cryptography and Network Security*, 2005.

[16] William J. Haga and Moshe Zviran. Question-and-Answer Passwords: An Empirical Evaluation. *Information Systems*, 16(3):335–343, 1991.

[17] Markus Jakobsson and Hossein Siadati. Improved visual preference authentication. *Workshop on Socio-Technical Aspects in Security and Trust (STAST)*, 2012.

[18] Markus Jakobsson, Erik Stolterman, Susanne Wetzel, and Liu Yang. Love and Authentication. *ACM SIGCHI Conference on Human Factors in Computing Systems*, 2008.

[19] Markus Jakobsson, Liu Yang, and Susanne Wetzel. Quantifying the Security of Preference-Based Authentication. *ACM Workshop on Digital Identity Management (DIM)*, 2008.

[20] Mike Just. Designing and Evaluating Challenge-Question Systems. *IEEE Security & Privacy Magazine*, 2(5), 2004.

[21] Mike Just and David Aspinall. Personal Choice and Challenge Questions: A Security and Usability Assessment. *SOUPS '09: The 5th Symposium on Usable Privacy and Security*, 2009.

[22] Chris Karlof, J. D. Tygar, and David Wagner. Conditioned-Safe Ceremonies and a User Study of an Application to Web Authentication. *SOUPS '09: The 5th Symposium on Usable Privacy and Security*, 2009.

[23] Hyoungshick Kim, John Tang, and Ross Anderson. Social Authentication: Harder than it Looks. *Financial Cryptography*, 2012.

[24] Jack Lindamood and Murat Kantarcioglu. Inferring Private Information Using Social Network Data. Technical Report UTDCS-21-08, University of Texas at Dallas Computer Science Department, 2008.

[25] A. Nosseir, R. Connor, and M.D. Dunlop. Internet Authentication Based on Personal History—A Feasibility Test. *ACM Customer Focused Mobile Services Workshop*, 2005.

[26] Rachael Pond, John Podd, Julie Bunnell, and Ron Henderson. Word Association Computer Passwords: The Effect of Formulation Techniques on Recall and Guessing Rates. *Computers & Security*, 2000.

[27] Ariel Rabkin. Personal knowledge questions for fallback authentication: Security questions in the era of Facebook. *SOUPS '08: The 4th Symposium on Usable Privacy and Security*, 2008.

[28] Stuart Schechter, A. J. Bernheim Brush, and Serge Egelman. It's No Secret: Measuring the security and reliability of authentication via 'secret' questions. *2009 IEEE Symposium on Security and Privacy*, 2009.

[29] Stuart Schechter, Serge Egelman, and Robert W. Reeder. It's Not What You Know, But Who You Know: A social approach to last-resort authentication. *ACM SIGCHI Conference on Human Factors in Computing Systems*, 2009.

[30] Victoria Schwanda-Sosik, Elie Bursztein, Sunny Consolvo, David A Huffaker, Gueorgi Kossinets, Kerwell Liao, Paul McDonald, and Aaron Sedley. Online microsurveys for user experience research. *CHI'14 Extended Abstracts on Human Factors in Computing Systems*, 2014.

[31] The Next Web. Microsoft can recycle your outlook.com email address if your account becomes inactive. `http://tnw.co/1sWsNAU`, 2013.

[32] Sarita Yardi, Nick Feamster, and Amy Bruckman. Photo-Based Authentication Using Social Networks. *WOSN '08: The 1st Workshop on Online Social Networks*, 2008.

[33] Moshe Zviran and William J. Haga. A Comparison of Password Techniques for Multilevel Authentication Mechanisms. *Computer Journal*, 36(3):227–237, 1993.

Supporting Ethical Web Research: A New Research Ethics Review

Anne Bowser
University of Maryland
2117 Hornbake Building, South Wing
College Park, MD 90740
abowser1@umd.edu

Janice Y. Tsai
Microsoft Research
One Microsoft Way
Redmond, WA 98052
janice.tsai@microsoft.com

ABSTRACT

Research ethics is an important and timely topic. In academia, federally regulated Institutional Review Boards (IRBs) protect participants of human subjects research, and offer researchers a mechanism to assess the ethical implications of their work. Industry research labs are not subject to the same requirements, and may lack processes for research ethics review. We describe the creation of a new ethics framework and a research ethics submission system (RESS) within Microsoft Research (MSR). This RESS is customized to the needs of web researchers. We describe our iterative development process, including our assessment of the current state of web research, developing a framework of methods based on a survey of 358 research papers; build and evaluate our system with 14 users to identify the benefits and pitfalls of full deployment; evaluate how our system matches with existing federal regulations; and, suggest next steps for supporting ethical web research.

Categories and Subject Descriptors

K.4.1. [**Computer and Society**]: Public Policy Issues-*Ethics;* H.4.M. [**Information Systems Applications**]: Miscellaneous

General Terms

Design, Human Factors, Legal Aspects

Keywords

Ethics; Ethics Review; Institutional Review Board (IRB); Research Methods

1. INTRODUCTION

In July 2014, researchers at Facebook published a controversial study exploring how the emotions of Facebook users influence the emotions expressed by their Facebook friends [14]. This research was conducted as an online A/B test, a method considered "the gold standard evaluation for web-based products" by some computer science researchers [9]. Despite the prevalence of this method, public outcry over Facebook's research was cutting and instantaneous. Some critics took issue with the lack of consent, which those conducting large scale-Internet research studies often find difficult to obtain [15, 17]. Others believed the emotional manipulation may have caused harm. Still others pounced on the realization that neither Facebook researchers nor collaborators at Cornell solicited a formal ethical review [26].

The controversy surrounding Facebook's study quickly grew beyond the ethics of a single company. The general practice of web research was called into question as critics articulated a "new privacy truth: legal compliance and sound security practices are not sufficient to meet societal expectations" [12]. In this way, Facebook's emotional contagion study proved a tipping point, bringing ethical concerns of web research to the mainstream, though web researchers have been grappling with these issues less publically for decades. New technologies, whether videotape in 1995 [16], or public displays in 2013 [15], consistently challenge how existing research methods develop. They also engender new methods, such as data mining, with new ethical considerations.

In academia and at medical institutions, research ethics review is governed by Institutional Review Boards (IRBs). These boards are backed by United States federal policy which dictates that researchers must secure approval for research sponsored by granting agencies such as the National Science Foundation (NSF). In contrast, many industry research labs—especially within the Information Technology sector—are not dependent on federal funding, and, hence, not required to support a formal IRB. Still, as the Facebook example illustrates, the requirement for ethical research crosses sectors. And while IRBs are designed to protect human subjects, they also benefit researchers [21]. They facilitate collaboration by setting common standards within an institution; provide researchers with a framework to critically contemplate the implications of their work; and illustrate the care a researcher takes in their study design to participants, peers, conference chairs, and society as a whole.

We developed a streamlined ethics review program for industry-based research. To do this, we developed a new ethics framework to elicit risk in the specific context of web research. To build this framework, we conducted a survey of methods used in 358 papers presented at 5 top computer science conferences in 2013. This framework was refined and implemented in a digital Research Ethics Submission System (RESS) for use within Microsoft Research (MSR). Our system streamlines the ethics review process with a score calculation and a capacity for automatic approval.

While several companies (including Facebook) have committed to developing a process for internal research review [22], we believe that ours is the first fully implemented system customized for and shared with a community of web researchers.

Specifically, our contribution is:

- A framework for characterizing and evaluating the ethics of the research methods used in web research.
- A digital research ethics submission system customized for the methods used in web research.

We begin by describing standards for ethical human subjects research. Based on these, we explore the current state of academic IRBs. We then describe the methodology used for developing our

WWW 2015, May 18–22, 2015, Florence, Italy.
ACM 978-1-4503-3469-3/15/05.
http://dx.doi.org/10.1145/2736277.2741654

ethics framework, provide an overview of the RESS, and report on an early user test with 14 participants. We compare our RESS to federal standards and conclude with limitations and future work: both for MSR, and for the web research community.

2. BACKGROUND

We focus on United States policy because the majority of our researchers work within the US, and because many other nations base their research policies on US law [21]. The guidelines for ethical human subjects research are advanced by the U.S. Department of Health and Human Services (HHS). This agency points to the Belmont Report [2] as a set of overarching ethical guidelines—*respect for persons*, *justice*, and *beneficence*—with applications. HHS also dictates that human subjects research conducted with federal funding must be evaluated by an IRB.

2.1 IRBs in the United States

IRBs assess the use of *informed consent*, an *assessment of risks and benefits*, and the *selection of subjects* to determine whether a research project should be proceed as proposed, proceed with modifications, or be rejected. Notably, not every research proposal must go through full IRB assessment. Federal regulations designate three types of review: exemption from full review, expedited review, and full board review [25]. A research proposal is considered "exempt" when an IRB official determines that the research poses minimal risk to participants, or fits a number of pre-defined parameters. Expedited review is appropriate in situations that involve human subjects *and* minimal risk. Expedited review may be conducted via a single review by the IRB official, or additional reviewers at the official's discretion. All other proposals require full IRB review by a 5-person board.

2.2 Common critiques

IRBs were created to regulate medical and behavioral science research, and researchers within these fields consider IRBs appropriate and effective safeguards [5]. Others argue that IRBs impose unnecessary and unjustified constraints. Schrag [21] posits that as social scientists have their own shared ethical code, the extension of IRB regulation to social science research constitutes "ethical imperialism." Schrag also argues that some generic questions posed by IRBs (e.g., does your research involve pregnant women?) are irrelevant outside of these contexts.

Others argue that while broad regulation *is* appropriate, the implementation of IRBs outside of medical and behavioral science is flawed. For example, the idea of "exempt" research, which includes "research involving collation or study of existing data, documents, records, or pathological or diagnostic specimens," is relatively straightforward in medical and behavioral research [23]. In contrast, "existing data" becomes convoluted in the context of web research (consider: is Twitter an "existing data" set?). Additionally, while research practices involving existing medical data typically poses a low risk to participants in face-to-face studies, research involving existing data in web research may threaten participants through re-identification, or through reuse of data in a new context [5]. Yet, the idea that web research is "exempt" from ethical consideration is supported by many disciplinary norms. Graduates of some traditional computer science programs, taught to study "systems and processes," may not understand their work as human subjects research [4]. This is a challenge for all ethics review processes, as those most in need of systematic support may be those least likely to seek it.

Additionally, existing IRBs may be a poor fit for web research if reviewers lack relevant expertise. In an early review of online psychology experiments, Peden [19] observed multiple ethical violations that IRBs failed to notice or correct, such as failing to discuss consent during web surveys. In a follow-up study of 334 IRBs, 62% of respondents reported that their IRBs lack guidelines for reviewing web research, and 74% reported that their IRBs fail to provide training on web research issues [4]. These respondents identified five areas as particularly problematic: privacy, data security, data sensitivity, models for confidentiality and anonymity, and models for consent.

Researchers themselves echo these concerns. Computer security researchers describe how "boilerplate" language such as "no others will have access to the data" may be taken at face value by an IRB without technical expertise, but challenged by a reviewer with domain knowledge [1]. Deciding whether a platform is public vs. private, or assessing the potential harm to re-identification, are similarly problematic issues [4]. Other researchers question: is acceptance of a corporation's Terms of Service proxy for informed consent [26]? What are reasonable expectations of online privacy [1, 4]?

Securing IRB approval requires that researchers invest their time gathering materials such as protocols and informed consent forms for submission, and also invest time awaiting a decision [23]. In some cases, securing IRB approval can take over a year—a timeline incompatible with the current practices in computer science research, where research is often carried out by students as classroom projects, or by summer interns [9]. Commercial IRBs advertise as time effective solutions to this conundrum, but come at a significant financial cost to the researcher.

Recognizing numerous concerns with the current IRB system, HHS published an advanced notice of proposed rulemaking to improve human subjects research regulations in 2011 [25]. Unfortunately, the proposed changes have neither been implemented, nor adequately address the range of concerns presented above. There have been additional broad efforts to add web research specific principles outside of HHS (e.g., [8]). And, a few researchers within computer science have proposed changes that would directly support the needs of web researchers. Garfinkel and Cranor [6] advocate for a self-serve IRB Kiosk in the form of a website posing a series questions about a proposed research design. This hypothetical kiosk would be able to identify exempt research, or approve expedited, low-risk proposals while helping researchers consider the ethics of their work, but would be unable to contend with proposals designated for full panel review.

In the following sections we introduce our ethics framework and RESS. Our system addresses a number of the concerns described above, by posing domain relevant questions [21], staffing review panels with web researchers [1, 5, 19], and supporting faster processes of submission and evaluation [19, 23].

3. A NEW TYPE OF REVIEW SYSTEM

To introduce ethics review in an environment where it had not existed in a systematic way, and to ensure minimal opposition and resistance, we needed to craft a new framework specific for the scope of research conducted by MSR. We are unable to adopt existing academic IRB system due to the critiques discussed above. Our system must also include an online submission system, and have a fast turnaround time.

3.1 Framework construction

We began by surveying the methodological landscape of web research to understand the most important questions and considerations to build into our RESS. Specifically, we reviewed the research methods described in 358 publications in 2013 from 5 conferences to create a framework of web research methods. This framework was refined through interviews with 11 researchers. We describe this work, the resulting framework, and key methodological considerations for web research below.

We considered using an existing taxonomy of computer science research, but rejected this idea on two grounds. First, we were unable to find a taxonomy produced since 2006 [11]. Second, we recognized that existing frameworks likely codify existing methodological, and thus, ethical assumptions, which may be problematic. Since our focus is the creation of an internal ethics review, we used the publication history of our research lab to define the research fields pursued (see: limitations).

Using the ACM Digital Library (http://dl.acm.org/dl.cfm), we identified the five conferences with the most publications with MSR authors in 2013. These were the SIGCHI Conference on Human Factors in Computing Systems (CHI), the International Conference on World Wide Web (WWW), the ACM SIGIR Conference on Research and Development in Information Retrieval (SIGIR), the ACM International Conference on Information & Knowledge Management (CIKM), and the ACM Conference on Electronic Commerce (EC). We sampled two *full* papers from each *unique* track (e.g., we did not review notes or posters, nor did we sample from a track called "Search I" and also a track called "Search II"). This yielded 358 papers for review, as summarized in Table 1. Note that this sample represents roughly 1.8% of all papers published in the ACM digital library in 2013.

Table 1. Research Contributions Reviewed

Conference	# Full Papers	# Unique Tracks	Sampled Papers
CHI	316	76	182 (58%)
WWW	137	31	62 (45%)
SIGIR	74	14	28 (38%)
CIKM	143	25	50 (40%)
EC	73	17	34 (47%)
Total	**743**	**163**	**358 (48%)**

We read, at a minimum, the abstract and methods of each paper, and recorded the methodologies used. These notes were compiled into a single document and analyzed via an iterative approach inspired by grounded theory [6]. Specifically, we began by conducting open coding to identify key phrases, then arranged key phrases into larger groups, and finally arranged emerging groups into a larger classification scheme, which we refined until satisfied. This process was designed to avoid classifying research based on historical distinctions, such as quantitative vs. qualitative, which may not accurately represent contemporary work.

3.2 Framework validation

We refined and validated our initial framework through semi-structured interviews with 11 MSR researchers in our research institution (again, see: limitations).

3.2.1 Participants

Participants were recruited to represent a range of research interests and geographies. For example, we interviewed researchers with interests including data mining, machine learning, privacy, ICT(4)D, media studies, economics, and socio-digital systems, to name a few. Participants were located in Asia, India, the United Kingdom, and the United States.

3.2.2 Procedure

After describing our research and obtaining consent, we presented each participant with a version of our framework in the form of a flow chart. These charts covered a range of research processes, as presented below. We asked participants questions to *"Think of a research project you are conducting or planning. Please use this decision tree to share your research methodologies with us."* After walking through the framework and answering questions, participants were thanked and debriefed. Our framework was altered after each of the first 7 reviews. After the 8th review, feedback did not merit additional changes.

3.3 Types of Human Subjects Research

Our framework identifies four general types of research involving human subjects along two axes, *participant awareness* and *environmental manipulation*.

3.3.1 Common types of human subjects research

Our defined research types the following:

- **Type I:** Participants are aware of the research, and researchers manipulate participant environment;
- **Type II:** Participants are aware of the research, **but** researchers **do not** manipulate participant environment;
- **Type III:** Participants are **not** aware of the research, but researchers manipulate participant environment;
- **Type IV:** Researchers collect or obtain personal information about participants **without** participant awareness or environmental manipulation.

Key definitions include the following:

- *Awareness* results from online or real life exchanges between researcher and participant, conducted asynchronously (e.g., through Mechanical Turk) or in real time;
- *Manipulation* characterizes situations in which a stimulus (e.g., an experimental manipulation; a request for data) is designed to produce a specific response. This does not include indirect manipulation, where a stimulus is a facet of the methodology (e.g., the presence of a researcher in a chat room; an observable recording device).

The types are elaborated in Table 2. Note that these research types are not mutually exclusive: any publication may describe research classified in multiple categories. For example, researchers may use data mining to examine the demographics of social media users (Type IV), then go on to recruit a separate set of participants for an interview study (Type II), presenting these as complementary facets of a single research project.

Table 2: Common Types of Web Research with Illustrative Examples

Type	Description	Illustrative Examples	Common methods for data collection
I	**Participant awareness:** Yes **Environmental manipulation:** Yes	Lab-based user study, modified data sets (e.g., annotated images) produced upon researcher request	Observation; surveys; interviews; behavioral trace data
II	**Participant awareness:** Yes **Environmental manipulation:** No	A diary study of daily habits; a survey on general attitudes towards social media; analysis of existing artifacts shared by participant (e.g., Instagram photos)	Observation; surveys interviews; artifact analysis; diary studies
III	**Participant awareness:** No **Environmental manipulation:** Yes	Experiments conducted without participant knowledge (e.g., most online A/B tests)	Online telemetry and usage data collection
IV	**Participant awareness:** No **Environmental manipulation:** No	Observation conducted without participant knowledge or consent; data mining studies that collect personal information (e.g., unique identifier; location)	Observation; data mining; artifact analysis

Our research review was designed to let categories naturally emerge from the data. After identifying and refining these categories, we began to critically evaluate how each category is distinct from the others. One important distinction is level of interaction between researcher and participant. While recognizing that this may not be true in every case, as a general rule, Type I research supports the closest interaction between researcher and participant, with levels of interaction progressively decreasing in Type II, Type III, and Type IV research.

Research types also vary regarding locus of control. Type II research often manifests as self-reported attitudes, behaviors, or beliefs. As conversations between a researcher and a participant, these methods generally allow participants a high degree of autonomy regarding how to interpret a particular question or decide exactly what information to disclose. In Type I research, participant autonomy is significant, but may be less strong than in Type II research (consider the degree of freedom afforded by the question "Please tell us about your Facebook use," typical of a Type II study, versus the question "Please tell us how you would use this perspective Facebook feature," which might be asked in Type I research). Types III and IV afford less autonomy, as participants are not even aware that research is being conducted. Finally, these categories vary in terms of how research is understood and presented. For example, in Type I and Type II research, authors often refer to *participants* or *subjects* in the *Methods* section of a conference paper. In contrast, Type III and Type IV researchers may describe *data* or *data sets* involved in *experimental manipulations* (referring to both real-time A/B tests and experiments run on archived data). Note that the linguistic conventions of Type III and Type IV researchers are often similar to those of researchers who conduct *experiments* or *modeling* with *real-life* or *synthetic* data in non-human-subjects research. Following constructivist theory, which suggests that human understanding of the world is shaped in part through dialogue, these distinctions are non-trivial.

3.4 The prevalence of different research types

Our classification of conference papers suggested a strong relationship between research type and publication venue. This is natural reflection of each conference's unique purpose. However, the topical nature of conferences increases the likelihood that researchers will rub shoulders with colleagues of similar epistemological and methodological perspectives, and decreases the likelihood that researchers will be exposed to radically different points of view.

3.4.1 Classification

In light of these considerations we decided to investigate the relationship between research type and venue more fully. Two researchers independently classified 10% of the 358 conference proceedings (*n*=36). Of 43 distinct research studies identified, there were 36 agreements and 7 disagreements (Cohen's Kappa= 0.79). Disagreements were resolved through closer readings of the papers in question. Note that this process confirms that our classification can be useful for characterizing computer science research to the extent that it is represented in these conferences. We classified the papers in our sample.

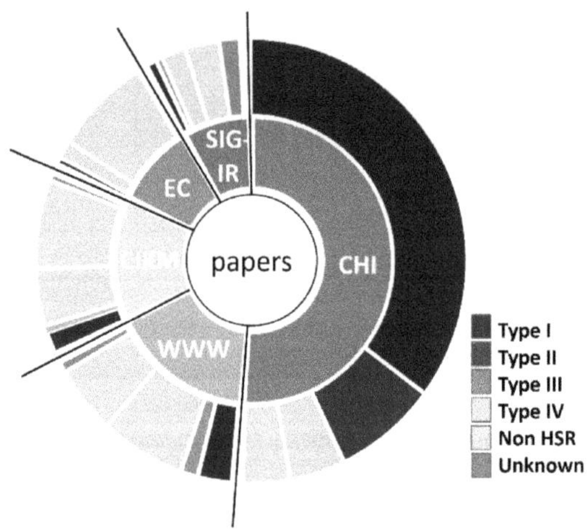

Figure 1: Conference Proceedings Reviewed

Of 358 publications, we identified 263 unique instances of human-subjects research reported in 251 papers (70%). In 96 publications, methods were described in such a way that we concluded these papers did not report human subjects research (27% of total). It was impossible to classify the remaining 3% of our sample. Papers considered non-human-subjects research covered topics ranging from discourse analysis of newspaper articles, to natural language processing of news archives, to evaluation of interfaces without human aid.

Of the 263 unique instances of human subjects research, 157 were considered Type I (60%), 30 were considered Type II (11%), 7 were considered Type III (4%), and 69 were considered Type IV (26%). (Note that these do not add up to 100% due to rounding.) As illustrated by Figure 1, these four types of research were not represented equally among the conferences we surveyed. CHI, for example, was dominated by Type I research (69% of total publications), and was also the *only* conference to publish research categorized as Type II. In contrast, Type IV and non-human subjects research dominated WWW and CIKM (with these types representing 41 papers, or 82% of total contributions in CIKM; and, 44 papers, or 71% of total contributions in WWW).

3.5 Risk Areas in Research

Using the framework, the evaluation of risk is built into the decision trees stemming from the classification of the research.[1] This section describes key areas for evaluating risk.

3.5.1 Research Settings

Research is conducted in controlled environments, or in naturalistic settings. Some research is conducted in physical environments; other research, online. These environments can be characterized as falling on a spectrum of private to public. For example, a digital ethnography of an exclusive online community is *online research* conducted in a *naturalistic, semi-private* environment.

3.5.2 Recruitment, Enrollment, and Screening

We define recruitment broadly, to refer to both active solicitation of participants and automatic enrollment in online studies. Recruitment may be done in advance of participation, in physical settings (e.g., fliers posted to a discussion board) or online. Note that online recruitment (especially via social media) must be conducted in accordance with site policies. This is an important consideration in both instances where recruitment is distinct from data collection (e.g., a participant is recruited for physical lab study via Facebook) and in instances where recruitment is tied to data collection (e.g., recruitment and data collection are simultaneous for researchers who mine Facebook).

3.5.3 Identifying Participants

While many researchers gather demographic data to support data analysis, we are interested in data gathered for the purpose of understanding whether participants may ethically participate in research. In some research, demographic data are collected for this purpose during recruitment or screening. In other cases, researchers believe that suitability is determined by external partners or platforms (including recruitment agencies, collaborators, and online platforms). In still other cases (including data mining), researchers believe it is impossible to conclusively identify demographic traits.

Generally, research may involve two populations with limited power to consent. Participants with low **capacity** may lack the situational ability to understand the risks and benefits involved in research, and to make an informed decision regarding whether to participate [20]. Participants with low capacity may include those who are socially or economically disadvantaged, e.g., homeless individuals; those with situational sensitivities, e.g., women suffering from abuse; and, those with physical or mental disabilities. Participants with low capacity may consent with the aid of surrogates such as caregivers, and consent from these participants need not be written.

Depending on age, children may also be unable to consent to research. Parental consent may be obtained for participants under 18 (or researchers may request a waiver), and *must* be obtained for participants under 13, as required by US federal law. Note that in some cases research with children conducted in "established or commonly accepted" educational settings may qualify from IRB exemption [13]. Of course, this begs the question of what constitutes a "commonly accepted" educational setting in the era of online courses, including massively open online courses (MOOCs).

3.5.4 Consent and Debriefing

Determining whether participants have capacity to consent is a separate process from obtaining consent. Participants are often informed about a study prior to data collection. In these cases researchers often (but not always) obtain consent at this point in time. We also identify instances where participants are debriefed, either in addition to or as substitute for information offered prior to participation. Deception plays a role in some computer science research, in the form of misleading information (e.g., regarding the true purpose of a study) or through omission (e.g., being informed that data collection was occurring, but not to what end).

3.5.5 Primary Data Collection for Type I and II

Researchers may document participant actions and behaviors, for example, through audio, video, visual recordings, or notes. In this type of data collection, the researcher is solely and actively responsible for determining what is captured and codified. Data are also collected through automatic recordings of participant behaviors. These recordings may capture data from digital interactions, such as search logs, or from physical interactions, such as biometric data. Type I and Type II research alike rely on participant self-report. The specific mechanism of self-report varies (surveys; interviews; focus groups). But, the type of data that we label as self-report is data provided by a participant about *that participant* (such as self-reported texting behaviors).

Data are also created as participants critically evaluate an existing technology, artifact, or environment. These data are generated in response to and are primarily about *an external environment, artifact, or other entity* (though such data may contain information about participants, as addressed below). Finally, participants may create new data sets. These data may be physical artifacts or data, such as Polaroid photos, or digital artifacts or data, such as digital photographs or image annotations. Note that in this case, data are *created* through intelligent processes rather than *generated.*

3.5.6 Primary Data Collection for Type III and IV

For those conducting Type III and Type IV research, one type of valuable data is generated via *utilitarian use* of artifacts, technologies, and environments. These data may be trace data from physical interactions, such as biometric data collected from sensors, or data from digital interactions. Data sets may be *quantitative*, measuring, for example, the number of books added to a shopping cart. They may also be *qualitative*, e.g., the names of books added to a shopping cart. Type III and Type IV researchers also may be interested in data *produced through intelligent processes* that involve creativity, judgment, or expertise (e.g., movie reviews). Again, these data sets may be quantitative or qualitative. Finally, researchers study data produced by or describing interactions between human beings. Examples of these data include declared relational data (e.g., LinkedIn Connections), data shared between parties (e.g., retweets), and reactions to shared content (e.g., Facebook likes).

3.5.7 Secondary Data Collection

Data about secondary participants may be embedded in data collected from primary participants. "Likes" of a Facebook post

[1] The complete framework can be found at http://aka.ms/MSREthicsFramework.

contain the name of that post's author, and A/B experiments analyzing the use of a particular browser may capture data from multiple family members. Additionally, non-sensitive data that are deliberately collected may be intrinsically linked to sensitive data. A data set listing the number of Foursquare check-ins at a *location* of interest also includes data about *humans* who checked in. In some cases, personal or sensitive secondary data can be removed. In other cases, such cleaning would render the data set useless.

3.5.8 Data sharing

Raw data sets are either kept private, or shared with colleagues, with other participants, or with the general public. Similarly, select raw data are shared with researchers outside the project team, with other participants, or with the public at large. Sharing select raw data is different from sharing data in aggregate form. For example, the content of a tweet posted as part of a digital disaster relief campaign is considered select raw data.

Researchers sometimes share raw data containing sensitive information, which we define as data that could damage participants through reconstruction of personal information or through use in a new context. This practice is especially prevalent when a raw data set stripped of sensitive information would lose its value. These key components of web research are codified in our digital research ethics submission system (RESS), described in Section 4.

3.6 Feedback via validation interviews

Interviews conducted with lab researchers allowed us to refine our framework, and helped shape our implementation based on early reactions to the emerging RESS system. On the positive side, multiple interviewees expressed that our process helped them understand the ethics and values inherent in their research. One even mentioned that he planned to follow up on our discussion by talking about ethics with others on his research team.

We recognize that some aspects of our process, such as the categorization of different data types, is unorthodox. Indeed, many of our researchers indicated that they tended to think of their research in terms of "I do data mining," or "I do ethnographic work." These conceptualizations are a poor fit for the process we present, and caused minor frustrations. But, it became clear through the interviews that pushing researchers outside of their comfort zones was precisely what allowed them to challenge existing assumptions regarding the ethics associated with certain topics, methodologies, or paradigms.

4. BUILDING A DIGITAL RESEARCH ETHICS REVIEW PROCESS

We use our framework to design the digital research ethics submission system (RESS) which calculates a risk score based on research type and risk area, determining the level of review needed for the research proposal. We provide an overview of the RESS, and then address three workflows in depth: the submission process, preliminary evaluation, and full board review.

4.1 Basic infrastructure

To initiate IRB review in academic contexts, a researcher submits a new project to the designated system. This submission includes a list of researchers, their credentials including certificates of ethics training completion, and a document describing the proposed research, in detail. IRB reviewers access each proposal, and may review the proposal independently prior to a real-time, virtual meeting. Following each meeting a proposal is approved, rejected pending modifications, or rejected. This process may be repeated until approval is obtained.

Our first departure from this system is our choice of platform. We decided against existing platforms, which can be expensive and time consuming to implement, for various reasons. Unlike their academic counterparts, Microsoft researchers are not subject to federal regulation of their research. Thus, our IRB will either need to be "opt in," or mandated through corporate policy. For this reason, there is a significant need to establish the value of our RESS by first initiating a small deployment, and then slowly scaling up.

The absence of federal regulations governing industry research also presents an opportunity, enabling us to address the limitations of current IRBs, and to customize our RESS to the needs of web researchers. For our system, we customized an existing conference paper submission system, Microsoft's Conference Management Toolkit (CMT).[2] Our customized system supports users in three roles:

- *Authors* submit proposals for ethics review by uploading documents (e.g., consent forms and other protocols) and completing a web form. Authors may also use the system to read reviews and download a letter of IRB approval.
- *Reviewers* evaluate research proposals via forms submitted to conference chairs. Reviewers may also use the system to collectively evaluate proposals through a hosted discussion forum.
- *Conference chairs* manage this process by conducting an initial review, assigning proposals to reviewers, moderating discussions, and notifying authors of evaluation outcomes.

4.2 Overview of MSR RESS process

The review process (Figure 2) is initiated when authors submit a research proposal. When prompted by an email notification, chairs conduct an initial review with three potential outcomes: approval through automated expedited review, approval through human expedited review, or designation for full board review (as described below). Authors of automatically approved proposals receive email notification of this decision. For expedited human review, the chair may elect to review the proposal, or to designate a small number of reviewers. Proposals that receive expedited review may be approved without modification, or pending modification. In the later case, authors are prompted to edit their submissions, and receive approval when edits are complete. Proposals designated for full review are sent to a review panel.

MSR has an IRB registered with HHS. All proposals that are approved by the MSR ethics review process receive an official letter of approval attached to their proposal submission, which authors may share with external parties, such as conference reviewers and academic IRBs, at their discretion.

4.3 Author submission

Our submission system is designed as a web form. Each researcher submits a title and abstract for their proposal, and optionally uploads either a consent form, or an application for a waiver of

[2] The Conference Management Toolkit, http://cmt.research.microsoft.com. Interest parties may request an implementation of their own RESS.

informed consent. Researchers then answer a series of questions based on our framework. These questions begin with a general categorization of research as Type I, Type II, Type III, or Type IV. This classification serves two purposes. First, it allows the system to ask users an abbreviated list of questions based on their research type. Second, it allows the system to present users with questions in a vocabulary consistent with their existing mental models.

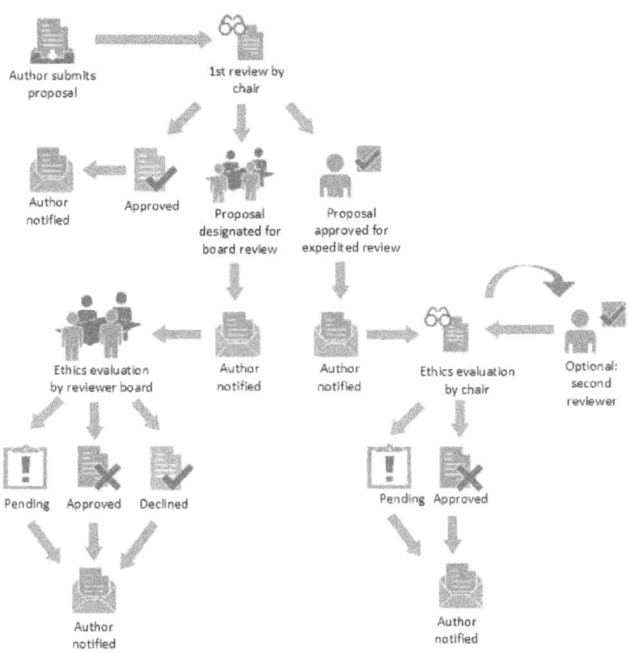

Figure 2. Overview of the research review process

After this initial classification, researchers answer a series of questions using branch logic based on key aspects of the framework described in Section 3. For example:

- For research settings, users are asked whether their research will be conducted in online and/or online settings.
- For recruitment, *enrollment,* and *screening*, users are asked whether they will recruit in advance of participation or during/after participation (e.g., some large display studies).
- Users indicate whether participants may include groups such as children under 13, children under 18, disabled populations, or others with a low capacity to consent.
- Users are asked whether they seek consent prior to research, and/or whether debriefing is utilized after.
- Users describe their primary data collection. For example, Type I and Type II studies may collect data through active documentation (e.g., interviews) or automatic recordings (e.g., biometric data); Type II and Type III studies may collect quantitative or qualitative behavioral trace data.
- For secondary data collection, users are asked whether data about secondary participants may be embedded in data about primary participants, and whether sensitive data is linked to non-sensitive data.
- For data sharing, users indicate whether raw and aggregate data is kept private to the research team, shared with other colleagues, shared with participants, and/or shared publicly.

An initial, automated review follows this submission; if needed, human expedited review or full review follow.

4.4 Initial review

Based on the data submitted by authors, a process of initial review should characterize research as minimal risk or greater than minimal risk. Note that some aspects of a research protocol, such as the use of deception, are risky in themselves. Other aspects, such as the collection of sensitive metadata, are less risky in some cases—e.g., if sensitive metadata is removed prior to analysis—and more risky in others, e.g., if sensitive metadata is collected from children under 13. CMT does not support an easy way to assess these risks, but does support a bulk export to excel. Therefore, we have designed a series of Excel macros to conduct the initial review.

Our process of initial review covers 124 cases where the ethics of a research study may be questionable. Drawing on the linguistic traditions of privacy researchers including [18], we refer to these cases as "flags." Of the 124 flags, 13 (10%) are associated with an author's single answer to a question- for example, an answer of "no" to the question "Is research conducted in accordance with site policy?" In addition, 111 flags (90%) are raised when each of two questions are answered in a particular way.

We have designated 3 levels of flags: red, orange, and yellow (Table 3). These flags are derived from three sources: our understanding of canonical ethical guidelines articulated in the Belmont Report, our understanding of ethical questions voiced by those studying web research, and our previous work.

Red flags designate potentially catastrophic aspects of a research protocol. Typically, protocols with red flags are ethically problematic in any environment, but are exacerbated by the nature of web research. Orange flags designate commonly recognized ethical grievances, such as the failure to obtain informed consent in face-to-face research. Yellow flags identify aspects of a proposal that may or may not be ethically problematic in this particular research context, but have been identified as problematic in *some* contexts. The majority of yellow flags are unique to web research, and do not apply to face-to-face contexts.

Table 3: The flagging system for initial review

Flag	Points	Description	Example
Red	15	Egregious ethical consideration; often unique to CS research	Sensitive PII embedded in public data set
Orange	5	Standard ethical consideration	Failure to gain consent in face to face studies
Yellow	1	Possible ethical consideration; likely unique to CS research	Publishing tweets may support re-identification

Each type of flag is associated with a certain number of points. The number of points accrued by each proposal designates the outcome of initial review. Our thresholds are set as:

- *Under 10 points:* Research is minimal risk, and automatically approved. Potential outcomes of review include: accept.
- *10-20 points:* Research is minimal risk, and designated for expedited human review. Potential outcomes of review include: accept; accept with modifications.
- *Over 20 points:* Research is **not** minimal risk, and is designated for full review. Potential outcomes of review include: accept; accept with modifications; reject.

This process is similar to the review via kiosk [9], where an automated system approves select research proposals and designates others for human review. We do believe that the opportunity for initial automated or semi-automated review adds value to a system such as ours, and provide an overview of our implementation for this reason. We also recognize that the implementation itself may be non-ideal, and that each institution seeking to duplicate our RESS (or implement a similar process) will need to carefully construct a framework for initial review suitable to their unique needs.

4.5 Full board review

As described earlier, initial review designates research as automatically approved, suitable for expedited review, or suitable for full board review. We discuss our full review process below.

Each meeting of our RESS is called when a chair selects the "email all reviewers" function, and sends a preloaded template calling the meeting to order. At this point, reviewers are asked to review the proposal submitted by an author, and fill out a form posing the following questions:

- Are the potential risks to participants minimized?
- Are the potential risks to participants reasonable, given the anticipated benefits to participants and/or society?
- Is the selection of subjects equitable?
- Do researchers obtain consent, or provide compelling evidence why consent should be waived?
- Do researchers protect participant safety and confidentiality?
- Please share any additional concerns.

These questions are presented as qualitative response, allowing each reviewer the ability to provide minimal (e.g., "no") or substantial feedback. In addition, reviewers are asked, "Do you vote to accept or reject the research as currently proposed?" Acceptable answers to this question are "yes" and "no."

We initially designated each board as "open" for a 48-hour period. This timeframe should allow researchers adequate opportunity to read and review each proposal, while also providing authors with timely feedback. During the 48-hour period, a discussion forum hosted by CMT is activated to allow researchers to discuss each proposal assigned. Following this period, an RESS chair reviews the submitted review forms and online discussions. If the chair observes consensus between reviewers, she decides whether to accept the proposal, reject the proposal, or request modifications. Authors are provided with notification of the RESS outcome, a copy of each review, and a summary of key points made in the discussion forum compiled by the RESS chair. If there is significant disagreement between reviewers, the panel is extended for a second 48-hour period. During this time the chair posts contentious issues to the forum and asks reviewers to discuss the severity of their concerns and brainstorm potential solution. After the second 48-hour period, the chair determines a review outcome by majority vote, and notifies the author.

5. SUBMISSION SYSTEM EVALUATION

We evaluated our proposal submission system through user testing with participants acting as authors (n=9) and reviewers (n=5). We also evaluated the degree our system adheres to HHS guidelines for the ethical evaluation of human subjects research.

5.1 Author evaluation of interface

Nine participants from our Redmond lab submitted 10 distinct research proposals. Each evaluation began with a meeting where researchers provided an overview of the review process, offered participants the chance to ask questions, and secured consent. Participants then used our system to submit a proposal of a current or planned project using a think-aloud protocol. Initial review and secondary review (as needed) was conducted through the process described above. Following this assessment, we invited participants to take an online survey describing their experiences with the RESS. This survey contained a mix of open-ended questions, including "What do you consider the value of research ethics evaluation at MSR?" and close-ended questions, such as "Would you submit another proposal for research review?"

Of the 10 proposals submitted, five were approved through automated expedited review; three were approved through human expedited review; and, two were designated for full board review. Though a few usability issues were noted, the majority of authors characterized the system as easy to use. Additionally, most appreciated the use of logic to avoid answering unnecessary questions: the order *"makes sense."* Participants had mixed reactions to the re-purposing of CMT as a system to support research ethics review. Some complimented the system, and appeared unaware that our RESS was not custom built. But a few objected to the use of legacy language, e.g. the word "abstract." Our next iteration will address these complaints.

5.2 Reviewer evaluation of interface

In accordance with HHS guidelines, we recruited three colleagues within MSR, one colleague from the legal group within Microsoft, and one external collaborator to act as reviewers. We convened our digital review board for a 48-hour period, asking each of our participants to a) read the two proposals designated for full review; b) submit a web form reviewing each proposal independently; and, c) make at least one post to a community discussion forum for each proposal reviewed (while not all reviewers will be required to post to forums in our implemented RESS, we wanted to evaluate this feature). Reviewers also completed a version of the author survey described above.

Of the five reviewers recruited for our panel, two submitted reviews and three contributed to the discussion forum during the designated 48-hour period. Additionally, two submitted comments and three submitted to the forum within the following 48 hours. This caused us to re-think our timeframe; future panels will unfold over a week, with additional time allocated to discuss contentious issues as needed.

In our user tests, the forums were extremely useful for full board discussion and generated significant and useful feedback for authors. For both proposals, the level of detail voiced through forum comments exceeded the level of detail provided in individual reviews. Regarding usability, reviewers found the RESS interface more difficult to navigate than authors. Some identified issues, such as the use of small and ambiguous icons, are easily corrected. Reviewers also questioned our process, for example asking why feedback was required in both a web form and a forum. This can only be clarified by explaining HHS regulations for ethics reviews in the case of contended proposals.

While we designed an abbreviated RESS to reduce the information burden on authors and reviewers alike, some reviewers wanted more information than our RESS system provided. Specifically, two asked to see consent forms describing the specific risks and benefits of participation (optional for authors), and multiple researchers asked for elaboration on key aspects of protocols. These requests shaped our future implementation, as discussed in Section 6.

5.3 Perceived value of MSR research review

Introducing a corporate research ethics review is a contentious process that may be met with resistance if researchers consider ethics review a bureaucratic hurdle to clear [21]. Only one of our nine researchers failed to find value in our system: "*I believe that most of my projects are pretty straightforward--I put a user in front of a computer and have them click, or deploy it to their workstations; therefore, I'm not too worried about 'ethics' issues.*" Still, this researcher contended that the system could have value for those "*sitting at the ethical margins*," or researchers submitting to conferences requiring a statement of ethical evaluation. In addition to this critique, two of our nine authors questioned why the system was not organized around specific research methods (e.g. online surveys). We address this question in our discussion.

Most participants saw value in implementing a process of research ethics review within MSR. First, participants saw personal value in the system. Some authors indicated that the submission process reminded them of *"forgotten"* best practices, such as debriefing. Others, including those conducting cooperative research with academic institutions, believed that our process could help them submit better applications to academic IRBs. Participants also understood how our RESS could support MSR as a whole. The controversy surrounding Facebook's emotional contagion study prompted many to comment on the reputational value of research review. For example, one tester considered our system could help *"Avoid an ethical breach (also a public relations disaster) like Facebook recently had."* Finally, participants saw value in a shared conversation and commitment to addressing ethical issues: *"The value of the review is the conversation it could generate as we all figure out how to do the most ethical work in this challenge space."*

Most participants familiar with existing IRBs characterized our system as an improvement for evaluating the ethical implications of MSR web research. Testers did share two concerns. One reviewer commented that our RESS is *"a lighter lift but that's appropriate for the initial program development. Hopefully, as the program evolves, it will become more robust."* Noting that our process *"feels like filing paperwork (and that's what usually leads people to misrepresent or miss the ethical concerns that are likely),"* and a second researcher advocated for a dialogical approach supporting conversation between *"fellow researchers."*

5.4 Compliance with HHS standards

While designing and implementing our system, one key consideration was the degree that our system should comply with HHS regulation for human subjects research. Even if problematic, HHS standards are considered best practices by some researchers.

5.4.1 Requirements for compliance

Federal regulations for the protection of human subjects are outlined in the HHS code of federal regulations under Title 45, Part 46 [25]. This policy applies to all research "supported or otherwise subject to regulation by any federal apartment or agency" (§46.103). Following a statement of scope and key definitions, HHS §45.46 begins with two conditions of compliance unrelated to IRBs. First, each complying institution must register their IRB, and then file a federal wide assurance (FWA) as a statement of compliance. Second, each institution must implement a statement of ethical principles. Following these conditions, the remainder of §45.46 outlines requirements for IRBs, including requirements for board membership (§46.107) and requirements for securing informed consent or applying for a waiver of consent (§46.116).

5.4.2 Evaluation of MSR RESS compliance

MSR partially complies with the second condition HHS §45.46, relating to registering the board and filing a FWA. Specifically, the MSR RESS is registered with HHS, but we have not submitted a FWA. This decision was made because we have decided to retain the flexibility to define an ethics review process in line with our specific research areas and corporate requirements, and not those mandated by federal process. MSR complies with the second condition of HHS §45.46 by advancing the Belmont Report as a statement of ethical principles. The MSR RESS complies with the vast majority of the remaining HHS requirements. In most cases, compliance is built into the system. For example, §46.115 requires documentation of all proposals and reviews; these are automatically saved by the RESS. In other cases, compliance is set by policy, or through other practices. §46.103 dictates requirements for publishing written procedures describing the review process.

Given our technical infrastructure, there is not a single requirement posed by HHS that **cannot** be met. Thus, it is entirely possible for an industry research lab using our system to fully comply with HHS requirements for the ethical review of human subjects research. Still, we note that some requirements may be problematic for institutions hoping to implement a fully compliant RESS. For example, one of our authors indicated that his research was confidential and should not be shared with reviewers outside of MSR; yet, HHS guidelines dictate that an external reviewer must sit on a full IRB board. Other industry research labs may share this constraint.

6. DISCUSSION

6.1 Key contributions to research and practice

We developed an ethics review system that includes a new framework for characterizing the methods used in web research. This framework serves as the underlying infrastructure for our digital research ethics submission system (RESS). Our framework supports the calculation of risk based on the classification of the research and answers to key questions. We evaluated this framework, and the resulting system, with MSR researchers.

While the majority of our evaluators saw value in the system, a few participants voiced concerns. Two researchers questioned whether research ethics review was truly necessary, given the nature of their work. This concern may be addressed by implementing our system as opt-in. It may also be addressed by designing the system carefully, so that researchers conducting truly low risk research are not required to undergo lengthy evaluation process. Our process of automated expedited review is designed to meet this challenge. Notably, both researchers who failed to see value of our system for their work submitted research proposals that were approved via automated expedited review.

In line with our early interviews, we were not surprised to hear some of our later evaluators advocate for a system that considers research methods as oppose to data types. As one participant who believed she was asked too many questions complained, "*It's just a survey.*" We respectfully disagree. A survey questioning experience with a prototype of an online discussion forum is not equivalent to a survey collecting information about experience with an existing forum for transgender teens. Our framework recognizes these nuances an classifies these two surveys differently (as Type I and Type II research respectively).Therefore, while we do not consider our system of eliciting data types as opposed to research methods the single best solution for those seeking to evaluate ethics in all contexts, we believe that this system meets our needs by recognizing the considerations unique to web researchers working at MSR.

6.2 Summary of key tensions

A number of tensions emerged during the implementation and evaluation of our system. First, our system is more effective at supporting the needs of authors, as opposed to reviewers. While we will continue to improve our reviewer interface, we believe that if an imbalance must occur, this is the correct direction: given our process of automated and human expedited review, we expect that a larger number of authors than reviewers will access our system overall.

Second, he intake portion of our system is biased to support complex research proposals over easy ones. However, we believe that asking researchers unnecessary questions is preferable to failing to sufficiently address ethically contentions aspects of a research proposal. We have implemented automated expedited review to balance this bias.

Third, we have designed a relatively conservative system that flags research as potentially problematic from an ethical perspective when, in fact, no significant ethical considerations may exist. Our conservatism is implemented in response to existing standards, which are biased towards classifying research as "exempt" that may, in fact, pose significant risk. We have no desire to stall ethically valid research, and anticipate that any unnecessary conservatism will be corrected via our processes of expedited human review or full board review.

6.3 Limitations and future work

Within MSR, the next step is to fully implement our RESS. We have selected two labs for initial deployment, and will implement full deployment as our system demonstrates the ability to scale. We are also implementing a research ethics training program customized to the needs of web researchers working in an industry setting. We hope that together, these initiatives will effectively support ethical research within MSR.

As we scale up our RESS system we may be able to address some of the concerns raised by our participants. For example, the researcher who advocated for a dialogical review process made a valid suggestion that could help our research community understand and embrace shared ethical best practices. CMT supports the option for reviewers to see evaluations from others; we will support this in future iterations. We may also invite authors to participate in discussions of their research in the online forum. The request for more rigorous review requires careful consideration. On one hand, we deliberately implemented a system that is customized for web research and uses branching logic; adding extra questions or requiring longer answers would mitigate some of the intended improvements to traditional IRB review. On the other hand, we wish to implement a process that is as effective at supporting ethical research as possible.

Finally, we recognize that the effectiveness of any process depends on the dedication of those who participate in it. To this end, our process will continue to prioritize the needs of MSR researchers as it evolves; we expect others who implement ethics review processes in industry settings will follow the same goal. We also note that when researcher needs conflict with established HHS guidelines, difficult decisions must be made.

There are a number of limitations to our work. Perhaps most significantly, our research and development process is biased towards the practices of Microsoft Research. While this is not a limitation for the implementation of our RESS, it is a limitation for the generalizability of our work to other industry and academic contexts. Note that our framework partially address this by including papers authored by students, academic researchers, and industry researchers alike. Yet, this sample itself is problematic, as we examined papers from only five conferences in the broad field of web research. We invite future researchers to challenge and improve upon our framework by applying it to a greater range of web research in various domains and sub-domains.

To this end, we suggest that supporting ethical web research is truly a community goal. Researchers often define their community based on their research area (e.g. the social science research community; the data mining community). Our classification of the conference papers we reviewed was designed to understand the degree that different types of research are represented in different conferences. We observed that in addition to hosting research around a particular topic, conferences overwhelmingly host research of a certain methodological type. On one hand, researchers within a community are uniquely qualified to evaluate the value of contributions to that community. This is true for research contributions, and may be true for ethical contributions as well [5]. On the other hand, holding discussions within a community of research and practice limits the cross-pollination of ideas. This is particularly significant when the ideas being shared deal with big, out-of-the box challenges—exactly the types of ethical challenges that computer science research provokes. And significant commonalities do exist between researchers conducting similar types of research (e.g., our Type IV research), and between researchers coming from different sub-domains. For example, researchers studying big data and ICT(4)D alike grapple with notions of consent and equity [7, 24].

Researchers agree that considering ethical practices in computer science is not a matter of "hammering offline ethics onto online experimentation" [3]. And, cultural standards should uphold ethical practices as best practices. There are two key barriers to supporting a holistic and shared understanding of ethical best practices within computer science. First, important ethical conversations are occurring within communities of research and practice, and may not be shared across sub-disciplinary divides. Second, the infrastructure that supports academic research will continue to determine how ethics is considered in this space. If industry researchers perceive these processes as outdated—and many do [5]—they will form and follow separate ethical practices.

These silos highlight the need for overarching guidelines that cross sub-disciplines and sectors. Some argue that standards must be truly enforceable, and thus come from a regulatory agency like HHS [24]. We join the call for updated HHS guidelines but also recognize that guidelines at this level are difficult to change, and new challenges are continually posed as technologies evolve. Others suggest that standards should be set or hosted by international associations such as IEEE and ACM [5]. We believe it is particularly important that formal guidelines and standards reflect the actual experiences and expertise of domain researchers, and join this call as well. Guidelines from such associations could be enforced in a number of ways. For example, it could be mandated that conference submissions include a statement of ethical evaluation of the research (ideally, one that is both proactive and retrospective).

ACKNOWLEDGMENTS

We thank Gaoxiang Xu and Vivek Narasayya for customizing CMT, and Carol Boston for reviewing an early version of this paper.

7. REFERENCES

[1] Aycock, J., Buchanan, E., Dexter, S. and Dittrich, D. 2011. Human subjects, agents, or bots: Current issues in ethics and

computer security research. In *Financial Cryptography and Data Security,* G. Danezis, S. Dietrich, and K. Sako Eds. Springer Verlag, Berlin, Germany, 138-145.

[2] The Belmont Report. http://www.hhs.gov/ohrp/humansubjects/guidance/belmont.html.

[3] Bernstein, M. 2014. The destructive silence of social computing researchers. https://medium.com/@msbernst/the-destructive-silence-of-social-computing-researchers-9155cdff659.

[4] Buchanan, E., Aycock, J., Dexter, S., Dittrich, D. and Hvizdak, E. 2011. Computer science security research and human subjects: Emerging considerations for research ethics boards. *Journal of Empirical Research on Human Research Ethics,* 6, 2 (Jun.2011), 71-83. DOI= 10.1525/jer.2011.6.2.71.

[5] Buchanan, E. and Ess, C. 2009. Internet research ethics and the institutional review board: Current practices and issues. *SIGCAS Computers and Society,* 39, 5 (Dec. 2009), 43-49.

[6] Corbin, C. and Strauss, S. 2008. *Basics of Qualitative Research.* Sage Publications, Thousand Oaks, CA.

[7] Dearden, A. 2012. See no evil? Ethics in interventionist ICTD. In *Proceedings of the 5th International Conference on Information and Communication Technologies and Development* (Atlanta, GA, Mar. 12-15, 2012), ICTD '12. New York: ACM Press, 46-55.

[8] Ethical decision-making and internet research: Recommendations from the AoIR ethics working committee. http://www.aoir.org/reports/ethics.html.

[9] Garfinkel, S. and Faith Cranor, L. 2010. Viewpoint: Institutional review boards and your research. *Communications of the ACM, 53,* 6 (Jun. 2010), 38-40.

[10] Gupta, P., Goel, A., Lin, J., Sharma, A., Wang, D. and Zadeh, R. 2013. WTF: The who to follow service at Twitter. In *Proceedings of the 22nd international conference on World Wide Web* (Rio de Janeiro, Brazil, May 13 – 17, 2013). WWW '13. ACM, New York, NY, 505-514.

[11] Holz, H., Applin, A., Haberman, B., Joyce, D., Purchase, H. and Reed, C. 2006. Research methods in computing: What are they, and how should we teach them? In *Proceedings of ITiCSE 2006* (Bologna, Italy, June 26-28, 2006). iTiCSE '11. ACM Press, New York, NY, 96-114.

[12] Hughes, J. T. and Tene, O. 2014. The truth is out there: Compliance and security are not enough. *Privacy Perspectives* (3 Oct. 2014). https://privacyassociation.org/news/a/the-truth-is-out-there-for-big-data-privacy-compliance-and-security-are-not-enough/

[13] IRBs and Assurances. http://hhs.gov/ohrp/assurances/index.html

[14] Kramer, A., Guillory, J. and Hancock, J. 2014. Experimental evidence of massive-scale emotional contagion through social networks. *PNAS, 111,* 24 (Jun. 2014), 8788-8790.

[15] Langheinrich, M., Schmidt, A., Davies, N. and Jose, R. 2013. A practical framework for ethics—the PD-net approach to supporting ethics compliance in public display systems. In *Proceedings of the 2nd ACM International Symposium on Pervasive Displays* (Mountain View, California, June 5 - 7, 2013), PerDis '13. ACM, New York, NY, 139-144. DOI= http://dx.doi.org/10.1145/2491568.2491598

[16] Mackay, M. 1995. Ethics, lies, and videotape…In *Proceedings of the SIGCHI Conference on Human Factors in Computing Systems* (Denver, Colorado, May 7-11, 1995). CHI '95. ACM, New York, NY, 138-145. DOI= http://dx.doi.org/10.1145/223904.223922

[17] McMillan, D., Morrison, A. and Chalmers, M. 2013. Categorized ethical guidelines for large scale mobile HCI. In *Proceedings of the SIGCHI Conference on Human Factors in Computing Systems* (Paris, France, April 27-May 2, 2013). CHI '13. ACM, New York, NY, 1853-1862. *Proc. CHI 2013,* ACM Press, New York, NY, 1853-1862. DOI= http://dx.doi.org/10.1145/2470654.2466245

[18] Nissenbaum, H. 2009. *Privacy in Context: Technology, Policy, and the Integrity of Social Life*. Stanford University Press, Stanford, CA.

[19] Peden, B. and Flashinski, D. 2004. Virtual research ethics: A content analysis of surveys and experiments. In *Readings in Virtual Research Ethics: Issues and Controversies,* E. Buchanan Ed. Idea Group, Hershey, PA, 1-26.

[20] Research involving individuals with questionable capacity to consent: Points to consider. http://grants.nih.gov/grants/policy/questionablecapacity.html.

[21] Schrag, D. 2010. *Ethical Imperialism: Institutional Review Boards and the Social Sciences, 1965-2009.* Johns Hopkins University Press, Baltimore, MD.

[22] Schroepfer, M. 2014. Research at Facebook. *Facebook Newsroom* (2 October 2014). http://newsroom.fb.com/news/2014/10/research-at-facebook/

[23] Silberman, G. and Kahn, K. 2011. Burdens on research imposed by institutional review boards: The state of the evidence and its implications for regulatory reform. *The Milbank Quarterly,* 89, 3 (Dec. 2011), 599-627.

[24] Solberg, L. 2012. Regulating human subjects research in the information age: Data mining on social networking sites. *Northern Kentucky Law Review, 39,* 2 (Oct. 2012), 327-358.

[25] U.S. Department of Health and Human Services 45 CFR 46.

[26] Verna, I. 2014. Editorial expression of concern: Experimental evidence of massive scale emotion contagion through social networks. *Proc. National Academies of Science USA, 111,* 29, 10779.

Sequential Hypothesis Tests for Adaptive Locality Sensitive Hashing

Aniket Chakrabarti
The Ohio State University
chakrabarti.14@osu.edu

Srinivasan Parthasarathy
The Ohio State University
srini@cse.ohio-state.edu

ABSTRACT

All pairs similarity search is a problem where a set of data objects is given and the task is to find all pairs of objects that have similarity above a certain threshold for a given similarity measure-of-interest. When the number of points or dimensionality is high, standard solutions fail to scale gracefully. Approximate solutions such as Locality Sensitive Hashing (LSH) and its Bayesian variants (BayesLSH and BayesLSHLite) alleviate the problem to some extent and provide substantial speedup over traditional index based approaches. BayesLSH is used for pruning the candidate space and computation of approximate similarity, whereas BayesLSHLite can only prune the candidates, but similarity needs to be computed exactly on the original data. Thus where ever the explicit data representation is available and exact similarity computation is not too expensive, BayesLSH-Lite can be used to aggressively prune candidates and provide substantial speedup without losing too much on quality. However, the loss in quality is higher in the BayesLSH variant, where explicit data representation is not available, rather only a hash sketch is available and similarity has to be estimated approximately. In this work we revisit the LSH problem from a Frequentist setting and formulate sequential tests for composite hypothesis (similarity greater than or less than threshold) that can be leveraged by such LSH algorithms for adaptively pruning candidates aggressively. We propose a vanilla sequential probability ratio test (SPRT) approach based on this idea and two novel variants. We extend these variants to the case where approximate similarity needs to be computed using fixed-width sequential confidence interval generation technique. We compare these novel variants with the SPRT variant and BayesLSH/BayesLSHLite variants and show that they can provide tighter qualitative guarantees over BayesLSH/BayesLSHLite – a state-of-the-art approach – while being upto 2.1x faster than a traditional SPRT and 8.8x faster than AllPairs.

WWW 2015, May 18–22, 2015, Florence, Italy.
ACM 978-1-4503-3469-3/15/05.
http://dx.doi.org/10.1145/2736277.2741665.

Categories and Subject Descriptors

H.2.8 [**Database Management**]: Database Applications—*Datamining*

Keywords

AllPairs Similarity Search; Locality Sensitive Hashing; Sequential Hypothesis Tests and Confidence Intervals;

1. INTRODUCTION

Similarity search in a collection of objects has a wide variety of applications such as clustering [17], semi-supervised learning [22], information retrieval [6], query refinement on websearch [1], near duplicate detection [21], collaborative filtering, and link prediction [15]. Formally, the problem statement is: *Given a collection of objects D and an associated similarity measure* $sim(.,.)$ *and a similarity threshold* t*, the problem is to find all pairs of objects* x, y*, such that* $sim(x, y) \geq t$*, where* $x, y \in D$.

The major challenge here is dealing with the large volume of data. The volume combined with high dimensionality of datasets can lead to inefficient solutions to this problem. Recent research has focused on reducing the candidate search space. The AllPairs [1] candidate generation algorithm builds a smart index structure from the vector representation of the points to compute exact similarity. Another approach is to do an approximate similarity calculation that involves sacrificing small accuracy for substantial speedup. The most popular technique is locality sensitive hashing (LSH) [11, 8] that involves projecting the high dimensional data into a lower dimensional space and similarity of a pair of points is approximated by the number of matching attributes in the low dimensional space.

A recent idea, BayesLSHLite [19], adopts a principled Bayesian approach on top of LSH and AllPairs to reason about and estimate the probability that a particular pair of objects will meet the user-specified threshold. Unpromising pairs are quickly pruned away based on these estimates realizing significant performance gains. The way BayesLSHLite works is, for a pair of data objects x, y, BayesLSHLite incrementally compares their hashes (in batches of size b) and infers after each batch, how likely is it that pair will have similarity above the threshold. If that probability becomes too low, then the candidate pair is pruned away. The above algorithm has a variant called BayesLSH, where after the candidate pruning is done, similarity is estimated approximately from the hash signatures instead of exact computation. This is useful in cases where exact similarity computation is infeasible. Exact similarity computation might be infeasible in cases where the original data was too large to store and the small hash sketch of the data was stored instead. Another scenario could be where the similarity measure-of-interest is a kernel function and exact representation of the data points in the kernel induced feature space is not possible as that space might be infinite dimensional (e.g. Gaussian RBF kernel). Additionally, the specialized kernel functions are extremely expensive to compute on the fly. In such cases, both candidate generation and similarity estimation has to be done approximately using the LSH hash sketches.

In this paper we adapt a Frequentist view of this idea and propose a fully principled sequential model to do the incremental pruning task with rigorous quality guarantees. Specifically, we model the problem of $sim(x, y) \geq t$ as a sequential hypothesis test problem and provide quality guarantees through Type I and Type II errors. We start with the traditional SPRT [20], and show that it is extremely inefficient in practice, making it unsuitable for large scale analytics. We then propose an alternate sequential hypothesis test procedure based on a one-sided fixed-width confidence limit construction technique. Finally we show that no single hypothesis testing strategy works well for all similarity values. Therefore, we propose a fine-grained hybrid hypothesis testing strategy, that based on a crude estimate of the similarity from the first batch of hash comparisons for that specific candidate pair, selects the most suitable test for that pair. *In other words, instead of using a single hypothesis test, we dynamically choose the best suited hypothesis test for each candidate pair.* We extend the above technique to develop a variant, that after candidate pruning, estimates the approximate similarity by using the fixed-width two-sided confidence interval generation technique [7]. Our ideas are simple to implement and we show that our hybrid method always guarantees the minimum quality requirement (as specified by parameters input to the algorithm), while being upto 2.1x faster than an SPRT-based approach and 8.8x faster than AllPairs while qualitatively improving on the state-of-the-art BayesLSH/Lite estimates.

2. BACKGROUND

2.1 Locality Sensitive Hashing

Locality sensitive hashing [11, 8] is a popular and fast method for candidate generation and approximate similarity computation within a large high dimensional dataset. Research has demonstrated how to leverage the key principles for a host of distance and similarity measures [2, 11, 5, 3, 17, 10]. Briefly, each data point is represented by a set of hash keys using a specific hash family for a given distance or similarity measure (sim). Such a family of hash function is said to have the locality sensitive hashing property if:

$$P_{h \in F}(h(x) == h(y)) = sim(x, y) \tag{1}$$

where x, y are any two points in the dataset, and h is a randomly selected hash function from within a family F of hash functions. Consequently, the approximate similarity between the pair can be estimated as:

$$\hat{sim(x, y)} = \frac{1}{n} \sum_{i=1}^{n} I[h_i(x) == h_i(y))]$$

where n is the total number of hash functions and I is the indicator function.

2.2 Candidate generation

We use AllPairs [1] candidate generation algorithm when the original data set is available. The AllPairs candidate generation algorithm is exact, hence all true positives (candidates with similarity above the threshold) will be present in the set of candidates generated. The AllPairs algorithm builds an index from the vector representation of data and instead of building a full inverted index, AllPairs only indexes the information that may lead to a pair having similarity greater than the specified threshold. The AllPairs algorithm can be used when the original dataset is small enough to be stored entirely and the similarity of interest is computed on the original feature space (unlike kernel similarity measures).

In cases where the entire dataset cannot be stored, rather a small sketch of it is available, AllPairs cannot be used. Additionally, if the similarity is a kernel function and the feature space of that kernel cannot be explicitly represented, AllPairs will not work as it relies on the explicit representation. However, in both scenarios we can use LSH to generate a low dimensional sketch of the dataset and use the probabilistic candidate generation algorithms [2, 11, 5, 3, 17, 10] to build the index. The advantage of such an index structure is that for a query point similarity search can be be done in sublinear time. LSH based index structures perform well compared to traditional indices when the dimensionality of the data set is very high. The algorithm is as follows:

1. *Using a LSH method for a given similarity measure, form l signatures for each data point, each signature having k hash keys.*
2. *Each pair of points that share at least one signature will stay in the same hash bucket.*
3. *During all pairs similarity search, for each point, only those points which are in the same bucket needs to be searched.*
4. *From [21], for a given k and similarity threshold t, the number of signatures l required for a recall $1 - \phi$,*

$$l = \lceil \frac{log(\phi)}{log(1 - t^k)} \rceil$$

2.3 Candidate Pruning using BayesLSH/Lite

Traditionally maximum likelihood estimators are used to approximate similarity of a candidate pair. For the candidate pair, if there are a total of n hashes and m of them match, then the similarity estimate is $\frac{m}{n}$. The variance of this estimator is $\frac{s(1-s)}{n}$ where s is the similarity of the candidate pair. Two issues to observe here are - 1) as n increases, the variance decreases and hence the accuracy of the estimator increases, 2) more importantly, the variance of the estimator depends on the similarity of the pair itself. This means for a fixed number of hashes, the accuracy achieved if the similarity of the candidate pair was 0.9 is higher than if the similarity was 0.5. In other words the number of hashes required for different candidate pairs for achieving the same level of accuracy is different. Therefore, the problem with fixing the number of hashes is - some of the candidate pairs can be pruned by comparing the first few hashes only. For example if the similarity threshold is 0.9 and 8 out of the first 10 hashes did not match, there is very low probability that the similarity of the pair is greater than 0.9. The BayesLSH/Lite[19] is among the earliest approaches to solve this problem of fixing the number of hashes. Instead it incrementally compares hashes until the candidate pair can be pruned with a certain probability, or the maximum allowed hash comparisons is reached. It will then compute exact or approximate similarity. To do the incremental pruning, BayesLSHLite solves the inference problem $P(sim(x,y) \geq t)$, where t is the similarity threshold. Additionally, the BayesLSH variant estimates the approximate similarity by creating an interval for the true similarity by the solving the inference $P(|sim(x,y) - \widehat{sim(x,y)}| \leq \delta)$. Both inferences are solved using a simple Bayesian model. These inferences help overcome the problem pointed above - number of hashes required to prune a candidate or build an interval around it adaptively set for each candidate pair.

Let us denote the similarity $sim(x,y)$ as the random variable S. Since we are counting the number of matches m out of n hash comparison, and the hash comparisons are i.i.d. with match probability S as per equation 1, the likelihood function becomes a binomial distribution with parameters n and S. If $M(m,n)$ is the random variable denoting m matches out of n hash bit comparisons, then the likelihood function will be:

$$P(M(m,n)|S) = \binom{n}{m} S^m (1-S)^{n-m} \tag{2}$$

In the Bayesian setting, the parameter S can be treated as a random variable. Let the estimate of S in this setting be $\hat{S}$. Using the aforementioned likelihood function, the two inference problems become:

Early pruning inference: given m matches out of n bits, what is the probability that the similarity is above threshold t:

$$P[S \geq t \,|\, M(m,n)] = \int_t^1 P(S \,|\, M(m,n))dS \tag{3}$$

Concentration inference: given the similarity estimate $\hat{S}$, what is the probability that it falls within δ of the true similarity:

$$\begin{aligned} P[|S-\hat{S}| < \delta \,|\, M(m,n)] &= P[\hat{S}-\delta < S < \hat{S}+\delta \,|\, M(m,n)] \\ &= \textstyle\int_{\hat{S}-\delta}^{\hat{S}+\delta} P(S \,|\, M(m,n))dS \end{aligned} \tag{4}$$

The BayesLSHLite algorithm works as follows:
For each pair x,y:

1. *Compare the next b hashes and compute the early pruning probability* $P[S \geq t \,|\, M(m,n)]$.
2. *If* $P[S \geq t \,|\, M(m,n)] < \alpha$*, then prune the pair and stop.*
3. *If maximum allowable hash comparisons have been reached, compute exact similarity and stop.*
4. *Go to step 1.*

The BayesLSH variant works as follows:
For each pair x,y:

1. *Compare the next b hashes and compute the early pruning probability* $P[S \geq t \,|\, M(m,n)]$.
2. *If* $P[S \geq t \,|\, M(m,n)] < \alpha$*, then prune the pair and stop.*
3. *If* $P[|S-\hat{S}| < \delta \,|\, M(m,n)] > 1-\gamma$*, then output pair* x,y *if* $\hat{S} \geq t$ *and stop.*
4. *If maximum allowable hash comparisons have been reached, then output pair* x,y *if* $\hat{S} \geq t$ *and stop.*
5. *Go to step 1.*

3. CASE FOR FREQUENTIST FORMULATION

The BayesLSH/Lite candidate pruning and approximate similarity estimation algorithms as described in the previous section, provide the basis for the current work. Specifically in this work we examine the same problems they attempt to solve but in a Frequentist setting. BayesLSH/Lite makes a simplifying assumption potentially leading to somewhat weak bounds on error. *Specifically, BayesLSH/Lite tries to model an inherently sequential decision process in a non-sequential way.* The inferences (equations 3 and 4) in the BayesLSH/Lite algorithms are done every b hash comparisons (this can be viewed as a bin of comparisons). Therefore, for a candidate pair, if the pruning inference is done once, then the error probability rate will α, but when it is done for the second time, probability of the pair getting pruned will be determined by getting pruned the first time (first bin) and the probability of getting pruned the second time (a cumulative of the first and second bin matches). Essentially, we argue that this error may propagate resulting in an accumulated error over multiple pruning inferences. The same scenario is true for the concentration inference as well (equation 4). Over multiple concentration inferences done incrementally, the coverage probability could fall below $1-\gamma$. We note that in practice this may not be a significant issue but the question remains can this problem be fixed (in the rare cases it may materialize) without significantly impacting the gains obtained by BayesLSH/Lite. We note that fixing this problem in a Bayesian setting remains open but in this work we show how this problem can be fixed to guarantee tighter error bounds in a Frequentist setting.

Another issue, again a minor one, is when a pair is unlikely to be above a certain similarity threshold, pruning it early saves hash comparisons, similarly when a pair is very likely to be above the threshold, hash comparison for it should stop immediately and it should be processed for exact/approximate similarity computation. This can also save a number of hash comparisons.

To overcome these problems, we propose to model the problem in a Frequentist setting as follows. In the frequentist setting let the similarity $sim(x,y)$ be denoted by the parameter s (instead of S as in Bayesian setting).

- We model the early pruning inference $s > t$ as a *sequential hypothesis test* problem that should be able to guarantee Type I and Type II errors under the sequential hash comparison setting and if possible, it should be able to early prune a pair or send a pair for exact/approximate similarity computation.
- We model the concentration inference $|s - \hat{s}| \leq \delta$ as a *sequential two-sided fixed-width confidence interval* creation problem that should be able to guarantee a certain coverage probability.

4. METHODOLOGY

In this section, we describe a principled way of doing the early pruning inference (equation 3) and the concentration inference (equation 4) under the sequential setting where the number of hash functions (n) is not fixed, rather it is also a random variable.

4.1 Early Pruning Inference

We use sequential tests of composite hypothesis for pruning the number of generated candidates, so that the cardinality of the remaining candidate set is very small. Therefore, exact similarity computation on the remaining set of candidate pairs becomes feasible in terms of execution time, provided the original data set is available and the similarity function can be computed on the feature space of the original data. Our pruning algorithm involves sequentially comparing the hashes for a pair of data objects and stop when we are able to infer with some certainty whether the similarity for the pair is above or below the user defined threshold. If, according to the inference, the similarity of the pair is below the threshold, then we prune away the pair, otherwise we compute exact or approximate similarity of the pair depending on which variant we are using. More formally, if the similarity of the pair is s and the user defined threshold is t, we need to solve the hypothesis test, where the null hypothesis is $H0 : s \geq t$ and the alternate hypothesis is $H1 : s < t$. Two interesting aspects of our problem formulation are:

1. For performance reasons as described in section 3, we do not want to fix the number of hashes to compare for the hypothesis test, but rather incrementally compare the hashes and stop when a certain accuracy in terms of Type I error has been achieved.

2. We focus on Type I error, i.e. we do not want to prune away candidate pairs which are true positives ($s \geq t$). We can allow false positives ($s < t$) in our final set, as either exact similarity computation or approximate similarity estimation will be done on the final set of candidate pairs and any false positives can thus be pruned away. In other words, we do not need to provide guarantees on Type II error of the hypothesis test. Of course keeping a low Type II error implies less false positives to process, resulting in better performance.

We discuss three strategies for formulating the hypothesis test. First, we cast our problem in a traditional Sequential Probability Ratio Test (SPRT) [20] setting and then discuss the shortcomings of such an approach. Second, we then develop a sequential hypothesis test based on a sequential fixed width one-sided confidence interval (CI) and show how it can overcome some of the limitations of traditional SPRT. We empirically find that even this test does not always perform better than the more traditional SPRT. Third, building on the above, we propose a hybrid approach (HYB), where we dynamically select the hypothesis test (SPRT or CI) based on the similarity of each candidate pair which we crudely estimate from the first few comparisons. In other words, *instead of using a single fixed hypothesis test, we select one which is best suited for the candidate pair being estimated.*

For a candidate pair x, y with similarity s, the probability of a hash matching is s for a locality sensitive hash function as described in equation 1. Therefore, given n hashes for the pair, the probability that m of them will match follows a binomial distribution with parameters n and s. This is because the individual hash matching probabilities are identically and independently distributed Bernoulli with parameter s. So our problem formulation reduces to doing sequential hypothesis test on a binomial parameter s.

4.1.1 *Sequential Probability Ratio Test*

We use the traditional sequential probability ratio test by Wald [20] as our first principled sequential model for matching LSH signatures, to decide between $s \geq t$ or $s < t$. For the purpose of this model we swap the null and alternate hypotheses of our formulation. We do this because the resulting formulation of the hypothesis test $H0 : s < t$ vs. $H1 : s \geq t$, where s is a binomial parameter, has a well known textbook solution (due to Wald). The important thing to recollect is that we care more about Type I error in our original formulation. Therefore under the swapped SPRT setting, we care about the Type II error. That is easily done as SPRT allows the user to set both Type I and Type II errors, and we set Type II error to be α. To solve a composite hypothesis test using SPRT for a binomial parameter s, the first step is to choose two points $t+\tau$ and $t-\tau$. Now the SPRT becomes a simple hypothesis test problem of $H0 : s = s_0 = t - \tau$ vs. $H1 : s = s_1 = t + \tau$. The algorithm works as follows:

1. Incrementally compare batches of size b hashes until

$$\frac{log(\frac{\alpha}{1-\beta})}{log(\frac{s_1}{s_0}) - log(\frac{1-s_1}{1-s_0})} + n\frac{log(\frac{1-s_0}{1-s_1})}{log(\frac{s_1}{s_0}) - log(\frac{1-s_1}{1-s_0})} < \hat{s}$$
$$< \frac{log(\frac{1-\alpha}{\beta})}{log(\frac{s_1}{s_0}) - log(\frac{1-s_1}{1-s_0})} + n\frac{log(\frac{1-s_0}{1-s_1})}{log(\frac{s_1}{s_0}) - log(\frac{1-s_1}{1-s_0})}$$

   Here n is the cumulative number of hash comparisons till now, and $\hat{s} = m/n$, where m is the cumulative number of hash matches up to that point.

2. Reject null hypothesis (conclude $s \geq t$) if,

$$\hat{s} \geq \frac{log(\frac{1-\alpha}{\beta})}{log(\frac{s_1}{s_0}) - log(\frac{1-s_1}{1-s_0})} + n\frac{log(\frac{1-s_0}{1-s_1})}{log(\frac{s_1}{s_0}) - log(\frac{1-s_1}{1-s_0})}$$

3. Fail to reject null hypothesis (conclude $s < t$) if,

$$\hat{s} \leq \frac{log(\frac{\alpha}{1-\beta})}{log(\frac{s_1}{s_0}) - log(\frac{1-s_1}{1-s_0})} + n\frac{log(\frac{1-s_0}{1-s_1})}{log(\frac{s_1}{s_0}) - log(\frac{1-s_1}{1-s_0})}$$

SPRT is a cumulative likelihood ratio test, and is an optimal test with guaranteed Type I and Type II errors, when the hypotheses are simple. In the case of composite hypothesis (across bins of hashes), no optimality guarantees can be given, and consequently, to make a decision, SPRT typically takes a large number of hash comparisons. This results in extremely slow performance as we will empirically validate. We next describe the confidence interval based test.

4.1.2 *One-Sided-CI Sequential Hypothesis Test*

4.1.2.1 *Constructing the confidence interval (CI).*

The true similarity s of pair of data objects x, y can be estimated as $\hat{s} = \frac{m}{n}$, where m is the number of hashes that matched out of n hash comparisons. It can be shown that $\hat{s}$ is the maximum likelihood estimate of s [18]. Following standard convention we denote this estimator as $\hat{S}$ (random variable, distinguished from its realization, $\hat{s}$). Here we describe the procedure for constructing a fixed-width (say w) upper confidence interval for s with $1-\alpha$ coverage probability. More formally, we want to continue comparing hashes and estimating similarity until,

$$P(s < \hat{S} + w) = 1 - \alpha \quad (5)$$

Here $\hat{s} + w$ is the upper confidence limit for s with $1 - \alpha$ coverage probability. We use an approach similar to Frey [7] to solve this problem.

Stopping rule for incremental hash comparisons: We use the Wald confidence interval for binomial as our stopping rule. Formally, for some value λ, and a fixed confidence width w, we incrementally compare batches of b hashes and stop when $z_\lambda\sqrt{\frac{\hat{s_a}(1-\hat{s_a})}{n}} \leq w$. Then the upper confidence limit can be reported as $min(\hat{s} + w, 1.0)$. Here $\hat{s_a} = \frac{m+a}{n+2a}$, where a is a very small number. $\hat{s_a}$ is used instead of $\hat{s}$ because, if the batch size is extremely small, and number of matches is 0 (or it is the maximum, i.e., all match), then the confidence width becomes 0 after the first batch if $\hat{s}$ is used.

Finding λ: In a non-sequential setting, the Wald upper confidence limit as described above will have a coverage probability of $1 - \lambda$. But in a sequential setting, where the confidence interval is tested after every batch of hash comparisons, the coverage probability could fall below $1 - \lambda$. Hence to ensure coverage probability of at least $1 - \alpha$, λ should be set less than α. Given the set of stopping points and a λ, we can compute the coverage probability CP(λ) of our one-sided confidence interval using the path-counting technique [9]. Suppose the stopping points are $(m_1, n_1), (m_2, n_2), \ldots.., (m_k, n_k)$ and $H(m, n)$ is the number of ways to do n hash comparisons with m matches, without hitting any of the stopping points. Therefore, the probability of stopping at stopping point (m_i, n_i) is $H(m_i, n_i)s^{m_i}(1-s)^{n_i-m_i}$. Since the incremental hash comparison process is guaranteed to stop, probability of stopping at all the stopping points should sum to 1. This implies

$$\sum_{i=1}^{k} H(m_i, n_i)s^{m_i}(1-s)^{n_i-m_i} = 1$$

Consequently, the coverage probability for similarity s will be

$$T(s, \lambda) = \sum_{i=1}^{k} H(m_i, n_i)s^{m_i}(1-s)^{n_i-m_i} I(s \leq \frac{m_i}{n_i} + w) \quad (6)$$

Here I is the indicator function of whether the stopping point is within the correct interval width w. Now the overall coverage probability can be computed as,

$$CP(\lambda) = min_{s\in[0,1]}T(s, \lambda) \quad (7)$$

For our one-sided confidence interval to have at least $1 - \alpha$ coverage probability, we need to find λ such that $CP(\lambda) \geq 1 - \alpha$. The function $H(m, n)$ can be solved using the path-counting recurrence relation:

$$\begin{aligned} H(m, n+1) =& H(m, n)ST(m, n) \\ &+ H(m-1, n)ST(m-1, n) \end{aligned}$$

Here $ST(m, n)$ is the indicator function of whether (m, n) is a non-stopping point. The base of the recursion is $H(0, 1) = H(1, 1) = 1$. With a fixed λ, $ST(m, n)$ can be computed using the Wald stopping rule as described before, and $H(m, n)$ can be hence computed by the aforementioned recurrence relation. Then we need to solve equation 7 to find out the confidence coefficient of our one-sided interval. $T(s, \lambda)$ is a piecewise polynomial in s with jumps at the points in the set $C = \{0, \frac{m_i}{n_i} + w, \forall i = 1 \; to \; k \; and \; \frac{m_i}{n_i} + w \leq 1\}$. $CP(\lambda)$ is then approximated numerically by setting $s = c \pm 10^{-10}$, where $c \in C$ and taking the minimum resulting $T(s, \lambda)$. Now that we know how to compute $CP(\lambda)$, we use bisection root-finding algorithm to find a λ for which $CP(\lambda)$ is closest to our desired coverage probability $1 - \alpha$.

4.1.2.2 *Constructing the Hypothesis Test.*

In the previous section we described a procedure for creating a fixed-width once-sided sequential upper confidence limit with coverage probability $1 - \alpha$. In this section, we describe the process to convert the one-sided upper confidence interval to a level-α hypothesis test using the duality of confidence intervals and hypothesis tests.

LEMMA 4.1. *If $\hat{s} + w$ be an upper confidence limit for s with coverage probability $1 - \alpha$, then a level $- \alpha$ hypothesis test for null hypothesis $H0 : s \geq t$ against alternate hypothesis $H1 : s < t$ will be to Reject H0, if $\hat{s} + w < t$, else Fail to Reject H0.*

PROOF. By equation 5,

$$\begin{aligned} &P(\hat{S} + w \geq s) = 1 - \alpha \\ &\implies P(\hat{S} + w \geq t | s \geq t) \geq 1 - \alpha \\ &\implies -P(\hat{S} + w \geq t | s \geq t) \leq -1 + \alpha \\ &\implies 1 - P(\hat{S} + w \geq t | s \geq t) \leq \alpha \\ &\implies P(\hat{S} + w < t | s \geq t) \leq \alpha \\ &\implies P(Reject \; H0 | H0) \leq \alpha \end{aligned}$$

□

4.1.2.3 *Choosing w.*

The fixed-width w of the one-sided upper confidence interval has a significant effect on the efficiency of the test. Intuitively, the larger the width w, the less the number of hash comparisons required to attain a confidence interval of that width. However, setting w to a very high value would result in a large Type II error for our test. Though our algorithm's quality is not affected by Type II error (since we compute exact or approximate similarity when alternate hypothesis is satisfied), but still a large Type II error will imply that many false positives (candidates which fall in alternate hypothesis, but are classified as null hypothesis). Exact/approximate similarity is computed and these candidates are pruned away. Therefore, a large Type II error will translate to lower efficiency. In other words, making w too high or too low will cause significant slowdown in terms of execution time.

We next describe a simple heuristic to select w. Suppose a candidate pair has similarity $s < t$, i.e. for this candidate pair, the null hypothesis should be rejected. So the upper confidence limit $\hat{s}+w$ can be as high as t, and our test statistic should still be able to reject it. Therefore, the maximum

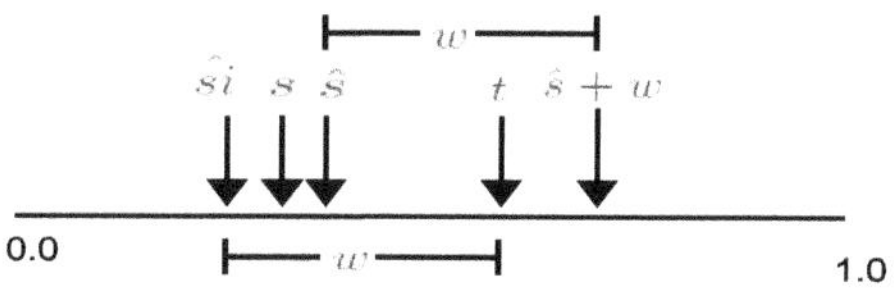

Figure 1: Estimating w

length of w is dictated by how large the upper confidence limit can be. So instead of presetting w to a fixed value, we dynamically set w according to the following heuristic. We compare the first batch of hashes and use the crude estimate of s, say $\hat{si}$ from the first batch to come up with w:

$$w = t - \hat{si} - \epsilon \quad (8)$$

The key insight here is, *instead of using a single hypothesis test for all candidate pairs, we choose a different hypothesis test based on an initial crude similarity estimate of the candidate pair being analyzed, so that w can be maximized, while still keeping Type II error in control, resulting in efficient pruning.* Note that every such test is a $level - \alpha$ test according to Lemma 4.1. We need the ϵ parameter as $\hat{si}$ is a crude estimate from the first batch of hash comparisons and it could be an underestimate, which would result in an overestimate of w. Consequently, the final test statistic $\hat{s}+w$ can go beyond t and the candidate cannot be pruned. Figure 1 explains the phenomenon. Of course, dynamically constructing the test for each candidate can make the candidate pruning process inefficient. We solve this issue by caching a number of tests for different w and during the candidate pruning step, the test that is closest to w (but smaller than or equal to it) is selected. Hence there is no need for online inference, making the algorithm very efficient.

4.1.3 Hybrid Hypothesis Tests

We found out empirically that the number of hash comparisons required by SPRT is very high for our composite hypothesis test problem. The one-sided CI based tests performed considerably better. Specifically we saw that the candidate pairs whose actual similarity s is quite far away from the threshold t were very quickly classified into the null or alternate hypothesis as the width w is quite large. But interestingly, for the candidate pairs which have similarity very close to the threshold, the estimated parameter w becomes very small. For such pairs, to attain the fixed-width confidence interval, the number of hash comparison requirement is very high. It is even higher than the more traditional SPRT. Therefore, to utilize the best of both worlds, we use a hybrid hypothesis testing strategy, where based on how far the true similarity is away from the threshold, we either select a one-sided CI based hypothesis test, or the SPRT. Formally, *we use a parameter μ, such that if the estimated fixed-width $w \geq \mu$, we use the one-sided CI based hypothesis test, else we use SPRT.* Again, in this hybrid strategy all the tests are $level - \alpha$, so we have guarantees on the overall Type I error, while minimizing the number of overall hash comparisons by smarty selecting the proper test for a specific candidate.

4.2 Concentration Inference

To solve the concentration inference of equation 4, we can create a two-sided fixed-width confidence interval for a binomial proportion under the sequential setting. The technique is very similar to the one we described in section 4.1.2 for the one-sided upper confidence limit. The major difference is, for two-sided confidence interval, the coverage probability equation 6 from section 4.1.2 becomes:

$$T(s, \lambda) = \sum_{i=1}^{k} H(m_i, n_i) s^{m_i} (1-s)^{n_i - m_i} I(|s - \frac{m_i}{n_i}| \leq \delta)$$

Now this equation can be solved in a manner similar to the one described in section 4.1.2 to find out the critical value λ and hence the stopping points in the sequential process. The stopping rule will also change to $z_{\frac{\lambda}{2}} \sqrt{\frac{\hat{s_a}(1-\hat{s_a})}{n}} \leq \delta$ (in the one-sided case λ was used instead of $\frac{\lambda}{2}$). The concentration inference is used to estimate the similarity with probabilistic guarantees under circumstances where exact similarity computation is infeasible.

Choosing maximum number of hashes: In our problem scenario, we do not need all candidates to converge to a fixed-width interval. Since we guarantee $1-\alpha$ recall, any candidate pair which has less than α probability of being greater than t can be ignored. In other words, we do not need to consider all the stopping points generated. We can choose the stopping points based on the user defined threshold t.

LEMMA 4.2. *If m_i, n_i are the stopping points decided by the fixed-width confidence interval method having coverage probability $1-\gamma$, the stopping points m_i, n_i, such that $\frac{m_i}{n_i} < t-\delta$ can occur with probability at most γ if the true similarity s is greater than threshold t.*

PROOF. By the fixed-width confidence interval guarantee,

$$P(\hat{S} - \delta \leq s \leq \hat{S} + \delta) = 1 - \gamma$$

$$\implies P(s > \hat{S} + \delta \text{ or } s < \hat{S} - \delta) = \gamma$$

$$\implies P(\hat{S} < s - \delta) \leq \gamma$$

This implies for $s > t$, the probability of $\hat{s} < t - \delta$ is less than γ. For all the stopping points m_i, n_i, $\hat{s} = \frac{m_i}{n_i}$. Hence the proof. □

COROLLARY 4.3. *If m_i, n_i are the set of stopping points, the maximum number of hashes n_{max} required by our algorithm to estimate any similarity above t while ensuring $1-\gamma$ recall is $n_{max} = max(n_i)$ s.t. $\frac{m_i}{n_i} \geq t - \delta$.*

If we set $\gamma = \alpha$, the above lemma will ignore points which have less than α probability of being a true positive. In other words, our algorithm is able to guarantee $1-\alpha$ recall.

4.3 Similarity Measures

The proposed techniques in this paper can be used with similarity measures for which a locality sensitive hash function exists. Previous work has developed locality sensitive hash functions for a wide range of similarity measures [2, 11, 5, 3, 17, 10] as well as for arbitrary kernel functions [12]. In this paper, we show that our methods work well with two of the most popular similarity measures - i) Jaccard similarity and ii) Cosine similarity.

4.3.1 *Jaccard Similarity*

The locality sensitive hash function relevant to Jaccard similarity is *MinWise Independent Permutation*, developed by Broder *et al* [2]. This hash function can approximate the Jaccard coefficient between two sets x, y. Formally,

$$P(h(x) == h(y)) = \frac{|x \cap y|}{|x \cup y|}$$

The estimate of Jaccard similarity between x, y will be:

$$\hat{s} = \frac{1}{n}\sum_{i=1}^{n} I[h_i(x) == h_i(y))]$$

As described earlier in equation 2, the likelihood function for getting m matches out n hashes is a binomial with parameters n, s. Note that n is also a random variable here. Hence we can directly use our proposed methods for doing inference on s.

4.3.2 *Cosine Similarity*

The locality sensitive hash function for cosine similarity is given by the *rounding hyperplane algorithm*, developed by Charikar [4]. However, the similarity given by the above algorithm is a little different from cosine similarity. Specifically, such a hash function gives:

$$P(h(x) == h(y)) = 1 - \frac{\theta}{\pi}$$

where θ is the angle between the two vectors. Let the above similarity be defined as s and let the cosine similarity be r. The range of s is therefore, 0.5 to 1.0. To convert between s and r, we need the following transformations:

$$r = cos(\pi(1 - s)) \tag{9}$$

$$s = 1 - \frac{cos^{-1}(r)}{\pi} \tag{10}$$

Consequently, we need to adapt our proposed algorithms to handle these transformations. Handling the pruning inference is quite simple. If the user sets the cosine similarity threshold as t, before running our pruning inference, we change the threshold to the value of the transformed similarity measure. So the pruning inference becomes $s \geq (1 - \frac{cos^{-1}(t)}{\pi})$ instead of $s \geq t$.

The transformation of the concentration inference is trickier. We need to transform the confidence interval of s (our algorithm will generate this) to the confidence interval of r (for cosine similarity). The user provides an estimation error bound δ, implying that we need to generate an estimate $\hat{r}$ within a confidence interval of 2δ with $1-\gamma$ coverage probability. Since we can only estimate $\hat{s}$, we need to create a level-$(1-\gamma)$ confidence interval $2\delta_s$ around $\hat{s}$, such that, if $l_s \leq s \leq u_s$ and $l_r \leq r \leq u_r$ then,

$$u_s - l_s \leq 2\delta_s \implies u_r - l_r \leq 2\delta$$

If we create, a $2\delta_s$ fixed-width confidence interval, then the upper and lower confidence limits will be $\hat{s} + \delta_s$ and $\hat{s} - \delta_s$ respectively. Since r is a monotonically increasing function of s, hence the upper and lower confidence limit of r (cosine similarity) will be $cos(\pi(1-min(1.0, \hat{s}+\delta_s)))$ and $cos(\pi(1-max(0.5, \hat{s}-\delta_s)))$ respectively. The interval for the estimate of cosine similarity will be $cos(\pi(1 - min(1.0, \hat{s} + \delta_s))) - cos(\pi(1-max(0.5, \hat{s}-\delta_s)))$. We have to choose δ_s such that

$$cos(\pi(1-min(1.0, \hat{s}+\delta_s)))-cos(\pi(1-max(0.5, \hat{s}-\delta_s))) \leq 2\delta$$

Dataset	Vectors	Dimensions	Avg. Len	Nnz
Twitter	146,170	146,170	1369	200e6
WikiWords100K	100,528	344,352	786	79e6
RCV	804,414	47,236	76	61e6
WikiLinks	1,815,914	1,815,914	24	44e6
Orkut	3,072,626	3,072,66	76	233e6

Table 1: Dataset details

The above function is monotonically decreasing in $\hat{s}$. So the interval will be largest when $\hat{s}$ is smallest (0.5). So we set $\hat{s}$ to 0.5 and numerically find out largest δ_s such that the inequality of the above expression is still satisfied.

5. EXPERIMENTAL EVALUATION

5.1 Experimental Setup and Datasets

We ran our experiments on a single core of a AMD Opteron 2378 machine with 2.4GHz cpu speed and 32GB of RAM. We only use one core as our application is a single threaded C++ program. We use five real world datasets to evaluate the quality and efficiency of our allpairs similarity search algorithms. Details are given in Table 1

Twitter: This is a graph representing follower-followee links in Twitter [13]. Only users having at least 1000 followers are selected. Each user is represented as an adjacency list of the users it follows.

WikiWords100K and WikiLinks: These datasets are derived from the English Wikipedia Sep 2010 version. The WikiWords100K is a preprocessed text corpus with each article containing at least 500 words. The Wikilinks is a graph created from the hyperlinks of the entire set of articles weighted by tf-idf.

RCV: This is a text dataset consisting of reuters articles [14]. Each document is represented as a set of words. Some basic preprocessing such as stop-words removal and stemming is done.

Orkut: The Orkut dataset is a friendship graph of 3 million users weighted by tf-idf [16].

5.2 Results

As explained in section 4 (methodology), we expect BayesLSH/Lite variants to be very fast, however those could potentially suffer a loss in the qualitative guarantees as they model an inherently sequential process in a non-sequential manner. Since the sequential confidence interval based methods have provable guarantees about quality (lemmas 4.1 and 4.2), they are always expected to be qualitatively better. The SPRT and hence the Hybrid methods should qualitatively perform very well, however under the composite hypothesis testing scenario, SPRT cannot provide strong guarantees. In the next two sections we will evaluate these premises.

5.2.1 *Algorithms using Early Pruning and Exact Similarity Computation*

We compare the following four strategies for computing all pairs with similarity above a certain user defined threshold. All of these algorithms assume that the original dataset is available (instead of the smaller sketch). These algorithms use the exact candidate generation technique AllPairs [1] and an early pruning technique and finally exact similarity computation.

BayesLSHLite: BayesLSHLite [19] is the state-of-the-art candidate pruning algorithm which is known to perform better than AllPairs [1] and PPJoin [21].
SPRT: We use the traditional Sequential Probability Ratio Test to do the early pruning of candidates. We set $\tau = 0.025$.
One-Sided-CI-HT: We compare against our model, which is the fixed-width one-sided upper confidence interval based hypothesis testing technique. We set $\epsilon = 0.01$. The choice of ϵ is done by empirically evaluating several values – we found values in the neighborhood of $0.01 - 0.05$ worked best. We set $a = 4$ as it seems to work well in practice [7].
Hybrid-HT: This is the second model we propose, where based on the candidate in question, we either choose a One-Sided-CI-HT or SPRT. We set $\mu = 0.18$, that is the threshold of w below which our Hybrid-HT algorithm switches from a One-Sided-CI-HT to SPRT. Again, we selected μ, empirically by trying different thresholds. For all the tests above, we set the Type I error or recall parameter $1 - \alpha = 0.97$. We also compare with the AllPairs algorithm which uses exact similarity computation right after the candidate generation step (no candidate pruning).

The performance and quality numbers are reported in Figure 2. We measure performance by total execution time and we measure quality by recall (since we are giving probabilistic guarantees on recall). An added advantage of these methods is that since we compute exact similarity for all candidates that are retained and check whether they are above the threshold using exact similarity computation, all the strategies yield full precision (100%). Further more, the sequential hypothesis tests we do are truncated tests, i.e. we compute at most $h = 256$ hashes, after which if a decision cannot be made, we send the pair for exact similarity computation. We report results on all the aforementioned datasets on both Jaccard and cosine similarity measures. For Jaccard, we vary the similarity threshold from $0.3 - 0.7$ and for cosine, we vary the threshold from $0.5 - 0.9$. These are the same parametric settings used in the original BayesLSHLite work.

Results indicate that the pattern is quite similar for all datasets. BayesLSHLite is always substantially faster in case of cosine similarity while in case of Jaccard similarity, AllPairs is marginally faster at times. At high values of the similarity threshold, SPRT is the slowest, while both One-Sided-CI-HT and Hybrid-HT performs very close to BayesLSHLite. This performance benefit comes from the one-sided tests. More precisely, choosing the width w of the test based on the estimate from the first bin of hash comparisons makes each test optimized for the specific candidate being processed. Those tests are extremely efficient at pruning away false positive candidates whose true similarities are very far from the similarity threshold t. The reason is these tests can allow a larger confidence width w and hence less number of hash comparisons. Obviously the Hybrid-HT performs very well at such high thresholds because it chooses one of the one-sided tests. However, at the other end of the spectrum, at very low similarity thresholds, the allowable confidence interval width w becomes too small and a large number of trials is required by the one-sided tests, making them inefficient. SPRT performs reasonably well under these situations. Under these conditions, the Hybrid-HT strategy is able to perform better than both (SPRT and One-Sided-CI-HT) as it able to smarty delegate pairs with true similarity close to threshold to SPRT instead of one-sided tests. In summary, the green lines (Hybrid-HT) can perform well through the whole similarity threshold range. For the WikiWords100K dataset in Figure 2(k) Hybrid-HT gave 8.8x speedup over AllPairs and 2.1x speedup of SPRT at 0.9 threshold and at 0.5 threshold, it gave 3.4x speedup over AllPairs and 1.3x speedup over SPRT.

In terms of quality, our proposed method One-Sided-CI-HT guarantee at least 97% recall ($\alpha = 0.03$). In all results we see the recall of One-Sided-CI-HT, as expected, is above 97%. In spite of the fact that SPRT does not have strong guarantees in case of composite hypothesis, we see that SPRT performs quite well in all datasets. Since Hybrid-HT uses the One-Sided-CI-HT and SPRT, its quality numbers are also extremely good. Only BayesLSHLite, which does not model the hash comparisons as a sequential process, falls marginally below the 97% mark at some places. In summary, our tests can provide rigorous quality guarantees, while significantly improving the performance by over traditional SPRT.

5.2.2 *Algorithms using Early Pruning and Approximate Similarity Estimation*

The previous section discussed the algorithms that can be used when the explicit representation of the original data is available. We now describe results on two algorithms for which only the hash signatures needs to be stored rather than the entire dataset. These algorithms use the LSH index generation followed by candidate pruning, followed by approximate similarity estimation. We compare the following two techniques:
BayesLSH: This uses the same pruning technique as BayesLSHLite along with the concentration inference for similarity estimation.
Hybrid-HT-Approx: This is our sequential variant. It uses Hybrid-HT's pruning technique along with the sequential fixed-width confidence interval generation strategy as described in section 4.2. We set $\tau = 0.015$.

We use the same parametric settings as before. The additional parameters required here are the estimation error bound δ and the coverage probability $1 - \gamma$ for the confidence interval. We set $\delta = 0.05$ and $\gamma = \alpha$. Again we measure performance by execution time. Here we measure quality by both recall and estimation error as we provide probabilistic guarantees on both.

Figure 3 reports both the performance and recall numbers. We do not list the estimation error numbers as the avg. estimation error for each algorithm on each dataset was within the specified bound of 0.05. Results indicate that Hybrid-HT-Approx is slower than BayesLSH as expected, however is qualitatively better than BayesLSH. More importantly, in all cases, Hybrid-HT-Approx has a recall value which is well above the 97% guaranteed number. BayesLSH on an average performs quite well, however it does fall below the guaranteed recall value quite a few times. In summary, our method provides rigorous guarantees of quality without losing too much performance over BayesLSH.

6. CONCLUSIONS

In this paper we propose principled approaches of doing all pairs similarity search on a database of objects with a given similarity measure. We describe algorithms for handling two different scenarios - i) the original data set is available and the similarity of interest can be exactly computed from the

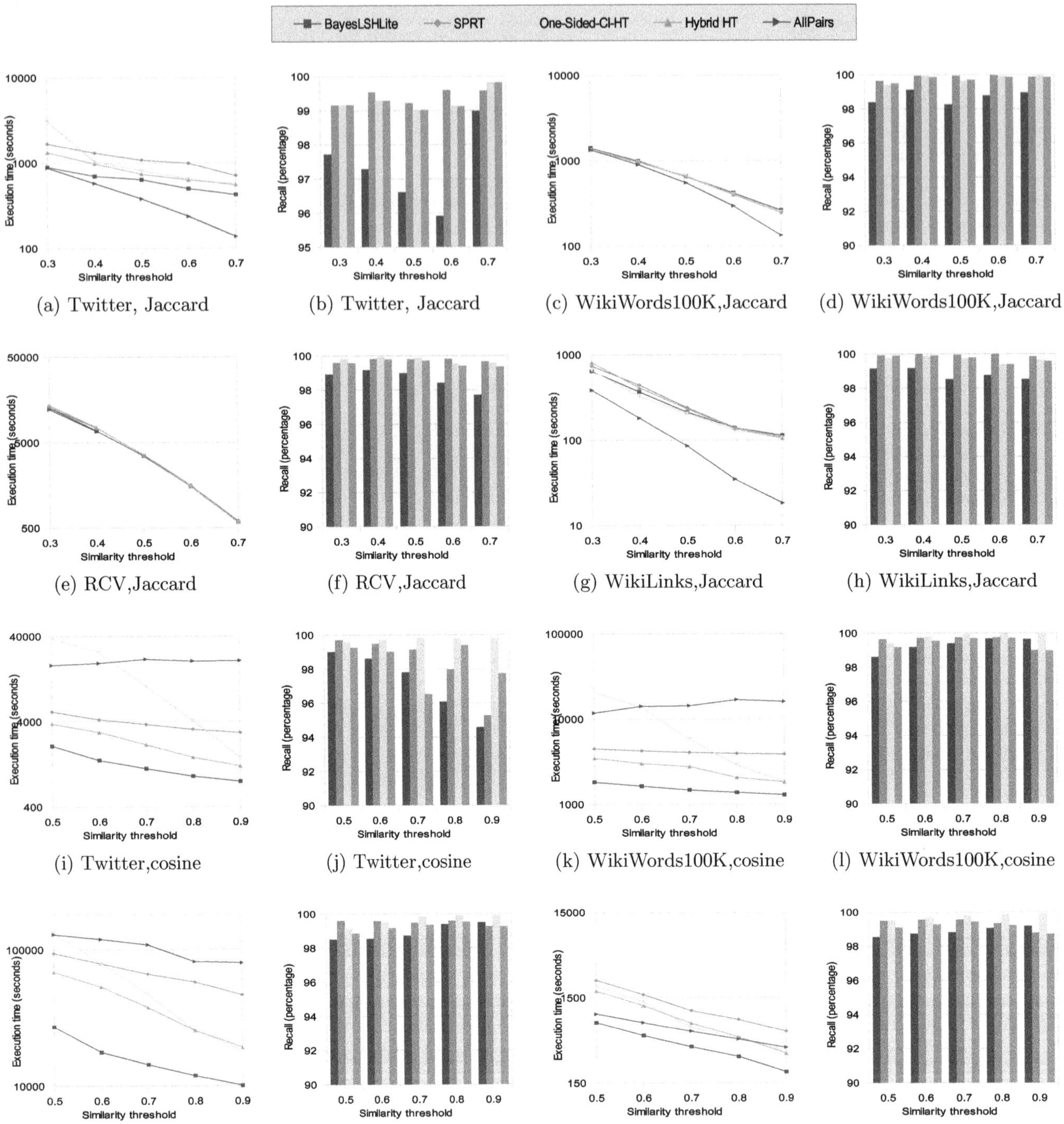

(a) Twitter, Jaccard (b) Twitter, Jaccard (c) WikiWords100K,Jaccard (d) WikiWords100K,Jaccard

(e) RCV,Jaccard (f) RCV,Jaccard (g) WikiLinks,Jaccard (h) WikiLinks,Jaccard

(i) Twitter,cosine (j) Twitter,cosine (k) WikiWords100K,cosine (l) WikiWords100K,cosine

(m) RCV,cosine (n) RCV,cosine (o) WikiLinks,cosine (p) WikiLinks,cosine

Figure 2: Comparisons of algorithms with exact similarity computation.

explicit representation of the data points and ii) instead of the original dataset only a small sketch of the data is available and similarity needs to be approximately estimated. For both scenarios we use LSH sketches (specific to the similarity measure) of the data points. For the first case we develop a fully principled approach of adaptively comparing the hash sketches of a pair of points and do composite hypothesis testing where the hypotheses are similarity greater than or less than a threshold. *Our key insight is a single test does not perform well for all similarity values, hence we dynamically choose a test for a candidate pair, based on a crude estimate of the similarity of the pair.* For the second case we additionally develop an adaptive algorithm for estimating the approximate similarity between the pair. Our methods are based on finding sequential fixed-width confidence intervals. We compare our methods against state-of-the-art allpairs similarity search algorithms – BayesLSH/Lite that does not precisely model the adaptive nature of the prob-

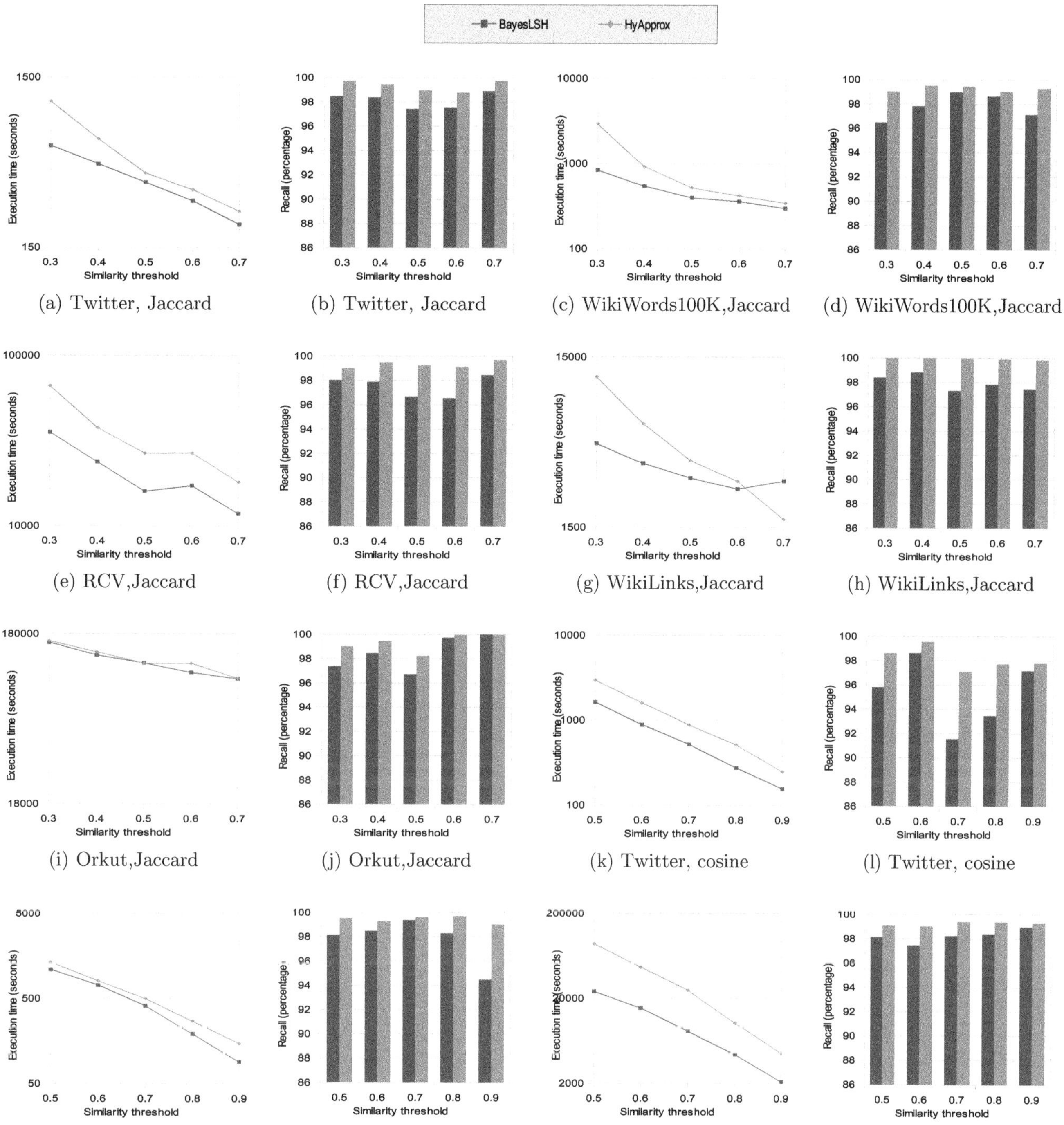

Figure 3: Comparisons of algorithms with approximate similarity estimations.

lem. We also compare against the more traditional sequential hypothesis testing technique – SPRT. We conclude that if quality guarantee is paramount, then we need to use our sequential confidence interval based techniques, and if performance is extremely important, then BayesLSH/Lite is the obvious choice. Our Hybrid models give a very good trade-off between the two extremes. We show that our hybrid methods always guarantee the minimum-prescribed quality requirement (as specified by the input parameters), while being upto 2.1x faster than SPRT and 8.8x faster than AllPairs. Our hybrid methods also improve the recall by up to 5% over BayesLSH/Lite, a contemporary state-of-the-art adaptive LSH approach.

Acknowledgments: We thank the anonymous reviewers for helpful comments. This work is supported in part by the following NSF grants: CCF 1217353, IIS-1141828, IIS-0917070, IIS-1111182 and IIS-1111118.

7. REFERENCES

[1] R. Bayardo, Y. Ma, and R. Srikant. Scaling up all pairs similarity search. In *WWW*, 2007.

[2] A. Z. Broder, M. Charikar, A. M. Frieze, and M. Mitzenmacher. Min-wise independent permutations (extended abstract). In *STOC '98*, pages 327–336, New York, NY, USA, 1998. ACM.

[3] A. Z. Broder, S. C. Glassman, M. S. Manasse, and G. Zweig. Syntactic clustering of the web. In *WWW*, 1997.

[4] M. S. Charikar. Similarity estimation techniques from rounding algorithms. In *STOC '02*, 2002.

[5] M. Datar, N. Immorlica, P. Indyk, and V. Mirrokni. Locality-sensitive hashing scheme based on p-stable distributions. In *SOCG*, pages 253–262. ACM, 2004.

[6] W. B. Frakes and R. Baeza-Yates. Information retrieval: data structures and algorithms. 1992.

[7] J. Frey. Fixed-width sequential confidence intervals for a proportion. *The American Statistician*, 64(3), 2010.

[8] A. Gionis, P. Indyk, and R. Motwani. Similarity search in high dimensions via hashing. In *VLDB*, 1999.

[9] M. Girshick, F. Mosteller, and L. Savage. Unbiased estimates for certain binomial sampling problems with applications. In *Selected Papers of Frederick Mosteller*, pages 57–68. Springer, 2006.

[10] M. Henzinger. Finding near-duplicate web pages: a large-scale evaluation of algorithms. In *SIGIR*, 2006.

[11] P. Indyk and R. Motwani. Approximate nearest neighbors: towards removing the curse of dimensionality. In *STOC*, 1998.

[12] B. Kulis and K. Grauman. Kernelized locality-sensitive hashing. *Pattern Analysis and Machine Intelligence, IEEE Transactions on*, 34(6):1092–1104, 2012.

[13] H. Kwak, C. Lee, H. Park, and S. Moon. What is Twitter, a social network or a news media? In *WWW*, 2010.

[14] D. Lewis, Y. Yang, T. Rose, and F. Li. Rcv1: A new benchmark collection for text categorization research. *JMLR*, 5:361–397, 2004.

[15] D. Liben-Nowell and J. Kleinberg. The link-prediction problem for social networks. *J. Am. Soc. Inf. Sci. Technol.*, 58:1019–1031, May 2007.

[16] A. Mislove, M. Marcon, K. P. Gummadi, P. Druschel, and B. Bhattacharjee. Measurement and Analysis of Online Social Networks. In *IMC*, 2007.

[17] D. Ravichandran, P. Pantel, and E. Hovy. Randomized algorithms and nlp: using locality sensitive hash function for high speed noun clustering. In *ACL*, 2005.

[18] J. A. Rice. *Mathematical statistics and data analysis.* Cengage Learning, 2007.

[19] V. Satuluri and S. Parthasarathy. Bayesian locality sensitive hashing for fast similarity search. *Proceedings of the VLDB Endowment*, 5(5):430–441, 2012.

[20] A. Wald. *Sequential analysis.* Courier Corporation, 1973.

[21] C. Xiao, W. Wang, X. Lin, J. X. Yu, and G. Wang. Efficient similarity joins for near duplicate detection. *ACM Transactions on Database systems*, 2011.

[22] X. Zhu and A. Goldberg. Introduction to semi-supervised learning. *Synthesis Lectures on Artificial Intelligence and Machine Learning*, 3(1):1–130, 2009.

Opinion Spam Detection in Web Forum: A Real Case Study

Yu-Ren Chen and Hsin-Hsi Chen
Department of Computer Science and Information Engineering, National Taiwan University
No. 1, Sec. 4, Roosevelt Road, Taipei, 10617 Taiwan
+886-2-33664888ext311
chenaren@gmail.com; hhchen@ntu.edu.tw

ABSTRACT

Opinion spamming refers to the illegal marketing practice which involves delivering commercially advantageous opinions as regular users. In this paper, we conduct a real case study based on a set of internal records of opinion spams leaked from a shady marketing campaign. We explore the characteristics of opinion spams and spammers in a web forum to obtain some insights, including subtlety property of opinion spams, spam post ratio, spammer accounts, first post and replies, submission time of posts, activeness of threads, and collusion among spammers. Then we present features that could be potentially helpful in detecting spam opinions in threads. The results of spam detection on first posts show: (1) spam first posts put more focus on certain topics such as the user experiences' on the promoted items, (2) spam first posts generally use more words and pictures to showcase the promoted items in an attempt to impress people, (3) spam first posts tend to be submitted during work time, and (4) the threads that spam first posts initiate are more active to be placed at striking positions. The spam detection on replies is more challenging. Besides lower spam ratio and less content, replies even do not mention the promoted items. Their major intention is to keep the discussion in a thread alive to attract more attention on it. Submission time of replies, thread activeness, position of replies, and spamicity of first post are more useful than content-based features in spam detection on replies.

Categories and Subject Descriptors

H.3.3 [INFORMATION STORAGE AND RETRIEVAL]: Information Search and Retrieval –*Information filtering.*

General Terms

Algorithms, Design, Experimentation, Human Factors.

Keywords

Fake Web Review; Opinion Spam Detection; Web Forum.

1. INTRODUCTION

Mining opinions from heterogeneous resources attract much attention due to their practical applications in various domains. More and more customers refer to opinions spreading on the web before purchasing items, reserving hotel rooms, and so on. To affect customers' buying decisions, fake opinions are generated for purpose to promote special targets and/or denounce their competitors. How to filter out untrustful information becomes an important issue in opinion mining.

WWW 2015, May 18–22, 2015, Florence, Italy.
ACM 978-1-4503-3469-3/15/05.
http://dx.doi.org/10.1145/2736277.2741085

To prepare datasets for the study of opinion spam detection is indispensable. However, it is more difficult than the preparation of the datasets for the other types of spam detection tasks such as email spams and web spams due to the subtlety nature of opinion spams. Crowdsourcing is introduced to annotate opinion spams. The major problem is the context cannot be fully rebuilt for the workers to make correct annotations.

In this paper, we study a real case: Samsung probed in Taiwan over 'fake web reviews', reported by BBC on 16 April 2013 [1]. This case happened in *Mobile01*, a web forum in Taiwan, which mainly features discussion about mobile phones, hand-held devices, and other consumer electronics. In April 2013, a poster submitted a thread in which several confidential documents of a covert marketing campaign that had been conducted under the table were disclosed. The campaign instructed hired writers and designated employees to post disingenuous comments on some web forums including *Mobile01*. This revelation created a big stir at that time, since it was the first time such strong evidence supporting what most folks had considered as a "conspiracy theory" came to light.

Generally speaking, web forums provide platforms for people with similar interests to interact and share experiences with each other. Since people normally believe posts on legit forums to be based on genuine personal opinion and experience, it is considered unethical to use them to promote things for personal gain without disclaimer, and take advantage of the inherent mutual trust between forum users. As a matter of fact, such marketing malpractice violated the fair trade law, and the company in charge of the campaign was fined by the *Fair Trade Commission* (*FTC*) in Taiwan, after the investigation was completed.

The confidential documents, along with relevant articles describing the campaign, are listed on Taiwansamsungleaks.[2] In this campaign, hired posters were asked to promote a certain brand and denounce its rivals on web forums such as *Mobile01*, while disguised as normal consumers. Among the disclosed documents, there are two spreadsheets that appear to be internally-kept records of the spam posts incurred by the

[1] http://www.bbc.com/news/technology-22166606.
[2] http://taiwansamsungleaks.org/.

campaign from 2011 to 2012. Each row in these spreadsheets is a record of an incentivized forum post and consists of the poster's username, the time of posting, the url to the post, the product that was discussed in the post, and some other details.

In this research, we leverage the spreadsheets to generate ground truth of deceptive forum spams. To the best of our knowledge, this is the first real case study of opinion spam detection in web forum. The real spammers' behaviors in a thread consisting of first post and replies are investigated. This paper is organized as follows. Section 2 surveys the related work of opinion spam detection. Section 3 gives a detail description of the real dataset. Section 4 analyzes the dataset from various perspectives. Section 5 presents spam opinion detection in first post and replies in threads. Section 6 concludes the remarks and shows some future works.

2. RELATED WORK

2.1 Opinion Spam

Spam, whose definitions usually center on the concept of *unsolicited message* [8], has been bothering Internet users for a long time. Email spam is one of the most prevalent types of spams that could be dated back to long ago [1]. Web spam is another form of spams whose objective is to game the ranking algorithm of a search engine in order to get an undeserved high ranking [5]. As social media gained its popularity in recent years, social network spam came along [15]. One of the variants involves throwaway accounts created in batch to somehow bait regular users to clicks certain link for personal gain.

Opinion spam is different from the above types of spams from various perspectives. One of the most prominent differences is that opinion spam is arguably the most "subtle" kind of spams. This is because it is not only completely ineffective, but also very harmful to the reputation of the target that it promotes, when it gets caught. Therefore, opinion spammers would generally try their best to disguise their opinion spams as genuine opinions. Carefully-written opinion spams have caused great challenges in manually identifying the spams and annotating the ground truth, which is in concert with the finding that human are poor judge of deception [20]. Ott et al. [17] reported a very low annotator agreement score when annotating the opinion spams from a review corpus. In contrast, most of the email spams, web spams, or social network spams are fairly easy to spot by an experienced user of the respective platform.

One of the earliest researches on opinion spam is Jindal and Liu [10]. They attempt to detect fake product reviews on *Amazon.* Since then, this topic has been drawing increasing attention. Jindal et al. [11], Lim et al. [14], Mukherjee et al. [16], Wang et al. [21] and Xie et al. [22], are some of the researches.

2.2 Targets of Detection

The task of opinion spam detection can be seen as a binary classification problem. A detection model aims at detecting whether a given instance is a spammy or not. Naturally, an instance would be a post. Spam and non-spam post would be the two classes. Alternatively, an instance could be a user account, where spammer and non-spammers would be the classes. In this paper, we attempt to deal with the former type of targets in web forum with a real case study.

In spam post detection, the goal of a detection model is to identify whether a forum post, a product review, a store review, etc. is a spam post. Many of the previous researches on opinion spam aimed at detecting spam reviews, which can be seen as a type of post [7, 10, 11, 17]. Nonetheless, even if the target of detection is spam, we can still utilize features derived from information about the corresponding spammers, and vice versa.

Lim et al. [14] and Wang et al. [21] are two of the previous researches that focused on identifying spammers, while Mukherjee et al. [16] considered a variation by making groups of spammers who worked together to write fake reviews as their detection target.

2.3 Features Used

A number of features have been proposed with some common supervised learning models such as *SVM* (*Support Vector Machine*), or alternatively, in some ad-hoc models designed for the specific purpose. Most of these features fall into two categories: the ones derived from the textual contents of opinion spams, and the ones not directly related to them.

For the features derived from textual contents, Jindal and Liu [10] counted the percentage of opinion-bearing words, brand name mentions, numerals, capitals, etc. Mukherjee et al. [16] computed content similarity between reviews to examine if there are duplicate or near-duplicate reviews, which are suspicious of being spam reviews. Ott et al. [17] used bag-of-n-grams and slightly improved the performance with psychologically meaningful dimensions in *LIWC* [19]. Harris [7] took cues such as word diversity, proportion of first person pronouns and mention of brand names. Feng et al. [3] went a step further by adopting deep syntactic features, which were derived from the production rules involved in parsing the contents based on the PCFG, in addition to the basic bag-of-words.

Speaking of features not directly related to textual contents, Lim et al. [14] and Feng et al. [3] both made extensive use of various characteristics of user rating patterns on *Amazon.* Mukherjee et al. [16] derived features from bursts in the amount of reviews, how early the reviews was post, and rating deviation, with respect to either groups or individuals. Wang et al. [21] iteratively computed the trustiness of reviewers, honesty of reviews and reliability of stores based on a graph model which utilized non-content-centric features such as average rating and number of reviews.

2.4 Ground Truth Acquisition

One of the major obstacles in studies of opinion spam is the difficulty in acquiring ground truth, since spammers try their best to keep it secret, and manual annotation is ineffective because of the subtlety nature of opinion spam mentioned in Section 2.1.

A lot of efforts had been put into obtaining ground truth in studies of opinion spam. Jindal and Liu [10] assumed near-duplicate reviews were likely to be spam and followed this heuristic to build an annotated dataset. More recently, collective annotations using crowdsourcing platform like *Amazon Mechanical Turk* had become a popular approach. Gokhman et al. [4] discussed various techniques of obtaining ground truth in studies of deception, and argued that realistic deceptive contents could be generated from crowdsourcing, if the context of deception in practice is replicated on the crowdsourcing platform. On the other hand, it is ineffective to annotate existing deceptive contents. In fact, one of the quality indicators of fabricated opinion spams is that they should not be recognizable by crowdsourced annotations. Ott et al. [17] scraped truthful opinions from *TripAdvisor* and synthesized deceptive opinion with the help of *Amazon Mechanical Turk*.

Thus far, most of the previous researches on opinion spams adopted some sort of approximations of the actual ground truth. On the contrary, we study a real case in this paper. We extract ground truth from the confidential records leaked directly from a covert advertising campaign.[3] The Fair Trade Commission (FTC) in Taiwan, the central competent authority in charge of competition policy and Fair Trade Act in Taiwan, announced a decision on October 31, 2013 based on the leaked information and other documents, "the Samsung Taiwan, OpenTide Taiwan, and Sales & Profit International Co. concealed their identity and pretended to be regular private citizens to market their products on the Internet by making comparisons with and comments on the products of other enterprises. The deceptive conduct was able to affect trading order in violation of Article 24 of the Fair Trade Act. In addition to ordering the three companies to immediately cease the unlawful act, the FTC also imposed on them administrative fines of NT$10 million, NT$3 million and NT$50,000 respectively."[4]

3. DATASET

3.1 Leaked Spreadsheets

The leaked spreadsheets *HHP-2011.xlsx* and *HHP-2012.xlsx* keep the histories of the opinion spam posts made in 2011 and 2012, respectively. Several discussion platforms were spammed, but for simplicity, we consider only the opinion spams and the corresponding spammers on *Mobile01*, which make up the majority of the records contained in the spreadsheets.

From the spreadsheets, urls to the spam posts and usernames of the spammers[5] are extracted. Some typos and inconsistent ways of presenting the usernames are manually checked and fixed. Furthermore, urls linked to pages on *Mobile01* might appear in different forms. To reliably match the posts we scraped later, a 3-tuple (*fid*, *thid*, *pnum*) are extracted from each url, where *fid*, *thid* and *pnum* refers to forum id, thread id and page number, respectively. These 3-tuples serve as unique identifiers of a page in a thread on *Mobile01*.

Since we regard a user who has ever posted a spam post as a spammer, any account contained in the spreadsheets is considered to be spammer. Thereafter, we have a set of 2-tuples, each consisting of a spammer's username and a nested 3-tuples identifier leading to the page containing one or more spamming posts of the spammer.

3.2 Mobile01 Corpus

A large portion of past related studies used dataset scraped from product or store review websites such as *Amazon* or *TripAdvisor*, whereas our corpus is scraped from a **web forum**. Another difference is that the contents on *Mobile01* are mostly written in Traditional Chinese, with little bit of English phrases scattered around, rather than predominantly written in English as in previously used corpora.

Since more than 70% of the recorded spams were submitted to the *Samsung* (*Android*) board on *Mobile01*, we decide to focus our analysis on this board. We fetched all the threads along with the contained posts accessible by a regular member on the *Samsung* (*Android*) board on May, 2014. In addition, profiles of users who have ever posted in this board are also retrieved.

Table 1 lists the statistics of POSTS, THREADS and PROFILES, which correspond to the post messages, the threads they belong, and the posters who post the messages. Total 632,234 messages belonging to 41,759 threads were posted by 58,531 posters. Of these, there are 300 spammers and 3,116 spam posts. Tables 2-4 show the attributes of a post, a thread, and a poster, respectively. Note that the data we scraped from *Mobile01* is the May-2014 version, while the spam activities we investigate happened during 2011 and 2012. Ideally, a snapshot at the end of the 2012 may suit our need best. When we collected the dataset, some posts could have been edited or removed. Besides, profiles could have evolved with time. That will affect if users still stay active. The dataset is available at http://nlg.csie.ntu.edu.tw/m01-corpus/.

Table 1. Statistics of *Mobile01* corpus

Table	Total Instances	Spammer/Spam
PROFILES	58,531	300
POSTS	632,234	3,116
THREADS	41,759	Non-applicable

Table 2. Attributes of POSTS

Attribute	Description
thid	id of the thread to which the post belong
time	submission time of the post
uid	id of the poster who made the post
uname	username of the poster
nfloor	position relative to other posts in the thread
pnum	page number on which the post is
content	structured content in *HTML*

Table 3. Attributes of THREADS

Attribute	Description
thid	id of the thread
fid	id of the forum (board) in which the thread is
title	title of the thread
pages	number of pages in the thread
clicks	number of clicks (views) on this thread
time	submission time of the thread (=first post time)

Table 4. Attributes of PROFILES

Attribute	Description
uid	id of the user
reg_time	time of registration on the site
login_time	last time the user logged in
n_threads	number of threads initialized by the user
n_eff_posts	number of effective posts
n_posts	number of all posts
n_replies	number of replies, i.e., n_posts - n_threads
score	karma given by other users to the threads
p_phone	proportion of posts made on the smart phone

[3] http://taiwansamsungleaks.org/.

[4] http://www.ftc.gov.tw/internet/english/doc/docDetail.aspx?uid=179&docid=13035

[5] Whenever the word **spammer** or **user** is used hereafter without further details, we are talking about **spammer account** or **user account**, respectively, since we cannot tell out who is the actual human poster behind a user account.

3.3 Product Information

Because the spams related to cell phones, we scrape product information of all cell phones and tablets of the top brands. People use a wide variety of aliases to refer to cell phone or tablets products on *Mobile01*. To be able to match as many product mentions as possible, we take unigrams and bigrams from the full name as the aliases. If the name contains Roman numerals, we convert them to the respective Arabic numbers.

Many products of the same brand share aliases. For example, people often use *Note* to refer to a *Samsung* product, but there are a dozen of *Samsung* products with such alias. Since we care about only the brand the product belongs to, we just deem it as a mention of an arbitrary *Samsung* product of the *Note* series.

3.4 Data Splitting

We split the posts into training set and test set for spam detection based on their temporal orders. Posts submitted between Jan 2011 and Dec 2011 are placed into training set, and those submitted between Jan 2012 and May 2012 are put into test set.

The posts in test set may be posted by the same user in training set. To avoid the possible effects of the writing style of the spammers on spam detection, we remove all the posts by user accounts whose posts are included in training set from the test set, and call the resulting set "test set*". As a result, there do not exist any posts submitted by the same user account between training set and test set*. Table 5 shows the statistics of training set, test set and test set* for spam detection.

Table 5. Training, test set and test set* for spam detection

	#spam posts	#all posts	spam ratio
training set	1,883	159,432	1.12%
test set	1,233	92,552	1.33%
test set*	414	32,932	1.26%

4. CORPUS ANALYSIS

4.1 Subtlety Property

One of the properties we observed is that most of the spam posts do not really look suspicious, which echoes the discussion in Section 2.1. Spammers usually deliver their opinions about brands in a subtle way. Some spam posts (mostly replies) do not even carry opinion about any brand. They may only keep the discussion alive to attract more attention to the specific topics of the thread that meet the goal of the campaign. Replying to a thread would bump it to the top place of a board, since threads are ordered by the time of the last reply on most web forums. In this paper, we still deem these spam posts as opinion spam, but we probably should come up with an appropriate name for such spam posts.

Figure 1 shows a real thread in Chinese. The first post, i.e., "#1: *can NDSL stylus be shared with GALAXY NOTE*", intended to initiate a discussion about a *Samsung* product. It does not contain any opinion about any brand. The subsequent posts translated in English as follows are replies to the thread initiated by spam post.

#5: *Who says girls must pretend to be cute! I prefer to buy GALAXY R!*

#42: *The best way to celebrate her birthday is to send her a SII and push her down the valley!*

#24: *Please sign in if you are eager to get Galaxy Nexus.*

#24: *Through i9100 lens, we share a little happiness of life.*

#7: *Do White SII + Pink SGP protector glass look good?*

These posts only serve the purpose of heating up the discussion or just keep it alive. Since the intended messages may already be delivered by the first post or some other replies in the thread, the spammers avoid stating any strong opinions about the brands directly to make these posts even less suspicious. Such carefully written spam posts may make the automatic detection very challenging, because the content-centric features could be ineffective.

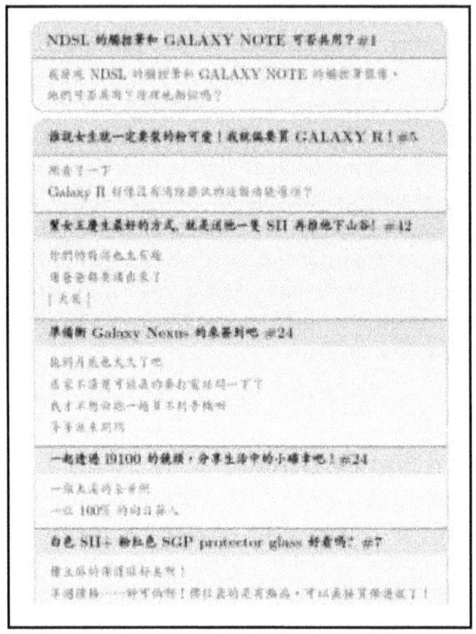

Figure 1. An example thread containing spam posts

4.2 Spam Post Ratio

Spammers are those posters who had submitted any spam post recorded in the leaked spreadsheets, as defined in Section 3.1. When we inspect the posts from the training set specified in Section 3.4, only about 33% of the posts by spammers are recorded as spam. Figure 2 shows the distribution of the spam post ratio among spammers. It demonstrates that a large number of spammers actually rarely spammed.

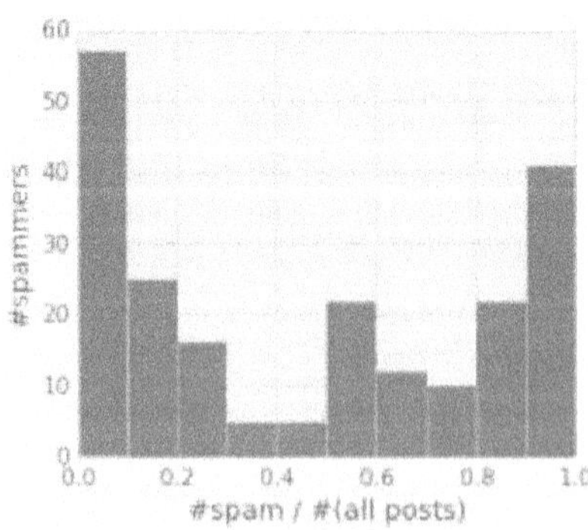

Figure 2. Distribution of the spam post ratios

4.3 Spammer Accounts

There are two possible spammer accounts in this dataset: reputable accounts and throwaway accounts. Figure 3 plots the spam post ratio vs. total number of threads made by the spammers.

We can see that most of the spammers with a high #spams/#posts ratio have initialized very few threads. It could be a clue that these are the throwaway accounts created for the sole purpose of spamming. On the other hand, accounts with a lower ratio show a larger variance in #threads. Some of them are likely to be reputable posters who usually make lots of threads.

Throwaway accounts are often created in mass within a short period of time, as it takes much more effort and patience to spread out the daunting task of registering throwaway accounts, especially if a large number of them are needed. To test if this postulation is applicable in our dataset, we adopt a simple heuristic to categorize accounts initiating less than 35 threads as throwaway accounts, and reputable accounts otherwise. Figure 4 shows the number of spammer accounts registered within each two weeks after 2009.

Indeed, there are three short periods in which large numbers of throwaway spammer accounts were registered, i.e., January 2010, April 2011 and October 2011. On the other hand, registration time for reputable accounts spreads quite evenly.

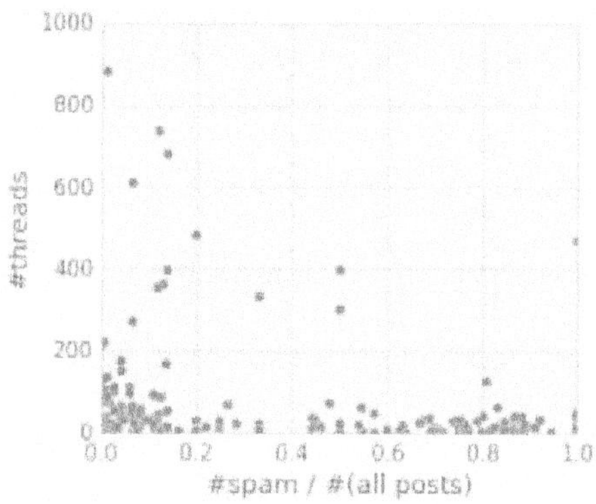

Figure 3. Spam posts ratio vs. number of threads

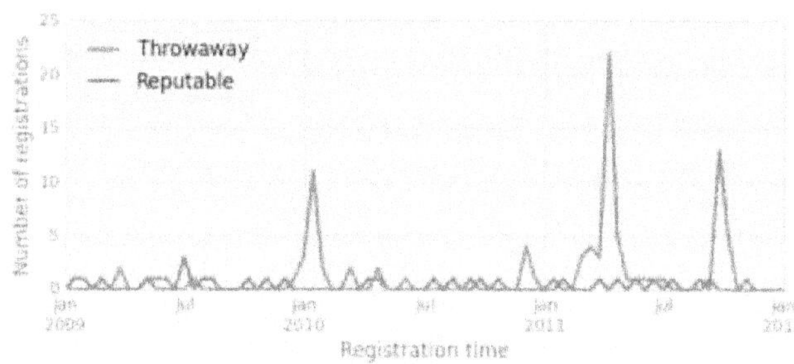

Figure 4. Number of spam accounts created in each 2 weeks

4.4 First Post vs. Replies

In the online web forums, first post, also known as original post, in a thread is written by the user submitting the thread. First posts are relatively richer in content as they serve the critical role in initializing a discussion on a specific topic. On the other hand, replies are often quite concise, and sometimes do not carry any opinion.

First posts and replies in threads display different characteristics in many aspects. Figure 5 shows that first posts tend to contain more characters. Moreover, at least one image is embedded in 19.2% of first posts, but only in 4.1% of replies.

Table 6 shows the spam counts and proportions for first posts and replies in training set. The ratio of spams in first posts is as high as 4.99%. In other words, for every 20 threads in the training set, one of them is created for covert marketing! In contrast, %spam is much lower for replies, i.e., 0.90%.

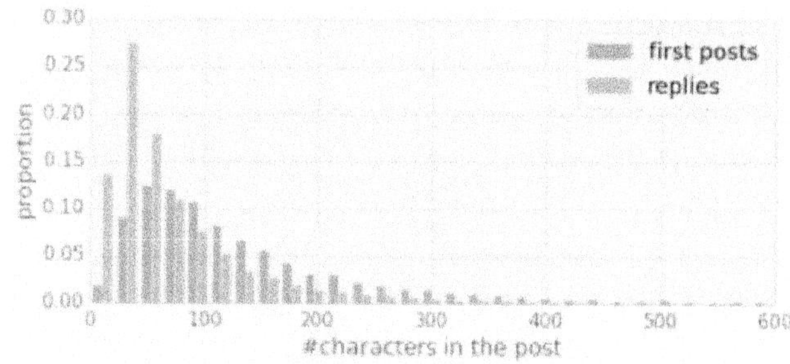

Figure 5. #Characters in first posts and replies

Table 6. Spams in first posts and replies

Type	#posts	#spams	%spams
First posts	10,951	546	4.99%
Replies	148,481	1,337	0.90%
All posts	159,432	1,883	1.18%

4.5 Submission Time of Posts

Because making spam posts is a job rather than a leisure activity for spammers, we postulate that a higher percentage of spam posts would be submitted during work time, compared to non-spam posts.

To verify our postulation, we plot the distribution of submission time of spam and non-spam. In Figure 6, the submission time of non-spam posts distributes pretty evenly over each day of week, whereas the amount of spam posts drops drastically on Saturday, and has a moderate decrease on Sunday. In Figure 7, we can observe that more spam posts are submitted during work hour, especially between 10 a.m. and 11 a.m., while non-spam posts are more often made during the spare hours. Hence, we see there is more or less a trend that spam posts are more often made during work time than leisure time, in comparison with non-spam posts.

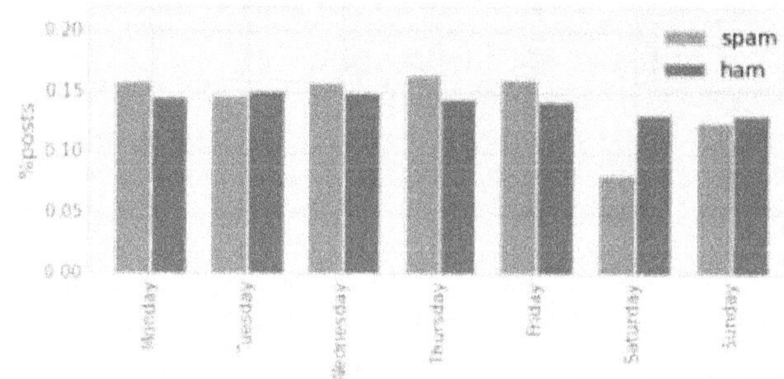

Figure 6. Proportion of spams submitted throughout a week

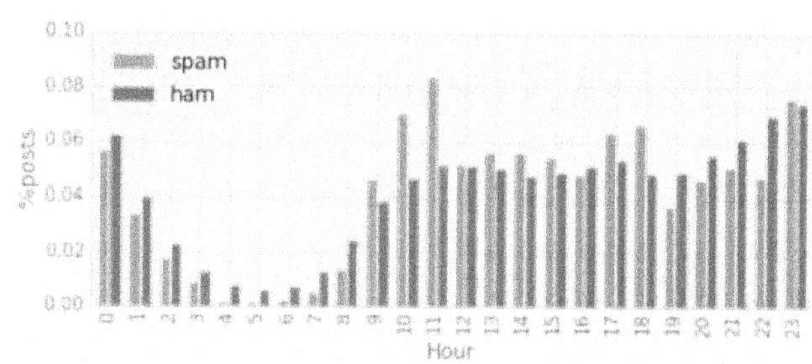

Figure 7. Proportion of spams submitted throughout a day

4.6 Activeness of Threads

The threads started by spam first posts are expected to be more active, since those are written to draw attention and exposure, while non-spam threads may or may not be created with such intent in mind.

One intuitive way to measure the activeness of a thread would be counting the total number of posts in the thread, which is equal to 1 (first post) + #replies. Figure 8 plots the numbers of posts in spam and non-spam threads. Clearly, spam threads tend to attract more replies, which could be either spam replies or non-spam replies.

Another way to measure the activeness of a thread is the number of clicks. Figure 9 shows that spam threads tend to get more clicks in comparison with normal threads.

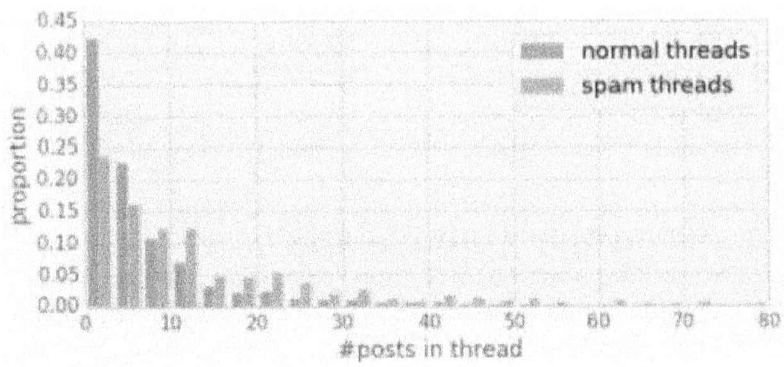

Figure 8. #posts in spam threads vs. normal threads

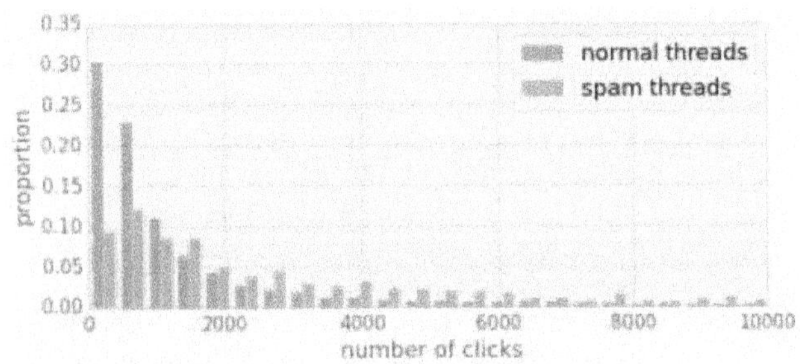

Figure 9. #clicks in spam threads vs. normal threads

4.7 Collusion among Spammers

Looking into the leaked spreadsheets, we note that a few threads contain multiple spam posts submitted by different accounts. It may be an indication of collusion going on among multiple spammers. These spammers would usually express similar opinions in the same thread to reinforce the credibility, or it could be just a result of multiple spammers bumping the same thread in an attempt to attract more attention to it.

Sometimes, it could be just the same person submitting posts with different spammer accounts in a thread, but it can still be regarded as collusion between multiple spammer accounts on the surface. In Figure 10, we could observe that there are threads containing 2 or more spam posts. In fact, 67% of the spam posts occur in threads containing at least 2 spam posts.

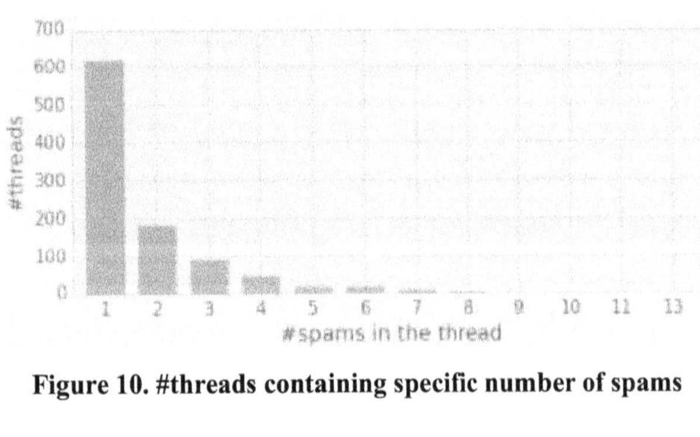

Figure 10. #threads containing specific number of spams

5. SPAM DETECTION

5.1 Models for First Post

At first, we will train a detection model specifically for first posts in thread. Thus we only use first posts from the training set and test set of posts introduced in Section 3.4. Counts and ratios of spam for first posts are listed in Table 7 for reference. Due to the low ratio of spam posts in training set, we randomly remove 60% of the non-spam posts from training set beforehand.

Table 7. Training and test set for spam detection for first posts

	#spam posts	#all posts	spam ratio
training set	546	10,951	4.99%
test set	208	5,870	3.54%
test set*	70	3,035	2.30%

In our dataset, spam posts ratio is quite low. Therefore, accuracy is not a good metric since it is dominated by the majority non-spam class. High precision on the spam class is desired because we do not want to falsely incriminate an innocent forum post as a spam; high recall on the spam class is also desired because we would like to find as many opinion spams as possible. Depending on the application, precision could be more important than recall, or vice versa. For instance, in an application where the detection system is used in an initial filtering stage narrowing down the set of suspicious posts for a later stage of manual classification, high recall might be preferred since misclassifying a spam post as normal one completely rules out the possibility of identifying the instance, while identifying a normal post as spam could still be corrected in the later stage of the pipeline. Because no particular application is aimed at, we do not have a prior preference on either precision or recall. Therefore, our evaluation metric would be the harmonic mean of precision and recall, also known as F-measure.

We adopt *Scikit-Learn* library [18] and explore various learning algorithms such as *Logistic Regression*, *SVM with linear kernel*, *SVM with RBF kernel*, *SVMperf*, etc. Most of the time, *SVM with RBF kernel* seems to win out by a non-negligible margin. *SVMperf* claims to somehow directly optimize the F-measure [12], but the F-measure in our experiments is not better than that using *SVM with RBF kernel*, Besides, *SVMperf* takes much longer time to train a model. Therefore, we decide to stick with *SVM with RBF kernel* from *Scikit-Learn*, which is actually a *Python* wrapper for the widely-used LibSVM [2], to conduct our experiments. As suggested in Hsu et al. [9], we scale each feature to zero mean and unit variance before feeding it to *SVM.*

There are two primary hyperparameters C and γ to be tuned in *SVM with RBF kernel*. For this purpose, whenever a model is to be learned, we first run 5-fold cross-validation multiple times on the training set to facilitate a grid search on C and γ with F-measure as the metric to optimize. The grid to search is represented below.

$$(C,\gamma) \in \{10^x \mid -3 \le x \le 3, x \in \mathbb{Z}\} \times \{10^y \mid -5 \le y \le 2, y \in \mathbb{Z}\}$$

Various feture combinations were explored in the experiments. Tables 8 and 9 summarize the experimental results using test set and test set*, respectively. Precision (**P**), Recall (**R**), and F-measuere (**F1**) are listed. The detail of each model will be discussed in the following sections.

Table 8. Spam detection for first post using test set

Model	P	R	F1
M1: random baseline	0.0343	0.4904	0.0642
M2: content bag-of-words	0.6289	0.4808	0.5450
M3: content + title bag-of-words	0.5912	0.5144	0.5501
M4: M3+content characteristics	0.7305	0.4952	0.5897
M5: M4+time+thread	**0.7237**	**0.5288**	**0.6111**
M6: M5+sentiment on brands	0.7097	0.5288	0.6061

Table 9. Spam detection for first post using test set*

Model	P	R	F1
M1: random baseline	0.0252	0.5571	0.0482
M2: content bag-of-words	0.5000	0.5143	0.5070
M3: content + title bag-of-words	0.5616	0.5857	0.5734
M4: M3+content characteristics	0.6491	0.5286	0.6032
M5: M4+time+activeness	**0.6667**	**0.5714**	**0.6154**
M6: M5+sentiment on brands	0.6557	0.5714	0.6107

5.1.1 Random Baseline

As an absolute baseline, the model M1 predicts whether a first post is spam based on the result of flipping a fair coin. As expected, the precision is about equal to ratio of the spams, which is 0.0354 and 0.0230 on test set and test set*, respectively. The recall is around 0.50, which reflects that fact that there is a half chance we correctly identify a spam as such by flipping a fair coin.

5.1.2 Bag-of-Words

After Chinese word segmentation on the HTML-stripped cleansed content from each post with *Jieba* (https://github.com/fxsjy/jieba), we count the occurrence of each word in training set, and construct a vocabulary. Next, rare words with less than 5 occurrences are removed from the vocabulary, since these would be the sparse bag-of-words features and might cause overfitting. On the other hand, words appearing in over 30% of the posts are also removed, as these are likely to be stop words or the like. After the vocabulary is set up, we represent each post as a vector of occurrences of each word in the vocabulary, where the occurrences are normalized by the length of the post.

In bag-of-words, each word in the vocabulary corresponds to a feature. Since the high number of features could slow down the training process significantly and may cause overfitting, we apply randomized PCA [6] on the #posts×#words bag-of-words matrix to reduce the word dimension. The desired number of dimension to reduce with PCA is tuned by looking at the average F-measure from 5-fold cross-validation on the training set, as plotted in Figure 11.

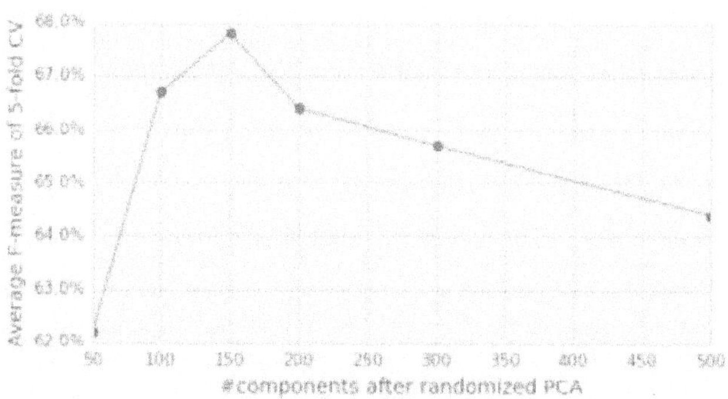

Figure 11. F-measures as #components in PCA changes

As shown in the plot, reducing to 50 components may cause too much information loss and thus deteriorating the average F-measure. On the other hand, too many components may cause some degree of overfitting which also worsens the performance. The average F-measure is the highest when the bag-of-words is reduced to 150 components, so we adopt it to train our model on the whole training set and see how it performs on test set.

Referring to M2 in Tables 8 and 9, the performance is surprisingly good. Our observation on subtlety of the spam posts in Section 4.1 gives us a hunch that the contents of the posts might not give strong clues about whether a post is spam, since the contents of spam posts are well-disguised. We are curious about what happens under the hood. To dive deeper into it, we would like to get the importance of each feature in order to observe what types of words are the decisive factors in the model predictions. However, for a non-linear model like *SVM with RBF kernel*, there is no simple way of computing importance of each feature. Nevertheless, by falling back to linear kernel, the model suffers around 10% performance loss in F-measure on test set, but we are able to see the relative importance of each word by looking at the coefficients after inverse-transformed with PCA.

Figure 12 is a word cloud containing the words with the highest coefficients, that is, words that are the strongest spam indicators, where the font size of a word is positively correlated with its weight. Figure 13 shows word cloud for words with the lowest weights, that is, words that are the strongest non-spam posts indicators. We can observe the distinctive difference between the two word clouds at the first glance. The first one is mainly about Samsung's top products (*galaxy*, *nexus*, *note*, *sii*) and the user experiences in terms of words such as "體驗" (experience), "看到" (see), and "覺得" (feel), while focusing on the multimedia aspect such as "照片" (photo), "拍照" (photograph), and "影片" (movie). On the other hand, the second word cloud is more about seeking help with words "問題" (problem), "解決" (solve), and "無法" (unable), and involves more polite words such as "謝謝" (thanks), "大大" (big brother and big sister), "and "小弟" (I) and technicalities such as rom, "開機" (boot), and "設定" (set up).

Figure 12. Words with the highest weights

Figure 13. Words with the lowest weights

The previous bags-of-word features were based on only contents of the posts. There is also much information lying in the titles of the threads, so we create another 50 dimension-reduced bags-of-word features based on the titles, and combine these with the content parts to yield 200 features. We prefer not to have them mixed together because title and content may have distinct groups of spam keywords.

M3 in Tables 8 and 9 shows that the addition of title bag-of-words improves F-measure further. The dimension-reduced bags-of-word features turned out to be surprisingly helpful. The model is able to accomplish over 0.55 in F-measure while the ratio of spam is only around 3% on the test sets for first posts. Compared to the random baseline, it boosts the F-measure by as much as 0.45, which implies that the contents of posts actually give some strong clues about whether a first post is spam. Although each spam post looks rather unsuspicious on its own, spam posts put more emphasis on certain topics, in comparison with non-spam posts. Our model trained with bag-of-words features is able to exploit this distinction.

5.1.3 Content Characteristics

A set of features derived from basic characteristics of the contents of the post is introduced in Table 10. In regard to the naming of these features, the *n_* prefix means *number of*, while the *p_* prefix means *proportion of*, i.e., divided by the number of characters in the post. Most features are self-explanatory.

Table 10. Description of content characteristics

Attribute	Description
n_all	number of characters used in the post
n_words	number of words in the post
n_lines	number of lines in the post
n_hyperlinks	number of hyperlinks in the post
n_img	number of images added to the post
n_emoticon	number of emoticons used in the post
n_quote	number of quotations from previous posts
p_digit	proportion of digits
p_english	proportion of English characters
p_punct	proportion of punctuation characters
p_special	proportion of non-alphanumeric characters
p_wspace	proportion of white space characters
p_immediacy	proportion of first person pronouns
p_ntusd_pos	proportion of positive words in *NTUSD*
p_ntusd_neg	proportion of negative words in *NTUSD*
p_emoticon_pos	proportion of positive emoticons
p_emoticon_neg	proportion of negative emoticons

We compute symmetric KL divergence to find out which features exhibit the most different distributions between spams and hams. The formula of symmetric KL divergence is defined as follows.

$$D_{KL}(P_{spam}(f)\|Q_{ham}(f)) + D_{KL}(Q_{ham}(f)\|P_{spam}(f))$$

where P_{spam} and Q_{ham} are the distributions of the features under all spam and all non-spam first posts, respectively. The higher the symmetric KL divergence is, the more different the two distributions are. That makes the features more useful in discriminating between spam and non-spam first posts.

Figure 14 shows symmetric KL divergence between spams and hams. The top four features that distinguish spam and non-spam first posts best are *n_all*, *n_imgs*, *n_words* and *n_lines*, which are all related to the quantity of content. This is not surprising because many of the spam first posts are essentially advertisements in disguise, e.g., unboxing posts and positive experience with *Samsung* product posts, they would generally use lots of words and pictures to showcase *Samsung* products in an attempt to impress people.

On top of the bag-of-words features, we add these 17 numerical features that characterize the contents of the first posts. The resulting performance is shown in M4 in Tables 8 and 9. F-measure increases by about 0.03 on both test set and test set*, so these features do provide extra information that helps detect spam first posts.

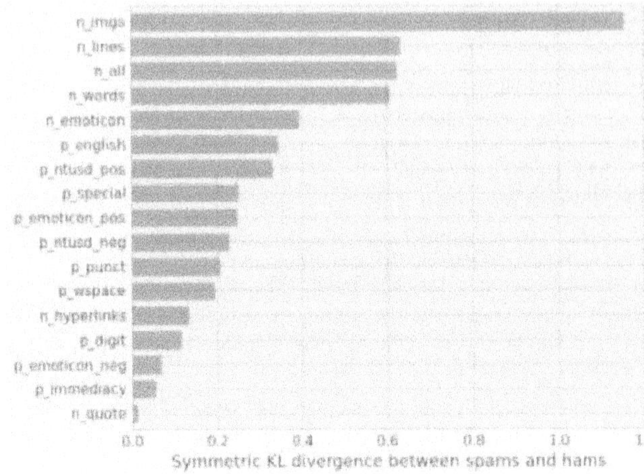

Figure 14. Content characteristics features

5.1.4 Submission Time and Thread Activeness

Besides content-centric features, we also incorporate some non-content-centric features. As discussed in Section 4.5, spam posts have a tendency of being submitted more often during work time. To make use of this observation, we add a binary feature for each hour in a day and each day in a week, in total 24+7=31 new features. If the first post was submitted during the hour or the day a feature corresponds to, then its value is 1; otherwise it is 0.

Moreover, we use number of posts in the thread started by the first post as another feature, which can serve as a measure of the activeness of the thread, as discussed in Section 4.6. Tables 8 and 9 show that incorporating these non-content-centric features (i.e., M5) further improves the F-measure on both test set and test set*.

5.1.5 Sentiment Scores toward the Brands

The main objective of the covert marketing campaign is to promote a certain brand and sometimes denounce its competitor's brands in order to give it an unfair edge. Hence, we expect spam posts to show a positive attitude when it comes to *Samsung*, and possibly a negative attitude toward the competitors. We devise a simple method to capture the sentiment toward brands in posts. Basically, we just add up the polarity of sentiment words in NTU sentiment dictionary (*NTUSD*) [13] and emoticons near mention of a brand or a product.

M6 in Tables 8 and 9 shows that the F-measure of the approach with the sentiment scores toward brands dropped a little on both test set and test set*. The possible reasons why the polarity of our estimated sentiment score fails to reflect the true opinion polarity are listed as follows. First, as discussed in Sections 2.1 and 4.1, the spam posts are carefully written to subtly deliver the messages, so they might avoid using sentiment words to some degree. Second, *NTUSD* has been released for some years, while the community on *Mobile01* may give some words new meanings, and even invent new words in their subculture. For example, the following post "orz 只能說 S2 真的是怪物" (orz We can only say S2 is really a monster) used negative emoticon such as orz, and word like 怪物 (monster) to compliment a *Samsung* product in a dramatic manner. Third, sarcasm is heavily used on *Mobile01*. The following is a first post in Chinese. The corresponding English translation is also shown. In this example, *Note* and *XL* are products of *Samsung* and *HTC*, respectively. They are competitors in cell phone domains.

我比較推薦 Note
(*I comparatively recommend Note*)
因為 htc 好像把 XL 當精品賣..哈
(*Because htc seems to sell XL as boutique .. Ha*)
現在單核心的手機還敢賣那麼貴的..而且還很多人讚賞
(*Now single-core phone is sold so expensive bravely.. and a lot of people are appreciated*)
真的只有 HTC
(*Really only HTC*)
XL 真的不錯啦
(*XL is really good*)

5.2 Models for Replies

Following the discussion for first posts, we consider spam detection for replies. In the experimental setup, we remove all the replies in a thread containing any posts (first post and replies) in the training set from the test set in Table 5. Table 11 shows the spam counts and ratios for replies. The ratio of spam posts for replies is even lower than that for first posts. Thus, we randomly remove 90% of the non-spam post for downsampling. Tables 12 and 13 list the experimental results of different models with test set and test set*. The detail will be discussed in the following sections.

Table 11. Training and test set for spam detection for replies

	#spam posts	#all posts	spam ratio
training set	1,337	148,841	0.90%
test set	1,020	67,025	1.52%
test set*	343	25,165	1.36%

Table 12. Spam detection for replies using test set

Model	P	R	F1
M1: random baseline	0.0147	0.4833	0.0285
M2: content bag-of-words	0.1731	0.2451	0.2029
M3: content + title bag-of-words	0.1560	0.2647	0.1963
M4: M3+content characteristics	0.1770	0.2520	0.2079
M5: M4+time+activeness+position	0.1966	0.3098	0.2406
M6: M5+spamicity of the first post	0.2559	0.2961	0.2745

Table 13. Spam detection for replies using test set*

Model	P	R	F1
M1: random baseline	0.0138	0.5015	0.0268
M2: content bag-of-words	0.1185	0.1983	0.1483
M3: content + title bag-of-words	0.1028	0.2216	0.1405
M4: M3+content characteristics	0.1232	0.1983	0.1520
M5: M4+time+activeness+position	0.1465	0.2507	0.1849
M6: M5+spamicity of the first post	0.2110	0.2682	0.2362

5.2.1 Random Baseline

The performance of random baseline for replies, i.e., M1, is worse in comparison with the random baseline for first posts. It reflects the fact that spam ratio is much lower for replies, as observed in Section 4.4.

5.2.2 Bag-of-Words

We repeat the procedure in Section 5.1.2. The optimal number of dimensions to reduce the bag-of-words features is 250, according to the F-measure of 5-fold cross-validation. The evaluation result shown in M2 in Tables 12 and 13 does not looks as nice as bag-of-words for first posts. Besides, the performance on test set is significantly better than that on test set*, so the writing style of the users might partially contribute to the F-measure on test set.

We explain such discrepancy between the performance with bag-of-words features for first posts and for replies as follows. In addition to the fact that spam ratio is lower and content is less for replies, as observed in Section 4.4, many of the spam replies are the vacuous ones with the sole intention of keeping the discussion in the thread alive to attract more attention to the thread, which is probably started by a spam first post, as mentioned in Section 4.1. They are concise and contain little opinion on the brands, so it would be very difficult to distinguish them from non-spam posts. On the other hand, because first posts are the posts that initiate the threads, it cannot be used for such "keeping a thread alive" purpose obviously. In this case, adding title bag-of-words features shown in M3 in Tables 12 and 13 does not help. It is probably due to the fact that title is per thread (also per first post), rather than per reply. A title is shared by all the replies in the thread.

5.2.3 Content Characteristics

As in Section 5.1.3, we compute the symmetric KL divergence of the content characteristics features for replies to find out which of them are the most useful. Figure 15 shows the content characteristics features. Interestingly, replies seem to use more emoticons in general. Spam replies often have either positive or negative attitude explicitly expressed to side with the previous "pro-Samsung" posts (first post in the thread or some previous replies, compared to non-spam replies). Tables 12 and 13 show the performance is slightly improved with the addition of content characteristics features, i.e., M4.

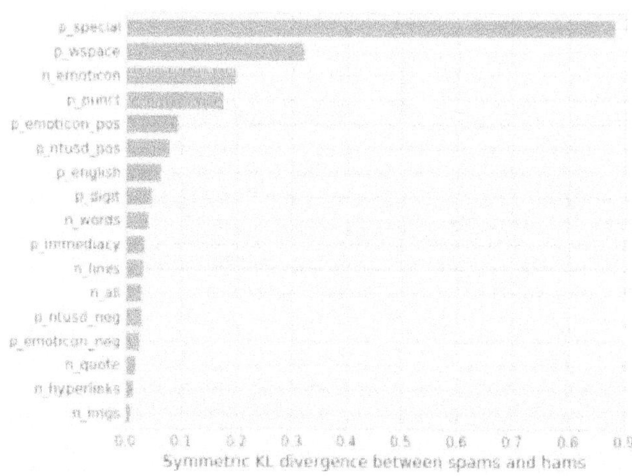

Figure 17. Content characteristics features

5.2.4 Non-Content-Centric Features

As in Section 5.1.4, non-content-centric features indicating the hour/day of the submission time, and the number of posts in the thread in which the reply is, are added. Moreover, the two attributes about the position of a post (reply) in the thread, i.e., *nfloor* and *pnum*, as described in Table 2, are also incorporated as non-content-centric features. M5 in Tables 12 and 13 shows these non-content-centric features are quite helpful in spam detection for replies. F1 is increased 0.0327 and 0.0329 on the test set and test set*, respectively.

5.2.5 Spamicity of the First Post in the Thread

When a thread is started by a spam first post, we could envision more spam activities to follow (as spam replies to the thread), due to the collusion discussed in Section 4.7. To measure the spamicity of first post in the thread in which the reply occur, we leverage our best model for spam detection for first posts, i.e., M5 in Tables 8 and 9. We include its probabilistic prediction on the first post in the thread as an additional feature. M6 in Tables 12 and 13 show its effectiveness. F1 is further increased 0.0339 and 0.0513 on the test set and the test set*, respectively

6. CONCLUSION AND FUTURE WORKS

In this paper, we conduct a real case study of opinion spams with a dataset containing the "true" ground truth. We obtain decent results on opinion spam detection for first posts with features derived from the contents of first posts. Seemingly contradictory to the observation that spam posts are carefully written to avoid getting caught (Section 4.1), our investigation demonstrated that spam first posts tend to put more focus on certain topics that are not that suspicious per se (Section 5.1.2), and we also saw the unusually rich contents of spam first posts could also be a giveaway (Section 5.1.3). Non-content based features such as submission time and thread activeness are useful clues (Section 5.1.4). On the other hand, performance has more room for improvement for spam detection for replies. Spamicity of first post has significant effect on identifying spams from replies.

In our study, the sentiment postulation, i.e., spam posts might show certain attitudes toward their competitors, does not have clear effect. The coverage of sentiment dictionary and the uses of sarcasm are some of major reasons. How to successfully grasp sentiment score toward the brands need to be further investigated.

The interaction between forum posters is also interesting. In comparison to product reviews sites like *Amazon* or *TripAdvisor*, the activities of users on a web forum involve more interactions one another. It may be in an explicit form such as quoting a previous post directly or mentioning a poster's username, or in an implicit form that requires deep natural language understanding. The ways in which spammers interact with each other or with other posters may be worthy of studying to improve the performance of spam detection for replies.

Opinion spammer detection is another interesting task. On the one hand, we can utilize the maximum spamicity of first posts by the poster as a feature, where the spamicity is estimated by the model we devised for spam first post detection. On the other hand, we can also use the spamicity of the posters to help in detection of spam posts. A unified model to integrate spam and spammer detection together can be explored.

7. ACKNOWLEDGMENTS

This research was partially supported by National Taiwan University under grants NTU-ERP-103R890858 and NTU-ERP-104R890858, and Ministry of Science and Technology, Taiwan, under grant MOST 102-2221-E-002-103-MY3.

8. REFERENCES

[1] Enrico Blanzieri and Anton Bryl. A survey of learning-based techniques of email spam filtering. *Artificial Intelligence Review*, 29(1):63–92, 2008.

[2] Chih-Chung Chang and Chih-Jen Lin. LIBSVM: A library for support vector machines. *ACM Transactions on Intelligent Systems and Technology*, 2:27:1–27:27, 2011.

[3] Song Feng, Ritwik Banerjee, and Yejin Choi. Syntactic stylometry for deception detection. In *Proceedings of the 50th Annual Meeting of the Association for Computational Linguistics: Short Papers-Volume* 2, pages 171–175. Association for Computational Linguistics, 2012.

[4] Stephanie Gokhman, Jeff Hancock, Poornima Prabhu, Myle Ott, and Claire Cardie. In search of a gold standard in studies of deception. In *Proceedings of the Workshop on Computational Approaches to Deception Detection*, pages 23–30. Association for Computational Linguistics, 2012.

[5] Zoltan Gyongyi and Hector Garcia-Molina. Web spam taxonomy. In *Proceedings of First International Workshop on Adversarial Information Retrieval on the Web* (*AIRWeb* 2005), 2005.

[6] Nathan Halko, Per-Gunnar Martinsson, and Joel A Tropp. Finding structure with randomness: Probabilistic algorithms for constructing approximate matrix decompositions. *SIAM review*, 53(2):217–288, 2011.

[7] Christopher G. Harris. Detecting deceptive opinion spam using human computation. In *Proceedings of AAAI Workshops at the Twenty-Sixth AAAI Conference on Artificial Intelligence*, pages 87-93, 2012. AAAI, 2008.

[8] Pedram Hayati, Vidyasagar Potdar, Alex Talevski, Nazanin Firoozeh, Saeed Sarenche, and Elham A Yeganeh. Definition of spam 2.0: New spamming boom. In *Proceedings of 2010 4th IEEE International Conference on Digital Ecosystems and Technologies* (*DEST*), pages 580–584. IEEE, 2010.

[9] Chih-Wei Hsu, Chih-Chung Chang, Chih-Jen Lin, et al. A practical guide to support vector classification, 2003.

[10] Nitin Jindal and Bing Liu. Opinion spam and analysis. In *Proceedings of the 2008 International Conference on Web Search and Data Mining*, pages 219–230. ACM, 2008.

[11] Nitin Jindal, Bing Liu, and Ee-Peng Lim. Finding unusual review patterns using unexpected rules. In *Proceedings of the 19th ACM International Conference on Information and Knowledge Management*, pages 1549–1552. ACM, 2010.

[12] Thorsten Joachims. A support vector method for multivariate performance measures. In *Proceedings of the 22nd International Conference on Machine Learning*, pages 377–384. ACM, 2005.

[13] Lun-Wei Ku, Hsiu-Wei Ho and Hsin-Hsi Chen. Opinion mining and relationship discovery using CopeOpi opinion analysis system. *Journal of the American Society for Information Science and Technology*, 60(7):1486–1503, 2009.

[14] Ee-Peng Lim, Viet-An Nguyen, Nitin Jindal, Bing Liu, and Hady Wirawan Lauw. Detecting product review spammers using rating behaviors. In *Proceedings of the 19th ACM International Conference on Information and Knowledge Management*, pages 939–948. ACM, 2010.

[15] M McCord and M Chuah. Spam detection on twitter using traditional classifiers. In *Proceedings of the 8th International Conference on Autonomic and Trusted Computing (ATC* 2011), pages 175–186. Springer, 2011.

[16] Arjun Mukherjee, Bing Liu, Junhui Wang, Natalie Glance, and Nitin Jindal. Detecting group review spam. In *Proceedings of the 20th International Conference on World Wide Web*, pages 93–94. ACM, 2011.

[17] Myle Ott, Yejin Choi, Claire Cardie, and Jeffrey T Hancock. Finding deceptive opinion spam by any stretch of the imagination. In *Proceedings of the 49th Annual Meeting of the Association for Computational Linguistics: Human Language Technologies-Volume 1*, pages 309–319. Association for Computational Linguistics, 2011.

[18] Fabian Pedregosa, Ga¨el Varoquaux, Alexandre Gramfort, Vincent Michel, Bertrand Thirion, Olivier Grisel, Mathieu Blondel, Peter Prettenhofer, Ron Weiss, Vincent Dubourg, Jake Vanderplas, Alexandre Passos, David Cournapeau, Matthieu Brucher, Matthieu Perrot, and Edouard Duchesnay. Scikitlearn: Machine learning in Python. *Journal of Machine Learning Research*, 12:2825–2830, 2011.

[19] James W Pennebaker, Cindy K Chung, Molly Ireland, Amy Gonzales, and Roger J Booth. The development and psychometric properties of liwc2007. Austin, TX, LIWC. Net, 2007.

[20] Aldert Vrij, Ronald Fisher, Samantha Mann, and Sharon Leal. A cognitive load approach to lie detection. *Journal of Investigative Psychology and Offender Profiling*, 5(1-2):39–43, 2008.

[21] Guan Wang, Sihong Xie, Bing Liu, and Philip S Yu. Review graph based online store review spammer detection. In *Proceedings of 2011 IEEE 11th International Conference on Data Mining (ICDM*), pages 1242–1247. IEEE, 2011.

[22] Sihong Xie, Guan Wang, Shuyang Lin, and Philip S Yu. Review spam detection via temporal pattern discovery. In *Proceedings of the 18th ACM SIGKDD International Conference on Knowledge Discovery and Data Mining*, pages 823–831. ACM, 2012.

Summarizing Entity Descriptions for Effective and Efficient Human-centered Entity Linking

Gong Cheng
gcheng@nju.edu.cn

Danyun Xu
dyxu@smail.nju.edu.cn

Yuzhong Qu
yzqu@nju.edu.cn

State Key Laboratory for Novel Software Technology, Nanjing University, Nanjing 210023, PR China

ABSTRACT

Entity linking connects the Web of documents with knowledge bases. It is the task of linking an entity mention in text to its corresponding entity in a knowledge base. Whereas a large body of work has been devoted to automatically generating candidate entities, or ranking and choosing from them, manual efforts are still needed, e.g., for defining gold-standard links for evaluating automatic approaches, and for improving the quality of links in crowdsourcing approaches. However, structured descriptions of entities in knowledge bases are sometimes very long. To avoid overloading human users with too much information and help them more efficiently choose an entity from candidates, we aim to substitute entire entity descriptions with compact, equally effective structured summaries that are automatically generated. To achieve it, our approach analyzes entity descriptions in the knowledge base and the context of entity mention from multiple perspectives, including characterizing and differentiating power, information overlap, and relevance to context. Extrinsic evaluation (where human users carry out entity linking tasks) and intrinsic evaluation (where human users rate summaries) demonstrate that summaries generated by our approach help human users carry out entity linking tasks more efficiently (22–23% faster), without significantly affecting the quality of links obtained; and our approach outperforms existing approaches to summarizing entity descriptions.

Categories and Subject Descriptors

H.3.1 [**Information Storage and Retrieval**]: Content Analysis and Indexing—*abstracting methods*; H.1.2 [**Models and Principles**]: User/Machine Systems—*human factors, human information processing*; H.5.2 [**Information Interfaces and Presentation**]: User Interfaces—*user-centered design*

WWW 2015, May 18–22, 2015, Florence, Italy.
ACM 978-1-4503-3469-3/15/05.
http://dx.doi.org/10.1145/2736277.2741094.

General Terms

Algorithms, Experimentation, Human Factors

Keywords

Class vector model, entity summarization, human-centered entity linking, quadratic multidimensional knapsack

1. INTRODUCTION

The Web is embracing an increasing number of entity-centric knowledge bases, like Google's Knowledge Graph, Facebook's Open Graph, and W3C's Linked RDF Data. To bridge such structured data and traditional unstructured data (i.e. text in webpages) and form a unified Web, a fundamental task is to link entity mentions in text to their corresponding entities in a knowledge base, called entity linking, as illustrated in Fig. 1. Whereas a large body of work has been devoted to automatically generating candidate entities, or ranking and choosing from them [16], manual efforts are still needed for at least two reasons. Firstly, to evaluate automatic approaches to entity linking, human experts need to define gold-standard links by manually carrying out entity linking tasks [4, 10]. Secondly, some crowdsourcing approaches to entity linking directly solicit links from human users via entity linking tasks [5]. However, to the best of our knowledge, *no attention has been focused on facilitating human-centered entity linking*, and thus our aim is to *help human users effectively and more efficiently carry out entity linking tasks.* Thereafter, human users' productivity can be improved, and/or the payment can be reduced.

As illustrated in Fig. 1, when carrying out an entity linking task, the human user is usually provided with a set of candidate entities in the knowledge base, and is responsible for choosing one from them to be linked to, based on the context of the entity mention and the descriptions of candidate entities. The structured description of an entity comprises a set of property-value pairs, called features, and it is often the case that an entity in a modern knowledge base (e.g. Freebase and DBpedia [12]) has hundreds of or even more features. To avoid overloading human users with too much information and help them *more efficiently* choose an entity from candidates, in this paper we attack the problem of *how to summarize descriptions of candidate entities* by selecting and presenting only a subset of features. The selected features are expected to *effectively* substitute entire entity descriptions, without significantly affecting the quality of links produced by human users.

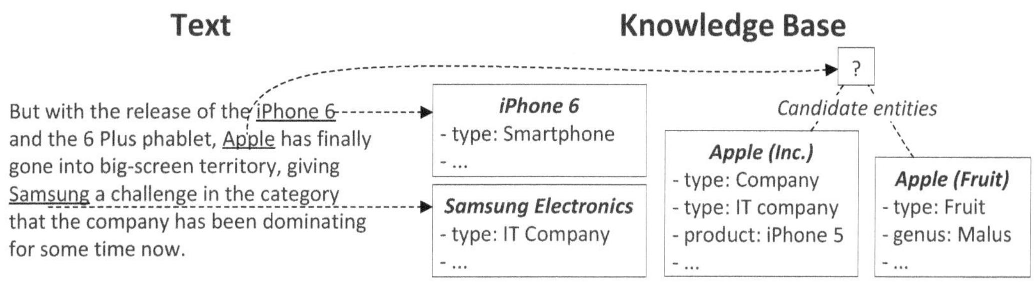

Figure 1: In this example, "iPhone 6" and "Samsung" in text have been linked to corresponding entities in the knowledge base. For "Apple", two candidate entities have been found to be chosen by human users.

To achieve it, we analyze entity descriptions in the knowledge base and the context of entity mention from three perspectives, and propose to automatically generate *characteristic*, *differential*, and *contextual* summaries by selecting features based on their characterizing and differentiating power, the information overlap between them, and their relevance to the context of entity mention. Accordingly, we develop three approaches from different perspectives, and finally combine them. To evaluate the proposed approaches, we carry out extrinsic evaluation by inviting human users to carry out entity linking tasks based on descriptions of candidate entities or their summaries generated by different approaches, and also carry out intrinsic evaluation by inviting human users to directly rate and comment on summaries generated by different approaches.

The remainder of this paper is structured as follows. Section 2 gives some preliminaries and defines the problem. Section 3, 4, and 5 describe three approaches from different perspectives. Section 6 combines the three approaches into a more powerful one. Section 7 presents experiments. Section 8 discusses related work. Section 9 concludes the paper with future work.

2. PROBLEM STATEMENT

A knowledge base is characterized by an eight-tuple $KB = \langle E, C, P, D, \sqsubseteq_C, \sqsubseteq_P, dom, d\rangle$, where

- E is a set of entities,
- C is a set of classes (a.k.a. entity types),
- P is a set of properties,
- D is a set of data values,
- $\sqsubseteq_C$ is a reflexive and transitive binary relation on C characterizing the subclass-superclass relation,
- $\sqsubseteq_P$ is a reflexive and transitive binary relation on P characterizing the subproperty-superproperty relation,
- $dom : P \to C$ is a function returning the domain of a property, which is a class, and
- $d : E \to 2^{P\times(D\cup C\cup E)}$ is a function returning the structured description of an entity comprising a set of property-value pairs (called features) where a value is a data value (e.g. string, integer), a class (if the property is `type`), or an entity.

For convenience, given a feature f, let $p(f)$ and $v(f)$ return the property and the value of this feature, respectively.

Each entity, class, and property is assumed to have a human-readable name. When presenting a feature to human users, for each entity, class, or property involved, its name will be shown; for a data value, its string form will be shown. The length of a feature f, denoted by $l(f)$, is defined as the total number of characters in the name of $p(f)$ and in the name or string form of $v(f)$.

Figure 1 illustrates four entity descriptions in a knowledge base. In practical human-centered entity linking tasks, features in descriptions of candidate entities are sometimes too long to be completely presented without overloading human users with too much information. To help human users more efficiently choose an entity from candidates, a compact, length-limited summary of entity descriptions is expected. Given k candidate entities $e_1, e_2, \ldots, e_k \in E$ to be chosen from and linked to from an entity mention, a structured *summary* of their descriptions consists of a subset of features selected from each entity description, or formally, $\langle S_1, S_2, \ldots, S_k\rangle$ subject to $S_i \subseteq d(e_i)$ for $i = 1, 2, \ldots, k$. Given a length limit L, a *feasible summary* $\langle S_1, S_2, \ldots, S_k\rangle$ satisfies

$$\sum_{f\in S_i} l(f) \leq L, \text{ for } i = 1, 2, \ldots, k. \quad (1)$$

There could be many different feasible summaries. In the next sections, we will discuss, from three perspectives, what kinds of features will be selected to form a feasible summary that is effective in facilitating human-centered entity linking.

3. GENERATING CHARACTERISTIC SUMMARIES

Our first approach facilitates human-centered entity linking by selecting features and generating summaries that help human users determine the identity of each candidate entity. In the following, we introduce the basic idea of this approach, and then formulate it, at a high level, as a combinatorial optimization problem and solve it. Finally we discuss a low-level implementation of the measures used in the high-level problem formulation.

3.1 Basic Idea

To help human users choose an entity from k candidates to be linked to, we assume that the user has determined the identity of the entity mention based on its context. Then, entity linking will be successfully carried out if the user is able to correctly determine the identity of each candidate entity. To this end, we propose to generate a summary that can best reflect the identity of each candidate entity, i.e., to select features that can best characterize each candidate entity or, in other words, have the highest *characterizing power*. For instance, in Fig. 1, the feature "product: iPhone 5" has a very high characterizing power because it is a unique feature of the entity "Apple (Inc.)". We will measure the characterizing power of a feature by using information theory (cf. Sect. 3.3).

Further, we observe that features in an entity description may carry overlapping information, e.g. "type: Company" and "type: IT company" of the entity "Apple (Inc.)" in Fig. 1. To provide more information to the user within a limited length, we improve the diversity of the generated summary by selecting features from each entity description that not only are characteristic but also share not much *information overlap* between each other. We will measure the information overlap between two features by using logical inference and string/numerical similarity (cf. Sect. 3.3).

Next we will formulate the selection of features as a combinatorial optimization problem that maximizes the characterizing power of and minimizes the information overlap between selected features.

3.2 High-level Problem Formulation

Given k candidate entity descriptions to be summarized, our goal is to maximize the total characterizing power of selected features and also minimize the total information overlap between features selected from the same entity description. Generally, the two objectives could be conflicting; that is, sometimes no single feasible summary can simultaneously optimize both objectives. Optimal summaries need to be formed in the presence of a trade-off between the two objectives. We solve such a multi-objective optimization problem by quantifying the trade-off in satisfying the two objectives by formulating a linear scalarization to be maximized. Formally, let $ch(f) \in [0,1]$ be the characterizing power of feature f, and let $ov(f_m, f_n) \in [0,1]$ be the information overlap between feature f_m and f_n. We define the goodness of a feasible summary $\langle S_1, S_2, \ldots, S_k \rangle$ as

$$g_{\text{chr}}(\langle S_1, S_2, \ldots, S_k \rangle) = \alpha \cdot \sum_{i=1}^{k} \sum_{f \in S_i} ch(f) + \beta \cdot \sum_{i=1}^{k} \sum_{\substack{f_m, f_n \in S_i \\ f_m \neq f_n}} (-ov(f_m, f_n)), \quad (2)$$

where $\alpha, \beta > 0$ are the weights of the objectives to be tuned in the specific application, and an implementation of *ch* and *ov* will be given in the next subsection. Now our goal is to find a feasible summary that maximizes g_{chr}.

We observe that g_{chr} can be reformulated as k independent sub-objectives to be simultaneously optimized:

$$g_{\text{chr}}(\langle S_1, S_2, \ldots, S_k \rangle) = \sum_{i=1}^{k} g'_{\text{chr}}(S_i), \quad (3)$$

where

$$g'_{\text{chr}}(S_i) = \alpha \cdot \sum_{f \in S_i} ch(f) + \beta \cdot \sum_{\substack{f_m, f_n \in S_i \\ f_m \neq f_n}} (-ov(f_m, f_n)), \quad (4)$$

that is, features can be selected from each candidate entity description separately.

The optimization of g'_{chr} can be formulated as an instance of the binary quadratic knapsack problem (QKP) [14]. Specifically, given a candidate entity e_i, we number the features in its description $d(e_i)$ from f_1 to $f_{|d(e_i)|}$. By introducing a series of binary variables x_m for $m = 1, 2, \ldots, |d(e_i)|$ to indicate whether feature f_m is selected into the optimal summary, the optimization of g'_{chr} is reformulated as:

$$\begin{aligned} \text{maximize} \quad & \sum_{m=1}^{|d(e_i)|} \sum_{n=m}^{|d(e_i)|} p_{m,n} \cdot x_m \cdot x_n \\ \text{subject to} \quad & \sum_{m=1}^{|d(e_i)|} l(f_m) \cdot x_m \leq L, \\ & x_m \in \{0,1\},\ m = 1, 2, \ldots, |d(e_i)|, \end{aligned} \quad (5)$$

where $l(f_m)$ and L (cf. Eq. (1)) are regarded as the "weight" of feature f_m and the "capacity" of the knapsack, respectively, and $p_{m,n}$ is the "profit" achieved if both feature f_m and f_n are selected, which is defined as:

$$p_{m,n} = \begin{cases} \alpha \cdot ch(f_m) & \text{if } m = n, \\ \beta \cdot (-ov(f_m, f_n)) & \text{if } m \neq n. \end{cases} \quad (6)$$

A QKP with positive and negative profits, as in our case, does not have any polynomial-time approximation algorithm with a constant approximation ratio unless P=NP [14]. So we solve it by using a state-of-the-art heuristic method [20]. Basically, this GRASP-based method consists of iterations made up of successive constructions of a greedy randomized solution and subsequent iterative improvements of it through local search. In particular, a greedy randomized solution is generated by adding elements (i.e. features) to the solution (i.e. the summary) from a list of features ranked by the following greedy function:

$$\frac{g'_{\text{chr}}(S'_i \cup \{f_x\})}{\sum_{f \in S'_i \cup \{f_x\}} l(f)}, \quad (7)$$

where S'_i is the set of features having been added to the summary in previous iterations and f_x is an unselected candidate feature being evaluated. It represents the profit per unit of weight that will be achieved if f_x is added to the summary.

3.3 Low-level Implementation

Now we give an implementation of *ch* and *ov*.

To measure $ch(f) \in [0,1]$, the characterizing power of a feature f, we follow information theory and compute the normalized amount of self-information contained in the probabilistic event of observing f in an entity description. We estimate probabilities based on the knowledge base $KB = \langle E, C, P, D, \sqsubseteq_C, \sqsubseteq_P, dom, d \rangle$:

$$\begin{aligned} ch(f) &= \frac{-\log \frac{|\{e \in E : f \in d(e)\}|}{|E|}}{\log |E|} \\ &= 1 - \frac{\log |\{e \in E : f \in d(e)\}|}{\log |E|}, \end{aligned} \quad (8)$$

that is, a feature will have high characterizing power if it is shared by a small number of entities in KB.

To measure $ov(f_m, f_n) \in [0,1]$, the information overlap between feature f_m and f_n, we perform logical inference based on the ontological semantics of classes and properties in KB, and also employ a range of similarity measures.

Firstly, we will define $ov(f_m, f_n) = 1$, i.e. maximize the information overlap between f_m and f_n, if one of them can be inferred from the other based on the schema level of KB, namely C, P, $\sqsubseteq_C$, $\sqsubseteq_P$, and *dom*. The following rules of inference are used.

- If $p(f_m) = p(f_n) = \texttt{type}$, $v(f_m), v(f_n) \in C$, and $v(f_m) \sqsubseteq_C v(f_n)$, then f_n can be inferred from f_m.
- If $p(f_m) \sqsubseteq_P p(f_n)$ and $v(f_m) = v(f_n)$, then f_n can be inferred from f_m.
- If $p(f_n) = \texttt{type}$, $v(f_n) \in C$, and $dom(p(f_m)) \sqsubseteq_C v(f_n)$, then f_n can be inferred from f_m.

Secondly, if none of the above rules can be applied, we will measure the similarity between properties ($psim$) and the similarity between property values ($vsim$). For $psim$, we measure the ISub string similarity [17] between the names of $p(f_m)$ and $p(f_n)$, which is in the range [-1,1]. For $vsim$, we also measure the string similarity between $v(f_m)$ and $v(f_n)$, but specially handle numerical values. Specifically, if both $v(f_m)$ and $v(f_n)$ are numerical data values, we define $vsim(f_m, f_n) \in [-1, 1]$ as follows.

1. If $v(f_m) = v(f_n)$, then $vsim(f_m, f_n) = 1$;
2. otherwise, if $v(f_m) \cdot v(f_n) < 0$, then $vsim(f_m, f_n) = -1$;
3. otherwise, $vsim(f_m, f_n) = \frac{\min\{|v(f_m)|, |v(f_n)|\}}{\max\{|v(f_m)|, |v(f_n)|\}}$.

If at least one of $v(f_m)$ and $v(f_n)$ is not a numerical data value, we will use the ISub string similarity between their names or string forms to define $vsim(f_m, f_n)$, which is in the range [-1,1]. Finally, we define

$$ov(f_m, f_n) = \max\{psim(f_m, f_n), vsim(f_m, f_n), 0\}\,. \quad (9)$$

4. GENERATING DIFFERENTIAL SUMMARIES

Our second approach facilitates human-centered entity linking by selecting features and generating summaries that help human users identify the difference between candidate entities. In the following, we introduce the basic idea of this approach, and then formulate it, at a high level, as a combinatorial optimization problem and solve it. Finally we discuss a low-level implementation of the measures used in the high-level problem formulation.

4.1 Basic Idea

Similar to our first approach described in Sect. 3, here we also assume that the user has determined the identity of the entity mention based on its context. Then, to help the user correctly determine the identity of each candidate entity and choose one from them, we propose to generate a summary that can best differentiate candidate entities from each other, i.e., to select features that can best reflect the difference between candidate entities or, in other words, have the highest *differentiating power*. For instance, in Fig. 1, the feature "type: Company" of the entity "Apple (Inc.)" and the feature "type: Fruit" of the entity "Apple (Fruit)" have a very high differentiating power because they provide very different values of the same property. We will measure the differentiating power of a pair of features from different entity descriptions in a way similar to the measurement of information overlap between features given in Sect. 3.3, by using logical inference, string/numerical similarity, and even more (cf. Sect. 4.3).

Next we will formulate the selection of features as a combinatorial optimization problem that maximizes the differentiating power of selected features.

4.2 High-level Problem Formulation

Given k candidate entity descriptions to be summarized, our goal is to maximize the total differentiating power of features selected from different entity descriptions. Formally, let $di(f_m, f_n) \in [0, 1]$ be the differentiating power of a pair of features f_m and f_n. We define the goodness of a feasible summary $\langle S_1, S_2, \ldots, S_k\rangle$ as

$$g_{\text{dff}}(\langle S_1, S_2, \ldots, S_k\rangle) = \sum_{i=1}^{k} \sum_{j=i+1}^{k} \sum_{\substack{f_m \in S_i \\ f_n \in S_j}} di(f_m, f_n)\,. \quad (10)$$

An implementation of di will be given in the next subsection. Now our goal is to find a feasible summary that maximizes g_{dff}.

The optimization of g_{dff} can be formulated as an instance of the binary quadratic multidimensional knapsack problem (QMKP), namely QKP with multiple constraints. Specifically, given k candidate entities $e_1, e_2, \ldots, e_k$, we number the features in $d(e_i)$, for $i = 1, 2, \ldots, k$, from $f_{i,1}$ to $f_{i,|d(e_i)|}$. By introducing a series of binary variables $x_{i,m}$ for $i = 1, 2, \ldots, k$ and $m = 1, 2, \ldots, |d(e_i)|$ to indicate whether feature $f_{i,m}$ is selected into the optimal summary, the optimization of g_{dff} is reformulated as:

$$\begin{aligned} \text{maximize} \quad & \sum_{i=1}^{k} \sum_{j=i+1}^{k} \sum_{m=1}^{|d(e_i)|} \sum_{n=1}^{|d(e_j)|} p_{i,m,j,n} \cdot x_{i,m} \cdot x_{j,n} \\ \text{subject to} \quad & \sum_{m=1}^{|d(e_i)|} l(f_{i,m}) \cdot x_{i,m} \le L,\ i = 1, 2, \ldots, k\,, \\ & x_{i,m} \in \{0, 1\},\ i = 1, 2, \ldots, k,\ m = 1, 2, \ldots, |d(e_i)|\,, \end{aligned} \quad (11)$$

where $l(f_{i,m})$ and L (cf. Eq. (1)) are regarded as the "weight" of feature $f_{i,m}$ and the "capacity" of each of the k knapsacks, respectively, and $p_{i,m,j,n}$ is the "profit" achieved if both feature $f_{i,m}$ and $f_{j,n}$ are selected, which is defined as:

$$p_{i,m,j,n} = di(f_{i,m}, f_{j,n})\,. \quad (12)$$

QMKP is at least as hard as QKP. To solve it, we adapt the heuristic method for solving QKP proposed in [20]. One basic modification to the method is to consider multiple constraints throughout the method. Besides, we develop a new greedy function to rank features:

$$\frac{\gamma \cdot g_{\text{dff}}(\langle S'_1, S'_2, \ldots, S'_x \cup \{f_{x,y}\}, \ldots, S'_k\rangle) + \delta \cdot \text{Potential}}{\sum_{i=1}^{k} \sum_{f \in S'_i} l(f) + l(f_{x,y})}\,, \quad (13)$$

where $\langle S'_1, S'_2, \ldots, S'_k\rangle$ represents the sets of features having been added to the summary in previous iterations, $f_{x,y}$ is an unselected candidate feature being evaluated, $\gamma, \delta \in [0, 1]$ are weights to be tuned in the specific application, and

$$\text{Potential} = \sum_{\substack{i=1 \\ i \neq x}}^{k} \sum_{f \in d(e_i) \setminus S'_i} di(f, f_{x,y}) \,. \quad (14)$$

If $\gamma = 1$ and $\delta = 0$, i.e. ignoring Potential, the greedy function given by Eq. (13) will be similar to the one given by Eq. (7), representing the profit per unit of weight that will be achieved if $f_{x,y}$ is added to the summary. In general cases, Potential gives the maximum profit that can be achieved by pairing $f_{x,y}$ with other unselected candidate features, representing the potential profit to achieve with $f_{x,y}$. We introduce Potential because we observe that, different from the definition of profit in Eq. (6) where features can contribute independently, here in the definition of profit in Eq. (12), features will contribute only if they are paired. If Potential is not considered, an arbitrary feature will be selected at the start of iterations, and will direct the selection of features in subsequent iterations. So Potential is introduced to direct the selection toward promising features.

4.3 Low-level Implementation

Now we give an implementation of *di*.

To measure $di(f_{i,m}, f_{j,n}) \in [0, 1]$, the differentiating power of a pair of features $f_{i,m}$ and $f_{j,n}$, we perform logical inference based on the ontological semantics of classes and properties in KB, and also employ a range of dissimilarity measures.

Firstly, we will define $di(f_{i,m}, f_{j,n}) = 0$, i.e. minimize the differentiating power of $f_{i,m}$ and $f_{j,n}$, if one of them can be inferred from the other based on the schema level of KB, namely C, P, $\sqsubseteq_C$, $\sqsubseteq_P$, and *dom*. We reuse the rules of inference presented in Sect. 3.3.

Secondly, if none of the rules of inference can be applied, we will measure the dissimilarity between property values by reusing $vsim$, the similarity between property values given in Sect. 3.3. Given a pair of features $f_{i,m}$ and $f_{j,n}$, we will define $di(f_{i,m}, f_{j,n}) = 0$ unless all the following conditions are satisfied.

- $p(f_{i,m}) = p(f_{j,n})$, i.e., they have the same property.
- $f_{i,m} \notin d(e_j)$ and $f_{j,n} \notin d(e_i)$, i.e., they are not shared by the two entities but are unique to the entity descriptions they belong to.
- $vsim(f_{i,m}, f_{j,n}) < 0$, i.e., the two property values are dissimilar.

If all the above conditions are satisfied, we will define

$$di(f_{i,m}, f_{j,n}) = vu(p(f_{i,m})) \cdot |vsim(f_{i,m}, f_{j,n})| \,, \quad (15)$$

where $vu(p(f_{i,m})) \in [0, 1]$ is to weight the result by $p(f_{i,m})$'s value uniqueness, namely how likely $p(f_{i,m})$ takes at most one value for an entity. We estimate it by the reciprocal of the average number of values taken by $p(f_{i,m})$ in an entity description in $KB = \langle E, C, P, D, \sqsubseteq_C, \sqsubseteq_P, dom, d \rangle$:

$$vu(p(f_{i,m})) = \frac{|\{e \in E : \exists f \in d(e), (p(f) = p(f_{i,m}))\}|}{\sum_{e \in E} |\{f \in d(e) : p(f) = p(f_{i,m})\}|} \,. \quad (16)$$

That is, the fewer values a property usually takes for an entity, the bigger difference an observation of its different values indicates.

5. GENERATING CONTEXTUAL SUMMARIES

Our third approach facilitates human-centered entity linking by selecting features and generating summaries that help human users determine the relevance of each candidate entity to the entity mention and its context. In the following, we introduce the basic idea of this approach, and then propose a class vector model for representing features of candidate entities and the context of entity mention as vectors of classes. Finally we present a way of computing weights in vectors and an algorithm for selecting features.

5.1 Basic Idea

Different from the two approaches described in Sect. 3 and 4, here we do not assume that the user has determined the identity of the entity mention in text. Rather, to help the user choose an entity from candidates, we propose to generate a summary that can best reflect the *relevance* of each candidate entity to the entity mention and its context. For instance, in Fig. 1, the feature "type: IT Company" of the entity "Apple (Inc.)" is highly relevant to the context of entity mention because another entity mention "Samsung" in the context has been linked to the entity "Samsung Electronics" which is also an "IT Company". We will measure relevance based on a model representing both features of candidate entities and the context of entity mention as vectors of classes (cf. Sect. 5.2) that are appropriately weighted (cf. Sect. 5.3).

Further, instead of simply selecting top-ranked relevant features, we will improve the diversity of the generated summary by diversity-based re-ranking, which is also based on the class vector model (cf. Sect. 5.4).

5.2 Class Vector Model

Term vector model (a.k.a. vector space model or VSM) has been extensively used for relevance ranking in information retrieval [15]. It represents both documents and queries as vectors of terms, and then defines the relevance of each document to a query as the cosine of the angle between the two corresponding vectors (called their cosine similarity). Inspired by this, we propose to represent both features of candidate entities and the context of entity mention as vectors. In our *class vector model* (CVM), each dimension corresponds to not a separate term but a class in the knowledge base. If a class, its subclass, or its instance occurs in a feature (or the context of entity mention), its weight in the vector is non-zero. In CVM, the similarity between two vectors is also defined as their cosine similarity. The relevance of a feature to the context of entity mention is then defined as the cosine similarity between the corresponding vectors.

5.3 CF-IIF Weighting

We weight classes in vectors in CVM by class frequency-inverse instance frequency (CF-IIF), which is adapted from the term frequency-inverse document frequency (TF-IDF) which is often used with VSM.

Let $I(c) \subseteq E$ be the set of class c's instances in $KB = \langle E, C, P, D, \sqsubseteq_C, \sqsubseteq_P, dom, d \rangle$:

$$I(c) = \{e \in E : \exists f \in d(e), (p(f) = \texttt{type}, v(f) \sqsubseteq_C c)\} \,. \quad (17)$$

The number of times a class c, its subclass, or its instance occurs in a feature f of a candidate entity is called c's class frequency (cf) in f. Since a property value could be a class, an entity, or a data value, we formalize cf in different cases:

$$cf(c,f) = \begin{cases} 1 & \text{if } v(f) \in C \text{ and } v(f) \sqsubseteq_C c, \\ 1 & \text{if } v(f) \in E \text{ and } v(f) \in I(c), \\ 0 & \text{otherwise.} \end{cases} \quad (18)$$

To calculate c's class frequency in the context of entity mention, denoted by $cf_{cnt}(c)$, we assume that a set of entities E_{cnt} have been linked to from other entity mentions in the context, and count the number of c's instances within this set:

$$cf_{cnt}(c) = |I(c) \cap E_{cnt}| . \quad (19)$$

The inverse instance frequency (iif) of a class c is a measure of how much information c provides, i.e., whether c is common or rare across all entities. It is obtained by dividing the total number of entities in KB by the number of c's instances, and then taking the logarithm of this quotient:

$$iif(c) = \log \frac{|E|}{|I(c)|} . \quad (20)$$

Finally, for a class c in a vector representing a feature f of a candidate entity, its CF-IIF weight is

$$cf(c,f) \cdot iif(c) , \quad (21)$$

and for a class c in a vector representing the context of entity mention, its CF-IIF weight is

$$cf_{cnt}(c) \cdot iif(c) . \quad (22)$$

5.4 Summary Generation

Instead of simply selecting top-ranked relevant features, we diversify generated summaries by maximizing marginal relevance (MMR) in the selection of features. MMR [1] is a widely used framework for integrating relevance and diversity. According to MMR, features are iteratively selected. In each iteration, unselected candidate features are re-ranked according to a linear combination of their relevance scores and their similarity to previously selected features, and the one having the highest re-ranking score will be added to the summary. Iterations will stop if adding any of the unselected candidate features exceeds the length limit (i.e. L). Specifically, let V_{cnt} and $V(f)$ be the vector in CVM representing the context of entity mention and the vector representing a feature f, respectively. Let S' be the set of features having been added to the summary in previous iterations, and let f_x be an unselected candidate feature being evaluated. The re-ranking score of f_x is defined as its marginal relevance:

$$\epsilon \cdot cs(V(f_x), V_{cnt}) - (1-\epsilon) \cdot \max_{f \in S'} cs(V(f_x), V(f)) , \quad (23)$$

where cs returns the cosine similarity between two vectors which is in the range [0,1], and $\epsilon \in [0,1]$ is a weight to be tuned in the specific application.

6. COMBINATION OF APPROACHES

The three proposed approaches select features and generate summaries from different, complementary perspectives. We combine them by integrating the two approaches presented in Sect. 3 and 5 using harmonic mean, and then incorporating the result into an extension of the formulation of QMKP presented in Sect. 4.

Specifically, given k candidate entities $e_1, e_2, \dots, e_k$, we number the features in $d(e_i)$, for $i = 1, 2, \dots, k$, from $f_{i,1}$ to $f_{i,|d(e_i)|}$. By introducing a series of binary variables $x_{i,m}$ for $i = 1, 2, \dots, k$ and $m = 1, 2, \dots, |d(e_i)|$ to indicate whether feature $f_{i,m}$ is selected into the optimal summary, we formulate an instance of QMKP as:

$$\begin{aligned} \text{maximize} \quad & \sum_{i=1}^{k} \sum_{j=i}^{k} \sum_{m=1}^{|d(e_i)|} \sum_{n=1}^{|d(e_j)|} p_{i,m,j,n} \cdot x_{i,m} \cdot x_{j,n} \\ \text{subject to} \quad & \sum_{m=1}^{|d(e_i)|} l(f_{i,m}) \cdot x_{i,m} \le L, \; i = 1, 2, \dots, k, \\ & x_{i,m} \in \{0,1\}, \; i = 1, 2, \dots, k, \; m = 1, 2, \dots, |d(e_i)| , \end{aligned} \quad (24)$$

where $l(f_{i,m})$ and L (cf. Eq. (1)) are regarded as the "weight" of feature $f_{i,m}$ and the "capacity" of each of the k knapsacks, respectively, and $p_{i,m,j,n}$ is the "profit" achieved if both feature $f_{i,m}$ and $f_{j,n}$ are selected, which is defined as:

$$p_{i,m,j,n} = \begin{cases} \alpha' \cdot hm(ch(f_{i,m}), cs(V(f_{i,m}), V_{cnt})) & \text{if } i = j \text{ and } m = n, \\ -\beta' \cdot (1 - hm(1 - ov(f_{i,m}, f_{j,n}), 1 - cs(V(f_{i,m}), V(f_{j,n})))) & \text{if } i = j \text{ and } m \ne n, \\ \zeta' \cdot di(f_{i,m}, f_{j,n}) & \text{if } i \ne j, \end{cases} \quad (25)$$

where hm returns the harmonic mean of two values, ch and ov are defined in Sect. 3, di is defined in Sect. 4, cs, V, and V_{cnt} are defined in Sect. 5, and $\alpha', \beta', \zeta' > 0$ are the weights to be tuned in the specific application.

To solve it, we accordingly extend the greedy function in Eq. (13), considering both the profit that will be immediately achieved if adding a feature to the summary and the potential profit that can be achieved by this feature in subsequent iterations. The extension is straightforward, and its details are omitted.

7. EXPERIMENTS

To evaluate the proposed approaches, we carried out both extrinsic and intrinsic evaluation. In extrinsic evaluation, we invited human users to carry out entity linking tasks based on structured descriptions of candidate entities or their summaries generated by different approaches, and then analyzed the accuracy of linking as well as the time used. In intrinsic evaluation, we invited human users to directly rate and comment on summaries generated by different approaches, and then analyzed the ratings and comments received. We also tested the running time of our approach.

7.1 Data Sets

Documents from two text corpora widely adopted for evaluating entity linking were used in our experiments to provide entity mentions, which had been linked to Wikipedia articles and were then mapped to entities in the DBpedia knowledge base [12] as the gold standard for linking.

- **AQUAINT**. The AQUAINT Corpus of English News Text [9] consists of newswire text data in English drawn from the Xinhua News Service, the New York Times News Service, and the Associated Press Worldstream News Service. The authors of [13] randomly selected

50 short documents from this corpus, and then manually linked entity mentions in these documents to corresponding Wikipedia articles.[1] These documents, entity mentions, and links were used in our experiments.

- **IITB**. The authors of [11] built IITB by collecting 104 documents linked to from homepages of popular sites belonging to a handful of domains including sports, entertainment, science and technology, and health, and then manually linked entity mentions in these documents to corresponding Wikipedia articles.[2] All of these documents, entity mentions, and links were used in our experiments.

We used DBpedia (version 3.9-en[3]) as the knowledge base to be linked to, which provided four million entity descriptions of various types extracted from Wikipedia. To form gold-standard links, Wikipedia articles linked to from entity mentions in the above text corpora were mapped to corresponding entities in DBpedia according to DBpedia's "Links to Wikipedia Article" data set. Structured descriptions of these entities were obtained by combining eight of DBpedia's major data sets, including Mapping-based Types, Mapping-based Properties, Titles, Geographic Coordinates, Homepages, Persondata, PND, and YAGO types. Features containing non-English data values were removed from entity descriptions because subjects in the experiments might not read them. The schema level of the knowledge base was obtained by combining a set of ontologies/schemas used in these entity descriptions, including the DBpedia ontology,[4] YAGO type hierarchy,[5] schema.org terms,[6] and FOAF vocabulary.[7]

7.2 Tasks

An entity linking task to be carried out by subjects consisted of a document randomly selected from a text corpus (i.e. AQUAINT or IITB), an entity mention randomly selected from the document, and three candidate entities in the knowledge base (i.e. DBpedia) to be chosen from and linked to. The three candidate entities included one entity (called the target entity) that was expected to be chosen from and linked to according to the gold standard, and the other two entities (called noise entities) that were randomly selected from a set of entities in DBpedia that shared a common name with the target entity. Such noise entities were obtained from DBpedia's "Disambiguation links" data set, which was extracted from Wikipedia's disambiguation pages.

We required the three candidate entities in a task to have at least twenty features in their descriptions, so that it was possible for different approaches to generate significantly different summaries. Only 155 entity mentions from 45 documents in AQUAINT and 487 entity mentions from 98 documents in IITB satisfied this requirement, and were to be used in the experiments.

[1] `http://www.nzdl.org/wikification/docs.html`
[2] `http://www.cse.iitb.ac.in/soumen/doc/CSAW/Annot/`
[3] `http://wiki.dbpedia.org/Downloads39`
[4] `http://wiki.dbpedia.org/Downloads39?dbpedia-ontology`
[5] `http://wiki.dbpedia.org/Downloads39?yago-type-hierarchy`
[6] `http://schema.rdfs.org/all.rdf`
[7] `http://xmlns.com/foaf/spec/`

7.3 Approaches

Subjects chose entities to be linked to based on their structured descriptions or summaries generated by six approaches to be compared.

- **DESC** returns the entire description of each entity, without performing summarization.
- **CHR** generates characteristic summaries according to Sect. 3.
- **DFF** generates differential summaries according to Sect. 4.
- **CNT** generates contextual summaries according to Sect. 5.
- **COMB** combines the above three approaches according to Sect. 6.
- **RELIN** [3] is a state-of-the-art approach to summarizing entity descriptions for generic purposes. Similar to CHR, it prefers to select characteristic features from each entity description. It also considers relatedness between features, whereas CHR measures information overlap between features.

In CHR, DFF, CNT, COMB, and RELIN, the length limit L in Eq. (1) was set to 100 characters, whereas the average total length of all candidate entity descriptions in all possible tasks was 680.36 characters; that is, the expected space savings produced by summarization was 85.30%. Other parameters in RELIN were set according to [3]. Other parameters in CHR, DFF, CNT, and COMB were empirically tuned based on three tasks randomly selected from each of the two text corpora (which were kept separate from those to be used in subsequent experiments): in CHR, $\alpha = 2$ and $\beta = 5$ in Eq. (6); in DFF (and COMB), $\gamma = 0.8$ and $\delta = 0.2$ in Eq. (13); in CNT, $\epsilon = 0.7$ in Eq. (23); and in COMB, $\alpha' = 2$, $\beta' = 5$, and $\zeta' = 4$ in Eq. (25). In CNT (and COMB), when calculating class frequency in the context of entity mention according to Eq. (19), we let E_{cnt} be the set of all other entities linked to from entity mentions in the document according to the gold standard.

7.4 Extrinsic Evaluation

In extrinsic evaluation, 30 students majoring in computer science and technology were paid to carry out entity linking tasks based on structured descriptions of candidate entities or their summaries generated by different approaches. Each subject was assigned a total of 72 tasks, or 36 tasks from each of the two text corpora. Tasks were randomly selected and were controlled to share no common document in order to minimize the correlation between them. Specifically, based on each of the six approaches that were arranged in random order, the subject was assigned 6 consecutive tasks without knowing the name of the approach (i.e., approaches were blinded). The 6 tasks comprised 1 task as a warmup whose result was not included in subsequent analysis, and 5 tasks whose results were to be analyzed. In each of these tasks, the subject was asked to choose one of the three candidate entities to be linked to from a given entity mention in the document, based on the context of the entity mention (i.e. the content of the document) and the descriptions of candidate entities or their summaries. The subject could

Table 1: Accuracy of Linking and Time per Task on AQUAINT

	Mean (SD)						$F(5,145)$ (p-value)	LSD post-hoc ($p < 0.05$)
	DESC	CHR	DFF	CNT	COMB	RELIN		
Accuracy	**0.91** (0.13)	0.80 (0.17)	0.75 (0.22)	0.71 (0.19)	**0.88** (0.13)	0.75 (0.25)	6.586 (0.000)	(1) DESC,COMB > CHR,DFF,CNT,RELIN. (2) CHR > CNT.
Time (s)	59.37 (26.27)	51.26 (24.22)	**39.28** (19.77)	52.23 (19.07)	**45.63** (16.49)	51.57 (35.36)	3.998 (0.006)	(1) DFF < CHR,CNT,RELIN,DESC. (2) COMB < DESC.

Table 2: Accuracy of Linking and Time per Task on IITB

	Mean (SD)						$F(5,145)$ (p-value)	LSD post-hoc ($p < 0.05$)
	DESC	CHR	DFF	CNT	COMB	RELIN		
Accuracy	**0.89** (0.16)	0.80 (0.18)	0.75 (0.16)	0.78 (0.19)	**0.85** (0.17)	0.77 (0.21)	2.598 (0.028)	(1) DESC > CHR,DFF,RELIN. (2) COMB > DFF.
Time (s)	53.88 (19.34)	**40.01** (17.94)	47.61 (22.04)	44.23 (18.79)	**41.90** (16.34)	43.82 (18.33)	3.335 (0.012)	(1) CHR,CNT,COMB,RELIN < DESC. (2) CHR < DFF.

also respond "not sure" if the provided information was considered insufficient for making a decision.

We defined the accuracy of linking as the percentage of tasks in which the subject chose the target entity instead of a noise entity or "not sure". Table 1 and 2 present the mean and standard deviation (SD) of the accuracy of linking achieved and the time per task used by all the subjects based on entity descriptions or their summaries generated by each of the six approaches on AQUAINT and IITB, respectively. Repeated measures ANOVA (F and p) revealed that the differences in mean accuracy and mean time based on different approaches on the two text corpora were all statistically significant ($p < 0.05$). In particular, higher accuracy but more time were, as expected, observed on DESC than all the other approaches to summarization. On AQUAINT, Fisher's Least Significant Difference (LSD) post-hoc analysis revealed that, compared with DESC, the loss of accuracy on CHR, DFF, CNT, and RELIN was statistically significant ($p < 0.05$); that is, summaries generated by the three proposed approaches from different single perspectives and the state-of-the-art generic approach could not effectively substitute entire entity descriptions. By comparison, the loss of accuracy on COMB ($0.91 - 0.88 = 0.03$) was not statistically significant ($p < 0.05$) according to LSD post-hoc analysis; that is, summaries generated by the proposed combined approach were as effective as entire entity descriptions. Meanwhile, compared with DESC, the mean time used for a task on COMB decreased from 59.37 to 45.63 seconds, or by 23%, and LSD post-hoc analysis revealed that this difference was statistically significant ($p < 0.05$). Similar results were observed on IITB. In particular, compared with DESC, the mean time used for a task on COMB significantly ($p < 0.05$) decreased from 53.88 to 41.90 seconds, or by 22%, whereas the loss of accuracy ($0.89 - 0.85 = 0.04$) was not statistically significant ($p < 0.05$). *To conclude, summaries generated by our combined approach helped human users carry out entity linking tasks more efficiently (22–23% faster), without significantly affecting the quality of links obtained, whereas existing approaches to summarizing entity descriptions like RELIN could not achieve this.*

7.5 Intrinsic Evaluation

In intrinsic evaluation, the 30 students directly rated and commented on summaries generated by different approaches. Each subject was assigned a total of 10 tasks, or 5 task from each of the two text corpora. Tasks were randomly selected and were controlled to share no common document in order to minimize the correlation between them. In each task, summaries generated by CHR, DFF, CNT, COMB, and RELIN were all presented, and the subject was blind to the correspondences between summaries and approaches. The subject was asked to compare these summaries and rate each of them on a scale of 1 to 5, indicating its effectiveness in helping make a decision. The subject was also encouraged to comment on summaries having very high or low ratings.

We calculated the average rating given by each subject to the summaries generated by each approach. Table 3 presents the mean and standard deviation (SD) of the average rating given by all the subjects to different approaches on AQUAINT and IITB. Repeated measures ANOVA (F and p) revealed that the differences in rating on the two text corpora were both statistically significant ($p < 0.05$). In particular, COMB received the highest rating on both text corpora, followed by CHR. Both of their ratings were higher than the other three approaches (namely DFF, CNT, and RELIN). LSD post-hoc analysis revealed that these differences were statistically significant ($p < 0.05$). *To conclude, summaries generated by our combined approach were considered more effective in helping human users carry out entity linking tasks than existing approaches to summarizing entity descriptions like RELIN. In particular, characterizing power and information overlap (which make up CHR) were dominating factors. Differentiating power and relevance to context were also complementary factors.*

We also summarized all the major comments that were made by at least fifteen subjects (50%).

- As to CHR, on IITB, 16 subjects (53%) commented that their decision was facilitated by some highly distinguishing features.

- As to DFF, on IITB, 15 subjects (50%) commented that different types helped them filter out noise entities easily. However, on AQUAINT, 18 subjects (60%)

Table 3: Ratings of Summaries on AQUAINT and IITB

	Mean (SD)					$F(4, 116)$ (p-value)	LSD post-hoc ($p < 0.05$)
	CHR	DFF	CNT	COMB	RELIN		
AQUAINT	**3.75** (0.60)	2.78 (0.98)	3.03 (0.82)	**4.02** (0.52)	3.20 (0.75)	18.499 (0.000)	(1) COMB > CHR > DFF,CNT,RELIN.
IITB	**4.01** (0.55)	2.86 (0.89)	2.84 (0.87)	**4.27** (0.48)	3.29 (0.76)	35.890 (0.000)	(1) COMB > CHR > RELIN > DFF,CNT.

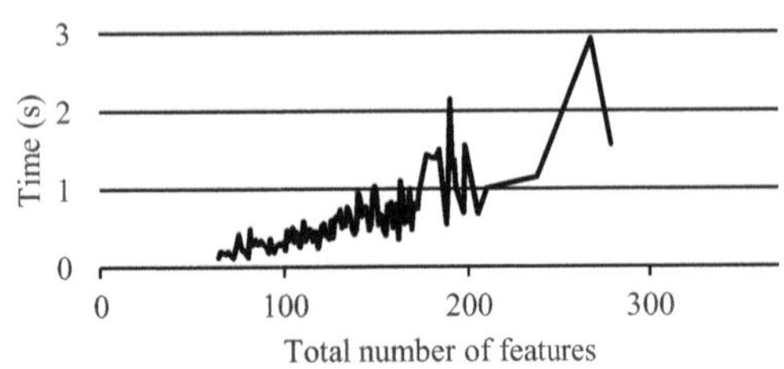

Figure 2: Average running time of the heuristic solution to QMKP in COMB on a task from AQUAINT.

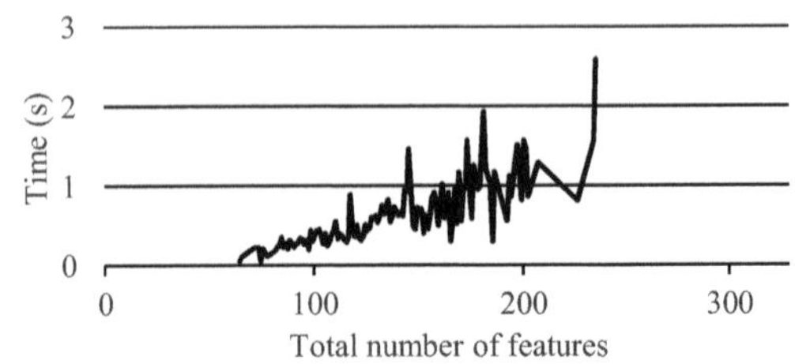

Figure 3: Average running time of the heuristic solution to QMKP in COMB on a task from IITB.

commented that, apart from different types, almost no useful information was provided.

- As to COMB, on AQUAINT and IITB, 24 subjects (80%) and 27 subjects (90%) commented that their decision was facilitated by some highly distinguishing features, respectively. On IITB, 16 subjects (53%) also commented that comprehensive information was provided, which was very helpful.

7.6 Discussion

We conclude extrinsic and intrinsic evaluation with the following insights.

Firstly, as shown in both Table 1 and 2, in extrinsic evaluation, the mean accuracy of linking achieved based on DESC was high but did not reach 1.00; that is, subjects sometimes made wrong decisions even based on entire entity descriptions. A major reason was that some entity linking tasks were inherently difficult. For instance, in some task, an entity mention "Nice" was expected to be linked to the city in France but not the town in California, because in the document, Saint-Laurent-du-Var was also mentioned and this town was a suburb of the city of Nice in France. Subjects made wrong decisions in this task because they neither had the above background knowledge nor could find it in the document or in Nice's entity description. To solve it, more information needs to be provided to the subject by, for instance, expanding entity descriptions wisely.

Secondly, in intrinsic evaluation, more than half (53%) of subjects commented that "comprehensive" information was provided by COMB on IITB. Here we tend to interpret comprehensive information as multiple paths that could lead to decision. COMB achieved this because it combined three different perspectives, generating characteristic, differential, and contextual summaries. Also for this reason, in extrinsic evaluation, it outperformed CHR, DFF, and CNT, all of which were only from single perspectives.

Thirdly, whereas the expected space savings produced by summarization in our experiments was 85.30%, in extrinsic evaluation, the mean time used for a task based on COMB decreased by only 22–23% compared with DESC. A major reason was that, apart from descriptions of candidate entities or their summaries, subjects consistently needed to spend time reading the context of entity mention, which could be the entire document typically containing thousands of characters in our experiments. Therefore, it motivates us to summarize not only candidate entity descriptions but also the context of entity mention in future work.

7.7 Running Time

We tested the running time of our approach, although summaries could be generated off-line in practical applications and thus its running time would not be a main concern. We only tested the running time of COMB, the most complex approach we proposed. It was written in Java and ran on an Intel Xeon E3-1225 v2 with 512MB memory for JVM. We found that its running time was dominated by the heuristic solution to QMKP. Figure 2 and 3 show the average running time of this computation on 500 random tasks from AQUAINT and IITB, respectively; and the results are grouped by the total number of features of all the three candidate entities in a task. Our implementation of COMB was reasonably fast, since it took less than 3 seconds in all the cases and less than 2 seconds in most cases.

8. RELATED WORK

8.1 Entity Linking

Entity linking is the task of linking an entity mention in text to its corresponding entity in a knowledge base. A large body of work has been devoted to automatically generating candidate entities, or ranking and choosing from them [16]. However, here we will not discuss any of these specific automatic approaches to entity linking, because the goal of our work is orthogonal to all of them and we focus on human-centered entity linking. Nevertheless, *our work can be beneficial to the evaluation of automatic approaches to entity linking* because such evaluation is usually based on manually defined gold-standard links obtained from human experts carrying out entity linking tasks [4, 10], and our approach can facilitate human-centered entity linking by substituting entire descriptions of candidate entities with compact, equally effective summaries, thereby improving human experts' productivity.

Another line of research involves humans in the loop, and combines algorithmic and manual efforts instead of pursuing a fully automatic solution. For instance, ZenCrowd [5] dynamically generates entity linking tasks and publishes them on an online crowdsourcing platform, and employs a probabilistic framework to integrate links contributed by human users which are possibly inconsistent. *Our work well complements existing crowdsourcing techniques for entity linking* because ZenCrowd does not focus on tool support on the user side for carrying out each single entity linking task, whereas our approach exactly targets this issue, and improves user experience by largely reducing the amount of information that needs to be consumed by human users, without significantly affecting the quality of links obtained. Therefore, the payment can also be reduced.

8.2 Summarizing Entity Descriptions

Summarizing structured descriptions of entities, a.k.a. entity summarization, has proven to be useful in many applications. For instance, in entity search engines, entity descriptions in search results pages are summarized to concisely indicate their relevance to the keyword query, by selecting features that contain query keywords [2] or by selecting features via more sophisticated machine learning techniques [21]. In interactive entity resolution, entity descriptions are summarized to help human users more efficiently judge whether they refer to the same real-world entity, by selecting features that reflect commonalities shared by and conflicts between them, and that carry characteristic and diverse information about them [19]. Different from all these efforts, *our work aims to summarize entity descriptions for a different task*, namely human-centered entity linking. Accordingly, *our approach deals with different types of data (e.g. context of entity mention) and thus employs different techniques (e.g. class vector model).*

Another line of research aims to summarize entity descriptions for generic use, i.e. not for any specific task. For instance, RELIN [3] employs a random surfer model to rank features based on their informativeness as well as the relatedness between them. DIVERSUM [18] improves the diversity of a summary by not selecting features sharing a common property. In the database community, all data held in a database about a particular data subject is summarized based on affinity of relations and attributes [6, 7, 8]. Although summaries generated by these approaches can also be used or adapted for the task of human-centered entity linking, *summaries generated by our specifically developed approach have proven to be more effective* according to the accuracy of linking achieved and the ratings given by human users in extrinsic and intrinsic evaluation, respectively.

9. CONCLUSIONS AND FUTURE WORK

To facilitate human-centered entity linking, we have proposed to substitute entire descriptions of candidate entities with compact summaries. Extrinsic evaluation demonstrates that summaries generated by our approach help human users carry out entity linking tasks more efficiently (22-23% faster), without significantly affecting the quality of links obtained. Next, we are interested in whether and how our summaries are also beneficial to automatic approaches to entity linking, which will be explored in future work.

Our characteristic, differential, and contextual summaries select features based on their characterizing and differentiating power, the information overlap between them, and their relevance to the context of entity mention. This multi-perspective approach outperforms approaches from single perspectives and a state-of-the-art generic approach, in terms of accuracy of and time for linking in extrinsic evaluation, and in terms of rating in intrinsic evaluation. For future work, our experimental design can be extended in several directions, e.g., to test with different numbers of candidate entities (including not-in-the-list) in extrinsic evaluation, and to solicit multi-dimensional ratings in intrinsic evaluation. Another attempt will be to create gold-standard summaries to enable automatic evaluation without humans in the loop.

10. ACKNOWLEDGMENTS

This work was supported in part by the 863 Program under Grant 2015AA015406, in part by the NSFC under Grants 61223003, 61170068, and 61370019, and in part by the JSNSF under Grant BK2012723. The authors would like to thank all the participants and anonymous reviewers.

11. REFERENCES

[1] J. Carbonell and J. Goldstein. The use of MMR, diversity-based reranking for reordering documents and producing summaries. In *Proc. SIGIR*, pages 335–336, August 1998.

[2] G. Cheng and Y. Qu. Searching linked objects with Falcons: Approach, implementation and evaluation. *Int'l J. Semant. Web Inf. Syst.*, 5(3):49–70, July–September 2009.

[3] G. Cheng, T. Tran, and Y. Qu. RELIN: Relatedness and informativeness-based centrality for entity summarization. In *Proc. ISWC*, pages 114–129, October 2011.

[4] M. Cornolti, P. Ferragina, and M. Ciaramita. A framework for benchmarking entity-annotation systems. In *Proc. WWW*, pages 249–260, May 2013.

[5] G. Demartini, D. Difallah, and P. Cudré-Mauroux. ZenCrowd: Leveraging probabilistic reasoning and crowdsourcing techniques for large-scale entity linking. In *Proc. WWW*, pages 469–478, April 2012.

[6] G.J. Fakas. A novel keyword search paradigm in relational databases: Object summaries. *Data Knowl. Eng.*, 70(2):208–229, February 2011.

[7] G.J. Fakas. Size-l object summaries for relational keyword search. *Proc. VLDB Endowment*, 5(3):229–240, November 2011.

[8] G.J. Fakas, Z. Cai, and N. Mamoulis. Versatile size-l object summaries for relational keyword search. *IEEE Trans. Knowl. Data Eng.*, 26(4):1026–1038, April 2014.

[9] D. Graff. The AQUAINT corpus of English news text LDC2002T31. Linguistic Data Consortium, September 2002.

[10] B. Hachey, W. Radford, J. Nothman, M. Honnibal, and J. Curran. Evaluating entity linking with Wikipedia. *Artif. Intell.*, 194:130–150, January 2013.

[11] S. Kulkarni, A. Singh, G. Ramakrishnan, and S. Chakrabarti. Collective annotation of Wikipedia

entities in Web text. In *Proc. KDD*, pages 457–466, June–July 2009.

[12] J. Lehmann, R. Isele, M. Jakob, A. Jentzsch, D. Kontokostas, P. Mendes, S. Hellmann, M. Morsey, P. van Kleef, S. Auer, and C. Bizer. DBpedia - A large-scale, multilingual knowledge base extracted from Wikipedia. *Semant. Web J.*, to appear.

[13] D. Milne and I. Witten. Learning to link with Wikipedia. In *Proc. CIKM*, pages 509–518, October 2008.

[14] D. Pisinger. The quadratic knapsack problem - A survey. *Discrete Appl. Math.*, 155(5):623–648, March 2007.

[15] G. Salton, A. Wong, and C. Yang. A vector space model for automatic indexing. *Commun. ACM*, 18(11):613–620, November 1975.

[16] W. Shen, J. Wang, and J. Han. Entity linking with a knowledge base: Issues, techniques, and solutions. *IEEE Trans. Knowl. Data Eng.*, 27(2):443–460, February 2015.

[17] G. Stoilos, G. Stamou, and S. Kollias. A string metric for ontology alignment. In *Proc. ISWC*, pages 624–637, November 2005.

[18] M. Sydow, M. Pikuła, and R. Schenkel. The notion of diversity in graphical entity summarisation on semantic knowledge graphs. *J. Intell. Inf. Syst.*, 41(2):109–149, October 2013.

[19] D. Xu, G. Cheng, and Y. Qu. Facilitating human intervention in coreference resolution with comparative entity summaries. In *Proc. ESWC*, pages 535–549, May 2014.

[20] Z. Yang, G. Wang, and F. Chu. An effective GRASP and tabu search for the 0-1 quadratic knapsack problem. *Comput. Oper. Res.*, 40(5):1176–1185, May 2013.

[21] L. Zhang, Y. Zhang, and Y. Chen. Summarizing highly structured documents for effective search interaction. In *Proc. SIGIR*, pages 145–154, August 2012.

Semantic Tagging of Mathematical Expressions

Pao-Yu Chien and Pu-Jen Cheng
Department of Computer Science and Information Engineering
National Taiwan University, Taiwan
b97901186@gmail.com, pjcheng@csie.ntu.edu.tw

ABSTRACT

Semantic tagging of mathematical expressions (STME) gives semantic meanings to tokens in mathematical expressions. In this work, we propose a novel STME approach that relies on neither text along with expressions, nor labelled training data. Instead, our method only requires a mathematical grammar set. We point out that, besides the grammar of mathematics, the special property of variables and user habits of writing expressions help us understand the implicit intents of the user. We build a system that considers both restrictions from the grammar and variable properties, and then apply an unsupervised method to our probabilistic model to learn the user habits. To evaluate our system, we build large-scale training and test datasets automatically from a public math forum. The results demonstrate the significant improvement of our method, compared to the maximum-frequency baseline. We also create statistics to reveal the properties of mathematics language.

Categories and Subject Descriptors

H.3.3 [**Information Storage and Retrieval**]: Information Search and Retrieval

Keywords

Mathematics language processing; Semantic enrichment; Semantic tagging

1. INTRODUCTION

As mathematics-related materials on the web surge rapidly, mathematics language processing (MLP) becomes an important issue. Like what nature language processing (NLP) does to text documents and words, MLP should help computers understand the meaning of mathematical expressions and tokens for further retrieval such as mathematical search and mathematics-answering systems.

Besides being displayed as images directly, there are two types of mathematical expression representations: content-

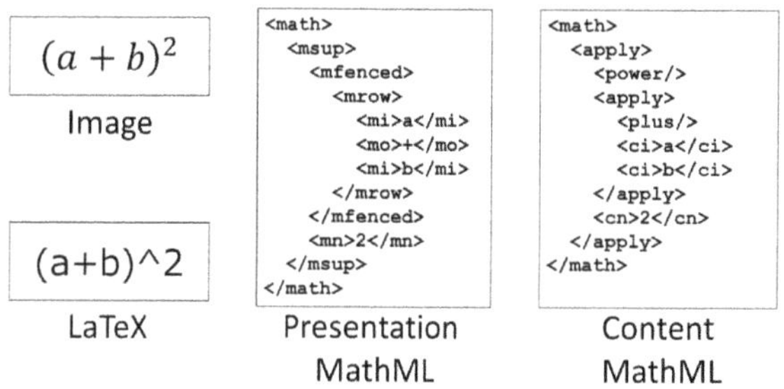

Figure 1: The same expression in different representations. The presentation-based methods use token "^" and "<msup>" to indicate that "2" is a superscript, while the token "<power/>" in the content-based methods further implies that such superscript means an exponent.

based and presentation-based. The former, such as *Content MathML* and *OpenMath*[1], encodes the syntax tree of an expression as well as the semantics of tokens into representation. The latter, such as *Presentation MathML* and LaTeX, only contains the appearance information about an expression. Figure 1 illustrates an example of these representations. Although the semantic information in content-based representation benefits MLP, its tree structure and tedious tags are too complicated for humans. In contrast, presentation-based representation is simpler and more convenient. Consequently, most documents on the web encode expressions with presentation-based representation, including *Wikipedia*[2] and *MathOverflow*[3].

The goal of *semantic tagging of mathematical expressions* (STME) is to mark the semantic tags for tokens in (presentation-based) expressions, especially variables [4] like "f" and "p". The semantic tag of a variable should show whether it denotes a number, a function, a matrix, or even more complicated data types. STME plays an important role in all MLP tasks dealing with presentation-based expressions.

However, the state-of-the-art STME algorithms are not good enough. For instance, if a user types "$M^{-1} = M^T$" in Google[5] search bar, the user may be disappointed with the search results. One reason is that modern search engines

[1]http://www.openmath.org/standard/om20
[2]http://en.wikipedia.org/
[3]http://mathoverflow.net/
[4]The word *variable* has different meanings in elementary and advanced mathematics. In this work, a *variable* is simply a symbol denoting some data, which may or may not be a number.
[5]http://www.google.com/

WWW 2015, May 18–22, 2015, Florence, Italy.
ACM 978-1-4503-3469-3/15/05.
http://dx.doi.org/10.1145/2736277.2741108.

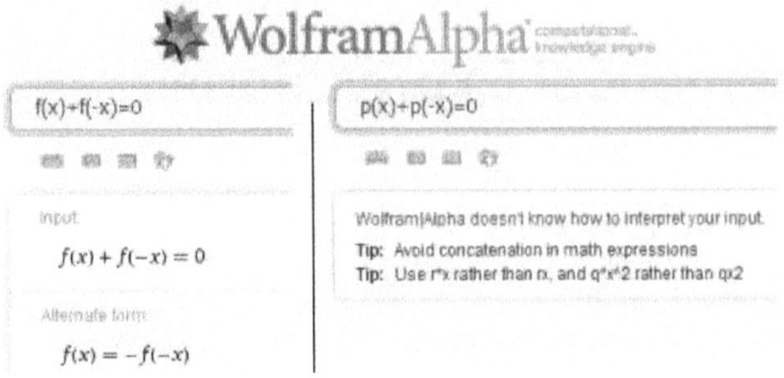

Figure 2: Resulting answers of Wolfram Alpha (on June 4, 2014)

usually ignore punctuation marks in the query, but more significant reason is that search engines cannot figure out the intent of the user: The alphabet "M" denotes a matrix, and "T" denotes the transposition operation of a matrix.

Take a returning answer of Wolfram Alpha [6] as another example. If one queries an expression "$x^2 = x(1+\sqrt{2})$" to Wolfram Alpha, it provides the plot, alternate forms, and the solutions of the equation. However, if one queries the same expression but replaces "x" with "f", Wolfram Alpha only returns an alternate form: "$f^2 - f(1+\sqrt{2}) = 0$" without further deduction. Still another example is that Wolfram Alpha returns several results to the query "$f(x) + f(-x) = 0$", but if one queries "$p(x) + p(-x) = 0$" instead, Wolfram Alpha will argue that it does not know how to interpret the input, as shown in Figure 2.

In this work, we propose a STME approach to LaTeX representations. Our solution is inspired by how people understand expressions (without explanatory text). First, the restrictions of the grammar of mathematics imply most of token semantics. The variable "p" in expression "$p(x+1)$" can represent either a function or a number, but not a set. In our approach, we build a context-free grammar (CFG) of mathematics that satisfies such restrictions. Parsing an expression with CFG will output all parse trees of the expression. Our self-built CFG consists of hundreds of LaTeX tokens and rules that cover most of the fundamentals of the grammar of mathematics.

Second, it is believed that a variable usually denotes the same data all the time when it appears in an expression, or even in a document. So if there is the expression "$p = 3$" directly after "$p(x+1)$", we can clearly state that both "p's" represent a number, rather than a function. This property, named the *consistency property* in our work, is the main difference between STME and other tagging problems. It is also why variables are special tokens in mathematical expressions. Due to the assumption that the consistency property holds in the whole document, our approach further reduces the number of possible parse trees of expressions.

After such deduction, if there are still multiple candidates for token semantics, then the user habits are introduced to determine the most probable one. These user behaviors include not only preferred letters for specific types of variables, but also how likely a grammar rule of mathematics is applied. For instance, the token "P" frequently represents a polynomial in elementary mathematics, but it will be reserved for the probability function in probability theorem. The expression "$(0,1)$" is more likely to be an open interval in some fields, yet denotes a point on the plane in others. As one can see, the user habits depend on the education levels, field of study, and writing purposes of both readers and writers.

The Wolfram Alpha examples mentioned above reveal that Wolfram Alpha overfits the preferred letters such that it refuses to admit that the token "p" can denote the same type of data as "f" in the expression. In our solution, we propose a probabilistic model, which is related to *probabilistic context-free grammar* (PCFG), to learn the user habits in the targeted corpus. The probabilistic model considers preferred letters as well as the probability of applying a grammar rule. Since most of the expressions on the web are presentation-encoded, and it is also expensive and time-consuming to manually build the labelled dataset for every targeted corpus, the probabilistic model of STME should be trained by an unsupervised method.

The proposed STME approach has the following different features from existing STME-aware systems. First, we show the importance of consistency property, while other systems usually treat variables in an expression or a document independently. Second, we solve the STME problem by only using the expressions themselves. This makes our solution practical for the documents that contain only expressions like web queries or equation-based questions. Our solution demonstrates that expressions themselves contain sufficient information about their meanings. Third, we notice that user habits, which vary according to different corpora, should be considered when mining the semantics of tokens. Finally, we adopt unsupervised learning in our approach, making our approach flexible to apply on different corpora without labelled data.

We build our training and test datasets from the math forum *AOPS* [7]. Our training dataset is composed of millions of expressions written by forum users. The test dataset is generated automatically from the same corpus by mining clues from the text part of a document. We conduct an experiment to evaluate the performance of our approach and compare it with a frequency-based baseline. We show that our approach increases the accuracy of correct tagging from 87% to 94%. Error analysis of both the baseline method and ours are provided as well. Furthermore, we show several interesting statistics of the mathematics language such as the *Zipf's law* for consistent tokens. These observations will be helpful for designing MLP algorithms.

Section 2 reviews the related works of STME. Section 3 presents the STME problem and the overall framework of our approach, whose details, including preprocessing and model learning are described in Sections 4 and 5, respectively. The experimental results and in-depth analyses are given in Sections 6 and 7. Section 8 concludes the work.

2. RELATED WORK

2.1 Mathematical Search

Given a mathematical expression as a query, *mathematical search* is to retrieve documents that contain relevant expressions to the query. Mathematical search methods can be classified as presentation-based and content-based.

[6]Wolfram Alpha, an question-answering engine developed by Wolfram Research that can deal with mathematical inputs. https://www.wolframalpha.com/

[7]http://www.artofproblemsolving.com/

Presentation-based methods only consider the variables, numbers and operators appearing in an expression, with no idea about the semantic meanings behind the tokens [10, 19, 20, 7]. For example, one can treat the expression as an ordinary sentence in NLP after proper preprocessing. The technique of keyword search can then be applied.

Content-based methods, on the other hand, consider both the semantic meaning of a token, and the syntax tree of an expression [8, 1, 18, 14]. Content-based methods usually estimate the similarity of two expressions based on their syntax trees in various ways. Nghiem et al. [12] compared the performance of presentation-based and content-based methods. They concluded that the semantic information is helpful to mathematical search, especially when the query has a specific meaning.

2.2 Semantic Enrichment

Content-based mathematical search methods usually need an extra transformation from presentation representation to content representation. Such transformation, like turning Presentation MathML into Content MathML, is called the *semantic enrichment* of mathematical expressions. As one can see, the objective of semantic enrichment is similar to STME. In fact, our system can determine the most probable syntax tree of an expression.

Although semantic enrichment is important to MLP, there are few studies on semantic enrichment. SnuggleTeX[8] is a open-source toolkit that converts math mode LaTeX into Presentation MathML, and further semantically enriches it to Content MathML. Many works [14, 9] apply SnuggleTeX for semantic enrichment directly. However, SnuggleTeX is based on manually-encoded rules, instead of learning from datasets.

Grigore et al. [6] and Quoc et al. [15] both proposed approaches to mine the semantic meaning of an expression based on the surrounding text. Mining the meaning of an expression from text is impractical on expression-only documents. It does not work if the writer does not rigorously define variables in text.

Nghiem et al. [13, 11] proposed a series of semantic enrichment approaches. They trained the translation rules (that translate sub tree of Presentation MathML to sub tree of Content MathML) and segmentation rules automatically. However, it requires MathML parallel markup corpora, i.e., expressions encoded in both content MathML and presentation MathML, for supervised learning.

2.3 Part-of-Speech Tagging

One may find the STME problem similar to part-of-speech tagging (POST), a well-explored topic in NLP.

POST can be solved by either supervised or unsupervised methods. The state-of-the-art supervised methods reach a high accuracy while the unsupervised methods are relatively hard. Goldwater and Griffiths [5] showed that a fully Bayesian approach improves the accuracy of the Expectation Maximization (EM) algorithm with a 3-gram model. Goldberg et al. [4] showed EM can learn a good POS Tagger when provided with good initial conditions. Ravi et al. [16] further improved the accuracy to 91.6% by integer programming, which searches for the smallest model, and EM training.

[8]http://www2.ph.ed.ac.uk/snuggletex/

Table 1: A tiny example of the token set, tag set and CFG. The tag comp stands for complement in set theory.

W	{A,B,-,1,2}	$\bar{v}$	#Init
T	{var, set, comp, minus, number}	V	{#Init, #Exp, #SExp }
W_t	$W_{\texttt{var}}$ = {A,B} $W_{\texttt{set}}$ = {A,B} $W_{\texttt{comp}}$ = {-} $W_{\texttt{minus}}$ = {-} $W_{\texttt{number}}$ = {1,2}	R	#Exp → #Exp minus var #Exp → number var #Exp → var #SExp → #SExp comp set #SExp → set #Init → #Exp #Init → #SExp
C	{A,B}		

The main difference between STME and POST is that the latter does not obey the consistency property, or at least not as intuitively [17]. Two identical words in a sentence can have distinct part of speeches, e.g. the word "saw" in the sentence "I saw a man with a saw". Moreover, the sequential model performs well in POST, but the syntax tree structure is more important to STME.

3. PROBLEM & SYSTEM FRAMEWORK

3.1 Mathematics Grammar

Due to the lack of available mathematics grammar, we build a simple context-free grammar (CFG) manually for our system. A more general and advanced grammar should be constructed for MLP in the future, while the main ideas of our approach rarely depend on the type of used grammar and can easily adapt to a more advanced one.

A CFG is denoted as $G = (V, T, R, \bar{v})$, where V is the set of **non-terminal symbols**, T is the set of **terminal symbols** (or **terminals**), R is the set of **rules**, and $\bar{v} \in V$ is the start symbol. A rule $r = v \to S$ denotes that we can substitute the sequence of symbols S for the non-terminal symbol v. Length of r is defined as the length of S. In our CFG, we ensure that r has non-zero length.

A **derivation** $\mathcal{T}$ is a series of substitutions based on R that starts at $\bar{v}$ and eventually generates a string of terminals S. In this case, we say that $\mathcal{T}$ *yields* S. We can depict a derivation as a **parse tree**. Two derivations are equivalent if they have identical parse trees.

A string of terminals S may have multiple derivations. Define $\mathcal{T}_S$ as the set of derivations that yield S. All the parse trees in $\mathcal{T}_S$ will tangle and turn into a **parse forest**. *Probabilistic context-free grammar* (PCFG) is to give a probability distribution over $\mathcal{T}_S$, so that the most probable derivation of S can be determined. Table 1 shows a tiny example of CFG. More details of our practical grammar will be given in Section 6.1.

3.2 Problem Formalization

The STME problem is defined here. Let W be the set of tokens and T be the set of tags. Each tag $t \in T$ has a **legal token set** $W_t \subset W$. In addition, there is a subset of tokens $C \subset W$ called **consistent tokens**, which should obey consistency property described later. $G = (V, T, R, \bar{v})$ is a CFG, whose terminal set is the tag set T. We assume that W, W_t, C, T and G are all known as background knowledge.

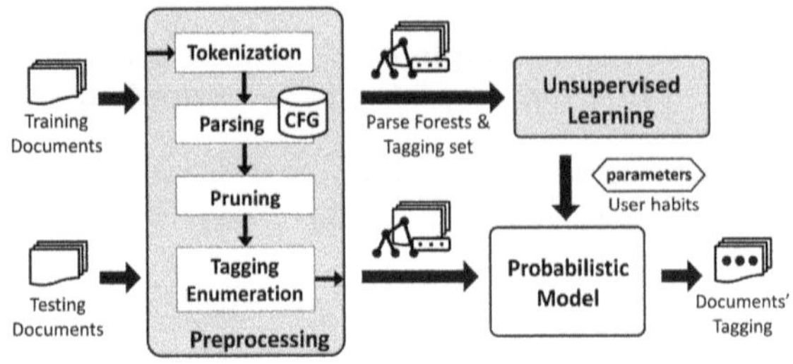

Figure 3: System Diagram of Our STEM Solution

An **expression** is a sequence of tokens. A derivation $\mathcal{T}$ is able to **produce** an expression $E = w_1 w_2 \cdots w_k$ if $\mathcal{T}$ yields tag sequence $S = t_1 t_2 \cdots t_k$, and w_i is a legal token of t_i for all i's. We say that the tag of w_i is t_i in this case.

A **document** D consists of a list of expressions $(E_1, \cdots, E_n)$. $C_D \subset C$ is denoted as the set of consistent tokens appearing in D. A list of derivations $L = (\mathcal{T}_1, \cdots, \mathcal{T}_n)$ (based on grammar G) is a **stamp** of D if it satisfies following conditions:

1. $\mathcal{T}_i$ can produce E_i.
2. **Consistency property**: each consistent token $w \in C_D$ must has its own tag, which should be the same every time it appears in D. In other words, there is a mapping $K(w) : C_D \rightarrow T$ such that the tag of every consistent token w in D must be $K(w)$. Such mapping $K(w)$ is called a **tagging** of D or the **tagging** of L. Two stamps of D may share same tagging.

The goal of SMTE is to determine the most probable stamp, or the most probable tagging, of the given document D. Table 1 shows a tiny example, where there are two derivations producing the expression "$A - B$". One yields "`var comp var`" while the other yields "`set comp set`".

3.3 System Framework

Figure 3 introduces the framework of our STME system. When receiving document D, we perform four preprocessing steps on it. First, we **tokenize** each expression in D from text into tokens. Then we **parse** expressions into parse forests based on the mathematics grammar G. Next, we **prune** the parse forests based consistency property. And finally, we **enumerate taggings** of D in order to narrow down the search space of learning.

The result of preprocessing is the parse forest of each expression, as well as a tagging pool consisting of all possible taggings. The whole preprocessing is deterministic and does not involve any machine learning.

After preprocessing, we will train a probabilistic model to score all stamps of D. The top-ranked one will be outputted as the stamp of D, and its tagging will be regarded as the most probable tagging of D. The parameters of the model are trained by unsupervised learning according to an unlabelled training dataset.

4. PREPROCESSING

4.1 Tokenization

We first tokenize every expression from a stream of text into a series of tokens. In our dataset, LaTeX is used to represent expressions. Here we state some details when tokenizing LaTeX representation. We remove tokens that are used for display and do not contain mathematical meanings, e.g., "`\left`" for changing the size of delimiter, "`\,`" for spacing, and "`\color`" for changing the color of characters. We also remove "`\text{}`" that enables user to insert text into an expression since we do not handle text contents.

Besides, we find that lots of users type the names of standard mathematics functions directly; however, these functions usually have specific tokens in LaTeX. For example, the sine function should be written as the token "`\sin`" instead of "`sin`", since the latter means multiplication of variables s, i and n from the viewpoint of LaTeX. As we will discuss in Section 7.4.3, this kind of typo violates the assumption of the consistency property. We, therefore, replace the name of the standard function with its corresponding token directly.

4.2 Parsing

Our parsing algorithm is analogous to a well-known parsing algorithm of CFG [3] with a slight modification. Given an expression $E = w_1 \cdots w_k$, the algorithm uses a boolean $\mathcal{N}(i, j, v)$ to denote if there is a derivation that starts at symbol v and yields $w_i \cdots w_j$. The base case $\mathcal{N}(i, i, v)$ is true if v is a terminal and w_i is a legal token of v. Other values $\mathcal{N}(i, j, v)$ can then be calculated by the dynamic programming technique. More specifically, we try every rule $r = v \rightarrow v_1 v_2 \cdots v_k$ to substitute for v. To yield $w_i \cdots w_j$ (after such substitution), each v_x should yield a sub-interval of $w_i \cdots w_j$ in order. Hence, $\mathcal{N}(i, j, v)$ is true if there exists a rule $r = v \rightarrow v_1 v_2 \cdots v_k$ and indexes $i = i_1 < i_2 < \cdots < i_{k+1} = j + 1$ such that all elements in the tuple

$$(\mathcal{N}(i_1, i_2 - 1, v_1), \mathcal{N}(i_2, i_3 - 1, v_2), \cdots, \mathcal{N}(i_k, i_{k+1} - 1, v_k))$$

are true. When we link $\mathcal{N}(i, j, v)$ to all tuples satisfying such condition, these $\mathcal{N}$ and links become the nodes and edges of the parse forest of E. The root of the parse tree is $\mathcal{N}(1, k, \bar{v})$.

The length-1 rules in mathematics CFG are usually used for embedding operation priority or synonym into grammar. Two derivations $v_1 \rightarrow v_2 \rightarrow v_3$ and $v_1 \rightarrow v_3$ are regarded distinct in ordinary CFG, but they usually have no difference from the viewpoint of mathematics. Some effort should be made to eliminate such false ambiguities. One possible solution is splitting links and dividing each node $\mathcal{N}(i, j, v)$ into two levels: $\mathcal{N}_1(i, j, v)$ and $\mathcal{N}_2(i, j, v)$. The node $\mathcal{N}_1(i, j, v)$ can only link to $\mathcal{N}_2(i, j, u)$ if u can be substituted for v with a series of substitutions based on length-1 rules. On the other hand, $\mathcal{N}_2(i, j, v)$ links to $\mathcal{N}_1(i_x, i_{x+1} - 1, v_x)$ just like what original $\mathcal{N}(i, j, v)$ does, except that length-1 rules are not considered here.

In practice, we also apply the technique of the *CYK algorithm* [3] to parse more efficiently. In other words, we split the rule $v \rightarrow v_1 v_2 \cdots v_k$ into $k - 1$ rules $v \rightarrow v_1 v_1^*, v_1^* \rightarrow v_2 v_2^*, \cdots$, and $v_{k-1}^* \rightarrow v_{k-1} v_k$ if $k > 2$, where v_i^* are pseudo-symbols and will not be reused in anywhere else.

4.3 Parse Forest Pruning

Now we are going to remove the derivations that violate the consistency property. Recall that for an expression $E = w_1 \cdots w_k$, $\mathcal{N}$ and their links form the parse forest of E. If a node $\mathcal{N}(i, i, t)$ is not in the parse forest, i.e., the node and the root node $\mathcal{N}(1, k, \bar{v})$ are disconnected, it implies that t cannot be the tag of token w_i.

For a document D with parse forests, we repeatedly check each consistent token w. w may appear in D multiple times. If t can be the tag for some of them but not for the others (due to the deduction from parse forest mentioned above), by consistency property we know that t must not be the tag of w. That is to say, there is no tagging K of D that satisfies $K(w) = t$. Thus we remove all nodes in parse forests representing that w's tag is t, as well as all links connected to them. The process of removing nodes goes recursively. Removing a node may cause other nodes in parse forests to have no links or to be disconnected from the parse forest. It may also eliminate candidate tags of another consistent token due to the consistency property. This process continues until all parse forests in D become stable.

4.4 Tagging Enumeration

The last step of preprocessing is to enumerate all possible taggings of the document D. This step is for reducing search space of our learning algorithm described in Section 5.3. We want to find the restriction between consistent tokens based on the consistency property again. Consider a simple document that contains one expression "$a + b$". The token "a" can have, says, five kinds of tags: "`num`", "`function`", "`set`", "`vector`", and "`matrix`". All these tags obey the consistency property since "a" only appears once in D, and so does the token "b". At first glance, D might have 25 taggings in total. But of course we know that only 5 of them are possible, since "a" and "b" must be compatible to be summed up.

We enumerate all tag combinations of consistent tokens as a tagging before launching the learning algorithm. By tracing the parse forests of D, we carefully verify whether there is a stamp with such a tagging. If so, this tagging will be put into a set called **tagging pool**. Every tagging in the tagging pool must belong to a stamp of D.

The time complexity of this step is exponential, and one can use a more efficient search algorithm instead of enumerating all tag combinations to expedite the process. In practice, we find that there are not too many tag combinations for a document, so the computational cost is acceptable.

5. PROBABILISTIC MODEL

After preprocessing, we obtain parse forests that embed all stamps of the document D, as well as a tagging pool consisting of all possible taggings of D. This section introduces our probabilistic model and learning algorithm.

5.1 Two Steps of Writing Expressions

If we look deeper at how people write down an expression, we can separate such process into two steps. Imagine that a person would like to define a set containing all square numbers. She may first come up with the most common format to define a set with specific condition:

$$\text{set} = \{\text{number}|\text{condition}\}$$

the condition in this case is that the number is square of another number, so the format becomes:

$$\text{set} = \{\text{number}|\text{number} = \text{number2}^\wedge\text{constant}\} \quad (1)$$

After the format is decided, she then chooses tokens to present each noun in Eq. (1). For example, lots of people are used to denoting two related real numbers as "x" and "y". Furthermore, people tend to use an uppercase letter to represent a set, especially "S" because it is the first letter of "set". Therefore, the resulting expression becomes

$$S = \{x|x = y^2\} \quad (2)$$

(We omit the condition that y should be an integer to keep the example clear).

The example shows that writing down an expression can be separated into the decisions of (1) *which format (derivation) to be used*, i.e., Eq. (1), and (2) *which token to be used*, i.e., Eq. (2). (The example is still simplified. In the real model, she has to first come up with the tag "`equal`" in Eq. (1), then realize there is only one token "=" that can be used to represent "`equal`". So do the other tokens). These two steps will correspond to two types of parameters involved in our probabilistic model.

5.2 Model Definition

For a document $D = (E_1, \cdots, E_n)$, we would like to find the most probable stamp L^* of D that maximizes the probability $P(L|D)$:

$$L^* = \underset{L}{\text{argmax}}\ P(L|D) \quad (3)$$

It is reasonable to regard the tagging of L^* as the most probable tagging of D. Let $L = (\mathcal{T}_1, \cdots, \mathcal{T}_n)$ be a stamp of D. According to Bayes' theorem, we have

$$P(L|D) = \frac{P(D|L)P(L)}{P(D)} \propto P(D|L)P(L) \quad (4)$$

since D is fixed. By assuming that the probabilities of expressions in D are independent, Eq. (4) becomes

$$P(L|D) \propto \prod_{i=1}^{n} P(E_i|\mathcal{T}_i)P(\mathcal{T}_i) \quad (5)$$

Based on the explanation in Section 5.1, $P(\mathcal{T}_i)$ in Eq. (5) relates to *which format to be used* and $P(E_i|\mathcal{T}_i)$ relates to *which token to be used*. Thus our probabilistic model matches the discussion in Section 5.1.

Let's focus on the conditional probability $P(E|\mathcal{T})$ first, i.e., the probability that a derivation produces the expression $E = w_1 w_2 \cdots w_k$. Denote $S = t_1 t_2 \cdots t_k$ as the tag sequence yielded by $\mathcal{T}$. We assume that the probability only depends on S and that the tokens are independent from each other. Then $P(E|\mathcal{T})$ becomes

$$P(E|\mathcal{T}) = P(E|S) = \prod_{i=1}^{k} P(w_i|t_i) \quad (6)$$

$P(w_i|t_i)$ is the first type of parameters in our probabilistic model that should be learned. It refers to the user habits that which token people prefer to use to represent such tag. For some tags, the token is unique, like the tag "`equal`" has only one token "=". Other tags may have multiple choices. Some of them are used more frequently than the others, like tag "`set`" and token "S" in the example given in Section 5.1.

Now we turn to dealing with $P(\mathcal{T})$, i.e., the probability that a derivation $\mathcal{T}$ is generated under the given grammar. Consider all substitutions in $\mathcal{T}$ and denote them as a set $R_{\mathcal{T}}$. We estimate the probability of $\mathcal{T}$ as

$$P(\mathcal{T}) = \prod_{r \in R_{\mathcal{T}}} P(r|h(r)) \quad (7)$$

where $h(r)$ is the prior knowledge for conditional probability. $P(r|h(r))$ is the second type of parameters that should be learned. A regular PCFG sets $h(r) = h_1(r) = v$ for the rule $r = v \to S$. In this case, $P(r|h(r))$ measures how frequently the rule r is used. It does not consider any dependencies between the rules. We then call $h_1(r)$ a **unigram model**.

Integrating more information into $h(r)$ results in a more advanced probabilistic model. Here we modify the idea of the bigram model to fit the tree-based structure. That is, $h(r) = h_2(r)$ is a tuple of a rule and a number (r_f, c), denoting that the substitution r is applied to the c-th outputted symbol of substitution r_f. We call $h_2(r)$ a **bigram model**. Take the expression

$$A \cup B = \{x|2|x\} \tag{8}$$

as instance. One derivation $\mathcal{T}$ for Eq. (8) is shown in the left of Figure 4. If we use the bigram model, i.e., $h(r) = h_2(r)$, the probability of $\mathcal{T}$ will be:

$$\begin{aligned} P(\mathcal{T}) = & P\left(r_{\text{equal}}|\emptyset\right) \times P\left(r_{\text{union}}|(r_{\text{equal}}, 1)\right) \times \\ & P\left(r_{\text{condSet}}|(r_{\text{equal}}, 3)\right) \times P\left(r_{\text{divisible}}|(r_{\text{condSet}}, 4)\right) \end{aligned} \tag{9}$$

In practice, the length-1 rules are frequently used for handling the priority of operations or synonyms. Such rules rarely contain any mathematical meanings. The right part of Figure 4 shows the derivation $\mathcal{T}$ for Eq. (8) by considering the length-1 rules. These rules make the bigram model meaningless. Consequently, we always ignore length-1 rules when calculating the probability of a derivation.

5.3 Obtaining the Most Probable Stamp

The next problem is how to compute Eq. (3), i.e., obtaining the most probable stamp L^* among all possible stamps of document D.

We enumerate the taggings from the tagging pool generated in Section 4.4. Once tagging K is fixed, expressions E_i in D become independent. Hence we turn to finding the most probable derivation $\mathcal{T}$ for every expression $E = w_1 \cdots w_k$ in D. Here we use dynamic programming to solve the problem. One may associate our algorithm with the *inside-outside algorithm* [2] of PCFG.

Define $\mathcal{Q}(i, j, v, r)$ as the maximum possibility among all sub-trees whose root is v and first substitution is r. And the sub-trees should be able to yield $w_i \cdots w_j$. The base case $\mathcal{Q}(i, i, v, r)$ has non-zero value $P(w_i|v)$ iff $r = \emptyset$ and either $K(w_i) = v$ for consistent token w_i or $w_i \in W_v$ for inconsistent token w_i. For $i < j$, we can calculate its value with dynamic programming. There are length-1 and length-2 rules in practice. Let $r = u \to v_l v_r$. The value of $\mathcal{Q}(i, j, v, r)$ is zero if $v \neq u$ and there is no derivation generating u from v; otherwise, $\mathcal{Q}(i, j, v, r)$ can be calculated as follows:

$$\begin{aligned} \mathcal{Q}(i, j, v, r) = \max_{k, r_l, r_r} & \left(P\left(r_l|(r, 1)\right) \mathcal{Q}(i, k, v_l, r_l) \times \right. \\ & \left. P\left(r_r|(r, 2)\right) \mathcal{Q}(k+1, j, v_r, r_r)\right) \end{aligned}$$

The maximum possibility of derivations with stamp K becomes:

$$\max_{L\text{'s tagging is} K} P(L|D) = \max_{r} \mathcal{Q}(1, k, \bar{v}, r) \tag{10}$$

With dynamic programming, the most probable derivation of E can also be obtained. Combining the most probable derivations of expressions in D, it becomes the most probable stamp among all stamps having the tagging K.

5.4 Learning the Probabilistic Model

Due to the scarcity of labelled training data, unsupervised learning is more appropriate for training the probabilistic model. We implement the EM algorithm to maximize the overall probability among documents in a training dataset.

After training, a stamp will be selected and assigned to each document, and the parameters of the probabilistic model will be set as:

$$P(w|t) = \frac{n_{(w,t)} + \alpha}{n_{(t)} + \alpha|W_t|} \tag{11}$$

$$P(r|(r_f, c)) = \frac{n_{(r,r_f,c)} + \beta}{n_{(r_f,c)} + \beta|R|} \tag{12}$$

where $n_{(r,r_f,c)}$ is the number of occurrences that the substitution r is applied to the c-th outputted symbol of substitution r_f in the training data, and $n_{(w,t)}$ is the number of occurrences that the tag of w is t in the training data. α and β are constants for smoothing, $|W_t|$ is the size of legal token set of t, and $|R|$ is the number of rules.

To train the model by EM, we first randomly assign a stamp to each document. The E-step scans through all possible taggings of document D to find the most likely stamp under current parameters. The M-step re-computes the parameters based on Eq. (11), Eq. (12) and current numbers of occurrences, e.g., $n_{(r,r_f,c)}$.

6. EXPERIMENTS

6.1 Setting

Since most of the mathematical expressions are represented in LaTeX form, the token set W and grammar G in this work are constructed based on LaTeX. To the best of our knowledge, there does not exist a publicly available CFG for a mathematics grammar. Therefore, we build the CFG grammar G manually, containing 294 LaTeX tokens and 814 rules. These rules cover most of the fundamental mathematics. 109 out of 294 tokens (including English alphabets, Greek letters, and Hebrew letters) are consistent. These consistent tokens are frequently used as variables in mathematical expressions. All consistent tokens have three legal tags: "`num`", "`function`", and "`set`" in this work. Some consistent tokens have additional legal tags like the tokens "`e`" and "`i`" can be "`constant`" (i.e. Euler's number and imaginary number), and "Σ" can be the "`summation`" symbol.

6.2 Dataset

Our dataset is collected from the *Art of Problem Solving* (AOPS), a forum mainly for discussing the various problems of high school and college mathematics as well as mathematical contests. There are 56 sub-forums in AOPS (unrelated sub-forums like *Chemistry* and *Games* are ignored). We collect all topics posted before May 30, 2013. Each topic consists of a *post*, which usually contains a mathematical problem and several *replies*, which may be discussions or solutions to the problem. Both post and reply in a topic can contain text as well as mathematical expressions. We treat all expressions in a topic, including the post and the first few replies (up to 19), as a document. It leads to 227,948 documents and 3,979,588 expressions in total.

We preprocess expressions whose length is between 7 and 300, and those failing to tokenize or parse will be removed.

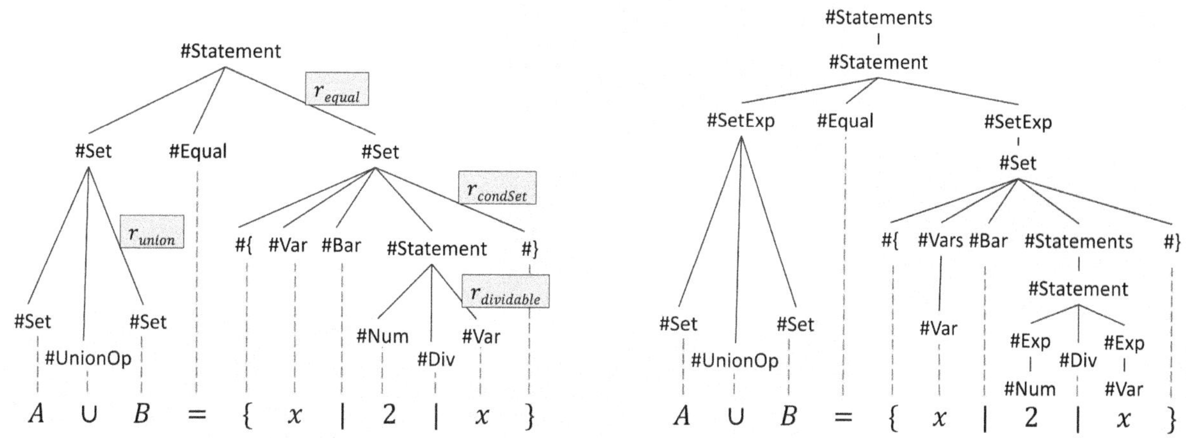

Figure 4: Derivation of Eq. (8). Left: ignore length-1 rules. Right: consider length-1 rules.

Also, documents that have no expressions left or do not have any possible taggings will be removed from the dataset. Eventually, there are 186,364 documents and 2,914,085 expressions in the dataset. The average length of expressions is 12.93. 33% of the expressions have more than one derivation. 53% of the documents have more than one possible tagging.

6.3 Test Dataset and Ground Truth

To make the size of our test dataset larger, we generate the test dataset with ground truth automatically. Let $D = (E_1, \cdots, E_k)$ be a document in the AOPS forum and D_i be the pseudo document containing only one expression E_i. Assume that D_i has multiple taggings, which means that the tags of consistent tokens in E_i are ambiguous. These tags, on the other hand, may be determined if we look back to the original document D since the consistency property makes some restrictions. We add D_i into our test dataset if D_i has multiple taggings yet D has only one tagging. The ground truth of D_i is given from the tagging of D. Note that all documents in the test data contain only one expression.

Unfortunately, the resulting test dataset has a serious bias. That is, over 97% of consistent tokens are "`num`" in the test dataset. It is because that those tokens having the tag "`num`" are much more easily determined than those having the tag "`function`" or "`set`". For example, the tag of the token "`x`" in the expression "$x+1$" or "e^x" is definitely "`num`" (at least in fundamental mathematics). In contrast, "`function`" is the hardest tag to be determined in preprocessing. Unless clearly specified like "$f\colon \mathbb{R} \to \mathbb{R}$", a function in all other expressions can also be explained as a number without any conflict. As a result, an extra effort must be taken to balance the test dataset.

To do this, we seek for clues in the text part of the retrieved documents. We first list a few specific keywords for each tag. The text part of the topic is divided into *chunks* with punctuations (such as comma and period) and prepositions (such as *to, of* and *with*). If an expression consisting of only one token is included in a chunk with a specific keyword, the tag corresponding to the keyword will be directly assigned to the token. For example, consider the text "*Assume S is the non-empty set of integer that satisfies...*". Both "*set*" and "*integer*" are keywords, and their corresponding tags are "`set`" and "`num`". But the keyword "*integer*" is not in the same chunk with expression "`S`" due to the preposition "*of*". Therefore, we assign the tag of token "`S`" as "`set`" instead of "`num`".

These assignments will be used in the parse-forest-pruning step when preprocessing document D. It makes documents containing "`set`" and "`function`" more likely to be unambiguous and be added into the test dataset. Note that there are other works that semantically enrich expressions by text [6, 15], but here we only need a naive solution that is workable in our dataset. Finally, there are 20,297 documents in total in the test dataset. Among 53,493 consistent tokens in the test dataset, the percentages of "`num`", "`function`", and "`set`" are about 64%, 23%, and 12%, respectively.

In brief, we build the tagging of test data as the ground truth based on the consistency property. Other kinds of ground truth, such as the tag of non-consistent tokens or the stamp of the document, cannot be generated in a similar way, because the consistency property does not hold. Consequently, even though our method returns the most probable stamp of a document, only the performance of outputting the correct tagging (or equivalently, outputting the correct tag of consistent tokens) can be evaluated in this work.

6.4 Competitive Methods

We compare the performance of the following methods:

1. `PR`: After preprocessing, the outputted tagging is randomly chosen from all possible taggings. No model training is involved.

2. `S`: To each consistent token w, this method always outputs the most frequent tag t that w has in the training data. The method requires labelled training data. However, our dataset does not have any labels, and using labelled data from other sources will allow `S` to learn the user habits different from those of our dataset. Therefore, we allow `S` to be trained based on 10% of our (automatically labelled) test data. Learning from the test dataset makes `S` overfit the test dataset. The reported performance of `S`, as a baseline, will be higher than it should actually be.

Table 2: **Accuracy of different methods that 1) output correct tagging to a document, 2) output correct tag to a (consistent) token and 3) output correct tag to each type of token**

Method	Document	Token	Type of token		
			"num"	"func"	"set"
PR	0.458	0.686	0.701	0.505	0.914
S	0.876	0.880	0.899	0.853	0.780
PW	0.890	0.931	0.930	0.920	0.961
PW1G	0.935	0.962	0.989	0.901	0.944
PW2G	0.945	0.968	0.986	0.912	0.929

3. `PW`: This method basically follows our approach, but it only calculates $P(E_i|S_i)$ instead of $P(E_i|S_i)P(S_i)$ in Eq. (5). In other words, `PW` considers neither derivations nor the grammar of mathematics. It degenerates from a tree-based model into a sequential model.

4. `PW1G`: This method implements our approach completely, where the unigram model, i.e. $h(r) = h_1(r)$, is used in Eq. (7).

5. `PW2G`: Same as `PW1G`, this method implements our approach completely. But the bigram model, i.e. $h(r) = h_2(r)$, is used in Eq. (7).

7. EXPERIMENTAL RESULTS

7.1 Overall Performance

We calculate the accuracy of each method that 1) outputs the correct tagging of a document and 2) outputs the correct tag of a consistent token. Results are reported in Table 2.

The random method `PR` obtains 45.8% accuracy, showing that most documents in the test dataset have only two to three possible taggings (after preprocessing). The baseline method `S`, which always assigns the maximum-frequency tag to a consistent token, obtains 87% accuracy. It reveals that `S` is a simple solution of STME with acceptable performance. It might be the reason why available systems such as Snuggletex adopt rule-based methods as their STEM solutions. However, there are still 12% of tokens that `S` cannot correctly handle. Note that the performance of `S` for token type "`set`" is worse than that of the random method, meaning that the data type "`set`" can often be determined in preprocessing.

We test the performance of our solution with different probabilistic models. Even the weakest one (`PW`) beats the baseline `S` in both document and token accuracy. `PW` learns the user habit of preferred letters. By further taking the rule likelihood (i.e., the unigram and bigram models) into consideration, the accuracy increases from 89% to 94.5%. The result shows that preferred letter habits and rules likelihood are helpful to STME.

Although we cannot evaluate the accuracy of our method that outputs the correct stamp, we show that the resulting tagging of STME can help reduce the derivation ambiguity of an expression. In our dataset, there are 973, 270 (33%) expressions that have more than one derivation. If the tagging of documents is decided (by our method), the proportion of ambiguous expressions decreases to 10%. The proportion of documents containing ambiguous expressions also decreases from 72% to 39%. That is, nearly two thirds of derivation ambiguities can be eliminated.

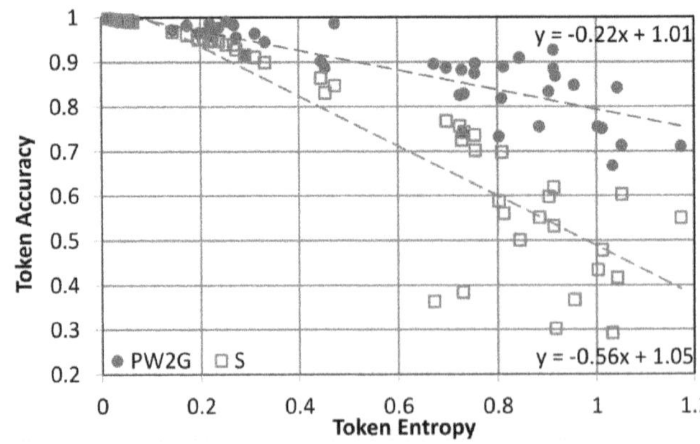

Figure 5: The relation between tag entropy and the resulting accuracy. Each point represents an English alphabet token. We also show the linear regression of both methods.

7.2 Performance of Each Token

For a consistent token w, we calculate the tag entropy of w in the test dataset to measure the diversity of w's semantic meaning, i.e.,

$$Entropy(w) = -\sum_t p_{(w,t)} \log p_{(w,t)} \tag{13}$$

where $p_{(w,t)}$ is the probability that w has tag t in the test dataset. We plot the relation between $Entropy(w)$ and the accuracy (of `S` and `PW2G`) on w in Figure 5.

Both `S` and `PW2G` perform well on low-diversity tokens. As the tag entropy increases, the semantic meaning of the token becomes diverse, making the STME problem on these tokens harder. Therefore, both methods' accuracies drop on high-diversity tokens, but `S` drops more seriously than `PW2G`. Actually, for a fixed level of tag entropy, `PW2G` performs strictly better than `S` over all tokens in that level.

7.3 Error Analysis

We observe closely the test data that our method `PW2G` answers correctly but `S` fails to tag. We briefly classify the reasons as follows:

1. The method `S` may return tagging that is unreasonable from the point of view of mathematics grammar. It relates to the example "$p(x) + p(-x) = 0$" of Wolfram Alpha in Section 1.

2. The method `S` performs poorly on high-entropy tokens. For example, `S` always marks tokens "`p`" and "`h`" as "`num`", but both of these two tokens are also used frequently as "`function`".

3. The method `S` treats a document as a *bag of tokens*, but it does not consider the relation between these tokens. Therefore, the expressions "$3(x + h)$" and "$h(x + 3)$" are identical to `S`.

We also observe the test data that `PW2G` fails to predict, and briefly classify the reasons as following:

Table 3: Examples in the test dataset. We show the actual tag t_i of token w_i in the expression, and the tags outputted by three methods S, PW and PW2G.

Expression	w_i	t_i	S	PW	PW2G
$B = \{1\}$	B	set	var	func	set
$p(x) + p(-x) = 0$	p	func	var	var	func
$U + V = U + W$	U	set	var	set	set
$P(x, y, z) \geq 0$	P	func	func	prob	prob
$\Phi^n = 0$	Φ	func	func	func	var
$f_n + f_{7n} = 14,379$	f	var	func	func	func

1. The tokens "P" and "E" have special tag "prob" that represents function of probability and expected value. We distinguish probability-related functions from ordinary functions because the former must use the fixed tokens "P" and "E", and have a different behavior from ordinary function. However, our method PW2G does not learn the difference of the behaviors. To make matters worse, it overfits probability-related functions too much. It almost marks "prob" to all tokens P's, which may be a normal function actually.

2. We do not have tag "matrix" in our grammar. A matrix can be operated like a number as well as a linear transformation (function). It allows a matrix "A" to be defined as a function "$A : \mathbb{R}^n \rightarrow \mathbb{R}^n$" yet multiply to a vector without parenthesis, i.e., "Ax", in a document. We find that many documents that lead PW2G to a fail are matrix-related. However, the tags of such tokens themselves are arguable.

3. In some situation, the consistency property does not hold. We will discuss this in more detail in Section 7.4.3.

We find few automatically-generated ground truth of test documents wrong. Most of them are caused by informal usage of operation. For example, lots of users in *AOPS* write function composition as "$fg(x)$", while the correct usage is "$f \circ g(x)$" or "$f(g(x))$". Since our grammar does not support the usage "$fg(x)$" for function, "f" and "g" will be recognized as "num" instead.

7.4 Issues of Mathematics Language

7.4.1 Document Frequency and Zipf's Law

Recall that the *Zipf's Law* [21] in NLP states that the frequency f of a word and its rank r follow the relationship $f = a/r^s$, where a and s are constants that vary with different languages. We are curious whether the language of mathematics also follows the Zipf's law.

We count the *document frequency* of each consistent token, i.e., the number of documents containing such a token (note that the *term frequency* of a consistent token is meaningless, since each consistent token always represents identical thing no matter how many times it appears in a document). We sort all of the consistent tokens by their frequencies, and plot the result on a *log-log graph*, as shown in Figure 6.

As one can see, the plot consists of two segments: high-frequency tokens and low-frequency tokens, with the boundary of 6,500 times. The statistical results of them are different. If we look closer at the two classes of tokens, the 43 high-frequency tokens are all English alphabet letters except "\pi" (14,704 times), obviously because π is a mathematical constant. The top-5 most frequent consistent tokens are "x", "a","n", "b", and "y". The 50 low-frequency tokens are all Greek and Hebrew letters, except for the 10 English alphabet letters (the frequencies of these 10 alphabets are from 1,353 to 6,362 times). The other consistent tokens do not appear in any documents.

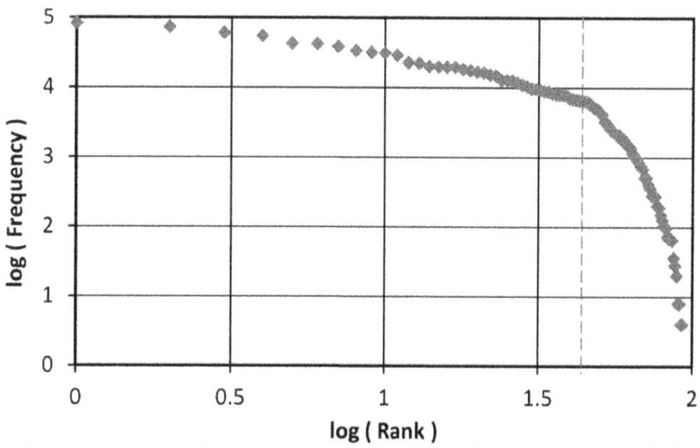

Figure 6: The document frequency of consistent tokens

The analysis shows that the usages of English alphabets and Greek letters are significantly different. People not only prefer to use English alphabets but also follow the Zipf's law with different values of a and s. Therefore, it may be proper to treat them as different language systems when processing mathematics expressions.

7.4.2 Merging Standard Function

In the first step of tokenization, we directly replace a standard function name by its corresponding token, like "log" to token "\log". It is reasonable to believe that multiplying three variables that are also assembled exactly as a standard function name rarely happens. We now demonstrate the validation of such a replacement. For a stream of characters S that form a standard function name, if more than half of the characters in S only appear in S, we believe that S is really a token of standard function; otherwise, such a replacement is doubtful. We have applied such combinations in 11,159 out of 227,948 (4.9%) documents. Only 732 out of 11,159 (6.6%) combinations are doubtful. The most common doubtful combination is "max", since "m", "a", and "x" are frequently-used tokens. Therefore, we believe the combination is valid.

7.4.3 Issue of Mathematics Language

Although mathematics emphasizes rigorous deduction, the language of mathematics is relatively loose. Mathematicians like to simplify expressions in order to clarify them, especially when the concepts become more abstruse and abstract. It highly increases the complexity of the mathematics language. Here we provide some examples found in our dataset to illustrate the limitation of our problem formalization, as well as why MLP like STME is challenging.

First, CFG cannot fully model the mathematics language. One reason is that some types of data are based on other types, like the concept of *template types* in programming language. A token "S" can be a set of numbers, a set of pairs, or even a set of sets, so we actually learn nothing about variable "a" from expression "$a \in S$". CFG does not support template types and it is impossible to enumerate all data types into grammar rules.

Even though the types of the input and output of a function are clearly defined, it can take another type of variable as input once the meaning is somehow intuitive to everyone. For example, the function "$f(x) = x^2$" can also take a set of numbers as input and output like "$f([-1, 2]) = [0, 4]$". Although such usage is informal, it is still widely used since it is easy to understand.

Mathematicians always create new rules. Rules in specific fields are similar to the various dialects in nature languages. For example, the keyword "cyc" is frequently used for cyclic sum in high school mathematics competitions like $\sum_{\text{cyc}}(x + xy)$ equals $(x + xy) + (y + yz) + (z + zx)$. Even worse, these rules may be so local. They might only be used by an individual mathematician or appear in an article or even a proof. This flexibility makes the mathematics language too dynamic to fit any rule-based models.

Finally, the consistency property does not always hold. For example, the summation, integration or set definition can contain a **local variable**. Take "$\int_t t^2 dt$" as an example. Token "t" is only used in *integration* to represent a temporary number. One can use the same token "t" in *summation* somewhere else in the same expression. Tokens may also be confused with the characters of a function name, like the first "n" in "$sinx/n$" is a part of the sine function, while the second one is a number. If we insist the consistency of "n", we will recognize "sin" as the product of numbers "s","i", and "n". Although LaTeX has a special token "\sin" for the sine function and a token "\operatorname" for user-defined function names, lots of writers forget to use them when writing. The last example that violates the consistency property is that some variables consist of multiple tokens. One can define "p" in "$p(n)$" as a function and "$p_0 = p(0)$" as a number. Now p_0("p_0") is an atomic variable, which has different type to "p".

8. CONCLUSIONS

In this work, we propose a novel approach to labelling semantic tags to mathematical expressions. We show two key points of the STME problem: the consistency property and the user habits. The former is a special property that does not hold in common tagging problems. The latter is a common concept to NLP, but it has not been introduced to MLP in the past. Our experimental results indicate that by considering the two key points, the performance of STME can be increased significantly. Also, the existence of the Zipf's law in mathematics language reveals that it is possible to introduce the concepts and methodologies of NLP into MLP.

As for future work, it is necessary to find a more general grammar than CFG to simulate advanced mathematics grammar such as supporting template types. It is also useful if there are hierarchical tags for the same tokens, e.g., we can mark a token as a "function" as well as a "polynomial".

9. ACKNOWLEDGMENTS

This work was partially sponsored by the Ministry of Science and Technology, Taiwan, under Grant 103-2221-E-002-182.

10. REFERENCES

[1] M. Adeel, H. S. Cheung, and S. H. Khiyal. Math go! prototype of a content based mathematical formula search engine. *Journal of Theoretical & Applied Information Technology*, 4(10):1002–1012, 2008.

[2] J. K. Baker. Trainable grammars for speech recognition. *The Journal of the Acoustical Society of America*, 1979.

[3] J. Cocke and J. T. Schwartz. *Programming languages and their compilers: Preliminary notes.* Courant Institute of Mathematical Sciences, New York University, 1970.

[4] Y. Goldberg, M. Adler, and M. Elhadad. Em can find pretty good hmm pos-taggers (when given a good start). In *Proc. of Annual Meeting of the ACL*, pages 746–754, 2008.

[5] S. Goldwater and T. Griffiths. A fully bayesian approach to unsupervised part-of-speech tagging. In *Proc. of Annual Meeting of the ACL*, pages 744–751, 2007.

[6] M. Grigore, M. Wolska, and M. Kohlhase. Towards context-based disambiguation of mathematical expressions. In *Proc. of the Joint Conference of ASCM*, pages 262–271, 2009.

[7] S. Kamali and F. W. Tompa. Retrieving documents with mathematical content. In *Proc. of ACM SIGIR Conference*, pages 353–362. ACM, 2013.

[8] M. Kohlhase and I. Sucan. A search engine for mathematical formulae. In *Artificial Intelligence and Symbolic Computation*, pages 241–253. Springer, 2006.

[9] G. Y. Kristianto, M.-Q. Nghiem, and A. Aizawa. The mcat math retrieval system for ntcir-10 math track. In *Proc. of the NTCIR Conference*, pages 680–685, 2013.

[10] R. Munavalli and R. Miner. Mathfind: a math-aware search engine. In *Proc. of ACM SIGIR Conference*, pages 735–735. ACM, 2006.

[11] M.-Q. Nghiem, G. Y. KRISTIANTO, and A. Aizawa. Using mathml parallel markup corpora for semantic enrichment of mathematical expressions. *IEICE Transactions on Information and Systems*, 96(8):1707–1715, 2013.

[12] M.-Q. Nghiem, G. Y. Kristianto, G. Topic, and A. Aizawa. Which one is better: presentation-based or content-based math search? *Intelligent Computer Mathematics*, pages 200–212, 2014.

[13] M.-Q. Nghiem, G. Yoko, Y. Matsubayashi, and A. Aizawa. Automatic approach to understanding mathematical expressions using mathml parallel markup corpora. In *Proc. of Annual Conference of the Japanese Society for Artificial Intelligence*, 2012.

[14] T. T. Nguyen, K. Chang, and H. S. Cheung. A math-aware search engine for math question answering system. In *Proc. of ACM CIKM Conference*, pages 724–733, 2012.

[15] M. N. Quoc, K. Yokoi, Y. Matsubayashi, and A. Aizawa. Mining coreference relations between formulas and text using wikipedia. In *Workshop on NLP Challenges in the Information Explosion Era*, pages 69–74, 2010.

[16] S. Ravi and K. Knight. Minimized models for unsupervised part-of-speech tagging. In *In Proc. of the Joint Conference of Annual Meeting of the ACL and IJCNLP of AFNLP*, pages 504–512, 2009.

[17] A. M. Rush, R. Reichart, M. Collins, and A. Globerson. Improved parsing and pos tagging using inter-sentence consistency constraints. In *Proc. of the Joint Conference of EMNLP and CoNLL*, pages 1434–1444, 2012.

[18] K. Yokoi and A. Aizawa. An approach to similarity search for mathematical expressions using mathml. *Towards a Digital Mathematics Library*, pages 27–35, 2009.

[19] A. S. Youssef. Methods of relevance ranking and hit-content generation in math search. In *Towards Mechanized Mathematical Assistants*, pages 393–406. Springer, 2007.

[20] R. Zanibbi and B. Yuan. Keyword and image-based retrieval of mathematical expressions. In *Proc. of Document Recognition and Retrieval*, pages 1–9, 2011.

[21] G. K. Zipf. *Human behavior and the principle of least effort.* Addison-Wesley Press, 1949.

Collaborative Ranking with a Push at the Top

Konstantina Christakopoulou
Dept. of Computer Science & Engineering
University of Minnesota, Twin Cities
christa@cs.umn.edu

Arindam Banerjee
Dept. of Computer Science & Engineering
University of Minnesota, Twin Cities
banerjee@cs.umn.edu

ABSTRACT

The goal of collaborative filtering is to get accurate recommendations at the top of the list for a set of users. From such a perspective, collaborative ranking based formulations with suitable ranking loss functions are natural. While recent literature has explored the idea based on objective functions such as NDCG or Average Precision, such objectives are difficult to optimize directly. In this paper, building on recent advances from the learning to rank literature, we introduce a novel family of collaborative ranking algorithms which focus on accuracy at the top of the list for each user while learning the ranking functions collaboratively. We consider three specific formulations, based on collaborative p-norm push, infinite push, and reverse-height push, and propose efficient optimization methods for learning these models. Experimental results illustrate the value of collaborative ranking, and show that the proposed methods are competitive, usually better than existing popular approaches to personalized recommendation.

Categories and Subject Descriptors

H.3.3 [**Information Storage and Retrieval**]: Information Search and Retrieval; I.2.6 [**Computing Methodologies**]: Artificial Intelligence—*Learning*

Keywords

Recommender systems; collaborative ranking; infinite push

1. INTRODUCTION

Personalized recommendation has become popular in a wide range of applications, such as electronic commerce, web search, news discovery, and more [2, 6, 13, 23]. Typically, the recommendation system selects a small set from the underlying pool of items (e.g., news, movies, books) to recommend to the user. The user can either like (e.g., read, click, buy, etc.) or dislike the items in the list, or take no action. Ideally, we want each user to like the items presented towards the top of the ranked list, since these are the ones she will actually get to see.

Collaborative filtering is a popular approach for recommendations systems. Typically such techniques assume that the user-item rating matrix R is low-rank, and they collaboratively learn the latent factors U and V for the users and the items correspondingly [19, 25]. Probabilistic matrix factorization type of approaches, widespread especially after the Netflix challenge [6], pose the problem of personalized recommendation as a rating prediction or matrix completion problem, trying to predict the ratings of unrated items [1, 19, 25, 31, 33]. Such approaches consider the square loss or variants as a measure of prediction accuracy. In reality, for a 5-point rating scale, predicting a true 5 as a 3 is often more costly than predicting a 3 as a 1, although their square loss is the same. More generally, what matters in a recommendation system is the ranking of items, especially the ranking performance at the top of the list, i.e., the items the user will actually see.

In this paper, we consider the recommendation problem as a collaborative ranking (CR) problem, such that the ranking loss focuses on accuracy at the top of the list for each user. The consideration is inspired by recent results [5, 38, 39] which support the hypothesis that posing recommendation problems as a ranking problem, as opposed to matrix completion or ratings prediction, leads to better performance. While existing CR models do optimize certain classical ranking metrics [34, 35, 36, 39], most of these metrics are non convex, so one works with a relaxation of the original problem, e.g., CofiRank [39] optimizes a convex upper bound of a loss based on Normalized Discounted Cumulative Gain (NDCG) [17], CLiMF [34] optimizes a smoothed version of the Reciprocal Rank [4] via a lower bound, etc. Moreover, certain CR models [22] consider the entire list, rather than focusing on accuracy at the top of the list.

We build on two good ideas respectively from the collaborative filtering and the learning to rank literature. First, the low rank representation with latent factor for users and items is indeed a simple and powerful idea. Second, the convex loss functions developed in the recent literature on learning to rank, such as p-norm push, infinite push, and reverse-height push [3, 28, 30], perform well to get accurate rankings at the top of the list. In our work, we use low rank representations for CR while working with ranking losses for individual users which focus on accuracy at the top of the list for each user. The result is a flexible new family of approaches for CR based on collaborative p-norm push, infinite

WWW 2015, May 18–22, 2015, Florence, Italy.
ACM 978-1-4503-3469-3/15/05.
http://dx.doi.org/10.1145/2736277.2741678.

push, and reverse-height push. We propose efficient alternating minimization methods for iteratively updating the latent factors, including a new approach for the non-smooth problem in infinite push based on gradient mapping for minimax problems [26]. Empirical evaluation carefully considers three key questions: (i) Between square loss and ranking loss with focus at the top of the list, which does better with recommendations at the top of the list? (ii) Between individual ranking and collaborative ranking, which does better for recommendations across all users, and (iii) Are the new collaborative ranking methods competitive with related existing ideas? Through extensive experiments, we illustrate that ranking loss indeed performs better than squared loss, collaborative ranking outperforms individual ranking, and the proposed set of algorithms are competitive, usually better than existing baselines.

The rest of the paper is organized as follows. We briefly review related work in Section 2. In Section 3, we combine the ideas of push and collaborative ranking, and propose three algorithms for collaborative ranking with a push at the top of the list. We empirically evaluate the proposed methods in Section 4, and conclude in Section 5.

2. RELATED WORK

In Information Retrieval (IR), the Learning To Rank (LTR) problem considers a set of training queries, where for each query a set of retrieved documents along with their relevance scores are given [8, 9, 10, 11, 24, 32]. The goal is to learn a ranking function which maps the features of the documents to a relevance score, based on which the documents will be ranked by degree of predicted relevance. A vast literature for LTR exists, and the categories of the methods proposed to approach the problem are *pointwise* [12], *pairwise* [3, 7, 8, 9, 30, 32] and *listwise* [10, 40]. The *pointwise* techniques require fitting to the actual relevance values, which is analogous to optimizing for the AUC metric. Thus, pointwise techniques try to predict the exact relevance scores of unseen documents instead of just capturing the correct ordering between them. The *pairwise* approach avoids these drawbacks by predicting the preference order between data. The two LTR approaches we employ, i.e., P-Norm Push [30] and Infinite Push [3] both lie in the category of pairwise LTR approaches. Their main disadvantage is the computational complexity, which is however not prohibitive when being applied to recommender systems, because of the sparsity of ratings for the users. *Listwise* approaches learn a ranking model for the entire set of documents.

Inspired by the analogy between query-document relations in IR and user-item relations in recommender systems, many CR approaches have been proposed over the past few years for personalized recommendations [5, 20, 22, 29, 34, 35, 36, 38, 39]. The majority of them optimize one of the (top-N) ranking evaluation metrics by exploiting advances in structured estimation [37] that minimize convex upper bounds of the loss functions based on these metrics [21]. CofiRank is one of the state-of-the-art listwise CR approaches which optimizes a convex relaxation of the NDCG measure for explicit feedback data (i.e., ratings) [39]. CLIMF and xCLIMF respectively optimize a smooth lower bound for the mean reciprocal rank on implicit (based on user behavior) feedback data [34], and expected reciprocal rank for data with multiple levels of relevance [36]. GAPfm [35] has been proposed to optimize Graded Average Precision, in order to address the concerns with Average Precision in multiple-relevance graded data. Recent work in [38], in the same spirit as [5], argued the need to bridge the ideas in the LTR community with Collaborative Filtering (CF). For that, they used a novel approach of generating features for the LTR task using CF techniques, i.e., neighborhood-based and model-based techniques, so that the problem can be transformed to a classic pairwise LTR problem. Recently, [22] introduced a method for Local Collaborative Ranking (LCR) where ideas of local low-rank matrix approximation were applied to the pairwise ranking loss minimization framework. A special case of this framework is Global Collaborative Ranking (GCR) where global low-rank structure is assumed, as is usually done in the ranking counterpart of Probabilistic Matrix Factorization (PMF)-type methods [1, 25, 31, 33], although equal importance is given to the whole ranked list.

3. PUSH COLLABORATIVE RANKING

Consider a collaborative ranking setting with m users $\{\rho_1, \ldots, \rho_m\}$ and n items $\{x_1, \ldots, x_n\}$, where the items can be movies, books, news articles, etc. Each user ρ_i is assumed to have rated a total of $n_i \leq n$ items, of which n_i^+ items are rated as 'relevant' and n_i^- items are rated as 'not relevant.' Let L_i^+ denote the set of relevant items and L_i^- denote the set of non-relevant items for user ρ_i, so that $|L_i^+| = n_i^+$ and $|L_i^-| = n_i^-$. For convenience, for a given user ρ_i, we will denote the relevant items as x_k^+ (not $x_k^{i,+}$ to avoid clutter) and the non-relevant items as x_j^-.

The goal is to construct ranking/scoring functions $f_i(x)$ over the items for each user ρ_i such that relevant items for ρ_i get a higher rank/score. From a ranking perspective, $f_i(x)$ induces a ranking over all items, and the goal is to make sure relevant items are ranked higher than non-relevant items. To accomplish the goal, our algorithms focus on two aspects: the ranking functions $f_i(x)$ for users will be

(i) trained with focus on accuracy at the top of the list for each user, and
(ii) constructed collaboratively across all the users, rather than separately for each user.

The working hypothesis that emphasis on these two aspects for collaborative ranking lead to better performance will be carefully evaluated in Section 4, where we consider alternative approaches which give equal importance to the entire list, or train the ranking functions individually on each user. We start with a discussion on how these two aspects are realized in our algorithms.

3.1 Push and Collaborative Ranking

Ranking with a Push: The idea of ranking with emphasis on the top of the list has been explored in the learning to rank literature [3, 7, 28, 30]. We build on a specific idea, originally due to [30]. For any user ρ_i, the "height" of a non-relevant item x_j^- is the number of relevant examples x_k^+ ranked below it by the learned ranking function f_i, i.e.,

$$H_i(x_j^-) = \sum_{k \in L_i^+} \mathbb{1}[f_i(x_k^+) \leq f_i(x_j^-)] , \qquad (1)$$

where $\mathbb{1}[\cdot]$ is the indicator function. The vector $H_i \in \mathbb{R}_+^{n_i^-}$ contains the height of all non-relevant items. A high value of $H_i(x_j^-)$ implies that several relevant items are ranked below the non-relevant x_j^- according to $f_i(\cdot)$. The learning of $f_i(\cdot)$ needs to focus on making the heights of non-relevant items small, i.e., *push* the non-relevant items down, with more emphasis on the large entries in H_i, i.e., non-relevant items towards the top of the list. One can consider learning $f_i(\cdot)$ by minimizing the L_p-norm of H_i [30] (p-norm push), or, the L_∞-norm of H_i (infinite push), which simply focuses on the largest element [3]. Other such suitable functions of H_i, which focus on pushing down non-relevant items from the top of the list, can also be considered.

An alternative approach involves pushing the relevant examples up, rather than pushing the non-relevant examples down. For any user ρ_i, the "reverse height" of a relevant item x_k^+ is the number of non-relevant examples x_j^- ranked above it by the learned ranking function f_i, i.e.,

$$R_i(x_k^+) = \sum_{j \in L_i^-} \mathbb{1}[f_i(x_k^+) \leq f_i(x_j^-)] \ . \tag{2}$$

The vector $R_i \in \mathbb{R}_+^{n_i^+}$ contains the reverse height of all relevant items. A high value of $R_i(x_k^+)$ implies that several non-relevant items are ranked above the relevant x_k^+ according to $f_i(\cdot)$. The learning of $f_i(\cdot)$ needs to focus on making the reverse heights of relevant items small, i.e., *push* the relevant items up. As before, one can choose objective functions on R_i which put more emphasis on relevant items with high reverse heights, e.g., one can use p-norm or infinite push.

The use of indicator functions $\mathbb{1}[f_i(x_k^+) \leq f_i(x_j^-)]$ to define heights, while conceptually convenient, is not suitable for optimization purposes. As a result, we will use a surrogate for the indicator function. For the paper, with$\Delta_i(k,j) = f_i(x_k^+) - f_i(x_j^-)$, we use the logistic loss of the difference as the surrogate:

$$\ell(\Delta_i(k,j)) = \log(1 + \exp(-\Delta_i(k,j))) \ , \tag{3}$$

noting that it forms a convex upper bound to the indicator function. In the sequel, we refer to the height (reverse height) computed using the surrogate, as surrogate height $\tilde{H}_i$ (surrogate reverse height $\tilde{R}_i$).

Collaborative Ranking: Instead of learning the functions $f_i(\cdot)$ separately for each user, we focus on learning them collaboratively. Towards this end, we build on the existing approach of low-rank or latent factor based representation of the scores, widely used in the collaborative filtering literature [25, 39]. Let $U \in \mathbb{R}^{d \times m}$ be the latent factor corresponding to the users, where the ith column $\mathbf{u}_i \in \mathbb{R}^d$ is the latent factor for user ρ_i. Similarly, let $V \in \mathbb{R}^{d \times n}$ be latent factor for the items, where j^{th} column $\mathbf{v}_j \in \mathbb{R}^d$ is the latent factor for item x_j. Then, we assume the scoring function $f_i(x_j) = \mathbf{u}_i^T \mathbf{v}_j$, so that the overall score matrix $F = U^T V \in \mathbb{R}^{m \times n}$ is of rank d, where d is a user specified parameter. Based on such a representation, we have

$$\Delta_i(k,j) = f_i(x_k^+) - f_i(x_j^-) = \mathbf{u}_i^T(\mathbf{v}_k - \mathbf{v}_j) \ . \tag{4}$$

Plugging the above form to compute the surrogate height of a non-relevant sample from (1) gives

$$\tilde{H}_i(x_j^-) = \sum_{k \in L_i^+} \log\left(1 + \exp(-\mathbf{u}_i^T(\mathbf{v}_k - \mathbf{v}_j))\right) \ . \tag{5}$$

Similarly, we obtain the form of the surrogate reverse height for a relevant sample from (2) as

$$\tilde{R}_i(x_k^+) = \sum_{j \in L_i^-} \log\left(1 + \exp(-\mathbf{u}_i^T(\mathbf{v}_k - \mathbf{v}_j))\right) \ . \tag{6}$$

In the rest of the section, we discuss three different loss functions which work with such surrogate heights and put emphasis on accuracy at the top of the list. We outline algorithms for minimizing such loss functions over the latent factors (U, V).

3.2 P-Norm Push Collaborative Ranking

The main idea in p-norm push collaborative ranking (`P-Push CR`), building on [30], is to consider the L_p norm of the surrogate height vector $\tilde{H}_i$ with elements as in (5), and construct an objective function as a suitable scaled sum of such norms over all users. In particular, we consider the objective

$$\mathcal{E}_{\text{p-push}}(U,V) = \sum_{i=1}^{m} \frac{\|\tilde{H}_i\|_p^p}{n_i} = \sum_{i=1}^{m} \frac{1}{n_i} \sum_{j \in L_i^-} \left(\tilde{H}_i(x_j^-)\right)^p \tag{7}$$

$$= \sum_{i=1}^{m} \frac{1}{n_i} \sum_{j \in L_i^-} \left(\sum_{k \in L_i^+} \log\left(1 + \exp(-\mathbf{u}_i^T(\mathbf{v}_k - \mathbf{v}_j))\right) \right)^p \ .$$

The optimization is done by alternating minimization [16], i.e., updating U while keeping V fixed, and then updating V while keeping U fixed. The objective function is bi-convex, i.e., convex in one argument while keeping the other fixed. The updates of the latent factors for each user and each item can be done using gradient descent. In each iteration $t+1$:

$$\mathbf{u}_i^{t+1} \leftarrow \mathbf{u}_i^t - \eta \nabla_{\mathbf{u}_i} \mathcal{E}_{\text{p-push}}(U^t, V^t) \ , \quad i = 1, \ldots, m, \tag{8}$$

$$\mathbf{v}_h^{t+1} \leftarrow \mathbf{v}_h^t - \eta \nabla_{\mathbf{v}_h} \mathcal{E}_{\text{p-push}}(U^{t+1}, V^t) \ , \quad h = 1, \ldots, n. \tag{9}$$

The gradients can be obtained by a direct application of chain rule. For compact notation, let

$$\sigma(x) = \frac{1}{1 + \exp(x)} \ . \tag{10}$$

From (3) and (4), we get the gradients

$$\nabla_{\Delta_i(k,j)} \ell(\Delta_i(k,j)) = -\sigma(\Delta_i(k,j)) \ , \tag{11}$$

$$\nabla_{\mathbf{u}_i} \Delta_i(k,j) = (\mathbf{v}_k - \mathbf{v}_j) \ , \tag{12}$$

$$\nabla_{\mathbf{v}_h} \Delta_i(k,j) = \begin{cases} \mathbf{u}_i \ , & \text{if } h = k \ , \\ -\mathbf{u}_i \ , & \text{if } h = j \ . \end{cases} \tag{13}$$

By chain rule, the gradient of the objective w.r.t. $\mathbf{u}_i$ is

$$\nabla_{\mathbf{u}_i} \mathcal{E}_{\text{p-push}}(U,V)$$

$$= \frac{p}{n_i} \sum_{j \in L_i^-} \left\{ (\tilde{H}_i(x_j^-))^{p-1} \sum_{k \in L_i^+} \sigma(\Delta_i(k,j))(\mathbf{v}_j - \mathbf{v}_k) \right\} .$$

The latent factors $\mathbf{v}_h$ play different roles for different users, depending on whether x_h is relevant or non-relevant for user ρ_i. For item x_h, let Γ_h^+ be the set of users for which x_h is relevant, and letΓ_h^- be the set of users for which x_h is non-relevant. There may be additional users who have no (announced) preference on item x_h, and the optimization of $\mathbf{v}_h$ will not depend on these users. Then, by dividing the sum over all users into sums overΓ_h^+ andΓ_h^- and noting the gradients of$\Delta_i(k,j)$ w.r.t. $\mathbf{v}_h$ for the two cases from (13), by chain rule we have

$$\nabla_{\mathbf{v}_h}\mathcal{E}_{\text{p-push}}(U,V)$$

$$= \sum_{i\in\Gamma_h^-}\frac{p}{n_i}\sum_{j\in L_i^-}\left\{(\tilde{H}_i(x_j^-))^{p-1}\sum_{k\in L_i^+}\sigma(\Delta_i(k,j))\mathbf{u}_i\right\}$$

$$-\sum_{i\in\Gamma_h^+}\frac{p}{n_i}\sum_{j\in L_i^-}\left\{(\tilde{H}_i(x_j^-))^{p-1}\sum_{k\in L_i^+}\sigma(\Delta_i(k,j))\mathbf{u}_i\right\} .$$

In practice, instead of summing over all users inΓ_h^+,Γ_h^-, one can pick a mini-batch of users to do the update on, in the flavor of stochastic or mini-batch gradient descent.

3.3 Infinite Push Collaborative Ranking

The main idea in infinite push collaborative ranking (`Inf-Push CR`), building on [3], is to consider the L_∞ norm, i.e., the largest element, of the surrogate height vector $\tilde{H}_i$, and construct an objective function as a suitable scaled sum of such norms over all users. In particular, we consider the objective

$$\mathcal{E}_{\text{inf-push}}(U,V) = \sum_{i=1}^{m}\frac{\|\tilde{H}_i\|_\infty}{n_i} = \sum_{i=1}^{m}\frac{1}{n_i}\max_{j\in L_i^-}\tilde{H}_i(x_j^-) \quad (14)$$

$$= \sum_{i=1}^{m}\frac{1}{n_i}\max_{j\in L_i^-}\left(\sum_{k\in L_i^+}\log\left(1+\exp(-\mathbf{u}_i^T(\mathbf{v}_k-\mathbf{v}_j))\right)\right) .$$

From an optimization perspective, the infinite push objective above is non-smooth, since it considers the maximum over all elements in $\tilde{H}_i$. One can consider a sub-gradient descent approach, or add auxiliary variables to handle the non-smoothness, and possibly consider the dual problem. Such approaches, however, can be slow in practice, and ignore the specific type of non-smoothness in the problem. In our approach we observe that fixing any one variable U or V, the problem is a smooth minimax problem in the other variable, for which efficient gradient-like first order methods exist [26]. We discuss such efficient updates for U, while keeping V fixed, noting that similar updates are possible for V, leading to suitable alternating minimization algorithms.

Consider the latent factor $\mathbf{u}_i$ corresponding to user ρ_i. Assuming V is fixed, the objective function to minimize for $\mathbf{u}_i$ is given by the max-type function

$$f(\mathbf{u}_i) = \max_{j\in L_i^-} f_j(\mathbf{u}_i) \quad (15)$$

where

$$f_j(\mathbf{u}_i) \triangleq \sum_{k\in L_i^+}\log\left(1+\exp(-\mathbf{u}_i^T\mathbf{a}_{kj})\right) , \quad (16)$$

with $\mathbf{a}_{kj} = (\mathbf{v}_k - \mathbf{v}_j)$ being a fixed vector. Note that $f_j(\mathbf{u}_i) = \tilde{H}_i(x_j^-)$, and we are using a more suitable notation for the current discussion illustrating the dependency on $\mathbf{u}_i$. For the development, we assume that each $f_j(\mathbf{u}_i)$ are α-strongly convex and β-smooth [26]. For the current setting, the assumptions are satisfied as long as $\mathbf{u}_i, \mathbf{v}_j$ are bounded.

Following [26], we define the linearization of the max-type function $f(\mathbf{u}_i)$ at $\bar{\mathbf{u}}_i$ as

$$f(\bar{\mathbf{u}}_i;\mathbf{u}_i) = \max_{j\in L_i^-}\left[f_j(\bar{\mathbf{u}}_i) + \langle\nabla f_j(\bar{\mathbf{u}}_i), \mathbf{u}_i - \bar{\mathbf{u}}_i\rangle\right] . \quad (17)$$

In order to define a gradient mapping, we consider a proximal operator of the linearization, given by

$$f_\gamma(\bar{\mathbf{u}}_i;\mathbf{u}_i) = f(\bar{\mathbf{u}}_i;\mathbf{u}_i) + \frac{\gamma}{2}\|\mathbf{u}_i - \bar{\mathbf{u}}_i\|^2 , \quad (18)$$

where $\gamma > 0$. Based on the proximal operator, let

$$f^*(\bar{\mathbf{u}}_i;\gamma) = \min_{\mathbf{u}_i} f_\gamma(\bar{\mathbf{u}}_i;\mathbf{u}_i) , \quad (19)$$

$$\mathbf{u}_i^*(\bar{\mathbf{u}}_i;\gamma) = \operatorname*{argmin}_{\mathbf{u}_i} f_\gamma(\bar{\mathbf{u}}_i;\mathbf{u}_i) , \quad (20)$$

$$\mathbf{g}_f(\bar{\mathbf{u}}_i;\gamma) = \gamma(\bar{\mathbf{u}}_i - \mathbf{u}_i^*(\bar{\mathbf{u}}_i;\gamma)) , \quad (21)$$

where $\mathbf{g}_f(\bar{\mathbf{u}}_i;\gamma)$ is the gradient mapping of the max-type function f at $\bar{\mathbf{u}}_i$ [26, Section 2.3]. Assuming the individual functions f_j, the gradient method for the minimax problem is given by the simple iterative update:

$$\mathbf{u}_i^{t+1} \leftarrow \mathbf{u}_i^t - \eta\mathbf{g}_f(\mathbf{u}_i^t;\gamma) , \quad (22)$$

where η is the learning rate and $\mathbf{u}_i^t$ serves as the linearization point $\bar{\mathbf{u}}_i$. Since each function $f_j(\mathbf{u}_i)$ is β-smooth, we can set $\gamma = \beta$. With any $\eta \leq \frac{1}{\beta}$, the gradient method has an exponential convergence rate [26, Theorem 2.3.4], which is substantially better than just treating the problem as non-smooth optimization and using sub-gradient descent [26].

The key step in obtaining the gradient mapping in (21) is to solve the optimization problem in (19). Using the definition of the linearization and the proximal operator [27], we get the following optimization problem:

$$\min_{\mathbf{u}_i}\left\{\max_{j\in L_i^-}[f_j(\bar{\mathbf{u}}_i) + \langle\nabla f_j(\bar{\mathbf{u}}_i), \mathbf{u}_i - \bar{\mathbf{u}}_i\rangle] + \frac{\gamma}{2}\|\mathbf{u}_i - \bar{\mathbf{u}}_i\|^2\right\} . \quad (23)$$

The above problem is the proximal operator of a piecewise linear function. The problem can be rewritten as a constrained optimization problem:

$$\begin{aligned}\min_{\mathbf{u}_i,t}\ & t + \frac{\gamma}{2}\|\mathbf{u}_i - \bar{\mathbf{u}}_i\|^2 \\ \text{s.t.}\ & f_j(\bar{\mathbf{u}}_i) + \langle\nabla f_j(\bar{\mathbf{u}}_i), \mathbf{u}_i - \bar{\mathbf{u}}_i\rangle \leq t .\end{aligned} \quad (24)$$

A direct calculation shows that the dual of the constrained problem is equivalent to a quadratic minimization problem over the probability simplex:

$$\min_{\mathbf{y}}\mathbf{y}^TQ\mathbf{y} + \mathbf{b}^T\mathbf{y} \quad \text{s.t.} \quad \sum_j y_j = 1,\ \ y_j \geq 0 , \quad (25)$$

where Q is a positive semi-definite matrix. The dual objective is concave, and simply the negative of the above quadratic form, and $\mathbf{y}$ corresponds to the Lagrange multipliers. The quadratic problem with simplex constraints can be solved by a projected gradient or exponentiated gradient method [15, 18]. In practice, we use early stopping of the dual projected gradient descent, compute the gradient mapping, and update $\mathbf{u}_i$ based on (22).

3.4 Reverse-Height Push Collaborative Ranking

We now consider a formulation based on the reverse height $R_i(x_k^+)$ of positive items x_k^+ for user ρ_i as in (2). As discussed in [30], the reverse height is similar to the rank of a positive item x_k^+, but only considering the negative items x_j^- which are above it, and disregarding the other positive items. By treating reverse height as a surrogate for rank, one can follow the existing literature on learning to rank, and consider maximizing objectives such as reciprocal rank or discounted cumulative gain (DCG), e.g., for each user ρ_i,

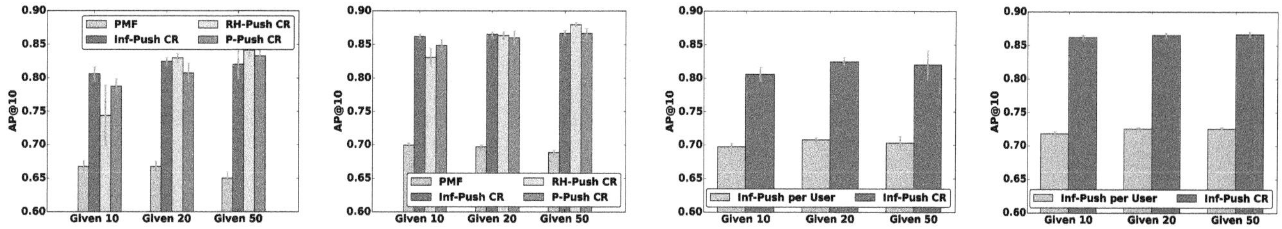

(a) MovieLens 100K (b) MovieLens 1M (c) MovieLens 100K (d) MovieLens 1M

Figure 1: (a),(b): Ranking vs. Rating Prediction (PMF) for the two MovieLens datasets. All Push CR methods outperform PMF in terms of AP@10. (c),(d): `Inf-Push CR` vs. Infinite Push per User for the two MovieLens datasets. Collaboratively learning ranking function results in better top 10 performance than constructing different ranking model per user.

maximize

$$\sum_{k \in L_i^+} \frac{1}{R_i(x_k^+)} \quad \text{or} \quad \sum_{k \in L_i^+} \frac{1}{\log(1 + R_i(x_k^+))} .$$

However, these objectives are difficult to directly maximize. Instead, staying in the spirit of these objectives, we consider the following objective

$$\sum_{k \in L_i^+} \log \left(\frac{1}{1 + R_i(x_k^+)} \right) ,$$

which decreases with increasing rank.

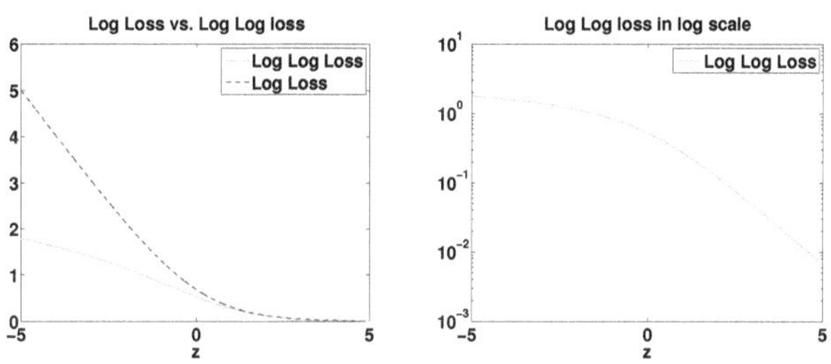

(a) Log-log vs. logistic loss (b) Log-log loss in log-scale

Figure 2: (a) A comparison of log-log loss with the logistic loss, and (b) the log-log loss with a y-log scale.

To maintain consistency with the earlier formulations, we consider minimizing the negative of the objective. Further, using the surrogate reverse height $\tilde{R}_i(x_k^+)$ as in (6), and considering the objective over all users, we focus on minimizing the following objective for reverse height push collaborative ranking:

$$\mathcal{E}_{\text{rh-push}}(U, V) = \sum_{i=1}^{m} \frac{1}{n_i} \sum_{k \in L_i^+} \log(1 + \tilde{R}_i(x_k^+)) \qquad (26)$$

where

$$\tilde{R}_i(x_k^+) = \sum_{j \in L_i^-} \log \left(1 + \exp(-\mathbf{u}_i^T(\mathbf{v}_k - \mathbf{v}_j)) \right) . \qquad (27)$$

Denoting$\Delta_i(k, j) = z$ for simplicity, the above loss has components of the form $\log(1 + \log(1 + \exp(-z))$, which we refer to as log-log loss. Interestingly, while the log-log loss is not convex, it is quasi-convex and monotonic decreasing, as shown in Figure 2. Further, the objective is more robust than the logistic loss for negative z, and stays closer to the 0-1 loss for which it acts as a surrogate. Related non-convex losses have been explored in the literature, e.g., in the context of t-logistic regression [14].

As in Section 3.2, we use alternating minimization of the objective in (26), i.e., updating U keeping V fixed, and updating V keeping U fixed. In the current setting, the alternating minimization will reach a stationary point, possibly a local minimum of the objective. As we discuss in Section 4, the empirical results from the log-log loss are surprisingly good along with fairly stable parameter sensitivity, which implies the need for further study of the loss. For alternating minimization, the updates can be done using gradient descent:

$$\mathbf{u}_i^{t+1} \leftarrow \mathbf{u}_i^t - \eta \nabla_{\mathbf{u}_i} \mathcal{E}_{\text{rh-push}}(U^t, V^t) , \quad i = 1, \dots, m, \qquad (28)$$

$$\mathbf{v}_h^{t+1} \leftarrow \mathbf{v}_h^t - \eta \nabla_{\mathbf{v}_h} \mathcal{E}_{\text{rh-push}}(U^{t+1}, V^t) , \quad h = 1, \dots, n. \qquad (29)$$

As before, the gradients can be obtained by chain rule. Using (11) and (12), from (26) we have

$$\nabla_{\mathbf{u}_i} \mathcal{E}_{\text{rh-push}}(U, V)$$

$$- \frac{1}{n_i} \sum_{k \in L_i^+} \left\{ \frac{1}{1 + \tilde{R}_i(x_k^+)} \sum_{j \in L_i^-} \sigma(\Delta_i(k, j))(\mathbf{v}_j \quad \mathbf{v}_k) \right\} .$$

Recall that the latent factors $\mathbf{v}_h$ play different roles for different users, depending on whether x_h is relevant or not for user ρ_i. As before, for item x_h, let Γ_h^+ be the set of users for which x_h is relevant, and letΓ_h^- be the set of users for which x_h is non-relevant. There may be additional users who have no (announced) preference on item x_h, and the optimization of $\mathbf{v}_h$ will not depend on these users. Then, by dividing the sum over all users into sums overΓ_h^+ and Γ_h^- and noting the gradients of$\Delta_i(k, j)$ w.r.t. $\mathbf{v}_h$ for the two cases from (13), from (26), by chain rule we have

$$\nabla_{\mathbf{v}_h} \mathcal{E}_{\text{rh-push}}(U, V)$$

$$= \sum_{i \in \Gamma_h^-} \frac{1}{n_i} \sum_{j \in L_i^-} \left\{ \frac{1}{1 + \tilde{R}_i(x_k^+)} \sum_{k \in L_i^+} \sigma(\Delta_i(k, j)) \mathbf{u}_i \right\}$$

$$- \sum_{i \in \Gamma_h^+} \frac{1}{n_i} \sum_{j \in L_i^-} \left\{ \frac{1}{1 + \tilde{R}_i(x_k^+)} \sum_{k \in L_i^+} \sigma(\Delta_i(k, j)) \mathbf{u}_i \right\} .$$

Again, in practice, instead of summing over all users in Γ_h^+, Γ_h^-, one can pick a mini-batch of users to do the update on, in the flavor of stochastic or mini-batch gradient descent.

Remark: For all of our proposed formulations we consider an additional regularization term $\frac{\lambda}{2}(\|U\|^2+\|V\|^2)$. The gradient term for the $\mathbf{u}_i$ updates then has an additional term $\lambda\mathbf{u}_i$, and similarly for the $\mathbf{v}_h$ updates. Also, the computational complexity for computing the gradients for a user ρ_i in one iteration is $\mathcal{O}(n_i^+ n_i^-)$, which is small in practice since $n_i^+, n_i^- \ll n$, the total number of items.

4. EXPERIMENTS

We conducted extensive experiments in order to validate the performance of the three proposed collaborative ranking approaches (`P-Push CR`, `Inf-Push CR`, `RH-Push CR`) on real world datasets. We have divided our experiments into three sets in order to address the following questions: (i) What is the impact of posing the problem as a rating prediction problem versus a ranking one, i.e., optimizing for the square loss versus a ranking loss with focus on the top of the list? (ii) Is learning the ranking functions *collaboratively* across all users more effective than constructing a separate ranking model per user? (iii) Do the proposed push collaborative ranking approaches outperform state-of-the-art CR approaches for recommendation systems? After discussing the experimental setup, we evaluate these questions empirically in Sections 4.2, 4.3, and 4.4 respectively.

4.1 Experimental Setting

Datasets. We used four publicly available datasets for our experiments: three movie datasets MovieLens 100K, MovieLens 1M, EachMovie and a musical artist dataset from Yahoo! which contains user ratings of music artists [41]. The two MovieLens datasets were kept in their original form. The EachMovie dataset used was a subset of the original EachMovie including the ratings of 30,000 randomly selected users with 20 or more ratings[1]. The Yahoo! dataset was subsampled to speed up the experiments, since the original dataset had close to 2 million users and 100,000 items. For the Yahoo! dataset, we first selected the 1,000 most popular items and then selected the 6,000 most heavy users (with the most ratings). In addition to the subsampling we removed the user ratings of the special value 255 ('never play again') and rescaled user ratings from 0-100 to the 1-5 interval. The rescaling was done by mapping 0-19 to 1, 20-39 to 2, etc. The procedure followed for the Yahoo! dataset is close to the one described in [38]. The users, items and ratings statistics are summarized in Table 1.

Dataset	# Users	# Items	# Ratings
MovieLens 100K	943	1,682	100,000
MovieLens 1M	6,040	3,706	1,000,209
EachMovie	30,000	1,623	2,109,780
Yahoo! R1	6,000	1,000	3,522,232

Table 1: Dataset Statistics

Data Split. Throughout our experiments we adopted the "weak" generalization setting which has become standard practice in the literature [5, 22, 38, 39]. In this setting, we fix the number of training ratings per user $n_i = \{10, 20, 50\}$ and randomly choose n_i ratings for each user for training, 10 ratings for validation, and test on the remaining ratings. The experimental setting facilitates the comparison with the state-of-the-art approaches and allows the study of the ranking algorithms' sensitivity to the number of available training ratings per user. Users with less than $n_i + 20$ ratings are removed to ensure that we can evaluate on at least 10 ratings for each user. Note that the number of test items vary significantly across users, with many users having many more test ratings than training ones, thus simulating the real life recommendation scenario [38]. For each setting of 'given n_i' ratings per user we repeated the whole procedure 10 times and reported the mean and standard deviation of the results.

Setup. In the evaluation phase, for each user, we compare pairs of items $(x_h, x_{h'})$ belonging to the test set for that user, such that each of these items have appeared in the training set of some users. Using such items ensures that the latent factors of the items have been updated during training, and we are not working with their randomly initialized value. In addition, in order to simulate the setup of two-level relevance ratings (Section 3), we transformed the ratings of all datasets from a multi-level relevance scale to a two-level scale $(+1, -1)$, i.e., using 4 as relevance threshold for MovieLens 100K, MovieLens 1M and Yahoo!, and 5 for EachMovie. In particular, for the two MovieLens datasets and the Yahoo! dataset, ratings of the value 4-5 are marked as relevant, and 1-3 are marked as non-relevant. For the EachMovie dataset 5-6 are marked as relevant, and 1-4 are marked as non-relevant. Also, we removed users with no positive (relevant) or no negative (non-relevant) ratings in the training set, so that there is at least one positive example to "pull up" or at least one negative example to "push down". The exact same input was given to all algorithms.

Evaluation Metrics. Since our goal is to achieve accuracy towards the top of the ranked list, we chose two evaluation metrics which reflect this and have been widely used in the learning to rank literature [7, 11, 21].

In the definitions below, we assume that the items are enumerated according to the decreasing order of their scores. We will denote with k the truncation threshold, reflecting the number of recommendations we want to consider. Let r be the index ranging over positions in the ranked list ($r = \{1, \ldots, k\}$), and $rel(r)$ denote the relevance of the r-th item for the user. For the definition of *Average Precision@k*, $rel(r) = 0$ if this is a non-relevant item for the user, $rel(r) = 1$ otherwise. For the computation of *NDCG@k*, $rel(r)$ equals to the user's observed rating from the multi-level scale, i.e., 1-6 for EachMovie, 1-5 for the rest of the datasets. The latter choice was made for the sake of consistency with the state-of-the-art literature [38, 39], though during training all approaches have access just to the two-level relevance scale ratings.

Average Precision@k (*AP@k*) is defined as the average of Precisions computed at each relevant position in the top k items of the user's ranked list. *Precision@r* (*P@r*) equals the fraction of relevant items out of the top r ranked items.

$$AP@k = \sum_{r=1}^{k} \frac{P@r \cdot rel(r)}{\min(k, \#\text{ of relevant items})} \tag{30}$$

DCG@k captures the importance of finding the correct ordering among higher ranked items compared to that among lower ranked items, by discounting the importance weight with the item's position in the ranked list. *DCG@k* is formally given by

$$DCG@k - \sum_{r=1}^{k} \frac{2^{rel(r)} - 1}{\log_2(r+1)} \tag{31}$$

[1] http://mlcomp.org/datasets/350

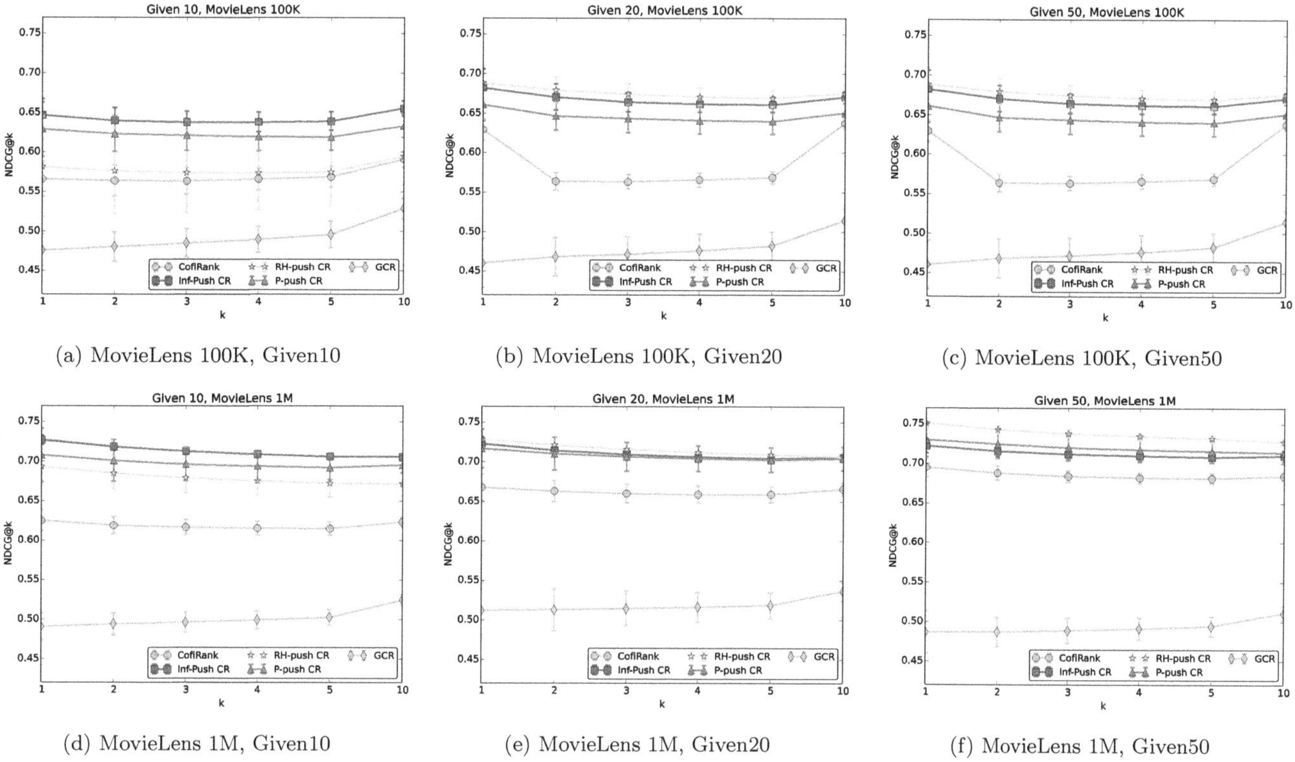

(a) MovieLens 100K, Given10 (b) MovieLens 100K, Given20 (c) MovieLens 100K, Given50

(d) MovieLens 1M, Given10 (e) MovieLens 1M, Given20 (f) MovieLens 1M, Given50

Figure 3: Comparison of performance of the proposed Push CR models against CofiRank and GCR in NDCG@k for $k = \{1, 2, 3, 4, 5, 10\}$ for the two MovieLens datasets. All of our proposed Push CR methods outperform CofiRank and GCR.

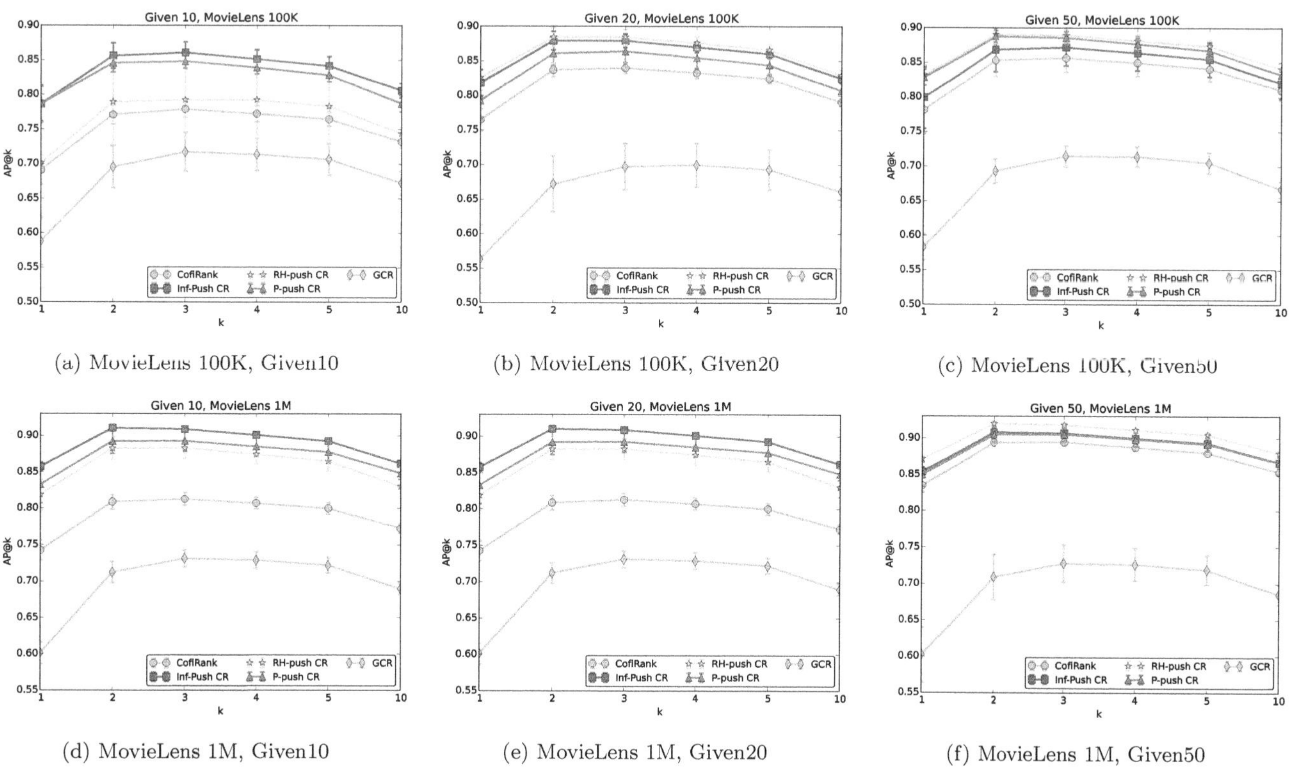

(a) MovieLens 100K, Given10 (b) MovieLens 100K, Given20 (c) MovieLens 100K, Given50

(d) MovieLens 1M, Given10 (e) MovieLens 1M, Given20 (f) MovieLens 1M, Given50

Figure 4: Comparison of performance of the proposed Push CR models against CofiRank and GCR in Average Precision@k for $k = \{1, 2, 3, 4, 5, 10\}$ for the two MovieLens datasets. All of our proposed Push CR methods outperform CofiRank and GCR.

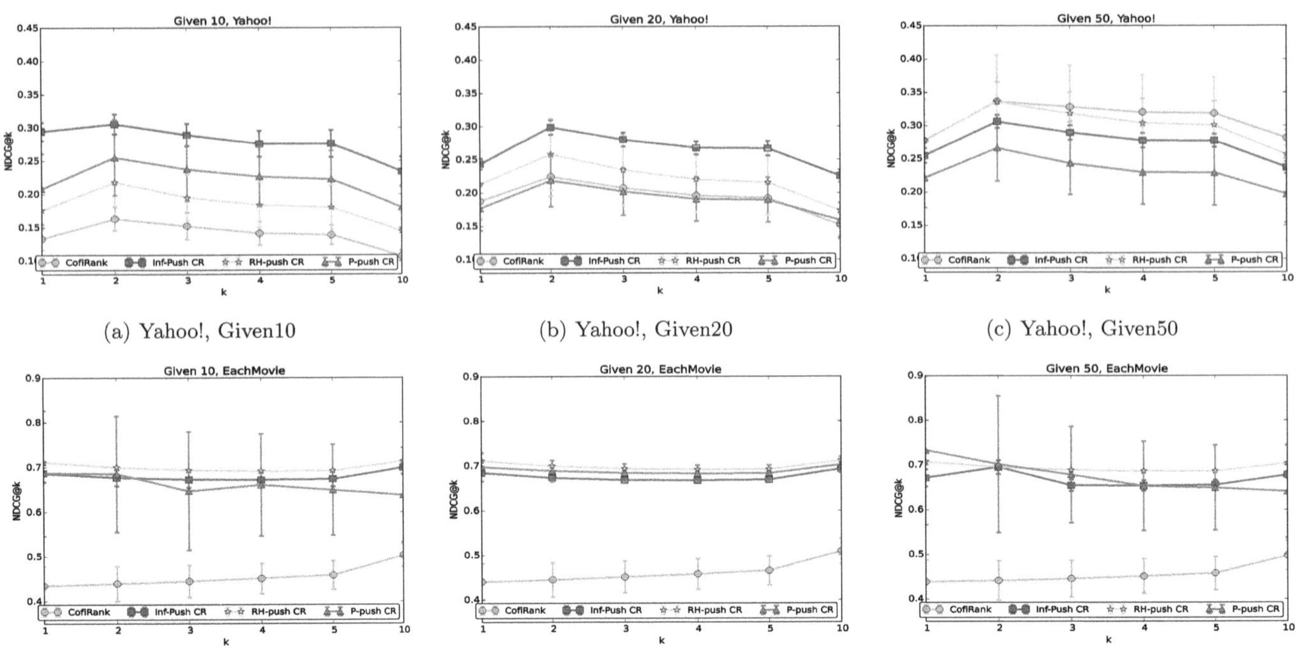

(a) Yahoo!, Given10 (b) Yahoo!, Given20 (c) Yahoo!, Given50

(d) EachMovie, Given10 (e) EachMovie, Given20 (f) EachMovie, Given50

Figure 5: Comparison of performance of the proposed Push CR models vs. CofiRank in NDCG@k for the Yahoo! and EachMovie datasets. In most cases at least one (usually all) of our proposed Push CR methods outperforms CofiRank.

$NDCG@k$ is the ratio of $DCG@k$ to the Ideal $DCG@k$ for that user, i.e the $DCG@k$ obtained had the user's recommendation list been sorted according to the ground truth ratings given by the user.

In our experiments, after computing the metrics per user, we averaged the results over all users and reported the results for Mean Average Precision@k (MAP@k) and Mean NDCG@k. We varied k from 1 to 10 as this is usually the size of a recommendation list fitting a device's screen.

Model Parameters. The validation set was used for selecting the best model parameters. We varied the regularization coefficient λ in the range $\{10^{-4}, 10^{-3}, 10^{-2}, 10^{-1}, 1\}$ and the rank of the latent factors in {5, 10, 20, 30, 50, 70, 90}. We fixed the learning rate for the gradient based updates to be $\eta = 10^{-4}$ for MovieLens 1M and Yahoo!, and $\eta = 10^{-3}$ for MovieLens 100K and EachMovie. In addition, the validation set was used to determine early stopping. We stopped either after 200 iterations or when the improvement in MAP@5 in the validation set got smaller than some threshold (10^{-4}).

For the `p-Push CR` method we set the parameter $p = 2$, which gives a small push towards the top of the list. The reason we chose a small p was because of numerical instabilities which appeared for higher values of p. For the inner optimization problem (23) of the `Inf-Push CR` approach, we used the following parameter setting: We set γ of the proximal operator equal to 10, learning rate equal to 0.01 and regularization coefficient $1/\gamma = 0.1$. Early stopping was used, since there was no need to solve the inner problem fully as in the next outer iteration the same optimization problem would have to be solved. We stopped either when the improvement in the value of the optimization problem was smaller than 0.01 or after 25 iterations.

4.2 Validation: Ranking vs. Rating Prediction

In the first set of experiments, we validate the effect of optimizing for a ranking based loss function versus the square loss. Since such a comparison has been explored in the recent literature [5, 39], we limit the set of experiments to a direct comparison between Probabilistic Matrix Factorization (PMF) [25] (*rating prediction*) and the proposed Push CR approaches (*ranking*) in terms of AP@10. For the experiments, we used the two MovieLens datasets, with the number n_i of training ratings per user set to vary in the range of $\{10, 20, 50\}$. Figures 1(a) and 1(b) illustrate the superiority of optimizing a ranking based loss function compared to the square loss. The results support the effectiveness of posing recommendation systems as a ranking problem rather than a rating prediction problem based on squared loss. Thus, in the sequel we focus on comparing ranking approaches.

4.3 Validation: Collaborative vs. Individual

The second set of experiments is conducted to examine whether collaborative ranking, i.e., learning latent factors for the users and items from the rating matrix, results in higher ranking accuracy compared to training separate ranking functions per user. For this task, we compare the proposed collaborative model for Infinite Push (`Inf-Push CR`) with the approach of building a separate Infinite Push model per user (Inf-Push per User). We again used the two MovieLens datasets, varying the number n_i of training ratings per user in the range of $\{10, 20, 50\}$ and reported the mean and standard deviation of AP@10. For Inf-Push per User we implemented Infinite Push as in [3] and used the feature vectors of the items (movie genre) in order to learn the linear ranking function [1, 33]. Note that according to [33], genre seems to be the most informative feature among other types

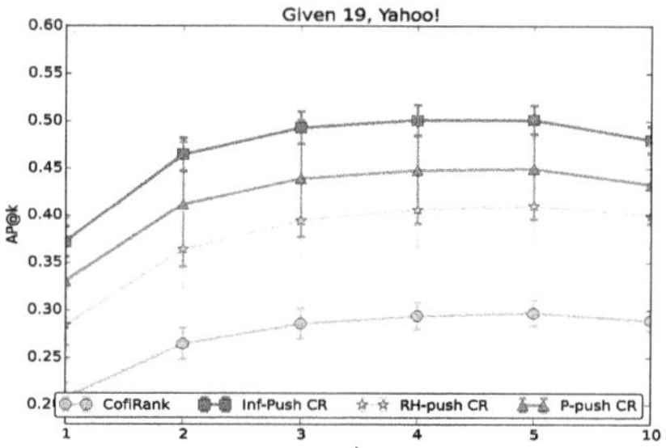

(a) Yahoo!, Given10

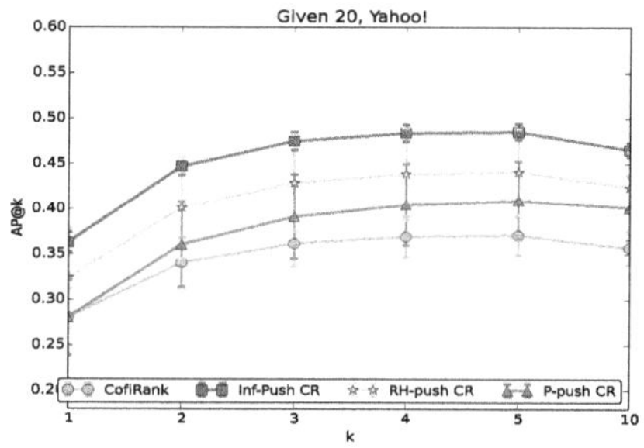

(b) Yahoo!, Given20

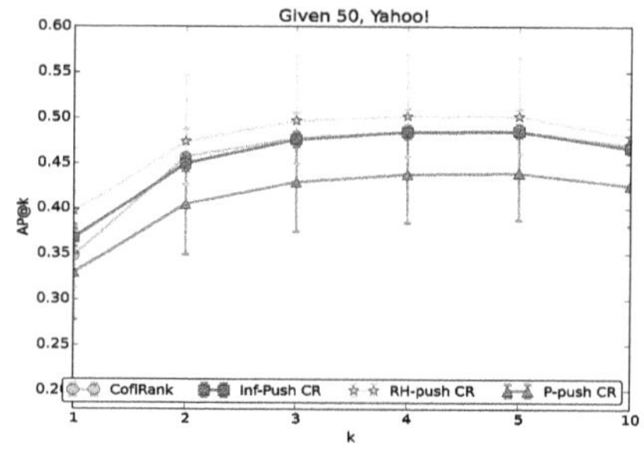

(c) Yahoo!, Given50

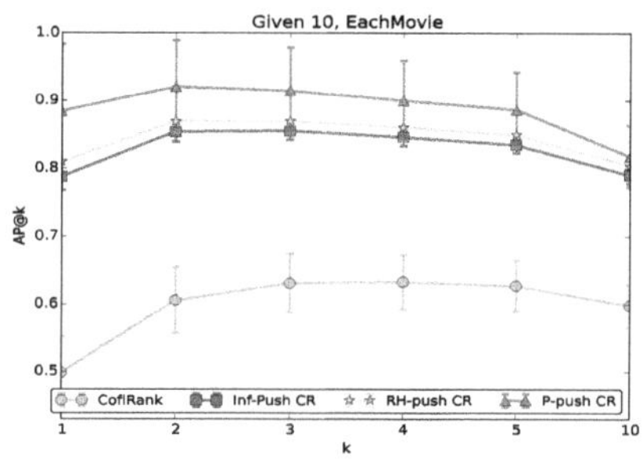

(d) EachMovie, Given10

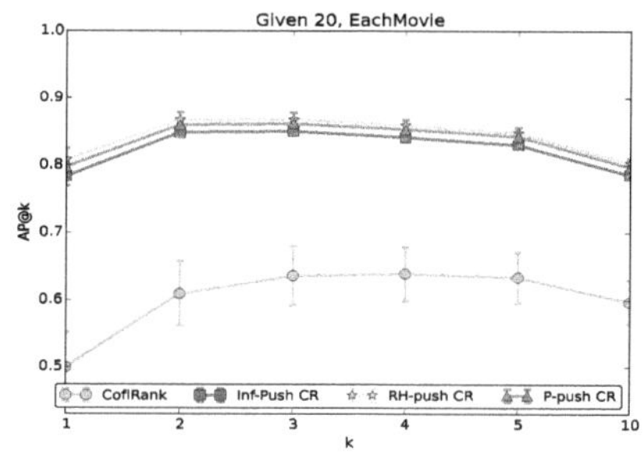

(e) EachMovie, Given20

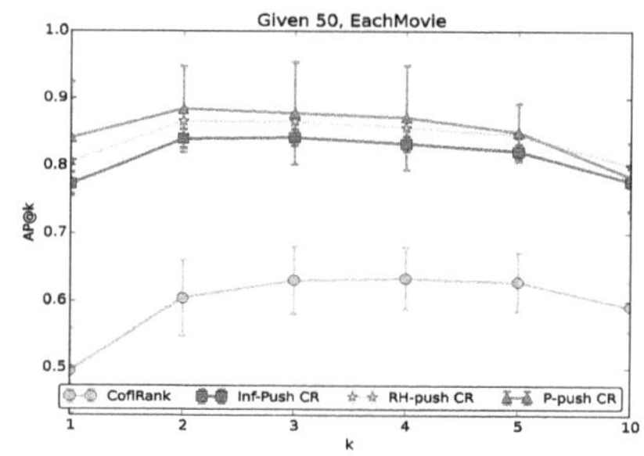

(f) EachMovie, Given50

Figure 6: Comparison of performance of the proposed Push CR models vs. CofiRank in AP@k for the Yahoo! and EachMovie datasets. In all cases at least one (usually all) of our proposed Push CR methods outperforms CofiRank.

of side information. Further, any helpful feature one can add for the items, the collaborative model can also be extended to take advantage of such features. Figures 1(c) and 1(d) show that learning the latent factors collaboratively clearly outperforms learning a separate ranking function per user using the rated items' features. The experiment validates the effectiveness of the collaborative ranking framework and allows us to focus on CR approaches for recommendation for the rest of the paper.

4.4 Comparison of Proposed Approaches

In the third set of experiments, we address the question: Do our three proposed CR approaches, i.e., `p-Push CR`, `Inf-Push CR`, `RH-Push CR` outperform the state-of-the-art CR methods? We compare the Push CR methods with CofiRank [39], which is considered a very popular baseline in the CR literature and with Global Collaborative Ranking (GCR) [22] which is the ranking counterpart of PMF-type methods. For CofiRank, we used the publicly available package[2] and set the same parameter values provided in the original paper [39] (rank = 100 and $\lambda = 10$), and default values provided in the source code for unstated parameters. For GCR, we implemented the source code based on the publicly available package[3] since the original code used slightly different experimental setting than ours, making the comparison of the different methods difficult. In the GCR experiments, we chose the local model rank in the validation set, varying it in the range $\{5, 10, 15, 20\}$ and the regularization parameter λ in $\{10^{-3}, 10^{-2}, 10^{-1}\}$, and kept the rest of the parameters in their default values given in the package. Also, we optimized for the average number of mis-ordered pairs (0-1 error) [22, Eq (6)] and we stopped the algorithm either when the improvement in the 0-1 error in the validation set got smaller than some threshold (0.001) or after 200 iterations.

Results and Discussion. We report the mean and standard deviation of AP@top and NDCG@top over 10 runs, where 'top' varies in the range of {1, 2, 3, 4, 5, 10} and the fixed number of training ratings per user (n_i) varies in {10, 20, 50}. Recall that the parameters, such as rank, regularization parameter, and early stopping, for the Push CR methods were all chosen based on performance on AP@5 in the validation set. Figures 3(a)-(c), 3(d)-(f), 5(a)-(c), 5(d)-(f) compare the competing methods in terms of NDCG@top for the MovieLens 100K, 1M, EachMovie and Yahoo! datasets respectively, whereas figures 4(a)-(c), 4(d)-(f), 6(a)-(c), 6(d)-(f) show the corresponding AP@top comparison.

Based on the experimental results illustrated in Figures 3, 4, 5, 6 we conclude that in most cases at least one (usually all) of our proposed Push CR methods outperforms CofiRank in terms of both ranking metrics. The only case where the mean of NDCG@top of CofiRank outperforms the proposed approaches is for Yahoo!, Given 50. For the same case, the mean of AP@top of CofiRank almost coincides with that of `Inf-Push CR`, is higher than that of `P-Push CR` but is outperformed by `RH-Push CR`. For the case of Yahoo!, Given 20, the NDCG@ top of CofiRank outperforms that of `P-Push CR` but lags behind `Inf-Push CR` and `RH-Push CR`. So, overall, our Push CR approaches significantly outperform CofiRank. In addition, from our experiments in the two MovieLens datasets, we observe that CofiRank and all proposed Push CR methods always outperform GCR in terms of the two top-k ranking metrics.

We can also compare the performance among the proposed Push CR methods. The improvement of `Inf-Push CR`

[2] www.cofirank.org [3] prea.gatech.edu

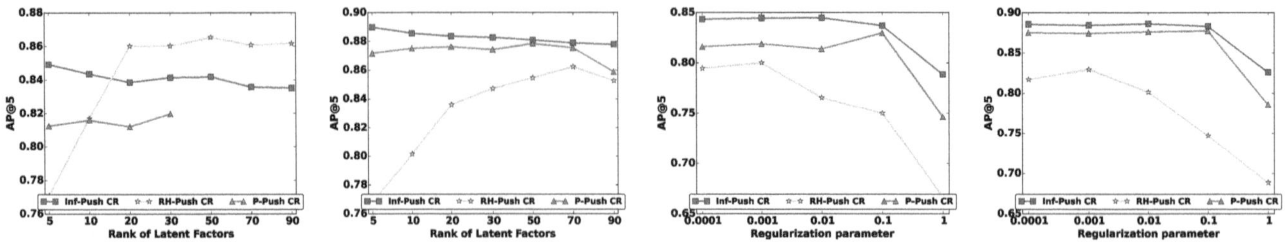

(a) MovieLens 100K (b) MovieLens 1M (c) MovieLens 100K (d) MovieLens 1M

Figure 7: Effect of Rank of Latent Factors and Regularization parameter on AP@5 for MovieLens 100K and MovieLens 1M, for $n_i = 10$. (a)(b) The rank varies in $\{5, 10, 20, 30, 50, 70, 90\}$ while the regularizer is fixed to 0.0001. (c)(d) The regularizer λ varies in $\{0.001, 0.001, 0.1, 1\}$ while rank= 10. For high values of rank and λ, AP@5 decreases.

is particularly notable when the amount of available training points (n_i) is small. For n_i=10, **Inf-Push CR** outperforms all other methods in terms of both AP@top and NDCG@top, in all datasets apart from EachMovie (where it lags behind `P-Push CR`). In contrast, the improvement of **RH-Push CR** is particularly notable when the amount of available training points (n_i) grows larger. For n_i=50, **RH-Push CR** outperforms the rest of Push CR methods in both AP@top and NDCG@top, except for EachMovie, where the mean of AP@top lags behind that of `P-Push CR`. Also, `P-Push CR` has the most variability in its performance across the ten runs.

Comparison with CLiMF

For completeness, we also compare the proposed Push CR methods with another state-of-the-art method, CLiMF [34]. Such a comparison is tricky as CLiMF uses implicit binary ratings data while Push CR methods use explicit binary ratings. We train CLiMF on the explicit feedback datasets by binarizing the rating values using 4 as the relevance threshold, treating ratings of value 1-3 as 0 (not observed). Otherwise, we evaluate CLiMF using exactly the same setup as in the rest of the methods. For this experiment, we use the MovieLens 100K and 1M datasets, fix the number of training ratings per user $n_i = 20$, choose best parameters (λ: $\{10^{-4}$, 10^{-3}, 10^{-2}, 10^{-1},1}, rank: {5, 10, 20, 30, 50, 70, 90}) in the validation set and report the mean of AP@5 and NDCG@5 over ten random runs. Results are reported in Table 2 and show that the Push CR methods are competitive, usually better on AP@5 and NDCG@5 compared to CLiMF. Similar trends were observed for different values of 'top' and for $n_i = 10$, $n_i = 50$, and are thus omitted.

	MovieLens 100K		MovieLens 1M	
Method	AP@5	NDCG@5	AP@5	NDCG@5
CLiMF	0.8446	0.6424	0.8787	0.6982
`Inf-Push CR`	0.8605	0.6612	**0.8938**	0.7042
`RH-Push CR`	**0.8665**	**0.6693**	0.8926	**0.7092**
`P-Push CR`	0.8443	0.6402	0.8865	0.7028

Table 2: Comparison of `Push CR` methods with CLiMF.

4.5 Parameter Sensitivity Analysis

Figures 7(a)-(d) show how the Push CR models behave with different combinations of parameters. We used the two MovieLens datasets, fixing the number of training ratings per user n_i=10. To study the effect of the rank of the latent factors on the model performance, we varied it in the range of $\{5, 10, 20, 30, 50, 70, 90\}$ while keeping the regularizer λ fixed to 0.0001. Figures 7(a)-(b) show that there is a decrease in AP@5 for high values of rank (70, 90). For `P-Push CR`, in the MovieLens 100K dataset, higher values of rank resulted in numerical instability issues. Also, in order to study the effect of the regularizer on the model performance, we varied λ in the range of $\{0.0001, 0.001, 0.01, 1\}$ while keeping the rank fixed to 10. Figures 7(c)-(d) show that for all three methods there is a decrease in AP@5 for high values of λ (0.1, 1). Note that we have performed early stopping based on the validation set, which leads to robustness of our methods to different parameter choices.

5. CONCLUSION

The paper builds on and merges two keys themes from the collaborative filtering and learning to rank literature: the use of a low rank representation for collaborative scoring, and the use of ranking losses which focus on the accuracy at the top of the list, by pushing down non-relevant items and/or pulling up relevant items. The merge results in a family of novel collaborative ranking algorithms with a push at the top of the ranked list for each user. The proposed algorithms are simple and scalable from an optimization perspective and are shown to be competitive to state-of-the-art baselines through extensive experiments. The modular structure of the develoment shows that other representations, beyond low rank, and other ranking losses, beyond the three considered here, can be considered with simple changes to the ideas presented.

Our methods are applicable in a variety of settings where (i) explicit binary relevance ratings are available (i.e., helpfulness of a review, like/dislike of a song) and (ii) implicit binary ratings are treated as explicit (i.e., considering non-clicks as non-relevant [13], using proxies such as dwell time as a threshold to quantify item relevance [42]). However, we plan to extend Push CR methods to handle multi-level relevance ratings as well. Future work will also consider developing parallel versions of the updates as well as incorporating feature information from users and items when available.

Acknowledgments. We thank the anonymous reviewers for the detailed comments. We thank Suju Rajan and her team at Yahoo! for helpful discussions related to the paper. The work was supported in part by NSF grants IIS-1447566, IIS-1422557,CCF-1451986, CNS-1314560, IIS-0953274, IIS-1029711, NASA grant NNX12AQ39A, and a gift from Yahoo!. We also acknowledge technical support from the University of Minnesota Supercomputing Institute.

6. REFERENCES

[1] D. Agarwal and B.-C. Chen. Regression-based latent factor models. In *KDD*, 19–28, 2009.

[2] D. Agarwal, B.-C. Chen, P. Elango and R. Ramakrishnan. Content recommendation on web portals. In *Communications of the ACM*, 56(6): 92–101, 2013.

[3] S. Agarwal. The infinite push: A new support vector ranking algorithm that directly optimizes accuracy at the absolute top of the list. In *SDM*, 839–850, 2011.

[4] R. Baeza-Yates and R-N. Berthier. Modern information retrieval. In *ACM*, (463), 1999.

[5] S. Balakrishnan and S. Chopra. Collaborative ranking. In *WSDM*, 143–152, 2012.

[6] R. M. Bell and Y. Koren. Lessons from the netflix prize challenge. In *ACM SIGKDD Explorations Newsletter*, 9(2): 75–79, 2007.

[7] S. Boyd, C. Cortes, M. Mohri, and A. Radovanovic. Accuracy at the top. In *NIPS*, 953–961, 2012.

[8] C. JC Burges, T. Shaked, E. Renshaw, A. Lazier, M. Deeds, N. Hamilton and G. Hullender. Learning to rank using gradient descent. In *ICML*, 89–96, 2005.

[9] C. JC Burges. From RankNet to LambdaRank to LambdaMART: An overview. In *Learning*, 11: 23–581, 2010.

[10] Z. Cao, T. Qin, T.-Y. Liu, M.-F. Tsai, and H. Li. Learning to rank: from pairwise approach to listwise approach. In *ICML*, 129–136, 2007.

[11] O. Chapelle and Y. Chang. Yahoo! Learning to Rank Challenge Overview. In *Yahoo! Learning to Rank Challenge*, 1–24, 2011.

[12] K. Crammer and Y. Singer. Pranking with ranking. In *NIPS*, 14: 641–647, 2011.

[13] A. S Das, M. Datar, A. Garg and S. Rajaram. Google news personalization: scalable online collaborative filtering. In *WWW*, 271–280, 2007.

[14] N. Ding, SVN Vishwanathan, M. Warmuth and V. S. Denchev. T-logistic regression for binary and multiclass classification. In *JMLR*, (5): 1–55, 2013.

[15] J. Duchi, S. Shalev-Shwartz, Y. Singer, and T. Chandra. Efficient projections onto the l1-ball for learning in high dimensions. In *ICML*, 272–279, 2008.

[16] P. Jain, P. Netrapalli, Y. Singer, and S. Sanghavi. Low-rank matrix completion using alternating minimization. In *ACM symposium on Theory of computing*, 665–674, 2013.

[17] K. Järvelin and J. Kekäläinen. IR evaluation methods for retrieving highly relevant documents In *SIGIR*, 41–48, 2000.

[18] J. Kivinen and M. K. Warmuth. Exponentiated gradient versus gradient descent for linear predictors. *Information and Computation*, 132(1): 1–63, 1997.

[19] Y. Koren, R. Bell and C. Volinsky. Matrix factorization techniques for recommender systems. In *Computer IEEE*, 42(8): 30–37, 2009.

[20] Y. Koren and J. Sill. Ordrec: an ordinal model for predicting personalized item rating distributions. In *RecSys*, 117–124, 2011.

[21] Q. Le, and A. Smola. Direct optimization of ranking measures. In *arXiv preprint arXiv:0704.3359*, 2007.

[22] J. Lee, S. Bengio, S. Kim, G. Lebanon, and Y. Singer. Local collaborative ranking. In *WWW*, 85–96, 2014.

[23] G. Linden, B. Smith and J. York. Amazon. com recommendations: Item-to-item collaborative filtering. In *Internet Computing, IEEE*, 7(1): 76–80,2003.

[24] T.-Y. Liu. Learning to rank for information retrieval. *Foundations and Trends in Information Retrieval*, 3(3): 225–331, 2009.

[25] A. Mnih and R. Salakhutdinov. Probabilistic matrix factorization. In *NIPS*, 1257–1264, 2007.

[26] Y. Nesterov. *Introductory lectures on convex optimization: A basic course*, volume 87. Springer, 2004.

[27] N. Parikh and S. Boyd. Proximal algorithms. *Foundations and Trends in Optimization*, 1(3): 123–231, 2013

[28] A. Rakotomamonjy. Sparse support vector infinite push. *arXiv preprint arXiv:1206.6432*, 2012.

[29] S. Rendle, C. Freudenthaler, Z. Gantner, and L. Schmidt-Thieme. BPR: Bayesian personalized ranking from implicit feedback. In *UAI*, 452–461, 2009.

[30] C. Rudin. The p-norm push: A simple convex ranking algorithm that concentrates at the top of the list. In *JMLR*, 10: 2233–2271, 2009.

[31] R. Salakhutdinov and A. Mnih. Bayesian probabilistic matrix factorization using markov chain monte carlo. In *ICML*, 880–887, 2008.

[32] D. Sculley. Large scale learning to rank. In *NIPS Workshop on Advances in Ranking*, 1–6, 2009.

[33] H. Shan, and A. Banerjee. Generalized probabilistic matrix factorizations for collaborative filtering. In *ICDM*, 1025–1030, 2010.

[34] Y. Shi, A. Karatzoglou, L. Baltrunas, M. Larson, N. Oliver, and A. Hanjalic. CLIMF: learning to maximize reciprocal rank with collaborative less-is-more filtering. In *RecSys*, 139–146, 2012.

[35] Y. Shi, A. Karatzoglou, L. Baltrunas, M. Larson, and A. Hanjalic. GAPfm: Optimal top-n recommendations for graded relevance domains. In *CIKM*, 2261–2266, 2013.

[36] Y. Shi, A. Karatzoglou, L. Baltrunas, M. Larson, and A. Hanjalic. xCLIMF: optimizing expected reciprocal rank for data with multiple levels of relevance. In *RecSys*, 431–434, 2013.

[37] I. Tsochantaridis, T. Joachims, T. Hofmann, and Y. Altun. Large margin methods for structured and interdependent output variables. In *JMLR*, 1453–1484, 2005.

[38] M. Volkovs and R. S. Zemel. Collaborative ranking with 17 parameters. In *NIPS*, 2294–2302, 2012.

[39] M. Weimer, A. Karatzoglou, Q. V. Le, and A. Smola. CofiRank: Maximum margin matrix factorization for collaborative ranking. In *NIPS*, 2007.

[40] J. Xu and H. Li. Adarank: a boosting algorithm for information retrieval. In *SIGIR*, 391–398, 2007.

[41] Yahoo! R1 dataset `webscope.sandbox.yahoo.com`

[42] X. Yi, L. Hong, E. Zhong, N.N. Liu and S. Rajan. Beyond Clicks: Dwell Time for Personalization. In *RecSys*, 2014.

Parallel Streaming Signature EM-tree: A Clustering Algorithm for Web Scale Applications

Christopher M. De Vries
Game Analytics ApS
Berlin, Germany
cdevries@gameanalytics.com

Lance De Vine
Queensland University of Technology
Brisbane, Australia
l.devine@hdr.qut.edu.au

Shlomo Geva
Queensland University of Technology
Brisbane, Australia
s.geva@qut.edu.au

Richi Nayak
Queensland University of Technology
Brisbane, Australia
r.nayak@qut.edu.au

ABSTRACT

The proliferation of the web presents an unsolved problem of automatically analyzing billions of pages of natural language. We introduce a scalable algorithm that clusters hundreds of millions of web pages into hundreds of thousands of clusters. It does this on a single mid-range machine using efficient algorithms and compressed document representations. It is applied to two web-scale crawls covering tens of terabytes. ClueWeb09 and ClueWeb12 contain 500 and 733 million web pages and were clustered into 500,000 to 700,000 clusters. To the best of our knowledge, such fine grained clustering has not been previously demonstrated. Previous approaches clustered a sample that limits the maximum number of discoverable clusters. The proposed EM-tree algorithm uses the entire collection in clustering and produces several orders of magnitude more clusters than the existing algorithms. Fine grained clustering is necessary for meaningful clustering in massive collections where the number of distinct topics grows linearly with collection size. These fine-grained clusters show an improved cluster quality when assessed with two novel evaluations using ad hoc search relevance judgments and spam classifications for external validation. These evaluations solve the problem of assessing the quality of clusters where categorical labeling is unavailable and unfeasible.

Categories and Subject Descriptors

H.3.3 [**Information Storage and Retrieval**]: Information Search and Retrieval—*Clustering*; I.5.3 [**Computing Methodologies**]: Pattern Recognition—*Clustering, Algorithms, Similarity measures*; D.1.3 [**Software**]: Programming Techniques—*Concurrent Programming, Parallel Programming, Distributed Programming*

WWW 2015, May 18–22, 2015, Florence, Italy.
ACM 978-1-4503-3469-3/15/05.
http://dx.doi.org/10.1145/2736277.2741111.

General Terms

Algorithms, Experimentation, Performance, Theory

Keywords

Document Clustering; Large Scale Learning; Parallel and Distributed Algorithms; Random Projections; Hashing; Document Signatures; Search Tree; Compressed Learning

1. INTRODUCTION

Clustering is a fundamental process for applications such as Content Analysis, Information Integration, Information Retrieval, Web Mining and Knowledge Discovery. The proliferation of the internet has driven the need for unsupervised document clustering for analyzing natural language without having to label all possible topics such as in supervised learning approaches. Other web data exists with the potential of generating millions of clusters from billions of examples. For example, sensor data, images, video, audio, customer data, smart grid data, and, data produced by everyday physical objects such as in the web of things. Clustering algorithms are essential for these emerging web applications, and it is challenging due to heavy computational requirements. It may be possible to achieve web-scale clustering using a high performance distributed architecture, but the cost is prohibitive for many applications. Additionally, high-performance computing platforms are limited to organizations with large budgets and highly skilled employees. Additionally, achieving fine-grained clustering poses difficulties even with high-performance architectures. We found no examples of clustering near a billion natural language documents.

Information Retrieval utilizes document clustering for pre-clustering collections on to multiple machines for distributed search. Collection distribution uses clustering for organization into thematic groups. These clusters are ranked by collection selection to determine which clusters to search. Collection selection selects a few relevant thematically related clusters for each query and therefore improves search performance. Only the top k documents that are returned by the initial search are considered for further analysis when ranking search results. By contrast, global pre-clustering of documents captures the thematic association of documents on the basis of shared content. Documents that may not contain the search terms, but are thematically related to documents that are initially retrieved by keywords search, can be found in re-ranking and query expansion. Finding hidden thematic relationships based on the initial keyword search provides added motivation to pre-clustering document collections.

We are not aware of any solutions to the problem of clustering a billion web pages on standard hardware, other than by sampling to produce a relatively small number of clusters. It is not possible to cluster a collection into numerous small clusters with only a small sample. Clustering algorithms require redundancy in the data, and a small number of documents in the sample means reduced redundancy; this does not allow for discovery of small clusters. The size of the final clusters produced by sampling is relatively large because of distribution of the entire collection over the learned clusters. For instance, Kulkarni and Callan [23] have clustered a 0.1% sample of ClueWeb09 into 1,000 clusters and then mapped all 500 million documents onto these clusters, yielding an average cluster size of 500,000 documents. These large clusters work for collection distribution and selection, but we later demonstrate the advantage of finer grain clusters. Furthermore, coarse clusters are not useful for topical clustering of documents, where topic cluster size is expected to be several of orders of magnitude smaller. Fine grained clustering is not achievable through aggressive subsampling in web-scale collections.

This paper introduces the parallel streaming EM-tree algorithm for clustering web-scale collections on low-cost standard hardware. The quality of clustering solutions and processing efficiency depend on the representation of objects. Therefore, we present a useful data model using random projections [18] for representation of the document collection as binary signatures. We apply the parallel streaming EM-tree clustering algorithm that is specialized for binary signatures to segment the collection into fine grained clusters. The proposed method is evaluated with the web scale collections, ClueWeb09[1] and ClueWeb12[2], containing 500 and 733 million English language documents respectively.

Document clusters are often evaluated by comparison to a ground truth set of categories for documents. No topical labels are available for ClueWeb, and it is nigh impossible to generate the labels for a large scale web crawl for millions of categories. We present two novel methods for external cluster validation: (1) ad hoc relevance; and (2) spam classification. We used relevance judgements from the TREC Web Track in 2010, 2011, 2012 and 2013 [7, 8, 9, 31] and spam classifications created by Cormack et. al. [11] for the evaluation of document clustering.

Extensive analysis reveals that the clusterings with 500,000 to 700,000 clusters were found to improve the quality using this evaluation. We emphasize that there are no earlier reports in the open literature of document clustering of this magnitude, and there are no standard benchmark resources or comparative evaluation results.

This paper makes two novel contributions: (1) we introduce the novel parallel streaming signature EM-tree algorithm that can cluster documents at scales not previously reported; and (2) we solve the problem of cluster validation in web-scale collections where creating a ground truth set of categories is a near impossible task for human assessors.

Section 2 discusses related research on web scale clustering. The generation of a document representation is discussed in Section 3. Section 5 discusses the complexity of the proposed method and section 4 introduces the EM-tree algorithm. The evaluation of cluster validity is presented in Section 6. The discussion of potential applications and conclusions are contained in Sections 7 and 8.

2. RELATED RESEARCH

Few clustering algorithms can scale to web collections on modest hardware platforms. They rely on supercomputing resources or imposed constraints such as: (1) using a small sample for clustering and then mapping the entire collection to these clusters; (2) by reducing the number of target clusters.

MapReduce has been used to implement clustering algorithms by Jin [21] and Kumar [24]. The experiments created a small number of clusters using small data sets several gigabytes in size. Esteves and Rong [16] investigated using the open source Mahout library implemented using MapReduce for the clustering of Wikipedia. The k-means algorithm took two days to cluster the 3.5 million Wikipedia articles into 20 clusters using ten compute nodes. In comparison, we increase *both* the number of documents and clusters by two to three orders of magnitude. We analyze the complexity of k-means and EM-tree in Section 5.

Broder et. al. [5] describe an approach to scaling up k-means by the use of inverted indexes. It reverses the process of assigning points to clusters and assign clusters to points. The authors also highlight the need for fine-grained clustering of high dimensional data such as web pages, users, and, advertisements. They indicate that k-means may take thousands of hours to converge when using parallel and distributed programming techniques such as MapReduce. While the authors show improvements to k-means, they only experiment with clustering millions of examples into thousands of clusters. We far exceed this scale.

Bahmani et. al. [2] present a scalable parallel approach to the D^2 seeding approach from k-means++ [1] called k-means||. The experiments run k-means to complete convergence after initialization. It is often impractical to run the optimization to complete convergence. Typically, more than 95% of the optimization happens in the first few iterations, and further iterations offer very little improvement. We observed this with EM-tree in prior work [12]. The EM-tree can be seeded with k-means||. However, for fine-grained clustering of ClueWeb using signatures we found no advantage to more computationally expensive initializations. It may be due to the smoothing properties of random projections, but analysis of this is beyond the scope of this paper. However, when such an approach does help, our approach is complementary to k-means||. We can leverage the advantages of both approaches by the use of the scalable initialization procedure and the scalable optimization of EM-tree. As with other approaches, the experiments were run on data sets orders of magnitude smaller and much lower dimensionality.

Zhang et. al. [36] present the BIRCH algorithm that incrementally constructs a tree as data is streamed from disk. It is similar to the K-tree algorithm except that not all data points are kept in the tree [13]. The BIRCH algo-

[1] `http://ktree.sf.net/emtree/clueweb09`
[2] `http://ktree.sf.net/emtree/clueweb12`

rithm performs updates along the insertion path like K-tree. When using signatures it has been reported to cause scalability problems because the signature bits are continually unpacked and repacked [12]. Furthermore, the EM-tree has immutable tree state at each iteration leading to scalable parallel implementations. We were unable to find any reference to BIRCH clustering near 1 billion documents.

We have only found a few other examples of clustering near a billion examples. These reports were on lower dimensional data sets of images, image patches, low dimensional generic point sets and weather patterns. Liu et. al. [27] used 2000 CPUs, MapReduce and commodity hardware to cluster 1.5 billion images into 1 million clusters for near duplicate detection. Similarly to our approach, they used random projections and a tree structure. Wang et. al. [34] also describe an approach to clustering images for duplicate detection using a 2000 core cluster for clustering 2 billion images. Bisgin and Dalfes [4] used 16,000 CPUs and a top500 supercomputer to cluster weather data into 1000 clusters. Wu et. al. [35] report on the speedup obtained when using GPUs instead of multicore CPUs, to cluster billions of low dimensional point sets of upto 8 dimensions. These approaches rely on high-performance computing resources that put it out of reach for most application developers. Additionally, we found no examples of clustering web-scale document collections into fine-grained clusters.

The ClueWeb collections are some of the largest document collections used for research. These web crawls have been used at TREC to evaluate ad hoc retrieval and other Web search tasks. While it is clear that retrieval systems can scale to these collections, there has been little investigation of clustering such large document collections.

3. DOCUMENT REPRESENTATION WITH SIGNATURES

The first task in clustering documents is the definition of a representation. We use a binary signature representation called TopSig[3] [18]. It offers a scalable approach to the construction of document signatures by applying random indexing [30], or random projections [3] and numeric quantization. Signatures derived in this manner have been shown to be competitive with state of the art retrieval models at early precision, and also to clustering approaches. The binary signature vectors faithfully preserve the mutual similarity relationships between documents in the original representation. The Johnson Lindenstrauss lemma [22] states that if points in a high dimensional space are projected into a randomly chosen subspace then the distances between the points are approximately preserved. The lower dimensionality required is asymptotically logarithmic with respect to the original high dimensional space.

This signature generation is similar to that of SimHash [6]. However, we use a different term weighting scheme, use signatures more than an order of magnitude larger, and, much sparser random codes. SimHash has predominantly been applied to nearest duplicate detection where relatively short signatures are used to find the few nearest neighbors of a document. We refer the reader to [18] for the specific details of the signature generation process.

We removed stop words, and stemmed words using the Porter algorithm. We use 4096-bit signatures because that choice was previously shown to be sufficient to produce the same quality clustering as the original real-valued representation of documents [18]. We derived the signatures used to represent the ClueWeb collections on a single 16 core machine. Our approach uses a fixed amount of memory while indexing and can process a collection without keeping the entire index in memory. Each document is indexed independently of all other documents leading to massive parallelization.

It is important to understand that the focus of this paper is efficient, scalable document clustering, not to compare different approaches of the generation of document signatures. There have been numerous approaches reported that fall under the general category of similarity preserving hashing [33].

The use of signatures is advantageous for increased computational efficiency of document to document similarity. It has been shown to provide a one to two orders of magnitude increase in processing speed for document clustering over traditional sparse vector representations with sacrificing quality [18]. In prior research [18], we used an algorithm similar to k-means designed especially for signatures. We specifically designed the proposed EM-tree algorithm for signatures. All documents and cluster representatives are binary signatures. Therefore, traditional vector space clustering approaches can not be applied to these signatures without expanding them into a larger representation such as integer or floating point vectors.

[3]`http://topsig.googlecode.com`

4. CLUSTERING WITH EM-TREE

The EM-tree algorithm can cluster vast collections into numerous fine-grained clusters. K-means is one of the earliest and most popular clustering algorithms due to its quick convergence and linear time complexity. However, it is not suitable for web scale collections that have a vast diversity of content resulting in an enormous number of topics as elaborated in the previous section. EM-tree solves this previously unaddressed issue.

4.1 M-Way Nearest Neighbor Search Tree

A m-way nearest neighbor search tree is a recursive data structure that indexes a set of n binary signatures in d dimensions where, $X = \{x_1, \ldots, x_n\}$, $X \subset \{+1, -1\}^d$ and $|X| = n$. Each node contains a list of *records* that are $(key, value)$ pairs. The *keys* are binary signatures that are cluster representatives of the associated subtree. Each iteration of the optimization updates the *keys*. The *record* values are the nodes associated with the *keys* that are one level deeper. The data structure also generalizes to all vector space representations in $\mathbb{R}^d$. However, in the case of the EM-tree, we have specialized the data structure for binary signatures. It is not a traditional vector space clustering algorithm.

Applying the k-means clustering algorithm recursively is known as Tree-Structured Vector Quantization (TSVQ) [17], repeated k-means, or for clusters of size two, bisecting k-means. It generates a m-way tree in $\mathbb{R}^d$.

4.2 The EM-tree Algorithm

The EM-tree algorithm iteratively optimizes a randomly initialized m-way tree until convergence. In contrast, the repeated k-means algorithm initially creates k clusters using k-means [17]. It recursively clusters each partition in a layer wise fashion until reaching a desired tree depth or node size.

The EM-tree builds a cluster tree in a different manner [12]. The collection is initially partitioned by selecting a random set of data points as cluster prototypes. Unlike repeated k-means, clustering is not applied at this point. Instead, the data points are recursively distributed to random partitions until a desirable tree depth is reached. At this point, the initial tree is complete. Now cluster means are updated in a bottom-up fashion. The entire process of tree insertion and tree update forms an iteration of the optimization and has been proven to converge [12]. The entire tree is recomputed with each insert update cycle. It is different from repeated k-means in which the optimization process is run to completion at each node before proceeding deeper into the tree. The EM-tree algorithm includes an additional pruning step in for removing empty branches of the tree. The EM-tree is not a standard vector space clustering algorithm in this context. It works directly with binary vectors where all documents and cluster prototypes are binary vectors.

The EM-tree algorithm can optimize any m-way tree such as a tree produced by a low-cost algorithm with poor cluster quality. The algorithm can be applied to any subtree in a m-way tree. In a setting where a changing data set is being clustered, branches of the tree affected by insertions and deletions can be restructured to the data independently of the rest of the tree.

By a process of insertion (Expectation), update (Maximization), and pruning, the m-way tree model adapts to the underlying data as the clusters converge as seen in Figure 1.

The procedure SEED initializes the EM-tree algorithm where m is the tree order, X is the set of data points to cluster and *depth* is the tree depth. It produces a height-balanced tree where all leaves are at the same depth. The INSERT procedure inserts a set of vectors into a m-way tree. Points are inserted by following the nearest neighbor search path, where at each node in the tree, the branch with the nearest key is followed.

The UPDATE procedure updates the means in the tree according to the current assignment of data points in the leaves. Since we work with binary vectors, the bits in each signature assigned to a given leaf node are unpacked and accumulated into an integer vector. This vector is then used in two different ways. It is quantized to a binary vector to form a new cluster mean for a given leaf node, and it is also propagated up the tree so that new cluster centroids higher in the tree can be computed. The updating of cluster centroids is performed for all levels of the tree.

The PRUNE procedure removes any branches with no associated data points. It is completed bottom up where leaf nodes are removed first. The empty branches are removed once UPDATE and INSERT have completed. It allows the tree structure to adapt to the data.

The optimization error of EM-tree is robust with respect to different initializations when producing fine-grained clusters of ClueWeb. A tree with random initialization and subsequent optimization was found to minimize the objective function on par with more computationally expensive approaches. A 10% sample is used to seed the tree because it is large enough to produce meaningful centroid representations for a large number of clusters. This initial seeding only consumes a small percentage of the compute time.

```
EMTREE(m, depth, X)
root = SEED(m, depth, X)
converged = false
while not converged
    root′ = root
    INSERT(root′, X)
    PRUNE(root′)
    UPDATE(root′)
    if root == root′
        converged = true
    else
        root = root′
return root
```

Figure 1: EM-tree

Additionally, approximation guarantees can be achieved by initializing with the D^2 approach as in k-means++ [1] but analysis of this is beyond the scope of this paper.

In summary, the EMTREE procedure initializes and iteratively optimizes an EM-tree of order m that is *depth* levels deep.

4.3 Streaming EM-tree

One of the key constraints in scaling clustering algorithms to large data sets is the availability of computer memory. One way to approach this problem is to adopt a streaming paradigm in which the data points are streamed sequentially, and only a small portion of them are ever kept in memory at one time. The approach used in the streaming EM-tree is only to keep internal nodes in memory. The data points are collected in accumulators associated with each leaf node. The data points inserted are, therefore, added into the accumulators but are then discarded.

At each iteration of the optimization, all signatures are read from disk and inserted into the tree as seen in Figure 2. Bits are unpacked from the signature and added into the accumulators. A count is kept of the number of points added into the accumulator. When all inserts have been performed, the values of the accumulators in the leaf nodes are propagated up the tree and new centroids are calculated in the UPDATE step. The centroids, which are now vectors of integers, are quantized to produce new bit signatures. The PRUNE step is then performed.

Large datasets can be clustered on a single machine with limited memory. The algorithm is compute bound on typical hardware architectures the data is streamed from disk.

4.4 Parallelizing EM-tree

The EM-tree algorithm is particularly amenable to large scale parallel and distributed implementations due to the nature of the optimization process. The key property that ensures scalability is that the entire tree is immutable at each iteration, and the data points can be concurrently inserted according to the nearest neighbor search path.

The EM-tree algorithm has been parallelized using threads via the use of loop parallelization and producer-consumer pipelines. The accumulators in the leaf nodes are locked when updated, although the chance of multiple threads attempting to update the same accumulator at the same time is small due to the typically very large number of leaf nodes.

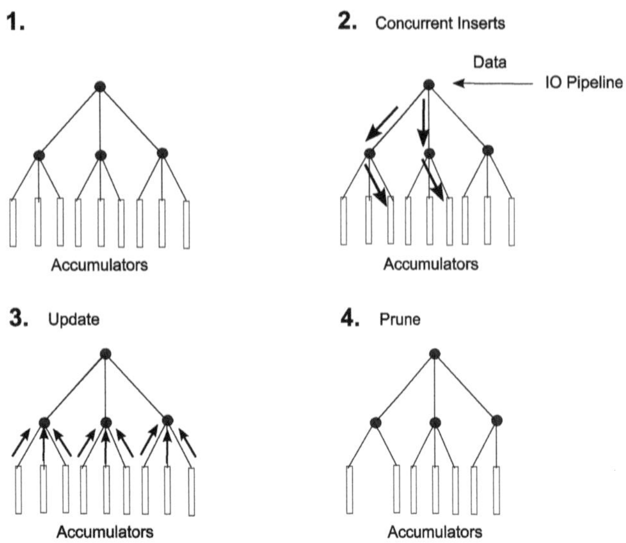

Figure 2: Streaming EM-tree Iteration

This property ensures that EM-tree scales almost linearly with regards to the number of threads. For thread implementation, we use Intel's Threading Building Blocks (TBB).

A parallel threaded implementation can be executed on a single machine in which case the entire tree structure with accumulators is shared between threads. The bottleneck for the streaming EM-tree is the insertion step, primarily because of nearest neighbor calculations and bit unpacking of accumulators. The UPDATE and PRUNE steps require much less computation.

Figure 3 contains the results of an experiment to test how EM-tree scales with the number of threads used. We tested EM-tree on a machine with 16 CPU cores. The speedup is measured relative to the execution in a single thread on the same hardware. The CPUs support two hyper-threads per core, and we have stepped through the number of threads in the program from 1 up to 34. The top curve in Figure 3 shows the speedup that could be obtained if speedup exactly followed the number of threads. It is not achievable in practice when using hyper-threads. The bottom curve shows the actual execution speedup as the number of threads is increased. The middle curve depicts the number of cores used – when there are fewer threads than cores the threads are mapped to idle cores. After that point, all CPU cores are utilized, and threads are mapped to busy cores using their second hyper thread. In summary, on a machine with 16 cores we were able to achieve a 16 fold speedup through conventional multi-threading. In this experiment, we used a 10 million document sample from the ClueWeb09 collection. It is large enough to eliminate any caching effects and small enough that the single threaded experiment does not take weeks to run.

4.5 Software

EM-tree and Streaming EM-tree have been implemented by the authors as part of the open source LMW-tree C++ software package[4]. The software has been built on Linux, Mac OS and Windows. The clusters and tree structure have

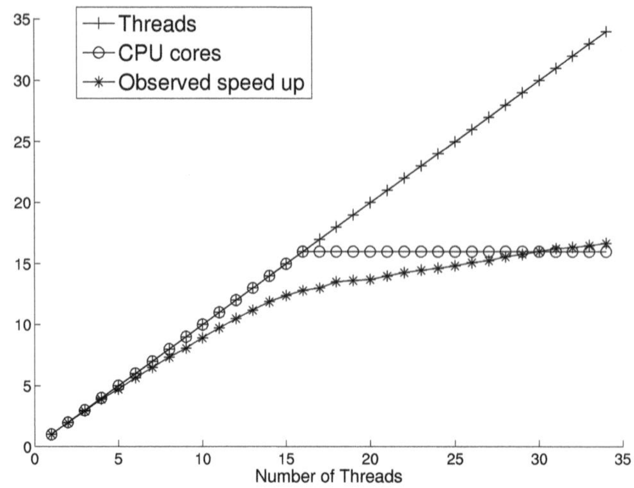

Figure 3: Scaling EM-tree to 16 CPU cores

been made available online[5]. It is important to have these openly available since any alternative solution can be compared.

5. COMPLEXITY ANALYSIS

The time complexity of the k-means algorithm is linear with respect to all its inputs, $O(nki)$ [5]. Where n is the number of non-zero entries in the document-term matrix, k is the number of clusters, and, i is the number of iterations. The number of iterations, i, is limited to some small fixed amount of iterations as k-means converges quickly in practice. Fine grained clustering pushes k much closer to n. As $k \to n$, the complexity of k-means approaches $O(n^2 i)$. It makes k-means impractical for fine-grained clustering of web-scale collections containing billions of examples. Algorithms using height balanced trees such as EM-tree, K-tree [13] and BIRCH [36] alleviate this problem by reducing the time complexity associated with the number of clusters to $O(\log(k))$. The complexity of EM-tree approaches $O(n \log(n) i)$ as $k \to n$ for fine-grained clustering.

Three nontrivial computer architecture considerations contribute to the efficiency of our approach. We process 64 dimensions of the binary signatures at a time in a single CPU operation. While it is a constant speedup, it is certainly not negligible. Our approach only uses integer operations that are faster and have higher throughput in instructions per cycle on modern processors than floating point operations used for k-means clustering. Furthermore, due to the extremely concise representation of our model as binary signatures, we observe more cache hits. Cache misses are extremely costly on modern processors with main memory accesses taking more than 100 cycles. When using traditional sparse representations, the cluster means in the root of the tree contain many millions of terms, quickly exceeding processor cache size. With signatures a cluster means always consumes 4096 bits.

By the use of efficient representations and algorithms we turn the problem of fine grained clustering of the entire web into a tractable problem.

[4]http://github.com/cmdevries/LMW-tree

[5]http://sf.net/projects/ktree/files/clueweb_clusters/

6. EMPIRICAL ANALYSIS

We ran the experiments on a dual-socket Xeon E5-2665 based system. Each CPU package has 8×2.4 GHz CPU cores connected in a ring topology, for a total of 16 CPU cores. The program used 64GB of memory to store the tree in memory where the data set is 240GB to 350GB on disk. We streamed the data points from a 7200rpm 3TB SATA disk providing 150MB per second of sequential read performance, although this much bandwidth was not needed. A mid-range machine like this can be purchased for around 5,000 USD.

The ClueWeb 09 and 12 collections took approximately two and three days to index and resulted in 240GB and 350GB signatures indexes. It is a concise representation of the collections that measure in tens of terabytes when uncompressed. The EM-tree processes these document signatures to produce document clusters. Clustering the ClueWeb 09 and 12 signatures took approximately 15 and 20 hours. Both ran for five iterations and produced 700,000 and 600,000 clusters respectively.

Most of the literature on cluster evaluation focuses on evaluating document clusters by comparison to the ground truth set of categories for documents. It poses problems when evaluating large-scale collections containing millions to billions of documents. Human assessors are required to label the entire collection into many thousands of potential topics. Even if a small percentage of the collection is labeled, how does an assessor choose between many thousands of potential topics in a general purpose document collection such as the World Wide Web? The experience of labeling large test collections such as RCV1 [26] demonstrate that categorizing a general purpose document collection such as the web is a daunting task for humans. RCV1 contains 800,000 short newswire articles with hundreds of categories. Even though this collection is many orders of magnitude simpler than the web, assessors still struggled with categorization.

There are no topical human generated labels available for ClueWeb. Therefore, we propose novel uses of external sources of information as proxies for cluster validation: (1) ad hoc relevance; and (2) spam classification. The information retrieval evaluation community has already dealt with the problem of assessor load in ad hoc relevance evaluation via the use of pooling [32]. Pooling reduces assessor load and topics evaluated are specific and well defined. The issue of assessor load is alleviated by using ad hoc relevance to assess document clustering, instead of category labels for every document in a collection.

We also present another alternative evaluation based upon spam classification produced in earlier research by Cormack et. al. [11]. The goal in this case is to place documents with the same spam score into the same cluster. It measures how consistent the clustering is with respect to the external measure of spam learned from 4 different spam classifications. We of course conjecture that there is some underlying topical vocabulary that spammy documents use. Clustering, grouping documents on the basis of shared vocabulary, should show a correlation with spam detection scores – which are, of course, independently derived.

Before we present results of these two cluster validation experiments, we present some qualitative evaluation by inspection of partial documents content in the final trees in Tables 1, 2 and 3.

6.1 Ad Hoc Relevance Based Evaluation

The use of ad hoc relevance judgments for evaluation of document clusters is motivated by the cluster hypothesis [20]. It states that relevant documents tend to be more similar to each other than non-relevant documents for a given query. The cluster hypothesis connects ad hoc information retrieval and document clustering. Documents in the same cluster behave similarly with respect to the same information need [28, 29, 15]. It is due to the clustering algorithm grouping documents with similar vocabularies together. There may also be some higher order correlation due to effects caused by the distributional hypothesis [19] and limitation of the analysis to the size of the document.

6.1.1 *Oracle Collection Selection*

We have evaluated document clustering solutions by creating plots for the optimal ordering of clusters for ad hoc queries. This ordering is created by an *oracle collection selection* ranking that has full knowledge of relevant documents. Clusters are ordered by the number of relevant documents they contain. Cumulative recall is calculated by traversing the cluster ranking in descending order. Then the percentage of recall and documents visited is averaged across all queries. It represents the optimal ordering of the given clusters for a given query and represents an upper bound on recall ranking performance for the given set of clusters. Relevant documents group together in clusters when the cluster hypothesis holds. Additionally, this grouping is better than expected from randomly distributing documents into clusters of the same size. In summary, we assign to any clustering solution the performance of the oracle in collection selection. The better the clustering solution, the better the oracle performs in collection selection. Fewer clusters have to be searched to recall relevant documents.

There are no baselines available for clustering the ClueWeb collections into the order of a million clusters. Therefore, we compare our clustering solutions against a random partitioning baseline. A common problem when comparing different clustering solutions is that, by nature, different clustering solutions are produced by different methods. It can introduce structural bias to the evaluation. Unequal cluster sizes can lead to different performance measurements. In order to compare any given clustering solution against an equivalent random partitioning, we impose the same cluster structure on the random solution. We assign documents randomly to the same cluster structure obtained from clustering. In this manner, there is no structural bias to either solution, random or derived through clustering [14]. It eliminates advantages of ineffective clustering solutions. For example, if almost all documents are placed in a single cluster except for one document being placed in every other cluster, then the large cluster will almost always contain all the relevant documents to any query. An evaluation that tests to see if collection selection discovers the correct cluster to search concludes that the dysfunctional solution is indeed the best – it almost always finds the right cluster. On the other hand, if the same ineffective solution is compared to a random baseline having the same dysfunctional structure then the clustering solution it is found to offer no improvement.

Weight Loss 9f08ef2b0 220 documents	**Investment** 9f06c7770 1169 documents	**Language** 9f0476410 106 documents	**Politics** 9f0a77b10 1213 documents	**SciFi and Fantasy** 9f0b871e0 198 documents
383 bits – find a meetup group near you weight loss meetups pelham	463 bits – find a meetup group real estate buying investing meetups alexandria	386 bits – find a meetup group linguistics meetups aurora	637 bits – find a meetup group democratic underground meetups portland	667 bits – find a meetup group star trek meetups long beach
417 bits – find a meetup group weight loss meetups englewood	587 bits – find a meetup group real estate buying investing meetups decatur	630 bits – find a meetup group near you language lovers meetups naperville	851 bits – find a meetup group democratic underground meetups worcester	706 bits – find a meetup group star trek meetups allendale
474 bits – find a meetup group fitness meetups staten island	801 bits – find a meetup group investing meetups lake jackson	941 bits – find a meetup group near you scandinavian languages meetups skokie	1097 bits – find a meetup group near you dennis kucinich meetups lakewood	1009 bits – find a meetup group near you comic books meetups reading
550 bits – find a meetup group fitness meetups new rochelle	998 bits – find a meetup group near you real estate buying investing meetups soulsbyville	1252 bits – find a meetup group near you hungarian language meetups libertyville	1671 bits – harford county democrats	1157 bits – find a meetup group buffy meetups london
580 bits – find a meetup group weight loss meetups clinton	1752 bits – westfield group mergers and acquisitions alacrastore-com	1844 bits – algebra 1 terms and practice problems chapter 1 lesson 1 flash cards quizlet	1911 bits – welsh statutory instruments 2005	1804 bits – fleet registration station archive star trek online forums

`http://ktree.sourceforge.net/emtree/clueweb09/9f033ca50.html`

Table 1: ClueWeb09 – Sample From Meetup.com Cluster

Hepatitis a5b5f0820 774 documents	**HIV Vaccine** a5ae2f420 165 documents	**Treating HIV** a5b62af80 752 documents	**Disease Research** a5b48c900 288 documents	**Bacteria** a5b88ca20 126 documents

`http://ktree.sourceforge.net/emtree/clueweb09/a5acc38a0.html`

Table 2: ClueWeb09 – Sample From Diseases Clusters

The performance of different clustering solutions is normalized against the performance of a random baseline solution having an identical clustering structure.

6.1.2 ClueWeb Results

For the ClueWeb09 collection, we have evaluated three different clustering solutions. The first approach is by Kulkarni and Callan [23] using KL-divergence and k-means and the other two by the EM-tree algorithm. First we describe the approaches, and then compare their quality.

Kulkarni and Callan describe an experiment with ClueWeb09 where a 500,000 document sample of the ClueWeb09 collection was clustered using k-means with a KL-divergence similarity measure to produce 1000 clusters. It maps the 500 million documents onto these clusters. We have chosen this analysis for a direct comparison with EM-tree, even though it does not represent fine-grained clustering. However, it allows us to perform a side by side comparison with a published baseline. We processed the entire ClueWeb with an EM-tree containing two levels of tree nodes of order $m = 1000$. The first level contained 1000 clusters and the second 691,708 clusters due to pruning. The first level of the EM-tree and the method of Kulkarni and Callan using k-means both produced 1000 clusters. Therefore, these clustering solutions are directly comparable. We also compare solution quality of fine grained clusters, using the second level of the EM-tree. We demonstrate that using many more fine-grained clusters can produce higher quality clusters with respect to ad hoc relevance. Furthermore, the EM-tree can produce higher quality clusters with respect to spam, even at 1000 clusters. Direct comparison KL-divergence k-means approach is not possible for 691,708 clusters. It does not scale to produce this many clusters.

We generate cumulative recall plots for the three methods using the oracle collection selection approach. Each of the 3 approaches appear in separate plots in Figures 4, 5, and 6. We place most relevant documents first using the oracle ranking process. We visit clusters in descending order of recall. The average percentage of total documents in the collection contained in the first n clusters is display along the x-axis. The y-axis is the average percentage of recall included in the first n clusters when averaged over all topics. Visiting a cluster produces a mark on the curve. So, after seeing 2 marks, 2 clusters have been visited in the order specified by the oracle ranking.

Each clustering has a unique random baseline created where the cluster size distribution matches that of each clustering solution. In all cases, there is a difference between the random baseline and the clustering solution. Useful learning has occurred. The baseline normalization removes any effect of random chance or ineffective cluster size distributions. Therefore, all three clustering solutions support the

Logistics Software	Video Surveillance	Computer Security	Wireless	Enterprise Software
a7aded0e0	a7b3b8f60	a7b145970	a7b5417c0	a7b361450
213 documents	818 documents	2007 documents	326 documents	415 documents

http://ktree.sourceforge.net/emtree/clueweb09/a7aa623c0.html

Table 3: ClueWeb09 – Sample From Information Technology Cluster

cluster hypothesis that relevant documents tend to cluster together.

In comparison to the 1000 clusters produced by the first level of EM-tree in Figure 5, the KL-divergence k-means approach in Figure 4 clearly groups relevant documents better. It achieves total recall after 2.81% of the collection is visited, whereas the EM-tree approach does not achieve this until 4.19%. Figure 7 highlights difference between the two approaches. All three approaches are plotted on one graph without their baselines. We note that this is not a surprising result – k-means is superior to EM-tree in terms of quantization distortion rates. However, this is a trade off as it is also much more computationally intensive. If a particular application requires 1000 clusters then, the KL-divergence with k-means approach is clearly better at grouping relevant documents together. A 500,000 document sample provides adequate statistics for learning 1000 clusters. However, suppose that fine granularity clustering is sought after and applying k-means recursive clustering to the entire collection is necessary. We clustered 500,000 documents into 1000 clusters using a sparse vector approach using k-means, and it took approximately ten hours using a very fast implementation. If each of these 1000 clusters are clustered into another 1000 clusters using the recursive k-means approach, then each subset requires another 500,000 document sample to learn another 1000 subclusters. As there are 1000 partitions, taking ten hours per partition, it would take another 10,000 hours to produce a similar number of clusters as EM-tree, making this k-means based approach infeasible.

EM-tree can produce many more clusters in the second level that group relevant documents much more tightly. In Figures 7 and 8, the second level of EM-tree reaches total recall after 0.06% of the collection has been visited. Because these clusters still group relevant documents together, and support the cluster hypothesis, we also conclude they are highly topical. Relevant documents for a given query are related to the same topic because they satisfy the same information need. Many applications can benefit from identifying small clusters of highly topical documents. This is discussed further in Section 7.

The random baseline for the second level of EM-tree looks surprisingly effective. It achieves total recall after only visiting 0.22% of the collection. It is not unexpected because this baseline is close to the worst case possible, where each relevant document for a given query appears in a separate cluster. There are on average 80 relevant documents per query for the 148 queries. So the oracle returns an average of 80 clusters per query to achieve 100% recall. Indeed, the first cluster in the random baseline contains 4.3% or 3.44 relevant documents on average. It decreases to below the average of one document per cluster by the 15th cluster. Some clusters still contain more than one relevant document on average because the cluster size distribution in the random baseline matches that of clustering. Large clusters can receive more relevant documents due to their size.

In contrast, the first EM-tree cluster in the second level contains 25% or 20 relevant documents on average. Additionally, the first EM-tree cluster contains 450 documents on average, whereas the first random baseline cluster contains 30,000 documents on average. We calculate precision by dividing the number of relevant documents by the number of documents in the cluster. The first EM-tree cluster has a precision of 4.44% on average, whereas the first random baseline cluster has a precision of 0.011% on average. It is some 400 times worse.

Furthermore, clusters in the random baseline contain a mixture of relevant documents with mostly random off topic documents. It makes it much harder for a non-oracle ranker to find them using vocabulary statistics. There are on average 3.4 documents mixed with 30,000 random other off-topic documents in the first cluster in the random baseline.

The plots of EM-tree level 1 and 2 in Figures 5 and 6 look very similar when the x-axis scale is ignored. It indicates that the same relationships between the random baseline and the clustering exist in both levels of the EM-tree. While the same relationships exist, the 2nd level contains 691 times more clusters. The cluster hypothesis holds in the same way, even though the size of the clusters is reduced by almost three orders of magnitude. It verifies that there is no significant loss of fidelity in fine granularity clustering.

We conducted the same experiments on ClueWeb12. We were unable to compare the KL-divergence approach [23] as clusters have not been made available for this recent collection. However, the same trends for the EM-tree emerge as shown in Figure 9. All the corresponding plots were highly similar but were left out for brevity. The relevance judgments from the 2013 TREC Web Track have much deeper pooling, increasing our confidence in the results.

6.2 Spam Based Evaluation

We have performed another evaluation using external knowledge in the form of spam scores. These spam scores have been produced by an approach by Cormack et. al. [11] using a supervised learning approach that combines training from 4 different labeled spam datasets. It quantizes the spam scores into 100 values. A score of 99 is the least spammy and 0 the most. For instance, a document score of 99 indicates that 99% of the collection is more spammy than the said document. These spam scores have shown to be useful for improving search quality in ad hoc retrieval [11].

If a perfect document clustering exists with respect to spam, it places documents with the same spam score in the same cluster. We have evaluated clusters by taking the average spam score for documents in the cluster. Clusters are sorted and traversed by descending spam score. We then observe the percentage of the documents contained in the clusters visited so far. Again, we create a random baseline for each clustering solution. As expected, almost all clusters average out to a spam score of 50. We display the best possible oracle solution by ordering documents according to their

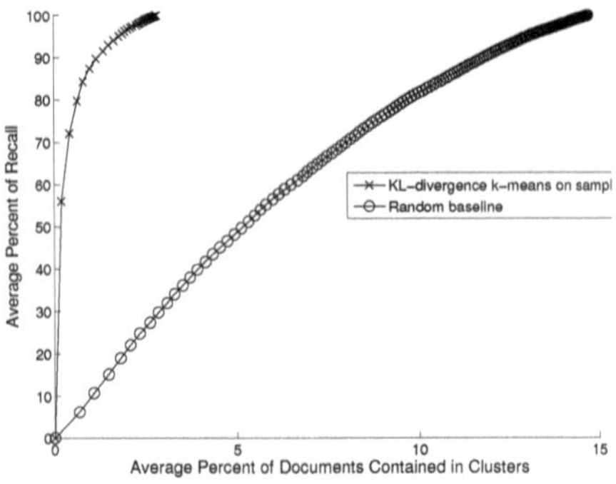

Figure 4: ClueWeb09 – 1000 KL-divergence k-means clusters

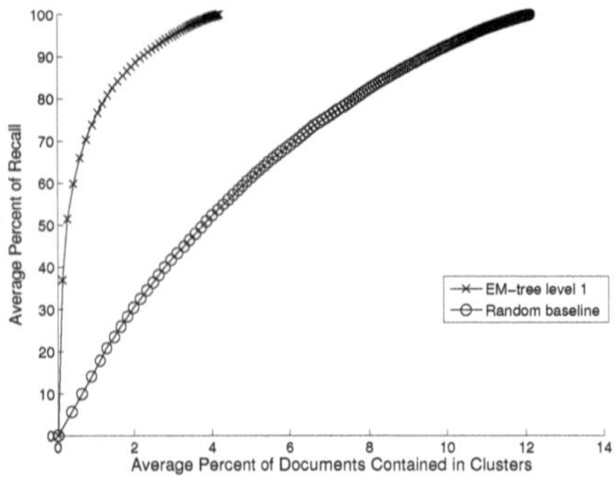

Figure 5: ClueWeb09 – 1000 EM-tree level 1 clusters

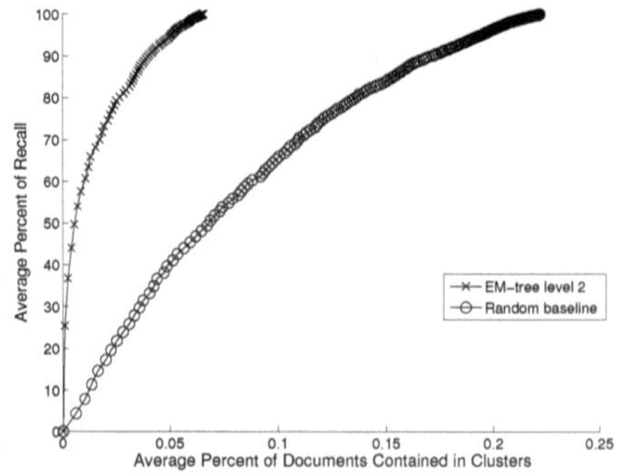

Figure 6: ClueWeb09 – 691,708 EM-tree level 2 clusters

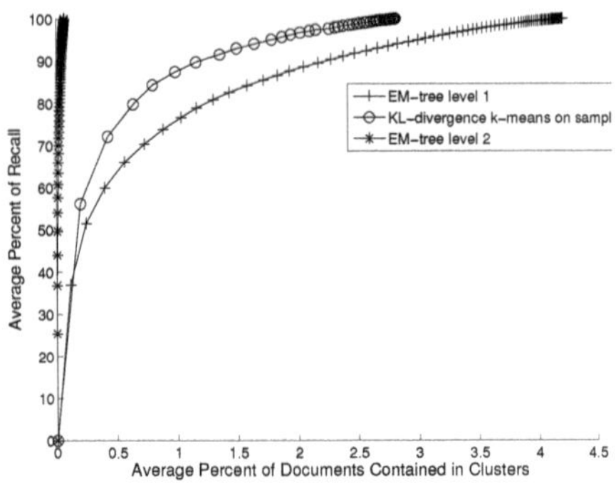

Figure 7: ClueWeb09 – Comparing all approaches

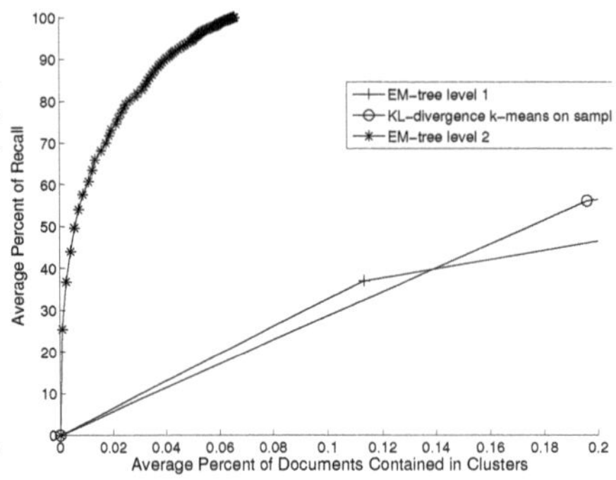

Figure 8: ClueWeb09 – Comparing all approaches – Zoomed

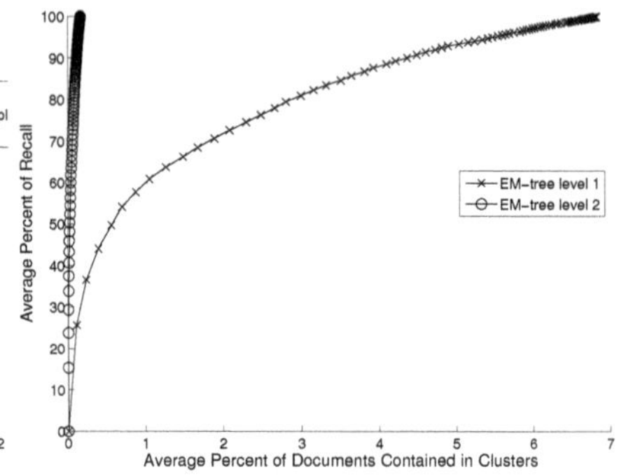

Figure 9: ClueWeb12 – Comparing all approaches

spam score; i.e. all documents with a score of 99, then 98 and so on. It is a straight line where the first ranked cluster contains all documents with a spam score of 99, then those with a spam score of 98, and so forth. Therefore, the closer an actual clustering solution comes to this straight line from the top left to the bottom right, the better the clustering is with respect to the spam scores.

We evaluated the same clustering solutions as in Section 6.1. These are KL-divergence k-means [23] and the two clusterings produced by level 1 and 2 of the EM-tree. For the ClueWeb09 collection, the results of this experiment can be seen in Figure 13. Each of the clusterings have been plotted separately with random baselines and optimal document ordering in Figures 10, 11 and 12.

The signature-based approach with EM-tree better groups documents according to spam score than the KL-divergence k-means approach when producing 1000 clusters. It is the opposite result to using ad hoc relevance judgments where KL-divergence k-means was superior. The finer grained clustering in the 2nd level of EM-tree allows more pure clusters with respect to spam.

For ClueWeb12, we have only created the final plot comparing all approaches for brevity in Figure 14. We omitted the random baselines because they behave in exactly the same manner. The plots look very similar for ClueWeb12 and ClueWeb09.

7. APPLICATIONS

Recent results in computer vision demonstrate the usefulness of scalable algorithms for unsupervised feature learning [25, 10]. The EM-tree algorithm using signatures could be advantageous in computer vision applications where the generation of many clusters from large amounts of data is desirable.

Near duplicate object detection is another application for large scale fine-grained clustering, particularly for eliminating near-duplicate web pages. In fact, we found many near duplicate pages in ClueWeb 2012.

Most existing cluster based re-ranking and query expansion approaches use fine-grained clusters of the top k results returned by a search engine. It limits the analysis to documents returned by the search engine, and usually it is based solely on the keywords in the query. With fine-grained clusters of web-scale collections made available by the EM-tree algorithm, re-ranking and query expansion of documents that do not contain the keywords becomes a possibility. Common cluster membership associates documents based on other keywords that appear in relevant documents. Such documents do not necessarily contain the query keywords. Another area of information retrieval, collection selection, is apt for the application of our approach. Kulkarni and Callan [23] have demonstrated the effectiveness of selective search using collection selection and 1000 clusters of ClueWeb09. It only visits the first few clusters per query. Our results indicate that relevant results cluster in the same way, even when there are almost three orders of magnitude more clusters.

The clustering solutions produced by EM-tree may be useful for scaling classification applications. Nearby points contained in a few fine-grained clusters can be used to build a

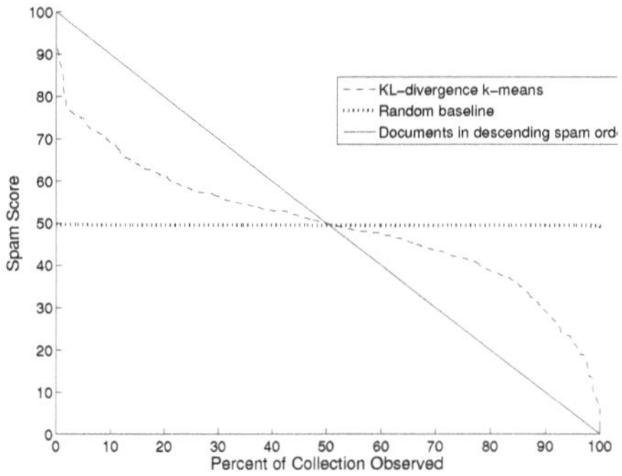

Figure 10: ClueWeb09 – 1000 KL-divergence k-means clusters

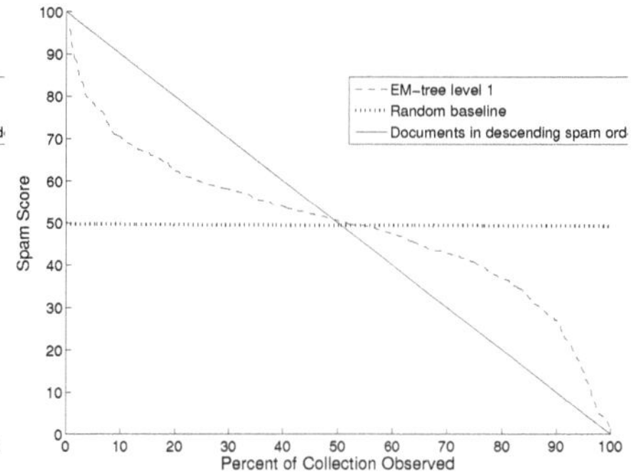

Figure 11: ClueWeb09 – 1000 EM-tree level 1 clusters

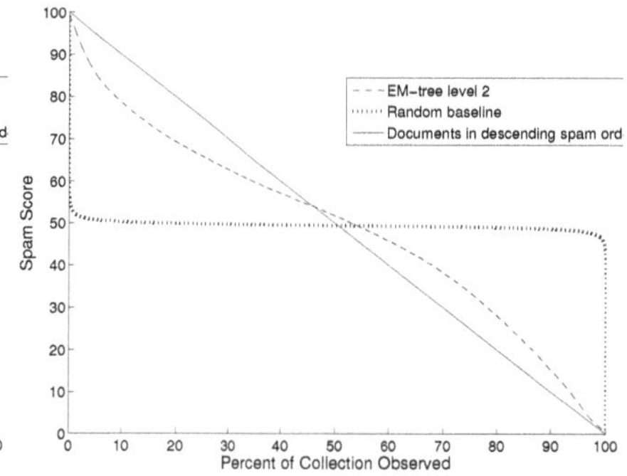

Figure 12: ClueWeb09 – 691708 EM-tree level 2 clusters

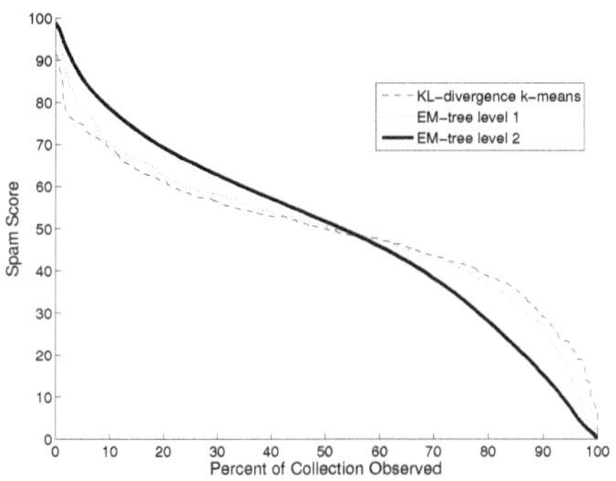

Figure 13: ClueWeb09 – Comparing all approaches

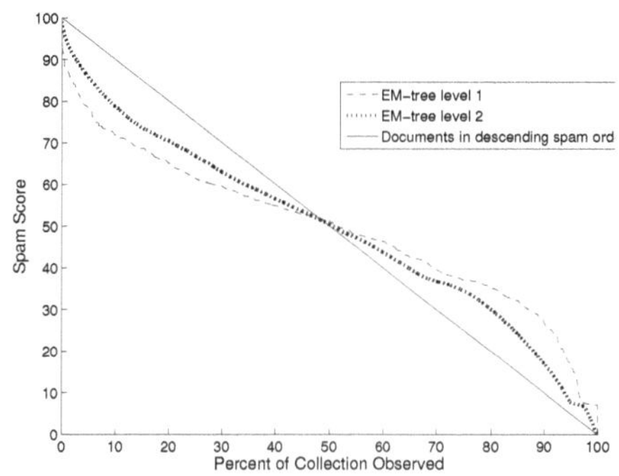

Figure 14: ClueWeb12 – Comparing all approaches

classifier. Alternatively, clusterings can be used for classification directly.

Sub-document clustering is now a possibility for large-scale document collections where splitting documents into fragments creates even more objects to cluster. It makes sense to split larger documents since such documents probably contain multiple sub-topics. However, splitting documents in web-scale collections certainly push it well beyond the capability of standard commodity hardware. However, with EM-tree it may be possible to consider such clustering of document fragments.

8. CONCLUSION

In this paper, we presented solutions for two major problems in web-scale document clustering – scalable and efficient document clustering and evaluation of cluster validity where categorical labeling of collections is unavailable and unfeasible.

The proposed EM-tree algorithm can cluster hundreds of millions of documents into hundreds of thousands of clusters on a single 16 CPU core machine in under 24 hours. It is standard hardware available to organizations of all sizes. To the best of our knowledge, clustering on a single machine at this scale has not been reported in the literature. To the contrary, the few published attempts at this scale have used high-performance computing resources, well beyond reach of most organizations. These attempts were also on lower dimensional non-document data. For document clustering, this is far beyond any examples we have been able to find. The largest scale approach we could find sampled 500,000 documents to produce 1,000 clusters. It then maps the 500 million documents onto these clusters [23]. The closest comparison we could find is a method that clusters the same order of magnitude of images into a similar order of magnitude of clusters using 2000 CPUs [27, 34]. However, this approach does not cluster documents that are sparse and high dimensional. Another approach parallelized k-means using 16,000 CPUs on a super computer to produce 1,000 clusters of 1 billion much lower dimensional weather data [4].

We presented two novel evaluations using ad hoc relevance and spam classifications to assess the validity of clusters where no category labels are available. This evaluation demonstrated that the fine-grained clustering created by EM-tree led to higher quality clusters. Additionally, we expect this approach to clustering to be applicable to many different types of web scale data emerging from sources such as images, sound recordings, sensors, positioning systems, genome research, marketing data and many more fields.

9. REFERENCES

[1] D. Arthur and S. Vassilvitskii. k-means++: The advantages of careful seeding. In *Proceedings of the eighteenth annual ACM-SIAM symposium on Discrete algorithms*, pages 1027–1035. Society for Industrial and Applied Mathematics, 2007.

[2] Bahman Bahmani, Benjamin Moseley, Andrea Vattani, Ravi Kumar, and Sergei Vassilvitskii. Scalable k-means++. *Proceedings of the VLDB Endowment*, 5(7):622–633, 2012.

[3] E. Bingham and H. Mannila. Random projection in dimensionality reduction: applications to image and text data. In *KDD 2001*, pages 245–250. ACM, 2001.

[4] H. Bisgin and H.N. Dalfes. Parallel clustering algorithms with application to climatology. In *Geophysical Research Abstracts*, volume 10, 2008.

[5] A. Broder, L. Garcia-Pueyo, V. Josifovski, S. Vassilvitskii, and S. Venkatesan. Scalable k-means by ranked retrieval. In *Proceedings of the 7th ACM international conference on Web search and data mining*, pages 233–242. ACM, 2014.

[6] M.S. Charikar. Similarity estimation techniques from rounding algorithms. In *STOC*, pages 380–388, New York, NY, USA, 2002. ACM.

[7] C.L.A. Clarke, N. Craswell, I. Soboroff, and G.V. Cormack. Overview of the TREC 2010 web track. Technical report, DTIC Document, 2010.

[8] C.L.A. Clarke, N. Craswell, I. Soboroff, and E.M. Voorhees. Overview of the TREC 2011 web track. Technical report, DTIC Document, 2011.

[9] C.L.A. Clarke, N. Craswell, and E.M. Voorhees. Overview of the TREC 2012 web track. Technical report, DTIC Document, 2012.

[10] A. Coates, A. Karpathy, and A. Ng. Emergence of object-selective features in unsupervised feature learning. In *NIPS 25*, page 2690–2698, 2012.

[11] G.V. Cormack, M.D. Smucker, and C.L.A. Clarke. Efficient and effective spam filtering and re-ranking for large web datasets. *Information retrieval*, 14(5):441–465, 2011.

[12] C.M. De Vries. *Document clustering algorithms, representations and evaluation for information retrieval.* PhD thesis, Electricial Engineering and Computer Science, Queensland University of Technology, Brisbane, Australia, 2014.

[13] C.M. De Vries and S. Geva. K-tree: large scale document clustering. In *Proceedings of the 32nd international ACM SIGIR conference on Research and development in information retrieval*, pages 718–719. ACM, 2009.

[14] C.M. De Vries, S. Geva, and A. Trotman. Document clustering evaluation: Divergence from a random baseline. *WIR-2012, Dortmund, Germany.*, 2012.

[15] C.M. De Vries, R. Nayak, S. Kutty, S. Geva, and A. Tagarelli. Overview of the INEX 2010 XML mining track: Clustering and classification of XML documents. In *INEX 2010*, pages 363–376, 2011.

[16] R.M. Esteves and C. Rong. Using mahout for clustering wikipedia's latest articles: a comparison between k-means and fuzzy c-means in the cloud. In *IEEE CloudCom*, pages 565–569. IEEE, 2011.

[17] A. Gersho and R.M. Gray. *Vector quantization and signal compression.* Kluwer Academic Publishers, 1993.

[18] S. Geva and C.M. De Vries. Topsig: topology preserving document signatures. CIKM '11, pages 333–338, New York, NY, USA, 2011. ACM.

[19] Z.S. Harris. Distributional structure. *Word*, 1954.

[20] N. Jardine and C.J. van Rijsbergen. The use of hierarchic clustering in information retrieval. *Information storage and retrieval*, 7(5):217–240, 1971.

[21] R. Jin, C. Kou, R. Liu, and Y. Li. Efficient parallel spectral clustering algorithm design for large data sets under cloud computing environment. *Journal of Cloud Computing: Advances, Systems and Applications*, 2(1):18, 2013.

[22] W.B. Johnson and J. Lindenstrauss. Extensions of Lipschitz mappings into a Hilbert space. *Contemporary mathematics*, 26(189-206):1–1, 1984.

[23] A. Kulkarni and J. Callan. Document allocation policies for selective searching of distributed indexes. In *CIKM 2010*, pages 449–458. ACM, 2010.

[24] A. Kumar and S. Mukherjee. Verification and validation of mapreduce program model for parallel k-means algorithm on hadoop cluster. *International Journal of Computer Applications*, 72, 2013.

[25] Q.V. Le, M.A. Ranzato, R. Monga, M. Devin, K. Chen, G.S. Corrado, J. Dean, and A.Y. Ng. Building high-level features using large scale unsupervised learning. *arXiv preprint arXiv:1112.6209*, 2011.

[26] D.D. Lewis, Y. Yang, T.G. Rose, and F. Li. RCV1: A new benchmark collection for text categorization research. *The Journal of Machine Learning Research*, 5:361–397, 2004.

[27] T. Liu, C. Rosenberg, and H.A. Rowley. Clustering billions of images with large scale nearest neighbor search. In *WACV'07*, pages 28–28. IEEE, 2007.

[28] C.D. Manning, P. Raghavan, and H. Schutze. An introduction to information retrieval. 2008.

[29] R. Nayak, C.M. De Vries, S. Kutty, S. Geva, L. Denoyer, and P. Gallinari. Overview of the INEX 2009 XML mining track: Clustering and classification of XML documents. *Focused Retrieval and Evaluation*, pages 366–378, 2010.

[30] M. Sahlgren. An introduction to random indexing. In *TKE 2005*, 2005.

[31] K.C. Thompson, P Bennett, F. Diaz, C.L.A. Clarke, and E.M. Voorhees. Overview of the TREC 2013 web track. Technical report, DTIC Document, 2013.

[32] E.M. Voorhees. The philosophy of information retrieval evaluation. In *Evaluation of cross-language information retrieval systems*, pages 143–170. Springer, 2002.

[33] J. Wang, H.T. Shen, J. Song, and J. Ji. Hashing for similarity search: A survey. *arXiv preprint arXiv:1408.2927*, 2014.

[34] Xin-Jing Wang, Lei Zhang, and Ce Liu. Duplicate discovery on 2 billion internet images. In *Computer Vision and Pattern Recognition Workshops (CVPRW), 2013 IEEE Conference on*, pages 429–436. IEEE, 2013.

[35] Ren Wu, Bin Zhang, and Meichun Hsu. Clustering billions of data points using gpus. In *Proceedings of the combined workshops on UnConventional high performance computing workshop plus memory access workshop*, pages 1–6. ACM, 2009.

[36] Tian Zhang, Raghu Ramakrishnan, and Miron Livny. Birch: an efficient data clustering method for very large databases. In *ACM SIGMOD Record*, volume 25, pages 103–114. ACM, 1996.

Network-based Origin Confusion Attacks against HTTPS Virtual Hosting

Antoine Delignat-Lavaud
Inria Paris-Rocquencourt
antoine@delignat-lavaud.fr

Karthikeyan Bhargavan
Inria Paris-Rocquencourt
karthikeyan.bhargavan@inria.fr

ABSTRACT

We investigate current deployment practices for virtual hosting, a widely used method for serving multiple HTTP and HTTPS origins from the same server, in popular content delivery networks, cloud-hosting infrastructures, and web servers. Our study uncovers a new class of HTTPS origin confusion attacks: when two virtual hosts use the same TLS certificate, or share a TLS session cache or ticket encryption key, a network attacker may cause a page from one of them to be loaded under the other's origin in a client browser. These attacks appear when HTTPS servers are configured to allow virtual host fallback from a client-requested, secure origin to some other unexpected, less-secure origin. We present evidence that such vulnerable virtual host configurations are widespread, even on the most popular and security-scrutinized websites, thus allowing a network adversary to hijack pages, or steal secure cookies and single sign-on tokens. To prevent our virtual host confusion attacks and recover the isolation guarantees that are commonly assumed in shared hosting environments, we propose fixes to web server software and advocate conservative configuration guidelines for the composition of HTTP with TLS.

1. INTRODUCTION

Web applications are increasingly being moved to the cloud or deployed on *distributed content delivery networks* (CDNs), raising new concerns about their security. The cloud environment requires the sharing of servers and network addresses between many unrelated, mutually distrusting principals. On the client side, the problem of securely isolating websites from each other within the browser has been a core topic of security research in recent years, producing a rich literature centered around the notion of *security origin*. Yet, on the server side, the security implications of hosting large numbers of websites from the same web servers has gathered relatively little attention, even though cloud infrastructures constitute a prime target for attacks, both from criminals and from governmental adversaries [1].

WWW 2015, May 18–22, 2015, Florence, Italy.
ACM 978-1-4503-3469-3/15/05.
http://dx.doi.org/10.1145/2736277.2741089.

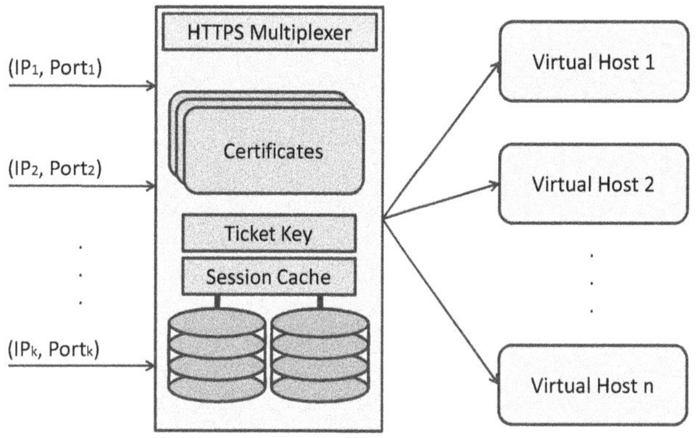

Figure 1: HTTPS server with multiple virtual hosts

The Transport Layer Security (TLS) protocol [2], as used within HTTP over TLS (HTTPS) [3], remains the only defense against network-layer attacks on the web. It provides authentication of the server (and optionally, of the client), as well as confidentiality and integrity of HTTP requests and responses, against attackers that control both the network and malicious websites visited by the client.

While the precise security guarantees of TLS have been extensively studied [4–6], these formal works all consider a simple deployment model, where each server only has one network interface and one certificate valid for a single domain that matches the server identity. This model does not reflect current practices, especially in the cloud, but also in many mainstream web servers.

Sharing TLS Server Credentials Many web servers employ *virtual hosting* to serve multiple HTTPS domains behind the same TLS server. To do this, the TLS server needs to decide which certificate to present to an incoming connection. This decision is either based on the incoming IP address, or increasingly often, on the server identity requested within the TLS *server name indication* (SNI) extension [7]. Even when different domains use different certificates, by using the same TLS server, they often implicitly share the TLS session cache that is used for fast session resumption.

Moreover, the same certificate may be used across multiple domains on different servers. Recent measurement studies of TLS certificate issuance [8, 9] show that a majority of newly issued certificates are valid for more than one domain name, with a significant number of them containing at least one wildcard. For example, all the front-end Google servers share a certificate that covers `*.google.com` as well as 50 other DNS names, many with wildcards.

Finally, the same certificate may be used on multiple ports on the same domain. For example, web servers often listen for HTTP-based protocols such as WebSocket [10] on non-traditional ports, but reuse the same IP address, domain name, and TLS certificate as the main website.

When TLS credentials are shared between different HTTP server entities, how do the security guarantees provided by TLS relate to those desired by HTTPS? In this paper, we investigate this question with regard to the origin-based security policies commonly used in modern web applications.

Same Origin Policy Web browsers identify resources by the *origin* from which they were loaded, where an origin consists of the *protocol, domain name* and *port number*, e.g. **`https://y.x.com:443`**. The *same-origin policy* [11] allows arbitrary sharing between pages on the same origin, but strictly regulates cross-origin interactions. Hence, if any page on a given origin is compromised, either by a cross-site scripting (XSS) flaw [12], or because the server is under attacker control, the whole origin must be considered compromised as well. Consequently, prudent websites divide their content into different subdomains at different security levels, so that the compromise of one (e.g. **`blog.x.com`**) does not affect another (e.g. **`login.x.com`**).

In the presence of a network attacker, the same origin policy only protects HTTPS origins, for which the underlying TLS protocol can guarantee that the browser is connected to a server that owns a certificate for the desired origin. However, when TLS server credentials, such as certificates and cached sessions, are shared across servers, the isolation guarantees of the same origin policy crucially rely on the routing of HTTP requests to the correct origin server.

Routing Requests to Virtual Hosts The server-side counterpart of the notion of *origin* is the *virtual host*, whose role is to produce the response to an HTTP request given its *path* and *query parameters* (i.e. what appears in the URL after the origin). Virtual hosts used to correspond to directories on the server's filesystem, but with the widespread use of rewriting rules and dynamically generated pages, virtual hosts are now best treated as abstract request processors.

Figure 1 depicts the process that a web server uses to choose a virtual host for a given HTTPS request. The decision depend on parameters gathered at various levels: the IP address and port that the TCP connection was accepted on, the SNI extension received during the TLS handshake, and the `Host` header received in the HTTP request. On the client, all these parameters are derived from the request URL (a DNS request yields the IP address). On the server, each parameter is considered separately in a manually configured set of complex rules to determine the virtual host that will handle the request (see Section 3 for more detail).

In particular, most web servers will pick a *fallback* virtual host when the normal routing rules fail. In plain HTTP, routing fallback can be quite useful, for instance to access a website by its IP address or former domain name, or to use the same request handler for all subdomains. However, HTTPS routing fallback can be extremely dangerous, since it may allow a request for a client-requested secure origin to be processed by the virtual host for some unexpected, less-secure origin.

Virtual Confusion Attacks The main contribution of this paper is the identification of a new class of attacks on virtual hosts that share TLS credentials, either on the same or on different web servers. In these attacks, a network attacker can take an HTTPS connection meant for one of these virtual hosts and redirect it to the other. The TLS connection succeeds because of the shared TLS credentials; then, because of virtual host fallback, the request is processed by a virtual host that was never intended to serve contents for the domain in the `Host` header.

In particular, we show that a network attacker can always break the same-origin policy between different ports on the same domain, by redirecting connections from one port to another. Moreover, if two servers serving two independent domains share a common certificate (covering both domains), or a cached TLS session, the network attacker can cause pages from one server to be loaded under the other's origin. In all these cases, the attacker subverts the browser's intended origin of the request, often with exploitable results.

Concrete Website Exploits Origin confusion attacks between two HTTPS domains are particularly dangerous when one of them is less secure than the other, for example, if one has an XSS flaw or an insecure redirection. We detail five exemplary instances of origin confusion attacks that demonstrate different attack vectors and illustrate the applicability and impact of this class of attacks:

1. We show how HTTPS requests to many websites hosted by the Akamai CDN can be hijacked by a server controlled by an attacker (Section 2).
2. We show how single sign-on access tokens on Yahoo (and several other major websites) can be stolen by exploiting an unsafe redirector on Yahoo (Section 4.1).
3. We describe a combined network- and web-based XSS attack on Dropbox that exploits malicious hosted content and cookie forcing (Section 4.2).
4. We show how HTTPS requests to highly-trusted Mozilla websites such as **`bugzilla.mozilla.org`** can be redirected to user-controlled pages on **`git.mozilla.org`**, by exploiting shared TLS session caches (Section 4.3).
5. We show how TLS session reuse in the SPDY protocol [13] can be exploited to impersonate any HTTPS website in Chrome (Sections 6).

These attacks were responsibly disclosed, acknowledged, and fixed in the relevant websites, CDNs, browsers, and web servers. They have been awarded bug bounties by HackerOne, Chromium, and Mozilla. More worryingly, the attacks show the dangerous consequences of seemingly innocuous routing decisions within widely used web servers, TLS terminators, and reverse proxies. Section 7 discusses some countermeasures, and we hope this paper will trigger a more systematic study of server-side HTTPS multiplexing, and research on new robust designs that can prevent such attacks.

2. IMPERSONATING WEBSITES SERVED BY THE AKAMAI CDN

Akamai is the leading content delivery network (CDN) on the web, claiming to be responsible for up to 20% of the total Internet traffic [14]. Like other CDNs, Akamai has a large network of *points of presence* (PoP) distributed all around

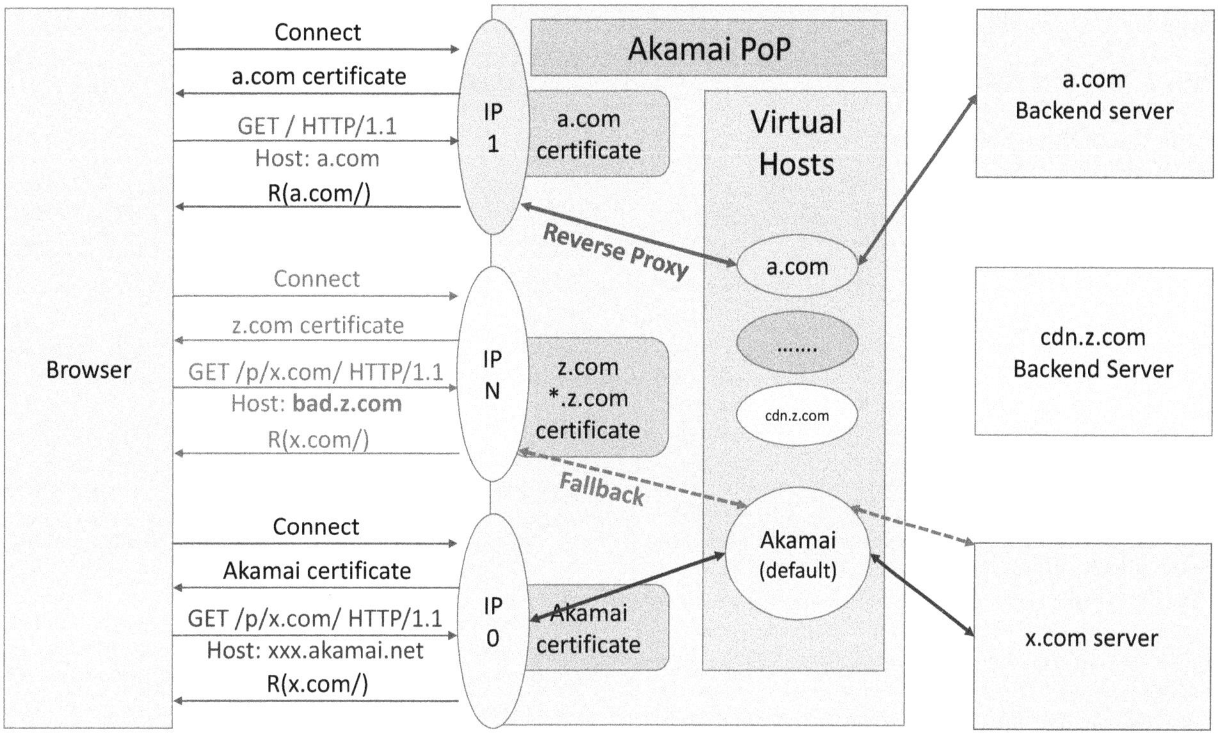

Figure 2: Akamai Point-of-Presence (POP) server design

the world, whose job is to cache static contents from the websites of Akamai customers, to reduce latency and distribute load. Akamai serves varied customers, including popular social networks like `linkedin.com` and sensitive websites like `nsa.gov` that are often accessed over HTTPS. We will see how virtual host fallback on Akamai's PoPs leads to a serious origin confusion attack on such websites.

CDNs use one of two strategies to deploy HTTPS for customer websites; an extensive survey of real-world practices appears in [15]. Some CDNs (e.g. CloudFlare) use *shared certificates* that are fully managed by the CDN operator with no involvement from its customer. Shared certificates are valid for a large number of customer domains and may be deployed on all the PoPs of the CDN; their private keys remain under the CDN provider's control. Other CDNs (e.g. Akamai) require customers to obtain *custom certificates* for their HTTPS domains from certification authorities. The CDN must be given access to the private keys of these certificates, so that they can be installed on the PoPs allocated to the customer. On a PoP with custom certificates, the choice of server certificate on a TLS connection may depend on the incoming IP address or on the server name in the TLS SNI extension. CDNs increasingly prefer SNI, but it is not available on some legacy clients (e.g. Windows XP).

Virtual Host Fallback in Akamai PoPs The Akamai CDN uses a uniform virtual host configuration on its PoPs, all of which run a custom HTTP server implementation called "AkamaiGhost". Figure 2 depicts how HTTPS requests are processed by Akamai: each PoP has `N` custom certificates installed for `N` virtual hosts, and each certificate is served on a dedicated IP address. Therefore, if a client connects to IP 1, it will be given the certificate for `a.com`, whereas if it connects to IP 2, it will be given the certificate for `*.z.com`. After the TLS connection is complete, the PoP inspects the HTTP `Host` header and routes the request to the appropriate virtual host.

Each PoP also serves a special Akamai virtual host, which is also the fallback default. Hence, if the `Host` header of a request (received on any IP address) isn't one of the `N` configured customer domains, it is routed to this default host. Interestingly, the Akamai virtual host acts as a universal proxy: when a request for `/p/a.com/path` is received, for a certain well-known prefix `p`, the PoP forwards the request to `a.com/path`, along with all HTTP headers sent by the client (including cookies and HTTP authentication). Then, it caches and forward the response from `a.com` to the client. Providing an open proxy for HTTP connections to any website is a perfectly reasonable design decision and may even be considered a generous gesture[1]. Unfortunately, the impact of this proxy on HTTPS connections to customer domains is severe.

Server Impersonation Attack We now consider a concrete example. LinkedIn uses Akamai only for the domain `static.linkedin.com`, but the certificate it provides to Akamai is valid for `*.linkedin.com`. Suppose a user is logged in to LinkedIn from her browser. The attack (shown for `bad.z.com` in Figure 2) proceeds as follows:

1. A network attacker gets the browser to visit: `https:`

[1] `http://www.peacefire.org/bypass/Proxy/akamai.html`

Figure 3: Outcome of the attack against nsa.gov

//www.linkedin.com/p/attacker.com/ by injecting JavaScript on some HTTP page loaded by the browser.

2. The attacker redirects the resulting TLS connection to the LinkedIn IP address on some Akamai PoP.
3. The TLS connection succeeds since the certificate returned from the PoP is valid for `*.linkedin.com`.
4. The PoP only has a virtual host configured for `static.linkedin.com`; hence, the request falls back to the Akamai virtual host, which triggers the open proxy to `attacker.com`.
5. The user's browser loads the attacker's website under the `https://www.linkedin.com` origin (no certificate warning). It also sends the user's `Secure`, `HttpOnly` LinkedIn cookies to the attacker.

This is an instance of an *origin confusion attack* that leads to full server impersonation. It defeats all existing HTTPS protections: it leaks all cookies, it allows the attacker to disable HSTS and content security policy. Worse, it does not leave any trace on the impersonated server (which is never involved during the attack). In the PoP's HTTP log, the request looks like a harmless caching query to the proxy.

Responsible Disclosure This critical flaw existed in Akamai servers for nearly 15 years without getting noticed. Based on domains in the Alexa list, we estimate that at least 12,000 websites have been vulnerable to this attack, including 7 out of the top 10 websites in the USA. For example, Figure 3 depicts the server impersonation attack on the `nsa.gov` domain. Following our report, Akamai changed its default virtual host to one that only returns an error page.

3. MULTIPLEXING HTTPS CONNECTIONS

In this section, we investigate how real-world HTTPS implementations decide which certificate and virtual host to use when processing an incoming request. This problem applies to all popular web servers such as Apache, Nginx or IIS, but also to *SSL terminators*, CDN frontend servers and other reverse proxy software.

Virtual Host Parameters There are three layers of identity involved in the processing of HTTPS request: the network layer identity corresponds to an IP address and port; the transport/session layer identity consists of a server certificate and TLS session database and/or ticket encryption key; lastly, the application layer identity is conveyed in the

```
ssl_session_ticket_key "/etc/ssl/ticket.key";
ssl_session_cache shared:SSL:1m;

server { #1
        listen 1.2.3.4:443 ssl;
        server_name www.a.com;
        ssl_certificate "/etc/ssl/a.pem";
        root "/srv/a";
}
server { #2
        listen 4.3.2.1:443 ssl;
        server_name ~^(?<sub>api|dev)\.a\.com$;
        ssl_certificate "/etc/ssl/a.pem";
        root "/srv/api";
}
server { #3
        listen 2.1.4.3:443 ssl;
        server_name www.learn-a.com;
        ssl_certificate "/etc/ssl/learn-a.pem";
        root "/srv/learn";
}
```

Figure 4: Sample virtual host configuration

`Host` header of HTTP requests (however, there is no equivalent header in responses, which are origin-unaware).

Concretely, each web server implements some *multiplexing* logic based on a configuration file that defines how to route an incoming HTTPS connection to the right virtual host. While each server software has its own configuration syntax, there is a common set of parameters that are used to define new TLS-enabled virtual hosts:

1. A *listen* directive that specifies at least one pair of IP address and port number on which the virtual host accepts connections. It is possible to use a wildcard in the IP address to accept connections to any address, whereas a port must be specified.
2. A *server name* directive that may contain one or more fully qualified domain names or regular expressions defining a class of domain names. Without loss of generality, we assume that the server name is always given as a single regular expression.
3. A *certificate* directive which points to the certificate and private key to use for this virtual host.
4. A *session cache* directive, that optionally describes how to store the data structures for session identifier based resumption, either in memory, or on a hard drive or external device. This directive may also specify the encryption key for ticket-based resumption.

If any of the last three items is not defined in the configuration of the virtual host, its value is typically inherited from the server-wide configuration settings, if available. Figure 4 shows an example virtual host configuration for Nginx.

Request Routing The process of selecting the virtual host to use for a given incoming connection can be broken up as follows (see [16, 17] for implementation-specific references):

1. First, the server initializes the list of candidates with every virtual host defined in the configuration.
2. Then, the server inspects the IP address and port on which the client connected. Virtual hosts defined on a different IP address (save for wildcards) or port are removed from the list of candidates.

3. The server next inspects the TLS handshake message sent by the client.
   (a) if the client hello message does not include the SNI extension, the server will return the certificate configured in the virtual host that has been marked as default for the given IP address and port, or if no default is defined, in the first one;
   (b) if an SNI value is specified, the server returns the certificate from the first virtual host whose server name matches the given SNI. If no server name matches, once again, the certificate from the default host is used.
4. Next, the web server finishes the handshake and waits for the client to send its request to inspect the `Host` HTTP header. If it includes a port number, it is immediately discarded. Then, the server picks either the first virtual host from the candidate list whose server name matches the HTTP `Host`. If none matches, it picks either the default virtual host, if one is defined, or the first host from the candidate list otherwise.

There are multiple problems with this virtual host selection process: for instance, it may allow the server to pick TLS settings (including certificate and session cache) from one virtual host, but route the incoming request to a different one (this behavior may be justified by the SPDY optimization described in Section 6).

Port Routing Even though the requested port is included in the `Host` header, and thus reflects the actual port that the browser will use to enforce the same-origin policy, is ignored by all the implementations we tested in favor of the port the connection was received on, which is unauthenticated. This means that it is *always* possible for an attacker to redirect requests from one port to another, and confuse the two origins. Because of this observation, *we strongly recommend to remove the port number from the same-origin policy*, considering that cross-port origin isolation simply does not work in practice (it is already known not to work with cookies).

Fallback Most dangerously, fallback mechanisms open a wide range of unexpected behaviors, and they often depend on the order in which the virtual hosts have been written in the configuration file. The configuration in Figure 4 includes one of the most widespread vulnerable patterns. A certificate valid for two subdomains of `a.com` is used in virtual hosts on different IP addresses (possibly on different physical machines). If an attacker intercepts a connection to `www.a.com` and redirects it to `4.3.2.1:443`, a page from `api.a.com` will be loaded under the `www.a.com` origin, because the host selected during routing must match the IP address and port of the connection.

TLS Session Cache Similarly, the TLS session caching behavior appears to have serious pitfalls in several popular web servers (unlike the request processing algorithm, session caching mechanisms can significantly differ between implementations). For instance, in Nginx:

- By default, only ticket-based session caching is enabled. If no ticket key has been configured, a fresh one is generated for each IP address and port (but not for each virtual host). On the other hand, if a ticket key is specified in the global configuration of the server, all tickets created by any virtual host can be resumed on any other. If a ticket key is given in the configuration of a given virtual host, it will also replace the key on all previously defined hosts on the same IP address.
- Session identifier-based resumption must be explicitly enabled by configuring a session cache database on the server. In-memory shared caches (shared in the sense of threads), which carry an identifier, are commonly used. Sessions from all virtual hosts that use the same identifier in their shared cache can be resumed on each other, regardless of IP address, SNI or certificate.

Once again, it is easy to mis-configure a server to allow sessions to be resumed across virtual hosts. For instance, the configuration in Figure 4 has a global ticket key: if the user has a TLS session created with `www.a.com`, a resumption attempt can be redirected by the attacker to `4.3.2.1:443`: the TLS session ticket will be accepted but because of fallback, a page from `www.learn-a.com` gets loaded under the wrong origin, even thought they don't use the same certificate. Such an attack is enabled by the lack of authentication during the abbreviated TLS handshake: indeed, resumption is purely based on the session identifier or session ticket, regardless of the original SNI or server certificate.

In the next section, we demonstrate various classes of exploit that rely on virtual host confusion, illustrated by concrete attacks against popular websites.

4. ORIGIN CONFUSION EXPLOITS

In itself, virtual host confusion does not sound like a big problem: fundamentally, it only allows a network attacker to load a page under an unexpected, but related (in certificate or session cache), origin. The interesting question is, what can an attacker do with this capability? We found a variety of possible exploits that always follow the same pattern: the loaded page contains bad HTTP characteristics that can break the security of the confused origin.

In the case of Akamai, the loaded page was under complete attacker control. We found similar cases where the loaded page is controlled by the adversary. However, weaker forms of control are a lot more common, but can be still exploited. For instance, if the page sets the `X-Frame-Options` header to `allow`, the confused origin can be loaded in an `iframe`, even though the confused origin might have relied on that header to block clickjacking. Similarly, the origin may have relied on the `Content-Security-Policy` [18] header to block the execution of injected inline scripts, but this can be broken if the loaded page contains a more relaxed CSP. In the rest of this section, we present three more exploits that rely on more creative uses of a network attacker's capabilities.

4.1 Cross-Protocol Redirections: OAuth

The first class of exploits relies on the observation that many websites only use HTTPS on the security-critical parts of their website (for instance, the login form). If, on a low-security virtual host, there exists a page that redirects either to plain HTTP, or to an arbitrary page on another origin (open redirector), then, by confusing a request on a high trust virtual host to such a page, an attacker may learn some secret parameters from the query string or URL fragment by intercepting the redirection.

The prime candidate for this type of exploit is single sign-on access tokens, used by Facebook, Twitter, Google or Yahoo on a large proportion of websites as a replacement for

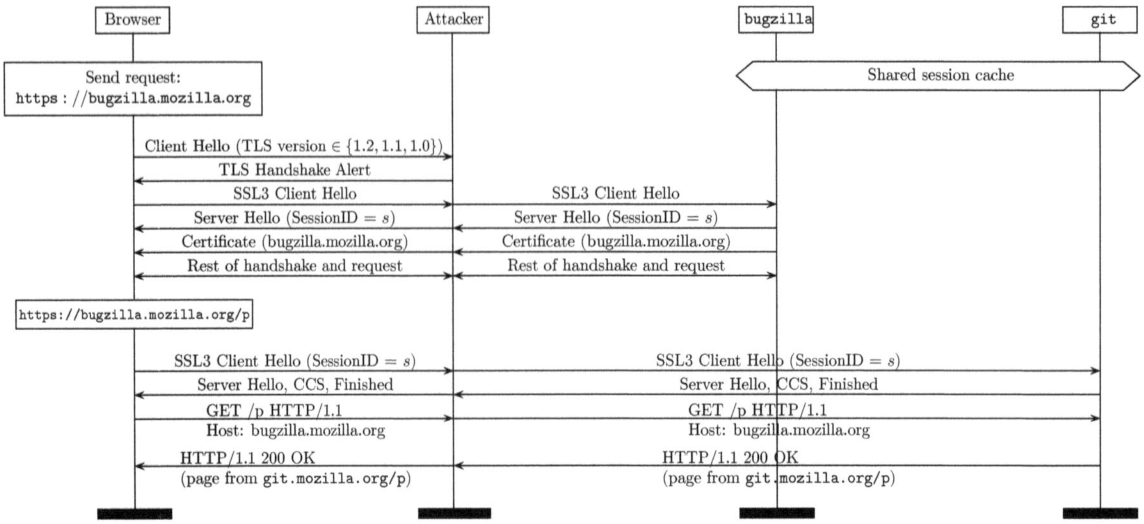

Figure 5: Session cache sharing attack against two Mozilla servers

login forms. For instance, in the OAuth 2.0 protocol [19], a client website registers its origin with the identity provider (e.g. Google), and can obtain an access token to access the user credentials by sending the user to the authorization page on the identity provider's website. This request includes a redirection URL on the registered high-trust origin of the client website. The access token is included in the redirection response in the URL fragment.

Assume `X=https://oauth.a.com` is the registered OAuth origin, served by a virtual host that can be confused with the one for `https://www.a.com` (e.g. because they share a wildcard certificate for `*.a.com`). If the attacker finds a page on `www.a.com` that redirects to HTTP or to his own website, say on the path `/p`, then it can send the user to the URL: `https://idp.com/token?redirect_url=X/p`, which in turn redirects to: `https://oauth.a.com/p#token`. The attacker redirects the request to `oauth.a.com` to point to the server that handles `www.a.com`. The request is thus redirected to, say, `http://attacker.com/#token` which leaks the access token to the attacker. We found that many of the top Alexa websites that use single sign-on systems are vulnerable to these origin confusion exploits based on cross-protocol redirections in practice (including Pinterest and Yahoo).

Responsible Disclosure We discussed this attack with leading identity providers such as Facebook. We agree it is inherently caused by the weakness of OAuth to redirection attacks, a problem that is well known and can only be avoided by properly following recommendations regarding redirections on OAuth-enabled websites.

4.2 Hosted Contents: Dropbox

Dropbox allows users to share their public files on the low-trust origin `dropboxusercontent.com`, whereas it deploys state of the art HTTP security protections on its high-trust origin `www.dropbox.com`, including HSTS to prevent any network attack. However, non-public files cannot be served from this low-trust origin when the user wants to download data from her account, because they require access to the session cookie to prove that the user is authorized to view the file. Thus, the `dl-web.dropbox.com` origin is used for the purpose of displaying files from the user's own Dropbox account while he is logged in. This origin uses the same wildcard certificate as `www.dropbox.com`.

Using virtual host confusion, an attacker is able to load a page from the `dl-web` subdomain under the `www` origin. To turn this into an exploit, the attacker can take advantage of the complete lack of integrity guarantee for cookies [20, 21]. The attacker then performs the following steps:

1. store a malicious HTML page on his own Dropbox account (on `https://dl-web.dropbox.com/m`);
2. trigger request to `http://attacker.dropbox.com` (not protected by HSTS) and inject a `Set-Cookie` header in the response with `domain=.dropbox.com` and a very low `max-age`, that contains his own session identifier;
3. trigger request to `https://www.dropbox.com/m`, but forward the connection to the `dl-web` server. The `Cookie` header of the request contains (depending on browser) the user's session identifier, followed by the attacker's; the Dropbox server authenticates the latter and returns the malicious page.
4. wait for the delay specified in `max-age` until the forced cookie expires;
5. perform arbitrary requests on the user's Dropbox account (same impact as a XSS flaw on `www.dropbox.com`).

Responsible Disclosure We reported this attack to the Dropbox security team, who immediately confirmed the attack and fixed their virtual host configuration.

4.3 Shared TLS Cache: Mozilla

When two different servers or virtual hosts share a TLS session cache or session ticket encryption keys, an HTTPS connection to one host may be redirected to the other (using session resumption). If one of these hosts has a lower trust level than the other, this amounts to a cross-site scripting attack. We found multiple interesting examples of servers on the web that share TLS session caches, most of which can be found in cloud infrastructures, such as Amazon Web Services, Yahoo or Google. Google is an interesting case: every single Google front-end server uses the same session cache and ticket key. However, because they also have the exact same virtual host configuration, we found no exploit against Google servers.

We found shared session caches to be a lot more common than shared ticket keys within the sample of cloud servers we tested, which we assume to be caused by improperly configured, global-scoped caches. We observed that these global caches are often too small to store the large amounts of sessions created on these cloud services for more than a few seconds, a sufficiently long time window for attacks. However, most of these servers also implement ticket-based resumption, even though ticket keys are often not synchronized across servers (e.g. on Yahoo). Exploiting shared caches when tickets are enabled requires another tool in the network attacker arsenal.

Browsers attempt to maximize their compatibility with buggy TLS implementations by retrying failed handshakes with downgraded TLS versions, all the way from TLS 1.2 to SSL3. There have been concerns about downgrading; in fact, browsers are moving away from the practice because of another TLS attack (see Section 7 for details). By intercepting connections and injecting TLS alerts on strong protocol versions, an attacker is able to ensure that the browser will connect to its target website with SSL 3.0. Hence, features that rely on TLS extensions, such as SNI and ticket-based resumption, become unavailable.

We put this attack into practice to exploit origin confusion on Mozilla servers hosted on the Amazon cloud. We first noticed that a number of Mozilla domains serve dangerous content. For instance, `git.mozilla.org` or `hg.mozilla.org` contain many third party files, as well as a number of test HTML pages for the Firefox browser, some of which deliberately include XSS flaws. Even though these domains use dedicated certificates, their server share a server-side session cache with several other Mozilla domains, including high-security ones such as the one used for bug reports `bugzilla.mozilla.org`.

Figure 5 depicts the virtual host confusion exploit, which translate to the following steps for the attacker:

1. find a vulnerable page `/p` on low-trust origin `git`;
2. trigger a request to `https://bugzilla.mozilla.org/` (which has a single-domain, extended-validation certificate), while downgrading the connection to SSL 3.0, ensuring the lack of a TLS session ticket;
3. trigger request to `https://bugzilla.mozilla.org/p`, forwarding the connection to `git` server. The browser resumes the previous TLS sessions, even though the `git` server uses a completely different certificate. Despite the wrong `Host` header, the request is processed by the `git` virtual host;
4. compromise `bugzilla` origin with the XSS flaw on `/p`.

As usual, the whole attack can occur in the background without any user involvement (besides visiting any HTTP website on the attacker network).

Responsible Disclosure We reported this attack to Mozilla in bug 1004848. It was traced to a session cache isolation vulnerability in the Stingray Traffic Manager, which was fixed in version 9.7. We learned that a similar attack presented at Black Hat 2010 [22] had described how to transfer an XSS flaw from one Mozilla domain to another, also using virtual host confusion. Surprisingly, the hackers who described the attack consider it too targeted to be serious.

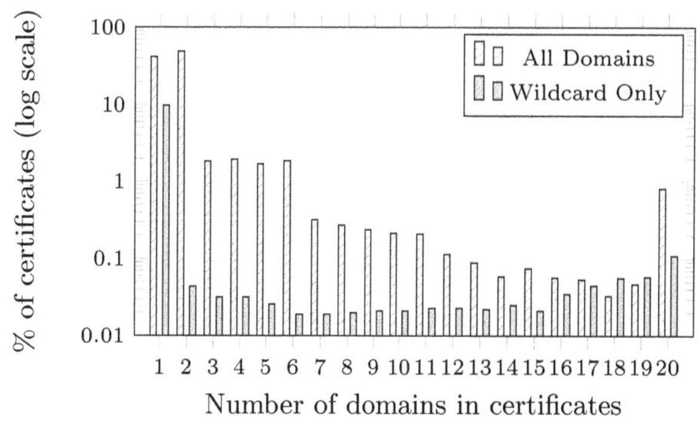

Figure 6: Issuance of multi-domain certificates

5. IMPACT MEASUREMENT

We have described four different exploits of virtual host confusion against major websites. However, these particular exploits do not give a clear picture of the general proportion of all websites vulnerable to similar attacks.

Virtual Host Fallback The main ingredient of our origin confusion attacks is virtual host fallback. We tested the top three most popular HTTPS implementations according to the September 2014 Netcraft Web Survey[2] with a configuration similar to the one in Figure 4 (without any deliberate effort to defend against virtual host confusion) and found that fallback was indeed possible on IIS (36% of servers), Apache (35%), and Nginx (14%).

Multi-Domain Certificates The issuance of new certificates by certification authorities is monitored fairly closely, including by the academic community [23]. We can easily build statistics about the number of domains found in publicly trusted certificates issued between July 2012 and July 2013 based on data collected in [9]. The results, depicted in Figure 6, show that about 40% of issued certificates are valid for a single domain; however, about 10% of them contain a wildcard. Many certificates are valid for two domains, but among them, over 95% list the same top-level domain with and without the `www` prefix (which can already lead to confusion attacks, but in most cases, both are be served by the same virtual host).

Shared TLS Cache Evaluating TLS session cache sharing is very difficult: any two servers on the web can potentially share their session ticket key or session database, regardless of their IP addresses and certificates. We were able to find several examples of shared session caches by manually testing servers within the same IP ranges known to be used by cloud services. Still, the actual number of vulnerable servers remains mostly unknown.

Cross-Protocol Redirections We have shown in Section 4.1 that a network attacker can impersonate users on websites that use single sign-on protocols based on token redirection to a secure registered origin, if this origin can be confused for another which contains redirections to any plain HTTP URL. To evaluate this scenario, we considered the HTTPS-enabled subset of the Alexa Top 10,000 websites [24], and simply sent a request for the path `/404`. In

[2] `http://news.netcraft.com/archives/2014/09/24/september-2014-web-server-survey.html`

about 1 out of 6 cases, this request was redirected to HTTP. Next, we decided to manually inspect the top 50 Alexa websites in the US that implement a single sign-on system. We found that 15 of them had in fact registered an HTTP origin with their identity provider (allowing a network to get an access token to impersonate the user without any effort). In 21 other cases, we found a page that redirects to HTTP within the secure registered origin (in such cases, the attacker can obtain access tokens without virtual host confusion). Finally, we found 11 instances where virtual host confusion could be used to recover the access tokens.

Overall, the results of our study on the 50 most popular websites in the US show that access tokens are for the most part not adequately protected against network attacks, which is consistent with previous results [25–28]. In particular, the dangers of cross-protocol redirections appears to be widely underestimated, especially on websites that implement single sign-on protocols.

6. CONNECTION SHARING IN SPDY AND HTTP/2

We have demonstrated in the previous sections that there exists a significant gap between the models used to analyze the security of TLS and the actual deployment of HTTPS in practice. However, web technologies are evolving so quickly that even the HTTPS multiplexer model presented in this paper fails to capture all current uses of TLS on the web.

In this section, we investigate the next-generation web protocols: SPDY [13] (which is already implemented major browsers such as Chrome, Firefox and Internet Explorer), and its derived IETF proposal for HTTP 2.0 [29]. An important design goal of these new protocols is to improve request latency over HTTPS. To this end, SPDY attempts to reduce the number of non-resumption TLS handshakes necessary to load a page by allowing browsers to reuse previously established sessions that were negotiated with a different domain, under certain conditions. In current HTTP2 drafts, this practice is called *connection reuse* [29, Section 9.1.1], but we also use the expression *connection sharing*.

Connection Sharing Recall that in normal TLS resumption, the browser caches TLS sessions indexed by domain and port number. On the client-side, there is no confusion between the different notions of identity: the origin of the request matches the SNI sent by the client, its HTTP Host header, the index of the session in the cache, and the origin used by the same-origin policy (assuming the client is not buggy). Thus, when accessing a website `https://w.com`, the browser may resume its session to download a picture at `https://w.com/y`, but it needs to create a fresh session if the picture is loaded from `https://i.w.com`, even if the domains `w.com` and `i.w.com` are served by the same server, on the same IP, and using the same certificate.

Connection reuse in SPDY and HTTP2 is a new policy that allows the browser to send the request to `i.w.com` on the session that was established with `w.com`, because it satisfies the two following conditions:

1. the certificate that was validated during the handshake of the session being reused also covers the domain name of the new request;
2. the original and new domain names both point to the same IP address.

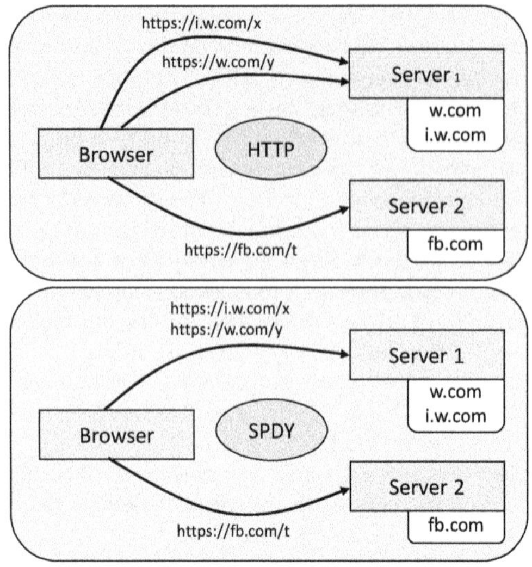

Figure 7: Connection Reuse in SPDY

Figure 7 illustrates connection reuse in SPDY: each arrow represents the TLS session used for the request(s) in its label. Because `w.com` and `i.w.com` point to the same IP or Server 1, which uses a certificate that covers both names, the same TLS session can be reused for requests to both domains.

Security Impact Connection sharing negates important assumptions used in several TLS and HTTPS mechanisms, such as TLS client authentication [30], Channel ID and Channel Bindings [31, 32] or certificate pinning [33, 34]. Concretely, every feature derived from the TLS handshake may no longer be considered to apply to the domain for which the session was created, but instead, to potentially any name present in the certificate used during the handshake. It is tempting to argue that the fact these domains appear in the same certificate is a clue that their sharing of some TLS session-specific attributes could be acceptable, but we stress that it is in fact not the case. For instance, recall from Section 2 that CloudFlare uses shared certificates that cover dozens of customers' domains [9, 35]. In fact, it is common on today's web to *connect to a website whose certificate is shared with a malicious, attacker-controlled domain.* With connection reuse, requests for the honest and malicious domain not only use the same TLS session, but possibly *the same connection* as well.

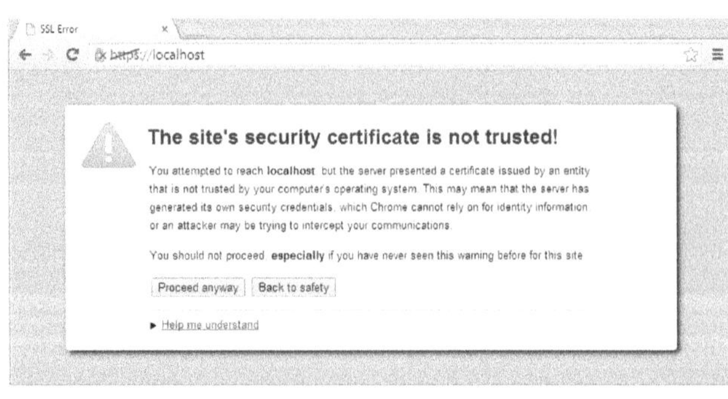

Figure 8: Interstitial Certificate Warning in Chrome

Exploit against Chrome With connection reuse, when a certificate is accepted by the browser during a TLS handshake, the established session can potentially be used for requests to all the domains listed in the certificate. The condition about the IP address of all these domains being the same doesn't matter to a network attacker who is anyway in control of the DNS.

In Chrome up to version 36, if a network attacker can get a user to click through a certificate warning for any unimportant domain (users may be used to ignore such warnings when connecting to captive portals, commonly found in hotels and other public network), he may be able to impersonate an arbitrary set of other domains, by listing them in the subject alternative name extension of the certificate (which has no displayed feedback in the interstitial warning, as shown in Figure 8). If the user attempts to connect to any of these added domains (say, `facebook.com`), the attacker can tamper with the DNS request for `facebook.com` to return his own IP address, which tells the browser it can reuse the SPDY connection established with the attacker when the self-signed malicious certificate was accepted. Although Chrome will keep the red crossed padlock icon in the address bar because of the invalid certificate of the original session, the attacker can still collect the session cookies for any number of websites in the background.

Figure 9: Compromise of Pinned, HSTS Origin

Interestingly, since the only trust decision made by the browser occurs when the bad certificate is accepted, this attack is able to bypass all security protections in Chrome against TLS MITM attacks. For instance, when a domain enables HSTS, certificate warning on this domain can not longer be clicked through by the user. Similarly, the Chrome browser includes a pinning list of certificates used by top websites, which successfully detected at least two man-in-the-middle attacks that were using improperly issued trusted certificates recently. Since these checks are only performed when a certificate is validated, they fail to trigger on reused connections, as shown in Figure 9. The user isn't shown any further certificate warning after the one caused by the attacker on an innocuous domain.

Responsible Disclosure This bug (CVE-2014-3166) was fixed by a security update for Chrome 36.

7. COUNTERMEASURES AND MITIGATION

Thorough this paper, we have pointed out multiple flaws both at the transport and application levels that prevent proper virtual host isolation on the server, and break the same origin policy on the client as a result. In this section, we summarize the possible countermeasures and mitigations that can prevent this class of attacks at each network layer.

Preventing Virtual Host Fallback Our evaluation shows

```
server {
       listen 1.2.3.4:443 ssl default_host;
       server_name "";
       # Used if no SNI is present in client hello
       ssl_certificate "/etc/ssl/a.com.pem";
       return 400;
}
```

Figure 10: Preventing virtual host fallback

that the fallback mechanism of the virtual host selection algorithm in current HTTPS servers is by far the leading factor in exploiting confusion vulnerabilities. For instance, even though all the services hosted by Google suffer from TLS session confusion, it cannot be directly exploited because all the front-end servers serve the same set of virtual hosts without fallback. We propose that upon receiving a request with a `Host` header that doesn't match any of the configured virtual host names, the server should immediately return an error. In particular, a request without a `Host` header would always be rejected (thus breaking compatibility with HTTP/1.0 clients). While this change only needs to apply to requests received over TLS, it does break backwards compatibility and may cause improperly configured websites to stop working. Therefore, none of the vendors we contacted are willing to implement such a change.

Authenticating Port in Host Header Currently, web servers ignore the port indicated by the client in the `Host` header, thus making it useless for the purpose of origin isolation. We propose that for requests received over TLS, a web server should compare the port included in the `Host` header with the one the request was sent to. We argue that unless this change is implemented in all HTTPS server software, browsers should stop using the port for origin isolation purposes, given that this isolation is mostly illusionary. This is the approach currently adopted by Internet Explorer.

Preventing Cross-Virtual Host Resumption In HTTP 1.1, there is no circumstance under which a session negotiated on a given virtual host would ever be resumed on another host with a different name or certificate. However, this invariant was broken with the introduction of SPDY and HTTP2 connection sharing. Thus, our initial suggestion to cryptographically bind TLS sessions with the virtual host they were created for was rejected. However, since connection sharing is only supposed to happen on the same IP address, it still makes sense to strictly block resumption across hosts on different TCP sockets. We convinced Nginx to implement such an isolation both for their server-side cache and session ticket implementation, starting from version 1.7.5 (CVE-2014-3616).

Preventing SSL Downgrading The attack we present in Section 4.3 was first to demonstrate that SSL downgrading can be taken advantage of by a network attacker to exploit virtual host confusion attacks. The recent POODLE attack (CVE-2014-3566) also exploits downgrading to mount a padding oracle attack; as a result, Chrome and NSS have removed downgrading to SSL3. A draft has also been submitted to the TLS working group of the IETF to introduce a new extension that prevents the attacker from downgrading the TLS version [36].

Configuration Guidelines for Current Web Servers Even without modifying web server software or the TLS library, there are some safe usage guidelines that website administrators can use to mitigate the attacks described in this paper. As a general rule, we recommend that only domains with the same trust levels should be allowed to share a certificate. It is best to avoid wildcard certificates, as they are valid even for non-existing subdomains, which increases the likelihood of a virtual host fallback. Anytime a certificate is used on a virtual host, it is necessary to ensure that all the domain names it contains have a matching virtual host configured on the same IP address and port; or at least a default one that returns an error. The same check applies to every other pair of IP address and port where this certificate is used. For domains with wildcards, the associated virtual host must use a regular expression that reflects all possible names. In cases where only some of the domains in the certificate are served on this IP, it is necessary to configure an explicit default host similar to the one given in Figure 10.

Session caches should be configured on a per-virtual host basis. Furthermore, all the ticket keys and shared cache names must be different in every virtual host where they are defined, unless SPDY connection sharing is used.

Cross-protocol redirections should be avoided in all TLS-enabled virtual hosts. When plaintext and encrypted versions of the same virtual host need to coexist, protocol-relative URLs (such as `//x.a.com/p`) should be used.

Finally, whenever possible, it is best to avoid cookies altogether, in particular to implement sessions: the origin-bound `localStorage` provides a safer alternative. If cookie-based sessions cannot be avoided (e.g. because a session cookie must be available to multiple subdomains), the page that sets the cookie should be served from the top-level domain using the `includeSubdomains` option of HSTS.

8. RELATED WORK

Origin confusion attacks may target the same-origin policy at various levels in the browser. The policy for cookies (which are always attached to requests regardless of their source origin) is often abused to mount cross-site request forgery attacks [20]. Implementations of single sign-on protocols [37] have been found to suffer from many flavors of origin confusion, sometimes on the messaging between frames by `postMessage` [38], sometimes because of JavaScript bugs [39], and often because of dangerous redirections [26, 40].

Among the documented network attack on HTTPS [34], the easiest is to trick clients into using HTTP instead; a method called SSL stripping [41]. To prevent such attacks, browsers and servers now implement Strict Transport Security (HSTS) [42], which can itself be sometimes attacked [32, 43]. Virtual host confusion attacks apply even to websites that use HSTS, since they rely on TLS credential sharing. However, some of the concrete exploits in this paper rely on some domains not requiring HSTS, for instance the exploit against Dropbox from Section 4.2.

Typical man-in-the-middle attacks on HTTPS rely on DNS rebinding [22, 44] or cache poisoning [45, 46] and on fooling the client into accepting a bogus, mis-issued, or compelled certificate [47, 48]. The goal is for a network attacker to impersonate a trusted HTTPS server [49]. Our attacks rely on shared server credentials to obtain similar impact, but do not require buggy clients [50], or on users clicking through certificate warnings [51] on the attacked origin. Our threat model, which mixes web and network attacks, is similar to those of recent cryptographic attacks on HTTPS, notably BEAST [52], CRIME [53] and FREAK [54], but the attacks in this paper do not rely on cryptographic weaknesses.

There have been many proposals to improve the PKI such as pinning [33], certificate transparency [55], or ARPKI [56], but they fail to prevent our attacks, which rely on bad certificate practices (in particular, the use of wildcard and shared certificates) by honest websites.

9. CONCLUSION

In this paper, we have have shown that the isolation between HTTPS origins in various kinds of shared environments (shared or overlapping certificate, content delivery networks, shared session cache, different ports on the same domain) can be broken by weaknesses in the handling of HTTP requests and the isolation of TLS session caches, resulting in high impact exploits. Preventing all virtual host confusion attacks requires vendors of HTTP servers to stop virtual host fallback when processing requests over TLS. However, from the feedback we received when we disclosed these attacks, such a change is unlikely to occur. In fact, virtual host confusion may become more common when HTTP2 gets deployed, and features such as connection sharing introduce a new "same-certificate policy" approach that can interfere badly with the same-origin policy enforced by browsers. We leave to future work the question of how to redesign HTTPS deployment to improve security isolation in the presence of shared credentials and connections.

10. REFERENCES

[1] S. Landau, "Highlights from making sense of Snowden, part II: What's significant in the NSA revelations," *IEEE Security & Privacy*, vol. 12, pp. 62–64, 2014.

[2] T. Dierks and E. Rescorla, "The Transport Layer Security Protocol Version 1.2," RFC 5246, 2008.

[3] E. Rescorla, "HTTP over TLS," RFC 2818, 2000.

[4] K. G. Paterson, T. Ristenpart, and T. Shrimpton, "Tag size does matter: attacks and proofs for the TLS record protocol," in *ASIACRYPT*, 2011.

[5] H. Krawczyk, K. G. Paterson, and H. Wee, "On the security of the TLS protocol: a systematic analysis," in *CRYPTO*, 2013.

[6] K. Bhargavan, C. Fournet, M. Kohlweiss, A. Pironti, and P. Strub, "Implementing TLS with verified cryptographic security," in *IEEE S&P*, 2013.

[7] S. Blake-Wilson, M. Nystrom, D. Hopwood, J. Mikkelsen, and T. Wright, "Transport Layer Security (TLS) Extensions," IETF RFC 3546, 2003.

[8] Z. Durumeric, J. Kasten, M. Bailey, and J. A. Halderman, "Analysis of the HTTPS certificate ecosystem," in *IMC*, Oct. 2013.

[9] A. Delignat-Lavaud, M. Abadí, M. Birrell, I. Mironov, T. Wobber, and Y. Xie, "Web PKI: closing the gap between guidelines and practices," in *NDSS*, Feb 2014.

[10] I. Fette and A. Melnikov, "The WebSocket protocol," RFC 6455, 2011.

[11] M. Zalewski, "Browser Security Handbook," Web: http://code.google.com/p/browsersec/, undated.

[12] J. Grossman, *XSS Attacks: Cross-site scripting exploits and defense*. Syngress, 2007.

[13] M. Belshe and R. Peon, "The SPDY protocol," IETF draft-mbelshe-httpbis-spdy-00, 2012.
[14] Akamai Technologies, "Visualizing akamai," akamai.com/html/technology/dataviz3.html, 2014.
[15] J. Liang, J. Jiang, H. Duan, K. Li, T. Wan, and J. Wu, "When HTTPS meets CDN: A case of authentication in delegated service," in *IEEE S&P*, 2014.
[16] I. Sysoev and B. Mercer, "How nginx processes requests," nginx.org/docs/http/request_processing.html, 2012.
[17] Apache Foundation, "Virtual host documentation," http://httpd.apache.org/docs/current/vhosts/, 2014.
[18] S. Stamm, B. Sterne, and G. Markham, "Reining in the web with content security policy," in *WWW*, 2010.
[19] E. Hammer-Lahav, D. Recordon, and D. Hardt, "The OAuth 2.0 Authorization Protocol," IETF Draft, 2011.
[20] A. Barth, C. Jackson, and J. C. Mitchell, "Robust defenses for cross-site request forgery," in *CCS*, 2008.
[21] A. Bortz, A. Barth, and A. Czeskis, "Origin cookies: session integrity for web applications," in *W2SP*, 2011.
[22] R. Hansen and J. Sokol, "MitM DNS rebinding SSL wildcards and XSS," http://goo.gl/23Yt9l, 2010.
[23] M. Schloesser, B. Gamble, J. Nickel, C. Guarnieri, and H. D. Moore, "Project sonar: IPv4 SSL certificates," https://scans.io/study/sonar.ssl, 2013.
[24] Alexa Internet Inc., "Top 1,000,000 sites (updated daily)," http://goo.gl/OZdT6p, 2014.
[25] S. Pai, Y. Sharma, S. Kumar, R. M. Pai, and S. Singh, "Formal verification of oauth 2.0 using alloy framework," in *CSNT*. IEEE, 2011.
[26] S.-T. Sun and K. Beznosov, "The devil is in the (implementation) details: an empirical analysis of OAuth SSO systems," in *CCS*. ACM, 2012.
[27] C. Bansal, K. Bhargavan, and S. Maffeis, "Discovering concrete attacks on website authorization by formal analysis," in *CSF*. IEEE, 2012.
[28] D. Akhawe, A. Barth, P. Lam, J. Mitchell, and D. Song, "Towards a formal foundation of web security," in *CSF*, 2010, pp. 290–304.
[29] M. Belshe, R. Peon, and M. Thomson, "Hypertext transfer protocol version 2," 2012. [Online]. Available: http://tools.ietf.org/html/draft-ietf-httpbis-http2-14
[30] A. Parsovs, "Practical issues with TLS client certificate authentication," in *NDSS*, 2014.
[31] M. Dietz, A. Czeskis, D. Balfanz, and D. S. Wallach, "Origin-bound certificates: a fresh approach to strong client authentication," in *Usenix Security*, 2012.
[32] K. Bhargavan, A. Delignat-Lavaud, C. Fournet, , A. Pironti, and P.-Y. Strub, "Triple handshakes and cookie cutters: Breaking and fixing authentication over TLS," in *IEEE S&P*. IEEE, 2014.
[33] C. Evans and C. Palmer, "Certificate pinning extension for HSTS," 2011. [Online]. Available: http://tools.ietf.org/html/draft-evans-palmer-hsts-pinning-00
[34] C. Meyer and J. Schwenk, "SoK: Lessons learned from SSL/TLS attacks," in *Information Security Applications*, ser. LNCS. Springer, 2014, pp. 189–209.
[35] J. Liang, J. Jiang, H. Duan, K. Li, T. Wan, and J. Wu, "When HTTPS meets CDN: A case of authentication in delegated service," in *IEEE Symposium on Security & Privacy 2014 (Oakland'14)*. IEEE, 2014.
[36] B. Moeller and A. Langley, "TLS Fallback Signaling Cipher Suite Value (SCSV) for Preventing Protocol Downgrade Attacks," Internet Draft (v.01), 2014.
[37] R. Wang, S. Chen, and X. Wang, "Signing me onto your accounts through Facebook and Google: A traffic-guided security study of commercially deployed single-sign-on web services," in *IEEE S&P*, 2012.
[38] D. Fett, R. Kusters, and G. Schmitz, "An expressive model for the web infrastructure: definition and application to the BrowserID SSO system," in *IEEE S&P*, 2014.
[39] K. Bhargavan, A. Delignat-Lavaud, and S. Maffeis, "Language-based defenses against untrusted browser origins," in *Usenix Security*, 2013.
[40] C. Bansal, K. Bhargavan, and S. Maffeis, "Discovering concrete attacks on website authorization by formal analysis," in *CSF*, 2012.
[41] M. Marlinspike, "More tricks for defeating SSL in practice," *Black Hat USA*, 2009.
[42] J. Hodges, C. Jackson, and A. Barth, "HTTP Strict Transport Security (HSTS)," IETF RFC 6797, 2012.
[43] J. Selvi, "Bypassing http strict transport security."
[44] C. Jackson, A. Barth, A. Bortz, W. Shao, and D. Boneh, "Protecting browsers from DNS rebinding attacks," *TWEB*, vol. 3, no. 1, 2009.
[45] S. Son and V. Shmatikov, "The hitchhiker's guide to DNS cache poisoning," in *SecureComm*, 2010.
[46] D. Dagon, M. Antonakakis, P. Vixie, T. Jinmei, and W. Lee, "Increased DNS forgery resistance by 0x20-bit encoding: security via leet queries," in *CCS*, 2008.
[47] N. Karapanos and S. Capkun, "On the effective prevention of TLS man-in-the-middle attacks in web applications," in *Usenix Security*, 2014.
[48] C. Soghoian and S. Stamm, "Certified lies: setecting and defeating government interception attacks against SSL," in *FC*, 2012.
[49] C. Karlof, U. Shankar, J. D. Tygar, and D. Wagner, "Dynamic pharming attacks and locked same-origin policies for web browsers," in *CCS*, 2007.
[50] M. Georgiev, S. Iyengar, S. Jana, R. Anubhai, D. Boneh, and V. Shmatikov, "The most dangerous code in the world: validating SSL certificates in non-browser software," in *ACM CCS*, 2012.
[51] D. Akhawe, B. Amann, M. Vallentin, and R. Sommer, "Here's my cert, so trust me, maybe? understanding TLS errors on the web," in *WWW*, 2013.
[52] T. Duong and J. Rizzo, "Here come the XOR ninjas," *White paper, Netifera*, 2011.
[53] J. Rizzo and T. Duong, "The CRIME attack," in *EKOparty Security Conference*, vol. 2012, 2012.
[54] B. Beurdouche, K. Bhargavan, A. Delignat-Lavaud, C. Fournet, M. Kohlweiss, A. Pironti, P.-Y. Strub, and J. K. Zinzindohoue, "A messy state of the union: taming the composite state machines of TLS," in *IEEE S&P*, 2015.
[55] B. Laurie, "Certificate transparency," *Commun. ACM*, vol. 57, no. 10, 2014.
[56] D. Basin, C. Cremers, T. H.-J. Kim, A. Perrig, R. Sasse, and P. Szalachowski, "ARPKI: Attack resilient public-key infrastructure," in *CCS*, 2014.

The Dynamics of Micro-Task Crowdsourcing

The Case of Amazon MTurk

Djellel Eddine Difallah*, Michele Catasta†, Gianluca Demartini‡,
Panagiotis G. Ipeirotis◇, Philippe Cudré-Mauroux*
* eXascale Infolab, University of Fribourg, Switzerland
† EFPL, Switzerland
‡ University of Sheffield, UK
◇ New York University, USA

ABSTRACT

Micro-task crowdsourcing is rapidly gaining popularity among research communities and businesses as a means to leverage Human Computation in their daily operations. Unlike any other service, a crowdsourcing platform is in fact a marketplace subject to human factors that affect its performance, both in terms of speed and quality. Indeed, such factors shape the *dynamics* of the crowdsourcing market. For example, a known behavior of such markets is that increasing the reward of a set of tasks would lead to faster results. However, it is still unclear how different dimensions interact with each other: reward, task type, market competition, requester reputation, etc.

In this paper, we adopt a data-driven approach to (A) perform a long-term analysis of a popular micro-task crowdsourcing platform and understand the evolution of its main actors (workers, requesters, and platform). (B) We leverage the main findings of our five year log analysis to propose features used in a predictive model aiming at determining the expected performance of any batch at a specific point in time. We show that the number of tasks left in a batch and how recent the batch is are two key features of the prediction. (C) Finally, we conduct an analysis of the demand (new tasks posted by the requesters) and supply (number of tasks completed by the workforce) and show how they affect task prices on the marketplace.

Categories and Subject Descriptors

H.4 [**Information Systems Applications**]: Miscellaneous

General Terms

Design; Experimentation; Human Factors

Keywords

Crowdsourcing; trend identification; tracking; forecasting

WWW 2015, May 18–22, 2015, Florence, Italy.
ACM 978-1-4503-3469-3/15/05.
http://dx.doi.org/10.1145/2736277.2741685.

1. INTRODUCTION

While general data availability increases, its quality is not necessarily perfect and manual data pre-processing is often necessary before using it to create value or to support decisions. To this end, outsourcing data-processing tasks like, for example, image tagging, audio transcription, translation, etc. to a large crowd of individuals on the Web has become more popular over time.

To perform such Human Intelligence Tasks (HITs), crowdsourcing platforms have been developed. Such platforms serve as a place where the crowd (*workers*) willing to perform small tasks (so called *micro-tasks*) in exchange of a small monetary reward and work providers (also known as *requesters*) meet.

The micro-task crowdsourcing market has seen a rapid growth in the last five years. This is also explained by the fact that large amounts of data are today available in companies, which are increasingly seen as a key asset for optimizing all business processes.

The micro-task crowdsourcing process works as follows. First, the requesters design the HIT based on their data and required task. Next, they publish batches of HITs on the crowdsourcing platform specifying their requirements and the monetary amount rewarded to workers in exchange of the completion of each HIT. Then, the workers willing to perform the published HITs complete the tasks and submit their work back to the requester who obtains the desired results and pays workers accordingly.

In this paper, we analyze the evolution of a very popular micro-task crowdsourcing platform (i.e., Amazon MTurk[1]) over a five-year time span and report key findings about how the market behaves with regards to demand and supply. Using features derived from a large-scale analysis of observations made on the platform, we propose methods to predict the throughput of the crowdsourcing platform for a batch of HITs published by a given requester at a certain point in time. This prediction is based on different features including the current platform load and the task type. Using this prediction method, we try to understand the impact of each feature that we consider, and its scope over time.

The main findings of our analysis are: 1) the type of tasks published on the platform has changed over time with content creation HITs being the most popular today; 2) the HIT pricing approach evolved towards larger and higher paid HITs to better attract workers in a competitive market; 3) geographical restrictions are applied to certain task types

[1] `http://mturk.com`

(e.g., surveys for US workers); 4) we observe an organic growth in the number of new requesters who use the platform, which is a sign of a healthy market; 5) we identify *size of the batch* as the main feature that impacts the progress of a given batch; 6) we observe that supply (the workforce) has little control over driving the price of demand.

In summary, the main contributions of this paper are:

- An analysis of the evolution of a popular micro-task crowdsourcing platform looking at dimensions like topics, reward, worker location, task types, and platform throughput.
- A large-scale classification of 2.5M HIT types published on Amazon MTurk.
- A predictive analysis of HIT batch progress using more than 29 different features.
- An analysis of the crowdsourcing platform as a market (demand and supply).

The rest of the paper is structured as follows. In Section 2, we overview recent work on micro-task crowdsourcing specifically focusing on how micro-task crowdsourcing has been used and on how it can be improved. Section 3 presents how Amazon MTurk has evolved over time in terms of topics, reward, and requesters. Section 4 summarizes the results of a large-scale analysis on the types of HIT that have been requested and completed over time. Based on the previous findings, Section 5 presents our approach to predicting the throughput of the crowdsourcing platform for a batch of published HITs. Section 6 studies the Amazon MTurk market and how different events correlate (e.g., new HITs attracting more workers to the platform). We discuss our main findings in Section 7 before concluding in Section 8.

2. RELATED WORK

The objective of this piece of work is to understand and characterize how a micro-task crowdsourcing platform behaves as a marketplace. Thus, we first start by reviewing related work on human computation and micro-task crowdsourcing, before turning to related work on market analysis and on how to improve crowdsourcing platforms.

Micro-task Crowdsourcing.

Crowdsourcing is defined as the outsourcing of tasks to a crowd of individuals over the Web. Crowdsourcing has been used for a variety of purposes, from innovation to software development [23]. Early crowdsourcing examples leveraged the fun or community belonging incentives (e.g., Wikipedia) instead of monetary rewards. Examples of crowdsourcing systems based on gamification include the ESP game [21] where players must agree on tags to use for a picture without the possibility to interact with each other. An extension of the ESP game is Peekaboom: a game that asks players to annotate specific objects within an image [22].

In this work, we focus on *paid micro-task crowdsourcing*, where the crowd is asked to perform short tasks, also known as Human Intelligence Tasks (HITs), in exchange for a small monetary reward per unit. Popular examples of such tasks include: spell checking of short paragraphs, sentiment analysis of tweets, rewriting product reviews, or transcription of scanned shopping receipts.

Micro-task crowdsourcing is often used to improve the quality of machine-run algorithms in order to combine both the scalability of machines over large amounts of data as well as the quality of human intelligence in processing and understanding data [21]. Many examples of such hybrid human-machine approaches exist. Crowd-powered databases [9] leverage crowdsourcing to deal with problems like data incompleteness, data integration, graph search, and joins [24, 18, 25]. Semantic Web systems leverage the crowd for tasks like schema matching [19], entity linking [4], and ontology engineering [17]. Information Retrieval systems have used crowdsourcing for evaluation purposes [1]. Models and paradigm for hybrid human-machine systems have been proposed on top of crowdsourcing platforms [15], also including the design of hybrid workflows [16].

In this work, we specifically focus on micro-task crowdsourcing and analyze the dynamics of a very popular platform for this purpose: Amazon MTurk. This platform provides access to a crowd of workers distributed worldwide but mainly composed of people based in the US and India [12]. Many Amazon MTurk workers share their experience about HITs and requesters through dedicated web forums and ad-hoc websites [13]. Requester 'reviews' serve as a way to measure the reputation of the requesters among workers and it is assumed to influence the latency of the tasks published [20], as workers are naturally more attracted by HITs published by requesters with a good reputation.

Because of the complex mechanisms connecting the workers to the requesters and to the platform itself, characterizing the dynamics and evolution of micro-task crowdsourcing platforms is key in order to understand the impact of the various components and to design better human computation systems. The goal of our work is to understand the evolution of a micro-task crowdsourcing platform over time and to identify key properties of such platform.

Market Analysis.

An initial work analyzing the Amazon MTurk market was done in [12]. Our paper extends this work by considering the time dimension and analyzing long term trends. Faradani et al. [7] proposed a model to predict the completion time of a batch. Our prediction endeavor is however different, in the sense that we aim at predicting the immediate throughput based on current market conditions and to understand what features have more impact than others.

Improving Crowdsourcing Platforms.

In [14] authors give their view on how the crowdsourcing market should evolve in the future, specifically focusing on how to support full-time crowd workers. Likewise, our goal is to identify ways of improving crowdsourcing marketplaces by understanding the dynamics of such platforms—based on historical data and models.

Recent contributions on novel crowdsourcing platforms have proposed methods for identifying the best workers in the crowd for specific tasks [6, 2]. Given the diverse task types being published on micro-task crowdsourcing platforms, such functionalities could be used to improve the work experience of the crowd and the quality of the results returned to the requesters.

One way to improve the efficiency of the crowdsourcing process is to use custom HIT *pricing schemes*. For example, in [11] authors propose models to set the HIT reward given some latency and budget constraints. In [5], we studied how worker retention can improve the latency of a batch by leveraging varying bonus schemes.

Our work is complementary to existing work as we present a data-driven study of the evolution of micro-task crowdsourcing over five years. Our work can be also used to support requesters in publishing HITs on these platforms and getting results more rapidly.

3. THE EVOLUTION OF AMAZON MTURK FROM 2009 TO 2014

In this section, we start by describing our dataset and extract some key information and statistics that we will use in the rest of the paper.

3.1 Crowdsourcing Platform Dataset

Over the past five years, we have periodically collected data about HITs published on Amazon MTurk. The data that we collect from the platform is available at `http://mturk-tracker.com/`.

In this work, we consider hourly aggregated data that includes the available HIT batches and their metadata (title, description, rewards, required qualifications, etc.), in addition to their progress over time, that is, the temporal variation of the set of HITs available. In fact, one of the main metrics that we leverage (see Section 5) is the throughput of a batch, i.e., how many HITs get completed between two successive observations. In Figure 1, we plot the number of HITs available in a given batch versus its throughput. An interesting observation that can be made is that large batches can achieve high throughput (thousands of HITs per minute).

In total, our dataset covers more than 2.5M different batches with over 130M HITs. We note that the tracker reports data periodically only and does not reflect fine-grained information (e.g., real-time variations). We believe however that it captures enough information to perform meaningful, long-term trend analyses and to understand the dynamics and interactions within the crowdsourcing platform.

3.2 A Data-driven Analysis of Platform Evolution

First, we identify trends obtained from aggregated information over time, keywords, and countries associated to the published HITs. Each of the following analyses is also available as an interactive visualization over the historical data on `http://xi-lab.github.io/mturk-mrkt/`.

Topics Over Time.

First, we want to understand how different topics have been addressed by means of micro-task crowdsourcing over time. In order to run this analysis, we look at the keywords associated with published HITs. We observe the evolution of keyword popularity and associated reward on Amazon MTurk. Figure 2 shows this behavior. Each point in the plot represents a keyword associated to the HITs with its frequency (i.e., number of HITs with this keyword) on the x-axis, and the average reward in a given year on the y-axis. The path connecting data points indicates the time evolution, starting in 2009, with one point representing the keyword usage over one year.

We observe that the frequency of the 'audio' and 'transcription' keywords (i.e., blue and red paths from left to right) have substantially increased over time. They have become the most popular keywords in the last two years and are paid more than $1 on average. HITs with the 'video' tag have also increased in number with a reward that has reached a peak in 2012 and decreased after that. HITs tagged as 'categorization' have been paid consistently in the range of $0.10-$0.30 on average, except in 2009 where they were rewarded less than $0.10 each. HITs tagged as 'tweet' have not increased in number but have been paid more over the years, reaching $0.90 on average in 2014: This can be explained by more complex tasks being offered to workers, such as sentiment classification or writing of tweets.

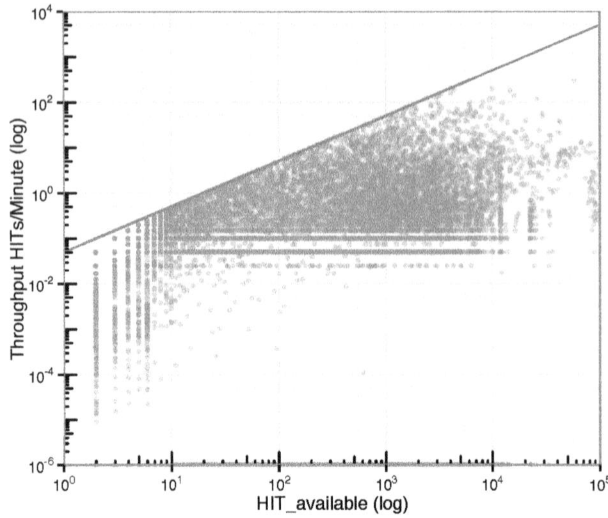

Figure 1: Batch throughput versus number of HITs available in the batch. The red line corresponds to the maximum throughput we could have observed due to the tracker periodicity constraints. For readability, this graph represents a subset of 3 months (January-March 2014), and HITs with rewards $0.05 and less.

Preferred Countries by Requesters Over Time.

Figure 3 shows the requirements set by requesters with respect to the countries they wish to select workers from. The left part of Figure 3 shows that most HITs are to be completed exclusively by workers located in the US, India, or Canada. The right part of Figure 3 shows the evolution over time of the country requirement phenomenon. The plot shows the number of HITs with a certain country requirement (on the y-axis) and its time evolution (on the x-axis) with yearly steps. The size of the data points indicates the total reward associated to those HITs.

We observe that US-only HITs dominate, both in terms of their large number as well as in terms of the reward associated to them. Interestingly, we notice how HITs for workers based in India have been decreasing over time. On the other hand, HITs for workers based in Canada have been increasing over time, becoming in 2014 larger than those exclusively available to workers based in India. We also see that the reward associated to them is smaller than the budget for India-only HITs. As of 2014, both HITs for workers based in Canada or UK are more numerous that those for workers based in India. Overall, 88.5% of the HIT batches

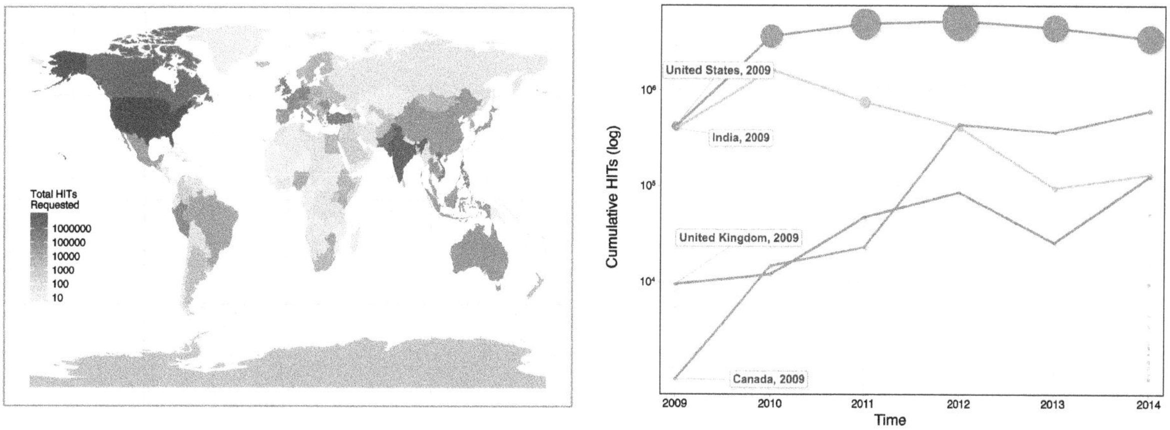

Figure 3: HITs with specific country requirements. On the left-hand side, the countries with the most HITs dedicated to them. On the right-hand side, the time evolution (x-axis) of country-specific HITs with volume (y-axis) and reward (size of data point) information.

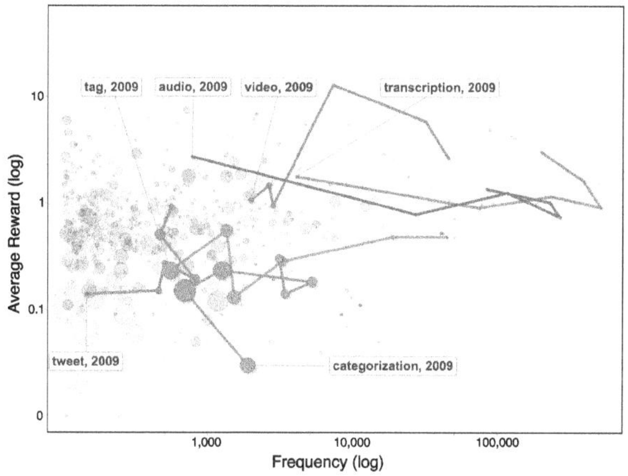

Figure 2: The use of keywords to annotate HITs. *Frequency* corresponds to how many times a keyword was used, and *AverageReward* corresponds to the average monetary reward of batches that listed the keyword. The size of the bubbles indicates the average batch size.

that were posted in the considered time period did not require any specific worker location. 86% of those which did, imposed a constraint requesting US-based workers.

Figure 4 shows the top keywords attached to HITs restricted to specific locations. We observe that the most popular keywords (i.e., 'audio' and 'transcription') do not require country-specific workers. We also note that US-only HITs are most commonly tagged with 'survey'.

HIT Reward Analysis.

Figure 5 shows the most frequent rewards assigned to HITs over time.[2] We observe that while in 2011 the most popular reward was $0.01, recently HITs paid $0.05 are getting more frequent. This can be explained both by how workers search for HITs on Amazon MTurk and by the Amazon MTurk fee scheme. Requesters now prefer to publish more complex HITs possibly with multiple questions in them and grant a higher reward: This also attracts those workers who are not willing to complete a HIT for small rewards and reduces the fees paid to Amazon MTurk, which are computed based on the number of HITs published on the platform.

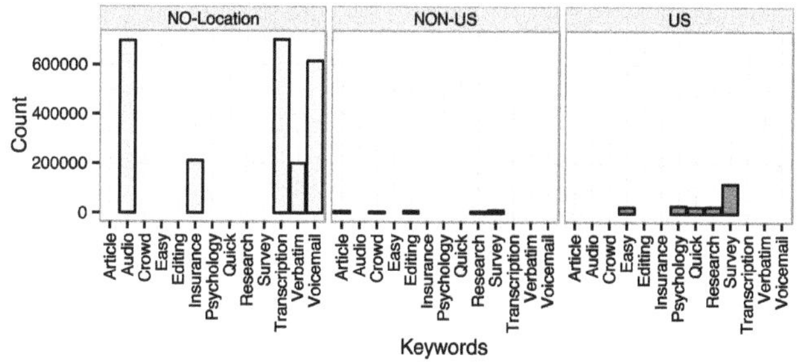

Figure 4: Keywords for HITs restricted to specific countries.

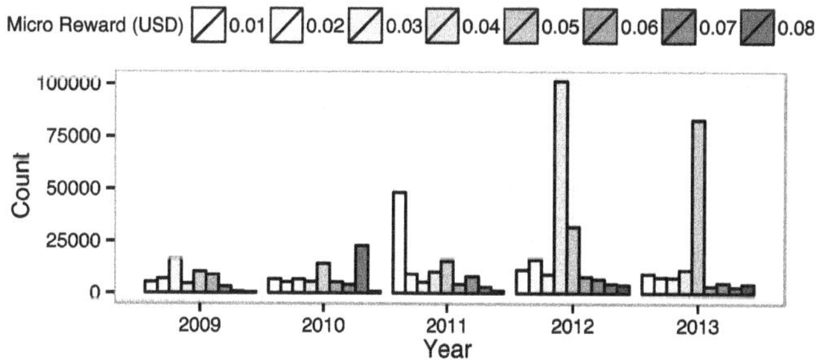

Figure 5: Popularity of HIT reward values over time.

Requester Analysis.

In order to be sustainable, a crowdsourcing platform needs to retain requesters over time or get new requesters

[2] Data for 2014 has been omitted as it was not comparable with other year values.

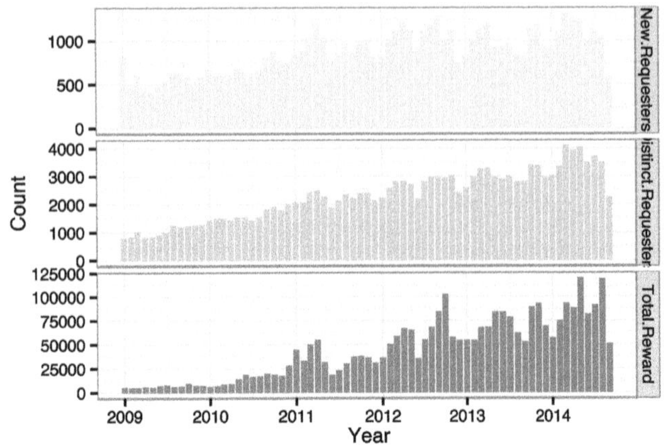

Figure 6: Requester activity and total reward on the platform over time.

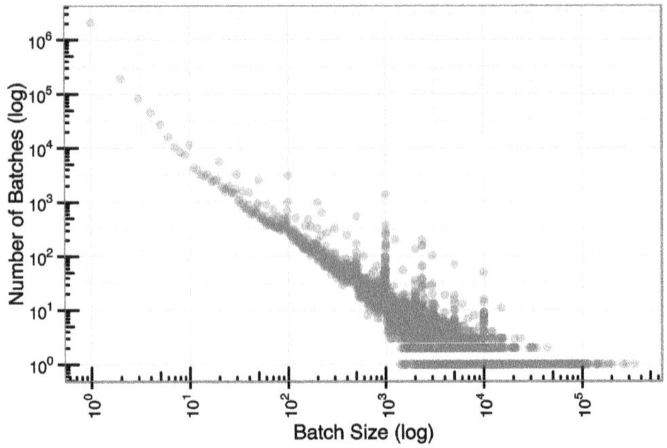

Figure 7: The distribution of batch sizes.

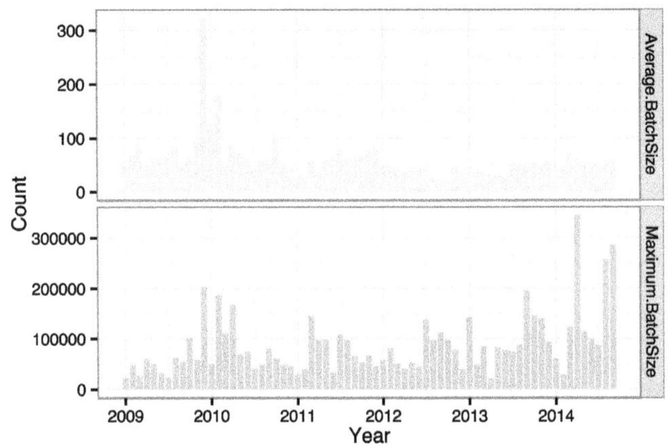

Figure 8: Average and maximum batch size per month. The monthly median is 1.

to replace those who do not publish HITs anymore. Figure 6 shows the number of new requesters who used Amazon MTurk and the overall number of active requesters at a certain point in time. We can observe an increasing number of active requesters over time and a constant number of new requesters who join the platform (at a rate of 1,000/month over the last two years).

It is also interesting to look at the overall amount of reward for HITs published on the platform, as platform revenues are computed as a function of HIT reward. From the bottom part of Figure 6, we observe a linear increase in the total reward for HITs on the platform. Interestingly, we also observe some seasonality effects over the years, with October being the month with the highest total reward and January or February being the month with minimum total reward.

HIT Batch Size Analysis.

When a lot of data needs to be crowdsourced (e.g., when many images need to be tagged), multiple tasks containing similar HITs can be published together. We define a batch of HITs as a set of similar HITs published by a requester at a certain point in time.

Figure 7 shows the distribution of batch sizes in the period from 2009 to 2014. We can observe that most of the batches were of size 1 (more than 1M), followed by a long tail of larger, but less frequent, batch sizes.

Figure 8 shows how batch size has changed over time. We observe that the average batch size has slightly decreased. The monthly median is 1 (due to the heavily skewed distribution). Another observation that can be made is that in 2014 very large batches containing more that 200,000 HITs have appeared on Amazon MTurk.

4. LARGE-SCALE HIT TYPE ANALYSIS

In this section, we present the results of a large-scale analysis of the evolution of HIT types published on the Amazon MTurk platform. For this analysis, we used the definition of HIT types proposed by [10] in which authors perform an extensive study involving 1,000 crowd workers to understand their working behavior, and categorize the types of tasks that the crowd perform into six top-level "goal-oriented" tasks, each containing further sub-classes. We briefly describe the six top-level classes introduced by [10] below.

- Information Finding (IF): Searching the Web to answer a certain information need. For example, "Find the cheapest hotel with ocean view in Monterey Bay, CA".
- Verification and Validation (VV): Verifying certain information or confirming the validity of a piece of information. Examples include checking Twitter accounts for spamming behaviors.
- Interpretation and Analysis (IA): Interpreting Web content. For example, "Categorize product pictures in a predefined set of categories", or "Classify the sentiment of a tweet".
- Content Creation (CC): Generating new content. Examples include summarizing a document or transcribing an audio recording.
- Surveys (SU): Answering a set of questions related to a certain topic (e.g., demographics or customer satisfaction).
- Content Access (CA): Accessing some Web content. Examples include watching online videos or clicking on provided links.

4.1 Supervised HIT Type Classification

Using the various definitions of HIT types given above, we trained a supervised machine learning model to classify HIT types based on their metadata. The features we used to train the Support Vector Machine (SVM) model are: HIT title, description, keywords, reward, date, allocated time, and batch size.

To train and evaluate the supervised model, we created labelled data: We uniformly sampled 5,000 HITs over the entire five-year dataset and manually labelled their type by means of crowdsourcing. In detail, we asked workers on MTurk to assign each HIT to one of the predefined classes by presenting them with the title, description, keywords, reward, date, allocated time, and batch size for the HIT. The instructions also contained the definition and examples for each task type. Workers could label tasks as 'Others' when unsure or when the HIT did not fit in any of the available options.

After assigning each labelling HIT to three different workers in the crowd, a consensus on the task type label was reached in 89% of the cases (leaving 551 cases with no clear majority). A consensus was reached when at least two out of three workers agreed on the same HIT type label. The other cases, that is, when the workers provided different labels or when they where not sure about the HIT type, have then been removed from our labelled dataset.

Using the labelled data, we trained a multi-class SVM classifier for the 6 different task types and evaluated its quality with 10-fold cross validation over the labelled dataset. Overall, the trained classifier obtained a Precision of 0.895, a Recall of 0.899, and an F-Measure of 0.895. Most of the classifier errors (i.e., 66 cases) were caused by incorrectly classifying IA instances as CC jobs.

Performing feature selection for the HIT type classification problem, we observed that the best features based on information gain are the HIT allotted time and reward: This indicates that HITs of different types are associated with different levels of reward as well as different task durations (i.e., longer and better paid tasks versus shorter and paid worse). The most distinctive keywords for identifying HIT types are 'transcribe', 'audio', and 'survey', which clearly identify CC and SU HITs.

Using the classifier trained over the entire labelled dataset, we then performed a large-scale classification of the types for all 2.5M HITs in our collection. This allows us to study the evolution of the task types over time on the Amazon MTurk platform, which we describe next.

4.2 Task Type Popularity Over Time

Using the results of the large-scale classification of HIT types, we analyze which types of HITs have been published over time. Figure 9 shows the evolution of task types published on Amazon MTurk. We can observe that, in general, the most popular type of task is Content Creation. In terms of observable trends, we note that–while there is a general increase in the volume of tasks on the platform—CA tasks have been decreasing over time. This can be explained by the enforcement of Amazon MTurk terms of service, which state that workers should not be asked to create accounts on external websites or be identified by the requester. In the last three years, SU and IA tasks have seen the biggest increase.

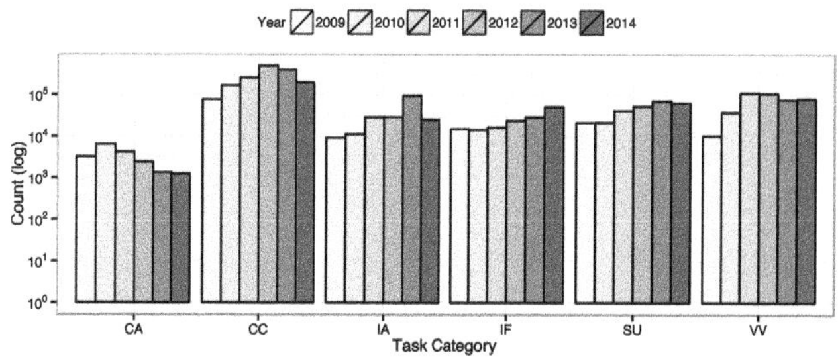

Figure 9: Popularity of HIT types over time.

5. ANALYZING THE FEATURES AFFECTING BATCH THROUGHPUT

Next, we turn our attention to analyzing the factors that influence the progress (or the pace) of a batch, how those factors influence each other and how their importance changes over time.

In order to conduct this analysis, we carry out a prediction experiment on the batch's *throughput*, that is, the number of HITs that will be completed for a given batch within the next time frame of 1 hour (i.e., the $DIFF\_HIT$ feature is the target class). Specifically, we model this task as a regression problem using 29 features; some of them were used in the previous section to classify the HIT type; we describe the remaining ones in Appendix A.

5.1 Throughput Prediction

To predict the throughput of a batch at time T, we train a Random Forest Regression model with samples taken in the range $[T-\delta, T)$ where δ is the size of the time window that we are considering directly prior to time T. The rationale behind this approach is that the throughput should be directly correlated to the current and recent market situations.

We considered data from June to October 2014, and hourly observations (see Section 3.1), from which we uniformly sampled 50 test time points for evaluation purposes. In our experiments, the best prediction results, in terms of R-squared[3], were obtained using $\delta = 4hours$. For that window, our predicted versus actual throughput values are shown in Figure 10. The figure suggests that the prediction works best for larger batches having a large momentum.

In order to understand which features contribute significantly to our prediction model, we proceed by feature ablation. For this experiment, we computed the prediction evaluation score R-squared, for 1,000 randomly sampled test time points and kept those where the prediction worked reasonably, i.e., having R-squared>0, that is 327 samples. Next, we reran the prediction on the same samples by removing one feature at a time. The results revealed that the features $HIT\_available$ (i.e., the number of tasks in the batch) and $Age\_minutes$ (i.e., how long ago the batch was created) were the only ones having a statistically significant impact on the prediction score with $p < 0.05$ and $p < 0.01$ respectively.

[3]`http://scikit-learn.org/stable/modules/generated/sklearn.metrics.r2_score.html`

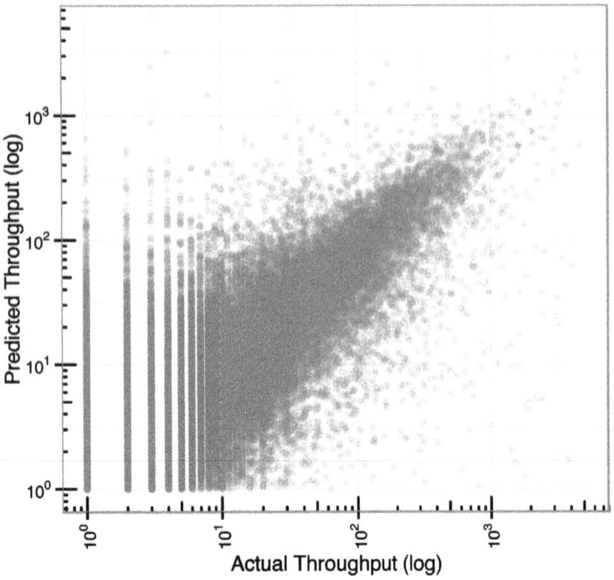

Figure 10: Predicted vs actual batch throughput values for $\delta = 4hours$. The prediction works best for larger batches having a large momentum.

Table 1: Gini importance of the top 2 features used in the prediction experiment. A large mean indicates a better overall contribution to the prediction. A positive slope indicates that the feature is gaining in importance when the considered time window is larger.

Feature	mean	stderr	slope	intercept
HIT_available	29.8606	13.4247	-0.0257	34.4940
Age_minutes	12.9087	8.1967	-0.0050	13.8181

5.2 Features Importance

In order to better grasp the characteristics of the batch throughput, we examine the computed Gini importance of the features [3]. In this experiment, we varied the training time frame δ from 1 hour to 24 hours for each tested time point. Figure 11 shows the contribution of our 2 top features (as concluded from the previous experiment, i.e., *HIT_available* and *Age_minutes*) and how their importances varied when we increased the training time-frame. These features are again listed in Table 1, the slope indicates whether the feature is gaining importance over time (positive value) or decreasing in importance (negative value).

The most important feature is *HIT_available*, that is, the current size of the batch. Indeed, as observed by previous work, larger batches tend to attract more workers [12, 9]. This feature becomes less important when we consider longer periods, partly because of noise, and because other features start to encode additional facts. On the other hand, *Age_minutes* importance suggests that the crowd is sensitive to newly posted HITs, or how *fresh* the HITs are. To better understand this phenomenon, we conduct an analysis on what attracts the workforce to the platform in the next section.

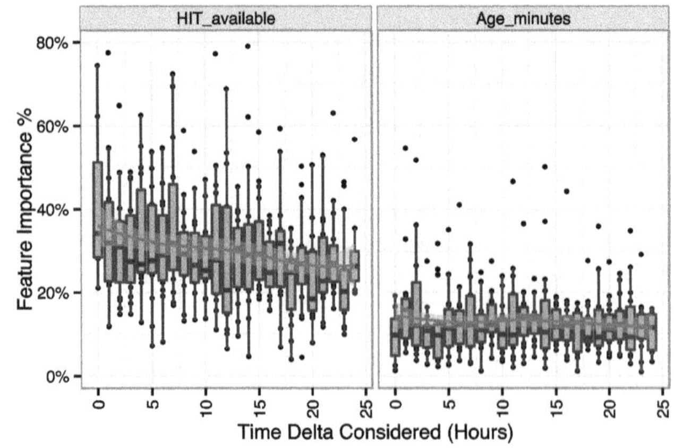

Figure 11: Computed feature importance when considering a larger training window for batch throughput prediction.

6. MARKET ANALYSIS

Finally, we study the demand and supply of the Amazon MTurk marketplace. In the following, we define *Demand* as the number of new tasks published on the platform by the requesters. In addition, we compute the average reward of the tasks that were posted. Conversely, we define *Supply* as the workforce that the crowd is providing, concretized as the number of tasks that got completed in a given time window by the workers. In this section we use hourly collected data for the time period spanning June to October 2014.

6.1 Supply Attracts New Workers

We start by analyzing how the market reacts when new tasks arrive on the platform, in order to understand the degree of elasticity of the supply. If the supply of work is inelastic, the amount of work done over time should be independent of the demand for work. So, if the amount of tasks available in the market ("demand") increases, then the percentage of work that gets completed in the market should drop, as the same amount of "work done" gets split among a higher number of tasks. To understand the elasticity of the supply, we regressed the percentage of work done in every time period (measured as the percentage of HITs that are completed) against the number of new HITs that are posted in that period. Figure 12 shows the scatterplot for those two variables.

Our data reveals that an increase in the number of arrived HITs is positively associated with a higher percentage of completed HITs. This result provides evidence that the new work that is posted is more attractive than the tasks previously available in the market, and attracts "new work supply".[4]

Our regression[5] of the "Percent Completed" against "Hits Arrived (in thousands)" indicates an intercept of 2.5 and a slope of 0.05. To put these numbers in context: On average, there are 300K HITs available in the market at any given time, and on average 10K new HITs arrive every hour. The

[4]From the data available, it is not possible to tell whether the new supply comes from distinct workers, from workers that were idle, or from an increased productivity of existing workers.

[5]We use Ordinary Least Squares regression.

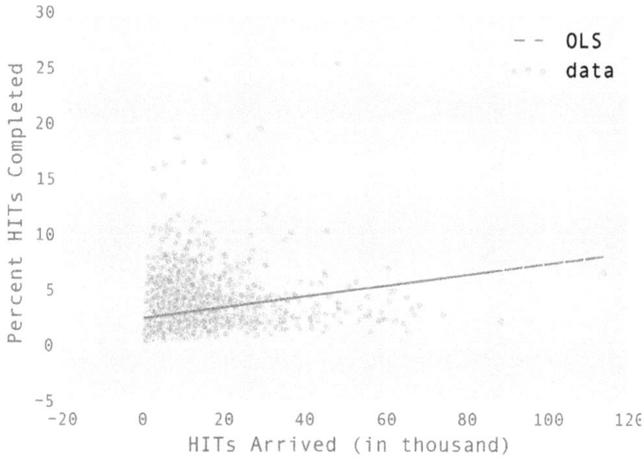

Figure 12: The effect of new arrived HITs on the work supplied. Here, the supply is expressed as the percentage of HITs completed in the market.

intercept of 2.5 means that 2.5% of these 300K HITs (i.e., 7.5K per hour) get completed, as a baseline, assuming that no new HIT gets posted. The slope is 0.05, meaning that if 10K new HITs arrive within an hour, then the completion ratio increases by 0.5%, to 3% (i.e., 9K HITs per hour). When 50K new HITs arrive within an hour, then the completion percentage increases to 5% indicating that 15K to 20K HITs get completed. In other words, approximately 20% of the *new* demand gets completed within an hour of being posted, indicating that new work has almost 10x higher attractiveness for the workers than the remaining work that is available on the platform. This result could be explained by how tasks are presented to workers by Amazon MTurk. Workers, when not searching for tasks using specific keywords, are presented with the most recently published tasks first.

6.2 Demand and Supply Periodicity

On the demand side, some requesters frequently post new batches of recurrent tasks. Hence, we are interested in the periodicity of such demand in the marketplace and the supply it drives. To look in this, we consider both the time-series of available HITs and the rewards completed.

First, we observe that the demand exhibits a strong weekly periodicity, which is reflected by the autocorrelation that we compute from the number of available HITs on Amazon Mturk (See Figure 13a and 13c). The market seems to have a significant memory that lasts for approximately 7-10 days. This indicates that future transactions are highly predictable using simple algorithms [8].

Conversely, and to check for the periodicity in the supply, we compute an autocorrelation on the weekly moving average of the completed HITs reward. Figure 13b and 13d show that there is a strong weekly periodicity effect, as we observe high values in the range 0-250 hours.

7. DISCUSSION

In this section, we summarize the main findings of our study and present a discussion of our results. We extracted several trends from the five years data, summarized as follows:

- Tasks related to audio transcription have been gaining momentum in the last years and are today the most popular tasks on Amazon MTurk.
- The popularity of Content Access HITs has decreased over time. Surveys are however becoming more popular over time especially in the US.
- While most HITs do not require country-specific workers, most of such HITs require US-based workers.
- HITs that are exclusively asking for workers based in India have strongly decreased over time.
- Surveys are the most popular type of HITs for US-based workers.
- The most frequent HIT reward value has increased over time, and reaches $0.05 in 2014.
- New requesters constantly join Amazon MTurk, making the total number of active requesters and the available reward increase over time.
- The average HIT batch size has been stable over time; however, very large batches have recently started to appear on the platform.

Our batch throughput prediction (Section 5) indicates that the throughput of batches can be best predicted based on the number of HITs available in the batch,i.e., its size; and its freshness, i.e., for how long the batch has been on the platform.

Finally, we analyzed Amazon MTurk as a marketplace in terms of demand (new HITs arriving) and supply (HITs completed). We observed some strong weekly periodicity both in demand and in supply. We can hypothesize that many requesters might have repetitive business needs following weekly trends, while many workers work on Amazon MTurk on a regular basis during the week.

8. CONCLUSIONS

We studied data collected from a popular micro-task crowdsourcing platform, Amazon MTurk, and analyzed a number of key dimensions of the platform, including: topic, task type, reward evolution, platform throughput, and supply and demand. The results of our analysis can serve as a starting point for improving existing crowdsourcing platforms and for optimizing the overall efficiency and effectiveness of human computation systems. The evidence presented above indicate how requesters should use crowdsourcing platforms to obtain the best out of them: By engaging with workers and publishing large volumes of HITs at specific points in time.

Future research based on this work might look at different directions. On one hand, novel micro-task crowdsourcing platforms need to be designed based on the findings identified in this work, such as the need for supporting specific task types like audio transcription or surveys. Additionally, analyses that look at specific data could provide a deeper understanding of the micro-task crowdsourcing universe. Examples include per-requester or per-task analyses of the publishing behavior rather than looking at the entire market evolution as we did in this work. Similarly, a worker-centered analysis could provide additional evidence of the existence of different classes of workers, e.g., full-time vs casual workers, or workers specializing on specific task types as compared to generalists who are willing to complete any available task.

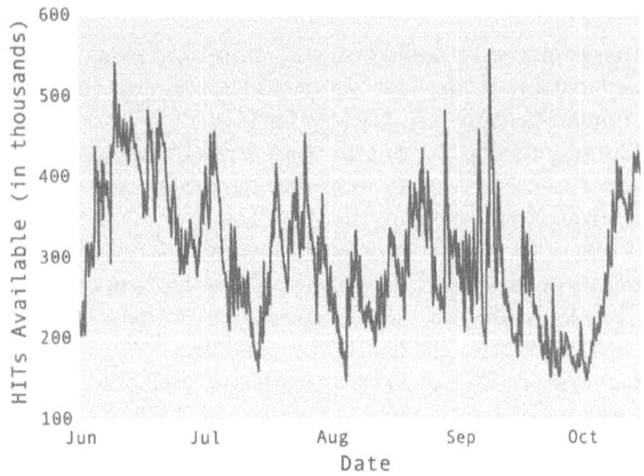

(a) HITs Available.

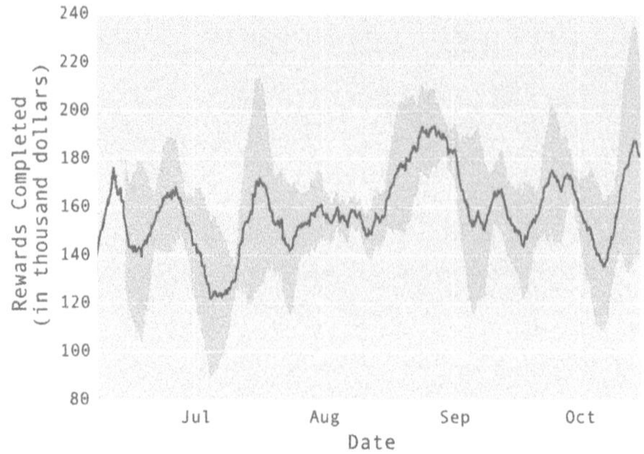

(b) Weekly moving average on rewards completed.

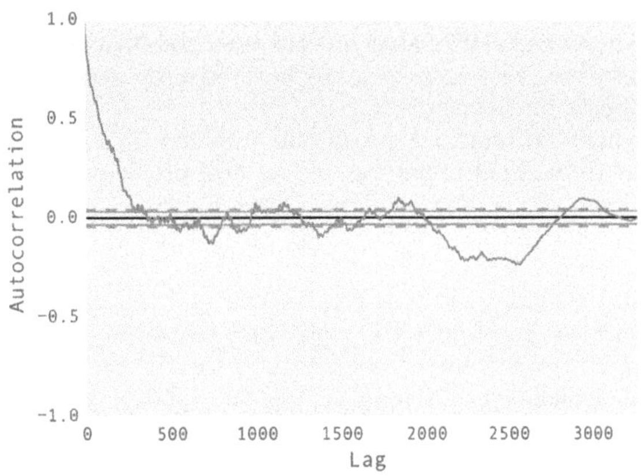

(c) Autocorrelation on HITs available.

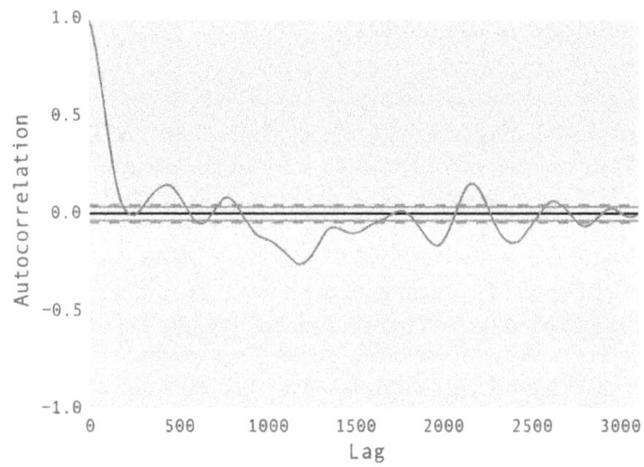

(d) Autocorrelation on moving average of rewards completed.

Figure 13: Computed autocorrelation on the number of HITs available and on the weekly moving average of the completed reward (N.B., autocorrelation's Lag is computed in Hours). In both cases, we clearly see a weekly periodicity (0-250 Hours).

9. ACKNOWLEDGMENTS

We thank the reviewers for their helpful comments. This work was supported by the Swiss National Science Foundation under grant number PP00P2_128459.

APPENDIX

A. MACHINE LEARNING FEATURES USED TO PREDICT THROUGHPUT

The following is the list of features associated to each batch. We used these features in our machine learning approach to predict batch throughput for the next hourly observation (see Section 5):

- **HIT_available:** Number of available HITs in the batch.
- **start_time:** The time of an observation.
- **reward:** HIT Reward in USD.
- **description:** String length of the batch's description.
- **title:** String length of the batch's title.
- **keywords:** Keywords (space separated).
- **requester_id:** ID of the requester.
- **time_alloted:** Time allotted per task.
- **tasktype:** Task class (as per our classification in 4).
- **ageminutes:** Age since the Batch was posted (minutes).
- **leftminutes:** Time left before expiration (minutes).
- **location:** The requested worker's Location (e.g., US).
- **totalapproved:** Batch requirement on the number of total approved HITs.
- **approvalrate:** Batch requirement on the percentage of workers approval.
- **master:** Worker is a master.
- **hitGroupsAvailableUI:** Number of batches as reported on Mturk dashboard.
- **hitsAvailableUI:** Number of HITs available as reported on Mturk dashboard.
- **hitsArrived:** Number of new HITs arrived.
- **hitsCompleted:** Number of HITs completed.
- **rewardsArrived:** Sum of rewards associated with the HITs arrived.
- **rewardsCompleted:** Sum of rewards associated with the HITs completed.
- **percHitsCompleted:** Ratio of HITs completed and total HITs available.
- **percHitsPosted:** Ratio of new HITs arrived and total HITs available.
- **diffHits:** hitsCompleted-hitsArrived.

- **diffHitsUI:** Difference in HITs observed from Mturk dashboard.
- **diffGroups:** Computed difference in number of completed and arrived batches.
- **diffGroupsUI:** Difference in number of completed and arrived batches observed from Mturk dashboard.
- **diffRewards:** Difference in rewards = (rewardsArrived-rewardsCompleted).
- **DIFF_HIT:** Number of HITs completed since the last observation.

B. REFERENCES

[1] O. Alonso and S. Mizzaro. Using crowdsourcing for TREC relevance assessment. *Inf. Process. Manage.*, 48(6):1053–1066, 2012.

[2] A. Bozzon, M. Brambilla, S. Ceri, M. Silvestri, and G. Vesci. Choosing the right crowd: Expert finding in social networks. In *Proceedings of the 16th International Conference on Extending Database Technology*, EDBT '13, pages 637–648, New York, NY, USA, 2013. ACM.

[3] L. Breiman and A. Cutler. Random Forests. `https://www.stat.berkeley.edu/~breiman/RandomForests/cc_home.htm`. Accessed: 2015-03-04.

[4] G. Demartini, D. E. Difallah, and P. Cudré-Mauroux. ZenCrowd: Leveraging Probabilistic Reasoning and Crowdsourcing Techniques for Large-scale Entity Linking. In *Proceedings of the 21st International Conference on World Wide Web*, WWW '12, pages 469–478, New York, NY, USA, 2012. ACM.

[5] D. E. Difallah, M. Catasta, G. Demartini, and P. Cudré-Mauroux. Scaling-up the Crowd: Micro-Task Pricing Schemes for Worker Retention and Latency Improvement. In *Second AAAI Conference on Human Computation and Crowdsourcing*, 2014.

[6] D. E. Difallah, G. Demartini, and P. Cudré-Mauroux. Pick-a-crowd: Tell me what you like, and i'll tell you what to do. In *Proceedings of the 22Nd International Conference on World Wide Web*, WWW '13, pages 367–374, Republic and Canton of Geneva, Switzerland, 2013. International World Wide Web Conferences Steering Committee.

[7] S. Faradani, B. Hartmann, and P. G. Ipeirotis. What's the right price? pricing tasks for finishing on time. *Human Computation*, 11, 2011.

[8] J. D. Farmer, A. Gerig, F. Lillo, and S. Mike. Market Efficiency and the Long-Memory of Supply and Demand: Is Price Impact Variable and Permanent or Fixed and Temporary. *Quant. Finance*, 6(2):107–112, 2006.

[9] M. J. Franklin, D. Kossmann, T. Kraska, S. Ramesh, and R. Xin. CrowdDB: Answering Queries with Crowdsourcing. In *Proceedings of the 2011 ACM SIGMOD International Conference on Management of Data*, SIGMOD '11, pages 61–72, New York, NY, USA, 2011. ACM.

[10] U. Gadiraju, R. Kawase, and S. Dietze. A taxonomy of microtasks on the web. In *Proceedings of the 25th ACM Conference on Hypertext and Social Media*, HT '14, pages 218–223, New York, NY, USA, 2014. ACM.

[11] Y. Gao and A. G. Parameswaran. Finish them!: Pricing algorithms for human computation. *PVLDB*, 7(14):1965–1976, 2014.

[12] P. G. Ipeirotis. Analyzing the amazon mechanical turk marketplace. *XRDS*, 17(2):16–21, Dec. 2010.

[13] L. C. Irani and M. S. Silberman. Turkopticon: Interrupting Worker Invisibility in Amazon Mechanical Turk. In *Proceedings of the SIGCHI Conference on Human Factors in Computing Systems*, CHI '13, pages 611–620, New York, NY, USA, 2013. ACM.

[14] A. Kittur, J. V. Nickerson, M. Bernstein, E. Gerber, A. Shaw, J. Zimmerman, M. Lease, and J. Horton. The future of crowd work. In *Proceedings of the 2013 Conference on Computer Supported Cooperative Work*, CSCW '13, pages 1301–1318, New York, NY, USA, 2013.

[15] P. Kucherbaev, S. Tranquillini, F. Daniel, F. Casati, M. Marchese, M. Brambilla, and P. Fraternali. Business processes for the crowd computer. In M. La Rosa and P. Soffer, editors, *Business Process Management Workshops*, volume 132 of *Lecture Notes in Business Information Processing*, pages 256–267. Springer Berlin Heidelberg, 2013.

[16] A. Kulkarni, M. Can, and B. Hartmann. Collaboratively crowdsourcing workflows with turkomatic. In *Proceedings of the ACM 2012 Conference on Computer Supported Cooperative Work*, CSCW '12, pages 1003–1012, New York, NY, USA, 2012. ACM.

[17] J. Mortensen, M. A. Musen, and N. F. Noy. Crowdsourcing the verification of relationships in biomedical ontologies. In *AMIA*, 2013.

[18] A. Parameswaran, A. D. Sarma, H. Garcia-Molina, N. Polyzotis, and J. Widom. Human-assisted graph search: It's okay to ask questions. *Proc. VLDB Endow.*, 4(5):267–278, Feb. 2011.

[19] C. Sarasua, E. Simperl, and N. F. Noy. Crowdmap: Crowdsourcing ontology alignment with microtasks. In *Proceedings of the 11th International Conference on The Semantic Web - Volume Part I*, ISWC'12, pages 525–541, Berlin, Heidelberg, 2012. Springer-Verlag.

[20] M. S. Silberman, L. Irani, and J. Ross. Ethics and tactics of professional crowdwork. *XRDS*, 17(2):39–43, Dec. 2010.

[21] L. von Ahn and L. Dabbish. Designing games with a purpose. *Commun. ACM*, 51(8):58–67, Aug. 2008.

[22] L. von Ahn, R. Liu, and M. Blum. Peekaboom: a game for locating objects in images. In *Proceedings of the SIGCHI Conference on Human Factors in Computing Systems*, CHI '06, pages 55–64, New York, NY, USA, 2006. ACM.

[23] M. Vukovic. Crowdsourcing for enterprises. In *Services-I, 2009 World Conference on*, pages 686–692. IEEE, 2009.

[24] J. Wang, T. Kraska, M. J. Franklin, and J. Feng. CrowdER: Crowdsourcing Entity Resolution. *Proc. VLDB Endow.*, 5(11):1483–1494, July 2012.

[25] J. Wang, G. Li, T. Kraska, M. J. Franklin, and J. Feng. Leveraging transitive relations for crowdsourced joins. In *Proceedings of the 2013 ACM SIGMOD International Conference on Management of Data*, pages 229–240. ACM, 2013.

Hierarchical Neural Language Models for Joint Representation of Streaming Documents and their Content

Nemanja Djuric*†, Hao Wu*‡, Vladan Radosavljevic†, Mihajlo Grbovic†, Narayan Bhamidipati†
†Yahoo Labs, Sunnyvale, CA, USA, {nemanja, vladan, mihajlo, narayanb}@yahoo-inc.com
‡University of Southern California, Los Angeles, CA, USA, hwu732@usc.edu

ABSTRACT

We consider the problem of learning distributed representations for documents in data streams. The documents are represented as low-dimensional vectors and are jointly learned with distributed vector representations of word tokens using a hierarchical framework with two embedded neural language models. In particular, we exploit the context of documents in streams and use one of the language models to model the document sequences, and the other to model word sequences within them. The models learn continuous vector representations for both word tokens and documents such that semantically similar documents and words are close in a common vector space. We discuss extensions to our model, which can be applied to personalized recommendation and social relationship mining by adding further user layers to the hierarchy, thus learning user-specific vectors to represent individual preferences. We validated the learned representations on a public movie rating data set from MovieLens, as well as on a large-scale Yahoo News data comprising three months of user activity logs collected on Yahoo servers. The results indicate that the proposed model can learn useful representations of both documents and word tokens, outperforming the current state-of-the-art by a large margin.

Categories and Subject Descriptors

I.2.7 [**Artificial Intelligence**]: Natural Language Processing—*Language Models*; I.5.4 [**Pattern Recognition**]: Applications—*Text processing*; I.7.m [**Document and Text Processing**]: Miscellaneous

Keywords

Machine learning; document modeling; distributed representations; word embeddings; document embeddings.

1. INTRODUCTION

Text documents coming in a sequence are common in real-world applications and can arise in various contexts. For example, consider Web pages surfed by users in random walks along the hyperlinks, streams of click-through URLs associated with a query in search engine, publications of an author in chronological order, threaded posts in online discussion forums, answers to a question in online knowledge-sharing communities, or e-mails in a common thread, to name a few. The co-occurrences of documents in a temporal sequence may reveal relatedness between them, such as their semantic and topical similarity. In addition, sequences of words within the documents introduce another rich and complex source of the data, which can be leveraged together with the document stream information to learn useful and insightful representations of both documents and words.

In this paper, we introduce algorithm that can simultaneously model documents from a stream and their residing natural language in one common lower-dimensional vector space. Such algorithm goes beyond representations which consider each document as a separate bag-of-words composition, most notably Probabilistic Latent Semantic Analysis (PLSA) [10] and Latent Dirichlet Allocation (LDA) [3]. We focus on learning continuous representations of documents in vector space jointly with distributed word representations using statistical neural language models [2], whose success was previously shown in a number of publications [6]. More precisely, we propose hierarchical models where document vectors act as units in a context of document sequences, and also as global contexts of word sequences contained within them. The probability distribution of observing a word depends not only on some fixed number of surrounding words, but is also conditioned on the specific document. Meanwhile, the probability distribution of a document depends on the surrounding documents in stream data. Our work is most similar to [13] as it also considers document vectors as a global context for words contained within, however the authors in [13] do not model the document relationships which brings significant modeling strength to our models and opens a plethora of application areas for the neural language models. In our work, the models are trained to predict words and documents in a sequence with maximum likelihood. We optimize the models using stochastic gradient learning, a flexible and powerful optimization framework suitable for the considered large-scale problems in an online setting where new samples arrive sequentially.

Vector representations of documents and words learned by our model are useful for various applications of critical importance to online businesses. For example, by means of simple nearest-neighbor searches in the joint vector space between document and word representations, we can address a number of important tasks: 1) given a query keyword,

*Authors contributed equally. This work was done while Hao Wu was an intern at Yahoo Labs in Sunnyvale, USA.

WWW 2015, May 18–22, 2015, Florence, Italy.
ACM 978-1-4503-3469-3/15/05.
http://dx.doi.org/10.1145/2736277.2741643.

search for similar keywords to expand the query (useful in the search product); 2) given a keyword, search for relevant documents such as news stories (useful in document retrieval); 3) given a document, retrieve similar or related documents (useful for news stream personalization and document recommendation); and 4) automatically generate related words to tag or summarize a given document (useful in native advertising or document retrieval). All these tasks are essential elements of a number of online applications, including online search, advertising, and personalized recommendation. In addition, as we show in the experimental section, learned document representations can be used to obtain state-of-the-art document classification results.

The proposed approach represents a step towards automatic organization, semantic analysis, and summarization of documents observed in sequences. We summarize our main contributions below:

- We propose hierarchical neural language model which takes advantage of the context of document sequences and the context of each word within a document to learn their low-dimensional vector representations. The document contexts can act as an empirical prior which helps learn smoothed representations for documents. This is useful for learning representations of short documents with a few words, for which [13] tends to learn poor document representations as separately learned document vectors may overfit to a few words within a specific document. Conversely, the proposed model is not dependent on the document content as much.

- The proposed approach can capture inherent connections between documents in the data stream. We tailor our models to analyze movie reviews where a user's preferences may be biased towards particular genres, as well as Yahoo News articles for which we collect click-through logs of a large number of users and learn useful news article representations. The experimental results on retrieval and categorization tasks demonstrate effectiveness of the proposed model.

- Our learning framework is flexible and it is straightforward to add more layers in order to learn additional representations for related concepts. We propose extensions of the model and discuss how to learn explicit distributed representations of users on top of the basic framework. The extensions can be applied to personalized recommendation and social relationship mining.

2. RELATED WORK

The related work is largely centered on the notion of neural language models [2], which improve generalization of the classic n-gram language models by using continuous variables to represent words in a vector space. This idea of distributed word representations has spurred many successful applications in natural language processing. More recently, the concept of distributed representations has been extended beyond pure language words to a number of applications, including modeling of phrases [15], sentences and paragraphs [13], relational entities [4, 20], general text-based attributes [12], descriptive text of images [11], online search sessions [7], smartphone apps [1], and nodes in a network [19].

2.1 Neural language models

Neural language models take advantage of a word order, and state the same assumption as n-gram models that words closer in a sequence are statistically more dependent. Typically, a neural language model learns the probability distribution of next word given a fixed number of preceding words which act as the context. More formally, given a word sequence $(w_1, w_2, \dots, w_T)$ in a training data, the objective of the model is to maximize log-likelihood of the sequence,

$$\mathcal{L} = \sum_{t=1}^{T} \log \mathbb{P}(w_t | w_{t-n+1} : w_{t-1}), \tag{1}$$

where w_t is the tth word in the sequence, and $w_{t-n+1} : w_{t-1}$ represents a sequence of successive preceding words $(w_{t-n+1}, \dots, w_{t-1})$ that act as the context to the word w_t. A typical model architecture to approximate probability distribution $\mathbb{P}(w_t | w_{t-n+1} : w_{t-1})$ is to use a neural network [2]. The neural network is trained by projecting the concatenation of vectors for context words $(w_{t-n+1}, \dots, w_{t-1})$ into a latent representation with multiple non-linear hidden layers and the output soft-max layer comprising W nodes, where W is a size of the vocabulary, where the network attempts to predict w_t with high probability. However, a neural network of large size is challenging to train, and the word vectors are computationally expensive to learn from large-scale data sets comprising millions of words, which are commonly found in practice. Recent approaches with different versions of log-bilinear models [16] or log-linear models [14] attempt to modify the model architecture in order to reduce the computational complexity. The use of hierarchical soft-max [18] or noise contrastive estimation [17] can also help speed up the training complexity. In the following we review two recent neural language models [14, 15] which directly motivated our work, namely continuous bag-of-words (CBOW) and skip-gram (SG) model.

2.2 Continuous bag-of-words

The continuous bag-of-words model is a simplified neural language model without any non-linear hidden layers. A log-linear classifier is used to predict a current word based on its preceding and succeeding words, where their representations are averaged as the input. More precisely, the objective of the CBOW model is to maximize the log-likelihood,

$$\mathcal{L} = \sum_{t=1}^{T} \log \mathbb{P}(w_t | w_{t-c} : w_{t+c}), \tag{2}$$

where c is the context length, and $w_{t-c} : w_{t+c}$ is the subsequence $(w_{t-c}, \dots, w_{t+c})$ excluding w_t itself. The probability $\mathbb{P}(w_t | w_{t-c} : w_{t+c})$ is defined using the softmax,

$$\mathbb{P}(w_t | w_{t-c} : w_{t+c}) = \frac{\exp(\bar{\mathbf{v}}^\top \mathbf{v}'_{w_t})}{\sum_{w=1}^{W} \exp(\bar{\mathbf{v}}^\top \mathbf{v}'_w)}, \tag{3}$$

where $\mathbf{v}'_{w_t}$ is the output vector representation of w_t, and $\bar{\mathbf{v}}$ is averaged vector representation of the context, found as

$$\bar{\mathbf{v}} = \frac{1}{2\,c} \sum_{-c \le j \le c, j \ne 0} \mathbf{v}_{w_{t+j}}. \tag{4}$$

Here $\mathbf{v}_w$ is an input vector representation of word w. It is worth noting that CBOW takes only partial advantage of the word order, since any ordering of a set of contextual words will result in the same vector representation.

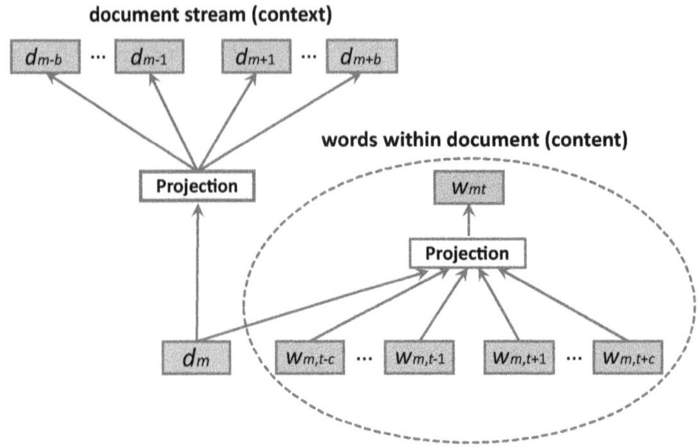

Figure 1: The proposed hierarchical model architecture with two embedded neural languages models (orange/left - document vectors; green/right - word vectors)

2.3 Skip-gram model

Instead of predicting the current word based on the words before and after it, the skip-gram model tries to predict the surrounding words within a certain distance based on the current one. More formally, skip-gram defines the objective function as the exact counterpart to the continuous bag-of-words model,

$$\mathcal{L} = \sum_{t=1}^{T} \log \mathbb{P}(w_{t-c} : w_{t+c} | w_t). \tag{5}$$

Furthermore, the model simplifies the probability distribution, introducing an assumption that the contextual words $w_{t-c} : w_{t+c}$ are independent given current word w_t,

$$\mathbb{P}(w_{t-c} : w_{t+c} | w_t) = \prod_{-c \leq j \leq c, j \neq 0} \mathbb{P}(w_{t+j} | w_t), \tag{6}$$

with $\mathbb{P}(w_{t+j}|w_t)$ defined as

$$\mathbb{P}(w_{t+j}|w_t) = \frac{\exp(\mathbf{v}_{w_t}^\top \mathbf{v}'_{w_{t+j}})}{\sum_{w=1}^{W} \exp(\mathbf{v}_{w_t}^\top \mathbf{v}'_w)}, \tag{7}$$

where $\mathbf{v}_w$ and $\mathbf{v}'_w$ are the input and output vectors of w. Increasing the range of context c would generally improve the quality of learned word vectors, albeit at the expense of higher computation cost. Skip-gram assumes that the surrounding words are equally important, and in this sense the word order is again not fully exploited, similarly to the CBOW model. A wiser strategy to account for this issue would be to sample training word pairs in (7) less from relatively distant words that appear in the context [14].

3. HIERARCHICAL LANGUAGE MODEL

In this section we present our algorithm for joint modeling of streaming documents and the words contained within, where we learn distributed representations for both the documents and the words in a shared, low-dimensional embedding space. The approach is inspired by recently proposed methods for learning vector representations of words which take advantage of a word order observed in a sentence [14]. However, and unlike similar work presented by the authors of [13], we also exploit temporal neighborhood of the streaming documents. In particular, we model the probability of observing a particular document by taking into account its temporally-close documents, in addition to conditioning on the content of the document.

3.1 Model architecture

In the considered problem setting, we assume the training documents are given in a sequence. For example, if the documents are news articles, a document sequence can be a sequence of news articles sorted in a chronological order in which the user read them. More specifically, we assume that we are given a set $\mathcal{S}$ of S document sequences, with each sequence $s \in \mathcal{S}$ consisting of N_s documents, $s = (d_1, d_2, \ldots, d_{N_s})$. Moreover, each document in a stream d_m is a sequence of T_m words, $d_m = (w_{m1}, w_{m2}, \ldots, w_{m,T_m})$. We aim to simultaneously learn low-dimensional representations of streaming documents and language words in a common vector space, and represent each document and word as a continuous feature vector of dimensionality D. If we assume that there are M unique documents in the training corpus and W unique words in the vocabulary, then during training we aim to learn $(M + W) \cdot D$ model parameters.

The context of a document sequence and the natural language context are modeled using the proposed hierarchical neural language model, where document vectors act not only as the units to predict their surrounding documents, but also as the global context of word sequences contained within them. The architecture consists of two embedded layers, shown in Figure 1. The upper layer learns the temporal context of a document sequence, based on the assumption that temporally closer documents in the document stream are statistically more dependent. We note that temporally does not need to refer to the time of creation of the document, but also to the time the document was read by the user, which is the definition we use in our experiments. The bottom layer models the contextual information of word sequences. Lastly, we connect these two layers by adopting the idea of paragraph vectors [13], and consider each document token as a global context for all words within the document.

More formally, given set $\mathcal{S}$ of sequences of documents, the objective of the hierarchical model is to maximize log-likelihood of the streaming data,

$$\mathcal{L} = \sum_{s \in \mathcal{S}} \Big(\alpha \sum_{d_m \in s} \sum_{w_{mt} \in d_m} \log \mathbb{P}(w_{mt} | w_{m,t-c} : w_{m,t+c}, d_m) + \sum_{d_m \in s} \big(\alpha \log \mathbb{P}(d_m | w_{m1} : w_{mT}) + \sum_{-b \leq i \leq b, i \neq 0} \log \mathbb{P}(d_{m+i} | d_m) \big) \Big), \tag{8}$$

where α is the weight that specifies a trade-off between focusing on minimization of the log-likelihood of document sequence and of the log-likelihood of word sequences (we set $\alpha = 1$ in the experiments), b is the length of the training context for document sequences, and c is the length of the training context for word sequences. In this particular architecture, we are using the CBOW model in the lower, sentence layer, and the skip-gram model in the upper, document layer. However, we note that either of the two models can be used in any level of the hierarchy, and a specific choice depends on the modalities of the problem at hand.

Given the architecture illustrated in Figure 1, probability of observing one of the surrounding documents based on the current document $\mathbb{P}(d_{m+i}|d_m)$ is defined using the soft-max function as given below,

$$\mathbb{P}(d_{m+i}|d_m) = \frac{\exp(\mathbf{v}_{d_m}^\top \mathbf{v}'_{d_{m+i}})}{\sum_{d=1}^{M} \exp(\mathbf{v}_{d_m}^\top \mathbf{v}'_d)}, \tag{9}$$

where $\mathbf{v}_d$ and $\mathbf{v}'_d$ are the input and output vector representations of document d. Furthermore, probability of observing a word depends not only on its surrounding words, but also on a specific document that the word belongs to. More precisely, probability $\mathbb{P}(w_{mt}|w_{m,t-c} : w_{m,t+c}, d_m)$ is defined as

$$\mathbb{P}(w_{mt}|w_{m,t-c} : w_{m,t+c}, d_m) = \frac{\exp(\bar{\mathbf{v}}^\top \mathbf{v}'_{w_{mt}})}{\sum_{w=1}^{W} \exp(\bar{\mathbf{v}}^\top \mathbf{v}'_w)}, \tag{10}$$

where $\mathbf{v}'_{w_{mt}}$ is the output vector representation of w_{mt}, and $\bar{\mathbf{v}}$ is the averaged vector representation of the context (including the specific document d_m), defined as follows,

$$\bar{\mathbf{v}} = \frac{1}{2c+1}(\mathbf{v}_{d_m} + \sum_{-c \leq j \leq c, j \neq 0} \mathbf{v}_{w_{m,t+j}}). \tag{11}$$

Lastly, we define probability of observing a document given the words contained within $\mathbb{P}(d_m|w_{m1} : w_{m,T_m})$ in a similar way, by reusing equations (10) and (11) and replacing the appropriate variables.

3.2 Variants of the model

In the previous section we presented a typical architecture where we specified language models in each layer of the hierarchy. However, in real-world applications, we could vary the language models for different purposes in a straightforward manner. For example, a news website would be interested in predicting on-the-fly which news article a user would read after a few clicks on some other news stories, in order to personalize the news feed. Then, it could be more reasonable to use directed, feed-forward models which estimate $\mathbb{P}(d_m|d_{m-b} : d_{m-1})$, probability of the mth document in the sequence given its b preceding documents. Or, equivalently, if we want to model which documents were read prior to the currently observed sequence, we can use feed-backward models which estimate $\mathbb{P}(d_m|d_{m+1} : d_{m+b})$, probability of the mth document given its b succeeding documents.

Moreover, it is straightforward to extend the described model for problems that naturally have more than two layers. Let us assume that we have a data set with streaming documents specific to a different set of users (e.g., for each document we also know which user generated or read the document). Then, we may build more complex models to simultaneously learn distributed representations of users by adding additional user layer on top of the document layer. In this setup a user vector could serve as a global context of streaming documents pertaining to that specific user, much like a document vector serves as a global context to words pertaining to that specific document. More specifically, we would predict a document based on the surrounding documents and its content, while also conditioning on a specific user. This variant models $\mathbb{P}(d_m|d_{m-b} : d_{m-1}, u)$, where u is an indicator variable for a user. Learning vector representations of users would open doors for further improvement of personalized services, where personalization would reduce to simple nearest-neighbor search in the joint embedding space.

3.3 Model optimization

The model is optimized using stochastic gradient ascent, which is very suitable for large-scale problems. However, computation of gradient $\nabla \log \mathbb{P}(w_{mt}|w_{m,t-c} : w_{m,t+c}, d_m)$ in (8) is proportional to the vocabulary size W, and of gradients $\nabla \log \mathbb{P}(d_{m+i}|d_m)$ and $\nabla \log \mathbb{P}(d_m|w_{m1} : w_{m,T_m})$ is proportional to the number of training documents M. This is computationally expensive in practice, since both W and M could easily reach millions in our applications.

An efficient alternative that we use is hierarchical soft-max [18], which reduces the time complexity to $\mathcal{O}\big(R \log(W) + bM \log(M)\big)$ in our case, where R is the total number of words in the document sequence. Instead of evaluating every distinct word or document during each gradient step in order to compute the sums in equations (9) and (10), hierarchical softmax uses two binary trees, one with distinct documents as leaves and the other with distinct words as leaves. For each leaf node, there is a unique assigned path from the root which is encoded using binary digits. To construct a tree structure the Huffman encoding is typically used, where more frequent documents (or words) in the data set have shorter codes to speed up the training. The internal tree nodes are represented as real-valued vectors, of the same dimensionality as word and document vectors. More precisely, hierarchical soft-max expresses the probability of observing the current document (or word) in the sequence as a product of probabilities of the binary decisions specified by the Huffman code of the document as

$$\mathbb{P}(d_{m+i}|d_m) = \prod_l \mathbb{P}(h_l|q_l, d_m), \tag{12}$$

where h_l is the lth bit in the code with respect to q_l, which is the lth node in the specified tree path of d_{m+i}. The probability of each binary decision is defined as follows,

$$\mathbb{P}(h_l = 1|q_l, d_m) = \sigma(\mathbf{v}_{d_m}^\top \mathbf{v}_{q_l}), \tag{13}$$

where $\sigma(x)$ is the sigmoid function, and $\mathbf{v}_{q_l}$ is the vector representation of node q_l. It can be verified that $\sum_{d=1}^{M} \mathbb{P}(d_{m+i} = d|d_m) = 1$, and hence the property of probability distribution is preserved. We can compute $\mathbb{P}(d_m|w_{m1} : w_{m,T_m})$ in the same manner. Furthermore, we similarly express $\mathbb{P}(w_{mt}|w_{m,t-c} : w_{m,t+c}, d_m)$, but with construction of a separate Huffman tree pertaining to the words.

Table 1: Movie classification accuracy

Algorithm	drama	comedy	thriller	romance	action	crime	adventure	horror
LDA	0.5544	0.5856	0.8158	0.8173	0.8745	0.8685	0.8765	0.9063
paragraph2vec	0.6367	0.6767	0.7958	0.7919	0.8193	0.8537	0.8524	0.8699
word2vec	0.7172	0.7449	0.8102	0.8204	0.8627	0.8692	0.8768	0.9231
HDV	**0.7274**	**0.7487**	**0.8201**	**0.8233**	**0.8814**	**0.8728**	**0.8854**	**0.9872**

Table 2: Nearest word neighbors of selected keywords

boxing	university	movies	batman	woods	hijack	tennis	messi
welterweight	school	characters	superman	tiger	hijacked	singles	neymar
knockouts	college	films	superhero	masters	whereabouts	masters	ronaldo
fights	professor	studio	gotham	holes	transponders	djokovic	barca
middleweight	center	audiences	comics	golf	autopilot	nadal	iniesta
ufc	students	actors	trilogy	hole	radars	federer	libel
heavyweight	national	feature	avenger	pga	hijackers	celebration	atletico
bantamweight	medical	pictures	sci	classic	turnback	sharapova	cristiano
greats	american	drama	sequel	par	hijacking	atp	benzema
wrestling	institute	comedy	marvel	doral	decompression	slam	argentine
amateur	california	audience	prequel	mcilroy	baffling	roger	barcelona

4. EXPERIMENTS

In this section we describe experimental evaluation of the proposed approach, which we refer to as *hierarchical document vector* (HDV) model. First, we validated the learned representations on a public movie ratings data set, where the task was to classify movies into different genres. Then, we used a large-scale data set of user click-through logs on a news stream collected on Yahoo servers to showcase a wide application potential of the HDV algorithm. In all experiments we used cosine distance to measure the closeness of two vectors (either document or word vectors) in the common low-dimensional embedding space.

4.1 Movie genre classification

In the first set of experiments we validated quality of the obtained distributed document representations on a classification task using a publicly available data set. We note that, although we had access to a proprietary data set discussed in Section 4.2 which served as our initial motivation to develop the HDV model, obtaining a similar public data set proved to be much more difficult. To this end, we generated such data by combining a public movie ratings data set MovieLens 10M[1], consisting of movie ratings for around 10,000 movies generated by more than 71,000 users, with a movie synopses data set from Internet Movie DataBase (IMDB) that was found online[2]. Each movie in the data set is tagged as belonging to one or more genres, such as "action", "comedy", or "horror". Then, following terminology from the earlier sections, we viewed movies as "documents" and synopses as "document content". The document streams were obtained by taking for each user the movies that they rated 4 and above (on the scale from 1 to 5), and ordering them in a sequence according to a timestamp of the rating. The described preprocessing resulted in 69,702 document sequences comprising 8,565 distinct movies, with an average synopsis length of 190.6 words.

[1]grouplens.org/datasets/movielens/, accessed March 2015
[2]ftp.fu-berlin.de/pub/misc/movies/database/, March 2015

Let us discuss several explicit assumptions that we made while generating the movie data set. First, we retained only high-rated movies for each user in order to make the data less noisy, as the assumption is that the users are more likely to enjoy two movies that belonged to the same genre, than two movies coming from two different genres. Thus, by removing low-rated movies we aim to keep only similar movies in a single user's sequence. As we show in the remainder of the section, the experimental results indicate that the assumption holds true. In addition, we used the timestamp of a rating as a proxy for a time when the movie was actually watched. Although this might not always hold in reality, the empirical results suggest that the assumption was reasonable for learning useful movie and word embeddings.

We learned movie vector representations for the described data set using the following methods: 1) LDA [3], which learns low-dimensional representations of documents (i.e., movies) as a topic distribution over their synopses; 2) paragraph vector (paragraph2vec) [13], where an entire movie synopsis is taken as a single paragraph; 3) word2vec [15], where movie sequences are used as "sentences" and movies are used as "words"; and 4) the proposed HDV method. We used publicly available implementations of online LDA training [9][3] and word2vec[4], and used our implementations of paragraph2vec and HDV algorithms. Note that LDA and paragraph2vec take into account only the content of the documents (i.e., movie synopses), word2vec only considers the movie sequences and does not consider the movie synopses and contained natural language in any way, while HDV combines the two approaches and jointly considers and models both the movie sequences and the content of movie synopses.

Dimensionality of the embedding space was set to $D = 100$ for all low-dimensional embedding methods (in the case of LDA this amounts to using 100 topics). The neighborhood of the neural language methods was set to 5 for both document and word sequences, and the models were trained for

[3]hunch.net/~vw/, accessed March 2015
[4]code.google.com/p/word2vec, accessed March 2015

Table 3: Most related news stories retrieved for a given keyword

movies	tennis
'American Hustle,' 'Wolf of Wall Street' Lead Nominations	Tennis-Venus through to third round, Li handed walkover
3 Reasons 'Jurassic World' Is Headed in the Right Direction	Nadal rips Hewitt, Serena and Sharapova survive at Miami
Irish Film and TV academy lines up stellar guest list for awards	Williams battles on at Sony Open in front of empty seats
10 things the Academy Awards won't say	Serena, Sharapova again on Miami collision course
I saw Veronica Mars, thanks to $35 donation, 2 apps & $8 ticket	Wawrinka survives bumpy start to Sony Open
boxing	**hijack**
Yushin Okami's Debut for WSOF 9 in Las Vegas	Thai radar might have tracked missing plane
UFC Champ Jon Jones Denies Daniel Cormier Title Shot Request	Criminal probe under way in Malaysia plane drama
UFC contender Alex Gustafsson staring at a no-win situation	Live: Malaysia asks India to join the expanding search
Alvarez back as Molina, Santa Cruz defend boxing titles	Malaysia dramatically expands search for missing jet
Anthony Birchak Creates MFC Championship Ring	Malaysia widening search for missing plane, says minister
university	**entertainment**
The 20 Public Colleges With The Smartest Students	'American Hustle,' 'Wolf of Wall Street' Lead Nominations
Spring storm brings blizzard warning for Cape Cod	Madison Square Garden Company Buys 50% Stake in Tribeca
U.S. News Releases 2015 Best Graduate Schools Rankings	Renaissance Technologies sells its Walt Disney position
No Friday Night Lights at $60 Million Texas Stadium	News From the Advertising Industry
New Orleans goes all in on charter schools	10 things the Academy Awards won't say

Table 4: Top related words for news stories

News articles	Related keywords
Serena beats Li for seventh Miami crown	hardcourts biscayne sharapova nadal nishikori aces unforced walkover angelique threeset
This year's best buy ISAs	isas pensioners savers oft annuity isa pots taxfree nomakeupselfie allowance
Galaxy S5 will get off to a painfully slow start in Samsung's home market	mwc quadcore snapdragon oneplus ghz appleinsider samsung lumia handset android
'Star Wars Episode VII': Actors Battle for Lead Role (EXCLUSIVE)	reboot mutants anthology sequels prequel liv helmer vfx villains terminator
Western U.S. Republicans to urge appeals court to back gay marriage	lesbian primaries rowse beshear legislatures schuette heterosexual gubernatorial stockman lgbt
Russian forces 'part-seize' Ukrainian missile units	postcold rulers aipac redrawn eilat warheads lawlessness blockaded czechoslovakia ukranian
Pope marks anniversary with prayer and a tweet	catholics pontiff curia dignitaries papacy xvi halal theology seminary bishops
Uncle Sam buying mortgages? Who knew?	berkowitz moelis erbey gse cios lode ocwen nationstar fairholme subsidizing
5 Foods for Healthier Skin	carbs coconut cornstarch bundt vegetarian butter tablespoons tsp dieters salad
Dwyane Wade on pace to lead all guards in shooting	beverley bynum vogel spoelstra shootaround dwyane nuggets westbrook bledsoe kobe

5 iterations. Once we obtained the document vectors using the abovementioned methods, we used linear Support Vector Machine (SVM) [5] to predict a movie genre. Note that we chose a linear classifier, instead of some more powerful non-linear one, in order to reduce the effect of variance of non-linear methods on the classification performance and help with the interpretation of the results.

The classification results after 5-fold cross-validation are shown in Table 1, where we report results on eight binary one-vs-rest classification tasks for eight most frequent movie genres in the data set. We can see that the neural language models on average obtained higher accuracy than LDA, although LDA achieved very competitive results on the last six tasks. It is interesting to observe that the word2vec algorithm obtained higher accuracy than paragraph2vec despite the fact that word2vec only considered sequences in which the movies were seen without using the movie synopses, and that, unlike word2vec, the paragraph2vec model was specifically designed for document representation. This result indicates that the users have strong genre preferences that exist in the movie sequences which was utilized by word2vec, validating our assumption discussed earlier. Furthermore, we see that the proposed approach achieved higher accuracy than the competing state-of-the-art methods, obtaining on average 5.62% better performance over the paragraph2vec and 1.52% over the word2vec model. This can be explained by the fact that the HDV method successfully exploited both the document content and the relationships in a stream between them, resulting in improved performance.

4.2 Large-scale document representation

In this section we evaluate the proposed algorithm a large-scale data set collected on Yahoo servers. The data consists of nearly 200,000 distinct news stories, viewed by a subset of company's users from March to June, 2014. After pre-processing where the stopwords were removed, we trained the HDV model on more than 80 million document sequences generated by users, containing a total of 100 million words with a vocabulary size of 161,000. Considering that the used data set is proprietary and that numerical results may carry business-sensitive information, we first illustrate a wide potential of the proposed method for numerous

Table 5: Titles of retrieved news articles for given news examples

Russian forces 'part-seize' Ukrainian missile units
Russia says cannot order Crimean 'self-defense' units back to base
Russia says Ukraine "hallucinating" in warning of nuclear risks
Lavrov snubs Ukrainian but says talks will continue
Kiev must have say in Crimea's future: US
Crisis in Ukraine: After day of Paris talks, a dramatic change in tone
Galaxy S5 will get off to a slow start in Samsung's home market
New specs revealed for one of 2014's most intriguing Android phones
LG G Pro 2 review: the evolutionary process
[video] HTC wins smartphone of the year
Samsung apparently still has a major role in Apple's iPhone 6
Samsung's new launch, the Galaxy S5, lacks innovative features
This year's best buy ISAs
Savings rates 'could rise' as NS&I launch new products
How to use an Isa to invest in property
Pensions: now you can have a blank canvas - not an annuity
Ed Balls' Budget Response Long on Jokes, a Bit Short on Analysis
Half a million borrowers to be repaid interest and charges
Western U.S. Republicans to urge appeals court to back gay marriage
Ky. to use outside counsel in gay-marriage case
Disputed study's author testifies on gay marriage
Texas' Primary Color Battle Begins
Eyes on GOP as Texas holds nation's 1st primary
Michigan stumbles in court defending same-sex marriage ban

online applications using qualitative experiments, followed by the document classification task where we show relative performance improvements over the baseline method.

4.2.1 Keyword suggestion

An important task in many online applications is finding similar or related words given an input word as a query. This is useful in the setting of, for example, search retargeting [8], where advertisers bid on search keywords related to their product or service and may use the proposed model to expand the list of targeted keywords with additional relevant keywords. Table 2 shows example keywords from the vocabulary, together with their nearest word neighbors in the embedding space. Clearly, meaningful semantic relationships and associations can be observed within the closest distance of the input keywords. For example, for the query word "batman", the model found that other superheroes such as "superman" and "avengers" are related, and also found keywords related to comics in general, such as "comics", "marvel", or "sequel".

4.2.2 Document retrieval

Given a query word, one may be interested in finding the most relevant documents, which is a typical task of an online search engine or news webservice perform. We consider the keywords used in the previous section, and find the titles of the closest document vectors in the common embedding space. As can be seen in Table 3, the retrieved documents are semantically related to the input keyword. Interestingly, in some cases it might seem that the document is irrelevant, as, for example, in the case of keyword "university" and headlines "Spring storm brings blizzard warning for Cape Cod" and "No Friday Night Lights at $60 Million Texas Stadium". However, after closer inspection and a search for the headlines in a popular search engine, we can see that the snow storm from the first headline affected school operations and the article includes a comment by an affected student. Similar search also confirmed that the second article discussed school facilities and an education fund. Although the titles may be misleading, we can see that the both articles are of interest to users interested in the keyword "university", as our model correctly learned from the actual user sessions.

We note that the proposed approach differs from the traditional information retrieval methods due to the fact that retrieved documents do not necessarily need to contain the query word, as examplified in Table 3 in a case of the keyword "boxing". As we can see, the HDV method found that the articles discussing UFC (Ultimate Fighting Championship) and WSOF (World Series of Fighting) events are related to the sport, despite the fact that neither of them specifically mentions the word "boxing".

4.2.3 Document tag recommendation

An important task in online news services is automatic document tagging, where, given a news article, we assign a list of relevant keywords (called *tags*) that explain the article content. Tagging is very useful in improving the document retrieval systems, document summarization, document recommendation, contextual advertising (tags can be used to match display ads shown alongside the article), and many other applications. Our model is suitable for such tasks due to the fact that document and word vectors reside in the same feature space, which allows us to reduce complex task of document tagging to a trivial K-nearest-neighbor search in the joint embedding space.

Using the trained model, we retrieved the nearest words given a news story as an input. In Table 4 we give the results, where titles of the example news stories are shown together with their lists of nearest words. We can see that the retrieved keywords often summarize and further explain the documents. For example, for the news article "This year's best buy ISAs", related to Individual Savings Account (ISA), the keywords include "pensioners" and "taxfree", while in the mortgage-related example ("Uncle Sam buying mortgages? Who knew?") keywords include several financial companies and advisors (e.g., Nationstar, Moelis, Berkowitz).

Table 6: Relative improvement over LDA

Algorithm	Avg. accuracy improvement
LDA	0.00%
paragraph2vec	0.27%
word2vec	2.26%
HDV	**4.39%**

4.2.4 *Document recommendation*

In the document recommendation task, we search for the nearest news articles given a news story. The retrieved articles can be provided as a reading recommendations for users viewing the query news story. We give the examples in Table 5, where we can see that relevant and semantically related documents are located nearby in the latent vector space. For example, we can see that the nearest neighbors for article related to the 2014 Ukraine crisis are other news stories discussing the political situation in Ukraine, while for the article focusing on Samsung Galaxy S5 all nearest documents are related to the smartphone industry.

4.2.5 *News topic classification*

Lastly, we used the learned representations to label news documents with 19 first-level topic tags from the company's internal interest taxonomy (e.g., taxonomy includes "home & garden" and "science" tags). We used linear SVM to predict each topic separately, and the average improvement over LDA after 5-fold cross-validation is given in Table 6. We see that the proposed method outperformed the competition on this large-scale problem, strongly confirming the benefits of HDV for representation of streaming documents.

5. CONCLUSION

We described a general unsupervised learning framework to model the latent structure of streaming documents, that learns low-dimensional vectors to represent documents and words in the same latent space. Our model exploits the context of documents in streams and learns representations that can capture temporal co-occurrences of documents and statistical patterns of the words contained within The method was verified on a movie classification task, outperforming the current state-of-the-art by a large margin. Moreover, experiments on a large-scale data set comprising click-through logs on Yahoo News demonstrated effectiveness and wide applicability of the proposed neural language approach.

6. REFERENCES

[1] R. Baeza-Yates, D. Jiang, F. Silvestri, and B. Harrison. Predicting the next app that you are going to use. In *Proceedings of the 8th ACM international conference on Web search and data mining*. ACM, 2015.

[2] Y. Bengio, R. Ducharme, P. Vincent, and C. Jauvin. A neural probabilistic language model. *Journal of Machine Learning Research*, 3:1137–1155, 2003.

[3] D. M. Blei, A. Y. Ng, and M. I. Jordan. Latent dirichlet allocation. *the Journal of machine Learning research*, 3:993–1022, 2003.

[4] A. Bordes, N. Usunier, A. Garcia-Duran, J. Weston, and O. Yakhnenko. Translating embeddings for modeling multi-relational data. In *Advances in Neural Information Processing Systems*, pages 2787–2795, 2013.

[5] C.-C. Chang and C.-J. Lin. LIBSVM: A library for support vector machines. *ACM Transactions on Intelligent Systems and Technology*, 2:27:1–27:27, 2011.

[6] R. Collobert and J. Weston. A unified architecture for natural language processing: Deep neural networks with multitask learning. In *Proceedings of the 25th international conference on Machine learning*, pages 160–167. ACM, 2008.

[7] N. Djuric, V. Radosavljevic, M. Grbovic, and N. Bhamidipati. Hidden conditional random fields with distributed user embeddings for ad targeting. In *IEEE International Conference on Data Mining*, 2014.

[8] M. Grbovic and S. Vucetic. Generating ad targeting rules using sparse principal component analysis with constraints. In *International World Wide Web Conference*, pages 283–284, 2014.

[9] M. Hoffman, F. R. Bach, and D. M. Blei. Online learning for Latent Dirichlet Allocation. In *Advances in Neural Information Processing Systems*, pages 856–864, 2010.

[10] T. Hofmann. Probabilistic latent semantic indexing. In *Proceedings of the 22nd annual international ACM SIGIR conference on Research and development in information retrieval*, pages 50–57. ACM, 1999.

[11] R. Kiros, R. Zemel, and R. Salakhutdinov. Multimodal neural language models. In *Proceedings of the 31th International Conference on Machine Learning*, 2014.

[12] R. Kiros, R. S. Zemel, and R. Salakhutdinov. A multiplicative model for learning distributed text-based attribute representations. *arXiv preprint arXiv:1406.2710*, 2014.

[13] Q. V. Le and T. Mikolov. Distributed representations of sentences and documents. *arXiv preprint arXiv:1405.4053*, 2014.

[14] T. Mikolov, K. Chen, G. Corrado, and J. Dean. Efficient estimation of word representations in vector space. *arXiv preprint arXiv:1301.3781*, 2013.

[15] T. Mikolov, I. Sutskever, K. Chen, G. S. Corrado, and J. Dean. Distributed representations of words and phrases and their compositionality. In *Advances in Neural Information Processing Systems*, pages 3111–3119, 2013.

[16] A. Mnih and G. Hinton. Three new graphical models for statistical language modelling. In *Proceedings of the 24th international conference on Machine learning*, pages 641–648. ACM, 2007.

[17] A. Mnih and Y. W. Teh. A fast and simple algorithm for training neural probabilistic language models. *arXiv preprint arXiv:1206.6426*, 2012.

[18] F. Morin and Y. Bengio. Hierarchical probabilistic neural network language model. In *AISTATS*, volume 5, pages 246–252, 2005.

[19] B. Perozzi, R. Al-Rfou, and S. Skiena. Deepwalk: Online learning of social representations. *arXiv preprint arXiv:1403.6652*, 2014.

[20] R. Socher, D. Chen, C. D. Manning, and A. Ng. Reasoning with neural tensor networks for knowledge base completion. In *Advances in Neural Information Processing Systems*, pages 926–934, 2013.

Future User Engagement Prediction and Its Application to Improve the Sensitivity of Online Experiments

Alexey Drutsa
Yandex
Moscow, Russia
adrutsa@yandex.ru

Gleb Gusev
Yandex
Moscow, Russia
gleb57@yandex-team.ru

Pavel Serdyukov
Yandex
Moscow, Russia
pavser@yandex-team.ru

ABSTRACT

Modern Internet companies improve their services by means of data-driven decisions that are based on online controlled experiments (also known as A/B tests). To run *more* online controlled experiments and to get statistically significant results *faster* are the emerging needs for these companies. The main way to achieve these goals is to improve the sensitivity of A/B experiments. We propose a novel approach to improve the sensitivity of user engagement metrics (that are widely used in A/B tests) by utilizing prediction of the future behavior of an individual user. This problem of prediction of the exact value of a user engagement metric is also novel and is studied in our work. We demonstrate the effectiveness of our sensitivity improvement approach on several real online experiments run at Yandex. Especially, we show how it can be used to detect the treatment effect of an A/B test faster with the same level of statistical significance.

Categories and Subject Descriptions: H.1.2 [User/Machine Systems]: Human information processing; H.5.2 [User interface]: Evaluation/methodology

General Terms: Measurement, Experimentation

Keywords: User engagement; engagement prediction; online controlled experiment; sensitivity; quality metrics

1. INTRODUCTION

Online controlled experiments, or A/B testing, have become the state-of-the-art technique to improve web services based on data-driven decisions [16]. It is utilized by many web companies, e.g., web search engines such as Bing [6, 16] and Google [28], social networks like Facebook [1], etc. The largest ones have designed special experimental platforms that allow them to run A/B tests at large scale (e.g., hundreds of concurrent experiments per day) [28, 15].

An A/B test compares two variants of a service[1] at a time by exposing them to two user groups and by measuring the difference between them in terms of a key metric (e.g., the revenue, the number of visits, etc.), also known as an overall evaluation criterion [18]. The ability of the metric to detect the statistically significant difference when the treatment effect exists is referred to as the *sensitivity* of the test. Improvement of the sensitivity is quite challenging, because the better it is, the smaller changes of the service could be detected by an experiment.

The straightforward way to improve the sensitivity, or the *power*, of a controlled experiment is to increase the amount of the observed statistical data that could be done either by increasing the population of users, participating in the experiment, or by conducting the experiment for a sufficient period of time. Both approaches have disadvantages. First, the amount of data is upper-bounded by the available web service traffic, and the growth of traffic per experiment reduces the number of experiments conducted per year [28, 7]. Second, increasing the size of a treatment group in the treatment group is always not desirable, as any treatment may have a negative effect[2]. Third, the sooner an experiment finishes, the sooner the treatment variant of the system is shipped or is returned for rework. So, the described ways of improving the sensitivity of an A/B test are not preferred, because they are contrary to the main purposes of an experimentation platform: to run many experiments and to get their results fast [28].

The power of a controlled experiment depends on the variance of the key metric used in the test [18], hence, a variance reduction could serve as another way to improve the sensitivity. The basic examples of such approaches are discussed in [18]: the use of a key metric with lower variance and the elimination of users who were not affected by the service change in the treatment group[3]. The applicability of these approaches is limited and strongly depends on the case of a conducted experiment. Namely, an experimental platform usually has a standardized success criteria, which utilizes a small set of key metrics to make the final decision on the treatment variant of the service [15]. These metrics are usually selected with respect to some business-related criteria of a considered service and are aligned with its long-term goals (like the number of sessions per user for a search engine [14]). Hence, finding an alternative for them is non-trivial

[1]e.g., a current version of the service (the control variant) and a new one (the treatment variant)

[2]Actually, experiments with negative result form a noticeable fraction among all experiments [13].

[3]For instance, if an update of the ranking algorithm of a search engine is made only for the small amount of queries, then only the users submitted these queries should be kept in the treatment group.

WWW 2015, May 18–22, 2015, Florence, Italy.
ACM 978-1-4503-3469-3/15/05.
http://dx.doi.org/10.1145/2736277.2741116.

and challenging [4], that is why a modification of an existing standardized metric is preferred.

The variance reduction techniques (the stratification and control variates), used in Monte Carlo simulations, were also applied [7] in the A/B testing. Though, they do not have the above-mentioned drawbacks and lead to a noticeable variance reduction, these techniques are based on the utilization of pre-experiment data and, hence, are limited in their applicability as well.

In our paper, we propose a novel method to improve sensitivity of online controlled experiments that exploits the prediction of the future behavior of an *individual* user based solely on the user's behavior observed during the experiment. The intuition of this method is the following. We know (as mentioned above) that the longer an A/B experiment is conducted, the higher its sensitivity. Therefore, we can try to peek into the future behavior of each user participated in the experiment, and, based on the predicted user behaviors, calculate the evaluation metric for the experiment as if it was conducted beyond its actual time period. Hence, we expect improvement of the sensitivity as if the experiment was extended, while the actual experiment duration was not increased.

While our approach could be applied to any online metric of system performance (which is calculated over user data) we investigate it for the case of user engagement metrics. User engagement reflects how often the user solves her needs (e.g., to search something) by means of the considered service (e.g., a search engine). On the one hand, these metrics are measurable in the short-term experiment period, and, on the other hand, they are predictive of the long-term success of the company [14, 15, 16, 25]. That is why engagement metrics are often considered to be most appropriate for online evaluation. In this study, we pay special attention to the metrics that reflect the loyalty aspect of engagement: the state-of-the-art *number of sessions per user* metric [14, 27] (which is accepted as the "North-star" for A/B testing evaluation in major search engine companies like Bing [15, 16]) and the recently proposed *absence time* metric [9]. Our approach raises the problem of prediction of the future individual user engagement. To the best of our knowledge, no existing study on user engagement investigated such a prediction problem[4].

Finally, our approach could be used simultaneously with other sensitivity improvement methods (i.e., with stratification, control variates [7], transformation of the metric, filtration of the treatment group [18], etc.) and, hence, is not an a substitute, but rather a complement to them.

To sum up, our study considers the problem, which coincides with the *emerging Internet companies' needs*: to run *more* online controlled experiments and to get their results on a significant level *faster*. Specifically, the major contributions of our work include:

- The solution to the problem of predicting the exact future values of engagement metrics of individual user behavior.
- Utilization of this predictor for the sensitivity improvement of online controlled experiments.
- Validation of our sensitivity improvement approach on real online experiments run at Yandex, first, demonstrating the growth of the number of statistically significant A/B experiments and, second, detecting the treatment effect of an A/B test faster (up to 50% of saved time) with the same level of statistical significance.

[4]The only study [27] was devoted to the binary prediction of user engagement increase/decrease in the future week. In our study, we focus on predicting the exact values of the user engagement metrics.

The rest of the paper is organized as follows. In Section 2, the related work on A/B testing and user engagement is discussed. In Section 3, our sensitivity improvement approach is presented. In Section 4, the six studied user engagement measures are introduced and a brief analysis of them is presented. In Section 5, our user engagement prediction problem is stated and its solution is evaluated by a large series of experiments. In Section 6, we show the results of applying our sensitivity improvement approach to several A/B experiments and discuss its possible extensions. In Section 7, the study's conclusions and our plans for the future work are presented.

2. RELATED WORK

We compare our research with other studies in two aspects. The first one relates to online controlled experiments and, specifically, to the sensitivity improvement. The second one concerns user engagement with web services.

Online controlled experiment studies. The theoretical details of the online controlled experiment methodology were widely described in the existing works [22, 17, 18], and we conduct our experiments in accordance with them. A rich practical experience of using this methodology for different evaluation cases in many web companies was studied recently [13, 19, 28, 15]. These studies concern, inter alia, experiments with different components of a web service (the user interface [13, 8], ranking algorithms [27, 8], etc.), large-scale experimental infrastructure [28, 15], different aspects of user behavior and interaction with a web service (clicks [14, 16], speed [19, 16], abandonment [16], periodicity [8], etc.), and so on. Some of existing works focused on the study of the trustworthiness of the results of an A/B test. Various pitfalls and puzzling results of online controlled experimentation were shared in [4, 14] and several "rules of thumb" were discussed in [16]. In our work, we were aware of all these experiences and pitfalls during our A/B experimentation.

Basic sensitivity improvement techniques for an online controlled experiment were concerned in [18]: increasing of the experiment duration or of the user population, participated in the experiment [5]; the use of another evaluation metric with lower variance [8]; and the elimination of users who were not affected by the service change in the treatment group [27]. More sophisticated variation reduction techniques were proposed in [7]: the stratification and the usage of control variates based on pre-experiment data. The authors of [16] noted that the reduction of skewness of the evaluation metric used in an A/B experiment could also improve the sensitivity (e.g., transformation of the metric or capping its values [16]). The sensitivity improvement for two-stage online controlled experiments was proposed in [6]. All these methods have their own disadvantages and limitations in their applicability (as discussed in Section 1). We propose an alternative approach to improve the sensitivity, which is based on predicting future user behavior and does not possess the limitations of the ones described above: no use of pre- or post-experiment data; no dependance on the particular case of the service change (or comparison) under evaluation; and applicability to a wide range of metrics that could be predicted for an individual user.

User engagement with web services. Existing studies of user engagement with a web service and, particularly, a search engine are three-fold. First, several studies focused on analysis of user behavior. Some of them discovered the relationship between search success and search engine reuse [30, 11]. Some others concerned behavioral patterns of users (e.g., simultaneous usage of several search engines [30] or periodicity of user engagement with a search engine usage [8]) and models of web sites with respect to user behavior (e.g., w.r.t. multitasking user behavior [20] or w.r.t. popularity, activity, and loyalty among users [21]). In our work, we present a brief analysis of the correlations between several user engagement metrics including the state-of-the-art "number of sessions" and the recently proposed "absence time".

Second, some studies focused on the prediction of future changes in user engagement. Prediction of how a user switches (no switch, persistent switch, or oscillating behavior) between search engines during 26 weeks was studied in [30]. The authors of [27] predict user engagement increase/decrease in the future week (they did not attempt to put this into any practical use, e.g., for sensitivity improvement). Among the features of the classifier they built, there were both engagement measures (the numbers of sessions, queries, clicks) and some non-engagement ones (query types, user satisfaction, etc.) observed during either one or three preceding weeks. The output of such a classifier could not be straightforwardly integrated in the A/B testing methodology to improve the sensitivity of evaluation metric due to the lack of the interpretable quantity of that output (see Sec. 3 for details). The prediction of the exact values of a user engagement metric provides an approximation of the original evaluation metric, which thus can serve as an interpretable metric itself, but it was not investigated in existing studies to the best of our knowledge. In our work, we introduce such prediction methodology for different user engagement metrics including the commonly used numbers of sessions, queries, clicks, and the recently proposed absence time.

Third, there are papers devoted to user engagement as an evaluation metric in online controlled experiments. In [14, 15, 16] the number of sessions per user was stated to be one of the key metrics used in Bing's experimentation platform. The authors of [27] evaluated different changes in search relevance of a popular search engine by means of A/B testing with respect to this engagement metric and several non-engagement measures reflecting query types and user satisfaction. The absence time (the time between two user visits) on a par with other engagement metrics was applied to compare different ranking algorithms used at Yahoo! Answers [9] and to evaluate a web search engine changes in ranking algorithm and user interface [3]. The novel periodicity engagement metrics of user behavior (resulted from the Discrete Fourier transform of 4 state-of-the-art engagement measures) were applied in [8] to evaluate, by means of A/B experiments, different changes of the search engine ranking algorithm, changes of the user interface, and changes of the engine's efficiency. In our work, we study the sensitivity improvement of controlled experiments with several user engagement metrics that are widely used in the described literature (see details in Sec. 4).

3. FRAMEWORK

Background. In A/B testing, users, participated in an experiment, are randomly exposed to one of two variants of the service, the control (A) and the treatment (B) variants (e.g., the current production version of the service and its update), in order to compare them [18, 14, 16]. The comparison is based on *the evaluation metric* (also known as the online service quality metric, the overall evaluation criterion, etc.). In this paper, we consider "per user metrics" [4], which are calculated for each individual user and, then, are averaged over all users in each experiment variant[5]. Namely, let us consider a measure $\mathtt{M}(u,\mathbb{T})$ of user interaction with the service (e.g., the number of clicks) during the experiment period $\mathbb{T}$. For each user group $\mathcal{U}_A$ and $\mathcal{U}_B$, we calculate the average values[6] $\mathtt{M}^X(\mathbb{T}) = \mathrm{avg}_{u\in\mathcal{U}_X}\mathtt{M}(u,\mathbb{T}), X = A, B$. After that, their absolute and relative differences are calculated[7]: $\Delta_\mathbb{T} = \mathtt{M}^B(\mathbb{T}) - \mathtt{M}^A(\mathbb{T})$ and $\mathrm{Diff}_\mathbb{T} = \chi \cdot \Delta_\mathbb{T}/\mathtt{M}^A(\mathbb{T})$.

Nonetheless, the quantities $\Delta_\mathbb{T}$ and $\mathrm{Diff}_\mathbb{T}$ could not serve themselves as indicators of positive or negative consequences of the evaluated treatment variant of the service. The difference between the evaluation metrics over groups should be controlled by a statistical significance test. In our study, we utilize widely applicable *two-sample t-test* (as in [7, 27, 6]) to decide weather the metric of the treatment user group B is significantly larger or smaller than that of the control one. This test is based on *t-statistic*:

$$\Delta_\mathbb{T}/\sqrt{\sigma_A^2(\mathtt{M}(\mathbb{T}))\cdot|\mathcal{U}_A|^{-1} + \sigma_B^2(\mathtt{M}(\mathbb{T}))\cdot|\mathcal{U}_B|^{-1}}, \quad (1)$$

where $\sigma_X^2(\mathtt{M}(\mathbb{T}))$ is the standard deviation of the measure $\mathtt{M}(\cdot,\mathbb{T})$ over users $\mathcal{U}_X, X = A, B$. The larger the absolute value of the t-statistic, the lower the probability (also known as *p-value*) of *the null hypothesis*, which assumes that the observed difference is caused by random fluctuations, and the variants are not actually different. If the p-value is lower than the threshold $p_{\mathrm{val}} \leq 0.05$ (commonly used [18, 14, 7, 27, 16]), then the test rejects the null hypothesis, and the difference $\Delta_\mathbb{T}$ is assumed to be statistically significant. The additional details of the A/B testing framework could be found in the survey and practical guide [18].

The future user behavior prediction approach. As it was shown above, any evaluation metric is calculated based on some time period $\mathbb{T} = [0, T)$, i.e., on the experiment period. One way to improve the sensitivity of an A/B test is to conduct it longer [18], i.e., to increase the length of the period $\mathbb{T}$. *The main idea of this paper is to make it virtually by peeking into the future user behavior.*

Suppose that, for a considered measure M and for each user $u \in \mathcal{U}$, we are able to forecast the value of the measure M, calculated over some forecast T_f-day period based on some user behavior data $\mathbf{F}_{T_p}(u)$ observed during the first T_p days of the target period. We denote this predicted value of the true measure by $\mathtt{P}_{\mathtt{M},T_f}(\mathbf{F}_{T_p}(u))$. If the length T of an A/B experiment equals to T_p, then we are able to predict the user

[5]This type of metrics (e.g., the number of sessions per user) is very popular in the online controlled experimentation [14]. However, there are also frequently used non-per user metrics [4] like the annual revenue [16].

[6]In order to distinguish the method of calculating the value $\mathtt{M}(u,\mathbb{T})$ for a user, from the value $\mathtt{M}^X(\mathbb{T})$, calculated for a user group X, the first one is referred to as *a measure* and the second one is referred to as *a metric* in our work.

[7]The factor χ is randomly chosen once in our study in order to hide real values for confidentiality reasons.

measure $\mathtt{M}(u,\cdot)$ over *the post-experiment period* $\mathbb{T}_f = [0, T_f)$ and calculate the evaluation metric $\mathtt{M}^X(\cdot), X = A, B$, (based on the predicted values) as if the A/B test was conducted beyond its actual time period. We will use the notations $\widetilde{\mathtt{M}}(u, \mathbb{T}_f) = \mathrm{P}_{\mathtt{M},T_f}(\mathbf{F}_T(u)) \approx \mathtt{M}(u, \mathbb{T}_f)$ and $\widetilde{\mathtt{M}}^X(\mathbb{T}_f) \approx \mathtt{M}^X(\mathbb{T}_f)$ for the predicted user measure and its average values over the user groups $X = A, B$ respectively. Thereby, we forecast the metric $\mathtt{M}(\cdot, \mathbb{T}_f)$, which would be calculated, if the A/B test period has been $[0, T_f)$ instead of $[0, T_p)$. We refer to this method of improving an evaluation metric as *the future user behavior prediction approach* (***FUBPA***).

First, our approach differs from the naive one, where prediction of the metric value $\mathtt{M}^X(\mathbb{T}_f)$ for each group $X = A, B$, (or of their difference $\Delta_{\mathbb{T}}$) is based on their trends, observed during the A/B experiment (i.e., on the metric values $\mathtt{M}^X([0, t))$ for some $t \leq T$) [14]. This method does not provide the significance level of the forecast difference due to the absence of data per experimental unit (i.e., per user in our case), and, thus, could not be used to improve sensitivity of A/B tests. On the contrary, our approach provides data for each user and, therefore, allows to calculate t-statistic.

Second, our approach differs from the utilization of a binary classifier of increase/decrease of a considered user measure in a post-experiment period (as it is proposed in [27] for the number of sessions). A fundamental shortcoming of such a classifier is that it could not be straightforwardly integrated in the A/B testing methodology. In fact, its outputs should be transformed to an evaluation metric first. One clear solution is to take the fraction of users whose engagement is predicted to grow. Another solution could be the averaged probability of growth estimated by the classifier. In any case, there is no reason why the obtained metric will correlate with the original user engagement metric accepted in the company. Hence, its difference $\mathrm{Diff}_{\mathbb{T}}$ could not provide an insight on the difference of the original metric, which may be fatal both for understanding the A/B experiment's result and for the taken decision. For instance, a drop in the fraction of users with increased number of clicks on ads could be observed simultaneously with a growth in the number of clicks per user. The latter evaluation metric has the direct connection with the annual revenue of a considered company. On the contrary, in our approach, the approximation $\widetilde{\mathtt{M}}^X(\mathbb{T}_f)$ is trained to be as close as possible to the baseline metric $\mathtt{M}$.

Finally, the approximation is a surrogate of different simple measures $\mathbf{F}_{T_p}(u)$ (which are used as features in the predictor). Therefore, *the FUBPA could be also treated as a method to combine a series of evaluation metrics ([4]), targeting the combined metric to be similar to a desirable evaluation metric in future.* The rest of this section is devoted to the theoretical analysis of the FUBPA approach.

Relation between prediction quality and sensitivity. Denote $m(u) = \mathtt{M}(u, \mathbb{T}_f)$ the metric over users $u \in \mathcal{U}$. Denote $\widetilde{m}(u) = \widetilde{\mathtt{M}}(u, \mathbb{T}_f)$ its predictor. W.l.o.g., we assume that the mean value $\mathbb{E}(m)$ equals 0. We also assume that our prediction is unbiased, i.e., its mean value $\mathbb{E}(\widetilde{m})$ is also equal to zero. In this case, the standard deviation σ_e of the prediction error $e := m - \widetilde{m}$ is, by definition, the Root Mean Square Error (RMSE) of the predictor $\widetilde{m}$. We have

$$\sigma_m^2 = \sigma_e^2 + \sigma_{\widetilde{m}}^2 + 2\mathrm{Cov}(e, \widetilde{m}), \qquad (2)$$

where σ_ξ^2 denotes the standard deviation of a variable ξ.

Note that, for any predictor m', the optimal predictor in the class $\{cm' \mid c \in \mathbb{R}\}$ is $\widehat{m'} := (\mathrm{Cov}(m, m')/\sigma_{m'}^2)m'$, since it provides the minimum of the mean squared error $\sigma_{m-cm'}^2 = c^2\sigma_{m'}^2 - 2c\mathrm{Cov}(m, m') + \sigma_m^2$. Therefore, if the class of prediction models is closed under scalar multiplication[8], for the optimal predictor $\widetilde{m}$, we have $\mathrm{Cov}(m, \widetilde{m}) = \sigma_{\widetilde{m}}^2$, and thus

$$\mathrm{Cov}(e, \widetilde{m}) = \mathrm{Cov}(m - \widetilde{m}, \widetilde{m}) = \mathrm{Cov}(m, \widetilde{m}) - \sigma_{\widetilde{m}}^2 = 0.$$

Therefore, the identity (2) implies that, in the case of an optimal predictor, the RMSE and the standard deviations of the metric σ_m and its predictor $\sigma_{\widetilde{m}}$ are connected by the following identity

$$\sigma_{\widetilde{m}}^2 = \sigma_m^2 - \mathrm{RMSE}^2(m, \widetilde{m}). \qquad (3)$$

This implies the following clear finding. The better the prediction quality in terms of RMSE, the greater the variance of the obtained surrogate measure $\widetilde{m}$. On the one hand, increasing of the prediction quality provides a better approximation of the original measure $m(u)$ and may lead to a better online metric $\mathtt{M}(\mathbb{T}_f)$. On the other hand, better prediction implies greater variance, which may affect the sensitivity of the metric (see t-statistics in Eq. (1)). Hence, we conclude that the prediction quality does not directly translate into the growth of the metric sensitivity. For example, we may expect that a 10% growth of prediction quality over a baseline may lead to a significant sensitivity improvement, while further growth of quality does not improve the obtained metric.

4. USER ENGAGEMENT

Engagement measures. We use the logs of Yandex[9], one of the most popular global search engines, in order to study user engagement. For each user[10], we study 6 popular engagement measures, which represent both loyalty and activity aspects of user engagement. For a considered period of time (a day, a week, a month, etc.), we study the following engagement measures calculated over this time period:

- the number of sessions (`S`);
- the number of queries (`Q`);
- the number of clicks (`C`);
- the presence time (`PT`);
- the number of clicks per query (`CpQ` or `CTR`);
- the absence time per session (`ATpS`).

Following common practice [12, 14, 9, 27, 3, 8], we define a session as a sequence of user actions whose dwell times are less than 30 minutes. The presence time `PT` is measured as the sum of all session lengths (in seconds) observed during the considered time period, while the total absence time is measured as the length of the considered time period minus the presence time. Note that the measures `S`, `Q`, `C`, and `PT` are additive with respect to the time period. The measure `ATpS` is calculated as the total absence time divided by the

[8]This condition is satisfied by a wide range of prediction models including linear model and the state-of-the-art Friedman's gradient boosting decision tree model [10], which are applied in Section 5.

[9]`http://www.yandex.com`

[10]We use cookie IDs [18] to identify users as done in other studies on user engagement [9, 20, 27, 8].

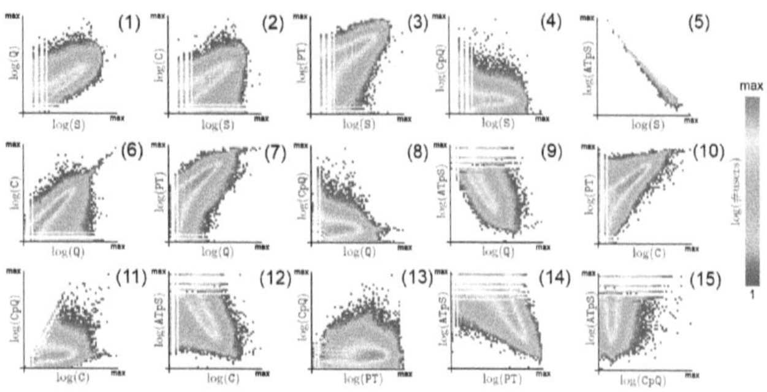

Figure 1: The joint distributions of users $\mathcal{U}$ w.r.t. each pair of the studied measures $\mathfrak{M}$ calculated over a 2-week period.

number of user sessions S[11]. The number of clicks per query CpQ could be regarded as *the CTR of the search engine result pages* as well. The measures S and ATpS represent the *user loyalty* [25, 14, 9, 27, 8], whereas the measures Q, C, PT, and CpQ represent the *user activity* [18, 25, 9, 7, 8] aspects of user engagement [25]. The set of all measures is denoted by $\mathfrak{M} = \{\texttt{S}, \texttt{Q}, \texttt{C}, \texttt{PT}, \texttt{CpQ}, \texttt{ATpS}\}$. Before proceeding to the main problems studied in this paper, we present a brief analysis of these measures. We investigate the relationships between them and their persistence across time in order to have a better interpretation of the prediction quality obtained in the next section.

Correlation between measures. We calculate the correlations between the studied measures in the following way. Let one consider two measures $\texttt{M}_1, \texttt{M}_2 \in \mathfrak{M}$, a certain set of users $\mathcal{U}$, and a certain time period $\mathbb{T}$. Then, these measures $\texttt{M}_i(u, \mathbb{T}), i = 1, 2$, are calculated for each user $u \in \mathcal{U}$ *over the whole* time period $\mathbb{T}$ (e.g., the total number of sessions during the entire period). We consider a user as a random event and calculate the Pearson's correlation coefficient $\mathrm{Corr}_{\mathcal{U}}$ over users $\mathcal{U}$.

In the analysis of this section, we use a *2-week period*[12] from March, 2013 as the time period $\mathbb{T}$, and we consider all active users of the search engine during the period $\mathbb{T}$ as the set $\mathcal{U}$ (its size $|\mathcal{U}| \gg 10^7$). Table 1 reports the values of the correlations $\mathrm{Corr}_{\mathcal{U}}$ between all measures from $\mathfrak{M}$. We highlighted in **boldface** the ones with the highest absolute value in each column, while the smallest ones are underlined. First, one sees that all additive measures S, Q, C, and PT are noticeably well correlated ($\mathrm{Corr}_{\mathcal{U}} \geq 0.81$). Second, the measure CpQ has low correlation with other measures ($|\mathrm{Corr}_{\mathcal{U}}| \leq 0.083$) except with the number of clicks C ($\mathrm{Corr}_{\mathcal{U}} = 0.175$). Third, the absence time ATpS is mostly negatively correlated with the other measures. This observation coincides with the intuition that the more frequently a user utilizes the service (higher the number of sessions, queries, etc.), the lower the absence time.

Next, we plot the joint distributions[13] of users $\mathcal{U}$ w.r.t. each pair of the studied measures $\mathfrak{M}$ calculated over the 2-week period $\mathbb{T}$ (i.e., 15 heat maps in total) in Fugure 1. First, the previously observed close relationships between all additive measures S, Q, C, and PT are also seen in their joint distributions: the user population is concentrated near the main diagonal in the heat maps in Fig. 1 (1, 2, 3, 6, 7, and 10). The most consistent pattern is observed for the distribution of the number of queries Q and the number of clicks C (Fig. 1 (6)), which reveals a clear linear dependence between their logarithms. The maps Fig. 1 (4, 8, 11, 13, and 15) explain the very small correlation of CpQ with other measures reported in Table 1. Second, the negative correlation of the absence time ATpS with the other measures is also seen in Fig. 1 (5, 9, 12, 14, and 15), where the user population is concentrated along the secondary diagonal of the heat maps.

Table 1: Correlations $\mathrm{Corr}_{\mathcal{U}}$ between all engagement measures $\mathfrak{M}$ calculated over a 2-week period.

$\mathrm{Corr}_{\mathcal{U}}$	S	Q	C	PT	CpQ	ATpS
S	—	0.843	0.810	0.831	0.028	**−0.595**
Q	**0.843**	—	0.888	**0.910**	−0.001	−0.483
C	0.810	0.888	—	0.904	**0.175**	−0.478
PT	0.831	**0.910**	**0.904**	—	0.081	−0.461
CpQ	0.028	−0.001	0.175	0.081	—	−0.083
ATpS	−0.595	−0.483	−0.478	−0.461	−0.083	—

Long-term measure persistence. We also identify the relationship between the values of the same measure calculated over two different time periods. Namely, the Pearson's correlation coefficient over users $\mathcal{U}$ is calculated for the values $\texttt{M}(\cdot, \mathbb{T}_1)$ and $\texttt{M}(\cdot, \mathbb{T}_2)$ of each measure $\texttt{M} \in \mathfrak{M}$, where $\mathbb{T}_1$ and $\mathbb{T}_2$ are two *consecutive 2-week periods*[14]. The correlation are presented at the bottom of Fig. 2. The highest value is highlighted in **boldface**, and the lowest one is underlined. The joint distributions of users $\mathcal{U}$ w.r.t. each engagement measure from $\mathfrak{M}$ calculated over the 2-week periods are also captured in Fig. 2. Almost all measures (except for CpQ) have a high persistence over time ($\mathrm{Corr}_{\mathcal{U}} \geq 0.61$). Hence, *we expect that the values of these measures over the future may be better predicted by their values over the observed period than the ones of* CpQ.

In this section, we presented the main user engagement measures under our study and briefly analyzed them in different ways. These observations will help us clearly understand the findings in the next section devoted to the prediction of user engagement.

5. USER ENGAGEMENT PREDICTION

In our work, we study the user engagement prediction problem in the following setting. We suppose that one has user data observed during a period of time $\mathbb{T}_p$ (the *past*, or the *observed time period*), and, based on these data, one needs to predict *the exact value* of a target engagement measure calculated over an increased period of time $\mathbb{T}_f \supseteq \mathbb{T}_p$ (the *forecast time period*) for each *individual user*. We consider the 6 engagement measures $\mathfrak{M}$ presented in the previous section as our targets.

The models. We utilized two models to predict the exact values of the targets. The first one is a state-of-the-art Friedman's gradient boosting decision tree model [10]. We used a proprietary implementation of the machine learning algo-

[11] In our study, we also considered another definition of this measure: the sum of times between consecutive user sessions divided by the number of absences (i.e., by S − 1), and, if only one session is observed, then it is equal to 0. However, such variant of measure demonstrated lower persistence over time, noticeably lower predictability, and the OEC based on it failed unacceptable number of A/A tests.

[12] It is a popular length of A/B experiments [14, 27, 16, 8].

[13] We hide all absolute values for confidentiality reasons.

[14] In our study, we consider all users $\mathcal{U}$ that used the search engine during the period $\mathbb{T}_1$ (and may use it during the forecast period), while users who started using it in the period $\mathbb{T}_2$ are not included in the set $\mathcal{U}$.

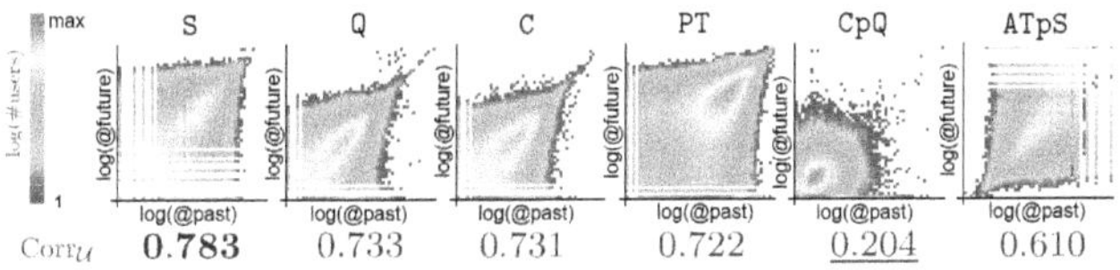

Figure 2: Correlations and the joint distributions of users $\mathcal{U}$ w.r.t. to each engagement measure from the set $\mathfrak{M}$ between two consecutive 2-week periods.

rithm with 1000 iterations and 1000 trees, which appeared to be the best settings during validation. The second model is a linear regression model with L_2 regularization. The learning rate of the decision tree model and the regularization parameter of the linear model were adjusted by means of cross-validation technique during optimization. The optimal settings were found with respect to *the mean squared error* used as the loss function.

The data. In order to conduct our experiments, we used the logs of user search activity on the popular search engine Yandex. We collected user data from two non-intersecting 34-day periods of 2013 year, the earlier period was used to form the training data set and the later one was used to collect the test data set. Since the day of the week may have a considerable impact on the user behavior, we would not like the data set to be biased to some particular day of the week the observed period $\mathbb{T}_p$ begins. Therefore, for each of the 34-day periods, each user is represented by 7 feature vectors in the data set (treated as 7 different examples) that are calculated based on the raw user behavior data truncated at $0, 1, \ldots, 6$ first days, so that the observed period begins on the 1st, 2nd, ..., 7th day of the 34-day period. Further, we randomly sampled these data sets 20 times, obtaining smaller training and test data sets of equal size (of $> 10^5$ users) in order to, first, reduce the data size, which should comply with computational constrains, and, second, apply *the paired two-sample t-test* to measure the significance level of the obtained results.

The performance measure. Let us consider the naive average prediction model ($\text{avg}_{\mathcal{U}}$), which, for each user from the test data set, predicts the target value as *the average* of the values of that target *over all users* in the training data set. One could treat it as a model, which utilizes *zero features*. Denote the RMSE value calculated over the test set for a given observed and forecast periods ($\mathbb{T}_p$ and $\mathbb{T}_f$), for a given target (**tg**), for a given prediction model (m), and for a given feature set (Φ), by $\text{RMSE}(\mathbb{T}_p, \mathbb{T}_f, \mathbf{tg}, m, \Phi)$. In the results reported below, we use the *normalized RMSE* (nRMSE) defined as

$$\text{nRMSE}(\mathbb{T}_p, \mathbb{T}_f, \mathbf{tg}, m, \Phi) = \frac{\text{RMSE}(\mathbb{T}_p, \mathbb{T}_f, \mathbf{tg}, m, \Phi)}{\text{RMSE}(\mathbb{T}_p, \mathbb{T}_f, \mathbf{tg}, \text{avg}_{\mathcal{U}}, \varnothing)}.$$

This performance measure allow us, first, to hide the RMSE values due to confidential reasons, second, to compare the prediction quality between different targets and forecast periods, and, finally, to improve our understanding of weather a studied prediction model is better or not than a naive baseline model (the average prediction) by comparing the nRMSE w.r.t. 1.

The observed and target periods. In our experimentation, we compare different feature sets and prediction models for 14-day observed periods $\mathbb{T}_p$ and for 28-day forecast period $\mathbb{T}_f$. We remind that these are popular lengths of A/B experiments [14, 27, 16, 8]. However, the dependence of the prediction quality on the period lengths is analyzed at the end of this section.

Table 2: The top-20 features w.r.t. the improvement over the baseline feature set in terms of RMSE for the measure S with $|\mathbb{T}_p| = 14$ and $|\mathbb{T}_f| = 28$.

Decision Trees			Linear Regression		
M	Feature	Impr.	M	Feature	Impr.
S	lg**avg**	−0.43%	S	$\mathbf{DFT_A}$[1]	−0.28%
ATpS	lg$\mathbf{TS_c}$[14]	−0.40%	S	lg$\mathbf{DFT_A}$[1]	−0.25%
ATpS	$\mathbf{Ent_{Perm}}$[5]	−0.20%	C	$\mathbf{GrPos_1}$	−0.24%
S	$\mathbf{Ent_{Ap}}$[2]	−0.20%	PT	$\mathbf{GrPos_1}$	−0.23%
ATpS	lg$\mathbf{TS_c}$[13]	−0.19%	PT	$\mathbf{GrPos_2}$	−0.23%
S	$\mathbf{sum_2}$	−0.18%	S	lg**max**	−0.22%
ATpS	lg$\mathbf{Ent_{Perm}}$[5]	−0.18%	S	**std**	−0.21%
Q	$\mathbf{Ent_{Smpl}}$[6]	−0.18%	Q	$\mathbf{GrPos_1}$	−0.21%
ATpS	$\mathbf{Ent_{Perm}}$[6]	−0.17%	S	$\mathbf{GrPos_1}$	−0.21%
ATpS	lg**avg**	−0.17%	Q	lg$\mathbf{GrPos_1}$	−0.21%
S	$\mathbf{DFT_A}$[1]	−0.17%	S	lg$\mathbf{GrPos_1}$	−0.21%
Q	$\mathbf{Ent_{Ap}}$[2]	−0.16%	PT	$\mathbf{Ent_{Sh}}$	−0.20%
ATpS	$\mathbf{Ent_{Perm}}$[8]	−0.16%	ATpS	$\mathbf{Ent_{Sh}}$	−0.20%
ATpS	$\mathbf{Ent_{Perm}}$[8]	−0.15%	S	lg**std**	−0.20%
S	lg$\mathbf{Ent_{Ap}}$[2]	−0.14%	ATpS	lg$\mathbf{Ent_{Sh}}$	−0.19%
S	lg$\mathbf{sum_2}$	−0.14%	S	$\mathbf{Ent_{Ap}}$[2]	−0.18%
ATpS	$\mathbf{Ent_{Sort}}$[8]	−0.13%	ATpS	$\mathbf{DFT_A}$[1]	−0.18%
Q	$\mathbf{Ent_{Ap}}$[6]	−0.13%	S	lg**max**	−0.18%
S	$\mathbf{GrPos_4}$	−0.13%	PT	lg$\mathbf{Ent_{Sh}}$	−0.17%
ATpS	$\mathbf{Ent_{Perm}}$[7]	−0.13%	ATpS	$\mathbf{Ent_{Perm}}$[2]	−0.17%

Features. Now we discuss the features we utilize in the user engagement prediction. Each engagement measure $\mathtt{M} \in \mathfrak{M}$ can be translated into several scalar features in different ways. Specifically, we consider the following *calculation and transformation methods.*

The total feature. First, we calculate the measure M over the observed time period $\mathbb{T}_p$ (e.g., for $\mathtt{M} = \mathtt{S}$, it is the total number of sessions over the time period $\mathbb{T}_p$). This is the same as the predicted target, but over the observed time period $\mathbb{T}_p$ instead of the forecast one $\mathbb{T}_f$. We denote this feature by **Total**.

The time series. Second, we calculate the measure M over each day of the time period $\mathbb{T}_p$ and obtain a daily time series of length $|\mathbb{T}_p|$. We denote such feature vector by $\mathbf{TS_d}$. Then, for each day $t \in \mathbb{T}_p$, we calculate the measure M over the time period that starts on the first day of $\mathbb{T}_p$ and finishes on the day t. Thus, we obtain a cumulative time series of length $|\mathbb{T}_p|$. This feature vector is denoted by $\mathbf{TS_c}$.

The statistics features. Next, we consider the daily time series $\mathbf{TS_d} = \{x_t\}_{t=1}^{|\mathbb{T}_p|}$ and get basic statistics over it: the minimal (**min**), maximal (**max**), average (**avg**) values, the standard deviation (**std**), the median (**med**), the sum (**sum**), the sum of squares ($\mathbf{sum_2}$), and the sum of cubes ($\mathbf{sum_3}$) over days. Additionally, we calculate the variation of the time series (i.e., $\mathbf{var} := \sum_{t=1}^{|\mathbb{T}_p|-1} |x_{t+1} - x_t|$) and the number ($\mathbf{GrPos_\tau}$) of the values of the series not less than the threshold τ, which is chosen from among $1, 2, 4, 10, 20, 40$, and 100. Thus, we consider here 16 scalar features in total.

The derivative features. We calculate the finite differences of the first order $\mathbf{FD_1} := \{x_{t+1} - x_t\}_{t=1}^{|\mathbb{T}_p|-1}$ and of the second order $\mathbf{FD_2} := \{x_{t+2} - 2x_{t+1} + x_t\}_{t=1}^{|\mathbb{T}_p|-2}$ over the daily time series $\mathbf{TS_d}$. These $2|\mathbb{T}_p| - 3$ scalar features are analogs of the first and second derivatives in the discrete case. Similar first order finite differences over weekly time series were used in the classifier [27] and had one of the highest weights in the prediction settings. We also sort in descending order the differences $\mathbf{FD_1}$ ($\mathbf{FD_2}$) and replace each difference by its index in the original series, obtaining the integer sequence

$\mathbf{FD}_1^{\text{rank}}$ ($\mathbf{FD}_2^{\text{rank}}$), which describes the day of the highest difference, the day of the lowest difference, etc.

The periodicity features. We apply the *discrete Fourier transform (DFT)* [29] to the daily time series $\mathbf{TS_d}$: $X_k = \sum_{t=1}^{|\mathbb{T}_p|} x_t e^{-i\omega_k(t-1)}$, $\omega_k = \frac{2\pi k}{|\mathbb{T}_p|}$, $k \in \mathbb{Z}_{|\mathbb{T}_p|}$. Thus, we obtain $|\mathbb{T}_p|$ complex numbers (**DFT**), then we get their real parts (amplitudes $\mathbf{DFT_A}$) and their imaginary parts (phases $\mathbf{DFT_{Ph}}$). These $2|\mathbb{T}_p|$ scalar features encode periodicity in user engagement and were studied in the paper [8], where their long-term persistence is found to be better than the one of the daily time series. We also sort in descending order the amplitudes $\mathbf{DFT_A}$ and replace each amplitude by its index in the original series, obtaining the integer sequences $\mathbf{DFT_A^{rank}}$. This sequence describes which frequencies $\omega_k, k \in \mathbb{Z}_{|\mathbb{T}_p|}$, dominate among others, which one has the lowest amplitude, etc.

The entropy features. In order to get the average amount of information contained in daily user engagement series, we calculate entropy for our series $\mathbf{TS_d}$ in the following ways: (a) the Shannon entropy $\mathbf{Ent_{Sh}}$ as in [26]; (b) the Permutation entropies $\mathbf{Ent_{Perm}}$ as in [2], and the Sorting entropies $\mathbf{Ent_{Sort}}$ as in [2] of orders $n = 2, .., |\mathbb{T}_p| - 1$; (c) the Approximate entropies $\mathbf{Ent_{Ap}}$ as in [23, 24], and the Sample entropies $\mathbf{Ent_{Smpl}}$ as in [24] for $m = 2, .., |\mathbb{T}_p| - 2$.

Thus, we consider $14|\mathbb{T}_p| + 2$ scalar features for each of 6 engagement measures $\mathfrak{M}$ (i.e., 1188 in total). All features described above are considered both in normal and in logarithmic (where applicable) scales in order to better catch the differences between values of different magnitudes. Besides, we consider the day-of-the-week of the first day of the observed period $\mathbb{T}_p$ as an additional categorical feature **DoW** in order to better catch the influence of the position of the period w.r.t. the week cycle.

Feature selection. Note that statistics, derivative, periodicity, and entropy features are derivable from the source time series. Therefore, we expect that not all these features could provide a significant profit in prediction quality w.r.t. the source time series. Besides, utilization of the large number of features may lead to overfitting of the model[15] and unreasonable consumption of computational resources. Hence, we conduct feature selection by studying the profit in prediction quality of each scalar feature w.r.t. a baseline feature set. We consider the set $\{\mathbf{Total}, \mathbf{TS_d}\}$ calculated for all user engagement measures $\mathfrak{M}$ as the baseline feature set (it consists of $6|\mathbb{T}_p| + 6 = 90$ scalar features) in our feature selection procedure. Then, we train our models under the setup described at the beginning of this section for the baseline set and for this set extended by one of the other scalar features. We present the top-20 features w.r.t. the improvement of the baseline prediction quality in terms of RMSE for the number of sessions measure S in Table 2[16].

We see that both the periodicity and entropy features improve prediction quality, contrariwise, none of the derivative features shows any significant improvement with p-value $\leq$ 0.05. We selected the features that showed noticeable and significant improvement in several prediction tasks (i.e., targets and models) or for several user engagement measures. These features are: $\lg\mathbf{TS_d}[13-14]$, $\mathbf{TS_c}[12-13]$, $\lg\mathbf{TS_c}[12-14]$, $\mathbf{GrPos}_\tau$ for $\tau = 1, 2, 4, 10, 20, 40$, and 100, **min**, **max**, **lgmax**, **avg**, **lgavg**, **std**, **med**, $\mathbf{sum_2}$, $\mathbf{lgsum_2}$, $\mathbf{sum_3}$, **var**, *Re*$\mathbf{DFT}[1]$, *Im*$\mathbf{DFT}[1]$, $\mathbf{DFT_A}[1]$, $\mathbf{DFT_A^{rank}}[1]$, $\mathbf{Ent_{Sh}}$, $\mathbf{Ent_{Perm}}[3-6]$, $\mathbf{Ent_{Sort}}[2, 3, 4-8]$, $\mathbf{Ent_{Ap}}[2-9]$, $\mathbf{Ent_{Smpl}}[3-6]$, and **DoW**. All these features together with the baseline ones (**Total** and $\mathbf{TS_d}$) calculated over all user engagement measures are denoted by **Best** (307 scalar features in total).

Table 3: Comparison of feature sets in terms of nRMSE (relative improvement w.r.t. the first column) of prediction of each of the measures $\mathfrak{M}$ for $|\mathbb{T}_p| = 14$ and $|\mathbb{T}_f| = 28$.

Measures:		Target measure		All (i.e., $\mathfrak{M}$)		
Features:		Total	Total, $\mathrm{TS_d}$	Total	Total, $\mathrm{TS_d}$	Best
Target & Model		1 feat.	15 feat.	6 feat.	90 feat.	307 feat.
S	LR	0.334	−4.92%	−0.12%	−5.11%	−5.58%
	DT	0.34	−6.38%	−0.32%	−6.48%	−7.59%
Q	LR	0.37	−2.65%	−0.64%	−3.59%	−5.04%
	DT	0.411	−4.49%	−1.17%	−4.28%	−5.62%
C	LR	0.375	−2.52%	−1.12%	−4.21%	−5.4%
	DT	0.394	−5.31%	−1.9%	−5.23%	−6.49%
PT	LR	0.372	−2.49%	−1.35%	−4.47%	−4.94%
	DT	0.388	−4.82%	−1.86%	−5.41%	−6.57%
CpQ	LR	0.423	0%	−0.12%	−0.08%	−0.46%
	DT	0.44	−0.03%	−1.18%	−1.02%	−2.5%
ATpS	LR	0.458	−0.3%	−0.2%	−0.64%	−1.78%
	DT	0.456	−1.9%	−0.67%	−2.63%	−2.96%

Comparison of feature sets and prediction models. We evaluate the feature set **Best** for both the linear regression model and the decision tree model with respect to the following 4 baselines. The first baseline set consists of one scalar feature **Total** calculated for the target measure we predict. The second baseline includes 6 scalar features **Total** calculated for each user engagement measure from $\mathfrak{M}$. The last two baseline sets contain both **Total** and the daily time series $\mathbf{TS_d}$ calculated either for the target measure (15 scalar features in total), or for each measure from $\mathfrak{M}$ (90 scalar features). The nRMSE values for these 5 feature sets, for 2 models, and for 6 different targets are presented in Table 3, all differences are significant with p-value $\leq$ 0.05.

First, we see that our feature set **Best** outperforms all baselines. Second, we see that the feature set **Best** provides a higher improvement over the fourth baseline set than the addition of each scalar feature individually, what we did in our feature selection procedure (compare the top of Table 2 and two first rows in Table 3). Therefore, we conclude that the new features carry different information for prediction and are not interchangeable.

Third, the decision trees and the linear models show similar results. On the one hand, the linear regression model sometimes outperforms the former one for several targets, especially for a low number of features. On the other hand, we see that the decision tree model demonstrates a higher rate of improvement with the growth of the size of the feature set than the linear one. In the next experiments we mostly report the results only for the decision trees model, because it demonstrates the best results for loyalty measures (S and ATpS) and it is the state-of-the-art model.

Fourth, we see that the number of sessions S is the most predictable target measure in terms of nRMSE for any used feature set (e.g., the use of only one feature **Total** reduces

[15]In our work, we tried to train models based on all features. However, these models were outperformed by the models based on the time series features solely.

[16]We removed the identical features, such as **avg**, *Re*$\mathbf{DFT}[0]$, $\mathbf{DFT_A}[0]$, etc. from the lists.

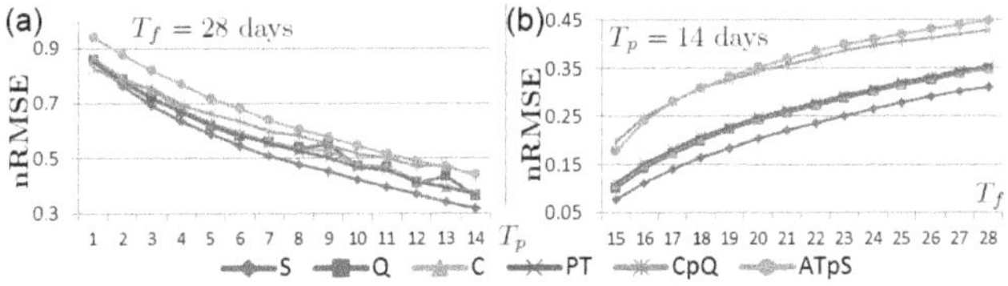

Figure 3: The dependence of prediction performance on (a) different $T_p = 1, .., 14$ for $T_f = 28$ and (b) different $T_f = 15, .., 28$ for $T_p = 14$ in terms of nRMSE.

the RMSE of the naive average baseline by 66.6%). The other additive target measures `Q`, `C`, and `PT` have almost the same nRMSE values and they are a little bit worse than the ones of `S`. The ratio target measures `CpQ` and `ATpS` have the worst prediction quality w.r.t. the naive average baseline. Moreover, the prediction quality for these two targets is very difficult to improve in comparison with the others. These observations coincide with our findings on the measures' persistence across time (compare the correlations $\mathrm{Corr}_{\mathcal{U},\mathbb{T}_{p/f}}$ in Fig. 2 and the first column of Table 3).

Fifth, the most noticeable quality improvement is observed, when we add the daily time series $\mathbf{TS_d}$ into the feature set (see col. 2 and 4 in the table) for all additive engagement measures (`S`, `Q`, `C`, and `PT`). This effect is expected, because all our novel features are derived from these time series (even the cumulative time series due to additivity of these measures). Note also that the quality for `CpQ` is improved noticeably when the feature set is extended by the other measures or the novel features, while the quality for `ATpS` also increases with the addition of the daily time series $\mathbf{TS_d}$ in the feature set.

At last, in order to understand the dependence of the prediction quality on the UE measures $\mathfrak{M}$ used in the set of features, we conduct the experiments to evaluate the drop in the performance caused by removal of each measure $\mathtt{M} \in \mathfrak{M}$. For all targets, we observe the highest performance drop, when we remove the features calculated for the target measure (e.g., ablation of all `S`-features decreases the nRMSE for prediction of the number of session `S` by 0.94%). In the other cases, the ablation of one of the measures connected with the activity aspect of user engagement (`Q`, `C`, `PT`, and `CpQ`) does not have a noticeable effect on the quality, while the user loyalty measures `S` and `ATpS` have a noticeable and significant influence on the prediction of any studied target (e.g., the ablation of all `S`-features decreases the nRMSE for prediction of the presence time `PT` by 0.24%). Finally, Fig. 3 demonstrates the nRMSE values for our best predictors learned for different combinations of the length T_p of the observed time period and the length T_f of the forecast one. We see that the closer these lengths are, the better the prediction quality.

To sum up, in this section, we studied the problem of prediction of the exact value of one of the six user engagement measures. We investigated the dependance of the prediction quality on the utilization of different user engagement measures, on the calculation/transformation techniques of translation them into features, and on the sizes of the observed and the forecast time periods. We conclude that *the use of almost all studied features could significantly improve the quality of user engagement prediction, and the dependance of this quality on the parameters of the prediction task agrees with the user engagement analysis provided in Section 4.*

6. A/B EXPERIMENTS

Experimental setup. In our paper, we consider 32 A/B experiments conducted on *real users* of the search engine (Yandex) in order to validate our approach of improving the sensitivity of key metrics (FUBPA, see Section 3 for details). Each experiment ran for at least two weeks. The user samples used in the A/B tests are all uniformly randomly selected, and the control and the treatment groups are of approximately the same size (at least, hundreds of thousands of users). Each experiment evaluates a change in one of the main components of the search engine: a change in the ranking algorithm, the engine response time, or a change in the user interface. During our A/B experimentation, 23 control experiments (so-called A/A tests) were conducted in order to check the correctness of the experimentation [18, 4]. We considered a commonly used threshold $p_{\mathrm{val}} = 0.05$ for the p-value of the statistical significance test (i.e., of two-sample t-test [7, 27, 6], see Sec. 3 for details).

In this section, the per-user metrics based on six user engagement measures from $\mathfrak{M}$ (introduced and analyzed in Sec. 4) are considered as our baseline evaluation criteria. Then, we study the modified variants of these metrics obtained by means of *the future user behavior prediction approach* (FUBPA) described in Sec. 3. Namely, for each user participated in an A/B test, we predict her future engagement based only on the data observed during the A/B test's period by means of the best decision tree model from Sec. 5, that have been trained in advance[17]. We consider forecast time periods up to the 28-th day since the experiment start, and, hence, we get several novel modifications for each metric $\mathtt{M} \in \mathfrak{M}$. In this section, we refer to them as $\mathtt{FUBPA}_{X \to Y}$, where X is the considered duration of the experiment in days and Y is the length of the forecast period in days. For instance, $\mathtt{FUBPA}_{7 \to 21}$ is the evaluation metric, which predicts (based on the first 7 days of the experiment) the value of the considered metric `M` over 21 days since the experiment start, as if it was conducted for 21 days. Additionally, we predicted the metric value at the post-experiment periods. Such metric modifications, which are referred to as $\mathtt{FUBPA}^{post}_{X \to Y}$, predict the value of `M` over $(Y - X)$ days after the end of X-day experiment period.

A/A tests. First of all, we check our metrics against 23 A/A tests. An A/A test should be failed about 5% of the time for the p-value threshold 0.05 [18, 4], which is used in our work. Each of the metrics `C`, `PT`, `CpQ`, each of all their FUBPA modifications, and each of the post-experiment modifications (i.e., $\mathtt{FUBPA}^{post}_{X \to Y}$) of `ATpS` failed one A/A test. All other metrics and all other modifications did not fail any A/A test. Hence, all our metrics and all our modifications have an acceptable rate of A/A fails.

Example. We start our study from consideration of an example A/B experiment. It evaluates a treatment, which is an improvement of the ranking algorithm of the search engine. We look at the absence time metric `ATpS`. The results for this experiment are presented in Fig. 4. We see that the metric does not detect the treatment effect during the first 7 days of the experiment. However, its modification $\mathtt{FUBPA}_{4 \to 17}$ shows a statistically significant difference -0.4%

[17]They have been trained on the data obtained during the time period of February and March, 2013, before all our A/B experiments that were conducted from April, 2013 to September, 2014.

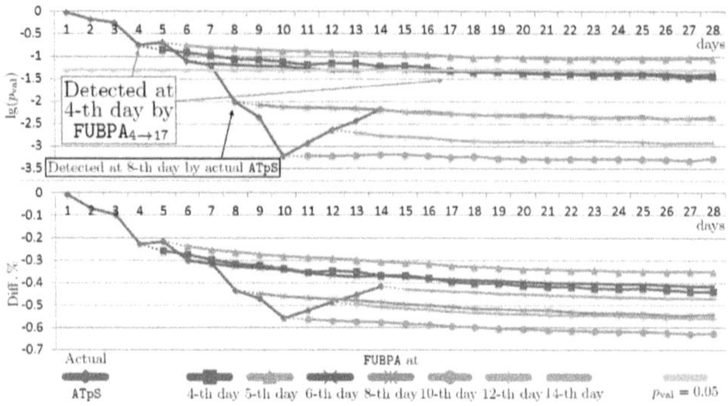

Figure 4: The Diff and p_{val} of ATpS observed during an example A/B test and of the estimations of ATpS by the $\mathtt{FUBPA}_{X\to Y}$ with different values of X and Y.

($p_{val} \le 0.048$). Thus, *the treatment effect is correctly*[18] *detected at the 4-th day since the experiment start by means of FUBPA, while the baseline metric* ATpS *does not detect the effect till the 8-th day* (i.e., one saves 50% of the time for this example). Note that the signs of the actual and the predicted differences Diff are the same. Moreover, it is observed for all FUBPA modifications. The magnitudes of the predicted Diff for $\mathtt{FUBPA}_{X\to Y}$ are also of the same order. However, their exact values are sometimes far from the actual ones and depend noticeably on the difference observed at the X-day for the actual metric. This finding correlates with the fact that the information from the last days of the observation period has a large impact on the prediction quality (see Sec. 5).

Overall detection of the treatment effect. Next, we discuss the results of application of our approach to our six user engagement metrics $\mathfrak{M}$ in order to improve sensitivity of 32 studied A/B experiments with 14-day duration. Table 4 summarizes the number of A/B experiments, whose treatment effect is detected (i.e., $p_{val} \le 0.05$) by each of the actual key metrics and each of its FUBPA modifications[19]. The best result in each column is underlined. Additionally, the number of A/B experiments, whose treatment effect is detected by a considered modification and is not detected by the corresponding baseline metric, is indicated in brackets. First, we see that the metrics based on the number of sessions measure S (i.e., the actual per-user metric and its FUBPA modifications) detect the treatment effects in a fewer number of A/B tests than the ones based on the absence time measure ATpS, which is assumed to be a novel alternative to S [9]. Thus, *the absence time appears to be more sensitive than the state-of-the-art number of sessions per user.* Second, the click-based metrics (i.e., the number of clicks per user C and the number of clicks per query per user CpQ) are more sensitive than the others. This observation is expected and exactly correlates with the "rule of thumb" #5 in [16], which states that clicks are easy to shift, while the number of sessions is hard to change.

Third, one could note that, for instance, the actual metric C detects the treatment effects in 8 A/B tests, while its modification $\mathtt{FUBPA}^{post}_{14\to 21}$ detects the ones in 8 A/B tests also, but one of them is new (i.e., it is not detected by C). It means that a FUBPA modification does not always detect the treatment effect in a test, where the baseline metric detects it. On the one hand, if the change of the service is already detected in such experiments, then we do not need to utilize sensitivity improvement approaches. On the other hand, one could use the FUBPA technique to ensure that the treatment effect will not disappear in the future (see further in this section). Nonetheless, in all those treatment effects that were detected both by a baseline metric and its FUBPA modifications, the sign and the magnitude of the relative difference value Diff are *the same.* This means that our modifications at least do not harm the decision taken after a successful experiment: to accept the evaluated change of the web service, or to reject it. In total, the baseline metrics detected the treatment effects in 17 A/B experiments (i.e., $p_{val} \le 0.05$ for at least one of the metrics), while, *after applying the FUBPA, we additionally detect the treatment effect in 3 tests.* Thereby, the FUBPA metrics increase this number from 53.125% to 62.5%, w.r.t. the number of all A/B tests. Thus, we conclude that *our FUBPA technique improves the sensitivity of the studied user engagement metrics and helps us to detect the treatment effect in more online controlled experiments.*

Discover of future metric sensitivity. Let us see how the FUBPA detects the actual future sensitivity of a baseline metric. We consider the metric CpQ, which detected the largest number of treatment effects. For these purposes, we consider our 32 A/B experiments as if they ran only for the first 7 days of their duration, and, based on these observations, we apply the FUBPA to our baseline metric. Further, we *consider only those A/B tests* that *have no detected* treatment effect w.r.t. the baseline metric over 7 days. For each FUBPA modification and for each A/B test, we look at the FUBPA modification and check if it expects appearing of the treatment effect in the future measurement of the baseline metric (i.e., in the future 7 days, 14 days, etc., depending on the type of the FUBPA). After that, we check it against the actual effect in the baseline metric measured for the considered A/B test over the 14 days of its duration. Finally, Table 5 summarizes this information over considered A/B tests and the baseline metric CpQ obtaining the statistics for each type of the FUBPA modification. Thus, we are interested in how good our approach is at prediction of the detection of the treatment effect in the future (i.e., at the 14-th day of an A/B test) in the case of the non-significant difference observed at the current moment (i.e., at the 7-th day of an A/B test). From Table 5, one sees that almost all FUBPA modifications have very good positive and negative predictive values (i.e., Col. 1 and Col. 4). So, one could conclude that *our FUBPA technique can be used in practice as an additional flag* to make the decision (e.g., at a half of time period of an A/B test which had not detected a

Table 4: The number of A/B tests whose treatment effect is detected by each UE metric and its FUBPA modifications.

Metric	S	Q	C	PT	CpQ	ATpS
Actual@14 day	2	$\underline{1}$	8	$\underline{4}$	$\underline{15}$	$\underline{4}$
$\mathtt{FUBPA}_{14\to 15}$	$\underline{3}$ (+1)	$\underline{1}$	$\underline{9}$ (+1)	$\underline{4}$	14	$\underline{4}$
$\mathtt{FUBPA}_{14\to 18}$	$\underline{3}$ (+1)	0	$\underline{9}$ (+1)	$\underline{4}$	14	$\underline{4}$
$\mathtt{FUBPA}_{14\to 21}$	$\underline{3}$ (+1)	0	$\underline{9}$ (+1)	$\underline{4}$	$\underline{15}$ (+1)	$\underline{4}$
$\mathtt{FUBPA}_{14\to 25}$	$\underline{3}$ (+1)	0	$\underline{9}$ (+1)	$\underline{4}$	$\underline{15}$	$\underline{4}$
$\mathtt{FUBPA}_{14\to 28}$	$\underline{3}$ (+1)	0	$\underline{9}$ (+1)	3	14	$\underline{4}$
$\mathtt{FUBPA}^{post}_{14\to 21}$	2	0	8 (+1)	2	8	1
$\mathtt{FUBPA}^{post}_{14\to 28}$	2	0	6	3	8	3

[18]The absence time should decrease for an improvement [9].

[19]We present several representative forecast period lengths Y, because the results for all the other are similar to them.

Table 5: The prediction of appearing of the treatment effect of 17 A/B tests w.r.t. CpQ.

Actual 14-day effect:	appears (1)		none (16)	
FUBPA expects:	appears	none	appears	none
$\mathtt{FUBPA}_{7\to 8}$	0 (0%)	1	1	15 (94%)
$\mathtt{FUBPA}_{7\to 11}$	0 (0%)	1	1	15 (94%)
$\mathtt{FUBPA}_{7\to 14}$	0	1	0	16 (94%)
$\mathtt{FUBPA}_{7\to 21}$	0	1	0	16 (94%)
$\mathtt{FUBPA}_{7\to 28}$	0 (0%)	1	1	15 (94%)
$\mathtt{FUBPA}^{post}_{7\to 14}$	0 (0%)	1	1	15 (94%)
$\mathtt{FUBPA}^{post}_{7\to 21}$	1 (50%)	0	1	15 (100%)
$\mathtt{FUBPA}^{post}_{7\to 28}$	1 (50%)	0	1	15 (100%)

Table 6: The persistence of the treatment effect of 15 A/B tests w.r.t. CpQ.

Actual 14-day effect:	remains (14)		disappears (1)	
FUBPA expects:	remains	disappears	remains	disappears
$\mathtt{FUBPA}_{7\to 8}$	13 (93%)	1	1	0 (0%)
$\mathtt{FUBPA}_{7\to 11}$	13 (93%)	1	1	0 (0%)
$\mathtt{FUBPA}_{7\to 14}$	13 (93%)	1	1	0 (0%)
$\mathtt{FUBPA}_{7\to 21}$	14 (93%)	0	1	0
$\mathtt{FUBPA}_{7\to 28}$	14 (93%)	0	1	0
$\mathtt{FUBPA}^{post}_{7\to 14}$	8 (**100%**)	6	0	1 (14%)
$\mathtt{FUBPA}^{post}_{7\to 21}$	9 (**100%**)	5	0	1 (**17%**)
$\mathtt{FUBPA}^{post}_{7\to 28}$	9 (**100%**)	5	0	1 (**17%**)

treatment effect at this time): to stop the experiment (and, hence, *save some experimentation platform's resources for other A/B tests*, e.g., a fraction of an experimentation traffic) or to continue it.

Control of the current effect persistence. On the contrary, we can consider the opposite situation. Suppose that a key metric detects the treatment effect at the 7-th day of an A/B test, then we are interested to know if this effect remains at the 14-th day or disappears. This case is very important in practice, because the statistically significance difference in the first days of an A/B experiment may be caused by the *Primacy* and *Novelty* effects [18, 14, 16], and, as a result, the true treatment effect might be delayed or be absent at all. In order to check the persistence of the treatment effect observed at the 7-th day to the 14-th day, we apply our FUBPA technique in the same way as in the previous paragraph, but we *consider only those A/B tests* that *have detected* treatment effect w.r.t. to the baseline metric over 7 days. We present these results for predicting the current treatment effect persistence in Table 6 for the metric CpQ. First, one sees that all types of the FUBPA have a very good precision (i.e., $\geq 93\%$, see Col. 1), however the negative predictive values (i.e., Col. 4) are very low, i.e. the biggest one is 17%. The recall values (Col. 1 divided by the sum of Col. 1 and Col. 2) for all types of the FUBPA are higher than 57%, and the best recall value 93% is observed for $\mathtt{FUBPA}_{7\to Y}$, $Y = 8, 11$, and 14. So, one could conclude that *our FUBPA technique can be used in practice as an additional flag* to make the decision after obtaining a treatment effect earlier than the predefined experiment duration: to continue the experiment (e.g., *to ensure the result against the Primacy and Novelty effects*), or to stop the experiment (and, hence, *save some experimentation platform's resources for other A/B tests*, e.g., a fraction of an experimentation traffic).

Possible extensions and combinations with other techniques. Our future user behavior prediction approach could be applied in many cases and could be combined with other sensitivity improvement techniques. For example, we could combine the FUBPA with the stratification technique, which is proposed in [7]. On the one hand, we could directly apply stratification of users (e.g., w.r.t. the used browser) to the FUBPA modification of the key metric. On the other hand, we could stratify users in the training set of the user behavior predictor and obtain an individual predictor for each stratum (e.g., own predictor for each user preference to a particular browser). After that, during an A/B test, we would apply the proper predictor for each stratum.

Besides, a FUBPA modification of a metric could be regarded as a self-sufficient evaluation metric, because it is the average value of a user's feature, which is calculated based on the data observed in the experiment period solely (as it is shown in Sec. 3). The only difference between this feature and a simple measure, like the number of sessions, consists in that the first one is calculated in a sophisticated way by means of the predictor. Therefore, we can apply any previously proposed approaches of sensitivity improvement, treating a FUBPA modification as a key metric. For instance, one can (a) remove those users from the treatment group, who were not affected by the evaluated change [18, 5]; (b) transform or cap this metric [16]; and (c) consider this metric in two-stage controlled experiments, applying proper variation reduction techniques, that are proposed in [6]. Finally, note, that some techniques (e.g., the point (b)) could be applied during the prediction training stage (i.e., train a future predictor of an improved metric).

7. CONCLUSIONS AND FUTURE WORK

In our work, we consider the problem of prediction of user engagement in terms of exact values of several state-of-the-art UE metrics. To the best of our knowledge, this problem is assumed to be novel and never investigated in existing studies. We performed a deep study of the influence on the prediction quality of utilized engagement measures and their transformations. Then, we applied the obtained predictor for the purpose of improving the sensitivity of online controlled experiments. We found that this approach increases the number of online controlled experiments with detected a treatment effect. The evaluations on real online experiments run at Yandex show that the approach can be used to detect the treatment effect of an A/B test faster (up to 50% of saved time) with the same level of statistical significance. Our technique can also be used in practice as an additional flag to make the decision during an A/B test to continue or to stop it based on the probabilities of obtaining the significant treatment effect. Hence, the results of our study coincide with the emerging needs of modern web companies to run more and fast controlled experiments on a limited number of their users.

Future work. We believe that our sensitivity improvement approach will be of interest to researchers and practitioner in online controlled experiments. As future work we can, first, extend the set of user engagement measures and other user behavior data for further improvement of the user engagement prediction quality and, hence, the controlled experiment sensitivity. Second, we can study more sophisticated prediction models to be applied in our sensitivity improvement approach. Finally, it would be interesting to combine different sensitivity improvement techniques with our approach.

8. REFERENCES

[1] E. Bakshy and D. Eckles. Uncertainty in online experiments with dependent data: An evaluation of bootstrap methods. In *KDD'2013*, pages 1303–1311, 2013.

[2] C. Bandt and B. Pompe. Permutation entropy: a natural complexity measure for time series. *Physical review letters*, 88(17):174102, 2002.

[3] S. Chakraborty, F. Radlinski, M. Shokouhi, and P. Baecke. On correlation of absence time and search effectiveness. In *SIGIR'2014*, pages 1163–1166, 2014.

[4] T. Crook, B. Frasca, R. Kohavi, and R. Longbotham. Seven pitfalls to avoid when running controlled experiments on the web. In *KDD'2009*, pages 1105–1114, 2009.

[5] A. Deng and V. Hu. Diluted treatment effect estimation for trigger analysis in online controlled experiments. In *WSDM'2015*, pages 349–358, 2015.

[6] A. Deng, T. Li, and Y. Guo. Statistical inference in two-stage online controlled experiments with treatment selection and validation. In *WWW'2014*, pages 609–618, 2014.

[7] A. Deng, Y. Xu, R. Kohavi, and T. Walker. Improving the sensitivity of online controlled experiments by utilizing pre-experiment data. In *WSDM'2013*, pages 123–132, 2013.

[8] A. Drutsa, G. Gusev, and P. Serdyukov. Engagement periodicity in search engine usage: analysis and its application to search quality evaluation. In *WSDM'2015*, pages 27–36, 2015.

[9] G. Dupret and M. Lalmas. Absence time and user engagement: evaluating ranking functions. In *WSDM'2013*, pages 173–182, 2013.

[10] J. H. Friedman. Greedy function approximation: a gradient boosting machine. *Annals of Statistics*, 2001.

[11] V. Hu, M. Stone, J. Pedersen, and R. W. White. Effects of search success on search engine re-use. In *CIKM'2011*, pages 1841–1846, 2011.

[12] B. J. Jansen, A. Spink, and V. Kathuria. How to define searching sessions on web search engines. In *Advances in Web Mining and Web Usage Analysis*, pages 92–109. Springer, 2007.

[13] R. Kohavi, T. Crook, R. Longbotham, B. Frasca, R. Henne, J. L. Ferres, and T. Melamed. Online experimentation at microsoft. *Data Mining Case Studies*, page 11, 2009.

[14] R. Kohavi, A. Deng, B. Frasca, R. Longbotham, T. Walker, and Y. Xu. Trustworthy online controlled experiments: Five puzzling outcomes explained. In *KDD'2012*, pages 786–794, 2012.

[15] R. Kohavi, A. Deng, B. Frasca, T. Walker, Y. Xu, and N. Pohlmann. Online controlled experiments at large scale. In *KDD'2013*, pages 1168–1176, 2013.

[16] R. Kohavi, A. Deng, R. Longbotham, and Y. Xu. Seven rules of thumb for web site experimenters. In *KDD'2014*, 2014.

[17] R. Kohavi, R. M. Henne, and D. Sommerfield. Practical guide to controlled experiments on the web: listen to your customers not to the hippo. In *KDD'2007*, pages 959–967, 2007.

[18] R. Kohavi, R. Longbotham, D. Sommerfield, and R. M. Henne. Controlled experiments on the web: survey and practical guide. *Data Mining and Knowledge Discovery*, 18(1):140–181, 2009.

[19] R. Kohavi, D. Messner, S. Eliot, J. L. Ferres, R. Henne, V. Kannappan, and J. Wang. Tracking users' clicks and submits: Tradeoffs between user experience and data loss, 2010.

[20] J. Lehmann, M. Lalmas, G. Dupret, and R. Baeza-Yates. Online multitasking and user engagement. In *CIKM'2013*, pages 519–528, 2013.

[21] J. Lehmann, M. Lalmas, E. Yom-Tov, and G. Dupret. Models of user engagement. In *User Modeling, Adaptation, and Personalization*, pages 164–175. Springer, 2012.

[22] E. T. Peterson. *Web analytics demystified: a marketer's guide to understanding how your web site affects your business*. Ingram, 2004.

[23] S. M. Pincus. Approximate entropy as a measure of system complexity. *Proceedings of the National Academy of Sciences*, 88(6):2297–2301, 1991.

[24] J. S. Richman and J. R. Moorman. Physiological time-series analysis using approximate entropy and sample entropy. *American Journal of Physiology-Heart and Circulatory Physiology*, 278(6):H2039–H2049, 2000.

[25] K. Rodden, H. Hutchinson, and X. Fu. Measuring the user experience on a large scale: user-centered metrics for web applications. In *CHI'2010*, pages 2395–2398, 2010.

[26] C. E. Shannon. A mathematical theory of communication. *ACM SIGMOBILE Mobile Computing and Communications Review*, 5(1):3–55, 2001.

[27] Y. Song, X. Shi, and X. Fu. Evaluating and predicting user engagement change with degraded search relevance. In *WWW'2013*, pages 1213–1224, 2013.

[28] D. Tang, A. Agarwal, D. O'Brien, and M. Meyer. Overlapping experiment infrastructure: More, better, faster experimentation. In *KDD'2010*, pages 17–26, 2010.

[29] W. W.-S. Wei. *Time series analysis*. Addison-Wesley Redwood City, California, 1994.

[30] R. W. White, A. Kapoor, and S. T. Dumais. Modeling long-term search engine usage. In *User Modeling, Adaptation, and Personalization*, pages 28–39. Springer, 2010.

Enriching Structured Knowledge with Open Information

Arnab Dutta, Christian Meilicke, Heiner Stuckenschmidt
Data and Web Science Research Group
Chair of Artificial Intelligence, University of Mannheim
Mannheim, 68159, Germany
{arnab, christian, heiner}@informatik.uni-mannheim.de

ABSTRACT

We propose an approach for semantifying web extracted facts. In particular, we map subject and object terms of these facts to instances; and relational phrases to object properties defined in a target knowledge base. By doing this we resolve the ambiguity inherent in the web extracted facts, while simultaneously enriching the target knowledge base with a significant number of new assertions. In this paper, we focus on the mapping of the relational phrases in the context of the overall workflow. Furthermore, in an open extraction setting identical semantic relationships can be represented by different surface forms, making it necessary to group these surface forms together. To solve this problem we propose the use of markov clustering. In this work we present a complete, ontology independent, generalized workflow which we evaluate on facts extracted by NELL and REVERB. Our target knowledge base is DBPEDIA. Our evaluation shows promising results in terms of producing highly precise facts. Moreover, the results indicate that the clustering of relational phrases pays off in terms of an improved instance and property mapping.

Categories and Subject Descriptors

I.2.4 [**Knowledge Representation Formalisms and Methods**]: [Representations (procedural and rule-based)]; I.2.3 [**Deduction and Theorem Proving**]: [Uncertainty, fuzzy, and probabilistic reasoning]

Keywords

Data Integration, Markov Clustering, Enriching Knowledge Bases, Probabilistic Inference

1. INTRODUCTION

State-of-the art information extraction systems like NELL [8], REVERB [16] or OLLIE [25] work on web-scale text corpora. They are based on the general paradigm of *open* information extraction (OIE) [3]. Systems that follow this paradigm are not constrained by the boundaries of encyclopedic knowledge or a corresponding fixed schemata. On the contrary, approaches like YAGO [40], DBPEDIA [1] or FREEBASE [4] follow a different paradigm and extract knowledge from partially structured resources. The facts stored in these knowledge bases (KBs) are, unlike extracts by OIE systems, assertions that use an URI scheme to uniquely identify both instances and concepts in its ontology.

In our work, we focus on the task of mapping the facts extracted by an OIE system to a target ontology, DBPEDIA for instance. The results of such a mapping process are precise and unambiguous KB assertions, compared to the raw, ambiguous OIE facts. From the perspective of the target KB, an automated mapping approach allows to extend the KB, or a poorly covered sub-domain of the KB, significantly.

Our approach is not limited to any domain and is applicable to any natural language text extracted from the web having the general form $rel(s, o)$; where rel defines a binary relation between the subject term s and object term o. For instance, consider the following REVERB fact [1]:

is a town in (Croydon, London)

If we want to map this fact to an ontology, like DBPEDIA, the relational phrase might possibly map to `dbo:county`, and the terms should be mapped to `db:Croydon` and `db:London` respectively[2]. The task of pinpointing to the exact instance is difficult since both *Croydon* and *London* are extremely polysemous. *Croydon* refers to 59 different entities and *London* to 441 entities in WIKIPEDIA. Given these respective correct mappings, we can translate the original fact to a KB property assertion as

`dbo:county(db:Croydon, db:London)`

It must be noted that instance and property matching tasks are not independent. If we correctly map "*is a town in*", we know that subject and object term will refer to geographical entities. Inversely, a fact that involves two geographical entities increases the probability that the relational phrase refers to a property relating locations. Our approach derives and leverages such dependencies within the overall task of generating new semantified facts.

In an open extraction scenario, different relational phrases often capture the same meaning and might still refer to the

[1]Croydon is large town to the south of London.
[2]`db`: DBPEDIA instances with the namespace http://dbpedia.org/resource/
`dbo`: defines the namespace http://dbpedia.org/ontology/ and can be used either with concepts or properties. We use this nomenclature in the rest of the paper.

WWW 2015, May 18–22, 2015, Florence, Italy.
ACM 978-1-4503-3469-3/15/05.
http://dx.doi.org/10.1145/2736277.2741139.

same property in the target ontology. For instance, "*is located in*", or "*is a village in*" can nevertheless be translated into a correct assertion using the more general property. So, it is important to first cluster such phrases [24] instead of computing a mapping for each one individually. A relational phrase that appears only rarely in the data set can thus profit from its cluster membership, leveraging comprehensive statistics available via all members of its cluster.

Our main contributions in this paper include (i) a modularised workflow for solving the general task of mapping OIE facts to a target KB, (ii) proposing markov clustering technique to group OIE relational phrases, and (iii) a feedback based approach to improve the overall quality of the assertions that are finally generated. In Section 2 we discuss some of the major related works from this area, followed by a brief overview of our framework in Section 3. In Section 4 we explain the clustering and the property matching techniques in detail where we propose markov clusters for the clustering problem. Empirical results and analysis are presented in Section 5. Finally we conclude in Section 6, with insights into our approach, limitations and scopes of improvements.

2. RELATED WORK

Matching Instances: The task of instance matching has been dealt with previously under the notion of entity linking. Major work in this area was done by Bunescu and Paşca [7] and Cucerzan [9] who focused on the usage of Wikipedia categories and global contexts, respectively. Systems like DBpedia Spotlight [26], AIDA [21], exploit mainly context of the entities. However in our problem setting. context is usually missing within the facts generated by OIE systems, making the task bit harder. In our approach, we apply a method that uses Wikipedia anchor text as surface forms as introduced by Bunescu and Paşca [7]. This allows us to derive the probability of a candidate based on the frequency associated to this surface form.

Knowledge Base Constructions and Debugging: There has been some development towards scalable knowledge base creation with a minimal amount of human intervention. Chen et.al. [44] introduced a system called ProbKB, performing deductive reasoning on web extracted facts by a set of first order logic rules and solving as an inference task in MLN. As a follow up work [43], ProbKB was used for automated KB construction. Our work does not target creation but rather using the open information for extending an already existing structured KB. Also, considerable work has explored unsupervised methods for tasks like acquisition of binary relations [5], facts [14], and instances [30]. Pujara et. al. [32] have used probabilistic soft logic to detect inconsistencies in knowledge graphs by exploiting dependencies within the graph. These works aim at reasoning within a given structure, provided, for example, by the concept and property hierarchy of NELL. In our work, the instance mapping module exploits OIE reasoning to a considerable degree in the context of a target KB like DBpedia and Yago to disambiguate OIE terms. Our assumption is that the source facts might be unstructured and do not maintain a concept/role hierarchy. This makes our approach independent of the existence of a source ontology. Moreover, we do not aim at refining the OIE itself, but use the OIE data in its given form to generate semantified facts.

Distant Supervision based Approaches: On a different note, there has been a lot of work on distant supervision based approaches since the early 90s. Work like DIPRE [6] was first of its kind to use a set of seed KB facts to discover patterns all across the web. Those patterns were used to discover more facts, furthermore, bootstrap these two to learn more facts and more patterns. The idea was also seen in systems like SOFIE [38], where natural language texts were excavated for entities and relationship patterns and most likely entity references were solved as a joined satisfiabilty problem. In particular, systems like PATTY [28] provide a taxonomy of relations. This is yet another example of a system which exploits relational patterns between entities and uses them to create a hierarchy of relational phrases. The authors of PATTY tried to paraphrase DBpedia and Yago entity relations with multiple paraphrases. This is different, since our approach tries to find a mapping given a set of paraphrases. Even Nell [8] and Reverb [17, 15] bear a similar architecture in identifying and finding relationships across the web. More recently, there has been clustering based works by Moro et.al [27], Sun et.al. [41]. This genre of work primarily focuses on the relations from open domain extractions; it extracts them, clusters them and finally disambiguates them. They exploit distributional semantics of relational phrases to aid their clustering (which is based on shortest path kernel method). Eventually, their goal is to disambiguate OIE facts based on the context, for instance "*is part of*" may be used in the sense of a location part of a larger place, or a person part of a band or organization. However, we have a different objective. We want to fully semantify an OIE triple in terms of a target KB, i.e., we want to select the correct property from the KB given an ambiguous relational phrase (and we have to solve a similar mapping task for subject and object terms). In this context, we should also mention the work by Augenstein et. al [2] cater to the classical problem of relation extraction from web texts and attempts to improve upon state of the art methods.

Semantifying Open Information: Soderland et.al. [36] worked on ontologizing OIE, by both mapping subject and object terms that occur Reverb facts to WordNet, additionally learning relations, such as entailment, between property phrases. This allows to derive a property taxonomy expressed in a normalized vocabulary of the OIE system, while the object and subject terms are mapped to an existing target vocabulary. It is thus partially similar to our approach, however, the mapping of relational phrases is not covered. Moreover, this approach has only been applied to the domain of health and nutrition. We found close resemblance of our work to the work of Soderland et.al [37], which aims at mapping the relational phrases from Reverb to "domain relations". They adopt a two step approach: first, by finding a suitable class recognizer for the OIE terms, second, learning a mapping of the relation under the constraints of the classes recognized. However, they used NFL (National Football League) as the target KB, unlike broader DBpedia in our case. The concept of a "Universal Schema" as introduced by [35] is interesting as they solve the task by defining an union of schemas from source inputs, in an attempt to fix incompleteness generated in mapping to target schemas. They used Freebase as the target KB and use matrix factorization to rectify both structured and unstructured data. However, we exploit the unstructured sources to enrich the structured KB. PARIS [39] is another well known tool which needs to be mentioned in this context. It performs proba-

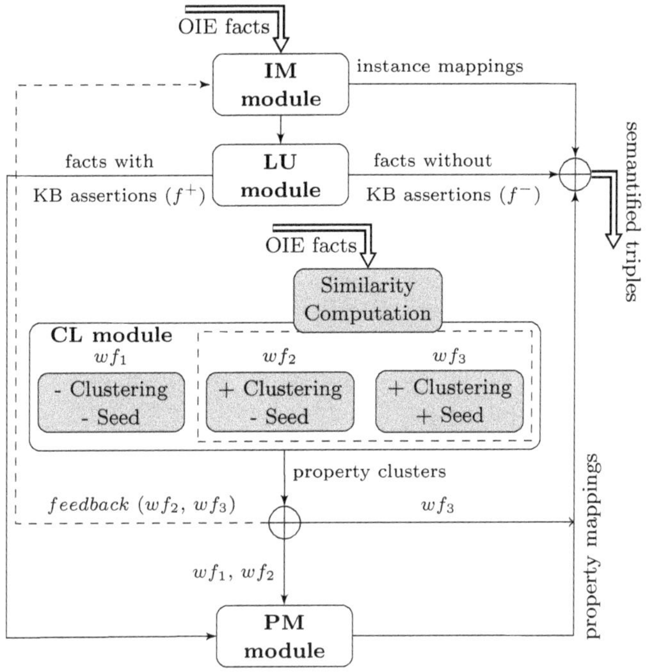

Figure 1: The system architecture.

bilistic alignment of relations, instances and schema across ontologies. This work focuses particularly on aligning two ontologies, for instance the authors of PARIS matched YAGO and DBPEDIA. However, we align an unstructured source to a structured target ontology. The key aspect of our methodology is the assumption that source is without an ontology and thereby making our approach applicable to any kind of source input. More recently, work by Presutti et. al [31] discovers semantic relations from inter wiki page links. However, they have a very simplistic edit distance based entity matching scheme and they exploit the available sentence to create a RDF graph representation. We have a more general framework capable of working without context.

3. OVERVIEW

In Figure 1, we depict the framework for translating OIE facts to assertions in the target knowledge base. It consists of four primary interacting components.

The **instance matching (IM)** module takes as input facts from OIE systems. Additionally, it may also accept groups of OIE facts, clustered together based on their relational phrases. The aim is to find the correct or most probable KB reference to every subject and object term in a REVERB fact. The outcome of the IM module is a mapping of the subject and object terms to DBPEDIA instances. This module is not the core contribution of the paper, but we present its working mechanism in brief. Every REVERB instance term (not the relational phrase) can be considered as a surface form representation of the actual entity in context. For instance, *"london"* might refer to the cricket stadium "The Oval", the capital city of UK, or even the poem by William Blake. Hence, there is a considerable amount of ambiguity involved in finding the correct entity reference. We exploited the English Wikipedia and looked for all the anchor texts along with their respective directed article links. We used Wikiprep [18, 19] for the pre-processing, resulting in tuples like <*anchor, article, #link*>, for instance <London, University of London, 118> or <London, London, 121299>. From such a collection of tuples, it is easy to get a probabilistic ranking of the possible referred entities. This simple but robust approach originates from [7], was applied to mapping OIE facts in [13], and has further been used in [11]. The algorithm considers top-k possible DBPEDIA candidates and exploits, for a particular relation pattern like *"is a suburb of* ($*$, $*$)", a probabilistic distribution over the likely domain/range. For this pattern, `dbo:City` is more likely to be a domain than `dbo:Scientist`, and so for the range. A more likely domain/range restriction enhances the candidate matching. This mutual reinforcement cycle is embedded in Markov logic network [34], and the improbable mappings are filtered out by finding a MAP[3] state of the network, where a maximum number of correct mappings hold true under a set of constraints.

The **look up (LU)** module searches for facts that are already stated in the target KB, DBPEDIA in this case. The input to this module is a set of instance mappings generated by IM module. Particularly, for each OIE fact, f, if the subject maps to x and object to y, we search for assertions in DBPEDIA that relate x and y. Multiple property assertions involving x and y is also likely[4]. Some of the assertions in this set might correspond to the given OIE fact. These are called f^+; facts with KB assertions and are fed into the PM module as evidences for mapping, which will be explained later on. If the set is empty, the facts are classified as f^-; facts without KB assertions. These facts are, at the end of the overall workflow, translated into the DBPEDIA vocabulary. The idea for this module is to separate OIE facts which can be used for knowledge base extension(f^-) from those which can serve as evidence(f^+). This is especially important since we do not intend to generate a KB assertion like `dbo:country(db:London, db:United_Kingdom`, which already exists in the KB.

The **clustering (CL)** module generates as output clusters of relational phrases having similar meaning, i.e., that can be correctly mapped to the same property. We implemented three different clustering methods including the trivial case for which we treat each relational phrase as a one element cluster. There are two non-trivial clustering methods. One works with DBPEDIA input seeds and the other one works without DBPEDIA seeds. Both methods are explained in detail in Section 4.3. These two methods require a similarity score computed for each pair of relational phrases in the input OIE data set. The similarity computation module is hence applied only on these two non-trivial clustering methods. As illustrated in Figure 1, we execute three different workflows wf_1, wf_2 and wf_3 that differ with respect to the applied clustering technique. The output of this module is clusters of relational phrases, which includes the simplest case where the phrases constitute a one element cluster, i.e for wf_1. The clusters generated by wf_2 and wf_3 are forwarded to the IM module (dashed arrow in Figure 1), which is executed again to improve the instance mapping due to better statistical coverage of clusters compared to the coverage of individual relational phrases.

[3]Maximum a Posteriori

[4]`dbo:location(db:London, db:United_Kingdom)`
`dbo:capital(db:London, db:United_Kingdom)`

The **property mapping (PM)** module tries to map a relation phrase or clusters of such phrases to a target KB object property. It must be noted, the PM module tries to map OIE properties to KB object properties[5]. The underlying mechanism for this module is an association rule mining based approach, which attempts to mine for the frequent rule pattern of the form *rel* → (*domain*, *range*) (described in [12]). Observe that the output f^+ from the LU module is also an input, serving as evidences for the association rules formation. Every OIE fact which is also "observed" in the target KB in some relational form, can be considered to be a strong evidence for a likely mapping. For example, consider the OIE fact "'*is the voice of(Glenn Tilbrook, Squeeze)*" the analogous fact we observed in DBPEDIA was "`dbo:associatedBand(db:Glenn_Tilbrook, db:Squeeze_(band))`". This provides a possibility that "*is the voice of*" might be mapped to "`dbo:associatedBand`". The rule we generate is *is the voice of* → (`dbo:MusicalArtist`, `dbo:Band`)

In general, the whole set of f^+ facts provides evidences for a possible mapping. This module exploits the domain and range of a DBPEDIA property in the stated assertion. The first workflow wf_1 involves a direct application of this technique on REVERB. We extend the algorithm for workflow wf_2 to treat clusters of relational phrases as well. Eventually, this module outputs a set of property mappings. Note that clustering with DBPEDIA properties as seeds (wf_3) implicitly solves the property mapping problem, since each relational phrase is mapped to the DBPEDIA seed in that cluster. Thus, the PM module is not used by wf_3.

Given the instance and property mappings for a certain fact, each component of the fact can be translated directly to an assertion formulated in the vocabulary of the target knowledge base. Since we apply this translation to f^- only, we know that each generated assertion is completely new. For instance, we started from the OIE fact "*originated in(Japanese honeysuckle, Japan)*", and generated the new assertion "`dbo:origin(db:Lonicera_japonica, db:Japan)`", with the guarantee that there are no pre-existing assertions in DBPEDIA with some other object property.

4. CLUSTERING AND MAPPING

In this section, we focus on the methodology for solving the clustering of relational phrases and the resulting mapping task. Often, the same relationship might be expressed by the use of different relational phrases. For instance, phrases like *"is the partner of"*, *"was the spouse of"*, *"is married to"* denote the same relationship. Hence, it is rational to group these phrases into a cluster which can then be treated as one collective unit.

For computing these clusters, we apply a graph based approach in which nodes represent relational phrases and edges weigh the degree of similarity of the connected phrases. We first explain how to compute the pairwise similarity in Section 4.1. In Section 4.2 we introduce the clustering techniques that we apply on the undirected edge-weighted graphs. Finally, we explain the property mapping technique in Section 4.3.

[5]properties defined between entities in the KB, for instance, `dbo:author` which is defined for `dbo:Work` and `dbo:Person`. This is different from data type properties which have literals as objects/subjects, like `dbo:foundationDate` defined between `dbo:PopulatedPlace` and `xsd:date`

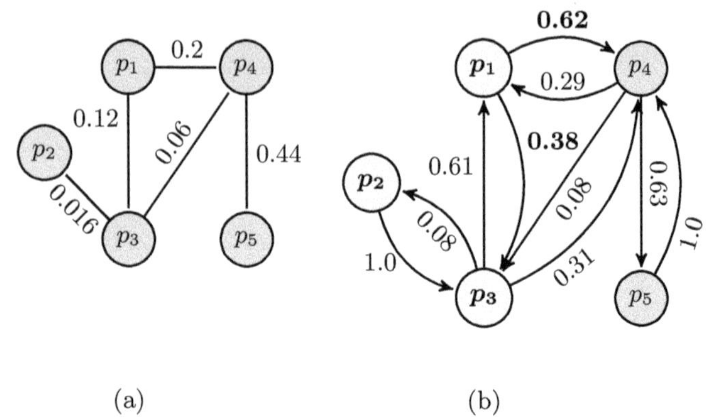

Figure 2: (a): A weighted undirected graph representing similarities between nodes. (b): same graph showing the transition probabilities. The directed edges represent the probability of moving to the connecting node. Note that the bold values add up to 1. p_1: ***is a village in***; p_2: ***is a town in***; p_3: ***is a suburb of***; p_4: ***currently resides in***; p_5: ***currently lives in***; **nodes of same color are eventually in the same cluster.**

4.1 Similarity Metrics

We introduce a similarity measure $sim(r_i, r_j)$ which captures the degree of similarity between any two property phrases $r_i, r_j (i \neq j)$. The measure is defined as,

$$sim(r_i, r_j) = \beta * jac(r_i, r_j) + (1 - \beta) * wn(r_i, r_j)$$

where, $jac(r_i, r_j)$ denotes a jaccard similarity and $wn(r_i, r_j)$ denotes a WORDNET similarity, and *beta*, β, is a weighing factor ($0 \leq \beta \leq 1$). All similarity scores are normalized between 0 and 1. In Section 5.3.2, we present an empirical analysis for our choice of β.

The jaccard similarity $jac(r_i, r_j)$ is defined as follows. Let f_{r_i} and f_{r_j} be the set of facts having the relational phrase r_i and r_j respectively. If n denotes the number of instance pairs where both the subject and object terms are in common across both sets, then the jaccard similarity is, in our context, defined by, $jac(r_i, r_j) = n/|f_{r_i} \cup f_{r_j}|$. For computing the WORDNET score we used a similarity API[6] which internally uses a hybrid approach involving statistics from a large corpus [23, 20]. We added jaccard co-efficient, which has been proven effective in document clustering[22, 29], to incorporate a component involving the data set characteristics. Applying the measure to the phrases r_i = *is the capital of* and r_j = *is the capital city of*, for example, we obtain the score 0.505 with $wn(r_i, r_j) = 0.829$ and $jac(r_i, r_j) = 0.181$ if we set $\beta = 0.5$.

4.2 Markov Clustering

We apply markov clustering (MCL) to generate the clusters that we finally map to the properties in the target ontology. MCL works well with large inputs and it has been applied successfully for finding semantically similar words [10]. The primary work on MCL was done by van Dongen [42]. In Figure 2(a), we depict an example for a set of five REVERB properties p_1 to p_5. The nodes represent individual property phrases. A weighted edge connecting

[6]http://swoogle.umbc.edu/SimService/

two nodes denotes their affinity score (introduced as *sim* in Section 4.1). A missing edge denotes absolute dissimilarity, for instance, there exists no edge between p_5 and p_3. These weights are converted to probabilities. For instance, node p_1, is connected to p_3 and p_4, hence the transition probability to p_3 is given by $0.12/(0.12 + 0.2) = 0.38$ as shown in Figure 2(b) with a directed edge. The sum of all the transition probabilities from a particular node has to be 1.0.

A graph with n nodes will have a probability matrix, $\mathcal{P} \in \mathbb{R}^{nXn}$. An element $p_{ij} \in \mathcal{P}$ represents the probability of node j transiting to node i. And so essentially

$$\sum_{i=1}^{n} p_{ij} = 1.0$$

thereby making $\mathcal{P}$ a column stochastic matrix. Donjen et. al. have simulated the concept of random walk using markov chains, where the steady state probability distribution is obtained by an iterative product of the probability matrix. Hence the nth state probability is given by $\mathcal{P}^n$. The idea is to make a stronger link even stronger and weaker ones even weaker, with these repetitive steps. Computing matrix products and re-normalizing them is called *inflation* and is controlled by the parameter *inflation factor*, I. We used the available implementation[7] for our experiments.

There are two major challenges in applying the method successfully. First, the choice of the inflation factor I is crucial. Setting it too small, makes the cluster too coarse and vice versa. And second, our initial experiments showed that with a reasonable I, some of the final clusters had further local sub-clusters. We implemented an extension to the algorithm which allows to find these local sub-clusters. For a given I, we apply markov clustering on each of the cluster, ignoring the influences from all other clusters. In Section 5.3.2, we report about experiments to automatically determine the optimal choice of I, which avoids a random selection of this parameter.

4.3 Property Mapping Strategies

We aim at mapping REVERB relational phrases or clusters of such phrases to DBPEDIA object properties. The abstract algorithm for the complete framework is presented in Algorithm 1. It accepts as input the different workflow modes and performs the mapping task accordingly. In workflow wf_1, we treat each REVERB relational phrase individually and map it to a DBPEDIA property. This involves a direct application of the rule based approach described in [12].

The second workflow wf_2, is an extension of the former, but involves clustering (Algorithm 1, line 14) the REVERB relational phrases. Once the relational phrases are clustered, we apply the rule based technique on the clusters. Here we treat each cluster as a single property for which the set of associated facts is the union of all facts containing one of the relational phrases in the cluster. The output of this workflow is a set of clusters, where each cluster is mapped to a DBPEDIA property. Each phrase in a cluster is eventually mapped to the cluster specific DBPEDIA property. For instance, "*is a city in*" and "*is a village in*", belonging to same cluster, are mapped both to `dbo:isPartOf`.

In workflow wf_3, we opt for a purely cluster based approach in which the mapping task is automatically solved by computing the clusters. Here, we *add* DBPEDIA properties

Algorithm 1 Algorithm for Semantfying Web Facts

Require: F: facts from OIE system; *mode*
1: **function** GENFACTS
2: $i_{maps} \leftarrow null$ ▷ instance mappings collection
3: $p_{maps} \leftarrow null$ ▷ property mappings collection
4: $phrases \leftarrow relational\ phrases\ from\ F$
5: $cl \leftarrow cluster(phrases)$ ▷ call to line 14
6: $i_{maps} \leftarrow IM(cl)$ ▷ call to IM module
7: f^-, f^+ using $LM(i_{maps})$ ▷ call to LU module
8: **if** $mode = wf_1$ *or* wf_2 **then**
9: $p_{maps} \leftarrow PM(f^+)$ ▷ call to PM module
10: **else**
11: $p_{maps} \leftarrow from\ cl$
12: $newFacts \leftarrow combine\ i_{maps}, p_{maps}, and\ f^-$
13: **return** $newFacts$

14: **function** CLUSTER(p)
15: $c \leftarrow null$
16: **if** $mode = wf_1$ **then**
17: $c \leftarrow one\ element\ cluster$
18: **else** ▷ wf_2 and wf_3
19: **if** $mode = wf_3$ **then**
20: $p \leftarrow p$+DBPEDIA *seeds*
21: $simCompute(P)$ ▷ similarity scores
22: $c \leftarrow markov\ cluster\ on\ p$
23: **return** c

as seeds and allow them to be clustered with the REVERB phrases using the markov clustering technique. Pairwise similarity scores (Algorithm 1, line 21) between the newly fed DBPEDIA properties and the REVERB relational phrases need to be computed in that setting. Applying clustering on this heterogeneous mixture of REVERB phrases and DBPEDIA properties results in clusters where most of the clusters had a DBPEDIA property along with a set of other REVERB properties. For instance, {`dbo:origin`, "*originated in*", "*is the source of*", "*is a source of*"} is one of the clusters. However, the major drawback of this approach is that, we cannot ensure that every final cluster contains a DBPEDIA property. There can be clusters without any DBPEDIA property, for instance {"*is ideal for*", "*is perfect for*"}. This might be the effect of an unsuccessful clustering or, DBPEDIA might not have an analogous property capturing the similar sense of a cluster of REVERB phrases.

5. EXPERIMENTS

In the following we present our experiments and discuss their results. In Section 5.1 we describe the used datasets. In Section 5.2 we refer to the procedure we applied to evaluate the results of our approach. In Section 5.3 we explain how we searched for the optimal parameter setting. Finally, we present and discuss the results in Section 5.4.

5.1 Experimental Settings

We used the latest REVERB ClueWeb Extractions dataset[8], consisting of approximately 15 million facts annotated with a confidence score. Unlike the smaller REVERB Wikipedia extractions data set (0.4 million), ClueWeb is larger and contains more domain independent facts, thereby providing

[7] http://www.micans.org/mcl/index.html?sec_software

[8] reverb.cs.washington.edu/reverb_clueweb_tuples-1.1.txt.gz

ReVerb fact	DBpedia assertion	fact clear?	subject correct?	property correct?	object correct?
is a kind of(Croatia, country)	`dbo:type(db:Croatia, db:List_of_sovereign_states)`	✓	✓	✓	×
is located in(Yekaterinburg, Ural Federal District)	`dbo:region(db:Yekaterinburg, db:Ural_Federal_District)`	✓	✓	✓	✓
could not be reached for(Jacob, comment	`dbo:knownFor(db:Jacob, db:Comment_(computer_programming)`	×	-	-	-

Table 1: Sample annotation schemes. (✓= correct; × = incorrect; - = not annotated)

a generalized setting for our approach. For our experiments we considered only triples with at least 95% confidence and removed facts that contain numeric expressions, (e.g. *saw the start of(1609, ceasefire)*, *were spotted in(161 tornadoes, last month)*), since we are only interested in facts that can be mapped to object property assertions. The filtered dataset contains 3.5 million triples with 474325 different relational phrases. We selected the facts that use the 500 most frequent property phrases, which consisted of 1072215 facts, i.e., approximately 31% of the filtered dataset. It was quite interesting to observe that selecting the top 0.1% relational phrases (500 out of 474325) covers nearly one-third of all facts. As target knowledge base we used DBpedia (Version 3.9). With respect to wf_3, we used the most frequent 100 object properties of DBpedia as input to the clustering.

As already mentioned, we applied the algorithm of [11] for the instance matching task. This algorithm decides between different matching candidates based on their types. Since some DBpedia instances do not have a specified type in DBpedia we additionally exploited the type information available in Yago. As experimentally verified with cross-validation in [11] (Section Experiments: Learning α), we set α to 0.5, the only parameter of the IM module.

Note that we include in our results presentation numbers reported in [12]. These results are based on running workflow wf_1 on a Nell dataset. Nell uses already a controlled set of distinct relations in its facts. Thus, the clustering problem does not exist. It is thus interesting to see whether it is possible to achieve similar results for the harder ReVerb problem scenario, where we cluster property phrases in the context of our overall workflow.

All experiments were conducted on a 64-bit Linux machine with 4GB physical memory and 2 cores. However, for the similarity computation module, we implemented it as an asynchronous and multi-threaded application, allowing us to exploit the multiple cores of a 8-core machine.

5.2 Evaluation

A random sample of 500 new facts was extracted from the final output of each workflow and annotated. The first question we ask to the annotator is, if the whole of ReVerb fact is fully comprehensible. If so, only then it is possible to determine the correctness of the candidate mappings. Marking a fact as ambiguous is important since we do not consider those facts for evaluation. Since for such facts the annotator was unable to determine the correct references to the terms in the first place and hence a mapping, if generated, would still remain dubious about its correctness. One such fact is the third example of Table 1 where it is impossible to determine "*which Jacob?*" the fact is talking about.

If the triple is decipherable, we ask the subsequent set of questions: Is the mapping of the subject term, the mapping of the object term, and the mapping of the relational phrase correct in the given context of the fact? Based on these annotations, a fully mapped ReVerb fact was considered to be translated correctly, if all the three questions were answered positively. If one of the mappings is annotated as incorrect, the whole translation was considered wrong. This can be seen with the first example in Table 1, where a wrong mapping for *country* makes the whole translation wrong, while the second fact is considered to be a correct translation. Likewise the "-" marks denote that the mappings were not annotated on account of the ReVerb fact being ambiguous. Note that, there are no ambiguous annotations, there are only ambiguous input ReVerb triples.

The annotation result allows us to compute approximated precision scores based on the evaluated sample. Assuming our method outputs only the three facts presented in Table 1, instance precision will be 3/4 or 75%, since one of the instance matching (*country* → **`db:List_of_sovereign_states`**) was wrong out of the 4 mappings. Similarly, the property precision will be, 2/2 or 100% and fact precision will be 1/2 or 50%. Note, that the ambiguous fact was not considered for evaluation.

5.3 Cluster Analysis

5.3.1 Metric

A substantial part of this work deals with different clustering strategies. We had two parameters in our overall approach, I and β, that have probably an effect on the cluster quality. To quantify this, we define a cluster quality score, which considers two factors, intra-cluster and inter-cluster sparseness. For a set of clusters, $C = \{c_1, \dots, c_{|C|}\}$, we measure the cluster outputs in terms of a quality measure [33], denoted by S and defined as,

$$S = \left(\sum_{c_i \in C} \frac{comp(c_i)}{iso(C)}\right)^{-1}$$

where, $comp(c_i)$ denotes compactness and is defined as

$$comp(c_i) = min(sim(r_i, r_j)); \forall r_i, r_j \in c_i$$

It measures how tightly any two arbitrary phrases r_i and r_j are connected in cluster c_i by looking at the minimum pairwise score between all elements in c_i. Note that $comp(c_i)$ is defined only if a cluster has at least two elements. Otherwise, we set it to zero. The metric $iso(\mathcal{C})$ measures isolation. It is defined as

$$iso(\mathcal{C}) = max(sim(r_i, r_j)); \forall r_i \in c_i; \forall r_j \in c_j; c_i \neq c_j$$

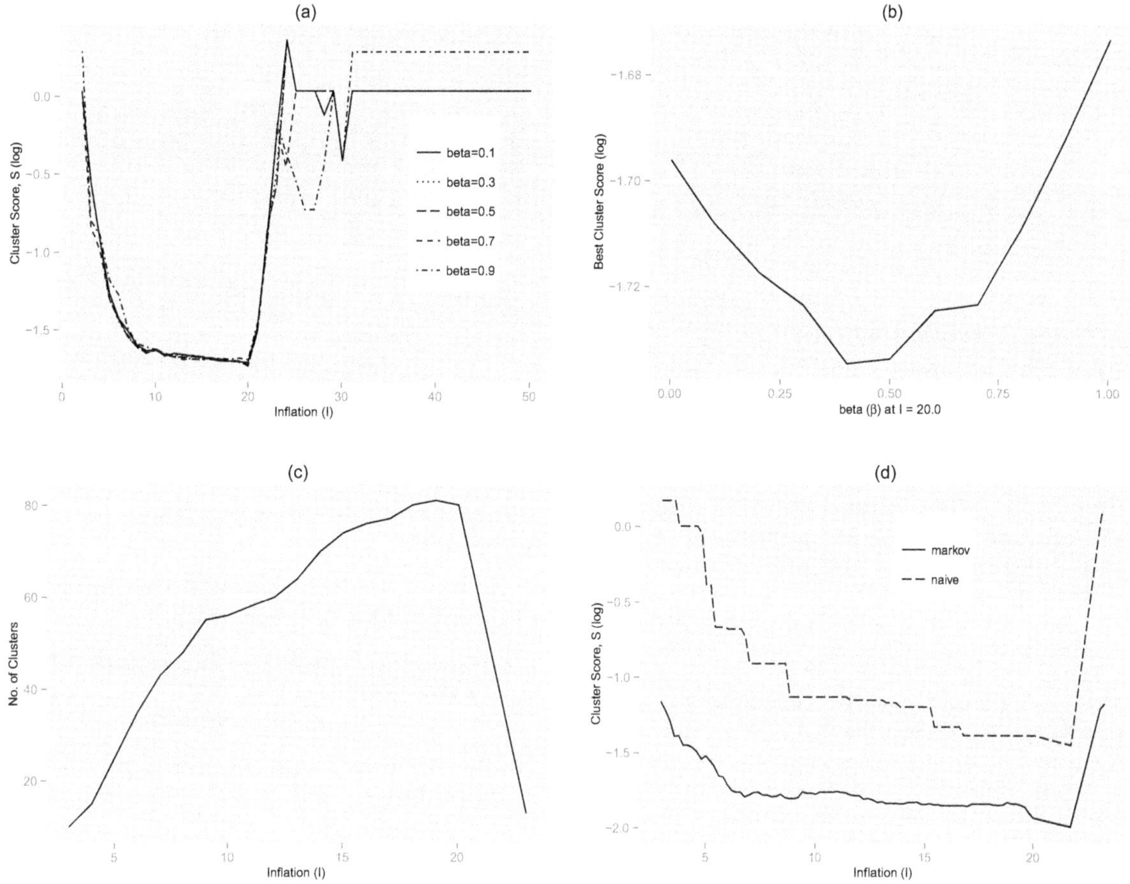

Figure 3: (a) Cluster scores for the range of I, for varying values of β (b) Best cluster scores (minimum score) for various β at I=20 (c) Number of clusters generated depending on I (d) Comparison of the Markov clustering based scheme with a naive mediod based scheme (N.B. All the cluster scores are presented in log10 scale, for making the finer differences more prominent)

It denotes how sparsely the elements are distributed across clusters in C. Ideally, for a good cluster scheme, every cluster c_i should contain very similarly elements i.e high compactness and there should very low similarity between elements across different clusters, i.e. low isolation. This tends to make S low for good clustering schemes.

5.3.2 Parameter Search

In this section we present a principled way of choosing the optimal parameters for our experimental settings. In this initial setup, we alter β in steps of 0.1 starting from 0 to 1.0. For each of these settings, we obtain different pairwise scores for our set of top-500 REVERB relational phrases. For every given β, we alter the inflation factor I (introduced in Section 4.2) in steps of 1.0 ranging from 2.0 to 50.0. We started by setting this factor to 1.0, but the clustering process did not terminate. The choice of the upper limit is not strict but empirical. It was chosen high enough to observe the general trend over a large range of values. We ran the clustering 11 * 49 times (11 data points for $0 \leq \beta \leq 1.0$; 49 data points for I) and we present the results in Figure 3(a). For clarity, we omitted some of the intermittent values for β from the figure. From the notion of quality, we must remember, the lower the score, better is the cluster quality. In general, we observed a similar pattern across different beta values. This can be generalized into trend sections as follows: a sharp improvement in the cluster quality ($\approx 2 \leq I \leq 10$), a marginal improvement phase ($\approx 10 \leq I \leq 20$), followed by a sharp deterioration and some randomness ($\approx I \geq 20$) and eventually saturation ($\approx I \geq 30$). Furthermore, Figure 3(a) also shows that irrespective of the β, at $I = 20$ we have the best cluster score.

We are interested in a score of β, which would be optimal for the given set of REVERB relational phrases. However, in an attempt to present the pattern over a wide range of values, Figure 3(a) fails to capture the exact β value (at I=20.0) which results in the lowest cluster score and hence the best cluster configuration. For this reason we *zoom-in* the results from Figure 3(a) at I=20, and investigate them further for all the β values and their corresponding cluster score. We present them in Figure 3(b). We achieved the best cluster score for $\beta = 0.4$. This was a two step approach to find the two parameters I and β, by deciding the former first, fixing it and and then deciding the later. In all the subsequent experiments, we used these parameter values.

	NELL wf_1	REVERB wf_1	wf_2	wf_3
matched rel. phrases	22	26	29	212
matched KB properties	25	52	29	41
new facts generated	1455	59,526	48,212	78,085
instance precision	97%	86.48%	89.88%	95.12%
property precision	96%	59.46%	75.28%	86.18%
fact precision	77%	43.24%	57.30%	78.05%

Table 2: Comparison of workflows.

5.3.3 *Comparison with Naive Clustering*

We compared the performance of the Markov cluster approach with a variant of k-means clustering. We refer to this method as naive clustering. It selects k random relational phrases from an input set (in our case, $k < 500$) and tries to assign the rest (i.e. 500-k) of the phrases closest to one of these k feed relational phrases. Note that, for the naive clustering, there is no direct influence of I. However, we have chosen the number of clusters generated by the Markov technique, and feed it as k for the naive clustering. Thus we ensure that the number of clusters generated by the two schemes is comparable. In Figure 3(c) we report about the change in the number of clusters generated with an increasing inflation factor. We observe that after a point, there is a sharp drop, denoting that higher I does not necessarily generate higher number of clusters.

However, higher number of clusters does not guarantee a good cluster. Hence, we measure the score S, as introduced above, for capturing the individual qualities of the two schemes. These behaviors are reported in Figure 3(d), where we compare both schemes by plotting I vs S. Since the naive approach is based on random feeds, we perform a repeated random sampling ($\approx$1000 times) for each step of I, and get the best score from them. As discussed in Section 4.2, we try to reduce the granularity of clusters by iteratively re-clustering. For this step, we try to find sub-clusters for clusters with more than 10 elements. While doing this, I was kept the same. It often happened that a sub-division was not possible and the iteration was terminated. The cluster sizes and quality scores reported here are the numbers measured after performing this refinement step. We had an average cluster size of 5.204 at the optimal inflation.

It must be observed that for all values of I, the Markov scheme generates always lower scores than the naive approach. And more interestingly, after the threshold (at I=20) both values tend to go up for both schemes, denoting deterioration in quality. The purpose of these preliminary experiments was to measure the effectiveness of the Markov clustering technique compared to the naive approach. In the following experiments we adopt Markov clustering and run it with different sets of inputs; only on REVERB in wf_2 and on a mixture of REVERB and DBPEDIA in wf_3.

5.4 Main Results

Table 2 summarizes the results for all workflows discussed in the paper. The table header denotes the following:

1. wf_1: considering every relational phrase uniquely, i.e. without any clustering, and applying association rule mining techniques for property mapping
2. wf_2: clustering relational phrases and applying rule mining for mapping the resulting clusters
3. wf_3: clustering relational phrases with DBPEDIA object properties as seeds without applying any rule mining

We compare these different workflows based on the following aspects:

1. *matched relational phrases*: the number of unique OIE relations that have been mapped
2. *matched KB properties*: unique target KB properties to which relational phrases have been mapped, in this case DBPEDIA object properties.
3. *new facts generated*: number of new KB assertions generated
4. *instance precision*: for each completely translated OIE fact, this denotes the fraction of subject and object mappings actually correct
5. *property precision*: similar as above, but fraction of relational phrase mappings actually correct
6. *fact precision*: fraction of translated KB assertions actually correct. A KB assertion is actually correct if all of the subject, object and relational phrases are mapped correctly

For a detailed comparison, we also present the numbers obtained for the NELL data set under the column header "NELL (wf_1)". These are the results as reported by Dutta et al. [12]. As the first step, we ran the full workflow under the simplistic scenario, i.e. wf_1. This is the trivial setting where the rule based mapping technique was applied on the REVERB data. Given that, REVERB is few magnitudes larger than the NELL data set, it was not surprising to observe a greater number of generated facts while applying wf_1 on REVERB. However, the precision suffered heavily. Overall, fact precision was 43.24%. This was mainly caused by a low property precision. This indicates the drawbacks of a rule mining based approach to find a correct mapping for the relational phrases. Note that, in this setting, every relational phrase was reasoned and dealt with individually, completely disregarding the effect of its synonymous sibling phrases. Furthermore, out of top-500 relational phrases, we could match only 26. These 26 relational phrases have been mapped to 52 different DBPEDIA object properties. Often, it was the case that a relation was mapped to almost two or more ($\approx$ 52/26) target KB properties. And during the annotation process, it was found that one or more options were wrong. For instance, the phrase *"is a city in"* was mapped to the following DBPEDIA properties: `dbo:councilArea`, `dbo:district`, `dbo:isPartOf`, `dbo:leade-rName`, `dbo:timeZone` and more. Clearly, `dbo:leaderName` and `dbo:timeZone` are wrong, and it made the whole translated KB assertion incorrect.

The next improvement was to jointly deal the relational phrases. We clustered the top-500 phrases from REVERB and performed the instance mapping and property mapping using the rule mining technique. With this workflow (wf_2), we expected that the clustering would push the instance matching precision higher due to the feedback loop we incorporated. Our expectation was also to observe a positive impact on the property mapping phase. Results were interesting in this setting, since we achieved a marginal improvement in the instance mapping and quite a lot in the property mapping. This speaks in favor of the clustering approach. We further analyzed the complete set of output mappings for the same relation phrase as we did in wf_1, i.e. *"is a city in"*. It had no incorrect mappings to `dbo:leaderName` or `dbo:timeZone`, instead had more valid mappings generated like: `dbo:ceremonialCounty`, `dbo:principalArea` and so on. This is also reflected in the numbers: the number of matched KB properties, reduced from 52 to 29, and precision was raised to almost 75%. Combined with a better instance and property precision, we could achieve much better fact precision of 57% compared to wf_1. Clustering looked promising, but still we were suffering from low recall in the sense that hardly any of the phrases were actually mapped, given that we started with 500 of them.

Finally, we choose the Markov clustering approach but with DBPEDIA properties as cluster seeds (workflow wf_3). We also re-run the instance mapping module using a feedback loop. We observe an increase in instance mapping precision compared to wf_2. We also observe that the property mapping is much better compared to all previous workflows. The improved instance mapping precision combined with a better property mapping precision leads to a higher number of new facts which are of the same quality as that achieved with NELL. Adding DBPEDIA properties as seed also helped to achieve better instance mappings. We had higher numbers both in terms of quality and quantity. Significantly, a higher number of different relational phrases were matched, resulting in almost 78K new KB assertions. Furthermore, the number of different target properties is increased. Thus, wf_3 is not only the workflow with the highest precision, but also the workflow that achieves the highest recall values. Analyzing further, the phrase *"is a city in"* was matched to `dbo:city`, `dbo:county`, `dbo:region`, `dbo:state`, Since we considered top-100 DBPEDIA properties, entries like `dbo:principalArea` or `dbo:canton` were absent. Even more interesting was to observe that `dbo:city` was actually a mapping for *is a city in, is a city of, is a suburb of, is a region in, is a town in, is the capital city of* and also *is the county seat of*. A large cluster of relational phrases was mapped correctly to properties in the target KB. Mathematically, every DBPEDIA property is mapped to approximately 5 (=212/41) relational phrases. The mappings for the property `dbo:city` are thus a typical example. Similarly, for `dbo:location`, there were 11 REVERB phases mapping to it, including *is located in, is situated in* and *lies in*.

Even though with wf_3 we achieved better recall, we observed that there is often a limitation on the number of phrases which could be mapped. We had clusters of phrases, which could not be mapped or actually had no analogous DBPEDIA property to be mapped to. Out of 500 REVERB phrases, 274 of them were assigned to some cluster that was not mapped to any DBPEDIA property. Examples are phrases like {*is an essential part of, is essential for, is essential to, is the essence of, is vital to, are essential for, are essential to*}, which were in the same cluster, but had no KB property to be mapped to. In this case our approach is right in not generating any mappings for this cluster, because there exists just no counterpart for this cluster in DBPEDIA. However, the clustering itself worked fine, since these relational phrases have obviously similar meanings.

Our approach generated also the cluster {*is similar to, are similar to, is very similar to*}. The analogous DBPEDIA property is `dbo:similar`, however, it was not in our top-100 seed properties. Including more DBPEDIA properties can help to map some of these 274 non-mapped relational phrases. We roughly sampled 10 clusters (containing 31 phrases) from the set of output clusters involving these 274 relations. The idea was to get a very rough number about the fraction which can be mapped. We manually investigated each of these samples, and found that out of the 10 clusters, 7 had no analogous DBPEDIA property, while we might have been able to map 3 if we would had included more DBPEDIA seeds. Note that in these 10 clusters there was no relational phrase for which a counterpart in the top-100 seeds existed. It seems that our algorithm matched all matchable relational phrases given the restriction of using the top-100 seed of DBPEDIA properties only.

Note that the fact precision for NELL (wf_1) and REVERB (wf_3) are comparable. This indicates that the clustering approach with DBPEDIA properties as input seed is better suited for mapping REVERB facts and produces a large number of precise facts. Whereas, the rule mining approach seemed to perform equally well for NELL but REVERB achieved worse performance with that same technique (wf_1). This highlights the importance of applying an appropriate clustering technique within an overall framework that deals with OIE systems like REVERB or similar ones having raw non-normalized textual relational phrases.

6. CONCLUSION AND FUTURE WORK

While these results are promising, we identify few areas which could be improved and highlight some key aspects of our method.

- Our approach considers a Wikipedia-like textual corpus work. But, it is not indispensable. We need a ranked list of entity-candidate mappings as input, irrespective of how that was generated.
- Our framework is robust to KB incompleteness and can easily handle missing types for instances and missing domain/range restrictions for the properties. It is always better to have them but A-box completeness is never an absolute necessity.
- We consider the number of facts generated ($\approx$ 78K) still to be low, given that we started with 1072215 REVERB facts. The generation factor is approximately 7.8% of the input data size. This bar can be raised by selecting a larger REVERB corpus, not just selecting the

top-500 relations. Also we are considering additional input sources, from text corpora like news archives.

- For the IM module, it is sometimes difficult to make a choice between the candidates of the same type, for e.g. `db:Vienna,_Maryland` and `db:Vienna,_Illinois`, both of type `dbo:Place`. Kernel based density estimation can help in this scenario.
- We will try to use another target KB like YAGO and compare the property phrase mappings generated by our system to those generated by PATTY [28].
- We have created a gold standard and working towards finalizing its release. We also extended our framework to incorporate an evaluation module, developed as an easily plug-able framework to our existing framework. We are planning to release the source code and the framework.
- Our current experiments with complete REVERB and DBPEDIA properties did not yield any scalability issues. Several internal modules are designed to work on distributed nodes. Only bottleneck is the MAP state computation with RockIt inference engine, used in IM module. It cannot work in distributed setting and can sometimes raise issues with large inputs.
- Our target is to generate A-box knowledge and not T-box. This is something we would like to investigate more, since, often several OIE relations capture interesting relationships which are completely missing in the target KB. Presutti et.al [31] tackles this problem, but on a custom ontology, we would like to define new properties on the target KB available.

We presented a general framework for generating new knowledge from a large corpus of web extracted facts in terms of a target knowledge base vocabulary. We applied our framework to the facts generated by REVERB in order to enrich DBPEDIA. In doing so, we analyzed three different workflows. In particular, we used Markov clustering as a means for clustering relational phrases and showed its effectiveness in improving instance matching and property mapping in a bootstrapped way. In our experiments, we showed that best results were achieved by using the target properties of DBPEDIA as seed for the clustering process. In particular, we were able to generate 78,085 new facts with an estimated precision of 78.05%.

7. ACKNOWLEDGMENTS

The authors gratefully acknowledge the support of a Google Faculty Research Award (see http://dws.informatik.uni-mannheim.de/en/projects/current-projects/). We would also like to extend our gratitude to Dr. Mathias Niepert from University of Washington, for sharing his valuable ideas in the initial phases of this work.

8. REFERENCES

[1] S. Auer, C. Bizer, G. Kobilarov, J. Lehmann, R. Cyganiak, and Z. Ives. Dbpedia: A nucleus for a web of open data. In *Proc. of the 6th International Semantic Web Conference*, pages 722–735, 2007.

[2] I. Augenstein, D. Maynard, and F. Ciravegna. Relation extraction from the web using distant supervision. In *Knowledge Engineering and Knowledge Management - 19th International Conference, EKAW 2014, Linköping, Sweden, November 24-28, 2014. Proceedings*, pages 26–41, 2014.

[3] M. Banko, M. J. Cafarella, S. Soderland, M. Broadhead, and O. Etzioni. Open information extraction from the Web. In *Proc. of IJCAI-07*, pages 2670–2676, 2007.

[4] K. Bollacker, C. Evans, P. Paritosh, T. Sturge, and J. Taylor. Freebase: a collaboratively created graph database for structuring human knowledge. In *Proc. of the 2008 ACM SIGMOD international conference on Management of data*, 2008.

[5] S. Brin. Extracting patterns and relations from the World Wide Web. In *Proc. of WebDB Workshop at EDBT-98*, 1998.

[6] S. Brin. Extracting patterns and relations from the world wide web. In *In WebDB Workshop at 6th International Conference on Extending Database Technology, EDBTâĂŹ98*, pages 172–183, 1998.

[7] R. Bunescu and M. Paşca. Using encyclopedic knowledge for named entity disambiguation. In *Proc. of EACL-06*, 2006.

[8] A. Carlson, J. Betteridge, B. Kisiel, B. Settles, E. R. Hruschka, and T. M. Mitchell. Toward an architecture for never-ending language learning. In *Proc. of AAAI*, 2010.

[9] S. Cucerzan. Large-scale named entity disambiguation based on Wikipedia data. In *Proc. of EMNLP-CoNLL-07*, 2007.

[10] B. Dorow, D. Widdows, K. Ling, J.-P. Eckmann, D. Sergi, and E. Moses. Using Curvature and Markov Clustering in Graphs for Lexical Acquisition and Word Sense Discrimination. *eprint arXiv:cond-mat/0403693*, Mar. 2004.

[11] A. Dutta, C. Meilicke, and S. P. Ponzetto. A probabilistic approach for integrating heterogeneous knowledge sources. In *ESWC-14*, pages 286–301, 2014.

[12] A. Dutta, C. Meilicke, and H. Stuckenschmidt. Semantifying triples from open information extraction systems. In *Frontiers in Artificial Intelligence and Applications*, volume 264. IOS Press, 2014.

[13] A. Dutta, M. Niepert, C. Meilicke, and S. P. Ponzetto. Integrating open and closed information extraction : Challenges and first steps. In *Proc. of the ISWC-13 NLP and DBpedia workshop*, 2013.

[14] O. Etzioni, M. Cafarella, D. Downey, S. Kok, A.-M. Popescu, T. Shaked, S. Soderland, D. S. Weld, and A. Yates. Web-scale information extraction in KnowItAll (Preliminary results). In *WWW*, 2004.

[15] O. Etzioni, A. Fader, J. Christensen, S. Soderland, and M. Mausam. Open information extraction: The second generation. In *Proceedings of the Twenty-Second International Joint Conference on Artificial Intelligence - Volume Volume One*, IJCAI'11, pages 3–10. AAAI Press, 2011.

[16] A. Fader, S. Soderland, and O. Etzioni. Identifying relations for open information extraction. In *Proc. of EMNLP-11*, 2011.

[17] A. Fader, S. Soderland, and O. Etzioni. Identifying relations for open information extraction. In *Proc. of EMNLP-11*, 2011.

[18] E. Gabrilovich and S. Markovitch. Overcoming the brittleness bottleneck using wikipedia: Enhancing text categorization with encyclopedic knowledge. In *Proc. of AAAI-06*, 2006.

[19] E. Gabrilovich and S. Markovitch. Computing semantic relatedness using wikipedia-based explicit semantic analysis. In *Proc. of IJCAI-07*, 2007.

[20] L. Han, A. Kashyap, T. Finin, J. Mayfield, and J. Weese. Umbc ebiquity-core: Semantic textual similarity systems. *2nd Joint Conf. on Lexical and Computational Semantics, Association for Computational Linguistics*, page 44, 2013.

[21] J. Hoffart, M. A. Yosef, I. Bordino, H. Fürstenau, M. Pinkal, M. Spaniol, B. Taneva, S. Thater, and G. Weikum. Robust disambiguation of named entities in text. In *Proc. of EMNLP'11*, 2011.

[22] A. Huang. Similarity Measures for Text Document Clustering. In J. Holland, A. Nicholas, and D. Brignoli, editors, *New Zealand Computer Science Research Student Conference*, pages 49–56, Apr. 2008.

[23] A. Kashyap, L. Han, R. Yus, J. Sleeman, T. Satyapanich, S. Gandhi, and T. Finin. Meerkat mafia: Multilingual and cross-level semantic textual similarity systems. *SemEval 2014*, page 416, 2014.

[24] D. Lin and P. Pantel. Dirt @sbt@discovery of inference rules from text. In *Proc. of KDD '01*, KDD '01, pages 323–328. ACM, 2001.

[25] Mausam, M. Schmitz, R. Bart, S. Soderland, and O. Etzioni. Open language learning for information extraction. In *Proc. of (EMNLP-CONLL)*, 2012.

[26] P. N. Mendes, M. Jakob, A. García-Silva, and C. Bizer. DBpedia Spotlight : Shedding light on the web of documents. In *Proc. of I-Semantics'11*, 2011.

[27] A. Moro and R. Navigli. Integrating syntactic and semantic analysis into the open information extraction paradigm. In *Proceedings of the Twenty-Third International Joint Conference on Artificial Intelligence*, IJCAI '13, pages 2148–2154. AAAI Press, 2013.

[28] N. Nakashole, G. Weikum, and F. M. Suchanek. PATTY: A taxonomy of relational patterns with semantic types. In *Proceedings of the 2012 Joint Conference on Empirical Methods in Natural Language Processing and Computational Natural Language Learning, EMNLP-CoNLL 2012, July 12-14, 2012, Jeju Island, Korea*, pages 1135–1145, 2012.

[29] S. Niwattanakul, J. Singthongchai, E. Naenudron, and S. Wanapu. Using of jaccard coefficient for keywords similarity. In *Proceedings of the International MultiConference of Engineers and Computer Scientists 2013 Vol I*, 2013.

[30] M. Paşca and B. Van Durme. Weakly-supervised acquisition of open-domain classes and class attributes from Web documents and query logs. In *Proc. of ACL-08*, 2008.

[31] V. Presutti, S. Consoli, A. G. Nuzzolese, D. R. Recupero, A. Gangemi, I. Bannour, and H. Zargayouna. Uncovering the semantics of wikipedia pagelinks. In *Knowledge Engineering and Knowledge Management - 19th International Conference, EKAW 2014, Linköping, Sweden, November 24-28, 2014. Proceedings*, pages 413–428, 2014.

[32] J. Pujara, H. Miao, L. Getoor, and W. Cohen. Large-scale knowledge graph identification using psl. In *AAAI Fall Symposium on Semantics for Big Data*, 2013.

[33] B. Raskutti and C. Leckie. An evaluation of criteria for measuring the quality of clusters. In *Proceedings of the Sixteenth International Joint Conference on Artificial Intelligence*, IJCAI '99, pages 905–910, San Francisco, CA, USA, 1999. Morgan Kaufmann Publishers Inc.

[34] M. Richardson and P. Domingos. Markov logic networks. *Machine Learning*, 62(1-2), 2006.

[35] S. Riedel, L. Yao, B. M. Marlin, and A. McCallum. Relation extraction with matrix factorization and universal schemas. In *(HLT-NAACL '13)*, 2013.

[36] S. Soderland and B. Mandhani. Moving from textual relations to ontologized relations. In *AAAI Spring Symposium: Machine Reading*, pages 85–90. AAAI, 2007.

[37] S. Soderland, B. Roof, B. Qin, S. Xu, Mausam, and O. Etzioni. Adapting open information extraction to domain-specific relations. *AI Magazine*, 31(3):93–102, 2010.

[38] F. Suchanek, M. Sozio, and G. Weikum. SOFIE: A self-organizing framework for information extraction. In *WWW'09 : proceedings of the 18th International World Wide Web Conference*, pages 631–640, Madrid, Spain, 2009. Association for Computing Machinery (ACM), ACM.

[39] F. M. Suchanek, S. Abiteboul, and P. Senellart. PARIS: Probabilistic Alignment of Relations, Instances, and Schema. *PVLDB*, 5(3):157–168, 2011.

[40] F. M. Suchanek, G. Kasneci, and G. Weikum. Yago: A Core of Semantic Knowledge. In *Proc. of WWW-07*, 2007.

[41] A. Sun and R. Grishman. Semi-supervised semantic pattern discovery with guidance from unsupervised pattern clusters. In *Proceedings of the 23rd International Conference on Computational Linguistics: Posters*, COLING '10, pages 1194–1202, Stroudsburg, PA, USA, 2010. Association for Computational Linguistics.

[42] S. van Dongen. *Graph Clustering by Flow Simulation*. PhD thesis, University of Utrecht, Utrecht, May 2000.

[43] D. Z. Wang, Y. Chen, S. Goldberg, C. Grant, and K. Li. Automatic knowledge base construction using probabilistic extraction, deductive reasoning, and human feedback. In *Proceedings of the Joint Workshop on*, AKBC-WEKEX '12, pages 106–110, 2012.

[44] D. Z. W. Yang Chen. Web-scale knowledge inference using markov logic networks. *ICML workshop on Structured Learning: Inferring Graphs from Structured and Unstructured Inputs*, June 2013.

A Multi-View Deep Learning Approach for Cross Domain User Modeling in Recommendation Systems

Ali Elkahky*
Department of Computer Science
Columbia University
New York, NY 10027, USA
ame2154@columbia.edu

Yang Song, Xiaodong He
Microsoft Research
One Microsoft Way
Redmond, WA 98052, USA
{yangsong,xiaohe}@microsoft.com

ABSTRACT

Recent online services rely heavily on automatic personalization to recommend relevant content to a large number of users. This requires systems to scale promptly to accommodate the stream of new users visiting the online services for the first time. In this work, we propose a content-based recommendation system to address both the recommendation quality and the system scalability. We propose to use a rich feature set to represent users, according to their web browsing history and search queries. We use a Deep Learning approach to map users and items to a latent space where the similarity between users and their preferred items is maximized. We extend the model to jointly learn from features of items from different domains and user features by introducing a multi-view Deep Learning model. We show how to make this rich-feature based user representation scalable by reducing the dimension of the inputs and the amount of training data. The rich user feature representation allows the model to learn relevant user behavior patterns and give useful recommendations for users who do not have any interaction with the service, given that they have adequate search and browsing history. The combination of different domains into a single model for learning helps improve the recommendation quality across all the domains, as well as having a more compact and a semantically richer user latent feature vector. We experiment with our approach on three real-world recommendation systems acquired from different sources of Microsoft products: Windows Apps recommendation, News recommendation, and Movie/TV recommendation. Results indicate that our approach is significantly better than the state-of-the-art algorithms (up to 49% enhancement on existing users and 115% enhancement on new users). In addition, experiments on a publicly open data set also indicate the superiority of our method in comparison with transitional generative topic models, for modeling cross-domain recommender systems. Scalability analysis show that our multi-view DNN model can easily scale to encompass millions of users and billions of item entries. Experimental results also confirm that combining features from all domains produces much better performance than building separate models for each domain.

*Work done at Microsoft Research during the author's summer internship.

WWW 2015, May 18–22, 2015, Florence, Italy.
ACM 978-1-4503-3469-3/15/05.
http://dx.doi.org/10.1145/2736277.2741667.

General Terms

User Modeling

Keywords

User Modeling; Recommendation System; Multi-View Learning; Deep Learning

1. INTRODUCTION

Recommendation systems and content personalization play increasingly important role in modern online web services. Many recent web services work on finding the most relevant content to their users in order to maximize the engagement with the site and minimize the time for finding the relevant content. A major approach to this task is called Collaborative Filtering (CF) [3, 19, 22, 21, 23, 6], which uses user's previous history of interaction in the web site to predict the most relevant content for recommendation. Another common approach is content-based recommendation [14, 15], which uses features about items and/or users to recommend new items to users based on the similarity between features. While both approaches work well in many practical applications [6], they usually face certain limitations and challenges especially with the increasing demand of personalization and recommendation quality.

Specifically, CF needs a considerable amount of previous history of interaction with the site before it can give high quality recommendation. This problem is known as user cold start problem [24]. In a newly established online service, the problem becomes more severe since users have little or no history of interaction with the site. Therefore, traditional CF methods often fail to produce high quality recommendation for new users. On the other hand, content-based recommendation methods extract features from each user and/or item and use those features to make recommendations. For example, if two News articles N_i and N_j share the same topic and a user liked article N_i, the system may recommend article N_j to the user. Similarly, if two users U_i and U_j share certain similarities like their location, age or gender, the system may recommend to user U_j the items that user U_i liked before. In practice, research has shown that content-based approach can handle the cold start problem for new items well [32]. However, its effectiveness is questionable when applying to recommendations for new users since user-level features are usually more difficult to acquire and often generated from a limited information in user online profiles, which failed to accurately capture the actual user's interests.

To address these limitations, we propose a recommendation system that leverages both user and item features. To build user features, unlike many user profile-based approaches, we propose to extract rich features from user's browsing and search histories to model user's interests. The underlying assumption is that, users' historical online activities reflect a lot about user's background and preference, and therefore provide a precise insight of what items and topics users might be interested in. For example, a user with many infant-related queries and website visits (e.g., toysrus.com) may suggest that she is a mom for a new-born baby. With these abundantly available user online activities, recommending relevant items can be achieved more efficiently and effectively.

In our work we propose a novel deep learning approach extended from the Deep Structured Semantic Models (DSSM) [9] to map users and items to a shared semantic space and recommend items that have maximum similarity with users in the mapped space. To achieve this, our model projects the users and items, each of which is represented by a rich feature set, through non-linear transformation layer(s) to a compact shared latent semantic space where the similarity between the mapping of the user and mappings of items liked by the user is maximized. This allows the model to learn interesting mappings such as people who visited *fifa.com* will like to read News articles about the *World Cup* and play *soccer games* on PC or Xbox. The rich features in the user side enable modeling the user's behavior and thus overcome many limitations in the content-based recommendation. It also addresses the user cold start problem effectively since the model allows us to capture user interests from queries and recommend related items (say music) even if they do not have any history on using music services. Our deep learning model has a ranking based objective which aims at ranking positive examples (items that users like) higher than negative examples. This ranking based objective has shown to be better for recommendation systems [9].

Furthermore, we extend the original DSSM model, which is referred to as *single-view* DNN in this paper since it learns from user features and items that come from a single domain, to jointly learn features of items from different domains. We name the new model *Multi-View* Deep Neural Network (MV-DNN). In literature, multi-view learning is a well-studied area which learns from data that do not share common feature space [27]. We consider MV-DNN as a general Deep learning approach in the multi-view learning setup. Specifically, in our data sets with News, Apps and Movie/TV logs, instead of building separate models for each of the domain that naively maps the user features to item features within the domain, we build a novel multi-view model that discovers a single mapping for user features in the latent space such that it is jointly optimized with features of items from all domains. MV-DNN allows us to learn a better user representation that leverages more data across domains and tackles the data sparsity problem in a principled way by leveraging user preference data from all domains. We show in our experiments that this multi-view extension improves the recommendation quality across all the domains at the same time. In addition, it is worth mentioning that the non-linear mapping in the deep learning models enables us to find a compact representation of users in the latent space which makes it much easier to store the learnt user mapping and share the information among different tasks.

One challenge in using deep learning to model rich user features is the high dimension of the feature space which makes the learning inefficient and may impact the generalization ability of the model. We propose several effective and scalable dimensionality reduction techniques that reduce the dimension to a reasonable size without the loss of much information.

To summarize, the contributions in this work are: (1) use rich user features to build a general-purpose recommendation system, (2) propose a deep learning approach for content-based recommendation systems and study different techniques to scale-up the system, (3) introduce the novel Multi-View Deep learning model to build recommendation systems by combining data sets from multiple domains, (4) address the user cold start issue which is not well-studied in literature by leveraging the semantic feature mapping learnt from the multi-view DNN model, and (5) perform rigorous experiments using four real-world large-scale data set and show the effectiveness of the proposed system over the state-of-the-art methods by a significantly large margin.

The rest of this paper is organized as following, first we review major approaches in recommendation systems including papers that focus on the cold start problem in Section 2; in Section 3, we describe the data sets we work with and detail the type of features we use to model the user and the items in each domain, respectively. We then review the basic DSSM model and discuss how it could be extended for our setting in Section 4; in Section 5, we introduce the multi-view deep learning model in details and discuss its advantages; in Section 6, we discuss the dimension reduction methods to scale-up the model; in Section 7, 8, 9 & 10, we present a comprehensive empirical study; we finally conclude in Section 11 and suggest several future work.

2. RELATED WORK

There has been extensive study on recommendation systems with a myriad of publications. In this section, we aim at reviewing a representative set of approaches that are mostly related to our proposed approach.

In general, recommendation systems can be divided into collaborative recommendation and content based recommendation. Collaborative Recommendation systems recommend an item to a user if similar users liked this item. Examples of this technique include nearest neighbor modeling [3], Matrix Completion [19], Restricted Boltzmann machine [22], Bayesian matrix factorization [21] etc. Essentially, these approaches are user collaborative filtering, item collaborative filtering or both item and user collaborative filtering. In user collaborative filtering such as [3], the algorithm computes the similarity between users based on items they liked. Then, the scores of user-item pairs are computed by combining scores of this item given by similar users. Item based collaborative filtering [23], computes similarity between items based on users who like both items, then recommend the user items similar to the ones she liked before. User-item based collaborative filtering finds a common space for items and users based on user-item matrix and combines the item and user representation to find a recommendation. All matrix factorization approaches like [19] and [21] are examples of this technique. CF can be extended to large-scale setups like in [6]. However, CF is generally unable to handle new users and new items, a problem which is often referred to as cold-start issue.

The second approach for recommendation systems is content-based recommendation. This approach extracts features from item's and/or user's profile and recommend items to users according to these features. The underlying assumption is that similar users tend to like items similar to the items they liked previously. In [14], a method is proposed to construct a search query with some features of items the user liked before to find other relevant items to recommend. Another example is presented in [15] where each user is modeled by a distribution over News topics that is constructed from articles she liked with a prior distribution of topic preference computed using all users who share the same location. This approach can handle new items (News articles) but for new users the system used location feature only which implies that new users are expected to see most frequent topics in their location. This might be a good features to recommend News but in other domains, for example Apps recommendation, using only location information may not work as a good prior over user's preferences.

Recently, researchers have developed approaches that combine both collaborative recommendation and content based recommendation. In [16], the author used item features to smooth user data before using collaborative filtering. In [7], the authors used Restricted Boltzmann Machine to learn similarity between items, and then combined this with collaborative filtering. A Bayesian approach was developed in [32] to jointly learn the distribution of items, research papers in their case, over different components (topics) and the factorization of the rating matrix.

Handling the cold start issue in recommendation systems is studied mainly for new items (items that have no rating by any user). As we mentioned before, all content based filtering can handle cold start for item, and there are some methods that were developed and evaluated specifically for this issue like in [24] and [7]. The work in [18] studied how to learn user preferences for new users incrementally by recommending items that give the most information about user preferences while minimizing the probability of recommending irrelevant content. User modeling via rich features have been studied a lot recently. For example, it has been shown that user search queries can be used to discover the similarities between users [25]. Rich features from user search history has also been used for personalized web search [26]. For recommendation systems, the authors in [2] leveraged the user's historical search queries to build personalized taxonomy for recommending Ads. On the other hand, researchers have discovered that a user's social behaviors can also be used to build the profile of the user. In [1], the authors used user's tweets in Twitter data to recommend News articles.

Most traditional recommendation system research focused on data within a single domain. Recently, there has been an increasing interest in cross domain recommendation. There are different approaches for addressing cross domain recommendation. One approach is to assume that different domains share similar set of users but not the items, as illustrated in [20]. In their work, the authors augmented data from rating of movies and books from datasets that have common users. The augmented data set was then used to perform collaborative filtering. They showed that this in particular helped the cases where users with little profile information in one of the domains (cold-start users). The second approach addressed the scenarios where the same set of items shared different types of feedbacks in different domains like user clicks or user explicit rating. As shown in [17], the authors introduced a coordinate system transfer method for cross domain matrix factorization. In [12], the authors studied the cross domain recommendation in the case where there existed no shared users or items between domains. They developed a generative model to discover common clusters between different domains. However, a challenge in their approach is its ability to scale beyond medium datasets due to the computational cost. A different approach was introduce in [28] for author collaboration recommendation where they built a topic model to recommend authors to collaborate from different research fields.

For many approaches in recommendation systems the objective function is to minimize the root mean squared error on the user-item matrix reconstruction. Recently, ranking based objective function has shown to be more effective in giving better recommendation as shown in [11].

Deep learning has recently been proposed for building recommendation systems for both collaborative and content based approaches. In [22], an RBM model was used for collaborative filtering. Deep learning for content based recommendation has been done for example in [30] where deep learning was applied to learn embedding for music features. This embedding was then used to regularize matrix factorization in collaborative filtering.

3. DESCRIPTION OF THE DATA SETS

In this section introduces the data sets. We describe the data collection process and the feature representations for each data set, as well as some basic statistics of the data.

The four data sets used in this study were collected from user logs of several Microsoft products, including (1) Search engine logs from Bing Web vertical, (2) News article browsing history from Bing News vertical, (3) App download logs from Windows AppStore, and (4) Movie/TV view logs from Xbox. All the logs were collected between December 2013 and June 2014, with primary focus on English-speaking markets including United States, Canada and Great Britain.

(**User Features**) We collected users' search queries and their clicked URLs from Bing to form user features. Queries were first normalized, stemmed and then split into unigram features and URLs were shorten into domain-level only (e.g., www.linkedin.com) to reduce the feature dimension. We then used TF-IDF scores to keep only the most popular and non-trivial features. Overall, we selected 3 million unigram features and 500K domain features, leading to a total length of 3.5-million user feature vector.

(**News Features**) We collected news article clicks from Bing News vertical. Each News item is represented by three parts of features. The first part is the title features encoded using letter tri-gram representation as we will describe in the next section. Secondly, the top-level category of each News (e.g., Entertainment) is encoded as binary features. Finally, the Named Entities in each article, extracted using

Type	DataSet	UserCnt	Feature Size	Joint Users
User View	Search	20M	3.5M	/
Item View	News	5M	100K	1.5M
	Apps	1M	50K	210K
	Movie/TV	60K	50K	16K

Table 1: Statistics of the four data sets used in this paper. The *Joint Users* column indicates the number of common users between each item view and the user view.

an internal proprietary NLP parser, is encoded using letter tri-gram as well. This results in a 100K feature vector.

(**App Features**) Users' App download histories were collected from Windows AppStore logs. The title of each App is represented using letter tri-gram, combining with its category (e.g., Game) features in the binary format. Do to the nature of constant change of App descriptions, we decided not to include that as part of the feature space. This results in a 50K feature vector for Apps.

(**Movie/TV Features**) From Xbox logs, we collected the Movie/TV view history for each Xbox user. The title and description of each item were combined into text features and then encoded using letter tri-gram. The genre is also used as binary features. This results in a 50K feature vector for Movie/TV.

In our neural network framework, user features are mapped into the user view and the rest is mapped into different item views. For training purpose, each user view is matched with an item view which contains the exact set of users. To achieve this, we sub-sampled logged-in users (i.e., users with uniquely annonymized and hashed Microsoft User IDs) from each user-item view pair and performed inner join based on their IDs. This results in different number of users for each user-item view pair. Table 1 depicts some basic statistics of the data used in this paper.

4. DSSM FOR USER MODELING IN RECOMMENDATION SYSTEMS

A deep structured semantic model (DSSM) is introduced in [9] to enhance query document matching in the web search context. Given the close relationship to our proposed multi-view deep neural network, we briefly review DSSM here.

The typical architecture of the DSSM is shown in Fig. 1.The input (raw text features) to the DNN is a high dimensional term vector, e.g., raw counts of terms in a query or a document without normalization. Then the DSSM passes its input through two neural networks, one for each of the two different inputs, respectively, and maps them into semantic vectors in a shared semantic space. For Web document ranking, DSSM computes the relevance score between a query and a document as the cosine similarity of their corresponding semantic vectors, and ranks documents by their similarity scores to the query.

More formally, if we denote x as the input term vector, y as the output vector, $l_i, i = 1, ..., N-1$, as the intermediate hidden layers, W_i as the i-th weight matrix, and b_i as the i-th bias term, we have

$$\begin{aligned} l_1 &= W_1 x \\ l_i &= f(W_i l_{i-1} + b_i), i = 2, ..., N-1 \\ y &= f(W_N l_{N-1} + b_N) \end{aligned} \quad (1)$$

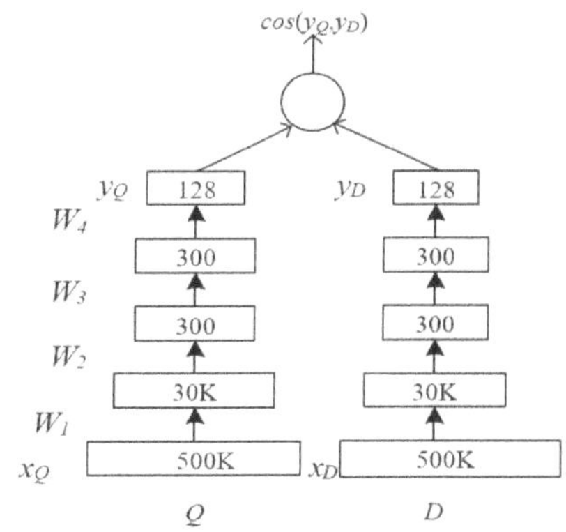

Figure 1: The illustration of the deep structured semantic model (DSSM).

where we use the *tanh* function as the activation function at the output layer and the hidden layers $l_i, i = 2, ..., N-1$:

$$f(x) = \frac{1 - e^{-2x}}{1 + e^{-2x}} \quad (2)$$

The semantic relevance score between a query Q and a document D is then measured as:

$$R(Q, D) = cosine(y_Q, y_D) = \frac{{y_Q}^T y_D}{||y_Q|| \cdot ||y_D||} \quad (3)$$

where y_Q and y_D are the semantic vectors of the query and the document, respectively. In Web search, given the query, the documents are sorted by their semantic relevance scores.

Conventionally, each word w is represented by a one-hot word vector where the dimensionality of the vector is the size of the vocabulary. However, the vocabulary size is often very large in real-world Web search tasks, and the one-hot vector word representation makes model learning very expensive. Therefore, the DSSM uses a *word hashing* layer to represent a word by a letter trigram vector. For example, given a word (e.g. *web*), after adding word boundary symbols (e.g. *#web#*), the word is segmented into a sequence of letter-n-grams (e.g. letter-tri-grams: *#-w-e, w-e-b, e-b-#*). Then, the word is represented as a count vector of letter-tri-grams. For example, the letter-trigram representation of *web* is:

In Figure 1, the first layer matrix W_1 denotes the letter-trigram matrix transforming from a term-vector to its letter-trigram count vector, which requires no learning. Even though the total number of English words may grow to be extremely large, the total number of distinct letter-trigrams in English (or other similar languages) is often limited. Therefore, it can generalize to new words unseen in the training data.

In training, it is assumed that a query is relevant to the documents that are clicked on for that query, and the parameters of the DSSM, i.e., the weight matrix W_i, are trained using this signal. I.e., first the posterior probability of a document given a query is estimated from the semantic relevance score between them through a softmax function

$$P(D|Q) = \frac{exp(\gamma R(Q, D))}{\sum_{D' \in \mathbf{D}} exp(\gamma R(Q, D'))} \quad (4)$$

where γ is a smoothing factor in the softmax function, which is usually set empirically on a held-out data set in our experiment. **D** denotes the set of candidate documents to be ranked. Ideally, **D** should contain all possible documents. In practice, for each (query, clicked-document) pair, denoted by (Q, D^+) where Q is a query and D^+ is the clicked document, we approximate **D** by including D^+ and N randomly selected unclicked documents, denote by $\{D_j^-; j = 1,, N\}$.

In training, the model parameters are estimated to maximize the likelihood of the clicked documents given the queries across the training set.

$$L(\Lambda) = -\log \prod_{(Q,D^+)} P(D^+|Q) \tag{5}$$

where Λ denotes the parameter set of the neural networks.

5. MULTI-VIEW DEEP NEURAL NETWORK

The DSSM can be viewed as a multi-learning framework where it maps two different views of the data into a shared view. In that sense, it can be viewed in a more general setting to learn a shared mapping between two different views.

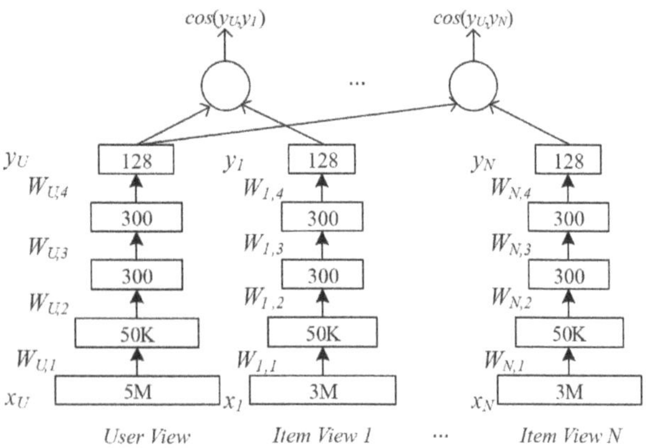

Figure 2: Multi-view DNN for multiple domain recommendation. It uses a DNN to map high-dimensional sparse features (e.g., raw features of users, News, App) into low-dimensional dense features in a joint semantic space.. The first hidden layer, with 50k units, accomplishes word hashing. The word-hashed features are then projected through multiple layers of non-linear projections. The final layer's neural activities in this DNN form the feature in the semantic space. Note that the input feature dimension x (5M and 3M) in this figure is hypothetical as in practice each view can have arbitrary number of features. See text for details.

In this work, we propose an extension to the DSSM where we have more than two views of the data and we call this Multi-view DNN (MV-DNN). In this setting, we have $v+1$ views, one pivot view called X_u and other v auxiliary views X_1 through X_v and each X_i has its own input domain $X_i \in R^{d_i}$. Each view also has its own non-linear mapping layer(s) $f_i(X_i, W_i)$ which transforms X_i into shared semantic space Y_i. The training data contains a set of samples. The jth sample has an instance of the pivot view $X_{u,j}$ and one active auxiliary view $X_{a,j}$ where a is the index of the active view in sample j. All other views input $X_{i:i \neq a}$ are set to 0 vectors. The objective of is finding a non-linear mapping for each view such that the sum of similarities, in the semantic space between mapping of the pivot view Y_u and mappings of all other views $Y_1, ...Y_v$ is maximized. Formally, we have:

Algorithm 1 Training Multi-View DNN

Input: $N = \#$ of view pairs, $M = \#$ of training iterations,
U_A = user view architecture,
$I_A = \{I_{A1}, ...I_{AN}\}$ item view architecture,
$U_D = \{U_{D1}, ...UDN\}$ user input files,
$I_D = \{I_{D1}, ...I_{DN}\}$ item input files,
$\mathbf{W_U}$ = user view weight matrix,
$\mathbf{W_I} = \{W_{I1}, ...W_{IN}\}$ item view weight matrices
Initialization
Initialize $\mathbf{W_U}$ and $\mathbf{W_I}$ using U_A and I_A
for $m = 1$ to M
  for $v = 1$ to N
    $T_U \leftarrow U_{Dv}$
    $T_I \leftarrow I_{Dv}$
    train $\mathbf{W_U}$ and $\mathbf{W_I}$ using T_U and T_I
  end for
end for
Output: $\mathbf{W_U}$ = final user weight matrix,
$\mathbf{W_I}$ = final set of item view weight matrices

$$p = \arg \max_{W_u, W_1, ..W_v} \sum_{j=1}^{N} \frac{e^{\alpha_a \cos(Y_u, Y_{a,j})}}{\sum_{X' \in R^{d_a}} e^{\alpha \cos(Y_u, f_a(X', W_a))}} \tag{6}$$

The architecture of MV-DNN is shown in figure 2. In our recommendation systems setup, we set the pivot view X_u to user features and create auxiliary view for each different type of items we aim to recommend.

The intuition for having this objective function is to try to find a single mapping for user's features, namely W_u, that can transform users features into a space that matches all different items the user liked in different views/domains. This way of sharing parameters allows the domains that do not have enough information to learn good mapping through other domains which have more data. It should work well if the assumption that users who have similar News articles taste also have similar taste in other domains which means those domains can benefit from user mapping learned by News domain. If this assumption is valid, then samples from any domain will help in grouping similar users more accurately in all domains. The empirical results showed that the assumption is reasonable in the domains we experimented on, which we elaborate more in the experiment sections.

5.1 Training MV-DNN

MV-DNN can be trained using Stochastic Gradient Decent (SGD). In practice, each training example contains a pairs of inputs, one for the user view and one for the data views. Therefore, despite the fact that there exists only one user view in our model, it is often more convenient to have N user feature files, each of which corresponds to an item feature file, where N is the total number of user-item view pairs. In Algorithm 1, we sketch the high-level process of training MV-DNN. When taking the derivative with respect to all $W_i \in \{W_u, W_1, ..W_v\}$ we end up with only two non-zero derivatives $\frac{\partial p}{\partial W_u}$ and $\frac{\partial p}{\partial W_a}$ which allow us to apply the same update rules for DSSM as in [9] substituting q by X_u and d by X_a.

5.2 Advantages of MV-DNN

Although MV-DNN is extended from the original DSSM framework, it has several unique characteristics that makes it superior than its predecessor. First of all, the original DSSM model uses for both the query view and document view the same size of feature dimensions, and preprocessed using the same representation (letter tri-gram for example). This poses a huge restrictions in the feature composition step. Due to the heterogeneity nature of recommendation systems, it is quite likely that the user view and item view pose different input features. Also, many types of features cannot be optimally represented using letter trigram. For example, the URL domain feature often contains prefix and suffix like www, com, org which will be mapping to the same feature if letter tri-gram is applied. In practice, we have discovered that the letter tri-gram representation works ideally in the case that the input raw text is short (e.g., query text and document title in the original DSSM model), but becomes inappropriate to model user level features which often contain a large collection of queries and URL domains. By removing this constraint, the new MV-DNN model can incorporate categorical features such as movie genre and app category, geospatial features such as country and region, as well as raw text features represented using uni-grams or bi-grams from user inputs.

Secondly, MV-DNN has the capability of scaling up to many different domains which the original DSSM framework is unable to. By performing pair-wise training between each user-item view pair as described in Algorithm 1, our model can easily adopt new sets of view pairs which may contain completely independent sets of users and items at any stage of the training process, e.g., adding a new data set from Xbox games. By alternating user-view pairs during each training iteration, our model can eventually converge to an optimal embedding of user view that is trained through all item views. Note that although we can have different user sets in different item views in theory, during our experiment, we choose to keep the same set of users across all views with the consideration of both convenience and the ease of feature normalization.

6. DIMENSION AND DATA REDUCTION

In practice, the proposed deep learning approach often needs to handle a huge amount of training examples in high dimensional feature spaces for the user view. In order to scale the system up, we propose several dimensionality reduction techniques to reduce the number of features in the user view. Then, we propose an idea to compact and summarize user training examples which reduces the number of training data to be linear to the number of users.

6.1 Top Features

One simple dimensionality reduction approach for user features is to select the top-K most frequent features. We select all features that have a probability of 0.001 or greater to be picked by a user. The main underlying hypothesis is that users can be described well using a relatively small set of frequent features that explains the users' common online behavior. Note that as described in Section 3, the user's raw features are preprocessed using TF-IDF scores so that the top features we select no longer contains common stop words in search queries. This resulted in 83K user features.

6.2 K-means

K-means [8] is a well-known clustering technique aims at creating a number of clusters such that the sum of distances between each point and its nearest cluster is minimized:

$$\arg\min_{C_1,..C_k} \sum_{i=1}^{N} \min_{C_j \in \{C_1,..C_k\}} distance(X_i, C_j), \tag{7}$$

Where X_i is a data point and C_j indicates a cluster centroid. K-means has shown good performance as a way to learn unsupervised features in vision [5]. The basic idea is to group similar features together into one cluster and generate a new feature vector Y which has the size equal to number of clusters K and has number of appearances of features in cluster i as value of its ith component. To do this we represent each feature using a vector f_i of length U where U is the number users in the training data and $f_i(j)$ equals to the number of times user i has feature j. f_i are then normalized to have length 1. One important aspect in running K-means is that the relevant distance here is the angle between different feature vectors which can be computed using cosine similarity. Then the reduced dimensional vector Y_i is created for each user vector f_i as follows: denote $1 \leq Cls(a) \leq K$ the cluster assigned to feature a, we can compute Y_i using:

$$Y_i(j) = \sum_{a:X_i(a)>0 \& Cls(a)=j} f_i(a) \tag{8}$$

To be able to extract a reasonable number of features using K-means we need to have a relatively large number of clusters, since a small number of clusters (say 100) will results in large chunk of features to be in the same cluster considering the size of user features to be 3.5M. This will hence generate features that are difficult to learn useful pattern from. In order to mitigate this issue, we set the number of clusters to be $10k$. This means that on average there are 350 features per cluster. The large size of clusters and raw features makes K-means computationally expensive to run. In our experiment, we use a cloud-based Map-Reduce implementation for K-means [4].

6.3 Local sensitive Hashing

Local Sensitive Hashing (LSH) [10] works by projecting the data using a random projection matrix into a much lower dimensional space such that the pairwise cosine distance in the original space is still preserved in the new space. LSH requires a transformation matrix $A \in R^{d \times k}$, where d is the number of features in the original space and k is the number of random projections used. This means That A contains k different projection, indicated by A_i, each of which takes X vector and output a single hash value Y_i. The output vector $Y \in R^k$ of LSH can be found by concatenating all different hash values of Y_i. Specifically, to compute each Y_i we use the following equation:

$$Y_i = \begin{cases} 1 & \text{if } A_i X \geq 0 \\ 0 & else. \end{cases} \tag{9}$$

The cosine similarity between two vectors $X_1, X_2 \in R^d$ can be approximated by $cos\left(\frac{H(Y_1,Y_2)}{k}\pi\right)$ where $H(Y_1, Y_2)$ is the hamming distance between the LSH of input vectors. In order to preserve cosine similarity with higher accuracy we need to increase the number of projections used k. We used $k = 10,000$, the same as used for K-means clusters. While LSH can be applied to each vector independently and all projection can be computed independently which makes the algorithm highly distributable under the

Map-Reduce framework, the algorithm requires the generation of the transformation matrix A which is our case has $3.5M \times 10^4$ entries generated from $N(0,1)$, requiring about 300GB storage. Also, A must be stored on each node during the computation of LSH vectors. These issues make LSH prohibitively expensive in the Map-Reduce framework.

Many solutions have been proposed to address this problem. A lot of them are based on generating sparse A [13]. Here, we used the pooling trick introduced in [31]. The idea is to keep a pool B of size m of random numbers generated from $N(0,1)$ where m is usually significantly smaller than the size of a transformation matrix A. To get the entry in A_{ij} one simply applies consistent hash function of i, j to get an index in B and look up the value. In our experiments we set $m = 1,000,000$ which is more than $10,000$ times reduction in memory requirement and can be easily stored in each node in during Map-Reduce using only 10M storage.

6.4 Reduce the Number of Training Examples

The training data for each view contains a set of pairs $(User_i, Item_j)$ such that $User_i$ liked $Item_j$. In practice, a user may like many items which sometimes cause the training data to be very large. For example, in our News recommendation data set, the number of pairs is well over 1 billion and causes the training to be very slow even when using an optimized GPU implementation.

To alleviate this problem, we compress the training data so that it includes a *single* training example per user per each view. Specifically, the compressed training example includes the user features paired with the features with an *average* score of all items the user liked in that view. This reduces the number of training examples per view to the number of users in the training data, which greatly reduce the training data size. Note that a concern of this technique is that the objective function now becomes maximizing the similarity between user features and the average features of items the user liked. There is a slight difference when it comes to evaluation since during test time each user is given only one single item. However, this approximation is necessary to make the system scale up well. Also, experimental results will show that this approximation still generates very promising results in practice.

7. EXPERIMENTAL SETUP

In this section, we explain the process of our empirical study and briefly review several recommendation algorithms we compared to as baselines.

For each data set, we aim at evaluating the system performance on users who already have previous interaction in this domain (old users) and users who did not have any previous interaction but have some search and browsing history that can be encoded into user view (new users). For evaluation, the data sets were split into training and test sets using the following criteria:

First, each user is randomly assigned a label of either "train" or "test" with the probability ratio of 0.9:0.1. Then, for each user with a "test" label, we further label them as "old" or "new" user with the probability ratio of 0.8:0.2. For those labeled as "old" users, 50% of their items are used for training and the rest for test. On the other hand, for "new" users, their items are only used for testing as the user-item pairs are guaranteed to never appear in the training process. This way, these users are indeed completely *new* to the system. The details of the dataset breakdown is in table 2.

In terms of performance evaluation, for each $(user_i, item_j)$ pair in the training data we select 9 other random items $item_{r1}, ...item_{r9}$, where $r1$ though $r9$ are random indices, and create 9 testing pairs $(user_i, item_{rk}), 1 \leq k \leq 9$ and added to the testing data set. The evaluation criteria is to measure of how well the system ranks the correct pair $(user_i, item_j)$ against the other random items for the same user $(user_i, item_{rk})$. Therefore, we employed two metrics for this: (1) the Mean Reciprocal Rank (MRR), which computes the inverse of the rank of the correct item among other items and average the score across the whole testing data, and (2) Precision@1 (P@1) which computes the percentage of times the system ranks the correct item as the top item.

We compared to several baseline systems described below:

Standard SVD Matrix decomposition: In this baseline, we construct the user/item matrix and perform matrix decomposition using SVD. This is a standard baseline for collaborative filtering techniques that does not use any features from items or users. In practice, this baseline is computationally feasible only on relatively small data set (in our case, the Apps data). In addition, this approach cannot give recommendation on new users since they do not appear in the user-item matrix.

Most Frequent Items: Since SVD is unable to handle new user recommendation, this approach is used as trivial baseline for new users. It works by first computing the frequency of each item in the training data, and then for each testing sample it ranks $(user_i, item_j)$ with respect to other random items according to their frequency in training set.

Canonical Correlation Analysis (CCA): CCA [29] is a traditional multi-view learning technique aims at finding two pairs of linear transformations, one for each input view, such that the correlation between transformed data is maximized. It is similar to DSSM with two main differences: (1) CCA often uses linear transformation, despite there exists non-linear transformations through kernel versions of CCA, which is often computationally prohibited in large-scale experiments, and (2) CCA maximizes the correlation under certain fixed variance constraints while DSSM maximizes the rank of the correct pairs. The ranking objective has shown be to a better objective recommendation systems. In our experiment for CCA, we only used top-k users features since the other two dimension reduction techniques, K-means and LSH, produce a non-sparse feature vectors which make the correlation matrix too dense to be efficiently computed.

Collaborative Topic Regression (CTR): CTR [32] is a recently-developed recommendation system that combines both Bayesian matrix factorization and items features to create a recommendation for items. It has shown to be successful in academic paper recommendations. In the CTR model, two inputs are given: a collaborative matrix and items features (represented using bag-of-words). The model matches users to items by maximizing the reconstruction error of the collaborative matrix and leveraging item features as an extra signal. This helps to model new items that did not appear before in the training data. For new user recommendation in our scenario, we take the transpose of the collaborative matrix A as input and supply user features instead of items features.

For our proposed approach, for both Apps and News data sets, we first run three sets of experiments to train single-view DNN models, each of which corresponds to a dimension reduction method in Section 6 (SV-TopK,SV-Kmeans and SV-LSH). Then we run another three sets of experiments for MV-DNN. The first two combine Apps and News data using TopK and Kmeans user features (MV-TopK and MV-Kmeans). The third set of experiments train a joint model between Apps, News and Movie/TV features with TopK user features (MV-TopK w/Xbox).

8. RESULTS AND DISCUSSION

Table 3 and 4 shows results obtained from different approaches in App and News data respectively[1]. We separate the algorithms into three types for clarification: Type *I* are baseline algorithms; Type *II* are our single-view models and Type *III* are multi-view DNN models. We see that the naive most-frequent-item baseline performs very poorly which confirms that the simple solutions to new users will not work well in our cases. It is also shown that standard SVD matrix factorization is not good enough in this task even for the current users that have entries in the collaborative filtering matrix. Surprisingly, the CCA model performed no better than random guess in Apps data which shows that using the non-linear mapping in DSSM plus the ranking based objective are important to the system. The CTR model [32] performed reasonably well for current users but not as good for the new users.

For the single-view DNN (shown as Type *II*), the results indicated that the performance is dependent on the dimensionality reduction approach used. It can be seen that the best one for both Apps and News data was the top-K feature dimension method which outperformed other two by a large margin. This can be viewed as a confirmation of the hypothesis that users can be model with a relatively small set of informative features. It also indicates that K-means and LSH are less effective to capture the semantics of the user behavior correctly. As a head-to-head comparison between our single-view models (Type *II*) and traditional recommendation methods (Type *I*), our best model (SV-TopK) outperformed the best baselines CTR [32], which also leveraged item features for recommendation, by 11% for all users (0.497 vs. 0.448 MRR score), and 36.7 % for new users (0.436 vs. 0.319 MRR score), relatively. For P@1, we see a much larger improvement: 13% for all users and 88.7%for new users, which shows the effectiveness of our system on recommending top-rated items.

Furthermore, for MV-DNN, results showed that adding more domains indeed helps to improve all domains at the same time. Specifically, by combining both News view and App view for training, we see a significant improvement on both News and App data sets in both metrics. Specifically, for the App data shown in Table 3, the MRR score increased from 0.497 to 0.517 for all users when comparing to the best single-view model, which is a 4% relative increase comparing to the single-view model. More importantly, we see a much bigger improvement on new users where one view's lack of new user data can be compensated by the data from other views. This is demonstrated by the 7% MRR (from 0.436 to 0.466) and 11% P@1 (from 0.268 to 0.297) relative improvement on the new users of App data set. Therefore, we are eager to know: can we safely conclude that more views can indeed improve the performance of the system? To find the answer to this hypothesis, we further added the Xbox data into the framework and trained a MV-DNN model with three user-item view pairs. The results are quite encouraging: MRR scores are further improved by 6% for all users and 8% for new users in App data, relatively. On the other hand, by comparing to the state-of-the-art algorithm, our best MV-DNN (with Xbox view) with top-K features performed 25.2% better than the CTR model for all users (from 0.277 to 0.347) , and 115% better for new users (from 0.142 to 0.306), for P@1.

Similar results can also be observed for the News data in Table 4, where MV-DNN scored 49% better for all users and 101% better for new users than the CTR model, relatively. Note that in this table, the results for CCA and SVD are missing. Due to the extreme size of the training data which contains 1.5 Million users with over 1 Billion entries, these two traditional algorithms failed miserably to handle such big data. We will detail our discussion on the scalability in the next section but it is quite evident here that our DNN based approach can easily scale up to billion-entry computing capacity while yield excellent recommendation results.

In order to explore the effectiveness of the learned pattern from the system, we perform the following experiment to test the recommendation performance with *single-feature inputs*. Specifically, we took the best performing system (MV-DNN with top-k features) and construct user features with only one domain feature turned on. The resulting user feature thus has only one value which is the ID of the domain. We then run our model for prediction against other views in order to find the top-matched News and Apps among all existing items. Table 5 shows some of those results. It can be seen that the learned recommendation system is indeed quite effective. In the first example, we assume a user has only visited *brackobama.com*. The top matched news show all related information regarding *President Obama* and *Obamacare health*, which are all relevant to the website. On the other hand, the top matched Apps are also related to health in this case. In the second example, we have a user who visited *www.spiegel.de*, a major online German News Website, which is not telling a lot about users except they can read German. The system matches articles for them on *FIFA world cup 2014* which seems to be a common interest for Germans in this time span. In last example where the user seems to have interests in *baby-related* information, both the top matched News and Apps are quite relevant to *baby, pregnancy* and etc.

9. EXPERIMENTS ON PUBLIC DATA

To further show the strength of our approach in modeling cross-domain users, we perform a set of experiments on the public data[2] by the authors in [28]. The data set contains authors from different research fields and the objective is to recommend authors from another field for cross-domain collaboration. The data contains 33,739 authors from five domains (data mining, theory etc.), where each data entry specifies the name of the research field, the title and abstract of a paper, the list of authors and the year the paper got published. We use a single-view DNN to model this cross-domain collaboration (e.g., collaboration between data

[1]Due to the sensitivity of Xbox data, we are unable to show the individual results for Movie/TV recommendation performance. However, in the tables, we still show how Xbox view can be used to enhance the performance of other views.

[2]Available at http://arnetminer.org/billboard/collaboration

Data Set	Training			Testing		
	Number Of unique users	Number of unique items	Number of training pairs	Number of new users	Number of test pairs for old users	Number of test pairs for new users
Apps Data	200K	55k	2.5M	1K	11K	2K
News Data	1.5M	5M	> 1B	5K	50K	10K
Xbox Data	16K	10K	45K	1K	10K	3K

Table 2: Details of the Train/Test breakdown for the three data sets used to evaluate our proposed approach.

User View with Single Domain ID Feature	Top Matched News	Top Matched Apps
barackobama.com	Obama to Delay Obamacare Again to Help Democrats Froma Harrop: Democrats should not run away from Obamacare Democratic Senator: I am willing to defy Obama Governor Jindal proposes Republican alternative to Obamacare	7 Minutes Fitter Relax Meditate Escape Sleep Sleep Tracker U.S. Constitution
spiegel.de	Nazi-Era Jerseys on View in World Cup Exhibit 2014 World Cup Day 3 Lessons: Colombia Fun In The Sun... Belgium Vs. Algeria World Cup 2014: Live Stream... Colombia vs. Ivory Coast: Tactical Preview ...	ESPN Cricinfo Golf News RSS Pulse News Dinamalar - Tamil News Paper
linkedin.com	RectorSeal, ... Acquires Assets of Resource Conservation... Berkshire Partners Teams With Glen T. Senk To Co-Invest ... TF Financial: National Penn Bancshares, Inc. to Acquire ... H.I.G. Capital Portfolio Company Surgery Partners to Acquire ...	LinkedIn App LinkedIn Touch The Economist on Windows The Wall Street Journal
babycenter.com	Jenelle Evans' Baby Name: What We Know Catelynn Lowell ... Are Reportedly Pregnant With Baby #2! Jenelle Evans Can Take Drugs During Pregnancy If She Wants Pregnant Jenelle Evans: What Should She Name Her Baby?	Parents Pregnancy & Baby Guide ANIMALS FOR KIDS GAME Minecraft Fan Hub GS Preschool Games

Table 5: Examples of learned mapping between URL domains, News articles and Apps. For the domains, only their feature IDs are used for training. The underlying domain names are unknown to the target applications.

	Algorithm	All Users		New Users	
		MRR	P@1	MRR	P@1
I	Most Frequent	0.298	0.103	0.303	0.119
	CF	0.337	0.142	/	/
	CCA (TopK) [29]	0.295	0.105	0.295	0.104
	CTR [32]	0.448	0.277	0.319	0.142
II	SV- Kmeans	0.359	0.159	0.336	0.154
	SV-LSH	0.372	0.169	0.339	0.158
	SV-TopK	**0.497**	**0.315**	**0.436**	**0.268**
III	MV-Kmeans	0.362	0.16	0.339	0.156
	MV-TopK	0.517	0.335	0.466	0.297
	MV-TopK w/ Xbox	**0.527**	**0.347**	**0.473**	**0.306**

Table 3: Results for different algorithms on Windows Apps Data Set. Type *I* algorithms are baseline methods we compare with. Type *II* are single user-item view methods trained using the original DSSM framework. Type *III* are multi-view DNN models we proposed. The best performance is achieved by training a MV-DNN on all three user-item views with TopK as feature selection method.

	Algorithm	All Users		New Users	
		MRR	P@1	MRR	P@1
I	Most Frequent	0.301	0.111	0.305	0.111
	CTR [32]	0.427	0.215	0.276	0.123
II	SV-Kmeans	0.386	0.192	0.294	0.143
	SV-LSH	0.45	0.247	0.34	0.186
	SV-TopK	**0.486**	**0.286**	**0.358**	**0.208**
III	MV-Kmeans	0.391	0.194	0.296	0.145
	MV-TopK	0.494	0.303	0.368	0.222
	MV-TopK w/ Xbox	**0.503**	**0.321**	**0.398**	**0.245**

Table 4: Results for the News Data Set. Similarly, the best performance is achieved by our multi-view models. Note that due to the extreme big size of this data set (> 1B entries), traditional algorithms like CF (SVD) and CCA failed to handle it due to memory constraint.

mining and theory researchers). In this case, both the user view and item view share the same feature representations. Specifically, we use the unigram words from the titles and abstracts of the papers that an authors published during the training period (1990 to 2001) as features, which results in a feature dimension of 31,932. Similar to the original authors evaluation approach, we randomly selected a set of authors who have already had cross-domain collaboration during the training period and have at least five cross-domain collaborations during testing period to be our evaluation set. For each set of collaboration between different fields, we train a separate single-view DNN model in 100 iterations.

Table 6 shows the results. Overall, our method performs significantly better than the CTL method in all four cross-domain data sets except for the metric of P@20. In particular, we achieve a much higher recall at 100, with the best improvement of 96% in the DM to theory recommendation performance. The results indicate that using rich user features with non-linear deep neural models can indeed capture lots of semantics that cannot be accurately modeled

Cross Domain	ALG	P@10	P@20	MAP	R@100
DM to Theory	CTL	37.7	**36.4**	40.6	35.6
	SV-DNN	**40.0**	24.2	**41.2**	**69.8**
MI to DB	CTL	32.5	**30.0**	36.9	59.8
	SV-DNN	**35.7**	20.6	**39.7**	**70.9**
MI to DM	CTL	30.0	**24.0**	35.6	49.6
	SV-DNN	**37.2**	21.5	**41.8**	**63.3**
Visual to DM	CTL	28.3	**26.0**	32.8	36.3
	SV-DNN	**35.2**	20.8	**37.8**	**64.4**

Table 6: Recommendation performance on the cross-domain collaboration public data [28].

using traditional word-based co-occurrence models such as generative topic models. We believe the performance can be further improved using multi-view DNN models but we leave that to future investigation.

In terms of efficiency, the authors reported 12-15 hours training time for the CTL method for the entire data set. Our algorithm runs much fast in that each model finished 100 iterations training within only 5-7 minutes on the same amount of data on a GPU machine. We will detail the scalability of our framework in the next section.

10. ALGORITHM SCALABILITY

This section we compare the performance of varies algorithms in terms of their training time. Recall that in the previous section, we mentioned that (in Table 4) for the News data, SVD (CF) and CCA were unable to handle the user-item matrix which has 1 Billion entries. This shows one of the strengths of our deep learning framework which is trained using SGD and thus able to handle massive amount of data using distributed training. The detail of the performance is shown in Table 7. We can observe that for the relatively small Apps data set, SVD and CCA finished relatively fast (around 4 hours, but yielded quite poor recommendation performance). The single-view DNN model (SV-TopK) finished 100 training iterations in 33 hours. The content-based CTR model, however, took a long time to train. The reason is that CTR requires an initial seed of topic proportion (θ) and topic distribution (β) trained using an LDA model. CTR then took these files and optimized the correlation between users and item features. Therefore, it turned out to be more expensive to train CTR than our deep learning model, for both data sets. On the other hand, we saw that both SV-TopK and MV-TopK exhibited (sub)linear training time to the data size, since usually SGD runs less epochs to converge when more data become available.

Figure 3 shows the training error during each iteration of the MV-TopK model for both News and Apps views. In our experiment, we manually specify the training iterations to be 100. One reason is that we continue to see improved performance for all views even though the improvement becomes smaller and smaller over time. On the other hand, we discovered that in practice the convergence of some views is faster than others. For example, for that particular model in Figure 3, the News view converged quickly after 20 iterations, while it took around 70 iterations for the Apps view to reach convergence. Due to the process of alternating user-item view pairs during training as well as the different convergence speed for different views, performing early stopping to further improve the scalability of our model becomes a critical future work.

Algorithm	Data Set: Apps	Data Set: News
CF	4 hours	OutOfMemory
CCA [29]	4 hours	OutOfMemory
CTR [32]	40 hours	120 hours
SV-TopK	33 hours	50 hours
MV-TopK	60 hours	
MV-TopK w/ Xbox	62 hours	

Table 7: Training time for all algorithms in comparison. The CTR model using Bayesian approach takes twice longer to finish than our most expensive DNN model.

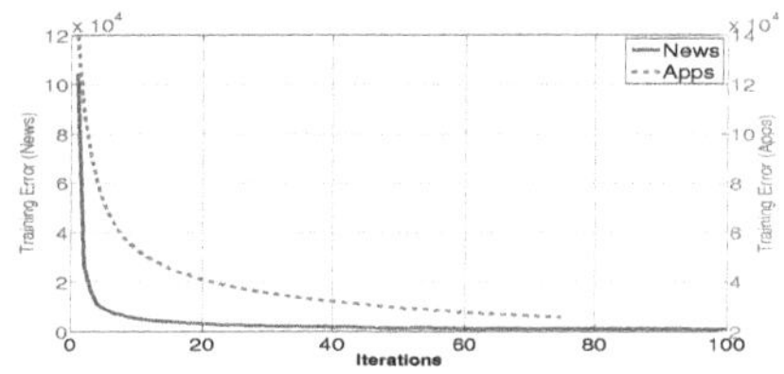

Figure 3: Training errors for two views in MV-TopK model.

11. CONCLUSION AND FUTURE WORK

In this work, we presented a general recommendation framework that uses deep learning to match rich user features to items features. We also showed how to extend this framework to combine data from different domains to further improve the recommendation quality. We then discussed different ways to make this approach scalable to large data sets through dimensionality reduction. The proposed model can handle both existing user and new user recommendation. Experiments on several large-scale real-world data sets indicated that the proposed approach worked much better than other systems by large margin.

As a pilot study, we believe that this work has opened a new door to recommendation systems using deep learning from multiple data sources. Despite the fact that most of the evaluation in this paper used proprictary data, the framework should be able to generalize to other data sources without much additional effort as shown in Section 9 using a small public data set. For example, recommending music to users based on their tweets, recommending restaurants according to Facebook status updates, or recommending images and videos based on user search queries.

For future work, we aim at incorporating more user features into the user view. We want to make our DNN learning more scalable so that eventually the entire set of user features can be used for training without dimension reduction. We also aim at adding more domains into our multi-view framework and further analysis its performance in details. Another important direction is to investigate how to incorporate collaborative filtering with our approach which currently running only as content-based filtering approach.

12. ACKNOWLEDGEMENTS

We greatly appreciate the authors in the KDD'12 paper [28] for making their data public. In particular, Sen Wu for his great support in discussion of the data set. We also want to thank anonymous reviewers for their invaluable feedback.

13. REFERENCES

[1] Fabian Abel, Qi Gao, Geert-Jan Houben, and Ke Tao. Twitter-based user modeling for news recommendations. In *IJCAI'13*, pages 2962–2966.

[2] Amr Ahmed, Abhimanyu Das, and Alexander J Smola. Scalable hierarchical multitask learning algorithms for conversion optimization in display advertising. In *WSDM'14*, pages 153–162.

[3] Robert M Bell and Yehuda Koren. Improved neighborhood-based collaborative filtering. In *KDD'13 CUP*, 2007.

[4] Cheng Chu, Sang Kyun Kim, Yi-An Lin, YuanYuan Yu, Gary Bradski, Andrew Y Ng, and Kunle Olukotun. Map-reduce for machine learning on multicore. 2007.

[5] Adam Coates, Andrew Y Ng, and Honglak Lee. An analysis of single-layer networks in unsupervised feature learning. In *AISTATS'11*, pages 215–223.

[6] Abhinandan S Das, Mayur Datar, Ashutosh Garg, and Shyam Rajaram. Google news personalization: scalable online collaborative filtering. In *WWW'07*, pages 271–280.

[7] Asela Gunawardana and Christopher Meek. Tied boltzmann machines for cold start recommendations. In *RECSYS'08*, pages 19–26.

[8] John A Hartigan and Manchek A Wong. Algorithm as 136: A k-means clustering algorithm. *Applied statistics*, pages 100–108, 1979.

[9] Po-Sen Huang, Xiaodong He, Jianfeng Gao, Li Deng, Alex Acero, and Larry Heck. Learning deep structured semantic models for web search using clickthrough data. In *CIKM'13*, pages 2333–2338.

[10] Piotr Indyk and Rajeev Motwani. Approximate nearest neighbors: towards removing the curse of dimensionality. In *STOC'98*, pages 604–613.

[11] Joonseok Lee, Samy Bengio, Seungyeon Kim, Guy Lebanon, and Yoram Singer. Local collaborative ranking. In *WWW'14*, pages 85–96.

[12] Bin Li, Qiang Yang, and Xiangyang Xue. Transfer learning for collaborative filtering via a rating-matrix generative model. In *ICML'09*, pages 617–624.

[13] Ping Li, Trevor J Hastie, and Kenneth W Church. Very sparse random projections. In *KDD'06*, pages 287–296.

[14] Greg Linden, Brent Smith, and Jeremy York. Amazon. com recommendations: Item-to-item collaborative filtering. *Internet Computing, IEEE*, 7(1):76–80, 2003.

[15] Jiahui Liu, Peter Dolan, and Elin Rønby Pedersen. Personalized news recommendation based on click behavior. In *IUI'10*, pages 31–40.

[16] Prem Melville, Raymond J Mooney, and Ramadass Nagarajan. Content-boosted collaborative filtering for improved recommendations. In *AAAI'02*.

[17] Weike Pan, Evan Wei Xiang, Nathan Nan Liu, and Qiang Yang. Transfer learning in collaborative filtering for sparsity reduction. In *AAAI'10*, 2010.

[18] Al Mamunur Rashid, George Karypis, and John Riedl. Learning preferences of new users in recommender systems: an information theoretic approach. *ACM SIGKDD Explorations Newsletter*, 10(2):90–100, 2008.

[19] Jasson DM Rennie and Nathan Srebro. Fast maximum margin matrix factorization for collaborative prediction. In *ICML'05*, pages 713–719.

[20] Shaghayegh Sahebi and Peter Brusilovsky. Cross-domain collaborative recommendation in a cold-start context: The impact of user profile size on the quality of recommendation. In *User Modeling, Adaptation, and Personalization*, pages 289–295. Springer, 2013.

[21] Ruslan Salakhutdinov and Andriy Mnih. Bayesian probabilistic matrix factorization using markov chain monte carlo. In *ICML'08*, pages 880–887.

[22] Ruslan Salakhutdinov, Andriy Mnih, and Geoffrey Hinton. Restricted boltzmann machines for collaborative filtering. In *ICML'07*, pages 791–798.

[23] Badrul Sarwar, George Karypis, Joseph Konstan, and John Riedl. Item-based collaborative filtering recommendation algorithms. In *WWW'01*, pages 285–295. ACM, 2001.

[24] Andrew I Schein, Alexandrin Popescul, Lyle H Ungar, and David M Pennock. Methods and metrics for cold-start recommendations. In *SIGIR'02*, pages 253–260.

[25] Yang Song, Weiwei Cui, Shixia Liu, and Kuansan Wang. Online behavioral genome sequencing from usage logs: decoding the search behaviors. In *WWW'14*, pages 91–94.

[26] Yang Song, Hongning Wang, and Xiaodong He. Adapting deep ranknet for personalized search. In *WSDM'14*, pages 83–92.

[27] Shiliang Sun. A survey of multi-view machine learning. *Neural Computing and Applications*, 23(7-8):2031–2038, 2013.

[28] Jie Tang, Sen Wu, Jimeng Sun, and Hang Su. Cross-domain collaboration recommendation. In *KDD'12*, pages 1285–1293.

[29] Bruce Thompson. Canonical correlation analysis. *Encyclopedia of statistics in behavioral science*, 2005.

[30] Aaron Van den Oord, Sander Dieleman, and Benjamin Schrauwen. Deep content-based music recommendation. In *NIPS'13*, pages 2643–2651.

[31] Benjamin Van Durme and Ashwin Lall. Online generation of locality sensitive hash signatures. In *ACL'10 Short Papers*, pages 231–235.

[32] Chong Wang and David M Blei. Collaborative topic modeling for recommending scientific articles. In *KDD'11*, pages 448–456.

Cookies That Give You Away: The Surveillance Implications of Web Tracking

Steven Englehardt
Princeton University
ste@princeton.edu

Dillon Reisman
Princeton University
dreisman@princeton.edu

Christian Eubank
Princeton University
cge@princeton.edu

Peter Zimmerman
Princeton University
peterz@princeton.edu

Jonathan Mayer
Stanford University
jmayer@stanford.edu

Arvind Narayanan
Princeton University
arvindn@princeton.edu

Edward W. Felten
Princeton University
felten@princeton.edu

ABSTRACT

We study the ability of a passive eavesdropper to leverage "third-party" HTTP tracking cookies for mass surveillance. If two web pages embed the same tracker which tags the browser with a unique cookie, then the adversary can link visits to those pages from the same user (i.e., browser instance) even if the user's IP address varies. Further, many popular websites leak a logged-in user's identity to an eavesdropper in unencrypted traffic.

To evaluate the effectiveness of our attack, we introduce a methodology that combines web measurement and network measurement. Using OpenWPM, our web privacy measurement platform, we simulate users browsing the web and find that the adversary can reconstruct 62—73% of a typical user's browsing history. We then analyze the effect of the physical location of the wiretap as well as legal restrictions such as the NSA's "one-end foreign" rule. Using measurement units in various locations—Asia, Europe, and the United States—we show that foreign users are highly vulnerable to the NSA's dragnet surveillance due to the concentration of third-party trackers in the U.S. Finally, we find that some browser-based privacy tools mitigate the attack while others are largely ineffective.

1. INTRODUCTION

How much can an adversary learn about an average user by surveilling web traffic? This question is surprisingly tricky to answer accurately, as it depends on four things: the structure of the web, the mapping of web resources to the topology of the global Internet, the web browsing behavior of a typical user, and the technical capabilities and policy restrictions of the adversary. We introduce a methodology for quantifying the efficacy of passive surveillance. Our technique combines web measurement, network measurement, a client model (that incorporates user browsing behavior, web browser policies and settings, and privacy-protecting extensions), and an adversary model.

More specifically, the adversary has the ability to inspect packet contents and wishes to either track an individual target user or surveil users *en masse*. A key challenge for the adversary is the lack of persistent identifiers visible on the network (in Section 3 we discuss why IP addresses are inadequate). However, the adversary can observe HTTP cookies in transit. Indeed, both the NSA and GCHQ are known to use such cookies for surveillance (Section 3).

Our work starts with three insights. First, the presence of *multiple unrelated* third-party cookies on most web pages, albeit pseudonymous, can tie together most of a user's web traffic without having to rely on IP addresses (Figure 1). Thus the adversary can separate network traffic into clusters, with each cluster corresponding to only one user (or more precisely, one browser instance). A single user's traffic may span more than one cluster if the linking is imperfect.

Second, a significant portion of a typical user's traffic traverses U.S. borders even when the user is outside the U.S. and browses local content. As it turns out, such sites frequently include third-party resources such as analytics scripts, tracking pixels, and advertisements from U.S. servers. This leaves foreign users particularly vulnerable to the NSA's wiretaps within the U.S. under the "one-end foreign" rule (Section 3).

Third, although most popular websites now deploy HTTPS for authentication, many web pages reveal an already logged-in user's *identity* in plaintext. Thus, an adversary that can wiretap the network can not only cluster together the web pages visited by a user, but can then attach real-world identities to those clusters. This technique relies on nothing other than the network traffic itself for identifying targets.

Figure 1 illustrates the basis for our work. The adversary observes the user visit three different web pages which embed trackers X, Y or both. The user's IP address may change between visits to each page, though we assume it is consistent for the request to site A and the request to A's embedded tracker X. But there is no way to tie together her visits to pages A and B until she visits C after which all three visits can be connected. The unique cookie from X connects A and C while the one from Y connects B and C. We assume here that the user has visited pages with both trackers before so that cookies have already been set in her browser and will be sent with each request. While IP address is a *convenient* method to link a request to a first party page to the corresponding request to an embedded third party tracker, it is not necessary. In Section 6.1 we show how this linkage can be achieved even if the IP address cannot be observed at all or if an IP address is shared by many users.

Contributions. Our contributions are both conceptual and empirical. First, we identify and formalize a new pri-

WWW 2015, May 18–22, 2015, Florence, Italy.
ACM 978-1-4503-3469-3/15/05.
http://dx.doi.org/10.1145/2736277.2741679.

Figure 1: Illustration of link between each of a single browser's visits to three first-party pages using two different third-party tracking cookies. The user accesses the web at three different times, behind three different IP addresses.

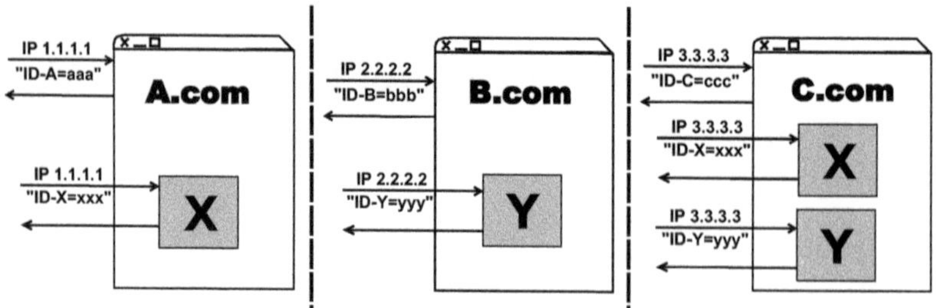

vacy threat from packet sniffing. While the technique of utilizing cookies to target users is well known, we formulate the attack concretely in terms of the following steps: (1) automatically classifying cookies as unique identifiers (2) using multiple ID cookies to make *transitive* inferences and *clustering* HTTP traffic, (3) geographically tagging the flow of traffic, and (4) inferring real-world identity from HTTP request and response bodies. We believe this attack to be the strongest known way for a passive adversary to utilize web traffic for surveillance.

Second, we rigorously evaluate the above attack model using a novel methodology that combines web measurement, network measurement, a user model, and an adversary model (Section 4). We simulate realistic browsing behavior and measure the actual cookie ecosystem. This requires nuanced techniques along several fronts: (1) a crawling infrastructure based on *browser automation* to more closely simulate real users (2) a model of browsing history derived from real user behavior, and (3) network measurements to help verify the robustness of geolocation data.

Third, we present an exhaustive empirical evaluation of browser privacy settings and privacy extensions to discover how well a proactive user can protect himself against the attack model we've defined. Specifically, we measure how each of the following privacy measures affect the effectiveness of the attack: blocking all third-party cookies, blocking only those from sites not visited directly, setting Do Not Track (DNT), using Ghostery, and using HTTPS Everywhere.[1]

Results. We simulate users that make 0 to 300 web page visits spread out over a 2–3 month period. We consider users located in several possible countries. For each such set of visits, we perform clustering using the method described above and find the "giant connected component." For non-U.S. users, we consider an adversary with wiretaps in the target user's country as well as one with wiretaps in the U.S.

At a high level, our results show that for a U.S. user, over 73% of visits fall into this connected component. The clustering effect is extremely strong and is robust to differences in the models of browsing behavior. Clustering even occurs when the adversary is able to observe only a small, random subset of the user's requests.

Non-U.S. locations show a lower degree of clustering due to a lower number of embedded third-parties: over 59% of traffic falls into the giant connected component. If the adversary is further restricted to be in the U.S., the clustering level does drop significantly (12% – 20%), but this is still surprisingly high given that these users are browsing local content.

Second, we measure the presence of identifying information in plaintext among popular (Alexa Top 50 U.S.) websites. 56% of sites transmit some form of identifying information in plaintext once a user logs in, whether first name, first and last name, username, or email address. The majority of these (42% of websites overall) present *unique* identifiers (username or email address) in the clear.

Third, we show that many built-in browser protections are able to reduce but not fully mitigate the attack. The most effective blocking solution, Ghostery, still allows 24.2% of a user's traffic to be clustered, while alternative solutions have far less of an impact.

Implications An adversary interested in targeted surveillance can proceed as follows: (1) Either scan for the target's identity in plaintext HTTP traffic, or use auxiliary methods to obtain the target's cookie ID on some first-party page (2) From this starting point, transitively connect the target's known first-party cookie to other third-party and first-party cookies of the target. On the other hand, an adversary interested in *en masse* surveillance can first cluster all observed HTTP traffic, albeit at a high computational cost, and then attach identities to these clusters using the methods above. Our attacks show the feasibility of either adversary's goal.

What can the adversary do after attaching an identity to a cluster of web traffic? First, browsing history itself could be the information of interest, as in the NSA plan to discredit 'radicals' based on browsing behavior, such as pornography [4]. Second, further sensitive information might be found in unencrypted web content such as preferences, purchase history, address, etc. Finally, it can enable active attacks such as delivering malware to a targeted user [47, 19].

2. RELATED WORK

Our work draws from two previously independent bodies of research. The first analyzes the privacy implications of third-party cookies and the second analyzes the ability of a network eavesdropper to infer sensitive information. We describe each in turn. To our knowledge, the two sets of ideas have not been combined before.

Third-party tracking: prevalence and privacy implications. There have been several notable results uncovering or quantifying various types of online tracking: cookies [28, 45], flash cookies (LSOs) including respawning behavior [46, 9, 38, 6], and browser fingerprinting [41, 7, 6]. The ability of trackers to compile information about users is further aided by PII leaks from first parties to third parties [29, 30, 27] and "cookie syncing", or different third-party trackers linking their pseudonymous cookies to each other [42, 6].

While this body of research helps us understand what trackers themselves can learn, it does not address the question we are interested in, which is what an *eavesdropper* can learn through cookies and identifier leaks. The latter is influenced by many additional factors including geographic location of the trackers and the adoption of HTTPS by websites.

Yen et al. show how IP, cookies and usernames can be combined to track devices reliably even when any one of

[1]DNT: `http://donottrack.us/`, Ghostery: `https://www.ghostery.com`, HTTPS-E: `https://www.eff.org/https-everywhere`

these identifiers may be individually unreliable [50]. The similarities to our work are superficial: we study linkage by an eavesdropper who utilizes third-party cookies rather than a website that uses its first-party cookies. The goals are also different: learning users' web histories vs. ID-ing devices.

There are various client-side tools to block, limit or visualize third-party tracking. These are too numerous to list exhaustively, but a sampling include Adblock Plus, Ghostery, ShareMeNot [1], Lightbeam, and TrackingObserver [2]. Studies that have quantified the privacy effect of these tools include [35, 11, 20].

Surveillance: attacks, defenses, and measurement. While there is a large body of work on what a passive adversary can infer about users, virtually all of it concerns attacks arising from side-channels in encrypted traffic, particularly Tor. While Tor is insecure against a global passive adversary, traffic analysis attacks have been studied with respect to passive and active adversaries with less comprehensive access to the network [39, 40]. *Website fingerprinting* allows a local eavesdropper to determine which of a set of web pages the user is visiting, even if the connection is encrypted, by observing packet lengths and other features [25, 24, 43]. Other side-channel attacks include timing attacks on SSH [48], leaks in web forms, [15] and inferring spoken phrases from VoIP [49].

By contrast, we study users who do *not* use a properly configured Tor browser. The adversary's main challenge is not linking origin and destination, but rather linking different traffic flows to the same (real-world) identity.

Closer to our work, Arnbak and Goldberg studied how the NSA could actively redirect U.S. traffic abroad, so as to bring it within broader surveillance authorities [8].[2] The IXMaps tool allows users to interactively view the routes taken by their traffic and intersection with known NSA wiretapping sites [16].

3. BACKGROUND AND THREAT MODEL

In recent years, a combination of technical research, leaks, and declassifications has provided unprecedented transparency into Internet surveillance by governments. Some nations, such as Iran and Bahrain [17], practice near-total Internet monitoring. Others, including the United States and Britain, have large-scale technical capacity—but subject to legal limits. This section explains how the National Security Agency (NSA) and Government Communication Headquarters (GCHQ) have used third-party cookies in their respective surveillance programs, as well as briefly discusses the laws that govern surveillance of Internet traffic within the United States. It then sets out a threat model that motivates our study.

NSA and GCHQ use of third-party cookies. Leaked documents reflect at least three ways in which the NSA has used third-party cookies obtained from its Internet intercepts. First, the agency has investigated passively identifying Tor users by associating cookies with non-Tor sessions. Specifically, the NSA attempted to link a Google third-party advertising cookie between Tor and non-Tor sessions [5].

Second, the agency has an active, man-in-the-middle system ("QUANTUMCOOKIE") that induces cookie disclosure [5]. Applications include identifying Tor users and targeting malware delivery.

Third, the agency has used passively obtained cookies to target active man-in-the-middle exploitation. On at least one occasion, the NSA offered a Google cookie to single out a user for exploitation [47].

In addition to these specific applications, HTTP analytical tools (such as "XKEYSCORE") incorporate cookie data. An analyst could easily take advantage of third-party cookies when querying intercepted data [21].

Several leaked documents also reveal two GCHQ programs for surveilling and targeting users via third-party tracking data, both from web browsers and mobile applications. One program, "MUTANT BROTH", a repository of tracking cookies linked with additional metadata such as IP addresses and User-Agent strings. This repository is reported to have been used for targeted malware delivery [19].

The other program, "BADASS", offers a similar repository and search interface for querying information leakage from mobile apps. The system collects and extracts leaked identifiers, device and operating system details, and additional information transmitted in plaintext [31].

United States Internet monitoring. The law surrounding NSA authority derives from a complex mixture of constitutional doctrine, statutory restrictions, and executive regulation. One emergent property is that, when at least one party to a communication is outside the United States, it is eligible for warrantless surveillance.[3] "Upstream" interception devices, controlled by the NSA and foreign partners, are exposed to large volumes of this "one-end foreign" Internet traffic. While the details remain classified, it also appears that a substantial quantity of one-end foreign traffic is temporarily retained. Leaks indicate that at least some installations of "XKEYSCORE," a distributed analysis system, maintain a multi-day buffer of Internet traffic [12].

Threat model. In developing a threat model, there are two extremes, neither of which is desirable. The first is to assume that the adversary is all-powerful, as in cryptographic security arguments. Such a model is both uninteresting and largely irrelevant to the real world. The other extreme is to focus too closely on the NSA or GCHQ's activities. Such a model may not yield insights that apply to other surveillance programs and the results may be invalidated by changes to the respective agency's programs. We seek a careful middle ground and arrive at a model that we believe is realistic enough to influence policy debates and privacy tool development, yet general enough for our analyses and algorithms to be of independent scientific interest and for our results to hold up well over time.

We consider only passive attacks for several reasons. First, passive attacks appear to be more powerful than generally realized, and we wish to highlight this fact. Second, even an active attack must usually begin with passive eavesdropping. An adversary must have refined criteria for targeting the active attack. Finally, almost all active attacks carry some

[2]It is not apparent whether the NSA has redirected traffic in this manner, nor is it apparent whether the agency would consider the practice lawful.

[3]One-end foreign wireline interceptions inside the United States are generally governed by Section 702 of the FISA Amendments Act [22]. Two-end foreign interceptions and one-end foreign wireless interceptions inside the United States are generally governed by Executive Order 12333. Interceptions outside the United States are also generally governed by Executive Order 12333 [3].

risk of detection. Passive attacks much easier to mount, especially at large scale.

We consider a powerful adversary with the ability to observe a substantial portion of web traffic on the Internet backbone. The adversary's view of a given user's traffic may be complete or partial. We model partial coverage in two ways: by assuming that a random subset of the user's HTTP requests and responses flows through one of the adversary's wiretaps, or that the adversary taps the portion of the user's traffic that traverses United States borders. While the NSA has many interception points outside U.S. borders as well, the U.S.-only model provides a useful, approximate lower bound of the agency's abilities. We also assume that the adversary cannot routinely compromise HTTPS, so cookies or other identifying information sent over HTTPS are of no use.

The adversary may have one of two goals: first, he might want to target a specific individual for surveillance. In this case the adversary knows either the target's real-world identity or a single ID cookie known to belong to the target (whether on a first or third party domain). Second, the adversary might be engaged in mass surveillance. This adversary would like to "scoop up" web traffic and automatically associate real-world identities with as much of it as possible.

The adversary's task is complicated by the fact that the IP addresses of the target(s) may change frequently. A user's IP address could change because she is physically mobile, her ISP assigns IP addresses dynamically, or she is using Tor. Leaked GCHQ documents show that their search interface even warns analysts to take care when selecting data on dynamic IPs [19]. Browsing from a smartphone is a case worth highlighting: Balakrishnan et al. find that "individual cell phones can expose different IP addresses to servers within time spans of a few minutes" and that "cell phone IP addresses do not embed geographical information at reasonable fidelity" [10].

To link users across different networks and over time, the adversary aims to utilize first-party and third-party unique cookies assigned to browser instances by websites. He can easily sniff these on the network by observing the "Cookie" field in HTTP request headers and the "Set-Cookie" field in HTTP response headers. Cookies set by an "origin" (roughly, a domain) that have not expired are automatically sent as part of requests to the same origin.

4. METHODOLOGY

In this study, we wish to simulate real users browsing over a period of time, detect the creation of unique identifiers, and measure the flow of both unique pseudonymous and real-world identifiers to adversaries with differing collection capabilities. We present a summary of our methodology below, and provide detailed descriptions of our measurement and analysis methodology in the following subsections.

1. Define all clients and adversaries to be studied, according to the following models:
   - client: (location, browsing model, browser configuration) which encodes the client's geographic and network location, which sites the client visits, and the browser settings and plugins the client browses with.
   - adversary: (location, policy restrictions) which encodes the adversary's geographic and network location, and the policy restrictions on data use and collection.
2. For each unique (user location, browsing model) pair of interest, generate N simulated browsing profiles as defined in Section 4.1 and create a corresponding client instance for each one.
3. Use the measurement infrastructure (Section 4.2) to simulate the users defined in Step 2 and collect all network traffic (i.e. HTTP requests, responses, and cookies). Our measurements are summarized in Section 4.3.
4. For each (client location, web resource) pair of interest, determine the geographic path of traffic using the procedure described in Section 4.4.
5. Run the ID cookie detection algorithm detailed in Section 4.5 to flag identifying cookies
6. For each (client, adversary) pair of interest, do the following for all instances of the client and average the results:
   - filter the list of requests based on the geographic location and policy restrictions of the adversary using the geographic mapping created in Step 4.
   - run the cookie linking algorithm detailed in Section 4.6 using the ID cookies detected in Step 5.
   - report the size of the connected components in the linking graph (as a ratio of total number of visits)
   - report the number of sites known to leak real-world identifiers (Section 4.7) contained in each component.

4.1 Browsing models

We use two browsing models to create simulated user profiles. One of our models was a naive one – the user visits random subsets of the Alexa top 500 sites local to the location of the measurement instance. For example, a measurement instance in Japan would sample the Alexa top-500 sites for users in Japan, while a measurement instance in Ireland would sample from the Alexa top-500 sites for users in Ireland.

Our other browsing model aims for realism by making use of the AOL search query log dataset. The dataset contains queries made by 650,000 anonymous users over a three month period (March–May 2006). We create a browsing profile from a user's search queries as follows. First, we remove repeated queries. Next, for every search query performed by the user, we submit the query to Google search and retrieve the links for the first five results. Users were selected on the basis that they performed between 50 to 100 unique queries which resulted in browsing profiles of 250 to 500 URLs. This is almost identical to the method that was used in [32].

Of course, only a subset of real users' web browsing results from web searches. Nevertheless, we hypothesize that our profiles model two important aspects of real browsing histories: the distribution of popularity of web pages visited, and the topical interest distribution of real users. Popular websites may embed more trackers on average than less popular sites, and websites on the same topic may be more interconnected in terms of common embedded trackers. Failure to model these aspects correctly could skew our results.

The reason we recreate the users' searches on a current search engine rather than simply using the sites visited by the AOL users (available in the dataset) is that the distribution of websites visited by real users changes over time as websites rise/fade in popularity, whereas the distribution of users' interests can be expected to be more stable over time.

4.2 Measurement infrastructure

We built our study on top of a web measurement platform, OpenWPM [18], which we developed in earlier work. The platform has the ability to drive full browsers, such as Firefox, with any set of browser extensions and collects a wide range of measurement data as it visits sites.[4] In our study, we use version 0.1.0 of OpenWPM to drive Firefox measurement instances from which we record all HTTP data for analysis. We configure the measurement instances to browse with profiles generated from the models described in Section 4.1, and deploy the crawls on cloud machines in the United States, Japan, and Ireland.

4.3 Measurements

We deployed OpenWPM on Amazon EC2[5] instances in three regions: Northern Virginia, United States, Dublin, Ireland, and Tokyo, Japan. We chose these to achieve as much geographic diversity as possible from Amazon's limited set of regions. Each measurement took place on an m3.medium instance of Ubuntu 14.04 in June 2014. All measurements were ran using 25 simulated profiles for each (user location, browsing model, browser configuration) combination.

When making measurements from within the U.S., we were able to utilize the more realistic AOL browsing model. We used it under serveral browser configurations: no cookie blocking, blocking third-party cookies from sites which the user has not yet visited as a first-party, blocking all third-party cookies, setting the DNT flag, browsing with HTTPS Everywhere installed, and browsing with Ghostery installed and configured to block all possible entities.

For measurements outside of the Unites States, we were not able to utilize the AOL browsing model as the search terms and results are likely biased towards U.S. users. Instead, we fall back to the Alexa browsing model when doing comparisons between geographic locations. To compare measurements between the United States, Japan, and Ireland we used an Alexa browsing model localized to the most popular sites within each country.

To run the identifying cookie detection algorithm described in Section 4.5, we also require synchronized measurements of each site visit from two separate machines. We ran these measurements from the Northern Virginia location and visited all of the links which may be visited by any other measurement instance (13,644 links total).

For all measurements, web pages were visited approximately once every ten seconds. We set a 60 second timeout per visit and restarted the browser with consistent state in the event of a crash.

4.4 HTTP Traffic geolocation

In order to determine the if an HTTP request is bound for a specific location of interest, we augment commercially available geolocation data with additional measurement data. After each measurement instance finished browsing, we ran a `traceroute`[6] to each unique hostname and recorded the full output. All IPs returned in each hop of the traceroute were geo-located with the `MaxMind GeoLite2`[7] country databases.

The mapping between IP and physical location is not one-to-one. Instead, there may be many servers in different locations which all share the same IP address for various purposes. One such example is *anycasting*, the process by which several nodes share the same address and the user is routed to the nearest node.[8]

Thus, when determining if an HTTP request enters a specific country it is not sufficient to simply geolocate the IPs returned from a traceroute to that host. As a solution, we implement a simplified version of the *geo-inconsistency* check proposed by Madory, et.al. [33]. We check that the minimum round-trip time (RTT) returned by a traceroute to each hop is greater than the physical minimum RTT assuming a direct fiber-optic connection between the two locations.

Algorithm 1 summarizes the steps we take to perform this origin-specific geolocation check. Broadly, if the geolocation of a specific hop returns as being within the country of interest, we find the travel time between the (latitude, longitude) pairs of the origin server and the geolocated IP. If geolocated IP's location is on the country level, we choose the closest point in the geolocated country from the origin location. We then use the haversine forumla to calculate the distance between the two points and find the minimum RTT:

$$minRTT = 2 * \frac{\text{haversine distance} * n}{c}$$

where c is the speed of light in units matching the distance measurement and n is the optical index of the fiber. In our study, we use $n = 1.52$ as the reference optical fiber index.

```
Data: httpRequest, testCountry
Result: True/False if httpRequest enters testCountry
origin ← latitude/longitude of origin server
hostname ← parse httpRequest.url
for each hop in hostname traceroute do
    location ← geolocate(hop.IP)
    if location not in testCountry then
        continue
    if location not city code then
        location ← closest point to origin within country
    dist ← haversine(origin,location)
    minRTT ← 2 * minimum time to travel dist
    if hop.RTT > minRTT then
        return True
end
return False
```

Algorithm 1: Origin-specific geolocation check

This check does not guarantee that a specific request enters a country, as network delays could artificially push a traceroute RTT above the threshold. Our assumption of a straight-line connection and optical fiber index is also unlikely to hold in practice. Instead, this check provides a more realistic upper-bound on the amount of traffic an adversary at a specific geographic location can monitor. For example, this check eliminated the numerous examples we observed of traceroutes originating in Ireland and Japan having geolocations within the United States with RTTs of <5ms.

We use a simplified version of this check when examining if requests are exiting the United States. Since a request can be bound for any non-U.S. destination, we do not attempt to find the closest point in each country. Instead, we only check that the observed RTT is greater than the minimum RTT to the geolocation point regardless of the point's location.

4.5 Detecting unique identifier cookies

[4]`https://github.com/citp/OpenWPM`

[5]`https://aws.amazon.com/ec2/`

[6]Our traceroutes were configured to use a single probe per hop with a maximum of 25 hops.

[7]`http://dev.maxmind.com/geoip/geoip2/geolite2/`

[8]CloudFlare, for example, claims to use anycasting as part of their content delivery network: `https://www.cloudflare.com/features-cdn`

An essential task to quantifying our attack is the ability to detect which cookies are identifying. Identifiers can be stored in many locations (e.g. HTTP cookies, Flash cookies), but to be sent back to trackers the identifiers must be included in HTTP cookies or query parameters of the request. We choose to focus HTTP cookies as they are included in every request and thus provide a generic approach that does not necessitate the parsing of URL parameters for all sites under surveillance. Furthermore, non-cookie tracking techniques are ordinarily paired with tracking cookies; our approach indirectly incorporates an adversary's capabilities against those technologies.

For our analysis, we are interested in the host (the domain that set the cookie), name, and value fields of a cookie and determine if the data stored in the value field is identifying. This algorithm is a modified version of one we used in a previous study [6].

To be useful to the adversary as identifiers, cookie values must have two important properties: persistence over time and uniqueness across different browser instances. Based on these criteria we develop an algorithm that classifies cookies as identifiers. Our algorithm is intentionally conservative, since false positives risk exaggerating the severity of the attack. Our method does have some false negatives, but this is acceptable since it is in line with our goal of establishing lower bounds for the feasibility of the attack.

We define a cookie to be an identifier cookie if it meets the following criteria: (1) It is *long-lived*, with expiry times longer than three months. The three month cut-off matches our AOL dataset three month window. (2) It's value is *stable*, and remains constant through all page visits. Dynamic value strings may be timestamps or other non-identifiers. (3) Has a *constant-length* across all our datasets. (4) Is *user-specific*, so the values are unique across different browser instances in our dataset. (5) Has a *high-entropy* value string, with values sufficiently different between machines to enable unique identification. To test for this, we used the Ratcliff-Obershelp [13] algorithm to compute similarity scores between value strings. We filtered out all cookies with value strings that were more than 55% similar to value strings from the corresponding cookies of different measurements.

We run our detection algorithm on the synchronized measurement data described in Section 4.3. By using synchronized measurements, we avoid the problem of sites changing their cookie interaction behavior depending on a user's browsing time. For instance, in relation to the entropy heuristic, cookies with values that depend on time stamps will be easier to detect and ignore if the crawls have nearly the same timestamps for all actions. For other measurements, we extract identifying cookie values by searching for cookies which match the identifying (host, name) pairs classified in the synchronized measurements.

4.6 Transitive Cookie Linking

Building the graph. Once we determine which cookies contain unique identifiers, we use the `http_requests`, `http_responses`, and `http_cookies` tables of the OpenWPM crawl database to cluster traffic. From these tables, we construct cookie linking graph using Algorithm 2, which creates a graph with two node types: *URL* nodes and *Cookie* nodes. URL nodes are identified by the tuple (U, <node url>, <request's geographic destination>) and cookie nodes consisting of the tuple (C, <cookie_value>).

Edges are created under the assumption that a network adversary will be able to link all requests and responses for a single page visit together if he can both follow the chain of referrer and redirect headers for HTTP requests from a single IP. URL — URL edges are created under two conditions: (1) one url node was observed as the `referer` on a request to the connected url node or (2) one url node was returned in the location field of a `301` or `302` redirect response to the request for the connected url. An adversary is only able to link together different page visits by the shared cookie values loaded on each page. As such, URL — Cookie edges are created whenever a cookie value is observed in the `Cookie` field of an HTTP Request header or the `Set-Cookie` field of an HTTP Response header. Notice that the only linking between separate page visits in the graph occurs when two HTTP requests/responses happen to link to the same Cookie node, while referrer and redirection chaining provides linking within a page visit.

```
Data: httpRequests and httpResponses for user_i
Result: Graph G_i for user_i with URL & Cookie nodes
for each visited url do
    for httpRequest do
        if HTTPS then
            continue
        urlNode ← createNode (U, req.url, req.inUS)
        G.addNode(urlNode)
        if req.referer is not empty then
            refNode ← createNode (U, ref.url)
            G.addNode(refNode)
            G.addEdge(refNode, urlNode, req.inUS)
        if req.cookie is not empty and is identifying
        then
            cookieNode ← createNode (C, cookie.value)
            G.addNode(cookieNode)
            G.addEdge(cookieNode, urlNode, req.inUS)
    end
    for httpResponse with Set-Cookie do
        if HTTPS then
            continue
        if cookie is identifying then
            cookieNode ← createNode (C, cookie.value)
            urlNode ← node for requested url
            G.addNode(cookieNode)
            G.addEdge(cookieNode, urlNode, req.inUS)
    end
    for httpResponse with location field do
        if HTTPS then
            continue
        urlNode ← node for requested url
        locNode ← createNode (U, loc.url)
        G.addNode(locNode)
        G.addEdge(locNode, urlNode, req.inUS)
    end
end
```

Algorithm 2: Cookie Linking algorithm

Analyzing the graph. In our analysis all graphs only contain traffic for a single user. This allows us to find the connected components within the graph and utilize the giant connected component (GCC) to find the amount of a single user's traffic an adversary is able to link. Once the GCC is found, we take the intersection of the set of URLs contained in the GCC with the set of URLs visited during the measurement to find the amount of top-level page visits an adversary is able to observe. When the adversary applies the attack in a multi-user setting, they will have many disjoint subgraphs per user of varying size. Depending on the adversary's goal, these clusters could be processed to link them individually to real world identities, or disambiguated by identifying disjoint sets of cookies for the same sites.

When evaluating adversaries restricted by policy or geographic constraints, an additional pre-processing step is required before finding the GCC. Utilizing the geolocation data from Section 4.4, we are able to filter nodes from the cookie linking graph based on geographic restrictions. In order to determine the amount of traffic for a specific user that a U.S. restricted adversary has access to, we filter all edges from the cookie linking graph that were not added due to U.S. bound requests. We create a subgraph from this filtered edge list and continue the normal linking analysis.

4.7 Identity leakage in popular websites

We conducted a manual analysis of identity leaks on the most popular pages which allow account creation. The top-50 pages are a useful representation for how heavily-used sites with user accounts manage data, and are more likely to be visited by a real user. We identified 50 of the Alexa top 68 U.S. sites that allow for account creation and signed up test accounts when possible. We then examined the homepage, account page, and several random pages on each site to see if any of identifiers are displayed on an HTTP page. If so, an adversary collecting HTTP traffic for that user could inspect the contents of the page to find the identifier and link it to any tracking identifiers also loaded on the page.

5. RESULTS

In the course of our measurements we make nearly 100,000 page visits to 13,644 distinct sites under several client and adversary models. Of these 13,644 sites, nearly all of them (13,266) make requests for external content from a host different than the domain of the host visited.

5.1 Clustering

In this section, we evaluate the effectiveness of our proposed attack under several (adversary, client) models. We are primarily interested in the number of web pages visited by a user which are located in the giant connected component (GCC) relative to the number of pages with embedded third-parties. We focus on large connected components because the probability that a cluster will have at least one page visit that transmits the user's real-world identity in plaintext increases with the size of the cluster. Manual inspection shows that page visits not in the large connected components belong to small clusters, typically singletons, and are thus unlikely to be useful to the adversary.

An adversary's incomplete view. We must consider that the adversary's position on the network may not give them a full view of any user's traffic. The adversary's view may be limited due to its policy or geographic restrictions as described in Section 3, however even with these considerations an adversary may not see all of a user's traffic. A user may change locations on the network or alternative routes taken by packets through the network might result in gaps in the adversary's data collection. To model the adversary's partial view of the user's browsing activity, we repeat our analysis with random subsets of web pages of various sizes.

For illustration, Figure 2a shows how the GCC of a single AOL user's page visits (y-axis) grows as we vary the completeness of the adversary's view of the user's HTTP traffic (x-axis). Each data point was computed by taking 50 independently random samples of page visits. For each sample we apply the clustering algorithm and compute the fraction contained in the GCC. We then average the fractions across the 50 samples. Since we wish to simulate these page visits being spread out over time, only cookies with expiration times at least three months into the future were included when computing the clusters.

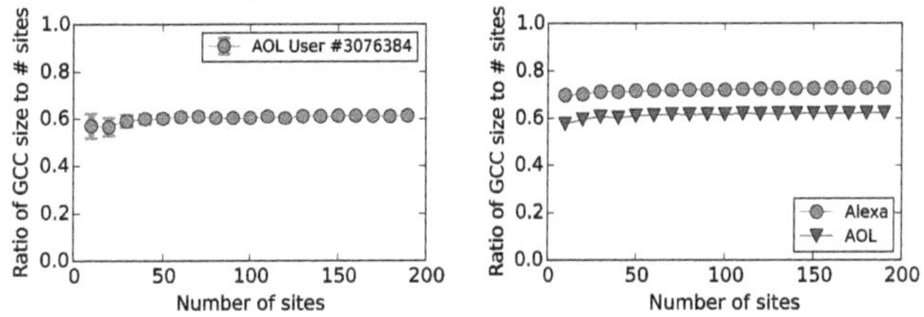

(a) Individual AOL User (b) Average AOL & Alexa Users

Figure 2: Clustering, random subsets of traffic

Thus for each (x, y) pair we can say that if the adversary captures x web page visits by a user in the course of a wiretap, they could link approximately $y\%$ of those visits into a single cluster. The numbers we see for this user are typical — the fraction is around 55% for even very small clusters and exceeds 60% as the cluster size increases. As discussed in Section 4, we average all results over $N = 25$ client instances for all (client, adversary combinations).

We alternatively examined an adversary who sees subsets of web pages that the user visited in chronological order (perhaps the adversary only observed the user for a short period of time). These results had no statistically significant differences from random subsets. As such, we present the remainder of the graphs using random subsets.

Unrestricted Adversary — AOL User Profiles We first examine the level of clustering an adversary can achieve when it is not subject to any policy or geographic restriction. The results for users simulated under the AOL browsing model and no blocking tools are included in Figure 2b. These results show that the clustering remains very similar to the single user case of Figure 2a, except that no inconsistencies remain. After just 55 web page visits observed by the adversary, the growth of the GCC flattens out to $62.4 \pm 3.2\%$ after 200 sites. For the remaining results, we will only present values for this asymptotic case of 200 sites, as the shape of the GCC growth is nearly identical in all cases.

Unrestricted Adversary — Alexa profiles Next we examine the effect of the browser model on the ability of an unrestricted adversary to cluster user data. We hold the user location and browser configuration set to browsing within the U.S. with no blocking settings. Figure 2b compares the results for Alexa profiles for U.S. users against the AOL profiles. The Alexa clustering shows a similar growth pattern with an offset around 10% higher on average, with an overall level of clustering after two sites of $72.9 \pm 1\%$.

5.2 U.S. Users Under One-End Foreign

We now consider an adversary located within the United States who is constrained by the "one-end foreign" rule when collecting data on U.S. users. The client model used in evaluating this adversary is U.S.-based users browsing random subsets of the Alexa top-500 U.S. sites with no blocking tools. The size of the largest cluster observed reduces to just 0.9±0.2% of visited sites averaged across all instances.

To understand why this occurs, we must look at the composition of HTTP traffic. For the average user in this (adversary, client) pair, at least one non-U.S. sub-resource request occurs for 31.7% of the Alexa top-500 sites in the U.S. However, the overall number of HTTP Requests leaving the United States is comparatively small, accounting for just 2.0% of all requests. Only considering traffic where an adversary could learn the top-level domain through the referrer headers, this reduces to 22.7% of visits and 1.6% of requests.[9] Although nearly a quarter of a user's browsing history is visible to the adversary, we show that cookie linking is an ineffective method to cluster this traffic.

5.3 Cookie Linking in Non-U.S. Traffic

We now explore the level of clustering that is possible for traffic with a non-U.S. origin. We examine two different cases in this section: we first show the level of clustering possible under the assumption that the adversary will see all web requests that occur for a specific page visit and then we show what an adversary observing U.S.-bound traffic would see. A key point to note is that even if the majority of a website's resources are requested from a local server, embedded third-parties may cause U.S.-bound requests to occur which have the domain of the first-party as a referrer.

User Location	Unrestricted Adver.	US-based Adver.
Japan	59.6±1.2%	20.9±0.7%
Ireland	63.8±1.2%	12.8±1.1%

Table 1: Clustering of non-U.S. users by an adversary with no restrictions vs. one restricted to U.S. bound traffic.

Unrestricted Adversary — non-U.S. profiles When all requests are considered, the level of clustering is similar to that of the U.S.-based Alexa user simulations. Table 1 shows amount of clustering that occurs for users in Ireland and Japan under the random subset clustering model. Simulated users in Ireland can expect around 63% of traffic to be clustered, while users in Japan can expect nearly 60%. We believe the differences between user simulations generated using Alexa's top U.S., Japan, and Ireland lists arises from the difference in the number of included third parties on the first party (i.e., 62, 38, and 30 on average, respectively).

U.S. based Adversary — non-U.S. profiles We then restrict the clustering to only consider requests which are U.S. bound, and cluster based on the information available to a geographically restricted adversary. This could include an adversary within the United States, or an adversary sitting at the entrance to undersea cables returning to the United States. Table 1 shows clustering capabilities of an adversary restricted to these conditions. In Ireland, we see a reduction to around 13% of page visits and in Japan we see a less severe decrease to 20% of visited sites.

5.4 Cookie Linking Under Blocking Tools

We now investigate several ways users may mitigate a clustering attacking using currently available consumer tools. For all blocking configurations, we make measurements using the AOL browsing model and we examine the ability of an unrestricted adversary to cluster traffic. Measurements are run using several different privacy settings within the browser and two popular privacy and security add-ons.

[9]These results are broadly consistent with measurements taken by several of this paper's authors in past work [36].

Baseline displays the level of clustering with no privacy settings or blocking tools enabled. This represents an upper bound on the level of tracking we would expect to see under the other configurations.

DNT had a negligible effect on clustering, showing no statistically significant difference than without blocking.

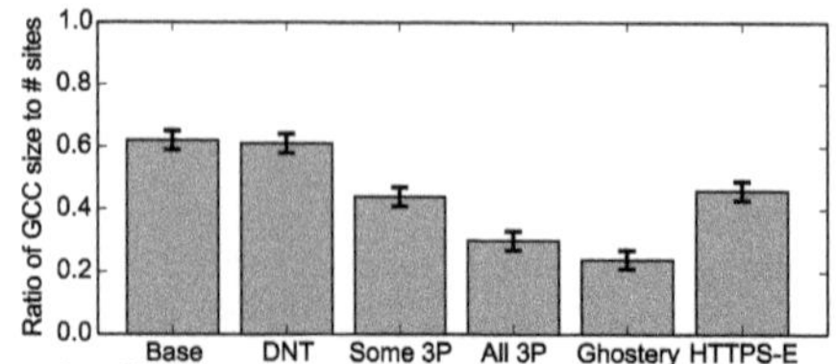

Figure 3: Clustering under several privacy settings.

Cookie blocking policies are more effective, particularly when an adversary sees a low number of page visits. We block cookies for sites that have not been visited in a first-party context by setting "Accept third-party cookies: From visited" in Firefox (this is also the default in Safari). When set, the level of clustering reduces to 43.9±3.2%. Blocking all third-party cookies further reduces this to 30.2±3.0%.

HTTPS Everywhere is an extension created by the EFF to force HTTPS connections whenever available. Since HTTPS requests are not visible to an attacker, and HTTP requests from HTTPS origins will not include a *referer* (preventing the attacker from linking requests back the the original site). A site can fall into one of four categories: no support for HTTPS, supported but not the default, supported and used by default, and finally, HTTPS-only. This measurement provides a picture of what happens as more sites support and use HTTPS by default. Under our browsing model, the number of HTTPS requests increases from 12.7% to 34.0% and the level of clustering is reduced to 46.1±3.2%.

Ghostery is a popular list-based browser extension for blocking third-party requests to domains considered to be trackers. This proves to be the most effective solution for users, reducing the level of clustering to 24.2±2.8% of visited sites. Enabling Ghostery and configuring it to block as much as possible reduces the average number of inclusions from external hosts to just 5.2 per first-party.

5.5 Identity Leakage

Table 2 summarizes our results from a manual survey of the Alexa U.S. sites. We picked the top 50 sites that support account creation. 44 of the 50 websites used HTTPS to secure login pages.[10] Only 19 of those sites continued to use HTTPS to secure future interactions with the user after logged in. We summarize the cleartext identity leaks for the websites which no longer continue to use HTTPS after login.

Although a majority of sites secure user credentials on login pages, personally identifying information (name, username, email address) is transmitted much more frequently via HTTP. Over half of the surveyed sites leak at least one type of identifier, and 42% (not shown in table) leak either username or email address, which can be used to uniquely infer the user's real-world identity. Past work [34, 29] has found a roughly equivalent level of leakage to occur through the Request-URI and Referer.

A representative example of the web's identity-leak problem is `imdb.com`. IMDB provides a secure login page, but

[10]5 of the remaining 6 made POSTs with credentials and 1 made a GET with the credentials as a URL query parameter

once logged in, users return to an HTTP page. This page includes the user's full name on the homepage of the site. Every time a user visits the site while logged in, a passive attacker can extract the name from the unencrypted traffic.

Plaintext Leak Type	Percentage of Sites
First Name	28%
Full Name	14%
Username	36%
Email Address	18%
At least one of the above	56%

Table 2: Leakage on Alexa Top 50 supporting user accounts

Furthermore, we verified that pages from these popular sites that leak identity occur in the clusters of web pages found in our attack. Specifically, at least 5 (and an average 9.92) of the 28 sites we found to leak some type of identity were found in the giant connected component of every one of the 25 Alexa U.S. users. Due to global popularity of the top-50 U.S. sites, an average of 4.4 and 6.4 of these identity leaking sites are found in the GCC's of the Alexa Japan and Alexa Ireland users, respectively. Additionally, for the AOL profiles with no blocking, 9 of the 25 simulated users had at least 1 identity leaker in the GCC. Of course, there are likely also many sites outside the top 50 that leak identity and are found in these clusters, but we did not measure these.

Taken together with our results on clustering, our measurements show that a passive attack is highly feasible: after observing only a fraction of a user's web traffic the adversary will be able to link the majority of the user's web requests together and furthermore, use the contents of the responses to infer the user's real-world identity.

6. DISCUSSION

6.1 Linking without IP address

So far we have assumed that the adversary sees the same source IP address on a request to a first-party site and its corresponding third-party tracker, and that this can be used to link the two requests. There are at least two scenarios in which this assumption is problematic. The first is a NAT. If two users, Alice and Bob, behind the same NAT visit the same web page at roughly the same time, the adversary sees the same IP address on all ensuing HTTP requests. The other scenario is when the user employs Tor without proper application layer anonymization, and the adversary is able to sniff cookies only on the path from the exit node to the web server. (If the user is using a properly configured Tor setup, such as the Tor browser bundle, this attack does not work at all). Since Tor will, in general, use different circuits for communicating with different servers, the adversary will see different source IPs for the two requests (or may be able to observe only one of the requests).

However the well-known "intersection attack" can be used to link requests without using the IP address: if a cookie value a associated with page A's domain and a cookie value x associated with an embedded tracker domain X are observed *multiple times* near-simultaneously (e.g. within 1 second of each other), then a and x are probably associated with the same user. Intuition suggests that for all but the busiest of web pages, two or three visits may be sufficient to link the first-party and tracker cookies with each other. However, this claim cannot be rigorously evaluated without access to large-scale HTTP traffic and so we leave this as a hypothesis.

6.2 NSA Surveillance

Our results bear directly on the NSA's technical capabilities, against individuals both within and external to the United States. For non-U.S. individuals, our data indicates that the agency could have access to a majority of a person's browsing history (71.3% of visits in Ireland and 61.1% of visits in Japan), without ever collecting data outside the United States.[11] Furthermore, we show that the agency can link a non-trivial portion of this traffic through cookies.

Nearly a quarter of U.S. page visits are visible outside the U.S. through third parties and referers. While we show that linking is infeasible, this does not imply that U.S. users browsing domestic sites are safe from NSA surveillance. Passive tracking techniques, or a static IP address, could cause the user's traffic to be just as vulnerable.

6.3 Mitigation by users

Figure 3 shows that users can minimize their exposure to surveillance through cookies, but can not eliminate it all together. Since the identifiers of advertising networks play a key part in the transitive linking of page visits, ad filtering lists (e.g. Ghostery) are currently the most effective solution for users. However even after blocking these lists, ISP level identifiers like Verizon's UIDH would cause the vulnerability to persist [26]. Firefox's built-in cookie blocking can also be effective in reducing the level of traffic clustering, though even the most restrictive option leaves nearly a third of a user's traffic vulnerable to clustering.

Users have very little control over identity leakage outside of stopping the use of services. Forcing HTTPS connections after login can help (i.e. using HTTPS Everywhere), but as we show in our measurements, two-thirds of sites still do not support HTTPS after this step is taken. Users can also be careful to not reuse usernames between sites as this could provide an additional identifier to link page visits.

6.4 Mitigation by trackers

Trackers can prevent a passive eavesdropper from piggybacking on their unique identifiers if they are only transmitted over HTTPS. Some trackers have already deployed HTTPS to avoid mixed content warnings when embedding in HTTPS pages. There are also subtle issues, such session tickets used for TLS session resumption, which can be used by an eavesdropper to link multiple HTTPS connections to the same browser instance similar to a cookie.

Unfortunately, a large fraction of trackers would need to deploy such mitigation strategies for them to make a dent in the adversary's overall chances. As we showed in Section 5.4 with our HTTPS Everywhere measurements, the feasibility of traffic clustering only drops by 23% when the amount requests occurring over HTTPS more than doubles.

6.5 Limitations

A couple of important limitations of the attack must be pointed out. First, using the Tor browser bundle likely defeats it. "Cross-origin identifier unlinkability" is a first-order design goal of the Tor browser, which is achieved through a variety of mechanisms such as double-keying cookies by first-party and third-party [44]. In other words, the same tracker

[11] Alternatively, the agency could rely on collection points just outside the U.S. That approach would fall under Executive Order 12333, which affords more latitude than Section 702 of the FISA Amendments Act.

on different websites will see different cookies. However, our measurements on identifier leakage on popular websites apply to Tor browser usage as well. Preventing such leakage is not a Tor browser design goal.

Simply disabling third-party cookies will also deter the attack, but it is not clear if it will completely stop it. There are a variety of stateful tracking mechanisms in addition to cookies [14, 23, 51, 37, 6], although most are not as prevalent on the web as cookies are.

We also mention two limitations of our study. First, while a significant fraction of popular sites transmit identities of logged-in users in the clear, we have not actually measured how frequently typical users are logged in to the sites that do so. Anecdotal evidence suggests that this number must be high, but experiments on actual user sessions are required for an accurate estimation of vulnerability.

Second, we use commercial geolocation data with an additional custom metric to determine if requests enter the United States for users in Japan and Ireland, and to determine if requests leave the United States for users within the U.S. Even with this additional check, two scenarios can occur: requests outside the U.S. can be marked as entering the U.S. due to an incorrect geolocation and high network latency, and requests inside the U.S. can be marked as staying in the U.S. if they are incorrectly geolocated as being further away than the actual location of the destination (which may still be external to the U.S.).

6.6 Other applications of our methodology

Stated in general terms, we study an adversary with a given set of technical capabilities, network positions, and policy restrictions, and ask, for a given user browsing model, how much of her activity is vulnerable. Our general algorithm in Section 4 can be easily adapted to study a variety of questions that fit this framework. For example, we might assume an adversary who can can compel certificate creation and uses this to spoof some third parties on secure websites to launch active attacks. Here the relevant measurement would be the prevalence of active third-party content on websites visited by typical users and the geographic distribution of third parties serving such content.

7. CONCLUSION

While much has been said from a legal, ethical and policy standpoint about the recent revelations of NSA tracking, many interesting *technical* questions deserve to be considered. In this paper we studied what can be inferred from the surveillance of web traffic and established that utilizing third-party tracking cookies enables an adversary to attribute traffic to users much more effectively than methods such as considering IP address alone. We hope that these findings will inform the policy debate on tracking, raise user awareness of subtle, inferential privacy breaches, and lead to the development of better defenses and greater adoption of existing ones.

8. ACKNOWLEDGMENTS

We would like to thank Jennifer Rexford, Doug Madory, Harlan Yu, and our anonymous reviewers for their insightful comments, as well as Andrew Clement and Colin McCann for their willingness to share data related to this study.

9. REFERENCES

[1] ShareMeNot: Protecting against tracking from third-party social media buttons while still allowing you to use them. `https://sharemenot.cs.washington.edu`.

[2] TrackingObserver: A Browser-Based Web Tracking Detection Platform. `http://trackingobserver.cs.washington.edu`.

[3] Executive Order 12333–United States intelligence activities. `http://www.archives.gov/federal-register/codification/executive-order/12333.html`, 1981.

[4] NSA 'planned to discredit radicals over web-porn use'. `http://www.bbc.co.uk/news/technology-25118156`, November 2013.

[5] 'Tor Stinks' presentation - read the full document. `http://www.theguardian.com/world/interactive/2013/oct/04/tor-stinks-nsa-presentation-document`, October 2013.

[6] G. Acar, C. Eubank, S. Englehardt, M. Juarez, A. Narayanan, and C. Diaz. The Web never forgets: Persistent tracking mechanisms in the wild. In *Conference on Computer and Communications Security (CCS)*. ACM, 2014.

[7] G. Acar, M. Juarez, N. Nikiforakis, C. Diaz, S. Gürses, F. Piessens, and B. Preneel. FPDetective: dusting the web for fingerprinters. In *Conference on Computer and Communications Security (CCS)*. ACM, 2013.

[8] A. Arnbak and S. Goldberg. Loopholes for circumventing the constitution: Warrantless bulk surveillance on americans by collecting network traffic abroad, 2014.

[9] M. Ayenson, D. J. Wambach, A. Soltani, N. Good, and C. J. Hoofnagle. Flash cookies and privacy II: Now with HTML5 and ETag respawning. *World Wide Web Internet And Web Information Systems*, 2011.

[10] M. Balakrishnan, I. Mohomed, and V. Ramasubramanian. Where's that phone?: geolocating IP addresses on 3G networks. In *Internet Measurement Conference (IMC)*. ACM, 2009.

[11] R. Balebako, P. Leon, R. Shay, B. Ur, Y. Wang, and L. Cranor. Measuring the Effectiveness of Privacy Tools for Limiting Behavioral Advertising.

[12] J. Ball. NSA stores metadata of millions of web users for up to a year, secret files show. `http://www.theguardian.com/world/2013/sep/30/nsa-americans-metadata-year-documents`, 2013.

[13] P. E. Black. Ratcliff/Obershelp pattern recognition. `http://xlinux.nist.gov/dads/HTML/ratcliffObershelp.html`, December 2004.

[14] E. Bursztein. Tracking users that block cookies with a HTTP redirect. `http://www.elie.net/blog/security/tracking-users-that-block-cookies-with-a-http-redirect`, 2011.

[15] S. Chen, R. Wang, X. Wang, and K. Zhang. Side-channel leaks in web applications: A reality today, a challenge tomorrow. In *Security and Privacy (S&P)*. IEEE, 2010.

[16] A. Clement. IXmaps–Tracking your personal data through the NSA's warrantless wiretapping sites. In *International Symposium on Technology and Society (ISTAS)*. IEEE, 2013.

[17] B. Elgin and V. Silver. The Surveillance Market and Its Victims. `http://www.bloomberg.com/data-visualization/wired-for-repression/`, 2011.

[18] S. Englehardt, C. Eubank, P. Zimmerman, D. Reisman, and A. Narayanan. Web Privacy Measurement: Scientific principles, engineering platform, and new results. Manuscript, 2014.

[19] R. Gallagher. Operation Socialist: The Inside Story of How British Spies Hacked BelgiumâĂŹs Largest Telco. `https://firstlook.org/theintercept/2014/12/13/belgacom-hack-gchq-inside-story/`, 2014.

[20] Ghostery. Are we private yet? `http://www.areweprivateyet.com/`.

[21] S. Gorman and J. Valentino-Devries. New Details Show Broader NSA Surveillance Reach. `http://online.wsj.com/news/articles/SB10001424127887324108204579022874091732470`, 2013.

[22] G. Greenwald and S. Ackerman. How the NSA is still harvesting your online data. `http://www.theguardian.com/world/2013/jun/27/nsa-online-metadata-collection`, 2013.

[23] M. Hastak and M. J. Culnan. Persistent and unblockable cookies using HTTP headers. `http://www.nikcub.com/posts/persistant-and-unblockable-cookies-using-http-headers`, 2011.

[24] D. Herrmann, R. Wendolsky, and H. Federrath. Website Fingerprinting: Attacking Popular Privacy Enhancing Technologies with the Multinomial Naive-Bayes Classifier. In *Workshop on Cloud Computing Security (CCSW)*. ACM, 2009.

[25] A. Hintz. Fingerprinting Websites Using Traffic Analysis. In *Privacy Enhancing Technologies*. Springer, 2003.

[26] J. Hoffman-Andrews. Verizon Injecting Perma-Cookies to Track Mobile Customers, Bypassing Privacy Controls. `https://www.eff.org/deeplinks/2014/11/verizon-x-uidh`, 2014.

[27] B. Krishnamurthy, K. Naryshkin, and C. Wills. Privacy leakage vs. Protection measures: the growing disconnect. In *Web 2.0 Security & Privacy (W2SP)*. IEEE, 2011.

[28] B. Krishnamurthy and C. Wills. Privacy diffusion on the Web: a longitudinal perspective. In *International Conference on World Wide Web (WWW)*. ACM, 2009.

[29] B. Krishnamurthy and C. E. Wills. On the Leakage of Personally Identifiable Information Via Online Social Networks. In *Workshop on Online Social Networks (WOSN)*. ACM, 2009.

[30] B. Krishnamurthy and C. E. Wills. Privacy leakage in mobile online social networks. In *Conference on Online Social Networks (COSN)*. USENIX, 2010.

[31] M. Lee. Secret "BADASS" Intelligence Program Spied on Smartphones. `https://firstlook.org/theintercept/2015/01/26/secret-badass-spy-program/`, 2015.

[32] B. Liu, A. Sheth, U. Weinsberg, J. Chandrashekar, and R. Govindan. AdReveal: Improving Transparency Into Online Targeted Advertising. In *Workshop on Hot Topics in Networks (HotNets)*. ACM, 2013.

[33] D. Madory, C. Cook, and K. Miao. Who Are the Anycasters? In *Proceedings of NANOG59*, 10 2013.

[34] D. Malandrino, A. Petta, V. Scarano, L. Serra, and R. Spinelli. Privacy awareness about information leakage: Who knows what about me? In *Workshop on Privacy in the Electronic Society (WPES)*. ACM, 2013.

[35] J. Mayer. Tracking the Trackers: Self-Help Tools. `https://cyberlaw.stanford.edu/blog/2011/09/tracking-trackers-self-help-tools`, September 2011.

[36] J. Mayer and E. W. Felten. The Web is Flat. `http://webpolicy.org/2013/10/30/the-web-is-flat/`, 2013.

[37] J. R. Mayer and J. C. Mitchell. Third-party web tracking: Policy and technology. In *Security and Privacy (S&P)*. IEEE, 2012.

[38] A. M. McDonald and L. F. Cranor. Survey of the use of Adobe Flash local shared objects to respawn HTTP cookies. *ISJLP*, 7:639, 2011.

[39] S. J. Murdoch and G. Danezis. Low-cost traffic analysis of Tor. In *Security and Privacy (S&P)*. IEEE, 2005.

[40] S. J. Murdoch and P. Zieliński. Sampled Traffic Analysis by Internet-Exchange-Level Adversaries. In *Privacy Enhancing Technologies*. Springer, 2007.

[41] N. Nikiforakis, A. Kapravelos, W. Joosen, C. Kruegel, F. Piessens, and G. Vigna. Cookieless monster: Exploring the ecosystem of web-based device fingerprinting. In *Security and Privacy (S&P)*. IEEE, 2013.

[42] L. Olejnik, T. Minh-Dung, C. Castelluccia, et al. Selling Off Privacy at Auction. 2013.

[43] A. Panchenko, L. Niessen, A. Zinnen, and T. Engel. Website Fingerprinting in Onion Routing Based Anonymization Networks. In *Workshop on Privacy in the Electronic Society (WPES)*. ACM, 2011.

[44] M. Perry, E. Clark, and S. Murdoch. The design and implementation of the Tor browser [DRAFT]. `https://www.torproject.org/projects/torbrowser/design`, November 2014.

[45] F. Roesner, T. Kohno, and D. Wetherall. Detecting and Defending Against Third-Party Tracking on the Web. In *Networked Systems Design and Implementation (NDSI)*. USENIX, 2012.

[46] A. Soltani, S. Canty, Q. Mayo, L. Thomas, and C. J. Hoofnagle. Flash Cookies and Privacy. In *AAAI Spring Symposium: Intelligent Information Privacy Management*, 2010.

[47] A. Soltani, A. Peterson, and B. Gellman. NSA uses Google cookies to pinpoint targets for hacking. `http://www.washingtonpost.com/blogs/the-switch/wp/2013/12/10/nsa-uses-google-cookies-to-pinpoint-targets-for-hacking`, December 2013.

[48] D. X. Song, D. Wagner, and X. Tian. Timing Analysis of Keystrokes and Timing Attacks on SSH. In *Security Symposium*. USENIX, 2001.

[49] A. M. White, A. R. Matthews, K. Z. Snow, and F. Monrose. Phonotactic reconstruction of encrypted VoIP conversations: Hookt on fon-iks. In *Security and Privacy (S&P)*. IEEE, 2011.

[50] T.-F. Yen, Y. Xie, F. Yu, R. P. Yu, and M. Abadi. Host fingerprinting and tracking on the web: Privacy and security implications. In *Network and Distributed System Security Symposium (NDSS)*. IEEE, 2012.

[51] M. Zalewski. Rapid history extraction through non-destructive cache timing (v8). `http://lcamtuf.coredump.cx/cachetime/`.

Efficient Densest Subgraph Computation in Evolving Graphs

Alessandro Epasto*
Brown University, Providence
alessandro_epasto@brown.edu

Silvio Lattanzi
Google, New York
silviol@google.com

Mauro Sozio†
Institut Mines–Télécom,
Télécom ParisTech,
CNRS LTCI, Paris
sozio@telecom-paristech.fr

ABSTRACT

Densest subgraph computation has emerged as an important primitive in a wide range of data analysis tasks such as community and event detection. Social media such as Facebook and Twitter are highly dynamic with new friendship links and tweets being generated incessantly, calling for efficient algorithms that can handle very large and highly dynamic input data. While either scalable or dynamic algorithms for finding densest subgraphs have been proposed, a viable and satisfactory solution for addressing both the dynamic aspect of the input data and its large size is still missing.

We study the densest subgraph problem in the the dynamic graph model, for which we present the first scalable algorithm with provable guarantees. In our model, edges are added adversarially while they are removed uniformly at random from the current graph. We show that at any point in time we are able to maintain a $2(1+\epsilon)$-approximation of a current densest subgraph, while requiring $O(\text{poly}\log(n+r))$ amortized cost per update (with high probability), where r is the total number of update operations executed and n is the maximum number of nodes in the graph. In contrast, a naïve algorithm that recomputes a dense subgraph every time the graph changes requires $\Omega(m)$ work per update, where m is the number of edges in the current graph. Our theoretical analysis is complemented with an extensive experimental evaluation on large real-world graphs showing that (approximate) densest subgraphs can be maintained efficiently within hundred of microseconds per update.

Categories and Subject Descriptors

H.2.8 [**Database Management**]: Database Applications—*Data mining*; E.1 [**Data Structures**]: Graphs and networks; G.2.2 [**Discrete Mathematics**]: Graph Theory—*Graph algorithms*

Keywords

Densest Subgraph; Dynamic Graph; Approximation Algorithm

*Work partially supported by a Google Europe Ph.D. Fellowship in Algorithms, 2011; Google Focused Award; PRIN Ars TechnoMedia and NSF Award IIS-1247581. Work partially done while at Sapienza University of Rome.

†Work partially supported by a Google Faculty Research Award.

WWW 2015, May 18–22, 2015, Florence, Italy.
ACM 978-1-4503-3469-3/15/05.
http://dx.doi.org/10.1145/2736277.2741638.

1. INTRODUCTION

Finding dense subgraphs has emerged as an important primitive in a wide range of data analysis tasks such as community detection [17, 19, 26], event detection [7], link spam detection [20], computational biology [34], distance query indexing [4, 18], etc. Densely connected users in a social network might correspond to communities, i.e., sets of users sharing similar interests or being affiliated with a same organization such as a university or a company. Entities such as city, person and company names, starting suddenly to co-occur in tweets might indicate that an interesting event involving the corresponding entities is taking place. Dense subgraphs have also been employed to give a compact representation of node distances in a graph, so as to efficiently compute distances between any two nodes given in input.

In the aforementioned application scenarios, data is large and inherently dynamic. In Facebook, users join and leave the social network frequently, with new friendship links being established or removed all the time. In Twitter, tweets are generated incessantly making older tweets less interesting. As a result, communities evolve over time, new events trigger new dense subgraphs in the corresponding entity-relationship graph, while changing distances between nodes in a graph requires frequent re-indexing.

This calls for efficient algorithms that can cope with large and highly dynamic streams of input data. While either scalable [10] or dynamic algorithms [6] for finding densest subgraphs have been proposed, a viable and satisfactory solution for addressing both the dynamic aspect of the input data and its large size is still missing.

We present the first scalable algorithm for the computation of a densest subgraph in the dynamic graph model [23] with provable guarantees. We focus on the average degree density, which is defined as the ratio between the number of edges and the number of nodes of a given undirected graph. The input of our problem consists of an undirected graph as well as a sequence of update operations on such a graph (namely edge additions and deletions), describing its evolution over time. At each point in time in the sequence, we would like to maintain a subgraph of the current graph with near-optimal average degree density.

We consider a model similar to the one studied in [9], where edges are added adversarially while they are removed uniformly at random from the current graph. We show that at any point of the sequence of updates, we are able to maintain a $2(1+\epsilon)$-approximation of a current densest subgraph, while requiring $O(\text{poly}\log(n+r))$ amortized cost per update (with high probability), where r is the total number of update operations executed and n is the maximum number of nodes in the graph. Observe that a naïve algorithm, which recomputes the densest subgraph every time the graph changes, would require $\Omega(m)$ work per update, where m is the number of edges in the current graph.

Our theoretical analysis is complemented with an extensive experimental evaluation on real world graphs showing the effectiveness of our approach. In particular, we evaluate our algorithms in the sliding window model, where the most recent edges (e.g. generated in the last hour or day) define the current graph. This entails frequent updates with the most recent edges being added to the current graph and the less recent ones being removed. We show that approximate densest subgraphs can be maintained within hundreds of microseconds per update (on average) on large graphs requiring more than one billion of update operations, making our algorithms an effective tool for studying the evolution of communities in a social network, for finding events automatically in Twitter, as well as, for efficiently maintaining node distance indexes.

The rest of the paper is organized as follows. In Section 2 we review the relevant literature. In Section 3 we define formally the problem. Then, in Section 4 we introduce our algorithms and prove their approximation guarantees and amortized cost bounds. Later, in Section 5 we evaluate experimentally our algorithms on several large scale datasets. Finally, in Section 6 we recap and hint at possible interesting research directions stemming from our work.

2. RELATED WORK

In recent years, there have been significant efforts in devising efficient algorithms for finding densest subgraphs. Due to the large amount of work that has been done in this research area, our survey might not be comprehensive.

Densest subgraph problem. Several definitions of density have been studied in literature including cliques and quasi-cliques [13], α-β-communities [32], minimum degree density [39], k-cores [38] and the densest subgraph [21]. Among these, the average degree density stands outs as a natural definition of density. Given an undirected graph, its average degree density is defined as the ratio between the number of edges and the number of nodes in such a graph. Charikar [16] devised a linear-programming based approach as well as a linear 2-approximation algorithm for such a problem. Bahmani et al. [10] provided a $2(1+\epsilon)$ approximation algorithm that can be implemented in $O\left(\frac{\log(n)}{\epsilon}\right)$ streaming passes over the graph (for a total cost of $O\left(m\frac{\log(n)}{\epsilon}\right)$). More recently, Bahmani et al. [8] provided a near-optimal algorithm in the MapReduce model of computation. In [11], authors study the problem of finding several subgraphs with maximum total density and limited overlap. In [40], heuristics for finding quasi-cliques [40] are presented. All previously mentioned results hold for undirected graphs, while in [25] authors study the densest subgraph problem in directed graphs.

Applications. Finding dense subgraphs in large input graphs has emerged as an important subroutine used to tackle a host of real-world problems [29]. Saha et al. [35] showed how finding dense subgraphs might help in identifying interesting and novel patterns in gene annotation networks. Chen et al. [17] devise a graph partitioning algorithm based on some definition of density and applied it extensively on social and biological networks. Finding dense regions in web graphs has received large attention recently [19,20] as those regions might represent some link-spam activity. Dourisboure et al. [19] proposed an efficient heuristic for such a problem. Similarly Kumar et al. [27] cast the problem of finding communities of web-pages as the problem of mining dense bipartite subgraphs. Densest subgraph computation is an important subroutine in graph indexing for efficient reachability and distance queries [18,24], as well as for graph compression [14]. Angel et al. [6] show how dense subgraphs represent interesting events in Twitter.

Dynamic settings. Das Sarma et al. [37] studied the densest subgraph problem in a dynamic version of the congest model for distributed computation [33], which presents significantly different challenges. In this model, authors develop a $(2+\epsilon)$-approximation algorithm which requires $O\left(D\frac{\log(n)}{\epsilon}\right)$ parallel rounds where D is the diameter of the network. Contrary to our work, there is no guarantee that the amortized cost be poly-log(n). Angel et al. [6] study the problem of efficiently maintaining dense subgraphs under streaming edge weight updates, so as to find interesting events in Twitter. Authors consider a different definition of density, while they focus on finding small dense subgraphs (with at most 10 nodes). In our work, we would like not to restrict our attention to graphs with small number of nodes given that this is not the case in many cases of interest (such as communities in a social network). Moreover, in contrast to our work there is no guarantee that the amortized cost be poly-log(n) per update. Valari et al. [41] study the problem of computing the top-k densest subgraphs, when the densest subgraph is removed recursively at each time. They address such a problem in dynamic graph collections, where at each step graphs might arrive or be removed from the collection. Other authors have studied other definitions of density in dynamic graphs. Lee et al. [28] used (k,d)-cores to discover new stories from social streams and track their evolution. Several authors [5, 31, 36] addressed the related problem of maintaining a k-core decompositions in graphs subject to dynamic changes and in streaming. In [23] authors study the problem of efficiently answering queries on the properties of an evolving graph.

None of the previous approaches maintains an approximation of the densest subgraph in amortized poly-log(n) time per update and can cope with billions of edge additions or removals. Recently, independently from our work, Bhattacharya et al. [12] (unpublished at the time of preparation of this paper) studied the densest subgraph problem in the streaming model of computation achieving strong theoretical guarantees.

3. PROBLEM DEFINITION

Preliminaries. Let $G=(V,E)$ be an undirected graph. For any set of vertices $S\subseteq V$, we let $E(S)$ to be the set of edges induced by S, i.e., $E(S)=\{(u,v):(u,v)\in E\wedge u,v\in S\}$. The average degree density $\rho_G(S)$ is defined as: $\rho_G(S)=$

$\frac{|E(S)|}{|S|}$. In the rest of the paper we omit the subscript G in $\rho_G(S)$ when it is clear from the context, while we use the term density instead of average degree density, for simplicity. We denote by ρ_O the density of a densest subgraph. We say that an algorithm computes an α-approximation of a densest subgraph $S \subseteq V$ if such an algorithm computes a subgraph $S' \subseteq V$ such that $\rho(S) \leq \alpha\rho(S')$. We say that an algorithm has amortized time $O(\mathcal{T}(n))$ per update, if for any sequence of ℓ update operations such an algorithm completes in time $O(\ell \cdot \mathcal{T}(n))$. We denote by polylog$(n)$ a polynomial in the logarithm, such as $\log^2 n$.

Problem definition. We study the densest subgraph problem in the dynamic graph model [23], where a sequence of update operations on an input graph describes the evolution of such a graph over time. Our input consists of an undirected graph $G = (V, E)$ as well as an online sequence of update operations on the input graph, namely edge additions and deletions. Every edge in such a sequence is either added adversarially (i.e. so as to cause maximum discomfort to the algorithm) or is removed uniformly at random from the current graph. We assume that the edges to be added (adversarially) are chosen without taking into account the set of removed edges. Our graph-evolution model is similar to the model in [9]. Our goal is to maintain at any point in time in the sequence a $2(1+\epsilon)$-approximation of a densest subgraph with amortized time of $O(\text{polylog}(|V|)$, for any $\epsilon > 0$. In particular, at any point in time in the sequence, the output of our algorithm consists of a collection of subsets of V, with the last among such subsets inducing a $2(1+\epsilon)$-approximation of a densest subgraph in the current graph. The amortized cost must include the time required to produce such subgraphs in output.

4. ALGORITHMS

In this section, we present several algorithms to compute an approximation of a densest subgraph. We start by considering the static case to warm-up, then, we generalize our solution to a dynamic setting. For simplicity, we initially consider a model with edge addition only which is then generalized to the most general case with both edge addition and removal.

4.1 Warm-up: Static Case

We first design an approximation algorithm for the static case, which is perhaps not interesting per se but it is pivotal in dealing with the dynamic case.

Consider the following algorithm inspired by the algorithm introduced in [10]. Given rational numbers $\beta > 0, \epsilon > 0$, we start from the input graph G and remove iteratively all nodes with degree $< 2(1+\epsilon)\beta$ from the current graph, until the graph becomes empty or the total number of iterations becomes larger than $\lceil \log_{1+\epsilon}(n) \rceil$ — notice that $\log_{1+\epsilon}(n) = O\left(\log(n)\epsilon^{-1}\right)$. We then return the subgraph with maximum density among all subgraphs computed throughout the execution of the algorithm. It can be shown that if the density ρ_O of a densest subgraph is known then one can run such an algorithm with $\beta = \frac{\rho_O}{2(1+\epsilon)}$ (i.e. at each step we remove nodes with degree smaller than ρ_O) to quickly find an approximate densest subgraph. See Algorithm 1 for a pseudo-code.

Unfortunately ρ_O is usually not known in advance, so in order for Algorithm 1 to be useful we need to understand

Algorithm 1 Find($G(V, E)$, $\beta > 0$, $\epsilon > 0$)

> $S_0, \bar{S} \leftarrow V, t \leftarrow 0$.
> **while** $S_t \neq \emptyset$ and $t \leq \lceil \log_{1+\epsilon}(n) \rceil$ **do**
>   Let $A(S_t)$ be the set of nodes with degree $< 2(1+\epsilon)\beta$ in $G_t = (S_t, E(S_t))$.
> $S_{t+1} \leftarrow S_t \setminus A(S_t)$.
>   If $\rho(S_{t+1}) > \rho(\bar{S})$ then $\bar{S} \leftarrow S_{t+1}$.
> $t \leftarrow t+1$.
> **end while**
> **return** $\bar{G} = (\bar{S}, E(\bar{S}))$.

its behavior when executed with an arbitrary $\beta > 0$. This is clarified by the following lemma, whose proof goes along the lines of the proofs in [10].

LEMMA 1. *If $0 < \beta \leq \frac{\rho_O}{2(1+\epsilon)}$, Algorithm 1 finds a subgraph with density at least β, while if $\beta > \rho_O$ a subgraph with density strictly less than β is found.*

PROOF. If $\beta > \rho_O$, then the claim follows by definition of ρ_O. We show that in the case when Algorithm 1 does not find a subgraph with density at least β, with $0 < \beta \leq \frac{\rho_O}{2(1+\epsilon)}$, the density of a densest subgraph is strictly less than ρ_O, leading to a contradiction.

Let $S_t \subseteq V$ be the set of nodes active at rounds t of the algorithm and $A(S_t)$ be the set of nodes with degree $< 2(1+\epsilon)\beta$ in $G_t = (S_t, E(S_t))$. We have

$$2|E(S_t)| = \sum_{v \in S_t \setminus A(S_t)} \delta_{G_t}(v) + \sum_{v \in A(S_t)} \delta_{G_t}(v).$$

Furthermore if Algorithm 1 does not find a graph with density at least β then $\rho(S_t) < \beta$ for every t, otherwise the algorithm would have found a subgraph with density at least β. So by considering only the first summation term in the previous equation we derive

$$2|E(S_t)| \geq 2\beta(1+\epsilon)|S_t \setminus A(S_t)| > 2\rho(S_t)(1+\epsilon)|S_t \setminus A(S_t)|,$$

where the second inequality follows from $\beta > \rho(S_t)$. Then

$$2|E(S_t)| > 2(1+\epsilon)|S_t \setminus A(S_t)|\frac{|E(S_t)|}{|S_t|},$$

which implies $|S_{t+1}| = |S_t \setminus A(S_t)| < \frac{1}{1+\epsilon}|S_t|$, for every step $t \geq 1$. Hence, Algorithm 1 terminates at step $t \leq \lceil \log_{1+\epsilon}(n) \rceil$ with all nodes and edges being removed from the input graph G.

We now show that if at the end of the algorithm all edges are removed and $\beta \leq \frac{\rho_O}{2(1+\epsilon)}$, then the density of a densest subgraph in G is strictly less than ρ_O leading to a contradiction.

We define a directed graph H, obtained by finding an orientation of the edges in the input graph G as follows. At every step $t \geq 1$ of Algorithm 1, for every node v in $A(S_t)$ we assign all edges of v in G_t, to v (breaking ties arbitrarily). Let $\delta_H(v)$ be the in-degree of v in the directed graph H. From the fact that all nodes and edges have been removed at the end of the algorithm, it follows that all edges are assigned to some node. We can then write:

$$\rho(S_O) = \frac{|E(S_O)|}{|S_O|} \leq \frac{\sum_{v \in S_O} \delta_H(v)}{|S_O|} < 2(1+\epsilon)\beta \leq \rho_O,$$

which leads to a contradiction. Therefore, our algorithm would have found a subgraph with density at least β, when executed with $\beta \leq \frac{\rho_O}{2(1+\epsilon)}$. □

The following lemma can be proved in a very similar way to Lemma 1, its proof is omitted for brevity and deferred to the full version of the paper.

LEMMA 2. *Let $\beta, \epsilon > 0$. Let $\bar{G}$ and S_k be, respectively, the subgraph and the k-th set found by Algorithm 1 with input β,ϵ, where $k = \lceil \log_{1+\epsilon}(n) \rceil$. If $\rho(\bar{G}) < \beta$, then $S_k = \emptyset$. Moreover, if $S_k = \emptyset$ then $\rho_O < 2(1+\epsilon)\beta$.*

Lemma 1 suggests the following natural algorithm for finding an approximate densest subgraph in the static case: Starting from a "sufficiently small" value for β, we run Algorithm 1 with different values of β (namely all integral powers of $(1+\epsilon)$) outputting the subgraph with maximum density among those we found. Algorithm 2 shows a pseudo-code for such an algorithm, where $\bar{\rho}$ is a lower bound for the density of a densest subgraph (this parameter will be used in the next sections).

Algorithm 2 *FindDensest*$(G(V,E), \bar{\rho}, \epsilon > 0)$

```
Ḡ = ∅.
β ← max(1/(4(1+ε)), (1+ε)ρ̄).
while (true) do
    G' ← Find(G, β, ε).
    if ρ(G') ≥ β then
        Ḡ ← G'.
        β ← (1+ε)ρ(Ḡ).
    else
        return (β, Ḡ).
    end if
end while
```

While Algorithm 2 might perform worse than other known algorithms for the static case, it will be a key ingredient for our dynamic algorithms. We conclude this section by proving its performance guarantees.[1]

THEOREM 1. *For any $\epsilon > 0$, FindDensest$(G, 0, \epsilon)$ computes a $2(1+\epsilon)^2$-approximation of a densest subgraph.*

PROOF. If the input graph is not empty then $\rho_O \geq \frac{1}{2}$. Therefore, it follows from Lemma 1 that Algorithm 2 executed with $\beta = \frac{1}{4(1+\epsilon)}$ finds in the first step a set of density at least β.

The loop in Algorithm 2 terminates as soon as a subgraph with density β is not found, while outputting a subgraph with density $\frac{\beta}{1+\epsilon}$. From Lemma 1 it follows that $\rho_O \leq 2(1+\epsilon)\beta$, which proves the approximation guarantee. □

THEOREM 2. *For any $\epsilon > 0$, FindDensest$(G, 0, \epsilon)$ requires $O(m \log(n) \epsilon^{-1})$ operations.*

PROOF. From the fact that $\rho_O \leq n$ and from Lemma 1, it follows that the while loop of Algorithm 2 is executed at most $\lceil \log_{1+\epsilon} n \rceil$ times. Since the input graph in undirected, Algorithm 1 can be implemented in $O(n+m)$ using the same method described in [25] for computing densest subgraphs in an undirected graph. □

[1]For simplicity, we express the approximation guarantee of our algorithms as $2(1+\epsilon)^2$, for any $\epsilon > 0$. Observe that this is equivalent to say that its approximation guarantee is $2(1+\epsilon)$, for any $\epsilon > 0$. The asymptotic amortized cost does not change.

4.2 Dynamic Case: Edge Insertion Only

In this section, we describe how to maintain a $2(1+\epsilon)^2$-approximation of a densest subgraph with amortized cost of $O\left(\frac{\log(n)^2}{\epsilon^2}\right)$ per edge insertion. We first assume that the set V of all the nodes appearing in the evolving graph is known in advance, then we show how to remove such assumption.

The core idea is to maintain the main properties of the *Find* and *FindDensest* algorithms, without having to rerun the algorithm from scratch every time the graph is updated.

Consider the first call to Algorithm 2. Let $S_0, \ldots, S_k$, $k = \lceil \log_{1+\epsilon}(n) \rceil$ be the sets computed by the last call to *Find* in Algorithm 2. Our algorithm will maintain throughout the execution the following invariant:

INVARIANT 1. *Given $\beta, \epsilon > 0$ and the current graph $G = (V, E)$, the nodes in V are organized as a collection of sets $S_0, \ldots, S_k$, $k = \lceil \log_{1+\epsilon}(n) \rceil$, where*

- *$S_0 = V$;*
- *S_{t+1} is obtained from S_t by removing all nodes with degree less than $2(1+\epsilon)\beta$ in $G_t = (S_t, E(S_t))$, $t = 0, \ldots, k-1$;*
- *$S_k = \emptyset$.*

Note that Invariant 1 is satisfied at the end of any call to Algorithm 2 (it follows from Lemma 2), while we maintain it as follows. Given an edge (u, v) being added to the current graph $G = (V, E)$ and a collection of sets $S_0, \ldots, S_k$ satisfying Invariant 1, we first check whether adding (u, v) to G does not violate the invariant. If this is the case we add (u, v) to G while leaving the sets S_t's unchanged. Otherwise, let $u \in V$, and let t be such that $u \in S_t \setminus S_{t+1}$ and $\delta_{G_t}(u) \geq 2(1+\epsilon)\beta$, while let $\hat{t} > t$ be the smallest index such that $\delta_{G_{\hat{t}}}(u) < 2(1+\epsilon)\beta$. If $\hat{t} = \lceil \log_{1+\epsilon}(|V|) \rceil$ then we rebuild the sets S_t's from scratch, which is done by running Algorithm 2 and using the sets S_t's computed in the last call to *Find*.

Otherwise, we add u to the sets $S_{t+1}, \ldots, S_{\hat{t}}$. In turn, we might need to move the neighbors of u to other sets and so on. This is iterated for u and v until the invariant becomes satisfied or we need to move some node to a set $S_{\hat{t}}$, with $\hat{t} = \lceil \log_{1+\epsilon}(|V|) \rceil$. In the latter case, we rebuild the sets S_t's from scratch.

A pseudo-code of the algorithm is shown in Algorithm 3. The algorithm returns *true* if the sets S_t's need to be rebuilt, which is done in Algorithm 4. Note that maintaining the invariant might be costly sometimes, as moving nodes from one set to the other might trigger a chain effect involving a large part of the nodes in the current graph. However, we are able to prove that this does not happen "often" (see Theorem 4).

Armed with an algorithm for maintaining our invariant, we now present the main algorithm which is executed continuously. Algorithm *Main* (Algorithm 4) receives an initial graph $G = (V, E)$ (potentially with no edges) in input and runs *FindDensest* to build a collection of sets $S_0, \ldots, S_k$ satisfying Invariant 1. Then the algorithm outputs our approximation of the densest subgraph $\bar{G}$. When a new edge (u, v) is added to the current graph G, algorithm *Add* is executed and the sets S_t's are updated so as to maintain the invariant. If this can be done, then the density of the densest

Algorithm 3 $Add((u,v),(S_0,\dots,S_k),G=(V,E),\beta,\epsilon)$

Require: $S_0,\dots,S_k$ must satisfy Invariant 1
Ensure: $S_0,\dots,S_k$ are updated so to satisfy Invariant 1 after adding (u,v), if this is not possible return a flag $Rebuild = true$ signaling that such sets must be rebuilt.

```
E ← E ∪ {(u, v)}.
Update degrees of u and v.
Stack ← ∅.
Push(u, v, Stack).
while Stack is not empty do
    w ← Pop(Stack).
    Let S_t be such that w ∈ S_t \ S_{t+1}.
    If δ_{G_t}(w) < 2(1 + ε)β continue.
    Let t̂ > t be smallest such that δ_{G_t̂}(w) < 2(1 + ε)β.
    If t̂ = ⌈log_{1+ε}(|V|)⌉ return true.
    Add w to the sets S_{t+1}, ..., S_t̂.
    Push all neighbors of w to the Stack.
end while
return false.
```

subgraph has not increased significantly (this follows from Lemma 2). In this case the previously computed subgraph $\bar{G}$ is still a good approximation of the densest subgraph.

Otherwise, we rebuild the sets from scratch by running *FindDensest* as in this case the density of the densest subgraph might have increased. After this operation *Main* outputs a new dense subgraph $\bar{G}$. Notice that although rebuilding the S_t's is an expensive operation (as it requires to process the whole input graph), this is performed only a poly-log number of times (as β is multiplied each time by a factor of $(1+\epsilon)$ and never decreases).

Algorithm 4 $Main(G=(V,E),\epsilon)$

```
(β, Ḡ) ← FindDensest (G, 0, ε) and let S_0, ..., S_k be the
sets computed by Find.
Output Ḡ.
while (true) do
    Wait for a new edge (u, v).
    Rebuild ← Add((u, v), S_0, ..., S_k, G, β, ε).
    if (Rebuild) then
        (β, Ḡ) ← FindDensest (G, β, ε) (update S_0 ... S_k).
        Output Ḡ.
    end if
end while
```

We now study the approximation guarantee of our algorithm.

THEOREM 3. *The algorithm always maintains a* $2(1+\epsilon)^2$ *approximation of the densest subgraph.*

PROOF. From Lemma 2 it follows that Invariant 1 holds at the end of *FindDensest*. Moreover, it either holds at the end of *Add* or *FindDensest* is executed right after that, so as to maintain such an invariant. Therefore, at any point in time the subgraph $\bar{G}$ found by *Main* has density at least $\frac{\beta}{1+\epsilon}$, while from Lemma 2 it follows that $\rho_O < 2(1+\epsilon)\beta$. This proves the approximation guarantee. □

The following lemma is useful for analyzing the amortized cost of the algorithm. Its proof is omitted for brevity and deferred to the full version of the paper.

LEMMA 3. *At any point in time, let n be the number nodes in the current graph $G=(V,E)$. The total number of FindDensest calls in the algorithm, up to this point is* $O(\log(n)\epsilon^{-1})$.

The following theorem shows that the algorithm has amortized cost $O(\log^2(n)\epsilon^{-2})$ per edges in the graph.

THEOREM 4. *At any point in time, let n and m be the number of nodes and edges in the current graph $G=(V,E)$, respectively. The total number of operations of the algorithm, up to this point, is $O(m\log^2(n)\epsilon^{-2})$ while the algorithm requires $O(m+n)$ space.*

PROOF. Notice that to implement the algorithm, it is sufficient to store the current graph and some additional bookkeeping information of cost $O(n)$ (we do not need to store the sets S_t's explicitly but only which is the last set in which each node is present).

We now bound the total number of operations performed by *Main*. We start by proving that the total number of operations executed between two consecutive calls to *FindDensest* is $O(m\log(n)\epsilon^{-1})$. Consider any call to *FindDensest* and any node v. Let t and $\hat{t}$ be such that v belongs to some set $S_t \setminus S_{t+1}$ right after such a call and v belongs to $S_{\hat{t}} \setminus S_{\hat{t}+1}$ right before the next call to *FindDensest*. By construction, it must be $\hat{t} \geq t$. Moving a node from S_t to $S_{\hat{t}}$ requires at most $\delta_G(u)\cdot(\hat{t}-t)$ operations, while the number of sets S_t's is at most $\lceil \log_{1+\epsilon}(n) \rceil$. Therefore, the total number of operations between two consecutive calls to the procedure *FindDensest* is at most $\sum_{v\in V}\delta_G(v)\log_{1+\epsilon}(n) = O(m\log(n)\epsilon^{-1})$. From Lemma 3, it follows that there are $O(\log(n)\epsilon^{-1})$ calls to *FindDensest*, with each of them requiring $O(m\log(n)\epsilon^{-1})$ operations.

This concludes the proof. □

Handling node insertions. In this section we have assumed for simplicity to know the set V of all nodes that will appear in the graph. This is not necessary as simple changes are sufficient to adapt the algorithm to the general case. Each time a new node v is introduced, we first assign it to the set S_0 (a node of degree 0 is always removed at the first iteration), then the algorithm proceed as usual. Notice as well that we use the cardinality of V only to determine the threshold $k = \lceil \log_{1+\epsilon}(|V|) \rceil$ for the maximum number of sets S_t's. It is easy to see that as $|V|$ can only grow we can simply keep track of the current cardinality of V and always use the current value when necessary. The monotonicity of $|V|$ ensure that the algorithm remains consistent and that the theorems continue to hold.

4.3 Fully dynamic case

In this section, we show how to adapt the previous algorithm to the fully dynamic model with both adversarial edge insertions and random removals as described in Section 3. For this case we provide an approximation algorithm that handles both operations in amortized poly-log time, in the size of the graph and the number of operations, with high probability. We stress that the approximation guarantees of our algorithm holds for adversarially chosen edge insertions and removals. We rely on the randomness of removals only for showing the amortized complexity bounds. In the experimental section (Section 5.2), we conduct an extensive empirical evaluation showing the effectiveness of our algorithm in the sliding window model as well.

We start from an initial graph $G=(V,E)$. We first assume that the set V of all nodes appearing in the graph is known in advance, while we show later on in this section how to relax this requirement. Let A be the total number of (possibly repeated) edges that are inserted in the graph, i.e. A counts both the edges in the initial graph and the edge addition operations. Let R be the number of edge deletions executed. We have that $A + R = O(A)$. We will bound the total cost of this sequence of operations in the probability space defined by the random choices of the edge removals. We say that an event happens with high probability (w.h.p.) if it happens with probability $\geq 1 - A^{-c}$ for some constant $c > 1$.

The main idea of our algorithm is to lazily maintain a data structure (the sets S_t's presented in the previous section) from which we can extract a dense subgraph, while requiring a small number of operations (on average). To this purpose we maintain a slightly weaker invariant (Invariant 2) which is defined as follows:

INVARIANT 2. *Given $\beta, \epsilon > 0$ and the current graph $G = (V, E)$, the nodes in V are organized as a collection of sets $S_0, \ldots, S_k$, $k = \lceil \log_{1+\epsilon}(n) \rceil$, where*

- *$S_0 = V$;*
- *For $t = 0, \ldots, k-1$, $S_{t+1} \subseteq S_t$ and if $v \in S_t$ has degree larger than or equal to $2(1+\epsilon)\beta$ in $G_t = (S_t, E(S_t))$ then $v \in S_{t+1}$;*
- *$S_k = \emptyset$.*

Notice that this invariant is weaker than the previous one, in that, we only require that high degree nodes in S_t are also part of set S_{t+1} (no condition is placed on the removal of low degree nodes). Similar to the previous section, the sets S_t's are first defined as the ones obtained in the last call to *Find* in *FindDensest* and then are later updated as described in the algorithm.

Unfortunately, after many update operations such data structure might become corrupted and must be reconstructed from scratch by means of a costly procedure (*FindDensest*). Our goal is to minimize the number of times that such a costly procedure is executed. To this purpose we divide the execution of the algorithm in rounds, with each round containing all the operations required to maintain Invariant 2 between two consecutive calls to the costly procedure *FindDensest*. We say that a round is *good* if the total number of edge removal operations in the round is larger than or equal to a threshold R^*, while it is *bad* otherwise. R^* is defined as follows:

$$R^* := \frac{m_0 \epsilon}{6(1+\epsilon)^2 \log_{1+\epsilon}(|V|)}, \tag{1}$$

where m_0 is the number of edges in the graph at the beginning of the round. Notice that R^* might not be an integer.

The main intuition is that in good rounds the number of maintenance operations is "justified" by a large number of update operations, causing no issues in our amortized cost analysis. We will then show that the bad rounds are not too many with respect to the good ones.

Given a parameter $\epsilon > 0$, our algorithm works with a parameter $\epsilon' = 2\epsilon + \epsilon^2$. The algorithm starts with round 1 where *FindDensest* is executed so to construct the sets S_t's. At round s, the execution of such a procedure starts a new round $s + 1$. A counter R' keeps track of the number of removals that have been been executed in the current round so to be able to determine whether the current round is good or bad. When a new edge is added to the current graph, our algorithm executes the same algorithm *Add* described in the previous section, while when an edge is removed our algorithm executes the algorithm *Remove* (see Algorithm 6 for a pseudo-code). In either case, Invariant 2 is maintained. Both algorithms return a flag *Rebuild* signaling whether the S_t's must be rebuilt, in which case, *FindDensest* is executed. See Algorithm 5 for a pseudo-code of *MainFullyDyn*. For efficiency reasons we maintain a graph $\ddot{G}$ which is a super graph of the current graph.

Algorithm 5 *MainFullyDyn* $(G = (V, E), \epsilon)$

```
ε' ← 2ε + ε², R' ← 0.
s ← 1 // Begin round 1.
(β_1, Ḡ) ← FindDensest (G, 0, ε').
Let S_0, ..., S_k be the sets computed by Find.
G̃ = (V, Ẽ) ← G. //supergraph of G maint. for efficiency.
Let R* as in Equation 1, where m_0 = |E|.
Output Ḡ.
while (true) do
   Wait for update (Op, u, v), Op ∈ {Add, Remove}.
   if Op = Add then
      if R' < R* then Ẽ ← Ẽ ∪ (u, v).
      Rebuild ← Add((u, v), (S_0, ..., S_k), G, β_s, ε').
   else
      Rebuild ← Remove((u, v), G, Ḡ, β_s, ε').
      R' ← R' + 1.
   end if
   if (Rebuild) then
      if R' < R* then
         Let H ← Find (G̃, β_s, ε')
         if ρ_G(H) ≥ ρ_G(Ḡ) then Ḡ ← H
      end if
      s ← s + 1. //begin round s + 1.
      (β_{s+1}, H) ← FindDensest(G, ρ_G(Ḡ), ε') (update
S_0 ... S_k as the sets computed by Find).
      G̃ = (V, Ẽ) ← G.
      if ρ_G(H) ≥ ρ_G(Ḡ) then Ḡ ← H.
      Output Ḡ.
      Let R* as in Equation 1, where m_0 = |E|.
      R' ← 0.
   end if
end while
```

We now prove the approximation guarantees of our algorithm.

THEOREM 5. *The algorithm always maintains a $2(1+\epsilon)^6$ approximation of a densest subgraph.*

PROOF. Notice that algorithm *Remove* ensures that any time we have a set S of density $\rho(S) \geq \frac{\beta}{(1+\epsilon')^2}$. Furthermore by Invariant 2 we know that if we execute *Find* (G, β, ϵ') on the current graph all nodes are removed in at most $\log_{1+\epsilon'}(|V|)$ iterations. Hence, by Lemma 2 it follows that $\rho_O < 2(1+\epsilon')\beta$ and this proves the approximation guarantee $2(1+\epsilon')^3 = 2(1+\epsilon)^6$. $\square$

We now state the following theorem that proves that our algorithm has amortized cost $O(\log(A)\log^2(n)\epsilon^{-2})$ for edge addition and $O(\log(A)\log^3(n)\epsilon^{-4})$ for edge removal, w.h.p.

THEOREM 6. *For any $\epsilon > 0$, at any point in time, let A and R be the number of edge insertion and deletion operations. The total number of operations of the algorithm is w.h.p $O\left(A\log(A)\log^2(|V|)\epsilon^{-2} + R\log(A)\log^3(|V|)\epsilon^{-4}\right)$, while the algorithm requires $O(n + m)$ space.*

Algorithm 6 *Remove*$(u, v, G(V,E), \bar{G}, \beta, \epsilon > 0)$

Ensure: $\rho(\bar{G}) \geq \frac{\beta}{(1+\epsilon)^2}$ after removing (u, v), if this is not true return a flag *Rebuild* = *true* signaling that the densest subgraph must be recomputed.

$E \leftarrow E \setminus \{(u, v)\}$.
Update degrees of u and v.
if $\rho(\bar{G}) < \frac{\beta}{(1+\epsilon')^2}$ **then**
  return *true*
else
  return *false*
end if

Proof of Theorem 6

Our proof strategy for Theorem 6 is the following. We analyze separately the case of bad ($R' < R^*$) and good ($R' \geq R^*$) rounds. In the former case we show that the density of the densest subgraph is unlikely to be affected significantly, so we can use similar arguments to the ones used in the previous subsection. In the latter case, we amortize the cost of the re-computation of the densest subgraph using the large number of edge update operations.

The next lemma shows that many random edge removals are required to decrease significantly the density of any given subgraph. Such a lemma is used to prove that, we cannot have many (more than poly-log) consecutive bad rounds, w.h.p. Finally, we will use this result to bound the average cost of each operation.

LEMMA 4. *Given an undirected graph $G = (V, E)$, let H be a subgraph of G while let G' be a graph obtained by removing R' edges uniformly at random from G, with $0 \leq R' < R^*$. If $\rho_G(V(H)) \geq \beta$ then, $\rho_{G'}(V(H)) \geq \frac{\beta}{(1+\epsilon)}$, with probability at least $p = 1 - (6 \log_{1+\epsilon}(|V|))^{-1}$.*

PROOF. The probability of removing an edge from H is smaller than $\frac{|E(H)|}{|E(V)|-R^*}$. Let X be the random variable that counts the number of edges removed from H. We can bound $E[X]$ as follows:

$$E[X] \leq R^* \frac{|E(H)|}{|E(V)| - R^*} \leq \frac{|E(H)|\epsilon}{6(1+\epsilon)\log_{1+\epsilon}(|V|)}$$

Furthermore, note that $|E(H)| \geq \beta|V(H)|$ and that in order to decrease the density of H to $\frac{\beta}{(1+\epsilon)}$ at least $\beta|V(H)|(1 - \frac{1}{1+\epsilon}) = \frac{\beta|V(H)|\epsilon}{1+\epsilon}$ edges must be removed.
Hence, from Markov inequality it follows:

$$P\left(X > \frac{\beta|V(H)|\epsilon}{1+\epsilon}\right) \leq \frac{E[X]}{\frac{\beta|V(H)|\epsilon}{1+\epsilon}} \leq \frac{1}{6\log_{1+\epsilon}(|V|)}.$$

Hence, with probability at least $1 - \frac{1}{6\log_{1+\epsilon}(|V|)}$ the graph H has density $\geq \frac{\beta}{1+\epsilon}$. □

We now state a lemma is deferred to the full version of the paper

LEMMA 5. *For any bad round s of MainFullyDyn, $\beta_{s+1} \geq \beta_s(1+\epsilon)$ with probability at least $1 - \frac{1}{3\log_{1+\epsilon}(|V|)}$, independently of the previous rounds.*

We now prove the following lemma that can be used to show that we cannot have many consecutive bad rounds.

LEMMA 6. *Let $\epsilon > 0$. At any point in time during the execution of MainFullyDyn, let A be the total number of edge additions. There are less than $O(\log(|V|)\log(A)\epsilon^{-1})$ consecutive bad rounds, with high probability.*

PROOF. Consider an arbitrary sequence of k consecutive bad rounds $s_1, \ldots, s_k$, with $k \geq 6\lceil \log_{1+\epsilon}(|V|) \log_{3/2}(A) \rceil$. Let $p = \frac{1}{3\log_{1+\epsilon}(|V|)}$ and $t = 2\lceil \log_{1+\epsilon}(|V|) \rceil$. Let β_i be the value of β at round s_i. From Lemma 5 and union bound, it follows that the probability that there is $i < t$ such that $\beta_{i+1} < (1+\epsilon)\beta_i$ is at most $p \cdot t < \frac{2}{3}$. Therefore, with probability at least $1 - \frac{2}{3}^{3\log_{3/2}(A)} = 1 - O(A^{-3})$ there are t consecutive bad rounds $s_{i+1}, s_{i+2}, \ldots, s_{i+t}$, with $i + t < k$ such that $\beta_{j+1} \geq (1+\epsilon)\beta_j$ for any $j \in [i+1, i+t-1]$. However, by definition the β_j's are bounded by $|V|$ and therefore cannot increase by a factor of $(1+\epsilon)$ more than $\log_{1+\epsilon}(|V|) < t$ times. From the above observations, it follows that if there are more than k consecutive bad rounds then the latter condition is not satisfied with probability at least $1 - O(A^{-3})$. From the fact that there are at most $A + R = O(A)$ rounds in total and from a union-bound argument it follows that throughout the execution of the algorithm there are at most $6\lceil \log_{1+\epsilon}(|V|) \log_{3/2}(A) \rceil = O(\log(|V|)\log(A)\epsilon^{-1})$ consecutive bad rounds, w.h.p. □

We can now provide a proof sketch of the main theorem. The proof is omitted for brevity and deferred to the full version of the paper.

PROOF SKETCH OF THEOREM 6. Similarly to the algorithm in the previous section, it is easy to see that the algorithm can be implemented in space $O(n+m)$ (for storing the nodes and edges in the current graph) plus some additional space for bookkeeping information of cost $O(n)$.

We now bound the amortized cost of our algorithm. From Lemma 6, it follows that at any point in time we can partition (w.h.p.) all rounds of *MainFullyDyn* in *super-rounds*, such that every super-round, except possibly the last one, contains $O(\log_{1+\epsilon}(|V|)\log(A))$ consecutive bad rounds followed by one final good round, while the last super-round contains $O(\log_{1+\epsilon}(|V|)\log(A))$ consecutive bad rounds which might or might not be followed by one final good round. We prove our bound on the amortized cost for any such super-round, which will prove the desired claim.

We first consider any super-round $\mathcal{S}$ containing both good and bad rounds. Let a and r be the total number of edge additions and deletions in $\mathcal{S}$. By using similar arguments to the ones in the proof of Theorem 4 and using the fact that we have at most $O(\log_{1+\epsilon}(|V|)\log(A))$ rounds in a given super-round, it follows that the total number of operations performed throughout $\mathcal{S}$ is $O\left((m_0 + a + r)\log(A)\log^2(|V|)\epsilon^{-2}\right)$, where m_0 is the number of edges at the beginning of $\mathcal{S}$.

Let a' and r' be, respectively, the total number of additions and removals in the bad rounds of $\mathcal{S}$, while let a'', r'' be the total number of additions and removals in the final good round of $\mathcal{S}$, respectively. We now use the fact that in any good round a large number of removal operations is performed.

By definition of good round, $r'' \geq R^* \in \Theta\left(\frac{m'\epsilon}{\log_{1+\epsilon}(|V|)}\right)$, where m' is the number of edges at the beginning of the good round. Using the fact that $m' = m_0 + a' - r'$ and after some

Graph	$\|V\|$	$\|E\|$	Time
DBLP	938,609	4,541,961	1959-2014
Patent (Co-Aut.)	1,162,227	3,660,945	1975-1999
Patent (Cit.)	2,745,762	13,965,410	1975-1999
LastFm	681,387	43,518,693	2005-2009
Yahoo! Answer	2,432,573	1.21×10^9	2006

Table 1: Properties of the dynamic graphs analysed. $|V|$, $|E|$, refer to the number nodes appearing in the graph and number of edge additions, respectively. Time indicates when evolution took place.

simple algebra, we derive $m_0 \in O\left(r\frac{\log(|V|)}{\epsilon^2}\right)$. Therefore, we can bound the total number of operations $C_{\mathcal{S}}$ performed in the super-round $\mathcal{S}$ as follows

$$\begin{aligned} C_{\mathcal{S}} &= O\left((m_0 + a + r)\log(A)\log^2(|V|)\epsilon^{-2}\right) \\ &= O\left(a\log(A)\log^2(|V|)\epsilon^{-2} + r\log(A)\log^3(|V|)\epsilon^{-4}\right). \end{aligned}$$

By summing up over all super-rounds we prove the desired claim. Notice that if $\mathcal{S}$ does not contain any good round then there is an additional term $O\left((A+R)\log(A)\log^2(|V|)\epsilon^{-2}\right)$. As this might happen only for the last super-round this does not change the asymptotic cost. □

Handling node insertions. Similar consideration of the previous section holds in this context. When a node is added we can assign it to the first set S_0 only. Moreover, if we define V as the set of all nodes ever inserted in the graph, then $|V|$ is again monotone increasing. So the algorithm remains consistent.

5. EXPERIMENTS

In this section, we provide an extensive experimental evaluation of our algorithms on large real-world graphs some of which contain more than one billion edges. From each dataset, we extracted an undirected graph with each edge being associated with a timestamp.

Datasets & Experimental setup.

We start by describing our publicly available datasets. See Table 1 for a summary of their features.

DBLP. The *DBLP* graph is obtained from a snapshot [1] of a coauthorship graph, constructed from 2.5 million scientific publications in computer science published between 1959 and 2014. Nodes in this graph represent authors, while an edge with timestamp t between two nodes indicates that the corresponding authors published an article in year t. To take into account only strong scientific collaborations, we restrict our attention to papers with at most 10 authors.

Patent (Co-Aut.) & Patent (Cit.). The *Patent (Co-Aut.) & Patent (Cit.)* graphs are obtained from a dataset [22] containing about 2 million U.S. patents granted between '75 and '99. In the *Patent (Co-Aut.)* graph, nodes represent inventors while an edge with timestamp t connects two inventors of the same patent granted in year t. In the *Patent (Cit.)* graph, nodes represent patents while an undirected edge with timestamp t connects two patents if one received a citation from the other in year t.

LastFm. The LastFm graph is obtained from a dataset [2, 15] of song listenings of `last.fm` users. The dataset contains about ≈ 20 million listenings of ≈ 1 million songs from ≈

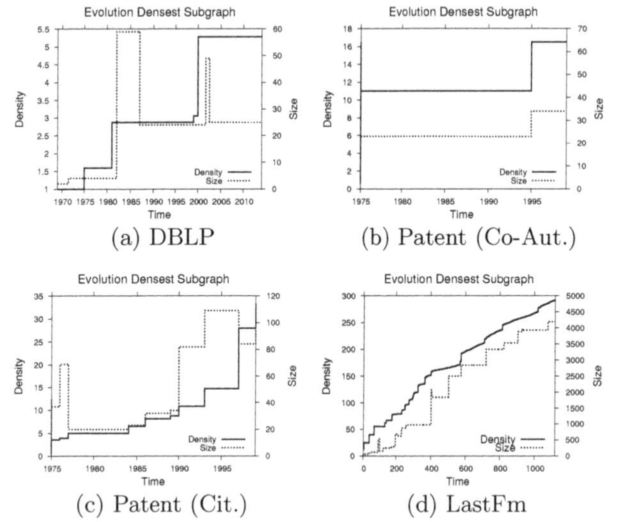

(a) DBLP (b) Patent (Co-Aut.)

(c) Patent (Cit.) (d) LastFm

Figure 1: Evolution of the densest subgraph — edge addition only.

1000 users. In this graph, nodes represent songs while an edge with timestamp t connects two songs if they where *both* listed by the same 3 or more users in the same day t.

Yahoo! Answer. This graph is obtained from a sample of ≈ 160 million answers to ≈ 25 millions questions in Yahoo! Answer [3]. From this dataset, we derived an undirected graph where nodes represent users and an edge connects two users at time $max(t_1, t_2)$ if they both answered the same question at times t_1, t_2 respectively. We removed 6 outliers questions with more than > 5000 answers.

Experimental setup. All our experiments have been run using in-house developed C++ code compiled with `g++` and `-O4` optimization option. We used a machine equipped with Intel(R) Xeon(R) E7-4870 CPUs with 2.40GHz clock and approximately 50GB of main memory. Each run employs a single core of the machine while using less than 10% of the available main memory.

5.1 Edge insertion only

In this subsection, we show our results for the case with edge additions only. First, we show the evolution over time of the properties of the densest subgraph for some of our datasets, when edges are introduced according to their timestamps. Then, we study the tradeoff between running time and accuracy of our algorithm as a function of our accuracy parameter ϵ. Finally, we consider the natural variant of state-of-the-art approaches for static densest subgraph computation, where a densest subgraph is recomputed every time k update operations are performed. Our experimental evaluation shows that our dynamic algorithm is up to 3 orders of magnitude faster than such a natural variant.

Evolution of the densest subgraph.

In our first experiment, edges are first sorted according to their timestamps in a non-decreasing order. Then, starting from an empty graph they are added one at a time[2] while our algorithm maintains an approximate densest subgraph

[2]Notice that in our experiments we ignore trivial update operations (e.g. inserting an edge already present).

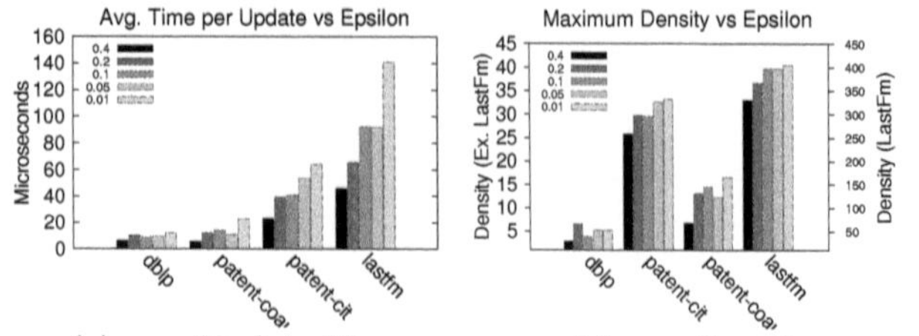

(a) ϵ vs Update Time (b) ϵ vs Density

Figure 2: Trade-offs between the average updated time in microseconds and the density of the densest subgraph found— edge addition only. Notice how in all the graph the average update times are in the hundreds of microseconds at most. Smaller the ϵ values results in higher update time and densities.

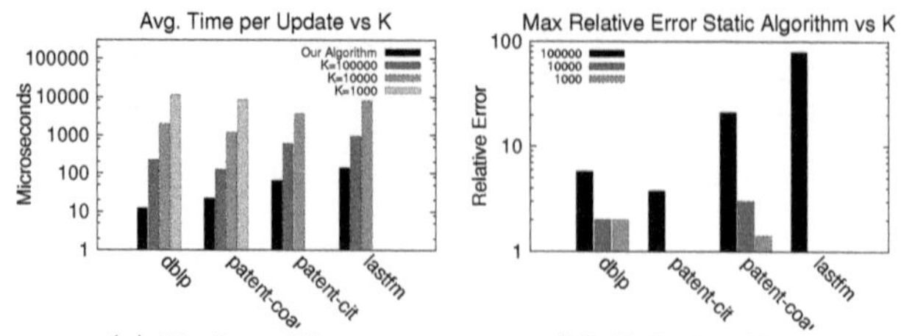

(a) Update Time (b) Relative Error

Figure 3: Comparison between our approach and re-computing the densest subgraph every K updates with a static graph algorithm. Notice that both plots are in log scale. Our algorithm outperforms static graph algorithms by orders of magnitude even when allowed to run very infrequently and output up to 80 times more dense clusters.

of the current graph. Figure 1, illustrates the evolution of the density as well as the size of the densest subgraph found by our algorithm over time. For the DBLP and Patent graph the time is in years, while for LastFm is in days.

For this experiment we used parameter $\epsilon = 0.01$ which provides a ≈ 2.04-approximation. Notice how the density of the densest subgraph grows in a stepwise fashion, which is expected as the algorithm does not recompute the densest subgraph unless a sufficiently larger one emerges. The largest densest subgraphs found in our datasets range in size between ≈ 60 and ≈ 4000 nodes, while having density between ≈ 5 and ≈ 400. In particular we observe very dense subgraphs for our LastFm dataset where node represents songs.

Efficiency accuracy trade-offs. We now turn our attention to the tradeoff between running time and density of the densest subgraph as a function of our accuracy parameter ϵ. Figure 2(a) shows average time per update in microseconds for our algorithm. We can observe that on average a few hundreds of microseconds are sufficient for handling any update. This implies that our algorithm can handle between ≈ 7000 and ≈ 80000 edge update operations per second with very small error ($\epsilon = 0.01$). These results highlight that our algorithm can be employed effectively in a very dynamic context. Figure 2(b) illustrates how the density of the densest subgraph is affected by our accuracy parameter ϵ. Notice that, as expected, smaller values of ϵ results in denser subgraphs. However, our algorithm seems to find very dense subgraphs even for relatively large values of ϵ suggesting that our algorithm finds denser subgraphs than those predicted by our worst case analysis.

Comparison with static algorithms. To the best of our knowledge, no approximation algorithm has been designed to efficiently maintain a densest subgraph in a dynamic graph, while requiring time $o(|V| + |E|)$ per update (i.e. without recomputing the solution from scratch every time). Therefore, we study a natural variant of the algorithm proposed by Bahmani et al. [10]), where the densest subgraph is recomputed every time K update operations are performed. As it is not clear how to fix K a priori we consider several different values for K. Notice that, even though the algorithm presented by Bahmani et al. [10] provides a $2(1 + \epsilon)$ approximation, recomputing the densest subgraph every K update operations does not give any meaningful approximation guarantee. This follows from the fact that densest subgraphs might emerge very quickly, before the densest subgraph is recomputed. Indeed, this is what we observe in our experimental evaluation.

Figure 3(a) shows the comparison of the running time of our algorithm vs that of Bahmani et al. [10]. Both algorithms are set to provide an approximation guarantees of $2(1 + \epsilon)^2$ with $\epsilon = 0.01$. It is possible to see that our algorithm is up to 3 orders of magnitude faster than the one that recomputes the densest subgraph periodically, even when this is done every 100000 updates. Times in Figure 3(a) are in microseconds per update. For the dataset LastFm and Patent (Cit.) with $K = 10000$ we stopped the computation of the algorithm after few hours so the result is a lower-bound of the total time required.

We remark that an average update time in the order of tens of milliseconds is far from being practical. As an illustrative example, if each update requires 10 milliseconds, the analysis of datasets with one billion updates would require at least 100 days. Hence, it is crucial to design algorithms with an update time in the order of tens to hundreds of microseconds or less to scale to such datasets.

Moreover, recomputing the subgraph periodically may also lead to poor results, because, dense subgraphs that emerge and disappear quickly might be missed. This is illustrated in Figure 3(b), showing that the naive approach might find subgraphs that are up to ≈ 80 times less dense than the one found by our algorithm (essentially providing no guarantees in terms of accuracy). In comparison our algorithm, is guaranteed to find a subgraph that is always within 2.04 factor from the optimum. In Figure 3(b), we report only the results for the runs that completed in the allotted time.

5.2 Fully dynamic case

In this section, we evaluate our fully dynamic algorithm in datasets containing both edges additions and removals. To show the viability and effectiveness of our approach, we evaluate our algorithm in the *sliding window model*, where a sliding window of the most recent edges (say in the last hour or day) defines the current graph. Over time new recent edges might be added to the current graph, while old ones are being removed. This might results in high rate update operations. The dynamic graphs in this section are obtained in the following way. For DBLP, and Patent (Co-Aut.) & (Cit.) we keep in the sliding window the edges generated

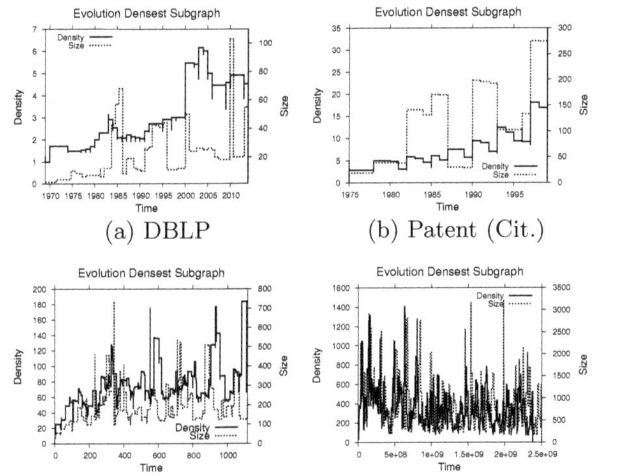

(a) DBLP (b) Patent (Cit.) (c) LastFm (d) Yahoo! Answer

Figure 4: Evolution of the densest subgraph — fully dynamic case.

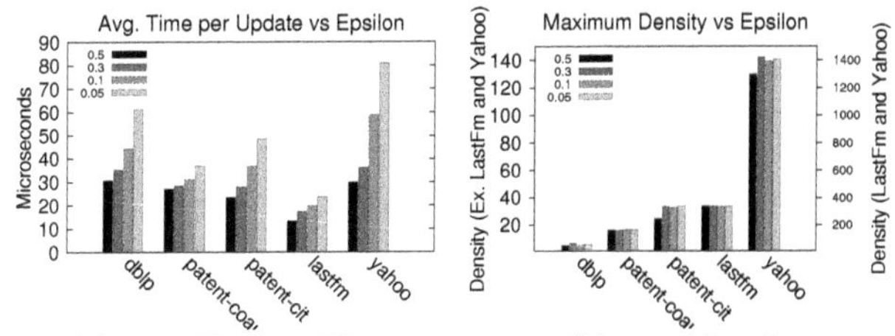

(a) ϵ vs Update Time (b) ϵ vs Density

Figure 5: Trade-offs between the average updated time in microseconds and the density of the densest subgraph found— fully dynamic case.

in the last 5 years, while for LastFm we keep the edges generated in the last 30 days. For our larger graph Yahoo! Answer, instead we keep in the sliding window the last 10 millions edges. In case of a tie the corresponding edges are sorted randomly. We experimented with different sizes for the sliding windows, leading to very similar results (which are omitted for space issues).

Evolution of the densest subgraph. Figure 4 shows the evolution of the densest subgraph in the sliding window model. Notice that in the case of LastFm and Yahoo! Answer both size and density varies very quickly, while for the other graphs we observe less pronounced variations. This is expected as, for instance in Yahoo! Answer, the appearance of new popular topic can trigger the rapid emergence of very large (albeit shortly lived) dense communities of users. In the context of co-authorships graphs, instead, we clearly expect slower variations in the community structure (introducing an edge requires the authorship of a research paper). In our co-authorhsip graphs (DBLP and Patent) we observe a clear trend of densification of the communities over time, which is consistent with previous observations [30]. However, notice that in our work we are able to study for the first time the evolution of the density of the densest subgraphs (as opposed to the density of the whole graph), which is possible thanks to the ability of our algorithm to process efficiently very large dynamic graphs. This pattern is less clear in LastFm and Yahoo! Answer but our analysis of these graphs is limited to significantly smaller periods of times, with other transient phenomena possibly prevailing.

These results highlight that our algorithm can be a valuable tool in studying the evolution of communities in a social network over time.

Efficiency accuracy trade-offs. Figure 5(a) shows the average time per update in microseconds of our algorithm as a function on the parameter ϵ for some our datasets. We can consistently observe that a densest subgraph can be maintained within hundreds of microseconds per update on average. This is the case also for our larger datasets requiring billions of updates, allowing the computation of densest subgraphs in evolving graphs at these scales.

Figure 5(b), instead, shows how the density of the densest subgraph found is affected by our accuracy parameter ϵ. Similar considerations of the insertion only graph section holds in this case.

By comparing Figure 4 and Figure 5(a), we observe higher update times in the most highly dynamic datasets, such as LastFm and Yahoo!, Answer) as opposed to DBLP, Patent. This is expected as frequent changes in the density of the densest subgraph requires the frequent executions of the costly *FindDensest* procedure. Notice, however, that our algorithm scales very well in very large and highly dynamic datasets like Yahoo! Answer.

6. CONCLUSIONS AND FUTURE WORKS

We studied the problem of maintaining an approximate densest subgraph problem in dynamic graphs. We give the first algorithm that maintains a constant factor approximation when edges are added adversarially and removed randomly, while ensuring amortized cost being poly-log per update on average. Our extensive experimental evaluation shows that our algorithm can cope with more than one billion of update operations within a few hundreds of microseconds per update, on average.

An interesting direction for future work is to adapt into a dynamic environment the algorithm developed in [11] for finding several dense subgraphs with limited overlap. It would also be interesting to improve the approximation factor of our algorithm by using a technique similar to the one presented in [8], as well as, to design algorithms that work under adversarial edge deletion.

Acknowledgments.

We thank Flavio Chierichetti, Ravi Kumar and Alessandro Panconesi for their many insightful comments and suggestions.

7. REFERENCES

[1] DBLP dataset (October 2014). `http://dblp.uni-trier.de/xml/`.

[2] Last.fm song network dataset - KONECT. `http://konect.uni-koblenz.de/networks/lastfm_song`.

[3] Yahoo! Answers browsing behavior version 1.0. - Yahoo! Research Webscope Datasets. `http://webscope.sandbox.yahoo.com`.

[4] T. Akiba, Y. Iwata, and Y. Yoshida. Fast exact shortest-path distance queries on large networks by pruned landmark labeling. In *SIGMOD*, 2013.

[5] H. Aksu, M. Canim, Y.-C. Chang, I. Korpeoglu, and O. Ulusoy. Distributed k -core view materialization and maintenance for large dynamic graphs. *IEEE Trans. Knowledge and Data Eng.*, 2014.

[6] A. Angel, N. Koudas, N. Sarkas, D. Srivastava, M. Svendsen, and S. Tirthapura. Dense subgraph maintenance under streaming edge weight updates for real-time story identification. *The VLDB Journal*, 2014.

[7] A. Angel, N. Sarkas, N. Koudas, and D. Srivastava. Dense subgraph maintenance under streaming edge weight updates for real-time story identification. *PVLDB*, 2012.

[8] B. Bahmani, A. Goel, and K. Munagala. Efficient primal-dual algorithms for mapreduce. *Manuscript*, 2012.

[9] B. Bahmani, R. Kumar, M. Mahdian, and E. Upfal. Pagerank on an evolving graph. In *KDD*, 2012.

[10] B. Bahmani, R. Kumar, and S. Vassilvitskii. Densest subgraph in streaming and mapreduce. *PVLDB*, 2012.

[11] O. D. Balalau, F. Bonchi, T.-H. Chan, F. Gullo, and M. Sozio. Finding subgraphs with maximum total density and limited overlap. In *WSDM*, 2015.

[12] S. Bhattacharya, M. Henzinger, D. Nanongkai, and C. E. Tsourakakis. Space- and Time-Efficient Algorithm for Maintaining Dense Subgraphs on One-Pass Dynamic Streams. In *STOC*, (to appear), 2015.

[13] M. Brunato, H. H. Hoos, and R. Battiti. On effectively finding maximal quasi-cliques in graphs. In *Learning and Intelligent Optimization*. 2008.

[14] G. Buehrer and K. Chellapilla. A scalable pattern mining approach to web graph compression with communities. In *WSDM*, pages 95–106. ACM, 2008.

[15] Ò. Celma Herrada. Music recommendation and discovery in the long tail. Technical report, 2009.

[16] M. Charikar. Greedy approximation algorithms for finding dense components in a graph. In *Approximation Algorithms for Combinatorial Optimization*. 2000.

[17] J. Chen and Y. Saad. Dense subgraph extraction with application to community detection. *IEEE Trans. on Knowledge and Data Eng.*, 2012.

[18] E. Cohen, E. Halperin, H. Kaplan, and U. Zwick. Reachability and distance queries via 2-hop labels. *SIAM Journal on Computing*, 2003.

[19] Y. Dourisboure, F. Geraci, and M. Pellegrini. Extraction and classification of dense communities in the web. In *WWW*, 2007.

[20] D. Gibson, R. Kumar, and A. Tomkins. Discovering large dense subgraphs in massive graphs. In *VLBD*, 2005.

[21] A. V. Goldberg. *Finding a maximum density subgraph*. UC Berkeley, 1984.

[22] B. H. Hall, A. B. Jaffe, and M. Trajtenberg. The NBER patent citation data file: Lessons, insights and methodological tools. Technical report, National Bureau of Economic Research, 2001.

[23] G. F. Italiano, D. Eppstein, and Z. Galil. Dynamic graph algorithms. *Algorithms and Theory of Computation Handbook*, 1999.

[24] R. Jin, Y. Xiang, N. Ruan, and D. Fuhry. 3-hop: a high-compression indexing scheme for reachability query. In *SIGMOD*, 2009.

[25] S. Khuller and B. Saha. On finding dense subgraphs. In *Automata, Languages and Programming*. 2009.

[26] R. Kumar, J. Novak, and A. Tomkins. Structure and evolution of online social networks. In *KDD*, 2006.

[27] R. Kumar, P. Raghavan, S. Rajagopalan, and A. Tomkins. Trawling the web for emerging cyber-communities. *Computer networks*, 1999.

[28] P. Lee, L. V. Lakshmanan, and E. Milios. CAST: A Context-Aware Story-Teller for Streaming Social Content. In *CIKM*, 2014.

[29] V. E. Lee, N. Ruan, R. Jin, and C. Aggarwal. A survey of algorithms for dense subgraph discovery. In *Managing and Mining Graph Data*. Springer, 2010.

[30] J. Leskovec, J. Kleinberg, and C. Faloutsos. Graph evolution: Densification and shrinking diameters. *ACM Trans. KDD*, 2007.

[31] R.-H. Li, J. Yu, and R. Mao. Efficient core maintenance in large dynamic graphs. *IEEE Trans. Knowledge and Data Engineering*, 2014.

[32] N. Mishra, R. Schreiber, I. Stanton, and R. E. Tarjan. Finding strongly knit clusters in social networks. *Internet Mathematics*, 2008.

[33] D. Peleg. Distributed computing. *SIAM Monographs on discrete mathematics and applications*, 2000.

[34] B. Saha, A. Hoch, S. Khuller, L. Raschid, and X. Zhang. Dense subgraphs with restrictions and applications to gene annotation graphs. In *RECOMB*, 2010.

[35] B. Saha, A. Hoch, S. Khuller, L. Raschid, and X.-N. Zhang. Dense subgraphs with restrictions and applications to gene annotation graphs. In *Research in Computational Molecular Biology*, 2010.

[36] A. E. Saríyüce, B. Gedik, G. Jacques-Silva, K.-L. Wu, and Ü. V. Çatalyürek. Streaming algorithms for k-core decomposition. *PVLDB*, 2013.

[37] A. D. Sarma, A. Lall, D. Nanongkai, and A. Trehan. Dense subgraphs on dynamic networks. In *Distributed Computing*. 2012.

[38] S. B. Seidman. Network structure and minimum degree. *Social networks*, 1983.

[39] M. Sozio and A. Gionis. The community-search problem and how to plan a successful cocktail party. In *Proceedings of the 16th ACM SIGKDD, 2010*, pages 939–948, 2010.

[40] C. Tsourakakis, F. Bonchi, A. Gionis, F. Gullo, and M. Tsiarli. Denser than the densest subgraph: Extracting optimal quasi-cliques with quality guarantees. In *KDD*, 2013.

[41] E. Valari, M. Kontaki, and A. N. Papadopoulos. Discovery of top-k dense subgraphs in dynamic graph collections. In *Scientific and Statistical Database Management*, 2012.

A Practical Framework for Privacy-Preserving Data Analytics

Liyue Fan*
Integrated Media Systems Center
University of Southern California
Los Angeles, CA, USA
liyuefan@usc.edu

Hongxia Jin
Samsung R&D Research Center
San Jose, CA, USA
hongxia@acm.org

ABSTRACT

The availability of an increasing amount of user generated data is transformative to our society. We enjoy the benefits of analyzing big data for public interest, such as disease outbreak detection and traffic control, as well as for commercial interests, such as smart grid and product recommendation. However, the large collection of user generated data contains unique patterns and can be used to re-identify individuals, which has been exemplified by the AOL search log release incident. In this paper, we propose a practical framework for data analytics, while providing *differential privacy* guarantees to individual data contributors. Our framework generates differentially private aggregates which can be used to perform data mining and recommendation tasks. To alleviate the high perturbation errors introduced by the differential privacy mechanism, we present two methods with different sampling techniques to draw a subset of individual data for analysis. Empirical studies with real-world data sets show that our solutions enable accurate data analytics on a small fraction of the input data, reducing user privacy risk and data storage requirement without compromising the analysis results.

Categories and Subject Descriptors

H.2.7 [**Database Management**]: Database Administration—*Security, integrity, and protection*; H.2.8 [**Database Management**]: Database Applications—*Data mining*

Keywords

Data Analytics, Differential Privacy, Sampling

1. INTRODUCTION

We live in the age of big data. With an increasing number of people, devices, and sensors connected with digital networks, individual data now can be largely collected and analyzed to understand important phenomena. One example is Google Flu Trends [1], a service that estimates flu activity by aggregating individual search queries. In the retail market, individual purchase histories are used by recommendation tools to learn trends and patterns. Performing analytics on private data is clearly beneficial, such as early detection of disease and recommendation services. However, user concerns rise from a privacy perspective, with sharing an increasing amount of information regarding their health, location, service usage, and online activities.

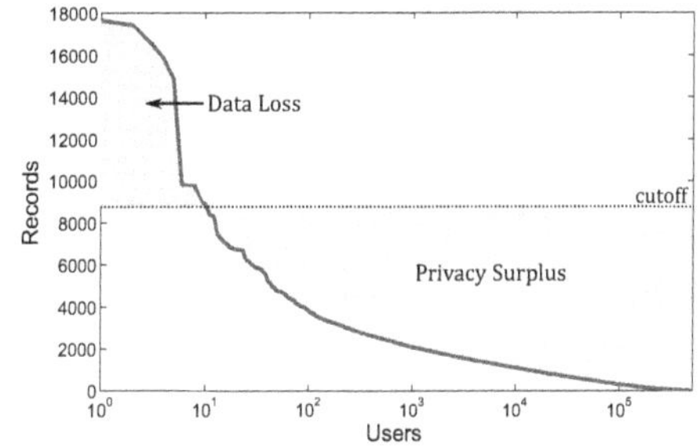

Figure 1: Record Distribution of *Netflix* Users

As a matter of fact, the uniqueness of each user is increased by the big collection of individual data. The AOL data release in 2006 is an unfortunate example of privacy catastrophe [1], in which the search logs of an innocent citizen were quickly identified by a newspaper journalist. A recent study by de Montjoye et al. [9] concludes that human mobility patterns are highly unique and four spatio-temporal points are enough to uniquely identify 95% of the individuals. In order to protect users from re-identification attacks, their private data must be transformed prior to release for analysis.

The current state-of-the-art paradigm for privacy-preserving data analysis is *differential privacy* [10], which allows un-trusted parties to access private data through aggregate queries. The aggregate statistics are perturbed by a randomized algorithm, such that the output remains roughly the same even if any user is added or removed in the input data. Differential privacy provides a strong guarantee: given the output statistics, an adversary will not be able to infer whether any user is present in the input database. However, this indistinguishability can be only achieved at high perturbation cost. Intuitively, the more data a user contributes to the analysis process, the more perturbation noise is needed to hide his/her presence. In some cases, a user could generate an *unbounded* amount of data, such as purchase or check-in history, the addition or removal of which may result in unlimited impact on the output.

The challenge of enforcing differential privacy is that it incurs a surplus of privacy cost, i.e. high perturbation error, being designed to protect each user according to the highest possible data contribution. In reality, only a very small number of users generate large amount of personal data, while the rest contribute little data each. As shown in Figure 1, out of 500K users from Netflix prize com-

*work done while interning with Samsung.
[1]http://www.google.org/flutrends/

WWW 2015, May 18–22, 2015, Florence, Italy.
ACM 978-1-4503-3469-3/15/05.
http://dx.doi.org/10.1145/2736277.2741122.

petition [2], only 1 user generated around 17K data records, while the majority of users generated much less personal data, less than 2K data records each. If a upper bound is imposed on individual user data contribution, the surplus of privacy, e.g. high perturbation noise, can be reduced at the cost of data loss, i.e. part of data from those users who contributed more than the threshold.

To limit individual data contribution, some strategies have been adopted by several works [16][25]. The authors of [16] used the first d search queries submitted by each user, and the work in [25] reduced the number of items contained in each transaction to l with "smart" truncation. However, there has been no discussion on the choice of the bounds, i.e., d and l. Furthermore, the choice of actual user records (or items in a single transaction) remains non-trivial, for generic applications.

With a rigorous privacy notion, we consider how to analyze individually contributed data to gain a deep understanding of service usage and behavior patterns, for various application domains. We would like to understand the impacts of privacy and data loss on the resulting data analytics, and design algorithms to draw private data accordingly. Example data analytical questions are: "Which places do people visit on Thursdays?" and "What are the most popular movies with female watchers under age 25?" We formally define the tasks as database queries and details are provided in Section 3.

Contributions. In this paper, we address the problem of differentially private data analytics, where each user could contribute a large number of records. We propose a generic framework to generate analysis results on a sampled database, and study two sampling methods as well as the sampling factor in order to achieve a balance between data loss and privacy surplus. We summarize the contributions of this paper as follows:

(1) We propose a generic, sampling-based framework for an important class of data analytical tasks: top-K mining and context-aware recommendation. We consider the problem of releasing a set of *count* queries regarding the domain-specific items of interest as well as customizable predicates to answer deep, analytical questions. The count queries are perturbed prior to release such that they satisfy differential privacy.

(2) We design two algorithms that draw a sample of user records from the raw database and generate analysis results on the sampled data. The `SRA` algorithm randomly samples up to l records per user. The `HPA` algorithm selects up to l records from each user that are most useful for the specific analytical tasks. The utility of each record can be customized based on the actual application domain. We outline each sampling method and provide pseudo code for easy implementation.

(3) We provide analysis on the accuracy of random sampling, i.e. Mean Squared Error of released counts, with respect to the sampling factor l. We conclude that the optimal l value is positively correlated the privacy constraint. We show that performing record sampling on individual user's data does not inflict extra privacy leakage. We formally prove that both sampling algorithms satisfy differential privacy.

(4) We conduct extensive empirical studies with various real-world data sets. We compare our approaches with existing differentially private mechanisms and evaluate the accuracy of released count data with three utility metrics. The experimental results show that although performed on a small sampled database, our methods provide comparable performance to the best existing approaches in MSE and KL-divergence, and superior performance in top-K discovery and context-aware recommendation tasks. The `HPA` algorithm yields higher precision, while the `SRA` algorithm preserves well the distributional properties in released data. We believe that our privacy-preserving framework will enable data analytics for a variety of services, reducing user privacy cost and data storage requirement without compromising output utility.

The rest of the paper is organized as follows: Section 2 briefly surveys the related works on privacy-preserving data publishing and analytics. Section 3 defines the problem and privacy notion. Section 4 presents the technical details of the proposed framework and two sampling algorithms. Theoretical results of privacy guarantees are provided in Section 5. Section 6 describes the data set and presents a set of empirical studies. Finally, Section 7 concludes the paper and states possible directions for future work.

2. RELATED WORKS

A plethora of differentially private techniques have been developed since the introduction of ϵ-differential privacy in [12]. Here we briefly review the most recent, relevant works to our problem.

Differential Privacy. Dwork et al. [12] first proposed ϵ-differential privacy and established the Laplace mechanism to perturb aggregate queries to guarantee differential privacy. Since then, two variants have been proposed and adopted by many works as relaxations of ϵ-differential privacy. The (ϵ, δ)-probabilistic differential privacy [19] achieves ϵ-differential privacy with high probability, i.e. $\geq (1-\delta)$. The (ϵ, δ)-indistinguishability [11, 21] relaxes the bound of ϵ-differential privacy by introducing an additive term δ. Our work adopts the strict definition of ϵ-differential privacy and the Laplace mechanism to release numeric data for analysis.

Data Publication Techniques. A plethora of works have been proposed to publish sanitized data with differential privacy. To list a few representatives among them, there is histogram publication for range queries [7], for a given workload [24], and for sparse data [8]. The majority of data publication methods consider settings where each user contributes only one record, or affects only one released *count*. In contrast, we focus on those services where each individual may contribute a large number of records and could even have unbounded influence on the released *count* queries.

Bounding Individual Contribution. Here we review works established in a similar problem setting, i.e. where individual data contribution is high, i.e. high *global sensitivity*. The work of Nissim et al. [21] proposed *smooth sensitivity*, which measures individual impact on the output statistics in the neighborhood of the database instance. They showed that smooth sensitivity allows a smaller amount of perturbation noise injected to released statistics. However, it does not guarantee ϵ-differential privacy. Proserpio et al. [22] recently proposed to generalize ϵ-DP definition to weighted datasets, and scale down the weights of data records to reduce sensitivity. Rastogi and Nath [23], Fan and Xiong [13] and Chan et. al [5] studied the problem of sharing time series of counts with differential privacy, where the maximum individual contribution is T, the number of time points. The authors of [23] proposed to preserve only k discrete Fourier coefficients of the original count series. The FAST framework in [13] reduced the sensitivity by sampling M points in a count series and predicts at other points. The work [5] proposed the notion of p-sum to ensure each item in the stream only affects a small number of p-sum's. Two works by Korolova et al. [16] and Hong et al. [14] addressed the differentially private publication of search logs, where each user could contribute a large search history. The work of [16] keeps the first d queries of each user, while the work of [14] explicitly removes those users whose data change the optimal output by more than a certain threshold. Zeng et al. [25] studied frequent itemset mining with differential privacy and truncated each individual transaction to contain up to l items. Recently, Kellaris and Papadopoulos [15]

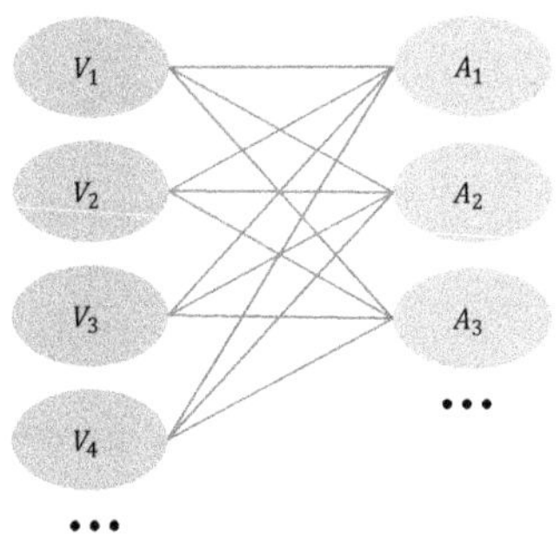

Figure 2: Releasing Counts for Data Analytics

proposed to release non-overlapping count data by grouping similar columns, i.e. items in our definition. In their work, each user is allowed to contribute no more than one records to each column, thus the maximum individual contribution is bounded by the number of columns. However, the binary representation of user data may not truly convey information about each column, i.e. place of interest or product. For example, when the bit for a user and a location is set, we cannot distinguish whether it was an accidental check-in or the user went there many times due to personal preference.

Sampling Differential Privacy. There have been a few works which studied the relationship between sampling and differential privacy. Chaudhuri and Mishra [6] first showed that the combination of k-anonymity and random sampling can achieve differential privacy with high probability. Li et al. [17] proposed to sample each record with a calibrated probability β and then perform k-anonymity on the sampled data, to achieve (ϵ, δ)-indistinguishability. Both works adopt the random sampling technique which samples a data record with certain probability. However, when applied in our setting, no guarantee is provided on bounding the individual data in the sampled database.

Our Competitors. After reviewing existing differentially private technique, we identify three works that allow high individual contribution, release aggregate statistics, and satisfy ϵ-differential privacy. The first is a straight-forward application of Laplace perturbation mechanism [12] to each released count, denoted as `LPA`. The second is the Fourier transform based algorithm from [23], which can be adapted to share count vectors, denoted as `DFT`. The third is `GS`, which is the best method proposed in [15].

3. PRELIMINARIES

3.1 Problem Formulation

Suppose a database D contains data records contributed by a set of n users about m items of interest. Each item could represent in reality a place or a product. Each record in dataset D is a tuple $(rID, uID, vID, attrA)$, where rID is the record ID, uID corresponds to the user who contributed this record, vID is the item which the record is about, and $attrA$ represents contextual/additional information regarding this record. In reality, various information is often available in the actual database, such as transaction time, user ratings and reviews, and user demographic information. In our problem setting, $attrA$ can be an attribute, e.g. *dayOfWeek*, or a set of attributes, e.g. *(Gender, Age)*, which can be customized to offer deep insight in a specific application domain. Let h denote the number of possible $attrA$ values.

To be more concrete, we select two analytic tasks, i.e. *top-K discovery* and *context-aware recommendation*, to illustrate the usability of our solutions. The first task answers questions as "What are the most popular places in city X?", while the second task aims more specifically at "Recommend good places to visit on a Tuesday!". Moreover, we consider the problem of performing the above tasks on released *count* data. As in Figure 2, each V_i's represents an item of interest, e.g. a restaurant, and each A_j represents a value of the context, e.g."Monday". For each V_i, the number of records containing V_i is released. For each edge connecting V_i and A_j, the number of records containing V_i and A_j is released. As a result, top-K discovery can be performed on the item counts and context-aware recommendation on the edge counts connected to any context A_j. We formally state the problem to investigate below.

DEFINITION 1 (ITEM COUNTS). *For each item V_i in database D, release*

$$c_i(D) \leftarrow \text{select} * \text{from } D \quad \text{where } vID = V_i \tag{1}$$

DEFINITION 2 (EDGE COUNTS). *For each edge connecting item V_i and attribute A_j, release*

$$c_{i,j}(D) \leftarrow \text{select} * \text{from } D \quad \text{where } vID = V_i \text{ and } attrA = A_j \tag{2}$$

PROBLEM 1 (PRIVATE DATA ANALYTICS). *Given database D and privacy parameter ϵ, release a sanitized version of item counts and edge counts, such that the released data satisfies ϵ-differential privacy.*

Note that the problem definition, i.e. the counting queries to release, can be customized according to the analytical task to perform. For instance, to understand the correlation between items, the bipartite graph in Figure 2 can be adapted as follows: A_* nodes will be replaced by items, i.e. V_* nodes; and each edge (V_i, V_j) represents "the number of times that V_j is purchased/watched/visited by users who also purchase/watch/visit V_i". Similarly, those counts can be released privately with slight adaption of our proposed solutions below.

3.2 Privacy Definition

The privacy guarantee provided by our work is *differential privacy* [4]. Simply put, a mechanism is differentially private if its outcome is not significantly affected by the removal or addition of any user. An adversary thus learns approximately the same information about any individual, irrespective of his/her presence or absence in the original database.

DEFINITION 3 (ϵ-DIFFERENTIAL PRIVACY). A non-interactive privacy mechanism $\mathcal{A} : \mathcal{D} \rightarrow \mathcal{T}$ satisfies ϵ-differential privacy if for any neighboring databases D_1 and D_2, and for any set $\widetilde{D} \in \mathcal{T}$,

$$Pr[\mathcal{A}(D_1) = \widetilde{D}] \leq e^{\epsilon} \cdot Pr[\mathcal{A}(D_2) = \widetilde{D}] \tag{3}$$

where the probability is taken over the randomness of $\mathcal{A}$.

The privacy parameter ϵ, also called the *privacy budget* [20], specifies the degree of privacy offered. Intuitively, a lower value of ϵ implies stronger privacy guarantee and a larger perturbation noise, and a higher value of ϵ implies a weaker guarantee while possibly achieving higher accuracy. The neighboring databases D_1 and D_2 differ on at most one user.

Laplace Mechanism. Dwork et al. [12] show that ϵ-differential privacy can be achieved by adding i.i.d. noise to query result $q(D)$:

$$\tilde{q}(D) = q(D) + (\tilde{N}_1, \ldots, \tilde{N}_z)^{\mathsf{T}} \tag{4}$$

$$\tilde{N}_i \sim Lap(0, \frac{GS(q)}{\epsilon}) \text{ for } i = 1, \ldots, z \tag{5}$$

Symbol	Description
$D/\mathcal{D}$	Input database / Domain of all databases
T_k	Set of records contributed by user u_k in D
$D_R/\mathcal{D_R}$	SRA sampled database / Domain of D_R
$D_G/\mathcal{D_G}$	HPA sampled database / Domain of D_G
$D_E/\mathcal{D_E}$	HPA sampled database / Domain of D_E
$\mathbf{q_1}/\tilde{\mathbf{q}}_1$	Query of all item counts / Noisy output of $\mathbf{q_1}$
$\mathbf{q_2}/\tilde{\mathbf{q}}_2$	Query of all edge counts / Noisy output of $\mathbf{q_2}$
$\mathbf{p}/\tilde{\mathbf{p}}$	Popularity vector for all items / Estimation of $\mathbf{p}$
M	Max records per user allowed in D
l	Max records per user allowed in D_R and D_G
d	Max records per user allowed in D_E

Table 1: Summary of notations

where z represents the dimension of $q(D)$. The magnitude of $\tilde{N}$ conforms to a Laplace distribution with 0 mean and $GS(q)/\epsilon$ scale, where $GS(q)$ represents the *global sensitivity* [12] of the query q. The global sensitivity is the maximum L1 distance between the results of q from any two neighboring databases. Formally, it is defined as follows:

$$GS(q) = \max_{D_1,D_2} ||q(D_1) - q(D_2)||_1 . \quad (6)$$

Sensitivity Analysis. Let M denote the maximum number of records any user could contribute and $\mathcal{D}$ denote the domain of database D. Let $\mathbf{q_1} = \{c_1, \ldots, c_m\}$ output the item counts for every V_i. Let $\mathbf{q_2} = \{c_{1,1}, c_{1,2}, \ldots, c_{m,h}\}$ output the edge counts for every V_i and A_j. The following lemmas establish the global sensitivity of $\mathbf{q_1}$ and $\mathbf{q_2}$, in order to protect the privacy of each individual user. The proof is quite straightforward thus omitted here for brevity.

LEMMA 1 (ITEM COUNTS SENSITIVITY). *The global sensitivity of* $\mathbf{q_1} : \mathcal{D} \rightarrow \mathbb{R}^m$ *is* M, *i.e.*

$$GS(\mathbf{q_1}) = M. \quad (7)$$

LEMMA 2 (EDGE COUNTS SENSITIVITY). *The global sensitivity of* $\mathbf{q_2} : \mathcal{D} \rightarrow \mathbb{R}^{mh}$ *is* M, *i.e.*

$$GS(\mathbf{q_2}) = M. \quad (8)$$

Composition.. The composition properties of differential privacy provide privacy guarantees for a sequence of computations, which can be applied to mechanisms that require multiple steps.

THEOREM 1 (SEQUENTIAL COMPOSITION [20]). Let $\mathcal{A}_i$ each provide ϵ_i-differential privacy. A sequence of $\mathcal{A}_i(D)$ over the dataset D provides $(\sum_i \epsilon_i)$-differential privacy.

4. PROPOSED SOLUTIONS

Below we describe two sampling-based solutions to privacy-preserving data analytics. The notations used in the problem definition and our proposed solutions are summarized in Table 1.

4.1 Simple Random Algorithm (SRA)

Our first solution has been inspired by the fact that the maximum number of records contributed by each user, i.e. M, could be rather large in real applications. For example, the *Netflix* user who contributed the most data submitted 17,000 reviews, as shown in Table 4. In fact, a user could contribute as many records as the domain size, i.e. m, as in the total number of movies on Netflix. As a result of the large magnitude of M, a very high perturbation noise is required to provide differential privacy, according to the Laplace mechanism. Furthermore, the number of records contributed by each user can be unbounded for many applications, as a user could repeatedly check in at the same location or purchase the same product. In that case, M may not be known without breaching individual user privacy.

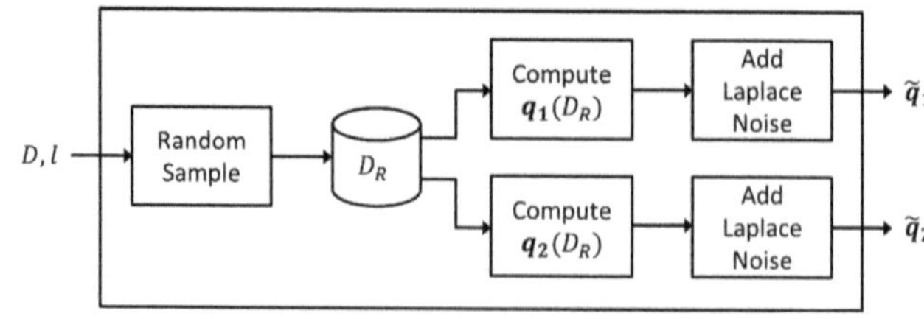

Figure 3: Outline of SRA Algorithm

Algorithm 1 Simple Random Algorithm (SRA)

Input: raw dataset D, sampling factor l, privacy budget ϵ
Output: sanitized answer $\tilde{q}_1$ and $\tilde{q}_2$

```
/* Simple Random Sampling */
D_R ← ∅
for k = 1, ..., n do
  T_k ← σ_{uID=u_k}(D)   /* T_k: records of user u_k */
  if |T_k| ≤ l do
    D_R ← D_R ∪ T_k
  else do
    T'_k ← random sample l records from T_k
    D_R ← D_R ∪ T'_k
/* Generate Private Item Counts */
q1(D_R) ← compute count c_i(D_R) for every i
Output q̃1(D_R) = q1(D_R) + ⟨Lap(l/ε1)⟩^m
/* Generate Private Edge Counts */
q2(D_R) ← compute count c_{i,j}(D_R) for every i, j
Output q̃2(D_R) = q2(D_R) + ⟨Lap(l/ε2)⟩^{mh}
```

In order to mitigate the effect of very large or unbounded individual data contribution, we propose to sample the raw input dataset D and allow up to l records per user in the sampled database. Therefore, the individual contribution to the sampled database is bounded by the fixed constant l. The aggregate statistics will be generated from the sampled data and then perturbed correspondingly in order to guarantee differential privacy. The sampling technique used in our solution is simple random sampling without replacement, after which our solution is named. An outline of the algorithm is provided in Figure 3.

Given the input database D and a pre-defined sampling factor l, the SRA method generates a sampled database D_R by random sampling without replacement at most l records for each user in input database D. The sampled database D_R could be different every time the algorithm is run, due to the randomness of sampling. However, it is guaranteed that for every possible sample D_R, any user could have no more than l records. The following lemma establishes the sensitivity of $\mathbf{q_1}$ and $\mathbf{q_2}$ under such constraint.

LEMMA 3 (SAMPLE SENSITIVITY). *In the domain of* D_R, *it holds that* $GS(\mathbf{q_1}) = l$ *and* $GS(\mathbf{q_2}) = l$.

Subsequently, the SRA method computes the query answers to $\mathbf{q_1}$ and $\mathbf{q_2}$ from the sampled database D_R, where all individual count queries c_i and $c_{i,j}$ are evaluated based on the data records in D_R. According to the Laplace mechanism, it is sufficient to add perturbation noise from $Lap(\frac{l}{\epsilon_1})$ to each item count $c_i(D_R)$ to guarantee ϵ_1-differential privacy. Similarly, adding perturbation noise from $Lap(\frac{l}{\epsilon_2})$ to each edge count $c_{i,j}(D_R)$ guarantees ϵ_2-differential privacy. The pseudocode of SRA method is provided in Algorithm 1.

rID	uID	vID	Day-Of-Week
r_1	Alice	Gym	Monday
r_2	Alice	Mary's house	Tuesday
r_3	Alice	de Young Museum	Friday
r_4	Alice	Golden Gate Bridge	Saturday

Table 2: Example Check-in Records

To sum up, SRA injects low Laplace noise into released query results, due to reduced sensitivity in the sampled database. However, the accuracy of released query results is affected by only using D_R, a subset of the input data D. Intuitively, the more we sample from each user, the closer $\mathbf{q_1}(D_R)$ and $\mathbf{q_2}(D_R)$ are to the true results $\mathbf{q_1}(D)$ and $\mathbf{q_2}(D)$, respectively, at the cost of a higher Laplace perturbation error to achieve differential privacy. Below we formally analyze the trade-off between accuracy and privacy for query $\mathbf{q_1}$ to study the optimal choice of l. Similar analysis can be conducted for query $\mathbf{q_2}$ and is thus omitted here for brevity.

DEFINITION 4 (MEAN SQUARED ERROR). *Let $\tilde{c}_i$ denote the noisy count released by $\tilde{\mathbf{q}}_1(D_R)$ and c_i denote the real count computed by $\mathbf{q_1}(D)$, for each item V_i. The Mean Squared Error of the noisy count $\tilde{c}_i$ is defined as follows:*

$$MSE(\tilde{c}_i) = Var(\tilde{c}_i) + (Bias(\tilde{c}_i, c_i))^2 . \quad (9)$$

THEOREM 2. *Given D_R is a simple random sample of D and $\tilde{\mathbf{q}}_1(D_R) = \mathbf{q_1}(D_R) + \langle Lap(\frac{l}{\epsilon_1})\rangle^m$, the value of l that minimizes MSE is a monotonically increasing function of ϵ_1^2.*

PROOF. *See Appendix A.* □

The above theorem provides a guideline to choose the l value given the privacy budget ϵ_1: when the privacy budget is higher, we can afford to use more private data to overcome the error due to data loss; When privacy budget is limited, a small number of data records should be taken from each user to reduce the perturbation error by the differential privacy mechanism.

4.2 Hand-Picked Algorithm (HPA)

Observing that a majority of data analytical tasks depend on "popular" places or products, such as in traffic analysis and recommendation services, data related to popular items should preferably be preserved in the sample database. In other words, some records generated by one user might be more useful for data analytics than the rest. The following example illustrates the concept of record "usefulness".

EXAMPLE 1. *Table 2 illustrates Alice's check-in records in the raw database. Among the 4 places Alice has been, de Young Museum and the Golden Gate Bridge are places of interest and attract a large number of visitors. On the other hand, gym and Mary's house are local and personal to Alice and may not interest other people. Therefore we consider r_3 and r_4 more useful than r_1 and r_2 for data analytics. However, r_1 and r_2 may be chosen by SRA over r_3 and r_4, due to the simple random sampling procedure.*

From Example 1, it can be seen that r_3 and r_4 should be picked by the sampling procedure over r_1 and r_2, in order to generate meaningful recommendation results. Therefore, we define the following popularity-base utility score for each private data record and propose to preserve records with highest scores for each user.

DEFINITION 5 (UTILITY SCORE). *Given record r and $r.vID = V_i$, the utility score of r is defined as follows:*

$$score(r) = p_i \quad (10)$$

where p_i represents the underlying popularity of item V_i.

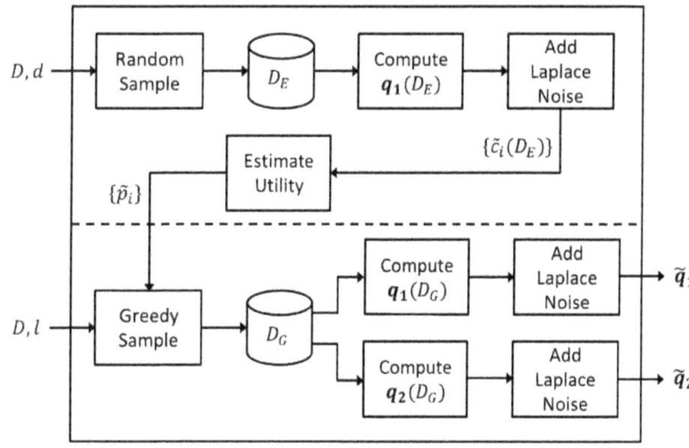

Figure 4: Outline of HPA Algorithm

rID	uID	vID	Day-Of-Week	Utility
r_4	Alice	Golden Gate Bridge	Saturday	0.2
r_3	Alice	de Young Museum	Friday	0.1
r_1	Alice	Gym	Monday	0.001
r_2	Alice	Mary's house	Tuesday	0.0001

Table 3: Example Check-in Records Sorted by Utility Score

Note that the record utility can be defined in other ways according to the target analytical questions. Our choice of the popularity-based measure is motivated by the tasks of discovering popular places or products, as well as the fact that popular items are less personal/sensitive to individual users.

In order to maximize the utility of the sampled database, we propose to greedily pick up to l records with highest utility scores for each user. Note that a user's records with the same score will have equal chance to be picked. The outline of HPA is provided in Figure 4. Below we describe (1) private estimation of record utility and (2) greedy sampling procedure.

Popularity Estimation. For each item V_i, the popularity p_i represents the probability of any record r having $r.vID = V_i$, which is often estimated by the relative frequency of such records. However, the estimation of p_i's from the private user data must not violate the privacy guarantee. We present our privacy-preserving utility estimation in Algorithm 2 from Line 1 to Line 7, which is outlined in the upper half of Figure 4.

The utility estimation is also conducted on a sampled database D_E with sampling factor d. D_E is obtained by randomly choosing up to d records per user from the raw database D. We adopt randomly sampling here because we do not have prior knowledge about the database at this point. The query $\mathbf{q_1}$ is computed based on D_E and each count is perturbed with Laplace noise from $Lap(\frac{d}{\epsilon_0})$. The perturbed counts $\{\tilde{c}_i(D_E)\}$ are used to estimate the popularity for each item V_i by the following normalization:

$$\tilde{p}_i = \frac{max(\tilde{c}_i(D_E), 0)}{\sum_{i=1}^{m} max(\tilde{c}_i(D_E), 0)} . \quad (11)$$

Since the Laplace perturbation noise is a random variable and therefore could be negative, we replace the negative counts with 0's in computing item popularity. The resulting $\tilde{p}_i$ is used to estimate the utility score of each record r with $r.vID = V_i$.

The following lemma establishes the sensitivity of $\mathbf{q_1}$ and $\mathbf{q_2}$ where each user can contribute up to d records. The proof is straightforward and is thus omitted.

LEMMA 4. *In the domain of D_E, it holds that $GS(\mathbf{q_1}) = d$.*

Greedy Sampling. The greedy sampling procedure hand-picks up to l records with highest utility scores among each user's data in

Algorithm 2 Hand-Picked Algorithm (HPA)

Input: raw dataset D, sampling factor l
Output: sanitized answer $\tilde{q}_1$ and $\tilde{q}_2$

/* *Popularity Estimation* */
/* *Random Sample* */
1: $D_E \leftarrow \emptyset$
2: **for** k = 1, ..., n **do**
3: $T_k \leftarrow \sigma_{uID=u_k}(D)$ /* T_k: *records of user* u_k */
4: Random sample d record from T_k, add to D_E
/* *Generate Private Item Counts* */
5: $\mathbf{q_1}(D_E) \leftarrow$ compute count $c_i(D_E)$ for every i
6: $\tilde{\mathbf{q}}_1(D_E) = \mathbf{q_1}(D_E) + \langle Lap(\frac{d}{\epsilon_0})\rangle^m$
/* *Estimate Popularity* */
7: $\tilde{\mathbf{p}} \leftarrow$ normalize histogram $\tilde{\mathbf{q}}_1(D_E)$
/* *Greedy Sampling* */
8: $D_G \leftarrow \emptyset$
9: **for** k = 1, ..., n **do**
10: $T_k \leftarrow \sigma_{uID=u_k}(D)$
11: **if** $|T_k| \leq l$ **do**
12: $D_G \leftarrow D_G \bigcup T_k$
13: **else do**
14: **for** record r in T_k **do**
15: assign $score(r) = \tilde{p}_i$ iff $r.vID = V_i$
16: $T'_k \leftarrow$ pick l records with highest scores from T_k
17: $D_G \leftarrow D_G \bigcup T'_k$
/* *Generate Private Item Counts* */
18: $\mathbf{q_1}(D_G) \leftarrow$ compute count $c_i(D_G)$ for every i
19: Output $\tilde{\mathbf{q}}_1(D_G) = \mathbf{q_1}(D_G) + \langle Lap(\frac{l}{\epsilon_1})\rangle^m$
/* *Generate Private Edge Counts* */
20: $\mathbf{q_2}(D_G) \leftarrow$ compute count $c_{i,j}(D_G)$ for every i, j
21: Output $\tilde{\mathbf{q}}_2(D_G) = \mathbf{q_2}(D_G) + \langle Lap(\frac{l}{\epsilon_2})\rangle^{mh}$

D. The pseudo code is provided in Algorithm 2 from Line 8 to Line 17. Table 3 illustrates Alice's records sorted by utility score. Since "Gym" and "Mary's House" do not interest greater public, their scores are likely to be much lower than "Golden Gate Bridge" and "de Young Museum". Then the top l records on the sorted list will be put in the sampled database D_G. This step is performed on every user's data in the raw database D.

LEMMA 5. *In the domain of D_G, it holds that $GS(\mathbf{q_1}) = l$ and $GS(\mathbf{q_2}) = l$.*

After the greedy sampling step, the results to $\mathbf{q_1}$ and $\mathbf{q_2}$ will be computed on the sampled database D_G. Each individual item count and edge count will be perturbed by Laplace noise from $Lap(\frac{l}{\epsilon_1})$ and $Lap(\frac{l}{\epsilon_2})$, respectively. We will provide proof of privacy guarantee in the next section.

The advantage of HPA is that it greedily picks the most valuable data records from each user, without increasing the sample data size, i.e. l records per user. The utility of each data record is estimated privately from the overall data distribution. Records with high utility have higher chance to be picked by greedy sampling. Since the sampled data greatly depends on the relative usefulness among each user's records, it is difficult to analyze the accuracy of released counts. We will empirically evaluate the effectiveness of this approach in Section 6.

5. PRIVACY GUARANTEE

In this section, we prove that both SRA and HPA algorithms are differentially private. We begin with the following lemma, which states that record sampling on each user does not inflict differential privacy breach.

Dataset	*Gowalla*	*Foursquare*	*Netflix*	*MovieLens*
Users	12,579	45,289	480,189	6,040
Items	15,200	17,967	17,700	3,706
$\|D\|$	739,600	1,276,988	100,480,507	1,000,209
max $\|T_k\|$	14,380	1,303	17,000	2,314
avg $\|T_k\|$	58.8	60.2	209.2	165.6
min $\|T_k\|$	1	1	1	20

Table 4: Data Sets Statistics

LEMMA 6. *Let $\mathcal{A}$ be an ϵ-differentially private algorithm and $\mathcal{S}$ be a record sampling procedure which is performed on each user individually. $\mathcal{A} \circ \mathcal{S}$ is also ϵ-differentially private.*

PROOF. *See Appendix B.* □

THEOREM 3. *SRA satisfies $(\epsilon_1 + \epsilon_2)$-differential privacy.*

PROOF. *Let $S_{rand,l}$ denote the random sampling procedure in SRA. $S_{rand,l}$ is therefore a function that takes an raw database and outputs a sampled database, i.e. $S_{rand,l} : \mathcal{D} \rightarrow \mathcal{D_R}$.*

According to the Laplace mechanism and Lemma 3, $\tilde{\mathbf{q}}_1 : \mathcal{D_R} \rightarrow \mathbb{R}^m$ is ϵ_1-differentially private. By the above Lemma 6, the item counts by SRA, i.e. $\tilde{\mathbf{q}}_1 \circ S_{rand,l} : \mathcal{D} \rightarrow \mathbb{R}^m$ is ϵ_1-differentially private. Similarly, $\tilde{\mathbf{q}}_2 : \mathcal{D_R} \rightarrow \mathbb{R}^{mh}$ is ϵ_2-differentially private. The edge counts by SRA, i.e. $\tilde{\mathbf{q}}_2 \circ S_{rand,l} : \mathcal{D} \rightarrow \mathbb{R}^{mh}$ is also ϵ_2-differentially private. Therefore, the overall SRA computation satisfies $(\epsilon_1 + \epsilon_2)$-differential privacy by Theorem 1. □

THEOREM 4. *HPA satisfies $(\epsilon_0 + \epsilon_1 + \epsilon_2)$-differential privacy.*

PROOF. *Let $S_{rand,d}$ denote the random sampling procedure in HPA for popularity estimation, i.e. $S_{rand,d} : \mathcal{D} \rightarrow \mathcal{D_E}$. Let $S_{grd,l}$ denote the greedy sampling procedure, i.e. $S_{grd,l} : \mathcal{D} \rightarrow \mathcal{D_G}$.*

According to the Laplace mechanism and Lemma 4, $\tilde{\mathbf{q}}_1 : \mathcal{D_E} \rightarrow \mathbb{R}^m$ is ϵ_0-differentially private. By Lemma 6, the HPA popularity estimation step, i.e. $\tilde{\mathbf{q}}_1 \circ S_{rand,d} : \mathcal{D} \rightarrow \mathbb{R}^m$ is ϵ_0-differentially private. Similarly, we can prove that the HPA item counts $\tilde{\mathbf{q}}_1 \circ S_{grd,l} : \mathcal{D} \rightarrow \mathbb{R}^m$ is ϵ_1-differentially private, and the HPA edge counts $\tilde{\mathbf{q}}_2 \circ S_{grd,l} : \mathcal{D} \rightarrow \mathbb{R}^{mh}$ is ϵ_2-differentially private. Therefore, by Theorem 1, the overall HPA satisfies $(\epsilon_0 + \epsilon_1 + \epsilon_2)$-differential privacy. □

6. EXPERIMENTS

Here we present a set of empirical studies. We compare our solutions SRA and HPA with three existing approaches: 1) LPA, the baseline method that injects Laplace perturbation noise to each count, 2) DFT, the Discrete Fourier Transform based algorithm proposed in [23], applied to a vector of counts, and 3) GS, the best method with grouping and smoothing proposed in [15], applied to count histograms. Given the overall privacy budget ϵ, we set $\epsilon_{1,2} = \frac{\epsilon}{2}$ for SRA method, and $\epsilon_0 = \frac{\epsilon}{10}$ and $\epsilon_{1,2} = 0.45\epsilon$ for HPA method. Without speculating about the optimal privacy allocation, we set ϵ_0 to a small fraction of ϵ, because it is used to protect a small sample of private data for utility score estimation. To achieve the same privacy guarantee, we apply LPA, DFT, and GS to item counts and edge counts separately, with privacy budget $\frac{\epsilon}{2}$ for each application.

Data sets. We conducted our empirical studies with four real-world data sets referred to as *Gowalla*, *Foursquare*, *Netflix*, and *MovieLens*, each named after its data source. The first two data sets consist of location check-in records. *Gowalla* is collected among users based in Austin from Gowalla location-based social network by

Berjani and Strufe [3] between June and October 2010. Similarly, *Foursquare* is collected from Foursquare by Long et al. [18] between February and July 2012. In these two data sets, each record contains a user, a location, and a check-in time-stamp. Since a user can check-in at one location many times, the check-in data sets can represent a class of services which value the returning behavior, such as buying or browsing. The other two data sets consist of movie ratings, where a movie may not be rated more than once by a user. *Netflix* is the training data set for the Netflix Prize competition. *MovieLens* is collected from users of MovieLens website [2]. Each rating corresponds to a user, a movie, a rating score, and a time-stamp. Moreover, *MovieLens* also provides user demographic information, such as gender, age, occupation, and zipcode. The properties of the data sets are summarized in Table 4. Note that the minimum individual contribution in *MovieLens* is 20, as opposed to 1 for other data sets. This is because *MovieLens* was initially collected for personalized recommendation, thus users with fewer than 20 records were excluded from the published data set.

Setup. We implemented our SRA and HPA methods, as well as the baseline LPA and DFT in Java.We obtained Jave code of GS from the authors of [15]. All experiments were run on a 2.9GHz Intel Core i7 PC with 8GB RAM. Each setting was run 20 times and the average result was reported.

The default settings of parameters are summarized below: the overall privacy $\epsilon = 1$, the sampling parameter d for HPA popularity estimation $d = \min |T_k|$, the sampling parameter $l = 10$ for *Gowalla*, *Foursquare*, and *Netflix* and $l = 30$ for *MovieLens*. Our choice of parameter settings is guided by analytical results and minimal knowledge about the data sets and thus might not be optimal. For LPA and DFT, we set M to be equal to $\max |T_k|$. However, this value may not be known *a priori*. Strictly speaking, M is unbounded for check-in applications. In this sense, we *overestimate* the performance of LPA and DFT.

6.1 HPA-Private Popularity Estimation

We first examine the private popularity estimation step of HPA method regarding the ability to discover top-K popular items from the noisy counts $\tilde{\mathbf{q}}_1(D_E)$. Recall that D_E is generated by randomly sampling d records per user and the output of $\mathbf{q}_1(D_E)$ is then perturbed with noise from $Lap(\frac{d}{\epsilon_0})$ to guarantee privacy. Given a small privacy budget ϵ_0, it is only meaningful to choose a small d value for accuracy, according to Theorem 2. Therefore, we set d equal to the minimum individual contribution, i.e. $\min |T_k|$, in every data set.

In this experiment, we sort all items according to $\tilde{\mathbf{q}}_1(D_E)$ output and K items with highest noisy counts are evaluated against the ground truth discovered from the raw data set. Figure 5 reports the precision results with various K values on *Foursquare* and *Netflix* data. As can be seen, from the output of $\tilde{\mathbf{q}}_1(D_E)$, we are able to discover more than 60% of top-20 popular locations in *Foursquare* and 70% top-20 popular movies on *Netflix*. When looking at $K = 100$, the output of $\tilde{\mathbf{q}}_1(D_E)$ captures 40% of the real popular locations and almost 80% popular movies. We conclude that HPA popularity estimation provides a solid step stone for subsequent greedy sampling, at very small cost of individual data as well as privacy.

6.2 Impact of Sampling Factor l

Here we look at the upper bound l of individual data contribution required by our solutions and study its impact on the accuracy of $\tilde{\mathbf{q}}_1$ and $\tilde{\mathbf{q}}_2$ output. Mean Squared Error(MSE) is adopted as the

[2]http://movielens.org

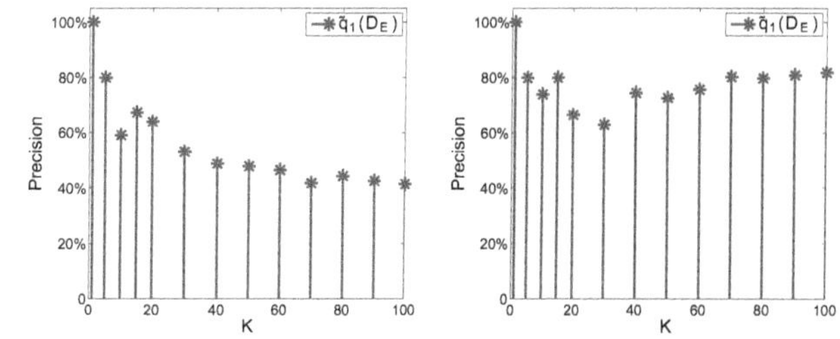

(a) *Foursquare* (b) *Netflix*

Figure 5: Estimation of Item Popularity by HPA

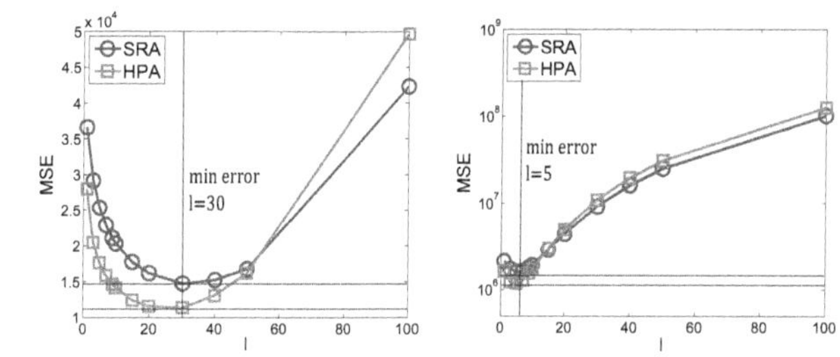

(a) MSE of $\tilde{\mathbf{q}}_1$ (b) MSE of $\tilde{\mathbf{q}}_2$

Figure 6: Impact of l with *Foursquare* Data Set

metric for accuracy and is calculated between the noisy output by our methods and the true results of $\mathbf{q}_1$ and $\mathbf{q}_2$ from the raw input data D. We ran our SRA and HPA methods varying the value of l, in order to generate sampled database D_R and D_G with different sizes. Figure 6(a) summarizes the results from *Foursquare* data for item counts, i.e. $\tilde{\mathbf{q}}_1$, and Figure 6(b) for edge counts, i.e. $\tilde{\mathbf{q}}_2$.

In both figures of Figure 6, when l value increases, the MSE of the noisy output by our methods first drops as sampled database gets larger. For example, we observe a decreasing trend of MSE as l is raised to 30 in Figure 6(a) and as l is raised to 5 in Figure 6(b). Beyond these two points, when further increasing l, the MSE grows due to the perturbation noise from $Lap(\frac{l}{\epsilon_1})$. Clearly, there is a trade-off between sample data size and the perturbation error. The optimal value of l depends on actual data distribution and the privacy parameter ϵ_1, according to Theorem 2. This set of results show that both SRA and HPA achieve minimum MSE with relatively small l values, i.e. $l = 30$ for $\tilde{\mathbf{q}}_1$ and $l = 5$ for $\tilde{\mathbf{q}}_2$. Our findings in Theorem 2 are confirmed and we conclude that choosing a small upper bound l on individual data contribution is beneficial especially when privacy budget is limited.

6.3 Comparison of Methods

Here we compare our SRA and HPA methods with existing approaches, i.e. LPA, DFT, and GS on all data sets. The utility of item counts and edge counts released by all private mechanisms are evaluated with three metrics. Note that for *Gowalla*, *Foursquare*, and *Netflix* data, each edge connects an item with a *day-of-week*, from "Monday" to "Sunday". For *MovieLens* data set, each edge connects a movie with a (*Gender*, *Age*) pair. The domain of *Gender* is {"M", "F"} and the domain of *Age* is {"Under 25", "25-34", "Above 34"}. Below we review the results regarding the released item counts and edge counts, for each utility metric.

Mean Squared Error (MSE). This metric provides a generic utility comparison of different methods on the released counts. Figure 7(a) and Figure 8(a) summarize the MSE results for item counts and edge counts, respectively. As can be seen, the baseline LPA yields the highest error in both item counts and edge counts. The

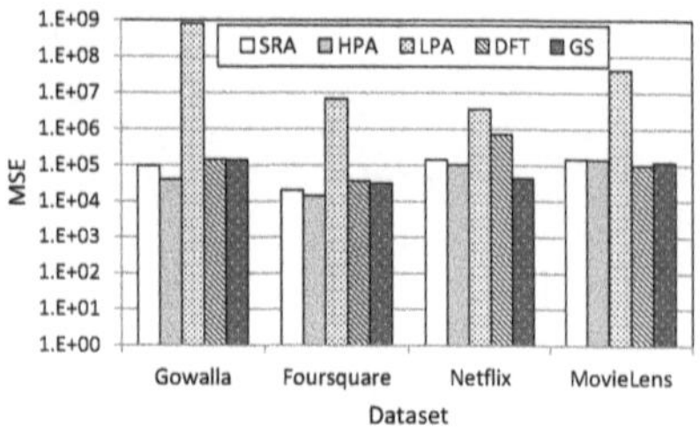

(a) Mean Squared Error

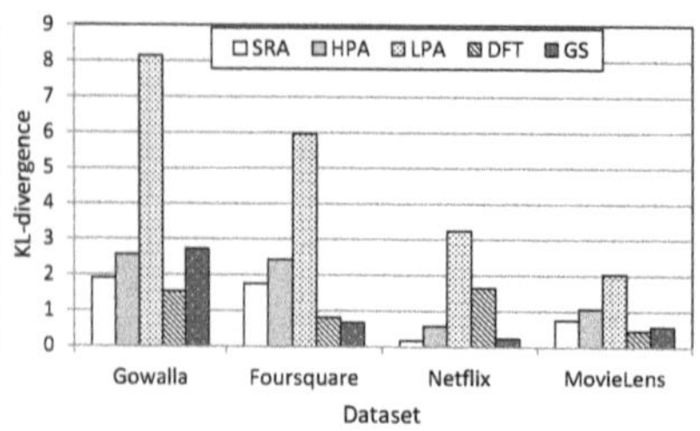

(b) KL-Divergence

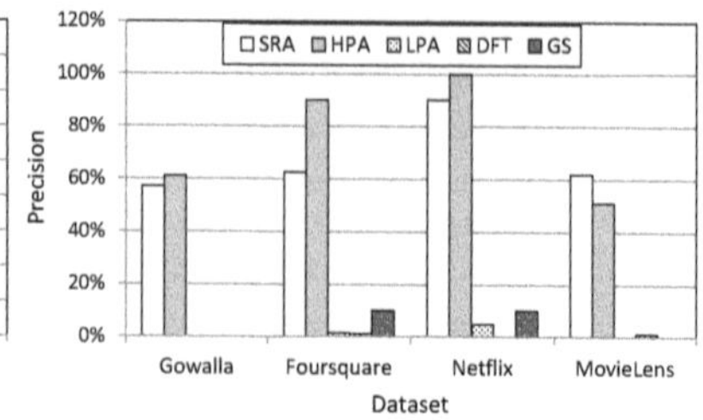

(c) Top-10 Precision

Figure 7: Utility of Released Item Counts

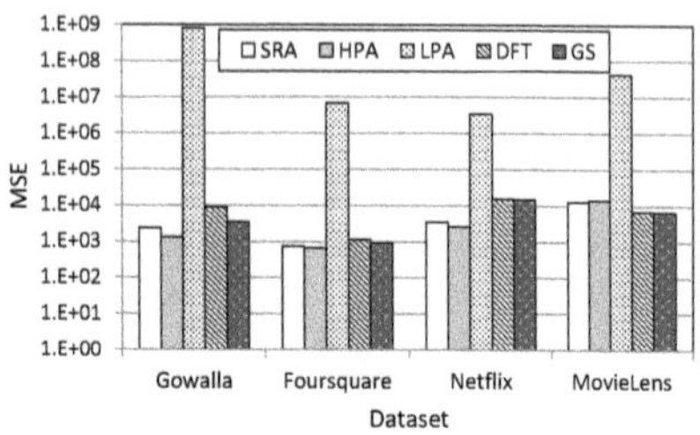

(a) Mean Squared Error

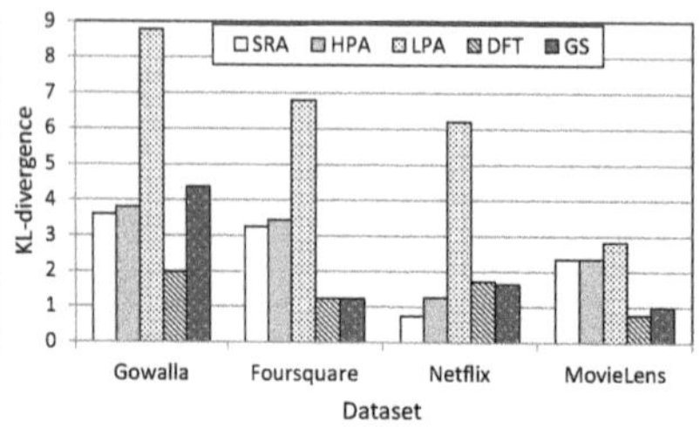

(b) KL-Divergence

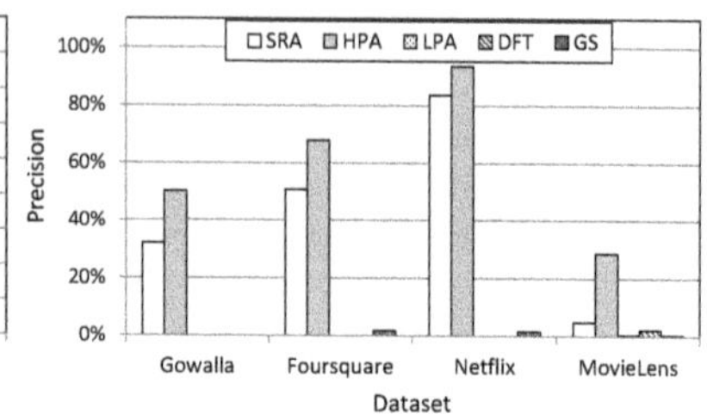

(c) Average Top-10 Precision

Figure 8: Utility of Released Edge Counts

GS method, as studied in the original work [15], is no worse than DFT in every case except for *MovieLens* item counts. Our methods SRA and HPA provide the lowest MSE error except in three cases, i.e. *Netflix* item counts and *MovieLens* item/edge counts. This can be interpreted by the high average user contribution in these two data sets, where our methods inflict more data loss by limiting individual data in the sampled database.

KL-divergence. The KL-divergence is a common metric widely used to measure the distance between two probability distributions. In this set of experiments, we consider the item/edge counts as data record distributions over the domain of items/edges. Both the released counts and original counts are normalized to simulate probability distributions. Note that prior to that, zero or negative counts are replaced with 0.01 for continuity without generating many false positives. We compute the KL-divergence of the released distribution with respect to the original distribution for each query and present the results in Figure 7(b) and Figure 8(b).

The released distributions by LPA are further from original data distributions than those of other methods for every data set. As expected, DFT and GS preserve the count distributions well in general, because: 1) the DFT method is designed to capture major trends in data series, and 2) the GS method generates smooth distributions by grouping similar columns. However, in several cases, those two methods fail to provide similar distributions, e.g. on *Gowalla* and *Netflix* data. We believe that their performance depends on the actual data distribution, i.e. whether significant trend or near-uniform grouping exists and can be well extracted. On the other hand, our solutions SRA and HPA provide comparable performance to the best existing methods, although not optimized to preserve distributional similarities. Furthermore, SRA constantly outperforms HPA in approximating the true distributions, thanks to the nature of simple random sampling technique.

Top-K Discovery. In this set of experiments, we examine the quality of top-10 discovery retrieved by all privacy-preserving mechanisms. For item counts, the top-10 popular items are evaluated. For edge counts, the top-10 popular items associated with each attribute value are evaluated and the average precision is reported, to simulate discoveries for each day-of-week and each user demographic group. In Figure 7(c), we observe that existing methods fail to preserve the 10 most popular items in any dataset. The reason is the baseline LPA suffers from high perturbation error, and DFT and GS yield over-smoothed released counts and thus cannot distinguish the most popular items from those ranked next to them. When K is large enough, we will see that their performance in top-K discovery slowly recovers in a subsequent experiment. On the other hand, our methods SRA and HPA greatly outperform existing approaches and HPA even achieves 100% precision for *Netflix* data. Similarly, our methods show superior performance in Figure 8(c), with the absolute precision slightly dropped due to sparser data distributions. Overall, HPA outperforms SRA by preserving user records with high popularity scores. The only exception where SRA is better than HPA is in finding the top-10 most popular movies on *MovieLens*. The reason is that those users who contribute less than 20 records were excluded from the data set and no movies were preferred by the majority of the rest users. As for finding top-10 movies for each demographic group, HPA greatly improves over SRA, since users within a demographic group show similar interests.

We further look at top-K precision of the released item counts by all methods, with K ranging from 1 to 1000. The results are provided in Figure 9. We can see that the performance of our greedy approach HPA is 100% when $K = 1$ and drops as K increases, since the sampling step only picks a small number of records, i.e. l records, from each user with highest utility score, i.e. item popularity. Our random approach SRA also shows decreasing precision as K increases, due to the data loss caused by sampling. However, the decreasing rate is much slower compared to that of HPA, because records of a user have equal chance to be selected by random sampling. On the contrary, LPA, DFT, and GS show 0% precision when $K = 1$ and higher precision as K increases. We conclude that SRA and HPA can discover the most popular items, superior to existing approaches up to $K = 100$, but do not distinguish less popular items due to lack of information in the sampled database.

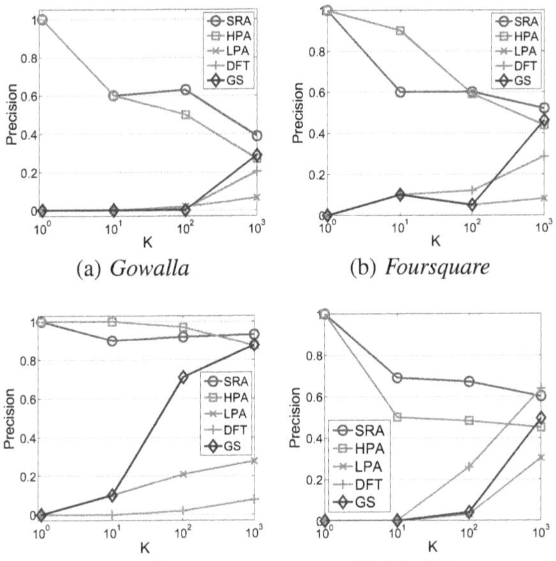

(a) *Gowalla* (b) *Foursquare*

(c) *Netflix* (d) *MovieLens*

Figure 9: Comparison of Methods: Top-K Mining

The existing approaches fail to distinguish the most popular items, e.g. top-10, because of perturbation or the smoothing effect of their methods, but might provide good precision for large K, e.g. $K \geq 1000$.

6.4 Additional Benefits

Data Reduction. One beneficial side effect of limiting individual data contribution is the reduction of data storage space by generating analytics from a sampled database. Figure 10 shows the number of records in the sampled databases used by SRA and HPA compared to that of the raw input. As can be seen, the sampled data is much smaller than the raw input for every data set. For *Netflix* data set, our methods perform privacy-preserving analytics and generate useful results on sample databases with less than 5% of the original data, reducing the data storage requirement without compromising the utility of output analytics.

Weekly Distribution. We also examine the sampled database by SRA and HPA by the weekly distribution of data records. The percentage of *Foursquare* check-in records on each day of week is plotted in Figure 11. As is shown, the percentage of Friday, Saturday, and Sunday check-ins is higher in the sampled databases generated by our methods than in the original data set, while the percentage of Monday-Thursday check-ins is lower than the original. Since the majority of the users are occasional users and contribute less than l records, our methods preserve their data completely in the sampled databases. We may infer that the occasional users are more likely to use the check-in service on Friday-Sunday. Moreover, the SRA sampled data is constantly closer to the original data distribution, compared to HPA. We can further infer that users are more likely to check-in popular places on Friday-Sunday.

Movie Recommendation. A example of context-aware, fine-grained recommendation is to suggest items based on the common interest demonstrated among the user group with similar demographics, such as age and gender. We illustrate the top-10 movie recommendation to male users under the age of 25 with released edge counts by our solutions on *MovieLens* data set. The first column in Table 5 shows the top-10 recommended movies using original data, while the second and third columns list movies recommended by our privacy-preserving solutions. We observe that some movies

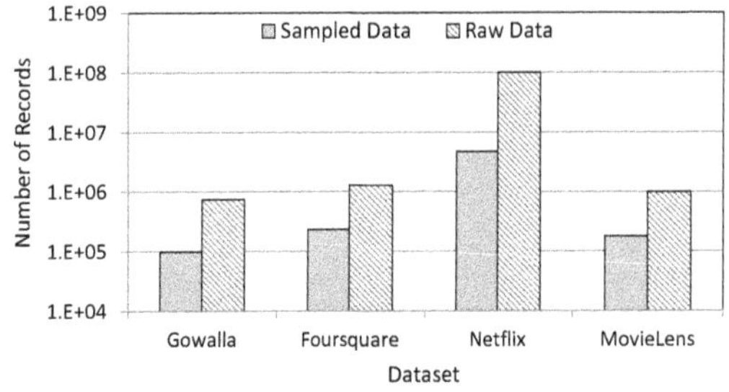

Figure 10: Data Reduction

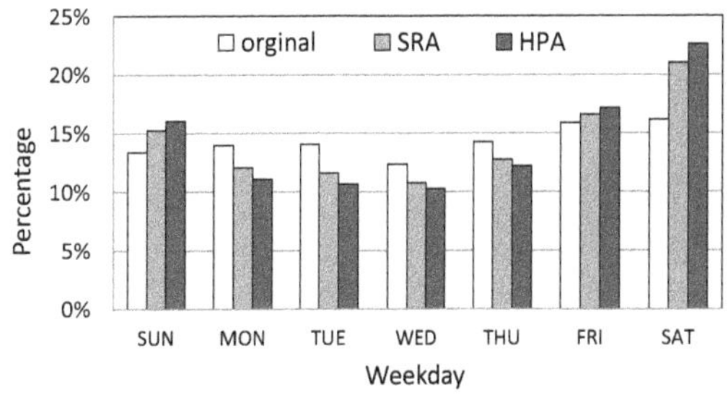

Figure 11: Weekly Distribution with *Foursquare* Data

Top 10 Movies	SRA Output	HPA Output
American Beauty	Phantasm II	American Beauty
Star Wars VI	Marvin's Room	Star Wars VI
Star Wars V	All Dogs Go to Heaven	Terminator 2
The Matrix	In the Line of Duty 2	Star Wars V
Star Wars IV	Star Wars V	Jurassic Park
Terminator 2	The Slumber Party Massacre III	The Matrix
Saving Private Ryan	The Story of Xinghua	Men in Black
Jurassic Park	American Beauty	The Fugitive
Star Wars I	Shaft	Braveheart
Braveheart	Star Wars I	Saving Private Ryan

Table 5: Movie Recommendations to Male, Under 25.

recommended by SRA may not interest the target audience, such as "Marvin's Room" and "The story of Xinghua". Furthermore, the top movie on SRA list, i.e. "Phantasm II", is a horror movie and not suitable for underage audience. On the other hand, the movies recommended by HPA are quite consistent with the original top-10 except for two movies, i.e. "Men in Black" and "The Fugitive", which may interest the target audience as well. We believe that HPA captures more information by greedy sampling and thus can make better recommendations than SRA, especially when users have very diverse interests.

7. CONCLUSION AND DISCUSSION

We have proposed a practical framework for privacy-preserving data analytics by sampling a fixed number of records from each user. We have presented two solutions, i.e. SRA and HPA, which implement the framework with different sampling techniques. Our solutions do not require the input data be preprocessed, such as removing users with large or little data. The output analysis results are highly accurate for performing top-K discovery and context-aware recommendations, closing the utility gap between no privacy and existing differentially private techniques. Our solutions benefit from sampling techniques that reduce the individual data contribution to a small constant factor, l, and thus reducing the perturbation error inflicted by differential privacy. We provided analysis results about the optimal sampling factor l with respect to the privacy requirement. We formally proved that both mechanisms satisfy ϵ-differential privacy. Empirical studies with real-world data sets confirm that our solutions enable accurate data analytics on a small fraction of the input data, reducing user privacy cost and data storage requirement without compromising utility.

Potential future work may include the design of a hybrid approach between SRA and HPA which could have the benefits of both. For real-time applications, we would like to consider how to dynamically sample user generated data, in order to further reduce the data storage requirement. Another direction is to apply the proposed sampling framework to solving more complex data analytical tasks, which might involve multiple, over-lapping count queries or other statistical queries.

8. ACKNOWLEDGMENTS

We thank the anonymous reviewers for the detailed and helpful comments to the manuscript.

9. REFERENCES

[1] M. Barbaro and T. Zeller. A face is exposed for aol searcher no. 4417749. *The New York Times*, Aug. 2006.

[2] J. Bennett and S. Lanning. The netflix prize. In *Proceedings of KDD cup and workshop*, volume 2007, page 35, 2007.

[3] B. Berjani and T. Strufe. A recommendation system for spots in location-based online social networks. In *Proceedings of the 4th Workshop on Social Network Systems*, SNS '11, pages 4:1–4:6, New York, NY, USA, 2011. ACM.

[4] A. Blum, K. Ligett, and A. Roth. A learning theory approach to non-interactive database privacy. In *Proceedings of the 40th annual ACM symposium on Theory of computing*, pages 609–618, New York, 2008. ACM.

[5] T.-H. H. Chan, E. Shi, and D. Song. Private and continual release of statistics. *ACM Trans. Inf. Syst. Secur.*, 14(3):26:1–26:24, Nov. 2011.

[6] K. Chaudhuri and N. Mishra. When random sampling preserves privacy. In *Proceedings of the 26th annual international conference on Advances in Cryptology*, CRYPTO'06, pages 198–213, Berlin, Heidelberg, 2006. Springer-Verlag.

[7] R. Chen, G. Acs, and C. Castelluccia. Differentially private sequential data publication via variable-length n-grams. In *Proceedings of the 2012 ACM conference on Computer and communications security*, CCS '12, pages 638–649, 2012.

[8] G. Cormode, C. Procopiuc, D. Srivastava, and T. T. L. Tran. Differentially private summaries for sparse data. In *Proceedings of the 15th International Conference on Database Theory*, ICDT '12, pages 299–311, New York, NY, USA, 2012. ACM.

[9] Y.-A. de Montjoye, C. A. Hidalgo, M. Verleysen, and V. D. Blondel. Unique in the Crowd: The privacy bounds of human mobility. *Scientific Reports*, Mar.

[10] C. Dwork. Differential privacy. In M. Bugliesi, B. Preneel, V. Sassone, and I. Wegener, editors, *Automata, Languages and Programming*, volume 4052 of *Lecture Notes in Computer Science*, pages 1–12. Springer Berlin Heidelberg, 2006.

[11] C. Dwork, K. Kenthapadi, F. McSherry, I. Mironov, and M. Naor. Our data, ourselves: privacy via distributed noise generation. In *Proceedings of the 24th annual international conference on The Theory and Applications of Cryptographic Techniques*, EUROCRYPT'06, pages 486–503, Berlin, Heidelberg, 2006. Springer-Verlag.

[12] C. Dwork, F. Mcsherry, K. Nissim, and A. Smith. Calibrating noise to sensitivity in private data analysis. In *In Proceedings of the 3rd Theory of Cryptography Conference*, pages 265–284, Heidelberg, 2006. Springer-Verlag.

[13] L. Fan and L. Xiong. An adaptive approach to real-time aggregate monitoring with differential privacy. *Knowledge and Data Engineering, IEEE Transactions on*, 26(9):2094–2106, Sept 2014.

[14] Y. Hong, J. Vaidya, H. Lu, and M. Wu. Differentially private search log sanitization with optimal output utility. In *Proceedings of the 15th International Conference on Extending Database Technology*, EDBT '12, pages 50–61, New York, NY, USA, 2012. ACM.

[15] G. Kellaris and S. Papadopoulos. Practical differential privacy via grouping and smoothing. In *Proceedings of the 39th international conference on Very Large Data Bases*, PVLDB'13, pages 301–312, 2013.

[16] A. Korolova, K. Kenthapadi, N. Mishra, and A. Ntoulas. Releasing search queries and clicks privately. In *Proceedings of the 18th international conference on World wide web*, WWW '09, pages 171–180, 2009.

[17] N. Li, W. Qardaji, and D. Su. On sampling, anonymization, and differential privacy or, k-anonymization meets differential privacy. In *Proceedings of the 7th ACM Symposium on Information, Computer and Communications Security*, ASIACCS '12, pages 32–33, 2012.

[18] X. Long, L. Jin, and J. Joshi. Towards understanding traveler behavior in location-based social networks. In *Global Communications Conference (GLOBECOM), 2013 IEEE*, 2013.

[19] A. Machanavajjhala, D. Kifer, J. Abowd, J. Gehrke, and L. Vilhuber. Privacy: Theory meets practice on the map. In *Data Engineering, 2008. ICDE 2008. IEEE 24th International Conference on*, pages 277–286, 2008.

[20] F. McSherry. Privacy integrated queries: an extensible platform for privacy-preserving data analysis. volume 53, pages 89–97, 2010.

[21] K. Nissim, S. Raskhodnikova, and A. Smith. Smooth sensitivity and sampling in private data analysis. In *Proceedings of the thirty-ninth annual ACM symposium on Theory of computing*, STOC '07, pages 75–84, New York, NY, USA, 2007. ACM.

[22] D. Proserpio, S. Goldberg, and F. McSherry. Calibrating data to sensitivity in private data analysis: A platform for differentially-private analysis of weighted datasets. *Proc. VLDB Endow.*, 7(8):637–648, Apr. 2014.

[23] V. Rastogi and S. Nath. Differentially private aggregation of distributed time-series with transformation and encryption. In *Proceedings of the 2010 ACM SIGMOD International Conference on Management of data*, pages 735–746, 2010.

[24] G. Yuan, Z. Zhang, M. Winslett, X. Xiao, Y. Yang, and Z. Hao. Low-rank mechanism: optimizing batch queries under differential privacy. *Proc. VLDB Endow.*, 5(11):1352–1363, July 2012.

[25] C. Zeng, J. F. Naughton, and J.-Y. Cai. On differentially private frequent itemset mining. *Proc. VLDB Endow.*, 6(1):25–36, Nov. 2012.

APPENDIX

A. PROOF OF THEOREM 2

PROOF. For item V_i, let c'_i denote the true count computed by $\mathbf{q}_1$ from the sample D_R. Therefore, the noisy count $\tilde{c}_i$ is derived by adding a Laplace noise to c'_i as follows:

$$\tilde{c}_i = c'_i + \nu_i \,, \tag{12}$$

$$\nu_i \sim Laplace(0, l/\epsilon_1) \,. \tag{13}$$

The MSE of $\tilde{c}_i$ can be re-written as:

$$\begin{aligned} MSE(\tilde{c}_i) &= Var(c'_i + \nu_i) + (E(c'_i + \nu_i - c_i))^2 \\ &= Var(c'_i) + Var(\nu_i) + (E(c'_i) - E(c_i))^2 \,. \end{aligned} \tag{14}$$

Note that c'_i and ν_i are mutually independent.

Let p_i denote the popularity of item V_i, i.e. the probability of any record having $vID = V_i$. For simplicity, we assume that users are mutually independent, records are mutually independent, and every user has M records in the raw data set D. To obtain D_R, l records out of M are randomly chosen for each user in D. Thus for any item V_i, c'_i can be represented as the sum of independent random variables:

$$c'_i = \sum_{k=1}^{n} \sum_{r \in T_k} \delta_{r,i} \tag{15}$$

$$\delta_{r,i} = \begin{cases} 1 & \text{if } r.vID = V_i \;\&\; r \in D_R \,, \\ 0 & \text{otherwise} \,. \end{cases} \tag{16}$$

The event of $\delta_{r,i} = 1$ is equivalent to the event of record r is about V_i and r is sampled in D_R by chance:

$$Pr[\delta_{r,i} = 1] = Pr[r.vID = Vi \;\&\; r \in D_R] = p_i \frac{l}{M} \,. \tag{17}$$

Therefore, we can obtain the following expectation and variance for c'_i:

$$\begin{aligned} E(c'_i) &= \sum_{k=1}^{n} \sum_{r \in T_k} E(\delta_{r,i}) \\ &= \sum_{k=1}^{n} \sum_{r \in T_k} p_i \frac{l}{M} \\ &= nlp_i \end{aligned} \tag{18}$$

$$\begin{aligned} Var(c'_i) &= \sum_{k=1}^{n} \sum_{r \in T_k} Var(\delta_{r,i}) \\ &= \sum_{k=1}^{n} \sum_{r \in T_k} p_i \frac{l}{M}(1 - p_i \frac{l}{M}) \\ &= nlp_i(1 - p_i \frac{l}{M}) \end{aligned} \tag{19}$$

Similarly, we can obtain the expectation of c_i:

$$E(c_i) = nMp_i \,. \tag{20}$$

From the above results, we can re-write Equation 14 as follows:

$$MSE(\tilde{c}_i) = nlp_i(1 - p_i \frac{l}{M}) + 2\frac{l^2}{\epsilon_l^2} + (nlp_i - nMp_i)^2 \tag{21}$$

and we can perform the standard least square method to minimize the MSE. The optimal l value is thus:

$$l = \frac{2n^2 p_i^2 M - np_i}{4/\epsilon_1^2 - 2np_i^2/M + 2n^2 p_i^2} \tag{22}$$

We conclude that the optimal l value is a monotonically increasing function of ϵ_1^2. □

B. PROOF OF LEMMA 6

PROOF. By definition of differential privacy, we are to prove that for any neighboring raw databases D_1 and D_2, $\mathcal{A} \circ \mathcal{S}$ satisfies the following inequality for $\widetilde{D} \in Range(\mathcal{A} \circ \mathcal{S})$:

$$Pr[\mathcal{A} \circ \mathcal{S}(D_1) = \widetilde{D}] \leq e^{\epsilon} Pr[\mathcal{A} \circ \mathcal{S}(D_2) = \widetilde{D}] \,. \tag{23}$$

Without loss of generality, we assume D_2 contains one more user than D_1. Let u denote the user that is contained in D_2 but not D_1 and T be user u's set of records in D_2. By definition of neighboring databases, we can rewrite $D_2 = D_1 \oplus T$ [3].

Let $\hat{D}_1$ denote any possible sampling output of $\mathcal{S}(D_1)$. We have:

$$\begin{aligned} & Pr[\mathcal{A} \circ \mathcal{S}(D_1) = \widetilde{D}] \\ &= \sum_{\hat{D}_1} Pr[\mathcal{A} \circ \mathcal{S}(D_1) = \widetilde{D} | \mathcal{S}(D_1) = \hat{D}_1] Pr[\mathcal{S}(D_1) = \hat{D}_1] \\ &= \sum_{\hat{D}_1} Pr[\mathcal{A}(\hat{D}_1) = \widetilde{D}] Pr[\mathcal{S}(D_1) = \hat{D}_1] \end{aligned} \tag{24}$$

Let $\hat{T}$ denote any possible sampling output of $\mathcal{S}(T)$. We note that $\hat{T}$ can take values from the entire domain, in general:

$$\sum_{\hat{T}} Pr[\mathcal{S}(T) = \hat{T}] = 1 \,. \tag{25}$$

Since $\mathcal{S}$ is performed independently on each user, we can derive:

$$\begin{aligned} & Pr[\mathcal{S}(D_1) = \hat{D}_1] \\ &= \sum_{\hat{T}} Pr[\mathcal{S}(D_1) = \hat{D}_1] Pr[\mathcal{S}(T) = \hat{T}] \\ &= \sum_{\hat{T}} Pr[\mathcal{S}(D_1 \oplus T) = \hat{D}_1 \oplus \hat{T}] \,. \end{aligned} \tag{26}$$

Note that since D_1 and T are disjoint, the sampling output on D_1 and T are also independent and disjoint. Therefore,

$$\begin{aligned} & Pr[\mathcal{A} \circ \mathcal{S}(D_1) = \widetilde{D}] \\ &= \sum_{\hat{D}_1} Pr[\mathcal{A}(\hat{D}_1) = \widetilde{D}] \sum_{\hat{T}} Pr[\mathcal{S}(D_1 \oplus T) = \hat{D}_1 \oplus \hat{T}] \\ &= \sum_{\hat{D}_1, \hat{T}} Pr[\mathcal{A}(\hat{D}_1) = \widetilde{D}] Pr[\mathcal{S}(D_1 \oplus T) = \hat{D}_1 \oplus \hat{T}] \\ &\leq \sum_{\hat{D}_1, \hat{T}} e^{\epsilon} Pr[\mathcal{A}(\hat{D}_1 \oplus \hat{T}) = \widetilde{D}] Pr[\mathcal{S}(D_1 \oplus T) = \hat{D}_1 \oplus \hat{T}] \end{aligned} \tag{27}$$

$$= e^{\epsilon} \sum_{\hat{D}_2} Pr[\mathcal{A}(\hat{D}_2) = \widetilde{D}] Pr[\mathcal{S}(D_2) = \hat{D}_2] \tag{28}$$

$$= e^{\epsilon} Pr[\mathcal{A} \circ \mathcal{S}(D_2) = \widetilde{D}] \,. \tag{29}$$

Line 27 is due to the fact that $\mathcal{A}$ is ϵ-differentially private and $\hat{D}_1$ and $\hat{D}_1 \oplus \hat{T}$ are neighboring databases. In line 28 we change notation and let $\hat{D}_2$ represent $\hat{D}_1 \oplus \hat{T}$. The proof is hence complete. □

[3] $\oplus$ is used to denote a co-product, or disjoint union of two databases.

Compressed Indexes for String Searching in Labeled Graphs

Paolo Ferragina Francesco Piccinno Rossano Venturini
Dipartimento di Informatica, University of Pisa
{ferragina, piccinno, rossano}@di.unipi.it

ABSTRACT

Storing and searching large labeled graphs is indeed becoming a key issue in the design of space/time efficient online platforms indexing modern social networks or knowledge graphs. But, as far as we know, all these results are limited to design compressed graph indexes which support basic access operations onto the *link structure* of the input graph, such as: *given a node u, return the adjacency list of u*.

This paper takes inspiration from the Facebook Unicorn's platform and proposes some *compressed-indexing* schemes for large graphs whose *nodes are labeled with strings of variable length*— i.e., node's attributes such as user's (nick-)name— that support sophisticated *search operations* which involve both the linked structure of the graph and the string content of its nodes.

An extensive experimental evaluation over real social networks will show the time and space efficiency of the proposed indexing schemes and their query processing algorithms.

Categories and Subject Descriptors

H.3.2 [**Information Storage and Retrieval**]: Information Storage; E.4 [**Coding and Information Theory**]: Data Compaction and Compression

Keywords

Compression; Data structures; Social Networks

1. INTRODUCTION

In a recent paper [11], Facebook's engineers introduced the Unicorn system as an online, in-memory social graph-aware indexing platform designed to search huge graphs distributed over many commodity servers. In that paper the authors claimed that *"Unicorn is based on standard concepts in information retrieval, but it includes features to promote results with good social proximity"*.

Storing and searching large labeled graphs is indeed becoming a key issue in the design of space/time efficient online platforms indexing modern social networks or knowledge graphs [35]. However, as far as we know, all these results are limited to design compressed graph-indexes (see e.g., [5, 6, 8, 10, 30]) which support only basic access operations onto the *link-structure* of the input graph, such as: *given a node u, return the adjacency list of u*. Other results consider more sophisticated access-patterns to the graph structure, but do not deal with compression issues or labeled nodes [12, 33].

In this paper we take inspiration from the Unicorn's platform and make one step forward in the design of *compressed-indexing* schemes for large graphs whose *nodes are labeled with strings of variable length*, i.e., node's attributes such as user's (nick-)name or country or any other information the user has input for its profile or the system has drawn from user behavior, and support (i) basic access operations into the link-structure of the graph (as above), plus (ii) novel sophisticated *search operations* which involve both the linked structure of the graph and the string content of its nodes.

As an example, we aim at designing a compressed graph index that efficiently supports the Facebook's typeahead search (Section 6 of [11]). Typeahead enables Facebook users to find other users by typing the first few characters of the person's name. For example, if a user is typing in the name of "Jon Jones" the typeahead backend sequentially receives queries for "J", "Jo", "Jon", "Jon ", "Jon J", etc. For each prefix, the system has to return a list of individuals for whom the user might be searching for. Some of these individuals will be within the user's explicit circle of friends or they will be Friends-of-Friends (shortly, FoF).

A simple implementation for the typeahead query among the FoF of a given user could be based on standard information retrieval algorithms in which users' adjacency lists are treated as posting lists. The idea is to solve the query into two main steps: (1) the former step identifies a set of candidate users in the graph having the queried string as a prefix of their names; (2) the latter step reports those candidates which are in the FoF's network of the given user. Step 1 is implemented by searching the queried-prefix in a dictionary containing all users' names; step 2 is implemented by scanning the adjacency list of the given user u and, for each friend of u, looking at her friends (FoF of u) by checking whether they occur also in the candidate set. This solution is consistent with the proposal in [11], where the authors claim that *"The index server stores adjacency lists and performs set operations on those lists, the results of which are returned to the aggregators. In the index server, intersection, union,*

WWW 2015, May 18–22, 2015, Florence, Italy.
ACM 978-1-4503-3469-3/15/05.
http://dx.doi.org/10.1145/2736277.2741140.

and difference operations proceed as is described in standard information retrieval texts".

But unfortunately this simple approach may be computationally expensive because both the candidate set to be generated in step 1 and the FoF's network searched in step 2 could turn out to be very large. A strategy to partially mitigate the cost of step 1 consists in precomputing and storing as posting lists the results of step 1 for short or frequently searched prefixes. For example, the solution in [11] precomputes results for prefixes of few characters. Despite this simple trick, we are not aware of any other solution which is able to answer a query without processing the whole FoF network.

In [11] the authors also discuss variants of this FoF query, by introducing a *social relevance* score (Section 6.1 in [11]) which allows to *rank the FoF users* whose names are prefixes by the queried string. In this case too, the query is answered by scanning the FoF for prefix-match and then ranking the results, thus inheriting the limitations above.

The problem of answering FoF queries has been addressed also in a distributed setting in which a large graph has to be distributed among several servers, with the goal of reducing the traffic among them. Authors in [36] proposed a graph partitioning approach to relocate nodes while respecting strict shard balancing constraints. Even in this distributed setting, we are faced with the problem of answering queries on a single in-memory shard whose inefficient solution may become the dominant cost and may impact on the traffic induced by the partial results sent among machines.

Notation and problems definition. In the following we will refer to a graph $G = (V, E)$ with $n = |V|$ nodes and $m = |E|$ edges. Without loss of generality we focus on social graphs made up of users $u \in V$ which have associated a name $\mathsf{name}(u)$ which is either the user's *screen name* or her *real name*. The dictionary of strings $\mathcal{D}$ contains the names associated with all users in the graph. Graphs representing a (social) network may have types for both nodes — e.g., users, pages, photos, posts, etc. - and edges — e.g., friends, followers, live-in, likers, etc.. Even if, in the rest of the paper, we will restrict our attention to the case in which nodes are labeled with users' names and edges represent their friendships, our solutions can be easily adapted to deal with several other node or edge types, simultaneously.

In this kind of graphs (either directed or undirected) a link between two users u and v exists if both users know each other or are in some sort of relationship (e.g., user u is a follower of v, u liked the posts of v, u is a friend of v, and so on). For the sake of clarity we will refer to this situation as *friendship*: u is friend of v.

For each user u, we use $N_1(u)$ to denote the adjacency list of node u in G, namely, the list of u's friends, and use $d(u)$ to denote the number of nodes in this list or, equivalently, the degree of u. A friend-of-friend (FoF) of a user u is any user which is either a direct friend of u or a friend of a friend of u. In graph terminology, a FoF of u is a node at distance at most 2 from u in G. In the following we will use $N_2(u)$ to denote the list of FoF of u (i.e., $N_2(u) = N_1(u) \cup (\cup_{v \in N_1(u)} N_1(v))$).

Finally, we will assume that each user u is associated with a *relevance score*, denoted $\mathsf{score}(u)$, which quantifies the importance of u in the social network (e.g., the PageRank of u, the number of likes she got, etc.). This score will be used to restrict our graph-search operations on the k neighbors of a given node (e.g., $k = 10$) that match the prefix-query and have the highest scores.

Given Table 1 in [11] (see also Table 1 in our paper), the size of $N_1(u)$ can go from hundreds (`friends`) to thousands or millions (`likers` or `live-in`); and the size of $N_2(u)$ may even blow up to three or more order of magnitudes than the size of $N_1(u)$. This poses challenging efficiency concerns about the storage and brute-force scanning/intersection of those lists for the queries above, even in the in-memory storage of the graph or its parts. Let us then introduce the problems we attack in our paper.

Prefix-search over friends: Given a node u and a string P, search for all friends v of u (i.e., $v \in N_1(u)$) such that $\mathsf{name}(v)$ is prefixed by P.

Prefix-search over FoF: Given a node u and a string P, search for all FoF v of u (i.e., $v \in N_2(u)$) such that $\mathsf{name}(v)$ is prefixed by P.

Top-k prefix-search over friends (or FoF): Given a node u, a string P and a positive integer k, return the top-k *scoring* nodes which are friends (or FoF) of u and are prefixed by P.

In our paper we wish to design a compressed-indexing scheme for labeled graphs which guarantees efficient time and compressed space for all queries mentioned above. Our proposal combines, in a principled way, string searching and graph storage solutions, so that it can be looked at as a basic block upon which one could design more sophisticated queries and compressed graph-indexing platforms.

Our Contributions. In this paper we introduce and efficiently solve the problems above both theoretically and in practice via an extensive experimental analysis over (a large part) of three real networks of increasing size: namely, Dblp of about 1.4 mln nodes and 12 mln edges, LiveJournal of about 4.8 mln nodes and 68.5 mln edges, and Twitter of about 41.6 mln nodes and 1.4 billion edges.

Prefix-search over friends. We propose a simple renumbering of the nodeIDs which takes into account the alphabetic ordering of node's strings and allows to turn the implementation of this query-type from a series of list intersections over spread out integers (a là [11]) to a single (thus fast) range query over an adjacency list. Our experiments on prefix-search over friends show that our solution significantly outperforms baselines based on standard IR approaches. In particular, it improves the approach based on intersections by at least a factor 62, and the approach based on scanning by a factor up to 33 depending on the dataset and the queried-pattern length.

Prefix-search over FoF. Building upon the best approaches for the problem on friends, we turn to range-queries also the problem on FoF and show an improvement of a factor up to 38 over the best IR-based approach. Even if the gain of our solution varies depending on the pattern length and network size, we provide a careful analysis which gives a precise and clear explanation of all our experiments.

Top-k prefix-search over friends and FoF. We propose to augment the previous solutions with a Range-Maximum-Query data structure built over the scores of the friends of every node u in the graph, at the cost of $2 + o(1)$ bits per edge [19]. Then, taking inspiration from [28], we turn the top-k prefix search over friends and FoF of u into a specifically designed intermingled execution of RMQ-queries. We also investigate an hybrid solution based on a principled combination of this RMQ-approach with *early termination* approaches, which are typically used in IR search engines. This allows us to devise a pretty clear solution which significantly beats a strong baseline hinging on an approach that scans and scores the query results. Experiments show that our approach improves the query time by a factor up to 20.

Before proceeding further a comment is in order. The string-matching literature is full of results regarding the *prefix-search* problem on dictionary of strings and labeled trees, possibly compressed (see e.g., [15, 16, 18], and refs therein). About thirty years ago some (theoretical) work has been done also on the topic *pattern-matching on labeled DAGs* (see e.g., [2, 24, 29]), in which queries asked to search for a labeled path in those DAGs.

The problem we propose in our paper is the *first one* addressing the string-matching issue with *some neighbor constraints in labeled and general graphs, with significant practical applications.* Additionally, our extensive experimental tests on large and real graphs will show that our algorithms are not only theoretically valid but also efficient in practice.

2. RELATED WORK

Because of space limitations we refer the reader to the Introduction for other related works on this subject and for the notation we adopt in this paper.

Here we dig a little bit more on the Unicorn system [11]. Since a Unicorn instance (or vertical) may store an index that is too large to fit into the memory of a single machine, the index is broken up into multiple shards such that each shard can fit in a single index server. Queries to Unicorn are broadcast to all index servers, each index server retrieves entities from its shard and returns it to an Aggregator server, which then combines all these entities and returns them to the caller. As a result, queries may require multiple round-trips in order to retrieve objects that are more than one edge away from source nodes.

In order to reduce the round-trips over thousands of machines, and thus optimize the performance, the authors of [36] presented a label-propagation algorithm for finding 'joints' in graphs of particularly massive proportions, with an emphasis on the Facebook social graph. Specifically the goal was to perform graph sharding such that, as often as possible, whenever $v \in N_1(u)$ both u and v belong to the same shard. By doing this well, they reduced the number of other machines that need to be queried, and also reduced the total amount of data that need to be transferred over the network, consequently increasing overall system throughput and latency.

In this paper we introduce a *new re-assignment algorithm for node-IDs and proper compressed data structure and searching algorithms* that may be used either on the FB-graph as a whole, or inside every single FB-shard (as computed by [36]) with the goal of offering guaranteed performance in query time, reduced hops among machines, and compressed space occupancy.

3. BACKGROUND

Social networks (e.g., Facebook [21, 37]) have hubs and a surprisingly large number of FoF per individual. This neighbor structure has substantial algorithmic implications for graph traversals. In particular BFS out to distance two (i.e., touching $N_2(u)$'s neighbors) will potentially query a large number of individuals who may match a prefix-query especially if either the degree of u is large or if P is short. This is the reason why services on social networks show only few (e.g., five or ten) most promising users that match a prefix-query (such as the Typeahead tool in Facebook).

It is therefore obvious that compression issues and properly structured (string-matching) computations come into play if we wish to solve efficiently (in time and space) the problems we stated in the introduction. For the sake of space, we recall here few algorithmic techniques on which our solutions will hinge upon. For each of them, we will make use of state-of-the-art algorithms and their implementations which are available around the Web.

Prefix-search on a dictionary of strings. This is undoubtedly the most well-known problem in data-structural design for strings. It asks for preprocessing a set $\mathcal{D}$ of n strings, having total length L, in such a way that, given a query-pattern P, all strings in $\mathcal{D}$ having P as a prefix can be returned efficiently in time and space. Efficiently means in time proportional to P's length, and in space proportional to L or to the empirical entropy of $\mathcal{D}$'s strings. As far as the output size (i.e., number and length of returned strings) is concerned, we notice that returned strings are contiguous (if dictionary is alphabetically sorted) so they can be represented via a *range* $\langle l_P, r_P \rangle$ of their IDs. Just two integers suffice to encode the *occ* strings prefixed by P, where $occ = r_P - l_P + 1$. If the explicit strings are required by the underlying application, then a scan of that interval suffices, taking $O(occ)$ time.

The first solution to the prefix-search problem dates back to Fredkin ('60s) [20], who introduced the notion of (compacted) trie to solve it. After this seminal paper, a plethora of different solutions have been introduced to address different issues, namely, compression, I/O-efficiency, cache-obliviousness, and so on (see e.g., [7, 17, 18] and refs therein). We will not dig into these algorithmic details, we content ourselves, for the purposes of this paper, to remind the reader that the prefix-search problem on a dictionary of strings can be solved *optimally in time (I/Os) and in compressed space* [18].

Our solutions will be oblivious w.r.t. the particular data structure used to solve prefix-search queries over $\mathcal{D}$; in the experiments, we adopt the Compressed Permuterm index of [17] because of its compressed space occupancy (up to h-th order entropy of $\mathcal{D}$), very efficient prefix-query time complexity (i.e., $O(|P|)$ time), and appealing practical performance.

Accessing compressed sequences of integers. Representing strictly monotone sequences of integers in compressed space is a crucial problem, studied since the '50s with its most important application in inverted indexes [25]. Here the goal is to minimize the space occupancy of the posting lists with a compression scheme that guarantees the efficient processing of users' queries. Of course, the obvious sequential scan may be slow, so that engineers resort to *skipping* strategies. The basic idea is to divide a posting list in small blocks that are compressed independently, and to store the maximum integer present in each block. This allows to find and decode only the block that possibly contains the sought integer by scanning the sublist of maxima, thus skipping a potentially large number of useless blocks.

Compression is achieved by delta-encoding the integers within each block, i.e., representing the differences between consecutive integers. These differences may be encoded by any of the known variable-length binary codes: such as *unary codes*, *Elias Gamma/Delta codes*, *Golomb/Rice codes* [32], or the faster *Variable byte codes* (Vbyte) [32,34], *PForDelta* (PFD) [40] or OptPFD [39]. A completely different integer-encoding approach is taken by *Binary Interpolative Coding* [27], but experiments [30] have shown that, although this produces the most compressed sequence, when the sequence is highly clustered, it results very slow in decoding and thus it is less appealing for posting-list storage and in our setting too.

In the present paper we will concentrate on the *Elias-Fano* representation of monotone sequences [13, 14], which has been applied recently and successfully to the compression of inverted indexes [30, 38], showing both excellent space occupancy and query performance thanks to its efficient random access into a compressed posting list. More precisely, given a monotonically increasing sequence of n integers drawn from an *universe* $[m] = \{0, 1, \ldots, m-1\}$, Elias-Fano can be used to represent the sequence by using at most $n\lceil \log \frac{m}{n} \rceil + 2n + o(n)$ bits and to solve efficiently two key operations Access and NextGEQ by decoding only a small portion of the indexed sequence (see e.g., [30] and refs therein for more details). The Access(i) operation returns the ith element of the sequence. The NextGEQ(d) operation returns the smallest integer in the sequence that is greater than or equal to a given value d. Elias-Fano representation supports constant-time Access and logarithmic-time NextGEQ operations.

These compressed encodings will be at the core of the storage and access to the adjacency lists N_1 of the following known/new solutions.

Range Maximum Queries over integer sequences. Given an integer array $S[1, n]$ the Range-Maximum-Query problem asks to build a data structure that supports efficiently the following query: Given a range $[l, r]$, return the position p of the maximum value in $S[l, r]$. Notice that the value of the maximum can then be computed by accessing $S[p]$. There exist data structures that solve the RMQ-problem in constant-query time and $O(n)$ space in addition to S's storage [4]. By distinguishing the maximum value $S[p]$ from its position p, some authors were able to achieve the optimality in space occupancy without sacrificing the constant query-time [19]. The net result is a solution that takes $2+o(1)$ bits per integer, and still supports RMQ in constant time.

Our solution to the top-k query will deploy this data structure upon the scores of the nodes in the adjacency list N_1. By combining the Elias-Fano storage scheme for adjacency lists and a global array of nodes' scores, we will be able to plug RMQ-query support over NextGEQ operation, by paying only 2 additional bits per integer. Details below.

4. PROBLEMS AND ALGORITHMS

We start by presenting a possible solution to prefix searching over friends (or FoF) that uses standard information retrieval techniques. This approach is consistent with the solution described in [11], and makes use of the following two data structures.

1. The dictionary $\mathcal{D}$ of users' names is indexed with any data structure solving string-prefix searches.
2. The adjacency lists $N_1(u)$, of every node u in the graph, are indexed with compressed representation for integer sequences, supporting efficient Access and NextGEQ operations.

Given a pattern P and a target node u, let us start with solving the *prefix-search over friends* problem. This requires just to scan the friends of u in the graph checking whether their string name(u) is prefixed by P, thus taking $O(|P| \times |N_1(u)|)$ time.

Alternatively, one could resort standard list-intersection operations as follows.

1. Prefix search for P in $\mathcal{D}$ in order to obtain the set $V_P \subseteq V$ of all the nodes v in the graph whose name is prefixed by P.
2. Nodes in V_P are sorted by their identifiers, and the resulting list is intersected with $N_1(u)$.

Step 1 takes $O(|P|)$ time and step 2 requires $O(|V_P| \log |V_P|)$ time to sort V_P and $\min(|V_P|, |N_1(u)|)$ calls to the NextGEQ-operations to intersect nodes. The sorting of V_P is required to speed up the series of NextGEQ-operations over $N_1(u)$, which are faster when querying non-decreasing values. Obviously, the larger is the candidate set V_P, the worse is this solution which, nevertheless, may be appealing because of its simplicity.

More costly is to scale this solution to the *prefix-search over FoF* problem because $N_1(u)$ is substituted by $N_2(u)$ with a consequent significant increase in the total number of nodes to be intersected in step 2. In particular, we observe that checking whether a node of V_P occurs in $N_2(u)$ needs either to materialize $N_2(u)$ and execute $\min(V_P, |N_2(u)|)$ calls to the NextGEQ-operation over it, or it needs to perform $d(u)$ calls to NextGEQ, one call per adjacency list of a friend of u (without thus materializing $N_2(u)$). The former approach is faster, but it incurs in a huge space occupancy (see comments above on FB FoF's network, and our Table 1); the latter approach saves space but it incurs in a total of $O(|V_P| \times d(u))$ executions of NextGEQ.

As far as the *top-k* variant of the two problems above is concerned, it could be solved by keeping only the k nodes with the highest scores during the list intersections. An alternative approach could mimic the *early termination* strategies in inverted indexes (e.g., WAND [9]) and thus compute these top-k nodes without generating the score of all of them. Indeed, the idea could be to store for each node v the maximum score $M(v)$ among the nodes in its adjacency list. At query time, instead of processing all the neighbors of u at once, we can start from the most promising ones (i.e., the ones with the largest values of M), and then immediately exclude the adjacency list of a node v as soon as we recognize that the kth largest score discovered so far is larger than $M(v)$ and, thus, none of v's neighbors may enter in the top-k ones.

Overall these solutions have some serious efficiency drawbacks. The first solution has to decode and scan $N_1(u)$ (and possibly $N_2(u)$) regardless of the size of the final output and pattern length. This may be a problem because of u's degree and the typical size of FoF. The second solution incurs into two other drawbacks. One concerns with the need of materializing (and, possibly, sorting) the set V_P of candidate nodes. This list may be huge, especially if the pattern P is short.[1] This has been recognized as a problem also in [11] and, indeed, they precompute and store the sets V_P for all the patterns P of length at most few characters (e.g., two). Of course, this strategy trades space occupancy for time efficiency but it does not scale with the pattern's length. The other drawback is the need to check, for each element in the (sorted) set V_P, its presence within the friend- or the FoF-list of u. This task is computational demanding whenever the set V_P or the degree of u are, even moderately, large. In fact, although we discussed the similarity with traditional query-processing approaches in posting lists, their adaptation on our problems is slower for two main reasons: (i) a SE-query is usually solved by processing the posting lists of the *few terms* which compose the query, while in our case we have to process the *possibly many* adjacency lists of the neighbors of nodes in $N_1(u)$ (in case of query over $N_2(u)$); (ii) our query can be re-phrased in terms of AND or OR operators in SE-query processing terminology— i.e., V_P AND ($N_1(u)$ OR $N_1(v_1)$ OR ... OR $N_1(v_{d(u)})$), where $v_i \in N_1(u)$— but unfortunately the OR operator is more than 20 times slower than AND [30].

In Section 5 we will investigate the time and space efficiency of all these proposals that will constitute the baselines against which we will compare our novel algorithmic solutions (described below) to the four problems in this paper.

4.1 Prefix-search over friends (or FoF)

Our novel compressed scheme hinges on a simple yet crucial step, that is the *renumbering* of the nodesIDs: *Each node $u \in V$ has assigned a new identifier* rank(u), *which is the rank of* name(u) *within the alphabetic ordering of all nodes' names in $\mathcal{D}$.* This renumbering bridges nodeIDs with their names so that a node u is prefixed by a pattern P if and only if rank(u) is within the range $\langle l_P, r_P\rangle$ (see Section 3).

We store any data structure that solves prefix-search queries over the dictionary $\mathcal{D}$ of users' names; and we adopt the new nodeIDs for storing the adjacency list $N_1(u)$ of every node u in the graph. This way, we guarantee the following two key properties.

- For any pattern P, all the nodes prefixed by P in $N_1(u)$ will form a consecutive range, if any: i.e., $\langle l_P, r_P\rangle$. This range can be identified by searching for P in the prefix-search data structure built on the $\mathcal{D}$'s strings, taking $O(|P|)$ time.
- The range can be identified in $N_1(u)$ with only two NextGEQ-operations: it starts at position $l =$ NextGEQ(l_P) and ends at position $r =$ NextGEQ$(r_P + 1) - 1$. The range is empty whenever $r < l$.

[1]Table 1 shows that the average size of $N_2(u)$ is from 269 (Dblp) to about 153,445 (Twitter). This means that patterns of few characters will likely occur more often than these numbers.

This simple solution can be generalized to solve FoF queries in either $2d(u)$ NextGEQ-operations, by querying the adjacency list $N_1(v)$ of each friend v of u, or only 2 NextGEQ-operations by materializing and indexing the whole $N_2(u)$.

As a final remark, we notice that, once we renamed the nodes, the query we are solving becomes a well-known *range* reporting query. The problem of designing efficient data structures to answer these types of queries has been studied in the literature where the best (theoretical) data structure [1] is able to retrieve all the, say *occ*, elements within any range in optimal $O(occ)$ time and linear space. Our use of Elias-Fano representation solves that query in slightly suboptimal time (i.e., $O(\log |N_1(u)| + occ)$ worst-case time) but has the great advantage of being very efficient in practice and offer compressed space, as we will show in the experiments.

4.2 Top-k prefix-search over friends (or FoF)

We start by considering the top-k prefix-search queries over friends, and assume that the scores of the nodes are stored in a global table indexed by the new nodeIDs.

For each user u, we define the array $S_1(u)$ that stores the scores of u's friends according to their order in $N_1(u)$ (i.e., for any $1 \le i \le d(u)$, $S_1(u)[i] =$ score$(N_1(u)[i])$). On top of $S_1(u)$ we build a RMQ data structure that takes $2 + o(1)$ bits per edge, hence almost 2 bits per node in $N_1(u)$ (see Section 3). The crucial observation here is that $S_1(u)$ does not need to be stored because, if the RMQ-query returns position p in $N_1(u)$, we can retrieve the corresponding nodeID by accessing $N_1(u)$ and then using it to get its score from the global table above.

Given these data structures, answering a top-k prefix-search P over the friends of u proceeds as follows.

- We search for P in the data structure built over $\mathcal{D}$, and thus identify the range $\langle l_P, r_P\rangle$ of nodes in the graph that are prefixed by P.
- We map this range onto $N_1(u)$ by computing the positions $l =$ NextGEQ(l_P) and $r =$ NextGEQ$(r_P + 1) - 1$.
- We finally identify the k nodes with the largest score in $N_1(u)[l, r]$ by adopting two different approaches. The former is trivial: it scans and scores all the nodes in that range taking time proportional to its size (i.e., $O(r - l + 1)$ time). The latter approach is more sophisticated and computes the k results in $O(k \log k)$ time, hence independent of the range size, by adapting an algorithm originally introduced by Muthukrishnan [28] to solve a different problem, and then extended by various authors to solve top-k strings in a dictionary (see e.g., [22] and refs therein). Here we adapt these approaches to our node-scoring setting as follows:

(1) The algorithm is recursive and uses an auxiliary max-heap of at most $2k$ elements, each being a triple of integers. The heap is initialized by computing in $O(1)$ time the value $m =$ RMQ(l, r), which is the position (hence node) in $N_1(u)$ storing the largest score within the range $N_1(u)[l, r]$. Then the triple $\langle l, m, r\rangle$ is inserted in the heap, with priority equal to the score of node $N_1(u)[m]$.

(2) The algorithm proceeds by repeating three main steps for k times: (i) It picks from the heap the triple with maximum priority (score), say $\langle l, m, r\rangle$; (ii) it

then splits the range (l, r) in two parts: $(l, m-1)$ and $(m+1, r)$ and, recursively, computes the maximum scoring node into each of them: $m' = \mathsf{RMQ}(l, m-1)$ and $m'' = \mathsf{RMQ}(m+1, r)$; (iii) finally, it inserts the two triples $\langle l, m', m-1\rangle$ and $\langle m+1, m'', r\rangle$ in the heap with priorities given by the scores of nodes $N_1(u)[m']$ and $N_1(u)[m'']$, respectively. Hence, each step extracts one triple and inserts two triples in the heap, overall taking $O(k \log k)$ time.

It is clear that the latter method is better than the former one whenever the range becomes slightly larger than k.

A top-k prefix-search query over the FoF of a user u can be obviously computed by running the above algorithm over all the $d(u)$ friends of u and inserting the (at most) top-k results from each friend of u in the max-heap mentioned above. This algorithm has to manage at most $k \times d(u)$ candidates and, thus, it requires $O(k \times d(u) \log(k \times d(u)))$ time in the worst case. This worst-case analysis is quite precise: it suffices that a fraction of u's friends reports $\Theta(k)$ results to match this time complexity.

However a smarter approach is possible that offers the same worst-case time complexity but with a possibly better performance in real scenarios. The idea is to initialize the Max-Heap with the top-1 result from each friend of u (not the top-k), and then repeat the three steps above until k *distinct* nodes have been extracted from the max-heap. We notice that these nodes may come from different adjacency lists and in multiple copies from them. So from the one hand this approach guarantees that an adjacency list is examined only if it may potentially include one of the top-k final results; but, from the other hand, this algorithm may subtly induce more than k steps because of the presence of duplicates in the adjacency lists of the friends of u. These duplicates are clearly at most $k \times d(u)$ but they may be significantly less depending on the graph's structure. This is the algorithmic approach to top-k over FoF we will experiment in the following sections.

5. EXPERIMENTAL RESULTS

All the algorithms were implemented in C++11 and compiled with GCC 4.9.1 with the highest optimization settings. The tests were performed on a machine with 24 Intel Xeon E5-2697 Ivy Bridge cores (48 threads) clocked at 2.70Ghz, with 64GiB RAM, running Linux 3.12.7.

The data structures were saved to disk after construction, and memory-mapped to perform the queries. The timings for each query are derived by averaging the last three measurements out of four total measurements. In the following all reported query times are in microseconds (μs) and spaces are in megabytes (MBytes).

The source code is available at `http://github.com/nopper/compressed-indexes-string/tree/www15` for the reader interested in replicating the experiments.

Datasets. We used the following three networks.

- Dblp. The co-authorship network built from a DBLP data downloaded from `http://dblp.uni-trier.de/xml` in October 2014. The graph is available at `http://zola.di.unipi.it/rossano/dblp.tgz`.
- LiveJournal is a snapshot of the friendship network of LiveJournal blogging community crawled in 2006 [3]. In this graph, there exists a directed edge from u to v when u is a friend of v.
- Twitter is a snapshot crawled starting on June 6th and lasting until June 31st, 2009 [23]. In this graph, there exists a directed edge from node u to node v when u *follows* v in Twitter.

We preferred these datasets among other freely available ones because they were the most complete. In particular, we excluded a Facebook snapshot [21] because about 51 million nodes, out of its about 59 million nodes, have degree 1, which is very far from being a realistic characteristic of this social network.

Table 1 reports some basic statistics on our datasets. The column $|\mathcal{D}|$ indicates the size in characters of the dictionary of string names of graph nodes. We notice that the size of N_2 makes unfeasible any approach which attempts its indexing directly. Indeed, the number of elements in N_2's lists w.r.t. N_1's ones grows by a factor ≈ 32 on Dblp, a factor ≈ 49 on LiveJournal, and a factor ≈ 4380 on Twitter, which in turn induce similar increases in the index space.

Implementation of the key step. It is the one that searches the pattern P in the adjacency list of a given node u. We used this step to solve prefix-search for P over Friends of u, and to solve FoF-query by iterating it over all the adjacency lists of the friends of u (for details see Section 4).

According to what we discussed in the previous sections, we provide the following three implementations.

- Intersect answers the query via standard information retrieval approaches by weakly intersecting V_P and the adjacency list of u.
- Scan answers the query by decompressing and scanning the adjacency list of u and by checking whether the queried prefix P prefixes the name of each processed node. Instead of comparing the pattern and each name character-by-character, we store in a global array the rank of each name in the alphabetic ordering. Thus, it suffices to report any node whose rank belongs to the interval $\langle l_P, r_P\rangle$. This is a necessary and sufficient condition for a name to be prefixed by P (see beginning of Subsection 4.1).
- Range answers the query by executing two NextGEQ operations (one for l_P and one for $r_P + 1$) over the adjacency list of u to identify the contiguous range of nodes which are prefixed by P. Reporting those nodes requires the scan of this range.

In all solutions we represent the adjacency lists with any of the compression schemes for integer sequences described in Section 3. In our experiments we tried four of them (namely, Elias-Fano, Interpolative, OptPFD, and Varint-G8IU) since they offer various space/time trade-offs[2].

We remark that there exist compression schemes specifically designed to achieve higher compression on graphs, especially Web graphs [6,8]. But these representations support basic operations onto the link-structure of the input graph, such as the retrieval of the whole adjacency list of a

[2]Code is available at `http://github.com/ot/partitioned_elias_fano`. See [30] for more details.

Dataset	$\|V\|$	$\|E\|$	Avg. Degree	$\|N_2\|$	$\|N_2\|/\|V\|$	$\|\mathcal{D}\|$ in chars
Dblp	1,420,763	12,005,120	8.5	383,444,104	269.9	20,054,749
LiveJournal	4,846,608	68,475,391	14.1	3,370,481,580	695.4	56,269,582
Twitter	41,652,229	1,468,365,182	35.3	6,391,337,859,405	153,445.3	406,349,035

Table 1: Basic statistics on our three datasets.

		Pattern length $\|P\|$				
Dataset	Space	1	2	3	4	5
Dblp	14.43	0.41	0.50	0.51	0.54	0.56
LiveJournal	42.74	0.42	0.52	0.54	0.57	0.60
Twitter	316.63	0.50	0.58	0.59	0.63	0.64

Table 2: Space occupancy (in MBytes) and average query time (in μs) of CPI.

	Dblp		LiveJournal		Twitter	
Encoding	Space	bpe	Space	bpe	Space	bpe
Varint-G8IU	33.86	22.87	163.49	19.57	3836.72	21.70
Interpolative	29.77	20.04	139.40	16.63	3067.45	17.32
OptPFD	33.70	22.76	160.26	19.17	3440.63	19.44
Elias-Fano	33.94	22.93	177.35	21.26	3513.07	19.86
Varint-G8IU	38.43	26.04	208.02	25.00	4271.63	24.18
Interpolative	32.06	21.63	170.50	20.42	3441.41	19.45
OptPFD	38.23	25.90	204.57	24.58	3856.98	21.82
Elias-Fano	33.94	22.93	177.35	21.26	3513.07	19.86

Table 3: Index space occupancies in MBs and bits per edge (bpe) for each dataset by varying the compression scheme. The top part refers to the compression of original nodeIDs, the bottom part refers to the compression of *alphabetic* nodeIDs, according to our renumbering scheme at the beginning of Section 4.1.

given node. Therefore the only way to solve our queries over these representations would be to scan the whole list and check for possible results. Experiments in [8] on LiveJournal show that the fastest representations scan an adjacency list by taking 2 μs per node; this is much higher than what we aim for in our setting where baselines achieve timings in the order of tens of nanoseconds per node on the same dataset. For this reason we do not experiment with them.

Prefix Search in $\mathcal{D}$. The first step of any solution is to perform a prefix-search for a given pattern P in the dictionary $\mathcal{D}$. As we mentioned in Section 3 this is a very well-studied problem and several solutions exist. Comparing the plethora of solutions known for this problem is out of the scope of this paper. We only report the time/space efficiency of the compressed permuterm index (CPI) described in [17][3]. This is a compressed solution that is competitive in query time w.r.t. uncompressed ones (e.g., tries) [17]. Anyway, we remark that any other prefix-search data structure could be plugged in without jeopardizing the conclusions of this paper.

Table 2 reports CPI's space occupancy and its average query time by varying the pattern length from 1 to 5 characters. Experiments were performed by searching 1000 patterns for each length which were randomly selected from $\mathcal{D}$ (i.e., succesful searches). In the subsequent experiments we do not account for the prefix-search time and space occupancy.

Space occupancy. In Table 3 we report the space occupancy to represent the adjacency lists of each graph with different compression schemes. Note that both Intersect and Scan work on lists encoding the original nodeIDs; conversely, Range renames nodeIDs accordingly to the alphabetic rank of the corresponding names.

Interpolative is always the most performant encoder, with a gain between $11\% - 21\%$ on original nodeIDs, and $4\% - 28\%$ on alphabetic nodeIDs.

We point out that all integer encoders require more space when alphabetic nodeIDs are used, except for Elias-Fano which is independent on the renumbering of nodeIDs because of its properties. This is a very important outcome of this experiment because we have shown theoretically (and we will prove experimentally) that alphabetic nodeIDs are crucial to achieve efficient time performance on our prefix-queries on friends and FoF. Consequently Elias-Fano will be the winning encoding choice in terms of time efficiency in our solutions, and this will come at the cost of loosing a small percentage (i.e., $2\% - 6\%$) in space occupancy wrt Interpolative which however may be significantly slower (i.e., $2.2 \div 4.0$ times).

Prefix-search over friends. Our first experiment reports the query time of each solution in solving prefix-search over friends (space has been given in Table 3). In order to run our experiment we need a pattern P and a node u. We selected 1000 patterns of length from 1 to 5 at random from $\mathcal{D}$, and we selected 10,000 nodes u as follows.

For each graph, we identified the 11-quantiles in its degree distribution. For each pair of consecutive 11-quantiles, we selected uniformly at random a group of 1000 nodes having degree between two consecutive quantiles. This way, we have 10 groups of 1000 nodes each, hence 10,000 nodes in total. This selection is very close to a uniform selection of 10,000 nodes from V, and the subdivision in groups will be useful in the subsequent experiments where our goal will be to study the impact of node degree on query time.

We report in Table 4 the average query time in microseconds of the three solutions mentioned at the beginning of this section, and study how this time depends onto the pattern length and the compression scheme in use. Due to space limitations, we only report results for LiveJournal and Twitter. We observed similar results on Dblp.

These results lead us to three main conclusions which are inspired by the three main horizontal bands in which the Table 4 can be divided according to the proposed approaches.

The first conclusion concerns with Intersect. Since this solution has to process each element in V_P, its poor performance is not surprising when answering queries for short patterns because they induce a large V_P. Interestingly, even if its

[3] An implementation of CPI is available at `http://code.google.com/p/cpi00`

		LiveJournal					Twitter				
	Encoding	$\lvert P\rvert = 1$	$\lvert P\rvert = 2$	$\lvert P\rvert = 3$	$\lvert P\rvert = 4$	$\lvert P\rvert = 5$	$\lvert P\rvert = 1$	$\lvert P\rvert = 2$	$\lvert P\rvert = 3$	$\lvert P\rvert = 4$	$\lvert P\rvert = 5$
Intersect	Varint-G8IU	26,350.37	2166.34	425.54	101.27	41.54	219,029.26	20,280.51	3436.84	776.84	295.10
	Interpolative	26,314.67	2164.79	426.07	102.26	42.61	220,805.02	20,366.81	3472.17	799.64	313.35
	OptPFD	26,318.48	2164.56	425.81	101.97	42.30	220,816.15	20,356.54	3460.55	788.96	304.41
	Elias-Fano	26,307.03	2161.47	424.05	100.58	40.94	220,466.91	20,333.70	3452.83	782.82	298.50
Scan	Varint-G8IU	1.77	1.54	1.52	1.52	1.51	29.27	27.59	27.59	27.41	27.48
	Interpolative	2.75	2.51	2.49	2.49	2.49	39.25	37.93	37.80	37.76	37.86
	OptPFD	2.68	2.44	2.41	2.40	2.40	28.60	27.21	26.93	26.74	26.77
	Elias-Fano	1.75	1.51	1.48	1.48	1.48	43.95	42.21	42.20	42.09	42.19
Range	Varint-G8IU	1.14	0.99	0.97	0.97	0.98	2.20	1.42	1.31	1.27	1.27
	Interpolative	1.95	1.79	1.77	1.77	1.77	5.72	3.57	3.36	3.30	3.30
	OptPFD	1.82	1.67	1.65	1.64	1.64	3.77	2.47	2.31	2.26	2.25
	Elias-Fano	0.87	0.70	0.68	0.67	0.67	2.04	1.02	0.88	0.84	0.83
	Avg. $\lvert V_P\rvert$	431,055	41,869	8896	2326	975	3,135,085	330,600	60,828	14,810	5769
	Avg. # results	9.68	1.76	1.15	1.04	1.02	131.09	14.38	4.43	2.12	1.59

Table 4: Average query time (in μs) to answer a prefix-search over the friends of a node u in either dataset LiveJournal or Twitter, by varying the length of the pattern P.

performance improves rapidly, Intersect is noncompetitive for longer patterns as well: when $|P| = 5$, Intersect is always slower than Range by at least 62 times on LiveJournal, and 360 times slower on Twitter. One may consider to precompute sets V_P and augment them to support fast NextGEQ operations. This would certainly speed up intersections and, thus, the overall query processing of this solution. However, due to the space overhead introduced by augmentation, this approach can be applied only on short patterns, thus inheriting the slow performance on long patterns. This leads us to exclude Intersect from the next experiments because such limitations cannot be reverted on the next, more difficult, types of queries involving FoF and top-k.

The second conclusion is about Scan, for which Varint-G8IU, except for few exceptions, is the fastest encoding. This leads us to choose Varint-G8IU as integer compressor for the approach Scan in the next experiments.

The third and last conclusion is about Range. Elias-Fano exhibits the best performance on any dataset. This leads us to use Elias-Fano as integer compressor for the approach Range in the next experiments.

In conclusion we can observe that Range (with Elias-Fano) is faster than Scan (with Varint-G8IU) by a factor ranging from 2 to 2.25 on LiveJournal, and from 14.3 to 33.1 on Twitter. Observe that this gap increases as the pattern length increases too. This is a virtue of Range which requires just two NextGEQ operations to identify the range in N_1 that contains all the query results, then it needs to decode only values within this range. This implies that its query time decreases as the number of query results decreases too (which occurs when P's length increases). This favorably compares with Scan that always needs to decode and scan the whole list N_1, regardless the number of query results.

As far as space occupancy is concerned, Range with Elias-Fano (8th row in Table 3) is $\approx 10\%$ better than Scan with Varint-G8IU (1st row) on Twitter, but it is $\approx 8\%$ worse than Scan (with Varint-G8IU) on LiveJournal.

Prefix-search over FoF. In the next experiments we compare Range and Scan in answering prefix-search over FoF, given their best performance above. Recall that in this type of query, given a prefix P and a node u, we use one of these two solutions to process the adjacency lists of each friend of u to identify those nodes which are prefixed by P. By the considerations above, we expect that the performance gap between Range and Scan will be amplified because each solution is run over the adjacency lists of the, potentially many, friends of u. We report in Table 5 the query time to answer prefix-search query on FoF over our datasets, and we also specify the average number of results returned for each query. We run this experiment by using the same patterns (1000) and nodes (10,000) of the previous paragraph, now prefix-querying over their FoF. The results adhere to our expectations: Range is significantly faster than Scan on any dataset for any pattern-length. The space occupancy remains the one discussed in the previous paragraph. The smallest gain is on Dblp where Range is faster than Scan by a factor from 1.9 to 2.2, the largest gain is on Twitter where the improvement is by a factor from 4 to 38 depending on the pattern length. Again, the gain factor increases with the pattern length and on the network size.

In Figure 1 we plot the average query time of Range and Scan on Twitter for patterns of length 1 and 5. Nodes are divided into 10 groups accordingly to the 11-quantiles as described at the beginning of the previous paragraph. The largest gain is on the second group (a factor 5.4 for $|P| = 1$ and a factor 201 for $|P| = 5$) while the smallest gain is on the last group (a factor 3.8 for $|P| = 1$ and a factor 35 for $|P| = 5$).

A more careful analysis of the query time of the two solutions provides a precise and clear explanation of all our experiments. Given a pattern P and a queried-node u, the query time $T_{\mathsf{Range}}(u, P)$ of Range is approximately equal to the sum of three cost terms. The first one is the cost of identifying the range on nodes prefixed by P in each u's friend lists, which is equal to $2\, T_{\mathsf{EFNextGEQ}} \times d(u)$ time, where $T_{\mathsf{EFNextGEQ}}$ is the time of a NextGEQ with Elias-Fano. Second, the cost of decoding nodes within each of these ranges, which equals $T_{\mathsf{EFAccess}} \times |R_u(P)|$, where T_{EFAccess} is the cost of an Access operation with Elias-Fano and $|R_u(P)|$ is total length of these

Dblp

Solution	Pattern length $\|P\|$ 1	2	3	4	5
Scan (Varint-G8IU)	48	43	42	41	40
Range (Elias-Fano)	25	21	20	19	18
Avg. # results	98.80	45.37	25.06	14.65	3.38

LiveJournal

Solution	Pattern length $\|P\|$ 1	2	3	4	5
Scan (Varint-G8IU)	206	147	146	145	145
Range (Elias-Fano)	123	68	66	65	66
Avg. # results	551.81	21.13	4.41	2.14	1.70

Twitter

Solution	Pattern length $\|P\|$ 1	2	3	4	5
Scan (Varint-G8IU)	133,006	103,560	99,895	99,666	99,540
Range (Elias-Fano)	33,019	5924	2998	2783	2635
Avg. # results	90,017	12,573	1925	896	385

Table 5: Average query time (in μs) to answer a prefix-search over the FoF of a node u in all datasets, by varying the length of the pattern P.

ranges (i.e., the number nodes in u's friends lists which are prefixed by P). Third, the time $T_{\mathsf{Report}}(u,P)$ to manage and report query-results (i.e., sort them and remove duplicates), which is independent on the particular solution in use, and depends only on size of the candidate-list of results.

The query time of Scan is approximately $T_{\mathsf{Scan}}(u,P) = T_{\mathsf{VIAccess}} \times \hat{N}_2(u) + T_{\mathsf{Report}}(u,P)$, where T_{VIAccess} is the time of a Access operation with Varint-G8IU and $\hat{N}_2(u)$ is the number nodes in u's friends lists. The number $\hat{N}_2(u)$ is always at least the size of the FoF network of u (i.e., $N_2(u)$), and it may be larger because it accounts also for duplicates.

Even if T_{VIAccess} is smaller than T_{EFAccess}, which, in turn, is smaller than $T_{\mathsf{EFNextGEQ}}$ [30], the large difference in size between $R_u(P)$ and $\hat{N}_2(u)$ significantly favours Range query time, especially in larger graphs.

By increasing the pattern length, $T_{\mathsf{Range}}(u,P)$ decreases because both $R_u(P)$ and $T_{\mathsf{Report}}(u,P)$ decrease too. Instead, the first term in $T_{\mathsf{Scan}}(u,P)$ remains fixed and only $T_{\mathsf{Report}}(u,P)$ decreases. Thus, T_{Range} decreases more rapidly than T_{Scan} by increasing the pattern length and, in fact, its gain improves as shown in Table 5.

Finally, we observed a significant drop in the gain of $T_{\mathsf{Range}}(u,P)$ versus $T_{\mathsf{Scan}}(u,P)$ when the pattern length is fixed but u's degree grows. At a first glance, one would be temped to think that this is due to the first term $2\ T_{\mathsf{EFNextGEQ}} \times d(u)$ in $T_{\mathsf{Range}}(u,P)$ that, obviously, increases with u's degree. However this is not the case, just look at the query times of Range for the last bins in Figure 1: in average Range requires 215,436 μs for $|P| = 1$ and 17,122 μs for $|P| = 5$. Thus, since Range executes exactly the same number of NextGEQ operations in solving queries with different pattern lengths on the same node u, the time cost of all these operations cannot be larger than 17,122 μs. Surprisingly, experiments show that more than half of the query time is spent in managing and reporting query-results (i.e., the term $T_{\mathsf{Report}}(u,P)$). For example, $T_{\mathsf{Report}}(u,P)$ is roughly 110,000 μs in the last bin of Figure 1 for $|P| = 1$, where queries have 3,227,675 results on average. These considerations explain the drop in the gain

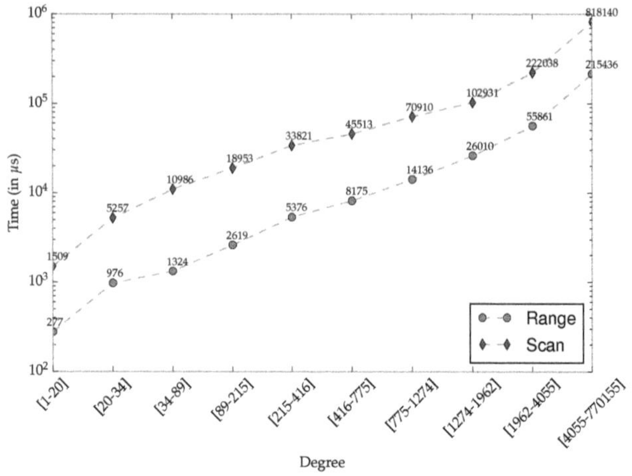

(a) $|P| = 1$

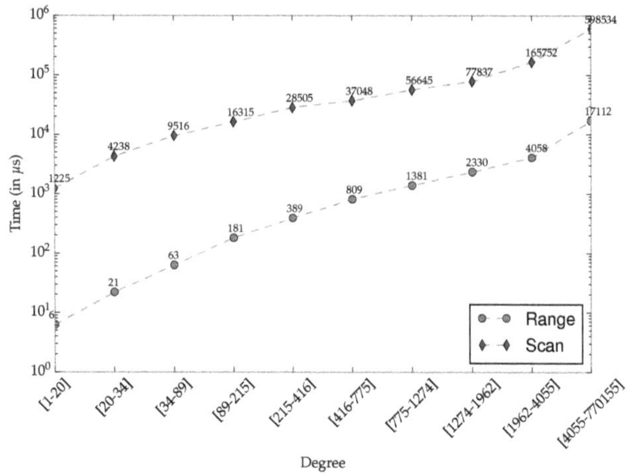

(b) $|P| = 5$

Figure 1: Average query time (in μs) to answer a prefix-search over FoF on Twitter for $|P| = 1$ and $|P| = 5$. The queried nodes are divided into 10 groups based on their degrees. The y-axis is in log-scale.

achieved by Range over Scan when querying higher degree nodes, because of an increase in the number of candidate results to process and report; and, furthermore, they motivate the interest for efficient solutions to the top-k variant of the problem because the reporting step is absent there since the reporting is confined to just k nodes (and thus it is independent of the range size).

Top-k prefix-search over FoF. The previous experiments established that Range is the clear winner. In this paragraph we make a step forward by experimenting over the algorithms proposed in Subsection 4.2 for retrieving top-k results. Due to space limitations, we focus on answering top-k prefix-search over FoF. We experiment the following solutions.

- Range+Score implements the simple strategy which retrieves and scores all the results identified by applying Range over the friends of the queried node u. A Max-Heap is used to keep only the k largest scores. This

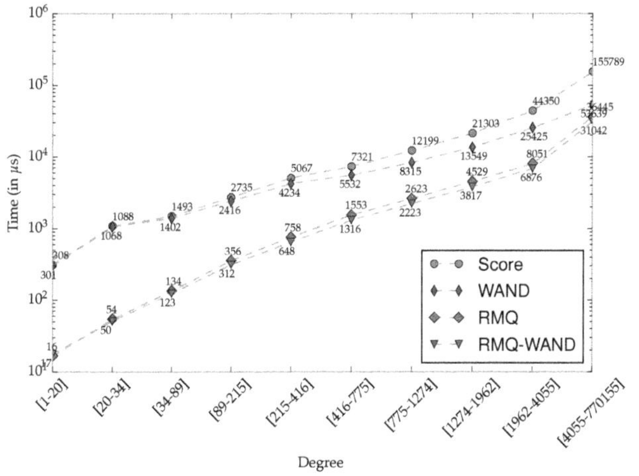

Figure 2: Average query time (in μs) to answer a Top-k ($k = 10$) prefix-search over the FoF on Twitter for the nodes divided into 10 groups based on their degrees and patterns of length 1. The y-axis is in log-scale. All solutions are based on Range which is then dropped from the legend.

solution serves as a baseline to show the improvement induced by strategies targeted to the top-k problem.

- Range+WAND implements a solution inspired by early termination strategies in Search Engines. The solution keeps a global array M, entry $M[v]$ stores the maximum score of a node in $N_1(v)$. This way, we process the friends of u by starting from the most promising ones (i.e., the nodes v with largest values of $M[v]$). This gives the chance of early stopping the processing of u's friends.

- Range+RMQ implements the solution described in Subsection 4.2, which uses an intermingled execution of RMQ-queries to speed up the detection of top-k nodes.

- Range+RMQ+WAND is an hybrid approach that has been inspired by experimental results, which show the complementary characteristics of the previous two approaches. First, the solution runs Range+RMQ on nodes with a degree larger than a threshold D, thus computing and inserting their top-k in the Max-Heap; then, it processes the remaining low-degree nodes with the WAND strategy. In our experiments the threshold D has been fixed to 1000.

In our experiments we use the degree of a node as its score. We remark that our solutions are indenpendent of the scoring functions. Indeed, we obtained the same results with a random scoring generation. We run our experiments by using the same set of patterns and nodes as in the previous paragraphs. In Figure 2 we plot the query time on Twitter by varying the node degree and by fixing $k = 10$ and the pattern length to 1. Due to space limitations, we do not show pictures for other experiments which are, nevertheless, commented below.

We notice that, albeit Range+Score is the same solution as in Figure 1, the performance here are improved on nodes with larger degrees. This is because in solving top-k there is no need to sort and deduplicate all the matching results (as observed at the end of the previous paragraph). However, all these matching results need to be scored, which is a non-negligible task. This explains the limited improvement on high-degree nodes and the slightly worse performance on low-degree ones.

In any case our algorithm based on RMQ gives a significant improvement over Range+Score. The gain is a factor ranging from 2.9 to 20.2. The gain decreases with the increasing of the queried-node degree.

A comment is in order now. Even if Range+WAND seems to be noncompetitive w.r.t. Range+RMQ, intuition suggests that these two strategies complement each other. Indeed, Range+RMQ is very efficient on high-degree friends of u because they are likely to have much more than k matching results and, thus, RMQ operations allow us to skip most of them. Range+WAND, instead, is more likely to exclude low-degree friends of u which will have lower maxima on average. Experiments confirm this intuition: Range+RMQ+WAND improves Range+RMQ by a factor up to 1.7. The largest improvements are on large degree nodes where Range+RMQ has the smallest gain with respect to the baseline Range+Score. This way, our solutions improve the gain over the baseline Range+Score, which is now at least a factor 5.0 instead of 2.9.

We finally report that the time gain of the best solutions decreases on longer patterns, vanishing with patterns of length $|P| = 5$. This is due to the fact that the pattern's occurrences are few enough that Range+Score is sufficiently fast to identify the top-k nodes among them. We remark that the reduced time gain of Range+RMQ over long patterns does not occur for graphs of average degree smaller than Twitter and, we foresee that, this will not occur for a larger snapshot of Twitter where we expect more pattern's results to be scanned, so that Range+Score will turn out to be slower than Range+RMQ on par of what happens on our snapshot for shorter patterns.

6. FUTURE WORK

First of all we would like to experiment our solutions on much larger networks. As shown in our experiments, the gain of our solutions increase with the social network size.

Second, we would like to extend our solutions to the case of queries over *multi-attribute* nodes, such as age, geographic location, preferences, and so on. The simplest approach to deal with this scenario would be to apply our node-renumbering scheme onto each attribute, thus blowing-up the space by a factor proportional to the number of indexed attributes. We foresee to design solutions which do not pass through an *explicit replication* of the graph, but rather exploit information-theoretic ideas to encode succinctly different *permutations* of the same adjacency lists.

Finally we remark that our graphs were *static* so that every node/edge change would require a reconstruction of the corresponding part of the index. In a more realistic setting, we would need to update efficiently the index by e.g. any known dynamization technique [26,31]. An experimental evaluation on real graph-update traces is foreseen.

Acknowledgments

We wish to warmly thank Domenico Dato and Daniele Vitale (Istella, Tiscali) for exposing us to some of the problems we addressed in this paper and for fruitful discussions. This work was partially supported by MIUR PRIN ARS-Technomedia.

7. REFERENCES

[1] S. Alstrup, G. S. Brodal, and T. Rauhe. Optimal static range reporting in one dimension. In *STOC*, pages 476–482, 2001.

[2] A. Amir, M. Lewenstein, and N. Lewenstein. Pattern matching in hypertext. In *WADS*, LNCS 1272, pages 160–173, 1997.

[3] L. Backstrom, D. P. Huttenlocher, J. M. Kleinberg, and X. Lan. Group formation in large social networks: membership, growth, and evolution. In *KDD*, pages 44–54, 2006.

[4] M. A. Bender and M. Farach-Colton. The LCA problem revisited. In *LATIN*, pages 88–94, 2000.

[5] P. Boldi, M. Santini, and S. Vigna. Permuting web and social graphs. *Internet Mathematics*, 6(3):257–283, 2009.

[6] P. Boldi and S. Vigna. The webgraph framework I: compression techniques. In *WWW*, pages 595–602, 2004.

[7] N. Brisaboa, R. Cánovas, F. Claude, M. Martínez-Prieto, and G. Navarro. Compressed string dictionaries. In *SEA*, LNCS 6630, pages 136–147, 2011.

[8] N. R. Brisaboa, S. Ladra, and G. Navarro. k2-trees for compact web graph representation. In *SPIRE*, pages 18–30, 2009.

[9] A. Z. Broder, D. Carmel, M. Herscovici, A. Soffer, and J. Y. Zien. Efficient query evaluation using a two-level retrieval process. In *CIKM*, pages 426–434, 2003.

[10] F. Chierichetti, R. Kumar, S. Lattanzi, M. Mitzenmacher, A. Panconesi, and P. Raghavan. On compressing social networks. In *ACM SIGKDD*, pages 219–228, 2009.

[11] M. Curtiss and *et al.* Unicorn: A system for searching the social graph. *VLDB*, 6(11):1150–1161, Aug. 2013.

[12] B. B. Dalvi, M. Kshirsagar, and S. Sudarshan. Keyword search on external memory data graphs. *VLDB Endow.*, 1(1):1189–1204, 2008.

[13] P. Elias. Universal codeword sets and representations of the integers. *IEEE Transactions on Information Theory*, 21(2):194–203, 1975.

[14] R. M. Fano. On the number of bits required to implement an associative memory. *Memorandum 61, Computer Structures Group, MIT, Cambridge, MA*, 1971.

[15] P. Ferragina and R. Grossi. The String B-tree: A new data structure for string search in external memory and its applications. *J. ACM*, 46(2):236–280, 1999.

[16] P. Ferragina, F. Luccio, G. Manzini, and S. Muthukrishnan. Compressing and indexing labeled trees, with applications. *J. ACM*, 57(1), 2009.

[17] P. Ferragina and R. Venturini. The compressed permuterm index. *ACM Transactions on Algorithms*, 7(1):10, 2010.

[18] P. Ferragina and R. Venturini. Compressed cache-oblivious String B-tree. In *ESA*, pages 469–480, 2013.

[19] J. Fischer. Optimal succinctness for range minimum queries. In *LATIN*, pages 158–169, 2010.

[20] E. Fredkin. Trie memory. *Communication of the ACM*, 3(9):490–499, Sept. 1960.

[21] M. Gjoka, M. Kurant, C. Butts, and A. Markopoulou. Walking in facebook: a case study of unbiased sampling of osns. In *IEEE Conference on computer communications*, 2010.

[22] B. P. Hsu and G. Ottaviano. Space-efficient data structures for top-k completion. In *WWW*, pages 583–594, 2013.

[23] H. Kwak, C. Lee, H. Park, and S. Moon. What is Twitter, a social network or a news media? In *WWW*, pages 591–600, 2010.

[24] U. Manber and S. Wu. Approximate string matching with arbitrary costs for text and hypertext. In *Proc. IAPR Workshop on Structural and Syntactic Pattern Recognition*, pages 22–33, 1992.

[25] C. D. Manning, P. Raghavan, and H. Schülze. *Introduction to Information Retrieval.* Cambridge University Press, 2008.

[26] K. Mehlhorn and M. H. Overmars. Optimal dynamization of decomposable searching problems. *Inf. Process. Lett.*, 12(2):93–98, 1981.

[27] A. Moffat and L. Stuiver. Binary interpolative coding for effective index compression. *Inf. Retr.*, 3(1):25–47, 2000.

[28] S. Muthukrishnan. Efficient algorithms for document retrieval problems. In *SODA*, pages 657–666, 2002.

[29] G. Navarro. Improved approximate pattern matching on hypertext. In *LATIN*, Lecture Notes in Computer Science, Vol. 1380, pages 352–357, 1998.

[30] G. Ottaviano and R. Venturini. Partitioned Elias-Fano indexes. In *SIGIR*, pages 273–282, 2014.

[31] M. H. Overmars. *The Design of Dynamic Data Structures.* Lecture Notes in Computer Science #156, Springer, 1983.

[32] D. Salomon. *Variable-length Codes for Data Compression.* Springer, 2007.

[33] P. Sarkar and A. W. Moore. Fast nearest-neighbor search in disk-resident graphs. In *ACM SIGKDD*, pages 513–522, 2010.

[34] A. A. Stepanov, A. R. Gangolli, D. E. Rose, R. J. Ernst, and P. S. Oberoi. Simd-based decoding of posting lists. In *CIKM*, pages 317–326, 2011.

[35] F. M. Suchanek and G. Weikum. Knowledge bases in the age of big data analytics. *PVLDB*, 7(13):1713–1714, 2014.

[36] J. Ugander and L. Backstrom. Balanced label propagation for partitioning massive graphs. In *WSDM*, pages 507–516, 2013.

[37] J. Ugander, B. Karrer, L. Backstrom, and C. Marlow. The anatomy of the facebook social graph. In *Preprint* `arXiv:1111.4503v1`, 2011.

[38] S. Vigna. Quasi-succinct indices. In *WSDM*, pages 83–92, 2013.

[39] H. Yan, S. Ding, and T. Suel. Inverted index compression and query processing with imized document ordering. In *WWW*, pages 401–410, 2009.

[40] M. Zukowski, S. Heman, N. Nes, and P. Boncz. Super-scalar RAM-CPU cache compression. In *ICDE*, pages 59–70, 2006.

Improving Paid Microtasks through Gamification and Adaptive Furtherance Incentives

Oluwaseyi Feyisetan
University of Southampton
Southampton, UK
oof1v13@soton.ac.uk

Elena Simperl
University of Southampton
Southampton, UK
e.simperl@soton.ac.uk

Max Van Kleek
University of Southampton
Southampton, UK
emax@ecs.soton.ac.uk

Nigel Shadbolt
University of Southampton
Southampton, UK
nrs@ecs.soton.ac.uk

ABSTRACT

Crowdsourcing via paid microtasks has been successfully applied in a plethora of domains and tasks. Previous efforts for making such crowdsourcing more effective have considered aspects as diverse as task and workflow design, spam detection, quality control, and pricing models. Our work expands upon such efforts by examining the potential of adding gamification to microtask interfaces as a means of improving both worker engagement and effectiveness. We run a series of experiments in image labeling, one of the most common use cases for microtask crowdsourcing, and analyse worker behavior in terms of number of images completed, quality of annotations compared against a gold standard, and response to financial and game-specific rewards. Each experiment studies these parameters in two settings: one based on a state-of-the-art, non-gamified task on CrowdFlower and another one using an alternative interface incorporating several game elements. Our findings show that gamification leads to better accuracy and lower costs than conventional approaches that use only monetary incentives. In addition, it seems to make paid microtask work more rewarding and engaging, especially when sociality features are introduced. Following these initial insights, we define a predictive model for estimating the most appropriate incentives for individual workers, based on their previous contributions. This allows us to build a personalised game experience, with gains seen on the volume and quality of work completed.

Categories and Subject Descriptors

H.4 [**Information Systems Applications**]: Miscellaneous

General Terms

algorithms; experimentation; theory

WWW 2015, May 18–22, 2015, Florence, Italy.
ACM 978-1-4503-3469-3/15/05.
http://dx.doi.org/10.1145/2736277.2741639.

Keywords

crowdsourcing; microtasks; gamification; incentives engineering

1. INTRODUCTION

Crowdsourcing offers a powerful and scalable way of outsourcing knowledge-intensive tasks to a large group of remote contributors over the Internet. Eight years since the concept was first introduced [10], it seems to have found global adoption; virtually any industry, science discipline, or public sector agency could tell a story about how they reached out to the wisdom of the crowds to improve their services and react more flexibly to customer demand, run comprehensive data collection and analysis projects, or collect ideas and views for a better informed policy making [3]. However, with every such success story, it has also become apparent that running crowdsourcing projects effectively is not straightforward and requires in-depth insight into a wide range of topics, including interface design, statistical data analysis, and incentives engineering [15, 16].

One of the most popular forms of online crowdsourcing are paid microtasks. People have tried to understand how to make microtask projects more effective, looking at aspects as diverse as task and workflow design, spam detection, quality control, and pricing models. Our work shares similar aims. We explore the use of gamification in combination with paid microtasks as a means to improve both task performance and worker experience.

We run a series of experiments in image labeling, one of the most common use cases for paid microtask crowdsourcing[1] on platforms such as Amazon Mechanical Turk[2] and CrowdFlower[3], and analyse worker behavior in terms of number of images completed, quality of annotations compared against a golden standard, as well as monetary and game-specific rewards. Each experiment studies these parameters in two settings: one based on a state-of-the-art, non-gamified 'job' on CrowdFlower (i.e., the unit of work on this platform); and another one using an alternative interface incorporating several game elements. The second setting uses CrowdFlower as well, but only to seek contributors; it offers the same reward for the same amount of work as the baseline task, but points to an external page where the gamified version of the task is deployed. More specifically, in the second condition, CrowdFlower

[1]See `http://www.behind-the-enemy-lines.com/2010/10/what-tasks-are-posted-on-mechanical.html`.
[2]Amazon Mechanical Turk - `https://www.mturk.com`
[3]CrowdFlower - `http://www.crowdflower.com`

workers are asked to engage with a game-with-a-purpose (GWAP) [27] called Wordsmith, which was developed for the purpose of these experiments.[4]

When creating Wordsmith, our primary focus was not on coming up with a fundamentally novel game experience to collect image labels, but on building an experimental framework to test our research hypotheses regarding the interplay between monetary and gamification-centric rewards. Overall, our design choices were guided by the four traits that define games: a goal, rules, a feedback system, and voluntary participation [21]. The game elements we implemented are some of the most common in the literature [31]: points, levels, leaderboards, and badges. These components provide feedback and reinforcement, while helping workers judge their progress relative to the end-goal of the task, as well as relative to other workers. We also included progress bars and alerts, which informed on their proximity to level goals. Finally, we put in place elements that enforced the game rules, for example, modules that check for spam, duplicates, and non-English words.

Our basic hypothesis is that by designing a playful interface for the image labeling task - as opposed to the functional style common to most microtask platforms - we will encourage workers to engage with the task more, independently of the actual monetary reward. This hypothesis was confirmed by our findings, which revealed better accuracy (an improvement of almost 10% compared to the baseline condition) and significantly lower costs per annotated image (5,708 unique labels collected via the game vs. 111 unique labels contributed through equivalent, non-gamified microtasks, see Experiment 1 in Section 5). We tested this hypothesis on different variations of image labeling tasks, in which we increased the complexity of the task and adjusted the prices accordingly, observing a similar trend.

Then we looked into the impact of different game elements and related incentives on the behavior of the workers, following the *SAPS framework* (Status, Access, Power, Stuff) presented by [31]. Besides studying how people responded to the primary gamification components (leaderboard, levels, points, and badges), we also introduced a sociality aspect, which was originally missing from the game and allowed contributors to view each others' achievements. Our final incentive dimension was additional cash payment for more work, once the goals of the initial task had been achieved.

These new experiments produced clear evidence of the positive effects of game mechanics on both task performance and crowd engagement; up to five times more unique labels were generated while preserving a comparable level of accuracy (see Experiment 2 in Section 5). This is true particularly for sociality features, which are largely absent on microtask platforms.

Following these insights, we went on to create a predictive model that estimates the most suitable set of incentives for individual workers, based on their previous contributions. This allowed us to build a personalized game experience, with positive results on the volume and quality of work completed. With this model, we were able to obtain 19% more concordant image keywords (4849 vs. 4091) while maintaining the same average pair-wise agreement score. We also recorded a significant uptake in image tagging (with 77% of players tagging an extra image when confronted with targeted incentives against 27% in the experiments using a randomly selected incentive).

Overall, the results of these experiments shed light on possible design improvements of paid microtasks environments in order to achieve better task performance and make the overall experience more fair and rewarding for the workers. While we are not necessarily arguing for a fully-fledged gamification of microtask platforms, considering specific game mechanics [31], or in fact, any social design features that are widely discussed on online communities literature [17] is worth further investigations. This is important not just for purely utilitarian motives on the side of the task requesters, but also in the context of the ongoing debate on ethical and fair crowdsourcing [11].

Previous work has approached such aspects through studies of crowd motivations [14], discussing the rich repertoire of extrinsic and intrinsic reasons that drive people to contribute to microtask projects. Our experiments quantify some of these insights. We deliberately chose a task that is well-known in the crowdsourcing literature, as we were aiming for task-independent findings, which were only minimally influenced by interface or quality control aspects. For the same reasons, we opted for average market prices to reward participation; lower pays would have been less attractive (and unfair) for workers, higher ones might have appealed to people who were primarily financially incentivised. We believe more research needs to be done to build microtask platforms that reflect and support the values and motivations of the crowd as an integral part of their functionality. Our experiments give evidence that such efforts could be be beneficial both workers, and for requesters.

2. BACKGROUND

In this section, we briefly review some of the most relevant prior work pertaining to maximising the effectiveness of incentivised crowdsourcing. In particular, we focus on approaches that use game mechanics in human computation, and on methods that aim to optimize the performance of crowd workers, be that by offering bespoke incentives, or by assigning tasks to those workers who are likely to be able or willing to complete them accurately. As much of this background literature is inspired by, and explained using, theories of human motivation, we touch on fundamental work in that space as well.

2.1 Motivation and incentives

While efforts at designing successful crowdsourcing projects have considered a variety of dimensions, including end-user interfaces, spam detection, and quality control, some of the most influential works in recent crowdsourcing literature have approached this problem by looking at crowd engagement. This is seen as an effective way to achieve better productivity and ensure the sustainability of crowdsourcing platforms over time. Research on crowd engagement covers various aspects, from studies of motivations of contributors to specific projects to applications of theoretical models from economics to the newer scenarios of online labor markets.

Intrinsic and extrinsic motivation Frameworks such as the Self Determination Theory [4] make the distinction between *intrinsic* and *extrinsic* motivation to study the reasons why individuals decide to contribute to a task. The former covers those types of tasks which are perceived as interesting, enjoyable, or rewarding in themselves, and is seen as responsible for engagement in many on and off-line activities, including reading books, socialisation, or participation in virtual worlds and volunteering projects. Extrinsic motives, by contrast, are related to factors that are not inherently related to the actual task, but are appealing for some external reason such as status or reputation within a group. Equally powerful, they underpin a fair share of our contributions to social networks, discussion forums, or community projects.

Theories of external reward and incentivisation
Yet for many classes of tasks, the most reliable way for getting crowd workers engaged remains through explicit external rewards, in particular monetary payment [13]. However, studies have shown

[4]Wordsmith - `http://seyi.feyisetan.com/wordsmith`

that such models are no guarantee for effective crowdsourcing. Where in some cases higher rewards are likely to expedite task completion, they do not necessarily lead to an improved worker performance and attract more spammers [20, 19, 30]. Such scenarios have to consider anchoring effects, caused by discrepancies between perceived work value and actual remuneration, and drop-off effects, where they stop after hitting their self-defined targets no matter how high the additional gains might be [20, 30].

Gamification and its effects Gamification refers to "the use of game design elements in non-game contexts" [7]. It often includes adding game-like rewards, and may also include competitive and social elements, such as leaderboards, explicit competitions, as well as group and individual performance feedback to encourage engagement. Many projects have already demonstrated substantial success in applying this idea to crowdsourcing settings; this applies most prominently for *games-with-a purpose* (GWAPs) [27], which build a game narrative around human computation tasks such as image labeling [26], protein folding,[5] or language translation.[6]

Similarly to the concerns raised in the context of external rewards and incentivisation [18], gamification has been seen, in some context, to undermine intrinsic benefits by subjugating and trivialising contributions into simple game goals and achievements.[7] This effect has been called *overjustification* and has been the subject of various studies with intriguing results; while some negative effects of overjustification have been recurrently reproduced, current research acknowledges the fact that its prevalence seems to be highly dependent on context and that, in most cases, extrinsic rewards complement rather than hamper intrinsic motivations for participating [5, 22].

Comparative studies

Several works have explored such effects by undertaking comparative studies of different forms of crowdsourcing to solve specific tasks. In [25] the authors analysed paid microtasks and a game-with-a-purpose to build a conceptual schema from topics of Wikipedia articles. They reported similar levels of task performance for both approaches, and were concerned by the costs associated with the development and maintenance of a sustainable community of GWAP players. Similarly, a comparison of a purely gamified environment (with no monetary reward) vs standard paid microtasks by Jurgens et al. showed that while comparable quality was achieved from both conditions, the former yielded an overall cost savings (when game development costs were factored in) of 63% overall to achieve task completion [12]. However, the cost savings came at an expense of timely completion; results from the paid microtask platforms were completed in hours, while results from the game approach (Puzzle Racer) trickled in over two weeks.

Meanwhile, a few previous studies have also looked at supplementing monetary reward with gamification, as we do in this paper. A study of crowdsourced judgements on relevance assessments and clustering compared traditional HITs and gamified HITs across the dimensions of quality (compared against a gold standard), efficiency (time required to collect judgements) and incentives (financial vs fun)[8]. Their results show that adding gamification yielded quicker judgements at a higher quality over purely financial incentives. Our work offers a more in-depth study of different types of incentives, alongside a model to predict the most effective type of reward. Other relevant studies in literature include a comparison of crowd-based, game-based, and machine-based approaches by [9].

[5]Fold It - `http://fold.it`

[6]Duolingo - `https://www.duolingo.com/`

[7]Criticisms of Gamification - `http://radar.oreilly.com/gamification-criticism`

2.2 Methods to make crowdsourcing more effective

While in the previous section we primarily looked at prior studies of motivation and incentives aspects in particular scenarios, we will now give an overview of methods which help make crowdsourcing projects more effective by optimizing key components of such projects.

A number of descriptive frameworks have been proposed in the literature to capture the nuances of incentives engineering beyond simplistic *'fun or money'* considerations. Some of these include *MICE* (Money, Ideology, Coercion, Excitement) [2], *RASCLS* (Reciprocation, Authority, Scarcity, Commitment, Liking, Social Proof) [2], and *SAPS* [31]. SAPS represents Status, Access, Power and Stuff, intended to represent a system of incentives from the most desired to the least desired, and the cheapest to the most expensive. We adopted this framework in our experiments.

Mechanisms for effective allocation of incentives have been studied in market and auction platforms, wireless and peer-to-peer networks and corporate organisations. In the context of crowdsourcing, a number of studies have been carried out, applying *game-theory* techniques to incentive design [28, 29]. These two pieces of work focus on financial incentives and a premise of inter-player strategy dependency. Not all crowdsourcing tasks can be modelled in this way; we adopt a probabilistic approach based on prior player behaviours to predict appropriate incentives beyond the purely financial. Similar techniques are used for various purposes in crowdsourcing design, in particular to inform the assignment of tasks to workers or to predict task completion [6, 24].

A large body of work has been dedicated to task and workflow design, as well as quality control (see, for instance, [23] for a recent compilation). We take their findings into account when implementing the basic interfaces published on CrowdFlower as well as the means to check quality and validate results.

3. CROWDSOURCING IMAGE LABELING: OUR APPROACH

In this section, we introduce a high level overview of our approach to crowdsource image labeling. We present our microtask design model and strategies for undertaking crowd work. This involves the use of an external platform, CrowdFlower, and our bespoke game *Wordsmith*.

3.1 Task model

We now describe our model for maximising the output from crowd assigned tasks while maintaining quality.

Task. Each HIT (Human Intelligence Task) consists of n images, $x = \{x_1, ..., x_n\}$, which can each be described by a set of m keywords $k = \{k_1, ..., k_m\}$, where m is a large unknown number. Each task seeks to capture new keywords that correctly describes each image.

Requester. The requester desires to have as many image annotations as possible, without compromising on the quality of the describing keywords. The requester requires the help of human agents to carry out the tasks.

Strategy. We define two requester strategies for presenting tasks. The *crowd* strategy relies on traditional crowdsourcing techniques in a standard "image field - text fields" layout. The *game* strategy employs game mechanisms, and a game based interface to capture keywords. Our nomenclature defines human agents in the crowd strategy as *workers*, and those in the game as *players*.

Crowd $\rightarrow$ Worker. Each worker provides judgement on a task by assigning m keywords $\{k_1, ..., k_m\}$ to n images $\{x_1, ..., x_n\}$ in a traditional crowdsourcing system. We used CrowdFlower as our crowdsourcing platform, presenting each task using the standard image annotation template provided. In this strategy, n and m are defined and fixed by the requester.

Game → Player. Each player provides judgements on a task in a fashion similar to workers in the *crowd* strategy. However, in the *game* strategy, players can tag a variable number of images as they progress through more levels.

Quality. Is defined by consensus. The number of keywords matching a quasi-gold standard bank, gives an overview of the quality of annotations. This was extended to also cover consensual annotations within workers and players - as this suggests probable new keywords for the image.

3.2 Recruitment

We sourced all our human agents from CrowdFlower. For each experiment, we created 2 jobs which channelled task resources to the crowd strategy and game strategy. We used identical settings for each experiment set, consisting of the following parameters:

Geography - limited to the top 15 English speaking countries, and the top CrowdFlower contributor countries.
Skills - we chose *Level 2 Contributors*, which account for 36% of monthly judgements.
Judgements - 3 per unit, which meant each image would be annotated by at least 3 human agents.
Behaviour - each human agent was paid for 1 task, i.e., paid to tag m images, with n keywords, each as determined by the requester. For this, CrowdFlower tracks the IPs and aliases created by the agents.
Reward/Time Limits - reward payment and completion time limits were experimentally set as described later.

3.3 Game design

We designed an image-labelling game called *Wordsmith* for our experimental game conditions. The design was heavily borrowed from the ESP game, with variations described below. The basic elements of Wordsmith consisted of an image frame and text fields for inputting keywords. We describe Wordsmith in terms of the four defining properties of games [21]) as follows: its goal, rules, feedback mechanisms and participation.

Game goal
The goal of the game was to annotate as many images as possible (up to the maximum in the dataset) with descriptive keywords. In designing Wordsmith, we incorporated several elements to engage the player in achieving the goal. We added a colour coded progress timer on each image task and progress bars to track level completion. We also incorporated feed forward alerts to nudge players on when a goal (such as the next level or a new badge) is within reach.

Rules and constraints
Due to the simplicity of Wordsmith as an image labeling game, the rules of Wordsmith merely consist of constraints designed to prevent cheating and input from spam-bots. These constraints consist of a service based English word verification, a restricted-word list to ban common words as players advanced through levels, duplicate checking, and a simple CAPTCHA-like question (e.g. 'What is the current day of the week?') after every 10 image labeling rounds to filter automated processes.

Feedback mechanisms
Feedback consists of information provided to players on their progress and current standing in the game. Providing feedback has been shown to improve player retention and engagement by enhancing intrinsic feelings of accomplishment as players advance. Both social and non-social feedback elements were added to Wordsmith as follows:

1. Leaderboard - showed the hourly scores and level of the top 5 players.
2. Levels - the game consisted of a total of 9 levels from Newbie to Wordsmith. A player's level advancement was a function of how many images were tagged.
3. Badges - were awarded based on the number of images tagged.
4. Feedback Alerts - informed a player how a bonus point or badge was attained and how it can be re-attained.
5. Bonus Points - were awarded when players submitted keywords that matched 1, 2, or 3 known images tags.
6. Treasure Points - were awarded when players got multiples of 10 bonus points.
7. Activities Widget - displayed in realtime, what other players were doing in the game.

Voluntary participation
The final trait was to present the task within the game as what the player chose to do rather than what they were mandated to do. In this regard, Wordsmith supported player freedom in three ways; first, participation of course was purely optional and anonymous, and they could join without registering (filling out a form or providing any personal details). Second, players could terminate at any time; finally, an image skip feature was provided so they could freely skip images they were not interested in.

3.4 Furtherance incentives

In Experiment 2, we introduce "*furtherance incentives*" to Conditions 3 and 4, which is a reward or concession presented to a player when they attempt to exit the game to induce them to stay and play more levels. We selected our incentives based on the SAPS framework presented by [31].

In our experiment, we expanded *Status* from SAPS to encompass the 3 game status elements mentioned by [31], i.e., badges, leaderboard and levels. We interpreted the SAPS incentives as a popup messages presented to the player at the point of attempted exit. Each incentive began with the message: Would you like to tag the next *"target number"* images? If the player had tagged less than 21 images, the "*target number*" of additional images was 5, otherwise it was 11.

The specific messages appended to each incentive is as follows:

- **Badges** - You would automatically be rewarded with The 'Ultimate' Badge. Get upgraded to a shiny new avatar
- **Leaderboard** - You would automatically be advanced on The Global Leaderboard. Get seen globally on the leaderboard
- **Levels** - You would automatically be advanced to The Next Level. Advance to the next level.
- **Access** - You would be given quicker access to Treasure Points. Get more treasure in half the time.
- **Power** - You would be rewarded with the power to View Other Players Tags. Power to see other players image tags.
- **Stuff** - You would be rewarded with a bonus of 5 cents extra. More cash for your effort.

At each point of attempted exit, a player was shown one of the 6 furtherance incentives

$V = \{badges, leaderboard, levels, access, power, money\}$

The choice of the incentive to be shown was decided by drawing a random variable $V \backsim U([0,1])$

At the moment of incentive offer, we record the incentive offered, the requested target number, the number of images tagged so far (as start_tags and end_tags) and the current timestamp. We then recorded the player's game state after the incentive was presented i.e., the player could ignore the incentive and exit the game (*state=out*), or the player could go on playing the game (*state=in*).

If the player remains in *state = in*, we keep track of game play (updating the number of images tagged as end_tags) until the player has tagged an additional "target images". At this point, the offered incentive is activated. Players can then transition into state in or out. If a player attempts to exit the game at this point, we do not show any furtherance incentive. However, if the player remains in the game, we continue to keep track of the number of images tagged, and therefore update the value for end_tags.

3.5 Adjusting incentives probabilistically

In the final condition (Experiment 4), we posit that certain furtherance incentives are more effective at different stages of gameplay. To test this hypothesis, we computed a probabilistic model that estimates, at every potential game exit point, the incentive that would maximize the probability of the player remaining in the game. To do this, our probabilsitic model computes *a priori* state transitions at previous attempted exit points, to predict what incentive a player would accept given the number of images they have tagged. This model is computed from:

1. ***the prior probability*** of the incentive given the incentive distribution obtained from the results of the random incentives condition (Experiment 4 Condition 3)
2. ***the likelihood probability*** of the player remaining in the game after tagging the current number of images given a certain offered incentive and
3. ***the likelihood probability*** of the player remaining in the game after tagging a set of images (defined over a numeric range), given a certain offered incentive.

The details of the reasoning approach is detailed in the next few sections.

Our probabilistic reasoning approach to computing the maximum a posteriori incentive given our selected feature (the number of tagged images) is similar to the method of determining the correctness of worker results by [6].

We compute the posterior as the maximum conditional probability of the incentive *v* at a given point *x* using Bayesian inferencing as shown in the equation below:

$$\Pr(v|x, s = in) = \frac{\Pr(x|v, s = in) \Pr(v|s = in)}{\Pr(x|s = in)} \quad (1)$$

where:
v is a potential incentive to be shown to the player.
x is the number of images a player has tagged so far.
s is the state of a player being in or out of the game.
Pr(v|x,s=in) is the posterior of the incentive given the number of images the player has tagged.
Pr(v|s=in) is the prior probability of the incentive i.e., the probability of any player at any given point accepting this incentive.
Pr(x|v,s=in) is the likelihood at the current game point that the player would accept the given incentive.

3.5.1 Definitions

Image point
$x \in X = \{1, ..., N\} where N = 2,200$.
Represents the number of images a player has tagged at the point of an attempted game exit.

Game states
$s \in S = \{out, in\}$
Represents the state a game player is in after attempting to exit the game at an image point.

Incentive
$v \in V = \{badges, leaderboard, levels, access, power, money\}$
Represents the set of incentives from which v is drawn to be presented to the player at the point of attempted exit.

Image Band
$b = (x_i, x_j) = \{b \in \mathbb{R} \mid x_i < b < x_j\}$
Represents a range over image points x_i to x_j over which players exhibit similar exit pattern behaviours.

3.5.2 Prior distributions

Our prior distributions come from the results of random incentives presented to players. We compute the *objective prior* of the incentive *v* as given by the sum and product rule in Bayes Theorem:

$$\Pr(v|s = in) = \frac{\sum_{x=1}^{N} \Pr(s = in|v, x)}{\sum_{x=1}^{N} \sum_{v \in V}^{V} \Pr(s = in|v, x)} \quad (2)$$

This represents the number of players that remained in state *s = in*, at image point *x* after being shown incentive v over all image points x ∈ X, compared with all the players that remained in state *s = in*, at image point *x* after being shown any incentive v in the set of all incentives V over all image points x ∈ X.

As an example, given that 100 players remained in state *s = in* after they were shown any incentive v ∈ V over all image points x ∈ X = {1, ..., 2,200}. If 29 of such players (who remained in the game) were shown incentive v = "*power*", then the prior of the incentive "*power*" over all image points is 29/100 or 29%.

3.5.3 Likelihood distributions

We also compute the likelihood at each image point x, of a worker remaining in state *s = in* given an incentive v. The likelihood represents the conditional probability

$$P(x|v, s = in)$$

at image point x. Our likelihood function was a product of 2 variables: (a) the image point likelihood and (b) the image band likelihood.

Image point likelihood
For each incentive v, we calculate the image point likelihood at point x as:

$$\Pr(x|v, s = in) = \frac{\Pr(s = in, x|v)}{\sum_{s \in S}^{S} \Pr(s, x|v)} \quad (3)$$

This represents how many players remained in state *s = in*, at image point *x* after being shown incentive *v* at image point *x*, compared with all observations of state changes at image point *x* after being shown incentive *v*.

As an example, given that 3 players attempted to stop playing the game after tagging 11 images (image point x = 11) and the 3 players were all shown the incentive v = "*power*". If 2 of the players go on to tag the 12th image, then we calculate the likelihood of a player remaining in state s=in, at the 11th image, when shown "power" as 2/3.

For image points where we do not have any observed behaviours, i.e., where no player had attempted to exit the game at a certain image point x, we apply the principle of indifference (*principle of maximum entropy*) to accommodate these latent variables.

$$P(x|v, s = in) = 1/N \ \forall \ x \in N = \{1, ..., N\} \quad (4)$$

The variable x here represents the image point while N = 2, representing 2 possible states s = {in, out}. Therefore, for unobserved image points,

$$P(x|v, s = in) = P(s = in) = P(s = out) = 0.5 \quad (5)$$

Image band likelihoods
To further accommodate for latent variables and present an expressive picture of how players behave after tagging a certain numbered range of images, we introduced image band likelihoods.

Image Band
$b = (x_i, x_j) = \{b \in \mathbb{R} \mid x_i < b < x_j\}$
Represents a range over image points x_i to x_j over which players exhibit similar exit pattern behaviours.

The image bands b ∈ B were elicited by observations over the results from the randomised incentive condition and they are:

$$B = \{0 - 11, 12 - 60, 61 - 100, 101 - 200, 201 - 2200\}$$

The image band likelihoods were computed on an incentives basis, as such:

$$\sum_{b \in B}^{B} \Pr(s = in, b|v) = 1 \quad (6)$$

For each incentive v, we calculate the image band likelihood over band b as:

$$\Pr(b|v, s = in) = \frac{\Pr(s = in, b|v)}{\sum_{s \in S}^{S} \Pr(s, b|v)} \quad (7)$$

This represents how many players remained in state $s = in$, within image band b, after being shown incentive v, compared with all players who remained in state $s = in$, over all image bands b ∈ B, after being shown incentive v.

As an example, given that 100 players remained in state $s = in$ after they were shown incentive v = "*power*" over all image points x ∈ X = 1, ..., 2,200. If 16 players go on to tag 1 more image within the range of image points x_i, x_j = (12,60) = 12 < b < 60, then the image band likelihood of "12-60" given incentive v = "*power*" is 16/100 or 16%.

3.5.4 Updating the likelihoods

As the experiment runs, we continuously take into account the behaviour of players at each image point. With each new observation at an image point, we recalculate the likelihood of remaining in state $s = in$, at image point x after being shown incentive v. Therefore, our probabilistic model iteratively updates the likelihoods by constantly learning and taking into account new data based on player interaction. This is of particular importance in filling in revised parameters for the earlier unobserved image points.

As an example, given an image point $x = 20$, where there had been no earlier observations in *experiment 4* of a player exit after being shown incentive v = "*power*". The image point likelihood would be assigned the default of 0.5 (*principle of maximum entropy*), computed as 2 observations with 1 observation at state $s = in$. If a new observation occurs (for any given player) at the image point $x = 20$ for incentive v = "*power*" and the player transitions to state $s = out$, the image point likelihood is updated to 3 observations with 1 observation at state $s = in$ = 0.33.

3.5.5 Computing the posteriors

Given the incentive prior P(v|s=in) when a player remains in the game, the image point likelihood $\Pr(x|v, s = in)$ and the image band likelihood $\Pr(b|v, s = in)$, we are able to compute the best incentive to offer a player at image point x as the incentive that maximizes the posterior given as

$$\arg\max_v \Pr(v|x) = \Pr(j|v, s = in) \Pr(v|s = in) \quad (8)$$

where the joint likelihood of the image point and the image band is given as:

$$\Pr(j|v, s = in) = \Pr(x|v, s = in) \Pr(b|v, s = in)$$

The incentive is then offered to the player and the ensuing state transition is recorded as a new observation point to update the image point likelihood given that incentive.

3.5.6 Algorithms

We now present the algorithm for the image point likelihoods for an incentive and the algorithm for calculating the incentive posteriors at any given image point.

Result: Likelihood P(x|v) = inx/obv
Parameter: v = incentive;
Initialize Latent Variables;
Image Points: x = {1,...,N};
Observations at x: obv = 2;
State = in at x: inx = 1;
for *x in Image Points* **do**
    if *state = in at x* **then**
        obv += 1;
        inx += 1;
    else
        obv += 1;
    end
end

Algorithm 1: Image point likelihoods for incentive v

4. EXPERIMENT DESIGN

This section details the experiments we carried out. We ran 2 experiments. Experiment 1 had 2 conditions - (a) CrowdFlower (non gamified) condition; (b) Wordsmith (gamified) condition. Experiment 2 had 4 conditions - (a) Non gamified condition; (b) Gamified condition (without furtherance incentives); (c) Gamified condition (with random furtherance incentives); (d) Gamified condition (with targeted furtherance incentives).

4.1 Research hypotheses

Our work was centered around 3 potential ways in which gamification can be used to improve paid microtasks:

1. Gamifying paid micro-tasks leads to increased worker engagement, culminating in more work done for less cost.
2. Gamifying paid micro-tasks leads to higher inter-annotator agreement, yielding higher quality results than without.
3. Targeting incentives when a player attempts to quit leads to increased engagement.

Result: Posterior Incentive: $\arg\max_v \Pr(v|x)$
Parameter: x = image point;
Initialize Latent Variables;
Incentive v at x: vx = { };
Posteriors Tracker: pt = {levels = 0, ..., power = 0};
Min Tags: min = 11;
Max Tags: max = 2,200;
for *image tag x from min to max* **do**
  $\Pr(v|x)\ \forall\ v \in V$;
  $\Pr(v|x) = \Pr(v).\Pr(b|v).\Pr(x|v)$;
  Incentive Identifier iid = 0;
  Selected Incentive vx = $\Pr(v|x)$ at iid;
  Update Posteriors Tracker $ptatvx+ = 1$;
  Max Incentive Assignment $mia = \Pr(v) * (max - min)$
  if *pt at vx < mia* **then**
    return vx;
  else
    return vx = $\Pr(v|x)$ at iid + 1;
  end
end

Algorithm 2: Incentive posteriors at image point x

To test these hypothesis, we carried out 2 experiments in image labelling. Workers were shown an image, and asked to assign keywords that describe the image. To test the first two hypotheses, we chose a between-subjects design where the control condition consisted of a standard, non-gamified interface, using CrowdFlower's image labelling job; while the experimental condition, consisted of a gamified interface incorporating several game elements. Both conditions relied on CrowdFlower for worker recruitment, but while workers performed tasks directly within CrowdFlower for the control condition, workers assigned the experimental were redirected to an external game site. Participants in both setups were paid the same amount.

To test the 3rd hypothesis, we carried out 2 additional condition setups on our gamified interface, again with players sourced and redirected from CrowdFlower. In the control condition, workers were shown a randomly-selected incentive to stay when they attempted to leave the game. In the experimental condition, an incentive was shown selected based upon a predictive model constructed from the previous worker's task history. The details of this predictive model was presented earlier in Section 3.5.

4.2 Dataset

For our experiments, we used the ESP game dataset from [26]. This comprises of 100,000 images and about 1.4 million image tags. For each experiment, we selected the images in the dataset which had the highest number of keyword tags associated with it. This was used as a sort of quasi-ground truth, for checking basic tagging quality and assigning bonus points.

4.3 Evaluation metrics

To evaluate worker performance, we measured both the volume of work completed and work quality. To assess the volume of work completed, we simply measured the average number of keywords provided per image. To assess work quality, we used two measures: overlap with the gold standard keywords in the dataset, and a standard measure of inter-annotator agreement from [1] to determine the degree of the pairwise consensus of image labels which were not in the gold standard datset.

For Experiment 2 condition 4, we sought to evaluate the effectiveness of targeted incentives over random ones. To do this, we used as a measure the number of players that tagged at least 1 more image after they were shown each particular incentive. The incentive was shown when they attempted to stop playing the game.

4.4 Experimental conditions

In this section, we summarise both experiments and their conditions in detail.

Experiment 1: *Task: Tag 1 Image with at least 2 keywords; Source dataset size: 200 images; Workers: 600; Payment: $0.02; Platforms: CrowdFlower and Wordsmith.* In the first experiment, workers in either condition were required to tag 1 image with 2 keywords. In Wordsmith, the gamified condition, this corresponded to advancing 1 level into the game. Players in Wordsmith could continue playing the game (tagging more images) after completing the required annotation. There were 200 images in the dataset. Participants were paid 2 cents for the image tagged.

Experiment 2: *Task: Tag 11 images with at least 2 images each; Source dataset size: 2,200; Workers: 600; Payment: $0.10; Platforms: Crowdflower and Wordsmith; Furtherance Incentives:none, random or targeted.* In experiment 2, workers were required to tag 11 images with keywords. However, the dataset size was increased 11 fold (from 200 to 2,200) to allow players to play for longer without seeing repeated images. Intermediate results had shown a number of players tagged the entire dataset of 200 images. This experiment consisted of 4 conditions detailed below. In addition, for conditions 3 and 4, furtherance incentives, defined in Section 3.4 are introduced when players attempt to quit.

Experiment 2 - Condition 1: *Platform: CrowdFlower; Furtherance Incentives: none.* This was a non gamified setup where workers were required to tag 11 images from a dataset of 2,200 images for 10 cents.

Experiment 2 - Condition 2: *Platform: Wordsmith; Furtherance Incentives: none.* In this gamified setup, players were required to tag 11 images from a dataset of 2,200 images for 10 cents. This advanced them 2 levels into the game. The players could continue tagging (playing the game) if they wished.

Experiment 2 - Condition 3: *Platform: Wordsmith; Furtherance Incentives: Random.* Identical to Condition 2, except a random furtherance incentive is presented when a player attempted to exit the game.

Experiment 2 - Condition 4: *Platform: Wordsmith; Furtherance Incentives: Targeted.* Identical to Condition 3, except that the furtherance incentive was selected according to the maximum likelihood of user retention using the probabilistic model presented in Section 3.5.

5. RESULTS

The result of Experiment 1 is summarised in Table 1. The results show that players (participants in the game condition) supplied more keywords than those in the CrowdFlower condition on average (97 per image vs 2), and labeling more images overall (32 per worker vs 1), resulting in an overall yield of 41,206 total keywords vs 1,200 in the control condition. We note that, since the control condition restricted workers to supply up to two keywords for a single image, it is unsurprising that individuals in the control condition provided only two keywords for a single image. However, in both conditions, individuals were rewarded only up through the same amount of work (completing the task of supplying 2 keywords for a single image), and thus the additional work done in the Wordsmith condition was not financially incentivised and done for free. Moreover, compared to the control, the experimental condition yielded significantly more *new keywords*, which we define to be keywords that were not in the original gold standard seed, but achieved the requisite threshold of inter-annotator agreement. The average inter-annotator agreement, computed as described in 4.3 over all images for the control condition was also much less than that of the experimental condition (5.72% vs 37.7%). The control condition achieved 42.9% coverage of the original gold standard label set, while the experimental condition covered 52.5%.

Table 2 summarises the results for Experiment 2. Again, compared with the CrowdFlower interface, all game conditions saw much greater output, both in terms of labels per image (average 40,510 keywords across game conditions vs 13,200 in the control condition) and number of images tagged (30 images labeled per worker across game conditions vs 11) despite monetary compensation being held constant between conditions (10 cents to complete 11 images with 2 labels each). Examining the game conditions only, conditions 3 and 4 which featured furtherance incentives on exit attempt resulted in players performing more labels on average (31.5 vs 27) than condition 2, which had no furtherance incentives. We note that due to the much larger source dataset of images, the likelihood that two workers would be presented the same image is much lower, resulting overall in noisier inter-rater agreement and lower coverage of gold-standard labels.

To analyse player response to furtherance incentives, Table 4 shows the number of players who responded to each furtherance incentive stimulus type at various levels of play (image bands). To clarify, we considered a player to be *responding to the incentive stimulus* when, upon attempting to quit the game *and* being presented with a furtherance incentive, decided to tag at least 1 extra image prior to exiting. The table shows the number of responses of the number of presentations of each stimuli for each (C3 random and C4 targeted) condition at 5 image image bands, corresponding to the number of images previously tagged when attempting to exit. Comparing randomised to targeted incentive, the results show greater response to furtherance incentives when delivered in the targeted incentive condition (C4) than randomised (C3). In the targeted incentives condition, 77% of players went on to tag at least 1 more image, compared with only 27% in the randomised condition.

With respect to furtherance incentive type, direct comparison is in Table 4 due to the fact that the number of stimulus presentations differ for different types and conditions. We constructed Table 3 to make this comparison further, which simply shows a breakdown, by type, of all successful furtherance incentive stimulus responses. As can be seen, in both C3 (Randomised) and C4 (Targeted), the Power and Money incentives made up the top two successful incentives, with Money comprising the largest share of the targeted successes. We discuss these results in the next section.

Experiment 1		
Metric	CrowdFlower (control)	Wordsmith (experimental)
Total workers	600	423
Total keywords	1,200	41,206
New keywords	111	5,708
Avg. agreement	5.72%	37.7%
Gold keywords	42.92%	52.53%
Mean Imgs/person	1	32
Max Imgs/person	1	200

Table 1: *Experiment 1 Results* - High level results for Experiment 1, comparing number of keywords and images tagged in the gamified (Wordsmith) condition compared to the standard CrowdFlower interface.

Incentive	C3: Randomised	C4: Targeted
Power	26.09%	30.16%
Money	19.65%	46.17%
Leaderboard	16.59%	5.71%
Levels	13.01%	7.34%
Badges	13.04%	5.98%
Access	11.61%	4.35%

Table 3: *Incentive Response Distribution* - Successful furtherance incentives stimuli broken down by type, for both C3 (randomised) and C4 (targeted) conditions.

6. DISCUSSION AND CONCLUSION

In this section, we first briefly re-visit our results in the context of the research hypotheses, discussing limitations in the process. We then discuss implications of our findings to crowdsourcing, and conclude with a summary of ongoing and future work.

The results show support for all three of our research hypotheses. With respect to H1, players in the game condition unilaterally performed more tasks even when they were not explicitly incentivised with monetary reward to do so. In addition, output was of higher quality, showing support for H2, both when measured in terms of diversity (new words with high agreement) and achieved consistent coverage of the gold standard labels than the control condition. In particular, we saw no support for overjustification in these results, which would have been manifest in reduced productivity with the introduction of game elements.

One limitation of our experimental design is that, since the number of contributions in the control interface was clamped while the game condition was not (meaning they could contribute indefinitely), it is not meaningful to quantify the increased volume of work between the control and gamification conditions. However, we can compare quality differences (which showed significant gains), and volume differences among just the game conditions in Experiment 2, when targeted furtherance incentives were shown to yield higher volumes of work than randomised ones (H3).

However, perhaps more significantly, this study demonstrated that even simple furtherance incentivisation methods do work towards getting players to complete more tasks. In all but the Money furtherance incentive condition, such methods worked to increase output at no extra cost. Moreover, we found that among furtherance incentivisation strategies, those that were more social generally fared better than those that were personal; for example, the Power incentive was presented "*You would be rewarded with the power to view other players' tags*", while the Leaderboard incentive promised participants a higher place on the leaderboard, which was visible to everyone. This agrees with previous work in GWAPs such as the the ESP Game, in particular [26]) in which social incentives were shown to be among the most powerful. Most human computation environments, like Mechanical Turk, CrowdFlower and citizen science projects still lack elements that promote social visibility that might improve engagement.

The effectiveness of money as an effective furtherance incentive was somewhat surprising, given the fact that most participants already performed free labour, that is, work beyond the minimum that was asked of them to get their initial reward. Therefore, it could be concluded that these participants were motivated to do this additional work for other reasons. However, when financial reward is re-introduced as a furtherance incentive, it effectively motivated people to complete more work. Further analysis is required to understand to what extent such monetary rewards could compel con-

Experiment 2				
	CrowdFlower (Non-gamified)	Wordsmith (Gamified)		
	C1: No furtherance	C2: No furtherance	C3: Random furtherance	C4: Targeted furtherance
Total workers	600	514	543	454
Total keywords	13,200	35,890	47,418	38,223
New keywords	1,323	4,091	5,435	4,849
Avg. agreement	6.32%	10.90%	10.16%	9.86%
Gold keywords	48.42%	45.02%	41.21%	47.10%
Mean Imgs/person	11	27	33	30
Max. Imgs/person	11	351	501	540

Table 2: *Experiment 2 Results* - High level summary of work output and quality comparing non-gamified (C1) and gamified (C2, C3, C4) conditions.

Image Band	11		12-60		61-100		101-200		201-2,200	
	Random	Targeted	Random	Targeted	Random	Targeted	Random	Targeted	Random	Targeted
Power	26.67% (4/15)	70.97% (22/31)	33.33% (9/27)	74.68% (59/79)	55.55% (5/9)	80.95% (17/21)	25.00% (2/8)	100.00% (5/5)	100.00% (3/3)	61.54% (8/13)
Money	23.53% (4/17)	88.24% (75/85)	34.78% (8/23)	77.57% (83/107)	66.67% (2/3)	100.00% (2/2)	40.00% (2/5)	100.00% (6/6)	0.00% (0/0)	100.00% (5/5)
Leaderboard	21.43% (3/14)	0.00% (0/1)	10.00% (3/30)	70.00% (7/10)	33.33% (1/3)	100.00% (1/1)	70.00% (7/10)	57.14% (12/21)	75.00% (3/4)	100.00% (1/1)
Levels	13.04% (3/23)	40.00% (2/5)	18.18% (6/33)	69.57% (16/23)	75.00% (3/4)	100.00% (3/3)	16.67% (1/6)	100.00% (3/3)	100.00% (2/2)	100.00% (3/3)
Badges	0.00% (0/0)	0.00% (0/1)	22.22% (4/18)	63.63% (7/11)	16.67% (1/6)	100.00% (3/3)	66.67% (4/6)	90% (9/10)	66.67% (2/3)	75.00% (3/4)
Access	11.76% (2/17)	0.00% (0/0)	17.24% (5/29)	33.33% (5/15)	33.33% (3/9)	50.00% (2/4)	20.00% (1/5)	100.00% (3/3)	100.00% (1/1)	100.00% (6/6)

Table 4: *Furtherance Incentive responses (Results of Experiment 2 Condition 3 & 4)* Percentage of players in who responded to each Furtherance Incentive broken down by type (Power, Money, Leaderboard, Levels, Badges and Access), and condition (randomised vs targeted). The number of incentive prompts delivered for each type are listed by the responded percentage.

tinued participation, and the optimal amounts of reward for doing so.

As our experiments only tested one type of crowdsourced task and GWAP, namely image labeling, the results may not necessarily apply to all task types. In particular, tasks that require high cognitive load, require significant time investment or creative thought may not benefit from game mechanics due to their intensive nature. Moreover, those kinds of crowdsourced tasks driven by strong intrinsic motivations (such as citizen science, disaster relief, and so on) are unlikely to substantially benefit from these results because such motivations will probably overshadow the simpler incentives tested here. Moreover, such intrinsic motivation settings have been shown to be more prone to overjustification effects, and thus may result in actually reduced participation. We wish to test whether such effects will become present in such settings in future experiments.

Among our ongoing efforts, we wish to better understand how and why the incentives work in the ways and to the extent that they do. In particular, we believe that furtherance incentives could be more effective if carefully distributed within the game mechanics so that they appear at appropriate intervals when motivation begins to wane, not only after the participant has initiated an attempt to leave.

Second, we wish to the improve the probabilistic model to take into account other aspects of players' performance, task history and demographic, and to understand the ways in estimating appropriate rewards. In particular, we wish to run further experiments to determine whether incentives are more effective for particular demographics than for others, or for workers at particular skill levels or task completion histories.

In addition, we would like to investigate further social effects of furtherance incentives. In this experiment, levels and badges were merely to mark a player's own progress; however, these might be made more effective if such rewards were made visible to other players and seen as a form of status. Such status has been shown to effectively encourage participation in online communities [17] and may translate well to microtask environments as well. Moreover, all of the incentives we applied in this experiment were positive, individual incentives; we next wish to explore the effectiveness of other types of incentives such as positive social incentives (e.g., members of an entire group get a reward), as well as negative incentives both as in-game elments and furtherance incentives. Finally, we would like to understand the span of furtherance incentives, and potential avenues for extending the effects of such incentives in various ways.

In summary, our results have shown that very adding gamification to crowdsourced micro-tasks that already have external incentives can improve the quality and quantity of work completed. Our results complement previous work comparing purely gamified and paid crowdsourcing, and extend previous results with a look at multiple kinds of furtherance incentives, combined with reward adaptation. Although we have shown social incentives and supplemental monetary rewards outperform other such incentives, and demonstrated a simple probabilistic model able to outperform a randomised strategy, we believe that we have only begun to understand the relationships that such incentives have on subjective worker experience and sustained engagement in the long term, and plan to continue to pursue such investigations in the future.

7. REFERENCES

[1] P. K. Bhowmick, P. Mitra, and A. Basu. An agreement measure for determining inter-annotator reliability of human judgements on affective text. In *Proceedings of the Workshop on Human Judgements in Computational Linguistics*, pages 58–65. Association for Computational Linguistics, 2008.

[2] R. Burkett. An alternative framework for agent recruitment: From mice to rascls. In *Studies in Intelligence*, volume 57 of *1*, pages 7–17, mar 2013.

[3] R. Dawson and S. Bynghall. *Getting Results from Crowds*. Advanced Human Technologies, 2012.

[4] E. Deci and R. Ryan. *Intrinsic Motivation and Self-Determination in Human Behavior*. Perspectives in Social Psychology. Springer, 1985.

[5] E. L. Deci, R. Koestner, and R. M. Ryan. A meta-analytic review of experiments examining the effects of extrinsic rewards on intrinsic motivation. *Psychological bulletin*, 125(6):627, 1999.

[6] G. Demartini, D. E. Difallah, and P. Cudré-Mauroux. Large-scale linked data integration using probabilistic reasoning and crowdsourcing. *The VLDB Journal*, 22(5):665–687, Oct. 2013.

[7] S. Deterding, R. Khaled, L. Nacke, and D. Dixon. Gamification: Toward a definition. In *CHI 2011 Gamification Workshop Proceedings*, pages 12–15, 2011.

[8] C. Eickhoff, C. G. Harris, A. P. de Vries, and P. Srinivasan. Quality through flow and immersion: Gamifying crowdsourced relevance assessments. In *Proceedings of the 35th International ACM SIGIR Conference on Research and Development in Information Retrieval*, SIGIR '12, pages 871–880, New York, NY, USA, 2012. ACM.

[9] C. Harris and P. Srinivasan. Comparing crowd-based, game-based, and machine-based approaches in initial query and query refinement tasks. In P. Serdyukov, P. Braslavski, S. Kuznetsov, J. Kamps, S. RÃijger, E. Agichtein, I. Segalovich, and E. Yilmaz, editors, *Advances in Information Retrieval*, volume 7814 of *Lecture Notes in Computer Science*, pages 495–506. Springer Berlin Heidelberg, 2013.

[10] J. Howe. The rise of crowdsourcing. *Wired magazine*, 14(6):1–4, 2006.

[11] L. C. Irani and M. Silberman. Turkopticon: Interrupting worker invisibility in amazon mechanical turk. In *Proceedings of the SIGCHI Conference on Human Factors in Computing Systems*, pages 611–620. ACM, 2013.

[12] D. Jurgens and R. Navigli. It's All Fun and Games until Someone Annotates: Video Games with a Purpose for Linguistic Annotation. *Transactions of the Association for Computational Linguistics (TACL)*, 2:449–464, 2014.

[13] N. Kaufmann, T. Schulze, and D. Veit. More than fun and money. worker motivation in crowdsourcing - a study on mechanical turk. In *AMCIS'11*, pages –1–1, 2011.

[14] N. Kaufmann, T. Schulze, and D. Veit. More than fun and money. worker motivation in crowdsourcing: a study on mechanical turk. In *Proceedings of the Seventeenth Americas Conference on Information Systems*, pages 1–11, 2011.

[15] M. Kearns. Experiments in social computation. *Commun. ACM*, 55(10):56–67, 2012.

[16] A. Kittur, E. H. Chi, and B. Suh. Crowdsourcing user studies with mechanical turk. In *Proceedings of the SIGCHI Conference on Human Factors in Computing Systems*, CHI '08, pages 453–456, 2008.

[17] R. E. Kraut, P. Resnick, S. Kiesler, M. Burke, Y. Chen, N. Kittur, J. Konstan, Y. Ren, and J. Riedl. *Building successful online communities: Evidence-based social design*. Mit Press, 2012.

[18] M. R. Lepper, D. Greene, and R. E. Nisbett. Undermining children's intrinsic interest with extrinsic reward: A test of the" overjustification" hypothesis. *Journal of Personality and social Psychology*, 28(1):129, 1973.

[19] A. Mao, E. Kamar, Y. Chen, E. Horvitz, M. E. Schwamb, C. J. Lintott, and A. M. Smith. Volunteering versus work for pay: Incentives and tradeoffs in crowdsourcing. In B. Hartman and E. Horvitz, editors, *HCOMP*. AAAI, 2013.

[20] W. Mason and D. J. Watts. Financial incentives and the "performance of crowds". In *Proceedings of the ACM SIGKDD Workshop on Human Computation*, HCOMP '09, pages 77–85, New York, NY, USA, 2009. ACM.

[21] J. McGonigal. *Reality Is Broken: Why Games Make Us Better and How They Can Change the World*. Penguin Group , The, 2011.

[22] C. Mellström and M. Johannesson. Crowding out in blood donation: was titmuss right? *Journal of the European Economic Association*, 6(4):845–863, 2008.

[23] P. Michelucci. *Handbook of human computation*. Springer, 2013.

[24] V. S. Sheng, F. Provost, and P. G. Ipeirotis. Get another label? improving data quality and data mining using multiple, noisy labelers. In *Proceedings of the 14th ACM SIGKDD international conference on Knowledge discovery and data mining*, pages 614–622. ACM, 2008.

[25] S. Thaler, E. Simperl, and S. Wölger. An experiment in comparing human-computation techniques. *IEEE Internet Computing*, pages 52–58, 2012.

[26] L. von Ahn and L. Dabbish. Labeling images with a computer game. In *Proceedings of the SIGCHI Conference on Human Factors in Computing Systems*, CHI '04, pages 319–326, New York, NY, USA, 2004. ACM.

[27] L. von Ahn and L. Dabbish. Designing games with a purpose. *Commun. ACM*, 51(8):58–67, Aug. 2008.

[28] H. Xie and J. C. Lui. Modeling crowdsourcing systems: Design and analysis of incentive mechanism and rating system. *SIGMETRICS Perform. Eval. Rev.*, 42(2):52–54, Sept. 2014.

[29] D. Yang, G. Xue, X. Fang, and J. Tang. Crowdsourcing to smartphones: Incentive mechanism design for mobile phone sensing. In *Proceedings of the 18th Annual International Conference on Mobile Computing and Networking*, Mobicom '12, pages 173–184, New York, NY, USA, 2012. ACM.

[30] M. Yin, Y. Chen, and Y. Sun. The effects of performance-contingent financial incentives in online labor markets. In *Proceedings of the Twenty-Seventh AAAI Conference on Artificial Intelligence, July 14-18, 2013, Bellevue, Washington, USA.*, 2013.

[31] G. Zichermann and C. Cunningham. *Gamification by Design: Implementing Game Mechanics in Web and Mobile Apps*. 2011.

Tagging Personal Photos with Transfer Deep Learning

Jianlong Fu [1]*, Tao Mei [2], Kuiyuan Yang [2], Hanqing Lu [1], and Yong Rui [2]
[1]National Laboratory of Pattern Recognition, Institute of Automation, Chinese Academy of Sciences
No. 95, Zhongguancun East Road, Beijing 100190, China
[2]Microsoft Research, No. 5, Dan Ling Street, Haidian District, Beijing 10080, China
[1]{jlfu, luhq}@nlpr.ia.ac.cn, [2]{tmei, kuyang, yongrui}@microsoft.com

ABSTRACT

The advent of mobile devices and media cloud services has led to the unprecedented growing of personal photo collections. One of the fundamental problems in managing the increasing number of photos is automatic image tagging. Existing research has predominantly focused on tagging general Web images with a well-labelled image database, e.g., ImageNet. However, they can only achieve limited success on personal photos due to the domain gaps between personal photos and Web images. These gaps originate from the differences in semantic distribution and visual appearance. To deal with these challenges, in this paper, we present a novel transfer deep learning approach to tag personal photos. Specifically, to solve the semantic distribution gap, we have designed an ontology consisting of a hierarchical vocabulary tailored for personal photos. This ontology is mined from 10,000 active users in Flickr with 20 million photos and 2.7 million unique tags. To deal with the visual appearance gap, we discover the intermediate image representations and ontology priors by deep learning with bottom-up and top-down transfers across two domains, where Web images are the source domain and personal photos are the target. Moreover, we present two modes (single and batch-modes) in tagging and find that the batch-mode is highly effective to tag photo collections. We conducted personal photo tagging on 7,000 real personal photos and personal photo search on the MIT-Adobe FiveK photo dataset. The proposed tagging approach is able to achieve a performance gain of 12.8% and 4.5% in terms of NDCG@5, against the state-of-the-art hand-crafted feature-based and deep learning-based methods, respectively.

Categories and Subject Descriptors

H.3.1 [**Information Storage and Retrieval**]: Content Analysis and Indexing; I.2.6 [**Artificial Intelligence**]: Learning

General Terms

Algorithm, Performance, Experimentation

* This work was performed when Jianlong Fu was visiting Microsoft Research as a research intern.

WWW 2015, May 18–22, 2015, Florence, Italy.
ACM 978-1-4503-3469-3/15/05.
http://dx.doi.org/10.1145/2736277.2741112.

Figure 1: Compared with Web images, the user-provided tags of personal photos are more subjective and the visual appearances are more complex. Here the personal photos are collected from real users, while Web images are from ImageNet.

Keywords

Personal photo, image tagging, deep learning, transfer learning, ontology.

1. INTRODUCTION

Recent years have witnessed the emergence of mobile devices (e.g., smart phones, digital cameras, tablets, etc.) and cloud storage services. This has led to an unprecedented growth in the number of personal photos. People are taking photos using their smart devices every day and everywhere. One of the fundamental challenges to managing this ever-increasing number of photos is providing appropriate tags for each photo. Therefore, image tagging has become an active research topic in the last few years, in order to label images with human-friendly *concepts*[1]. Before we dive into the details of various image tagging techniques, we first define *personal photos* and introduce their characteristics.

We define *personal photos* as photos that are usually captured by amateur users with personal digital devices (e.g., smart phones, digital cameras, etc.). Compared with general Web images, personal photos have several unique properties: 1) Personal photos lack accurate text descriptions in general as users are unlikely to label their photos. 2) The semantic distribution of personal photos is only a subset of a general vocabulary of Web images. For example, some celebrities such as "Barack Obama" and specific terms such as "mammal" and "placental," are not likely to appear in personal photos of common users. Moreover, the semantic distribution in personal photos is typically biased toward the concepts related to "landscape," "family," and so on. 3) The appearance of personal photos is more complex due to occlusion, lighting variation, clut-

[1]"concept" and "tag" are considered as interchangeable terms, and we don't differentiate them in this paper.

tered background, and considerable camera motion. The tags, if there are any, are very subjective. This has led to the challenge of understanding personal photos. If we refer to Fig. 1, we can see that the Web images collected from ImageNet[2] are more likely to reflect a concept. In personal photos, however, various objects such as people, tree, grass, and sunlight appear in Fig. 1(b), and a blur effect and lighting variation appear in Fig. 1(c). Additionally, the photo labelled with "airport" may be very subjective. 4) There is rich metadata (e.g., time, geo-location) that can be exploited for analyzing personal photos.

The extensive research on image tagging can be divided into model-based and model-free approaches. The model-based approaches heavily rely on pre-trained classifiers with machine learning algorithms [17] [19] [27] [30], while the model-free approach propagates tags through the tagging behavior of visual neighbors [18][29]. The two streams of approaches both assume that there is a well-labelled image database (source domain) that has the same or at least a similar data distribution as the target domain, so that the well-labelled database can ensure good generalization abilities for both classifier training and tag propagation. However, the well-labelled database is hard to obtain in the domain of personal photos. On one hand, although some photo sharing websites such as Flickr[3] can provide a huge number of personal photos and user-contributed tags, this data is not appropriate as supervised information, as half of the user-contributed tags are noises to the image content [4]. On the other, although ImageNet [6] can provide accurate supervised information, the two significant gaps, i.e., the semantic distribution and visual appearance gaps between the two domains pose grand challenges to personal photo tagging.

To address the above issues, we present a novel transfer deep learning approach with ontology priors to tag personal photos. First, we have designed an ontology specific for personal photos from 10,000 active users in Flickr. Although previous methods (e.g., [3][12]) defined about a dozen common types as concepts (e.g., "beach fun," "ball games," and "wedding") in the domain of personal photos, they are not enough to comprehensively describe the variety of content. Furthermore, the correlations between different concepts have not been fully exploited in previous research.

Second, we propose reducing the visual appearance gap by applying deep learning techniques. Existing image tagging methods often leverage hand-crafted features, e.g., Scale-Invariant Feature Transform (SIFT) [20], GIST [23], Histogram of Oriented Gradients (HOG) [5], and so on. Based on these features, visual representation algorithms (e.g., Bag-of-Features [24]) have been proposed to describe image content and assign keywords. However, these hand-crafted descriptors are designed for general tasks to capture fixed visual patterns by pre-defined feature types and are not suitable for detecting some middle-level features that are shared and meaningful across two specific domains. With the recent success in many research areas [1], deep learning techniques have attracted increasing attention. This method can automatically learn hierarchical deep networks from raw pixels and produce adaptive middle-level feature representations for a specific task, especially in computer vision. For example, deep convolutional neural networks achieved a winning top-5 test error rate of 15.3%, compared to the 26.2% achieved by the second-best approach which combines scores from many classifiers trained by a set of hand-crafted features [14]. Another breakthrough was achieved in [15], where the algorithm automatically learned the concepts of cat faces and human bodies from unlabelled data. Motivated by such promising performances, we have proposed to discover middle-level feature abstractions from raw image pixels (i.e., called "bottom-up transfer" in this paper) and high-level ontology priors (i.e., called "top-down transfer" in this paper) using deep learning techniques. Both the middle-level and high-level representations are shared and meaningful across the two domains and thus can facilitate algorithms to reduce the visual differences between the two domains. As a result, a type of deep network learned from the source domain can be transferred to the target with good generalization abilities.

To the best of our knowledge, this paper is one of the first attempts to design a domain-specific ontology for personal photos and solve the tagging problem by transfer deep learning. The main contributions of this paper can be summarized as follows:

- We design a domain-specific ontology for personal photos, which is the most comprehensive ontology in this domain.
- We propose a novel transfer deep learning approach with ontology priors to effectively discover intermediate image representations from deep networks and ensure good generalization abilities across the two domains (Web images as the source domain and personal photos as the target).
- We propose two modes, including a single-mode and a batch-mode, to highly efficiently tag personal photos by leveraging the discriminative visual descriptors and rich metadata in the personal photos.

The rest of this paper is organized as follows. Section 2 describes related work. Section 3 first presents the ontology collection scheme for personal photos, then Section 4 formulates the transfer deep learning approach. Section 5 further describes two modes to efficiently tag personal photos. Section 6 provides empirical evaluations, followed by the conclusion in Section 7.

2. RELATED WORK

In this section, we briefly review research related to our approach in two categories. Image tagging aims to automatically assign concepts to images and has been studied intensively in the past decade, while transfer deep learning has drawn a great deal of attention recently with the success of deep learning techniques.

2.1 Image Tagging

A large body of work on image tagging proceeds along two dimensions, i.e., model-based and model-free approaches [7]. Model-based approaches heavily rely on pre-trained classifiers with machine learning algorithms. Tag ranking estimates initial relevance scores for tags by using probability density functions and performs a random walk process to refine the tagging results [19]. To address the problem of large-scale annotation of Web images, Visual synset applies multi-class one-vs-all linear Support Vector Machine models, which are learned from the automatically generated visual synsets of a large collection of Web images [27]. In [13], Ji *et al.* exploit both low-level visual features and high-level semantic context into a unified conditional random fields (CRF) model for solving the image tagging problem, which achieves significant improvement and more robustness results on two benchmarks. Although the model-based approach can achieve good performance, it may suffer from a limited vocabulary and less scalability on large-scale datasets.

In contrast to the model-based approach, the model-free approach [11][18][29] was developed to learn visual concepts from Web images. The intuition is that we can measure the relevance between an image and tags by searching and voting from its visual duplicates in

[2]www.image-net.org

[3]www.flickr.com

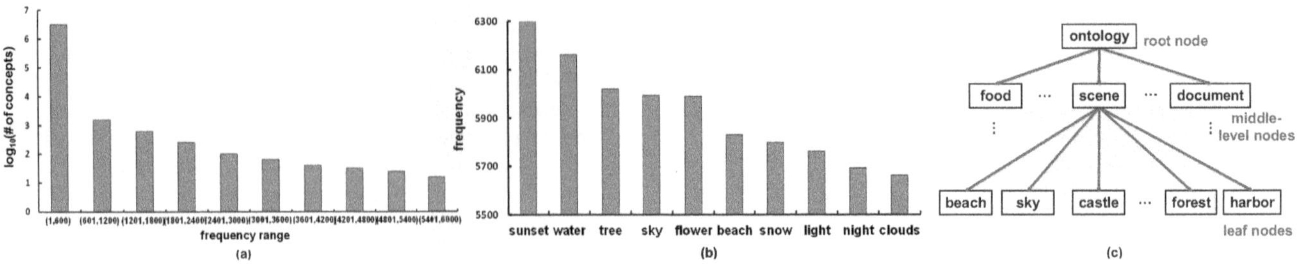

Figure 2: The statistics from 10K active users in Flickr and an illustration of the defined ontology. (a) Distribution of concepts on frequency ranges. (b) The top 10 concepts with frequencies. (c) An illustration of the curated ontology in the domain of personal photos. The concepts in the leaf nodes are the focus of the subsequent tagging procedure.

a well-labelled image database. Note that the model-free approach does not impose any model training. In [18], Li *et al.* leverage such techniques to measure social tag relevance by neighbor voting. In [29], Wang *et al.* adopt web-scale images to reformulate the image tagging problem as a search for semantically and visually similar images. In [11], Guillaumin *et al.* propose a novel nearest neighbor voting scheme that predicts tags by taking a weighted combination of the tag absence or presence among neighbors. However, the size of the well-labelled image database is limited in practice, and thus irrelevant tags may be propagated by mistake due to the well-known "semantic gap."

However, these works, in both dimensions, only leverage hand-crafted features. For example, in [18] and [29], global features (e.g., color correlogram, texture moment) are widely used as global similarity metrics. In [11] and [27], local shape descriptors and face signatures are employed, respectively. Although the approaches based on these hand-crafted features have achieved good results, it is still unclear how they should be selected to achieve better results for a desired task. Additionally, prior research for personal photos only focuses on event recognition for about 10 common types that have relatively small datasets [3][12]. A vocabulary of such size is less descriptive and comprehensive for a variety of personal photos. The goal of this paper is to show that a deep network can automatically learn image representations on a large domain-specific ontology for personal photos, which removes the need for engineered feature representations and can transfer to new tasks.

2.2 Transfer Deep Learning

Deep learning began emerging as a new area of machine learning research in 2006 [1]. The techniques developed from deep learning research exploit many layers of non-linear information processing for supervised or unsupervised feature extraction and for pattern analysis and classification, and they have shown many promising and exciting results [14].

Transfer deep learning targets the transfer of knowledge from a source domain to a target domain using deep learning algorithms. In [22], transfer learning problems are divided into two categories. One class tries to improve the classification performance of categories that have deficit training examples by discovering other similar categories and transferring knowledge among them (e.g., [25]). Other works aim to solve the different data distribution problems, so as to effectively transfer the knowledge learned from the source domain to the target (e.g., [22]).

Compared to the above methods, our task is more challenging, because there are few labelled images for all categories in the domain of personal photos. The approaches of [22] and [25], which all need labelled training images in the target domain, are unsuitable for our task. More similar to our work, Bengio *et al.* learn to extract a meaningful representation for each review text for different products using a deep learning approach in an unsupervised fashion [9]. In contrast to [9], which is applied to text applications, we need to handle the high-dimensional problem of images, which results in more difficulties. Furthermore, unlike [9], which only uses a bottom-up transfer, we propose both a bottom-up transfer and a top-down transfer in a unified framework to better reduce the domain gap.

3. ONTOLOGY FOR PERSONAL PHOTOS

We propose to design an ontology for personal photos, since the vocabulary of general Web images is often too large and not specific to personal photos. To obtain the ontology, we explored the semantic distributions in the domain of personal photos by mining frequent tags from active users in Flickr. Although Flickr cannot provide us with accurate tags to image content, we can mine a set of semantic words frequently used in personal photos by common users and collect them into this ontology. We collected more than $30,000$ users and selected about $10,000$ active users who had uploaded more than 500 photos in the most recent six months and with a registration time of more than two years. There are about 20 million photos and 2.7 million unique tags in total. For each user, we crawled all the photos and considered each user-contributed tag as a concept. After eliminating the stop words, we aggregated the concepts among all the users, ranked these concepts in the decreasing order by frequency and selected the top concepts whose frequencies were larger than $3,000$. Finally, we obtained 272 concepts, which forms the vocabulary in the subsequent image tagging. Fig. 2(a) and Fig. 2(b) show the distribution of concepts in terms of frequency and the top 10 concepts mined from the 10,000 active users, respectively.

To reflect the correlations between different concepts, we construct a three-layer ontology which consists of a hierarchical vocabulary. The top is a root node, followed by 20 human-curated middle-level nodes which represent various topics in personal photos. These topics are defined as: entertainment, social activity, daily routine, home, public places, people, plant, animal, transportation, clothing, regular items, furniture, kitchen ware, electronics, food, beverage, instrument, public facilities, scene, and document. The 272 concepts are considered as leaf nodes in the ontology and eventually grouped into the 20 middle-level nodes according to the word similarity in WordNet[4]. For example, as shown in Fig. 2(c), "beach," "sky," "castle," etc. are grouped into the topic of "scene." This ontology embeds the relationships of concepts, which can be considered as prior probabilities to improve tagging performance.

As we aim to conduct transfer learning from ImageNet to personal photos, the concepts in the source and target domains should be matched. However, there is a "label bias" between the two do-

[4]http://wordnet.princeton.edu/

mains [26]. To solve this problem, we calculated the word similarity between the 272 concepts and the ImageNet-22K labels by using WordNet. As a result, each concept in the domain of personal photos can be mapped to the closest label in the ImageNet. The images corresponding to these labels in the ImageNet form the training data in the source domain.

4. TRANSFER DEEP LEARNING WITH ONTOLOGY PRIORS

In this section, we propose a six-layer deep neural network for simultaneously harnessing the labelled images in the source domain and the unlabelled images in the target to reduce the visual appearance gap across the two domains. Fig. 3 shows an overview of the proposed approach, which consists of three components, i.e., (a) the training set, (b) the network of the transfer deep learning with ontology priors and (c) the ontology. In the testing stage, the personal photos that have been input in (d) can be annotated by the transferred network in (b) and the resultant tags are shown in (e).

First, the stacked convolutional autoencoders (CAES) are pre-trained on both the source and target domains in an unsupervised manner, from which the shared deep feature representations can be discovered from raw pixels. A fine-tuning process is then implemented using the supervision in the source domain to give the network stronger discriminability. Note that although the fine-tuning is guided by the supervision in the source domain, it starts with the network parameters discovered across the two domains. Therefore, the fine-tuned network can still produce the shared feature representations across domains. Once the shared deep feature representations are fine-tuned, the top layer, i.e., a fully connected layer with ontology priors (FCO), is further trained. Since the shared deep feature representations and the ontology take effect across the two domains, the resultant parameters can be transferred to the target domain in the testing stage to obtain middle-level feature representations (a bottom-up transfer) and high-level confidence scores (a top-down transfer).

Let $\mathbf{X} = [\mathbf{x}_1, ..., \mathbf{x}_N] \in \mathbb{R}^{d \times N}$ be a set of N training data with d dimensions and $\mathbf{Y} = [\mathbf{y}_1, ..., \mathbf{y}_N] \in \mathbb{R}^{K \times N}$ be the corresponding label matrix. Here the labels in the target domain are unknown, while in the source domain each label $\mathbf{y}_i$ is a K dimensional output for leaf nodes. The value of 1 is for the correct concept in the defined ontology and 0 otherwise. Let $\mathbf{W}$ denote the set of parameters of CAES (i.e., weights and biases), and $\mathbf{B}$ denote parameters of the top FCO layer, $\mathbf{B} \in \mathbb{R}^{K \times D}$. Here D represents the dimension of the transformed feature after CAES. Given $\mathbf{X}$, the parameter learning is determined by a conditional distribution over $\mathbf{Y}$, which can be formulated as:

$$\max_{\mathbf{W},\mathbf{B}}\{P(\mathbf{Y}|\mathbf{X})\} = \max_{\mathbf{W},\mathbf{B}}\left\{\sum_{\mathbf{W},\mathbf{B}} P(\mathbf{Y}|\mathbf{X},\mathbf{W},\mathbf{B})P(\mathbf{W})P(\mathbf{B})\right\}, \tag{1}$$

where $\mathbf{W}$ and $\mathbf{B}$ need to be optimized in the subsequent transfer deep learning procedures.

4.1 Deep Learning with Bottom-Up Transfer

To ensure good generalization abilities in transfer learning, a shared middle-level feature abstraction is first learned in an unsupervised pre-training and a supervised fine-tuning from both the source and target domains, in which $\mathbf{W}$ is optimized.

The autoencoder (AE) is one of the methods to build deep networks that is often used for learning an effective encoding of the original data without using supervised labels [1]. An autoencoder consists of an encoder function $f_{\mathbf{W}}(\mathbf{x}_i)$ and a decoder function $g_{\mathbf{W}'}(\mathbf{x}_i)$, where $\mathbf{x}_i$ is an input, $\mathbf{W}$ and $\mathbf{W}'$ are the parameters of the encoder and decoder, respectively. The fully connected AE is a basic form of an autoencoder. However, the fully connected AE ignores the high dimensionality and spatial structure of an image. Inspired by convolutional neural networks (CNN) [14], the convolutional autoencoder (CAE) has been proposed [21]. In contrast to the full connected AE, weights of the CAE are shared among all locations in the input. Therefore, CAE scales better to the realistic-sized high-dimensional images. For the input $\mathbf{x}_i$, the hidden representation of the jth feature map is given by:

$$\mathbf{h}_j = f_{\mathbf{W}_j}(\mathbf{x}_i) = \sigma(\mathbf{x}_i * \mathbf{W}_j), \tag{2}$$

where σ is an activation function and $*$ denotes the two-dimensional convolution. The reconstruction of $\mathbf{x}_i$, i.e., $\mathbf{r}_i$, is obtained by:

$$\mathbf{r}_i = g_{\mathbf{W}'}(f_{\mathbf{W}}(\mathbf{x}_i)) = \sigma\Big(\sum_{j \in \mathbf{H}} \mathbf{h}_j * \mathbf{W}'_j\Big), \tag{3}$$

where $\mathbf{H}$ denotes the set of all the hidden feature maps and $\mathbf{W}'$ is usually forced to be the transpose of $\mathbf{W}$. A cost function is defined to minimize the reconstruction error over all the training data using mean squared error (MSE):

$$cost(\mathbf{W}) = \frac{1}{2N}\sum_{i=1}^{N}(\mathbf{x}_i - \mathbf{r}_i)^2. \tag{4}$$

The cost function can be solved using the back propagation algorithm [14] as standard networks.

To build deep networks, we cascade several convolutional autoencoders to form a stacked CAES. The input of each layer is the encoding of the layer below. The unsupervised training can be implemented in a greedy layer-wise fashion. Although unsupervised pre-training can guide the learning and support better generalizations from the training set, the discriminability can be further enhanced through a supervised fine-tuning. Therefore, based on the learned unsupervised architecture, a fine-tuning procedure is conducted using the supervision in the source domain. For the sake of simplicity, we denote $\mathbf{W}$ as the overall parameter of the five layers after fine-tuning. Note that the fine-tuned network not only retains the shared architecture across the two domains, but is more discriminative than the unsupervised network. The architecture of the five-layer stacked convolutional autoencoders (CAE1 to CAE5) is shown in Fig. 3(b).

Once $\mathbf{W}$ has been learned, we can obtain a transformed feature representation for $\mathbf{X}$, and thus Eqn. (1) can be further represented by:

$$\max_{\mathbf{B}}\{P(\mathbf{Y}|\mathbf{X})\} = \max_{\mathbf{B}}\left\{\sum_{\mathbf{B}} P(\mathbf{Y}|f_{\mathbf{W}}(\mathbf{X}),\mathbf{B})P(\mathbf{B})\right\}. \tag{5}$$

4.2 Deep Learning with Top-Down Transfer

Following the CAES, an FCO layer with ontology priors is learned on the shared feature abstractions in the source domain and transferred to the target. An ontology is a high-level semantic structure reflecting whether concepts are close to each other or not. Such priors with respect to this relationship can be more discriminative to different concepts, especially those with great differences. For example, "beach" and "sky" belong to the same middle-level node "scene," while "dog" belongs to "animal." Therefore, the priors of "beach" and "sky" are similar, but very different from that of "dog." In this paper, we have defined an ontology curated for the domain of personal photos. For the concepts in this defined ontology, the relationship among different concepts is inherited across the two

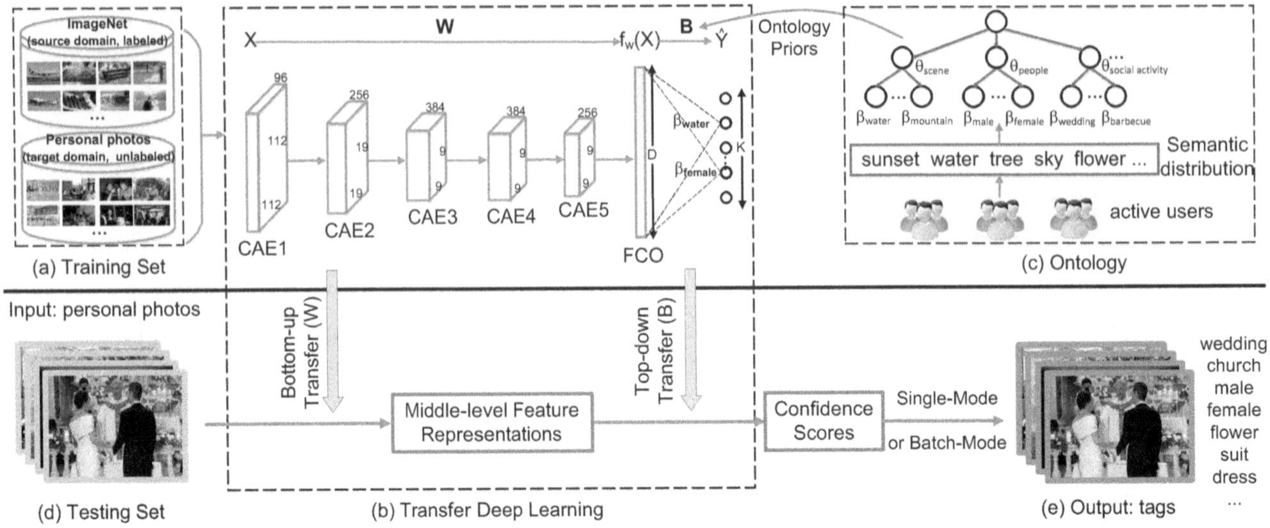

Figure 3: The network of the proposed transfer deep learning. (a) The training set contains the labelled source images and the unlabelled target images. (b) The network of the transfer deep learning with ontology priors. It is first trained on both ImageNet (the source domain) and personal photos (the target domain) by pre-training and fine-tuning for discovering shared middle-level feature abstractions across domains. Once the shared feature abstractions are learned, the top layer with ontology priors is further trained. In the testing stage, the resultant parameters $\mathbf{W}$ and $\mathbf{B}$ can be transferred to the target domain to obtain the middle-level feature representations (a bottom-up transfer) and high-level confidence scores (a top-down transfer). (c) An illustration of the ontology collecting scheme. (d) The input, in the testing stage, is highly flexible which can either be a single photo or a photo collection. (e) The tagging result.

domains. For example, a middle-level node "animal" is composed of the same leaf nodes (e.g., "cow," "bird," etc.) in both domains. Therefore, based on the shared feature abstractions and the inherited relationship, the parameters of the FCO layer can be learned from the source domain and transferred to the target without much of a gap. The ontology priors can enhance the correlations among close concepts and weaken those among dissimilar ones, and thus boost the prediction accuracy. Meanwhile an ontology built upon the shared feature abstractions across domains can help reduce the domain gap, which is the main difference between our approach and some single-domain learning methods, e.g., [25].

As $\mathbf{W}$ has been learned, we fix $\mathbf{W}$ and introduce the ontology priors into Eqn. (5) to maximize:

$$P(\mathbf{Y}|\mathbf{X}) = \sum_{\mathbf{B},\mathbf{\Theta}} P(\mathbf{Y}|f_{\mathbf{W}}(\mathbf{X}),\mathbf{B})P(\mathbf{B}|\mathbf{\Theta})P(\mathbf{\Theta}), \quad (6)$$

where $\mathbf{B} = [\boldsymbol{\beta}_1, ..., \boldsymbol{\beta}_K]^T \in \mathbb{R}^{K\times D}$ and $\mathbf{\Theta} = [\boldsymbol{\theta}_1, ..., \boldsymbol{\theta}_M]^T \in \mathbb{R}^{M\times D}$ are the priors of the leaf nodes and the middle-level nodes in the defined ontology, respectively. The M and K are the number of middle-level nodes and leaf nodes, respectively. The prior over a leaf node is constrained by its immediate middle-level node (i.e., parent node) in the form of a conditional probability. We define a function $parent(\cdot)$ as a mapping from leaf nodes to their middle-level nodes, i.e., if k and m are indexes of a leaf node and a middle-level node separately, then $parent(k) = m$.

The typical choice for priors $\mathbf{B}$ and $\mathbf{\Theta}$ is Gaussian distribution. We thus define the following forms for $\mathbf{B}$ and $\mathbf{\Theta}$:

$$\boldsymbol{\beta}_k \sim \mathcal{N}(\boldsymbol{\theta}_{parent(k)}, \frac{1}{\lambda_1}\mathbf{I}_D), \boldsymbol{\theta}_{parent(k)} \sim \mathcal{N}(0, \frac{1}{\lambda_2}\mathbf{I}_D), \quad (7)$$

where $\boldsymbol{\beta}_k \in \mathbb{R}^D$ denotes the prior for the kth leaf node, whose mean is determined by its parent $\boldsymbol{\theta}_{parent(k)}$ and $\mathbf{I}_D$ is a diagonal covariance. Let $\boldsymbol{\theta}_m$ be a prior of the mth middle-level node in the ontology. $\boldsymbol{\theta}_m$ consists of a set of $\boldsymbol{\beta}_k$ where $parent(k) = m$. λ_1 and λ_2 are the scale factors of the two covariance matrix. We define $C_m = |\{k|parent(k) = m\}|$, where $|\cdot|$ denotes the cardinality of a set. As $\boldsymbol{\beta}_k$ and $\boldsymbol{\theta}_m$ are Gaussian distributions, given $\boldsymbol{\beta}_k$, $\boldsymbol{\theta}_m$ can be represented as in [25], which is:

$$\boldsymbol{\theta}_m = \frac{1}{C_m + \lambda_2/\lambda_1} \sum_{parent(k)=m} \boldsymbol{\beta}_k, \quad (8)$$

where $\boldsymbol{\theta}_m \in \mathbb{R}^D$. In general, we resort to MAP estimation to determine the value of the FCO layer's parameters $\mathbf{B}$ and $\mathbf{\Theta}$, which is to maximize:

$$\log P(\mathbf{Y}|f_{\mathbf{W}}(\mathbf{X}),\mathbf{B}) + \log P(\mathbf{B}|\mathbf{\Theta}) + \log P(\mathbf{\Theta}). \quad (9)$$

By selecting the mean squared error (MSE) as loss, the loss function can be expressed as:

$$\min_{\mathbf{B},\mathbf{\Theta}} \left\{ ||\mathbf{B}\, f_{\mathbf{W}}(\mathbf{X}) - \mathbf{Y}||^2 + \frac{\lambda_1}{2}\sum_{k=1}^{K} ||\boldsymbol{\beta}_k - \boldsymbol{\theta}_{parent(k)}||^2 + \frac{\lambda_2}{2}||\mathbf{\Theta}||^2 \right\} \quad (10)$$

4.3 Optimization for Top-Down Transfer

To efficiently solve the above loss function, we propose to transform the $\mathbf{\Theta} \in \mathbb{R}^{M\times D}$ matrix into the same dimension as $\mathbf{B}$. Let $\mathbf{\Theta} = [\boldsymbol{\theta}_{parent(1)}, \boldsymbol{\theta}_{parent(2)}, ..., \boldsymbol{\theta}_{parent(K)}]^T \in \mathbb{R}^{K\times D}$, then Eqn. (10) can be simplified into the following form:

$$\min_{\mathbf{B},\mathbf{\Theta}} \left\{ ||\mathbf{B}\, f_{\mathbf{W}}(\mathbf{X}) - \mathbf{Y}||^2 + \frac{\lambda_1}{2}||\mathbf{B} - \mathbf{\Theta}||^2 + \frac{\lambda_2}{2}||\mathbf{\Theta}||^2 \right\}. \quad (11)$$

By fixing $\mathbf{\Theta}$, we set the derivative of $\mathbf{B}$ of the above loss function to zero, then $\mathbf{B}$ can be updated according to the following rules:

$$\mathbf{B} = \left(2\mathbf{Y}\, f_{\mathbf{W}}(\mathbf{X})^T + \lambda_1\mathbf{\Theta}\right)\left(2f_{\mathbf{W}}(\mathbf{X})f_{\mathbf{W}}(\mathbf{X})^T + \lambda_1\mathbf{I}\right)^{-1}, \quad (12)$$

where $\mathbf{I}$ is an identity matrix. Once we obtain an updated $\mathbf{B}$, we can recalculate $\mathbf{\Theta}$ using Eqn. (8) and transform it again. Therefore, Eqn. (11) can be optimized by iteratively updating $\mathbf{B}$ and $\mathbf{\Theta}$ until the difference between two successive iterations is below a threshold, e.g., 10^{-4}.

5. PERSONAL PHOTO TAGGING

Once the deep network is trained, we describe two tagging modes to highly efficiently tag personal photos, i.e., a single-mode for tagging a single photo and a batch-mode for tagging a photo collection. The single-mode only takes visual content into account, while the batch-mode further combines visual content with time constraints in a photo collection since the time information has been demonstrated as an essential constraint in the domain of personal photos [8].

5.1 Tagging with Single-Mode

Let $\mathbf{x} \in \mathbb{R}^d$ be the raw pixels of a single photo. We feed $\mathbf{x}$ into the learned stacked convolutional autoencoders and obtain a transformed feature representation $f_{\mathbf{W}}(\mathbf{x}) \in \mathbb{R}^D$. Then the tagging problem can be formulated as the following objective function:

$$\min_{\mathbf{y}} ||\mathbf{B}\, f_{\mathbf{W}}(\mathbf{x}) - \mathbf{y}||^2, \tag{13}$$

where $\mathbf{y} \in \mathbb{R}^K$ denotes the label vector indicating a confidence score for each concept. We can directly obtain a closed formed solution of $\mathbf{y}$, which is

$$\mathbf{y} = \mathbf{B}\, f_{\mathbf{W}}(\mathbf{x}). \tag{14}$$

Typically, we can utilize $\mathbf{y}$ in two ways. One way is to sort concepts according to their scores in $\mathbf{y}$ in decreasing order and select the top k concepts as the tagging results. An alternative way is to set a threshold and concepts whose scores are above the threshold can be selected as the tagging results.

5.2 Tagging with Batch-Mode

One of the most distinct characteristics of personal photos is the metadata stored in the digital photo files. This metadata includes the timestamp when the photo was taken and the geo-location of the photo. The metadata can be very useful in bridging the semantic gap in multimedia understanding. The single-mode only considers the visual content of a single photo, because an absolute timestamp is not very useful for understanding a photo via algorithms. However, a series of timestamps of a photo collection can be exploited for discovering the relationship among photos and boosting the tagging performance. For example, if the timestamps of two photos have a short interval between them, we can infer that the two photos were taken at the same event and the tagging results of the two photos should be highly correlated. Since geo-location information is not always available, we only leverage the time information in this paper.

Suppose there is a photo collection $\mathbf{X} \in \mathbb{R}^{d\times N}$ containing N photos and a label matrix $\mathbf{Y} \in \mathbb{R}^{K\times N}$. To reflect the time constraints, we construct an affinity matrix $\mathbf{S} \in \mathbb{R}^{N\times N}$ by:

$$S_{i,j} = \begin{cases} \exp\{-\frac{||t_i - t_j||^2}{\gamma^2}\}, & |t_i - t_j| < T, \\ 0, & \text{otherwise}, \end{cases} \tag{15}$$

where t_i denotes the timestamp of photo i, γ is a free parameter to control the decay rate and T is a threshold. In a photo collection, if the difference of timestamps between two photos is smaller than T, the two photos are likely to share the tagging results. Considering the time constraints and visual clues simultaneously, the objective function of the batch-mode is formulated as:

$$\min_{\mathbf{Y}} \left\{ Tr[\mathbf{Y}^T\mathbf{L}\mathbf{Y}] + ||\mathbf{B}\, f_{\mathbf{W}}(\mathbf{X}) - \mathbf{Y}||^2 \right\}, \tag{16}$$

where $\mathbf{L} = \mathbf{A}^{-1/2}(\mathbf{A}-\mathbf{S})\mathbf{A}^{-1/2}$ and $\mathbf{A}$ is a degree matrix defined as the diagonal matrix with the degrees $a_1, ..., a_N$ on the diagonal and $a_i = \sum_{j=1}^{N} S_{i,j}$. By setting the derivative of $\mathbf{Y}$ to zero, the above optimization has a closed formed solution:

$$\mathbf{Y} = 2\mathbf{B}\, f_{\mathbf{W}}(\mathbf{X})(\mathbf{L} + \mathbf{L}^T + 2\mathbf{I})^{-1}, \tag{17}$$

where $\mathbf{I}$ is an identity matrix and the matrix $\mathbf{Y}$ indicates the tagging results of the whole collection, where each column is a set of confidence scores of a single photo.

6. EXPERIMENTS

In this section, we evaluate the proposed approach on two datasets. Personal photo tagging with single-mode and batch-mode is evaluated on a real personal photo dataset collected from 25 volunteers. Besides, an application of personal photo search is conducted on the public MIT-Adobe FiveK photo dataset [2], as it covers a broad range of topics in personal photos.

6.1 Dataset

Training: For each of the 272 concepts, we randomly selected about 650 images and obtained 180,000 images in total from ImageNet as the training data in the source domain. Although the user tags are subjective and noisy, to learn the intermediate feature representation across the two domains, we selected about 180, 000 photos tagged with the 272 concepts (650 photos for each) from the 10, 000 active users in Flickr as the training data in the target domain. The training set contained about 0.36 million images in total.

Testing: In photo tagging, the testing photos were collected from 25 volunteers. The 25 volunteers, including 17 males and 8 females, were from different educational backgrounds, including computer science, mathematics, physics, business, management science, art and design. All the volunteers were familiar with photography and liked taking photos. Among the volunteers, 19 of them were students ranging from 20 to 28 years old, while the rest were employees ranging from 30 to 45 years old. Each volunteer was asked to contribute at least 500 photos of his/her own and all volunteers contributed 35,217 testing photos in total.

As there is no well-labelled datasets in the domain of personal photos, to conduct the evaluation and comparison with other approaches, we organized a ground-truth dataset with manual labeling. Since the labeling procedure was very time-consuming, the 25 volunteers were asked to randomly annotate one fifth of their own personal photos. The 272 concepts were annotated for each photo on three levels: 2–Highly Relevant; 1–Relevant; 0–Non Relevant. Before labeling a photo, each volunteer was strictly requested to browse the 272 concepts, from middle-level nodes to leaf nodes in the ontology. Finally, we obtained 7,000 annotated personal photos in total, which were used in the following evaluations. The distribution of the 7,000 photos on the different topics (represented by middle-level nodes) is shown in Fig. 4. The top five topics of the personal photos were related to "scene," "public places," "plant," "people," and "home," which demonstrates the semantic bias in the domain of personal photos. Fig. 5 further shows the statistics of the number of concepts in photos. Each column expresses the number of photos for a given number of concepts. Among the 7,000 photos, there were 10 photos having 15 relevant or highly relevant

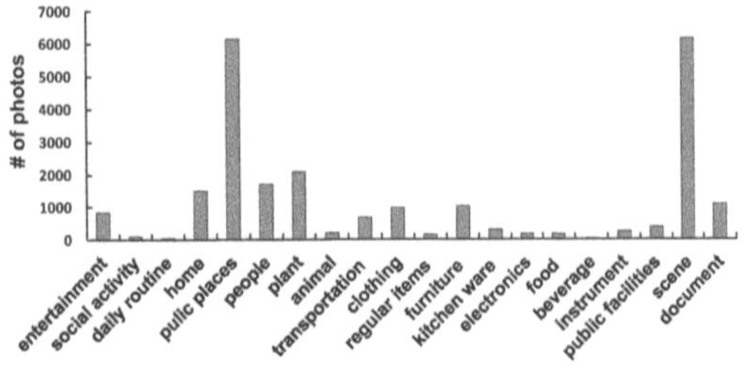

Figure 4: The photo distribution on middle-level nodes in our ontology. Each photo can contain multiple concepts.

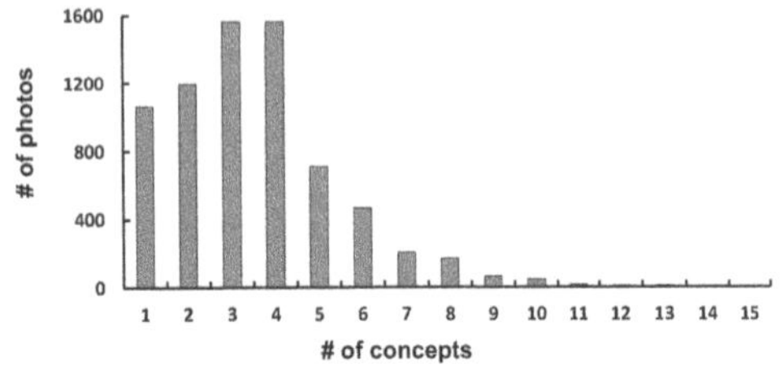

Figure 5: The concept distribution for personal photos.

concepts and about 70% of the photos present more than three relevant or highly relevant concepts which indicates the complexity in the visual appearances of personal photos.

6.2 Experiment Settings

Compared approaches: The following approaches were compared for the performance evaluation:

1. Tag ranking [19]: A typical approach uses hand-crafted features (225-d color moment and 128-d wavelet feature). It estimates initial relevance with concepts by a Gaussian kernel function and refines them by random walk. The kernel function is learned on ImageNet with 1,000 images for each concept, and the tag graph is built as in [19].
2. Dyadic Transfer Learning (DTL) [28]: A nonnegative matrix tri-factorization based transfer learning framework for image tagging, where the same hand-crafted features are extracted as in Tag ranking.
3. Transfer Learning with Geodesic Flow Kernel (GFK) [10]: An unsupervised approach to learn domain-invariant features by leveraging the subspaces that lie on the geodesic flow. Hand-crafted features are extracted as in Tag ranking and the nearest neighbor classifier is adopted as in [10]. We selected GFK because of its best performance over other hand-crafted feature-based transfer learning methods.
4. Deep learning with no transfer (DL) [14]: A deep learning approach with five convolutional layers and three fully connected layers. The networks are trained in the source domain (i.e., ImageNet), with about 650 images for each of the 272 concepts and about 180,000 training images in total.
5. Deep learning with **Flickr** training data (DL(Flickr)): We trained the same network as DL except for using the 180, 000 Flickr training data in the target domain.
6. Deep learning with top-down transfer (DL+TT): The same architecture and training set as DL except for the ontology priors embedded in the top, fully connected layer.
7. Deep learning with bottom-up transfer (DL+BT): A deep learning approach with five-layer CAES and one fully connected layer. The networks are trained on both domains.
8. Deep learning with full transfer (DL+FT) (i.e., bottom-up and top-down transfer): The same architecture and training set as DL+BT except for the ontology priors embedded in the top, fully connected layer.

Note that DL+TT, DL+BT, and DL+FT are proposed in this paper.

Network architecture: The architecture of our network is summarized in Fig. 3(b) and contains five convolutional layers and one fully connected layer with detailed specifications, CAE1 including 96 filters of size $7 \times 7 \times 3$ with a stride of 2 pixels, CAE2 including 256 filters of size $5 \times 5 \times 96$ with a stride of 2 pixels, CAE3 including 384 filters of size $3 \times 3 \times 256$ with a stride of 1 pixel, CAE4 including 384 filters of size $3 \times 3 \times 384$ with a stride of 1 pixel and CAE5 including 256 filters of size $3 \times 3 \times 384$ with a stride of 1 pixel. The input photos were color images of size $224 \times 224 \times 3$. To achieve higher computational efficiency and robustness, max-pooling layers were used following CAE1, CAE2 and CAE5 with the same window size of 3×3 and strides of 3, 2, 2, respectively. In the convolutional layers, rectifier linear unit $max(0, x)$ was adopted as the activation function, while in the top layer a linear activation function was used. The parameters λ_1 and λ_2 related to the prior distributions in the top layer were learned on a validation set in the source domain and set as $\lambda_1 = 30$ and $\lambda_2 = 10$.

Evaluation metrics: we adopted Normalized Discounted Cumulative Gain (NDCG) as metrics to evaluate photo tagging and Precision@K to evaluate photo search. The NDCG measures multi-level relevance and assumes the relevant tags are more useful when appearing higher in a ranked list. This metric at the position of p in the ranked list is defined by:

$$NDCG@p = Z_p \sum_{i=1}^{p} \frac{2^{r^i} - 1}{log(1 + i)}, \tag{18}$$

where 2^{r^i} is the relevance level of the ith tag and Z_p is a normalization constant such that $NDCG@p = 1$ for the perfect ranking. Additionally, the top-N error rates were adopted in tagging as they are more intuitional for common users. For example, the top-5 error rate is the ratio of testing photos whose top-5 tags are all irrelevant.

6.3 Evaluation of Tagging with Single-Mode

The problem of tagging with single-mode is to assign one or more relevant concepts to a given personal photo based on its visual content. As presented in Section 6.1, the 7,000 photos of real users with ground truth were evaluated. Fig. 6 shows the NDCG of different approaches for tagging personal photos. Obviously, we can see that DL(Flickr) is even far below than the method DL trained on ImageNet without transfer learning, which indicates the large percentage of noises in the user-provided tags in Flickr. Fig. 7 shows the error rates of different approaches over the 7,000 personal photos and an ideal performance of the DL approach (denoted as "DL+withinDomian") which is trained and tested on ImageNet. Overall, the tagging performances across domains were inferior to that within the same domain. The results verify our observation that there are significant domain gaps between Web images and personal photos.

It can also be observed from Fig. 6 and Fig. 7 that the existing tagging approach (Tag ranking) using hand-crafted features was the worst to bridge the domain gaps. It indicates that pre-defined feature types have difficulty discovering the shared feature representations across the two domains. By adopting cross-domain learning ideas, DTL [28] and GFK [10] were superior to the Tag ranking, but were inferior to the deep learning-based approach (DL). This shows stronger learning and generalization abilities of deep learning than the hand-crafted features. When further integrating transfer learning to deep learning, DL+TT, DL+BT and DL+FT achieve better performance than the DL approach. DL + FT achieved the best re-

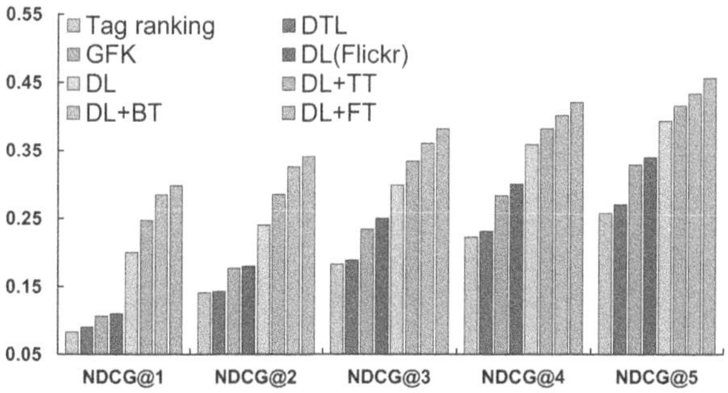

Figure 6: The NDCG of different approaches for tagging personal photos.

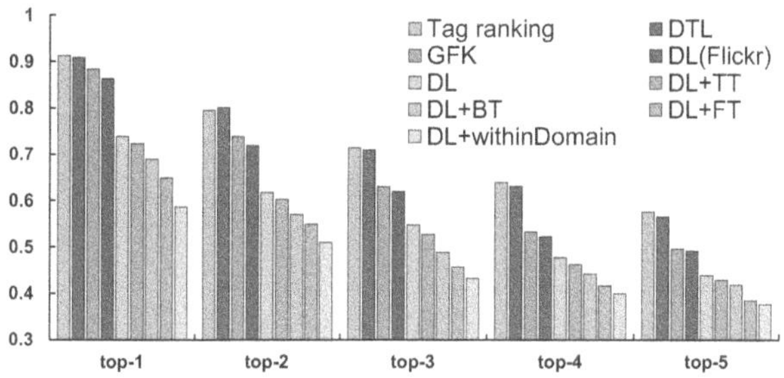

Figure 7: The top-N error rates of different approaches for tagging personal photos and an ideal performance obtained by training and testing on ImageNet (denoted as DL+withinDomain).

sult. The NDCG@5 of the full transfer network increased 12.8% and 4.5% against the GFK and the DL approach, respectively. The top-5 error rate of the full transfer network was 40.0%, which is very close to the top-5 error rate 37.6% within the domain. The superior performance derives from the fact that the full model can discover the shared feature abstractions from low-level raw pixels and the shared ontology from semantic structures across the two domains. In Fig. 7, we can observe that DL+FT (guided by the ontology) relatively decreased about 8.0% (in terms of top-5 "error" rate), compared to DL+BT. By extending the ontology beyond the three hierarchies with deeper networks, the top-down transfer can get further improvement. For the full model (DL+FT), we also varied the relative percentage of the labelled training set (source domain) as other typical transfer learning methods. The result is drawn in Fig. 13.

Fig. 10 shows the tagging results of different approaches ranked by confidence scores. We can observe that the typical approaches with hand-crafted features work well for "simple" photos with a clean background and few objects (e.g., the first photo in the left column), because of the limited descriptive power of these features. However, personal photos are always captured in the real world with uncontrolled environments, which are more likely to present complex visual patterns. This challenge can deteriorate the performance of the hand-crafted feature-based approaches. On the other hand, the deep learning-based approaches show stronger generalization abilities. However, it is still challenging for algorithms to predict the correct tags, since the photos are annotated by owners so that the ground truth is sometimes very subjective. For example, in Fig. 10, the content of the first photo in the right column is very similar to an "exhibition hall" or an "office," but the owner of the photo considers the two tags are wrong, because he took the photo in a restaurant. We will resort to the batch-mode to solve this problem.

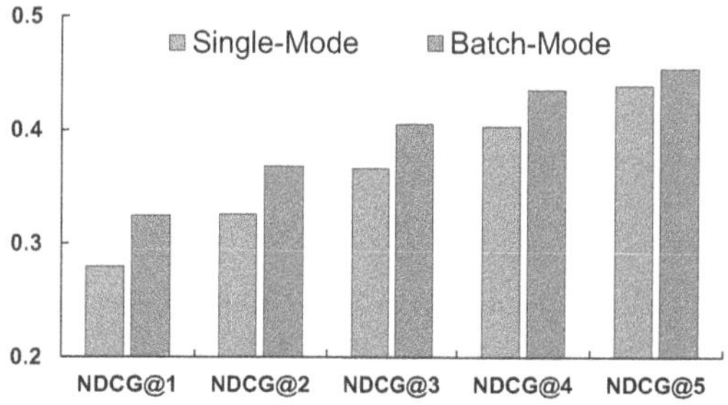

Figure 8: The NDCG of single-mode and batch-mode for tagging personal photos.

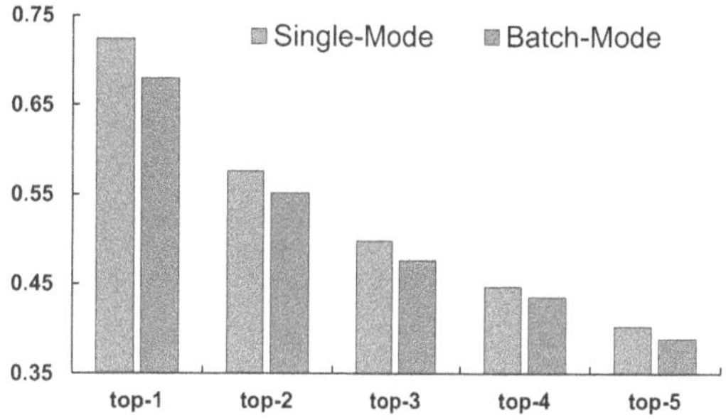

Figure 9: The top-N error rates of single-mode and batch-mode for tagging personal photos.

6.4 Evaluation of Tagging with Batch-Mode

The problem of tagging with batch-mode is how to assign concepts to a given photo collection, where the visual content and rich metadata embedded in personal photos is exploited simultaneously. As the geo-locations are not always available for photos, we only leverage the time information in this paper. Since the personal photos have been organized into several folders when submitted by the 25 volunteers, we considered the photos in each folder as a photo collection. We randomly selected three photo collections with various sizes (from 10 to 600 photos) from each user. In total, about 4,000 photos from 75 photo collections were evaluated.

Empirically, we set $\gamma = 2$ in Eqn. (15) to make $S_{i,j}$ in a proper scale, and we counted t_i by hours. Fig. 8 and Fig. 9 show the NDCG and error rates by using the DL+FT network with single-mode and batch-mode, respectively. In the single-mode, each photo in a photo collection was annotated individually by algorithms. While in the batch-mode, we ran the photo collection at one time. Compared to the single-mode, the batch-mode could consistently achieve a better performance, with gains of 4.4%, 4.3%, 3.9%, 3.2% and 1.5% from the NDCG@1 to NDCG@5. The improvement partly benefited from the idea to formulate the photo collection as a group, so that a photo can contribute its tags to others and vice versa depending on their time consistency. In our experiment, we set T at one hour. The shorter and longer time intervals led to inferior results over a validation set. Our analysis shows that, the shorter interval limited the tag propagation within a photo collection as the event in a photo collection usually lasts three to four hours. However, the longer interval inevitability led to noise.

Fig. 11 shows the tagging results for the same photo collections with single-mode and batch-mode, respectively. We found that tagging with batch-mode was more affective and could partially solve the problem of subjective annotation. For example, in the case of photo(c) of user #1, collection #3, the tagging algorithm with single-mode merely predicted "library," and "conference room" based on visual content. However, the batch-mode simul-

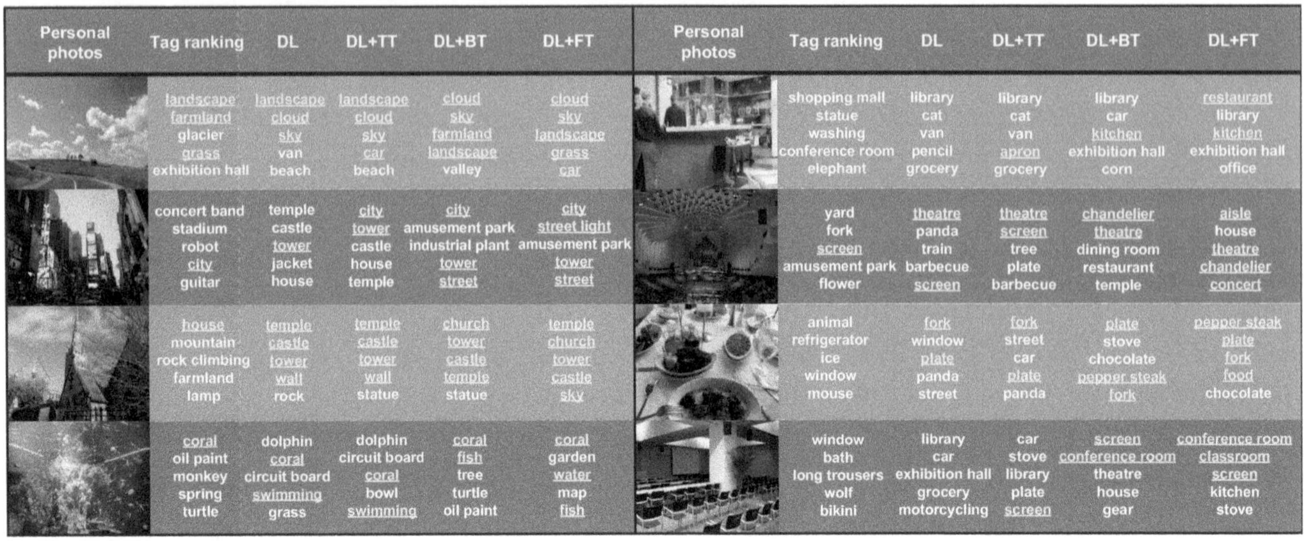

Figure 10: Example tagging results for eight personal photos by different approaches. Tag ranking and DL are produced by [19] and [14], respectively. The DL+TT, DL+BT and DL+FT are proposed in this paper. The top five tags are listed for each approach and the correct tags are highlighted in yellow and underlined.

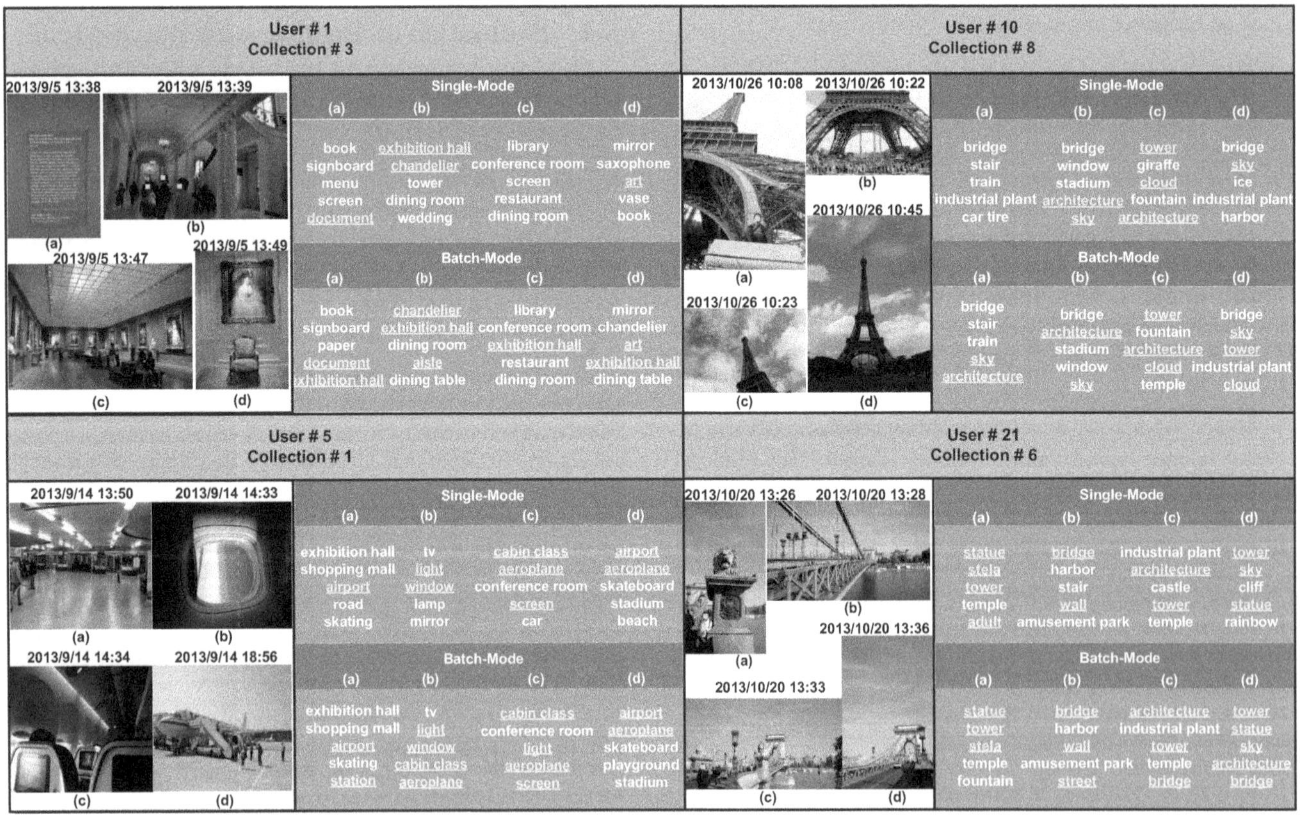

Figure 11: The tagging results for four example photos in each of four collections by single-mode and batch-mode, respectively. We adopted the network of DL+FT to produce the results for both modes. In single-mode, each photo was annotated individually. In batch-mode, we ran a photo collection at one time. The top five tags are listed for each photo and the correct tags are highlighted in yellow and underlined.

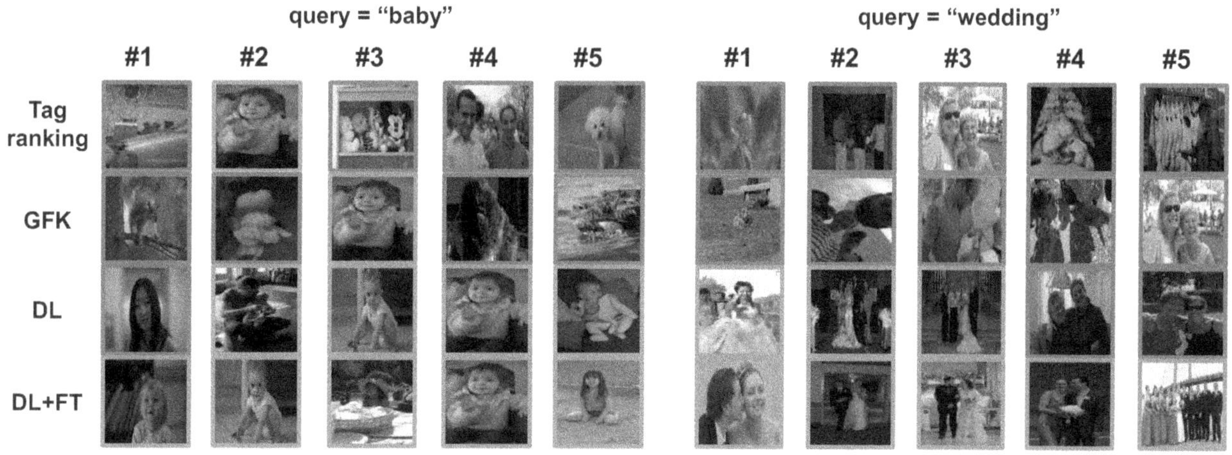

Figure 12: Photo search results on two exemplary queries for four typical compared approaches in the MIT-Adobe FiveK photo dataset. The green and red rectangles mark relevant and irrelevant photos, respectively. [best viewed in color]

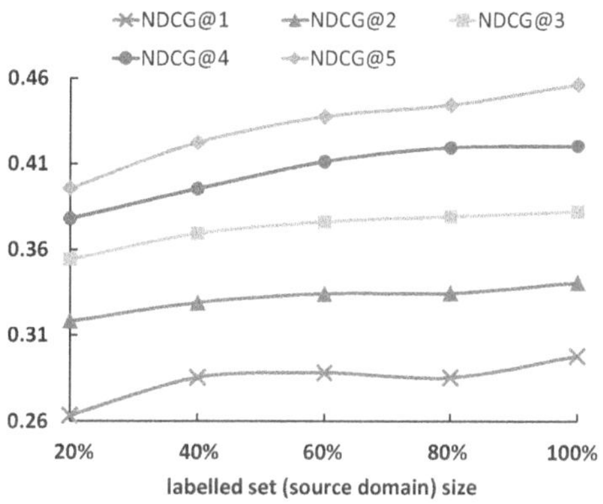

Figure 13: NDCG@1 to NDCG@5 with different percentages of the labelled training set.

Table 1: The average precision@K of photo search in the MIT-Adobe FiveK dataset.

	Tag ranking	GFK	DL(Flickr)	DL	DL+TT	DL+BT	DL + FT
P@1	0.34	0.41	0.42	0.55	0.61	0.71	0.77
P@5	0.28	0.32	0.31	0.46	0.52	0.62	0.74
P@10	0.22	0.26	0.25	0.40	0.45	0.56	0.72

taneously considered visual content and correlations from time-adjacent photos. Therefore, "exhibition hall" was propagated from time-adjacent neighbors. The batch-mode with time constraints complements the visual content analysis and enhances the robustness of our tagging algorithm.

6.5 Evaluation of Personal Photo Search

One of the most useful features of photo tagging is to help users recall and reconstruct the situation what he (or she) experienced. It can be conducted by photo search and ranking [16] with the user-typed queries. MIT-Adobe FiveK photo dataset was used in this evaluation. As there is no specific time information in this public dataset, we annotated photos by the proposed single-mode to generated the top-1 tag for each photo. Each tag was associated with a probability score produced by the deep learning networks. We used each of the 272 concepts in the personal photo ontology as queries. A photo is returned to users if its top-1 tag can be matched to the query. For each query, photos are ranked in the decreasing order according the probability scores. We retrieved ten photos for each query and manually judged the relevance of each photo. We calculated the average precision@K on all queries for different compared methods. The result is in Tab. 1. We can see that our proposed approach achieves much better performance compared to the other baselines. DL+FT achieves the best results, which demonstrates that DL+FT can build more accurate links between visual features and tags through the bottom-up and top-down transfer. Fig. 12 further illustrates some exemplary photo search results. For each query, the top-5 photos are returned. We can clearly see that the retrieved photos by the proposed approach can provide users with better results.

6.6 Complexity Analysis

We trained the six-layer network through the training set of 0.36 million images, which took three to four days on a NVIDIA GTX 580 GPU. For tagging with single-mode, the algorithm took less than 10 milliseconds on a PC with Intel Core Quad CPU with 2.83GHz and 4GB RAM. For tagging with batch-mode, it took three seconds for a photo collection of 200 photos (800*600 pixels). The high efficiency ensures an immediate response, and thus the transfer deep learning approach with two modes can be adopted as a prototype model for real-time mobile applications, such as photo tagging and event summarization on mobile devices.

7. CONCLUSIONS

In this paper, we have studied the problem of tagging personal photos. To effectively leverage supervised Web resource and reduce the domain gap between general Web images and personal photos, we have proposed a transfer deep learning approach to discover the shared representations across the two domains. Such representations can guide knowledge transfer from the source to the target domain. We conducted personal photo tagging on 7,000 real personal photos and personal photo search on the MIT-Adobe FiveK photo dataset. Experiments demonstrated the superiority of the transfer deep learning approach over the state-of-the-art hand-crafted feature-based methods and deep learning-based methods.

8. ACKNOWLEDGMENTS

This work was supported by 863 Program (2014AA015104), and National Natural Science Foundation of China (61273034, and 61332016).

9. REFERENCES

[1] Y. Bengio. Learning deep architectures for AI. *Found. Trends Mach. Learn.*, 2(1):1–127, Jan. 2009.

[2] V. Bychkovsky, S. Paris, E. Chan, and F. Durand. Learning photographic global tonal adjustment with a database of input / output image pairs. In *CVPR*, pages 97–104, 2011.

[3] L. Cao, J. Luo, H. A. Kautz, and T. S. Huang. Annotating collections of photos using hierarchical event and scene models. In *CVPR*, pages 1–8, 2008.

[4] T. Chua, J. Tang, R. Hong, H. Li, Z. Luo, and Y. Zheng. Nus-wide: A real-world web image database from national university of singapore. In *Proc. of ACM Conf. on Image and Video Retrieval*, pages 1–9, 2009.

[5] N. Dalal and B. Triggs. Histograms of oriented gradients for human detection. In *CVPR*, pages 886–893, 2005.

[6] J. Deng, W. Dong, R. Socher, L.-J. Li, K. Li, and L. Fei-Fei. ImageNet: A Large-Scale Hierarchical Image Database. In *CVPR*, pages 248–255, 2009.

[7] J. Fu, J. Wang, Y. Rui, X.-J. Wang, T. Mei, and H. Lu. Image tag refinment with view-dependent concept representations. In *IEEE Transactions on Circuits and Systems for Video Technology*. IEEE, 2014.

[8] A. C. Gallagher, C. Neustaedter, L. Cao, J. Luo, and T. Chen. Image annotation using personal calendars as context. In *ACM Multimedia*, pages 681–684, 2008.

[9] X. Glorot, A. Bordes, and Y. Bengio. Domain adaptation for large-scale sentiment classification: A deep learning approach. In *ICML*, pages 513–520, 2011.

[10] B. Gong, Y. Shi, F. Sha, and K. Grauman. Geodesic flow kernel for unsupervised domain adaptation. In *CVPR*, pages 2066–2073, 2012.

[11] M. Guillaumin, T. Mensink, J. Verbeek, and C. Schmid. Tagprop: Discriminative metric learning in nearest neighbor models for image auto-annotation. In *ICCV*, pages 309–316, 2009.

[12] N. Imran, J. Liu, J. Luo, and M. Shah. Event recognition from photo collections via pagerank. In *ACM Multimedia*, pages 621–624, 2009.

[13] C. Ji, X. Zhou, L. Lin, and W. Yang. Labeling images by integrating sparse multiple distance learning and semantic context modeling. In *ECCV*, pages 688–701, 2012.

[14] A. Krizhevsky, I. Sutskever, and G. E. Hinton. Imagenet classification with deep convolutional neural networks. In *NIPS*, pages 1106–1114, 2012.

[15] Q. V. Le, M. Ranzato, R. Monga, M. Devin, G. Corrado, K. Chen, J. Dean, and A. Y. Ng. Building high-level features using large scale unsupervised learning. In *ICML*, 2012.

[16] C. Li, Q. Liu, J. Liu, and H. Lu. Learning ordinal discriminative features for age estimation. In *CVPR*, pages 2570–2577, 2012.

[17] T. Li, T. Mei, I.-S. Kweon, and X.-S. Hua. Contextual bag-of-words for visual categorization. *IEEE Transactions on Circuits and Systems for Video Technology*, 21(4):381–392, Apr. 2011.

[18] X. Li, C. G. Snoek, and M. Worring. Learning tag relevance by neighbor voting for social image retrieval. In *Proc. ACM International Conference on Multimedia Information Retrieval*, pages 180–187, 2008.

[19] D. Liu, X.-S. Hua, L. Yang, M. Wang, and H.-J. Zhang. Tag ranking. In *WWW*, pages 351–360, 2009.

[20] D. G. Lowe. Distinctive image features from scale-invariant keypoints. *Int. J. Comput. Vision*, 60(2):91–110, Nov. 2004.

[21] J. Masci, U. Meier, D. C. Ciresan, and J. Schmidhuber. Stacked convolutional auto-encoders for hierarchical feature extraction. In *ICANN*, pages 52–59, 2011.

[22] O. Maxime, B. Leno, L. Ivan, and S. Josef. Learning and transferring mid-level image representations using convolutional neural networks. In *CVPR*, pages 1717–1724, 2014.

[23] A. Oliva and A. Torralba. Building the gist of a scene: The role of global image features in recognition. *Visual Perception, Progress in Brain Research*, 155, 2006.

[24] J. Sivic and A. Zisserman. Video google: A text retrieval approach to object matching in videos. In *ICCV*, pages 1470–1477, 2003.

[25] N. Srivastava and R. Salakhutdinov. Discriminative transfer learning with tree-based priors. In *NIPS*, pages 2094–2102, 2013.

[26] A. Torralba and A. A. Efros. Unbiased look at dataset bias. In *CVPR*, pages 1521–1528, 2011.

[27] D. Tsai, Y. Jing, Y. Liu, H. A. Rowley, S. Ioffe, and J. M. Rehg. Large-scale image annotation using visual synset. In *ICCV*, pages 611–618, 2011.

[28] H. Wang, F. Nie, H. Huang, and C. Ding. Dyadic transfer learning for cross-domain image classification. In *ICCV*, pages 551–556, 2011.

[29] X.-J. Wang, L. Zhang, F. Jing, and W.-Y. Ma. Annosearch: Image auto-annotation by search. In *CVPR*, pages 1483–1490, 2006.

[30] P. Wu, S. C.-H. Hoi, P. Zhao, and Y. He. Mining social images with distance metric learning for automated image tagging. In *WSDM*, pages 197–206, 2011.

MobInsight: On Improving the Performance of Mobile Apps in Cellular Networks

Vijay Gabale
IBM Research, India
vijay.gabale@gmail.com

Dilip Krishnaswamy
IBM Research, India
dilikrish@in.ibm.com

ABSTRACT

It is well-known that the performance of Web-browsing as well as mobile applications (or apps) suffers on today's cellular networks. In this work, we perform a systematic measurement study of more than 50 popular apps and 2 cellular networks, and discover that while cellular networks have predictable latency, it is the path between exit points of cellular networks (e.g., GGSN) and cloud-servers that degrades apps performance. High latency and unpredictability over this path affects browsing and activity completion times of apps, worsening the performance by several magnitudes. Furthermore, we find that as the number of apps on mobile devices increases, cellular networks in turn suffer due to large number of active connections, primarily used for push notifications, experiencing heavy signaling overhead in the network. Towards accelerating the performance of apps and improving their operational efficiency, we envision an easy to deploy operator-managed platform, and study two architectural optimizations that sit at vantage points inside cellular networks: virtual app-server (vApp) and network-assisted, virtual push-notification server (vPNS). vApps improve apps' browsing experience while vPNSs take the burden of carrying periodic message off cellular networks. Using trace-driven simulations, we find that vApps can improve activity completion times by more than 3-fold, whereas vPNS can reduce the signaling load by a factor of 6 in cellular networks and reduce energy consumption by a factor of 2 on mobile devices.

1. INTRODUCTION

Due to increasing popularity of smart-phones, tablets and other mobile devices, cellular data networks are fast becoming the defacto standard for information access. At the same time, the ecosystem of mobile applications (or apps) has evolved rapidly and is fast replacing the traditional web-browsing over mobile devices. There are more than 1 million apps [20] hosted in Google and Apple app-stores, and this number is growing at a rapid pace. This unprecedented scale as well as diversity of apps has posed several challenges towards desired app performance and operational efficiency in cellular networks.

WWW 2015, May 18–22, 2015, Florence, Italy.
ACM 978-1-4503-3469-3/15/05.
http://dx.doi.org/10.1145/2736277.2741138.

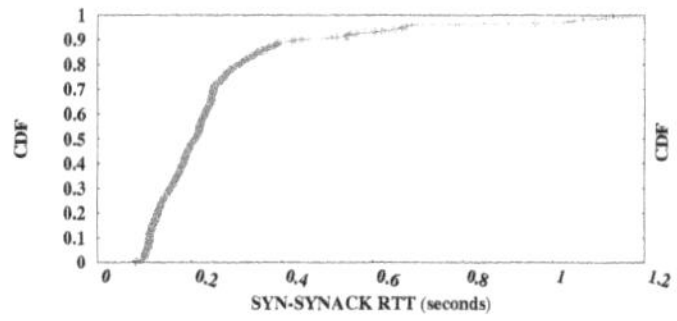

Figure 1: SYN-SYNACK Cellular

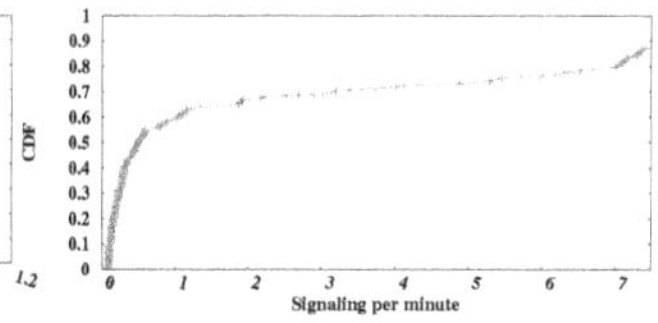

Figure 2: Signaling cellular

Today's mobile users broadly access two types of networks, WiFi and cellular. While cellular networks provide pervasive access, users experience poorer quality of access over these networks [15]. In fact, our analysis shows that the time to load app-pages almost doubles over cellular networks. Figure 1 shows a preview of our measurement study, a CDF of TCP SYN-SYNACK latency experienced by more than 50 apps for over a period of 2 months on 2 major cellular operators in India. The median app latency is about 200ms while more than 20% flows experience a latency of more than 300ms. Such high value of latency is undesirable and affects browsing experience of many apps such as news, banking, augmented reality. Several studies from search-advertisement to online-stores businesses have emphasized the ill-effects of high latency of transactions on business revenues [16]. Cellular operators thus need innovative solutions to remain relevant and match performance experienced over WiFi networks [10].

While apps experience poor performance over cellular networks, the scale and diversity of apps causes several operational challenges in cellular networks. Most of the app-clients on mobile devices today maintain long-lived app-level connections to cloud-servers. While managing such high number of simultaneous connections is a significant provisioning challenge, these connections exhibit "chatty" behavior, wherein apps run in the background and periodically generate or receive small amount of traffic (keep-alive messages or polling messages) even when users are not actively using their mobile devices. Such apps include real-time alerts, instant messaging, cloud enabled sync and push, social networking etc. The keep-alive (or polling) messages primarily help the apps to maintain connections in active state which otherwise could be torn down due to inactivities by a firewall (or NAT) timer [31]. Cellular networks also exercise a timeout mechanism on radio access network (called dormancy or inactivity timer), which puts a mobile device into sleep state from active state if there is no net-

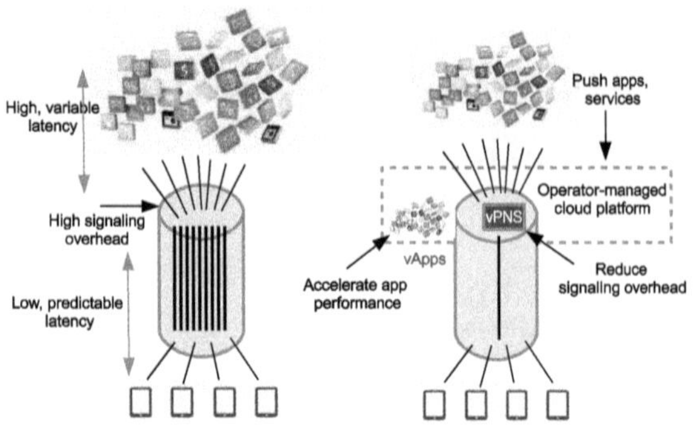

Figure 3: Cellular-operator-managed platform to improve user experience and enhance operational efficiency

work activity for a timeout period. Typically, firewall timers operate over a coarse time-scale of order of minutes (15 to 30 minutes) while dormancy timers operate over a short time-scale of order of seconds (5 to 10 sec), and this mismatch causes frequent state-switches in mobile devices which induces heavy signaling in the network.

Figure 2 shows a CDF of signaling instances resulting from such periodic messages by a mix of popular apps operating on a mobile device in our measurement study. The figure shows that more than 30% of times, a mobile device with a set of popular apps generates at least 8 signaling message per minute. A thought experiment on signaling channel capacity implies that just 323 mobile devices with a mix of popular apps can jam the signaling channel[12] of an LTE base station, while none of the apps or devices are attempting to misbehave. Several catastrophic instances on real networks [19, 18] emphasis the challenge of mitigating such signaling storms. Admittedly, setting dormancy and firewall timeouts to appropriate values may alleviate the signaling overhead; however, the timeout settings depends on multitude of factors such as periodicity of different applications, capacity to handle active connections, and effects on device energy consumption.

In this context, *our primary goal in this work is to study architectural alternatives for next generation cellular networks that accelerate app performance and reduce signaling (and energy) overload.* Specifically, we want to study optimizations that are transparent to mobile apps as well as to application servers. While there are prior attempts to accelerate browsing performance [2, 30, 26] or to reduce signaling overhead [23, 8], we argue that these approaches are not scalable since either individual apps need to be patched or individual mobile devices need to get an OS update with improved mechanisms built in. Contrary to wired networks which are completely distributed, cellular networks are owned and controlled by a single entity, and hence designing and deploying network-centric (and cloud-based) services, as opposed to mobile-centric solutions, is the need of the hour.

In this context, we suggest mechanisms for operator cloud support. Fig. 3 describes the state of the art and the operator-managed cloud scenario. While several Content Distribution Network (CDN) servers are already hosted today inside operator networks, we envision a generic cloud-platform which can enable external entities to push apps and services "into" operator-managed clouds. In this work, we study and evaluate instances of such apps and services that can be "pushed" into such cloud-platforms to enhance user experience and operational efficiency in cellular networks.

Specifically, we make the following contributions in this paper.

- *Measuring and analyzing cellular network support for popular apps.* We experimentally characterize latency performance and signaling impact of more than 50 apps in Android and iOS ecosystem using packet traces collected from a diverse set of smart-phone users over cellular and WiFi networks. Through passive measurements over cellular networks, we discover that the path between exit points of cellular networks (e.g., GGSN (Gateway GPRS Support Node) in a 3G cellular network), and cloud-servers is the major contributor to high end-to-end latencies and poor performance of apps. While such variation also exists on paths through WiFi-based networks (albeit with low intensity), from a cellular-networks perspective we find that paths between mobile devices and exit points have predictable (and tolerable) values of latency. Diagnosing and attributing causes of high variations over paths in core ISP networks is an interesting problem. However, in this work, we focus optimizing performance of apps over cellular networks. Based on this observation, we design and evaluate optimizations to push apps and services at vantage points inside cellular networks to improve performance of apps,
- *Study apps-performance by pushing app-servers close to users.* We design and study an architectural optimization of hosting scaled-down instances of app-servers (vApps) closer to mobile devices, in operator-managed clouds (see Fig. 3). To serve requests and hence to maintain the freshness of content at vApps, we design a learning-based low-overhead mechanism to update content for different apps. While the benefits of lower latency are intuitive and such architectures are proposed in the past [2], note that different apps have different network-access patterns (e.g., number of RTTs or processing times). Using real packet-traces, we then quantify the activity completion times of different apps. Our evaluation shows that activity completion times of apps can be improved by more than 3-fold using vApps after imposing realistic latencies observed inside cellular networks.
- *Design and study of a novel signaling-proxy.* To mitigate the ill-effects of periodic keep-alive messages, we design a novel cloud-based proxy to manage long-lived connections. Using such network-assisted proxy, push notification service (PNS) providers (Google, Apple, Yahoo) can host their local instances (vPNS) as signaling-proxies inside operator's network (see Fig. 3). vPNS helps in off-loading the periodic messages of active connections from cellular access network. This design dramatically reduces the signaling overhead by a factor of 6, while reducing energy consumption by a factor of 2.

We believe that our propositions of vApps and vPNS are attractive not only to cellular network operators but also to application service providers since user experience is of utmost importance to cellular network operators as well as to app-developers. Furthermore, our network-centric solutions are easy to deploy with no modifications to cloud-servers or to mobile-clients. The rest of the paper is organized as follows. In Sec. 2 we describe our measurement setup and analysis. Based on the measurement observations, we give a detailed design of vApps and vPNS in Sec. 3. We evaluate our approach in Sec. 4 using trace-driven simulations. We compare state-of-the-art with our approach in Sec. 5, and conclude the paper in Sec. 6.

2. MEASUREMENT-DRIVEN APP ANALYSIS

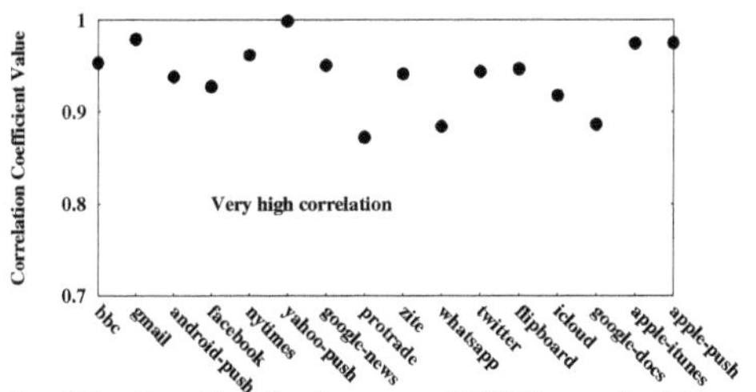

Figure 4: Similarity between WiFi and 3G packet traces

In this section, we describe our measurement setup, data collection procedure and data analysis of more than 50 mobile apps [1] over 2 cellular networks (named OperatorA, OperatorB to maintain anonymity) [2] and WiFi networks over 2 months time period. Through analysis, our goal is to demonstrate the effects of high end-to-end latency on mobile apps, and the intensity of signaling overload in cellular networks. Using analysis and observations, we then derive several new and important insights which guide the design of our system.

2.1 Measuring app-performance

A desirable way to collect traffic data of apps is to access their packet traces in operator's network. However, we do not have access to such data as it is typically not published by network operators. Hence we considered the alternative of collecting packet-level traces on individual devices operated by real users. This is possible only if the device is rooted (Android) or jailbroken (iOS). We rooted 3 devices (two HTC Desire phones running Android 2.3, and one Samsung Galaxy Duos running Android 4.2) and collected packet traces on cellular networks by logging packets in the device using tcpdump tool. Operated by active users, two phones were connected to cellular network A and one phone was connected to cellular network B. We connected the phones from two cell locations with roughly equal time distribution between the two. We collected the traces for over 3 weeks between 9am and 6pm. For elaborate data collection, we installed a set of 50 smart phone apps that fall into categories such as news, email, social networking, cloud sync, finance, free games (with ads) and instant messaging on each device.

We collected 120 hours worth of data among all phones with phones transmitting and receiving over 700K packets. We now define key terms related to our data set. *Session:* Session denotes all packets transmitted or received by a single user in a single day most of the times corresponding to a single IP address. *Flow:* Flow denotes all packets that are grouped under the five tuple <source ip, destination ip, source port, destination port, protocol>. Note that a session can have multiple flows and flows do not cross session boundaries. *Application:* Applications are identified using deep packet inspection of URLs for HTTP flows or by mapping protocol, port numbers and server subnets for known server subnets and port numbers. For encrypted flows, URLs are identified by processing the DNS request and response packets generated before the corresponding encrypted data flow begins. This procedure identifies apps for more than 89% of flows in our data set. In our entire data set, we have 57 sessions each of which lasts for at least 5 hours continuously, and account for 11783 flows.

Our primary goals behind the data collection activity were two-fold: (1) analyze the performance of various apps over cellular network, (2) collect network access pattern of various apps which can be used for trace-driven simulation. To collect more data to help in mining network access patterns, we asked 15 volunteers to let us capture the traffic of apps on their mobile devices. However, rooting or jailbreaking was not acceptable for most of the volunteers on account of several privacy and update issues. We then considered an approach of connecting devices to a WiFi access point (AP) and logging packet traces at the AP. This approach does not require devices to be rooted or jailbroken and can accommodate large number of users. However, we needed to validate this approach by comparing the behavior of packet traces collected on WiFi access point to the packet traces on cellular network.

Fig. 4 shows the correlation between the time series of vectors of the form {sequence number, packet size, packet direction} for different apps when the phones operated over WiFi and cellular networks. We observe that for majority of the apps the correlation is above 95%. We thus collected data from rest of the volunteers by capturing packet traces on WiFi network. The users had a mix of smart phones ranging from top-end Android phones (Samsung Galaxy S4 running Android 4.1) to basic Android phones (HTC Desire running Android 2.3) as well as Apple iPhone 4S running iOS 7.1. We conducted this data collection procedure for over a period of 45 days with 15 smart-phone users. In total, we collected over 762 hours worth of data among all users with users transmitting and receiving over 3.3 million packets.

Due to lack of space, we report our analysis results for the following app categories and a popular app in each category: (1) News: Flipboard, (2) Augmented reality: Layar, (3) Instant messaging: Skype, (4) Social networks: Facebook, (5) Banking: Bank-ServiceApp, (6) Service: OperatorA-ServiceApp, (7) Analytics: Crittercism, (8) Trading: Protrade, (9) Push-notification: Android-Push, (10) Mobile-games: Zynga-draw-something. We mark the following activities for each app during our evaluation: (1) Flipboard: loading of news page, (2) Layar: text response to a video image captured by the app, (3) Viber: connection establishment, (4) Facebook: loading of user feed, (5) BankApp: balance check enquiry, (6) OperatorApp: loading operator-hosted video portal, (7) Crittercism: upload of analytics data, (8) Protrade: refresh of a page to load stock prices, (9) Android-Push: connection establishment, (10) Zinga-draw-something: delivery of a drawing to online users.

2.2 Measuring network-latency

A desirable way to measure latency in operators network is to deploy active probes in the network. However, we do not have access to such active probing mechanism. Hence,

[1]Account-Samsung,Account-Google, Accuweather, Alchemy, Apple-push-notification, Apple-itunes, Android-push-notification, BBC, Bookstore, Boxcar, Camfind, Cloudfront, Crittercism, Docs-Google, Dowjones, Dropbox, Economictimes, Evernote, Facebook, Flickr, Flipboard, Flurry, Gmail, Google-analytics, Google-drive, Huffington-post, IBNLive, BankX, iCloud, Layar, Localytics, Mail-Yahoo, NDTV, NYTimes, Picassa, Protrade, Yahoo-push-notification, Yahoo-analytics, Sharekhan, Skype, Techcrunch, TimesOfIndia, Picsart, Twitter, Tumblr, Viber, Whatsapp, Youtube, Zite, Zynga-draw-something, OperatorA

[2]each having 100 million subscribers

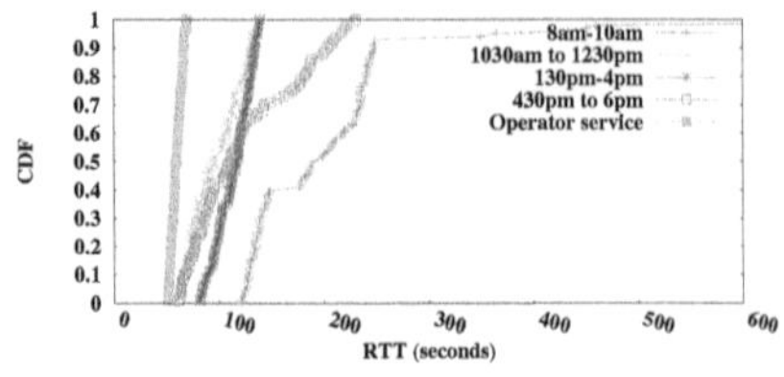

Figure 5: Ping Latency for a cell for operator A over 2 weeks

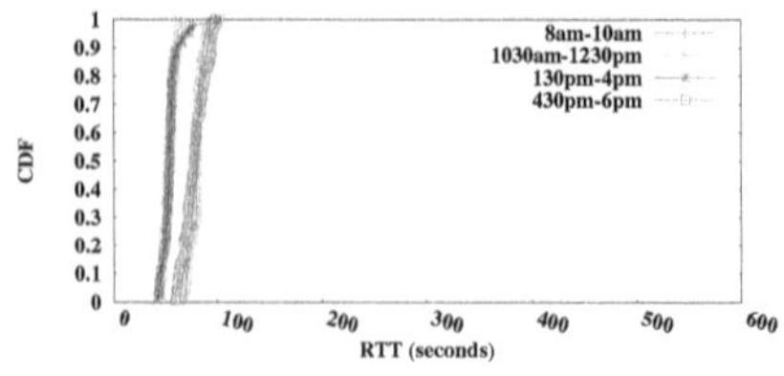

Figure 6: Ping Latency for a WiFi AP over 2 weeks

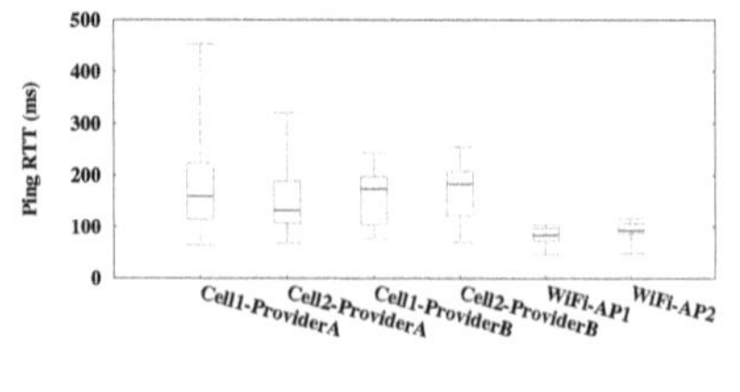

Figure 7: Ping Latency comparison over 2 weeks

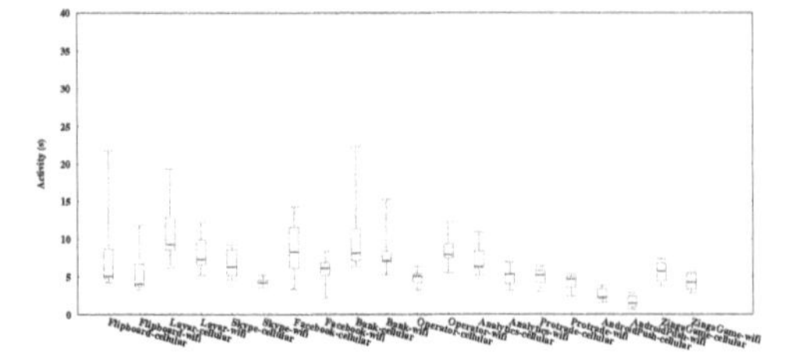

Figure 8: Apps main-activity completion time

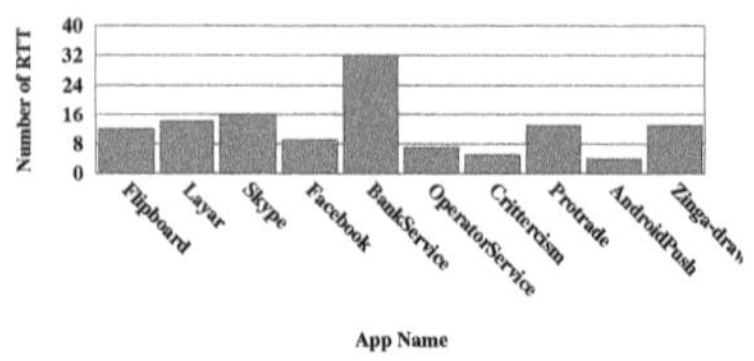

Figure 9: Number of request-response in activity

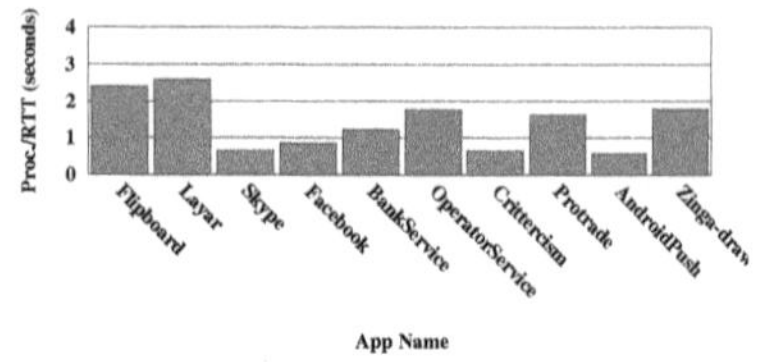

Figure 10: Average request-response processing latency

we rely on passive probes from mobile devices. We use two phones connected to cellular network A and one phone connected to cellular network B. We connected the phones from two cell locations with almost equal time distribution between the two. We also connected these phones to WiFi networks from two access points: one in an office-environment and other in a home-network. To measure latency, we installed Traceroute [22] and Ping [21] apps on mobile devices. We primarily measure latency between mobile device and google.com, mobile device and yahoo.com, and mobile device and GGSN. We discover GGSN as the last-hop with IP address in the same IP address range as that allocated to the mobile device over a Traceroute path. Using geo-ip services, we confirm that the IP-addresses indeed match the known locations of operator GGSNs. We consistently receive Traceroute measurements from exit points of cellular networks and cloud-servers. Not all the middleboxes in between respond to Traceroute measurements (mostly due to port blocking for security reasons). These measurements primarily help us analyze the two paths: from mobile devices to exist points, and exit points to cloud-servers.

2.3 Observations

We use the following metrics for our analysis.

• *Latency.* For each activity of an app, we measure SYN-SYNACK latency of the corresponding TCP flow. We further measure activity completion time from the corresponding flow completion duration. Note that, for the above activities, the corresponding app spawns a separate TCP connection. We further measure the number of application-level request-response instances for each activity.

• *Load.* We also measure the number of active connections at every 2 minute boundary over a session. To quantify the signaling overhead due to app-level keep-alive messages, we first identify such messages by observing their packet sizes and arrival time difference between itself and its predecessor packet. We then assume a dormancy timer of 5s [8] and compute sleep-to-active and active-to-sleep transitions caused by keep-alive messages.

Based on the measurement study, we now make the following observations.

• *Apps experience higher latencies over cellular networks.* From Fig. 5 and Fig. 7, we see that the first quartile latency observed over cellular network is about 120ms while on WiFi it is 75ms. Furthermore, the gap between median and 95% value shows a high variation, especially during peak-times (morning or evening rush hours) which typically leads to poor apps performance. We observed such high values of latency for the two operator networks under measurements, and two other operator networks on which we conducted limited ping tests. This is in contrast to latencies observed over WiFi networks as shown in Fig. 6 where absolute value and variation in latency is quite low.

• *However, latency to servers hosted inside operator's network is low and stable.* From Fig. 5, we observed that the ping latency to a service hosted inside operator's network (OperatorA app accessing operatorA's video store) is as low as 60ms and it remains stable even during peak time periods. This measurement observation corroborates our discussions with operators where they claim their networks to be over-provisioned. We observe similar behavior for Google servers hosted inside OperatorA's data centers. *Implication.* This observation of low and predictable latency inside operators network motivates us to study and evaluate effects of operator-managed apps-servers on apps performance.

We wish to note that it is an interesting study for future work to explaining the differences between latencies over WiFi and cellular networks. Such study can also lead to atttributing high latencies over end-to-end paths to specific causes (such as router overloads, or latency over peering links). However, focus of this work is to measure network characteristics over different network configurations and study performance improvements through optimized network designs based on existing network characteristics. For instance, we wish to utilize predictable latencies inside operators network to host apps and services inside an operator hosted cloud platform. We also note that the observations may vary for cellular service providers in different parts of the world.

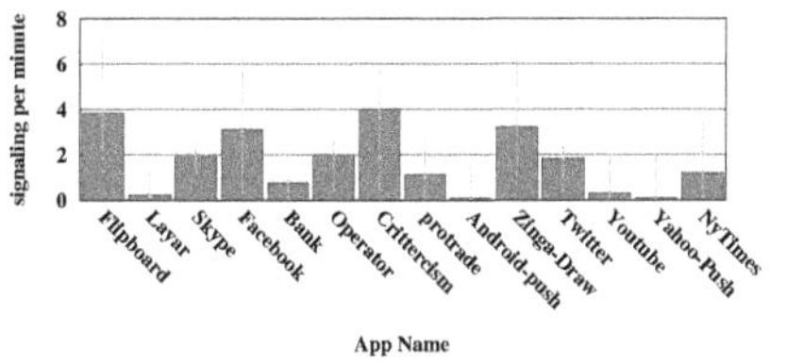

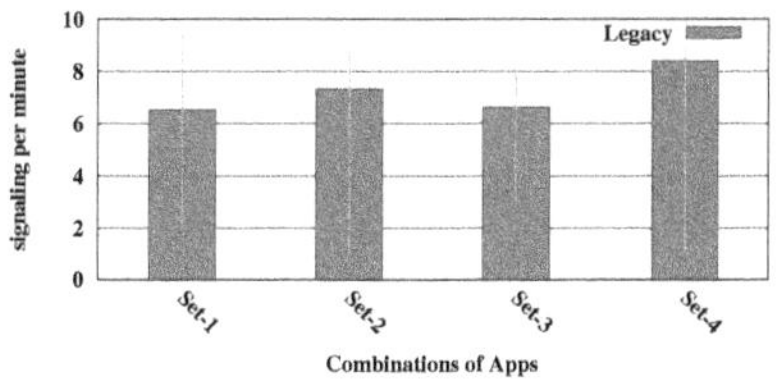

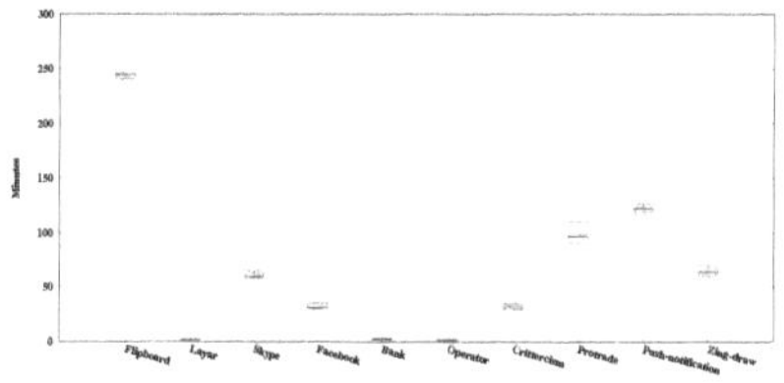

Figure 11: Signaling per minute for different apps

Figure 12: Signaling generated by a mix of apps on mobile devices

Figure 13: Connection durations of apps

• *Performance of apps worsens by a factor of 2 over cellular networks as compared to WiFi netwoks.* From Fig. 8, we see that activity completion times (such as app-page loading time, or a feed loading time) of apps on cellular networks are much higher as compared to completion times on WiFi networks, with high variations. This result can be attributed to high ping-latencies, and hence high end-to-end latencies, which we verify by measuring the latency between SYN and SYNACK packets of the corresponding TCP connections (See Fig. 1). Furthermore, WiFi networks do not add connection setup and access network latencies, that cellular networks have to add by virtue of their design. From latency measurements we see that, SYN-SYNACK latencies are about 1.5 to 2 times higher on cellular networks as compared to over WiFi networks. Also from Fig. 9 and Fig. 10, we see that different apps have different number of RTTs, and different processing times, and hence variation in latencies affects different apps by different factors. *Implication.* This observation motivates our data-driven simulation approach to analyze apps-performance for different latencies to systematically compute effects varying latencies on activity completion times.

• *The primary component of latency is the path between operator's edge and servers deployed in the cloud.* In Tab. 1, we show a break-up of the components involved in the end-to-end latency for a set of apps hosted in cloud data centers outside operators' networks. These components are computed based on Traceroute latencies to different nodes in the network, SYN-SYNACK latencies of apps, and appropriate accounting for processing times that are computed by subtracting end-to-end latency from a request-response transfer latency. There are two primary components to network latency: intra-cellular and extra-cellular. As the table shows, we see that the latency observed inside cellular networks is lower as compared to the latency over the path from exit points to cloud-servers. Furthermore, we see that apps experience high latency and high variations over the path between exit points of cellular networks and cloud-servers. The response-request activities of apps experience high and unpredictable end-to-endlatency between 1000ms (typically during non-peak period) to 300ms (typically during peak period) while DNS-look-up and cellular latency remains predictable. We also see that the variance on the path inside cellular networks is much lower as compared variance over exit paths.

In our study, we also observe that WiFi based paths too experience variations in latency between WiFi-AP and cloud-servers. However, the end-to-end latency is lower as compared to cellular networks (see Fig. 7) which results in a comparatively better apps-performance. As we mentioned earlier, focus of this work is to design and study optimization for cellular networks and performance improvement in user experience. *Implication.* In this work, we seek to utilize predictable (and tolerable) values of latency inside operators network to accelerate apps-performance on cellular networks.

• *Unaware to users or networks, only a few tens of legitimate mobile devices running a mix of popular apps in the background can bring down the signaling channel.* We find that a mobile device with a popular mix of apps installed can have 10 to 20 number of active connections at any given time. Fig. 11 shows signaling instances for different app-connections when apps are run in isolation on a mobile device. Fig. 12 shows a device-level measurement of signaling caused by a mix of apps running on the device. As shown in Fig. 13, most of the apps maintain long-tailed flows and have flow duration from 15 minutes to 2 hours except transaction-oriented apps such as mobile banking. By looking at the number of signaling instances, we see that most of the long-tailed flows are chatty and result in large number of signaling instances.

We now quantify the effects of chatty mobile devices on the capacity of signaling channel as follows. Note that this quantification is based on thought-experiments. We consider an LTE network where random access channel (RACH) is used to initiate signaling to setup connections inside an operators network, and hence to support a network flow. RACH is a random access channel where mobile devices contend to get access to the channel to send a signaling message. To compute RACH collision probability, we assume eNodeB in an LTE network is configured using a typical PRACH configuration index 6 that can provide about 200 RACH opportunities per second per preamble. There are in total 64 preambles of which 10 are reserved. So the number of RACH attempts that can cause RACH collision probability to exceed 1% is about 108 [12]. RACH attempts are caused by a variety of signaling exchanges between the mobile and the radio access network that includes attach/detach attempts, PDP context setup/release, radio up/down, paging, etc. Out of all type of signaling exchanges, radio up/down accounts for more than 40% of signaling exchanges [12]. So the number of state transitions attempts that can be allowed in an eNodeB is about 43 per second (40% of 108). As shown in Fig. 12, using 9 state transition attempts per mobile per minute, we see that *as few as 286 mobiles can cause congestion in RACH* when radio-bearer dormancy timer is 5s.

Implication. This observation motivates us to design a service to manage long-lived connections which can reduce the associated signaling overhead of keep-alive messages.

3. DESIGN

In the previous section, we observed that while application performance suffers over cellular networks due to high latencies between exit points and cloud locations, cellular networks in turn are exposed to high operational overhead due to large number of active connections and periodic message exchanges thereof. In this section, we describe two opti-

Table 1: Components of end-to-end latency, median latency (standard deviation)

App	DNS look-up	Cellular	Core	Processing
Flipboard	198.49ms (16.75ms)	83.42ms (6.75ms)	105.74ms (28.46ms)	2.23s (0.45s)
Facebook	175.58ms (12.57ms)	98.57ms (9.29ms)	126.30ms (32.73ms)	1.74s (0.23s)
Bank	224.80ms (6.84ms)	85.84ms (10.40ms)	116.94ms (25.93ms)	3.43s (0.67s)
Protrade	241.32ms (16.33ms)	88.53ms (7.43ms)	99.53ms (22.34ms)	0.98s (0.18s)

mizations which accelerate application performance and alleviate operational overhead in cellular networks. Our overall idea is for application providers to engage with cellular operators and host scaled-down versions of their app-servers (vApps) in operator-managed clouds. We describe a low-overhead mechanism for vApps to sync user-centric as well as content-centric information from cloud-servers. Furthermore, we propose a novel push notification service (PNS) proxy that significantly reduces the overhead number of active connections and hence the associated signaling overload in the network.

3.1 Placing App Servers in Operator Managed Data Centers

Our measurement study reveals that the latency inside cellular networks is low (order of 80ms) and predictable. It is hence clear that hosting applications inside operators networks can significantly improve apps-performance. To enable such operator-hosted applications, we make the following design choices.

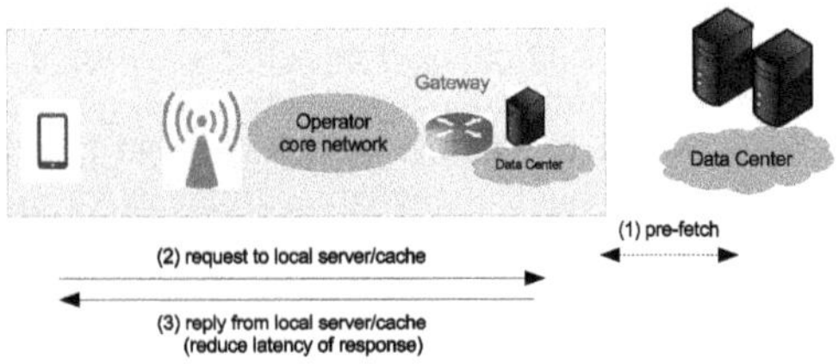

Figure 14: App server hosted close to users

Cellular-gateways as the aggregation points. While hosting applications close to users such as at cellular base stations can improve the performance dramatically, such distributed architecture poses significant management challenges. We instead propose to host apps at the most common aggregation point where we get predictable latency. Cellular gateways (GGSN, or P-GW) thus become a natural choice to host app-servers. Cellular gateways then sit between app-servers and user devices so that activities such as billing, or packet filtering which are typically performed at the gateways in cellular networks remain unaffected. This is shown in Fig. 15.

vApps: App-servers as VMs. Network Function Virtualization (NFV) [17] has emerged as a promising tool for cellular operators to virtualize network functions and to host app-servers. NFV proposes to virtualize monolithic boxes in cellular service providers network by introducing data centers at key locations where serving-gateway (SGSN or S-GW) and packet-gateway (GGSN or P-GW) are hosted. We propose that small, medium, large app providers get into an agreement with cellular service providers at a nominal rate per resource (thus ensuring fairness in terms of resource usage) to host their applications (vApps) close to users. vApps can be considered as smaller-scale instances of main applications (e.g., a small MVC-based instance [4] in an operator network of a large MVC-based instance in the cloud). We build on a prior work in Dealer [13] which splits sample applications across multiple tiers. Similar to design in [13], vApps inside operators network can sync up with cloud-servers to fetch content in local databases to serve requests locally, thus improving activity completion times of apps.

The placement of vApps is similar to the popular approaches such as Content Distribution Networks (CDN) and Cloudlets [2]. In effect, we propose to generalize CDN archiectures into a cloud-based framework to enable operators to host apps and servers inside the network. In comparison to Cloudlets, we specifically wish to observe the performance improvement in different mobile applications by using such architecture. We use packet-level traces from 50 different apps and latencies over cellular networks to quantify performance improvement in different apps using vApps. Note that, typically CDNs are used to serve static content (such as images of a web page), while dynamic content (such as comment section of a web page) is still served from cloud-servers. In vApps, our idea is to serve the entire request from local cloud platforms.

To serve content from local servers, fresh content has to be available at local servers all the time. A naive solution to tackle this challenge is for each cloud-server to sync information synchronously, i.e., as and when it gets updated. Clearly, this solution is not scalable, since, for instance, for user-centric content either each cloud-server has to sync content for all the relevant users, or vApps have to continuously poll updates for each user. Depending on the activity patterns of users, most of the hard work of getting the content may not be fruitful since such content may never get accessed instantaneously. Furthermore, we find that most of the updates for user-centric apps are of small size (more than 90% updates have less than 20KB of transfer) and fetching such content continuously may create a high computation overhead at vApps or at cloud-servers. Thus, there is a trade-off between maintaining freshness of the content at vApps and the computation or bandwidth overload in the cloud.

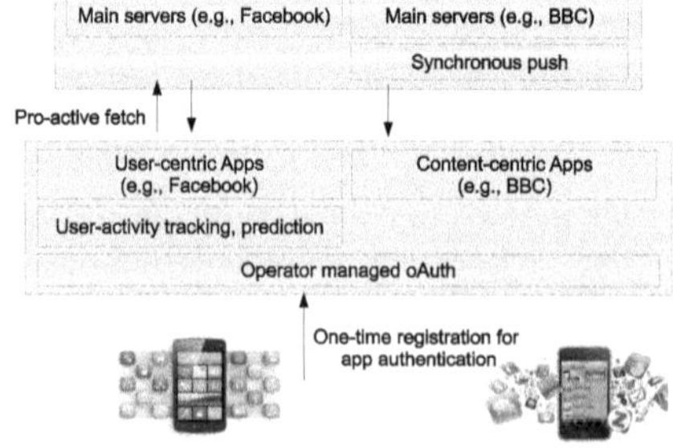

Figure 15: vApps at operators data center

Mining user-activity patterns to prefetch user-centric content. Many studies in the literature observe unique activity patterns for each user. For instance, users typically access news websites in morning or evening hours, while social networking websites at periodic intervals [27]. We answer the above trade-off (of computation overhead vs. content freshness) by predicting the activity patterns and fetching the the content on per-user per-app basis.

Operator provided opt-in service for apps acceleration. We assume a one-time registration by network users to declare their intent to receive accelerated app-performance. Thus, users can register apps with operators to let app-agents fetch the content at vApps. Such registration and fetching on behalf of users can be achieved using oAuth protocol [11]. Thus, operator-hosted agents can prefetch content at vApps using cloud-apps through activity patterns. Due to the use of oAuth service, the cloud-apps perceive app-agents as the app-users and thus respond with a fresher state. This approach thus does not require any modification to cloud-servers or app-clients. Requests can be first redirected to vApps by introducing a set of rules in DNS server. If vApps have fetched content in the recent past to serve the request, then those requests can be served locally; otherwise requests can be forwarded to main cloud-servers. To touch upon the privacy aspect, we feel that users are increasingly and willingly subscribing to services which enhance their quality of experience. Furthermore, the data for individual users is processed by machines to be protected from privacy violations.

To improve app-performance, it is essential that most of the times content is served through vApps. Thus, app-agents in operator-hosted services have to predict and fetch content to match user activity patterns with a reasonably high accuracy. To predict a user accessing an application at a given time, we thus want to learn a function $f(user-app, t) \rightarrow (0, 1)$.

We now describe an approach to learn such a function. Given a set of access timestamps over a day for a user and for an app, we first discretize the time into 5-minute time intervals. We then mark an interval as busy if the user accesses the app in that interval. We repeat the above exercise for 'p' number of days and count the number of busy instances b_i for every time interval t_i. Now, for every user U and app A, we compute the probability of access for a time interval $P_{t_i,U,A}$ as $P_{t_i,U,A} = \frac{b_i}{n}$. For each user and app, we thus maintain a list of probabilities for each 5-minute time period for a weekday and weekend each. We then predict an access using these probabilities.

Learning-based approach. The above approach does not take into account temporal relationship between user activity patterns. For instance, it is likely that if user U has accessed app A at time t, U might access app B at time $t + \delta$. To take into account such relationship, we use a simple supervised-learning algorithm to fetch content appropriately. We discretize the intervals as before and mark them as busy or free. We then describe each (user,app,interval) row via a feature vector F. F contains the following features: (1) $x_1 : P_{t_i,U,A}$ as before, (2) x_2 : the probability of user U accessing app A at any time interval, (3) x_3 : whether user is active in the last time interval, (4) x_4 : number of times user has been active in last T time intervals which captures the fact that user is more likely to access an app when he/she is active. In our evaluation, we set empirically set T to be 3 by observing user activity patterns. We then model the chance of user U accessing app A in time t_i using logistic regression.

$$Y_{t_i,UA} = \frac{1}{1 + e^{Z_{t_i,U,A}}}$$
$$Z_{t_i,U,A} = w_1x_1 + w_2x_2 + w_3x_3 + w_4x_4$$

We learn the weights of these features while applying a classifier based on logistic regression.

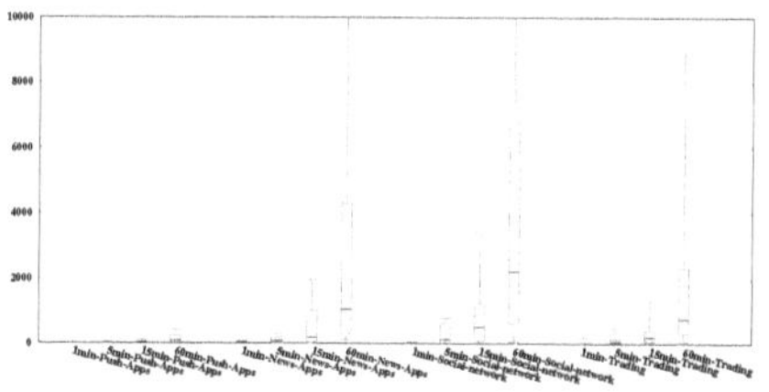

Figure 16: Change in content size of apps

As we mentioned earlier, there are user-centric apps (e.g., Facebook, Twitter, Flipbaord) and there are content-centric apps (e.g., BBC, Push notifications). Content of content-centric apps is broadcast to all the users and Fig. 16 shows the change in the size of the content for different content-centric apps. From the plots, the change content size is mostly small, of order of few tens of KBs per minute, or of similar order for every 5 minutes. Assuming 1000 applications hosted on operator managed data centers, this implies that for a periodic push from cloud-servers to vApps the total inflow of traffic vApps would be few tens of MBs per minute for every 5 minutes. Since such content update would not be per-user, content-centric apps don't suffer from the computation and scaling overhead with increase in number of users.

3.2 Operator Cloud Messaging

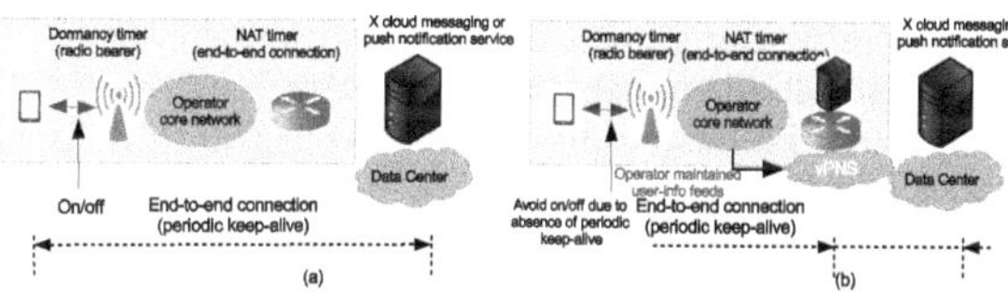

Figure 17: vPNS taking signaling load off cellular network

Push notification services have become very popular among mobile app users to get real-time notifications from different apps. Popular mobile platforms (e.g., Android, iOS, Windows Phone) provide platform specific push notification services [1, 3]. There already exists a push notification client in mobile devices running in the background talking to a cloud hosted push notification server to obtain notifications. Different application providers register with the push notification server and push notifications in real time. The push notification server then routes the notificiations to all the mobile users who have subscribed for notification from different apps. Note that, the push notification client running on mobile devices has to maintain periodic keep-alive messages to the server so that the stateful firewall in cellular networks does not close the connection between the client and the server. Furthermore, the periodicity of keep alive messages is typically configurable and specified by the server.

These periodic keep-alive messages increase signaling load in the cellular network as the mobile has to establish a radio bearer to send the keep-alive message even when there are no notifications for the mobile. More signaling overhead occurs when the periodicity of keep-alive messages is shorter. To minimize this signaling overhead in the network, we propose a signaling proxy optimization for cellular network operators.

vPNS: Virtual Push Notification Service: We propose that every platform specific push notification service (PNS) (such as Google, or Apple) has a virtual micro instance of the service (vPNS) running behind the stateful firewall within the operator's network. This is shown in Fig. 17. This virtual instance serves are a proxy to all push notification clients that connect via the cellular network. Note that, there can be multiple vPNSs, one for each GGSN in the cellular network, proxying all the mobiles that are connected via the corresponding GGSN. The vPNSs can be transparently added in the middle of the mobile client and the cloud server by modifying the operator's DNS servers to point to the vPNS. When push notification clients on mobile devices attempt to connect to the push notification service, the clients mobiles assume vPNS as the actual push notification service.

When a mobile client connects to vPNS, vPNS provides a response with the configurable keep-alive message timer value to be a very large one (say in the order of few hours). Since the vPNS is within the stateful firewall of the operator's network, the connection is not closed even when there are not packets for a long time. The vPNS on the other hand acts as a proxy for the mobile client and sends periodic keep-alive messages to the real push notification service in the cloud. From the push notification server's point of view, this change is transparent. Whenever there is a notificiation from any app, the cloud based push notification server pushes the notifiation to vPNS which is then forwared to the mobile client. Note that, by having vPNS we have eliminated the frequent keep-alive messages from mobile clients that cause large number of signaling connections that can overload the cellular network.

When a mobile device disconnects from the cellular network or hands off to WiFi network, the vPNS coordinates with its corresponding GGSN to get the latest state of the mobile and then disconnects from the cloud based push notification service transparently. If the mobile device makes a new connection (say in a WiFi network) before it breaks from the cellular network, the cloud server may reject the first request. However, the mobile client on the device typically makes more than one attempts to connect to the server which acts as fall-back mechanism to connect to the network server in subsequent attempts.

4. EVALUATION

In this section, we evaluate the benefits of hosting applications at network exit points of networks using a trace driven simulation. We also evaluate the design of a signaling-proxy and measure the signaling load in the network and related energy consumption on mobile devices.

Simulation setup In our simulation study, we use the packet traces collected as a part of our measurement study as described in Sec. 2. By looking at sequence numbers of the packets, we curate the packet traces by removing the retransmitted packets. The curated packet traces thus model the application behavior as observed on real networks. To analyze the effects of latency, we modify the one-way delays (in both directions) for every TCP segment, and measure its effects on app performance. To take into account processing times at the server, we appropriately adjust the timestamps of each request-response packet transfer by looking at the corresponding latency (if it is higher than 95% of end-to-end latency) to model back-end server processing. Note that, this does not affect the TCP behavior or its congestion control algorithm since TCP simply reacts to round-trip times to clock subsequent segments of a connection. We validate the results of our simulator by imposing latencies as observed in packet traces and then measuring correlation between the timestamps of packet arrivals and flow completion times. We get above 96% (very high) correlation. We consider the same set of apps and activities as those consider in Sec. 2 to show a set of representative results.

4.1 Activity prediction

In Sec. 3, we presented a design of vApps and associated low-overhead content-fetch mechanism which predicts user-activities. To evaluate the accuracy of this prediction model, we employ a K-fold cross-validation approach and randomly divide each of the 20 session-level traces per user, for 6 users, into $K = 10$ partitions. We use $K - 3$ partitions to train the models and remaining ones to test the model. We also evaluate user-activity prediction model proposed in [27].

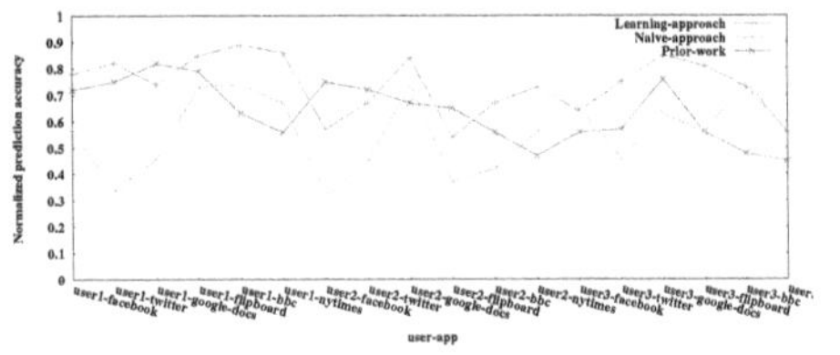

Figure 18: Access prediction errors of different models

Fig. 18 shows the median prediction accuracy over a set of representative apps for 6 users for our prediction models and a prediction model in [27]. As the figure indicates, our learning-based model is reasonably robust to different users and applications and results in 15% to 25% of prediction errors. This model matches and sometimes exceeds the accuracy of a method in the prior work [27], which results in large prediction errors for a subset of apps. While naive approach results in 25% to 40% of prediction errors, it highlights the importance of considering historical features such as last device access and correlation between times of inter-app access patterns. Our model also gives high precision (87%) and high recall (91%).

4.2 App Performance

To evaluate activity performance of different apps, we compare following two cases: (1) traditional networks using packet traces observed on real networks, and (2) apps hosted at exit points of cellular networks by imposing ping latencies observed in our measurement study. For the latter case, we impose a ping latency of 80ms (median latency observed in Sec. 2) with a random variation of 10ms. We primarily compare the activity completion times of different applications. As noted in Sec. 2, completion of activities is equivalent to page-load times or transaction completion for relevant applications.

For our evaluation, we first predict the presence of content at vApps using the output of our prediction model. If the model has not pre-fetched any content, we simulate a content-fetch from main cloud-servers by imposing an additional latency of 120ms with a random variation of 30ms (median observations in our measurement study). As shown in Fig. 19, hosting applications inside cellular networks improves application performance substantially. Note that, different apps experience different number of round-trip times, and hence the improvements in latency vary across apps. In particular, most of the apps see 2 to 3 fold improvement in median activity completion times, and while the 95th percentile decreases by several folds. This establishes the benefits of vApps hosting at exit points of cellular networks. Most of the apps experience a performance improvement of 2 to 8 seconds, which is a significant improvement for any delay-sensitive user or app.

In comparison to measurements over WiFi networks in Sec. 2, we see that the performance of optimized cellular networks matches and sometimes exceeds the performance over WiFi networks. Thus, by hosting apps-servers in operator-managed clouds at exit points, cellular network operators can indeed improve user quality of experience and match it or even exceed the experience over WiFi-based networks.

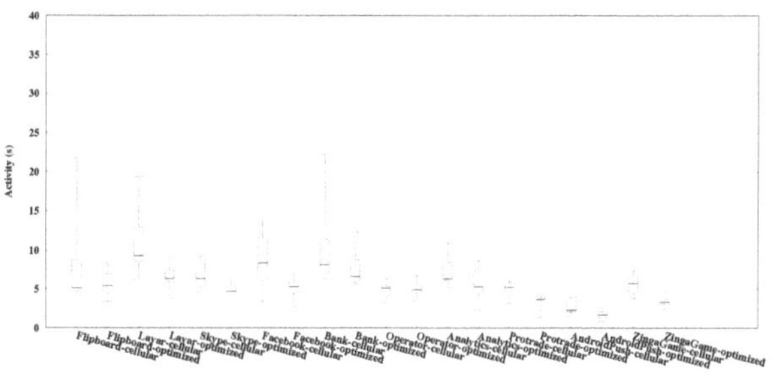

Figure 19: Latency comparison

In Fig. 20, 21, 22, we show latency improvements for different activities for three representative apps: Layar, Flipboard and BankService. As shown in the plots, the text response for an image in case of Layar improves from 14 sec median to 6 sec median with tail time dropping substantially. This is mostly because of short round-trip-times which enables a speedy upload of image to app server, leading to a faster response time. Although not as dramatic as Layar, the activities such as logging, refresh or loading a new item in case of Flipboard too see improvements of several seconds. In case of the bank application, we evaluate 4 different activities: login, balance check, money transfer and payment for a utility. For all the activities we see at least 50% reduction in activity completion. Note that since apps such as banking apps have high processing overhead, the improvements in activity completion times may not be as dramatic as other apps, such as augmented reality (e.g., Layar).

4.3 Signaling-proxy performance

To compare the benefits of a signaling-proxy, we evaluate following three cases: (1) traditional network using packet traces observed on real networks, (2) firewall timer tuned to a high value to reduce the frequency of keep-alive messages, and (3) signaling-proxy where apps (whether hosted inside or outside operators network) use the proxy to maintain connections with user devices, the proxy obviates unnecessary keep-alive or polling messages from user devices.

To compare the above three cases, we consider the dormancy timer settings of 5sec as mentioned in [14]. Note that every keep-alive message after dormancy timeout results in a signaling activity. Thus, it is intuitive to expect that any long-lived apps that frequently (period greater than the dormancy timeout) send keep-alive messages will cause heavy signaling overhead in the network, and a signaling-proxy will show significant improvements in their signaling load. A high signaling load also implies that the device has to transition frequently from 'sleep' to 'active' state which incurs energy consumption. Hence, we also evaluate energy consumption of the three cases using an energy model mentioned in [14].

4.3.1 Signaling comparison

Fig. 23 shows signaling per minute our representative set of apps. As we observe from the plot, when apps react to firewall-timer, and when firewall-timer is set to a high value, it substantially reduces signaling per minute for most of the apps. In particular, for apps having long-lived background connections such as Skype and Facebook, a high value of firewall timeout reduces the signaling overhead by more than a factor of 4. In comparison, in case of a signaling-proxy, the signaling per minute reduces by more than a factor of 6 and reaches almost close to 0 for a subset of apps.

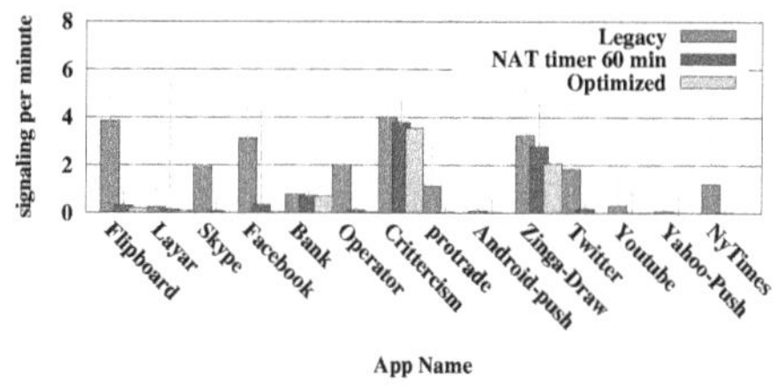

Figure 23: Signaling improvement

Signaling for a device, however, is not dictated by a single app but by a mix of apps. In Fig. 11 we plot the signaling per minute observed from a device having a set of apps installed. We consider 4 combinations of apps (from each from 4 different users) in out dataset. As shown in the plot, signaling per minute from a phone decreases substantially when a signaling-proxy is used.

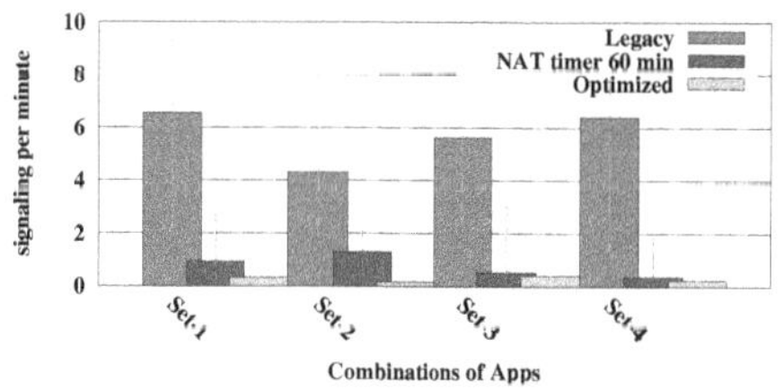

Figure 24: Signaling over different combination of apps

4.3.2 Energy comparison

Given the reductions in signaling messages from a device, the number of switches between 'sleep' and 'active' states, as well as the time spent in 'active' state also reduces. Hence, the energy consumed by a device is also expected to decrease. We use the energy model for different states as measured in [14], and in Fig. 25, show energy reduction in mobile devices having 4 representative mix of apps. As the figure shows, having a signaling-proxy improves device energy consumption by 100% (i.e., it reduces energy consumption by a factor of 2). Note that the reduction in energy consumption need not be not proportional to reduction in signaling instances, since the calculation of energy consumption also accounts for the time intervals when the device is in active

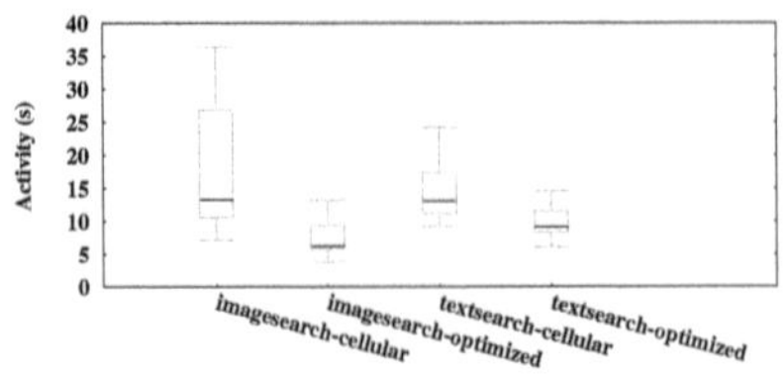

Figure 20: Layar

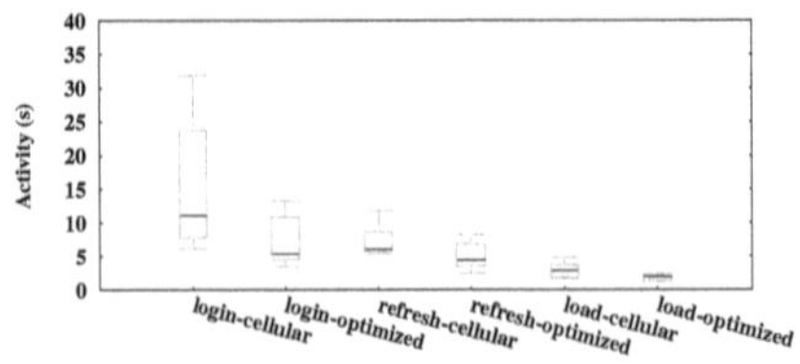

Figure 21: Flipboard

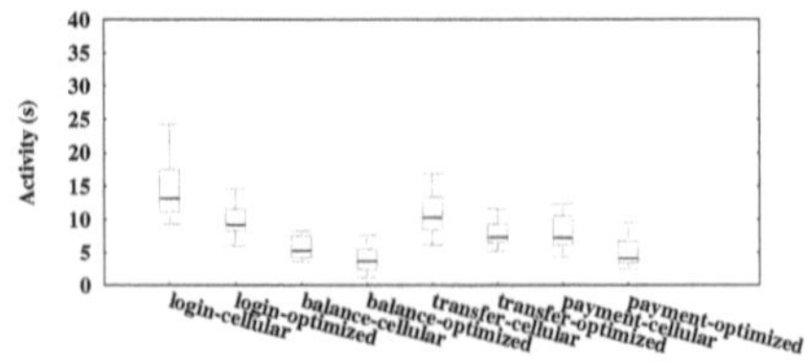

Figure 22: BankService

state due to foreground apps or due to activities (e.g., push messages) on background apps.

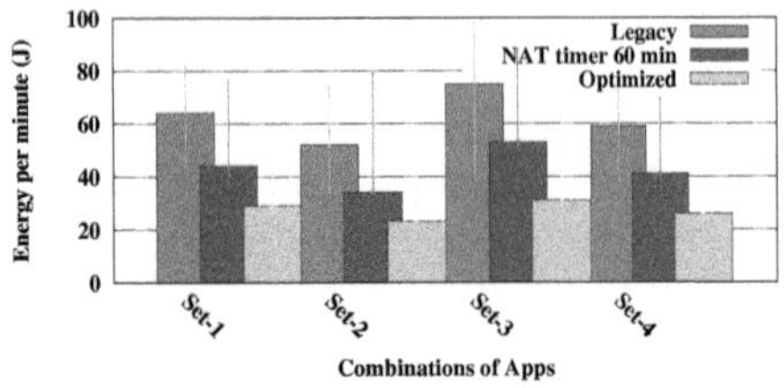

Figure 25: Energy consumption over different combination of apps

5. RELATED WORK

We classify the prior work related to our work into the following categories.

Mobile app performance. [25] explores a device-centric approach to quantify the quality of apps. This approach needs to instrument app binaries and quantifies the behavior of apps on mobile devices in terms of critical paths in user transactions etc. We instead take a network-centric solution approach where, we look at the packet-level traces of applications and quantify the effects of latency without instrumenting devices. The authors in [29] focus on page load times in mobile-browser and develop a lightweight in-browser profiler to attribute performance to different causes. In [30], the authors evaluate the effectiveness of a client-only solutions such as caching, prefetching for web browsing. In contrast, we focus on the performance of mobile apps instead of mobile web browsing, and evaluate the benefits of placing app-servers at an aggregate point close to user devices.

Design for performance boost. [26] presents a system to allow applications to achieve consistent response times in the face of variable delays such as DNS resolution, radio wake-up, and server-client-side processing delays. The authors proposition is for servers to adapt its processing time to control the end-to-end delay for a request while occasionally trading the quality of results. However, implementing this system requires modifications to cloud-servers as well as mobile-clients. In [2], the authors propose 'data center in a box' to bring the cloud closer to users. Our work is complementary to [2] in following way. Similar [2], we believe that server-apps would soon be hosted as virtual CDNs (vCDN) on VMs inside operators network [9]. However, we conduct a systematic measurement study to design our system based on predictable latency values inside cellular networks. Furthermore, we propose a new architecture for users to host images of their apps inside cellular networks for seamless and transperant performance boost.

Mobile energy consumption. [6] points out the tail energy overhead due to the time spent in high power states after completing a transfer, and develops a model for energy consumption. [28] explicitly focuses on the web pages, web browsers and relevant energy consumption, and do not consider mobile apps which are becoming dominant. The authors in [5] and [8] propose to change the radio state from IDLE to ACTIVE, by learning the traffic patterns and predicting traffic bursts. Compared to these works, we consider more than 50 popular apps, and specifically focus on keep-alive or polling messages caused by long-lived apps which results in energy drain on mobile devices. We propose and evaluate design of a novel network-assisted signaling-proxy that is transparent to apps-services to eliminate signaling overhead and reduce associated energy consumption by reducing switches between high-power and low-power states.

Network signaling. In [23], the authors point out the effects of periodic transfers on network signaling and evaluate device-based strategies such as piggybacking or batching. The authors in [7], seek appropriate values of dormancy timer based on application-level traffic and show the effect of signaling messages generated by different applications. However, they conclude that it is not trivial to arrive at a solution especially considering a mix of apps. The authors in [24] design and implement an Application Resource Optimizer (ARO) that exposes the cross-layer interactions between among application layer and radio layer. This work advises developers to practice solutions such as batching and prefetching etc to develop network-friendly applications. In this work, we show that it is indeed possible to manage and reduce signaling overhead from a mix of apps by designing and evaluating a clean-slate, network-centric artifact.

6. CONCLUSION

Cellular networks have been largely acting as bit-pipes for over-the-top applications, and such ecosystem is performing poorly in terms of apps-performance as well as operational efficiency. We believe that cellular networks have to evolve to support the unprecedented increase in mobile apps and provide a high-quality browsing experience. Towards such evolution, in this work, we proposed and evaluated designs to improve application performance and operational efficiency in cellular networks. Through systematic measurements, we attributed the poor response time of mobile-apps browsing to high and variable latency over the path between exit points and app-servers. Using predictions of user-activity patterns, we then designed and evaluated a low-overhead system to host app-servers at exit points, and showed that apps can receive significant performance boost on account of lower end-to-end latencies. We also presented design of a novel, lightweight signaling proxy to eliminate the ill-effects of periodic messages on cellular networks. The signaling proxy reduced signaling load by a factor of 6, and reduce energy expenditure on mobile devices by a factor of 2. We are currently working towards implementing and evaluating these mechanisms on real networks and attributing latencies to specific network configurations.

7. REFERENCES

[1] Apple push notification service. http://bit.ly/1iP08v6.

[2] Elijah: Cloudlet-based mobile computing. http://elijah.cs.cmu.edu/.

[3] Google cloud messaging for android. https://developer.android.com/google/gcm/index.html.

[4] Model-view-controller. http://en.wikipedia.org/wiki/Model_view_controller.

[5] P. K. Athivarapu, R. Bhagwan, S. Guha, V. Navda, R. Ramjee, D. Arora, V. N. Padmanabhan, and G. Varghese. Radiojockey: Mining program execution to optimize cellular radio usage. In *Mobicom '12*, 2012.

[6] N. Balasubramanian, A. Balasubramanian, and A. Venkataramani. Energy consumption in mobile phones: A measurement study and implications for network applications. In *Proceedings of the 9th ACM SIGCOMM Conference on Internet Measurement Conference*, IMC '09, 2009.

[7] S. Christian, H. Tobias, L. Frank, and T.-G. Phuoc. Angry apps: The impact of network timer selection on power consumption, signalling load, and web qoe. *Journal of Computer Networks and Communications*, 2013, Article ID 176217, 13 pages, 2013, 2013.

[8] S. Deng and H. Balakrishnan. Traffic-aware techniques to reduce 3g/lte wireless energy consumption. In *CoNext '12*, 2012.

[9] Ericsson. The real-time cloud. www.ericsson.com/res/docs/whitepapers/wp-sdn-and-cloud.pdf.

[10] Forbes. Time to scale public wifi in india. http://forbesindia.com/blog/no-wires-attached/time-to-scale-public-wifi-in-india/.

[11] google. oauth for web 1.0. https://developers.google.com/accounts/docs/OAuth.

[12] S. group. 3rd generation partnership project; technical specification group radio access network; study on ran improvements for machine communications; (release 11). www.qtc.jp/3GPP/Specs/37868-b00.pdf.

[13] M. Hajjat, S. P. N, D. Maltz, S. Rao, and K. Sripanidkulchai. Dealer: Application-aware request splitting for interactive cloud applications. In *Proceedings of the 8th International Conference on Emerging Networking Experiments and Technologies*, CoNEXT '12, 2012.

[14] J. Huang, F. Qian, A. Gerber, Z. M. Mao, S. Sen, and O. Spatscheck. A close examination of performance and power characteristics of 4g lte networks. In *MobiSys '12*, 2012.

[15] Huawei. Smartphone solutions: white paper. www.huawei.com/ilink/en/download/HW_193034.

[16] Kissmetrics. How loading time affects your bottom line. https://blog.kissmetrics.com/loading-time/.

[17] D. Krishnaswamy, R. Krishnan, D. Lopez, P. Willis, and A. Qamar. An open nfv and cloud architectural framework for managing application virality behavior. In *IEEE Consumer Communications and Networking Conference (CCNC) 2015, to appear.*

[18] News. How Smart Phones are Bogging Down Some Wireless Carriers? http://tinyurl.com/kt7a8qu.

[19] NSN. Signaling is growing 50% faster than data traffic. http://tinyurl.com/kdlhuwt.

[20] Phonearea. Android's google play beats app store with over 1 million apps, now officially largest. http://www.phonearena.com/news/Androids-Google-Play-beats-App-Store-with-over-1-million-apps-now-officially-largest_id45680.

[21] G. play. Ping app. https://play.google.com/store/apps/details?id=com.ulfdittmer.android.ping.

[22] G. play. Traceroute, ping apps. https://play.google.com/store/apps/details?id=com.scan.traceroute.

[23] F. Qian, Z. Wang, Y. Gao, J. Huang, A. Gerber, Z. Mao, S. Sen, and O. Spatscheck. Periodic transfers in mobile applications: Network-wide origin, impact, and optimization. In *Proceedings of the 21st International Conference on World Wide Web*, WWW '12, 2012.

[24] F. Qian, Z. Wang, A. Gerber, Z. Mao, S. Sen, and O. Spatscheck. Profiling resource usage for mobile applications: A cross-layer approach. In *MobiSys '11*, 2011.

[25] L. Ravindranath, J. Padhye, S. Agarwal, R. Mahajan, I. Obermiller, and S. Shayandeh. Appinsight: Mobile app performance monitoring in the wild. In *Proceedings of the 10th USENIX Conference on Operating Systems Design and Implementation*, OSDI'12, 2012.

[26] L. Ravindranath, J. Padhye, R. Mahajan, and H. Balakrishnan. Timecard: Controlling user-perceived delays in server-based mobile applications. In *Proceedings of 24th ACM Symposium on Operating Systems Principles*, SOSP'13, 2013.

[27] V. Srinivasan, S. Moghaddam, A. Mukherji, K. K. Rachuri, C. Xu, and E. M. Tapia. Mobileminer: Mining your frequent patterns on your phone. In *Proceedings of the 2014 ACM International Joint Conference on Pervasive and Ubiquitous Computing*, UbiComp '14, 2014.

[28] N. Thiagarajan, G. Aggarwal, A. Nicoara, D. Boneh, and J. P. Singh. Who killed my battery?: Analyzing mobile browser energy consumption. In *Proceedings of the 21st International Conference on World Wide Web*, WWW '12, 2012.

[29] X. S. Wang, A. Balasubramanian, A. Krishnamurthy, and D. Wetherall. Demystifying page load performance with wprof. In *Proceedings of the 10th USENIX Conference on Networked Systems Design and Implementation*, nsdi'13, 2013.

[30] Z. Wang, F. X. Lin, L. Zhong, and M. Chishtie. How far can client-only solutions go for mobile browser speed? In *Proceedings of the 21st International Conference on World Wide Web*, WWW '12, 2012.

[31] Z. Wang, Z. Qian, Q. Xu, Z. Mao, and M. Zhang. An Untold Story of Middleboxes in Cellular Networks. *SIGCOMM Comput. Commun. Rev.*, 41(4), 2011.

Rethinking Security of Web-Based System Applications

Martin Georgiev
University of Texas at Austin
mgeorgiev@utexas.edu

Suman Jana
University of Texas at Austin
suman@cs.utexas.edu

Vitaly Shmatikov
University of Texas at Austin
shmat@cs.utexas.edu

ABSTRACT

Many modern desktop and mobile platforms, including Ubuntu, Google Chrome, Windows, and Firefox OS, support so called Web-based system applications that run outside the Web browser and enjoy direct access to native objects such as files, camera, and geolocation. We show that the access-control models of these platforms are (a) incompatible and (b) prone to unintended delegation of native-access rights: when applications request native access for their own code, they unintentionally enable it for untrusted third-party code, too. This enables malicious ads and other third-party content to steal users' OAuth authentication credentials, access camera on their devices, etc.

We then design, implement, and evaluate POWERGATE, a new access-control mechanism for Web-based system applications. It solves two key problems plaguing all existing platforms: security and consistency. First, unlike the existing platforms, POWERGATE correctly protects native objects from unauthorized access. Second, POWERGATE provides uniform access-control semantics across all platforms and is 100% backward compatible. POWERGATE enables application developers to write well-defined native-object access policies with explicit principals such as "application's own local code" and "third-party Web code," is easy to configure, and incurs negligible performance overhead.

Categories and Subject Descriptors

D.4.6 [**Security and Protection**]: Access controls

Keywords

Web Security; Mobile Security; Firefox OS

1 Introduction

Web-based system applications, as defined by the W3C Working Group [47], are Web applications with comparable capabilities to native applications. They are implemented in languages such as HTML5 and JavaScript but operate outside the Web browser sandbox, with direct access to the operating system on the host machine. Many modern operating systems, including Ubuntu, Google Chrome, Windows, and Firefox OS, provide runtime environments to support Web-based system applications, eroding the distinction between desktop, mobile, and Web-based software.

Web-based system applications offer several attractive features. First, they are implemented in platform-independent Web languages and thus are portable, in contrast to native applications. In theory, the developer can write the application once and it will run on many desktop and mobile platforms. Second, they have access to native functionality such as local files, camera, microphone, etc., in contrast to conventional Web applications. Third, after they are installed by the user, they can work offline, also in contrast to conventional Web applications. Fourth, they are easy to maintain and update by changing the Web code hosted on the developer's site, instead of requiring all users to update their local copies. Fifth, even though they use runtime Web-browser libraries, they do not rely on browsers' user interfaces, which can take up valuable display space on mobile devices and make applications less responsive.

Our contributions. We first analyze the security models of the existing platforms for Web-based system applications: Ubuntu, Chrome, Windows, and Firefox OS. These platforms have different access-control semantics for native objects, making it difficult to implement secure, portable applications even when the language and API are platform-independent (e.g., Open Web APIs in HTML5).

Another problem with the existing platforms is that their access-control policies are expressed in terms of system components and thus do not map naturally onto the applications' privilege separation requirements. For example, in Ubuntu and Windows, native-access capabilities are granted not to the application per se but to specific browser instances. Consider a Web-based system application created from a conventional Web application that combines its own content with untrusted third-party advertising in the same browser instance (e.g., WebView). When the platform gives native-access rights to this WebView object, it effectively grants them not only to the application's own code, but also to unauthorized third-party code sharing the same WebView.

We demonstrate several security vulnerabilities caused by the unintentional delegation of native-access rights on the existing platforms. These vulnerabilities have not been reported in previous work [20]. For example, a malicious iframe included into an Ubuntu HTML5 app can use the privileges of the browser's main frame to steal the user's OAuth credentials for Gmail, Facebook, etc. Similarly, a malicious iframe in a Windows Runtime app can get unfettered access to geolocation. Google Chrome has a different but related problem, where messages sent by the app's local code to the app's Web code can be intercepted by malicious third-party content, thereby enabling content injection attacks.

We then design, implement, and evaluate POWERGATE, a new access-control mechanism for Web-based system applications. In contrast to the existing mechanisms, POWERGATE provides both

WWW 2015, May 18–22, 2015, Florence, Italy.
ACM 978-1-4503-3469-3/15/05.
http://dx.doi.org/10.1145/2736277.2741663.

security and consistency by defining and correctly enforcing uniform access-control semantics for all native objects.

POWERGATE enables application developers to express access restrictions on native objects in terms of explicit principals such as "application's own local code," "application's own remote code," and "third-party remote code." Crucially, these policies do not rely on the risk-prone delegation of access capabilities to WebViews and other system components.

We implemented a prototype of POWERGATE based on Firefox OS. Our evaluation shows that the performance overhead of POWERGATE is very small vs. stock Firefox OS. We also demonstrate how POWERGATE can automatically emulate the access-control semantics of conventional Ubuntu, Google Chrome, Windows, and Firefox OS, thus ensuring 100% backward compatibility: any existing Web-based system application will run on a POWERGATE-enabled platform without any changes to the application's code.

2 Software stack

The software stack for Web-based system applications is shown schematically in Fig. 1. All platforms in our study implement some version of this stack; individual variations are explained in the corresponding sections. We divide the layers of this stack into two categories: those managed by the platform OS and those managed by individual applications.

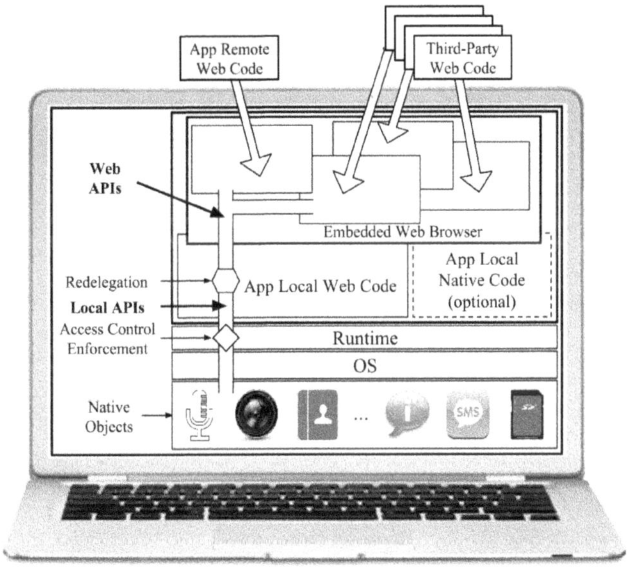

Figure 1: Software stack of Web-based system applications

2.1 Platform components

Native objects. These are the native resources and functionalities that the platform makes available to Web-based system applications. Depending on the platform, native objects may include hardware components (e.g., camera or GPS), special files (e.g., contacts list on a mobile device), and platform-level functionality (e.g., notifications or authentication credentials).

Local API to native objects. To enable applications to access native objects, each platform provides a runtime environment with special APIs. Different APIs may be available depending on the application's level of privilege. Even on platforms where local APIs are implemented in Web languages such as JavaScript, the platform may make them available only to the application's local code, i.e., the part already installed on the machine, but not to the remote Web code running inside a browser instance.

Web API to native objects. In contrast to the local API, Web API to native objects is available to the application's remote Web code. Web API is implemented via special browser objects or other mechanisms that enable Web content executing inside a browser to make calls outside the browser sandbox—either to the application's local code, or directly to the platform. Often, the Web API is a subset of the local API.

2.2 Application components

Manifest. The application's manifest lists what the application needs from the platform. The key part of the manifest is an explicit list of native objects that the application wants to access. In all platforms in our study, this list must be approved by the user when the application is installed. The platform's runtime environment is responsible for ensuring that an application cannot access a native object via the local or Web API unless this object has been approved by the user as part of the manifest.

Local code. Web-based system applications typically have a component which is installed on the host machine as a local program.

In the simplest case, the local component consists solely of the application's manifest and content caches, but in many applications it also includes executable code. This local code (1) creates embedded browser instances that execute the application's remote Web code (see below), (2) "links" the platform's local API and the browser's Web API so that the application's remote code, too, can access native objects, and/or (3) provides some offline functionality. Depending on the platform, the local code may be implemented in a Web language such as JavaScript, but it runs outside the browser, is not subject to the standard browser sandboxing policies, and has direct access to the platform's local API.

Own remote code. The bulk of the code of a Web-based system application is typically hosted at a remote, developer-controlled domain (we call it the app's *Web-home* domain). Hosting application code remotely allows developers to re-use the same code across multiple platforms, update it without involving the users, and dynamically generate new content.

This code runs on the user's machine inside an embedded browser instance (e.g., WebView) created by the application's local code. Consequently, it can access native objects via the Web API but not via the platform's local API.

Third-party remote code. Web-based system applications may also incorporate third-party Web code from origins other than the developer's own domain. For example, an advertising-supported application may include an iframe which dynamically fetches ads from different origins while the application is executing.

2.3 Threat model

For the purposes of this paper, we assume that the hardware, operating system, and the application (both the local and remote code written by the application developer, as well as the developer-specified privilege separation policies) are trusted. The main threat is third-party remote content included into the application. The origins of this content are not known statically, e.g., due to syndicated and auction-based advertising. It may be malicious and attempt to gain unauthorized access to camera, file system, etc.

The security of the software stack shown in Fig. 1 thus fundamentally depends on the platform's correct separation between the privileges granted to the application's local code, application's own remote code, and third-party remote code.

3 Existing platforms

Web-based system applications need to expose native objects to parts of the application's code (e.g., Web code hosted at the developer's own site) while hiding them from other parts (e.g., third-party ads). Standard OS access control works at the granularity of individual applications and cannot provide the required privilege separation. Platforms supporting Web-based system applications thus implement new access-control mechanisms for native objects.

In this section, we analyze the access-control models and enforcement mechanisms in Ubuntu, Google Chrome, Windows, and Firefox OS (summarized in Table 1). We show that native-access semantics are inconsistent across the platforms, explain the pros and cons of each approach, and demonstrate several security problems caused by the design flaws in access-control models.

3.1 Ubuntu

Overview. Ubuntu provides isolation between the app's local and remote Web code and also enforces the same origin policy on the remote Web code from different origins. The app's local code is treated as a distinct origin. Ubuntu uses a mix of install-time and runtime access control to protect access to native objects.

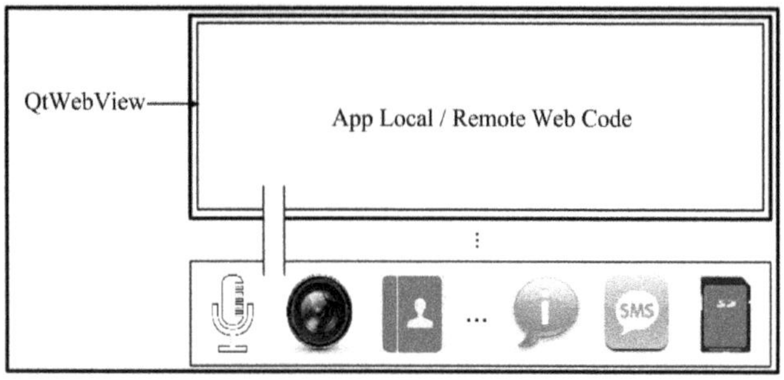

Figure 2: Ubuntu HTML5 apps: software stack

Privilege hierarchy. Ubuntu supports two classes of applications: HTML5 apps and regular Web apps. The latter execute inside a Web browser and have access to a very limited set of native objects. By contrast, HTML5 apps execute inside a Web "container" without the browser UI elements. The overall architecture of Ubuntu HTML5 apps is shown in Fig. 2.

Ubuntu supports three different API classes for HTML5 apps: Ubuntu platform APIs (Unity), W3C APIs, and Cordova APIs. Ubuntu platform APIs provide access to OS services such as notification, messaging, media player, launcher, etc. The W3C APIs follow W3C specifications and provide access to a very limited set of device resources such as geolocation. The Cordova APIs [10] provide access to a wide range of OS resources such as accelerometer, camera, capture, contacts, device, file, geolocation, and storage. Cordova uses a plugin framework to expose device-level functionality via a JavaScript interface. Ubuntu requires app developers to either package their own copies of the Cordova runtime with the app, or use the one offered by the platform.

Principals and access-control implementation. Ubuntu uses the open-source AppArmor utility to sandbox each app. An app developer can either use pre-existing templates to configure the sandbox for the resources her app needs, or customize the templates by adding her own set of "policy groups," roughly analogous to Android permissions. Sample policy groups include accounts, audio, calendar, camera, connectivity, contacts, and location, etc. [3]

The Cordova API is accessible to Web code from any origin [20]. Even though Cordova supports origin whitelisting, Ubuntu does not expose it to app developers, thus there is no way to restrict native-object accesses to a particular origin(s). On the other hand, Ubuntu ensures that most of the Unity API is only accessible to the app's local code and not to any Web code. Unfortunately, this policy has exceptions which lead to serious security vulnerabilities.

Pros. Ubuntu relies on AppArmor and hides most of the fine-grained, origin-based access control from the user.

Cons. As mentioned above, Ubuntu exposes the Cordova API to all Web origins, allowing untrusted Web code to access camera, microphone, etc. [20] Furthermore, Ubuntu lets users link their online accounts such as Google and Facebook to their OS account. Once linked, the login credentials are accessible via the OnlineAccounts API [36]. Even though untrusted Web code inside iframes cannot query this API directly, it can navigate the top frame to its own origin, steal the user's OAuth credentials via the API (since access is granted to a particular *frame*, not to a particular Web origin), and redirect the main frame back to the original page to keep the attack stealthy. This attack enables malicious Web content to hijack users' Google and Facebook accounts.

3.2 Chrome

Overview. The software stack of Google Chrome apps is shown in Fig. 3. Chrome provides isolation between the app's local code, which it treats as a distinct origin different from all Web origins, and remote content, to which it applies the same origin policy. Chrome uses install-time access control for the native objects declared in the app's manifest, but developers can add stricter runtime checks by coding them in the app's JavaScript shim.

Chrome also supports optional permissions,[1] which are declared in the app's manifest but must be approved by the user at runtime when the object is accessed. Optional permissions are not the focus of this paper because they apply only to a handful of native objects, not including the more sensitive ones such as camera.

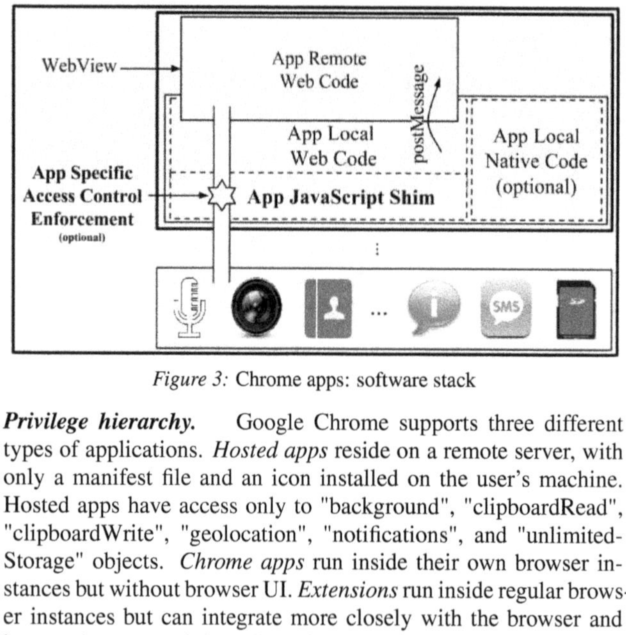

Figure 3: Chrome apps: software stack

Privilege hierarchy. Google Chrome supports three different types of applications. *Hosted apps* reside on a remote server, with only a manifest file and an icon installed on the user's machine. Hosted apps have access only to "background", "clipboardRead", "clipboardWrite", "geolocation", "notifications", and "unlimitedStorage" objects. *Chrome apps* run inside their own browser instances but without browser UI. *Extensions* run inside regular browser instances but can integrate more closely with the browser and bypass the same origin policy. Chrome apps and extensions have access to most of the native objects.

Principals. The local Web code of Chrome apps cannot include third-party resources such as scripts and embedded objects. Unlike Firefox OS (described below), Chrome does not allow iframes pointing to third-party content. Instead, such content must be put into WebView tags. Unlike iframes, these WebViews are separate browser instances, thus their rendering engines run in separate processes. Even if malicious content compromises the rendering pro-

[1] `https://developer.chrome.com/apps/permissions`

Platform	Privilege hierarchy	Install-time access control	Runtime access control	Each tuple defines a principal
Ubuntu	Yes (2 levels)	Yes	Yes	(app, local/remote code)
Chrome	Yes (3 levels)	Yes	(optional) in JavaScript shim	(app, local/remote code, Web origin*)
Windows	No	Yes	Yes	(app, local/remote code)
Firefox OS	Yes (4 levels)	Yes	Yes	(app, browser instance, Web origin)

Table 1: Access control enforcement on different platforms.
*Code for origin-based access control enforcement is the responsibility of the app developer.

cess of its WebView, the other browser instances are still protected by the OS-level process isolation.

By default, native objects in Chrome are exposed only to local app code, but developers can implement JavaScript shims that expose certain objects via Web API to the remote code executing inside WebView instances. The developer is responsible for ensuring that this access is not abused by untrusted third-party code executing in the same WebViews. This is a problem because, when enabled, a WebView API to a native object can be accessed by any content inside this WebView, regardless of its origin.

Access-control implementation. Each Chrome app must request via its manifest the permissions for all native objects it accesses [9]. Sensitive permissions (videoCapture, audioCapture, etc.) are shown to the user for approval when the app is installed. Once approval is granted, the app can access all requested native objects without any further user interaction.

Pros. Chrome hides its fine-grained, origin-based isolation from the user. Individual Web APIs are not activated by default, but must be explicitly requested by the app.

Cons. Conceptually, Chrome relies on delegating native-access rights not to named principals (explicitly specified Web origins) but to system components (WebView instances). This is risky because a given component may include code from untrusted principals. Security thus completely depends on the developers correctly implementing origin checks for each resource request coming from a WebView instance. These checks can rely on *WebRequestEventInteface*,[2] or use various match patterns.[3] In either case, the access-control code is subtle and difficult to write correctly [43]. The sample WebView app distributed by Google Chrome via GitHub [8], which is supposed to serve as a coding guidance for other apps, is missing any such checks and consequenly exposes the native objects to all Web origins.

Furthermore, even correctly implemented checks can be bypassed. For example, the current implementation of the "pointer lock" object incorrectly reports the source of the request to be the origin of the main frame even when the request comes from inside an iframe, rendering all origin checks ineffectual.

Another problem inherent in Chrome apps is their use of HTML5 postMessage for communication between the app's local Web code and its remote Web code. By design, the remote Web code running inside WebView does not have a reference to the parent app's window. It must first receive a postMessage from the local side of the application before it can send a message to it. Unfortunately, the local code of some existing Chrome apps (e.g., Lucidchart Diagrams) sends postMessage with "*" as the destination, i.e., without restricting the receiver's origin. Malicious third-party Web code running inside an iframe can "frame-bust" (i.e., navigate the main frame of its WebView to the attacker's URL), capture the message and its contents, and change the main frame to its old URL. Once it obtains a reference to the parent app's window in this way, malicious code can also send messages to the app's local code. This makes content injection attacks possible.

3.3 Windows

Overview. Windows 8.1 supports Windows Runtime apps written in HTML5 and JavaScript. These apps have access to native objects such as camera, removable storage, and geolocation via the Windows.* API. Remote Web content included in an app cannot access the namespace of these native objects directly. The overall architecture of Windows Runtime apps is shown in Fig. 4

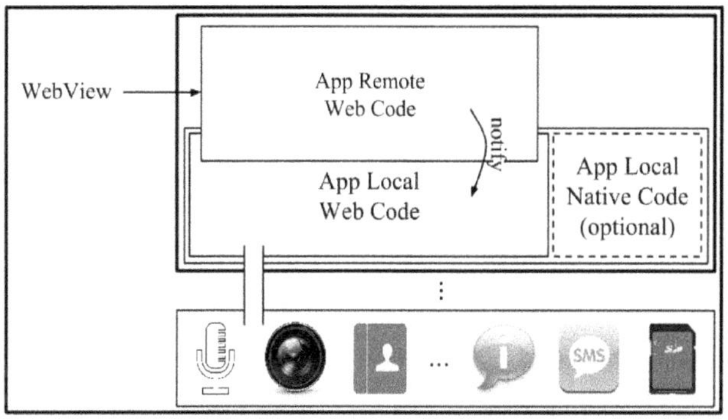

Figure 4: Windows Runtime apps: software stack

Principals and access-control implementation. A Windows Runtime HTML5 application can include remote Web content in two ways: in an iframe embedded into an internal application page or in a WebView object. If remote content is loaded in an iframe, the developer must whitelist its domain in order for the content to be fetched and loaded successfully. Windows allows only HTTPS domains to be whitelisted. No whitelisting is needed if the content is to be displayed inside WebView. Windows also requires that if the main WebView frame is fetched over HTTPS, all inner iframes must be fetched over HTTPS as well.

Windows uses 20 capability groups [51] to protect native objects. Developers must declare all capabilities needed by their apps in the manifests. The user is prompted when an app wants to use a given permission for the first time; all subsequent requests are granted or denied based on this decision.

The permission prompt shows the name of the app but not the origin of the request (e.g., "Can TestApp use your location?"). This does not affect native objects managed by Windows Runtime because they are not visible to remote Web code, but it affects the W3C geolocation API which is exposed to Web code by Windows. If an internal application page requests access to the geolocation object and the user approves, all third-party Web content included in this app will implicitly get access to geolocation.

Pros. Windows exposes access to the Windows Runtime library only to local application code, thus reducing the security risks of running untrusted remote Web code in embedded browser instances.

Cons. Windows does not provide origin-based access control for native device resources. This access-control model is inadequate

[2] `https://developer.chrome.com/apps/tags/webview.html#type-WebRequestEventInteface`

[3] `https://developer.chrome.com/apps/match_patterns.html`

for objects such as geolocation that are available through both Windows Runtime and W3C API. As a result, malicious third-party content can surreptitiously obtain the user's location.

Due to lack of built-in mechanisms for intra- and inter-principal communications, developers of Windows Runtime apps must rely on custom schemes—for example, the app's Web code can use the *window.external.notify()* API to talk to the app's local code outside the browser. The domain of this Web code must be whitelisted; if there are multiple domains in the whitelist, then each of them can send a *window.external.notify()* message. In this case, the developer must write (error-prone) code that checks *sender.callingUri* and disambiguates calls made by different senders.

3.4 Firefox OS

Overview. Firefox OS supports fine-grained access control for native objects. Principals are defined by the application instance, embedded browser instance, and Web origin [16]: each combination of these has its own distinct access rights. Firefox OS uses a mix of install-time and runtime, prompt-based access control.

The software stack of Firefox OS applications is shown in Fig. 5. The OS part of the stack (not shown in detail in the picture) consists of three major components: Gaia front-end responsible for maintaining the UI, the underlying operating system layer called Gonk that provides abstractions for accessing the device hardware, and an intermediate layer called Gecko which includes the runtime engines for HTML, CSS, and JavaScript and is responsible for enforcing all security policies regarding access to native objects.

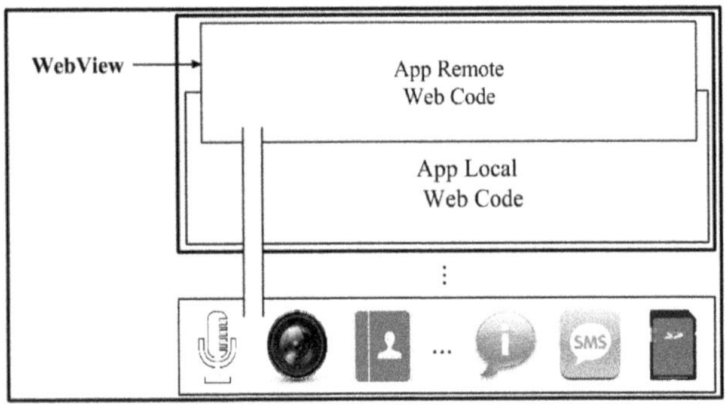

Figure 5: Firefox OS apps: software stack

Privilege hierarchy. There are two types of applications (apps) in Firefox OS: hosted and packaged. *Hosted apps* have no local content and their manifest file is hosted at a remote server. This file may also contain instructions for caching or offline usage of the app. Isolation of hosted apps is based on the Web origins [4] of their manifest files, defined by the protocol, domain, and port number. Firefox OS allows only one hosted app per origin since it cannot isolate distinct hosted apps if they have the same origin. To prevent arbitrary files from being interpreted as manifests, Firefox OS requires manifest files to be served with a specific MIME type ("application/x-web-app-manifest+json").

Unlike hosted apps, packaged apps store local content on the user's machine during installation. Packaged apps can be further categorized into three categories, in increasing order of privilege: regular, privileged, and certified apps.

Regular packaged apps have the same privileges as hosted apps. The only difference is that they can work offline because their contents are stored locally on the user's machine.

Privileged packaged apps contain an explicit list of assets in a ZIP archive, reviewed and signed by the app store. All assets are verified during installation and stored locally.

Certified packaged apps are special apps with elevated privileges, similar to setuid binaries in UNIX. In contrast to privileged apps, almost all permissions for certified apps are implicit and not controllable by the user. Certified apps are signed with the same key as the OS and distributed solely by the device manufacturer.

Principals. As mentioned above, each tuple of (application instance, browser instance, Web origin) defines a unique access-control principal. Firefox OS allows different browser instances to coexist inside a single application. The application can use them to render Web content from the same origin, yet prevent the sharing of cookies and other browser state.

The local content of an application is treated by Firefox OS as a special principal whose origin is different from all Web origins. All application code is written in HTML5 and JavaScript; Firefox OS applications do not have local native code. The application's local code cannot include content from other origins via tags like *embed* or *script*. It can include third-party content using *iframe*, but in this case the included content is isolated from the local content by the same origin policy [4] since its origin is different from that of local content. Firefox OS uses content security policies (CSP) to enforce these restrictions.

Access-control implementation. Depending on the application's privilege level (i.e., hosted, regular, privileged, or certified), certain permissions are implicit and the rest are explicit; also, certain objects are not available to certain classes of applications. For example, contacts and device storage API are not available to regular applications. The application developer must list all permissions the application needs, whether explicit or implicit, in its manifest. When enumerating individual permissions in the manifest, the developer must supply a short description of why the application needs this permission and how it will be used. This description is displayed to the user when the user is asked to authorize access to the underlying object and on other UI screens concerning the application's management and integration with the OS.

Once the application is installed, the implicit permissions are granted without any user interaction. The explicit permissions generate user prompts when the corresponding objects are requested. The user grants or denies access and can optionally instruct the system to remember her decision for subsequent requests of the same type coming from the same principal.

Local APIs to some native objects have an additional "access" property, which lets the developer specify the access rights he wishes the application to have with respect to the corresponding object, such as "readonly", "createonly", "readcreate", and "readwrite". These properties are specified in the manifest but not shown to the user. Firefox OS lets users monitor permission state and change applications' permissions via special UI. More details about the Firefox OS permission system can be found in [15].

Pros. The access control mechanism in Firefox OS helps developers implement flexible, fine-grained isolation between application components without writing any extra code.

Cons. Firefox OS bombards the user with permission requests for each (application, browser, origin) tuple. For example, suppose an app requests access to geolocation from both its local HTML5 code and remote HTML5 code hosted at the developer's domain. The user will be prompted twice: once with the name of the app and second time with the domain name. To make matters more confusing, suppose that this app uses two different browser instances, both of which render content from the same domain that needs access to geolocation (e.g., both show the same geotargeted ad). In this case, the user will be prompted twice with the same domain name.

4 Design of POWERGATE

The purpose of POWERGATE is to help developers of Web-based system applications write access-control and privilege separation policies that (1) support inclusion of untrusted third-party content such as Web advertising, and (2) restrict this third-party content to an explicitly enumerated subset of native objects.

The common case in all existing Web-based system applications is that the application requests native access only for its own code, which may be hosted on the device itself and/or provided from the application's remote Web server. All third-party code included into these applications is conventional Web content such as ads and "Like" buttons, intended for conventional browsers without native-access APIs. Therefore, no third-party code—even if included into the application's own code (for example, as a syndicated ad in an iframe)—should be able to access native objects, except possibly geolocation which may be needed for geotargeted advertising.

To support this common case, POWERGATE gives developers an easy way to "name" all external domains so that they can be blocked en masse from native access. For applications with more fine-grained native-access policies, POWERGATE can also support different rights for different third-party domains. This takes a single line per domain in the application's policy specification.

Access-control principals. POWERGATE policies are expressed in terms of native objects and access-control principals, as opposed to the platform components (shims, browser instances, etc.). We chose this approach because the distinction between the application's own code and third-party code does not map neatly onto the platform components. For example, on some platforms the application's own code is split into a local part hosted on the user's machine and a remote part hosted on the developer's server. At the same time, certain components such as embedded Web browsers combine the application's own code with third-party code.

Web origins are natural access-control principals in many scenarios—for example, when implementing privilege separation inside pure Web applications [2, 29]—but they are often too fine-grained for developers' purposes. Consider the developer of an ad-supported application who wants to allow all ads in her application to access the user's location for better geotargeting. In the case of syndicated or auction-based advertising, the origins of these ads are determined dynamically and enumerating them in advance as part of the access-control policy is not feasible.

There are four main principals in POWERGATE: *application's local native code*, *application's local Web code*, *application's remote Web code*, and *third-party Web code*. In Section 6.1 we show that these principals are sufficient to emulate the access-control models of all existing platforms. Optionally, individual domains can be specified as sub-principals of "third-party Web code."

The developer specifies a static "Web-home" domain hosting the application's remote Web code. All other Web origins are treated as sources of untrusted code and thus—for the purposes of native access only—are clustered into the "third-party Web code" principal. This lumping does not introduce any security vulnerabilities because the same origin policy is still enforced by the browser, thus individual Web origins within the "third-party Web code" principal still cannot access each other's Web resources. Furthermore, by default, this joint principal is blocked from accessing any native objects. Therefore, third-party Web origins have strictly fewer rights when they are combined into this joint principal than they have individually on any existing platform.

Access-control policies. In a POWERGATE policy, every native object is associated with an ACL-style list of privileges for each principal. POWERGATE has a very simple hierarchy of privileges. The default setting is *deny*: the principal has no access to the object. A principal may be *allowed* to access the object unconditionally, or the system may *prompt* the user for permission. For complex native objects (e.g., contacts, external storage, etc.), POWERGATE supports the access qualifiers of *readonly*, *readwrite*, *readcreate*, and *createonly*, same as stock Firefox OS.

The app's remote Web code is associated with a specific Web origin which, by definition, includes the protocol (HTTP or HTTPS). If the protocol is not specified in the manifest, POWERGATE assumes HTTPS. If access to a particular native object is allowed unconditionally for third-party Web code, then POWERGATE restricts it to HTTPS origins to prevent network attacks.

This simple system of principals and privileges can express rich, yet conceptually straightforward policies. For example, the application's local native and Web code may access the contacts, videos, and pictures, the application's remote Web code may access only videos and pictures, and third-party code may access geolocation but only if the user explicitly approves.

To enable secure communication between the app's local Web code and its remote Web code, POWERGATE introduces new API functions *sendToAppLocalWebPrincipal(String msg)*, *receiveFromAppLocalWebPrincipal()*, *sendToAppRemoteWebPrincipal(String msg)*, and *receiveFromAppRemoteWebPrincipal()*. Messaging between other pairs of principals can be supported in a similar fashion, if needed. These new messaging APIs deliver messages to explicitly named principals rather than individual system components. Therefore, applications that use them do not suffer from the vulnerabilities affecting current Web-based system applications whose intra-application communication is based on HTML5 postMessage. In many such applications, the recipient's origin is specified as "*" and messages can thus be intercepted by any third-party code running in the same browser.

Centralized enforcement and backward compatibility. All access-control decisions in POWERGATE are made in a single place in the code. Access-control logic is independent of the actual native object being accessed and does not depend on the platform-specific implementation details. POWERGATE is thus "future-proof": it protects access not only to all native objects in today's platforms, but also to any objects added in future releases.

POWERGATE ensures that existing applications behave as before when ported to POWERGATE. In Section 6.1, we show how the manifest of any existing application can be rewritten to emulate the access-control semantics of any of the platforms described in Section 3. In Section 6.2, we show that all existing Web-based system applications can run without any code modifications on a POWERGATE-capable platform and, if needed, preserve the same access-control semantics they currently have.

Limitations. By design, POWERGATE only protects access to native objects. To protect and isolate Web resources such as DOM, POWERGATE relies on the Web browser's implementation of the same origin policy. Like all other OS and browser access-control policies, POWERGATE's policies are binary: access is denied or allowed, but there is no notion of "rate-limiting" (e.g., allowing an app to access a certain object only 5 times). We did not observe the need for such richer policies in the existing apps.

Remote principals are defined by their Web origin or a set of origins, since this is the only information about them that is readily available to the host platform. POWERGATE thus cannot express policies such as "only domains belonging to local businesses can access geolocation" because there is no feasible way for the platform to determine whether a particular domain truly belongs to a local business. This is a generic limitation of the entire Web model and not specific to POWERGATE.

POWERGATE does not control what happens to information after it has been accessed by an authorized principal. For example, the user may grant access to the contacts list to the application's own code, which then sells this data to an advertiser. This is a generic limitation of host-based access control and cannot be solved without radically restructuring the existing host and network infrastructure to enforce Internet-wide information flow control.

5 Implementation of POWERGATE

The design of POWERGATE is platform-independent, but our proof-of-concept prototype implementation is based on Firefox OS. Implementations on other platforms would be essentially identical since all of them, except Chrome, have permission managers that are similar to Firefox OS and can be modified identically. In Chrome, native access is controlled inside the app, not the OS, thus POWERGATE would be provided as a library. The alternative is to add a Firefox-OS-style permission manager to Chrome.

The key data structure in POWERGATE is *PowerGateStore*, an in-memory hash map indexed by app id which stores the access privileges of currently running apps. We also use the same term for the file from which this hash map is populated when a new app is launched. The in-memory *PowerGateStore* is used to make access-control decisions at runtime, whereas the *PowerGateStore* file is used to persist apps' access-control settings between host restarts. *PowerGateStore* is managed internally by the OS and cannot be accessed by applications unless the OS is compromised, which is beyond our threat model.

The implementation of POWERGATE consists of two parts. The first part parses the app's manifest when the app is installed and updates the *PowerGateStore* file accordingly. The second part decides at runtime whether to unconditionally allow, prompt the user for permission, or deny a given access request to a native object.

At app installation time. POWERGATE parses the app's manifest file and creates a *Preference* object for each (native object, principal) pair declared in the manifest. This object's string representation is prefixed with the app's id, which is assigned by the underlying system at install time. A *Preference* object is also created for the app's own Web-home domain.

The set of all *Preference* objects for the app being installed is then stored in the *PowerGateStore* file. For example, if the app's system id is 32, its Web-home domain is `www.example.com`, and the app allows only Web code from `adserver.com` to access the *geolocation* object (with explicit user approval), then POWERGATE will create the following entries in *PowerGateStore*:

```
32.webhome: https://www.example.com
32.geolocation.third-party-web-code.prompt.true.domain:
    https://adserver.com
```

The user can manually overwrite these policies, if needed.

At app runtime. The in-memory representation of the access-control policies of all apps currently running on the host is kept in the *PowerGateStore* hash map, keyed by app id. Each entry in this map includes the app's Web-home domain and a *Policy* object defining the policies for all native objects to which the app has requested access via its manifest file. These *Policy* objects are hash maps keyed by the native object's name and enumerating the access rights of each principal.

Access-control policies. The possible values for the *principals* tag in a policy are *local-native-code*, *local-web-code*, *app-web-code*, or *third-party-web-code*. The current version of Firefox OS does not allow applications to include native code, thus all existing ap-

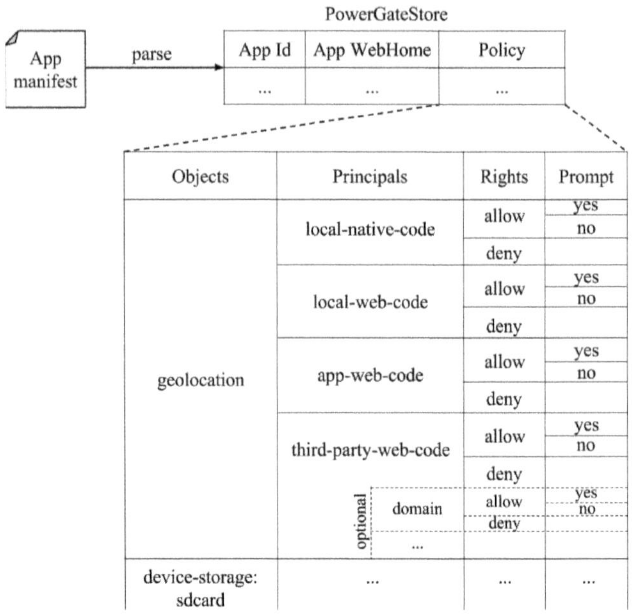

Figure 6: PowerGateStore

plications are implemented exclusively in Web languages such as HTML5, JavaScript, and CSS. On other platforms, however, applications can include local native code, necessitating support for the *local-native-code* principal. Optionally, individual domains can be specified as sub-principals of the *third-party-web-code* principal.

The *prompt* tag allows developers to specify whether the user should be prompted for permission when access to a given native object is attempted. The default value of this tag is *"yes"*. In POWERGATE, the user can instruct the GUI to remember her choice. By explicitly incorporating user prompts into access-control policies, POWERGATE can emulate the following access-control semantics: *prompt: no*, *prompt: always* (the user instructs the system to *not* remember her choice), *prompt: first-time-use* (the user instructs the system to remember her choice).

Access-control enforcement. POWERGATE's enforcement mechanism is shown schematically in Fig. 7. It is implemented in 366 lines of C++ code. Specifically, in *nsPermissionManager.cpp*, POWERGATE modifies the internal implementation of

```
CommonTestPermission(nsIPrincipal * aPrincipal,
                     const char * aType,
                     uint32_t   * aPermission,
                     bool  aExactHostMatch,
                     bool  aIncludingSession)
```

with a function call to:

```
uint32_t * aPermission
PowerGate::GetAction(uint32_t appId,
                     const char * aType,
                     string prePath)
```

defined in *PowerGate.cpp*. Since the *CommonTestPermission()* function is the central location used by Firefox OS to make access-control decisions about any native object, *PowerGate::GetAction()* effectively assumes this responsibility.

In POWERGATE, the decision to allow or deny access is based on the app id, the name of the object being requested, and the requesting principal. The app id and the principal are determined from the information provided by the platform's runtime environment for every request. The name of the object is conveyed by the platform's local API. Specifically, POWERGATE derives the values of *appId* and *prePath* from the *aPrincipal* object and uses *aType* as the native object name. POWERGATE does not use *ExactHostMatch* be-

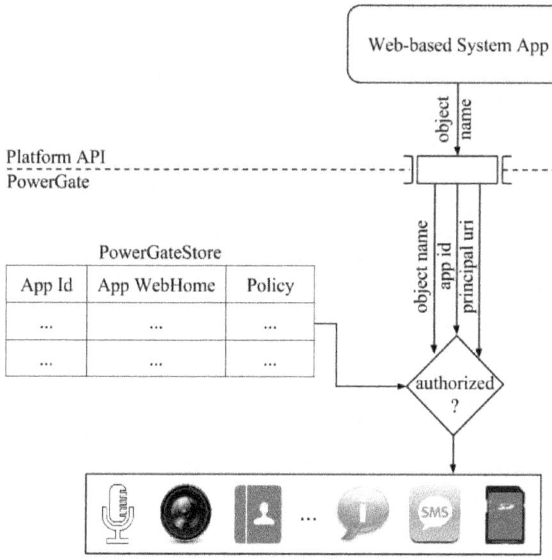

Figure 7: Access-control enforcement at runtime

cause it always assumes this flag to be true when the request comes from the app's Web code or a third-party origin explicitly defined in the app's manifest, and false in all other cases. POWERGATE then looks up the app id in *PowerGateStore*. If a match is found, POWERGATE retrieves the app's policy object. POWERGATE internally computes the value of *aIncludingSession* based on the prompt part of the policy and/or user's choice (if the user was previously prompted). Finally, POWERGATE uses the policy to decide whether to allow the request, deny it, or prompt the user.

Inter-principal communication. To enable secure communication between the app's local Web code and its remote Web code, POWERGATE provides a new messaging API. This API can be implemented via a new, distinct native object, but our current proof-of-concept prototype implementation is based on a sandboxed variant of the existing *Alarms* object, which we called *Communicator*. When the local Web code wants to talk to its remote counterpart, it invokes *sendToAppRemoteWebPrincipal(String msg)*. The local Web code then sends a *postMessage("pending message", "*")* to the browser instance executing remote code to notify the latter that a message is waiting for it. Upon receiving this notification, the remote Web code retrieves the pending message by invoking *receiveFromAppLocalWebPrincipal()*. Note that there is no need to protect the content of the postMessage since it does not contain any sensitive information. Even if malicious third-party code intercepts this postMessage, the POWERGATE access-control mechanism will prevent it from retrieving the actual message since it is not the *app-web-code* principal. Messaging from the app's remote Web code to the app's local Web code works similarly by using the *sendToAppLocalWebPrincipal(String msg)* and *receiveFromAppRemoteWebPrincipal()* API.

6 Evaluation

For the evaluation of the existing platforms described in Section 3, we used a Dell Latitude E6500 laptop executing Windows 8.1 with Windows Phone Simulator; a MacBook Pro laptop executing OS X 10.9.4 with Google Chrome 34.0.1847 and two virtual machines installed inside VMware Fusion 5.0.4, running Ubuntu 13.10 and Ubuntu 14.04, respectively; and a Dell PowerEdge 2950 running Ubuntu 12.10 LTS and the Firefox OS version 1.3 simulator. To evaluate our proof-of-concept implementation of POWERGATE, we modified the Firefox OS simulator with scripts that automate user interaction and thus generate deterministic sequences of native-access requests. All performance evaluation of POWERGATE was done on the Dell PowerEdge 2950 running Ubuntu 12.10 LTS.

6.1 Backward compatibility

POWERGATE can emulate the access-control policies of all four platforms analyzed in our study. This is done by automatically rewriting the application's manifest, without any changes to the application's code.

Ubuntu. In Ubuntu HTML5 apps (see Section 3.1), local code has access to the Unity API [49], allowing apps to reserve a spot on the Launcher or integrate with Messaging and Music menus. This API is not available to either the app's own, or third-party Web code. The corresponding POWERGATE policy is as follows:

```
In Ubuntu:
  Allowed

In PowerGate:
  "policy_groups": [
    "unity": {
      "principals": {
        "local-web-code": {"prompt": "no"}}}]
```

For objects that are likely to be useful to HTML5 apps, such as the *OnlineAccounts* object, Ubuntu grants access (without user interaction) to all Web content loaded in the main frame of the app's WebView, but not to third-party content loaded in iframes. This corresponds to the following POWERGATE policy:

```
In Ubuntu:
  "policy_groups": ["accounts"]

In PowerGate:
  "policy_groups": [
    "accounts": {
      "principals": {
        "local-web-code": {"prompt": "no"},
        "app-web-code": {"prompt": "no"}}}]
```

Cordova on Ubuntu (see Section 3.1) comes with a set of 16 plugins [10], enabled by default. Access is implicitly granted to all Web content regardless of its origin [20]. In POWERGATE-enabled Ubuntu, this policy is implemented by instrumenting each plugin's native object with the appropriate access attributes. For example, the policy for the camera object is expressed as:

```
In Ubuntu:
  "policy_groups": ["camera"]

In PowerGate:
  "policy_groups": [
    "camera": {
      "principals": {
        "local-web-code": {"prompt": "no"},
        "app-web-code": {"prompt": "no"},
        "third-party-web-code": {"all": {"prompt": "no"
            }}}}]
```

Chrome. In Chrome (see Section 3.2), the application's local Web code—but not its remote code—has access to the local API. Chrome does not require that application developers declare their intention to use the local API in the manifest. In POWERGATE, a new object called "locals" represents the local API in Chrome. The declaration in the manifest is as follows:

```
In Chrome:
  Allowed

In PowerGate:
  "locals": {
    "principals": {
        "local-web-code": {"prompt": "no"}}}
```

Using its access to the local API, the application's local Web code can enable Web API for individual native objects. If this API is enabled, the application's remote Web code—as well as any third-party Web code in the same browser—can use it to access the corresponding object. For instance, the access policy for the video capture object can be expressed as:

```
In Chrome:
  "permissions": {"videoCapture"}

In PowerGate:
  "permissions": {
    "videoCapture": {
      "principals": {
        "local-web-code": {"prompt": "no"},
        "app-web-code": {"prompt": "no"},
        "third-party-web-code": {"all": {"prompt": "no"
            }}}}}
```

Windows. In Windows Runtime apps (see Section 3.3), only local application files have access to the Windows.* native objects and the user is prompted on the first use of each native object [51]. Therefore, in POWERGATE-enabled Windows, the access policy for each object is listed individually. For instance, the manifest entry for the camera object is expressed as:

```
In Windows:
  <DeviceCapability Name="webcam" />

In PowerGate:
  <DeviceCapability Name="webcam"
    Principal="local-native-code" Prompt="Yes"/>
  <DeviceCapability Name="webcam"
    Principal="local-web-code" Prompt="Yes"/>
```

Firefox OS. In Firefox OS (see Section 3.4), all requests to native objects can be categorized into four categories: *denied*, *granted*, *prompt: first-time-use*, and *prompt: always*. While different native objects have different access policies [15], they can all be expressed in POWERGATE's terms using one of the *local-web-code*, *app-web-code*, or *third-party-web-code* principals. For example, here is the policy for the desktop-notification object:

```
In Firefox OS:
"permissions": {
  "desktop-notification": {
    "description": "Notify the user.", }}

In PowerGate:
"permissions": {
  "desktop-notification": {
    "description'': "Notify the user.",
      "principals": {
        "local-web-code": {"prompt": "no"},
        "app-web-code": {"prompt": "yes"},
        "third-party-web-code": {"all": {"prompt" : "yes
            "}}}}}
```

6.2 Deployment

By design, POWERGATE augments the application's manifest on all platforms with information about the application's Web home and the access rights it grants to various principals with respect to the platform's native objects. To disambiguate between manifest formats, POWERGATE increments the version number of the manifest file by 1. For instance, the current version number of the manifest in Chrome apps is 2, whereas POWERGATE-compatible Chrome apps have manifest version 3. Similarly, current Ubuntu HTML5 apps have policy group version 1, whereas POWERGATE-compatible Ubuntu HTML5 apps have policy group version 2.

At application installation time, POWERGATE checks the version number of the application's manifest. If it matches POWERGATE's manifest version number for the given platform, the manifest is parsed as described in Section 5. Otherwise, POWERGATE assumes that the application is not aware of POWERGATE and cannot take advantage of its facilities. In this case, POWERGATE rewrites the manifest with appropriate settings to ensure backward compatibility with the original platform, as described in Section 6.1.

POWERGATE does not change the API used to access native objects and is thus fully transparent to all existing applications. Any application that currently runs on stock Firefox OS will run on POWERGATE, too. We developed a test suite and verified that in 100% of the tests, API access to native objects from legacy code returns exactly the same results with and without POWERGATE.

6.3 Performance

Micro benchmarks. Table 2 compares how long it takes to make access-control decisions in POWERGATE vs. stock Firefox OS on individual accesses to native objects. All numbers are in microseconds and averaged over 3000 runs.

	Firefox OS	PowerGate	Overhead
ALLOW_ACTION	39.76 μs	42.34 μs	1.0649X
DENY_ACTION	18.19 μs	18.65 μs	1.0253X

Table 2: Micro benchmark: Performance overhead per native-object access as visible to the Permissions Manager

Macro benchmarks. Table 3 compares the overall performance of POWERGATE with stock Firefox OS on individual accesses to native objects from JavaScript. All numbers are in milliseconds and averaged over 3000 runs.

	Firefox OS	PowerGate	Overhead
ALLOW_ACTION	66.5733 ms	67.3916 ms	1.0123X
DENY_ACTION	1.0527 ms	1.0533 ms	1.0006X

Table 3: Macro benchmark: Performance overhead per native-object access as visible to JavaScript

7 Related work

Origin-based access control for Web content. Origin-based access control [4] in Web browsers isolates content from different origins, defined by domain, protocol, and port. Zalewski [52] and Singh et al. [42] describe several flaws in browsers' implementations of origin-based access control.

Browsers conforming to the HTML5 specifications provide the postMessage API for communication between frames from different origins. Prior work [5, 43] found security flaws in cross-origin communication that can be used to bypass origin-based access control by exploiting incorrect authentication of the sender, certain frame navigational policies, etc..

Wang et al. [50] investigated cross-origin communication channels, such as intent, scheme, and Web-accessing utility classes, on Android and iOS, and found that they are vulnerable to cross-origin attacks from malicious apps and malicious links clicked by users. Their proposed defense, Morbs, labels every message with its origin and uses this information to enforce developer-specified security policies. In contrast to Morbs, which protects Web resources from malicious apps, POWERGATE protects native resources from malicious third-party content inside benign apps.

Origin-based access control for native-access APIs. Modern mobile platforms, including Android and iOS, allow applications to embed instances of Web browsers and equip them with interfaces or "bridges" that let Web code access resources outside the browser. For example, 'addJavascriptInterface' is used to add such interfaces to Android's WebView. In older versions of Android, these interfaces can be exploited by malicious Web code to compromise the host via reflection attacks [1, 34, 39]. Luo et al. [31] observed that these WebView interfaces can be accessed by any script regardless of its origin. Chin et al. [7] found instances of this problem in several Android applications. Other papers [22, 44] investigated how Android advertising libraries expose device resources via 'addJavascriptInterface' to Web advertisements.

Hybrid application development frameworks such as PhoneGap and Web Marmalade use these bridges to equip apps written mostly in JavaScript and HTML5 with native access to the host platform. Hybrid apps are somewhat similar to Web-based system applications, but the native-access capabilities and the corresponding access control are provided by an application-level framework, not by the platform itself. Georgiev et al. [20] showed how untrusted Web content can bypass this access control in popular hybrid frameworks. Jin et al. [26, 27] demonstrated how naive uses of the framework-supplied functionality, such as reading from 2D barcodes and scanning Wi-Fi access points, can expose hybrid apps to code injection attacks. MobileIFC [41] leverages hybrid-framework APIs to enforce a fine-grained, information flow-based permission model that controls what an untrusted application can do with the data received through the framework API.

In this paper, we consider a different layer of the software stack and investigate the native-access APIs provided by the platform to the applications, not compiled into the application via a third-party library. The APIs we study (1) are not based on 'addJavaScriptInterace', (2) are exposed to code *outside* the Web browser, and (3) access control is performed by the platform, not by the application. Since the platform is responsible for access-control enforcement, defenses that are suitable for hybrid frameworks (such as NoFrak [20]) do not apply, necessitating modifications to the platform. In general, platform-level native access is more attractive for app developers than relying on hybrid frameworks because the developers do not need to update, repackage, and redistribute their applications every time the framework is updated. Furthermore, platform support obviates the need to include a copy of the framework in every application, thus reducing code bloat.

As an alternative to browser interfaces for native access, Gibraltar [28] exposes hardware resource via a Web server hosted on localhost and accessible via AJAX.

Isolating untrusted advertisements. Several privilege separation techniques aim to minimize the risks of untrusted advertisements included into Web applications [2, 29, 40, 44]. These approaches either isolate advertisements inside iframes, or else run them in separate processes and control communication between the application and the confined content using developer-specified policies. For example, AdSplit [40] puts Web-based advertisements into separate WebView instances and relies on the application to restrict invocations of privileged APIs from these WebViews.

A key purpose of Web-based system applications studied in this paper is to enable the developers to integrate already deployed Web applications with new Web code that accesses system resources. Web-based system applications are thus effectively mashups, with multiple principals executing together in the same browser instance. Applying solutions like [2, 29, 40, 44] requires re-engineering of the existing code. By contrast, POWERGATE does not require modifications to advertising-supported legacy Web code.

An alternative to platform-based isolation is language-based isolation [17, 32, 37, 48]. Language-based solutions, such as Caja [33], require the app developer to fetch all third-party JavaScript and rewrite it to satisfy the developer's security policy before serving it to the client. In contrast to language-based approaches, POWERGATE works with legacy apps and lets unmodified third-party JavaScript execute directly on the client machine. This reduces the burden on the app since the app's server does not need to fetch, rewrite, and serve all ads shown to the users. Note that deploying language-based isolation on the platform (as opposed to the server) would have been challenging because different apps have different isolation policies for native objects, while the platform presumably has a single JavaScript rewriting engine.

Vulnerable Firefox OS applications. DeFreez et al. [12] used lightweight static analysis to automatically find XSS (cross-site scripting) and other vulnerabilities in Firefox OS applications. Their focus and techniques are complementary to this paper, which investigates access control for native objects exposed to Firefox OS applications and similar applications on other platforms. We do analyze the exposure of native objects to untrusted Web origins, but the vulnerabilities we found are related to the unintended delegation of access rights, not XSS bugs in individual applications.

Permission re-delegation on Android. Many Android applications suffer from permission re-delegation vulnerabilities [11, 14]. This is an instance of the "confused deputy" problem [24], caused by a privileged application exposing sensitive operations without properly checking the credentials of the invoking application and thus enabling the latter to bypass the permission system.

While vulnerabilities analyzed in this paper are also of the general "confused deputy" type, they involve exposure of sensitive native APIs at the OS level, not at the application level. Furthermore, they are unrelated to Android permissions and affect platforms other than Android. Consequently, previously proposed defenses against re-delegation [6, 13, 14, 23, 30] do not solve the problems investigated in this paper.

Sandboxing for protecting OS resources. Many research projects [18, 19, 21, 25, 38, 45] and commercial products [35, 46] provide solutions for restricting an untrusted application to a subset of system resources. Unlike POWERGATE, these approaches do not differentiate between content from different Web origins as long as it is running inside the same application.

8 Conclusions

We analyzed the access-control models of the existing platforms for Web-based system applications and demonstrated semantic inconsistencies between the platforms, as well as design flaws that result in security vulnerabilities such as unauthorized access to OAuth tokens from untrusted Web code.

We then designed and implemented POWERGATE, a new access-control mechanism for Web-based system applications that allows developers to specify access policies for native objects in terms of high-level principals. POWERGATE policies are platform-independent and enforced uniformly and securely on all platforms. POWERGATE imposes a tiny performance overhead and is backward-compatible with all existing Web-based system applications.

Acknowledgments. This work was partially supported by the NSF grants CNS-0746888 and CNS-1223396, a Google research award, NIH grant R01 LM011028-01 from the National Library of Medicine, and Google PhD Fellowship to Suman Jana.

References

[1] Abusing WebView JavaScript bridges. http://50.56.33.56/blog/?p=314.

[2] D. Akhawe, P. Saxena, and D. Song. Privilege separation in HTML5 applications. In *USENIX Security*, 2012.

[3] AppArmor. http://developer.ubuntu.com/publish/apps/security-policy-for-click-packages/, 2014.

[4] A. Barth. The Web origin concept. http://tools.ietf.org/html/rfc6454.

[5] A. Barth, C. Jackson, and J. Mitchell. Securing frame communication in browsers. In *USENIX Security*, 2009.

[6] E. Chin, A. Felt, K. Greenwood, and D. Wagner. Analyzing inter-application communication in Android. In *MobiSys*, 2011.

[7] E. Chin and D. Wagner. Bifocals: Analyzing WebView vulnerabilities in Android applications. In *WISA*, 2013.

[8] Chrome app samples. `https://github.com/GoogleChrome/chrome-app-samples`, 2014.

[9] Permissions in Chrome apps and extensions. `https://developer.chrome.com/apps/declare_permissions`, 2014.

[10] Cordova platform support. `http://cordova.apache.org/docs/en/3.4.0/guide_support_index.md.html`, 2014.

[11] L. Davi, A. Dmitrienko, A. Sadeghi, and M. Winandy. Privilege escalation attacks on Android. In *ISC*, 2010.

[12] D. DeFreez, B. Shastry, H. Chen, and J. Seifert. A first look at Firefox OS security. In *MoST*, 2014.

[13] M. Dietz, S. Shekhar, Y. Pisetsky, A. Shu, and D. Wallach. QUIRE: Lightweight provenance for smart phone operating systems. In *USENIX Security*, 2011.

[14] A. Felt, H. Wang, A. Moshchuk, S. Hanna, and E. Chin. Permission re-delegation: Attacks and defenses. In *USENIX Security*, 2011.

[15] Firefox OS app permissions. `https://developer.mozilla.org/en-US/Apps/Build/App_permissions`, 2014.

[16] Firefox OS security model. `https://developer.mozilla.org/en-US/Firefox_OS/Security/Security_model`, 2014.

[17] M. Finifter, J. Weinberger, and A. Barth. Preventing capability leaks in secure JavaScript subsets. In *NDSS*, 2010.

[18] B. Ford and R. Cox. Vx32: Lightweight user-level sandboxing on the x86. In *USENIX ATC*, 2008.

[19] T. Garfinkel, B. Pfaff, and M. Rosenblum. Ostia: A delegating architecture for secure system call interposition. In *NDSS*, 2004.

[20] M. Georgiev, S. Jana, and V. Shmatikov. Breaking and fixing origin-based access control in hybrid Web/mobile application frameworks. In *NDSS*, 2014.

[21] I. Goldberg, D. Wagner, R. Thomas, and E. Brewer. A secure environment for untrusted helper applications: Confining the wily hacker. In *USENIX Security*, 1996.

[22] M. Grace, W. Zhou, X. Jiang, and A. Sadeghi. Unsafe exposure analysis of mobile in-app advertisements. In *WiSec*, 2012.

[23] M. Grace, Y. Zhou, Z. Wang, and X. Jiang. Systematic detection of capability leaks in stock Android smartphones. In *NDSS*, 2012.

[24] N. Hardy. The Confused Deputy: (or why capabilities might have been invented). *ACM SIGOPS Operating Systems Review*, 1988.

[25] S. Jana, D. Porter, and V. Shmatikov. TxBox: Building secure, efficient sandboxes with system transactions. In *S&P*, 2011.

[26] X. Jin, X. Hu, K. Ying, W. Du, Y. Heng, and G. Peri. Code injection attacks on HTML5-based mobile apps: Characterization, detection and mitigation. In *CCS*, 2014.

[27] X. Jin, T. Luo, D. Tsui, and W. Du. Code injection attacks on HTML5-based mobile apps. In *MoST*, 2014.

[28] K. Lin, D. Chu, J. Mickens, L. Zhuang, F. Zhao, and J. Qiu. Gibraltar: Exposing hardware devices to Web pages using AJAX. In *WebApps*, 2012.

[29] M. Louw, K. Ganesh, and V. Venkatakrishnan. AdJail: Practical enforcement of confidentiality and integrity policies on Web advertisements. In *USENIX Security*, 2010.

[30] L. Lu, Z. Li, Z. Wu, W. Lee, and G. Jiang. Chex: Statically vetting Android apps for component hijacking vulnerabilities. In *CCS*, 2012.

[31] T. Luo, H. Hao, W. Du, Y. Wang, and H. Yin. Attacks on WebView in the Android system. In *ACSAC*, 2011.

[32] S. Maffeis and A. Taly. Language-based isolation of untrusted javascript. In *CSF*, 2009.

[33] M. Miller, M. Samuel, B. Laurie, I. Awad, and M. Stay. Caja: Safe active content in sanitized JavaScript. `http://google-caja.googlecode.com`, 2008.

[34] WebView addJavascriptInterface remote code execution. `https://labs.mwrinfosecurity.com/blog/2013/09/24/webview-addjavascriptinterface-remote-code-execution/`.

[35] NSA. Security-enhanced linux. `http://www.nsa.gov/research/selinux/`.

[36] Ubuntu OnlineAccounts API. `http://developer.ubuntu.com/api/html5/sdk-14.04/OnlineAccounts.OnlineAccounts/`, 2014.

[37] J. Politz, S. Eliopoulos, A. Guha, and S. Krishnamurthi. ADsafety: Type-based verification of JavaScript sandboxing. In *USENIX Security*, 2011.

[38] N. Provos. Improving host security with system call policies. In *USENIX Security*, 2003.

[39] E. Shapira. Analyzing an Android WebView exploit. `http://blogs.avg.com/mobile/analyzing-android-webview-exploit/`.

[40] S. Shekhar, M. Dietz, and D. Wallach. AdSplit: Separating smartphone advertising from applications. *USENIX Security*, 2012.

[41] K. Singh. Practical context-aware permission control for hybrid mobile applications. In *RAID*, 2013.

[42] K. Singh, A. Moshchuk, H. Wang, and W. Lee. On the incoherencies in Web browser access control policies. In *S&P*, 2010.

[43] S. Son and V. Shmatikov. The postman always rings twice: Attacking and defending postMessage in HTML5 websites. In *NDSS*, 2013.

[44] R. Stevens, C. Gibler, J. Crussell, J. Erickson, and H. Chen. Investigating user privacy in Android ad libraries. In *MoST*, 2012.

[45] W. Sun, Z. Liang, V. Venkatakrishnan, and R. Sekar. One-way isolation: An effective approach for realizing safe execution environments. In *NDSS*, 2005.

[46] SUSE. AppArmor Linux application security. `https://www.suse.com/support/security/apparmor/`.

[47] System applications working group charter. `http://www.w3.org/2012/09/sysapps-wg-charter`, 2014.

[48] A. Taly, U. Erlingsson, J. Mitchell, M. Miller, and J. Nagra. Automated analysis of security-critical JavaScript APIs. In *S&P*, 2011.

[49] Ubuntu Unity Web API. `http://developer.ubuntu.com/api/devel/ubuntu-13.10/javascript/web-docs/`, 2014.

[50] R. Wang, L. Xing, X. Wang, and S. Chen. Unauthorized origin crossing on mobile platforms: Threats and mitigation. In *CCS*, 2013.

[51] App capability declarations (Windows Runtime apps). `http://msdn.microsoft.com/en-us/library/windows/apps/hh464936.aspx`, 2014.

[52] M. Zalewski. Browser security handbook. `https://code.google.com/p/browsersec/wiki/Main`.

Cardinal Contests

Arpita Ghosh
Cornell University
Ithaca, NY, USA
arpitaghosh@cornell.edu

Patrick Hummel
Google Inc.
Mountain View, CA, USA
phummel@google.com

ABSTRACT

Contests are widely used as a means for effort elicitation in settings ranging from government R&D contests to online crowdsourcing contests on platforms such as Kaggle, Innocentive, or TopCoder. Such rank-order mechanisms—where agents' rewards depend only on the relative ranking of their submissions' qualities—are natural mechanisms for incentivizing effort when it is easier to obtain ordinal, rather than cardinal, information about agents' outputs, or where absolute measures of quality are unverifiable. An increasing number of online contests, however, rank entries according to some numerical evaluation of their absolute quality—for instance, the performance of an algorithm on a test dataset, or the performance of an intervention in a randomized trial. Can the contest designer incentivize higher effort by making the rewards in an ordinal rank-order mechanism contingent on such *cardinal* information?

We model and analyze cardinal contests, where a principal running a rank-order tournament has access to an absolute measure of the qualities of agents' submissions in addition to their relative rankings, and ask how modifying the rank-order tournament to incorporate cardinal information can improve incentives for effort. Our main result is that a simple threshold mechanism—a mechanism that awards the prize for a rank if and only if the absolute quality of the agent at that rank exceeds a certain threshold—is *optimal* amongst all mixed cardinal-ordinal mechanisms where the fraction of the jth prize awarded to the jth-ranked agent is any arbitrary non-decreasing function of her submission's quality. Further, the optimal threshold mechanism uses exactly the same threshold for each rank. We study what contest parameters determine the extent of the benefit from incorporating such cardinal information into an ordinal rank-order contest, and investigate the extent of improvement in equilibrium effort via numerical simulations.

WWW 2015, May 18–22, 2015, Florence, Italy.
ACM 978-1-4503-3469-3/15/05.
http://dx.doi.org/10.1145/2736277.2741652.

Categories and Subject Descriptors

J.4 [**Computer Applications**]: Social & Behavioral Sciences.

General Terms

Economics.

Keywords

Contests; Optimal contest design; Crowdsourcing; Game theory.

1. INTRODUCTION

Contests have a long history as a means for procuring innovations, with government-sponsored contests for research and development dating back to at least 1714.[1] Contests provide an effective incentive structure for eliciting effort in settings where the quality of an agent's output as well as her effort are unverifiable or difficult to measure, making conventional contracts based on input or output-dependent rewards infeasible—either by virtue of being too costly for the sponsor to implement, or because they cannot be credibly enforced due to unverifiability of output ([8], [41]). In several such situations an *ordinal* comparison—identifying a relative ranking of agents' submissions—might nonetheless be feasible, allowing the principal to commit to an enforceable contract that awards rank-based prizes to some subset of entrants in a contest. This has led to a large literature on the optimal design of rank-order mechanisms for effort elicitation; see §1.1.

In contrast with more traditional settings, however, an increasing number of online contests procure innovations whose quality is evaluated and ranked via verifiable *cardinal* measurements. For instance, the well-known Netflix contest, designed to procure improved algorithms for movie recommendations, evaluated entries according to how well they predicted user preferences on a test subset of its user database, with the algorithm that obtained the highest score being declared the winner. In a different context, contests for designing mobile apps for health or education might compute scores for submissions based on their performance on metrics of efficacy in randomized trials[2], and rank entries

[1]The British parliament ran a contest with a 20000 pound prize for a method for determining longitude-at-sea to within half a degree.
[2]See, for one example, http://www.robinhood.org/prize

based on these scores. A third example is the contest platform Kaggle, which hosts contests where the innovation being procured is a data-mining algorithm: again, submissions are typically evaluated on a test dataset provided by the requesters and ranked according to the score they obtain. A number of other such contests abound. In summary, there is an increasingly large family of contests where submissions can be assigned a meaningful numerical quality score that reflects their value to the principal.

Suppose a principal running a contest has access to such *cardinal* measurements of the qualities of agents' submissions, in addition to the ordinal ranking of their outputs. What effect does making prizes contingent on absolute performance, in addition to relative ranking, have on contestants' incentives for effort, and what is the optimal way to incorporate such cardinal measurements of output into an ordinal rank-order contest?

Our contributions. We model and analyze *cardinal contests*, where a principal, who wants to maximize some increasing function of the quality of received submissions, can evaluate the quality of each submission via a real-valued score in addition to observing the rank-ordering of contestants' outputs. We ask whether and how such a principal can improve her utility by incorporating such cardinal information to determine agents' rewards.

Specifically, consider a rank-order tournament with prizes $(A_1, A_2, \dots, A_n)$ for ranks $1, \dots, n$, in a model where contestants are strategic and have a cost to effort. Can the principal modify the rank-order mechanism $\mathcal{M}(A_1, A_2, \dots, A_n)$, using participants' quality scores q_j in addition to their ranks j to decide how much of the prize A_j to actually award, to improve incentives for effort? And if so, how should the function $g_j(q_j)$ that determines the fraction of the prize A_j to be awarded to the jth-ranked contestant based on her output quality q_j (such as fractions that grow linearly or as a convex function of quality) be chosen to create the optimal incentives for the agents?

Our main result is that a very simple threshold mechanism—a mechanism that awards the prize for a rank if and only if the output of the agent at that rank exceeds a certain threshold—is *optimal* amongst all mechanisms induced by any increasing functions $g_j(\cdot)$: We show that for any given rank-order mechanism $\mathcal{M}(A_1, A_2, \dots, A_n)$, the functions $g_j(q_j)$ that incentivize the highest effort are precisely step functions that increase from 0 to 1 at a threshold score (Theorem 3.1). Additionally, if the noise density that stochastically maps an agent's effort into her output quality is single-peaked at 0, we find that the optimal threshold mechanism also uses exactly the *same threshold* for each rank. Interestingly, real-world contests where prizes are made contingent on cardinal information measuring absolute performance seem to commonly use such threshold-based prize structures.[3]

After deriving comparative statics for the optimal threshold and equilibrium effort in such mechanisms in §3.2, we ask to what extent does incorporating cardinal information (via an optimal threshold mechanism) improve equilibrium effort relative to using only ordinal information. We address this question via numerical simulations as well as theory, and find that the extent to which cardinal information incentivizes higher effort depends on the contest parameters: the most substantial improvements are achieved in contests with a smaller number of participants, contests with participants whose cost functions are 'not too convex' (in a sense made precise in §4), and contests that award a larger rather than smaller number of prizes.

We note that we ask the question of how to optimally *modify* a given rank-order mechanism $\mathcal{M}(A_1, A_2, \dots, A_n)$, rather than the question of choosing the overall optimal reward structure $(A_1(q_1, \dots, q_n), \dots, A_n(q_1, \dots, q_n))$ that incorporates all available cardinal information in determining the reward for each rank. There are a number of reasons we address this question rather than the more general mechanism design problem, the foremost of which is practical: a principal announcing a contest might choose, or be committed to, a certain rank-based prize structure for reasons such as sponsorship constraints, publicity, simplicity, cost of precise evaluations of a full rank-order due to scale, and so on.[4] However, the principal might still want, and more easily be able to, incorporate an entry's absolute quality in determining whether, and how much of the announced rank-based prize to actually award (for instance, she may wish to award no prize if the highest-ranked submission performs worse than the current state-of-the-art innovation). See §2 and §5 for further discussion.

1.1 Related Work

There is a large body of work on contest design in the economics literature. In addition to foundational work on the theory of contests ([18], [24], [26], [27], [28], [29], [33], [34], [35], [36], [37], [38], [39], [40]), there has also been a variety of work motivated by specific applications. [17], [21], [23], and [31] address the design of rank-order tournaments for the purpose of incentivizing employees to work hard. [8] and [41] study contest design in the context of research tournaments. And there is a growing literature motivated by online crowdsourcing contests ([1], [6], [7], [11], [16]). There is also an extensive empirical literature analyzing observed strategic behavior by real subjects in contests in a variety of settings ([2], [3], [4], [5], [9], [10], [12], [13], [22], [25], [30]).

This work addresses a variety of questions related to the economics of contests such as comparing tournaments to incentive schemes that are based solely on an individual's personal performance ([18], [21], [31], [34]), relationships between contests and all-pay auctions ([7], [8], [11]), taxing entry to improve the quality of contributions ([16], [41]), dynamic contests in which agents dynamically decide how much effort to exert when they continuously get information about how they are doing in the contest compared to their competitors ([14], [20]), and incentives for agents to work hard in teams [19]. The most relevant subset of this literature to our paper is that relating to optimal contest design ([1], [17], [24], [26], [27], [28], [29], [40]), which asks how to best choose the rank-based rewards for each rank under various models of effort and constraints on the rewards.

The key difference between this literature and our work is that this literature almost exclusively studies contests that are structured as *rank-order* mechanisms, where the

[3]For example, one of the largest contests hosted on Kaggle awarded prizes to the top three entries, provided their scores were above a minimum baseline.

[4]Similar contests on the same platform (e.g. Kaggle) with similar total prize money do sometimes differ in how they split the total prize across ranks, suggesting that the choice of the rank-order mechanism might perhaps not be driven only by optimality of effort incentives.

announced prizes depend only on the *rank* of an agent's output relative to that of her competitors, whereas we consider mixed cardinal-ordinal mechanisms of the form described in §2. Specifically, rather than ask which ordinal rewards $(A_1, A_2, \ldots, A_n)$ incentivize optimal outcomes, we ask how cardinal information about an agent's output can be optimally incorporated into a *given* ordinal reward mechanism $\mathcal{M}(A_1, A_2, \ldots, A_n)$ to incentivize the highest effort, a question that has not been addressed previously in this literature. The only relevant exception, to the best of our knowledge, is the work in [7] which does address the question of optimal contest design using both cardinal and ordinal information, albeit in a completely different model of output and for risk-*neutral* agents only. Interestingly, although the models are completely different, the optimal mechanism in that model also turns out to use cardinal information via a threshold.

In addition to this key difference, we also note that we do not make any of a variety of simplifying assumptions used in several papers in this literature, such as risk-neutrality of the agents, linearity of agents' cost functions, the assumption that there is no stochastic component that affects the final quality of an agent's contribution, or assuming a particular functional form for the principal's objective function.

2. MODEL

We consider a setting where a pool of agents competing in a contest strategically choose their effort levels which stochastically determines their submission qualities, and each agent receives a prize based on the relative rank of her output as well as possibly its absolute quality. The model is a natural extension of [23].

Agents. There are n agents who compete in a contest. Each agent simultaneously chooses a level of effort $e_i \geq 0$ to exert. The quality q_i of agent i's output is determined both by her effort, and a random noise term ϵ_i as $q_i = e_i + \epsilon_i$, where each ϵ_i is an independent and identically distributed draw from a cumulative distribution function $F(\epsilon)$. The noise ϵ_i has a number of possible interpretations. Most simply, ϵ_i could model the fact that a given amount of effort (for example, the time spent working on a research problem) does not deterministically guarantee a certain level of output, but rather only influences its expected value. As another interpretation, the noise ϵ could also model randomness in the measurement, or perception, of an agent's output quality by the principal. Most interestingly, ϵ_i could be thought of as modeling heterogeneity amongst agents' abilities to solve the specific problem or execute the specific task required for the contest; we discuss this in detail at the end of this section. We will assume throughout that the probability density function $f(\epsilon)$ corresponding to F is a bounded continuously differentiable function of ϵ with a bounded first derivative, and the distribution F and the number of agents n are known to all agents.

Utilities. An agent's utility is the difference between her benefit from any prize she wins and her cost of effort. An agent who receives a prize A_i derives a benefit of $v(A_i)$, where $v(\cdot)$ is a strictly increasing and concave function satisfying $v(A) \geq 0$ for all $A \geq 0$ and $v(0) = 0$. Exerting effort e_i incurs a cost $c(e_i)$, where $c(\cdot)$ is a strictly increasing and convex function satisfying $c(0) = 0$ and $c'(0) = 0$.

The utility to an agent who exerts effort e_i and receives prize A_i is the difference between this benefit and cost, $u_i = v(A_i) - c(e_i)$. We assume that each agent chooses e_i to maximize her expected utility $E[v(A_i)] - c(e_i)$, where the expectation is over the n random draws of $\epsilon_{i'}$ that determine each agent's output quality (and therefore their prizes). Our model allows for both risk-neutral and risk-averse agents, as $v(A)$ may either be a linear function of A (for risk-neutral agents) or a strictly concave function of A (risk-averse agents).

Mechanisms. We suppose that the principal running the contest can observe the quality q_i of each agent's output. (Our results extend immediately to a model where the principal's observations of output qualities are noisy, as long as the noise in each observation is an IID draw for each agent). We use $\mathcal{M}(A_1, A_2, \ldots, A_n)$ to denote a rank-order mechanism which assigns a reward A_j to the agent with the jth-highest output regardless of its absolute quality, and assume throughout that $A_1 \geq \ldots \geq A_n \geq 0$.[5]

Mixed cardinal-ordinal mechanisms. Let q_j denote the quality of the jth-ranked submission. We consider mixed cardinal-ordinal modifications of a rank-order mechanism $\mathcal{M}(A_1, A_2, \ldots, A_n)$ of the form $\mathcal{M}(g_1(q_1)A_1, \ldots, g_n(q_n)A_n)$, which awards the agent with the jth-ranked submission of quality q_j a prize $P_j = g_j(q_j)A_j$, where $g_j(q)$ is a non-decreasing function of q satisfying $0 \leq g_j(q) \leq 1$. That is, $g_j(q)$ represents the fraction of the 'maximum' prize A_j for achieving rank j that an agent obtains if she produces a contribution with absolute quality q. Note that the rank-order mechanism $\mathcal{M}(A_1, A_2, \ldots, A_n)$ corresponds to setting g_j to be the constant function $g_j(q) = 1$ for all j.

We note that a principal with access to cardinal measurements of the qualities of each submission could conceivably use more general mechanisms by allowing the function g_j to depend not only on the quality of the corresponding j^{th}-ranked submission, but rather on the entire vector of qualities $(q_1, \ldots, q_n)$. We restrict ourselves to mechanisms that use functions $g_j(q_j)$ for simplicity, both of analysis and implementation. In addition to leading to simpler mechanisms, a principal might, practically speaking, prefer to announce a contest where the prize awarded to a winner is contingent on the absolute quality *only* of her own submission, and not on the absolute qualities of the submissions produced by her competitors; see also the discussion in §1.

Principal's objective. We assume that the principal's objective is to maximize some utility function $W(q_1, \ldots, q_n)$ of agents' output qualities in equilibrium, where W is non-decreasing in its arguments, *i.e.*, $W(q_1, \ldots, q_n)$ is such that if $q'_i \geq q_i$ for all i, then $W(q'_1, \ldots, q'_n) \geq W(q_1, \ldots, q_n)$. We will be interested throughout in symmetric pure-strategy Nash equilibria. If agents all use the same level of effort in equilibrium, then the principal's expected utility is non-decreasing in the effort choice of the agents: therefore, all such increasing objectives are simultaneously improved by mechanisms which elicit higher equilibrium effort from agents, assuming a symmetric equilibrium.

Heterogeneity. Our model, with noise terms ϵ_i all drawn from the same distribution $F(\cdot)$ and costs to effort given by the same function $c_i(\cdot) = c(\cdot)$, suggests contributors who are *a priori* homogeneous, corresponding to a pool of contestants who all have similar skills or ability for the subject of the contest (for example, programmers with similar levels of expertise or graphic designers with similar skill levels).

[5]It is worth noting, however, that most of the proofs and results in this paper will continue to hold even if this assumption on the monotonicity of rewards is relaxed.

Such a model captures scenarios where it is predominantly differences in effort, rather than differences in ability, that dominate differences in the quality produced. It also captures scenarios where the set of potential contestants may be self-selected to have rather similar abilities or expertise levels, and therefore similar costs to producing a particular quality.

Our model nonetheless allows capturing agent heterogeneity in two different ways. First, two contestants with the same effort choice will still come up with solutions of different qualities depending on their draws of ϵ_i, corresponding to situations where agents with similar skills nonetheless produce different outputs for the *specific* task posed by a particular contest. Second, the incentives of agents in contests where there is indeed heterogeneity in abilities that affects agents' final output qualities, but where agents do not know these abilities (beyond their distribution) prior to making their strategic effort choices, are identical to those in our model with 'abilities' drawn from $F(\cdot)$ after the agents choose their effort levels. Therefore, this model of heterogeneity includes many situations with non-homogeneous contributors, *as long as* agents do not learn their abilities prior to choosing their effort levels.

In a different model of heterogeneity amongst agents that appears in the contest design literature, an agent's output q_i is her ability-scaled effort $a_i e_i$, where agents' abilities are all randomly drawn from a single distribution F: a logarithmic transformation of variables from $q_i = a_i e_i$ in those models yields exactly our model where $q_i = e_i + \epsilon_i$. The key difference between these two models of heterogeneity is *timing of information*—agents observe their random draws of a_i *before* making their strategic effort choices in those models, whereas agents do *not* observe their draws of ϵ_i prior to making their effort choices in our model (for instance, as with a graphic designer who does not know exactly how good a design she will produce until she attempts it).

3. OPTIMAL CARDINAL MODIFICATIONS OF ORDINAL MECHANISMS

A contestant's cardinal quality score can be incorporated into a given rank-order mechanism in many different ways. A mechanism might choose to increase the reward for each rank linearly with an agent's output; more generally, the reward might increase as some convex function of her cardinal quality score up to some maximum reward. The reward scheme could also vary discontinuously with the quality of the agent's output, for instance so that the reward for a particular rank is determined by which of several intervals the corresponding quality score lies in. *A priori*, each of these cardinal modifications to a rank-order mechanism might create stronger incentives for effort than a purely ordinal mechanism by making reward more strongly dependent on the absolute quality. What choice of functions $g_j(\cdot)$ creates the strongest incentives for effort amongst all possible non-decreasing functions g_j?

While analyzing this question, we make two mild simplifying assumptions throughout. First, we assume that there is a symmetric pure strategy equilibrium in which all agents exert the same effort level e in the game; we show in the full version of the paper [15] that such symmetric pure strategy equilibria will exist under the fairly standard assumption that a player's cost function is sufficiently convex. Second, we consider functions $g_j(q)$ for which there is some small $\delta_j > 0$ such that $g_j(q)$ may only assume values that are integral multiples of δ_j. While this assumption is purely for technical simplicity and our results continue to hold without this assumption (albeit with a more complex proof), we note that this assumption is realistic because in any practical application there will be some minimum unit of a currency that represents the smallest possible amount by which one can change the value of an agent's prize. (For example, if prizes were paid in US dollars, any prize would necessarily have to be some integral multiple of some small fraction of a penny, as a principal would not be able to divide an agent's prize further than this).

Our main result, Theorem 3.1, shows that the question of how to choose the functions $g_j(q)$ to optimally modify any given rank-order mechanism using cardinal information has a strikingly simple answer: For any given rank-order mechanism $\mathcal{M}(A_1, A_2, \ldots, A_n)$, no other functions $g_j(q)$ can incentivize higher equilibrium effort than the optimal step functions that increase from 0 to 1 at some threshold score. We refer to such mechanisms as *threshold mechanisms.*

THEOREM 3.1. *Consider a rank-order tournament in which the agent who finishes in j^{th} place is awarded a prize $g_j(q)A_j$, where $g_j(q)$ is a non-decreasing function satisfying $0 \leq g_j(q) \leq 1$ for all q. There exist functions $g_j(q)$ of the form $g_j(q) = 0$ for $q < q_j^*$ and $g_j(q) = 1$ for $q \geq q_j^*$ for some constants q_j^* that incentivize the highest equilibrium effort amongst all possible mechanisms characterized by some functions $g_j(q)$.*

PROOF. Consider a set of *ladder* functions $l_j(q)$ that are characterized by a set of m_j cutoffs $q_{1,j}^* < q_{2,j}^* < \ldots < q_{m_j,j}^*$ for each of the j prizes such that $g_j(q) = r_{0,j}$ for $q < q_{1,j}^*$, $g_j(q) = r_{m,j}$ for all $q \in [q_{m,j}^*, q_{m+1,j}^*)$, and $g_j(q) = r_{m_j,j}$ for $q \geq q_{m_j,j}^*$, where $0 \leq r_{0,j} < r_{1,j} < \ldots < r_{m_j,j} \leq 1$. Note that any non-decreasing function $g_j(q)$ such that $g_j(q)$ is an integral multiple of δ_j and $0 \leq g_j(q) \leq 1$ for all q can be written in this form. Thus in order to prove that threshold mechanisms are optimal amongst the set of all mechanisms, it suffices to show that threshold mechanisms are also optimal amongst the set of all mechanisms induced by ladder functions.

Let $y_j(e, e_i, \epsilon_i)$ denote the probability that agent i finishes in j^{th} place for a given realization of ϵ_i given that agent i exerts effort e_i and all other agents exert effort e. If the prize for being ranked in the jth place with a contribution of quality q is $l_j(q)A_j$ for some ladder function $l_j(q)$, then an agent i's expected utility from exerting effort e_i when all other agents are exerting effort e is

$$E[u_i] = \sum_{j=1}^{n} \int_{-\infty}^{\infty} v(g_j(e_i + \epsilon_i)A_j) y_j(e, e_i, \epsilon_i) f(\epsilon_i)\, d\epsilon_i - c(e_i)$$

$$= \sum_{j=1}^{n} \sum_{k=0}^{m_j} \int_{q_{k,j}^* - e_i}^{q_{k+1,j}^* - e_i} v(r_{k,j}A) y_j(e, e_i, \epsilon_i) f(\epsilon_i)\, d\epsilon_i - c(e_i)$$

where we abuse notation by letting $q_{0,j}^* \equiv -\infty$ and $q_{m_j+1,j}^* \equiv \infty$. In a symmetric pure-strategy equilibrium, all agents, and specifically agent i, choose effort e, and this is a best response, *i.e.*, the derivative of u_i with respect to e_i must be zero at $e_i = e$. That is, the equilibrium effort e must satisfy the first order conditions given below:

$$c'(e) = \sum_{j=1}^{n}\sum_{k=0}^{m_j} v(r_{k,j}A)[y_j(e,e,q^*_{k,j}-e)f(q^*_{k,j}-e)$$
$$-y_j(e,e,q^*_{k+1,j}-e)f(q^*_{k+1,j}-e)$$
$$+\int_{q^*_{k,j}-e}^{q^*_{k+1,j}-e} \left.\frac{\partial y_j(e,e_i,\epsilon_i)}{\partial e_i}\right|_{e_i=e} f(\epsilon_i)\, d\epsilon_i]. \quad (1)$$

But note that the right-hand side of this equation is a linear function of $v(r_{k,j}A)$ for all k and j. From this it follows that for all $k \leq m_j$, the right-hand side of this equation is either non-decreasing in $r_{k,j}$ or non-increasing in $r_{k,j}$. Thus if $m_j \geq 2$, then one can instead set the value of $r_{1,j}$ to either be equal to $r_{0,j}$ or $r_{2,j}$ without decreasing the right-hand side of equation (1), meaning that one can make this change without decreasing equilibrium level of effort.

But setting the value of $r_{1,j}$ to equal to $r_{0,j}$ or $r_{2,j}$ would be equivalent to replacing the ladder function $l_j(q)$ with a ladder function that has $m_j - 1$ points of discontinuity rather than m_j points of discontinuity. From this it follows that if one is using a mechanism based on ladder functions $l_j(q)$ such that some $l_j(q)$ has $m_j \geq 2$ points of discontinuity, then the mechanism designer can induce at least as large a level of effort by instead using some mechanism based on ladder functions such that $l_j(q)$ has $m_j - 1$ points of discontinuity. By induction, it then follows that the mechanism designer can also induce at least as large a level of effort by instead using some mechanism based on ladder functions such that each $l_j(q)$ has no more than one point of discontinuity.

To complete the proof, it suffices to show that if the mechanism designer is using a mechanism based on ladder functions $l_j(q)$ that each have no more than one point of discontinuity, then these single-step ladder functions must correspond to threshold mechanisms, *i.e.*, that $r_{0,j} \in \{0,1\}$ and $r_{1,j} \in \{0,1\}$. Since equilibrium effort is again given by the solution to equation (1), and the right-hand side of this equation is a linear function of $v(r_{k,j}A)$ for all k and j, we again have that the right-hand side of this equation is either non-decreasing in $r_{0,j}$ or non-increasing in $r_{0,j}$. Thus if $l_j(q)$ has exactly one point of discontinuity, then one can set the value of $r_{0,j}$ to either be equal to 0 or $r_{1,j}$ without decreasing the right-hand side of equation (1), meaning that one can make this change without decreasing equilibrium effort.

Now if $r_{0,j} = 0$, then the same argument illustrates that one can set the value of $r_{1,j}$ to either be equal to 0 or 1 without decreasing the right-hand side of equation (1), meaning that one can make this change without decreasing equilibrium effort. And if $r_{0,j} = r_{1,j}$, then $l_j(q)$ has no points of discontinuity, and the same argument again illustrates that one can set the value of $r_{0,j} = r_{1,j}$ to be either 0 or 1 without decreasing the right-hand side of equation (1), meaning that one can make this change without decreasing equilibrium effort. Thus the mechanism designer can induce the agents to exert at least as much effort in equilibrium by using a threshold mechanism in which $r_{0,j} \in \{0,1\}$ and $r_{1,j} \in \{0,1\}$. □

While there are potentially a variety of far more nuanced ways to incorporate cardinal information in determining agents' prizes in a mixed cardinal-ordinal mechanism, Theorem 3.1 says that there is always an optimal mechanism with an exceedingly simple form—it awards the entire value of the jth prize to the agent who finishes in j^{th} place if this agent's output quality meets some threshold, and awards her no prize at all otherwise. This result may be surprising, since it would seem far more natural to use a mechanism where an agent's prize varies smoothly with the quality of her output than one where it exhibits a sharp discontinuity with respect to quality, especially if agents are risk-averse—risk-averse agents are likely to prefer a prize structure in which they have a good chance of receiving a moderate prize over one in which they have a high chance of receiving nothing and a high chance of receiving a large prize. Nonetheless, Theorem 3.1 shows that such threshold mechanisms can always incentivize agents to choose optimal effort levels.[6]

3.1 Optimal Thresholds

Our main result shows that the optimal mechanism is a threshold mechanism. We now ask what the optimal thresholds are. To do this, we will need an equilibrium analysis of threshold mechanisms.

Since we are interested in symmetric equilibria in which all players exert effort e, we begin by computing a player's expected utility from a given threshold mechanism when the player exerts effort e_i and all other players exert effort e. Consider a given threshold mechanism $\mathcal{M}(A_1, t_1, A_2, t_2, \ldots, A_n, t_n)$, where the jth-ranked agent receives the prize A_j if and only if her output quality exceeds the threshold t_j. Agent i's expected utility in $\mathcal{M}(A_1, t_1, A_2, t_2, \ldots, A_n, t_n)$ from choosing effort e_i, when all other agents are exerting effort e, is the difference between i's expected prize minus the cost of her effort $c(e_i)$, where i's prize depends both on the rank of the quality of her output $q_i = e_i + \epsilon_i$ relative to the qualities of the other agents' outputs $q_{i'} = e_{i'} + \epsilon_{i'}$, and whether her output q_i exceeds the threshold t_j specified for her rank j. We thus begin by considering the probability that agent i's output has rank j when she chooses effort e_i and all other agents choose effort e.

If $\epsilon_{[j]}$ denotes the jth-largest of the noise terms ϵ drawn by the $n-1$ *remaining* agents, then agent i will have the jth-highest quality output if and only if $e + \epsilon_{[j]} \leq e_i + \epsilon_i \leq e + \epsilon_{[j-1]}$. The probability of this event, for a *given* draw of ϵ_i, is the probability that the number $e_i + \epsilon_i - e$ lies between the random values of $\epsilon_{[j]}$ and $\epsilon_{[j-1]}$. Thus the probability of this event is equal to the probability that exactly $j-1$ of $n-1$ randomly drawn values from the cumulative distribution function $F(\cdot)$ exceed $e_i + \epsilon_i - e$. Using standard expressions for binomial probabilities, we know that this event takes place with probability

$$\binom{n-1}{j-1}(1 - F(e_i - e + \epsilon_i))^{j-1} F(e_i - e + \epsilon_i)^{n-j}. \quad (2)$$

Now suppose agent i produces output $q_i = e_i + \epsilon_i$. To actually receive the prize A_j in the threshold mechanism $\mathcal{M}(A_1, t_1, A_2, t_2, \ldots, A_n, t_n)$, i's output must also exceed the threshold t_j, *i.e.*, satisfy $e_i + \epsilon_i \geq t_j$. Therefore, the probability that agent i finally receives the jth prize, unconditional on the realization of ϵ_i, is the integral of the probability in equation (2) over $\epsilon_i \geq t_j - e_i$, *i.e.*,

[6]It is worth noting that this result will also hold even if there is a common shock to the agents' output in the sense that $q_i = e_i + \epsilon_i + \eta$ for some randomly drawn value of η that is common to all agents. A substantively identical proof can be used to prove Theorem 3.1 in this slightly more general model.

$$\int_{t_j-e_i}^{\infty}\binom{n-1}{j-1}(1-F(e_i-e+\epsilon_i))^{j-1}F(e_i-e+\epsilon_i)^{n-j}f(\epsilon_i)\,d\epsilon_i.$$

Thus an agent's total expected utility from exerting effort e_i, when other agents choose e, is the sum of her expected benefit over all ranks j minus her cost $c(e_i)$ or

$$E[u_i]=\sum_{j=1}^{k}v(A_j)\int_{t_j-e_i}^{\infty}\binom{n-1}{j-1}(1-F(e_i-e+\epsilon_i))^{j-1}\times F(e_i-e+\epsilon_i)^{n-j}f(\epsilon_i)\,d\epsilon_i-c(e_i).$$

We now address the question of what the optimal thresholds are. The proof of optimality of threshold mechanisms does not say anything about how the thresholds corresponding to each rank j vary with j, and thus allows for the possibility that the thresholds that are optimal for each rank might be substantially different for each rank. However, while it might seem intuitive that the optimal threshold could either consistently increase or consistently decrease across ranks, this turns out not to be the case, as we show below:

THEOREM 3.2. *Suppose the noise density $f(\cdot)$ is single-peaked at 0. Then the optimal threshold mechanism $\mathcal{M}(A_1,t_1^*,\ldots,A_n,t_n^*)$ applies the same threshold to each rank j for any monotone mechanism $\mathcal{M}(A_1,A_2,\ldots,A_n)$, i.e., $t_j^*=t^*$ for $j=1,\ldots,n$.*

PROOF. If the mechanism designer uses a threshold mechanism in which the agent who finishes in j^{th} place receives a prize if and only if this agent's observed quality exceeds t_j, then an agent i's expected utility from exerting effort e_i when all other agents are exerting effort e is given by

$$E[u_i]=\sum_{j=1}^{n}\int_{t_j-e_i}^{\infty}v(A_j)y_j(e,e_i,\epsilon_i)f(\epsilon_i)\,d\epsilon_i-c(e_i)$$

where we let $y_j(e,e_i,\epsilon_i)\equiv\binom{n-1}{j-1}(1-F(e_i-e+\epsilon_i))^{j-1}F(e_i-e+\epsilon_i)^{n-j}$ denote the probability that agent i finishes in j^{th} place given that all other agents exert effort e, agent i exerts effort e_i, and the value of agent i's noise term is ϵ_i. From this it follows that the derivative of the agent's utility with respect to e_i is given by the following expression:

$$\sum_{j=1}^{n}v(A_j)[y_j(e,e_i,t_j-e_i)f(t_j-e_i)+\int_{t_j-e_i}^{\infty}\frac{\partial y_j(e,e_i,\epsilon_i)}{\partial e_i}f(\epsilon_i)\,d\epsilon_i]-c'(e_i)$$

By setting this derivative equal to zero when $e_i=e$, it then follows that it is an equilibrium for all agents to exert effort e if and only if $c'(e)$ is equal to

$$\sum_{j=1}^{n}v(A_j)[y_j(e,e,t_j-e)f(t_j-e)+\int_{t_j-e}^{\infty}\left.\frac{\partial y_j(e,e_i,\epsilon_i)}{\partial e_i}\right|_{e_i=e}f(\epsilon_i)\,d\epsilon_i].\tag{3}$$

In the optimal threshold mechanism, the thresholds t_j must be chosen in such a way as to make the expression in equation (3) as large as possible for a given e. A necessary condition for this is that the derivative of this equation with respect to t_j must be zero for all j. When we differentiate this equation with respect to t_j, the only term that remains is

$$v(A_j)y_j(e,e,t_j-e)f'(t_j-e).\tag{4}$$

Now note that the principal would never have an incentive to choose a value of t_j that is equal to $-\infty$ or ∞ for all j. To see this, note that for values of t_j that are arbitrarily negative, it must be the case that $t_j-e<0$ in equilibrium, meaning $f'(t_j-e)>0$ and the derivative of equation (3) with respect to t_j is positive. Thus for any sufficiently negative values of t_j, the principal can always increase the expression in equation (3) by increasing t_j, and thereby increase the equilibrium level of effort. From this it follows that a threshold of $t_j=-\infty$ can never be optimal for any j. A similar argument shows that a threshold of $t_j=\infty$ can also never be optimal. Thus there is some large finite value of $T>0$ such that all thresholds $t_j\notin[-T,T]$ are dominated by some threshold $t_j\in[-T,T]$ for all j. Since this set of feasible thresholds is compact, and the equilibrium level of effort varies continuously with the thresholds, it then follows that some set of optimal thresholds exists.

Now if the optimal threshold t_j is not equal to $-\infty$ or ∞, then it must be the case that the derivative in equation (4) is zero at the optimal t_j. Now we know that $f(\cdot)$ is single-peaked at 0, so when t_j is not equal to $-\infty$ or ∞, the above derivative is only zero when $t_j=e$. Thus the optimal thresholds satisfy $t_j=e$ for all j and the optimal thresholds are always equal for all prizes. □

Theorem 3.2 says that optimally incorporating cardinal scores into a rank-order contest to maximize effort is, in fact, even simpler than the method suggested by Theorem 3.1—a mechanism designer only needs to compare all agents' outputs against the *same* baseline, reducing the problem of finding the optimal modification of $\mathcal{M}(A_1,A_2,\ldots,A_n)$ to one of choosing a single optimal threshold t^* for $\mathcal{M}(A_1,A_2,\ldots,A_n)$. Our proof of Theorem 3.2 also contains a proof of the following result, which we state here since it is used repeatedly in the remainder of our analysis:

COROLLARY 3.1. *Suppose that $f(\cdot)$ is single-peaked at 0. Then the optimal threshold that induces the highest equilibrium effort in the threshold mechanism is equal to the equilibrium level of effort at that threshold.*

3.2 Comparative Statics

We now address the question of how the optimal threshold t^* varies with changes in the problem parameters, specifically with the number of contestants and changes in the prize structure. First we consider comparative statics with respect to the number of agents. Our mechanisms $\mathcal{M}(A_1,A_2,\ldots,A_n)$ so far have been specified in terms of the prizes for each of the n ranks, where n is the number of players. Since we want to now vary n, we assume that there is a fixed number k of prizes, $A_1,A_2,\ldots,A_k$, and the number of players n is greater than or equal to k. In this scenario, we prove the following result:

THEOREM 3.3. *Consider any given rank-order mechanism $\mathcal{M}$ with prizes $A_1,\ldots,A_k$, and let $t^*(n)$ denote the optimal threshold for $\mathcal{M}$ when there are n agents in the contest. If the noise density $f(\cdot)$ is single-peaked at 0, then the optimal threshold $t^*(n)$ is decreasing in the number of players n*

for all $n \geq k$. Further, the equilibrium effort in the optimal threshold mechanism also decreases with n.

PROOF. Note that a player i's expected value for her prize from exerting effort e_i when all other players are exerting effort e is just equal to the sum, over all $j = 1, \ldots, k$, of the difference between the value the player obtains from receiving the jth prize A_j and her value from the $j+1^{th}$ prize A_{j+1}, multiplied by the probability that she finishes in at least j^{th} place and meets the threshold t. Now let $G_j(q)$ denote the probability that no more than $j-1$ of the $n-1$ values of $\epsilon_{i'}$ are greater than q. Then the probability that agent i finishes in at least j^{th} place for any given realization of ϵ_i when she exerts effort e_i and all other players are exerting effort e is $G_j(e_i - e + \epsilon_i)$. From this it follows that the probability agent i finishes in at least j^{th} place and meets the threshold t unconditional on the realization of ϵ_i is

$$\int_{t-e_i}^{\infty} G_j(e_i - e + \epsilon_i) f(\epsilon_i)\, d\epsilon_i.$$

By using the insights in the previous paragraph, it follows that player i's expected utility from exerting effort e_i when all other players are exerting effort e is

$$\sum_{j=1}^{k}(v(A_j) - v(A_{j+1})) \int_{t-e_i}^{\infty} G_j(e_i - e + \epsilon_i) f(\epsilon_i)\, d\epsilon_i - c(e_i)$$

By differentiating this expression with respect to e_i, setting the derivative equal to zero, and using the fact that $e_i = e$ must hold in any symmetric pure strategy equilibrium, it follows that at the equilibrium level of effort e, $c'(e)$ must equal

$$\sum_{j=1}^{k}(v(A_j) - v(A_{j+1}))[G_j(t-e)f(t-e) + \int_{t-e}^{\infty} \frac{dG_j(\epsilon)}{d\epsilon} f(\epsilon)\, d\epsilon].$$

From Corollary 3.1, the equilibrium effort e at the optimal threshold t will satisfy $t - e = 0$. Thus equilibrium effort in the *optimal* threshold mechanism is the solution to

$$\sum_{j=1}^{k}(v(A_j) - v(A_{j+1}))[G_j(0)f(0) + \int_{0}^{\infty} \frac{dG_j(\epsilon)}{d\epsilon} f(\epsilon)\, d\epsilon] = c'(e). \quad (5)$$

Here $\frac{dG_j(\epsilon)}{d\epsilon}$ represents the density corresponding to this distribution. Write $G_j(\epsilon; n)$ to denote the dependence of G_j on n. Then, the distribution $G_j(\epsilon; n')$ first order stochastically dominates $G_j(\epsilon; n)$ for all $n' > n$. Further, $f(\epsilon)$ is non-increasing in ϵ for all $\epsilon \geq 0$, since we assumed that $f(\cdot)$ is single-peaked at 0. From this it follows that increasing n decreases the value of the expression

$$G_j(0)f(0) + \int_{0}^{\infty} \frac{dG_j(\epsilon)}{d\epsilon} f(\epsilon)\, d\epsilon = E_{\epsilon \sim G_j}[f(\max\{0, \epsilon\})]$$

for all j (by stochastic dominance). Therefore, for equality to hold in equation (5), the equilibrium effort $e(n)$ must be such that $c'(e(n))$ also decreases with n, *i.e.*, $e(n)$ decreases with n. Since the equilibrium effort in the optimal threshold mechanism decreases with the number of players, and the optimal threshold equals equilibrium effort in the optimal threshold mechanism, by Corollary 3.1, the optimal threshold $t^*(n)$ is also decreasing in n. □

Next we ask how the optimal threshold varies with the number of prizes awarded. To formulate this question meaningfully, we consider contests where the top k participants who meet the threshold all receive the same prize, for some k, and consider two ways that the total number of prizes might increase—first, where the total prize pool stays the same, but the prizes are split amongst a larger number of players, and second, where the value of each prize stays the same, but more prizes of this value are awarded (contingent on meeting the threshold). The optimal threshold varies predictably with these changes in the prize structure, as the following theorem illustrates:

THEOREM 3.4. *Suppose that $f(\cdot)$ is single-peaked at zero and the number of prizes is less than the number of players.*
(1) The optimal threshold t^* in a contest with k equal prizes of value A increases with k.
(2) The optimal threshold t^* in a contest with k equal prizes of value A/k each also increases with k if players are sufficiently risk-averse in the sense that the coefficient of absolute risk aversion on $v(\cdot)$ is sufficiently large.

PROOF. We know from equation (5) in the proof of the previous theorem that if $G_j(q)$ denotes the probability that no more than $j-1$ of the $n-1$ other values of $\epsilon_{i'}$ are greater than q, then the following condition must be satisfied by the equilibrium level of effort e in the optimal threshold mechanism:

$$\sum_{j=1}^{k}(v(A_j) - v(A_{j+1}))[G_j(0)f(0) + \int_{0}^{\infty} \frac{dG_j(\epsilon)}{d\epsilon} f(\epsilon)\, d\epsilon] = c'(e)$$

Substituting in the fact that $A_j = A_k$ for $j \leq k$ and $A_j = 0$ for $j > k$, it then follows that the equilibrium level of effort e satisfies the following equation:

$$v(A_k)[G_k(0)f(0) + \int_{0}^{\infty} \frac{dG_k(\epsilon)}{d\epsilon} f(\epsilon)\, d\epsilon] = c'(e),$$

which can be rewritten as

$$v(A_k) E_{\epsilon \sim G_k}[f(\max\{0, \epsilon\})] = c'(e). \quad (6)$$

Now if one increases the number of prizes by awarding additional prizes that are the same as those originally awarded to agents who finished in the top k and met the threshold, then $v(A_k)$ is independent of k. And if one increases the number of prizes by splitting the same total prize pool amongst a larger number of players, then in the limit as the coefficient of absolute risk aversion on $v(\cdot)$ becomes arbitrarily large, $\frac{v(A_k)}{v(A)}$ becomes arbitrarily close to 1, and $v(A_k)$ approaches a function that is also independent of k.

But we also know that $E_{\epsilon \sim G_k}[f(\max\{0, \epsilon\})]$ is increasing in k since the fact that $G_k(\epsilon)$ is a distribution corresponding to the probability that no more than $k-1$ of the $n-1$ values of ϵ_j are greater than ϵ implies that G_j first order stochastically dominates G_k for all $j < k$. And we also know that $f(\max\{0, \epsilon\})$ is decreasing in ϵ for all $\epsilon > 0$. By combining these facts, it follows that $E_{\epsilon \sim G_k}[f(\max\{0, \epsilon\})]$ is increasing in k. Thus under either of the conditions of the theorem, it must be the case that $v(A_k) E_{\epsilon \sim G_k}[f(\max\{0, \epsilon\})]$ is increasing in k. By combining this fact with equation (6), it then follows that under either of these conditions, equilibrium effort in the optimal threshold mechanism is increasing in k. Since the optimal threshold is equal to equilibrium effort in the optimal threshold mechanism, it then follows that the optimal threshold is also increasing in k. □

The intuition for this result has to do with how an agent's incentives to try to meet the threshold vary with the number of prizes. As the number of prizes increases in either of the two manners considered in Theorem 3.4, the expected value of the prize that an agent obtains for meeting the threshold unambiguously increases. Thus agents have a stronger incentive to try to meet the threshold when the number of prizes increases, and agents will thus exert more effort in equilibrium when there are a larger number of prizes. Since the optimal threshold is equal to the equilibrium level of effort (from Corollary 3.1), it then follows that increasing the number of prizes also increases the optimal threshold.

4. HOW USEFUL IS CARDINAL INFORMATION?

Our results thus far show that making the award of the prizes in a rank-order contest $\mathcal{M}(A_1, A_2, \ldots, A_n)$ contingent on submission qualities exceeding a suitable threshold creates the strongest incentives for effort, and in particular, outperforms the contest that ignores cardinal information. In this section, we briefly address the question of *how much* of an improvement is obtained from using this cardinal information relative to $\mathcal{M}(A_1, A_2, \ldots, A_n)$, which awards prizes based only on relative rankings.

We first present simulation results to obtain a quantitative sense for the size of the improvement in equilibrium effort as a function of the number of contestants, the nature of participants' cost functions, the reward structure $(A_1, A_2, \ldots, A_n)$, and the noise distribution governing the stochastic perturbations that influence an agent's output. We ask to what extent the size of these gains are affected by changes in these underlying parameters, and discuss these results in the context of typical parameter values in online contests. Finally, we conclude with a result (proven in the full version of the paper [15]) that formalizes the observations from these simulations.

Simulations. We simulate contests where n players each have cost function $c(\hat{e}) = \frac{\hat{e}^a}{a}$ for some constant $a > 1$ (a larger a corresponds to a more convex cost function). We assume that players are risk-neutral with values $v(A) = A$ for prize A. For the distribution of the noise terms ϵ_i that randomly influence a player's submission quality as $q_i = e_i + \epsilon_i$, we consider IID draws from (i) a standard normal distribution and (ii) a standard Laplace distribution. For the set of prize structures, we consider contests with prizes of A_1 and A_2 for the top two ranks and $A_j = 0$ for all lower ranks for simplicity and brevity. Each of n, a, and the split into A_1 and A_2 are parameters describing the contest that we will vary in our simulations.

Computing equilibrium effort. To quantify the extent of improvement in equilibrium effort from using cardinal information in a contest $\mathcal{M}(A_1, A_2, \ldots, A_n)$, we first need to calculate the equilibrium level of effort both with no threshold and with the optimal threshold. When there is no threshold, the equilibrium level of effort is the same as it would be if the threshold were $t = -\infty$. Applying equation (3) to the special case in which $t = -\infty$, we see that the equilibrium level of effort e^*_ϕ with no thresholds must satisfy

$$\sum_{j=1}^{n} v(A_j)\left[\int_{-\infty}^{\infty}\left[\frac{(n-1)!}{(j-1)!(n-j-1)!}(1-F(\epsilon_i))^{j-1}F(\epsilon_i)^{n-j-1} - \frac{(n-1)!}{(j-2)!(n-j)!}(1-F(\epsilon_i))^{j-2}F(\epsilon_i)^{n-j}\right]f^2(\epsilon_i)\,d\epsilon_i\right] = e^{*\,a-1}_\phi$$

where we abuse notation by defining $\frac{(n-1)!}{(j-2)!(n-j)!}$ to be zero when $j = 1$.

When the mechanism designer uses the *optimal* threshold t^*, we know from Corollary 3.1 that the equilibrium level of effort e^*_O equals the optimal threshold. Therefore, setting $t = e$, we see that e^*_O must satisfy

$$e^{*\,a-1}_O = \sum_{j=1}^{n} v(A_j)\left[\binom{n-1}{j-1}\left(\frac{1}{2}\right)^{n-1} f(0) + \int_0^{\infty}\left[\frac{(n-1)!}{(j-1)!(n-j-1)!}(1-F(\epsilon_i))^{j-1}F(\epsilon_i)^{n-j-1} - \frac{(n-1)!}{(j-2)!(n-j)!}(1-F(\epsilon_i))^{j-2}F(\epsilon_i)^{n-j}\right]f^2(\epsilon_i)\,d\epsilon_i\right] \quad (7)$$

We can compute the percentage increase in equilibrium effort for a particular set of contest parameters by using the equations above to compute e^*_ϕ and e^*_O. We compute these improvements for a wide range of different parameters to observe how the various parameters affect the extent of the increase in equilibrium effort from using cardinal information via the optimal threshold mechanisms. While we cannot present the full results for want of space, we summarize the results for a few parameter values in Tables 1, 2, and 3.

n	Normal distribution	Laplace distribution
2	20.71%	50.00%
3	4.95%	16.67%
4	1.59%	7.14%
5	0.58%	3.33%
6	0.23%	1.61%
7	0.10%	0.80%
8	0.04%	0.40%
9	0.02%	0.19%

Table 1: Percentage increase in equilibrium effort from using the optimal threshold under a winner-take-all contest when the cost to effort $\hat{e}$ is $c(\hat{e}) = \frac{\hat{e}^2}{2}$ for different noise distributions and varying values of the number of players n.

Discussion of simulation results. The simulations lead to a number of interesting insights. First, they show that when the number of players is larger, the benefit to setting the optimal threshold is relatively smaller. We also see that when the parameter a in the exponent of the cost function $c(\hat{e}) = \frac{\hat{e}^a}{a}$ increases, so that players' cost functions are more convex, less is gained by using the optimal threshold. Finally, when more of the prizes are given to the lower-ranked players, there is again a larger benefit from using the optimal threshold.

These observations all have intuitive explanations. Since equilibrium effort equals the optimal threshold (Corollary 3.1), when there are a large number of players, the final realized quality of the winning player is likely to far exceed

a	Normal distribution	Laplace distribution
1.25	6.51%	31.78%
1.5	3.21%	14.80%
1.75	2.12%	9.64%
2	1.59%	7.14%
3	0.79%	3.51%
4	0.53%	2.33%
5	0.40%	1.74%
6	0.32%	1.39%

Table 2: Percentage increase in equilibrium effort from using the optimal threshold for different noise distributions and varying values of the the term a in the cost function $c(\hat{e}) = \frac{\hat{e}^a}{a}$, under a winner-take-all contest with $n = 4$.

(A_1, A_2)	Normal distribution	Laplace distribution
$(1, 0)$	0.58%	3.33%
$(0.9, 0.1)$	1.06%	5.17%
$(0.8, 0.2)$	1.59%	7.14%
$(0.7, 0.3)$	2.20%	9.26%
$(0.6, 0.4)$	2.90%	11.54%
$(0.5, 0.5)$	3.72%	14.00%

Table 3: Percentage increase in equilibrium effort from using the optimal threshold for different noise distributions and varying distributions of the top prizes, with five players when $c(\hat{e}) = \frac{\hat{e}^2}{2}$.

the threshold, so the threshold provides little incentive to exert additional effort. By contrast, when there are only a small number of players, there is a significant risk that even the winning player's final realized quality will be in the same range as the threshold, and the threshold may therefore provide significant incentives to exert effort. Thus using the optimal threshold should have a relatively smaller effect when there are a larger number of players.

We note that both regimes with large numbers of players and small numbers of players are relevant empirically. For example, in Kaggle contests, there are typically at least dozens and usually hundreds of participants, so in such a contest setting the optimal threshold is likely to have little effect on incentives to exert effort. By contrast, many tasks on TaskCN and Topcoder[7] only attract a few participants[8], so in such contests, using the optimal threshold is likely to significantly improve effort. There are also online contests with elimination rounds leading up to a final round with a few finalists (such as the Robin Hood Foundation Prize[9]). In such settings, our results would suggest that using an optimal threshold to award prizes is likely to significantly improve effort in the final round of the contest.

To understand why convexity affects equilibrium effort, note that when the players' cost functions are more convex, a change in a player's effort does relatively more to increase the player's marginal cost of exerting effort, which in turn implies that a player can only increase his effort by a smaller amount in response to improved incentives before the player's marginal cost from exerting more effort will equal his marginal benefit. Thus using the optimal threshold will have less effect when the players' cost functions are more convex.

Finally we address the effect of the distribution of prizes on effort. The lower-ranked players are more likely to have final realized qualities that are close to the threshold, so the threshold provides a greater incentive for a lower-ranked player to exert effort than a higher-ranked player. Thus when a relatively greater amount of the prize pool is given to the lower-ranked players, this has the effect of shifting prizes from players who will be less strongly incentivized by the thresholds to players who will be more strongly incentivized by the thresholds. Thus using the optimal threshold has a relatively greater effect when a larger amount of the prize pool is distributed amongst lower ranks.

The insights from these simulations are, in fact, more general than this. In the full version of the paper [15], we prove the following result under some technical assumptions:

THEOREM 4.1 (INFORMAL). *The absolute and relative differences between the equilibrium effort elicited in the optimal threshold mechanism and an ordinal rank-order mechanism with no threshold is (i) decreasing in the number of players, (ii) increasing in the number of prizes if all the prizes are equal, and (iii) decreasing in the convexity of the cost function, where the degree of convexity of the cost function is measured by the ratio* $\frac{c''(e)}{c'(e)}$.

5. DISCUSSION AND FURTHER WORK

In this paper, we addressed the problem of how a principal running a contest might optimally incorporate cardinal information regarding the absolute qualities of contestants' entries into an existing rank-order tournament, motivated by the observation that an increasing number of contests today evaluate entries according to some numerical metric. We found that threshold mechanisms, which compare a submission's score against an absolute threshold—in fact, the *same* threshold for each prize—are optimal amongst the class of all mixed cardinal-ordinal mechanisms which award the agent with the jth-ranked submission with quality q_j an arbitrary quality-dependent fraction $g_j(q_j)$ of the prize A_j. Therefore, using cardinal information as coarsely as by comparing against a single threshold provides the optimal modification of a rank-order mechanism in terms of incentives for effort. Finally, we saw that gains from incorporating cardinal information relative to using only ordinal information are highest for small contests with more than one prize and with participants whose costs to effort are not too convex.

Further results. There are a number of interesting questions regarding incentives in cardinal contests that we address in the full version of this paper [15].

Endogenous entry. A first natural question is how the results would be affected by the possibility of endogenous entry. While we have assumed throughout this paper that the number of players in the contest is known and fixed,

[7]http://community.topcoder.com/tc?module=CompList&pt=35

[8]For example, [25] notes that most programming tasks on TaskCN attracted fewer than six participants and [42] notes that it is far more common to receive a small number of solutions for a task on TaskCN than some larger number of solutions.

[9]https://www.robinhood.org/prize

there are many real-world situations in which participation, even with very low effort, is costly and an agent must strategically decide whether to participate at all. We address how the possibility of endogenous entry affects the equilibrium in [15], and show that the choice of threshold in a threshold mechanism results in an interesting participation-effort tradeoff: the equilibrium level of participation may increase as a result of decreasing the threshold, but such equilibria will result in the agents exerting lower levels of effort. How the principal resolves this tradeoff will then depend on how much the principal values participation versus effort.

Optimal rank-based prizes. Another interesting question relates to whether the optimal division of prizes would change as a result of optimally incorporating cardinal information into a contest. In particular, suppose that the optimal division of the total prize pool A amongst the n places for a rank-order mechanism is $(A_1, \ldots, A_n)$. Is it still the case that this is the optimal division of the prizes amongst the n places for the optimal mixed cardinal-ordinal mechanism that makes use of the optimal threshold? We address this question in [15] as well, and show that the answer to this question depends crucially on whether the agents are risk-averse: if agents are risk-neutral in the sense that $v(A)$ varies linearly with A, then the optimal division of prizes will be the same for both a pure rank-order mechanism and the optimal threshold mechanism. However, if agents are risk-averse in the sense that $v(A)$ is strictly concave in A, then this need not be the case. Instead, the principal will typically want to reward a larger percentage of the prize pool to the lower ranks under the optimal threshold mechanism than in a purely ordinal tournament.

Learning optimal thresholds. A number of questions also arise from practical considerations regarding uncertainty. For instance, the optimal threshold t^* for a given rank-order contest depends on the parameters of the population, which the designer might typically not have access to. As such, it might be difficult for a mechanism designer to set the optimal threshold in a contest. How could a mechanism designer who intends to run multiple iterations of a contest learn what the optimal threshold is from the earlier iterations of the contest? We show in [15] how a mechanism designer without complete knowledge of the contest population could make probabilistic inferences about whether the threshold selected was too high or too low from the results of previous contests and use this information to better set the threshold in future iterations.

Open questions. A number of open questions remain for further research. First, the specific question we ask about modifying given rank-order mechanisms to incorporate cardinal information is motivated by the fact that practical considerations beyond incentives for effort—such as simplicity, sponsorships of various prize levels, media or publicity considerations—might cause a principal to choose a particular prize structure for his contest. However, it is also very interesting to study the more general optimal contest design problem in such contests with access to absolute measurements of quality. What mechanism $\mathcal{M}(q_1, \ldots, q_n)$ incentivizes the highest effort over all mechanisms with access to cardinal, and not just ordinal, information about outputs?[10] And how does the answer to this question depend on the specifics of the model such as agents' risk preferences and the objective function of the mechanism designer?

A second intriguing theoretical question regards a connection to optimal auctions and reserve pricing. There is a formal connection between auctions and contests ([7], [8], [11]) in an *alternative* model for contests where effort deterministically translates into output (see §2 for a discussion regarding the difference with our model). At first glance, this might suggest a mapping between the model and analysis in our paper and that in the literature on sponsored search auctions [32]. However, this simplified mapping is a fallacious analogy in contests where output is a stochastic perturbation of effort, because the fact that an agent's output is determined by a noise-perturbed version of effort completely changes both the structure of the problem and all the underlying analysis relative to auctions. Nevertheless, the parallels between the results on optimality of threshold-like structures in these two settings—contests and auctions—raises the intriguing question of whether there is indeed a way to formally relate our results on optimalities of thresholds in contests to optimality of reserve prices in auctions. A deeper understanding of the connection between threshold mechanisms and optimal auctions is an interesting open direction for further research.

[10][7] addresses this question in a specific (but different) model; see §1.1.

6. REFERENCES

[1] N. Archak. Money, glory and cheap talk: analyzing strategic behavior of contestants in simultaneous crowdsourcing contests on TopCoder.com. In *Proceedings of the 19th International Conference on the World Wide Web (WWW)*, pages 21–30, 2009.

[2] N. Archak, A. Sundararajan. Optimal design of crowdsourcing contests. In *Proceedings of the 30th International Conference on Information Systems (ICIS)*, pages 1–16, 2009.

[3] K.J. Boudreau, N. Lacetera, K.R. Lakhani. Incentives and problem uncertainty in innovation contests: an empirical analysis. *Management Science*, 57(5): 843–863, 2011.

[4] C.B. Cadsby, C. Bram, F. Song, F. Tapon. Sorting and incentive effects of pay-for-performance: an experimental investigation. *Academy of Management Journal*, 50(2): 387–405, 2007.

[5] J. Carpenter, P.H. Matthews, J. Schirm. Tournaments and office politics: evidence from a real effort experiment. *American Economic Review*, 100(1): 504–517, 2010.

[6] R. Cavallo, S. Jain. Winner-take-all crowdsourcing contests with stochastic production. In *Proceedings of the First AAAI Conference on Human Computation and Crowdsourcing (HCOMP)*, pages 34–41, 2013.

[7] S. Chawla, J.D. Hartline, B. Sivan. Optimal crowdsourcing contests. In *Proceedings of the 23rd ACM-SIAM Symposium of Discrete Algorithms (SODA)*, pages 856–868, 2012.

[8] Y.-K. Che, I. Gale. Optimal design of research tournaments. *American Economic Review*, 93(3): 646–671, 2003.

[9] Y. Chen, T.-H. Ho, Y.-M. Kim. Knowledge market design: a field experiment at Google Answers. *Journal of Public Economic Theory*, 12(4): 641–664, 2010.

[10] S.M. Chowdhury, R.M. Sheremeta, T.L. Turocyd. Overbidding and overspreading in rent-seeking experiments. *Games and Economic Behavior*, 87: 224–238, 2014.

[11] D. DiPalantino, M. Vojnović. Crowdsourcing and all-pay contests. In *Proceedings of the 10th ACM Conference on Electronic Commerce (EC)*, pages 119–128, 2009.

[12] T. Dohmen, A. Falk. Performance pay and multidimensional sorting: productivity, preferences, and gender. *American Economic Review*, 101(2): 556–590, 2011.

[13] T. Eriksson, M.C. Villeval. Performance pay, sorting, and social motivation. *Journal of Economic Behavior and Organization*, 68(2): 412–421, 2008.

[14] Q. Fu, J. Lu. The optimal multi-stage contest. *Economic Theory*, 51(2): 351–382, 2012.

[15] A. Ghosh, P. Hummel. Cardinal contests. Mimeo, 2015.

[16] A. Ghosh, R.P. McAfee. Crowdsourcing with endogenous entry. In *Proceedings of the 20th International World Wide Web Conference (WWW)*, pages 137–146, 2012.

[17] A. Glazer, R. Hassin. Optimal contests. *Economic Inquiry*, 26(1): 133–143, 1988.

[18] J.R. Green, N.L. Stokey. A comparison of tournaments and contracts. *Journal of Political Economy*, 91(3): 349–364, 1983.

[19] B. Holmstrom. Moral hazard in teams. *Bell Journal of Economics*, 13(2): 324–340, 1982.

[20] K.A. Konrad. Dynamic contests. Max Planck Institute for Intellectual Property Typescript, 2010.

[21] E.P. Lazear. Pay equality and industrial politics. *Journal of Political Economy*, 97(3): 561–580, 1989.

[22] E.P. Lazear. Performance pay and productivity. *American Economic Review*, 90(5): 1346–1361, 2000.

[23] E.P. Lazear, S. Rosen. Rank-order tournaments as optimum labor contracts. *Journal of Political Economy*, 89(5): 841–864, 1981.

[24] B. Liu, J. Liu, R. Wang, J. Zhang. Prize and punishment: optimal contest design with incomplete information. National University of Signapore Typescript, 2013.

[25] T.X. Liu, J. Yang, L.A. Adamic, Y. Chen. Crowdsourcing with all-pay auctions: a field experiment on Taskcn. *Management Science*, 60(8): 2020–2037, 2014.

[26] D.B. Minor. Increasing revenue through rewarding the best (or not at all). Northwestern University Typescript, 2013.

[27] B. Moldovanu, A. Sela. The optimal allocation of prizes in contests. *American Economic Review*, 91(3): 542–558, 2001.

[28] B. Moldovanu, A. Sela. Contest architecture. *Journal of Economic Theory*, 126(1): 70–96, 2006.

[29] B. Moldovanu, A. Sela, X. Shi. Contests for status. *Journal of Political Economy*, 115(2): 338–363, 2007.

[30] J. Morgan, H. Orzen, M. Sefton. Endogenous entry in contests. *Economic Theory*, 51(2): 435–463, 2012.

[31] B.J. Nalebuff, J.E. Stiglitz. Prizes and incentives: towards a general theory of compensation and competition. *Bell Journal of Economics*, 14(1): 21–43, 1983.

[32] M. Ostrovsky, M. Schwarz. Reserve prices in Internet advertising auctions: a field experiment. Stanford Graduate School of Business Typescript, 2009.

[33] S. Parreiras, A. Rubinchik. Contests with three or more heterogeneous agents. *Games and Economic Behavior*, 68(2): 703–715, 2010.

[34] C. Riis. Efficient contests. *Journal of Economics and Management Strategy*, 19(3): 643–665, 2010.

[35] R. Siegel. All-pay contests. *Econometrica*, 77(1): 71–92, 2009.

[36] R. Siegel. Asymmetric contests with conditional investments. *American Economic Review*, 100(5): 2230–2260, 2010.

[37] R. Siegel. Participation in deterministic contests. *Economics Letters*, 116(3): 588–592, 2012.

[38] R. Seigel. Asymmetric contests with productive effort. *American Economic Journal: Microeconomics*, 6(3): 59–105, 2014.

[39] R. Siegel. Contests with productive effort. *International Journal of Game Theory*, 43(3): 515–523, 2014.

[40] S. Szymanski, T.M. Valletti. Incentive effects of second prizes. *European Journal of Political Economy*, 21(2): 467–481, 2005.

[41] C.R. Taylor. Digging for golden carrots: an analysis of research tournaments. *American Economic Review*, 85(4): 872–890, 1995.

[42] J. Yang, L.A. Adamic, M.S. Ackerman. Crowdsourcing and knowledge sharing: strategic user behavior on TaskCN. In *Proceedings of the 9th ACM Conference on Electronic Commerce (EC)*, pages 246–255, 2008.

Accessible On-Line Floor Plans

Cagatay Goncu
Monash University, Australia
cagatay.goncu@monash.edu

Anuradha Madugalla
Monash University & NICTA
Victoria, Australia
amad29@student.monash.edu

Simone Marinai
Universita degli Studi di
Firenze, Italy
simone.marinai@unifi.it

Kim Marriott
Monash University & NICTA
Victoria, Australia
Kim.Marriott@monash.edu

ABSTRACT

Better access to on-line information graphics is a pressing need for people who are blind or have severe vision impairment. We present a new model for accessible presentation of on-line information graphics and demonstrate its use for presenting floor plans. While floor plans are increasingly provided on-line, people who are blind are at best provided with only a high-level textual description. This makes it difficult for them to understand the spatial arrangement of the objects on the floor plan. Our new approach provides users with significantly better access to such plans. The users can automatically generate an accessible version of a floor plan from an on-line floor plan image quickly and independently by using a web service. This generates a simplified graphic showing the rooms, walls, doors and windows in the original floor plan as well as a textual overview. The accessible floor plan is presented on an iPad using audio feedback. As the users touch graphic elements on the screen, the element they are touching is described by speech and non-speech audio in order to help them navigate the graphic.

Categories and Subject Descriptors

H.5.2 [**Information Interfaces and Presentation**]: User Interfaces; I.7.5 [**Document And Text Processing**]: Document Capture—*Graphics recognition and interpretation*; K.4.2 [**Computers And Society**]: Social Issues—*Assistive technologies for persons with disabilities*

General Terms

Human Factors, Design

Keywords

graphics; accessibility; vision impairment; transcription; graphics recognition

WWW 2015, May 18–22, 2015, Florence, Italy.
ACM 978-1-4503-3469-3/15/05.
http://dx.doi.org/10.1145/2736277.2741660.

1. INTRODUCTION

One of the most disabling consequences of being blind (by whom we mean any person whose level of vision does not allow them to easily read printed text or graphics even when magnified) is a lack of access to information presented graphically, such as maps, plans, diagrams and illustrations in instruction manuals. Such graphics are increasingly accessed on the web. However, on-line graphics are typically not accessible to users who are blind because despite accessibility guidelines [1] the vast majority either do not include an alternative text description of the graphic or the text is very general and not helpful [16]. While in theory a blind person might request an audio description or a tactile graphic version of an on-line graphic from a support organisation such as Vision Australia this is expensive and may take weeks for the accessible version to be produced.

We present a new model for providing access to on-line information graphics: automatic transcription from an on-line image to an accessible graphic designed for presentation on a portable touch screen device such as an iPad. The accessible graphic can be viewed immediately by using audio feedback, and can also be improved by a transcriber with semi-automatic transcription. We believe this model has the potential to dramatically improve access to a wide range of on-line information graphics.

We describe and evaluate the use of the model for provision of accessible on-line floor plans. The reason for focusing on floor plans is that the fear of leaving the safety of home and having to find one's way in a new environment is another great disabling consequence of blindness. Navigation in buildings and public spaces such as hotels, conference venues, airports or shopping centres is particularly challenging. When visiting a building for the first time it is difficult to find doors, elevators, stairs or the location of the desired destination. Accessible floor plans help with this task by allowing a person who is blind to plan their visit beforehand and to identify if they will need help to reach their location. Floor plans are not only useful for navigation. For most sighted people they are an important part of the decision making process when finding an apartment or house for renting or buying. However, if you are blind it is currently virtually impossible to access floor plans that are available on most on-line real estate sites, making renting or buying that much more difficult.

Nowadays floor plans of buildings and public spaces are usually accessed on the web. Thus, there is a real practical

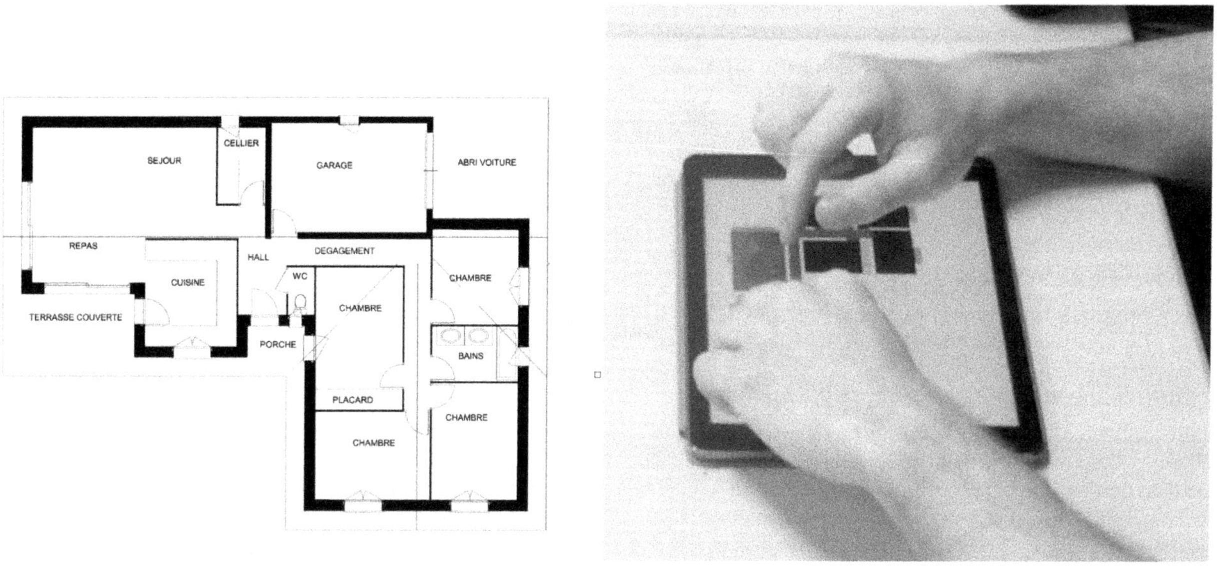

Figure 1: The web service can be used to convert an on-line image of an apartment or house floor plan (for instance the one the left) to an accessible version that is being read by a blind person using the iPad app (shown on the right).

need to provide better access to such on-line floor plans. Our model, illustrated in Figure 1, addresses both presentation and automatic production of accessible floor plans from on-line images. It allows a blind person to immediately view building and floor plans that they encounter on-line and does not require printing expensive tactile graphics. This potentially provides much greater access to such information and removes a significant barrier to travel by blind people. Our approach relies on two innovations.

The first innovation is that we present an accessible version of the floor plan on an iPad using audio feedback. This is based on prior research into audio and audio-haptic presentation of street maps on mobile devices. We have implemented a new application that we call GraViewer. The presentation is not a simple VoiceOver labelling of the objects in the floor plan. As the users move their fingers over the accessible floor plan they receive carefully chosen feedback, e.g sharp clicks as a finger moves through a wall. Based on transcription guidelines used for tactile floor plans we also include a high level description of the floor plan that allows the user to obtain an overview when they first open the floor plan.

Our approach is in contrast to research on producing accessible versions of on-line bar charts and line graphs which has focused on producing a textual description of the on-line graphic [6, 7]. While a textual description can provide an overview of the building's layout, such a description necessarily loses information and it is also difficult to use it to build a mental model of the layout. For this reason accessibility guidelines recommend the use of tactile graphics for presenting graphics such as floor plans in which spatial relationships are important, e.g. [24]. Unfortunately tactile graphics are relatively expensive and require specialised printing devices and/or paper: touch screen mediated presentation potentially provides the spatial benefits of a tactile graphic but at a fraction of the cost.

Currently accessible versions of a graphic such as a floor plan are created manually, typically by trained transcribers. This is expensive and time consuming. It is not practical to manually transcribe floor plans in order to support travel by blind people and completely infeasible to provide manual transcription of the dozens of floor plans encountered when searching on an on-line real estate site. Thus, some sort of automatic transcription is required. In the case of maps, accessible graphics can be generated from GIS data. Unfortunately, equivalent geospatial data is not available for most buildings or public spaces. What is required is automatic transcription from on-line floor plan images.

Our second innovation is to have developed a web service, called GraFloor, that automatically creates an accessible graphic in SVG format from a floor plan image. This uses sophisticated graphics recognition algorithms and OCR to recognise the rooms, walls, windows, doors and furniture. From this GraFloor generates a simplified graphic for display on the GraViewer which shows the rooms, walls, doors and windows. This graphic also includes an automatically generated textual overview.

Robust floor plan recognition is a very difficult problem. While GraFloor is very effective, in applications where manual transcription is not cost prohibitive (such as for the web pages of a hotel or convention center) manual transcription will typically produce a better result. In order to support manual transcription we have also integrated GraFloor with GraAuthor, a web application which is designed to create content for the GraViewer. GraAuthor takes the output of GraFloor web service and allow the transcriber to correct/edit the accessible version. Such semi-automatic transcription is much faster than traditional manual transcription which can take many hours.

We provide two preliminary empirical evaluations of our approach. The first is a user-study with 8 blind participants to show that GraViewer's audio-only presentation allows blind users to understand an accessible floor plan and use it in common tasks such as planning how to get from one room to another or identifying the number of bedrooms. The second is an evaluation of the quality of the automatic transcription provided by GraFloor.

In the next section we discuss related work. In Section 3 we describe the presentation app GraViewer, in Section 4 we describe the authoring tools GraFloor and GraAuthor, and in Section 5 we provide the evaluations.

2. RELATED WORK

Related work falls into three categories: presentation technologies, graphics recognition and automatic transcription.

Presentation Technologies for Accessible Graphics

Presentation technologies fall into four main categories: tactile graphics, audio only presentation which is either based on a textual description of the graphic or sonification, e.g. [14, 4]; tactile overlay on top of a pressure-sensitive screen which provides audio feedback when a graphic element is pressed, e.g. IVEO or TTT [9, 15]; haptic presentation using devices like the phantom, e.g. TeDUB [21] or the VTPlayer tactile mouse with a graphics tablet [28]; or presentation on a touchscreen device using a mixture of haptic or audio feedback as the user explores the graphic, e.g. GraVVITAS [11] or [10]. The advantage of the last approach is that it does not rely on expensive tactile graphics or overlays but still allows the user to use both hands to explore the graphic and build up a mental model of it. This is the approach we use.

Our implementation of GraViewer is based on that of GraVVITAS [11]. The main difference is that GraVVITAS provides haptic feedback using a custom data glove that used small vibrators attached to fingers to indicate when an element was touched. In this project we focussed on audio-only feedback because most users do not have access to a data glove and we wanted to create an application that could be easily downloaded and deployed on any iPad.[1] Our work extends earlier work on GraVVITAS by demonstrating that an audio only presentation of a complex graphic such as a floor plan can be understood and by the use of automatic transcription to create the graphic.

Our approach is also similar to audio-only and haptic-audio presentation of on-line street maps on mobile devices, e.g. [23, 13]. Here the main difference is that we are focussing on floor plans which have different characteristics and tasks to street maps (which are primarily used for way-finding) and the use of automatic transcription from an image rather than an on-line GIS. We also note a mobile app being developed for generating textual directions for blind users when navigating large public spaces [25]. This does not provide a graphical representation or consider automatic transcription from an image.

Graphics Recognition

The second field of research is graphic recognition. Graphics recognition has proven to be extremely difficult and most previous research has focussed on recognising particular visual notations such as tables, charts, music, CAD drawings, floor plans etc [17]. Traditionally graphics recognition has dealt with scanned images, but some recent work has dealt with recognition of born-digital, i.e. computer generated, images from PDF documents [8]. We also only consider born-digital images and not scanned images as information graphics are increasingly born-digital. This means that recognition is easier as the images are clean and so few ambiguities arise in low-level image pre-processing and state-of-the-art OCR tools recognize text with few errors.

Our automatic transcription tool is based on a state-of-the-art application for vectorizing and recognising images of floor-plans [2]. The original application integrated open-source image processing tools with Markov Logic Networks to achieve robust identification of walls, doors, stairs, windows and furniture as well as identification of the room type and function based on furniture. We have extended the recognition software to handle text and to use this to aid in room identification and also added functions to determine the geometry of rooms including multi-use open plan areas.

Automatic Transcription

Researchers at the University of Washington have built an image processing tool (TGA) that can be used by transcribers to extract and replace text from scanned graphics by the equivalent braille [12]. ViewPlus have a vectorization and OCR-to-speech tool for constructing presentations for IVEO [9], while TMAP and Talking TMAP are tools for creating tactile maps from a geographic database [19]. However, all of these tools employ relatively simple image processing, OCR and vectorization technologies and cannot perform anything like the sort of complex transcription provided in our tool.

There has been some previous research into automatic generation of accessible graphics from on-line images. This has focussed on automatically generating a textual summary or audio presentation of on-line bar charts (Interactive SIGHT) [6] and (iGraph-LITE) line graphs [7]. Our work differs from this because of its focus on floor plans rather than bar or line charts and because we generate a simplified spatial representation as well as a textual summary. Because of the more open ended tasks performed with floor plans and the fact that they are inherently spatial in nature we feel that it is important to provide a graphical representation.

3. FLOOR PLAN PRESENTATION

The most common ways to provide an accessible version of a floor plan are either to provide a textual description or a tactile graphic. While a textual description can provide an overview of the building's layout such a description necessarily loses information and it is also difficult to use it to build a mental model of the layout. Research has shown that touch allows blind people to build internal spatial representations that are functionally equivalent to those obtained from visual input [3] and tactile maps have been shown to help blind children and adults build a survey-like representation of their environment, thus facilitating navigation [27]. For this reason a tactile graphic together with a textual overview is the preferred presentation approach [24].

The disadvantage of tactile graphics as a presentation medium is that they are relatively expensive to produce and require specialised printing devices and/or paper. Thus, it

[1]However, we note that it is likely that in the near future touch screen devices will provide haptic feedback natively through technologies such as Tactus (`http://www.tactustechnology.com/technology.html`), in which case it would be straightforward to modify GraViewer to take advantage of this.

is not practical to use them to present accessible versions of most on-line floor plans. Instead we decided to use touch screen with audio feedback. As we have noted, this approach has previously been used to present street maps to blind users.

We have built an iPad application called GraViewer for accessible presentation of information graphics. When the blind user touches a graphic element on the display, audio feedback describes the element and is also provided in order to help with navigation. The great advantage of this approach is that it does not require the use of expensive tactile overlays or additional haptic presentation devices like the phantom, yet allows the user to explore the graphic with both hands using strategies similar to those used with tactile graphics.

The user interface of GraViewer and the presentation model for floor plans was developed using a participatory design methodology with blind end-users. The GraViewer user interface is designed to be consistent with that of iOS accessibility framework: it utilises standard iOS accessibility gestures for menu navigation and application control as well as using VoiceOver for speech.

When the accessible floor plan is first displayed an overview of the graphic is read to the user. This describes the rooms in the floor plan. If required again the overview can be accessed through the menu items that appear when the user double taps with two fingers. This menu also allows the user to open files and change application settings.

Components in the floor-plan–rooms, walls, windows and doors–have both a textual description and non-speech audio associated with them. The colour of the object determines which non-speech audio is associated with it. Initially we experimented with high-affordance non-speech audio with different rooms (such as the sound of cutlery in the dining room) but feedback from blind-users was that they preferred more neutral non-speech audio and so we now simply use different frequencies for different colours.

GraViewer displays the accessible floor plan on the iPad. While people who are totally blind obviously cannot see this image, it is useful to provide a visible graphic with distinct colours and thick simple lines for users who have low-vision. Furthermore it is useful to have a visible graphic in a classroom like environment where a sighted instructor might wish to see what the blind person is doing.

When a floor plan component is first touched its associated textual description is read aloud using VoiceOver. This is read again if the user double taps the component to "query" it or if the user's fingers leave the component and then reenter it. One subtlety in floor plans are open plan areas which may contain multiple functionally different spaces that do not have clear boundaries. Our convention is to associate a description of form "Open plan: kitchen" and "Open plan: dining" to the different areas in the open plan room.

One of the most difficult tasks for blind-users is following the boundary of a graphic element or following thin-lines such as those indicating walls in a floor plan. To help this we use a sharp click to indicate when a graphic element is entered or left and use a volume gradient along the boundary to reduce the non-speech audio as the user's fingers are about to leave the room or wall. Junction points such as where two walls meet are also indicated with a different sharp click sound to the user.

Users can use multiple fingers at once. However our earlier studies found that using more than two fingers simultaneously was confusing because of the multiple speech and non-speech feedback. Furthermore it was quite common for the user to inadvertently touch the screen with their thumb or another fingers and then to become quite confused by the associated feedback. Therefore, GraViewer now lets the users know when they are touching the screen with more than two fingers by using a short non-speech audio warning. It also warns the user when one of their fingers leaves the display area and enters the surrounding bezel area using another distinct non-speech audio. If the users use two fingers, they simultaneously receive separate audio feedback for each finger if they are touching different objects but if both fingers are touching the same object the non-speech audio feedback is amplified.

GraViewer displays graphic content specified in SVG (the W3C standard for Scalable Vector Graphics) on a graphic canvas which is part of the iOS framework. The canvas loads a SVG file and uses metadata associated with the shapes to control the interaction. The metadata associated with a shape is: its ID, audio volume level for the interior of the shape and for its boundary, the text string to be read out when the shape is queried, and the name of a (non-speech) audio file and/or the color code for generating the sound associated with the shape during navigation. Figure 2 shows an example floor plan and the associated meta data. The metadata also includes the title, category, and the overview summary of the graphic.

While we have focussed on the presentation of floor plans, GraViewer is a generic technology that can be used to display accessible web graphics. Because it displays an SVG file it fits well with HTML5 and current web technologies. Web authors can choose to link or embed SVG files in their web pages that are suitable for display using GraViewer and so provide an accessible alternative to the default web page graphic. This is most suitable for use in situations where a tactile graphic would be preferred to a textual description, i.e. when the spatial layout of graphic elements is important. This is true for floor plans but also maps and many scientific and technical drawings in on-line educational material and instruction manuals.

4. FLOOR PLAN CREATION

While GraViewer provides an exciting new technology for displaying accessible graphics it is unfortunately not realistic to expect that most web page authors will have the time or recognise the need to create an accessible version of an on-line floor plan or other graphic. We know that it is still rare for web authors to provide even the most rudimentary accessibility information for a graphic such as a detailed alternative text description. Thus, in practice we need an automated method for creating an accessible floor plan from an on-line image that can be used by both blind and non-blind web authors when creating a web page or blind people when they encounter a floor plan image on the web. We have created a web service called GraFloor to do this.

GraFloor has two main components: the *graphics recognition module* and the *transcription module*. The graphics recognition module takes an floor plan image in common formats such as png and jpg, and produces a text file with a high level specification of the rooms, walls, windows, doors and furniture in the floor plan including textual labels and

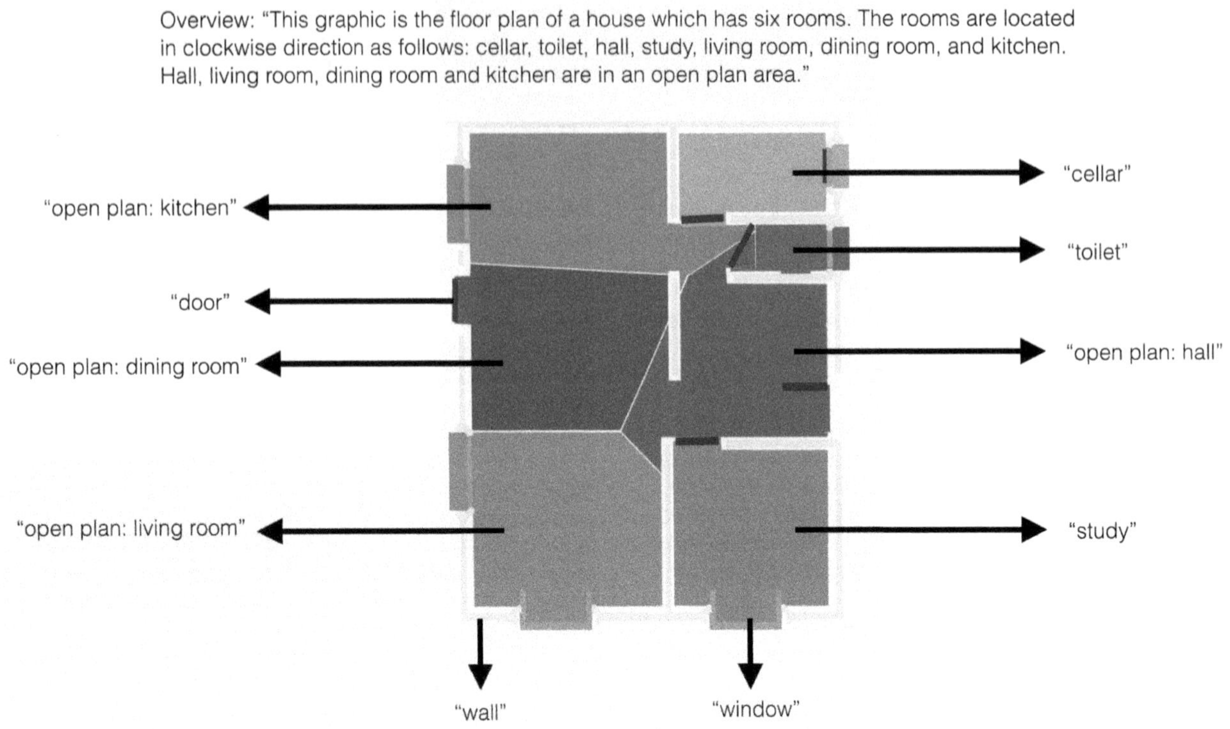

Figure 2: A floor plan annotated with the associated textual descriptions and overview. Different coloured regions have different associated non-audio feedback.

their geometry. The transcription module gets the output of the recognition module in JSON format and generates an SVG file with additional meta data information that is suitable for display on the GraViewer.

4.1 Graphics Recognition Module

The application developed to recognize the floor plan images is based on the following main steps. They are illustrated in Figure 3.

1. Preprocessing. Thin dashed and solid lines are removed as they usually describe items on other levels of the house (e.g. the shape of the roof).
2. Text recognition. Text regions are identified and recognized by `tesseract`, a state-of-the-art Optical Character Recognition (OCR) tool (`https://code.google.com/p/tesseract-ocr/`). These regions are also removed from the input image.
3. Image representation. The floor plan image is described by means of a *region adjacency graph* whose nodes correspond to connected components in the image while edges connect touching components.
4. Object recognition is performed by means of an inexact graph matching algorithm on the region adjacency graph. Objects include furniture and windows.
5. Wall identification and vectorization. This includes determining the location of stairs.
6. Door recognition and removal from the floor plan image.
7. Room identification and sub-division of open-plan areas into separate "virtual" rooms.

Our implementation extends that described in [2]. We use the image preprocessing and the floor plan representation and object retrieval provided in the first release of the tool and have extended wall, door, and room identification. While the focus of [2] was identifying the purpose of a room from its furniture and without considering textual labels, the main aim of the floor plan analysis system in GraFloor is the delineation of the geometry and function of rooms as well as their mutual arrangement. In the rest of this section we describe the above mentioned steps more important for the extraction of the floor plan structure.

Text Localization and Recognition

Text strings are identified in the image by looking for connected components (CC) with "character-like" features. The latter are CCs having dimensions (width and height) close to a square and with neighbouring CCs with similar features. A text string is hypothesized if there are at least three character-like objects aligned. Additional smaller components in the neighbourhood of the string can be added to the string in order to recover punctuation marks that could be skipped in the first check.

All the potential text strings (Figure 3(b))are then processed with the OCR tool in order to identify the room function and the position of the corresponding text string.

Wall Identification

In the preprocessing step the use of adaptive thresholding allows us to obtain a black-and-white image with empty walls

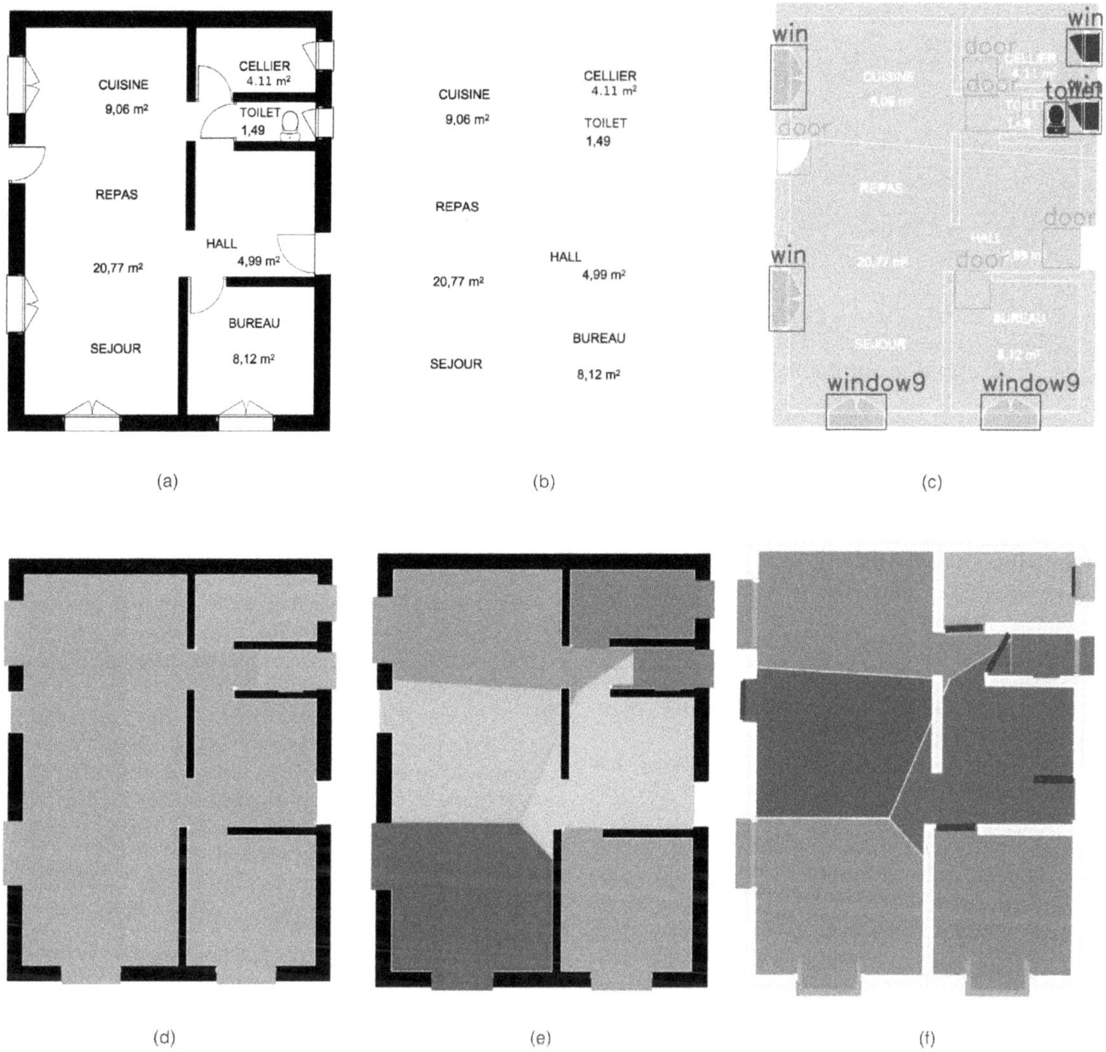

Figure 3: Main processing steps in automatic floor plan transcription: (a) input floor plan; (b) text extraction using OCR; (c) object recognition; (d) wall recognition; (e) room identification and sub-division of open plan area; (f) accessible graphic produced for display on GraViewer.

even when the input image has black walls. This is achieved by smoothing the image with a 3×3 Gaussian Filter and then thresholding the resulting image with a fixed-size moving window where the binarization threshold is adapted in each position on the basis of the average pixel intensity in the window. operations are then performed to fill black components opened by the previous operations. After this step the objects are identified with an inexact graph matching algorithm [2]. Among objects, we consider also windows that are recognized with the same algorithm. For example, Figure 3(c) represents the objects found in Figure 3(a) including doors and windows.

Walls are then searched among components not recognized as objects. To this purpose we first identify the skeleton of the component and then look for straight lines formed by pixels of the skeleton with the Hough transform (HT). Potential walls correspond to segments in the output of HT and are verified by means of the standard deviation of the local thickness of the component along the segment. Segments are stored as walls If the standard deviation is low and the component is dense.

After recognizing the walls, the corresponding connected component is represented by means of a poligonalization of its skeleton that is computed with the Douglas-Peucker algorithm. The description of walls by means of their skeleton allows us to adapt the wall thickness to the needs of the final visualization so that different users can modify the wall thickness.

Door Identification

In floor plans, doors are often represented with one segment that denotes the door in the opened position and one circular arc that represents the doorway. In our system we analyze the contour of large connected components (Figure 4(a)) and search potential doors (short segments, Figure 4(b)). To verify whether one potential door is a real one we search the

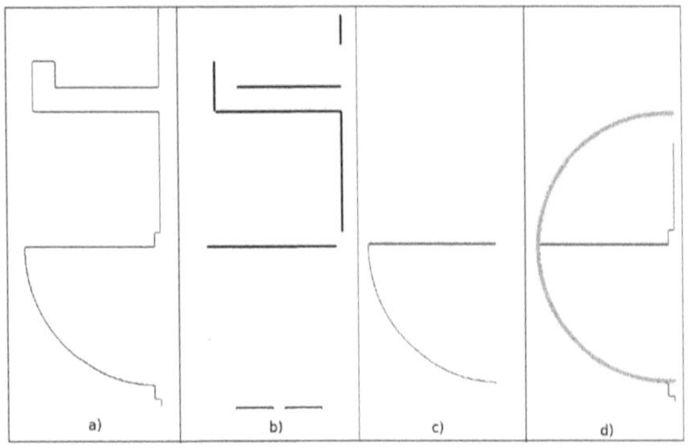

Figure 4: Steps in door identification.

doorway by first extracting the pixels of the contour closer to the segment (Figure 4(c)) and then verifying whether these points belong to a circle by using the Hough transform for circles (Figure 4(d)).

With this procedure it is possible to identify also the opening direction of the door. This can be represented in the accessible floor plan.

Room Identification

Room identification is made more difficult because modern houses and flats frequently contain multi-purpose rooms where open-plan living spaces share different functions that are sometimes identified by suitable text strings. In this case, in Figure 3(a) one room has three labels: "CUISINE" (kitchen), "REPAS" (meal room), and "SEJOUR" (living room). For a sighted reader this makes it clear that while this is a single large room it is split into three different regions whose approximate location is given by the textual label.

In order to extract the shape of rooms we need to remove the objects and the doors identified in each room. A room is recognised as a region completely enclosed by walls, windows and doors. In Figure 3(d) initially four rooms are identified since "CUISINE", "REPAS", "SEJOUR" and "HALL" are not separated by doors and so GraFloor recognises them as a single open space room. In GraFloor open-plan rooms with multiple functions are split in virtual sub-rooms by considering the Voronoi partition of the original open-plan room by using the barycenters of the text strings as the central points. In Figure 3(e) we show the partition of the larger room on the basis of the four text strings.

While the Voronoi partition provides a reasonable first approximation to how to split the rooms we plan to explore this further by better taking into account natural boundaries between regions induced by stub walls and kitchen benches.

At the end of the room extraction, the polygonal approximation of its contour is stored, together with the furniture objects and structural items (doors and windows) extracted from the floor plan input image.

4.2 Semi-Automatic Transcription

Robust floor plan recognition is a difficult problem and while evaluation in Section 5 shows that GraFloor is quite effective the generated images typically contain small errors, such as not recognising small internal walls or mis-recognized doors or windows. In situations where manual transcription is not cost prohibitive (such as for a hotel or convention center) this will typically produce a better result. To support such manual transcription we have created another web-service, GraAuthor, for manual production of accessible versions of floor plans designed for display on GraViewer. Importantly, GraAuthor can take the output of GraFloor and allow the transcriber to correct/edit the accessible version. Such semi-automatic transcription is much faster than fully automatic transcription. An example of its use is shown in Figure 5.

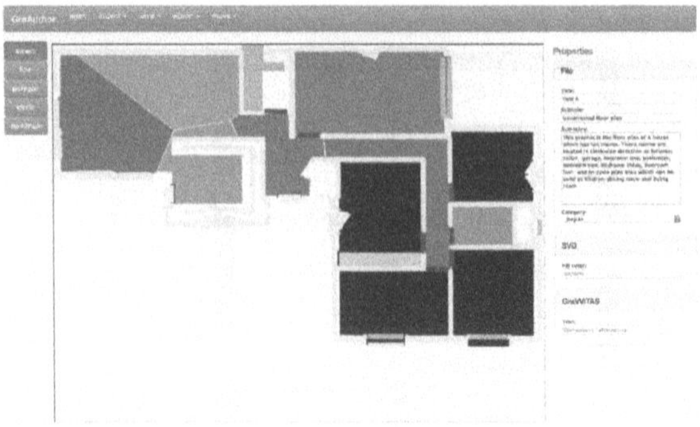

Figure 5: GraAuthor: The web application which is designed for creating content for GraViewer.

The use of a JSON intermediate floor plan description also allows other ways of generating accessible floor plans. It is possible to specify a floor plan textually say by hand or to generate it from CAD or some other digital representation of the building and then use the transcription module to generate an accessible version.

5. EVALUATION

We have conducted two preliminary evaluations of our approach. The first is a user-study with blind participants to investigate whether GraViewer's audio-only presentation allows blind users to understand an accessible floor plan and to use it in common tasks. The second is an evaluation of the quality of the automatic transcription using GraFloor.

5.1 User Study

As discussed previously GraViewer has been developed using a participatory design methodology with blind students and adults. We believe participatory design with blind participants is vital for any project of this kind since our experiences, and those of other researchers in the field, suggest that people who have been blind from an early age may have quite different strategies for understanding graphics to people who are sighted. It has been reported that congenitally blind children perform significantly poorer than other blindfolded and late-blind children in unfamiliar spatial tasks [20].

The main aim of the user study was to evaluate whether blind people could understand a floor plan of a house or apartment generated using GraFloor and displayed using GraViewer and use the plan to help them perform a number of simple tasks.

Participants

Eight participants, all legally blind (2 born blind and 6 late blind), between the ages of 25 to 55 participated in the user study. It is worth pointing out that since there are relatively few blind people and it is often hard for them to travel, it

Figure 6: Test graphics: Input images (a, d), uncorrected graphics (b, e), and corrected graphics (c, f).

is quite difficult to find blind participants (also pointed out in [26, 22]). Hence the number of participants in any such study is necessarily quite small.

The participants had previously been recruited to participate in the design of GraViewer through an email list for print disabled people in Australia. They had prior experience with tactile graphics and most had some prior training in the accessibility features of iOS and had used GraViewer to view simply geometric shapes: polygons and lines.

Procedure and Materials

The experiments were performed in a private room at Monash University or at one of the offices of Vision Australia, with a single participant at a time. Each study took about one hour.

Participants were asked to sign a consent form which had previously been sent by email. This also provided a short explanation of the user study and what type of information would be collected.

Participants were then asked some background questions to clarify:

- Their prior experience in understanding tactile floor plans,
- Whether they wanted to be reminded how the GraViewer system works.

Next they were trained in the use of GraViewer for viewing floor plans. This had two parts: If they wanted, first they reviewed the common iOS accessibility gestures and interface, e.g. accessing menus and turning VoiceOver on and off, and the use of GraViewer for viewing an image containing a simple geometric shape. In the second stage of training participants were shown a simple floor plan on GraViewer and asked to explore it and answer questions similar to those used in the subsequent study. They were encouraged to use a rapid sweeping gesture with one finger across the screen to obtain an initial overview of the spatial layout while using the other finger as an anchor.

In the evaluation proper, the participants were shown two floor plans on GraViewer one after the other. For each floor plan they were asked to explore it and to let the experi-

Participant	Training 1	Training 2	Corrected Floor Plan A					Uncorrected Floor Plan B				
	Exp.	Exp.	Exp.	Q1	Q2	Q3	Q4	Exp.	Q1	Q2	Q3	Q4
P1	40	210	112	49	24	125	66	446	50 (X)	44	77	33
P2	60	120	127	5	5	61	30	127	5 (X)	5	22	61
P3	32	225	363	4	13	62	26	342	3	21	40	37
P4	23	305	164	1	7	45	97	167	1	2	36	103
			Uncorrected Floor Plan A					Corrected Floor Plan B				
P5	94	321	215	51	5	140	89	110	10	41	184	30
P6	45	170	210	10	13	89	170	424	7	12	38	152
P7	70	160	95	1	30	210	65	420	20	11	80	40
P8	67	83	46	38	35	71	37	219	27	28	29	65

Table 1: User study results: Task completion times for training and test graphics are given in seconds (X: incorrect answer, Exp: Exploration, Qn: Question n).

menter know when they felt that they knew the basic layout. They were then asked to answer the following questions:

Q1 How many bedrooms are there in the house?

Q2 Point to where the kitchen is on the floor plan?

Q3 What is the shortest route from the kitchen to the bathroom and which rooms do you pass through?

Q4 Can you describe the layout of the house?

The time taken for the initial exploration and to answer each question was recorded as well as the answers to the question.

The two floor plans (A and B) used in the evaluation are shown in Figure 6. Both were generated by GraFloor from a floor plan in the corpus from [18] with English room names replacing the original French names. Two versions of each floor plan were created. The first version was corrected manually in GraAuthor to remove any errors arising from mis-recognition while the second was the actual output from GraFloor and contained several transcription errors. The reason for using the results from both semi-automatic and fully automatic transcription was to better understand whether any difficulties in understanding were the result of the presentation on GraViewer or whether they were the result of imperfect transcription by GraFloor. Participants were either shown the the corrected version of A and then the uncorrected version of B or else the corrected version of B then the uncorrected version of A.

Finally the participants were asked how the tools and presentation could be improved and whether they thought automatic transcription of on-line floor plans would be useful.

Results

For the first two participants the fully automatic transcription of Floor Plan B did not include the overview and different bedrooms where all labelled as "Bedroom" while the manually corrected transcription of Floor Plan A included a textual overview and also bedrooms were labelled "Bedroom 1", "Bedroom 2", etc. As a result participants P1 and P2 did not correctly determine the number of bedrooms in the uncorrected Floor Plan B. In response to this and their suggestions we modified the transcription module to automatically generate a textual overview and also to label bedrooms "Bedroom 1", "Bedroom 2", etc. This modified version was used in the subsequent experiments.

We see that apart from this problem all participants could correctly answer the 4 questions for both the fully automatic and manually corrected floor plans. The task completion times are given in Table 1.

Feedback from the participants included suggestions to help navigation: "It will be good to query where the rooms are located relative to the finger" and "There might be different sound themes which can represent the rooms better" and also "I like the overview summary. You can not picture the image in your mind, but it gives you an idea of what to expect."

All participants felt that access to on-line floor plans would be useful and that the tool provided a good approach to provide this. In fact one participant described how they had recently been searching for a house to buy and had paid Vision Australia to provide tactile versions of the on-line floor plans that he/she was interested in. They felt that this tool would have been very useful.

5.2 Quality of Automatic Transcription

Recognition of floor plans is a difficult task and so it is not realistic to expect 100% accuracy for even well-structured images. One of the great difficulties in robust floor plan recognition is that there are many different graphical conventions: for instance walls can be drawn as thick black lines or as two thin parallel lines.

In order to verify the effectiveness of GraFloor we evaluated the errors made in the automatic transcription of one benchmark dataset of floor plan images. The dataset [18] is composed of 90 images that contain floor plans with some basic furniture objects and rooms labelled with textual descriptions. These images have been provided by an architectural office and cover a period of more than ten years.

In our first experiment we evaluated how well GraFloor recognised rooms including open plan rooms. This was the primary purpose of the tool, to provide the blind user with an understanding of the rooms in the floor plan and their spatial arrangement. The results are summarized in Table 2. For each room (including regions in an open-plan area) in each floor plan in the corpus we manually determined if the room/region had been correctly recognised and included in the generated image. Full recognition meant that the room and its regions (if an open-plan room) was correctly recognised and displayed at the correct location in the generated image; partial recognition meant that though the room's extent was determined the kind of room was not (usually because the associated text was too short to be recognised). We see that GraFloor is quite effective and recognises nearly 95% of rooms at least partially. This is

Recognition	Open Plan Room	Non-Open Plan Room
Full	85% (82)	77%(718)
Partial	8%(8)	15%(138)
Failed	7%(6)	8%(77)

Table 2: Percentage and total number of items correctly recognized by the floor plan analysis system for the entire dataset.

Recognition	Door	Window	Sink	Tub	Cupboard	Toilet	Table	Shower	Stairs
Full	78%(162)	50%(90)	29%(9)	50%(5)	67%(37)	60%(12)	86%(6)	0%(0)	0%(0)
Partial	16%(33)	17%(31)	13%(4)	20%(2)	0%(0)	15%(3)	14%(1)	75%(3)	90%(9)
Failed	6%(12)	33%(60)	58%(18)	30%(3)	33%(18)	25%(5)	0%(0)	25%(1)	10%(1)

Table 3: Percentage and total number of items correctly recognized by the floor plan analysis system for 20 randomly chosen images.

comparable with other state of-the-art floor plan recognition software [5] where a detection rate of 94.76 % and a recognition accuracy of 94.29 % are reported. It is important to notice that [5] is not aimed at recognizing the type of room and does not address the subdivision of open-plan areas.

In a second experiment we evaluated how well other objects in the floor plan were recognised. In this case because of the time required to manually check all components of a floor plan we only considered 20 randomly chosen floor plans. The results are summarized in Table 3. Full recognition meant that the object was correctly recognised and displayed at the correct location in the generated image; partial recognition meant that it was either recognised as another kind of object, e.g. window as a door, or in the case of stairs its extent was not fully determined. While the results are not outstanding recognition rates are reasonable for most objects apart from showers (which are confused with sinks) and stairs because only some of the stairs in a staircase were recognised. We are currently working on improving this: however for the purpose of providing an overview, accurate object recognition is not required.

6. CONCLUSION AND FUTURE WORK

We have presented a new model for providing blind users with accessible on-line graphics: automatic transcription from an on-line image to an accessible graphic designed for presentation on a touch screen device such as an iPad that can be viewed using audio feedback with semi-automatic transcription as a back-up. We believe this approach can be used to handle a wide variety of information graphics including statistical charts, tables, simple maps, chemical structural diagrams etc. Thus it has the potential to dramatically improve accessibility of a wide range of on-line information graphics.

We have described and evaluated the use of this model for on-line floor plans. An empirical evaluation of our approach shows that it can provide an accurate overview of the layout of the rooms in a floor plan and that this presentation can be used by a blind person to understand the layout. The great advantage of our approach is that it allows a blind person to immediately view building and floor plans that they encounter on-line and does not require printing expensive tactile graphics. This potentially provides much greater access to such information and removes a significant barrier to travel by blind people.

However, while the initial evaluations presented in this paper are very promising there is some additional work required before we have a full-fledged system ready for mainstream use:

- We need to investigate how to include panning and zooming so that we can present large floor plans of buildings and public spaces.
- We would like to provide more advanced interaction searching and filtering features so that users can, for instance, be presented with a route to their desired destination.
- The recognition system has been tailored to work with a particular corpus of examples and the graphic conventions used in that corpus. We are now modifying the system so that given some initial training it can robustly identify floor plans using other conventions.

Acknowledgements

We acknowledge the support of ARC through LP110200469 and of our project partners the Statewide Vision Resource Center, Vision Australia, jTribe and the Catholic Education Office (Melbourne). In particular we wish to thank Deb Lewis, Armin Kroll, Leona Holloway and the participants who have helped in the development of GraViewer and GraFloor. NICTA is funded by the Australian Government through the Department of Communications and the Australian Research Council through the ICT Centre of Excellence Program.

7. REFERENCES

[1] Web content accessibility guidelines (WCAG) 2.0. 2008.

[2] A. Barducci and S. Marinai. Object recognition in floor plans by graphs of white connected components. In *21st International Conference on Pattern Recognition (ICPR)*, pages 298–301. IEEE, 2012.

[3] Z. Cattaneo et al. Imagery and spatial processes in blindness and visual impairment. *Neuroscience and Biobehavioral Reviews*, 32(8):1346–1360, 2008.

[4] G. Daunys and V. Lauruska. Sonification system of maps for blind. In *Universal Access in Human-Computer Interaction. Ambient Interaction*, pages 349–352. Springer, 2007.

[5] L.-P. de las Heras, S. Ahmed, M. Liwicki, E. Valveny, and G. Sánchez. Statistical segmentation and structural recognition for floor plan interpretation. *International Journal on Document Analysis and Recognition (IJDAR)*, 17:221–237, 2014.

[6] S. Demir, D. Oliver, E. Schwartz, S. Elzer, S. Carberry, K. F. Mccoy, and D. Chester. Interactive sight: textual access to simple bar charts. *New Review of Hypermedia and Multimedia*, 16(3):245–279, 2010.

[7] L. Ferres, G. Lindgaard, L. Sumegi, and B. Tsuji. Evaluating a tool for improving accessibility to charts and graphs. *ACM Transactions on Computer-Human Interaction (TOCHI)*, 20(5):28, 2013.

[8] R. P. Futrelle, M. Shao, C. Cieslik, and A. E. Grimes. Extraction, layout analysis and classification of diagrams in pdf documents. In *2013 12th International Conference on Document Analysis and Recognition*, volume 2, pages 1007–1007. IEEE Computer Society, 2003.

[9] J. Gardner and V. Bulatov. Scientific Diagrams Made Easy with IVEO. *Computers Helping People with Special Needs*, 4061:1243–1250, 2006.

[10] N. A. Giudice, H. P. Palani, E. Brenner, and K. M. Kramer. Learning non-visual graphical information using a touch-based vibro-audio interface. In *Proceedings of the 14th international ACM SIGACCESS conference on Computers and accessibility*, pages 103–110. ACM, 2012.

[11] C. Goncu and K. Marriott. Gravvitas: Generic multi-touch presentation of accessible graphics. In *Proc. INTERACT'11*, pages 30–48. Springer, 2011.

[12] C. Jayant, M. Renzelmann, D. Wen, S. Krisnandi, R. Ladner, and D. Comden. Automated tactile graphics translation: in the field. In *Proceedings of the 9th international ACM SIGACCESS conference on Computers and accessibility*, pages 75–82. ACM, 2007.

[13] N. Kaklanis, K. Votis, and D. Tzovaras. Touching openstreetmap data in mobile context for the visually impaired. In *Proceedings of the 3rd Workshop on Mobile Accessibility-ACM SIGCHI Conference on Human Factors in Computing Systems*, 2013.

[14] A. R. Kennel. Audiograf: a diagram-reader for the blind. In *Proceedings of the second annual ACM conference on Assistive technologies*, pages 51–56. ACM, 1996.

[15] S. Landau and K. Gourgey. Development of a Talking Tactile Tablet. *Information Technology and Disabilities*, 7(2), 2001.

[16] J. Lazar, A. Allen, J. Kleinman, and C. Malarkey. What frustrates screen reader users on the web: A study of 100 blind users. *International Journal of human-computer interaction*, 22(3):247–269, 2007.

[17] Llados, Josep and Rusinol, Marcal. Graphics recognition techniques. In D. Doermann and K. Tombre, editors, *Handbook of Document Image Processing and Recognition*, pages 489–521. Springer London, 2014.

[18] S. Mace, H. Locteau, E. Valveny, and S. Tabbone. A system to detect rooms in architectural floor plan images. In D. S. Doermann, V. Govindaraju, D. P. Lopresti, and P. Natarajan, editors, *Document Analysis Systems*, ACM International Conference Proceeding Series, pages 167–174. ACM, 2010.

[19] J. A. Miele, S. Landau, and D. Gilden. Talking TMAP: Automated generation of audio-tactile maps using Smith-Kettlewell's TMAP software. *British Journal of Visual Impairment*, 24(2):93–100, 2006.

[20] S. Millar. *Space and sense.* Psychology Press, 2008.

[21] H. Petrie et al. TeDUB: A system for presenting and exploring technical drawings for blind people. *Computers helping people with special needs*, pages 47–67, 2002.

[22] H. Petrie, F. Hamilton, N. King, and P. Pavan. Remote usability evaluations with disabled people. In *Proceedings of the SIGCHI conference on Human Factors in computing systems*, pages 1133–1141. ACM, 2006.

[23] B. Poppinga, C. Magnusson, M. Pielot, and K. Rassmus-Gröhn. Touchover map: audio-tactile exploration of interactive maps. In *Proceedings of the 13th International Conference on Human Computer Interaction with Mobile Devices and Services*, pages 545–550. ACM, 2011.

[24] Round Table on Information Access for People with Print Disabilities Inc., Australia & New Zealand. *Guidelines on Conveying Visual Information (2005)*, 2005.

[25] M. Spindler, M. Weber, D. Prescher, M. Miao, G. Weber, and G. Ioannidis. Translating floor plans into directions. In *Computers Helping People with Special Needs (ICCHP)*, pages 59–66. Springer, 2012.

[26] H. Takagi, S. Saito, K. Fukuda, and C. Asakawa. Analysis of navigability of Web applications for improving blind usability. *ACM Trans. on Computer-Human Interaction*, 14(3):13, 2007.

[27] S. Ungar. Cognitive mapping without visual experience. *Cognitive mapping: Past, Present and Future*, pages 221–248, 2000.

[28] S. Wall and S. Brewster. Feeling what you hear: tactile feedback for navigation of audio graphs. In *Proc. of the SIGCHI Conference on Human Factors in Computing Systems*, pages 1123–1132. ACM, 2006.

Network A/B Testing: From Sampling to Estimation

Huan Gui† Ya Xu‡ Anmol Bhasin‡ Jiawei Han†
† University of Illinois at Urbana-Champaign, Urbana, IL 61801 USA
‡ LinkedIn Corporation, Mountain View, CA 94043 USA
†{huangui2, hanj}@illinois.edu ‡{yaxu, abhasin}@linkedin.com

ABSTRACT

A/B testing, also known as bucket testing, split testing, or controlled experiment, is a standard way to evaluate user engagement or satisfaction from a new service, feature, or product. It is widely used in online websites, including social network sites such as Facebook, LinkedIn, and Twitter to make data-driven decisions. The goal of A/B testing is to estimate the treatment effects of a new change, which becomes intricate when users are interacting, *i.e.*, the treatment effects of a user may spill over to other users via underlying social connections. When conducting these online controlled experiments, it is a common practice to make the Stable Unit Treatment Value Assumption (SUTVA) that each individual's response is affected by their own treatment only. Though this assumption simplifies the estimation of treatment effects, it does not hold when network interference is present, and may even lead to wrong conclusion.

In this paper, we study the problem of network A/B testing in real networks, which have substantially different characteristics from the simulated random networks studied in previous works. We first examine the existence of network effects in a recent online experiment conducted at LinkedIn; Secondly, we propose an efficient and effective estimator for Average Treatment Effect (ATE) considering the interference between users in real online experiments; Finally, we apply our method in both simulations and a real world online experiment. The simulation results show that our estimator achieves better performance with respect to both bias and variance reduction. The real world online experiment not only demonstrates that large-scale network A/B test is feasible but also further validates many of our observations in the simulation studies.

Categories and Subject Descriptors

G.3 [**Probability and Statistics**]: Experimental design

WWW 2015, May 18–22, 2015, Florence, Italy.
ACM 978-1-4503-3469-3/15/05.
http://dx.doi.org/10.1145/2736277.2741081.

Keywords

A/B testing; controlled experiments; network A/ B testing; design of experiments; peer effects; network effects; balanced graph partition.

1. INTRODUCTION

A/B testing, also called controlled experimentation, is widely used in many consumer facing web technology companies to guide product development and data-driven decisions, including Amazon, eBay, Etsy, Facebook, Google, Groupon, LinkedIn, Microsoft, Netflix and Yahoo. It has become the gold standard for testing out new product strategies and approaches [14, 13].

The theory of A/B test is simple and dates back to Sir Ronald A. Fisher's experiments at the Rothamsted Agricultural Experimental Station in England in the 1920s [29]. Rubin causal model [23], a standard machinery of testing framework, is usually adopted in conducting and analyzing A/B tests. A key assumption made in Rubin causal model is the *Stable Unit Treatment Value Assumption* (SUTVA), which states that the behavior of each user in the experiment depends only on their own treatment and not on the treatments of others.

However, in a social network setting, a user's behavior is likely impacted by that of his/her social neighborhood [12, 27, 28]. In most cases, a user would find a new feature more valuable and hence more likely to adopt it if more of his/her neighbors adopt it. For example, video chat is a useless feature unless one's friends use it too. The phenomenon that an individual's behavior has a non-trivial effect on his/her social neighborhood is called *network effects*, also known as *social interactions*, *peer influence*, or *social interference* [2, 8]. In an A/B experiment, this implies that if the treatment has a significant impact on a user, the effect would spill over to his/her social circles, regardless whether his/her neighbors are in treatment or control.

To understand how network effects introduces challenges for A/B testing, consider the *Average Treatment Effect* (ATE), a primary quantity of interest defined as the difference of the average outcomes between applying treatment to the *entire* user population and applying control to the *entire* user population. Define $\mathcal{U}$ as the set of users and $|\mathcal{U}| = N$, where N is the total number of users. Let $\boldsymbol{Z} \in \mathcal{M}^N$, a vector of length N, as the experiment assignment vector for all users, where $\mathcal{M}$ is the set of variants. Without loss of generality, for the rest of the paper, we assume the experiment only has two variants that $\mathcal{M} = \{0, 1\}$, where 1 stands for treatment and 0 for control. We let $Y_i(\boldsymbol{Z} = \mathbf{z})$ be the response function of user i given $\boldsymbol{Z} = \mathbf{z}$. The response can be any user metrics the experiment tries to optimize, such as number of pageviews or clicks. The ATE can be expressed as

$$\delta(\mathbf{1}, \mathbf{0}) = \frac{1}{N} \cdot \sum_i \mathbb{E}\big[Y_i(\boldsymbol{Z} = \mathbf{1}) - Y_i(\boldsymbol{Z} = \mathbf{0})\big], \quad (1)$$

where $\mathbf{1}$, and $\mathbf{0}$ are the treatment assignment where all users receive the control variant and treatment variant respectively.

Of course, a user can only receive one treatment at a time in reality. So in classical A/B experiments, we randomly select N_0 users to receive the control variant, and N_1 users to receive treatment. The ATE can then be estimated by

$$\hat{\delta} = \frac{1}{N_1} \cdot \sum_{\{i;\mathbf{z}_i=1\}} Y_i(\boldsymbol{Z} = \mathbf{z}) - \frac{1}{N_0} \cdot \sum_{\{i;\mathbf{z}_i=0\}} Y_i(\boldsymbol{Z} = \mathbf{z}), \quad (2)$$

where $\mathbf{z}_i$ is the experiment assignment of user i. Under SUTVA and the Law of Large Numbers [11], we have $\hat{\delta} \to \delta(\mathbf{1}, \mathbf{0})$ when $N_1, N_0 \to \infty$. However, when there are network effects, STUVA is no longer valid, and the convergence does not hold any more.

This poses a special challenge for running A/B tests in many online social and professional networks like Facebook, Twitter and LinkedIn. Many features tested there through A/B experiments are likely to have network effects. For example, a better recommendation algorithm in treatment for the People You May Know module on LinkedIn encourages a user to send more invitations. However, users who receive such invitations can be in the control variant and when they visit LinkedIn to accept the invitation they may discover more people they know. If the primary metric of interest is the total number of invitations sent, we would see a positive gain in both the treatment and the control groups. The ATE estimated ignoring network effects would be biased and not fully capturing the benefit of the new algorithm. Such bias exists in testing almost any features that involve social interactions, which is truly ubiquitous in a social network environment.

In this paper, we define the problem of A/B testing when there are network effects as *Network A/B Testing*. Specifically, we study the problem in large real social networks, which have substantially different properties and characteristics than simulated random networks studied in previous works. Our work aims at bridging the gap among theoretical analysis on casual analysis in the Statistical literature, recent works on network bucket testing [3, 8, 28], and real-world applications of online controlled experiments. Our main contributions are as follows:

1. As far as we know, we are the first to extensively study the problem in real social networks.

2. We propose a simple yet efficient network sampling algorithm that is able to overcome an important challenge presented in sampling real social networks.

3. We propose a new estimation model that not only generalizes the existing methods, but also produces smaller bias and variance in our extensive simulation studies.

4. We are the first to study how the overall traffic split between treatment and control impacts the performance of various ATE estimators.

5. We run a large-scale network A/B test with a real application at LinkedIn. The results from the experiment not only help us compare the various models but also further validate many of the observations from the simulation studies.

The rest of the paper is organized as follows. Related work is discussed in Section 2. In Section 3 we take a close look at possible network effects in a recent A/B experiment conducted at LinkedIn to motivate our study. Section 4 is where we introduce our framework for network A/B testing and propose our new network sampling and estimation methods. Extensive simulations and online experimental results are included in Section 5. Section 6 concludes our study, summarizing our approach and motivating future work in this area.

2. RELATED WORK

In this section, we will introduce some related work on network A/B testing, mainly including two parts, interference analysis in Statistics, and network bucket testing in Computer Science.

There are two parts of related work on interference, one is based on group-level interference analysis, where there is interference within each group, and no interference across groups [10, 22, 24, 26]; the other one is based on unit-level interference analysis, where interference between any two units may be non-trivial [2, 8, 16, 27, 28]. [22] explores methods of inverting distribution-free randomization tests for Fisher's sharp null hypothesis based on group-level interference analysis. [24] considers the potential bias for ATE estimation when SUTVA is assumed, and further defines several causal estimands including direct and indirect effects that might be identifiable. This work is further extended by [10] by defining direct, indirect, total and overall causal effects, and relationship between these estimands are established. Hudegens *et al.* [10] also propose unbiased estimators of the proposed estimands by a two-stage randomization procedure experimental design that first perform randomization at the group level, then at the individual level within groups. [26] gives conservative variance estimators, and proposes a new framework of finite sample inference analysis and inverse probability weighting estimators considering interference.

Regarding arbitrary interference of known form between units, [2] proposes randomization based methods to estimate ATE, and further refines the estimator by covariance adjustment, besides analysis of conservative estimators of the ATE estimators. [16] explores the identification of users' responses under different constraints and assumptions, considering that social interference will influence users' behaviors. To quantify the causal effect of peer influence, [27] introduces new randomization based causal estimand of peer influence, by extending the potential responses with social interference. [8, 28] focus on estimating the ATE in networks, in which a new randomization scheme is proposed, called graph clustering randomization. Extensive simulations are conducted on random networks. We further this work by studying the ATE estimation on *real* networks, which have drastically different topologies and structures.

Another line of research that is quite related to our work is network bucket testing [3, 12], in which the new feature will take effect only if some minimal number of treated users' social neighbors are also in treatment. [3] proposes a walk-based sampling method to generate the core set of users which are internally well-connected while approximately uniform over the whole network. This work is generalized by [12], which introduces a general framework for network A/B testing, which first generate the core set based on different algorithms, and then gives out the corresponding variance bound based on the core set generation function.

Our work takes both the sampling (design) and estimation (analysis) into consideration, by proposing a realistic sampling method that works well in real networks and a new estimation framework that generalizes the existing ones.

3. NETWORK EFFECTS IN REAL EXPERIMENT

There is a line of research studying social interference, also known as information diffusion [6, 9, 21]. Whenever information can be propagated from a user to his/her social neighborhood, there is likely to be network effects. In particular, we are interested in studying how such information propagates between the treatment and control groups in an A/B test setting. With that in mind, we first take a close look at a real A/B experiment recently conducted at LinkedIn on homepage Feeds. By incorporating components that are specific to one's social neighborhood, we show using a linear model that there are significant network effects present in this experiment.

3.1 Feed Experiment

Feed is an important part of LinkedIn homepage experience. It provides users with stories that they may be interested in reading, updates from their network (such as a job change), and more. One can click on a feed, or interact with it through social gestures such as "like", "comment" or "share".

The Feed team strives to surface the most relevant items to users by constantly testing new recommendation algorithms. One important evaluation criterion is whether the new algorithm has improved the total number of user interactions with the feeds. In a recent experiment, users are randomly split into two equal groups, one receives the production algorithm (control) and the other receives a new experimental algorithm (treatment) that is supposed to provide more relevant feeds.

Because the sampling is uniformly random, users in treatment have neighbors in both treatment and control. Therefore, users in the control group will not only receive the set of recommended feeds from the control recommendation algorithm, but also the set of feeds shared/liked from their neighbors in treatment group, and vice versa. If the new algorithm is indeed better, and users are interacting more with the more relevant content discovered in their feeds, those good content pieces will leak into the control group and hence makes the control algorithm look better that it actually is.

In the following section, we will show that such concerns of information "leaking" is not vacuous and there is indeed significant network effects present in this feed experiment. We verify by extending the classical framework used to estimate ATE to incorporate components that are specific to one's social neighborhood.

3.2 Presence of Network Effect

Two-sample t-test is the most commonly used framework to analyze online experiment [7]. Suppose we are interested in some response metric Y (e.g. pageviews per user). The null hypothesis is that treatment and control have the same mean for this metric (i.e. ATE $= 0$) and the alternative is that they do not (i.e. ATE $\neq 0$) . The t-test is based on the t-statistic

$$\frac{\hat{\delta}}{\sqrt{\operatorname{var}\left(\hat{\delta}\right)}}, \tag{3}$$

and under SUTVA, $\hat{\delta}$ defined in (2) is an unbiased estimator of the ATE and the t-statistic is a normalized version of that estimator. This framework is in fact equivalent to the following linear model

$$Y_i(\boldsymbol{Z}) = \alpha + \beta \boldsymbol{Z}_i \tag{4}$$

where $\boldsymbol{Z}_i \in \{0, 1\}$ is user i's experiment assignment and the least square estimator for β turns out to be $\hat{\delta}$.

In order to take into consideration of possible network effects, we introduce two additional components to the linear model above, social interference and homophily [15, 17]. The social interference component aims at capturing the "spillover" treatment effects from one's neighbors, and is therefore modeled based on the total number of treated neighbors, *i.e.*, $\boldsymbol{A}_{\cdot i}^{\top}\mathbf{Z}$, where $\mathbf{A}$ is the adjacency matrix, and $\boldsymbol{A}_{\cdot i}$ is the ith column of $\mathbf{A}$. The homophily refers to the observation that one's social network is homogeneous considering different sociodemographic, behavioral, and intrapersonal traits, *i.e.*, people are more likely to connect with others who are similar (birds of a feather). To this end, a user's behavior can be partially explained by the behavior of his/her neighbors. Therefore, homophily is approximated by the average behavior of i's neighborhood, *i.e.*, $\boldsymbol{A}_{\cdot i}^{\top}\boldsymbol{Y}/\mathbf{D}_{ii}$, where $\mathbf{D}$ is the diagonal matrix that $\mathbf{D}_{ii} = \sum_{j=1}^{N} A_{ij}$. Putting the three pieces together, we have

$$Y_i(\boldsymbol{Z}) = \alpha + \beta Z_i + \gamma \boldsymbol{A}_{\cdot i}^{\top}\boldsymbol{Z} + \eta \boldsymbol{A}_{\cdot i}^{\top}\boldsymbol{Y}/D_{ii}. \tag{5}$$

Note that linear additive models have been widely used in other works on causal analysis [15, 27]. The three parameters β, γ and η aim at capturing treatment effects, network effects and homophily respectively. Under this simple linear model, we can estimate the size of each effect and test whether each effect is statistically significant. The results are shown in Table 1 where we can see that users' responses are positively correlated with treatment effects (*primary effects*), network effects, and homophily.

Metric	β	γ	η
# of interactions	0.0486	0.1252	0.0626

Table 1: The linear regression results of the feed experiment. All the p-value are $< 10^{-16}$, and thus omitted.

It is important to point out that this experiment is conducted with fully uniform random sampling, and hence the number of treated neighbors and the neighborhood size are highly correlated. This means that the network effects we measure here could be confounded with one's popularity in the network. To control for that, we have also tried a model that includes one's neighborhood size as the fourth component, as follows:

$$Y_i(\boldsymbol{Z}) = \alpha + \beta Z_i + \gamma \boldsymbol{A}_{\cdot i}^\top \boldsymbol{Z} + \eta \boldsymbol{A}_{\cdot i}^\top \boldsymbol{Y} / D_{ii} + \kappa D_{ii}.$$

The coefficient γ for the network effects stays significantly positive. Also note that because the sampling is done uniformly random, every user in the experiment has about the same percentage of neighbors in treatment. This means that we cannot expect to remove such confounding effects by using the percent of treated neighbors instead of the absolute number.

4. NETWORK A/B TESTING

The framework of A/B testing usually involves two parts: sampling, which determines who gets what treatment; and estimation, which provides a framework to compute the ATE.

Uniform random sampling is the most commonly used sampling method in most web facing applications. It is simple and sufficient in most cases when the sample size is large. However, as we have mentioned in the last section, uniform random sampling makes it difficult to separate out the contribution of the network effects from other confounding factors such as neighborhood size. To this end, we look for a sampling solution in Section 4.1 that is able to take into consideration the network structure. The idea is to remove information diffusion between treatment and control groups as much as we can. However, as we will see, network sampling itself poses special challenges in *real* social networks because of their sizes and structures. We propose a sampling method that is able to overcome several of these challenges in Section 4.1.2. With the new sampling algorithm, we then study the problem of estimation, where we propose an exposure model and the corresponding estimators in Section 4.2 and show that they are a generalization of the existing estimators.

4.1 Network Sampling

Sampling is the process where we decide which users get assigned into what variant. At a high level, we try to split users into treatment and control so that there is as little information flow between the variants as possible. The sampling scheme we adopt here is called *cluster randomized sampling*, which is a sampling method where clusters of users are randomized together [18, 20]. It is a two-stage procedure:

1. Partition the users into clusters;
2. Treat each cluster as a unit and randomize at the cluster level, so that all the users in the same cluster are assigned to the same variant.

The advantages of cluster randomized sampling include the ability to study the interference within the same cluster and the ability to control for "contamination" across clusters [8]. In this section, we will start with a recent proposal called ϵ-net [28]. We examine its performance in a real social network. We then propose a new sampling algorithm that can overcome an important limitation and hence reduce the bias of the ATE estimator.

4.1.1 *Graph Cluster Randomization*

Graph clustering, also known as community detection, graph cutting, and graph partition, is a well-researched area [1, 4, 19]. However, clustering real social networks is challenging due to their special structure and topology. [28] proposes a local clustering algorithm, ϵ-net, that overcomes some of those challenges and the idea is as follows:

1. Find k cluster centers that are at least $2\epsilon - 1$ apart;-
2. Assign the nodes to their nearest center, and break the tie randomly if needed.

To study how this clustering algorithm works on real networks, we extract a sub-network from LinkedIn's social graph by taking all the users who have ever worked at a leading internet technology company with a global presence. The sub-network (employee network) is constructed by extracting the connections among them. After removing nodes with no connections, we get a network of about 70K users. The basic statistics of this sub-network are given in Table 2. We

Nodes #	Edges #	max$\{d_i\}$	mean $\{d_i\}$	var$\{d_i\}$
7.26e4	2.88e6	3997	39.67	1.27e4

Table 2: Basic statistics of a employee network.

then apply the 3-net clustering algorithm to partition this sub-network into 100 shards. The distribution of the cluster sizes in logarithmic scale is given in Figure 1.

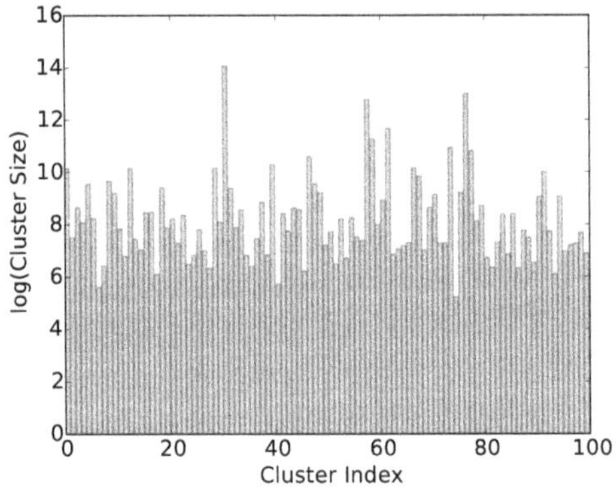

Figure 1: Cluster sizes of 3-net Network Clustering. Y axis specifies the $\log_2$ of cluster sizes.

It is not surprising to find out that the cluster sizes vary quite a lot. Intuitively, the ϵ-net algorithm constructs clusters of radius at least $\epsilon - 1$ around each center node, which implies that the size of each cluster is largely determined by the degrees of the center node. Because degrees are heterogeneous in real networks, so are the cluster sizes. But how would this influence the estimation of ATE?

According to bias analysis in [18], the ATE estimator given in (2) has the following bias

$$\mathbb{E}[\hat{\delta}] - \delta = -\frac{N_c}{N}\left[\frac{1}{|\mathcal{J}_1|}\text{Cov}\left(\frac{\sum_{j\in\mathcal{J}_1}\sum_{i=1}^{n_j} Y_{ij}}{\sum_{j\in\mathcal{J}_1} n_j}, \sum_{j\in\mathcal{J}_1} n_j\right) - \frac{1}{|\mathcal{J}_0|}\text{Cov}\left(\frac{\sum_{j\in\mathcal{J}_0}\sum_{i=1}^{n_j} Y_{ij}}{\sum_{j\in\mathcal{J}_0} n_j}, \sum_{j\in\mathcal{J}_0} n_j\right)\right],$$

where $\mathcal{J}_1$ ($\mathcal{J}_0$) is the set of clusters that are assigned to treatment (control), $N_c = |\mathcal{J}_0| + |\mathcal{J}_1|$ is the number of clusters, Y_{ij} is the response of i-th user in the j-th cluster, n_j is the size of cluster j, and $\text{Cov}(\cdot,\cdot)$ is the covariance function.

To get an unbiased estimator, we need to have $\mathbb{E}[\hat{\delta}] - \delta = 0$, *i.e.*,

$$\begin{aligned} \text{Cov}\left(\frac{\sum_{j\in J_1}\sum_{i=1}^{n_j} Y_{ij}}{\sum_{j\in J_1} n_j}, \sum_{j\in J_1} n_j\right) = 0, \\ \text{Cov}\left(\frac{\sum_{j\in J_0}\sum_{i=1}^{n_j} Y_{ij}}{\sum_{j\in J_0} n_j}, \sum_{j\in J_0} n_j\right) = 0. \end{aligned} \tag{6}$$

There are two scenarios under which (6) can hold. Scenario (i): users' responses Y_{ij}'s are independent of cluster size n_j; Scenario (ii): n_j's are constant. When there are network effects, we expect users in larger treatment clusters to get more social influence, and hence scenario (i) is unlikely to hold. Therefore, we need a network sampling method that is able to produce equal size clusters. Based on this observation and the large scale of real online social networks, we propose a simple yet efficient balanced graph partition algorithm, called *randomized balanced graph partition.*

4.1.2 Randomized Balanced Graph Partition

In this section, we introduce the randomized balanced graph partition algorithm with the goal of producing clusters that are of equal size and that can be computationally feasible to be applied to real, large-scale social networks.

We start with an initial feasible partition where all the clusters are of the same size. Our goal is to maintain the balance of the cluster sizes while maximize the number of edges within each cluster. To do that, we iteratively update the cluster label of each node based on the majority vote from its neighbors. The balance of the cluster sizes is achieved by swapping the cluster label of a pair of nodes, instead of simply changing them. The challenge, of course, is to decide which and how many pairs of labels should be swapped.

It is worth noting that the balanced graph partitioning problem is proven to be NP complete even for the case with only two clusters [1]. We propose a greedy algorithm with randomization, which is effective and efficient and can be easily parallelizable. Our algorithm alternates the two steps below till convergence:

1. *Label Propagation.* Define "gain" as an increase of the number of edges between nodes of the same cluster. For every pair of nodes, switch their cluster labels in a greedy way until the gain cannot be increased any more.

2. *Random Shuffling.* Randomly select $\zeta\%$ pairs of nodes, and swap their labels.

By randomly shuffling the cluster labels, we can break the local optimum, and increase the number of links within the same cluster. As shown in Table 3, we can improve the baseline label propagation by 8.9% with shuffling. In experiments, we set $\zeta = 5$[1]. Since the sub-network is not very large, we are also able to compare our proposal with Modularity Maximization [5][2], which is known to have good performance but computationally expensive for large networks. Our proposed method achieves comparable results yet is scalable and can be easily parallelized.

[1]The choice of ζ may be of independent interest. However it is beyond the scope of this paper.

Methods	LP	RSLP	MM
# of links in clusters ($\times 10^6$)	2.161	2.355	2.359

Table 3: Clustering results for **L**abel **P**ropagation (LP) and **R**andom **S**huffling on **L**abel **P**ropagation (RSLP), as well as one based on **M**odularity **M**aximization (MM).

4.2 Estimation

In this section, we study the problem of how to estimate ATE. To do that, we need to first decide how we model users' exposure to network effects. As we will see, the assumptions of existing exposure models are hard to satisfy in real networks and under the new sampling scheme we proposed in Section 4.1.2.

To address this problem, we propose a new exposure model that we describe in Section 4.2.4 and the corresponding estimators. Through a linear additive model, we are able to show that our exposure model and estimator is a generalization of the existing ones.

4.2.1 Framework

Suppose $\mathbf{z} = (\mathbf{z}_1, \mathbf{z}_2, \cdots, \mathbf{z}_N)'$ where $\mathbf{z}_i \in \{0,1\}$, and the probability of seeing a particular value of $\mathbf{z}$ is $p_\mathbf{z}$. Let $\mathcal{Z} = \{\mathbf{z} : p_\mathbf{z} > 0\}$, so that $\mathbf{Z} = (\mathbf{Z}_1, ..., \mathbf{Z}_N)'$ is a random vector with support $\mathcal{Z}$ and probability $\mathbb{P}(\mathbf{Z} = \mathbf{z}) = p_\mathbf{z}$. Define a unit-specific onto function that maps an assignment vector and unit specific traits $\xi_i \in \mathcal{E}$ (such as one's local neighborhood structure) to an *expected* user response $f : \mathcal{Z} \times \mathcal{E} \to \Delta$. The codomain of Δ contains all the expected treatment responses that might be induced in the experiment.

Instead of being determined by the entire treatment assignment vector, users' responses are determined by different treatment exposures, which are resulted from the interaction of sampling design ($\mathbf{Z}$) and the traits of users ξ_i. The key step of causal inference, as well as treatment effects estimation, is to specify f.

The ATE can be expressed as

$$\begin{aligned} \delta &= \frac{1}{N} \cdot \sum_{i=1}^{N} f_i(\mathbf{Z} = \mathbf{1}, \xi_i) - \frac{1}{N} \cdot \sum_{i=1}^{N} f_i(\mathbf{Z} = \mathbf{0}, \xi_i) \\ &= \tau_1 - \tau_0 \end{aligned} \tag{7}$$

where τ_1 is the expected response when treatment is applied *globally*, similarly for τ_0. We will start with two existing exposure models and their corresponding ATE estimators.

4.2.2 SUTVA

Under the Stable Unit Treatment Value Assumption, also known as Individual Treatment Response, f is defined as

$$f_i^S(\mathbf{Z}, \xi_i) = \mathbf{I}(\mathbf{Z}_i = 1) \cdot \tau_1 + \mathbf{I}(\mathbf{Z}_i = 0) \cdot \tau_0. \tag{8}$$

In other words, (i) user i's treatment exposure depends only on his/her own treatment, regardless of the treatment as-

[2]The Modularity Maximization algorithm does not generate clusters with equal sizes, so that we constrained the maximum cluster size during each iteration.

signments of other users in the network; (ii) user i's expected response under treatment (control) is the same as if everyone were in treatment (control). It is easy to see that under this response function $f^S(\cdot)$, the ATE can be estimated based on (2).

4.2.3 Neighborhood Exposure

There are two basic Neighborhood Exposure models, one based on the percent of treated neighbors and the other based on the absolute number of treated neighbors. We assume the former in our discussion here as it is more robust to the heterogeneity of users' degrees, though the analysis for the latter is similar.

Given a threshold $\theta \in [0,1]$, the expected response function f for the neighborhood exposure model is defined as

$$f_i^N(\mathbf{Z}, \xi_i) = \mathbf{I}(\mathbf{Z}_i = 1, \sigma_i \geq \theta) \cdot \tau_1 + \mathbf{I}(\mathbf{Z}_i = 0, \sigma_i \leq 1-\theta) \cdot \tau_0 \\ +(\mathbf{I}(\mathbf{Z}_i = 0, \sigma_i \geq 1-\theta) + \mathbf{I}(\mathbf{Z}_i = 1, \sigma_i \leq \theta)) \cdot x_i(\mathbf{Z}, \xi_i),$$

where $x_i(\mathbf{Z}, \xi_i)$ is an unknown function and σ_i is the percent of i's neighbors in treatment. Define $\mathcal{T}_i^\theta = \{\mathbf{Z}|\mathbf{Z}_i = 1, \sigma_i \geq \theta\}$. Then we have that $\forall\ \mathbf{Z} \in \mathcal{T}_i^\theta$, i is *neighborhood exposed to treatment.* Similarly, define $\mathcal{C}_i^\theta = \{\mathbf{Z}|\mathbf{Z}_i = 0, \sigma_i \leq 1-\theta\}$. We have that $\forall\ \mathbf{Z} \in \mathcal{C}_i^\theta$, i is *neighborhood exposed to control.*

Under the neighborhood exposure model, we have (i) user i's treatment exposure depends on not just his/her own treatment but also his/her neighbors' treatment assignment; (ii) user i's expected response when he/she is network exposed to treatment (control) is τ_1 (τ_0), the same as if everyone were in treatment (control).

For i to be neighborhood exposed to treatment, i should be in treatment and at least θ fraction of i's neighbors are also in treatment. For users who are not neighborhood exposed to either treatment or control, their responses, $x_i(\mathbf{Z}, \xi_i)$ are considered invalid and are hence removed from estimation. Again, we can estimate τ_1 and τ_0 based on the sample means of the network-exposed users and hence the ATE as

$$\hat{\delta}^N = \frac{1}{N_1^\theta} \cdot \sum_{\{i;\mathbf{Z}\in\mathcal{T}_i^\theta\}} Y_i - \frac{1}{N_0^\theta} \cdot \sum_{\{i;\mathbf{Z}\in=\mathcal{C}_i^\theta\}} Y_i, \quad (9)$$

where N_0^θ, N_1^θ are the number of users that are network-exposed to control, treatment with threshold θ respectively.

A key step of applying Neighborhood Exposure model is to select θ, the threshold for σ_i that determines which nodes meet the condition of being neighborhood exposed. To see how θ affects the estimation, we first apply the randomized graph partition to the employee network in Table 2. After randomly assigning 50 of the 100 clusters to treatment, we have an empirical cumulative distribution function of σ_i for the nodes in treatment (Figure 2).

By setting different θ's, we have the following observations.

- If we set $\theta = 0.9$, we have $\Pr(\sigma_i \leq \theta) = 0.79$. A larger θ means a weaker assumption for the exposure model and hence smaller bias. However, about 79% observations are "invalid" and cannot be used to estimate the ATE, which leads to larger variance;

- If we set $\theta = 0.3$, we have $\Pr(\sigma_i \leq \theta) = 0.07$. 93% of the observations can be used in the estimation. However, a smaller θ means a stronger assumption and hence a larger bias.

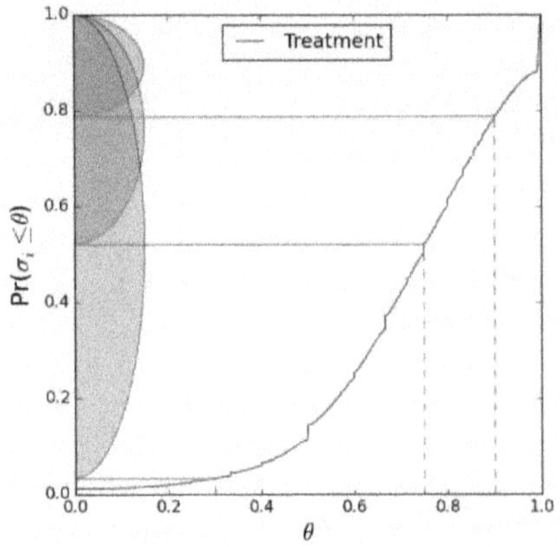

Figure 2: Empirical cumulative distribution function of σ_i for nodes in treatment.

The bias and variance trade-off presented in the choice of θ leads us to propose a new estimator that is able to take into consideration the level of exposure, and hence utilize all observations regardless whether they are network exposed. The new model also turns out to be a generalization of the exposure models and estimators discussed so far.

4.2.4 Fraction Neighborhood Exposure

In this section, we propose a new estimator based on what we call the *Fraction Neighborhood Exposure* model. We define $f(\cdot)$ the expected response function to be any function that depends only on the user's experiment assignment and the fraction of his treated neighbors σ_i:

$$f_i^F(\mathbf{Z}, \xi_i) = g(\mathbf{Z}_i, \sigma_i). \quad (10)$$

It is easy to see that the ATE in (7) becomes

$$\delta = g(\mathbf{1}, 1) - g(\mathbf{0}, 0). \quad (11)$$

Various response function $g(\cdot)$ can be chosen to model users' behavior. We demonstrate using two linear additive models.

Linear Additive Model I.

The first model we consider is as follows:

$$g(\mathbf{Z}_i, \sigma_i) = \alpha + \beta\mathbf{Z}_i + \gamma\sigma_i, \quad (12)$$

where β captures the treatment effects and γ the network effects. α, β, γ can be estimated from users' responses, as $\hat{\alpha}, \hat{\beta}, \hat{\gamma}$. The additive assumption of various effects is also made by previous works, such as the "linear-in-mean" model [15]. By (11), the ATE can be estimated as

$$\hat{\delta}_{L_I} = \hat{\beta} + \hat{\gamma}.$$

Linear Additive Model II.

The linear model in (12) can be further generalized by considering different response functions for users in treatment and control groups:

$$g(\mathbf{Z}_i, \sigma_i) = \begin{cases} \alpha_0 + \gamma_0\sigma_i, & \text{if } \mathbf{Z}_i = 0 \\ \alpha_1 + \gamma_1\sigma_i, & \text{if } \mathbf{Z}_i = 1 \end{cases} \quad (13)$$

where α_0, γ_0 are learned from observation data of users in control group, while α_1, γ_1 are learned from observation data of users in treatment group. By (11), the ATE can be estimated as

$$\hat{\delta}_{L_{II}} = \hat{\alpha}_1 + \hat{\gamma}_1 - \hat{\alpha}_0.$$

4.2.5 Comparison of Exposure Models

While comparing the three exposure models we discussed so far, we show in this section that the SUTVA and neighborhood exposure model are special cases of the fraction neighborhood exposure model.

Lemma 1. *SUTVA is a special case of fraction neighborhood exposure model in* (12).

Proof. It can be trivially proved by setting $\gamma = 0$, *i.e.*, set the network effects to be zero. □

For the case of neighborhood exposure model, we only need to show that the assumption of the response function is a special case of the linear model in (12).

Lemma 2. *The neighborhood exposure model is a special case of the fraction neighborhood exposure model in* (12).

Proof. The response function in neighborhood exposure model can be defined as follows:

$$f_i^N(\mathbf{Z}, \xi_i) = \begin{cases} \tau_0 & \text{if } \mathbf{Z}_i = 0, \sigma_i < 1-\theta \\ \tau_1 & \text{if } \mathbf{Z}_i = 1, \sigma_i > \theta \\ \text{invalid} & \text{otherwise} \end{cases}$$

which is equivalent to

$$f_i^N(\mathbf{Z}, \xi_i) = \begin{cases} \alpha + \beta\mathbf{Z}_i & \text{if } \mathbf{Z}_i = 0, \sigma_i < 1-\theta \\ \alpha + \beta\mathbf{Z}_i & \text{if } \mathbf{Z}_i = 1, \sigma_i > \theta \\ \text{invalid} & \text{otherwise} \end{cases},$$

by re-parameterizing $\alpha = \tau_0, \beta = \tau_1 - \tau_0$. In other words, $f_i^N(\mathbf{Z}, \xi_i) = \alpha + \beta\mathbf{Z}_i$ restricted to only users who are network-exposed. □

5. EXPERIMENTAL RESULTS

In order to demonstrate the effectiveness and efficiency of fraction neighborhood model, we performed various experiments including extensive simulations and a real online experiment. These two types of experiments are complementary. We can obtain ground truth in the simulation study, so it is possible to evaluate methods under various conditions based on their bias and variance. On the other hand, real experiment offers special insights into how models compare in practice. Also note that all simulations here are based on real social network, so we only need to simulate user responses.

5.1 Simulations

Considering the heterogeneity of degrees of nodes in real social networks, we will use the Randomized Balanced Graph Partition algorithm proposed in Section 4.1.2 to determine the experiment assignment and focus on comparing the estimation models. To be more specific, we aim at answering the following questions based on the simulations:

1. How does the percentage of units under treatment (or control) influence the estimation?

2. How do different estimation models compare with respect to both bias and variance?

All simulations are based on the employee network summarized in Table 2, which has a heterogeneous degree distribution with a high variance. We have also run similar simulation analysis on different networks extracted from LinkedIn's social network graph, but the results are similar.

5.1.1 Simulation Model

The observed user response is generated based on the following probit model [8][3]

$$\begin{aligned} \widetilde{Y}_{i,t} &= \lambda_0 + \lambda_1 \cdot \mathbf{Z}_i + \lambda_2 \cdot \frac{\mathbf{A}_{\cdot i}^\top \cdot \mathbf{Y}_{t-1}}{D_{ii}} + U_{i,t} \\ Y_{i,t} &= \mathbf{I}(\widetilde{Y}_{i,t} > 0), \end{aligned} \quad (14)$$

where $Y_{i,t}$ is the response of i at time t and $U_{i,t} \sim \mathcal{N}(0,1)$ is a stochastic component capturing user specific traits. λ_0 is a constant that $\lambda_0 = -1.5$. λ_1 captures the strength of treatment effects, and λ_2 is for the network effects. We initialize $Y_{i,0} = 0$ for all users, and then run the iterative process to generate users' responses for T steps with different combinations of λ_1 and λ_2 where $\lambda_1 \in \{0.25, 0.5, 0.75, 1.0\}$, and $\lambda_2 \in \{0, 0.1, 0.5, 1.0\}$. The step length is set to $T = 3$.

It is worth noting that in this data generation model, one's response depends directly on the behavior of his/her neighbors at the previous time stamp, not simply the neighbors' experiment assignments, which is quite realistic.

5.1.2 Estimators

We have discussed different estimators in Section 4.2.1 according to different exposure models. In addition to these discussed, we will also include in the comparison the *Hajek estimator*[2]. Specifically, we will study the following five estimators:

1. Under SUTVA, the sample mean estimator as in (2).

2. Under the Neighborhood Exposure Model, the sample mean estimator as in (9).

3. Under the Neighborhood Exposure Model, the *Hajek estimator*[2] defined as follows

$$\begin{aligned} \widehat{\tau}_{0,H} &= \frac{\sum_{i=1}^N \mathbf{I}(\mathbf{z}_i = 0, \sigma_i < 1-\theta) \cdot Y_i / \pi(\mathcal{C}_i^\theta)}{\sum_{i=1}^N \mathbf{I}(\mathbf{z}_i = 0, \sigma_i < 1-\theta) \cdot 1/\pi(\mathcal{C}_i^\theta)} \\ \widehat{\tau}_{1,H} &= \frac{\sum_{i=1}^N \mathbf{I}(\mathbf{z}_i = 1, \sigma_i > \theta) \cdot Y_i / \pi(\mathcal{T}_i^\theta)}{\sum_{i=1}^N \mathbf{I}(\mathbf{z}_i = 1, \sigma_i > \theta) \cdot 1/\pi(\mathcal{T}_i^\theta)} \\ \hat{\delta}_H^N &= \widehat{\tau}_{1,H} - \widehat{\tau}_{0,H} \end{aligned} \quad (15)$$

where $\pi(\mathcal{C}_i^\theta)$ and $\pi(\mathcal{T}_i^\theta)$ are the probabilities for user i to be neighborhood exposed to control and treatment given the cluster level randomization and threshold θ. We set $\theta = 0.75$.

4. Under the Fraction Neighborhood Exposure Model, the linear model I estimator (12).

5. Under the Fraction Neighborhood Exposure Model, the linear model II estimator (13).

[3]For fair comparison, the simulation process is exactly the same as [8] except that we use real networks while [8] uses simulated random networks.

We did 1000 simulations to compute both bias and variance for each of these estimators. For each simulation, the true ATE is estimated by putting all users in treatment or all in control.

5.1.3 *Percentage of Users in Treatment*

When running an A/B test, how to split the traffic between treatment and control is one of the key questions one has to decide. This is even more crucial if there are network effects, as the overall percentage of users in treatment (ρ) will substantially influence the fraction of one's neighbors in treatment, which leads to different level of treatment exposure. This is demonstrated by how the empirical cumulative distribution function of σ_i changes with different ρ's in Figure 3.

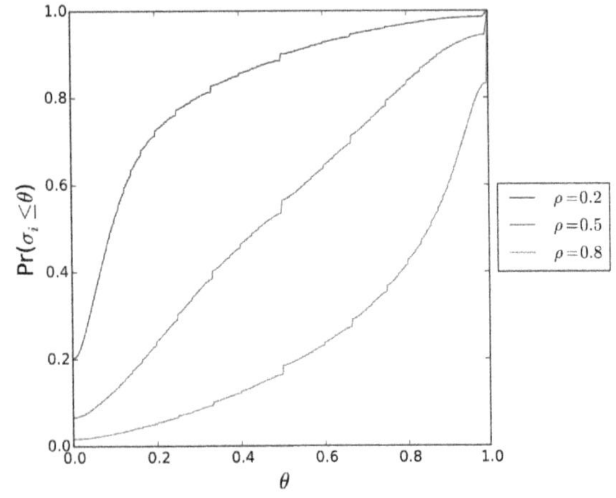

Figure 3: By changing the percentage of units in treatment ρ, the distribution of σ_i changes significantly.

A more interesting question is how the performance of different estimators change with ρ. As far as we know, we are the first one to study this problem and the results are shown in Figure 4. We have the following observations. (i) The bias of each estimator does not change much as ρ changes, but the variance changes significantly and reaches the smallest when $\rho = 0.5$ (as expected since Var $\sim 1/\sqrt{1/N_0 + 1/N_1}$). (ii) For $\rho < 0.3$ and $\rho > 0.7$, the variance of the Hajek estimator is large because the scale factors π_i's (probabilities of being neighborhood exposed) are small. (iii) The Hajek estimator performs worse than sample mean estimator under the same neighborhood exposure model. It is interesting to note that, in random networks such difference is minimal [8], showing the importance of the network structure when evaluating estimators. (iv) Our linear estimators under the Fraction Neighborhood Exposure model achieve the smallest bias and variance. The L_I estimator achieves smaller variance, while L_{II} estimator achieves smaller bias. The different between L_I estimator and L_{II} is minimal when $\rho = 0.5$.

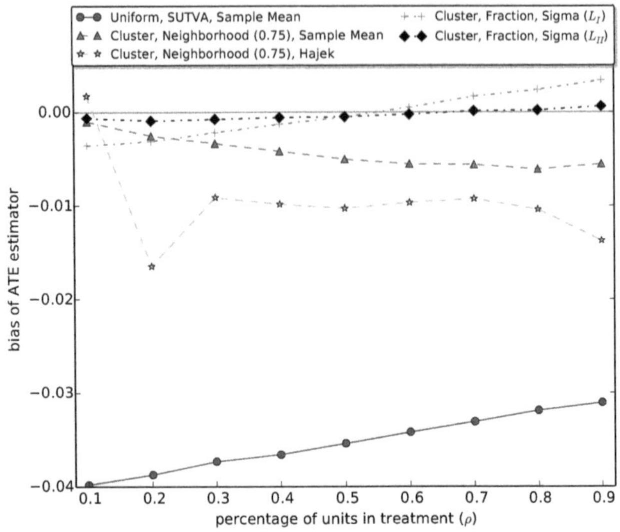

(a) The bias of different estimators

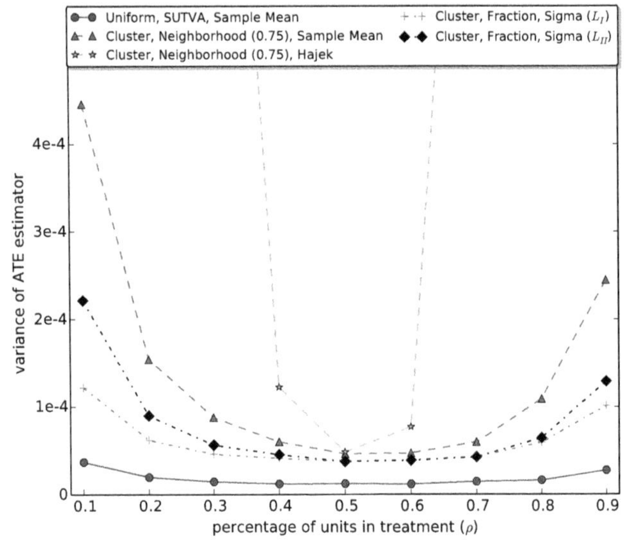

(b) The variance of different estimators

Figure 4: Behavior of different estimators with different percentage of neighbors in treatment.

5.1.4 *Network Effect*

We now compare the performance of different ATE estimators under different levels of treatment effects and network effects, by changing the values of λ_1 and λ_2 in the simulation model (14). We use $\rho = 0.5$ and the results are shown in Figure 5. The results with $\rho = 0.1$ are similar and hence omitted.

We have the following observations. (i) The bias of both sample mean and Hajek estimators under the neighborhood exposure model becomes larger as the network effects and treatment effects become larger; (ii) The variance of the estimators is fairly consistent across different levels of treatment effects and network effects. This is because the number of observations used in estimation does not change as λ_1 and λ_2 change. In addition, the linear estimators under our fraction neighborhood exposure model achieve a smaller variance than the estimators under the neighborhood exposure model because all the observations are included in the estimation. (iii) Our linear estimators achieve the best bias and variance across different levels of network effects and treatment effects.

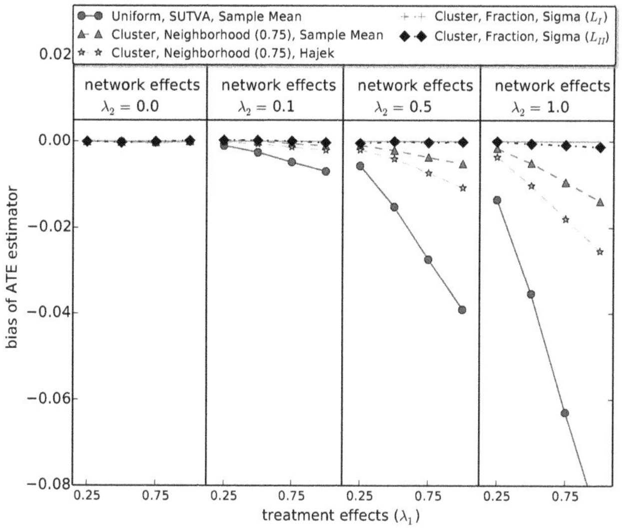

(a) The bias of different estimators

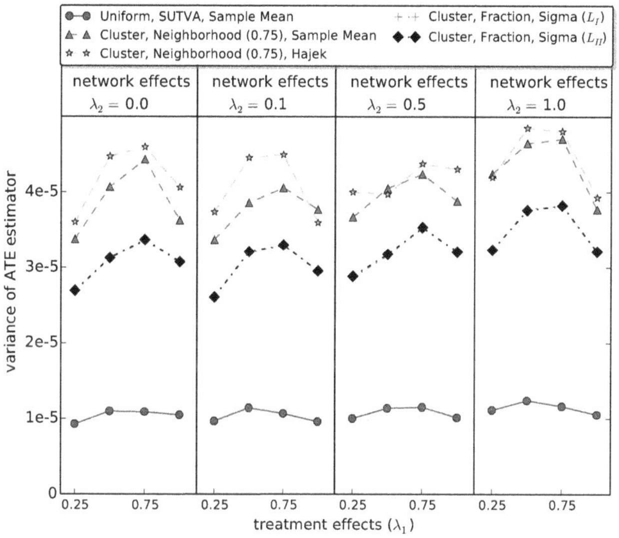

(b) The variance of different estimators

Figure 5: Behavior of different estimators with different parameters, which controls the strength of treatment effects (λ_1) and network effects (λ_2), in the simulation model. The overall percentage of nodes in treatment $\rho = 0.5$.

5.2 Real Online Experiment

In addition to the extensive simulations, we have also conducted a real online experiment at LinkedIn using the network A/B testing framework we have proposed. Specifically, we have done the following:

1. Select a country as the sub-network to experiment on.

2. Apply our randomized balanced graph partition algorithm to assign users from this country into treatment and control groups.

3. Apply different Feed algorithms to the treatment and control groups. Estimate the ATE after running the experiment for two weeks.

Country	$N_\mathcal{S}$ ($\times 10^6$)	$R_\mathcal{S}$	$\overline{d_\mathcal{S}}$
Brazil	19.9	0.932	41.6
United States	119.3	0.910	54.3
Netherlands	**6.1**	**0.868**	**93.0**
Chile	2.8	0.866	38.4
New Zealand	1.3	0.654	29.4

Table 4: Basic statistics about several countries. $N_\mathcal{S}$ is the size of the subnetwork, selected by the corresponding country; $R_\mathcal{S}$ is the self-containment measure defined in (16); $\overline{d_\mathcal{S}}$ is the average degree of the selected subnetwork defined in (17).

We note that unlike simulations, there is no ground truth for this real world experiment. The Feed team has, however, compared these two Feed algorithms globally in a uniformly randomized A/B test, and the treatment Feed algorithm was significantly better than control.

Our goal for the real world experiment is two-fold. First, we would like to compare results from different estimators in a real application setting to complement the observations from simulations. In particular, we want to compare results with and without taking into consideration of the network effects, and further, how our fraction neighborhood exposure model compares with the neighborhood exposure model. Second, as far as we know, we are the first to run a real network A/B test. We would like to establish a process for running network A/B test in practice. As we have seen how the conclusions can differ drastically in real networks compared to simulated networks, we hope this can bridge the gap and encourage more research focusing on real applications in the area of network A/B testing.

5.2.1 *Country Selection*

We would like to select a country that has a well self-contained LinkedIn social network. Ideally, It should be an isolated sub-network that has as few connections to the outside of the country as possible to prevent network influence to and from users outside. We use the following ratio to quantify such "self-containment" for a set $\mathcal{S}$ of users:

$$R_\mathcal{S} = \frac{\sum_{i,j \in \mathcal{S}} A_{i,j}}{\sum_{i \in \mathcal{S}} \sum_{j \in \mathcal{S} \cup \mathcal{S}^c} A_{i,j}}, \tag{16}$$

where $\mathcal{S}^c$ is the complement of $\mathcal{S}$ in the population network. Remark that $R_\mathcal{S}$ is the ratio between the edge count within the set $\mathcal{S}$ and all the edges with one end in $\mathcal{S}$.

In addition, we consider the average internal degree such that the selected subnetwork is well connected. Considering selected sub-network $\mathcal{S}$, the average internal degree is defined as

$$\overline{d_\mathcal{S}} = \frac{\sum_{i,j \in \mathcal{S}} A_{i,j}}{|\mathcal{S}|}. \tag{17}$$

We calculate $R_\mathcal{S}$ and $\overline{d_\mathcal{S}}$ for all countries on LinkedIn, and among the ones with top $R_\mathcal{S}$ ratios (shown in Table 4), we decide to pick Netherlands as it has the highest average internal degrees and a reasonably large sized network (around 6 million users).

After selecting the Netherlands as the sub-network, we applied the randomized balanced graph partition algorithm to divide it into 600 shards and randomly picked 300 of them to receive treatment while the rest 300 to receive control. Before performing the A/B test, we have also conducted an A/A test, which is a controlled experiment where treatment is identical to control. This was to confirm that no bias was introduced during the experiment assignment process.

5.2.2 Online Results

We let the experiment run for two weeks before we collected data for analysis. The metric we use for evaluation is the average number of social gestures on Feed, such as "like", "comment" or "share".

We compute the ATE based on the various estimators described in Section 5.1.2. The results are shown in Table 5. We have the following observations. (i) The ATE estimators with consideration of network effects are all larger than the estimate under SUTVA. This is yet another good confirmation that there are indeed network effects presented in the A/B experiment. (ii) The choice of θ in the neighborhood exposure model matters. The sample mean estimator almost doubles when θ changes from 0.75 to 0.9. On the other hand, the Hajek estimator gives a smaller estimate when θ changes from 0.75 to 0.9, this is due to small values of π_i's when θ is large. (iv) The fraction neighborhood exposure model gives larger estimates than existing methods.

Method	ATE for social gestures
SUTVA	0.168
Neighbor. Exposure $\theta = 0.75$	0.264
Neighbor. Exposure $\theta = 0.9$	0.520
Hajek. Exposure $\theta = 0.75$	0.625
Hajek. Exposure $\theta = 0.9$	0.133
Fraction Exposure (I)	0.687
Fraction Exposure (II)	0.714

Table 5: ATE estimates from different models for the online Feed experiment.

6. CONCLUSION AND FUTURE WORK

In this paper, we study the problem of network A/B testing in real networks. We start by examining a recent A/B experiment conducted on LinkedIn without considering network structures, which motivates us to set up a framework to study both the sampling and the estimation aspects of the network A/B testing problem. To address the challenge of degree heterogeneity in real social networks, we come up with a new randomization scheme based on balanced graph partitioning, for which an efficient and distributed algorithm is proposed. Based on new sampling scheme, we propose a new method to estimate the average treatment effect (ATE) that is able to take into consideration of the level of network exposure. Extensive simulations are conducted to evaluate these methods and the results show that our new proposals can achieve both a smaller bias and a smaller variance. We have also conducted a real online experiment under the framework we have proposed and the results further validate many observations from simulations.

On the other hand, there are still many open problems in the field of network A/B testing that remain to be addressed, especially with respect to real world applications. First of all, we did not consider the influence strength between pairs of nodes, which may have significant impact on determining users exposure status; Secondly, real social networks are growing all the time, leading to rapid change of network structures, which makes network A/B testing even more challenging considering the effects of newly added edges and nodes. To further complicate the problem, many real experiments on social networks are aiming at increasing network density, making the temporal variability a real, noticeable issue. Thirdly, there are different forms of network interference to be considered. For instance, in discussion *groups*, information propagates from one user to all other users of the same group, so every group acts as a fully connected sub-network. However each user can belong to multiple groups. In this case, the graph clustering randomization can no longer split users into treatment and control under the new information propagation structure. Lastly, our focus here has been on ATE estimation, and we have not touched upon how virality works and how to preserve it in a network A/B testing setting. Given the complex structure of real social networks and the way viral information propagates, the framework proposed here may not be sufficient.

A/B testing in general is widely used and also well studied in the industry as it offers the best scientific approach to understand the causal impact of product changes on end user behavior. However, the problem of A/B testing in a social network setting is no where near solved. A lot of work still remains to be done to make it a well-understood problem in real world applications. We hope our work here can bridge some of the gaps and encourage more research in this area.

Acknowledgement

Firstly, we wish to thank our colleagues and friends who have held many enlightening discussions with us: Deepak Agarwal, Mathieu Bastian, Evion Kim, Wayne Tai Lee, Haishan Liu, Mitul Tiwari, Xiaolong Wang, and many members of the A/B testing team at LinkedIn. Secondly, we wish to thank Bee-Chung Chen, Liang Zhang, Pannagadatta Shivaswamy, Cory Hicks and Caroline Gaffney for working with us to run the network A/B test on LinkedIn Feeds. Lastly, we wish to thank the anonymous reviewers for their valuable comments and suggestions to improve the quality of the paper.

References

[1] K. Andreev and H. Racke. Balanced graph partitioning. *Theory of Computing Systems*, 39(6):929–939, 2006.

[2] P. M. Aronow and C. Samii. Estimating average causal effects under general interference. Citeseer, 2012.

[3] L. Backstrom and J. Kleinberg. Network bucket testing. In *Proceedings of the 20th international conference on World wide web*, pages 615–624. ACM, 2011.

[4] D. A. Bader, H. Meyerhenke, P. Sanders, and D. Wagner. *Graph partitioning and graph clustering*, volume 588. American Mathematical Soc., 2013.

[5] V. D. Blondel, J.-L. Guillaume, R. Lambiotte, and E. Lefebvre. Fast unfolding of communities in large networks. *Journal of Statistical Mechanics: Theory and Experiment*, 2008(10):P10008, 2008.

[6] J. Cheng, L. Adamic, P. A. Dow, J. M. Kleinberg, and J. Leskovec. Can cascades be predicted? In *Proceedings of the 23rd international conference on World wide web*, pages 925–936. International World Wide Web Conferences Steering Committee, 2014.

[7] N. Cressie and H. Whitford. How to use the two sample t-test. *Biometrical Journal*, 28(2):131–148, 1986.

[8] D. Eckles, B. Karrer, and J. Ugander. Design and analysis of experiments in networks: Reducing bias from interference. *arXiv preprint arXiv:1404.7530*, 2014.

[9] H. Gui, Y. Sun, J. Han, and G. Brova. Modeling topic diffusion in multi-relational bibliographic information networks. In *Proceedings of the 23rd ACM International Conference on Conference on Information and Knowledge Management*, pages 649–658. ACM, 2014.

[10] M. G. Hudgens and M. E. Halloran. Toward causal inference with interference. *Journal of the American Statistical Association*, 103(482), 2008.

[11] K. L. Judd. The law of large numbers with a continuum of iid random variables. *Journal of Economic theory*, 35(1):19–25, 1985.

[12] L. Katzir, E. Liberty, and O. Somekh. Framework and algorithms for network bucket testing. In *Proceedings of the 21st international conference on World Wide Web*, pages 1029–1036. ACM, 2012.

[13] R. Kohavi, A. Deng, B. Frasca, T. Walker, Y. Xu, and N. Pohlmann. Online controlled experiments at large scale. In *Proceedings of the 19th ACM SIGKDD international conference on Knowledge discovery and data mining*, pages 1168–1176. ACM, 2013.

[14] R. Kohavi, A. Deng, R. Longbotham, and Y. Xu. Seven rules of thumb for web site experimenters. *Proceedings of the 14th ACM SIGKDD international conference on Knowledge discovery and data mining*, 2014.

[15] C. F. Manski. Identification of endogenous social effects: The reflection problem. *The review of economic studies*, 60(3):531–542, 1993.

[16] C. F. Manski. Identification of treatment response with social interactions. *The Econometrics Journal*, 16(1):S1–S23, 2013.

[17] M. McPherson, L. Smith-Lovin, and J. M. Cook. Birds of a feather: Homophily in social networks. *Annual review of sociology*, pages 415–444, 2001.

[18] J. A. Middleton and P. M. Aronow. Unbiased estimation of the average treatment effect in cluster-randomized experiments. *Available at SSRN 1803849*, 2011.

[19] M. E. Newman. Modularity and community structure in networks. *Proceedings of the National Academy of Sciences*, 103(23):8577–8582, 2006.

[20] S. W. Raudenbush. Statistical analysis and optimal design for cluster randomized trials. *Psychological Methods*, 2(2):173, 1997.

[21] M. G. Rodriguez, J. Leskovec, D. Balduzzi, and B. Schölkopf. Uncovering the structure and temporal dynamics of information propagation. *Network Science*, 2(01):26–65, 2014.

[22] P. R. Rosenbaum. Interference between units in randomized experiments. *Journal of the American Statistical Association*, 102(477), 2007.

[23] D. B. Rubin. Estimating causal effects of treatments in randomized and nonrandomized studies. *Journal of educational Psychology*, 66(5):688, 1974.

[24] M. E. Sobel. What do randomized studies of housing mobility demonstrate? causal inference in the face of interference. *Journal of the American Statistical Association*, 101(476):1398–1407, 2006.

[25] L. Tang, R. Rosales, A. Singh, and D. Agarwal. Automatic ad format selection via contextual bandits. In *Proceedings of the 22nd ACM international conference on Conference on information & knowledge management*, pages 1587–1594. ACM, 2013.

[26] E. J. T. Tchetgen and T. J. VanderWeele. On causal inference in the presence of interference. *Statistical Methods in Medical Research*, 21(1):55–75, 2012.

[27] P. Toulis and E. Kao. Estimation of causal peer influence effects. In *Proceedings of The 30th International Conference on Machine Learning*, pages 1489–1497, 2013.

[28] J. Ugander, B. Karrer, L. Backstrom, and J. Kleinberg. Graph cluster randomization: network exposure to multiple universes. In *Proceedings of the 19th ACM SIGKDD international conference on Knowledge discovery and data mining*, pages 329–337. ACM, 2013.

[29] F. Yates. Sir ronald fisher and the design of experiments. *Biometrics*, 20(2):307–321, 1964.

User Session Identification Based on Strong Regularities in Inter-activity Time

Aaron Halfaker[1] Oliver Keyes[1] Daniel Kluver[2] Jacob Thebault-Spieker[2]
Tien Nguyen[2] Kenneth Shores[2] Anuradha Uduwage[2] Morten Warncke-Wang[2]

[1]Wikimedia Foundation
149 New Montgomery St.
6th Floor
San Francisco, CA 94105
{ahalfaker,okeyes}@wikimedia.org

[2]GroupLens Research
Computer Science and Engineering
University of Minnesota
Minneapolis, MN 55455
{kluver,thebault,tien,shores,uduwage,morten}@cs.umn.edu

ABSTRACT

Session identification is a common strategy used to develop metrics for web analytics and perform behavioral analyses of user-facing systems. Past work has argued that session identification strategies based on an inactivity threshold is inherently arbitrary or has advocated that thresholds be set at about 30 minutes. In this work, we demonstrate a strong regularity in the temporal rhythms of user initiated events across several different domains of online activity (incl. video gaming, search, page views and volunteer contributions). We describe a methodology for identifying clusters of user activity and argue that the regularity with which these activity clusters appear implies a good rule-of-thumb inactivity threshold of about 1 hour. We conclude with implications that these temporal rhythms may have for system design based on our observations and theories of goal-directed human activity.

Categories and Subject Descriptors

H.4 [**Information Systems Applications**]: Miscellaneous; H.1.1 [**Coding and Information Theory**]: Formal models of communication

General Terms

Theory, Measurement, Human Factors

Keywords

User session; Activity; Human behavior; Regularities; Metrics; Modeling; Analytics

1. INTRODUCTION

In 2012, we had an idea for a measurement strategy that would bring insight and understanding to the nature of work in an online community. While studying volunteer participation in Wikipedia, the open, collaborative encyclopedia, we found ourselves increasingly curious about the amount of time that volunteer contributors invested into the encyclopedia's construction. Past work measuring Wikipedia editor engagement relied on counting the number of contributions made by a user[1], but we felt that the amount of time editors spent editing might serve as a more appropriate measure.

The measurement strategy we came up with was based on the clustering of Wikipedia editors' activities into "edit sessions" with the assumption that the duration of an edit session would represent a lower bound of the amount of time invested into Wikipedia contributions [9]. Through our ethnographic work in Wikipedia we had found the notion of a work session to be intuitive, yet there did not appear to be a consensus in the literature on how to identify work sessions from timestamped user activities. This led us to look to the data for insight about what might be a reasonable approach to delineating users' editing activity into sessions. The regularities we found in inter-activity time amazed us with their intuitiveness and the simplicity of session demarcation they implied. It is that work that led us to look for such regularities in other systems and to write this paper to share our results.

We are not the first to try our hands at identifying a reasonable way to measure user session behavior in human-computer interaction. User sessions have been used extensively to generate metrics for understanding the performance of information resources [11] – especially in the domain of search [7, 8] and content personalisation [10, 20]. Despite this interest in understanding the nature and manifestation of user sessions, no clear consensus about how to perform session identification has emerged.

Some have have even argued that human behavior is best understood as a series of goal-driven tasks as opposed to activity sessions and that the common strategy of choosing a global inactivity threshold is ineffective at identifying the boundaries of such tasks [12]. We draw from Activity Theory [16] to conceptualize tasks as sub-session activities and argue that both are are important for undertanding goal-oriented human behavior.

WWW 2015, May 18–22, 2015, Florence, Italy.
ACM 978-1-4503-3469-3/15/05.
http://dx.doi.org/10.1145/2736277.2741117.

[1]for example, "Wikipedian is first to hit 1 million edits" `http://www.dailydot.com/news/wikipedian-first-1-million-edits`

In this paper, we describe a strategy for identifying user sessions from log data and demonstrate how the results match both intuition and theory about goal-directed human activity. We also show how this strategy yields consistent results across many different types of systems and user activities. First, we summarize previous work which attempts to make sense of user session behavior from log data. Then we discuss theoretical arguments about how goal-directed user behavior ought to manifest in the data. Third, we discuss a generalized version of the inactivity threshold identification strategy we developed in previous work [9] and present strategies for identifying optimal inactivity thresholds in new data. Then, we introduce 6 different systems from which we have extracted 10 different types of user actions for analysis and comparison. Finally, we conclude with discussions of the regularities and irregularities between datasets and what that might imply for both our understanding of the measurement of human behavior and the design of user-facing systems

2. RELATED WORK

2.1 Human activity sessions

The concept of an activity session is an intuitive one, but it's surprisingly difficult to tie down a single definition of what a session *is*. A "session" may refer to "(1) a set of queries to satisfy a single information need (2) a series of successive queries, and (3) a short period of contiguous time spent querying and examining results." [12]

(1) is referred to, particularly in search-related literature [8, 12], not as a session but as a task–a particular information need the user is trying to fulfil. Multiple tasks may happen in a contiguous browsing period, or a single task may be spread out over multiple periods. (2) is unclear. It may refer to a series of contiguous but unrelated queries (in which case it is identical to the third definition), or a series of contiguous queries based on the previous query in the sequence (in which case it is best understood as a sequence of tasks). (3) is the most commonly-used definition in the literature we have reviewed [11, 15, 20, 22]. This contrasts with the notion of *task* and is the definition of "session" that we have chosen for this paper. It's also the definition used by the W3C [21].

We found inspiration in thinking about how to model user session behavior in two distinct, but related threads: the empirical modeling work of cognitive science and the theoretical frameworks of human consciousness as applied to "work activities".

The lack of purely random distribution in the time between logged human actions has been the topic of recent studies focusing on the cognitive capacity of humans as information processing units. Notably, Barbasi showed that, by modeling communication activities with decision-based priority queues, he could show evidence for a mechanism to explain the heavy tail in time between activities [1] – a pattern he describes as bursts of rapid activity followed by long periods of inactivity. Wu et al. built upon this work to argue that short-message communication patterns could be better described by a "bimodal" distribution characterized by Poisson-based initiation of tasks and a powerlaw of time inbetween task events[23].

In contrast, Nardi calls out this cognitive science work for neglecting context in work patterns, motivation and community membership – thereby inappropriately reducing a human to a processing unit in a vacuum [16] (p21). Instead, Nardi draws from the framework of Activity Theory (AT) to advocate for an approach to understanding human-computer interaction as a conscious procession of *activities*. AT describes an activity as a goal-directed or purposeful interaction of a subject with an object through the use of tools. AT further formalizes an *activity* as a collection of *actions*[2] directed towards completing the activity's goal. Similarly, *actions* are composed of *operations*, a fundamental, indivisible, and unconscious movement that humans make in the service of performing an *action*.

For an example application of AT, let us examine Wikipedia editing. Our ethnographic work with Wikipedia editors suggests that it is common to set aside time on a regular basis to spend doing "wiki-work". AT would conceptualize this wiki-work overall as an *activity* and each unit of time spent engaging in the wiki-work as an "activity phase" – though we prefer the term "activity session".

The *actions* within an activity session would manifest as individual edits to wiki pages representing contributions to encyclopedia articles, posts in discussions and messages sent to other Wikipedia editors. These edits involve a varied set of *operations*: typing of characters, copy-pasting the details of reference materials, scrolling through a document, reading an argument and eventually, clicking the "Save" button.

In this work we draw from both the concepts of the *operation-action-activity* heirarchy of Activity Theory and the empirical modeling strategies of cognitive science as applied to time between events.

2.2 Session identification

User sessions have been used as behavioral measures of human-computer interaction for almost two decades, and for this reason, strategies for session identification from log data have been extensively studied [8].

Cooley et al. [5] and Spiliopoulou et al. [20] contast two primary strategies for identifying sessions from activity logs: "navigation-oriented heuristics" and "time-oriented heuristics".

Time-oriented heuristics refer to the assignment of an inactivity threshold between logged activites to serve as a session delimiter. The assumption implied is that if there is a break between a user's actions that is sufficiently long, it's likely that the user is no longer *active*, the session is assumed to have ended, and a new session is created when the next action is performed. This is the most commonly-used approach to identify sessions, with 30 minutes serving as the most commonly used threshold [8, 20, 17]. Both threshold and approach appear to originate in a 1995 paper by Catledge & Pitkow [4] that used client-side tracking to examine browsing behavior. In their work, they reported that the mean time between logged events 9.3 minutes. They choose to add 1.5 standard deviations to that mean to achieve a 25.5 minutes inactivity threshold. Over time this threshold has simplified to 30 minutes.

[2]We see Jones' conceptualization of tasks [12] as analogous to AT's conceptualization of *action*.

The utility and universality of this 30-minute inactivity threshold is widely debated; Mehrzadi & Feitelson [13] found that 30 minutes produced artefacts around long sessions, and could find no clear evidence of a global session inactivity threshold[3], while Jones & Klinkner [12] found the 25.5 minute threshold performed "no better than random" in the context of intentifying search tasks. Other thresholds have been proposed, but Montgomery and Faloutsos [14] concluded that the actual threshold chosen made little difference to how accurately sessions were identified.

Navigation-oriented heuristics involve inferring browsing patterns based on the HTTP referers and URLs associated with each request by a user. When a user begins navigating (without a referer), they have started a session; when a trail can no longer be traced to a previous request based on the referers and URLs of subsequent requests, the session has ended. This approach was pioneered by Cooley et al in 2002 [5]. While it demonstrated utility in identifying "tasks", and has been extended by Nadjarbashi-Noghani et al. [15], it shows poor performance on sites with framesets due to implicit assumptions about web architecture [3]. Further, the sheer complexity of this strategy and it's developmental focus on *task* over *session* make it unsuitable as a replacement for time-oriented heuristics in practical web analytics of user sessions.

In this work, we will challenge the assertion by prior works that (1) no reasonable cutoff is identifiable from the empirical data and (2) a global inactivity threshold is inappropriate as a session identification strategy. To our knowledge, we are the first to apply a general session identification methodology to a large collection of datasets and to conclude that not only are global inactivity thresholds an appropriate strategy for session identification, but also that, for most user-initiated actions, an inactivity threshold of 1 hour is most appropriate.

3. METHODS

This section is intended to both serve as a description of our methodology as well as to instruct readers on how to apply the same methods to their own datasets. First, we will discuss how we recommend applying our methodology for fitting interactivity clusters to a dataset. Then, we describe the origin of our datasets and the cleanup we performed in order to remove artifacts.

3.1 Fitting inter-activity times

First, we must gather a dataset of user-initiated actions with timestamps of at least *seconds* resolution. We generate inter-activity times on a per-user basis, so a relatively robust user identifier is necessary. While a persistent user identifier such as one associated with a user account is preferable, we have found that in the case of request logs, a fingerprint based on the request's IP and User-agent seems to be sufficient.

Once we have generated per-user inter-activity times, we plot a histogram based on the logarithmically scaled inter-activity time and look for evidence of a valley. Given the observations we have seen (and report in section 4), we expect to see a valley around 1 hour with peaks around 1 minute and 1 day. It is at this time that anomalies in the data should be detected and removed. For example, we found that the time between Wikimedia Mobile Views (described in the next section) had an unreasonably large spike at exactly 18 minutes of inter-activity time caused by a few (likely automated) users and removed their activities from the dataset.

Next, we try to fit a two component gaussian mixture model using expectation maximization [2] and visually inspect the results[4]. When the simple bimodal components did not appear to fit the data appropriately, we explored the addition of components to the mixture model with careful skepticism and repeated visual inspection.

Finally, if we have found what appears to be an appropriate fit, we identify a theoretically optimal inter-activity threshold for identifying sessions by finding the point where inter-activity time is equally likely to be within the gaussians fit with sub-hour means (within-session) and gaussians fit with means beyond an hour (between-session).

3.2 Datasets

To test this approach to session identification, we used a variety of datasets covering multiple sites, user groups, and types of action.

Wikimedia sites. One of the broadest groups of datasets comes from the Wikimedia websites (such as Wikipedia) and covers both page views (read actions) and edits. For the page views, we gather three datasets, each consisting of randomly-sampled page view events from the Wikimedia request logs. These covered app views (page views from the Wikimedia's official mobile app), mobile views (page views to the mobile site) and desktop views (page views to the desktop site). 100,000 IP addresses (or UUIDs, in the case of the mobile app) were selected, and all requests from those IPs/UUIDs for the month of October 2014 were retrieved. For desktop and mobile views, a UUID was produced by hashing the IP address, the User agent, and the accept_language provided with each request. After filtering out known crawlers and automata using tobie's ua-parser[5], we arrived at three page view datasets consisting of 2,376,891(app), 932,754(mobile) and 2,285,521(desktop) pageviews. These came from 100,000, 235,067 or 247,269 UUIDs. We also extracted inter-edit times from the English Wikipedia using the methodology we employed in previous work [9] – randomly selecting 1 million edits from 157,342 registered users.

AOL search. Contrasting with the Wikimedia datasets we used the (now infamous) AOL search logs[6] (aol, search)

[3]Note that this conclusion was reached using the same AOL search dataset that we analyze in this paper

[4]Note that we tried several strategies for statistically confirming the most appropriate fit – of which we found Davies–Bouldin index(DBI) [6] to be most reasonable – but none were as good as a simple visual inspection, so we employ and recommend the same.

[5]`https://github.com/tobie/ua-parser`

[6]These logs are controversial due to their inclusion of search terms containing private information, and there has historically been an ethical debate about their use. We have modified the dataset to strip search terms so that it consists solely of unique IDs and timestamps, as has been used in the past.[13] See `https://en.wikipedia.org/wiki/AOL_search_data_leak` for more discussion.

Table 1: Fit and threshold information for clusters. Note that fits correspond to logarithmically scaled (base 2) seconds between events. For example, $2^{6.7} = 104$ seconds. It's important to report these values in log scale because, while the mean can be re-exponentiated, the standard deviation of log values doesn't make sense that way.

dataset	theshold (min)	short within			within			between			break		
		μ	σ	λ	μ	σ	λ	μ	σ	λ	μ	σ	λ
aol search	115				6.7	2.9	0.70	16.8	2.2	0.30			
cyclo. route	89				5.0	2.5	0.87	18.6	3.1	0.13			
wiki. app	29				5.2	2.3	0.74	15.7	2.5	0.26			
wiki. mobile	50				6.4	2.6	0.65	15.8	2.5	0.35			
wiki. desktop	46				5.5	2.6	0.75	15.7	2.5	0.25			
osm change	101				8.6	2.1	0.68	15.5	2.5	0.30	22.7	2.0	0.02
wiki. edit	80				6.8	2.5	0.83	15.4	2.7	0.16	22.6	1.9	0.01
mov. rating	33	3.0	1.3	0.58	5.2	1.9	0.34	18.0	3.0	0.07			
mov. search	52	4.0	0.8	0.30	5.7	2.5	0.50	17.1	3.1	0.20			
lol game	14				8.3	0.5	0.59	14.1	2.8	0.41			
s. o. answer	91				10.2	1.7	0.30	16.6	2.9	0.63	23.0	1.5	0.06
s. o. quest.	335				12.7	1.7	0.10	18.5	2.1	0.63	22.4	1.7	0.26

consisting of 36,389,567 search actions from 657,427 unique IDs. These actions span from March through May of 2006.

Cyclopath. We also gathered a dataset from Cyclopath, a computational geowiki leveraging cyclists' local knowledge to collabortively build a map [18]. The dataset consists of HTTP requests to the Cyclopath server that are automatically labelled by type. We filtered these requests to include only those that represent a request for a cycle route between two points (cyclopath, route get). This came to 6,123 requests from 2,233 distinct registered users.

Movielens. To explore different types of search and contributory behavor, we also extracted logs from the MovieLens movie recommender system, which has been in use since 1997. As of November 2014 there are 225,543 unique users who have provided more than 21 million movie ratings for more than 25,000 movies. From MovieLens, we extracted two datasets: (movielens, rating) consists of movie rating actions from between 1997 until 5 November 2014, and (movielens, search) consists of search actions from 19 December 2007 to 1 January 2014.

StackOverflow. This popular question/answer system relating to programming and software engineering regularly releases public data dumps. For our analysis, we extracted questions asked and answers posted between July 2008 and September 2013. The question dataset (stack overflow, question) consists of 6,397,301 questions from 1,191,748 distinct users, while the answer dataset (stack overflow, answer) consists of 11,463,991 answers from 790,713 distinct users.

OpenStreetMap (OSM). This open-source alternative mapping service also publishes regular database dumps. We downloaded a full history dump of OSM contributions as of 24 February 2014, restricting this to the North American region as defined by Geofabrik[7], which consists of the United States, Canada and Greenland. OSM groups individual changes to the map into *changesets*[8] when an editor saves their work. We used the timestamp of the last revision in a changeset as the time that the user saved the changeset. The resulting dataset (osm, changeset) contains 13,388,923 million changesets from 46,595 distinct users. We found that more than 75% of changesets occured with less than 5 seconds of inter-activity time and assume that this is only possible in the case of a data import – not human behavior – and filtered them from the dataset.

League of Legends. This widely-played online multiplayer game supports an extension tha logs game data and play times for all users of the extension. Notably, we used this dataset in previous work to study the effect of deviant behaviour on player retention [19]. The dataset consists of roughly 2.5 million unique players participating in almost 166 million games. We extracted the time between when a user finished a game and started playing the next game as an inter-activity time (lol, game). Though not all games were captured in the dataset provided via this extension (see [19] for more details), missing data is believed to be most prevalent around newer players with less consistent play habits.

Taken together, these datasets represent seven different systems and include different interaction mechanisms (mobile apps, mobile devices, desktop devices and a video game interface), and different classes of interaction (web search & route finding, contributions to collaboratively edited artifacts, page reads, and games played).

4. RESULTS & DISCUSSION

In this section, we present and discuss the result of applying our proposed inactivity threshold identification method to the datasets described in the previous section. We start with datasets that were well fit with two clusters. Then we move to more complicated fits and discuss the implications of additional clusters. Finally, we demonstrate datasets with less suitable fits and discuss what this implies about the nature of participation in these systems. Reference table 1 for fitted values and thresholds.

[7]`http://download.geofabrik.de/north-america.html`
[8]`http://wiki.openstreetmap.org/wiki/API_v0.6#Changesets_2`

4.1 Simple bimodal fits

Most of the datasets of user-initiated inter-activity times that we observed display a simple bimodal distribution when their histograms are plotted on a logarithmically scaled X axis. Figure 1 plots a log inter-activity time histogram overlaid with expectation maximization fits of a mixture of two log-normal cluster components. Notably, the AOL search logs represent one of the most clear fits to this bimodal distribution. This suggests that, counter to Mehrzadi & Feitelson's conclusions [13], there *does* seem to to be a clear location for an inactivity cutoff in this dataset – at approximately one hour.

Figure 1 also demonstrates the striking regularity of inter-activity time clusters between systems. All of the systems presented show a clear fit for a theoretical *within-session* cluster with a mode around one minute and a theoretical *between-session* cluster with a mode at one day. Each fit intersects at approximately one hour – with Wikimedia app views displaying the lowest intersection at 29 minutes while AOL searches display the highest intersect at 115 minutes – nearly two hours. Despite this variance in the intersection points, a visual inspection of the empirical distribution does not suggest that the choice of a one hour cutoff for either of these datasets would be inappropriate. Indeed, many of the *between-session* clusters appear to be left shifted due to a lack of longitudinal data, and it is only in these cases that the intersection falls below the one hour mark.

Also of note in these results is the spike of probability of a 24 hour inter-activity time for all but the cyclopath dataset. This suggests that, for reading Wikimedia sites and searching in AOL, there is a strong tendency to return on a daily basis. The curious lack of such a day-spike for cyclopath route searches could be explained by the type of usage the site sees. Bicycle route searching may be less of a daily information need than web search and Wikimedia's reference content.

4.2 Fits with extended breaks

In some cases, we found that the data were fit better by adding a third component to the mixture model that represents very low frequency events. Figure 2 shows the fits for the inter-activity time between OpenStreetMap's changesets and English Wikipedia edits. Note that, like the bimodal fits above, we again see modes for the *within-session* cluster around one minute and modes for the *between-session* cluster around one day. However, we found that we could more cleanly fit these datasets with an additional cluster with a mode of around 2.5 months.

As we noted in our past work [9], we believe that this low frequency cluster represents an extended break from contributing that corresponds to a life event – like getting married, buying a house, going to school or getting a job. Wikipedia editors refer to this phenomena in volunteer participation as a "wikibreak"[9]. We suspect that the reason for the tiny scale of this cluster is two-fold: (1) contributors who work on Wikipedia or OpenStreetMap for long enough to take an extended break are rare compared to the rate of higher frequency activity and (2) breaks at the scale of 2-3 months often result in total abandonment of participation in the project.

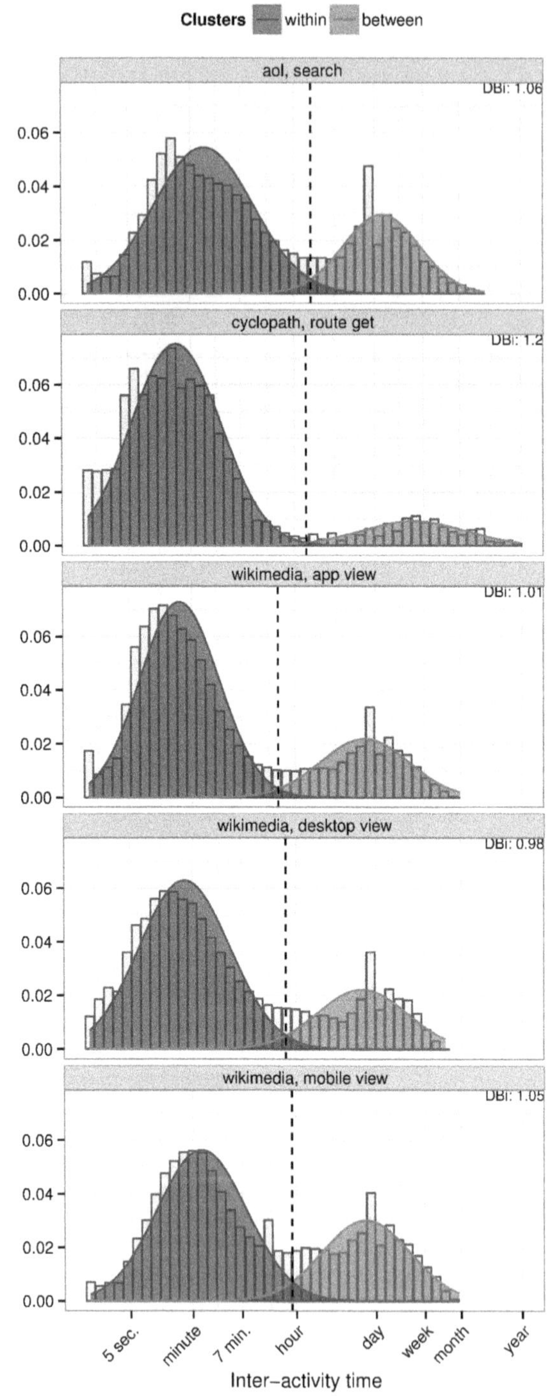

Figure 1: Bimodal clusters. Empirical inter-activity density (bars) and fitted mixture models of gaussians are plotted for datasets where two clusters appeared to sufficiently explain the observed data.

[9]https://en.wikipedia.org/wiki/Wikipedia:Wikibreak

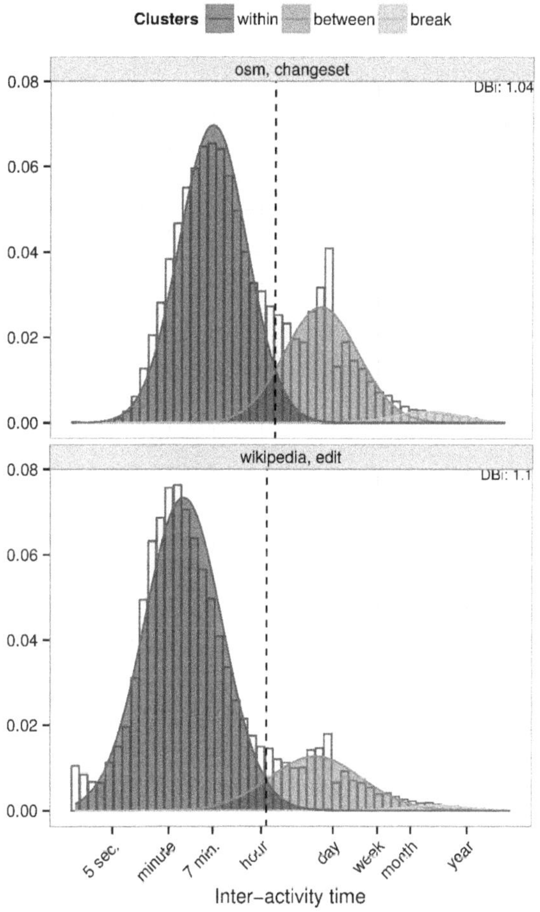

Figure 2: Trimodal clusters. Empirical inter-activity density (bars) and fitted mixture models of gaussians are plotted for datasets where an additional, "break" cluster was needed to fit the data.

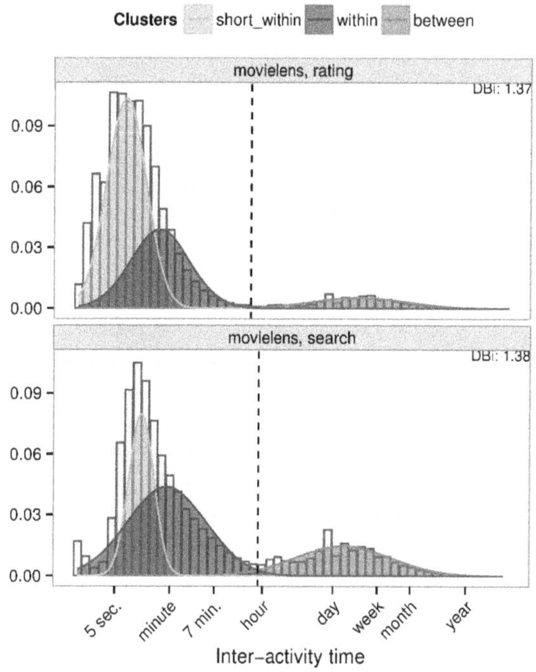

Figure 3: High frequency activity clusters. Empirical inter-activity density (bars) and fitted mixture models of gaussians are plotted for datasets where an additional, high-frequency inter-activity cluster was needed to fit the data.

4.3 Fits with a high frequency component

When observing the distribution of inter-activity times for ratings and searches in Movielens, we found that both these events occurred with higher frequency than the other datasets. This made us suspect that there could be an additional cluster component at a high frequency time interval. Figure 3 shows how the two datasets lent themselves to this additional "short within" component. Like in previous mixture models, we see a within-session cluster with a mode around one minute and a between-session cluster with a mode around one day. However, in these datasets we also observed a pattern in inter-activity times that suggested a faster component with a mode around 15 seconds.

Given that this component occurs at shorter intervals than the within-session component, we assume that it also represents within-session activity. In the case of rating, this high frequency component could represent the rapid rating behavior that the MovieLens interface affords – a user can rate several movies from a list without leaving a page. However, we are less sure on how to explain the high frequency component of MovieLens searches. It could be that, unlike when performing a web search (AOL) or reading encyclopic content (Wikimedia), users' movie searches are more likely to benefit from more rapid iteration.

4.4 Unusual fits

While the fits described so far follow a clear pattern with somewhat minor nuance as to the nature of the gaussian fitting strategy, other datasets did not seem to fit at all. This

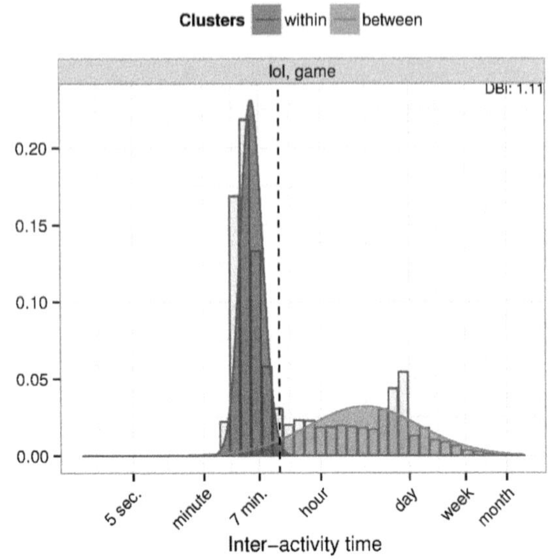

Figure 4: Inter-game clusters. Empirical inter-activity density (bars) and fitted mixture models of gaussians are plotted for time between League of Legends games.

suggest that our strategy for identifying session thresholds is not universally suitable for all user-intiated log events.

League of Legends. Figure 4 shows the two cluster fit for League of Legends game playing. Here, we see a very high density component with a mode around five minutes and a very wide component with a mode around five hours. The intersection of these components place the threshold at approximately 14 minutes. It is important to note that the tightness of the dense component may be an artifact of the way that inter-game times differ from the inter-activity times observed in the other datasets. In the case of this dataset, only the time between games is accounted for – the time between the end of one game and the beginning of the next.

There also may be constraints inherent to the system that limit the potential time spans in which a user could possibly act. For example, League of Legends employs a queuing mechanism for matching teammates with opponents that takes approximately 5 minutes to complete most of the time. Our own experience with the game suggests that many users will often finish one game and immediately get into the queue for another. It is likely that these system limitations are the reason for infrequent between-game times under 1 minute. It seems clear from this result that understanding a system's limitations on user behavior is important when interpreting cluster fit.

Stack overflow. Unlike the other datasets observed, the time between Stack Overflow posts does not suggest a clear valley from which to draw intuition about where to draw a session cutoff. Figure 5 shows the (non-convergent) fits of question asking and answering activities. In this case, there is a dramatic reduction in the scale of the higher frequency time components and what appears to be a shift of the within-session component to the right.

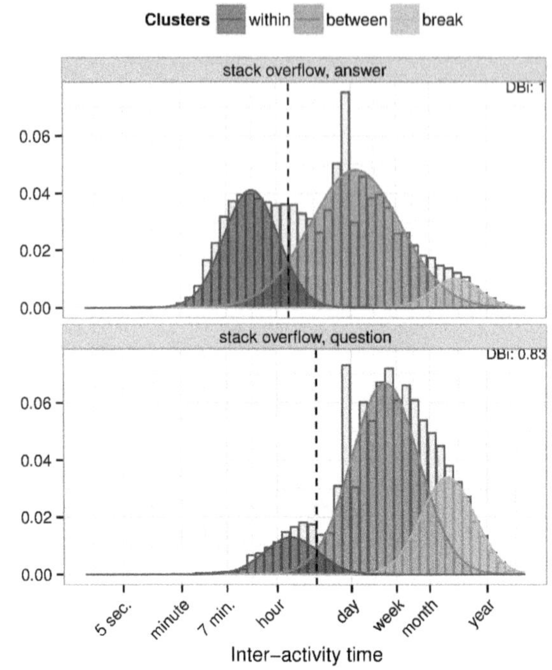

Figure 5: Low frequency clusters. Empirical inter-activity density (bars) and (non-convergent) fitted mixture models of gaussians are plotted for time between posts on Stack Overflow.

If we are to interpret the fit of these clusters as meaningful, the right shift of the within-session component could be due to the time needed to produce a high quality question or answer. Stack Overflow's incentive structure is designed to encourage high quality posts. High quality posts are more likely to be reviewed positively by other users, and a user's score within Stack Overflow is largely dependent on how other users rate the quality of their posts[10]. It seems likely that producing a high quality post would take a substantial amount of time and that this time investment would make it difficult to complete posts with a high enough frequency to produce a short inter-activity time component like we saw in other systems. In this case, it seems that either our strategy for identifying a suitable inactivity threshold is insufficient or that Stack Overflow users rarely post more than one question or answer within an *activity session*.

5. IMPLICATIONS & FUTURE WORK

In this paper, we have challenged previous literature that suggests no apparent global inactivity threshold exists for identifying user sessions from logs. From our results, we propose a simple, yet apparently robust, rule of thumb and a methodology for checking this rule in other datasets. The rule of thumb is easy to apply; our analysis suggests that setting an inactivity threshold to demarcate the end of a session at *one hour* will be appropropriate for most kinds of activity log analysis.

[10] `http://meta.stackexchange.com/help/whats-reputation`

We suspect that this strategy will be robust to new datasets since (1) it is grounded in empirical observations of a natural valley in activity times that corresponds to our intuitions about users' activities and (2) it holds constant across a wide range of systems and activity types. Even when our threshold detection strategy deviated from one hour, the devations were relatively small given the scale of activities, and in some cases, this deviation could be explained by limitations in the data used to fit our models. However, we still advise that any new application of session identification using an hour as an inactivity threshold is preceeded by a plot of a histograph of log-scaled inter-activity times and visual inspection for a natural valley between 1 minute and 1 day.

These results and our recommendations stand in the face of a long and nuanced discussion of the nature of user sessions as can be extracted from logged interactions with a computer system. We place our criticisms of previous work into two categories: (1) previous empirical work did not attempt to look for log-normally distributed patterns and therefore concluded that no obvious separation between within- and between-session inter-activity times exists[13][4] and (2) other work exploring *task driven* behavior conflates "task" with "session". We challenge (1) on the basis of the clear trends represented in the results of this work and (2) by drawing a distinction between goal-directed tasks and activity sessions which often represent a collection of heterogenious goal-directed tasks.

Further, given the strong regularities we see between different types of human-computer interactions, our results suggest something more fundimental about human activity itself. As discussed in section 2.1, Activity Theory(AT) conceptualizes human consciousness as a sequence of *activitie sessions* which represent a heirarchical relationship with *actions* and *operations*. We suspect that the fact that *operations* and *actions* must be performed in a sequence explains the temporal rhythm we observe. While it's hard to say conclusively, we suspect that the "short_within" clusters we observe represent *operation*-level events, the "within" clusters represent *action*-level events, and the "between" clusters represent *activity*-level events.

If this application of AT to the observed patterns is accurate, this could have substantial implications for the design of systems. System designers may be able to take advantage of the regularities observed by constructing systems that afford operations, actions and activity sessions at timescales that humans will find natural. Our analysis suggests that operations should exist at the timescale of about 5-20 seconds, actions should be completable at a timescale of 1-7 minutes and activities should be supported at daily to weekly time intervals. We suspect that systems that do not allow users to work at these time scales may be frustrating or may otherwise limit the ability of their users to function at full capacity.

These ruminations about human behavior and its manifestation in well designed systems are only speculation at this point. New work will need to be done to explore whether our predictions hold and whether limiting or enabling certain types of activity rhythms substantially affects user experience or performance.

6. ACKNOWLEDGMENTS

We thank Stuart Geiger for his involvement in our previous work and for the inspiration he provided toward pushing for measurements that more accurately represent human activity. This work has been funded in part by the National Science Foundation (grants 0808692, 0964695, 0968483, 1017697, 1111201, 1218826, 1319382). We are grateful to Dror Feitelson for agreeing to share the AOL search dataset with us. Individual authors would also like to thank Katie Horn and Margret Wander for their feedback and inspiration. Our data[11] and source code[12] are openly available.

7. REFERENCES

[1] A.-L. Barabasi. The origin of bursts and heavy tails in human dynamics. *Nature*, 435(7039):207–211, 2005.

[2] T. Benaglia, D. Chauveau, D. R. Hunter, D. S. Young, et al. mixtools: An r package for analyzing finite mixture models. *Journal of Statistical Software*, 32(6):1–29, 2009.

[3] B. Berendt, B. Mobasher, M. Nakagawa, and M. Spiliopoulou. The impact of site structure and user environment on session reconstruction in web usage analysis. In *WEBKDD 2002-Mining Web Data for Discovering Usage Patterns and Profiles*, pages 159–179. Springer, 2003.

[4] L. D. Catledge and J. E. Pitkow. Characterizing browsing strategies in the world-wide web. *Computer Networks and ISDN systems*, 27(6):1065–1073, 1995.

[5] R. Cooley, B. Mobasher, and J. Srivastava. Data preparation for mining world wide web browsing patterns. *Knowledge and information systems*, 1(1):5–32, 1999.

[6] D. L. Davies and D. W. Bouldin. A cluster separation measure. *Pattern Analysis and Machine Intelligence, IEEE Transactions on*, (2):224–227, 1979.

[7] D. Donato, F. Bonchi, T. Chi, and Y. Maarek. Do you want to take notes?: identifying research missions in yahoo! search pad. In *Proceedings of the 19th international conference on World wide web*, pages 321–330. ACM, 2010.

[8] C. Eickhoff, J. Teevan, R. White, and S. Dumais. Lessons from the journey: a query log analysis of within-session learning. In *Proceedings of the 7th ACM international conference on Web search and data mining*, pages 223–232. ACM, 2014.

[9] R. S. Geiger and A. Halfaker. Using edit sessions to measure participation in wikipedia. In *Proceedings of the 2013 conference on Computer supported cooperative work*, pages 861–870. ACM, 2013.

[10] S. Gomory, R. Hoch, J. Lee, M. Podlaseck, and E. Schonberg. Analysis and visualization of metrics for online merchandizing. In *Proceedings of WEBKDD'99*, 1999.

[11] K. Goševa-Popstojanova, A. D. Singh, S. Mazimdar, and F. Li. Empirical characterization of session–based workload and reliability for web servers. *Empirical Software Engineering*, 11(1):71–117, 2006.

[12] R. Jones and K. L. Klinkner. Beyond the session timeout: automatic hierarchical segmentation of search topics in query logs. In *Proceedings of the 17th ACM conference on Information and knowledge management*, pages 699–708. ACM, 2008.

[11] `http://dx.doi.org/10.6084/m9.figshare.1291033`

[12] `https://github.com/halfak/Activity-sessions-research`

[13] D. Mehrzadi and D. G. Feitelson. On extracting session data from activity logs. In *Proceedings of the 5th Annual International Systems and Storage Conference*, SYSTOR '12, pages 3:1–3:7, New York, NY, USA, 2012. ACM.

[14] A. L. Montgomery and C. Faloutsos. Identifying web browsing trends and patterns. *Computer*, 34(7):94–95, 2001.

[15] M. Nadjarbashi-Noghani and A. A. Ghorbani. Improving the referrer-based web log session reconstruction. In *Communication Networks and Services Research, 2004. Proceedings. Second Annual Conference on*, pages 286–292. IEEE, 2004.

[16] B. A. Nardi. *Context and consciousness: activity theory and human-computer interaction.* Mit Press, 1996.

[17] J. L. Ortega and I. Aguillo. Differences between web sessions according to the origin of their visits. *Journal of Informetrics*, 4(3):331–337, 2010.

[18] R. Priedhorsky and L. Terveen. The computational geowiki: what, why, and how. In *Proceedings of the 2008 ACM conference on Computer supported cooperative work*, pages 267–276. ACM, 2008.

[19] K. B. Shores, Y. He, K. L. Swanenburg, R. Kraut, and J. Riedl. The identification of deviance and its impact on retention in a multiplayer game. In *Proceedings of the 17th ACM conference on Computer supported cooperative work & social computing*, pages 1356–1365. ACM, 2014.

[20] M. Spiliopoulou, B. Mobasher, B. Berendt, and M. Nakagawa. A framework for the evaluation of session reconstruction heuristics in web-usage analysis. *Informs journal on computing*, 15(2):171–190, 2003.

[21] W. W. W. C. (W3C). Web characterization terminology & definitions sheet, May 1999.

[22] R. W. White and J. Huang. Assessing the scenic route: measuring the value of search trails in web logs. In *Proceedings of the 33rd international ACM SIGIR conference on Research and development in information retrieval*, pages 587–594. ACM, 2010.

[23] Y. Wu, C. Zhou, J. Xiao, J. Kurths, and H. J. Schellnhuber. Evidence for a bimodal distribution in human communication. *Proceedings of the national academy of sciences*, 107(44):18803–18808, 2010.

Incentivizing High Quality Crowdwork

Chien-Ju Ho*
University of California, Los Angeles
cjho@ucla.edu

Aleksandrs Slivkins
Microsoft Research
slivkins@microsoft.com

Siddharth Suri
Microsoft Research
suri@microsoft.com

Jennifer Wortman Vaughan
Microsoft Research
jenn@microsoft.com

ABSTRACT

We study the causal effects of financial incentives on the quality of crowdwork. We focus on *performance-based payments* (PBPs), bonus payments awarded to workers for producing high quality work. We design and run randomized behavioral experiments on the popular crowdsourcing platform Amazon Mechanical Turk with the goal of understanding *when*, *where*, and *why* PBPs help, identifying properties of the payment, payment structure, and the task itself that make them most effective. We provide examples of tasks for which PBPs do improve quality. For such tasks, the effectiveness of PBPs is not too sensitive to the threshold for quality required to receive the bonus, while the magnitude of the bonus must be large enough to make the reward salient. We also present examples of tasks for which PBPs do not improve quality. Our results suggest that for PBPs to improve quality, the task must be *effort-responsive*: the task must allow workers to produce higher quality work by exerting more effort. We also give a simple method to determine if a task is effort-responsive *a priori*. Furthermore, our experiments suggest that all payments on Mechanical Turk are, to some degree, *implicitly* performance-based in that workers believe their work may be rejected if their performance is sufficiently poor. Finally, we propose a new model of worker behavior that extends the standard principal-agent model from economics to include a worker's subjective beliefs about his likelihood of being paid, and show that the predictions of this model are in line with our experimental findings. This model may be useful as a foundation for theoretical studies of incentives in crowdsourcing markets.

Categories and Subject Descriptors

J.4 [**Social and Behavioral Sciences**]: Economics

*Much of this research was conducted while Ho was visiting Microsoft Research.

WWW 2015, May 18–22, 2015, Florence, Italy.
ACM 978-1-4503-3469-3/15/05.
http://dx.doi.org/10.1145/2736277.2741102.

General Terms

Economics, Experimentation

Keywords

Crowdsourcing; Performance-Based Payments; Incentives

1. INTRODUCTION

Crowdsourcing markets are platforms on which workers around the world perform tasks for pay. In a crowdsourcing market like Amazon Mechanical Turk, requesters post tasks along with the amount of money that they are willing to pay workers for their task's completion. Workers can then browse the available tasks and choose tasks to work on.

Crowdsourcing markets are used to conduct user studies [22], run behavioral experiments [18, 28], collect data [17, 35], test or even build business applications [1, 31], and more. While these markets are effective at recruiting diverse labor pools, the quality of work produced varies widely across tasks and workers. The prevalence of low quality crowdwork has inspired a growing literature on techniques to boost accuracy, for example, by using redundant assignments for labeling tasks [15, 19, 21, 26, 34], smartly assigning tasks to workers [14, 15], introducing social incentives [30, 33], or altering financial incentives [4, 10, 12, 29, 30, 33, 36, 37]. These solutions have had mixed success, and how to improve the quality of work in general is still not well understood.

In this paper, we study the use of financial incentives to encourage high quality crowdwork on Amazon Mechanical Turk. In particular, we focus on the use of *performance-based payments* (PBPs), bonus payments awarded to workers for producing high quality work. Previous empirical studies of performance-based payments in crowdsourcing markets have produced mixed and somewhat contradictory recommendations. Harris [12] and Yin et al. [37] suggested that PBPs can improve work quality, while Shaw et al. [33] found no improvement and Yin et al. [36] found no difference in quality when varying bonus size.

Our results explain these disparities in prior work. Furthermore, we show how to generalize previous findings beyond the particular tasks that were studied. We design and run experiments with the goal of understanding not just whether PBPs improve work quality for a specific task or bonus size, but *when*, *why*, and *where* they improve work quality. We identify properties of the payment, payment structure, and the task itself that make PBPs effective.

In our experiments, we first identified a task (proofreading an article) for which PBPs improve workers' performance. We tested the robustness of this finding by varying the payment structure and amount. We found that using PBPs with a wide range of quality thresholds improved work quality provided the bonus awarded for exceeding the threshold was sufficiently high. We also found that even when standard, unconditional payments are used and no explicit acceptance criteria is specified, workers may behave as if the payments are *implicitly* performance-based since they believe their work may be rejected if its quality is sufficiently low.

We examined potential reasons why PBPs improve quality. We found that simply increasing the amount of the base payment without offering any bonus significantly improved quality, contradicting several previous studies [2, 4, 10, 29, 30]. However, PBPs led to improved quality and lower cost compared to a guaranteed payment of the same amount. We also found that whether the opportunity to receive a bonus or higher base payment is revealed before or after the task is accepted does not make a difference in the quality of crowdwork, ruling out the possibility that the increased quality we observed was due (at least in part) to the reciprocity caused by workers' joy at receiving an unexpected bonus, as discussed by Gilchrist et al. [10].

Finally, we investigated which properties of a particular *task* allow PBPs to have an effect. We examined the conjecture that PBPs are more likely to improve quality on *effort-responsive* tasks, tasks for which workers can produce higher quality work by exerting additional effort. We ran experiments on four different tasks. By taking the amount of time workers spent on the task as the proxy measure for their effort, we found that additional effort was correlated with improved quality for the tasks for which PBPs helped, but not for the tasks for which PBPs did not help. This observation yields a simple method for requesters to determine whether or not a given task is likely to benefit from PBPs.

Based on our experimental results, we propose a simple theoretical model of worker behavior. The model is a variant of the standard principal-agent model from economics that additionally incorporates workers' subjective beliefs about the quality of work required to be paid. We show that this model can be used to explain our key empirical observations which cannot be explained using the principal-agent model alone. This model may be useful as a more realistic foundation for future theoretical work on crowdsourcing markets.

Related Work. Performance-based payments have been studied extensively outside of crowdsourcing markets. Lazear [24] conducted a highly influential analysis of observational data from an autoglass company that switched from paying workers a fixed hourly rate to paying workers based on the number of units installed, and showed that workers' performance significantly improved when payments were contingent on work done. As another example, Gneezy and Rustichini [11] gave college students fifty questions from IQ tests to answer and found that their performance increased when they received a bonus for answering questions correctly as long as the bonus was sufficiently high. On the other hand, when the bonus payment was very small, quality decreased compared with not offering a bonus at all. The psychology literature suggests that this is perhaps due to a decrease in workers' intrinsic motivation (enjoyment, responsibility, pride) for performing well, though this theory is not universally accepted [6, 8, 9].

Camerer and Hogarth [5] performed a meta-analysis of 74 papers examining the effect of using payments contingent on performance in lab experiments. They showed that using payments contingent on performance improved the average performance of subjects for tasks in which increased effort leads to improved performance, such as memory or recall tasks, clerical tasks such as coding words or building things, and problem-solving tasks. Similar meta-analyses were performed by Jenkins Jr. et al. [20], Bonner et al. [3], and Hertwig and Ortmann [13]. We build on and extend this work by showing that PBPs have a causal impact on work quality in a field setting, specifically, a crowdsourcing environment in which eliciting high quality work is a main concern for requesters. Moreover, we give evidence to support the conjecture of Camerer and Hogarth [5] that PBPs work in tasks that are effort-responsive.

The results of studies on performance-based payments in crowdsourcing markets have been mixed and sometimes discouraging. On the positive side, in an early workshop paper, Harris [12] showed that when asking workers to evaluate the relevance of resumes, PBPs increased both performance and the time workers spent on the task. In very recent work, Yin et al. [37] studied a setting in which workers switched back and forth between two types of tasks, and showed that PBPs improved performance, especially when used immediately after a task switch.

On the negative side, Shaw et al. [33] compared fourteen different incentive schemes, including four using PBPs,[1] and saw little variation in their effects on quality of work. However, the bonuses offered were extremely small, only 10% ($0.03) on base payments of $0.30. One might hypothesize that the lack of effect stems from decreased intrinsic motivation as in Gneezy and Rustichini [11], or that obtaining the small bonus is simply not worth the costly additional effort that would be required. More recently, Yin et al. [36] studied the effect of varying the bonus size of PBPs and found that the size of the bonus did not impact the quality of work. In their case, all bonuses offered were large compared with the base payment ($0.04, $0.08, $0.16, or $0.32 on a base payment of $0.01 per task), so it is possible that even their smallest bonus was large enough to elicit the workers' maximum effort; since Yin et al. did not include a treatment without PBPs, there is no way to know whether PBPs boosted quality compared with offering base payments alone. In Section 4, we give a unifying explanation for these results. We show small bonuses in a PBP result in little to no effect on work quality, and that it can be hard to detect the effect between two large PBP bonuses. However, the overall trend is that using PBPs with sufficiently high bonuses yields better quality work.

Several additional studies have examined financial incentives in crowdsourcing markets. Horton and Chilton [17] empirically estimated workers' reservation wages and found

[1]The differences in these four treatments were whether payments were described in terms of rewards for high quality or punishments for low quality, and whether quality was measured objectively or in terms of agreement with other workers' responses. Of these, the only treatment that resulted in performance statistically significantly different than the control was punishing workers when their responses did not agree with others.

that many workers aim to hit payment targets (such as multiples of $0.05). Mason and Watts [29] found that paying workers more increased the number of tasks workers chose to complete, but did not increase performance on each task. That increased pay did not increase performance was observed by other authors as well [4, 10, 25, 30]. In this paper, we found that paying workers more can actually increase their performance for some types of tasks. This disparity can be explained by considering workers' subjective beliefs on how much work they must do to get their work accepted. In prior work, workers either already performed well even with low pay since the tasks were easy or were given additional instructions which could have primed their subjective beliefs. In our experiments, workers are uncertain about how much work they should do to get paid. Therefore, they are willing to produce higher quality work to increase their chance of having their work accepted when the payments are higher.

Gilchrist et al. [10] showed that the manner in which the payment is presented can influence quality. In particular, they found that on oDesk, a crowdsourcing market for larger tasks, initially telling workers they would receive $3 per hour and increasing this payment to $4 after the job was accepted led to higher performance than paying either $3 or $4 per hour without the surprise. We show in Section 5 that this result did not translate to the Mechanical Turk setting.

Ho et al. [16] studied the algorithmic problem of adaptively optimizing PBPs in crowdsourcing markets, modeling the problem as a dynamic variant of the standard principal-agent model from contract theory. Their model assumed that each worker chooses how much effort to exert in order to maximize his expected utility, which is simply his expected payment minus the cost of his effort. In Section 7, we propose a variant of this worker model that is in line with our experimental observations. The results of Ho et al. [16] still apply when our worker model is used in place of theirs.

2. PRELIMINARIES

Before describing our experiments, we briefly describe the setting in which they were conducted. All of our experiments were run on Amazon Mechanical Turk[2] (henceforth MTurk), one of the most popular crowdsourcing platforms. On MTurk, requesters post tasks (HITs) for workers to complete. When a worker browses a task, he sees a description of the work to be done along with the amount of money that the requester has offered as a base payment. A worker can then choose whether to accept the task. After the worker completes the chosen task, the requester may evaluate the worker's submission and choose to either approve or reject the work. Each worker has an approval rating which is simply the fraction of HITs he has submitted that have been accepted. If the work is rejected, the worker is not paid and his approval rating, which serves as a *de facto* reputation score, suffers. If the work is accepted, the worker receives the base payment for the task and his approval rating increases. Requesters also decide at this time whether or not to award a bonus payment on top of the base, and how much of a bonus to award. The possibility of such a bonus may or may not be included in the task description.

HITs can also have qualifications associated with them. Only those workers who have the appropriate qualifications can do a HIT. These qualifications are specified by the requester. For example, we used a geographic qualification to restrict our tasks to workers located in the United States, and used qualifications to disallow workers from completing the same type of task more than once. We also used qualifications for random assignment in one of our experiments; how and why we did this is described in Section 5.

Our experiments focus on the use of threshold-based PBPs. A threshold-based PBP is specified by a base payment, a bonus payment, and a threshold. The base payment specifies the amount of money a worker receives from completing the task; this is fixed at $0.50 USD in all of our experiments.[3] The bonus payment specifies the amount the worker can potentially receive as a bonus. The threshold determines what the worker must do in order to obtain the bonus.

All of the experiments in this paper were approved by the Microsoft Research IRB.

3. DOES PBP WORK?

Our first experiment was designed with two goals in mind. The first was to verify that PBPs can lead to higher quality crowdwork and identify a task for which this happens. The second was to determine if there exists what we call an *implicit PBP effect*: even if the requester offers a guaranteed payment, MTurk workers have subjective beliefs on the quality of work they must produce in order to receive this payment, and therefore behave as if the payments were (implicitly) performance-based. We measure these subjective beliefs by the difference in the quality of crowdwork when base payments are explicitly guaranteed, effectively resetting the workers' subjective beliefs, compared to when base payments are not guaranteed.

3.1 Experiment Design

In this experiment, workers were asked to proofread an article of 500 to 700 words and correct spelling errors. For each article, we randomly inserted 20 typos from a list of common spelling errors. Workers were asked to input the line number of each typo, the misspelled word, and the correct spelling of the word.

This task has two key properties. First, we would expect that workers could produce better work by exerting more effort—the more carefully a worker reads or the more passes a worker takes over the text, the more typos he will find—and that this would open up the possibility of PBPs improving quality. (We study this conjecture in more detail in Section 6.) Second, since we injected the typos into the text, the quality of each worker's output could be measured objectively, though this was not known to the workers.

Before accepting the HIT, each worker saw a preview consisting of the instructions, an example article with typos, and the base payment of $0.50 USD. The preview was the same for all workers. After workers accepted the HIT, they were randomly assigned to different treatments and then shown treatment-specific instructions, when applicable. Our experiment had a 2×3 design, with 2 treatments governing the base payment and 3 treatments governing the bonus payment (if any). We discuss the bonus treatments first:

[2]https://mturk.com

[3]The base payment of $0.50 was chosen so that workers could obtain a $6 hourly rate from the base payment alone with a reasonable amount of effort in each of our tasks.

- *No Bonus:* This is the control group. It had no bonus and no mention of a bonus.
- *Bonus for All:* All workers earned a \$1 bonus after submitting the HIT.
- *PBP:* Workers earned a \$1 bonus if they found 75% of the typos found by the other workers.

The purpose of the control group was to allow us to measure the baseline number of typos workers found. The purpose of the Bonus for All treatment was to test if simply paying more resulted in higher quality work. The purpose of the PBP bonus treatment was to test if specifically incentivizing for quality improved the number of typos found.

As mentioned, we are also interested in whether workers have subjective assumptions on how much effort they must exert to get their work accepted. Workers may be afraid that if they do not find a sufficient number of typos their work will be rejected, resulting in no pay and a negatively affected MTurk reputation. To estimate this, we designed a treatment in which workers were explicitly guaranteed acceptance provided that they completed a very small amount of work. We had two treatments for the base payment:

- *Non-Guaranteed:* There were no extra instructions. This is the control and emulates most MTurk tasks.
- *Guaranteed:* Workers were told they would get paid if they found at least one typo.

The first typo appeared before line 3 in each article. Thus a worker would only have to do a trivial amount of work to ensure they got paid in the guaranteed base treatment.

3.2 Results

The HIT was completed by 1,000 unique workers, who were each assigned uniformly to one of the six treatments. We conducted a chi-squared test to check for significant differences in the number of participants who finished the six treatments and found none ($p = 0.38$). The primary dependent variable (or outcome measure) we were interested in is the number of true typos found. In the analysis we made six comparisons that we spell out below. We performed this analysis using an ANOVA with one-sided, planned comparisons [32] and report p-values that have been corrected for these multiple (six) comparisons. The results of this experiment are shown in Figure 1 and described below.

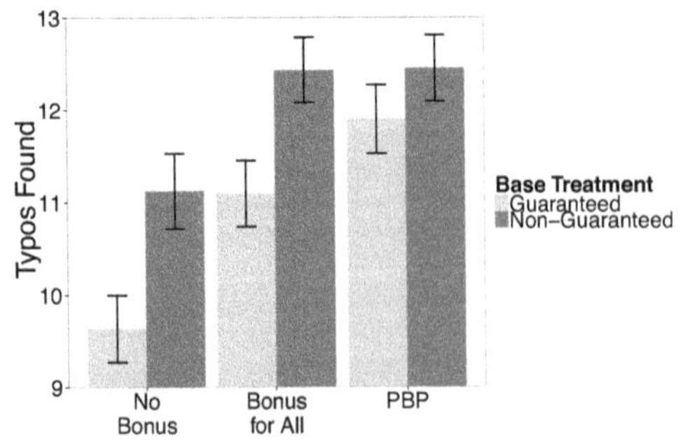

Figure 1: The effect of different payment schemes on work quality in the proofreading task. Error bars indicate the mean ± one standard error.

PBPs improve quality. To determine whether PBPs increase quality for this task, we focus on the non-guaranteed base treatments since almost all HITs on MTurk do not explicitly guarantee any kind of acceptance criteria. Workers in the PBP bonus treatment found on average 1.3 more typos than workers in the No Bonus treatment ($p = 0.042$), showing that PBPs did improve quality for this task.

All payment schemes may be implicitly performance-based. In the No Bonus treatment, the guaranteed base resulted in 1.5 fewer typos found on average compared with the non-guaranteed base ($p = 0.015$). Similarly, in the Bonus for All treatment, the guaranteed base resulted in 1.3 fewer typos found on average ($p = 0.024$). While there may be other explanations, this suggests that workers do have subjective beliefs on the amount of work that needs to be done for their work to be accepted, lending support to our conjecture that payments on MTurk are already implicitly performance-based. We discuss this further in Section 7.

In the PBP bonus treatment, we did not see a significantly different effect between the guaranteed base and non-guaranteed base treatments. We offer two related explanations of this finding. First, the only way to grant a bonus using the MTurk API is to first accept the work. This means that in the PBP bonus treatment, workers would likely believe that finding 75% of typos would almost certainly result in their work being accepted, already altering their subjective beliefs. Second, the treatment might have made this 75% threshold more salient to the workers. This gave a clear goal for the workers to strive for.

Simply paying more improves quality. Focusing again on the non-guaranteed base treatment, workers in the Bonus for All treatment found on average 1.3 more typos than workers in the No Bonus treatment ($p = 0.036$). Thus offering an unconditional bonus—which is essentially just paying more—increased quality.

This finding is perhaps surprising since it appears to contradict the results of prior work [4, 29, 30]. We give two potential explanations. First, since the announcement of the bonus came after workers accepted the HIT, the workers may be exhibiting reciprocity by doing higher quality work [10], rewarding the requester for this pleasant surprise. We further test and refute this hypothesis in Section 5. Second, this could be explained by the implicit PBP effect described above. That is, workers might have subjective beliefs about the number of typos they must find to get paid. If we increase the bonus payment, workers might be willing to put in more effort to increase their probability of earning this higher amount.

This observation is not inconsistent with previous work. In most prior work, either easy tasks were chosen which might cause workers to perform well even for low pay [4, 30] or additional instructions or tutorials were provided which may have primed workers' subjective beliefs [29].

PBPs can save money compared with high unconditional payments. In the non-guaranteed base treatment, the difference in the number of typos found in the PBP and Bonus for All treatments is not significant. Both resulted in higher quality work than the control. However, we spent much less money on the PBP treatment. We paid each worker \$1.50 in the Bonus for All treatment, while we paid each worker only \$0.97 on average in the PBP treatment with non-guaranteed base and \$0.96 on average in the PBP treatment with guaranteed base. Therefore, it may still be advantageous for requesters to offer PBPs even if they could achieve the same quality work with unconditional payments.

4. WHEN DOES PBP WORK?

Having established that PBPs can improve quality for the proofreading task, we investigated the effect of varying two parameters of the payment scheme, the bonus threshold and the bonus amount, to better understand when PBPs help.

4.1 Bonus Thresholds: Experiment Design

We first tested the effect of varying the threshold of quality that must be met in order for workers to receive the bonus. We used the same proofreading task described in Section 3.1, with the same base payment of \$0.50 and bonus of \$1. Workers were randomly assigned to treatments in which they were told they could earn the bonus if they found at least 5 typos or at least 25%, 75%, or 100% of the typos found by the other workers. In the control, workers did not receive any bonus or see any mention of a bonus.

4.2 Bonus Thresholds: Results

The results from 585 unique workers are presented in Figure 2. As before, we ran an ANOVA with one-sided, planned comparisons [32] and report p-values that have been corrected for the multiple (five) comparisons we describe below.

PBPs improve quality for a wide range of bonus thresholds. Improvements in quality over the control can be observed in both the 25% and 75% treatments. The 25% treatment resulted in workers finding, on average, 1.1 more typos than the control ($p = 0.082$). Similarly, the 75% treatment resulted in workers finding, on average 1.2 more typos, than the control ($p = 0.049$). We conjecture that setting a threshold anywhere between 25% and 75% would yield similar results, so the improvements from PBPs are not overly sensitive to the threshold. However, the 100% typo condition was neither significantly different than the 75% treatment or control, so our results suggest that if the bonus threshold is set too high, then workers' average performance slightly decreases. This could be due to some workers giving up because they do not believe the bonus is attainable.

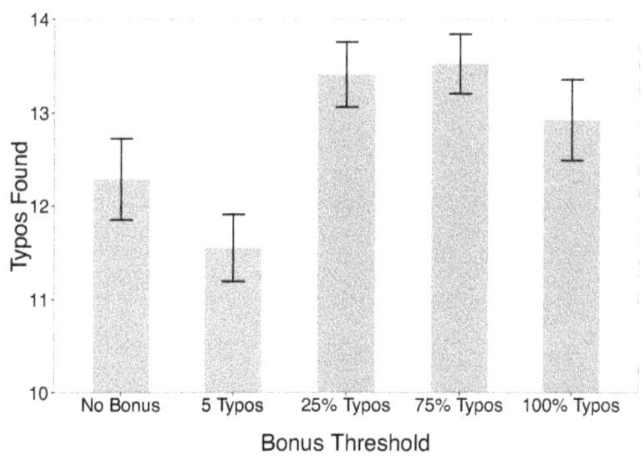

Figure 2: The effect of the bonus threshold on work quality in the proofreading task. Error bars indicate the mean ± one standard error.

Subjective beliefs on the quality thresholds can improve work. Since each article contains 20 typos in total, 25% of the typos found by other workers is at most 5 typos and will be exactly 5 typos if the number of workers is sufficiently large. In this sense, the two thresholds are roughly equivalent. However, workers in the 25% treatment performed much better than workers in the 5 typos treatment. Workers in the 25% treatment found, on average, 1.9 more typos than those in the 5 typo treatment ($p < .001$). An analysis of the line numbers in which typos were found showed that workers in the 5 typo treatment did not stop reading before workers in the 25% treatment; however, there may be a variety of other explanations for this. For example, it is possible that workers in the 25% group had different subjective beliefs and thought that they would need to find more than 5 typos to receive the bonus. After all, workers did not know the total number of typos in the article.

4.3 Bonus Amounts: Experiment Design

We next examined the effect of varying the bonus amount. We used the same proofreading task with a base payment of \$0.50. Workers were assigned to treatments in which they could earn either \$0.05, \$0.50, or \$1 if they found 75% of the typos found by other workers. Once again, workers in the control did not receive or see any mention of a bonus.

As an implementation detail, we note that these experiments were run simultaneously with those described in Section 4.1, allowing us to share two treatments (the control and the \$1 for 75%) and run only seven treatments in total instead of nine. We excluded workers who had already participated in the experiment from Section 3. We collected results from 815 unique workers assigned uniformly to the seven treatments. A chi-squared test showed no significant differences between the number of workers who completed the seven treatments ($p = 0.23$)

4.4 Bonus Amounts: Results

We collected data from 451 unique workers. Figure 3 shows the overall trend: PBPs lead to higher quality work only when the bonus is sufficiently large, but increasing the bonus amount has diminishing returns. Indeed, regressing the number of typos found on the bonus amount shows that an extra \$1 of bonus results in finding 1.4 more typos ($p = 0.002$) on average.

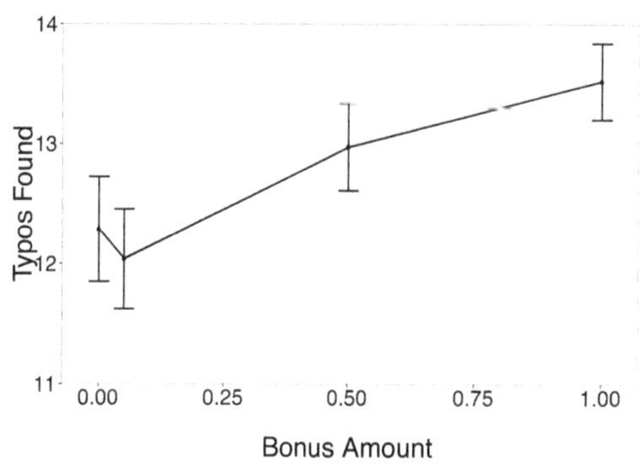

Figure 3: The effect of the bonus amount on work quality in the proofreading task. Error bars indicate the mean ± one standard error.

This may help to explain previous negative results on PBPs in crowdsourcing markets. Shaw et al. [33] reported little or no quality improvement using PBPs compared with fixed payments. However, they offered a bonus payment of only \$0.03, 10% of their \$0.30 base. As we observe from the leftmost two points in Figure 3, PBPs do not improve quality when the bonus is very small. Yin et al. [36] tested PBPs with several bonus sizes and reported that bonus size alone did not significantly impact quality. However, their study did not include a control with fixed payments, and the bonus sizes that they tested were all significantly larger than their base payment (\$0.04, \$0.08, \$0.16, and \$0.32 on a base payment of \$0.01). As we observe from the rightmost two points in Figure 3, increasing the bonus size only leads to minor improvements in quality once the bonus is already sufficiently large. It is only when we view the whole picture that we can see that PBPs do help.

Taken as a whole, the results in this section show that PBPs improve quality for a wide range of possible thresholds, provided that the requester offers a bonus that is high enough to make the extra reward salient.

5. WHY DOES PBP WORK?

There are two primary motivations for our next experiment. First, we wanted to verify that PBPs are useful in other tasks beyond finding typos. Second, we wanted to explore potential reasons why PBPs work. In particular, as pointed out in Section 3.2, simply increasing the amount of the bonus payment led to almost as much of an improvement as using PBPs in the proofreading experiment. While it could be that workers are responding rationally to the provided incentives, it could also be the case that workers are increasing their effort due to a reciprocity effect; workers are pleasantly surprised to discover the opportunity to receive a (performance-based or unconditional) bonus after accepting the HIT, and reward the requester for this kind action by working harder. Indeed, Gilchrist et al. [10] found, in a different crowdsourcing context, that workers who accept a task and then receive an unexpected bonus do higher quality work than workers who are paid the same amount total but are told up front. This experiment is designed to test whether this "unexpected bonus effect," is the (partial) cause of the observed increases in performance using PBPs.

5.1 Experiment Design

In this task, workers were shown twenty pairs of images. Ten of the pairs were identical images, while the other ten pairs contained minor differences. Workers were asked to specify whether each pair was identical or not, and were not told how many pairs of images were identical in advance. Again, this task has two key properties we desire. First, we speculated that workers would be more likely to spot the differences between images if they spent more time and effort looking. Second, we can objectively measure the quality of workers' output by the number of correctly answered pairs. A similar task was used in experiments by Yin et al. [36].

To test our research questions, we wished to vary the bonus amount and bonus rules as well as the amount of the base payment. Obviously, if we launched two HITs that differed only in the base payment amount, the majority of workers would choose the HIT with the higher base payment, resulting in selection bias. To avoid this, we used the following method for randomly assigning treatments. We first posted a qualification HIT in which workers were paid a small amount (\$0.05) if they agreed to receive notifications about our future tasks. We made it clear that they were under no obligation to do the future tasks. We then randomly assigned the workers who completed this recruitment task to different treatments. For each treatment, we posted a separate HIT. Workers were only qualified to see and do the HIT corresponding to their assigned treatment. Finally, we used the notifyWorkers API call to send notification emails to workers with a link to their assigned HITs (treatments). While others have suggested using qualifications to filter out workers for experiments [7] or recruiting a panel of workers in advance [28], we believe that the approach described here is novel and of independent interest.

We next describe the treatments:

- *Low Base:* The base payment was \$0.50. No opportunity for a bonus was given. This was our control.
- *High Base:* The base payment was \$1.50. No opportunity for a bonus was given.
- *Unexpected Bonus:* The base payment was \$0.50. After accepting the HIT, workers were told they would receive an additional bonus of \$1.
- *PBP:* The base payment was \$0.50. In addition to the base payment, workers could earn a bonus of \$1 if they correctly labeled 80% of the image pairs as identical or not. Workers were informed of the bonus and rules for receiving the bonus before accepting the HIT.

Note that the payment amounts in the High Base and Unexpected Bonus treatments are the same. The difference is only how and when the payments were described.

5.2 Results

We randomly chose 800 workers from the pool that completed the qualification HIT and randomly assigned them to the four treatments, 200 workers per treatment. After assigning qualifications corresponding to each treatment, we posted the HITs for each simultaneously and sent each worker a notification with a link to their treatment's HIT. We conducted a chi-squared test to check for significant differences in the number of participants who finished the four treatments and found none ($p = 0.90$). In the analysis we make six comparisons, described below. We did this analysis using an ANOVA with one-sided, planned comparisons [32] and report p-values that have been corrected for these multiple comparisons. The results are shown in Figure 4.

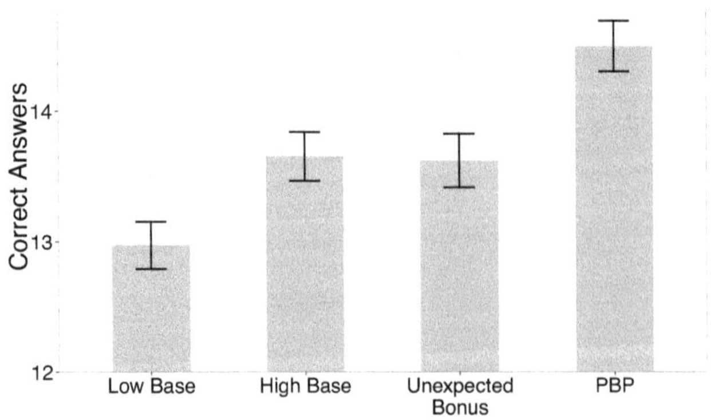

Figure 4: The effect of different payment schemes on work quality in the spot the differences task. Error bars indicate the mean ± one standard error.

Similar to the proofreading experiment described in Section 3, simply paying more resulted in higher quality work. The High Base treatment had a significantly higher number of correct answers than the Low Base treatment ($p = 0.030$). Similarly, the Unexpected Bonus treatment had a significantly higher number of correct answers than the Low Base treatment ($p = 0.047$). Figure 4 shows no significant difference between the High Base and the Unexpected Bonus treatments. This suggests that there was no "unexpected bonus effect" in contrast to Gilchrist et al. [10][4] The absence of any reciprocity effect due to the unexpected bonus suggests that workers were doing better work to increase the probability (according to their prior assumptions) that their work got accepted and thus earn the higher pay.

We also observe that workers in the PBP treatment outperformed workers in all other treatments ($p < 0.005$). This suggests that workers are rational to some degree and are willing to exert more effort to increase their chances of receiving higher payments. Note that in this experiment workers knew *before* they accepted the HIT that they could earn a bonus, in contrast to the experiment described in Section 3 in which workers were informed of the opportunity to earn a bonus only *after* they accepted the HIT. We have therefore shown that PBPs can work whether or not the opportunity for a bonus is unexpected.

6. WHERE DOES PBP WORK?

We have shown that PBPs incentivize higher quality crowdwork on two specific tasks, proofreading and spotting differences in images. It is natural to ask whether our results generalize, and in particular, what properties of a task open up the possibility of performance improvements with PBPs.

Camerer and Hogarth [5] note that in the context of economics lab experiments, performance-based incentives tend to improve quality for *effort-responsive* tasks, tasks for which it is possible to generate higher quality work by exerting additional effort (presumably without requiring *too much* effort). One might ask if the same is true in a crowdsourcing setting. More specifically, we investigate a hypothesis that whether, and to what extent, a task is effort-responsive is an important reason for whether or not PBPs work for this task. We find an empirical correlation between the two, which we interpret as a strong evidence in favor of this hypothesis. Since it is difficult to directly measure how much effort a worker has put into a task, we use the time a worker spent on a HIT as a proxy measure for effort, and examine the relationship between time spent and quality of work.

Figures 5(a) and 5(b) illustrate this correlation for the proofreading and spot-the-difference tasks respectively. Each shows the amount of time that a worker spent on the HIT versus the quality of his work (measured as number of typos found or number of correctly labeled image pairs as before). For the proofreading task, regressing the number of correct typos found on the amount of time a worker spent shows that every minute is correlated with finding another 0.42 typos on average ($p < 0.001$). Similarly, for the spot-the-difference task, regressing the number of pairs correctly identified on the amount of time a worker spent shows that every minute is correlated with another 0.17 correct answers ($p < 0.001$). We see that, in general, workers who spent more time on our tasks generated better quality work. We observe similar trends in all treatments, but include only workers in the control groups in the plots since they are most comparable across tasks. This is evidence that the tasks on which we observed improvements from PBPs are effort-responsive.

To further explore this hypothesis and the generalizability of our results, we examined the effects of PBPs on two additional tasks, handwriting recognition and audio transcription. For consistency with our previous experiments, we maintained a base payment of \$0.50 (adjusting the task lengths to maintain an hourly rate of roughly \$6) and a bonus of \$1 when applicable. Workers were randomly assigned to treatments after accepting the HIT in the same way as in the experiments described in Sections 3 and 4.

6.1 Handwriting Recognition: Design

For the handwriting recognition task, workers were shown two images containing handwritten text and asked to transcribe the text. The images were collected from the IAM Handwriting Database [27]. One contained 89 words and the other 74. As in our other experiments, workers in the control treatment received only the base payment. We also used a PBP treatment in which workers were told that for one of the images, their transcription would be compared against a gold standard solution and they would receive the bonus if they correctly transcribed 90% of the words in the image. They were not told which image would be used to assess their accuracy. This payment rule was used to make the task appear more like a realistic MTurk task.

6.2 Handwriting Recognition: Results

Data was collected from 220 workers. As shown in Figure 5(c), the quality of work produced was not significantly correlated with the time a worker spent on the task. In other words, this task does not appear to be effort-responsive. Moreover, we did not find a significant difference between the accuracy of workers in the control group versus the PBP treatment via a one-sided t-test. We note that one of the two images given to workers was chosen because it was especially difficult for workers in a pilot study. Restricting our analysis to just this image did show a marginal effect, with workers in the control group averaging 92.3% accuracy and workers in the PBP treatment averaging 93.5% ($p = 0.055$). Since PBPs only had a small, marginal effect on even the most difficult handwriting recognition image, we conclude that PBPs only have a small effect on this task in general.

One reason why PBPs did not have a strong effect on quality for this task may be that there was a ceiling effect, as discussed in the context of incentives in lab experiments by Camerer and Hogarth [5]. As Figure 5(c) shows, the average accuracy over the two articles of the workers in the control group was 95.2%, leaving little room for PBPs to have impact. A related explanation is that most of handwritten words in our data sets were trivial to recognize. Over 80% of words were correctly transcribed by over 90% of workers.

It is possible that PBPs would have improved performance if we had chosen a different threshold. However, since the average performance was already very high, there was little room for experimentation. If a better threshold exists, it would be difficult for a requester to identify.

[4]Note that our experimental setting is not the same as theirs. They ran experiments on oDesk for tasks with much longer working hours (3 hours) while our experiment is on MTurk and our tasks only last for on average 8.8 minutes.

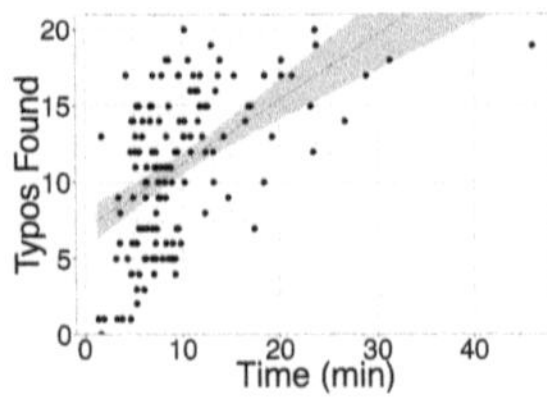

(a) Proofreading

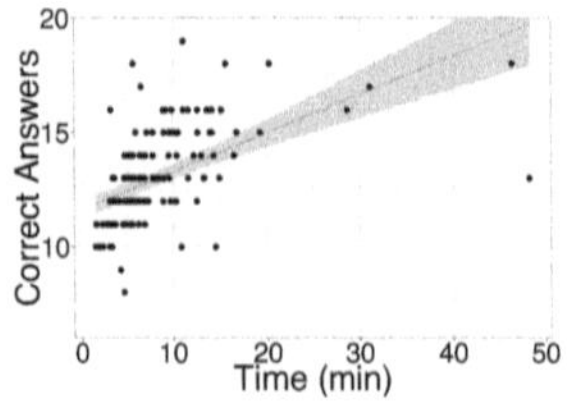

(b) Spot-the-Difference

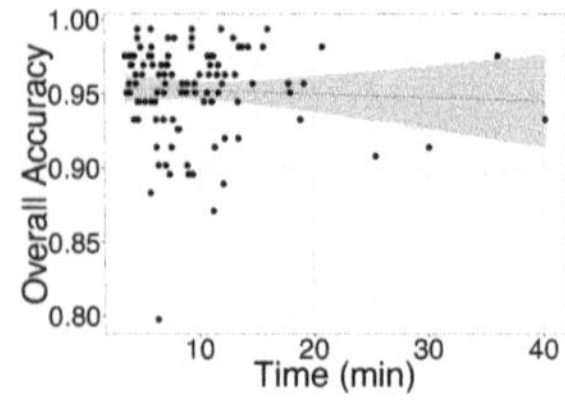

(c) Handwriting Rec.

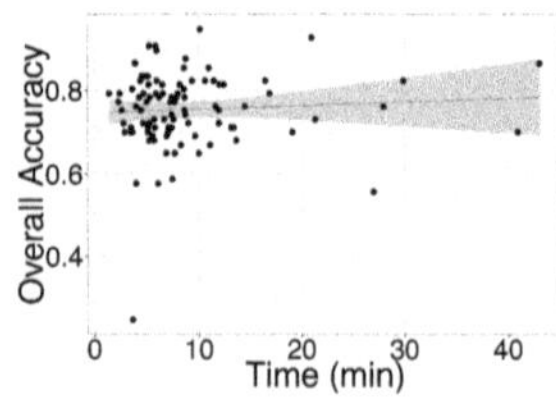

(d) Audio Transcription

Figure 5: Time vs. quality for effort responsive tasks in panels 5(a) and 5(b), and non-effort responsive tasks in panels 5(c) and 5(d). The blue lines indicate the regression line and the shaded areas represent the 95% confidence interval around it. Results are similar when outliers are excluded from the analysis.

6.3 Audio Transcription: Design

For the audio transcription task, workers were asked to transcribe 10 audio clips, each of which contained approximately 5 seconds of speech. The audio clips were collected from VoxForge[5] and we intentionally chose clips from speakers with heavy accents to increase the difficulty of the task and avoid the ceiling effect. Once again workers in the control treatment received only the base payment. We additionally included three PBP treatments with different thresholds of quality required to receive the bonus. In these treatments, workers were told that their answers for 5 of the 10 clips would be compared against gold standard answers, and that they would receive the bonus if they correctly transcribed 80%, 85%, or 90% of the words respectively. These threshold values were chosen based on quality observed in a pilot experiment on this task in order to cover the range of thresholds that we believed would be most likely to lead to quality improvements with PBPs. We note that audio transcription is one of the most common tasks on MTurk.

6.4 Audio Transcription: Results

We collected data from 400 workers. As Figure 5(d) shows, quality and time are not significantly correlated. That is, audio transcription does not appear to be effort-responsive. Furthermore, we did not find a significant difference between any of the three PBP treatments and the control group. Since the average accuracy in the control group was only 75.4%, this cannot be fully explained by a ceiling effect as may have been the case for handwriting recognition. One might ask if there are certain hard words for which PBPs did improve performance. We took a closer look at the data and found that this does not appear to be the case. Of the 97 words included in the 10 clips, workers' combined accuracy was better in the 85% threshold PBP treatment compared with the control on 52 words, and better in the control than the 85% threshold PBP treatment on 44; essentially these differences appear to be mostly due to noise. We observe a similar pattern for the other PBP treatments. Additionally, for more than 80% of the words, the percentage of workers correctly transcribing the word when PBPs were offered is close (within ±5%) to the percentage in the control group. This could suggest that workers' performance is limited by their abilities and cannot be improved through PBPs.

6.5 A Practical Recommendation

While the results in this section are not causal, they are in line with the hypothesis that the extent to which a task is effort-responsive is an important reason for whether or not PBPs help improve quality for this task. This suggests an approach that requesters can use when deciding whether or not to employ PBPs in their own HIT. A requester could run a pilot of their HIT with a small number of workers and a fixed (not performance-based) payment and plot the time that workers spend on the task versus the quality of their work to determine whether and to what extent the task is effort-responsive. A requester may be able to incentivize higher quality using PBPs only if the task is (sufficiently) effort-responsive. In this case, the requester must determine whether the boost in quality is worth the extra cost of PBPs.

[5]http://www.voxforge.org/

7. A THEORY OF WORKER INCENTIVES

The worker model in the well-known *principal-agent* framework [23] assumes that a worker chooses a level of effort or quality to maximize his expected utility, which is simply the expected payment he receives minus the expected cost of doing the work at the chosen effort level. In this section, we show that incorporating the worker's subjective beliefs about how much quality is required to earn the base and bonus payments into the worker model allows us to explain the main observations from our experiments in a parsimonious way. Furthermore, it is not clear how one might capture our experimental results using the traditional worker model *without* incorporating the worker's subjective beliefs. Our model can be used to reason about the possible consequences of using performance-based payments.

We assume that a worker views a task and chooses to produce work at a particular quality level in order to maximize his expected utility, defined as his *perceived* expected payment minus the perceived cost of doing the task at a given quality level. In our model, when workers are offered performance-based payments with base payment p and bonus payment b, the worker's expected utility is

$$U_{\mathtt{pbp}}(q) = p\Pr(\mathtt{base}|q) + b\Pr(\mathtt{bonus}|q) - c(q), \quad (1)$$

where q is the quality level, $\Pr(\mathtt{base}|q)$ and $\Pr(\mathtt{bonus}|q)$ denote the worker's perceived probabilities of receiving the base and bonus payments with work of quality q, and $c(q)$ is the worker's perceived cost of producing quality q. We posit that q comes from a totally ordered set, and assume that $\Pr(\mathtt{base}|q)$ and $\Pr(\mathtt{bonus}|q)$ are non-decreasing in q.

While we typically think of the cost of producing work as positive, capturing the effort the worker must exert to produce work of the chosen quality level, it could in some cases be negative, capturing the subjective intrinsic utility the worker receives from his enjoyment of the task or his satisfaction from a job well done. To allow for such effects, we make no assumptions on the monotonicity of $c(q)$.

We make a minor *consistent tie-breaking* assumption. If multiple quality levels maximize the expected utility for a pair of base and bonus payments, we assume the tie is broken consistently in the sense that the worker chooses the same quality level for any payments leading to this particular tie.

7.1 Consequences of the Worker Model

Given the worker model, we are able to provide a coherent explanation of our key observations, including some that are not explained by the standard principal-agent model. To explain the key observations from our experiments we compare Equation 1, which describes the worker's utility when there are both a base payment and a bonus payment, with the utility of a worker with subjective beliefs under the "standard" payment scheme in which workers are offered a base payment only. The standard payment scheme was used in the control group in our experiments. In this case, the worker's expected utility is simply

$$U_{\mathtt{std}}(q) = p\Pr(\mathtt{base}|q) - c(q). \qquad (2)$$

Let $q_{\mathtt{std}}$ be the quality level chosen by the worker under this utility function, so $q_{\mathtt{std}} \in \arg\max_q U_{\mathtt{std}}(q)$, and $q_{\mathtt{pbp}}$ be the quality chosen under Equation 1, so $q_{\mathtt{pbp}} \in \arg\max_q U_{\mathtt{pbp}}(q)$.

Subjective beliefs about acceptance criteria increase quality. In Section 3, we experimentally showed that the quality of work produced is higher when workers have subjective beliefs about acceptance criteria than when the base payment is explicitly guaranteed. We called this an *implicit PBP*. It is easy to explain in our model.

Consider the standard setting (no PBPs). With a guaranteed base payment, the worker's utility becomes $p - c(q)$. Let q^* be a maximizer of this expression. It follows that q^* is a minimizer of $c(q)$, thus $c(q^*) \leq c(q)$ for all q. For any $q < q^*$, we have $p\Pr(\mathtt{base}|q) \leq p\Pr(\mathtt{base}|q^*)$ given the monotonicity of $\Pr(\mathtt{base}|q)$. Therefore, for any $q < q^*$, $U_{\mathtt{std}}(q) \leq U_{\mathtt{std}}(q^*)$. Given the consistent tie-breaking assumption, the worker will not choose to generate work of quality q if $q < q^*$. Therefore, if $q_{\mathtt{std}}$ is the maximizer of Equation 2 then $q_{\mathtt{std}} \geq q^*$. Thus $q_{\mathtt{std}}$, the optimal quality level with no guaranteed base payment, is greater than or equal to q^*, the optimal quality level with guaranteed base payment, which we observed experimentally in Figure 1. It is possible to strengthen this result to strict inequality ($q_{\mathtt{std}} > q^*$) with a few additional assumptions.[6] Similar arguments can be made for the setting with PBPs.

Higher payments increase quality. The experiments in Sections 3 and 4 demonstrated that increasing the base payment (or the unconditional bonus) can increase quality. This is also easy to explain in our model. Consider increasing the base payment in the standard setting (no PBPs). Let q_δ be the maximizer of $U_\delta(q) = (p+\delta)\Pr(\mathtt{base}|q) - c(q)$, the utility of the worker if the base payment were $p+\delta$ instead of p, where $\delta > 0$. By optimality of $q_{\mathtt{std}}$, for all q,

$$p\Pr(\mathtt{base}|q) - c(q) \leq p\Pr(\mathtt{base}|q_{\mathtt{std}}) - c(q_{\mathtt{std}}).$$

Since $\Pr(\mathtt{base}|q)$ is non-decreasing in q, $q < q_{\mathtt{std}}$ implies $\delta\Pr(\mathtt{base}|q) \leq \delta\Pr(\mathtt{base}|q_{\mathtt{std}})$. Combining the last two inequalities, $U_\delta(q) \leq U_\delta(q_{\mathtt{std}})$ for all $q < q_{\mathtt{std}}$. Therefore, given the consistent tie-breaking assumption, q_δ, the optimal quality level under higher pay, is greater than or equal to $q_{\mathtt{std}}$, the optimal quality level under the standard setting. Again, strict inequality is achievable with the additional assumptions from Footnote 6. Similar arguments can be made for increasing the base payment with PBPs, and for increasing the bonus payment.

These conclusions hold only when uncertainty about receiving the payment is included. They would not hold in the standard principal-agent model, where increasing a guaranteed payment does not increase quality.

Performance-based payments (significantly) increase quality. A key result from our experiments in Sections 3-5 is that PBPs can, in fact, increase quality in a significant way. This can be explained from our model too.

We have that the quality improves ($q_{\mathtt{pbp}} \geq q_{\mathtt{std}}$, or $q_{\mathtt{pbp}} > q_{\mathtt{std}}$ with additional assumptions) as a special case of the argument above. However, this statement is relatively weak, as it does not say anything about the magnitude of the improvement, i.e., the difference $q_{\mathtt{pbp}} - q_{\mathtt{std}}$. We would like this difference to be large; a requester might not want to take on the extra costs of PBPs if the increase in quality is small. In order to gain some intuition for when it is or is not possible to obtain a sufficiently large improvement in quality, we consider several special cases as examples.

As a first example, consider the case in which the worker does not have fine-grained control over the precise quality of his work, but can only choose between two options: high-quality, denoted $q_{\mathtt{high}}$, or low quality, $q_{\mathtt{low}}$. Then PBPs work if and only if the worker's optimal quality level is $q_{\mathtt{low}}$ without PBPs, and $q_{\mathtt{high}}$ with PBPs. In formulas, $U_{\mathtt{std}}(q_{\mathtt{high}}) < U_{\mathtt{std}}(q_{\mathtt{low}})$ and $U_{\mathtt{pbp}}(q_{\mathtt{high}}) > U_{\mathtt{pbp}}(q_{\mathtt{low}})$, or

$$\begin{aligned} p\left(\Pr(\mathtt{base}|q_{\mathtt{high}}) - \Pr(\mathtt{base}|q_{\mathtt{low}})\right) &< c(q_{\mathtt{high}}) - c(q_{\mathtt{low}}) \\ &< p\left(\Pr(\mathtt{base}|q_{\mathtt{high}}) - \Pr(\mathtt{base}|q_{\mathtt{low}})\right) + \\ &\quad b\left(\Pr(\mathtt{bonus}|q_{\mathtt{high}}) - \Pr(\mathtt{bonus}|q_{\mathtt{low}})\right). \end{aligned}$$

In words, the extra cost to produce high-quality work must be less than the extra benefit the worker would receive in terms of expected payments if the bonus is included, and bigger than the extra benefit he would receive with standard payments. Examining this expression gives us intuition about when we might expect PBPs to help. First, $c(q_{\mathtt{high}}) - c(q_{\mathtt{low}})$ cannot be too large. It must be possible for the worker to substantially increase his quality with additional effort (and at a reasonable cost)—essentially, the task must be effort-responsive, as conjectured in Section 6. Second, $c(q_{\mathtt{high}}) - c(q_{\mathtt{low}})$ cannot be too small (in particular, compared with $\Pr(\mathtt{base}|q_{\mathtt{high}}) - \Pr(\mathtt{base}|q_{\mathtt{low}})$ and p) or PBPs are unnecessary to achieve high quality. This is a partial explanation for why we did not see improvements from PBPs in the handwriting recognition task when the cost of producing high quality was already small. Third, the bonus b must be set large enough. This could partially explain our observation that PBPs did not help in the proofreading task with a very small bonus. Finally, the difference

[6]In multiple places in this section, to make inequalities on quality strict, we could first assume that q takes values on some interval $[q_{\min}, q_{\max}]$ such that $c(q_{\max}) > b+p$, and that $\Pr(\mathtt{base}|q)$, $\Pr(\mathtt{bonus}|q)$, and $c(q)$ are differentiable on this interval. We must then also assume that the subjective probabilities $\Pr(\mathtt{base}|q)$ and $\Pr(\mathtt{bonus}|q)$ are strictly increasing in q. In this particular instance, under these assumptions, since $c'(q^*) = 0$, we have $U'_{\mathtt{std}}(q^*) > 0$, which implies that q^* cannot be the maximizer of $U'_{\mathtt{std}}(q^*)$, so $q_{\mathtt{std}} > q^*$.

$\Pr(\texttt{bonus}|q_{\texttt{high}}) - \Pr(\texttt{bonus}|q_{\texttt{low}})$ must be high enough. This could explain why we observed that PBPs did not help when the threshold for receiving a bonus is set too low.

As a second tractable example, suppose that the worker has fine-grained control over quality, but has no uncertainty over whether the bonus will be obtained, i.e.,

$$\Pr(\texttt{bonus}|q) = \begin{cases} 1 & \text{if } q \geq \bar{q} \\ 0 & \text{otherwise} \end{cases}$$

for some threshold value $\bar{q}$. It is easy to show that either $q_{\texttt{pbp}} = q_{\texttt{std}}$ (if the worker prefers to do less work and pass up the bonus) or $q_{\texttt{pbp}} \geq \bar{q}$ (if the worker prefers to do more work to receive the bonus). PBPs are useful if and only if $\bar{q}$ is sufficiently higher than $q_{\texttt{std}}$ (according to the needs of the requester), and for some $q \geq \bar{q}$, $U_{\texttt{pbp}}(q) > U_{\texttt{pbp}}(q_{\texttt{std}})$, or equivalently

$$c(q) - c(q_{\texttt{std}}) < p(\Pr(\texttt{base}|q) - \Pr(\texttt{base}|q_{\texttt{std}})) + b. \quad (3)$$

Again we see that for PBPs to help it must be possible for the worker to increase his quality with additional effort at a reasonable cost, and the bonus must be set sufficiently large.

Equation 3 provides a concrete and simple way to think about whether it would help to increase the bonus threshold $\bar{q}$. For fixed payments p and b, it is optimal to choose as $\bar{q}$ the largest q which satisfies Equation 3. However, $\bar{q}$ is a *perceived* threshold and cannot always be controlled directly. Instead, it may help to alter workers' perception, perhaps without even changing the objective bonus rule. For example, in the proofreading experiment from Section 4 the "5 typos" bonus rule is roughly equivalent to the "25%" bonus rule in terms of when bonus payments are awarded, yet workers react differently. One possible explanation for this general phenomenon is a difference in the perceived value $\bar{q}$.

7.2 Comparison with Principal-Agent Model

In the standard principal-agent model, a worker maximizes his payment minus the intrinsic cost of his effort. We deviate from the standard model in that we include the worker's subjective beliefs about how high quality his work must be to be paid. In particular, while the objective probability of receiving the base payment is often 1, the subjective probability may be much smaller, depending on the quality level. This feature allows us to capture some effects that are not captured by the standard model, e.g., that increasing the base payment may increase the quality of work that the worker chooses to produce, while removing uncertainty about the base payment may decrease quality.

Our model may be useful as a more realistic foundation for theoretical work. As an example, consider Ho et al. [16], a recent theoretical paper on the optimization of PBPs. While that paper posits the standard principal-agent model, all results carry over to our model. (A proof of this fact is omitted due to space constraints.)

8. CONCLUSIONS AND DISCUSSION

We describe the results of a series of experiments studying the effect of performance-based payments on the quality of crowdwork on Amazon Mechanical Turk. Our goal is to identify properties of the payment, payment structure, and task that allow for quality improvements using PBPs.

We find that PBPs can improve the quality of submitted work for some tasks, but are not likely to for others. We identify the extent to which a task is *effort-responsive* as a potential important reason for whether or not PBPs work for this task. This leads to an actionable insight for requesters. When considering whether or not to use PBPs, one could first run a pilot experiment to determine whether a task is effort-responsive by examining the correlation between time spent and quality. If additional time spent leads to a sufficiently high boost in quality, we would expect PBPs to improve performance.

We find strong evidence for what we call the *implicit PBP effect*: workers may have their own subjective beliefs about the quality of work they must submit to have their work accepted, which makes them view fixed payments as implicitly performance-based. Workers may also have subjective beliefs about the likelihood of receiving the bonus when payments are explicitly performance-based. This should be taken into account when designing a payment scheme. For example, we find that in some cases a requester can incentivize higher quality work by defining the bonus threshold relative to other workers or with respect to gold standard data that the workers do not have access to.

We show that in order for PBPs to improve quality, the bonus payment offered must be sufficiently large, but that there are diminishing returns for further increasing this payment. This partially explains existing negative results on the effectiveness of PBPs in crowdsourcing markets. We provide evidence that when PBPs improve quality, they do so for a wide range of quality thresholds.

Finally, we suggest a theoretical model of workers' behavior that captures all of the above effects and explains several outcomes we observed in our experiments. We believe this model may be useful in further work on crowdsourcing markets, both as a concrete way to think about the consequences of using this or that payment scheme in practice, and as a more realistic foundation for theoretical work compared to the standard principal-agent model.

Acknowledgements

This research was partially supported by the National Science Foundation under grant IIS-1054911.

References

[1] O. Alonso. Implementing crowdsourcing-based relevance experimentation: An industrial perspective. *Information Retrieval*, 16(2):101–120, 2013.

[2] R. M. Araujo. 99designs: An analysis of creative competition in crowdsourced design. In *HCOMP*, 2013.

[3] S. E. Bonner, R. Hastie, S. G. B., and S. M. Young. A review of the effects of financial incentives on performance in laboratory tasks: Implications for management accounting. *Journal of Management Accounting Research*, 12(1):19–64, 2000.

[4] M. Buhrmester, T. Kwang, and S. D. Gosling. Amazon's Mechanical Turk: A new source of inexpensive, yet high-quality, data? *Perspectives on Psychological Science*, 2011.

[5] C. F. Camerer and R. Hogarth. The effects of financial incentives in economics experiments: A review and capital-labor-production framework. *Journal of Risk and Uncertainty*, 19(1):7–42, 1999.

[6] J. Cameron and W. D. Pierce. Reinforcement, reward, and intrinsic motivation: A meta-analysis. *Review of Educational Research*, 64(3):363–423, 1994.

[7] J. Chandler, P. Mueller, and G. Paolacci. Nonnaïveté among Amazon Mechanical Turk workers: Consequences and solutions for behavioral researchers. *Behavior Research Methods*, 46(1):112–130, 2014.

[8] R. Eisenberger and J. Cameron. Detrimental effects of reward: Reality or myth? *American psychologist*, 51 (11):1153, 1996.

[9] B. S. Frey and F. Oberholzer-Gee. The cost of price incentives: An empirical analysis of motivation crowding-out. *The American Economic Review*, pages 746–755, 1997.

[10] D. Gilchrist, M. Luca, and D. Malhotra. When 3+1 > 4: Gift structure and reciprocity in the field. Technical report, 2014. Working Paper.

[11] U. Gneezy and A. Rustichini. Pay enough or don't pay at all. *Quarterly Journal of Economics, August*, pages 791–810, 2000.

[12] C. G. Harris. You're hired! An examination of crowdsourcing incentive models in human resource tasks. In *WSDM 2011 Workshop on Crwdsourcing for Search and Data Mining*, 2011.

[13] R. Hertwig and A. Ortmann. Experimental practices in economics: A methodological challenge for psychologists? *Behavioral and Brain Sciences*, 24(3): 383–403, 2001.

[14] C.-J. Ho and J. W. Vaughan. Online task assignment in crowdsourcing markets. In *AAAI*, 2012.

[15] C.-J. Ho, S. Jabbari, and J. W. Vaughan. Adaptive task assignment for crowdsourced classification. In *ICML*, 2013.

[16] C.-J. Ho, A. Slivkins, and J. W. Vaughan. Adaptive contract design for crowdsourcing markets: Bandit algorithms for repeated principal-agent problems. In *ACM EC*, 2014.

[17] J. J. Horton and L. B. Chilton. The labor economics of paid crowdsourcing. In *ACM EC*, 2010.

[18] J. J. Horton, D. Rand, and R. Zeckhauser. The online laboratory: Conducting experiments in a real labor market. *Experimental Economics*, 14(3):399–425, 2011.

[19] P. G. Ipeirotis, F. Provost, and J. Wang. Quality management on Amazon Mechanical Turk. In *HCOMP*, 2010.

[20] G. D. Jenkins Jr., N. Gupta, A. Gupta, and J. D. Shaw. Are financial incentives related to performance? A meta-analytic review of empirical research. *Journal of Applied Psychology*, 83(5):777–787, 1998.

[21] D. Karger, S. Oh, and D. Shah. Iterative learning for reliable crowdsourcing systems. In *NIPS*, 2011.

[22] A. Kittur, E. Chi, and B. Suh. Crowdsourcing user studies with Mechanical Turk. In *CHI*, 2008.

[23] J.-J. Laffont and D. Martimort. *The Theory of Incentives: The Principal-Agent Model.* Princeton University Press, 2002.

[24] E. P. Lazear. Performance pay and productivity. *American Economic Review*, pages 1346–1361, 2000.

[25] L. Litman, J. Robinson, and C. Rosenzweig. The relationship between motivation, monetary compensation, and data quality among US- and India-based workers on Mechanical Turk. *Behavioral Research Methods*, 2014. To appear.

[26] Q. Liu, J. Peng, and A. Ihler. Variational inference for crowdsourcing. In *NIPS*, 2012.

[27] U.-V. Marti and H. Bunke. The iam-database: an english sentence database for offline handwriting recognition. *International Journal on Document Analysis and Recognition*, 5(1):39–46, 2002.

[28] W. Mason and S. Suri. Conducting behavioral research on Amazon's Mechanical Turk. *Behavior Research Methods*, 44(1):1–23, 2012.

[29] W. Mason and D. J. Watts. Financial incentives and the "performance of crowds". In *HCOMP*, 2009.

[30] J. Rogstadius, V. Kostakos, A. Kittur, B. Smus, J. Laredo, and M. Vukovic. An assessment of intrinsic and extrinsic motivation on task performance in crowdsourcing markets. In *ICWSM*, 2011.

[31] D. Schall. *Service-Oriented Crowdsourcing - Architecture, Protocols and Algorithms.* Springer Briefs in Computer Science. Springer, 2012.

[32] H. J. Seltman. Experimental design and analysis. `http://www.stat.cmu.edu/~hseltman/309/Book`, 2014.

[33] A. D. Shaw, J. J. Horton, and D. L. Chen. Designing incentives for inexpert human raters. In *CSCW*, 2011.

[34] V. Sheng, F. Provost, and P. Ipeirotis. Get another label? Improving data quality using multiple, noisy labelers. In *KDD*, 2008.

[35] C. Wah, S. Branson, P. Welinder, P. Perona, and S. Belongie. The Caltech-UCSD Birds-200-2011 Dataset. Technical Report CNS-TR-2011-001, California Institute of Technology, 2011.

[36] M. Yin, Y. Chen, and Y.-A. Sun. The effects of performance-contingent financial incentives in online labor markets. In *AAAI*, 2013.

[37] M. Yin, Y. Chen, and Y.-A. Sun. Monetary interventions in crowdsourcing task switching. In *HCOMP*, 2014.

Skolemising Blank Nodes while Preserving Isomorphism

Aidan Hogan *
Department of Computer Science
University of Chile
ahogan@dcc.uchile.cl

ABSTRACT

In this paper, we propose and evaluate a scheme to produce canonical labels for blank nodes in RDF graphs. These labels can be used as the basis for a Skolemisation scheme that gets rid of the blank nodes in an RDF graph by mapping them to globally canonical IRIs. Assuming no hash collisions, the scheme guarantees that two Skolemised graphs will be equal if and only if the two input graphs are isomorphic. Although the proposed scheme is exponential in the worst case, we claim that such cases are unlikely to be encountered in practice. To support these claims, we present the results of applying our Skolemisation scheme over a diverse collection of 43.5 million real-world RDF graphs (BTC–2014); we also provide results for some nasty synthetic cases.

Categories and Subject Descriptors

H.4 [**Information Systems Applications**]: Miscellaneous; G.2.2 [**Discrete Mathematics**]: Graph Theory—*Graph labeling*

Keywords

RDF; blank nodes; Skolemisation; isomorphism

1. INTRODUCTION

Blank nodes have been a thorny issue in the Semantic Web standards for well over a decade [10]. In the original 1999 specification of RDF [14], blank nodes (then simply called "anonymous nodes") made the assignment of URIs to nodes in an RDF graph optional. This enabled, e.g., convenient shortcuts for containers and reification in the RDF/XML syntax of the time, allowing parsers to generate anonymous nodes where necessary when reconstructing the RDF graph.

Blank nodes were later formalised as local existential variables in the 2004 RDF Semantics specification [7]. Unlike IRIs or literals, they do not point to something specific in the world described. Rather they denote the *existence* of something. Thus one can, for example, perform a one-to-one relabelling of the blank nodes in an RDF graph without affecting its meaning: two RDF graphs that are the same modulo a one-to-one rewriting of blank nodes are called *isomorphic*. Existential blank nodes also give rise to other semantic conditions involving simple entailment (checking if one RDF graph permits a subset of the interpretations of another RDF graph), simple equivalence (checking if two RDF graphs permit the same interpretations), leanness (checking if an RDF graph contains redundancy), and so forth [8, 6].

Blank nodes thus add theoretical complexity to RDF. No polynomial-time algorithms are known for deciding whether or not two RDF graphs are isomorphic. Likewise, checking simple entailment, simple equivalence and leanness of RDF graphs have all been proven to be intractable specifically due to the presence of existential blank nodes [6].

Blank nodes also introduce practical problems when dealing with RDF [10]. Although theoretical worst-case scenarios are unlikely to be encountered in real-world data [10], algorithms and tools handling RDF must still either account for all such cases or apply a pragmatic but non-standard fudge with respect to blank nodes. Fundamental operations, like checking what changed between two versions of an RDF graph [21], are often greatly complicated by blank nodes. In SPARQL, blank nodes cannot be directly referenced by a query, making them difficult to get data about [10]. In Linked Data, blank nodes cannot be externally linked and their use is thus discouraged [9]. And so forth [10].

Although blank nodes add complexity for consumers, their convenience for publishers means that they are widespread in real-world data. Our recent survey [10] found that in the BTC–2012 corpus – a crawl of 8.4 million RDF documents from the Web – 44.9% of the documents mentioned at least one blank node, 25.9% of the unique RDF terms were blank nodes, and 66.2% of pay-level-domains used blank nodes. Hence even if blank nodes were to be deprecated, the question of what to do with legacy data would remain open.

Ten years on from the previous release, an updated set of RDF 1.1 W3C Recommendations were recently published. The issue of blank nodes was a core topic within the working group. Since blank nodes have been in widespread use for

*This work was supported by the Millennium Nucleus Center for Semantic Web Research under Grant No. NC120004 and by Fondecyt Grant No. 11140900. The author would also like to thank Marcelo Arenas and Carsten Lutz for their valuable input as well as the anonymous referees whose detailed comments helped improve the paper.

WWW 2015, May 18–22, 2015, Florence, Italy.
ACM 978-1-4503-3469-3/15/05.
http://dx.doi.org/10.1145/2736277.2741653.

over a decade, major changes would have lead to too drastic a cost in terms of current adoption [10]. Instead, for scenarios where blank nodes are considered undesirable, RDF 1.1 now endorses an abstract scheme whereby blank nodes can be replaced with "fresh" IRIs, called *Skolem IRIs* [5, § 3.5].

The name "Skolem" refers to the process of *Skolemisation* whereby existential variables appearing in a first-order formula can be replaced with a function whose function symbol is "fresh" and whose arguments include the terms upon which the existential variable (loosely speaking) depends. If the variable being replaced does not depend on another term – as is the case in RDF – it can be replaced by a constant (a zero-arity function). Although Skolemisation can change the possible interpretations of the formula, it does not affect the satisfiability of the formulae in question.[1]

Likewise, RDF 1.1 systems creating Skolem IRIs "SHOULD *mint a new, globally unique IRI for each blank node so replaced*" [5].[2] Using this process Skolemising an RDF graph does not affect its satisfiability. However, guaranteeing *equisatisfiability* – that the Skolemised RDF graph is satisfiable if and only if the input graph is satisfiable – is vacuous since all RDF graphs are satisfiable until semantic conditions for datatypes or built-in vocabularies like RDFS or OWL are considered [8]. Skolemisation is rather a practical heuristic rubber-stamped by the recommendation for use in scenarios where blank nodes would otherwise be problematic.

However, the Skolemised versions of two isomorphic RDF graphs (or two copies of the same graph) are no longer isomorphic, nor do they entail each other. This means that it could not be known if two Skolemised graphs originated from isomorphic RDF graphs or even the same RDF graph.[3]

In this paper, we propose a method for producing a canonical labelling of blank nodes in an RDF graph that preserves isomorphism. We foresee two main use-cases for this scheme:

1. checking the isomorphism of RDF graphs or identifying groups of isomorphic RDF graphs from a large collection without requiring pair-wise isomorphism checks;
2. Skolemising RDF graphs such that the output graphs are equal if and only if the input graphs are isomorphic.

This paper continues with some preliminaries on RDF isomorphism. We then introduce a cheap but naive algorithm for computing a canonical labelling. Thereafter, we present illustrative cases where the naive algorithm fails and introduce a complete but exponential solution inspired by an existing canonical labelling algorithm that we adapt for RDF. We then address some issues relating to the generation of Skolem IRIs. Later evaluating our approach, we show that although the proposed scheme is efficient over a large collection of real-world RDF graphs, it can – as expected for an exponential algorithm – struggle for some modestly-sized synthetic cases. We wrap-up the contribution with discussion of related work and a brief conclusion.

[1]Which is used in FOL, e.g., to simplify theorem proving.

[2]In fact, minting globally unique IRIs is an unfeasible guarantee to make since any Web location may mention any IRI, but one can at least mint IRIs that are almost certainly unique, at least at the time of creation.

[3]One option would be to convert Skolem IRIs back to blank nodes, but this is problematic since there is nothing to restrict using Skolem-like IRIs in the input graph.

2. BACKGROUND

We first provide some formal preliminaries for RDF graphs, with a particular focus on blank nodes and the problem of checking if two RDF graphs are isomorphic.

Definition 1. Let $\mathbf{I}$ be the set of *IRIs*, $\mathbf{B}$ the set of *blank nodes*, and $\mathbf{L}$ the set of *literals*. The sets $\mathbf{I}$, $\mathbf{B}$, and $\mathbf{L}$ are infinite and pair-wise disjoint; collectively we call them *RDF terms*. An *RDF triple* $t := (s, p, o)$ is a member of the set $(\mathbf{I} \cup \mathbf{B}) \times \mathbf{I} \times (\mathbf{I} \cup \mathbf{B} \cup \mathbf{L})$; s is called the *subject*, p the *predicate* and o the *object* of t. An *RDF graph* G is a finite set of RDF triples. We denote by terms(G) the set of all RDF terms in some triple of G. An RDF graph G is *ground* if terms(G) contains no blank nodes.

In order to understand appropriate solutions to get rid of blank nodes from RDF graphs, we need to (perhaps unfortunately) first understand them in some detail. We first define two operations on the blank nodes in an RDF graph.

Definition 2. Let μ denote a mapping from RDF terms to RDF terms that is the identity on IRIs and literals. We call μ a *blank node mapping*. Slightly abusing notation, given a triple $t := (s, p, o)$, we let $\mu(t) := (\mu(s), \mu(p), \mu(o))$, and given an RDF graph G, we let $\mu(G) := \{\mu(t) \mid t \in G\}$. If μ is restricted to map from blank nodes to blank nodes in a one-to-one manner, we call it a *blank node bijection*.

Definition 3. Two RDF graphs G and H are *isomorphic*, denoted $G \cong H$, if and only if there exists a blank node bijection μ such that $\mu(G) = H$, in which case we call μ an *isomorphism* between G and H.

Two isomorphic RDF graphs can be intuitively considered as containing the same "structure" [5]. If G and H are both ground, then $G \cong H$ if and only if $G = H$. Next, an *RDF merge*, denoted $G + H$, uses isomorphism to avoid blank node clashes when combining RDF graphs.

Definition 4. An *RDF merge* of two RDF graphs, denoted $G + H$, is defined as $G' \cup H'$ where G' and H' are isomorphic copies of G and H resp. that share no blank nodes.

The RDF 1.1 Semantics recommendation [8] formalises the meaning of RDF graphs in terms of their *interpretations* (the possible worlds that they describe). The notion of *simple interpretations*, which consider existential blank nodes but no built-in vocabulary, gives rise to semantic concepts such as simple entailment, simple equivalence and leanness.

It is known from works by, e.g., Gutierrez et al. [6], that the problem of checking simple entailment/equivalence of RDF graphs is NP-COMPLETE, and that the problem of checking if G is lean is coNP-COMPLETE.

Regarding isomorphism, it is folklore – hinted at by, e.g., Carroll [4] – that deciding RDF isomorphism is of the same complexity as the standard GRAPH ISOMORPHISM problem[4] and hence is GI-COMPLETE.[5] However, to the best of our knowledge, the result has not been formally stated or proved. Though the GI-HARDNESS of RDF isomorphism is quite trivial to prove (since one can easily encode the structure of a

[4]Herein we call "simple graphs" "standard graphs" to avoid a naming clash with the simple semantics of RDF.

[5]GRAPH-ISOMORPHISM–COMPLETE: problems in this class are in NP but are not known to be NP-COMPLETE nor to have polynomial-time algorithms.

standard graph in RDF by representing each undirected edge $a - b$ as two RDF triples $a \overset{p}{\leftrightarrow} b$ for some arbitrary p), showing that it is *within* GI appears non-immediate. Hence we now formalise this result.

THEOREM 1. *Deciding if $G \cong H$ is GI-complete.*

PROOF. The proof relies on a polynomial-time many-one reduction both to and from the GI-COMPLETE problem of deciding GRAPH ISOMORPHISM for standard graphs.

The reduction from standard graph isomorphism to RDF graph isomorphism can be done straightforwardly by encoding the standard graph as an RDF graph as previously discussed. Hence RDF graph isomorphism is GI-HARD.

The reduction from RDF graph isomorphism to standard graph isomorphism is more tricky. We need a polynomial-time method to encode two RDF graphs G and H as standard graphs enc(G) and enc(H) such that $G \cong H$ (under RDF isomorphism) if and only if enc(G) $\cong$ enc(H) (under standard isomorphism). We now provide an example of one such encoding mechanism that satisfies the proof.

First, let SO denote the set of literals and IRIs that appear in the subject and/or object position of some triple in G and let P denote the set of IRIs appearing as a predicate in G. We assume that the sets SO and P correspond for both G and H, otherwise isomorphism can be trivially rejected.

We first give an example input and output. The encoding scheme we propose would encode the RDF graph on the left as the standard graph on the right (we keep the intuitive "shape" of both graphs intact for reference).

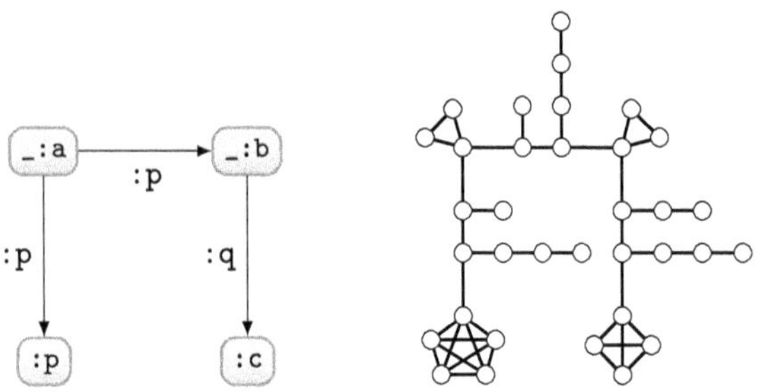

We start with an empty standard graph G into which we will encode the RDF graph G. The encoding adds cliques and path graphs to G to represent nodes and edges in the original RDF graph. Each clique and path graph has a fixed *external node* chosen to connect it to other parts of G; for path graphs, the external node is a terminal node.

First add a fresh 3-clique to G for every blank node in G.

Define a total ordering $\leq$ over SO (e.g., lexical) such that for all $x \in SO$, we can compute sorank(x) := card$\{y \mid y \in SO$ and $y \leq x\}$. In the example above, taking a lexical ordering, sorank(:c) = 1 and sorank(:p) = 2. Add a fresh (sorank(x) + 3)-clique to G for each term $x \in SO$.

Next we must encode the RDF edges, capturing labels and directionality. Again define a total ordering over P and let prank(p) denote the rank of p in P such that prank(p) := card$\{q \mid q \in P$ and $q \leq p\}$ (e.g., with a lexical ordering, prank(:p) = 1, prank(:q) = 2). For each $(s, p, o) \in G$, add two fresh path graphs of length prank(p) + 1 and $|P| + 1$ to G and connect their external nodes. Connect the external nodes of the clique of s and the short path, and connect the external nodes for the clique of o and the long path.

Once all triples are processed, the encoding is completed in time polynomial to the size of G.[6] Letting G and H denote the graphs encoded from G and H – where we again assume that SO and P are fixed for G and H – we now argue why $G \cong H$ (under RDF isomorphism) if and only if $\mathsf{G} \cong \mathsf{H}$ (under standard isomorphism).

$G \cong H$ implies $\mathsf{G} \cong \mathsf{H}$ since if $G \cong H$, then G and H differ only in blank node labels, which the encoding ignores.

To show that $\mathsf{G} \cong \mathsf{H}$ implies $G \cong H$, we show that each RDF graph has an encoding that's unique up to homomorphism. In particular, G can be decoded back to a G' such that $G \cong G'$. The decoding relies on two main observations:

1. No (≥ 3)-cliques can be unintentionally created in the encoding other than as part of a bigger clique for another vocabulary term. Nor can such a clique grow. Maximal cliques can thus be detected in G and mapped back to fresh blank nodes or to terms in SO.

2. No nodes with a degree of 1 can be introduced other than as the terminals of the paths used to encode RDF edges. Such nodes can thus be detected and walked back (to the node with degree 3) to decode the predicate in P and the direction.

This unambiguous decoding shows that the encoding (w.r.t. P and SO) is one-to-one modulo isomorphism. Hence two non-isomorphic RDF graphs cannot be encoded to isomorphic standard graphs under fixed vocabulary.[7]

This encoding thus completes the proof of Theorem 1. □

Finding a polynomial-time algorithm for RDF isomorphism is unlikely: it would imply GI = P, where all known algorithms for GRAPH ISOMORPHISM are exponential. However, isomorphism can be efficiently computed for many graphs; e.g., Babai showed that isomorphism for the vast majority of randomly generated graphs can be performed efficiently using a naïve algorithm [1]. Hence, despite exponential worst cases, many practical algorithm exist.

One of the most famous graph isomorphism algorithms – due to McKay [17] – is called NAUTY. This algorithm derives a canonical labelling Can such that for two standard graphs G and H, Can(G) = Can(H) if and only if $\mathsf{G} \cong \mathsf{H}$. In fact, this is quite close to our own use-case, where we wish to find a canonical mapping from blank nodes to IRIs.

Definition 5. We call a blank node mapping μ a *blank node grounding* if it maps blank nodes exclusively to IRIs.

One of our main goals herein is to find a blank node grounding μ such that $\mu(G) = \mu(H)$ if and only if $G \cong H$. When computing $\mu(G)$, only information from G is used; nothing is known from H. Our problem is similar to that of canonically labelling standard graphs, where our proposals are inspired by NAUTY. However, the presence of directed edges and ground labels (IRIs and literals) on both vertexes and edges in RDF suggests the need for custom methods.

[6]Expressing the exact size of G w.r.t. G is trivial but long. It suffices to observe that the number of nodes added to G has a (loose) upper-bound of $(so+3)^2 + 3b + g(2p+3)$ where $so := |SO|$, $b := |\text{terms}(G) \cap \mathbf{B}|$, $g := |G|$ and $p := |P|$. The number of edges added to G is bounded by the square of this number, and is thus bounded polynomially by $|G|$.

[7]Note: the decoding is not part of the reduction. In particular, listing all maximal cliques may not be possible in polynomial time. However, our goal is to merely demonstrate the *existence* of an unambiguous decoding.

3. NAIVE ALGORITHM

To generate a canonical labelling of a standard graph, NAUTY depends on *invariants* that must be preserved by isomorphism. An example is node degree: an isomorphism can only map two nodes with the same degree. Such invariants thus help to narrow the search. In RDF, ground terms offer a rich invariant. Our first step is thus to *colour* the blank nodes in an RDF graph with the ground information surrounding them such that blank nodes of different colours cannot be mapped to one another by an isomorphism.

In Algorithm 1, we propose a hashing scheme for colouring the blank nodes. A colour map is initialised in lines 2–5; IRIs and literals are assigned static hash-based colours, whereas blank nodes hashes are computed iteratively later. For now, we assume one-to-one perfect hashing (practical hashing issues will be discussed later). Lines 9–18 iteratively compute the blank node colours, where $hashTuple(\cdot)$ is order dependant and $hashBag(\cdot)$ is commutative and associative. The '+' and '-' symbols distinguish edge direction. The computed colours form a partition of blank nodes. The loop terminates when the partition does not change in an iteration (though the colour values may have changed).

Algorithm 1 Colouring blank nodes

1: **function** COLOUR(G) ▷ G an RDF graph
2: initialise $\mathsf{clr}_0[]$ ▷ a map from terms to colours
3: **for** $x \in \mathrm{terms}(G)$ **do** ▷ all terms in G
4: **if** $x \in \mathbf{B}$ **then**
5: $\mathsf{clr}_0[x] \leftarrow 0$ ▷ initial colour
6: **else**
7: $\mathsf{clr}_0[x] \leftarrow hashTerm(x)$ ▷ static colour
8: $i \leftarrow 0$
9: **repeat**
10: i++
11: initialise $\mathsf{clr}_i[]$ with $\mathsf{clr}_{i-1}[]$ ▷ copy map
12: **for** $(b, p, o) \in G : b \in \mathbf{B}$ **do** ▷ $o \in \mathbf{IBL}$
13: $c \leftarrow hashTuple(\mathsf{clr}_{i-1}[o], \mathsf{clr}_{i-1}[p], \text{'+'})$
14: $\mathsf{clr}_i[b] \leftarrow hashBag(c, \mathsf{clr}_i[b])$
15: **for** $(s, p, b) \in G : b \in \mathbf{B}$ **do** ▷ $s \in \mathbf{IB}$
16: $c \leftarrow hashTuple(\mathsf{clr}_{i-1}[s], \mathsf{clr}_{i-1}[p], \text{'-'})$
17: $\mathsf{clr}_i[b] \leftarrow hashBag(c, \mathsf{clr}_i[b])$
18: **until** $\forall x, y : \mathsf{clr}_i[x] = \mathsf{clr}_i[y] \Leftrightarrow \mathsf{clr}_{i-1}[x] = \mathsf{clr}_{i-1}[y]$
19: **return** $\mathsf{clr}_i[]$ as Clr ▷ final map of terms to colours

EXAMPLE 1. *We now exemplify how Algorithm 1 works. Blank nodes are "coloured" with hashes, but here we illustrate the process using Greek letters (upper-case for static hashes, lower-case for dynamic hashes). The iteration is given by i.*

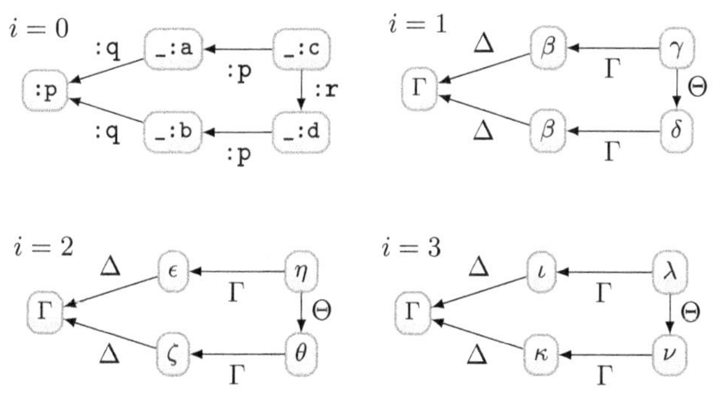

In the initial state ($i = 0$), assume that an initial hash α is assigned to all blank nodes and static hashes to all IRIs and literals. In the iterations that follow, blank nodes are coloured according to their neighbourhood; e.g., for _:d *at $i = 1$, the hash is computed as:*

$$\begin{aligned}\mathsf{clr}_1[\text{\_:d}] \leftarrow hashBag(&\mathsf{clr}_0[\text{\_:d}],\\ &hashTuple(\mathsf{clr}_0[\text{\_:b}], \mathsf{clr}_0[\text{:p}], \text{'+'}),\\ &hashTuple(\mathsf{clr}_0[\text{\_:c}], \mathsf{clr}_0[\text{:r}], \text{'-'}))\end{aligned}$$

All blank nodes are distinguished by $i = 2$. At $i = 3$, we see that for each pair of blank nodes (x, y), $\mathsf{clr}_2[x] = \mathsf{clr}_2[y]$ if and only if $\mathsf{clr}_3[x] = \mathsf{clr}_3[y]$; the process thus terminates.

In fact, in the case of Example 1, the last iteration is unnecessary since once the unit partition is reached (all blank nodes are distinguished), we can end the process knowing no new blank nodes can be distinguished thereafter. Since this case is quite common, we apply this early termination heuristic in the implementation of the colouring method.

Algorithmic characteristics.

We now show that in the general case, the algorithm terminates in a bounded number of iterations, and that the computed colours preserve isomorphism.

LEMMA 1. *Assuming a perfect hashing scheme, in Algorithm 1, if $\mathsf{clr}_i[x] \neq \mathsf{clr}_i[y]$, then $\mathsf{clr}_j[x] \neq \mathsf{clr}_j[y]$ for $j \geq i$.*

PROOF. (*Sketch*) Can be proven by induction observing that if $i < j$, then $\mathsf{clr}_i[x]$ is encoded in the hash of $\mathsf{clr}_j[x]$. □

THEOREM 2. *Let $B := \mathbf{B} \cap \mathrm{terms}(G)$ denote the set of blank nodes mentioned in an RDF graph G. Algorithm 1 terminates in $\Theta(|B|)$ iterations for G in the worst case.*

PROOF. Colours form a partition of B. Algorithm 1 terminates if the partition doesn't change. Per Lemma 1, partitions can only split. Hence only $|B| - 1$ splits can occur before the unit partition is reached. The tight asymptotic bound is given, for example, by the $\lfloor \frac{1}{2} \cdot |B| \rfloor + 1$ iterations needed for a regular path graph. □

Letting T denote terms(G), and assuming for simplicity that clr has constant insert/lookup and linear copy performance, then Algorithm 1 runs in $\Theta(|B| \cdot (|T| + |G|))$ in a worst-case analysis. In terms of space, the input graph and two colour maps of size T are stored. Ground triples in G can be pre-filtered to reduce space and time.

THEOREM 3. *Let Clr_G denote the map from RDF terms to colours produced by Algorithm 1 for G. Let $G \cong H$ be two isomorphic RDF graphs. Let b be a blank node of G and c be a blank node of H. If there exists a blank node bijection μ such that $\mu(G) = H$ and $\mu(b) = c$, then $\mathrm{Clr}_G(b) = \mathrm{Clr}_H(c)$.*

PROOF. (*Sketch*) The main observations are that (i) Algorithm 1 is agnostic to lexical blank node labels, (ii) the commutativity and associativity of $hashBag(\cdot)$ ensures order-independent hashing over sets of triples, and (iii) the number of iterations is deterministic modulo isomorphism. □

A nuance of the algorithm is that when there are disconnected sub-graphs of blank nodes in the input RDF graph, the colouring of some of those sub-graphs may continue longer than necessary. Specifically, let's say we use Clr_G as the basis of a blank node grounding μ_G, where output colours would be used to mint fresh IRIs. Given two RDF graphs G and H, then $\mu_G(G)$ may not equal $\mu_{G+H}(G)$; alternatively, $\mu_G(G)$ may not be a subset of $\mu_{G+H}(G + H)$.

EXAMPLE 2. *In the following, G will require one fewer iteration than H or $G+H$ to terminate. Hence the colourings of graph G would no longer correspond with the colourings of the corresponding sub-graph of $G + H$.*

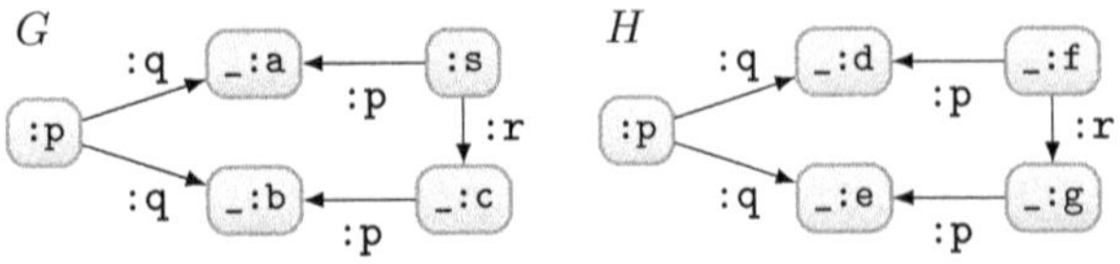

Since this may be undesirable in certain applications, we propose an optional step prior to Algorithm 1 that breaks up the input RDF graph according to its blank nodes.

Definition 6. For an RDF graph G, let $\mathcal{G} := (\mathcal{V}, \mathcal{E})$ denote a standard undirected graph where $\mathcal{V} = G$ and $\mathcal{E}$ is a set of unordered pairs of triples from G such that $\{t, u\}$ is in $\mathcal{E}$ if and only if $\{t, u\} \subseteq G$ and $\text{terms}(\{t\}) \cap \text{terms}(\{u\}) \cap \mathbf{B} \neq \emptyset$. Let $t \sim_{\mathcal{G}} v$ denote that t and v are reachable from each other in $\mathcal{G}$, and let $G/\sim_{\mathcal{G}}$ denote the partition of G based on reachability in $\mathcal{G}$. We define a *blank node split* of G as $\text{split}(G) := \{G' \in G/\sim_{\mathcal{G}} \mid G' \text{ is not ground}\}$.

The *blank node split* of G contains a set of non-overlapping subgraphs of G, where each subgraph G' contains all and only the triples for a given group of "connected blank-nodes" in G; e.g., in Example 2, $\text{split}(G + H) = \{G, H\}$. Now, instead of passing a raw RDF graph G to Algorithm 1, to ensure that $\mu_G(G)$ is a subset of $\mu_{G+H}(G+H)$, we can pass the individual split sub-graphs to Algorithm 1. This process is outlined in Algorithm 2. On line 2, we compress the details of computing $\text{split}(G)$: a standard UNION–FIND algorithm with $O(n \cdot \log n)$ runtime suffices. The results of each split are computed and joined; a regular join operation suffices since two splits cannot disagree on the colour of a given term: colours for IRIs and literals are static and no blank node can appear in two splits. Versus Algorithm 1, Algorithm 2 may produce different colours for blank nodes due to running fewer iterations over split graphs (per Example 2) and may miss colours for ground terms (we are only interested in blank node colours). The added cost of the split computation is offset by the potential to parallelise and reduce iterations when colouring individual sub-graphs.

Algorithm 2 Colouring split graphs

```
1: function COLOUR'(G)                  ▷ G a non-ground RDF graph
2:     {G_1, ..., G_n} ← split(G)         ▷ use, e.g., Union–Find
3:     Clr ← COLOUR(G_1)                  ▷ calls Algorithm 1
4:     for 1 < i ≤ n do
5:         Clr ← Clr ⋈ COLOUR(G_2)        ▷ ⋈ indicates a join
6:     return Clr                         ▷ final colours
```

4. COMPLETE ALGORITHM

For many real-world RDF graphs, the algorithm described in the previous section would probably suffice to compute distinct colours/labels for all blank nodes. However, the naive algorithm is tractable and we would expect a complete algorithm to be exponential (since it could solve a GI-COMPLETE problem per Theorem 1). Indeed, there are various cases in which the naive approach fails; e.g., non-trivial *automorphisms* cause problems for the naive approach.

Definition 7. An *automorphism* of an RDF graph G is an isomorphism from G to itself; i.e., μ is an automorphism of G if $\mu(G) = G$. If μ is not the identity mapping on blank nodes in G then μ is a *non-trivial automorphism*. We denote the set of all automorphisms of G by $\text{Aut}(G)$.

EXAMPLE 3. *We give the automorphisms for two RDF graphs. Trivial automorphisms are in grey. Applying any of the automorphisms shown for the graph in question would lead to the same graph (and not just an isomorphic copy).*

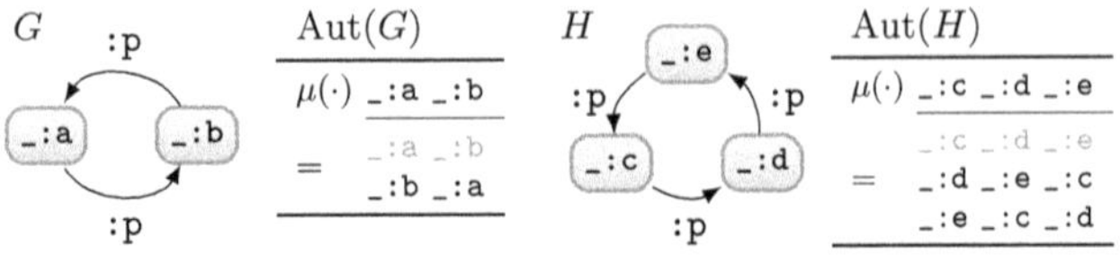

If we input G into our naive colouring algorithm, the process would terminate after two iterations and no blank nodes will be distinguished by colour. The same holds for H. This is due to the presence of automorphisms that make G and H vertex transitive *(in an RDF sense): for any two vertexes u and v, there exists an automorphism μ such that $\mu(u) = v$.*

In fact, the blank nodes of G and H would both have the same global colour. To see this, imagine that a blank node is coloured blue in $i = 1$ if it is grey in $i = 0$ and has both an inlink and an outlink with label `:p` *to a grey blank node in $i = 0$; likewise, a blank node is coloured green in $i = 2$ if it is blue in $i = 1$ and has both an inlink and an outlink with label* `:p` *to a blue blank node in $i = 1$. All blank nodes in G and H – or any directed cycle with that predicate – would be green in the result. If we were to use the naive colouring to ground the triples in $G+H$, the result would be single triple: $(g,$ `:p`$, g)$ for g the IRI generated from green.*

Thus the naive approach can be problematic in certain (not-so-exotic) cases. To overcome these problems, we first define a sound canonical version of an RDF graph.

Canonicalising RDF graphs.

Assume a total ordering of all RDF terms (e.g., lexical), of all RDF triples (e.g., lexicographic) and of all RDF graphs (e.g., $G < H$ if and only if $G \subset H$ or there exists a triple $t \in G \setminus H$ such that no triple $t' \in H \setminus G$ exists where $t' < t$). Assume that κ is a blank node bijection that labels all k blank nodes in a graph G from `:b1` to `:b`k.[8] We denote by $\mathcal{K}$ the $k!$ possible κ-mappings for G. Since we have a total ordering of graphs, there is a unique graph $\min\{\kappa(G) \mid \kappa \in \mathcal{K}\}$, which we denote by $\lfloor G \rfloor$. We now show that $\lfloor G \rfloor$ is a canonical graph with respect to isomorphism.

LEMMA 2. $G \cong H$ IF *and* ONLY IF $\lfloor G \rfloor = \lfloor H \rfloor$.

PROOF. (IF) Observe that $G \cong \lfloor G \rfloor$ and $H \cong \lfloor H \rfloor$ since κ-mappings are blank node bijections. Given the premise $\lfloor G \rfloor = \lfloor H \rfloor$, then $G \cong \lfloor G \rfloor = \lfloor H \rfloor \cong H$, which gives $G \cong H$.

(ONLY IF) Suppose the result does not hold: suppose (without loss of generality) that $\lfloor G \rfloor > \lfloor H \rfloor$ may hold if $G \cong H$. Since $G \cong H$, there exists a blank node bijection μ such that $\mu(G) = H$. Let κ be a mapping such that $\kappa(H) = \lfloor H \rfloor$. Now $\kappa \circ \mu(G) = \lfloor H \rfloor$. Since $\kappa \circ \mu$ is a valid κ-mapping for G and $\lfloor G \rfloor > \kappa \circ \mu(G)$, we arrive at a contradiction. □

[8] Any such scheme would do. We use an instance for brevity.

EXAMPLE 4. *Take graph H from Example 7. We have* 3! *possible κ-mappings as follows.*

$\kappa(\cdot)$	_:c	_:d	_:e	H {(_:c, :p, :d), (_:d, :p, :e), (_:e, :p, :c)}
	_:b1	_:b2	_:b3	{(_:b1, :p, _:b2), (_:b2, :p, _:b3), (_:b3, :p, _:b1)}
	_:b1	_:b3	_:b2	{(_:b1, :p, _:b3), (_:b3, :p, _:b2), (_:b2, :p, _:b1)}
=	_:b2	_:b1	_:b3	{(_:b2, :p, _:b1), (_:b1, :p, _:b3), (_:b3, :p, _:b2)}
	_:b2	_:b3	_:b1	{(_:b2, :p, _:b3), (_:b3, :p, _:b1), (_:b1, :p, _:b2)}
	_:b3	_:b1	_:b2	{(_:b3, :p, _:b1), (_:b1, :p, _:b2), (_:b2, :p, _:b3)}
	_:b3	_:b2	_:b1	{(_:b3, :p, _:b2), (_:b2, :p, _:b1), (_:b1, :p, _:b3)}

The six mappings produce two distinct graphs. Assuming a typical lexical ordering, the first, fourth and fifth mappings produce $\lfloor H \rfloor$. One could (bijectively) relabel `_:c`, `_:d`, `_:e` *in the original graph without affecting the result: the result would be the same for any $\lfloor H' \rfloor$ such that $H \cong H'$.*

This suggests a correct and complete brute force algorithm for canonicalising RDF graphs: search all κ-mapping of G for one that gives $\lfloor G \rfloor$. However, optimisations to improve upon trying all $k!$ possible mappings are not obvious.

Instead we use similar notions of ordering to refine the results of the naive algorithm, distinguishing blank nodes that would otherwise have the same colour, similar in principle to standard graph isomorphism methods like NAUTY [17].

Ordering colour partitions.

We assume a set of totally ordered colours $\mathbf{C}$ (in our case hashes). Let Clr be a map from blank nodes to colours computed, e.g., by the naive methods described previously. If Clr maps all blank nodes in G to a unique colour, we are done. However, as discussed, this may not always be the case. Initial colourings may assign the same colour to different blank nodes, forming a partition of blank nodes.

Definition 8. Let $\backsim$ denote an equivalence relation between two blank nodes $b_1, b_2 \in B$ such that $b_1 \backsim b_2$ if and only if $\text{Clr}(b_1) = \text{Clr}(b_2)$. We define a *coloured partition* P of a set of blank nodes B with respect to Clr as the quotient set of B with respect to $\backsim$, i.e., $P := B/\backsim$. We call $B' \in P$ a *part* of P. We call B' *trivial* if $|B'| = 1$; otherwise we call it *non-trivial*. We call P *fine* if it contains only trivial parts and *coarse* if it contains only one part.

Our goal is to thus use a deterministic process – avoiding arbitrary choices and use of blank node labels – to compute a colouring for the RDF graph G that results in a fine partition of blank nodes. The general idea is to manually distinguish individual blank nodes in non-trivial partitions. Since there is no deterministic way to choose one such blank node, we must try all equal choices. However, we can use an ordering of the partition to narrow the choices insofar as possible.

Definition 9. Given $P = \{B_1, \ldots B_n\}$, a partition of B w.r.t. the colouring Clr, we call a sequence of sets of blank nodes $\mathcal{P} := (B_1, \ldots B_n)$ an *ordered partition* of B w.r.t. Clr.

Thus given P and an associated colouring Clr, $\mathcal{P}$ encodes an ordering of the parts of P. To deterministically compute an initial $\mathcal{P}$ from an input P and Clr, we use a total ordering $\leq$ of parts such that $B' < B''$ if $|B'| < |B''|$, or in the case that $|B'| = |B''|$, then $B' < B''$ if and only if $\text{Clr}(b') < \text{Clr}(b'')$ for $b' \in B'$ and $b'' \in B''$ (recall that all elements of B' have the same colour; likewise for B'').

We can then *refine* $\mathcal{P}$ by recursively distinguishing blank nodes in its lowest non-trivial part, knowing the same part will likewise be selected for all isomorphic graphs.

Definition 10. Let $\mathcal{P} := (B_1, \ldots, B_n)$, $\mathcal{P}' := (B'_1, \ldots, B'_m)$ be two ordered partitions. We say that $\mathcal{P}'$ is *finer* than $\mathcal{P}$, or equivalently that $\mathcal{P}$ is *coarser* than $\mathcal{P}'$, if and only if:

- for every part $B'_i \in \mathcal{P}$ there exists a $B_j \in \mathcal{P}$ such that $B'_i \subseteq B_j$; *and*
- if $B'_i, B'_j \in \mathcal{P}'$ such that $i \leq j$ and such that $B'_i \subseteq B_k$ and $B'_j \subseteq B_l$ for $B_k, B_l \in \mathcal{P}$, then $k < l$.

In other words, $\mathcal{P}'$ is finer than $\mathcal{P}$ if $\mathcal{P}'$ splits some of the parts of $\mathcal{P}$ and leaves those splits "in place". We call any function that takes as input an ordered partition and provides as output a finer partition a *refinement*.

EXAMPLE 5. *Take these four ordered partitions:*

- $\mathcal{P} := (\{b_1, b_2\}, \{b_3, b_4\})$
- $\mathcal{P}_1 := (\{b_1\}, \{b_3\}, \{b_2, b_4\})$
- $\mathcal{P}_2 := (\{b_1\}, \{b_3\}, \{b_2\}, \{b_4\})$
- $\mathcal{P}_3 := (\{b_1, b_2\}, \{b_4\}, \{b_3\})$.

The last part of $\mathcal{P}_1$ is not a subset of any part of $\mathcal{P}$; hence it is neither finer nor coarser than $\mathcal{P}$. Likewise, since $\mathcal{P}_2$ "swaps" the order of b_2 and b_3, it is neither finer nor coarser than $\mathcal{P}$ (it is finer than $\mathcal{P}_1$). Only $\mathcal{P}_3$ is finer than $\mathcal{P}$.

Exploring partition refinements.

Algorithm 3 thus takes as input an initial ordered partition $\mathcal{P}$ with respect to a naive colouring Clr and deterministically explores possible refinements. For now we assume that the algorithm accepts an RDF graph with one connected component of blank nodes and no ground triples (i.e., a single blank node split). As discussed, the algorithm first computes an initial ordered partition in the entry function CANONICALISE. Next in DISTINGUISH, the algorithm recursively tries distinguishing, in turn, each blank node from the lowest non-trivial part of the current ordered partition. The colour of the distinguished blank node is marked and the result is fed as input along with G into the naive graph colouring method, which is run until fixpoint: this propagates the changes caused by distinguishing the blank node through the graph. The fixpoint colouring returned is passed to the REFINE function to compute a refinement of the previous ordered partition, dividing parts according to the new colouring while maintaining the prior precedence of parts. If the resulting refinement distinguishes all blank nodes, a labelling function uses the colours as a basis to label the blank nodes in G. Throughout the recursive process of distinguishing blank nodes, the lowest labelled graph seen thus far – $\underline{G}$ – is tracked. When all possibilities have been explored, $\underline{G}$ serves as a canonical version of G: the lowest graph found during the deterministic exploration of refinements.

The algorithm thus explores a directed labelled search-tree $T = (V, E, L)$, where the set of vertices V are ordered partitions, edges E connect ordered partitions to their direct refinements, and L labels edges with an ordered list of blank nodes manually distinguished for that refinement. More specifically, let $\mathcal{P} \in V$ be a node in the tree and $\text{lin}(\mathcal{P})$ denote the label of its inlink (or an empty list for the root

Algorithm 3 Finding a canonical version of G

function CANONICALISE(G) ▷ G an RDF graph
  Clr ← COLOUR(G)
  $B \leftarrow \text{terms}(G) \cap \mathbf{B}$
  compute partition P of B w.r.t. Clr
  $\mathcal{P} \leftarrow$ order P by $\leq$
  $\underline{G} \leftarrow$ DISTINGUISH(G, Clr, $\mathcal{P}$, $\emptyset$, B)
  return $\underline{G}$ ▷ canonical graph

function DISTINGUISH(G, Clr, $\mathcal{P}$, $\underline{G}$, B) ▷ $\underline{G}$: min. graph
  $B_i \leftarrow$ lowest non-trivial part of $\mathcal{P}$
  for $b \in B_i$ **do**
    Clr(b) ← *hashTuple*(Clr(b), '@') ▷ '@' a marker
    Clr′ ← COLOUR(G, Clr) ▷ initialise clr_0 with Clr
    $\mathcal{P}_{[b]} \leftarrow$ REFINE($\mathcal{P}$, Clr′, b, B)
    if $|\mathcal{P}_{[b]}| = |B|$ **then** ▷ all nodes distinguished
      $G_C \leftarrow$ *label*(G, Clr) ▷ gen. bnodes from Clr
      if $\underline{G} = \emptyset$ or $G_C < \underline{G}$ **then** $\underline{G} \leftarrow G_C$
    else $\underline{G} \leftarrow$ DISTINGUISH(G, Clr′, $\mathcal{P}_{[b]}$, $\underline{G}$, B)
  return $\underline{G}$ ▷ canonical graph

function REFINE($\mathcal{P}$, Clr, b, B)
  denote $\mathcal{P} = (B_1, \ldots, B_i, \ldots, B_n)$ s.t. $b \in B_i$
  $\mathcal{P}_{[b]} \leftarrow (B_1, \ldots, B_{i-1}, \{b\})$ ▷ init. refined partition
  compute partition P' of B w.r.t. Clr
  $\mathcal{P}' \leftarrow$ order P' by $\leq$
  for $B^+ \in (B_i \setminus \{b\}, B_{i+1}, \ldots, B_n)$ **do**
    $\mathcal{P}^+ := ()$ ▷ empty list
    for $B' \in \mathcal{P}'$ **do**
      if $B^+ \cap B' \neq \emptyset$ **then**
        $\mathcal{P}^+ \leftarrow \mathcal{P}^+ \,\|\, (B^+ \cap B')$ ▷ $\|$: concatenate
    $\mathcal{P}_{[b]} \leftarrow \mathcal{P}_{[b]} \,\|\, \mathcal{P}^+$
  return $\mathcal{P}_{[b]}$ ▷ refined partition

node). Let B be the first non-trivial part of $\mathcal{P}$ (if $\mathcal{P}$ is fine, it has no children). Then, for every $b \in B$, an edge extends from $\mathcal{P}$ with label $\text{lin}(\mathcal{P}) \,\|\, [b]$ (where $\|$ denotes concatenation) to the refinement of $\mathcal{P}$ computed by distinguishing b and rerunning the colouring to a fixpoint. Algorithm 3 explores this refinement tree in a depth-first manner looking for a leaf that corresponds to the lowest labelled graph.

EXAMPLE 6. *We adapt the canonical example of the canonical labelling of a 2D-grid-like graph – used for example by McKay and Piperno [18] – to an RDF version as follows:*

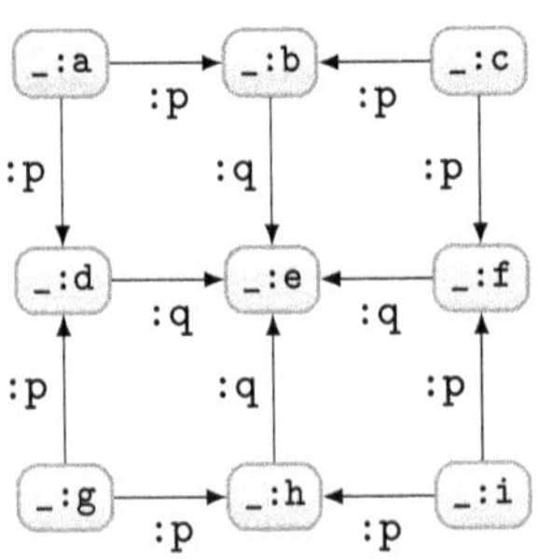

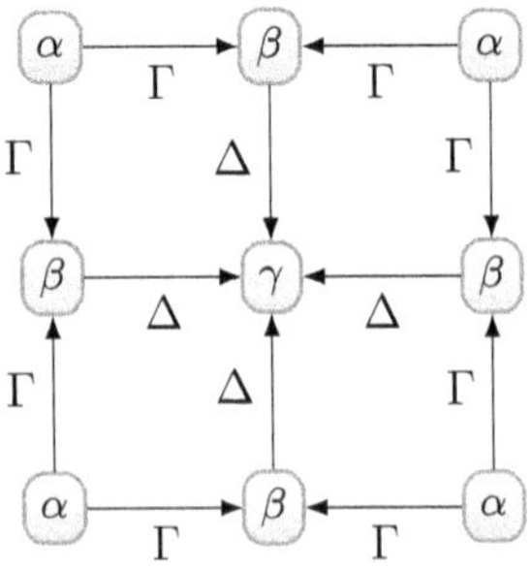

The graph on the right depicts the fixpoint of the naive colouring. The ordered partition resulting from this would be $\mathcal{P} = (\{$`_:e`$\}, \{$`_:a`, `_:c`, `_:g`, `_:i`$\}, \{$`_:b`, `_:d`, `_:f`, `_:h`$\})$ *assuming* $\alpha < \beta$. *So now we distinguish blank nodes in the first non-trivial part. The following graph to the left shows the result of distinguishing* `_:a` *and colouring to fixpoint:* $\mathcal{P}_{[\texttt{\_:a}]} = (\{$`_:e`$\}, \{$`_:a`$\}, \{$`_:i`$\}, \{$`_:c`, `_:g`$\}, \{$`_:b`, `_:d`$\}, \{$`_:f`, `_:h`$\})$.

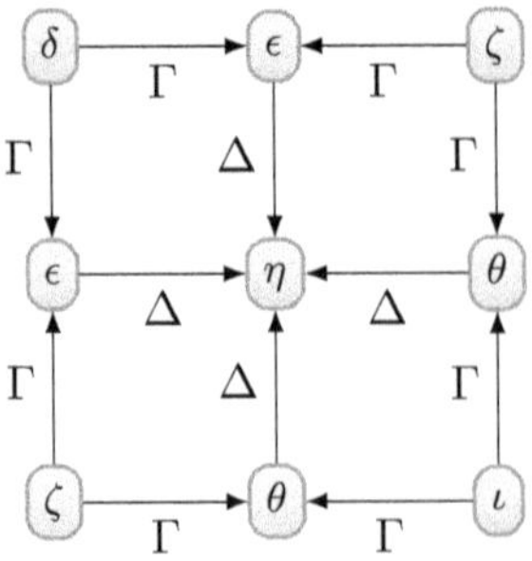

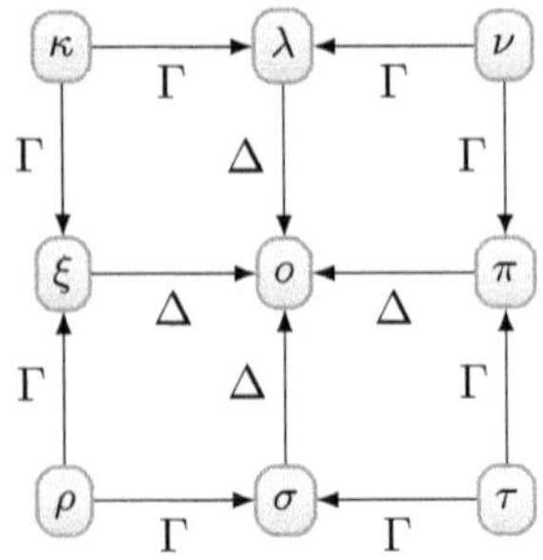

$\mathcal{P}_{[\texttt{\_:a}]}$ *is still not a fine partition. Hence we proceed by distinguishing one of the blank nodes in the first non-trivial part* $\{$`_:c`, `_:g`$\}$. *If we distinguish, e.g.,* `_:c`, *then* $\mathcal{P}_{[\texttt{\_:a},\texttt{\_:c}]}$ *would be a fine ordered partition, as shown on the right. We can then imagine a deterministic labelling for the blank nodes of the graph based on the colours computed (e.g.,* `_:kappa`, *etc.) where only the minimum such graph is kept.*[9]

This example illustrates traversing one path down the refinement tree to a leaf: [`_:a`, `_:c`]. *Next the algorithm would try* [`_:a`, `_:g`], *then* [`_:c`, `_:a`], [`_:c`, `_:i`], *and so on until all eight leaves of the tree are checked. Figure 1 depicts the refinement tree with the ordered partition resulting at every step where the first non-trivial part of each partition is shaded (other greyed-out parts of the tree will be discussed later). For every leaf, the corresponding labelled graph is computed and the minimum such graph is kept.*

In this particular example, every leaf of the tree will result in the same labelled graph: consider, e.g., the path [`_:c`, `_:a`]. *The result would be the same as for* [`_:a`, `_:c`] *(but mirrored on the vertical axis): all edges, like* (ρ, Γ, σ), *will appear in every such graph produced by a leaf (in this example).*

Pruning by automorphisms.

As observed in the previous example, traversing the entire tree may involve unnecessary repetitions of orientations due to automorphisms. In the given grid graph, there are two large *orbits* – sets of nodes mappable by an automorphism – namely $\{$`_:a`, `_:c`, `_:g`, `_:i`$\}$ and $\{$`_:b`, `_:d`, `_:f`, `_:h`$\}$. As such, exploring each leaf is redundant. The NAUTY algorithm – and similar canonical labelling methods such as TRACES [20] or BLISS [12] – keep track of automorphisms found while exploring the search tree. If two leaves produce the same labelled graph, then the mapping between the generating ordered partitions represents an automorphism.

EXAMPLE 7. *Taking Example 6, consider the two partitions* $\mathcal{P}_{[a,c]} = (\{$`e`$\}, \{$`a`$\}, \{$`i`$\}, \{$`c`$\}, \{$`g`$\}, \{$`b`$\}, \{$`d`$\}, \{$`f`$\}, \{$`h`$\})$ *and* $\mathcal{P}_{[a,g]} = (\{$`e`$\}, \{$`a`$\}, \{$`i`$\}, \{$`g`$\}, \{$`c`$\}, \{$`d`$\}, \{$`b`$\}, \{$`h`$\}, \{$`f`$\})$.[10] *Since both partitions generate the same labelled graph, we can assert the following bidirectional automorphism:* $\{$`e`$\} \leftrightarrow \{$`e`$\}$, $\{$`a`$\} \leftrightarrow \{$`a`$\}$, $\{$`i`$\} \leftrightarrow \{$`i`$\}$, $\{$`c`$\} \leftrightarrow \{$`g`$\}$, $\{$`b`$\} \leftrightarrow \{$`d`$\}$, $\{$`f`$\} \leftrightarrow \{$`h`$\}$.

Automorphisms can thus be used to prune the refinement tree [18] where we employ one such strategy. Let $\mathcal{P}$ be a node in the tree with children $\mathcal{P}'$ and $\mathcal{P}''$ derived by distinguishing b' and b'' respectively. Assume that $\mathcal{P}'$ has been visited and we are considering visiting $\mathcal{P}''$ next. If we can find an

[9]We could equivalently (modulo isomorphism) consider a labelling based on the index of the part containing the blank node in the ordered partition.

[10]Dropping underscores for formatting reasons.

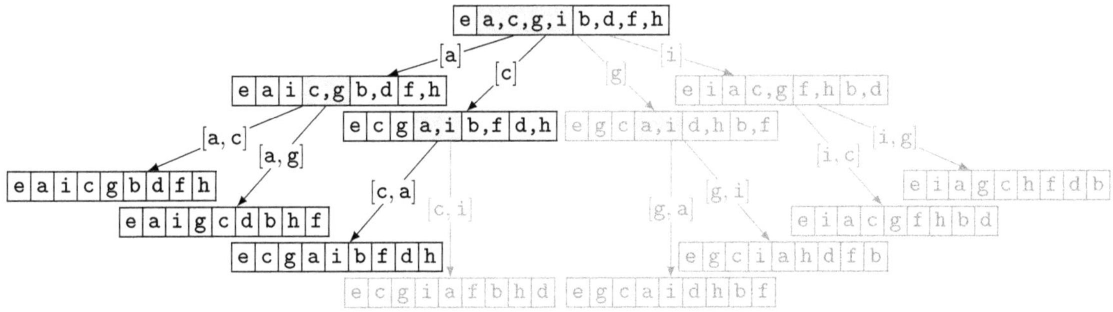

Figure 1: Refinement tree for Example 6

automorphism μ that is the *pointwise stabiliser* for all the blank nodes in $\text{lin}(\mathcal{P})$ (i.e., $\mu(b) = b$ for all $b \in \text{lin}(\mathcal{P})$) and that maps $\mu(b') \to \mu(b'')$, then we need not visit $\mathcal{P}''$ [18].

EXAMPLE 8. *In Figure 1, the greyed-out sub-tree need not be explored if automorphisms are tracked and used to prune branches (for now, we include* [c, i]*). After discovering that the* [a, c], [a, g], [c, a] *and* [c, i] *leaves form the same graph, automorphisms can be formed, per Example 7, by mapping the leaf nodes (in the same column) from the following table:*

[a, c]	e	a	i	c	g	b	d	f	h
[a, g]	e	a	i	g	c	d	b	h	f
[c, a]	e	c	g	a	i	b	f	d	h
[c, i]	e	c	g	i	a	f	b	h	d

Assume we are now considering visiting [g] *from the root. No nodes need be stabilised at the root, so we need not restrict the automorphisms considered. Take the automorphism derived from, e.g.,* [c, a] $\to$ [a, g]*, which gives* e $\to$ e, c $\to$ a, g $\to$ i, a $\to$ g*, and so on. We can use this automorphism to map to* [g] *from its sibling* [a]*, which has already been visited. We can now compute the sub-tree below* [g] *by applying the same automorphism to the sub-tree of* [a] *where we would ultimately end up with the same leaf graphs. Hence we know we can prune* [g]*. We need not visit* [i] *along the same lines.*

In fact, going back a little, as hinted at by Figure 1, in theory we need not have visited [c, i] *either. When considering visiting* [c, i]*, we must look for automorphisms that root* c*, but no such automorphism is computable from the first three leaves. However, if we look at a higher level, after visiting the* [c, a] *leaf, we have found an automorphism that makes visiting the higher branch at* [c] *redundant. Thus we need not continue with the* [c] *branch any further.*

A major challenge associated with the pruning phase is that naively materialising and indexing the entire automorphism group as it is discovered can consume lots of space. Our current implementation thus computes automorphisms on-the-fly as needed, lazily generating and caching orbits with pointwise stabilisers relevant for a given level of the tree. For this reason, in the previous example we would not prune [c, i]: instead of checking pruning possibilities at every level for all steps, we only check on the current level of the depth-first search. Thus we would run [c, i] without checking at the [c] level. When the depth-first-search returns to the higher level, we would prune at [g] and [i].

In general, a variety of pruning and search strategies have been explored in the graph isomorphism literature that are not considered in this current work (see, e.g., [18] for more details, explaining how different strategies may work better for different types of graphs). However, such strategies only become crucial when considering larger instances of difficult cases which, as we will put forward later, are unlikely to be of concern when dealing with real-world RDF data.

Algorithmic characteristics.

We briefly remark on two properties of the algorithm.

THEOREM 4. *Algorithm 3 terminates.*

PROOF. The search tree, though exponential, is finite. The search follows standard depth-first recursion. □

THEOREM 5. *The graph produced by Algorithm 3 is a canonical version of G with respect to isomorphism.*

PROOF. (*Sketch*) Follows from the fact that the output is isomorphic with G and, coupled with Lemma 2, that the process provides a deterministic ordering of the isomorphs of G without considering blank node labels. □

With respect to RDF graphs containing a blank node split with multiple graphs, we can perform the split per Algorithm 2 and then run Algorithm 3 over each split. We can then compare the resulting canonical graphs. If two or more graphs contain the same blank node label, we can distinguish all blank nodes in said graphs by hashing with an arbitrary fresh symbol to separate them, taking the union with the ground triples for output. (Another option would be to run Algorithm 3 directly over the full RDF graph, but this would lead to products in the orbits and thus a larger search tree.)

5. SKOLEMISATION: GENERATING IRIS

Thus far we've discussed the general principles of canonically labelling an RDF graph to preserve isomorphism. In this context, it is only important that the labels produced from the colouring are locally unique. However, if we were to use such a scheme to Skolemise the blank nodes and produce IRIs, these IRIs would have to be globally unique. This raises two important aspects that we now discuss.

Hashing.

Table 1 presents the estimated risk of collisions for hypothetical hashing schemes of various lengths (represented in bits, hexadecimal strings and Base64, rounding up the number of characters where necessary). In particular, we present the approximate number of inputs needed to reach the given

Table 1: **Approximate number of elements needed to reach the given probability of hash collision for the given length hash (assuming perfect uniformity)**

Bits	Hex	B64	Probability			
			2^{-1}	2^{-4}	2^{-16}	2^{-64}
32	8	6	77,163	22,820	362	< 2
64	16	11	5.1×10^{09}	1.5×10^{09}	2.4×10^{07}	< 2
128	32	22	2.2×10^{19}	6.4×10^{18}	1.0×10^{17}	6.1×10^{09}
160	40	27	1.1×10^{24}	4.2×10^{23}	6.7×10^{21}	4.0×10^{14}
256	64	43	4.0×10^{38}	1.1×10^{38}	1.9×10^{36}	1.1×10^{29}
512	128	86	1.4×10^{77}	4.0×10^{76}	6.4×10^{74}	3.8×10^{67}

probability of collision, where 2^{-1} indicates a $\frac{1}{2}$ probability, 2^{-4} a $\frac{1}{16}$ probability, etc. We assume hashing schemes with perfect uniformity, i.e., we assume that the schemes produce an even spread of hashes across different inputs.

We see a trade-off: longer hashes require longer string labels but increase tolerance to collisions. When considering the Web, we could be talking about billions or trillions of inputs to the scheme. As such, we can rule out hashes of 32 or 64 bits, where even relatively modest inputs cause a 50% or greater chance of a collision. However, if we use a very long labelling scheme, the resulting labels would be cumbersome and slow down transmission times, clog up storage, etc. For reference, we previously found that the average length of IRIs found in a large RDF crawl was about 52 characters [11]. Even in Base64, a 512- or 256-bit hash would produce a relatively cumbersome IRI. Hence we propose that the sweet-spot is around 128-bit (MD5 or MURMUR3_128) or 160-bits (SHA1): in this range, the likelihood of collisions – even assuming very large inputs in the trillions – are negligible when compared with the risk of, say, a comet wiping out life as we know it in the meantime.

Global colours.

When generating Skolem IRIs, we would like to guarantee that these IRIs are globally unique with respect to the graph they originate from. This requires an additional step.

EXAMPLE 9. *Consider the following two RDF graphs:*

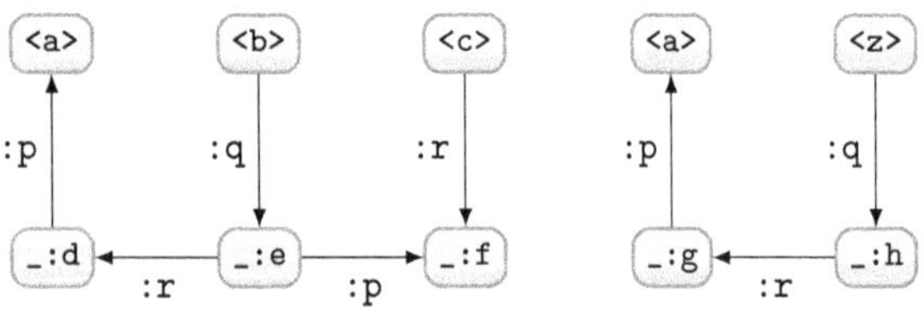

Both graphs would have distinguished colours after one iteration of Algorithm 1 but nodes `_:d` *and* `_:g` *would have the same colour:* `_:d` *would not yet have "encoded" the information from* `<b>` *and* `_:f`*. The Skolem IRIs produced for* `_:d` *and* `_:g` *would (problematically) thus be the same.*

As such, we need an additional step to ensure that Skolem IRIs are unique with respect to a given graph, modulo isomorphism. Our solution is to compute a hash of the entire canonicalised graph – which assuming perfect hashing, is unique to that graph modulo isomorphism – and combine that hash with the hash of each blank node. The hash of each blank node then includes a hash signature unique (modulo hash collisions) to the structure of the entire graph.

Table 2: **BTC–14 runtimes for three hash functions**

Hash	Bits	Runtime (h)	Adjusted (h)
MD5	128	16.4	12.4
MURMUR3_128	128	13.6	9.6
SHA1	160	16.5	12.5

6. EVALUATION

We implemented our methods as a Java package we call BLABEL.[11] We now present evaluation in two main parts. First we look at real-world graphs: given that our complete algorithm is indeed exponential (as expected from the outset), we want to see if bad cases occur in reality; we also wish to compare the performance of different possible hashing schemes in the 128/160-bit range as previously justified. Second we stress-test our algorithm for some nasty cases known from the graph isomorphism literature to illustrate the types of graphs for which our algorithm can struggle.

Real-world RDF graphs.

We ran our complete algorithm for the BTC–14 dataset: a collection of 43.6 million RDF graphs crawled from Web documents spanning 47,560 pay-level-domains [13].[12] The dataset contains around 4 billion quadruples, taking up about 1.1 TB uncompressed in N-Quads format [3]. Experiments were run in a single-threaded manner on an Intel® E5-2407 Quad-Core 2.2GHz machine with 30 GB of heap space.

We first sorted the data according to context to group the triples of documents together (this took 20.8 hours). We then scanned the sorted file, loading each RDF graph individually into memory and computing a canonical labelling before moving onto the next graph. We kept a hash for every graph to identify isomorphic duplicates. We also ran a control that just parsed the data and loaded the graphs without canonicalisation; this took almost precisely 4 hours.

We then ran canonicalisation tests with three suitable hashing schemes: results are provided in Table 2. We present the arity of the hash scheme, the total runtime and the runtime adjusted to subtract the control overhead. We see that the total time taken to canonicalise all of the graphs, minus the control, was between 9.6–12.5 hours, where MURMUR3_128 was the fastest. Given that there were 9.9 million graphs containing blank nodes, this averages to 3.5–4.5 ms per graph. The slowest graph took 31–40 seconds, mainly due to its size: 7.3 million triples with 254 thousand blank nodes.[13] Of the 9.9 million graphs with blank nodes, 9.4 million (95%) were left after removing isomorphic duplicates.

These results show that our canonicalisation scheme is indeed practical for a large collection of real-world graphs.

Synthetic cases.

We also tried some difficult synthetic cases from the BLISS benchmark [12] for standard graph isomorphism.[14] We took five well-known classes of standard graphs at various sizes and represented them as RDF graphs (using a single predicate with edges in both directions). We also took a set of

[11] See http://aidanhogan.com/skolem/ for code/data.

[12] Although many such domains only provide "vacuous" RDFa metadata extracted from HTML pages.

[13] http://www.berkeleybop.org/ontologies/ncbitaxon.owl

[14] http://www.tcs.hut.fi/Software/bliss/benchmarks/index.shtml

Table 3: Results for synthetic graphs

Class	k	Triples	BNodes	Time (ms)
GRID 2D	15	840	225	955
	100	39,600	10,000	58,482
GRID 3D	7	1,764	343	938
	19	38,988	6,589	37,402
CLIQUE	16	240	16	719
	55	2,970	55	578,830
	56	3,080	56	—
LATTICE	6	360	36	532
	18	11,016	324	371,073
	19	12,996	361	—
TRIANGLE	9	504	36	656
	29	21,924	406	507,036
	30	24,360	435	—
MIYAZAKI	2	120	40	140
	8	480	160	195,770
	10	600	200	—

MIYAZAKI graphs known to be a particularly tough case for graph isomorphism [19]. A timeout of ten minutes was set. The experiments were run on a laptop with 1GB of heap-space and an Intel® i3 Dual-Core 2.4GHz processor. We use MURMUR3_128: the fastest hashing method per Table 2.

Table 3 summarises the results. For each class, we present the largest graph run under one second, the largest graph under the ten minute timeout, and for classes with graphs that did not succeed, the smallest graph that hit the timeout ("—" indicates a timeout). We see that our algorithm struggles for even modest sizes of certain synthetic graphs, with MIYAZAKI graphs being the hardest tested. However, we argue that such structures would be rare in real-world graphs: we speculate these cases would require an "adversary" deliberately creating them to be problematic in reality. Likewise we take encouragement from the fact that, e.g., cliques of size 16 can be processed in under a second.

7. RELATED WORK

In 2003, Carroll [4] proposed methods to canonicalise RDF graphs with blank nodes in such a manner that they could be signed. Carroll had quite similar aims to this work, albeit with a different use-case in mind: Carroll's aim was to generate a digital signature of the entire graph rather than to label individual blank nodes. The method he proposes for signing the graph is based on writing it to N-Triples, temporarily mapping all blank nodes to a global blank node, sorting the triples lexically, and then relabelling the blank nodes sequentially as the sorted file is scanned, preserving a bijection between the original input and output blank nodes. In cases where blank nodes are not distinguished by this method, Carroll proposes to inject new triples on such blank nodes that uniquely "mark" them but in such a way that the semantics ignores these triples. This is a weakness of the approach: it modifies the signed graph in an ad hoc way.

Jena [16] offers a method for checking isomorphism between two RDF graphs. However, the method is designed for pairwise isomorphism-checks rather than for producing a (globally-unique) canonical labelling.

Tzitzikas at al. [21] compute minimal deltas between RDF graphs based on an edit distance metric. They propose two algorithms: one views the computation as a combinatorial optimisation problem to which the Hungarian method can be applied; the other is based on computing a signature for blank nodes based on the constant terms in their direct neighbourhood. Although the goals of Tzitzikas at al. and our goals differ somewhat, the signature method that they propose for blank nodes is similar to a non-recursive version of our naive colouring algorithm.

We recently conducted a survey of blank nodes [15, 10], covering their theory and practice, their semantics and complexity, how they are used in the standards and in published data, etc. Some of the main conclusions were that blank nodes are common in RDF data published on the Web (as previously discussed), and that although RDF graphs can sometimes contain connected blank nodes with treewidths as high as 6, most graphs do not contain cycles of blank nodes, which makes various tasks involving them easier. We also found that in a merge of the BTC–12 corpus, 6% of the blank nodes were redundant under simple entailment [10]; for this, we used a signature method similar to the naive algorithm proposed earlier, but only for a fixed depth: we used the method to initially cluster potentially isomorphic graphs rather than to generate a full canonical labelling.

Popular RDF syntaxes like Turtle or RDF/XML are tree-based and require explicit blank node labels for blank nodes to form cycles. The observation that many RDF graphs have acyclical blank nodes and that the complexity of (implementing) various operations over such graphs drops significantly has led to calls for defining a profile of RDF that disallows cyclical blank nodes [15, 2]. Booth calls this profile "Well Behaved RDF" [2]. Recent discussion on the public mailing lists have centred around "deterministic naming" of blank nodes (which is what we tackle here) for such "well-behaved graphs". Although removing consideration of blank node cycles would simplify matters, in this paper we show that in terms of deterministically labelling blank nodes, many real-world graphs, even with cycles, can be labelled cheaply. Our results support the conjecture that exponential cases are unlikely to be found in "real-world" RDF graphs.

8. CONCLUSION

In this paper, we presented methods to compute a canonical labelling of RDF graphs. First we proved that RDF isomorphism is GI-COMPLETE: hence we would expect such an algorithm to be exponential. We then presented an efficient naive colouring method that we would expect to cover many common cases, and showed why it could fail to distinguish blank nodes. Inspired by graph isomorphism algorithms like NAUTY, we then presented a sound algorithm for producing a canonical labelling, which can be used to check isomorphism between RDF graphs or to cluster isomorphic RDF graphs within a collection. We also addressed issues regarding use of the algorithm to compute global Skolem IRIs that deterministically replace blank nodes. Though our algorithm is exponential, we found that we could process 9.9 million real-world RDF graphs (with blank nodes) in approximately 9.6 hours: on average, about 3.5 ms a graph. We showed that some synthetic cases can cause performance problems but argued that such cases seem unlikely to occur "naturally". We thus see our proposal as being both well-founded in theory and (hopefully) useful in practice.

9. REFERENCES

[1] L. Babai, P. Erdös, and S. M. Selkow. Random graph isomorphism. *SIAM J. Comput.*, 9(3):628–635, 1980.

[2] D. Booth. Well Behaved RDF: A Straw-Man Proposal for Taming Blank Nodes, 2012. http://dbooth.org/2013/well-behaved-rdf/Booth-well-behaved-rdf.pdf.

[3] G. Carothers. RDF 1.1 N-Quads. W3C Recommendation, 2014. http://www.w3.org/TR/n-quads/.

[4] J. J. Carroll. Signing RDF graphs. In *International Semantic Web Conference*, pages 369–384, 2003.

[5] R. Cyganiak, D. Wood, and M. Lanthaler. RDF 1.1 Concepts & Abstract Syntax. W3C Recommendation, Feb. 2014. http://www.w3.org/TR/rdf11-concepts/.

[6] C. Gutierrez, C. A. Hurtado, A. O. Mendelzon, and J. Pérez. Foundations of Semantic Web databases. *J. Comput. Syst. Sci.*, 77(3):520–541, 2011.

[7] P. Hayes. RDF Semantics. W3C Recommendation, 2004. http://www.w3.org/TR/2004/REC-rdf-mt-20040210/.

[8] P. Hayes and P. F. Patel-Schneider. RDF 1.1 Semantics. W3C Recommendation, 2014. http://www.w3.org/TR/2014/REC-rdf11-mt-20140225/.

[9] T. Heath and C. Bizer. *Linked Data: Evolving the Web into a Global Data Space*, volume 1. Morgan & Claypool, 2011.

[10] A. Hogan, M. Arenas, A. Mallea, and A. Polleres. Everything you always wanted to know about blank nodes. *J. Web Sem.*, 27:42–69, 2014.

[11] A. Hogan, J. Umbrich, A. Harth, R. Cyganiak, A. Polleres, and S. Decker. An empirical survey of Linked Data conformance. *J. Web Sem.*, 14:14–44, 2012.

[12] T. A. Junttila and P. Kaski. Engineering an efficient canonical labeling tool for large and sparse graphs. In *Workshop on Algorithm Engineering and Experiments (ALENEX)*, 2007.

[13] T. Käfer and A. Harth. Billion Triples Challenge data set. http://km.aifb.kit.edu/projects/btc-2014/, 2014.

[14] O. Lassila and R. R. Swick. Resource Description Framework (RDF) Model and Syntax Specification. W3C Recommendation, 1999. http://www.w3.org/TR/1999/REC-rdf-syntax-19990222/.

[15] A. Mallea, M. Arenas, A. Hogan, and A. Polleres. On blank nodes. In *International Semantic Web Conference*, pages 421–437, 2011.

[16] B. McBride. Jena: A Semantic Web Toolkit. *IEEE Internet Computing*, 6(6):55–59, 2002.

[17] B. McKay. Practical Graph Isomorphism. In *Congressum Numerantium*, volume 30, pages 45–87, 1980.

[18] B. D. McKay and A. Piperno. Practical graph isomorphism, II. *J. Symb. Comput.*, 60:94–112, 2014.

[19] T. Miyazaki. The Complexity of McKay's Canonical Labeling Algorithm. In *Groups and Computation, II*, pages 239–256, 1997.

[20] A. Piperno. Search Space Contraction in Canonical Labeling of Graphs (Preliminary Version). *CoRR*, abs/0804.4881, 2008.

[21] Y. Tzitzikas, C. Lantzaki, and D. Zeginis. Blank Node Matching and RDF/S Comparison Functions. In *International Semantic Web Conference*, pages 591–607, 2012.

Scalable Methods for Adaptively Seeding a Social Network

Thibaut Horel
Harvard University
thorel@seas.harvard.edu

Yaron Singer
Harvard University
yaron@seas.harvard.edu

ABSTRACT

In recent years, social networking platforms have developed into extraordinary channels for spreading and consuming information. Along with the rise of such infrastructure, there is continuous progress on techniques for spreading information effectively through influential users. In many applications, one is restricted to select influencers from a set of users who engaged with the topic being promoted, and due to the structure of social networks, these users often rank low in terms of their influence potential. An alternative approach one can consider is an adaptive method which selects users in a manner which targets their influential neighbors. The advantage of such an approach is that it leverages the friendship paradox in social networks: while users are often not influential, they often know someone who is.

Despite the various complexities in such optimization problems, we show that scalable adaptive seeding is achievable. In particular, we develop algorithms for linear influence models with provable approximation guarantees that can be gracefully parallelized. To show the effectiveness of our methods we collected data from various verticals social network users follow. For each vertical, we collected data on the users who responded to a certain post as well as their neighbors, and applied our methods on this data. Our experiments show that adaptive seeding is scalable, and importantly, that it obtains dramatic improvements over standard approaches of information dissemination.

Categories and Subject Descriptors

H.2.8 [**Database Management**]: Database Applications—*Data Mining*; F.2.2 [**Analysis of Algorithms and Problem Complexity**]: Nonnumerical Algorithms and Problems

Keywords

Influence Maximization; Two-stage Optimization

WWW 2015, May 18–22, 2015, Florence, Italy.
ACM 978-1-4503-3469-3/15/05.
http://dx.doi.org/10.1145/2736277.2741127.

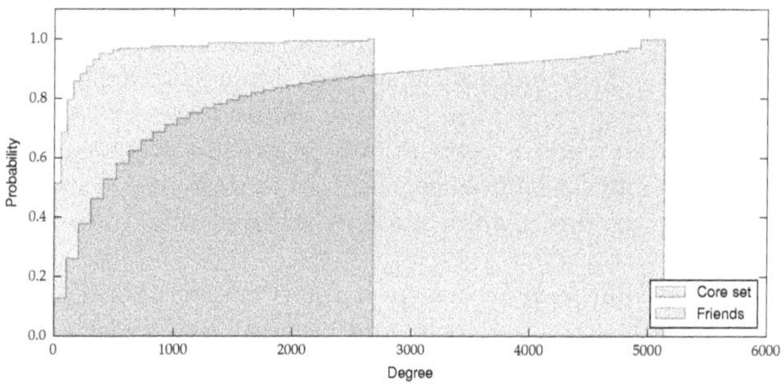

Figure 1: CDF of the degree distribution of users who liked a post by Kiva on Facebook and that of their friends.

1. INTRODUCTION

The massive adoption of social networking services in recent years creates a unique platform for promoting ideas and spreading information. Communication through online social networks leaves traces of behavioral data which allow observing, predicting and even engineering processes of information diffusion. First posed by Domingos and Richardson [7, 25] and elegantly formulated and further developed by Kempe, Kleinberg, and Tardos [14], *influence maximization* is the algorithmic challenge of selecting a fixed number of individuals who can serve as early adopters of a new idea, product, or technology in a manner that will trigger a large cascade in the social network.

In many cases where influence maximization methods are applied one cannot select any user in the network but is limited to some subset of users. As an example, consider an online retailer who wishes to promote a product through word-of-mouth by rewarding influential customers who purchased the product. The retailer is then limited to select influential users from the set of users who purchased the product. In general, we will call the *core set* the set of users an influence maximization campaign can access. When the goal is to select influential users from the core set, the laws that govern social networks can lead to poor outcomes. Due to the heavy-tailed degree distribution of social networks, high degree nodes are rare, and since influence maximization techniques often depend on the ability to select high degree nodes, a naive application of influence maximization techniques to the core set can become ineffective.

An adaptive approach. An alternative approach to spending the entire budget on the core set is an adaptive two-stage approach. In the first stage, one can spend a fraction of the budget on the core users so that they invite their friends to participate in the campaign, then in the second stage spend the rest of the budget on the influential friends who hopefully have arrived. The idea behind this approach is to leverage a structural phenomenon in social networks known as the friendship paradox [9]. Intuitively, the friendship paradox says that individuals are not likely to have many friends, but they likely have a friend that does ("your friends have more friends than you"). In Figure 1 we give an example of such an effect by plotting a CDF of the degree distribution of a core set of users who responded to a post on Facebook and the degree distribution of their friends. Remarkably, there are also formal guarantees of such effects. Recent work shows that for any network that has a power law degree distribution and a small fraction of random edges, there is an asymptotic gap between the average degree of small samples of nodes and that of their neighbors, with constant probability [18]. The implication is that when considering the core users (e.g. those who visit the online store) as random samples from a social network, any algorithm which can use their neighbors as influencers will have dramatic improvement over the direct application of influence maximization.

Warmup. Suppose we are given a network, a random set of core users X and a budget k, and the goal is to select a subset of nodes in X of size $t \leq k$ which has the most influential set of neighbors of size $k - t$. For simplicity, assume for now that the influence of a set is simply its average degree. If we take the $k/2$ highest degree neighbors of X, then surely there is a set S of size at most $k/2$ in X connected to this set, and selecting S would be a two-approximation to this problem. In comparison, the standard approach of influence maximization is to select the k highest degree nodes in X. Thus, standard influence maximization would have k of the most influential nodes in X while the approximation algorithm we propose has $k/2$ of the most influential nodes from its set of neighbors. How much better or worse is it to use this approach over the standard one? If the network has a power-law degree distribution with a small fraction of random edges, and influence is measured in terms of sum of degrees of a set, then the results of [18] discussed above imply that the two-stage approach which allows seeding neighbors can do asymptotically (in the size of the network) better. Thus, at least intuitively, it looks as if two-stage approaches may be worth investigating.

In this paper, our goal is to study the potential benefits of adaptive approaches for influence maximization. We are largely motivated by the following question.

Can adaptive optimization lead to significant improvements in influence maximization?

To study this question we use the adaptive seeding model recently formalized in [27]. The main distinctions from the caricature model in the warmup problem above is that in adaptive seeding the core set X can be arbitrary (it does not have to be random), and every neighbor of X is assumed to arrive with some independent probability. These probabilities are used to model the uncertainty we have in that the neighbors would be interested in promoting the product, as they are not in the core set. The goal in adaptive seeding is to select a subset of nodes in X such that, in expectation over all possible arrivals of its neighbors, one can select a maximally influential set of neighbors with the remaining budget.[1] It is worth noting that using X to be the entire set of nodes in the network we get the Kempe-Kleinberg-Tardos model [14], and thus adaptive seeding can be seen as a generalization of this model.

Scalability. One of the challenges in adaptive seeding is scalability. This is largely due to the stochastic nature of the problem derived from uncertainty about arrival of neighbors. The main result in [27] is a constant factor approximation algorithm for well-studied influence models such as independent cascade and linear threshold which is, at large, a theoretical triumph. These algorithms rely on various forms of sampling, which lead to a significant blowup in the input size. While such techniques provide strong theoretical guarantees, for social network data sets which are often either large or massive, such approaches are inapplicable. The main technical challenge we address in this work is how to design scalable adaptive optimization techniques for influence maximization which do not require sampling.

Beyond random users. The motivation for the adaptive approach hinges on the friendship paradox, but what if the core set is not a random sample? The results in [18] hold when the core set of users is random but since users who follow a particular topic are not a random sample of the network, we must somehow evaluate adaptive seeding on representative data sets. The experimental challenge is to estimate the prominence of high degree neighbors in settings that are typical of viral marketing campaigns. Figure 1 is a foreshadowing of the experimental methods we used to show that an effect similar to the friendship paradox exists in such cases as well.

Main results. Our main results in this paper show that adaptive seeding is a scalable approach which can dramatically improve upon standard approaches of influence maximization. We present a general method that enables designing adaptive seeding algorithms in a manner that avoids sampling, and thus makes adaptive seeding scalable to large size graphs. We use this approach as a basis for designing two algorithms, both achieving an approximation ratio of $(1 - 1/e)$ for the adaptive problem. The first algorithm is implemented through a linear program, which proves to be extremely efficient over instances where there is a large budget. The second approach is a combinatorial algorithm with the same approximation guarantee which can be easily parallelized, has good theoretical guarantees on its running time and does well on instances with smaller budgets. The guarantees of our algorithms hold for linear models of influence, *i.e.* models for which the influence of a set can be expressed as the sum of the influence of its members. While this class does not include models such as the independent cascade and the linear threshold model, it includes the well-studied *voter model* [12, 8] and measures such as node degree, click-through-rate or retweet measures of users which serve as natural proxies of influence in many settings [30]. In comparison to submodular influence functions, the rel-

[1] The model can be extended to the case where nodes take on different costs, and results we present here largely generalize to such settings as well. Although it seems quite plausible that the probability of attracting neighbors could depend on the rewards they receive, the model deliberately assumes unit costs, consistent with the celebrated Kempe-Kleinberg-Tardos model [14]. Of course, if the likelihood of becoming an early adopter is inversely proportional to one's influence, then any influence maximization model loses substance.

ative simplicity of linear models allows making substantial progress on this challenging problem.

We then use these algorithms to conduct a series of experiments to show the potential of adaptive approaches for influence maximization both on synthetic and real social networks. The main component of the experiments involved collecting publicly available data from Facebook on users who expressed interest ("liked") a certain post from a topic they follow and data on their friends. The premise here is that such users mimic potential participants in a viral marketing campaign. The results on these data sets suggest that adaptive seeding can have dramatic improvements over standard influence maximization methods.

Paper organization. We begin by formally describing the model and the assumptions we make in the following section. In Section 3 we describe the reduction of the adaptive seeding problem to a non-adaptive relaxation. In Section 4 we describe our non-adaptive algorithms for adaptive seeding. In Section 5 we describe our experiments, and conclude with a brief discussion on related work.

2. MODEL

Given a graph $G = (V, E)$, for a node $v \in V$ we denote by $\mathcal{N}(v)$ the neighborhood of v. By extension, for any subset of nodes $S \subseteq V$, $\mathcal{N}(S) \equiv \bigcup_{v\in S} \mathcal{N}(v)$ will denote the neighborhood of S. The notion of influence in the graph is captured by a function $f : 2^{|V|} \to \mathbf{R}_+$ mapping a subset of nodes to a non-negative influence value.

The adaptive seeding model. The input of the *adaptive seeding* problem is a *core set* of nodes $X \subseteq V$ and for any node $u \in \mathcal{N}(X)$ a probability p_u that u realizes if one of its neighbor in X is seeded. We will write $m = |X|$ and $n = |\mathcal{N}(X)|$ the parameters controlling the input size. The seeding process is the following:

1. *Seeding:* the seeder selects a subset of nodes $S \subseteq X$ in the core set.
2. *Realization of the neighbors:* every node $u \in \mathcal{N}(S)$ realizes independently with probability p_u. We denote by $R \subseteq \mathcal{N}(S)$ the subset of nodes that is realized during this stage.
3. *Influence maximization:* the seeder selects the set of nodes $T \subseteq R$ that maximizes the influence function f.

There is a budget constraint k on the total number of nodes that can be selected: S and T must satisfy $|S| + |T| \leq k$. The seeder chooses the set S before observing the realization R and thus wishes to select optimally in expectation over all such possible realizations. Formally, the objective can be stated as:

$$\begin{aligned} &\max_{S\subseteq X} \sum_{R\subseteq\mathcal{N}(S)} p_R \max_{\substack{T\subseteq R\\|T|\leq k-|S|}} f(T) \\ &\text{s.t. } |S| \leq k \end{aligned} \tag{1}$$

where p_R is the probability that the set R realizes, $p_R \equiv \prod_{u\in R} p_u \prod_{u\in\mathcal{N}(S)\setminus R}(1 - p_u)$.

It is important to note that the process through which nodes arrive in the second stage is *not* an influence process. The nodes in the second stage arrive if they are willing to spread information in exchange for a unit of the budget. Only when they have arrived does the influence process occur. This process is encoded in the influence function and occurs after the influence maximization stage without incentivizing nodes along the propagation path. In general, the idea of a two-stage (or in general, multi-stage) approach is to use the nodes who arrive in the first stage to recruit influential users who can be incentivized to spread information. In standard influence maximization, the nodes who are not in the core set do not receive incentives to propagate information, and cascades tend to die off quickly [29, 3, 10, 6].

Influence functions. In this paper we focus on *linear* (or additive) influence models: in these models the value of a subset of nodes can be expressed as a weighted sum of their individual influence. One important example of such models is the *voter model* [26] used to represent the spread of opinions in a social network: at each time step, a node adopts an opinion with a probability equal to the fraction of its neighbors sharing this opinion at the previous time step. Formally, this can be written as a discrete-time Markov chain over opinion configurations of the network. In this model influence maximization amounts to "converting" the optimal subset of nodes to a given opinion at the initial time so as to maximize the number of converts after a given period of time. Remarkably, a simple analysis shows that under this model, the influence function f is additive:

$$\forall S \subseteq V,\ f(S) = \sum_{u\in S} w_u \tag{2}$$

where $w_u, u \in V$ are weights which can be easily computed from the powers of the transition matrix of the Markov chain. This observation led to the development of fast algorithms for influence maximization under the voter model [8].

NP-Hardness. In contrast to standard influence maximization, adaptive seeding is already NP-Hard even for the simplest influence functions such as $f(S) = |S|$ and when all probabilities are one. We discuss this in the full version of the paper [13].

3. NON-ADAPTIVE OPTIMIZATION

The challenging aspect of the adaptive seeding problem expressed in Equation 1 is its adaptivity: a seed set must be selected during the first stage such that in expectation a high influence value can be reached when adaptively selecting nodes on the second stage. A standard approach in stochastic optimization for overcoming this challenge is to use sampling to estimate the expectation of the influence value reachable on the second stage. However, as will be discussed in Section 5, this approach quickly becomes infeasible even with modest size graphs.

In this section we develop an approach which avoids sampling and allows designing adaptive seeding algorithms that can be applied to large graphs. We show that for additive influence functions one can optimize a relaxation of the problem which we refer to as the *non-adaptive* version of the problem. After defining the non-adaptive version, we show in sections 3.1 that the optimal solution for the non-adaptive version is an upper bound on the optimal solution of the adaptive seeding problem. We then argue in Section 3.2 that any solution to the non-adaptive version of the problem can be converted to an adaptive solution, losing an arbitrarily small factor in the approximation ratio. Together, this implies that one can design algorithms for the non-adaptive problem instead, as we do in Section 4.

Non-adaptive policies. We say that a policy is *non-adaptive* if it selects a set of nodes $S \subseteq X$ to be seeded in the first stage and a vector of probabilities $\mathbf{q} \in [0,1]^n$, such that each neighbor u of S which realizes is included in the solution independently with probability q_u. The constraint will now be that the budget is only respected in expectation, *i.e.* $|S| + \mathbf{p}^T\mathbf{q} \leq k$. Formally the optimization problem for non-adaptive policies can be written as:

$$\begin{aligned} \max_{\substack{S\subseteq X\\ \mathbf{q}\in[0,1]^n}} & \sum_{R\subseteq\mathcal{N}(X)} \Big(\prod_{u\in R} p_u q_u \prod_{u\in\mathcal{N}(X)\setminus R}(1-p_u q_u)\Big) f(R) \\ \text{s.t. } & |S| + \mathbf{p}^T\mathbf{q} \leq k,\ q_u \leq \mathbf{1}\{u\in\mathcal{N}(S)\} \end{aligned} \tag{3}$$

where we denote by $\mathbf{1}\{E\}$ the indicator variable of the event E. Note that because of the condition $q_u \leq \mathbf{1}\{u\in\mathcal{N}(S)\}$, the summand associated with R in (3) vanishes whenever R contains $u \in \mathcal{N}(X)\setminus\mathcal{N}(S)$. Hence, the summation is restricted to $R \subseteq \mathcal{N}(S)$ as in (1).

3.1 Adaptivity Gap

We will now justify the use of non-adaptive strategies by showing that the optimal solution for this form of non-adaptive strategies yields a higher value than adaptive ones. For brevity, given a probability vector $\pi \in [0,1]^m$ we write:

$$F(\pi) \equiv \sum_{R\subseteq\mathcal{N}(X)} \left(\prod_{u\in R}\pi_u \prod_{u\in\mathcal{N}(X)\setminus R}(1-\pi_u)\right) f(R) \tag{4}$$

as well as $\mathbf{p}\otimes\mathbf{q}$ to denote the component-wise multiplication between vectors $\mathbf{p}$ and $\mathbf{q}$. Finally, we write $\mathcal{F}_A \equiv \{S \subseteq X : |S| \leq k\}$, and $\mathcal{F}_{NA} \equiv \{(S,\mathbf{q}), |S| + \mathbf{p}^T\mathbf{q} \leq k, q_u \leq \mathbf{1}_{\{u\in\mathcal{N}(S)\}}\}$ to denote the feasible regions of the adaptive and non-adaptive problems, respectively.

Proposition 1. *For additive functions given by (2), the value of the optimal adaptive policy is upper bounded by the optimal non-adaptive policy:*

$$\begin{aligned} \max_{S\subseteq X} \sum_{R\subseteq\mathcal{N}(S)} p_R \max_{\substack{T\subseteq R\\ |T|\leq k-|S|}} f(T) &\leq \max_{\substack{S\subseteq X\\ q\in[0,1]^n}} F(\mathbf{p}\otimes\mathbf{q}) \\ \text{s.t. } S\in\mathcal{F}_A \qquad\qquad & \qquad \text{s.t. } (S,\mathbf{q})\in\mathcal{F}_{NA} \end{aligned}$$

The proof of this proposition can be found in the full version of the paper [13] and relies on the following fact: the optimal adaptive policy can be written as a feasible non-adaptive policy, hence it provides a lower bound on the value of the optimal non-adaptive policy.

3.2 From Non-Adaptive to Adaptive Solutions

From the above proposition we now know that optimal non-adaptive solutions have higher values than adaptive solutions. Given a non-adaptive solution $(S,\mathbf{q})$, a possible scheme would be to use S as an adaptive solution. But since $(S,\mathbf{q})$ is a solution to the non-adaptive problem, Proposition 1 does not provide any guarantee on how well S performs as an adaptive solution.

However, we show that from a non-adaptive solution $(S,\mathbf{q})$, we can obtain a lower bound on the adaptive value of S, that is, the expected influence attainable in expectation over all possible arrivals of neighbors of S. Starting from S, in every realization of neighbors R, sample every node $u \in R\cap\mathcal{N}(S)$ with probability q_u, to obtain a random set of nodes $I_R \subseteq R\cap S$. $(S,\mathbf{q})$ being a non-adaptive solution, it could be that selecting I_R exceeds our budget. Indeed, the only guarantee that we have is that $|S| + \mathbb{E}\big[|I_R|\big] \leq k$. As a consequence, an adaptive solution starting from S might not be able to select I_R on the second stage.

Fortunately, the probability of exceeding the budget is small enough and with high probability I_R will be feasible. This is exploited in [28] to design a randomized rounding method with approximation guarantees. These rounding methods are called *contention resolution schemes.* Theorem 1.3 of this paper gives us a contention resolution scheme which will compute from $\mathbf{q}$ and for any realization R a *feasible* set $\tilde{I}_R$, such that:

$$\mathbb{E}_R\big[f(\tilde{I}_R)\big] \geq (1-\varepsilon)F(\mathbf{q}) \tag{5}$$

What this means is that starting from a non-adaptive solution $(S,\mathbf{q})$, there is a way to construct a random *feasible* subset on the second stage such that in expectation, this set attains almost the same influence value as the non-adaptive solution. Since the adaptive solution starting from S will select optimally from the realizations $R \subseteq \mathcal{N}(S)$, $\mathbb{E}_R[f(\tilde{I}_R)]$ provides a lower bound on the adaptive value of S that we denote by $A(S)$.

More precisely, denoting by OPT_A the optimal value of the adaptive problem (1), we have the following proposition whose proof can be found in the full version of this paper [13].

Proposition 2. *Let $(S,\mathbf{q})$ be an α-approximate solution to the non-adaptive problem (3), then* $\mathrm{A}(S) \geq \alpha\mathrm{OPT}_A$.

4. ALGORITHMS

Section 3 shows that the adaptive seeding problem reduces to the non-adaptive problem. We will now discuss two approaches to construct approximate non-adaptive solutions. The first is an LP-based approach, and the second is a combinatorial algorithm. Both approaches have the same $(1-1/e)$ approximation ratio, which is then translated to a $(1-1/e)$ approximation ratio for the adaptive seeding problem (1) via Proposition 2. As we will show in Section 5, both algorithms have their advantages and disadvantages in terms of scalability.

4.1 An LP-Based Approach

Note that due to linearity of expectation, for a linear function f of the form given by (2) we have:

$$\begin{aligned} F(\mathbf{p}) = \mathbb{E}_R\big[f(R)\big] &= \mathbb{E}_R\left[\sum_{u\in\mathcal{N}(X)} w_u \mathbf{1}_{\{u\in R\}}\right] \\ &= \sum_{u\in\mathcal{N}(X)} w_u \mathbb{P}[u\in R] = \sum_{u\in\mathcal{N}(X)} p_u w_u \end{aligned} \tag{6}$$

Thus, the non-adaptive optimization problem (3) can be written as:

$$\begin{aligned} \max_{\substack{S\subseteq X\\ \mathbf{q}\in[0,1]^n}} & \sum_{u\in\mathcal{N}(X)} p_u q_u w_u \\ \text{s.t. } & |S| + \mathbf{p}^T\mathbf{q} \leq k,\ q_u \leq \mathbf{1}\{u\in\mathcal{N}(S)\} \end{aligned}$$

The choice of the set S can be relaxed by introducing a variable $\lambda_v \in [0,1]$ for each $v \in X$. We obtain the following

LP for the adaptive seeding problem:

$$\begin{aligned} \max_{\substack{\mathbf{q}\in[0,1]^n\\ \boldsymbol{\lambda}\in[0,1]^m}} \ & \sum_{u\in\mathcal{N}(X)} p_u q_u w_u \\ \text{s.t.}\ & \sum_{v\in X}\lambda_v + \mathbf{p}^T\mathbf{q} \le k,\ q_u \le \sum_{v\in\mathcal{N}(u)}\lambda_v \end{aligned} \tag{7}$$

An optimal solution to the above problem can be found in polynomial time using standard LP-solvers. The solution returned by the LP is *fractional*, and requires a rounding procedure to return a feasible solution to our problem, where S is integral. To round the solution we use the pipage rounding method [2]. We defer the details to the full version of the paper [13].

LEMMA 1. *For* ADAPTIVESEEDING-LP *defined in (7), any fractional solution $(\boldsymbol{\lambda},\mathbf{q})\in[0,1]^m\times[0,1]^n$ can be rounded to an integral solution $\bar{\boldsymbol{\lambda}}\in\{0,1\}^m$ s.t. $(1-1/e)F(\mathbf{p}\circ\mathbf{q})\le A(\bar{\lambda})$ in $O(m+n)$ steps.*

4.2 A Combinatorial Algorithm

In this section, we introduce a combinatorial algorithm with an identical approximation guarantee to the LP-based approach. However, its running time, stated in Proposition 5 can be better than the one given by LP solvers depending on the relative sizes of the budget and the number of nodes in the graph. Furthermore, as we discuss at the end of this section, this algorithm is amenable to parallelization.

The main idea is to reduce the problem to a monotone submodular maximization problem and apply a variant of the celebrated greedy algorithm [24]. In contrast to standard influence maximization, the submodularity of the non-adaptive seeding problem is not simply a consequence of properties of the influence function; it also strongly relies on the combinatorial structure of the two-stage optimization.

Intuitively, we can think of our problem as trying to find a set S in the first stage, for which the nodes that can be seeded on the second stage have the largest possible value. To formalize this, for a budget $b\in\mathbf{R}^+$ used in the second stage and a set of neighbors $T\subseteq\mathcal{N}(X)$, we will use $\mathcal{O}(T,b)$ to denote the solution to:

$$\begin{aligned} \mathcal{O}(T,b)\equiv \max_{\mathbf{q}\in[0,1]^n} & \sum_{u\in\mathcal{N}(X)\cap T} p_u q_u w_u \\ \text{s.t. } & \mathbf{p}^T\mathbf{q}\le b \end{aligned} \tag{8}$$

The optimization problem (3) for non-adaptive policies can now be written as:

$$\max_{S\subseteq X} \mathcal{O}\big(\mathcal{N}(S),k-|S|\big) \quad \text{s.t. } |S|\le k \tag{9}$$

We start by proving in Proposition 3 that for fixed t, $\mathcal{O}(\mathcal{N}(\cdot),t)$ is submodular. This proposition relies on lemmas 2 and 3 about the properties of $\mathcal{O}(T,b)$.

LEMMA 2. *Let $T\subseteq\mathcal{N}(X)$ and $x\in\mathcal{N}(X)$, then $\mathcal{O}(T\cup\{x\},b)-\mathcal{O}(T,b)$ is non-decreasing in b.*

The proof of this lemma can be found in the full version of the paper [13]. The main idea consists in writing:

$$\mathcal{O}(T\cup\{x\},c)-\mathcal{O}(T\cup\{x\},b) = \int_b^c \partial_+\mathcal{O}_{T\cup\{x\}}(t)dt$$

where $\partial_+\mathcal{O}_T$ denotes the right derivative of $\mathcal{O}(T,\cdot)$. For a fixed T and b, $\mathcal{O}(T,b)$ defines a fractional Knapsack problem over the set T. Knowing the form of the optimal fractional solution, we can verify that $\partial_+\mathcal{O}_{T\cup\{x\}}\ge\partial_+\mathcal{O}_T$ and obtain:

$$\mathcal{O}(T\cup\{x\},c)-\mathcal{O}(T\cup\{x\},b)\ \ge\ \mathcal{O}(T,c)-\mathcal{O}(T,b)$$

LEMMA 3. *For any $b\in\mathbf{R}^+$, $\mathcal{O}(T,b)$ is submodular in T, $T\subseteq\mathcal{N}(X)$.*

The proof of this lemma is more technical. For $T\subseteq\mathcal{N}(X)$ and $x,y\in\mathcal{N}(X)\setminus T$, we need to show that:

$$\mathcal{O}(T\cup\{x\},b)-\mathcal{O}(T,b)\ge\mathcal{O}(T\cup\{y,x\},b)-\mathcal{O}(T\cup\{y\},b)$$

This can be done by partitioning the set T into "high value items" (those with weight greater than w_x) and "low value items" and carefully applying Lemma 2 to the associated subproblems. The proof is in the full version of the paper [13].

Finally, Lemma 3 can be used to show Proposition 3 whose proof can be found in the full version [13].

PROPOSITION 3. *Let $b\in\mathbf{R}^+$, then $\mathcal{O}(\mathcal{N}(S),b)$ is monotone and submodular in S, $S\subseteq X$.*

We can now use Proposition 3 to reduce (9) to a monotone submodular maximization problem. First, we note that (9) can be rewritten:

$$\max_{\substack{S\subseteq X\\ t\in\mathbb{N}}} \mathcal{O}\big(\mathcal{N}(S),t\big) \quad \text{s.t. } |S|+t\le k \tag{10}$$

Intuitively, we fix t arbitrarily so that the maximization above becomes a submodular maximization problem with fixed budget t. We then optimize over the value of t. Combining this observation with the greedy algorithm for monotone submodular maximization [24], we obtain Algorithm 1, whose performance guarantee is summarized in Proposition 4.

Algorithm 1 Combinatorial algorithm

$S\leftarrow\emptyset$
for $t=1$ **to** $k-1$ **do**
  $S_t\leftarrow\emptyset$
  for $i=1$ **to** $k-t$ **do**
    $x^*\leftarrow\text{argmax}_{x\in X\setminus S_t}\ \mathcal{O}(\mathcal{N}(S_t\cup\{x\}),t)-\mathcal{O}(\mathcal{N}(S_t),t)$
    $S_t\leftarrow S_t\cup\{x^*\}$
  end for
  if $\mathcal{O}(\mathcal{N}(S_t),t)>\mathcal{O}(\mathcal{N}(S),k-|S|)$ **then**
    $S\leftarrow S_t$
  end if
end for
return S

PROPOSITION 4. *Let S be the set computed by Algorithm 1 and let us denote by $\mathrm{A}(S)$ the value of the adaptive policy selecting S on the first stage. Then $\mathrm{A}(S)\ge(1-1/e)\mathrm{OPT}_A$.*

Parallelization. The algorithm described above considers all possible ways to split the seeding budget between the first and the second stage. For each possible split $\{(t,k-t)\}_{t=1\dots,k-1}$, the algorithm computes an approximation to the optimal non adaptive solution that uses $k-t$ nodes in the first stage and t nodes in the second stage, and returns the solution for the split with the highest value (breaking ties arbitrarily). This process can be trivially parallelized across $k-1$ machines, each performing a computation of a single split. With slightly more effort, for any $\epsilon > 0$ one can parallelize over $\log_{1+\epsilon} n$ machines at the cost of losing a factor of ϵ in the approximation guarantee (see full version of the paper [13] for details).

Implementation in MapReduce. While the previous paragraph describes how to parallelize the outer `for` loop of Algorithm 1, we note that its inner loop can also be parallelized in the MapReduce framework. Indeed, it corresponds to the greedy algorithm applied to the function $\mathcal{O}(\mathcal{N}(\cdot), t)$. The SAMPLE&PRUNE approach successfully applied in [17] to obtain MapReduce algorithms for various submodular maximizations can also be applied to Algorithm 1 to cast it in the MapReduce framework. The details of the algorithm can be found in the full version of the paper [13].

Algorithmic speedups. To implement Algorithm 1 efficiently, the computation of the argmax on line 5 must be dealt with carefully. $\mathcal{O}(\mathcal{N}(S_t \cup \{x\}), t)$ is the optimal solution to the fractional Knapsack problem (8) with budget t and can be computed in time $\min(\frac{t}{p_{\min}}, n)$ by iterating over the list of nodes in $\mathcal{N}(S_t \cup \{x\})$ in decreasing order of the degrees. This decreasing order of $\mathcal{N}(S_t)$ can be maintained throughout the greedy construction of S_t by:

- ordering the list of neighbors of nodes in X by decreasing order of the degrees when initially constructing the graph. This is responsible for a $O(n \log n)$ preprocessing time.
- when adding node x to S_t, observe that $\mathcal{N}(S_t \cup \{x\}) = \mathcal{N}(S_t) \cup \mathcal{N}(\{x\})$. Hence, if $\mathcal{N}(S_t)$ and $\mathcal{N}(\{x\})$ are sorted lists, then $\mathcal{O}(\mathcal{N}(S_t \cup \{x\}), t)$ can be computed in a single iteration of length $\min(\frac{t}{p_{\min}}, n)$ where the two sorted lists are merged on the fly.

As a consequence, the running time of line 5 is bounded from above by $m \min(\frac{t}{p_{\min}}, n)$. The two nested for loops are responsible for the additional k^2 factor. The running time of Algorithm 1 is summarized in Proposition 5.

PROPOSITION 5. *Let* $p_{min} = \min\{p_u, u \in \mathcal{N}(X)\}$, *then Algorithm 1 runs in time* $O(n \log n + k^2 m \min(\frac{k}{p_{min}}, n))$.

5. EXPERIMENTS

In this section we validate the adaptive seeding approach through experimentation. Specifically, we show that our algorithms for adaptive seeding obtain significant improvement over standard influence maximization, that these improvements are robust to changes in environment variables, and that our approach is efficient in terms of running-time and scalable to large social networks.

5.1 Experimental setup

We tested our algorithms on three types of datasets. Each of them allows us to experiment on a different aspect of the adaptive seeding problem. The Facebook Pages dataset that we collected ourselves has a central place in our experiments since it is the one which is closet to actual applications of adaptive seeding.

Synthetic networks. Using standard models of social networks we generated large-scale graphs to model the social network. To emulate the process of users following a topic (the core set X) we sampled subsets of nodes at random, and applied our algorithms on the sample and their neighbors. The main advantage of these data sets is that they allow us to generate graphs of arbitrary sizes and experiment with various parameters that govern the structure of the graph. The disadvantages are that users who follow a topic are not necessarily random samples, and that social networks often have structural properties that are not captured in generative models.

Real networks. We used publicly available data sets of real social networks available at [21]. As for synthetic networks, we used a random sample of nodes to emulate users who follow a topic, which is the main disadvantage of this approach. The advantage however, is that such datasets contain an entire network which allows testing different propagation parameters.

Facebook Pages. We collected data from several Facebook Pages, each associated with a commercial entity that uses the Facebook page to communicate with its followers. For each page, we selected a post and then collected data about the users who expressed interest ("liked") the post and their friends. The advantage of this data set is that it is highly representative of the scenario we study here. Campaigns run on a social network will primarily target users who have already expressed interests in the topic being promoted. The main disadvantage of this method is that such data is extremely difficult to collect due to the crawling restrictions that Facebook applies and gives us only the 2-hop neighborhood around a post. This makes it difficult to experiment with different propagation parameters. Fortunately, as we soon discuss, we were able to circumvent some of the crawling restrictions and collect large networks, and the properties of the voter influence model are such that these datasets suffice to accurately account for influence propagation in the graph.

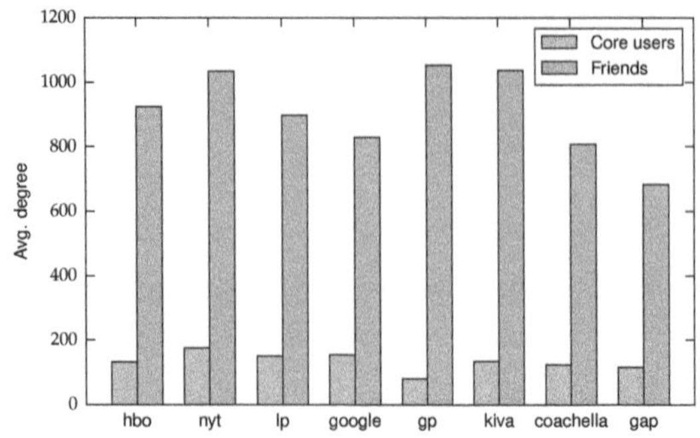

Figure 2: Comparison of the average degree of the core set users and the average degree of their friends.

Data collection. We selected Facebook Pages in different verticals (topics). Each page is operated by an institution or an entity whose associated Facebook Page is regularly used for promotional posts related to this topic. On each of these pages, we selected a recent post (posted no later than January 2014) with approximately 1,000 *likes*. The set of users who liked those posts constitute our core set. We then crawled the social network of these sets: for each user, we collected her list of friends, and the degrees (number of friends) of these friends.

Data description. Among the several verticals we col-

Vertical	Page	m	n
Charity	Kiva	978	131334
Travel	Lonely Planet	753	113250
Fashion	GAP	996	115524
Events	Coachella	826	102291
Politics	Green Party	1044	83490
Technology	Google Nexus	895	137995
News	The New York Times	894	156222
Entertainment	HBO	828	108699

Table 1: Dataset statistics. m: number of users in the core set, n: number of friends of core set users.

lected, we select eight of them for which we will report our results. We obtained similar results for the other ones. Table 1 summarizes statistics about the selected verticals. We note that depending on the privacy settings of the core set users, it was not always possible to access their list of friends. We decided to remove these users since their ability to spread information could not be readily determined. This effect, combined with various errors encountered during the data collection, accounts for an approximate 15% reduction between the users who liked a post and the number of users in the datasets we used. Following our discussion in the introduction, we observe that on average, the degrees of core set users is much lower than the degrees of their friends. This is highlighted on Figure 2 and justifies our approach.

5.2 Performance of Adaptive Seeding

For a given problem instance with a budget of k we applied the adaptive seeding algorithm (the combinatorial version). Recall from Section 2 that performance is defined as the expected influence that the seeder can obtain by optimally selecting users on the second stage, where *influence* is defined as the sum of the degrees of the selected users. We tested our algorithm against the following benchmarks:

- *Random Node* (RN): we randomly select k users from the core set. This is a typical benchmark in comparing influence maximization algorithms [14].
- *Influence Maximization* (IM): we apply the optimal influence maximization algorithm on the core set. This is the naive application of influence maximization. For the voter model, when the propagation time is polynomially large in the network size, the optimal solution is to simply take the k highest degree nodes [8]. We study the case of bounded time horizons in Section 5.5.
- *Random Friend* (RF): we implement a naive two-stage approach: randomly select $k/2$ nodes from the core set, and for each node select a random neighbor (hence spending the budget of k rewards overall). This method was recently shown to outperform standard influence maximization when the core set is random [18].

5.3 Performance on Facebook Pages

Figure 3 compares the performance of *adaptive seeding*, our own approach, to the afore-mentioned approaches for all the verticals we collected. In this first experiment we made simplifying assumptions about the parameters of the model. The first assumption is that all probabilities in the adaptive seeding model are equal to one. This implicitly assumes that every friend of a user who followed a certain topic is interested in promoting the topic given a reward. Although

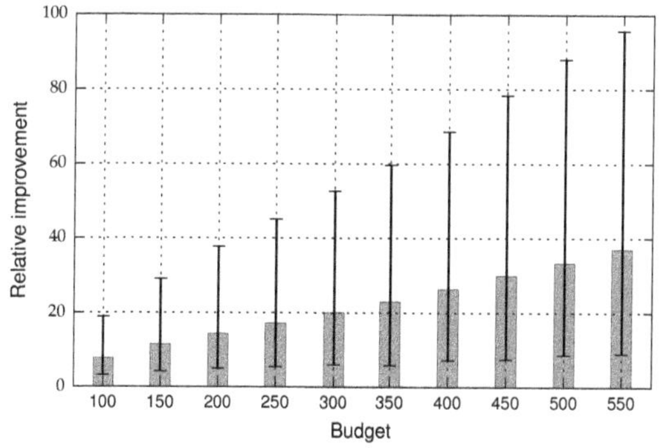

Figure 4: Ratio of the performance of adaptive seeding to IM. Bars represents the mean improvement across all verticals, and the "error bar" represents the range of improvement across verticals.

this is a strong assumption that we will revisit, we note that the probabilities can be controlled to some extent by the social networking service on which the campaign is being run by showing prominently the campaign material (sponsored links, fund-raising banners, etc.). The second assumption is that the measure of influence is the sum of the degrees of the selected set. This measure is an appealing proxy as it is known that in the voter model, after polynomially many time steps, the influence of each node is proportional to its degree with high probability [8]. Since the influence process cannot be controlled by the designer, the assumption is often that the influence process runs until it stabilizes (in linear thresholds and independent cascades for example, the process terminates after a linear number of steps [14]). We perform a set of experiments for different time horizons in Section 5.5.

It is striking to see how well adaptive seeding does in comparison to other methods. Even when using a small budget (0.1 fraction of the core set, which in these cases is about 100 nodes), adaptive seeding improves influence by a factor of at least 10, across all verticals. To confirm this, we plot the relative improvements of *adaptive seeding* over IM in aggregate over the different pages. The results are shown in Figure 4. This dramatic improvement is largely due to the friendship paradox phenomenon that adaptive seeding leverages. Returning to Figure 3, it is also interesting to note that the RF heuristic significantly outperforms the standard IM benchmark. Using the same budget, the degree gain induced by moving from the core set to its neighborhood is such that selecting at random among the core set users' friends already does better than the best heuristic restricted only on the core set. Using *adaptive seeding* to optimize the choice of core set users based on their friends' degrees then results in an order of magnitude increase over RF, consistently for all the pages.

5.4 The Effect of the Probabilistic Model

The results presented in Section 5.2 were computed assuming the probabilities in the adaptive seeding model are one. We now describe several experiments we performed with the Facebook Pages data set that test the advantages of adaptive seeding under different probability models.

Impact of the Bernouilli parameter. Figure 5a shows the impact of the probability of nodes realizing in the second stage. We computed the performance of *adaptive seeding* when each friend of a seeded user in the core set joins

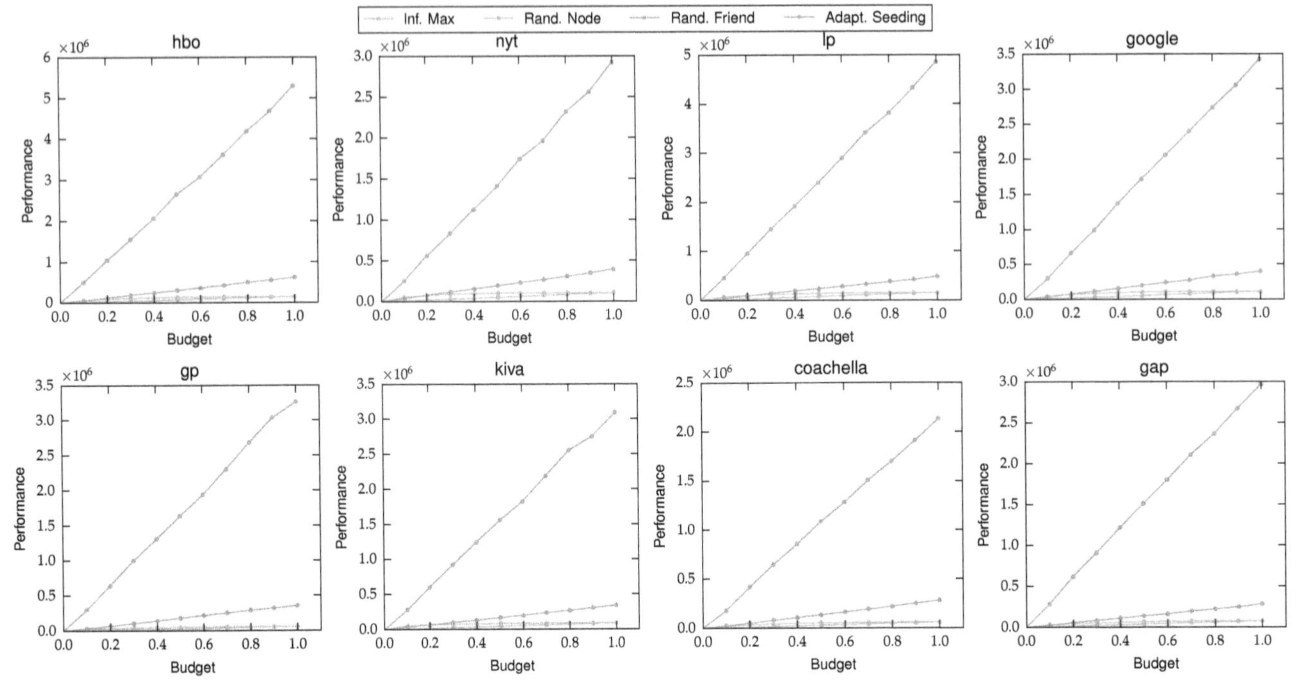

Figure 3: Performance of adaptive seeding compared to other influence maximization approaches. The horizontal axis represents the budget used as a fraction of the size of the core set. The vertical axis is the expected influence reachable by optimally selecting nodes on the second stage.

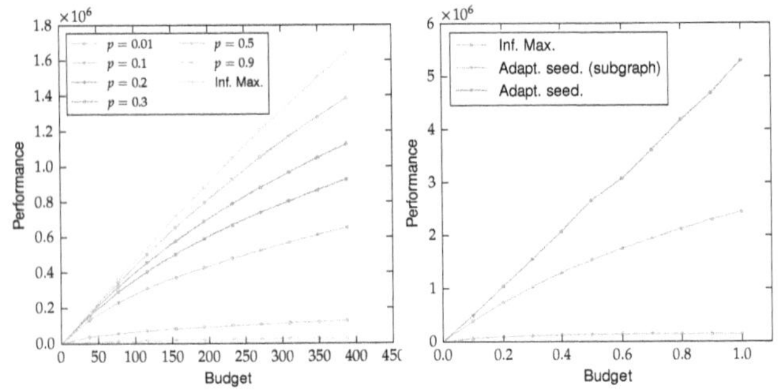

(a) (b)

Figure 5: (a) Performance of adaptive seeding for various propagation probabilities. (b) Performance of *adaptive seeding* when restricted to the subgraph of users who *liked* HBO (red line).

during the second stage independently with probability p, using different values of p. We call p the *Bernouilli* parameter, since the event that a given user joins on the second stage of adaptive seeding is governed by a Bernouilli variable of parameter p. We see that even with $p = 0.01$, *adaptive seeding* still outperforms IM. As p increases, the performance of *adaptive seeding* quickly increases and reaches 80% of the values of Figure 3 at $p = 0.5$.

Coarse estimation of probabilities. In practice, the probability a user may be interested in promoting a campaign her friend is promoting may vary. However, for those who have already expressed interest in the promoted content, we can expect this probability to be close to one. We therefore conducted the following experiment. We chose a page (HBO) and trimmed the social graph we collected by only keeping on the second stage users who indicated this page (HBO) in their list of interests. This is a coarse estimation of the probabilities as it assumes that if a friend follows HBO she will be willing to promote with probability 1 (given a reward), and otherwise the probability of her promoting anything for HBO is 0. Figure 5b shows that even on this very restricted set of users, *adaptive seeding* still outperforms IM and reaches approximately 50% of the unrestricted adaptive seeding.

Impact of the probability distribution. In order to test scenarios where users have a rich spectrum of probabilities of realizing on the second stage. We consider a setting where the Bernouilli parameter p is drawn from a distribution. We considered four different distributions; for each distribution for fixed values of the budget and the parameter p, we tuned the parameters of the distribution so that its mean is exactly p. We then plotted the performance as a function of the budget and mean p.

For the Beta distribution, we fixed $\beta = 5$ and tuned the α parameter to obtain a mean of p, thus obtaining a unimodal distribution. For the normal distribution, we chose a standard deviation of 0.01 to obtain a distribution more concentrated around its mean than the Beta distribution. Finally, for the inverse degree distribution, we took the probability of a node joining on the second stage to be proportional to the inverse of its degree (scaled so that on average, nodes join with probability p). The results are shown in Figure 6.

We observe that the results are comparable to the one we obtained in the uniform case in Figure 5a except in the case of the inverse degree distribution for which the performance is roughly halved. Remember that the value of a user v on the second stage of adaptive seeding is given by $p_v d_v$ where d_v is its degree and p_v is the its probability of realizing on the second stage. Choosing p_v to be proportional to $1/d_v$ has the effect of normalizing the nodes on the second stage and is a strong perturbation of the original degree distribution of the nodes available on the second stage.

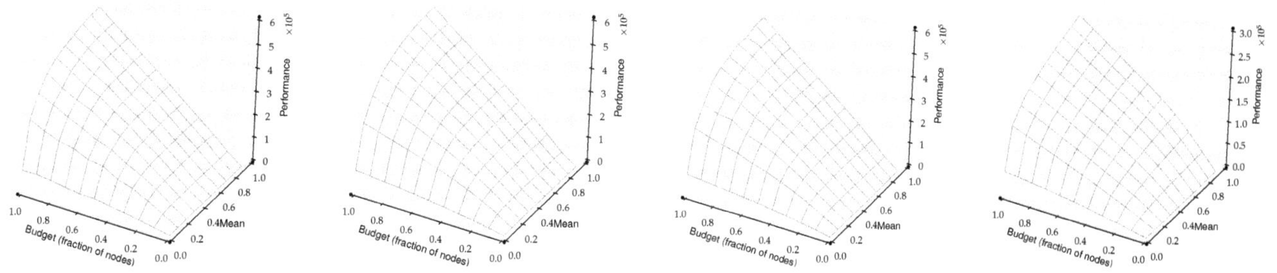

(a) Beta distribution (b) Normal Distribution (c) Power-law distribution (d) Inverse degree

Figure 6: Performance of adaptive seeding as a function of the budget and the mean of the distribution from which the Bernouilli parameters are drawn. The details of the parameters for each distribution can be found in Section 5.4.

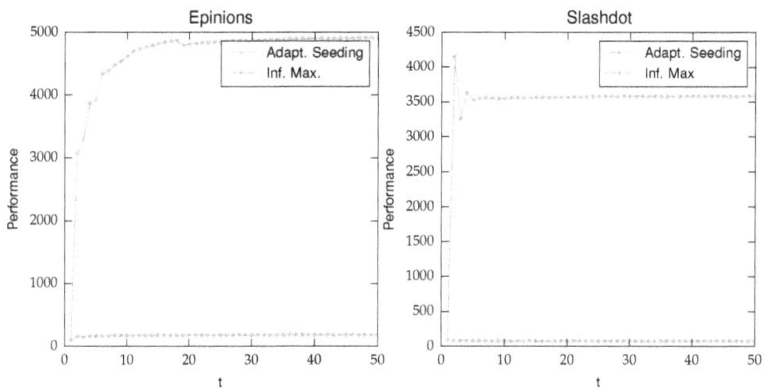

Figure 7: Performance of adaptive seeding compared to IM for the voter influence model with t steps.

5.5 Impact of the Influence Model

The Facebook Pages data set we collected is limited in that we only have access to the 2-hop neighborhood around the seed users and we use the degree of the second stage users as a proxy for their influence. As proved in [8], in the voter model, the influence of nodes converges to their degree with high probability when the number of time steps become polynomially large in the network size.

In order to analyze the expected number of nodes influenced according to the voter model that terminates after some fixed number of time steps, we use publicly available data sets from [21] where the entire network is at our disposal. As discussed above, we sample nodes uniformly at random to model the core set. We then run the voter model for t time steps to compute the influence of the second stage users. Figure 7 shows the performance of adaptive seeding as a function of t compared to the performance of the IM benchmark. In this experiment, the budget was set to half the size of the core set.

We see that the performance of adaptive seeding quickly converges (5 time steps for Slashdot, 15 time steps for Epinions). In practice, the voter model converges much faster than the theoretical guarantee of [8], which justifies using the degree of the second stage users as measure of influence as we did for the Facebook Pages data sets. Furthermore, we see that similarly to the Facebook data sets, adaptive seeding significantly outperforms IM.

5.6 Performance on Synthetic Networks

In order to analyze the impact of topological variations we generated synthetic graphs using standard network models. All the generated graphs have 100,000 vertices, for each model, we tuned the generative parameters to obtain when possible a degree distribution (or graph density otherwise) similar to what we observed in the Facebook Pages data sets.

- *Barabási-Albert:* this well-known model is often used to model social graphs because its degree distribution is a power law. We took 10 initial vertices and added 10 vertices at each step, using the preferential attachment model, until we reached 100,000 vertices.
- *Small-World:* also known as the Watts-Strogatz model. This model was one of the first models proposed for social networks. Its diameter and clustering coefficient are more representative of a social network than what one would get with the Erdős–Rényi model. We started from a regular lattice of degree 200 and rewired each edge with probability 0.3.
- *Kronecker:* Kronecker graphs were more recently introduced in [19] as a scalable and easy-to-fit model for social networks. We started from a star graph with 4 vertices and computed Kronecker products until we reached 100,000 nodes.
- *Configuration model:* The configuration model allows us to construct a graph with a given degree distribution. We chose a page (GAP) and generated a graph with the same degree distribution using the configuration model.

The performance of adaptive seeding compared to our benchmarks can be found in Figure 8. We note that the improvement obtained by adaptive seeding is comparable to the one we had on real data except for the *Small-World* model. This is explained by the nature of the model: starting from a regular lattice, some edges are re-wired at random. This model has similar properties to a random graph where the friendship paradox does not hold [18]. Since adaptive seeding is designed to leverage the friendship paradox, such graphs are not amenable to this approach.

5.7 Scalability

To test the scalability of adaptive seeding we were guided by two central questions. First, we were interested to witness the benefit our non-sampling approach has over the standard SAA method. Secondly, we wanted to understand when one should prefer to use the LP-based approach from Section 4.1 over the combinatorial one from Section 4.2. The

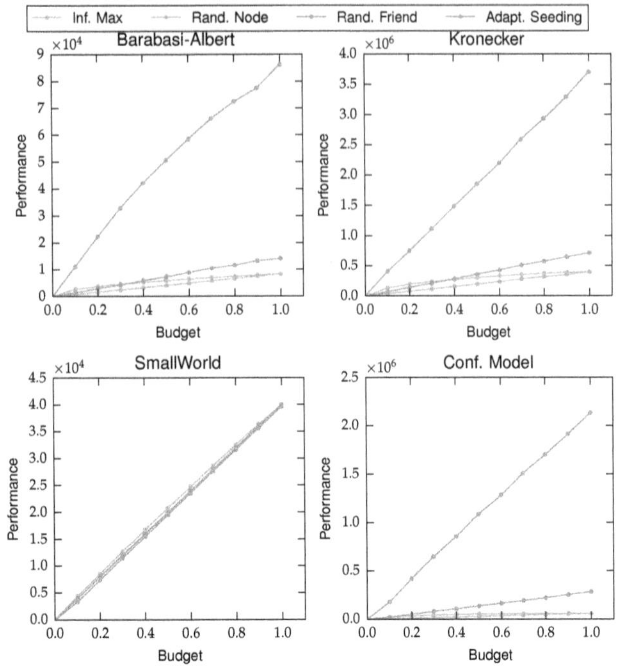

Figure 8: Performance of adaptive seeding on synthetic networks.

computations in this section were run on Intel Core i5 CPU 4x2.40Ghz. For each computation, we plot the time and number of CPU cycles it took.

Comparison with SAA. The objective function of the non-adaptive problem (3) is an expectation over exponentially many sets, all possible realizations of the neighbors in the second stage. Following the sampling-based approach introduced in [27], this expectation can be computed by averaging the values obtained in $O(n^2)$ independent sample realizations of the second stage users (n is the number of neighbors of core set users). One important aspect of the algorithms introduced in this paper is that in the additive case, this expectation can be computed exactly without sampling, thus significantly improving the theoretical complexity.

In Figure 9, we compare the running time of our combinatorial algorithm to the same algorithm where the expectation is computed via sampling. We note that this sampling-based algorithm is still simpler than the algorithm introduced in [27] for general influence models. However, we observe a significant gap between its running time and the one of the combinatorial algorithm. Since each sample takes linear time to compute, this gap is in fact $O(n^3)$, quickly leading to impracticable running times as the size of the graph increases. This highlights the importance of the *sans-sampling* approach underlying the algorithms we introduced.

Combinatorial vs. LP algorithm. We now compare the running time of the LP-based approach and the combinatorial approach for different instance sizes.

Figure 10 shows the running time and number of CPU cycles used by the LP algorithm and the combinatorial algorithm as a function of the network size n. The varying size of the network was obtained by randomly sampling a varying fraction of core set users and then trimming the social graph by only keeping friends of this random sample on the second stage. The LP solver used was CLP [1].

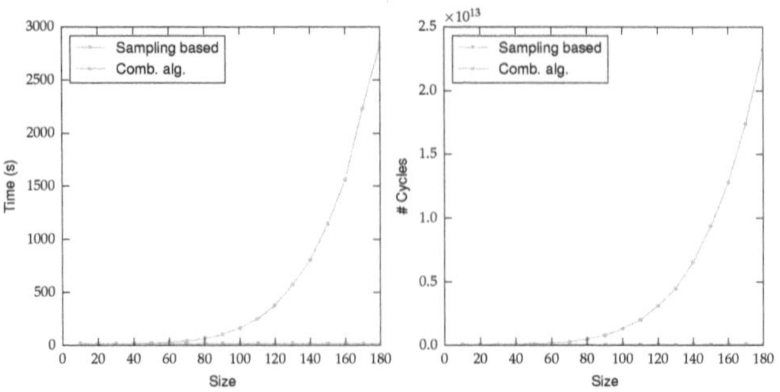

Figure 9: Running time and number of CPU cycles used by the sampling-based algorithm and the combinatorial adaptive seeding algorithm for different sizes of the core set.

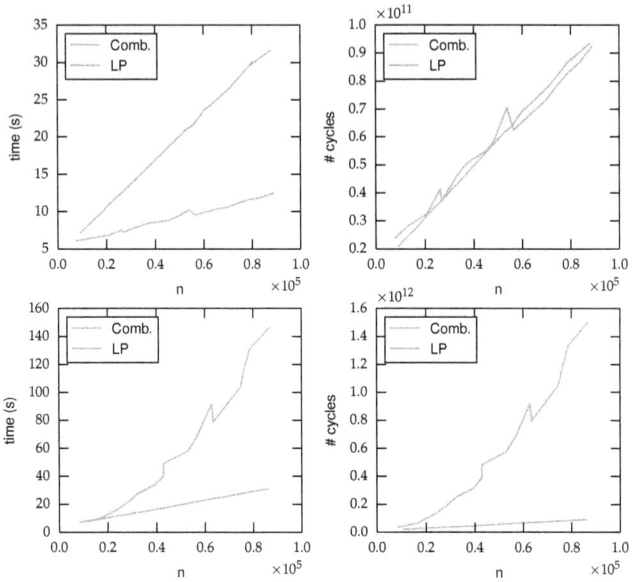

Figure 10: Running time and number of CPU cycles of the combinatorial algorithm and the LP algorithm as a function of the number of nodes n. First row with budget $k = 100$, second row with budget $k = 500$.

We observe that for a *small* value of the budget k (first row of Figure 10), the combinatorial algorithm outperforms the LP algorithm. When k becomes *large* (second row of Figure 10), the LP algorithm becomes faster. This can be explained by the k^2 factor in the running time of the combinatorial algorithm (see Proposition 5). Even though the asymptotic guarantee of the combinatorial algorithm should theoretically outperform the LP-based approach for large n, we were not able to observe it for our instance sizes. In practice, one can choose which of the two algorithms to apply depending on the relative sizes of k and n.

6. RELATED WORK

Influence maximization was introduced by Domingos and Richardson [7, 25], formulated by Kempe, Kleinberg and Tardos [14, 15], and has been extensively studied since [23, 5, 20, 23, 5, 22, 4]. The main result in [14, 15] is a characterization of influence processes as submodular functions, which implies good approximation guarantees for the influence maximization problem. In [8], the authors look at the special case of the voter model and design efficient algorithms in this setting.

Our two-stage model for influence maximization is related to the field of stochastic optimization where problems are commonly solved using the *sample average approximation* method [16]. Golovin and Krause [11] study a stochastic sequential submodular maximization problem where at each step an element is chosen, its realization is revealed and the next decision is made. We note that contrary to adaptive seeding, the decision made at a given stage does not affect the following stages as the entire set of nodes is available as potential seeds at every stage.

Acknowledgement

This research is supported in part by a Google Research Grant and NSF grant CCF-1301976.

7. REFERENCES

[1] https://projects.coin-or.org/Clp.

[2] A. A. Ageev and M. Sviridenko. Pipage rounding: A new method of constructing algorithms with proven performance guarantee. *J. Comb. Optim.*, 8(3):307–328, 2004.

[3] E. Bakshy, J. M. Hofman, W. A. Mason, and D. J. Watts. Everyone's an influencer: quantifying influence on twitter. In *WSDM*, 2011.

[4] C. Borgs, M. Brautbar, J. Chayes, and B. Lucier. Maximizing social influence in nearly optimal time. In *SODA*, volume 14. SIAM, 2014.

[5] N. Chen. On the approximability of influence in social networks. In *SODA*, pages 1029–1037, 2008.

[6] J. Cheng, L. Adamic, P. A. Dow, J. M. Kleinberg, and J. Leskovec. Can cascades be predicted? WWW '14, pages 925–936, New York, NY, USA, 2014. ACM.

[7] P. Domingos and M. Richardson. Mining the network value of customers. In *KDD*, pages 57–66, 2001.

[8] E. Even-Dar and A. Shapira. A note on maximizing the spread of influence in social networks. In *WINE*, pages 281–286, 2007.

[9] S. L. Feld. Why your friends have more friends than you do. *American Journal of Sociology*, pages 1464–1477, 1991.

[10] S. Goel, D. J. Watts, and D. G. Goldstein. The structure of online diffusion networks. In *EC '12, Valencia, Spain, June 4-8, 2012*, pages 623–638, 2012.

[11] D. Golovin and A. Krause. Adaptive submodularity: Theory and applications in active learning and stochastic optimization. *Journal of Artificial Intelligence Research*, 42(1):427–486, 2011.

[12] R. A. Holley and T. M. Liggett. Ergodic theorems for weakly interacting infinite systems and the voter model. *The annals of probability*, pages 643–663, 1975.

[13] T. Horel and Y. Singer. Scalable methods for adaptively seeding a social network. *CoRR*, abs/1503.01438, 2015.

[14] D. Kempe, J. M. Kleinberg, and É. Tardos. Maximizing the spread of influence through a social network. In *KDD*, pages 137–146, 2003.

[15] D. Kempe, J. M. Kleinberg, and É. Tardos. Influential nodes in a diffusion model for social networks. In *ICALP*, pages 1127–1138, 2005.

[16] A. J. Kleywegt, A. Shapiro, and T. Homem-de Mello. The sample average approximation method for stochastic discrete optimization. *SIAM Journal on Optimization*, 12(2):479–502, 2002.

[17] R. Kumar, B. Moseley, S. Vassilvitskii, and A. Vattani. Fast greedy algorithms in mapreduce and streaming. In G. E. Blelloch and B. Vöcking, editors, *SPAA 2013*, pages 1–10. ACM, 2013.

[18] S. Lattanzi and Y. Singer. The power of random neighbors in social networks. *WSDM*, 2015.

[19] J. Leskovec, D. Chakrabarti, J. M. Kleinberg, and C. Faloutsos. Realistic, mathematically tractable graph generation and evolution, using kronecker multiplication. In *PKDD 2005*, volume 3721 of *Lecture Notes in Computer Science*, pages 133–145. Springer, 2005.

[20] J. Leskovec, A. Krause, C. Guestrin, C. Faloutsos, J. M. VanBriesen, and N. S. Glance. Cost-effective outbreak detection in networks. In *KDD*, pages 420–429, 2007.

[21] J. Leskovec and A. Krevl. SNAP Datasets: Stanford large network dataset collection. http://snap.stanford.edu/data, June 2014.

[22] M. Mathioudakis, F. Bonchi, C. Castillo, A. Gionis, and A. Ukkonen. Sparsification of influence networks. In *KDD*, 2011.

[23] E. Mossel and S. Roch. On the submodularity of influence in social networks. In *STOC*, pages 128–134, 2007.

[24] G. L. Nemhauser, L. A. Wolsey, and M. L. Fisher. An analysis of approximations for maximizing submodular set functions—i. *Mathematical Programming*, 14(1):265–294, 1978.

[25] M. Richardson and P. Domingos. Mining knowledge-sharing sites for viral marketing. In *KDD*, pages 61–70, 2002.

[26] M. Richardson and P. Domingos. Mining knowledge-sharing sites for viral marketing. In *KDD*, pages 61–70. ACM, 2002.

[27] L. Seeman and Y. Singer. Adaptive seeding in social networks. In *FOCS*, 2013.

[28] J. Vondrák, C. Chekuri, and R. Zenklusen. Submodular function maximization via the multilinear relaxation and contention resolution schemes. In *STOC*, pages 783–792. ACM, 2011.

[29] J. Yang and S. Counts. Predicting the speed, scale, and range of information diffusion in twitter. In *ICWSM*, 2010.

[30] T. R. Zaman, R. Herbrich, J. V. Gael, and D. Stern. Predicting information spreading in twitter, 2010.

User Review Sites as a Resource for Large-Scale Sociolinguistic Studies

Dirk Hovy
Center for Language Technology
University of Copenhagen, Denmark
Njalsgade 140
dirk@cst.dk

Anders Johannsen
Center for Language Technology
University of Copenhagen, Denmark
Njalsgade 140
ajohannsen@hum.ku.dk

Anders Søgaard
Center for Language Technology
University of Copenhagen, Denmark
Njalsgade 140
soegaard@hum.ku.dk

ABSTRACT

Sociolinguistic studies investigate the relation between language and extra-linguistic variables. This requires both representative text data and the associated socio-economic *meta*-data of the subjects. Traditionally, sociolinguistic studies use small samples of hand-curated data and meta-data. This can lead to exaggerated or false conclusions. Using social media data offers a large-scale source of language data, but usually lacks reliable socio-economic meta-data. Our research aims to remedy both problems by exploring a large new data source, international review websites with user profiles. They provide more text data than manually collected studies, and more meta-data than most available social media text. We describe the data and present various pilot studies, illustrating the usefulness of this resource for sociolinguistic studies. Our approach can help generate new research hypotheses based on data-driven findings across several countries and languages.

Categories and Subject Descriptors

I.2.7 [**Artificial Intelligence**]: Natural Language Processing

General Terms

Human Factors; Experimentation

Keywords

Language-analysis techniques; Multi-lingual and cross-lingual analysis and mining; Social science research based on social media; Insights from natural-language analysis of social media; Novel applications

1 Introduction

Sociolinguistic studies investigate the relation between language use and extra-linguistic socio-economic variables, such as regional origin, gender, social class, or age [17, 29, 25, 27, 9]. These studies thus require both a representative corpus of text data *and* meta-data about the socio-economic variables. Traditionally, these studies have relied on individual interviews and questionnaires and their manual transcriptions to collect data and meta-data. Due to the effort in curating them, the resulting corpora are often of moderate size, and sometimes include less than five subjects [27]. However, small sample sizes may lead to false research findings, as elaborated on in [8] (albeit for neuro-sciences). Sociolinguistic studies, in other words, often lack statistical power to either establish relationships between language use and socio-economic variables (because they are limited to detect only large effects), or are liable to present exaggerated claims (if they report spurious effects due to a small sample size).

Web data, on the other hand, presents a source of large amounts of text data. In addition, a lot of web data is personalized text (i.e., not canonical), such as blogs and other social media texts. I.e., they represent *actual* language use, rather than a prescriptively normed (standard) variant. This allows sociolinguistic studies with sufficient statistical power, but requires a web-mining approach. Indeed, the natural language processing (NLP) community has recently shown a growing interest in sociolinguistic research questions, applying modern data-driven methods to social media data. This interest was in part driven by the availability of *some* meta-data (e.g., location and time) in social media platforms such as Twitter [14, 13, 12, 5].

The meta-data for social media, however, is partial at best and often unreliable, and so most previous work has only considered regional origin and time as extra-linguistic variables. This severely limits the types of sociolinguistic research questions that can be addressed, because most traditional studies are concerned with socio-economic factors such as age, gender, or class, which are not present in social media meta-data. To remedy this problem of incomplete meta-data, a whole branch of previous work has thus focused on building predictive models for age and gender [7, 4, 10] to add user information. Some social media data sets, like Facebook, contain more meta-data, but are difficult or impossible to obtain.

This paper proposes a novel source of data for sociolinguistic studies, namely user-review sites. We show that these sites contain textual data (reviews) that is linked to various extra-linguistic information, namely age, gender, and location of the reviewer, as well as time-stamps. The language in the reviews, while not as informal as e.g., Twitter, is much

WWW 2015, May 18–22, 2015, Florence, Italy.
ACM 978-1-4503-3469-3/15/05.
http://dx.doi.org/10.1145/2736277.2741141.

less canonical than newswire, and thus likely to reflect the socio-economic background of the user. More importantly, some user-review sites contain up to millions of user reviews and thus provide the statistical power to study the influence of socio-economic variables on language use.

In our case, we extract data from the website of Trustpilot[1]. On Trustpilot, users review online and brick-and-mortar companies they shopped at, and leave a one to five star rating, as well as a written review. The website offers reliable information about the time the review was posted, so it can be used to track some diachronic development. In addition, users often supply information about their location, age, and gender. The data is available for 24 countries, using 13 different languages (Danish, Dutch, English, Finnish, French, German, Italian, Norwegian, Polish, Portuguese, Russian, Spanish, Swedish), and thus contains comparable text across socio-economic variables in several languages, spanning several years.

We explore this new data source and its usefulness to test sociolinguistic hypotheses with sufficient statistical power.

Our contributions

We show how publicly available user-review sites can be used for large-scale sociolinguistic experiments. The size of the corpus allows for statistically more powerful analyses than manually-collected corpora. The sites also contain more meta-data (information about the speaker, including age, gender, and location) than social media data.

We describe the process of collecting data from the Trustpilot website, and how to augment missing information. The scripts for harvesting and preprocessing the corpora are made publicly available.[2]

We analyze the resulting corpus with respect to representativeness for all age ranges, both genders, and various regions. Since the data consists of user reviews, we also study the distribution of ratings across socio-economic variables.

We then present a series of pilot studies across several languages. The studies are based on hypotheses found in sociolinguistic literature and include gender-specific lexical differences, the distribution of regional/dialect markers, the decline of grammatical constructions, and spelling variations. Our results indicate that user-review sites can provide informative data for large-scale sociolinguistic studies.

2 Related Work

Sociolinguistic and variational studies have a long tradition, correlating speakers' linguistic traits with socio-economic background and variables such as origin, social class, age, and gender.

Labov's seminal studies [19] investigated the influence of regional origin and class on phonology. In recent years, sociolinguistic studies have investigated the influence of age [27], gender [17, 27], class [24, 22, 23], and ethnicity [9, 27]. All of them find that language use is highly influenced by these factors, although a statistical correlation is sometimes tenuous or absent.

With the widespread availability of Twitter, recent studies in NLP have focused on exploring linguistic features such as phonological, lexical, and morphological variation, and how they are influenced by spatial resolution [14, 13, 28, 12, 5], gender [6], and ethnicity [32]. Some of these research questions, such as which phonological features influence written language on social media, are interesting on their own, and NLP offers tools for answering these questions [13]. Other sociolinguistic research questions coincide with important topics in NLP, e.g., language change, which challenges the robustness of the predictive models used in the field [14, 30]. While Twitter provides a large amount of constantly updated data, it is notoriously difficult to verify sociolinguistic traits of the speakers. Some inferences can be made by correlating linguistic differences to census data [13]. In this work, we use a resource that provides *both* textual and meta-data.

There is also an active research area in predicting sociolinguistic traits of authors, mainly focusing on age and gender [4, 10, 21] using information such as linguistic choice and names as input. [26] presented a study where they caution that humans apparently use various other factors to assess a user's age and gender. [20] recently presented a relation-extraction inspired approach to inferring a user's spouse, education, and job by using distant supervision from various social networks. While interesting, these "acquired" features are only secondary to language use.

Areal studies of language variation across time have existed systematically at least since the neo-grammarians. Georg Wenker collected 30k transcriptions of dialect variations in the 1880s. However, they do not include meta-information about the speakers themselves, other than the name of the transcriptor (local school teachers). The results were mapped out to show regional variations and have recently been published along with the questionnaires by [29]. Similar work, but with a focus on computer-aided clustering and mapping of Dutch dialects, has been undertaken by [25]. A more historical approach to data-driven areal linguistic studies and language phylogeny was presented by [11].

Other studies that investigate linguistic variation, albeit across languages and stylistic variation, include [16] and [18].

3 Data collection

3.1 Data format

Users	Name, ID, profile text, location (city and country), gender, year of birth
Reviews	Title, text, rating (1–5), User ID, Company ID, Date and time of review
Company	Name, categories (e.g., electronics), number of ratings, description, address, location (city and country)

Table 1: Meta-information available in the TRUSTPILOT CORPUS

The TRUSTPILOT CORPUS consists of user reviews from the Trustpilot website. In order to make the data usable for our purposes, we crawl the website and extract publicly available information into JSON format with objects (dictionaries) that correspond to the various entities. Apart from the **reviews**, these are **users** and **companies**. Table 1 contains a list of the fields that are available for each type of entity.

[1] `http://trustpilot.com`

[2] `http://www.lowlands.dk/results`

	Users	Age	Sex	Place	All
United Kingdom	1,424k	7%	62%	5%	4%
France	741k	3%	53%	2%	1%
Denmark	671k	23%	87%	17%	16%
United States	648k	8%	59%	7%	4%
Netherlands	592k	9%	39%	7%	5%
Germany	329k	8%	47%	6%	4%
Sweden	170k	5%	64%	4%	3%
Italy	132k	10%	61%	8%	6%
Spain	56k	6%	37%	5%	3%
Norway	51k	5%	50%	4%	3%
Belgium	36k	13%	42%	11%	8%
Australia	31k	8%	36%	7%	5%
Finland	16k	6%	36%	5%	3%
Austria	15k	10%	43%	7%	5%
Switzerland	14k	8%	41%	7%	4%
Canada	12k	10%	19%	9%	4%
Ireland	12k	8%	30%	7%	4%

Table 2: Number of users for a given variable per country (after applying augmentations). Table contains only countries with 10,000+ registered Trustpilot users.

Users need to register with a username in order to leave reviews, but many also opt to fill in a public profile. There are no mandatory fields – other than the name – but many users also supply their birth year, gender, and location, as well as a short profile text.

Companies are represented in our data with their location, a short description (presumably self-supplied), and a classification based on the type of business (e.g., *electronics*).

We assign unique identifiers to both users and companies and use those to link up reviews. Reviews further contain a star-rating, the review text, and a time-stamp. We did not include any replies to reviews written by the companies.

We collect data that spans a period of seven years. The fields we are most interested in here are the socio-economic variables supplied by the users, i.e., age, gender, and location, in combination with the written reviews.

Note that the countries differ in the amount and type of information available. Table 2 gives an overview. In our experiments, we restrict ourselves to the countries with more than 250k users: Denmark, France, Germany, the United Kingdom and the United States.

The high number of users in Denmark (one tenth of the country's population) might be due to the fact that Trustpilot is Danish company and thus existed there longer than in other countries. Danish users provide (in relative terms) more information about themselves than any other country, so that even in absolute numbers, there is oftentimes more available information than for larger countries like France, where users are more reluctant to disclose information.

For these reasons, and due to a higher level of linguistic expertise on that language in our group, we use Danish as a case-study.

3.2 Data augmentation

We augment the retrieved data set in two ways, namely by adding 1. gender information based on first names, and 2. geotagging information (latitude and longitude).

In order to add gender information when it is not supplied, we collect statistics for each occurrence of the name where gender information is available. This provides us with a distribution over genders for each name. If a name is found with sufficient frequency in our data, and predominantly for one gender, we propagate this information to all occurrences of the name that *lack* gender information. In our experiments, we used a gender-ratio of 0.95 (name occurs with one gender at least 95% of the time) and a minimum frequency of 3 (name appears at least 3 times with gender information in the data). Since the gender of some names is country-specific (e.g., *Simone* is a male name in Italy, but female in Germany or France), we repeat this step for each country separately. This augmentation step typically doubles the amount of available data with gender information for any language, while minimizing the risk of introducing false positives.

To add geographical information, we use the Geonames database[3] to attach latitude and longitude information to the user. This allows areal distribution analysis of the data.

Since the place names are entered as free text by the user, we apply various heuristics to get an acceptable match percentage. We remove short suffixes (e.g., "k" from "københavn *k*"), spaces, and punctuation, spell out abbreviations, and try to correct misspellings with an edit distance of 1 from a known place name. Latitude and longitude values allow us to precisely place the user review on a map.

One problem with locations is the ambiguity of some place names, say "Nykøbing", "Neustadt", or "Springfield". In many cases there is a "canonical" town with this name in a country, typically the largest one (one such example is "Kastrup" in Denmark, which refers to two cities on Sealand, as well as several villages in Jutland, but is generally understood to refer to the one close to the eponymous airport in Copenhagen). We determine the canonical location using a set of heuristics based on a population database. When the heuristics fail (e.g. when towns are of similar size, or more than one town has a population above a certain threshold), the location is left out of the analysis. Another, for now unanswered, problem is that the stated location most likely refers to the current residence of the user, and thus provides no information about their birthplace or where they grew up (typically important variables in variational linguistics).

4 Representativeness

Since the user information is given voluntarily and not verified, some birth years are presumably spurious (it seems unlikely that 2-year-olds or 110-year-olds review businesses on the Internet). In our experiments involving age, we thus restrict ourselves to the range from 16 to 80.

Apart from the outliers, the age distributions for both genders follow a reasonable distribution (see Figure 1). Additionally, the median age in our data is typically close to the country's median value according to the CIA World Factbook [3] (see Table 3), deviating slightly to both sides. For women, our mean-absolute error (MAE) over all countries is 0.74, for men 0.44. This indicates that the distributions are reasonably representative for the generations as a whole.

For gender, however, the differences are larger. Within each country, the gender distributions look similar, but there

[3] `www.geonames.org`

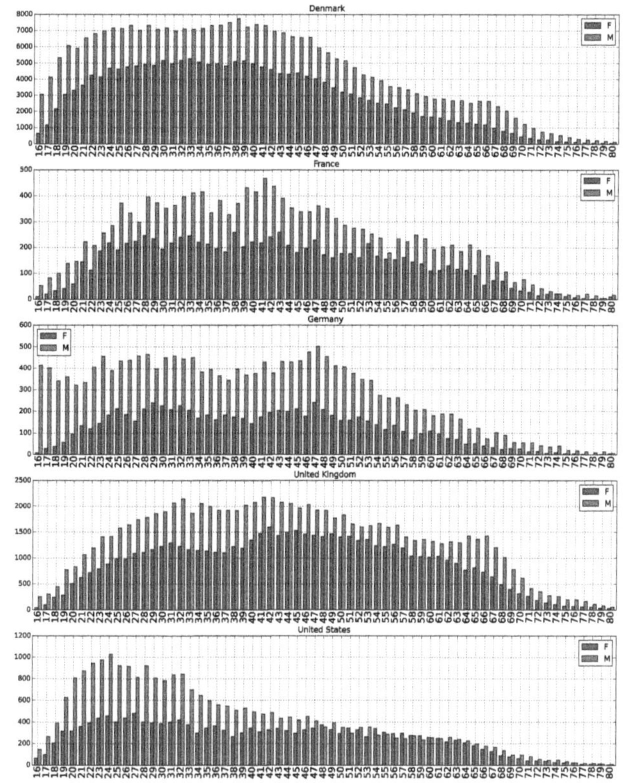

Figure 1: Age distribution per gender for all countries

are always more male than female users. The exact distributions differ from country to country: in Germany and the US, the distributions are skewed towards younger men. Naturally, this does not reflect the actual demographics. However, it is easy to control for this bias in our data, for example by downsampling the male data.

We note a slight dip around the mid-thirties for both genders and in most countries (except the US), which is consistent with the actual age distribution of those countries.

While most users tend to leave only one or two reviews, the average number of reviews per user is around 4 due to some prolific reviewers. Very few users did either not leave a review after setting up an account, or were not captured during our crawl.

For the EU countries, we can compare the population per region in our data (as given by the geocodes) to the official statistics. Figure 2 shows the comparison. Again, we see that our data is a reasonable approximation of the underlying distribution.

5 Pilot studies

In the following, we present a series of pilot studies to explore the usefulness of our resource. All of the studies are based on sociolinguistic problems, yet use a solely data-driven approach.

We first conduct several language-independent studies across five different languages (Danish, French, German, and English from both the US and the UK) (Section 6), before we explore some language dependent questions for Danish (Section 7) and German (Section 8).

In all studies, our methodology is to use the reviews to extract lexical variation and compute correlations of the variants with a socio-economic variable, i.e., gender, age, or region. E.g., we count how often a certain word X and its variant Y are used by a certain socio-economic group, and how much the variation is correlated with the group. In the case of gender, we compute χ^2 over the contingency matrix. For correlation of variants with age and region, we use the Spearman coefficient. We are only interested in highly significant correlations, so we set our $p < 0.001$.

6 General

6.1 Discovering gender-specific words

If we already have a pre-defined sociolinguistic hypothesis, it is easy to verify it with enough data. However, such hypotheses require already-existing knowledge about the target variables. This limits what we can explore, and can also introduce bias from the researcher, by restricting the alternatives that are considered. One of the advantages of a large data collection is the ability to discover variations in a purely data-driven manner. [15] presented a data-driven approach to discover ethnicity-specific words using $l_{1,\infty}$-regularization. In this pilot study, we look at gender, and use a simpler method (*tf-idf*) to learn salient expressions.

In order to find the most gender-specific words, we separate the reviews from each language into two sub-corpora, based on the reviewers stated or inferred gender. We then compute *tf-idf* on each sub-corpus separately and normalize them. *Tf-idf* weighs content words that occur in fewer documents higher than common words (prepositions, forms of *to be*, etc.). We can now compare the relative *tf-idf* scores for both genders and compute the difference by subtracting one from the other. This gives us a gradient, with predominantly "female" words on one and predominantly "male" words on the other end of the spectrum.

Table 4 gives an overview of the 10 most gender-specific words for each language. In general, women tend to express satisfaction ("tilfreds", "satisfaite", "content" "pleased") in all languages (except German), while men seem to talk more about problems ("problemer", "problème") and agreement ("aftalt", "conforme"). For French, where adjectives in sentences like "I am ADJ" are inflected according to the gender of the speaker, we see that the word for "satisfied" appears in both top 10. For both varieties of English, we find that certain words are associated more with women than with men ("loved', "pleased").

We do not attempt to interpret these findings any further, but point out that this might be a valuable approach to collect information about gender-specific differences in a data-driven way.

6.2 Emoticons, age, and gender

Emoticons have traditionally been seen as markers of adolescent language. We thus expect to see emoticons of all sorts used more by younger speakers.

We correlate emoticon usage with age and gender. We define emoticons to be a combination of eyes (such as `:`, `;`, or `X`), nose (`-`, or none), and mouth (`)`, `(`, `[`, `*`, etc). Overall, we check for 66 variations and record the ratio of emoticons in the overall number of words used in the category.

	WOMEN			MEN		
	mean	median	off. median	mean	median	off. median
Denmark	38.80	38	41.6	39.07	38	39.8
France	42.03	41	41.2	41.92	41	38.2
Germany	40.64	40	45.3	38.97	38	42.3
United Kingdom	44.51	45	41.5	43.87	43	39.4
United States	40.79	40	38.1	36.70	33	35.5

Table 3: Mean and median age for both genders over all countries, in data and official median

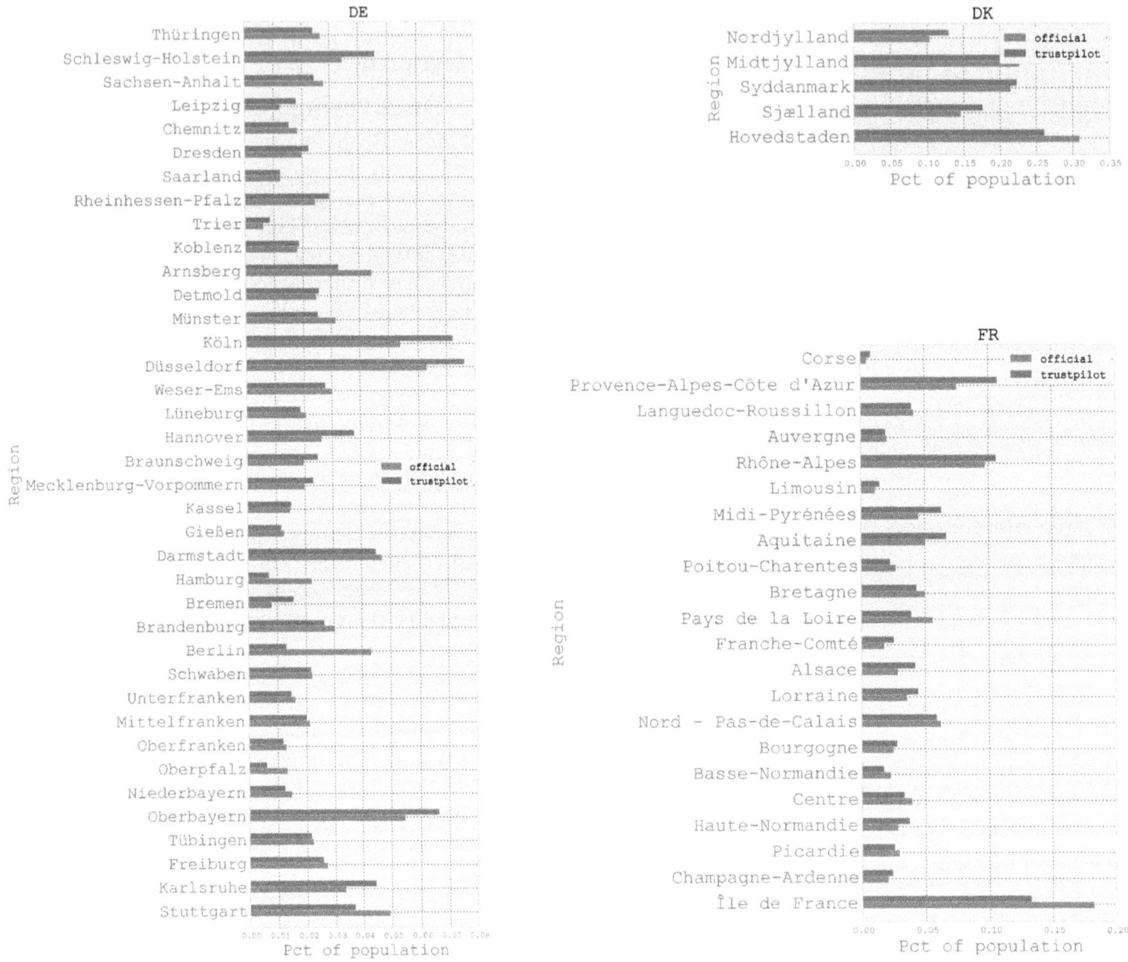

Figure 2: Regional coverage of our data. The figure compares geographical distribution of the population by region with the distribution in our dataset. Source: [2].

We find that for all countries, use of emoticons is strongly anti-correlated with age (Spearman $\rho = -0.99$ over all countries, see Table 5) at $p < 0.001$. In other words, as expected, the older a user is, the less likely they are to use emoticons.

For gender, we find that women use emoticons almost twice as often as men do (0.10% vs 0.18% of the respective words across all languages). The difference in the ratios is significant for all languages but French and German, although for the aggregated total of all languages, it is significant.

The presence or absence of a nose is a distinguishing feature of emoticon use, and seems to vary a lot. We suspect that this is correlated with user age. We select the most frequent emoticons (`:-)`, `;-)`, and `:-D`) and collect counts over the occurrences with and without a nose.

We find that for all ages, the use of a nose is highly anti-correlated with age (at $p < 0.001$). Figure 3 shows the distribution over all languages, which shows a different interesting fact: there are two distributions at work. Use of a nose increases steadily with age, until at around 34, it overtakes the use of no nose. Given that there are fewer older

	DENMARK	FRANCE	GERMANY	UK	US
female	nemt	**satisfaite**	gerne	flowers	customer_service
	bestille	**contente**	qualität	really	**love**
	varer	suis	tolle	**pleased**	we
	tilfreds	produits	wir	thank_you	**pleased**
	rigtig	chaussures	ware	definitely	really
	handle	étiquettes	bestellen	lovely	petflow
	dejligt	sont	sind	**love**	free_shipping
	nem	ma	karten	quickly	thank_you
	hjemmeside	été	bestellung	received	our
	mine	spartoo	vielen_dank	impressed	food
male	lovet	**problème**	keys	wife	these_guys
	deres	rien	günstig	parts	parts_geek
	problemer	bonne	service	deal	fast
	alt	matériel	mmoga	product	partsgeek
	aftalt	**conforme**	support	00	prices
	virker	ldlc	weiter_so	an	best
	tiden	service	top	first_class	shipping
	ok	sans	key	tyres	customer
	pris	bon	guter	could_find	part
	00	satisfait	gerne_wieder	best	parts

Table 4: The 10 most gender-specific words per language, based on relative *tf-idf*

	AGE		GENDER		
country	Spearman ρ	signif.	male	female	signif.
Denmark	-0.96	yes	0.24%	0.47%	yes
France	-0.93	yes	0.06%	0.05%	no
Germany	-0.95	yes	0.14%	0.15%	no
UK	-0.98	yes	0.04%	0.06%	yes
US	-0.93	yes	0.03%	0.05%	yes
Total	-0.99	yes	0.10%	0.18%	yes

Table 5: Correlation of emoticons with age, and % of words for gender in different countries. Significance tests at $p < 0.001$

users and that the use of emoticons declines with age, this effect is likely to be even more distinct.

With respect to gender, we find that women tend to use the noseless variant significantly more than men, except for France, where the difference between genders is not statistically significant at the chosen level.

	AGE		GENDER
country	Spearman ρ	significant	significant
Denmark	0.89	yes	yes
France	0.63	yes	no
Germany	0.83	yes	yes
UK	0.83	yes	yes
US	0.82	yes	yes

Table 6: Correlation of nose-use in emoticons for age and gender in different countries. All correlations significant at $p < 0.001$

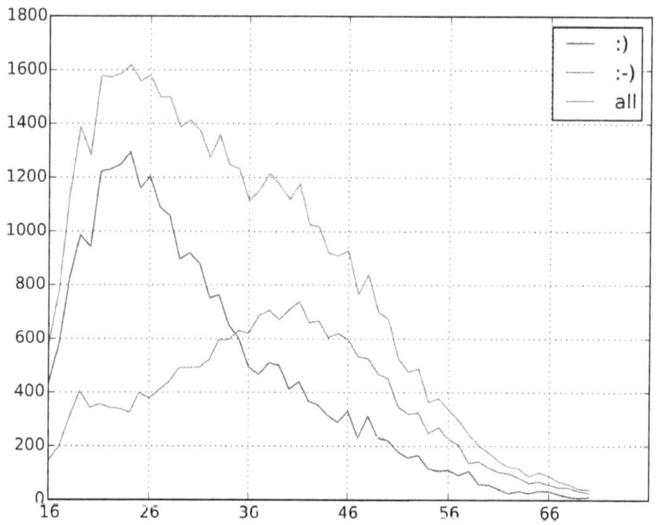

Figure 3: Usage of emoticons with and without nose by age group, aggregated over all countries

6.3 Ratings, categories, gender, and age

Gender Apart from the linguistic data, we also have ratings associated with the reviews. Users rate the business on a 5-point Likert scale. We restrict ourselves to 1, 3 and 5-start ratings (borrowed from the sentiment analysis categories *positive*, *negative*, *neutral*) and record the distribution for each gender to see whether any differences emerge.

Table 7 shows the distributions of labels over gender and age. We find that men tend to vote slightly more negative than women, using fewer 5-star and more 1-star reviews. While the difference between genders on those two ratings

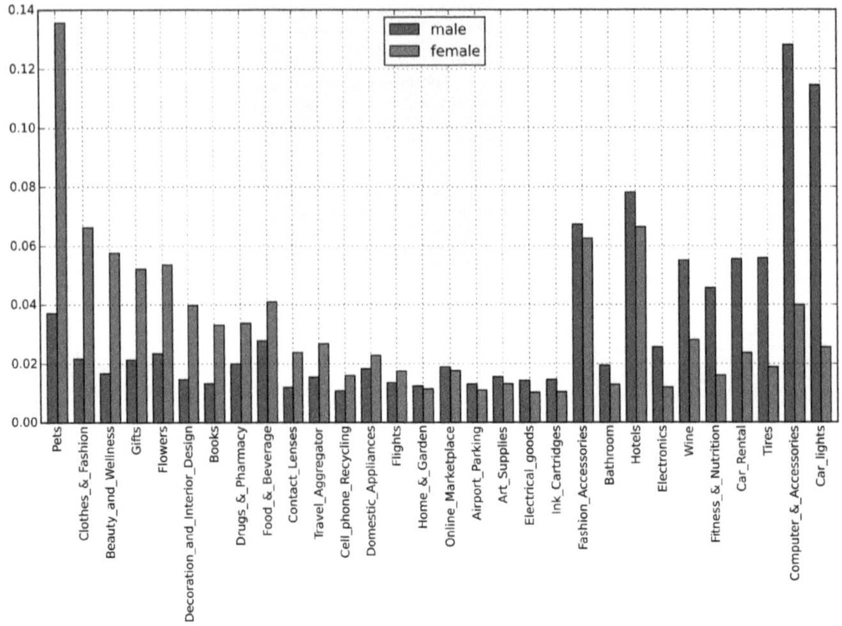

Figure 4: Distribution of the 30 most frequent categories per gender

LABEL	MALE	FEMALE	U35	O45
negative	5.92	4.09	12.56	9.96
neutral	4.46	4.21	4.72	3.82
positive	89.61	91.70	82.72	86.23

Table 7: Percentage of labels for each sub-group

is statistically significant, the overall difference between the two distributions is not.

Similarly, people in the younger group are more likely to use negative ratings than people in the older group (see Table 7). While the differences are small, they show that there are measurable differences worth modeling.

The categories used to classify businesses show a very different behavior. Figure 4 shows that the categories are highly gender-specific. With the exception of *Hotels* and *Fashion Accessories*, the two distributions are almost opposites.

Age We also hypothesized that users of different age would exhibit different rating behavior. Again, we collected all available data. Rather than mapping a distribution for each age, we compute the average rating score.

While all ages have an average rating above 4, we find that older users tend to be more generous (or satisfied), which is reflected in a Spearman ρ of 0.92, i.e., a a strong correlation between user age and average rating. The correlation is significant at $p < 0.001$.

7 Denmark

7.1 Reflexive possessive pronouns

One of the distinguishing features of the western Danish dialect of Jutland is the missing distinction between the reflexive possessive pronouns *sin/sit* ("his/her own") and the non-reflexives *hans/hendes/dens/dets* ("his"). I.e., there is no distinction between "He met his (own) wife" and "He met his (=someone else's) wife".

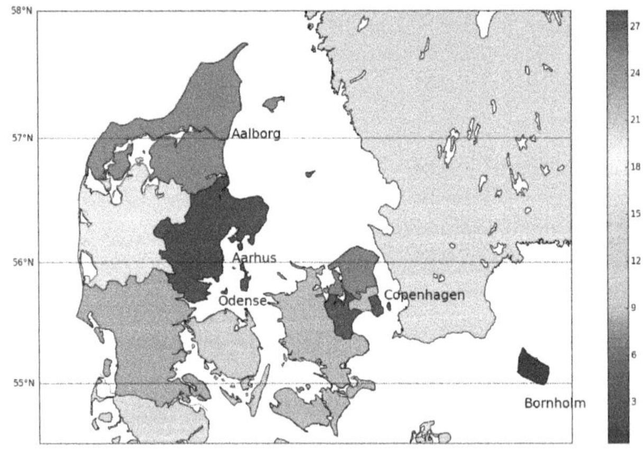

Figure 5: Regional distribution of "sin/sit" (ratio of all pronouns per NUTS-2 region)

In order to investigate this phenomenon in a data-driven way, we record the frequency of *sin/sit* and the joint frequency of all possessive pronouns. We then compute the ratio of the former in all pronouns. That is

$$r = \frac{count(\text{sin, sit})}{count(\text{sin, sit, hans, hendes, dens, dets})} \quad (1)$$

If the merger is still reflected in written language, we should expect to see a higher ratio of *sin/sit* in areas that do *not* make the distinction (i.e, in the western part of Denmark), because it is used in all contexts.

Overall, we find 420 locations that contain reviews with the possessive pronouns. Note that if the reviews for a location do not include *sin/sit*, the ratio is 0. If these are the only pronouns recorded for a location, the ratio is 1.

In order to find a regional distribution, we divide our data into NUTS-2 regions. Figure 5 shows the regional distribution according to these regions.

The map shows two distinct parts, at a line drawn at 11 degrees longitude. It approximately divides the country into two even parts, with Sealand (with the capital, Copenhagen) and Bornholm in the east, and Fyn and Jutland in the west. We have 159 data points in the eastern part, 261 in the western. Aggregating over all ratios for each of the two part, we find a ratio of 0.27 in the west, and of 0.21 in the east. The χ^2 test on the contingency matrix comes out highly significant, i.e., the ratio of *sin/sit* among the possessive pronouns is highly correlated with regions. This is likely due to the merger in the west, and is in line with the traditional dialectological distinction.

In this case, we were able to confirm a dialectological distinction with our data-driven approach.

7.2 Swear words across location, gender, and age

Traditionally, dialectal language is tightly linked with the region where it is natively spoken, to the degree that it is rarely heard (or understood) outside that region. One way this happens is when speakers of a dialect change to the standard language when addressing non-dialect speakers. On the internet, however, it is not always obvious whether the audience is local or global. The question is whether people still use dialect when they are writing reviews, which will be publicly available on the internet.

We consider the word *træls*, which is primarily found in the Jutland dialect. Used as an adjective, it suggests that some situation or state of affairs is unpleasant or unwanted. Interestingly, the word has no exact translation equivalent in standard language, which might make it harder for people to abandon the use of the word as they move outside their home region, virtually or physically.

Figure 6 maps out the regional distribution of the word following NUTS-2 regions. The map shows that the word is mostly found in the western part of the country. Of the 841 reviews with at least one occurrence of *træls*, 84% were written by people living west of the 11 degrees longitude line dividing Sealand and Funen. The word is also used by people living in Copenhagen; the number of users there, however, is small compared to the population of the city. These are most likely Jutlandic citizens living in Copenhagen.

Furthermore, *træls* has a gender and age distribution which deviates from the population as a whole. Notably, as can be seen in Figure 7, it is much more prevalent in the younger age groups, and the rate of usage falls sharply off as people get older. This might be explained by the fact that the word does not belong to the standard language, and as people grow older, they tend to use more conservative language.

Finally, for comparison, we plot the age and gender distribution of the word *lort*. *Lort* is a curse word (literally: *feces*), although not strong enough to be considered offensive in most contexts, and is frequently used to characterize the same types of situations as *træls*. Here, too, we see that the principal users of the word are young people, although women use this stronger version less than the men of the

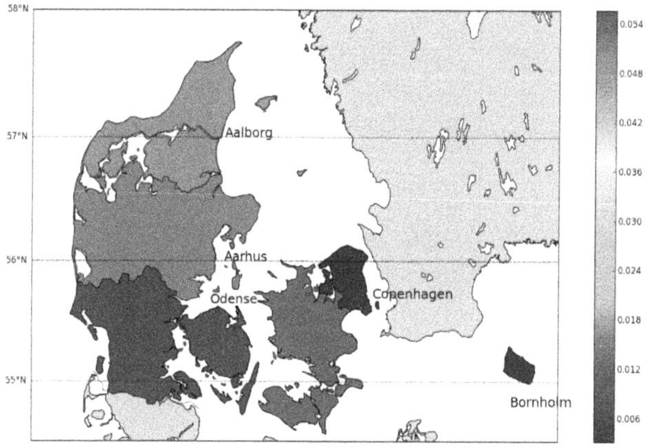

Figure 6: Regional distribution of the word *træls* (ratio of all words per NUTS-2 region).

same age group. This is in line with the findings of [31] that the use of swear words/expletives reduces with age. However, contrary to her study, we *do* find gender differences, with women using the "softer" (and more dialectal) version more than men.

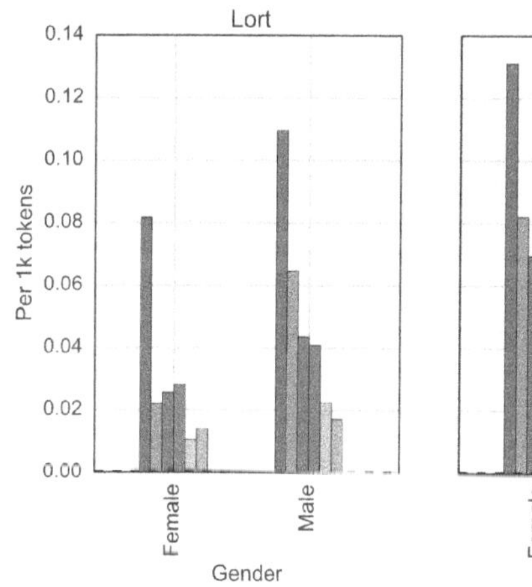

Figure 7: Two words expressing negative emotions. *Lort* is stronger than *træls*.

7.3 Compounds and multi-word expressions

In Danish, a considerable part of lexicon entries are multi-word units, such as the words for "today" (*i dag*), "yesterday" (*i går*), or "furthermore" (*i øvrigt*). These expressions have traditionally been written apart, i.e., with an intervening white space between the two words. However, in daily use, these expressions are no longer identified by the speakers as composed of two elements, but *grammaticized*, i.e., they are interpreted as a single linguistic unit.

Compound words, on the other hand, are officially *always* written in one word, i.e., without white space. They are often made up on the spot and thus usually analyzable as two elements. Compounds are a productive source of new words in Danish, and potentially unlimited. In English, in contrast, compounds are almost always written with white

	translation	% sep.	% joint	ρ
selv om	even though	0.28	**0.72**	0.98
i går	yesterday	**0.61**	0.39	0.82
ud over	apart from	0.47	**0.53**	0.79
i dag	today	**0.67**	0.33	0.78
i orden	alright	**0.84**	0.16	0.74
i øvrigt	furthermore	**0.66**	0.34	-0.52
inden for	inside	**0.54**	0.46	-0.54
hjemme side	home page	0.03	**0.97**	-0.59
ind til	into	0.38	**0.62**	-0.70
lyn hurtig	lightning fast	0.17	**0.83**	-0.77
super service	super service	**0.97**	0.03	-0.79
i det	in that	**0.73**	0.27	-0.86
super hurtig	super fast	**0.94**	0.06	-0.88
super god	super good	**0.95**	0.05	-0.90

Table 8: Frequency of spelling variations and Spearman correlation of *separate* spelling with age. Positive $\rho =$ older users prefer separate spelling. Correlations significant at $p < 0.001$

space between the nouns, and this seems to influence how young Danes write compounds. To complicate matters, the official spelling has been reformed within the last 50 years, and many words that used to be written together are now written apart.

As a result, there is a multitude of different spellings in Danish for both compounds and multiword adverbial expressions. We hypothesize that there are age-related differences in the preference for one the various spelling variants. Specifically, we expect younger Danes to split noun compounds more often than older ones, due to the influence of English, while grammaticizing multiword adverbial expressions such as *i dag*. We expect older language users to maintain the separate writing for adverbials and to not split noun compounds.

In order to analyze this, we collect all combinations of two words (*bigrams*) that occur more than 10 times in our corpus, and record for each age how often they are written apart or together. We exclude all bigrams that contain the article suffixs *-en* or *-et*, as well as all verb forms of "to be", and function words. This filters out some false positives (such as *var**en*** ("**the** goods") vs. *var **en*** ("was **a**")).

For the resulting list, we compute the ratio of the two-word spelling for each expression and analyze its correlation with respect to age via Spearman correlation. Table 8 shows the Spearman correlation of the separate spelling with age for some of the results, together with the overall distribution of the two spellings in the language.

We find that the separate spelling variant of *i dag* ("today") and *i går* ("yesterday") are strongly correlated with age, i.e., older speaker prefer to write it in two words. However, surprisingly, for *i øvrigt* (furthermore), we see a slight anti-correlation (Spearman $\rho = -0.52$). This means that older speakers tend to write it in one single word. This goes against our expectations. Comparison to a dictionary from 1957 [1], however, reveals that these were indeed the prescribed spellings, with *i øvrigt* written in one word. Older speakers thus seem to continue to use prescriptive writing norms acquired in their youths.

For compounds, we find that the most distinct cases involve the extremely productive adjectival prefix *super-*, either as an adjective intensifier, or as an adjectival modifier of a noun. Interestingly, older speakers also prefer to use the one-word spelling, while younger speakers tend to prefer the separate spelling. There are three examples in our top 20, and in all of them the separate spelling is strongly anti-correlated with age (see Table 8).

In German, where compounds famously abound, words can be combined with a hyphen or simply by concatenation. However, while there are some words that show variation, we do not find any significant correlations with age or gender. This seems to indicate that in German, compound spelling is not as free as in Danish.

8 German

8.1 Spelling reform "ss" vs. "ß"

Germany underwent a spelling reform in 1996, with the main goal to simplify spelling. After a transition period, the new spelling was legally binding for schools from 2007 on. One of the most pervasive (and contentious) changes was the replacement of *ß* with *ss* after short vowels. Two of the most frequent words affected by this reform were the conjunction *dass/daß*, "that", and the modal *müssen/müßen*, "to must".

Younger people (born after 1980) were thus predominantly taught the new spelling in school, so we expect to see predominant use of *dass/müssen*, with occasional uses of the old form (depending on at which age the new spelling was acquired), while older speakers retain the traditional spelling they acquired in their youth to a much greater extent.

Again, we collect frequency counts for the two variants of the conjunction, and expect to see a correlation of the traditional spelling (with ß) with older users.

Indeed, when we run significance tests, we see that usage of the old spelling (*daß/müßen*) is significantly correlated with age (Spearman ρ 0.84). Most occurrences of the old spelling crop up for users older than 30, i.e., people who started school in 1990 and encountered the new spelling only after they had left elementary school (when most of spelling is learned). If we divide the data into two bins, the most significant difference between the usage in the two groups occurs when splitting at the age of 40. We do note, though, that use of the old form is lower than use of the new form for all ages.

Our findings indicate that while the spelling reform has been largely accepted, there is a residual use of the old forms, significantly correlated with age. We do not find a gender effect for this spelling variation.

9 Conclusion

Traditional sociolinguistic studies often lack statistical power to draw valid conclusions, while big-data approaches to language studies mostly lack extra-linguistic information that would enable sociolinguistic studies.

In this paper, we presented user-review sites as a possible solution to this dilemma. The data provides a combination of non-canonical textual information with meta-information about the authors, including age, gender, and location, as well as time-stamps.

We presented several pilot studies that show how linguistic features are highly correlated with these socio-economic variables. This includes the use of emoticons (with and without nose), detection of gender-specific words, and rating behavior, as well as phenomena in Danish (reflexive pronouns, swear words, and compounding) and German (spelling reform).

The focus of this work has been to evaluate the suitability of the resource. Given the robustness of our findings, we plan on investigating the consequences of language variation among groups for NLP tools. More concretely, do NLP tools perform equally well for all demographic groups, and if not, can we use the findings of our study to improve them?

We also plan to a) relate the data to extra-linguistic information and b) augment it with information on the grammatical information.

10 Acknowledgements

This research is funded by the ERC Starting Grant LOWLANDS No. 313695. The authors would like to thank the anonymous reviewers for their helpful suggestions.

11 References

[1] *Ordbog over det danske sprog.* Gyldendal, 2nd edition edition, 1967.

[2] *EUROSTAT regional yearbook 2013.* EUROSTAT, 2013.

[3] C. I. Agency. Field Listing – Median Age, 2014.

[4] J. S. Alowibdi, U. A. Buy, and P. Yu. Empirical evaluation of profile characteristics for gender classification on twitter. In *Machine Learning and Applications (ICMLA), 2013 12th International Conference on*, volume 1, pages 365–369. IEEE, 2013.

[5] D. Bamman, C. Dyer, and N. A. Smith. Distributed representations of geographically situated language. In *Proceedings of the 52nd Annual Meeting of the Association for Computational Linguistics*, pages 828–834. ACL, 2014.

[6] D. Bamman, J. Eisenstein, and T. Schnoebelen. Gender identity and lexical variation in social media. *Journal of Sociolinguistics*, 18(2):135–160, 2014.

[7] C. Boulis and M. Ostendorf. A quantitative analysis of lexical differences between genders in telephone conversations. In *Proceedings of ACL*, pages 435–442. Association for Computational Linguistics, 2005.

[8] K. Button, J. Ioannidis, C. Mokrysz, B. Nosek, J. Flint, E. Robinson, and M. Munafo. Power failure: why small sample size undermines the reliability of neuroscience. *Nature Reviews Neuroscience*, 14:365–376, 2013.

[9] P. M. Carter. Shared spaces, shared structures: Latino social formation and african american english in the us south. *Journal of Sociolinguistics*, 17(1):66–92, 2013.

[10] M. Ciot, M. Sonderegger, and D. Ruths. Gender inference of twitter users in non-english contexts. In *Proceedings of the 2013 Conference on Empirical Methods in Natural Language Processing, Seattle, Wash*, pages 18–21, 2013.

[11] H. Daumé III. Non-parametric bayesian areal linguistics. In *Proceedings of NAACL*, pages 593–601. Association for Computational Linguistics, 2009.

[12] G. Doyle. Mapping dialectal variation by querying social media. In *EACL*, 2014.

[13] J. Eisenstein. Phonological factors in social media writing. In *Workshop on Language Analysis in Social Media, NAACL*, 2013.

[14] J. Eisenstein. What to do about bad language on the internet. In *NAACL*, 2013.

[15] J. Eisenstein, N. Smith, and E. Xing. Discovering sociolinguistic associations with structured sparsity. In *ACL*, 2011.

[16] J. Ganitkevitch, B. Van Durme, and C. Callison-Burch. Ppdb: The paraphrase database. In *Proceedings of NAACL-HLT*, pages 758–764, 2013.

[17] J. Holmes. Women, language and identity. *Journal of Sociolinguistics*, 1(2):195–223, 1997.

[18] R. Jones and A. Irvine. The (un)faithful machine translator. In *ACL Workshop on Language Technology for Cultural Heritage, Social Sciences, and Humanities (LaTeCH)*, 2013.

[19] W. Labov. *The social stratification of English in New York City.* PhD thesis, Columbia university, 1964.

[20] J. Li, A. Ritter, and E. Hovy. Weakly supervised user profile extraction from twitter. In *ACL*, 2014.

[21] W. Liu and D. Ruths. What's in a name? using first names as features for gender inference in twitter. In *Analyzing Microtext: 2013 AAAI Spring Symposium*, 2013.

[22] R. Macaulay. You're like 'why not?' the quotative expressions of glasgow adolescents. *Journal of Sociolinguistics*, 5(1):3–21, 2001.

[23] R. Macaulay. Extremely interesting, very interesting, or only quite interesting? adverbs and social class. *Journal of Sociolinguistics*, 6(3):398–417, 2002.

[24] L. Milroy and J. Milroy. Social network and social class: Toward an integrated sociolinguistic model. *Language in society*, 21(01):1–26, 1992.

[25] J. Nerbonne. Linguistic variation and computation. In *Proceedings of EACL*, pages 3–10. Association for Computational Linguistics, 2003.

[26] D. Nguyen, D. Trieschnigg, A. S. Dogruöz, R. Gravel, M. Theune, T. Meder, and F. D. Jong. Predicting Author Gender and Age from Tweets: Sociolinguistic Theories and Crowd Wisdom. In *Proceedings of COLING 2014*, 2014.

[27] J. Rickford and M. Price. Girlz ii women: Age-grading, language change and stylistic variation. *Journal of Sociolinguistics*, 17(2):143–179, 2013.

[28] R. B. Russ. *Examining Regional Variation Through Online Geotagged Corpora.* PhD thesis, The Ohio State University, 2013.

[29] J. E. Schmidt and J. Herrgen. Digitaler Wenker-Atlas (DiWA). Bearbeitet von Alfred Lameli, Tanja Giessler, Roland Kehrein, Alexandra Lenz, Karl-Heinz Müller, Jost Nickel, Christoph Purschke und Stefan Rabanus. Erste vollständige Ausgabe von Georg Wenkers "Sprachatlas des Deutschen Reichs", 2001.

[30] A. Søgaard. Zipfian corruptions for robust pos tagging. In *NAACL*, 2013.

[31] A.-B. Stenström. Taboos in teenage talk. *Stockholm studies in English*, 85:71–79, 1995.

[32] I. Stewart. Now we stronger than ever: African-american syntax in twitter. *EACL 2014*, page 31, 2014.

When Does Improved Targeting Increase Revenue?

Patrick Hummel
Google Inc.
Mountain View, CA, USA
phummel@google.com

R. Preston McAfee
Microsoft Corp.
Redmond, WA, USA
preston@mcafee.cc

ABSTRACT

In second price auctions with symmetric bidders, we find that improved targeting via enhanced information disclosure decreases revenue when there are two bidders and increases revenue if there are at least four bidders. With asymmetries, improved targeting increases revenue if the most frequent winner wins less than 30.4% of the time, but can decrease revenue otherwise. We derive analogous results for position auctions. Finally, we show that revenue can vary non-monotonically with the number of bidders who are able to take advantage of improved targeting.

Categories and Subject Descriptors

J.4 [**Social and Behavioral Sciences**]: Economics

General Terms

Economics, Theory

Keywords

Targeting, Revenue, Online Auctions, Position Auctions, Advertising

1. INTRODUCTION

There has been substantial concern in the Internet advertising business over whether improvements in targeting technology will reduce revenue from online advertising. The intuition underlying these concerns runs as follows. Improvements in targeting enable advertisers to more accurately identify the interests of consumers. If a consumer's interests are so accurately identified that advertisers know there is only one product this consumer would ever buy, wouldn't this process result in only a single advertiser who is willing to advertise to this consumer, meaning this advertiser can bid without competition? A more nuanced version of this argument relies on a quantity effect. Since advertisers will no longer purchase ads that reach consumers who will not be interested in their products, the total demand for advertisements will go down. If the supply of advertising opportunities remains unchanged, revenue from selling ads will decline.

The question of whether enhanced targeting increases revenue is important because of two powerful trends. First, media consumption is moving online, and print newspapers and radio have waned. The survival of much of the existing media appears to depend on the ability to monetize online content with advertising. Second, Internet advertising is increasingly using sophisticated targeting through extensive online databases on customers. Thus the likely survival of existing publishers turns on whether enhanced targeting will increase advertising revenue. Furthermore, since advertising exchanges typically take a constant fraction of a publisher's revenue, there is a direct correspondence between whether revenue increases for intermediaries and for publishers.

The argument that improvements in targeting will result in only a single relevant advertiser for each consumer is likely misplaced. The argument assumes that the purchase of the customer is a foregone conclusion, which ignores one of the main purposes of advertising: to influence the consumer's choice. While there is some advertising that is informational in nature—alerting consumers to the existence of a product and its features—the majority of advertising is intended to sway the consumer's perception of the product. This kind of advertising is commonly called emotional branding, and it is the most common kind by revenue. Coca-Cola advertises extensively to people already aware of its products. Similarly, how many American television watchers are unaware of Proctor and Gamble's Tide?

But the fact that the demand for advertisements to an individual consumer will not decline to one as a result of improved targeting does not invalidate the argument that targeting might reduce revenue. Enhanced targeting will typically increase advertiser welfare, by making advertising more effective, while reducing competition through specialization.[1] The effect of improving targeting in online advertising is exactly the reverse of pure bundling for a monopolist, where the monopolist requires consumers to purchase a bundle of objects or none at all. Targeting permits advertisers to distinguish unlike consumers, whereas pure bundling or the lack of targeting forces advertisers to treat different types of consumers as if they were the same.

[1][5] and [24] also note that such a trade-off is likely to arise as a result of improved targeting.

WWW 2015, May 18–22, 2015, Florence, Italy.
ACM 978-1-4503-3469-3/15/05.
http://dx.doi.org/10.1145/2736277.2741079.

Thus to analyze whether improvements in targeting technology increase revenue from auctions for advertisements, we can analyze whether enabling advertisers to learn more detailed information about their value before bidding would increase revenue from the auction. In particular, under targeting, we assume that the targeting information enables an advertiser to learn his exact value for advertising to a consumer before deciding how much to bid for an advertisement. By contrast, when an advertiser is unable to target, the advertiser only knows that his value for advertising to this consumer will be a random draw from some distribution, where the distribution reflects the different values the advertiser might place on advertising to different types of consumers. We compare a seller's expected revenue from auctions under these two different scenarios.

Throughout we consider a model in which bidders have private values and bidders' values are independently distributed. While this is not the only possible modeling choice, it is a natural one. There is empirical evidence that there is little correlation in bidder values within auctions on Microsoft's Ad Exchange [10], which [10] indicates implies that "bidder valuations are private, driven by idiosyncratic match quality, rather than a common component". Furthermore, if there is a common component to bidders' values that is not known to any participant and the bidders have private values that are independent conditional on the common value, then the results of this paper for the zero reserve price will continue to hold since the results are attained for each realization of the common component.[2]

We also frequently make use of the standard hazard rate condition on the cumulative distribution of the buyers' values. Although this assumption is not completely innocuous, it is satisfied by many distributions frequently encountered in empirical studies.

In this environment, when advertisements are being sold via second price auctions, we first demonstrate a result analogous to that in [8], [18], and [30] which illustrates that targeting decreases revenues when there are two bidders, even if there are asymmetries in the distributions of the bidders' values. We next show that when bidders' values are drawn from identical distributions, then improved targeting has an ambiguous effect on revenue when there are three bidders, but improved targeting increases revenue if there are at least four bidders. These results are virtually unaffected by the possibility that a seller can set reserve prices. Finally, we address the question of what happens when the bidders' values are drawn from different distributions. Here we find that if the strongest firm wins the auction less than 30.4% of the time, then improved targeting increases revenue, but targeting can reduce revenue when the two strongest bidders win a disproportionate percentage of the time.

While second price auctions for a single advertising opportunity are used by most publishers, we also consider position auctions, as these are frequently used by search engines as well as a smaller number of publishers. Here we find that targeting unambiguously decreases revenue when there are only a small number of bidders, increases revenue when there are a large number of bidders, and has an ambiguous effect on revenue when there are an intermediate number of bidders. When there are an intermediate number of bidders, improved targeting increases revenue if and only if the click-through rates of the top positions are sufficiently large compared to the click-through rates of the lower positions.

Finally, we address the question of how improved targeting affects revenue when only some advertisers are able to make use of the targeting information. In this setting we show that even when there are symmetric bidders whose values are drawn from a distribution satisfying standard regularity conditions, it could be the case that a seller's revenue may vary non-monotonically with the number of bidders who are able to make use of the targeting information. That is, the seller may be indifferent between targeting and bundling when only one bidder can target, prefer targeting to bundling when two bidders can target, and prefer bundling to targeting when three bidders can target. We also illustrate how improved targeting affects revenue when there is exactly one bidder who can make use of the targeting information. We find that this decreases revenue when the strongest bidder is making use of the targeting information, increases revenue when the weaker bidders are making use of the targeting information, and has an ambiguous effect on revenue for bidders of intermediate strength.

Our paper relates to two distinct strands of literature. First, our paper relates to the literature on whether a mechanism designer should provide information to bidders in a private value auction that would better help them assess their values for an object. Here [16] provides examples that illustrate that improving targeting may decrease revenue in a private value auction and [17] illustrates that an auctioneer may have an incentive to release less than full information to the bidders when the auctioneer has the ability to release partial information. [6] considers the optimal information structure in a joint design problem in which there may be a direct tie between the information the seller discloses and the mechanism the seller then uses to sell the object, [14] addresses the question of how much information the mechanism designer should provide under the optimal mechanism which may possibly involve charging the bidders in the auction for providing the information, and [12] considers questions related to how information disclosure affects the ultimate prices advertisers would charge for their products. Finally, [7] analyzes the value of targeting data to advertisers, [18] provides general methods of classifying the informativeness of signals to bidders in private value auctions, and [31] conducts field experiments analyzing the effect of information disclosure on wholesale auto auctions.

The second related strand of literature is work analyzing when sellers would want to bundle goods and sell them together. [4] and [15] both study a standard bundling framework in which a monopolist considers selling bundles of goods to buyers, but these papers do not consider situations in which the goods are sold via an auction. [2], [23], and [26] study mixed bundling in which a monopolist offers buyers both the option of buying various goods individually and the option of buying multiple goods at the same time, possibly for a discount. [11] studies a model in which a seller sells two objects via an auction and the seller must decide whether to sell them separately or via bundling. [20] studies how a seller's revenue from selling two objects separately or from only offering to sell the objects together compares to the seller's revenue from an optimal mechanism, which may

[2]In addition, we already know from [28] that if there is a common component to all bidders' values, then the seller has an incentive to reveal this common component. [1] further discusses when information asymmetries in common value auctions can lead to revenue losses.

not involve either of these approaches. [25] and [33] study questions related to when a monopolist's optimal mechanism involves take-it or leave-it mechanisms that set a price for each possible collection of goods. Finally, [3] studies questions related to optimal bundling with multiple sellers.

While these papers are all interesting, they all differ from our work in significant ways. Our paper differs from the work on bundling goods together in that very few of these papers consider models of bundling in an auction setting, whereas we focus on auctions throughout our paper. Our paper also differs from the literature on information provision by a mechanism designer in that these papers do not attempt to derive the detailed results in this paper on how the number and sizes of the various bidders affects the suitability of bundling compared to targeting for a fixed auction format. Furthermore, none of the above papers consider the problem of whether to sell goods using targeting or bundling when the seller must use a position auction, and these papers also do not consider scenarios in which some of the buyers buy objects using bundling while other buyers buy the objects separately. Our paper thus makes a number of new contributions to the literature on information provision by a mechanism designer and bundling.

2. THE MODEL

Each buyer $i \in \{1, 2, \dots, n\}$ has a value v_i that is an independent draw from the cumulative distribution function $F_i(v)$ with finite mean and variance, and a corresponding continuous density $f_i(v)$ on its support $[0, \overline{v}_i)$, where $\overline{v}_i$ may be infinite. These bidders compete in an auction, and bid either before their value is realized (bundling) or after their value is realized (targeting). The model also applies to situations in which bidders do not learn their exact values under targeting but instead learn estimates v_i that are correct in expectation. Each bidder i's expected value under bundling is $\int_0^\infty v f_i(v)\, dv = \int_0^\infty 1 - F_i(v)\, dv$. For convenience we name the bidders in decreasing order of their expected values so $\int_0^\infty 1 - F_i(v)\, dv \geq \int_0^\infty 1 - F_{i+1}(v)\, dv$ for all i.

Throughout this manuscript we consider two possible auction formats that the bidders may compete in. First we consider standard second price auctions in which there is one object for sale and the bidder who makes the highest bid wins the object and pays the second highest bid. The results with symmetric buyers for this format will also extend to first price auctions by the revenue equivalence theorem.

The second auction format we consider is a position auction. Position auctions differ from the setting considered above in that there are s positions, where s is a positive integer satisfying $1 \leq s < n$. Each position $k \leq s$ has a click-through-rate $c_k > 0$, where c_k is non-increasing in k for all $k \leq s$. Bidders compete by submitting bids per clicks. The top position then goes to the bidder with the highest bid, the second position goes to the bidder with the second highest bid, and so on, with ties broken randomly.

We consider two methods for setting prices in position auctions. The first pricing method we consider is a generalized second price (GSP) auction. In this setting, the kth highest bidder pays a price per click that is equal to the bid submitted by the $k+1^{th}$ highest bidder. Thus if $v_{(k)}$ denotes the value of the kth highest bidder and $b_{(k+1)}$ denotes the bid submitted by the $k+1^{th}$ highest bidder, then the final payoff of the kth highest bidder is $c_k(v_{(k)} - b_{(k+1)})$. This is the same basic model of generalized second price auctions without clickability of ads that is considered in [13] and [32].

The second possibility we consider is the Vickrey-Clarke-Groves (VCG) mechanism. Under VCG pricing, each advertiser pays a total cost equal to the externality he imposes on other bidders by bidding in the auction. Thus under VCG pricing, the bidder who wins the kth position pays a total cost of $\sum_{j=k}^{s}(c_j - c_{j+1})b_{(j+1)}$ and a total price per click equal to $\frac{1}{c_k}\sum_{j=k}^{s}(c_j - c_{j+1})b_{(j+1)}$, where we abuse notation by letting $c_{s+1} \equiv 0$.

Finally we also sometimes allow for the possibility of reserve prices. If there is a reserve price of r, then only bidders who bid at least r will be considered in the auction. Under standard second price auctions, if there is only one bidder who bids more than the reserve, then this bidder pays r for the object. Under GSP auctions, if there are only $k \leq s$ bidders who bid more than the reserve price, then the payoffs of the first $k-1$ of these bidders are unaffected by the reserve price, but the kth highest bidder pays a price of r per click and obtains a payoff of $c_k(v_{(k)} - r)$.

Finally, under position auctions using VCG pricing, we introduce reserve prices in the following manner: If at least $s+1$ bidders submit a bid in the auction that is greater than the reserve price, then the reserve price has no effect on the outcome of the auction. If $K \leq s$ bidders submit a bid in the auction that is greater than the reserve price, then only the bidders who submitted a bid greater than the reserve price have their ads shown and these bidders pay a price per click equal to the price they would pay if there were exactly K positions available and there were an additional bidder who submitted a bid equal to the reserve price. [21] has noted in a more general setting that this method of introducing reserve prices into the VCG mechanism both preserves the incentive for advertisers to bid truthfully and also ensures that any advertisers who have their ads shown pay a price per click that is greater than or equal to the reserve price.

3. SECOND PRICE AUCTIONS WITHOUT RESERVE PRICES

We begin by comparing bundling to targeting in a standard second price auction setting with no reserve price. Under bundling, all bidders have a weakly dominant strategy of bidding their expected values. Thus the bidder with the highest expected value wins and pays the second highest bid, and the seller's revenue under bundling is the second highest expected value or $\int_0^\infty 1 - F_2(v)\, dv$.

Under targeting bidders bid their exact values after learning their values, and the seller's revenue is the second highest realized value. The second highest realized value is less than or equal to v when either the highest value is no greater than v, or the highest value exceeds v but all other values are less than or equal v. Thus if $v_{(2)}$ denotes the realization of the second highest value, the distribution of this realization is given by the following cumulative distribution function:

$$\begin{aligned} Pr(v_{(2)} \leq v) &= \prod_{j=1}^{n} F_j(v) + \sum_{j=1}^{n}(1 - F_j(v)) \prod_{i \neq j} F_i(v) \\ &= \sum_{j=1}^{n} \prod_{i \neq j} F_i(v) - (n-1) \prod_{j=1}^{n} F_j(v) \end{aligned}$$

From this it follows that the difference between the seller's expected revenue under targeting and bundling is $\Delta_n =$

$$\int_0^\infty 1 - \sum_{j=1}^{n} \prod_{i \neq j} F_i(v) + (n-1) \prod_{j=1}^{n} F_j(v) - (1 - F_2(v))\, dv$$

$$= \int_0^\infty F_2(v) - \sum_{j=1}^{n} \prod_{i \neq j} F_i(v) + (n-1) \prod_{j=1}^{n} F_j(v)\, dv$$

First we illustrate that the insight in [18] and [30] that the seller prefers bundling to targeting when there are two bidders extends to cases where the values of the bidders are not drawn from identical distributions:

THEOREM 1. *Suppose there are $n = 2$ bidders. Then the seller prefers bundling to targeting.*

PROOF. The difference between the seller's expected revenue under targeting and bundling when there are $n = 2$ bidders is $\Delta_2 =$

$$\int_0^\infty F_2(v) - \sum_{j=1}^{2} \prod_{i \neq j} F_i(v) + (2-1) \prod_{j=1}^{2} F_j(v)\, dx$$

$$= \int_0^\infty -F_1(v) + F_2(v) F_1(v)\, dv = \int_0^\infty (F_2(v) - 1) F_1(v)\, dv < 0.$$

Thus the seller prefers bundling to targeting when there are $n = 2$ bidders. □

Next we consider cases in which the bidders' values are drawn from the same distributions. When $F_i(v) = F(v)$ for all v, the difference between the seller's expected revenue under targeting and bundling is

$$\Delta_n = \int_0^\infty F_2(v) - \sum_{j=1}^{n} \prod_{i \neq j} F_i(v) + (n-1) \prod_{j=1}^{n} F_j(v)\, dv$$
$$= \int_0^\infty F(v) - nF^{n-1}(v) + (n-1) F^n(v)\, dv$$

Now we use this expression for the difference between the seller's expected revenue under targeting and bundling to show that the seller prefers targeting to bundling when there are $n \geq 4$ bidders. Throughout the remainder of this manuscript, we let $f(v)$ denote the density corresponding to the cumulative distribution function $F(v)$, and let $\overline{v}$ denote the upper bound of the support of $F(\cdot)$.

THEOREM 2. *Suppose $F_i(v) = F(v)$ for all i, $\frac{1-F(v)}{f(v)}$ is nonincreasing in v throughout its support, and $n \geq 4$. Then the seller prefers targeting to bundling.*

PROOF. First note that if $n \geq 4$, then $\phi(y) \equiv \frac{y^2}{2} + \frac{y^3}{3} + \ldots + \frac{y^{n-1}}{n-1} - \frac{n-1}{n} y^n \geq 0$ for all $y \in [0,1]$. $\phi(y) = y^n(\frac{y^{2-n}}{2} + \ldots + \frac{y^{n-n}}{n} - 1)$, so $\phi \geq 0$ if and only if $\frac{y^{2-n}}{2} + \ldots + \frac{y^{n-n}}{n} - 1 \geq 0$. And since $\frac{y^{2-n}}{2} + \ldots + \frac{y^{n-n}}{n} - 1$ is decreasing in y, $\phi \geq 0$ for all $y \in [0,1]$ if and only if $\frac{1}{2} + \ldots + \frac{1}{n} - 1 \geq 0$, which holds for all $n \geq 4$. Thus $\phi(y) \geq 0$ for all $y \in [0,1]$ if $n \geq 4$.

Now the difference between the seller's expected revenue under targeting and bundling when there are n bidders and $F_i(v) = F(v)$ for all i is $\Delta_n =$

$$\int_0^{\overline{v}} F(v) - nF^{n-1}(v) + (n-1)F^n(v)\, dv$$

$$= \int_0^{\overline{v}} \left(\frac{1-F(v)}{f(v)}\right) (F(v) + \ldots + F^{n-2}(v) - (n-1)F^{n-1}(v)) f(v)\, dv$$

$$= \left(\frac{1-F(v)}{f(v)}\right) \left(\frac{F^2(v)}{2} + \ldots + \frac{F^{n-1}(v)}{n-1} - \frac{n-1}{n} F^n(v)\right) \Big|_0^{\overline{v}}$$

$$- \int_0^{\overline{v}} \left(\frac{1-F(v)}{f(v)}\right)' \left(\frac{F^2(v)}{2} + \ldots + \frac{F^{n-1}(v)}{n-1} - \frac{n-1}{n} F^n(v)\right) dv$$

$$= \left(\lim_{v \to \overline{v}} \frac{1-F(v)}{f(v)}\right) \left[\frac{1}{2} + \ldots + \frac{1}{n-1} - \frac{n-1}{n}\right]$$

$$- \int_0^{\overline{v}} \left(\frac{1-F(v)}{f(v)}\right)' \left[\frac{F^2(v)}{2} + \ldots + \frac{F^{n-1}(v)}{n-1} - \frac{n-1}{n} F^n(v)\right] dv$$

By the result in the first paragraph of this proof, both the terms in square brackets are positive for all v. Also, the term $\lim_{v \to \overline{v}} \frac{1-F(v)}{f(v)}$ is non-negative since $\frac{1-F(v)}{f(v)}$ is non-negative for all v, and the term $\left(\frac{1-F(v)}{f(v)}\right)'$ is non-positive by assumption. Thus $\Delta_n \geq 0$ and the seller prefers targeting to bundling. □

Thus, in the symmetric case, when there are at least four bidders and the usual hazard rate condition is satisfied, targeting dominates bundling. The reason for this is that the second highest realized value (the revenue under targeting) when there are at least four bidders is greater than the average value of these bidders (the revenue under bundling) as long as the distribution does not have fat tails. The possibility of fat tails is ruled out by the standard hazard rate condition, so targeting dominates bundling when there are $n = 4$ bidders in this case.[3] A similar approach can illuminate the case of three bidders.

THEOREM 3. *Suppose $F_i(v) = F(v)$ for all i and there are $n = 3$ bidders. Then the seller prefers targeting to bundling if $f(v)$ is increasing in v on its support, prefers bundling to targeting if $f(v)$ is decreasing in v on its support, and is indifferent between targeting and bundling if $f(v)$ is constant on its support.*

PROOF. The difference between the seller's expected revenue under targeting and bundling when there are $n = 3$ bidders is $\Delta_3 =$

$$\int_0^{\overline{v}} F(v) - 3F^2(v) + 2F^3(v)\, dv$$

$$= \int_0^{\overline{v}} \frac{1}{f(v)} (F(v) - 3F^2(v) + 2F^3(v)) f(v)\, dv$$

$$= \frac{1}{f(v)} \left(\frac{F^2(v)}{2} - F^3(v) + \frac{F^4(v)}{2}\right) \Big|_0^{\overline{v}}$$

$$- \int_0^{\overline{v}} \left(\frac{1}{f(v)}\right)' \left(\frac{F^2(v)}{2} - F^3(v) + \frac{F^4(v)}{2}\right) dv$$

$$= \frac{F^2(v)}{2f(v)} (1 - F(v))^2 \Big|_0^{\overline{v}} - \int_0^{\overline{v}} \left(\frac{1}{f(v)}\right)' \frac{F^2(v)}{2} (1 - F(v))^2\, dv$$

Now if $f(v)$ is increasing in v on its support or $f(v)$ is constant on its support, then $\frac{F^2(v)}{2f(v)} (1 - F(v))^2 \big|_0^{\overline{v}} = 0$ and

[3]For any finite number of players, there exists a distribution with sufficiently fat tails such that the seller prefers bundling to targeting.

$\Delta_3 = -\int_0^{\overline{v}} (\frac{1}{f(v)})' \frac{F^2(v)}{2} (1-F(v))^2 \ dv$. Thus if $f(v)$ is increasing in v on its support, then $\Delta_3 > 0$, and if $f(v)$ is constant on its support, then $\Delta_3 = 0$. Similarly, if $f(v)$ is decreasing in v on its support and $\frac{F^2(v)}{2f(v)} (1-F(v))^2 \Big|_0^{\overline{v}} = 0$, then $\Delta_3 = -\int_0^{\overline{v}} (\frac{1}{f(v)})' \frac{F^2(v)}{2} (1-F(v))^2 \ dv < 0$.

If $f(v)$ is decreasing in v and $\frac{F^2(v)}{2f(v)} (1-F(v))^2 \Big|_0^{\overline{v}} \neq 0$ (which implies $\overline{v} = \infty$), then consider what Δ_3 would equal if the players' values were instead random draws from the distribution $F(v|\theta)$ satisfying $F(v|\theta) = \frac{F(v)}{F(\theta)}$ for $v \leq \theta$ and $F(v) = 1$ for $v > \theta$. For any finite $\theta > 0$, it is necessarily the case that $\frac{F^2(v|\theta)}{2f(v|\theta)} (1-F(v|\theta))^2 \Big|_0^{\overline{v}|\theta} = 0$, where $f(v|\theta)$ denotes the density corresponding to $F(v|\theta)$ and $\overline{v}|\theta$ denotes the upper bound on the support of $F(v|\theta)$. Moreover, $f(v|\theta)$ is decreasing in v on its support, so $\Delta_3 < 0$ when the players' values are random draws from $F(v|\theta)$. Furthermore, Δ_3 must be bounded away from 0 for all $\theta \geq \theta^*$, where θ^* is some constant in the interior of the support of $F(\cdot)$.

But in the limit as θ becomes arbitrarily large, the value of Δ_3 when the values of the players are random draws from the distribution $F(v|\theta)$ becomes arbitrarily close to the value of Δ_3 when the values of the players are random draws from the distribution $F(v)$. From this it follows that if $f(v)$ is decreasing in v on its support, then $\Delta_3 < 0$ even if $\frac{F^2(v)}{2f(v)} (1-F(v))^2 \Big|_0^{\overline{v}} \neq 0$. The result then follows. □

The fact that a seller may either prefer bundling or targeting when there are three bidders is intuitive. When there are three bidders, the second highest value is the median value, so the seller's expected revenue under targeting is just the median value of the bidders. The seller's expected revenue under bundling is the expected value of the bidders. Whether a seller prefers targeting to bundling simply depends on whether the mean or the median of a certain distribution is greater.

In summary, when the buyers' values are drawn from identical continuous distributions, the seller typically prefers targeting to bundling when there are four or more bidders, while the seller prefers bundling to targeting when there are two bidders. The seller's exact preferences in the case where there are three bidders depend on the distribution, but since most natural distributions of values have a density $f(v)$ that is decreasing on most of its support, the seller is also likely to prefer bundling to targeting when there are three bidders.

4. RESERVE PRICES

When there is more than one bidder, in symmetric settings appropriate reserve prices favor targeting. Adding reserve prices does not improve the seller's revenue under bundling since the seller's revenue is equal to the bidders' expected values regardless of whether the seller uses a reserve price, but reserve prices do increase the revenue from targeting. Thus when there are four or more bidders, targeting with reserve prices dominates bundling with reserve prices.

However, while reserve prices increase the revenue from targeting but not the revenue from bundling, it is still the case that the seller typically prefers bundling to targeting when there are two bidders. This is illustrated below:

THEOREM 4. *Suppose there are $n = 2$ bidders, $F_i(v) = F(v)$ for all i, and the density $f(v)$ is non-increasing in v. Then the seller prefers bundling to targeting with the optimal reserve price.*

PROOF. We know from [9] that when $f(v)$ is non-increasing in v, the seller's expected revenue in an auction with two bidders and the optimal reserve price is lower than the seller's expected revenue in an auction with three bidders and no reserve price. However, we know from Theorem 3 that when $F_i(v) = F(v)$ for all i, and the density $f(v)$ is non-increasing in v, then the seller prefers bundling to targeting when there are $n = 3$ bidders and no reserve price. Since the seller's expected revenue under targeting when there are two bidders with the optimal reserve price is even lower than the seller's expected revenue under targeting when there are three bidders and no reserve price, it then follows that the seller prefers bundling to targeting when there are $n = 2$ bidders, even if the seller uses the optimal reserve price. □

In addition to bundling still typically being optimal in the case where there are two bidders, it is also the case that the seller will sometimes want to use bundling even when there are three bidders. Although the seller now prefers targeting to bundling in the case where the buyers' values are drawn from a uniform distribution, the seller still prefers bundling to targeting when the buyers' values are drawn from an exponential distribution, even if the seller uses the optimal reserve price:

THEOREM 5. *Suppose there are $n = 3$ bidders and $F_i(v) = F(v)$ for all i. Then the seller prefers targeting to bundling when the bidders' values are drawn from the uniform distribution, but the seller prefers bundling to targeting when the bidders' values are drawn from the exponential distribution.*

PROOF. When there are $n = 3$ bidders and each bidder's value is an independent and identically distributed draw from the uniform distribution, we know from Theorem 3 that the seller is indifferent between bundling and targeting when there is no reserve price. Since setting the optimal reserve price increases the seller's revenue under targeting but not under bundling, it then follows that when there are $n = 3$ bidders and the seller sets the optimal reserve price, the seller obtains greater revenue under targeting than under bundling when the bidders' values are drawn from the uniform distribution.

Now suppose there are $n = 3$ bidders and the bidders' values are independent and identically distributed draws from the exponential distribution with cumulative distribution function $F(v) = 1 - e^{-v}$. If there is no targeting, then all bidders bid their expected value of 1, and the seller's revenue will be 1. If there is targeting, then the seller's optimal reserve price r satisfies $r = \frac{1-F(r)}{f(r)} = 1$, and the seller's expected revenue is

$$\begin{aligned} & \int_r^\infty \left(v - \frac{1-F(v)}{f(v)}\right) nF(v)^{n-1} f(v) \ dv \\ = & \int_1^\infty (v-1)nF(v)^{n-1} f(v) \ dv \\ = & -(v-1)(1-F(v)^n)\Big|_1^\infty + \int_1^\infty 1 - F(v)^n \ dv \\ = & \int_1^\infty 1-(1-e^{-v})^3 \ dv = \frac{2 - 9e + 18e^2}{6e^3} < 1. \end{aligned}$$

Thus the seller prefers bundling to targeting when the bidders' values are drawn from the exponential distribution. □

5. ASYMMETRIC BIDDERS WITHOUT RESERVE PRICES

We now consider a scenario in which the values of the bidders are not all drawn from the same distribution. In particular, we consider a scenario in which there is some cumulative distribution function $F(v)$ and some values $\alpha_1, \ldots, \alpha_n$ satisfying $\alpha_1 \geq \alpha_2 \geq \ldots \geq \alpha_n > 0$ such that $F_i(v) = F(v)^{\alpha_i}$ for all i. This formulation is useful because the values of α_i have a natural interpretation in terms of the bidders' probabilities of winning the auction. If $A \equiv \sum_{j=1}^{n} \alpha_j$, then the probability bidder j has the highest value is

$$Pr(v_j > v_i \; \forall \, i \neq j) = \int_0^\infty \prod_{i \neq j} F_i(v) \alpha_j F(v)^{\alpha_j - 1} f(v)\, dv = \frac{\alpha_j}{A}$$

We now give a result that expresses the circumstances under which targeting is preferred to bundling as a function of the probabilities the various bidders win the auction.

LEMMA 1. *Suppose that $F_i(v) = F(v)^{\alpha_i}$ for some $\alpha_1, \ldots, \alpha_n$ satisfying $\alpha_1 \geq \alpha_2 \geq \ldots \geq \alpha_n > 0$, α_2 is sufficiently large, $n \geq 3$, and $\frac{1-F(v)}{f(v)}$ is nonincreasing in v. Then if $\frac{\alpha_2}{A} \leq \left(1 - \frac{\alpha_1}{A}\right)\left(1 - \frac{\alpha_2}{A}\right)^{\frac{1-\alpha_1/A}{\alpha_2/A}}$, the seller prefers targeting to bundling.*

We defer the proof of this result to the full version of the paper [22]. The inequality in Lemma 1 is a function only of two variables, $\frac{\alpha_1}{A}$ and $\frac{\alpha_2}{A}$, and indicates that we can give conditions under which targeting is preferred to bundling solely in terms of the probabilities the strongest bidders will win the auction. We now seek to show when this inequality is satisfied given that α_1 and α_2 must meet the constraints $0 \leq \frac{\alpha_2}{A} \leq \min\{\frac{\alpha_1}{A}, 1 - \frac{\alpha_1}{A}\}$.

THEOREM 6. *The inequality in Lemma 1 is satisfied if $\frac{\alpha_1}{A} \leq 0.30366$. If $\frac{\alpha_1}{A} > 0.30366$, there exists some $y^* \in (0, \min\{\frac{\alpha_1}{A}, 1 - \frac{\alpha_1}{A}\})$ such that this inequality is satisfied if and only if $\frac{\alpha_2}{A} \leq y^*$. Furthermore, if this key value of y^* is taken as a function of $\frac{\alpha_1}{A}$, $y^*(\frac{\alpha_1}{A})/(1 - \frac{\alpha_1}{A})$ is increasing in $\frac{\alpha_1}{A}$ and as $\frac{\alpha_1}{A} \to 1$, $y^*(\frac{\alpha_1}{A})/(1 - \frac{\alpha_1}{A}) \to 1$.*

PROOF. First we show that there is some $y^* \in (0, 1 - \frac{\alpha_1}{A})$ such that the inequality in Lemma 1 is satisfied if and only if $\frac{\alpha_2}{A} \leq y^*$. Note that $\frac{\alpha_2}{A} \leq \left(1 - \frac{\alpha_1}{A}\right)\left(1 - \frac{\alpha_2}{A}\right)^{\frac{1-\alpha_1/A}{\alpha_2/A}}$ holds if and only if $\frac{\alpha_2/A}{1-\alpha_1/A} \leq \left(1 - \frac{\alpha_2}{A}\right)^{\frac{1-\alpha_1/A}{\alpha_2/A}}$. Now let $\beta \equiv \frac{\alpha_2}{A}$ and let $\gamma \equiv 1 - \frac{\alpha_1}{A}$. We can rewrite this inequality in terms of β and γ as $\frac{\beta}{\gamma} \leq (1-\beta)^{\gamma/\beta}$ or $(\beta/\gamma)^{(\beta/\gamma)} \leq 1 - \beta$. And if $x \equiv \frac{\beta}{\gamma}$, then we can further rewrite this inequality as $x^x \leq 1 - \gamma x$ or $x^x + \gamma x \leq 1$. Now $g(x;\gamma) \equiv x^x + \gamma x$ is a convex function of x that satisfies $g(0;\gamma) = 1$, $g(1;\gamma) = 1 + \gamma$ and $g'(0) = -\infty$. Thus $g(x;\gamma) \leq 1$ if x is sufficiently close to 0, $g(x;\gamma) > 1$ if x is sufficiently close to 1, and there is some $x^*(\gamma) \in (0,1)$ such that $g(x;\gamma) \leq 1$ if and only if $x \leq x^*(\gamma)$. From this it follows that this inequality is satisfied if and only if $\frac{\alpha_2}{A} \leq y^*$ for some $y^* \in (0, 1 - \frac{\alpha_1}{A})$.

The result in the previous paragraph implies that if the inequality in Lemma 1 is satisfied when $\frac{\alpha_2}{A} = \frac{\alpha_1}{A}$, then this inequality is also satisfied for any values of $\frac{\alpha_2}{A} \leq \frac{\alpha_1}{A}$. Now the inequality in Lemma 1 is satisfied when $\frac{\alpha_2}{A} = \frac{\alpha_1}{A}$ if and only if $\frac{\alpha_1}{A} \leq \left(1 - \frac{\alpha_1}{A}\right)\left(1 - \frac{\alpha_1}{A}\right)^{\frac{1-\alpha_1/A}{\alpha_1/A}}$, which holds if and only if $\frac{\alpha_1/A}{1-\alpha_1/A} \leq \left(1 - \frac{\alpha_1}{A}\right)^{\frac{1-\alpha_1/A}{\alpha_1/A}}$. Thus if $\delta \equiv \frac{\alpha_1}{A}$, then this holds if and only if $\frac{\delta}{1-\delta} \leq (1-\delta)^{\frac{1-\delta}{\delta}}$ or $(\frac{\delta}{1-\delta})^{\delta/(1-\delta)} + \delta \leq 1$. Now $h(\delta) \equiv (\frac{\delta}{1-\delta})^{\delta/(1-\delta)} + \delta$ satisfies $h(0) = 1$, $h(1) = \infty$, and $h'(0) = -\infty$. Thus $h(\delta) \leq 1$ for δ sufficiently close to 0, $h(\delta) > 1$ if δ is sufficiently close to 1, and there is some $\delta^* \in (0,1)$ such that $h(\delta^*) \leq 1$ if and only if $\delta \leq \delta^*$. Thus the inequality in Lemma 1 is satisfied for all $\frac{\alpha_2}{A} \leq \frac{\alpha_1}{A}$ if and only if $\frac{\alpha_1}{A} \leq \delta^*$, where δ^* is the unique $\delta \in (0,1)$ satisfying $h(\delta) = 1$. Computationally it follows that $\delta^* = 0.30366$, so the inequality in Lemma 1 is satisfied if $\frac{\alpha_1}{A} \leq 0.30366$, and if $\frac{\alpha_1}{A} > 0.30366$, then there is some $y^* \in (0, \min\{\frac{\alpha_1}{A}, 1 - \frac{\alpha_1}{A}\})$ such that this inequality is satisfied if and only if $\frac{\alpha_2}{A} \leq y^*$.

Furthermore, since $g(x;\gamma)$ is increasing in γ, the critical value of $x^*(\gamma)$ given in the first paragraph of this proof is decreasing in γ, meaning x^* is increasing in $\frac{\alpha_1}{A}$. From this it follows that for the key value of y^* above, it must be the case that $y^*(\frac{\alpha_1}{A})/(1 - \frac{\alpha_1}{A})$ is increasing in $\frac{\alpha_1}{A}$. Furthermore, when $\gamma = 0$, $x^*(\gamma) = 1$ since $g(1;0) = 1$. Thus as $\frac{\alpha_1}{A} \to 1$, $y^*(\frac{\alpha_1}{A})/(1 - \frac{\alpha_1}{A}) \to 1$ as well. □

The above result indicates that when $\frac{\alpha_1}{A} \leq 0.30366$ and the strongest firm wins the auction less than 30.366% of the time, there is automatically enough competition in the auction that targeting will increase revenue. When the largest firm is larger than this, then improved targeting will increase revenue if and only if the second largest firm is sufficiently small and there is enough competition from other firms.

Interestingly, the result that $y^*(\frac{\alpha_1}{A})/(1 - \frac{\alpha_1}{A})$ is increasing in $\frac{\alpha_1}{A}$ indicates that as the strongest firm becomes more dominant, the second strongest firm can be relatively stronger compared to the weaker firms without changing the result that targeting increases revenue. Furthermore, as $\frac{\alpha_1}{A} \to 1$ and the strongest firm becomes arbitrarily strong, $y^*(\frac{\alpha_1}{A})/(1-\frac{\alpha_1}{A}) \to 1$, indicating that the second strongest firm can also become arbitrarily strong relative to the weaker firms and still ensure that targeting increases revenue. This makes sense intuitively since when the strongest firm becomes more dominant, there is a greater need to allow targeting to increase the chances that the strongest firm will be given a substantial challenge in the auction.

6. POSITION AUCTIONS

Having discussed whether targeting is preferred to bundling in the case of a single object auction, we now consider how the results would be affected by using position auctions. We focus on the case where $F_i(v) = F(v)$ for all i, and $F(v)$ has compact support $[0, \overline{v}]$.

In this symmetric case, if the seller uses bundling, and all bidders bid before learning the realizations of their values, then all bidders have an expected value for a click that equals $\int_0^{\overline{v}} 1 - F(v)\, dv$ and it is an equilibrium for all bidders to bid this expected value regardless of whether we use GSP or VCG pricing. Total revenue for the seller under bundling is therefore equal to $\sum_{k=1}^{s} c_k \int_0^{\overline{v}} 1 - F(v)\, dv$.

Next we consider the case in which bidders bid after learning the realizations of their values. We assume that when bidders bid that they know their own values but they do not know the bids or the values of any of the other bidders.

Throughout our analysis of targeting, we assume that there is a symmetric pure strategy equilibrium in which bidders follow monotonic bidding strategies. This assumption is a mild assumption for two reasons. First, we show in [22] that when bidders are restricted to making bids in discrete increments of ϵ for some small $\epsilon > 0$ that there exists a symmetric pure strategy equilibrium in which bidders follow the same monotonic bidding strategies. This assumption that bidders bid in discrete increments is realistic in situations in which bidders cannot adjust their bids by less than some very small amount (such as a small fraction of a penny).

Second, [19] has already illustrated that for a wide variety of cases, there exists a symmetric pure strategy equilibrium in which bidders follow strictly monotonic bidding strategies, even if the players may submit bids along a continuous scale. We thus take symmetric monotonic equilibria as a starting point and use this to address the question of whether targeting is preferred to bundling for the seller.

When bidders follow a symmetric monotonic bidding strategy in equilibrium, the seller's expected revenue in the GSP auction is pinned down by the following lemma:

LEMMA 2. *Suppose $F_i(v) = F(v)$ for all i and the bidders use a symmetric and strictly monotonic bidding strategy $b(v)$ in equilibrium. Then expected revenue in GSP auctions equals $n \int_r^{\overline{v}} \sum_{k=1}^{s} c_k \binom{n-1}{k-1}(1-F(v))^{k-1} F(v)^{n-k}(v - \frac{1-F(v)}{f(v)}) f(v)\, dv$.*

We defer the proof of this result to the full version of the paper [22]. The above result illustrates that there is a natural correspondence between the seller's expected revenue in a single auction setting and the seller's revenue in a generalized second price auction with private values. In a standard private values auction setting, the seller's expected revenue is just the expectation of the highest virtual valuation $v - \frac{1-F(v)}{f(v)}$. In a GSP auction, the only difference is that the seller's expected revenue is now the sum of the expectations of the jth highest virtual valuations $v - \frac{1-F(v)}{f(v)}$ weighted by the various click-through rates.

The seller's revenue in GSP auctions also turns out to be the exact same as the seller's revenue in position auctions using VCG pricing. [21] has characterized the seller's revenue in a more general class of position auctions when prices for advertising are set according to VCG pricing. In the special case of [21] corresponding to the model considered in the present paper, the seller's revenue under VCG pricing is the exact same as the seller's revenue in Lemma 2.

Now we use the above result to address the question of whether the seller prefers targeting or bundling when there are no more than s positions in the auction for some fixed s. Our characterization of the circumstances under which the seller prefers targeting to bundling illustrates that there are some natural similarities between the situations in which the seller prefers targeting to bundling in position auctions and standard auctions for a single object. When there is a relatively small number of players, the seller prefers bundling to targeting, and when there is a larger number of players, the seller prefers targeting to bundling. For intermediate numbers of players, it is ambiguous whether the seller prefers targeting to bundling. This result is formalized in the following theorem:

THEOREM 7. *Suppose $F_i(v) = F(v)$ for all i, $v - \frac{1-F(v)}{f(v)}$ is increasing in v, the bidders use a symmetric and strictly monotonic bidding strategy $b(v)$ in equilibrium under GSP pricing, and the reserve price is either zero or the optimal reserve. Then the following hold regardless of whether the seller uses GSP or VCG pricing:*

(1). There exists some $n^* \geq 2$ such that bundling is always preferred to targeting if and only if $n \leq n^*$.

(2). There exists some $n^{**} > n^*$ such that targeting is always preferred to bundling if and only if $n \geq n^{**}$.

(3). For values of $n \in (n^*, n^{**})$, there exists some positive integer $k^* < s$ such that targeting is preferred to bundling if and only if the values of c_k for $k \leq k^*$ are sufficiently large compared to the values of c_k for $k > k^*$. Moreover, this k^* is nondecreasing in n.

PROOF. The seller's expected revenue from targeting under the conditions of the theorem can be rewritten as $\sum_{k=1}^{s} c_k E\left[v_{(k)} - \frac{1-F(v_{(k)})}{f(v_{(k)})} | v_{(k)} \geq r\right] Pr(v_{(k)} \geq r)$, where $v_{(k)}$ denotes the kth highest value of n draws from the distribution F. We use this to prove each of the three results.

First note that in the limit as $n \to \infty$, $E\left[v_{(k)} - \frac{1-F(v_{(k)})}{f(v_{(k)})} | v_{(k)} \geq r\right] Pr(v_{(k)} \geq r) \to \overline{v}$ for all k since in the limit as $n \to \infty$, $v_{(k)} \to \overline{v}$ and $\frac{1-F(v_{(k)})}{f(v_{(k)})} \to 0$ with probability arbitrarily close to 1 for all k. Thus in the limit as $n \to \infty$, the expected revenue from the mechanism under targeting approaches $\sum_{k=1}^{s} c_k \overline{v}$. By contrast, under bundling, all bidders bid $w \equiv \int_0^{\overline{v}} 1 - F(v)\, dv < \overline{v}$, and the total expected revenue under bundling is $\sum_{k=1}^{s} c_k w < \sum_{k=1}^{s} c_k \overline{v}$. From this it follows that for sufficiently large values of n, the expected revenue from targeting exceeds the expected revenue from bundling for all values of c_k.

Also note that $E\left[v_{(k)} - \frac{1-F(v_{(k)})}{f(v_{(k)})} | v_{(k)} \geq r\right] Pr(v_{(k)} \geq r)$ is increasing in n for all k since the distribution of the kth highest of $n+1$ draws from the cumulative distribution function F first order stochastically dominates the distribution of the kth highest of n draws from the cumulative distribution function F and the kth highest virtual valuation $v_{(k)} - \frac{1-F(v_{(k)})}{f(v_{(k)})}$ is strictly increasing in the kth highest value $v_{(k)}$. From this it follows that the expected revenue from the mechanism under targeting is strictly increasing in n. But we have seen the expected revenue from the mechanism under bundling is $\sum_{k=1}^{s} c_k w$, which is independent of n. Combining this with the results in the previous paragraph shows that there is some n^{**} such that targeting is always preferred to bundling if and only if $n \geq n^{**}$.

Next note that if $n = 2$, then bundling is strictly preferred to targeting. If $n = 2$, then it must be the case that $s = 1$ and the position auction is equivalent to a standard second price auction. But we have already seen that under the standard second price auction that bundling is strictly preferred to targeting when $n = 2$. Thus bundling is also preferred to targeting in position auctions when $n = 2$. And we have also seen that the seller's expected revenue from targeting is strictly increasing in n, while the seller's expected revenue from bundling is independent of n. Combining these facts shows that there is some $n^* \geq 2$ such that bundling is always preferred to targeting if and only if $n \leq n^*$.

Finally consider values of $n \in (n^*, n^{**})$ for which it is neither the case that targeting is always preferred to bundling or that bundling is always preferred to targeting. The seller's expected revenue under targeting is $\sum_{k=1}^{s} c_k E\left[v_{(k)} - \frac{1-F(v_{(k)})}{f(v_{(k)})} | v_{(k)} \geq r\right] Pr(v_{(k)} \geq r)$, whereas the seller's expected revenue under bundling is $\sum_{k=1}^{s} c_k w$, where $w \equiv \int_0^{\overline{v}} 1-F(v)\,dv < \overline{v}$. Thus the difference between the seller's expected revenue under targeting and the seller's expected revenue under bundling is $\sum_{k=1}^{s} c_k(E\left[v_{(k)} - \frac{1-F(v_{(k)})}{f(v_{(k)})}|v_{(k)} \geq r\right] Pr(v_{(k)} \geq r) - w)$. But $E\left[v_{(k)} - \frac{1-F(v_{(k)})}{f(v_{(k)})}|v_{(k)} \geq r\right] Pr(v_{(k)} \geq r)$ is decreasing in k since the distribution of the kth highest of n draws from the cumulative distribution function F first order stochastically dominates the distribution of the $k+1^{th}$ highest of n draws from the cumulative distribution function F and the kth highest virtual valuation $v_{(k)} - \frac{1-F(v_{(k)})}{f(v_{(k)})}$ is strictly increasing in the kth highest value $v_{(k)}$. Thus there is some $k^* \in [1, s)$ such that $E\left[v_{(k)} - \frac{1-F(v_{(k)})}{f(v_{(k)})}|v_{(k)} \geq r\right] Pr(v_{(k)} \geq r) > w$ if and only if $k \leq k^*$.

But from this it follows that the difference between the seller's expected revenue under targeting and the seller's expected revenue under bundling, $\sum_{k=1}^{s} c_k(E\left[v_{(k)} - \frac{1-F(v_{(k)})}{f(v_{(k)})}|v_{(k)} \geq r\right] Pr(v_{(k)} \geq r) - w)$, is strictly decreasing in c_k for all $k > k^*$ and strictly increasing in c_k for all $k \leq k^*$. From this it follows that for values of $n \in (n^*, n^{**})$, there is some $k^* \in [1, s)$ such that targeting is preferred to bundling if and only if the values of c_k for $k \leq k^*$ are sufficiently large compared to the values of c_k for $k > k^*$. Moreover, since $E\left[v_{(k)} - \frac{1-F(v_{(k)})}{f(v_{(k)})}|v_{(k)} \geq r\right] Pr(v_{(k)} \geq r)$ is increasing in n for all k, the relevant value of $k^* \in [1, s)$ for which $E\left[v_{(k)} - \frac{1-F(v_{(k)})}{f(v_{(k)})}|v_{(k)} \geq r\right] Pr(v_{(k)} \geq r) > w$ if and only if $k \leq k^*$ is nondecreasing in n. Thus the $k^* \in [1, s)$ for which targeting is preferred to bundling if and only if the values of c_k for $k \leq k^*$ are sufficiently large compared to the values of c_k for $k > k^*$ is also nondecreasing in n. □

To understand the intuition behind this result, note that the number of players in position auctions never has any effect on seller revenues under bundling because the players always bid their (identical) expected values under bundling. But seller revenues are increasing in the number of bidders in position auctions because the expectations of the kth highest virtual valuations $v - \frac{1-F(v)}{f(v)}$ are all increasing in the number of players. This explains the observed comparative statics results with respect to the number of players in Theorem 7.

The comparative statics results in part (3) of Theorem 7 follow from the difference between the seller's expected revenue from each position in the position auction under targeting and bundling. Under targeting, the seller's expected revenue per click from the top positions is greater than the seller's expected revenue per click from the bottom positions, but the seller's expected revenue per click is independent of position under bundling. Thus situations in which the top positions contribute a disproportionate percentage of revenues compared to bottom positions make targeting a better choice, whereas situations in which the bottom positions contribute a substantial percentage of revenues may make bundling a better choice. This gives the comparative statics results given in part (3) of Theorem 7.

Finally we give an example to give a sense of the values n^* and n^{**} that arise in Theorem 7. When the players' values are drawn from the uniform distribution and there is no reserve price, we obtain the following result:

THEOREM 8. *Suppose the bidders' values are independent draws from the uniform distribution on $[0, 1]$ and there is no reserve price. Then the appropriate values for n^* and n^{**} in Theorem 7 are $n^* = 3$ and $n^{**} = 2s + 1$.*

PROOF. Under position auctions, the seller's expected revenue from targeting equals the seller's expected revenue under the VCG mechanism, which is $\sum_{k=1}^{s} k(c_k - c_{k+1})E[v_{(k+1)}]$, where $v_{(k)}$ denotes the value of the bidder with the kth highest value, and $c_{s+1} \equiv 0$. Now when the bidders' values are draw from the uniform distribution on $[0, 1]$, it is necessarily the case that $E[v_{(k+1)}] = 1 - \frac{k+1}{n+1} = \frac{n-k}{n+1}$, so the seller's revenue under targeting is $\sum_{k=1}^{s} \frac{k(n-k)}{n+1}(c_k - c_{k+1})$. Also, since the bidders all make a bid of $\frac{1}{2}$ under bundling, the seller's revenue under bundling is $\frac{1}{2}\sum_{k=1}^{s} c_k$.

Now if $n = 3$, then $s \leq 2$, and the seller's revenue under targeting reduces to $\frac{1}{2}(c_1 - c_2) + \frac{1}{2}c_2 = \frac{1}{2}c_1$, while the seller's revenue under bundling is $\frac{1}{2}(c_1 + c_2)$. From this it follows that if $n = 3$, then bundling dominates targeting. If $n = 4$, then $s \leq 3$, and the seller's revenue under targeting reduces to $\frac{3}{5}(c_1 - c_2) + \frac{4}{5}(c_2 - c_3) + \frac{3}{5}c_3 = \frac{3}{5}c_1 + \frac{1}{5}(c_2 - c_3)$, but the seller's revenue under bundling is $\frac{1}{2}(c_1 + c_2 + c_3)$. From this it follows that if $c_2 = c_3 = 0$, then the seller's revenue under targeting is greater than the seller's revenue under bundling, but if $c_2 = c_3 = c_1$, then the seller's revenue under bundling is greater than the seller's revenue under targeting. Thus the key value of n^* in Theorem 7 is $n^* = 3$.

Now by part (3) of Theorem 7, we know that if the seller's revenue under targeting is greater than the seller's revenue under bundling when $c_2 = \ldots = c_s = c_1$, then the seller's revenue under targeting is greater than the seller's revenue under bundling for all possible values of the click-through rates. Now when $c_1 = c_2 = \ldots = c_s$, the seller's revenue under targeting is $\sum_{k=1}^{s} \frac{k(n-k)}{n+1}(c_k - c_{k+1}) = \frac{s(n-s)}{n+1}c_1$, and the seller's revenue under bundling is $\frac{s}{2}c_1$, so the seller's revenue under targeting is greater than the seller's revenue under bundling if and only if $\frac{n-s}{n+1} \geq \frac{1}{2}$, which holds if and only if $n \geq 2s + 1$. From this it follows that the seller's revenue under targeting is only guaranteed to be greater than the seller's revenue under bundling if $n \geq 2s + 1$.

By combining the results in the previous two paragraphs, it follows that, under the conditions of the theorem, the critical values n^* and n^{**} in Theorem 7 are $n^* = 3$ and $n^{**} = 2s + 1$ respectively. □

7. WHAT IF NOT ALL BIDDERS CAN TARGET?

So far in this manuscript we have compared scenarios in which all bidders can target with scenarios in which not all bidders can target. While this an important baseline, there may also be some important scenarios in which certain targeting information would only help some bidders more accurately assess the values they have for a particular advertisement. Additionally, a seller may want to experiment with making targeting information available to certain advertisers but not to others. This section explores the consequences of only allowing certain bidders to target.

As before, we consider a model in which there are n bidders, and bidder i's value, v_i, is an independent draw from the cumulative distribution function F_i with corresponding density f_i. If bidder i is able to target, he learns his value before placing a bid, but if bidder i is not able to target, then the bidder simply knows that his expected value for a click equals $\int_0^\infty v f_i(v)\, dv = \int_0^\infty 1 - F_i(v)\, dv$. For notational convenience, we assume throughout that $\int_0^\infty 1 - F_i(v)\, dv \geq \int_0^\infty 1 - F_{i+1}(v)\, dv$ for all i.

First we address whether the types of comparative statics results that we obtained in the previous sections continue to hold when only some of the bidders are able to target. Previously we obtained results that suggested that targeting is more likely to be preferred to bundling when there are more bidders who can target. While one might expect this result to continue to hold when only some bidders can target, this is not the case, as the following result illustrates:

THEOREM 9. *A seller's expected revenue from targeting need not be monotonic in the number of bidders that can target in an auction for a single object.*

PROOF. Suppose there are $n = 4$ bidders and each bidder's value is an independent and identically distributed draw from the lognormal distribution with parameters $\mu < 0$ and $\sigma^2 = -2\mu$. Note that if no bidders are able to target, then each bidder has an expected value of $e^{\mu+\sigma^2/2} = 1$, each bidder bids this amount, and the seller's revenue is 1. If exactly one bidder is able to target, then three of the bidders only know that they have an expected value equal to 1, these three bidders all bid this amount, and the seller's revenue is again 1.

If exactly two bidders are able to target, then the two bidders that are not able to target both only know that they have an expected value equal to 1, these two bidders both bid this amount, and the seller's revenue is always at least 1. At the same time, there is a strictly positive probability that both sellers that are able to target will learn that their values are greater than 1, these sellers will both bid more than 1, and the seller's revenue will be greater than 1. Thus if exactly two bidders are able to target, then the seller's expected revenue in the auction is strictly greater than 1.

Now consider what happens when exactly three bidders are able to target in the limit as $\mu \to -\infty$ and $\sigma^2 = -2\mu$. Note that if exactly one of the three bidders who is able to target learns that his value is greater than 1 and the other bidders who are able to target learn that their values are less than or equal to 1, then the the seller's revenue will be the exact same as it would be if no bidders were able to target. Thus whether it is beneficial for the seller to allow targeting depends on the relative costs and benefits from circumstances in which all three bidders who are able to target learn that their values are less than 1 with the circumstances under which at least two bidders learn that their values are greater than or equal to 1.

Note that the probability that a given bidder has a value less than c for any $c > 0$ goes to one in the limit as $\mu \to -\infty$ when $\sigma^2 = -2\mu$. From this it follows that, conditional on a buyer having a value less than 1, the expectation of the buyer's value goes to zero in the limit as $\mu \to -\infty$ when $\sigma^2 = -2\mu$. Similarly, if $p(\mu)$ denotes the probability that a buyer has a value greater than 1 for a given $\mu < 0$ when $\sigma^2 = -2\mu$, it follows that $\lim_{\mu\to-\infty} p(\mu) = 0$. Thus when exactly three bidders are able to target, in the limit as $\mu \to -\infty$ and $\sigma^2 = -2\mu$, the probability all three bidders that are able to target learn that their values are less than or equal 1 goes to 1, and conditional on this event taking place, the expectation of the highest of these three bidders' values goes to 0.

Now a bidder's expected value is $(1 - p(\mu))E[v|v \leq 1] + p(\mu)E[v|v > 1]$. And we know that in the limit as $\mu \to -\infty$ when $\sigma^2 = -2\mu$, we have $p(\mu) \to 0$ and $E[v|v \leq 1] \to 0$. Thus since each bidder has an expected value of 1, it follows that in the limit as $\mu \to -\infty$ when $\sigma^2 = -2\mu$, we must have $p(\mu)E[v|v > 1] \to 1$, meaning $E[v|v > 1] = \Theta(\frac{1}{p(\mu)})$. But the probability that at least two of the bidders who are allowed to target learn that their values are greater than or equal to 1 is $O(p(\mu)^2)$ in the limit as $\mu \to -\infty$. And the expectation of the second highest of these bidders' values given that at least two of these bidders have values greater than 1 is no greater than $E[v|v > 1] = \Theta(\frac{1}{p(\mu)})$. From this it follows that the total expected benefit to allowing exactly three bidders to target from the circumstances in which at least two bidders learn that their values are greater than or equal to 1 is $O(p(\mu)^2 \frac{1}{p(\mu)}) = O(p(\mu))$, which goes to zero in the limit as $\mu \to -\infty$ when $\sigma^2 = -2\mu$.

But we have seen that the total expected costs to the seller from allowing exactly three bidders to target that result from the circumstances in which all three bidders who are able to target learn that their values are less than 1 is roughly 1 unit of revenue in expectation in the limit as $\mu \to -\infty$ when $\sigma^2 = -2\mu$. It thus follows that for sufficiently negative values of μ and $\sigma^2 = -2\mu$, a seller's expected revenue from allowing exactly three bidders to target is lower than the seller's expected revenue from not allowing any bidders to target. From this it follows that a seller's expected revenue from targeting need not be monotonic in the number of bidders that can target. □

Theorem 9 illustrates that a seller's expected revenue from targeting need not increase in the number of bidders who are able to target when we fix the number of bidders and vary the number of bidders that are allowed to target. In fact, our proof illustrates a stronger result. It is possible that whether a seller will want to allow targeting may vary nonmonotonically with the number of bidders that are able to target. It may be the case that the seller is indifferent between targeting and bundling when exactly one bidder can target, the seller strictly prefers targeting to bundling when exactly two bidders can target, and the seller strictly prefers bundling to targeting when exactly three bidders can target.

These non-monotonicities are especially likely to arise in cases where the values of the bidders are drawn from distributions with fat tails. Then if there are four bidders but only one bidder can target, the second highest price in the auction is always the same as it would be if there were no targeting. If two bidders can target, this second highest price is always at least this high and sometimes strictly larger, so targeting is preferred to bundling. But if three bidders can target, then it is very likely that these bidders will all learn they have a very small value, the seller's revenue is likely to be very small, and bundling will be preferred to targeting.

Now we turn to the question of how allowing just one bidder to target would affect seller revenues when the buyers' values are drawn from different distributions. This situation is important because some targeting information may only affect one bidder's estimate of the bidder's value for advertising to a certain user.

THEOREM 10. *Suppose that only one bidder will be able to make use of certain targeting information in an auction for a single object. Then the following results hold:*

(1). The seller strictly prefers bundling to targeting if the bidder with the highest expected value is the only bidder that can target.

(2). The seller strictly prefers targeting to bundling if a bidder with the kth highest expected value for some $k \geq 3$ is the only bidder that can target.

(3). If a bidder with the second highest expected value is the only bidder that can target, then the seller prefers targeting to bundling if and only if the values of the highest and third highest expected bids are sufficiently high.

PROOF. If the bidder with the highest expected value is the only bidder that can target and this bidder learns that his value exceeds the second highest expected value, then the seller's revenue is unaffected by targeting. But if this bidder learns that his value is lower than the second highest expected value, then allowing targeting decreases the seller's revenue. Thus the seller prefers bundling to targeting if the bidder with the highest expected value is the only bidder that can target.

Similarly, if a bidder with the kth highest expected value for some $k \geq 3$ is the only bidder that can target and this bidder learns that his value is less than or equal to the second highest expected value, then the seller's revenue is unaffected by targeting. But if a bidder with the kth highest expected value for some $k \geq 3$ learns that his value is greater than the second highest expected value, then targeting increases the seller's revenue. Thus the seller prefers targeting to bundling if a bidder with the kth highest expected value for some $k \geq 3$ is the only bidder that can target.

Finally, if a bidder with the second highest expected value is the only bidder that can target, then the second highest bid is the value of the bidder with the second highest expected value (if this value is between the highest expected value and the third highest expected value), the highest expected value (if this value is less than the value of the bidder with the second highest expected value), or the third highest expected value (if this value is greater than the value of the bidder with the second highest expected value). Thus the seller's expected revenue is $\int_0^{w_{(3)}} w_{(3)} f_2(v)\, dv + \int_{w_{(3)}}^{w_{(1)}} v f_2(v)\, dv + \int_{w_{(1)}}^{\infty} w_{(1)} f_2(v)\, dv$, where $w_{(1)}$ denotes the highest expected value and $w_{(3)}$ denotes the third highest expected value. This expression is increasing in both $w_{(1)}$ and $w_{(3)}$. Furthermore, in the limit as $w_{(3)} \to w_{(2)}$, where $w_{(2)}$ denotes the second highest expected value, and $w_{(1)} \to \infty$, $\int_0^{w_{(3)}} w_{(3)} f_2(v)\, dv + \int_{w_{(3)}}^{w_{(1)}} v f_2(v)\, dv + \int_{w_{(1)}}^{\infty} w_{(1)} f_2(v)\, dv$ approaches $\int_0^{w_{(2)}} w_{(2)} f_2(v)\, dv + \int_{w_{(2)}}^{\infty} v f_2(v)\, dv > \int_0^{\infty} v f_2(v)\, dv = w_{(2)}$. And in the limit as $w_{(3)} \to 0$ and $w_{(1)} \to w_{(2)}$, $\int_0^{w_{(3)}} w_{(3)} f_2(v)\, dv + \int_{w_{(3)}}^{w_{(1)}} v f_2(v)\, dv + \int_{w_{(1)}}^{\infty} w_{(1)} f_2(v)\, dv$ approaches $\int_0^{w_{(2)}} v f_2(v)\, dv + \int_{w_{(2)}}^{\infty} w_{(2)} f_2(v)\, dv < \int_0^{\infty} v f_2(v)\, dv = w_{(2)}$. Combining these results shows that if a bidder with the second highest expected value is the only bidder that can target, then the seller prefers targeting to bundling if and only if the values of the highest and third highest expected bids are sufficiently high. □

Theorem 10 suggests that it is not in a seller's interest to enable targeting if only the strongest bidder will be able to make use of the targeting information, it is in a seller's interest to improve targeting if only the weakest bidders will be able to make use of the targeting information, and it may or may not be in a seller's interest to improve targeting if only intermediate-strength bidders will be able to make use of the targeting. These results are somewhat related to Myerson's [29] insights on optimal auctions. [29] finds that when asymmetric bidders are competing in an auction, a seller can increase revenue by giving an artificial bonus to the weaker bidders. In this setting, the seller can likewise increase revenue when the weaker bidders have the advantage of being able to target. We show in the full version of the paper [22] that this insight extends to position auctions as well.

8. CONCLUSION

This paper has analyzed circumstances under which improved targeting increases revenue. We have generally found that improved targeting increases revenue when there are a sufficiently large number of serious bidders, but targeting can hurt revenue when there are just a few dominant bidders. These types of results tend to hold regardless of whether we are in a standard second price auction or a position auction, and regardless of whether the seller uses reserve prices. We now discuss several possible avenues for future research.

In this paper, we have considered multiple scenarios in which the bidders' values are drawn from asymmetric distributions, but have not considered what happens under position auctions with asymmetric bidders when each bidder has private information about his or her value. A natural question to ask is how the results would extend to position auctions when bidders' values are drawn from different distributions. In addition, throughout this paper we have restricted attention to cases in which the bidders have private values, and not considered models of common value auctions. There is little that is known about the equilibria of position auctions when there is a common component to bidders' values, so it is natural ask whether a seller would want to reveal information that affects a common component to bidder preferences in position auctions. We leave this question for future work.

Acknowledgments

We thank Pierre Grinspan, Vahab Mirrokni, Uri Nadav, Prabhakar Raghavan, and seminar attendees at Google and University of British Columbia for helpful discussions.

9. REFERENCES

[1] I. Abraham, S. Athey, M. Babaioff, and M. Grubb. Peaches, lemons, and cookies: designing auction markets with dispersed information. *Microsoft Research Typescript*, 2014.

[2] W. J. Adams and J. L. Yellen Commodity bundling and the burden of monopoly. *Quarterly Journal of Economics*, 90(3): 475–498, 1976.

[3] M. Armstrong A more general theory of commodity bundling. *Journal of Economic Theory*, 148(2): 448–472, 2013.

[4] Y. Bakos and E. Brynjolfsson. Bundling information goods: pricing, profits, and efficiency. *Management Science*, 45(12): 1613–1630, 1999.

[5] D. Bergemann and A. Bonatti. Targeting in advertising markets: implications for offline versus online media. *RAND Journal of Economics*, 42(3): 417–443, 2011.
[6] D. Bergemann and M. Pesendorfer. Information structures in optimal auctions. *Journal of Economic Theory*, 137(1): 580–609, 2007.
[7] K. Bhawalkar, P. Hummel, and S. Vassilvitskii. Value of targeting. In *Proceedings of the 7th International Symposium on Algorithmic Game Theory (SAGT)*, pages 194–205, 2014.
[8] S. Board Revealing information in auctions: the allocation effect. *Economic Theory*, 38(1): 125–135, 2009.
[9] J. I. Bulow and P. D. Klemperer. Auctions versus negotiations. *American Economic Review*, 86(1): 180–194, 1996.
[10] L. E. Celis, G. Lewis, M. M. Mobius, and H. Nazerzadeh. Buy-it-now or take-a-chance: a simple sequential screening mechanism. In *Proceedings of the 20th International Conference on the World Wide Web (WWW)*, pages 147–156, 2011.
[11] I. Chakraborty. Bundling decisions for selling multiple objects. *Economic Theory*, 13(3): 723–733, 1999.
[12] A. De Cornière and R. De Nijs. Online advertising and privacy. *RAND Journal of Economics* (forthcoming).
[13] B. Edelman, M. Ostrovsky, and M. Schwarz. Internet advertising and the generalized second price auction: selling billions of dollars of keywords. *American Economic Review*, 97(1): 242–259, 2007.
[14] P. Eső and B. Szentes. Optimal information disclosure in auctions and the handicap auction. *Review of Economic Studies*, 74(3): 705–731, 2007.
[15] H. Fang and P. Norman. To bundle or not to bundle. *RAND Journal of Economics*, 37(4): 946–963, 2006.
[16] H. Fu, P. Jordan, M. Mahdian, U. Nadav, I. Talgam-Cohen, and S. Vassilvitskii. Ad auctions with data. In *Proceedings of the 5th International Symposium on Algorithmic Game Theory (SAGT)*, pages 184–189, 2012.
[17] J. Ganuza. Ignorance promotes competition: an auction model with endogenous private valuations. *RAND Journal of Economics*, 35(3): 583–598, 2004.
[18] J. Ganuza and J. S. Penalva. Signal orderings based on dispersion and the supply of private information in auctions. *Econometrica*, 78(3): 1007–1030, 2010.
[19] R. Gomes and K. Sweeney. Bayes-Nash equilibria of the generalized second price auction. *Games and Economic Behavior*, 86: 421–437, 2014.
[20] S. Hart and N. Nisan. Approximate revenue maximization with multiple items. *Hebrew University of Jerusalem Typescript*, 2012.
[21] P. Hummel. Position auctions with dynamic resizing. *Google Inc. Typescript*, 2014.
[22] P. Hummel and R. P. McAfee. When does improved targeting increase revenue? *Google Inc. Typescript*, 2015.
[23] P. Jehiel, M. Meyer-ter-Vehn, and B. Moldovanu. Mixed bundling auctions. *Journal of Economic Theory*, 134(1): 494–512, 2007.
[24] J. Levin and P. Milgrom. Online advertising: heterogeneity and conflation in market design. *American Economic Review: Papers and Proceedings*, 100(2): 603–607, 2010.
[25] R. P. McAfee and J. McMillan. Multidimensional incentive compatibility and mechanism design. *Journal of Economic Theory*, 46(2): 335–354, 1988.
[26] R. P. McAfee, J. McMillan, and M. D. Whinston. Multiproduct monopoly, commodity bundling, and correlation of values. *Quarterly Journal of Economics*, 104(2): 371–383, 1989.
[27] P. R. Milgrom. *Putting Auction Theory to Work.* New York, Cambridge University Press, 2004.
[28] P. R. Milgrom and R. J. Weber. A theory of auctions and competitive bidding. *Econometrica*, 50(5): 1089–1122, 1982.
[29] R. B. Myerson. Optimal auction design. *Mathematics of Operations Research*, 6(1): 58–73, 1981.
[30] T. Palfrey. Bundling decisions by a multiproduct monopolist with incomplete information. *Econometrica*, 51(2): 463–483, 1983.
[31] S. Tadelis and F. Zettelmeyer. Information disclosure as a matching mechanism: theory and evidence from a field experiment. *American Economic Review*, 105(2): 886–905, 2015.
[32] H. Varian. Position auctions. *International Journal of Industrial Organization*, 25(6): 1163–1178, 2007.
[33] D. R. Vincent and A. Manelli. Bundling as an optimal selling mechanism for a multiple-good monopolist. *Journal of Economic Theory*, 127(1): 1–35, 2006.

Social Status and Badge Design

Nicole Immorlica
Microsoft Research
nicimm@microsoft.com

Greg Stoddard
Northwestern University
gregs@u.northwestern.edu

Vasilis Syrgkanis
Microsoft Research
vasy@microsoft.com

ABSTRACT

Many websites encourage user participation via the use of virtual rewards like badges. While badges typically have no explicit value, they act as symbols of social status within a community. In this paper, we study how to design virtual incentive mechanisms that maximize total contributions to a website when users are motivated by social status. We consider a game-theoretic model where users exert costly effort to make contributions and, in return, are awarded with badges. The value of a badge is determined endogenously by the number of users who earn an equal or higher badge; as more users earn a particular badge, the value of that badge diminishes for all users.

We show that among all possible mechanisms for assigning status-driven rewards, the optimal mechanism is a leaderboard with a cutoff: users that contribute less than a certain threshold receive nothing while the remaining are ranked by contribution. We next study the necessary features of approximately optimal mechanisms and find that approximate optimality is influenced by the convexity of status valuations. When status valuations are concave, any approximately optimal mechanism must contain a coarse status partition, i.e. a partition of users into status classes whose size will grow as the population grows. Conversely when status valuations are convex, we prove that fine partitioning, that is a partition of users into status classes whose size stays constant as the population grows, is necessary for approximate optimality.

Categories and Subject Descriptors

J.4 [**Social and Behavioral Sciences**]: Economics

Keywords

Social Computing, Game Theory, Mechanism Design

WWW 2015, May 18–22, 2015, Florence, Italy.
ACM 978-1-4503-3469-3/15/05.
http://dx.doi.org/10.1145/2736277.2741664.

1. INTRODUCTION

A number of popular websites are driven by user-generated content. Review sites such as Yelp and TripAdvisor need users to rate and review restaurants and hotels, social news aggregators like Reddit rely on users to submit and vote upon articles from around the web, and question and answer sites like Stack Overflow and Quora depend on their users to ask good questions and provide good answers. One threat to the success of such sites is the free-rider problem, that not enough users will expend the effort to meaningfully contribute. Many popular websites address this problem using incentive systems like badges, reputation points, or leaderboards, e.g. the badge system on StackOverflow or the reviewer leaderboard on Amazon.

Given the diversity in design of virtual reward systems, one natural question is how should a site design their reward system to incentivize desired behavior, such as answering more questions on StackOverflow or contributing more to class discussions on Coursera. Is it more effective to use a leaderboard or to award badges? Should a badge be awarded for answering 10 questions or 100 questions? A number of recent papers address these questions using a game-theoretic analysis; assuming that users strategically choose their efforts to maximize the reward they receive minus the cost of their efforts, what is the best way to design a virtual reward system?

A general theme of this literature is that different features of online communities should influence these design choices. For example, the quality of a contribution may be directly observable such as the number of edits on StackOverflow, or may be observed noisily or subjectively such as the quality of an answer to a question [13]. Or perhaps the site only values the best contribution instead of the number of contributions, or has some complex valuation for the set of contributions received [21, 6]. In other cases, the number of participants in the platform may be exogenous as in Wikipedia or MOOCs where there is a stable userbase of primary contributors, or the number of participants may be highly dependent on the parameters of the design [10, 16]. Finally, users' values for rewards may be exogenous, e.g., when the reward is associated with a monetary prize or other privilege, or endogenous, e.g., when the value is derived from a social status within the community [10].

In this work we focus on settings where users primarily value rewards because of the *social status* they confer within their community, and characterize the optimal and approximately optimal reward mechanisms for incentivizing contributions. Empirical work on understanding user motivations to contribute to such systems finds that although intrinsic factors, such as learning or enjoyment, are a prominent motivation, the acquisition of reputation and social comparisons are frequently identified as motivations [17, 2]. In practice many virtual rewards have a status element in their design. Top level rewards, such as "gold" badges on StackOverflow or the "SuperUser" badge on the Huffington Post, are described as difficult to earn and only awarded to the most committed users. For status-motivated users, the value for a badge depends on the number of other users that have earned it. As more users earn that badge, it loses its ability to distinguish a member within the community and thus becomes less valuable. Our goal is to formally model these status concerns and to study the design of optimal virtual incentive schemes in their presence.

Current systems use a variety of social-psychological incentive schemes such as awarding badges, ranking users on a leaderboard, or awarding points. Each of these schemes induces a partitioning of users into an ordered set of status classes; users that earn no reward are in the lowest status class while users that earn the highest reward are in the top status class. We abstract away the details of rewards and focus on the induced assignment of users into status classes. For the sake of convenience, we generically refer to a *badge* as the assigned status class of a user.

The high level question we address is how should a designer award badges to maximize the amount of content contributed by the users of a website. Our goal is to give a broad characterization of the design of badge mechanisms with social status concerns. To do so, we modify a canonical model of contests [22] and study the following questions: What is the badge mechanism that maximizes effort contributed by users and how does the nature of status valuations affect the design of good mechanisms? This stylized model enables us to fully explore a very general environment of status concerns and badge design and to compare different mechanisms such as leaderboard and achievement badges.

1.1 Our Contributions

We model and analyze a game of incomplete information where users simultaneously make costly contributions to a site. Users have some privately-known ability that determines their cost of contributing to the site. Based on their contributions, each user is assigned a single *badge* out of an ordered set of badges. Users derive value because of the *status* the badges confer, where a user's status is defined by the fraction of users that have earned an equal or better badge. A user's value for this status is given by some function $S(\cdot)$.

The objective of the designer is to maximize the expected sum of contributions received from all users. We analyze this problem by using tools from Bayesian optimal mechanism design theory and the connection between contests and all-pay auctions. The nature of status valuations precludes a straightforward application of mechanism design techniques because of the negative status externalities that users impose on each other. These negative externalities constrain the set of outcomes the designer can implement in equilibrium.

We first prove that the optimal mechanism, the one that maximizes expected total contributions, is a leaderboard with a cutoff. This mechanism assigns the lowest badge to any user whose contribution falls below a certain threshold, and assigns unique badges to the remaining users in increasing order of their contribution. This optimality holds for any status value function $S(\cdot)$.

While we derive a strong optimality result, the optimal badge mechanism has some drawbacks. First, setting the cutoff optimally requires knowledge of the distribution of user abilities. Second, the induced equilibrium behavior is a complex function of the ability distribution, so small errors in a user's beliefs could dramatically change the total contribution that would arise in practice.

We therefore study two common types of mechanisms that each circumvent one of these drawbacks, and prove that they can be approximately optimal. A mechanism is an α-approximation if it induces agents to contribute at least a $1/\alpha$-fraction of the contributions generated by the optimal mechanism. The first class of mechanisms we study are absolute threshold mechanisms, defined by a vector of thresholds $\boldsymbol{\theta}$ such that agents who contribute at least θ_i are awarded the badge associated with threshold i. The second mechanism we study is the leaderboard mechanism, which assigns a unique badge to each user in increasing order of contribution (i.e. positions on a leaderboard). As we'll discuss in section 7, absolute badge mechanisms with small number of thresholds have simple equilibrium behavior and the leaderboard mechanism places no informational requirements on the designer.

The study of these mechanisms also reveals that the essential features of an approximately optimal mechanism depends strongly on the "shape" of status values, i.e. whether $S(\cdot)$ is concave or convex with respect to status. When $S(\cdot)$ is concave, an absolute threshold mechanism with just a single threshold is a 4-approximation to the optimal mechanism but cannot achieve any constant approximation for examples of convex status functions. By contrast, the leaderboard mechanism is a 2-approximation whenever status is convex, but cannot achieve any finite approximation for examples of concave status functions. In section 7, we discuss the general properties of these mechanisms that prove necessary for approximately optimal performance.

1.2 Related Work

There's a growing literature on the role and design of incentives systems [1, 9, 14, 16, 8, 10, 4, 23, 15]. These papers consider how to award badges, virtual points, a monetary prize, or viewer attention on a website in order to maximize either the total quantity of contributions or the quality of the best contribution. While the design of the exactly optimal mechanism depends on modeling assumptions, one general takeaway of this literature is that the winner-take-all mechanism, i.e. allocating the entire prize budget to the agent with the best contribution, does well at maximizing these objectives. These informational assumptions include: abilities of users are private [3, 6] or publicly known [9], noisy observations as to the size or quality of the contribution [14, 10]. However, most of these papers assume an exogenous and well-defined user value for the associated rewards.

The paper most closely related to ours is that of [23]; we adopt the same contest model and a similar definition of social status.[1] They analyze a particular class of badge mechanisms, where agents are separated in status classes only based on relative contribution comparisons, e.g. top 10% of contributors get the first badge, next 20% the second

[1]There's a technical difference in our definition of status regarding the way that users value users with equal status

badge etc. For instance, absolute threshold mechanisms or the leaderboard with an absolute contribution threshold are not considered. They also assume that a user's value is linear in status. They prove that fine partitioning (leaderboard) is optimal in their model, and show that a coarse partitioning of agents is a 2-approximation (under certain distributional assumptions). We consider general status value functions and in doing so, develop a more general theory of optimal mechanisms for status contests. Notably, we prove that the optimal mechanism in their setting can be arbitrarily bad for a large class of status valuations. On a technical level, [19] use the mathematical connection between allocation in a first-price auction and a consumer's expected social status to analyze a game of consumer choice, and [6, 8] use optimal mechanism design techniques to study contest design.

Also highly related is the paper of [10], which studies badge mechanisms with only on a single absolute or relative threshold in a setting where participation is endogenous and contributions are observed noisily. They find that awarding a badge to the top k% of all potential contributors is more robust than awarding to the top k% of actual contributors. Among other results, they also study a model of convex vs concave status concerns and show that disclosing the number of winners of a contest can increase or decrease aggregate effort depending on the convexity of the status function. However, they do not address the design of the optimal badge mechanism or the use of multiple badges.

There is a growing empirical literature that studies the motivations of online volunteers in diverse settings such as open-source software [29], Wikipedia [25], and citizen science websites [26, 11]. The more recent literature on "gamification" studies how virtual rewards mediate and enhance those motivations. This literature shows that the primary roles of virtual rewards include displaying a user's progress [2, 20], signaling that the site values the user's contributions [28], and allowing users to establish reputation via the accrual of virtual rewards [12, 11]. Observational and experimental studies have consistently shown that users alter their behavior in the presence of a badge or leaderboard, or when given information regarding the contributions of other users [26, 28, 17, 12].

2. MODEL

We now introduce our formal model. There is a population of n *users* and an ordered set of $m+1$ *badges*, where badges are ordered such that $m \succ m-1 \ldots \succ 1 \succ 0$. Each user simultaneously makes a contribution $b_i \in \mathbb{R}^+$ to a *badge mechanism* and we denote with $\mathbf{b} = (b_1, \ldots, b_n)$ the profile of contributions. The badge mechanism maps this profile to an assignment of badges for each user. More formally:

DEFINITION 1 (BADGE MECHANISM). *A badge mechanism specifies an ordered set of $m+1$ badges $m \succ m-1 \ldots \succ 1 \succ 0$ and a function $r : \mathbb{R}^+ \times (\mathbb{R}^+)^{n-1} \rightarrow \{0, ..., m\}$. Given a user's contribution b_i and vector of other contributions $\mathbf{b}_{-i}$, the user earns badge $r(b_i, \mathbf{b}_{-i})$.*

Informally, a badge mechanism sets a number of badges and how they should be awarded to agents based on their contributions. For convenience, this definition assumes that all users receive a badge. Thus low contributing agents will simply receive the lowest possible badge rather than awarded nothing (our assumptions on status valuations imply that agents receive no value from the lowest badge).

While this definition of a badge mechanism allows for a number of ways to award social status as a function of contributions, we study a few canonical mechanisms in this paper.

DEFINITION 2 (ABSOLUTE THRESHOLD MECHANISM). *An absolute threshold mechanism is defined by a set of m thresholds $\boldsymbol{\theta} = (\theta_1, \ldots, \theta_m)$, with $\theta_1 \leq \ldots \leq \theta_m$, such that user i is awarded badge $j \in \{0, \ldots, m\}$ if $b_i \in [\theta_j, \theta_{j+1})$. By convention, $\theta_0 = 0$ and $\theta_{m+1} = \infty$.*

DEFINITION 3 (LEADERBOARD MECHANISM). *The leaderboard mechanism assigns each user a distinct badge among a set of $m = n$ badges in increasing order of their contributions. If user i contributes the jth lowest amount (where m is highest amount and 1 is the lowest), he is assigned badge j. In the event that two users submit equal levels of contributions, the tie is broken randomly.*

The key difference between the above two mechanisms is that the badge that user i receives in an absolute threshold mechanism depends only on his own contribution b_i and not on the contributions of the remaining players. By contrast, the badge that a player earns in a leaderboard mechanism depends only on the position of his contribution within the ordered list of all contributions, but not on the amount of his contribution. The next mechanism is a hybrid of these two mechanisms.

DEFINITION 4 (LEADERBOARD WITH A CUT-OFF). *The leaderboard with a cut-off mechanism is defined by a single threshold θ such that any user who submits $b_i < \theta$ is assigned badge 0. The remaining users are assigned badges in increasing order of contributions, as in the leaderboard mechanism.*

This is not an exhaustive list of mechanisms, nor are we the first to construct such definitions. For example, another common mechanism is a relative threshold badge, studied in [23] and [10], where a top percentage of users will receive the unique badge. We focus on the three mechanisms defined above because they give a good sketch of the properties of (approximately) optimal mechanisms across a range of environments.

Status Value and User Utility. A user's utility is a function of his *status*, which determines his value, and his *ability*, which determines his cost. The *status* of a user i is defined as the fraction of users who have earned an equal or better badge. We denote this fraction by $t_i(\mathbf{b})$. A user's *status value* is given by a function $S(\cdot) : [0,1] \rightarrow \mathbb{R}^+$ of $t_i(\mathbf{b})$. We assume that $S(1) = 0$, i.e. users in the lowest status class derive a status value of 0. The *ability* v_i of user i is private information and drawn independently and identically from a common distribution F with support over $[0, \bar{v}]$ and density f. We assume F is atomless and regular.[2] If a user with ability v_i contributes b_i, then he incurs a cost of $\frac{b_i}{v_i}$. A user's utility for contributing b_i is quasi-linear in his status value and his cost of contribution:

$$u(b_i, \mathbf{b}_{-i}; v_i) = S(t_i(\mathbf{b})) - \frac{b_i}{v_i} \tag{1}$$

We will find later that the performance of the mechanisms mentioned above depends heavily on the "shape" of

[2]This is a weaker assumption than the *monotone hazard rate* condition, assumed in Moldovanu et al. [23]; see Section 3 for a formal definition.

the status function. We divide status valuation functions into the classes of linear functions, concave functions, and convex functions. Each regime has a natural interpretation; for concave status, a user's marginal gain in status value decreases as he increases his standing in society. For convex, the marginal gain in status value increases as a user increases his standing, and in linear, the marginal gain in status value is constant.

As a solution concept, we assume that agents bid according to a Bayesian Nash equilibrium. In a Bayesian Nash equilibrium (BNE), user i's strategy is a function $b_i(\cdot)$ which maps his ability v_i to a contribution $b_i(v_i)$. A profile of strategies $\mathbf{b}()$ is a BNE if each agent maximizes his utility in expectation over the realizations of abilities and strategies of other agents, i.e., for all v_i, b_i':

$$\mathrm{E}_{v_{-i}}\left[u_i\left(\mathbf{b}(\mathbf{v}); v_i\right)\right] \geq \mathrm{E}_{v_{-i}}\left[u_i(b_i', \mathbf{b}_{-i}(\mathbf{v}_{-i}); v_i)\right].$$

Designer Objective. The goal of the designer is to maximize the sum of the contributions of all users $\sum_i b_i$.[3]

2.1 Illustrative Example

We illustrate the main insights of our results through the lens of a simple example. Suppose that the abilities of users are distributed uniformly in $[0,1]$ and that the *status value* of a user is simply the proportion of opponents that earn a lower badge than her, i.e. $S(t) = 1 - t$.

Let's first analyze the simplest possible badge mechanism: the designer sets a single absolute contribution threshold θ and all users that contribute more than θ are assigned the top badge, while the remaining are assigned the low badge.

How do users behave? In equilibrium higher ability users contribute more, since it costs them less effort (c.f. Theorem 10 for a formal claim). Moreover, users only contribute 0 or θ because other contribution levels win the same badge at a higher cost. Thus at equilibrium, users above some ability threshold v_* contribute θ and users below v_* contribute 0. *What is this ability threshold v_* and is v_* unique for each θ?* The ability threshold is derived by the observation that a user with ability v_* should be indifferent between getting the low or the top badge. By the linearity of the status function, her *status value* at the top badge is simply $\mathrm{E}[S(t)] = F(v_*) = v_*$. Thus her utility from the top badge is $v_* - \frac{\theta}{v_*}$, while her utility at the low badge is 0, leading to $v_* = \sqrt{\theta}$. This equilibrium behavior is unique and we show in Theorem 10 that this is a property that holds more generally in our model.

What is the optimal contribution threshold? Since, we showed that each θ corresponds to a unique v_*, instead of picking the optimal contribution threshold, the designer can instead pick an optimal ability threshold v_*. This is a general principle that we will follow throughout the paper, i.e. choose a target expected status as a function of the ability of a user and then find a badge mechanism that implements that function at equilibrium.

For a target v_*, each user makes an expected contribution of $\theta \cdot (1 - F(v_*)) = v_*^2 \cdot (1 - v_*)$ and by symmetry the expected total contribution is n times this amount. This is maximized at $v_* = 2/3$, leading to an expected per-user contribution of $4/27 \approx .15$. Thus the designer has to set the contribution threshold in such a way that at equilibrium $1/3$ of the users occupy the top badge in expectation.

[3]Alternative objectives could be maximizing the quality of the single best solution such as in [6] and [3]. We note that we can extend this framework to incorporate objectives such as maximizing contributions that are at least of a certain quality (to mitigate agents submitting large amounts of low quality content) by redefining what a contribution constitutes.

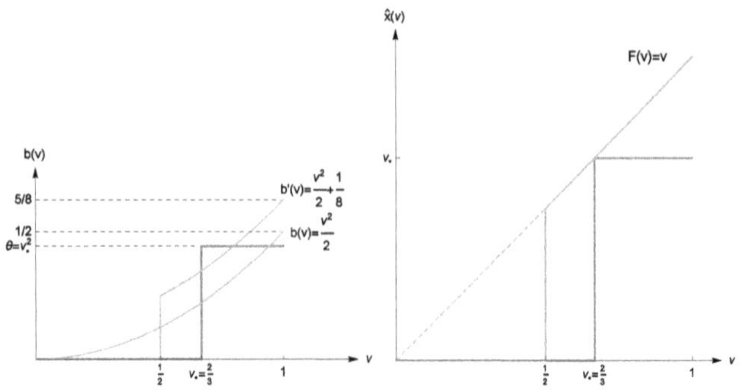

Figure 1: Equilibrium bid and expected status under the three different mechanisms: single absolute contribution threshold (blue), leaderboard (orange), leaderboard with a cut-off (green).

What if a leaderboard is used? Each user is assigned a badge in increasing order of his contribution. It still holds that at equilibrium higher ability users contribute more (c.f. Theorem 9 for a formal proof). However, the contribution of each user is now a complex, continuous, and increasing function $b(v)$ of his ability.

How do users contribute? Under the assumption that equilibrium contribution is increasing in ability, users are assigned a badge in increasing order of ability. Thus the expected proportion of opponents ranked below a user with ability v is simply $F(v) = v$. At equilibrium a user with ability v should not prefer to contribute as if he had some other ability z, which would lead to utility $z - \frac{b(z)}{v}$. Based on this fact we can derive that the equilibrium contribution of a user with ability v is $b(v) = \frac{v^2}{2}$. Thus the expected contribution of a user is, $\frac{1}{6} \approx .16$, slightly higher than the expected contribution under the optimal single absolute threshold. This is not always the case in our model, and especially when the status function is very concave (c.f. Example 6).

What if a leaderboard is combined with an absolute contribution threshold? Suppose that the designer uses the following mechanism: every user who contributes more than $1/4$ is ranked in a leaderboard in increasing order of contribution. As we will show in Section 4 (for our general model), the unique equilibrium of this mechanism takes the following form: users with ability below $1/2$ don't contribute, while users with ability $v \geq 1/2$ contribute $b(v) = \frac{v^2}{2} + \frac{1}{8}$. When compared to the *leaderboard* mechanism, this mechanism incentivizes higher ability users to contribute more, due to their fear of falling in the lowest status class and getting a zero utility. However, the lower half of the users contribute nothing. The gain from high ability users outweighs the loss from low ability ones, and each user now contributes $5/24 \approx .2$ in expectation, which is higher than the leaderboard mechanism.

Can we do better? As we show in Theorem 9, the latter mechanism is the optimal mechanism among all possible badge mechanisms, i.e. *in our example, no badge mechanism can induce an expected user contribution of more than* $5/24$. In the general model, the contribution threshold of the optimal mechanism depends on the distribution of abilities and the form of the status function.

Can the single threshold or leaderboard mechanisms do much worse? Even though the single threshold and leaderboard mechanisms where suboptimal, they generated more than half of the optimal contribution. In Theorem 13, we show that the leaderboard mechanism always achieves at least half of the optimal when the status function is convex. In Theorem 12, we show that the best single-threshold mechanism always achieves a fourth of the optimal when status is concave. In fact this is achieved by the simple absolute contribution threshold mechanism that induces half of the population to get the top badge. These approximation guarantees hold for any ability distribution.

3. CONNECTION TO OPTIMAL AUCTION DESIGN

We begin the analysis by converting the contest framework into a mathematically equivalent auction. In the contest setting, agents first make costly, unrecoverable efforts and then later receive their prizes (if any). When their contributions are perfectly observable, a contest is equivalent to an *all-pay auction*, an auction in which agents first announce and pay their bids and then receive their item (if they won the auction).

In Bayes-Nash equilibrium, an agent with ability v_i contributes b_i such that b_i maximizes his utility, written on the left-hand side of the equation below. From the perspective of agent i, v_i is a constant, so the b_i which maximizes the equation on the left also maximizes the function on the right equation.

$$\arg\max_{b_i} E[S(t_i(\mathbf{b}))] - \frac{b_i}{v_i} = \arg\max_{b_i} v_i \cdot E[S(t_i(\mathbf{b}))] - b_i \quad (2)$$

So we can equivalently assume that agents have the utility function on the right hand side. This form of the utility function falls into the class of quasi-linear utility functions used in mechanism design, and has the advantage that we can study the optimal contest design question using tools from optimal mechanism design which we briefly introduce in the remainder of the section.

Optimal Mechanism Design. In the standard auction design problem, the n agents are competing for a single unit of a divisible good. The goal is to design an auction that maximizes *revenue* or total payments.

Quantiles. Each agent i has a *value* v_i per unit of the good (equivalent to ability in contests), drawn IID from an atomless distribution F with support $[0, \bar{v}]$ and density $f(\cdot)$. There is a one-to-one correspondence between an agent's value v_i and his *quantile* q_i:

$$q(v_i) = 1 - F(v_i) \in [0,1] \text{ and } v(q_i) = F^{-1}(1-q_i).$$

Intuitively, the quantile denotes the probability that a random sample from F has higher value than agent i, thus *lower quantile corresponds to higher value.* Furthermore quantiles are uniformly distributed in $[0,1]$. *As it is often more convenient to work in quantile space, we will use the quantile terminology for the remainder of this paper.*

Equilibrium and Revenue Characterization. A direct revelation auction solicits bids $\mathbf{b} = (b_1, \ldots, b_n)$ from the agents and computes an *allocation* $\{x_i(\mathbf{b})\}$ and set of payments $\{p_i(\mathbf{b})\}$ such that agent i receives an $x_i(\mathbf{b})$ fraction of the good (or is allocated the good with probability $x_i(\mathbf{b})$) and pays $p_i(\mathbf{b})$. The resulting utility for agent i with quantile q_i is then

$$u_i(\mathbf{b}; q_i) = v(q_i) \cdot x_i(\mathbf{b}) - p_i(\mathbf{b}). \quad (3)$$

The Bayes-Nash equilibria of this setting are characterized by classic results of Myerson [24] and Bulow and Roberts [5]. Letting $\tilde{x}_i(\mathbf{q}) = x_i(\mathbf{b}(\mathbf{q}))$, $\hat{x}_i(q_i) = \mathrm{E}_{\mathbf{q}}[\tilde{x}_i(\mathbf{q}); q_i]$ and $\hat{p}_i(q_i) = \mathrm{E}_{\mathbf{q}}[p_i(\mathbf{b}(\mathbf{q})); q_i]$ denote the *ex-post* allocation, *interim* allocation and interim payment rules respectively, the lemma states:

LEMMA 5 ([24], [5]). *A profile of bidding functions $\mathbf{b}(\cdot)$ and an implied profile of interim allocation and payment rules $\hat{\mathbf{x}}(\cdot)$ and $\hat{\mathbf{p}}(\cdot)$ are a BNE only if (1) $\hat{x}_i(q_i)$ is monotone non-increasing in q_i and (2):*

$$\hat{p}_i(q_i) = v(q_i) \cdot \hat{x}_i(q_i) + \int_{q_i}^{1} \hat{x}_i(z) \cdot v'(z) \cdot dz$$

These two conditions are sufficient for $\mathbf{b}(\cdot)$ to be a BNE if each bid function $b_i(\cdot)$ spans the whole region of feasible bids. Otherwise, they only imply that each player doesn't want to deviate to any other bid in the set of bids spanned by $b_i(\cdot)$.

Simple manipulations of these identities allows one to characterize the revenue of a mechanism concisely in terms of the quantiles of the agents. Let $R(q) = q \cdot v(q)$ denote the *revenue function*[4] of the value distribution F, and $R'(q_i)$ the *virtual value* of a player with quantile q_i. Then,

LEMMA 6 ([24], [5]). *The expected total payment of a mechanism is equal to the expected* virtual surplus*:*

$$\mathrm{E}_{\mathbf{q}}\left[\sum_i p_i(q_i)\right] = \mathrm{E}_{\mathbf{q}}\left[\sum_i R'(q_i) \cdot \tilde{x}_i(\mathbf{q})\right].$$

while the expected payment of each player is his expected virtual surplus allocation: $\mathrm{E}_{q_i}[p_i(q_i)] = \mathrm{E}_{q_i}[R'(q_i) \cdot \hat{x}_i(q_i)]$.

A consequence of Lemma 6 is that the optimal mechanism is the mechanism that maximizes the expected virtual surplus. This reduces mechanism design to a constrained optimization problem.

Regular Distributions. A distribution F is *regular* if the revenue function $R(q) = q \cdot v(q)$, is a concave function, or equivalently, the virtual value of a player $R'(q)$ is non-increasing in his quantile. Our assumption that F has support $[0, \bar{v}]$ also implies that $R(0) = R(1) = 0$. Hence, the virtual value is positive up until some quantile κ^*, and negative afterwards. Quantile κ^*, where $R'(\kappa^*) = 0$, is defined as the *monopoly quantile* of the value distribution.

4. OPTIMAL BADGE MECHANISM

We can now easily see the mapping between the contest and auction environments. The (virtual) ability of a user equates with the (virtual) value of an agent in an auction and the contribution $b_i(q_i)$ each agent makes equates with their expected payment $\hat{p}_i(q_i)$. Most importantly, by comparing equations (2) and (3), we see that the expected status an agent receives from the contest $\mathrm{E}[S(t_i(\mathbf{b}))]$ is equivalent to their expected allocation in an auction $\hat{x}_i(q_i)$. Designing the optimal status-contest is equivalent to designing an all-pay auction that maximizes revenue but with important

[4]Intuitively, the revenue function computes the revenue a seller can generate by selling the (entire) item with probability q.

distinctions introduced by social status concerns. In a standard auction environment the designer chooses the allocation function but in the status contest setting the set of feasible allocations is highly constrained by the form of the status function $S(\cdot)$ and by the externalities that a user's status imposes on others. Feasible allocations also exhibit some ill-behaved properties. For example the total amount of allocation, i.e., $\sum_i S(t_i)$ is not constant as it is in a standard auction setting.

The optimal auction framework states that the optimal mechanism chooses an ex-post allocation rule which maximizes expected virtual surplus and then computes payments which support the implied interim allocations in equilibrium (see Section 3). Following this reasoning, we first compute the ex-post virtual surplus-maximizing badge allocation. We then argue that this allocation is implemented in a BNE by a *leaderboard with a contribution cutoff*. Finally, we show that the derived BNE is unique.

Virtual Surplus-Maximizing Badge Allocation. Maximizing virtual surplus for some instantiation of a quantile profile $\mathbf{q}$ is simply an optimization problem, subject to the constraints that are implicit in the way that users derive status. The optimization problem asks: given a vector of virtual abilities $R'(q_1), \ldots, R'(q_n)$, assign badges $\mathbf{r} = (r_1, \ldots, r_n)$ to the users so as to maximize: $\sum_i R'(q_i) \cdot S(t_i(\mathbf{r}))$. The following lemma states that the optimal solution assigns users distinct badges in decreasing order of their quantile so long as their quantile is below the *monopoly quantile* κ^*, and assigns all other users a badge of 0.

LEMMA 7. *Let $q_1 \leq \ldots \leq q_k \leq \kappa^* < q_{k+1} \leq \cdots \leq q_n$ be a profile of quantiles. Then the optimal virtual surplus is achieved by assigning a distinct decreasing badge to all users $\{1, \ldots, k\}$ with non-negative virtual ability and badge 0, to all negative virtual ability users $\{k+1, \ldots, n\}$, i.e. $r_1 = n, r_2 = n-1, \ldots, r_k = n-k+1$, and $r_{k+1} = \ldots = r_n = 0$.*

PROOF. The allocation of badges must be monotone non-increasing in quantile, since if $R'(q_i) > R'(q_j)$ (i.e. $q_i < q_j$) and $r_i < r_j$ then we can increase virtual welfare by swapping the status class of player i and player j (this wouldn't affect the status of other players). Therefore, it holds that $r_1 \geq r_2 \geq \ldots, \geq r_n$ and it remains to show that $r_1 > \ldots > r_k > 0$ and that $r_{k+1} = \ldots = r_n = 0$. If for some $i < k$ it holds that $r_i = r_{i+1} = \ldots = r_{i+t}$, then by discriminating player i above the remaining players, will increase virtual welfare. More concretely, by setting $r'_j = r_j - 1$ for all $j > i$ (for a moment let's allow for negative badges, since at the end we can always shift the badge numbers), then the satisfaction of all players $j > i$ doesn't change since the number of people that have badge at least as high as them remains the same. Additionally, the status allocation of player i strictly increases, since the number of people ranked at least as high as him, strictly decreased. A recursive application of this reasoning implies that $r_1 > \ldots > r_k > r_{k+1} \geq \ldots \geq r_n$. Now we show that it must be that $r_{k+1} = \ldots = r_n$. Any other allocation to these players would allocate positive status to a negative virtual ability user, which would only decrease virtual welfare. Moreover, by grouping together negative virtual ability players, the status allocation of all non-negative virtual ability players is unaffected. ■

Implementation. We now show that the ex-post virtual surplus maximizing allocation of badges is implemented at the unique equilibrium of the *leaderboard with a cutoff* mechanism as defined in section 2. To do so, we need to show two things: first, we must describe the interim status allocation rule implied by the ex-post allocation rule in Lemma 7. Then we must compute the corresponding equilibrium contributions using the payment identity of the optimal auction framework and check that these contributions do indeed give rise to the interim allocation, under the rules of the aforementioned badge mechanism.

The interim status allocation of a user is the expected status value he receives from the mechanism given his quantile q_i. To compute it, let T_i be the random variable denoting the number of opponents with quantile smaller than q_i. Observe that if $q_i \leq \kappa^*$, then under the optimal ex-post allocation of badges in Lemma 7, user i will be ranked at the $T_i + 1$ position. Thus the implied interim status of a user with $q_i \leq \kappa^*$ is $\mathbb{E}_{\mathbf{q}_{-i}}\left[S\left(\frac{T_i}{n-1}\right)\right]$ and 0 if $q_i > \kappa^*$. T_i is distributed as a binomial distribution of $n-1$ independent random trials, each with success probability of q_i.[5] For convenience, we introduce the following notation

$$S_n(q_i) = \sum_{\nu=0}^{n-1} S\left(\frac{\nu}{n-1}\right) \cdot \beta_{\nu,n-1}(q_i) \tag{4}$$

where $\beta_{\nu,n}(q) = \binom{n-1}{\nu} \cdot q^{\nu} \cdot (1-q)^{n-1-\nu}$, denotes the Bernstein basis polynomial and $S_n(q)$ is the Bernstein polynomial approximation of the status function $S(\cdot)$. By properties of Bernstein polynomials (see [27]), if $S(\cdot)$ is a strictly decreasing function then $S_n(\cdot)$ is also strictly decreasing and if $S(\cdot)$ is convex or concave then so is $S_n(\cdot)$. Additionally, $S_n(\cdot)$ is continuous and differentiable and $S_n(0) = S(0)$ and $S_n(1) = S(1) = 0$.

Using this notation, we can express the interim status allocation for each user. This expression will be useful throughout the course of this paper, so we formalize it in the following proposition.

PROPOSITION 8. *In the optimal badge mechanism, the interim status allocation of a user with quantile q is*

$$\hat{x}(q) = \begin{cases} S_n(q) & q \leq \kappa^* \\ 0 & q > \kappa^* \end{cases} \tag{5}$$

If the interim allocation of status of a user has the form presented in Equation 5, then for his contribution to constitute an equilibrium of the badge mechanism, it must satisfy the payment characterization of Lemma 5:

$$b(q) = \begin{cases} v(q) \cdot S_n(q) + \int_q^{\kappa^*} S_n(z) \cdot v'(z) \cdot dz & q \leq \kappa^* \\ 0 & q \geq \kappa^* \end{cases} \tag{6}$$

Moreover, by Lemma 6 the expected user contribution under the optimal mechanism is:

$$\text{OPT} = \mathbb{E}_q[b(q)] = \int_0^{\kappa^*} R'(q) \cdot S_n(q)\, dq \tag{7}$$

We now show that the above pair of interim allocation and equilibrium contribution, given in Equations (5) and (6), constitute the unique equilibrium of a badge mechanism that takes the form of a leaderboard with a cutoff.

[5]Recall that quantiles are distributed uniformly in $[0, 1]$.

THEOREM 9. *The optimal badge mechanism assigns a distinct badge to each user in decreasing order of contribution (breaking ties at random) as long as they pass a contribution threshold of $\theta = v(\kappa^*) \cdot S_n(\kappa^*)$. Users that don't pass the contribution threshold are assigned a badge of 0. The mechanism has a unique equilibrium.*

PROOF. The proof consists of two parts: First we show that the interim allocation of status $\hat{x}(\cdot)$, given in Equation (5) and the contribution function given in (6), constitute an equilibrium of the proposed badge mechanism. Second, we argue this mechanism has no other equilibria by showing that it falls into the class of anonymous order-based auctions defined by Chawla and Hartline [18], where it is shown that such auctions have unique equilibria.

Observe that the contribution function in Equation (6) is strictly decreasing in the region $[0, \kappa^*]$, since $b'(q) = v(q) \cdot S_n'(q)$, and $v(\cdot)$ is positive and $S_n'(\cdot)$ is negative by assumption that status value is decreasing. Moreover, observe that $b(\kappa^*) = v(\kappa^*) \cdot S_n(\kappa^*) = \theta$. Since all quantiles are distributed uniformly in $[0, 1]$, under the above bid function, a user with quantile $q \le \kappa^*$ is assigned a better badge than every user with higher quantile and a worse badge than every user with lower quantile, while the event of a tie has zero measure. Therefore this bid function $b(\cdot)$ gives rise to the optimal interim allocation of status given in Equation (5). We next prove that no user will contribute any positive amount outside the range $[\theta, b(0)]$. Contributing $b_i > b(0)$ is strictly worse than $b(0)$ as it yields the same expected status but at a higher cost. Similarly, any $b_i \in (0, \theta)$ yields the same expected status as $b_i = 0$ but at a higher cost. Thus any positive equilibrium contribution must be in the range $[\theta, b(0)]$. Combining this fact with Lemma 5 yields that $b(\cdot)$ is a BNE.

The fact that the mechanism has a unique equilibrium follows from the results of [18], which shows that mechanisms in which a player's ex-post expected allocation depends only on his bid and the rank of his bid (defined as the pair of the number of players with equal bid and strictly higher bid) have unique BNE. To show that the leaderboard with a cutoff falls into this framework, we need to argue that for any contribution profile $\mathbf{b}$ (even in the case of tied contributions), the ex-post expected allocation of status of a user depends only on his own contribution, on the number of users that have a higher contribution $n_g(\mathbf{b})$ and on the number of users that have the same contribution $n_e(\mathbf{b})$. Since, ties are broken uniformly at random, a user is ranked above another user with an equal contribution with probability of 1/2. Thus the expected ex-post status allocation is:

$$\sum_{\nu=0}^{n_e(\mathbf{b})} S\left(\frac{n_g(\mathbf{b}) + \nu}{n-1}\right) \cdot \beta_{\nu, n_e(\mathbf{b})}(1/2)$$

when his contribution $b_i \ge \theta$ and 0 otherwise. It is clear that this ex-post allocation only depends on the quantities required by the framework of [18]. ■

5. ABSOLUTE THRESHOLD MECHANISMS

In this section, we explore the approximate optimality of absolute threshold mechanisms as formally described in Definition 2. We show that for concave status valuations (including linear), the expected contributions of a mechanism with a single threshold is a 4-approximation to the expected user contribution of the optimal mechanism. This threshold is set such that any user with ability greater than the median ability will earn the top badge while the other half of the population earns nothing. We also show an example of a convex status valuation where no mechanism with a constant number of thresholds can achieve any constant approximation to the optimal mechanism.

We begin by characterizing the unique symmetric BNE[6] of an absolute threshold mechanism with thresholds $\boldsymbol{\theta}$.

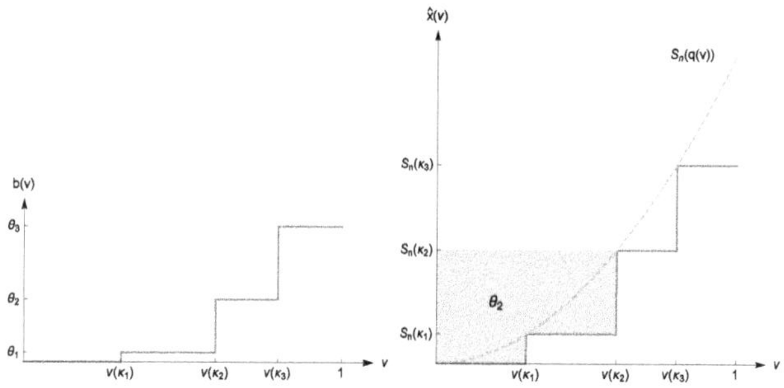

Figure 2: Equilibrium contribution (left), interim status allocation (right, solid line) and depiction of contribution threshold (shaded area), in a multi-level absolute threshold mechanism.

THEOREM 10 (EQUILIBRIUM STRUCTURE). *Any absolute threshold mechanism with contribution thresholds $\boldsymbol{\theta} = (\theta_1, \ldots, \theta_m)$ has a unique symmetric BNE $b(\cdot)$ characterized by a vector of quantile thresholds $\boldsymbol{\kappa} = (\kappa_1, \ldots, \kappa_m)$ with $\kappa_1 \ge \kappa_2 \ldots \ge \kappa_m$ such that a user with ability quantile q_i will make a contribution of (c.f. Figure 2):*

$$b(q_i) = \begin{cases} 0 & q_i > \kappa_1 \\ \theta_t & q_i \in (\kappa_{t+1}, \kappa_t] \\ \theta_m & q_i \le \kappa_m \end{cases}$$

These quantile thresholds can be computed by a system of m equations.

Furthermore, for any vector of quantile thresholds $\boldsymbol{\kappa} = (\kappa_1, \ldots, \kappa_m)$ there exists a vector of contribution thresholds $\boldsymbol{\theta}$, characterized by (c.f. Figure 2):

$$\forall t \in [1, \ldots, m] : \theta_t = \sum_{j=1}^{t} v(\kappa_j) \cdot (S_n(\kappa_j) - S_n(\kappa_{j-1})), \quad (8)$$

under which the unique symmetric BNE implements $\boldsymbol{\kappa}$.

PROOF. Observe that if a player earns badge r_i, her contribution b_i should be exactly the threshold to win that badge, θ_{r_i}, since contributing more would be more costly but will not increase her status value. Additionally, the equilibrium is monotone in quantile, i.e. if a player with quantile q_1 contributes θ_{r_1} and with value $q_2 < q_1$ he contributes θ_{r_2} then it must be that $r_1 \le r_2$.[7]

[6]Asymmetric equilibria do exist in absolute threshold badge mechanisms.

[7]Suppose the contrary. For simplicity, denote with x_r the expected status that a player gets from bidding θ_r, assuming the rest of the players follow strategy $b(\cdot)$. Since, $r_1 > r_2$ we have $\theta_{r_1} > \theta_{r_2}$. Since $b(q_1)$ is an equilibrium for a player with value q_1, it must be that $v(q_1)(x_{r_1} - x_{r_2}) \ge \theta_{r_1} - \theta_{r_2} > 0$. Thus $x_{r_1} > x_{r_2}$ and since $v(q_2) > v(q_1)$ we get: $v(q_2)(x_{r_1} - x_{r_2}) > v(q_1)(x_{r_1} - x_{r_2}) \ge \theta_{r_1} - \theta_{r_2}$. But the latter implies, $v(q_2) \cdot x_{r_1} - \theta_{r_1} > v(q_2) \cdot x_{r_2} - \theta_{r_2}$ and therefore $b(v_2)$ cannot be an equilibrium for a player with quantile q_2.

Since the equilibrium mapping is a monotone step function of quantile, it is defined by a set of thresholds in the quantile space $\kappa_1, \ldots, \kappa_p$, for some $p \le m$, such that if player i has quantile $q_i \in (\kappa_{t+1}, \kappa_t]$ then he contributes $b(q_i) = \theta_t$. If $q_i > \kappa_1$ then $b(q_i) = 0$ and if $q_i \le \kappa_p$ then $b(q_i) = \theta_p$. For notational convenience we will denote with $\kappa_0 = 1$ and $\kappa_{p+1} = 0$. Observe that it is not necessarily true that $p = m$, since some contribution thresholds might be too high.

To characterize the BNE, it remains to compute those quantile thresholds and show that they are unique. A player's status value is a function of the proportion of other players with a weakly better badge. A player with quantile $q_i \in [\kappa_{t+1}, \kappa_t]$ earns the badge associated with quantile κ_t; thus, because the equilibrium is a monotone step function, any player that has a quantile less than κ_t will earn a weakly better badge than player i. By definition, a player has a lower quantile than κ_t with probability κ_t. This allows us to compute the interim status value of player i with quantile $q_i \in [\kappa_{t+1}, \kappa_t]$ as:

$$\hat{x}(q_i) = S_n(\kappa_t) \tag{9}$$

where $S_n(\cdot)$ is given by Equation (4).

By the payment identity of Lemma 5, for the vector of quantiles $\boldsymbol{\kappa}$ to be an equilibrium they must satisfy the following equation:

$$\forall t \in [1, \ldots, p] : \theta_t = \sum_{j=1}^{t} v(\kappa_j) \cdot (S_n(\kappa_j) - S_n(\kappa_{j-1})) \tag{10}$$

This relationship is depicted in Figure 2. Equivalently, the above set of conditions can be re-written as:

$$\forall t \in [1, \ldots, p] : \ v(\kappa_t) \cdot (S_n(\kappa_t) - S_n(\kappa_{t-1})) = \theta_t - \theta_{t-1} \tag{11}$$

This set of equalities has an intuitive interpretation as saying that the players with quantiles at the boundary of two badges should be indifferent between getting either of the two badges. Additionally, to ensure that the latter is an equilibrium we also need to make sure that if $p < m$, then the highest ability player doesn't prefer being on badge $p+1$ alone, rather than being on badge p:

$$\text{if } p < m : v(0) \cdot (S_n(0) - S_n(\kappa_p)) \le \theta_{p+1} - \theta_p \tag{12}$$

To show uniqueness of the symmetric equilibrium we need to show that the above set of conditions have a unique solution.

LEMMA 11. *There exists a unique $p \le m$ and a unique vector $\boldsymbol{\kappa} = (\kappa_1, \ldots, \kappa_p)$, that satisfies the system of Equations (11) and (12).*

PROOF. Given a profile of badge thresholds $\boldsymbol{\theta}$, we show recursively that there is a unique set of quantile thresholds which satisfies the set of equations. For $t = 1$, Equation (11) becomes: $\theta_1 = v(\kappa_1) \cdot S_n(\kappa_1)$. Observe that $v(0) \cdot S_n(0) = \bar{v} \cdot S(0)$, $v(1) \cdot S_n(1) = 0$, $v(x) \cdot S_n(x)$ is continuous decreasing. If $\theta_1 < \bar{v} \cdot S(0)$ then a unique solution exists (recall that $\bar{v}$ is the upper bound of the ability distribution). Otherwise, no player is willing to bid as high as θ_1 (or any θ_t for $t > 1$) and the recursion stops with $p = 0$. Subsequently, find the solution a_2 to the equation: $\theta_2 - \theta_1 = v(\kappa_2)(S_n(\kappa_2) - S_n(\kappa_1))$. For similar reason, either a unique such solution exists or no player (not even a player with ability $\bar{v}$) is willing to bid θ_2 rather than bid θ_1 and we can stop the recursion, setting $p = 1$. Then solve for $\kappa_3, \ldots, \kappa_p$ in the same way. ■

The latter Lemma completes the proof of the uniqueness and characterization of the equilibrium. The inverse part of the theorem, is trivial based on the previous discussion. ■

Single Threshold Mechanism. We now analyze the approximate optimality of absolute threshold mechanisms that use a single threshold. Let θ be the contribution threshold and let κ be the corresponding equilibrium quantile threshold. The interim status allocation of a player who gets the top badge is $S_n(\kappa)$. Any user with quantile $q_i = \kappa$ must be indifferent between earning the top badge and earning nothing, so κ and θ must satisfy $\theta = v(\kappa) \cdot S_n(\kappa)$. The expected contribution of a user is equal to the probability that she has a quantile $q_i \le \kappa$, times θ.

$$\text{APX} = E[b_i] = \kappa \cdot \theta = \kappa \cdot v(\kappa) \cdot S_n(\kappa) = R(\kappa) \cdot S_n(\kappa) \tag{13}$$

This gives a simple expression for the expected user contribution of a single threshold mechanism as a function of the quantile threshold implemented in equilibrium.

THEOREM 12 (MEDIAN ABSOLUTE BADGE MECHANISM). *When the status function $S(\cdot)$ is concave, the expected total contribution of an absolute threshold mechanism with a single quantile threshold $\kappa = \frac{1}{2}$ is a 4-approximation to the expected total contribution of the optimal badge mechanism.*

PROOF. Setting a quantile threshold of $\kappa = 1/2$, by Equation (13), yields an expected user contribution of

$$\text{APX} = R(1/2) \cdot S_n(1/2).$$

Our first step is to upper bound the expected user contribution of the optimal mechanism, and then to show that $R(1/2) \cdot S_n(1/2)$ is a 4-approximation of this upper bound. An approximation of the expected user contribution implies the same approximation to the expected total contribution.

By Equation 7 and using the fact that $S_n(q) \le S_n(0)$ and that $R'(q) \ge 0$ for any $q \le \kappa^*$:

$$\begin{aligned} \text{OPT} = & \int_0^{\kappa^*} R'(q) \cdot S_n(q)\, dq \\ & \le S_n(0) \int_0^{\kappa^*} R'(q) dq \le S_n(0) \cdot R(\kappa^*) \end{aligned}$$

Now we prove $R\left(\frac{1}{2}\right) \cdot S_n\left(\frac{1}{2}\right) \ge \frac{1}{4} R(\kappa^*) \cdot S_n(0)$. By the concavity of $S_n(\cdot)$ and the fact that $S_n(1) = 0$, we get

$$S_n\left(\tfrac{1}{2}\right) \ge \tfrac{1}{2} S_n(0) + \tfrac{1}{2} S_n(1) = \tfrac{1}{2} S_n(0)$$

From the concavity of the revenue function $R(\cdot)$ and Jensen's inequality, we get

$$R\left(\tfrac{1}{2}\right) \ge \int_0^1 R(q) dq \ge \tfrac{1}{2} R(\kappa^*)$$

where the first inequality follows from Jensen's inequality and the last inequality follows from concavity and the fact that $R(0) = R(1) = 0$ and $R(\kappa^*)$ is the maximum. [8] ■

Thus a designer can implement a good incentive mechanism by setting the threshold of a single badge such that half of the user base earns the badge.

[8] The latter is the same property of regular distributions employed for proving Bulow-Klemperer's result that the revenue of the optimal single item auction with one bidder yields at most the revenue of a second price auction with two i.i.d bidders. See Figure 1 of [7] or Figure 5.1 in [18].

Lower Bound. While absolute threshold mechanisms can provide a good approximation with just a single badge for concave status functions, the next example demonstrates that no absolute threshold mechanism with a constant number of thresholds can achieve any constant approximation to the optimal badge mechanism, for convex status functions.

Example. [Logarithmic loss for convex status] Suppose that the status of a user is inversely proportional to the proportion of users (including the user himself) with a weakly better badge (normalized so that $S(1) = 0$):

$$S(t) = \frac{n}{(n-1)t+1} - 1 \tag{14}$$

Assume that abilities are distributed uniformly in $[0, 1]$. The ability function is then $v(q) = 1-q$ and the revenue function is $R(q) = q(1-q)$, with derivative $R'(q) = 1 - 2 \cdot q$ and a monopoly quantile of $1/2$. The interim status allocation of a user with quantile q under the optimal mechanism ends up being after simplifications $S_n(q) = \frac{1-(1-q)^n}{q} - 1$, if $q \leq 1/2$ and 0 otherwise. The optimal expected user contribution is:

$$\begin{aligned}
\text{OPT} &= \int_0^{1/2}(1-2\cdot q)S_n(q)\,dq \\
&= \int_0^{1/2}(1-2\cdot q)\tfrac{1-(1-q)^n}{q}dq - \tfrac{1}{2}\int_0^{1/2}(1-2\cdot q)dq \\
&\geq \int_0^{1/2}(1-2q)\tfrac{1-e^{-nq}}{q}dq - \tfrac{1}{8} = \Theta(\log(n))
\end{aligned}$$

Leading to a total expected contribution of $\Theta(n\log(n))$. On the other hand, the virtual surplus, and hence total contribution, achievable by any mechanism that uses m badges is at most $n\cdot(m-1)$: even if all users have a maximum virtual ability of 1, the virtual surplus from any badge mechanism with m badges at any contribution profile $\mathbf{b}$ is simply:

$$\begin{aligned}
&\sum_{k=1}^{m} |\{i : r(b_i, \mathbf{b}_{-i}) = k\}| \left(\tfrac{n}{|\{i:r(b_i,\mathbf{b}_{-i})\geq k\}|} - 1\right) \leq \\
&\quad \sum_{k=1}^{m} n - \sum_{k=1}^{m} |\{i : r(b_i, \mathbf{b}_{-i}) = k\}| = n\cdot m - n
\end{aligned}$$

As $n \to \infty$ the approximation to the optimal total contribution achievable with m badges grows as $\Theta\left(\frac{\log(n)}{m-1}\right)$. ■

6. COMPLETE LEADERBOARDS

In this section we explore the approximation power of the complete leaderboard mechanism, i.e. the mechanism that assigns each user a distinct badge in increasing order of their contributions (see section 2 for a formal definition). We prove that the leaderboard mechanism is a good approximation to the optimal mechanism when the status function is convex. In contrast, it may be an unboundedly bad approximation for concave status functions.

THEOREM 13. *For any convex status function, the leaderboard mechanism is a 2-approximation to the optimal mechanism.*

PROOF. The complete leaderboard is a special case of the leaderboard with a cutoff mechanism for $\kappa^* = 1$ (equiv. $\theta = 0$), so Theorem 9 proves it has a unique symmetric monotone equilibrium, under which, the expected contribution is:

$$\text{APX} = \int_0^1 R'(q)\cdot S_n(q)\,dq \tag{15}$$

whereas the expected user contribution of the optimal mechanism, OPT, is given in Equation (7). We will show that the convexity of the status function and the regularity of the ability distribution imply that $\text{OPT} \leq 2\cdot\text{APX}$.

By convexity of $S_n(\cdot)$, $S_n(t\cdot k + (1-t)\cdot 1) \leq tS_n(k) + (1-t)S_n(1)$. Instantiating this for $t = (1-q)/(1-\kappa^*)$ and recalling that $S_n(1) = 0$, we get that for any $q \geq \kappa^*$: $S_n(q) \leq S_n(\kappa^*)\cdot(1-q)/(1-\kappa^*)$. By definition $R'(q)$ is non-positive for any $q \geq \kappa^*$, we can lower bound the negative part of APX as follows:

$$\begin{aligned}
\int_{\kappa^*}^{1} R'(q)\cdot S_n(q)\,dq &\geq \int_{\kappa^*}^{1} R'(q)\frac{S_n(\kappa^*)}{1-\kappa^*}(1-q)dq \\
&= \frac{S_n(\kappa^*)}{1-\kappa^*}\int_{\kappa^*}^{1} R'(q)(1-q)dq \\
&= \frac{S_n(\kappa^*)}{1-\kappa^*}\left(\int_{\kappa^*}^{1} R(q)dq - R(\kappa^*)(1-\kappa^*)\right) \\
&\geq -\tfrac{1}{2}\cdot S_n(\kappa^*)\cdot R(\kappa^*)
\end{aligned}$$

where the last inequality follows since, by the fact that $R(q)$ is concave non-increasing in the region $[\kappa^*, 1]$ and the assumption that $R(1) = 0$, we have that $\int_{\kappa^*}^1 R(q)dq \geq \frac{1}{2}R(\kappa^*)\cdot(1-\kappa^*)$. We can now lower bound APX, using integration by parts:

$$\begin{aligned}
\text{APX} &\geq \int_0^{\kappa^*} R'(q)\cdot S_n(q)\,dq - \tfrac{1}{2}\cdot S_n(\kappa^*)\cdot R(\kappa^*) \\
&= \tfrac{1}{2}\cdot R(\kappa^*)\cdot S_n(\kappa^*) - \int_0^{\kappa^*} R(q)\cdot S_n'(q)\,dq \\
&\geq \tfrac{1}{2}\cdot R(\kappa^*)\cdot S_n(\kappa^*) - \tfrac{1}{2}\int_0^{\kappa^*} R(q)\cdot S_n'(q)\,dq \\
&= \tfrac{1}{2}\int_0^{\kappa^*} R'(q)\cdot S_n(q)\,dq = \tfrac{1}{2}\text{OPT}
\end{aligned}$$

where in the last inequality we used that $S_n'(q) \leq 0$. ■

On the other hand the following example shows that for concave status, the total contribution achieved by the leaderboard mechanism, can be arbitrarily worse than the optimal total contribution. Hence a cut-off threshold is necessary.

Example. Consider the concave status function of $S(t) = (1-t)^\alpha$ with a uniform $[0, 1]$ distribution of abilities, i.e., $F(x) = x$. We consider $\alpha \to 0$ such that the status function is an almost constant function. Intuitively, this means that a player is very easily satisfied by being simply ranked above a small portion of the population and any other portion yields almost no extra status value. We also consider the number of players $n \to \infty$ implying that $S_n(q) \to (1-q)^\alpha$. In this setting, the revenue function $R(q) = q\cdot F^{-1}(1-q) = q(1-q)$ and the expected per-player contribution of the leaderboard mechanism converges to 0:

$$\begin{aligned}
&\lim_{\alpha\to 0}\lim_{n\to\infty}\text{APX} = \lim_{\alpha\to 0}\int_0^1 R'(q)\cdot\lim_{n\to\infty} S_n(q)\,dq \\
&= \lim_{\alpha\to 0}\int_0^1 (1-2\cdot q)\cdot(1-q)^\alpha dq = \lim_{\alpha\to 0}\frac{\alpha}{\alpha^2+3\alpha+2} \to 0
\end{aligned}$$

where the interchange of the limit and the integration is justified by the uniform convergence of Bernstein polynomials. On the other hand the optimal mechanism is a leaderboard with quantile threshold of $\kappa^* = 1/2$ yielding an expected per-player contribution which converges to a constant of $1/4$:

$$\begin{aligned}
&\lim_{\alpha\to 0}\int_0^{1/2} R'(q)\cdot\lim_{n\to\infty} S_n(q)\,dq = \\
&\lim_{\alpha\to 0}\int_0^{1/2} (1-2\cdot q)\cdot(1-q)^\alpha dq = \lim_{\alpha\to 0}\frac{\alpha+2^{-\alpha-1}}{\alpha^2+3\alpha+2} \to \frac{1}{4}
\end{aligned}$$

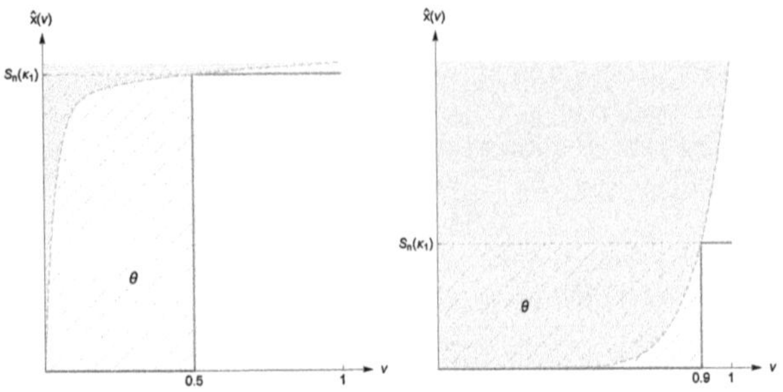

(a) Inability of leaderboards to induce high contribution. (b) Inability of a single absolute badge to induce high contribution.

Figure 3: Graphical representation of main approximation results, assuming uniform distribution of abilities in [0, 1].

■

7. DISCUSSION

Convex/Concave status and approximate optimality. The intuition behind our lower bound examples can be more easily understood via picture. Figure 3a shows an example where the status function is concave and the ability distribution is uniform over [0,1]. The solid blue line depicts the expected status allocation for an agent with ability v_i in the median badge mechanism and the dashed orange line displays his expected status in the leaderboard mechanism. The light shaded region shows the contribution made by an agent with ability $v_i = 1$ in the leaderboard mechanism (this graphic representation can be derived by manipulating the payment identity from lemma 5). The expected status of a low-ability user is very close to that of a high-ability user, so consequently the high ability users will not contribute much more than the low ones. In the median badge mechanism, the difference between the expected status of high and low ability users is much larger than in the leaderboard mechanism, so the mechanism can elicit more contributions from the high ability agents. Figure 3b shows a convex status function, and in this case, the difference in expected status between agents grows as their abilities gets higher. Thus competition between high ability agents generates a lot of contributions for the leaderboard mechanism. A mechanism with only a single absolute threshold does not create competition amongst the very high ability agents because they receive the same expected status. In both cases, as the status function gets more convex or concave, the approximation ratio of a single absolute threshold mechanism or the leaderboard mechanism, respectively, degrades.

Coarse vs Fine status partitions. This exploration of approximately optimal mechanisms highlights the interesting relationship between the convexity of the status value function and the size of induced status classes of agents. A status class is *coarse* if the expected number of agents partitioned into that status class grows with the number of agents in the game; the median badge mechanism induces coarse partitions because the expected number of agents in each status class is $n/2$. A status class is *fine* if the expected number of agents partitioned into that class does not grow with the number of agents; the leaderboard induces fine classes since there will only ever be a single agent in each position on the leaderboard. Coarse partitioning is a necessary property of approximate optimality when status is concave, while fineness is a necessary property when status is convex. The optimal mechanism, which does not depend on the properties of the status function, uses both fine and coarse partitioning.[9]

Convex vs Concave in practice. Intuitively, a concave status function can be understood as modeling situations where users are simply striving for a "sense of community", i.e. they get all their satisfaction by not being in the bottom 10% of contributions, since it shows that they care contributing to the online community, but any further increase in their perceived ranking within the community doesn't give them much more satisfaction. This seems a good fit for collaborative environments, such as Q&A forums or Wikipedia. It is noteworthy that a small number of absolute achievement badges are indeed ubiquitous in such settings (though factors exogenous to our model could also be contributing to this fact). On the other hand, a convex status function models more competitive scenarios where the closer you are to the top the more you want to surpass other users, i.e. whether you are the first, second or third highest contributor really makes a difference in your satisfaction. Such settings are for instance, online gaming communities, where indeed leaderboards seem more prevalent in practice.

Simplicity vs Optimality. Our approximation results are also interesting from a "simplicity vs optimality" viewpoint. The optimal mechanism requires both knowledge of the ability distribution from the designer and complex equilibrium behavior from the users. The leaderboard mechanism can be implemented with no knowledge of the distribution and thus places a lower informational requirement. The median badge mechanism reduces the strategic reasoning of each user to a simple contribute-or-not decision, which only requires from them to know whether they are in the top 50% of users in terms of ability.[10]

8. CONCLUSION

In this paper, we considered the design of badge mechanisms when badge values were endogenously determined by the social status they confer to its recipients. In addition to deriving the optimal mechanism, we studied the necessary properties of approximately optimal mechanisms and found an interesting relationship between the size of status classes and the convexity of status valuations.

The high level goal of this paper is to enhance the theory of designing virtual incentive systems by introducing and studying an alternative utility model. An interesting future direction is incorporating more theories of human motivation from psychology and human-computer interaction into formal game theory and mechanism design problems. Finally, given the increasing ease of online experimentation, one of the more important directions is empirically testing the efficacy of virtual incentive schemes in the wild [30, 20].

9. REFERENCES

[1] Ashton Anderson, Daniel Huttenlocher, Jon Kleinberg, and Jure Leskovec. Steering user behavior with badges. In *Proceedings of the 22nd international conference on World Wide Web*, pages 95–106.

[9]The coarse vs fine distinction is also discussed in [23].

[10]The recent paper [15] conducts a rigorous analysis of contest design with simple agent reasoning.

International World Wide Web Conferences Steering Committee, 2013.

[2] Ashton Anderson, Daniel Huttenlocher, Jon Kleinberg, and Jure Leskovec. Engaging with massive online courses. In *Proceedings of the 23rd international conference on World wide web*, pages 687–698. International World Wide Web Conferences Steering Committee, 2014.

[3] Nikolay Archak and Arun Sundararajan. Optimal design of crowdsourcing contests. In *ICIS*, page 200, 2009.

[4] Yoram Bachrach, Vasilis Syrgkanis, and Milan Vojnovic. Incentives and efficiency in uncertain collaborative environments. In *WINE*, 2013.

[5] Jeremy Bulow and John Roberts. The simple economics of optimal auctions. *The Journal of Political Economy*, pages 1060–1090, 1989.

[6] Shuchi Chawla, Jason D Hartline, and Balasubramanian Sivan. Optimal crowdsourcing contests. In *Proceedings of the Twenty-Third Annual ACM-SIAM Symposium on Discrete Algorithms*, pages 856–868. SIAM, 2012.

[7] Peerapong Dhangwatnotai, Tim Roughgarden, and Qiqi Yan. Revenue maximization with a single sample. In *Proceedings of the 11th ACM Conference on Electronic Commerce*, EC '10, pages 129–138, New York, NY, USA, 2010. ACM.

[8] Dominic DiPalantino and Milan Vojnovic. Crowdsourcing and all-pay auctions. In *Proceedings of the 10th ACM conference on Electronic commerce*, pages 119–128. ACM, 2009.

[9] Pradeep Dubey and John Geanakoplos. Grading exams: 100, 99, 98,ï£¡ or a, b, c? *Games and Economic Behavior*, 69(1):72–94, 2010.

[10] David Easley and Arpita Ghosh. Incentives, gamification, and game theory: An economic approach to badge design. In *Proceedings of the fourteenth ACM conference on Electronic commerce*, pages 359–376. ACM, 2013.

[11] Alexandra Eveleigh, Charlene Jennett, Stuart Lynn, and Anna L Cox. I want to be a captain! i want to be a captain!: gamification in the old weather citizen science project. In *Proceedings of the First International Conference on Gameful Design, Research, and Applications*, pages 79–82. ACM, 2013.

[12] Rosta Farzan, Joan M DiMicco, David R Millen, Casey Dugan, Werner Geyer, and Elizabeth A Brownholtz. Results from deploying a participation incentive mechanism within the enterprise. In *Proceedings of the SIGCHI Conference on Human Factors in Computing Systems*, pages 563–572. ACM, 2008.

[13] Arpita Ghosh and Patrick Hummel. Implementing optimal outcomes in social computing: a game-theoretic approach. In *Proceedings of the 21st international conference on World Wide Web*, pages 539–548. ACM, 2012.

[14] Arpita Ghosh and Patrick Hummel. Learning and incentives in user-generated content: Multi-armed bandits with endogeneous arms. In *ITCS*, 2013.

[15] Arpita Ghosh and Robert Kleinberg. Optimal contest design for simple agents. In *Proceedings of the fifteenth ACM conference on Economics and computation*, pages 913–930. ACM, 2014.

[16] Arpita Ghosh and Preston McAfee. Crowdsourcing with endogenous entry. In *WWW*, 2012.

[17] F Maxwell Harper, Yan Chen, Joseph Konstan, and Sherry Xin Li. Social comparisons and contributions to online communities: A field experiment on movielens. *The American economic review*, pages 1358–1398, 2010.

[18] Jason Hartline. *Approximation in Economic Design*. 2012.

[19] Ed Hopkins and Tatiana Kornienko. Running to keep in the same place: Consumer choice as a game of status. *American Economic Review*, pages 1085–1107, 2004.

[20] Panagiotis G Ipeirotis and Evgeniy Gabrilovich. Quizz: Targeted crowdsourcing with a billion (potential) users. In *Proceedings of the 23rd international conference on World wide web*, pages 143–154. International World Wide Web Conferences Steering Committee, 2014.

[21] Shaili Jain, Yiling Chen, and David C Parkes. Designing incentives for online question-and-answer forums. *Games and Economic Behavior*, 2012.

[22] Benny Moldovanu and Aner Sela. The optimal allocation of prizes in contests. *American Economic Review*, pages 542–558, 2001.

[23] Benny Moldovanu, Aner Sela, and Xianwen Shi. Contests for status. *Journal of Political Economy*, 115(2):338–363, 2007.

[24] R. Myerson. Optimal auction design. *Mathematics of Operations Research*, 6(1):58–73, 1981.

[25] Oded Nov. What motivates wikipedians? *Communications of the ACM*, 50(11):60–64, 2007.

[26] Oded Nov, Ofer Arazy, and David Anderson. Scientists@ home: what drives the quantity and quality of online citizen science participation? *PloS one*, 9(4):e90375, 2014.

[27] George McArtney Phillips. *Interpolation and approximation by polynomials*, chapter 7, pages 247–290. CMS books in mathematics. Springer, New York, 2003.

[28] Chris Preist, Elaine Massung, and David Coyle. Competing or aiming to be average?: normification as a means of engaging digital volunteers. In *Proceedings of the 17th ACM conference on Computer supported cooperative work & social computing*, pages 1222–1233. ACM, 2014.

[29] Jeffrey A Roberts, Il-Horn Hann, and Sandra A Slaughter. Understanding the motivations, participation, and performance of open source software developers: A longitudinal study of the apache projects. *Management science*, 52(7):984–999, 2006.

[30] Haiyi Zhu, Amy Zhang, Jiping He, Robert E Kraut, and Aniket Kittur. Effects of peer feedback on contribution: a field experiment in wikipedia. In *Proceedings of the SIGCHI Conference on Human Factors in Computing Systems*, pages 2253–2262. ACM, 2013.

Mapping Temporal Horizons

Analysis of Collective Future and Past related Attention in Twitter

Adam Jatowt
Kyoto University
adam@dl.kuis.kyoto-u.ac.jp

Émilien Antoine
Kyoto Sangyo University
first.last@cc.kyoto-su.ac.jp

Yukiko Kawai
Kyoto Sangyo University
kawai@cc.kyoto-su.ac.jp

Toyokazu Akiyama
Kyoto Sangyo University
akiyama@cc.kyoto-su.ac.jp

ABSTRACT

Microblogging platforms such as Twitter have recently received much attention as great sources for live web sensing, real-time event detection and opinion analysis. Previous works usually assumed that tweets mainly describe "what's happening now". However, a large portion of tweets contains *time expressions* that refer to time frames within the past or the future. Such messages often reflect expectations or memories of social media users. In this work we investigate how microblogging users collectively refer to time. In particular, we analyze half a year long portion of Japanese and four months long collection of US tweets and we quantify *collective temporal attention* of users as well as other related temporal characteristics. This kind of knowledge is helpful in the context of growing interest for detection and prediction of important events within social media. The exploratory analysis we perform is possible thanks to the development of visual analytics framework for robust overview and easy detection of various regularities in the past and future-oriented thinking of Twitter users. We believe that the visualizations we provide and the findings we outline can be also valuable for sociologists and computer scientists to test and refine their models about time in natural language.

Categories and Subject Descriptors

H.5.m [**Information Interfaces and Presentation**]: Miscellaneous

Keywords

Time Mention; Twitter; Social Network; Temporal Analysis; Visualization

1. INTRODUCTION

Memory of past actions or events as well as expectations or predictions about future occupy much of our thinking every day. Rather than constantly focusing on the present, human thoughts tend to stray over different time perspectives within near or more distant time. Memory is useful for analyzing the past and for understanding the present, while future expectations and future-focused thinking serve an important role of arranging our actions and preparing for what may come.

As both remembering and expecting represent significant amount of human cognitive activities, not surprisingly, also in social media, users tend to leave traces of expressions related to the past and future. Such temporal expressions constitute a wealth of information about what users are going to do or what they expect to happen, as well as, which past events played important roles in their lives or what they recall from the past. Recently, there has been significant interest in building models for prediction of real-world outcomes using social media. For example, it has been shown that movie box-office revenues can be successfully forecasted using Twitter [4]. Most of the proposed approaches relied on detecting periodical patterns or trends of user activities and extrapolate to forecast the future. We advocate here another approach to directly analyze expectations expressed by users for judging their future actions. For example, when users tweet about a meeting scheduled in the evening, they leave a strong signal about a future activity at the end of the day. We believe that the traces of future-related thoughts are valuable to be mined and analyzed as they can be used for recommendation, targeted advertising, predictive user assistance and group behavior forecasting or even for tracking user whereabouts in case of sudden, massive disasters.

Similarly, we consider past-related expressions to carry high significance for assessing self-reported importance of events and activities users had in the past, or, in general, to characterize remembering and reminiscing patterns. In social sciences the concept of *collective memory* as a shared remembrance of the past has been known for quite a long time. However, it was usually measured in small scale or through controlled studies. It has become possible now to investigate the memory decay on the collective of social media users.

In this work, we advocate the concept of *memory and expectation sensing* as a complement to the well-known notion of *social sensing* in microblogging and social media. As we are aware that human memory and futuristic thinking are inherently complex matters, we thus first attempt to uncover any observable regularities and patterns in data through exploratory analysis of the way in which social media users

WWW 2015, May 18–22, 2015, Florence, Italy.
ACM 978-1-4503-3469-3/15/05.
http://dx.doi.org/10.1145/2736277.2741632.

collectively refer to the future and the past. By this we hope to shed more light on the feasibility of implementing effective future prediction solutions through improved feature engineering and for understanding the importance of future and past events for users.

In particular, we focus on Twitter which is commonly used in the nascent field of *computational social science* [20]. First, we collect tweets with any explicit temporal references treating them as reflections of user thoughts on the future and the past. We make use of a half year long portion of Japanese tweets from mid-July 2013 to mid-January 2014; and a four month long collection of tweets in the USA from end of September 2013 to mid-January 2014. Then we map any detected temporal expressions to their corresponding time points. This allows us to determine the *time mention* (disambiguated time expression) of tweets. Next, we manipulate the two temporal signals: tweet timestamp (when the user sends the tweet) and *time mention* (to what time period the user refers) in tweets. Finally, we allow uncovering several findings through the visual analytics process.

Note that we choose two culturally different regions in order to perform comparative analysis of the way in which users refer to both the past and the future in Japan and in the USA. We find many commonalities in the shape of temporal attention but, at the same time, we also pinpoint certain differences.

To sum up, we make the following contributions in this paper. We are the first to analyze the way in which microblogging users refer to the past and to the future, and to propose the idea of *memory and expectation sensing* in social media. Our focus is on two distinct countries and on tweets written in different languages. For enabling visual analytics, we build an *interactive system* that collectively visualizes historical and future-oriented perspectives in microblogging. The system is available online [41, 42] for anyone interested in a quick overview or in detailed exploration of temporal aspects in shared messages. Lastly, we discuss the analysis results and outline several avenues for further research.

The reminder of this paper is structured as follows. In the next section we review the related work. Section 3 describes the data processing model, while Section 4 introduces our methodological approach for visualizing temporal patterns in tweets and overviews findings from this study. We formally describe the technical aspects in Section 5 and summarize our findings as well as their implications in the subsequent section. Finally, Section 7 concludes the paper and outlines our future work.

2. RELATED WORK

Numerous research works have shown the usefulness of microblogging for real-time information analysis in many domains, ranging from detecting natural disaster [36] and disease outbreaks [17]; via analyzing how the popularity of topics emerge and evolve on time [40] and space [3]; to opinion detection and analysis of the crowd about events [37]. An increasing number of users leave numerous traces of their daily life activities [20], especially, in social networks. Some works then exploit this new flow of personal data to predict upcoming activities in the near future [4, 38] or hot emerging topics [7].

Our work is also related to the subset of socio-psychological sciences about the study of memory and expectations. *Collective memory* is a term introduced in social sciences by Halbwachs [11] to define the collective view of society on the past. Russell Jacoby [13] also coined the term *collective amnesia* for describing forcible repression of memories when whole groups or nations "forget" events from the past. In parallel to *collective memory*, Ebbinghaus [9, 10] investigated the characteristics of personal memory and the forgetting process. Both the social and individual-focused memory studies were limited to small samples of users and had subjective character. Thus, computer science approaches could already offer a significant complement to manual investigations exploiting large data and high coverage. Already, some recent works started investigating collective memory [8, 18] or estimating collective predictions in news [14], and on the web [15, 31, 32]. Unlike those works, in our research, we focus on social media and we perform large scale analysis on the way in which microblogging platform users refer to time.

Memories and predictions rely on temporal analysis of text that models and leverage temporal expressions as well as their uncertainty [5, 14]. After prior detection and disambiguation, the temporal expressions can be included in the Temporal Information Retrieval (TIR) process [2, 5, 16, 19]. The objective of TIR is to improve the effectiveness of information retrieval methods by exploiting temporal information in documents and queries and by extending the traditional notion of *topical relevance* with *temporal relevance* [2, 6]. In fact, quite a significant fraction of Web queries have been found to contain explicit temporal expressions such as dates or names of calendar events [30, 34], while many other queries are known to have implicit temporal intent [26]. The importance of time comes from the fact that the value of information and its quality are intrinsically time-dependent, as shown in [25] that consider timeliness or currency as one of the five key aspects that determine a document's quality; the others being relevance, accuracy, objectivity, and coverage. Studies in TIR have actually shown that the retrieval effectiveness of temporal queries can be significantly improved by modelling and taking into account publication timestamps and time mentions of documents [5, 16, 19]. Through this work we hope to provide better outlook on different ways in which users refer to diverse time periods and by this to offer clues for solving the challenge of designing effective TIR systems and for understanding society and humans.

Finally, regarding event detection within microblogging data, time analysis has been a major field of research as shown in [39, 34, 21]. Also, studies in [1, 23, 36] provide a suite of visualization capabilities to explore tweets from different dimensions relating to specific application like fire combat and earthquake detection. More generic platforms have been designed with visualization tools to portray time perspectives [24, 28, 29].

3. DATA MODEL

This section describes our model to organize the data to make it usable for visualization. The following entities are of our interest: *users*: people sharing messages; *time-referring messages*: atomic interactions of users with others that contain temporal expressions including expectations and memories about subjects; and *subjects*: objects mentioned in time-referring messages. Our field of study is a portion of Japanese and US Twitter data. Therefore, in our context the users are Twitter registered users, the messages are tweets written in Japanese and English and the subjects are topics of tweets. A tweet is a short message limited to 140 characters used to communicate with others but also to react to certain events. We are particularly interested in time-referring tweet messages from which we can extract temporal expressions. The temporal expressions allow us to categorize tweets into those about future and those about past as well as to map them on timeline after prior disambiguation. We further describe the datasets in Section 4.1.

3.1 Data Structure

Each tweet is first represented as a tuple of raw data:

< *user id, tweet content, timestamp* >

The *user id* is the Twitter identification number, the *tweet content* is the text of the tweet and the *timestamp* is the time when the tweet has been published on Twitter. Based on these attributes, the information related to time is extracted and is represented by two additional attributes:

< *time mention, time diff* >

The *time mentions* are extracted and disambiguated from the *tweet content* by applying temporal entity-recognition techniques further detailed in Section 3.2. The *time diff* is then computed as the difference between the time mention and the timestamp. Intuitively, the quintuple of attributes should allow to answer simple but fundamental questions such as:

- *timestamp*: what people tend to say at the same time ?
- *time mention*: what people tend to say about the same time ?
- *time diff*: what people tend to say before or after the same time ?

The goal of our data model is to allow a combination of attributes to be contrasted leading us to infer information about the global and per user behavior of microblogging users.

3.2 Time Mention Extraction

As mentioned above we consider only tweets with time mentions. Note that while there are ready temporal taggers for English, to the best of our knowledge, none is available for extracting and anchoring temporal expressions from Japanese. Therefore, we use the Stanford CoreNLP tagger [22] for US dataset whereas we built our own tagging system for Japanese. We match tokens in the tweet content with a dictionary of the lexical expressions related to time in Japanese. For this we provide a set of common time expressions in Japanese accumulated from diverse resources such as the list of temporal expressions given by Japan Meteorological Agency [1] and others. The list we made includes different time-related phrases that refer either to near or distant time, both in future and in the past. We also asked 3 native speakers to ensure that no common temporal expressions have been missed and included their new suggestions. In addition, we defined a set of regular expressions to capture mentions of hours, days, including names of weekdays, months, seasons, national holidays and years. Eventually, the numbers of tweets containing time mentions detected in both datasets are comparable, as shown in Section 4.1, indicting that our dedicated system for Japanese language seems to be rather reliable.

We emphasize that differently to previous studies on analyzing or visualizing collective time references [14, 15], in this work, we use not only absolute temporal expressions (e.g., "January 2012" or "December 2, 2013") but also we extract and disambiguate relative temporal references (e.g., "next week" or "three months ago"). Intuitively, the latter are quite common in spoken and colloquial language and should be thus included in the analysis.

Lastly, we note that our model assumes the entire tweet content to be related to temporal expression that appears in the tweet. This assumption is reasonable given the short length of tweets.

Time Mention Disambiguation.

Each temporal expression is mapped to an absolute time period value in the past or in the future. The process is straightforward for absolute time expressions. Relative time expressions are resolved based on tweet timestamps.

Time Granularity Shifts.

It is known that humans tend to perceive time using scale similar to a logarithmic one [12]. When the time distance measured from the speaking time point increases, the granularity of temporal expressions used becomes coarser. For example, when someone talks about far future (e.g., several months or years ahead) he or she usually refrains from pinpointing exact hours, minutes or even days. On the other hand, when referring to near future, such as to actions in the same day or few days later, humans tend to use finer granularity time-references (hours or even minutes). This have been also confirmed by the analysis of time expressions extracted from large collections of news articles and then related to the article timestamps [14]. In our model we thus apply the logarithmic scale of time using three main time granularity levels inherent to human speech: minutes, hours and days depending on the distance to the start time of the disambiguated temporal expressions measured from the tweet timestamp (*time diff*). Below we show a sample of the mapping used in our model emphasizing heterogeneity of time granularity and the phenomenon of *granularity shifts* in natural language:

"Now"	→	timestamp (granularity of minutes)
"Tomorrow"	→	subsequent day of the timestamp (granularity of hours)
"Next month"	→	subsequent month of the timestamp (granularity of days)

Mapping Time Expressions.

Usually time mentions in human language do not express a specific point in time but rather a period. For example, for the time mention in the following tweet: "I will fly to Okinawa next week" the model should reflect the fact that the next week is a seven days long period, while the action (flight) may take place on any of them. To do this we represent time mentions by a uniform probability distribution over its time duration. For example, "tomorrow" is mapped into probability distribution over hours in the next day, while "next month" is converted to the uniform distribution spanning each day of the following month and so forth. For the Japanese dataset, we provide a set of this kind of mappings for each temporal expression based on the Japan Meteorological Agency guidelines[2]. Figure 1 shows a sample of temporal expressions, translated from Japanese, referring to different time frames of a day (hour granularity) and their mappings to the absolute time values.

[1] http://www.jma.go.jp/jma/kishou/know/yougo_hp/toki.html

[2] http://www.jma.go.jp/jma/kishou/know/yougo_hp/saibun.html

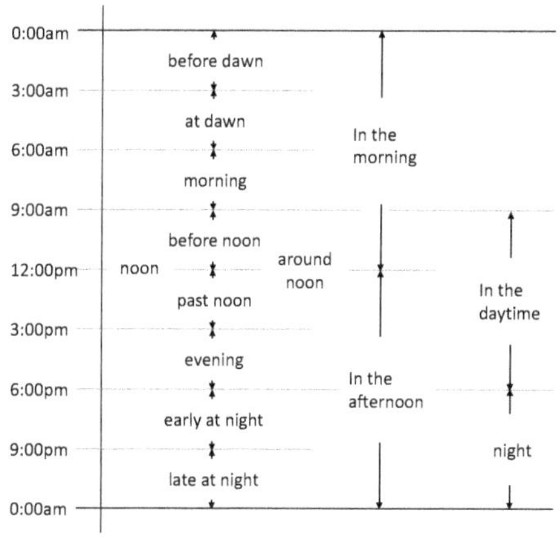

Figure 1: Sample of time expression mappings referring to different times of a day

For the US dataset we consider as a *time expression*, annotated expressions recognized as a *time* or *date* entity by the Stanford Name Entity Recognizer with some additional manually added ones to fit the same mapping style as the one for the Japanese dataset and to handle the granularity shift effect.

To sum up, in this work, the weight coming from a single time-referenced tweet on a particular time point is determined using the uniform probability distribution over the period defined by the temporal expression in the tweet and according to the selected granularity level for this expression. Following, the weight of the time point coming from several temporal expressions that cover this time point is calculated as the sum of their corresponding probabilities. The technical details of this probabilistic mapping are formally described in Section 5.1. Note that some previous works [14] adopted a more refined approaches to map activities occurring within a time period using either exponential, Gaussian or uniform distributions depending on temporal modifiers. However, deciding parameters of the probability distributions for different messages requires deeper NLP processing such as analyzing the character of events and activities, which is outside the scope of this work. Such processing would be also slow and require considerable computing resources for large datasets.

4. ANALYSIS

In this section we describe our visualization framework and detail findings we could obtain from the analysis. We defer the detailed description of the technical details until Section 5 to focus first on the conceptual way of portraying the data and on any observable patterns.

The following discussion will be mainly based on 2D plots called heat maps containing colored cells. A cell is the timespace on 2D time pane. The cell color represents the *intensity*, detailed in Section 5.1, with which tweets in the datasets refer to that cell. Below each graph, we display the color scale ranging from dark blue (the lowest *intensity*) to dark red (the highest *intensity*).

4.1 Distribution of Time References

First, we report the overall statistics of the data we use. The Japanese dataset has been build retrieving 31.6M tweets posted from Japan between July 21, 2013 and January 12, 2014; and the US dataset has been made by collecting 198M tweets between September 25, 2013 and January 17, 2014. Unfortunately, due to technical obstacles and the lack of resources the data crawling was disrupted at certain times. This explains the blank sections in Figures 3 and 4.

We use the language detection method[3], which is based on Naïve Bayesian filter and has nearly 99% precision, to select roughly 25M (millions) tweets written in Japanese in the Japanese dataset and 158M written in English from the US dataset. Among them we found 4M (16%) Japanese tweets and 30M (18%) English tweets that have temporal expressions. It means that a considerable fraction of messages contain some temporal clues. The slightly lower ratio of temporal expression usage in Japanese is more likely to be caused by our custom Japanese NLP parsing that may not be as efficient as the Stanford CoreNLP for English rather than by an actual difference within the datasets. The difference is rather small that indicates our custom Japanese *time expression* detection should work reasonably well.

In the table shown below, we report the overall strength of *temporal attention* of users towards the past, the present and the future as portrayed by the usage of temporal expressions towards each temporal class. Note that the present is determined by several words denoting the concept of "now" in Japanese and English.

	Japan	US
# time-referenced tweets	3.96M	29.92M
about past	38%	26%
about present	22%	16%
about future	40%	58%

These numbers seems to indicate that the overall *temporal attention* of Japanese Twitter users is equally distributed between the future and the past while the US Twitter users seem to be more oriented to future. This might be a language related difference since Japanese does not have an explicit future tense or difference related to the culture. However, we cannot rule out possible bias comming from different efficiency of parsers used for English and Japanese.

Next, we examine per user statistics. Figure 2 shows the distribution of users according to the frequency with which they use the *time mentions*. The horizontal axis is the ratio

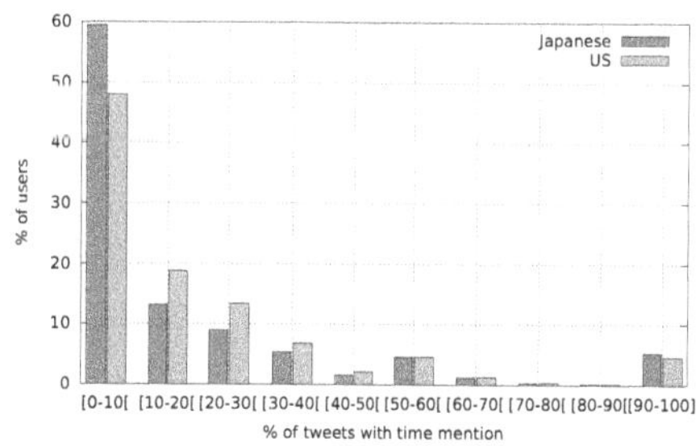

Figure 2: Rate of temporal expression usage in the tweets per user

between tweets with *time mentions* and the total number of tweet of a given user. The vertical axis denotes the percentage of users for each different usage rate of *time mentions*. We can notice that the ratio of users that at least once submitted a time-referenced tweet is 50% for Japanese and 65% for US. The value for the first bin $[0 - 10\%]$ shows that about

[3]http://code.google.com/p/language-detection

40% of Japanese users and over 50% of US users add time mentions in more than 10% of their tweets. This indicates that temporal expressions are relatively commonly used in Twitter and can be used as a signal for measuring temporal orientation of user messages. The small bump (5.2% for US and 4.6% for Japan) in the last bin, which groups users who send more than 90% of tweets containing *time references*, is likely due to the presence of bots or automatically created accounts.

4.2 Scope of Temporal Attention

We expect the way in which users refer to the future or the past differs depending on whether the temporal perspective is near- or far-fetching. In particular, we expect that forecasting and remembering attention should drop over time. By this we mean that the amount of predictions and remembrances about near future and near past should be greater than the ones associated with more distanced events. Previous studies [14, 15] conducted on news article and web page collections have demonstrated the drastic drop in the count of references that point to time periods far away from document timestamps.

For testing this and other hypotheses we use the visualizations in Figure 3 to show the difference between the time mentioned in tweets and their timestamps. The top graph (Fig. 3(a)) displays the Japanese dataset and the bottom one (Fig. 3(b)) is for the US dataset. The timestamp values of tweets published on a particular day are given on the abscissa and their agglomerated time differences are shown in ordinate in logarithmic scale. Each graph in Figure 3 is composed of two parts, the top one showing the map of future-related expressions and the bottom one portraying the expressions about the past. For example, when looking at the future-related parts of the graphs, the cells falling into the segment of 1 - 7 days represent aggregate tweets that contain time references pointing to the period from 1 to 7 days later when counting from their timestamps. Similarly, the same segment on the past-related graph part represents the aggregate of tweets with time references referring to the span from 1 to 7 days ago from tweet timestamps. Since the horizontal line denotes the tweet timestamps, we should be able to observe fluctuations in the *temporal attention* over the whole time frame of our dataset. Note that as discussed in Section 4.1 data is missing at certain time points (indicated in the graphs in Figure 3 as blank columns).

To observe any potential calendar effect we indicate by black horizontal lines the start points of each week (dashed black lines) as well as the start points of each month (solid black lines). Below the graph we also display the curve of the total number of tweets crawled (in blue) and the percentage of the tweets with time mentions (in orange) to compare the visualization on particular day with the total amount of data used to visualize that day. On the right-hand side of the graph, the blue, vertical curve shows the amount of tweets mapped to every *time diff* interval (i.e. the sum of all the cell values on each lines).

We note that our system allows fine-grained investigation of tweets constituting any selected cell. Upon clicking on a given cell a new tab is opened in a browser with the list of top words, top temporal expressions and the table detailing all the attributes of tweets associated with the cell including their text. Similarly, selecting any gray cell on the right-hand side or on the top line will trigger pop-up window with ranked top terms for the cell. The computation of top words will be described in Section 5.4.

Looking at both the future and the past related heat map graphs in both the datasets we observe the pronounced color gradation with some abrupt changes in color drawing parallel to the abscissa which indicate intensity levels that vary depending on the temporal scope of future and past references. This shows the tendency in human speech to use landmark expressions such as "today", "this afternoon", "next year" or "next week". It appears that the strongest *temporal attention* seems to be mainly related to actions within the period up to the next 1 day in the future and down to 1 day in the past for both the languages (orange and yellow colors). Within these horizons, the activities up to the next hour and down to the past 10-15min seem to be even more often referenced, as especially visible in the US dataset. We then observe significant decline in the amount of temporal attention further above or below the lines of 1 day as marked by green or light yellow color areas. In the US dataset we can also observe the effect of Fridays and Saturdays during which users seem to make slightly more plans and forecasts up to 6-12h ahead (note the periodical, horizontal stripes in orange color) than on other days. In the Japanese dataset this is more blurred.

Lastly, we note that in general the far past and distant future are characterized by fewer references what confirms our initial hypothesis that the attention decreases the farther one looks into the past and the future.

4.3 Similarity of Past and Future

Perhaps, the most striking pattern one can observe is the relatively high similarity in the temporal attention related to the future and to the past. Thus, at this point, it is difficult to say that Twitter users have significantly different pattern of interest in the future than in the past or vice versa. future were only slightly more common than the ones pointing to the near past. Of course, the symmetry is not perfect. There are certain differences noticeable such as curvy lines within the time frame further than several days from the timestamps (more visible in the US dataset). In general, the similarity between the past and future views is rather striking.

Next, we describe the periodical decreasing yellow or green curves in the future and the past-related parts of the graphs. After manual investigation of their top words, we found that they represent the tendency of people to use expressions referring to the end of a week. This is also confirmed by the fact that such lines last for a week when measured on abscissa and that they are vertically symmetrical based on dashed black lines indicating the change of the week. We note that in both the datasets the periodical curves are stronger in future (upper parts of the graphs) than in the past. When setting the different coloring scale (not shown in this paper) we managed also to observe similar situation for months. In addition, few curves longer than weekly or monthly curves can be noticed. As we observed they are due to tweets referring to significant temporal landmarks within our dataset such as Christmas (see the "Christmas" label in both the graphs).

Interestingly, we can notice another intriguing symmetry in the future and past-related areas of the graphs centered around the start of the New Year (see areas indicated with labels 1 and 2). In the past-related part (area with label 2 in both the graphs) we interpret it as the process of *re-*

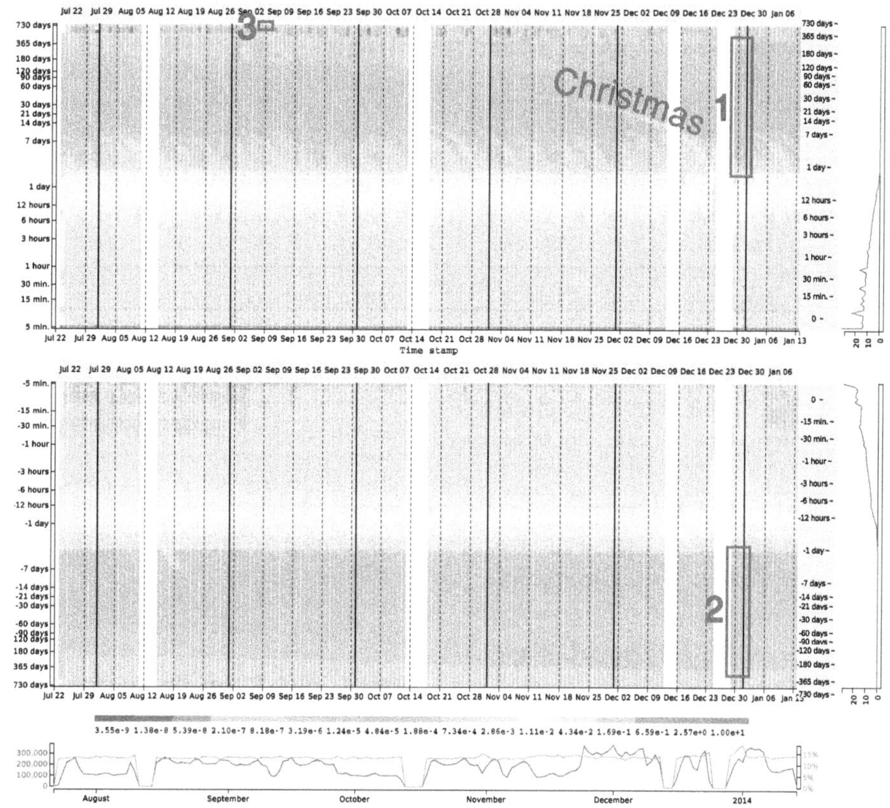

(a) Snapshot of Japanese dataset available online [43]

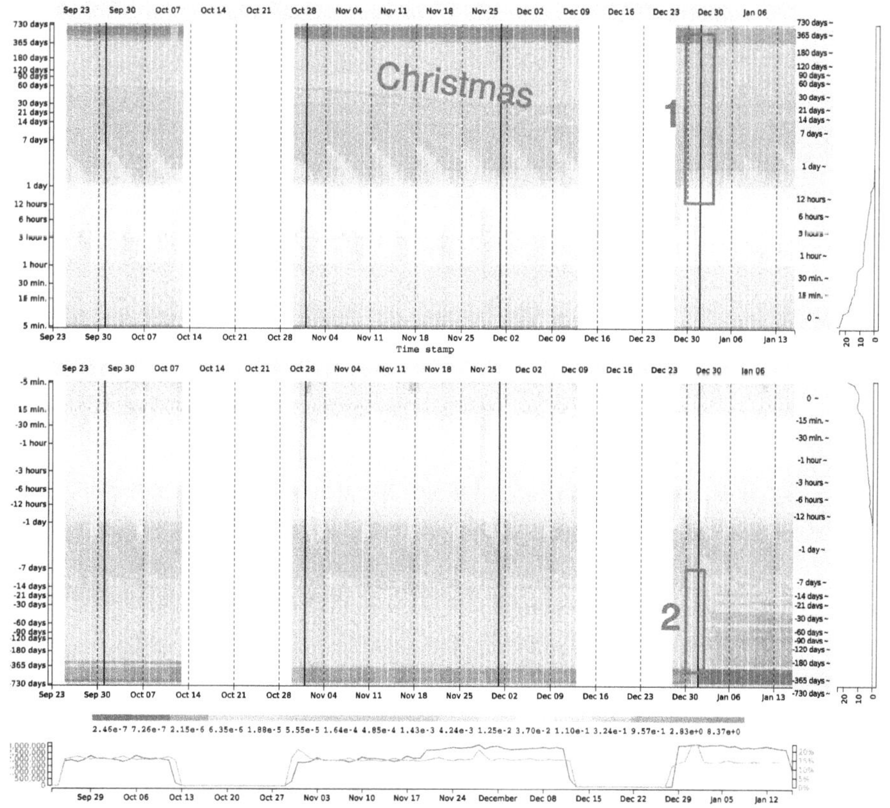

(b) Snapshot of US dataset available online [44]

Figure 3: Heat maps of relative mentions of future and past along time (best viewed in color)

calling things that happened throughout the last year. This phenomenon starts to surface several days (and is especially evident just one day) before the end of the year[4]. We can observe the continuous green color of the cells on the column representing Dec 31, 2013. Note the rather drastic decrease in the past mentions referring to the time older than one day during the first days of 2014 what emphasizes that people tend to "forget" or, at least, to reminiscence less the events and things of the previous year, right after the new year has come. When looking on the part of the graphs representing the future (label 1 in both the graphs) we conclude that the process of *making plans for the next year* starts also few days before the end of the year but is the strongest on the first day of the next year (Jan 1, 2014) and then lasts for several subsequent days. Same as in the past part of the graphs on Dec 31, 2013, the column representing the first day of the new year in the future area (see area with label 1) has the pattern of green cells spanning almost the whole year (cells on the column of that day and also several next days). It is likely due to users discussing plans and wishes for their future activities to be done in various time periods of the new year.

4.4 Variation of Patterns in Temporal Mentions over Time

The next observation is the apparent stability of temporal attention both for the future and for the past, if one neglects the effect of major calendar events such as the Christmas and the New Year's Eve. It means that the time horizons of users are essentially unchanging over the time period of our datasets.

When zooming in graphs by changing the upper limit of *intensity* used by the color scale, we were able to find some collective expectations of future events, such as announcement of Tokyo city as a host of Olympics 2020 that was made public on Sunday of Sep 8, 2013 (area with label 3 in the Japanese graph). In the snapshot in Figure 3(a), this is not so obvious due to cell normalization effect, described latter in Section 5.3. To observe this effect the cell normalization can be deactivated in the options. Another collective expectation can be found on top cell of Jan 13, 2014 which is due to the *Coming of Age Day* in Japan[5]. The celebrating students are expected to graduate from their schools after two years, hence many tweets on that day refer to the time two years later.

4.5 Topics of Expectations and Memories

We hypothesize that, on average, different expressions should be found when someone refers to events or actions in very near time (e.g., expecting breakfast or remembering lunch meeting at the end of the day) as opposed to happenings associated with more distant time (e.g., planning a vacation trip well ahead or reminiscing it some time later).

We examine then key terms related to different temporal scopes. Our system allows seeing the representative words used in tweets that refer to given time frames. These appear in a pop-up window upon pointing mouse pointer over gray buttons on the right-hand side of both future-related and past-related plots. The calculation of word scores is detailed in Section 5. Similarly, for exploration purposes it is possible to see representative words chosen from all the time-refereed tweets on a given week by selecting the gray buttons on the top (bottom) of the future-related (past-related) plots.

Table 1 shows the top representative words for tweets mentioning selected time frames both in the past and the future in the case of the Japanese dataset (we skip the US dataset due to space constraints). We can observe that there are few expressions about the weather conditions for the near future (6-12h ahead), while the far future is dominated by the information about IOC decision to hold 2020 Olympics in Japan. The near past (6-12h ago) is about common things people have just done (ate lunch, studied, returned home, etc.), while the distant past expressions associate with tweets containing recollections and reminiscences.

future over 730 days	Olympics, marriage, live, good luck, Olympics (kanji), Japan, hold, words, decide, imagination
future 6-12 hours	weather, good morning, announcement, forecast, sleep, lunch, information, caution, exam, school
past 6-12 hours	weather, lunch, arrive, practice, sleep, study, announcement, good job (well done), leisure, tired
past over 730 days	nostalgic, change, recall, in those days, I, old, young, remember, know, period

Table 1: Top words in tweets related to near/distant future/past

Then, in Table 2 (future) and Table 3 (past) we show top words from aggregated predictions and memories for two different weeks, one in summer (Aug 19-25) and one at the change of the year (Dec 30-Jan 5). We see that for example, in the summer period, that the tweets about future often concern weather predictions, plans for summer vacations or about sports matches. For the past related words in the summer we observe memories of Obon vacation period (Aug 13-16) and some fireworks events. There are also some words about the earthquakes that happened at that time. Looking at the top words for the predictions and memories at the time of the year change we observe many customary expressions for greeting the new year, remembering the old year and visiting shrines to celebrate the new year and to thank for the good things in the old year.

Aug 19-25	high temperature, °C, caution, thunders, information, sports match, summer vacation, hot, beach, rain
Dec 30-Jan 5	start of the new year, celebrate, (the new year) begins, first visit of the year to a shrine (typical custom in Japan), new year, welcome the new year and forget the old, shrine, kind regards, new year (kanji), welcome

Table 2: Top words in future related tweets in Aug 19-25 and Dec 30-Jan 5 in the Japanese dataset

4.6 Comparison of Time Mentions and Timestamps

We investigate here to which days tweets written on a particular day refer to. Intuitively, the majority of tweets written on a given day should refer to the actions during that day. We test this hypothesis using the visualization shown in the graphs in Figure 4. Figure 4(a) refers to the Japanese and Figure 4(b) to the US dataset. The horizontal axis in the graphs denotes tweet timestamps, while the horizontal

[4]Unfortunately, due to data loss this pattern cannot be seen in its entirety

[5]http://en.wikipedia.org/wiki/Coming_of_Age_Day

Aug 19-25	obon (holiday period in Japan on Aug 12-16), scary, fireworks, km, happen, deep, earthquake, hot, beach, breaking news
Dec 30-Jan 5	greetings, thank you (for everything this past year), farewell to the old year, new year, old year, (the new year) begins, the last year, congratulations, various things (of this year), year-crossing

Table 3: Top words in past related tweets in Aug 19-25 and Dec 30-Jan 5 in the Japanese dataset

one denotes tweet mentions, both represented in days. Note that these matrix-like graphs have been computed based on all *time expressions* in our datasets, hence, not only on *time expressions* of daily granularity. We perform a Jaccard-style normalization, further described in Section 5.2, that is mix of column-wise and row-wise normalization, allowing us to avoid the effect of a non-uniform distribution of the tweet *timestamps* and *time mentions*. Below the matrix graphs of Figure 4 we also display for reference the cumulative "popularity" of days mentioned in tweets, and on the right-hand side we show the frequency of tweets.

When looking at the graphs, indeed, we observe the strong impact of timestamp on the time mentions in tweets in the form of pronounced diagonal (red and orange colors) of a width of about 3 cells. This means that many tweets refer to the same day as their timestamp or just 1 day before or after it. In addition, we observe light blue periodical rectangles which fit inside the week cells. A week cell is bounded by dashed line. Keeping in mind that all the cells above the diagonal represent tweets about future and below the diagonal tweets about the past, we conclude that these periodical rectangles portray expectations or memories within the same week as the one of the tweet timestamp. This again confirms the usage of *temporal landmarks* in natural language. Users tend to relate to the future and the past in a way which is bounded by the start and the end of the current week. Also, as seen in the graphs, there seems to be more attention put on the future than on the past by the users.

Lastly, the three light blue vertical lines in the Japanese and the US datasets correspond to the long awaited major calendar events: Obon holiday (Aug 13-16), Halloween, Christmas and Halloween, Thanksgiving, Christmas, respectively.

5. TECHNICAL ASPECTS

The system has been implemented in SCALA programming language on the server side and using D3 graphical library for enabling the web interface. The Japanese morphological analyzer Kuromoji [6] was used for text processing tasks and Stanford CoreNLP [22] was used for text parsing and for detecting time expressions in English.

In the following of this section we present the definitions of the main aspects of the system. Formally, let T be the set of all the tweets in the dataset, $t \in T$ be a tweet characterized by a bag of words W_t. Visualizations are heat maps discretized in cells. Let also CEL be the set of all the cells in a heat map and $C \in CEL$ be one cell in the heat map. Finally, $C_{i,j}$ is a cell in row i and column j of a heat map with ROW and COL are respectively the number of lines and columns of a heat map.

[6] http://www.atilika.org/

5.1 Probability Mass Function

According to time mentions in a tweet t the cell $C_{i,j}$ is associated with the probability $P(C_{i,j}|t)$ such that $t \in C_{i,j}$ when the time expression is a point in time, $P(C_{i,j}|t) \rightarrow \{0,1\}$. Otherwise, for a time period, $P(C_{i,j}|t) \rightarrow \{w \in \mathbb{R} : 0 \leq w \leq 1\}$ following a uniform distribution of the weight w of the tweet over the time period discretized according to the granularity described in Section 3.2. Intuitively, $P(C_{i,j}|t)$ is the amount of the probability mass that the tweet assigns to the cell. Hence, the sum of the weight of a tweet t in all the cells of a heat map, must be 1 (i.e. $\sum_{C \in CEL} P(t|C) = 1$).

Let $I(C_{i,j}) = \sum_{t \in T} P(C_{i,j}|t)$ be the *intensity* I of a cell $C_{i,j}$. This *intensity* value controls the color displayed in Figure 3 and 4.

5.2 Normalization

When looking at the blue curves at the bottom of graphs in Figure 3 and right of graphs in Figure 4, one can remark that the number of tweets issued each day is significantly varying. Hence, the system provides three possible normalizations to remove the effect of peak time. First, the row-wise normalization allows comparing the cells on the same row: $\text{Score}(r,c) = \frac{I(C_{r,c})}{\sum_{i \in ROW} I(C_{i,c})}$
Second, the column-wise normalization allows comparing the cells on the same column: $\text{Score}(r,c) = \frac{I(C_{r,c})}{\sum_{j \in COL} I(C_{r,j})}$
The third one, a Jaccard coefficient normalization offers a way to "combine" both normalizations on the same visualization:

$$\text{Score}(r,c) = \frac{I(C_{r,c})}{\sum\limits_{i \in ROW} I(C_{i,c}) + \sum\limits_{j \in COL} I(C_{r,j}) - I(C_{r,c})}$$

The Jaccard coefficient is a ratio to measure the similarity between two sets. It is computed as the ratio between the intersection and the union of the two sets. In this application, for a given cell $C_{r,c}$ the two sets are, the set of all the tweets in the cells of row r, and the set of all the tweets in the cells of column c. Hence, it measures how much the cell is representative for the two values r and c on the axis x and y of the heat map.

These normalizations are parameters, allowing the user to change the visualizations to spot different kind of patterns.

5.3 Normalization of Logarithmic Scale

Here we address the problem of time visualization on a logarithmic scale. To illustrate the problem let's consider an extreme case where all the tweets at a given timestamp ts have the time expression "this month". In such case we would expect that the column ts would have cells spanning from beginning of this month until the end displayed in one uniform color and all the rest of cells in white. However, due to the ordinate axis drawn in a logarithmic scale the cells farther from the origin (more distant past or future) represent a larger time range than cells closer to the origin (near past or future). They will thus aggregate much more tweet's weights and, consequently, will be represented with a much stronger color, giving the false impression than the far future and past are stronger referred to than they actually are. This is because the weight of the tweets will be uniformly distributed over time covered by the expression "this month".

Let $I(C_{i,j}) = \sum_{t \in T} P(C_{i,j}|t)$ be the *intensity* I of a cell $C_{i,j}$. Intensity represents a raw measurement, as the sum of the probability of the tweets in the dataset to affect a cell.

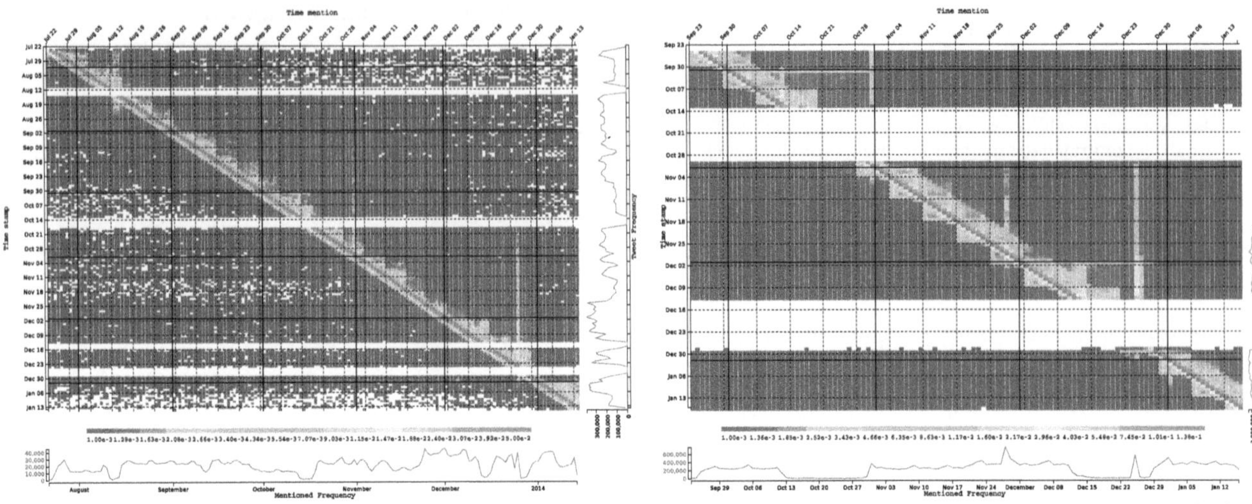

(a) Snapshot of Japanese dataset available online [45]　　(b) Snapshot of US dataset available online [46]

Figure 4: Heat map of timestamp vs. time mention matrix (best viewed in color)

Therefore, intensity should not be used directly to represent colors. Instead, we normalize it according to the scale of the axis. The color of a cell is then quantified as the *intensity* of that cell divided by time range of that cell:

$$color(C_{i,j}) = \frac{I(C_{i,j})}{size(C_{i,j})}$$

This normalization is called cell normalization and can be deactivated in the visualization options online.

5.4 Ranking Words

For each visualization, the system provides a ranking of the words in an arbitrarily defined area on the heat map called a region. The goal is to keep a top-k list of the most characteristic words for the region. The weight of each word is based on a TF-iDF weighting scheme to represent how much the word is characteristic for the given region. Intuitively, TF-iDF assigns high scores to terms that often appear in tweets associated with a given cell, while appearing infrequently in other cells. The novelty in our approach is in the count of term frequency using probability and in the definition of document based on the two levels of granularity defined for the regions: *cell* and *segment.* They are described in the subsequent paragraphs.

Cell.

In order to find the most relevant words appearing in tweets for each cell we measure the word relevance using a modified TF-iDF score where a term is a word and a document is a set of tweets corresponding to a given cell. The score to rank a word w in a cell $C_{i,j}$ using the whole set of tweets T is:

$$\text{Score}(w, C_{i,j}, T) = \frac{\sum_{t \in T} P(C_{i,j}|t) : w \in W_t}{\sum_{t \in T} P(C_{i,j}|t)} \times \log \frac{|CEL|}{|C \in CEL : \exists t \in C : w \in W_t|}$$

Segment.

In the visualization in Figure 3, the gray cells on the top or bottom line and on the right-hand side are regarded as virtual documents that represent *segments.* For instance, the top left gray cell in Figure 3 with label "Jul 22" gathers all the cells between column July 22 to 28 on every row. The *segments* are either row-wise or column-wise; they are sets of cells that span, respectively, all columns covered by the width of the selected rows, or all rows covered by the width of the selected columns.

A second level TF-iDF score is computed to rank top words in *segments.* The content of a virtual document (segment) is the set of words W_{S_i} built from all the words of the cells in that *segment.*

Let SEG be the set of all the horizontal segments in a heat map and $S \in SEG$ be one horizontal segment in the heat map that is s set of all the tweets affecting the cells of that segment. Finally, S_i is a horizontal segment in position i in a heat map. The weight of a word w in a segment is the sum of the weights of the tweets in which the word w appears.

$$\text{Score}(w, S_i, T) = \frac{\sum_{t \in T} P(C|t) : C \in S_i : w \in W_C}{\sum_{t \in T} P(C|t) : C \in S_i} \times \log \frac{|SEG|}{|S \in SEG : \exists t \in S : w \in W_t|}$$

6. DISCUSSION

We will first list the key observations we noticed using our system. Then we enumerate several directions for future research.

6.1 Key Findings

Amount of Temporal Expressions. We have found quite many temporal expressions in tweets. They can be used for anchoring tweet content on the timeline useful for many tasks including information retrieval, summarization, trend detection and so on.

Short Time Horizons and Supremacy of the Present. As expected, tweets exhibit clear temporal constraints. The attention to distant time periods as measured by the amount of extracted temporal references is significantly lower than the one to the near time. The present when more generally defined by yesterday, today and tomorrow, dominates the time-span of the temporal attention. This observation confirms conclusions from some related studies on news articles or on the open web [14, 15].

Similarity of Remembering and Expecting. We have noticed strong symmetry in the visual maps of temporal references to the past and to the future. The time horizons and the patterns of temporal attention are quite similar with the future taking however more attention of the users than the past.

Temporal Landmarks. As observed users tend to use temporal landmarks such as the start and end of weeks or months. The strongest landmark is the end and the start of the year.

Relative Stability of Temporal Horizons. We observed that the patterns of attention are more or less stable over time apart from few exceptions (e.g., the time periods just before and after the New Year's Eve). That is, for different periods of collected data there is relatively little variation in the distribution of temporal attention and the lengths of temporal horizons.

Diversity of Discussed Topics over Time. We observe certain variations in words used when referring to diverse time distances. Different time segments are characterized by differing sets of activities. The day life activities dominate the present, as shown in Table 1 but some popular events can be noticed for far future and past.

Cultural Differences. Some cultural variations can be observed by comparing views of the two datasets. The most obvious ones relates to different calendar events (e.g., Thanksgiving day in the USA). Nevertheless, on average more similarities can be observed.

Lastly, we note that our study is limited to only tweets containing temporal expressions. We also analyze only half a year long time period for the Japanese dataset and 4 months long period in case of the US dataset. It would be advantageous to analyze more implicit ways in which people can refer to future or past and to compare the results over longer datasets such as ones spanning a year or even few years. We plan to work on these issues in the future.

6.2 Applications and Future Extensions

Combined spatio-temporal analysis. The addition of location mentions and location stamps to the analysis should help to more precisely discover commonly remembered or expected events. We could also investigate time-space orthogonality through the comparative analysis of the temporal and spatial attention.

Future Prediction. As mentioned before, the expressed expectations can be utilized for predicting user activities to support any pro-active, reactive or adaptive systems. By studying the visualization graphs the feature engineering for classifiers can be improved for any activity prediction systems. For example, to predict user future mobility (e.g., holiday travel) we would expect the references to the travel to appear long before the departure date. Thus, any evidence data hinting travel plans to be used for creating classifier features should be searched within certain time ahead of the start of the travel with corresponding granularity. Also, the typical variations in temporal attention that we observe in the graphs of Figure 3 suggest particular division of time into units from where features can be extracted. Instead of uniform time division one could use the one adopted to the significant changes occuring in temporal attention as portrayed by our visualizations. Obviously, different time divisions will result in different classification features collected and should impact prediction accuracy.

Recommendation. Based on captured user memories or expectations future systems could better suggest particular activities, products, services or locations to visit.

Sentiment analysis. Humans tend to retain positive memories more than negative ones (*rosy retrospection* [27]) and favor positive future views than negative ones (*valence effect* [35]). It is then interesting to perform sentiment analysis to confirm any potential sentiment biases.

Verifying expectations and predictions. It should be possible to evaluate the predictability of future expressions and credibility of future plans. For example, for a user tweeting about travelling to Hawaii in the next month, we might search for any tweets by this user with GPS location within Hawaii to confirm the fact of visiting the islands one month later.

Social computing. As future work we plan to extend our system to accept any datasets for visualization. This should be useful for social scientists who lack efficient means for making sense of their data. Also, a more precise name entity recognizer [33] designed to deal with the noisy nature of twitter will replace Stanford CoreNLP.

7. CONCLUSIONS

In this paper we studied the dynamics of expecting and remembering processes characteristic to social media users based on data collected over nearly half a year long time-span for the Japanese and 4 months for the US datasets. Our focus is a large population of microblogging users who continuously share online information about their daily lives and things that matter to them. We have demonstrated visual framework to portray particular ways in which users refer to the past and to the future. Our methodological approach allows observing the scope of temporal attention of users, temporal horizons of their perspectives, the typical expressions and topics associated with references to given time frames (e.g., near, distant past or near, distant future) and other related features. In the future we plan to work on the previously listed directions.

8. ACKNOWLEDGMENTS

This work was supported by the Strategic Information and Communications R&D Promotion Programme (SCOPE) of the Ministry of Internal Affairs and Communications of Japan, the JSPS KAKENHI Grant Number 26280042 and the JST research promotion program Sakigake: "Analyzing Collective Memory and Developing Methods for Knowledge Extraction from Historical Documents".

References

[1] Fabian Abel, Claudia Hauff, Geert-Jan Houben, Richard Stronkman, and Ke Tao. "Twitcident: Fighting Fire with Information from Social Web Streams". In: *WWW Companion*. 2012.

[2] Omar Alonso, Ricardo Baeza-yates, Jannik Strötgen, and Michael Gertz. "Temporal Information Retrieval: Challenges and Opportunities". In: *TempWeb*. 2011.

[3] Sebastien Ardon, Amitabha Bagchi, Anirban Mahanti, Amit Ruhela, Aaditeshwar Seth, Rudra Mohan Tripathy, and Sipat Triukose. "Spatio-temporal and Events Based Analysis of Topic Popularity in Twitter". In: *CIKM*. 2013.

[4] Sitaram Asur and Bernardo A. Huberman. "Predicting the Future with Social Media". In: *WI-IAT*. Vol. 1. Aug. 2010.

[5] Klaus Berberich, Srikanta Bedathur, Omar Alonso, and Gerhard Weikum. "A Language Modeling Approach for Temporal Information Needs". In: *ECIR*. 2010.

[6] Ricardo Campos, Gaël Dias, Alípio M. Jorge, and Adam Jatowt. "Survey of Temporal Information Retrieval and Related Applications". In: *ACM Comput. Surv.* 47.2 (2014), 15:1–15:41.

[7] Yan Chen, Hadi Amiri, Zhoujun Li, and Tat-Seng Chua. "Emerging Topic Detection for Organizations from Microblogs". In: *SIGIR*. 2013.

[8] Au Yeung Ching-man and Adam Jatowt. "Studying How the Past is Remembered: Towards Computational History Through Large Scale Text Mining". In: *CIKM*. 2011.

[9] Hermann Ebbinghaus. "Uber das Gedchtnis. Untersuchungen zur experimentellen Psychologie." In: (1885).

[10] Hermann Ebbinghaus. *Memory: A Contribution to Experimental Psychology*. Columbia University. Teachers College. Educational reprints. no. 3. 1913.

[11] Maurice Halbwachs. *La mémoire collective*. Les Presses universitaires de France. 1950.

[12] Christoph Hoerl and Teresa McCormack. *Time and memory : issues in philosophy and psychology*. No.1. 2001.

[13] R. Jacoby. *Social Amnesia: A Critique of Contemporary Psychology*. 1997.

[14] Adam Jatowt and Ching-man Au Yeung. "Extracting collective expectations about the future from large text collections". In: *CIKM*. 2011.

[15] Adam Jatowt, Hideki Kawai, Kensuke Kanazawa, Katsumi Tanaka, Kazuo Kunieda, and Keiji Yamada. "Analyzing Collective View of Future, Time-referenced Events on the Web". In: *WWW*. 2010.

[16] Nattiya Kanhabua, Klaus Berberich, and Kjetil Nørvåg. "Learning to Select a Time-aware Retrieval Model". In: *SIGIR*. 2012.

[17] Nattiya Kanhabua and Wolfgang Nejdl. "Understanding the Diversity of Tweets in the Time of Outbreaks". In: *WWW*. 2013.

[18] Nattiya Kanhabua, Tu Ngoc Nguyen, and Claudia Niederee. "What triggers human remembering of events? A large-scale analysis of catalysts for collective memory in Wikipedia". In: *JCDL*. Sept. 2014.

[19] Nattiya Kanhabua and Kjetil Nørvåg. "Determining Time of Queries for Re-ranking Search Results". In: *ECDL*. 2010.

[20] David Lazer, Alex (Sandy) Pentland, Lada Adamic, Sinan Aral, Albert Laszlo Barabasi, Devon Brewer, et al. "Life in the network: the coming age of computational social science". In: *Science* 323.5915 (Feb. 6, 2009), pp. 721–723.

[21] Chenliang Li, Aixin Sun, and Anwitaman Datta. "Twevent: Segment-based Event Detection from Tweets". In: *CIKM*. 2012.

[22] Christopher D. Manning, Mihai Surdeanu, John Bauer, Jenny Finkel, Steven J. Bethard, and David McClosky. "The Stanford CoreNLP Natural Language Processing Toolkit". In: *ACL*. 2014.

[23] Adam Marcus, Michael S. Bernstein, Osama Badar, David R. Karger, Samuel Madden, and Robert C. Miller. "Twitinfo: Aggregating and Visualizing Microblogs for Event Exploration". In: *CHI*. 2011.

[24] Andrew J. McMinn, Daniel Tsvetkov, Tsvetan Yordanov, Andrew Patterson, Rrobi Szk, Jesus A. Rodriguez Perez, and Joemon M. Jose. "An Interactive Interface for Visualizing Events on Twitter". In: *SIGIR*. 2014.

[25] M. J. Metzger. "Making sense of credibility on the Web: Models for evaluating online information and recommendations for future research". In: *JASIST* 58.13 (2007), pp. 2078–2091.

[26] Donald Metzler, Rosie Jones, Fuchun Peng, and Ruiqiang Zhang. "Improving Search Relevance for Implicitly Temporal Queries". In: *SIGIR '09*. 2009.

[27] Terence R. Mitchell, Leigh Thompson, Erika Peterson, and Randy Cronk. "Temporal Adjustments in the Evaluation of Events: The "Rosy View"". In: *Journal of Experimental Social Psychology* 33.4 (1997), pp. 421–448.

[28] Fred Morstatter, Shamanth Kumar, Huan Liu, and Ross Maciejewski. "Understanding Twitter Data with TweetXplorer". In: *KDD*. 2013.

[29] Mashaal Musleh. "Spatio-temporal Visual Analysis for Event-specific Tweets". In: *SIGMOD*. 2014.

[30] Sérgio Nunes, Cristina Ribeiro, and Gabriel David. "Use of Temporal Expressions in Web Search". In: *ECIR*. 2008.

[31] Kira Radinsky, Sagie Davidovich, and Shaul Markovitch. "Learning Causality for News Events Prediction". In: *WWW*. 2012.

[32] Kira Radinsky and Eric Horvitz. "Mining the Web to Predict Future Events". In: *WSDM*. 2013.

[33] Alan Ritter, Sam Clark, Mausam, and Oren Etzioni. "Named Entity Recognition in Tweets: An Experimental Study". In: *EMNLP*. 2011.

[34] Alan Ritter, Mausam, Oren Etzioni, and Sam Clark. "Open Domain Event Extraction from Twitter". In: *KDD*. 2012.

[35] David Rosenhan and Samuel Messick. "Affect and expectation". In: *Journal of Personality and Social Psychology* 3.1 (1966), pp. 38–44.

[36] Takeshi Sakaki, Makoto Okazaki, and Yutaka Matsuo. "Earthquake shakes Twitter users: real-time event detection by social sensors". In: *WWW*. 2010.

[37] George Valkanas and Dimitrios Gunopulos. "How the Live Web Feels About Events". In: *CIKM*. 2013.

[38] W. Weerkamp and M. de Rijke. "Activity Prediction: A Twitter-based Exploration". In: *TAIA*. 2012.

[39] Jianshu Weng and Bu-Sung Lee. "Event Detection in Twitter." In: *ICWSM*. 2011.

[40] Jaewon Yang and Jure Leskovec. "Patterns of Temporal Variation in Online Media". In: *WSDM*. 2011.

Online Resources

[41] *Portal to visualizations of the Japanese dataset.* URL: `http://scope13.cse.kyoto-su.ac.jp/JP4/chartlist.html`.

[42] *Portal to visualizations of the USA dataset.* URL: `http://scope13.cse.kyoto-su.ac.jp/US4/chartlist.html`.

[43] *Time difference for Japanese dataset.* URL: `http://scope13.cse.kyoto-su.ac.jp/JP4/timediff.html`.

[44] *Time difference for US dataset.* URL: `http://scope13.cse.kyoto-su.ac.jp/US4/timediff.html`.

[45] *Time transition matrix for Japanese dataset.* URL: `http://scope13.cse.kyoto-su.ac.jp/JP4/timematrix.html`.

[46] *Time transition matrix for US dataset.* URL: `http://scope13.cse.kyoto-su.ac.jp/US4/timematrix.html`.

Path Sampling: A Fast and Provable Method for Estimating 4-Vertex Subgraph Counts*

Madhav Jha[†]
Zenefits
San Francisco, CA 94107
mjha@zenefits.com

C. Seshadhri
University of California, Santa Cruz
Santa Cruz, CA 95064
scomandu@ucsc.edu

Ali Pinar
Sandia National Laboratories
Livermore, CA 94550
apinar@sandia.gov

ABSTRACT

Counting the frequency of small subgraphs is a fundamental technique in network analysis across various domains, most notably in bioinformatics and social networks. The special case of triangle counting has received much attention. Getting results for 4-vertex patterns is highly challenging, and there are few practical results known that can scale to massive sizes. Indeed, even a highly tuned enumeration code takes more than a day on a graph with millions of edges. Most previous work that runs for truly massive graphs employ clusters and massive parallelization.

We provide a sampling algorithm that provably and accurately approximates the frequencies of all 4-vertex pattern subgraphs. Our algorithm is based on a novel technique of *3-path sampling* and a special pruning scheme to decrease the variance in estimates. We provide theoretical proofs for the accuracy of our algorithm, and give formal bounds for the error and confidence of our estimates. We perform a detailed empirical study and show that our algorithm provides estimates within 1% relative error for all subpatterns (over a large class of test graphs), while being orders of magnitude faster than enumeration and other sampling based algorithms. Our algorithm takes less than a minute (on a single commodity machine) to process an Orkut social network with 300 million edges.

*This work was funded by the GRAPHS Program at DARPA and by the Applied Mathematics Program at the U.S. Department of Energy. Sandia National Laboratories is a multi-program laboratory managed and operated by Sandia Corporation, a wholly owned subsidiary of Lockheed Martin Corporation, for the U.S. Department of Energy's National Nuclear Security Administration under contract DE-AC04-94AL85000.

†Work done while the author was a postdoc at Sandia National Laboratories, Livermore.

WWW 2015, May 18–22, 2015, Florence, Italy.
ACM 978-1-4503-3469-3/15/05.
http://dx.doi.org/10.1145/2736277.2741101.

Categories and Subject Descriptors

G.2.2 [**Discrete Mathematics**]: Graph Theory—*Graph algorithms*; G.2.1 [**Discrete Mathematics**]: Combinatorics—*Counting problems*; E.1 [**Data Structures**]: Graphs and networks; H.2.8 [**Database Management**]: Database Applications—*Data mining*; G.3 [**Probability and Statistics**]: Probabilistic algorithms (including Monte Carlo)

General Terms

Algorithms, Theory

Keywords

Subgraph counting; sampling algorithms; path sampling; motif counting; graphlet distribution

1. INTRODUCTION

Counting the number of occurrences of small subgraphs in a graph is a fundamental network analysis technique used across diverse domains: bioinformatics, social sciences, and infrastructure networks studies [18, 10, 25, 23, 7, 26, 13, 19, 2, 14, 33, 40, 32]. The subgraphs whose counts are desired are variously referred as "pattern subgraphs," "motifs," or "graphlets." It is repeatedly observed that certain small subgraphs occur substantially more often in real-world networks than in a randomly generated network [18, 39, 23]. Motifs distributions have been used in bioinformatics to evaluate network models [26, 19]. Analysis of triadic (3-vertex) motifs has a long history in social network analysis and modeling [18, 7, 13, 30, 12]. Work in the data mining community has applied motif frequencies for spam detection and group classification of sets of nodes [2, 37].

The main challenge of motif counting is combinatorial explosion. Even in a moderately sized graph with millions of edges, the subgraph counts (even for 4-vertex patterns) is in the billions. Any exhaustive enumeration method (no matter how cleverly designed) is forced to touch each occurrence of the subgraph, and cannot truly scale. One may apply massive parallelism to counteract this problem, but that does not avoid the fundamental combinatorial explosion. An alternative approach is based on *sampling*. Here, we try to count the number of subgraphs using a randomized algorithm. The difficulty is in designing a fast algorithm that also provides an accurate estimate. The holy grail is to get mathematically provable bounds on accuracy with quantifiable error bars.

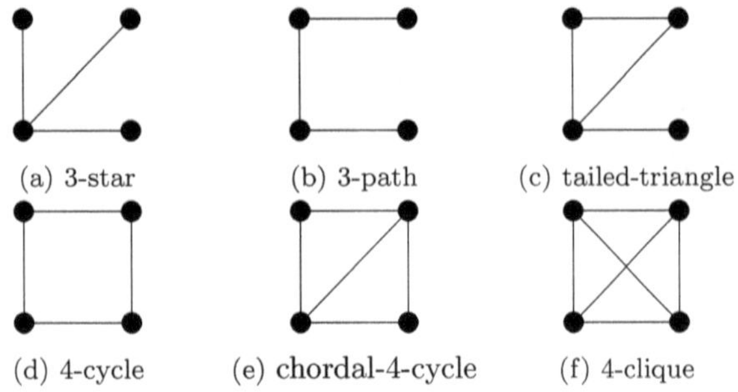

Figure 1: List of all connected 4-vertex motifs

Sampling approaches have been employed for triangle counting with good success [28, 34, 36, 35, 31]. There also exists work for counting larger motifs, as we shall discuss later. Most methods (especially in bioinformatics) [19, 4, 41, 27] work for graphs of at most 100K edges, much smaller than the massive social networks we encounter.

1.1 The main problem

We focus on estimating frequency of all connected 4-vertex subgraphs on massive input graphs. There are six connected 4-vertex graphs (Fig. 1): (i) the 3-path, (ii) the 3-star, (iii) the tailed-triangle, (iv) the 4-cycle, (v) the chordal-4-cycle, and (vi) the 4-clique. Throughout this work, we refer to these motifs by their numbering in this list. For example the "6-th motif" is the 4-clique.

Our aim is to give an accurate and fast estimate of all 4-vertex subgraph counts. Triadic analysis is now a standard aspect of network analysis. Recent work of Ugander et al [37] specifically use 4-vertex pattern counts to provide a "map" of egonets, and show significant patterns among these counts. Such analyses require fairly precise frequency counts.

1.2 Related Work

Motif counting for bioinformatics was arguably initiated by a seminal paper of Milo *et al.* [23]. This technique has been used for graph modeling [26, 19], graph comparisons [26, 16], and even decomposing a network [20]. Refer to [4, 41] for more details.

Triangle counting has a rich history in social sciences and related analyses, that we simply refer the reader to the related work sections of [35, 31]. The significance of 4-vertex patterns was studied in recent work of Ugander et al. [37], who propose a "coordinate system" for graphs based on the motifs distribution. This is used for improved network classification, and the input graphs were comparatively small (thousands of vertices).

Previous studies tailored to 4-vertex patterns [15, 22] provide both exact and approximation algorithms. However, the asymptotic bounds in these graphs are far from practical, and they are only applied to small graphs. For example, a graph with 90K edges requires 40 minutes of processing [22]. Color coding [1], Monte-Carlo Markov Chain sampling [5], and edge sampling to speedup edge iteration based algorithms [27] have been adopted to count patterns in graphs. We will provide 'detailed comparisons with these methods in §6.1. To exploit more powerful computing platforms, incremental pattern building algorithms for Map-Reduce have been described in [24, 6].

Most relevant to this work are previous studies on *wedge sampling* [28, 31, 21]. This method samples paths of length 2 to estimate various triangle statistics. Our method of 3-path sampling can be seen as building on wedge sampling. We employ new path pruning techniques to improve the algorithm's efficiency. These pruning techniques are inspired by degeneracy ordering algorithms for triangle counting [9, 29]. We can actually provide mathematical error bars for real runs and instances (as opposed to just a theoretical proof of convergence of estimate).

1.3 Summary of our contributions

We design a new randomized algorithm, based on *3-path sampling*, that outputs accurate estimates of all 4-vertex subgraphs counts. The algorithm is provably correct and makes no distributional assumption on the graph. All probabilities are over the internal randomness of the algorithm itself (which is independent of the instance). We run detailed simulations on a large variety of datasets, including product co-purchasing networks, web networks, autonomous systems networks, and social networks. All experiments are done on a single commodity machine using 64GB memory.

Extremely fast. Our algorithm relies on a sampling based approach making it extremely fast even on very large graphs. Indeed, there are instances where a finely tuned enumeration code takes almost a day to compute counts of 4-vertex motifs whereas our algorithm only takes less than a minute to output accurate estimates. Refer to Fig. 2a for speedup over a well-tuned enumeration code. Our algorithm takes less a minute on an Orkut social network with 200 million edges, where the total count of each motif is over a billion (and most counts are over 10 billion). An input Flickr social network has more than 10 billion 4-cliques; we get estimate of this number with less than 0.5% error within 30 seconds on a commodity machine. We do not preprocess any of the graphs, and simply read them as a list of edges.

Excellent empirical accuracy. We empirically validate our algorithm on a large variety of datasets, and it consistently gives extremely accurate answers. Refer to Fig. 2b. We get $< 1\%$ relative error *for all subgraph counts on all datasets*, even those with more than 100M edges. (Exact counts were obtained by brute-force enumerations that took several days.) This is much more accurate than any existing method to count such motifs. We compare with existing sampling methods, and demonstrate that our algorithm is faster and more accurate than the state-of-the-art.

Provable guarantees with error bars. Our algorithm has a provable guarantee on accuracy and running time. Furthermore, we can quantify the accuracy/confidence on real inputs and runs of our algorithm. For a given number of samples, we can have a method to put an explicit error bar on our estimate, based on asymptotically tight versions of Chernoff's bound. While these error bars are not as tight as the real errors in Fig. 2b, we can still mathematically prove that the errors are mostly within 5% and always within 10%.

Trends in 4-vertex pattern counts: Given the rapid reporting of 4-vertex pattern counts, our algorithm can be used as a tool for motif analysis. We detect common trends among a large variety of graphs. Not surprisingly, the 3-star is the most frequent 4-vertex motif in all graphs we experimented upon. The least frequent is either the 4-cycle or the 4-clique. The chordal-4-cycle frequency is always more than that of the 4-cycle or 4-clique. Ugander et al [37] study

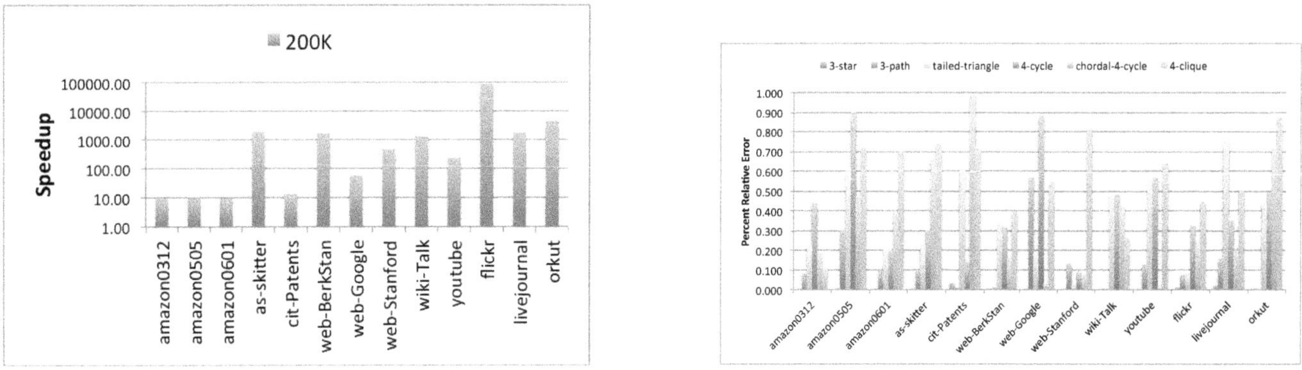

(a) Speedup

(b) Relative error

Figure 2: Summary of 3-path sampling algorithm behavior over a large variety of datasets: The left figure shows speedup over a tuned enumeration code. The right figure shows the relative error of each estimate, which is always less than 1% (and mostly much smaller).

what trends are merely implied by graph theory, and what are actually features of real-world graphs. Such analyses require accurate estimates quickly, which our algorithm can provide. It is a promising direction to use our algorithm to provide more input to such studies.

2. FORMAL DESCRIPTION OF THE PROBLEM

Our input is an undirected simple graph $G = (V, E)$, with n vertices and m edges. For vertex v, d_v is the degree of v.

It is critical to distinguish subgraphs from *induced subgraphs.* A subgraph is simply some subset of edges. An induced subgraph is obtained by taking a subset V' of vertices, and consider *all edges* among these vertices. Refer to Fig. 3. The edges $(v_1, v_2), (v_2, v_3), (v_3, v_4), (v_4, v_1)$ form a 4-cycle, but the vertex set $\{v_1, v_2, v_3, v_4\}$ induces a chordal-4-cycle. We collectively refer to the 4-vertex subgraphs as "motifs".

It is technically convenient to think of induced subgraph counts. We denote the number of induced occurrences of the i-th subgraph (of Fig. 1) by C_i. So, C_4 is the number of induced 4-cycles in G, which is the number of distinct subsets of 4 vertices that induce a 4-cycle. When we talk of a "vanilla" subgraph, we mean the usual subgraph setting (a subset of edges). In general, if we do not say "induced", we mean vanilla.

Our aim is to get an estimate of all C_i values. Let N_i denote the number of (vanilla) subgraph occurrences of the ith subgraph, There is a simple linear relationship between induced and non-induced counts, given below. The (i, j) entry of the matrix A below is simply the number of distinct copies of the ith subgraph in the jth subgraph (so $A_{2,4} = 4$, the number of 3-paths in the 4-cycle).

$$\begin{pmatrix} 1 & 0 & 1 & 0 & 2 & 4 \\ 0 & 1 & 2 & 4 & 6 & 12 \\ 0 & 0 & 1 & 0 & 4 & 12 \\ 0 & 0 & 0 & 1 & 1 & 3 \\ 0 & 0 & 0 & 0 & 1 & 6 \\ 0 & 0 & 0 & 0 & 0 & 1 \end{pmatrix} \cdot \begin{pmatrix} C_1 \\ C_2 \\ C_3 \\ C_4 \\ C_5 \\ C_6 \end{pmatrix} = \begin{pmatrix} N_1 \\ N_2 \\ N_3 \\ N_4 \\ N_5 \\ N_6 \end{pmatrix}. \tag{1}$$

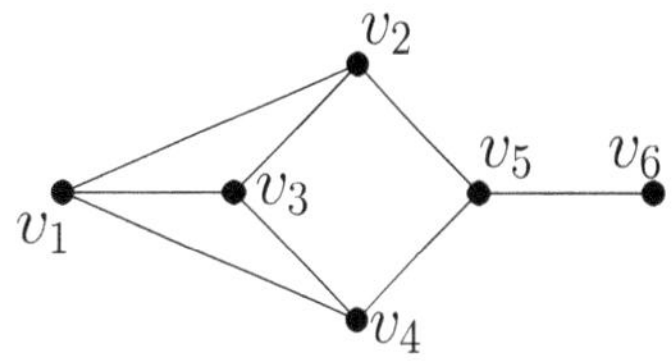

Figure 3: An example graph.

3. THE BASIC ALGORITHM: ESTIMATING COUNTS VIA 3-PATH SAMPLING

Our algorithm for estimating counts of 4-vertex motifs is based on 3-path sampling. In this section, we discuss a basic version of this method. In the next section, we enhance it to improve accuracy.

We begin with a simple procedure that samples a uniform (vanilla) random 3-path. For each edge $e = (u, v) \in E$, denote $\tau_e = (d_u - 1)(d_v - 1)$. We denote $W = \sum_e \tau_e$.

Algorithm 1: `sample`

1 Compute τ_e for all edges and set $p_e = \tau_e / W$.
2 Pick edge $e = (u, v)$ with probability p_e.
3 Pick uniform random neighbor u' of u *other than* v.
4 Pick uniform random neighbor v' of v *other than* u.
5 Output the three edges $\{(u', u), (u, v), (v, v')\}$.

Observe that the output of `sample` can either be a triangle (if $u' = v'$) or a 3-path.

CLAIM 3.1. *Fix any 3-path. The probability that* `sample` *outputs this 3-path is exactly* $1/W$.

PROOF. Fix a 3-path $(u', u), (u, v), (v, v')$ (u, u', v, v' are all distinct). The probability that $e = (u, v)$ is selected as the middle edge (in Step 2) is exactly $(d_u - 1)(d_v - 1)/W$. Conditioned on this event, the probability that u' is selected as a neighbor of u is $1/(d_u - 1)$ (note that the neighbor v is excluded). Similarly, v' is selected with probability $1/(d_v - 1)$. Putting it all together, the 3-path is chosen with probability $[(d_u - 1)(d_v - 1)/W] \cdot [1/(d_u - 1)] \cdot [1/(d_v - 1)] = 1/W$. The probability is the same for all 3-paths, proving our claim. □

All motifs of Fig. 1, except the 3-star, contain a 3-path. So one can perform the following experiment. Run **sample** to get a collection of edges, and hence a set of (at most 4) vertices. Check the motif induced by this set of vertices. Repeat this experiment many times to estimate the true counts C_i ($i \in [2,6]$). Finally, we use the formula of (1) to estimate C_1. This is exactly the algorithm **3-path-sampler**, as given in Alg. 2. We remind the reader that $A_{2,i}$ is the number of 3-paths in the ith motif.

Algorithm 2: 3-path-sampler
Input: graph $G = (V, E)$, samples k

Run **sample** k times to get k sets of edges. Let S_ℓ denote the set of corresponding vertices for the ℓth set.
Initialize $count_i = 0$ for $i \in [2,6]$.
For $\ell \in [1,k]$,
    Determine subgraph induced by S_ℓ.
    If this is the ith motif, increment $count_i$.
For each $i \in [2,6]$,
    Set $\widehat{C}_i = (count_i/k) \cdot (W/A_{2,i})$.
Set $N_1 = \sum_{v \in V} \binom{d_v}{3}$.
Set (induced 3-stars) $\widehat{C}_1 = N_1 - \widehat{C}_3 - 2\widehat{C}_5 - 4\widehat{C}_6$.

We prove that **3-path-sampler** outputs unbiased estimates for all C_is.

THEOREM 3.2. *For every $i \in [1,6]$, $\mathbf{E}[\widehat{C}_i] = C_i$.*

PROOF. First, let use deal with subgraphs other than the 3-star, so fix some $i \neq 1$. For each $\ell \in [k]$, let X_ℓ be the indicator random variable for S_ℓ inducing the ith motif. So X_ℓ is 1 iff the ℓth call to **sample** outputs a 3-path contained in a copy of the ith motif. The total number of (distinct) such 3-paths is exactly $A_{2,i} \cdot C_i$. By Claim 3.1, the probability that $X_\ell = 1$ is $A_{2,i} \cdot C_i/W$. Hence, $\mathbf{E}[X_\ell] = C_i \cdot A_{2,i}/W$.

We have $\mathbf{E}[count_i] = \sum_{\ell=1}^{k} \mathbf{E}[X_\ell] = (kC_iA_{2,i})/W$, by linearity of expectation. Hence, $\mathbf{E}[\widehat{C}_i] = C_i$. Now, we detail with $\widehat{C}_1$. Note that N_1, the number of 3-star subgraphs, is exactly $\sum_{v \in V} \binom{d_v}{3}$. By linearity of expectation, $\mathbf{E}[\widehat{C}_1] = N_1 - \mathbf{E}[\widehat{C}_3] - 2\mathbf{E}[\widehat{C}_5] - 4\mathbf{E}[\widehat{C}_6]$, which is $N_1 - C_3 - 2C_5 - 4C_6$ $= C_1$ (as given by (1)). □

We can also prove concentration results using the Hoeffding bound [17]. This is useful as a proof of concept, but does not give useful bounds in practice. (We give more details later.) This analysis is analogous to that of wedge sampling results [29, 31].

THEOREM 3.3 (HOEFFDING [17]). *Let $X_1, X_2, \ldots, X_k$ be independent random variables with $0 \leq X_i \leq 1$ for all $i = 1, \ldots, k$. Define $\bar{X} = \frac{1}{k}\sum_{i=1}^{k} X_i$. Let $\mu = \mathbf{E}[\bar{X}]$. Then for $\varepsilon \in (0,1)$, we have*

$$\Pr[|\bar{X} - \mu| \geq \varepsilon] \leq 2\exp(-2k\varepsilon^2).$$

We can derive concentration results quite directly from this bound. Note that the bound is for a fixed $i \in [2,6]$, i.e., a fixed motif that is not the 3-star.

THEOREM 3.4. *Fix $\delta, \varepsilon \in (0,1)$ and $i \in [2,6]$. Set $k = \lceil (2\varepsilon)^{-2} \ln(2/\delta) \rceil$. For all $i \in [2,6]$: with probability at least $1 - \delta$, $|\widehat{C}_i - C_i| < \varepsilon W/A_{2,i}$. With probability at least $1-\delta$, $|\widehat{C}_1 - C_1| < \varepsilon W$.*

PROOF. We have fixed $i \neq 1$. For each $\ell \in [k]$, define X_ℓ to be the indicator random variable for S_ℓ inducing the ith motif. Observe that *when i is fixed*, each X_ℓ is independent, since it is simply the result on an independent sample. In other words, the chance of the ℓth sample inducing the ith motif is independent over the sample index ℓ.

Apply Theorem 3.3 to $X_1, \ldots, X_k$. With probability at most δ, $|\bar{X} - \mathbf{E}[\bar{X}]| \geq \varepsilon$ (we use the notation from Theorem 3.3). It remains to interpret $\bar{X}$. Note that $\widehat{C}_i = (count_i/k) \cdot (W/A_{2,i})$. Since $count_i = \sum_{\ell=1}^{k} X_\ell$, $\widehat{C}_i = \bar{X} \cdot (W/A_{2,i})$. So $|\bar{X} - \mathbf{E}[\bar{X}]| \geq \varepsilon$ implies $|\widehat{C}_i - C_i| \geq \varepsilon$, as desired.

Since $\widehat{C}_1$ is obtained by subtracting out other terms, it appears that the errors could add up. With a little care, we can get the same bound as the other $\widehat{C}_i$'s. Define random variable Y_ℓ as follows: if S_ℓ induces a tailed triangle, $Y_\ell = 1/A_{2,3} = 1/2$. If S_ℓ induces a chordal-4-cyle, $Y_\ell = 2/A_{2,5} = 2/6$. If S_ℓ induces a 4-clique, $Y_\ell = 4/A_{2,6} = 4/12$. In all other cases, $Y_\ell = 0$. We have constructed this random variable, so that $\mathbf{E}[Y_\ell] = (C_3 + 2C_5 + 4C_6)/W$.

Observe that $\widehat{C}_1$ can also be expressed as $N_1 - (\sum_\ell Y_\ell/k)W$. The additive error $|\widehat{C}_1 - C_1|$ is the same as $W \cdot |\bar{Y} - \mathbf{E}[\bar{Y}]|$. Applying Theorem 3.3, with probability at least $1-\delta$, $|\widehat{C}_1 - C_1| < \varepsilon W$. □

To get error bounds for obtaining all estimates, we take the union bound. Hence, with probability at least $1 - 6\delta$, we get the same accuracy guarantee of Theorem 3.4 simultaneously for all counts.

THEOREM 3.5. *The running time (including all preprocessing) of* **3-path-sampler** *is $O(m + k\log k)$. The total storage is $O(m+k)$.*

PROOF. We store the graph as an adjacency list. We assume that each list is a hash table, so we can access the degree d_v, find a random neighbor of v, and check for existence of edge (u,v) in (expected over hash table) constant time.

The preprocessing required to determine each value of τ_e is linear in m. Generating k 3-path samples can be done by sorting k random numbers in $(0,1)$ and merging with a list of partial sums of τ_e. This takes $O(k\log k)$ time. (It is possible to get these samples in $O(k)$ using Walker's alias method [38], but it rarely gives a benefit in practice.) Checking the motif induced by the path takes $O(1)$ time by the hash table representation. The total running time is bounded by $O(m+k\log k)$. The only additional storage over the graph are the values τ_e and the various counts. Hence, the storage can be bounded by $O(m+k)$. □

3.1 The challenge of cycle-based motifs

Theorem 3.2 and Theorem 3.4 seem to give us all we want, so why aren't we done? The catch is that the concentration bound of Theorem 3.4 is actually too weak to give reasonable estimates for real world graphs. Let us do some rough calculations, ignoring the constants. To get an estimate such that $|\widehat{C}_i - C_i| < \varepsilon W$, we require $k \approx 1/\varepsilon^2$. But for such an estimate to be useful, we need to understand how W relates to C_i. So ε needs to be of the order of C_i/W, and consequently, k needs to be $(W/C_i)^2$.

Refer to Tab. 1 for the values of W and a few C_is. (For convenience, we just give the order of magnitude of each

Table 1: W vs C_i: counts given as orders of magnitude.

Graph	W	C_2	C_3	C_4	C_6
amazon0312	E+09	E+08	E+08	E+06	E+06
as-skitter	E+12	E+11	E+11	E+10	E+08
orkut	E+13	E+13	E+12	E+10	E+09

number. Full numbers are given later.) For $i \in \{1, 2, 3\}$ (3-star, 3-path, and tailed triangle), $(W/C_i)^2$ is usually $< 10^4$. This is fairly reasonable number of samples to take, and leads to an efficient and accurate algorithm. On the other hand, for $i \in \{4, 5, 6\}$ (4-cycle, chordal-4-cycle, and 4-clique), $(W/C_i)^2$ is often $> 10^8$, which is too many samples to take.

In other words, `3-path-sampler` does not perform well for motifs containing a 4-cycle. This leads us to a new algorithm for dealing with these motifs, as described in the next section.

4. IMPROVED ESTIMATION OF 4-CYCLE-BASED MOTIFS VIA *CENTERED* 3-PATHS

We denote the 4-cycle, chordal-4-cycle, and 4-clique as *cycle-based* motifs. We design a better algorithm to estimate them. While the algorithm is provably correct for any graph, the fact that it gives a significant improvement is dependent on the structure of real-world graphs.

Our aim is to find a subset $\mathcal{S}$ of 3-paths with the following properties:

- Every cycle-based motif is guaranteed to contain a fixed number of 3-paths from $\mathcal{S}$.
- It is possible to quickly generate uniform random samples from $\mathcal{S}$.
- $|\mathcal{S}|$ is significantly smaller than $W = \sum_{e=(u,v)} (d_u - 1)(d_v - 1)$.

Let us go back to `sample`, and think of enumerating all 3-paths. For edge (u, v), we take every neighbor of u and every neighbor of v to generate a 3-path. We basically take the Cartesian product of the adjacency lists of u and v. Could we prune the adjacency lists so this product is smaller?

Suppose we order all vertices based on degree and vertex id. So we say $u \prec v$ if: $d_u < d_v$ or, if $d_u = d_v$, the vertex id of u is less than that of v. We could prune the lists using this ordering. When looking for 3-paths where (u, v) is the middle edge, we only look at the portion of u's list "greater" than v, and the portion of v's list greater than u. In general, many 3-paths are generated when d_u and d_v are large. But in that case, we hope that many neighbors of u and v are of lower degree. The pruning ignores such vertices and (hopefully) reduces the set of 3-paths considered. Let us define the set $\mathcal{S}$ of centered 3-paths.

DEFINITION 4.1 (CENTERED 3-PATH). *A 3-path formed by edges $\{(t, u), (u, v), (v, w)\}$ is* centered *if: $v \prec t$, $u \prec w$, and the edge (t, w) exists in the graph (so t, u, v, w form a 4-cycle).*

We prove the important property that every cycle-based motif contains a fixed number of centered 3-paths.

LEMMA 4.2. *Every induced 4-cycle and chordal-4-cycle contains exactly one centered 3-path. Every induced 4-clique contains exactly three centered 3-paths.*

PROOF. Consider any (vanilla) 4-cycle, formed by vertices (in order) t, u, v, w. Pick the smallest vertex, say u. Pick the neighbor of u that is smaller, say v. We show that the 3-path $\{(t, u), (u, v), (v, w)\}$ is the only centered 3-path in this 4-cycle.

By the choice of (u, v), $v \prec t$ and $u \prec w$. Hence, we see that $\{(t, u), (u, v), (v, w)\}$ is centered. The only other possible centered 3-path is $\{(u, t), (t, w), (w, v)\}$. Because $v \prec t$, this path cannot be centered. That completes the proof for the induced 4-cycle case.

Now, suppose t, u, v, w forms an induced chordal-4-cycle. The extra 3-paths contain the chord in the middle, and such 3-paths do not lie on a 4-cycle. So there only exists one centered 3-path.

A 4-clique contains three 4-cycles that partition the 12 different 3-paths. Each of these 4-cycles has a centered 3-path, yielding a total of three such 3-paths. □

We now show how to sample a uniform random centered 3-path. It is quite analogous to `sample`. First, some notation. Let $L_{u,v}$ be the number of neighbors of u greater than v. By sorting all adjacency lists according to vertex degree and id, we can compute for every edge $e = (u, v)$, the value $\lambda_e = L_{u,v} L_{v,u}$. Let $\Lambda = \sum_e \lambda_e$.

Algorithm 3: `sample-centered`

```
Compute λ_e for all edges and set p_e = λ_e/Λ.
Pick edge e = (u, v) with probability p_e.
Pick uniform random neighbor u' of u such that v ≺ u'.
Pick uniform random neighbor v' of v such that u ≺ v'.
Output the three edges {(u', u), (u, v), (v, v')}.
```

Note that it is possible that `sample-centered` outputs a 3-path that is not centered (if the 3-path does not lie on a 4-cycle). Nonetheless, analogous to Claim 3.1, we have the following.

CLAIM 4.3. *Fix any centered 3-path. The probability that* `sample-centered` *outputs this 3-path is exactly* $1/\Lambda$.

Now, we give the algorithm that estimates the number of cycle-based motifs. It is analogous to `3-path-sampler`, only using centered 3-paths. For convenience, let B_i denote the number of centered 3-paths in the ith motif. So $B_4 = B_5 = 1$ and $B_6 = 3$, by Lemma 4.2.

Algorithm 4: `centered-sampler`
Input: graph $G = (V, E)$, samples k

```
Run sample-centered k times to get k set of edges. Let
  T_ℓ denote the set of corresponding edges for the ℓth set.
Initialize count_i = 0 for i ∈ [4, 6].
For ℓ ∈ [1, k],
    If T_ℓ is a centered 3-path,
        Determine subgraph induced by S_ℓ.
        If this is the ith motif, increment count_i.
For each i ∈ [4, 6],
    Set Ĉ_i = (count_i/k) · (Λ/B_i).
```

Analogous to Theorem 3.4, we can prove the following. Observe how W is replaced by Λ.

THEOREM 4.4. *Fix $\delta, \varepsilon \in (0,1)$ and set $k = \lceil (2\varepsilon)^{-2} \ln(2/\delta) \rceil$. For all $i \in [4,6]$: with probability at least $1-\delta$, $|\widehat{C}_i - C_i| < \varepsilon\Lambda/B_i$.*

For the same number of samples, the performance of `centered-sampler` requires an additional logarithmic factor because of additional preprocessing. In general, d_v is much smaller than n (and is effectively constant for most vertices), so the additional logarithmic factor is not too expense. We require fewer samples for the same accuracy, so `centered-sampler` wins at scale.

THEOREM 4.5. *The running time of* `centered-sampler` *is $O(\sum_v d_v \log d_v + k \log k)$ and the total storage is $O(m+k)$.*

PROOF. As discussed earlier, we need to sort the adjacency lists to determine each value of λ_e. That leads the running time bound. We store adjacency lists as (variable sized) array. This allows us to sort a list of size d_v in time $O(d_v \log d_v)$. The total running time of this step is $O(\sum_v d_v \log d_v)$. Once the lists are sorted, the remaining analysis is identical to that of Theorem 3.5 for `3-path-sampler`. □

4.1 Why centered 3-paths help

We put the value of W and Λ for various real world networks in Tab. 2. Observe how Λ is at least an order of magnitude smaller than W. This is a huge difference when it comes to the sampling bounds in Theorem 3.4 and Theorem 4.4. These bounds show that *two orders of magnitude less samples* suffice for the same error (in estimating cycle-based motifs). This improvement is extremely significant for getting good accuracy with fewer samples.

Table 2: Difference between the number of 3-paths and the number of centered 3-paths.

Graph	W	Λ	W/Λ
amazon0312	1.40E+09	9.36E+07	15
amazon0505	1.59E+09	1.02E+08	16
amazon0601	1.57E+09	1.01E+08	15
as-skitter	1.43E+12	9.05E+10	16
cit-Patents	9.16E+09	8.78E+08	10
web-BerkStan	1.69E+12	1.28E+11	13
web-Google	2.05E+10	6.34E+08	32
web-Stanford	1.85E+11	1.36E+10	14
wiki-Talk	1.31E+12	9.08E+09	144
youtube	1.19E+11	1.68E+09	71
flickr	1.31E+13	8.42E+11	16
livejournal	1.67E+12	1.14E+11	15
orkut	2.22E+13	9.48E+11	23

The final algorithm is simply obtained by running both `3-path-sampler` and `centered-sampler`. The former gives estimates for C_1, C_2, C_3 (we simply discard the remaining estimates), and the latter estimates C_4, C_5, C_6.

5. GETTING PRACTICAL ERROR BARS

While the Hoeffding bound used above provides theoretical convergence, we do not get practical error bars from it. In this section, we show how to get useful error bars for our algorithm on real instances.

All of our sampling algorithms have the same underlying primitive: try to estimate the expectation p of a Bernoulli random variable. We generate a binomial random variable $X \sim B(k,p)$ (by performing k i.i.d. Bernoulli trials), and hope that the outcome is close enough to the expectation.

We employ a standard Bayesian viewpoint to generate an error bar. Suppose, our outcome of the binomial draw is $X = r$. Conditioned on a choice of p, we calculate the probability that $X = r$. This gives a prior on p. Of course, this cannot be done explicitly because of computational issues, but we can use tail bounds for $B(k,p)$ to get appropriate estimates. We use the following theorem of Chernoff [8] (we use notation of Equation 1.4 from [11]) that gives good tail bounds for $B(k,p)$.

THEOREM 5.1 (CHERNOFF). *Suppose $X \sim B(k,p)$. Fix $\alpha \in (0,1)$.*

$$\Pr[X/k \geq \alpha] \leq \exp(-D(\alpha,p)k) \quad \text{if } \alpha > p$$
$$\Pr[X/k \leq \alpha] \leq \exp(-D(\alpha,p)k) \quad \text{if } \alpha < p$$

where $D(a,b) = a\ln(a/b) + (1-a)\ln((1-a)/(1-b))$ (the KL-divergence between Bernoulli distributions with expectation a and b).

Suppose the outcome of $X/k = \alpha$. We can use the Chernoff bound to get a range of likely values of p. Think of $\exp(-D(\alpha,p)k)$ as a function of p. The basic properties of the KL-divergence (and simple algebra) imply that $\exp(-D(\alpha,p)k)$ is a unimodal function with a maximum value of 1 at $p = \alpha$ and a minimum of 0 at $p = 0, 1$. That motivates the following definition.

DEFINITION 5.2. *Fix parameters $k, \alpha, x \in (0,1)$. Then $p_l(k,\alpha,x)$ (lower) and $p_u(k,\alpha,x)$ (upper) are the two unique values of p such that $\exp(-D(\alpha,p)k) = x$.*

With this definition, we can give precise error bars. In other words, given the outcome of a binomial random variable $B(k,p)$, we can give an interval of plausible values (up to any desired confidence δ) for p.

COROLLARY 5.3 (BINOMIAL DISTRIBUTION ERROR BAR). *Fix binomial distribution $B(k,p)$, and $\alpha, \delta \in (0,1)$ Then, for any $p \notin [p_l(k,\alpha,\delta), p_u(k,\alpha,\delta)]$,*

$$\Pr_{X \sim B(k,p)}[X/k = \alpha] \leq \delta$$

How does this relate to our algorithms? Observe that in both Alg. 2 and Alg. 4, the variables $count_i$ are binomial random variables. So we can produce errors bars for $count_i/k$ using the above corollary. The final estimates are of the form $\widehat{C}_i = (count_i/k) \cdot K_i$ ($i \neq 1$, and K_i is some fixed scaling, depending on the algorithm and i). So error bars for $count_i/k$ directly translate to error bars for $\widehat{C}_i$. For $i = 1$ (3-stars), we simply add up the errors (in `3-path-sampler`) for $\widehat{C}_3$, $2\widehat{C}_5$, and $4\widehat{C}_6$.

6. EXPERIMENTAL RESULTS

Preliminaries: We implemented our algorithms in `C` and ran our experiments on a computer equipped with a 2x2.4GHz Intel Xeon processor with 6 cores and 256KB L2 cache (per core), 12MB L3 cache, and 64GB memory. We performed our experiments on 13 graphs from SNAP [43]. In all cases, directionality is ignored, and duplicate edges are omitted.

Tab. 3 has the properties of these graphs, where $|V|$ and $|E|$ are the numbers of vertices and edges, respectively.

Exact counts for the motifs are obtained by a well-tuned enumeration (counts and runtime given in Tab. 3). This algorithm only enumerates the 4-cycle, the chordal-4-cycle, and the 4-clique, and uses direct approaches to get other counts. For convenience, we refer to this the *enumeration code*. We do not get into details, but note that this code processes million edge Amazon networks in only 5 seconds[1]. It uses vertex orderings for speedup, analogous to using degeneracy orderings for triangle enumeration [9, 29]. For getting 3-path sampling estimates, we run both **3-path-sampler** and **centered-sampler** as described earlier, with $k = 200K$. We use the outputs of $\widehat{C}_1, \widehat{C}_2, \widehat{C}_3$ as given by **3-path-sampler**, and $\widehat{C}_4, \widehat{C}_5, \widehat{C}_6$ from **centered-sampler**. The runtimes are in the last column of Tab. 3.

Convergence of estimates: To show convergence, we perform detailed runs on the as-skitter graph. We choose this because it is the most difficult to get accurate estimates, since the cycle-based motif counts are small relative to the graph size. We vary the numbers of samples in increments of 2.5K. For each choice of the number of samples, we perform 50 runs of our algorithm. We plot those results in Fig. 4 for tailed-triangles, chordal-4-cycles, and 4-cliques. (Other patterns are omitted due the space considerations, and had even better convergence.) The output of each run (for a given number of samples) is depicted by a blue dot. For 4-clique counts, we can see the spread of outputs reducing. The figure only goes up to 35K samples. (The convergence is so rapid that at around 50K samples, the spread is impossible to see.)

Accuracy: Fig. 2b presents the relative errors for all 13 graphs and all 6 motifs, using 200K samples for both **3-path-sampler** and **centered-sampler**. *All relative errors are less than 1% in all instances.* As expected the relative errors tend to be larger for the less frequent patterns such as 4-cycles and 4-cliques.

Speedup: Fig. 2a presented the speedups achieved over full enumeration by using our path sampling algorithm. Enumeration for flickr and orkut takes order of a day. Since the motifs counts are in the order of tens of billions, there is no hope of getting any scalability. Our algorithms takes less than a minute (even including I/O) for all these graphs.

The benefit of centered 3-paths: We could simply use the basic 3-path sampling given in **3-path-sampler** to approximate all counts. We compare this approach to our final algorithm that use **centered-sampler** for C_4, C_5, C_6 estimates. Comparisons between the relative errors for C_4, C_5, C_6 are given in Fig. 5. ("Basic" denotes simply using **3-path-sampler**, and "centered" is the main algorithm.) We used 200K samples for both algorithms. Some instances of using **3-path-sampler** give somewhat large errors, and **centered-sampler** really cuts these errors down. It shows the power of centered 3-path sampling.

Error bounds: We use Corollary 5.3 (as explained in §5) to compute 99% confidence error bounds for all of our runs. So, for a single run of our algorithm on a candidate graph, we have a mathematical bound on the error that is solely based on output estimates. (These are critical in the situation where we do not know the true answer, and need confidence that the estimates are accurate.) Fig. 6 shows the accuracy of our error bounds with 99% confidence, so $\delta = 0.01$ in Corollary 5.3. In all cases, the provable bounds on the error are always less than 10% and mostly at most 5%. (We stress that the actual error is much smaller.) To the best of our knowledge, no previous sampling based algorithm for motif counting comes with hard mathematical error bars that are practically reasonable.

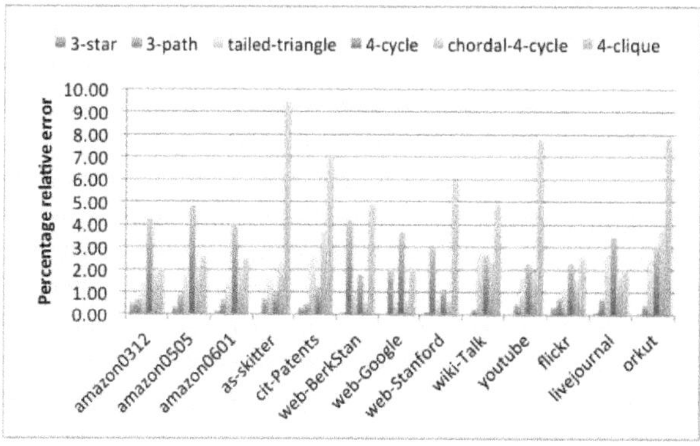

Figure 6: Provable error bounds

Trends in patterns: The most frequent connected induced motif is the 3-star. The least frequent is either the 4-cycle or the 4-clique. We find it intriguing that (among cycle-based motifs) the chordal-4-cycle is the most frequent. (The orkut graph is a notable exception in that 4-cycles are more frequent.) A future direction is to connect these counts with the subgraph frequency approaches of [37].

6.1 Comparison with previous work

Here we present an empirical comparison between our proposed methods and other sampling based algorithms. We focus on color coding methods [19, 4, 42], MCMC based sampling algorithms [5], and edge sampling algorithms [27]. These methods are specifically designed for practicality and scalability. We give a short synopsis of these methods.

GUISE [5]: This employs a Markov Chain Monte Carlo (MCMC) method to uniformly sample a motif from the space of all (induced) occurrences of motifs of sizes 3, 4, and 5. We use the implementation of GUISE from `http://cs.iupui.edu/~alhasan/software.html`.

GRAFT [27]: This algorithm samples a set of edges uniformly at random from the input graph and then counts the number of occurrences of each motif that uses any of these sampled edges. These counts can then be scaled appropriately to obtain unbiased estimates. Observe that if edges are sampled with probability 1, this gives an algorithm for exact counting using an edge iteration. For our experiments, we have used our own implementation.

Color Coding [1, 19, 4, 42]: This is a general technique for pattern counting, which samples to prune the enumeration search tree. We randomly color the vertices of the graph and then only enumerate over motifs all of whose vertices have distinct colors. These counts can be appropriately scaled to get unbiased estimates for the true frequencies. For our experiments, we implemented color coding (with 4 colors), and used the same algorithmic techniques that we used for our enumeration algorithm.

[1]This is quite competitive with the best existing numbers in the literature of [22], whose algorithm takes 40 minutes on a 90K autonomous systems graph.

Table 3: Exact values of pattern counts and runtimes (in seconds).

Datasets	$\|V\|$	$\|E\|$	3-star	3-path	Tailed triangle	4-cycle	Chordal 4-cycle	4-clique	Enum. time	3-path time
amazon0312	4.01E+5	2.35E+6	1.07E+10	8.44E+08	1.90E+08	3.23E+06	1.71E+07	3.98E+06	4.42	0.47
amazon0505	4.10E+5	2.44E+6	1.21E+10	9.63E+08	2.19E+08	3.30E+06	1.91E+07	4.36E+06	4.75	0.48
amazon0601	4.03E+5	2.44E+6	1.11E+10	9.41E+08	2.17E+08	3.22E+06	1.92E+07	4.42E+06	4.74	0.48
as-skitter	1.70E+6	1.11E+7	9.64E+13	8.19E+11	1.62E+11	4.27E+10	1.96E+10	1.49E+08	5128.93	2.7
cit-Patents	3.77E+6	1.65E+7	6.11E+9	6.54E+09	5.52E+08	2.69E+08	6.28E+07	3.50E+06	46.46	3.33
flickr	1.86E+6	1.56E+7	1.90E+13	6.89E+12	1.18E+11	1.18E+11	2.30E+11	2.67E+10	217274.39	2.53
livejournal	5.28E+6	4.87E+7	4.46E+12	1.14E+12	1.26E+11	5.21E+09	1.90E+10	1.14E+10	11894.63	6.86
orkut	3.07E+6	2.24E+8	9.78E+13	1.86E+13	1.51E+12	7.01E+10	4.78E+10	3.22E+09	70966.96	16.24
web-BerkStan	6.85E+5	6.65E+6	3.82E+14	3.14E+10	4.76E+11	2.53E+10	9.86E+10	1.07E+09	6462.56	3.77
web-Google	8.76E+5	4.32E+6	6.50E+11	4.06E+09	6.72E+09	3.80E+07	3.82E+08	3.99E+07	52.29	0.88
web-Stanford	2.82E+5	1.99E+6	2.51E+13	1.28E+10	5.08E+10	4.48E+09	8.60E+09	7.88E+07	831.50	1.76
wiki-Talk	2.39E+6	4.66E+6	1.92E+14	1.17E+12	6.41E+10	9.24E+08	1.03E+09	6.49E+07	1346.76	1.04
youtube	1.16E+6	4.95E+6	5.73E+12	9.15E+10	1.24E+10	2.32E+08	2.22E+08	4.99E+06	141.78	0.61

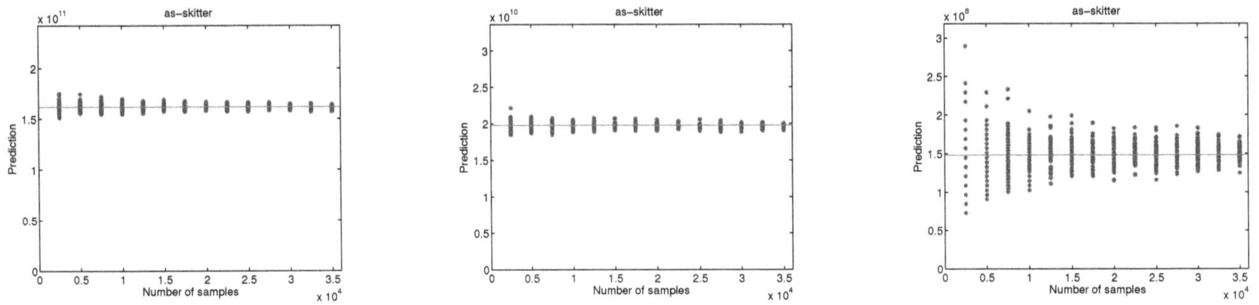

(a) tailed-triangle (b) chordal-4-cycle (c) 4-clique

Figure 4: Increasing number of samples decreases error: Each blue dot is an output of a run of the algorithm with the number of samples in the x-axis. The red line is the true count.

All these methods are quite general and work for motifs of any size. These algorithms are more general than our approach. But our focus on the specific six subgraphs in Fig. 1 allows for the design of faster and more accurate algorithms, that work better than these generic methods.

For a fair comparison, all running times for previous algorithms are for estimating frequencies of only the cycle-based motifs. (We are being conservative here, since we compare with the entire time for 3-path sampling.) Both GUISE and GRAFT take as input a number of samples. We ran GUISE for 10 million samples, since for fewer samples, the errors were usually around 100%. At 10 million samples, the running time was more than the enumeration cost (usually over 5 times that), so we simply terminated. We increased the number of samples for GRAFT until the errors were within 5% or the running time became larger than 5 times the enumeration cost. For moderately sized graphs, the enumeration running time is typically 2-3 orders of magnitude more than that of 3-path sampling. Color coding takes no parameters, and uses 4 colors.

Our results are summarized in Fig. 7 (running time comparison) and Tab. 4 (accuracy comparison). For ease of presentation, we focus on 4 graphs: as-skitter, cit-patents, web-Stanford, and wiki-Talk. These range from a million to 10 million edges. Our results were similar on other graphs. We present results for a single run of each algorithm. (We ran for numerous iterations, and all results were consistent.) In summary, our algorithm is many orders of magnitude faster and more accurate than these methods. We stress that these results are consistent with the literature, where previous methods were only employed on graphs with about 100K edges.

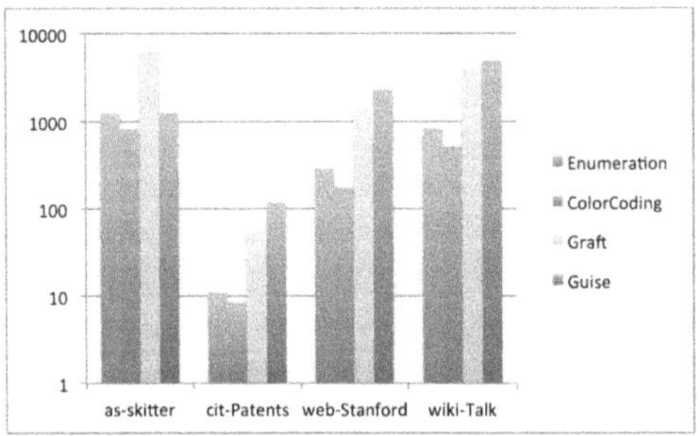

Figure 7: Runtimes of the existing algorithms normalized with respect to runtimes of 3-path sampling algorithm

Scalability and speed. Previous works either leverage Map-Reduce clusters or max out at a million (or so) edges. Our 3-path sampler runs on a single commodity machine with 64GB memory, and easily handles graphs with more than a hundred million edges.

Running time comparisons are in Fig. 7, where for each graph, we normalize by the running time of 3-path sampler. This figure is limited to only moderate sized graphs due to large runtimes of the other algorithms. At about a million edges, 3-path sampling is already hundreds of times faster than other algorithms. (As we explain in the next section and

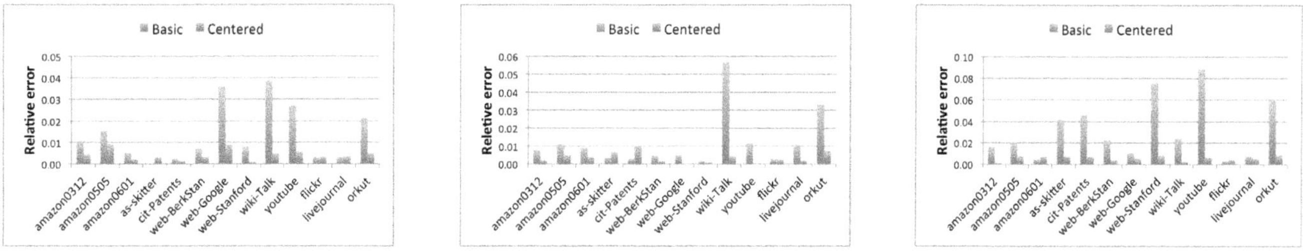

(a) 4-cycle (b) Chordal 4-cycle (c) 4-clique

Figure 5: Comparing the accuracy of estimations using basic 3-path sampling and centered 3-path sampling

Tab. 4, the accuracy of 3-path sampling is much better than GRAFT and GUISE, and comparable to color coding.) We note that our enumeration code is actually competitive with existing sampling algorithms. Color coding is consistently (a little) faster than enumeration. GUISE and GRAFT do not yield accurate approximations even when run for many multiples of the enumeration time. We believe that this is an issue of scale, since previous algorithm were not run for graphs with many millions of edges.

We provide some explanations for these runtimes. GRAFT provides a speedup over edge iteration enumeration procedures. However, edge-iteration algorithms are not the best methods for enumeration, as is well-known for triangle enumeration [29, 3]. Enumeration using vertex orderings is significantly faster. The same principles to apply to counting 4-vertex patterns. For small sizes (100K edges or less), GRAFT may give improvements over the best enumeration, but this is not true for larger sizes.

GUISE estimates the relative frequencies of the motifs, not the exact frequencies. GUISE has to perform relatively long random walks before it can obtain samples from the stationary distribution. This limits the number of samples that can be made. More problematically, the universe from which GUISE samples from uniformly is prohibitively large. In particular, focusing only on 4-vertex motifs, we see that (say for as-Skitter), the fraction of cliques in the universe of 4-vertex motifs is less than 10^{-6}. This means that roughly a million samples are needed to witness a single 4-clique, and the square of a million samples to estimate accurately.

Color coding is hindered by the sheer size of the output. Color coding cuts down the set of motifs by enumerating only polychromatic motifs (i.e. all vertices with distinct colors), but this set is still quite large. In particular, for 4-vertex motifs, the reduction of the output is only of the order of one-tenth (or 3/32 to be precise – the probability that four vertices of a motif all get different colors when using 4 colors). This means enumerating over a billion motifs in as-skitter, for example. There is also the extra overhead of actually searching through neighborhoods to perform this enumeration. We do see that color coding provides some benefit over enumeration, and is probably the best algorithm for 4-vertex pattern counting among previous work.

Accuracy. We present the accuracies of the various algorithms in Tab. 4. We focus on 4-clique counts for brevity. Even after running for times more than enumeration, GRAFT and GUISE give low accuracies. GUISE generally fails to even find a 4-clique, and GRAFT has not processed enough samples to converge. Color coding is extremely accurate, and 3-path sampling is competitive. But the running time of color coding is a hundred to thousand times that of 3-path sampling on these instances.

Table 4: Relative error in 4-clique count. For GUISE, we choose 10M samples. For GRAFT, we report the errors after running the algorithm for up to 5 times the enumeration time.

	3-path	Color Coding	Graft	Guise
as-skitter	0.7	0.1	95	99
cit-Patents	0.7	0.4	78	54
web-Stanford	0.8	0.8	29	99
wiki-Talk	0.3	0.5	5	99

7. CONCLUSIONS AND FUTURE WORK

We get accurate results for all 4-vertex motif frequencies on a large number of graphs, and believe this is useful for motif analyses. Previous work usually focuses on a small, specific set of larger motifs [19, 4, 42], or gives coarser approximations for more motifs [5]. It is natural to ask if we can extend this sampling scheme further to estimate counts of 5-vertex (or even higher order) motifs.

8. REFERENCES

[1] N. Alon, R. Yuster, and U. Zwick. Color-coding: A new method for finding simple paths, cycles and other small subgraphs within large graphs. In *Proceedings of the Twenty-sixth Annual ACM Symposium on Theory of Computing*, STOC '94, pages 326–335, New York, NY, USA, 1994. ACM.

[2] L. Becchetti, P. Boldi, C. Castillo, and A. Gionis. Efficient semi-streaming algorithms for local triangle counting in massive graphs. In *KDD'08*, pages 16–24, 2008.

[3] J. W. Berry, L. K. Fostvedt, D. J. Nordman, C. A. Phillips, C. Seshadhri, and A. G. Wilson. Why do simple algorithms for triangle enumeration work in the real world? In *Proceedings of the 5th Conference on Innovations in Theoretical Computer Science*, ITCS '14, pages 225–234, New York, NY, USA, 2014. ACM.

[4] N. Betzler, R. van Bevern, M. R. Fellows, C. Komusiewicz, and R. Niedermeier. Parameterized algorithmics for finding connected motifs in biological networks. *IEEE/ACM Trans. Comput. Biology Bioinform.*, 8(5):1296–1308, 2011.

[5] M. Bhuiyan, M. Rahman, M. Rahman, and M. A. Hasan. Guise: Uniform sampling of graphlets for large

graph analysis. In *Proceedings of International Conference on Data Mining*, pages 91–100, 2012.

[6] M. A. Bhuiyan and M. A. Hasan. Mirage: An iterative mapreduce based frequent subgraph mining algorithm. Technical report, arXiv, 2013. `http://arxiv.org/pdf/1307.5894.pdf`.

[7] R. Burt. Structural holes and good ideas. *American Journal of Sociology*, 110(2):349–399, 2004.

[8] H. Chernoff. A measure of asymptotic efficiency for test of a hypothesis based on the sum of observations. *Annals of mathematical statistics*, 23:493–507, 1952.

[9] N. Chiba and T. Nishizeki. Arboricity and subgraph listing algorithms. *SIAM J. Comput.*, 14:210–223, 1985.

[10] J. Coleman. Social capital in the creation of human capital. *American Journal of Sociology*, 94:S95–S120, 1988.

[11] D. Dubhashi and A. Panconesi. *Concentration of Measure for the Analysis of Randomized Algorithms.* Cambridge University Press, 2009.

[12] N. Durak, A. Pinar, T. G. Kolda, and C. Seshadhri. Degree relations of triangles in real-world networks and graph models. In *CIKM'12*, 2012.

[13] G. Fagiolo. Clustering in complex directed networks. *Phys. Rev. E*, 76:026107, Aug 2007.

[14] K. Faust. A puzzle concerning triads in social networks: Graph constraints and the triad census. *Social Networks*, 32(3):221–233, 2010.

[15] M. Gonen and Y. Shavitt. Approximating the number of network motifs. *Internet Mathematics*, 6(3):349–372, 2009.

[16] D. Hales and S. Arteconi. Motifs in evolving cooperative networks look like protein structure networks. *NHM*, 3(2):239–249, 2008.

[17] W. Hoeffding. Probability inequalities for sums of bounded random variables. *J. American Statistical Association*, 58:13–30, 1963.

[18] P. Holland and S. Leinhardt. A method for detecting structure in sociometric data. *American Journal of Sociology*, 76:492–513, 1970.

[19] F. Hormozdiari, P. Berenbrink, N. Pr̆ulj, and S. C. Sahinalp. Not all scale-free networks are born equal: The role of the seed graph in ppi network evolution. *PLoS Computational Biology*, 118, 2007.

[20] S. Itzkovitz, R. Levitt, N. Kashtan, R. Milo, M. Itzkovitz, and U. Alon. Coarse-graining and self-dissimilarity of complex networks. 71(016127), January 2005.

[21] T. G. Kolda, A. Pinar, T. Plantenga, C. Seshadhri, and C. Task. Counting triangles in massive graphs with MapReduce. *SIAM Journal of Scientific Computing*, 2013. To appear.

[22] D. Marcus and Y. Shavitt. Efficient counting of network motifs. In *ICDCS Workshops*, pages 92–98. IEEE Computer Society, 2010.

[23] R. Milo, S. Shen-Orr, S. Itzkovitz, N. Kashtan, D. Chklovskii, and U. Alon. Network motifs: Simple building blocks of complex networks. *Science*, 298(5594):824–827, 2002.

[24] T. Plantenga. Inexact subgraph isomorphism in mapreduce. *Journal of Parallel and Distributed Computing*, (0), 2012.

[25] A. Portes. Social capital: Its origins and applications in modern sociology. *Annual Review of Sociology*, 24(1):1–24, 1998.

[26] N. Przulj, D. G. Corneil, and I. Jurisica. Modeling interactome: scale-free or geometric?. *Bioinformatics*, 20(18):3508–3515, 2004.

[27] M. Rahman, M. A. Bhuiyan, and M. A. Hasan. Graft: An efficient graphlet counting method for large graph analysis. *IEEE Transactions on Knowledge and Data Engineering*, PP(99), 2014.

[28] T. Schank and D. Wagner. Approximating clustering coefficient and transitivity. *Journal of Graph Algorithms and Applications*, 9:265–275, 2005.

[29] T. Schank and D. Wagner. Finding, counting and listing all triangles in large graphs, an experimental study. In *Experimental and Efficient Algorithms*, pages 606–609. Springer Berlin / Heidelberg, 2005.

[30] C. Seshadhri, T. G. Kolda, and A. Pinar. Community structure and scale-free collections of Erdös-Rényi graphs. *Physical Review E*, 85(5):056109, May 2012.

[31] C. Seshadhri, A. Pinar, and T. G. Kolda. Fast triangle counting through wedge sampling. In *Proceedings of the SIAM Conference on Data Mining*, 2013.

[32] S. Son, A. Kang, H. Kim, T. Kwon, J. Park, and H. Kim. Analysis of context dependence in social interaction networks of a massively multiplayer online role-playing game. *PLoS ONE*, 7(4):e33918, 04 2012.

[33] M. Szell and S. Thurner. Measuring social dynamics in a massive multiplayer online game. *Social Networks*, 32:313–329, 2010.

[34] C. Tsourakakis, P. Drineas, E. Michelakis, I. Koutis, and C. Faloutsos. Spectral counting of triangles in power-law networks via element-wise sparsification. In *ASONAM'09*, pages 66–71, 2009.

[35] C. Tsourakakis, M. N. Kolountzakis, and G. Miller. Triangle sparsifiers. *J. Graph Algorithms and Applications*, 15:703–726, 2011.

[36] C. E. Tsourakakis, U. Kang, G. L. Miller, and C. Faloutsos. Doulion: counting triangles in massive graphs with a coin. In *Knowledge Data and Discovery (KDD)*, pages 837–846, 2009.

[37] J. Ugander, L. Backstrom, and J. M. Kleinberg. Subgraph frequencies: mapping the empirical and extremal geography of large graph collections. In D. Schwabe, V. A. F. Almeida, H. Glaser, R. A. Baeza-Yates, and S. B. Moon, editors, *WWW*, pages 1307–1318. International World Wide Web Conferences Steering Committee / ACM, 2013.

[38] A. Walker. Walker, a. j. (1977). "an efficient method for generating discrete random variables with general distributions. *ACM Transactions on Mathematical Software (TOMS)*, 3(3):253–256, 1977.

[39] D. Watts and S. Strogatz. Collective dynamics of 'small-world' networks. *Nature*, 393:440–442, 1998.

[40] B. Welles, A. Van Devender, and N. Contractor. Is a friend a friend?: Investigating the structure of friendship networks in virtual worlds. In *CHI-EA'10*, pages 4027–4032, 2010.

[41] E. Wong, B. Baur, S. Quader, and C.-H. Huang. Biological network motif detection: principles and practice. *Briefings in Bioinformatics*, 13(2):202–215, 2012.

[42] Z. Zhao, G. Wang, A. Butt, M. Khan, V. S. A. Kumar, and M. Marathe. Sahad: Subgraph analysis in massive networks using hadoop. In *Proceedings of International Parallel and Distributed Processing Symposium (IPDPS)*, pages 390–401, 2012.

[43] Stanford Network Analysis Project (SNAP). Available at `http://snap.stanford.edu/`.

Automatic Online Evaluation of Intelligent Assistants

Jiepu Jiang[1*], Ahmed Hassan Awadallah[2], Rosie Jones[2], Umut Ozertem[2], Imed Zitouni[2], Ranjitha Gurunath Kulkarni[2] and Omar Zia Khan[2]

[1] Center for Intelligent Information Retrieval, University of Massachusetts Amherst
[2] Microsoft Redmond, WA USA

jpjiang@cs.umass.edu, {hassanam, rosie.jones, umuto, izitouni, raguruna, omarzia.khan}@microsoft.com

ABSTRACT

Voice-activated intelligent assistants, such as Siri, Google Now, and Cortana, are prevalent on mobile devices. However, it is challenging to evaluate them due to the varied and evolving number of tasks supported, e.g., voice command, web search, and chat. Since each task may have its own procedure and a unique form of correct answers, it is expensive to evaluate each task individually. This paper is the first attempt to solve this challenge. We develop consistent and automatic approaches that can evaluate different tasks in voice-activated intelligent assistants. We use implicit feedback from users to predict whether users are satisfied with the intelligent assistant as well as its components, i.e., speech recognition and intent classification. Using this approach, we can potentially evaluate and compare different tasks within and across intelligent assistants according to the predicted user satisfaction rates. Our approach is characterized by an automatic scheme of categorizing user-system interaction into task-independent dialog actions, e.g., the user is commanding, selecting, or confirming an action. We use the action sequence in a session to predict user satisfaction and the quality of speech recognition and intent classification. We also incorporate other features to further improve our approach, including features derived from previous work on web search satisfaction prediction, and those utilizing acoustic characteristics of voice requests. We evaluate our approach using data collected from a user study. Results show our approach can accurately identify satisfactory and unsatisfactory sessions.

Categories and Subject Descriptors

H.5.2 [**Information Interfaces and Presentation**]: User Interfaces – *evaluation/methodology, interaction styles, voice I/O.*

Keywords

Voice-activated intelligent assistant; evaluation; user experience; mobile search; spoken dialog system.

1. INTRODUCTION

Intelligent assistants are becoming a prevalent feature on mobile devices. They provide voice control and feedback to mobile device functions (e.g., making phone calls, calendar management, finding places). Users can also search the web or even chat with intelligent assistants. While these novel applications are useful and attractive for users, it is challenging to evaluate and compare them due to the large variability of tasks.

Evaluation is a central component of many related applications, e.g., search engines, Q&A systems, and recommendation systems. These applications are usually evaluated by comparing system-generated answers with "correct" answers labeled by human annotators. For example, in web search, we annotate relevant webpages and evaluate using metrics such as mean average precision (MAP) and normalized discounted cumulative gain (nDCG) [14].

However, intelligent assistants differ from these applications in that they can involve a wide variety of tasks, ranging from making phone calls and managing calendars, to finding places, finding answers to general questions, and web search. These tasks have different forms of "correct" answers. It is expensive to evaluate each task separately using different human judgments and metrics. It is also difficult to use one single setup to evaluate all tasks. In addition, the tasks performed can be personal in nature and the performance of the system depends heavily on users. These factors make it challenging to conduct manual ground-truth-based evaluation.

To solve these challenges, we adopt approaches similar to recent studies of user satisfaction prediction in web search [1, 3, 6, 7, 17, 32]. These studies developed alternative evaluation approaches by finding and using correlation between explicit ratings of user experience and implicit behavioral signals such as click and dwell time [4, 7]. However, we cannot simply apply user behavior signals in web search to evaluate intelligent assistants due to the wider range and different nature of tasks. These tasks may involve a variety of user intents, diverse topics, and distinct user interaction modes. For example, the process of making a phone call, or navigating to a place, involves a dialog style conversation between user and system, with user requests and system responses very different from those in web search. In addition, intelligent assistants heavily use voice interactions, and it is important to consider the voice signal to assess user experience.

We introduce a model for evaluating user experience in voice-activated intelligent assistants. We consider satisfaction as the major indicator of user experience because our study shows that it is consistently correlated with changes in user interests towards the system. Our model predicts whether the user has satisfactory or unsatisfactory experience with an intelligent assistant based on user interaction patterns. Once the model is trained, it can evaluate real traffic of intelligent assistants without human judgments of correct answers for tasks. This makes it a useful and cheap evaluation approach for intelligent assistants' developers, who have abundant user traffic and user logs. Our model includes a sub-model for automatically classifying user-system interaction into dialog actions, a Markov model over action transitions, as well as features related to requests, responses, clicks, and those using acoustic signals.

Our contributions can be summarized as follows:

- An accurate model for predicting user satisfaction with an intelligent assistant and its components, i.e., speech recognition and intent classification.
- A scheme of categorizing user-system interaction into task-independent dialog actions, and a model to automatically map different actions to this scheme.
- Analysis of user behavior and patterns indicating user experience in intelligent assistants.

---

* Work done during an internship at Microsoft Research

WWW 2015, May 18–22, 2015, Florence, Italy.
ACM 978-1-4503-3469-3/15/05.
http://dx.doi.org/10.1145/2736277.2741669

2. RELATED WORK

There are a number of areas of related work relevant to the research described in this paper. These include (1) methods and metrics for the evaluation of search systems, (2) inferring satisfaction from observed search behavior and (3) dialog act modeling and classification in conversational speech. We cover these in turn in this section.

User behavior modeling has been used extensively for evaluating search systems [1, 4, 6, 7]. Traditionally search system have been evaluated using retrieval metrics such as MAP and nDCG [14], where a collection of documents, queries and human labeled relevance judgments are used to evaluate search system performance. These metrics are expensive to collect and potentially noisy, given that third-party judges have limited knowledge of the individual user's intent. Additionally, these metrics are query-based. Previous research has shown that search tasks often contain multiple queries related to the same information need [7]. Unfortunately the connections between these queries are ignored by these metrics. Session-based DCG (sDCG) [15] does consider the session-context, but still requires manual relevance judgments.

Another line of research has focused on using implicit feedback from user behavior to evaluate search engine. These methods have lower cost, are more scalable, and sourced from the actual users.

Early research on implicit feedback [4] used an instrumented browser to determine if there was an association between explicit ratings of user satisfaction and implicit measures of user interest and identified the measures that were strongly associated with user satisfaction. Huffman and Hochster [13] found a strong correlation with session satisfaction using a linear model encompassing the relevance of the first three results returned for the first query in a search task, whether the information need was navigational, and the number of events in the session. Hassan et al. [7] developed models of user behavior to accurately estimate search success using action sequences of user behavior and showed that this yields better performance compared to models derived from the query-URL relevance of top-ranked results for the first query in a task. Follow-up studies showed that satisfaction ratings can be collected in-situ from users [9] and that action sequence models can be learned in a semi-supervised manner from both labeled and unlabeled data [6]. Ageev and colleagues [1] augmented this approach with additional search features. They also used a game-like strategy for collecting labeled data by asking participants to find answers to questions using web search. All these methods focus on analyzing user behavior when interacting with traditional search systems.

In this work, we extend this line of work by presenting the first study, to the best of our knowledge, of user behavior patterns when interacting with intelligent assistants. We study the action sequences performed by the users and jointly model them with the actions performed by the system to predict user satisfaction. We also study features specifically related to voice input and propose methods to analyze the root cause of dissatisfaction.

Perhaps the biggest difference between traditional web search and intelligent assistants is their conversational nature. In many scenarios, intelligent assistants can refer to the previous requests to understand the user better; e.g. "show me weather in mountain view" followed by "how about in palo alto", or "Italian restaurants nearby" and "which ones are 4-stars or above". Therefore spoken dialog systems research is closely related to intelligent assistants. Spoken dialog systems interpret and respond to spoken commands by implementing dialog strategies [2], and the field has seen steady progress over the past two decades [29]. Since they use speech as the primary (or only) form of user communication, they provide error correction mechanisms to account for the potential errors in the automatic speech recognizer (ASR) output. Recently, partially observable Markov decision Processes (POMDP) has established itself as a solid foundation for managing dialogues, and a comprehensive review can be found in [33].

Since they also support other forms of interactions, intelligent assistants differ from traditional spoken dialog systems. In addition to voice system response, intelligent assistants provide answers or options in the display, and users can type in the requests and select a displayed result or option. In this sense, intelligent assistants are related to multi-modal conversational systems [11, 20, 30].

Note that many different taxonomies of dialog acts have been proposed [28]. We do not intend here to propose a new one, but rather to model user and system interaction with the goal of predicting user satisfaction. Our model of system interaction and user is designed independently from any dialog model the system uses. Hence, it is independent of any specific implementation. In contrast with work on learning dialog model transitions [27] we do not attempt to model the most likely dialog sequence, but to use the dialog sequence to model user satisfaction. Our work differs from previous work in offline evaluation of dialog systems [31], as we do not require manual transcription of speech, and thus once trained, our models can be run online, at-scale, evaluating voice assistants in an automated, unsupervised fashion.

3. INTELLIGENT ASSISTANTS

Intelligent assistants are emerging and evolving applications lacking a precise definition. Related products are usually referred to as "intelligent personal assistants", "mobile assistant", "virtual personal assistant", "voice assistant" etc. Also it is unclear to what ends and how frequently people use them. To clarify the goal of evaluation, we need to first study their functionalities and the scenarios they support. This section studies these questions. Due to too many related applications, we restrict our scope as follows:

1. We only consider intelligent assistants on mobile devices.
2. We do not consider proactive suggestions based on personal information, such as displaying flight status automatically if the user received an email about it, or showing traffic and time-to-leave reminders based on daily commute patterns. Evaluating this functionality is outside our scope since it requires long term studies to collect personal information from users' emails, GPS signal, etc.

3.1 Functionality

We picked five representative intelligent assistant products, including Apple Siri, Google Now, Microsoft Cortana, Samsung S Voice, and Nuance Dragon. After extensive usage of these applications, we summarize three major functionalities of intelligent assistants:

1. Device+dialog. This includes using voice commands to access device functions and other tasks using dialog style interaction. For example, users can say "call James" to make a phone call, or ask "do I have any meetings tomorrow?" to check calendars directly. Rich information dialogs, such as "weather in Florence" to check the weather, are also included here. All the five products provide this functionality, but the specific supported features may differ.
2. Web search. All the five products support web search using voice input. Apart from Siri, the other four support a combination of voice and text input. Also, it is usually the last resort to handle user requests: if the intelligent assistant fails to understand a request, it will handle it as a query for web search.
3. Chat. Users can talk to intelligent assistants for fun. Many intelligent assistants have pre-defined interesting responses for popular user questions. For example, if the user asks Cortana "who is your father", the response could be "technically speaking, that'd be Bill Gates. No big deal." All products apart from Google Now support chat.

Another angle of comparison is the types of input they support. All five products support voice input, and all except Siri support text input.

Table 1. Top 5 requests (speech recognition results) and proportion of each domain in a sample of Cortana user logs in April, 2014. Web search and other requests takes 30.7% and 0.6% of the data (do not show examples of requests here due to limited space).

Chat (21.4%)	Device Control (13.3%)	Communication (12.3%)	Location (9.2%)	Calendar (8.7%)	Weather (3.8%)
tell me a joke	play music	call	where am I	set alarm	in Celsius
do you like clippy	play	call mom	find a library	show my alarms	do I need a coat
hello	open facebook	call my wife	I'm hungry	wake me up	what's the weather
sing me a song	open whatsapp	text	where I am	wake me up in twenty minutes	what's the weather like
what's your name	stop music	call my mom	take me home	remind me	what's the weather today

3.2 Usage Analysis

We further study the scenarios of using intelligent assistants. We limit our scope to Cortana due to data access. We randomly sampled 70K sessions from Cortana's user logs during April, 2014. Note that during this time-range, Cortana was demonstrated for the first time, was not yet commercially available, and early-adopter developers were trying out Cortana to explore the functionality. Here a session refers to a sequence of requests from the same user, in which the interval of two adjacent requests does not exceed 30 minutes. This setting is similar to many previous web search studies [10, 23]. We annotated the underlying tasks of the user requests and summarized them into several domains. Web search and chat are two open domains. We also categorize requests to device+dialog functions into the following topics:

- Device control, e.g. launch apps, and play music.
- Communication, e.g. make phone calls, send text message.
- Location, i.e., find or navigate to certain places.
- Calendar, e.g. check calendar, create reminder, and set alarm.
- Weather, i.e., check weather conditions.
- Other: all other supported requests, e.g. taking notes.

Table 1 shows the five most frequent requests and proportion of requests for each domain in the sampled Cortana log (we do not show examples of web search and other requests due to limited space). About half of the requests (47.9%) are accessing device+dialog functions. Web search and chat take 30.7% and 21.4% respectively. In the following discussion, we also refer to them as "device+dialog function tasks", "web search tasks", and "chat tasks".

Note that the domains of requests and their popularity largely depend on the features supported by specific intelligent assistants and the way they are implemented. Therefore, the statistics in Table 1 may not be generalized to other intelligent assistants. Besides, they are also not necessarily representative of Cortana's requests today because the log is sampled from the very early period when Cortana was first put to public test. However, this is the best we can access at the time of the study. Despite the limitations, these domains and topics are still representative because all the five products support them (except that Google Now does not support chat). Therefore, our approach should cover these tasks and domains.

3.3 Goal of Evaluation

Based on the analysis in this section, we come to the following goals of evaluating intelligent assistants.

1. The evaluation approach should be able to work well on the three major tasks as well as the five popular domains.

2. We should evaluate not only the intelligent assistant as a whole, but also its important components separately. Intelligent assistants need to first recognize user requests (may include voice input) and then classify the intent (e.g., identify task and context information). We consider two components in this paper, i.e., automatic speech recognition (ASR) and intent classification.

3. The evaluation measure should be generic and task-independent. This is important because, unlike many applications, it is difficult and expensive to collect ground truth data to evaluate intelligent assistants, since they do not have a consistent form of correct answers for different tasks. For example, for "call James", the correct answer is to understand the intent and the correct person, but for "remind me for a meeting tomorrow at 3pm", the correct answer is the intent and the event information (e.g., theme and time). Without a task-independent evaluation measure, we would need to collect ground truth data for each scenario, which is expensive.

Table 2. Examples of task descriptions.

Type	Description
Device-Dialog Function	You are stuck in very heavy traffic and it seems you will be late for your meeting with James. Use Cortana to send James a text message explaining the situation (James is a contact stored in your phone).
Web Search	Check the exchange rate between US dollars and Australian dollars.
Chat	Talk to Cortana as if she is a real person. Try to make a conversation with her for about 2 minutes.

To make the approach task-independent, we evaluate intelligent assistants by solving the following classification problem:

Given user interaction information of a session, can we identify whether the user is satisfied or not with the intelligent assistant (or its speech recognition and intent classification)?

Using this approach, we can evaluate and compare intelligent assistants by the predicted percentage of satisfactory sessions. This makes the evaluation measure task-independent. As Section 6 will show, user satisfaction is a user experience measure with consistent correlation with changes in user interests towards the product. We conduct a user study to collect user behavior and satisfaction ratings in intelligent assistant tasks, which will be introduced in Section 4.

4. USER STUDY

This section introduces a user experiment to collect user behavior and ratings in different intelligent assistant tasks.

4.1 Participants

We recruited 60 participants through emails sent to a mailing list of an IT company located in the United States. All participants were college or graduate students interning at the company. Their average age was 22.97 (SD=3.45). Among these participants, 35% were female and 58.3% were native English speakers. We asked the participants to rate their spoken English proficiency on a 5-point Likert scale (5 means the highest). For those who are not English native speakers, the average rating was 4.24 (SD=0.66). They were reimbursed $10 gift card for participating in a half-hour experiment.

4.2 Tasks

Each participant finished 10 tasks, including: 4 web search tasks, 1 chat task, and 5 device+dialog function tasks (1 for each of the five domains). This makes the distribution of tasks and domains similar to those shown in Table 1. In total we developed 12 web search tasks, 15 device+dialog function tasks (3 for each domain), and 1 chat task. We rotated the assignment of web search tasks and device+dialog function tasks such that 20 participants worked on each unique task. The chat task is usually open-ended, so we assigned the same chat task (presented in Table 2) to all participants. We also rotated task sequence using a Latin Square. Table 2 shows examples of task descriptions. Detailed descriptions of tasks can be accessed at http://aka.ms/intelligent_assistant_tasks.

Table 3. An example of user requests, system responses, and annotated action types in a satisfactory (SAT) session.

#	User Request	System Response	User Action	System Action
1	"Cortana call James"	"Sure, call James Smith mobile, is that right?"	Command	Confirm
2	"Yes"	"Calling James Smith, mobile." [call the contact]	Yes	Execute

Table 4. An example of user requests, system responses, and annotated action types in a dissatisfactory (DSAT) session.

#	User Request	System Response	User Action	System Action
1	"Where is the nearest pharmacy"	"Here are 8 pharmacies near you." [show options on the screen]	Command	Option
2	"Send me the directions to block sponsee" (Show me the directions to Clark's pharmacy)	"Sorry, I couldn't find anything for 'Send me the directions to block sponsee.' Do you wanna search the web for it?"	Select	Confirm
3	"No"	"Here are 8 pharmacies near you." [show options on the screen]	No	Option
4	"Directions to Clark's pharmacy"	"OK, getting you directions to Clark's Pharmacy." [navigation]	Select	Execute

4.3 Device and Environment

Participants worked on the tasks using a Windows phone with the latest version of Windows Phone 8.1 and Cortana installed. If the task needed to access some device resources or functions, they were installed to make sure users would not encounter problems. The experiment was conducted in a quiet room, so that we can reduce the disturbance of environment noise. Although real application environment often involves noise and interruption, we eliminated those factors to simplify the experiment.

4.4 Procedure

The participants were first asked to watch a video introducing Cortana (about 3 minutes long) and to complete a background survey. Then, they worked on a training task and 10 formal tasks. We instructed them that they could stop a task when they had accomplished the goal or if they became frustrated and wanted to give up. Finally, they answered a feedback survey and a short interview. The total experiment time was about 30 minutes.

For each task, we first verbally described the task scenario to the participants. The participants were not shown the task description while they are working on the task, because in an earlier pilot study, many participants directly read the sentences shown in task descriptions as requests. To encourage them to use free form commands and queries, we switched to verbal descriptions. When the participants worked on the task, they were allowed to issue both voice and text requests, reformulate requests, and interact with results (e.g., tapping a result to read more details). After terminating a task, they answered questions regarding their experience in this task session. In this paper, we mainly used their answers to the following three questions:

- How satisfied are you with your experience in this task?
- How well did Cortana recognize what you said?
- How well did Cortana understand your intent?

Responses to the three questions are referred to as ratings of user satisfaction, ASR quality, and intent classification quality. We did not specifically instruct participants the definition of intent classification, and the ratings are purely based on user's own understanding. Our goal is to predict these ratings in order to evaluate intelligent assistants. Participants answered these questions using a 5-point Likert scale (5 is the best and 1 the worst). In addition, we collected user ratings of frustration, goal success, and effort in each task. We also asked participants to report their interests in using Cortana twice: before they started with any task, and after they finished all the tasks. This helps us understand the relationship between user experience in individual tasks and changes in user interests towards an intelligent assistant product over time.

5. METHOD

This section introduces our approach. We assume the existence of a classifier that can accurately classify user sessions into three task types, i.e., device+dialog function, web search, and chat tasks. This assumption is reasonable because such classifiers have been readily implemented in most intelligent assistant products (such that they can handle requests for different types of tasks). We do not discuss how to implement such a classifier in this paper, because we focus on the evaluation models for different tasks. We train separate evaluation models for each task due to large task variability. When evaluating a session, we first classify its task type and then adopt the task's evaluation model to predict user satisfaction and the quality of ASR and intent classification.

This section introduces approaches and features for evaluating intelligent assistants. First, we introduce a way of characterizing user interaction in device+dialog function tasks. We classify requests and responses into action types and use action sequence to predict user satisfaction. Then, we introduce generic features for all tasks. We put more focus on device+dialog function tasks because few previous work addressed the challenge.

5.1 User and System Action

In device+dialog function tasks, users interact with intelligent assistant in a way similar to spoken dialog systems. A task session includes one to many rounds of user-system interactions. In each round the user issues a request and the system gives a response.

Table 3 shows an example of a satisfactory (SAT) device+dialog function task session. The user completed the task without any obstacles. In contrast, the system makes mistakes in speech recognition and/or intent classification in dissatisfactory (DSAT) sessions. It requires extra user interaction to correct the mistakes. Table 4 shows an example. The system did not recognize the user request in the second round and gave a useless suggestion for web search. It costs the user two more rounds to correct the error.

We categorize requests and responses into different types. We refer to these types as action types. Table 3 and Table 4 also show annotated action types. These action types are high level characterization of requests and responses ignoring the detailed contents. For example, we annotate both "Cortana call James" and "Where is the nearest pharmacy" as "Command", i.e., commanding the intelligent assistant to execute certain operations, despite the details of the operation are different.

These actions may indicate the status of the session. For example, when the system asks the user to confirm an operation (e.g. to call someone), a "Yes" action conveys the user's positive attitude to the system's response in the previous round and is indicative of SAT sessions, and vice versa. We show more analysis in Section 7.

Following previous work on dialog acts modeling [27], we define the following system (intelligent assistant) actions:

- **Execute**: executes an operation in this round.
- **Confirm**: asks the user whether or not to execute an operation.
- **Question**: asks the user a question for specific information.
- **Option**: provides a list of options and wait for user selection.
- **WebSearch**: searches the web using request content.
- **Error**: reports system error to the user, e.g., cannot understand the request, cannot find an answer, network error, etc.
- **NoAction**: does nothing and returns to the default interface. In Cortana, it happens when user declines to execute an operation.

And the following user actions:

- **Command**: commands the system to perform an operation.
- **Yes/No**: agrees or declines the system's confirmation.
- **Answer**: answers the system's questions.
- **Select**: selects an option provided by the system.

Here we define system actions based on the actual operation of the intelligent assistants in each round. For a specific product, one can simply define a rule to map operations to action types. In contrast, we only know limited content of user request. We need a classifier to identify user action types. For this purpose, we annotate the collected data and train a classifier for user action types using the following features:

- **QLength**: the number of words in the user request (ASR result). QLength is useful because we notice that "Yes/No" and "Select" are usually short, while "Command" and "Answer" are longer.
- **HasWordX**: whether the request (ASR result) includes a specific word X. We handcraft a list of "Yes" and "No" words for Cortana. The "Yes" words include: yes, yep, right, yeah, send, and call. The "No" words include: no, nope, and cancel.
- **PercWordX**: the percentage of a specific word X in the request. We use the "Yes" and "No" word list in PercWordX features.
- **IsPrevActionX and IsNextActionX**: whether the previous/next system action is X. This feature is important because user action is usually triggered by the previous system action, or triggers the next system action.

Note that different intelligent assistants may implement these actions differently. For example, they can notify the user a list of options by voice, or displaying on the screen, or both. When asking for user's confirmation of an operation, some assistants consider the user as agreeing with the operation if the user does not respond after a few seconds. Similarly, user behavior for each action may be distinct in different system. Therefore, it requires different rules and classifiers to predict action types in different systems. Whereas we believe these action types are generalizable to other products.

5.2 Modeling Action Patterns

We infer the quality of a session by modeling action patterns in the session. We assume that SAT and DSAT sessions (or sessions with SAT or DSAT ASR/intent classification quality) have different action patterns, e.g., "No" may be more common in DSAT sessions.

We represent a session S as a series of user and system actions, i.e., $S\{u_1, s_1, \ldots, u_n, s_n\}$, where u_i and s_i are the user and system action in the ith round. We model action pattern using a 3-gram model, i.e., each action depends on previous two actions. We also add START and END to the beginning and the end of a session.

Let L be a target session quality label (e.g., SAT or DSAT). The evaluation problem can be solved by inferring the most likely label L for an observed action sequence S, as shown in Equation (1). We use θ_L for the 3-gram action model of sessions with label L. Then, we can calculate $P(S|L)$ as Equation(2), where u_0 and s_0 are START and u_{n+1} and s_{n+1} are END. Let (s, u, v) be three successive actions, we estimate $P(v|s, u)$ from the dataset as Equation(3), where: $c(s, u, v)$ is the raw count of (s, u, v); $P(v|u)$ and $P(v)$ are the bigram and unigram probabilities of v; α and β are smoothing parameters.

$$P(L\mid S)\propto P(S\mid L)P(L) \quad (1)$$

$$P(S\mid L)=\prod_{i=1}^{n+1}P(u_i\mid s_{i-1},u_{i-1};\theta_L)\cdot\prod_{i=1}^{n+1}P(s_i\mid u_i,s_{i-1};\theta_L) \quad (2)$$

$$\hat{P}(v\mid s,u)=\frac{c(s,u,v)+\alpha\cdot P_{ML}(v\mid u)+\beta\cdot P_{ML}(v)}{\sum_{v_i\in U}c(s,u,v_i)+\alpha+\beta} \quad (3)$$

The action sequence model itself can evaluate a session. We can use it with or without the prior probability factor $P(L)$. We found that using $P(L)$ can lead to better accuracy while dropping $P(L)$ can result in better F-measure. To combine with other features, we use the log probability of a session's action sequence as features, i.e., $\log P(S|\text{SAT})$, $\log P(S|\text{DSAT})$, $\log P(\text{SAT}|S)$, and $\log P(\text{DSAT}|S)$.

5.3 Generic Features

In addition to action sequence features, we introduce other features in this section. Most of the features are applicable to all three tasks, with only a few exceptions. Some of these features (e.g., click features) come from previous studies of user satisfaction and success in web search. Besides, we also adopt acoustic features due to the prevalence of voice interaction in intelligent assistants.

5.3.1 Click Features

In web search, click and click dwell time are useful indicators of document relevance [21, 22] as well as query and session level search success [1, 6, 7, 17, 32]. Here "click" means tapping a result item. The item can be a search result in web search tasks or in other types in device+dialog function tasks (e.g., a best answer from a list of candidates). Click features are not applicable to chat tasks. We include the following click features:

#click	Number of clicks per session and per request.
#click longer or shorter than *t*	Number of clicks by dwell time. We count clicks longer than 30s and those shorter than 15s.
rank_click	Average rank of clicks.
click_dwelltime	Average click dwell time.
time_firstclick	Average time to the first click of a request.

5.3.2 Request Features

Previous studies found some query characteristics are useful for predicting search success or difficulty. We use similar request features here. We first consider request type in a session. Shokouhi et al. [26] found that switching from voice to text queries correlates with low search quality in mobile search. Studies also found increased usage of query suggestions in difficult topics [24] and complex tasks [18]. Therefore, we use the number of requests by type (voice, text, suggestion) and voice-to-text switch as features.

Request content may also indicate user experience. For example: Hassan et al. found that high similarity of queries is an indicator of unsuccessful task [8, 10]; Jiang et al. [19] found that user may repeat a voice query if ASR error happens, and long queries are more likely to have ASR errors. We use request length and the similarity of adjacent requests (by ASR results) as features.

Another information we make use of is request dwell time. It is calculated as the time interval of adjacent requests. We consider average request dwell time as well as the number of requests with dwell time longer or shorter than certain thresholds.

#request	Total number of requests in a session.
#request_type	Number of requests of a specific type.
#request longer or shorter than *t*	Number of requests whose dwell time is longer or shorter than *t* (set to 30s, 50s, or 100s).
request_length	Average request length (by word).
request_dwell	Average request dwell time.
#voice2text	Number of transition from voice to text request.
edit_distance	Average edit distance of adjacent requests.
#common_word	Average number of common words in adjacent requests.
#common_req	Number of adjacent requests with the same ASR output.

5.3.3 Response Features

We consider responses of a specific type as features. In device+dialog function tasks and chat tasks, we use the number and percentage of voice responses. In web search tasks, we use the number and percentage of responses the intelligent assistant can provide instant answers as features. This is because in some tasks, user may prefer certain types of responses. For example, users may be frustrated if the intelligent assistant cannot respond them in voice in device+dialog tasks and chat tasks. Similarly, users may prefer responses of instant answers when searching for factual questions.

We also incorporate features considering the content of response. We use the Jaccard similarity of results between adjacent responses as a feature. This helps us measure request similarity at result level. In addition, we consider the time to achieve the first execute action in the session in device+dialog function tasks. Intuitively, if it requires many rounds of interaction to command an intelligent assistant, the task session is unlikely satisfactory.

instant_answer/ voice_response	Number and percentage of responses provide instant answers/voice responses to the user.
jaccard_result	Jaccard similarity of results or items.
first_execute	Time (number of rounds) to the first "execute".

5.3.4 Acoustic Features

Since intelligent assistant involves lots of voice interaction, we also adopt acoustic features as a component of our approach. When encountering ASR errors, user may slow down the speed of speaking in requests [16, 19]. To detect such behavior, we compare the speaking rate in adjacent voice requests. The speaking rate is measured as the number of words (in ASR output) divided by the duration of the request. We measure the number and percentage of requests with speaking rate below a certain ratio as compared to the previous request. We set the ratio to 0.25, 0.5, and 0.75.

The second acoustic feature is the similarity of metaphone code between adjacent requests. Metaphone [25] is a way of indexing words by their pronunciation and it can help us detect ASR errors and enhance the accuracy of request similarity measures. For example, a request "WhatsApp" may be incorrectly recognized as "what's up", but their Metaphone codes are both "WTSP". In such cases, this phonetic similarity feature helps us detect repeated or similar requests that are missed by normal request similarity features (based on ASR outputs).

Besides, we adopt Huang et al.'s method [12] to measure ASR confidence and use the confidence of the voice requests as a feature. In short, ASR confidence gets higher when both acoustic and language model scores of the selected recognition hypothesis are significantly higher than the remaining hypotheses.

asr_confidence	Voice request speech recognition confidence score.
metaphone_sim	Metaphone code similarity between adjacent requests.
slow_request	The number and percentage of requests with slower speaking rates comparing to previous requests.

6. DATA

We collected information of 60 users in 600 sessions. We use the dataset to test how well our approach can correctly evaluate an intelligent assistant and its components in different types of tasks. Table 5 shows some data statistics. We consider the evaluation as binary classification and divide the sessions into binary classes by user ratings. Due to the large difference of rating distributions, we set the thresholds differently for each task type and rating type such that we can balance the proportion of positive and negative classes.

We compute the correlation of user satisfaction with the quality of ASR and intent classification. Results in **Error! Reference source not found.** suggest that the quality of the two components do affect overall user satisfaction. Comparing two components, satisfaction relies more on the quality of intent classification but less on ASR quality. The degree of correlation also differs a lot in three tasks. We observed a moderate correlation (r=0.54) in device function tasks, but a weaker one in web search tasks (r=0.37), and an insignificant correlation in chat tasks ($p \geq 0.05$). This indicates different types of tasks rely differently on the two components. This also confirms our objective that it is necessary to evaluate not only the overall experience, but also each components in order to diagnose the system in deeper details.

Table 5. Some statistics of the collected user study data.

Statistics / Task Type	Device Function	Web Search	Chat
# Sessions	300	240	60
Average # requests in a session	2.44	2.59	8.95
Satisfaction vs. ASR Quality	0.54	0.37	-
Satisfaction vs. Intent Quality	0.77	0.76	0.70
ASR Quality vs. Intent Quality	0.49	0.35	-
Satisfaction vs. Frustration	-0.63	-0.75	-0.76
Satisfaction vs. Goal Success	0.69	0.67	0.70
Satisfaction vs. Effort	-0.67	-0.71	-0.63

"-" means the correlation is statistically insignificant ($p \geq 0.05$)
all other correlations are significant ($p < 0.05$)

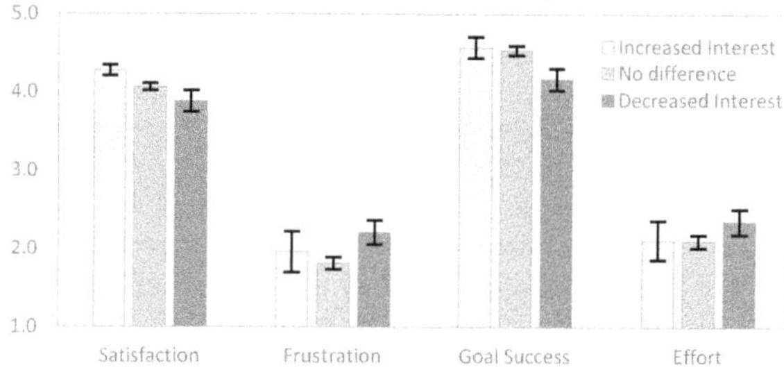

Figure 1. Average task-level ratings for users with increased, equal, or decreased interests after the experiments (10 tasks).

In this paper, we use user satisfaction as measure for the overall quality of a session. There are other user-based measures, such as goal success [6, 7] and user frustration [3]. We do not know much about their differences and validity. Table 5 shows the correlation of satisfaction with frustration, goal success, and effort in three task types. Satisfaction is positively correlated with goal success, and negatively correlated with frustration and effort. The correlations are rather strong, showing these measures are related to each other.

We further examine how task-level user experience relate to the changes of user interests in using the product. We measured user interests in using Cortana twice: at the beginning and the end of the user study. We divide the users into groups with increased, equal, or decreased interests. Figure 1 shows that three groups have significantly different task-level satisfaction ($p < 0.05$). But we only observed significant differences in frustration, goal success, and effort between users with decreased interests and others. This indicates that satisfaction is a task-level measure consistently correlate to the changes of long term user adoption, but other three measures may only correlate with decreased user interests. This confirms that we should adopt user satisfaction as the measure for session quality.

7. DEVICE+DIALOG FUNCTION TASKS

This section evaluates our model in device+dialog function tasks. We first evaluate the action sequence model described in Section 5.2. Then, we evaluate other features. In all experiments, we generate 10 random divisions of the data and perform 10-fold cross validation on each division. This generates results for 100 folds in total. We report the mean value of F-measure and accuracy in the 100 folds. We test for significant difference using Welch t-test.

7.1 Action Type Classification

We first evaluate how well we can predict user action type. We manually labeled all the user actions to train a classifier and evaluate its accuracy. We use multi-class logistic regression for classification. Table 6 reports the effectiveness of the classifier. It shows that we can achieve satisfactory performance in predicting user action types. The average F-measure is as high as about 0.9. Comparatively it is less effective in identifying the "No" and "Select" actions (but it still has over 0.8 F-measure). This is probably due to there is limited data (only 2.8%) to train models for "No" and we

Table 6. Effectiveness of user action type classification.

Action Type	Proportion	F_1	Precision	Recall
Command	67.6%	0.956	0.973	0.940
Yes	6.7%	0.956	0.984	0.929
No	2.8%	0.815	0.867	0.768
Select	13.9%	0.849	0.793	0.913
Answer	9.0%	0.910	0.870	0.953
Micro-averaged	-	0.932	0.932	0.932
Macro-averaged	-	0.897	0.897	0.901

did not make a word list for "Select". This shows that, provided certain amount of training data, we can automatically identify action types defined in Section 5 accurately. If not specified, we use predicted user action types in following experiments.

7.2 Action Sequence Model

Table 7 shows results for action sequence model without using the prior probability of classes with both the human annotated and the predicted action types. The results show that using predicted actions can be as effective as using human annotated actions in all three prediction tasks. We did not observe significant difference of the two in predicting user satisfaction and the intent classification quality. The action sequence model using the predicted action types has only slightly worse average F-measure comparing to that using human annotated action types when predicting ASR quality (0.699 vs. 0.713, $p<0.05$). Again, this shows that the prediction of user action type is accurate and does not affect much on the performance of the action sequence model.

Due to few baseline approaches for evaluating device-dialog function tasks, we do not directly compare action sequence model to other approaches. But according to Wang et al.'s studies [32], state-of-the-art approaches predict user satisfaction in web search with the average F-measures ranging from 0.7 to 0.8. The action sequence model achieves similar performance in evaluating device function tasks of intelligent assistants. The model is relatively more effective in prediction of user satisfaction and intent classification quality (with 0.79 and 0.76 average F-measures), but worse in evaluating ASR quality (but still can achieve about 0.7 average F-measure). It is probably because many action patterns indicating SAT and DSAT sessions are not equally predictive of ASR quality. We will show examples in Section 7.1.3. Using the prior probability of classes leads to 2%-3% improvement in accuracy, but about 2% decline in F-measure. We do not further show details here.

7.3 Action Sequence Patterns

We further analyze typical action sequence patterns indicative of SAT or DSAT sessions. We look into the following four patterns:

- actions prior to the end of a session, i.e., (*, *, END)
- actions next to a user command, i.e., (Command, *, *)
- actions after system execution, i.e., (Execute, *, *)
- actions before system execution, i.e., (*, *, Execute)

For each action sequence, we calculate its probabilities in SAT and DSAT sessions. We use the probability ratio as an indicator of to what degree its occurrence favors the session is satisfactory. If the ratio is greater than one, occurrence of action sequence favors the session is satisfactory. We use human annotated action types for the accuracy of analysis. Table 8 shows results.

The (*, *, END) pattern helps us analyze how SAT and DSAT sessions terminate. It shows that SAT sessions are more likely to end with a system execution. The probability ratio for (Command, Execute, END), (Yes, Execute, END), and (Select, Execute, END) are all above 1. In comparison, ending with a system action other than "Execute" is a strong indicator of DSAT sessions. This is not surprising since by our definition, "Execute" is the only way to achieve the task goal in device-dialog function tasks. If the session terminates with other actions, it probably means that the user gives

Table 7. Effectiveness using action sequence (without prior probability of classes) to evaluate device-dialog function tasks.

User Satisfaction	Avg F_1	Pos F_1	Neg F_1	Accuracy
Human Annotated Action	0.785	0.861	0.709	0.813
Predicted Action	0.793	0.866	0.719*	0.820
ASR Quality	**Avg F_1**	**Pos F_1**	**Neg F_1**	**Accuracy**
Human Annotated Action	0.713	0.873	0.553	0.804
Predicted Action	0.699*	0.877	0.522**	0.805
Intent Classification Quality	**Avg F_1**	**Pos F_1**	**Neg F_1**	**Accuracy**
Human Annotated Action	0.772	0.886	0.658	0.831
Predicted Action	0.764	0.883	0.645	0.825

* and ** means $p<0.05$ and $p<0.01$ comparing to "Human Annotated Action".

up without achieving the goal. However, note that even in DSAT sessions, the chances of ending with "Execute" is still much higher than other actions (not shown in the table). Therefore, this pattern can only be applied to a limited number of DSAT sessions (high precision but low recall).

Since it relies on correct "Execute" to achieve the task goal, we further analyze action sequence prior to and next to "Execute", i.e., (*, *, Execute) and (Execute, *, *). Results show that it is a strong indicator of SAT sessions if the user successfully commands the system to execute an operation at the first round (the ratio is as high as 3.84). "Execute" next to "Yes" or "Select" are weaker, but still indicative of SAT sessions. In comparison, if (Command, Execute) does not happen at the beginning of a session, it is an indicator of DSAT sessions, e.g., (Option, Command, Execute) and (Execute, Command, Execute) all have lower than 1 ratio. These sequences indicate errors in the previous rounds. For example, when intelligent assistant provides a list of options ("Option"), normally user should select one option ("Select"). If the user issues a new command instead, it means the options are not useful at all. This also supports using time_first_execute as a feature (Section 5.5.3).

We further analyze action sequence patterns next to "Execute". It shows that if the session does not terminate after an "Execute", it is nearly always an indicator of DSAT sessions. This is because that any further interactions after an "Execute" means that the executed operation is incorrect (such that the user needs to correct it or retry).

The last pattern is actions next to user commands. Results show that if the user confirms to execute an operation after "Command", it is a very strong indicator of SAT sessions (the ratio is 4.47). (Command, Execute, END) is also a strong indicator. In contrast, it indicates DSAT sessions if user continuously issues two commands in adjacent requests, e.g., (Command, Execute, Command). This pattern suggests system did not correctly understand the previous command so that user needs to retry a new command. Besides, providing an option list or asking users for questions after a user command probably means negative user experience. On the one hand, this is probably because "Option" and "Question" indicate partial understanding of previous user commands in Cortana. For example, in Table 4, user asks for the closest pharmacy, but system does not understand "closest" and just returns a list of pharmacies nearby. On the other hand, this may suggest limited user experience for such interaction style, because (Command, Option, Select) and (Command, Question, Answer) increases the time to "Execute" and the effort to achieve the task goal by involving more interactions.

However, comparing to Table 8, some action patterns suggest distinct information in predicting of ASR and intent classification quality. Table 9 shows the probability ratios for action patterns with large differences in the three evaluation scenarios. Some patterns indicating SAT sessions do not suggest positive ASR quality, e.g., (Confirm, Yes, Execute) and (Yes, Execute, END). Similarly, some frequent patterns in DSAT sessions do not indicate negative ASR quality. This probably explains why action sequence model is less effective in evaluating ASR quality. Similar differences were found

Table 8. Action sequence (using human annotated action types) probability ratio in SAT and DSAT sessions for four patterns.

(*, *, END)			Ratio
Command	Execute	END	3.43
Yes	Execute	END	1.76
Select	Execute	END	1.34
Answer	Confirm	END	0.21
Command	WebSearch	END	0.08
Command	Error	END	0.00

(*, *, Execute)			Ratio
START	Command	Execute	3.84
Confirm	Yes	Execute	1.64
Option	Select	Execute	1.06
Option	Command	Execute	0.85
Execute	Command	Execute	0.70
Execute	Select	Execute	0.57
WebSearch	Command	Execute	0.34

(Execute, *, *)			Ratio
Execute	END	END	2.39
Execute	Command	Execute	0.70
Execute	Select	Execute	0.57
Execute	Command	WebSearch	0.28
Execute	Command	Confirm	0.00
Execute	Command	Option	0.00
Execute	Command	Question	0.00
Execute	Command	Error	0.00

(Command, *, *)			Ratio
Command	Confirm	Yes	4.47
Command	Execute	END	3.43
Command	Option	Select	0.85
Command	Execute	Command	0.51
Command	Question	Answer	0.40
Command	WebSearch	Command	0.23
Command	Option	Command	0.04

Table 9. Action sequence probability ratio difference in prediction of user satisfaction, ASR quality, and intent classification quality.

Action Sequence			Ratio		
			SAT	ASR	Intent
Yes	Execute	END	1.76	0.83	1.68
Confirm	Yes	Execute	1.64	0.78	1.54
Command	Option	Select	0.85	1.48	0.96
Execute	Command	Execute	0.70	1.10	0.77
Answer	Confirm	Yes	0.66	0.38	1.27
Question	Answer	Question	0.47	0.27	1.44
START	Command	WebSearch	0.39	1.26	0.19
Question	Answer	Confirm	0.37	0.28	1.33
Answer	Question	Answer	0.34	0.27	1.44
No	Option	Select	0.21	0.12	2.31
Confirm	No	Option	0.17	0.16	1.73
Answer	Confirm	No	0.09	0.12	1.35

Table 10. Effectiveness of using action sequence to predict user satisfaction and the quality of ASR and intent classification.

Features	User Satisfaction				ASR Quality				Intent Classification Quality			
	Avg F_1	Pos F_1	Neg F_1	Accuracy	Avg F_1	Pos F_1	Neg F_1	Accuracy	Avg F_1	Pos F_1	Neg F_1	Accuracy
Click	0.524**	0.825**	0.222**	0.718**	0.561**	0.880**	0.242**	0.795**	0.533**	0.844**	0.222**	0.743**
Request	0.815	0.901	0.729	0.856	0.743*	0.903	0.583*	0.846	0.796	0.904	0.688*	0.858
Response	0.758**	0.850**	0.665**	0.796**	0.673**	0.884**	0.463**	0.810**	0.695**	0.880	0.511**	0.812*
Acoustic	0.743**	0.849**	0.638**	0.790**	0.703**	0.882**	0.525**	0.815**	0.745*	0.875*	0.616*	0.813*
Action Sequence	0.819	0.892	0.746	0.850	0.763	0.903	0.623	0.848	0.776	0.892	0.660	0.839
Best Feature Set	All Features				Action + Request + Acoustic				Action + Request + Acoustic			
	0.852**	0.920**	0.783*	0.886**	0.786	0.909	0.664*	0.859	0.825**	0.913*	0.736**	0.874**

* and ** means p<0.05 and p<0.01 comparing to "Action Sequence"; shaded cells indicate the best results among those using individual feature set.

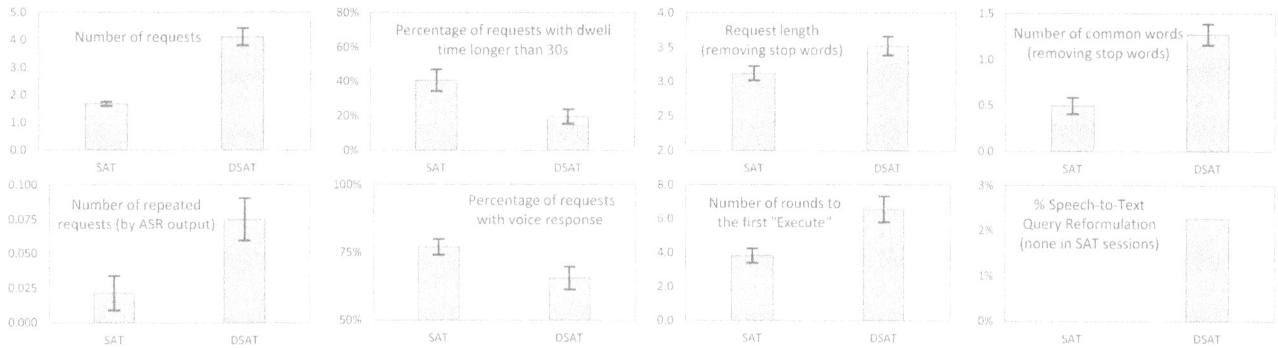

Figure 2. User behavior statistics (with standard error) in SAT and DSAT sessions. All differences are significant at 0.05 level.

between satisfaction and intent classification quality. However, we still found many patterns indicating ASR and intent classification quality. This is why action sequence model can effectively evaluate ASR and intent classification quality. The differences suggest it is necessary to train different models for each evaluation scenario.

To conclude, results in this section show that the action sequence model is an effective approach for evaluating intelligent assistants in device-dialog function tasks. Besides, analysis of action patterns is a helpful tool to diagnose effective and ineffective interactions.

7.4 Other Features

We further evaluate and compare the effectiveness of generic features. We first evaluate each individual feature set separately. Then, we evaluate combinations of feature sets. We use gradient boosted decision tree for classification [5]. Table 10 shows the results.

7.4.1 Request Features

Request features and action sequence are the two best performed feature sets. They have comparable effectiveness in predicting user satisfaction. Action sequence features are relatively more effective in predicting ASR quality, but less accurate in prediction of intent classification quality. They outperform other features significantly in both F-measure and accuracy. They are also more effective than the naive action sequence model approach, especially in predicting ASR quality (average F-measure improved by about 10%).

Figure 2 further shows comparison of user behavior statistics in SAT and DSAT sessions. It shows that significant differences exist in many request characteristics between SAT and DSAT sessions, including: the number of requests in a session (1.68 vs. 4.12), the percentage of requests with dwell time longer than 30 seconds (40.7% vs. 19.6%), request length after removing stop words (3.12 vs. 3.53), the number of common words between adjacent requests (0.50 vs. 1.27), and the number of repeated requests (simply count by whether two adjacent requests have same ASR outputs; 0.022 vs. 0.075). These statistics explain why request features have strong performance in predicting user satisfaction.

In prediction of ASR and intent classification quality, we observed similar differences. However, the distinction between sessions with SAT and DSAT ASR quality are less significant in terms of request length (3.21 vs. 3.53, p=0.09) and the number of common words between adjacent requests (0.91 vs. 1.14, p=0.08). This explains why request features are relatively less effective in predicting ASR quality (but still achieved 0.743 F-measure).

7.4.2 Response Features

Response features are useful for predicting user satisfaction (the average F-measure is 0.758), but relatively less indicative of the

Table 11. Effectiveness of features for predicting user satisfaction, ASR and intent classification quality in web search tasks.

Features	User Satisfaction				ASR Quality				Intent Classification Quality			
	Avg F_1	Pos F_1	Neg F_1	Accuracy	Avg F_1	Pos F_1	Neg F_1	Accuracy	Avg F_1	Pos F_1	Neg F_1	Accuracy
Click	0.536**	0.749**	0.324**	0.649**	0.493**	0.687**	0.299**	0.579**	0.533**	0.695**	0.370**	0.595**
Request	0.796	0.840	0.751	0.810	0.721**	0.754*	0.689**	0.730**	0.755	0.742	0.769	0.765
Response	0.614**	0.764**	0.465**	0.679**	0.509**	0.714**	0.305**	0.601**	0.587**	0.722**	0.452**	0.639**
Acoustic	0.721**	0.771**	0.671**	0.732**	0.752*	0.754*	0.749	0.758	0.715**	0.728**	0.702**	0.725**
Best Feature Set	All Features				Click + Request + Acoustic				Request + Acoustic			
	0.798	0.858	0.738	0.822	0.772	0.784	0.76	0.777	0.769	0.766	0.772	0.777

* and ** means p<0.05 and p<0.01 comparing to "Best Feature Set"; shaded cells indicate the best results among those using individual feature set.

quality of ASR and intent classification (with average F-measure 0.673 and 0.695). As shown in Figure 2, we also found significant differences between SAT and DSAT sessions in the percentage of requests with voice responses (76.9% vs. 65.5%) and the number of rounds to the first "Execute" action in the session (3.82 vs. 6.56). However, we did not find the Jaccard similarity of results useful, probably due to the fact that only about 10% of the responses in device+dialog function tasks include a result list (counting both the web search results and answer items).

We found similar and significant differences in response features and related user behavior in predicting intent classification quality. However, we only observed a slightly significant difference in the number of rounds to the first "Execute" action between sessions with and without satisfactory ASR quality (4.38 vs. 5.75, p=0.07). Other response features are not very indicative of the ASR quality. This is probably why response features perform relatively worse in predicting ASR quality comparing evaluating user satisfaction and intent classification quality.

7.4.3 Acoustic Features

Results suggest that acoustic features can also effectively predict user satisfaction as well as the quality of ASR and intent classification in device function tasks. We found significant differences in speech recognition confidence scores between SAT and DSAT sessions, as well as between those with SAT and DSAT quality of ASR and intent classification. This suggests that Huang et al.'s approach [12] is not only effective for predicting ASR quality of utterances, but also correlate well with user ratings of ASR quality at session level for intelligent assistant tasks. This is also why it is effective for predicting user satisfaction and intent classification considering the correlations between them.

In addition, we found that detecting requests with slower speaking rates are predictive of sessions with dissatisfactory ASR quality. Figure 3 shows the percentage of requests with slower speaking rates at different slower ratios (with standard error). The percentage of slower speaking requests ("% request" in Figure 3) are consistently higher in session with dissatisfactory ASR quality when we set the slower ratio r below 70%. The differences are significant at 0.05 level when we set r to 0.15, 0.6 or 0.65. Similar differences exist between the SAT and DSAT sessions, but are less significant. However, we did not observe such differences between sessions with satisfactory and dissatisfactory intent classification quality. This suggests that slowing-down is probably only a strategy of the user to deal with speech recognition error, but not necessarily for intent classification errors.

7.4.4 Click Features

Click features have the worst performance comparing to others, despite they are important in predicting satisfaction in web search. We found this is mainly because users do not "click" results very often in device+dialog function tasks. Here click means to tap a result on the screen. The result can be a search result or an answer item returned in device+dialog function tasks (e.g., it can be a place answer when looking for locations). One possible reason is that intelligent assistants allow users to interact with result items through

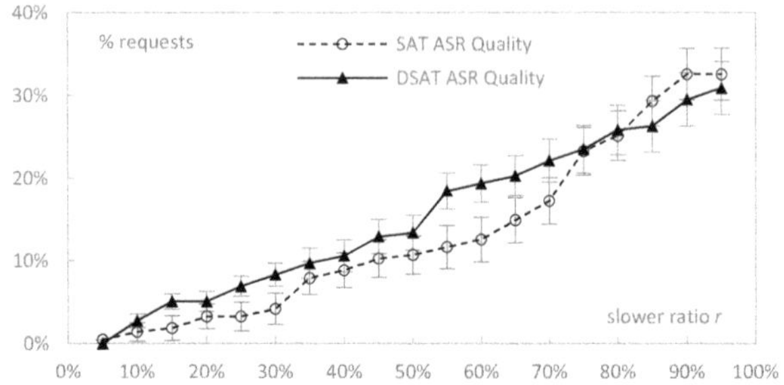

Figure 3. Percentage of requests (y-axis) whose speaking rate comparing to the previous requests falls below ratio *r* (x-axis).

voice interaction, e.g., the "Option" and "Select" action. In such case, users may rely less on tapping or other touch based interaction. Also, we did not observe significantly different user behavior related to click features. Thus, it is not surprising that click features are not as effective as they are in web search.

7.4.5 Using Multiple Features

After combining multiple features, we significantly improved the prediction of user satisfaction and intent classification quality by about 4%-6% in F-measure and accuracy (comparing to using the action sequence features). We finally achieved about 0.8 F-measure and 0.85 accuracy in all three evaluation scenarios. This confirms that our approach can effectively evaluate overall quality of intelligent assistants as well as its components.

8. WEB SEARCH AND CHAT TASKS

We further evaluate the effectiveness of features in web search and chat tasks. Table 11 shows the results for web search tasks.

Similar to the findings in device+dialog function tasks, results in Table 11 show that click features have very weak predictive powers for overall satisfaction and ASR and intent classification quality in web search tasks. The chances of clicking results remains low in web search tasks on intelligent assistants. Still, we did not observe significant differences in click features between SAT and DSAT sessions. However, different from the device+dialog function tasks, we cannot simply explain this by the availability of voice interaction to make selections, because Cortana did not provide users such function in web search scenario (e.g., at the time of the study, Cortana will not understand requests such as "open the first webpage").

One possible reason is that user becomes less willing to click and read details of a result page on mobile devices. Instead, they may prefer knowing answers directly, either displayed on the result webpage, or responded by Cortana in voice. Some participants' responses in the interview support this explanation: "For example with the scores it would have been nice if I just said San Francisco Giants and it just came up with a list of scores ... Rather than a website where I have to check it or a sports blog." [sic] Another evidence supporting this claim is that 14.8% requests in SAT sessions have voice responses (an indicator that Cortana provides extracted instant answers to the query in web search tasks), which is significantly higher than only 6.6% in the DSAT sessions.

Table 12. Effectiveness of evaluating chat tasks.

	Avg F_1	Pos F_1	Neg F_1	Accuracy
User Satisfaction	0.673	0.563	0.783	0.715
ASR Quality	0.702	0.767	0.637	0.724
Intent Classification Quality	0.590	0.329	0.851	0.761

Request features and acoustic features are also very effective for evaluating web search tasks. Request features are the strongest feature set in predicting user satisfaction and intent classification quality. In comparison, acoustic features outperforms others in predicting ASR quality. Further analysis found differences of related user behavior similar to those in device+dialog function tasks. Comparing to DSAT sessions, SAT sessions of web search tasks have significantly less (1.83 vs. 3.68) and shorter queries (4.34 vs. 4.72 words), as well as longer query dwell time (43% queries' dwell time is longer than 30s vs. 23% in DSAT sessions). ASR confidence score and queries with slower speaking rates also differ significantly in SAT and DSAT sessions. However, we did not find significant differences in query similarity (i.e., the number of common words) between SAT and DSAT sessions in web search tasks.

Besides, our results also confirm Shokouhi et al.'s findings [26] that switching from voice to text input is a signal of dissatisfactory user experience. As shown in Figure 2, among all the SAT sessions of web search tasks, we observed no voice-to-text switches. In comparison, 2.3% of the query reformulations in DSAT sessions are from voice to text. This suggests that voice-to-text is a highly precise indicator for DSAT sessions (but the coverage is limited).

After combining multiple features, we achieved better prediction results. The best approach has 0.798 average F-measure predicting user satisfaction, which is comparable to those reported for state-of-the-art approaches in normal web search scenario [32].

We further apply request, response, and acoustic features to chat tasks (because it seems meaningless to apply click features to chat tasks). Table 12 shows that these features are still predictive of user satisfaction and ASR quality in chat tasks, although less accurate than they are device+dialog function and web search tasks. They have limited effectiveness in evaluating intent classification quality in chat tasks. This suggests that automatic evaluation of chat quality is more challenging due to its open-ended nature.

To conclude, results suggest that we can apply features adopted in previous web search satisfaction studies (e.g., most of the click, request, and response features), as well as those newly designed for intelligent assistants (e.g., acoustic features, voice-to-text, etc.) to evaluate web search tasks and chat tasks in intelligent assistants. However, some of them are less effective in intelligent assistant, e.g., click features. Besides, our results show that using the same features, we can train different models to effectively predict ASR and intent classification quality as well. In addition, the effectiveness of acoustic features suggests that we can use voice interaction and related user behavior to improve modeling of applications in voice enabled scenario, e.g., intelligent assistant.

9. DISCUSSION AND CONCLUSION

This paper studied the topic of user behavior based evaluation of intelligent assistants. This is a challenging problem due to the variability of tasks and topics involved when interacting with an intelligent assistatn. We developed task-independent approaches to address the challenge and proved their effectiveness in experiments. Results demonstrate that using the same approach, we can evaluate not only intelligent assistant itself, but also its main components: speech recognition and intent classification. Results of a user study show the quality of both components affect user experience with intelligent assistants.

Admittedly, our study is limited in the coverage of tasks and the way data is collected. Due to the sensitivity and difficulty of data collection, we did not study a popular function of many intelligent assistants, i.e., proactive suggestions. This function requires lots of personal information, while in our lab study it is difficult to prepare such data for participants to perform tasks. Besides, we develop our tasks based on an early sample of the beta version of a commercial intelligent assistant. These tasks are not necessarily representative this intelligent assistant today, not of other products. Additionally, using a lab study to collect data is a double-bladed sword. An alternative approach usually adopted is to ask third-party judger to assess session quality. In comparison, a lab study can collect first-party user judgments, but cannot simulate the real environment of using intelligent assistants, which may affect user interaction pattern. For example, we may observe a longer dwell time when user is driving, and user may not repeat requests but switch to text more often when it is noisy. Although many user behavior signals may change, this should not affect the effectiveness of our approach, as long as we can detect and train models for the environment.

Another issue we did not consider in this paper is the variability of interface and interaction. Comparing to well-studied applications (e.g., web search and the "10 blue links"), there is no "standard" interface or interaction mode in intelligent assistants, especially in device+dialog function tasks. On the one hand, there are different ways of implementing the same action, e.g., the intelligent assistant can ask user to confirm and wait for user response, or simply assumes that the user agrees if there is no explicit response after a few seconds. When asking users for more information, it can use voice and wait for voice response, or show an input box on the screen and wait for text input. On the other hand, the set of actions may evolve in the future, although we found it is enough to characterize interaction in existing products. Depending on the availability of actions and their implementation, we may observe different action patterns, and we may need to retrain models to evaluate new interface designs. This suggests we should be cautious to use implicit feedback-based models to evaluate systems with different interface designs.

Comparing the three types of tasks, our approach works the best in device function tasks, and the worst in chat tasks. We suspect it is due to the number of features applicable to each task. As analyzed in Section 7.3, many action patterns indicate positive or negative user experience in device function tasks, but they are not available in web search and chat. Comparing to web search, it is meaningless to use click features as well as many other features in chat tasks, such as request type, voice-to-text, result similarity, etc. Additionally, this may also be caused by the subjectivity of tasks. That device+dialog function tasks are the least subjective one, because the goal is clear and straight-forward, i.e., commanding intelligent assistant to do something. In contrast, some of the web search tasks are more open-ended and complex, e.g., finding flight schedule. Chat is the most open-ended task, since different users may judge chat quality differently, e.g., some may prefer funny responses, while some others may expect the conversation to be as natural as talking to real person. We suspect the more open-ended a task is, the more difficult we can train a unified model to evaluate the task, because the subjectivity of the task may result in distinct user behavior.

Our study also assumes the existence of an accurate classifier for the three task types. Although this is reasonable, it is unclear how actual accuracy of the classifier would affect the effectiveness of the overall evaluation process. In addition, we only adopt satisfaction as the user experience measure in this study. It is unclear how well our approach can predict other user experience measures such as task success and efforts. These are left for future work. Despite these limitations, we push forward studies of intelligent assistant as well as modeling of user satisfaction and evaluation.

First, we are the first study to address the challenge of evaluating intelligent assistants. Although similar studies exist in web search, the diversity of tasks and interaction are not comparable to those in intelligent assistants. Our approach is task-independent. Although some features (e.g., action sequence) only apply to device+dialog function tasks, the majority of features are shared among all the tasks, making it a generalizable approach for other products and future changes.

Second, our results demonstrate that, using the same approach, we can train models to evaluate not only overall user satisfaction in intelligent assistant, but also the quality of speech recognition and intent classification. This contributes to more detailed diagnosis of intelligent assistants in evaluation, as well as a user-centric way of evaluating related techniques (e.g., ASR) in specific applications.

Third, through user behavior analysis, we found many patterns and behavioral signals indicating user experience in intelligent assistants. Although some of them may be affected by system design, most of the patterns are potentially generalizable to similar applications, e.g., the session does not terminate with an Execute can be a strong signal of user abandon. These patterns are useful for related studies and evaluation of other systems.

As we discussed, There are several directions of future work to advance this study, e.g., to consider uncovered tasks, environments, and variability of interface designs, to examine the effects of task type classification accuracy on the effectiveness of the approach, to correlate with other user experience measures, and to compare native and non-native speakers. Solutions to these issues will further improve the performance and reliability of our approach.

REFERENCES

[1] Ageev, M., Guo, Q., Lagun, D. and Agichtein, E. (2011). Find it if you can: a game for modeling different types of web search success using interaction data. *Proc. SIGIR '11*, 345–354.

[2] Smith R.W. and Hipp, D.R. (1995). *Spoken Natural Language Dialog Systems: A Practical Approach.* Oxford University Press.

[3] Feild, H.A., Allan, J. and Jones, R. (2010). Predicting searcher frustration. *Proc. SIGIR '10*, 34–41.

[4] Fox, S., Karnawat, K., Mydland, M., Dumais, S. and White, T. 2005. Evaluating implicit measures to improve web search. *ACM TOIS*, 23(2), 147–168.

[5] Friedman, J., Hastie, T., Tibshirani, R. (2000). Additive logistic regression: a statistical view of boosting (with discussion and a rejoinder by the authors). *The Annals of Statistics.*

[6] Hassan, A. (2012). A semi-supervised approach to modeling web search satisfaction. *Proc. SIGIR '12*, 275–284.

[7] Hassan, A., Jones, R. and Klinkner, K.L. (2010). Beyond DCG: user behavior as a predictor of a successful search. *Proc. WSDM '10*, 221–230.

[8] Hassan, A., Shi, X., Craswell, N. and Ramsey, B. (2013). Beyond clicks: query reformulation as a predictor of search satisfaction. *Proc. CIKM '13*, 2019–2028.

[9] Hassan, A., Song, Y. and He, L. (2011). A task level metric for measuring web search satisfaction and its application on improving relevance estimation. *Proc. CIKM '11*, 125–134.

[10] Hassan, A., White, R.W., Dumais, S.T. and Wang, Y.M. (2014). *Proc. WSDM '14*, 53–62.

[11] Heck, L.P., Hakkani-Tür, D., Chinthakunta, M., Tür, G., Iyer, R., Parthasarathy, P., Stifelman, L., Shriberg, E. and Fidler, A. (2013). Multi-modal conversational search and browse. *Proceedings of the First Workshop on Speech, Language and Audio in Multimedia*, 96–101.

[12] Huang, P.S., Kumar, K., Liu, C., Gong, Y. and Deng, L. (2013). Predicting speech recognition confidence using deep learning with word identity and score features. *Proc. ICASSP*, 7413–7417.

[13] Huffman, S.B. and Hochster, M. (2007). How well does result relevance predict session satisfaction? *Proc. SIGIR '07*, 567–574.

[14] Järvelin, K. and Kekäläinen, J. (2002). Cumulated gain-based evaluation of IR techniques. *ACM TOIS,* 20(4), 422–446.

[15] Järvelin, K., Price, S., Delcambre, L.L. and Nielsen, M. (2008). Discounted Cumulated Gain Based Evaluation of Multiple-Query IR Sessions. *Proc. ECIR '08*, 4–15.

[16] Jeng, W., Jiang, J. and He, D. (2013). Users' Perceived Difficulties and Corresponding Reformulation Strategies in Voice Search. *Proc. HCIR 2013.*

[17] Jiang, J., Hassan Awadallah, A., Shi, X. and White, R.W. (2015). Understanding and Predicting Graded Search Satisfaction. *Proc. WSDM '15*, 57–66.

[18] Jiang, J., He, D. and Allan, J. (2014). Searching, browsing, and clicking in a search session. *Proc. SIGIR '14*, 607–616.

[19] Jiang, J., Jeng, W. and He, D. (2013). How do users respond to voice input errors? lexical and phonetic query reformulation in voice search. *Proc. SIGIR '13*, 143–152.

[20] Johnston, M., Bangalore, S., Vasireddy, G., Stent, A., Ehlen, P., Walker, M., Whittaker, S. and Maloor, P. (2002). MATCH: An architecture for multimodal dialogue systems. *Proc. ACL '02*, 376–383.

[21] Kim, Y., Hassan, A., White, R.W. and Zitouni, I. (2014). Comparing client and server dwell time estimates for click-level satisfaction prediction. *Proc. SIGIR '14*, 895–898.

[22] Kim, Y., Hassan, A., White, R.W. and Zitouni, I. (2014). Modeling dwell time to predict click-level satisfaction. *Proc. WSDM '14*, 193–202.

[23] Kotov, A., Bennett, P.N., White, R.W., Dumais, S.T. and Teevan, J. (2011). Modeling and analysis of cross-session search tasks. *Proc. SIGIR '11*, 5–14.

[24] Niu, X. and Kelly, D. (2014). The use of query suggestions during information search. *IP&M*, 50(1), 218–234.

[25] Philips, L. (1990). Hanging on the Metaphone. *Computer Language*, 7(12), 39–44.

[26] Shokouhi, M., Jones, R., Ozertem, U., Raghunathan, K. and Diaz, F. 2014. Mobile query reformulations. *Proc. SIGIR '14*, 1011–1014.

[27] Stolcke, A., Ries, K., Coccaro, N., Shriberg, E., Bates, R., Jurafsky, D., Taylor, P., Martin, R., Van Ess-Dykema, C. and Meteer, M. (2000). Dialogue act modeling for automatic tagging and recognition of conversational speech. *Computational linguistics*, 26(3), 339–373.

[28] Traum, D.R. (2000). 20 questions on dialogue act taxonomies. *Journal of semantics*, 17(1), 7–30.

[29] Tur, G. and De Mori, R. (2011). *Spoken language understanding: Systems for extracting semantic information from speech.* John Wiley & Sons.

[30] Wahlster, W. (2006). *SmartKom: foundations of multimodal dialogue systems.* Springer.

[31] Walker, M.A., Litman, D.J., Kamm, C.A. and Abella, A. (1997). PARADISE: A framework for evaluating spoken dialogue agents. *Proc. ACL '97*, 271–280.

[32] Wang, H., Song, Y., Chang, M.W., He, X., Hassan, A. and White, R.W. (2014). Modeling action-level satisfaction for search task satisfaction prediction. *SIGIR '14*, 123–132.

[33] Young, S., Gasic, M., Thomson, B. and Williams, J.D. (2013). POMDP-based statistical spoken dialog systems: A review. *Proc. IEEE*, 101(5), 1160–1179.

Incorporating Social Context and Domain Knowledge for Entity Recognition

Jie Tang†♯, Zhanpeng Fang†, and Jimeng Sun‡
†Department of Computer Science and Technology, Tsinghua University
♯Tsinghua National Laboratory for Information Science and Technology (TNList)
‡College of Computing, Georgia Institute of Technology, USA
jietang@tsinghua.edu.cn, fzp13@mails.tsinghua.edu.cn, jsun@cc.gatech.edu

ABSTRACT

Recognizing entity instances in documents according to a knowledge base is a fundamental problem in many data mining applications. The problem is extremely challenging for short documents in complex domains such as social media and biomedical domains. Large concept spaces and instance ambiguity are key issues that need to be addressed.

Most of the documents are created in a social context by common authors via social interactions, such as *reply* and *citations*. Such social contexts are largely ignored in the instance-recognition literature. How can users' interactions help entity instance recognition? How can the social context be modeled so as to resolve the ambiguity of different instances?

In this paper, we propose the SOCINST model to formalize the problem into a probabilistic model. Given a set of short documents (e.g., tweets or paper abstracts) posted by users who may connect with each other, SOCINST can automatically construct a context of subtopics for each instance, with each subtopic representing one possible meaning of the instance. The model is also able to incorporate social relationships between users to help build social context. We further incorporate domain knowledge into the model using a Dirichlet tree distribution.

We evaluate the proposed model on three different genres of datasets: ICDM'12 Contest, Weibo, and I2B2. In ICDM'12 Contest, the proposed model clearly outperforms (+21.4%; $p \ll 1e-5$ with t-test) all the top contestants. In Weibo and I2B2, our results also show that the recognition accuracy of SOCINST is up to 5.3-26.6% better than those of several alternative methods.

Categories and Subject Descriptors

J.4 [**Social Behavioral Sciences**]: Miscellaneous; H.3.3 [**Information Search and Retrieval**]: Text Mining

General Terms

Algorithms, Experimentation

Keywords

Instance recognition; Social network; Probabilistic model

WWW 2015, May 18–22, 2015, Florence, Italy.
ACM 978-1-4503-3469-3/15/05.
http://dx.doi.org/10.1145/2736277.2741135 .

1. INTRODUCTION

The rapid development of online social networks has significantly enriched our daily communications. People use blogs, forums, and product review sites to share opinions on topics such as politicians or experiences with products, and also use the online space as the main channel to acquire and share information. As a result, large volumes of unstructured short-text documents are created. One fundamental analytic operation is to recognize entity instances in the document that map to existing concepts in a knowledge base. In social media, when talking about a specific product, different users may use different words when they mention the product (e.g., S4 vs. Samsung Galaxy S4). In some cases, people may deliberately use some new words to name an event or a product, just for fun or for other purposes, such as using "Fruit company" to name Apple Inc. or "Peace West King" to refer to "Xilai Bo" (a sensitive Chinese politician). In the medical domain, we may want to identify diverse instances from a medical corpus such as PubMed abstracts that map to an existing medical knowledge base such as the Unified Medical Language System (UMLS)[1].

The problem of entity instance recognition and linking requires simultaneous entity recognition and entity matching, which is a much harder problem than either one by itself. Despite many studies on related topics including entity recognition [9, 25, 13, 23, 27], entity matching [2, 3, 21, 29], entity resolution [4, 18, 22, 32], and entity morph [17] such combination and leveraging of social context are largely absent in the literature. Specifically, most entity recognition methods treat messages independently, without considering shared social context. Entity matching and resolution aim at linking entities from different sources with the same meaning. Entity morph is a special case of entity resolution, with an emphasis on connecting those instances intentionally concealed by users, for example, for avoiding censorship. Unlike this paper, none of them explicitly consider the structure of the social network and external knowledge base.

Figure 1 illustrates the problem addressed in this paper. The left figure shows three users with friend relationships, and the middle shows one original microblog posted by user A, and one reply to the original microblog by B, and one retweeted by C. The underlined text indicates three instances recognized by the proposed model and linked to the corresponding concepts in the knowledge base. The problem is non-trivial. First, as each message is very short, traditional methods for entity recognition that deal with messages independently would lead to unsatisfactory results. Second, the social network provides rich structure information, which should be leveraged. Third, the knowledge base also encodes useful domain knowledge (e.g., hypernyms and hyponyms), which should be utilized in the instance recognition process.

[1] http://www.nlm.nih.gov/research/umls

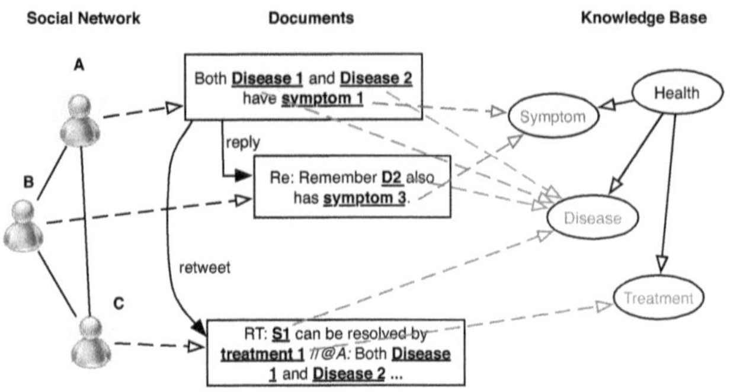

Figure 1: Example of entity instance recognition and linking in a microblogging network. The left figure shows three users with friend relationships, and the middle shows one original microblog from user A, and one reply from B, and a retweet from C. The underlined text indicates three instances recognized by the proposed model and linked to the corresponding concepts in the knowledge base

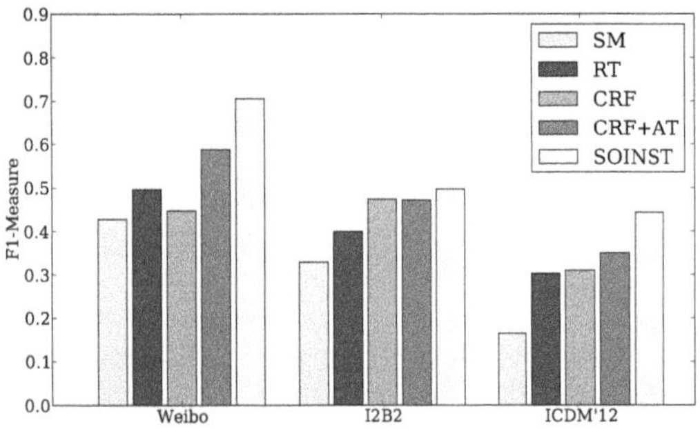

Figure 2: Performance comparison of SOCINST with comparative algorithms (in terms of F1-score). Please refer to § 5.1 for definitions of the comparative algorithms

In this paper, we study the problem of instance recognition and linking in a social context. We propose an SOCINST model to formalize the problem as a probabilistic topic model. Given a training set, the SOCINST method can automatically construct a context of subtopics for each instance by leveraging social relationships between users, with each subtopic representing one potential meaning of the instance. We further use a Dirichlet tree distribution to incorporate domain knowledge from the knowledge base into the topic model. We test the proposed model on three different genres of datasets: ICDM'12 Contest, Weibo, and I2B2. Our experimental results validate the effectiveness of the proposed SOCINST model in all three datasets. Our method improves the recognition accuracy by up to 5.3-26.6% compared with several alternative methods. Figure 2 shows the performance comparison of different methods on the three different datasets. Clearly, SOCINST performs much better than the other comparative algorithms. As an example, on the ICDM'12 Contest dataset, our method significantly outperforms (+21.4%; $p \ll 1e-5$ with t-test) the performance of the first place winner in the contest.

Organization. Section 2 formulates the problem; Section 3 enumerates preliminary considerations; Section 4 explains the proposed model and describes the algorithm for learning it; Section 5 presents the experimental results; Section 6 discusses related work and Section 7 concludes the work.

2. PROBLEM DEFINITION

We first provide necessary definitions and then formally formulate the problem.

Definition 1. **Social Network.** Let $G = (V, E)$ denote the social network, where V is a set of users and $E \subset V \times V$ is a set of relationships between users. We use $v \in V$ to represent a user and $e_{ij} \in E$ to represent a social relationship between users v_i and v_j.

Let D denote a set of M documents authored by users from V, each document $d \in D$ containing a vector $\mathbf{w}_d$ of N_d words, in which each $w_{di} \in \mathbf{w}_d$ is chosen from a vocabulary of size W. The authors of each document is denoted as $V_d \subset V$. The set of documents authored by v is denoted as D_v. Documents can also have links with each other. For example, in PubMed, the link between documents could be citation; in Weibo, the link between documents (tweets) can be retweet (or reply). For easy explanation of the algorithm, we use $IN(d)$ to indicate the subset of documents that have links to d and $OUT(d)$ to indicate the subset of documents to which document d has links. Moreover, we give a simple definition of the knowledge base.

Definition 2. **Knowledge Base.** A knowledge base is represented as a triple $KB = (C, R, X)$, where C represents a set of concepts; R represents a set of relations between concepts; and X represents a set of instances of those concepts.

In our problem, the instances X are to be recognized from the free text. The definition is a brief version of the definition of a knowledge base [10, 36]. In a general setting, relations fall into two broad types: *Taxonomies*, that organize concepts into sub- or super-concept hierarchy; and *Associative relations*, that relate concepts rather than the sub- or super-concepts. In this work, we mainly consider the taxonomy relation — i.e., sub-concept and super-concept relations — but the proposed model in the following section can be essentially extended to model the associative relations.

Instance recognition involves identifying instances X from free text, according to concepts C defined in the knowledge base, and then populating the knowledge base KB with the recognized instances X. Here, each instance $x_k \in X$ can be either a word or a phrase (multiple consecutive words). However, as the instances might be represented in different forms with different keywords, it is important to leverage the context information to aid in the recognition process. In this paper, we consider two types of context information — *social context* and *domain knowledge*. For a user, social context denotes information represented by friends or communities with which the user has been involved. Domain knowledge indicates information encoded in the knowledge base or information encoded in related documents. More specifically, we use topic models to model the context information.

Definition 3. **Topic models.** A topic model θ_i of a user v_i is a multinomial distribution of words $P(w|\theta_i)$. The assumption behind it is that words are sampled following a distribution corresponding to the user.

Thus the social context of user v_i can be represented as a mixture of user-specific topic models $\sum_{j \in NB(v_i)} \gamma\theta_j$, where $NB(v_i)$ is the set of neighbors of v_i and γ is the weight of the corresponding distribution. In practice, γ can be defined in different ways, for example, as the strength of the relationship between users v_i and v_j. Analogously, we can define the context for a concept as a mixture of instance-specific distributions. Given these definitions, we can formally formulate the problem studied in this work.

Table 1: Notations

SYMBOL	DESCRIPTION
K	Number of topics
W	Number of unique words
N_d	Number of words in document d
v_d	The author of document d
$\mathbf{w}_d$	Vector form of words in document d
w_{di}	The i-th word in document d
c^j_{di}	The corresponding concept at the j-th level in KB for word w_{di}
z_{di}	Topic sampled for the i-th word in document d
θ_v	Multinomial distribution over topics specific to author v
ϕ_z	Multinomial distribution of words specific to topic z
α	Dirichlet prior to multinomial distributions θ
β, η	Dirichlet (tree) prior to multinomial ϕ

Problem: The input of our problem consists of a labeled training set $\{(\mathbf{w}_d, \mathbf{y}_d)\}$, a social network G, and a knowledge base KB. The training set corresponds to a set of document $D = \mathbf{w}_d$ and the instance labeling results $\mathbf{y}_d$ for each document d (represented as $\mathbf{w}_d$), where $\mathbf{y}_d$ is a sequence of labels $\{y_{di}\}_i$, with each y_{di} indicating the label of the corresponding token. The author of each document is a user from G, and thus the social network G encodes the social context information and the labeled instances in D are mapped to concepts in KB. Thus the knowledge base provides domain knowledge.

Our goal is to learn a function from the given training dataset so as to extract from document d the set of instances $\{x_k\}$ for each concept $c_j \in C$. More specifically, we can define the problem as a sequential classification problem as follows:

$$f(\mathbf{w}_d, \theta, G, KB) \rightarrow \{(y_{di}, c_j)\}$$

where θ is the learned topic model from the input documents, y_{di} is a variable corresponding to w_{di} to represent whether w_{di} is (part of) an instance of concept c_j.

The fundamental challenge of this problem is how to capture the social context and the domain knowledge for recognizing each instance. In particular, for a specific concept/instance mentioned in someone's document (e.g., a microblog), which friends could share social context information, and on which topic?

3. PRELIMINARIES

We first introduce a baseline solution for this problem. To recognize instances from a free document, we can consider a sequential labeling model, for example, Conditional Random Fields (CRFs) [19]. Before proceeding, we first separate the document into tokens, then assign possible tags (e.g., concepts in C) to each token. The tokens form the basic units and the documents form the sequences of units in the tagging problem. Then given a training dataset, a CRF model is built with the labeled data by means of an iterative algorithm based on Maximum Likelihood Estimation, i.e.,

$$P(\mathbf{y}|\mathbf{x}) = \frac{1}{Z}\exp\left(\sum_i\sum_k \lambda_k f_k(x_i, y_i) + \sum_i\sum_j \mu_j f_j(\mathbf{x}, y_i, y_{i+1})\right) \quad (1)$$

where $\mathbf{x}$ denotes a sequence of the tokens, $\mathbf{y}$ is a label sequence, x_i is the i-th token in the sequence, and y_i is the label of the i-th token; $f_k(x_i, y_i)$ and $f_j(\mathbf{x}, y_i, y_{i+1})$ respectively represents the kth feature function defined for individual token x_i and the jth feature function defined for two consecutive tokens x_i and x_{i+1}. For example, a Boolean feature function can be defined for the token "Peace West King" and the label "politician". Finally, Z is a normalization factor to ensure that the distribution is normalized so that the sum of the probabilities equals 1. An example is illustrated in Figure 3(a).

In recognition, given a sequence of tokens $\mathbf{x}$, we determine the most likely corresponding sequence $\mathbf{y}^*$ of labels by using the trained CRF model, i.e., $\mathbf{y}^* = \max_{\mathbf{y}} P(\mathbf{y}|\mathbf{x})$.

4. SOCINST MODEL FRAMEWORK

The basic sequential labeling with CRFs only considers the linguistic information, but ignores the (topical) context information. This is very likely to result in high precision, but low recall performance (the results in § 5 confirm this). To alleviate this problem, we can resort to the topic modeling approach. However, traditional topic models cannot incorporate social context and domain knowledge information. To this end, we develop a new topic modeling called *Social Context-aware Instance Recognition (SOCINST)* to model social context and domain knowledge for entity instance recognition.

We begin with a brief introduction of the topic model and then describe the proposed method. Probabilistic topic models have been successfully applied to multiple text mining tasks to extract topics from text [5, 15, 30]. We employ an Author-Topic (AT) model [30], which utilizes the topic distribution to represent the interdependencies among authors and document content. The AT model can be considered as an extension of Latent Dirichlet Allocation (LDA) [5], but one that considers the collaborative relationships between users. The model simulates the process when people collaborate on a work, e.g., writing a scientific paper, using a series of probabilistic steps. In essence, for each object it estimates a mixture of topic distributions that represent the probability of the object associated with every topic. For example, for each author v, we have a set of probabilities $\{P(z_i|v)\}_i$ or $\{\theta_{vz_i}\}_i$, respectively denoting how likely author v is interested in topic z_i. Similarly, we have $\{P(w_j|z)\}_j$ or $\{\phi_{zw_j}\}_j$, the probability of word w_j given topic z. We use Gibbs sampling to learn the probabilities. The interested reader can refer to [30] and [28] for details. To model inter-dependencies among more categories of entities, one can also consider Author-Conference-Topic (ACT) model [35].

Based on the learned topic distributions, we define topic-based features and incorporate them into the sequential labeling method. An example is illustrated in Figure 3(b).

4.1 Model Description

The traditional topic modeling approach does not consider the social-structure information; also, it is difficult to incorporate domain knowledge into the model. As a result, the learned topical context cannot accurately represent the social context. We develop a new topic modeling approach called Social Context-aware Instance Recognition (SOCINST) to incorporate both social context and domain knowledge into the topic model. Regarding social context, the basic idea here is that if two users have strong relationships with each other, e.g., as shown by their having many interactions, then their topic distribution are likely to be similar. For incorporating domain knowledge, the idea is that if two words are instances of the same concept or two related concepts in the knowledge base, then the two words are likely to have the same topic.

Technically, the difference of the proposed model from the Author-Topic (AT) model lies in the way that θ and ϕ are generated. For modeling documents, the AT model treats each document separately, and topics in a document are sampled from the author-specific multinomial distribution θ. However, this ignores poten-

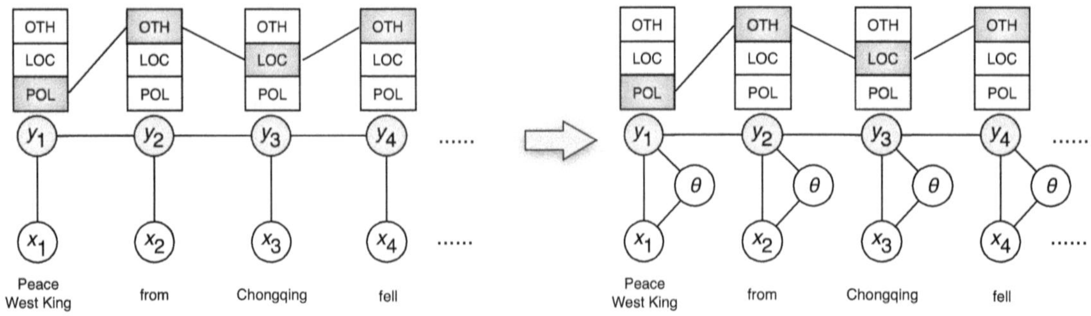

(a) Sequential Labeling with CRF (b) Sequential labeling with SOCINST

Figure 3: Graphical representation of the two sequential labeling models

tial relations between documents. Similarly, for modeling words, AT assumes that a document's words are interchangeable, and each word is sampled from a topic-specific multinomial distribution ϕ, which again ignores the potential relations between words. In the proposed SOCINST model, the multinomial distribution of instances is replaced with a tree-structured multinomial specific to the corresponding concept — e.g., $\phi \sim \text{DirichletTree}(\beta, \eta)$ — and the user-specific multinomial is replaced by a mixture of multinomials by combining neighbors' topic distributions. The advantage of this modeling method is that it smooths the learned model for instances where they belong to the same concept, which can significantly alleviate the ambiguity problem [4, 18].

Let us briefly introduce notations. d is a document and v_d is the author of the document[2]; θ_v is the topic model for author v; ϕ_z is a multinomial distribution over words specific to topic z; α and β are Dirichlet hyperparameters; η is the hyperparameter for the Dirichlet tree. Table 1 summarizes the notations used in the SOCINST model.

Modeling domain knowledge. Formally, the generative process of SOCINST is described in Algorithm 1. If a document d does not have any links to other documents or the author does not have any relationships with others, then for each word w_{di}, we draw a topic z_{di} from a topic distribution θ_v specific to author v and then use the topic to sample the word. In particular, for sampling word w_{di}, we check if the word is an instance of some concept $c \in KB$ in the training dataset. The generative process is described in Algorithm 2. If it is not, then we use a topic-specific multinomial distribution $\phi_{z_{di}}$ to generate the word. But if it is an instance of concept c, then we first sample the concept c from the multinomial $\phi_{z_{di}}$ and then sample the word from the concept-specific multinomial ψ_c. Intuitively, we replace the sampling of a word with a two-level generative process. At the first level, we select the corresponding concept according to a concept path distribution $multi(\pi)$; and at the second level, sample the word. Figure 4 shows an example of the sampling process. Theoretically, this process can be explained by the Dirichlet tree distribution [11, 31], a generalization of the Dirichlet distribution. In a Dirichlet distribution, all words in a document are treated independently; thus it is difficult to model dependencies between words. The Dirichlet tree distribution can be considered as a tree where words are leaf nodes, concepts are internal nodes, and the root node is the super concept of all nodes. Each tree edge encodes weight from the parent node to the child node. Let $S(c)$ be the immediate child of concept node c, $W(c)$ be the leaf nodes (words) in the subtree under concept c, W be all leaves

[2]For simplicity, we consider one author; but this can be easily extended to multiple authors by adding a uniform distribution for sampling an author to be responsible for each sampled topic [30].

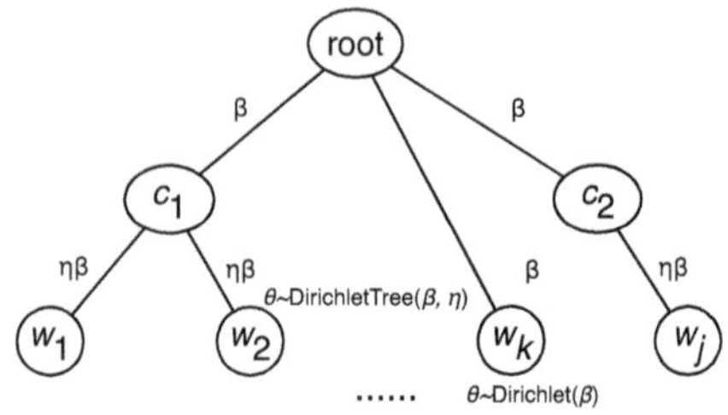

Figure 4: Example of sampling words from Dirichlet tree distribution. c is a concept and w is a word; β and η are two hyperparameters; root node is a super concept

in the tree and C be all the concepts (except the root concept). To generate a sample of multinomial distribution ϕ of a word (leaf node) from the Dirichlet tree distribution, we first sample a multinomial from the root node by using the edge weights from the root node to child nodes (concepts) as Dirichlet parameters, and further sample (re-distribute) the multinomial from the sampled internal (concept) node to its child nodes again, until we finally obtain the word. For simplicity, if we consider only one level of concepts, we can have the following Dirichlet tree distribution

$$\text{DirichletTree}(\beta, \eta) = \left(\prod_{i=1}^{W} \phi_{zw_i}^{\eta_{w_i}} \right) \times \left(\prod_{j, c_j \in C} \frac{\Gamma(\sum_{k, w_k \in W(c)} \eta_{w_k})}{\prod_{k, w_k \in W(c)} \Gamma(\eta_{w_k})} \left(\sum_{k, w_k \in W(c)} \phi_{zw_i}^{\eta_{w_i}} \right)^{\Delta(s)} \right) \quad (2)$$

where $\Gamma(.)$ is a gamma function; $\Delta(s) = \eta_c - \sum_{k, w_k \in W(c)} \eta_{w_k}$ denotes the difference between the weight of a concept and the sum of the weights of all instances under a concept. When $\Delta = 0$ for all concepts, the Dirichlet tree distribution reduces to a Dirichlet distribution.

Modeling social context. We mainly consider two types of social relationships: collaboration relationships and reference relationships. A collaboration relationship indicates that two users v_i and v_j collaborate with each other; for example collaboration on a scientific paper. A reference relationship indicates that v_i has a document that refers to one of v_j's documents. For example, in Twitter, if user v_i adds a post as a reply on v_j's microblog, then we create a reference relationship. The relationship can be either directed or undirected. For simplicity, here we consider only undirected relationships. For each relationship, (v, v'), and a new multinomial

Input: a social network G, a document set D, a knowledge base KB;
Output: estimated parameters θ,ϕ

For each author v, draw θ_v from Dirichlet prior α;
For each topic z, draw ϕ_z from Dirichlet prior β;
foreach *document* d **do**
    if v_d *does not have relationship with others* **then**
        foreach *word* $w_{di} \in \mathbf{w}_d$ **do**
            Draw a topic $z_{di} \sim multi(\theta_v)$ from the topic model of user v;
            Call SamplingWord(z_{di}, w_{di});
        end
    end
    else if v_d *have relationship with* v' **then**
        Construct a multinomial mixture $\vartheta_{v_d v'}$ by combining topics distributions specific to users v_d and v';
        foreach *word* $w_{di} \in \mathbf{w}_d$ **do**
            Draw a topic $z_{di} \sim multi(\vartheta)$ from the distribution specific to the pair;
            Call SamplingWord(z_{di}, w_{di});
        end
    end
end

Algorithm 1: Probabilistic generative process in SOCINST

SamplingWord(z_{di}, w_{di})
if w_{di} *is an instance of a concept* $c \in KB$ **then**
    Draw a concept path $\{c_k\}_k \sim multi(\pi)$ from a topic-specific concept path distribution;
    Draw word $w_{di} \sim multi(\psi_c)$ from a concept-specific multinomial distribution;
end
else
    Draw word $w_{di} \sim multi(\phi_{z_{di}})$ directly from a topic-specific multinomial distribution;
end

Algorithm 2: SamplingWord()

distribution $\vartheta_{vv'}$ is constructed by combining the two multinomial θ_v and $\theta_{v'}$ specific to the two users v and v'. The new distribution $\vartheta_{vv'}$ is then defined as $\tau(\theta_v + \theta_{v'})$, a simple mixture of the two expanded multinomials of θ_v and $\theta_{v'}$ [7], where τ is a normalization factor to guarantee that the sum of the distribution is 1. Finally, the word w_{di} is sampled from a topic z_{di} according to the new distribution $\vartheta_{vv'}$. By modeling the new distribution, SOCINST smooths the topic distribution of users who have social relationships. A similar strategy has been also used in [34] for modeling collaborations. Figure 5 gives an example of constructing multinomial mixtures based on social relationships. It is very flexible for incorporating hierarchical structure among users. For example, two users can form a pair, and the pair can be further combined with other pairs to form a group, and further combined with other groups to form a community. To do this, we only need to add more internal nodes to the constructed Dirichlet tree.

4.2 Model Learning

The Dirichlet tree distribution is also conjugate to the multinomial, thus we can use the Markov Chain Monte Carlo (MCMC) method to effectively train the model. In particular, we use Gibbs sampling to estimate the unknown parameters $\{\theta, \vartheta, \phi\}$ in the SOCINST model. We evaluate the posterior distribution on z for each word in the document; then use the sampling results of z to infer θ, ϑ and ϕ. More specifically, we begin with the joint probability of all documents, and then using the chain rule, we obtain the posterior probability of sampling the topic for each word.

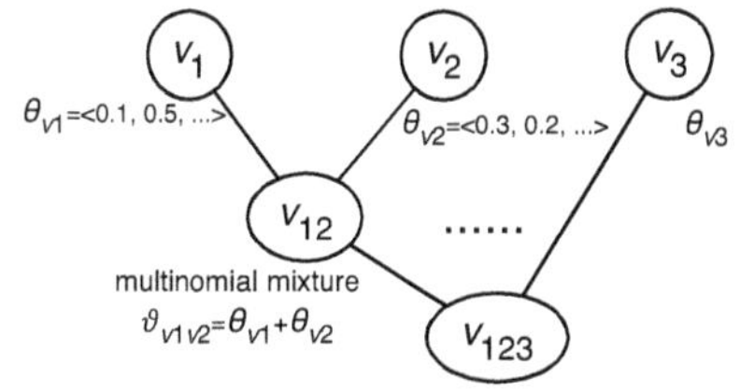

Figure 5: Example of constructing multinomial mixture based on social relationships

When we do not consider the social context, and the specific word w_{di} is not an instance of a concept in the knowledge base, we use a sampling equation similar to that in the Author-Topic model [30], i.e. with the posterior probability:

$$P(z_{di}|\mathbf{z}_{-di}, \mathbf{w}, \cdot) = \frac{n^{-di}_{vz_{di}} + \alpha}{\sum_z n^{-di}_{vz} + K\alpha} \times \frac{m^{-di}_{z_{di}w_{di}} + \beta}{\sum_w m^{-di}_{z_{di}w} + W\beta} \quad (3)$$

where n_{vz} is the number of times that topic z has been sampled from the multinomial distribution specific to the author v; m_{zw} is the number of times that word w has been generated by topic z; the number n^{-di} with the superscript $-di$ denotes a quantity, excluding the current instance; $\cdot$ indicates all the other parameters we should consider when calculating the probability.

If the word w_{di} is an instance of a concept, then based on the conjugate property between the Dirichlet tree distribution and the multinomial, we have (by assuming that we only have one level of concepts):

$$P(z_{di}|\mathbf{z}_{-di},\mathbf{w}, \cdot) = \frac{n^{-di}_{vz_{di}} + \alpha}{\sum_z n^{-di}_{vz} + W\alpha} \times \frac{m^{-di}_{z_{di}c_{di}} + W_c\beta}{\sum_c m^{-di}_{z_{di}c} + W\beta} \times \frac{m^{-di}_{c_{di}w_{di}} + \eta}{\sum_w m^{-di}_{c_{di}w} + W_c\eta} \quad (4)$$

where m_{zc} is the number of times that instances of concept c have been generated by z; W_c is the number of instances of concept c; m_{cw} is the number of times word w appears as an instance of c in all documents. As discussed before, the model can be easily extended by incorporating more levels of concepts. For example, we could consider concept-subconcept relationships by adding an internal node into the Dirichlet tree. Accordingly, the posterior probability can be generalized as:

$$P(z_{di}|\mathbf{z}_{-di}, \mathbf{w}, \cdot) = \frac{n^{-di}_{vz_{di}} + \alpha}{\sum_z n^{-di}_{vz} + W\alpha} \times \prod_{k=1}^{T} \frac{m^{-di}_{z_{di}c^k_{di}} + W_{c^k_{di}}\beta}{\sum_{c_s}(m^{-di}_{z_{di}c_s} + W_{c^k_s}\beta)} \times \frac{m^{-di}_{c_{di}w_{di}} + \eta}{\sum_w m^{-di}_{c_{di}w} + W_c\eta} \quad (5)$$

where $\{c^1_{di}, c^2_{di}, \cdots, c^T_{di}\}$ is a concept path from the root node to the leaf word node (excluding the end nodes); c_s indicates a child node of concept c.

To incorporate the social context further into the model, we use the constructed new distribution $\vartheta_{vv'}$ to replace the original multinomial distribution of user v and v', and then use the distribution $\vartheta_{vv'}$ to sample topic for each word. The posterior probability can be rewritten as:

$$P(z_{di}|\mathbf{z}_{-di}, \mathbf{w}, \cdot) = \frac{n_{vz_{di}}^{-di} + \gamma n_{v'z_{di}} + \alpha}{\sum_z (n_{vz}^{-di} + \gamma n_{v'z}) + W\alpha} \times \prod_{k=1}^{T} \frac{m_{z_{di}c_{di}^k}^{-di} + W_{c_{di}^k}\beta}{\sum_{c_s}(m_{z_{di}c_s}^{-di} + W_{c_s^k}\beta)} \times \frac{m_{c_{di}w_{di}}^{-di} + \eta}{\sum_w m_{c_{di}w}^{-di} + W_c\eta} \quad (6)$$

where γ is a tunable parameter to control the extent to which we want to smooth the distribution between v and v'. (Detailed derivation is given in Appendix.)

During the parameter estimation, the algorithm keeps track of an $|V| \times K$ (user by topic) count matrix, and an $C \times K$ (concepts by topic) count matrix. Given these matrices, we can estimate the probabilities of θ, ϑ, and ϕ.

Complexity Analysis. We analyze the complexity of the proposed model. The AT model has a complexity of $O(\bar{A}_d M \bar{N}_d KL)$, where M is the number of documents, $\bar{A}_d$ is the average number of authors for document d, L is the number of sampling iterations, K is the number of topics, and $\bar{N}_d$ is the average number of word tokens in document d. In our setting, we only consider one author, thus $\bar{A}_d$ can be ignored from the complexity. Then, by incorporating the domain knowledge, the complexity increases linearly with the height T of the Dirichlet tree. The height T is usually very small compared to the scale of the knowledge base, and can be considered as a constant. By incorporating the social context, the complexity increases linearly with the average number $|\bar{E}|$ of social relationships for each user in the social network G. By combining both of them, we obtain the final complexity $O(M\bar{N}_d L|\bar{E}|K)$. The complexity is acceptable, as in most cases, the average number of social relationships $|\bar{E}|$ is small comparing with M and N_d.

4.3 Applying to Instance Recognition

We now discuss how to combine the learned topic information into sequential labeling model for instance recognition. First, we apply the proposed SOCINST model to the document set to learn the topic distributions. Then we define feature functions in the sequential labeling method based on the topic distributions for instance recognition. Specifically, we define K topic-specific feature functions in the CRF model for each token, where K is the number of topics learned by the topic model. We use a threshold τ to determine whether a topic is relevant to an instance or not. If $P(z|v) > \tau$, then the value of the corresponding unit is 1, otherwise 0. Figure 3(b) shows the graphical representation of the sequential labeling process with SOCINST.

When training SOCINST, as for the hyperparameters α, β, and η, following [1, 5], we empirically take fixed values (i.e., $K = 15$, $\alpha = 0.1$, $\beta = 0.1$, and $\eta = 10$). γ is defined to represent our preference for smoothing the distributions between users with social relationships. We set it as $\gamma = 0.5$. We did try different settings and found that the estimated topic models are not very sensitive to the hyperparameters.

5. EXPERIMENTAL RESULTS

We conduct various experiments to evaluate the SOCINST method. All datasets and codes are publicly available.[3]

5.1 Experiment Setup

Dataset. We evaluate the proposed method on three datasets (as shown in Table 2): ICDM'12 Contest, Weibo, and I2B2.

[3]http://aminer.org/socinst/

Table 2: Statistics of the three datasets

Dataset	Weibo	I2B2	ICDM'12 Contest
#documents	1,800	899	2,110
#instances	545	2,400	565
#relationships	10,763	27,175	NA

Weibo. Weibo is the most popular microblogging service in China. The dataset is from [17]. The dataset includes 1,553,347 tweets crawled from Weibo from May 1st, 2013 to June 30th, 2013. Human annotations have been made on the dataset to label morph entities (e.g., "Fruit company") and their corresponding targets ("Apple Inc."). In total, there are 107 different morph entities. We view each distinct morph entity as a concept in the knowledge base. We randomly sampled 1,800 tweets that contain the morph entities. We use the following relationship to construct the relationship between users. Finally, we extracted 10,763 relationships. Our goal is to extract real morph instances in the dataset.

I2B2. This is a health care dataset from [37]. It was used in the 2006 Deidentification Challenge on automatically identifying private health information from medical discharge records.[4] The dataset comprises 899 medical records, with a total of 2,400 private health information instances in the records. We view each patient as a user and create a relationship between patients if they go to the same hospital. In total, we have 27,175 relationships. The knowledge base consists of eight concepts, such as Doctor, Location, and Hospital. Our goal here is to extract private health information instances in the dataset.

ICDM'12 Contest. This is a product forum dataset used in the ICDM'12 Contest[5]. The task is to automatically recognize product mentions in forum textual content and to also disambiguate which product(s) in product catalogs are being referenced. The dataset comprises 2,110 documents and a total of 565 labeled product mentions in these documents. We view each product catalog as a concept in the knowledge base and finally construct a large knowledge base of 15,367,328 concepts. The dataset does not provide the user information; thus, we mainly focus on evaluating the effect of incorporating domain knowledge for instance recognition. Our goal is to recognize product mentions in the dataset.

Comparison methods. We compare our model with the following methods for instance extraction:

Standard Matching (SM): Simply extracts all the terms/symbols that are annotated as extracted instances in the training data, then finds their occurrences in the test data and extracts them as target instances.

Rule Template (RT): Recognizes target instances from the test data by a set of rule templates. We design rules based on sentence position, special characters, and semantic patterns to extract instances.

Conditional Random Field (CRF): Trains a conditional random field (CRF) model using features associated with each token. Classifies each token into predefined labels, such as age, location, and phone in the I2B2 dataset. For CRF, we employ MALLET [24].

CRF+AT: Uses Author-Topic (AT) [30] to train a model for each document. Then it incorporates the topic distribution of each document as features in the CRF model for instance recognition. The

[4]https://www.i2b2.org/NLP/DataSets/Main.php

[5]http://icdm2012.ua.ac.be/content/contest

Table 3: **Performance of different methods on the three datasets (%)**

Data	Method	Recall	Precision	F1-Measure
Weibo	SM	55.34	34.92	42.82
	RT	39.62	66.31	49.60
	CRF	29.24	94.89	44.71
	CRF+AT	43.71	89.67	58.77
	SOCINST	**65.72**	76.27	**70.60**
I2B2	SM	39.58	28.24	32.96
	RT	39.60	40.29	39.94
	CRF	40.99	56.19	47.40
	CRF+AT	41.37	54.92	47.19
	SOCINST	**43.94**	**57.18**	**49.69**
ICDM'12 Contest	SM	9.47	62.50	16.46
	RT	23.69	42.01	30.30
	CRF	21.80	53.48	30.97
	CRF+AT	26.54	51.37	35.00
	SOCINST	**37.91**	53.33	**44.32**

difference between this method and CRF is that here we consider topic information.[6]

SOCINST: (Cf. § 4) This is the proposed method, which incorporates both domain knowledge and social context to extract topics. The topical information is then integrated into the sequential labeling method for instance recognition.

SM and RT only consider hard rules. In all the other comparison methods, we try to use the same linguistic features. Unlike CRF, CRF+AT and SOCINST incorporate topic-based features. The difference between AT and SOCINST lies in the way that topics are learned from the documents.

Evaluation Measures. In each dataset, we use the different methods to recognize instances and compare with ground-truth data. We evaluate the performance of different approaches in terms of Precision, Recall, and F1-Measure [6].

All algorithms are implemented in C++ and Python, and the experiments are performed on an x64 machine with E5-4650 2.70GHz Intel Xeon CPU (with 64 cores) and 128GB RAM. The operating system is Ubuntu 12.04. The proposed algorithm has tractable running times on the datasets and requires less than 120 minutes for training and prediction.

5.2 Performance Analysis

Table 3 lists the performance of instance recognition by the comparison methods on the three datasets. The proposed SOCINST method clearly outperforms the comparison methods (+5.3-26.6% in terms of F1-score, $p < 0.01$ with t-test). SM and RT use hard rules for recognizing instances, which often leads to suboptimal performance in F1-measure. CRF, considering the statistical linguistic information, improves recognition performance in terms of F1-measure. AT incorporates the topic information extracted from the input documents, and thus performs better than the standard CRF method. SOCINST incorporates both domain knowledge and social context into the topic model and obtains significant improvement over both CRF and CRF+AT methods. On the ICDM'12 Contest dataset, we further compare SOCINST with the method [38] of the first place in the contest. In the comparison, we use the same *blending strategy* as that of [38] to combine results of different models. Figure 6 shows a performance comparison of the two methods. SOCINST Blend is the result of our method with the blending strategy. It can be seen that our method significantly outperforms (+21.4%; $p \ll 1e-5$ with t-test) the performance of the first place in terms of all measures.

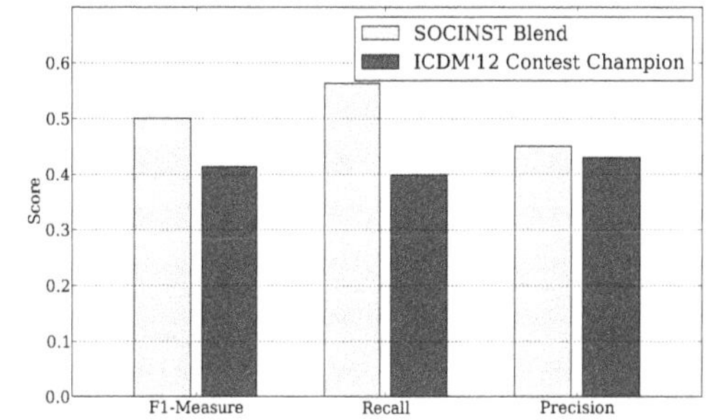

Figure 6: Performance comparison of SOCINST and the first place [38] in ICDM'12 Contest

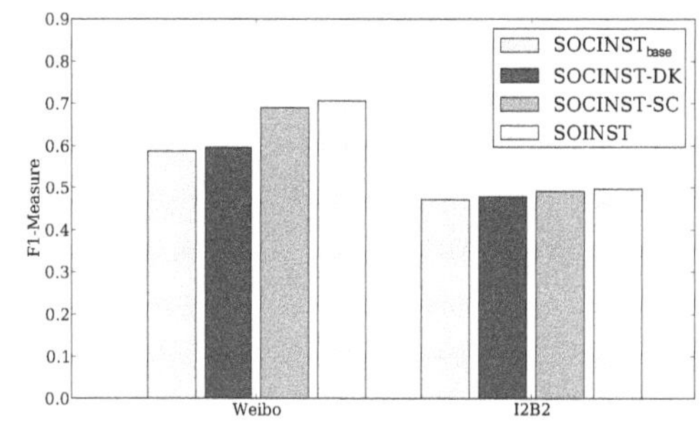

Figure 8: Effects of social context and domain knowledge. For SOCINST$_{base}$, we removed both social context and domain knowledge from our method. SOCINST-SC and SOCINST-DK are results in which we removed social context or domain knowledge information, respectively, from our method

Effects of social context and domain knowledge. We study how social context and domain knowledge can help instance recognition. Since the ICDM'12 Contest dataset does not consist of social relationships, we focus this analysis on the other two datasets: Weibo and I2B2. More specifically, we respectively remove domain knowledge and social context when training our proposed model, and then compare performance of instance recognition based on the trained models. Figure 8 shows the F1-Measure performance on the two datasets. SOCINST$_{base}$ means that we removed both social context and domain knowledge from our method. SOCINST-SC and SOCINST-DK indicate results from having removed social context or domain-knowledge information, respectively, from our method. We can clearly see that both social context and domain knowledge contribute significantly to the results for the two datasets. It is also interesting to see that social context seems to be more important for modeling the Weibo data. With social context information, the performance of instance recognition improved by up to 10% on Weibo, compared to an improvement of 5% on the I2B2 data.

Parameter analysis. We evaluate how different parameters (including number of topics, K, and hyperparameters α and η) affect

[6]The method is similar to T-NER [27], which considers both labeled information and topic information for instance recognition, but it does not model social context. We compare with this method to demonstrate the necessary to model social context and domain knowledge together.

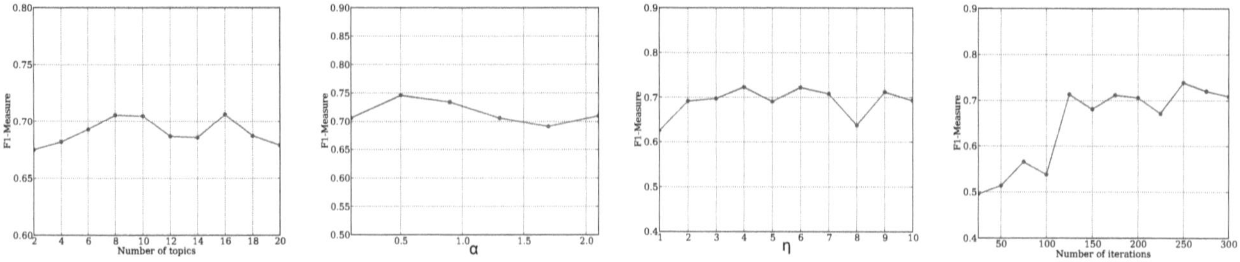

(a) number of topics K (b) Hyperparameter α (c) Hyperparameter η (d) Convergence analysis

Figure 7: Parameter analysis. (a) Performance of the SOCINST model by varying the number of topics K; (b) Performance of the SOCINST model is stable when varying α parameter; (c) Performance of SOCINST when varying the parameter η; (d) Convergence analysis of SOCINST model

the quality of the models learned by SOCINST. We performed the following analysis based on the Weibo data. For the number of topics, K, we perform an analysis by varying the number of topics in the proposed SOCINST method. Figure 7(a) shows its F1-Measure performance with the number of topics varied. We see that when the number is small (< 10), increasing the number often results in a performance improvement. The trend becomes stable when the number of topics is about 10. This demonstrates the stability of the SOCINST method with respect to the number of topics. Regarding the hyperparameter α, Figure 7(b) shows the performance of SOCINST with the parameter α varied (all the other hyperparameters fixed and the number of topics is set to $K = 15$). Although the performance changes when varying the value of α, the largest difference is less than 0.03. This confirms that the SOCINST method is not sensitive to the particular choice of α. Regarding the parameter η, Figure 7(c) shows the performance of SOCINST with the parameter η varied (with all the other hyperparameters fixed). It indicates that for a very small value for η, which means that we largely ignore the effect of social context, the performance varies quite a bit. However, as we increase η to 6 or more, the performance becomes much more stable.

Convergence analysis. We further investigate the convergence of the SOCINST learning algorithm. Figure 7(d) shows the convergence analysis of the algorithm on the Weibo dataset. We see that the algorithm converges within 300 Gibbs sampling iterations. This rapid fast convergence makes possible efficient training of the model on large scale datasets.

5.3 Discussions

Leveraging social context and domain knowledge, SOCINST clearly outperforms traditional instance recognition methods, such as Standard Matching (SM), Rule Template (RT), and Conditional Random Field (CRF). Several recently developed methods also considered using topic model to improve the performance of entity recognition. T-NER [27] is one of the most closely related methods. It considers labeled information and topic information for instance recognition. T-NER performs better than the Stanford NER system. In our comparison methods, CRF+AT can be considered as a counterpart of T-NER. CRF+AT considers labeled information, as well as topic information. However both T-NER and CRF+AT do not consider social context. CRF+AT underperforms the proposed SOCINST method by -2.5-11.9%. Liu et al. [23] presented another related method that incorporates additional (redundancy) information into a linear Conditional Random Fields (CRF) model for entity recognition. In principle, this method is similar to CRF or CRF+AT in our comparison methods, because the only difference between the method and CRF is that it combines the K-Nearest Neighbors (KNN) classified results into the CRF model to boost the recognition performance.

Based on the propose model, we are developing a new feature in ArnetMiner [35][7], an academic social network analysis and mining system. We are trying to automatically recognize instances from paper abstracts (or user queries) and map the the instances to a knowledge base from Wikipedia.

6. RELATED WORK

Considerable research has been conducted on entity recognition. Collins [9] proposed a ranking algorithm for entity extraction based on boosting and the voted perceptron. The method can obtain a performance similar to that of the Conditional Random Field (CRF) method. Finkel et al. [13] designed an entity extraction method by combining long-distance dependency information. A survey of entity recognition can be also found in [25]. However, all these works mainly focus on the linguistic information, and do not consider the social context or domain knowledge. Recently, Liu et al. [23] proposed to combine a K-Nearest Neighbors (KNN) classifier with a linear CRF model under a semi-supervised framework to deal with the unavailability of training data. This method can be considered as an extension of the CRF method, but it does not explicitly consider social context and domain knowledge information. Ritter et al. [27] used Labeled LDA [26] to exploit Freebase as a source of distant supervision to help named entity recognition in tweets by leveraging the redundancy in tweets. Again, they do not consider the social network information. Huang et al. [17] studied a special problem of entity recognition, entity morph. They try to identify those instances where authors deliberately hide the true entities due to Internet censorship. They defined several social-based features. They mainly focus on a special case of instance recognition and their method does not incorporate social context and domain knowledge in a unified model. Some other related references can be also found in [8, 20].

Our work is also relevant to entity resolution, where the task is to link entities of the same meaning or distinguish different entities with the same name. For example, Bhattacharya and Getoor [4] proposed a collective method for entity resolution in relational data. Kataria et al. [18] developed a hierarchical topic model for resolving different entities that have the same name. Li et al. [22] used network structure for named entity resolution. Tang et al.[32] studied the name resolution problem in digital libraries. However, in most entity resolution research, entity instances are assumed as input, so their focus is very different from the instance recognition studied in this work. Another line of loosely related research is en-

[7] `http://aminer.org`

tity matching [2, 3, 21, 29], which tries to find alignment between entities from different sources.

From the modeling aspect, substantial research has been conducted for topic models, such as [5, 15, 30]. Andrzejewski et al. [1] proposed a new method that incorporates must-links and cannot-links into the topic model. A must-link means that two words must be sampled from the same topic and a cannot-link means two words cannot be sampled from the same topic. Hu et al. [16] adopted the same strategy for modeling linguistic constraints in the topic model. In this paper, we propose a new method by combining social relationships and domain knowledge in a unified model.

7. CONCLUSION

In this paper, we study the problem of instance recognition by incorporating social context and domain knowledge. We precisely define the problem and propose a topic modeling approach to learn topics by considering social relationships between users and context information from a domain knowledge base. Experimental results on three different datasets validate the effectiveness and the efficiency of the proposed method.

The general idea in this paper, to incorporate social context and domain knowledge for entity instance recognition, represents an interesting and new research direction. There are many potential future directions for this work. A straightforward task would be to incorporate human feedback into the proposed model. Looking further ahead, we believe that combining the sequential labeling model and the proposed SOCINST into a unified model should be beneficial. Finally, further incorporating other social interactions, such as social influence [33], to help instance recognition is an intriguing direction for future research.

Acknowledgements. The work is supported by the National High-tech R&D Program (No. 2014AA015103), National Basic Research Program of China (No. 2014CB340506), Natural Science Foundation of China (No. 61222212), a research fund supported by Huawei Inc., and Beijing key lab of networked multimedia.

8. REFERENCES

[1] D. Andrzejewski, X. Zhu, and M. Craven. Incorporating domain knowledge into topic modeling via dirichlet forest priors. In *ICML'09*, pages 25–32, 2009.

[2] X. Bai, F. P. Junqueira, and S. H. Sengamedu. Exploiting user clicks for automatic seed set generation for entity matching. In *KDD'13*, pages 980–988, 2013.

[3] K. Bellare, S. Iyengar, A. G. Parameswaran, and V. Rastogi. Active sampling for entity matching. In *KDD'12*, pages 1131–1139, 2012.

[4] I. Bhattacharya and L. Getoor. Collective entity resolution in relational data. *ACM Transactions on Knowledge Discovery from Data*, 1(1):1–36, March 2007.

[5] D. M. Blei, A. Y. Ng, and M. I. Jordan. Latent dirichlet allocation. *JMLR*, 3:993–1022, 2003.

[6] C. Buckley and E. M. Voorhees. Retrieval evaluation with incomplete information. In *SIGIR'2004*, pages 25–32, 2004.

[7] W. Buntine and A. Jakulin. Applying discrete pca in data analysis. In *UAI'04*, pages 59–66, 2004.

[8] L. Chiticariu, R. Krishnamurthy, Y. Li, F. Reiss, and S. Vaithyanathan. Domain adaptation of rule-based annotators for named-entity recognition tasks. In *EMNLP'10*, pages 1002–1012, 2010.

[9] M. Collins. Ranking algorithms for named-entity extraction: boosting and the voted perceptron. In *ACL'02*, pages 489–496, 2002.

[10] M. Dean, G. Schreiber, S. Bechhofer, F. van Harmelen, J. Hendler, I. Horrocks, D. L. McGuinness, P. F. Patel-Schneider, and L. A. Stein. Owl web ontology language reference. w3c recommendation., Feb. 2004.

[11] S. Y. Dennis. On the hyper-dirichlet type 1 and hyper-liouville distributions. *Communications in Statistics - Theory and Methods*, 20:4069–4081, 1991.

[12] A. Doucet, N. de Freitas, K. Murphy, and S. Russell. Rao-blackwellised particle filtering for dynamic bayesian networks. In *UAI'00*, pages 176–183, 2000.

[13] J. R. Finkel, T. Grenager, and C. D. Manning. Incorporating non-local information into information extraction systems by gibbs sampling. In *ACL'05*, pages 363–370, 2005.

[14] G. Heinrich. Parameter estimation for text analysis. Technical report, University of Leipzig, Germany, 2004.

[15] T. Hofmann. Probabilistic latent semantic indexing. In *SIGIR'99*, pages 50–57, 1999.

[16] Y. Hu, J. Boyd-Graber, and B. Satinoff. Interactive topic modeling. In *HLT'11*, pages 248–257, 2011.

[17] H. Huang, Z. Wen, D. Yu, H. Ji, Y. Sun, J. Han, and H. Li. Resolving entity morphs in censored data. In *ACL'13*, pages 1083–1093, 2013.

[18] S. Kataria, K. S. Kumar, R. Rastogi, P. Sen, and S. H. Sengamedu. Entity disambiguation with hierarchical topic models. In *KDD'11*, pages 1037–1045, 2011.

[19] J. D. Lafferty, A. McCallum, and F. C. N. Pereira. Conditional random fields: Probabilistic models for segmenting and labeling sequence data. In *ICML'01*, pages 282–289, 2001.

[20] C. Li, J. Weng, Q. He, Y. Yao, A. Datta, A. Sun, and B.-S. Lee. Twiner: Named entity recognition in targeted twitter stream. In *SIGIR'12*, pages 721–730, 2012.

[21] J. Li, J. Tang, Y. Li, and Q. Luo. Rimom: A dynamic multi-strategy ontology alignment framework. *IEEE TKDE*, 21(8):1218–1232, 2009.

[22] Y. Li, C. Wang, F. Han, J. Han, D. Roth, and X. Yan. Mining evidences for named entity disambiguation. In *KDD'13*, pages 1070–1078, 2013.

[23] X. Liu, S. Zhang, F. Wei, and M. Zhou. Recognizing named entities in tweets. In *Proceedings of the 49th Annual Meeting of the Association for Computational Linguistics: Human Language Technologies - Volume 1*, ACL '11, pages 359–367, 2011.

[24] A. K. McCallum. Mallet: A machine learning for language toolkit. http://mallet.cs.umass.edu, 2002.

[25] D. Nadeau and S. Sekine. A survey of named entity recognition and classification. *Linguisticae Investigationes*, 30:3–26, 2007.

[26] D. Ramage, D. Hall, R. Nallapati, and C. D. Manning. Labeled lda: A supervised topic model for credit attribution in multi-labeled corpora. In *EMNLP '09*, pages 248–256, 2009.

[27] A. Ritter, S. Clark, Mausam, and O. Etzioni. Named entity recognition in tweets: An experimental study. In *EMNLP'11*, pages 1524–1534, 2011.

[28] M. Rosen-Zvi, T. Griffiths, M. Steyvers, and P. Smyth. The author-topic model for authors and documents. In *UAI'04*, pages 487–494, 2004.

[29] W. Shen, J. Wang, P. Luo, and M. Wang. Linking named entities in tweets with knowledge base via user interest modeling. In *KDD'13*, pages 68–76, 2013.

[30] M. Steyvers, P. Smyth, and T. Griffiths. Probabilistic author-topic models for information discovery. In *KDD'04*, pages 306–315, 2004.

[31] Y.-C. Tam and T. Schultz. Correlated latent semantic model for unsupervised lm adaptation. In *ICASSP?07*, volume 4, pages IV–41–IV–44, 2007.

[32] J. Tang, A. Fong, B. Wang, and J. Zhang. A unified probabilistic framework for name disambiguation in digital library. *IEEE TKDE*, 24(6):975–987, 2012.

[33] J. Tang, J. Sun, C. Wang, and Z. Yang. Social influence analysis in large-scale networks. In *KDD'09*, pages 807–816, 2009.

[34] J. Tang, S. Wu, J. Sun, and H. Su. Cross-domain collaboration recommendation. In *KDD'12*, pages 1285–1294, 2012.

[35] J. Tang, J. Zhang, L. Yao, J. Li, L. Zhang, and Z. Su. Arnetminer: Extraction and mining of academic social networks. In *KDD'08*, pages 990–998, 2008.

[36] K. M. Ting and I. H. Witten. Issues in stacked generalization. *Journal of Artificial Intelligence Research*, 10:271–289, 1999.

[37] O. Uzuner, Y. Juo, and P. Szolovits. Evaluating the state-of-the-art in automatic de-identification. *J Am Med Inform Assoc*, 14(5):550–563, 2007.

[38] S. Wu, Z. Fang, and J. Tang. Accurate product name recognition from user generated content. In *ICDM 2012 Contest*, pages 874–877, 2012.

9. APPENDIX

According to the generative process, we could integrate out the multinomial distributions θ, ϑ, ϕ, because the model only uses conjugate priors [12]. We use Eq. 6 as the example to explain its derivation, as it contains both social context and domain knowledge. First we write the joint probability:

$$\begin{aligned} & P(\mathbf{w},\mathbf{z},\mathbf{v}|\alpha,\beta,\eta,\gamma) \\ \propto & \int P(\mathbf{z}|(\mathbf{v},\mathbf{v}'),\vartheta)P(\vartheta|\alpha)d\vartheta \\ & \int P(\mathbf{w}|\mathbf{z},\phi)P(\phi|\pi_T)\prod_{k=1}^{T}P(\pi_{k+1}|\pi_k,\eta_c)P(\pi_1|\beta,\eta)d\phi d\pi \end{aligned} \tag{7}$$

The conditional of s_i is obtained by dividing the joint distribution of all variables by the joint with all variables but s_i (denoted by $\mathbf{s}_{-i}$) and canceling factors that do not depend on $\mathbf{s}_{-i}$.

$$\begin{aligned} P(z_{di}|\mathbf{z}_{-di},\mathbf{w},.) = & \frac{P(\mathbf{w},\mathbf{z},\mathbf{v}|\alpha,\beta,\eta,\gamma)}{P(\mathbf{w},\mathbf{z}_{di},\mathbf{v}|\alpha,\beta,\eta,\gamma)} \\ = & \frac{\int P(\mathbf{w}|\mathbf{z},\phi)P(\phi|\pi_T)\prod_{k=1}^{T}P(\pi_{k+1}|\pi_k,\eta_c)P(\pi_1|\beta,\eta)d\phi d\pi}{\int P(\mathbf{w}|\mathbf{z},\phi)P(\phi|\pi_T)\prod_{k=1}^{T}P(\pi_{k+1}|\pi_k,\eta_c)P(\pi_1|\beta,\eta)d\phi d\pi} \\ & \cdot\frac{\int P(\mathbf{z}|(\mathbf{v},\mathbf{v}'),\vartheta)P(\vartheta|\alpha)d\vartheta}{\int P(\mathbf{z}|(\mathbf{v},\mathbf{v}'),\vartheta)P(\vartheta|\alpha)d\vartheta} \end{aligned} \tag{8}$$

The first fraction of Eq. 8 is responsible for sampling word from topic and the second term is responsible for sampling topic from user (with social relationships). We start with the derivation of the second fraction. Specifically, as $P(\mathbf{z}|(\mathbf{v},\mathbf{v}',\vartheta)$ and $P(\vartheta|\alpha)$ are a conjugate pair of Multinomial-Dirichlet, we could solve the Multinomial-Dirichlet integral using Gibbs sampling [14]:

$$\begin{aligned} & \int P(\mathbf{z}|(\mathbf{v},\mathbf{v}'),\vartheta)P(\vartheta|\alpha)d\vartheta \\ = & \prod_d \frac{1}{\Delta(\alpha)}\prod_z \vartheta_{vv'z}^{n_{vz}+n_{v'z}+\alpha-1}d\vartheta_{vv'} \\ = & \prod_d \frac{\Delta(\vec{n_d}+\alpha)}{\Delta(\alpha)}, \\ & \text{with } \Delta(\alpha)=\frac{\Gamma(\alpha)^T}{\Gamma(T\alpha)} \text{ and } \vec{n_d}=\{n_{vz}+n_{v'z}\}_{z=1}^{T} \end{aligned}$$

where (v,v') denotes a social relationship between user v and v'; n_{vz} and $n_{v'z}$ are two numbers obtained when combining the two distributions θ_v and $\theta_{v'}$. Essentially, in this sampling, we smooth the sampled topic from a user v-specific topic distribution θ_v by the mixture $\vartheta_{vv'}$ of θ_v and $\theta_{v'}$. Accordingly, the second fraction of Eq. 8 can be written as:

$$\begin{aligned} & \frac{\int P(\mathbf{z}|(\mathbf{v},\mathbf{v}'),\vartheta)P(\vartheta|\alpha)d\vartheta}{\int P(\mathbf{z}_{-di}|(\mathbf{v},\mathbf{v}'),\vartheta)P(\vartheta|\alpha)d\vartheta} = \frac{\prod_d \frac{\Delta(\vec{n_d}+\alpha)}{\Delta(\alpha)}}{\prod_d \frac{\Delta(\vec{n}_{d,\neg i}+\alpha)}{\Delta(\alpha)}} \\ = & \frac{\frac{\Gamma(n_{vz}^{-di}+n_{v'z}+\alpha)}{\Gamma(\sum_{z'}(n_{vz'}^{-di}+n_{v'z'}+\alpha))}}{\frac{\Gamma(n_{vz}^{-di}+n_{v'z}+\alpha-1)}{\Gamma([\sum_{z'}(n_{vz'}^{-di}+n_{v'z'}+\alpha)]-1)}} = \frac{n_{vz_{di}}^{-di}+n_{v'z_{di}}+\alpha}{\sum_z(n_{vz_{di}}^{-di}+n_{v'z_{di}}+\alpha)} \end{aligned} \tag{9}$$

Here, we use the identity $\Gamma(x+1)=x\Gamma(x)$; the superscript $^{-di}$ denotes a quantity, excluding the current instance. By further considering a tunable parameter γ to balance the importance between n_{vz} and $n_{v'z}$, we can obtain the first term in Eq. 6. Analogously, we can derive the first fraction of Eq. 8. The difference is that ϕ is sampled from a Dirichlet tree distribution instead of a Dirichlet distribution as that used for sampling topic z. To make it more clear, let us assume that there is a concept path $\{c_{di}^1,\cdots,c_{di}^T\}$ from the root node to the leaf word node (excluding the leaf node). To sample the first level concept c^1, we have

$$\begin{aligned} P(c_{di}^1|\pi,\beta,\eta) = & \frac{\prod_i \frac{\Delta(\vec{m_z}+\alpha)}{\Delta(\beta)}}{\prod_i \frac{\Delta(\vec{m}_{z,\neg di}+\alpha)}{\Delta(\beta)}} \\ = & \frac{\frac{\Gamma(m_{zc_{di}^1}^{-di}+W_{c_{di}^1}\beta)}{\Gamma(\sum_{c_s}(m_{zc_s}^{-di}+W_{c_s}\beta))}}{\frac{\Gamma(m_{zc_{di}^1}^{-di}+\beta-1)}{\Gamma([\sum_{c_s}(m_{zc_s}^{-di}+W_{c_s}\beta)]-1)}} = \frac{m_{zc_{di}^1}^{-di}+W_{c_{di}^1}\beta}{\sum_{c_s}(m_{zc_s}+W_{c_s}\beta)} \end{aligned} \tag{10}$$

We continue to sample the child node in the concept path, until we get the last internal node in the Dirichlet tree. In this way, we could obtain

$$\prod_{k=1}^{T}\frac{m_{z_{di}c_{di}^k}^{-di}+W_{c_{di}^k}\beta}{\sum_{c_s}(m_{z_{di}c_s}^{-di}+W_{c_s^k}\beta)} \tag{11}$$

Then applying a similar sampling process for word from a topic-specific distribution to that in the standard LDA model, we can obtain the first term in Eq. 6.

$$\frac{m_{c_{di}w_{di}}^{-di}+\eta}{\sum_w m_{c_{di}w}^{-di}+W_c\eta} \tag{12}$$

Finally, by combining Eqs. 9, 11, and 12, we obtain Eq. 6.

Querying Web-Scale Information Networks Through Bounding Matching Scores

Jiahui Jin[†‡], Samamon Khemmarat[‡], Lixin Gao[‡], Junzhou Luo[†]
[†]School of Computer Science and Engineering, Southeast University, China
[‡]Department of Electrical and Computer Engineering, University of Massachusetts Amherst, USA
{jhjin, jluo}@seu.edu.cn; {khemmarat, lgao}@ecs.umass.edu

ABSTRACT

Web-scale information networks containing billions of entities are common nowadays. Querying these networks can be modeled as a subgraph matching problem. Since information networks are incomplete and noisy in nature, it is important to discover answers that match exactly as well as answers that are similar to queries. Existing graph matching algorithms usually use graph indices to improve the efficiency of query processing. For web-scale information networks, it may not be feasible to build the graph indices due to the amount of work and the memory/storage required.

In this paper, we propose an efficient algorithm for finding the best k answers for a given query without precomputing graph indices. The quality of an answer is measured by a matching score that is computed online. To speed up query processing, we propose a novel technique for bounding the matching scores during the computation. By using bounds, we can efficiently prune the answers that have low qualities without having to evaluate all possible answers. The bounding technique can be implemented in a distributed environment, allowing our approach to efficiently answer the queries on web-scale information networks. We demonstrate the effectiveness and the efficiency of our approach through a series of experiments on real-world information networks. The result shows that our bounding technique can reduce the running time up to two orders of magnitude comparing to an approach that does not use bounds.

Categories and Subject Descriptors

H.2.8 [**Database Management**]: Database Applications—*graph database*; C.2.4 [**Computer-Communication Networks**]: Distributed Systems—*distributed applications*

General Terms

Algorithms, Design, Performance

Keywords

Subgraph Matching, Graph Similarity, Billion-Node Graphs, Index-Free, Query Processing, Distributed System

WWW 2015, May 18–22, 2015, Florence, Italy.
ACM 978-1-4503-3469-3/15/05.
http://dx.doi.org/10.1145/2736277.2741131.

1. INTRODUCTION

Information networks such as Freebase [12] have become massive in recent years. Freebase, a collaborative knowledge graph, contains more than 43.9 million entities, interconnected by 2.4 billion facts. The Linked Open Data project [4] connects RDF datasets on the web, resulting in an information network containing 1.77 billion RDF triples. It is important to be able to extract information from these networks. However, performing query operations on such web-scale information networks can be challenging.

In this paper, we study the problem of identifying a set of unknown entities in an information network given a set of related entities and facts/relations. For example, a query on Freebase can be "find an actor who collaborated with the director of the movie *'Avatar'* and also performed in the movie *'Body of Lies'*". We can model an information network or a query as a graph that consists of entities and relationships (or facts) between entities. Answering queries on information networks then becomes a subgraph matching problem. While it is common to seek answers that match exactly to queries, it is equally important to discover an answer that is similar to the queries. Information networks are typically crawled from the web or a large collection of databases. Therefore, they can be incomplete and noisy. Further, a user might not know the schema of the information network well enough to specify a query. It is likely that a user describes a vague query that is similar in structure to the desired answer. Fig. 1(a) shows the query graph for the aforementioned example query. An answer to the query from Freebase, that the actor is DiCaprio and the director is Cameron, is shown in Fig. 1(b). Clearly, the answer is not an exact match to the query. In particular, actor DiCaprio does not connect to director Cameron or the movie *'Body of Lies'* directly in Freebase. Nevertheless, this is a good answer to the query. Therefore, it is crucial to be able to identify both *exact and similar matches* to a query for information networks.

The problem of subgraph matching has been studied extensively in the past decades [30, 28, 18, 19]. However, most of them utilize graph indices that require precomputation and storage size of super-linear to information network size [27]. It may be infeasible to build the graph indices for web-scale networks due to the amount of work and the memory/storage required. To address this problem, we propose an *index-free* approach for answering information queries. Our approach is able to identify all answers that have the same structure as the query as well as answers that are similar to the query. The quality of an answer is measured by

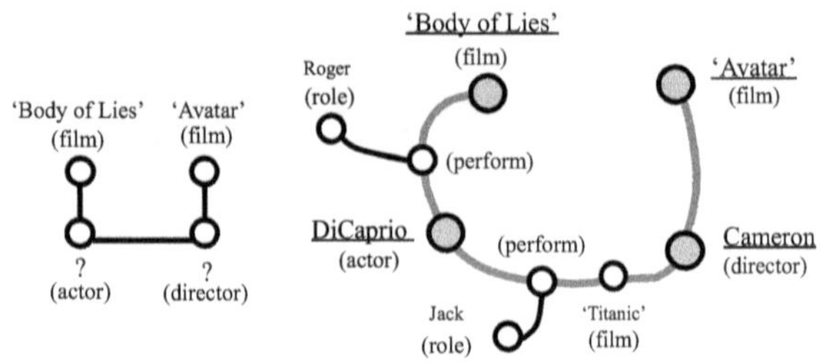

(a) Query (b) Answer from Freebase

Figure 1: A query on an information network

a matching score evaluated by comparing the structural signatures of the answer with that of the query. In contrast to the existing approaches, we compute matching scores online instead of precomputing the scores.

To speed up query processing, we propose GraB (Graph Matching using Bound), a novel technique for bounding the matching scores during the computation. By using the bounds, we can efficiently prune the low quality answers without evaluating all the possible answers. While we present the bounding technique in the context of a specific matching score function, it can be broadly applied to other functions as well. Furthermore, we implement the bounding technique in a distributed environment. Therefore, our approach can scale to answer the queries on web-scale information networks.

The key contributions of this paper are summarized as follows:

- We propose an algorithm for finding the k best answers. The algorithm can be applied to identify both exact and similar matches. The algorithm uses a novel heuristic to select only the promising candidates of the unknown entities, using the known entities as guides.
- In order to scale the algorithm to billions of nodes, we propose an index-free algorithm that computes matching scores online. Our index-free algorithm does not make assumptions about the extent of similarity between a query and the answers. Therefore, it is able to identify the top-k answers for every query. A novel technique for bounding the matching scores is used to efficiently find the top-k best answers.
- We implement our algorithm in a distributed environment. To evaluate the scalability, we deploy the distributed system on an Amazon EC2 cluster that contains hundreds of machines. The results show that our system can support querying on graphs with billions of nodes and scale to large queries.
- Our evaluation using real-world datasets shows that our algorithm can identify the top-k answers for every query and the answers are accurate. Additionally, our bounding technique can reduce the running time up to two orders of magnitude comparing to an approach that does not use bounds.

The rest of this paper is organized as follows. Section 2 describes the definition of the graph similarity matching problem. Section 3 provides the framework of our algorithm. In Section 4 an index-free algorithm is proposed. Section 5 discusses our distributed solution. In Section 6, we present the evaluation of our algorithm. We discuss related work in Section 7 and conclude the paper in Section 8.

2. PROBLEM DEFINITION

2.1 Preliminaries

We model an information network as a typed graph. A typed graph (V, E, T) is an undirected graph, where V is a set of nodes, E is a set of edges, and T is a set of node types. Each node v has a *node type* and a *name* that is a string. Generally, there are many nodes having the same node type, but a node name is usually unique or shared by only a few nodes. For simplicity, we assume the node names are unique and there are no types on the edges. However, our approach can be extended for graphs with shared names and typed edges. We represent an information network by a data graph $G = (V_G, E_G, T)$ and refer to its nodes as *data nodes.*

A query on an information graph aims to discover a set of *unknown entities* by providing related entities, or *known entities.* We model the query as a typed graph, $Q = (V_Q, E_Q, T)$. In the query graph, there are two types of nodes: (1) A *specific node* corresponds a known entity. Both the type and the name of a specific node are known. (2) A *query node* corresponds to an unknown entity. Only its type is known. In the query graph in Fig. 1, *'Avatar'* and *'Body of Lies'* are the specific nodes, and the two nodes with type *actor* and type *director* are the query nodes. We denote the set of specific nodes by V_Q^S and the set of queries nodes by V_Q^U.

To answer a query, we need to map every query node to a data node. The mapping is referred to as an *embedding.*

Definition 1 (Embedding). *Given a data graph G and a query graph Q, an embedding of Q in G is an injective function $f : V_Q \rightarrow V_G$ where (1) $\forall q \in V_Q$, q and $f(q)$ have the same type; (2) $\forall q^s \in V_Q^S$, q^s and $f(q^s)$ have the same name.*

The embeddings that result in the subgraphs with the same structure as the query graph are *exact matches.* Formally, we have the following definition.

Definition 2 (Exact Match). *An embedding f is an exact match of a query graph Q iff for each edge $(q_i, q_j) \in E_Q$, there is an edge $(f(q_i), f(q_j)) \in E_G$.*

Considering the noisiness and incompleteness of the information networks, to answer a given query we are interested in finding both the exact matches and similar matches. Therefore, we consider the top-k graph similarity matching problem, which returns the best k embeddings according to a similarity measure, as described in the next section.

2.2 Similarity Measure

In this section, we propose a similarity measure to quantify the structural similarity between a query graph and an embedding.

First, we introduce a closeness vector, which is used to represent a structural signature of a node's neighborhood in a graph. The closeness vector captures the graph structure around a node using the closeness between the node and the other nodes. For a node q_i in a query graph, its closeness vector specifies how close it is to each node in the query graph, defined formally as follows. Let the nodes in a query graph Q be $q_1, ..., q_m$. The *closeness vector* of q_i, denoted by $R_Q(q_i)$, is defined as

$$R_Q(q_i) = [\varphi_Q(q_i, q_1), ..., \varphi_Q(q_i, q_m)],$$

where $\varphi_Q(q_i, q_j)$ is a closeness score between q_i and q_j.

We design our closeness score function, which quantifies the closeness between two nodes, by aiming for two properties. (1) The closer the nodes are in terms of the shortest path distance, the higher the score. (2) When two pairs of nodes have the same shortest path distance, the pair having more shortest paths has a higher score. Based on these properties, the closeness between node u and v in a graph G, denoted by $\varphi_G(u,v)$, is defined by:

$$\varphi_G(u,v) = \begin{cases} 1, & u = v \\ \min\{n_{u,v}\alpha^{l_{u,v}}, N\alpha^{l_{u,v}}\}, & otherwise \end{cases} \tag{1}$$

where $l_{u,v}$ and $n_{u,v}$ are the length and the number of shortest paths between u and v, α is a constant between 0 and 1, and N is a constant smaller than $\frac{1}{\alpha}$. When $n_{u,v} > N$, the closeness score of u and v is bounded to $N\alpha^{l_{u,v}}$, which guarantees Property (1) since $N\alpha^{l_{u,v}} < \alpha^{l_{u,v}-1}$.

To quantify the similarity between a query graph and an embedding, we also represent a match of a query node in an embedding with a closeness vector. The closeness vector of a match specifies how close it is to the other matches in the data graph. Formally, the *closeness vector* $R_G(q_i, f)$ of a match of q_i in embedding f is defined as

$$R_G(q_i, f) = [\varphi_G(f(q_i), f(q_1)), ..., \varphi_G(f(q_i), f(q_m))].$$

Based on the closeness vectors, for a given embedding we quantify the cost of matching a node to a query node, or *node match cost*, using the difference between their closeness vectors. For a match of q_i in embedding f, the *node match cost* is computed as follows:

$$C(f, q_i) = \sum_{q_j \in V_Q} \Theta(\varphi_Q(q_i, q_j), \varphi_G(f(q_i), f(q_j))), \tag{2}$$

where Θ is a positive-difference function defined as

$$\Theta(a, b) = \begin{cases} a - b, & a > b \\ 0, & otherwise. \end{cases} \tag{3}$$

The node match cost is the sum of the difference in all the dimensions of the closeness vectors. The positive-difference function is used for two purposes: (1) To avoid penalizing the case where two matches are closer than their corresponding query nodes. The closer matches mean they are closely related. Intuitively, this should not degrade the quality of the answer. (2) To avoid the negative difference in one dimension canceling out the difference in the other dimensions of the vector, which can introduce false positive answers.

Based on the node match cost, we formulate a similarity measure for an embedding by combining the node match cost of all the nodes in the embedding as follows.

Definition 3 (Similarity Measure). *Given a data graph G, a query graph Q, and an embedding f, the match cost of f is defined as:*

$$\mathcal{C}(f) = \sum_{q_i \in V_Q} C(f, q_i) \tag{4}$$

The match cost of an embedding takes into account the structural difference between the query graph and the embedding. The more similar an embedding to the query graph, the lower its match cost. It is clear from the definition that the exact-match embeddings have zero matching cost and the match cost of any inexact match is greater than zero.

Our embedding match cost can be extended to support graphs with typed edges. When two nodes in a query graph are connected by a typed edge, their matches should be connected by the edge having the same type. Otherwise, the cost of matching the edge types should be added to the embedding matching costs.

Notation	Description
V_Q^U	A set of query nodes
V_Q^S	A set of specific nodes
q^s	A specific node
$\phi(q^s)$	An anchor node that is a match of specific node q^s (defined in Section 3)
$\varphi_G(u,v)$	The closeness score between u and v in data graph
$\varphi_Q(q_i,q_j)$	The closeness score between q_i and q_j in query graph
$\delta_{q_i,q_j}(u,v)$	A shortened form of $\Theta(\varphi_Q(q_i,q_j), \varphi_G(u,v))$
$\mathcal{C}(f)$	The embedding match cost of embedding f
$C^K(v,q)$	The known match cost of v as a candidate of q (defined in Section 3)
$\mathcal{M}^q$	The candidate match set of q (defined in Section 3)
$\mathcal{F}$	The candidate embedding set (defined in Section 3)

Table 1: Frequently used notations

Based on the defined match costs, the top-k graph similarity matching problem is defined as follows.

The top-k similarity matching problem. Given a data graph G and a query graph Q, identify k embeddings that have the smallest match costs.

To simplify the notation, in the rest of the paper, we let $\delta_{q_i,q_j}(u,v)$ denote $\Theta(\varphi_Q(q_i,q_j), \varphi_G(u,v))$. We list the frequently used notations in Table 1.

3. ALGORITHM FRAMEWORK

A naive approach for finding the top-k embeddings is to enumerate and rank all possible embeddings. From the definition, the candidate matches for each query node q include all the data nodes with the same type as q's. Thus, the number of all possible embeddings can be very large, especially in massive networks, and the naive approach can be very time-consuming. To speed up the computation, our approach reduces the search space by lessening the number of candidate matches for each query node while ensuring that the high quality (low matching cost) embeddings are still in the reduced search space.

In our approach, the candidate set for each query node is populated by selecting a small number of data nodes that are likely to produce high quality embeddings. For this, we need a measure that can evaluate the quality of the matches of each query node independently. To derive this measure, we decompose the embedding match cost as follows.

$$\mathcal{C}(f) = \underbrace{\sum_{q_i \in V_Q} \sum_{q_j \in V_Q^S} \delta_{q_i,q_j}(f(q_i), f(q_j))}_{\text{Part I}} + \underbrace{\sum_{q_i \in V_Q} \sum_{q_j \in V_Q^U} \delta_{q_i,q_j}(f(q_i), f(q_j))}_{\text{Part II}} \tag{5}$$

In the decomposition, Part I is the cost based on each match's closeness with the matches of specific nodes. Part II is the cost based on each match's closeness with the matches of query nodes. It can be seen that in Part I, the cost associated with each query node depends on only the matches of the specific nodes, independent of the other query nodes. Precisely, the cost of matching a data node v to a query node q in Part I, denoted by $C^K(v,q)$, is as follows:

$$C^K(v,q) = \sum_{q^s \in V_Q^S} \delta_{q^s,q}(\phi(q^s), v), \tag{6}$$

Algorithm 1: GraB

Input: data graph G, query graph Q, k
Output: top-k embeddings

// Phase 1: Identify the top-k^* candidate matches for each query node.
$\mathcal{M} \leftarrow$ IdentifyMatches(G, Q, k^*)
// Phase 2: Identify the top-k embeddings.
$\mathcal{F}_k \leftarrow$ IdentifyEmbs(G, Q, $\mathcal{M}$, k)
return $\mathcal{F}_k$

where $\phi(q^s)$ is an *anchor node*, the match of specific node q^s. We refer to $C^K(v, q)$ as *known match cost*.

We build a candidate set for each query node by selecting data nodes with the lowest known match cost. Because the selected candidates minimize a significant part of the total cost, the top embeddings are likely to be among the embeddings produced from these candidate sets. We show later through our experiments that this heuristic efficiently prunes search space but still provides accurate answers.

The overview of our approach, GraB, is shown in Algorithm 1. The approach consists of two phases. *In Phase 1, a candidate match set for each query node is created by selecting k^* best candidate matches, where k^* is a predefined constant. In Phase 2, the approach searches for k embeddings with the lowest match costs among the $k^{*|V_Q^U|}$ candidate embeddings.*

The value of k^* determines the accuracy of the algorithm. When k^* is larger, more candidate matches are selected for each query node; therefore, it is more likely that the real top-k answers are among the $k^{*|V_Q^U|}$ candidate embeddings. However, with larger k^* the algorithm will need longer time to enumerate the candidate embeddings in Phase 2. Intuitively, if each query node has more than k candidates, the accurate top-k answers are likely to be found. Therefore, we recommend to set k^* between k to $2k$. We discuss the selection of k^* further in the experiment. Note that in order to find all the embeddings that exactly match the query graph, we should select all the candidate matches whose known match costs are zero. In this case, the size of the candidate set may be larger than k^*.

4. ALGORITHM DESCRIPTION

From the algorithm framework, one solution that allows the results to be returned quickly is to create an index that stores a precomputed pairwise closeness scores and use the index in computing the known match cost and the embedding match cost. For fast access, the indexed closeness scores have to be stored in memory. However, the number of pairwise closeness scores is $|V_G|^2$, where $|V_G|$ is the number of data nodes; for a web-scale information network that contains billions of nodes, storing the pairwise closeness scores in memory is usually infeasible. In this section, we describe our index-free algorithm, which does not require the precomputed closeness scores but still can answer queries efficiently.

4.1 Algorithm Overview

As the algorithm described in Section 3, the index-free algorithm consists of two phases, *i.e.*, identifying the top-k^* candidate matches for each query node and identifying the top-k embeddings. While we can compute all the required closeness scores in both phases online, the computation is time-consuming. To obtain the results faster, our algorithm computes the bounds of the closeness scores and use the bounds to derive the top-k embeddings.

Algorithm 2: (Phase 1) IdentifyMatches(G, Q, k^*)

Input: data Graph G, query graph Q, k^*
Output: top-k^* candidate set for each query node $\mathcal{M}$
1 $Src \leftarrow$ all the anchor nodes
2 **foreach** $q \in V_Q^U$ **do**
3 **repeat**
4 BoundRefinement(Src,φ_G^+,φ_G^-, G) // Sec. 4.4
5 **until** TermPhase1(φ_G^+,φ_G^-,G,q) *is true* // Sec. 4.3.2
6 $\mathcal{M}_{k^*}^q \leftarrow$ the top-k^* candidate match set of q
$\mathcal{M} \leftarrow \mathcal{M} \cup \{\langle q, \mathcal{M}_{k^*}^q \rangle\}$
7 **return** $\mathcal{M}$

Algorithm 3: (Phase 2) IdentifyEmbs(G, Q, $\mathcal{M}$, k)

Input: data graph G, query graph Q, candidate match set $\mathcal{M}$, k
Output: top-k embedding set $\mathcal{F}_k$
1 $Src \leftarrow$ all the candidate matches
2 **repeat**
3 BoundRefinement(Src,φ_G^+,φ_G^-,G) // Sec. 4.4
4 **until** TermPhase2(φ_G^+,φ_G^-,$\mathcal{M}$) *is true* // Sec. 4.3.3
5 $\mathcal{F}_k \leftarrow$ the top-k embeddings
6 **return** $\mathcal{F}_k$

In this algorithm, the bounds of the closeness scores are computed by performing multiple Breadth-First Searches (BFSes). Each BFS iteratively refines the closeness score bounds (denoted by φ_G^+ and φ_G^-) between one data node (source node) and the other data nodes. As the BFSes are progressed, the bounds approach the exact scores. We refer to this process as *bound refinement*. In Phase 1, we need the closeness scores between each of the anchor node and the candidate matches of a query node q to compute the known match costs. Therefore, we perform $|V_Q^S|$ BFSes, each having an anchor node as a source node (line 4 of Algorithm 2). In Phase 2, the closeness scores among the candidate matches are required. Therefore, we perform the BFSes with each match as a source node (line 3 of Algorithm 3).

In both phases, while the bounds are being refined, the algorithm keeps checking whether the targeted results for those phases can be obtained with the current bounds. In Phase 1, for each query node, the algorithm checks whether the top-k^* candidate matches are found (line 5 of Algorithm 2). Once the top-k^* matches are found for all the query nodes, Phase 2 can be started. Similarly, in Phase 2, the algorithm keeps checking whether the top-k embeddings can be identified with the current bounds and returns the results as soon as they are found (line 4 of Algorithm 3). We refer to the process of checking whether the top-k^* candidate matches (or the top-k embeddings) can be identified with the bounds as *termination check*.

In the following sections, we describe the derivation of the closeness score bounds, the termination check process, and the bound refinement process in detail.

4.2 Deriving Closeness Score Bounds

As stated in the overview, we use a BFS to refine the closeness score bounds between one data node and the other data nodes. Here we describe how we compute the closeness score bounds in each BFS.

Given a source node, the BFS iteratively visits the data nodes in the source node's neighborhood. At iteration t, all the data nodes in the source node's t-hop neighborhood are visited by the search.

For the data nodes visited by the BFS in iteration t, we can compute its exact closeness scores. Suppose the source node is s. Let V_s^t denote the set of the data nodes that are visited in iteration t, *i.e.*, the nodes that are t hops away from s. Initially, we have $V_s^0 = \{s\}$ and $\varphi_G(s, s) = 1$. For the later iterations, the closeness score of a data node v in V_s^t is computed by aggregating the closeness scores of v's neighbors that are $t-1$ hops away from s, as shown in the following equation.

$$\varphi_G(s, v) = \min\{N\alpha^t, \textstyle\sum_{u \in V_s^{t-1} \cap \mathbb{N}(v)} \varphi_G(s, u) \cdot \alpha\} \quad (7)$$

where $\mathbb{N}(v)$ is v's adjacent neighbor set.

For the unvisited data nodes in iteration t, we know that they are at least $t+1$ hops away from the source node, which means that their closeness scores are in the range of $[0, N\alpha^{t+1}]$. Thus, at iteration t of the BFS starting from the source node s, we have the following closeness scores bounds for a data node v.

$$\begin{aligned}
\varphi_G^+(s, v) &= \begin{cases} \varphi_G(s, v), & v \text{ is visited} \\ N\alpha^{t+1}, & \text{otherwise} \end{cases} \\
\varphi_G^-(s, v) &= \begin{cases} \varphi_G(s, v), & v \text{ is visited} \\ 0, & \text{otherwise} \end{cases}
\end{aligned} \quad (8)$$

4.3 Termination Check

While the closeness score bounds are being refined by the BFSes, GraB periodically performs the termination check that tests whether the top-k^* candidate matches or the top-k embeddings are found. In this subsection, we describe how to use the bounds to identify the top-k^* candidate matches and the top-k embeddings.

4.3.1 Termination Check Using Bounds

First, we describe a strategy for finding the top-k embeddings from the candidate embedding set by using the upper bounds, $\mathcal{C}^+$, and lower bounds, $\mathcal{C}^-$, of the embedding match costs. The same strategy can be used to find the top-k^* candidates for each query node by using the upper bounds, C^{K+}, and lower bounds, C^{K-}, of the known match costs.

The top-k embedding identification consists of the following two steps.

1. Find k embeddings with the smallest cost upper bounds, $f_1, ..., f_k$.
2. Determine whether $f_1, ..., f_k$ are the top-k embeddings. Assuming that $\mathcal{C}^+(f_1) \le \mathcal{C}^+(f_2) ... \le \mathcal{C}^+(f_k)$, we check the following condition:

$$\mathcal{C}^+(f_k) < \mathcal{C}^-(f) \text{ for all } f \notin \{f_1, ..., f_k\} \quad (9)$$

Eq. (9) uses the cost lower bounds to ensure that every f that is not in $\{f_1, ..., f_k\}$ cannot have the cost lower than those of the tentative top-k items. If Eq. (9) is satisfied, it is guaranteed that $f_1, ..., f_k$ are the real top-k embeddings. Next, we discuss how to apply this strategy in each phase of the algorithm.

4.3.2 Termination Check for Top-k^* Candidates

In Phase 1, for each query node q, our task is to find k^* matches with the lowest known match costs. For each candidate, we derive its lower and upper bounds of known match costs.

Algorithm 4: TermPhase1(φ_G^+,φ_G^-,G, q)

Input: closeness score ub φ_G^+, closeness score lb φ_G^-, data graph G, query node q
Output: whether the top- k^* matches of q are found

1 $\mathcal{M}^q \leftarrow$ all the candidate matches of q
2 $\mathcal{M}_{k^*}^{q+} \leftarrow$ the k^* matches in $\mathcal{M}^q$ with the smallest C^{K+}.
3 $C^{K+}(v_{k^*}, q) \leftarrow$ the k^{*th} smallest known match cost ub
4 **foreach** $u \in \mathcal{M}^q - \mathcal{M}_{k^*}^{q+}$ **do**
5   **if** $C^{K-}(u, q) < C^{K+}(v_{k^*}, q)$ **then**
6   **return** false
    `//` $\mathcal{M}_{k^*}^{q+}$ `is the top-`k^* `candidate match set of` q.
7 **return** true

Algorithm 5: TermPhase2(φ_G^+,φ_G^-,$\mathcal{M}$)

Input: closeness score ub φ_G^+, closeness score lb φ_G^-, candidate match set $\mathcal{M}$
Output: whether the top-k embeddings are found

1 $\mathcal{F}_k^+ \leftarrow$ EmbGetUBTopK(φ_G^-,k)
2 **if** EmbCheckLB(φ_G^+, $\mathcal{C}^+(f_k)$) *is false* **then**
3   **return** false
    `//` $\mathcal{F}_k^+$ `is the top-`k `embedding set.`
4 **return** true

Bounds of known match cost. From Eq. (6), we derive the bounds of known match costs in terms of the bounds of closeness scores. For a candidate v of a query node q, the bounds of known match cost can be computed by the following equations.

$$\begin{aligned}
C^{K+}(v, q) &= \sum_{q^s \in V_Q^S} \Theta(\varphi_Q(q^s, q), \varphi_G^-(\phi(q^s), v)) \\
C^{K-}(v, q) &= \sum_{q^s \in V_Q^S} \Theta(\varphi_Q(q^s, q), \varphi_G^+(\phi(q^s), v))
\end{aligned} \quad (10)$$

Performing termination check. The termination check for Phase 1 is performed as shown in Algorithm 4. In the first step (line 1-3), we initialize a set $\mathcal{M}^q$ that contains all the data nodes having the same type as q. Then, the tentative top-k^* candidates, which have the smallest upper bound costs, are identified from $\mathcal{M}^q$. In the second step (line 4-7), we test whether the tentative top-k^* candidates are the real top-k^* candidates by checking the lower bound costs.

4.3.3 Termination Check for Top-k embeddings

In Phase 2, we find the top k embeddings with the lowest embedding match costs. The details are given as follows.

Bounds of embedding match cost. We derive the lower and upper bounds of embedding match costs, *i.e.*, $\mathcal{C}^-(f)$ and $\mathcal{C}^+(f)$, in terms of the bounds of closeness scores, as shown in the following equations.

$$\begin{aligned}
\mathcal{C}^+(f) &= \sum_{q_i \in V_Q} \sum_{q_j \in V_Q} \Theta(\varphi_Q(q_i, q_j), \varphi_G^-(f(q_i), f(q_j))) \\
\mathcal{C}^-(f) &= \sum_{q_i \in V_Q} \sum_{q_j \in V_Q} \Theta(\varphi_Q(q_i, q_j), \varphi_G^+(f(q_i), f(q_j)))
\end{aligned} \quad (11)$$

Performing termination check. The outline of the termination check is given in Algorithm 5. For the first step (line 1), we find the tentative top-k embeddings with the s-

Algorithm 6: BoundRefinement(S,φ_G^+,φ_G^-, G)

Input: source node set S, closeness score ub φ_G^+, closeness score lb φ_G^- and data graph G
Output: refined closeness score bounds φ_G^{*+} and φ_G^{*-}

```
1 s ← GetBestSrc(S)                      // By Eq. (15) or Eq. (13)
2 BFS(s).NextIteration()                 // By Eq. (7)
3 (φ*+_G, φ*-_G) ←UpdateBounds(φ+_G,φ-_G)  // By Eq. (8)
4 return φ*+_G and φ*-_G
```

mallest match cost upper bounds, computed from the closeness score lower bounds. In the second step (line 2), our task is to check whether there are no more than k embeddings f having $\mathcal{C}^-(f) < \mathcal{C}^+(f_k)$. However, in both steps, enumerating the entire embedding set from the candidate match sets and computing their match cost can be time-consuming. We accelerate the embedding enumeration with a branch-and-bound method. Due to lack of the space, readers are referred to [17] for the details of the branch-and-bound method.

4.4 Bound Refinement

In the two phases of our algorithm, multiple BFSes are performed to obtain all the required closeness score bounds. We progress the BFSes concurrently. The BFSes are selected one at a time, where each time the selected BFS is executed for one iteration, as shown in Algorithm 6.

How the BFSes are selected for execution is important for the efficiency of our algorithm. Naively performing the BFSes in a round-robin manner *i.e.,* one iteration in turn, can be inefficient. We illustrate the importance of choosing a proper order of the BFSes using Fig. 2. To identify the top-2 matches for query node q_3, we perform two BFSes starting from v_1 and v_2. We denote the two BFSes by BFS(v_1) and BFS(v_2), respectively. Consider two orders of execution: (1) perform BFS(v_2) two iterations and then BFS(v_1) one iteration and (2) perform BFS(v_1) and BFS(v_2) alternately for two iterations. The first order is more efficient since it only requires a total of three iterations to find the top-2 matches, as opposed to four iterations in the latter case.

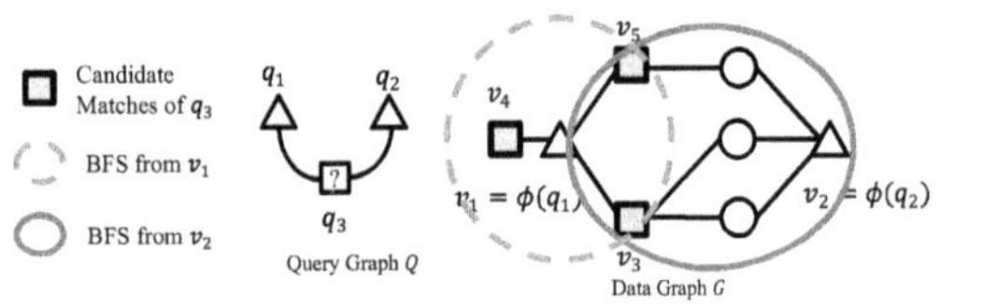

Figure 2: Identifying top-2 matches for a query node

To improve the efficiency, we dynamically assign priorities to the BFSes. We use a heuristic to quantify the benefit of performing each BFS. For Phase 1, intuitively, if the bounds of the known match costs are closer to the exact costs, we are more likely to find the top-k^* matches. Therefore, we should select the BFSes that are the most helpful in reducing the distance between the bounds and the exact known match costs of the candidate matches. Since the exact costs are not known, we use the difference between the upper bound and the lower bound, or the *bound gap*, to approximate the distance from the exact costs. For a candidate match v of query node q, the gap of the known match cost bounds is computed as follows.

$$C^{K+}(v) - C^{K-}(v) = \textstyle\sum_{q^s \in V_Q^S} \delta^+_{q^s,q}(\phi(q^s), v) - \delta^-_{q^s,q}(\phi(q^s), v) \tag{12}$$

From the equation, it can be seen that the BFS having $\phi(q^s)$ as a source node contributes the amount of $\delta^+_{q^s,q}(\phi(q^s), v) - \delta^-_{q^s,q}(\phi(q^s), v)$ to the bound gap. In order to approach the exact known match costs as quickly as possible, we select the BFS whose associated closeness scores contribute the most to the bound gaps of the candidate matches. Therefore, the priority of a BFS starting at an anchor node $\phi(q^s)$ is assigned by computing its total contribution to the bound gaps of all the candidate matches as follows.

$$\mathcal{P}_1(\phi(q^s)) = \sum_{v \in \widetilde{\mathcal{M}}^q} \delta^+_{q^s,q}(\phi(q^s), v) - \delta^-_{q^s,q}(\phi(q^s), v), \tag{13}$$

where $\widetilde{\mathcal{M}}^q$ is the set of q's candidates having the lower bound costs smaller than $C^{K+}(v_{k^*}, q)$. The nodes in $\widetilde{\mathcal{M}}^q$ are those eligible to be the top-k^* candidates of q in the future.

The priority of the BFSs in Phase 2 is assigned with a similar idea, but in Phase 2, we are interested in reducing the distance between the embedding match cost bounds and the exact costs of the candidate embeddings. The embedding match cost bound gap of an embedding f is computed as follows.

$$\begin{aligned}&\mathcal{C}^+(f) - \mathcal{C}^-(f)\\ &= \sum_{q_i \in V_Q} \sum_{q_j \in V_Q} \{\delta^+_{q_i,q_j}(f(q_i), f(q_j)) - \delta^-_{q_i,q_j}((f(q_i), f(q_j))\}\end{aligned} \tag{14}$$

Here the BFS starting from data node $f(q_i)$ contributes $\sum_{q_j \in V_Q} \delta^+_{q_i,q_j}(f(q_i), f(q_j)) - \delta^-_{q_i,q_j}(f(q_i), f(q_j))$ to the bound gap. Taking into account all the candidate embeddings, the priority $\mathcal{P}_2(u)$ of the BFS starting from u is computed as in the following equation.

$$\mathcal{P}_2(u) = \sum_{f \in \widetilde{\mathcal{F}}} \sum_{\substack{q_i \in V_Q \\ f(q_i)=u}} \sum_{q_j \in V_Q} \delta^+_{q_i,q_j}(u, f(q_j)) - \delta^-_{q_i,q_j}(u, f(q_j)), \tag{15}$$

where $\widetilde{\mathcal{F}}$ is the set of embeddings whose lower bounds are smaller than $\mathcal{C}^+(f_k)$. A high priority indicates that the BFS can efficiently reduce the distance between the bounds and the exact match costs of the candidate embeddings.

5. DISTRIBUTED IMPLEMENTATION

Since a single machine has limited memory and computation resources, we design a distributed system to store the web-scale information networks and execute our algorithm.

5.1 System Overview

Our system is implemented based on a distributed graph computation framework, Piccolo [24], which consists of one master process and multiple worker processes. Fig. 3 shows the architecture of the system. In our system, the master coordinates the workers to perform the bound refinement and the termination check in the two phases of the algorithm.

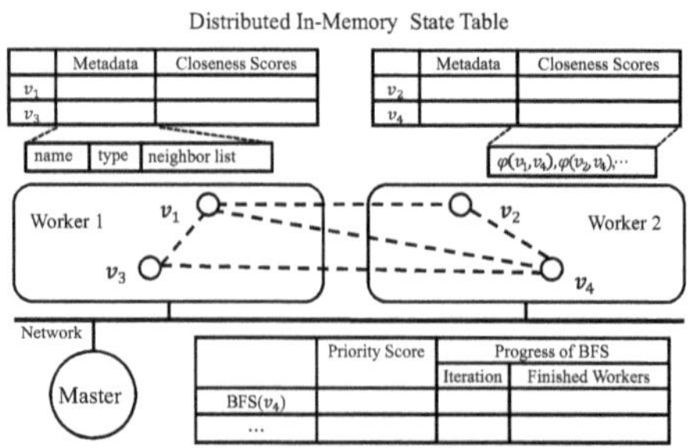

Figure 3: System architecture

Distributed in-memory state table. For efficiency, the data graph is stored in an *in-memory state table* that is distributed across the workers. Each data node corresponds to one row in the table. The row associated with a node v, row(v), stores the metadata of node v including the node name, the node type, and the neighbors' keys. Additionally, row (v) contains a hash map that stores the closeness scores associated with node v. Each worker stores a partition of the state table. In our implementation, we assign data nodes to the workers by applying a hash function to the node keys, but other partition strategies can also be applied. With the distributed in-memory state table, we next show how to perform the distributed bound refinement and the distributed termination check.

5.2 Distributed Bound Refinement

For the bound refinement, a total of $|V_Q^S|+k^*|V_Q^U|$ BFSes are performed simultaneously (from Phase 1 and Phase 2). To efficiently coordinate multiple workers to perform the BFSes is non-trivial. We explain our key designs as follows.

Computing priorities of BFSes. To schedule the BFSes, the master maintains the priority score of each BFS. The priority scores, as in Eq. (13) and Eq. (15), are computed distributedly. The computation is similar to the distributed termination check, which is explained in Section 5.3.

Expanding one BFS. The workers expand the BFS with the highest priority each time. Each iteration of a BFS finishes when all workers have finished processing for that iteration. The master keeps track of the workers that have finished the iteration and notifies the workers to expand the next BFS when the iteration is completed.

Aggressive expansion for multiple BFSes. When expanding a BFS, an iteration is not completed until all the workers have finished. This synchronization can degrade the efficiency, especially when the workloads are imbalanced among the workers. To solve this problem, we propose aggressive expansion. When a worker is idle, we let the worker aggressively expands the next BFS in the priority queue without waiting for the previous BFS's completion.

Multiple message queues. With aggressive expansion, an iteration may take longer time since multiple BFSes compete for the computation resources. We give an example as follows. Suppose there are two BFSes, BFS(v) and BFS(u). BFS(v) has the highest priority. When a worker, w, is working on BFS(v), it may receive the messages for BFS(u) from the workers that have finished processing BFS(v). Because w have to process the messages of both BFS(u) and BFS(v), the iteration of BFS(v) could be slowed down. Our solution is to implement multiple message queues in each worker, one message queue for each BFS. When processing messages, the message queues with higher priorities are processed earlier. With this design, the processing of the BFS with the highest priority is not interfered by the other BFSes.

5.3 Distributed Termination Check

We now discuss how to perform termination checks when the closeness scores are distributed across the workers.

Distributed termination check for Phase 1. We distribute the termination check workload among the workers. Each worker first finds its local top-k^* candidates (according to the upper bound costs) and send them to the master. The master finds the global top-k^* candidates among the local top-k^* candidates. Additionally, each worker is responsible for checking the top-k condition in Eq. (9) on its local nodes. Using the results from the workers, the master determines whether the real top-k^* candidates are found.

Distributed termination check for Phase 2. In Phase 2, the termination check is performed by the master. The master aggregates the closeness score bounds of the candidate pairs from the workers and performs the termination check by the branch-and-bound method [17]. In our implementation, the branch-and-bound method is accelerated by using multiple threads.

6. EVALUATION

6.1 Experiment Settings

System. We performed our experiments on two clusters: a local cluster and an Amazon EC2 cluster. The local cluster consisted of four machines connected by a 1Gb Ethernet switch. Each machine had 16GB RAM and one 1.86GHz Intel Xeon E5502 CPU with four cores. The Amazon EC2 cluster consisted of 100 m3.large instances, each of which had 2 vCPUs and 7.5GB RAM. All the experiments were implemented using C++.

Datasets. Two real-life networks, DBLP and Freebase, and several synthetic graphs were used in our experiments. (1) The DBLP graph [2] is a bibliography network containing three types of nodes: author, paper, and venue. There are 3.5 million nodes and 9.5 million edges in the DBLP graph. (2) A subset of Freebase containing film information was used in our experiments. The film dataset has five types of nodes: film, director, actor, perform, and role. There are 1.4 million nodes and 1.8 million edges. (3) Synthetic graphs were generated by duplicating the DBLP dataset. Each node in DBLP has several copies in the synthetic graphs. We varied the duplication factor from 30 to 300 to produce the synthetic graphs with different sizes ranging from 100 million nodes to 1 billion nodes.

Query graphs. Real-life and synthetic queries were used in the experiments. We selected the real-life queries that are representative of different patterns of query graphs, including a chain, a star, and a circuit. The real-life queries are listed in Table 2. Q1, Q2 are for DBLP. Q3 is for Freebase. The corresponding query graphs are shown in Fig. 4(a).

	Pattern	Content
Q1	Chain	Find an author of CIDR11 and an author of ISMB08 who have co-authored.
Q2	Star	Find an author who published papers in SIGMETRICS, IMC, and ICML between the years 2010 and 2012.
Q3	Circuit	Find two films that are directed by the director of 'A Beautiful Mind' and performed by an actor who performed in 'The Mask'.

Table 2: Real-life queries

The synthetic queries were composed based on a subgraph of a data graph. The size of the synthetic query is specified by two parameters: the number of specific nodes ($|V_Q^S|$) and the number of query nodes ($|V_Q^U|$), denoted in the form ($|V_Q^S|$,$|V_Q^U|$). To generate a query, we randomly selected a connected subgraph of specified size from a data graph and added noise to the query by inserting and deleting edges.

Parameter setting. We evaluated our index-free algorithm, GraB, and an index-based algorithm, GraB-Index. In our algorithms, α was set to 0.01. GraB-Index follows the algorithm framework shown in Section 3. In contrast to GraB, GraB-Index indexes the pairwise distances of nodes using the pruned labeling algorithm [5]. Since only the lengths of the

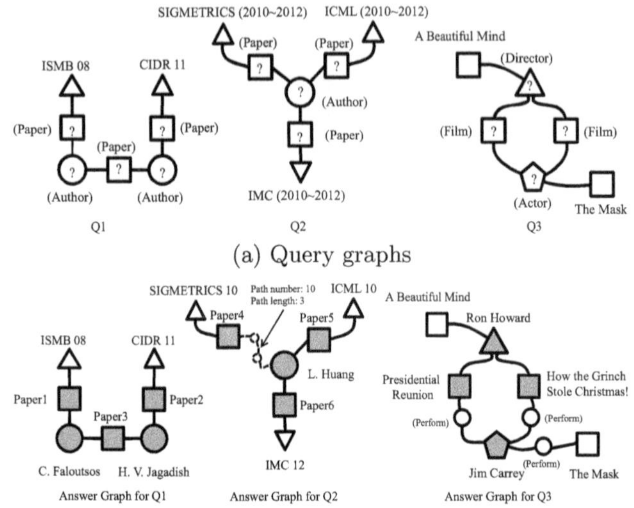

(a) Query graphs

(b) Top-1 answers (The gray nodes indicate the matches of the query nodes and the papers' titles are omitted.)

Figure 4: Query graphs and answers

shortest paths were indexed, N was set to 1 in GraB-Index. However, GraB considered the shortest path numbers and N was set to 99.

6.2 Answering Real-Life Queries

Here we show the effectiveness of our algorithm in answering real-life queries. The best embeddings obtained with our algorithm for the three queries in Table 2 are shown in Fig. 4(b). For Q1, there are multiple pairs of authors that can satisfy the query. Our algorithm found all of the authors and returned the exact matches of the query graph. For Q2, in DBLP no author published in all of the three conferences between 2010 and 2012, so there are no exact matches. However, our algorithm could still provide answers to the query with similar matches. As shown in Fig. 4(b), the algorithm found Ling Huang as the best answer because his coauthor published in SIGMETRICS 2010. Since they have coauthored ten papers, there are ten 3-hop paths between them. For Q3, the query does not conform with Freebase's schema. However, our algorithm found two films, *'Presidential Reunion'* and *'How the Grinch Stole Christmas!'*, as the best answer, which corresponds to the fact in real life. These results illustrate that our algorithm can provide answers to real-life queries effectively with both exact matches and similar matches.

6.3 Comparison with Existing Graph Matching Algorithms

We compared GraB-Index and GraB with four state-of-the-art graph matching algorithms, RDF-3X [23], Graph-Exploration-based subgraph matching (GE) [27], Ness [18], and NeMa [19]. RDF-3X is an index-based search engine that identifies exact matches on RDF documents. The RDF documents of DBLP and Freebase were used in our experiments. GE is an index-free subgraph matching algorithm that identifies exact matches in billion-node graphs. In contrast, Ness and NeMa identify the similar matches of a query graph using neighborhood similarity. The two algorithms are index-based; they precompute the structural signature of h-hop neighborhood for each graph node. Table 3 compares the supported features of the four algorithms with ours.

	Exact Match	Similarity Match	Schemaless	Index-Free
RDF-3X [23]	★			
GE [27]	★		★	★
Ness [18]	★	★	★	
NeMa [19]		★	★	
GraB-Index	★	★	★	
GraB	★	★	★	★

Table 3: The comparison of the supported features

	Finding Top-1 Answers			Finding Top-10 Answers		
	Q1	Q2	Q3	Q1	Q2	Q3
RDF-3X	0.263 s	×	×	0.263 s	×	×
GE	0.573 s	×	×	0.573 s	×	×
Ness	> 1 d	×	> 1 d	> 1 d	×	×
NeMa	×	×	0.21 s	×	×	×
GraB-Index	0.12 s	0.18 s	0.1 s	0.13 s	0.21 s	0.11 s
GraB	4.731 s	13.832 s	2.193 s	4.834 s	30.215 s	3.181 s

The symbol × indicates that an algorithm did not return k answers as requested.

Table 4: The comparison of running time (d=day, s=second)

In the following, we first compare the graph matching algorithms in terms of the effectiveness and the efficiency in answering real-life queries. Then, the costs of building indices on DBLP and billion-node graphs are shown.

6.3.1 *Effectiveness and Efficiency*

The performance comparison of the graph matching algorithms in finding the top-k answers for the real-life queries is shown in Table 6.3. The evaluation was performed in a single machine. For our algorithms, k^* were set to 10; for Ness and NeMa, we set $h = 2$, which was the recommended setting. First, we consider the capability in providing the answers to the queries. (1) RDF-3X and GE could only answer Q1 since they could not find similar matches. (2) NeMa could not find any answers for Q1. In Q1, there is a query node that is 3-hop away from the two specific nodes; therefore, NeMa could not find any matches for the query node. (3) Both Ness and NeMa could not find the answers for Q2. As shown in Fig. 4(b), the best answer of Q2 contains two nodes that are 3-hop away, but Ness and NeMa only considered 2-hop neighborhood. (4) Although Ness and NeMa could successfully find the top-1 answer for Q3, they could not find the top-10 answers. This is because actor Jim Carry only collaborated with director Ron Howard in two movies. If users need more answers, the movie nodes and the actor nodes that are more than 2 hops away should be considered. In contrast to the other algorithms, because GraB and GraB-Index consider node pairs of any distance, they found the top-1 and the top-10 answers for all the queries.

In terms of the running time, GraB-Index outperformed all the other algorithms, taking 0.14 seconds on average. As an index-free algorithm, GraB was slower than the index-based algorithms. The other index-free algorithm, GE, which finds only the exact matches, was also faster than GraB. However, without using indexes, GraB could answer queries with both exact and similar matches within only a few seconds, and the running time could be further reduced by increasing the worker number, as will be shown in Section 6.6. Next, we show the advantages of the index-free algorithms by comparing the costs of building indices

6.3.2 *Costs of Building Index*

We measured the cost of computing and storing the indices on DBLP and estimated the cost for a web-scale information network that had 1 billion nodes. The indices

	Time For Indexing		Data Size (Graph + Index)	
	DBLP	1B.Info.Net.	DBLP	1B.Info.Net.
RDF-3X	265 secs	> 9.2 days	0.93 GB	> 2.80 TB
NeMa (h=2)	1.53 hours	> 18 days	14.78 GB	> 5.17 TB
Ness (h=2)	5.34 hours	> 66 days	51.97 GB	> 15.59 TB
NeMa (h=3)	25.86 hours	> 1.2 years	289.81 GB	> 101.41 TB
Ness (h=3)	117.13 hours	> 4.9 years	1706 GB	> 597 TB
GraB-Index	2.12 hours	> 10 years	11.3 GB	> 400 TB
GE	0	0	0.2 GB	80 GB
GraB	0	0	0.2 GB	80 GB

Table 5: The costs of building indices

were built on a single machine. For NeMa and Ness, the 2-hop ($h = 2$) and the 3-hop ($h = 3$) neighborhoods were indexed. Table 6.3 shows the indexing cost. For GraB and GE, the indexing time is 0; the only data needed is an adjacency list. RDF-3X needs 9 days to index a 1-billion-node graph. For NeMa and Ness, the cost of building the indices increases significantly when the value of h increases from 2 to 3. When $h = 3$, it would require several years to build the 3-hop neighborhood index for the 1-billion-node information network. Although h can be limited to a small value, the bounded value of h may affect the capability of the index-based algorithms in finding the top-k answers. For GraB-Index, the index for the DBLP dataset could be created in less than 3 hours. However, it would take more than 10 years to index the 1-billion-node graph since the cost of building the index is super-linear to the graph size. This result illustrates that building indices for massive information networks may be infeasible.

6.4 The Selection of k^*

We evaluated the accuracy of the top-k answers using different settings of k^*. In the experiments, k was set to 10. We obtained baseline results by setting $k^* = 100$, assuming that finding the top-100 candidate matches for each query node is sufficient for finding the real top-10 embeddings. The accuracy of the top-k answers was measured as follows. Given the real top-10 embeddings, let $\mathcal{C}_{real}^k$ be the matching cost of the 10th embedding. From the top-10 embeddings found by GraB, let N_{acc} be the number of embeddings that have match costs less than or equal to $\mathcal{C}_{real}^k$. These embeddings are considered to be the accurate answers. The accuracy of the top-10 embeddings is computed as $\frac{N_{acc}}{10}$.

We generated 4 groups of queries for different query sizes. Each group contained 10 queries. We increased k^* from 5 to 30. For each setting of k^*, the average accuracy of each query group is shown in Fig. 5. It can been seen that 1) the accuracy increased significantly when k^* was changed from 5 to 10; 2) when $k^* = 10$, in most query groups, over 80% of the answers were accurate; 3) when $k^* = 30$, all the real top-10 answers were found. However, when k^* is larger, the running time of query processing is longer. Fig. 6 shows the average running time of each query group. When the query size is larger, the impact of k^* on the running time is more significant. For example, it requires 12.01 seconds to answer queries in group (5,10) in DBLP when k^* is 10, but when k^* is 20 and 30, it takes 18.10 and 34.31 seconds, respectively. Therefore, taking into account the accuracy and the running time, we recommend setting k^* to be between k and $2k$. In the rest of this section, we let k^* equal to k.

6.5 Performance

We evaluated the performance of our algorithm by measuring the running time. The experiments were performed on the local cluster. For each query size, we generated 10 queries and measured the average running time.

Effects of bounding technique. We set k to 10 and evaluated the efficiency of the bounding technique by comparing our algorithm with the naive algorithm that computes the exact matching costs of the embeddings. The running time of the two algorithms is shown in Fig. 7. It can be seen that our algorithm is 100 to 400 times faster than the naive algorithm. This result shows that using bounds can effectively reduce the running time. Additionally, the result demonstrates that our index-free algorithm can answer the top-10 queries within a few seconds.

Effects of priority scheduling. We show how the BFS priority scheduling policy introduced in Section 4.4 affects the running time. We set k to 10 and compared the priority scheduling policy with a round-robin scheduling policy. The running time of the two policies is shown in Fig. 8. When the query graph is larger, the priority scheduling is more efficient. We observe that DBLP benefits more from using the priority scheduling. Because the DBLP network is denser than Freebase, the priority scheduling greatly helps to reduce the expensive cost of performing BFSes on DBLP.

Effects of varying k. We studied how the value of k affects the running time. Fig. 9 shows the running time of finding the top-5, the top-10, and the top-20 answers for each query group. Because the running time is mainly determined by k^* and we set k^* to be equal to k, when k becomes larger, more embeddings have to be evaluated in Phase 2. Therefore, the running time is longer when k is larger.

6.6 Scalability

Scalability with worker number. We evaluated how our algorithm scales with the worker number using the Amazon EC2 cluster. For this experiment, the 100-million-node synthetic graph was used and k was set to 10. The worker number was varied from 20 to 100. We measured the average running time for each query group. Fig. 10(a) shows the running time for different numbers of workers. For the small queries, *i.e.*, group (4,2) and group (6,3), our algorithm could answer the queries within about 3 seconds. It can be seen that when the worker number increases, the running time of answering small queries is not significantly reduced. This is because using more workers introduce more communication overhead. However, for the large queries, *i.e.*, group (8,4) and group (10,5), the running time decreases as the worker number becomes larger. This is because the computation for answering larger queries is more intensive; using more workers could efficiently reduce the running time.

Scalability with graph size. To evaluate the scalability with graph size, we utilized 100 workers in the Amazon cluster. The graph size was varied from 200 million to 1 billion nodes. We let k be 10 and measured the average running time for each query group. Fig. 10(b) shows the running time for answering the queries on different sizes of data graph. The running time increases slowly with the data graph size. This result demonstrates the ability of our distributed system to scale for billion-node graphs.

7. RELATED WORK

Graph matching. Graph matching has been extensively studied over the past decades [26]. Some recent works [19, 18, 13, 10, 9, 7] studied how to perform subgraph matching on large graphs. However, the proposed approach-

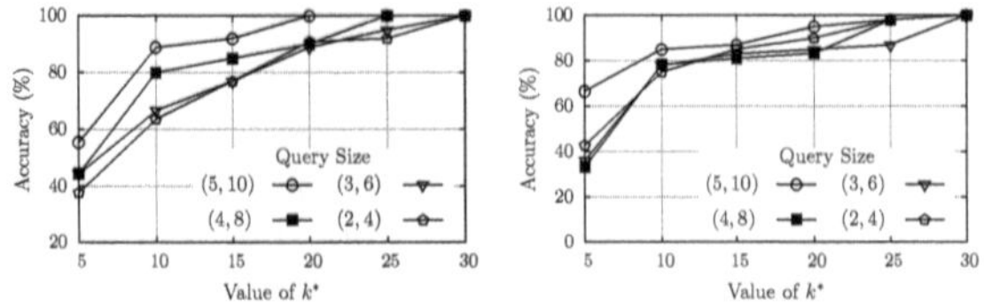

(a) DBLP (b) Freebase

Figure 5: The accuracy when varying k^*

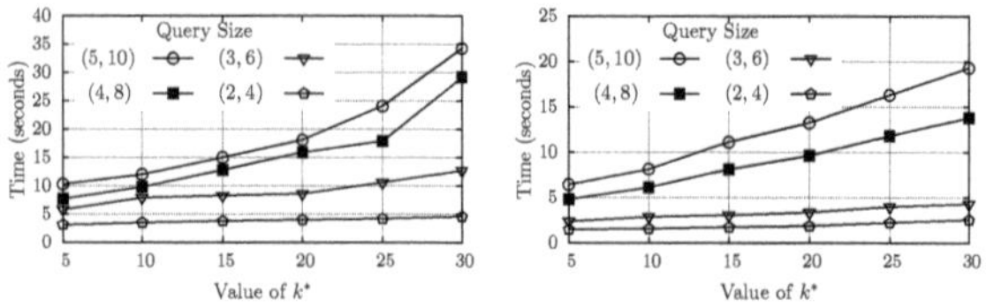

(a) DBLP (b) Freebase

Figure 6: The running time when varying k^*

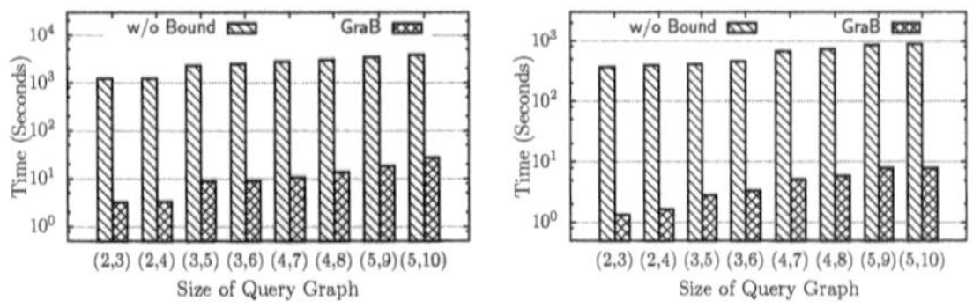

(a) DBLP (b) Freebase

Figure 7: Efficiency of bounding technique

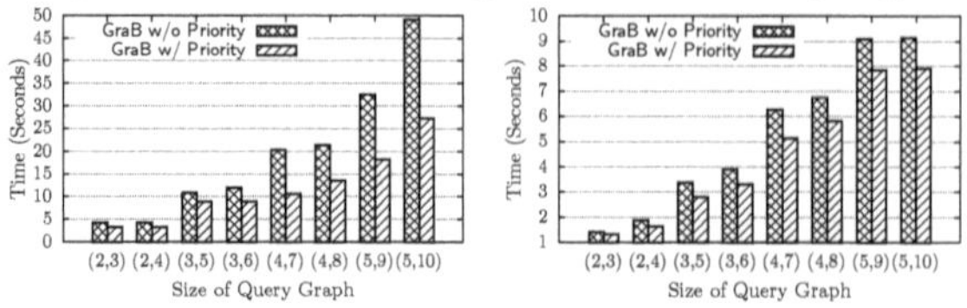

(a) DBLP (b) Freebase

Figure 8: Efficiency of priority scheduling

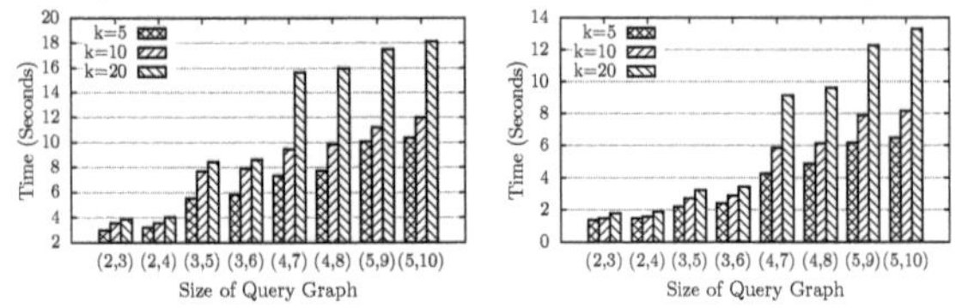

(a) DBLP (b) Freebase

Figure 9: The running time when varying k

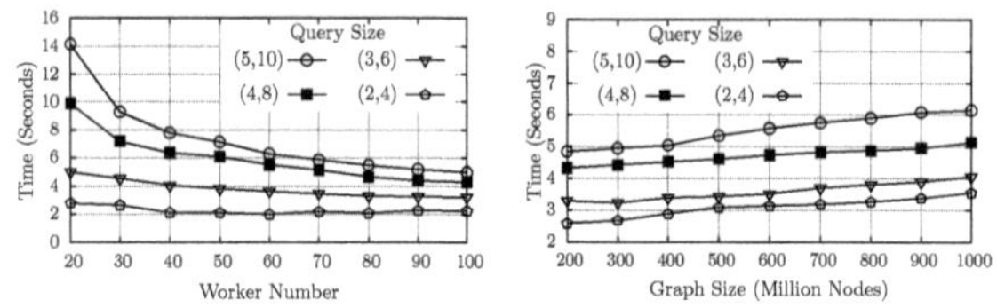

(a) Varying worker num. (b) Varying graph size

Figure 10: Scalability

es are not suitable for billion-node graphs due to expensive indexing costs. The graph-exploration-based subgraph matching algorithm by Sun et al. [27] finds exact matches in billion-node graphs. In contrast, our algorithm finds both exact matches and similar matches.

Top-k query. Top-k queries request the best-k answers for a given query [15]. The Threshold Algorithm and Fagin's Algorithm are commonly used to answer top-k queries [8]. However, they require precomputing sorted lists to derive the upper bounds and the lower bounds. For distributed graph databases, the top-k graph query problems studied in [20, 11, 16] query for one unknown entity that are highly relevant to a given set of entities, but the problem we studied considers the relationships among multiple unknown entities, which is more common in real life.

RDF query. RDF queries are important for discovering information on information networks. Some RDF query systems [1, 23, 6] have been developed. These systems build sophisticated indices on a single machine for query processing. In recent years, distributed RDF query systems [29, 14, 31] are proposed to support web-scale RDF graphs. However, the systems focus on finding the answers that exactly match queries. The flexible graph pattern queries have been studied in [25], which finds the answers similar to the RDF queries. The approach stores RDF triples on HDFS [3] and answers the queries by repeatedly joining intermediate results. In contrast, our approach does not produce a huge amount of intermediate join results.

Distributed graph computation. Since billion-node graphs are increasingly common, distributed graph computation frameworks [32, 21, 22, 24] have been developed to support graph operations, such as computing PageRank scores and computing shortest paths. Although our system is implemented based on Piccolo [24], it can also be implemented on any other frameworks that can support breadth-first search.

8. CONCLUSION

In this paper, we propose GraB, an index-free graph matching algorithm for answering top-k queries on web-scale information networks. Our approach provides meaningful answers via exact and similar matching. To obtain the answers quickly without indices, GraB utilizes a novel heuristic for selecting the top candidates of query nodes and computes the bounds of matching scores to derive the top-k answers instead of computing the exact matching scores. A distributed system for the algorithm is proposed to allow scalability. Our experiments demonstrate that the proposed approach can efficiently answer queries on billion-node information networks.

Acknowledgements

We would like to thank Dr. Xiang Cheng for useful discussion during the early stage of this work. This work is partially supported by U.S. NSF grants CNS-1217284 and CCF-1018114, National Natural Science Foundation of China under Grants No. 61320106007, No. 61370207, No. 61202449, No. 61300024, National High-tech R&D Program of China (863 Program) under Grants No. 2013AA013503, China Specialized Research Fund for the Doctoral Program of Higher Education under Grants No. 20110092130002, Jiangsu research prospective joint research project under Grants No. BY2012202, No.BY2013073-01, Jiangsu Provincial Key Laboratory of Network and Information Security under Grants No. BM2003201, Key Laboratory of Computer Network and Information Integration of Ministry of Education of China under Grants No. 93K-9. Jiahui Jin was a visiting student at UMass Amherst, supported by China Scholarship Council, when this work was performed. Any opinions, findings, conclusions or recommendations expressed in this paper are those of the authors and do not necessarily reflect the views of the sponsor.

References

[1] Apache Jena. http://jena.apache.org/.

[2] DBLP. http://www.informatik.uni-trier.de/~ley/db/.

[3] Hadoop Distributed File System. http://hadoop.apache.org/.

[4] Linked Open Data. http://www.w3.org/wiki/SweoIG/TaskForces/CommunityProjects/LinkingOpenData.

[5] T. Akiba, Y. Iwata, and Y. Yoshida. Fast exact shortest-path distance queries on large networks by pruned landmark labeling. In *SIGMOD'13*, pages 349–360, 2013.

[6] M. Atre, V. Chaoji, M. J. Zaki, and J. A. Hendler. Matrix "bit" loaded: a scalable lightweight join query processor for rdf data. In *WWW'10*, pages 41–50, 2010.

[7] J. Cheng, X. Zeng, and J. X. Yu. Top-k graph pattern matching over large graphs. In *ICDE'13*, pages 1033–1044, 2013.

[8] R. Fagin, A. Lotem, and M. Naor. Optimal aggregation algorithms for middleware. *J. Comput. Syst. Sci.*, pages 614–656, 2003.

[9] W. Fan, J. Li, S. Ma, N. Tang, Y. Wu, and Y. Wu. Graph pattern matching: From intractable to polynomial time. *PVLDB*, pages 264–275, 2010.

[10] W. Fan, X. Wang, and Y. Wu. Diversified top-k graph pattern matching. *PVLDB*, pages 1510–1521, 2013.

[11] Y. Fang, K. C.-C. Chang, and H. W. Lauw. Roundtriprank: Graph-based proximity with importance and specificity. In *ICDE'13*, pages 613–624, 2013.

[12] Google. "freebase data dumps". https://developers.google.com/freebase/data.

[13] M. Gupta, J. Gao, X. Yan, H. Cam, and J. Han. Top-k interesting subgraph discovery in information networks. In *ICDE'14*, pages 820–831, 2014.

[14] J. Huang, D. J. Abadi, and K. Ren. Scalable sparql querying of large rdf graphs. *PVLDB*, pages 1123–1134, 2011.

[15] I. F. Ilyas, G. Beskales, and M. A. Soliman. A survey of top-k query processing techniques in relational database systems. *ACM Comput. Surv.*, 2008.

[16] J. Jin, S. Khemmarat, L. Gao, and J. Luo. A distributed approach for top-k star queries on massive information networks. In *ICPADS'14*, pages 9–16, 2014.

[17] J. Jin, S. Khemmarat, L. Gao, and J. Luo. Querying web-scale information networks through bounding matching scores. Technical report, 2015. http://rio.ecs.umass.edu/mnilpub/papers/tech2015-jin.pdf.

[18] A. Khan, N. Li, X. Yan, Z. Guan, S. Chakraborty, and S. Tao. Neighborhood based fast graph search in large networks. In *SIGMOD'11*, pages 901–912, 2011.

[19] A. Khan, Y. Wu, C. C. Aggarwal, and X. Yan. Nema: Fast graph search with label similarity. *PVLDB*, pages 181–192, 2013.

[20] S. Khemmarat and L. Gao. Fast top-k path-based relevance query on massive graphs. In *ICDE'14*, pages 316–327, 2014.

[21] Y. Low, J. Gonzalez, A. Kyrola, D. Bickson, C. Guestrin, and J. M. Hellerstein. Distributed graphlab: A framework for machine learning in the cloud. *PVLDB*, pages 716–727, 2012.

[22] G. Malewicz, M. H. Austern, A. J. C. Bik, J. C. Dehnert, I. Horn, N. Leiser, and G. Czajkowski. Pregel: a system for large-scale graph processing. In *SIGMOD'10*, pages 135–146, 2010.

[23] T. Neumann and G. Weikum. Rdf-3x: a risc-style engine for rdf. *PVLDB*, pages 647–659, 2008.

[24] R. Power and J. Li. Piccolo: Building fast, distributed programs with partitioned tables. In *OSDI'10*, pages 293–306, 2010.

[25] P. Ravindra and K. Anyanwu. Scalable processing of flexible graph pattern queries on the cloud. In *WWW'13 (Companion Volume)*, pages 169–170, 2013.

[26] D. Shasha, J. T.-L. Wang, and R. Giugno. Algorithmics and applications of tree and graph searching. In *PODS'02*, pages 39–52, 2002.

[27] Z. Sun, H. Wang, H. Wang, B. Shao, and J. Li. Efficient subgraph matching on billion node graphs. *PVLDB*, pages 788–799, 2012.

[28] Y. Tian and J. M. Patel. Tale: A tool for approximate large graph matching. In *ICDE'08*, pages 963–972, 2008.

[29] R. Verborgh, M. V. Sande, P. Colpaert, S. Coppens, E. Mannens, and R. V. de Walle. Web-scale querying through linked data fragments. In *LDOW'14*, 2014.

[30] X. Yan, F. Zhu, P. S. Yu, and J. Han. Feature-based similarity search in graph structures. *ACM Trans. Database Syst.*, pages 1418–1453, 2006.

[31] K. Zeng, J. Yang, H. Wang, B. Shao, and Z. Wang. A distributed graph engine for web scale rdf data. *PVLDB*, pages 265–276, 2013.

[32] Y. Zhang, Q. Gao, L. Gao, and C. Wang. Priter: A distributed framework for prioritizing iterative computations. *IEEE Trans. Parallel Distrib. Syst.*, pages 1884–1893, 2013.

LN-Annote: An Alternative Approach to Information Extraction from Emails using Locally-Customized Named-Entity Recognition

YoungHoon Jung
Columbia University
jung@cs.columbia.edu

Karl Stratos
Columbia University
stratos@cs.columbia.edu

Luca P. Carloni
Columbia University
luca@cs.columbia.edu

ABSTRACT

Personal mobile devices offer a growing variety of personalized services that enrich considerably the user experience. This is made possible by increased access to personal information, which to a large extent is extracted from user email messages and archives. There are, however, two main issues. First, currently these services can be offered only by large web-service companies that can also deploy email services. Second, keeping a large amount of structured personal information on the cloud raises privacy concerns. To address these problems, we propose LN-Annote, a new method to extract personal information from the email that is locally available on mobile devices (without remote access to the cloud). LN-Annote enables third-party service providers to build a question-answering system on top of the local personal information without having to own the user data. In addition, LN-Annote mitigates the privacy concerns by keeping the structured personal information directly on the personal device. Our method is based on a named-entity recognizer trained in two separate steps: first using a common dataset on the cloud and then using a personal dataset in the mobile device at hand. Our contributions include also the optimization of the implementation of LN-Annote: in particular, we implemented an OpenCL version of the custom-training algorithm to leverage the Graphic Processing Unit (GPU) available on the mobile device. We present an extensive set of experiment results: beside proving the feasibility of our approach, they demonstrate its efficiency in terms of the named-entity extraction performance as well as the execution speed and the energy consumption spent in mobile devices.

Categories and Subject Descriptors

H.3.5 [**Online Information Services**]: Web-based services.

Keywords

NER; SNS; Personal Search; Information Extraction; Neural Network; OpenCL.

WWW 2015, May 18–22, 2015, Florence, Italy.
ACM 978-1-4503-3469-3/15/05.
http://dx.doi.org/10.1145/2736277.2741633.

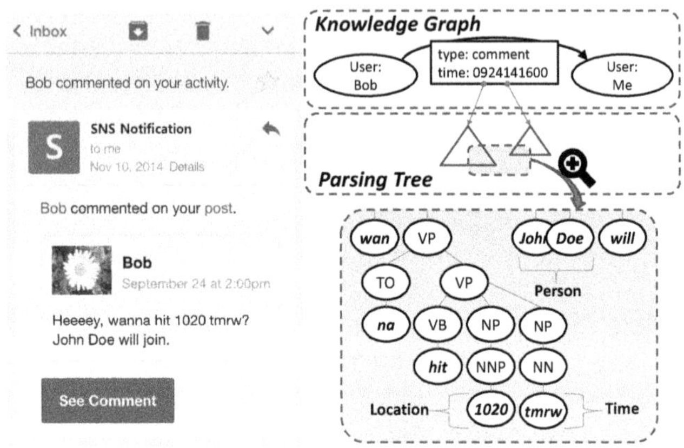

(a) An SNS Notification Email (b) Knowledge Graph and Parse Tree

Fig. 1: Parsing email to collect personal information.

1. INTRODUCTION

Recent advancements in personalized web-based services have enriched our daily lives. Intelligent personal assistant services such as Google Now [6] or Apple's Siri [7] can give "directions to home" or alert that "it's time to leave for your next meeting". Meanwhile, personal search services can answer queries based on the user's personal information. Googling "my flights", for instance, produces the upcoming flight reservations that the user has made. Personalized advertisement is another important (and most profitable) instance of personalized web services. The advertisement systems of Amazon, Facebook and Google [1, 4, 5] are known to utilize viewers' personal information such as previous purchase history.

What makes all these personalized services possible? The personal information collected by the service providers. Since its quality determines the quality of the personalized services, web service providers put in significant efforts to improve and extend its collection. One vast source of personal information is found in users' emails. Large web-service companies that provide also email services (like Google, Microsoft, and Yahoo) have the means to offer rich personalized services precisely thanks to the personal information they extract from the users' emails. The example of Fig. 1 illustrates this process. A notification email of a message posted on a Social Network Service (SNS) account by one of the user's friend is parsed through a sequence of steps to build structured data, including: 1) a knowledge graph indicating the subject, the object, a type of the action, and the contents of the comment; 2) the parsing tree of the comment; 3) various grammatical tags such as part-of-speech (e.g. Verbal Phrase and Noun Phrase) and Named-Entity Recognition (NER) labels (e.g. Person, Location, and Time). This kind of structured personal information is stored and used later in various ways: e.g. to improve personal search services by retrieving results that are relevant to the named-entities related to the user.

Thanks to the growing amount of personal data that are available to be collected, it is easy to predict that personalized services will continue to evolve and expand. There are, however, limitations and concerns. First, the current methods of information extraction are not feasible for any small company that doesn't have its own email service because they are based on accessing large data sets collected with proprietary email services. Second, keeping large amount of structured personal information on centralized remote cloud servers raises privacy and security concerns [10, 46].

To address these problems, we present LN-Annote (Locally-customized NER-based Annotation), a novel information-extraction subsystem that is designed and optimized to process the email data available *locally* on each personal mobile device. Our contributions include:

- a distributed learning model based on two phases: *universal training* to generate a common parameter set on the cloud and *custom training* to refine and optimize the shared common parameter set by using the email data locally available on each mobile device;
- a discussion on how to extend the architecture of a personal search system to integrate the LN-Annote subsystem;
- an implementation of LN-Annote using locally available information and optimization methods leveraging the GPU on the mobile device; and
- an extensive set of experimental results to prove the feasibility, effectiveness, and efficiency of our approach.

In Section 2 we describe a personal search service as an example of a personal information system where LN-Annote is employed as a subsystem. In particular, we compare two different approaches for information extraction, on the cloud and on the mobile. Also, we illustrate the workflow of LN-Annote to extract personal information from emails stored on smart devices, which can then be available for many personalized service providers. In Sections 3 and 4 we present how we implemented and optimized our system. In Section 5 we present a comprehensive set of experiment results to show the efficiency and the effectiveness of our approach. In particular, we show the advantages provided by the addition of custom training on top of universal training.

2. LN-Annote SYSTEM DESIGN

In this section we present the design of LN-Annote, its main components, and how these interact with other modules as part of a bigger system. LN-Annote is an NER-based system optimized to extract information from email messages, in particular those sent via SNSs. The focus on email is motivated by two observations: 1) email messages convey scads of personal information and 2) many web services send notification emails with very useful data such as reservations or recommendations.

2.1 Information Extraction and NER

Nowadays many companies send emails to their customers for various purposes such as discount offers, purchase history, appointment reminders, or activity updates on SNSs. As more companies integrate their services with email systems, these email messages contain a growing amount of personal information. Meanwhile, more and more people use their email to manage personal information [54]. Hence, the ability to extract personal information from emails becomes increasingly important. Nonetheless, existing extraction techniques have various limitations. One approach is to write vendor-specific parsing scripts; this, however, requires a large amount of manual labor to update the scripts whenever the vendor changes the email format. Another approach is to use Microdata embedded in the emails containing structured information [24]; this, however, is currently not very effective because the number of email messages that contain Microdata is very limited.

To overcome these problems, Natural Language Processing (NLP) techniques have been proposed to assist service providers in extracting useful information [37, 50]. Named-Entity Recognition (NER) is a popular NLP technique to classify given vocabularies into predefined categories [9, 36]. A wide variety of systems use NER for different text types such as queries, SNS posts, or résumés [23, 29, 38].

The performance of a NER system can be evaluated using various metrics. One of the most widely used metric is the F_1 *score* which is defined as the harmonic mean of *Precision* and *Recall*:

$$F_1 = 2 \cdot \frac{Precision \cdot Recall}{Precision + Recall} \qquad (1)$$

Precision, or *Positive Predictive Value*, is the correctness of the predicted classification and Recall, or *True Positive Rate*, is the coverage of the positive cases.

2.2 A Use Case: Personal Search Service

The service infrastructure that we present here is an example of a system where LN-Annote works as a key component subsystem in collaboration with other components.

A personalized search service provides answers based on the personal information that it has collected from the emails of the user who requested the query. The personal information of each user is collected periodically from the email database and stored into a structured database to simplify its retrieval. The diagrams of Fig. 2 illustrate two different approaches to implement this service. Each shaped object represents a processing component or a document database and each arrow indicates a direction of data flow. The users access the services through their smart devices, searching personal information through a *Personal Search App* and receiving emails through an *Email App*.

Fig. 2(a) shows an approach where the extraction happens in the cloud. Periodically, e.g. once a day, the extraction system accesses directly the email database to update the *Structured Personal Information Database*. When a user issues a personal query with the *Personal Search App*, the query is passed to the personal search where it is handled by the *Query Processor* to disambiguate it and augment it. The processed query is then passed to the *Personal Information Search Engine* which retrieves relevant documents from the Structured Personal Information Database. The retrieved documents are ranked by the *Search Result Ranking* system and returned to the particular app running on the mobile device, e.g. the Personal Search App, so that the user can see the results. This approach, however, has several disadvantages. First, it is feasible only for a very small group of service providers that own email services with a sufficient number of users. Hence, many service providers that do not

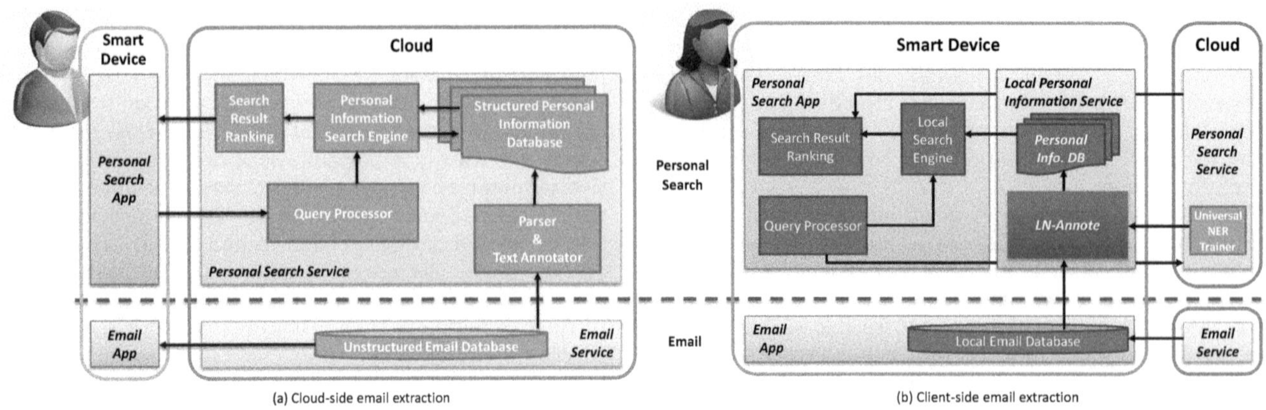

Fig. 2: An architectural comparison between two personal search systems.

have access to email services miss a major source of personal information. Second, it raises privacy and security concerns over the extraction, storage, and processing of very large amount of personal information in centralized remote cloud servers [28].

To address these challenges we propose the approach illustrated in Fig. 2(b). In this approach, the personal information extraction becomes a task that runs locally on the personal device of each user, where recently fetched emails are stored by the email app.[1] Our proposed LN-Annote in *Local Personal Information Service* is similar to the *Parser & Test Annotator* of Fig. 2(a) but uses NER and creates *Personal Information Database* on the local device. As shown in Fig 2(b) the local extraction of personal information resolves the dependency between the personalized service and the email service, thus allowing personalized service providers without their own emails services to access the local personal information database. Also, since the information remains local in the mobile device, privacy concerns and security issues are effectively alleviated [49]. Finally, the introduction of LN-Annote, a distributed NER subsystem, improves considerably the extraction accuracy while reducing the computation burden on the cloud servers (as discussed in more detail in Section 6). On the other hand, our approach requires that the mobile devices perform some additional amount of computation and this may have a negative impact on their overall performance and energy consumption. To minimize this impact, we have developed a method for custom training based on feature templates (as described in Section 4.1) and we have parallelized the key algorithms to run on the GPU present in each modern mobile device (Section 4.2).

2.3 The LN-Annote System Workflow

In this section, we describe the LN-Annote subsystem that we built to implement the approach shown in Fig. 2(b). To achieve more accurate prediction, we conceived a novel method that performs training for NER in two separate main steps, as illustrated in Fig. 3 (in this flowchart, a solid arrow represents a flow of data and a dashed arrow represents a sampling activity.) The first step, shown in the blue box (left), is *universal training*: this is essentially identical to traditional learning and returns learning parameters that will be **shared among all users**. The second step, shown in the red boxes (right), is *custom training*: it runs on each personal device, takes the learning parameters from the universal training, and enhances them by further training with the **locally accessible dataset which is specific to each user**. The main goal of our method is to produce locally-customized learning parameters that work well for the particular local environment. However, the parameters need to perform well also on the global texts, by preserving the knowledge from universal training.

As shown later, LN-Annote achieves extraction performance comparable to training for a combination of the global dataset and the personal dataset, while requiring a significantly smaller amount of computation. Next, we provide more details on the two main steps.

1. Universal Training in the Cloud. This step consists of two substeps:

1-a. *Data sampling and NER labeling* is a preparation activity that takes samples from a universal text database and creates labels for the sampled data to feed the supervised training of Substep 1-b. Choosing a representative dataset with an appropriate amount is an important task for the quality of the training [34]. The sampled data can be labeled using different methods: a) manual labeling, b) manual labeling and running semi-supervised learning, and c) running unsupervised learning [17, 51]. For the experiments of this paper we used the CoNLL03 dataset provided with manually labeled NER tags [47], while semi-supervised learning is commonly used for large datasets.

1-b. *NER universal training* uses supervised learning to process the labeled data produced by Substep 1-a. In traditional machine learning, the learning parameters created by this kind of algorithm are directly used to test the prediction of NER labels for the actual dataset. In our approach, instead, these learning parameters are shared to the multiple mobile devices for custom training.

2. Custom Training & Testing on the Mobile Device. This step consists of three substeps:

2-a. *Data sampling & semi-supervised NER labeling* works similarly to Substep 1-a to produce labeled data for Substep 2-b. Here, the inputs are text samples selected from the local email database used by the email app running on the mobile device. Also, in this case the manual labeling cannot be applied because it is infeasible to ask the user of the personal device to do it. Instead, we obtained *local gazetteers*, a list of named-entities from a reliable source [33]. This substep is performed automatically by using a semi-supervised learning

[1] Accessing other app's database is not trivial on smart platforms where each app runs in its own sandbox environment, but it is still possible through a couple of options. We have implemented email apps that share email data with other allowed apps through inter-app communication methods allowed in each platform, e.g. *Content-Provider* on Android [2]. The users can control which apps are allowed to access the emails.

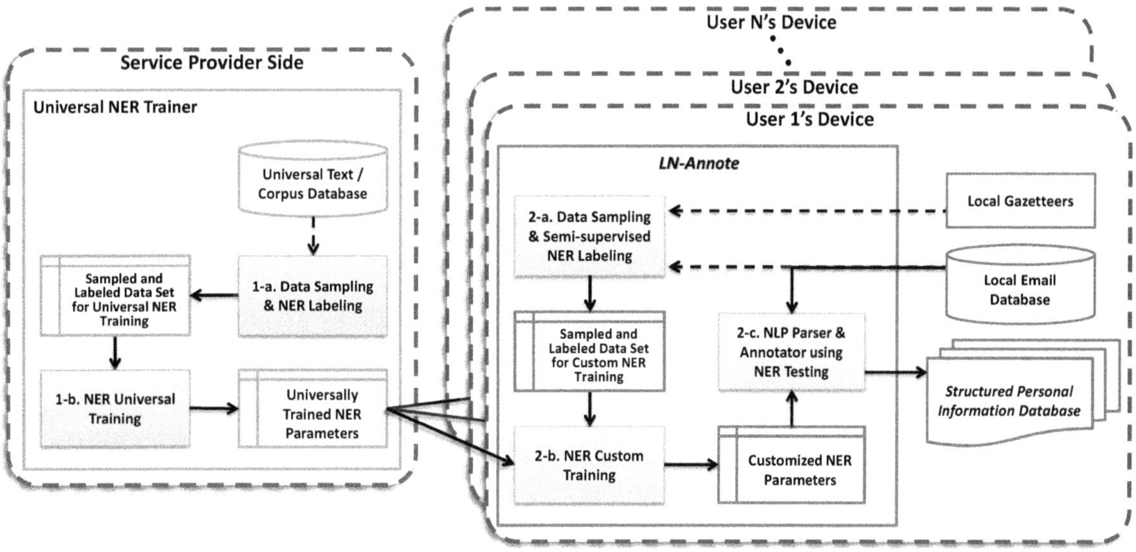

Fig. 3: The flowchart of LN-Annote.

algorithm based on the labels from the gazetteers. How to obtain gazetteers is explained in Section 3.3.

2-b. *NER Custom Training* updates the NER parameters by learning from the labeled dataset generated by the emails on the mobile device. The use of updated parameters is expected to keep the same performance as the use of universally trained parameters on the global dataset, while delivering better performance on the local emails.

2-c. *NLP Parser & Annotator using NER*, the final substep of LN-Annote processes the emails on the mobile device. This is done using NER based on the parameters created in the Substep 2-b. The outcome is stored in the Structured Personal Information Database where it can be used by any personal services running on the mobile device, as long as this is allowed by the user.

Notice that each substep of LN-Annote occurs with a different frequency: universal training (Substeps 1-a and 1-b) is done only once on the cloud servers; custom training (Substeps 2-a and 2-b), i.e. obtaining gazetteers, takes place periodically, e.g. once a week or a month; and finally, the actual information extraction (Substep 2-c) runs rather frequently, e.g. everyday.

3. NER SYSTEM IMPLEMENTATION

We designed the LN-Annote system to work with different types of incremental learning algorithms [27]. For instance, it can work as a framework running the universal training in the cloud and the custom training on the mobile while sharing the learning parameters between the two. In this section, we introduce as a showcase our *Neural Network* model for NER.

3.1 NER Algorithm Selection

NER systems may adopt a linguistic grammar-based model or a statistical learning model. We developed a system using a window-based neural network model for NER [13, 19]. Neural network learning algorithms learn the representation of multiple layers with increasing complexity and abstraction. A neural network works iteratively through *feed-forwarding*, a process to obtain the hypothesis and the cost objective (error), and *back-propagation*, a process to adjust the parameters according to the error.

Compared to various alternatives, neural network models are known to be difficult to understand with respect to the internals of the parameter optimization process. For this reasons, in many state-of-the-art NER systems programmers use other machine learning algorithms such as Conditional Random Fields [19, 52], Maximum-Entropy Markov Model [20], or Perceptron [12], which in many cases achieve pretty high F_1 score (over 90). Still, we chose to build a neural network model for NER for the following reasons. First, a neural network automatically chooses feature values through feed-forwarding and back-propagation. This makes the system free from the need of using carefully hand-crafted features that are required by other learning techniques. In particular, in our system it enables the automation of the preparation and training for the customized learning step. Second, neural network algorithms make heavy use of linear algebra and, particular, matrix operations: these can be easily parallelized and executed on the GPU of the mobile device, thereby reducing the time and energy spent on the computation in the custom training.

Neural network models are prone to *catastrophic forgetting* (or catastrophic interference), an extensive loss of previously learned information that may occur while learning new training data. This problem has its main causes in the representational overlap within the learning system and in the side-effects of the training methods used (rather than in the lack of sufficient computing resources in the system) [15]. In our system, catastrophic forgetting could manifest in a particular way: the customized NER parameters can recognize entities learned during custom training while losing the ability of identifying entities previously learned during universal training. There are several known solutions to mitigate catastrophic forgetting, including: conservative training and support vector rehearsal [8], multi-objective learning [26], sweep rehearsal [43], unsupervised neuron selection [22], fixed expansion layer [14], and ensemble of classifiers [40]. In our neural network model we avoid catastrophic forgetting by designing an incremental neural network model that introduces a scale factor to the weight adjustment [21, 53]. This leads to excellent results, as discussed in Section 5.

3.2 A Neural Network Model for NER

Both universal training and custom training are based on supervised learning and use the same neural network model. In fact, the two training algorithms are essentially the same

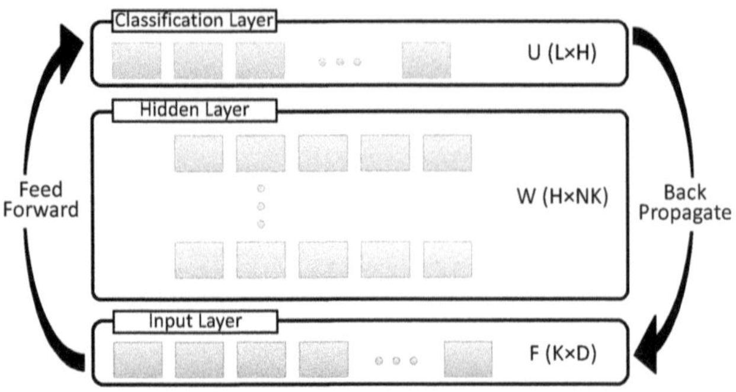

Fig. 4: The designed neural network architecture.

for consistency and compatibility of network parameters. The only differences are the number of iterations and the learning rate. We use a window-based network model with a fixed window size. This means that, while labeling a given word, a few nearby words are also processed to provide a local context that helps capturing the characteristics of the target word.

In the neural network we have three layers, as shown in Fig. 4: the input layer, the hidden layer, and the classification (output) layer. The input layer consists of feature vectors, or word representations, obtained from the unsupervised pre-training [25]. Each feature vector consists of K float values to represent a vocabulary in the dictionary of D vocabularies. The hidden layer, with a dimension of H, is used to derive hidden features by computing the input layer and the weight vectors. The dimension of weight vectors W for the hidden layer is $H \times NK$ where N is the size of window. On top of the hidden layer, there is the output layer for *softmax regression* to predict named-entities [16]. The weight vectors U for the output layer is of size $L \times H$, where L is the number of possible output classes.

Feed-Forwarding. Feed-forwarding in neural networks is a process to compute prediction values. We first calculate $z_i = Wx_i + b_1$ where x_i is the feature vectors of the words in the i-th window and b_1 is a bias vector. Then, we obtain $a_i = f(z_i)$ by applying a nonlinearity function f. Finally, we compute the hypothesis $h_i = g(U^T a_i + b_2)$, where b_2 is a bias for the softmax regression; the sigmoid function g makes the regression result fit smoothly into a classification result. The final prediction, h_i, is the probability that x_i be a named-entity of each class. Here, along with the feature vectors used as the input layer, the weight vectors and the bias vectors are considered as the NER parameters of Fig. 3.

Algorithm Configuration. We use the hyperbolic tangent function *tanh* as the nonlinearity function f. Note that its derivative can be expressed with the *tanh* function itself, i.e. $f'(x) = \frac{d}{dx}\tanh x = 1 - \tanh^2 x$. This greatly simplifies the back-propagation, thereby reducing the amount of computation for training and testing on the mobile side. The sigmoid function we use is $g(z) = \frac{1}{1-e^{-z}}$.

Training Objective. In both the universal training and the local training we minimize the same cost (objective) function which is the following cross-entropy error with a regularization factor:

$$J(\theta) = -\frac{1}{m}\sum_{i=1}^{m}\sum_{j=1}^{L}\left[1\{y^{(i)} = j\}\log\left(h_\theta^{(i)}\right)\right] + \frac{\lambda}{2}\sum_{i=1}^{k}\sum_{j=0}^{n}\theta_{ij}^2$$

Platform	API
Android	*ContactsContract.Contacts.CONTENT_URI*
iOS	*ABAddressBookCopyArrayOfAllPeople*
Windows Phone	*Microsoft.Phone.UserData.Contact.SearchAsync*

Table 1: Mobile APIs for *PER* entities.

Provider (Base URI)	REST API (PER) (ORG/LOC/MISC)
Facebook *http://graph.facebook.com*	*/v2.1/me/friendlists* */v2.1/me/feed?with=location*
Google+ *https://www.googleapis.com/plus*	*/v1/people/me/people/connected* */v1/people/me/activities/public*
Twitter *https://api.twitter.com*	*/1.1/followers/ids.json* */1.1/statuses/user_timeline.json*

Table 2: SNS open APIs for various entities.

where the model parameter θ includes the input values extracted by the current window, λ is a weight decay term (for any $\lambda > 0$) introduced for regularization, and $1\{condition\}$ is a function that returns 1 when *condition* is *true* and 0 otherwise. During back-propagation, we minimize this objective function using stochastic gradient descent, a first-order optimization method widely used for training a variety of models in machine learning.

3.3 Local Gazetteer from Mobile

Differently from universal training, which can benefit from the manually tagged corpus, the custom training on mobile devices cannot rely on any human effort to label the dataset. To automate the custom training while obtaining a high-quality training dataset, we used the idea of gazetteers [33] and developed a method to acquire gazetteers from local and external sources. Gazetteers are a named-entity list obtained from an external, reliable source. Our gazetteer-induction method uses the contact list, checked-in locations, and liked pages through the mobile platform and SNS open APIs. The available APIs for collecting this gazetteer information from mobile and SNS platforms are listed in Table 1 and Table 2, respectively. The labeled dataset is then fed into the semi-supervised learning algorithm to create a training set for the custom training.

4. OPTIMIZATION

The execution of custom training on the personal mobile device poses some challenges in terms of increased energy consumption and the possible slowdown of the overall device. To address these challenges we performed two major optimizations.

4.1 Feature Templates

Our neural network model for custom training is designed for enhancing accuracy by using the information available on the local device. Hence, it is important to capture the peculiar vocabularies observed during the custom training on the device. For example, non-standard words (frequently used on the web or in text messages as shown in Fig. 1) or abbreviated words (such as 'CROACC' [2]) are less likely to be part of a general dictionary and, therefore, less likely to have occurred during universal training. They, however, may occur frequently in the custom training with the database of a particular user. If so, for this user these words may be

[2] Cannot Rule Out Anything, Correlate Clinically.

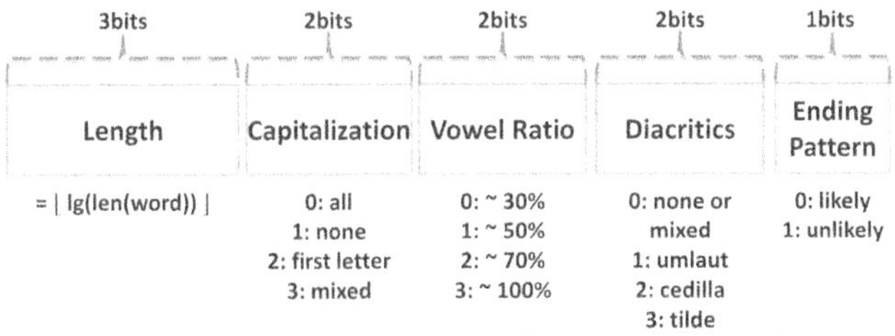

Fig. 5: The index of grouped feature templates.

named-entities or may be useful to determine nearby named-entities.[3] Thus, we capture the newly discovered words and add them to our vocabulary list, while also creating feature vectors for these new words. A performance concern, however, arises if we initialize the new feature vectors with random values. We keep the learning rate low in the custom training because it is additional training on top of the universal training and the scale factor of incremental back-propagation limits the learning rate to prevent catastrophic forgetting. Starting from parameters with the random values require more learning iterations, which slows down the training. To address this challenge, we developed a new technique to assign initial values to the feature vectors for the newly discovered words in the custom training. This technique copies template feature vectors from a group to which a new word belongs. Then, further training can converge with less learning iterations while keeping the learning rate low. As shown in Fig. 5, we use local features for grouping each word [30, 48]. The *Ending Pattern* is a boolean value representing if the word ends with one of the predefined postfixes, such as "ie", "son", "ng", or "a". These local features are then encoded to calculate the template group index for feature vectors, with a maximum index of $2^{10} - 1 = 1023$. For instance, the group index of a new word (*YoungHoon*) is 488. Then, the feature vectors for the word are copied from the template at index 488.

4.2 Hardware Acceleration

While feature templates can reduce the number of iterations to learn new vocabularies, the largest performance bottleneck still lies in the training algorithm. This leads into problems including: high energy consumption, CPU occupation, and delay in using the training results. In previous works, NER algorithms were accelerated by using some hardware units available on computer servers [18, 35]. Our goal, however, is to remove the performance bottleneck during the custom training on the mobile devices.[4] Furthermore, mobile devices are particularly prone to these problems due to their relatively slower CPUs and more limited energy budget. To accelerate the NER custom training and testing algorithm we exploit the GPU on the mobile device. Besides performance gains, GPU-based acceleration can also lower energy consumption due to the decreased execution time compared to the execution on the device CPU.

The implemented OpenCL kernel executes the entire training algorithm, e.g. window index extraction, hypothesis computation, and gradients calculation. Listing 1 shows an OpenCL kernel that computes the hypothesis of the softmax regression (the top layer in Fig. 4) for a NER class.[5]

[3] Notice that this is different from the case in universal training when newly discovered training vocabularies that have no corresponding feature vectors are discarded because they appear rarely.

[4] In most cases, training requires more computation than testing for the same size of dataset.

[5] This implementation is from our second version where each kernel computes a small portion of the algorithm.

```
/* Put product of global values to local mem */
if (gid * 4 < hiddenSize)
  partial_dot[lid] = U[gid] * a[gid];
else
  partial_dot[lid] = 0;
barrier(CLK_LOCAL_MEM_FENCE);

/* Repeatedly add values in local memory */
int nElem = group_size;
int i = (nElem + 1) / 2;
do {
  if(lid < i && lid + i < nElem) {
    partial_dot[lid] += partial_dot[lid + i];
  }
  barrier(CLK_LOCAL_MEM_FENCE);
  nElem = i;
  i = (i + 1) / 2;
} while (i != nElem);

/* Transfer final result to global memory */
if(lid == 0) {
  h[get_group_id(0)]
    = dot(partial_dot[0], (float4)(1.0f));
}

barrier(CLK_GLOBAL_MEM_FENCE);
if (gid == 0) {
  for (int i = 1; i < get_num_groups(0); i++)
    h[0] += h[i];
  h[0] += b2;
  h[0] = 1.0 + pow((float) M_E_F, -h[0]);
  h[0] = 1.0 / h[0];
}
```

Listing 1: A portion of OpenCL kernel that computes the hypothesis.

This kernel implementation uses a technique that first calculates the dot products of sub-matrices on the local memory storage shared among GPU thread blocks and then it sums up these partial dot products to quickly compute the dot product of the entire matrix. This exploitation of the local memory speeds up the summation process because for a GPU core accessing the local memory is faster than the global memory [55].

5. EXPERIMENTS

In the following experiments, we used the CoNLL03 shared task [47] in the universal training while we leveraged emails dataset in the custom training. CoNLL03 provides an English training dataset (*CoNLL03_train*) and two English test datasets (*CoNLL03_testa* and *CoNLL03_testb*). The actual email datasets used in the experiments were created with SNS notification emails, such as the example presented in Fig. 1(a), chosen from personally donated emails for research purposes. We created a training dataset and a testing dataset for each user and used these in Substeps 2-b and 2-c of Fig. 3, respectively. Let *email_traina* denote the training dataset from $user_a$ and *email_testa* denote the testing dataset from the same user. While a semi-supervised learning and gazetteers were used with the email datasets for training as explained in Section 2.3, the email datasets for testing were labeled following the CoNLL03 guidelines [47] for the experiments in this section. Each email dataset for custom training consists of 128,000 words out of which approximately 8,000 to 21,000 words are unique within that dataset. The used email dataset for testing contains around 64,000 words. Each measured value that has a possibility of variation, such as execution time and power consumption, was executed 10 times and averaged excluding the largest observation and the smallest observation.

(a) Random (b) Universal train on CoNLL03 (c) Custom train on email_traina (d) Custom train on email_trainb

Fig. 6: t-SNE plots of feature vectors.

	Training			Testing		
	Prec.	Recall	$F_{\beta=1}$	Prec.	Recall	$F_{\beta=1}$
LOC	84.28%	80.02%	82.10	83.15%	75.87%	79.34
MISC	79.24%	72.45%	75.69	73.86%	72.34%	73.10
ORG	85.58%	84.56%	85.07	78.64%	75.24%	76.91
PER	89.44%	86.43%	87.91	87.78%	83.44%	85.56
Overall	85.46%	81.88%	83.63	82.06%	77.54%	79.74

Table 3: CoNLL03 evaluation of universal training.

	Training			Testing		
	Prec.	Recall	$F_{\beta=1}$	Prec.	Recall	$F_{\beta=1}$
LOC	83.83%	80.58%	82.17	83.00%	77.27%	80.03
MISC	79.14%	72.02%	75.41	72.31%	69.96%	71.11
ORG	85.56%	84.41%	84.98	78.08%	75.17%	76.60
PER	89.28%	86.32%	87.77	87.21%	82.90%	85.00
Overall	85.25%	81.91%	83.55	81.48%	77.41%	79.39

Table 4: CoNLL03 evaluation of custom training.

5.1 Learning NER Feature Vectors

In this section, we compare how the feature vectors, the main learning parameter in our NER neural network model, change as we execute universal training and custom training.

One of the difficulties in using a neural network model is understanding its internal behavior. In many cases, visualizing how the learning iterations progress can help developers understand and improve the system. t-Distributed Stochastic Neighbor Embedding (t-SNE) is a nonlinear method to transform data with multiple dimensions into data with reduced dimensions. This technique is particularly popular for visualizing high-dimensional data on a two- or three-dimension plot. The idea of t-SNE is to minimize the difference between the two distance matrices across each point on the original space and the reduced space.

The diagrams in Fig. 6 visualize the feature vectors to investigate how they change through the universal training and the custom training. In these diagrams, each dot represents a word. A black dot is a word that was present in the initial vocabulary set. A red dot is a word newly encountered during custom training. Fig. 6(a) shows the randomly initialized values in the feature vectors before the pre-training. The values are mostly scattered in the two dimensional space without forming any specific patterns, with a few areas which are denser. The values in Fig. 6(b) are generated from the feature vectors which were originally copied from the pre-trained feature vectors and then universally trained on *CoNLL_train*. Here, the dots are spread around more than in the case of the random initial vector. We believe that across the many iterations of the training the values in each word representation have moved to establish a uniform distance from one another. Meanwhile, we can observe a new pattern: a few dots form short lines. This linear pattern can be also spotted in the following two figures. Fig. 6(c) shows the feature vectors obtained by copying the universally trained feature vectors in Fig. 6(b) and updating them by training on *email_traina*. The feature vectors in Fig. 6(d) are generated in the same way but trained with *email_trainb*. While these two figures maintain the forms and patterns of Fig. 6(b), the newly introduced red dots tend to stand close to some other red dots, thus forming a group. These groups likely incorporate named-entities that never existed in the initial vocabularies and that are very relevant to a particular user, such as the name of a friend or a local restaurant.

5.2 NER Performance Comparison

In LN-Annote, the universal training is done with supervised learning on the CoNLL03 training (or the *dev*) dataset. Table 3 shows the general NER performance of universal training. In particular, the left half of the table is tested with *CoNLL03_train* and the right half is tested with *CoNLL03_testa*. The results show that in general Precision is higher than Recall for every entity type and, based on Equation 1, the F_1 scores remain in the range $[70, 90]$. Obviously, all the NER performance results are a bit lower on the testing dataset than on the training dataset because the parameters used in this experiment are originally learned from the training dataset.

Meanwhile, Table 4 presents the NER performance of custom training. As described in Section 2.3, the parameters used in this experiment are the outcome of custom training, which takes as input the learning parameters from universal training. Then, the custom training further learns from a local email dataset (*email_traina*), updating the parameters. Like for Table 3, the results of Table 4 were tested on the CoNLL03 training (left) and testing dataset (right). Therefore, comparing the tables shows how much (negative) impact, such as catastrophic forgetting, was introduced in learning by custom training.

The results show that most values remain the same, with a slight decrease compared to the values in Table 3. Hence, catastrophic forgetting is avoided. Note that on both the training and testing datasets the recall value of *Location* (LOC) is higher (80.58 and 77.27) than before (80.02 and 75.87). This possibly means that the custom training with the local email dataset improves the parameters so that the algorithm can better recognize Location entities. For instance, there is no sentence that contains the two consecutive words "on Moscow" in the training dataset while the

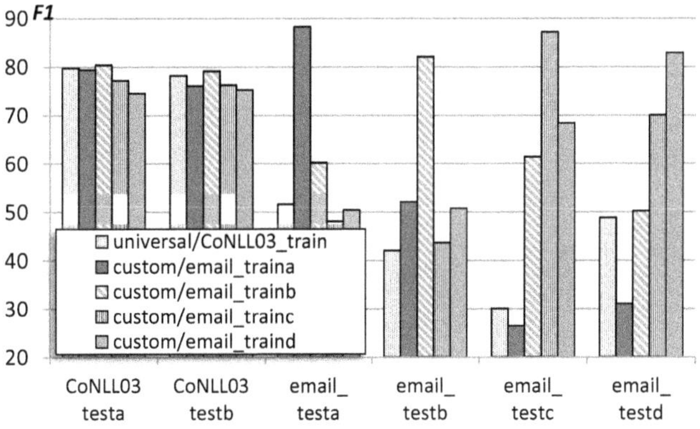

Fig. 7: F_1 scores of universal and custom training.

Platform	API
Model	Moto G
Chipset	Qualcomm MSM8226 Snapdragon 400
CPU	Quad-core 1.2GHz Cortex-A7 (Krait)
GPU	Adreno305 400Mhz
Main Memory	1GB
GPU Memory	441MB
Flash Storage	16GB
LCD Resolution	720 x 1280
Base OS	Linux-3.4.42 (LTS)
Platform	Android 4.4.4
OpenCL	Embedded Profile v1.1

Table 5: Device Specification.

testing dataset has it. The NER algorithm with the universally trained parameters tagged "Moscow" in that sentence in the CoNLL03 test dataset as *O* (non-entity). On the other hand, customized parameters which learned from a local email dataset made the NER algorithm tag "Moscow" in that sentence as *I-LOC* (Location). This implies that the custom training can improve the performance not only on the specific dataset for which it is trained but also on the general dataset.

5.3 Cross Evaluation of Learning

In this experiment, we use five parameter sets including: the one universal-trained with *CoNLL_train* and four parameter sets custom-trained with *email_train[a-d]*. The bars in Fig. 7 indicate evaluated values with different training and testing datasets. The evaluations are grouped by the six testing datasets: *CoNLL_test[ab]* and *email_test[a-d]*. For example, the leftmost bar indicates the F_1 score obtained from testing *CoNLL03_testa* with the parameters learned from *CoNLL03_train*. Likewise, the rightmost bar is obtained by testing *email_testd* on the parameters trained with *email_traind*. The first two groups present similar F_1 scores, ranging from 74 to 81. This shows that all these parameters can stably recognize entities in *CoNLL_train* even after custom training. In the next four groups, the customized parameters show a strong F_1 on the test datasets from the same user's emails on which the customized parameters were trained. In fact, in real systems a parameter set trained on a user's emails will never be used on a different user's emails. However, these evaluations across different custom datasets are conducted to analyze how custom training affects the performance of NER on different personal datasets. An interesting point is that the two bars, *email_testc* on *email_traind* and *email_testd* on *email_trainc*, have higher F_1 scores than other cross evaluations, e.g. *email_testb* on *email_trainc*. We speculate that this can happen when the two users share many named-entities, e.g. by having common friends or living close to one another. Similarly, the cross evaluation tends to have a certain level of correlation between the two customized parameter sets. This, however, does not mean that the relationship is always symmetric. For instance, the evaluation of *email_testb* with a parameter set from *email_trainc* has a low F_1 of 43.73 while the evaluation of *email_testc* with *email_trainb* has 61.5, close to the average cross evaluation score.

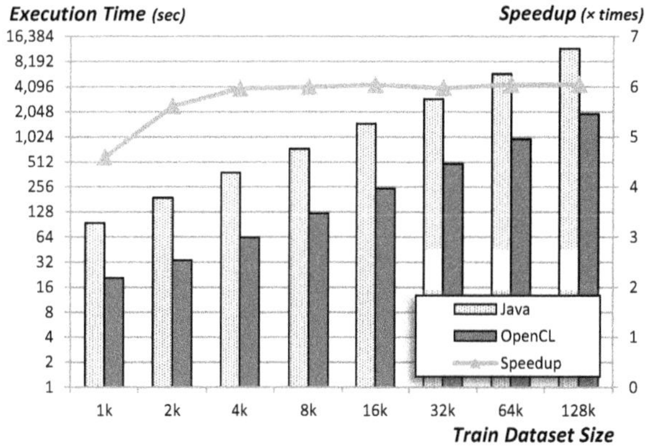

Fig. 8: Execution time comparison (H=64).

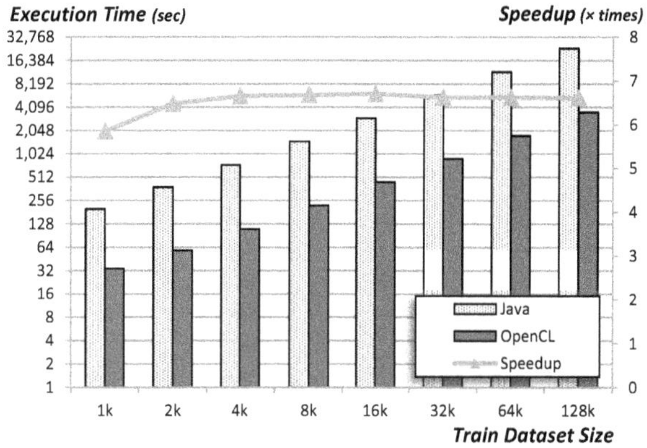

Fig. 9: Execution time comparison (H=128).

5.4 OpenCL Performance Speedup

In this section, we evaluate our efforts on executing the NER training algorithm to relieve the increased CPU occupation and power consumption caused from having more computations on the mobile devices. The experiments are done on a low-end Android phone. The detailed specification of the tested phone is listed in Table 5.

Fig. 8—10 compare the execution time of custom training by using the CPU and the GPU on the mobile device. The white bars represent the execution time of the CPU implementation written in Java. The red bars show the execution time of the GPU implementation written in OpenCL and embedded in the Java application through the Java Native Interface (JNI). The green curves indicate the speedup achieved by the OpenCL implementation (ran on the GPU) over the Java implementation (ran on the CPU).

Fig. 8 shows the execution time of the training algorithm when the hidden layer size H is set to 64. The execution times of both Java and OpenCL implementations grow proportional to the input size, i.e. the number of vocabularies in the training data set. In most cases, the speedup is close to 6, while the speedup is 4.5 and 5.5 for train dataset sized 1k and 2k, respectively. This interesting phenomenon occurs

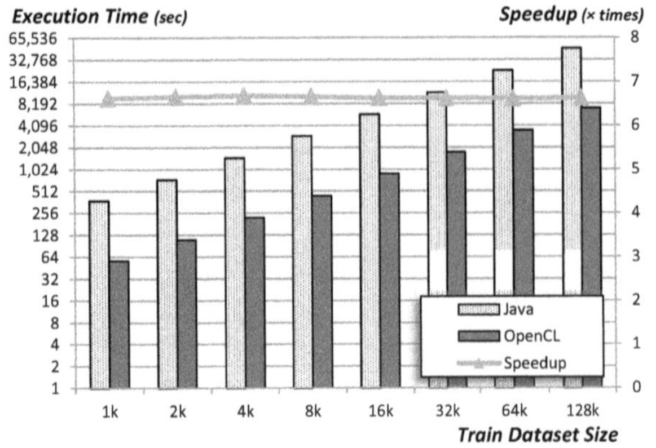

Fig. 10: Execution time comparison (H=256).

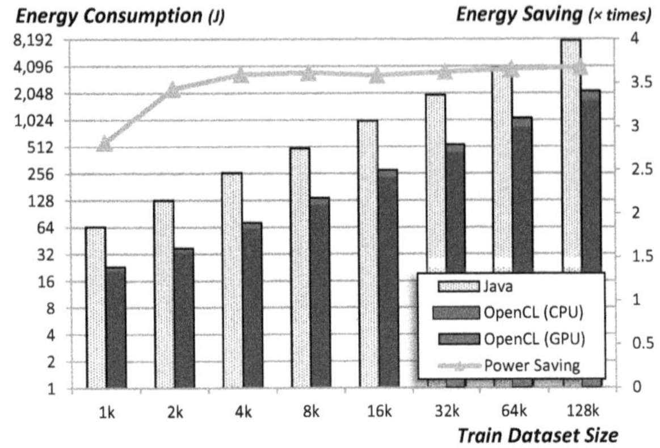

Fig. 11: Energy consumption comparison (H=64).

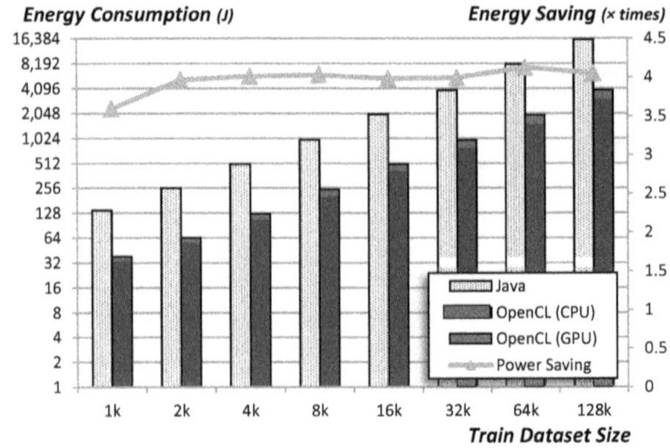

Fig. 12: Energy consumption comparison (H=128).

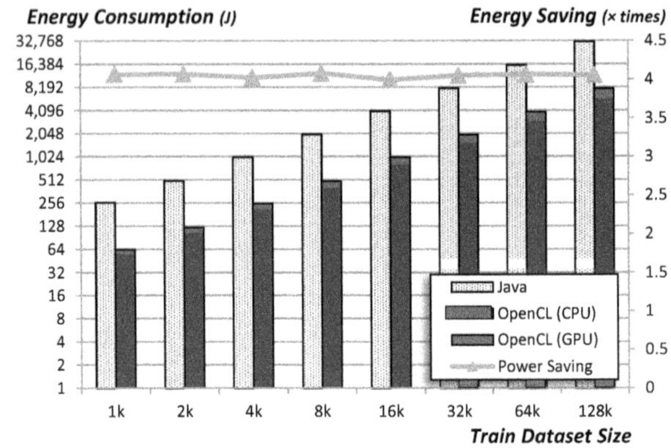

Fig. 13: Energy consumption comparison (H=256).

because for a small dataset the overhead from the OpenCL kernel invocation takes a large portion of the total execution time. This overhead includes the times for initializing the OpenCL context, compiling the OpenCL kernel, and copying kernel arguments.

Fig. 9 is the execution time when H is set to 128. While increasing H improves prediction performance, it takes more time to complete the computations. Compared to Fig. 8 the execution times are almost doubled. This means that the size of the hidden layer impacts the amount of computations proportionally. The lower points on the left end of the green curve are observed also in this figure. The bending slops is more gradual than in Fig. 8. The overall speedup from the previous figure is increased because the OpenCL performance gets better as H increases. This is because our OpenCL implementation exploits the benefit of the concurrent hardware threads, which execute the matrix operations parallelly.

Fig. 10 presents the execution time when H is 256. Since the amount of computations required in each iteration has increased because of the larger H value, the lower speedups observed in the previous figures do not appear in these experiments. The overall speedup remains the same without a large improvement with respect to the previous experiment.

5.5 OpenCL Energy Saving

Our next set of experiments is about energy consumption. Since we have achieved a good speedup by utilizing the mobile GPU, we also expect to see some reduction in energy consumption. To measure the power consumption of each application and component, we used an open source software called *PowerTutor* [56] and a profiling tool, called *Trepn*, provided by the chipset vendor [41].

Fig. 11 shows the energy consumed by the Java implementation executed on the CPU and by the OpenCL implementation run on the GPU. The red portion of the energy consumption of the OpenCL implementation is spent by the CPU while the rest is spent by the GPU. These experiments confirm that the energy consumed on the training for the same amount of input dataset could be reduced to one fourth by using the mobile GPU. This reduced energy consumption mostly came from the decreased execution time by the GPU. In fact, the power dissipation is even higher while the algorithm runs on the GPU. For instance, when the algorithm runs on the CPU the average power consumption by the CPU is approximately 0.682 Watt. On the other hand, the average power consumptions by the GPU and the CPU when the algorithm is executed on the GPU are around 1.02 Watt and 0.108 Watt, respectively. Another interesting point is that the power dissipation on the CPU, while the GPU is in use, is very low. This is because our OpenCL implementation is one consolidated kernel, thus not relying on the CPU during the entire iteration.[6] We speculate that the 0.108 Watt is mostly spent on the static power dissipation and on the maintenance of the Android app main thread, including event handling of the user interface.

Both Fig. 11 and Fig. 12 show lower energy savings for small datasets, i.e. 1k and 2k. Compared to the green curves in Fig. 8 and Fig. 9, the green curves in Fig. 11 and Fig. 12 stagger slightly. We presume that this is due to small errors introduced by the power measurement tools we used.

[6]There exist some GPUs that consume CPU resources even inside the GPU kernel, although the GPU we used in the experiments does not.

6. IMPACT ON MOBILE CLOUD SYSTEM DESIGN

One of the advantages of our approach is to decrease the computational burden in the cloud. Although the server computers in the cloud are faster than mobile devices by at least one order of magnitude, in some cases the large number of mobile devices hides the gap in computational power. This is important for the design of mobile cloud computing systems where many users access the cloud service with their own mobile devices. In this section, we discuss the design aspect of our extraction system by comparing two different approaches: 1) having the universal training and all the custom trainings on the cloud and 2) having the universal training on the cloud and the custom trainings on the mobile devices.

Let's assume that our system delivers a personalized service to ten million users who access it through their mobile devices. In general, the required number of computers depends largely on the characteristics of the service. The average number of users one server computer can handle for our service could fall in a range between 1,000 and 10,000. The lower bound, 1,000 users, is calculated as follows: according to the Amazon Web Services (AWS)'s Total Cost of Ownership (TCO) calculator, the cost for using 10,000 servers (thus making each server handle 1,000 users) is $9,224,460.[7] This would take a large portion, if not most, of the revenues that a service provider with ten million service users can make.[8] On the other hand, there are various factors that limit the processing scale of a server computer to stay under 10,000 concurrent users. One factor is the challenge imposed by the network connection capacity [39, 31].

Despite this considerable number of computers, performing all the custom training tasks only on the cloud will likely incur a large delay in the service preparation cycle. For instance, the previous experiment on custom training of 128,000 words with H=128 took 23301.93 seconds on the mobile CPU but only 3523.09 seconds on the mobile GPU, as shown in Fig. 9. The execution of the same training task on a server computer with an Intel Xeon E5-2690 CPU takes 2527.19 seconds. When each of 10,000 servers has 32 CPU cores, this will allow each CPU core to execute the custom training for 31.25 users. Suppose that we have a synchronous batch system (such as Hadoop) for the custom training where each CPU executes one custom training task for one user. Each user requests custom training everyday. The requests, however, arrive at a random time of the day. There are 32 synchronized execution time slots a day, thus making each slot be 2700 seconds. Note that this time slot is large enough for custom training on a cloud machine (2527.19 seconds) and 32 slots can sufficiently handle 31.25 users. However, when we assume that the user requests follow normal distribution across the 32 time slots, we get an average number of requests in each slot equal to 1.812. By applying *Little's law* [44], the average response time is derived as $1.812 * 2527.19 = 4579.27$ seconds. This is slower than the response time of 3523.09 seconds that is achieved with the training on the mobile devices, where there is no delay in response time for processing requests from other users. In other words, the training on the mobile devices may also lead to better performance. Finally, this approach will also reduce the computational burden on the cloud, thereby reducing the cloud cost.

[7] This cost includes 32 computing cores, 128 GB memory, and 16 TB storage space [3].

[8] The Average Revenue Per User (ARPU) varies across the companies, ranging from $1.21 (Facebook) to $12 (eBay) [32].

7. RELATED WORK

LN-Annote is related to some existing studies that focus on enhancing the model parameters for distinct cases. For instance, domain adaptation is an approach to transfer the feature vectors obtained on the source domain to the target domain [11]. In speech recognition, speaker adaptation is used to to improve the recognition performance by adapting the parameters of the acoustic models to better match the specific speaker's voice [45]. LN-Annote can be roughly categorized as distance supervision because the custom training uses the local contacts and SNS accounts to label the email datasets [42]. One of the characteristic differences between these approaches and LN-Annote is that LN-Annote uses information and computational capacity available on the local device. This addresses some privacy concerns and reduces the computational burden on the cloud as shown in Section 5 and 6.

8. CONCLUSIONS

We proposed and implemented Locally-customized NER-based Annotation (LN-Annote), a new method to extract personal information from emails stored locally on personal mobile devices. Our implementation is based on a newly-designed neural network model that works well for the two main phases of learning that characterize LN-Annote: universal training (performed in the cloud) and custom training & testing (performed on the mobile devices). We also developed two methods for optimizing the training of the neural network: one is based on the use of feature templates and the other on leveraging the GPUs that are present on the mobile devices. The experimental results show the feasibility and effectiveness of LN-Annote. In particular, they demonstrate how the use of custom trained parameters actually improves the performance of NER on the local email data without reducing its performance on the dataset used for universal training.

Acknowledgments

We gratefully thank Ethan Kim, Jinan Lou, and Younggyun Koh for their precious comments. This work is partially supported by the NSF (A#:1219001).

9. REFERENCES

[1] Amazon Product Ads: www.amazon.com/productads.
[2] Android Developers: developer.android.com.
[3] AWS Total Cost of Ownership Calculator awstcocalculator.com.
[4] Facebook Ads: www.facebook.com/ads.
[5] Google Adsense: www.google.com/adsense.
[6] Google Now: www.google.com/landing/now.
[7] Siri: www.apple.com/ios/siri.
[8] D. Albesano et al. Adaptation of artificial neural networks avoiding catastrophic forgetting. In *Proc. of the Int. Joint Conf. on Neural Networks*, pages 1554–1561, July 2006.
[9] H. Assal et al. Partnering enhanced-NLP with semantic analysis in support of information extraction. In *Proc. of the Int. Workshop on Ontology-Driven Software Engineering*, pages 9:1–9:7, Oct. 2010.
[10] D. Chaum. Security without identification: Transaction systems to make big brother obsolete. *Comm. of ACM*, 28(10):1030–1044, Oct. 1985.
[11] L. Chiticariu et al. Domain adaptation of rule-based annotators for named-entity recognition tasks. In *Proc. of the Conf. on Empirical Methods in Natural Language Processing*, pages 1002–1012, Oct. 2010.

[12] M. Collins. Discriminative training methods for Hidden Markov Models: Theory and experiments with Perceptron algorithms. In *Proc. of Conf. on Empirical Methods in NLP*, pages 1–8, July 2002.

[13] R. Collobert et al. Natural language processing (almost) from scratch. *Journal of Machine Learning Research*, 12:2493–2537, Nov. 2011.

[14] R. Coop and I. Arel. Mitigation of catastrophic interference in neural networks using a fixed expansion layer. In *Proc. of the Int. Symp. on Circuits and Systems*, pages 726–729, Aug. 2012.

[15] R. Coop and I. Arel. Mitigation of catastrophic forgetting in recurrent neural networks using a Fixed Expansion Layer. In *Proc. of the Int. Joint Conf. on Neural Networks*, pages 1–7, Aug. 2013.

[16] K. Duan et al. Multi-category classification by soft-max combination of binary classifiers. In *Proc. of the Int. Conf. on Multiple Classifier Systems*, pages 125–134, June 2003.

[17] D. Erhan et al. Why does unsupervised pre-training help deep learning? *The Journal of Machine Learning Research*, 11:625–660, Mar. 2010.

[18] H. Esmaeilzadeh, A. Sampson, L. Ceze, and D. Burger. Neural acceleration for general-purpose approximate programs. In *Proc. of the Int. Symp. on Microarchitecture*, pages 449–460, Dec. 2012.

[19] J. R. Finkel, T. Grenager, and C. Manning. Incorporating non-local information into information extraction systems by Gibbs sampling. In *Proc. of the Annual Meeting on Assoc. for Comp. Linguistics*, pages 363–370, June 2005.

[20] M. Fresko, B. Rosenfeld, and R. Feldman. A hybrid approach to NER by MEMM and manual rules. In *Proc. of the Int. Conf. on Info. and Knowledge Management*, pages 361–362, Oct. 2005.

[21] L. Fu, H.-H. Hsu, and J. C. Principe. Incremental backpropagation learning networks. *Trans. on Neural Network*, 7(3):757–761, May 1996.

[22] B. Goodrich and I. Arel. Unsupervised neuron selection for mitigating catastrophic forgetting in neural networks. In *Proc. of the Int. Symp. on Circuits and Systems*, pages 997–1000, Aug. 2014.

[23] J. Guo et al. Named entity recognition in query. In *Proc. of the Int. Conf. on Research and Development in Info. Retrieval*, pages 267–274, July 2009.

[24] M. Heinrich and M. Gaedke. Data binding for standard-based web applications. In *Proc. of the Symp. on Applied Comp.*, pages 652–657, Mar. 2012.

[25] E. H. Huang et al. Improving word representations via global context and multiple word prototypes. In *Proc. of the Annual Meeting of the Assoc. for Comp. Linguistics*, pages 873–882, July 2012.

[26] Y. Jin and B. Sendhoff. Alleviating catastrophic forgetting via multi-objective learning. In *Proc. of the Int. Joint Conf. on Neural Networks*, pages 3335–3342, July 2006.

[27] K.-H. Kim and S. Choi. Incremental learning to rank with partially-labeled data. In *Proc. of the Workshop on Web Search Click Data*, pages 20–27, Mar. 2009.

[28] A. Kobsa, B. P. Knijnenburg, and B. Livshits. Let's do it at my place instead?: Attitudinal and behavioral study of privacy in client-side personalization. In *Proc. of the Conf. on Human Factors in Comp. Sys.*, pages 81–90, Apr. 2014.

[29] C. Li et al. TwiNER: Named entity recognition in targeted twitter stream. In *Proc. of the Int. Conf. on Research and Development in Info. Retrieval*, pages 721–730, Aug. 2012.

[30] Q. Li and H. Ji. Incremental joint extraction of entity mentions and relations. In *Proc. of the Annual Meeting of the Assoc. for Comp. Linguistics*, pages 402–412, June 2014.

[31] D. Liu and R. Deters. The reverse C10K problem for server-side mashups. In *Workshops on Service-Oriented Computing*, volume 5472 of *Lecture Notes in Computer Science*, pages 166–177. 2009.

[32] P. R. L. Monica. 5 reasons to not 'like' Facebook's IPO. *CNN Money*, pages 1–1, May 2012.

[33] D. Nadeau, P. D. Turney, and S. Matwin. Unsupervised named-entity recognition: Generating gazetteers and resolving ambiguity. In *Proc. of the Int. Conf. on Advances in Artificial Intelligence*, pages 266–277, Dec. 2006.

[34] H. M. Nguyen et al. An alternative approach to avoid overfitting for surrogate models. In *Proc. of the Winter Sim. Conf.*, pages 2765–2776, Dec. 2011.

[35] E. Ordoñez Cardenas and R. d. J. Romero-Troncoso. MLP neural network and on-line backpropagation learning implementation in a low-cost FPGA. In *Proc. of the Symp. on VLSI*, pages 333–338, May 2008.

[36] S. Orlando, F. Pizzolon, and G. Tolomei. SEED: A framework for extracting social events from press news. In *Proc. of the Int. Conf. on World Wide Web Companion*, pages 1285–1294, May 2013.

[37] W. Paik et al. Applying natural language processing (NLP) based metadata extraction to automatically acquire user preferences. In *Proc. of the Int. Conf. on Knowledge Capture*, pages 116–122, Oct. 2001.

[38] S. Pawar, R. Srivastava, and G. K. Palshikar. Automatic gazette creation for named entity recognition and application to resume processing. In *Proc. of the Conf. on Intelligent & Scalable Syst. Tech.*, pages 15:1–15:7, Jan. 2012.

[39] A. Pintus, D. Carboni, and A. Piras. The anatomy of a large scale social web for internet enabled objects. In *Proc. of the Int. Workshop on Web of Things*, pages 6:1–6:6, June 2011.

[40] R. Polikar et al. Learn++: an incremental learning algorithm for supervised neural networks. *Trans. on Syst., Man, and Cybernetics*, 31(4):497–508, Nov. 2001.

[41] Qualcomm Technologies Inc. Trepn: Profiler starter edition user guide. In *Qualcomm Developer Network*, pages 1–46. Apr. 2014.

[42] A. Ritter et al. Modeling missing data in distant supervision for information extraction. *Trans. of the Association for Computational Linguistics*, pages 367–378, 2013.

[43] A. Robins. Catastrophic forgetting in neural networks: the role of rehearsal mechanisms. In *Proc. of the Int. Conf. on Artificial Neural Networks and Expert Syst.*, pages 65–68, Nov. 1993.

[44] K. Rust. Using little's law to estimate cycle time and cost. In *Proc. of the Conf. on Winter Sim.*, pages 2223–2228, Dec. 2008.

[45] G. Saon et al. Speaker adaptation of neural network acoustic models using i-vectors. In *Proc. of the Workshop on Automatic Speech Recognition and Understanding*, pages 55–59, Dec. 2013.

[46] E. Sarigol, D. Garcia, and F. Schweitzer. Online privacy as a collective phenomenon. In *Proc. of the Conf. on Online Social Networks*, pages 95–106, Oct. 2014.

[47] E. F. Tjong Kim Sang and F. De Meulder. Introduction to the CoNLL-2003 shared task: Language-independent named entity recognition. In *Proc. of the Conf. on Natural Lang. Learning*, pages 142–147, May 2003.

[48] M. Tkachenko and A. Simanovsky. Named entity recognition: exploring features. In *Proc. of NLP*, pages 118–127, Sept. 2012.

[49] V. Toubiana, V. Verdot, and B. Christophe. Cookie-based privacy issues on Google services. In *Proc. of the Conf. on Data and App. Security and Privacy*, pages 141–148, Feb. 2012.

[50] J. Tsujii. Generic NLP technologies: Language, knowledge and information extraction. In *Proc. of the Annual Meeting on Assoc. for Comp. Linguistics*, pages 12–22, Oct. 2000.

[51] J. Turian, L. Ratinov, and Y. Bengio. Word representations: A simple and general method for semi-supervised learning. In *Proc. of the Annual Meeting of the Assoc. for Comp. Linguistics*, pages 384–394, July 2010.

[52] S. N. V, P. Mitra, and S. K. Ghosh. Conditional random field based named entity recognition in geological text. *Int. Journal of Comp. Applications*, pages 119–122, 2010.

[53] J. H. Wang and H. Y. Wang. Incremental neural network construction for text classification. In *Proc. of the Int. Symp. on Comp., Consumer and Control*, pages 970–973, June 2014.

[54] S. Whittaker, V. Bellotti, and J. Gwizdka. Email in personal information management. *Comm. of the ACM*, 49(1):68–73, Jan. 2006.

[55] Y. Yang et al. Shared memory multiplexing: A novel way to improve GPGPU throughput. In *Proc. of the Int. Conf. on Parallel Arch. and Compilation Tech.*, pages 283–292, Sept. 2012.

[56] L. Zhang et al. Accurate online power estimation and automatic battery behavior based power model generation for smartphones. In *Proc. of the Int. Conf. on Hardware/Software Codesign and Syst. Synthesis*, pages 105–114, Oct. 2010.

Describing and Understanding Neighborhood Characteristics through Online Social Media

Mohamed Kafsi
EPFL
Lausanne, Switzerland
mohamed.kafsi@epfl.ch

Henriette Cramer
Yahoo Labs
Sunnyvale, CA, USA
henriette@yahoo-inc.com

Bart Thomee
Yahoo Labs
San Francisco, CA, USA
bthomee@yahoo-inc.com

David A. Shamma
Yahoo Labs
San Francisco, CA, USA
aymans@acm.org

ABSTRACT

Geotagged data can be used to describe regions in the world and discover local themes. However, not all data produced within a region is necessarily specifically descriptive of that area. To surface the content that is characteristic for a region, we present the *geographical hierarchy model* (GHM), a probabilistic model based on the assumption that data observed in a region is a random mixture of content that pertains to different levels of a hierarchy. We apply the GHM to a dataset of 8 million Flickr photos in order to discriminate between content (i.e., tags) that specifically characterizes a region (e.g., neighborhood) and content that characterizes surrounding areas or more general themes. Knowledge of the discriminative and non-discriminative terms used throughout the hierarchy enables us to quantify the uniqueness of a given region and to compare similar but distant regions. Our evaluation demonstrates that our model improves upon traditional Naive Bayes classification by 47% and hierarchical TF-IDF by 27%. We further highlight the differences and commonalities with human reasoning about what is locally characteristic for a neighborhood, distilled from ten interviews and a survey that covered themes such as time, events, and prior regional knowledge.

Categories and Subject Descriptors

H.3.3 [**Information Storage and Retrieval**]: Clustering; I.2.6 [**Artificial Intelligence**]: Learning—*Knowledge acquisition, Parameter learning*

Keywords

Geotagged Data; Probabilistic Hierarchical Model; Locally Characteristic; User Study; Survey

WWW 2015, May 18–22, 2015, Florence, Italy.
ACM 978-1-4503-3469-3/15/05.
http://dx.doi.org/10.1145/2736277.2741133.

1. INTRODUCTION

Finding characteristics that are specific to a geographic region is challenging because it requires local knowledge to identify what is particularly salient in that area. Knowledge of regional characteristics becomes critical when communicating about or describing regions, for instance in the context of a mobile travel application that provides country, city and neighborhood summaries. This knowledge is especially useful when comparing regions to make geo-based recommendations: tourists visiting Singapore, for example, might be interested in exploring the Tiong Bharu neighborhood if they are aware it is known for its coffee in the same way the San Francisco Mission district is.

Photo-sharing websites, such as Instagram and Flickr, contain photos that connect geographical locations with user-generated annotations. We postulate that local knowledge can be gleaned from these geotagged photos, enabling us to discriminate between annotations (i.e., tags) that specifically characterize a region (e.g., neighborhood) and those that characterize surrounding areas or more general themes. This is, however, challenging because much of the data produced within a region is not necessarily specifically descriptive for that area. Is the word "desert" specifically descriptive of Las Vegas, or rather of the surrounding area? Can we quantify to what extent the word "skyscraper" is descriptive of Midtown, Manhattan, New York City or the United States as a whole?

In this paper, we propose the geographical hierarchy model (GHM), a probabilistic hierarchical model that enables us to find terms that are specifically descriptive of a region within a given hierarchy. The model is based on the assumption that the data observed in a region is a random mixture of terms generated by different levels of the hierarchy. Our model further gives insight into the diversity of local content, for example by allowing for identification of the most unique or most generic regions amongst all regions in the hierarchy. The GHM is flexible and generalizes to both balanced and unbalanced hierarchies that vary in size and number of levels. Moreover, it is able to scale up to very large datasets because its complexity scales linearly with respect to the number of regions and the number of unique terms. To evaluate our model, we compare its performance with two methods: Naive Bayes [16] and a hierarchical variant of TF-IDF [23].

To investigate how well the descriptive terms surfaced by our model for a given region correspond with human descriptions, we focus on annotations of photos taken in neighborhoods of San Francisco and New York City. We apply our method to a dataset of 8 million geotagged photos described by approximately 20 million tags. We are able to associate to each neighborhood the tags that describe it specifically, and coefficients that quantify its uniqueness. This enables us to find the most unique neighborhoods in a city and to find mappings between similar neighborhoods in both cities.

We contrast the neighborhood characteristics uncovered by our model with their human descriptions by conducting a survey and a user study. This allows us not only to assess the quality of the results found by the GHM, but mainly to understand the human reasoning about what makes a feature distinctive (or not) for a region. Beyond highlighting individual differences in people's local experiences and perceptions, we touch topics such as the importance of supporting feature understanding, and consideration of adjacency and topography through porous boundaries.

The remainder of this paper is organized as follows. We first discuss related work in Section 2. We then present our geographical hierarchical model in Section 3, evaluate its performance in Section 4, and describe the user study in Section 5. We finally conclude the paper and present future outlooks in Section 6.

2. RELATED WORK

Human activities shape the perception of coherent neighborhoods, cities and regions; and vice versa. As Hillier and Vaughan [14] pointed out, urban spatial patterns shape social patterns and activity, but in turn can also reflect them. Classic studies such as those by Milgram and Lynch [17] on mental maps of cities and neighborhoods reflect that people's perceptions go well beyond spatial qualities. They illustrate individual differences between people, but also the effects of social processes affecting individual descriptions. People's conceptualization of region boundaries are fuzzy and can differ between individuals, even while they are still willing to make a judgement call on what does or does not belong to a geographic region [19]. Urban design is argued to affect the imageability of locales, with some points of interests for example may be well known, whereas other areas in a city provide less imageability and are not even recalled by local residents [17]. The perceived identity of a neighborhood differs between individuals, but can relate to their social identity and can influence behavior [27]. Various qualitative and quantitative methods, from surveys of the public to trained observation, have been employed over the years to gain such insights [19, 27, 11], with the fairly recent addition of much larger datasets of volunteered geographic information [12] and other community-generated content to benefit our understanding of human behavior and environment in specific regions. Geotagged photos and their tags are also an invaluable data source for research about social photography, recommendations, and discovery [8, 20].

We differentiate our approach from those aiming to discover new regions [29] or redefine neighborhood boundaries [9] using geotagged data. Backstrom et al. [3] presented a model to estimate the geographical center of a search engine query and its spatial dispersion, where the dispersion measure was used to distinguish between local and global queries. Ahern et al. [1] used k-means clustering to separate geotagged photos into geographic regions, where each region was described by the most representative tags. This work was followed up by Rattenbury and Naaman [23], in which the authors proposed new methods for extracting place semantics for tags. While these prior works principally attempted to identify new regions or arbitrary spaces, we instead aim to find the unique characteristics of regions in a known hierarchy. For each region at each level in the hierarchy we aim to find a specifically descriptive set of tags, drawn from the unstructured vocabulary of community-generated annotations.

Hollenstein and Purves [15] examined Flickr images to explore the terms used to describe city core areas. For example, they found that terms such as `downtown` are prominent in North America, `cbd` (central business district) is popular in Australia and `citycenter` is typical for Europe. The authors further manually categorized tags in the city of Zürich according to a geographical hierarchy; even with local knowledge they found that doing so was tedious because of tag idiosyncrasies and the diversity of languages. In contrast, our method enables us to automatically obtain such classifications. Moreover, we are not just able to distinguish between local and global content, but can classify a tag according to a geographical hierarchy with an arbitrary number of levels.

Hierarchical mixture models can be used for building complex probability distributions. The underlying hierarchy, that encodes the specificity or generality of the data, might be known a priori [18] or may be inferred from data by assuming a specific generative process, such as the Chinese restaurant process [6] for Latent Dirichlet Allocation [7, 2], where the regions and their hierarchy are learned from data. We emphasize that, in this paper, we do not try to learn latent geographical regions, but rather aim to describe regions that are known a priori. Moreover, these regions are structured according to a known hierarchy.

3. GEOGRAPHICAL HIERARCHY MODEL

Finding terms that are specifically descriptive of a region is a challenging task. For example, the tag `paname` (nickname for Paris) is frequent across many neighborhoods of Paris but is specific to the city, rather than to any of the neighborhoods in which the photos labeled with this tag were taken. The tag `blackandwhite` is also a frequent tag, which describes a photography style rather than any particular region in the world where the tag was used. The main challenge we face is to discriminate between terms that (i) specifically describe a region, (ii) those that specifically describe a sibling, parent or child region, and (iii) those that are not descriptive for any particular region. To solve this problem, we introduce a hierarchical model that is able to isolate the terms that are specifically descriptive of a given region by considering not only the terms used within the region, but also those used elsewhere. Our model goes beyond the distinction between only global and local content [21] by probabilistically assigning terms to a particular level in the hierarchy. In this paper we present our model from a geographic perspective, even though it is generic in nature: in principle any kind of hierarchy can be used where labeled instances are initially assigned to the leaf nodes.

3.1 Definitions

tag is the basic semantic unit and represents a term from a vocabulary indexed by $t \in \{1, \ldots, T\}$.

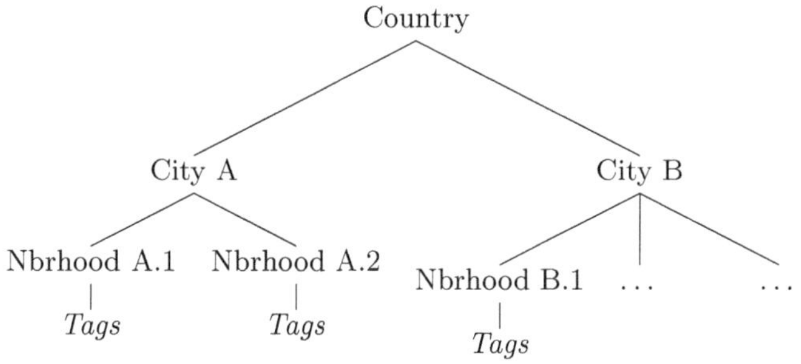

Figure 1: We represent the geographical hierarchy Country → City → Neighborhood as a geo-tree. Each node v of the geo-tree is associated to a multinomial distribution over tags θ_v.

neighborhood is the basic spatial unit. The semantic representation of a neighborhood is based on the collection of tags associated with the geotagged photos taken within the neighborhood. Consequently, we associate with each neighborhood $n \in \{1, \ldots, N\}$, where N is the number of neighborhoods, the vector $\boldsymbol{x}_n \in \mathbb{N}^T$, where x_{nt} is the number of times tag t is observed in neighborhood n.

geo-tree is the tree that represents the geographical hierarchy. Each node v of the geo-tree is associated with a multinomial distribution θ_v such that $\theta_v(t)$ is the probability to sample the tag t from node v. We designate the set of nodes along the path from the leaf n to the root of the geo-tree as R_n, whose cardinality is $|R_n|$. We use the hierarchy Country → City → Neighborhood, illustrated in Figure 1, as the leading example throughout this paper.

3.2 Model

The principle behind our model is that the tags observed in a given node are a mixture of tags specific to the node and of tags coming from different levels in the geographic hierarchy. We represent the tags as multinomial distributions associated with nodes that are along the path from leaf to root. This model enables us to determine the tags that are specifically descriptive of a given node, as well as quantify their level of specificity or generality. The higher a node is in the tree, the more generic its associated tags are, whereas the lower a node is, the more specific its tags are. The tags associated with a node are shared by all its descendants.

We can formulate the random mixture of multinomial distributions with respect to a latent (hidden) variable $z \in \{1, \ldots, |R_n|\}$ that indicates for each tag the level in the geo-tree from which it was sampled. For a tag t observed in neighborhood n, $z = 1$ means that this tag t was sampled from the root node corresponding to the most general distribution θ_{root}, whereas $z = |R_n|$ implies that the tag t was sampled from the most specific neighborhood distribution θ_n. This is equivalent to the following generative process for the tags of neighborhood n: (i) randomly select a node v from the path R_n with probability $p(v|n)$, and (ii) randomly select a tag t with probability $p(t|v)$. We suppose that tags in different neighborhoods are independent of each other, given the neighborhood in which they were observed. Consequently, we can write the probability of the tags $\boldsymbol{x}_1, \ldots, \boldsymbol{x}_n$ observed in the N different neighborhoods as

$$p(\boldsymbol{x}_1, \ldots, \boldsymbol{x}_n) = p(\boldsymbol{x}_1) \ldots p(\boldsymbol{x}_N). \tag{1}$$

We further assume tags are independent of each other given their neighborhood, such that we can write the probability of the vector of tags $\boldsymbol{x}_n$ as:

$$p(\boldsymbol{x}_n) = \prod_{t=1}^{T} p(t|n)^{x_{nt}}. \tag{2}$$

The probability of observing tag t in neighborhood n is then:

$$p(t|n) = \sum_{v \in R_n} p(t|v)\, p(v|n) = \sum_{v \in R_n} \theta_v(t)\, p(v|n), \tag{3}$$

which expresses the fact that the distribution of tags in neighborhood n is a random mixture over the multinomial distributions θ_v associated with the nodes along the path from the leaf n up to the root of the geo-tree. The random mixture coefficients are the probabilities $p(v|n)$. By combining (1), (2) and (3) we obtain the log-likelihood of the data:

$$\begin{aligned}
\log p(\boldsymbol{x}_1, \ldots, \boldsymbol{x}_N) &= \log \prod_{n=1}^{N} \prod_{t=1}^{T} p(t|n)^{x_{nt}} \\
&= \sum_{n=1}^{N} \sum_{t=1}^{T} x_{nt} \log p(t|n) \\
&= \sum_{n=1}^{N} \sum_{t=1}^{T} x_{nt} \log \sum_{v \in R_n} \theta_v(t)\, p(v|n). \qquad (4)
\end{aligned}$$

Classification. For a tag t observed in neighborhood n, we can compute the posterior probability that it was generated from a given level z of the geo-tree: we apply Bayes' rule to compute the posterior probability of the latent variable z

$$p(z|t,n) = \frac{p(t|n,z)p(z|n)}{\sum_{z=1}^{|R_n|} p(t|n,z)p(z|n)}. \tag{5}$$

Since we assume that the distribution of tags in neighborhood n is a random mixture over the distributions θ_v associated with nodes that forms the path R_n from leaf n up to the root of the geo-tree, the probability (5) is equal to

$$p(v'|t,n) = \frac{\theta_{v'}(t)\, p(v'|n)}{\sum_{v \in R_n} \theta_v(t)\, p(v|n)},$$

where v' is the node in R_n that is at level z. Classifying a tag t observed in leaf n amounts to choosing the node $v' \in R_n$ that maximizes the posterior probability $p(v'|t,n)$.

3.3 Learning

The parameters of our model are the multinomial distributions θ_v associated with each node v of our geo-tree and the mixture coefficients $p(v|n)$. In order to learn the model parameters that maximize the likelihood of data, given by (4), we use the Expectation-Maximization (EM) algorithm. This iterative algorithm increases the likelihood of the data by updating the model parameters in two phases: the E-phase and M-phase. The structure of our model allows us to derive closed form expressions for these updates. Due to lack of space, we omit to show our computations and refer the interested reader to Bishop [5]. If a node in the geo-tree might contain a tag that was not observed in the training set, maximum likelihood estimates of the multinomial parameters would assign a probability of zero to such a tag. In order to assign a non-zero probability to every tag, we "smooth" the multinomial parameters: we assume that the distributions θ_v are drawn from a Dirichlet distribution. The Dirichlet distribution is a distribution of T-dimensional discrete distributions parameterized by a vector $\boldsymbol{\alpha}$ of positive reals. Its support is the closed standard $(T-1)$ simplex, and it has the advantage of being the conjugate prior of the multinomial distribution. In other words, if the prior of a multinomial distribution is the Dirichlet distribution, the inferred distribution is a random variable distributed also as a Dirichlet conditioned on the observed tags. In order to avoid favoring one component over the others, we choose the symmetric Dirichlet distribution as a prior. We also assume a symmetric Dirichlet prior for the mixture coefficients $p(v|n)$.

Complexity. Learning the parameters of our model using EM algorithm has, for each iteration, a worst case running-time complexity of $\mathcal{O}(NTD)$, where N is the number of leaves of the tree, T the vocabulary cardinality and D the tree depth. GHM has therefore an important strength, as the time-complexity of training GHM scales linearly with respect to the number of leaves of the tree and the number of *unique* tags rather than the number of tag instances. Furthermore, the number of iterations needed for EM to converge, when trained on the Flickr dataset introduced in Section 4.1, is typically around 10.

4. EVALUATION

In this section, we apply our model to a large collection of geotagged Flickr photos taken in neighborhoods of San Francisco and New York City. The quality of the descriptive tags found by the GHM strongly supports the validity of our approach, which we further confirm using the results of the user study in Section 5: we approximate the probability that GHM classifies a tag "correctly" by the average number of times its classification matches the experts' classification. Moreover, the GHM allows us to quantify the uniqueness of these neighborhoods and to obtain a mapping between neighborhoods in different cities (Section 4.1), enabling us to answer questions such as "How unique is the Presidio neighborhood in San Francisco?" or "How similar is the Mission in San Francisco to East Village in New York City?". Finally, we compare the performance of our model with the performance of other methods in classifying data generated according to a given hierarchy (Section 4.2).

4.1 Dataset and classification

We now apply our model to a large dataset of user-generated content to surface those terms considered to be descriptive for different regions as seen through the eyes of the public.

Flickr dataset

Describing geographical areas necessitates a dataset that associates rich descriptors with locations. Flickr provides an ample collection of geotagged photos and their associated user-generated tags. We couple geotagged photos with neighborhood data from the city planning departments of San Francisco[1] and New York City[2], and focus on the neighborhoods of San Francisco (37 neighborhoods) and Manhattan (28 neighborhoods). Flickr associates an accuracy level with each geotagged photo that ranges from 1 (world level) to 16 (street level). In order to correctly map photos to neighborhoods, we only focus on photos whose accuracy level exceeds neighborhood level. We acquired a large sample of geotagged photos taken in San Francisco (4.4 million photos) and Manhattan (3.7 million photos) from the period 2006 to 2013. We preprocessed the tags associated with these photos by first filtering them using a basic stoplist of numbers, camera brands (e.g. Nikon, Canon), and application names (e.g Flickr, Instagram), and then by stemming them using the Lancaster[3] method. We further removed esoteric tags that were only used by a very small subset of people (less than 10). To limit the influence of prolific users we finally ensured no user can contribute the same tag to a neighborhood more than once a day. The resulting dataset contains around 20 million tags, of which 7,936 unique tags, where each tag instance is assigned to a neighborhood. These tags form the vocabulary we use for describing and comparing different regions. The geo-tree we build from this dataset has 3 levels: level one with a single root node that corresponds to the United States, level two composed of two nodes that correspond to San Francisco and Manhattan, and level three composed of 65 leaves that correspond to the neighborhoods of these cities.

Classifying tags

We applied our model to the Flickr dataset in order to find tags that are specifically descriptive of a region. We show the results for two neighborhoods in San Francisco—Mission and Golden Gate Park— and two neighborhoods in Manhattan—Battery Park and Midtown—in particular. In Table 1 we show the top 10 *most likely* tags for each of these four neighborhoods, where each tag is further classified to the *most likely* level that have generated it. Effectively, each tag observed in a neighborhood is ranked according to the probability $p(t|n)$. Then, we apply (5) to compute the posterior probability of the latent variable $p(z|t,n)$ and classify the tag accordingly. Recall that the value of the latent variable z represents the level of the geo-tree from which it was sampled. For example, a tag observed in neighborhood n is assigned to the neighborhood level if the most likely distribution from which it was sampled is the neighborhood distribution θ_n. We consider such a tag as being specifically descriptive of neighborhood n.

Despite the fact that the tag `california` is the most likely (frequent) tag in both Mission and Golden Gate Park, it is not assigned to the neighborhood distribution but rather to the city distribution (we presume, if we were to add a new State level to the geo-tree, that the tag `california` would most likely be assigned to it). This confirms the notion that the most frequent tag in a neighborhood does not necessarily describe it specifically. We see that `architecture` is applicable not only to the buildings in Golden Gate Park—notably the De Young—but it also is a descriptor for San Francisco in general. Our method is able to discriminate between frequent and specifically descriptive tags, whereas a

[1]`https://data.sfgov.org` (Accessed 11/2014)
[2]`http://nyc.gov` (Accessed 11/2014)
[3]`http://comp.lancs.ac.uk/computing/research/stemming/`(Accessed 11/2014)

Mission	GG Park	Battery Park	Midtown
california ‡	california ‡	newyork ‡	newyork ‡
mission	**flower**	manhattan ‡	manhattan ‡
sf ‡	**park**	*usa* †	*usa* †
usa †	sf ‡	**wtc**	**midtown**
graffiti	*usa* †	**brooklyn**	**skyscraper**
art	**museum**	**downtown**	**timessquare**
mural	**tree**	**bridge**	*light* †
valencia	**ggpark**	gotham ‡	**moma**
food	**deyoung**	**memorial**	**broadway**
car ‡	architecture ‡	*light* †	**rockefeller**

Table 1: For each neighborhood, we show the 10 most likely tags ranked according to their probability $p(t|n)$. We use the posterior probability $p(z|t, n)$ in order to assign each tag to the distribution that maximizes this posterior probability: country (†), city (‡) or neighborhood (bold).

Figure 2: Neighborhoods of San Francisco colored according to their local mixture coefficient $p(z|n)$, where $z = |R_n|$. A darker color indicates a larger local mixture coefficient ('uniqueness').

naive approach would still consider a very frequent tag in a neighborhood as being descriptive. The same observation is valid for the tags `usa` and `light`, which are tags that are too general and therefore not specifically descriptive of a neighborhood. The tag `car` may seem misclassified at the city level in San Francisco, until one realizes the city is well known for its iconic cable cars. Considering that the tags **`art`**, **`mural`** and **`graffiti`** are classified as being specific to Mission is not surprising, because this neighborhood is famous for its street art scene. The most probable tags that are specifically descriptive of Midtown in Manhattan include popular commercial zones, such as Rockefeller Center, Times Square and Broadway, as well as the museum of modern art (MoMa). The tag **`gotham`**, one of the most observed tags in Battery Park, is assigned to city level, which is not unexpected given that Gotham is one of New York City's nicknames.

Neighborhood uniqueness

If you are interested in visiting the most unique neighborhoods in San Francisco, which ones would you choose? With our framework, we can quantify the uniqueness of neighborhood n by using the probability $p(z|n)$ of sampling local tags, where $z = |R_n|$. In fact, a high probability indicates that we sample often from the distribution of local tags θ_n, and can therefore be interpreted as indicator of a more unique local character. We show a map of the city of San Francisco in Figure 2, in which each neighborhood is colored proportionally to its local-mixture coefficient. The darker the color is, the more unique the personality of the neighborhood is. The four most unique neighborhoods in San Francisco are Golden Gate Park (0.70), Presidio (0.67), Lakeshore (0.65) and Mission (0.60), which is not surprising if you know these neighborhoods. The Golden Gate park is the largest urban park in San Francisco, famous for its museums, gardens, lakes, windmills and beaches. The Presidio is a national park and former military base known for its forests, scenic points overlooking the Golden Gate Bridge and the San Francisco Bay. Lakeshore is known for its beaches, the San Francisco zoo and also for San Francisco State University. The Mission is famous for its food, arts, graffiti, and festivals.

Mapping neighborhoods between cities

Given a neighborhood in San Francisco, what is the most similar neighborhood in Manhattan? To answer such a question, we can use our framework to find a mapping between similar neighborhoods that are in different cities and even different countries. Recall that each neighborhood n is described by its local distribution θ_n. In order to compare two neighborhoods n and n', we compute the cosine similarity between their respective local distributions θ_n and $\theta_{n'}$, given by:

$$\text{sim}(\theta_n, \theta_{n'}) = \frac{\sum_{t=1}^{T} \theta_n(t)\, \theta_{n'}(t)}{\sqrt{\sum_{t=1}^{T} \theta_n(t)^2}\sqrt{\sum_{t=1}^{T} \theta_{n'}(t)^2}}. \quad (6)$$

The similarity range is $[0, 1]$, with $\text{sim}(\theta_n, \theta'_n) = 1$ if and only if $\theta_n = \theta'_n$. Table 2 shows the mapping from six San Francisco neighborhoods to the most similar neighborhoods in Manhattan respectively. We also include the second most similar neighborhood when the similarities are very close. In order to give some intuition about the mapping obtained, we also show the top five common local tags obtained by ranking the tags t according to the product of tag probabilities $\theta_n(t)\, \theta_{n'}(t)$. For example, the East Village in Manhattan is mapped to Mission in San Francisco; the strongest characteristics they share are graffiti/murals, food, restaurants and bars. Moreover, despite the major differences between San Francisco and Manhattan, their Chinatowns are mapped to each other and exhibit a highly similar distribution of local tags (cosine similarity of 0.85). Finally, it is not surprising that Treasure Island for San Francisco and Roosevelt Island for Manhattan are mapped to each other, since both are small islands located close to each city. We however emphasize that the top *common* local tags between neighborhoods are not necessarily most descriptive for the *individual* neighborhoods. The top tags may rather provide a shallow description (e.g. dragons in Chinatown, boats for island) and are useful to gain some insight into the mapping obtained, but we are aware that every Chinatown is unique and not interchangeable with another one.

San Francisco	Manhattan	Top common local tags
Mission	East Village (0.23)	graffiti, food, restaurant, mural, bar
Golden Gate Park	Washington Heights (0.26), Upper West Side (0.22)	park, museum, nature, flower, bird
Financial District	Battery Park (0.29), Midtown Manhattan (0.27)	downtown, building, skyscraper, city, street
Treasure Island	Roosevelt Island (0.38)	bridge, island, water, skylines, boat
Chinatown	Chinatown (0.85)	chinatown, chinese, downtown, dragons, lantern
Castro	West Village (0.06)	park, gay, halloween, pride, bar

Table 2: Mapping from San Francisco neighborhoods to the most similar ones in Manhattan. For each neighborhood pair n and n', we give the cosine similarity between their local distributions θ_n and $\theta_{n'}$, and list the top "common" local tags ranked according to the product of tag probabilities $\theta_n(t)\,\theta_{n'}(t)$.

4.2 Experimental evaluation

Evaluating models such as the GHM on user-generated content is hard because of the absence of ground truth. There is no dataset that associates, with objectivity, regions to specifically descriptive terms, or assigns terms to levels in a geographic hierarchy. This is due to the intrinsic subjectivity and vagueness of the human conception of regions and their descriptions [15]. In the absence of ground truth, a classic approach is to generate a dataset with known ground truth, and then use it to evaluate the performance of different classifiers. We follow the generative process presented in Algorithm 1 using the geo-tree (3 levels, 68 nodes) built from the dataset presented in Section 4.1. For each node v in our geo-tree, we sample the distribution of tags θ_v from the symmetric Dirichlet distribution $Dir(\alpha)$. We set $\alpha = 0.1$ to favor sparse distributions θ_v. If the node is a leaf, i.e. it represents a neighborhood, we also sample the mixture coefficient $p(z|v)$ from a symmetric Dirichlet distribution $Dir(\beta)$. We set $\beta = 1.0$ to sample the mixture coefficients uniformly over the simplex and have well-balanced distributions. Now that we have the different distributions that describe the geo-tree, we can start generating the tags in each neighborhood. We vary the number of samples per neighborhood in order to reproduce a realistic dataset that might be very unbalanced: data is sparse for some neighborhoods while very dense for some others. For each neighborhood n, we sample uniformly the continuous random variable γ, which represents the order of the number of tags in neighborhood n, from the interval $[3, 6]$. The endpoints of the support of γ are based on the the minimum and maximum values observed in the Flickr dataset presented in Section 4.1, such that an expected number of 18.8×10^6 tags will be generated, similar to the quantity of tags available in the Flickr dataset. Once the number of tags ν to be generated is fixed, we sample, for each iteration, a level of the geo-tree and then a tag from the distribution associated to the corresponding node.

We can now assess the performance of a model by quantifying its ability to correctly predict the level in the geo-tree from which a tag observed in a neighborhood was sampled. In addition to our model, we consider the following methods:

Naive Bayes (NB) is a simple yet core technique in information retrieval [16]. Under this model, we assume that the tags observed in a class (node) are sampled independently from a multinomial distribution. Each class is therefore described by a multinomial distribution learnt from the count of tags that are observed in that class. However, since we do not use the class membership to train our methods, we assign a tag t, observed in neighborhood n, to all the classes (nodes) along the the path R_n, which amounts to having a uniform prior over the classes.

Algorithm 1: Generating tags in neighborhoods

Input: Geo-tree V, neighborhoods $n \in \{1, \ldots, N\}$, tags $t \in \{1, \ldots, T\}$, hyper-parameters α, β.
Output: Tags observed in each neighborhood $\boldsymbol{x}_1, \ldots, \boldsymbol{x}_N$.

for $v \in V$ **do**
    Sample distribution $\theta_v \sim Dir(\alpha)$;
    if *v is a leaf* **then**
        Sample mixture coefficients $p(z|v) \sim Dir(\beta)$;
for $n \in \{1, \ldots, N\}$ **do**
    Initialize $\boldsymbol{x}_n = \boldsymbol{0}$;
    Sample order $\gamma \sim \mathcal{U}\,[3, 6]$;
    Set $\nu = \lfloor 2 \times 10^{\gamma} \rfloor$;
    while $\sum_t x_{nt} \leq \nu$ **do**
        Sample tree level $z \sim p(v|n)$;
        Sample tag $t \sim p(t|z, n)$;
        Increment tag count $x_{nt} \leftarrow x_{nt} + 1$;

Hierarchical TF-IDF (HT) is a variant of TF-IDF that incorporates the knowledge of the geographical hierarchy. This variant was used in the TagMaps method [23] to find tags that are specific to a region at a given geographical level. The method assigns a higher weight to tags that are frequent within a region (node) compared to the other regions at the same level in the hierarchy. We are able to represent each node with a normalized vector in which each tag t has a weight that encodes its descriptiveness.

For the classification, we map a tag t observed in the leaf n to the level $\hat{z}$ that maximizes the probability $p(z|t, n)$ (NB and GHM), or the tag weight (HT). Using our ground truth, we can then approximate the probability of correct classification $p(\hat{z} = z)$ by the proportion of tags that were correctly classified. In our evaluation, we repeat the following process 1000 times: we first generate a dataset, hold out 10% of the data for test purposes and train the model on the remaining 90%. For fair comparison, we initialize and smooth the parameters of each method similarly. Then, we measure the classification performance of each method. The final results, shown in Table 3, are therefore obtained by averaging the performance of each method over 1000 different datasets.

Our GHM model is the most accurate at classifying the tags to the correct level, greatly outperforming NB by 47% and HT by 27%. Even though both GHM and HT take ad-

	Classification Accuracy (std)
Random	0.33 (0.00)
NB	0.51 (0.02)
HT	0.59 (0.02)
GHM	**0.75** (0.01)

Table 3: The average classification accuracy is computed, for each method, over 1000 generated datasets. We also indicate this accuracy if we classify tags uniformly at random.

vantage of the geographical hierarchy in order to classify the tags, the probabilistic nature of GHM enables a more resilient hierarchical clustering of the data, while the heuristic approach of HT suffers from overfitting. For example, if the number of samples available for a neighborhood is low, HT might overfit the training data by declaring a frequent tag as being characteristic, although not enough samples are available to conclude this. This is not case for GHM, because the assumptions of random mixture enable us to obtain a resilient estimate of the distributions, which declare a tag as characteristic of a given level only if it has enough evidence for it. This observation is strengthened if we choose the maximum order γ of the number of tags per node to be 4 instead of 6: the classification accuracy of GHM decreases by 5% only (0.71), whereas the performance of HT decreases by 13% (0.51). Taken together, these results suggest that, if the data observed in a neighborhood is a mixture of data generated from different levels of a hierarchy that encodes the specificity/generality of the data, our method will be successfully able to accurately associate a tag to the level from which it was generated.

5. PERCEPTION FOCUSED USER STUDY

The results produced by our model might not necessarily be intuitive nor expected, especially in the light of people's differing individual geographic perspectives [19, 27, 11]. Trying to objectively evaluate these, without taking into account human subjectivity and prior knowledge, could be misleading. For the Castro neighborhood in San Francisco, for example, the GHM classified the tag `milk` as specifically descriptive. Someone who is not familiar with Harvey Milk, the first openly gay person to be elected to public office in California and who used to live in the Castro, would most probably not relate this tag to the neighborhood. We thus need to understand the correspondences and gaps between our model's results and human reasoning about regions.

We conduct a user-focused study to explore the premise that the posterior probability of a tag being sampled from the distribution associated with a region is indicative of the canonical descriptiveness of this region. We further aim to identify potential challenges in user-facing applications of the model, and to uncover potential extensions to our model. We held ten interviews and conducted a survey with local residents of the San Francisco Bay Area focusing on their reactions to the tags that our model surfaced. To assess the performance of our model while reducing the bias of subjectivity, we used the results of our user survey to obtain the human classification of tags to nodes in the hierarchy, allowing us to approximate the probability that our model classified a tag correctly by the average number of times it corresponded with human classification. We use the interviews to understand the reasons behind matches and mismatches.

5.1 Interview and survey methodology

Interviewees and survey respondents reacted to a collection of 32 tags per neighborhood. To ensure a certain diversity among the tags presented to the users, we select randomly a subset of tags that are classified by the GHM as being descriptive of (i) neighborhood level (e.g., `graffiti`), (ii) city level (e.g., `nyc`), (iii) country level (e.g., `usa`), or (iv) another neighborhood (e.g., `mission` for the Castro neighborhood). We selected these tags randomly, with the probability of choosing a given tag t proportional to the probability $p(t|n)$. The survey aims to highlight to which extent locals' perspectives match the results produced by our model, while the interviews highlight the reasons why and allow us to understand better the human perception of descriptiveness.

Interview procedure. Our semi-structured interviews focused on how people describe neighborhoods, and investigated their reasoning behind the level of specificity associated to a tag in a given neighborhood. Each one-to-one interview lasted 25–45 minutes. To ensure a wide range of (former) local to newcomer perspectives, we interviewed a total of 10 people (5F, 5M; ages 26–62, $\mu = 37$, $\sigma = 12$) that (had) lived in the San Francisco Bay Area from two months to 62 years. Three of the participants worked in the technology industry, two were students, one was a real estate agent, one a building manager and one a photographer. Each interview covered three different neighborhoods chosen by the participant out of 11 well-known San Francisco neighborhoods. However, one participant described only one neighborhood (due to time constraints), while another participant described four of them. Our interviews addressed:

1. Participants' characterization of the neighborhoods using their own words to get an understanding of the factors that are important to them.

2. Their considerations in whether a tag is perceived as specifically descriptive or not. Interviewees were first asked to classify the 32 tags presented to them as (not) specifically descriptive for the neighborhood, and explain the reasons. Then, they were shown the subset of tags that were classified by our model as specifically descriptive.

We emphasize the fact that the participants were not told about our model, nor that the terms presented to them were actually Flickr tags. This provided broader insight into the factors that led them to classify terms as (not) specifically descriptive of a neighborhood, and allowed for identification of factors not yet addressed by the model, without biasing their judgment towards the assumptions we made (i.e., hierarchical mixture of tags). The interviews were recorded, and transcriptions were iteratively analyzed, focusing on the identification of themes in interviewees' reasoning affecting classifications of tags as (non-)descriptive.

Survey procedure. A total of 22 San Francisco Bay Area residents (5F, 17M; ages 22–39, $\mu = 33$, $\sigma = 4.8$), who had lived there for an average of 5.6 years ($\sigma = 4.2$), participated in our survey about San Francisco and three of its neighborhoods (Mission, Castro and North Beach). Of these 22 respondents, 18 provided tag classifications for the Mission neighborhood, 12 for the Castro and 11 for North Beach. This resulted in 1291 tag classifications, of which 561 for the Mission, 381 for the Castro and 349 for North Beach. The survey asked respondents to describe each neighborhood with their own words using open text fields, and then to classify the 32 tags presented to them as descriptive for a given neighborhood, for a higher level (the city or country), or for another neighborhood. They could also indicate if they did not find the tag descriptive for any level, or did not understand its meaning.

5.2 Results

In this section, we present the results of the survey, and provide examples from the interviews to illuminate the reasoning processes on whether a tag is descriptive for a specific region. We compare the tag classifications provided by the GHM with those supplied by the participants, and we specifically focus on disagreements between neighborhood-level tag classifications in order to identify challenges in human interpretation of modeling results, and potential extensions to our model.

5.2.1 Participant and model congruency

The model's premise that locally frequent content is not necessarily specific to that locale was strongly supported by the interviews and the survey. None of the participants classified all of the tags that occurred *frequently* in a neighborhood as specifically *descriptive* of the given neighborhood. This supports the results of the GHM in classifications of very frequent but wide-spread tags as not being specifically descriptive of the neighborhood. Without prompting, interviewees mentioned terms as being too generic or specific for a given neighborhood. For example, one interviewee (F 28), when describing the Western Addition neighborhood, picked `haight` as a descriptive tag, "because there's Haight Street in this neighborhood", but not the tag `streets`, as "there's streets everywhere". Similar interview examples included: "`california` or `usa` is a generic, or general term" (F 28), "I don't think of ever describing Golden Gate Park as in the USA. Unless I'm somewhere far away, but then I wouldn't even say USA, I would say California or San Francisco" (F 41). This result implies that participants tend to classify tags according to a geographical hierarchy, which supports the validity of the assumptions we make about the hierarchy of tags: tag specificity/generality depends on the hierarchical level from which it was sampled.

We are aware that people will not agree with every classification made by our model. Tags classified by the GHM as specifically descriptive of a neighborhood, were not necessarily perceived as such by all respondents; variations occurred between neighborhoods and between participants. As a consequence, evaluating the results of an aggregate model 'objectively', as if there were only a single correct representation of a neighborhood, is difficult. However, to place the the GHM classification into context with human classification, we use the results of our survey to reduce subjective biases: we obtain a majority vote human classification by assigning each tag to the class that users have chosen most often. We then approximate the probability that the GHM classifies a tag 'correctly' by the average number of times its classification matches this human majority classification. For most tags the majority assignment is aligned with the assessment of the model (Table 5). We obtained an average classification correspondence of 0.77, with a highest classification accuracy of 0.84 for the Mission neighborhood. The alignment between the model and human classification for the Castro neighborhood was 0.81. Alignment was lowest for the North Beach neighborhood with a correspondence of 0.66, mainly caused by tag classifications as 'another neighborhood' (Table 4). Such mismatches occur for a multitude of reasons. First of all, as a very basic requirement, participants have to understand what a tag refers to, before they can assign it to a specific level. For example, in the survey, 8% of the answers given for the Mission neighborhood were "I don't know what this is" (Table 4). This issue occurred less for the selection of tags for the Castro (1%) and North Beach (0%). The terms that users understood were necessarily perceived as either descriptive (i.e. assignable to a level in the geographical hierarchy) or non-descriptive (i.e. not belonging to any level in the hierarchy). The proportion of individual answers that are "non-descriptive" is around 34%, which included answers to tags such as `cat`, `sticker` and `wall` for the Mission. The fact that these tags indeed describe content that occurs frequently in the Mission doesn't imply that they are perceived as descriptive per se by *all* users.

People's local experiences shape and differentiate their perceptions. The interviews illustrated how tags were interpreted in multiple ways; `church` was taken to refer to a church building, or to the streetcars servicing the J-Church light-rail line, and was not seen as descriptive by the majority of participants (see Castro in Table 5). Local terms surfaced by our model, such as `walls` in the Mission, represented the neighborhood's characteristic murals to a long-time local interviewee (M 49), whereas this term was a meaningless for others. While the majority of survey respondents classified `night` and `coffee` as unspecific for the Mission, the same interviewee (M 49) for example saw `night` as descriptive for its bars, restaurants and clubs and thought `coffee` referred to the copious amounts of coffee shops. Similarly, while one interviewee described North Beach as "party land" (M 46), another claimed "I don't believe there's much of a nightlife there" (F 26). While these results highlight an opportunity for discovery and recommendation of local content that users may not be aware of, it also means that a careful explanation might be necessary.

5.2.2 Model extensions

Beyond misunderstanding tags or finding them not specifically descriptive of a certain neighborhood, the interviews provided additional clues about the mismatches identified in our survey, as well as individual differences. They are organized below in potential opportunities for extensions of the GHM model.

Sub-region detection. According to the majority of our survey participants, 11 tags classified by the GHM as specifically descriptive of North Beach were actually descriptive of another neighborhood. From our interviews, we learned that the terms surfaced by our model for the North Beach neighborhood included references to the bay's waterside and to the tourist attraction Fisherman's Wharf (see for example `wharf`, `seal`, `crab`, `bay`, `pier` in Table 5). The locals

	Mission		Castro		North Beach	
Neighborhood-level tag count	17		17		17	
Neighborhood-level tag classifications	287	(100%)	201	(100%)	185	(100%)
Tags not understood	22	(8%)	3	(1%)	0	(0%)
Tags seen as non-descriptive for any level	116	(40%)	50	(25%)	62	(33%)
(Part of) neighborhood	109	(39%)	67	(33%)	37	(20%)
Higher-level node (CA/USA)	24	(8%)	38	(19%)	7	(4%)
Other neighborhood	16	(5%)	43	(22%)	79	(43%)

Table 4: The distribution of answers given by survey participants. The (rounded) percentages are computed with respect to the total number of answers given.

	Mission	Castro	North Beach
Tag count	32	32	32
Tag classications	561	381	349
GHM alignment	0.84	0.81	0.66
Misaligned tag count	5	6	11
Misaligned tags	`night, coffee, sidewalk cat, brannan`	`mission, streetcar, dolorespark church, sign, night`	`embarcadero, bridge, water alcatraz, seal, sea, crab, wharf, boat, bay, pier`

Table 5: Alignment of GHM tag assignments with the majority of survey respondents' assignment for each survey neighborhood. Misalignment would for example be a tag classified as neighborhood level by the GHM while the majority of survey respondents had assigned it to another neighborhood or another level.

that responded to our survey (see Table 4) and also the interviewees clearly made a distinction between Fisherman's Wharf and North Beach, whereas the set of administrative regions we used for our model did not: according to the data from the city planing department of San Francisco, Fisherman's Wharf is not a neighborhood in itself and is simply a sub-region of North Beach. Clarifications of region borders and detecting emerging sub-neighborhoods (e.g. "as you go further down south it's a totally different neighborhood"), would improve the quality of the neighborhood tags presented to the user. From the modeling perspective, the GHM already allows for considering predefined sub-regions in certain neighborhood, since the geo-tree can be unbalanced and have a different depth for certain sub-trees.

Permeable adjacency and topography. Using *permeable adjacency* by considering adjacent neighborhoods appears promising. For example, the mismatching tag `dolorespark` (see Table 5) refers to the park right on the edge of the Mission and Castro, which however was placed outside the Castro neighborhood by the majority of our survey respondents. Interviewees defined neighborhood boundaries differently, and sometimes indicated they didn't know neighborhoods well "It's a little difficult because it's right next to the Presidio. I kind of, maybe confuse them from each other" (F 26). Interviewees extended their reasoning about activities or points-of-interest that could spill over into adjacent neighborhoods. For example, the Golden Gate Bridge, officially part of the Presidio neighborhood, but photographed from a wide range of other neighborhoods was mentioned as a distant-but-characteristic feature: "you can see the Bay Bridge from there" (M 46). Extensions that consider wider topography and fuzzy boundaries could improve the quality of the results.

Representative lower levels. Interviewees at times cited neighborhoods' unique character as representative of wider regional developments, e.g. gentrification of neighborhoods, or "California is known for being... very liberal... and it's almost as if a lot it comes from Castro" (M 35). Hierarchical modeling offers opportunities beyond the identification of locally descriptive content; it could also help find neighborhoods that are representative of a higher level in the geographical hierarchy.

Temporality. Time of day, shifting character of a neighborhoods, events, long-term history, and even change itself were referenced by interviewees: "I think of night, ... there's a lot of activity during night time with the bars and the clubs... but before... you wouldn't be caught there at nighttime... 20 years ago it was a different neighborhood." (M 49). Since the Flickr tag collection we used spanned multiple years, some aspects of neighborhoods, represented in tags surfaced by our model, that were characteristic at one time but no longer as prominent at present (such as the Halloween celebrations in the Castro neighborhood), were considered out of place (M 32). Yet other interviewees still found such tags characteristic, and freely associated: "I think of outrageous costumes, and also the costumes that people see when it's not Halloween" (F 26). Combining hierarchical modeling with features detecting diurnal rhythms [13] or events [25] would provide additional insight in such content changes over time. However, we must be aware that this necessitates a dataset that is much more prolific than the one at hand: we need to have a sufficient number of geotagged samples per time period.

The non-tagged. More recent socio-economic developments were mentioned by the interviewees, but not represented in the dataset of tags. For example, one interviewee argued that, while the terms for SoMa did capture the neighborhood ("I think it's really descriptive and pretty accurate"), he would himself add "something about startups and expensive apartments that really aren't all that great. $3500 a month for one bedroom. That would be a good descriptor." (M 32). Note that even the absence of a feature could be characteristic: "There's not a lot to do around there." (M 35). Distinguishing however between what is absent in a neighborhood, and what is not represented in a dataset is a challenge [24]. Findings proxies for such features, such as proposed by Quercia et al. [22], requires rigor because it might introduce error and biases. Combining different data sources and model features can however provide additional opportunities.

6. DISCUSSION AND CONCLUSIONS

In this work we proposed a probabilistic model that allows for uncovering terms that are *specifically descriptive* of a region within a given geographical hierarchy. By applying our model to a large-scale dataset of 20 million tags associated with approximately 8 million geotagged Flickr photos taken in San Francisco and Manhattan, we were able to associate each node in the hierarchy to the tags that specifically describe it. Moreover, we used these descriptions to quantify the uniqueness of neighborhoods, and find a mapping between similar but geographically distant neighborhoods. We further conducted interviews and a survey with local residents in order to evaluate the quality of the results given by the GHM and its ability to surface neighborhood-characteristic terms, which span both terms known and unknown to locals. The classification accuracy of GHM, measured with respect to the classification of tags made by locals, provides strong support for the validity of our approach. However, the results of the interviews also highlighted the difference between the performance of a model at classifying community-generated data, and its performance as judged subjectively by an individual. This highlights the importance of taking user subjectivity into account, and the need for explanation and framing. As a consequence, the traditional evaluation of modeling approaches that are fed with user-generated data faces the challenge of both the representation and the subjectivity inherent to vernacular geography. It is important to note that the dataset itself was not formally labeled and rather only contained free-form, often noisy user-generated tags. While unstructured user-generated tags can be cleaned, for instance through canonicalization [28], one can utilize other structures inherent in the data to find meaning. Our work takes advantage of the latent geographical patterns exhibited by geotagged data, and shows how we can relate tags to regions within a geographical hierarchy.

Representation. We used a specific type of dataset (tags) in this paper to describe geographical regions. We are aware that the tags generated by other online communities that use different social photo sharing services, such as Instagram, may yield different descriptions of regions. For example, if tagging in such a service is more emotive rather than descriptive of the content, our method would surface different local qualities. User-generated data is only representative of the activity of a community within it, and not necessarily of all people in a certain region. Large-scale social media datasets, whether they consist of check-ins, status updates, or photos uploaded to a community-based service, are the result of communicative acts influenced by service design features and evolving community norms [24, 26, 8]. In our case, not all local features are captured and shared on Flickr. The content that is present can however be used as relative hints at local trends, and provide comparative insights. Consequently, when we here state locally descriptive, we therefore mean descriptive for the content generated in that locale, not necessarily for all human activity.

Vernacular geography. Spatial knowledge that is used to communicate about space and regions has been referred to as vernacular geography [15] or naive geography [11] that carries with it a certain intrinsic vagueness in its nature [10]. Individuals' descriptions of places are inherently subjective, as are interpretations of what is and what is not descriptive for a locale [4]. Towards any community, online or offline, the perception of place is considered to be of a shared frame of reference [19]. Photo tags generated by the Flickr community are no exception. However, our qualitative exploration is aimed at understanding *what factors come into play* when describing space, and how might they manifest into a probabilistic model. Fuzzy regional boundaries, temporal events, hidden landmarks all underscore types of regions and terms we surfaced through the interviews, as well as the kinds of tag descriptors discovered quantitatively. We find a mixed method approach brings a clearer understanding of online communities and naive geography alike.

Future work. As illustrated by our generative interviews, the presentation of our model's results ought to take into account subjective interpretations, support the discovery of new conceptual clusters and their explanation. The interviews also pointed to the possibility of using certain neighborhoods as embodying the spirit of its encompassing region, e.g., the Castro described as an influential San Francisco neighborhood, or technology companies moving into SoMa reflecting changes in the city as a whole. The relationship between the leaves of a geographical tree, temporal change and events, sub-regions, and fluid local boundaries that consider wider topographical features represent potential viable extensions to our model, conditioned on the fact that the dataset at hand includes enough data and spans a long period of time. For example, we could extend our model to account for the porosity of frontiers between neighborhoods and the fact that there is no consensus about the exact boundaries of a neighborhood: we define, for each region, a set that is composed of the regions that are adjacent to it. The probability of observing tag in a certain region then includes a new term that accounts for the possibility of sampling tags from adjacent regions. The learning procedure for this extension would be very similar to the GHM's learning procedure.

7. REFERENCES

[1] S. Ahern, M. Naaman, R. Nair, and J. Yang. World explorer: visualizing aggregate data from unstructured text in geo-referenced collections. In *Proceedings of Digital Libraries*, pages 1–10. ACM Press, 2007.

[2] A. Ahmed, L. Hong, and A. Smola. Hierarchical geographical modeling of user locations from social media posts. In *Proceedings of WWW'13*, 2013.

[3] L. Backstrom, J. Kleinberg, R. Kumar, and J. Novak. Spatial variation in search engine queries. In *Proceedings of WWW'08*, pages 357–366. ACM, 2008.

[4] F. Bentley, H. Cramer, S. Basapur, and W. Hamilton. Drawing the city. differing perceptions of the urban

environment. In *Proceedings of CHI 2012*. ACM Press, 2012.
[5] C. Bishop. *Pattern Recognition and Machine Learning (Information Science and Statistics)*. Springer-Verlag, New York, 2006.
[6] D. Blei, T. Griffiths, M. Jordan, and J. Tenenbaum. Hierarchical topic models and the nested Chinese restaurant process. In *NIPS*, 2003.
[7] D. Blei, A. Ng, and M. Jordan. Latent Dirichlet Allocation. *J. Mach. Learn. Res.*, 3:993–1022, March 2003.
[8] M. Cameron, M. Naaman, d. boyd, and M. Davis. HT06, tagging paper, taxonomy, Flickr, academic article, to read. In *Proceedings of HYPERTEXT'06*, pages 31–40. ACM Press, 2006.
[9] J. Cranshaw, R. Schwartz, J. Hong, and N. Sadeh. The livehoods project: utilizing social media to understand the dynamics of a city. In *Proceedings of ICWSM 2012*. AAAI, 2012.
[10] C. Davies, I. Holt, J. Green, J. Harding, and L. Diamond. User needs and implications for modelling vague named places. *Spatial Cognition & Computation*, 9(3):174–194, 2009.
[11] M. Egenhofer and D. Mark. *Naive geography*. Springer, 1995.
[12] S. Elwood, M. Goodchild, and D. Sui. Prospects for VGI research and the emerging fourth paradigm. In *Crowdsourcing Geographic Knowledge*, pages 361–375. Springer, 2013.
[13] N. Grinberg, M. Naaman, B. Shaw, and G. Lotan. Extracting diurnal patterns of real world activity from social media. In *ICWSM*, 2013.
[14] B. Hillier and L. Vaughan. The city as one thing. *Progress in Planning*, 67(3), 2007.
[15] L. Hollenstein and R. Purves. Exploring place through user-generated content: Using Flickr tags to describe city cores. *Journal of Spatial Information Science*, (1):21–48, 2010.
[16] D. D. Lewis. Naive (Bayes) at forty: The independence assumption in information retrieval. In *Proceedings of the 10th European Conference on Machine Learning*, ECML '98, pages 4–15, London, UK, UK, 1998. Springer-Verlag.
[17] K. Lynch. *The Image of the City*. MIT Press, 1960.
[18] A. McCallum, R. Rosenfeld, T. M. Mitchell, and A. Y. Ng. Improving text classification by shrinkage in a hierarchy of classes. In *Proceedings of the Fifteenth International Conference on Machine Learning*, ICML '98, pages 359–367, San Francisco, CA, USA, 1998. Morgan Kaufmann Publishers Inc.
[19] D. Montello, M. Goodchild, J. Gottsegen, and P. Fohl. Where's downtown?: Behavioral methods for determining referents of vague spatial queries. *Spatial Cognition & Computation*, 3(2-3):185–204, 2003.
[20] M. Naaman and R. Nair. Zonetag's collaborative tag suggestions: What is this person doing in my phone? *IEEE MultiMedia*, 15(3), 2008.
[21] Y. Pang, Q. Hao, Y. Yuan, T. Hu, R. Cai, and L. Zhang. Summarizing tourist destinations by mining user-generated travelogues and photos. *Comput. Vis. Image Underst.*, 115(3):352–363, March 2011.
[22] D. Quercia, H. Cramer, and N. O'Hare. Aesthetic capital: What makes London look beautiful, quiet, and happy. In *Proceedings of CSCW'14*, 2014.
[23] T. Rattenbury and M. Naaman. Methods for extracting place semantics from flickr tags. *ACM Transactions on the Web*, 3(1), 2009.
[24] M. Rost, L. Barkhuus, H. Cramer, and B. Brown. Representation and communication: Challenges in interpreting large social media datasets. In *Proceedings of CSCW'13*. ACM Press, 2011.
[25] D. A. Shamma, L. Kennedy, and E Churchill. Peaks and persistence: Modeling the shape of microblog conversations. In *Proceedings of CSCW'11*, 2011.
[26] D. A. Shamma, R. Shaw, P. Shafton, and Y. Liu. Watch what I watch: using community activity to understand content. In *Proceedings of MIR'07*, pages 275–284. ACM, 2007.
[27] R. Stedman. Toward a social psychology of place: Predicting behavior from place-based cognitions, attitude, and identity. *Environment & Behaviors*, 34(5), 2002.
[28] B. Thomee and G. De Francisci Morales. Automatic discovery of global and local equivalence relationships in labeled geo-spatial data. In *Proceedings of the ACM Conference on Hypertext and Social Media*, pages 158–168, 2014.
[29] B. Thomee and A. Rae. Uncovering locally characterizing regions within geotagged data. In *Proceedings of WWW'13*, pages 1285–1296, 2013.

Active Learning for Multi-relational Data Construction

Hiroshi Kajino[*]
The University of Tokyo
7-3-1, Hongo, Bunkyo
Tokyo, Japan
hiroshi_kajino@mist.i.u-tokyo.ac.jp

Akihiro Kishimoto
IBM Research - Ireland
Damastown Industrial Estate
Mulhuddart, Dublin 15, Ireland
AKIHIROK@ie.ibm.com

Adi Botea
IBM Research - Ireland
Damastown Industrial Estate
Mulhuddart, Dublin 15, Ireland
ADIBOTEA@ie.ibm.com

Elizabeth Daly
IBM Research - Ireland
Damastown Industrial Estate
Mulhuddart, Dublin 15, Ireland
elizabeth.daly@ie.ibm.com

Spyros Kotoulas
IBM Research - Ireland
Damastown Industrial Estate
Mulhuddart, Dublin 15, Ireland
Spyros.Kotoulas@ie.ibm.com

ABSTRACT

Knowledge on the Web relies heavily on multi-relational representations, such as RDF and Schema.org. Automatically extracting knowledge from documents and linking existing databases are common approaches to construct multi-relational data. Complementary to such approaches, there is still a strong demand for manually encoding human expert knowledge. For example, human annotation is necessary for constructing a common-sense knowledge base, which stores facts implicitly shared in a community, because such knowledge rarely appears in documents. As human annotation is both tedious and costly, an important research challenge is how to best use limited human resources, whiles maximizing the quality of the resulting dataset. In this paper, we formalize the problem of dataset construction as active learning problems and present the Active Multi-relational Data Construction (AMDC) method. AMDC repeatedly interleaves multi-relational learning and expert input acquisition, allowing us to acquire helpful labels for data construction. Experiments on real datasets demonstrate that our solution increases the number of positive triples by a factor of 2.28 to 17.0, and that the predictive performance of the multi-relational model in AMDC achieves the highest or comparable to the best performance throughout the data construction process.

Categories and Subject Descriptors

I.2.6 [**Artificial Intelligence**]: Learning—*Parameter learning*; I.2.4 [**Artificial Intelligence**]: Knowledge Representation Formalisms and Methods—*Semantic networks*

[*]JSPS Research Fellow.

WWW 2015, May 18–22, 2015, Florence, Italy.
ACM 978-1-4503-3469-3/15/05.
http://dx.doi.org/10.1145/2736277.2741103.

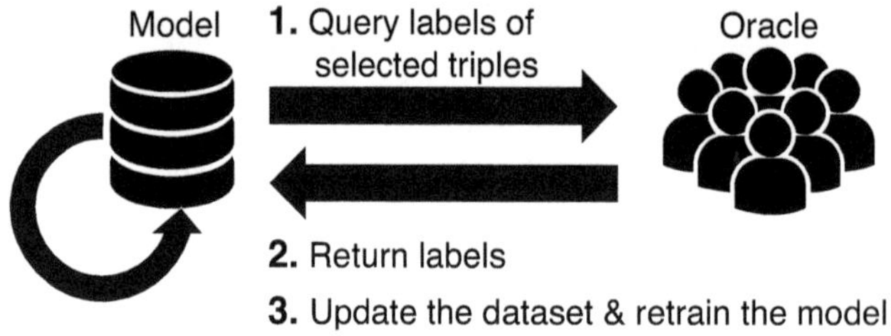

Figure 1: Overview of the AMDC method. Given an initial model, (i) the model asks the oracle to provide labels on a set of selected triples that will be beneficial to improve the model and the dataset, (ii) the oracle returns the labels to the model, and (iii) the model updates its dataset and retrains the model parameters on the updated dataset.

Keywords

Multi-relational data; active learning; human annotation

1. INTRODUCTION

Multi-relational data are commonly used to represent multiple types of relations between entities. In the Semantic Web, the Resource Description Framework (RDF) represents relations between Web or physical entities as directed labeled multi-graphs using a subject-predicate-object notion called a *triple*. Knowledge bases [22, 4, 12] represent information in a variety of domains, providing semantic and lexical relations between words, or relations between well-known entities such as people and places. Common sense knowledge databases are used to support AI tasks such as natural language processing, Web search, and question answering. Databases in bioinformatics [2, 1] store interactions between proteins, and the involvement of a protein into mechanisms such as the cell cycle. Such databases aim to integrate the diverse body of experimental evidence on protein-protein interactions into a single dataset enabling the scientific community to extract information providing deeper insights into the protein interaction networks.

Multi-relational learning [24, 6] is essential to increase the usefulness of multi-relational datasets. Learning a predictive model for a database allows knowledge inference not explicitly contained in it. For example, applying multi-relational learning to bioinformatics databases can reduce the need to perform experiments, predicting the results instead.

In this paper, we consider a fundamental problem in multi-relational learning: *How can we construct a dataset and a predictive model efficiently in a cold-start setting?* Some datasets can be automatically constructed or extracted from documents [3, 12, 10]. On the other hand, many multi-relational datasets depend crucially on human expert input, given that not all knowledge may be captured in documents. For example, the fact that "a banana is yellow" may not explicitly appear in documents. Similarly, undiscovered interactions between proteins cannot appear in scientific papers. However, employing human expertise to explicitly annotate such implicit knowledge is a time-consuming and costly process. In this light, there is strong demand in developing efficient human annotation methods to construct a multi-relational dataset.

We present the *Active Multi-relational Data Construction (AMDC) method*, a method to construct a multi-relational dataset and a predictive model efficiently. The main contribution is to make full use of human expertise by harnessing multi-relational learning as guidance, as shown in Fig. 1. We exploit a model of a multi-relational dataset to predict which triples need to be labeled by human experts (the *oracle*). AMDC repeats the following procedure. It trains the model using the current dataset and calculates a *query score* of each unlabeled triple based on the model. Feedback from a human expert about a triple with a low query score is helpful to enhance the model and the dataset. Then, the unlabeled triples with the lowest query scores are provided to the oracle for labeling. Finally, given the labels on the triples, it retrains the model with the updated dataset.

We apply an active learning algorithm to a multi-relational data model trained on the ROC-AUC (the Area Under the ROC Curve) loss function. The ROC-AUC loss function is commonly used to learn from an imbalanced dataset, in which the number of positive triples is much smaller than that of negative triples. As a multi-relational dataset is often imbalanced, many multi-relational learning techniques resort to it. Despite an attempt to apply active learning to another model trained on the ROC-AUC loss function [11], it is essentially difficult to apply active learning to a model trained on the ROC-AUC loss function. Active learning requires a decision boundary to discriminate positive triples from negative ones to compute query scores, but the ROC-AUC loss function does not provide the decision boundary. We resolve the issue by combining the ROC-AUC loss function with the classification error loss function, which provides a decision boundary. This enables us to perform active learning on an imbalanced dataset efficiently. Furthermore, we devise two modifications to improve the performance of an existing multi-relational learning algorithm. First, we extend the existing ROC-AUC loss function [21, 6] to make use of positive, negative, and unlabeled triples. The existing ROC-AUC loss function compares only scores of positive and non-positive triples, and it does not distinguish negative labels from unlabeled labels. We combine the existing ROC-AUC loss function with another ROC-AUC loss function that compares scores of negative and non-negative triples to explicitly handle negative triples. Second, we add two constraints to the RESCAL model [24] to increase the stability of learning. The two constraints decrease the model complexity, which helps to avoid overfitting.

We conduct two experiments with different scenarios to demonstrate the effectiveness of AMDC. The first scenario, called a *dataset construction problem*, aims to collect as many high-confidence positive triples as possible. The second scenario, called a *predictive model construction problem*, aims to learn a multi-relational model that has a high predictive ability on unlabeled triples. For each experimental setting, we use three real datasets to evaluate AMDC. Our experiments demonstrate the advantages of AMDC as a whole and the benefits of the separate components introduced in our work.

2. PRELIMINARIES

We first give our definition of multi-relational data and assumptions on the data. Then, we introduce the oracle that answers labeling queries. Finally, we define two problem settings that differ on the objectives of the dataset construction.

2.1 Multi-relational Data

We focus on directed binary relations between two entities, which is essentially the same as the RDF representation. Let $\mathcal{E}$ be a set of entities and $\mathcal{R}$ be a set of relations. A unit of the dataset is represented by (i, j, k) $(i, j \in \mathcal{E}, k \in \mathcal{R})$. We call (i, j, k) a *triple*. A triple (i, j, k) is positive if a directed relation k holds between entities i and j, and is negative if the relation does not hold. Let Δ be the set of all the possible triples, *i.e.*, $\Delta := \{(i, j, k) \mid i, j \in \mathcal{E}, k \in \mathcal{R}\}$. Then, a multi-relational dataset over Δ is defined as below, in Def 1.

DEFINITION 1 (MULTI-RELATIONAL DATASET). *A multi-relational dataset over Δ is defined as (Δ_p, Δ_n), in which Δ_p and Δ_n are sets of positive and negative triples, respectively, such that $\Delta_p \cup \Delta_n \subseteq \Delta$ and $\Delta_p \cap \Delta_n = \emptyset$.*

The number of positive triples in a multi-relational dataset is assumed to be much smaller than the total number of triples, *i.e.*, $|\Delta_p| \ll |\Delta|$. This holds true in many multi-relational datasets; some datasets (*e.g.*, the UMLS dataset we use in the experiment) have less than 1% positive triples.

2.2 Oracle

As an interactive environment, we have B (> 0) times access to the oracle, which provides the label of a triple. Letting positive and negative labels be 1 and 0, respectively, the oracle is defined as a function $\mathcal{O} : \mathcal{E} \times \mathcal{E} \times \mathcal{R} \to \{0, 1\}$. We call B a *budget*. We assume that the oracle is always correct with its labeling.

2.3 Problem Definitions

Finally, we define two problem settings with different objectives. The *dataset construction problem* (Problem 1) aims to collect as many correct positive triples as possible. As the set of positive triples is assumed to be a small fraction of the entire dataset, collecting as many positive triples as possible is essential to construct a useful dataset.

Problem 1. Given a set of entities $\mathcal{E}$, a set of relations $\mathcal{R}$, a budget B (> 0), and the oracle $\mathcal{O}$, the *dataset construction problem* is to construct a multi-relational dataset (Δ_p, Δ_n)

within the budget such that the number of positive triples is maximized.

The *predictive model construction problem* (Problem 2) aims to construct a model with high predictive performance. In order to construct a predictive model, not only positive triples, but also negative triples are informative. Therefore, the predictive model construction problem will lead to a different consequence from the dataset construction problem. We consider the model that outputs a predictive score $s_t \in \mathbb{R}$ given a triple $t \in \Delta$ such that a triple with a high score s_t is likely to be positive, and a triple with a low score s_t is likely to be negative. The predictive performance is measured by the Area Under the ROC Curve (ROC-AUC), which will be described in Section 4.2.

Problem 2. Given a set of entities $\mathcal{E}$, a set of relations $\mathcal{R}$, a budget B (> 0), and the oracle $\mathcal{O}$, the *predictive model construction problem* is to construct a predictive model $m : \mathcal{E} \times \mathcal{E} \times \mathcal{R} \to \mathbb{R}$ within the budget such that its ROC-AUC score on unlabeled triples is maximized.

3. ACTIVE MULTI-RELATIONAL DATA CONSTRUCTION

We present the Active Multi-relational Data Construction (AMDC) method to address Problems 1 and 2. Each problem is addressed with a slightly different instantiation of the generic AMDC method. An instantiation of AMDC implements a predictive model and a query score. The predictive model is a function $m : \mathcal{E} \times \mathcal{E} \times \mathcal{R} \to \mathbb{R}$ that assigns a predictive score s_t given a triple t. We use the same predictive model for both problem settings. The query score q_t ($t \in \Delta$) is used to select which triples should be given to the oracle for labeling. It is computed for each triple based on the predictive scores. We design two different query scores for the two problem settings, as discussed later.

AMDC first initializes its predictive model and then repeats the following three steps to create a multi-relational dataset and a predictive model. First, given the predictive model, it calculates query scores of unlabeled triples. Second, triples with the lowest query scores are provided to the oracle for labeling. Finally, it updates its dataset and retrains the predictive model.

In the following, we present the details of the predictive model and the query scores and the whole procedure of AMDC.

3.1 Predictive Model

We introduce a predictive model of multi-relational data based on the RESCAL model [24]. Our model assumes that each entity $i \in \mathcal{E}$ is modeled as a latent feature vector $\mathbf{a}_i \in \mathbb{R}^D$, and each relation $k \in \mathcal{R}$ is modeled as a linear operator in the latent feature space $R_k \in \mathbb{R}^{D\times D}$, where D (> 0) is the dimension of the latent feature space. We impose two constraints on these parameters. First, we fix the length of the latent feature vector to 1. Thus, we assume that for each $i \in \mathcal{E}$,

$$\|\mathbf{a}_i\|_2 = 1, \tag{1}$$

holds. Second, we introduce a new constraint, restricting the set of relation matrices to the set of rotation matrices. Thus, we assume that for each $k \in \mathcal{R}$,

$$R_k^\top R_k = I_D,\ |R_k| = 1, \tag{2}$$

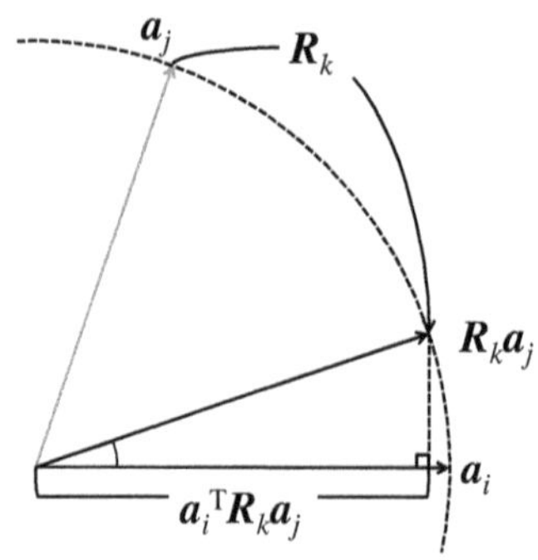

Figure 2: Geometrical illustration of our model. Positiveness of a triple $t = (i, j, k)$ is measured by the similarity between unit-length latent feature vectors $\mathbf{a}_i$ and $R_k\mathbf{a}_j$.

hold, where $I_D \in \mathbb{R}^{D\times D}$ is the D-dimensional identity matrix and $|\cdot|$ represents the determinant of a matrix. This reduces the degree of freedom of a relation matrix from $O(D^2)$ to $O(D)$. The second constraint ensures a relation matrix to be a closed operation on the ℓ_2 unit ball; for any $\mathbf{a}_j$ such that $\|\mathbf{a}_j\|_2 = 1$, $\|R_k\mathbf{a}_j\|_2 = 1$ holds. Given the latent representation, we further assume that a triple $t = (i, j, k)$ is positive if $\mathbf{a}_i = R_k\mathbf{a}_j$ holds, and the triple is negative if $\mathbf{a}_i = -R_k\mathbf{a}_j$ holds. Hence, a relation that the relation k does not hold is modeled as a relation matrix $-R_k$.

To measure the positiveness and negativeness of each triple, we define the predictive score s_t of each triple $t = (i, j, k)$ as

$$s_t = \mathbf{a}_i^\top R_k \mathbf{a}_j. \tag{3}$$

If the score is close to 1, the triple tends to be positive, and if the score is close to -1, the triple tends to be negative.

Letting $A = [\mathbf{a}_1 \ \dots \ \mathbf{a}_{|\mathcal{E}|}]^\top \in \mathbb{R}^{|\mathcal{E}|\times D}$ be a set of latent feature vectors and $R = [R_k]_{k\in\mathcal{R}} \in \mathbb{R}^{D\times D\times|\mathcal{R}|}$ be a set of relation matrices, we call the set of model parameters (A, R), a *model*.

3.1.1 Optimization Problem for Learning

We describe our optimization problem to learn the model explained in Section 3.1. The model is learned by solving the following optimization problem:

$$\begin{aligned}\min_{A,R} & \frac{1}{|\Delta_p||\Delta\setminus\Delta_p|}\sum_{t_p\in\Delta_p}\sum_{\bar{t}_p\in\Delta\setminus\Delta_p}[\gamma - s_{t_p} + s_{\bar{t}_p}]_+ \\ & + \frac{C_n}{|\Delta_n||\Delta\setminus\Delta_n|}\sum_{t_n\in\Delta_n}\sum_{\bar{t}_n\in\Delta\setminus\Delta_n}[\gamma - s_{\bar{t}_n} + s_{t_n}]_+ \\ & + C_e\left(\frac{1}{|\Delta_p|}\sum_{t_p\in\Delta_p}[\gamma' - s_{t_p}]_+ + \frac{1}{|\Delta_n|}\sum_{t_n\in\Delta_n}[\gamma' + s_{t_n}]_+\right),\end{aligned} \tag{4}$$

where $C_n, C_e, \gamma, \gamma'$ (> 0) are hyperparameters, and $[\cdot]_+ : \mathbb{R} \to \mathbb{R}$ is the hinge loss function such that

$$[x]_+ := \begin{cases} x & (x \geq 0), \\ 0 & (x < 0), \end{cases}$$

holds. Note that all the scores in the optimization problem (4) are functions of A and R as in Eq. (3).

The optimization problem comes from the following two assumptions on the scores. First, as relative relations between two scores, we assume that

$$s_{t_p} > s_{\bar{t}_p} \ (\forall t_p \in \Delta_p,\ \forall \bar{t}_p \in \Delta \backslash \Delta_p), \tag{5}$$
$$s_{t_n} < s_{\bar{t}_n} \ (\forall t_n \in \Delta_n,\ \forall \bar{t}_n \in \Delta \backslash \Delta_n), \tag{6}$$

hold. This induces the ROC-AUC loss functions, *i.e.*, the first and second terms in the objective function (4). Inequality (5) is a popular assumption when there are a small number of positive instances and a large number of unlabeled instances [26, 21, 6]. We newly introduce the relation between negative and non-negative triples as in Ineq. (6) in order to explicitly leverage negative triples. These two assumptions enable us to make full use of negative triples as well as positive triples. To the best of our knowledge, existing work does not take Ineq. (6) into account, and therefore, cannot effectively harness positive, negative, and unlabeled triples at the same time.

Second, as the sign of a score, we assume that

$$s_{t_p} > 0 \ (\forall t_p \in \Delta_p), \tag{7}$$
$$s_{t_n} < 0 \ (\forall t_n \in \Delta_n), \tag{8}$$

hold. This induces the classification error loss function, *i.e.*, the third term in the objective function (4). The second assumption enables us to discriminate positive triples from negative triples by threshold 0, while the first assumption does not provide such a decision boundary. As described later, a decision boundary is indispensable to define a query score called an uncertainty score. As far as we know, this is the first attempt to combine the ROC-AUC loss function and the classification error function to calibrate predictive scores to have threshold 0.

3.1.2 Learning Algorithm

We solve the optimization problem (4) by a stochastic gradient descent (SGD) algorithm in the same way as other related methods [26, 21, 6]. Rewriting the objective function (4) as

$$\frac{1}{|\Delta_p||\Delta\backslash\Delta_p|}\sum_{t_p,\bar{t}_p}\left(\left[\gamma - s_{t_p} + s_{\bar{t}_p}\right]_+ + C_e\left[\gamma' - s_{t_p}\right]_+\right)$$
$$+\frac{1}{|\Delta_n||\Delta\backslash\Delta_n|}\sum_{t_n,\bar{t}_n}\left(C_n\left[\gamma - s_{\bar{t}_n} + s_{t_n}\right]_+ + C_e\left[\gamma' + s_{t_n}\right]_+\right), \tag{9}$$

a SGD algorithm for Eq. (9) is derived as in Algorithm 1, where the Heaviside step function $H : \mathbb{R} \to \mathbb{R}$ is defined as

$$H(x) := \begin{cases} 0 & (x < 0), \\ 1 & (x \geq 0), \end{cases}$$

and for a matrix $R \in \mathbb{R}^{D \times D}$, SVD($R$) outputs the singular value decomposition of R, *i.e.*, U, Σ, V such that $R = U\Sigma V^*$. In the SGD algorithm, we set the maximum number of updates T (> 0). We also set the learning rate at the t-th iteration as $\alpha_0 \cdot t^{-1/2}$, where α_0 (> 0) is a hyperparameter.

3.1.3 Hyperparameter Tuning

Our multi-relational learning algorithm involves several hyperparameters that have to be determined manually in order to achieve high performance. In particular in AMDC, the dataset is updated at each iteration, and therefore, the best set of hyperparameters at the beginning is not necessarily the best at the ending. We resort to validation to address this issue as shown in Algorithm 2. We prepare multiple sets of hyperparameters and a validation dataset. All the models are trained on the current training dataset, and ROC-AUC scores of all the models are calculated on the validation dataset using ValScore, which outputs ROC-AUC scores on the validation dataset. We choose the model with the best validation score to calculate the query score, which we call a *default model*.

3.2 Query Scores

We calculate a *query score* q_t for randomly sampled Q ($>$ 0) unlabeled triple $t \in \Delta\backslash(\Delta_p \cup \Delta_n)$ and choose q ($< Q$) triples with the lowest scores for querying. We introduce two different query scores for the two problem settings.

1. Positiveness score
   Given the predictive scores $\{s_t\}_{t\in\Delta}$, the positiveness score of a triple $t \in \Delta$ is defined as
   $$q_t := -s_t.$$
   Choosing triples with the lowest query scores corresponds to choosing triples that the model believes to be positive.

2. Uncertainty score
   Given the predictive scores $\{s_t\}_{t\in\Delta}$, the uncertainty score of a triple $t \in \Delta$ is defined as
   $$q_t := |s_t|.$$
   This query score regards a triple whose predictive score close to 0 as uncertain. Such an interpretation is possible because we set a decision boundary between positive and negative triples on 0 as Eqs. (7) and (8). Querying the most uncertain samples is a standard heuristic to obtain a highly predictive model using less training data [28].

3.3 Active Learning Algorithm

We describe the entire procedure of the AMDC method in Algorithm 3. As inputs, AMDC is given a budget B (> 0), a budget for the validation set N_{val} (> 0), a small dataset $(\Delta_p^{(0)}, \Delta_n^{(0)})$, and multiple models with different hyperparameters.

The initialization consists of three parts. First, the validation set is created by randomly querying labels of N_{val} triples. Second, the models are trained on the initial dataset $(\Delta_p^{(0)}, \Delta_n^{(0)})$. Third, the validation scores of the models are calculated on the validation set, and the model with the best validation score is selected as the default model.

Then, the following steps are repeated until the budget B is exhausted. First, Q unlabeled triples are randomly sampled, the query scores are then calculated using the default model, and q triples with the lowest query scores are selected from the Q unlabeled triples. Second, the selected q unlabeled triples are provided to the oracle for labeling, and the dataset is updated using the labels given by the oracle. Third, all the models are retrained on the updated dataset, and the default model is re-selected using the validation step.

4. EXPERIMENTS

We conduct two experiments to show the effectiveness of AMDC in Problems 1 and 2. We investigate the effectiveness of our querying strategies, the constraints on the model

Table 1: Statistics of the datasets. $|\mathcal{E}|$ corresponds to the number of entities, $|\mathcal{R}|$ to that of relations, and $|\Delta_p|$ and $|\Delta_n|$ to the numbers of positive and negative triples in the original dataset.

	$\|\mathcal{E}\|$	$\|\mathcal{R}\|$	$\|\Delta_p\|$	$\|\Delta_n\|$
Kinships	104	26	10,790	270,426
UMLS	135	49	6,752	886,273
Nations	125	57	2,565	8,626

(Eqs. (1) and (2)), and the ROC-AUC loss function on negative and non-negative triples, which are part of the technical contributions implemented in AMDC. We first describe the datasets used in the experiments, the performance measures, evaluated methods, and the experimental setup. Then, we show experimental results on both problem settings.

4.1 Datasets

We use three real multi-relational datasets, which are also used by Bordes *et al.* [5] and Jenatton *et al.* [13]. Key statistics of the datasets are summarized in Table 1.

4.1.1 Kinships

The Kinships dataset describes kinship relations in Australian tribes that are famous for their complex kinship systems. The entities correspond to tribe members, and the relations correspond to kinship terms such as a brother, a son, and a wife (the Australian tribes often have more complex systems). A triple (i, j, k) is positive if member i calls member j by k. The dataset is fully-observed. This dataset was originally created by Denham [9], according to Kemp *et al.* [16]. We used the dataset distributed by Nickel *et al.* [24].

4.1.2 UMLS

The UMLS dataset is a biomedical semantic network constructed from the Unified Medical Language System, which was developed by McCray [20]. The entities correspond to high-level concepts, and the relations correspond to semantic relations. For example, a triple can be (Injury or Poisoning, Fully Formed Anatomical Structure, disrupts) and (Cell, Tissue, a part of) [20]. The dataset is fully-observed. We used the dataset distributed by Bordes *et al.* [6].

4.1.3 Nations

The Nations dataset contains both attributes of countries and relations between countries, which was originally curated by Rummel [27]. The entities correspond to countries, and the relations are, for example, the economical aid relation and the official visit relation. This dataset is partially-observed; there are positive, negative, and unlabeled triples in the original dataset. We only allow queries on the positive and negative triples in our experiments. We used the dataset distributed by Bordes *et al.* [6].

4.2 Performance Measures

The ROC-AUC is used to evaluate the performance of a predictive model. Given a test dataset $(\Delta_p^{(t)}, \Delta_n^{(t)})$, the ROC-AUC is calculated as

$$\frac{1}{\left|\Delta_p^{(t)}\right|\left|\Delta_n^{(t)}\right|} \sum_{t_p \in \Delta_p^{(t)}, t_n \in \Delta_n^{(t)}} \mathbb{I}[s_{t_p} > s_{t_n}],$$

where $\mathbb{I}[\text{condition}] = 1$ holds if the condition is true, and $\mathbb{I}[\text{condition}] = 0$ holds otherwise. In addition, the ratio of the positive triples the algorithm has collected so far to all the triples is used to evaluate the ability of the algorithm to collect positive triples. We call the latter performance measure a *completion rate*.

4.3 Methods Evaluated

Besides the fully-fledged AMDC, we evaluate three methods obtained by turning off, in each case, one feature of the full AMDC. AMDC_rand turns off our method of selecting the triples to be posed to the oracle, using a random querying strategy instead. AMDC_pos_only turns off the ROC-AUC loss function on negative and non-negative triples. AMDC_no_const ignores the additional constraints integrated into the model (Eqs. (1) and (2)). AMDC_rand can be derived by setting $Q = q$; we simply query labels on randomly sampled unlabeled triples. AMDC_pos_only corresponds to AMDC with $C_n = 0$. AMDC_no_const can be derived by skipping lines 13, 17, and 18 in Algorithm 1. However, without any constraints on the model parameters, the learning algorithm tends to be unstable. Therefore, we instead use regularized updates in Algorithm 1 by using regularization hyperparameters λ_A and λ_R for A and R, respectively. For example, the update rule in line 6 in Algorithm 1,

$$\mathbf{a}_{i_p} \leftarrow \mathbf{a}_{i_p} - \alpha\left[-(I_1 + I_2 C_e)\bar{R}_{k_p}\bar{\mathbf{a}}_{j_p}\right],$$

is modified into

$$\mathbf{a}_{i_p} \leftarrow \mathbf{a}_{i_p} - \alpha\left[-(I_1 + I_2 C_e)\bar{R}_{k_p}\bar{\mathbf{a}}_{j_p} + \lambda_A \bar{\mathbf{a}}_{i_p}\right].$$

We fix $\lambda_A = \lambda_R = 0.01$ in our experiments.

4.4 Protocol and Configuration

We design a protocol of an experiment as follows. Given the original dataset (Δ_p, Δ_n), we randomly divide the dataset into a test set $(\Delta_p^{(t)}, \Delta_n^{(t)})$ consisting of N_{test} triples, a validation set $(\Delta_p^{(v)}, \Delta_n^{(v)})$ consisting of N_{val} triples, the initial dataset $(\Delta_p^{(0)}, \Delta_n^{(0)})$ consisting of q triples, and the pool dataset $(\Delta_p^{(p)}, \Delta_n^{(p)})$ without overlaps between each other. Then, we run Algorithm 3 using the validation set, the initial dataset, and the pool dataset. Each algorithm is allowed to query the oracle, requesting labels for triples in the pool dataset. At each iteration of Algorithm 3, we calculate the performance measures introduced in Section 4.2, using the test set in case of the ROC-AUC score. We repeat this process 10 times and report the mean and the standard deviation of the scores at each iteration. For each dataset, we use the same experimental settings among the four tested methods, to evaluate the contribution of each individual feature turned on and off.

For the Kinships and UMLS datasets, we set $N_{\text{test}} = N_{\text{val}} = 1{,}000$, $B = 15{,}000$, $Q = 100{,}000$, and $q = 1{,}000$, and for the Nations dataset, we set $N_{\text{test}} = N_{\text{val}} = 100$, $B = 1{,}500$, $Q = 2{,}000$, and $q = 100$. This is because the number of labeled triples in the Nations dataset is much smaller than those in the Kinships and UMLS datasets. Other settings are the same across different datasets. The hyperparameter setting of the original AMDC method is $C = [5.0, 10.0, 30.0]$, $C_n = [1.0, 5.0, 30.0]$, $\gamma = 0.3$, $\gamma' = 0.9$, $D = [5, 10]$, $\alpha_0 = 0.1$, and $T = 50{,}000$. We use all the combinations of these subsets of hyperparameters; therefore the number of models L is 18. We override the hyperparameter setting when we use the other partial methods.

4.5 Experimental Results

We provide experimental results on the two problem settings in this section. We then discuss the properties of AMDC based on the experimental results.

4.5.1 *Dataset Construction Problem*

We provide experimental results as to the dataset construction problem (Problem 1). We run the four methods using the positiveness score to collect as many positive triples as possible. Figure 3 shows experimental results.

These charts emphasize four main conclusions. First, our querying strategy with the positiveness score enables us to collect many more positive triples than a random sampling strategy does. This strongly demonstrates the effectiveness of the positiveness score for the dataset construction problem. In particular, AMDC collected 6.18 times, 17.0 times, and 2.28 times more positive triples than AMDC_rand in the Kinships, UMLS, and Nations datasets, respectively.

Second, our querying strategy achieved the highest improvement on the UMLS dataset, the most imbalanced dataset. This shows that the AMDC method can successfully learn a model even from an imbalanced dataset.

Third, AMDC_pos_only had worse performance in the Kinships and UMLS datasets, but comparable performance with the other methods in the Nations dataset. This result can be explained by the property of the ROC-AUC loss function of negative triples. The contribution of the ROC-AUC loss function depends on the ratio between the number of unlabeled triples and positive triples. If the number of unlabeled triples is quite larger than that of positive triples, the ROC-AUC loss function has much influence on unlabeled triples. However, if the number of unlabeled triples decreases to be comparable to that of positive triples, it has less influence on unlabeled triples, and therefore, the effectiveness of the ROC-AUC loss function decreases. This can explain the fact that the increasing rate of the completion rate of AMDC_pos_only is comparable to that of other methods in the Kinships and UMLS datasets when the number of queries increases.

Fourth, the positiveness score is not beneficial to improve the predictive performance. AMDC achieved almost the same ROC-AUC scores as AMDC_rand on the UMLS and Nations datasets and achieved even worse ROC-AUC scores on the Kinships dataset. This supports our motivation to set two different problem settings.

4.5.2 *Predictive Model Construction Problem*

We then provide experimental results for the predictive model construction problem (Problem 2). We run the four methods using the uncertainty score to collect informative triples in order to improve the predictive performance. Figure 4 shows experimental results.

We present four conclusions drawn from these results. First, at every iteration, AMDC's ROC-AUC score is either the highest, or comparable to the highest, while the partial AMDCs are not always comparable to the highest one. In specific, AMDC performs the best on the Kinships and UMLS datasets, and is comparable to AMDC_rand on the Nations dataset. This demonstrates the benefits of the full AMDC method.

Second, AMDC_no_const resulted in the poorest score, and the standard deviations were the largest. This validates that the constraints we introduced helped to increase the stability of learning. By reducing the model complexity, we can successfully avoid overfitting.

Third, AMDC tends to outperform AMDC_rand in the middle of the active learning procedure. This illustrates the following active learning consequence. At the beginning, the predictive model shows insufficient active learning ability due to lack of labels. As the number of labels grows, the model is able to choose informative triples, and active learning becomes more effective. Towards the later iterations, the querying strategy benefits little when diminishing returns is observed in learning predictive models especially.

Fourth, the uncertainty score did not help improve the completion rate in the same way as the first experiment. This result, combined with the fourth finding in the previous section, shows that the dataset construction problem and the predictive model construction problem are essentially different problem areas. The predictive model construction problem needs both positive and negative labels, while the dataset construction problem aims to collect as many positive labels as possible.

5. RELATED WORK

The AMDC method is related to multi-relational data construction, multi-relational learning, and active learning in machine learning. We review existing studies and state the relationships with the AMDC method.

5.1 Multi-relational Data Construction

There are two main research directions in constructing a multi-relational dataset: manual construction and automatic construction by extracting data from documents.

ConceptNet [19], Cyc [18], and Wordnet [22] are constructed mainly by hand annotation. Von Ahn *et al.* [30] propose a game-with-a-purpose (GWAP) approach to use human resources efficiently. Unlike the AMDC method, these approaches do not make use of machine learning algorithms to facilitate manual dataset construction.

In bioinformatics, automatic extraction from scientific papers has been extensively studied. For example, Blaschke *et al.* [3] propose an automatic extraction method of protein-protein interactions from scientific abstracts. In the Semantic Web, knowledge bases are typically constructed from Web documents such as Wikipedia. DBpedia [17] and YAGO2 [12] have been built partly by extracting from Wikipedia. Dong *et al.* [10] combine automatic extraction methods and a machine learning method to construct a reliable knowledge base. The main difference between their method and ours is the objective of using machine learning. Dong *et al.* [10] utilize machine learning to improve the data reliability, while we apply machine learning to efficiently extract human knowledge that does not appear in documents.

5.1.1 *Multi-relational Data Learning*

Latent representation methods for multi-relational data learning have been broadly investigated because of their high predictive performance [7, 24, 25, 23, 5, 6, 31]. These approaches model entities as latent feature vectors and relations as operators on the vectors. In the RESCAL models [24, 25, 23], relations are modeled as asymmetric matrices that can be interpreted as operators on a latent feature vector of a tail of a triple. The models are learned by minimizing the squared loss function [24, 25] or the logistic loss function [23]. In the embedding models [7, 5, 6, 31], relations

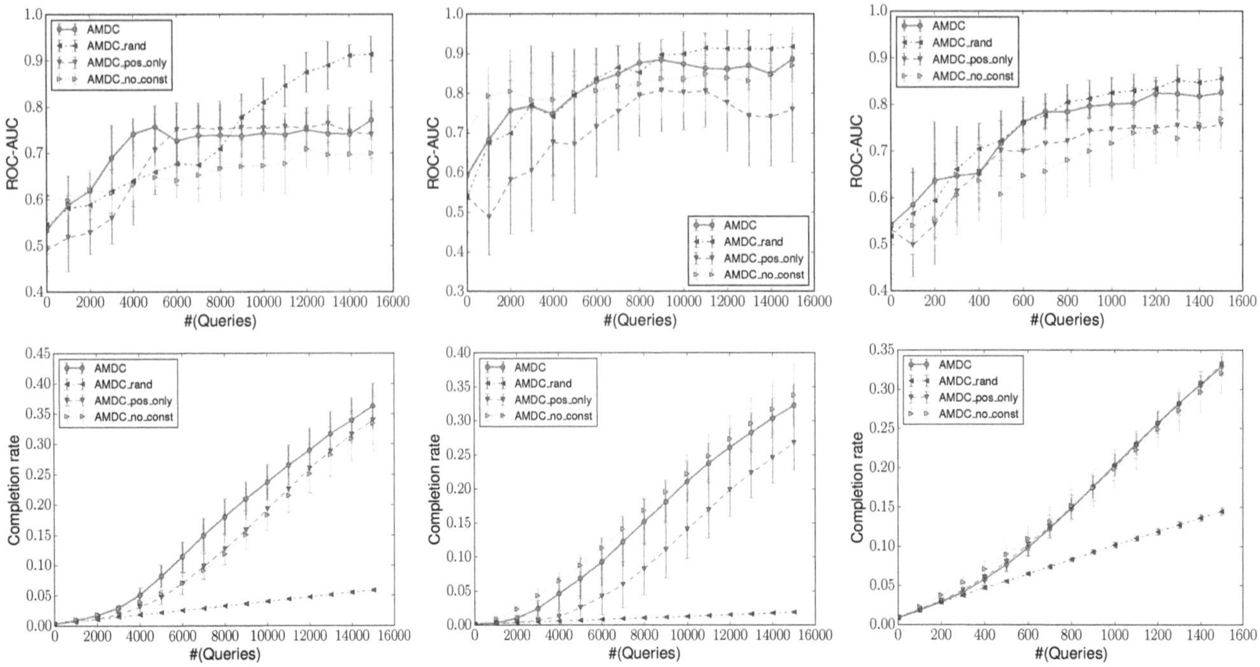

Figure 3: ROC-AUC scores and completion rates in the dataset construction problem (Problem 1). Upper-left, upper-middle, and upper-right figures correspond to the ROC-AUC scores on the Kinships, UMLS, and Nations datasets. Lower-left, lower-middle, and lower-right figures correspond to the completion rates on the Kinships, UMLS, and Nations datasets.

are modeled as matrices [7] or vectors [5, 6, 31]. The models are learned by minimizing the ROC-AUC loss function on positive and non-positive triples. We employ the RESCAL model in AMDC rather than the embedding models based on the initial experimental results.

The model complexity of the RESCAL models is high as compared to that of the embedding models. The RESCAL models assign $O(D^2)$ parameters to one relation while the embedding models [6, 31] assign $O(D)$ to one relation.

Our multi-relational data model has three crucial differences from the aforementioned existing models. First, by introducing additional constraints to the RESCAL model, we successfully develop a RESCAL-variant model with low model complexity. By fixing the length of latent feature vectors to 1 and restricting the set of relation matrices to the set of rotation matrices, we achieve the same model complexity with the embedding model [6]. Second, in order to make full use of negative triples, we combine the existing ROC-AUC loss function on positive and non-positive triples with another ROC-AUC loss function on negative and non-negative triples. Third, we further add the classification error loss function to the loss function in order to learn a decision boundary. The decision boundary plays a crucial role in active learning.

5.2 Active Learning

Active learning is a supervised learning scheme in which a learner is allowed to choose instances to be labeled. General techniques are summarized in the survey by Settles [28].

To the best of our knowledge, our approach is the first attempt to apply active learning to a multi-relational data model trained using the ROC-AUC loss function. Several research groups propose active learning algorithms for matrix factorization models [14, 15, 8, 29]. However, none of them employs the ROC-AUC loss function for learning, because these studies do not focus on imbalanced data. In order to achieve high predictive performance on an imbalanced multi-relational dataset, we develop an active learning algorithm for a model trained with the ROC-AUC loss function. Donmez *et al.* [11] propose an active learning algorithm on the learning-to-rank problem, in which a ranking model is learned using the ROC-AUC loss function. There are two main differences between Donmez *et al.*'s work and our work. The first difference is the model to be learned. Donmez *et al.* [11] employ RankSVM, while we develop a new multi-relational data model. The second difference is the method to estimate a decision boundary. Donmez *et al.* [11] assume that the decision boundary is between two scores whose difference is maximized. Our estimation method is believed to be more effective because it calibrates the predictive scores to satisfy the decision boundary 0 by incorporating the classification error loss function.

6. CONCLUSION

Constructing a multi-relational dataset can often benefit from human expert input, which can take the form of annotating triples whose positive/negative status is initially missing. While very valuable, human expert input is a limited resource, given that manually annotating a large amount of triples is a tedious and costly process. This research has focused on efficiently using human expert resources to construct a multi-relational dataset. We investigated two scenarios; a dataset construction problem and a predictive model construction problem.

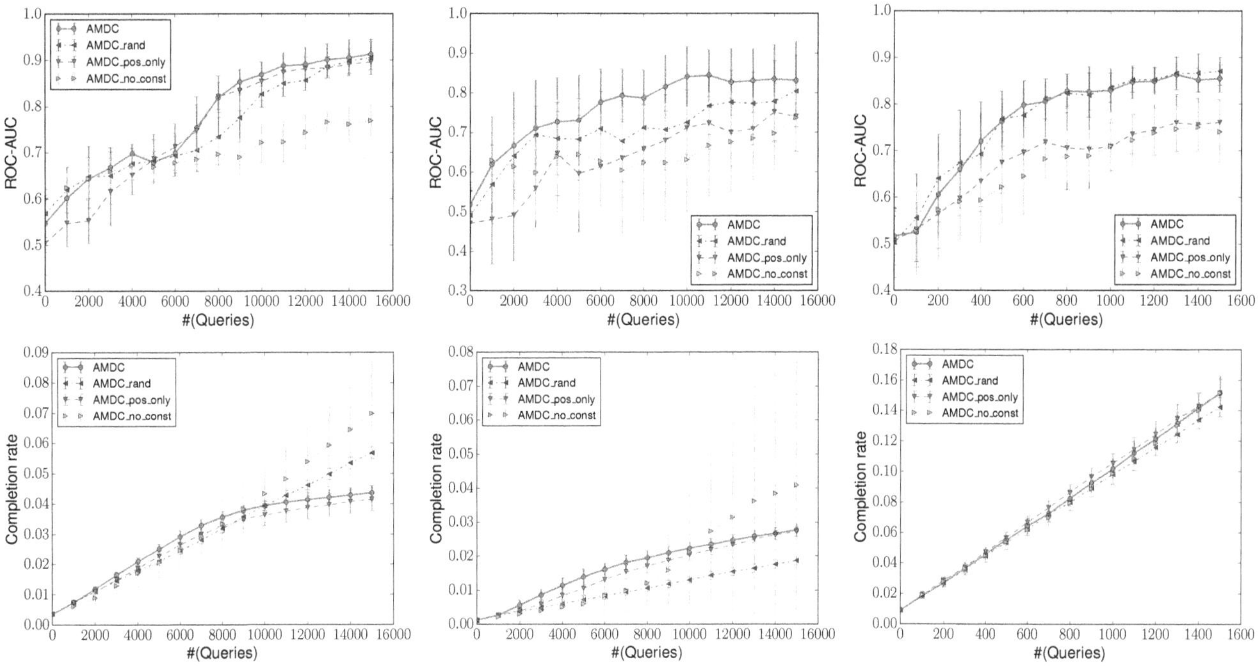

Figure 4: ROC-AUC scores and completion rates in the predictive model construction problem (Problem 2). Upper-left, upper-middle, and upper-right figures correspond to the ROC-AUC scores on the Kinships, UMLS, and Nations datasets. Lower-left, lower-middle, and lower-right figures correspond to the completion rates on the Kinships, UMLS, and Nations datasets.

We have introduced the AMDC method, our solution to this problem. AMDC performs active learning. It learns a model of a multi-relational dataset, and actively poses queries to an oracle, requesting labels to selected unlabeled triples. Our main technical contributions are three-fold. First, we developed active learning algorithms using the ROC-AUC loss function. Active learning cannot directly be applied to a model learned on the ROC-AUC loss function, because such a model does not have a decision boundary, which is necessary to select uncertain triples for querying. We resolved this issue by using a classification error loss function, which enabled the model to learn the decision boundary. Second, we presented a new ROC-AUC loss function utilizing negative triples to learn efficiently from abundant negative triples. Existing learning methods employ the ROC-AUC loss function only on positive and non-positive triples, which do not distinguish negative triples from unlabeled ones. We combined a ROC-AUC loss function on negative and non-negative triples to make full use of negative triples. Third, we added two constraints to the RESCAL model to reduce the model complexity. We fixed the length of latent feature vectors and restricted the set of model parameters associated with relations.

We conducted experiments to validate the effectiveness of AMDC. We evaluated the impact of each of the three technical contributions, comparing the full AMDC method with three other variants where each of these features were turned off. This allowed to identify strengths and limitations of each individual contribution. We found that the full AMDC has consistently good performance at every iteration, showing that the technical contributions implemented in AMDC work well in conjunction with each other.

An interesting direction for future work involves using crowdsourcing for annotation purposes. Crowdsourcing provides easy access to abundant human resources at low cost. However, it has been pointed out that labels obtained with crowdsourcing are sometimes of low quality. We believe that the quality issue can be resolved by combining quality control techniques [32].

Another research direction is to incorporate automatic extraction methods. By using a large dataset extracted from documents as the initial dataset, AMDC will be able to select more appropriate triples that contribute to efficient data construction. The key challenge is to estimate the reliability of each triple. As the reliability of an automatically extracted dataset is not always guaranteed, it is necessary to estimate it with help of human annotation.

7. REFERENCES

[1] E. Antezana, W. Blondé, M. Egaña, A. Rutherford, R. Stevens, B. De Baets, V. Mironov, and M. Kuiper. BioGateway: a semantic systems biology tool for the life sciences. *BMC Bioinformatics*, 10, 2009.

[2] F. Belleau, M.-A. Nolin, N. Tourigny, P. Rigault, and J. Morissette. Bio2RDF: towards a mashup to build bioinformatics knowledge systems. *Journal of Biomedical Informatics*, 41(5):706–716, 2008.

[3] C. Blaschke, M. A. Andrade, C. Ouzounis, and A. Valencia. Automatic extraction of biological information from scientific text: protein-protein interactions. In *Proceedings of the Seventh International Conference on Intelligent Systems for Molecular Biology*, pages 60–67, 1999.

[4] K. Bollacker, C. Evans, and P. Paritosh. Freebase: a collaboratively created graph database for structuring human knowledge. In *Proceedings of the 2008 ACM SIGMOD International Conference on Management of Data*, pages 1247–1249, 2008.

[5] A. Bordes, X. Glorot, J. Weston, and Y. Bengio. A semantic matching energy function for learning with multi-relational data. *Machine Learning*, 94(2):233–259, 2013.

[6] A. Bordes, N. Usunier, A. Garcia-Durán, J. Weston, and O. Yakhnenko. Translating embeddings for modeling multi-relational data. In *Advances in Neural Information Processing Systems 26*, pages 2787–2795, 2013.

[7] A. Bordes, J. Weston, R. Collobert, and Y. Bengio. Learning structured embeddings of knowledge bases. In *Proceedings of the Twenty-Fifth AAAI Conference on Artificial Intelligence*, pages 301–306, 2009.

[8] S. Chakraborty, J. Zhou, V. Balasubramanian, S. Panchanathan, I. Davidson, and J. Ye. Active matrix completion. In *Proceedings of 2013 IEEE 13th International Conference on Data Mining*, pages 81–90, 2013.

[9] W. W. Denham. *The detection of patterns in Alyawarra nonverbal behavior.* PhD thesis, University of Washington, 1973.

[10] X. L. Dong, E. Gabrilovich, G. Heitz, W. Horn, N. Lao, K. Murphy, T. Strohmann, S. Sun, and W. Zhang. Knowledge Vault: a web-scale approach to probabilistic knowledge fusion. In *Proceedings of the 20th ACM SIGKDD International Conference on Knowledge Discovery and Data Mining*, pages 601–610, 2014.

[11] P. Donmez and J. G. Carbonell. Active sampling for rank learning via optimizing the area under the ROC curve. In *Proceedings of the 31th European Conference on IR Research*, pages 78–89, 2009.

[12] J. Hoffart, F. M. Suchanek, K. Berberich, and G. Weikum. YAGO2: a spatially and temporally enhanced knowledge base from Wikipedia. *Artificial Intelligence*, 194:28–61, 2013.

[13] R. Jenatton, N. L. Roux, A. Bordes, and G. Obozinski. A latent factor model for highly multi-relational data. In *Advances in Neural Information Processing Systems 25*, pages 3167–3175, 2012.

[14] R. Karimi, C. Freudenthaler, A. Nanopoulos, and L. Schmidt-Thieme. Non-myopic active learning for recommender systems based on matrix factorization. In *Proceedings of 2011 IEEE International Conference on Information Reuse & Integration*, pages 299–303, 2011.

[15] R. Karimi, C. Freudenthaler, A. Nanopoulos, and L. Schmidt-Thieme. Exploiting the characteristics of matrix factorization for active learning in recommender systems. In *Proceedings of the Sixth ACM Conference on Recommender Systems*, pages 317–320, 2012.

[16] C. Kemp, J. B. Tenenbaum, T. L. Griffiths, T. Yamada, and N. Ueda. Learning systems of concepts with an infinite relational model. In *Proceedings of the 21st National Conference on Artificial Intelligence*, pages 381–388, 2006.

[17] J. Lehmann, R. Isele, M. Jakob, A. Jentzsch, D. Kontokostas, P. N. Mendes, S. Hellmann, M. Morsey, P. van Kleef, S. Auer, and C. Bizer. DBpedia – a large-scale, multilingual knowledge base extracted from Wikipedia. *Semantic Web*, 2014.

[18] D. B. Lenat. CYC : a large-scale investment in knowledge infrastructure. *Communications of the ACM*, 38(11):33–38, 1995.

[19] H. Liu and P. Singh. ConceptNet – a practical commonsense reasoning tool-kit. *BT Technology Journal*, 22(4):211–226, 2004.

[20] A. T. McCray. An upper-level ontology for the biomedical domain. *Comparative and Functional Genomics*, 4(1):80–84, 2003.

[21] A. K. Menon and C. Elkan. Link prediction via matrix factorization. In *Proceedings of the European Conference on Machine Learning and Principles and Practice of Knowledge Discovery in Databases 2011*, pages 437–452, 2011.

[22] G. A. Miller. WordNet: a lexical database for English. *Communications of the ACM*, 38(11):39–41, 1995.

[23] M. Nickel and V. Tresp. Logistic tensor factorization for multi-relational data. In *Proceedings of ICML 2013 Workshop - Structured Learning: Inferring Graphs from Structured and Unstructured Inputs*, 2013.

[24] M. Nickel, V. Tresp, and H.-P. Kriegel. A three-way model for collective learning on multi-relational data. In *Proceedings of the 28th International Conference on Machine Learning*, pages 809–816, 2011.

[25] M. Nickel, V. Tresp, and H.-P. Kriegel. Factorizing YAGO: scalable machine learning for linked data. In *Proceedings of the 21st International Conference on World Wide Web*, pages 271–280, 2012.

[26] S. Rendle, C. Freudenthaler, Z. Gantner, and L. Schmidt-Thieme. BPR: Bayesian personalized ranking from implicit feedback. In *Proceedings of the Twenty-Fifth Conference on Uncertainty in Artificial Intelligence*, pages 452–461, 2009.

[27] R. J. Rummel. Dimensionality of nations project: attributes of nations and behavior of nation dyads, 1950-1965.

[28] B. Settles. Active learning literature survey. Technical report, University of Wisconsin–Madison, 2009.

[29] D. J. Sutherland, B. Póczos, and J. Schneider. Active learning and search on low-rank matrices. In *Proceedings of the 19th ACM SIGKDD International Conference on Knowledge Discovery and Data Mining*, pages 212–220, 2013.

[30] L. von Ahn, M. Kedia, and M. Blum. Verbosity: a game for collecting common-sense facts. In *Proceedings of the SIGCHI Conference on Human Factors in Computing Systems*, pages 75–78, 2006.

[31] Z. Wang, J. Zhang, J. Feng, and Z. Chen. Knowledge graph embedding by translating on hyperplanes. In *Proceedings of the Twenty-Eighth AAAI Conference on Artificial Intelligence*, pages 1112–1119, 2014.

[32] J. Whitehill, P. Ruvolo, T. Wu, J. Bergsma, and J. Movellan. Whose vote should count more: optimal integration of labels from labelers of unknown expertise. In *Advances in Neural Information Processing Systems 22*, pages 2035–2043, 2009.

Algorithm 1 LEARN$((\Delta_p, \Delta_n), H)$

Input: multi-relational dataset (Δ_p, Δ_n) and hyperparameters $H = \{D, \gamma, \gamma', C_e, C_n, T, \alpha_0\}$.
Output: model (A, R).
Initialize: randomly initialize A, R to satisfy Eqs. (1) and (2), and set $\bar{A} = A, \bar{R} = R$, $t = 1$, $\alpha = \alpha_0$.

repeat
  Sample $v \sim$ Bernoulli(0.5)
  if $v = 1$ **then**
    Sample $t_p = (i_p, j_p, k_p)$ from Δ_p and $\bar{t}_p = (\bar{i}_p, \bar{j}_p, \bar{k}_p)$ from $\Delta \backslash \Delta_p$.
    Compute indicators as

$$I_1 \leftarrow H\left(\gamma - \mathbf{a}_{i_p}^\top R_{k_p} \mathbf{a}_{j_p} + \mathbf{a}_{\bar{i}_p}^\top R_{\bar{k}_p} \mathbf{a}_{\bar{j}_p}\right),$$
$$I_2 \leftarrow H\left(\gamma' - \mathbf{a}_{i_p}^\top R_{k_p} \mathbf{a}_{j_p}\right).$$

    Update model parameters as

$$\mathbf{a}_{i_p} \leftarrow \mathbf{a}_{i_p} - \alpha\left[-(I_1 + I_2 C_e)\bar{R}_{k_p}\bar{\mathbf{a}}_{j_p}\right],$$
$$\mathbf{a}_{j_p} \leftarrow \mathbf{a}_{j_p} - \alpha\left[-(I_1 + I_2 C_e)\bar{R}_{k_p}^\top\bar{\mathbf{a}}_{i_p}\right],$$
$$R_{k_p} \leftarrow R_{k_p} - \alpha\left[-(I_1 + I_2 C_e)\bar{\mathbf{a}}_{i_p}\bar{\mathbf{a}}_{j_p}^\top\right],$$
$$\mathbf{a}_{\bar{i}_p} \leftarrow \mathbf{a}_{\bar{i}_p} - \alpha\left[I_1 \bar{R}_{\bar{k}_p}\bar{\mathbf{a}}_{\bar{j}_p}\right],$$
$$\mathbf{a}_{\bar{j}_p} \leftarrow \mathbf{a}_{\bar{j}_p} - \alpha\left[I_1 \bar{R}_{\bar{k}_p}^\top\bar{\mathbf{a}}_{\bar{i}_p}\right],$$
$$R_{\bar{k}_p} \leftarrow R_{\bar{k}_p} - \alpha\left[I_1 \bar{\mathbf{a}}_{\bar{i}_p}\bar{\mathbf{a}}_{\bar{j}_p}^\top\right].$$

  else if $v = 0$ **then**
    Sample $t_n = (i_n, j_n, k_n)$ from Δ_n and $\bar{t}_n = (\bar{i}_n, \bar{j}_n, \bar{k}_n)$ from $\Delta \backslash \Delta_n$.
    Compute indicators as

$$I_3 \leftarrow H\left(\gamma - \mathbf{a}_{\bar{i}_n}^\top R_{\bar{k}_n} \mathbf{a}_{\bar{j}_n} + \mathbf{a}_{i_n}^\top R_{k_n} \mathbf{a}_{j_n}\right),$$
$$I_4 \leftarrow H\left(\gamma' + \mathbf{a}_{i_n}^\top R_{k_n} \mathbf{a}_{j_n}\right).$$

    Update model parameters as

$$\mathbf{a}_{i_n} \leftarrow \mathbf{a}_{i_n} - \alpha\left[(I_3 C_n + I_4 C_e)\bar{R}_{k_n}\bar{\mathbf{a}}_{j_n}\right],$$
$$\mathbf{a}_{j_n} \leftarrow \mathbf{a}_{j_n} - \alpha\left[(I_3 C_n + I_4 C_e)\bar{R}_{k_n}^\top\bar{\mathbf{a}}_{i_n}\right],$$
$$R_{k_n} \leftarrow R_{k_n} - \alpha\left[(I_3 C_n + I_4 C_e)\bar{\mathbf{a}}_{i_n}\bar{\mathbf{a}}_{j_n}^\top\right],$$
$$\mathbf{a}_{\bar{i}_n} \leftarrow \mathbf{a}_{\bar{i}_n} - \alpha\left[-I_3 C_n \bar{R}_{\bar{k}_n}\bar{\mathbf{a}}_{\bar{j}_n}\right],$$
$$\mathbf{a}_{\bar{j}_n} \leftarrow \mathbf{a}_{\bar{j}_n} - \alpha\left[-I_3 C_n \bar{R}_{\bar{k}_n}^\top\bar{\mathbf{a}}_{\bar{i}_n}\right],$$
$$R_{\bar{k}_n} \leftarrow R_{\bar{k}_n} - \alpha\left[-I_3 C_n \bar{\mathbf{a}}_{\bar{i}_n}\bar{\mathbf{a}}_{\bar{j}_n}^\top\right].$$

  end if
  for $i \in \mathcal{E}$ such that $\mathbf{a}_i \neq \bar{\mathbf{a}}_i$ **do**
    $\mathbf{a}_i \leftarrow \mathbf{a}_i / \|\mathbf{a}_i\|_2$.
    $\bar{\mathbf{a}}_i \leftarrow \mathbf{a}_i$.
  end for
  for $k \in \mathcal{R}$ such that $R_k \neq \bar{R}_k$ **do**
    $U_k, \Sigma_k, V_k \leftarrow \mathrm{SVD}(R_k)$.
    $R_k \leftarrow U_k V_k^*$.
    $\bar{R}_k \leftarrow R_k$.
  end for
  $\alpha \leftarrow \alpha_0 / \sqrt{t+1}$.
  $t \leftarrow t + 1$.
until $t \geq T$ holds.
return (A, R)

Algorithm 2 LEARNDEFAULT$((\Delta_p, \Delta_n), (\Delta_p^{(v)}, \Delta_n^{(v)}), \mathcal{H})$

Input: training dataset (Δ_p, Δ_n), validation dataset $(\Delta_p^{(v)}, \Delta_n^{(v)})$, and a set of models $\mathcal{H} = \{H^{(l)} \mid l \in \{1, \ldots, L\}\}$.
Output: default model (A, R).

for $l = 1, \ldots, L$ **do**
  $(A^{(l)}, R^{(l)}) \leftarrow$ LEARN$(\Delta_p, \Delta_n, H^{(l)})$.
  $v^{(l)} \leftarrow$ VALSCORE$(A^{(l)}, R^{(l)}, \Delta_p^{(v)}, \Delta_n^{(v)})$.
end for
$l^\star \leftarrow \arg\max_{l=1,\ldots,L} v^{(l)}$.
return $(A^{(l^\star)}, R^{(l^\star)})$.

Algorithm 3 Active Multi-relational Data Construction

Input: budget $B > 0$, budget for validation $N_{\text{val}} > 0$, initial dataset $(\Delta_p^{(0)}, \Delta_n^{(0)})$, a set of hyperparameters $\mathcal{H} = \{H^{(l)} \mid l \in \{1, \ldots, L\}\}$, the number of queries q, the number of unlabeled triples to calculate a query score Q, and a query score function.
Output: dataset (Δ_p, Δ_n) and model $(A^\star, R^\star)$.
Initialization:
$(\Delta_p, \Delta_n) \leftarrow (\Delta_p^{(0)}, \Delta_n^{(0)})$.
Create a validation dataset of size N_{val}, $(\Delta_p^{(v)}, \Delta_n^{(v)})$.
$(A^\star, R^\star) \leftarrow$ LEARNDEFAULT$((\Delta_p, \Delta_n), (\Delta_p^{(v)}, \Delta_n^{(v)}), \mathcal{H})$.
$t \leftarrow 0$.
Main algorithm:
while $tq \leq B$ **do**
  Randomly sample Q unlabeled triples to construct Δ_u.
  for each triple $t \in \Delta_u$ **do**
    Compute the query score q_t using the query score function.
  end for
  Choose q triples with the lowest query scores to construct $\Delta_q^\star$.
  for each triple $t \in \Delta_q^\star$ **do**
    $l \leftarrow \mathcal{O}(t)$.
    if $l = 1$ **then**
      $\Delta_p \leftarrow \Delta_p \cup \{t\}$.
    else
      $\Delta_n \leftarrow \Delta_n \cup \{t\}$.
    end if
  end for
  $(A^\star, R^\star) \leftarrow$ LEARNDEFAULT$((\Delta_p, \Delta_n), (\Delta_p^{(v)}, \Delta_n^{(v)}), \mathcal{H})$.
  $t \leftarrow t + 1$.
end while
return (Δ_p, Δ_n) and $(A^\star, R^\star)$.

The Social World of Content Abusers in Community Question Answering

Imrul Kayes
University of South Florida
Tampa FL, USA
imrul@mail.usf.edu

Nicolas Kourtellis
Yahoo Labs
Barcelona, Spain
kourtell@yahoo-inc.com

Daniele Quercia
Yahoo Labs
Barcelona, Spain
dquercia@yahoo-inc.com

Adriana Iamnitchi
University of South Florida
Tampa FL, USA
anda@cse.usf.edu

Francesco Bonchi
Yahoo Labs
Barcelona, Spain
bonchi@yahoo-inc.com

ABSTRACT

Community-based question answering platforms can be rich sources of information on a variety of specialized topics, from finance to cooking. The usefulness of such platforms depends heavily on user contributions (questions and answers), but also on respecting the community rules. As a crowd-sourced service, such platforms rely on their users for monitoring and flagging content that violates community rules.

Common wisdom is to eliminate the users who receive many flags. Our analysis of a year of traces from a mature Q&A site shows that the number of flags does not tell the full story: on one hand, users with many flags may still contribute positively to the community. On the other hand, users who never get flagged are found to violate community rules and get their accounts suspended. This analysis, however, also shows that abusive users are betrayed by their network properties: we find strong evidence of homophilous behavior and use this finding to detect abusive users who go under the community radar. Based on our empirical observations, we build a classifier that is able to detect abusive users with an accuracy as high as 83%.

Categories and Subject Descriptors

K.4.2 [**Computers and Society**]: Social Issues—Abuse and crime involving computers

Keywords

Community question answering; content abusers; crowdsourcing

1. INTRODUCTION

Community-based Question-Answering (CQA) sites, such as Yahoo Answers, Quora and Stack Overflow, are now rich and mature repositories of user-contributed questions and answers. For example, Yahoo Answers (*YA*), launched in December 2005, has more than one billion posted answers,[1] and Quora, one of the fastest growing CQA sites has seen three times growth in 2013.[2]

Like many other Internet communities, CQA platforms define community rules and expect users to obey them. To enforce these rules, published as community guidelines and terms of services, these platforms provide users with tools to flag inappropriate content. In addition to community monitoring, some platforms employ human monitors to evaluate abuses and determine the appropriate responses, from removing content to suspending user accounts.

To the best of our knowledge, this paper is the first to investigate the reporting of rule violations in *YA*, one of the oldest, largest, and most popular CQA platforms. The outcomes of this study could aid human monitors with automated tools in order to maintain the health of the community. Our sampled dataset contains 10 million editorially curated abuse reports posted between 2012 and 2013, and 1.5 million users who submitted content during the one-year observation period, with about 9% of the users having their accounts suspended. We use suspended accounts as a ground truth of bad behavior in *YA*, and we refer to these users as *content abusers*.

We discover that, although used correctly, flags do not tell accurately which users should be suspended: while 32% of the users active in our observation period have at least one flag, only 16% of them are suspended during this time. Even considering the top 1% users with the largest number of flags, only about 50% of them deserve account suspension. Moreover, we see that users with lots of flags contribute positively to the community in terms of providing (even best) answers. Complicating an already complex problem, we find that 40% of the suspended users have not received any flags.

To reduce this large gray area of questionable behavior, we employ social network analysis tools in an attempt to understand the position of content abusers in the *YA* community. We learned that the follower-followee social network tunnels user attention not only in terms of generating answers to posted questions, but also in monitoring user behavior.

WWW 2015, May 18–22, 2015, Florence, Italy.
ACM 978-1-4503-3469-3/15/05.
http://dx.doi.org/10.1145/2736277.2741674 .

[1]http://www.yanswersbloguk.com/b4/2010/05/04/1-billion-answers-served/
[2]http://www.goo.gl/MfK83y

More importantly, it turns out that this social network divulges information about the users who go under the community radar and never get flagged even if they seriously violate community rules. This network-based information, combined with user activity, leads to accurate detection of the "bad guys": our classifier is able to distinguish between suspended and fair users with an accuracy as high as 83%.

The paper is structured as follows. Section 2 discusses previous analysis of CQA platforms and the existing body of work on unethical behavior in online communities in general. Section 3 presents the *YA* functionalities relevant to this study and the dataset used. We introduce a deviance score in Section 4 that identifies the pool of bad users more accurately than the number of flags alone. Section 5 demonstrates that deviant users are not all bad: despite their high deviance score, in aggregate their presence in the community is beneficial. Section 6 shows the effects of the social network on user contribution and behavior. Section 7 shows the classification of suspended and fair users. We discuss the impact of these results in Section 8.

2. RELATED WORK

We collate past research on Community-based Question Answering (CQA) in five categories depending on whether it has dealt with content, users, new applications, bad behavior in online settings, or CQA communication networks.

Content. Research in this area has investigated textual aspects of questions and answers. In so doing, it has proposed algorithmic solutions to automatically determine: the quality of questions [14, 28] and answers [25, 1], the extent to which certain questions are easy to answer [9, 24], and the type of a given question (e.g., factual or conversational) [13].

Users. Research on CQA users has been mostly about understanding why users contribute content: that is, why users ask questions (askers are failed searchers, in that, they use CQA sites when web search fails [15]); and why they answer questions (e.g., they refrain from answering sensitive questions to avoid being reported for abuse and potentially lose access to the community [7]).

New applications. As for applications, research has proposed effective ways of recommending questions to the most appropriate answerers [23, 29], of automatically answering questions based on past answers [26], and of retrieving factual answers [4] or factual bits within an answer [31].

Bad behavior in online settings. Qualitative and quantitative studies of bad behavior in online settings have been done before including newsgroups [22], online chat communities [27], and online multiplayer video games [5]. A body of work also investigates the impact of the bad behavior. Researchers find that bad behavior has negative effects on the community and its members: it decreases community's cohesion [32], performance [10] and participation [6]. In the worst case, users who are the targets of bad behavior may leave or avoid online social spaces [6].

Communication networks. The communication networks behind CQA sites have been recently studied. More specifically, researchers have explored the relationship between content quality and network properties such as number of followers [30] and tie strength [21].

Research on CQA communication networks is quite recent, so it comes as no surprise that there has not been any work on how such networks mediate different types of behavior on CQA sites. This paper, for the first time, sheds light on bad behavior in CQA communities by studying *YA*, one of the largest and oldest such communities. It quantifies how *YA*'s networks channel user attention, and how that results in different behavioral patterns that can be used to limit bad behavior.

3. YAHOO ANSWERS

After 9 years of activity, *YA* has 56M monthly visitors (U.S. only).[3] The functionalities of the *YA* platform and the dataset used in this analysis are presented next.

3.1 The Platform

YA is a CQA platform in which community members ask and answer questions on various topics. Users ask questions and assign them to categories selected from a predefined taxonomy, e.g., *Business & Finance*, *Health*, and *Politics & Government*. Users can find questions by searching or browsing through this hierarchy of categories. A question has a title (typically, a short summary of the question), and a body with additional details.

A user can answer any question but can post only one answer per question. Questions remain open for four days for others to answer. However, the asker can select a best answer before the end of this 4-day period, which automatically *resolves* the question and archives it as a *reference* question. The best answer can also be rated between one to five, known as *answer rating*. If the asker does not choose a best answer, the community selects one through voting. The asker can extend the answering duration for an extra four days. The questions left unanswered after the allowed duration are deleted from the site. In addition to questions and answers, users can contribute comments to questions already answered and archived.

YA has a system of points and levels to encourage and reward participation.[4] A user is penalized five points for posting a question, but if she chooses a best answer for her question, three points are given back. A user who posts an answer receives two points; a best answer is worth 10 points. A leaderboard, updated daily, ranks users based on the total number of points they collected. Users are split into seven levels based on their acquired points (e.g., 1-249 points: level 1, 250-999 points: level 2, ..., 25000+ points: level 7). These levels are used to limit user actions, such as posting questions, answers, comments, follows, and votes: e.g., first level users can ask 5 questions and provide 20 answers in a day.

YA requires its users to follow the Community Guidelines that forbids users to post spam, insults, or rants, and the Yahoo Terms of Service [2] that limits harm to minors, harassment, privacy invasion, impersonation and misrepresentation, and fraud and phishing. Users can flag content (questions, answers or comments) that violates the Community Guidelines and Terms of Service using the "Report Abuse" functionality. Users click on a flag sign embedded with the content and choose a reason between violation of the community guidelines and violation of the terms of service. Reported content is then verified by human inspectors before it is deleted from the platform.

Users in *YA* can choose to follow other users, thus creating a follower-followee relationship used for information dissemination. The followee's actions (e.g., questions, an-

[3] http://www.listofsearchengines.org/qa-search-engines

[4] https://answers.yahoo.com/info/scoring_system

swers, ratings, votes, best answer, awards) are automatically posted on the follower's newsfeed. In addition, users can follow questions, in which case all responses are sent to the followers of that question.

3.2 Dataset

We studied a sample of 10 million abuse reports posted between 2012 and 2013 originating from 1.5 million active users. These users are connected via 2.6 million follower-followee relationships in a social network (referred to as FF in this study) that has 165,441 weakly connected components. The largest weakly connected component has 1.1M nodes (74.32% of the nodes) and 2.4M edges (91.37% of the edges). Out of the 1.5 million users, about 9% of the users have been suspended from the community. Figure 1(a) and Figure 1(b) plot the complementary cumulative distribution function (CCDF) for the degree of followers (indegree) and followees (outdegree), respectively. The indegree and outdegree follow power-law distributions [3], with an exponential fitting parameter α 3.53 and 2.95 respectively.

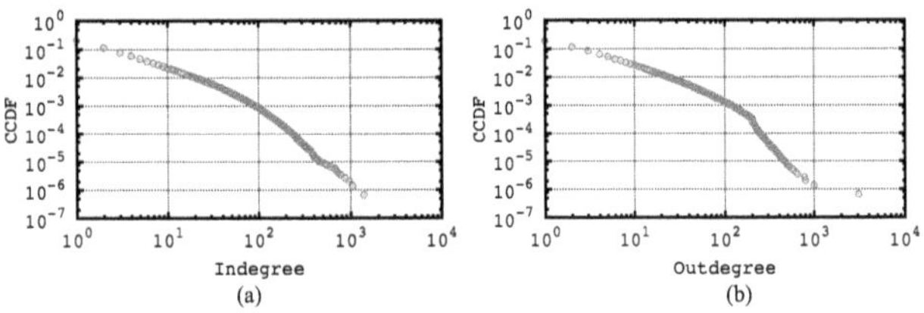

Figure 1: (a) Indegree distribution; (b) Outdegree distribution.

Along with the follower-followee social network, we built an activity network (AN) that connects users if they interacted with each other's content. In the AN network, nodes are users who answered other users' questions, directed edges point from the answerer to the asker. The activity network has 1.2M nodes and 45M edges, thus being 141 times denser (ratio of the number of edges to the number of possible edges) than the FF network.

4. FLAGGING IN YAHOO ANSWERS

In this section, we study whether flags (we use flags and abuse reports interchangeably) can be used as an appropriate proxy for content abuse. First, we investigate whether the flags reported from users are typically valid, i.e. if human inspectors remove the flagged content and further, how quickly this is done (Section 4.1). Then, we explore how the flags can be used to detect content abusers (Sections 4.2 and 4.3).

4.1 Abuse Reports

YA is a self-moderating community; the health of the platform depends on community contributions in terms of reporting abuses. Besides participating by providing questions and answers, *YA* users also contribute to the platform by reporting abusive content. Reporters serve as an intermediate layer in the *YA* moderation process since these abuse reports are verified by human inspectors. If the report is valid, the content is promptly deleted.

To check if valid abuse reports are indeed an accurate sensor for the correct monitoring of the platform, we look at how soon a report is curated. Figure 2 shows the distributions of the time interval between the time when a content (question or answer) is posted and when it is deleted due to abuse reports. About 97% of questions and answers marked as abusive are deleted within the same day they are posted. All reported abusive questions and answers are deleted within three days of posting.

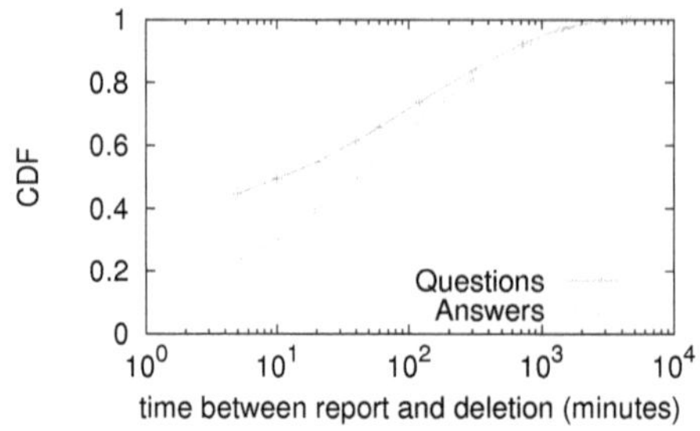

Figure 2: The CDF of the time delay between the posting of the content (questions or answers) and its deletion due to valid abuse reporting.

This result highlights two facts. First, the users monitoring the platform act very quickly on content: within 10 minutes from being posted, 50% of the bad posts are reported. Second, the validation of abuse reports happens within 3 days (and in vast majority within a day). Hence, in our dataset, if there are abuse reports that did not have the chance of being curated yet and thus we do not consider them, those are too few to impact our analysis.

However, the abuse reporting functionality might be abused as well, due to several reasons. First, reporting is an easy and fast process, requiring only a few steps. Second, a user is not penalized for misreporting content abuse, perhaps in an attempt to not discourage users from exercising good citizenship. And third, independent of their level in the *YA* platform (that limits the number of questions and answers posted per day), users can report an unlimited number of abuses.

To check whether users abuse the abuse reporting functionality, we compare the number of flags received/reported with the number of validated flags received/reported per user. Figure 3 shows a correlation heat map of the flags received and flags received that are valid, as well as flags reported and flags reported that are valid, on questions and for all contributors (results on answers are similar and are excluded for brevity). For questions (answers), we have a very high correlation between flags received by users and flags that are valid ($r = 0.90$ (0.87), $p < 0.01$) and between flags reported by users and that are valid ($r = 0.80$ (0.92), $p < 0.01$).

These high correlations indicate that, in general, users are not exploiting the abuse reporting functionality. When a user reports an abuse, it is very likely that the content is violating community rules. Another interesting finding from the correlation heat maps is that for both questions and answers, users have almost negligible or very weak correlation between the number of flags they reported that are valid and the number of flags they received that are valid. This hints that the good guys of the community are not bad guys at the same time: the users who correctly report a lot of content abuses are not posting abusive content themselves.

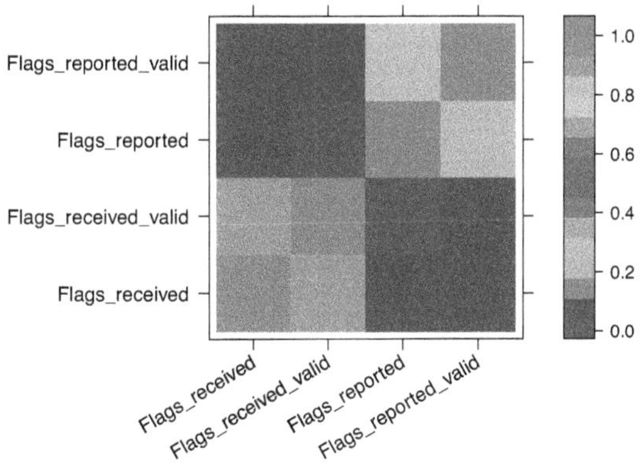

Figure 3: The Pearson correlation coefficient heat map of flags received, valid flags received, flags reported and valid flags reported on questions. All values are statistically significant (p-values <0.01).

4.2 Deviant Users

Given that flags are good proxies for identifying bad content, how should they be used to detect content abusers and thus determine which accounts to be suspended? Common wisdom might suggest that content abusers are those who receive a large number of flags. Of the top 1% flagged askers and answerers, we find 51.63% and 53.89%, respectively, are suspended. But finding a threshold on the number of flags received by a user is not likely to work accurately for content abuser detection: users with low activity who received flags for all their posts might go below this threshold. At the same time, highly active users may collect many flags even if for a small percentage of their posts, yet contribute significantly to the community.

This intuition motivated us to measure the correlation between a user's number of posts and the number of flags received. Indeed, we find that the correlation between the number of questions a user asks and the number of valid flags she receives from others is high ($r = 0.49$, $p < 0.05$). Similarly, the number of answers posted and the number of valid flags received per user are highly correlated ($r = 0.37$, $p < 0.05$). The distributions of the fraction of flagged questions and answers is shown in Figure 4. While about 27% users have more than 25% flagged questions, about 34% users have more than 25% flagged answers. Also, about 16% and 19% of users have more than 50% flagged questions and answers respectively.

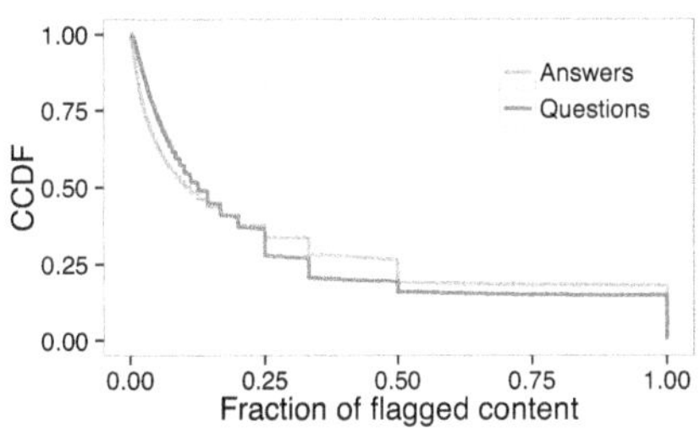

Figure 4: Distributions of fraction of flagged questions and answers.

So, instead of directly considering flags, we define a *deviance score* metric that indicates how much a user deviates from the norm in terms of received flags considering the amount of her activity. Deviant behavior is defined by actions or behaviors that are contrary to the dominant norms of the society [8]. Although social norms differ from culture to culture, within a context, they remain the same and they are the rules by which the members of the community are conventionally guided.

We define the deviance score for a user u as the number of correct abuse reports (flags) she receives over the total content (question/answer) she posted, after eliminating the expected average number of correct abuse reports given the amount of content posted:

$$\text{Deviance}_{\text{Q/A}}(u) = Y_{Q/A,u} - \hat{Y}_{Q/A,u} \tag{1}$$

where $Y_{Q/A,u}$ is the number of correct abuse reports received by u for her questions/answers, and $\hat{Y}_{Q/A,u}$ is the expected number of correct abuse reports to be received by u for those questions/answers.

To capture the expected number of the correct abuse reports a user receives for questions/answers, we considered a number of linear and polynomial regression models between the response variable (number of correct abuse reports) and the predictor variable (number of questions/answers) for all users. Among them, the following linear model was the best in explaining the variability of the response variable.

$$Y = \alpha + \beta X + \epsilon \tag{2}$$

where Y is the number of correct abuse reports (flags) received for the content, X is the number of content posts and ϵ is the error term.

In eq. (1), a positive deviance score reflects deviant users, i.e., those whose deviance cannot be only explained by their activity levels.

4.3 Deviance Score vs. Suspension

We found 105,340 users with positive *question* deviance scores and 121,705 users with positive *answer* deviance scores. Among the users with positive question deviance score, 31,891 users (30.27%) have been suspended. Similarly, among the users with a positive answer deviance score, 37,633 users (30.92%) have been suspended. The CDF of suspended and deviant (but not suspended) users' deviance scores for both questions and answers is shown in Figure 5. In both cases, suspended and deviant users are visibly characterized by different distributions: suspended users tend to have higher deviance scores than deviant (not suspended) users. While this difference is visually apparent, we also ensure it is statistically significant using two methods: 1) the two-sample Kolmogorov-Smirnov (KS) test, and 2) a permutation test, to verify that the two samples are drawn from different probability distributions.

We also find that 63.94% of top 1% deviant question askers' and 64.77% of top 1% deviant answerers' accounts have been suspended. This hints that the higher deviance score a user has, the more likely (s)he is to be removed from the community. Figure 6 shows the probability of a user being suspended as a function of its rank in the community as expressed by deviance score and number of flags. We observe that the more deviant a user is, the more probable is that she will be suspended. Also, in all cases, deviance score shows a higher probability of suspension compared to the number of flags.

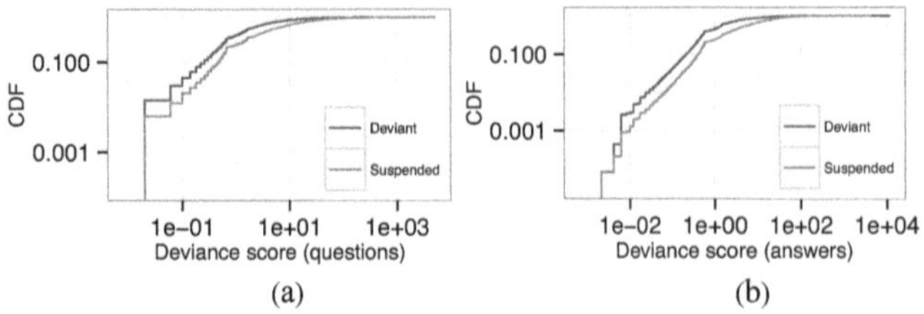

Figure 5: The CDF of suspended and deviant users' deviance scores for (a) questions; (b) answers. Distributions are different with $p<0.001$ for both KS and permutation tests (for questions: $D=0.22$, $Z=46.04$ and for answers: $D=0.28$, $Z=50.53$.)

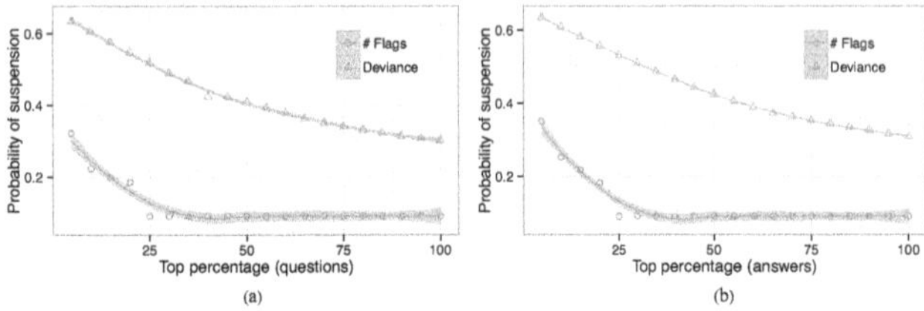

Figure 6: Probability of being suspended, given a user is within top x% of (a) question or (b) answer deviance scores and flags. Local polynomial regression fitting with 95% confidence interval area is also shown.

These results show that the deviance score is a better metric for identifying the content abusers than the number of flags is by itself. However, both metrics fail to identify content abusers who go under the community radar. We found that about 40% of the suspended users had never been flagged for the abusive content they certainly posted, thus maintaining a negative deviance score. Thus, our investigation into user behavior in the *YA* community continues.

5. DEVIANT VS. SUSPENDED USERS

Despite the fact that deviance score better identifies the pool of suspended users, it is clearly an imperfect metric. On one hand, there are high deviance score users who are not suspended, despite the fact that the platform seems to be fairly quick in responding to abuse reports. On the other hand, there are "ordinary" users, according to the deviance score (i.e., with a negative deviance score) who are never reported for abusive content, yet get suspended. These users may even be fair users for a long time, but sometimes their posted content can be highly abusive (e.g., vulgar language and images) that platform moderators immediately suspend them. To better understand these two groups of users—deviant but not suspended and suspended but not flagged—we analyze in more detail their activity. Note that the two groups are disjoint (i.e., deviant users have received at least one flag).

5.1 Deviance is Engaging

One of the success metrics of CQA platforms is *user engagement* [16], which can be measured by the number of contributions and by the number of users who respond to a particular content. Thus, we use the number of answers deviant users receive to their questions and the number of distinct users who respond to the deviant users' questions as measures of deviants' contribution to user engagement with the platform. To this end, for each category of users (typical, deviant but not suspended, and suspended) we randomly selected $500k$ questions they asked. For each question, we extracted all answers received and also the users who answered those questions. Table 1 presents the statistics of the number of answers received per category of users.

Table 1: Descriptive statistics of the number of answers received by typical, deviant but not suspended, and suspended users per question.

Type	Min.	1st Qu.	Med.	Mean	3rd Qu.	Max.
Typical	1.00	1.00	2.00	4.36	5.00	1296.00
Deviant	1.00	5.00	11.00	17.96	22.00	1205.00
Suspended	1.00	1.00	4.00	8.67	9.00	1144.00

Deviant users' questions get significantly more answers than typical users's questions get: on average, a question posted by a deviant user gets about 5 times more answers than the average question posted by a typical user. This difference is also seen in the CCDF of the number of answers received by typical, deviant and suspended users in Figure 7(a). The distributions (pairwise) are different with $p_{ks} < 0.01$ and $p_{perm} < 0.01$.

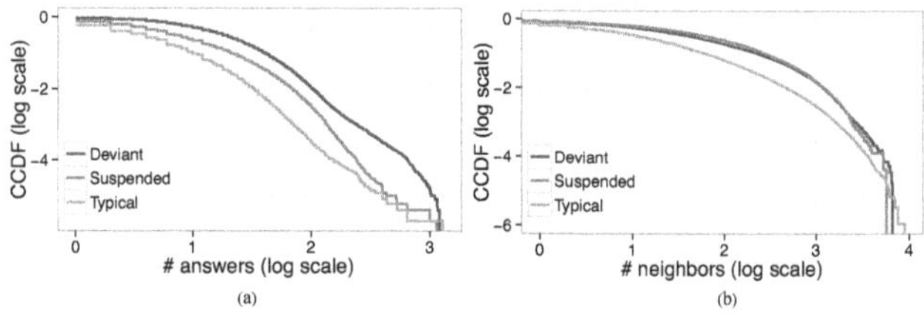

Figure 7: (a) CCDF of the number of answers received by the typical, deviant but not suspended, and suspended users on questions; (b) CCDF of the number of neighbors (distinct answerers) that typical, deviant but not suspended, and suspended users have.

Deviant users not only attract more answers, but also interact with more users than typical users do, as shown by Figure 7(b) and these two distributions are different ($p_{ks} < 0.01$, $p_{perm} < 0.01$).

This result from analyzing a random sample of $500k$ questions is confirmed when looking at the indegree of nodes in the activity network, which represents the number of users who answered that node's questions, as shown in Table 2 for typical and deviant users. Deviant askers have a higher number of neighbors than typical askers. An explanation might be, as shown in [13], that users who ask conversational questions tend to have more neighbors (with whom the asker has interaction) than users who ask informational questions. This suggests that deviant users tend to ask more conversational questions, which engage a larger number of responders.

5.2 Deviance is Noisy

We observed that deviant users impact the *quantity* of content in the system. Do they impact *quality*, too? To

Table 2: **Descriptive statistics of the number of neighbors askers have in the Activity Network.**

Type	Min.	1st Qu.	Med.	Mean	3rd Qu.	Max.
Typical	0.00	1.00	5.00	28.16	19.00	13270.00
Deviant	0.00	3.00	20.00	103.40	90.00	5698.00
Suspended	0.00	2.00	13.00	88.62	60.00	6576.00

address this question, we look at the percentage of the best answers with respect to the total number of answers submitted per user.

Figure 8 shows the CDF of the percentage of best answers for different classes of users: 1) typical, 2) deviant but not suspended, and 3) suspended. The results show that users who are moderately deviant but did not get suspended have higher percentage of best answers than suspended users (distributions are different $p_{ks} < 0.01$, $p_{perm} < 0.01$), but lower than that of typical users (distributions are different $p_{ks} < 0.01$, $p_{perm} < 0.01$).

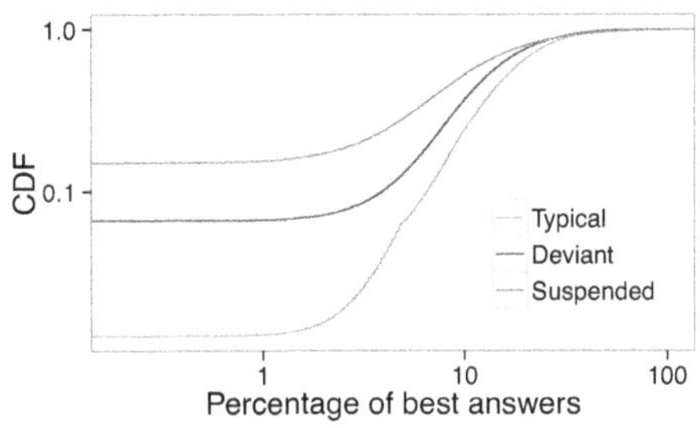

Figure 8: CDF of the percentage of best answers for typical, deviant but not suspended and suspended users.

To conclude, it turns out that while deviant users are beneficial in terms of platform success metrics, as they increase user engagement by attracting more answers and attracting more users who answer their questions, they do not contribute more than the norm-following users in terms of content quality.

5.3 The Suspended but Not Flagged Users

While the results above show how the deviant users differ from the suspended and from the typical users, we do not have yet an understanding of the behavior of the users who get suspended without other users flagging their abusive content. An initial analysis of these users—suspended but not flagged—shows the following particularities when compared to the fair users (all users, independent of their deviance status, who are not suspended).

First, they are followed by and follow significantly fewer other users. Figures 9 (a) and (b) show the distributions of indegree and outdegree of never-flagged-suspended users compared to those of fair users. Not only these users have smaller social circles, but they also have lower activity levels, as shown in Figure 9 (c). Of course, these results could be correlated: low activity may mean low engagement in the social platform. These results may also suggest that (some of) these users join the platform for particular objectives that are orthogonal to the platform purpose, such as spamming. More importantly, however, these results suggest directions that we present in the following.

6. MEMBERS OF THE NETWORK

We investigate how the social network defined by the follower-followee relationships impacts user activities and behaviors in *YA*. Our final goal is to understand how to separate fair users from users who should be suspended even in the absence of flags. We learn that users close in the *FF* network not only help each other by answering questions, but also monitor each other's behavior by reporting flags (Section 6.1). Thus, the social network allows users to implicitly coordinate their behavior so much so that users who are socially close exhibit not only similar behavior, but also a similar deviation from the typical behavior (Section 6.2).

6.1 Out of Sight, Out of Mind

We expect that users receive more answers from users that are close in the social network. To verify this intuition, we randomly selected 7M answers such that both parties of the interaction (the user who posted the question and the user who answered it) are in the social network, and measured the social distances between the two users. For a user u and a social distance h, the probability of receiving an answer from followers at distance h is the following:

$$p_h = \frac{\#\text{ of } u\text{'s followers at distance } h \text{ who answered } u\text{'s questions}}{\#\text{ of } u\text{'s followers at distance } h} \quad (3)$$

Figure 10 plots the geometric average of all these probabilities at a given distance as a function of social distance. The figure confirms that the probability of receiving answers from h-hop followers decreases with social distance.

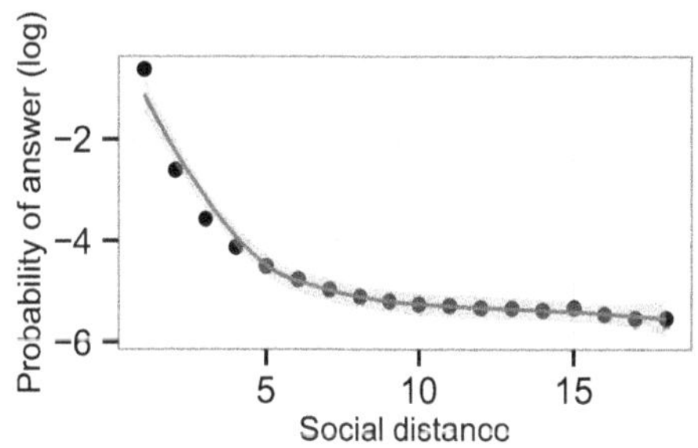

Figure 10: Probability of getting answers from h-hop followers. Local polynomial regression fitting with 95% confidence interval area is also shown.

Therefore, the *FF* network channels user attention, likely via its newsfeeds feature that sends updates to followers on the questions posted by the user. Does the same phenomenon hold true for abuse reports?

To answer this question we investigate both networks: along with the *FF* which is an explicit network, we also investigate the activity network (*AN*), which connects users based on their direct question-answer interactions. For each (reporter, reportee) pair in the editorially-curated abuse reports, we calculated the shortest path distance between them in the social network and the activity network. We compare our results with a null model that randomly assigns the abuse reports in our sample dataset to users in the two networks.

Figure 11 shows the percentage of abuse reports users receive from close distances (up to 8 hops) for both (social and

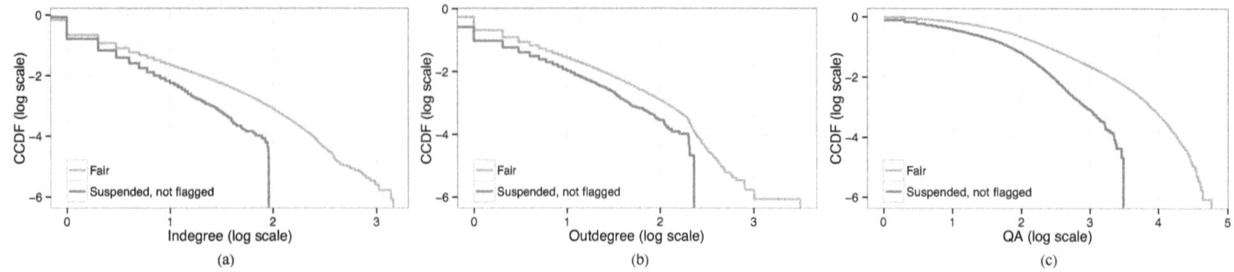

Figure 9: Distributions of (a) indegree; (b) outdegree and (c) number of questions and answers (QA) of never flagged suspended users and fair users (for outdegree: $D = 0.28$ and $Z = 27.40$, $p < 0.001$, for indegree: $D = 0.17$ and $Z = 15.86$, $p < 0.001$ and for activity: $D = 0.30$ and $Z = 40.30$, $p < 0.001$).

random) cases. About 75% of the reports that users receive are from reporters located within 5 social hops in the *FF* network. However, when reports are distributed randomly, about 9% are from within 5 social hops and very few from within 3 social hops.

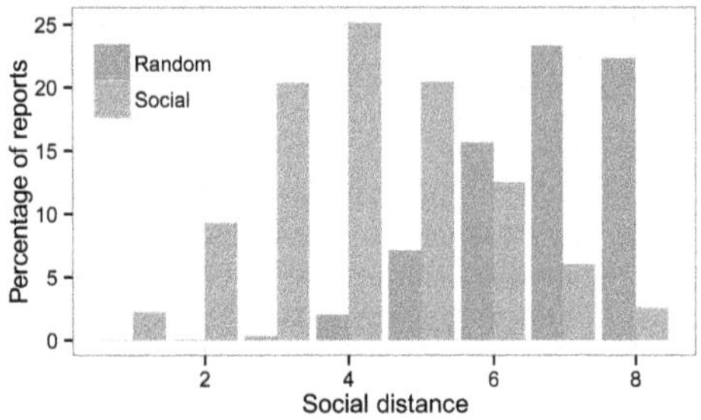

Figure 11: Percentage of the abuse reports received by users from different distances in the social network, for the observed case and a random case.

When comparing the percentage of abuse reports users receive with respect to distance in the *AN* (Figure 12), we notice that 94% of reports come from users within the first 3 hops, which is significantly higher than the social network (about 32%). We believe this is due to the high density of *AN*: most of the nodes are reachable from others within a few hops. However, even in this denser network, the null model has only about 10% of reports applied from within 3 hops.

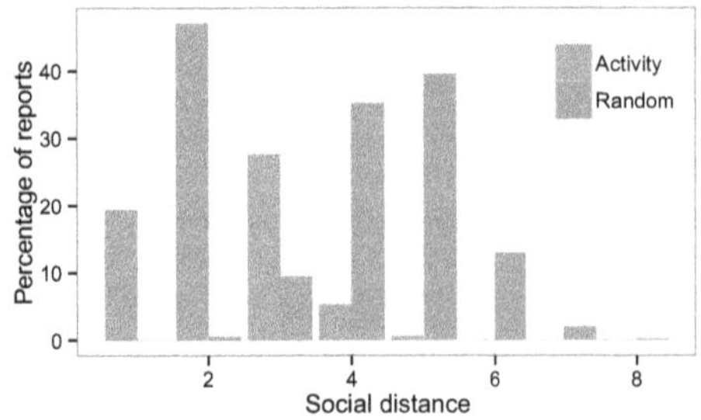

Figure 12: Percentage of the abuse reports received by users from different distances in the activity network, for the observed case and a random case.

To further quantify this phenomenon, we calculate the probability of being correctly flagged by users located at different network distances in the social and the activity network. For a user u and a social distance h, the probability of being flagged by followers at distance h is the following:

$$p_h = \frac{\#\text{ of } u\text{'s followers at distance } h \text{ who flagged } u}{\#\text{ of } u\text{'s followers at distance } h} \quad (4)$$

Figure 13 plots the geometric average of all probabilities at a given distance against the social distance for both networks. As expected, the probability decreases with social distance in both the social and the activity networks. The plot shows that users are likely to receive flags from others close to them in terms of social relationships and interactions.

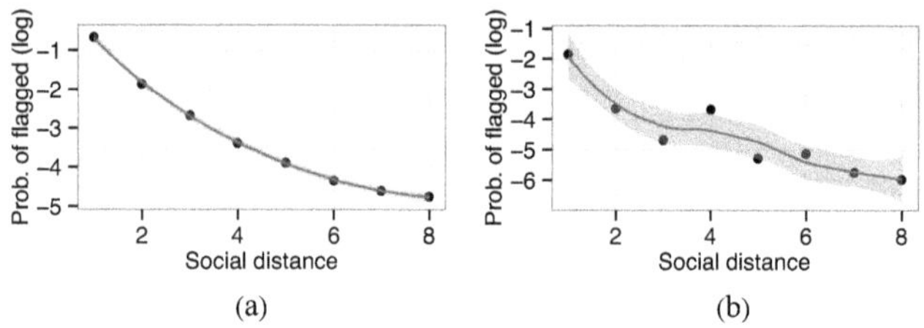

Figure 13: Probability of being flagged by h-hop followers in the: (a) social network, and (b) activity network. Local polynomial regression fitting with 95% confidence interval area is also shown.

These results confirm that the abuse reporting behavior is dominated by social relationships and interactions: users are reported for content abuse more from their close social or activity neighborhoods than from distant users. The underlying reason is likely content exposure: a user's contents (questions/answers) are disseminated to nearby followers, thus they get higher exposure to that content compared to more distant users in the social graph. Similarly, users who interact frequently with a user are more probable to view her contents and to report the inappropriate ones.

6.2 Birds of a Feather Flock Together

Similarity fosters connection– a principle commonly known as homophily, coined by sociologists in the 1950s. Homophily is our inexorable tendency to link up with other individuals similar to us [17]. In this section, we investigate whether homophily is also present in terms of deviance–that is, if

Table 3: Assortativity coefficient r for deviance scores in the *YA* network. Assortativity coefficients are also shown for other social networks from [19].

Yahoo! Answers	Other Social Networks
Question deviance $r = +0.11$	Mathematics coauthorship $r = +0.120$
Answer deviance $r = +0.13$	Biology coauthorship $r = +0.127$

deviant users tend to be close to each other in the social network.

One way to conclude about the homophily of a network is to compute the attribute assortativity of the network [20]. The assortativity coefficient is a measure of the likelihood for nodes with similar attributes to connect to each others. The assortativity coefficient ranges between -1 and 1; a positive assortativity means that nodes tend to connect to nodes of similar attribute value, while a negative assortativity means that nodes are likely to connect to nodes with very different attribute value from their own. If a network has positive assortativity coefficient, then it is often called assortative mixed by the attribute, otherwise called disassortative mixed.

In this work, we used question and answer-based deviant scores. We considered each of the scores as an attribute and calculated the assortativity coefficient r based on [19] for each type of deviance. The assortativity coefficients r are shown in Table 3 and are positive. In [19], Newman studied a wide variety of networks and concluded that social networks are often assortatively mixed (Table 3 offers two such examples), but that technological and biological networks (e.g., World Wide Web $r = -0.067$, software dependencies $r = -0.016$, protein interactions $r = -0.156$) tend to be disassortative. Comparing them quantitatively with the assortativity coefficients of the *YA* network, we conclude that the *YA* network is assortatively mixed in terms of deviance. So, users having contacts with (low)high deviance scores will also have (low)high deviance scores.

We next measure how similar the deviance scores of a user's contacts are with the user's, and how this similarity varies over longer social distances. For this, we randomly sampled $100k$ users from the social network for each social distance ranking from 1 hop to 4 hops. Let U_h be the set of all the users ($100k$) selected for the social distance h. We calculated the probability that user u's h-hop contacts (with $u \in U_h$) will have the same deviance score as:

$$p_u = \frac{\#\text{ of } u\text{'s followers at distance } h \text{ with same deviance score}}{\#\text{ of } u\text{'s followers at distance } h} \qquad (5)$$

Rather than computing the exact similarity between a user and her follower's deviance scores, we focused on whether their difference is small enough to be dubbed as the same. We considered two users' deviance scores are the same if their corresponding deviance score difference is less than a "similarity delta". More specifically, u will have *about the same* deviance score with user s located at distance h if:

$$|deviance_u - deviance_s| < \delta \qquad (6)$$

The same technique was used for both types of deviance scores.We experimented with two values for δ equal to one or two standard deviations of the distribution of deviance scores in the network. We report the geometric average of all p_u probabilities computed in each hop h.

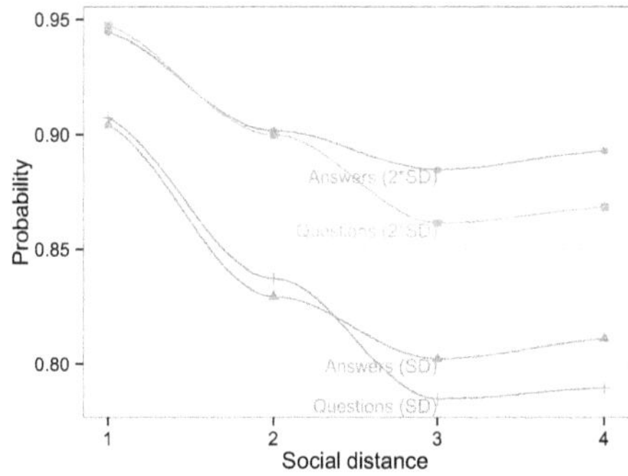

Figure 14: Probability that a h-hop follower has the same deviant score to the user for $\delta = \sigma$ and $\delta = 2\sigma$. SD: standard deviation.

Figure 14 shows the probability plots for both types of deviance, keeping similarity δ equal to one or two standard deviations. Although different values of the δ, the shapes of the figures are almost the same: up to 3-hops, the probability decreases gradually with the social distance.

7. SUSPENDED USER PREDICTION

Based on our previous analysis, we extract various types of features that we use to build predictive models. We formulate the prediction task as a classification problem with two classes of users: fair and suspended. Next, we describe the features used (Section 7.1) and the classifiers tested (Section 7.2), and demonstrate that we are able to automatically detect fair from suspended users on *YA* with an overall high accuracy (Section 7.3).

7.1 Features for Classification

Our predictive model has 29 features that are based on users' activities and engagements e.g., *social*, *activity*, *accomplishment*, *flag* and *deviance*. Table 4 shows the different categories of features used for the classification. *Social* features are based on the social network of the users, where *Activity* features are based on community contributions in the form of questions and answers. *Accomplishment* features acknowledge the quality of user contribution (e.g., points, best answers). *Flag* summarizes the flags of a user (both received and reported). *Deviance Score* features are the scores that we have computed based on users' flags and activities. Finally, *Deviance Homophily* represents the homophilous behavior with respect to deviance. Although most of the features are self-explanatory, below we clarify the ones which may not be.

Reciprocity. Reciprocity measures the tendency of a pair of nodes to form mutual connections between each other [12]. Reciprocity is defined as follows:

$$r = \frac{L}{L^*}$$

where L is number of edges pointing in both directions and L^* is the total number of edges. $r = 1$ holds for a network in which all links are bidirectional (purely bidirectional network), while a purely unidirectional network has $r = 0$.

Status. Defined as the ratio of the number of a user's followers to her followees.

Thumbs. The difference between the number of up-votes and the number of down-votes a user receives for all her answers.

Award Ratings. The sum of the ratings a user receives for her best answers.

Altruistic scores. The difference between a user's contribution and his takeaway from the community. For altruistic scores, we consider *YA*'s point system, which awards two points for an answer, 10 points for a best answer, and penalizes five points for a question:

$$\begin{aligned} \text{Altruistic scores}_u &= f(contribution) - f(takeaway) \\ &= 2.0 * A_u + 10.0 * BA_u - 5.0 * Q_u \end{aligned} \quad (7)$$

where Q_u is the number of questions posted by u, A_u is the number of answers posted by u, and BA_u is the number of best answers posted by u.

Table 4: Different categories of features used for fair vs. suspended user prediction. We create a reciprocated network from the reciprocated edges. CC: clustering coefficient.

Category	Number	Features
Social	6	Indegree Outdegree Status Reciprocity Reciprocated networks degree Reciprocated networks CC
Activity	4	#Questions #Answers #Flagged Questions #Flagged Answers
Accomplishment	5	Points #Best Answers Award Ratings Thumbs Altruistic scores
Flag	8	#Question Flag Received #Question Flag Received Valid #Question Flag Reported #Question Flag Reported Valid #Answer Flag Received #Answer Flag Received Valid #Answer Flag Reported #Answer Flag Reported Valid
Deviance Score	2	Question deviance score Answer deviance score
Deviance Homophily	4	Followers' question deviance score Followers' answer deviance score Followees' question deviance score Followees' answer deviance score

7.2 Experimental Setup and Classification

In our dataset, the percentage of fair users (about 91%) are high compared to the suspended users (about 9%). This leads to an unbalanced dataset. Various approaches have been proposed in the machine learning literature to deal with the problem of unbalanced datasets. We use the ROSE [18] algorithm to create a balanced dataset from the unbalanced one. ROSE creates balanced samples by random over-sampling minority examples, under-sampling majority examples or by combining over and under-sampling. Our prediction dataset has 250k users with 60-40% training–testing split. Using the under and over sampling technique of ROSE, we sample 150k users (fair and suspended each class has 75k users) to train the classifier. The testing set has 100k users, who are not present in the training dataset. They are drawn randomly and fair vs. suspended ratio in the testing dataset is the same as the original *YA* dataset.

We tested various classification algorithms, including Naive Bayes, K-Nearest Neighbors (KNN), Boosted Logistic Regression, and Stochastic Gradient Boosted Trees (SGBT). We use individual feature sets to investigate how successful each feature set is by itself, and then use all features for prediction. For evaluation, we measure widely used metrics in classification problems: Accuracy, Precision, Recall and F1-score. Table 5 shows a summary of our experimental setup.

Table 5: Details of experimental setup.

Dataset	250k sampled users
Class Balancing Alg.	Random Over-Sampling Examples (ROSE)
Classifiers	Stochastic Gradient Boosted Trees (SGBT) Naive Bayes, Boosted Logistic Regression K-Nearest Neighbors (KNN) Support Vector Machines RDF
Feature Sets	Social, Activity, Accomplishment Flag, Deviance Homophily, All features
Train-Test Split	150k users training, 100k users testing
Cross Validation	10-folds, repeated 10 times
Performance	Accuracy, precision, recall, F1 score

7.3 Classification Results and Evaluation

The performance results of various classifiers while using all features are shown in Table 6. The SGBT classifier outperforms other classifiers in all performance metrics. This classifier offers a prediction model in the form of an ensemble of weak prediction models [11]. In our setting, it achieves 82.61% accuracy in classifying fair vs. suspended users with a high precision (96.94) and recall (83.52). The confusion matrix of the classifier is shown in Table 7. The matrix shows that the SGBT classifier is able to correctly classify 83.52% of fair users and 73.39% of suspended users.

Table 6: Performance of various classifiers using all available features.

Classifier Name	Accuracy	Precision	Recall	F1 Score
Naive Bayes	47.21	96.93	43.34	59.89
Boosted Logistic Regression	71.61	96.62	71.28	82.03
KNN	73.81	96.41	73.97	83.71
SVM-RDF	75.92	95.62	77.06	85.34
SGBT	82.61	96.94	83.52	89.73

Table 7: Confusion matrix for the SGBT classifier.

		Actual	
		Fair	**Suspended**
Predicted	**Fair**	**83.52**%	26.60%
	Suspended	16.47%	**73.39**%

Figure 15 shows the performance (accuracy, precision, recall and F1 score) of the models trained with different subsets of features using the SGBT classifier, which performs the best among the tested classifiers. We observe that each feature set has a positive effect on the performance of the classifier across all performance metrics. This suggests that all our feature sets are important for prediction. Particularly, accomplishment, deviance, flags and activity features individually exhibit more than 70% accuracy with good precision, recall and F1 score. However, when all the features are used for classification, the performance metrics yield the best results, i.e., accuracy is improved by 4.11% compared to activity features.

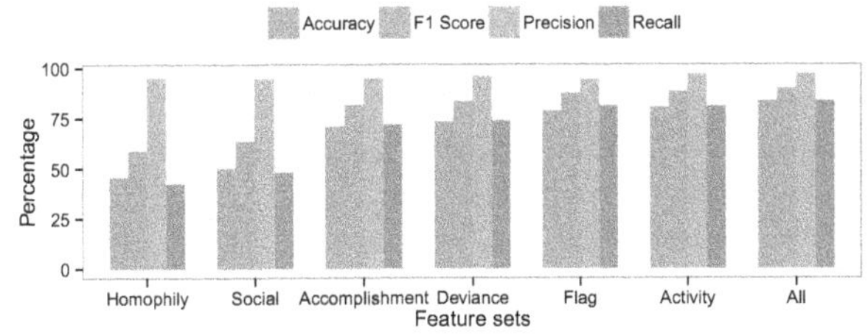

Figure 15: Performance of the SGBT while classifying fair and suspended users using different feature sets.

Figure 16 shows the most important features (top 15) in classification of fair vs. suspended users. The model uses a backwards elimination feature selection method for feature importance. For each feature, the model tracks the changes in the generalized cross-validation error and uses it as the variable importance measure.

We observe that the number of flagged content and deviance scores are the best predictors of fair and suspended users. Also, at least one feature from all feature sets is within the top 15 features. However, only activity and deviance score feature sets have all the features within the top 15 features.

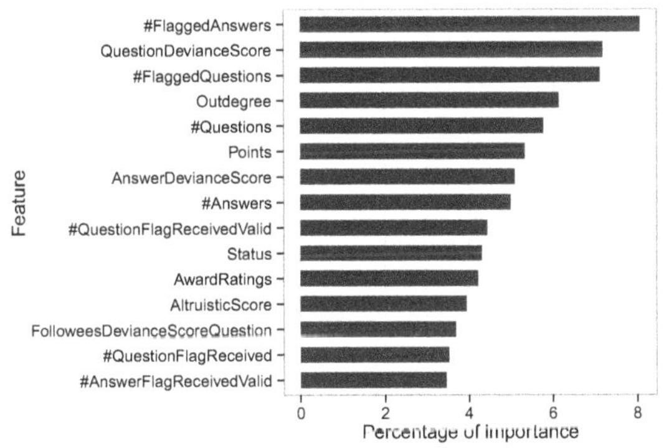

Figure 16: Relative importance (out of 100, how much a feature is contributing) of top 15 features in classifying fair and suspended users.

8. SUMMARY AND DISCUSSION

This paper is an investigation of the flagging of inappropriate content in Yahoo Answers, a popular and mature Community-based Question-Answering platform. Based on a sample of about 10 million flags in a population of about 1.5 million active users, our analysis revealed the following.

First, the use of flags is overwhelmingly correct, as shown by the large percentage of flags validated by human monitors. This is an important learning for crowd sourcing, as it shows for the first time (to the best of our knowledge) that crowdsourced monitoring of content functions well in CQA platforms. Moreover, although there are no explicit incentives (e.g., points) for flagging inappropriate content, users take the time to curate their environment. In fact, 46% of the users reported at least one abuse report, with the top abuse reporters flagging tens of thousands posts.

Second, we discovered that many users have collected a large number of flags, yet their presence is not deemed toxic to the community. Even more, their contributions are engaging, which is certainly a benefit to the platform: the questions asked by the users who deviate from the norm (in terms of number of flags received for their postings) receive many more answers and from many more users than the questions posted by ordinary users or by users who later had their accounts suspended. However, more content-based analysis is needed to understand how exactly the deviant users engage the community. We posit that they might ask conversational, rather than informative, questions, as this behavior is shown to increase community engagement.

Third, we showed the importance of the follower-followee social network for channeling attention and producing answers to questions. Less expected, perhaps, is the fact that this network also channels the attention of flaggers: we found that users in close social proximity are more likely to flag inappropriate content than distant users. Social neighborhoods, thus, tend to maintain their environment clean.

Fourth, a significant problem in *YA* is posed by the users who manage to avoid flagging, possibly by remaining at the outskirts of the social network. This relative isolation in terms of followers and in terms of interactions probably allows such users to remain invisible. They are likely caught by automatic spam-detection-like mechanisms and by paid human operators. However, our empirical investigation showed that classifiers that use activity- and social network-based features can successfully identify fair and suspended (40% of them are not flagged) users with accuracy as high as 83%.

This work leads to various promising directions for future work. Understanding what makes deviant users engaging can be helpful in designing strategies potentially applicable to a variety of communities. Quantifying the equivalent behavior in terms of content abuse reporting and in terms of bad users on different online platforms can help understand the relative importance of different features for the success of the platform. And finally, characterizing (e.g., activity and social network centrality) the pro-social users who report abusive content may help identify such potential volunteers and appropriately incentivize them.

9. ACKNOWLEDGMENTS

The work was funded by the National Science Foundation under the grant CNS 0952420, and by the Yahoo's Faculty Research and Engagement Program.

10. REFERENCES

[1] E. Agichtein, C. Castillo, D. Donato, A. Gionis, and G. Mishne. Finding high-quality content in social media. In *Proceedings of the International Conference on Web Search and Data Mining*, pages 183–194, 2008.

[2] Y. Answers. Yahoo answers community guidelines. `http://answers.yahoo.com/info/community_guidelines`, 2013.

[3] A.-L. Barabási and R. Albert. Emergence of scaling in random networks. *science*, 286(5439):509–512, 1999.

[4] J. Bian, Y. Liu, E. Agichtein, and H. Zha. Finding the right facts in the crowd: Factoid question answering over social media. In *Proceedings of the 17th International Conference on World Wide Web*, pages 467–476, 2008.

[5] J. Blackburn, R. Simha, N. Kourtellis, X. Zuo, M. Ripeanu, J. Skvoretz, and A. Iamnitchi. Branded with a Scarlet "C": Cheaters in a gaming social network. In *Proceedings of the 21st International Conference on World Wide Web*, pages 81–90, 2012.

[6] J. P. Davis. The experience of 'bad' behavior in online social spaces: A survey of online users. *Social Computing Group, Microsoft Research*, 2002.

[7] D. Dearman and K. N. Truong. Why users of Yahoo! Answers do not answer questions. In *Proceedings of the SIGCHI Conference on Human Factors in Computing Systems*, pages 329–332, 2010.

[8] J. D. Douglas and F. C. Waksler. *The sociology of deviance: An introduction.* Little, Brown Boston, MA, 1982.

[9] G. Dror, Y. Maarek, and I. Szpektor. Will my question be answered? predicting "question answerability" in community question-answering sites. In *The European Conference on Machine Learning and Principles and Practice of Knowledge Discovery in Databases*, pages 499–514. Springer, 2013.

[10] P. D. Dunlop and K. Lee. Workplace deviance, organizational citizenship behavior, and business unit performance: The bad apples do spoil the whole barrel. *Journal of Organizational Behavior*, 25(1):67–80, 2004.

[11] J. H. Friedman. Stochastic gradient boosting. *Computational Statistics & Data Analysis*, 38(4):367–378, 2002.

[12] D. Garlaschelli and M. I. Loffredo. Patterns of link reciprocity in directed networks. *Physical Review Letters*, 93(26):268701, 2004.

[13] F. M. Harper, D. Moy, and J. A. Konstan. Facts or friends?: distinguishing informational and conversational questions in social Q&A sites. In *Proceedings of the SIGCHI Conference on Human Factors in Computing Systems*, pages 759–768. ACM, 2009.

[14] B. Li, T. Jin, M. R. Lyu, I. King, and B. Mak. Analyzing and predicting question quality in community question answering services. In *Proceedings of the 21st International Conference Companion on World Wide Web*, pages 775–782, 2012.

[15] Q. Liu, E. Agichtein, G. Dror, Y. Maarek, and I. Szpektor. When web search fails, searchers become askers: Understanding the transition. In *Proceedings of the 35th International ACM Conference on Research and Development in Information Retrieval*, pages 801–810, 2012.

[16] L. Mamykina, B. Manoim, M. Mittal, G. Hripcsak, and B. Hartmann. Design lessons from the fastest Q&A site in the west. In *Proceedings of the SIGCHI Conference on Human Factors in Computing Systems*, pages 2857–2866, 2011.

[17] M. McPherson, L. Smith-Lovin, and J. M. Cook. Birds of a feather: Homophily in social networks. *Annual review of sociology*, pages 415–444, 2001.

[18] G. Menardi and N. Torelli. Training and assessing classification rules with imbalanced data. *Data Mining and Knowledge Discovery*, 28(1):92–122, 2014.

[19] M. E. Newman. Mixing patterns in networks. *Physical Review E*, 67(2):026126, 2003.

[20] M. E. J. Newman. *Networks: An Introduction.* Oxford University Press, 2010.

[21] K. Panovich, R. Miller, and D. Karger. Tie strength in question & answer on social network sites. In *Proceedings of the Conference on Computer Supported Cooperative Work*, CSCW, pages 1057–1066, New York, NY, USA, 2012. ACM.

[22] D. J. Phillips. Defending the boundaries: Identifying and countering threats in a usenet newsgroup. *The information society*, 12(1):39–62, 1996.

[23] M. Qu, G. Qiu, X. He, C. Zhang, H. Wu, J. Bu, and C. Chen. Probabilistic question recommendation for question answering communities. In *Proceedings of the 18th International Conference on World Wide Web*, pages 1229–1230, 2009.

[24] M. Richardson and R. W. White. Supporting synchronous social Q&A throughout the question lifecycle. In *Proceedings of the 20th International Conference on World Wide Web*, pages 755–764, 2011.

[25] C. Shah and J. Pomerantz. Evaluating and predicting answer quality in community qa. In *Proceedings of the 33rd International Conference on Research and Development in Information Retrieval*, pages 411–418, 2010.

[26] A. Shtok, G. Dror, Y. Maarek, and I. Szpektor. Learning from the past: Answering new questions with past answers. In *Proceedings of the 21st International Conference on World Wide Web*, pages 759–768, 2012.

[27] J. R. Suler and W. L. Phillips. The bad boys of cyberspace: Deviant behavior in a multimedia chat community. *CyberPsychology & Behavior*, 1(3):275–294, 1998.

[28] K. Sun, Y. Cao, X. Song, Y.-I. Song, X. Wang, and C.-Y. Lin. Learning to recommend questions based on user ratings. In *Proceedings of the 18th ACM Conference on Information and Knowledge Management*, pages 751–758, 2009.

[29] I. Szpektor, Y. Maarek, and D. Pelleg. When relevance is not enough: Promoting diversity and freshness in personalized question recommendation. In *Proceedings of the 22nd International Conference on World Wide Web*, pages 1249–1260, 2013.

[30] G. Wang, K. Gill, M. Mohanlal, H. Zheng, and B. Y. Zhao. Wisdom in the social crowd: An analysis of quora. In *Proceedings of the 22Nd International Conference on World Wide Web*, 2013.

[31] I. Weber, A. Ukkonen, and A. Gionis. Answers, not links: Extracting tips from Yahoo! Answers to address how-to web queries. In *Proceedings of the Fifth ACM International Conference on Web Search and Data Mining*, pages 613–622, 2012.

[32] J. M. Wellen and M. Neale. Deviance, self-typicality, and group cohesion the corrosive effects of the bad apples on the barrel. *Small Group Research*, 37(2):165–186, 2006.

The Lifecycles of Apps in a Social Ecosystem

Isabel Kloumann
Cornell University
Ithaca, NY
imk36@cornell.edu

Lada Adamic
Facebook Inc.
Menlo Park, CA
ladamic@fb.com

Jon Kleinberg
Cornell University
Ithaca, NY
kleinber@cs.cornell.edu

Shaomei Wu
Facebook Inc.
Menlo Park, CA
shaomei@fb.com

ABSTRACT

Apps are emerging as an important form of on-line content, and they combine aspects of Web usage in interesting ways — they exhibit a rich temporal structure of user adoption and long-term engagement, and they exist in a broader social ecosystem that helps drive these patterns of adoption and engagement. It has been difficult, however, to study apps in their natural setting since this requires a simultaneous analysis of a large set of popular apps and the underlying social network they inhabit.

In this work we address this challenge through an analysis of the collection of apps on Facebook Login, developing a novel framework for analyzing both temporal and social properties. At the temporal level, we develop a retention model that represents a user's tendency to return to an app using a very small parameter set. At the social level, we organize the space of apps along two fundamental axes — *popularity* and *sociality* — and we show how a user's probability of adopting an app depends both on properties of the local network structure and on the match between the user's attributes, his or her friends' attributes, and the dominant attributes within the app's user population. We also devolop models that show the importance of different feature sets with strong performance in predicting app success.

Categories and Subject Descriptors: H.2.8 [**Database Management**]: Database applications—*Data mining*
Keywords:apps; diffusion; social networks

1. INTRODUCTION

There is, or is likely soon to be, a webservice or app for virtually every component of modern life. They are diverse and ubiquitous; they constitute both a backdrop and chronicle of everyday experience. And they represent a broad change in overall patterns of Internet use — both the research community and the media have increasingly begun discussing the "appification of the Web" [1]. Yet empirical opportunities to consider them as a complete ecosystem have been limited, and as a result we still know very little about the population structure of apps — their inherent diversity, their lifecycles, and the ways in which users engage with them.

The high-level characteristics of app engagement as a form of Web use are still the subject of much discussion and refinement, but certain properties emerge independent of any one particular app's functionality — these include *temporal* properties, based on long-running patterns of individual usage and engagement over time, and *social properties*, in which an individual will typically be a user of many apps with overlapping functionality, in a broader social environment that is bootstrapped to create within-app social activity.

To address these issues, we study the collection of apps on Facebook Login, making use of anonymized aggregate daily usage logs of the apps and web services accessible through this mechanism. We undertake our analysis on two levels of scale — the individual level, focusing on the properties of user behavior over time and in relation to other users; and the app level, modeling the overall usage level of the app and the social structure on its users.

At the temporal level, we develop a user retention model, showing how with a small number of parameters we can approximate the probability that a user who adopts an app at time t will continue to be using it at a future time $t + \Delta$. The model exposes the ways in which usage decay has a time-dependent component, and provides us with a compact set of parameters representing a particular app's engagement profile that can then be used in higher-level tasks. When we consider the app's user population as a whole, we are led to natural lifecycle modeling and prediction questions — given an app's history up to a given point in time, how well can we predict its number of users going forward? Interesting recent work of Ribeiro [17] considered this question using time-series data for several large Web sites; we show how a broad range of feature categories — including our derived retention parameters, together with individual characteristics of the app's users and the social network structure on its full user population — can lead to strong prediction results across a wide diversity of apps.

At the level of app social structure, we show how the space of all the popular apps on Facebook Login can be organized in a two-dimensional representation whose axes correspond to *popularity* — the raw number of users — and *sociality* — the extent to which users of the app have friends who are also users of the app. This representation exposes certain global organizing principles in the full app population, including a pair of complementary "frontiers" to the space — one containing apps whose sociality is relatively fixed independent of their popularity, and one in which the sociality of the app's user population is not much greater than that of a random set of Facebook users of comparable size.

Finally, we perform an analysis of social characteristics at the individual user level, analyzing the Facebook users who are one step away from an app in the social network — a set we can think of

[1]`https://sites.google.com/site/appweb2012/`

WWW 2015, May 18–22, 2015, Florence, Italy.
ACM 978-1-4503-3469-3/15/05.
http://dx.doi.org/10.1145/2736277.2741684.

as the "periphery" of the app, containing people who are not yet users of the app, but have friends who are users. For a person in an app's periphery, we can attempt to predict future adoption of the app based on individual characteristics and network structure. We find that apps are diverse in the way in which the structure on a user's friends is related to adoption probabilities, and we find an interesting effect in the interactions among individual characteristics: a user's probability of adopting an app depends on the three-way relationship among their own attributes, the attributes of their friends who use the app, and the modal attributes of the full population of app users.

2. DATA

The data for this study comes from anonymized logs of Facebook Login daily activity, collected between January 2009 and June 2014. Facebook Login is a secure way for Facebook users to sign into their apps without having to create separate logins.

The various analyses in this paper required different slices of these logs, both considering the observation window and the apps being observed. Table 1 summarizes the different subsampled data sets that will be referred to throughout this work. The data for this study has granularity of one day; that is, we have logs about whether an individual uses a specific app on each day. All user level data is de-identified.

tag	selection criteria	time period	size
APPS_{RAND}	random $\propto$ DAU(2014-06)	Jan. 2014 - Jun. 2014	83,000 apps
APPS_{POP}	most popular by MAU(2013-06)	Jan. 2009 - Jun. 2014	2,319 apps 1.4×10^9 users

Table 1: Summary of data sets considered in this paper. DAU and MAU refer to Facebook Daily Active Users and Monthly Active Users, respectively. Our initial overview analyses consider APPS_{RAND}, while our subsequent and in-depth analyses consider APPS_{POP} and, as occasion permits, various subsets of it ($\text{APPS}_{POP\{X\}}$). Unless otherwise noted, subsampling in this work is done on apps, not on users.

The frequency with which the Facebook Login service is called, and hence daily activity is registered, depends on several factors. Web-based activity relies on authentication tokens that expire on the order of hours, while mobile apps can optionally request tokens that are valid for days, provided the user does not change their password. For some apps, we do see a periodic activity, typically 7 days apart, consistent with longer-term authentication tokens being refreshed. This periodicity is a small effect relative to the overall activity, as we show below. This is likely because other activity, such as posting updates or retrieving public profiles or friend lists, again requires reconnecting. Therefore, Facebook Login provides a reasonable proxy of daily use of the app. It allows us to characterize the app's adoption and retention.

3. SOCIAL PROPERTIES OF APPS

3.1 Popularity and sociality

One question that has been raised previously is how big of a role the social network plays in the adoption of apps. This parameter has been inferred indirectly by Onnela and Reed-Tsochas [15] in their study of the very early adoption of Facebook apps. It is also estimated in the model proposed by Ribeiro [18], where individuals can drive their friends' adoption and re-engagement.

However, these prior studies did not directly measure whether app adoption was in fact correlated on the network, and so we turn to this task presently. In particular, we would like to place apps in a low-dimensional space that can provide a view for how they are distributed across the social network of users.

To do this, we begin with two basic definitions

- We say that the *popularity* of an app, denoted $p(x)$, is the probability that an individual selected uniformly at random from Facebook's population is a user of the app.
- We say that the *sociality* of the app, denoted $p(x|y)$, is the probability that a member of Facebook is a user of the app given that they have at least one friend using the app.

Studying the distributions of $p(x)$ and $p(x|y)$, and how they are jointly distributed across apps, allows us to ask a number of questions. In particular, how socially clustered is the app? And how does it depend on the type of app, or characteristics of the app's users?

Note that if $p(x|y)$ is very high for an app, it means that its user population in a sense "conforms" to the structure of the underlying social network.

Moreover, $p(x|y)$ can in principle be high even when $p(x)$ is low — this would correspond to an app that is popular in a focused set of friendship circles, but not on Facebook more broadly. On the other hand, if $p(x|y)$ is not much more than $p(x)$, then it says that users of the app are spread out through the social network almost as though each member of Facebook independently flipped a coin of bias $p(x)$ in order to decide whether to become a user of the app — there would be no effect of the social network at all.

Plotting apps in popularity-sociality space

An appealing feature of this pair of parameters is that it provides a natural two-dimensional view of the space of all popular apps on Facebook. We show this view in Figure 1 — a heat map showing the density of apps at each possible (discretized) pair of values $(p(x), p(x|y))$.

We see in Figure 1 that the apps fill out a wedge-shaped region in the $p(x)$-$p(x|y)$ plane, and it is informative to understand what the boundaries of the region correspond to. First, note that if the social network had no relationship to app usage, we would see the diagonally sloping line $p(x) = p(x|y)$; in the plot this corresponds to a line that lies slightly below the diagonal lower boundary of the points in the heat map. Thus, there exists a frontier in the space of apps that is almost completely asocial — those apps that lie parallel to this diagonal line — but essentially no apps actually reach the line; even the most asocial apps exhibit some social clustering. We see this in the approximately horizontal top boundary of the points in the heat map — this is a frontier in the space of apps where knowing that a person x has a friend using the app gives you a fixed probability that x uses it, independent of the app's overall popularity on Facebook. The location of this horizontal line is interesting, since it provides an essential popularity-independent value for the maximal extent of social clustering that we see on Facebook.

Note that the wedge-shaped region in a sense has to come to a point on the right-hand side, as $p(x)$ becomes very large: once an app is extremely popular, there is no way to avoid having pairs of friends using it almost by sheer force of numbers. And given the crowding of app users into the network, there is also no way for the extent of social clustering to become significantly larger than one would see by chance.

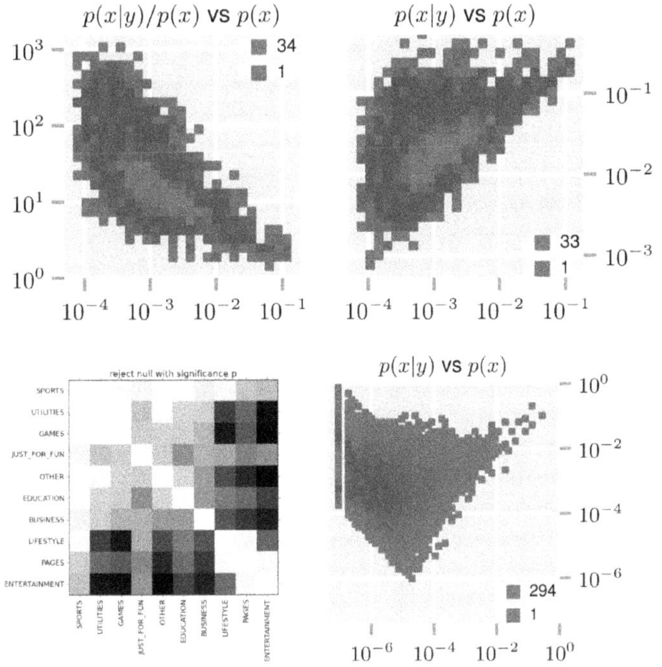

Figure 1: App sociality. Top left: Horizontal axis is app popularity, and vertical axis is the relative increase in adoption likelihood for people who have friends who also use the app. Right panels: Horizontal axis is app popularity, vertical axis is app sociality. The colors represent the number of apps falling within the given bin. The lower right panel uses APPS$_{RAND}$, while the other three panels use APPS$_{POP}$ (see Table 1 for details). The labeled colors indicate the relative frequencies of observations in each bin, such that the lowest values have been normalized to 1. Bottom left: Matrix indicating the p-values for the two sided Kolmogorov-Smirnov test comparing the distributions $p(x|y)/p(x)$ for apps within each pair of the nine listed categories. White indicates a lower p-value and black indicates a higher one.

The third, lower left boundary of the wedge is a manifestation of the Facebook friend limit of 5000: if a user is friends with someone who uses the app, at least 1/5000 of their friends use it. We approach this limit in the far left hand of this Figure with apps that have two users, one with 0 other friends using the app and the other with 1 of their nearly 5000, combining to approach the lower limit of $1/(2 * 5000)$. The lower bound decreases as $1/(n * 5000)$ as the number of users, n, increases.

3.2 Analysis of Social Neighborhoods

We saw in the previous section that app adoption can be localized in the social network. But what is the mechanism by which the app is adopted by friends? Is homophily driving both friendships and adoption of specific apps based on interests? Or is the primary mechanism one of exposure, where having even just a single friend who has installed the app now gives an opportunity to become familiar with the app and subsequently adopt it?

To answer these questions, we observe the Facebook friendship graph at time t. For each app, we consider everyone on Facebook who has friends using the app, but who has not used the app themselves by t. Are there features of the individual and their friends that will predict whether the individual will adopt the app at some point in the future?

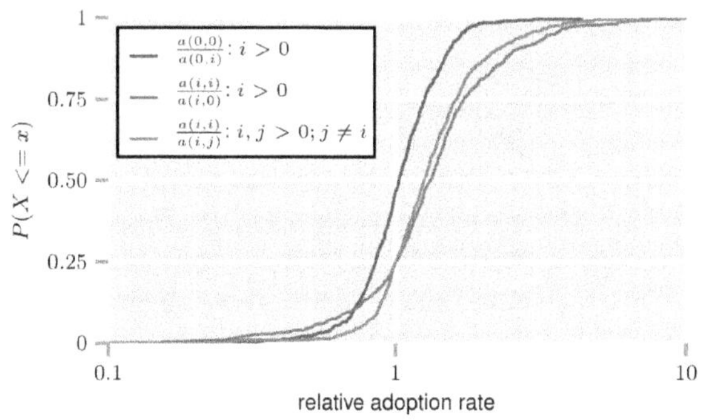

Figure 2: Relationship between national identity of potential app adopters, that of their current user friends, and the likelihood of their adopting the app. Blue: Relative adoption rates when a potential user and their current user friend are from the majority to when potential user is in majority and current user friend is in minority. Green: Relative rates when potential user and current user friend are in same minority to when potential user is in minority and current user friend is in majority. Red: Relative rates for when potential user and current user friend are in same minority to when they are in different minorities. The blue curve indicates that when a potential user is from the majority country, their current user friend could be from either the majority or a minority and they are still equally likely to adopt an app more often as less. In contrast, when the potential user is from a minority country, in 75% of apps they adopt more frequently when their current user friend is from the same country as them.

One-node neighborhoods

We begin with a question about homophily and its relation to app usage. Consider a Facebook user A who does not currently use the app, and suppose that has exactly one friend B who uses the app (that is, A has between 1 and 5000 friends on Facebook, but for our purposes here, exactly one of those friends is an app user). We choose some attribute on users (for example nationality, or age); we let $f(A)$ and $f(B)$ denote the value of this attribute for A and B, and we let f^* denote the modal (or median) value of the attribute across all app users.

Now the following question arises. Suppose that A is different from the typical user in this attribute, in the sense that $f(A) \neq f^*$. Is A more likely to adopt the app if the friend B is similar to A, or if B is similar to the typical app user? This is a basic question about the role of individual similarity in adoption decisions — if we're studying potential users who are outside the target demographic, is it more effective for their app-using friends to be similar to them, or similar to the target demographic?

We study this for nationality as an attribute in Figure 2 — given an app, we index nationalities so that the most common nationality among users of the app is labeled 0, and other nationalities are labeled by values $i > 0$. We now say that $a(i, j)$ is the adoption probability of a user A who has one friend B using the app, with $f(A) = i$ and $f(B) = j$. (Note that $f^* = 0$ according to our notation, since 0 is the most prevalent nationality in the app.) The figure shows that for a considerable majority of apps, we have

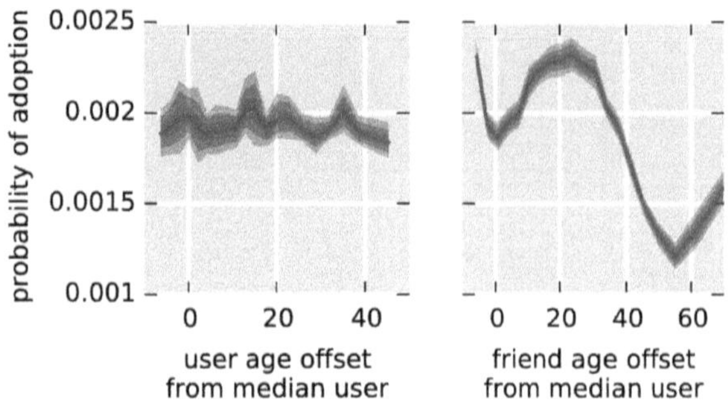

Figure 3: The probability that a user adopts the app given that they have one friend using the app. as a function of (left) the friend's age offset from the median and (right) the user's age offset from the median. The left plot indicates no apparent relationship between the age of the friend and that the user adopts. In contrast, the right plot illustrates that young users and users who are aged between 10 and 30 years above the median age are more likely to adopt. Users who are more than 40 years older than the median age are less likely to adopt. The probabilities were binned by age into 20 equally populated bins and the reported adoption probabilities are bootstrap estimates. The thick central line is the median bootstrap estimate of the mean, while the three outer bands indicate the 68%, 95%, and 99.7% confidence-intervals.

$a(i,i)/a(i,0) > 1$, indicating a clear aggregate tendency for the question in the previous paragraph: a user A is more likely to adopt the app in general when A's one friend using the app is similar to A, not to the typical app user. In contrast, when $f(A) = f^*$, the ratio $a(0,0)/a(0,i)$ is balanced around 1, so there is no clear tendency in adoption probabilities between the case $f(B) = f^*$ and $f(B) \neq f^*$: for users who have the modal attribute value, the attribute value of their friend does not have a comparably strong effect.

This style of question gives us a way of analyzing individual attributes in general, and we find that attributes differ in the way this effect manifests itself. For example, when we consider age as an attribute (in place of nationality), we see (Figure 3) that if A has a friend B using the app, the age of B has very little correlation with A's probability of adopting. However, the age of A is related to the adoption probability — users A who are much older or younger from the median age are relatively more likely to adopt the app if they have a friend who uses the app, compared to individuals who are near the median age themselves.

Two- and three-node neighborhoods

We can also use the population of apps, and the adoption decisions that people make about them, to address a recurring recent question in the literature on on-line diffusion. Given an individual A who is not currently using an app, but who has k friends $B_1, B_2, \ldots, B_k$ using it, how does A's adoption probability depend on the pattern of connections among these k friends? Is A more likely to adopt if there are many links among these friends, or very few?

Past work has suggested that the answer can depend on the adoption decision being studied. Consider the results observed by Backstrom et al. [1] with LiveJournal data, where conversion probability increases with the connectedness of one's friends, and contrast them with those observed by Ugander et al. [23] with Facebook e-mail invitations, where, for a fixed neighborhood size, one's probability of conversion strictly increased with the number of independent components. In both cases the result is non-obvious, as there is no a priori mathematical reason that the effect should be monotone with connectedness of one's neighbors.

Given the diverse answers arising in prior work, and the consequent suggestion that the result depends on the adoption decision, we consider how adoption probabilities vary with neighbor connectivity across a large sample of the most popular apps.

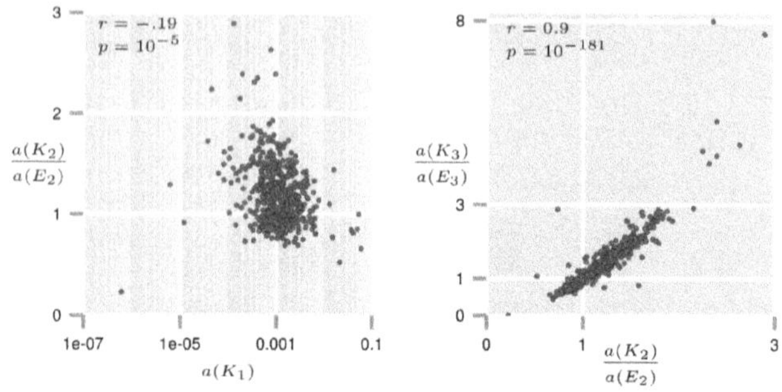

Figure 4: Right: the baseline rate of adoption given that a user has two friends using (horizontal) and the ratio of probability of adoption given friends are connected to probability given that friends are not connected (vertical). Apps above the line $y = 1$ exhibit the same trend as LiveJournal adoptions, and those below follow the trend observed in Facebook adoptions. Left: Closed to open conversion ratio for two-node neighborhoods (horizontal) and three node neighborhoods (vertical). Apps in the upper right quadrant follow the LiveJournal trend for two- and three-node neighborhoods, while apps in the lower left follow the Facebook trend. The correlation between these rates is 0.98 with $p << 0.01$, and there is a stark deficiency of apps in the diagonal quadrants.

We begin by considering the question just for two-node user neighborhoods, asking it separately for six hundred apps from APPS$_{POP}$: given that a non-user A has exactly two friends using the app at time t, how does A's adoption probability depend on the presence or absence of an edge between A's two friends? Note again that these users may have any number of Facebook friends between 2 and 5000, but that only two of those friends can be app users. We explore this question in Figure 4. We find that both possibilities — higher or lower adoption probability with the presence of an edge — occur in roughly comparable proportions across the population of apps, suggesting that at the level of two nodes, both possibilities are indeed prevalent.

As often happens in the analysis of phenomena on small social subgraphs, we begin to see some rich structure emerge in the question when we move to three-node neighborhoods. For a graph G, we let $a(G)$ denote the adoption probability of user A when A's neighbors induce the graph G, and note that on three nodes there are four possible graphs: the complete graph K_3, the three-node path P_3, the single-edge graph $P_2 \cup E_1$, and the empty graph E_3.

We find (Figure 4) that the ratio $a(K_3)/a(E_3)$ covaries closely with $a(K_2)/a(E_2)$ across the set of apps — in other words, when the adoption probability of an app is higher for a connected pair of friends, it is also higher for a connected triplet of friends. This indicates how properties of two-node neighborhoods provide strong information about the properties of larger neighborhoods — and it is an empirical regularity of the adoption decisions rather than a strictly mathematical one, since the property for three nodes does not follow from the property on two nodes. We find similar regu-

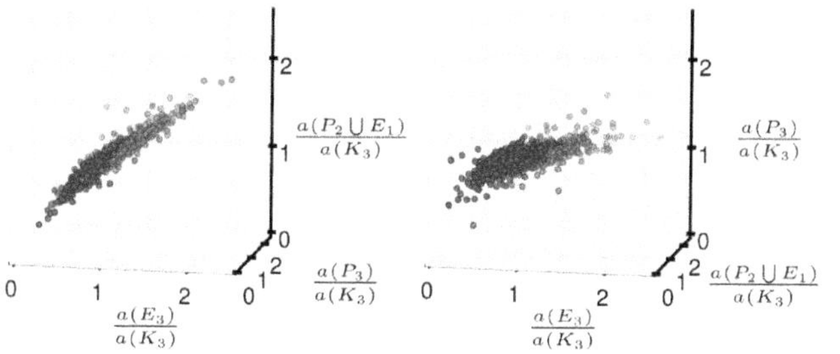

Figure 5: Two views of the same 3D point cloud: apps positioned according to the ratios $a(E_3)/a(K_3)$, $a(P_2 \bigcup K_1)/a(K_3)$, and $a(P_3)/a(K_3)$, and colored such that blue apps have $a(K_2)/a(E_2) \geq 1$, and red have $a(K_2)/a(E_2) < 1$. All adoption rates are reported relative to the rates for when a friend's user friends are a clique. Red apps have higher adoption rates with lower connectivity in the two-node graphs, and we see a near perfect correspondence in this trend for each possible combination of connectivity in three node graphs; this is demonstrated by the blue and red points falling naturally on either side of 1 in all three dimensions. In the left hand view the vertical extent of the cloud demonstrates the natural variation in relative adoption rates when a friend's user friends form two components (y-axis) compared to three (x-axis). In contrast, in the right hand view of this point cloud we observe more limited variation in relative adoption rates when the user friends are connected in one component. These differences are reflected in the Pearson correlation coefficients of 0.94 between $a(E_3)/a(K_3)$ and $a(P_2 \bigcup K_1)/a(K_3)$, and 0.57 between $a(E_3)/a(K_3)$ and $a(P_3)/a(K_3)$ ($p < 10^{-10}$ in both cases).

larities in the fact (Figure 5) that when adoption probabilities are higher for $a(E_3)$ relative to $a(K_3)$, they are also higher for the next-sparsest graph $a(P_2 \cup E_1)$. And we see comparatively much less variation between $a(P_3)$ and $a(K_3)$, which is consistent in interesting ways with the finding of Ugander et al. [23] that neighborhood topologies inducing the same number of connected components tended to lead to similar adoption probabilities.

4. TEMPORAL PATTERNS IN APPS

In addition to learning how the adoption of apps depends on friendship ties, we'd like to characterize the app's ability to retain those users who have adopted. These temporal features of an app's evolution hold some of the keys to its success.

To get a sense for what the retention of users looks like at a global level, we show the evolution of usage for a sample of apps in Figure 6. The images in this figure are heat maps in which the cell in the (i, j) entry records the density of users who first used the app at time i and last used it at time j. These maps thus show periods of heavy recruitment as horizontal bands — days when many individuals first started using the app. While there are a few vertical bands, denoting a narrow period of time when many users were last active, there is a clear concentration along the diagonal of many users departing soon after their first login, while some, located off-diagonal, remain active much longer. There are also sudden increases and decreases in density, as apps became more or less popular. With this type of global view of the diversity in usage and retention patterns, we next turn to modeling these retention patterns; our goal is to extract parameters from such a model to use as features in predicting an app's future engagement.

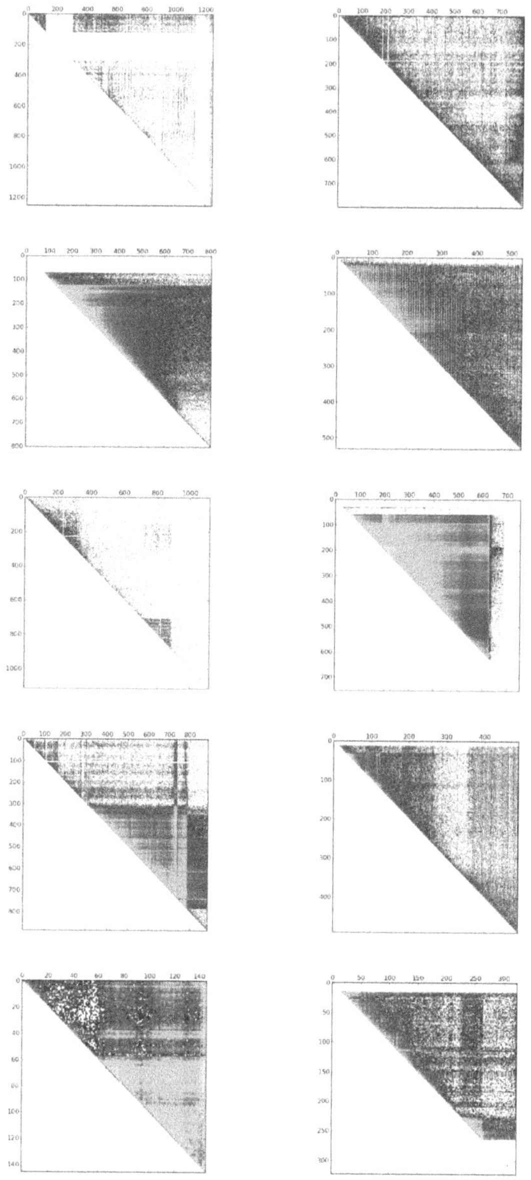

Figure 6: App adoption and departure dynamics. Heat maps of aggregate first and last login times for users of several examplar apps. The y-axis corresponds to the date of the first login and the x-axis to the last. The concentration is from blue (few) to yellow (many). Bright yellow and green horizontal or vertical bands correspond to periods of rapid adoption and departure, respectively. The color scale increases in density from white to blue, then yellow, then red.

4.1 Retention model

For an app to have long term success we expect that it needs to maintain a relatively high level of user retention. We would like to have a model of retention that characterizes not only whether an individual will log into the app the very next day, but for any day subsequent to their first login.

Past work on retention modeling (e.g. [8, 11, 29]) has been focused on a particular product/activity (mostly online games), trying to predict users' continous engagement with a wide selection

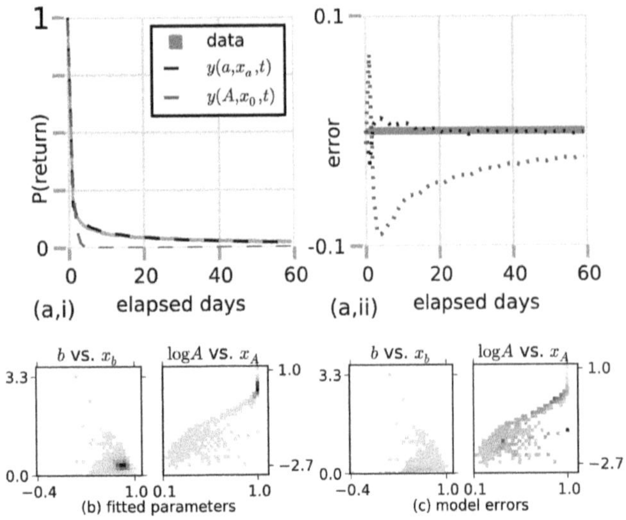

Figure 7: Empirical retention data, model predictions, and parameters. (a,i): Retention data and model predictions for an exemplar app. Error bars on the data (red solid curve) representing 99.999% confidence intervals ($4.4172\sqrt{p(1-p)/n}$). (a,ii): Error corresponding to fit shown in (a,i). (b): Distribution of fitted retention model parameters for the apps in APPS$_{POP}$. The shade represents the frequency of fitted parameter values falling into the given bin (darker being more frequent). (c): Mean error achieved by the model for apps with fitted parameters in the corresponding bin range. The same linear shade scale is used for both panels, with the lightest gray being 10^{-5} and black being 3 (white corresponds to no data). b and x_b denote the parameters in the time dependent model, and A and x_A those in the time indepdendent version.

of features, many of them are domain-spefic and computationally expensive. To study thousands of apps and billions of users, we want to propose a model that is easy to compute and highly generalizable.

Simplest model: exponential decay

We start with the population of newly installed users, $n(0)$, and assume that at every time step each user has a constant probability of leaving, x_0. This mechanism gives rise to exponential decay:

$$\frac{dn(t)}{dt} = -x_0 n(t) \rightarrow n(t) = n(0)\exp(-x_0 t), \qquad (1)$$

where $n(t)$ is the number of app users at time t. It turns out that this model does not yield a good fit to the data. However, the fit improves if we introduce a second parameter to the model by fitting from the second day; that is, we fit both for the decay rate, x_0, and the fraction of users that returned on day 2. With this relaxation from fitting day 1, the model becomes

$$n(t) = An(0)\exp(-x_0 t). \qquad (2)$$

It is interesting that the exponential decay model fits the day 2 and onward trend well while not fitting day 1: it is reasonable to expect that there is a discontinuous transition in the probability of returning given an install versus an install and a return the following day. Day 1 users are dominated by those who use the app exactly once, whereas all the other days contain a signal from users who exhibited at least some level of continued interest in the app. Despite its ability to capture this distinction, this model is unsatisfactory: it entirely ignores the day 1 users, and even in the two-parameter version it under-predicts retention at long times (Figure 7).

Introducing simple time dependence

Instead of assuming that people have a constant probability of leaving at every time step, let us assume that their probability is a simple function of time:

$$\frac{dn(t)}{dt} = -\frac{x_a}{t^a} n(t) \rightarrow n(t) = n(0)\exp\left(-\frac{x_a t^{1-a}}{1-a}\right). \qquad (3)$$

This model allows for the possibility that their likelihood of returning to the app could have a time dependent component, and it introduces this time dependence with the addition of only one parameter. Notice that by setting $a = 0$ we recover the traditional exponential decay model.

The parameters in this model have an interesting interpretation. Smaller values of a indicate that the app users have more momentum, that is, the app has more sticking power. The parameter x_a is still related to the familiar probability of depature: small x_a indicates that users are more likely to continue using the app.

4.2 Temporal analysis

After studying the temporal dynamics of individual apps through our retention model, we now look for regularities in the temporal patterns across multiple apps. We start this analysis by taking a random sample of all apps, and clustering their time series of daily active users using a k-means algorithm. All the time series are normalized by the number of active users on the app's peak day.

By varying k, we can get different sets of temporal clusters (see Figure 8). The two clusters generated for $k = 2$ already capture two dominant temporal trajectories of apps: one exhibits a clear rise and fall, while the other exhibits a slow but more sustainable rise. Note that the slow rise shown in the second cluster here may be misleading: as these apps keep growing and we normalize the time series by total volume, apps with a bigger user base will appear to have fewer fluctuations and slow growth/drop. When k increases, other small temporal clusters emerge, but they are not significantly different from the two typical ones.

Then, for all apps that existed on June 1 2013, we compute their monthly active users (MAU) on that day and one year out. We plot

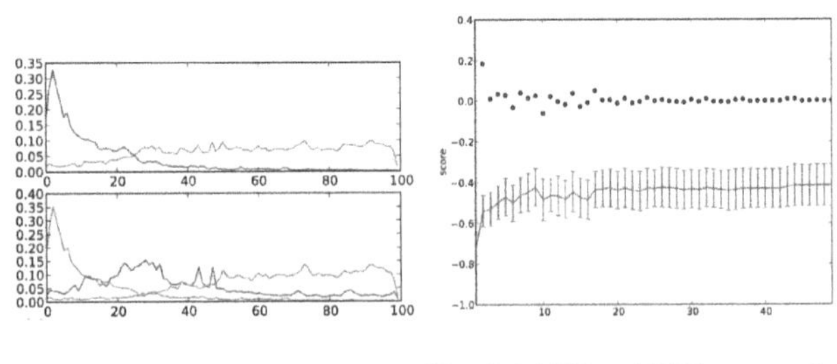

Figure 8: Left: k-means centroids of DAU for APPS$_{RAND}$, for $k = 2$ and $k = 3$. The clustering was done on the peak normalized time series of a 100-day observation window. Right: K-means scores (mean of distances from nearest centroid) for various values of k. Error bars represent 95% confidence intervals. Scatter plot is derivative of scores. Notice that no statistically significant improvement is gained for $k > 2$; that is, for all $k > 2$ the score of the resulting clustering is statistically significant different from that for $k = 2$. The scores were evaluated using a 75-25 train-test split, the clusters were generated with 100 restarts, and $L2$ was used as the distance metric.

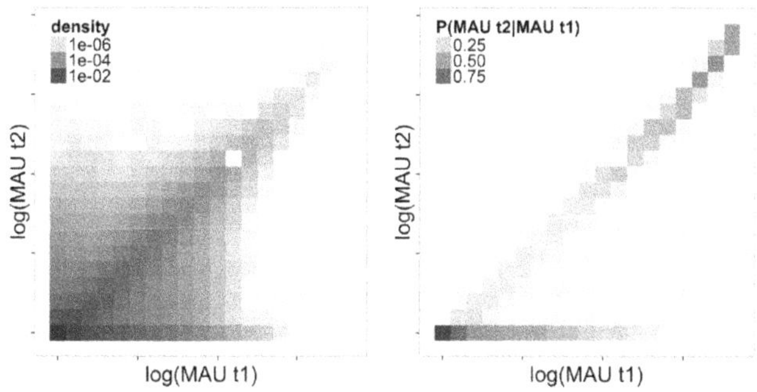

Figure 9: MAU of all apps in June 2013 (horizontal) and June 2014 (vertical). Left: Number of apps with MAU@t_1 and MAU@t_2 corresponding to the specified bins. Right: P(MAU@t_2| MAU@t_1) is the empirical probability of an app having y users at t_2 given that it had x users at t_1. At t_2 we observe that apps tend to either continue at the same level of popularity as they experienced at t_1 (bright diagonal) or exhibit a dramatic decrease in popularity (bright band on horizontal axis). Apps that are more populare have greater rates of continued success. However, when their popularity drops, the collapse tends to be complete.

those distributions against each other in Figure 9, where the color indicates the number of apps with the stated pairing of MAUs. The right-hand figure normalizes the columns, so that each bin column can be interpreted as the probability of ending up at the indicated MAU, given the current position. We can see that apps are most likely to stay at approximately the same MAU, but that, especially for very popular apps, there is a subpopulation that loses almost all of their users. This pattern suggests a natural underlying binary prediction problem: given that an app enjoys current success will it continue to be as popular one year later?

5. PREDICTING APP SUCCESS

In the previous sections we have seen that apps can be described in a variety of ways. We began by exploring the relationship between an individual's social network and their likelihood of adopting an app, and in general how app usage is clustered in the social network. We also related a user's likelihood of adopting an app to their individual characteristics relative to those of the current app's users. Next we observed that, though overall patterns of adoption can be quite complex, an app's retention properties are well described by a simple model with a small set of parameters. And finally we again saw that while the fine grained activity level for any app is complicated, in the long term apps tend to either continue at the same activity level or diminish in popularity.

In each analysis we considered either hundreds or thousands of popular apps from this ecosystem, and saw that these various low dimensional features had interesting and diverse distributions across the population.

This brings us to our final set of questions: can we use an app's social, demographic, retention, and temporal features to predict whether or not it will be successful in the long term?

5.1 Predicting the longevity of apps

Note that we have seen empirically that the question of an app's long term success is well approximated by a binary variable (see Figures 8 and 9). In this subsection and the next, we will consider two variations on a binary prediction task. One task is straightforward: given a collection of promising apps, we want to predict which apps will have persistent success over the next year. The other task is based on a pairwise evaluation: to compare a pair of similarly popular apps and predict which one will be more successful in the future.

First, we consider the task of predicting which apps in the entire population will continue to be successful. Based on the number of active users on June 2014, we label an app as a positive example if it has over 50% of the number of active users it had in June 2013, and we label it as a negative example if has lost more than 50% of its users. This labeling turns out to provide us with a balanced class distribution, with the guess-all-positive baseline being 50%. For this binary classification task we built and evaluated the model by training random forests on apps in APPS$_{POP}$, where each app is represented as a vector of the features in Table 2.

The prediction performance results are shown in Table 3, and the use of all the available features leads to performance above 70% on this binary task. We find that the temporal features are the best single set of features, with the most important features being the median number of users in months 8 and 9 of the 12 month observation period (June 1 2012-June 1 2013 – see Table 1). The apps that would continue to be successful also had a higher weekly minimum; given that the overall popularity of the apps between classes is evenly distributed, we interpret this high weekly minimum as a signal of stability, and that this stability was a positive predictor.

Individual user attributes yielded the second highest performance, with the most important class features being activity-based ones: $l_{5,7}$ and $l_{6,7}$ ($l_{k,7}$ is the fraction of app users that were also active Facebook users for past k out of 7 days). We observe that for $k = 0, \ldots, 6$, negative examples are correlated with greater values of $l_{k,7}$, whereas for $l_{7,7}$, the trend reverses, and the positive examples with more users who are active on Facebook every day. This means that having users who were also highly active Facebook users is a positive indicator of success.

Among all the retention features, the most important one was the fitted parameter x_A, which represents the "departure probability" in the exponential decay model of users leaving an app. Not surprisingly, we find that the positive examples tend to have lower x_A than negative examples, indicating that having users who continue using the app for an extended period of time (i.e. a lower leaving probability) is correlated with the app's long-term success.

Finally, the most important structural features were sociality, i.e., average user degree, and mean/max number of friends who used the app. For the latter two we could not notice any significant differences between the two classes, but we do notice that high sociality is a negative indicator of success. This is likely due to the fact that we normalize the sociality measure ($p(x|y)$) by the popularity of the app ($p(x)$); thus those apps with very high sociality score are relatively small, and tend to be the ones situated in a very specific, niche market. Indeed, we find that if we consider the separate distributions of the numerator and denominator, we observe that $p(x|y)$ is indistinguishable for the two classes, while $p(x)$ is a positive indicator, leaving $p(x|y)/p(x)$ as a negative indicator.

SIRS model

In general the task of predicting an app's time-series trajectory is a rich and interesting problem, but the binary nature of trajectories that we observed motivated our simplification to the binary prediction task. To explore the potential inherent in modeling richer properties of the time series, we also consider a model of app usage via a set of interacting reaction diffusion processes, much like a chemical reaction. The model we use was proposed by Ribeiro et al. [17], and falls into the well-known class of SIRS models. We

Temporal	
med /min/max $\text{DAU}_{mo.X}$	median, min, max number of daily users in month X of observation
med /min/max $\Delta\text{DAU}_{mo.X}$	median, min, max of change in daily users within month X ($\text{DAU}_X - \text{DAU}_{X-1}$)
med /min/max $\Delta^2\text{DAU}_{mo.X}$	median, min, max of second order change in daily users within month X
med /min/max DAU_{year}	median, min, max of DAU_X for $X \in 1, \ldots, 12$
med /min/max Δ DAU_{year}	median, min, max of ΔDAU_X for $X \in 1, \ldots, 12$
med /min/max Δ^2 DAU_{year}	median, min, max of $\Delta^2 DAU_X$ for $X \in 1, \ldots, 12$
Δ_{year} DAU	med DAU_{12} - med DAU_1
$\Delta_{year}\Delta$ DAU	med Δ DAU_{12} - med Δ^2 DAU_1
$\Delta_{year}\Delta^2$ DAU	med Δ^2 DAU_{12} - med Δ^2 DAU_1
*WAU, MAU, users, new users	Same statistics as listed for DAU above, considering instead weekly users, monthly users, total users, and new users
Demographic	
Country_X / $P(\text{Country}_X)$	Number, fraction of users from country X
Gender_X / $P(\text{Gender}_X)$	Number, fraction of users who stated their gender to be X
Age_X / $P(\text{Age}_X)$	Number, fraction of users who stated their age to be X
$l_{k,7}$ / $P(l_{k,7})$	Number, fraction of users who were active on Facebook for k out of 7 days
is30 / isnot30 / $P(is30)$	Number of users who are / aren't monthly active Facebook users; fraction of users who were monthly active Facebook users
Entropy(Country)	Entropy of country user distribution: $-\sum_{X \in \text{Countries}} P(\text{Country}_X) \log_2 P(\text{Country}_X)$
Entropy(Gender)	Entropy of gender user distribution: $-\sum_{X \in \text{Genders}} P(\text{Gender}_X) \log_2 P(\text{Gender}_X)$
Entropy(Age)	Entropy of age user probability distribution: $-\sum_{X \in \text{Ages}} P(\text{Age}_X) \log_2 P(\text{Age}_X)$
Entropy(l_7)	Entropy of l_7 distribution: $-\sum_{k \in 1,\ldots,7} P(l_{k,7}) \log_2 P(l_{k,7})$
Entropy(is30)	Entropy of is30 distribution: $-[P(is30) \log_2 P(is30) + (1 - P(is30)) \log_2(1 - P(is30))]$
Retention	
N(t)	Number of users who returned t days after their first login
P(t)	Empirical probability of a user returning t days after their first login
a, x_a	Parameters for best fits of time dependent model: $N(t) = N(0)exp\left[\frac{-x_a t^{1-a}}{1-a}\right]$
A, x_0	Parameters Least squares parameter fits of time independent model: $N(t) = AN(0)exp[-x_0 t]$
Social	
med / max deg	median and maximum number of friends of an app user
med / max using	median and maximum number of friends of an app user who also use the app
$p(x\|y)$	sociality: empirical probability of having adopted an app given that a friend has, i.e. mean fraction of an app user's friends who also use the app
$p(x\|y)/p(x)$	relative change in probability of a user adopting an app given that their friend has
SIRS model	
S_0	susceptible population size, i.e. number of Facebook users who are interested at this app
α	probability of a non-user adopting the app due to non-social reasons
β	probability of a non-user adopting the app through social process
γ	probability of active user becoming inactive
ϵ	probability of in-active user being drawn back by active users
$pred(day_k)$	the DAU prediction at day k for k between 2013-06-01 and 2014-06-01

Table 2: Features used for training and testing the binary app success prediction tasks. Features were measured for all apps in APPS_{POP} (see Table 1), with the exception of the SIRS model features due to issues of model convergence.

will briefly describe how we implemented this model, and when we return to our underlying prediction task, we will consider the predictions and parameters from this model as an additional set of features.

Ribeiro et al. [17] proposed a model describing the dynamics of a webservice of daily activity time series, derived from the classical epidemic model and comprised of a set of reaction diffusion processes. The model is specified by a set of parameters, including the estimate of the susceptible population, and the transition probabilities between different states. Ribeiro also outlines a framework for fitting these parameters given a window of time series activity levels, and then uses them to extrapolate and make a long term prediction of future activity levels. We implemented a model very similar to the one described in [17]. We fitted the model using a Monte Carlo process using time series from June 2, 2012 to May 25, 2013 (the same period from which we extract temporal features), and used the fitted model to generate predictions between May 26, 2013 and May 15, 2014.

There are two things we note about the SIRS model. First, as we try to predict the future of apps from a fixed time point, the apps we are studying can be in very different life stages. For example, some apps in our dataset had only existed for a short period of time by the observation day, and thus have very limited time series data to compute a good fit of the SIRS model. Second, some underlying assumptions in the SIRS model, such as the constant rate of user adoption through advertisement or word-of-mouth process, may not hold in reality. As a result, the model would not converge for certain apps, especially the ones that experienced large fluctuations in their lifecycles.

Nevertheless, we were able to fit over two-thirds of the apps in APPS_{POP}. Among them, 1100 apps had reasonable convergence and error estimates. We then used both the fitted parameters and the predicted time series as our features for this subset of 1100 apps. On that subset of 1100 apps, the relative performance of the other features sets was the same (all combined features yield the highest performance, followed by temporal, then demographic, retention, and finally social).

We find that the features from the SIRS model perform worse than the retention features but better than the social features. Thus, despite the richness of the time-series modeling made possible by the SIR framework, as a feature set it does not perform as well as other measures incorporating temporal properties, including the retention model from the previous section.

5.2 Predicting pairwise relative success

Next we formulate a separate but related prediction task, by constructing a pairwise comparison version of predicting app success. Given that two apps have approximately the same monthly active users at t_1 (MAU@t_1), and by t_2 they had diverged from each other, we want to predict at time t_1 which app is going to be more successful. We evaluate this problem with a variety of thresholds for what we considered "near-" and "long-"term predictions of MAU. This prediction task is particularly useful when investigating a set of competitive apps in the same market. Intuitively, it is difficult to tell similar apps apart at an early stage [18]. However, by looking at pairs whose outcomes at t_2 are successively farther apart, we can control for the difficulty of the task and understand when it becomes feasible to predict such divergence.

For the pairwise prediction task we begin by generating a 50-50 train-test split between apps, and represent each pair of apps as a concatenation of two feature vectors, again using the features from Table 2. We then introduce a subtle variation to make the setup

Feature set	*accuracy*	*prec: +;-*	*recall: +;-*	*top 2 features: {among all}; {within class}*
Baseline	0.50			
All	0.73	0.72; 0.74	0.74; 0.72	med users_8, med users_9 ; –
Temporal	0.71	0.72; 0.7	0.68; 0.74	$\Delta_{year}WAU$, $\min WAU_{11}$; med users_8 med users_9
Demographic	0.66	0.64; 0.68	0.70; 0.61	$l_{6,7}, l_{5,7}$; $l_{6,7}, l_{5,7}$
Retention	0.61	0.59; 0.64	0.70; 0.53	x_a, x_A; day 2 and 3 returns
Social	0.6	0.59; 0.61	0.60; 0.59	$\frac{p(x\|y)}{p(x)}$, ⟨user degree⟩; Mean and max # of friends using the app

Table 3: Prediction performance results for five combinations of features. Precision and recall: top and bottom rows are for positive and negative classes, respectively. Features are ranked by out-of-bag importance estimates while training the random forests. We trained the classifier using all the features, and report the most important ones in each category in the top row ("among all"), and train the classifier with only the features in each category, and report the top opens in lower row ("within class").

more relevant to a real-world scenario. The features and labels used in the training stage are generated using snapshots of our datasets at t_0 and $t_1 = t_0 + 6$ months, while those used for testing are generated using snapshots at t_1 and $t_2 = t_1 + 6$ months. This simulates the practical scenario of observing the app population at t_1, learning which characteristics of apps lead to their success, and using the learned knowledge to predict the future.

Two apps are considered to start off as being "comparable" if they fall into the same decile at $t_{0/1}$ (train/test), and are considered "distinct" if they are at least k deciles apart at $t_{1/2}$ (train/test). In Figure 10 we see that prediction accuracy increases monotonically with k, and that the best set of features (temporal) ultimately yield 75% prediction accuracy. The other most striking feature of Figure 10 is that for most of the threshold window, all the features yield approximately the same performance. Each set of features, besides demographic, takes a turn at being both the top performer and the lowest. The individual feature analysis that we did was consistent with the observation that this task is not highly sensitive to the choice of features. To analyze which features could best discriminate between positive and negative examples we used the two-sided Kolmogorov-Smirnov test to compare the distributions of each feature for positive and negative examples. We find that, with the exception of a few underpopulated demographic features, the Kolmogorov-Smirnov test finds that each feature is distinguishable between the negative and positive examples with p-values extremely close to zero.

6. RELATED WORK

Sociologists and economists have long studied the problem of product adoption and retention. Early work in this domain focused on the diffusion of innovations, as people proposed a series of mathematical models to describes the adoption of new products by consumers, such as the "S-shaped" adoption curve [7] and the

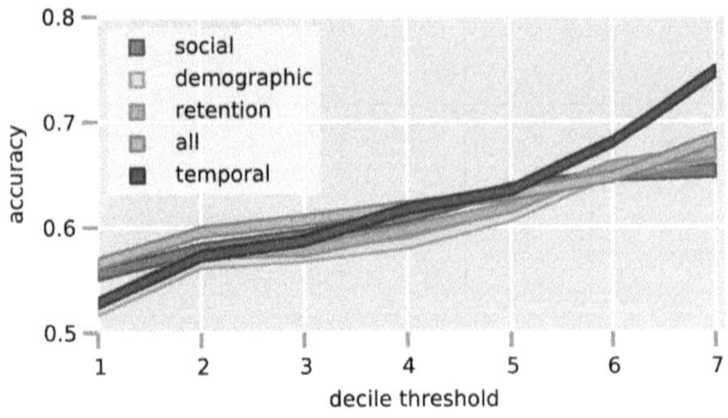

Figure 10: Prediction accuracy for the pairwise relative success prediction task, as a function of decile threshold, k.

Bass model [4]. These models have been successful in predicting the impact of advertising, especially the effect of advertising through mass-media and billboards. Other work has focused on the diffusion of innovations and products through social ties [19]. With the rise of social media and online social networks, there has been more and more evidence that the social influence, i.e. the word-of-mouth effect, is playing a increasingly important role at driving the adoption of products and services [3, 12, 14].

To understand how products and information spread in social networks, most existing work tries to predict the volume of popularity, such as the the size of online communities [1], the number of fans of Facebook pages [22], and the usage of hashtags on Twitter [2,20,25]. While these work showed the correlation between the scale of diffusion and its structural and topical properties, there has been a recent line of work questioning the predictability of large viral events [2, 21]. In response, Cheng et al. [5] showed that it is possible to predict how much more a cascade will grow by observing the temporal and other features of its spread up to the present time.

Besides being a key predictor for cascade size, the temporal dynamics of cascades have been an interesting research topic [6, 13, 28]. Upon the discovery of several robust temporal classes of cascades on different platforms, most studies on the temporal dynamics focused on bursty events [24], or the peak volume [6, 13]. Indeed, the majority of popular things spread on-line enjoy very short attention span: the popularity rises and drop quickly, usually within a few hours or a day [26, 28]. The persistence of interest, although rare, is rather intriguing. Wu et al. [26] found that the longevity of URLs on Twitter can be explained by the intrinsic cultural value of the content they link to. Follow-up work showed that information with positive sentiment is more likely to persist [27]. Ducheneaut et al.. discovered that smaller and denser guilds in World of Warcraft are more likely to survive longer [9].

While many papers correlate the temporal patterns of cascades with its empirical properties, some researchers have developed theoretical models on individuals' choice of adopting and engaging with a product or activity [17, 24]. These models are useful at depicting the mechanism behind the observed temporal dynamics, however, it is unclear how generalizable they are beyond the particular product or activity studied.

Our work contributes to current research in two major aspects.

First, we study the entire lifecycle of apps over a timespan as long as 5 years . Our focus is the persistency of growth other than the peak popularity. Different from a viral YouTube video or a meme photo, successful apps needs to engage with their users repeatedly. Therefore, we spent a significant amount of work analyzing and modeling the retention of apps, and showed its importance to the long-term success of apps.

Second, we study thousands of apps at once. Previously, most papers examined the adoption and retention of a single product/activity, thus their results might not be generalizable to other domains. By studying a large selection of apps on Facebook, we are able to control for app-specific features and understand how the characteristics of an app interact with its social and temporal dynamics.

Some work similar to ours includes a recent study of the growth and longevity of online communities [10], the modeling and prediction of the temporal pattern of membership-based websites [17], and a study of mobile app adoption over a small real-life social network [16]. Our study builds on these papers in both the scope and the variety of examples examined. Also, with the rich dataset we have about apps, users, and the underlying social graph, we are able to introduce several new theoretical and analytical models, and to compare them with recent formalisms [17]. By incorporating the parameters of a fitted model as part of the feature set, we are able to extend and compare different methodologies.

7. CONCLUSION

In this paper we studied the lifecycle of apps: as they grow and thrive, and, in some cases, as they decline. We studied differences in their development, looking for clues to their future fate. First, we sought parameters with which to model the interaction between the app and the individual. We found that a simple exponential decay, even with an adjustment for attrition after the first day of use, did not accurately capture user retention. Instead, those who keep using the app over a longer time period are less and less likely to stop. Modeling retention of individuals in this way is helpful in predicting app success.

Another dimension goes beyond the individual to whether the app is adopted socially. Apps vary widely in the sociality of their adoption, and we find heterogeneity in the apps based on how their adoption probabilities depend on the connectedness of friends who use the app and the similarities in attributes between an adopter and his or her friends.

The features most predictive of an app's future dynamics are those describing its past growth trajectory. More widely adopted apps that have recently been on a growth trajectory are more likely to persist. Given a range of features, we obtain over 20% absolute improvement over random guessing when it comes to making a binary prediction as to sustained activity for an app. We also obtain strong performance when we formulate the problem as one of matching two apps of roughly equal size which take different trajectories, and trying to distinguish the two with a much higher than random accuracy.

There are a number of further aspects of the app ecosystem that would be interesting to take into account in future work. First, app adoption is driven in part by the marketing and other recruitment strategies of the app owners. Although our models incorporate the numbers of new users coming to the app over time, they do not differentiate between organic growth and advertising-driven growth. Furthermore, it is not clear whether sociality of apps might accelerate growth or decline or both. Finally, it is unclear whether some features might be early harbingers of future behavior, e.g. whether the change in retention of long-time or recently acquired users is more useful in forecasting the eventual adoption of the app. We leave these and other questions for future work.

8. REFERENCES

[1] Lars Backstrom, Dan Huttenlocher, Jon Kleinberg, and Xiangyang Lan. Group formation in large social networks: membership, growth, and evolution. In *Proceedings of the 12th ACM SIGKDD International Conference on Knowledge Discovery and Data Mining*, pages 44–54. ACM, 2006.

[2] Eytan Bakshy, Jake M. Hofman, Winter A. Mason, and Duncan J. Watts. Everyone's an influencer: Quantifying influence on twitter. In *Proceedings of the Fourth ACM International Conference on Web Search and Data Mining*, WSDM '11, pages 65–74, New York, NY, USA, 2011. ACM.

[3] Eytan Bakshy, Itamar Rosenn, Cameron Marlow, and Lada Adamic. The role of social networks in information diffusion. In *Proceedings of the 21st international conference on World Wide Web*, pages 519–528. ACM, 2012.

[4] Frank Bass. A new product growth for model consumer durables. *Management Sciences*, 15(1):215–227, 1969.

[5] Justin Cheng, Lada Adamic, P. Alex Dow, Jon Michael Kleinberg, and Jure Leskovec. Can cascades be predicted? In *Proceedings of the 23rd International Conference on World Wide Web*, WWW '14, pages 925–936, New York, NY, USA, 2014. ACM.

[6] Riley Crane and Didier Sornette. Robust dynamic classes revealed by measuring the response function of a social system. *Proceedings of the National Academy of Sciences*, 105(41):15649–15653, 2008.

[7] G. de Tarde and E.W.C. Parsons. *The Laws of Imitation*. H. Holt, 1903.

[8] Thomas Debeauvais, Bonnie Nardi, Diane J Schiano, Nicolas Ducheneaut, and Nicholas Yee. If you build it they might stay: Retention mechanisms in world of warcraft. In *Proceedings of the 6th International Conference on Foundations of Digital Games*, pages 180–187. ACM, 2011.

[9] Nicolas Ducheneaut, Nicholas Yee, Eric Nickell, and Robert J. Moore. The life and death of online gaming communities: A look at guilds in world of warcraft. In *Proceedings of the SIGCHI Conference on Human Factors in Computing Systems*, CHI '07, pages 839–848, New York, NY, USA, 2007. ACM.

[10] Sanjay Ram Kairam, Dan J. Wang, and Jure Leskovec. The life and death of online groups: Predicting group growth and longevity. In *Proceedings of the Fifth ACM International Conference on Web Search and Data Mining*, WSDM '12, pages 673–682, New York, NY, USA, 2012. ACM.

[11] Marcel Karnstedt, Matthew Rowe, Jeffrey Chan, Harith Alani, and Conor Hayes. The effect of user features on churn in social networks. In *Proceedings of the 3rd International Web Science Conference*, page 23. ACM, 2011.

[12] Jure Leskovec, Lada A. Adamic, and Bernardo A. Huberman. The dynamics of viral marketing. In *16th ACM Conference on Economics and Computation*, pages 228–237, New York, NY, USA, 2006. ACM Press.

[13] Jure Leskovec, Lars Backstrom, and Jon Kleinberg. Meme-tracking and the dynamics of the news cycle. In *Proceedings of the 15th ACM SIGKDD International Conference on Knowledge Discovery and Data Mining*, KDD '09, pages 497–506, New York, NY, USA, 2009. ACM.

[14] Lev Muchnik, Sinan Aral, and Sean J Taylor. Social influence bias: A randomized experiment. *Science*, 341(6146):647–651, 2013.

[15] Jukka-Pekka Onnela and Felix Reed-Tsochas. Spontaneous emergence of social influence in online systems. *Proceedings of the National Academy of Sciences*, 107(43):18375–18380, 2010.

[16] Wei Pan, Nadav Aharony, and Alex Pentland. Composite social network for predicting mobile apps installation. *CoRR*, abs/1106.0359, 2011.

[17] Bruno Ribeiro. Modeling and predicting the growth and death of membership-based websites. In *Proceedings of the 23rd International Conference on World Wide Web*, WWW '14, pages 653–664, New York, NY, USA, 2014. ACM.

[18] Bruno Ribeiro and Christos Faloutsos. Modeling website popularity competition in the attention-activity marketplace. *arXiv preprint arXiv:1403.0600*, 2014.

[19] Everett M. Rogers. *Diffusion of Innovations, 5th Edition*. Free Press, August 2003.

[20] Daniel M. Romero, Brendan Meeder, and Jon Kleinberg. Differences in the mechanics of information diffusion across topics: Idioms, political hashtags, and complex contagion on twitter. In *Proceedings of the 20th International Conference on World Wide Web*, WWW '11, pages 695–704, New York, NY, USA, 2011. ACM.

[21] M.J. Salganik, P.S. Dodds, and D.J. Watts. Experimental Study of Inequality and Unpredictability in an Artificial Cultural Market. *Science*, 311(5762):854–856, 2006.

[22] Eric Sun, Itamar Rosenn, Cameron Marlow, and Thomas Lento. Gesundheit! Modeling Contagion through Facebook News Feed. In *International AAAI Conference on Weblogs and Social Media*, 2009.

[23] Johan Ugander, Lars Backstrom, Cameron Marlow, and Jon Kleinberg. Structural diversity in social contagion. *Proceedings of the National Academy of Sciences*, 109(16):5962–5966, 2012.

[24] Alexei Vázquez, João Gama Oliveira, Zoltán Dezsö, Kwang-Il Goh, Imre Kondor, and Albert-László Barabási. Modeling bursts and heavy tails in human dynamics. *Phys. Rev. E*, 73:036127, Mar 2006.

[25] L. Weng, F. Menczer, and Y.-Y. Ahn. Virality prediction and community structure in social networks. *Sci. Rep.*, 3(2522), 2013.

[26] Shaomei Wu, Jake M. Hofman, Winter A. Mason, and Duncan J. Watts. Who says what to whom on twitter. In *Proceedings of the 20th International Conference on World Wide Web*, WWW '11, pages 705–714, New York, NY, USA, 2011. ACM.

[27] Shaomei Wu, Chenhao Tan, Jon Kleinberg, and Michael Macy. Does bad news go away faster. In *In In Proceedings of the International Conference on Weblogs and Social (ICWSM*, 2011.

[28] Jaewon Yang and Jure Leskovec. Patterns of temporal variation in online media. In *Proceedings of the Fourth ACM International Conference on Web Search and Data Mining*, WSDM '11, pages 177–186, New York, NY, USA, 2011. ACM.

[29] Jiang Yang, Xiao Wei, Mark S Ackerman, and Lada A Adamic. Activity lifespan: An analysis of user survival patterns in online knowledge sharing communities. In *ICWSM*, 2010.

Getting More for Less: Optimized Crowdsourcing with Dynamic Tasks and Goals

Ari Kobren*
Google & UMass Amherst
akobren@cs.umass.edu

Chun How Tan
Google
chunhowt@google.com

Panagiotis Ipeirotis*
Google & NYU
panos@stern.nyu.edu

Evgeniy Gabrilovich
Google
gabr@google.com

ABSTRACT

In crowdsourcing systems, the interests of contributing participants and system stakeholders are often not fully aligned. Participants seek to learn, be entertained, and perform easy tasks, which offer them instant gratification; system stakeholders want users to complete more difficult tasks, which bring higher value to the crowdsourced application. We directly address this problem by presenting techniques that optimize the crowdsourcing process by jointly maximizing the user longevity in the system and the true value that the system derives from user participation.

We first present models that predict the "survival probability" of a user at any given moment, that is, the probability that a user will proceed to the next task offered by the system. We then leverage this survival model to dynamically decide what task to assign and what motivating goals to present to the user. This allows us to jointly optimize for the short term (getting difficult tasks done) and for the long term (keeping users engaged for longer periods of time).

We show that dynamically assigning tasks significantly increases the value of a crowdsourcing system. In an extensive empirical evaluation, we observed that our task allocation strategy increases the amount of information collected by up to 117.8%. We also explore the utility of motivating users with goals. We demonstrate that setting specific, static goals can be highly detrimental to the long-term user participation, as the completion of a goal (e.g., earning a badge) is also a common drop-off point for many users. We show that setting the goals dynamically, in conjunction with judicious allocation of tasks, increases the amount of information collected by the crowdsourcing system by up to 249%, compared to the existing baselines that use fixed objectives.

*Work done while at Google.

WWW 2015, May 18–22, 2015, Florence, Italy.
ACM 978-1-4503-3469-3/15/05.
http://dx.doi.org/10.1145/2736277.2741681.

1. INTRODUCTION

Crowdsourcing has become increasingly popular in recent years due to its proven success in a variety of domains including knowledge base construction, image labeling, language translation, and others. Despite its numerous successes, crowdsourcing remains more of an art than a science, as a system designer must attract users and keep them engaged in order to complete tasks. Various approaches for engaging users have been proposed, yet each of them has its shortcomings. Explicit monetary incentives, which are used by both Amazon Mechanical Turk (AMT) and oDesk, may incentivize participants to continue working even if they lack the necessary expertise. Systems like Duolingo [24] and Zooniverse[1] offer users an educational experience in exchange for tasks that are useful to the stakeholder. Finally, some crowdsourcing systems completely ignore the goal of user engagement, and use task completion as a pre-condition to access a valuable resource (e.g., ReCAPTCHA [25] or Google Consumer Surveys[2]).

One of the fundamental difficulties for engaging users in crowdsourcing tasks is the lack of alignment between the interests of crowd users and stakeholders. For example, users often prefer to work on simple tasks requiring low cognitive loads, while the stakeholders benefit when users complete difficult tasks that demand substantial effort to complete. For example, in Zooniverse, a user may prefer to work on easy cases, which provide the immediate gratification of successfully completing a task; however, such cases may not be the ones that contribute the most towards the goal of the Citizen Science project. In Duolingo, the user may spend a lot of time completing familiar exercises, as completing such exercises are an easy way to earn "experience points"; however, these exercises may not be the ones that lead to the best educational outcomes. In Quizz [10], users prefer to answer easy questions and drop out when facing hard quiz questions. However, the goal of the system is to leverage user answers to discover the answers to the hard questions; hence answers to the easy questions has significantly less value to the stakeholder than answers to the hard questions.

Past work has explored the use of goals (e.g., badges [2]) to improve user participation, and steer it towards more valuable tasks. In the setting of paid crowdsourcing, there are also previous works in determining the relationship between pricing and engagement [16]. In this work, we focus

[1]`https://www.zooniverse.org/`
[2]`https://www.google.com/insights/consumersurveys`

on the setting of volunteer crowdsourcing, building upon the paradigm of guided engagement and presenting two methods for *jointly maximizing* user engagement and the value of the data collected via a crowdsourcing campaign.

To this end, we first develop user *survival models*, which predict drop out events. By considering the user's preferred task subjects, appropriate difficulty level, and other joint characteristics of the user-task pair, it is possible to train models that predict drop out events up to 77% accuracy. Next, we present *survival-based dynamic task allocation*, which actively allocates tasks to users by balancing the value of the task with the likelihood of a user dropping out after being assigned to the task. Our method is framed as a Markov Decision Process [20] with an infinite state space and an action space consisting of all valid task allocations. Building upon [10], we model the contributions of each user as a noisy channel, and evaluate the quality of submitted responses using information theoretic metrics. We demonstrate that our survival-based task allocation strategy increases the amount of information collected from users (as measured by information gain) by up to 117.8%.

Our second technique is focused on optimized crowdsourcing via adaptive deployment of goals. Although goals aim to encourage users to be more participatory, we empirically demonstrate that the overall value of certain goals may have *negative net effects* on the volume of user contributions, compared to not having a goal at all. Somewhat counter-intuitively, we discovered that *not* setting short-term goals (e.g., showing the user how many tasks are left in a single session) actually increases overall participation. This happens because specific goals provide incentives for completing tasks, but at the same time they lead users to "fixate" on the goal completion and thus provide natural drop-out points after the user achieves the designated goal. Motivated by this discovery, we propose *survival-based dynamic goal deployment*—a strategy that dynamically sets reasonable goals for users who are at risk of dropping out, in order to encourage their continued participation. Similar to our proposed task allocation method, we formulate dynamic goal deployment as an MDP that optimally chooses between two possible actions: to set a goal or to leave all goals unspecified. We show that this strategy can result in an improvement of up to 249% in the amount of information collected from the users.

The contributions of this work are threefold. First, we show how to integrate user survival models into an active task allocation framework, in order to optimally assign tasks that balance user engagement and task value. Second, we present empirical results demonstrating how the presence of goals affects user participation in a crowdsourcing system. We show that setting specific goals may be detrimental to long-term user participation, as users tend to drop out immediately upon completing the goal. Finally, we propose an adaptive framework that dynamically sets goals for users in a way that significantly increases the amount of information contributed by the users. The experiments reported in this paper were performed on real-life tasks using the Quizz crowdsourcing platform [10], and involved over 13,000 users who contributed over 128,000 answers.

2. METHODOLOGY

User engagement plays a significant role in the effectiveness of most crowdsourcing applications. Despite this, formal models of *survival*—or a user's likelihood of continuing to work on a task—have been largely under-explored. Recently, Mao et al. [15] introduced models for predicting whether a user will *drop out*[3] (namely, stop working on a task) in the context of Galaxy Zoo, a citizen science crowdsourcing application.

In this section, we first introduce models of user survival, and then use those models to design dynamic approaches for task allocation and goal deployment. Throughout the paper, we use the term *task* to refer to a single multiple-choice question, and *quiz* to refer to a sequence of tasks. In our work, we focus on tasks that are in the form of multiple-choice questions but future work could extend to tasks into other formats such as validation questions (yes/no), annotation tasks, and free-text tasks. We note that prior work on survival models has primarily focused on longer term predictions, e.g., whether a user will drop out within the next 5 minutes [15]. On the other hand, models we develop have finer granularity and make shorter-term predictions, namely, whether a user will drop out given a specific task. Although we experimented with a number of models, we only present our logistic and fitted-Q models because they are fast to train and most accurate.

2.1 Logistic Survival Models

We present several logistic models to estimate the probability of a user dropping out given various signals derived from the user's state and the particular task. The complete list of signals is summarized at Table 1. Our models take the form:

$$P(x) = \frac{1}{1 + e^{-(\beta + w^T x)}}$$

where x is the feature vector representing the user's state and the current task, w are the learned weights and $P(x)$ is the probability of survival corresponding to that vector. All the models are L2-regularized and trained using scikit-learn [19]. The different models are trained on different subsets of the training data, as explained below.

2.1.1 Logistic-All Model (LA)

The Logistic-all model makes use of all available training data. This model was proposed in previous work [15].

2.1.2 Logistic-Middle Model (LM)

There is often high variance in user participation in crowdsourcing tasks: some users complete a single task while others complete many more tasks. The participation level of these users may be significantly biased by factors other than the task at hand: a user who completes a single task may be unwilling to complete additional ones regardless of their content; a user who completes hundreds of tasks may be generally interested in the application and would complete any task presented with the same vigor. To this end, we train the LM model by eliminating outliers and only use data from the users who complete between three and ten tasks, corresponding roughly to the middle 50 percentile of the users, in term of user engagement. This way, users whose interactions with the system are largely predetermined by external factors will not affect the model. These exclusions greatly reduces the size of the training data.

[3]In this work, the authors used the term *disengage* instead of drop out.

2.1.3 Logistic-Sequential Model (LS)

We develop the logistic-sequential model for modeling survival through a sequence of tasks. Unlike the previous models, the LS model is a sequence of models, one for each task in a sequence (first task, second and so on). Each model is trained using all data collected from users working on the corresponding task (e.g., the third model is trained using data collected from tasks served third in any quiz). Intuitively, there is a different prior probability of survival at each task index (i.e., it is more likely that a user survives a task if it is the final task separating the user from a goal/badge). In addition to accounting for this bias, the LS model is able to capture the relative importance of different features at each task index (e.g., to promote user engagement it is much more important for the first task to be easy than the ninth). The LS model requires splitting the training data into multiple groups of vastly different sizes.

2.2 Fitted-Q Survival Model (FQ)

We also train a regression model using fitted-Q iteration—a meta-algorithm borrowed from reinforcement learning [18]. Unlike the logistic models, the fitted-Q model predicts a real-valued *reward* for each training instance instead of a number between zero and one. While this model does not produce probabilities of survival, it can predict the relative utility of allocating different tasks to any user throughout interaction with a crowdsourcing application.

We allow the space of vectors describing a user's state (Table 1) to be infinite. Therefore the goal of training our FQ model is to learn a state-action function, $Q : S \times A \to \mathbb{R}$, i.e., a function whose input is a user's state and a task and whose output is a real value. To learn Q, we iteratively train a regression model using fitted-Q iteration.

We define a reward function $R : S \times A \to \mathbb{R}$ that takes a user's state and an action (i.e. a task to allocate) and returns the reward associated with being in state $s \in S$ and taking action $a \in A$. In our case,

$$R(s_u, a) = \begin{cases} 0, & \text{if user } u \text{ drops out after action } a \\ 1, & \text{otherwise} \end{cases}$$

Additionally, we define a value function $V : S \to \mathbb{R}$ that returns an estimate of the value of being in state s. Then, we iteratively learn the function $Q(s, a)$ by training a regression model to predict the sum of the reward function, R, and the discounted future reward, V, for taking action a and transitioning to state s'. We compute the value for $V(s)$ at iteration $k+1$ using the model, Q, learned at iteration k. Assuming the state-action function Q is parameterized by a vector θ, we iterate the following optimization:

$$\begin{aligned} \theta^{(k+1)} &= \arg\min_{\theta} l(Q(s, a; \theta), [R(s, a) + \gamma V^{(k)}(s')]) \\ &= \arg\min_{\theta} l(Q(s, a; \theta), [R(s, a) + \gamma Q(s', a'; \theta^{(k)})]) \end{aligned}$$

where s and s' are *consecutive* user states, a and a' are the tasks allocated to users in states s and s' respectively and $l(.)$ is some loss function defined by the choice of model for Q. In our work we model Q as ridge regression and initialize $Q^{(0)}(s, a) = 0$ for all states and actions. Each time we learn a new θ we refine our model; we iterate the training process until convergence.

The advantage of the FQ model is that it is trained to consider the *cumulative* reward of taking some action rather than the immediate reward (i.e. the logistic models, see Section 2.1). By considering future states, the FQ models could theoretically be used to construct a more engaging session for a user given his or her state.

2.3 Dynamic Task Allocation

Not all crowdsourcing tasks are created equal. Some tasks are more difficult than others; some tasks are interesting and others not; some tasks are more valuable to the system designer. Similarly, all users find tasks different in terms of interestingness, difficulty, etc. To account for this diversity, we develop models that dynamically allocate tasks to users in order to achieve higher user engagement and higher value for the task owner.

We formalize task allocation as a Markov Decision Process (MDP) [20]. An MDP is a tuple $\mathcal{M} = (S, A, P, R)$ where S is the state space, A is the action space, $P : S \times A \times S' \to [0, 1]$ is a transition function and $R : S \times A \times S' \to \mathbb{R}$ is the reward function. The (infinite) state space S contains vectors describing the state of a user in the midst of completing a sequence of tasks. The action space A is comprised of all tasks that the system can allocate to the user. P is a function that describes the likelihood of a user transitioning to state s' after being in state s and being allocated task a. R describes the reward associated with a user in state s and being allocated task a. The goal of task allocation is to learn a *policy* for allocating tasks to users that maximizes expected reward. In our work, we use the expected information gain (Section 3.4.1) to be our reward function.

A naive policy is to greedily allocate the task with the highest reward given the user. However, this fails to consider the probability that a user might not be interested in the task, find the task too difficult, etc. and choose to drop out. Allocating a task that causes a user to drop out is very costly; after dropping out, the user can produce no additional reward for the system.

We propose a *survival-based task allocation* framework for crowdsourcing tasks (e.g., quizzes consisting of multiple questions). Assuming a model of survival $\mathcal{M}_s$, survival-based task allocation computes the expected reward by considering the chance that a user will drop out after being served a task a:

$$\mathbb{E}[R(s_u, a)] = \mathcal{M}_s(s_u = 1|a) \cdot R(s_u, a)$$

where $\mathcal{M}_s(s_u = 1|a)$ is the probability that a user survives task a under model $\mathcal{M}_s$, and $R(s_u, a)$ is the reward that user u in state s provides to the system when allocated task a. This new reward function averages the case that a user survives the task with the case that a user does not survive the task and contributes no additional reward to the system. Under this framework, we can adopt a policy of allocating the task, a_u^*, with the highest *expected reward*:

$$a_u^* = \operatorname*{argmax}_{a \in A} \mathbb{E}[R(s_u, a)]$$

2.4 Dynamic Goal Deployment

Many crowdsourcing platforms introduce goals (e.g., badges) to motivate the users [2]. Assuming that goals motivate users to complete tasks, survival models can then be used to promote participation by setting attainable goals dynamically when users are at risk of dropping out. Similar to online task allocation, user participation can be improved through *survival-based dynamic goal deployment.*

Like task allocation (Section 2.3), we can formalize dynamic goal deployment as an MDP. The MDP for goal deployment consists of the same state space S as for task allocation, however, the action space now includes a set of goals. The transition function, P, and the reward function, R, are modified appropriately.

Again, we could employ a naive strategy and always use goals in an attempt to motivate additional participation. However, as we show empirically in Section 4.2, goals can also affect participation *negatively*. Therefore, we adopt a survival-based framework for deploying goals.

Although a system could have arbitrarily many goals, we consider a simplified action space consisting of two actions: deploying a goal or leaving the goal unspecified. Under this action space, we employ the following survival-based goal deployment policy:

$$g_u^* = \begin{cases} 0, & \text{if } P(s_u|\mathcal{M}_s) > \tau(\mathcal{M}_s) \\ 1, & \text{otherwise} \end{cases}$$

where $g_u^* = 1$ is the decision to deploy goal g to user u, $P(s_u|\mathcal{M}_s)$ is the probability of survival for user u in state s under the model $\mathcal{M}_s$, and $\tau(\mathcal{M}_s)$ is a survival model-based threshold. In practice, we set $\tau(\mathcal{M}_s)$ to be the empirical drop out rate of users at a particular task index. Thus, the policy only sets a goal if we predict the user is likely to drop out. This policy assumes that a goal deployed under appropriate circumstances will encourage a user to continue participating. We provide empirical support for this assumption in our experimentation (Section 4.2).

3. EXPERIMENTAL SETUP

To evaluate our proposed methodologies, we run experiments on Quizz—a gamified crowdsourcing platform that administers quizzes to volunteer users [10]. Quizz uses an advertising platform [4] to serve advertisements on search and display networks in order to recruit targeted volunteers [10]. When a user first arrives at the site, she is presented with a quiz, which is a collection of multiple choice, factual questions. After the user chooses an answer (or skips the given question), the system displays the correct answer to the question, which was either specified by the system designer in advance or computed using answer resolution techniques [7, 21, 27]. After answering a question, the system immediately presents the user with an additional question or signals the end of a quiz (quizzes are typically comprised of ten questions). Upon completion of a quiz, the system presents a summary of the user's performance and offers the user the option to begin another quiz. A user may *drop out*—or stop answering questions—at any time.

For each of our experiments, we apply the same advertising settings when recruiting volunteers. This is necessary to minimize the effects of specific volunteer groups biasing the final results. Settings that we explicitly control for include: advertising keywords, cost per click, total budget for each task, time and duration, geographical location, and etc.

[4]for more information about recruiting users for crowdsourcing through advertisements see [10].

3.1 Data Set

The training dataset (used to train the models described in Section 3.3) consists of question-answer pairs collected by crowdsourcing answers for question in four different domains: movie actors, musical artists, disease symptoms and effects of medical treatment. In total, there are 16,824 training instances—12,795 of them are positive instances (i.e., the user survives the question) and 4,029 are negative instances (i.e., the user drops out after seeing this question).

We collect a separate test dataset for each experiment. The datasets are comprised of question-answer pairs. There are (the same) 200 unique questions in each test set; these questions were drawn uniformly at random from question sets in the following nine domains: book authors, business CEOs, disease symptoms, soccer players, geography, movie actors, organization headquarters, American football players and effects of medical treatments. We term this set of 200 questions the *Mixed Quiz*. For some experiments we also collected test datasets using 200 questions drawn from a single domain. These additional datasets help us evaluate how well our models generalize across different tasks and question domains. In total, we collect 13,123 volunteer users and 128,466 answers in our system for the evaluation results.

3.2 Preprocessing

The set of typical Quizz users includes many users who answer a single question and then drop out. Since it is difficult to reason about users who contribute few answers, we exclude them from our evaluation results on the test dataset, unless otherwise specified. Specifically, we only compute our results using answers provided by users who submit *at least three* answers (not including skip actions).

3.3 Learning Survival Models for Quizz

We experiment with the Quizz crowdsourcing platform [10]. When interacting with Quizz a user answers an arbitrary, positive number of quiz questions. Our task is to learn a model that predicts whether a user will drop out given the user's state and a question (to serve the user). Therefore, we convert each displayed question into a training instance by representing it as the concatenation of features described in Table 1. The label of each training instance is a binary variable taking the value zero if the user drops out after seeing the question and the value one if the user survives (i.e. answers the current question seen). We construct training instances similar to those described in previous work except that our labels represent whether users drop out after the current task (i.e. Quizz question) while the previous work labels instances based on drop out after a number of additional tasks or minutes spent working [15].

3.3.1 Factors that Affect User Survival

We present features that are likely to affect user engagement in Table 1. Our *User* and *Question* features are inspired by those discussed in previous work [15]. We also include a number of platform specific features (i.e., features related to the Quizz platform) and features describing sequences of tasks served by the system. These additional features help to improve our ability to make accurate short term predictions (of users dropping out).

We divide the features affecting user survival into four main categories:

Quiz	User	Question	Sequential
1 more ques?	#, % correct answers	difficulty	prev. question difficulty
2 more ques?	#, % questions skipped	%correct answers (all users)	*prev. difficulty > avg. difficulty?*
3 more ques?	#, % incorrect answers	%skipped (all users)	log(prev. Freebase popularity)
4 more ques?	(#correct)/(#incorrect)	log(Freebase popularity)	*prev. popularity > avg. popularity?*
5 more ques?	(#skipped)/(#correct)	*difficulty > avg. difficulty?*	*prev. correct?*
6 more ques?	(#incorrect)/(#correct)	*popularity > avg. popularity?*	*prev. skipped?*
7 more ques?	log(ART)	*%skipped > avg. %skipped?*	*prev. ∧ curr. same category?*
8 more ques?	*ART <= 10s?*	*ART <= 10s?*	*prev. ∧ curr. same category ∧ prev. correct?*
9 more ques?	*10s < ART <= 20s?*	*10 < ART <= 20s?*	*prev. ∧ curr. same subcategory?*
10 more ques?	*20s < ART <= 30s?*	*20 < ART <= 30s?*	*prev. ∧ curr. same subcategory ∧ prev. correct?*
	30s < ART <= 40s?	*30 < ART <= 40s?*	*prev. ∧ curr. same Freebase mid?*
	40s < ART <= 50s?	*40 < ART <= 50s?*	*curr. popularity > prev. popularity?*
	50s < ART <= 60s?	*50 < ART <= 60s?*	*curr. ∧ prev. popularity > avg. popularity?*
	60s < ART?	*60 < ART?*	*curr. ∧ prev. difficulty > avg. difficulty?*
	%correct, %skip for category	*ART > user ART?*	*current ∧ prev. %skipped > avg. %skipped?*
	%correct, %skip for subcategory	log(ART)	
	%correct, %skip for mid		

Table 1: Features used to train survival models by feature group. Features in *italics* are binary features. All times are computed in seconds. We abbreviate average response time with ART. "Category" refers to the domain of the question (e.g. geography), "subcategory" refers to the notable type of the question subject (e.g. mountain, river) and "mid" refers to the question subject (e.g. Mount Everest).

- **Quiz**: features in this group capture the amount of a task that a user has completed.
- **User**: features in this group help represent a user working on a task. Some user features include: a user's average quality, domain expertise and average response time.
- **Question**: features in this group capture characteristics of a Quizz question. This group includes user-independent features (e.g., question difficulty, popularity, etc.) and user-dependent features (e.g., rate at which this question is skipped among all users, average response time, etc.).
- **Sequential**: features in this group represent question sequences and capture diversity of topic, difficulty, popularity, etc. in sequential questions.

3.4 Measuring Efficacy of Crowdsourcing

A crowdsourcing system designer strives to collect as much high quality data as possible at low cost. As such, we evaluate our methods using three metrics: information gain, efficiency, and user participation.

3.4.1 *Information Gain*

Previous work in crowdsourcing argues for information theoretic evaluation metrics (especially for tasks similar to question-answering) [10, 22, 26]. We adopt the notion of information gain presented in previous work on Quizz [10]. The entropy of a Quizz question is computed by:

$$H(q; A) = -\sum_{a \in A_q} P(a) \log P(a)$$

where q is the question, A_q is the set of multiple choice answers for q and $P(a)$ is the probability that answer choice a is correct. Theoretically, we can compute $P(a)$ using any arbitrary method (e.g. majority voting or other state of the art methods [7, 21, 27]). In practice we compute $P(a)$ using the number of votes collected for answer a in addition to the estimated *quality* of each user. Specifically, a user's quality, r_u, is the (smoothed) fraction of correct answers that user has submitted. When a user submits an answer $a \in A_q$ the user contributes $IG(r_u)$ bits in support of that answer, where the r_u is computed on the fly, based on her previous answers:

$$IG(r_u) = H(r_0) - H(r_u)$$

where $H(r_0) = \frac{1}{n}$ (i.e., the entropy of the distribution of answer submissions for a user who chooses answers at random). To compute $P(a)$ we simply divide the number of bits submitted in support of answer $a \in A_q$ by the total number of bits submitted for all answers in A_q. As we receive more contributions from the users, $P(a)$ is updated and the entropy of the question changes. The lower a question's entropy, the more confident we are in our prediction of its correct answer.

With these definitions, we can compute the initial entropy in a question set Q by summing the entropy of all questions (before any bits in support of answers have been contributed). We measure the improvement due to crowdsourcing via the *information gain* in the question set:

$$IG(Q, A) = \sum_{q \in Q} [H_0(q) - H(q; A_q)]$$

where Q is a set of questions and $H_0(q)$ is the initial entropy of question q (where all answers are equally probable).

Absolute information gain is significantly affected by the number of participants who submit responses. Therefore we compute the *average information gain* (AIG) per user when comparing two systems.

3.4.2 *Efficiency*

While a crowdsourcing application can achieve high AIG, it might not be *efficient* compared to the AIG it could theoretically achieve given the same user engagement and quality. For example, assigning a user with perfect quality in domain D to a question in domain D' could be wasteful (in terms of information gain). To measure how efficient our task allocation is, we define the *efficiency* of the system to be the quotient of the information gain obtained from crowdsourcing to the total information gain the users could have theoretically contributed:

$$EF = \frac{IG(Q,A)}{\sum_{u \in U} IG(u)}$$

where $IG(u)$ is the total information gain provided by the user u. We define the information gain of a user to be:

$$IG(u) = |A_u| \cdot IG(r_u)$$

where $|A_u|$ is the number of answers contributed by user u and $IG(r_u)$ is information gain for u with quality r.

3.4.3 User Participation

Significant user engagement (and participation) can improve the efficacy of a crowdsourcing application. As such, a system designer could craft a task to maximize the average contributions per user. However, the average can be highly skewed by users who submit an extraordinary large number of contributions. Therefore, we propose a metric that attempts to minimize such effects which we term *fractional participation* (FP):

$$FP_x(U,x) = \frac{|U_{\geq x}|}{|U|}$$

where $U_{\geq x}$ denotes the set of users who contribute at least x answers and U is the set of all users.

Sweeping the FP curve for x from $[0,\infty)$ yields a more complete profile of participation for a quiz. Comparing participation in two quizzes can then be done by plotting the FP curves for each and visually checking whether one strictly dominates the other (i.e. higher and to the right). We can also compare two FP curves by computing the area under the FP curve (FP-AUC) for each.

3.5 Methods Compared

We experiment with a number of dynamic task allocation and goal deployment strategies. We compare our model-based methods to a model-free, greedy baseline. The baseline operates by allocating the task with the highest entropy (i.e., largest potential for information gain) (note that the task with the highest entropy changes as users submit responses). We use the following notation when referring to our methods of task allocation:

- **TA**: the greedy baseline; quiz has length ten.
- **TA-INF**: the greedy baseline; quiz has unspecified length (i.e., potentially infinite length).
- **TA-x**: survival-based dynamic task allocation using model $x \in \{LA, LM, LS, FQ\}$; quiz has length ten.
- **TA-INF-x**: similar to TA-x, but quiz has unspecified length (i.e., potentially infinite length).
- **TA-INF-DG-x**: similar to TA-INF-x, but also employs survival-based dynamic goal deployment.

Quiz	TA-LA	TA-LM	TA-LS	TA-FQ
Geography	**93.1%**	71.5%	78.8%	24.8%
Symptom	23.3%	5.5%	**28.7%**	25.4%
Mixed	90.8%	48.4%	**117.8%**	73.3%

Table 2: Percent improvement of AIG for dynamic task allocation strategies over the baseline (TA).

4. EXPERIMENTAL RESULTS

4.1 Dynamic Task Allocation

We compare the performance of the greedy baseline and four dynamic task allocation strategies: TA-LA, TA-LM, TA-LS, and TA-FQ (Section 3.3). We evaluate all task allocation strategies on the Mixed Quiz and two other quizzes: one is comprised of questions about disease symptoms (Symptoms Quiz) and the other is comprised of geography question (Geography Quiz). Each of these additional quizzes tests how well the strategies generalize across different tasks with more specialized information. We recruit about 100 users for each quiz that answer at least three questions. We measure performance using all the three metrics described in Section 3.4.

4.1.1 Information Gain

We evaluate the information gain due to crowdsourcing under each task allocation strategy (including the baseline). Table 2 summarizes the percent improvement in AIG (Section 3.4) over the baseline for each task allocation strategy.

The results show that all four dynamic task allocation strategies improve upon the baseline, in some cases by more than 100%. Both the TA-LA and TA-LS models tend to perform the best while the TA-LM model tends to perform the worst. We believe the reason for this to be twofold: first, the TA-LM model is trained on less data than the other models and second, the data left out of the training set for the TA-LM model is important: many users (i.e. ~50%) drop out before question three and therefore selecting appropriate questions for them will dramatically enhance performance. Users who answer an extraordinary number of questions can also contribute significant information gain and should therefore not be left out of training. We believe that the TA-LS model performs well in part due to its ability to learn the bias at each question index.

The TA-FQ model works well compared to the baseline method but is not a top performer. Recall that in training this model the reward function returns the value one if the user does not drop out after being shown question q and zero otherwise. Thus our model is trained to predict a reward associated with the expected number of questions a user will answer but not the expected information gain. For future work, we believe that training the FQ model to predict expected information gain and then using a task allocation strategy that selects the question with the highest expected information gain (i.e. $\text{argmax}_{q \in Q} \mathcal{M}'(q,u)$) could perform much better and take advantage of the power of the fitted-Q meta-algorithm.

4.1.2 Efficiency

While all dynamic task allocation strategies achieve higher AIG than the baseline, it is important to understand the

Quiz	TA	TA-LA	TA-LM	TA-LS	TA-FQ
Geo.	0.40	0.45	**0.68**	0.53	0.41
Sym.	**0.55**	0.50	0.48	0.49	0.41
Mix.	0.35	0.64	0.62	0.62	**0.66**

Table 3: Efficiency of various task allocation strategies on the Geography, Symptoms and Mixed quizzes.

Quiz	TA	TA-LA	TA-LM	TA-LS	TA-FQ
Geo.	**17.4**	16.8	11.5	16.3	13.3
Sym.	19.1	20.9	20.4	22.2	**23.2**
Mix.	**17.3**	15.0	13.8	15.7	15.9

Table 4: FP-AUC of different task allocation strategies on the Geography, Symptoms and Mixed quizzes. Most of the task allocation strategies do worse than the TA baseline, suggesting that the improved information gain does not stem from more answers but rather better allocation of tasks to users.

theoretical improvement that can be achieved by a *perfect task allocation strategy* given the same user qualities and participation. Table 3 summarizes the efficiency of each task allocation strategy, defined in Section 3.4.2.

Our results show that none of the dynamic task allocation strategies are consistently top performers. This could be due to inaccuracies in our models of user quality and user information gain (Section 3.4.1), especially for users who submit few answers.

For dynamic task allocation strategies, efficiency tends to be higher for the Mixed Quiz. We believe that this is due to the dynamic strategies appropriately allocating tasks in different domains to users based on their inferred interests and expertise. This suggests that grouping crowdsourcing tasks by domain is not always optimal; instead, system designers should use dynamic methods to select a task from an appropriate domain for each user.

Finally, the highest efficiency achieved by any of our methods is 0.68, which is still far from the theoretical maximum efficiency (1.0). This suggests that it is possible to further improve the efficiency of our dynamic task allocation techniques and increase AIG by up to 50%.

4.1.3 User Participation

We also evaluate our methods in terms of user participation to understand whether the increase in AIG can be attributed to better task allocation or simply better user engagement. Table 4 presents the measured FP-AUC (Section 3.4.3) for each quiz.

We observe that none of the dynamic task allocation strategies have consistently higher FP-AUC than the baseline model, despite all dynamic methods achieving higher AIG. This implies that the higher AIG of the dynamic models is due to better task allocation rather than increased levels of participation. The dynamic methods are better able to balance asking appropriate questions on a per user basis and asking questions that are likely to yield high information gain.

Len.	Users	Users$\geq$3	Avg. Answers	FP-AUC
3	212	88	10.3	6.8
5	191	93	7.7	7.1
7	199	103	10.0	7.6
10	207	101	12.0	8.4
20	202	101	19.8	12.5
25	201	94	18.5	12.0
30	154	74	17.9	11.3
40	192	82	21.8	13.0
50	226	106	25.4	15.2
-1	184	88	26.2	15.5

Table 5: Effects of varying stated quiz length. Increasing the quiz length tends to increase the area under the FP curve. "Users$\geq$3" refers to users who answer $\geq$ 3 questions. The average number of answers submitted is highest when the quiz length is not specified (last row, labeled "-1").

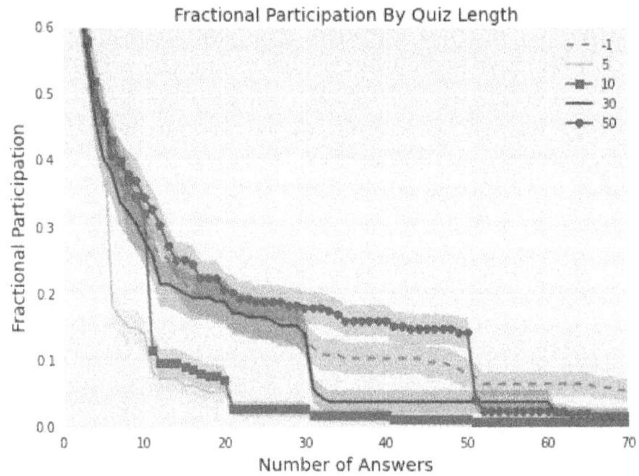

Figure 1: Fractional participation as a function of stated quiz length, plotted with shaded area representing one standard deviation away from the mean for both sides. Leaving quiz length unspecified ("-1") yields the highest fraction of users submitting more than 50 answers.

4.2 Static Goal Deployment

Quizz administers quizzes of length ten to incentivize users to contribute at least ten answers. Quiz length is clearly displayed to the users: a statistics bar on the task page reports the index of the current question out of ten. In this experiment we explore the effect of the displayed quiz length on user participation. We measure participation for quizzes of length up to 50 questions. We also repeat the experiment *without* displaying the quiz length at all. In each case, the stated length is the true length of the quiz; when no length is stated, questions are served until the user drops out. In all cases, when a user completes a quiz (i.e., answers ten questions in a quiz of length ten), the system immediately prompts the user to begin a new quiz. The results are summarized in Table 5 and Figure 1 (we omit displaying data for quizzes of lengths 3, 7, 20, 25 and 40 to improve readability; see Table 5 for all data).

Although previous research [2] suggests that humans work more effectively when trying to accomplish a goal, we find that, on average, users contribute the most answers when quizzes have an unspecified length (Table 5). Figure 1 shows that the FP curve corresponding to the quiz with unspecified length does not always dominate the other curves, but it has the highest fraction of users who contribute more than 50 answers. We find that our results are statistically significant using a sign test (with p-value <0.0001).

Figure 1 exhibits a clear trend that helps explain this surprising result: for all quizzes with a specified quiz length, the FP curve drops dramatically at the stated quiz length. For example, the curve that corresponds to quiz length 50 drops from about 0.15 to 0.04 between questions 50 and 51. Note that for the smaller quiz lengths (e.g., 10), there are similarly large drops at multiples of the quiz length (e.g., 20, 30 and so on). We hypothesize that this drop occurs because completing a quiz is a natural stopping point for users. The curve corresponding to the quiz of unspecified length has no large drops because there is no clear point at which users should stop working. In this way, leaving quiz length unspecified does not provide any encouragement to drop out for users with potential to answer a large number of questions.

However, in certain cases specifying quiz length does have some positive effects. As we can see in Figure 1, very few users drop off immediately before the stated quiz length. We hypothesize this happens because the goal seems so close and within reach. This implies that users are unlikely to drop out immediately before achieving goals. Although they provide natural points for users to drop out, in an appropriate context goals can be strong motivators for completing several additional tasks.

4.3 Dynamic Goal Deployment

Based on the results of the previous experiment (Section 4.2) we test dynamically setting quiz length (i.e. the goal) using the MDP for dynamic goal deployment (Section 2.4). In this experiment, setting a goal corresponds to specifying the number of questions remaining in the current quiz. We test setting the quiz length to an additional $x \in \{1, 2, 3, 4, 5\}$ questions (e.g. setting the goal to be completing three additional questions). We compare the results to two baselines: the TA baseline and the TA-INF baseline. It is important to compare our methods with the TA-INF baseline because the previous results (Section 4.2) show that leaving quiz length unspecified significantly boosts user participation. We recruit about 350 users for each experiment setting, which corresponds to about 150 users that submit at least three answers. We experiment with all task allocation strategies except for TA-LM (which does not perform well in practice).

4.3.1 Information Gain

Table 6 summarizes the improvement in AIG compared to the TA baseline method.

While all dynamic goal deployment strategies outperform the TA baseline, only a few of the dynamic strategies outperform the TA-INF baseline. Although setting goals dynamically can yield improvements in participation, inappropriately setting dynamic goals is *worse* than leaving goals unspecified. Intuitively, this result makes sense: setting a dynamic goal could trigger an early drop out.

Our results show that the TA-INF-DG-LS beats the TA-LS baseline regardless of the specific dynamic goal. This agrees with our information gain results in Section 4.1. The success of the LS model is in large part due to it being well calibrated (Section 4.4). A well calibrated model makes accurate estimates of a user's probability of survival allowing it to realistically compute expected information gain for task allocation.

Goal (Ques. Remaining)	LA	LS	FQ
-1	141.3%	133.7%	**147.8%**
1	42.5%	**249%**	102%
2	**156.4%**	154.7%	101.8%
3	127.4%	203.6%	27.6%
4	96.8%	232.9%	21.2%
5	122.6%	221.5%	74.4%

Table 6: Percent improvement in AIG for dynamic goal deployment over the TA baseline. "-1" corresponds to the TA-INF baseline.

Goal (Ques. Remaining)	LA	LS	FQ
static	16.0	16.0	16.0
-1	23.9	25.8	21.1
1	12.2	22.9	**23.9**
2	24.1	16.8	23.4
3	**27.2**	**26.8**	7.9
4	22.5	23.2	12.0
5	22.0	22.9	13.2

Table 7: FP-AUC under different models and adjustments in the dynamic goal deployment framework. "Static" corresponds to the TA baseline; "-1" corresponds to the TA-INF baseline.

Dynamic goal deployment using the FQ model performs the worst, with all the dynamic goals achieving lower information gain than leaving the goal unspecified. Upon further investigation, we discover that the FQ model triggers activating the dynamic goal *too eagerly*. Specifically, it deploys the dynamic goal five times as often as the other strategies. This causes 27.3% of the users to drop out immediately after the dynamic goal is triggered, compared to 11.5% in TA-INF-DG-LS model and 2.7% in TA-INF-DG-LA model. However, because the FQ model is not trained to predict a user's probability of survival, it is not well calibrated.

4.3.2 Effects of Dynamic Goal Deployments

Table 7 summarizes the affect of different dynamic goal deployment strategies on user participation.

The results show that not all the dynamic goal deployment strategies outperform the TA-INF baseline (i.e. no dynamic goal). We believe this to be the case for two reasons. First, these results are significantly impacted by model calibration (i.e. uncalibrated models can be highly detrimental). Second, dynamically setting goals that are difficult to attain (e.g. setting a goal to be answering five additional questions) can cause users to become frustrated and drop out prematurely. This hypothesis is supported by Figure 2, which shows the percent of users who drop out immediately after a dynamic goal is triggered.

Based on our results, dynamically setting quiz length to be three additional questions performs the best, with the ex-

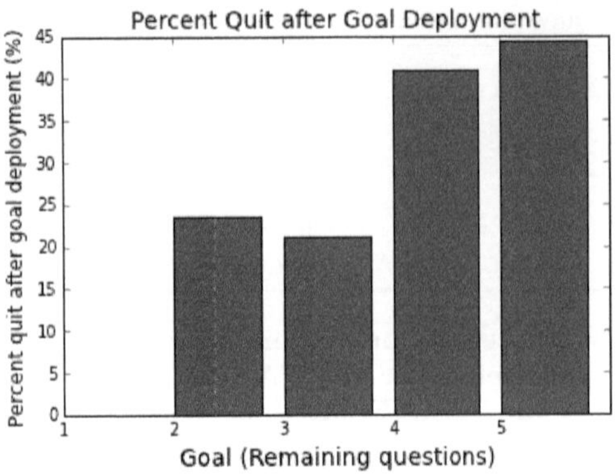

Figure 2: Percent of users who drop out after a dynamic goal is deployed. No users drop out if the dynamic goal is one additional question.

Model	Prediction accuracy
LA	77.5%
LM	69.8%
LS-1	65.2%
LS-2	70.8%
LS-3	71.9%
LS-4	71.0%
LS-5	70.9%
LS-6	75.3%
LS-7	69.8%
LS-8	73.3%
LS-9	70.8%
LS-10	74.3%

Table 8: Accuracy of survival model in 5-fold cross validation with instance reweighting to account for the imbalanced training data. Here, LS-N is the LS model trained for question N.

ception of the FQ model (as discussed previously, this could be due to the FQ model being uncalibrated for predicting survival probabilities).

4.4 Survival Models

As discussed in Section 3.3, our survival models are trained to predict the probability of a user dropping out given his or her state and the current question (except for the FQ model) . Table 8 summarizes the prediction accuracy of each survival model in 5-fold cross validation. The LA model performs the best with a prediction accuracy of 77.51%. The LS model also preforms well, with prediction accuracy ranging from 69.84% to 75.33%. We believe that the LS model has a worse prediction accuracy than the LA model because each of its ten predictors is trained with significantly less training data (than the LA model). The LM model performs the worst among the models presented and we believe it is because of the exclusion of the highly engaged users, where the prediction task could be easier.

We also examine how well each of the survival models is calibrated using Q-Q plots [28], which allows us to visualize two probability distributions by plotting their quantiles against each other. The results are shown in Figure 3. We find that all the models produce reasonable results in which the empirical survival probability increases almost monotonically with the model's output score. The LA and LS models are both better calibrated than the LM and FQ models. We present the Q-Q plot for LS-2 only (because of space limitations) but the Q-Q plots for the other LS models are similarly calibrated.

To better understand the performance of our survival models, we train a decision tree to evaluate the importance of each feature. The top five most important features are

- Whether there are 10 more questions in the quiz
- User's % correct for the current question's category
- The log(average response time) of the current question
- The log(average response time) of the user
- The % users who skipped the current question.

The importance of these features is intuitive. For example, average response time of a given question, if too long, might imply that the question is difficult and will negatively affect a user's probability of survival. If a user has an affinity for a particular question category, that user is likely to provide valuable contributions when served questions in that category.

5. RELATED WORK

One component of our work explores factors that affect user participation in crowdsourcing tasks. We focus on goals (e.g. quiz length) and dynamically adapting tasks based on models of user survival. Some recent work also builds models of user survival but does not use these models to inform task adaptation [15]. Other work proposes a variety of incentives and static task modifications to increase engagement without using user models. In one example, the authors introduce the notion of *micro-breaks*—short periods of time during which users participate in something other than the crowdsourcing task—and show that integrating them into long tasks can increase overall participation [23]. There has been some other work in user engagement with the web but these models are not immediately relevant for crowdsourcing [13]. Researchers have also studied participation patterns of Wikipedia editors [11].

A significant amount of recent work explores incentivizing participation with *badges*. Badges are awards that users earn through completion of arbitrary goals including both *absolute* goals (e.g., reaching some level of participation) and *relative* goals (e.g., becoming the top contributor in an online community). Researchers have analyzed the use of these badge types from an economic perspective in an effort to understand how to create mechanisms to encourage contributions [8]. In similar work, the authors build a model of user activity in the presence of badges and formalize a badge placement problem—a problem of creating a set of badges to incentivize users to participate according to the desires of a system designer [2]. Like our results, this work shows that users close to a goal are likely to work hard to achieve it (i.e., in our work, users are very unlikely to drop out when they are close to finishing a quiz). Unlike our work, these projects often do not focus on jointly incentivizing participation and the overall value of user contributions.

A related method of improving user engagement explored in the literature is that of personalization. Many researchers

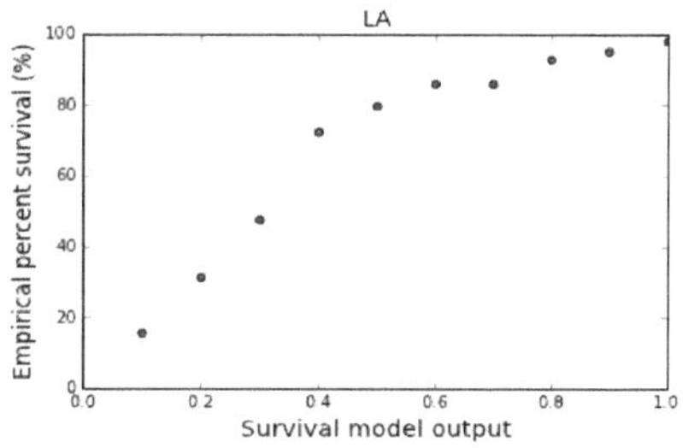

(a) Q-Q plot for LA model

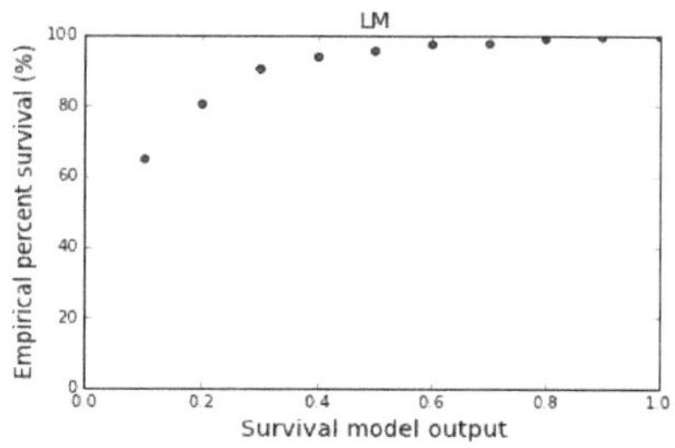

(b) Q-Q plot for LM model

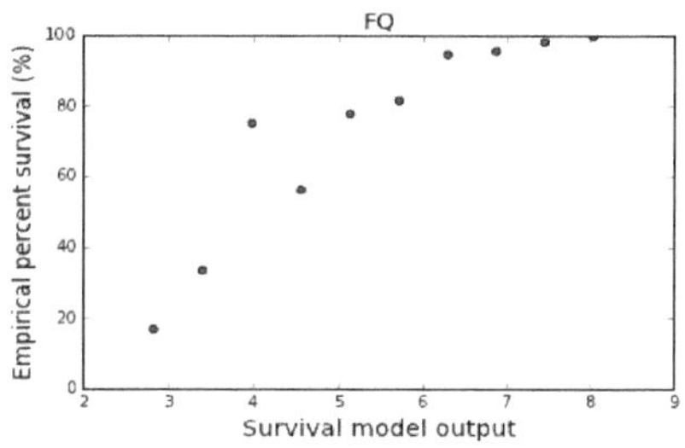

(c) Q-Q plot for FQ model

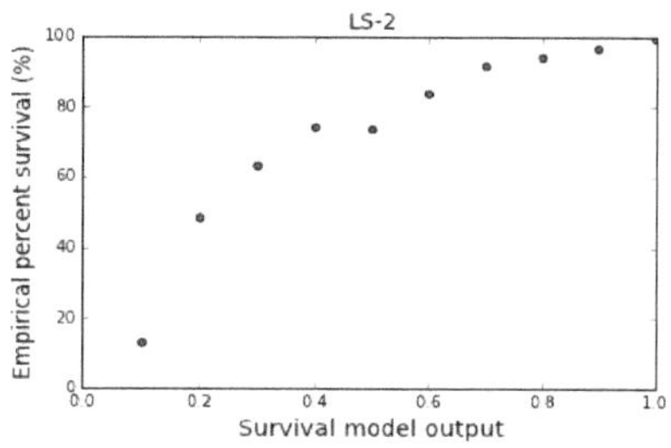

(d) Q-Q plot for LS-2 model

Figure 3: Q-Q plots for the survival models drawn by splitting the model output score into 10 buckets. The x-axis is the model output score and the y-axis is the empiricial survival probability of the data instances.

have identified the benefits of building human-computer interfaces that dynamically adapt to user preferences [17, 12]. This is similar to *computer adaptive testing* which describes tests in which questions are selected online based on the test-taker's performance. Adaptive testing can shorten tests, help gauge the user's ability quickly and make the test-taking experience better for the test-taker [14]. Our survival models facilitate a form of adaptive testing and personalization (i.e. dynamic task allocation) but our strategies consider more than task difficulty. There is also a significant body of work exploring various techniques for personalization of the web in order to improve user satisfaction [1, 9].

Like much of the recent crowdsourcing literature, our work focuses on improving user contribution quality. Like our work, there has been a significant amount of research developing methods for inferring user reliabilities and accuracy of collected labels. Some practitioners use expectation-maximization to jointly infer the reliability of users and the accuracy of the labels they submit [7, 27]. In another example, the authors propose a method for inferring the correct answers to multiple-choice questions by selecting answers that minimize a distance among all submitted answers (weighted by user reliability) [3]. Many of these studies have demonstrated the importance of modeling task difficulty [4] and user ability. Unlike our work, most of these methods are applicable after the data has been collected and thus cannot consider user participation.

Cosely et. al develop *intelligent task routing* for soliciting contributions from users for a movie database [5]. Their work is similar to our dynamic task allocation however each of their strategies is based on a single feature and none consider user survival. Other previous work makes use of a MDPs and partially observable MDPs (POMDPs) to actively modify crowdsourcing tasks. In one such project, the presented POMDP is used to actively modify crowdsourcing *workflows* to increase quality in the data collected [6]. Although this work does not explicitly focus on improving participation, it should be possible to train their POMDP considering both participation and contribution quality.

6. CONCLUSIONS

In this paper, we presented methods for realigning the interests of participants and designers of a crowdsourcing system. To this end, we introduced techniques that dynamically allocate tasks and goals in an optimal way in order to promote long-term user engagement. We presented four survival models for predicting when users will drop out from crowdsourcing tasks; these models form the basis of our dynamic techniques. We tested our survival-based dynamic task allocation in the context of Quizz a gamified crowdsourcing platform [10]. The results show that *survival-based task allocation* always yields higher information gain than the baseline that greedily allocates tasks with the highest entropy. With our best model we are able to improve upon the baseline by 117.8%.

This work also explored the effects of using specific goals on user participation. Surprisingly, we found that certain goals provide users with natural drop out points that decrease overall participation. We also found that users are very unlikely to drop out when close to achieving a goal. These findings inspired the development of *survival-based dynamic goal deployment*. In this approach, when users start a new quiz they are at first not shown any goal. When one of our models predicts that a user is likely to drop out, we deploy a goal in the form of an explicit limit on the quiz length (i.e., we show the user that she has only a few more tasks to complete). Coupling dynamic goal deployment with the our task allocation method, we jointly optimize user participation and quality. Using these techniques together, we increase the amount of information collection by the crowdsourcing system by up to 249% (compared to the baseline, as measured by the information gain).

7. REFERENCES

[1] S. S. Anand and B. Mobasher. Intelligent techniques for web personalization. In *Proceedings of the 2003 international conference on Intelligent Techniques for Web Personalization*, pages 1–36. Springer-Verlag, 2003.

[2] A. Anderson, D. Huttenlocher, J. Kleinberg, and J. Leskovec. Steering user behavior with badges. In *Proceedings of the 22nd international conference on World Wide Web*, pages 95–106. International World Wide Web Conferences Steering Committee, 2013.

[3] B. I. Aydin, Y. S. Yilmaz, Y. Li, Q. Li, J. Gao, and M. Demirbas. Crowdsourcing for multiple-choice question answering. In *Twenty-Sixth IAAI Conference*, 2014.

[4] Y. Bachrach, T. Graepel, T. Minka, and J. Guiver. How to grade a test without knowing the answers—a bayesian graphical model for adaptive crowdsourcing and aptitude testing. In *Proceedings of the 29th International Conference on Machine Learning (ICML-12)*, pages 1183–1190, 2012.

[5] D. Cosley, D. Frankowski, L. Terveen, and J. Riedl. Using intelligent task routing and contribution review to help communities build artifacts of lasting value. In *Proceedings of the SIGCHI conference on Human Factors in computing systems*, pages 1037–1046. ACM, 2006.

[6] P. Dai, C. H. Lin, D. S. Weld, et al. Pomdp-based control of workflows for crowdsourcing. *Artificial Intelligence*, 202:52–85, 2013.

[7] A. P. Dawid and A. M. Skene. Maximum likelihood estimation of observer error-rates using the em algorithm. *Applied statistics*, pages 20–28, 1979.

[8] D. Easley and A. Ghosh. Incentives, gamification, and game theory: an economic approach to badge design. In *Proceedings of the fourteenth ACM conference on Electronic commerce*, pages 359–376. ACM, 2013.

[9] M. Eirinaki and M. Vazirgiannis. Web mining for web personalization. *ACM Transactions on Internet Technology (TOIT)*, 3(1):1–27, 2003.

[10] P. G. Ipeirotis and E. Gabrilovich. Quizz: targeted crowdsourcing with a billion (potential) users. In *Proceedings of the 23rd international conference on World wide web*, pages 143–154. International World Wide Web Conferences Steering Committee, 2014.

[11] M. Krieger, E. M. Stark, and S. R. Klemmer. Coordinating tasks on the commons: designing for personal goals, expertise and serendipity. In *Proceedings of the SIGCHI Conference on Human Factors in Computing Systems*, pages 1485–1494. ACM, 2009.

[12] P. Langley. Machine learning for adaptive user interfaces. In *KI-97: Advances in artificial intelligence*, pages 53–62. Springer, 1997.

[13] J. Lehmann, M. Lalmas, E. Yom-Tov, and G. Dupret. Models of user engagement. In *User Modeling, Adaptation, and Personalization*, pages 164–175. Springer, 2012.

[14] J. M. Linacre et al. Computer-adaptive testing: A methodology whose time has come. *Chae, S.-Kang, U.-Jeon, E.-Linacre, JM (eds.): Development of Computerised Middle School Achievement Tests, MESA Research Memorandum*, (69), 2000.

[15] A. Mao, E. Kamar, and E. Horvitz. Why stop now? predicting worker engagement in online crowdsourcing. In *First AAAI Conference on Human Computation and Crowdsourcing*, 2013.

[16] W. Mason and D. J. Watts. Financial incentives and the performance of crowds. *ACM SigKDD Explorations Newsletter*, 11(2):100–108, 2010.

[17] S. McBurney, E. Papadopoulou, N. Taylor, and H. Williams. Adapting pervasive environments through machine learning and dynamic personalization. In *Parallel and Distributed Processing with Applications, 2008. ISPA'08. International Symposium on*, pages 395–402. IEEE, 2008.

[18] G. Neumann and J. R. Peters. Fitted q-iteration by advantage weighted regression. In *Advances in neural information processing systems*, pages 1177–1184, 2009.

[19] F. Pedregosa, G. Varoquaux, A. Gramfort, V. Michel, B. Thirion, O. Grisel, M. Blondel, P. Prettenhofer, R. Weiss, V. Dubourg, J. Vanderplas, A. Passos, D. Cournapeau, M. Brucher, M. Perrot, and E. Duchesnay. Scikit-learn: Machine learning in Python. *Journal of Machine Learning Research*, 12:2825–2830, 2011.

[20] M. L. Puterman. *Markov decision processes: discrete stochastic dynamic programming*, volume 414. John Wiley & Sons, 2009.

[21] V. C. Raykar, S. Yu, L. H. Zhao, G. H. Valadez, C. Florin, L. Bogoni, and L. Moy. Learning from crowds. *The Journal of Machine Learning Research*, 11:1297–1322, 2010.

[22] S. Robertson, M. Vojnovic, and I. Weber. Rethinking the esp game. In *CHI'09 Extended Abstracts on Human Factors in Computing Systems*, pages 3937–3942. ACM, 2009.

[23] J. M. Rzeszotarski, E. Chi, P. Paritosh, and P. Dai. Inserting micro-breaks into crowdsourcing workflows. In *First AAAI Conference on Human Computation and Crowdsourcing*, 2013.

[24] L. von Ahn. Duolingo: learn a language for free while helping to translate the web. In *Proceedings of the 2013 international conference on Intelligent user interfaces*, pages 1–2. ACM, 2013.

[25] L. Von Ahn, B. Maurer, C. McMillen, D. Abraham, and M. Blum. recaptcha: Human-based character recognition via web security measures. *Science*, 321(5895):1465–1468, 2008.

[26] T. P. Waterhouse. Pay by the bit: an information-theoretic metric for collective human judgment. In *Proceedings of the 2013 conference on Computer supported cooperative work*, pages 623–638. ACM, 2013.

[27] J. Whitehill, T.-f. Wu, J. Bergsma, J. R. Movellan, and P. L. Ruvolo. Whose vote should count more: Optimal integration of labels from labelers of unknown expertise. In *Advances in neural information processing systems*, pages 2035–2043, 2009.

[28] M. B. Wilk and R. Gnanadesikan. Probability plotting methods for the analysis for the analysis of data. *Biometrika*, 55(1):1–17, 1968.

Evolution of Conversations in the Age of Email Overload

Farshad Kooti
USC Information Sciences Institute, USA
kooti@usc.edu

Luca Maria Aiello
Yahoo Labs Barcelona, Spain
alucca@yahoo-inc.com

Mihajlo Grbovic
Yahoo Labs Sunnyvale, USA
mihajlo@yahoo-inc.com

Kristina Lerman
USC Information Sciences Institute, USA
lerman@isi.edu

Amin Mantrach
Yahoo Labs Barcelona, Spain
amantrac@yahoo-inc.com

ABSTRACT

Email is a ubiquitous communications tool in the workplace and plays an important role in social interactions. Previous studies of email were largely based on surveys and limited to relatively small populations of email users within organizations. In this paper, we report results of a large-scale study of more than 2 million users exchanging 16 billion emails over several months. We quantitatively characterize the replying behavior in conversations within pairs of users. In particular, we study the time it takes the user to reply to a received message and the length of the reply sent. We consider a variety of factors that affect the reply time and length, such as the stage of the conversation, user demographics, and use of portable devices. In addition, we study how increasing load affects emailing behavior. We find that as users receive more email messages in a day, they reply to a smaller fraction of them, using shorter replies. However, their responsiveness remains intact, and they may even reply to emails faster. Finally, we predict the time to reply, length of reply, and whether the reply ends a conversation. We demonstrate considerable improvement over the baseline in all three prediction tasks, showing the significant role that the factors that we uncover play, in determining replying behavior. We rank these factors based on their predictive power. Our findings have important implications for understanding human behavior and designing better email management applications for tasks like ranking unread emails.

Categories and Subject Descriptors

H.4.3 [**Information Systems**]: Information systems applications—*Communications Applications*

Keywords

Emailing behavior, information overload, prediction

1. INTRODUCTION

Electronic mail — email — remains an essential tool for social interactions and a popular platform for computer-mediated communication. It is used within organizations to exchange information and coordinate action, but also by ordinary people to converse with friends. Patterns of email interactions reveal circadian rhythms [32] and bursty dynamics of human activity [3], and the structure of evolving conversations [17]. Understanding how these patterns shape email use is necessary for designing the next generation of interaction tools that will improve the efficiency of communication and coordination in social groups.

Early studies of email examined how people process [12, 11], organize [40], and respond [34] to email messages. By surveying users within organizations, researchers uncovered common email triage strategies, with some users processing emails serially, while others read and reply to important messages first [34].

Those studies had relatively small sample sizes and were limited by their methodology to answering qualitative questions about email behavior. As a result, we do not have answers to a number of questions about how people use email. How many email conversations do people have? How long are these conversations and how do they end? When do people respond to a message in a conversation? Do they adapt their replies to the behavior of their conversation partner?

Furthermore, as the volume of email has increased steadily over the years, the concept of "email overload" has grown in prominence. Dabbish & Kraut [11] defined "email overload" as *"email users' perceptions that their own use of email has gotten out of control because they receive and send more email than they can handle, find, or process effectively."*. This motivates a whole set of questions that have been recently addressed in the setting of online social networks [21, 20], but never fully in the context of email. How does the volume of incoming email, information or email load, affect user behavior? How do people compensate for the increased load: do they take longer to reply, or do they send shorter replies that take less time to compose?

We address these questions with a largest study to date of email conversations (16B emails). We focus our analyses on the replying behavior within *dyadic interactions*, i.e., conversations between pairs of users. Specifically, we measure the time a user takes to reply to a message, the length of the reply, as well as the fraction of messages a user replies to. First, we empirically characterize replying behavior in email conversations in a large population of users, and also how these behaviors vary by gender and age. Although we find no significant variation due to gender, we find that younger email users reply faster and write shorter replies than older users.

Next, we study how email load, measured by the number of received email messages, affects replying behavior. We find that while users attempt to adapt to the rising information load by replying to more emails, they do not adequately compensate. As email load increases, they reply faster but to a decreasing fraction of in-

WWW 2015, May 18–22, 2015, Florence, Italy.
ACM 978-1-4503-3469-3/15/05.
http://dx.doi.org/10.1145/2736277.2741130.

coming emails. These findings suggest that email overload is a problem, with users generally unable to keep up with rising load.

We also study how replying behavior evolves over the course of a conversation. We find that users initially synchronize their behaviors, with reply times and length of replies becoming more similar in the first half of the conversation. However, they become desynchronized in the second half of the conversation. In contrast, users continue to coordinate their linguistic styles, as messages exchanged over the course of the entire conversation become more similar in content and style.

Finally, we develop a model to predict users' replying behavior in a conversation, namely, how long it will take the user to reply to a message, the length of the reply, and if the reply will end the thread. The features that we use for prediction include history of communication between the users, user demographics, email load, as well as the day of the week and time the message was received. Our predictive model considerably outperforms the baseline in all three cases. We obtain accuracy of 58.8% for reply time, which is a 67.1% relative improvement over the baseline, and 71.8% accuracy for length of replies (113.7% relative improvement over the baseline). We also predict the last email of the thread with accuracy of 65.9%, a 30.2% relative improvement over the baseline. Ability to accurately predict what messages a user will reply to can be used by email clients to rank emails in the users' inbox by their replying priority, thus helping ease the burden of information overload.

The key contributions of our work are:

1. We empirically characterize email *replying behavior* of users, focusing on reply time, length of the reply, and the correlation between them. We quantify how different factors, including the day and time the message was received, the device used, the number of attachments in the email, and user demographics affect replying.

2. We show that *email overload* is evident in email usage and has adverse effects, resulting in users replying to a smaller fraction of received emails. Users tend to send shorter replies, but with shorter delays when receiving many emails. We find that different age groups cope with overload differently: younger users shorten their replies, while older users reply to smaller fraction of received messages.

3. We find evidence of *synchronization* in dyadic interactions within a thread: users become more similar in terms of reply time and length of replies until the middle of a thread, and start acting more independently after that.

4. We can predict reply time and length, and the last email in a thread with a much higher accuracy than the baseline. This has important implications for designing future email clients.

2. DATASET

Yahoo Mail is one of the largest email providers in the world, with over 300M users (according to ComScore[1]), who generate an extremely high volume of messages. Obviously, not all the email addresses are associated with real people and are used instead by organizations or possibly bots to generate emails for commercial promotions and spam [25, 41, 22]. To meet the goal of studying social interactions, it is necessary to subsample the data to a set of interactions that are likely occurring between real people. For this reason, we apply a conservative filtering strategy and focus our study on user pairs (or *dyads*) that exhibit *reciprocal interaction*

[1]http://www.comscore.com

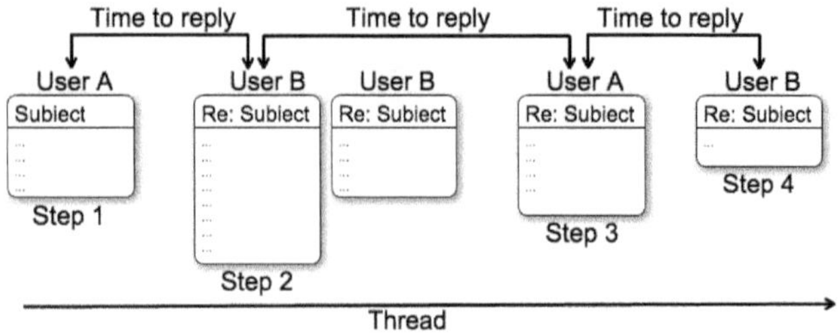

Figure 1: Illustration of an email thread.

(i.e., bi-directionality of emails sent) and exchange some minimum number of messages. This ensures that *i)* all the email addresses of the dyadic endpoints are likely associated with human users, and that *ii)* the emails sent between them are not automatically generated.

Accordingly, we selected a random subsample $\mathcal{E}$ of 1.3M dyads of Yahoo Mail users worldwide who have significant interactions with each other, sending at least five replies in each direction in the time span of undisclosed number of months. For privacy and policy reasons, the dataset includes messages belonging exclusively to users who voluntarily opted-in for such studies. Consequently, considering a pair of users who exchanged more than 5 emails, both users need to be opt-in users to be included in the study. These pairs comprise a set $\mathcal{N}$ containing 2M unique users exchanging 187M emails overall. We refer to the full sequence of emails flowing within the dyad as a *conversation*. Next, we gathered *all* incoming and outgoing emails of users in $\mathcal{N}$ over the same time period, a total of 16B emails. Note that these emails included only emails from commercial domains and emails to and from other opt-in Yahoo users. Due to Yahoo policy, the study did not include personal email messages between Yahoo users and other email clients. In addition, we excluded notifications from social network sites, such as Facebook or Twitter, which represent a considerable portion of commercial, automatically-generated emails.

We conduct our study at two different levels: at the dyadic level, we consider only the emails flowing between dyad endpoints; at the global level, we consider the entire dataset. In the latter case, commercial and spam messages will be likely be part of the incoming emails directed to users in $\mathcal{N}$. As one of the goals of this work is to study information overload in all its facets, we don't apply any *a priori* filter. Then, depending on the target of each part of the analysis, we apply ad-hoc filters to fit our specific goals.

Each email included the *sender ID*, *receiver ID*, *time sent*, *subject*, *body* of the email, and number of *attachments*. All data were anonymized to preserve user privacy and worked at the level of anonymized user ids and email ids. Given the data sensitivity, even with opt-in users, email bodies were not editorially inspected by humans. To extract statistics from email bodies (length, number of articles, email vectors, email ids in a thread, etc.), we made a MapReduce call with a specified function to a protected cluster.

To make sense of the conversation flow, we need to break down the dyadic conversations into *threads*. A thread is an ordered sequence of one or more emails, including the initial email, and the list of succeeding replies to it (if any). As our dataset does not keep track of the thread structure, we need to reconstruct it. We compose the threads using the subject line and the time each email was sent. Yahoo Mail automatically adds the token *"Re: "* to the subject line of all replies. For each pair of the users, we group all the exchanged emails that have the same subject line. If all the emails in the group start with "Re:", we also add the email that has the exact subject without the "Re:"; this email would be the first email of the thread. Then, in each group we order the emails based on the

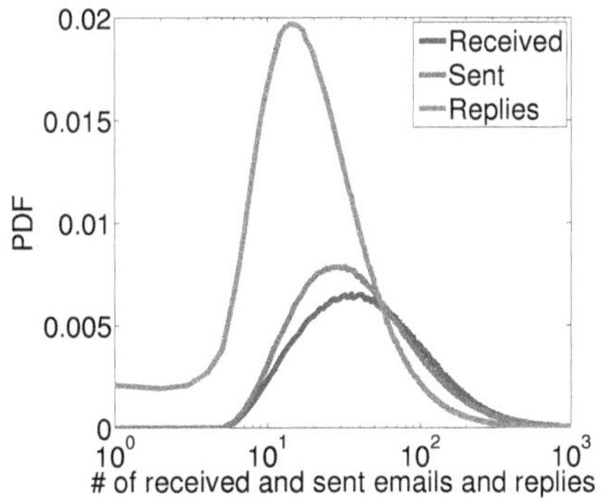

Figure 2: Distribution of number of received, sent, and replied emails.

sent time, and the time to replies could be calculated as the delay between the email from one user and the reply of the other user. In case of consecutive replies in one thread from one of the users, we just consider the first one (Figure 1).

Like most other email service providers, Yahoo Mail quotes the body of the original message at the end of the reply, unless manually removed. To get only the text of the last email sent, we search for standard string templates that occur before the quoted message, (e.g., "On Thursday May 1, 2014 a@yahoo.com wrote") and exclude any text from that point. We also looked for common mobile device signatures, such as "Sent from my iPhone" and exclude the text from the signature onwards.

Limitations. Our data comes with a few limitations. First, in case of an in-line reply, we would not be able to detect the quoted message, and it would be considered as a new message. The quoted message could be caught by comparison of reply and the email being replied to, but the string matching would be computationally expensive for the scale of our dataset. Second, we are not able to handle the emails that are sent to a group of users, and we consider all the emails as being dyadic. Moreover, for constructing the threads, we use the exact subject line and if there are two different threads between two users with the same subject, we will consider both of them as one thread. We believe these cases are special cases and a small fraction of emails, so our results would not be effected by these limitations.

Spam. One main concern with studying emails is the spam. To minimize the effect of spam, we conduct most of our analyses on dyadic email exchanges that occur between two users who have exchanged at least five emails with each other. We believe that the fact that two users have exchanged more than five emails means that neither of them is a spammer. In the analysis of the information load on users, we have to consider all the emails those users received, and many of them could be spam and should not be considered. To deal with this problem, we conduct the analysis once for all the received emails and once for emails received from contacts, i.e., others with whom the user had exchanged at least one email. Again, filtering users who have not received any replies from a user is a very conservative approach to eliminate spammers.

Figure 2 shows the distribution of the number of received, sent, and replied email messages for the 1.3M users for whom we have incoming and outgoing emails outside $\mathcal{E}$. Figure 3(a) shows the distribution of the number of emails in a thread across all conversations. This distribution has the expected heavy-tailed shape: most threads are very short, e.g., more than 30% of threads have only one step, which means, it's an email and a single reply to it. We also look at the number of the threads in a conversation (i.e., all

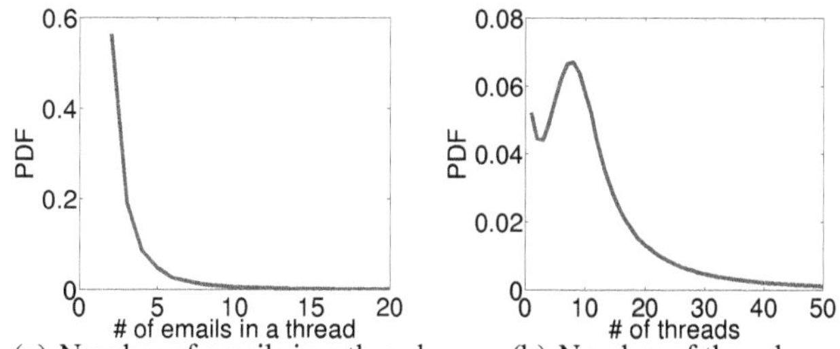

(a) Number of emails in a thread (b) Number of threads

Figure 3: Statistics of conversations. (a) Number of emails in a thread (mean 3.76 emails, median 2 emails) and (b) the number of threads in conversations (mean 13.94 emails, median 9 emails).

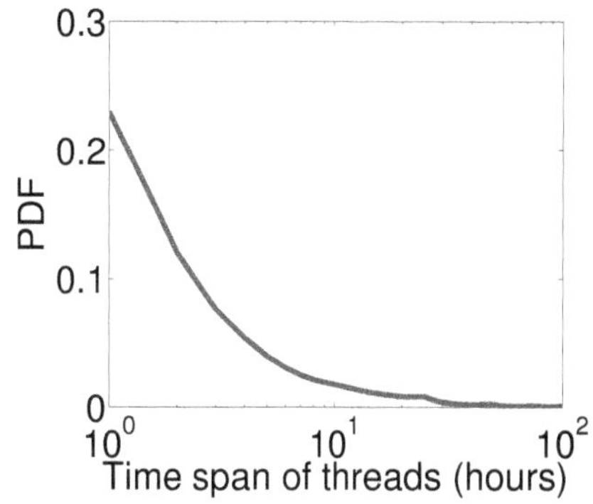

Figure 4: Distribution of time span of threads (mean 53.2 hours, median 3.5 hours).

the emails exchanged) during the considered period (Figure 3(b)). There is a small drop at the beginning, and then an increase up to 10 threads, after that users are less likely to have more threads. Also to better understand the time scale of communications, we measure the longevity of threads for all users (Figure 4). Many threads last for only a few hours; half of the threads last 3.5 hours or less. But, there is a considerable fraction of threads that last longer a day (22%).

3. REPLYING BEHAVIOR

We characterize the replying behavior of email users involved in dyadic interactions, focusing on reply time and the length of replies.

3.1 Reply time and length

Reply time is the period between the time the sender sends a message (e.g., "user A" in Figure 1) and the time the receiver ("user B") replies to it. When receiver replies after multiple consecutive emails are sent by the sender within the same thread, reply time is calculated from the time of the first message to the time the receiver replied. We experimented with different definitions of reply time, e.g., from the time of the last messages in a series of emails in a thread, but this did not significantly change the key properties of replying behavior, resulting only in slightly faster replies.

Figure 5 shows the probability distribution function (PDF) and the cumulative distribution function (CDF) of reply times. Most of the replies are very fast: more than 90% happen within a day of receiving the message, and the most likely reply time is just two minutes. Also, half of the replies are within 47 minutes of receiving the message. Interestingly, this distribution is very similar to the time it takes users to retweet a message on Twitter [24].

The length of a reply is the length of the message receiver sends

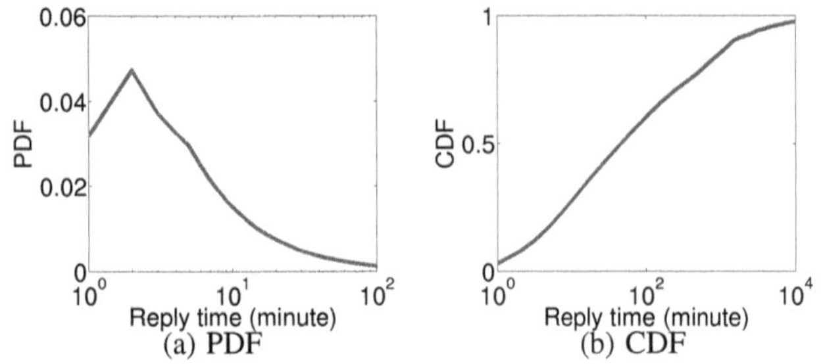

Figure 5: Distribution of reply times. In general, replies are very fast (mean:1157 minutes, median: 47 minutes, standard deviation: 19730).

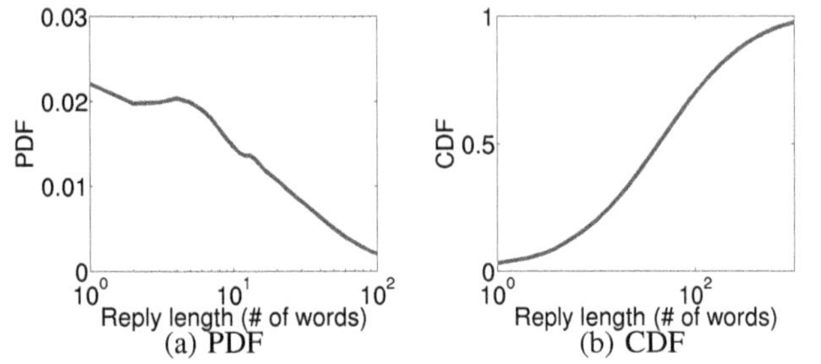

Figure 6: Distribution of reply lengths (mean 153 words, median 43 words, standard deviation 419).

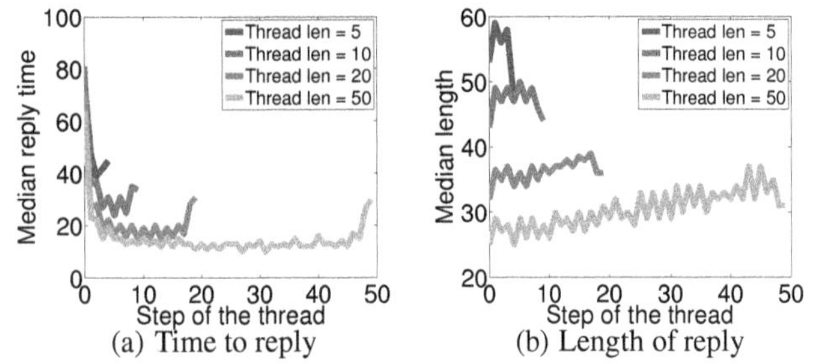

Figure 7: (a) Median reply time for different steps of threads for a given thread length. Replies become faster, except for the very last reply that is much slower. (b) Median length of reply for different steps of threads for a given thread length. Calculated on dyadic conversations.

back to the sender, excluding the body of the original message, which may have been quoted in the email. Figure 6 shows the PDF and CDF of the length of replies. Considerable fraction of replies are very short: the most likely reply length is only five words, with half of the replies being shorter than 43 words. However, there is a non-negligible fraction of long emails; 30% of emails are longer than 100 words.

3.2 Evolution of Conversations

Next, we investigate the effect of the position of the reply within a conversation (i.e., step in a thread) on the reply time and length. Figure 7(a) shows how reply time changes as a function of thread step, for threads of different length. Replies become faster as the conversation progresses, but the last reply is much slower than the previous replies. The long delay in a reply could be considered as a signal for the end of the conversation. Figure 7(b) shows the effect of thread step on the length of the reply. Replies get slightly longer as conversation progresses, although the last reply

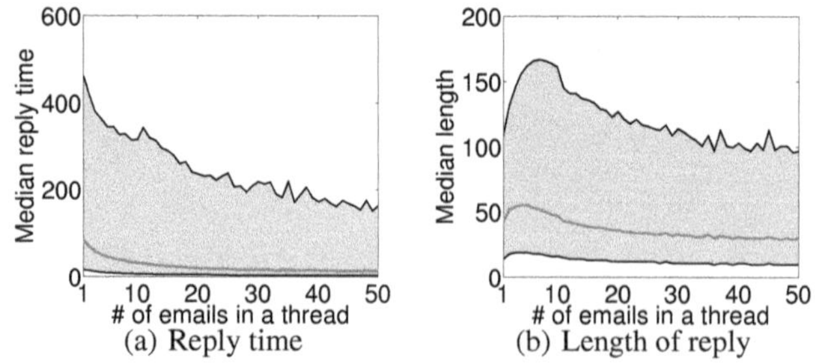

Figure 8: Reply time and length as a function of the length of a conversation for dyadic interactions with less than 50 steps in a thread, which are 99.7% of all threads. Each plot shows the median, 25th and 75th percentile of the measure vs. the number of messages in a thread. Longer threads have shorter reply delays and lengths.

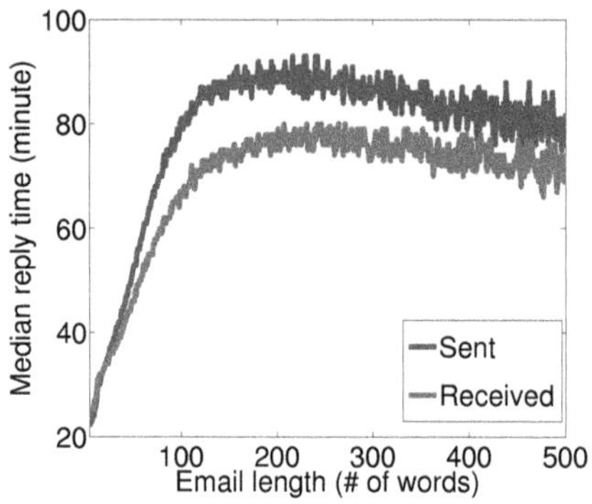

Figure 9: Correlation between time to reply and length of reply for outgoing and incoming emails for dyadic conversations. There is a strong correlation till the length of 200 words (more than 83% of all replies).

in a thread is much shorter than the previous replies. Moreover, we see that longer conversations (threads) have faster reply times and shorter reply lengths. To better quantify this effect, we calculate the median reply time and length for different thread lengths. We find that both reply times and length of replies are smaller in longer conversations (Figure 8). This would be expected if the data covered a very short time period, because the reply times would had to be small to fit a long conversation in a short period of time. But, this is not the case here, since we are covering several months.

Figure 9 shows how time to reply to an incoming (received) message varies as the function of the length of the received message and the length of the reply. There is a strong correlation between reply time and length, showing that longer replies take longer to be composed. However, replies longer than 200 words are slightly faster. This could be due to a number of reasons. First, we may not properly account for message length due to copy and pasted emails or missed quoted messages. Second, there could be systematic differences in the population of users who write replies longer than 200 words, e.g., such users may be more adept at writing. There is also a strong correlation between reply time and the length of received emails, showing that the longer the messages the users receive, the longer it takes them to reply. The slight decrease in reply time for messages longer than 200 words could be explained as above.

4. FACTORS AFFECTING REPLYING

A variety of factors affect replying behavior, most obviously the contents of the messages and who they are from. These are id-

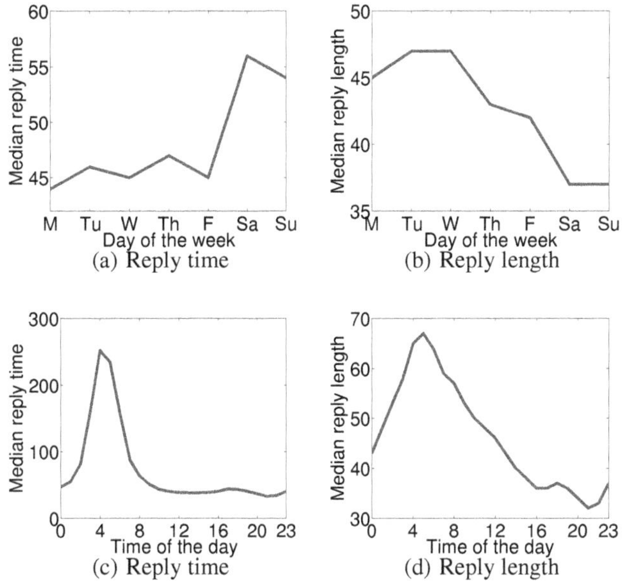

(a) Reply time (b) Reply length
(c) Reply time (d) Reply length

Figure 10: Day of the week and time of the day effects on email reply time and length. (a) Reply time in minutes and (b) length in number of words as a function of day of the week the message replied to was received. Emails received on weekends get shorter and slower replies, compared to the workdays. (c) Reply time and (d) length as a function of the hour of the day the email was received. Emails received during the night have considerably longer reply times.

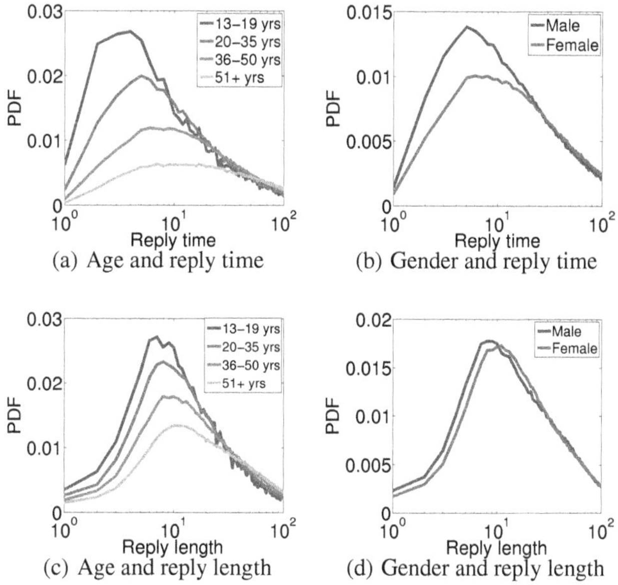

(a) Age and reply time (b) Gender and reply time
(c) Age and reply length (d) Gender and reply length

Figure 11: Demographics and email replying behaviors. PDF of reply time of users categorized by (a) age and (b) gender. Teens are fastest to reply, and as users get older their replies become slower. PDF of reply length of user populations divided by (c) age and (d) gender. Teenagers have the shortest replies, and as users get older their replies become longer.

iosyncratic and highly variable. Instead, in this section we examine universal factors that affect reply time and length, such as the time of the day the message was received, user's demographic characteristics, and volume of emails received. In Section 5, we show that these factors help predict user replying behavior even when email content is not known.

4.1 Circadian Rhythms

Email users are more active during the day than night time, and also on workdays rather than the weekend. These circadian cycles have a strong effect on email replying behavior. Figure 10 shows how the day of the week and the hour of the day the message was received, accounting for the time-zones, affect how quickly the email is replied to and the length of the reply. Emails received on weekends get substantially shorter replies compared to those received on workdays (Fig. 10(b)). The replies are also much slower (Fig. 10(a)). Messages received during the night get slower replies than those received during working hours (Fig. 10(c)). Interestingly, messages received in the morning get substantially longer replies than those received in the afternoon and evening (Fig. 10(d)).

4.2 Demographics of Users

Next, we investigate how demographic factors affect replying behavior. We categorize users based on their age and gender and compare email replying behavior across different populations. Results of demographic analysis of reply time are presented in Figure 11. Youngest email users, teens, have the fastest reply times; as users get older they become slower to reply to emails. Median reply time of different age groups was as follows: 13 minutes for teens, 16 minutes for young adults (20–35 years old), 24 minutes for adults (36–50 years old), and 47 minutes for mature users (51 and older). Gender does not seem to play as important a role in the replying

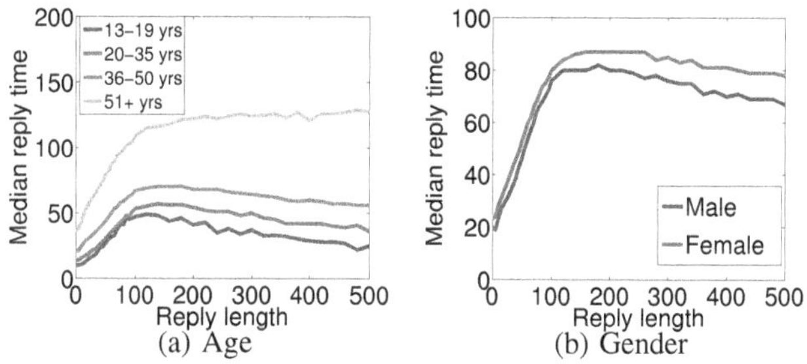

(a) Age (b) Gender

Figure 12: Median time to reply, given the length of the reply. Younger users are faster in composing the emails with the same length, compared to older users, and males are slightly faster than females.

behavior: females and males have very similar distributions of reply time, with men being slightly faster, with median reply time of 24 minutes, compared to 28 minutes for women.

The length of replies is also affected by demographics. Similar to reply time distribution, user groups who send faster replies, also send shorter replies: teens send the shortest replies and older users send longer ones. Teenagers' median reply length is only 17 words, while young adults' median reply length is 21 words, for adults it is 31 words, and for mature users it is 40 words. There is again no considerable difference between males and females, males having median length of 28 words, compared to females with median length of 30 words.

The older users are in general sending replies with longer delays, but they are also sending longer replies, which might explain their longer delays. To test if the difference in reply time is caused by the difference in length of replies, we compare the reply time of the users with different ages, while we account for the length of the reply. When plotting the median reply time for particular length of replies (Figure 12) the difference between young and older users becomes even clearer. Teenagers typically spend 39 minutes for sending a reply with 50 words, whereas older users (51+ years old) spend 79 minutes for the replies with the same length. Interestingly, as the length of the reply increases, the gap between the older users and younger users also increases. We repeat the same analysis for the gender of the users and the males are slightly faster than the females in composing replies of the same length.

4.3 Mobile Devices

We did not have access to email metadata, which had such useful information as the email client and the device used to send the email. However, we were able to reconstruct some of this information, because many mobile devices add a signatures, like "Sent from my iPhone", to the sent emails by default. Using such signatures, we were able to identify emails that were sent from smart phones or tablets and compare them with the emails from desktop computers. While this procedure does not detect all emails from mobile devices, the large size of our corpus gives us enough data to look for systematic differences in the replying behavior of mobile device users. Hence, to categorized emails as being sent from a phone, a tablet, or a desktop, we search for signatures such as "Sent from my iPhone" and "Sent from my iPad" (among others), after removing the quoted message, so that we would not catch a signature in the quoted message.

We find that replies sent from phones are the fastest, followed by emails sent from tablets, and finally replies from desktops. Emails from phones have a median reply time of only 28 minutes, compared to the 57 minutes for the replies from tablets, and 62 minutes for the desktop. This is expected since users often configure their phones to notify them of a received email, and they usually have their phones with them. Also, replies sent from mobile devices tend to be shorter than those sent from desktops. Replies from phones have a median length of 20 words, and tablets have a median length of 27 words, while desktops have median of 60 words.

Interestingly, adults (35–50 years old) represent the highest percentage of mobile device users, with 53% of them using a phone or a tablet at least once. Teens and young adults are the next largest populations of mobile users, with 49% and 48%, respectively. Mature adults use mobile devices the least: only 43% of them do. Also, more women use mobile devices than men (50% vs. 45%).

4.4 Attachments

We also study the effect of attachments in received emails on the time and length of replies. Replies to emails with attachments are much slower (median of 56 minutes) than replies to emails without any attachment (median of 32 minutes). The difference of almost a factor of two could be explained by the time needed for reading the attachment. Also, the emails with an attachment, get longer replies (median of 47 words) than emails without attachments (median of 33 words), which is probably due to the fact that the replier has to respond to more information.

4.5 Email Overload

How does replying behavior change as the number of incoming emails increases? In other words, as users receive more emails in a day, how do they adapt to the increased information load: do they become more active and reply to more emails, do they delay replying or fail to reply altogether?

We characterize a user's *email load* by the number of messages the user receives in a day, and the user *activity* by the number of sent emails. We divide users into two groups based on their activity: *low activity* and *high activity*. To do this, we rank users by their activity and consider the top third to be the *high activity* users and the bottom third as *low activity* users.

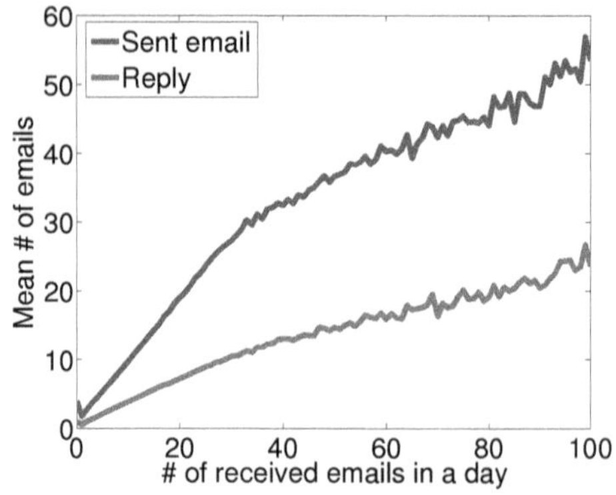

Figure 13: Change in behavior due to increased email load. Users send and reply to more emails, as they receive more emails in a day.

Email load affects user behavior. Users increase their activity as their email load, i.e., the number of emails received that day, grows. Figure 13 shows that user activity increases, both in terms of the number of sent emails and replied emails, as the number of emails they receive in a day grows. Here, we eliminate the users who sent more than 1,000 emails in a day, which is equivalent to sending more than one email in a minute for 16 hours straight. Such high activity is likely generated by bots, rather than humans.

While users increase their activity with higher email load, it appears that they are not able to adequately compensate for the increased load. Figure 14(a) shows that as the email load increases, users reply to a smaller fraction of their emails, from about 25% of all emails received in a day at low load to less than 5% of emails at high load (about 100 emails a day). However, highly active users are better able to keep up with the rising email load than low activity users.

Of course, not all emails require replies: spam, mailing list, advertisements, and purchase notifications are generally not replied to. As the number of such emails a user receives increases, the user might still be able to keep up with interactions with contacts, so the decreasing fraction of replies may not signal email overload. To address this question, we restrict analysis to emails received from contacts only, i.e., Yahoo mail users who emailed each other in our data set. The overall trend shown in Figure 14(b) is the same: as email load increases, users reply to an ever smaller fraction of emails. This suggests that information overload is a problem, and users are unable to keep pace with rising incoming email traffic. Note that we cannot compare figures 14(a) and 14(b) with each other, since a user with a particular load in Figure 14(a) would move to the left in Figure 14(b) and might bring down the fraction for the days with low email load.

Next, we categorize users based on their demographics to see how they respond to email overload. Figure 15(a) shows the result for different age groups. Younger users can deal with the increasing information load much better than older users. Teens seem to experience little overload, replying to a constant fraction of emails, even as the load increases. Email overload becomes progressively worse for older age groups. There is little difference in how different genders respond to email load, with women slightly more affected by the increase in the load of information than men (Figure 15(b)).

We also investigate how email load affects reply time and length.

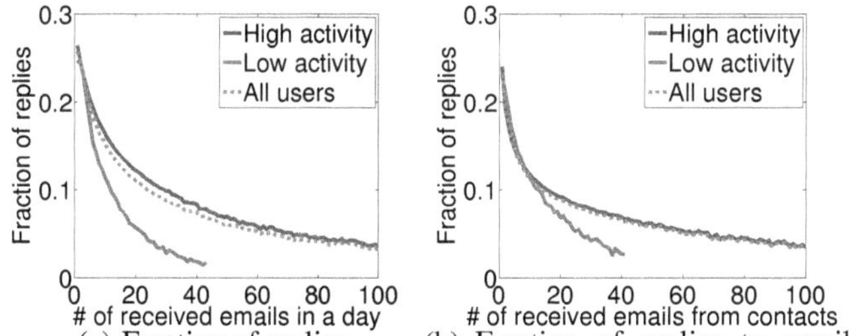

(a) Fraction of replies (b) Fraction of replies to email from contacts

Figure 14: Fraction of replies given the number of emails received in a day. (a) The number of received emails includes all emails. (b) Only emails received from contacts who the user had sent a message to are counted as received emails.

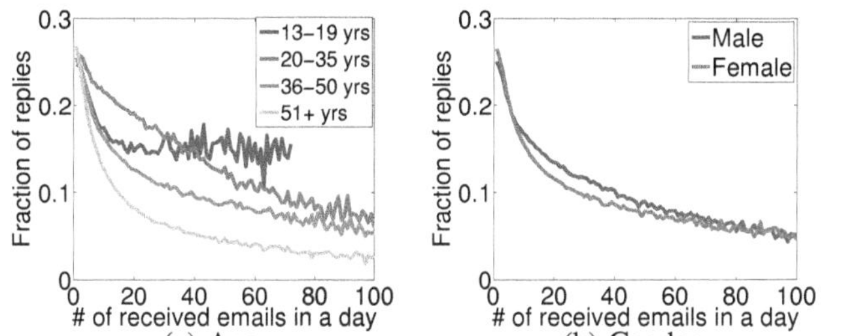

(a) Age (b) Gender

Figure 15: Fraction of replies given the number of emails received in a day for different demographic populations. Younger users are less sensitive to email overload than older users, while men are similar to women in their response. Reply time is for emails from dyadic interactions, but received emails include all emails.

Figure 16(a) shows the median reply time for messages sent on days with a given email load. Reply time decreases rapidly as information load increases. While this may seem counterintuitive at first, it makes sense in light of an earlier study [11], which found that a productive strategy for reducing the perception of email overload was to frequently check the email inbox. If users check email frequently, they are more likely to respond to more recent emails, decreasing the reply time. Interestingly, low activity users reply slightly faster as email load increases.

Moreover, the length of replies also decreases as email load grows (Figure 16(b)). This could be partially explained as a strategy to compensate for rising information load: users send shorter messages in order to reply to more messages, and since shorter messages take less time to write, reply time decreases as well. High activity users are not affected as much by overload as low activity users. They seem to compensate and send messages that are twice as long as what the low activity users are sending.

Finally, we investigate the effect of increased load of information on reply time and length of reply of users with different ages and genders. Figure 17 shows that younger users change their behavior more than older people, both for reply time and length of reply. When younger users become more overloaded they tend to send shorter and faster replies to cope with the increased load, on the other hand, older people are affected less with respect to reply time and length of reply, but as we have seen in the previous analyses, older users adapt to the increased load by replying to a smaller fraction of emails. Young users and old users cope with information overload differently, younger users try to reply to as many emails as they are supposed to at the expense of spending less time for each reply and sending shorter replies, whereas older users' replies do not become significantly faster nor shorter, but they do reply to a smaller fraction of emails.

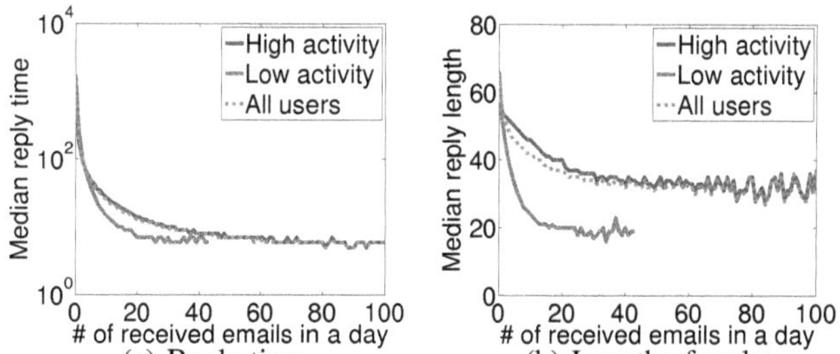

(a) Reply time (b) Length of reply

Figure 16: (a) Reply time and (b) length as a function of email load. Email load is measured by the number of all emails received in a day. As email load grows, users send shorter and faster replies.

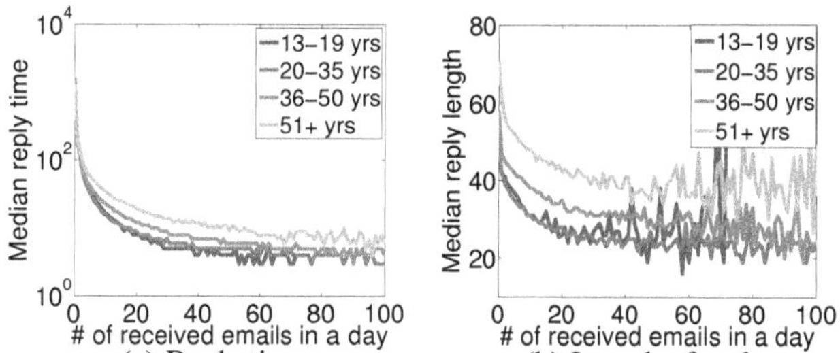

(a) Reply time (b) Length of reply

Figure 17: (a) Reply time and (b) length as a function of email load for users with different ages. Younger users decrease their reply time and length of reply more, to better handle the increased load.

4.6 Synchronization of Replying Behaviors

Do users coordinate their replies as the conversation evolves? In other words, do they become synchronized as their reply times and lengths become more similar over the course of the conversation, or do they act independently? To answer this question, we compare reply times at different stages in a thread. We do this by calculating the absolute difference in reply times in a thread, and then we divide the thread into 10 equal segments and report the mean difference within each segment. Since some users may be inherently fast, and we are interested in the change of behaviors rather than absolute value, we initially normalize the users' reply time by their median reply time. Median is used instead of the mean since reply time has a heavy-tailed distribution, and a single very long reply time would skew the mean, resulting in a very small normalized values.

Figure 18(a) shows evolution of reply times in a thread, along with the 95% confidence interval. Reply times become more similar until the middle of the conversation, and diverge afterwards: users become more synchronized until the mid-point of the conversation, then they start acting more independently. We repeat the analysis with the length of replies. Figure 18(b) shows a similar pattern: synchronization till the middle of the conversation and divergence afterwards. There is no significant difference in synchronization of behaviors between active and less active users.

Next, we study the content of emails in a thread, in particular, whether concepts converge over the course of a conversation. We divide each thread to 10 equal segments and calculate for each segment the cosine similarity between consecutive replies, and the average of cosine similarities at each step.

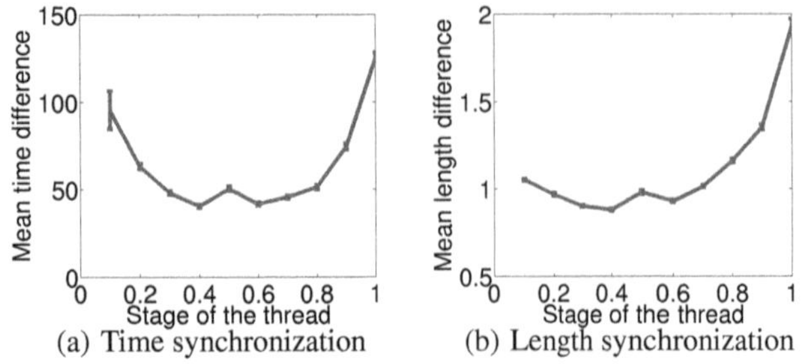

Figure 18: Synchronization of (a) reply times and (b) length of replies over the course of the conversation with 95% confidence interval. Users become more similar till the middle of conversation and become less similar till the end. For dyadic conversations.

We used a neural language model, known as paragraph2vec [31], to represent each email as a real-valued low dimensional vector. Introducing low dimensional embeddings of words by neural networks has significantly improved the state of the art in NLP [4]. These take advantage of word order in documents, and state the assumption that closer words in the word sequence are statistically more dependent. Typically, a neural language model learns the probability distribution of next word given a fixed number of preceding words which act as the context. A recently proposed scalable Continuous Bag-of-Words (CBOW) and scalable Continuous Skip-gram (SG) model [33] for learning word representations have shown promising results in capturing both syntactic and semantic word relationships in large news articles data. Their scalable open-source software is available online[2]. Word representations are typically learned from large collection of documents in a sliding window-fashion by updating the central word in the window such that it is capable of accurately predicting the surrounding words in the same window. In a followup publication, Le and Mikolov [31] addressed an open question of how to represent a document given word vectors. They introduced a notion of a global context vector. Each document is assigned a vector of its own, which was treated as global context of all the words in that document. Word vectors and document vectors are trained simultaneously. Training is conducted in the same manner as before, in a sliding window fashion, except that the document vector is updated with every word in a sequence, as global context.

We treated emails as "documents", and their vector representations were learned using the words in the email body. The dimensionality of the embedding space was set to $d = 300$, email vectors were treated as global context, thus updated with every word in its body, while the words vectors were updated using context neighborhood of length 5. We conducted 10 training iterations over the entire dataset of emails and words. With the resulting vector representation, we found that the emails get more similar as the conversation progresses. Figure 19 shows a considerably higher similarity of content in later stages of email threads.

Finally, we tested for linguistic style coordination. In social psychology, linguistic style coordination suggests that people mimic each other's linguistic style when they converse [14]. To quantify linguistic style, we use a set of "markers" [14], which are specific function words that have little semantic meaning and mostly represent the style of the language. We focus on six of the well-known markers: articles, auxiliary verbs, conjunctions, personal pronouns, prepositions, and quantifiers. Conventionally, style coordination is measured by comparing the counts of markers in a statement and a

[2]code.google.com/p/word2vec

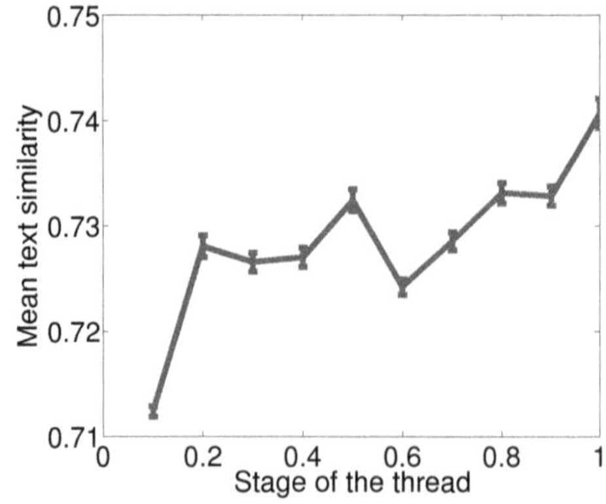

Figure 19: Cosine similarity of body of emails represented in a lower dimension. The topics of the conversation get more similar as the conversation progresses.

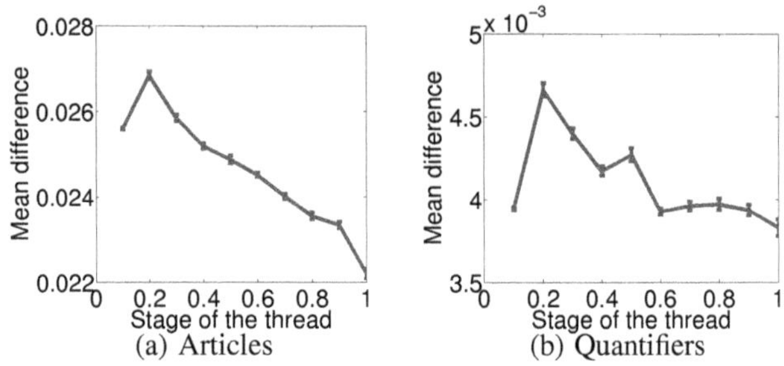

Figure 20: Synchronization in rate of usage of (a) articles and (b) quantifiers.

response. If the count in the response is correlated with the count in the original statement, coordination occurs. But, a recent study has shown that most of the linguistic coordination can be explained by the coordination in length of the response [19]. In other words, a long statement probably contains many articles, and its response is likely to be long as well, containing many articles, as well. Therefore, simply comparing the counts is not enough and the actual coordination happens only when the rate of the usage of the markers is similar. To account for this, we normalize the number of markers in an email.

We calculate the count of the six markers, normalized by the length of email, for each email and its reply. Then, we calculate the difference in the rate of marker usage at different stages of the thread. We observe the style coordination only for two out of the six markers, articles and quantifiers (Figure 20). For articles and quantifiers the difference in the rate of marker usage decreases in a conversations, meaning that users become more similar linguistically in later stages of a thread. But this is not the case for other four markers. So, our analysis does not show a clear style coordination in language of the users, and the coordination is only happening for some of the markers.

5. PREDICTING REPLIES

We test whether the features studied so far are suitable for predicting the behavior of users. In particular, we try to predict the *time* that a user will take to reply to a message, the *length* of the reply, and whether a message will *end the thread.* More than just measuring the performance in terms of accuracy, prediction allows us to quantify the importance of features in describing emailing behavior. We use the same features for the three analysis. Features in-

Rank	Feature	χ^2 value
1	Replier's median reply time	6,374
2	Receiver's median reply time	4,839
3	Replier's last reply time	4,528
4	Receiver's last reply time	4,157
5	Replier's 2nd to the last reply time	3,259

Table 1: Top 5 most predictive features for predicting reply time and their χ^2 value.

Rank	Feature	χ^2 value
1	Replier's average reply length	12,953
2	Replier's last reply length	12,509
3	Replier's median reply length	11,558
4	Replier's 2nd to the last reply length	9,476
5	Replier's 3rd to the last reply length	7,595

Table 2: Top 5 most predictive features for predicting length of reply and their χ^2 value.

Rank	Feature	χ^2 value
1	Receiver's avg # of words received/day	2,160
2	Replier's avg # of words received/day	1,981
3	Receiver's median # of words received/day	1,935
4	Receiver's avg # of words sent/day	1,884
5	Replier's median # of words received/day	1,872

Table 3: Top 5 most predictive features for predicting last email in a thread and their χ^2 value.

clude: mean, median, and earlier reply times and reply lengths between the pair of users (20 features), age and gender of the sender and receiver (4 features), step of the thread (1 feature), statistics on number of received, sent, and replied emails for sender and receiver (18 features), statistics on number of contacts of sender and receiver (18 features), statistics on length of all emails sent and received by the sender and receiver (18 features), the time of the day and day of the week that the email was received (2 features), number of attachments (1 feature), and if the user has used a phone, or tablet earlier (1 feature). Overall, we consider 83 features.

5.1 Predicting Reply Time

We start by predicting the reply time of emails within dyadic conversations. For each pair, we use the first 75% of the replies for training and the last 25% for testing, so that we are not using any of the future emails for predicting the current reply time. Predicting the exact reply time is a hard problem. We simplified the problem by considering classes of replies. In practice, knowing if we are going to receive a reply shortly or with a long delay would still be very helpful and we do not necessarily need the exact reply time. We consider three balanced classes of replies: immediate replies that happen within 15 minutes (33.5% of the data), fast replies that happen after 15 minutes, but before 164 minutes (33.1% of the data), and slow replies that take longer than 164 minutes (33.4% of the data). Here our baseline would be the largest class (majority vote), which contains 33.4% of the training data. We experiment with a variety of machine learning algorithms and bagging algorithm yields the best results with Root Mean Squared Error (RMSE) of 0.420 and accuracy of 55.8%, which is 22.4% absolute improvement and 67.1% relative improvement over the baseline. In case we want to just distinguish between immediate and slow replies in an application, we can eliminate our middle class and do the prediction only for the two class of immediate and slow replies. In this case, we achieve a much higher accuracy of 79.5% compared to the baseline of 50.1%.

We also rank the features based on their predictive power by computing the value of the χ^2 statistic with respect to the class. Table 1 shows the top 5 features with the highest predictive power, and all of them come from the history of the reply times between the users. The feature with the highest predictive power is the median reply time of the replier from earlier replies. So, if we want to use only one feature for guessing the reply time of a message, the typical reply time of the replier would be the most useful feature, which makes sense. Interestingly, if we select only 7 features from all the 83 features that have high predictive power and low overlap, the accuracy would be 58.3%, which is slightly less than the case that we consider all the features. All the 7 features represent earlier history of reply time between the pair of users.

5.2 Predicting Reply Length

Next, we take the same approach to predict the length of a reply that is going to be sent. We use the same set of features as the previous section and again use the first threads of emails between a pair of users for training and the rest for testing. Again, we divide our data to three balanced classes: short replies of 21 words or smaller (33.1% of the data), medium-length replies longer than 21 words, but shorter or equal to 88 words (33.6% of the data), and replies that are longer than 88 words (33.3%). A naive classifier that always predicts the largest class, would have a 33.6% accuracy, which is our baseline. Using the bagging classifier we achieve accuracy of 71.8%, which is much higher than the prediction of reply time. Our classifier has 38.2% absolute improvement and 113.7% relative improvement over the baseline. Similar to time to replies, we eliminate the middle class to calculate the accuracy for distinguishing short and long replies. Our classifier can successfully assign the correct class in 89.5% of cases, which is well above the 50.2% baseline.

We use the χ^2 statistics to rank the features based on their predictive power (Table 2). All the top 5 features are from the earlier reply lengths of the replier. Unlike reply time, there is no feature related to the receiver's activity in the top 5 features. This suggests that the length of the reply of the other person has a weaker effect on the length of the outgoing reply, compared to the effect of the reply time of the party on the reply time of the replier. We also try the 8 features that have high predictive power and these only top 8 features are just slightly less predictive than all the features (0.2%).

5.3 Predicting the End of the Thread

Finally, we use the same approach to predict whether a reply is the last reply in a thread or not. The baseline for this prediction problem is 50.6% and bagging classification yields accuracy of 65.9%, i.e. 15.3% absolute improvement and 30.2% relative improvement over the baseline. Table 3 shows the top 5 predictive features for predicting the last email in a thread and interestingly all the top features are related to the load of information in terms of number of words on the replier or receiver.

Table 4 summarizes our results for the three prediction problems. Besides the majority vote baseline, we also considered last reply and most used reply time and length as other baselines. These baselines perform better than the majority vote, but our classifier outperforms all three baselines: Relative improvement is 17.1% for last reply time and 5.3% for the last reply length. For most used baseline the relative improvement is 30.4% for reply time and 58.9% for reply length.

Prediction	Majority vote	Last reply	Most used	Our classifier	Absolute improvement	Relative improvement	AUC	RMSE
Reply time	33.4%	50.2%	45.1%	58.8%	22.4%	67.1%	0.715	0.420
Reply length	33.6%	68.2%	45.2%	71.8%	38.2%	113.7%	0.865	0.361
Last email	50.6%	–	–	65.9%	15.3%	30.2%	0.761	0.454

Table 4: Summary of the prediction results. Accuracy: percentage of correctly classified samples. AUC: Weighted average of Area Under the Curve for classes. RMSE: Root Mean Square Error. The improvements are reported over the majority vote baseline.

6. RELATED WORK

Online conversations were studied extensively in the context of social media, as they are important drivers of user *engagement* in online communities [23]. Research tried to identify common predictive models of the main traits of human communication. Previous work on Twitter investigated the *conventions* used to initiate and track conversations [6]. The evolution of conversational *norms* in time have been recently studied on Flickr and aNobii [1]. Similar to our study, previous work tried to predict the length of a discussion thread in Facebook using time and content features [2]. Models to reproduce some statistical properties of threads (e.g., size of thread, number of participants) were tested successfully in Twitter and Yahoo Groups [30]. Multimodal features of discussion threads can also predict its perceived interestingness [15]. Divergence of topics in Twitter group conversations was recently investigated [37]. The propensity to engage in conversation has been investigated under the light of the user personality traits such as openness to new experiences or emotional stability [10, 9]. The emotions conveyed in online conversations were also studied [26, 27, 7]. We believe ours is the first large scale analysis of email conversations and attempt to predict some of their main structural properties. Also, we do not focus on properties of the agents involved in conversations except for some demographic features like age and gender.

Emailing behavior was studied predominantly on small-scale data and often using qualitative methods. The attitude of email users towards work email was investigated through organizational surveys [13], finding that the social nature of the message is a stronger motivation to reply than the "importance" of the message. Also, survey respondents tended to reply to about only a third of the messages in their inbox. User studies and targeted interviews about rhythms in email usage, including intervals of replying, have uncovered the role of user expectation in relation with the replying behavior [39]. In particular, when a user perceives that the response has been delayed too much, the resulting *breakdown perception* triggers a follow-up action in the thread.

Quantitative studies targeted to specific application-oriented tasks such as classification of emails into folders [38, 28] were conducted mainly on the open Enron email data [29], which is one of the few complete temporal data on email communication whose structure has been studied extensively [16]. However, Enron's email communication patterns were very specific as they were limited to the context of the company and by its evolution and dramatic fall. This peculiarity held back researchers from drawing conclusions on general patterns of email use. Other less known, small-scale email datasets, such as the email corpora from OSS projects [5] can provide interesting traces on user interaction, but they do not allow any generalization of the findings. Email communication networks have been also used to investigate the propagation of computer viruses [35] and word-of-mouth advertising [36], or to solve specific tasks such as expert finding within organizations [8].

Information overload in email was studied since the 90's. In contrast to Whittaker and Sidner [40], who defined *email overload* as the use of email as a tool for task management, archival, and communication, we follow the definition of overload as not being able to keep up with the volume of incoming email [11, 18]. Unlike previous qualitative studies that focused on the perception of overload [11], we focus on quantitative measures of overload and its observed effects on users' behavior.

7. CONCLUSION

While email accounts for a considerable portion of interpersonal communication, emailing behavior is not well understood. We carried out a large-scale study of email replying behavior of more than 2M users. We studied how a variety of factors affects reply time and length. We found that users reply faster to emails received during weekdays and working hours, and that replies tend to become shorter later in the day and on weekends. In regard to demographics, younger users generally send faster and shorter replies, and men send slightly faster and shorter replies than women. Among other factors, replies from mobile devices were faster and shorter than from desktops, and emails without attachments typically got faster replies.

We investigated the effect of email overload on the replying behavior. We found that users increased their activity as they received more emails, but not enough to compensate for the higher load. This means that as users became more overloaded, they replied to a smaller fraction of incoming emails and with shorter replies. However, their responsiveness remained intact and may even be faster. Demographic factors affected information overload, too. Older users generally replied to a smaller fraction of incoming emails, but their reply time and length were not impacted by overload as much as younger users. In contrast, younger users replied faster, but with shorter replies and to a higher fraction of emails.

We also studied synchronization of replying behavior within a thread, and found that users tended to become more similar, both in reply time and length, until the middle of a thread. After that, their behavior became less similar. We also tested for coordination of linguistic styles using a variety of markers. Results were inconclusive: some markers suggested linguistic style coordination, but this was not the case for all.

Finally, to measure the predictive power of considered factors, we built classifiers to predict the time and length of replies, and whether an email was the last one in a thread. We obtained accuracy of 58.8%, 71.8%, and 65.9% for these tasks, which represented a relative improvement of 67.1%, 113.7%, and 30.2% respectively over the baselines. Our classifiers could be used to improve email client applications, to better classify and rank emails.

Acknowledgements

This work was supported in part by AFOSR (contract FA9550-10-1-0569), by DARPA (contract W911NF-12-1-0034), and by the NSF under grant SMA-1360058.

8. REFERENCES

[1] L. M. Aiello, R. Schifanella, and B. State. Reading the source code of social ties. In *Proceedings of the 2014 ACM Conference on Web Science*, WebSci '14, pages 139–148, New York, NY, USA, 2014. ACM.

[2] L. Backstrom, J. Kleinberg, L. Lee, and C. Danescu-Niculescu-Mizil. Characterizing and Curating Conversation Threads: Expansion, Focus, Volume, Re-entry. In *WSDM*, 2013.

[3] A. L. Barabasi. The origin of bursts and heavy tails in human dynamics. *Nature*, 435:207–211, 2005.

[4] Y. Bengio, H. Schwenk, J.-S. Senécal, F. Morin, and J.-L. Gauvain. Neural probabilistic language models. In *Innovations in Machine Learning*, pages 137–186. Springer, 2006.

[5] C. Bird, A. Gourley, P. Devanbu, M. Gertz, and A. Swaminathan. Mining email social networks. In *MSR*, pages 137–143, New York, NY, USA, 2006. ACM.

[6] d. boyd, S. Golder, and G. Lotan. Tweet, Tweet, Retweet: Conversational Aspects of Retweeting on Twitter. In *HICSS*, 2010.

[7] C. Budak and R. Agrawal. On Participation in Group Chats on Twitter. In *WWW*, 2013.

[8] C. S. Campbell, P. P. Maglio, A. Cozzi, and B. Dom. Expertise identification using email communications. In *CIKM*, pages 528–531, New York, NY, USA, 2003. ACM.

[9] F. Celli and L. Rossi. The Role of Emotional Stability in Twitter Conversations. In *Workshop on Semantic Analysis in Social Media*, 2012.

[10] T. Correa, A. W. Hinsley, and H. G. de Zúñiga. Who Interacts on the Web? The Intersection of Users' Personality and Social Media Use. *Computers in Human Behaviour*, 26(2), 2010.

[11] L. A. Dabbish and R. E. Kraut. Email overload at work: An analysis of factors associated with email strain. In *CSCW*, pages 431–440, 2006.

[12] L. A. Dabbish, R. E. Kraut, S. Fussell, and S. Kiesler. Understanding email use: Predicting action on a message. In *CHI*, 2005.

[13] L. A. Dabbish, R. E. Kraut, S. Fussell, and S. Kiesler. Understanding email use: Predicting action on a message. In *CHI*, pages 691–700, New York, NY, USA, 2005. ACM.

[14] C. Danescu-Niculescu-Mizil, L. Lee, B. Pang, and J. Kleinberg. Echoes of power: Language effects and power differences in social interaction. In *WWW*, pages 699–708. ACM, 2012.

[15] M. De Choudhury, H. Sundaram, A. John, and D. D. Seligmann. What Makes Conversations Interesting? Themes, Participants and Consequences of Conversations in Online Social Media. In *WWW*, 2009.

[16] J. Diesner, T. Frantz, and K. Carley. Communication Networks from the Enron Email Corpus: "It's Always About the People. Enron is no Different.". *Computational & Mathematical Organization Theory*, 11(3):201–228, 2005.

[17] J.-P. Eckmann, E. Moses, and D. Sergi. Entropy of dialogues creates coherent structures in e-mail traffic. *Proceedings of the National Academy of Sciences of the United States of America*, 101(40):14333–14337, Oct. 2004.

[18] D. Fisher, A. J. Brush, E. Gleave, and M. A. Smith. Revisiting whittaker & sidner's "email overload" ten years later. In *CSCW*, pages 309–312, New York, NY, USA, 2006. ACM.

[19] S. Gao, G. Ver Steeg, and A. Galstyan. Explaining away stylistic coordination in dialogues. In *WIN*, 2013.

[20] M. Gomez-Rodriguez, K. P. Gummadi, and B. Sch olkopf. Quantifying information overload in social media and its impact on social contagions. In *ICWSM*, 2014.

[21] B. Gonçalves, N. Perra, and A. Vespignani. Modeling users' activity on twitter networks: Validation of dunbar's number. *PLoS ONE*, 6(8), 2011.

[22] M. Grbovic, G. Halawi, Z. Karnin, and Y. Maarek. How many folders do you really need?: Classifying email into a handful of categories. In *Proceedings of the 23rd ACM International Conference on Conference on Information and Knowledge Management*, pages 869–878. ACM, 2014.

[23] F. M. Harper, D. Frankowski, S. Drenner, Y. Ren, S. Kiesler, L. Terveen, R. Kraut, and J. Riedl. Talk Amongst Yourselves: Inviting Users to Participate in Online Conversations. In *IUI*, 2007.

[24] N. O. Hodas and K. Lerman. How limited visibility and divided attention constrain social contagion. In *SocialCom*, 2012.

[25] T. N. Jagatic, N. A. Johnson, M. Jakobsson, and F. Menczer. Social phishing. *Commun. ACM*, 50(10):94–100, Oct. 2007.

[26] A. Java, X. Song, T. Finin, and B. Tseng. Why We Twitter: Understanding Microblogging Usage and Communities. In *WebKDD/SNA-KDD*, 2007.

[27] S. Kim, J. Bak, and A. Oh. Do You Feel what I Feel? Social Aspects of Emotions in Twitter Conversations. In *ICWSM*, 2012.

[28] B. Klimt and Y. Yang. The enron corpus: A new dataset for email classification research. In J.-F. Boulicaut, F. Esposito, F. Giannotti, and D. Pedreschi, editors, *ECML*, volume 3201, pages 217–226. Springer Berlin Heidelberg, 2004.

[29] B. Klimt and Y. Yang. Introducing the enron corpus. In *CEAS*, 2004.

[30] R. Kumar, M. Mahdian, and M. McGlohon. Dynamics of Conversations. In *KDD*, 2010.

[31] Q. V. Le and T. Mikolov. Distributed representations of sentences and documents. *arXiv preprint arXiv:1405.4053*, 2014.

[32] R. D. Malmgren, D. B. Stouffer, A. E. Motter, and L. A. N. Amaral. A poissonian explanation for heavy tails in e-mail communication. *Proceedings of the National Academy of Sciences*, 105(47):18153–18158, 2008.

[33] T. Mikolov, I. Sutskever, K. Chen, G. S. Corrado, and J. Dean. Distributed representations of words and phrases and their compositionality. In *NIPS*, pages 3111–3119, 2013.

[34] C. Neustaedter, A. J. B. Brush, and M. A. Smith. Beyond from and received: Exploring the dynamics of email triage. In *CHI*, 2005.

[35] M. E. J. Newman, S. Forrest, and J. Balthrop. Email networks and the spread of computer viruses. *Phys. Rev. E*, 66:035101, Sep 2002.

[36] J. E. Phelps, R. Lewis, L. Mobilio, D. Perry, and N. Raman. Viral marketing or electronic word-of-mouth advertising: Examining consumer responses and motivations to pass along email. *Journal of Advertising Research*, 44:333–348, 12 2004.

[37] H. Purohit, Y. Ruan, D. Fuhry, S. Parthasarathy, and A. Sheth. On Understanding Divergence of Online Social Group Discussion. In *ICWSM*, 2014.

[38] J. Shetty and J. Adibi. The Enron email dataset database schema and brief statistical report. *Information Sciences Institute Technical Report, University of Southern California*, 2004.

[39] J. Tyler and J. Tang. When can i expect an email response? a study of rhythms in email usage. In K. Kuutti, E. Karsten, G. Fitzpatrick, P. Dourish, and K. Schmidt, editors, *ECSCW*, pages 239–258. Springer Netherlands, 2003.

[40] S. Whittaker and C. Sidner. Email overload: Exploring personal information management of email. In *CHI*, pages 276–283, New York, NY, USA, 1996. ACM.

[41] L. Zhuang, J. Dunagan, D. R. Simon, H. J. Wang, and J. D. Tygar. Characterizing botnets from email spam records. In *LEET*, pages 2:1–2:9, Berkeley, CA, USA, 2008. USENIX Association.

Events and Controversies: Influences of a Shocking News Event on Information Seeking

Danai Koutra*
Carnegie Mellon University
Pittsburgh, PA
danai@cs.cmu.com

Paul N. Bennett
Microsoft Research
Redmond, WA
pauben@microsoft.com

Eric Horvitz
Microsoft Research
Redmond, WA
horvitz@microsoft.com

ABSTRACT

It has been suggested that online search and retrieval contributes to the intellectual isolation of users within their preexisting ideologies, where people's prior views are strengthened and alternative viewpoints are infrequently encountered. This so-called "filter bubble" phenomenon has been called out as especially detrimental when it comes to dialog among people on controversial, emotionally charged topics, such as the labeling of genetically modified food, the right to bear arms, the death penalty, and online privacy. We seek to identify and study information-seeking behavior and access to alternative versus reinforcing viewpoints following shocking, emotional, and large-scale news events. We choose for a case study to analyze search and browsing on gun control/rights, a strongly polarizing topic for both citizens and leaders of the United States. We study the period of time preceding and following a mass shooting to understand how its occurrence, follow-on discussions, and debate may have been linked to changes in the patterns of searching and browsing. We employ information-theoretic measures to quantify the diversity of Web domains of interest to users and understand the browsing patterns of users. We use these measures to characterize the influence of news events on these web search and browsing patterns.

Categories and Subject Descriptors: H.2.8 [Database Management]: Database Applications—*Data mining.*
Keywords: Controversies, Filter bubble, Log / behavioral analysis.

1. INTRODUCTION

How do people navigate webpages on polarizing topics? Are they isolated in their echo chambers? Do shocking news events burst their ideological bubbles and make them more likely to seek information on opposing viewpoints? These are the key questions we investigate.

With advances in personalization methods, search engines and recommendation systems increasingly adjust results to users' preferences, as inferred from their past searches and choices. In addition, users often input biased queries [38], which reflect their own positions, while personalized results have the potential to reinforce these opinions, acting as echo chambers. As a result, according to several recent studies [38, 15, 29], users remain within informational bubbles. The phenomenon is sometimes referred to as the "filter bubble" effect, where people get exposed only to opinions that align with their current views. This effect, where the world of viewpoints that people are exposed to on the web does not reflect the richness of views in the real world, may be especially strong for polarizing topics. We take as polarizing or controversial topics those linked to opposing perspectives, such as abortion, gun control vs. rights, labeling of genetically modified food, and death penalty.

To understand users' information seeking behaviors on polarizing issues, we focus on a highly controversial topic in the US: gun control and rights. At one end of the spectrum, extreme gun rights supporters argue an interpretation of the 2nd Amendment to the US Constitution that would prohibit any regulation of firearms. On the other side of the spectrum, extreme gun control supporters advocate the total ban of any private citizen ownership of firearms. Beyond these two extreme opinions are a spectrum of variations that lay between them (*e.g.*, more background checks, ban of fully automatic firearms). For our study we use web browser toolbar logs from November and December 2012, and primarily consider two time periods: before and after the Sandy Hook Elementary School Shooting (S.H.) in Newtown, Connecticut (December 14th), an event with broad news coverage and nationwide impact.

For a historical perspective, we summarize the event facts in [1] to aid readers in understanding why the event might be expected to broadly influence information consumption. The Sandy Hook shooting is the most deadly shooting in US history at a high, middle, or elementary school and the second deadliest in US History by a single perpetrator. The casualties included 20 children ages 6-7, six staff members, the perpetrator's mother (offsite), and the perpetrator – a 20-year-old male with no motive ever determined and a history of several psychological conditions. In a span of five minutes, the shooter entered the building and fired 156 rounds (one bullet every other second) causing all but one fatality during that span. The perpetrator committed suicide as the police arrived on the scene (five minutes after the shooter entered the building). Given the complexity and nature of the event, there was considerable political debate and media discussion following the event. Our focus here is on how this event may have influenced the general US population's information search and retrieval.

The event clearly had considerable influence on information seeking about gun control related topics as signified by the increased user activity in the days following the event (see Fig. 1). The first big spike in the figure, which corresponds to visits to on-topic websites on the day of the shootings, and other important spikes have been annotated. The effect on the quantity of information seeking is indisputable; so our focus is *not* on the increase in user activity, *but* on whether (and how) the event changed the *type* of activity.

*Work done during an internship at Microsoft Research.

WWW 2015, May 18–22, 2015, Florence, Italy.
ACM 978-1-4503-3469-3/15/05.
http://dx.doi.org/10.1145/2736277.2741099 .

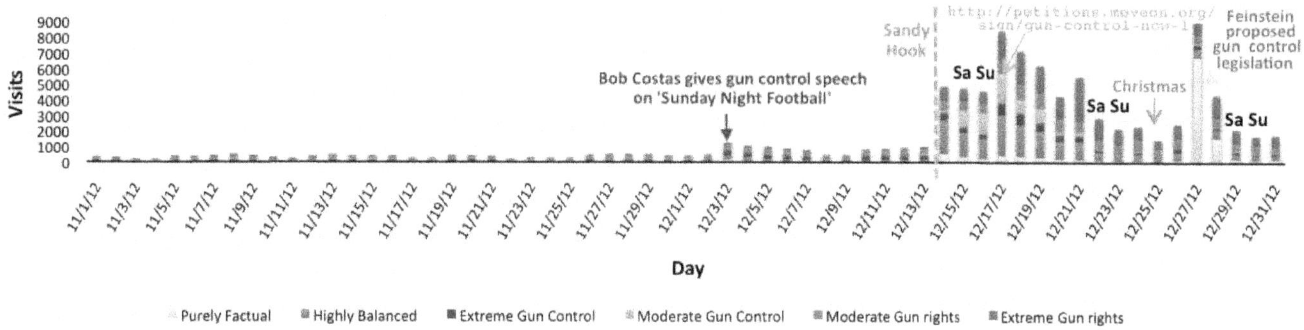

Figure 1: Number of visits to gun control/rights related webpages over time (November-December 2012). The colors correspond to webpage categories: gray for factual and balanced pages; blue for pages supporting gun control; and red for pages supporting gun rights. The categories and the labeling process are described in the Appendix and Sec. 3.2 respectively.

For the following analysis, we use raw web browser visitation logs from Internet Explorer, where users have given consent to logging all non-https URLs from URLs visited from search and those reached by direct entry or browsing. By employing techniques such as a two-step random walk on the query-click graph [11] and white-list and keyword-based classifiers, we extract –from this broad set of visitations– and label a large-scale dataset of user interaction data that is relevant to the gun debate, constituting about 61K users visiting 378K on-topic websites (Sec. 3). We first present evidence that websites are polarized with respect to individual topics in terms of their webpage content (Sec. 4). Then, we evaluate the diversity of the users and investigate to what extent ideological bubbles exist before and after the shootings (Sec. 5). Moreover, we explore the click trails of the users to understand how people transition among webpages of opposing views, and how news about the shootings influences such transitions (Sec. 6). Finally, we categorize users based on their browsing behavior (Sec. 7), and discuss the dynamics of the communities over the course of the time.

Contributions. This paper presents a case-study which is both interesting in its own right, but also highlights the computational tools and analysis methodology to answer questions such as : What type of websites offer the most diverse opinions? (Sec. 4); Do users desire diversity in opinions? (Sec. 5.1); Does a shocking event impact the user's desire for diversity? (Sec. 5.2); Is the polarity of a web page predictive of the polarity of the next domain on topic that a user will read a page from? (Sec. 6.1); Does a shocking event change the predictability of the polarity of the next domain on topic conditioned on the current one? (Sec. 6.2); Does a shocking news event permanently shift the user's topical view? (Sec. 7)

As a case-study the answers to these questions for this topic have implications for ranking scores for websites on polarizing topics based on predicted diversity, when diversity should be incorporated into search and recommendation results, how that diversity should change in the face of events, and for what duration of time a user's view should be persisted for personalization.

2. RELATED WORK

We first place our work in the context of related research, which includes studies on political controversies, conjectures about the so-called filter bubble, and the temporal evolution of knowledge.

Political Controversies. Munson et al. [25] focus on blog posts to study if people seek diverse information, while Balasubramanyan et al. [8] use an LDA-based methodology to predict how different communities respond to political discourse. Aktogla and Allan [6] show that diversification of search results in terms of sentiments to an explicit bias improves user satisfaction. The authors in [13] propose a model to mine contrastive opinions for political issues, and many research groups devise methods for polarity detection and political leaning classification [10, 36, 40, 30] or for understanding event dynamics and their relation to sentiment shifts [35]. In [23] and [39], the authors present work on extending sentiment analysis to match political text to parties. Awadallah et al. [7] mine the web to automatically map well-known people to their opinions on political controversies.

Filter Bubble. Pariser [26] points out the existence of the filter bubble, which he defines as "this unique, personal universe of information created just for you by an array of personalizing filters", and many works propose ways to mitigate its effects [15, 29]. For example, Munson et al. [24] build a browser widget that encourages the users to read diverse articles on political issues in order to avoid the selective exposure of users to political information. Yom-Tov et al. [38] focus on news outlet sites that people visit, quantify the filter bubble and study whether users browse webpages supporting disagreeable information when opposing views are introduced in their search results.

Temporal Evolution of Knowledge. White et al. [37] focus on the temporal search behavior of users to quantify the differences between experts and non-experts in terms of vocabulary, sites visited and search strategies. Kotov et al. [20] model and analyze user search behavior that spans multiple sessions in order to improve search for complex needs and support tasks which require cross-section searches. In a similar context, Liu et al. [22] study how the acquired user knowledge changes over time through performing multi-session information tasks.

This Work. In contrast to most previous work, which considers primarily news outlets and blogs, and studies whether people access sources of different political categories to get informed [24, 38], we put a particular topic under the microscope and study how *that* affects the browsing behavior of the users. Another major difference from prior efforts is that we separate the political orientation of the users from their orientation to the gun debate. For example, a Gallup poll in 2005 [2] indicated that 23%/27%/41% of, respectively, Democrats/Independents/Republicans own a gun for an overall average of 30% of US adults. Thus, while gun ownership correlates with political leanings, there is significant ownership in each population. Given that, it is quite likely that views toward the gun debate may differ from party affiliation as well. Thus, we do not engage in the common practice of characterizing websites as liberal and non-liberal. Rather, we define our own *content*-oriented labels (Appendix A). Finally, although our work is motivated by the findings of prior studies on the existence of the filter bubble, our focus is not limited to corroborating or opposing this view. Our goal is to understand the types of webpages people visit, as well as how they transition among content expressing different viewpoints.

We contribute an analysis of the temporal evolution of the users' *browsing* behaviors, and especially the *influence of specific external events with nationwide impact* on the shaping of the users' stances and their overall polarity. We also analyze the transitions of the users among webpages of different viewpoints.

3. THE GC-DEBATE DATA

We now present the dataset that we used for our study, focusing mainly on the data extraction and annotation.

3.1 Data Extraction

The data comes from users' anonymized search and browse behavior logged through Internet Explorer's instrumentation during November and December 2012. The data covers queries issued to a variety of search engines, as well as non-encrypted URLs that were visited, for more than 29 million users in the US-English market. While the sample of users in the log may not perfectly represent the distribution of the US population, independent studies [3] demonstrate that the user population of Internet Explorer contains significant representation from both genders and nearly all age and income levels of the US population. Thus, the changes we discuss at least indicate broad patterns of change across demographics and with respect to our user base.

Beyond the analysis of interaction on this particular topic, we seek to identify computational approaches to analyzing changes in patterns of information browsing given typical constraints on observation. To that end, we do not assume that our logs capture all of the user's on-topic activity across all devices but rather a random sample of the user's activity with respect to the topical content orientation. By random, we mean, that the user's selection of browser or device is independent of the topical polarity; for example, the user does not perform all of their browsing of gun rights on an alternative browser or device for which we would not have log information while all of their gun control activity on an instrumented browser on the desktop.

We consider primarily two time periods: before and after the Sandy Hook Elementary School shooting on December 14th. We note that we consider logs from a longer period of time before the event to develop a more robust estimate of users' habitual activity—a similar quantity of activity is observed in the period after the shooting because information seeking is more frequent after the event (Fig. 1). For the purposes of our study, we consider the URLs that are *on-topic*, i.e., websites that discuss gun control/rights issues. Hence, our first goal is to extract the relevant data with techniques that can be re-used in a programmatic manner for the analysis of other topics.

A naïve approach to obtaining a corpus of on-topic data is to consider all webpages containing the word "gun". Such an approach leads to numerous false positives, including websites about toys, video games, glue guns *etc.* We took an alternate approach that yielded a corpus with many fewer false positives. The extraction process focused on identifying on-topic seed queries with high precision and then expanding these to related URLs and queries to obtain high coverage of all of the on-topic activity. Specifically, the multi-step procedure, as illustrated in Fig. 2, does the following:

STEP 1. Identification of Relevant Queries: We start with easy to identify relevant queries through keyword matching, and automatically expand them to as many relevant queries as possible by exploiting usage data.

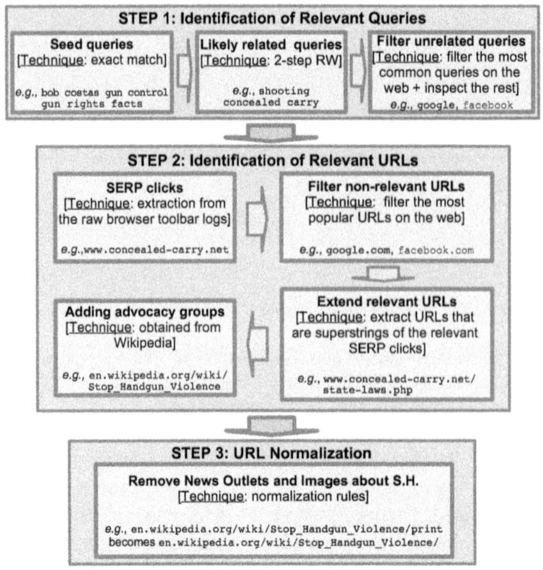

Figure 2: Illustration of the data extraction process.

Table 1: The most popular seed queries (col. 1), and relevant queries before and after the Sandy Hook shootings (col. 2 and 3).

Top 15 seed queries	Top 15 relevant queries before Sandy Hook	Top 15 relevant queries after Sandy Hook
Bob Costas gun control	Bob Costas gun control	Connecticut shooting
gun control petition	shooting	school shooting in Connecticut
Rupert Murdoch gun control	2nd amendment	school shooting
Piers Morgan gun control	gun control	Connecticut school shooting
gun control	nutnfancy	shooting in Connecticut
Feinstein gun control	Oregon shooting	elementary school shooting
gun control debate	second amendment	gun control petition
Rahm Emanuel gun control	concealed carry	Rupert Murdoch gun control
Murdoch gun control	National Rifle Association	Sandy Hook shooting
gun control laws	Obama gun control	shooting
obama gun control	home invasion	piers Morgan gun control
boehner on gun control	jason whitlock gun control	nra statement
ted nugent gun control	illinois gun laws	gun control
white house gun control petition	gun news	obama gun ban
piers morgan gun control debate	the second amendment	conneticut shooting

1A. Seed Queries. First, we identify seed queries by extracting those queries that contain the phrases "gun control" or "gun rights", but that are not related to electronic games. By doing this, we automatically filter out the queries that have an exact match with "xbox", "wii", "gun controller", "game", or "playstation". The resulting set consists of 6,878 queries, the 15 most popular of which are given in Table 1 (col. 1).

1B. Identifying Likely Related Queries. The second step consists of expanding the set of seed queries to relevant queries (misspelled, different expressions of the same intent, *etc.*). For this purpose, we create the query-click graph, a bipartite graph, where each query in the web logs is connected to the impression URLs that some user clicked; queries linked via a clicked URL are referred to as co-clicked. Starting from the seed set, we perform a two-step random walk [11], and expand the seed set to all the similar co-clicked queries, as evaluated by their character-trigram cosine similarity with the seed queries. The threshold for similarity is set to 0.5 to require relatively high similarity. Intuitively, the new queries are connected to the same URLs as the seed queries and have textual overlap. Thus, they are likely on-topic, and probably represent alternative ways of querying for highly related results.

1C. Filtering Non-Relevant Queries. Finally, from the likely relevant set of queries, after ordering them in decreasing order of popularity, we inspect and filter out the most common overall and seasonal queries, such as the navigational queries, *google* and *facebook*. Moreover, by manually inspecting the queries without the word "gun", we remove those queries that are not directly related to gun control, and lead to retrieval of numerous URLs unrelated to gun control (high recall/low precision) – e.g., *what do democrats and republicans stand for, conservative viewpoint.* The final, extended set, to which we will refer as set of *relevant* queries, consists of 7,778 queries. The most popular queries before and after Sandy Hook are given in Table 1 (col. 2 and 3).

STEP 2. Identification of Relevant URLs: Users reach URLs through many ways (*e.g.*, browsing, search, bookmarks). Our objective is to use the resulting on-topic *queries* to identify sessions of information-seeking behavior, which according to IR research tend to be topically coherent. Again, a naïve approach would be to extract any clicked URL from the search engine result page (SERP) of a topical query, as well as the pages browsed subsequently by consecutive clicks (click trail). However, users may click on ads and other contextual links (some of which may be topically relevant, but often not), and browse from a topical article to a non-topical one as they drift to a different topic. Therefore, similar to identifying relevant queries, we developed a semi-automated way of expanding to a broad topically relevant set without incorporating significant amounts of off-topic search and browsing:

2A. SERP Clicks. Starting from the relevant queries of the previous step, we obtain only the URLs users clicked directly from a topically relevant query's SERP.

2B. Filtering Non-Relevant URLs. Then, we filter URLs that are among the most popular URLs worldwide (e.g., `google.com`, `yahoo.com`, `youtube.com`, `facebook.com`), which reflect the way the users reached the on-topic URLs, but are not on-topic themselves. Although media analysis is interesting, we focus primarily on non-video web pages (*i.e.*, mainly text). We refer to this set of filtered URLs on gun control and gun rights as *seed* URLs.

2C. Extend Relevant URLs. We continue by extending the set of seed URLs to include more webpages that might not belong to the SERP clicks of relevant queries. To this end, we consider relevant all URLs that are superstrings of the seed URLs. The intuition is that those were either reached from or led to a seed URL, and have high overlap in the site organization – implying a topical relationship. Moreover, this process leads to higher recall, as it also extracts URLs entered in the toolbar, or saved as bookmarks.

2D. Adding Advocacy Groups. The method described above is *not* guaranteed to extract *all* the URLs that are relevant to gun control and rights. However, the procedure attempts to extract as many, highly related websites as possible, while maintaining neutral criteria with respect to the topic of study. Extracting all the webpages that are on-topic is challenging and is a distinct research problem. We seek to make sure that we capture visits to webpages for the most prevalent gun control and rights advocacy groups. Thus, we take compiled lists from Wikipedia[1], and explicitly extract user visits to both the advocacy group websites and their Wikipedia pages.

STEP 3. URL Normalization: Finally, we normalize the URLs so that different webpages with the same content, mobile versions of the websites, print requests of a page, user id encoding pages, *etc.* are considered the same.

The resulting dataset, GC-DEBATE, consists of records <user-id, session-id, URL, timestamp> (Table 2). In the following sections, we refer to the intersection between the sets of users before and after the shootings as **common users**. Studying them enables us to directly compare changes in user behavior by controlling for the set of users.

[1]Gun control / rights advocacy groups in the United States: http://en.wikipedia.org/wiki/Category:Gun_control_advocacy_groups_in_the_United_States http://en.wikipedia.org/wiki/Category:Gun_rights_advocacy_groups_in_the_United_States

Table 2: GC-DEBATE dataset. The last column holds the number of common users, URLs and domains between the two time periods.

	Before S.H.	After S.H.	Total	Overlap
Users	12,919	56,293	61,276	7,936
Unique URLs	6,081	20,788	25,201	1,668
Unique Domains	340	682	803	219
Total Visits	123,596	253,994	377,590	N/A

Table 3: Inter-rater agreement for the high-level labels (col. 1), and the expanded set of labels (col. 2). Overall agreement is simply the percent of labels on which the raters agree.

	Labels	
	High-level	**Expanded**
Overall agreement	86.10%	73.61%
free-marginal κ	82.64%	66.21%
fixed-marginal κ	77.53%	69.84%
chance-expected agreement	19.69 %	10.30%

3.2 Data Annotation

Answering the questions we have posed is not possible unless the webpages are labeled based on their stance on gun control/rights. Rather than focusing on alignment with a political party, we focus on the disposition of the content itself. Visits to a site that is predominantly affiliated with one party (*e.g.*, Democratic/Republican) or a particular pundit, does not by itself imply a lack of diversity in content; sites may contain content discussing a broad range of material. Considering the content also enables us to measure that extent to which sites provide information representing diverse views.

Manually labeling *all* the webpages is difficult. Our attempts to automate the labeling process by building *content*-centric classifiers failed to achieve high accuracy, revealing the challenges of classifying controversial pages by their stance. We could not apply the extensive work on detecting and labeling controversial topics [10, 40, 30], as our setting is different: we seek to characterize the presented *viewpoints* in documents on a *given controversial topic*. To overcome these challenges, we judged all webpages that had more than two unique visitors and sampled from the remaining webpages, obtaining this way 99.5% coverage of total visitations. The on-topic and accessible pages were initially judged by their content and classified into three high level categories: balanced, gun control, gun rights. Then, they were further classified into expanded categories that reflect the stance of the webpages at a finer granularity: purely factual and highly balanced, extreme and moderate gun control, and extreme and moderate gun rights. Details about the labels are provided in the Appendix.

Three expert assessors were provided with a subset of over 2,100 popular webpages, and were asked to classify them. One assessor self-identified as "moderate gun rights", while the other two self-identified as "moderate gun control". The inter-rater agreement [28], which already accounts for the chance-expected proportion of agreement between the assessors, is 82.64% for the high-level classification, and 66.21% for the expanded labels that reflect further key category distinctions. We note that these inter-rater agreements are high, since the chance-expected agreement [17] using the marginal distribution is 19.69% for the high-level labels, and 10.30% for the expanded labels.

By using a white-list and keyword-based classifier, we obtain all the URLs that correspond to news outlets. Among these, the news articles that are labeled as "Purely Factual" are not taken into account in the following analyses because they merely report news about the incident without discussing gun-related issues and policies, and do not serve the purpose of our study on exploring how users access information in reaction to a news event (versus how they are informed about the event). Although one can argue that some news sites are representative of specific ideological views, we do not rely on the latter, because often the political orientation differs from the orientation to the gun control issue [2].

4. DIVERSITY OF DOMAINS

Our first study seeks to characterize websites with respect to the diversity of opinions they present. Our findings help us label the large corpus we extracted, but also have broader implications on search: for example, they may be useful when considering how to rank search results to ensure that diversity is present. To evaluate the diversity of web domains, we use an information-theoretic measure, Shannon's entropy.

We identify domains with at least eight labeled webpages and give their label distribution in Fig. 3. It is evident that most of the web domains are one-sided, with almost all their webpages expressing similar opinions (e.g., supporting only gun rights). An exception to this finding is that user-generated content, such as that found on `wikipedia.org` and `answers.yahoo.com`, tends to be either balanced or diverse respectively.

To quantify the heterogeneity of the available information per domain in a principled way, we use Shannon's entropy [31], an information-theoretic measure of the uncertainty for a random variable. The higher the entropy associated with a random variable, the higher the uncertainty about its value, or, equivalently, the more diverse it is. Formally, for each domain d with entropy

$$H(X_d) = E[-\log P(X_d)] = -\sum_i P(X_d = x_i) * \log P(X_d = x_i),$$

we compute the *normalized entropy* for its webpage labels:

$$H^{norm}(X_d) = H_t(X_d)/H_t(X'_d|X'_d \sim \mathcal{U}),$$

where X_d, X'_d are the labels of the webpages with domain d, X'_d is uniformly distributed, and log is the base-2 logarithm. We note that $H_t(X'_d|X'_d \sim \mathcal{U})$ corresponds to the maximum entropy where the labels occur with equal probability.

We compute the *normalized* entropy for the labels of the URLs instead of the entropy for two reasons: (1) the normalized entropy handles comparisons across different event space sizes, which is needed when comparing high-level and expanded labels and (2) the normalized entropy ensures that comparisons between domains with different number of observations are at the same basis. Normalizing the measure helps to handle estimation error, as the entropy can have high variance when there are only a few observations.

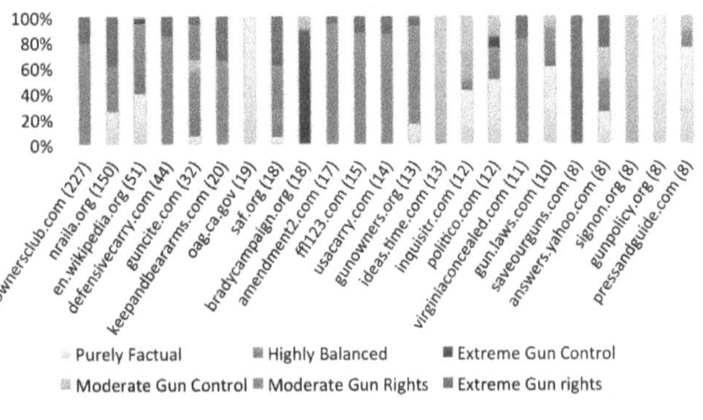

Figure 3: Label distribution per domain. The domains are in decreasing order of manually characterized URLs (in parentheses).

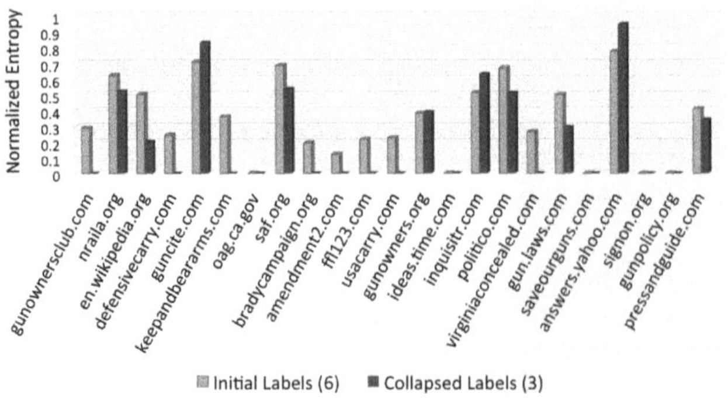

Figure 4: GC-DEBATE: Diversity of domains in terms of label entropy (for the manually labeled URLs).

Figure 4 depicts the normalized entropy in the labels of the webpages per domain, where we consider the 2,100 webpages that were manually labeled by expert assessors (Sec. 3.2). For each domain, the left and right bars correspond to the normalized label entropy for the expanded, and the high-level labels respectively. Overall, for the high-level labels, the normalized entropy is 0 (no diversity) for 54% of the domains, and smaller than or equal to 0.5 for 63% of the domains. The median normalized entropy is 0, and the mean 0.27. Similarly, for the expanded set of labels, 34% of the domains have entropy 0, and 73% have normalized entropy smaller than or equal to 0.5. The median and mean normalized entropy are 0.36 and 0.30 respectively.

The main finding is that the domains offer to the users mostly a single myopic view on gun control issues. Based on this observation, we were able to automatically label the remaining ~$23K$ webpages that were not labeled manually by the assessors, and obtain a rich, annotated dataset that can serve the purposes of our next analyses. We note that among those 23K webpages that we label automatically, 10,525 AND 4,398 URLs belong to the gun rights forums `gunownersclub.com` and `defensivecarry.com` respectively, while 4,221 URLs belong to the gun control petition page `signon.org`. That is, 82% of the webpages that we label automatically correspond to three domains with very clear stances. For the automatic labeling, we apply a label propagation approach from the webpages to their domains:

- **Forums.** We replace URLs that belong to a forum with its main page, and classify the latter based on the overall stance of its labeled webpages, (*i.e.*, the dominant category of the manual labeling).
- **Advocacy groups.** We label each domain based on the identified stance using Wikipedia's characterization.
- **Domains.** For the domains with normalized entropy smaller than 0.5, we first assign the dominant high-level category, and then the stance (moderate, extreme) of the majority of the labels. If we have a tie among the possible categories, we do not classify the domain, and keep the initial URLs and their labels for our analysis.

By following these rules, we obtain the final labeling of the *domains*, as well as the remaining URLs whose domain's stance could not be summarized succinctly by a single label. The distribution of the final labels is: 4% purely factual, 2% highly balanced, 58% and 16% moderate and extreme gun rights respectively, and 18% and 2% of moderate and extreme gun control.

Overall, this study indicates sites with user-generated content, such as Wikipedia and Q&A websites, are more diverse. In contrast, forums about controversial topics tend to be very polarized.

5. WITHIN-USER DIVERSITY

Our second study focuses on the diversity of information consumed by each user browsing controversial topics, and how the diversity in the information sought is influenced by a shocking news event. The within-user diversity can be expressed in terms of the number of different domains that a user browses, as well as the number of different *categories* (e.g., gun control, balanced webpages) of pages that she visits.

5.1 Examining the Existing Theories

We start by evaluating whether users desire diversity in opinions. As in Sec. 4, we use Shannon's entropy to quantify the diversity in the categories of webpages that each user visits. We note that this study may indicate whether recommendation systems and search results should be composed of diverse opinions in order to satisfy the user.

In the prior literature we find two contradictory theories, which we consider regarding the implications of using entropy to capture variance:

THEORY 1. "People use the web to access a variety of sources, and become more aware of political news and events." [18, 34].
IMPLICATION 1. If this assertion is true, we would expect users to visit domains with different labels regarding perspective, and that the associated normalized label entropy of the domains that the users browse would be high. In the case where users visit only a few domains, we would expect the label entropy of the domains to be high.

THEORY 2. "People use the web to access mostly agreeable political information" [5, 16, 14].
IMPLICATION 2. If this assessment is true, we would expect most users to access mostly domains supporting one side of the topic. Thus, the label entropy of the domains that the users access should be low.

We now analyze the diversity of information that users consume to explore the two assertions. We first focus on all users who visited at least three relevant domains during November and December.

From all the users, only 5% visited at least 4 relevant domains and news articles; the vast majority of these users, 50%, accessed exactly 4 domains, 24% browsed 5 domains, and 11% visited 6 domains. This observation, in combination with the low diversity of domains (Sec. 4), provide evidence that Theory 1 is unlikely. Most users appear too "narrow-minded" as far as the number of web domains is concerned, and the domains themselves are mostly one-sided.

To evaluate Theory 2, we need to examine the diversity of each user's consumed information by computing the entropy in the labels of the domains accessed. The intuition behind this need is that the number of domains does not provide enough information about the diversity of a user's exposure, as it does not fully characterize the type of information consumed. Two extreme cases would be a user who visited three websites supporting gun control, and another user who visited a website of each category: gun control, gun rights and balanced. Clearly, the second user's information stream is more diverse. Thus, for each user u who visited at least three different relevant domains during November and December, we compute a normalized label entropy

$$H^{norm}(X_u) = H(X_u)/H(X'_u|X'_u \sim \mathcal{U}) \qquad (1)$$

where X_u, X'_u are the labels of the domains visited by user u (thus, X_u, X'_u take values in {gun control, gun rights, balanced/factual}), and X'_u is uniformly distributed rendering $H(X'_u|X'_u \sim \mathcal{U})$ the maximum entropy.

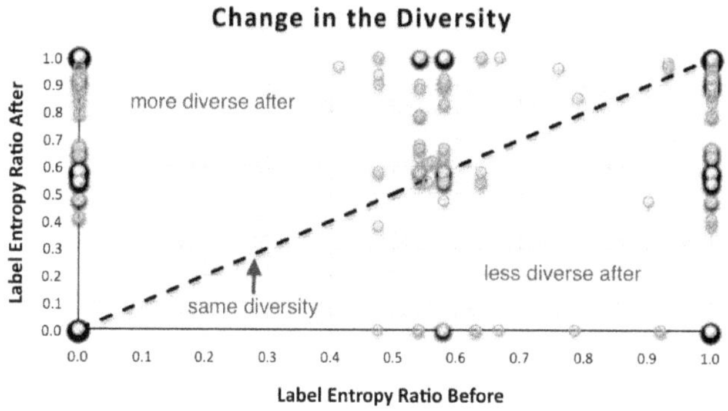

Figure 5: Change in the user diversity after S.H. for users who visited at least two different domains both before and after the event. Every point in the plot corresponds to a user.

Among the 5% of the users who accessed at least 4 domains, the average normalized entropy is 0.70, and the median is 0.66. Hence, from the users who access a considerable number of domains, the majority neither access webpages of a single stance (H^{norm} should be 0), nor websites of all possible labels (H^{norm} should be 1).

All in all, 5% of the users appears to seek diversity (Theory 1), while the vast majority seem to primarily get their information on a topic from one source and therefore are only exposed to that view.

5.2 Event: Change in Within-User Diversity

Although the diversity of information consumed by each user is low overall, we seek to understand if a *shocking event* with nationwide impact influences *a change* in the diversity of the information that users access. For this study, we use Shannon's entropy and assess the *change* in the label entropy of the information sought before and after the event. As in Sec. 5.1, this study may imply whether recommendation systems should adjust the diversity of their results after a shocking event to keep the user satisfied.

For a fair comparison of accesses before and after the shocking news event, we need to control for the users. Thus, we focus on the common users, *i.e.*, those who were active *both before and after* Sandy Hook (Table 2), as these are the only users whom we can characterize before and after the event. For each user u who visited at least two domains both before and after Sandy Hook, we compute per time period the normalized label entropy, $H^{norm}(X_u)$, as defined in Eq. (1). Then, to quantify the change in the within-user diversity, we compute the difference between the normalized entropies

$$H^{norm}_{AFTER}(X_u) - H^{norm}_{BEFORE}(X_u).$$

Next, we consider two cases for the data: (1) *all* the websites, and (2) all the webpages *except for* Feinstein's page about the new gun control legislation (gray spike on Dec. 27 in Fig. 1), which was heavily visited the day of its creation and, thus, corresponds to an "outlier" webpage. The reason for this two-fold analysis is to understand how much of the user diversity is attributed to a single page, which attracted the interest of many users the day of its creation.

With Feinstein's website. Figure 5 shows the change in the user diversity after the Sandy Hook shootings. On average, the normalized entropy increased by 12.54%. However, the results vary across users: for 30.20% of the users, the diversity remained the same; for 41.40% of the users, the entropy increased by 65.02%, and for 28.76% it decreased by 49.18%.

To understand what drove so many users to this site, we investigated more deeply. On Dec. 27, 2012, the Drudge Report, a primarily conservative link aggregation site, featured a gun rights re-

Table 4: Markov chain states for browsing history: Abbreviations for the high-level and expanded labels.

High-level States (3)		Expanded States (6)	
GC	Gun Control	EC	Extreme Gun Control
		MC	Moderate Gun Control
BF	Balanced/Factual	HB	Highly Balanced
		PF	Purely Factual
GR	Gun Rights	MR	Moderate Gun Rights
		ER	Extreme Gun Rights

action grabbing headline "Senate to Go For Handguns"[2]. Additionally, a summary underneath mentioned key sensitive points for gun rights supporters (gun registries and owner fingerprinting). 84% of the users who reached the Feinstein list came via the Drudge Report front page – nearly all of them had primarily consumed gun rights information prior to this. The implication is that when users consume information outside of their typical viewpoint the link comes from *within* their own sphere. Moreover, it suggests future research to redesign contextual link recommendation – which displays related-content to a page – may have a greater potential for changing the diversity of information a user browses than the composition of search results.

Without Feinstein's website. By repeating the analysis described above after removing the website which was heavily visited when the gun ban list was announced, we find that, on average, the normalized entropy of the users increased by 11.92%. That is, the increase is slightly smaller than in the previous analysis where we consider the outlier webpage. Specifically, for 32.87% of the users, the diversity remained the same; for 39.38% of the users, the entropy increased by 49.07%, and for 27.75% it decreased by 52.13%.

Based on our study, on average users do slightly increase the diversity of opinions they consume and peek outside of their bubble after a *shocking* event. One large motivator seems to be the the uncertainty and potential for change, which prompts speculatory reading on that change (*e.g.*, Feinstein's page).

6. WEB TRANSITIONS

Our third study addresses the way users navigate polarizing topics. Specifically, we seek insights about how the stance of content on the current website influences the type of webpage that users browse to next, when exploring polarizing political topics. What webpages are users more likely to visit after browsing a site supporting extreme gun control or rights? Although most of the users are not diverse in terms of the label entropy of the domains they visit (Sec. 5), many of them *do* transition between pages supporting opposing views. We seek to understand the most common transitions, as well as possible changes in the transitions due to the news on the Newtown shootings. By focusing on the influences of the stance of the current page on transitions to next pages, we obtain a micro-level view of information consumption patterns in distinction to the user-level view presented in Section 5.

For each user we represent her browsing history as a Markov chain with either the high-level or expanded labels as states X_i (Table 4). Then, we describe the distribution of the transition probabilities by an n-state transition matrix $\mathbf{P}^n$, with elements $p_{ij} = Prob(X_{t+1} = j|X_t = i)$. We note that the row-wise sums are equal to 1, $\sum_j p_{ij} = 1$. To make sense of the underlying trends of this matrix, we employ mobility indices that have been widely used in economics and sociology (e.g., credit mobility [19], social status mobility [9]).

[2]See `http://www.drudgereportarchives.com/data/2012/12/27/20121227_160126.htm` for an archive.

Table 5: *All* users: 6-state transition matrix $\mathbf{P}^6$ for November-December.

	EC	MC	HB	PF	MR	ER
EC	13.58%	18.57%	31.60%	12.45%	8.27%	15.53%
MC	10.67%	18.54%	33.06%	9.41%	7.70%	20.62%
HB	9.33%	15.10%	28.41%	16.94%	10.15%	20.08%
PF	6.06%	10.26%	34.46%	9.70%	12.55%	26.97%
MR	5.57%	9.39%	24.59%	13.00%	19.27%	28.17%
ER	5.18%	8.81%	19.40%	8.95%	12.08%	45.58%

Table 6: *All* users: 3-state transition matrix $\mathbf{P}^3$ for November-December.

	GC	BF	GR
GC	30.48%	43.15%	26.37%
BF	22.88%	45.12%	31.99%
GR	14.31%	31.34%	54.36%

6.1 Overall Transition Patterns

We start by studying whether the polarity of a web page can be predictive of the polarity of the next on-topic site that a user will browse, which might have implications for contextual search and recommendation. To that end, we use a specific type of mobility indices, called *Summary Mobility Indices*.

We consider the ~35,000 transitions of *all* users during November and December. We note that these are the users who visited at least two different domains, and, hence, we record for them at least one transition. The transitions are given in the form of a transition matrix in Tables 5 and 6.

We employ the Summary Mobility Indices, which describe the direction of the mobility:

- Immobility Ratio: $IR = \sum_{i=1}^{n} p_{ii}/n$
- Moving Up: $MU = \sum_{i<j} p_{ij}/n$
- Moving Down: $MD = \sum_{i>j} p_{ij}/n$,

where n is the number of states. The indices take values in $[0, 1]$. The immobility ratio represents the percent of same-state transitions (higher for more *im*mobility), while the other two indices give the percent of transitions from one extreme to the other, *i.e.*, the MU index captures the transitions from extreme gun control towards extreme gun rights, and the MD index describes the opposite directionality. The higher the MU and MD indices are, the more mobility is observed in the system.

The Summary Mobility Indices for all users during November and December are: (a) for the high-level states $IR = 0.4332$, $MU = 0.3384$, and $MD = 0.2284$, and (b) for the extended states $IR = 0.2251$, $MU = 0.4535$, and $MD = 0.3214$. Firstly, we observe that the overall system is characterized by mobility ($IR \ll 1$). Specifically, for the extended states, about 23% of the transitions are same state (and, thus, predictive), and 45% of the transitions occur in the direction from extreme gun control towards extreme gun rights. From the transitions in the opposite direction, the most dominant transitions are towards the "middle" states: from factual to balanced webpages (34.46%), from extreme gun rights to balanced pages (19.40%), and from moderate gun rights to balanced pages (24.59%).

6.2 Event: Change in Transition Patterns

We continue by studying whether a shocking event *changes* the predictivity of the polarity of the next on-topic domain conditioned on the current one – and, thus, implies changes in contextual search and recommendation. To evaluate the change, we restrict our analysis to the common users, and create two transition matrices, $\mathbf{P}_{before}$ and $\mathbf{P}_{after}$ (Table 7). For our analysis we employ both mobility indices and matrix distances.

Throughout our studies, we considered two different versions of our dataset: (i) GC-DEBATE: which contains all of the on-topic URLs that users visited during the two-month period that we are studying, and (ii) NONNEWS: contains the on-topic URLs excluding the news articles, which we separated from the rest URLs using a white list and keyword-based classifier (Sec. 3.2). The reason for this separation is to understand whether there are differences in the behaviors of the users when we consider different types of engagement; short-term interests in the topic (GC-DEBATE) vs. only long-term interests beyond news articles (NONNEWS). All the results we have presented up to this point refer to the dataset GC-DEBATE, because the results were very similar in NONNEWS and the conclusions were consistent. However, in this study, we observed that there are differences in the transitions of the users depending on the level of their engagement. Therefore, we present the results for both cases, and discuss the differences. Unless we explicitly state that the results consider the NONNEWS URLs, we refer to all the URLs (GC-DEBATE).

We start with the Summary Mobility Indices, as well as the eigenvalue-based indices [27, 32, 33, 19, 21] that quantify the amount of mobility in the system. This category includes the eigenvalue M_E, second eigenvalue M_2, determinant M_D indices. A value of 0 means to total immobility, and a value of 1 to perfect mobility.

The first observation on Table 9 is that, in all cases, the immobility ratio (IR) decreases after Sandy Hook signifying that users transition between different states more often after than before the event. The same can also be drawn from the eigenvalue-based indices, all of which increase. The direction of the transitions depends on the type of interests that we focus on. When we consider the transient interests (GC-DEBATE), the transitions towards extreme gun rights (MU) decrease, while the transitions towards extreme gun control (MD) increase. On the other hand, when we consider the long-term interests (NONNEWS), the system moves mainly towards extreme gun rights.

The indices described above are used to assess the underlying mobility behaviors in an *individual* transition matrix $\mathbf{P}^n$, but *not* the similarities between different transition matrices. To compute the latter, we need to introduce the notion of comparison between

Table 7: *Common* users: 6-state transition matrices $\mathbf{P}^6_{before}$ (top) and $\mathbf{P}^6_{after}$ (bottom).

	EC	MC	HB	PF	MR	ER
EC	28.35%	0.00%	21.13%	3.09%	30.93%	16.49%
MC	8.33%	0.00%	16.67%	4.17%	29.17%	41.67%
HB	12.53%	1.36%	28.07%	7.63%	25.61%	24.80%
PF	12.75%	1.96%	30.39%	3.92%	29.41%	21.57%
MR	8.33%	1.00%	12.83%	6.83%	40.33%	30.67%
ER	7.61%	0.60%	10.91%	2.70%	22.42%	55.76%

	EC	MC	HB	PF	MR	ER
EC	11.71%	20.42%	32.28%	9.76%	8.86%	16.97%
MC	9.06%	17.21%	28.91%	9.21%	11.17%	24.45%
HB	7.58%	16.00%	23.84%	17.56%	11.38%	23.64%
PF	4.61%	10.22%	26.45%	8.02%	13.83%	36.87%
MR	5.03%	11.95%	23.40%	15.72%	12.58%	31.32%
ER	4.04%	9.12%	17.41%	10.43%	12.06%	46.94%

Table 8: *Common* users: 3-state transition matrices $\mathbf{P}^3_{before}$ and $\mathbf{P}^3_{after}$.

	$\mathbf{P}^3_{before}$				$\mathbf{P}^3_{after}$		
	GC	BF	GR		GC	BF	GR
GC	26.15%	23.85%	50.00%	**GC**	28.23%	39.43%	32.35%
BF	14.07%	35.39%	50.53%	**BF**	21.78%	39.98%	38.24%
GR	8.63%	15.88%	75.48%	**GR**	14.17%	30.83%	55.00%

Table 9: *Common* users: Summary Mobility and Eigenvalue-based Indices for $\mathbf{P}^3_{before}$ and $\mathbf{P}^3_{after}$. The top (bottom) rows correspond to transitions between the 3 high-level (6 expanded) states. The rows annotated by NONNEWS refer to the version of the data that excludes news articles, while the rest refer to the whole dataset, GC-DEBATE.

	IR	MU	MD	M_E	M_2	M_D
Before-3	0.4567	0.4146	0.1286	0.8149	0.7483	0.9702
After-3	0.4107	0.3667	0.2226	0.8840	0.7994	0.9937
Before-3 NONNEWS	0.5342	0.3772	0.0886	0.6987	0.5780	0.9238
After-3 NONNEWS	0.4405	0.4362	0.1233	0.8393	0.7670	0.9794
Before-6	0.2607	0.5050	0.2342	0.8871	0.6868	<1
After-6	0.2005	0.4944	0.3051	0.9594	0.7642	1
Before-6 NONNEWS	0.3118	0.4988	0.1894	0.8259	0.5051	<1
After-6 NONNEWS	0.2197	0.5713	0.2091	0.9364	0.7042	1

Table 10: *Common* users: Distances of transition matrices from the immobility matrix **I**. The top (bottom) rows correspond to transitions between the 3 high-level (6 expanded) states. The rows annotated by NONNEWS refer to the version of the data that excludes news articles, while the rest refer to the whole dataset, GC-DEBATE, introduced in Sec. 3.

	L_1	L_2	D_1	D_3
Before-3	3.2594	1.2797	0.6575	0.0876
After-3	3.5359	1.2833		
Before-3 NONNEWS	2.7947	1.1386	-0.1546	-0.0202
After-3 NONNEWS	3.3571	1.3138		
Before-6	8.8713	2.1333	2.1419	0.4262
After-6	9.5941	2.2204		
Before-6 NONNEWS	8.2586	2.0464	-0.8122	-0.1632
After-6 NONNEWS	9.3639	2.2484		

matrices. The first step towards this goal is to have both matrices at the same base, which is achieved by computing their deviation from a perfectly immobile system described by the identity matrix **I**. Among the matrix distances in the literature, we use the L1-norm and L2-norm:

$$||\mathbf{P}-\mathbf{Q}||_1 = \sum_i \sum_j (p_{ij} - q_{ij})$$

$$||\mathbf{P}-\mathbf{Q}||_2 = \sqrt{\sum_i \sum_j (p_{ij} - q_{ij})^2},$$

where $\mathbf{P} = \mathbf{I}$ and $\mathbf{Q} = \mathbf{P}_{before}$ or $\mathbf{P}_{after}$. In addition to these standard matrix distances, we also use two "risk"-adjusted difference indices, D_1 and D_3, which have the advantage of comparing the two transition matrices directly and also detecting the direction of the transition –while weighing proportionally "close" and "far" transitions by the factor $(i - j)$:

$$D_1(\mathbf{P},\mathbf{Q}) = \sum_i \sum_j (i-j)(p_{ij} - q_{ij})$$

$$D_3(\mathbf{P},\mathbf{Q}) = \sum_i \sum_j (i-j) sign(p_{ij} - q_{ij})(p_{ij} - q_{ij})^2,$$

where $\mathbf{P} = \mathbf{P}_{after}$ and $\mathbf{Q} = \mathbf{P}_{before}$. The distances are given in Table 10. The L_1 and L_2 distances increase after Sandy Hook, showing that the users transition between different states more often after than before the event. As far as the D_1 and D_3 distances are concerned, we observe an interesting pattern: the two versions of data yield distances of different signs. The negative values in the NONNEWS data suggest that the long-term interests move from extreme gun control towards extreme gun rights after the event. On the other hand, the positive values in the GC-DEBATE data show that the transient interests due to the news about the event tend toward balanced and gun control stances. These conclusions are also corroborated by the MU and MD indices.

All in all, the event leads to more mobility in the system, and the way it affects the latter depends on the type of user interest (long-term vs. short term).

7. TIME-EVOLVING COMMUNITIES

In our last study we seek to understand whether a shocking news event permanently shifts the user's topical view, as the answer may be useful in conditioning personalization. To do that, we employ community analysis: we characterize the users based on their search and browsing patterns, and track the temporal evolution of their communities.

We introduce an approach that assigns to each user a score reflecting her stance for each time period, depending on the stance of the sites she visited. Let $X_{u,t}$ be the set of labels x of the webpages that user u visited during time period t, and $\mathcal{L}$ be the set of unique labels. Algorithm 1 finds the communities to which each user belongs at time t. For example, according to the algorithm, a user who visited 2 balanced, and 5 gun rights webpages before S.H., belongs to the gun rights community.

ALGORITHM 1: User Characterization and Assignment to Communities.

INPUT: set of labels $\mathcal{L}$
time period t
set of labels, X_t, of visited webpages
label function L

`//1: define the weight` w `for each label` $l \in \mathcal{L}$

$$w(l) = \begin{cases} -1 & \text{if } l = \text{gun rights} \\ 0 & \text{if } l = \text{balanced} \\ +1 & \text{if } l = \text{gun control} \end{cases}$$

for each user u **do**
for each label $l \in \mathcal{L}$ **do**
`//2: compute the number of webpages of label` l `browsed by user` u
$n_{u,t}(l) = \sum_{x \in X_{u,t}} \mathbb{1}_{x=l}$
end for
// 3: compute user's u score for time period t
$s_t(u) = \sum_{l \in \mathcal{L}} w(l) \cdot n_{u,t}(l)$
// 4: find user u's community for time period t

$$c_t(u) = \begin{cases} \text{gun rights} & \text{if } sign(s_t(u)) < 0 \\ \text{balanced} & \text{if } sign(s_t(u)) = 0 \\ \text{gun control} & \text{if } sign(s_t(u)) > 0 \end{cases}$$

end for
return the vector of user communities $\mathbf{c}_t$

To obtain the communities of the users who visited at least two on-topic webpages both before and after the event, we applied Algorithm 1 for $\mathcal{L}$ ={gun control, gun rights, balanced/factual} and t equal to the time period before and after Sandy Hook. As in Section 6.2, we analyze both GC-DEBATE and the NONNEWS data, because they exhibit differences. Our baseline is GC-DEBATE—we explicitly mention when we refer to NONNEWS.

First, we analyze the dynamics of the communities that we found. Table 11 shows that 76% and 75% of the users supporting gun control and gun rights respectively, stand firm after the event. The users who were part of the balanced community before the event split almost evenly among the three communities after Sandy Hook. This observation about the movement of users across communities naturally leads us to the question: Do the communities change size after the event? As shown in Fig. 6, the gun control community has almost 10% more users after S.H., while the gun rights community lost the same percent of users. The balanced community increased in size slightly, by about 2%.

If we focus on the users with long-term interest in the topic (NONNEWS), we observe that more of them remain loyal to their communities, consisting 79% and 91% of the gun control and gun rights community respectively. Moreover, the gun control and rights communities shrink by about 1%, while the balanced community expands by 2%. Therefore, the communities consisting of users with long-term interests are less prone to changes than users with transient interest in the topic.

Table 11: Transition matrix capturing the mobility between communities before (rows) and after (columns) Sandy Hook.

	GC	BF	GR
GC	76.32%	14.21%	9.47%
BF	29.94%	32.20%	37.85%
GR	12.25%	13.19%	74.56%

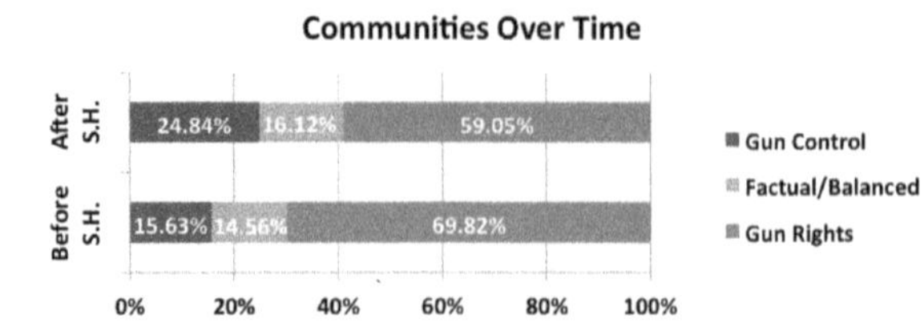

Figure 6: The gun control community increases in size, while the gun rights community shrinks after S.H.. For each community we give its size before and after S.H. in terms of the percentage of users belonging to them.

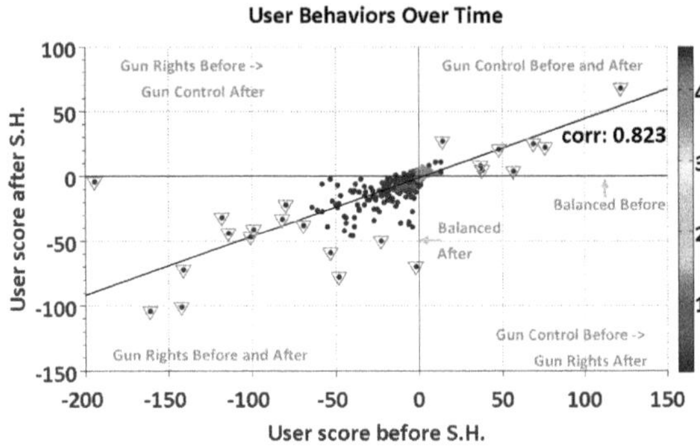

Figure 7: Heatmap of user scores before vs. user scores after Sandy Hook. Each point corresponds to one user. The points withing red triangles correspond to anomalous users (spotted by DBSCAN, a density-based spatial clustering method) with significantly different behavior from the rest.

We go beyond the aggregate user transitions and the community dynamics, and study the users' individual transitions to understand if and how they changed after the event. Figure 7 shows the score of each user, $s_t(u)$ (in Algorithm 1), before (x-axis) and after (y-axis) S.H. The bigger the absolute value of a score is, the more active and devoted is the user to the corresponding community. While most of the users have small or moderate activity, there are some very heavy users who are faithful supporters of their communities (either gun rights or gun control). Among them, we found some outlier users (noted in red triangles), using a density-based spatial clustering method, DBSCAN [12]. The outlier users that remain in the gun rights community after S.H. (third quadrant) are mostly members of some gun rights forums, including `gunownersclub.com` and `defensivecarry.com`. On the other hand, most of the outlier users who remained in the gun control community after the shootings, visited several times the webpage `childrensdefense.org`. About one third of the total users crossed communities after Sandy Hook (points in the second and fourth quadrant in Fig. 7). From the users with long-term interest in the topic, only 15% crossed communities, supporting our argument that they are less prone to changes than users with transient interests. In the data, there is no evidence for significant difference between the cross-over and loyal users with respect to their news consumption.

To sum up, it appears that the event affected people's browsing behavior: about 88% of the total users (and 61% of the NONNEWS users) browsed more balanced and factual webpages discussing gun control issues after the event, which indicates that the Sandy Hook shootings sparked their interest in the topic. As for the size of the communities, the change depends on the type of interest (long term vs. short term), as mentioned earlier.

8. LIMITATIONS

To understand the information-seeking behaviors of people about a controversial topic such as gun control, as well as the effect of an external, shocking event, we focused on the search and browsing patterns of 29 million users of Internet Explorer (IE) in the US-English market. The first limitation of our study is that we consider users of only one browser. However, during the time period that we studied (November-December 2012), the majority of users worldwide (54%) were using IE to browse the web [4]. Moreover, independent studies [3] show that the user population of IE is a broad representation of the US population covering both genders, and nearly all age and income levels. The second limitation of our study arises from the inherent differences in the browsing behavior of gun control and rights supporters. Before the Sandy Hook shootings, the observed activity comes mainly from users who support gun rights and are members of related forums. To compensate for the difference in browsing activity, we draw conclusions both for: a) the system as a whole, which includes users who have transient interests in the topic, and become active after the event, and b) the users who are active during the whole time period (mainly gun rights supporters), and have long-term interest in the topic.

9. CONCLUSIONS

We have examined the browsing behavior of searchers for the controversial and polarizing topic of gun control. We focused on the influence of a disruptive and shocking event involving the tragic mass shooting at the Sandy Hook Elementary School in December 2012. By starting from a large corpus of web logs from November and December 2012, we extracted a footprint of user information-seeking behavior on the URLs that are germane to the topic, and followed a multi-step labeling procedure. Our key findings are as follows:

- We find that people use the web to largely access information they agree with, as signified by the low diversity of labels capturing viewpoints expressed in visited domains.
- Domains provide a myopic view on the polarizing topic, showing low diversity in stances that are presented.
- When the external event threatens to influence users directly, they explore content outside their filter bubble.
- The overall system, including transient interests, largely moves mainly towards extreme gun control. However, the long-term interests in the topic, which are captured by visits to non-news webpages, tend to move towards the opposite direction and support extreme gun rights.
- The gun control and balanced communities grow after S.H., while the gun rights community shrinks.

We believe that the methods and results presented are a step toward leveraging log data to better understand how people navigate webpages on controversial topics. Future directions include devising studies exploring whether and how ranking and presentation procedures that expose users to a greater diversity of viewpoints can lead to increased user satisfaction. Other directions include predicting the changes in polarity in the information accessed via search and retrieval systems.

Acknowledgements. Thanks to Rebecca Hanson for her extensive support in labeling web pages.

APPENDIX

A. CATEGORIES OF WEBPAGES

We seek to label every page that is not "Off-Topic" or "Not Accessible". Thus, we define symmetric and objective categories:

A. Purely Factual: The page is on-topic, but only presents facts with no obvious interpretation or commentary on politics. This may include pages that give statistics regarding guns, laws in different locales about guns, or reporting on news events involving guns without additional commentary.

B. Discusses Policies and Issues: The page is on-topic and discusses gun policies and issues regarding legislation on gun ownership and usage, or ethical and historical justifications for gun control/rights. This includes pages that discuss how laws have been interpreted for application in court cases, as well as the personal/official pages of politicians, other persons, organizations, and entities whose stance on gun-related policy is well known even if the page does not feature content currently discussing the policy. The pages in this category are further classified into:

Extreme Gun Control: These pages present a view which favors extreme changes to the current gun laws in an area. This includes viewpoints that support laws banning any private citizen ownership of guns, as well as what would be viewed as major legislation changes relative to a locale that are not as sweeping. Pages that use derogatory and insulting language toward those supporting gun rights belong to this category. Discussion forums and blogs where most comments support this view, and webpages giving contact information about only anti-gun organizations belong here.

Moderate Gun Control: These pages present views that favor some to moderate changes to the current gun laws in an area. This includes views that may view private citizen ownership of guns as acceptable with appropriate conditions and limitations, but argue that the current laws are not sufficient in defining these conditions and limitations. Discussion forums and blogs where the preponderance of comments support this view fall in this category.

Highly Balanced: These pages either discuss both sides with no obvious bias, or present a straightforward discussion of how laws and policy have been interpreted in the past. For example, pages that discuss of court case reasoning involving guns would fall into this category. Likewise, educational texts that appear to fairly present both sides would also belong here.

Moderate Gun Rights: These pages present a view which favors little to no changes to the current gun laws in an area. This includes viewpoints that generally support private citizen ownership of guns with appropriate conditions and limitations, and argue that the current laws are generally sufficient. This includes pages selling guns that likely would be viewed acceptable for private ownership under appropriate limitations by a moderate gun control viewpoint. Discussion forums and blogs where the preponderance of comments support this view belong here.

Extreme Gun Rights: These pages present a view which favors no changes to the current gun laws in an area and argue that current laws may be overly restrictive and intrusive. This includes viewpoints that claim current laws are an intrusion on individual rights and argue for lessening of any current gun control policies. Pages that use derogatory and insulting language toward those supporting gun control are included in this category. This includes pages selling guns or providing information on guns limited not only to those guns viewed acceptable for private ownership under appropriate limitations by a moderate gun control viewpoint but also those falling under currently debated or proposed legislative control. Discussion forums and blogs where the preponderance of comments support this view, and webpages giving contact information about only pro-gun organizations belong to this category.

B. REFERENCES

[1] Sandy Hook elementary school shooting. `http://en.wikipedia.org/wiki/Sandy_Hook_Elementary_School_shooting`. Retrieved 6/10/14.

[2] Gun Ownership and Use in America. `http://www.gallup.com/poll/20098/gun-ownership-use-america.aspx`, 2005. Retrieved 7/10/14.

[3] Firefox vs. Internet Explorer. `http://www.comscore.com/Insights/Blog/Firefox-vs.-Internet-Explorer,Firefox-vs-Internet-Explorer-Part-2`, 2007. Retrieved 11/6/14.

[4] Usage share of web browsers. `http://thenextweb.com/apps/2012/10/01/internet-explorer-8-falls-25-market-share-firefox-15-passes-10-mark-chrome-loses-users`, 2012. Retrieved 3/7/15.

[5] Lada A. Adamic and Natalie Glance. The political blogosphere and the 2004 U.S. election: divided they blog. In *LinkKDD*, pages 36–43. ACM, 2005.

[6] Elif Aktolga and James Allan. Sentiment diversification with different biases. In *SIGIR*, pages 593–602. ACM, 2013.

[7] Rawia Awadallah, Maya Ramanath, and Gerhard Weikum. Harmony and dissonance: organizing the people's voices on political controversies. In *WSDM*, pages 523–532. ACM, 2012.

[8] Ramnath Balasubramanyan, William W. Cohen, Doug Pierce, and David P. Redlawsk. Modeling polarizing topics: When do different political communities respond differently to the same news? In *AAAI ICWSM*, 2012.

[9] P.M. Blau. *The American occupational structure*. Wiley, 1967.

[10] Ulrik Brandes, Patrick Kenis, Jürgen Lerner, and Denise van Raaij. Network analysis of collaboration structure in wikipedia. In *WWW*, pages 731–740, 2009.

[11] Nick Craswell and Martin Szummer. Random walks on the click graph. In *ACM SIGIR*, pages 239–246, 2007.

[12] Martin Ester, Hans peter Kriegel, Jörg S, and Xiaowei Xu. A density-based algorithm for discovering clusters in large spatial databases with noise. pages 226–231. AAAI Press, 1996.

[13] Yi Fang, Luo Si, Naveen Somasundaram, and Zhengtao Yu. Mining contrastive opinions on political texts using cross-perspective topic model. In *WSDM*, 2012.

[14] R Kelly Garrett. Politically motivated reinforcement seeking: Reframing the selective exposure debate. *Int. J. Comm.*, 59(4):676–699, 2009.

[15] R Kelly Garrett and Paul Resnick. Resisting political fragmentation on the internet. *Daedalus*, 140(4):108–120, 2011.

[16] Eric Gilbert, Tony Bergstrom, and Karrie Karahalios. Blogs are echo chambers: Blogs are echo chambers. In *HICSS*, pages 1–10, 2009.

[17] Kilem Li Gwet. *Handbook of Inter-Rater Reliability (3rd Edition): The Definitive Guide to Measuring the Extent of Agreement Among Multiple Raters.* Advanced Analytics Press, 3 edition.

[18] J.B. Horrigan, K. Garrett, and P. Resnick. *The Internet and Democratic Debate.* PIALP, 2004.

[19] Yusuf Jafry and Til Schuermann. Measurement, estimation and comparison of credit migration matrices. *J. Bank. Financ.*, 28(11):2603–2639, November 2004.

[20] Alexander Kotov, Paul N. Bennett, Ryen W. White, Susan T. Dumais, and Jaime Teevan. Modeling and analysis of cross-session search tasks. In *ACM SIGIR*, pages 5–14, 2011.

[21] Vasileios Koutras and Konstantinos Drakos. A migration approach for USA banks' capitalization: Are the 00s the same with the 90s? *IRFA*, 30(0):131 – 140, 2013.

[22] Jingjing Liu, Nicholas J. Belkin, Xiangmin Zhang, and Xiao-Jun Yuan. Examining users' knowledge change in the task completion process. *Inf. Process. Manage.*, 49(5):1058–1074, 2013.

[23] R. Malouf and T. Mullen. Taking Sides: User Classification for Informal Online Political Discourse. *Internet Res.*, 18(2):177–190, 2008.

[24] Sean A. Munson, Stephanie Y. Lee, and Paul Resnick. Encouraging reading of diverse political viewpoints with a browser widget. In *AAAI ICWSM*, 2013.

[25] Sean A. Munson and Paul Resnick. Presenting diverse political opinions: how and how much. In *CHI*, pages 1457–1466, 2010.

[26] Eli Pariser. *The Filter Bubble: What the Internet Is Hiding from You.* The Penguin Group, 2011.

[27] S. J. Prais. Measuring Social Mobility. *J. Roy. Statist. Soc. Ser. A*, 118(1):56–66, 1955.

[28] Justus J. Randolph. Free-Marginal Multirater Kappa (multirater K[free]): An Alternative to Fleiss' Fixed-Marginal Multirater Kappa. In *Joensuu Univ. Learn. Instruct. Symp.*, 2005.

[29] Paul Resnick, R. Kelly Garrett, Travis Kriplean, Sean A. Munson, and Natalie Jomini Stroud. Bursting your (filter) bubble: strategies for promoting diverse exposure. In *CSCW*, pages 95–100. ACM, 2013.

[30] Hoda Sepehri-Rad and Denilson Barbosa. Identifying controversial articles in wikipedia: A comparative study. In *8th Int. Symp. on Wikis & Open Collab.*, 2012.

[31] Claude E. Shannon. A mathematical theory of communication. *ATT Thec. J.*, 27:379–423, 623–656, July, October 1948.

[32] A. F. Shorrocks. The Measurement of Mobility. *Econometrica*, 46(5):1013–1024, 1978.

[33] PM Sommers and J Conlsk. Eigenvalue immobility measures for markov-chains. *J. Math. Sociol.*, 6(2):253–276, 1979.

[34] Jennifer Stromer-Galley. Diversity of political conversation on the internet: Users' perspectives. *J. Computer-Mediated Comm.*, 8(3), 2003.

[35] Mikalai Tsytsarau, Themis Palpanas, and Malu Castellanos. Dynamics of news events and social media reaction. In *KDD*, pages 901–910. ACM, 2014.

[36] Mikalai Tsytsarau, Themis Palpanas, and Kerstin Denecke. Scalable discovery of contradictions on the web. In *WWW*, pages 1195–1196, 2010.

[37] Ryen W. White, Susan T. Dumais, and Jaime Teevan. Characterizing the influence of domain expertise on web search behavior. In *WSDM*, pages 132–141, 2009.

[38] E. Yom-Tov, S.T. Dumais, and Q. Gao. Promoting civil discourse through search engine diversity. In *QPOL*, 2013.

[39] B. Yu, S. Kaufmann, and D. Diermeier. Classifying party affiliation from political speech. *JITP*, 5(1):33–48, 2008.

[40] Daniel Xiaodan Zhou, Paul Resnick, and Qiaozhu Mei. Classifying the political leaning of news articles and users from user votes. In *AAAI ICWSM*, 2011.

Statistically Significant Detection of Linguistic Change

Vivek Kulkarni
Stony Brook University, USA
vvkulkarni@cs.stonybrook.edu

Rami Al-Rfou
Stony Brook University, USA
ralrfou@cs.stonybrook.edu

Bryan Perozzi
Stony Brook University, USA
bperozzi@cs.stonybrook.edu

Steven Skiena
Stony Brook University, USA
skiena@cs.stonybrook.edu

ABSTRACT

We propose a new computational approach for tracking and detecting statistically significant linguistic shifts in the meaning and usage of words. Such linguistic shifts are especially prevalent on the Internet, where the rapid exchange of ideas can quickly change a word's meaning. Our meta-analysis approach constructs property time series of word usage, and then uses statistically sound change point detection algorithms to identify significant linguistic shifts.

We consider and analyze three approaches of increasing complexity to generate such linguistic property time series, the culmination of which uses distributional characteristics inferred from word co-occurrences. Using recently proposed deep neural language models, we first train vector representations of words for each time period. Second, we warp the vector spaces into one unified coordinate system. Finally, we construct a distance-based distributional time series for each word to track its linguistic displacement over time.

We demonstrate that our approach is scalable by tracking linguistic change across years of micro-blogging using Twitter, a decade of product reviews using a corpus of movie reviews from Amazon, and a century of written books using the Google Book Ngrams. Our analysis reveals interesting patterns of language usage change commensurate with each medium.

Categories and Subject Descriptors

H.3.3 [**Information Storage and Retrieval**]: Information Search and Retrieval

Keywords

Web Mining;Computational Linguistics

1. INTRODUCTION

Natural languages are inherently dynamic, evolving over time to accommodate the needs of their speakers. This effect is especially prevalent on the Internet, where the rapid exchange of ideas can change a word's meaning overnight.

WWW 2015, May 18–22, 2015, Florence, Italy.
ACM 978-1-4503-3469-3/15/05.
http://dx.doi.org/10.1145/2736277.2741627 .

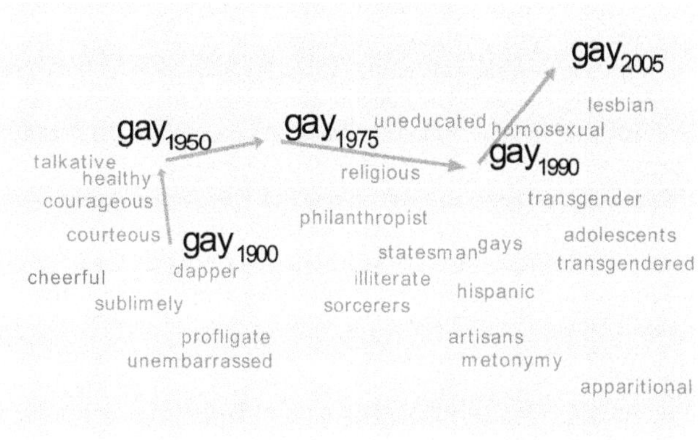

Figure 1: A 2-dimensional projection of the latent semantic space captured by our algorithm. Notice the semantic trajectory of the word gay transitioning meaning in the space.

In this paper, we study the problem of detecting such linguistic shifts on a variety of media including micro-blog posts, product reviews, and books. Specifically, we seek to detect the broadening and narrowing of semantic senses of words, as they continually change throughout the lifetime of a medium.

We propose the first computational approach for tracking and detecting statistically significant linguistic shifts of words. To model the temporal evolution of natural language, we construct a time series per word. We investigate three methods to build our word time series. First, we extract *Frequency* based statistics to capture sudden changes in word usage. Second, we construct *Syntactic* time series by analyzing each word's part of speech (POS) tag distribution. Finally, we infer contextual cues from word co-occurrence statistics to construct *Distributional* time series. In order to detect and establish statistical significance of word changes over time, we present a change point detection algorithm, which is compatible with all methods.

Figure 1 illustrates a 2-dimensional projection of the latent semantic space captured by our *Distributional* method. We clearly observe the sequence of semantic shifts that the word gay has undergone over the last century (1900-2005). Initially, gay was an adjective that meant `cheerful` or `dapper`. Observe for the first 50 years, that it stayed in the same general region of the semantic space. However by 1975, it had begun a transition over to its current meaning —a shift which accelerated over the years to come.

The choice of the time series construction method determines the type of information we capture regarding word usage. The difference between frequency-based approaches and distributional methods is illustrated in Figure 2. Figure 2a shows the frequencies of two words, **Sandy** (red), and **Hurricane** (blue) as a percentage of search queries according to Google Trends[1]. Observe the sharp spikes in both words' usage in October 2012, which corresponds to a storm called **Hurricane Sandy** striking the Atlantic Coast of the United States. However, only one of those words (**Sandy**) actually acquired a new meaning. Note that while the word **Hurricane** definitely experienced a surge in frequency of usage, it did not undergo any change in meaning. Indeed, using our distributional method (Figure 2b), we observe that only the word **Sandy** shifted in meaning where as **Hurricane** did not.

Our computational approach is scalable, and we demonstrate this by running our method on three large datasets. Specifically, we investigate linguistic change detection across years of micro-blogging using Twitter, a decade of product reviews using a corpus of movie reviews from Amazon, and a century of written books using the Google Books Ngram Corpus.

Despite the fast pace of change of the web content, our method is able to detect the introduction of new products, movies and books. This could help semantically aware web applications to better understand user intentions and requests. Detecting the semantic shift of a word would trigger such applications to apply focused sense disambiguation analysis.

In summary, our contributions are as follows:

- **Word Evolution Modeling**: We study three different methods for the statistical modeling of word evolution over time. We use measures of frequency, part-of-speech tag distribution, and word co-occurrence to construct time series for each word under investigation.(Section 3)
- **Statistical Soundness**: We propose (to our knowledge) the first statistically sound method for linguistic shift detection. Our approach uses change point detection in time series to assign significance of change scores to each word. (Section 4)
- **Cross-Domain Analysis**: We apply our method on three different domains; books, tweets and online reviews. Our corpora consists of billions of words and spans several time scales. We show several interesting instances of semantic change identified by our method. (Section 6)

The rest of the paper is structured as follows. In Section 2 we define the problem of language shift detection over time. Then, we outline our proposals to construct time series modeling word evolution in Section 3. Next, in Section 4, we describe the method we developed for detecting significant changes in natural language. We describe the datasets we used in Section 5, and then evaluate our system both qualitatively and quantitatively in Section 6. We follow this with a treatment of related work in Section 7, and finally conclude with a discussion of the limitations and possible future work in Section 8.

2. PROBLEM DEFINITION

Our problem is to quantify the linguistic shift in word meaning (semantic or context change) and usage across time. Given a temporal corpora $\mathcal{C}$ that is created over a time span

[1] `http://www.google.com/trends/`

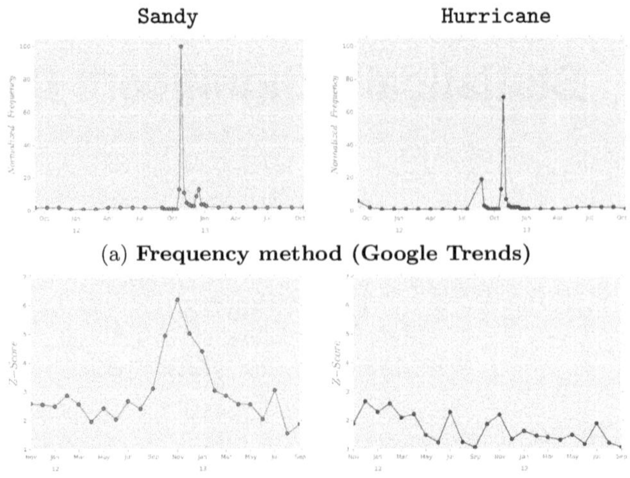

(a) **Frequency method (Google Trends)**

(b) **Distributional method**

Figure 2: Comparison between Google Trends and our method. Observe how Google Trends shows spikes in frequency for both **Hurricane** (blue) and **Sandy** (red). Our method, in contrast, models change in usage and detects that only **Sandy** changed its meaning and not **Hurricane**.

$\mathcal{S}$, we divide the corpora into n snapshots $\mathcal{C}_t$ each of period length P. We build a common vocabulary $\mathcal{V}$ by intersecting the word dictionaries that appear in all the snapshots (i.e, we track the same word set across time). This eliminates trivial examples of word usage shift from words which appear or vanish throughout the corpus.

To model word evolution, we construct a time series $\mathcal{T}(w)$ for each word $w \in \mathcal{V}$. Each point $\mathcal{T}_t(w)$ corresponds to statistical information extracted from corpus snapshot $\mathcal{C}_t$ that reflects the usage of w at time t. In Section 3, we propose several methods to calculate $\mathcal{T}_t(w)$, each varying in the statistical information used to capture w's usage.

Once these time series are constructed, we can quantify the significance of the shift that occurred to the word in its meaning and usage. Sudden increases or decreases in the time series are indicative of shifts in the word usage. Specifically we pose the following questions:

1. How statistically significant is the shift in usage of a word w across time (in $\mathcal{T}(w)$)?
2. Given that a word has shifted, at what point in time did the change happen?

3. TIME SERIES CONSTRUCTION

Constructing the time series is the first step in quantifying the significance of word change. Different approaches capture various aspects of a word's semantic, syntactic and usage patterns. In this section, we describe three approaches (*Frequency*, *Syntactic*, and *Distributional*) to building a time series, that capture different aspects of word evolution across time. The choice of time series significantly influences the types of changes we can detect —a phenomenon which we discuss further in Section 6.

3.1 Frequency Method

The most immediate way to detect sequences of discrete events is through their change in frequency. Frequency based methods are therefore quite popular, and include tools like Google Trends and Google Books Ngram Corpus, both of

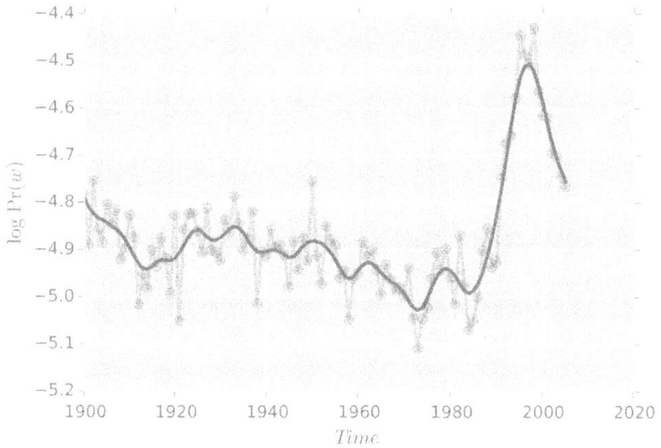

Figure 3: Frequency usage of the word **gay** over time, observe the sudden change in frequency in the late 1980s.

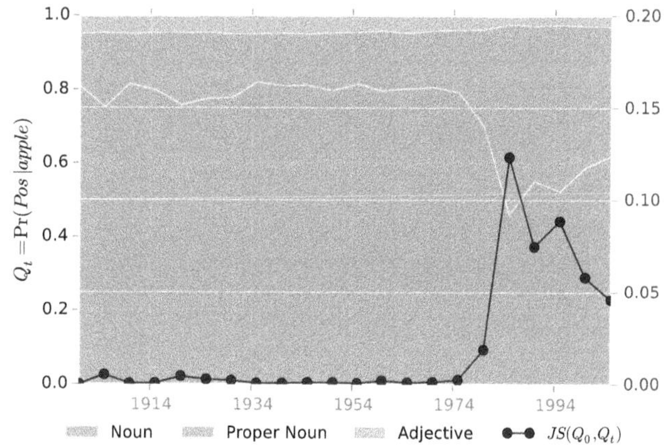

Figure 4: Part of speech tag probability distribution of the word **apple** (stacked area chart). Observe that the "Proper Noun" tag has dramatically increased in 1980s. The same trend is clear from the time series constructed using Jenssen-Shannon Divergence (dark blue line).

which are used in research to predict economical and public health changes [7, 9]. Such analysis depends on keyword search over indexed corpora.

Frequency based methods can capture linguistic shift, as changes in frequency can correspond to words acquiring or losing senses. Although crude, this method is simple to implement. We track the change in probability of a word appearing over time. We calculate for each time snapshot corpus $\mathcal{C}_t$, a unigram language model. Specifically, we construct the time series for a word w as follows:

$$\mathcal{T}_t(w) = \log \frac{\#(w \in \mathcal{C}_t)}{|\mathcal{C}_t|}, \quad (1)$$

where $\#(w \in \mathcal{C}_t)$ is the number of occurrences of the word w in corpus snapshot $\mathcal{C}_t$. An example of the information we capture by tracking word frequencies over time is shown in Figure 3. Observe the sudden jump in late 1980s of the word **gay** in frequency.

3.2 Syntactic Method

While word frequency based metrics are easy to calculate, they are prone to sampling error introduced by bias in domain and genre distribution in the corpus. Temporal events and popularity of specific entities could spike the word usage frequency without significant shift in its meaning, recall **Hurricane** in Figure 2a.

Another approach to detect and quantify significant change in the word usage involves tracking the syntactic functionality it serves. A word could evolve a new syntactic functionality by acquiring a new part of speech category. For example, **apple** used to be only a "Noun" describing a fruit, but over time it acquired the new part of speech "Proper Noun" to indicate the new sense describing a technology company (Figure 4). To leverage this syntactic knowledge, we annotate our corpus with part of speech (POS) tags. Then we calculate the probability distribution of part of speech tags Q_t given the word w and time snapshot t as follows: $Q_t = \Pr_{X \sim \text{POS Tags}}(X|w, \mathcal{C}_t)$. We consider the POS tag distribution at $t = 0$ to be the initial distribution Q_0. To quantify the temporal change between two time snapshots corpora, for a specific word w, we calculate the divergence between the POS distributions in both snapshots. We construct the time series as follows:

$$\mathcal{T}_t(w) = JSD(Q_0, Q_t) \quad (2)$$

where JSD is the Jenssen-Shannon divergence [21].

Figure 4 shows that the JS divergence (dark blue line) reflects the change in the distribution of the part of speech tags given the word **apple**. In 1980s, the "Proper Noun" tag (blue area) increased dramatically due to the rise of **Apple Computer Inc.**, the popular consumer electronics company.

3.3 Distributional Method

Semantic shifts are not restricted to changes to part of speech. For example, consider the word **mouse**. In the 1970s it acquired a new sense of "computer input device", but did not change its part of speech categorization (since both senses are nouns). To detect such subtle semantic changes, we need to infer deeper cues from the contexts a word is used in.

The distributional hypothesis states that words appearing in similar contexts are semantically similar [13]. Distributional methods learn a semantic space that maps words to continuous vector space $\mathbb{R}^d$, where d is the dimension of the vector space. Thus, vector representations of words appearing in similar contexts will be close to each other. Recent developments in representation learning (*deep learning*) [5] have enabled the scalable learning of such models. We use a variation of these models [28] to learn word vector representation (*word embeddings*) that we track across time.

Specifically, we seek to learn a temporal word embedding $\phi_t : \mathcal{V}, \mathcal{C}_t \mapsto \mathbb{R}^d$. Once we learn a representation of a specific word for each time snapshot corpus, we track the changes of the representation across the embedding space to quantify the meaning shift of the word (as shown in Figure 1).

In this section we present our distributional approach in detail. Specifically we discuss the learning of word embeddings, the aligning of embedding spaces across different time snapshots to a joint embedding space, and the utilization of a word's displacement through this semantic space to construct a distributional time series.

3.3.1 *Learning Embeddings*

Given a time snapshot $\mathcal{C}_t$ of the corpus, our goal is to learn ϕ_t over $\mathcal{V}$ using neural language models. At the beginning of the training process, the word vector representations are randomly initialized. The training objective is to maximize the probability of the words appearing in the context of word w_i. Specifically, given the vector representation $\mathbf{w}_i$ of a word

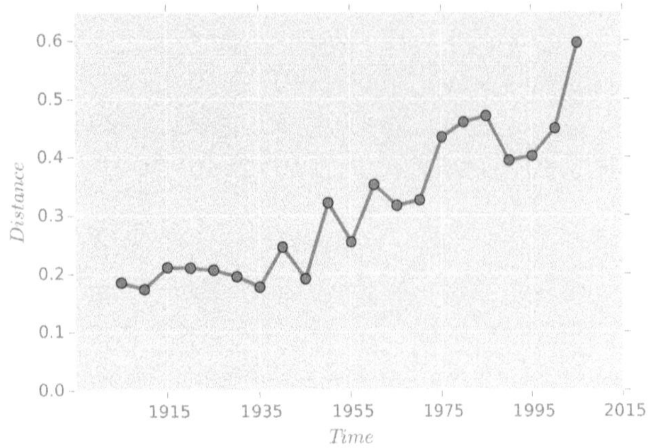

Figure 5: Distributional time series for the word **tape** over time using word embeddings. Observe the change of behavior starting in the 1950s, which is quite apparent by the 1970s.

w_i ($\mathbf{w}_i = \phi_t(w_i)$), we seek to maximize the probability of w_j through the following equation:

$$\Pr(w_j \mid \mathbf{w}_i) = \frac{\exp(\mathbf{w}_j^T \mathbf{w}_i)}{\sum_{w_k \in \mathcal{V}} \exp(\mathbf{w}_k^T \mathbf{w}_i)} \quad (3)$$

In a single epoch, we iterate over each word occurrence in the time snapshot $\mathcal{C}_t$ to minimize the negative log-likelihood J of the context words. Context words are the words appearing to the left or right of w_i within a window of size m. Thus J can be written as:

$$J = \sum_{w_i \in \mathcal{C}_t} \sum_{\substack{j=i-m \\ j!=i}}^{i+m} -\log \Pr(w_j \mid \mathbf{w}_i) \quad (4)$$

Notice that the normalization factor that appears in Eq. (3) is not feasible to calculate if $|\mathcal{V}|$ is too large. To approximate this probability, we map the problem from a classification of 1-out-of-$\mathcal{V}$ words to a hierarchical classification problem [30, 31]. This reduces the cost of calculating the normalization factor from $\mathcal{O}(|\mathcal{V}|)$ to $\mathcal{O}(\log |\mathcal{V}|)$. We optimize the model parameters using stochastic gradient descent [6], as follows:

$$\phi_t(w_i) = \phi_t(w_i) - \alpha \times \frac{\partial J}{\partial \phi_t(w_i)}, \quad (5)$$

where α is the learning rate. We calculate the derivatives of the model using the back-propagation algorithm [34]. We use the following measure of training convergence:

$$\rho = \frac{1}{|\mathcal{V}|} \sum_{w \in \mathcal{V}} \frac{\phi^{k^T}(w)\phi^{k+1}(w)}{\|\phi^k(w)\|_2 \|\phi^{k+1}(w)\|_2}, \quad (6)$$

where ϕ^k is the model parameters after epoch k. We calculate ρ after each epoch and stop the training if $\rho \leq 1.0^{-4}$. After training stops, we normalize word embeddings by their L_2 norm, which forces all words to be represented by unit vectors.

In our experiments, we use the **gensim** implementation of skipgram models[2]. We set the context window size m to 10 unless otherwise stated. We choose the size of the word embedding space dimension d to be 200. To speed up the training, we subsample the frequent words by the ratio 10^{-5} [27].

[2]https://github.com/piskvorky/gensim

3.3.2 Aligning Embeddings

Having trained temporal word embeddings for each time snapshot $\mathcal{C}_t$, we must now align the embeddings so that all the embeddings are in one unified coordinate system. This enables us to characterize the change between them. This process is complicated by the stochastic nature of our training, which implies that models trained on exactly the same data could produce vector spaces where words have the same nearest neighbors but not with the same coordinates. The alignment problem is exacerbated by actual changes in the distributional nature of words in each snapshot.

To aid the alignment process, we make two simplifying assumptions: First, we assume that the spaces are equivalent under a linear transformation. Second, we assume that the meaning of most words did not shift over time, and therefore, their local structure is preserved. Based on these assumptions, observe that when the alignment model fails to align a word properly, it is possibly indicative of a linguistic shift.

Specifically, we define the set of k nearest words in the embedding space ϕ_t to a word w to be k-NN$(\phi_t(w))$. We seek to learn a linear transformation $\mathbf{W}_{t' \mapsto t}(w) \in \mathbb{R}^{d \times d}$ that maps a word from $\phi_{t'}$ to ϕ_t by solving the following optimization:

$$\mathbf{W}_{t' \mapsto t}(w) = \underset{\mathbf{W}}{\operatorname{argmin}} \sum_{\substack{w_i \in \\ k\text{-NN}(\phi_{t'}(w))}} \|\phi_{t'}(w_i)\mathbf{W} - \phi_t(w_i)\|_2^2, \quad (7)$$

which is equivalent to a piecewise linear regression model.

3.3.3 Time Series Construction

To track the shift of word position across time, we align all embeddings spaces to the embedding space of the final time snapshot ϕ_n using the linear mapping (Eq. 7). This unification of coordinate systems allows us to compare relative displacements that occurred to words across different time periods.

To capture linguistic shift, we construct our distributional time series by calculating the distance in the embedding space between $\phi_t(w)\mathbf{W}_{t \mapsto n}(w)$ and $\phi_0(w)\mathbf{W}_{0 \mapsto n}(w)$ as

$$\mathcal{T}_t(w) = 1 - \frac{(\phi_t(w)\mathbf{W}_{t \mapsto n}(w))^T(\phi_0(w)\mathbf{W}_{0 \mapsto n}(w))}{\|\phi_t(w)\mathbf{W}_{t \mapsto n}(w)\|_2 \|\phi_0(w)\mathbf{W}_{0 \mapsto n}(w)\|_2} \quad (8)$$

Figure 5 shows the time series obtained using word embeddings for **tape**, which underwent a semantic change in the 1950s with the introduction of magnetic tape recorders. As such recorders grew in popularity, the change becomes more pronounced, until it is quite apparent by the 1970s.

4. CHANGE POINT DETECTION

Given a time series of a word $\mathcal{T}(w)$, constructed using one of the methods discussed in Section 3, we seek to determine whether the word changed significantly, and if so estimate the change point. We believe a formulation in terms of changepoint detection is appropriate because even if a word might change its meaning (usage) gradually over time, we expect a time period where the new usage suddenly dominates (tips over) the previous usage (akin to a phase transition) with the word **gay** serving as an excellent example.

There exists an extensive body of work on change point detection in time series [1, 3, 38]. Our approach models the time series based on the *Mean Shift* model described in [38]. First, our method recognizes that language exhibits a general stochastic drift. We account for this by first normalizing the time series for each word. Our method then attempts to

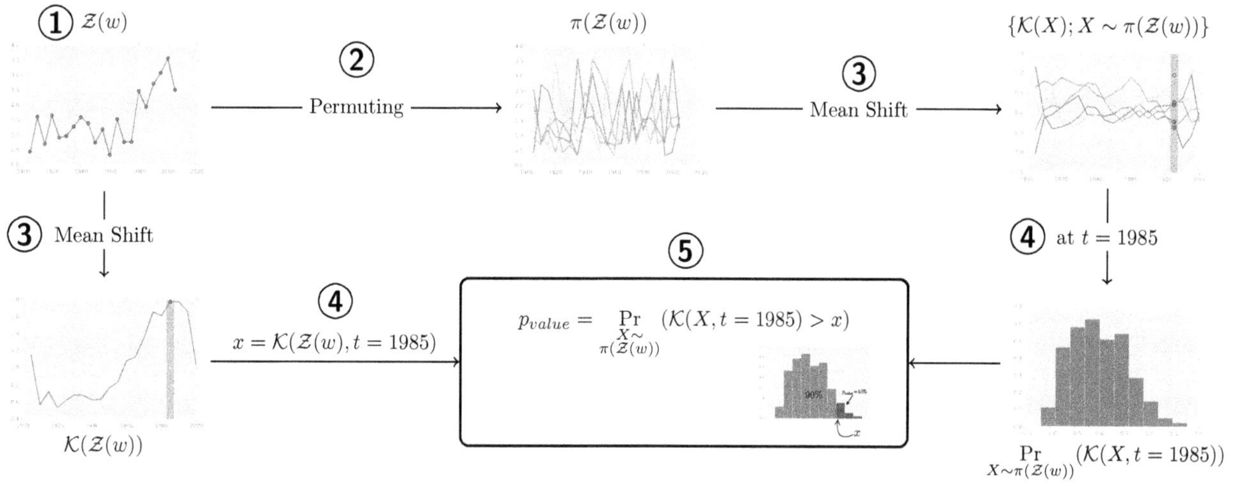

Figure 6: Our change point detection algorithm. In Step ①, we normalize the given time series $\mathcal{T}(w)$ to produce $\mathcal{Z}(w)$. Next, we shuffle the time series points producing the set $\pi(\mathcal{Z}(w))$ (Step ②). Then, we apply the mean shift transformation ($\mathcal{K}$) on both the original normalized time series $\mathcal{Z}(w)$ and the permuted set (Step ③). In Step ④, we calculate the probability distribution of the mean shifts possible given a specific time ($t = 1985$) over the bootstrapped samples. Finally, we compare the observed value in $\mathcal{K}(\mathcal{Z}(w))$ to the probability distribution of possible values to calculate the p-value which determines the statistical significance of the observed time series shift (Step ⑤).

Algorithm 1 CHANGE POINT DETECTION ($\mathcal{T}(w)$, B, γ)

Input: $\mathcal{T}(w)$: Time series for the word w, B: Number of bootstrap samples, γ: Z-Score threshold
Output: ECP: Estimated change point, p-value: Significance score.

```
    // Preprocessing
 1: Z(w) ← Normalize T(w).
 2: Compute mean shift series K(Z(w))
    // Bootstrapping
 3: BS ← ∅ {Bootstrapped samples}
 4: repeat
 5:   Draw P from π(Z(w))
 6:   BS ← BS ∪ P
 7: until |BS| = B
 8: for i ← 1, n do
 9:   p-value(w, i) ← (1/B) Σ_{P∈BS} [K_i(P) > K_i(Z(w))]
10: end for
    // Change Point Detection
11: C ← {j | j ∈ [1, n] and Z_j(w) >= γ}
12: p-value ← min_{j∈C} p-value(w, j)
13: ECP ← argmin_{j∈C} p-value(w, j)
14: return p-value, ECP
```

detect a shift in the mean of the time series using a variant of mean shift algorithms for change point analysis. We outline our method in Algorithm 1 and describe it below. We also illustrate key aspects of the method in Figure 6.

Given a time series of a word $\mathcal{T}(w)$, we first normalize the time series. We calculate the mean $\mu_i = \frac{1}{|\mathcal{V}|}\sum_{w\in\mathcal{V}} \mathcal{T}_i(w)$ and variance $Var_i = \frac{1}{|\mathcal{V}|}\sum_{w\in\mathcal{V}}(\mathcal{T}_i(w) - \mu_i)^2$ across all words. Then, we transform $\mathcal{T}(w)$ into a *Z-Score* series using:

$$\mathcal{Z}_i(w) = \frac{\mathcal{T}_i(w) - \mu_i}{\sqrt{Var_i}}, \tag{9}$$

where $\mathcal{Z}_i(w)$ is the Z-Score of the time series for the word w at time snapshot i.

We model the time series $\mathcal{Z}(w)$ by a *Mean shift model* [38]. Let $S = \mathcal{Z}_1(w), \mathcal{Z}_2(w), \ldots, \mathcal{Z}_n(w)$ represent the time series. We model $\mathcal{S}$ to be an output of a stochastic process where each $\mathcal{S}_i$ can be described as $\mathcal{S}_i = \mu_i + \epsilon_i$ where μ_i is the mean and ϵ_i is the random error at time i. We also assume that the errors ϵ_i are independent with mean 0. Generally $\mu_i = \mu_{i-1}$ except for a few points which are *change points*.

Based on the above model, we define the mean shift of a general time series S as follows:

$$\mathcal{K}(S) = \frac{1}{l-j}\sum_{k=j+1}^{l} S_k - \frac{1}{j}\sum_{k=1}^{j} S_k \tag{10}$$

This corresponds to calculating the shift in mean between two parts of the time series pivoted at time point j. Change points can be thus identified by detecting significant shifts in the mean.[3]

Given a normalized time series $\mathcal{Z}(w)$, we then compute the mean shift series $\mathcal{K}(\mathcal{Z}(w))$ (Line 2). To estimate the statistical significance of observing a mean shift at time point j, we use bootstrapping [12] (see Figure 6 and Lines 3-10) under the null hypothesis that there is no change in the mean. In particular, we establish statistical significance by first obtaining B (typically $B = 1000$) bootstrap samples obtained by permuting $\mathcal{Z}(w)$ (Lines 3-10). Second, for each bootstrap sample $\mathcal{P}$, we calculate $\mathcal{K}(P)$ to yield its corresponding bootstrap statistic and we estimate the statistical significance (p-value) of observing the mean shift at time i compared to the null distribution (Lines 8-10). Finally, we estimate the change point by considering the time point j with the minimum p-value score (described in [38]). While this method does detect significant changes in the mean of the time series, observe that it does not account for the magnitude of the change in terms of Z-Scores. We extend this approach to obtain words that changed significantly compared to other words, by considering only those time

[3] This is similar to the CUSUM based approach used for detecting change points which is also based on mean shift model.

	Google Ngrams	Amazon	Twitter
Span (years)	105	12	2
Period	5 years	1 year	1 month
# words	$\sim 10^9$	$\sim 9.9 \times 10^8$	$\sim 10^9$
$\lvert\mathcal{V}\rvert$	~50K	~50K	~100K
# documents	$\sim 7.5 \times 10^8$	$8. \times 10^6$	$\sim 10^8$
Domain	Books	Movie Reviews	Micro Blogging

Table 1: Summary of our datasets

points where the Z-Score exceeds a user-defined threshold γ (we typically set γ to 1.75). We then estimate the change point as the time point with the minimum p-value exactly as outlined before (Lines 11-14).

5. DATASETS

Here we report the details of the three datasets that we consider - years of micro-blogging from Twitter, a decade of movie reviews from Amazon, and a century of written books using the Google Books Ngram Corpus. Table 1 shows a summary of three different datasets spanning different modes of expression on the Internet: books, an online forum and a micro-blog.

The Google Books Ngram Corpus.

The Google Books Ngram Corpus project enables the analysis of cultural, social and linguistic trends. It contains the frequency of short phrases of text (*ngrams*) that were extracted from books written in eight languages over five centuries [25]. These ngrams vary in size (1-5) grams. We use the 5-gram phrases which restrict our context window size m to 5. The 5-grams include phrases like '`thousand pounds less then nothing`' and '`to communicate to each other`'. We focus on the time span from 1900 – 2005, and set the time snapshot period to 5 years (21 points). We obtain the POS Distribution of each word in the above time range by using the Google Syntactic Ngrams dataset [14, 22, 23].

Amazon Movie Reviews.

Amazon Movie Reviews dataset consists of movie reviews from Amazon. This data spans August 1997 to October 2012 (13 time points), including all 8 million reviews. However, we consider the time period starting from 2000 as the number of reviews from earlier years is considerably small. Each review includes product and user information, ratings, and a plain-text review. The reviews describe user's opinions of a movie, for example: '`This movie has it all. Drama, action, amazing battle scenes - the best I've ever seen. It's definitely a must see.`'.

Twitter Data.

This dataset consists of a sample that spans 24 months starting from September 2011 to October 2013. Each tweet includes the tweet ID, tweet and the geo-location if available. A tweet is a status message with up to 140 characters: '`I hope sandy doesn't rip the roof off the pool while we're swimming ...`'.

6. EXPERIMENTS

In this section, we apply our methods to each dataset presented in Section 5 and identify words that have changed usage over time. We describe the results of our experiments below. The code used for running these experiments is available at the first author's website.[4]

6.1 Time Series Analysis

As we shall see in Section 6.4.1, our proposed time series construction methods differ in performance. Here, we use the detected words to study the behavior of our construction methods.

Table 2 shows the time series constructed for a sample of words with their corresponding p-value time series, displayed in the last column. A dip in the p-value is indicative of a shift in the word usage. The first three words, `transmitted`, `bitch`, and `sex`, are detected by both the *Frequency* and *Distributional* methods. Table 3 shows the previous and current senses of these words demonstrating the changes in usage they have gone through.

Observe that words like `her` and `desk` did not change signifantly in meaning, however, the *Frequency* method detects a change. The sharp increase of the word `her` in frequency around the 1960's could be attributed to the concurrent rise and popularity of the feminist movement. Sudden temporary popularity of specific social and political events could lead the *Frequency* method to produce many false positives. These results confirm our intuition we illustrated in Figure 2. While frequency analysis (like Google Trends) is an extremely useful tool to visualize trends, it is not very well suited for the task of detecting linguistic shift.

The last two rows in Table 2 display two words (`apple` and `diet`) that *Syntactic* method detected. The word `apple` was detected uniquely by the *Syntactic* method as its most frequent part of speech tag changed significantly from "Noun" to "Proper Noun". While both *Syntactic* and *Distributional* methods indicate the change in meaning of the word `diet`, it is only the *Distributional* method that detects the right point of change (as shown in Table 3). The *Syntactic* method is indicative of having low false positive rate, but suffers from a high false negative rate, given that only two words in the table were detected. Furthermore, observe that *Syntactic* method relies on good linguistic taggers. However, linguistic taggers require annotated data sets and also do not work well across domains.

We find that the *Distributional* method offers a good balance between false positives and false negatives, while requiring no linguistic resources of any sort. Having analyzed the words detected by different time series we turn our attention to the analysis of estimated changepoints.

6.2 Historical Analysis

We have demonstrated that our methods are able to detect words that shifted in meaning. We seek to identify the inflection points in time where the new senses are introduced. Moreover, we are interested in understanding how the new acquired senses differ from the previous ones.

Table 3 shows sample words that are detected by *Syntactic* and *Distributional* methods. The first set represents words which the *Distributional* method detected (*Distributional* better) while the second set shows sample words which *Syntactic* method detected (*Syntactic* better).

Our *Distributional* method estimates that the word `tape` changed in the early 1970s to mean a "cassette tape" and not only an "adhesive tape". The change in the meaning of `tape` commences with the introduction of magnetic tapes in 1950s

[4]http://vivekkulkarni.net

Word	Time Series			p-value
	Frequency	*Syntactic*	*Distributional*	
transmitted				
bitch				
sex				
her				
desk				
apple				
diet				

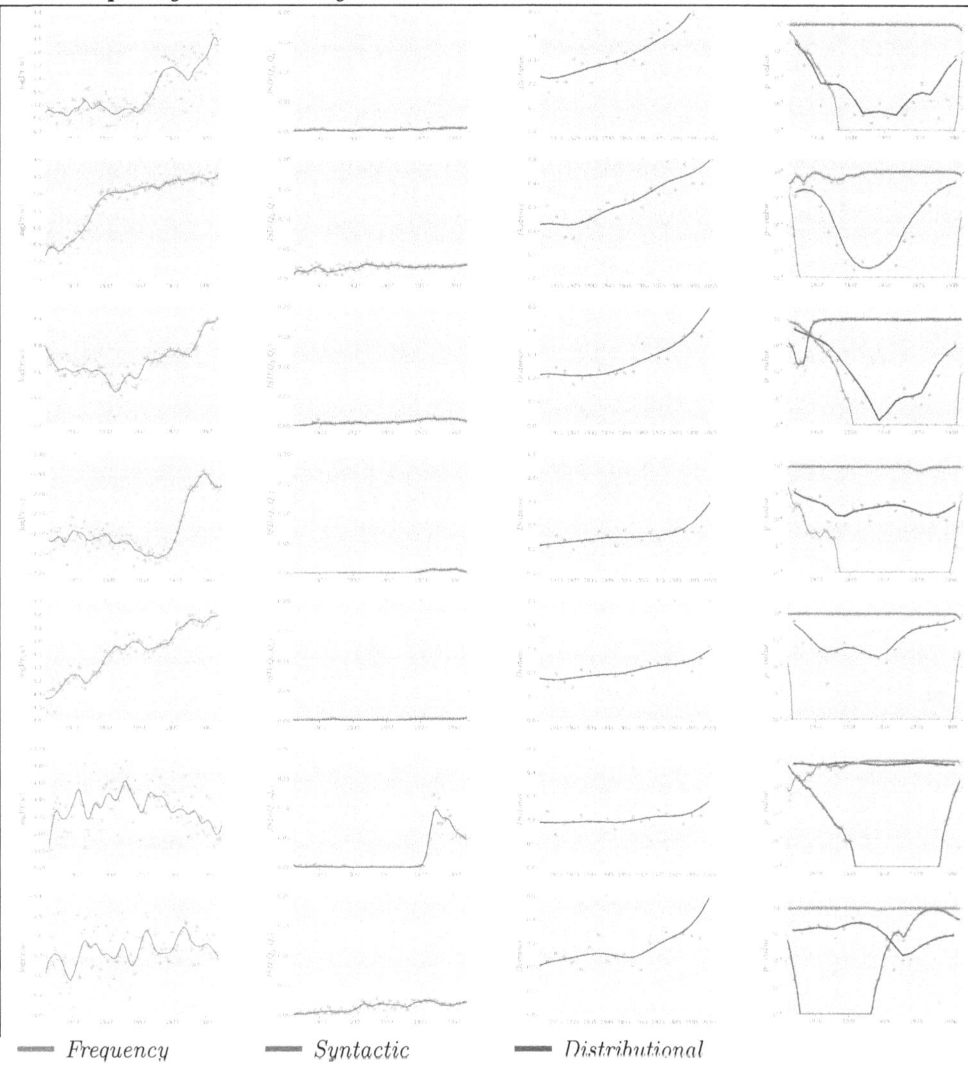

Table 2: Comparison of our different methods of constructing linguistic shift time series on the Google Books Ngram Corpus. The first three columns represent time series for a sample of words. The last column shows the p-value for each time step of each method, as generated by our change point detection algorithm.

(Figure 5). The meaning continues to shift with the mass production of cassettes in Europe and North America for pre-recorded music industry in mid 1960s until it is deemed statistically significant.

The word `plastic` is yet another example, where the introduction of new products inflected a shift in the word meaning. The introduction of Polystyrene in 1950 popularized the term "plastic" as a synthetic polymer, which was once used only to denote the physical property of "flexibility". The popularity of books on dieting started with the best selling book *Dr. Atkins' Diet Revolution* by Robert C. Atkins in 1972 [16]. This changed the use of the word `diet` to mean a life-style of food consumption behavior and not only the food consumed by an individual or group.

The *Syntactic* section of Table 3 shows that words like `hug` and `sink` were previously used mainly as verbs. Over time organizations and movements started using `hug` as a noun which dominated over its previous sense. On the other hand, the words `click` and `handle`, originally nouns, started being used as verbs.

Another clear trend is the use of common words as proper nouns. For example, with the rise of the computer industry, the word `apple` acquired the sense of the tech company Apple in mid 1980s and the word `windows` shifted its meaning to the operating system developed by Microsoft in early 1990s. Additionally, we detect the word `bush` that is widely used as a proper noun in 1989, which coincides with George H. W. Bush's presidency in USA.

6.3 Cross Domain Analysis

Semantic shift can occur much faster on the web, where words can acquire new meanings within weeks, or even days. In this section we turn our attention to analyzing linguistic shift on Amazon Reviews and Twitter (content that spans a much shorter time scale as compared to Google Books Ngram Corpus).

	Word	ECP	p-value	Past ngram	Present ngram
Distributional better	recording	1990	0.0263	*to be ashamed of recording that*	*recording, photocopying*
	gay	1985	0.0001	*happy and gay*	*gay and lesbians*
	tape	1970	<0.0001	*red tape, tape from her mouth*	*a copy of the tape*
	checking	1970	0.0002	*then checking himself*	*checking him out*
	diet	1970	0.0104	*diet of bread and butter*	*go on a diet*
	sex	1965	0.0002	*and of the fair sex*	*have sex with*
	bitch	1955	0.0001	*nicest black bitch* (Female dog)	*bitch* (Slang)
	plastic	1950	0.0005	*of plastic possibilities*	*put in a plastic*
	transmitted	1950	0.0002	*had been transmitted to him, transmitted from age to age*	*transmitted in electronic form*
	peck	1935	0.0004	*brewed a peck*	*a peck on the cheek*
	honey	1930	0.01	*land of milk and honey*	*Oh honey!*
				Past POS	**Present POS**
Syntactic better	hug	2002	<0.001	Verb (*hug a child*)	Noun (*a free hug*)
	windows	1992	<0.001	Noun (*doors and windows of a house*)	Proper Noun (*Microsoft Windows*)
	bush	1989	<0.001	Noun (*bush and a shrub*)	Proper Noun (*George Bush*)
	apple	1984	<0.001	Noun (*apple, orange, grapes*)	Proper Noun (*Apple computer*)
	sink	1972	<0.001	Verb (*sink a ship*)	Noun (*a kitchen sink*)
	click	1952	<0.001	Noun (*click of a latch*)	Verb (*click a picture*)
	handle	1951	<0.001	Noun (*handle of a door*)	Verb (*he can handle it*)

Table 3: Estimated change point (ECP) as detected by our approach for a sample of words on Google Books Ngram Corpus. *Distributional* method is better on some words (which *Syntactic* did not detect as statistically significant eg. sex, transmitted, bitch, tape, peck) while *Syntactic* method is better on others (which *Distributional* failed to detect as statistically significant eg. apple, windows, bush)

	Word	p-value	ECP	Past Usage	Present Usage
Amazon Reviews	instant	0.016	2010	*instant hit, instant dislike*	*instant download*
	twilight	0.022	2009	*twilight as in dusk*	*Twilight* (The movie)
	rays	0.001	2008	*x-rays*	*blu-rays*
	streaming	0.002	2008	*sunlight streaming*	*streaming video*
	ray	0.002	2006	*ray of sunshine*	*Blu-ray*
	delivery	0.002	2006	*delivery of dialogue*	*timely delivery of products*
	combo	0.002	2006	*combo of plots*	*combo DVD pack*
Twitter	candy	<0.001	Apr 2013	*candy sweets*	*Candy Crush* (The game)
	rally	<0.001	Mar 2013	*political rally*	*rally of soldiers* (Immortalis game)
	snap	<0.001	Dec 2012	*snap a picture*	*snap chat*
	mystery	<0.001	Dec 2012	*mystery books*	*Mystery Manor* (The game)
	stats	<0.001	Nov 2012	*sport statistics*	*follower statistics*
	sandy	0.03	Sep 2012	*sandy beaches*	*Hurricane Sandy*
	shades	<0.001	Jun 2012	*color shade, shaded glasses*	50 *shades of grey* (The Book)

Table 4: Sample of words detected by our *Distributional* method on Amazon Reviews and Twitter.

Table 4 shows results from our *Distributional* method on the Amazon Reviews and Twitter datasets. New technologies and products introduced new meanings to words like `streaming`, `ray`, `rays`, and `combo`. The word `twilight` acquired a new sense in 2009 concurrent with the release of the Twilight movie in November 2008.

Similar trends can be observed on Twitter. The introduction of new games and cellphone applications changed the meaning of the words `candy`, `mystery` and `rally`. The word `sandy` acquired a new sense in September 2012 weeks before Hurricane Sandy hit the east coast of USA. Similarly we see that the word `shades` shifted its meaning with the release of the bestselling book *"Fifty Shades of Grey"* in June 2012.

These examples illustrate the capability of our method to detect the introduction of new products, movies and books. This could help semantically aware web applications to understand user intentions and requests better. Detecting the semantic shift of a word would trigger such applications to apply a focused disambiguation analysis on the sense intended by the user.

6.4 Quantitative Evaluation

The lack of any reference (gold standard) data, poses a challenge to quantitatively evaluate our methods. Therefore, we assess the performance of our methods using multiple approaches. We begin with a synthetic evaluation, where we have knowledge of ground-truth changes. Next we create a

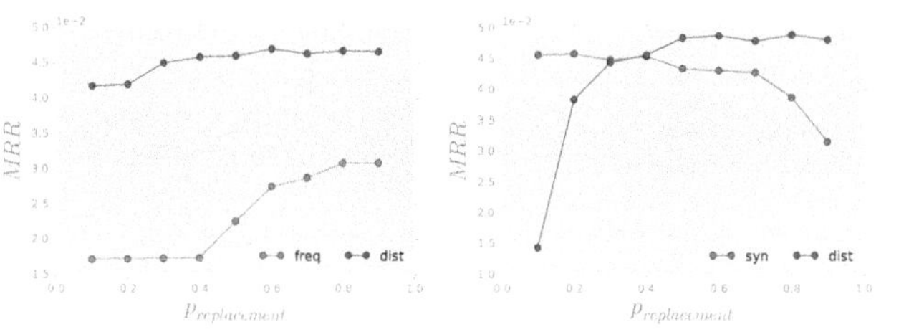

(a) Frequency Perturbation (b) Syntactic Perturbation

Figure 7: Performance of our proposed methods under different scenarios of perturbation.

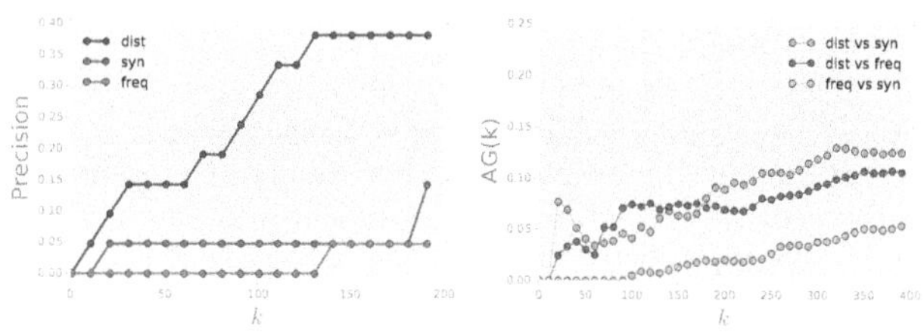

(a) Reference Dataset (b) Methods Agreement

Figure 8: Method performance and agreement on changed words in the Google Books Ngram Corpus.

reference data set based on prior work and evaluate all three methods using it. We follow this with a human evaluation, and conclude with an examination of the agreement between the methods.

6.4.1 Synthetic Evaluation

To evaluate the quantitative merits of our approach, we use a synthetic setup which enables us to model linguistic shift in a controlled fashion by artificially introducing changes to a corpus.

Our synthetic corpus is created as follows: First, we duplicate a copy of a Wikipedia corpus[5] 20 times to model time snapshots. We tagged the Wikipedia corpora with part of speech tags using the *TextBlob* tagger[6]. Next, we introduce changes to a word's usage to model linguistic shift. To do this, we perturb the last 10 snapshots. Finally, we use our approach to rank all words according to their p-values, and then we calculate the Mean Reciprocal Rank ($MRR = 1/|Q| \sum_{i=1}^{|Q|} 1/rank(w_i)$) for the words we perturbed. We rank the words that have lower p-value higher, therefore, we expect the MRR to be higher in the methods that are able to discover more words that have changed.

To introduce a single perturbation, we sample a pair of words out of the vocabulary excluding functional words and stop words[7]. We designate one of them to be a donor and the other to be a receptor. The donor word occurrences will be replaced with the receptor word with a success probability $p_{\text{replacement}}$. For example, given the word pair (`location`, `equation`), some of the occurrences of the word `location` (Donor) were replaced with the word `equation` (Receptor) in the second half snapshots of our temporal corpus.

Figure 7 illustrates the results on two types of perturbations we synthesized. First, we picked our (Donor, Receptor) pairs such that both of them have the same most frequent part of speech tag. For example, we might use the pair (boat, car) but not (boat, running). We expect the frequency of the receptor to change and its context distribution but no significant syntactic changes. Figure 7a shows the MRR of the receptor words on *Distributional* and *Frequency* methods. We observe that both methods improve their rankings as the degree of induced change increases (measured, here, by $p_{\text{replacement}}$). Second, we observe that the *Distributional* approach outperforms *Frequency* method consistently for different values of $p_{\text{replacement}}$.

Second, to compare *Distributional* and *Syntactic* methods we sample word pairs without the constraint of being from the same part of speech categories. Figure 7b shows that the *Syntactic* method while outperforming *Distributional* method when the perturbation statistically is minimal, its ranking continue to decline in quality as the perturbation increases. This could be explained by noting that the quality of the tagger annotations decreases as the corpus at inference time diverges from the training corpus.

It is quite clear from both experiments, that the *Distributional* method outperforms other methods when $p_{replacement} > 0.4$ without requiring any language specific resources or annotators.

6.4.2 Evaluation on a Reference Dataset

In this section, we attempt to gauge the performance of the various methods on a reference data set. We created a reference data set D of 20 words that have been suggested by prior work [15, 17, 19, 39] as having undergone a linguistic change[8]. For each method, we create a list L of its changed words ordered by the significance scores of the change, and evaluate the Precision@k with respect to the reference data set constructed. Specifically, the Precision@k between L and D can be defined as:

$$\text{Precision@}k(L, D) = \frac{|L[1:k] \cap D|}{|D|} \tag{11}$$

Figure 8a depicts the performance of the different methods on this reference data set. Observe that the *Distributional* method outperforms other methods with the *Frequency* method performing the poorest (due to its high false positive rate). The *Syntactic* method which does not capture semantic changes well also performs worse than the *Distributional* method.

6.4.3 Human Evaluation

We chose the top 20 words claimed to have changed by each method and asked 3 human evaluators to independently decide whether each word experienced a linguistic shift. For each method, we calculated the percentage of words each rater believes have changed and report the mean percentage. We observed that on an average the raters believe that only 13.33% of the words reported by *Frequency* method and only 21.66% of the words reported by *Syntactic* method changed. However, in the case of *Distributional* method we observed that on an average the raters believe that 53.33% of the words changed. We conclude thus from this evaluation that the *Distributional* method outperforms other methods.

[5] `http://mattmahoney.net/dc/text8.zip`
[6] `http://textblob.readthedocs.org/en/dev/`
[7] NLTK Stopword List: `http://www.nltk.org/`
[8] The reference data set and the human evaluations are available at `http://vivekkulkarni.net`

6.4.4 Method Agreement

In order to investigate the agreement between the various methods, we again consider the top k words that each method is most confident have changed. For each pair of methods, we then compute the fraction of words both methods agree on in their top k lists. Specifically given methods M_1 and M_2 let $M_1(k)$ and $M_2(k)$ represent the top k lists for M_1 and M_2 respectively. We define the agreement between these 2 lists as follows:

$$AG(M_1(k), M_2(k)) = \frac{|M_1(k) \cap M_2(k)|}{|M_1(k) \cup M_2(k)|} \quad (12)$$

which is the Jaccard Similarity between $M_1(k)$ and $M_2(k)$.

Figure 8b shows the agreement scores between each pair of methods for different values of k. We first note that the agreement between all methods is low, suggesting that the methods differ in aspects of word change captured. Observe that the agreement between *Distributional* and *Syntactic* is higher compared to that of *Syntactic* and *Frequency*. This can be explained by noting that *Distributional* method captures semantic changes along with elements of syntactic changes, and therefore agrees more with *Syntactic* method. We leave it to future work to investigate whether a single improved method can capture all of these aspects of word usage effectively.

7. RELATED WORK

Here we discuss the four most relevant areas of related work: linguistic shift, word embeddings, change point detection, and Internet linguistics.

Linguistic Shift: There has been a surge in the work about language evolution over time. Michel et al. [25] detected important political events by analyzing frequent patterns. Juola [18] compared language from different time periods and quantified the change. Lijffijt et al. [20] and Säily et al. [35] study variation in noun/pronoun frequencies, and lexical stability in a historical corpus. Different from these studies, we quantify linguistic change by tracking individual shifts in words meaning. This fine grain detection and tracking still allows us to quantify the change in natural language as a whole, while still being able to interpret these changes.

Gulordava and Baroni [15] propose a distributional similarity approach to detecting semantic change in the Google Book Ngram corpus between 2 time periods. Wijaya and Yeniterzi [39] study evolution of words using a topic modeling approach but do not suggest an explicit change point detection algorithm. Our work differs from the above studies by tracking word evolution through multiple time periods and explicitly providing a change point detection algorithm to detect significant changes. Mitra et al. [29] use a graph based approach relying on dependency parsing of sentences. Our proposed time series construction methods require minimal linguistic knowledge and resources enabling the application of our approach to all languages and domains equally. Compared to the sequential training procedure proposed by Kim et al. [19] work, our technique warps the embeddings spaces of the different time snapshots after the training, allowing for efficient training that could be parallelized for large corpora. Moreover, our work is unique in the fact that our datasets span different time scales, cover larger user interactions and represent a better sample of the web.

Word Embeddings: Bengio et al. [4] used word embeddings to develop a neural language model that outperforms traditional ngram models. These word embeddings have been shown to capture fine grain structures and regularities in the data [26, 27, 32]. Moreover, they have proved to be useful for a wide range of natural language processing tasks [2, 8, 10]. The same technique of learning word embeddings has been applied recently to graph representations [33].

Change Point Detection: Change point detection and analysis is an important problem in the area of time series analysis and modeling. Taylor [38] describes control charts and CUSUM based methods in detail. Adams and MacKay [1] presents a Bayesian approach to online change point detection. The method of bootstrapping and establishing statistical significance is outlined in [12]. Basseville and Nikiforov [3] provides an excellent survey on several elementary change point detection techniques and time series models.

Internet Linguistics: Internet Linguistics is concerned with the study of language in media influenced by the Internet (online forums, blogs, online social media) and also other related forms of electronic media like text messaging. Schiano et al. [36] and Tagliamonte and Denis [37] study how teenagers use messaging media focusing on their usage patterns and the resulting implications on design of e-mail and instant messaging. Merchant [24] study the language use by teenagers in online chat forums. An excellent survey on Internet Linguistics is provided by Crystal [11] and includes linguistic analyses of social media like Twitter, Facebook or Google+.

8. CONCLUSIONS AND FUTURE WORK

In this work, we have proposed three approaches to model word evolution through different time series construction methods. Our computational approach then uses statistically sound change point detection algorithms to detect significant linguistic shifts. Finally, we demonstrated our method's effectiveness on three different data sets each representing a different medium. By analyzing the Google Books Ngram Corpus, we were able to detect historical semantic shifts that happened to words like `gay` and `bitch`. Moreover, in faster evolving media like Tweets and Amazon Reviews, we were able to detect recent events like storms, game and book releases. This capability of detecting meaning shift, should help decipher the ambiguity of dynamical systems like natural languages. We believe our work has implications for the fields of Semantic Search and the recently burgeoning field of Internet Linguistics.

Our future work in the area will focus on the real time analysis of linguistic shift, the creation of better resources for the quantitative evaluation of computational methods, and the effects of attributes like geographical location and content source on the underlying mechanisms of meaning change in language.

Acknowledgments

We thank Andrew Schwartz for providing us access to the Twitter data. This research was partially supported by NSF Grants DBI-1355990 and IIS-1017181, a Google Faculty Research Award, a Renaissance Technologies Fellowship and the Institute for Computational Science at Stony Brook University.

References

[1] R. P. Adams and D. J. MacKay. Bayesian online changepoint detection. Cambridge, UK, 2007.

[2] R. Al-Rfou, B. Perozzi, and S. Skiena. Polyglot: Distributed word representations for multilingual nlp. In *CoNLL*, 2013.

[3] M. Basseville and I. V. Nikiforov. *Detection of Abrupt Changes: Theory and Application.* Prentice-Hall, Inc., Upper Saddle River, NJ, USA, 1993.

[4] Y. Bengio, H. Schwenk, et al. Neural probabilistic language models. In *Innovations in Machine Learning*, pages 137–186. Springer, 2006.

[5] Y. Bengio et al. Representation learning: A review and new perspectives. *IEEE Transactions on Pattern Analysis and Machine Intelligence*, 35(8):1798–1828, 2013.

[6] L. Bottou. Stochastic gradient learning in neural networks. In *Proceedings of Neuro-Nîmes. EC2*, Nimes, France, 1991. EC2.

[7] H. A. Carneiro and E. Mylonakis. Google trends: A web-based tool for real-time surveillance of disease outbreaks. *Clinical Infectious Diseases*, 49(10):1557–1564, 2009.

[8] Y. Chen, B. Perozzi, R. Al-Rfou, and S. Skiena. The expressive power of word embeddings. *CoRR*, abs/1301.3226, 2013.

[9] H. Choi and H. Varian. Predicting the present with google trends. *Economic Record*, 88:2–9, 2012.

[10] R. Collobert, J. Weston, et al. Natural language processing (almost) from scratch. *J. Mach. Learn. Res.*, 12: 2493–2537, Nov. 2011.

[11] D. Crystal. *Internet Linguistics: A Student Guide.* Routledge, New York, NY, 10001, 1st edition, 2011.

[12] B. Efron and R. J. Tibshirani. An introduction to the bootstrap. 1971.

[13] J. R. Firth. *Papers in Linguistics 1934-1951: Repr.* Oxford University Press, 1961.

[14] Y. Goldberg and J. Orwant. A dataset of syntactic-ngrams over time from a very large corpus of english books. In **SEM*, 2013.

[15] K. Gulordava and M. Baroni. A distributional similarity approach to the detection of semantic change in the google books ngram corpus. In *GEMS*, July 2011.

[16] D. Immerwahr. The books of the century, 2014. URL `http://www.ocf.berkeley.edu/~immer/books1970s`.

[17] A. Jatowt and K. Duh. A framework for analyzing semantic change of words across time. In *Proceedings of the Joint JCDL/TPDL Digital Libraries Conference*, 2014.

[18] P. Juola. The time course of language change. *Computers and the Humanities*, 37(1):77–96, 2003.

[19] Y. Kim, Y.-I. Chiu, K. Hanaki, et al. Temporal analysis of language through neural language models. In *ACL*, 2014.

[20] J. Lijffijt, T. Säily, and T. Nevalainen. Ceecing the baseline: Lexical stability and significant change in a historical corpus. VARIENG, 2012.

[21] J. Lin. Divergence measures based on the shannon entropy. *IEEE Transactions on Information Theory*, 37 (1):145–151, 1991.

[22] Y. Lin, J. B. Michel, E. L. Aiden, J. Orwant, W. Brockman, and S. Petrov. Syntactic annotations for the google books ngram corpus. In *ACL*, 2012.

[23] J. Mann, D. Zhang, et al. Enhanced search with wildcards and morphological inflections in the google books ngram viewer. In *Proceedings of ACL Demonstrations Track*. Association for Computational Linguistics, June 2014.

[24] G. Merchant. Teenagers in cyberspace: an investigation of language use and language change in internet chatrooms. *Journal of Research in Reading*, 24:293–306, 2001.

[25] J. B. Michel, Y. K. Shen, et al. Quantitative analysis of culture using millions of digitized books. *Science*, 331 (6014):176–182, 2011.

[26] T. Mikolov et al. Linguistic regularities in continuous space word representations. In *Proceedings of NAACL-HLT*, 2013.

[27] T. Mikolov et al. Distributed representations of words and phrases and their compositionality. In *NIPS*, 2013.

[28] T. Mikolov et al. Efficient estimation of word representations in vector space. *CoRR*, abs/1301.3781, 2013.

[29] S. Mitra, R. Mitra, et al. That's sick dude!: Automatic identification of word sense change across different timescales. In *ACL*, 2014.

[30] A. Mnih and G. E. Hinton. A scalable hierarchical distributed language model. *NIPS*, 21:1081–1088, 2009.

[31] F. Morin and Y. Bengio. Hierarchical probabilistic neural network language model. In *Proceedings of the international workshop on artificial intelligence and statistics*, pages 246–252, 2005.

[32] B. Perozzi, R. Al-Rfou, V. Kulkarni, and S. Skiena. Inducing language networks from continuous space word representations. In *Complex Networks V*, volume 549 of *Studies in Computational Intelligence*, pages 261–273. 2014.

[33] B. Perozzi, R. Al-Rfou, and S. Skiena. Deepwalk: Online learning of social representations. In *KDD*, New York, NY, USA, August 2014. ACM.

[34] D. E. Rumelhart, G. E. Hinton, and R. J. Williams. Learning representations by back-propagating errors. *Cognitive modeling*, 1:213, 2002.

[35] T. Säily, T. Nevalainen, and H. Siirtola. Variation in noun and pronoun frequencies in a sociohistorical corpus of english. *Literary and Linguistic Computing*, 26(2): 167 188, 2011.

[36] D. J. Schiano, C. P. Chen, E. Isaacs, J. Ginsberg, U. Gretarsdottir, and M. Huddleston. Teen use of messaging media. In *Computer Human Interaction*, pages 594–595, 2002.

[37] S. A. Tagliamonte and D. Denis. Linguistc Ruin? LOL! Instant messaging and teen language. *American Speech*, 83:3–34, 2008.

[38] W. A. Taylor. Change-point analysis: A powerful new tool for detecting changes, 2000.

[39] D. T. Wijaya and R. Yeniterzi. Understanding semantic change of words over centuries. In *DETECT*, 2011.

Replacing the Irreplaceable: Fast Algorithms for Team Member Recommendation

Liangyue Li
Arizona State University
liangyue@asu.edu

Hanghang Tong
Arizona State University
hanghang.tong@asu.edu

Nan Cao
IBM Research
nancao@us.ibm.com

Kate Ehrlich
IBM Research
katee@us.ibm.com

Yu-Ru Lin
University of Pittsburgh
yurulin@pitt.edu

Norbou Buchler
US Army Research Laboratory
norbou.buchler.civ@mail.mil

ABSTRACT

In this paper, we study the problem of TEAM MEMBER REPLACEMENT – given a team of people embedded in a social network working on the same task, find a good candidate to best replace a team member who becomes unavailable to perform the task for certain reason (e.g., conflicts of interests or resource capacity). Prior studies in teamwork have suggested that a good team member replacement should bring synergy to the team in terms of having both *skill matching* and *structure matching*. However, existing techniques either do not cover both aspects or consider the two aspects independently. In this work, we propose a novel problem formulation using the concept of graph kernels that takes into account the *interaction* of both skill and structure matching requirements. To tackle the computational challenges, we propose a family of fast algorithms by (a) designing effective pruning strategies, and (b) exploring the smoothness between the existing and the new team structures. We conduct extensive experimental evaluations and user studies on real world datasets to demonstrate the effectiveness and efficiency. Our algorithms (a) perform significantly better than the alternative choices in terms of both precision and recall and (b) scale *sub-linearly*.

Categories and Subject Descriptors

H.2.8 [**Database Management**]: Database applications—*Data mining*

Keywords

Team member replacement; graph kernel; scalability

1. INTRODUCTION

In his world-widely renowned book "The Science of the Artificial" [38], Nobel laureate Herbert Simon pointed out that it is more the complexity of the *environment*, than the complexity of the individual persons, that determines the complex behavior of humans. The emergence of online social network sites and web 2.0 applications provides a new connected environment/context, where people interact and collaborate with each other as a team to collectively perform some complex tasks.

Among others, the churn of team members is a common problem across many application domains. To name a few, an employee in a software or sales team might decide to leave the organization and/or be assigned to a new task. In a law enforcement mission, a SWAT team might lose certain task force due to the fatality or injury. In professional sports (e.g., NBA), the rotation tactic between the benches could play a key role on the game outcome. In all these cases, the loss of the key member (i.e., the irreplaceable) might bring the catastrophic consequence to the team performance. *How can we find the best alternate (e.g., from the other members within the organization), when a team member becomes unavailable?* This is the central question this paper aims to answer. However, despite the frequency with which people leave a team before a project/task is complete and the resulting disruption [44], replacements are often found opportunistically and are not necessarily optimal.

We conjecture there will be less disruption when the team member who leaves is replaced with someone with similar relationships with the other team members. This conjecture is inspired by some recent research which shows that team members prefer to work with people they have worked with before [22] and that distributed teams perform better when members know each other [10]. Furthermore, research has shown that specific communication patterns amongst team members are critical for performance [8]. Thus, in addition to factors such as skill level, maintaining the same or better level of familiarity and communication amongst team members before and after someone leaves should reduce the impact of the departure. In other words, for team member replacement, the similarity between individuals should be measured in the context of the team itself. More specifically, a good team member replacement should meet the following two requirements. First (*skill matching*), the new member should bring a similar skill set as the current team member to be replaced. Second (*structure matching*), the new member should have a similar network structure as the current team member in connecting the rest of the team members.

Armed with this conjecture, we formally formulate the TEAM MEMBER REPLACEMENT problem by the notation of

WWW 2015, May 18–22, 2015, Florence, Italy.
ACM 978-1-4503-3469-3/15/05.
http://dx.doi.org/10.1145/2736277.2741132.

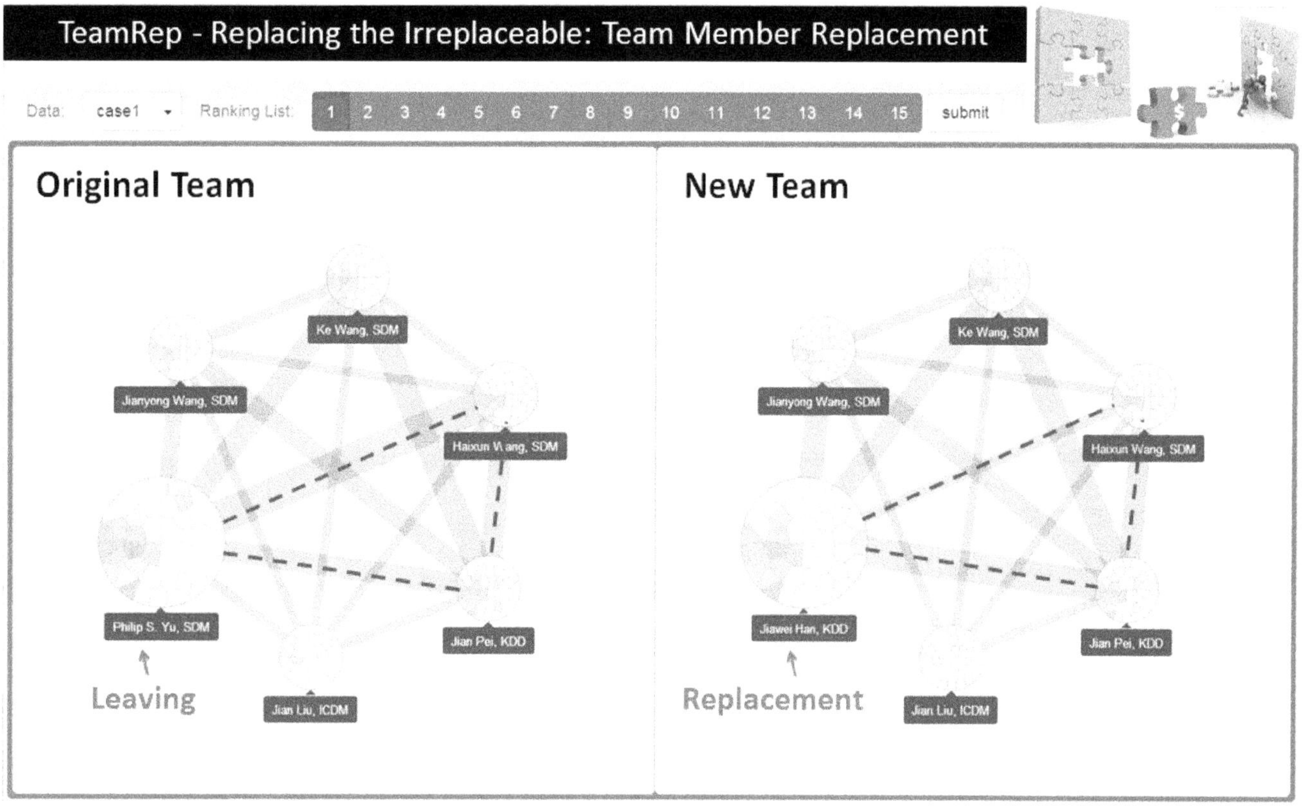

Figure 1: The team graphs before and after *Jiawei Han* takes *Philip S. Yu*'s place. See subsection 5.2 for detailed explanations.

graph similarity/kernel. By modeling the team as a labeled graph, the graph kernel provides a natural way to capture both the skill and structure match as well as the interaction of both. However, for a network with n individuals, a straightforward method would require $O(n)$ graph kernel computations for one team member replacement, which is computationally intractable. For example, for the *DBLP* dataset with almost 1M users (i.e., $n \approx 1,000,000$), we found that it would take 6,388s to find one replacement for a team of size 10. To address the computational challenges, we propose a family of fast algorithms by carefully designing the pruning strategies and exploring the smoothness between the existing and the new teams. We perform the extensive experimental evaluations to demonstrate the effectiveness and efficiency of our methods. Specifically, we find that (1) by encoding both the skill and structural matching, it leads to a much better replacement result. Compared with the best alternative choices, we achieve 27% and 24% *net increase* in average recall and precision, respectively; (2) our fast algorithms are orders of magnitude faster and scale *sub-linearly*. For example, our pruning strategy alone leads up to 1,709× speed-up, without sacrificing any accuracy.

The main contributions of this paper are as follows.

1 **Problem Formulation.** We formally define the TEAM MEMBER REPLACEMENT problem, to recommend a good candidate when a team member is unavailable in the context of networks where nodes carrying on multiple labels (skills) and edges representing social structures.

2 **Algorithms and Analysis.** We solve the problem by introducing graph kernels and propose a family of effective and scalable algorithms for TEAM MEMBER REPLACEMENT; and analyze its correctness and complexity.

3 **Experimental Evaluations.** We perform extensive experiments, including user studies and case studies, on real world datasets, to validate the effectiveness and efficiency of our methods. (See an example in Figure 1.)

The rest of the paper is organized as follows. Section 2 formally defines TEAM MEMBER REPLACEMENT problem. Section 3 presents our basic solutions. Section 4 addresses the computational challenges. Section 5 presents the experimental results. Section 6 reviews some related work. Section 7 concludes the paper.

2. PROBLEM DEFINITIONS

Table 1 lists the main symbols used throughout this paper. We describe the n individuals by a labelled social network $\mathbf{G} := \{\mathbf{A}, \mathbf{L}\}$, where $\mathbf{A}$ is an $n \times n$ adjacency matrix characterizing the connectivity among different individuals; and $\mathbf{L}$ is $n \times l$ skill indicator matrix. The ith row vector of $\mathbf{L}$ describes the skill set of the ith individual. For example, suppose there are only three skills in total, including {*data mining, databases, information retrieval*}. Then an individual with a skill vector $[1, 1, 0]$ means that s/he has both *data mining* and *databases* skills but no skill in terms of *information retrieval*. Also, we represent the elements in a matrix using a convention similar to Matlab, e.g., $\mathbf{A}(i, j)$ is the element at the ith row and j^{th} column of the matrix $\mathbf{A}$, and $\mathbf{A}(:, j)$ is the jth column of $\mathbf{A}$, etc.

Table 1: Table of symbols

Symbols	Definition
$\mathbf{G} := \{\mathbf{A}, \mathbf{L}\}$	the entire social network
$\mathbf{A}_{n \times n}$	the adjacency matrix of $\mathbf{G}$
$\mathbf{L}_{n \times l}$	skill indicator matrix
$\mathcal{T}$	the team member index
$\mathbf{G}(\mathcal{T})$	the team network indexed by its members $\mathcal{T}$
d_i	the degree of the ith node in $\mathbf{A}$
l	the total number of skills
t	the team size, i.e., $t = \|\mathcal{T}\|$
n	the total number of individuals in $\mathbf{A}$
m	the total number of connections in $\mathbf{A}$

We use the calligraphic letter $\mathcal{T}$ to index the members of a team, which includes a subset of $t = |\mathcal{T}|$ out of n individuals. Correspondingly, we can represent the team by another labelled team network $\mathbf{G}(\mathcal{T}) := \{\mathbf{A}(\mathcal{T}, \mathcal{T}), \mathbf{L}(\mathcal{T}, :)\}$. Note that $\mathbf{A}(\mathcal{T}, \mathcal{T})$ and $\mathbf{L}(\mathcal{T}, :)\}$ are sub-matrices of $\mathbf{A}$ and $\mathbf{L}$, respectively. If we replace an existing member $p \in \mathcal{T}$ of a given team $\mathcal{T}$ by another individual $q \notin \mathcal{T}$, the new team members are indexed by $\mathcal{T}_{p \to q} := \{\mathcal{T}/p, q\}$; and the new team is represented by the labelled network $\mathbf{G}(\mathcal{T}_{p \to q})$.

With the above notations and assumptions, our problems can be formally defined as follows:

Problem 1. Team Member Replacement

Given: *(1) A labelled social network* $\mathbf{G} := \{\mathbf{A}, \mathbf{L}\}$*, (2) a team* $\mathbf{G}(\mathcal{T})$*, and (3) a team member* $p \in \mathcal{T}$*;*

Output: *A "best" alternate* $q \notin \mathcal{T}$ *to replace the person* p*'s role in the team* $\mathbf{G}(\mathcal{T})$*.*

3. PROPOSED SOLUTIONS

In this section, we present our solution for Problem 1. We start with the design objectives for the Team Member Replacement problem, present graph kernel as the basic solution to fulfill such design objectives; and finally analyze the main computational challenges.

3.1 Design Objectives

Generally speaking, we want to find a *similar* person q to replace the current team member p who is about to leave the team. That is, a good replacement q should not only have a similar skill set as team member p; but also would maintain the good chemistry of the team so that the whole team can work together harmonically and/or be less disrupted. In other words, the similarity between individuals should be measured in the context of the team itself. Often, the success of a team largely depends on the successful execution of several sub-tasks, each of which requires the cooperation among several team members with certain skill configurations. For example, several classic tactics often recurringly find themselves in a successful NBA team, including (a) *triangle offense* (which is featured by a sideline triangle created by *the center*, *the forward*, and *the guard*), (b) *pick and roll* (which involves the cooperation between two players - one plays as 'pivot' and the other plays as 'screen', respectively), etc. Generally speaking, team performance arises from the shared knowledge and experience amongst team members and their ability to share and coordinate their work. As noted in the introduction, a specific pattern of communication is associated with higher team performance. Maintaining that communication structure should therefore be less disruptive to the team.

If we translate these requirements into the notations defined in Section 2, it naturally leads to the following two design objectives for a good Team Member Replacement:

- *Skill matching*: the new member should bring a similar skill set as the current team member p to be replaced that are required by the team.
- *Structural matching*: the new member should have a similar network structure as team member p in connecting the rest of the team members.

3.2 Basic Solutions

In order to fulfill the above two design objectives, we need a similarity measure between two individuals in the context of the team itself that captures both skill matching and the structural matching as well as the interaction of both. We refer to this kind of similarity as *team context aware similarity*. Mathematically, the so-called graph kernel defined on the current and new teams provides a natural tool for such a team context aware similarity. That is, we want to find a replacement person q as

$$q = \operatorname{argmax}_{j, j \notin \mathcal{T}} \ \operatorname{Ker}(\mathbf{G}(\mathcal{T}), \mathbf{G}(\mathcal{T}_{p \to j})) \quad (1)$$

In Eq. (1), $\mathbf{G}(\mathcal{T})$ is the labelled team graph; and $\mathbf{G}(\mathcal{T}_{p \to j})$ is the labelled team graph after we replace a team member p by another individual j; and Ker(.) is the kernel between these two labelled graphs. Generally speaking, the basic idea of various graph kernels is to compare the similarity of the *sub-graphs* between the two input graphs and then aggregate them as the overall similarity between the two graphs. As such, graph kernel is able to simultaneously capture both the skill matching and the structure matching, beyond the simple ad-hoc combination between the two (e.g., weighted linear combination, multiplicative combination, sequential filtering, etc). We would like to emphasize that this treatment is important - as we will show in the experimental section, it leads to much better performance over all the alternative choices. Let us explain the intuition/rationality of why graph kernel is a natural choice for team context aware similarity. Here, each subgraph in a given team (e.g., the dashed triangles in Figure 1) might reflect a specific skill configuration among a sub-group of team members that is required by a certain sub-task of that team. By comparing the similarity between two subgraphs, we implicitly measure the capability of the individual j to perform this specific sub-task. Thus, by aggregating the similarities of all the possible subgraphs between the two input graphs/teams, we get a goodness measure of the overall capability of the individual j to perform all the potential sub-tasks that team member p is involved in the original team. Note that the team replacement scenario is different from team formation [28, 1, 34]. This existing work on team formation aims to build a team from scratch by optimizing some pre-chosen metric (e.g., compatibility, diversity, etc). In contrast, we aim to find a new team member such that the new team resembles the original team as much as possible.

Having this in mind, many of the existing graph kernels can be adopted in Eq. (1), such as random walk based graph kernel, sub-tree based graph kernels (See section 6 for a review). In this paper, we focus on random walk based graph kernel due to its mathematical elegancy and superior empirical performance. Given two labelled graphs $\mathbf{G}_i := \{\mathbf{A}_i, \mathbf{L}_i\}$, $i = 1, 2$, the random walk based graph kernel between them can be formally computed as follows [40]:

$$\text{Ker}(\mathbf{G}_1, \mathbf{G}_2) = \mathbf{y}'(\mathbf{I} - c\mathbf{A}_\times)^{-1}\mathbf{L}_\times \mathbf{x} \quad (2)$$

where $\mathbf{A}_\times = \mathbf{L}_\times(\mathbf{A}_1' \otimes \mathbf{A}_2')$ is the weight matrix of the two graphs' Kronecker product, $\otimes$ represents the Kronecker product between two matrices, c is a decay factor, $\mathbf{y} = \mathbf{y}_1 \otimes \mathbf{y}_2$ and $\mathbf{x} = \mathbf{x}_1 \otimes \mathbf{x}_2$ are the so-called starting and stopping vectors to indicate the weights of different nodes and are set uniform in our case, $\mathbf{L}_\times$ is a diagonal matrix where $\mathbf{L}_\times(i,i) = 0$ if the ith row of $(\mathbf{A}_1' \otimes \mathbf{A}_2')$ is zeroed out due to label inconsistency of two nodes of the two graphs. $\mathbf{L}_\times$ can be expressed as $\mathbf{L}_\times = \sum_{k=1}^{l} \text{diag}(\mathbf{L}_1(:,k)) \otimes \text{diag}(\mathbf{L}_2(:,k))$.

3.3 Computational Challenges

Eq.(2) naturally suggests the following procedure for solving TEAM MEMBER REPLACEMENT problem (referred to as TEAMREP-BASIC): for each individual $j \notin \mathcal{T}$, we compute its score score(j) by Eq.(2); and recommend the individual(s) with the highest score(s). However, this strategy (TEAMREP-BASIC) is computationally intensive since we need to compute *many* random walk based graph kernels and each of such computations could be expensive especially when the team size is large. To be specific, for a team $\mathcal{T}$ of size t and a graph $\mathbf{G}$ with n individuals in total, its time complexity is $O(nt^6)$ since we need to compute a random walk based graph kernel for each candidate who is not in the current team, each of which could cost $O(t^6)$ [40] . Even if we allow some approximation in computing each of these graph kernels, the best known algorithms (i.e., by [24]) would still give an overall time complexity as $O(n(lt^2r^4 + mr + r^6))$, where r is reduced rank after low rank approximation, which is still too high. For example, on the *DBLP* dataset with 916,978 authors, for a team with 10 members, it would take 6,388s to find a best replacement.

In the next section, we present our solution to remedy these computational challenges.

4. SCALE-UP AND SPEED-UP

In this section, we address the computational challenges to scale-up and speed-up TEAMREP-BASIC. We start with an efficient pruning strategy to reduce the number of graph kernel computations, and then present two algorithms to speed-up the computation of individual graph kernel.

4.1 Scale-up: Candidate Filtering

Here, we propose an efficient pruning strategy to filter out those unpromising candidates. Recall that one of our design objectives for a good TEAM MEMBER REPLACEMENT is *structural matching*, i.e., the new member has a similar network structure as team member p in connecting the rest team members. Since p is connected to at least some of the rest members, it suggests that if an individual does not have any connection to any of the rest team members, s/he might not be a good candidate for replacement.

Pruning Strategy: Filter out all the candidates who do not have any connections to any of the rest team members.

LEMMA 1. Effectiveness of Pruning. *For any two persons i and j not in $\mathcal{T}$, if i is connected to at least one member in $\mathcal{T}/p$ and j has no connections to any of the members in $\mathcal{T}/p$, we have that*

$$Ker(\mathbf{G}(\mathcal{T}), \mathbf{G}(\mathcal{T}_{p\to i})) \geq Ker(\mathbf{G}(\mathcal{T}), \mathbf{G}(\mathcal{T}_{p\to j})).$$

PROOF. Suppose that $\mathbf{G}(\mathcal{T}) := \{\mathbf{A}_0, \mathbf{L}_0\}$. Let $\mathbf{G}(\mathcal{T}_{p\to i}) := \{\mathbf{A}_1, \mathbf{L}_1\}$, and $\mathbf{G}(\mathcal{T}_{p\to j}) := \{\mathbf{A}_2, \mathbf{L}_2\}$.

By Taylor expansion of Eq. (2), we have

$\text{Ker}(\mathbf{G}(\mathcal{T}), \mathbf{G}(\mathcal{T}_{p\to i})) = \sum_{z=0}^{\infty} c\mathbf{y}'(\mathbf{L}_{\times 1}(\mathbf{A}_0' \otimes \mathbf{A}_1'))^z \mathbf{x}$, where $\mathbf{L}_{\times 1} = \sum_{k=1}^{l} \text{diag}(\mathbf{L}_0(:,k)) \otimes \text{diag}(\mathbf{L}_1(:,k))$,

$\text{Ker}(\mathbf{G}(\mathcal{T}), \mathbf{G}(\mathcal{T}_{p\to j})) = \sum_{z=0}^{\infty} c\mathbf{y}'(\mathbf{L}_{\times 2}(\mathbf{A}_0' \otimes \mathbf{A}_2'))^z \mathbf{x}$, where $\mathbf{L}_{\times 2} = \sum_{k=1}^{l} \text{diag}(\mathbf{L}_0(:,k)) \otimes \text{diag}(\mathbf{L}_2(:,k))$.

Therefore, it is sufficient to show that $(\mathbf{L}_{\times 1}(\mathbf{A}_0' \otimes \mathbf{A}_1'))^z \geq (\mathbf{L}_{\times 2}(\mathbf{A}_0' \otimes \mathbf{A}_2'))^z$ for any $z > 0$, where two matrices $\mathbf{A} \geq \mathbf{B}$ if $\mathbf{A}_{ij} \geq \mathbf{B}_{ij}$ holds for all possible (i,j). We prove this by induction.

(Base Case of Induction) When $z = 1$, we have

$$\begin{aligned}
&\mathbf{L}_{\times 1}(\mathbf{A}_0' \otimes \mathbf{A}_1') \\
&= (\textstyle\sum_{k=1}^{l} \text{diag}(\mathbf{L}_0(:,k)) \otimes \text{diag}(\mathbf{L}_1(:,k)))(\mathbf{A}_0' \otimes \mathbf{A}_1') \quad (3)\\
&= \textstyle\sum_{k=1}^{l} (\text{diag}(\mathbf{L}_0(:,k))\mathbf{A}_0') \otimes (\text{diag}(\mathbf{L}_1(:,k))\mathbf{A}_1')
\end{aligned}$$

Because $(\text{diag}(\mathbf{L}_1(:,k))\mathbf{A}_1') \geq (\text{diag}(\mathbf{L}_2(:,k))\mathbf{A}_2')$, we have $\mathbf{L}_{\times 1}(\mathbf{A}_0' \otimes \mathbf{A}_1') \geq \mathbf{L}_{\times 2}(\mathbf{A}_0' \otimes \mathbf{A}_2')$.

(Induction Step) Assuming $(\mathbf{L}_{\times 1}(\mathbf{A}_0' \otimes \mathbf{A}_1'))^{z-1} \geq (\mathbf{L}_{\times 2}(\mathbf{A}_0' \otimes \mathbf{A}_2'))^{z-1}$, we have that

$$\begin{aligned}
(\mathbf{L}_{\times 1}(\mathbf{A}_0' \otimes \mathbf{A}_1'))^z &\geq (\mathbf{L}_{\times 2}(\mathbf{A}_0' \otimes \mathbf{A}_2'))^{z-1}(\mathbf{L}_{\times 1}(\mathbf{A}_0' \otimes \mathbf{A}_1')) \\
&\geq (\mathbf{L}_{\times 2}(\mathbf{A}_0' \otimes \mathbf{A}_2'))^z
\end{aligned}$$

where the first inequality is due to the induction assumption; and the second inequality is due to the base case. This completes the proof. $\square$

Remarks. By Lemma 1, our pruning strategy is 'safe', i.e., it will not miss any potentially good replacements. In the meanwhile, we can reduce the number of graph kernel computations from $O(n)$ to $O(\sum_{i\in\mathcal{T}/p} d_i)$, which is sub-linear in n.

4.2 Speedup Graph Kernel - Exact Approach

Here, we address the problem of speeding up the computation of an individual graph kernel. Let $\mathbf{G}(\mathcal{T}) := \{\mathbf{A}_1, \mathbf{L}_1\}$ and $\mathbf{G}(\mathcal{T}_{p\to q}) := \{\mathbf{A}_2, \mathbf{L}_2\}$, where $\mathbf{A}_1, \mathbf{A}_2$ are symmetric adjacency matrices of the two graphs.[1] Without loss of generality, let us assume that p is the last team member in $\mathcal{T}$. Compare $\mathbf{A}_1$ with $\mathbf{A}_2$, it can be seen that the only difference is their last columns and last rows. Therefore, we can rewrite $\mathbf{A}_2$ as $\mathbf{A}_2 = \mathbf{A}_c + \mathbf{A}_{d2}$, where $\mathbf{A}_c$ is $\mathbf{A}_1$ with its last row and column being zeroed out, and the nonzero elements of $\mathbf{A}_{d2}$ only appear in its last row and column reflecting the connectivity of q to the new team. Notice that $\mathbf{A}_{d2}$ has a rank at most 2, so it can be factorized into two smaller matrices as $\mathbf{A}_{d2} = \mathbf{E}_{t\times 2}\mathbf{F}_{2\times t}$.

Denote $\text{diag}(\mathbf{L}_1(:,j))$ as $\mathbf{L}_1^{(j)}$ and $\text{diag}(\mathbf{L}_2(:,j))$ as $\mathbf{L}_2^{(j)}$ for $j = 1, ..., l$. Compare $\mathbf{L}_1^{(j)}$ with $\mathbf{L}_2^{(j)}$, the only difference is the last diagonal element. Therefore, we can write $\mathbf{L}_2^{(j)}$ as $\mathbf{L}_2^{(j)} = \mathbf{L}_c^{(j)} + \mathbf{L}_{d2}^{(j)}$, where $\mathbf{L}_c^{(j)}$ is $\mathbf{L}_1^{(j)}$ with last element zeroed out, and $\mathbf{L}_{d2}^{(j)}$'s last element indicates q's strength of having

[1]Although we focus on the undirected graphs in this paper, our proposed algorithms can be generalized to directed graphs.

the jth skill. $\mathbf{L}_2^{(j)}$'s rank is at most 1, so it can be factorized as $\mathbf{L}_2^{(j)} = \mathbf{e}_{t\times 1}^{(j)} \mathbf{f}_{1\times t}^{(j)}$. Therefore, the exact graph kernel for the labelled graph can be computed as:

$$
\begin{aligned}
&\mathrm{Ker}(\mathbf{G}(\mathcal{T}), \mathbf{G}(\mathcal{T}_{p\to q})) \\
&= \mathbf{y}'(\mathbf{I} - c(\textstyle\sum_{j=1}^{l} \mathbf{L}_1^{(j)} \otimes \mathbf{L}_2^{(j)})(\mathbf{A}_1' \otimes \mathbf{A}_2'))^{-1}(\textstyle\sum_{j=1}^{l} \mathbf{L}_1^{(j)} \otimes \mathbf{L}_2^{(j)})\mathbf{x} \\
&= \mathbf{y}'(\underbrace{\mathbf{I} - c(\sum_{j=1}^{l} \mathbf{L}_1^{(j)} \otimes \mathbf{L}_c^{(j)})(\mathbf{A}_1 \otimes \mathbf{A}_c)}_{\mathbf{Z}\text{: invariant w.r.t. } q} \\
&\underbrace{-c(\sum_{j=1}^{l}(\mathbf{L}_1^{(j)} \otimes \mathbf{e}^{(j)})(\mathbf{I} \otimes \mathbf{f}^{(j)}))(\mathbf{A}_1 \otimes \mathbf{A}_c)}_{\mathbf{PQ}(\mathbf{A}_1 \otimes \mathbf{A}_c) = \mathbf{PY}_1} \\
&\underbrace{-c(\sum_{j=1}^{l} \mathbf{L}_1^{(j)} \otimes \mathbf{L}_c^{(j)})(\mathbf{A}_1 \otimes \mathbf{E})(\mathbf{I} \otimes \mathbf{F})}_{\mathbf{X}_1\mathbf{Y}_2} \\
&\underbrace{-c(\sum_{j=1}^{l}(\mathbf{L}_1^{(j)} \otimes \mathbf{e}^{(j)})(\mathbf{I} \otimes \mathbf{f}^{(j)}))(\mathbf{A}_1 \otimes \mathbf{E})(\mathbf{I} \otimes \mathbf{F})}_{\mathbf{X}_2\mathbf{Y}_2})^{-1} \\
&(\textstyle\sum_{j=1}^{l} \mathbf{L}_1^{(j)} \otimes \mathbf{L}_2^{(j)})\mathbf{x}
\end{aligned} \tag{4}
$$

Each $\mathbf{L}_1^{(j)} \otimes \mathbf{e}^{(j)}$ is a matrix of size t^2 by t and $\mathbf{I} \otimes \mathbf{f}^{(j)}$ is a matrix of size t by t^2. We denote the matrix created by concatenating all $\mathbf{L}_1^{(j)} \otimes \mathbf{e}^{(j)}$ horizontally as $\mathbf{P}$, *i.e.*, $\mathbf{P} = [\mathbf{L}_1^{(1)} \otimes \mathbf{e}^{(1)}, \ldots, \mathbf{L}_1^{(l)} \otimes \mathbf{e}^{(l)}]$; denote the matrix created by stacking all $\mathbf{I} \otimes \mathbf{f}^{(j)}$ vertically as $\mathbf{Q}$, *i.e.*, $\mathbf{Q} = [\mathbf{I} \otimes \mathbf{f}^{(1)}; \ldots; \mathbf{I} \otimes \mathbf{f}^{(l)}]$. Obviously, $(\sum_{j=1}^{l}(\mathbf{L}_1^{(j)} \otimes \mathbf{e}^{(j)})(\mathbf{I} \otimes \mathbf{f}^{(j)}))$ is equal to $\mathbf{PQ}$. We denote $(\sum_{j=1}^{l} \mathbf{L}_1^{(j)} \otimes \mathbf{L}_c^{(j)})(\mathbf{A}_1 \otimes \mathbf{E})$ by $\mathbf{X}_1$; denote $(\sum_{j=1}^{l}(\mathbf{L}_1^{(j)} \otimes \mathbf{e}^{(j)})(\mathbf{I} \otimes \mathbf{f}^{(j)}))(\mathbf{A}_1 \otimes \mathbf{E})$ by $\mathbf{X}_2$; denote $\mathbf{Q}(\mathbf{A}_1 \otimes \mathbf{A}_c)$ by $\mathbf{Y}_1$ and denote $(\mathbf{I} \otimes \mathbf{F})$ by $\mathbf{Y}_2$. Let $\mathbf{X}$ be $[\mathbf{P}, \mathbf{X}_1, \mathbf{X}_2]$ and $\mathbf{Y}$ be $[\mathbf{Y}_1; \mathbf{Y}_2; \mathbf{Y}_2]$.

With these additional notations, we can rewrite Eq. (4) as

$$
\begin{aligned}
&\mathrm{Ker}(\mathbf{G}(\mathcal{T}), \mathbf{G}(\mathcal{T}_{p\to q})) = \mathbf{y}'(\mathbf{Z} - c\mathbf{XY})^{-1}(\textstyle\sum_{j=1}^{l} \mathbf{L}_1^{(j)} \otimes \mathbf{L}_2^{(j)})\mathbf{x} \\
&= \mathbf{y}'(\mathbf{Z}^{-1} + c\mathbf{Z}^{-1}\mathbf{X}(\mathbf{I} - c\mathbf{Y}\mathbf{Z}^{-1}\mathbf{X})^{-1}\mathbf{Y}\mathbf{Z}^{-1}) \\
&((\textstyle\sum_{j=1}^{l} \mathbf{L}_1^{(j)} \otimes \mathbf{L}_c^{(j)})\mathbf{x} + (\sum_{j=1}^{l}(\mathbf{L}_1^{(j)} \otimes \mathbf{e}^{(j)})(\mathbf{I} \otimes \mathbf{f}^{(j)}))\mathbf{x})
\end{aligned} \tag{5}
$$

where the second equation is due to the matrix inverse lemma [19].

Remarks. In Eq. (5), $\mathbf{Z} = \mathbf{I} - c(\sum_{j=1}^{l} \mathbf{L}_1^{(j)} \otimes \mathbf{L}_c^{(j)})(\mathbf{A}_1 \otimes \mathbf{A}_c)$ does not depend on the candidate q. Thus, if we pre-compute its inverse $\mathbf{Z}^{-1}$, we only need to update $\mathbf{X}(\mathbf{I} - c\mathbf{Y}\mathbf{Z}^{-1}\mathbf{X})^{-1}\mathbf{Y}$ and $\mathbf{PQx}$ for every new candidate. Notice that compared with the original graph kernel (the first equation in Eq. (4)), $(\mathbf{I} - c\mathbf{Y}\mathbf{Z}^{-1}\mathbf{X})$ is a much smaller matrix of $(l+4)t \times (l+4)t$. In this way, we can accelerate the process of computing its inverse without losing the accuracy of graph kernel.

4.3 Speedup Graph Kernel - Approx Approach

Note that the graph kernel by Eq. (5) is exactly the same as the original method by the first equation in Eq. (4). If we allow some approximation error, we can further speed-up the computation.

Note that $\mathbf{A}_c$ is symmetric and its rank-r approximation can be written as $\hat{\mathbf{A}}_c = \mathbf{UV}$, where $\mathbf{U}$ is a matrix of size t by r and $\mathbf{V}$ is a matrix of size r by t. $\mathbf{A}_1$ can be approximated as $\hat{\mathbf{A}}_1 = \hat{\mathbf{A}}_c + \mathbf{A}_{d1} = \mathbf{UV} + \mathbf{E}_1\mathbf{F}_1 = \mathbf{X}_1\mathbf{Y}_1$, where $\mathbf{X}_1 = [\mathbf{U}, \mathbf{E}_1], \mathbf{Y}_1 = [\mathbf{V}; \mathbf{F}_1], \mathbf{E}_1 = [\mathbf{w}_1, \mathbf{s}], \mathbf{F}_1 = [\mathbf{s}'; \mathbf{w}_1']$, $\mathbf{s}$ is a zero vector of length t except that the last element is 1, and $\mathbf{w}_1$ is the weight vector from p to the members in $\mathcal{T}$. Similarly, after p is replaced by a candidate q, the weight matrix of the new team can be approximated as $\hat{\mathbf{A}}_2 = \mathbf{X}_2\mathbf{Y}_2$ where $\mathbf{X}_2 = [\mathbf{U}, \mathbf{E}_2], \mathbf{Y}_2 = [\mathbf{V}; \mathbf{F}_2], \mathbf{E}_2 = [\mathbf{w}_2, \mathbf{s}], \mathbf{F}_2 = [\mathbf{s}'; \mathbf{w}_2']$ and $\mathbf{w}_2$ is the weight vector from q to the members in the new team. The approximated graph kernel for labeled graphs can be computed as:

$$
\begin{aligned}
&\hat{\mathrm{Ker}}(\mathbf{G}(\mathcal{T}), \mathbf{G}(\mathcal{T}_{p\to q})) = \mathbf{y}^T(\mathbf{I} - c\mathbf{L}_\times(\hat{\mathbf{A}}_1' \otimes \hat{\mathbf{A}}_2'))^{-1}\mathbf{L}_\times\mathbf{x} \\
&= \mathbf{y}'(\mathbf{I} - c\mathbf{L}_\times(\mathbf{X}_1\mathbf{Y}_1) \otimes (\mathbf{X}_2\mathbf{Y}_2))^{-1}\mathbf{L}_\times\mathbf{x} \\
&= \mathbf{y}'(\mathbf{I} - c\mathbf{L}_\times(\mathbf{X}_1 \otimes \mathbf{X}_2)(\mathbf{Y}_1 \otimes \mathbf{Y}_2))^{-1}\mathbf{L}_\times\mathbf{x} \\
&= \mathbf{y}'(\mathbf{I} + c\mathbf{L}_\times(\mathbf{X}_1 \otimes \mathbf{X}_2)\mathbf{M}(\mathbf{Y}_1 \otimes \mathbf{Y}_2))\mathbf{L}_\times\mathbf{x} \\
&= \mathbf{y}'\mathbf{L}_\times\mathbf{x} + c\mathbf{y}'(\textstyle\sum_{j=1}^{l} \mathbf{L}_1^{(j)}\mathbf{X}_1 \otimes \mathbf{L}_2^{(j)}\mathbf{X}_2)\mathbf{M}(\mathbf{Y}_1 \otimes \mathbf{Y}_2)\mathbf{L}_\times\mathbf{x} \\
&= (\textstyle\sum_{j=1}^{l}(\mathbf{y}_1'\mathbf{L}_1^{(j)}\mathbf{x}_1)(\mathbf{y}_2'\mathbf{L}_2^{(j)}\mathbf{x}_2)) + c \\
&(\textstyle\sum_{j=1}^{l} \mathbf{y}_1'\mathbf{L}_1^{(j)}\mathbf{X}_1 \otimes \mathbf{y}_2'\mathbf{L}_2^{(j)}\mathbf{X}_2)\mathbf{M}(\sum_{j=1}^{l} \mathbf{Y}_1\mathbf{L}_1^{(j)}\mathbf{x}_1 \otimes \mathbf{Y}_2\mathbf{L}_2^{(j)}\mathbf{x}_2)
\end{aligned} \tag{6}
$$

where $\mathbf{M} = (\mathbf{I} - c(\sum_{j=1}^{l} \mathbf{Y}_1\mathbf{L}_1^{(j)}\mathbf{X}_1 \otimes \mathbf{Y}_2\mathbf{L}_2^{(j)}\mathbf{X}_2))^{-1}$, the second equation is due to the kronecker product property; the third equation is again due to the matrix inverse lemma, the fourth equation is by matrix multiplication distributivity and the last equation is due to the kronecker product property.

Remarks. The computation of $\mathbf{M}$ is much cheaper than the original graph kernel since it is a matrix inverse of size $(r+2)^2 \times (r+2)^2$. It was first proposed in [24] to explore the low-rank structure of the input graphs to speed-up graph kernel computations. However, in the context of TEAM MEMBER REPLACEMENT, we would need to estimate the low-rank approximation *many* times ($O(\sum_{i\in\mathcal{T}/p} d_i)$) when we directly apply the method in [24]. In contrast, we only need to compute top-r approximation *once* by Eq. (6). As our complexity analysis (subsection 4.4) and experimental evaluations (subsection 5.3) show, this brings a few times additional speed-up.

4.4 Putting Everything Together

Putting everything together, we are ready to present our algorithms for TEAM MEMBER REPLACEMENT. Depending on the specific methods for computing the individual graph kernels, we propose two variants.

4.4.1 *Variant #1:* TEAMREP-FAST-EXACT

We first present our algorithm using the exact graph kernel computation in Eq. (5). The algorithm (TEAMREP-FAST-EXACT) is summarized in Algorithm 1. We only need to pre-compute and store $\mathbf{Z}^{-1}$, $\mathbf{R}$, $\mathbf{b}$ and $\mathbf{l}$ for later use to compute each candidate's score (step 2 and 3). In the loop, the key step is to update $\mathbf{M}$ involving matrix inverse of size $(l+4)t \times (l+4)t$ which is relatively cheaper to compute (step 17).

The effectiveness and efficiency of TEAMREP-FAST-EXACT are summarized in Lemma 2 and Lemma 3, respectively. Compared with TEAMREP-BASIC, Algorithm 1 is much faster without losing any recommendation accuracy.

LEMMA 2. *Accuracy of* TEAMREP-FAST-EXACT. *Algorithm 1 outputs the same set of candidates as* TEAMREP-BASIC.

PROOF. (Sketch) First, according to Lemma 1, we will not miss a promising candidate during the pruning stage. Second, for each candidate after pruning, Algorithm 1 calculates its graph kernel exactly the same as Eq. (5), which is in turn the same as Eq. (4) and hence Eq. (2). Therefore, after ranking the scores, Algorithm 1 outputs the same set of candidates as TEAMREP-BASIC. □

Algorithm 1: TEAMREP-FAST-EXACT

Input: (1) The entire social network $\mathbf{G} := \{\mathbf{A}, \mathbf{L}\}$, (2) original team members $\mathcal{T}$, (3) person p who will leave the team, (4) starting and ending probability $\mathbf{x}$ and $\mathbf{y}$(be uniform by default), and (5) an integer k (the budget)

Output: Top k candidates to replace person p

1 Initialize $\mathbf{A}_c, \mathbf{L}_1^{(j)}, \mathbf{L}_2^{(j)}, j = 1, \ldots, l$;
2 Pre-compute $\mathbf{Z}^{-1} \leftarrow (\mathbf{I} - c(\sum_{j=1}^{l} \mathbf{L}_1^{(j)} \otimes \mathbf{L}_c^{(j)})(\mathbf{A}_1 \otimes \mathbf{A}_c))^{-1}$;
3 Set $\mathbf{R} \leftarrow (\sum_{j=1}^{l} \mathbf{L}_1^{(j)} \otimes \mathbf{L}_c^{(j)})\mathbf{x}$; $\mathbf{b} \leftarrow \mathbf{y}^T\mathbf{Z}^{-1}\mathbf{R}$; $\mathbf{l} \leftarrow c\mathbf{y}^T\mathbf{Z}^{-1}$;
4 **for** *each candidate* q *in* $\mathbf{G}$ *after pruning* **do**
5 Initialize $\mathbf{s} \leftarrow$ a zero vector of length t except the last element is 1;
6 Initialize $\mathbf{w} \leftarrow$ weight vector from q to the new team members;
7 Set $\mathbf{E} \leftarrow [\mathbf{w}, \mathbf{s}]; \mathbf{F} \leftarrow [\mathbf{s}'; \mathbf{w}']$;
8 Set $\mathbf{e}^{(j)} \leftarrow$ a t by 1 zero vector except the last element is 1, for $j = 1, \ldots, d_n$;
9 Set $\mathbf{f}^{(j)} \leftarrow$ a $1 \times t$ zero vector except the last element which is label j assignment for q;
10 Set $\mathbf{P} \leftarrow [\mathbf{L}_1^{(1)} \otimes \mathbf{e}^{(1)}, \ldots, \mathbf{L}_1^{(l)} \otimes \mathbf{e}^{(l)}]$;
11 Set $\mathbf{Q} \leftarrow [\mathbf{I} \otimes \mathbf{f}^{(1)}; \ldots; \mathbf{I} \otimes \mathbf{f}^{(l)}]$;
12 Compute $\mathbf{X}_1 \leftarrow (\sum_{j=1}^{l} \mathbf{L}_1^{(j)}\mathbf{A}_1 \otimes \mathbf{L}_c^{(j)}\mathbf{E})$;
13 Compute $\mathbf{X}_2 \leftarrow (\sum_{j=1}^{l} \mathbf{L}_1^{(j)}\mathbf{A}_1 \otimes \mathbf{e}^{(j)}\mathbf{f}^{(j)}\mathbf{E})$;
14 Compute $\mathbf{Y}_1 \leftarrow \mathbf{Q}(\mathbf{A}_1 \otimes \mathbf{A}_c)$;
15 Compute $\mathbf{Y}_2 \leftarrow (\mathbf{I} \otimes \mathbf{F})$;
16 Set $\mathbf{X} \leftarrow [\mathbf{P}, \mathbf{X}_1, \mathbf{X}_2], \mathbf{Y} \leftarrow [\mathbf{Y}_1; \mathbf{Y}_2; \mathbf{Y}_2]$;
17 Update $\mathbf{M} \leftarrow (\mathbf{I} - c\mathbf{Y}\mathbf{Z}^{-1}\mathbf{X})^{-1}$;
18 Compute $\mathbf{r}' \leftarrow \mathbf{Z}^{-1}\mathbf{P}\mathbf{Q}\mathbf{x}$;
19 Compute score$(q) = \mathbf{b} + \mathbf{y}^T\mathbf{r}' + \mathbf{l}\mathbf{X}\mathbf{M}\mathbf{Y}(\mathbf{Z}^{-1}\mathbf{R} + \mathbf{r}')$;
20 **end**
21 **Return** the top k candidates with the highest scores.

LEMMA 3. *Time Complexity of* TEAMREP-FAST-EXACT *Algorithm 1 takes* $O((\sum_{i \in \mathcal{T}/p} d_i)(lt^5 + l^3t^3))$ *in time.*

PROOF. (Sketch) After pruning, the number of potential candidates (the number of loops in Algorithm 1) is $O(\sum_{i \in \mathcal{T}/p} d_i)$. In every loop, computing $\mathbf{X}_1$,$\mathbf{X}_2$ and $\mathbf{Y}_1$ take $O(lt^5)$; computing $\mathbf{M}$ takes $O(lt^5 + l^3t^3)$ and computing the score(q) takes $O(lt^3)$. Putting everything together, the time complexity of Algorithm 1 is $O((\sum_{i \in \mathcal{T}/p} d_i)(lt^5 + l^3t^3))$. □

4.4.2 *Variant #2:* TEAMREP-FAST-APPROX

By using Eq. (6) to compute the graph kernel instead, we propose an even faster algorithm (TEAMREP-FAST-APPROX), which is summarized in Algorithm 2. In the algorithm, we only need to compute the top r eigen-decomposition for $\mathbf{A}_c$ once (step 2), and use that to update the low rank approximation for every new team. Besides, when we update $\mathbf{M}$, a matrix inverse of size $(r+2)^2 \times (r+2)^2$ (step 14), the time is independent of the team size.

The effectiveness and efficiency of TEAMREP-FAST-APPROX are summarized in Lemma 4 and Lemma 5, respectively. Compared with TEAMREP-BASIC and TEAMREP-FAST-EXACT, Algorithm 2 is even faster; and the only place it introduces

Algorithm 2: TEAMREP-FAST-APPROX

Input: (1) The entire social network $\mathbf{G} := \{\mathbf{A}, \mathbf{L}\}$, (2) original team members $\mathcal{T}$, (3) person p who will leave the team, (4) starting and ending probability $\mathbf{x}$ and $\mathbf{y}$ (be uniform by default), and (5) an integer k (the budget)

Output: Top k candidates to replace person p

1 Initialize $\mathbf{A}_c, \mathbf{L}_1^{(j)}, \mathbf{L}_2^{(j)}, j = 1, \ldots, l$;
2 Compute top r eigen-decomposition for $\mathbf{A}_c$: $\mathbf{U}\mathbf{\Lambda}\mathbf{U}' \leftarrow \mathbf{A}_c$;
3 Set $\mathbf{V} \leftarrow \mathbf{\Lambda}\mathbf{U}'$;
4 Initialize $\mathbf{s} \leftarrow$ a zero vector of length t except the last element is 1;
5 Initialize $\mathbf{w}_1 \leftarrow$ weight vector from p to $\mathcal{T}$;
6 Set $\mathbf{E}_1 \leftarrow [\mathbf{w}_1, \mathbf{s}], \mathbf{F}_1 \leftarrow [\mathbf{s}'; \mathbf{w}_1']$;
7 Set $\mathbf{X}_1 \leftarrow [\mathbf{U}, \mathbf{E}_1]$, $\mathbf{Y}_1 \leftarrow [\mathbf{V}; \mathbf{F}_1]$;
8 **for** *each candidate* q *in* $\mathbf{G}$ *after pruning* **do**
9 Initialize $\mathbf{w}_2 \leftarrow$ weight vector from q to the new team members ;
10 Set $\mathbf{E}_2 \leftarrow [\mathbf{w}_2, \mathbf{s}], \mathbf{F}_2 \leftarrow [\mathbf{s}'; \mathbf{w}_2']$;
11 Set $\mathbf{X}_2 \leftarrow [\mathbf{U}, \mathbf{E}_2]$, $\mathbf{Y}_2 \leftarrow [\mathbf{V}; \mathbf{F}_2]$;
12 Compute $\mathbf{S} \leftarrow \sum_{j=1}^{l} \mathbf{y}_1'\mathbf{L}_1^{(j)}\mathbf{X}_1 \otimes \mathbf{y}_2'\mathbf{L}_2^{(j)}\mathbf{X}_2$;
13 Compute $\mathbf{T} \leftarrow \sum_{j=1}^{l} \mathbf{Y}_1\mathbf{L}_1^{(j)}\mathbf{x}_1 \otimes \mathbf{Y}_2\mathbf{L}_2^{(j)}\mathbf{x}_2)$;
14 Update $\mathbf{M} \leftarrow (\mathbf{I} - c(\sum_{j=1}^{l} \mathbf{Y}_1\mathbf{L}_1^{j}\mathbf{X}_1 \otimes \mathbf{Y}_2\mathbf{L}_2^{j}\mathbf{X}_2))^{-1}$;
15 Set score$(q) = (\sum_{j=1}^{l}(\mathbf{y}_1'\mathbf{L}_1^{(j)}\mathbf{x}_1)(\mathbf{y}_2'\mathbf{L}_2^{(j)}\mathbf{x}_2)) + c\mathbf{SMT}$;
16 **end**
17 **Return** the top k candidates with the highest scores.

the approximation error is the low-rank approximation of $\mathbf{A}_c$ (step 2).

LEMMA 4. *Accuracy of* TEAMREP-FAST-APPROX. *If* $\mathbf{A}_c = \mathbf{U}\mathbf{\Lambda}\mathbf{U}'$ *holds, Algorithm 2 outputs the same set of candidates as* TEAMREP-BASIC.

PROOF. Omitted for brevity. □

LEMMA 5. *Time Complexity of* TEAMREP-FAST-APPROX *Algorithm 2 takes* $O((\sum_{i \in \mathcal{T}/p} d_i)(ll^2r + r^6))$ *in time.*

PROOF. Omitted for brevity. □

5. EXPERIMENTAL EVALUATIONS

In this section, we present the experimental evaluations. The experiments are designed to answer the following questions:

- *Effectiveness*: How accurate are the proposed algorithms for TEAM MEMBER REPLACEMENT?
- *Efficiency:* How scalable are the proposed algorithms?

5.1 Datasets

DBLP. DBLP dataset[2] provides bibliographic information on major computer science journals and proceedings. We use it to build a co-authorship network where each node is an author and the weight of each edge stands for the number of papers the two corresponding authors have co-authored. The network constructed has $n = 916,978$ nodes and $m = 3,063,244$ edges. We use the conferences (*e.g.,*

[2]http://arnetminer.org/citation

Table 2: Summary of Datasets.

Data	n	m	# of teams
DBLP	916,978	3,063,244	1,572,278
Movie	95,321	3,661,679	10,197
NBA	3,924	126,994	1,398

KDD, SIGMOD, CVPR, etc) to reflect authors' skills (*e.g., data mining, data base, computer vision, etc*) and for a given author and conference, we define his/her skill level as the percentage of the papers s/he publishes in that conference.. For a given paper, we treat all of its co-authors as a team. Alternatively, if a set of authors co-organize an event (such as a conference), we also treat them as a team.

Movie. This dataset[3] is an extension of MovieLens dataset, which links movies from MovieLens with their corresponding IMDb webpage and Rotten Tomatoes review system. It contains information of 10,197 movies, 95,321 actors/actress and 20 movie genres (*e.g.*, action, comedy, horror, etc.). Each movie has on average 22.8 actors/actress and 2.0 genres assignments. We set up the social network of the actors/actresses where each node represents one actor/actress and the weight of each edge is the number of movies the two linking actors/actresses have co-stared. We use the movie genres that a person has played as his/her skills. For a given movie, we treat all of its actors/actress as a team.

NBA. The NBA dataset[4] contains NBA and ABA statistics from the year of 1946 to the year of 2009. It has information of 3,924 players and 100 teams season by season. We use players' positions as their skill labels, including *guard, forward* and *center.* The edge weight of the player network stands for the number of seasons that the two corresponding nodes/individuals played in the same team.

The statistics of these three datasets are summarized in Table 2. All the experiments are run on a Windows machine with 16 GB memory and Intel i7-2760QM CPU.

Repeatability of Experimental Results. All the three datasets are publicly available. We will release the code of the proposed algorithms through authors' website.

5.2 Effectiveness Results

A. Qualitative Evaluations. We first present some case studies on the three datasets to gain some intuitions.

Case studies on DBLP. Let us take a close look at Fig. 1, which shows a screenshot of our current demo system. This prototype system has been developed to a fully functional system and deployed to real users [7]. The original team is shown on the left side and the person leaving the team (*Philip S. Yu*) is represented by a node (diagram) with larger radius. If the user clicks a replacement from the recommendation list (on the top), the system will show the new team on the right side. Here, we introduced a novel visualization technique to represent authors' relationships and their expertise within one unique graph visualization. Particularly, in this visualization, the authors are shown as voronoi diagrams [15]. The authors' expertise is visualized as the voronoi cells inside the diagram, that is, each cell indicates a type of expertise. We use different color hues to identify different expertise types and use the color saturations to encode the author's strength in that expertise type. For

[3]http://grouplens.org/datasets/hetrec-2011/

[4]http://www.databasebasketball.com

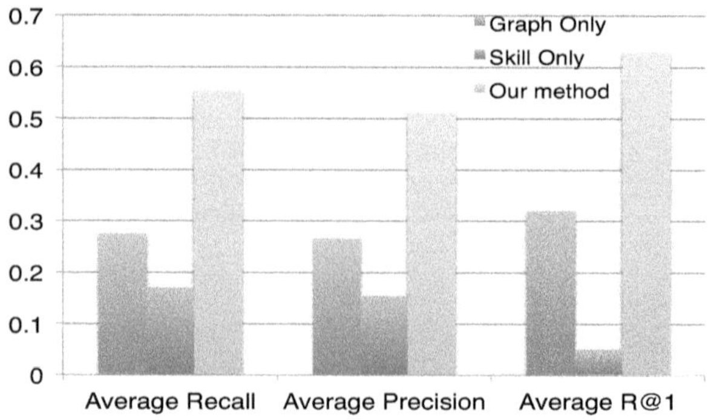

Figure 2: The average recall, average precision and R@1 of the three comparison methods. Higher is better.

example, if *KDD* is represented in orange, a bright orange cell in a voronoi diagram means the author has a strong expertise in *KDD*. In contrast, a white cell indicates the author's lacking of the corresponding expertise. To facilitate visual comparison of different authors, we fix the position of these expertise cells across different diagrams so that, for example, *KDD* is always shown at the left side of the author diagrams. These voronoi diagrams are connected by links indicating the authors' relationships. The strength of the relationship are presented by the line thickness.

Fig. 1 visualizes the team structures before and after *Philip S. Yu* becomes unavailable in the team writing [33]. Our algorithm's top recommendation is *Jiawei Han*. As we can see, both *Han* and *Yu* posses very similar skills and are renowned for their extraordinary contributions in the data mining and databases community. Moreover, *Han* has collaborated with almost each of the rest authors/team members. Looking more closely, we find *Han* preserves several key triangle substructures in the original team: one with *Ke Wang* and *Jian Pei*, and the other with *Haixun Wang* and *Jian Pei*. These triangle sub-structures might play a critical role in accomplishing sub-tasks in writing the paper.

We also consider a bigger team, i.e, the organizing committee of *KDD 2013*. After filtering those not in *DBLP*, we have 32 people in the committee team. We use their co-authorship network as their social network. Suppose one of the research track co-chairs *Inderjit Dhillon* becomes unavailable and we are searching for another researcher who can fill in this critical role in organizing *KDD 2013*. The top five candidates our algorithm recommends are *Philip S. Yu, Jiawei Han, Christos Faloutsos, Bing Liu* and *Wei Wang*. The results are consistent with the intuitions - all of these recommended researchers are highly qualified - not only have they made remarkable contributions to the data mining field, but also they have strong ties with the remaining organizers of *KDD 2013*. For example, *Liu* is the current chair of KDD executive committee; *Wang* is one of the research track program chairs for *KDD 2014*; and *Faloutsos* was the PC co-chair of *KDD 2003*, etc.

Case studies on Movie. Assuming actor *Matt Damon* became unavailable when filming the epic war movie *Saving Private Ryan* (1998) and we need to find an alternative actor who can play *Ryan*'s role in the movie. The top five recommendations our algorithm gives are: *Samuel L. Jackson, Steve Buscemi, Robert De Niro, Christopher Walken, Bruce Willis.* As we know, *Saving Private Ryan* is a movie

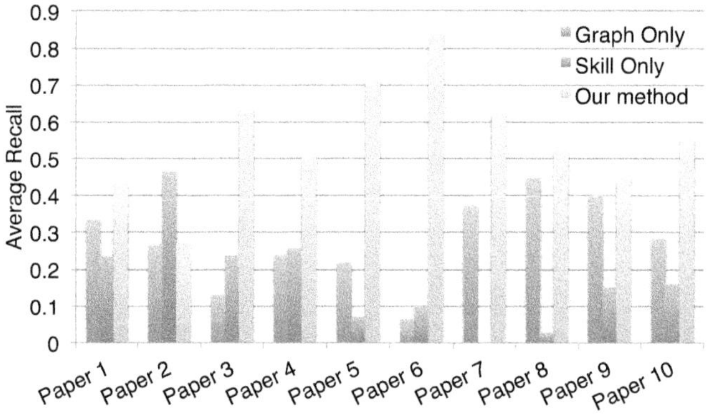

Figure 3: Recall for different papers. Higher is better.

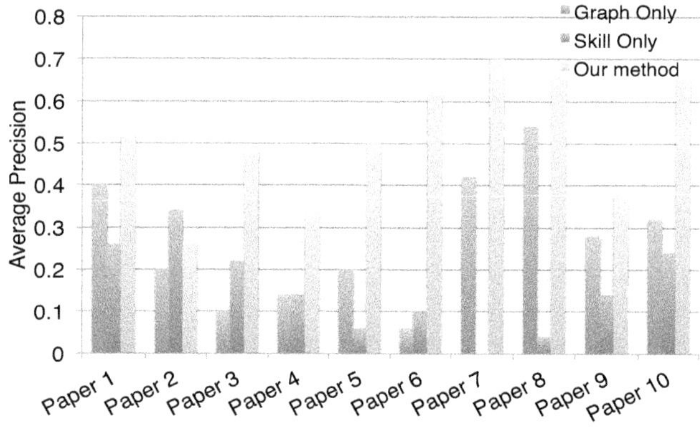

Figure 4: Precision for different papers. Higher is better.

of *action* and *drama* genres. Notice that both *Damon* and *Jackson* have participated in many movies of *drama*, *thriller* and *action* genres, hence *Jackson* has the acting skills required to play the role in this movie. Moreover, *Jackson* has co-played with *Tom Sizemore*, *Vin Diesel*, *Dale Dye*, *Dennis Farina*, *Giovanni Ribisi* and *Ryan Hurst* in the crew before. The familiarity might increase the harmony of filming the movie with others.

Case studies on NBA. Let us assume that *Kobe Bryant* in Los Angeles Lakers was hurt during the regular season in 1996 and a bench player is badly wanted. The top five replacements our algorithm recommends are: *Rick Fox*, *A.c. Green*, *Jason Kidd*, *Brian Shaw* and *Tyronn Lue*. As we know, *Bryant* is a guard in NBA. Among the five recommendations, *Kidd*, *Shaw* and *Lue* all play as guards. More importantly, *Jason*, *Brian* and *Tyronn* have played with 9, 7 and 9 of the rest team members on the same team in the same season for multiple times. Therefore, it might be easier for them to maintain the moment and chemistry of the team which is critical to winning the game.

B. Quantitative Evaluations. Besides the above case studies, we also perform quantitative evaluations. Recall that we have two design objectives for our TEAM MEMBER REPLACEMENT problem, including both the *skill match* and the *structural match*. Our quantitative evaluations focus on the following two aspects. First, we examine whether simultaneously considering both design objectives outperform only considering one of them. Second, we evaluate to what extent our graph kernel formulation outperforms other alternative choices, in order to fulfill both design objectives (i.e., the skill match and the structural match). To be specific, we compare to the following alternative methods, including (a) only with *structure matching* and not including $\mathbf{L}_{\times}$ in Eq. (2) (Graph Only),(b) only with *skill matching* and using cosine similarity of skill vectors as scores (Skill Only), (c) using the weighted sum of scores by 'Skill Only' and 'Graph Only' (Linear Combination), (d) using the multiplication of the two (Multiplicative Combination), and (e) first picking those with high 'Skill Only' scores and then ranking them by 'Graph Only' scores (Sequential Filtering).

User studies. We perform a user study with 20 people aged from 22 to 35 as follows. We choose 10 papers from various fields, replace one author of each paper, run our method and the first two comparison methods, and each of them recommends top five candidates. Then, we mix the outputs (15 recommendations in total) and ask users to (a) mark exactly one best replacement; (b) mark all good replacements from the list of 15 recommended candidates. The results are presented in Fig. 2, Fig. 3 and Fig. 4, respectively. As we can see from these figures, the proposed method (the green bar) is best in terms of both precision and recall. For example, the average recalls by our method, by 'Graph Only' and by 'Skill Only' are 55%, 28%, 17%, respectively. As for different papers, our method wins 9 out of 10 cases (except for 'paper 2' where 'Skill Only' is best).

Author alias prediction. In *DBLP*, some researchers might have multiple name identities/alias. For example, in some papers, *Alexander J. Smola* might be listed as *Alex J. Smola*, *Zhongfei (Mark) Zhang* might be listed as *Zhongfei Zhang*, etc. For such an author, we run the team replacement algorithm on those papers s/he was involved to find top-k replacement. If his/her other alias appears in the top-k recommended list, we treat it as a *hit*. The average accuracy of different methods is shown in Fig. 5. Again, our method performs best - it outperforms both the methods that consider only one design objective ('skill only' and 'graph only'); and that use alternative ad-hoc methods to combine both skill and structural match ('linear combination', 'multiplicative combination' and 'sequential filtering').

5.3 Efficiency Results

A. The speed-up by pruning. To demonstrate the benefit of our pruning strategy, we run TEAMREP-BASIC with and without pruning on the three datasets and compare their running time. For *DBLP*, we choose the authors of paper [29] (6 authors); for *Movie*, we select the film crew of *Titanic* (1997) (22 actors/actresses); for *NBA*, we pick the players on the Los Angeles Lakers in year 1996 (17 players). The result is presented in Fig. 6. As we can see, the pruning step itself brings significant savings in terms of running time, especially for larger graphs (e.g., *DBLP* and *Movie*). Notice that according to Lemma 1, we do not sacrifice any recommendation accuracy by pruning.

B. Further speedup. Next, we vary the team sizes and compare the running time of TEAMREP-BASIC with TEAMREP-FAST-EXACT(exact methods); and Ark-L [24] with TEAMREP-FAST-APPROX (approximate methods). For TEAMREP-BASIC and Ark-L, we apply the same pruning step as their preprocessing step. The results on *DBLP* are presented in Fig. 7 and Fig. 8, respectively. We can see that the proposed TEAMREP-FAST-EXACT and TEAMREP-FAST-APPROX are much faster than their alternative choices, especially when

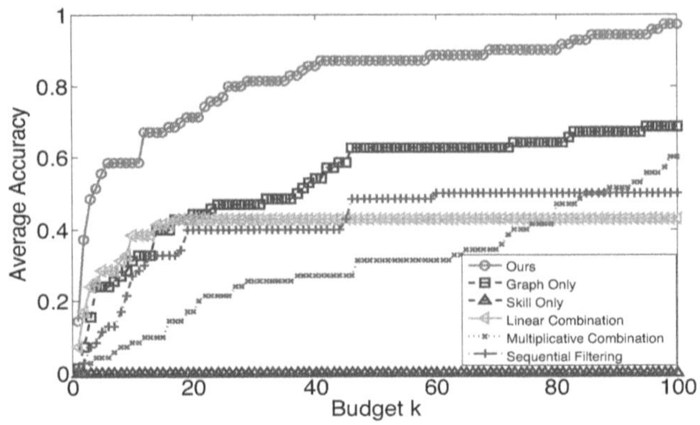

Figure 5: Average accuracy vs. budget k. Higher is better.

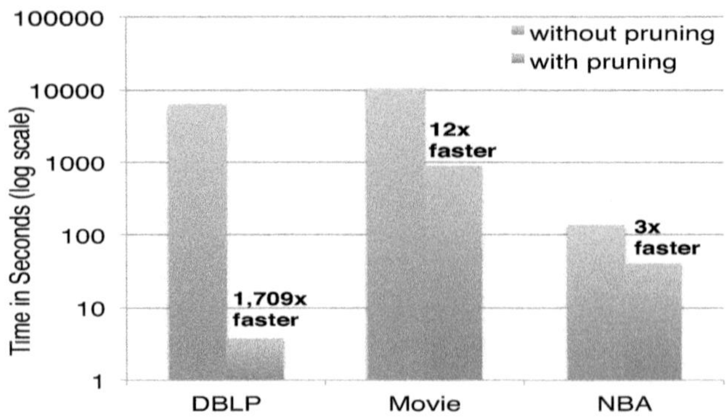

Figure 6: Time Comparisons before and after pruning on three datasets. Notice time is in log-scale.

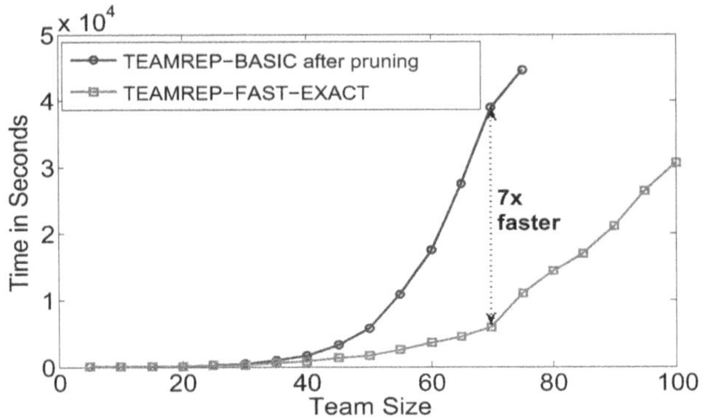

Figure 7: Time Comparison between TEAMREP-BASIC and TEAMREP-FAST-EXACT. TEAMREP-FAST-EXACT is on average 3× faster. TEAMREP-BASIC takes more than 10 hours when team size = 70.

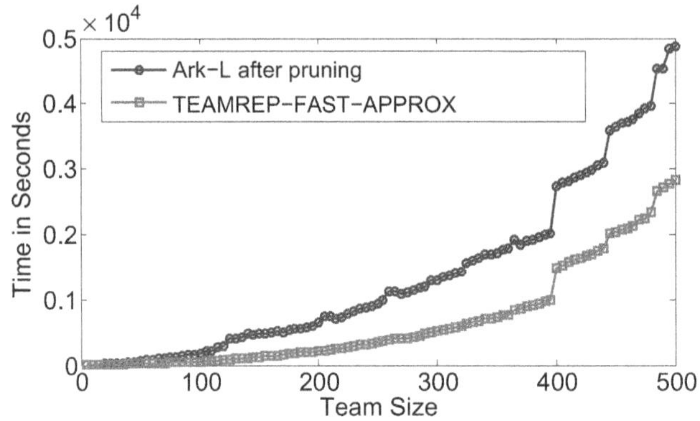

Figure 8: Time Comparisons between Ark-L[20] and TEAMREP-FAST-APPROX. TEAMREP-FAST-APPROX is on average 3× faster.

team size is large. Notice that Ark-L is the best known method for approximating random walk based graph kernel.

C. Scalability. To test the scalability of our TEAMREP-FAST-EXACT and TEAMREP-FAST-APPROX algorithms, we sample a certain percentage of edges from the entire *DBLP* network and run the two proposed algorithms on teams with different sizes. The results are presented in Fig. 9 and Fig. 10, respectively. As we can seen, both algorithms enjoy a *sub-linear* scalability w.r.t. the total number of edges of the input graph (m).

6. RELATED WORK

In this section, we review the related work in terms of (a) team formation, (b) recommendation and expert finding, and (c) graph kernel.

Team Formation. Team formation studies the problem of assembling a team of people to work on a project. To ensure success, the selected team members should possess the desired skills and have strong team cohesion, which is first studied in [28]. As follow-up work, Anagnostopoulos et al [1] studies forming teams to accommodate a sequence of tasks arriving in an online fashion and Rangapuram et al [34] allows incorporating many realistic requirements into team formation based on a generalization of the densest subgraph problem. With the presence of the underlying social network, the set cover problem is complicated by the goal of lowering the communication cost at the same time. Bogdanov et al [3] studies how to extract a diversified group pulled from strong cliques given a network; this ensures that the group is both comprehensive and representative of the whole network. Cummings and Kiesler [10] find that prior working experience is the best predictor of collaborative tie strength. To provide insights into designs of online communities and organizations, the systematic differences in appropriating social softwares among different online enterprise communities is analyzed in [32]. The patterns of informal networks and communication in distributed global software teams using social network analysis is also investigated in [9]. Specific communication structures are proven critical to new product development delivery performance and quality [8]. To assess the skills of players and teams in online multi-player games and team-based sports, "team chemistry" is also accounted for in [12, 11].

Recommendation and Expert Finding. Recommendation and expert finding is a very active research topic in data mining and information retrieval, either to recommend products a user is mostly interested in or to identify the most knowledgeable people in a field. Our work is related to this in the sense that we aim to recommend top candidates who are most suitable for the vacancy. A popular method in recommendation (collaborative filtering) is latent factor model [27, 14, 42]. The basic idea is to apply matrix factorization to user-item rating data to identify the latent factors. The factorization technique can be naturally

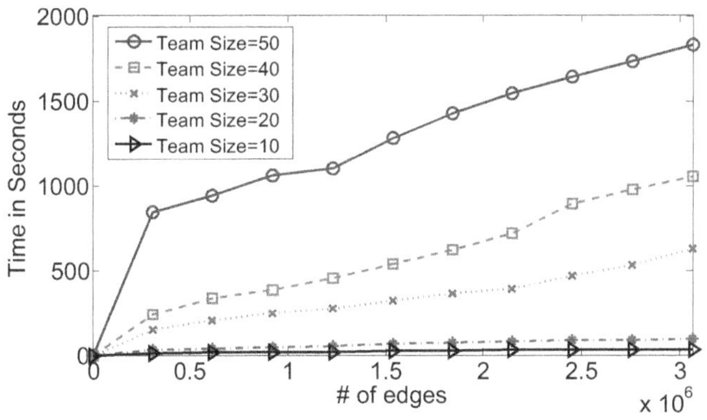

Figure 9: Running time of TEAMREP-FAST-EXACT vs. graph size. TEAMREP-FAST-EXACT scales sub-linearly w.r.t. the number of edges of the input graph.

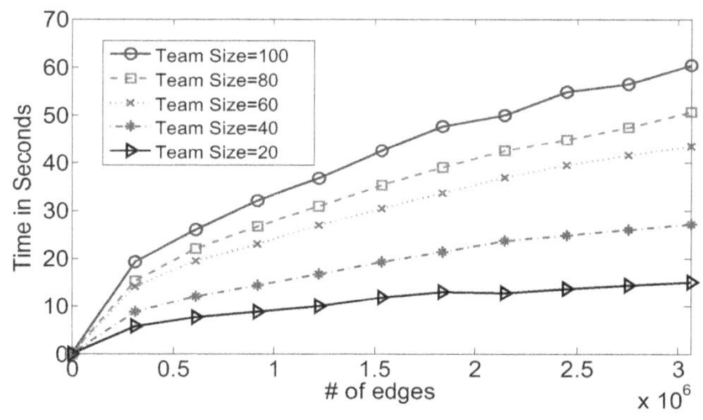

Figure 10: Running time vs. graph size. TEAMREP-FAST-APPROX scales sub-linearly w.r.t. the number of edges of the input graph.

extended by adding biases, temporal dynamics and varying confidence levels. In question-answering sites, *e.g.*, Quora and Stack Overflow, an important task is to route a newly posted question to the 'right' user with appropriate expertise and several methods based on link analysis have been proposed [45, 6, 46]. In academia, identifying experts in a research field is of great value, *e.g.*, assigning papers to the right reviewers in a peer-review process [31, 25], which can be done by either building the co-author network [29] or using language model and topic-based model [13, 20]. For enterprises, finding the desired specialist can greatly reduce costs and facilitate the ongoing projects. Many methods have been proposed to expert search through an organization's document repository [2, 43].

Graph Kernel. Graph kernel measures the similarity between two graphs. Typical applications include automated reasoning [39], bioinformatics/chemoinformatics [16, 36]. Generally speaking, graph kernels can be categorized into three classes: kernels based on walks [17, 40, 41, 18, 4], kernels based on limited-sized subgraphs [23, 37, 26] and kernels based on subtree patterns [30, 35, 21]. Graph kernels based on random walk is one of the most successful choices [5]. The idea is to perform simultaneous walks on the two graphs and count the number of matching walks. One challenge of random walk based graph kernel lies in computation. The straight-forward method needs $O(n^6)$ in time. For unlabelled graphs, the time complexity can be reduced to $O(n^3)$ by reducing to the problem of solving a linear system [40, 41]. With low rank approximation, the computation can be further accelerated with high approximation accuracy [24].

7. CONCLUSION

In this paper, we study the problem of TEAM MEMBER REPLACEMENT to recommend replacement when a critical team member becomes unavailable. To our best knowledge, we are the first to study this problem. The basic idea of our method is to adopt graph kernel to encode both *skill matching* and *structural matching*. To address the computational challenges, we propose a suite of fast and scalable algorithms. Extensive experiments on real world datasets validate the effectiveness and efficiency of our algorithms. To be specific, (a) by bringing skill matching and structural matching together, our method is significantly better than the alternative choices in terms of both average precision (24% better) and recall (27% better); and (b) our fast algorithms are orders of magnitude faster while enjoying a *sub-linear* scalability.

This paper has presented an efficient technique in addressing the team replacement challenge; however, the proposed method can be applied to general graph mining problem where the interaction of multiple objectives is critical, e.g., finding a similar multimedia object by considering both its content and relationship with other objects. In the future, we would like to expand team replacement to team enhancement and team composition. For instance, given the structure of a high-grossing movie (e.g., *Saving Private Ryan*) of a particular genre, we want to develop an effective algorithm to suggest a team of actors.

8. ACKNOWLEDGMENTS

This material is supported by the National Science Foundation under Grant No. IIS1017415, by the Army Research Laboratory under Cooperative Agreement Number W911NF-09-2-0053, by Defense Advanced Research Projects Agency (DARPA) under Contract Number W911NF-11-C-0200 and W911NF-12-C-0028, by National Institutes of Health under the grant number R01LM011986, Region II University Transportation Center under the project number 49997-33 25. The content of the information in this document does not necessarily reflect the position or the policy of the Government, and no official endorsement should be inferred. The U.S. Government is authorized to reproduce and distribute reprints for Government purposes notwithstanding any copyright notation here on.

References

[1] A. Anagnostopoulos, L. Becchetti, C. Castillo, A. Gionis, and S. Leonardi. Online team formation in social networks. In *WWW*, pages 839–848, 2012.

[2] K. Balog, L. Azzopardi, and M. de Rijke. Formal models for expert finding in enterprise corpora. In *SIGIR*, pages 43–50, 2006.

[3] P. Bogdanov, B. Baumer, P. Basu, A. Bar-Noy, and A. K. Singh. As strong as the weakest link: Mining diverse cliques in weighted graphs. In *ECML/PKDD (1)*, pages 525–540, 2013.

[4] K. M. Borgwardt and H.-P. Kriegel. Shortest-path kernels on graphs. In *ICDM*, pages 74–81, 2005.

[5] K. M. Borgwardt, H.-P. Kriegel, S. V. N. Vishwanathan, and N. Schraudolph. Graph kernels for disease outcome prediction from protein-protein interaction networks. In *Pacific Symposium on Biocomputing*, 2007.

[6] M. Bouguessa, B. Dumoulin, and S. Wang. Identifying authoritative actors in question-answering forums: the case of yahoo! answers. In *KDD*, pages 866–874, 2008.

[7] N. Cao, Y.-R. Lin, L. Li, and H. Tong. g-Miner: Interactive visual group mining on multivariate graphs. In *CHI*, 2015.

[8] M. Cataldo and K. Ehrlich. The impact of communication structure on new product development outcomes. In *CHI*, pages 3081–3090, 2012.

[9] K. Chang and K. Ehrlich. Out of sight but not out of mind?: Informal networks, communication and media use in global software teams. In *CASCON*, pages 86–97, 2007.

[10] J. N. Cummings and S. B. Kiesler. Who collaborates successfully?: prior experience reduces collaboration barriers in distributed interdisciplinary research. In *CSCW*, pages 437–446, 2008.

[11] C. DeLong and J. Srivastava. Teamskill evolved: Mixed classification schemes for team-based multi-player games. In *PAKDD (1)*, pages 26–37, 2012.

[12] C. DeLong, L. G. Terveen, and J. Srivastava. Teamskill and the nba: applying lessons from virtual worlds to the real-world. In *ASONAM*, pages 156–161, 2013.

[13] H. Deng, I. King, and M. R. Lyu. Formal models for expert finding on dblp bibliography data. In *ICDM*, pages 163–172, 2008.

[14] G. Dror, N. Koenigstein, and Y. Koren. Web-scale media recommendation systems. *Proceedings of the IEEE*, 100(9):2722–2736, 2012.

[15] Q. Du, V. Faber, and M. Gunzburger. Centroidal voronoi tessellations: applications and algorithms. *SIAM review*, 41(4):637–676, 1999.

[16] A. Feragen, N. Kasenburg, J. Petersen, M. de Bruijne, and K. M. Borgwardt. Scalable kernels for graphs with continuous attributes. In *NIPS*, pages 216–224, 2013.

[17] T. Gärtner, P. A. Flach, and S. Wrobel. On graph kernels: Hardness results and efficient alternatives. In *COLT*, pages 129–143, 2003.

[18] T. Gärtner, J. W. Lloyd, and P. A. Flach. Kernels and distances for structured data. *Machine Learning*, 57(3):205–232, 2004.

[19] G. Golub and C. Van Loan. Matrix computations. 1996.

[20] S. H. Hashemi, M. Neshati, and H. Beigy. Expertise retrieval in bibliographic network: a topic dominance learning approach. In *CIKM*, pages 1117–1126, 2013.

[21] S. Hido and H. Kashima. A linear-time graph kernel. In *ICDM*, pages 179–188, 2009.

[22] P. J. Hinds, K. M. Carley, D. Krackhardt, and D. Wholey. Choosing work group members: Balancing similarity, competence, and familiarity. In *Organizational Behavior and Human Decision Processes*, pages 226–251, 2000.

[23] T. Horváth, T. Gärtner, and S. Wrobel. Cyclic pattern kernels for predictive graph mining. In *KDD*, pages 158–167, 2004.

[24] U. Kang, H. Tong, and J. Sun. Fast random walk graph kernel. In *SDM*, pages 828–838, 2012.

[25] M. Karimzadehgan and C. Zhai. Constrained multi-aspect expertise matching for committee review assignment. In *CIKM*, pages 1697–1700, 2009.

[26] R. I. Kondor, N. Shervashidze, and K. M. Borgwardt. The graphlet spectrum. In *ICML*, page 67, 2009.

[27] Y. Koren, R. M. Bell, and C. Volinsky. Matrix factorization techniques for recommender systems. *IEEE Computer*, 42(8):30–37, 2009.

[28] T. Lappas, K. Liu, and E. Terzi. Finding a team of experts in social networks. In *KDD*, pages 467–476, 2009.

[29] J.-Z. Li, J. Tang, J. Zhang, Q. Luo, Y. Liu, and M. Hong. Eos: expertise oriented search using social networks. In *WWW*, pages 1271–1272, 2007.

[30] P. Mahé, N. Ueda, T. Akutsu, J.-L. Perret, and J.-P. Vert. Graph kernels for molecular structure-activity relationship analysis with support vector machines. *Journal of Chemical Information and Modeling*, 45(4):939–951, 2005.

[31] D. M. Mimno and A. McCallum. Expertise modeling for matching papers with reviewers. In *KDD*, pages 500–509, 2007.

[32] M. Muller, K. Ehrlich, T. Matthews, A. Perer, I. Ronen, and I. Guy. Diversity among enterprise online communities: collaborating, teaming, and innovating through social media. In *CHI*, pages 2815–2824, 2012.

[33] J. Pei, H. Wang, J. Liu, K. Wang, J. Wang, and P. S. Yu. Discovering frequent closed partial orders from strings. *IEEE Trans. Knowl. Data Eng.*, 18(11):1467–1481, 2006.

[34] S. S. Rangapuram, T. Bühler, and M. Hein. Towards realistic team formation in social networks based on densest subgraphs. In *WWW*, pages 1077–1088, 2013.

[35] N. Shervashidze and K. M. Borgwardt. Fast subtree kernels on graphs. *NIPS*, 2009.

[36] N. Shervashidze, P. Schweitzer, E. J. van Leeuwen, K. Mehlhorn, and K. M. Borgwardt. Weisfeiler-lehman graph kernels. *Journal of Machine Learning Research*, 12:2539–2561, 2011.

[37] N. Shervashidze, S. V. N. Vishwanathan, T. Petri, K. Mehlhorn, and K. M. Borgwardt. Efficient graphlet kernels for large graph comparison. *Journal of Machine Learning Research - Proceedings Track*, 5:488–495, 2009.

[38] H. A. Simon. *The Sciences of the Artificial (3rd Ed.)*. MIT Press, Cambridge, MA, USA, 1996.

[39] E. Tsivtsivadze, J. Urban, H. Geuvers, and T. Heskes. Semantic graph kernels for automated reasoning. In *SDM*, pages 795–803, 2011.

[40] S. V. N. Vishwanathan, K. M. Borgwardt, and N. N. Schraudolph. Fast computation of graph kernels. In *NIPS*, pages 1449–1456, 2006.

[41] S. V. N. Vishwanathan, N. N. Schraudolph, R. Kondor, and K. M. Borgwardt. Graph kernels. *The Journal of Machine Learning Research*, 99:1201–1242, 2010.

[42] C. Wang and D. M. Blei. Collaborative topic modeling for recommending scientific articles. In *KDD*, pages 448–456, 2011.

[43] S. Wu, J. Sun, and J. Tang. Patent partner recommendation in enterprise social networks. In *WSDM*, pages 43–52, 2013.

[44] R. Zadeh, A. D. Balakrishnan, S. B. Kiesler, and J. N. Cummings. What's in a move?: normal disruption and a design challenge. In *CHI*, pages 2897–2906, 2011.

[45] J. Zhang, M. S. Ackerman, and L. A. Adamic. Expertise networks in online communities: structure and algorithms. In *WWW*, pages 221–230, 2007.

[46] G. Zhou, S. Lai, K. Liu, and J. Zhao. Topic-sensitive probabilistic model for expert finding in question answer communities. In *CIKM*, pages 1662–1666, 2012.

Robust Group Linkage

Pei Li
University of Zurich
peili@ifi.uzh.ch

Xin Luna Dong
Google Inc.
lunadong@google.com

Songtao Guo
LinkedIn
songtao.gg@gmail.com

Andrea Maurino
University of Milan-Bicocca
maurino@disco.unimib.it

Divesh Srivastava
AT&T Labs-Research
divesh@research.att.com

ABSTRACT

We study the problem of *group linkage*: linking records that refer to multiple entities in the same group. Applications for group linkage include finding businesses in the same chain, finding social network users from the same organization, and so on. Group linkage faces new challenges compared to traditional entity resolution. First, although different members in the same group can share some similar *global* values of an attribute, they represent different entities so can also have distinct *local* values for the same or different attributes, requiring a high *tolerance* for value diversity. Second, we need to be able to distinguish local values from erroneous values.

We present a robust two-stage algorithm: the first stage identifies *pivots–maximal* sets of records that are very likely to belong to the same group, while being robust to possible erroneous values; the second stage collects strong evidence from the pivots and leverages it for merging more records into the same group, while being tolerant to differences in local values of an attribute. Experimental results show the high effectiveness and efficiency of our algorithm on various real-world data sets.

1. INTRODUCTION

Entity resolution aims at linking records that refer to the same real-world entity and has been extensively studied in the literature (surveyed in [7, 18]). In this paper we study a related but different problem that we call *group linkage*: linking records that refer to multiple entities in the same group.

One motivation for our work comes from the need to group the millions of social network users (*e.g.*, *LinkedIn*) by their organizations, which improves matching and recommendation activities in social networks. The organization information is often missing, incomplete, or simply too heterogeneous to be recognized as the same (*e.g.*, "International Business Machines Corporation", "IBM Corp.", "IBM", "IBM-Almaden", etc., all refer to the same organization). Contact phones, email addresses, and mailing addresses of people all provide extra evidence for group linkage, but they can also vary for different people even in the same organization.

We are also motivated by applications where we need to identify *business chains*, multiple business entities that share a brand name

WWW 2015, May 18–22, 2015, Florence, Italy.
ACM 978-1-4503-3469-3/15/05.
http://dx.doi.org/10.1145/2736277.2741118

Table 1: Identified top-5 US business chains. For each chain, we show the number of stores, distinct business names, distinct phone numbers, distinct URL domain names, and distinct categories.

Name	#Store	#Name	#Phn	#URL	#Cat
SUBWAY	21,912	772	21,483	6	23
Bank of America	21,727	48	6,573	186	24
U-Haul	21,638	2,340	18,384	14	20
USPS - United State Post Office	19,225	12,345	5,761	282	22
McDonald's	17,289	2401	16,607	568	47

and provide similar products and services (*e.g.*, *Walmart, McDonald's*). With the advent of the Web and mobile devices, we are observing a boom in *local search*: that is, searching local businesses under geographical constraints. Local search engines include *Google Maps, Yahoo! Local, YellowPages, yelp, ezlocal*, etc. The knowledge of business chains can have a big economic value to local search engines. However, business listings are rarely associated with specific chains explicitly stated in real-world business-listing collections. Sharing the same name, phone number, or URL domain name can all serve as evidence of belonging to the same chain. But the same value is often presented in different ways and there are many erroneous values, as we soon show.

Group linkage differs from entity resolution in the following aspects. First, the type of heterogeneity in groups is different from that in entities, which is mainly caused by typographical errors and different representations of the same value. Instead, different members in the same group can share some similar *global* values as group identifier, and meanwhile can have distinct *local* values of the same attribute as entity identifier. For example, many branches in the same business chain provide a primary company-wide phone number, while a significant number of branches may provide different local phone numbers. Traditional methods learn different weights for different attributes so they can be tolerant on value variety for some less coherent attributes; they fall short in our context since global values and local values often occur in the same attribute. Second, it is non-trivial to distinguish such differences from erroneous values in the data. Finally, a group can contain tens of thousands of members. Computation within such huge groups can be very expensive; thus, *scalability* is a big challenge. We use the following example throughout the paper for illustration.

EXAMPLE 1.1. *We consider a set of 18M real-world business listings in the US extracted from a local search engine, each describing a business by its name, phone number, URL domain name, location, and category. Our algorithm automatically finds 600K business chains and 2.7M listings that belong to these chains. Table 1 lists the five largest chains we found. We observe that (1) each chain contains up to 22K different branch stores, (2) different branches from the same chain can have a large variety of names,*

Table 2: Real-world business listings. We show only state for location and simplify names of category. There is a wrong value in italic font.

RID	name	phone	URL (domain)	location	category
r_1	Home Depot, The	808		NJ	furniture
r_2	Home Depot, The	808		NY	furniture
r_3	Home Depot, The	808	homedepot	MD	furniture
r_4	Home Depot, The	808	homedepot	AK	furniture
r_5	Home Depot, The	808	homedepot	MI	furniture
r_6	Home Depot, The	101	homedepot	IN	furniture
r_7	Home Depot, The	102	homedepot	NY	furniture
r_8	Home Depot, USA	103	homedepot	WV	furniture
r_9	Home Depot USA	808		SD	furniture
r_{10}	Home Depot - Tools	808		FL	furniture
r_{11}	Taco Casa		tacocasa	AL	restaurant
r_{12}	Taco Casa	900	tacocasa	AL	restaurant
r_{13}	Taco Casa	900	tacocasa, *tacocasatexas*	AL	restaurant
r_{14}	Taco Casa	900		AL	food
r_{15}	Taco Casa	900		AL	food
r_{16}	Taco Casa	701	tacocasatexas	TX	restaurant
r_{17}	Taco Casa	702	tacocasatexas	TX	restaurant
r_{18}	Taco Casa	703	tacocasatexas	TX	restaurant
r_{19}	Taco Casa	704		NY	food store
r_{20}	Taco Casa		tacodelmar	AK	restaurant

phone numbers, and URL domain names, and (3) even chains of similar sizes can have very different numbers of distinct URL domains (same for other attributes). Thus, rule-based linkage can hardly succeed and scalability is essential.

Table 2 shows 20 business listings (with some abstraction) in this data set. After investigating their webpages manually, we find that $r_1 - r_{18}$ *belong to three business chains:* $Ch_1 = \{r_1 - r_{10}\}$, $Ch_2 = \{r_{11} - r_{15}\}$, *and* $Ch_3 = \{r_{16} - r_{18}\}$*;* r_{19} *and* r_{20} *do not belong to any chain. Note the slightly different names for businesses in chain* Ch_1*; also note that* r_{13} *is integrated from different sources and contains two URLs, one (*tacocasatexas*) being wrong.*

Simple linkage rules do not work well on this data set. For example, if we require only high similarity on name *for chain linkage, we may wrongly decide that* $r_{11} - r_{20}$ *all belong to the same chain as they share a popular restaurant name* Taco Casa*. Traditional linkage strategies do not work well either. If we apply Swoosh-style linkage [25] and iteratively merge records with high similarity on* name *and shared* phone *or* URL*, we can wrongly merge* Ch_2 *and* Ch_3 *because of the wrong URL from* r_{13}*. If we learn different weights for different attributes, a high weight for* phone *would split* $r_6 - r_8$ *out of chain* Ch_1 *because of their different local phone numbers, but a low weight for* phone *would split* $r_9 - r_{10}$ *out of chain* Ch_1 *since sharing the primary phone number, the main evidence, is downweighted.* □

The key idea in our solution is to find *sufficient strong evidence* that can glue group members together, while being tolerant to differences in values specific for individual group members. For example, we wish to reward sharing of primary values, such as *primary phone numbers* or *URL domain names* for chain linkage, but would not penalize differences in local values, such as *locations* and *local phone numbers*. For this purpose, our algorithm proceeds in two stages. First, we identify *pivots* containing *maximal sets of* records that are very likely to belong to the same group. Second, we collect *strong evidence* from the resulting pivots, such as primary phone numbers and URL domain names in business chains, based on which we cluster the pivots and remaining records into groups. Whereas our approach shares insights with other two-stage clustering techniques in the literature [1, 19, 22, 26, 28, 4], our pivot identification step guarantees both *robustness* to presence of erroneous values, which is critical for high precision, and generation of *maximal* pivots, which is critical for high recall. The advantages of our approach are verified in our experiments.

The group linkage problem we study in this paper is different from the group linkage problems in [17, 23], which compute *group-level* similarity between *pre-specified* groups of records from the same entity. Our goal is to find records of multiple entities that belong to the same group and we make three contributions.

1. We study pivot generation in the presence of erroneous data. Our pivot is *robust*: even if we remove a few possibly erroneous records from a pivot, we still have sufficient strong evidence that the other records belong to the same group.
2. We then reduce the group linkage problem to clustering pivots and the remaining records. We learn different weights *at the value level*, such that our clustering algorithm can leverage strong evidence collected from pivots and meanwhile be *tolerant* to value variety of records in the same group.
3. Experiments on two real-world data sets based on our motivating applications show high efficiency and effectiveness of our proposed approach.

Note that this paper focuses on finding records that belong to the same group. It does not require applying entity resolution to identify records that refer to the same individual entity. However, we show empirically that combining our algorithm and entity resolution can improve the results of both.

In the rest of the paper, Section 2 discusses related work. Section 3 defines the problem and provides an overview of our solution. Sections 4-5 describe the two stages in our solution. Section 6 describes experimental results. Section 7 concludes. For reasons of space, all proofs are omitted, and can be found in [21].

2. RELATED WORK

Entity resolution has been extensively studied in the past (surveyed in [7, 18]). Traditional entity resolution techniques aim at linking records that refer to the same real-world entity, so implicitly assume value consistency between records that should be linked. Group linkage is different in that it aims at linking records that refer to different entities in the same group. The variety of individual entities requires better use of strong evidence and tolerance on different values even within the same group. These two features differentiate our work from any previous linkage technique.

For record clustering in entity resolution, existing work may apply the transitive rule [16], do match-and-merge [25], or reduce it to an optimization problem [15]. Our work is different in that our pivot-linkage algorithm aims at being robust to a few erroneous records; and our clustering algorithm emphasizes leveraging the strong evidence collected from the pivots.

For record-similarity computation, existing work can be distance based [6], rule based [16], or classification based [10]. There has also been work on weight (or model) learning from labeled data [10, 27]. Our work is different in that in addition to learning a weight for each attribute, we also learn a *separate weight for each value* based on whether it serves as important evidence for the group. Note that some previous works are also tolerant to different values, but they leverage evidence that may not be available in our contexts: [9] is tolerant to schema heterogeneity from different relations by specifying matching rules; [14] is tolerant to possibly false values by considering agreement between different data providers; [20] is tolerant to out-of-date values by considering time stamps; we are tolerant to value diversity within the same group.

Two-stage clustering has been proposed in DB and IR communities [1, 19, 22, 26, 28, 4]; however, they identify pivots in different ways. Techniques in [19, 26] consider a pivot as a single record, either randomly selected or selected according to the weighted degrees of nodes in the graph. Techniques in [28] generate pivots using agglomerative clustering but can be too conservative and miss strong evidence. Techniques in [1] identify pivots as *bi-connected components*, where removing any node would not disconnect the graph. Although this corresponds to the *1-robustness* requirement in our solution (defined in Section 4), they generate overlapping clusters; it is not obvious how to derive non-overlapping clusters in applications such as business-chain linkage and how to extend their techniques to guarantee k-robustness. Techniques in [19, 22] require knowledge of the number of clusters for one of the stages, so are inapplicable for linkage applications, where the number of clusters is not known a priori. Techniques in [4] generate pivots to collect evolution evidence for resolving entities that evolve over time, but may not be robust against erroneous values. We experimentally compare with these methods whenever applicable (Section 6), showing that our algorithm is robust in presence of erroneous values and consistently generates high-accuracy results on data sets with different features.

Link prediction [12, 24] aims to predict generic links (e.g., referring to the same entity, being in the same group) between a pair of records. However, link prediction itself can make mistakes, and clustering entities (into groups) by using straightforward methods (such as the transitivity rule in [24]) is undesirable. Combining link prediction with our robust techniques for group linkage is an interesting direction of future work.

Finally, we distinguish our work from *group linkage* in [17, 23], which has a different goal of matching groups of records associated with the same entity from multiple databases. On et al. [23] compute similarity between pre-specified groups of records based on *record-level similarity*. With the same goal, Huang [17] decides group-level similarity using network evolution analysis. Our goal is to find records of *multiple entities* that belong to the same group.

3. OVERVIEW

3.1 Problem Definition

Let $\mathbf{R}$ be a set of records describing entities by a set of attributes $\mathbf{A}$. For a record $r \in \mathbf{R}$, we denote by $r.A$ its value of attribute $A \in \mathbf{A}$. Records may contain erroneous or missing values.

Group linkage aims to find records that represent entities belonging to the same real-world group. We focus on non-overlapping groups, which often hold in applications. As an example application, we wish to find *business chains*–a set of business entities with the same or highly similar names that provide similar products and services (e.g., *Walmart*, *Home Depot*, *Subway* and *McDonald's*).

DEFINITION 3.1 (GROUP LINKAGE). *Given a set of records, denoted by* $\mathbf{R}$, group linkage *identifies a set of clusters* $\mathbf{CH}$ *in* $\mathbf{R}$, *such that records representing real-world entities in the same group belong to one and the same cluster, and vice versa.* □

EXAMPLE 3.2. *Consider the records in Example 1.1, where each record describes a business listing by attributes* name, phone, URL, location, *and* category.

The ideal solution to the group linkage problem contains 5 clusters: $Ch_1 = \{r_1 - r_{10}\}$, $Ch_2 = \{r_{11} - r_{15}\}$, $Ch_3 = \{r_{16} - r_{18}\}$, $Ch_4 = \{r_{19}\}$, *and* $Ch_5 = \{r_{20}\}$. *Among them,* Ch_2 *and* Ch_3 *represent two different chains with the same name.* □

3.2 Overview of Our Solution

Group linkage is related to but different from traditional entity resolution because it essentially looks for records that represent entities in the same group, rather than records that represent exactly the same entity. Different members in the same group often share a certain amount of commonality (*e.g.*, common name, primary phone, and URL domain of chain stores), but meanwhile can also have a lot of differences (*e.g.*, different addresses, local phone numbers, and local URL domains); thus, we need to allow much higher variety in some attribute values to avoid false negatives. On the other hand, as we have shown in Example 1.1, simply lowering our requirement on similarity of records or similarity of a few attributes in clustering can lead to a lot of false positives.

The key intuition of our solution is to distinguish between *strong* and *weak* evidence. For example, branches in the same business chain often share URL domain names and those in North America often share a few 1-800 phone numbers. Thus, a URL domain or phone number shared among many business listings can serve as strong evidence for chain linkage. In contrast, a phone number shared by only a couple of entities is much weaker evidence, since one might be an erroneous or out-of-date value.

To facilitate leveraging strong evidence, our solution consists of two stages. The first stage collects records highly likely to belong to the same group; for example, a set of business listings with the same name and phone number are very likely to be in the same chain. We call the results *pivots*; from them we can collect strong evidence such as name, primary phone number, and primary URL domain of chains. The goal is to be robust against erroneous values and make as few false positives as possible, so we can avoid causing incorrect ripple effect later; however, we need to keep in mind that being too strict can miss important strong evidence.

The second stage puts pivots and remaining records into groups according to the discovered strong evidence. It decides whether several pivots belong to the same group, and whether a record not in any pivot actually belongs to some group. It treats weak evidence differently from strong evidence. The intuition is to leverage strong evidence and meanwhile be tolerant to value diversity in the same group, so we can reduce false negatives in the first stage. We illustrate our approach for business-chain linkage as follows.

EXAMPLE 3.3. *Continue with the motivating example. In the first stage we generate three pivots:* $Cr_1 = \{r_1 - r_7\}, Cr_2 = \{r_{14}, r_{15}\}$, $Cr_3 = \{r_{16} - r_{18}\}$. *Records* $r_1 - r_7$ *form a pivot because they have the same name, five of them* ($r_1 - r_5$) *share phone number* 808 *and five of them* ($r_3 - r_7$) *share URL* homedepot. *Similar for the other two pivots. Note that* r_{13} *does not belong to any pivot, because one of its URLs is the same as that of* $r_{11} - r_{12}$, *and one is the same as that of* $r_{16} - r_{18}$, *but except name, there are no other common values between these two groups of records. To avoid mistakes, we defer the decision on* r_{13}. *Indeed, recall that* tacocasatexas *is a wrong value for* r_{13}. *For a similar reason, we defer the decision on* r_{12}.

In the second stage, we generate groups – business chains. We merge $r_8 - r_{10}$ *with pivot* Cr_1, *because they have similar names and share either the primary phone number or the primary URL. We also merge* $r_{11} - r_{13}$ *with pivot* Cr_2, *because (1)* $r_{12} - r_{13}$ *share the primary phone* 900 *with* Cr_2, *and (2)* r_{11} *shares the primary URL* tacocasa *with* $r_{12} - r_{13}$. *We do not merge* Cr_2 *and* Cr_3 *though, because they share neither the primary phone nor the primary URL. We do not merge* r_{19} *or* r_{20} *to any pivot, because there is again not much strong evidence. We thus obtain the ideal result.* □

We describe pivot identification in Section 4 and group linkage in Section 5. While we present the algorithms for the setting of one machine, many components of our algorithms can be easily parallelized in the Hadoop infrastructure [3]; we omit the details as it is not the focus of this paper. Before we proceed, we first introduce an important concept used in our algorithms, which typically exists for groups in practice.

3.3 Attribute categorization

To facilitate distinguishing between strong and weak evidence, we classify attributes into three categories, based on different relationship-cardinalities between attributes and groups.

- *Common-value attribute:* We call an attribute A a common-value attribute if there is an $m : 1$ relation between groups and A-values; that is, all entities in the same group have the same or highly similar A-values (*e.g.*, business-name for chain linkage and organization for organization linkage).
- *Primary-value attribute:* We call an attribute A a primary-value attribute if there is a $1 : n$ relation between groups and A-values; that is, entities in the same group often share one or a few primary A-values (but there can also be other values), and these values are seldom used by entities outside the group (*e.g.*, phone and URL-domain for chain, and phone-prefix and email-server for organization).
- *Multi-value attribute:* We call an attribute A multi-value attribute if there is a $m : n$ relation between groups and A-values (*e.g.*, category for chain linkage).

According to the definition, for each attribute A we define three measures to capture its features on labeled datasets. First, for each group Ch and its primary A-value v^A_{Ch} (*i.e.*, the A-value that occurs most often in Ch), we define m^A_{Ch} as the percentage of records in Ch that contain v^A_{Ch}, define s^A_{Ch} as the average similarity between v^A_{Ch} and other A-values in Ch, and define n^A_{Ch} as the percentage of other groups that contain v^A_{Ch}. Then, we compute m^A, s^A, n^A as the average of the top-k% values; to avoid being biased by small groups, we may filter groups of small sizes. According to the categorization, A is a common-value attribute if s^A is high; A is a primary-value attribute if m^A is high and n^A is low; and A is a multi-value attribute if n^A is high. We decide whether a measure is *high* or *low* using the largest gap between continuous measures.

Finally, we point out that despite the importance of attribute categorization, simply applying traditional entity resolution methods while treating the attributes of different categories differently does not work well (Figure 3).

4. PIVOT LINKAGE

The first stage creates pivots consisting of records that are very likely to be in the same group. To this end, we only consider common-value and primary-value attributes. This section starts with pivot definition (Section 4.1), then describes how we construct similarity graphs to facilitate pivot finding (Section 4.2), and finally gives the algorithm for pivot linkage (Section 4.3).

4.1 Criteria for a Pivot

At the first stage, we wish to make only decisions that are highly likely to be correct. First, we require that each pivot contains as many highly similar records as possible so as not to miss important strong evidence of a group, and different pivots are easily distinguishable from each other. Second, we wish that our results are robust even in the presence of a few erroneous values in the data. In Table 2, $r_1 - r_7$ form a good pivot, because *808* and *homedepot* are popular values among these records. In contrast, $r_{13} - r_{18}$ do not form a good pivot, because records $r_{14} - r_{15}$ and $r_{16} - r_{18}$ do not share any phone number or URL domain; the only "connector" between them is r_{13}, so they can be wrongly merged if r_{13} contains erroneous values. Also, considering $r_{13} - r_{15}$ and $r_{16} - r_{18}$ as two different pivots is risky, because (1) it is not very clear whether r_{13} is in the same chain as $r_{14} - r_{15}$ or as $r_{16} - r_{18}$, and (2) these two pivots share one URL domain name so are not fully distinguishable.

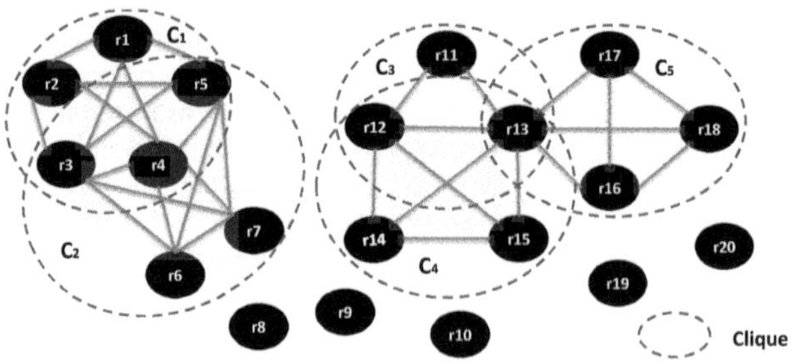

Figure 1: Similarity graph for records in Table 2.

We capture this intuition with *connectivity of a similarity graph*. We define the *similarity graph* of a set $\mathbf{R}$ of records as an undirected graph, where each node represents a record in $\mathbf{R}$, and an edge connects two nodes if they may contain strong evidence indicating a group. We consider two records sharing strong evidence if they agree on common-value attributes and (at least one) primary-value attribute. Note that our techniques are independent of the similarity criteria we apply. Figure 1 shows the similarity graph for Table 2.

Each pivot would correspond to a connected subgraph of the similarity graph. We would like such a subgraph to be *robust* such that even if we remove a few nodes the sub-graph remains connected; intuitively, even if there are some records with erroneous values, without them we still have enough evidence showing that the rest of the records should belong to the same group.

DEFINITION 4.1 (k-ROBUSTNESS). *A graph G is k-*robust *if after removing arbitrary k nodes and edges to these nodes, G is still connected. A clique or a single node is defined to be k-robust for any k.* □

In Figure 1, the subgraph with nodes $r_1 - r_7$ is 2-robust. It is not 3-robust as removing $r_3 - r_5$ can disconnect it.

According to the definition, we can partition the similarity graph into a set of k-robust subgraphs. As we do not wish to split any pivot unnecessarily, we require *maximal k-robust partitioning.*

DEFINITION 4.2 (MAXIMAL k-ROBUST PARTITIONING). *Let G be a similarity graph. A partitioning of G is a* maximal k-robust partitioning *if it satisfies the following properties.*

1. *Each node belongs to one and only one partition.*
2. *Each partition is k-robust.*
3. *The result of merging any partitions is not k-robust.* □

Note that a data set can have more than one maximal k-robust partitioning. Consider $r_{11} - r_{18}$ in Figure 1. There are three maximal 1-robust partitionings: $\{\{r_{11}\}, \{r_{12}, r_{14} - r_{15}\}, \{r_{13}, r_{16} - r_{18}\}\}$; $\{\{r_{11} - r_{12}\}, \{r_{14} - r_{15}\}, \{r_{13}, r_{16} - r_{18}\}\}$; and $\{\{r_{11} - r_{15}\}, \{r_{16} - r_{18}\}\}$. If we treat each partitioning as a possible world, records that belong to the same partition in all possible worlds have high probability to belong to the same group and so form a pivot. So, we define a pivot as follows.

DEFINITION 4.3 (k-PIVOT). *Let $\mathbf{R}$ be a set of records and G be the similarity graph of $\mathbf{R}$. The records that belong to the same subgraph in every maximal k-robust partitioning of G form a* k-pivot *of $\mathbf{R}$. A pivot contains at least 2 records.* □

PROPERTY 4.4. *A k-pivot is k-robust.* □

EXAMPLE 4.5. *Consider Figure 1 and assume $k = 1$. There are two connected sub-graphs. For records $r_1 - r_7$, the subgraph is 1-robust, so they form a 1-pivot. For records $r_{11} - r_{18}$, there are three maximal 1-robust partitionings, as we have shown. Two subsets of records belong to the same subgraph in each partitioning: $\{r_{14} - r_{15}\}$ and $\{r_{16} - r_{18}\}$; they form two 1-pivots.* □

Table 3: Simplified inverted index for the graph in Figure 1.

Record	V-Cliques	Represent
$r_{1/2}$	C_1	$r_1 - r_2$
r_3	C_1, C_2	r_3
r_4	C_1, C_2	r_4
r_5	C_1, C_2	r_5
$r_{6/7}$	C_2	$r_6 - r_7$
r_{11}	C_3	r_{11}
r_{12}	C_3, C_4	r_{12}
r_{13}	C_3, C_4, C_5	r_{13}
$r_{14/15}$	C_4	$r_{14} - r_{15}$
$r_{16/17/18}$	C_5	$r_{16} - r_{18}$

The higher the k, the stronger is the requirement for robustness; when $k = 0$, each connected subgraph is a pivot and the results would be vulnerable to erroneous values. In our motivating example, when $k = 0$, records $r_{11} - r_{18}$ would be wrongly considered as a pivot and thus belonging to the same chain. Our experiments show that a k in the range $[1, 4]$ is the best, improving the F-measure of the results by 10% over $k = 0$. Section 6.2.1 also shows that higher-precision, smaller-sized pivots with significantly lower recall can lead to low F-measure for the chains.

4.2 Constructing Similarity Graphs

Recall that we compare records by common-value and primary-value attribute values. All records agreeing on the common-value attributes and at least one value on a primary-value attribute form a clique, which we call a *v-clique*. We thus represent the similarity graph with a set of v-cliques, denoted by $\mathbf{C}$; for example, the graph in Figure 1 can be represented by five v-cliques ($C_1 - C_5$). In addition, we maintain an *inverted index* $\bar{L}$, where an entry corresponds to a record r and contains the v-cliques that r belongs to.

Given the sheer number of records in $\mathbf{R}$, it is not efficient to compare every pair of records, so we assume a *blocking* method [13] is applied to $\mathbf{R}$ to obtain a set of blocks. Still, the inverted index can be huge. In fact, according to Theorem 4.6, records in only one and the same v-clique belong to the same pivot, so we do not need to distinguish them. Thus, we simplify the inverted index such that for each v-clique we keep only a *representative* for nodes belonging only to this v-clique. Table 3 shows the simplified index for the similarity graph in Figure 1.

THEOREM 4.6. *Let G be a similarity graph and G' be a graph derived from G by merging nodes that belong to one and the same v-clique. Two nodes belong to the same pivot of G' if and only if they belong to the same pivot of G.* □

We can easily find v-cliques and construct the inverted index by scanning values of primary-value attributes. The running time is linear in the number of values from primary-value attributes.

Case study 1: On a data set with 18M records (Section 6), graph construction finished in 1.9 hours. The *original graph* contains 18M nodes and 4.2B edges. The *inverted index* is of size 89MB, containing 3.8M entries, each associated with at most 8 v-cliques; in total there are 1.2M v-cliques. The *simplified inverted index* is of size 34MB, containing 1.5M entries, where an entry can represent up to 11K records. The simplified inverted index reduces the size of the original graph by 3 orders of magnitude.

4.3 Identifying Pivots

We solve the pivot-linkage problem by reducing it to a Max-flow/Min-cut Problem. However, computing the max flow for a given graph G and a source-destination pair takes time $O(|G|^{2.5})$, where $|G|$ denotes the number of nodes in G; even the simplified inverted index can still contain millions of entries, so it can be very expensive. We thus first pre-process graph G in two steps (SCREEN in Section 4.3.1): (1) merging certain v-cliques according to a sufficient (but not necessary) condition for k-robustness and consider them as a whole in pivot linkage; then (2) splitting G into subgraphs according to a necessary (but not sufficient) condition for k-robustness. We find the max flow only on the resulting subgraphs, which are substantially smaller (SPLIT in Section 4.3.2). Section 4.3.3 gives the full algorithm, which iteratively applies SCREEN and SPLIT.

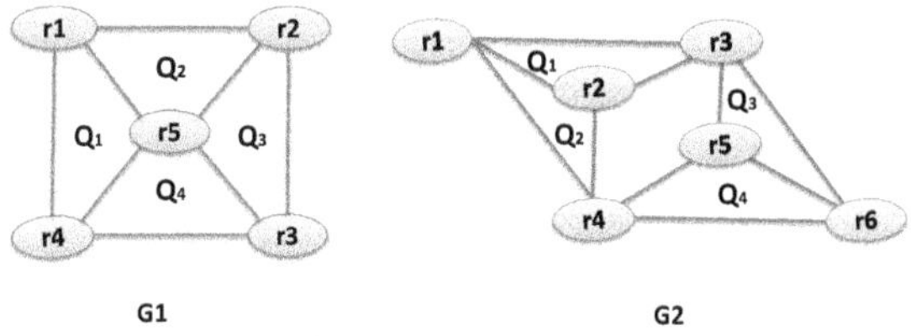

Figure 2: Two example graphs.

4.3.1 Screening

We explain how to reduce the search space for Max-flow by screening. Experiments show that we reduce the input size by 4 orders of magnitude on a real-world data set of 18M records.

A graph can be considered as a union of v-cliques, so essentially we need to decide if a union of v-cliques is k-robust. First, we can prove the following sufficient condition for k-robustness.

THEOREM 4.7 (($k+1$)-CONNECTED CONDITION). *Let G be a graph consisting of a union Q of v-cliques. If for every pair of v-cliques $C, C' \in Q$, there is a path of v-cliques between C and C' and every pair of adjacent v-cliques on the path share at least $k+1$ nodes, graph G is k-robust.* □

Given Theorem 4.7, we define a $(k+1)$-*connected v-union* as a maximal union of v-cliques that satisfies $(k+1)$-connected condition. A $(k+1)$-connected v-union (simplified as v-union) must be k-robust but not vice versa. In Figure 1, subgraph $\{r_1 - r_7\}$ is a 3-connected v-union, because the only two v-cliques, C_1 and C_2, share 3 nodes. Indeed, it is 2-robust. Graph G_1 in Figure 2 is 2-robust but not 3-connected (there are 4 v-cliques, where each pair of adjacent v-cliques share only 1 or 2 nodes). From Theorem 4.7, we have that a $(k+1)$-connected v-union is k-robust and accordingly a k-pivot. Therefore for pivot linkage we consider graph G as a set of v-unions instead of v-cliques.

Next, we present a necessary condition for k-robustness.

THEOREM 4.8 (($k+1$)-OVERLAP CONDITION). *Graph G is k robust only if for every $(k+1)$-connected v-union $Q \in G$, Q shares at least $k+1$ common nodes with the subgraph consisting of the rest of the v-unions.* □

Accordingly, we define a $(k+1)$-*overlap graph* as a graph that satisfies $(k+1)$-overlap condition. A k-robust graph must be a $(k+1)$-overlap graph but not vice versa. In Figure 1, subgraph $\{r_{11} - r_{18}\}$ is not a 2-overlap graph, because there are two 2-connected v-unions, $\{r_{11} - r_{15}\}$ and $\{r_{13}, r_{16} - r_{18}\}$, but they share only one node; indeed, the subgraph is not 1-robust. On the other hand, graph G_2 in Figure 2 satisfies the 3-overlap condition, as it contains four v-unions, $Q_1 - Q_4$, and each v-union shares 3 nodes in total with the others; however, it is not 2-robust (removing r_3 and r_4 disconnects it). According to Theorem 4.8, if graph G is not a $(k+1)$-overlap graph, it cannot be k-robust. Therefore we split G into a set of maximal $(k+1)$-overlap subgraphs, and check k-robustness by Max-flow on each subgraph.

Now the problem is to split G into $(k+1)$-overlap subgraphs. Let G be a graph where a $(k+1)$-connected v-union overlaps with the rest of the v-unions on no more than k nodes. We split G by removing these overlapping nodes. For subgraph $\{r_{11} - r_{18}\}$ in Figure 1, we remove r_{13} and obtain subgraphs $\{r_{11} - r_{12}, r_{14} - r_{15}\}$ and $\{r_{16} - r_{18}\}$ (recall from Example 4.5 that r_{13} cannot belong to any pivot). Note that the result subgraphs may not be $(k+1)$-overlap graphs (*e.g.*, $\{r_{11} - r_{12}, r_{14} - r_{15}\}$ contains two v-unions sharing one node), so we need to further screen them.

We now describe our screening algorithm, SCREEN, which takes a graph G, represented by a set $\mathbf{C}$ of v-cliques and inverted list $\bar{L}$, as input, finds $(k+1)$-connected v-unions in G and meanwhile decides if G is a $(k+1)$-overlap graph. If not, it splits G into subgraphs for further examination.

1. If G contains a single node, output it as a pivot if it represents records belonging only to one v-clique.
2. For each v-clique $C \in \mathbf{C}$, initialize a v-union $Q(C)$. We denote the set of v-unions by $\bar{Q}$, and the common nodes of C and C' by $\bar{B}(C, C')$.
3. For each v-clique $C \in \mathbf{C}$, we merge v-unions as follows.

   (a) For each unprocessed record $r \in C$, for every pair of v-cliques C_1 and C_2 in r's index entry, if they belong to different v-unions, add r to $\bar{B}(C_1, C_2)$.

   (b) For each v-union $Q \neq Q(C)$ where there exist $C_1 \in Q$ and $C_2 \in Q(C)$ such that $|\bar{B}(C_1, C_2)| \geq k+1$, merge Q and $Q(C)$.

   At the end, $\bar{Q}$ contains all $(k+1)$-connected v-unions.
4. For each v-union $Q \in \bar{Q}$, find its border nodes as $\bar{B}(Q) = \cup_{C \in Q, C' \notin Q} \bar{B}(C, C')$. If $|\bar{B}(Q)| \leq k$, split the subgraph it belongs to, denoted by $G(Q)$, into two subgraphs $Q \setminus \bar{B}(Q)$ and $G(Q) \setminus Q$.
5. Return the remaining subgraphs.

PROPOSITION 4.9. *Denote by $|\bar{L}|$ the number of entries in input $\bar{L}$. Let m be the maximum number of blocks a record belongs to, and a be the maximum number of adjacent v-unions a v-union has. Algorithm* SCREEN *finds $(k+1)$-overlap subgraphs in time $O((m^2 + a) \cdot |\bar{L}|)$ and the result is independent of the order in which we examine the v-cliques.* □

Note that m and a are typically very small, so SCREEN is basically linear in the size of the inverted index. For a similar reason as in Theorem 4.6, we further simplify G by keeping for each v-union a representative for all nodes that only belong to it.

EXAMPLE 4.10. *Consider Table 3 as input and $k = 1$. Step 2 creates five v-unions $Q_1 - Q_5$ for the input v-cliques.*

Step 3 starts with v-clique C_1. It has 4 nodes (in the simplified inverted index), among which 3 are shared with C_2. Thus, $\bar{B}(C_1, C_2) = \{r_3 - r_5\}$ and $|\bar{B}(C_1, C_2)| \geq 2$, so we merge Q_1 and Q_2 into $Q_{1/2}$. Examining C_2 reveals no other shared node.

Step 3 then considers v-clique C_3. It has three nodes, among which $r_{12} - r_{13}$ are shared with C_4 and r_{13} is also shared with C_5. Thus, $\bar{B}(C_3, C_4) = \{r_{12} - r_{13}\}$ and $\bar{B}(C_3, C_5) = \{r_{13}\}$. We merge Q_3 and Q_4 into $Q_{3/4}$. Examining C_4 and C_5 reveals no other shared node. We thus obtain three 2-connected v-unions: $\bar{Q} = \{Q_{1/2}, Q_{3/4}, Q_5\}$.

Step 4 then considers each v-union. For $Q_{1/2}$, $\bar{B}(Q_{1/2}) = \emptyset$ and we thus split subgraph $Q_{1/2}$ out and merge all of its nodes to one $r_{1/\dots/7}$. For $Q_{3/4}$, $\bar{B}(Q_{3/4}) = \{r_{13}\}$ so $|\bar{B}(Q_{3/4})| < 2$. We split $Q_{3/4}$ out and obtain $\{r_{11} - r_{12}, r_{14/15}\}$ (r_{13} is excluded). Similar for Q_5 and we obtain $\{r_{16/17/18}\}$. Therefore, we return three subgraphs for further screening. □

4.3.2 Reduction

Each result $(k+1)$-overlap subgraph is typically very small, and as we soon show, in practice the majority of them are already k-robust. Thus, in many cases SCREEN is adequate in finding pivots. For completeness, we next briefly describe SPLIT that *guarantees* k-robustness of the pivots.

Between two nodes a, b in G, consider the paths that do not share any node except a and b. We denote the maximal number of such paths between a and b by $\kappa(a, b)$. According to Menger's Theorem [2], $\kappa(a, b)$ is the minimum number of nodes removing which disconnects a and b. Obviously, G is k-robust if $\kappa(a, b) > k$ for any nodes a, b in G. Note that for two nodes a, b in a $(k+1)$-connected v-union, we have $\kappa(a, b) \geq k+1$. Theorem 4.11 further gives k-robustness condition of G on adjacent v-unions in G.

THEOREM 4.11 (k-ROBUSTNESS CONDITION). *Let G be a similarity graph. Graph G is k-robust if and only if for every pair of adjacent $(k+1)$-connected v-unions Q and Q', there exist two nodes $a \in Q \setminus Q'$ and $b \in Q' \setminus Q$ such that $\kappa(a, b) > k$.* □

Computing $\kappa(a, b)$ is reduced to a Max-flow Problem in [8], for which we apply the well-known Ford & Fulkerson Algorithm [11]. If a graph G is not k-robust, we shall get the set $\bar{S}$ of nodes that separate G, which we call *separator nodes*. Suppose the separator nodes separate G into $\bar{X}$ and $\bar{Y}$ (there can be more subgraphs). We split G into $\bar{X} \cup \bar{S}$ and $\bar{Y} \cup \bar{S}$ for further processing. Note that we need to include $\bar{S}$ in both sub-graphs to maintain the integrity of each v-union. As proved in [21], the separator nodes do not belong to any pivot, so we mark them as "separators" and eventually exclude them from the returned pivots.

Algorithm SPLIT takes a $(k+1)$-overlap subgraph G as input and decides if G is k-robust. If not, it splits G into subgraphs on which we will then re-apply screening.

1. For each pair of adjacent $(k+1)$-connected v-unions $Q, Q' \in G$, find $a \in Q \setminus Q', b \in Q' \setminus Q$. Apply Ford & Fulkerson Algorithm [11] to compute $\kappa(a, b)$.
2. Once we find nodes a, b where $\kappa(a, b) \leq k$, find separator nodes $\bar{S}$ that separate G. Remove $\bar{S}$ and obtain several subgraphs. Add $\bar{S}$ back to each subgraph and mark $\bar{S}$ as "separators". Return the subgraphs for screening.
3. Otherwise, G is k-robust and output it as a k-pivot.

EXAMPLE 4.12. *Consider graph G_1 in Figure 2 and $k = 2$. There are four 3-connected v-unions (actually four v-cliques) and six pairs of adjacent v-unions. For Q_1 and Q_2, we check nodes r_2 and r_4 and find $\kappa(r_2, r_4) = 3$. Similarly we check for every other pair of adjacent v-unions and decide that the graph is 2-robust.*

Now consider graph G_2 and $k = 2$. There are four 3-connected v-unions. When we check $r_1 \in Q_1$ and $r_6 \in Q_3$, we find $\bar{S} = \{r_3, r_4\}$. We then split G_2 into subgraphs $\{r_1 - r_4\}$ and $\{r_3 - r_6\}$, marking r_3 and r_4 as "separators". □

PROPOSITION 4.13. *Let p be the total number of pairs of adjacent v-unions, and g be the number of nodes in the input graph. Algorithm* SPLIT *runs in time $O(pg^{2.5})$.* □

Despite its high complexity, SPLIT is not expensive in practice as g is very small (**Case Study 2**).

4.3.3 Full Algorithm

We now present the full algorithm, PIVOTLINKAGE (Algorithm 1). It first initializes the working queue $\mathbf{Q}$ with only input G (Line 1). Each time it pops a subgraph G' from $\mathbf{Q}$ and invokes SCREEN

Algorithm 1 PIVOTLINKAGE(G, k)

Input: G: Simplified similarity graph, represented by $\mathbf{C}$ and $\bar{L}$.
k: Robustness requirement.
Output: $\bar{C}$ Set of pivots in G.

1: Let $\mathbf{Q} = \{G\}, \bar{C} = \emptyset$;
2: **while** $\mathbf{Q} \neq \emptyset$ **do**
3: Pop G' from $\mathbf{Q}$;
4: Let $\bar{P} =$ SCREEN($G', k, \bar{C}$);
5: **if** $\bar{P} = \{G'\}$ **then**
6: Let $\bar{S} =$ SPLIT($G', k, \bar{C}$);
7: add graphs in $\bar{S}$ to $\mathbf{Q}$;
8: **else**
9: add graphs in $\bar{P}$ to $\mathbf{Q}$;
10: **end if**
11: **end while**

Table 4: Step-by-step pivot linkage in Example 4.15.

Input	Method	Output
G	SCREEN	$G^1 = \{r_{1/.../7}\}, G^2 = \{r_{11}, r_{12}, r_{14/15}\}$, $G^3 = \{r_{16/17/18}\}$
G^1	SCREEN	Pivot $\{r_1 - r_7\}$
G^2	SCREEN	$G^4 = \{r_{11}\}, G^5 = \{r_{14/15}\}$
G^3	SCREEN	Pivot $\{r_{16} - r_{18}\}$
G^4	SCREEN	-
G^5	SCREEN	Pivot $\{r_{14} - r_{15}\}$

(Lines 3-4). If the output of SCREEN is still G' (so G' is a $(k+1)$-overlap subgraph) (Line 5), it invokes SPLIT on G' (Line 6). Subgraphs output by SCREEN and SPLIT are added to the queue for further examination (Lines 7, 9) and identified pivots are added to pivot set $\bar{C}$. It terminates when $\mathbf{Q} = \emptyset$.

THEOREM 4.14. *Let G be the input graph and q be the number of v-unions in G. Define a, p, g, m, and $|\bar{L}|$ as in Propositions 4.9 and 4.13. Algorithm* PIVOTLINKAGE *finds correct pivots of G in time $O(q((m^2 + a)|\bar{L}| + pg^{2.5}))$ and is order independent.* □

EXAMPLE 4.15. *Consider the motivating example, with the input shown in Table 3 and $k = 1$. Table 4 shows the step-by-step pivot linkage process. Originally, $\mathbf{Q} = \{G\}$. After invoking* SCREEN, *we obtain three subgraphs G^1, G^2, and G^3.* SCREEN *outputs G^1 and G^3 as 1-pivots since each contains a single node that represents multiple records. It further splits G^2 into two single-node graphs G^4 and G^5, and outputs the latter as a 1-pivot.* □

Case study 2: On the data set with 18M records, we found 3 pivots in 5.6 minutes. SCREEN was invoked 114K times and took 51 seconds (15%) in total. Except the original graph, an input to SCREEN contains at most 39.3K nodes; for 97% inputs there are fewer than 10 nodes and running SCREEN was very fast. SPLIT was invoked only 41 times; an input contains at most 58 nodes (8 v-unions) and on average 10 nodes (2.7 v-unions). Recall that the simplified inverted index contains 1.5M entries, so SCREEN reduced the size of the input to SPLIT by 4 orders of magnitude. Only 1 input graph to SPLIT did not passed the 3-robustness check.

5. GROUP LINKAGE

The second stage clusters the pivots and the remaining records, which together we call *elements*, into groups. We apply an efficient state-of-the-art hill-climbing algorithm for clustering (details in [21]). Note that in this stage we also consider multi-value attributes that may contain *weak* evidence. Comparing with clustering in traditional entity resolution, we make two changes in element-cluster similarity computation. First, in addition to weighting attributes, we weight *attribute values according to their popularities within a group* such that similarity on primary values (strong evidence) is rewarded more. Second, instead of learning weights for each attribute, we treat all primary-value attributes as a whole so that diverse local values in the same group are penalized less. Experiments in Section 6.2.2 show benefits of the two changes.

Collecting strong evidence: We identify popular values within a cluster as strong evidence. When we maintain the signature for a pivot or a cluster, we keep all values of an attribute and assign a high *weight* to a popular value. Specifically, let $\bar{R}$ be a set of records. Consider value v and let $\bar{R}(v) \subseteq \bar{R}$ denote the records in $\bar{R}$ that contain v. The weight of v is computed by $w(v) = \frac{|\bar{R}(v)|}{|\bar{R}|}$.

EXAMPLE 5.1. *Consider* phone *for pivot $Cr_1 = \{r_1 - r_7\}$ in Table 2. There are 7 business listings in Cr_1, 5 providing* 808 *($r_1 - r_5$), one providing* 101 *(r_6), and one providing* 102 *(r_7). Thus, the weight of* 808 *is $\frac{5}{7} = .71$ and the weight for* 101 *and* 102 *is $\frac{1}{7} = .14$, showing that* 808 *is the primary phone.* □

Allowing diverse values: When we compute the similarity between an element e and a cluster Ch, we consider all primary-value attributes together. To compute primary-value attribute similarity, denoted by $sim_{prm}(e, Ch)$, we reward sharing primary values (values with a high weight) but not penalizing different values, unless there is no shared value. Specifically, if the primary value of e is the same as that of Ch, we consider them having probability p to be in the same group. Since we use weights to measure whether the value is primary and allow slight difference on values, with a value v from e and v' from Ch, the probability becomes $p \cdot w_e(v) \cdot w_{Ch}(v') \cdot s(v, v')$, where $w_e(v)$ measures the weight of v in e, $w_{Ch}(v')$ measures the weight of v' in Ch, and $s(v, v')$ measures the similarity between v and v'.

We compute $sim_{prm}(e, Ch)$ as the probability that they belong to the same group given several shared values.

$$sim_{prm}(e, Ch) = 1 - \prod_{v \in e, v' \in Ch} (1 - p \cdot w_e(v) \cdot w_{Ch}(v') \cdot s(v, v')). \quad (1)$$

When there is no shared primary value, sim_{prm} can be close to 0; once there is one such value, sim_{prm} can be significantly increased, since we typically set a large p.

EXAMPLE 5.2. *Consider element $e = r_8$ and cluster $Ch_1 = \{r_1 - r_7\}$ in Example 1.1, where* phone *and* domain *are primary-value attributes. Assume $p = .9$. Element e and Ch_1 share the primary domain, with weight 1 and $\frac{5}{7} = .71$ respectively, but have different phone numbers (assuming similarity of 0). We compute $sim_{prm}(e, Ch_1) = 1 - (1 - .9 \cdot 1 \cdot .71 \cdot 1) \cdot (1 - 0) \cdot (1 - 0) \cdot (1 - 0) = .639$; essentially, we do not penalize the difference in phone numbers. However if* domain homedepot *appeared only once, so was not a primary value, its weight would be .14 and accordingly $sim_{prm}(e, Ch_1) = .126$, indicating a much lower similarity.*

If we treat phone *and* domain *separately and compute sim_{prm} as average of sim_{ph} and sim_{dm}, we have $sim_{prm}(e, Ch_1) = \frac{0 + .71}{2} = .355$, also indicating a lower similarity.* □

We then learn weights for each attribute (treating primary-value attributes as a whole), and compute element-cluster similarity as a weighted sum of attribute similarities (details in [21]).

6. EXPERIMENTAL EVALUATION

We experiment on two real-world data sets, showing advantages of our algorithm over rule-based or traditional machine-learning methods on accuracy, and high scalability of our techniques.

Table 5: Statistics of the experimental data sets.

	#Records	#Groups (size > 1)	Group size	#Singletons (size = 1)	Level of distinction
BizLow	2446	1	2446	0	low
BizAvg	2062	30	[2, 308]	503	average
BizHigh	1149	14	[33, 269]	0	high
SIGMOD	590	71	[2, 41]	162	average

6.1 Experiment Settings

Data and gold standard: We experimented on two real-world data sets. *Biz* contains 18M US business listings and each listing has attributes name, phone, URL, location and category; we decide which listings belong to the same business chain. In lieu of using a social network data set with user privacy issues, we use *SIGMOD*, which contains records of about 590 attendees of SIGMOD'98 and each record has attributes name, affiliation, address, phone, fax and email; we decide which attendees belong to the same institute.

We experimented on the whole *Biz* data set to study scalability of our techniques. We evaluated accuracy of our techniques on four sets of data with different properties (seen in Table 5). The first three are from *Biz*. (1) *BizLow* contains 2446 listings for the same business chain *Allstate Insurance*. These listings have the same name, but 1499 provide URL *"allstate.com"*, 854 provide another URL *"allstateagencies.com"*, while 130 provide both, and 227 listings do not provide any value for phone or URL. (2) *BizAvg* contains 2062 listings from *Biz*, where 1559 belong to 30 randomly selected business chains, and 503 do not belong to any chain; among the 503 listings, 86 are highly similar in name to listings in the business chains and the rest are randomly selected. (3) *BizHigh data set* contains 1149 listings with similar names and highly similar category values; they belong to 14 different chains. Among the listings, 708 provide the same wrong name *Texas Farm Bureau Insurance* and meanwhile provide a wrong *URL farmbureauinsurance-mi.com*. Among these three subsets, the latter two are hard cases; for each data set, we manually verified all the chains by checking store locations provided by the business-chain websites and used it as the gold standard. The last is the whole *SIGMOD* data set. It has very few wrong values, but the same affiliation can be represented in various ways and some affiliation names can be very similar (e.g., *UCSC* vs. *UCSD*). We manually identified 71 institutes with multiple attendees and 162 attendees who do not belong to any of these institutes.

Measure: We considered each group as a cluster and compared pairwise linking decisions with the gold standard. We measured the quality of the results by *precision* (P), *recall* (R), and *F-measure* (F). If we denote the set of true-positive pairs by TP, the set of false-positive pairs by FP, and the set of false-negative pairs by FN, then, $P = \frac{|TP|}{|TP|+|FP|}$, $R = \frac{|TP|}{|TP|+|FN|}$, $F = \frac{2PR}{P+R}$. We also reported execution time.

Implementation: We implemented the technique we proposed in this paper, and call it GROUP. Before applying GROUP, we merge records that share highly similar values on pre-selected attributes (i.e., name, city and address for *biz*). In pivot generation, by default we considered two records are similar for *Biz* if (1) their name similarity is above .95; and (2) they share at least one phone or URL domain name. For *SIGMOD* we require (1) affiliation similarity is above .95; and (2) they share at least one of phone prefix (3-digit), fax prefix (3-digit), or email server. We required 2-robustness for pivots. In clustering, (1) for blocking, we put records whose name similarity is above .8 in the same block; (2) for similarity computation, we computed string similarity by Jaro-Winkler distance [5], we set $p = .8$, and we learned attribute weights from 1000 records randomly selected from *BizAvg* data for *Biz*, and 300 records randomly selected from *SIGMOD*.

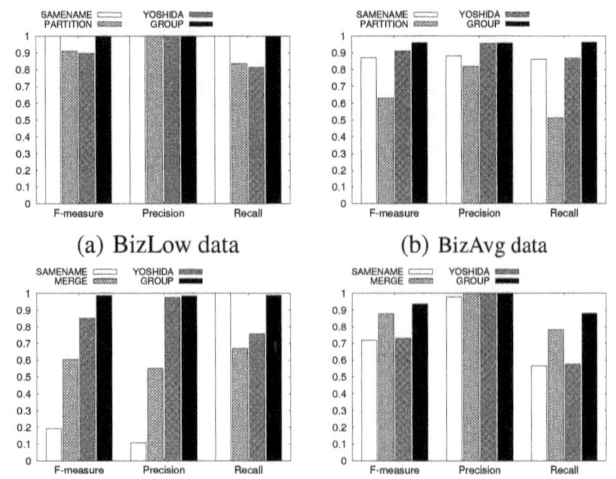

(a) BizLow data (b) BizAvg data

(c) Perturbed BizHigh data (d) SIGMOD data

Figure 3: Overall results on *Biz* and *SIGMOD* data sets.

For comparison, we implemented the following baselines:

- SAMENAME groups *Biz* records with highly similar names and groups *SIGMOD* records with highly similar affiliations (similarity above .95);
- Traditional machine-learning methods include PARTITION, CENTER and MERGE [15]; each computes record similarity as wighted sum of attribute similarities with learnt attribute weights, and applies a state-of-the-art clustering algorithm.
- Two-stage method YOSHIDA [28] generates pivots by agglomerative clustering with threshold .9 in the first stage, uses TF/IDF weights for features and applies linear algebra to cluster records in the second stage.

We implemented the algorithms in Java. We used a Linux machine with Intel Xeon X5550 processor (2.66GHz, cache 8MB, 6.4GT/s QPI) and 8GB main memory. We used MySQL to store the data and stored the index as a database table. Note that after blocking, we can fit each block of nodes or elements in memory, which is typically the case with a good blocking strategy.

6.2 Evaluating Effectiveness

We first evaluate effectiveness of our algorithms. Figure 3 compares GROUP with the baseline methods, where for the three traditional linkage methods we plot only the best results. On *BizHigh*, all methods put all records in the same chain because a large number (708) of listings have both a wrong name and a wrong URL. We manually perturbed the data as follows: (1) among the 708 listings with wrong URLs, 408 provide a single (wrong) URL and we fixed it; (2) for all records we set name to *"Farm Bureau Insurance"*, so removed hints from business names. Even after perturbing, this data set remains the hardest and we use it hereafter instead of the original one for other experiments.

We observe that (1) GROUP obtains the highest F-measure (above .9) on each data set. It has the highest precision most of the time as it applies pivot identification and leverages the strong evidence collected from resulting pivots. It also has a very high recall (mostly above .95) on each subset because the clustering phase is tolerant to diversity of values within chains. (2) The F-measure of SAMENAME is up to 80% lower than GROUP. It can have false positives when listings of highly similar names belong to different chains and can also have false negatives when some listings in a chain have fairly different names from other listings. It only performs well in the *easiest dataset BizLow*, where it happens that all listings have the same name and belong to the same chain. (3) The

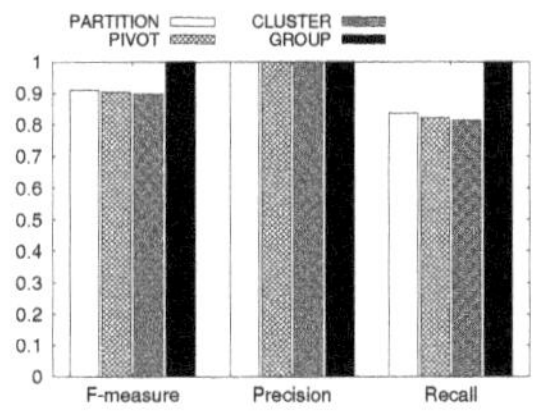

(a) BizLow data

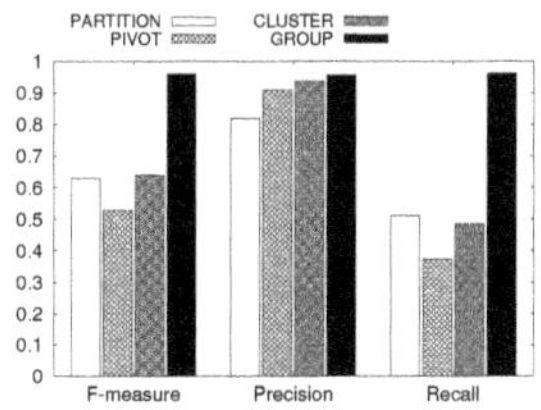

(b) BizAvg data

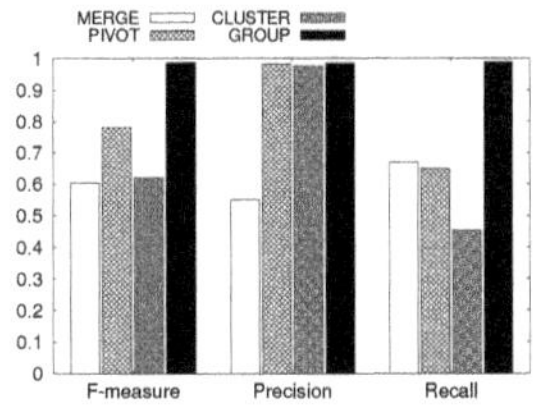

(c) Perturbed BizHigh data

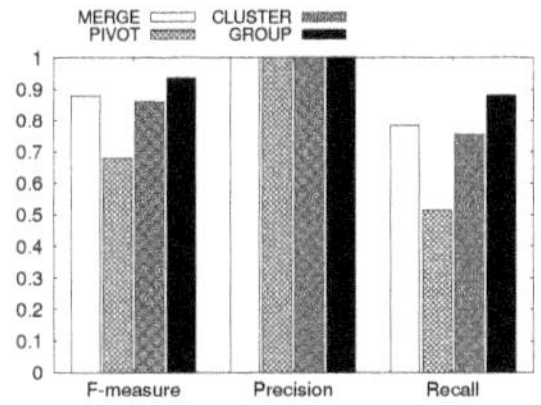

(d) SIGMOD data

Figure 4: Contribution of components on *Biz* and *SIGMOD*.

highest F-measure of traditional linkage methods can be 16-41% lower than SAMENAME. It requires higher similarity than sharing name values. As a result, it has a lower recall than SAMENAME. (4) YOSHIDA has comparable precision to GROUP since its first stage is conservative too, which makes it often improve over the best of traditional linkage methods on *Biz* dataset where reducing false positives is a big challenge; on the other hand, its first stage is often too conservative (requiring high record similarity) so the recall is 10-35% lower than GROUP, which also makes it perform worse than traditional linkage methods on *SIGMOD* dataset where reducing false negatives is challenging.

Contribution of different components: We compared GROUP with (1) PIVOT, which conducts only pivot identification, and (2) CLUSTER, which considers each individual record as a pivot (in the spirit of [19, 26]) and conducts only clustering. Figure 4 shows the results. First, we observe that PIVOT improves over traditional linkage methods on precision by up to 79% but has a lower recall (up to 34% lower) most of the time, because it sets a high requirement for merging records into groups. Note however that its goal is indeed to obtain a high precision such that the strong evidence collected from the pivots are trustworthy for the clustering phase. Second, CLUSTER often has higher precision (by up to 77%) but lower recall (by up to 32%) than the best traditional linkage methods; their F-measures are comparable on each data set. On *BizAvg* it can obtain an even higher precision than PIVOT, because PIVOT can make mistakes when too many records have erroneous values, but CLUSTER may avoid some of these mistakes by considering also weak evidence for similarity. However, applying clustering on the results of CLUSTER would not change the results, but applying clustering on the results of PIVOT can obtain a much higher F-measure, especially a higher recall (98% higher than CLUSTER on *BizAvg*). This is because the result of CLUSTER lacks the strong evidence collected from high-quality pivots so the final results would be less tolerant to diversity of values, showing the importance of pivot identification. Finally, we observe that GROUP obtains the best results in most of the data sets.

We next evaluate various choices in the two stages. Unless specified otherwise, we observed similar patterns on all data sets, and report the results on *BizAvg* or perturbed *BizHigh* data, whichever has more distinguishable results.

6.2.1 Pivot Identification

Pivot generation: We first compared three pivot-generation strategies: PIVOT iteratively invokes SCREEN and SPLIT, ONLYSCREEN only iteratively invokes SCREEN, and YOSHIDAI generates pivots by agglomerative clustering [28]. Recall that by default we apply PIVOT. Figure 5 compares them on the perturbed *BizHigh* data. First, we observe similar results of ONLYSCREEN and PIVOT on all data sets since most inputs to SPLIT pass the k-robustness test. Thus, although SCREEN in itself cannot guarantee soundness of the resulting pivots, it already does well in practice. Second, YOSHIDAI has lower recall in both pivot and clustering results, since it has stricter criteria in pivot generation.

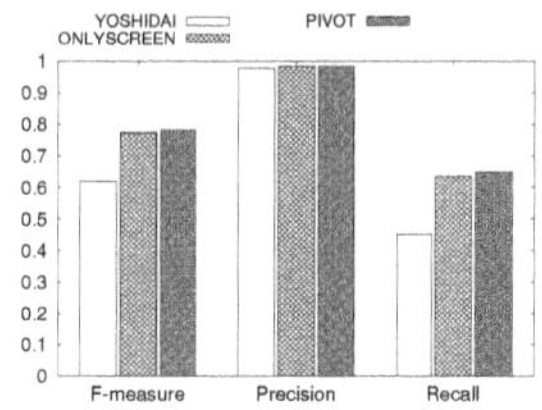

(a) Pivot quality.

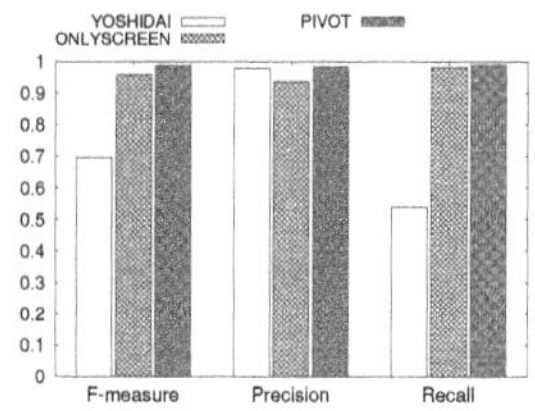

(b) Chain quality.

Figure 5: Pivot identification on perturbed *BizHigh* data.

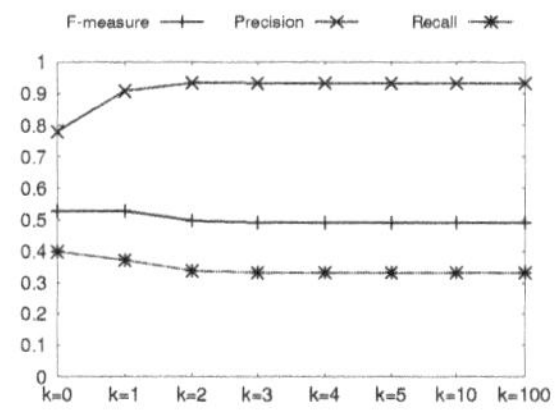

(a) Pivot quality.

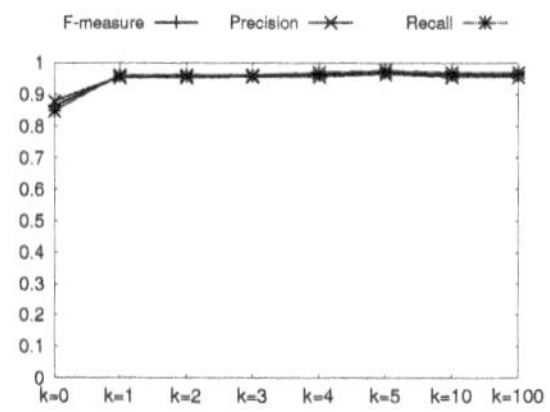

(b) Chain quality.

Figure 6: Effect of robustness requirement on *BizAvg* data.

Robustness requirement: We next studied how the robustness requirement can affect the results (Figure 6). We have three observations. (1) When $k = 0$, we essentially take every connected subgraph as a pivot, so the generated pivots can have a much lower precision; those false positives cause both a low precision and a low recall for the resulting chains because we do not collect high-quality strong evidence. (2) When we vary k from 1 to 4, the number of false positives decreases while that of false negatives increases for the pivots (Figure 6(a)), and the F-measure of the chains in Figure 6(b) increases but only very slightly. (3) When we continue increasing k, the results of pivots and clusters remain stable. This is because setting k=4 already splits the graph into single v-cliques, so further increasing k would not change the pivots. This shows that considering k-robustness is important, but k does not need to be too high.

Graph generation: We compared three edge-adding strategies for similarity graphs: SIM takes weighted similarity on each attribute except location and requires a similarity of over .8; TWODOM requires sharing name and at least two values on primary-value attributes; ONEDOM requires sharing name and one value on primary-value attributes. Recall that by default we applied ONEDOM. We observe that (1) SIM requires similar records so has a high precision, with a big sacrifice on recall for the pivots (0.00025); as a result, the F-measure of the chains is very low (.59); (2) TWODOM has the strongest requirements and so has even lower recall than SIM for the pivots (.00002), and in turn it has the lowest F-measure for the chains (.52). This shows that only requiring high precision for pivots with big sacrifice on recall can also lead to low F-measure for the chains.

6.2.2 Clustering

Clustering strategy: We first compared our clustering algorithm with two algorithms proposed for the second stage of two-stage clustering: LIUII [22] iteratively applies majority voting to assign each record to a cluster and collects a set of representative features

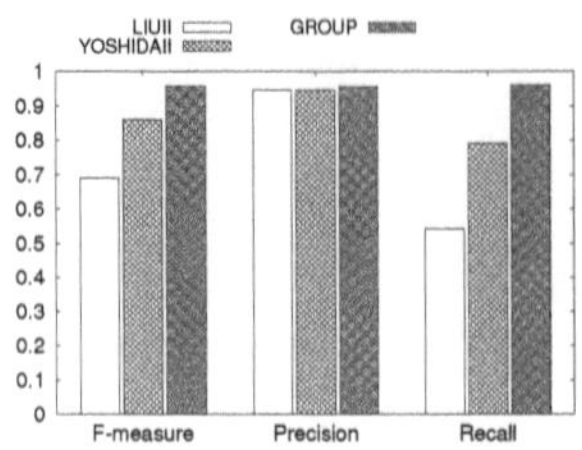

Figure 7: Clustering strategies on *BizAvg* data.

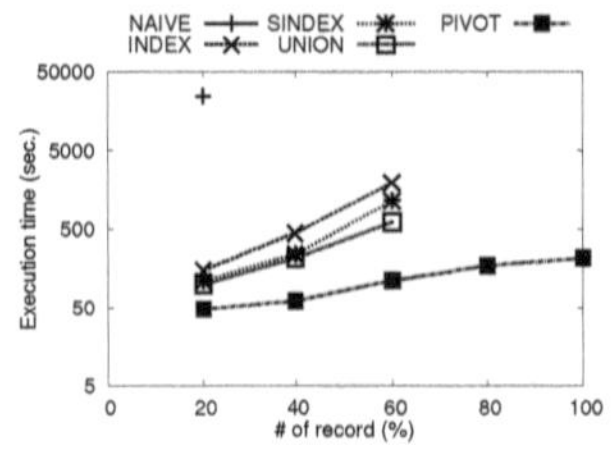

Figure 8: Execution time of pivot generation(we plot only those below 10 hours).

for each cluster using a threshold (we set it to 5, which leads to the best results); YOSHIDAII [28] is the second stage of YOSHIDA. Figure 7 compares their results. We observe that our clustering method improves the recall by 39% over LIUII and by 11% over YOSHIDAII. LIUII may filter strong evidence by the threshold; YOSHIDAII cannot handle records with null values well.

Value weight: We then compared the results with and without setting popularity weights for values. We observe that setting the popularity weight helps distinguish primary values from unpopular values, thus can improve the precision. Indeed, on perturbed *BizHigh* data it improves the precision from .11 to .98, and improves the F-measure by 403%.

Attribute weight: We next considered our attribute weight learning strategy. We first compared SEPARATEDPRIMARY, which learns separated weights for different primary-value attributes, and UNITEDPRIMARY (our default), which considers all such attributes as a whole and learns one single weight for them. On *BizAvg* the latter improves over the former by 95% on recall and obtains slightly higher precision, because it penalizes only if neither phone nor URL is shared and so is more tolerant to different values for primary-value attributes.

Robustness w.r.t. parameter p: We also ran experiments to test robustness against parameter setting. We observed very similar results when we ranged p from .8 to 1.

6.2.3 *Preprocessing*

Attribute categorization: We studied attribute categorization on both data sets. For *Biz* we used a labeled data set of 2062 records and identified name as a common-value attribute ($m = .94, s = .85, n = .001$); for *SIGMOD* we used a labeled data set of 369 records and identified affiliation as a common-value attribute ($m = .77, s = .85, n = 0$).

Then for *Biz* we used a set of randomly selected 166, 236 records and for *SIGMOD* we used all records. We considered only groups of size above 10; we averaged m, s, n among top 1% values for *Biz* and among all values for *SIGMOD*. For *Biz* data, we identify URL domain and phone as primary-value attributes, and state and category as multi-value attributes. For *SIGMOD* data, we identify phone-prefix, fax-prefix and email-domain as primary-value attributes, and state as a multi-value attribute.

Entity resolution vs group linkage: We studied the interaction between entity resolution and group linkage on *BizAvg*. We compared three strategies: NO-ER does not conduct entity resolution; PRE-ER (the default) conducts entity resolution before group linkage; FULL-ER first conducts entity resolution (merging records with highly similar name, address, city and the same phone or URL domain), then conducts group linkage, while removing duplicates within pivots or groups if they have highly similar address and city. We have three observations. First, the three approaches obtain similar results (F-measure all above .95). Second, applying entity resolution slightly improves group linkage (F-measure from .9639 to .9643). Third, among the 2062 records in *BizAvg*, PRE-ER identifies 21 pairs of duplicates while FULL-ER identifies 59 pairs, showing that group linkage can improve entity resolution too.

6.3 Evaluating Efficiency

Our algorithm finished in 8.3 hours on *Biz* data set with 18M listings on a single machine. Note that simpler methods (which we describe shortly) took over 10 hours for Stage I on 20% of the same data set. Also note that using Hadoop can reduce execution time for graph construction from 1.9 hours to 37 minutes.

Stage I: It spent 1.9 hours for graph construction and 2.2 minutes for pivot generation. To test scalability, we randomly divided the data set into five subsets of the same size; we started with one subset and gradually added the others. We compared five pivot generation methods: NAIVE applies SPLIT on the original graph; INDEX optimizes NAIVE by using an inverted index; SINDEX simplifies the inverted list by Theorem 4.6; UNION in addition merges v-cliques into v-unions by Theorem 4.7; PIVOT in addition splits the input graph by Theorem 4.8. Figure 8 shows the results and we have five observations. (1) NAIVE was very slow. Even though it applies SPLIT rather than finding the max flow for every pair of nodes, so already optimizes by Theorem 4.11, it took 6.8 hours on only 20% data and took more than 10 hours on 40% data. (2) INDEX improved NAIVE by two orders of magnitude just because the index simplifies finding neighborhood v-cliques; however, it still took more than 10 hours on 80% data. (3) SINDEX improved INDEX by 41% on 60% data as it reduces the size of the inverted index by 64%. (4) UNION improved SINDEX by 47% on 60% data; however, it also took more than 10 hours on 80% data. (5) PIVOT improved UNION significantly; it finished in 2.2 minutes on the whole data set so further reduced execution time by at least three orders of magnitude, showing importance of splitting.

Stage II: After Stage I we have .7M pivots and 17.3M remaining records. It spent 6.4 hours for Stage II: 1.7 hours for blocking and 4.7 hours for clustering. The long time for clustering is because of the huge number of blocks. There are 1.4M blocks with multiple elements (a pivot is counted as one element), with a maximum size of 22.5K and an average of 4.2. On only 35 blocks clustering took more than 1 minute and the maximum is 2.5 minutes, but for 99.6% blocks the size is less than 100 and CLUSTER took less than 60 ms. The average time spent on each block is only 9.6 ms.

6.4 Summary and Recommendations

We summarize our observations as follows.

1. Identifying pivots and leveraging strong evidence learned from the pivots is crucial in group linkage.
2. There are often erroneous values in real-world data and it is important to be robust against them; requiring k-robustness with $k \in [1, 4]$ already performs well on most data sets that have reasonable number of errors.
3. Setting weights of values according to their popularity is critical for obtaining good clustering results.
4. Our algorithm is efficient and scalable.

7. CONCLUSIONS

In this paper we studied how to link records to identify groups. We proposed a robust algorithm that is shown to be empirically scalable and accurate over two real-world data sets. Future work includes extending our techniques to find overlapping groups, and applying our framework in other contexts where tolerance to value diversity is critical, and erroneous data is prevalent.

8. REFERENCES

[1] N. Bansal, F. Chiang, N. Koudas, and F. W. Tompa. Seeking stable clusters in the blogosphere. In *VLDB*, pages 806–817, 2007.

[2] H. Bruhn, R. Diestel, and M. Stein. Menger's theorem for infinite graphs with ends. *J. Graph Theory*, 50:199–211, November 2005.

[3] C. Chambers, A. Raniwala, F. Perry, S. Adams, R. R. Henry, R. Bradshaw, and N. Weizenbaum. Flumejava: easy, efficient data-parallel pipelines. In *PLDI*, pages 363–375, 2010.

[4] Y.-H. Chiang, A. Doan, and J. F. Naughton. Tracking entities in the dynamic world: A fast algorithm for matching temporal records. *PVLDB*, 7(6):469–480, 2014.

[5] W. W. Cohen, P. Ravikumar, and S. E. Fienberg. A comparison of string distance metrics for name-matching tasks. In *IIWEB*, pages 73–78, 2003.

[6] D. Dey. Entity matching in heterogeneous databases: A logistic regression approach. *Decis. Support Syst.*, 44:740–747, 2008.

[7] A. K. Elmagarmid, P. G. Ipeirotis, and V. S. Verykios. Duplicate record detection: A survey. *IEEE Trans. Knowl. Data Eng.*, 19(1):1–16, 2007.

[8] S. Even and E. R. Tarjan. Network flow and testing graph connectivity. *SIAM Journal on Computing*, 4(4):507–518, 1975.

[9] W. Fan, X. Jia, J. Li, and S. Ma. Reasoning about record matching rules. *PVLDB*, 2(1):407–418, 2009.

[10] I. P. Fellegi and A. B. Sunter. A theory for record linkage. *Journal of the Americal Statistical Association*, 64(328):1183–1210, 1969.

[11] L. R. Ford and D. R. Fulkerson. *Flows in networks*. Princeton University Press, 1962.

[12] L. Getoor and C. P. Diehl. Link mining: A survey. *SIGKDD Explor. Newsl.*, 7(2):3–12, 2005.

[13] L. Getoor and A. Machanavajjhala. Entity resolution: Theory, practice & open challenges. *PVLDB*, 5(12):2018–2019, 2012.

[14] S. Guo, X. Dong, D. Srivastava, and R. Zajac. Record linkage with uniqueness constraints and erroneous values. *PVLDB*, 3(1):417–428, 2010.

[15] O. Hassanzadeh, F. Chiang, H. C. Lee, and R. J. Miller. Framework for evaluating clustering algorithms in duplicate detection. *PVLDB*, pages 1282–1293, 2009.

[16] M. A. Hernandez and S. J. Stolfo. Real-world data is dirty: Data cleansing and the merge/purge problem. *Data Mining and Knowledge Discovery*, 2:9–37, 1998.

[17] S. Huang. Mixed group discovery: Incorporating group linkage with alternatively consistent social network analysis. *International Conference on Semantic Computing*, 0:369–376, 2010.

[18] N. Koudas, S. Sarawagi, and D. Srivastava. Record linkage: similarity measures and algorithms. In *SIGMOD*, pages 802–803, 2006.

[19] B. Larsen and C. Aone. Fast and effective text mining using linear-time document clustering. In *KDD*, pages 16–22, 1999.

[20] P. Li, X. L. Dong, A. Maurino, and D. Srivastava. Linking temporal records. *PVLDB*, 4(11):956–967, 2011.

[21] P. Li, X. Luna Dong, S. Guo, A. Maurino, and D. Srivastava. Robust Group Linkage. http://arxiv.org/abs/1503.00604, Mar. 2015.

[22] X. Liu, Y. Gong, W. Xu, and S. Zhu. Document clustering with cluster refinement and model selection capabilities. In *SIGIR*, pages 191–198, 2002.

[23] B. W. On, N. Koudas, D. Lee, and D. Srivastava. Group linkage. In *ICDE*, pages 496–505, 2007.

[24] B. Taskar, M. fai Wong, P. Abbeel, and D. Koller. Link prediction in relational data. In *Advances in Neural Information Processing Systems*, 2003.

[25] S. E. Whang, D. Menestrina, G. Koutrika, M. Theobald, and H. Garcia-Molina. Entity resolution with iterative blocking. In *SIGMOD*, pages 219–232, 2009.

[26] D. T. Wijaya and S. Bressan. Ricochet: A family of unconstrained algorithms for graph clustering. In *DASFAA*, pages 153–167, 2009.

[27] W. E. Winkler. Methods for record linkage and bayesian networks. Technical report, U.S. Bureau of the Census, 2002.

[28] M. Yoshida, M. Ikeda, S. Ono, I. Sato, and H. Nakagawa. Person name disambiguation by bootstrapping. In *SIGIR*, pages 10–17, 2010.

Uncovering the Small Community Structure in Large Networks: A Local Spectral Approach

Yixuan Li
Cornell Unversity
yli@cs.cornell.edu

Kun He *
Huazhong University of Science and Technology
brooklet60@hust.edu.cn

David Bindel
Cornell University
bindel@cs.cornell.edu

John E. Hopcroft
Cornell University
jeh@cs.cornell.edu

ABSTRACT

Large graphs arise in a number of contexts and understanding their structure and extracting information from them is an important research area. Early algorithms on mining communities have focused on the global structure, and often run in time functional to the size of the entire graph. Nowadays, as we often explore networks with billions of vertices and find communities of size hundreds, it is crucial to shift our attention from macroscopic structure to microscopic structure when dealing with large networks. A growing body of work has been adopting local expansion methods in order to identify the community from a few exemplary seed members.

In this paper, we propose a novel approach for finding overlapping communities called *LEMON* (Local Expansion via Minimum One Norm). Different from PageRank-like diffusion methods, *LEMON* finds the community by seeking a sparse vector in the span of the local spectra such that the seeds are in its support. We show that *LEMON* can achieve the highest detection accuracy among state-of-the-art proposals. The running time depends on the size of the community rather than that of the entire graph. The algorithm is easy to implement, and is highly parallelizable.

Moreover, given that networks are not all similar in nature, a comprehensive analysis on how the local expansion approach is suited for uncovering communities in different networks is still lacking. We thoroughly evaluate our approach using both synthetic and real-world datasets across different domains, and analyze the empirical variations when applying our method to inherently different networks in practice. In addition, the heuristics on how the quality and quantity of the seed set would affect the performance are provided.

*Corresponding author.

WWW 2015, May 18–22, 2015, Florence, Italy.
ACM 978-1-4503-3469-3/15/05.
http://dx.doi.org/10.1145/2736277.2741676.

Categories and Subject Descriptors

H.3.3 [**Information Storage and Retrieval**]: Information Search and Retrieval - Clustering; G.2.2 [**Discrete Mathematics**]: Graph Theory - Graph Algorithms

General Terms

Algorithms

Keywords

Community detection; Local spectral clustering; Seed set expansion; Random walk; Minimum one norm

1. INTRODUCTION

Analyzing the structure and extracting information from complex networks is an important research area. Significant research has been carried out in finding the structure of networks and identifying communities [10].

In early work, researchers assumed that communities were disjoint and had more internal connections than external connections. Both assumptions have been discarded since it is clear that in most networks a vertex belongs to more than one community. For instance, in social networks, one might belong to a work community, a community of friends, and a community of individuals that share the same hobby such as golf; in co-purchased networks, one item might belong to multiple categories. Also since we are dealing with networks with hundreds of millions of vertices, an individual in a community of size 100[1] will certainly have more links outside the community than inside. These key insights have motivated researchers to identify communities from a new perspective.

Considerable researches on detecting communities have focused on the global structure. And these globally based detection algorithms usually run in time functional to the size of the entire graph, a major drawback in computational cost. Nowadays, we explore networks with billions of vertices to find communities of size a hundred. Thus, taking the entire graph into account might not serve as a practical solution in many situations. It is crucial to shift our attention from

[1]A statistical study on social networks done by Leskovec *et al.* [17] has shown that real-world communities with high quality are quite small and usually consist of no more than 100 vertices.

macroscopic structure to microscopic structure when dealing with large networks, and develop new approaches that enable finding communities in time functional to the size of the community.

Quite recently, there has been a growing interest in finding communities by locally expanding an exemplary seed set in the community of interest [6][14][25][27]. This type of algorithm usually starts with a few members that are already known to be in the target community, and the goal is to uncover the remaining members in the same community as the exemplary members. These known members are usually referred to as *seeds* in the literature, and the process of gradually growing the seed set into a larger set until the target community is revealed is called *seed set expansion*. The setting of seed set expansion can be widely applied to many real world applications. For example, in web search, with a few known pages that share similar information, we could generate a larger group of web pages that contain the relevant contents with respect to a certain search query; in product networks, seed set expansion enables the automatic categorization of products that are discovered to be in the same community as the labeled items.

The random walk technique has been extensively adopted as a subroutine for locally growing the seed set in the literature [6][12][14][21][23][25][27]. The dynamics of random walks are effective in finding a local community since they make non-uniform expansion decisions based on the structure revealed during the exploration of the neighborhood surrounding the seeds [6]. This implies that random walk based local expansion is able to trace the community members in a principled way that resembles the natural process of forming the local community structure. Very recently, Abrahao *et al.* [3] also experimentally verified that random walk produces communities that are most structurally similar to real-world communities amongst various algorithmic communities.

In this paper we propose a novel approach for finding overlapping communities called *LEMON* (Local Expansion via Minimum One Norm)[2] for finding overlapping communities in large networks. We systematically demonstrate that *LEMON* can achieve both high efficiency and effectiveness that significantly stand out amongst state-of-the-art proposals. Specifically, we consider the span of a few dimensions of vectors after the short random walk and use it as the approximate invariant subspace, which we refer as *local spectra*. What makes LEMON distinct from previous PageRank-like diffusion methods is by utilizing the subspace rather than a single probability vector. In contrast to the traditional spectral clustering methods, the local spectral method does not require the burdensome computation of a large number of singular vectors. In addition, as traditional spectral methods usually partition the vertices into disjoint communities, we make another fundamental change. Concretely, we mine the communities from the subspace by seeking a sparse approximate indicator vector in the span of the local spectral such that the seeds are in its support. In practice, this can be mathematically achieved by solving an ℓ^1-penalized linear programming problem.

We aim to develop a comprehensive understanding of the local spectral approach for identifying a community from a small seed set. Following the central idea of our approach, we seek to solve fundamentally important questions such as: what defines "good" communities and when do they emerge as we expand the seed set (Section 4.4)? How to find a small community in time functional to the size of the community rather than that of the entire graph (Section 4.3)? What defines "good" seeds and how many seeds could uniquely define a community (Section 5)? And given that networks are not all similar in nature, how the local expansion approach is suited for uncovering communities in different types of networks (Section 6.4)?

We thoroughly evaluate our approach using both synthetic and real-world datasets across different domains, and analyze the empirical variations when applying our method to inherently different networks in practice. We believe that the insights we gained from researching on these problems would provide valuable guidance for future investigation on this topic.

[2]Our demo code is publicly available at: `https://github.com/yixuanli/lemon`.

2. RELATED WORK

A considerable amount of literature has been published on finding communities in large social and information networks. We highlight a few ideas that have recently emerged in the literature to clarify how our method differs.

Globally based community finding algorithms. Various community detection algorithms have been developed in the past decade. And most of the algorithms fall into the category of global approach. One stream of global algorithms attempt to find communities by optimizing an objective function. For example, OSLOM [16] is based on the optimization of a fitness function, which expresses the statistical significance of clusters with respect to random fluctuations (i.e., the random graph generated by the configuration model [19] during community expansion). However, the communities identified by mathematical construction may structurally diverge from real communities as pointed out in [3]. Another main stream of research adopts the label propagation approach [22], which defines rules that simulate the spread of labels of vertices in the network. The DEMON algorithm [9], for example, democratically lets each vertex vote for the communities it sees surrounding it in its limited view of the global system using a label propagation algorithm, and then merges the local communities into a global collection. Other approaches such as Link Community (LC) [4] partitions the graph by first building a hierarchical link dendrogram according to the link similarity and then cutting the dendrogram at some threshold to yield link communities.

Random walk based detection algorithms. As noted in the preceding section, among the divergent approaches, random walks tend to reveal communities that bear the closest resemblance to the ground truth communities [3]. In the following, we briefly review some methods that have adopted the random walk technique in finding communities. Speaking of methods that focus on the global structure, Pons *et al.* [21] proposed a hierarchical agglomerative algorithm, *WalkTrap*, that quantified the similarity between vertices using random walks and then partitioned the network into non-overlapping communities. Meilă *et al.* [18] presented a clustering approach by viewing the pairwise similarities as edge flows in a random walk and studied the eigenvectors and values of the resulting transition matrix. A later successful algorithm, *Infomap*, proposed by Rosvall & Bergstrom [23] enabled uncovering hierarchical structures in networks by compressing a description of a random walker as a proxy for

Domain	Dataset	Vertices	Links	Average membership	Maximum membership	Community size mean
Product	Amazon	334,863	925,872	0.11	49	39
Collaboration	DBLP	317,080	1,049,866	0.22	11	251
Social	YouTube	1,134,890	2,987,624	0.05	41	79
Social	Orkut	3,072,441	117,185,083	9.56	504	83

Table 1: Statistics for the real networks.

real flow on networks. Variant of this technique such as biased random walk [28] has also been employed in community finding.

Seed set expansion based approaches. To interpret the problem of community detection from a local perspective, our work is in the same spirit as the seed set expansion algorithms in [6], [7], [11], [13], [14] and [25]. Specifically, Andersen & Lang [6] adapted the theoretical results from [24] to expand a set into a community with locally minimal conductance based on lazy random walks. However, the lazy random walk endured a much slower mixing speed and usually took more than 500 hundred steps before converging to a local structure, which is inefficient compared with several steps of rapid mixing in a regular random walk. Featuring on the seeding strategies, Whang *et al.* [25] established several sophisticated methods for choosing the seed set, and then used similar PageRank scheme as that in [5] to expand the seeds until a community with the optimal conductance is found. Nonetheless, the performance gained by adopting these intricate seeding methods was not significantly better than that by using random seeds. This implies that a better scheme of expanding the seeds is also needed aside from a good seeding strategy. A recent work by Kloumann & Kleinberg [14] provided a systematic understanding of variants of PageRank-based seed set expansions. They showed many insightful findings regarding the heuristics on seed set. However, the drawback of lacking a proper stop criterion has limited its functionality in practice. Even though a recently proposed heat kernel algorithm [13] advances PageRank by introducing a sophisticated diffusion method, the detection accuracy achieved by heat kernel approach is still much lower than that of *LEMON*, which is shown in Section 6.2.

3. PRELIMINARIES

3.1 Problem Statement

Given a network $G = (V, E)$ and a set of members $\mathcal{S}$ in the target community $\mathcal{C}$, where $|\mathcal{C}| \ll |V|$ and $|\mathcal{S}| \ll |\mathcal{C}|$, we are interested in discovering the remaining members in $\mathcal{C}$. Generally speaking, we focus on addressing the question of **how to accurately find a small community in time functional to the size of the community from a seed set?**

3.2 Datasets

3.2.1 Synthetic datasets

The LFR benchmark graphs [15] have been widely adopted for the purpose of evaluating the performance of community detection algorithms. LFR datasets are generated with built-in community structure that resembles the features found in most real-world networks with power-law degree distribution [8]. It provides researchers with rich flexibility to control the network topology through tuning different parameters, including the graph size n, the average degree $\bar{k}$, the maximum degree k_{max}, the minimum and maximum community size $|\mathcal{C}|_{min}$ and $|\mathcal{C}|_{max}$, the mixing parameter μ, the overlapping membership om and the number of vertices with overlapping membership on. Among these parameters, the mixing parameter μ has the most significant impact on the network topology, which controls the fraction of links for each vertex that cross to a community with which the vertex is not associated. Usually, larger μ would result in lower detection accuracy.

Xie et al. [26] have performed a thorough performance comparison of different state-of-the-art overlapping community detection algorithms on LFR benchmark datasets. To make the performance evaluation of our algorithm consistent with that in [26], we adopt the same parameters in our paper. In total, we generate two sets of networks with mixing parameter $\mu = 0.1$ and $\mu = 0.3$ respectively. We vary the parameter om from 2 to 8 for each μ and obtain a total of 14 networks. Table 2 lists the value of the parameters we have used for generating the LFR datasets.

Parameter	Description	Value
n	graph size	5000
μ	mixing parameter	{0.1, 0.3}
$\bar{k}$	average degree	10
k_{max}	maximum degree	50
$\|\mathcal{C}\|_{min}$	minimum community size	20
$\|\mathcal{C}\|_{max}$	maximum community size	100
τ_1	node degree distribution exp.	2
τ_2	community size distribution exp.	1
om	overlapping membership	{2, 3, ..., 8}
on	overlapping node	2500

Table 2: Parameters for the LFR datasets.

3.2.2 Real datasets

For the purpose of testing on real networks, we include four datasets with ground truth community membership from Stanford Network Analysis Project [2]. These datasets span various domains of network applications, including product networks (Amazon), collaboration networks (DBLP), and online social networks (YouTube and Orkut)[3]. Each network can be viewed as an undirected, connected graph. The statistical information of the datasets is summarized in Table 1.

[3]For all the four real datasets, we adopt the top 5000 communities that possess the highest quality according to [27].

3.3 Evaluation Metric

For the evaluation metric, we adopt F1 score to quantify the similarity between the algorithmic community $\mathcal{C}$ and the ground truth community $\mathcal{C}^*$. The F1 score for each pair of $(\mathcal{C}, \mathcal{C}^*)$ is defined by:

$$F_1(\mathcal{C}, \mathcal{C}^*) = \frac{2 \cdot Precision(\mathcal{C}, \mathcal{C}^*) \cdot Recall(\mathcal{C}, \mathcal{C}^*)}{Precision(\mathcal{C}, \mathcal{C}^*) + Recall(\mathcal{C}, \mathcal{C}^*)}, \quad (1)$$

where the precision and recall are defined as:

$$Precision(\mathcal{C}, \mathcal{C}^*) = \frac{|\mathcal{C} \cap \mathcal{C}^*|}{|\mathcal{C}|}, \quad (2)$$

$$Recall(\mathcal{C}, \mathcal{C}^*) = \frac{|\mathcal{C} \cap \mathcal{C}^*|}{|\mathcal{C}^*|}. \quad (3)$$

Throughout the paper, unless otherwise pointed out, the experimental results on synthetic data for each instance are given by the statistical mean and standard deviation based on 24 test cases[4]; and the experimental results on real datasets for each instance are based on 120 test cases. All the ground truth communities for testing are randomly chosen. The randomness of batch tests can guarantee the elimination of potential sampling bias in our tests.

4. LOCAL EXPANSION VIA MINIMIZING ONE NORM

4.1 Algorithm Overview

Spectral clustering makes use of a small number of singular vectors proportional to the number of communities in the network. If a graph has thousands of small communities, it is impractical to calculate a number of singular vectors greater than the number of communities. We are experimenting with a fundamentally new technique, which does not require the burdensome computation of a large number of singular vectors. Before explaining our local spectral approach for finding overlapping communities, it is necessary to make clear what we mean by "local spectra".

In traditional spectral clustering methods, one finds the first few singular vectors of the Laplacian matrix[5] of a graph G with n vertices. Suppose the first d singular vectors are obtained, one can form an $n \times d$ matrix as a latent space. Then one associates with each vertex a point in this latent space whose coordinates are given by the entries of the corresponding row in the matrix. Vertices are clustered using some method such as k-means clustering algorithm. This method is not likely to work well if the communities are small and heavily overlapping with each other.

We make two fundamental changes to this method. The first modification is to overcome the drawback of computing the singular vectors. Intuitively, the vertices around the seed members are more likely to be in the target community, thus a random walk serves as a natural subroutine to reveal these potential members. We start a random walk from several known members in the target community and run for a few steps. The number of random walk steps should be long enough to reach out to the vertices in the target community, but not too long to spread out to the entire graph. Instead of considering a single probability vector, we consider the span of a few dimensions of vectors after the short random walks and use it as the approximate invariant subspace (*local spectra*). The second is to handle the overlapping situation. Instead of using k-means to partition the points in the latent space into disjoint clusters, we look for the minimum 0-norm vector in the span of the invariant subspace obtained above, such that the seed members are in its support. We want to find rows in the invariant subspace that point in nearly the same direction as seed members. We will use 1-norm vector as a proxy for the minimum 0-norm vector since finding the 0-norm vector is an NP-hard problem.

In the following, we give a formal description of our local spectral approach *LEMON* for detecting the target communities from a small seed set. Given the input of a set of few vertices $\mathcal{S}$ that are already known to be in the target ground truth community $\mathcal{C}^*$, our algorithm would output the algorithmic community $\mathcal{C}$ such that the F1 measure for scoring the similarity between $\mathcal{C}$ and $\mathcal{C}^*$ is maximized.

Step 1. Generate the local spectra:

Let $\bar{\mathbf{A}} = \mathbf{D}^{-1/2}(\mathbf{A}+\mathbf{I})\mathbf{D}^{-1/2}$ be the normalized adjacency matrix of the graph where $\mathbf{D}$ is the diagonal matrix of vertex degree. Consider a random walk starting from exemplary vertices in $\mathcal{S}$. Let $\mathbf{p_0}$ denote the initial probability vector where the total probability is evenly distributed among the seed members. Consider the span of l-dimensional probability vectors which consist of probability vectors in l successive random walks

$$\mathbf{P}_{0,l} = [\mathbf{p}_0, \mathbf{p}_1, ..., \mathbf{p}_l]. \quad (4)$$

The initial invariant subspace is then obtained by calculating the orthonormal basis of the span $\mathbf{P}_{0,l}$, which we denote by $\mathbf{V}_{0,l}$. We then use the following recurrence to iteratively calculate the l-dimensional orthonormal basis $\mathbf{V}_{k,l}$ after k steps of random walk

$$\mathbf{V}_{k,l}\mathbf{R}_{k,l} = \mathbf{V}_{k-1,l}\bar{\mathbf{A}}, \quad (5)$$

where $\mathbf{R}_{k,l} \in \mathbb{R}^{n \times l}$ is chosen such that $\mathbf{V}_{k,l}$ is orthonormal. The orthonormal basis $\mathbf{V}_{k,l}$ will be used as the local spectra for clustering.

Step 2. Seek for a sparse vector

With the local spectra $\mathbf{V}_{k,l}$, we then solve the following linear programming problem [1].

$$\begin{aligned} \min \quad & \mathbf{e}^T\mathbf{y} = ||\mathbf{y}||_1 \\ s.t. \quad & \mathbf{y} = \mathbf{V}_{k,l}\mathbf{x}, \\ & \mathbf{y} \geq \mathbf{0}, \\ & \mathbf{y}(\mathcal{S}) \geq 1, \end{aligned}$$

where $\mathbf{e}$ is a vector of all ones, and both $\mathbf{x}$ and $\mathbf{y}$ are unknown vectors. The first constraint indicates that $\mathbf{y}$ is in the space of $\mathbf{V}_{k,l}$. The element in $\mathbf{y}$ indicate the likelihood for the corresponding vertex belong to the target community, which is non-negative. The third constraint enforces that seeds are in the support of sparse vector $\mathbf{y}$.

After sorting the elements in $\mathbf{y}$ in non-ascending order and getting a vector $\hat{\mathbf{y}}$, the vertices corresponding to the top $|\mathcal{C}|$ elements in $\hat{\mathbf{y}}$ are returned as the detected community with respect to the seed set $\mathcal{S}$.

[4]Each local expansion process from a seed set can be viewed as a test case.

[5]In the literature, several different definitions of graph Laplacian exist. Readers can refer to [20] for more details, which serves as a good introductory paper on spectral clustering.

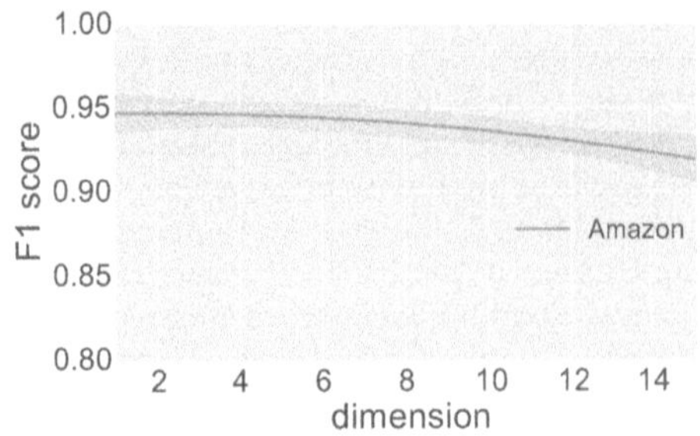

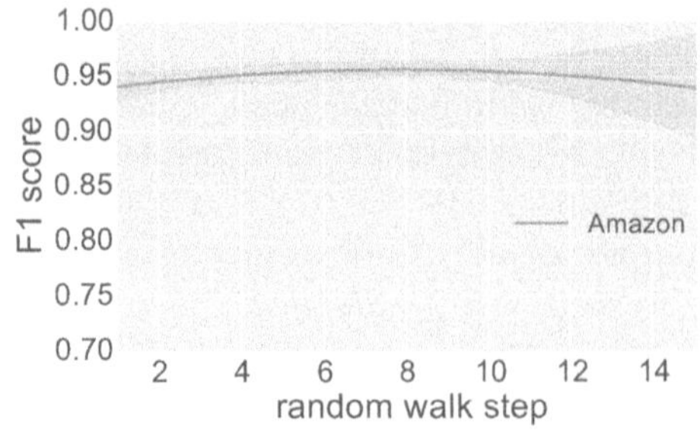

Figure 1: The average F1 score on Amazon network with varying dimensions l and random walk step k, respectively. The plots depict the statistical regression line with a 95% confidence interval.

Step 3. Reseeding
Augment the initial seed set by adding the vertices corresponding to the top t elements of $\hat{\mathbf{y}}$. Denote the augmented seed set as $\mathcal{S}'$. Then repeat step 1 and step 2 using the augmented seed set $\mathcal{S}'$. The detection accuracy can be improved through iterations via increasing t by a constant number s each time. We define s to be the seed expansion step, which is used as a tunable parameter for adjusting the convergence rate. Usually, the larger expansion step would result in lower performance but a faster running speed with less iterations. In the experiments, we fix the seed expansion step to be 6 for both synthetic and real datasets. The number of iterations for the seed expansion is determined by the stop criteria (Section 4.4).

4.2 Parameter Selection

The random walk step k and subspace dimension l are the key parameters in the local spectral clustering algorithm. We conduct parameter sensitivity study for these two parameters on the four real datasets.

4.2.1 *Subspace dimension*

To study the parameter of subspace dimension l, we fix the random walk step to be 3, and vary the number of dimension l from 1 to 15. Figure 1 (left panel) shows that changing the dimension l does not cause significant performance fluctuation. On one hand, choosing a large dimension l is undesirable because it would increase the computation cost of generating local spectra. On the other hand, when dimension degrades to $l = 1$, the standard deviation of F1 score becomes significant, making the detection accuracy unstable. In this paper, we fix $l = 3$ because the experiment suggests that setting $l = 3$ can statistically achieve both high and stable performance. Note that such observation holds not only for Amazon network, but for the remaining real datasets as well.

4.2.2 *Random walk step*

To investigate how the step of random walk affects the algorithm performance, we fix the dimension l to be 3, and vary the random walk step k from 1 to 15. Figure 1 (right panel) shows that the average F1 score plateaus as k increases, and 3-step random walk can yield the algorithm's full potential. The standard deviation, however, significantly increases when k exceeds 10. This indicates that longer random walk is undesirable for stably uncovering the local community structure. Throughout the paper, we fix the random walk step $k = 3$ for the real datasets[6].

4.3 Complexity Reduction by Sampling Method

If one wants to uncover a small community within a large network with billions of vertices, it would be very costly to take all the vertices into account. We want to discover the target community accurately while keeping the number of vertices examined small. Sampling method can effectively solve the memory consumption issue when one wants to find a local community within a large graph, since the whole graph does not have to be loaded into memory.

In practice, the unknown members in the target community are more likely to be around the seed members, and are usually a few steps away from the seeds. This observation motivates us to reduce the complexity by taking only a portion of the graph into consideration. Ideally, this partial graph should contain as many vertices in the target community as possible, and maintains a small size of the same scale as that of the target community.

To sample the graph, we expand the seed set using random walk. After a few steps of the random walk, vertices with large probability are more likely to be in the target community while vertices with small probability being reached would be treated as redundant ones. If the target community exists for the seed set, then according to [6], this target community would serve as a bottleneck for the probability to be spread out. It is worthwhile noting that other expansion methods such as breadth-first-search (BFS) would entirely ignore the bottleneck defining the community and rapidly mix with the entire graph before a significant fraction of vertices in the community have been reached. The subgraph returned by BFS usually contains less vertices in the target community than the subgraph of the same size obtained by random walk technique.

In the experiments on real datasets, we conduct a random walk starting from the seed set until the probability has been spread out to $\alpha \cdot |\mathcal{C}|_{\text{avg}}$ vertices, where α is some constant and $|\mathcal{C}|_{\text{avg}}$ is the average community size in the graph[7]. Note that $\alpha \cdot |\mathcal{C}|_{\text{avg}}$ should be large enough to be able to cover as many vertices in the ground truth community as possible.

[6]For LFR benchmark graphs, we adopt all together 6 combinations for the (step, dimension) tuple: $(2,3),(2,4),(2,5),(3,3),(3,4),(3,5)$ and return the highest F1 score among using these combinations.

[7]A fast implementation for updating the probability vector of the random walks is featured in detail in [6], Section 4.

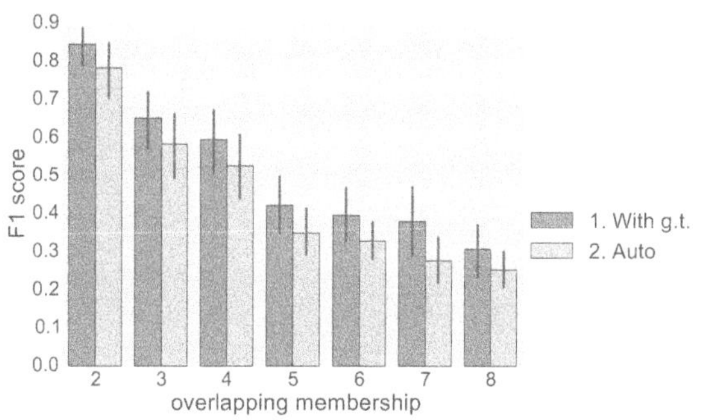

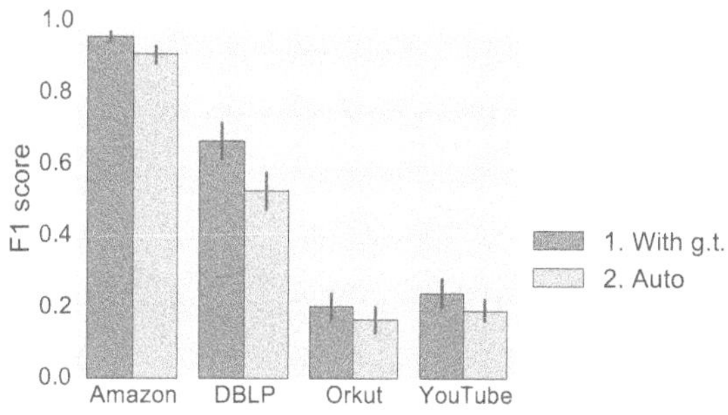

Figure 2: Comparison of the average F1 score with ground truth and automatic size determination. The left corresponds to the LFR datasets when $\mu = 0.3$ and the right corresponds to the real datasets.

This newly obtained subgraph will be used for the remaining computation.

Table 3 gives the statistics after applying sampling method to the real networks. For example, in DBLP network, setting α to be around 10 would yield a subgraph containing on average 98% vertices in the ground truth community. After sampling, we only need to deal with a subgraph of size around 2400 instead of 317,080, bringing a significant reduction of both temporal and spatial complexity.

Dataset	Coverage ratio	Sample rate	$\lvert\mathcal{C}\rvert_{\text{avg}}$	Subgraph size
Amazon	1.00	0.0087	39	2913
DBLP	0.98	0.0076	251	2409
YouTube	0.66	0.0033	79	3745
Orkut	0.64	0.0011	83	3379

Table 3: Statistics of the mean values for the sampling method on real datasets.

4.4 Stop Criteria

If there are ground truth communities available, the above algorithm is guaranteed to stop within few iterations since the seed set will no longer augment once its size exceeds that of the ground truth community. The algorithm would then return the community found with the highest F1 score during the iterations as the result. However, in real case, without knowing the exact size of the communities, most locally based detection algorithm has difficulty deciding when is the proper time to terminate expanding such that the discovered community is a "good" community. It is thus important to solve the two issues: 1) how to automatically determine the size of the community given a seed set $\mathcal{S}$, and 2) when to stop growing the seed set during the reseeding process.

4.4.1 Determine the size of the community

It has already been shown that random walks produce communities with conductance guarantees and ensure a small boundary defining a natural community in locally based detection algorithms [6]. The intuition is that adding irrelevant vertices to the target community would inevitably cause the conductance to increase, and finding a low-conductance community could ensure the closeness between the detected members and the known seed set. In [25], the authors also follow the same idea and adopt conductance as the metric for defining a good community found by the algorithm around a seed set. As we will see, the local conductance for a small group of vertices in the graph contains valuable information and enables designing effective stop criteria for our algorithm.

The definition of the conductance for a set of vertices $\mathcal{C}$ is given by

$$\phi(\mathcal{C}) = \frac{|\partial(\mathcal{C})|}{\min(\text{Vol}(\mathcal{C}), \text{Vol}(\bar{\mathcal{C}}))}, \tag{6}$$

where $|\partial(\mathcal{C})|$ denotes the cut size, and $\text{Vol}(\mathcal{C})$ is the sum of vertex degree in the set $\mathcal{C}$.

Suppose we have a rough estimation of the lower and upper bound for the size of communities in a graph, which we denote by $|\mathcal{C}|_{\min}$ and $|\mathcal{C}|_{\max}$ respectively. We could modify the original algorithm in the following way.

At step 2, after obtaining the sorted sparse vector $\hat{\mathbf{y}}$, we are hoping to truncate the sorted vector at some point y_g such that all the vertices corresponding to the elements no less than y_g are included in the algorithmic community. The crux lies in that we do not know yet what the best position is to truncate the vector $\hat{\mathbf{y}}$. To solve this issue, we denote Λ_i as the set of vertices corresponding to the top i elements in $\hat{\mathbf{y}}$. We then sweep over the sets from $\Lambda_{|\mathcal{C}|_{\min}}$ to $\Lambda_{|\mathcal{C}|_{\max}}$ and calculate the corresponding conductance for each of the sets. In practice, the value of the conductance with respect to varying size would usually change in a non-monotonic pattern that decreases first and then increases later on. We then adopt the first relative minimum conductance encountered on this curve as the estimated size of the community with respect to the seed set $\mathcal{S}$, which we denote by $\phi_{\mathcal{S}}^{\min}$.

4.4.2 Stop the reseeding process

As we keep augmenting the seed set through reseeding at step 3, a different seed set would result in a different sparse vector $\hat{\mathbf{y}}$ and thus lead to potentially different algorithmic communities. Practically, one of these seed sets during the augmenting process would achieve the highest F1 score. And it remains to address the issue of when to stop growing the seed set so that it finds the community that resembles most of the ground truth community. This issue can be solved in a similar fashion as that for determining community size.

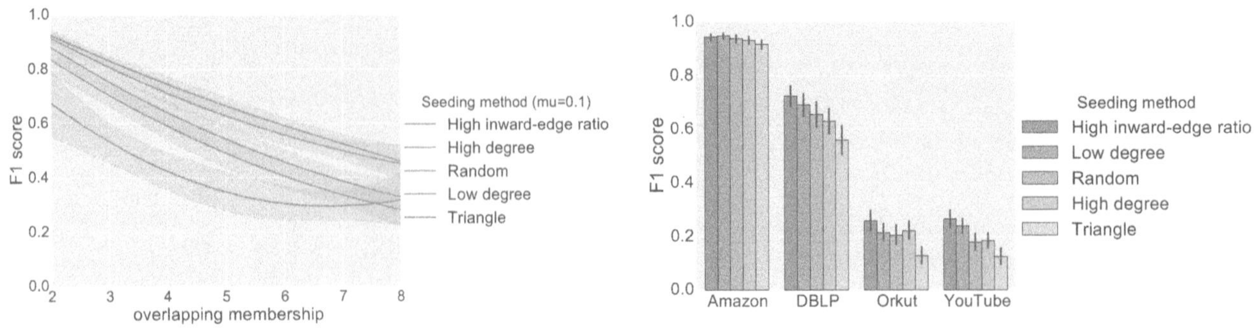

Figure 3: The average F1 score on LFR datasets ($\mu = 0.1$) and real datasets with different seeding methods.

Specifically, we keep track of the value of $\phi_S^{\min}$ for different seed set during the expansion, and stop to grow the seed set when $\phi_S^{\min}$ reaches a local minimum and starts to increase for the first time.

4.4.3 *Auto detect size vs ground truth size*

To verify our method, we compare the performance after applying the stop criteria with that obtained using ground truth communities. Figure 2 shows the statistical result of F1 score on both synthetic and real datasets. On both datasets, the F1 score with automatic size determination is only lowered by 10% on average compared with the performance with available ground truth. This implies that our method is applicable for finding communities that mostly resemble the ground truth communities on both synthetic and real datasets in different domains. It also suggests that our method can be applied in practice to uncover natural communities in the situation when no ground truth is available.

5. SEEDING

Since the initial seed set serves as a key component in our algorithm for uncovering the target community $\mathcal{C}$, it is crucial to consider how the quality of seed set affect the performance. In practice, there is not much control over how the seeds are selected. However, the alternative seeding methods we provide here can be strategically applied by the domain experts based on the availability of candidate seeds in different scenarios. In this section, we will focus on addressing two fundamentally important issues regarding the seed set: 1) What defines "good" seeds? and 2) How many seeds are needed in order to uniquely define a community?

5.1 Seeding Method

To give a well-rounded evaluation on this, we encompass in total five different seeding methods here. In this experiment, we adopt $|\mathcal{S}| = 3$ seeds for each of the seeding method listed below.

- **High degree seeding**: pick $|\mathcal{S}|$ vertices with degree ranked in the top one third among the degree of all vertices in $\mathcal{C}$.
- **Low degree seeding**: pick $|\mathcal{S}|$ vertices with degree ranked in the bottom one third among the degree of all vertices in $\mathcal{C}$.
- **Triangle seeding**: pick $|\mathcal{S}|$ vertices in $\mathcal{C}$ that form a triangle as the initial seed set.
- **Random seeding**: pick $|\mathcal{S}|$ vertices in $\mathcal{C}$ randomly.
- **High inward-edge ratio seeding**: the inward-edge ratio for a vertex v is defined by the fraction of links connecting to another vertex inside the target community $\mathcal{C}$ among all the links coming out from v. We pick $|\mathcal{S}|$ vertices with inward-edge ratio ranked in the top one third among all vertices in $\mathcal{C}$.

Figure 3 (left panel) gives the experimental results on LFR benchmark datasets with mixing parameter $\mu = 0.1$. It is interesting to note that the high-degree seeding method consistently achieves the highest F1 score in both groups of datasets. When $\mu = 0.1$, triangle seeding leads to the worst performance with low F1 score and high standard deviation. This implies that seeding from a compact core structure is less advantageous than seeding sporadically among vertices. The intuitive explanation behind this phenomenon is that it is more difficult for the probabilities to spread out when the random walk initiates from a cohesive structure.

Another interesting observation is that high inward-edge ratio seeding method can consistently lead to the best performance among different seeding methods on both synthetic and real datasets. In [14], the authors have the same observation as ours but did not give an explicit explanation on this phenomenon. In fact, when a large fraction of the seeds links connect to vertices within the same community, random walks starting from these seeds would be more likely to transit probabilities into the vertices within the community rather than spreading out to vertices outside the community. A higher detection accuracy can be thus achieved since the target community contains much of the probability after short random walks.

Moreover, it is also striking to note the difference between the test results on synthetic datasets and that on real datasets. Even though the high-degree seeding method can always bring higher performance than that of random seeding on synthetic datasets, the behavior of these seeding methods on real networks is quite different. In Figure 3 (right panel), we see that low-degree seeds lead to better result than that of high-degree seeds on DBLP and YouTube datasets. The degree of seeds does not have a significant impact on the performance in Amazon and Orkut networks since the performance of high-degree seeding and low-degree seeding almost tie with each other on these datasets. In [14], the authors compared the detection accuracy of PageRank based seed set expansion algorithm with high-degree seeding and random seeding on real networks, and concluded that random seeding method always outperforms high-degree seeding in all domains of real networks. However, we remark here that this observation does not apply to our algorithm as we find that high-degree seeding works slightly better than random seeding on Orkut and YouTube datasets.

5.2 Seed Set Size

It is also interesting to investigate how the size of the seed set affects the performance of our algorithm.

We first experiment on the LFR benchmark datasets with varying seed set size. We choose seed set of size proportional to the size of the target community $\mathcal{C}$. Specifically, we test with five different seeding ratios r: 2%, 4%, 6%, 8% and 10% respectively, and round $r \cdot |\mathcal{C}|$ to an integer if it is a fraction. Figure 4 shows the F1 scores when $\mu = 0.1$. The algorithm's performance can be improved in general as the seed set size increases. In the case when both mixing parameter and overlapping membership are small, e.g., $\mu = 0.1, om = 2$, increasing the seed set size does not seem to affect the performance significantly, and seed set consisting of a small percentage of vertices are sufficient to discover the target community with high accuracy. This implies that when the structure of a small community is well-defined, our algorithm only needs 2 to 3 seeds to reveal the remaining members in a community of size roughly 100. For general test purpose on LFR benchmark graphs, we adopt an 8% fraction of the vertices in the target community as seeds.

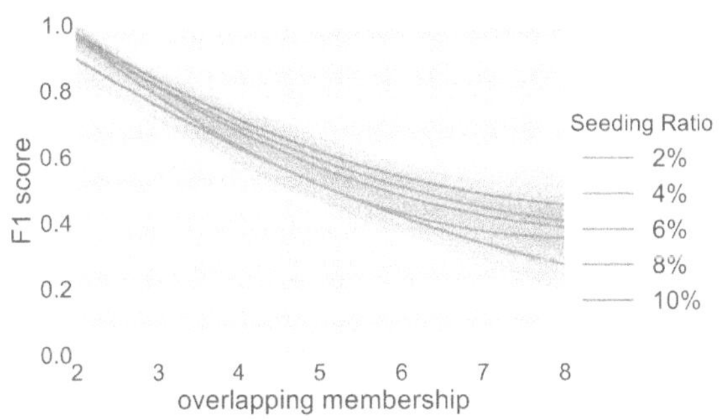

Figure 4: The average F1 score on LFR datasets ($\mu = 0.1$) with different seeding ratio.

We then carry out the similar experiment on the real datasets. The result on real networks is interesting because increasing the seed set size has little affect on the performance. Especially, using only 3 seeds can yield almost the same performance as using an 8% fraction of the vertices in the target community as seeds on real datasets.

Our algorithm is thus advantageous to many other seed set expansion algorithms that usually require a higher fraction of vertices to be known. For example, in [14], the authors perform a similar experiment on DBLP network. The performance of their algorithm achieves the maximum recall of 0.3 when seeding ratio is 10%, while *LEMON* can achieve an average F1 score of 0.66 with 3 vertices. This makes our algorithm practical for real networks when it is impossible to collect a large number of seeds.

5.3 Further Extension

As the results of using different seeding methods suggests, high-degree seeds can heuristically lead to better result on synthetic data. Such heuristic implies that a vertex with higher degree may exert higher impact on shaping the subspace we are looking for, and thus affect the performance by leading to different sparse vectors where we obtain the "candidates" of the target community from.

In practice, we usually have little control on the seed set. The chance we get a seed set of high-degree members is rare. More often than not, the degree of seeds is randomly distributed. We are therefore inspired to tailor our algorithm accordingly in order to emphasize the seeds with high degree. The modification is rather straightforward: when calculating the initial probability vector p_0 to start a random walk from, instead of evenly distributing the amount of probability to each seed, we initialize the probability vector according to the degree of each seed. Formally,

$$p_0(v_i) = \begin{cases} d(v_i)/\text{Vol}(\mathcal{S}) & \text{if } v_i \in \mathcal{S} \\ 0 & \text{otherwise} \end{cases} \quad (7)$$

where $d(v_i)$ denotes the degree of vertex v_i. In other words, we enforce a bias towards the high-degree vertices at the beginning of the random walk. Note that each time after the reseeding process, the initial probability vector also needs to be recalculated in the same way.

Figure 5 (left panel) depicts the experimental results on LFR benchmark graphs with and without degree normalized initialization for the random walk respectively. We can find that degree-normalization of the initial probability vector results in better performance.

We then perform the same experiments on real networks, and find that degree-normalization would on the contrary, lead to slightly worse statistical results (see the right panel of Figure 5). The completely different behavior of using degree normalization on real datasets is rather intriguing. In fact, this phenomenon accords with our previous observation in Section 5.1 that a high-degree seed set is less advantageous than random seeds on real datasets. And this explains why emphasizing on the high-degree vertices would worsen the performance on real datasets.

6. COMPARISON WITH THE STATE-OF-THE-ART ALGORITHMS

6.1 Baseline Algorithms

To give a well-rounded performance comparison with state-of-the-art algorithms, we compared our results to three localized community detection algorithms and four global community detection algorithms.

1. **Localized algorithms:** We encompass three locally based methods, Heat Kernel (HK) [13], PageRank (PR) [14] and Seed Set Expansion (SSE) [25].
2. **Global algorithms:** We also compare our local spectral clustering algorithm with four overlapping community detection methods that are based on the global structure: OSLOM[8] [16], DEMON[9] [9], and LinkCommunity[10] (LC) [4].

[8] `http://www.oslom.org/software.htm`
[9] `http://www.michelecoscia.com/?page_id=42`
[10] `https://github.com/bagrow/linkcomm`

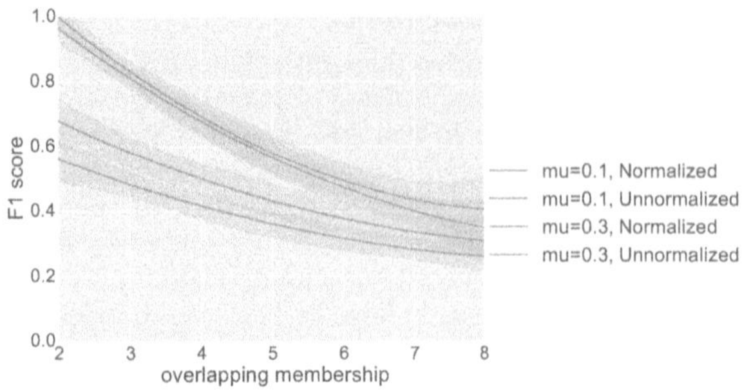

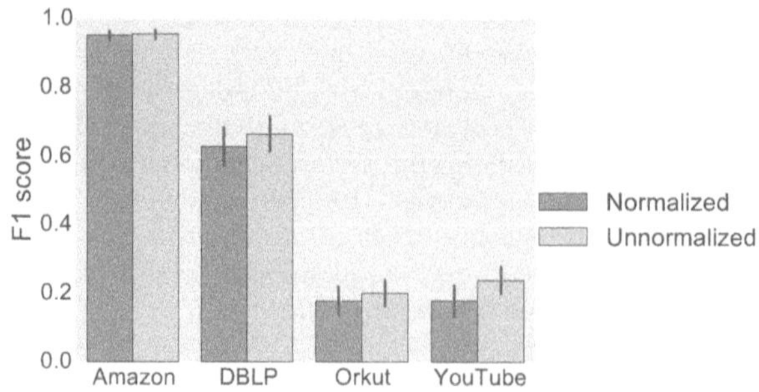

Figure 5: Comparison of the average F1 score with and without normalizing the initial probability vector by each seed's degree. The left corresponds to the LFR datasets and the right corresponds to the real datasets.

6.2 Comparison with Localized Algorithms

We refer to the experimental results reported in some recent publications on localized community detection algorithms [13][14][25]. Figure 6 illustrates the comparison of F1 scores on Amazon, DBLP, YouTube and Orkut datasets. We use "LEMON-auto" to denote the results obtained by applying the stop criteria in Section 4.4. Since the results on Orkut and YouTube datasets are missing in [25] and [14], we use empty bars to indicate them.

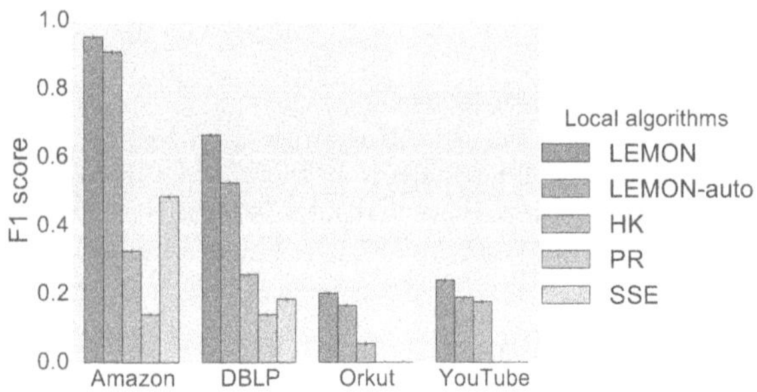

Figure 6: Comparison of the average F1 score with state-of-the-art local detection algorithms on real networks.

Figure 6 shows that *LEMON* achieves an F1 score of 0.910 on the Amazon dataset, far outperforming the other algorithms. The average F1 scores increases the performance by 3 times compared with the heat kernel algorithm [13] on Amazon, DBLP and Orkut networks. To compare with [25], we find that the average F1 score of our algorithm doubles their best performance achieved by the "spread hubs" method on Amazon dataset and triples the performance on the DBLP network. Also, note that in [14], the authors did not have an explicit stop criterion. Instead, they assumed using a budget for predicting the size of the target community. We compare with the F1 score at a budget of 100 for both Amazon and DBLP datasets. From the results on Amazon networks in [14], we notice that even granted a budget of 400, which is far beyond the average community size of 39 in Amazon network, only a recall of 0.45 can be achieved. And we infer the F1 score would be even lower than this value since the precision is dragged down by the large budget set.

It is also worth noting that we only use 3 randomly picked seeds for all the test cases on each dataset. Our algorithm requires very fewer seeds than other algorithms such as [14].

The experiment has verified that our algorithm is able to achieve high accuracy on large networks constituting communities of average size roughly hundred. This implies that our approach is well-suited for the task of detecting small communities in large networks.

6.3 Comparison with Global Algorithms

We also compare local spectral clustering with several state-of-the-art global based algorithms. Table 4 summarizes the running time as well as the average F1 score of each algorithm on real datasets. Among the baselines, OSLOM and LC fail to terminate within 10 days on the YouTube dataset. The OSLOM algorithm can achieve rather good performance but does not scale well.

In contrast, our algorithm can consistently return the result within few seconds irrespective of how large the entire graph is. Besides, our algorithm has small memory consumption, and a machine with 4GB RAM can afford to process networks as large as Orkut since the algorithm does not have to store the whole graph in memory. Moreover, our locally based algorithm is parallelizable because each seed set expansion can be computed independently. Such property can bring a further performance gain on running time with multi-threaded implementation.

Figure 7 compares the average F1 score with some state-of-the-art algorithms on LFR benchmark graphs. During the experimentation, we also incorporate the methods that can effectively improve the performance on synthetic datasets that are addressed in Section 5.3. We notice that our algorithm outperforms the baseline algorithms even when we use the random seeding strategy. When the mixing parameter $\mu = 0.3$, as is shown in Figure 7, *LEMON* brings about $30\% \sim 40\%$ relative improvement compared with the best results among the baselines. And we can expect the performance gain to be even more significant if the seeds possess the qualities discussed in Section 5.1.

Among the four baselines, we notice that LC and DEMON consistently perform poorly on both groups of the synthetic datasets. We further look into the communities found by LC and DEMON respectively, and find that LC tends to partition the graphs into very small pieces while DEMON, on the contrary, usually finds communities that are much larger

Algorithm	Implementation	Amazon		DBLP		YouTube		Orkut	
		F1 score	time	F1 score	time	F1 score	time	F1 score	time
LEMON	Python	0.953	<15s	0.665	<15s	0.240	<15s	0.202	<15s
LEMON-auto	Python	0.910	<15s	0.525	<15s	0.190	<15s	0.170	<15s
DEMON	Python/C++	0.164	4,562s	0.196	727,675s	0.031	22,395s	-	-
OSLOM	C++	0.766	885,867s	0.542	23,262s	-	>10d	-	-
LC	Python/C++	0.815	4,606s	0.527	49,045s	-	>10d	-	-

Table 4: Comparison with global algorithms on real datasets.

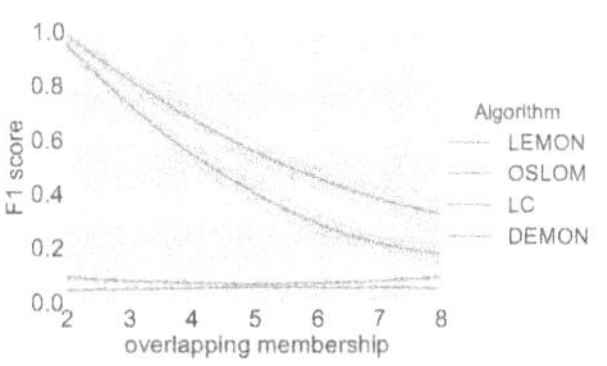

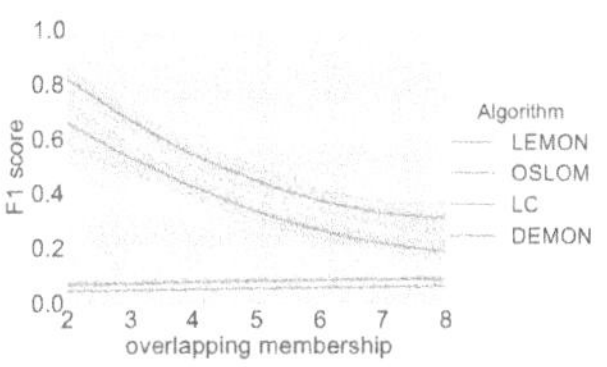

Figure 7: Comparison of the average F1 score on LFR datasets with baseline algorithms. The left corresponds to the datasets with mixing parameter $\mu = 0.1$ and the right corresponds to $\mu = 0.3$.

than the ground truth communities. This implies that both algorithms extract structures from networks that bear little resemblance to the natural formation of the communities. However, we remark here that even LC fails to recognize the communities well on the synthetic data, it perform better on real datasets as we see in Table 4 .

6.4 Empirical Comparison Between Synthetic and Real Data

Networks are not all similar and we cannot assume one algorithm works for finding communities in a network will behave the same on the other networks. Therefore, it is important to develop the understanding of how different types of networks affect the behavior of algorithms.

Our algorithm sustains a consistent performance on both LFR benchmark graphs and real networks though, we still want to summarize and call the attention to several subtle differences here.

First, *LEMON* is less sensitive to the parameter of random walk step k and subspace dimension l on real networks than that on LFR benchmark graphs. In practice, fixing (k, l) to be $(3, 3)$ for real networks can ensure a good performance.

Second, *LEMON* is less sensitive to the seed set size on real networks than that on LFR benchmark. In practice, a seed set size of 3 can guarantee a good performance on real networks. As for LFR, we adopt the seed set size to be proportional to the community size.

Third, *LEMON* is more sensitive to the high-degree seeds on real networks than that on LFR benchmark. In LFR graphs, the degree of a vertex is at most 50. Whereas in some large real networks such as YouTube, the degree of some vertices exceeds 1000, making the degree distribution much more screw than that seen in LFR graphs. And we expect that vertices with unusually high degree in real networks would have a stronger power in controlling the trend for the probabilities to spread out during the random walk, and thus have a higher risk to enter some other neighboring communities. Such an effect can be counterbalanced by putting less initial probabilities on these "super cores".

The above empirical analysis informs us that finding communities in real networks seems to be less parameterized than that on synthetic datasets for our algorithm. This indicates that our algorithm is better suited for uncovering those naturally well-formed communities than the artificially constructed communities in practice.

7. CONCLUSION

The problem of identifying small community structure in large networks has been gaining importance. In this paper, we have presented a method for finding overlapping communities by seeking a sparse vector in the span of local spectra where the seeds are in its support. To overcome the drawbacks of traditional spectral clustering methods, we propose a novel method to construct the local spectra based on the singular vector approximations drawn from short random walks. Our algorithm enables finding a small community in time functional to the size of the community, and it consistently returns the result within seconds even for a network with billions of vertices. We demonstrate the effectiveness and efficiency of our method for discovering communities on both synthetic and real-world datasets. As the experimental result shows, our algorithm achieves the highest detection accuracy amongst the state-of-the-art proposals.

Many other fundamentally important research questions remain to be addressed. First, the community detection algorithm based on local spectral clustering could be potentially applied to the membership detection problem, i.e., finding all the communities that an arbitrary vertex belongs to. Second, during the process of seed set expansion, we adopt the first low-conductance community as the target community, which usually yields a high resemblance to the ground truth community. It would also be interesting to look further into some larger low-conductance communities and see if a hierarchical structure exists. In this case, some large social group consisting of several small cliques is likely to be discovered.

Acknowledgements

The authors would like to thank Isabel Kloumann for valuable comments and discussions. This research has been supported in part by US Army Research Office W911NF-14-1-0477 and National Science Foundation of China 61173180, 61472147.

8. REFERENCES

[1] GNU linear programming kit. `http://www.gnu.org/software/glpk`.

[2] Stanford Network Analysis Project. `http://snap.stanford.edu`.

[3] B. Abrahao, S. Soundarajan, J. Hopcroft, and R. Kleinberg. A separability framework for analyzing community structure. *ACM Transactions on Knowledge Discovery from Data (TKDD)*, 8(1):5, 2014.

[4] Y.-Y. Ahn, J. P. Bagrow, and S. Lehmann. Link communities reveal multiscale complexity in networks. *Nature*, 466(7307):761–764, 2010.

[5] R. Andersen, F. Chung, and K. Lang. Local graph partitioning using pagerank vectors. In *FOCS*, pages 475–486. IEEE, 2006.

[6] R. Andersen and K. J. Lang. Communities from seed sets. In *WWW*, pages 223–232. ACM, 2006.

[7] M.-F. Balcan, C. Borgs, M. Braverman, J. Chayes, and S.-H. Teng. Finding endogenously formed communities. In *SIAM*, pages 767–783. ACM, 2013.

[8] A. Clauset, C. R. Shalizi, and M. E. Newman. Power-law distributions in empirical data. *SIAM review*, 51(4):661–703, 2009.

[9] M. Coscia, G. Rossetti, F. Giannotti, and D. Pedreschi. Demon: a local-first discovery method for overlapping communities. In *KDD*, pages 615–623. ACM, 2012.

[10] S. Fortunato. Community detection in graphs. *Physics Reports*, 486(3):75–174, 2010.

[11] T. J. Hansen and M. W. Mahoney. Semi-supervised eigenvectors for large-scale locally-biased learning. *Journal of Machine Learning Research*, 15:3691–3734, 2014.

[12] D. Jin, B. Yang, C. Baquero, D. Liu, D. He, and J. Liu. A markov random walk under constraint for discovering overlapping communities in complex networks. *Journal of Statistical Mechanics: Theory and Experiment*, 2011(05):P05031, 2011.

[13] K. Kloster and D. F. Gleich. Heat kernel based community detection. In *KDD*. ACM, 2014.

[14] I. M. Kloumann and J. M. Kleinberg. Community membership identification from small seed sets. In *KDD*. ACM, 2014.

[15] A. Lancichinetti, S. Fortunato, and F. Radicchi. Benchmark graphs for testing community detection algorithms. *Physical Review E*, 78(4):046110, 2008.

[16] A. Lancichinetti, F. Radicchi, J. J. Ramasco, and S. Fortunato. Finding statistically significant communities in networks. *PloS one*, 6(4):e18961, 2011.

[17] J. Leskovec, K. J. Lang, A. Dasgupta, and M. W. Mahoney. Statistical properties of community structure in large social and information networks. In *WWW*, pages 695–704. ACM, 2008.

[18] M. Meila and J. Shi. A random walks view of spectral segmentation. 2001.

[19] M. Molloy and B. Reed. A critical point for random graphs with a given degree sequence. *Random structures & algorithms*, 6(2-3):161–180, 1995.

[20] A. Y. Ng, M. I. Jordan, Y. Weiss, et al. On spectral clustering: Analysis and an algorithm. *Advances in neural information processing systems*, 2:849–856, 2002.

[21] P. Pons and M. Latapy. Computing communities in large networks using random walks. In *Computer and Information Sciences-ISCIS 2005*, pages 284–293. Springer, 2005.

[22] U. N. Raghavan, R. Albert, and S. Kumara. Near linear time algorithm to detect community structures in large-scale networks. *Physical Review E*, 76(3):036106, 2007.

[23] M. Rosvall and C. T. Bergstrom. Multilevel compression of random walks on networks reveals hierarchical organization in large integrated systems. *PloS one*, 6(4):e18209, 2011.

[24] D. A. Spielman and S.-H. Teng. Nearly-linear time algorithms for graph partitioning, graph sparsification, and solving linear systems. In *STOC*, pages 81–90. ACM, 2004.

[25] J. J. Whang, D. F. Gleich, and I. S. Dhillon. Overlapping community detection using seed set expansion. In *CIKM*, pages 2099–2108. ACM, 2013.

[26] J. Xie, S. Kelley, and B. K. Szymanski. Overlapping community detection in networks: The state-of-the-art and comparative study. *ACM Computing Surveys (CSUR)*, 45(4):43, 2013.

[27] J. Yang and J. Leskovec. Defining and evaluating network communities based on ground-truth. In *ICDM*, pages 10–13, 2012.

[28] V. Zlatić, A. Gabrielli, and G. Caldarelli. Topologically biased random walk and community finding in networks. *Physical Review E*, 82(6):066109, 2010.

Scalable Parallel EM Algorithms for Latent Dirichlet Allocation in Multi-Core Systems

Xiaosheng Liu[1,2], Jia Zeng[1,2,3,*], Xi Yang[1,2], Jianfeng Yan[1,2], Qiang Yang[3,4]
[1]School of Computer Science and Technology, Soochow University, Suzhou 215006, China
[2]Collaborative Innovation Center of Novel Software Technology and Industrialization
[3]Huawei Noah's Ark Lab, Hong Kong
[4]Department of Computer Science and Engineering, Hong Kong University of Science and Technology
*Corresponding Author: zeng.jia@acm.org

ABSTRACT

Latent Dirichlet allocation (LDA) is a widely-used probabilistic topic modeling tool for content analysis such as web mining. To handle web-scale content analysis on just a single PC, we propose multi-core parallel expectation-maximization (PEM) algorithms to infer and estimate LDA parameters in shared memory systems. By avoiding memory access conflicts reducing the locking time among multiple threads and residual-based dynamic scheduling, we show that PEM algorithms are more scalable and accurate than the current state-of-the-art parallel LDA algorithms on a commodity PC. This parallel LDA toolbox is made publicly available as open source software at mloss.org.

Categories and Subject Descriptors

H.4 [**Information Systems Applications**]: Miscellaneous; D.2.8 [**Software Engineering**]: Metrics—*complexity measures, performance measures*

Keywords

Latent Dirichlet allocation, parallel EM algorithms, multi-core systems, shared memory systems, scalability

1. INTRODUCTION

Latent Dirichlet allocation (LDA) [4, 3] is a popular probabilistic topic model for content analysis such as web mining [12]. It can automatically infer the hidden thematic groups of observed words called topics from a collection of documents represented as an input sparse document-word matrix. In the big data era, scalable parallel LDA algorithms have attracted intensive research interests because billions of tweets, images and videos on the web become increasingly common. The aim of this paper is to develop efficien parallel LDA algorithms for big data.

There are two widely available parallel architectures: 1) multi-processor [19] and 2) multi-core [29] systems, where the main difference lies in the way to use the memory. In the multi-processor architecture, all processes allocate independent memory space and communicate to synchronize LDA parameters at the end of each learning iteration [21, 27, 19, 15, 25, 1, 38]. The reduction of communication cost still remains an unsolved problem because this cost is often too big to be masked by computation time in web-scale applications. The experimental results confir that the communication cost may exceed the computation cost to become the primitive cost of large-scale topic modeling [27, 15]. In the multi-core architecture, all threads access the shared memory space so that the race condition is serious. A major scalability issue is the locking time among multiple threads. An example of shared memory architecture is GPU-LDA [29], which shares LDA document-topic and topic-word distribution parameters by multiple threads in multi-core GPU. To avoid access conflict in parameter matrices, the input document-word matrix is partitioned into independent data blocks with non-overlapping rows and columns. A preprocessing algorithm is used to balance the number of words in data blocks so that different threads can finis scanning non-conflictin blocks with almost the same time. However, it is difficul for absolute data block balancing and faster threads need to wait for the slowest one causing longer locking time. Yahoo!LDA [25, 1] presents a blackboard architecture that uses the *memcached* technique, a distributed shared cache service, to maintain LDA parameter matrices in the shared memory environment. Parallel processing of two or more corpus shards would lead to serious access conflicts Yahoo!LDA addresses this problem by locking accesses to conflictin shards, but this locking mechanism degenerates its scalability performance when the number of threads increases.

In this paper, we focus on developing more scalable LDA algorithms in shared memory systems, which can handle web-scale content analysis on just a commodity PC having the multi-core architecture. For example, our parallel solution can learn 1000 topics from 8 million documents on just a PC with 12 cores using around 3 hours. In contrast, previous parallel LDA algorithms on 1024 CPUs need around 4.5 hours to do the same task [19]. This result suggests that parallel LDA algorithms in multi-core system is not only competitive even compared to parallel processing over large clusters (multi-processor systems), but it is very affordable also. Generally, there are two main steps to develop scalable parallel LDA algorithms in shared memory systems. The firs step is to choose a batch/online LDA inference algorithm with the fast convergence speed on a single machine. The second step is to parallelize this algorithm in the shared memory system with small locking costs.

As far as the firs step is concerned, batch LDA inference algorithms include expectation maximization (EM) [7], variational Bayes (VB) [4], collapsed Gibbs sampling (GS) [10], collapsed variational Bayes (CVB) [26, 2], and belief propagation (BP) [35]. Most parallel inference solutions of LDA choose GS algorithms

WWW 2015, May 18–22, 2015, Florence, Italy.
ACM 978-1-4503-3469-3/15/05.
http://dx.doi.org/10.1145/2736277.2741106.

because they are more memory-efficien than other algorithms [21, 27, 19, 15, 25, 1]. For example, GS does not need to maintain the large posterior matrix in memory. In addition, GS stores LDA parameters using the integer type by sparse matrices, and often obtains higher topic modeling accuracy than VB [2]. So, GS is generally agreed to be a more scalable choice in many parallel LDA solutions. However, recent research [2] shows that EM [7], CVB0 [2] and BP [35, 34] converge much faster and produce higher topic modeling accuracy than GS. Online LDA inference algorithms [11, 16, 5, 9] become popular with two reasons. First, they combine the stochastic optimization framework [22] with the corresponding batch LDA algorithms, which theoretically can converge to the local optimal point of the LDA's objective function. Second, online algorithms are memory-efficien because they load each mini-batch of data in memory for online processing, and remove the processed mini-batch and local parameters from memory after one look. Although online algorithms converge slower than batch counterparts, they can process big data streams with a high velocity [23].

We choose EM [7] for LDA because of its fast convergence speed as well as high topic modeling accuracy. To justify this choice, we derive the batch EM (BEM), incremental EM (IEM) [18] and online EM (OEM) [6] algorithms for learning LDA, and compare them with other widely used LDA algorithms such as VB, GS, CVB and BP. Then, we parallelize EM algorithms in the multi-core systems called parallel EM (PEM). Inspired by the recent development of locking-free parallel stochastic gradient descent for matrix factorization [20, 39, 33], we further propose a residual-based scheduling method to reduce the locking time among multiple threads. In practice, this scheduling method can significantl speed up the convergence of PEM algorithms. Experiments confir that PEM algorithms converge significantl faster and scale up to more data and topics when compared with the current state-of-the-art parallel LDA algorithms [29, 25, 23] in multi-core systems. Note that the proposed PEM can be also deployed in multi-processor systems, similar to previous multi-core solutions that work in multi-processor systems [25, 33]. To summarize, we have the following contributions in this paper:

- We develop scalable PEM algorithms in both batch and online versions for LDA in shared memory environment. These efficien PEM algorithms can converge to the local maximum of the LDA log-likelihood function.
- We propose a residual-based scheduling method, which can reduce the locking time among multiple threads, and in the meanwhile speeds up the convergence of PEM in the multi-core architecture.
- Experiments on three large-scale data sets confir that the proposed PEM algorithms converge faster and are more scalable than the current state-of-the-art [29, 25, 23].

This paper is organized as follows: Section 2 discusses why we choose EM for LDA (Appendix shows the derivation of BEM, IEM, OEM and their convergence analysis). Section 3 describes scalable PEM algorithms by avoiding memory access conflicts reducing the locking time among multiple threads and residual-based dynamic scheduling. Section 4 shows extensive experiments on three large-scale data sets. Section 5 makes conclusions and envisions further work.

2. WHY EM INFERENCE FOR LDA?

LDA allocates a set of thematic topic labels, $\mathbf{z} = \{z^k_{w,d}\}$, to explain nonzero elements in the document-word co-occurrence matrix $\mathbf{x}_{W\times D} = \{x_{w,d}\}$, where $1 \leq w \leq W$ denotes the word index in the vocabulary, $1 \leq d \leq D$ denotes the document index in the corpus, and $1 \leq k \leq K$ denotes the topic index. Usually, the number of topics K is provided by users. The nonzero element $x_{w,d} \neq 0$ denotes the number of word counts at the index $\{w, d\}$. For each word token $x_{w,d,i} = \{0, 1\}, x_{w,d} = \sum_i x_{w,d,i}$, there is a topic label $z^k_{w,d,i} = \{0, 1\}, \sum_{k=1}^K z^k_{w,d,i} = 1, 1 \leq i \leq x_{w,d}$. Each nonzero element $x_{w,d} \neq 0$ is associated with a topic probability vector $\sum_k \mu_{w,d}(k) = 1$, which denotes the posterior probability of a topic label $z^k_{w,d} = 1$ given the observed word $\{w, d\}$. The objective of inference algorithms is to infer posterior probability from the full joint probability $p(\mathbf{x}, \mathbf{z}, \boldsymbol{\theta}, \boldsymbol{\phi}|\alpha, \beta)$, where $\mathbf{z}$ is the topic labeling configuration $\boldsymbol{\theta}_{K\times D}$ and $\boldsymbol{\phi}_{K\times W}$ are two non-negative matrices of multinomial parameters for document-topic and topic-word distributions, satisfying $\sum_k \theta_d(k) = 1$ and $\sum_w \phi_w(k) = 1$. Both multinomial matrices are generated by two Dirichlet distributions with hyperparameters α and β. For simplicity, we consider the smoothed LDA with fi ed symmetric hyperparameters [10]. Table 1 summarizes the important notations in this paper.

Table 1: Definition of Notation.

$1 \leq d \leq D$	Document index
$1 \leq w \leq W$	Word index in vocabulary
$1 \leq k \leq K$	Topic index
$1 \leq m \leq M \times M$	$M \times M$ data blocks
$1 \leq n \leq N$	Thread index
NNZ	Number of nonzero elements
$\mathbf{x}_{W\times D} = \{x_{w,d}\}$	Document-word matrix
$\mathbf{z}_{W\times D} = \{z^k_{w,d}\}$	Topic labels for words
$\boldsymbol{\theta}_{K\times D}$	Document-topic distribution
$\boldsymbol{\phi}_{K\times W}$	Topic-word distribution
$\boldsymbol{\mu}_{K\times NNZ}$	Responsibility matrix
α, β	Dirichlet hyperparameters

VB [4] infers the following posterior from the full joint probability,

$$p(\boldsymbol{\theta}, \mathbf{z}|\mathbf{x}, \boldsymbol{\phi}, \alpha, \beta) = \frac{p(\mathbf{x}, \mathbf{z}, \boldsymbol{\theta}, \boldsymbol{\phi}|\alpha, \beta)}{p(\mathbf{x}, \boldsymbol{\phi}|\alpha, \beta)}. \quad (1)$$

This posterior means that if we learn the topic-word distribution $\boldsymbol{\phi}$ from training data, we want to infer the best $\{\boldsymbol{\theta}, \mathbf{z}\}$ from unseen test data given $\boldsymbol{\phi}$, i.e., for the best generalization performance. However, computing this posterior is intractable because the denominator contains intractable integration, $\int_{\boldsymbol{\theta},\mathbf{z}} p(\mathbf{x}, \mathbf{z}, \boldsymbol{\theta}, \boldsymbol{\phi}|\alpha, \beta)$. So, VB infers an approximate variational posterior based on the variational EM algorithm [17]:

- Variational E-step:

$$\mu_{w,d}(k) \propto \frac{\exp[\Psi(\hat{\theta}_d(k) + \alpha)]\exp[\Psi(\hat{\phi}_w(k) + \beta)]}{\exp[\Psi(\sum_w [\hat{\phi}_w(k) + \beta])]}, \quad (2)$$

$$\hat{\theta}_d(k) = \sum_w x_{w,d}\mu_{w,d}(k). \quad (3)$$

- Variational M-step:

$$\hat{\phi}_w(k) = \sum_d x_{w,d}\mu_{w,d}(k). \quad (4)$$

In variational E-step, we update $\mu_{w,d}(k)$ and $\hat{\theta}_d(k)$ until convergence, which makes the variational posterior approximate the true posterior $p(\boldsymbol{\theta}, \mathbf{z}|\mathbf{x}, \boldsymbol{\phi}, \alpha, \beta)$ by minimizing the Kullback-Leibler (KL) divergence between them. In the variational M-step, we update $\hat{\phi}_w(k)$ to maximize the variational posterior. Here, we use

Table 2: Time and Space Complexities of LDA Inference Algorithms.

	Posterior	Time	Space (Memory)
VB [4]	$p(\boldsymbol{\theta}, \mathbf{z}\vert\mathbf{x}, \boldsymbol{\phi}, \alpha, \beta)$	$2 \times K \times NNZ \times digamma$	$2 \times K \times (D+W)$
GS [31]	$p(\mathbf{z}\vert\mathbf{x}, \alpha, \beta)$	$\delta_1 \times K \times ntokens$	$\delta_2 \times K \times W + ntokens$
CVB [26]	$p(\boldsymbol{\theta}, \boldsymbol{\phi}, \mathbf{z}\vert\mathbf{x}, \alpha, \beta)$	$\delta_3 \times 2 \times K \times NNZ$	$K \times (2 \times (W+D) + NNZ)$
BEM (Section 7.1)	$p(\boldsymbol{\theta}, \boldsymbol{\phi}\vert\mathbf{x}, \alpha, \beta)$	$2 \times K \times NNZ$	$2 \times K \times (D+W)$
Modifie IEM (Section 7.2)	$p(\boldsymbol{\theta}, \boldsymbol{\phi}\vert\mathbf{x}, \alpha, \beta)$	$2 \times K \times NNZ$	$K \times (D+W)$
OEM (Section 7.3)	$p(\boldsymbol{\theta}, \boldsymbol{\phi}\vert\mathbf{x}, \alpha, \beta)$	$2 \times K \times NNZ$	$K \times (D_s + W + NNZ_s)$

the notation $\hat{\phi}(k) = \sum_w \hat{\phi}_w(k)$ for the denominator in (2). Normalizing $\{\hat{\theta}, \hat{\phi}\}$ yields the multinomial parameters $\{\boldsymbol{\theta}, \boldsymbol{\phi}\}$. However, the variational posterior cannot touch the true posterior for inaccurate solutions [4]. In addition, the calculation of exponential digamma function $\exp[\Psi(\cdot)]$ is computationally complicated. As shown in Table 2, the time complexity of VB for one iteration is $\mathcal{O}(2 \times K \times NNZ \times digamma)$, where $digamma$ is the computing time for exponential digamma function, and NNZ is the number of nonzero elements in document-word sparse matrix. For each nonzero element, we need K iterations for variational E-step and K iterations for normalizing $\mu_{w,d}(k)$. The space complexity is $\mathcal{O}(2 \times K \times (D+W))$ for two multinomial parameters and temporary storage for variational M-step.

In contrast to VB, the collapsed GS [10] algorithm infers the posterior by integrating out $\{\boldsymbol{\theta}, \boldsymbol{\phi}\}$,

$$p(\mathbf{z}|\mathbf{x}, \alpha, \beta) = \frac{p(\mathbf{x}, \mathbf{z}|\alpha, \beta)}{p(\mathbf{x}|\alpha, \beta)} \propto p(\mathbf{x}, \mathbf{z}|\alpha, \beta). \quad (5)$$

This posterior means that we want to fin the best topic labeling configuratio $\mathbf{z}$ given the observed words $\mathbf{x}$. Because the multinomial parameters $\{\boldsymbol{\theta}, \boldsymbol{\phi}\}$ have been integrated out, the best labeling configuratio $\mathbf{z}$ is insensitive to the variation of $\{\boldsymbol{\theta}, \boldsymbol{\phi}\}$. Maximizing the joint probability $p(\mathbf{x}, \mathbf{z}|\alpha, \beta)$ is intractable (i.e., there are $K^{ntokens}$ configuration that increase exponentially), an approximate inference called Markov chain Monte Carlo (MCMC) EM [17] is used as follows:

- MCMC E-step:

$$\mu_{w,d,i}(k) \propto \frac{[\hat{\theta}_d^{-z_{w,d,i}^{k,old}}(k) + \alpha][\hat{\phi}_w^{-z_{w,d,i}^{k,old}}(k) + \beta]}{\sum_w [\hat{\phi}_w^{-z_{w,d,i}^{k,old}}(k) + \beta]}, \quad (6)$$

$$\text{Random Sampling } z_{w,d,i}^{k,new} = 1 \text{ from } \mu_{w,d,i}(k). \quad (7)$$

- MCMC M-step:

$$\hat{\theta}_d(k) = \hat{\theta}_d^{-z_{w,d,i}^{k,old}}(k) + z_{w,d,i}^{k,new}, \quad (8)$$

$$\hat{\phi}_w(k) = \hat{\phi}_w^{-z_{w,d,i}^{k,old}}(k) + z_{w,d,i}^{k,new}. \quad (9)$$

In the MCMC E-step, GS infers the topic posterior per word token, $\mu_{w,d,i}(k) = p(z_{w,d,i}^{k,new} = 1|\mathbf{z}_{w,d,-i}^{k,old}, \mathbf{x}, \alpha, \beta)$, and randomly samples a new topic label $z_{w,d,i}^{k,new} = 1$ from this posterior. The notation $-z_{w,d,i}^{k,old}$ means excluding the old topic label from the corresponding matrices $\{\hat{\theta}, \hat{\phi}\}$. In the MCMC M-step, GS updates immediately $\{\hat{\theta}, \hat{\phi}\}$ by the new topic label of each word token. In this sense, GS can be viewed as an incremental algorithm that learns parameters by processing data point sequentially. In Table 2, the time complexity of GS for one iteration is $\mathcal{O}(\delta_1 \times K \times ntokens)$, where $\delta_1 \ll 2$. The reason is that we require K iterations in MCMC E-step and less K iterations for normalizing $\mu_{w,d,i}(k)$. According to sparseness of $\mu_{w,d,i}(k)$, efficien sampling techniques [31, 13, 32] can make δ_1 even smaller. Practically, when K is larger than 1000, $\delta_1 \approx 0.05$. Generally, we do not need to store $\hat{\theta}_{K \times D}$ in memory because $\mathbf{z}$ can recover $\hat{\theta}_{K \times D}$. So, the space complexity is $\mathcal{O}(\delta_2 \times K \times W + ntokens)$ because $\hat{\phi}_{K \times W}$ can be compressed due to sparseness [31, 13]. When K is larger than 1000, $\delta_2 \approx 0.8$. Note that all parameters in GS are stored in integer type, saving half memory space than double type used by other algorithms.

Unlike VB and GS, CVB [26] infers the complete posterior given the observed data $\mathbf{x}$,

$$p(\boldsymbol{\theta}, \boldsymbol{\phi}, \mathbf{z}|\mathbf{x}, \alpha, \beta) \propto p(\mathbf{x}, \mathbf{z}, \boldsymbol{\theta}, \boldsymbol{\phi}|\alpha, \beta). \quad (10)$$

Maximizing this posterior means that we want to obtain the best combination of multinomial parameters $\{\theta, \phi\}$ for the best topic labeling configuratio $\mathbf{z}$. However, inference of this posterior is intractable so that the Gaussian approximation is used [26]. In this sense, CVB optimizes an approximate LDA model, which cannot achieve the best topic modeling accuracy. The variational E-step and M-step in CVB are similar to those in GS. The main difference is that the variational E-step requires multiplying an exponential correction factor containing variance update for each nonzero element rather than word token. In Table 2, the time complexity of CVB is $\mathcal{O}(\delta_3 \times 2 \times K \times NNZ)$, where $\delta_3 > 1$ denotes the additional cost for calculating exponential correction factor. The space complexity is $K \times (2 \times (W + D) + NNZ)$ because CVB needs to store one copy of matrix $\mu_{K \times NNZ}$, and two copies of matrices $\hat{\theta}_{K \times D}$ and $\hat{\phi}_{K \times W}$ in memory (one for the original and the other for the variance). Details can be found in [26, 2].

We advocate the standard EM [7] algorithm that infers the posterior by integrating out the topic labeling configuratio $\mathbf{z}$,

$$p(\boldsymbol{\theta}, \boldsymbol{\phi}|\mathbf{x}, \alpha, \beta) = \frac{p(\mathbf{x}, \boldsymbol{\theta}, \boldsymbol{\phi}|\alpha, \beta)}{p(\mathbf{x}|\alpha, \beta)} \propto p(\mathbf{x}, \boldsymbol{\theta}, \boldsymbol{\phi}|\alpha, \beta). \quad (11)$$

Unlike the posteriors of VB and GS, this posterior means that we want to fin the best parameters $\{\boldsymbol{\theta}, \boldsymbol{\phi}\}$ given observations $\mathbf{x}$, no matter what topic labeling configuratio $\mathbf{z}$ is. To this end, we integrate out the labeling configuratio $\mathbf{z}$ in full joint probability, and use the standard batch EM algorithm [8] to optimize this objective (11):

- E-step:

$$\mu_{w,d}(k) \propto \frac{[\hat{\theta}_d(k) + \alpha - 1][\hat{\phi}_w(k) + \beta - 1]}{\sum_w [\hat{\phi}(k) + \beta - 1]}, \quad (12)$$

- M-step:

$$\hat{\theta}_d(k) = \sum_w x_{w,d}\mu_{w,d}(k), \quad (13)$$

$$\hat{\phi}_w(k) = \sum_d x_{w,d}\mu_{w,d}(k). \quad (14)$$

In the E-step, EM infers the responsibility $\mu_{w,d}(k)$ conditioned on parameters $\{\hat{\theta}, \hat{\phi}\}$. In the M-step, EM updates parameters $\{\hat{\theta}, \hat{\phi}\}$ based on the inferred responsibility $\mu_{w,d}(k)$. Unlike VB, EM can touch the true posterior distribution $p(\boldsymbol{\theta}, \boldsymbol{\phi}|\mathbf{x}, \alpha, \beta)$ in the E-step for maximization. When compared with VB, the time complexity of EM for one iteration is $\mathcal{O}(2 \times K \times NNZ)$ without calculating exponential digamma functions. The space complexity of EM is the same as VB with $\mathcal{O}(2 \times K \times (D + W))$ because of storing $\{\hat{\theta}, \hat{\phi}\}$ as well as the temporary variables in the M-step.

In the past decade, VB and GS have been two main inference algorithms in LDA literatures, while EM has been rarely discussed and used in learning LDA. We show two main reasons to use EM:

1. **EM yields a higher topic modeling accuracy measured by predictive perplexity than both VB and GS.** Predictive perplexity is a standard performance measure for different LDA inference algorithms [4, 2, 35], which is calculated as follows: 1) We randomly partition the data set into training and test sets in terms of documents. 2) We estimate $\hat{\phi}$ on the training set by 500 iterations. 3) We randomly partition each document into 80% and 20% subsets on the test set. Fixing $\hat{\phi}$, we estimate $\hat{\theta}$ on the 80% subset by 500 iterations, and then calculate the predictive perplexity on the rest 20% subset,

$$\exp\left\{-\frac{\sum_{w,d} x_{w,d}^{20\%} \log\left[\sum_k \theta_d(k)\phi_w(k)\right]}{\sum_{w,d} x_{w,d}^{20\%}}\right\}, \quad (15)$$

where $\{\boldsymbol{\theta}, \boldsymbol{\phi}\}$ are multinomial parameters by normalizing $\{\hat{\theta}, \hat{\phi}\}$, and $x_{w,d}^{20\%}$ denotes the word counts in the the 20% subset. The lower predictive perplexity represents a better generalization ability. It is clear that Eq. (15) is a function of multinomial parameters $\{\boldsymbol{\theta}, \boldsymbol{\phi}\}$, and EM infers the best multinomial parameters $p(\boldsymbol{\theta}, \boldsymbol{\phi}|\mathbf{x}, \alpha, \beta)$ for the low predictive perplexity. By contrast, VB and GS produce higher predictive perplexity than EM because they infer different posteriors as discussed before.

2. **EM converges significantl faster than both VB and GS.** In Appendix (Section 7), we derive BEM [7], IEM [18] and OEM [6] algorithms for LDA. Convergence analysis shows that all these EM algorithms can converge to the local maximum of LDA's objective function, because in the E-step the lower-bound can touch the true posterior. The modifie IEM has a low space complexity, and OEM is able to process big data streams. We see that the zero-order approximation of CVB called CVB0 [2] and asynchronous BP [35, 34] are equivalent to IEM, which have been confirme empirically to converge faster than both VB and GS. Also, online BP (OBP) [37] and stochastic CVB (SCVB) [9] are implementations of OEM, which have been also confirme to be faster than some state-of-the-art online LDA algorithms.

3. SCALABLE PEM FOR LDA

Fig. 1 shows PEM for learning LDA with N threads in shared memory systems. First, we random shuffl and partition the input document-word matrix $\mathbf{x}_{W \times D}$ into $M \times M$ data blocks where $M > N$ (line 1). Second, we run N threads in parallel and each thread performs BEM, IEM and OEM in Figs. 9, 10 and 11 (line 5). Third, we update the residual $r^{m,t}$ (16) after sweeping each block and dynamically schedule the free threads to the free data blocks with the largest residual (lines 6 and 7). Finally, we synchronize the global parameter vector $\hat{\phi}(k)$ after some data blocks (e.g., N) are swept (line 8).

input : $\mathbf{x}, K, \alpha, \beta$.
output : $\hat{\boldsymbol{\phi}}_{W \times K}, \hat{\boldsymbol{\theta}}_{K \times D}$.
1 *random shuffl and partition* $\mathbf{x}_{W \times D}$ into blocks $\mathbf{x}^m, 1 \le m \le M \times M, M > N$;
2 *initialize* $\hat{\theta}_d(k)$, $\hat{\phi}_w(k)$, $\hat{\phi}(k)$;
3 **repeat**
4 **for** $n \leftarrow 1$ **to** N *thread in parallel* **do**
5 free block $\mathbf{x}^m$: do BEM/IEM/OEM ;
6 free block $\mathbf{x}^m$: update residual r^m ;
7 residual-based dynamic scheduling ;
8 synchronize $\hat{\phi}(k)$;
9 **until** *converged*;

Figure 1: Scalable PEM for LDA.

3.1 Residual-based Dynamic Scheduling

Multiple threads in parallel LDA algorithms have long locking time, which is a main factor that we should try to reduce [29]. This motivates us to develop the residual-based dynamic scheduling method. The document-word matrix is partitioned into multiple independent data blocks for parallel computation in different threads. PEM in shared-memory systems use all available N threads to perform E-step and M-step on different data blocks simultaneously. The challenge is that different threads may read and write the same elements in parameter matrices $\hat{\theta}_d(k)$, $\hat{\phi}_w(k)$ and $\hat{\phi}(k)$, which leads to a serious access conflic problem. The K-length parameter vector $\hat{\phi}(k)$ will be visited by all threads at the same time, so that the best method to avoid access conflict is to make N independent copies of vector $\hat{\phi}(k)$ for N threads [19]. After sweeping a certain number of data blocks (e.g., N), we synchronize the parameter vector by summing the updated parameter matrix $\hat{\phi}_w(k)$, i.e., $\hat{\phi}(k) = \sum_w \hat{\phi}_w(k)$. This synchronization cost is not the main bottleneck in PEM because the sum operation on the K-length vectors is very simple.

According to [29], we can avoid access conflict in $\hat{\theta}_d(k)$ and $\hat{\phi}_w(k)$ by partitioning the document-word matrix into $1 \le m \le M \times M$ blocks. In this case, the number of threads $N = M$. Fig. 2 shows an example of data blocks when $M = 4$ in the firs column. The second and third columns show the parameter matrices $\hat{\phi}_{W \times K}$ and $\hat{\theta}_{K \times D}$, respectively. We use four colors (red, yellow, blue and green) to denote four threads. Fig. 2A shows that four threads simultaneously process four data blocks in diagonal. In this way, four threads will visit only the independent rows in $\hat{\phi}_w(k)$ and independent columns in $\hat{\theta}_d(k)$ without conflicting After processing four diagonal data blocks, four threads will simultaneously move to another four data blocks as shown in Fig. 2B, which also use only the independent rows in $\hat{\phi}_w(k)$ and independent columns in $\hat{\theta}_d(k)$ without conflicting This continues in Fig. 2C and Fig. 2D until all 4×4 data blocks have been processed.

To avoid access conflicts all threads in Fig. 2A need to wait for the slowest thread before moving to the next data block in Fig. 2B. Due to data block imbalance (the number of nonzero elements is unequal in different data blocks), the locking time is the main bottleneck in PEM. There are currently two solutions to make data blocks more balanced. First, an approximate integer programming method is used to fin the better data partition efficien y before parallel computation [29]. Second, the random shufflin method works very well empirically [39], which randomly permutes documents (columns) and vocabulary words (rows) of document-word

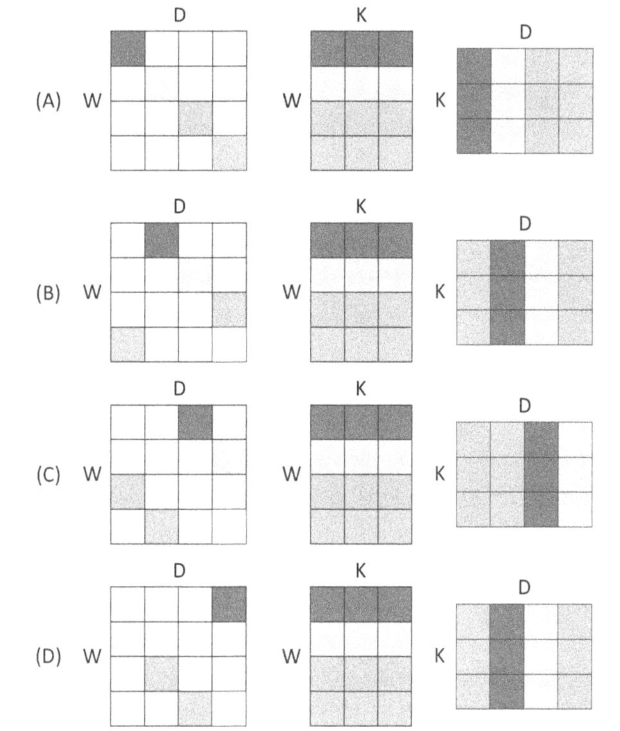

Figure 2: Locking problem occurs when four threads (red, yellow, blue and green) process four independent blocks. The first column denotes the document-word matrix. The second and third columns denote the parameter matrices $\hat{\phi}_w(k)$ and $\hat{\theta}_d(k)$.

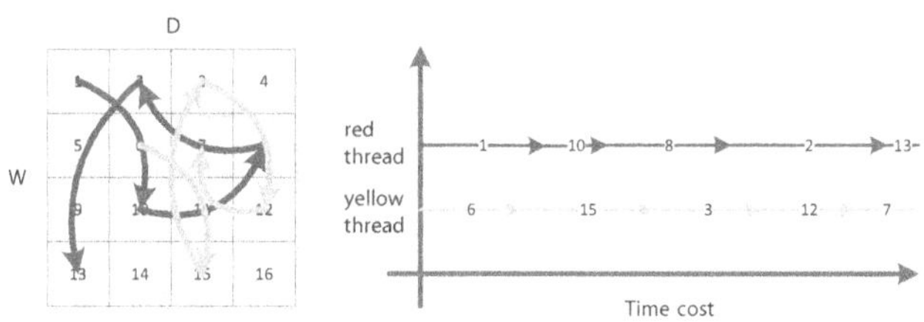

Figure 3: Residual-based dynamic scheduling of two threads (denoted by red and yellow) to process free data blocks without the locking time cost.

sparse matrix before processing. However, the locking problem still exists because NNZ in each data block may not be exactly the same, and there is also slight difference in computing efficien y among different threads.

Our approach is the residual-based scheduling to solve the locking problem in Fig. 3. First, we set $M > N$, i.e., the number of data blocks is more than the number of threads. For example in Fig. 3, we have $N = 2$ threads and partition data matrix into $M \times M = 4 \times 4$ blocks. As far as $N = 2$ threads are concerned, this will create more "free" data blocks without access conflicts On the left figure the red and yellow threads simultaneously process non-conflictin blocks 1 and 6. If the yellow thread finis sweeping block 6 earlier than the red thread, it can directly jump to process a free block 15 without waiting for the red thread. Then, the red thread can jump to process a free block 10 when the yellow thread is processing 15. On the right figure we show the scheduling order of red and yellow threads, where the overlapping data blocks in the time axis have no access conflicts For example, block 1

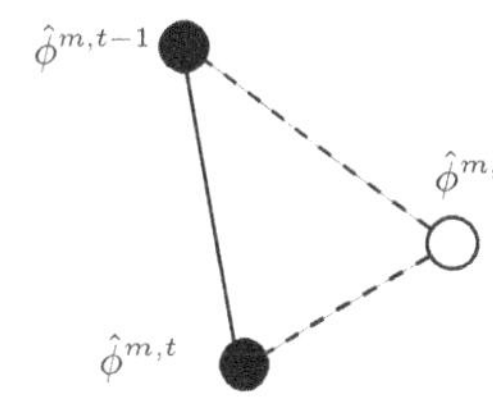

Figure 4: Residual reflect the convergence speed.

(red thread) has no access conflict with blocks 6 and 15 (yellow thread), and block 15 (yellow thread) has no access conflict with blocks 1, 10 and 8 (red thread). In this asynchronous parameter update strategy, there are little locking costs (i.e., few threads need waiting) but scheduling costs.

We propose an efficien residual-based scheduling method that can speed up convergence of PEM. For each data block m, we defin the residual as follows,

$$r^{m,t} = \sum_{w,k} \|\hat{\phi}_w^{m,t}(k) - \hat{\phi}_w^{m,t-1}(k)\|, \tag{16}$$

where $\hat{\phi}_w^{m,t}(k)$ is the updated parameter submatrix at sweep t and $\hat{\phi}_w^{m,t-1}(k)$ is the parameter submatrix before updating at sweep $t-1$. The residual implies the convergence speed when sweeping the current data block m. EM shows that the parameter submatrix $\hat{\phi}^{m,t}$ will converge to a stationary point $\hat{\phi}^{m,*}$ when $t \to \infty$. So, if we minimize the largest distance $\|\hat{\phi}^{m,t} - \hat{\phi}^{m,*}\|$ at higher priority, we will speed up convergence of PEM. However, we do not know this distance because the stationary point $\hat{\phi}^{m,*}$ is unknown. Alternatively, we turn to minimizing the lower bound (16) on this distance that can be calculated easily. Using the triangle inequality, we get the lower bound

$$\begin{aligned} r^{m,t} &= \|\hat{\phi}^{m,t} - \hat{\phi}^{m,t-1}\| \\ &\le \|\hat{\phi}^{m,t} - \hat{\phi}^{m,*}\| + \|\hat{\phi}^{m,t-1} - \hat{\phi}^{m,*}\|. \end{aligned} \tag{17}$$

Fig. 4 shows the definitio of residual (solid line), which is the lower bound of the distance to be minimized (dashed lines) according to the triangle inequality. In this way, the scheduling order is to sweep the free block with the largest residual first When $t \to \infty$, the residual $r^{m,t} \to 0$ due to convergence. This property ensures that the residual of each free block will become smaller when $t \to \infty$ so that all blocks have the chance to be swept in residual-based dynamic scheduling.

3.2 Implementation Issues

We fin that using single-precision floating-poin computation does not suffer from numerical error accumulation. Empirically, using single precision runs around 10% faster than using double precision by saving around 50% memory. Modern CPU provides Streaming SIMD Extension (SSE) instructions that can concurrently run floating-poin multiplications and additions. To speed up both E-step and M-step, we apply SSE instructions for vector inner products and additions in Fig. 9 (lines 5-6), Fig. 10 (lines 4-6), and Fig. 11 (lines 7-11). Using SSE reduces significantl the time cost of line 4 in Fig. 10.

4. EXPERIMENTS

In our experiments, we call parallel BEM as PBEM, parallel IEM as PIEM, and parallel OEM as POEM. We compare these PEM algorithms with the following state-of-the-art parallel LDA algo-

Table 3: Statistics of data sets.

Data	Pubmed	Wiki	Nytimes
W	$6,902$	$7,871$	$5,363$
D_{train}	$8,190,000$	$4,350,095$	$290,000$
D_{test}	$10,000$	$10,000$	$10,000$
NNZ_{tr}	$222,127,506$	$154,574,168$	$42,921,633$
NNZ_{te}	$271,871$	$360,140$	$1,457,642$

Table 4: Convergence time cost (second) when $K = 100$.

Algorithms	Pubmed	Wiki	Nytimes
PBEM-noScheduling	1162.04	630.75	176.8
PIEM-noScheduling	1280.12	613.69	271.30
PBEM	996.17	597.17	124.21
PIEM	976.96	535.08	192.68
PBGS	4370.29	2648.85	882.48
PBCVB0	2037.28	1317.25	550.48

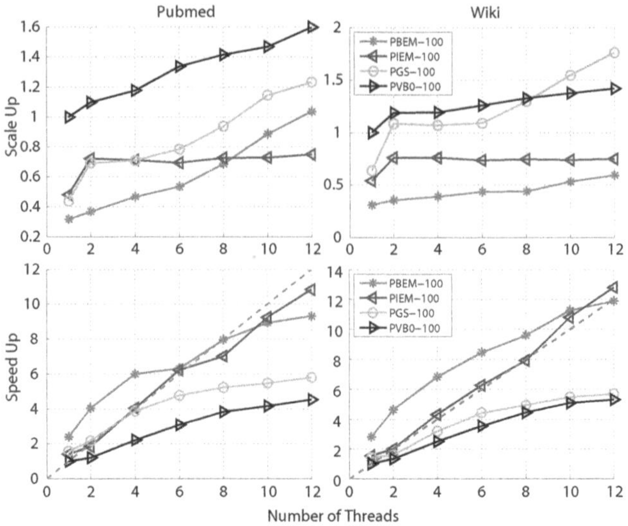

Figure 6: Scalability of PBEM and PIEM ($K = 100$).

rithms in shared memory systems: Yahoo!LDA[1] (parallel batch GS, PGS) [25, 1], GPU-LDA (parallel batch CVB0, PCVB0) [29, 2], parallel online VB[2] (POVB) [11], and distributed stochastic MCMC (parallel online GS, POGS) [23]. According to [2], for a fair comparison, we set Dirichlet hyperparameters $\{\alpha = \beta = 0.01\}$ in PGS, POGS and PCVB0, $\alpha - 1 = 0.01, \beta - 1 = 0.01$ in PEM, and $\alpha - 0.5 = 0.01, \beta - 0.5 = 0.01$ in POVB. We carry out experiments on a server with two Intel Xeon X5690 3.47G processors and 140G memory. There are 6 cores in each processor for a total of 12 cores (threads). Likewise to the previous studies [4, 2, 35], we use the predictive perplexity (15) to evaluate the topic modeling accuracy. The lower perplexity the higher topic modeling accuracy. If the difference of predictive perplexity between two consecutive iterations ≤ 5, the algorithm is considered to be converged [35]. In this way, we can compare the convergence time cost among all algorithms.

Table 3 shows publicly available training and held-out test sets in our experiments.[3] The infrequent words are removed from the vocabulary similar to [4] so that the number of nonzero elements in these data sets becomes smaller than that of the original sets. Among these data sets, Pubmed contains $8,200,000$, Wiki contains $4,360,095$, and Nytimes contains $300,000$ documents. These data sets are big enough for evaluating parallel LDA algorithms. For residual-based dynamic scheduling in PEM, we set $M = 2 \times N = 24$ for free data blocks similar to [39]. In benchmark algorithms without residual-based dynamic scheduling, we set $M = N = 12$ similar to [29].

4.1 PBEM and PIEM

In this subsection, we compare parallel batch LDA algorithms in multi-core systems (PBEM/PIEM v.s. PGS/PCVB0). Table 4 shows the convergence time cost of all algorithms when $K = 100$. We see that PBEM or PIEM converges around 1.2 or 1.3, 1.1 or 1.2, 1.4 or 1.4 times faster than PBEM-noScheduling or PIEM-noScheduling on Pubmed, Wiki and Nytimes, respectively. On average, residual-based dynamic scheduling can reduce around $10\% \sim 20\%$ running time for convergence excluding the speedup effects brought by implementations in Subsection 3.2. This confirm the effectiveness of the residual-based dynamic scheduling to reduce the overall locking time. In addition, we fin that PIEM benefi more from dynamic scheduling than PBEM. The major reason is that IEM often passes the influenc of data blocks with largest residuals more efficientl than BEM. Both PBEM and PIEM converge to almost the same perplexity level, which indicates almost the same topic modeling accuracy. On Nytimes data set, PIEM converges significantl slower than PBEM even after adding residual-based dynamic scheduling. Indeed, there is currently no theory that IEM always converges faster than BEM [18, 14], though some limited experiments [14] indicate that IEM converges faster than BEM. In our experiments, three data sets have quite different word distributions. We see that PIEM converges slightly faster than PBEM on Pubmed and Wiki, but it converges slower on Nytimes. This gives an example that BEM sometimes converges faster than IEM.

In Fig. 5, we compare the predictive perplexity of PBEM/PIEM and PGS/PCVB0 when $K \in \{50, 100, 150, 200, 250\}$ on three data sets. PBEM/PIEM always converges to a much lower predictive perplexity than PGS. On average, there is around $30\% \sim 50\%$ predictive perplexity improvement. Because PCVB0 is similar to PIEM, it converges to almost the same predictive perplexity as PIEM. Clearly, both PBEM and PIEM converge significantl faster than PGS and PCVB0. Their perplexity curves always locate on those of PGS/PCVB0's left. The speedup has been largely attributed to the residual-based dynamic scheduling methods as well as fast convergence speed of EM. In practice, PBEM and PIEM can process $820,000,000$ documents in Pubmed using no more than 16 minutes on a single PC, which is comparable with the previous multi-processor solution on 1024 CPUs (23 minutes) [19]. Therefore, parallel LDA algorithms in multi-core systems are not only competitive but also affordable in big data era.

To test scalability, we perform two types of experiments on both Pubmed and Wiki ($K = 100$): *Scale Up* and *Speed Up*. In *Scale Up*, we establish scalability in terms of the number of documents. We fi each thread to process 10M data and increase the number of threads from 1 to 12 (x-axis). Thus, the scale of processed data increases from 10M to 120M. The *Scale Up* (y-axis) is the division between the convergence time of all other algorithms and that of PCVB0 using 1 thread for 10M data. In *Speed Up*, we establish

[1] `https://github.com/shravanmn/Yahoo_LDA`
[2] `http://radimrehurek.com/2014/09/multicore-lda-in-\python-from-over-night-to-over-lunch/`
[3] `http://archive.ics.uci.edu/ml/datasets/Bag\%20of\%20Words`

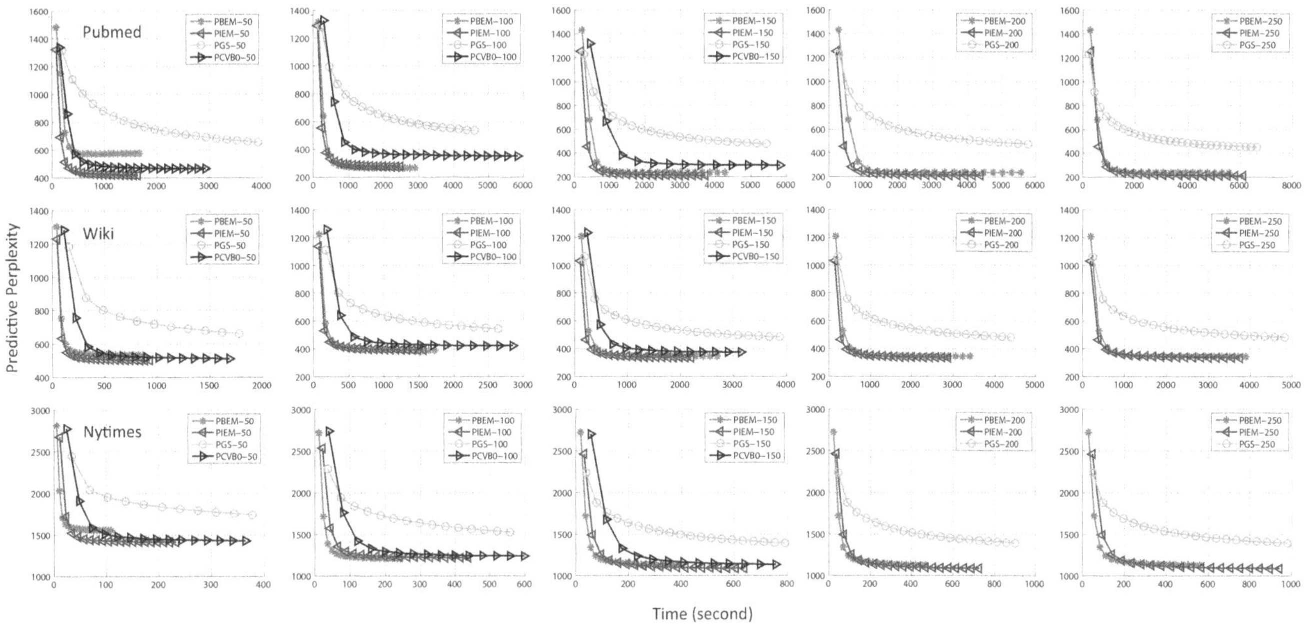

Figure 5: Comparisons of predictive perplexity when $K \in \{50, 100, 150, 200, 250\}$ on three data sets.

scalability in terms of a speedup in convergence time as we increase the number of threads available. We use the entire Pubmed and Wiki data sets, and increase the number of threads from 1 to 12 (x-axis). The *Speed Up* (y-axis) is the division between the convergence time of all other algorithms and that of PCVB0 using 1 thread for the entire data set.

Fig. 6 shows that PIEM performs the best in terms of *Scale Up* and *Speed Up*. The top row shows that the *Scale Up* curve of PIEM remains almost a horizontal line when the processed data increase. This means that PIEM uses a large fraction of runtime to do topic modeling when the volume of data increases. As a comparison, the *Scale Up* curves of PGS, PCVB0 and PBEM increase linearly with respect to the volume of processed data. The bottom row shows that the *Speed Up* curve of PIEM is almost linear with respect to the number of threads. This means that more threads will lead to faster speed. As a comparison, the *Speed Up* curves of PGS, PCVB0 and PBEM bend obviously when the number of threads increases. But PBEM's scalability is still much better than both PGS and PCVB0. The major reason why PIEM has the best scalability is that the residual-based dynamic scheduling performs very well in PIEM so that locking time has been significantl reduced. In this paper, we advocate PIEM in shared memory systems for large-scale data sets due to good scalability performance.

4.2 POEM

In this subsection, we compare POEM with two parallel online LDA algorithms: POVB (multi-core OVB with open source codes)[4] and POGS. Similar to previous work [11], we set the learning parameters as $\{\tau_0 = 64, \kappa = 0.5, D_s = 4096\}$. First, we compare parallel online LDA algorithms with batch algorithms: PBEM and PIEM. Fig. 7 (left panel) shows the convergence time costs (x-axis) and predictive perplexity (y-axis) achieved on three data sets Wiki (red color), Nytimes (blue color) and Pubmed (green color) when $K = 100$. If the algorithm locates in the left-bottom area, it

[4]http://radimrehurek.com/2014/
09/multicore-lda-in-python\
\-from-over-night-to-over-lunch/

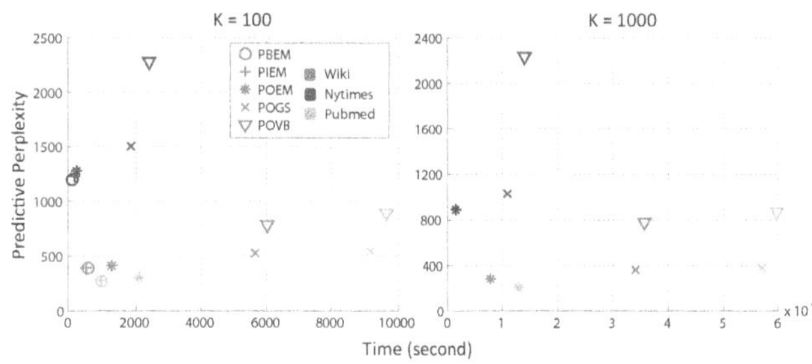

Figure 7: POEM convergence speed and predictive perplexity.

indicates the desirable topic modeling result (i.e., fast convergence speed as well as high topic modeling accuracy). We see that the batch algorithms converge faster than the online ones since they use the global gradient ascent of all data points while the online algorithms use only the local gradient ascent of each mini-batch to update parameters. This is consistent with the previous finding that the convergence rate of stochastic algorithms is often slower than that of batch algorithms [24]. POEM (star sign) can converge at almost the same predictive perplexity of PBEM (circle sign) and PIEM (plus sign), which confirm that POEM can converge to the local maximum of the LDA's log-likelihood function in Section 7.3. As a comparison, POGS (cross sign) and POVB (triangle sign) converge around $3 \sim 4$ times slower than POEM. The main reason is that POVB uses computationally complicated digamma functions in Table 2, while POGS uses much more iterations for learning each mini-batch due to its Markov Chain Monte Carlo (MCMC) nature. Also, we see that POVB and POGS converge at the higher level of predictive perplexity than POEM, supporting our analysis in Section 2 that EM yields a higher topic modeling accuracy because of its inferred posterior $p(\boldsymbol{\theta}, \boldsymbol{\phi}|\mathbf{x}, \alpha, \beta)$. Although [2] states that the topic modeling accuracy of different inference algorithms can be almost the same by tuning the hyperparameters $\{\alpha, \beta\}$, we still

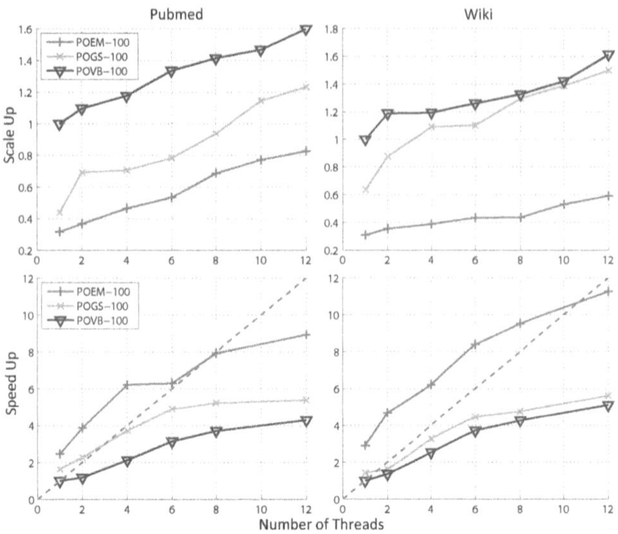

Figure 8: Scalability of POEM ($K = 100$).

advocate the standard EM framework because it converges much faster than both VB and GS.

Although POEM, POVB and POGS converge slower than PBEM and PIEM, they are more memory-efficien to handle larger scale topic modeling tasks on a single PC because they do not need to store the large matrix $\hat{\theta}_{K \times D}$. For example, PBEM and PIEM cannot efficientl process Pubmed data set when $K = 1000$, while POEM, POVB and POGS can do it. Fig. 7 (right panel) compares the convergence time costs and predictive perplexity of POEM, POVB and POGS when $K = 1000$. Similar to the results when $K = 100$, POEM performs significantl faster and achieves a lower perplexity than POVB and POGS. In practice, POEM processes Pubmed data set ($K = 1000$) using less than 3 hours, while PGS using 1024 CPUs requires around 4.5 hours on the same scale of data set [19].

Fig. 8 compares the *Scale Up* and *Speed Up* curves of POEM and POVB/POGS. In *Scale Up*, we f x each thread to process 30M data and increase the number of threads from 1 to 12 (x-axis). The *Scale Up* (y-axis) is the division between the convergence time of all other algorithms and that of POVB using 1 thread for 30M data. The perfect *Scale Up* curve is a horizontal line in the bottom area. Clearly, the *Scale Up* curve of POEM locates significantl lower than those of POGS and POVB, indicating a much better *Scale Up* performance. In *Speed Up*, we divide between the convergence time of all other parallel online LDA algorithms and that of POVB using 1 thread for the entire data set (y-axis). We increase the number of threads from 1 to 12 (x-axis) and see if the convergence speed increases. The perfect *Speed Up* curve is a linear line with a high slope without bending. We see that the *Speed Up* curve of POEM is significantl higher than those of POVB and POGS. This shows that POEM can reach a higher speedup when more threads are used. Both Fig. 6 and Fig. 7 confir that the proposed PEM algorithms are more scalable than the current state-of-the-art solutions.

5. CONCLUSIONS

Scalable LDA algorithms in shared memory systems are needed for big data on widely used multi-core systems. Unlike previous parallel solutions using batch/online VB and GS inference, we advocate the EM framework to build more scalable parallel LDA algorithms. Using the efficien residual-based dynamic scheduling, we propose scalable PEM algorithms for LDA with faster convergence speed and shorter locking time than the current state-of-the-art. Experiments show that the residual-based dynamic scheduling can effectively reduce the locking time and speed up convergence of PEM, which can be used in other latent variable models where EM inference works. In our future work, we shall study how to extend PEM from the multi-core systems to multi-processor systems [30, 28].

6. ACKNOWLEDGEMENTS

This work was supported by National Grant Fundamental Research (973 Program) of China under Grant 2014CB340304, NSFC (Grant No. 61373092 and 61033013), Hong Kong RGC project 620812, and Natural Science Foundation of the Jiangsu Higher Education Institutions of China (Grant No. 12KJA520004). This work was partially supported by Collaborative Innovation Center of Novel Software Technology and Industrialization.

7. APPENDIX

In this appendix, we derive BEM, IEM and OEM algorithms for LDA, which infer the posterior $p(\boldsymbol{\theta}, \boldsymbol{\phi}|\mathbf{x}, \alpha, \beta) \propto p(\mathbf{x}, \boldsymbol{\theta}, \boldsymbol{\phi}|\alpha, \beta)$ from the full joint probability of LDA. This objective is quite different from VB [4], GS [10] and CVB algorithms, which infer the posterior $p(\boldsymbol{\theta}, \mathbf{z}|\mathbf{x}, \boldsymbol{\phi}, \alpha, \beta)$, $p(\mathbf{z}|\mathbf{x}, \alpha, \beta)$, and $p(\boldsymbol{\theta}, \boldsymbol{\phi}, \mathbf{z}|\mathbf{x}, \alpha, \beta)$, respectively. The time and space complexity comparison of these algorithms has been shown in Table 2.

7.1 Batch EM (BEM)

We maximize the likelihood function of LDA in terms of multinomial parameter set $\lambda = \{\boldsymbol{\theta}, \boldsymbol{\phi}\}$ as follows,

$$p(\mathbf{x}, \boldsymbol{\theta}, \boldsymbol{\phi}|\alpha, \beta) = \prod_{w,d,i} \left[\sum_k p(x_{w,d,i} = 1, z^k_{w,d,i} = 1 |\theta_d(k), \phi_w(k)) \right] \prod_d p(\theta_d(k)|\alpha) \prod_k p(\phi_w(k)|\beta). \quad (18)$$

Employing the Bayes' rule and the definitio of multinomial distributions, we get the word likelihood,

$$\begin{aligned} &p(x_{w,d,i} = 1, z^k_{w,d,i} = 1|\theta_d(k), \phi_w(k)) = \\ &p(x_{w,d,i} = 1|z^k_{w,d,i} = 1, \phi_w(k)) \times p(z^k_{w,d,i} = 1|\theta_d(k)), \\ &= x_{w,d,i}\phi_w(k)\theta_d(k), \end{aligned} \quad (19)$$

input : $\mathbf{x}, K, T, \alpha, \beta$.
output : $\hat{\phi}_{W \times K}, \hat{\boldsymbol{\theta}}_{K \times D}$.
initialize $\hat{\theta}_d(k)$; $\hat{\phi}_w(k)$; $\hat{\phi}(k)$;
for $t \leftarrow 1$ **to** T **do**
  $\hat{\theta}^{\text{new}}_d(k) \leftarrow 0$; $\hat{\phi}^{\text{new}}_w(k) \leftarrow 0$; $\hat{\phi}^{\text{new}}(k) \leftarrow 0$;
  for $x_{w,d} \neq 0$ **do**
    $\mu_{w,d}(k) \leftarrow \text{normalize}([\hat{\theta}_d(k) + \alpha - 1][\hat{\phi}_w(k) + \beta - 1]/[\hat{\phi}(k) + W(\beta - 1)])$;
    $\hat{\theta}^{\text{new}}_d(k) \leftarrow \hat{\theta}^{\text{new}}_d(k) + x_{w,d}\mu_{w,d}(k)$;
    $\hat{\phi}^{\text{new}}_w(k) \leftarrow \hat{\phi}^{\text{new}}_w(k) + x_{w,d}\mu_{w,d}(k)$;
    $\hat{\phi}^{\text{new}}(k) \leftarrow \hat{\phi}^{\text{new}}(k) + x_{w,d}\mu_{w,d}(k)$;
  $\hat{\theta}_d(k) \leftarrow \hat{\theta}^{\text{new}}_d(k)$; $\hat{\phi}_w(k) \leftarrow \hat{\phi}^{\text{new}}_w(k)$;
  $\hat{\phi}(k) \leftarrow \hat{\phi}^{\text{new}}(k)$;

Figure 9: BEM for LDA.

which depends only on the word index $\{w, d\}$ instead of the word token index i. Then, according to the definitio of Dirichlet distributions, the log-likelihood of (18) is

$$\ell(\lambda) \propto \sum_{w,d,i} x_{w,d,i}\left[\log \sum_{k} \mu_{w,d}(k)\frac{\theta_d(k)\phi_w(k)}{\mu_{w,d}(k)}\right] + \sum_{d}\sum_{k} \log[\theta_d(k)]^{\alpha-1} + \sum_{k}\sum_{w} \log[\phi_w(k)]^{\beta-1}, \tag{20}$$

where $\mu_{w,d}(k)$ is some topic distribution over the word index $\{w, d\}$ satisfying $\sum_k \mu_{w,d}(k) = 1, \mu_{w,d}(k) \geq 0$. In (19), we observe that $\sum_{w,d,i}[x_{w,d,i} = 1] = \sum_{w,d} x_{w,d}$, so that we can cancel the word token index i in (20). Because the logarithm is concave, by Jensen's inequality, we have

$$\ell(\lambda) \geq \ell(\boldsymbol{\mu}, \lambda) = \sum_{w,d}\sum_{k} x_{w,d}\mu_{w,d}(k)\left[\log \frac{\theta_d(k)\phi_w(k)}{\mu_{w,d}(k)}\right] + \sum_{d}\sum_{k} \log[\theta_d(k)]^{\alpha-1} + \sum_{k}\sum_{w} \log[\phi_w(k)]^{\beta-1}, \tag{21}$$

which gives the lower bound of log-likelihood (20). The equality holds true if and only if

$$\mu_{w,d}(k) \propto \theta_d(k)\phi_w(k). \tag{22}$$

In EM, the K-length posterior probability vector $\mu_{w,d}(k)$ is the **responsibility** that the topic k takes for word index $\{w, d\}$ [17]. For this choice of $\mu_{w,d}(k)$, Eq. (21) gives a **tight lower bound** on the log-likelihood (20) we are trying to maximize. This is called the E-step in EM [8].

In the successive M-step, we then maximize (21) with respect to parameters to obtain a new setting of λ. Since the hyperparameters $\{\alpha, \beta\}$ are fi ed, without loss of generality, we derive the M-step update for the parameter $\theta_d(k)$. There is an additional constraint that $\sum_k \theta_d(k) = 1$ because $\theta_d(k)$ is parameter of a multinomial distribution. To deal with this constraint, we construct the Lagrangian from (21) by grouping together only the terms that depend on $\theta_d(k)$,

$$\ell(\theta) = \sum_{d}\sum_{k}\left[\sum_{w} x_{w,d}\mu_{w,d}(k) + \alpha - 1\right]\log\theta_d(k) + \delta\Big(\sum_{k}\theta_d(k) - 1\Big), \tag{23}$$

where δ is the Lagrange multiplier. Taking derivatives, we fin

$$\frac{\partial}{\partial_{\theta_d(k)}}\ell(\theta) = \frac{\sum_w x_{w,d}\mu_{w,d}(k) + \alpha - 1}{\theta_d(k)} + \delta. \tag{24}$$

Setting this to zero, we get

$$\theta_d(k) = \frac{\sum_w x_{w,d}\mu_{w,d}(k) + \alpha - 1}{-\delta}. \tag{25}$$

Using the constraint that $\sum_k \theta_d(k) = 1$, we easily fin that $-\delta = \sum_k[\sum_w x_{w,d}\mu_{w,d}(k) + \alpha - 1]$. We therefore have our M-step update for the parameter $\theta_d(k)$ as

$$\theta_d(k) = \frac{\hat{\theta}_d(k) + \alpha - 1}{\sum_k \hat{\theta}_d(k) + K(\alpha - 1)}. \tag{26}$$

where $\hat{\theta}_d(k) = \sum_w x_{w,d}\mu_{w,d}(k)$ is the expected sufficien statistics. Similarly, another multinomial parameter can be estimated by

$$\phi_w(k) = \frac{\hat{\phi}_w(k) + \beta - 1}{\hat{\phi}(k) + W(\beta - 1)}, \tag{27}$$

input : $\mathbf{x}, K, T, \alpha, \beta$.
output : $\hat{\boldsymbol{\phi}}_{W \times K}, \hat{\boldsymbol{\theta}}_{K \times D}$.
initialize $\hat{\theta}_d(k)$, $\hat{\phi}_w(k)$, $\hat{\phi}(k)$;
for $t \leftarrow 1$ **to** T **do**
  for $x_{w,d} \neq 0$ *in random order* **do**
    $\hat{\theta}_d(k) \leftarrow (1 - x_{w,d}/\sum_w x_{w,d})\hat{\theta}_d(k)$;
    $\hat{\phi}_w(k) \leftarrow (1 - x_{w,d}/\sum_d x_{w,d})\hat{\phi}_w(k)$;
    $\hat{\phi}(k) \leftarrow (1 - x_{w,d}/\sum_{w,d} x_{w,d})\hat{\phi}(k)$;
    $\mu_{w,d}(k) \leftarrow$ normalize($[\hat{\theta}_d(k) + \alpha - 1][\hat{\phi}_w(k) + \beta - 1]/[\hat{\phi}(k) + W(\beta - 1)]$);
    $\hat{\theta}_d(k) \leftarrow \hat{\theta}_d(k) + x_{w,d}\mu_{w,d}(k)$;
    $\hat{\phi}_w(k) \leftarrow \hat{\phi}_w(k) + x_{w,d}\mu_{w,d}(k)$;
    $\hat{\phi}(k) \leftarrow \hat{\phi}(k) + x_{w,d}\mu_{w,d}(k)$;

Figure 10: Modifie IEM for LDA.

where $\hat{\phi}_w(k) = \sum_d x_{w,d}\mu_{w,d}(k)$ is the expected sufficien statistics and $\hat{\phi}(k) = \sum_w \hat{\phi}_w(k)$. Note that the denominator of (26) is a constant. Replacing (26) and (27) into (22), we obtain the E-step in terms of sufficien statistics,

$$\mu_{w,d}(k) \propto \frac{[\hat{\theta}_d(k) + \alpha - 1] \times [\hat{\phi}_w(k) + \beta - 1]}{\hat{\phi}(k) + W(\beta - 1)}, \tag{28}$$

where the EM iterates the E-step and M-step to refin sufficien statistics $\hat{\theta}_d(k)$ and $\hat{\phi}_w(k)$, which can be normalized to be the multinomial parameters according to (26) and (27).

Fig. 9 shows BEM for LDA. We initialize three temporary matrices $\hat{\phi}_w^{new}(k), \hat{\theta}_d^{new}(k), \hat{\phi}^{new}(k)$ (line 3) to accumulate responsibilities in E-step for all words (line 6) without storing the large responsibility matrix $\boldsymbol{\mu}_{K \times NNZ}$ in memory. At the end of each iteration $t, 1 \leq t \leq T$, we copy the three temporary matrices back to $\hat{\phi}_w(k), \hat{\theta}_d(k), \hat{\phi}(k)$ in M-step (line 7). BEM iterates E-step and M-step repeatedly. Suppose λ^{t-1} and λ^t are the parameters from two successive iterations of EM. It is easy to prove that

$$\ell(\lambda^t) \geq \ell(\boldsymbol{\mu}^{t-1}, \lambda^t) \geq \ell(\boldsymbol{\mu}^{t-1}, \lambda^{t-1}) = \ell(\lambda^{t-1}), \tag{29}$$

which shows that EM always monotonically improves the LDA's log-likelihood (20) for convergence. The EM can be also viewed as a coordinate ascent on the lower bound $\ell(\boldsymbol{\mu}, \lambda)$ (21), in which the E-step maximizes it with respect to $\boldsymbol{\mu}$, and the M-step maximizes it with respect to λ.

7.2 Incremental EM (IEM)

In batch EM (BEM), the M-step is performed until the E-step updates all responsibilities $\mu_{w,d}(k)$, which slows down the convergence since the updated responsibility of each word in the E-step does not immediately influenc the parameter estimation in the M-step. This problem motivates incremental EM (IEM) [18]. When compared with BEM (28), IEM alternates a single E-step and M-step for each nonzero element $x_{w,d}$ sequentially. Thus, the E-step of IEM becomes

$$\mu_{w,d}(k) \propto \frac{[\hat{\theta}_{-w,d}(k) + \alpha - 1] \times [\hat{\phi}_{w,-d}(k) + \beta - 1]}{\hat{\phi}_{-(w,d)}(k) + W(\beta - 1)}. \tag{30}$$

The *expected sufficien statistics* are

$$\hat{\theta}_{-w,d}(k) = \sum_{-w} x_{w,d}\mu_{w,d}(k), \tag{31}$$

$$\hat{\phi}_{w,-d}(k) = \sum_{-d} x_{w,d}\mu_{w,d}(k), \tag{32}$$

$$\hat{\phi}_{-(w,d)}(k) = \sum_{-(w,d)} x_{w,d}\mu_{w,d}(k), \tag{33}$$

where $-w$, $-d$ and $-(w,d)$ denote all word indices except w, all document indices except d, and all word indices except $\{w,d\}$. After the E-step for each word, the M-step will update the sufficien statistics immediately by adding the updated posterior $\mu_{w,d}(k)$ (30) into (31), (32) and (33).

Comparing the E-step between BEM and IEM, we fin that the major difference between (28) and (30) is that IEM excludes the current posterior $x_{w,d}\mu_{w,d}(k)$ from sufficien statistics in (31), (32) and (33). As a result, IEM's space complexity is $\mathcal{O}(K \times (D+W+NNZ))$ by storing the large responsibility matrix $\boldsymbol{\mu}_{K\times NNZ}$. For example, if $K=100$, the responsibility matrix will occupy around 360GB (using double-precision floating-poin format) memory on the Pubmed data set [21] having 483, 450, 157 nonzero elements. This space is currently too large to be afforded by a single commodity PC. Note that CVB0 [2] and asynchronous BP [35, 36] are equivalent to IEM, which are also memory-consuming for big data on a single PC. So, we propose a modifie IEM in Fig. 10 that do not need to store the large responsibility matrix. After random initialization, we reduce the parameter matrices $\hat{\theta}_d(k), \hat{\phi}_w(k), \hat{\phi}(k)$ in a certain proportion (line 4). This avoids to subtract the current responsibility from parameter matrices in (31), (32) and (33). Then, the E-step of incremental EM becomes (28) rather than (30). In this way, we do not need to store the large responsibility matrix $\boldsymbol{\mu}_{K\times NNZ}$ in memory. After E-step (line 5) for each nonzero element, the parameter matrices can be compensated by the updated K-tuple responsibility $\mu_{w,d}(k)$ in M-step (line 6). In this way, the change of parameter matrix will immediately influenc the update of the responsibility for the next nonzero element (line 5). In anticipation, this incremental update method is more efficien to pass the influenc of the updated responsibility than batch EM in Fig. 9. Likewise, it is easy to see that IEM can also converge to the local stationary point of LDA's log-likelihood because

$$\begin{aligned}\ell(\lambda^t) = \ell(\boldsymbol{\mu}^t, \lambda^t) &\geq \ell(\mu^t_{w,d}, \boldsymbol{\mu}^{t-1}_{-(w,d)}, \lambda^t) \\ &\geq \ell(\mu^t_{w,d}, \boldsymbol{\mu}^{t-1}_{-(w,d)}, \lambda^{t-1}) \geq \ell(\boldsymbol{\mu}^{t-1}, \lambda^{t-1}) = \ell(\lambda^{t-1}). \end{aligned} \tag{34}$$

7.3 Online EM (OEM)

The basic idea of online algorithms is to partition a stream of D documents into small mini-batches with size D_s, and use the online gradient produced by each mini-batch to estimate topic distributions incrementally. OEM [6] combines IEM with the stochastic approximation, which achieves convergence to the stationary points of the likelihood function by interpolating between sufficien statistics based on a learning rate ρ_s satisfying Robbins-Monro conditions [22],

$$\rho_s = (\tau_0 + s)^{-\kappa}, \tag{35}$$

where τ_0 is a pre-define number of mini-batches, s is the mini-batch index and $\kappa \in (0.5, 1]$ is provided by users. Similar to (34), it is easy to observe that

$$\begin{aligned}\ell(\hat{\phi}^s) = \ell(\boldsymbol{\mu}^{s+1:\infty}, \mu^s, \hat{\phi}^s) &\geq \ell(\boldsymbol{\mu}^{s+1:\infty}, \mu^s, \hat{\phi}^{s-1}) \\ &\geq \ell(\boldsymbol{\mu}^{s:\infty}, \mu^{s-1}, \hat{\phi}^{s-1}) = \ell(\hat{\phi}^{s-1}), \end{aligned} \tag{36}$$

input : $x^s_{w,d}, D_s, \tau_0, \kappa, K, \alpha, \beta$.
output : $\hat{\phi}^S_{K\times W}$.
for $s \leftarrow 1$ **to** S **do**
  Load $x^s_{w,d}, d \in D_s$ in memory;
  $\rho_s = (\tau_0 + s)^{-\kappa}$; *initialize* $\boldsymbol{\mu}^s$;
  $\hat{\theta}^s_d(k) \leftarrow \sum_w x^s_{w,d}\mu^s_{w,d}(k), d \in D_s$;
  $\hat{\phi}^s_w(k) \leftarrow \hat{\phi}^s_w(k) + \sum_d x^s_{w,d}\mu^s_{w,d}(k), d \in D_s$;
  $\hat{\phi}^s(k) \leftarrow \hat{\phi}^s(k) + \sum_{w,d} x^s_{w,d}\mu^s_{w,d}(k), d \in D_s$;
  repeat
    for $x^s_{w,d} \neq 0$ *in random order* **do**
      $\hat{\theta}^s_{-w,d}(k) \leftarrow \hat{\theta}^s_d(k) - x^s_{w,d}\mu^s_{w,d}(k)$;
      $\hat{\phi}^s_{w,-d}(k) \leftarrow \hat{\phi}_w(k) - x^s_{w,d}\mu^s_{w,d}(k)$;
      $\hat{\phi}^s_{-(w,d)}(k) \leftarrow \hat{\phi}(k) - x^s_{w,d}\mu^s_{w,d}(k)$;
      $\mu^s_{w,d}(k) \leftarrow$ normalize($[\hat{\theta}^s_d(k) + \alpha - 1][\hat{\phi}^s_w(k) + \beta - 1]/[\hat{\phi}^s(k) + W(\beta - 1)]$);
      $\hat{\theta}^s_d(k) \leftarrow \hat{\theta}^s_d(k) + x^s_{w,d}\mu^s_{w,d}(k)$;
      $\hat{\phi}^s_w(k) \leftarrow \hat{\phi}^s_w(k) + x^s_{w,d}\mu^s_{w,d}(k)$;
      $\hat{\phi}^s(k) \leftarrow \hat{\phi}^s(k) + x^s_{w,d}\mu^s_{w,d}(k)$;
  until *converged*;
  $\hat{\phi}^s_w(k) \leftarrow (1-\rho_s)\hat{\phi}^{s-1}_w(k) + \rho_s[\sum_d x^s_{w,d}\mu^s_{w,d}(k)]$;
  $\hat{\phi}^s(k) \leftarrow (1-\rho_s)\hat{\phi}^{s-1}(k) + \rho_s[\sum_{w,d} x^s_{w,d}\mu^s_{w,d}(k)]$;
  Free $x^s_{w,d}$, $\hat{\boldsymbol{\theta}}^s_{K\times D_s}$, $\boldsymbol{\mu}^s_{K\times NNZ_s}$ from memory;

Figure 11: OEM for LDA.

where $\boldsymbol{\mu}^{s+1:\infty}$ denotes responsibilities of unseen mini-batches from $s+1$ to ∞. Note that the lower bound (36) will not touch the log-likelihood (20) until all responsibilities for data streams have been updated in (21). The inequality (36) confirm that OEM can improve $\hat{\phi}^s$ to maximize the LDA's log-likelihood (20). In practice, OEM reads each mini-batch $x^s_{w,d}$ into memory and runs IEM until $\boldsymbol{\mu}^s$ converged. Then, the sufficien statistics $\hat{\phi}^s$ is updated by a linear combination between previous $\hat{\phi}^{s-1}$ and the updated sufficien statistics $\sum_d x^s_{w,d}\mu^s_{w,d}(k)$,

$$\hat{\phi}^s = (1-\rho_s)\hat{\phi}^{s-1} + \rho_s\Big[\sum_d x^s_{w,d}\mu^s_{w,d}(k)\Big]. \tag{37}$$

Since OEM only stores the current mini-batch $x^s_{w,d}$, the local parameters $\boldsymbol{\mu}^s$, $\hat{\boldsymbol{\theta}}_{K\times D_s}$ and the global parameter $\hat{\phi}^s$ in memory, it is easy to process big data stream with low space complexities $\mathcal{O}(K \times (D_s + W + NNZ_s))$, where D_s is the number of documents and NNZ_s the number of nonzero elements in the sth mini-batch. Fig. 11 summarizes the OEM algorithm for LDA, where online BP [37] and stochastic CVB [9] are some implementations of OEM. Note that OEM can revisit previous processed mini-batch.

8. REFERENCES

[1] A. Ahmed, M. Aly, J. Gonzalez, S. Narayanamurthy, and A. Smola. Scalable inference in latent variable models. In *WSDM*, pages 123–132, 2012.

[2] A. Asuncion, M. Welling, P. Smyth, and Y. W. Teh. On smoothing and inference for topic models. In *UAI*, pages 27–34, 2009.

[3] D. M. Blei. Introduction to probabilistic topic models. *Communications of the ACM*, 55(4):77–84, 2012.

[4] D. M. Blei, A. Y. Ng, and M. I. Jordan. Latent Dirichlet allocation. *J. Mach. Learn. Res.*, 3:993–1022, 2003.
[5] T. Broderick, N. Boyd, A. Wibisono, A. C. Wilson, and M. I. Jordan. Streaming variational bayes. In *NIPS*, pages 1727–1735, 2013.
[6] O. Cappé and E. Moulines. Online expectation-maximization algorithm for latent data models. *Journal of the Royal Statistical Society: Series B*, 71(3):593–613, 2009.
[7] N. de Freitas and K. Barnard. Bayesian latent semantic analysis of multimedia databases. Technical report, University of British Columbia, 2001.
[8] A. P. Dempster, N. M. Laird, and D. B. Rubin. Maximum likelihood from incomplete data via the EM algorithm. *Journal of the Royal Statistical Society, Series B*, 39:1–38, 1977.
[9] J. R. Foulds, L. Boyles, C. DuBois, P. Smyth, and M. Welling. Stochastic collapsed variational bayesian inference for latent Dirichlet allocation. In *KDD*, pages 446–454, 2013.
[10] T. L. Griffith and M. Steyvers. Finding scientifi topics. *Proc. Natl. Acad. Sci.*, 101:5228–5235, 2004.
[11] M. Hoffman, D. Blei, and F. Bach. Online learning for latent Dirichlet allocation. In *NIPS*, pages 856–864, 2010.
[12] D. Jiang, K. W.-T. Leung, and W. Ng. Fast topic discovery from web search streams. In *WWW*, pages 949–960, 2014.
[13] A. Q. Li, A. Ahmed, S. Ravi, and A. J. Smola. Reducing the sampling complexity of topic models. In *KDD*, 2014.
[14] P. Liang and D. Klein. Online EM for unsupervised models. In *Human Language Technologies: The 2009 Annual Conference of the North American Chapter of the ACL*, pages 611–619, 2009.
[15] Z. Liu, Y. Zhang, E. Y. Chang, and M. Sun. PLDA+: Parallel latent dirichlet allocation with data placement and pipeline processing. *ACM Trans. Intell. Syst. Technol.*, 2(3):1–18, 2011.
[16] D. Mimno, M. D. Hoffman, and D. M. Blei. Sparse stochastic inference for latent Dirichlet allocation. In *ICML*, 2012.
[17] K. P. Murphy. *Machine Learning: A Probabilistic Perspective*. The MIT Press, 2012.
[18] R. M. Neal and G. E. Hinton. A view of the EM algorithm that justific incremental, sparse, and other variants. *Learning in Graphical Models*, 89:355–368, 1998.
[19] D. Newman, A. Asuncion, P. Smyth, and M. Welling. Distributed algorithms for topic models. *J. Mach. Learn. Res.*, 10:1801–1828, 2009.
[20] F. Niu, B. Recht, C. Re, and S. J. Wright. HOGWILD!: A lock-free approach to parallelizing stochastic gradient descent. In *NIPS*, pages 693–701, 2011.
[21] I. Porteous, D. Newman, A. Ihler, A. Asuncion, P. Smyth, and M. Welling. Fast collapsed Gibbs sampling for latent Dirichlet allocation. In *KDD*, pages 569–577, 2008.
[22] H. Robbins and S. Monro. A stochastic approximation method. *The Annals of Mathematical Statistics*, 22(3):400–407, 1951.
[23] B. S. S. Ahn and M. Welling. Distributed stochastic gradient mcmc. In *ICML*, 2014.
[24] M. W. Schmidt, N. L. Roux, and F. Bach. Minimizing finit sums with the stochastic average gradient. *CoRR*, abs/1309.2388, 2013.
[25] A. Smola and S. Narayanamurthy. An architecture for parallel topic models. In *PVLDB*, pages 703–710, 2010.
[26] Y. W. Teh, D. Newman, and M. Welling. A collapsed variational Bayesian inference algorithm for latent Dirichlet allocation. In *NIPS*, pages 1353–1360, 2007.
[27] Y. Wang, H. Bai, M. Stanton, W. Y. Chen, and E. Chang. PLDA: Parallel latent Dirichlet allocation for large-scale applications. In *Algorithmic Aspects in Information and Management*, pages 301–314, 2009.
[28] Y. Wang, X. Zhao, Z. Sun, H. Yan, L. Wang, Z. Jin, L. Wang, Y. Gao, C. Law, and J. Zeng. Peacock: Learning long-tail topic features for industrial applications. *ACM Transactions on Intelligent Systems and Technology*, 2015.
[29] F. Yan, N. Xu, and Y. Qi. Parallel inference for latent Dirichlet allocation on graphics processing units. In *NIPS*, pages 2134–2142, 2009.
[30] J.-F. Yan, J. Zeng, Z.-Q. Liu, and Y. Gao. Towards big topic modeling. page arXiv:1311.4150, 2013.
[31] L. Yao, D. Mimno, and A. McCallum. Efficien methods for topic model inference on streaming document collections. In *KDD*, pages 937–946, 2009.
[32] J. Yuan, F. Gao, Q. Ho, W. Dai, J. Wei, X. Zheng, E. P. Xing, T.-Y. Liu, and W.-Y. Ma. LightLDA: Big topic models on modest compute clusters. page arXiv:1412.1576 [stat.ML], 2014.
[33] H. Yun, H.-F. Yu, C.-J. Hsieh, S. V. N. Vishwanathan, and I. Dhillon. NOMAD: Nonlocking, stOchastic Multi-machine algorithm for Asynchronous and Decentralized matrix completion. In *PVLDB*, pages 975–986, 2014.
[34] J. Zeng. A topic modeling toolbox using belief propagation. *J. Mach. Learn. Res.*, 13:2233–2236, 2012.
[35] J. Zeng, W. K. Cheung, and J. Liu. Learning topic models by belief propagation. *IEEE Trans. Pattern Anal. Mach. Intell.*, 35(5):1121–1134, 2013.
[36] J. Zeng, Z.-Q. Liu, and X.-Q. Cao. A new approach to speeding up topic modeling. page arXiv:1204.0170 [cs.LG], 2012.
[37] J. Zeng, Z.-Q. Liu, and X.-Q. Cao. Online belief propagation for topic modeling. *arXiv:1210.2179 [cs.LG]*, 2012.
[38] K. Zhai, J. Boyd-Graber, and N. Asadi. Mr. LDA: A fl xible large scale topic modeling package using variational inference in MapReduce. In *WWW*, pages 879–888, 2012.
[39] Y. Zhuang, W.-S. Chin, Y.-C. Juan, and C.-J. Lin. A fast parallel SGD for matrix factorization in shared memory systems. In *ACM Recommender Systems*, 2013.

Grading the Graders: Motivating Peer Graders in a MOOC

Yanxin Lu, Joe Warren, Chris Jermaine, Swarat Chaudhuri and Scott Rixner
Department of Computer Science
Rice University
Houston, TX, 77007
{yanxin.lu,jwarren,cmj4,swarat,rixner}@rice.edu

ABSTRACT

In this paper, we detail our efforts at creating and running a controlled study designed to examine how students in a MOOC might be motivated to do a better job during peer grading. This study involves more than one thousand students of a popular MOOC. We ask two specific questions: (1) When a student knows that his or her own peer grading efforts are being examined by peers, does this knowledge alone tend to motivate the student to do a better job when grading assignments? And (2) when a student not only knows that his or her own peer grading efforts are being examined by peers, but he or she is also given a number of other peer grading efforts to evaluate (so the peer graders see how other peer graders evaluate assignments), do both of these together tend to motivate the student to do a better job when grading assignments? We find strong statistical evidence that "grading the graders" does in fact tend to increase the quality of peer grading.

1. INTRODUCTION

A *massive open online course* (MOOC) [24] is a web-based online course that is open to virtually all interested participants, with few restrictions to registration. Running a MOOC is challenging for many reasons, not the least of which is ensuring high-quality grading. The largest MOOCs have on the order of tens of thousands of participants who actually complete some fraction of the assignments and examinations. Clearly, grading at this scale is beyond even the largest team of instructors and TAs.

One solution to the problem of grading so many submissions is for the instructor to design assignments and examinations in such a way as to ensure that student work can be automatically graded. For example, multiple choice examinations can be given. For another example, in a computer programming class, student programs can be put through a test suite by an automated grader, and the number of test cases passed can be used to assign a student a grade.

The obvious problem with automated grading is that there exist courses for which purely automated grading is not possible. An example that we are intimately familiar with (and the course that is the subject of the experimental study described in this paper) is a course on interactive game programming in Python[1]. Since games by their very nature require a user to play them in order to test correctness, it is exceedingly difficult to utilize automated grading to score student-constructed games. Another example is a mathematics class where the construction of proofs is a key part of the course; fully automated grading of student proofs is not feasible at this time. Courses in the social sciences or languages are also not amenable to fully automated grading.

Peer Grading. The common way to scale up grading that cannot be automated is to rely on *peer grading* [21, 9, 30, 22, 8, 14, 15], where student submissions are distributed to other students in the class to be graded. Peer grading has many benefits. In addition to offering a way to crowdsource the grading of student work so as to achieve virtually infinite scalability, peer grading also has pedagogical benefits [6]. Students who grade other students' assignments can benefit from this activity. In particular, they are forced to carefully consider the validity of a wide variety of solutions to a problem. As a result, commonly used MOOC platforms such as Coursera [1] offer built-in facilities to support peer grading.

Peer grading, however, is not a panacea. Our personal experience is that in a MOOC, low quality peer grading can be a problem. The main reason for poor grading seems to be a simple lack of effort, rather than inability or maliciousness. On Coursera, for example, students are assessed a 20% penalty when they fail to peer grade. One unfortunate (and common) student response is simply to give all peers perfect scores. Consider the "An Introduction to Interactive Programming in Python" (IIPP) course that we have offered for a number of years on Coursera, and which serves as the subject of the study described in this paper. On the two assignments central to our study (Stopwatch and Memory), in those cases where we were able to automatically find an error that should have resulted in one or more points being deducted, the peer grader gave full credit 53% of the time (4,168/7,855 grades given). In contrast, in those cases where we could find no error automatically, only 2% of the time (292/16,427 grades given) did the grader take off more than one point.

This sets up the question that is at the heart of the paper:

How can an educator running a MOOC motivate students to do a better job of peer grading?

Our goal is to identify a simple and practical method for motivating students to perform high-quality peer grading, and to then rigorously test this method in a controlled experiment, in a real MOOC.

While we are primarily interested in MOOCs, we point out that answering this question definitively would have implications beyond MOOCs. Consider the task of ensuring high-quality peer re-

WWW 2015, May 18–22, 2015, Florence, Italy.
ACM 978-1-4503-3469-3/15/05.
http://dx.doi.org/10.1145/2736277.2741649.

[1]See https://www.coursera.org/course/interactivepython.

views of submissions to a competetive, academic conference. Reviewers agree to review submissions out of a sense of obligation or because they want to be associated with a prestigious conference, and often lack motivation to do a good job. Methods that work well in a MOOC might also help in motivating conference reviewers.

Motivating Peer Graders. One method for motivating peer graders that seems to have entered into the folklore is the method of "sentinels." Instructors or TAs pre-grade a few assignments, which are then added into the general population of assignments. These are called "sentinals." Since we know something of the ground-truth grade for the sentinels, it is possible to identify graders whose grades differ significantly from the expected score. Such off-target grading efforts could be identified, and students might be given some sanction for doing such a poor job grading the sentinels.

However, there are some inherent problems with the use of sentinels. Based on our experience in delivering several MOOCs, a substantial subset of the students enjoy discussing their peers' work in the class forums. Eventually, the sentinels themselves would be a popular topic for discussion. Of course, this knowledge would diminish the effectiveness of sentinels in motivating student effort during peer grading. Further, sentinels are meant to detect and presumably punish poor grading efforts. The idea of punishing students for poor grading seems counter-productive, especially when many students who are taking the MOOC are doing so simply to learn the topic. How does one punish a student who simply wants to learn the course material?

Perhaps a better approach would be to motivate students to do a better job. In this paper, we investigate a very different method for motivating peer graders. Rather than punishing (or rewarding) students for their peer grading, we examine the utility of crowdsourced examination of peer grading efforts. We ask two questions:

1. When a student knows that his or her own peer grading efforts are being examined by peers, *does this knowledge alone* tend to motivate the student to do a better job when grading assignments?

2. When a student not only knows that his or her own peer grading efforts are being examined by his or her peers, but he or she is also given a number of other peer grading efforts to evaluate (so the students see how other peer graders evaluate assignments), *do both of these together* tend to motivate the student to do a better job when grading assignments?

Crucially, there is no punishment or reward under either regime. There is only the knowledge that one's peers are going to examine one's grading efforts (case 1), and in addition, an exposure to how other peer graders have evaluated assignments (case 2).

Our Contributions. The idea of "grading the graders" is not revolutionary. In the context of peer review of scientific papers, this is often mentioned as a possible mechanism for ensuring high-quality peer review. However, most or all of the ideas along these lines rely on logical argument or thought experiment to demonstrate utility. Our efforts differ in that not only have we designed and implemented a system for grading the graders, but—far more importantly—we have also designed and run a large-scale, controlled experiment to evaluate the utility of the approach. Such studies should be considered mandatory as the community attempts to figure out the correct way to run a MOOC.

Our specific contributions are as follows:

1. We describe two easily-implementable and easily-deployable methods for motivating peer graders in a MOOC. These methods have the advantage that they require only moderate levels of effort from the MOOC community.

2. We conduct a carefully designed, controlled experimental evaluation of these methods in the context of a popular interactive (game programming) MOOC. We assert that such a controlled experiment is the only reliable way to collect data supporting or refuting the utility of a particular methodology in the context of a MOOC.

3. We find evidence that there are significant differences among the various study groups, even among the subset of students who are motivated enough to sign up for such a study.

Summary of Findings and Recommendations. Surprisingly, we found little evidence that simply knowing that one's grading efforts were going to be graded results in a superior grading effort. That is, those study participants who did not grade others, but only had their grading efforts graded, did not perform much better than those in the control group.[2] However, those who participated in the full regime—students who had their grading efforts graded *and* graded others' grading efforts—not only did a better job grading during the study (which lasted for two assignments), *but the positive effects were lasting*. That is, those who participated in the "grading the graders" regime continued to do a better job than those who did not participate in the full regime, even after the study ended.

Thus, the key to achieving better grading results seems to be actually seeing how other people grade, and not simply knowing that grading efforts are being monitored. As discussed in Section 6, we conjecture that actually seeing that other students put in the effort to do a good job helps provide the motivation that students need to do a good job when it is their turn to grade. In this case, simply showing examples of good grading is not enough; *students must be shown evidence that their peers are actually producing such high quality efforts*. This is exactly what the "grading the graders" regime does. Thus, our recommendation is that MOOCs that rely on peer grading should utilize the "grading the graders" regime for at least one or two assignments at the beginning of the class; our study seems to indicate that this should have a positive effect on grading quality.

2. BACKGROUND

IIPP is a 9-week course designed to help students with very little computing background learn the basics of writing simple interactive programs (games of various types) using the Python programming language. No prior programming experience is assumed. The course covers the basic syntax and semantics of Python, as well as object-oriented programming. Students learn the material of the course by completing a series of "mini-projects" including games such as Pong, Blackjack and Asteroids. We administered the study in the Fall 2013 session of the course. In that session, 120,000 students enrolled and 7,500 finished the course.

One challenging aspect of designing a Python programming MOOC for beginners is making sure that tens of thousands of inexperienced students are able to develop and run Python programs on their own machines. These students use a wide variety of machines and operating systems and there is no way of ensuring that they will all be willing or able to install the same version of any particular software package. Since IIPP relies on peer grading, these programs need to be completely portable. To facilitate this, IIPP

[2] As an aside, this would seem to argue *against* a sentinel-based approach, which by its nature relies on monitoring of grading efforts to increase grading quality.

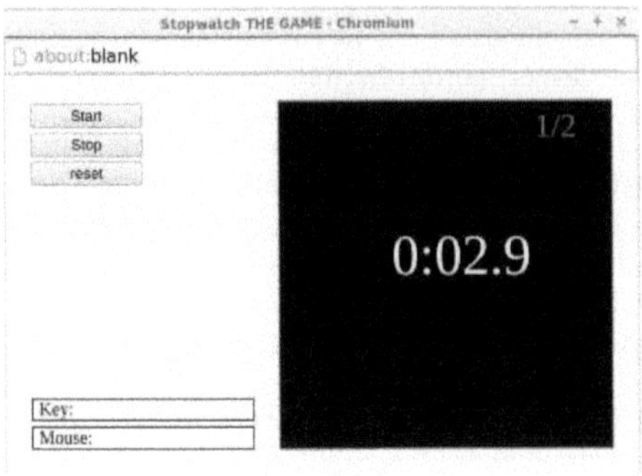

(a) Screen shot of Stopwatch assignment solution.

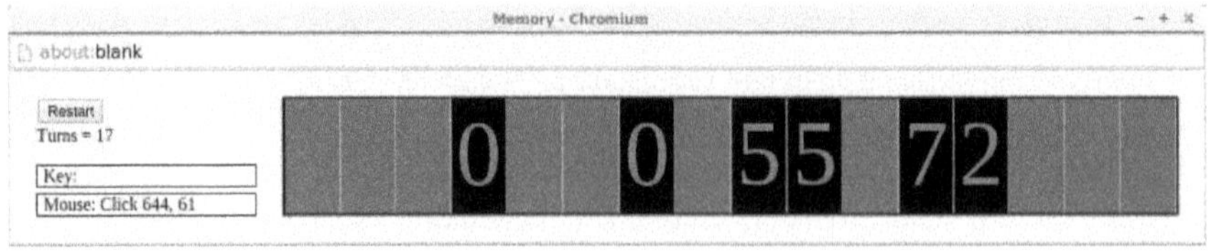

(b) Screen shot of Memory assignment solution.

Figure 1: Two IIPP programming assignments that are the subject of the study.

makes use of a browser-based programming environment called "CodeSkulptor" [29]. Any instructor or peer grader with access to the URL that points to the saved code can open and run the code, meaning that submitting a program is equivalent to submitting a URL.

```
import simplegui
# define global variables
minute = 0
second = 0
millisecond = 0
time = "0:00.0"
score = "0/0"
wins = 0
attempts = 0

#Function for the game
def score_keeper():
    ...

# define event handlers for buttons; "Start", "Stop", "Reset"
def timer_handler():
    ...

#Ensure there is a zero before the one
def second_string():
    ...

def reset_handler():
    timer.stop()
    time = "0:00:0"
    second = 0
    millisecond = 0
    minute = 0
    score = "0/0"
    attempts = 0
    wins = 0

# define draw handle
def draw_handler(canvas):
     global time
     canvas.draw_text(time, (100, 150), 50, 'White')
     canvas.draw_text(score, (230, 30), 30, 'Green')

# register event handlers
def start_handler():
     timer.start()

def stop_handler():
     timer.stop()
     score_keeper()

# create frame
frame = simplegui.create_frame("Stopwatch THE GAME", 300, 300)
button1 = frame.add_button('Start', start_handler, 100)
button2 = frame.add_button('Stop', stop_handler, 100)
button3 = frame.add_button('reset', reset_handler, 100)
timer = simplegui.create_timer(100, timer_handler)
frame.set_draw_handler(draw_handler)
# start frame
frame.start()
```

Figure 2: Source code listing of a submitted Stopwatch submission.

2.1 Assignments

The study described here concerns two different IIPP programming assignments, Stopwatch and Memory. We describe those programming assignments now.

Stopwatch. Stopwatch was assigned during the fourth week of the course. 10,500 students completed the regular version of the Stopwatch assignment, and 2,366 additional students participated in the study and completed the study version of the assignment.

In this project, students write the application whose screenshot is shown above in Figure 1a. Students must implement three buttons: a "start" button, a "stop" button, and a "reset" button. The application implements a simple game where a player presses the start button, which starts a timer that is accurate down to a tenth of a second. The player then attempts to press the stop button when the tenths position of the timer is zero (that is, the player attempts to hit "stop" at a whole second). The application should display the number of times that the user does this correctly. For example, displaying "3/4" means that the user has successfully stopped the timer at a whole second three out of four times. A partial listing of one student's code for this assignment is given in Figure 2.

Memory. Memory was assigned at the beginning of the sixth week of IIPP. 7,600 students completed the regular version of Memory, and 1,746 of the 2,366 students who completed the study version of Stopwatch also completed the study version of memory.

In this project, students build a game which first displays eight pairs of cards face down. A move consists of the player flipping over two cards. If they match, the game leaves them face up. Otherwise, they are flipped back face down. The goal is to flip all the cards face up in the minimum number of moves. Figure 1b shows a screenshot of a completed Memory assignment.

2.2 Peer Grading

Since submissions in IIPP are all interactive programs, they are very difficult to grade automatically, so IIPP utilizes Coursera's peer grading facilities.

Peer grading takes place after all students submit their programs. Students are required to assess five of their peers' programs and their own program. For each program, grading instructions are presented to the students followed by a series of rubric items. Figure 3 shows the rubric supplied to students for Stopwatch.

For each rubric item, students need to choose how many points to assign using a drop-down menu. After choosing a number of points from the drop-down menu, students can provide additional comments for that specific rubric item in a text area right below the drop-down menu. After grading the program, students can optionally provide a comment giving overall feedback on the submission.

Peer Grading Quality. We estimate that it takes an average grader about 10 minutes to do a reasonable job of grading a typical IIPP assignment, meaning that the grading load for each student is one hour per assignment. In our experience, some students voluntarily spend more time than that grading, but unfortunately, some students spend much less time. In fact, the amount of time and effort spent grading—and hence the accuracy of the peer grading effort as well as its utility to the students being graded—varies widely.

For just one example of this variance, consider Figure 4 which shows an average to above-average grading effort for one particular Stopwatch submission. The grader took off a few points for four of the eight rubric items (giving eight out of 13 points total), and for each of those items, reasonable comments were given.

In contrast, a second grader for this very same submission gave full credit (13 out of 13) to the submission. No comments at all were offered, except for a terse "Very fancy timer :) Great job." under the "Overall" category. Disparities in grading effort such as this are common, and are precisely our motivation for undertaking the study described in the remainder of the paper. We wish to ask the question: How might we motivate students to put in the effort required to produce an evaluation that is of equivalent quality to the evaluation depicted in Figure 4?

3. GRADING THE GRADERS

At the highest level, the approach we explore to motivating peer graders is to expose the peer graders themselves to grading, and ask them to grade others' grading efforts. Our hypothesis is that if graders know that they will be evaluated, and if they see the sort of grading efforts put forth by their peers, they will be more motivated to submit high quality evaluations.

In this section, we briefly describe the relatively simple software infrastructure that we implemented to evaluate this idea.

3.1 Stage One: Grading the Graders

A few days after students participating in the IIPP "grading the graders" regime finish their peer evaluations, they receive an email with a link to a web application. Following this link leads the student to a page where they are asked to evaluate a set of peer evaluations for five random submissions.

Following this link presents a simple web page that has a link to the assignment that is the subject of the various evaluations. A screen shot of the web page is shown in Figure 5. The web application allows students to cycle through the various rubric items, one at a time. For each rubric item, six different peer evaluations are shown. The application displays the score assigned by each of the six peer evaluators, as well as any comments. The student who is evaluating the evaluators is instructed to click a radio button next to each of the evaluations. The buttons are labeled with "good," "neutral," and "bad," referring to the quality of the evaluation. Typically, a student will look through the various evaluations and comments, and if the evaluators all give the rubric item full credit, the student will assign each a score of "good." If one of the evaluators has taken off some credit, the student will look at the submitted assignment to see if he/she agrees with the loss of credit, and evaluate each of the evaluations accordingly.

After the student evaluates each of the evaluations, the student clicks the "submit" button to move onto the next rubric item. After cycling through each of the rubric items, a final web page informs the student that he/she has completed the "grading the graders" process.

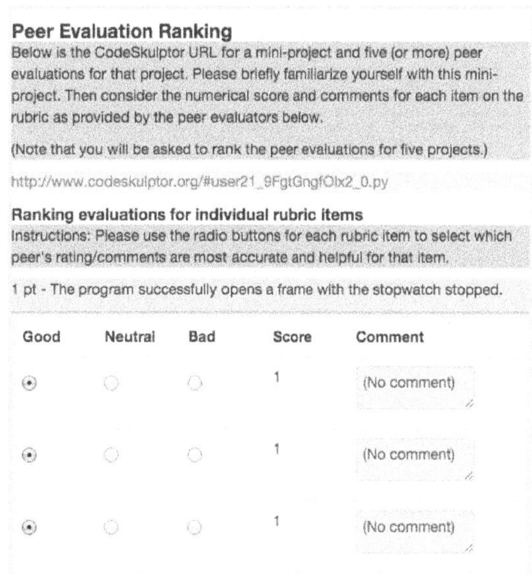

Figure 5: Screen shot of web page that students use to evaluate peer evaluations. A link to a particular submitted assignment is given, along with a listing of five different peer evaluations for that assignment, for a particular rubric item.

3.2 Stage Two: Examining Evaluations

Some time later, students who complete the "grading the graders" process will receive an email with a link to a web application that allows the student to see how others evaluated his or her *own* peer grading efforts. Since students are required to evaluate six assignments (five other students' assignments, as well as their own), following the link presents a web page that first lists links to six assignments that the student evaluated. For a particular rubric item, the web page lists each of the six evaluations that the student performed, along with the ratings supplied by those who participated in the "grading the graders" activity. Figure 6 shows a screenshot of the interface.

After cycling through the various rubric items, students are then given the opportunity to examine the grading of their own assignments. That is, the student can see how those who "graded the grader" viewed the quality of the grades for his or her own submission on the assignment. The student can choose to go to a screen that lists (for a particular rubric item) all of the evaluations of his or her own submission, along with the number of times that an examiner determined that the evaluation was "good," "neutral," or "poor."

4. EXPERIMENTAL DESIGN

Our central goal is to evaluate whether or not such a framework might have some utility in motivating students to perform high-quality peer evaluations. In this section, we describe in detail the study that we designed and executed to this effect.

4.1 Study Overview

The study was open to all participants in the Fall 2013 incarnation of the IIPP class. Because we would be asking participants to do a non-trivial amount of work, and (more importantly) because participants would have their work examined by others, participation needed to be voluntary. There was some concern that voluntary participation would skew the results, making it more difficult to detect effects. After all, those MOOC participants who are motivated

Item	Points	Description
1	1 pt	The program successfully opens a frame with the stopwatch stopped.
2	1 pt	The program has a working "Start" button that starts the timer.
3	1 pt	The program has a working "Stop" button that stops the timer.
4	1 pt	The program has a working "Reset" button that stops the timer (if running) and resets the timer to 0.
5	4 pt	The time is formatted according to the description in step 4 above. Award partial credit corresponding to 1 pt per correct digit. For example, a version that just draws tenths of seconds as a whole number should receive 1 pt. A version that draws the time with a correctly placed decimal point (but no leading zeros) only should receive 2 pts. A version that draws minutes, seconds and tenths of seconds but fails to always allocate two digits to seconds should receive 3 pts.
6	2 pt	The program correctly draws the number of successful stops at a whole second versus the total number of stops. Give one point for each number displayed. If the score is correctly reported as a percentage instead, give only one point.
7	2 pt	The "Stop" button correctly updates these success/attempts numbers. Give only one point if hitting the "Stop" button changes these numbers when the timer is already stopped.
8	1 pt	The "Reset" button clears the success/attempts numbers.

Figure 3: Rubric given to peer graders for Stopwatch program.

Rubric Item	Score	Comments
1	1	(No Comments)
2	1	(No Comments)
3	1	(No Comments)
4	0	you forgot use variable timer to stop the timer at reset button.
5	1	You used non-decimal number to count. The numbers for A, C and D was 0-9 and B was 0 - 6.The function format did not pass to the test numbers.
6	1	In the test, i stoped the clock 2.9 and the program showed 2.0 and count 1 correct attempt.I think some problems occurred because the way how you count the number with a non-integer number.
7	2	Update the numbers, but you need to look more deep how your time is increasing because sometimes the clock stop at time but it is not the real time counted. Just put a print time_elapsed at timer_handler an you will can see that behavior
8	1	(No Comments)
Overall	N/A	Remember to look more carefully to all the section "Mini-project development process". I think almost of all problems came from count time with a non-integer.Review format function an test it : http://www.codeskulptor.org/#examples-format_template.py. At "Discussion Forum" -> Code Clinic you always find great help to understand some things...use more discussion forum. Sorry about my poor english. =[google translator help me a lot hehehe

Figure 4: Reasonable quality peer grading effort for a Stopwatch submission. This grader gave eight out of 13 possible points for the submission. In contrast, for the same submission, another grader gave full credit, and the only comment offered was "Very fancy timer :) Great job." as an "Overall" comment.

enough to participate in a study are probably far more likely to already be motivated enough to submit high quality peer evaluations without the extra incentive (possibly) provided by a "grading the graders" regime. However, since the bias was far more likely to result in dampening of the significance of the study results (rather than creating positive results when none should have existed), in the end we considered this a necessary evil that we could live with.

Study participants were divided into three groups:

1. *Those receiving the full "grading the graders" treatment.* These participants evaluate other peer evaluations (as described in Section 3.1), and have their own peer evaluations evaluated. Then they are asked to examine the evaluations of the peer evaluations that they have performed (as described in Section 3.2), and hence receive the full treatment described in the previous section of the paper. We call this group G_1.

2. *Those who only have their peer examinations evaluated.* These participants do not actually evaluate any other peer evaluators, but they have their own evaluations examined by members of G_1. We included this group to try to understand whether there is a difference between being asked to evaluate others as is the case in G_1 (which necessarily imparts some knowledge of community standards in peer grading to the examiner) and being motivated by knowing that others will be examining one's peer evaluations. We call this group G_2.

3. *The control group.* These are people who sign up for the study, but then are not asked to do anything other than participate as usual in the IIPP class. We call this group G_3.

By design, we set the ratio of the sizes of three groups to be $G_1 : G_2 : G_3 = 8 : 1 : 1$. The reason for the large size of G_1 is that we needed the group to be large enough that it could produce enough evaluations so that members of G_2 could consume evaluations of their peer grading efforts, without contributing any evaluations of their own. We were concerned about the effect group size imbalance might have on the statistical power of any analyses that we would need to run, but again, this seemed necessary.

In order to enroll in the study, students were asked to complete a simple web consent form and submit their email address. The consent form described that there were three groups that students could be assigned to (including one where they would be asked to do nothing more than they would normally do in the IIPP class), but not the specific study goals nor what was being measured. Because students could easily communicate on the Coursera forums,

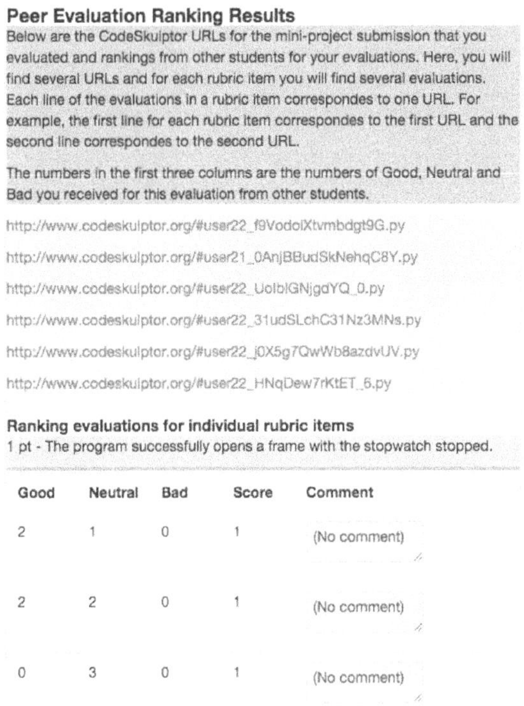

Figure 6: Screen shot of web page that allows students to see how others judged the quality of their peer evaluations.

there was little point in trying to blind the study so that students would not understand what group they were in. In fact, we decided that attempting to blind the study in this way would be worse than not, since we were concerned that it would encourage students to carefully compare notes on class forums regarding what they were seeing, possibly biasing the results.

To motivate students to sign up for the study—we were especially interested in attracting somewhat less motivated students from the general student population who might not have otherwise signed up—a Nexus tablet was promised to one randomly-selected student from each group.

4.2 Timeline and Details

All students who submitted the consent form were randomly assigned to groups. 3,015 students completed a consent form during the enrolling phase. 2,412 students were assigned to G_1, 301 students to G_2 and 302 students to G_3. All students received an email with information describing what they needed to do in the study.

It was expected that all students in the study would participate in the study during both the Stopwatch and Memory assignments. Here we detail the timeline that was used for both assignments.

Day 1. The assignment (Stopwatch/Memory) is posted and a special submission page for the study (separate from the normal submission page) is opened; study participants were asked to submit to that particular page. Students had nine days to submit.

Day 9. The assignment ends. If a study participant did not submit to the special submission page by day 9, he or she was removed from the study. Students begin peer evaluation. They have one week.

Day 16. Peer evaluation ends. At this point, the evaluation phase begins and emails are sent to all G_1 students pointing them to the web page where they can evaluate others' evaluations. Three days were allotted to this task. 201 students outside of the study (in the case of Stopwatch) and 421 students outside of the study (in the case of Memory) also (mistakenly) submitted to the special study submission page. We were happy to have extra evaluations to work with, so these students were treated as G_1 students and asked to "grade the graders," but they are not otherwise included in the study results. (Interestingly, 60 of the 201 "mistaken Stopwatch" students and 124 of the 421 "mistaken Memory" students actually completed the "grading the graders" task of Section 3.1).

Day 19. "Grading the graders" ends. In the case of Stopwatch, 1,891 out of 2,412 G_1 students and 244 out of 301 G_2 students (those who had successfully completed study requirements) receive emails pointing them to a URL where they can see what others thought of their submitted evaluations. In the case of Memory, 1,387 G_1 students and 192 G_2 students receive this email.

5. EXPERIMENTAL RESULTS

In this section, we describe in detail the results we obtained by analyzing the data that we collected.

5.1 Hypotheses Tested

Our goal was to determine whether or not there was some evidence that students enrolled in G_1 did a better job grading compared to either G_2 or G_3, or both. As we will discuss in detail shortly, if we find that G_1 generally does a better job, then it might be taken as evidence that the "grading the graders" regime does in fact motivate peer graders.

Thus, our data analysis task comes down to measuring the quality of students' grading efforts. We felt that (short of having a human expert review on the order of 10,000 peer grading submissions) the two best proxies for measuring quality are (1) whether or not an evaluator gets it right, and typically gives a high score to a good program and typically gives a low score to a bad program, and (2) how much time and effort are taken in writing comments.

However, it turns out that it is not trivial to measure either of those proxies. The problem with looking at score accuracy is that we do not actually know when a submission is in fact a good program, and when it is bad. These are, after all, interactive programs that are very difficult to grade automatically. This is why the IIPP course relies on peer grading. And without actually reading the comments, it is difficult to measure the effort level.

To address the first difficulty, we manually devised a number of assignment-specific program analyses that were able to automatically and roughly categorize student submissions as being good or bad. These methods simulated each submission on a large number of manually written "tests" — defined here as finite sequences of events — and recorded the program's executions on these tests. A large number of manually designed rules were then used to judge the correctness of these executions. The analyses that we ran were not perfect. However, we used deep knowledge about the assignments, as well as a large amount of effort, to make our tests and rules as accurate as possible. Moreover, any inaccuracy in the classification will tend to mask the accuracy (or inaccuracy) of a set of program grades in a systematic way (since a mis-categorized program will be graded by members of G_1, G_2 and G_3) and so such inaccuracies are unlikely to introduce bias into our analysis.

To address the second difficulty, we decided to use comment length as a reasonable measure of the quality of a comment. Of course, it is always possible for a grader to write a long but inane and useless comment, but in general, one would expect a longer comment to correlate with more care on the part of the grader.

H_0^1 = "The mean score for group A is no greater than the mean score for group B on good programs"

		Stopwatch			Memory		
Group A	Group B	Group A Mean	Group B Mean	p-value	Group A Mean	Group B Mean	p-value
G_1	G_2	12.91	12.91	0.5889	10.88	10.89	0.7781
G_1	G_3	12.91	12.88	**0.0255**	10.88	10.87	0.3501
G_2	G_3	12.91	12.88	**0.0477**	10.89	10.87	0.1987

H_0^2 = "The mean score for group A is no less than the mean score for group B on bad programs"

Group A	Group B	Group A Mean	Group B Mean	p-value	Group A Mean	Group B Mean	p-value
G_1	G_2	12.02	12.09	0.1095	10.29	10.36	0.1911
G_1	G_3	12.02	12.04	0.3543	10.29	10.39	0.0783
G_2	G_3	12.09	12.04	0.7527	10.36	10.39	0.3214

H_0^3 = "The median comment length for group A is no greater than the median comment length for group B on good programs"

Group A	Group B	Group A Median	Group B Median	p-value	Group A Median	Group B Median	p-value
G_1	G_2	11	10	0.6603	12	10	**0.0060**
G_1	G_3	11	11	0.7888	12	10	**0.0036**
G_2	G_3	10	11	0.8341	10	10	0.9356

H_0^4 = "The median comment length for group A is no greater than the median comment length for group B on bad programs"

Group A	Group B	Group A Median	Group B Median	p-value	Group A Median	Group B Median	p-value
G_1	G_2	83	78	0.3300	69	51.5	0.1014
G_1	G_3	83	74	0.2166	69	51	0.1348
G_2	G_3	78	74	0.4077	51.5	51	0.4700

H_0^5 = "The fraction of people doing a 'bad job' in group A is no less than the fraction doing a 'bad job' in group B"

Group A	Group B	Group A Mean	Group B Mean	p-value	Group A Mean	Group B Mean	p-value
G_1	G_2	0.3820	0.4007	0.0721	0.3477	0.4021	**0.0004**
G_1	G_3	0.3820	0.4091	**0.0191**	0.3477	0.4157	**0.0001**
G_2	G_3	0.4007	0.4091	0.3152	0.4021	0.4157	0.2504

H_0^6 = "The fraction of people doing a 'really bad job' in group A is no less than the fraction doing a 'really bad job' in group B"

Group A	Group B	Group A Mean	Group B Mean	p-value	Group A Mean	Group B Mean	p-value
G_1	G_2	0.04522	0.05051	0.1894	0.03404	0.04442	0.0691
G_1	G_3	0.04522	0.06133	**0.0057**	0.03404	0.04648	**0.0400**
G_2	G_3	0.05051	0.06133	0.0792	0.04442	0.04648	0.3896

Figure 7: Summary of study results, comparing G_1 (students who both "graded the graders" and viewed the peer evaluations of their own grading efforts), G_2 (students who only viewed the peer evaluations of their own grading efforts), and G_3 (students who neither "graded the graders" nor viewed the peer evaluations of their own grading efforts). Findings significant at the 0.05 level are shown in **bold**.

With this in mind, we developed six different null hypotheses that we would test in an attempt to differentiate the quality of any two groups of graders A and B. These null hypotheses are:

Hypothesis One: H_0^1 = "The mean score for group A is no greater than the mean score for group B on good programs"

If this hypothesis is refuted, then it means that group A is doing a better job than group B in recognizing good programs, which would be a strong indicator that group A does a better job grading good programs.

Hypothesis Two: H_0^2 = "The mean score for group A is no less than the mean score for group B on bad programs"

If this is refuted, it means that group A does a better job than B recognizing bad programs, which is again indicative that group A is doing a better job.

Hypothesis Three: H_0^3 = "The median comment length for group A is no greater than the median comment length for group B on good programs"

If this is refuted, it means that group A writes longer comments on high-quality submissions than group B. We use median rather than mean since the comment length appears to have a heavy-tailed distribution, making the mean quite unstable. Refuting this would be particularly interesting, because one might expect that it is very easy for a mediocre grader to simply give full credit to a high-quality submission. A careful grader would look at the code, even if the program works well, and offer comments on the style and substance of the implementation.

Hypothesis Four: H_0^4 = "The median comment length for group A is no greater than the median comment length for group B on bad programs"

Comments on bad programs are the most important feedback that a struggling student will receive, and so this is also an important hypothesis.

Hypothesis Five: H_0^5 = "The fraction of people doing a 'bad job' in group A is no less than the fraction doing a 'bad job' in B"

We define someone who has done a "bad job" to be a grader that either (a) gets the grade wrong, and gives a perfect score to a program that our code analysis engine thinks is flawed (or gives a non-perfect score to a program that our engine can find no fault with), or (b) writes no comment across all rubric items. If we are able to refute this hypothesis, it means that someone from group A is less likely to do a bad job than someone from group B.

Hypothesis Six: H_0^6 = "The fraction of people doing a 'really bad job' in group A is no less than the fraction doing a 'really bad job' in group B"

We define someone who has done a "really bad job" similarly to the way we define someone who has done a "bad job," but we replace the *or* with an *and*.

For each of these hypotheses, we perform six different statistical tests. For Stopwatch, we compare (1) G_1 vs. G_2, (2) G_1 vs. G_3, and (3) G_2 vs. G_3. We also make the same comparisons for Memory. The reason that we performed these particular tests is that we were looking for evidence that the "grading the graders" regime has a positive effect on peer grading, and so it makes sense to compare those who have undertaken the full "grading the graders" program (those in G_1) versus the other two groups. We are also interested in comparing G_2 and G_3 because we would like to see if there is any difference between the partial "grading the graders" program (those in G_2 only had their peer evaluations evaluated; they did not actually evaluate others' peer evaluations) and the control group.

5.2 Statistical Significance

Checking whether these various null hypotheses are refuted obviously requires some sort of statistical test of significance to obtain a p-value for each of the hypotheses. At first glance, the textbook test for this sort of experimental setup would be a paired t-test [4], since we have two groups, A and B, and in each case we are checking for a difference in the mean or the median of some statistic, computed across the groups. Further, a "paired" version of the test seems appropriate, since members of both groups are typically paired, grading the same program.

Unfortunately, a t-test, paired or otherwise, seems inappropriate when examined in detail. In fact, any sort of textbook test for significance, parametric or not, is likely going to be invalid in our experimental framework. The problem is that when we test a particular hypothesis (say, H_0^1) we have multiple sources of correlation across the scores that are being added. Not only are the graders grading the same programs (a source of correlation that is in fact handled by a paired test) but *more than one grader from each group* may be grading the same program. For example, when looking at a specific program, it can be the case that five graders from group A and three graders from group B graded the same program, leading to a very unique covariance structure. Another source of correlation among the observed scores is that *each grader will grade multiple programs*, so that the scores may be correlated because they came from the same grader.

As a result, we had two obvious options. We could resort to something like a t-test, being cognizant of its limitations, or else we could utilize a simulation-based solution that naturally takes into account such issues, such as the bootstrap [13]. In the end, we chose the latter option.

Briefly, the idea behind the bootstrap is to use a resampling-based algorithm to simulate a very large number of data sets from the collected data set. The null hypothesis is checked on each, and the fraction of the time that the null hypothesis holds is the p-value.

To apply the bootstrap in our own setting, we generate a simulated data set as follows. Given a set of n programs called P for which one or more peer graders participating in the study actually graded, let $cnt(A, p)$ denote the number of graders from group A who graded program $p \in P$, and let $scores(A, p)$ denote the set of peer grading efforts created by those graders from group A. Then to bootstrap resample our data set, we first resample n programs from P by sampling n times from P with replacement. Call these sampled programs $p_1, p_2, ..., p_n$. For each p_i, we then create a new set of grading efforts for group A by resampling $cnt(A, p_i)$ grades from $scores(A, p_i)$. We then create a new set of grading efforts for group B by resampling $cnt(B, p_i)$ grades from $scores(B, p_i)$. By unioning all of the grading efforts across all $p_1, ..., p_n$, we create a new, simulated version of our data set. This simulated version respects the correlations induced by having multiple graders grade the same program (because there will be multiple grades of the same program in the simulated data set), and it also respects correlations induced by having the same grader grade multiple programs (since this will also happen in the simulated data set).

5.3 Results

We ran the resulting bootstrap tests across all of the hypotheses defined above. All results are given above in Figure 7. For each group and for each hypothesis, we give the p-value with which we reject the relevant null hypothesis, according to the bootstrap test. In general, a p-value of less than or equal to 0.05 (or possibly 0.1) is considered to be statistically significant. We **bold** all p-values that are significant at ≤ 0.05. Just as important, we give the mean or median value of the relevant statistic for each group that is being tested. For example, for H_0^1 = "The mean score for group A is no greater than the mean score for group B on good programs," we give the mean program score for good programs for group A and group B. These values are there to let the reader judge whether any differences are of practical significance.

In the remainder of the section, we highlight and explain a few of the results. In the next full section of the paper, we discuss the conclusions that we might draw from them.

Many of the Findings Are Statistically Significant. If, for a moment, we restrict ourselves to comparisons of G_1 vs. G_2 and G_1 vs. G_3, for Memory (which is the second assignment; hence, any gains from undertaking the "grading the graders" regime on Stopwatch would have had a chance to manifest themselves), 12 different null hypotheses were checked. Of those 12, 5 were rejected with a p-value ≤ 0.05, and the other 2 at a p-value ≤ 0.1. While there is certainly something of a multiple-hypothesis testing problem here given that 12 tests were run [23], the fact so many result in rejection of the null hypothesis seems strongly indicative of a positive effect of the full "grading the graders" regime compared to students in G_2 and the control group G_3.

Might We Have Hurt Statistical Power By Partitioning $\bar{G}_1$ into G_2 and G_3? Often, if the effect one is looking for is stronger in one segment of the population, it makes sense to stratify into subpopulations and run multiple tests, but since it results in multiple tests that each have a smaller number of samples, power is reduced.

To investigate this a bit, we re-ran each of the hypothesis tests, this time comparing G_1 vs. $\bar{G}_1$. The results are summarized in Figure 8. Again restricting ourselves to Memory, 3 of 6 null hypotheses are rejected with a p-value ≤ 0.02, and another 2 of 6 with a p-value ≤ 0.056.

No Significant Difference Between G_2 and G_3. Of the twelve comparisons between G_2 and G_3 shown in Figure 7, only one rejects the null hypothesis at a p-value ≤ 0.05. This seems to be strong evidence for the position that simply knowing that one's grading efforts are going to be examined does not help to increase grading quality—an issue we will consider subsequently.

H_0^1 = "The mean score for group A is no greater than the mean score for group B on good programs"

		Stopwatch			**Memory**		
Group A	Group B	Group A Mean	Group B Mean	p-value	Group A Mean	Group B Mean	p-value
G_1	G_2 and G_3	12.912094	12.898951	0.1305	10.875696	10.878788	0.5824

H_0^2 = "The mean score for group A is no less than the mean score for group B on bad programs"

		Stopwatch			**Memory**		
Group A	Group B	Group A Mean	Group B Mean	p-value	Group A Mean	Group B Mean	p-value
G_1	G_2 and G_3	12.021513	12.069231	0.1610	10.286411	10.373171	0.0557

H_0^3 = "The median comment length for group A is no greater than the median comment length for group B on good programs"

		Stopwatch			**Memory**		
Group A	Group B	Group A Median	Group B Median	p-value	Group A Median	Group B Median	p-value
G_1	G_2 and G_3	11	10	0.7088	12	10	**0.0009**

H_0^4 = "The median comment length for group A is no greater than the median comment length for group B on bad programs"

		Stopwatch			**Memory**		
Group A	Group B	Group A Median	Group B Median	p-value	Group A Median	Group B Median	p-value
G_1	G_2 and G_3	83	76.5	0.2111	69	51.5	0.0540

H_0^5 = "The fraction of people doing a 'bad job' in group A is no less than the fraction doing a 'bad job' in group B"

		Stopwatch			**Memory**		
Group A	Group B	Group A Mean	Group B Mean	p-value	Group A Mean	Group B Mean	p-value
G_1	G_2 and G_3	0.382037	0.40477	**0.0132**	0.347659	0.408338	**0**

H_0^6 = "The fraction of people doing a 'really bad job' in group A is no less than the fraction doing a 'really bad job' in group B"

		Stopwatch			**Memory**		
Group A	Group B	Group A Mean	Group B Mean	p-value	Group A Mean	Group B Mean	p-value
G_1	G_2 and G_3	0.045217	0.05577	**0.0087**	0.034042	0.045371	**0.0182**

Figure 8: Summary of study results, comparing G_1 (students who both "graded the graders" and viewed the peer evaluations of their own grading efforts) versus those who did not "grade the graders". Findings significant at the 0.05 level are shown in **bold**.

Many of the Findings Are of Practical Significance. It is often easy to conflate statistical significance with practical significance. When one runs a large-scale study involving thousands of participants, there are often statistically significant results that are of no practical significance. Is that the case here? Many of the results in Figure 7 and Figure 8 appear to be of practical significance as well. For one example, consider the Memory assignment results in Figure 8. We found that the percentage of graders who did a "really bad job" decreased from 4.5% for those who do not receive the full "grading the graders" treatment down to 3.4% for those who did. The percentage of those who do a "bad job" decreased from 41% to 35% under the regime. These reductions are perhaps more significant when one considers that the students who voluntarily signed up for the study are likely to be far more motivated already than those who did not.[3]

The Effects Were Lasting. Students completed three more assignments after the study ended. To see whether there were any lasting effects from the "grading the graders" regime, we analyzed the median comment lengths of student grading efforts on those assignments (as a sanity check, we also analyzed the comment lengths on the assignment immediately before Stopwatch). Figure 9 summarizes the results. We find that there is actually a significant, persistent effect of participating in the "grading the graders" regime.

6. CONCLUSIONS

It is easy to do a poor job peer grading. Intuitively, if a grader spends little time grading, then the grader will not find any problems. This leads to artificially inflated numerical grades and little feedback. As intimated in the introduction of the paper, we found that it was much more likely that a grader would give a perfect score to an imperfect program than the other way around, which supports this intuition. The students who did not do well on an assignment and most need quality feedback are the ones who suffer the most from poor grading.

Our study results corroborate the expectation that peer graders have no problem assigning high numerical scores to good assignments. There was little evidence of a difference among study groups at assigning numerical grades to good IIPP programs. While there were statistically significant results showing that both groups G_1 and G_2 did a better job at assigning a grade to good Stopwatch programs, the actual differences in scores among all the groups for both Stopwatch and Memory were in the hundredths of points. Further note that the Stopwatch program was actually simpler to grade, as Memory requires a more complex set of actions to be performed by the grader to verify correctness. More than anything, this indicates that all groups graded good programs well.

Ultimately, this suggests that with no intervention, it should be expected that peer grading will bias towards higher scores. However, while little effort is required to give high scores, effort is required provide feedback. Here we found the "grading the graders" regime to be useful for motivating the graders, even on good programs. We found that group G_1 did provide longer comments than both G_2 and G_3 on such programs.

In fact, the study supports the hypothesis that the full regime leads to better peer grading in general. Those in group G_1 *did* consistently do a better job grading, according to most of our metrics. Consider the Stopwatch results in Figure 8, where in 5 of 6 analyses, the null hypothesis was rejected with a p-value ≤ 0.056. The only case where the null hypothesis was *not* rejected was when checking whether those in G_1 did no better in scoring good programs. But this is not surprising, as discussed above.

[3]Along those lines, we did a bit of data analysis on the students who did not agree to participate in the study but managed to accidentally submit their grading efforts to the study. We found, for example, that the median comment length for everyone who signed up for the study was 47, while for the non-study group the median length was 17. Thus, there is a lot more room to improve the grading efforts of non-study participants.

		Before Study			After Study		
H_0 = "The median comment length for group A is no greater than the median comment length for group B on all programs"							
Group A	Group B	Group A Median	Group B Median	p-value	Group A Median	Group B Median	p-value
G_1	G_2	46	56.5	0.9472	21	16	**0.0437**
G_1	G_3	46	47.5	0.5650	21	16	**0.0184**
G_2	G_3	56.5	47.5	0.0991	16	16	0.5595
G_1	G_2 and G_3	46	52	0.8950	21	16	**0.0072**

Figure 9: Analyzing comment lengths in the assignment before the study began (at left) and for the three assignments after the study ended. Findings significant at the 0.05 level are shown in **bold**.

Not only were the results immediately noticeable, they also seemed to be lasting. In Figure 9 we see that the median comment length for those in G_1 stays greater for the final three assignments in the class, compared to the other study participants. Significantly, this was after the end of the study, when students had no reason to expect that the median comment length was going to be monitored.

One might easily believe that peer graders can be motivated to do a better job simply by telling them that their evaluations will themselves be evaluated. However, we found no evidence that this is effective. In particular, those in G_2 tended to do no better than those in G_3 throughout the study. This strongly suggests that knowing that one is being monitored by one's peers is not a strong enough motivation to do a good job grading others' assignments. We suspect that this extends to other forms of monitoring, such as the use of sentinels to catch bad grading.

Another surprising result is that there were some significant differences between G_1 and both of the other two groups not only on the Memory assignment, but also on the Stopwatch assignment (see Figure 8). This was surprising because Stopwatch grading took place *after* students agreed to participate in the study (and after they had been assigned to groups), but *before students had actually participated in the study in any meaningful way.* At the point that the data were collected, the participants had yet to actually participate in the protocol described in Sections 3.2 and Section 3.1, so they had not yet examined any other students' grading efforts, and yet the differences between groups were still significant.

The most likely explanation is that those students in G_1 were aware that they were participating in the full version of the study and hence they were enthusiastic and felt motivated to do well by this simple fact they somehow felt "special," which turned out to be highly motivational by itself. The comments on the Coursera forums seem to corroborate this explanation. This observation is one source of our belief that high quality grading is likely as much related to good motivation as it is to good information.

Given all of this, we believe that motivation is a key component of high-quality grading, and that actually seeing cases where other students put in the effort to do a good job (or, conversely, seeing how unhelpful it is when other students do not put in such effort) helps provide motivation to student graders. Thus, we would recommend that MOOCS which utilize peer grading should consider using something like the "grading the graders" regime early on in a class, in order to help train and motivate students to do a good job grading subsequent assignments.

7. RELATED WORK

Peer evaluation has a long history in education. Many researchers have demonstrated that peer evaluation can be a beneficial part of the learning process [27, 10, 16]. Further, controlled studies have shown that peer evaluation can be a good proxy for instructor feedback [15, 30]. In addition to lessening the grading burden on instructors, peer evaluation is a valuable learning activity for the peer grader [14]. Grading someone else's work requires retrieval and evaluation of core concepts—activities known to boost learning and retention [11].

In the context of a MOOC, peer evaluation offers some unique challenges compared to a traditional classroom environment. The first is the lack of a gating function. In a traditional classroom, most students will have taken the same preparatory classes and/or been admitted to the same school. This is not the case in a typical MOOC, where one can assume no core competence on the part of the evaluators. A second challenge is the lack of centralized oversight. There is much mention in the online education research community of the necessity of "teaching presence" [25, 28]: the need for participants to feel as if an instructor is present and monitoring the proceedings. In a traditional environment where peer evaluation may be applied, a teacher is present to settle disputes and monitor the fairness of the proceedings. The incentive system that we investigate can be seen as a decentralized, bottom-up simulation of teacher presence.

Student behavior in an online education setting has been studied before. Specifically, Davies and Graff [7] studied correlation between students' performance and the level of interaction between other students. They discovered that greater online interaction did not lead to significantly higher performance, but they did find that students who failed the course tend to interact less.

User performance and behavior patterns have been studied in the context of MOOCs. Breslow et al. [5] did a broad study with the data gathered from edX 6.002x. Their study looked at resource usage, student demographics, achievement, persistence and success. Hew and Cheung [18] discovered several challenges in MOOCs. One of the challenges is low student engagement rate. Anderson et al. [3] examined student behavior patterns and engagement styles in MOOCs. They found some correlations between different engagement styles and student performance. Kizilcec et al. [20] clustered engagement patterns and discovered four prototypical categories of engagement consistently across three different MOOCs.

A recent paper by Kulkarni et al. [21] considers ways to improve grading accuracy in MOOCs. Specifically, The authors consider data on self and peer assessment from two iterations of a MOOC. Their solutions to improving grading accuracy include giving feedback to students about the bias in their peer grading, and using more precise rubric items.

Some online knowledge-sharing forums such as StackOverflow and Y! Answers use incentives to motivate people to contribute. Recognizing contributions by awarding badges has proved effective in motivating contribution [12]. Anderson et al. [2, 3] studied the effect of using badges to motivate participation in a MOOC. They have found that using badges indeed increases the level of engagement.

8. REFERENCES

[1] Susan Adams. Is coursera the beginning of the end for traditional higher education? *Higher Education*, 2012.

[2] Ashton Anderson, Daniel Huttenlocher, Jon Kleinberg, and Jure Leskovec. Steering User Behavior with Badges. In *Proceedings of WWW*, pages 95–106, 2013.

[3] Ashton Anderson, Daniel Huttenlocher, Jon Kleinberg, and Jure Leskovec. Engaging with Massive Online Courses. In *Proceedings of WWW*, pages 687–698, 2014.

[4] George EP Box, William Gordon Hunter, J Stuart Hunter, et al. *Statistics for experimenters*. John Wiley and sons New York, 1978.

[5] Lori B. Breslow, David E. Pritchard, Jennifer DeBoer, Glenda S. Stump, Andrew D. Ho, and Daniel T. Seaton. Studying learning in the worldwide classroom: Research into edX's first mooc. *Research & Practice in Assessment*, 8:13–25, 2013.

[6] D. Casey, E. Burke, C. Houghton, L. Mee, R. Smith, D. Van Der Putten, H. Bradley, and M. Folan. Use of peer assessment as a student engagement strategy in nurse education. *Nursing & Health Sciences*, 13(4):514–520, 2011.

[7] Jo Davies and Martin Graff. Performance in e-learning: online participation and student grades. *British Journal of Educational Technology*, 36(4):657–663, July 2005.

[8] J.P. Dineen, H.B. Clark, and T.R. Risley. Peer tutoring among elementary students: Educational benefits to the tutor. *Journal of Applied Behavior Analysis*, 10(2):231, 1977.

[9] A. DiPardo and S.W. Freedman. Peer response groups in the writing classroom: Theoretic foundations and new directions. *Review of Educational Research*, 58(2):119–149, 1988.

[10] F. Dochy, M. Segers, and D. Sluijsmans. The use of self-, peer and co-assessment in higher education: A review. *Studies in Higher Education*, 24(3):331–350, 1999.

[11] J. Dunlosky, K. A. Rawson, E. J. Marsh, M. J. Nathan, and D. T. Willingham. Improving students' learning with effective learning techniques: Promising directions from cognitive and educational psychology. *Psychological Science in the Public Interest*, 2012.

[12] David Easley and Arpita Ghosh. Incentives, Gamification, and Game Theory: An Economic Approach to Badge Design. In *Proceedings of the Fourteenth ACM Conference on Electronic Commerce*, EC '13, pages 359–376, New York, NY, USA, 2013. ACM.

[13] Bradley Efron and B Efron. *The jackknife, the bootstrap and other resampling plans*, volume 38. SIAM, 1982.

[14] P.A. Ertmer, J.C. Richardson, B. Belland, D. Camin, P. Connolly, G. Coulthard, K. Lei, and C. Mong. Using peer feedback to enhance the quality of student online postings: An exploratory study. *Journal of Computer-Mediated Communication*, 12(2):412–433, 2007.

[15] N. Falchikov and J. Goldfinch. Student peer assessment in higher education: A meta-analysis comparing peer and teacher marks. *Review of educational research*, 70(3):287–322, 2000.

[16] Nancy Falchikov. Peer feedback marking: Developing peer assessment. *Innovations in Education and Training International*, 32(2):175–187, 1995.

[17] Lisa E. Gueldenzoph and Gary L. May. Collaborative peer evaluation: Best practices for group member assessments. *Business Communication Quarterly*, 65(1):9–20, 2002.

[18] Khe Foon Hew and Wing Sum Cheung. StudentsâĂŹ and instructorsâĂŹ use of massive open online courses (moocs): Motivations and challenges. *Educational Research Review*, 12(0):45 – 58, 2014.

[19] James A Keaten and M. Elizabeth Richardson. A field investigation of peer assessment as part of the student group grading process, 1993.

[20] René F. Kizilcec, Chris Piech, and Emily Schneider. Deconstructing Disengagement: Analyzing Learner Subpopulations in Massive Open Online Courses. In *Proceedings of the International Conference on Learning Analytics and Knowledge*, LAK '13, pages 170–179. ACM, 2013.

[21] Chinmay Kulkarni, Koh Pang Wei, Huy Le, Daniel Chia, Kathryn Papadopoulos, Justin Cheng, Daphne Koller, and Scott R. Klemmer. Peer and self assessment in massive online classes. *ACM Trans. Comput.-Hum. Interact.*, 20(6):33:1–33:31, December 2013.

[22] Y. Lai. Which do students prefer to evaluate their essays: Peers or computer program. *British Journal of Educational Technology*, 41(3):432–454, 2009.

[23] Rupert G Miller. *Simultaneous statistical inference*, volume 196. Springer, 1966.

[24] Laura Pappano. The year of the mooc. *The New York Times*, 2(12):2012, 2012.

[25] J.C. Richardson and K. Swan. *Examing social presence in online courses in relation to students' perceived learning and satisfaction*. 2003.

[26] D. Sluijsmans, F. Dochy, and G. Moerkerke. Creating a learning environment by using self-, peer- and co-assessment. *Learning Environments Research*, 1(3):293–319, 1998.

[27] Hugh Somervell. Issues in assessment, enterprise and higher education: the case for self-peer and collaborative assessment. *Assessment and Evaluation in Higher Education*, 18(3):221–233, 1993.

[28] K. Swan and L.F. Shih. On the nature and development of social presence in online course discussions. *Journal of Asynchronous Learning Networks*, 9(3):115–136, 2005.

[29] Terry Tang, Scott Rixner, and Joe Warren. An environment for learning interactive programming. In *Proceedings of the 45th ACM technical symposium on Computer science education*, pages 671–676. ACM, 2014.

[30] K. Topping. Peer assessment between students in colleges and universities. *Review of Educational Research*, 68(3):249–276, 1998.

Measurement and Analysis of Mobile Web Cache Performance

Yun Ma[1], Xuanzhe Liu[1*], Shuhui Zhang[1], Ruirui Xiang[1], Yunxin Liu[2], Tao Xie[3]
[1] School of Electronics Engineering and Computer Science, Peking University, Beijing, China
[2] Microsoft Research, Beijing, China
[3] University of Illinois at Urbana-Champaign, Urbana, USA
{mayun, liuxuanzhe, zhangshuhui, xiangrr0512}@pku.edu.cn; yunxin.liu@microsoft.com; taoxie@illinois.edu

ABSTRACT
The Web browser is a killer app on mobile devices such as smartphones. However, the user experience of mobile Web browsing is undesirable because of the slow resource loading. To improve the performance of Web resource loading, caching has been adopted as a key mechanism. However, the existing passive measurement studies cannot comprehensively characterize the performance of mobile Web caching. For example, most of these studies mainly focus on client-side implementations but not server-side configurations, suffer from biased user behaviors, and fail to study *"miscached"* resources. To address these issues, in this paper, we present a proactive approach for a comprehensive measurement study on mobile Web cache performance. The key idea of our approach is to proactively crawl resources from hundreds of websites periodically with a fine-grained time interval. Thus, we are able to uncover the resource update history and cache configurations at the server side, and analyze the cache performance in various time granularities. Based on our collected data, we build a new cache analysis model and study the upper bound of how high percentage of resources could potentially be cached and how effective the caching works in practice. We report detailed analysis results of different websites and various types of Web resources, and identify the problems caused by unsatisfactory cache performance. In particular, we identify two major problems – ***Redundant Transfer*** and ***Miscached Resource***, which lead to unsatisfactory cache performance. We investigate three main root causes: ***Same Content***, ***Heuristic Expiration***, and ***Conservative Expiration Time***, and discuss what mobile Web developers can do to mitigate those problems.

Categories and Subject Descriptors
C.4 [**Computer Systems Organization**]: Performance of Systems — *Design studies*

Keywords
Mobile Web; Cache; Measurement

1. INTRODUCTION
The Web browser is a killer and arguably the most frequently used app on mobile devices such as smartphones and tablet computers. According to a study [26], Web browsers occupy 63% of the window focus time on the subjects' mobile devices. However, the user experience of mobile Web browsing is far from satisfaction. Resource loading is one of the key factors influencing Web browsing performance. It is reported that 65% of page load time is spent on resource loading [21]. Such problem becomes even worse on mobile devices because of the unreliable network conditions, particularly when the network is congested or the user is moving around. Furthermore, more resource downloading may consume more energy, which is the scarcest resource on battery-powered mobile devices.

Caching is a widely adopted mechanism to accelerate Web resource loading[1]. By saving the resources of visited webpages into the local storage (memory or disk), these webpages may be served from the local storage rather than being re-fetched from the Web servers when the webpages are visited again. As a result, caching reduces the quantity of downloaded resources and thus can improve Web browsing performance. Caching is particularly beneficial to mobile devices because it not only reduces page load time, but also reduces network traffic and energy consumption.

It is critical to understand how mobile Web browsing could benefit from caching and how well caching takes effect in practice. To this end, several measurement studies have been made by analyzing user access traces gathered from ISPs or instrumented client devices [11][15][16][17][24]. These studies have already revealed the performance problems of mobile Web caching caused by imperfect client-side implementations. However, they cannot comprehensively characterize the end-to-end Web cache performance involving not only Web clients but also Web servers and user behaviors. In particular, existing measurement studies on mobile Web cache have the following three main limitations.

- ***These existing studies suffer from biased user behaviors.*** The traces collected from ISPs or instrumented client devices are passive observations on users' Web access behaviors. These traces are just fragmented snapshots of the websites and thus cannot cover the full resource update history of these websites. As a result, measurements based on these traces could imply only how caching works on the sampled access of the sampled users, but cannot reflect how the websites themselves can essentially benefit from caching.
- ***These existing studies do not investigate the influences of server-side caching configurations on cache performance.*** Similar to the first issue, as the passively collected data traces cannot cover the full resource update history of the websites, these studies concentrate on client-side implementations but not server-side configurations. Although how the browsers support caching on mobile devices is important, Web cache performance is largely determined by the cache configurations at the server side. For example, if resources are configured as *no-cache* (indicating that they should not be cached), client-

* Corresponding author

WWW 2015, May 18–22, 2015, Florence, Italy.
ACM 978-1-4503-3469-3/15/05.
http://dx.doi.org/10.1145/2736277.2741114

[1] "Caching" and "cache" are often used interchangeably. Usually, "caching" denotes the mechanism defined by specifications, and "cache" represents the browser component that could store resources temporally. "Cache" is also used as a verb, denoting putting something in the cache. In this paper, caching and cache have the same meaning if not specifically stated.

side caching cannot help at all. It is desirable to examine how server-side configurations may impact Web caching.

- ***These existing studies do not investigate the problem of miscached resources.*** Miscached resources are those that have already been updated on the server, but the browser wrongly uses the expired resources from the cache rather than fetching the updated ones from the server. The passive data collection approaches cannot capture miscached resources because the passive approaches collect only the resources actually fetched by browsers. However, miscached resources may significantly affect user experience. In particular, if the functional resources (e.g., JavaScript or CSS) are miscached, the corresponding website may not work correctly. Therefore, there is a strong need of studying miscached resources.

To address the preceding issues faced by the existing studies, in this paper, we present a proactive approach for comprehensive measurement and analysis of mobile Web cache performance. In our approach, we proactively crawl resources from hundreds of websites periodically with a fine-grained time interval for a long time duration. In this way, we are able to uncover the resource update history and cache configurations at the server side, and analyze the cache performance in various time granularities, without bias caused by limited samples of users' behaviors. Furthermore, we build an analysis model to answer three research questions. The first one is *how much of a website can be cached,* giving an upper bound of how caching could help improve mobile Web browsing experience. More cacheable resources indicate more performance improvements that the website can benefit from caching. The second question is *how well caching has been supported to reach the upper bound,* providing comprehensive characterization of the state-of-the-art of mobile Web caching. The third question is *what causes the gap between the upper bound and the actual performance.* For various reasons, resources that can be cached may not be actually cached and there exist miscached resources.

To make a quantitative study, we measure the performance of Web caching in both the **resource size** and **resource number**. Larger size of resources loaded from the cache indicates less data traffic that needs downloading from the network. However, the resource size itself cannot fully quantify the performance of Web caching. Given the same total size of resources, a larger number of small resources loaded from the cache indicates fewer network connections to the server and less energy consumption, compared to a small number of large resources. Therefore, we consider both the resource size and resource number as the evaluation metrics on how caching influences mobile Web browsing experience in terms of page load time, data traffic, and energy consumption.

This paper makes the following main contributions:

- ***A proactive approach to acquire resource update history.*** We choose two sets of websites for a comparative study to uncover both the state-of-the-art and ordinary status of mobile Web cache performance. One set (Top) comes from Alexa Top 100 list. The other set (Random) comes from 100 websites randomly chosen from Alexa Top 1,000,000 list. We periodically crawl their resource update history for one week, forming the basis of our analysis.

- ***An analysis model for cache performance.*** Based on the resource update history, we formally define the metrics to quantitatively measure cache performance. We then build a cache behavior taxonomy to correlate cache configurations to resource updates. Such taxonomy maps each possible case to one of the four behavior patterns: Positive Hit (PH), Negative Hit (NH), Positive Miss (PM), and Negative Miss (NM).

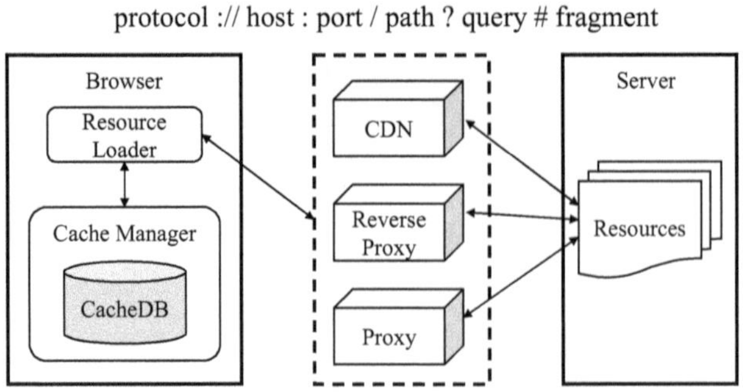

Figure 1. Architecture of Web caching

- ***Empirical results for showing the gap between ideal and actual mobile Web cache performance.*** On average, more than half of the total resources can be cached and the Random websites are more cacheable than the Top ones. However, in practice, only a limited portion of the cacheable resources are cached, not more than 50% for the Random websites. Different types of resources have different cacheabilities.

- ***Empirical results for highlighting two main problems caused by undesirable cache performance.*** The ***Redundant Transfer*** problem comes from NM resources (the resources that can be served from the cache but are actually downloaded from the network). The median Negative Miss Ratios in terms of the resource size of Top and Random websites are 10% and 52% for one-day revisiting interval, respectively. The ***Miscached Resource*** problem comes from NH resources (the resources that have been updated on the server but are actually served from the cache). NH resources have a similar proportion in both Top and Random websites.

- ***Root causes for undesirable mobile Web cache performance.*** Three main root causes are identified: ***Same Content*** (the same resources that have different URLs when requested at different times), ***Heuristic Expiration*** (the caching policy is not explicitly defined by the server and thus it depends on browsers to infer an expiration time), and ***Conservative Expiration Time*** (the expiration time is set to be too short).

- ***Implications and recommendations on how to improve cache performance by better cache policies.*** For example, the Application Cache of HTML 5 can be used to make the resource updates visible to clients.

The remainder of this paper is organized as follows. Section 2 motivates our study by analyzing how caching works and identifying three research questions. Section 3 describes our data set and data-collection approach. Section 4 presents the analysis methodology and Section 5 presents the detailed measurement results. Based on the findings, we provide implications and recommendations for Web developers in Section 6. Section 7 surveys related work and Section 8 concludes this paper.

2. BACKGROUND AND GOAL

In this section, we first describe the background on how Web caching works and then present the three research questions that we seek to answer, as the goal of this paper.

2.1 How Web Caching Works

Figure 1 shows a simplified procedure to illustrate how Web caching works. A webpage consists of a set of resources, such as

HTML, CSS, JavaScript, and images. When users type in a URL and press the "*Go*" button or click through a hyperlink, the browser will load the target webpage by acquiring the corresponding resources from the Resource Loader module.

The Resource Loader will first try to load resources from the local cache through the Cache Manager module. According to RFC 2616 [9], HTTP/1.1 defines a cache expiration model and a cache validation model. The cache expiration model allows a Web server to set an expiration time for each resource, indicating how long the resource can be cached by a client device. Setting expiration time is not mandatory. If a resource does not have an expiration time explicitly set by the server, browsers may apply their own heuristic algorithms to decide the cache expiration time of the resource. Such mechanism is called Heuristic Expiration.

The Cache Manager checks whether the requested resource (identified by its URL's protocol, host, port, path, and query) can be found in the Cache Database. If not, the browser will set up a HTTP connection to fetch the resource from the remote Web server. If the resource is found and not expired according to the cache expiration model, it will be returned directly from the cache. If the resource is expired, the HTTP/1.1 cache validation model requires the browser to check with the server whether the resource is changed or not (via the last modified time or Etag identifier). If the server decides the corresponding resource has not changed, it responds with a "*304 Not Modified*" message and the resource will be fetched from the cache of the client. Otherwise, the server sends the updated resource back to the browser.

It is worth mentioning that a website may be much more complex than a single Web server. A large website (e.g., Google) may have many backend Web servers. There may also be Content Delivery Network (CDN) servers to enable scalability and geographical distributions. In such a case, a URL's query part often contains a hash code to indicate which CDN server should process the request, and thus the same resource may have different URLs served by different CDN servers. Furthermore, proxy servers and reverse proxies often act in the middle to route the requests to different backend servers for workload balance. Different backend servers could also attach different URLs to the same resource. As discussed in Section 5.3, this "multiple URLs of the same resource" problem causes undesirable Web cache performance and should be investigated.

2.2 Research Questions to Answer

Our goal is to conduct a comprehensive study on the performance of mobile Web caching. Specifically, we intend to answer the following three research questions.

RQ1: What percentage of Web resources can be cached ideally? By answering this question, we study the upper bound of the benefit of Web caching. We consider not only the redundant transmission of the same resource (identified by its unique URL), but also the redundancy of the resources with different URLs.

RQ2: What percentage of the cacheable Web resources are actually cached if the client is perfectly implemented according to the specification? By answering this question, we uncover how well developers leverage the caching mechanism in practice, and reveal the gap between the ideal and actual performance of mobile Web caching.

RQ3: What causes the gap between ideal and actual performance? By answering this question, we investigate the root causes of the undesirable actual performance of Web caching, and give Web developers recommendations on how to improve the performance of mobile Web caching.

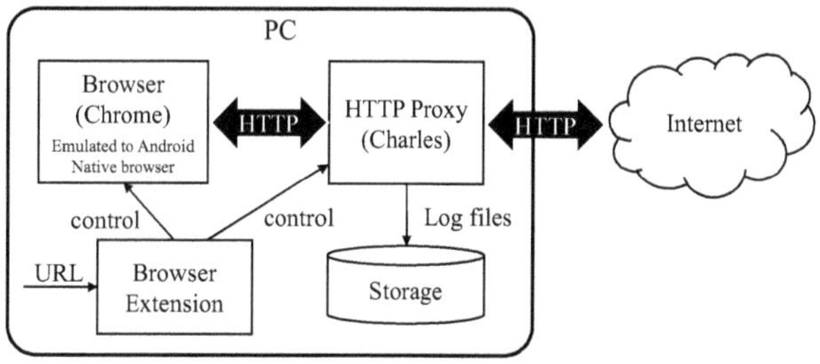

Figure 2. Data collection tool

Answering these questions requires tracking the whole resource update history of websites. This requirement cannot be met by existing passive data collection approaches. Therefore, we propose a new proactive data collection approach and next present how it works.

3. DATA COLLECTION

In this section, we describe how we proactively crawl Web resources and what data sets are used to conduct our study.

3.1 Proactive Data Collection Approach

We propose a proactive approach to capture the resource update history of a specific website. For a given URL, we periodically visit the corresponding webpage with a short time interval and for a long time duration. For each visit, we first clean the cache and then record all the returned resources. The short revisiting interval not only makes it possible to obtain the complete resource update history, but also enables us to make flexible analysis with various time granularities. The long data-collection time duration ensures enough samples and lowers the bias. We develop a tool to realize our approach and Figure 2 shows its architecture.

Our tool runs on a PC using the Chrome browser. We enable the Chrome browser's emulation mode to make it act as a mobile browser (Android 4.2 native browser in our case) so that a website will return its mobile-version webpages (if the website has a mobile version). It is important to use a real browser to crawl data. The reason is that many websites embed JavaScript, and more resources may be loaded by the JavaScript execution. Only when the webpage is actually *rendered* by a browser, can we obtain the whole set of resources. Furthermore, using a PC-version browser helps us leverage the programmability of the browser, which is not easy on Android smartphones.

We use the Charles proxy [3], a commercial product, to act as the middle tier for data collection. Charles can record each TCP connection passed through it and save HTTP traces in structured data. The data structures split HTTP protocol elements into different fields, making it easy to perform further analysis. In addition, Charles has a programming interface to ease the data recording and saving. We install Charles on the same PC and configure the Chrome browser to use Charles as the proxy.

We build a Chrome extension to automate our data collection. The extension takes a list of URLs and controls the Chrome browser to visit the URLs one by one. Before each visit, the browser cache is cleaned in order to ensure that all the resources are loaded from the network. When a Chrome *TabComplete* event is detected, the extension will regard that the website has finished loading. Note that some websites utilize lazy loading, and thus there will still be resource requests after *TabComplete* is fired. To mitigate such resource incompleteness, the extension is set to wait for two seconds after a *TabComplete* event. Finally, the extension invokes the Charles programming interface to save all the resource request records on the disk. We can also configure the extension to periodically crawl a list of URLs with a given time interval.

3.2 Data Sets

For a comparative study, we choose two sets of websites from Alexa [1] ranking list in January 2014. The first set (Top) contains Alexa top 100 websites. We expect that their cache performance is highly optimized and regard them as the state-of-the-art of Web caching. The other set (Random) contains 100 websites randomly selected from Alexa top 1,000,000 list. We assume that their cache performance is not fully optimized and regard them as the average level of cache performance.

We manually checked each website in the two sets and filtered out the following ones.

- Unreachable websites. Some websites were not reachable because they were shut down at the time that we visited. Unreachable websites occurred in only the Random data set.
- Same websites with different domain names. For example, in the Top data set, Google appears 16 times such as google.in, google.de, and google.jp. Since they have the same function and appearance, we keep only google.com in our Top data set. However, we treat yahoo and yahoo.jp as two different websites because their contents are totally different.
- HTTPS-only websites. As HTTPS prevents us from capturing the Web resources transmitted over the encrypted network connection, we exclude those websites that support only the HTTPS protocol.

After the filtering, 146 websites remain in total, 55 in the Top data set, and 91 in the Random data set. Note that not all of the 146 websites have a mobile version customized for mobile browsing. According to our manual checking, 7 of the 55 Top websites and 56 of the 91 Random websites do not have their mobile versions. However, the goal of our measurement is to study how Web caching performs on mobile devices for all websites, not only the ones with a mobile version. Therefore, we do not distinguish mobile or non-mobile websites.

For these 146 websites, we used our data-collection tool to periodically crawl their homepages for one week. The crawling time interval was 30 minutes, being short enough to capture all the resource changes. One week means that we visited each website for more than 300 times. In total we crawled 157 GB data, 73 GB for the Top websites, and 84 GB for the Random websites.

4. MEASUREMENT METHODOLOGY

In this section, we formally define the measurement metrics used to study Web cache performance. We also design a taxonomy to map the relationship between cache specifications and actual resource updates.

4.1 Metrics Definition

Cache only works when a website is revisited. So we consider two visits. At the first visit, the browser cache is empty and all the resources needed to render the website have to be loaded from the network. After a given Revisiting Interval (RI) Δt, the same website is visited for the second time, where some of the resources are loaded from the browser cache while others are loaded from the network. We examine how the browser cache behaves for the second visit.

Define $S_t = \{r_t\}$ as the resource set fetched by the browser at time t under the condition that the browser cache is empty. $r_t \in <URL, Content>$ is a resource entry, where URL (including the domain, port, path, and query) identifies the resource, and $Content$ is its actual entity. A resource can be updated when time goes on. S_t represents the up-to-date resources of the website at time t.

Define

$$CA_t(\Delta t) = \{r_t \in S_t | \exists r_{t-\Delta t} \in S_{t-\Delta t}, r_t.Content = r_{t-\Delta t}.Content\}$$

as the resources (at time t) that have already been loaded from the network at the previous visit before Δt. Note that we do not enforce whether the resource's URL is the same or not. We consider only the resource's content that is actually used by browsers to render websites. In fact, $CA_t(\Delta t)$ are the resources that can benefit from caching.

Based on the preceding definitions, cacheablity $\Psi(\Delta t)$ can be formulated as the proportion of $CA_t(\Delta t)$ in S_t:

$$\Psi(\Delta t) = \frac{CA_t(\Delta t)}{S_t}$$

$\Psi(\Delta t)$ measures what percentage of a website can be cached after Δt. Larger $\Psi(\Delta t)$ means more resources are cacheable. It should be pointed out that cacheablity depends on Δt because resource updates are different when a website is revisited after different Δt.

Define

$$C_t(\Delta t) = \{r_{t-\Delta t} \in S_{t-\Delta t} | r_{t-\Delta t}\ is\ configured\ to\ be\ cached\}$$

as the resource set in the browser cache at time t. $C_t(\Delta t)$ represents the resources stored into the cache on the previous visit at time $t - \Delta t$. Note that $C_t(\Delta t) \subseteq S_{t-\Delta t}$ because some resources in $S_{t-\Delta t}$may be configured not to be stored in the browser cache.

According to the cache mechanism, $C_t(\Delta t) = EX_t \cup FR_t$, indicates that some of the cached resources are expired (denoted as EX_t) while others are still fresh (denoted as FR_t). The browser will first load a resource from the cache if its URL is found in FR_t, in which case we say the resource is *hit*. Define $H_t = \{r_t \in S_t | \exists r \in FR_t, r_t.URL = r.URL\}$ as the resource set loaded from the cache. Otherwise, no matter when the resource URL is found in EX_t or cannot be found in $C_t(\Delta t)$, the browser will load it from the network, in which case we say the resource is *miss*. Define $M_t = \{r_t \in S_t | (\exists r \in EX_t, r_t.URL = r.URL) \vee (\forall r \in C_t(\Delta t), r_t.URL \neq r.URL)\}$ as the resource set loaded from the network.

However, the cache policy may not be set properly so that expired resources could still be up-to-date. In addition, only considering the resource URL can bring mistakes as the content is what actually matters for rendering websites. Therefore, we further define positive and negative patterns for H_t and M_t, respectively.

Positive Hit ($PH_t(\Delta t)$). Given $r_t \in H_t$, $r_t \in PH_t(\Delta t) \Leftrightarrow \exists r_{t-\Delta t} \in S_{t-\Delta t}, r_t.URL = r_{t-\Delta t}.URL \wedge r_t.Content = r_{t-\Delta t}.Content$, which means that the resource is loaded from the cache and it is the same with the up-to-date version on the server. Larger $PH_t(\Delta t)$ means more resources are correctly served from the cache.

Negative Hit ($NH_t(\Delta t)$). Given $r_t \in H_t$, $r_t \in NH_t(\Delta t) \Leftrightarrow \exists r_{t-\Delta t} \in S_{t-\Delta t}, r_t.URL = r_{t-\Delta t}.URL \wedge r_t.Content \neq r_{t-\Delta t}.Content$, which means that the resource is loaded from the cache but its content has already been updated on the server. In this case, the browser should acquire the updated resource. Larger $NH_t(\Delta t)$ means more stale resources are used to render the website, and wrong behaviors are more likely to happen.

Positive Miss ($PM_t(\Delta t)$). Given $r_t \in M_t$, $r_t \in PM_t(\Delta t) \Leftrightarrow \forall r_{t-\Delta t} \in S_{t-\Delta t}, r_t.Content \neq r_{t-\Delta t}.Content$, which means that the resource is loaded from the network and its content has never occurred in $S_{t-\Delta t}$. It is either a new resource or an update of a cached resource. Larger $PM_t(\Delta t)$ indicates more resources are newly involved by the website or changed during the time.

Table 1. Cache performance metrics

Metric	Description
$PH(\Delta t)$	The proportion of resources that are correctly served by the cache when the website is revisited after Δt.
$NH(\Delta t)$	The proportion of resources that should have been fetched from the server but are actually provided by the cache when the website is revisited after Δt.
$PM(\Delta t)$	The proportion of resources that are correctly fetched from the server when the website is revisited after Δt.
$NM(\Delta t)$	The proportion of resources that should have been provided by the cache but are actually fetched from the server when the website is revisited after Δt.
$\Psi(\Delta t)$	Cacheability of a website with revisiting interval Δt, giving an upper bound of how much a website can benefit from caching.
$\Phi(\Delta t)$	Actual cache performance of a website with revisiting interval Δt, showing how well a website has utilized caching.
$\Omega(\Delta t)$	Negative Miss Ratio with revisiting interval Δt, indicating how much data traffics are wasted by redundant transfers.

Negative Miss ($NM_t(\Delta t)$). Given $r_t \in M_t$, $r_t \in NM_t(\Delta t) \Leftrightarrow \exists r_{t-\Delta t} \in S_{t-\Delta t}, r_t.Content = r_{t-\Delta t}.Content$, which means that the resource is loaded from the network but its content has ever been loaded by the browser before. It is either stored in the cache or configured not to be cached. In this case, the browser should directly use the previously loaded resource. Larger $NM_t(\Delta t)$ indicates more redundant transfers.

Based on the preceding definitions, we can formulate the actual cache performance $\Phi(\Delta t)$ as the proportion of $PH_t(\Delta t)$ in $PH_t(\Delta t) \cup NM_t(\Delta t)$:

$$\Phi(\Delta t) = \frac{PH_t(\Delta t)}{PH_t(\Delta t) \cup NM_t(\Delta t)}$$

In addition, we can measure the problems of redundant transfer by Negative Miss Ratio $\Omega(\Delta t)$:

$$\Omega(\Delta t) = \frac{NM_t(\Delta t)}{PM_t(\Delta t) \cup NM_t(\Delta t)}$$

Larger Ω indicates more resources loaded from network can actually be loaded from the cache.

Table 1 summarizes the metrics and their meanings to measure mobile Web cache performance. Meanwhile, as we choose resource size and number as the quantitative parameters, subscript s and n will be attached to the metrics representing which parameter is used to calculate the metric values. For example, Ψ_s and Ψ_n denote the cacheability calculated by resource size and number, respectively.

4.2 Cache Behavior Taxonomy

In order to calculate the preceding metrics, we correlate the cache configurations and resource updates by building a cache behavior taxonomy (Figure 3).

When a web page is visited, the browser will look up in its cache table for each resource represented by the URL.

If the URL is found in the cache table (*URLHit*), the cache mechanism is ready to work. The browser will first check expiration to determine the freshness of the cached resources. There are two expiration policies. One is the server-specified expiration relying on the origin server to provide an explicit expiration time. The other is the heuristic expiration relying on the browser to assign an estimated value for those without explicit server-specified expiration time.

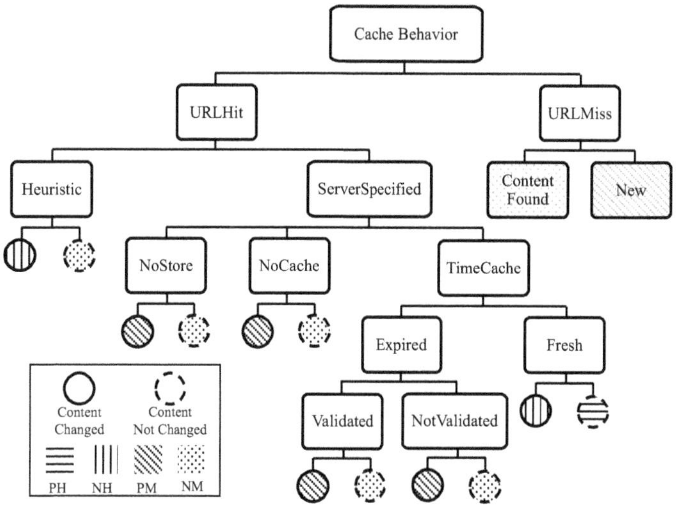

Figure 3. Cache behavior taxonomy

For the heuristic expiration, no matter whether the resource content is changed or not, any of the four cache behavior patterns is possible to happen as its freshness cannot be explicitly determined. In the worst case, we can assume the *ContentChanged* state of heuristic expiration as NH and the *ContentNotChanged* state as NM. In the following parts, all the analyses are for the worst case unless specially stated.

For the server-specified expiration, there are three possible policies. The first is *NoStore*, indicating that the resources cannot be persistently stored on the hard disk. The second is *NoCache*, indicating that although the resources should not be cached by the browser, they can be persistently stored on the hard disk. The *ContentChanged* and *ContentNotChanged* states of both *NoStore* and *NoCache* are classified as PM and NM, respectively. In the third case, according to the expiration time, we can determine whether the cached resources get expired or stay fresh. If expired, two further branches *Validated* and *NotValidated* can be derived from the cache validation model, where the last modified time or Etag is used for the freshness check with the origin server. Combined with resource update states, we can classify each leaf node with the *ContentChanged* state as PM or *ContentNotChanged* state as NM. For the *Fresh* node, NH happens if the content is changed, while PH happens if the content is not actually changed.

If the URL is not found in the cache table (*URLMiss*), it does not mean that the resource cannot be served by the cache. As aforementioned, resources with different URLs may have the same content. We use *ContentFound* to denote such case and classify its cache behavior pattern as NM. The last branch of *New* indicates completely new resources that have to be downloaded from the network, and thus we classify it as PM.

5. MEASUREMENT RESULTS

This section presents our detailed measurement results from three aspects: the gap between the ideal and the actual cache performance (Section 5.1), the problems caused by undesirable cache performance (Section 5.2), and the root cause analysis (Section 5.3).

5.1 Ideal and Actual Cache Performance

We first show the cacheability of websites and then present how much cacheability is realized in practice, uncovering the gap between the ideal and actual cache performance.

Table 2. Ψ of aggregated websites and resource types

	24h		6h		0.5h	
	Ψ_s	Ψ_n	Ψ_s	Ψ_n	Ψ_s	Ψ_n
All_{Top}	56.4%	69.5%	64.7%	76.0%	72.7%	83.2%
$\text{All}_{\text{Random}}$	63.2%	72.1%	73.5%	78.8%	79.0%	84.5%
HTML_{Top}	4.5%	34.2%	7.2%	39.6%	9.1%	41.1%
$\text{HTML}_{\text{Random}}$	22.4%	44.0%	27.8%	49.3%	32.7%	51.0%
CSS_{Top}	74.6%	86.9%	79.5%	86.9%	82.4%	89.4%
$\text{CSS}_{\text{Random}}$	72.0%	90.3%	81.7%	89.8%	84.8%	91.4%
JS_{Top}	70.9%	84.5%	69.7%	82.4%	72.3%	83.4%
$\text{JS}_{\text{Random}}$	54.1%	69.8%	66.6%	77.4%	72.1%	80.6%
$\text{Image}_{\text{Top}}$	51.0%	67.2%	68.3%	78.3%	81.4%	88.8%
$\text{Image}_{\text{Random}}$	74.0%	76.0%	83.7%	82.8%	91.4%	89.7%

5.1.1 Potential Benefits of Caching

To answer the first research question of "*What percentage of Web resources can be cached ideally*", we calculate Ψ of the websites in the two data sets, as shown in Table 2. From Table 2, we make the following observations.

A high percentage of the total resources are cacheable and thus caching may be substantially helpful. For the Top websites, 56.4%-72.7% of the total resource size (Ψ_s) and 69.5%-83.2% of the total resource number (Ψ_n) are cacheable, depending on the values of RI. For the Random websites, the percentages are even higher: 63.2%-79.0% in Ψ_s and 72.1%-84.5% in Ψ_n. These results demonstrate that caching has great potential to help improve the performance of mobile Web browsing if caching is correctly configured and implemented. For the websites that users visit daily or even more frequently (e.g., news websites and search engines), caching can substantially reduce the cost of Web browsing on mobile devices, in terms of network bandwidth, computation, and energy. Furthermore, as RI increases, Ψ declines. This phenomenon is reasonable because resources are more likely to change when users revisit a website after a longer period and thus the probability of cache hit becomes lower.

Caching is more helpful for the Random websites than for the Top websites. No matter what value RI has, Ψ_s and Ψ_n of the Random websites are always larger than those of the Top websites. For example, when RI is 24 hours, Ψ_s of the Random set is 6.8% higher than Ψ_s of the Top set. In other words, the Random websites are more cacheable than the Top websites. The reason is that resources are less likely to change for ordinary websites than for popular websites.

Next, we examine how different types of resources can benefit from caching.

HTML is the least likely to benefit from caching. Interestingly, HTML is the least cacheable type of Web resources. For example, Ψ_s of HTML for the Top websites is as small as 4.5%-9.1%. This result may be due to that modern websites are becoming increasingly dynamic to meet the ever-growing user requirements. Rich client technologies, such as Asynchronous JavaScript + XML (AJAX) programming, can change HTML DOM trees on-the-fly and make HTML less cacheable. Ψ_n of HTML (34.2%-41.1% for the Top websites) is larger than Ψ_s of HTML, because small HTML pages are less likely dynamic. In addition, Ψ of HTML for the Random websites is larger than the one for the Top websites, indicating that the Random websites are relatively more stable than the Top websites.

CSS is the most cacheable resources. Compared to other types of resources, Ψ of CSS is the highest: 74.6%-89.4% for the Top websites, and 72.0%-91.4% for the Random websites. This observation can be explained by the nature of CSS: although the content of a webpage may change frequently, the layout and style of the webpage may be more stable.

JS of the Top websites benefits more than that of the Random websites. The cacheability of JS for the Top and Random websites is very different from overall results and other resource types. Given an RI, Ψ of JS for the Top websites is always larger than that of the Random websites. Furthermore, Ψ of JS for the Top websites does not change much as RI changes (70.9% to 72.3%), but the variance of Ψ of JS is rather large for the Random websites (54.1% to 72.1%). This observation reflects that the Top websites remain more stable on functionalities than the Random websites.

Images mostly benefit from caching for short RI. As RI increases, Ψ of images decreases a lot (about 30% for the Top websites and 20% for the Random websites). This phenomenon is reasonable since new images may take place of old ones after a longer time.

Table 3. Φ of aggregated websites and resource types

	24h		6h		0.5h	
	Φ_s	Φ_n	Φ_s	Φ_n	Φ_s	Φ_n
All_{Top}	80.7%	48.8%	85.2%	56.6%	88.5%	64.9%
$\text{All}_{\text{Random}}$	42.4%	32.7%	48.9%	39.6%	53.8%	44.4%
HTML_{Top}	2.8%	3.8%	2.1%	4.9%	16.4%	12.9%
$\text{HTML}_{\text{Random}}$	39.4%	11.2%	40.9%	13.0%	47.2%	19.2%
CSS_{Top}	82.6%	52.7%	87.3%	55.9%	88.1%	67.7%
$\text{CSS}_{\text{Random}}$	44.6%	23.5%	55.2%	42.3%	57.9%	45.7%
JS_{Top}	74.9%	37.8%	76.9%	44.5%	83.7%	52.4%
$\text{JS}_{\text{Random}}$	51.6%	29.4%	63.2%	38.9%	69.2%	48.8%
$\text{Image}_{\text{Top}}$	84.5%	55.7%	90.8%	63.3%	93.0%	70.6%
$\text{Image}_{\text{Random}}$	36.6%	35.4%	41.9%	42.3%	45.2%	45.4%

5.1.2 Actual Cache Performance

We further calculate Φ of the two data sets, to explore "*What percentage of the cacheable Web resources are actually cached*" for the websites that we captured. Table 3 shows the results and we have the following findings.

Compared to the Top websites, the Random websites do not make best use of caching. Φ of Random is always smaller than Φ of Top. More than 80% of the cacheable bytes for Top have been actually cached in all cases, but just above 50% of the cacheable bytes for Random have been actually cached in the best case within 0.5 hour RI.

Small-size resources are not taken into consideration very well. Although Φ_s of Top is high, Φ_n is relatively low. For 24 hours RI, Φ_s is above 80% while Φ_n is just not more than 50%. This observation implies that the Top websites pay more attention on larger-size resources but there are still a number of resources not being considered. They occupy small proportion in the total resource size but constitute the large proportion of the total resource number. Network connections may be wasted to download these small resources, not being energy efficient.

The cacheability of HTML is almost not utilized at all. Both Φ_s and Φ_n of HTML for Top are smaller than those of Random. In the worst case with 24 hours RI, Φ_s of Top is just 2.8%. For Random, Φ_s is not above 50% in the best case with 0.5 hours RI. Generally, it seems not possible to make HTML cached as it can hardly be predicted when the HTML will be changed. Therefore, popular websites give up the cacheability of HTML.

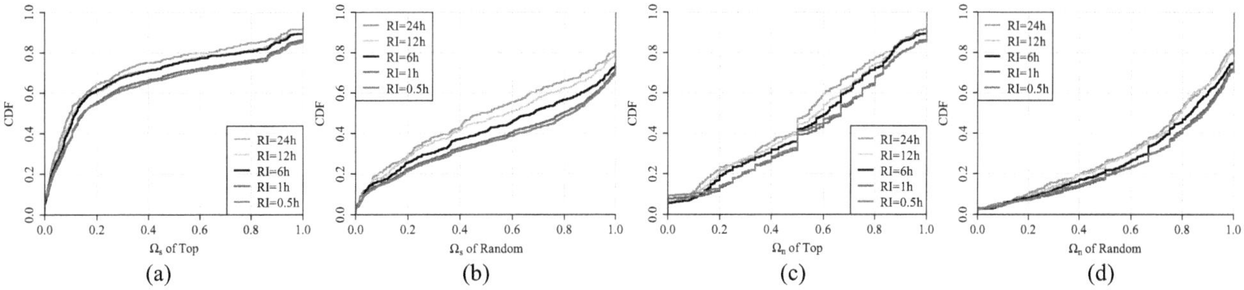

Figure 4. Overall Negative Miss Ratio

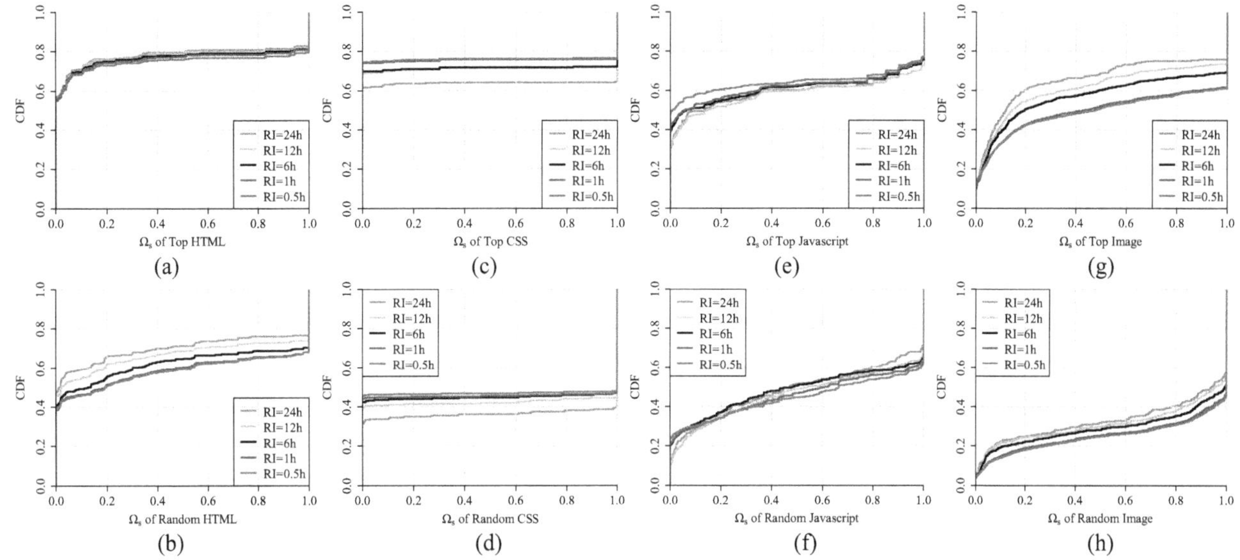

Figure 5. Ω_s of different resource types for Top and Random

The resource type with the highest cache performance is Image for Top and JS for Random. It is surprising that images of the Random websites do not make the best use of cache, where both Φ_s and Φ_n are even not above 50% in the best cases.

In summary, there is a big gap between ideal and actual cache performance. For the Top websites, the gap is mostly originated from the large number of small-size resources. For the Random websites, all types of resources' cacheability have not been properly considered.

5.2 Problems Caused by Undesirable Cache Performance

We then identify two major problems caused by undesirable cache performance: *Redundant Transfer* introduced by NM and *Miscached Resource* introduced by NH. These problems can negatively affect the experience of mobile Web browsing.

5.2.1 Redundant Transfer

The Redundant Transfer problem comes from NM when resources could be fetched from the cache but are actually downloaded from the network. Figure 4 shows the CDF of Ω_s and Ω_n of the Top and Random websites with different RIs.

Redundant Transfer is a significant issue for mobile Web browsing and the issue is worse for the Random websites than the Top ones. Considering 24 hours RI, the medium Ω_s of Top is about 10% while it reaches more than 40% for Random, i.e., 40% of the transferred bytes are redundant. The result indicates that Redundant Transfer is a common problem for mobile Web browsing while the Top websites indeed make some efforts to reduce it. However, in terms of the resource number, Ω_n of both Top and Random is relatively high where the medium value is about 50% and 75%, respectively.

Redundant Transfer is worse for short RI. Ω becomes higher as RI decreases for both Top and Random, represented by CDF curves shift to the right when RI decreases in Figure 4. In the worst case, the medium Ω_s of Random is more than 80% with 0.5 hour RI. As a result, a larger proportion of resources requested from the network are redundant when users revisit a website after a shorter interval. However, as discussed earlier, caching is more effective when RI is shorter. Therefore, caching is far from its capacity and it could be improved a lot if NM was reduced.

Some websites have 100% Ω, indicating that all the requested resources are redundant for these websites. For example, about 10% of Top and 20% of Random have 100% Ω with 24 hours RI. Table 4 lists the websites of 100% Ω for Top considering 24 hours RI. It is surprising that some popular websites are in the list, such as Baidu, Wikipedia, and Apple. Since users may visit these popular websites many times every day, the waste of data traffic and energy could be very large.

We then examine the Redundant Transfer problem for different resource types. Figure 5 shows Ω_s's CDF with different RIs for both Top and Random, corresponding to the resource types of HTML, CSS, JavaScript, and Image.

For all kinds of resources, Ω of Random is larger than that of Top, represented by CDF curves shift to the right bottom by comparing the two figures of the same resource type for Top and

Table 4. Top websites with 100% Ω

Website	Rank	Category
Baidu	5	Search
wikipedia	6	News & Reference
Wordpress	20	Misc
360	22	Corporation
Soso	29	Search
Ask	35	Search
Instagram	37	Entertainment
Apple	45	Corporation
Alibaba	68	E-commerce

Table 5. NH of aggregated websites and resource types

	24h		6h		0.5h	
	NH_s	NH_n	NH_s	NH_n	NH_s	NH_n
All_{Top}	6.4%	2.3%	7.8%	3.0%	8.1%	3.0%
All_{Random}	7.7%	2.9%	7.9%	2.7%	9.0%	2.8%
$HTML_{Top}$	35.7%	18.7%	35.8%	18.8%	40.0%	19.9%
$HTML_{Random}$	24.6%	10.3%	23.2%	8.9%	21.5%	9.1%
CSS_{Top}	8.3%	5.6%	13.4%	9.3%	12.1%	7.7%
CSS_{Random}	13.5%	2.8%	9.8%	2.7%	10.5%	2.9%
JS_{Top}	4.8%	2.1%	10.2%	3.7%	10.4%	4.1%
JS_{Random}	10.5%	4.3%	13.4%	3.7%	16.6%	5.3%
$Image_{Top}$	0.1%	0.3%	0.1%	0.3%	0.1%	0.2%
$Image_{Random}$	1.0%	1.3%	0.6%	0.9%	0.5%	0.8%

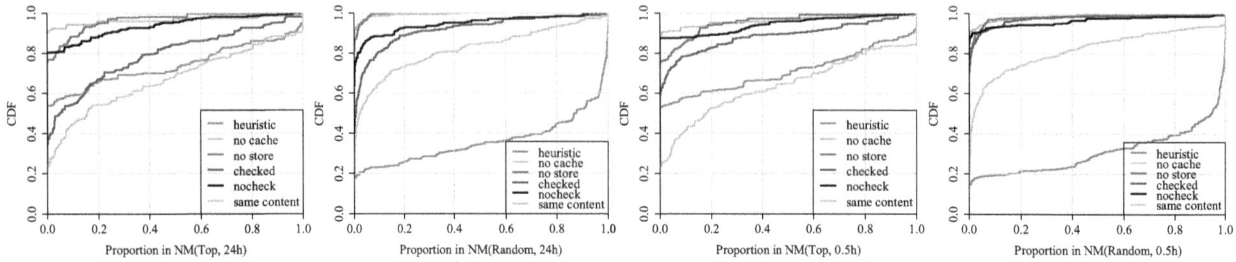

(a) (b) (c) (d)

Figure 6. Breakdown of NM

Random. This result implies that ordinary websites do not consider cache much for each kind of resources.

For HTML (5(a) and 5(b)), Ω of Top does not vary a lot while Ω of Random decreases as RI increases. This observation implies that HTML of the Top websites is more dynamic while HTML of the Random gets updated in a fixed period.

For CSS (5(c) and 5(d)), when RI increases, Ω of both Top and Random increases, implying that more redundant transfers could occur after a longer RI. The reason may be that both Top and Random leverage the cache expiration model for CSS but the expiration time is too conservative. As a result, when the CSS is revisited after a shorter interval, it will be served by the cache. In contrast, the CSS will be loaded from the network when the page is revisited after a longer interval, but the resource is actually not changed. It is also interesting that CDF of CSS is a traverse line, indicating a polar effect that some websites' CSS are no NM while others are all NM.

For JS (5(e) and 5(f)), Ω of both Top and Random does not vary so much, indicating there are a fixed set of NM in JS.

For image (5(g) and 5(h)), when RI increases, the Ω decreases. Random decreases in a small margin while Top decreases larger, implying that images of the Top websites change more frequently than the Random websites.

5.2.2 Miscached Resource

Due to the expiration model, it is likely to provide the out-of-date resources from the browser cache. In most cases, developers expect that users would tolerate these miscached resources such as acquiring information that is not the latest. However, in some circumstances, miscached resources could lead to incorrect functionalities. For example, during the evolution of Baidu, it changes many JS and CSS resources to improve its user interaction. However, some previous JS and CSS resources are configured to a considerable long expiration period. Therefore, users are even not able to use Baidu's search functionality until the users clear the browser cache, or force to refresh the page, or wait until the expiration time comes. It is worth exploring the Miscached Resource problem. In fact, NH measures the extent of this problem. Table 5 shows the result of NH.

NH takes a small proportion but we cannot ignore it. NH of Top and Random share a similar proportion. Although NH of the resource number is no more than 3%, NH of resource size is about 7%. Note that NH of Top and Random share a similar proportion, implying that both Top and Random have not considered much for NH.

NH of HTML is relatively large. NH introduces a lot of expired content. Developers may think that users could bare the expired content so that temporally expired content is also acceptable.

NH of image is the lowest but not zero because some functional images (such as border and button) may change when websites get updated.

5.3 Analysis of Root Causes

To study the third research question "*What causes the gap between ideal and actual performance*", we break down the cache behaviors of NM and plot the CDF of each case in Figure 6. As explained in Section 4.2, there are six cache behaviors belonging to the NM pattern. We calculate the proportion of each cache behavior in the total NM and plot them on a CDF graph. Figure 6 shows the cases of the resource size for Top and Random with 24 hours and 0.5 hours RI.

Heuristic and Same Content are the top two causes to NM for both Top and Random. For Top, Same Content is the most significant issue. For Random, Heuristic is the most significant issue while Same Content is in the second place. The distributions of Heuristic and Same Content are not affected by RI. For Heuristic, as we consider the worst case, RI is not an influencing factor and thus it occupies the same proportion in each RI. For Same Content, the distribution is similar because the same resources have different URLs at every visit.

Checked is the third reason for NM. Checked happens when the resources are expired in the cache (but actually are up-to-date on the server) and validated with the original server by last-modified

Table 6. Resources of Heuristic Expiration

		HTML	CSS	JS	Image	Others	Total
Top	Pct.	37.4%	1.9%	3.8%	2.6%	2.6%	6.0%
	Cycle	3.7 h	1.0 h	7.2 h	1.0 h	4.0 h	5.9 h
Random	Pct.	29.9%	37.3%	20.4%	45.2%	24.5%	33.7%
	Cycle	29 h	134 h	143 h	133 h	90 h	107 h

time or Etag identifiers. Although the validation is successful to eliminate sending a full response, the protocol overheads account for some redundant size. Therefore, validating each resource's status may be harmful for mobile Web browsing. The reason of Checked is that the expiration time is configured too short.

No-store and No-cache occupy small proportion, indicating that developers are careful when configuring resources to no store or no cache. Therefore it is less important to consider such cases to improve mobile Web cache performance.

We next analyze Same Content, Heuristic Expiration, and Conservative Expiration Time in detail.

5.3.1 Same Content

We first study the Same Content issue, as it has a significant influence on both Top and Random. As we described earlier, Same Content represents a case that a resource's content is found in the cache but the URL is different. Since the HTTP specification regards the URL as the index of resources for caching, there is no means to use the cached resource if the URL cannot be found in the cache. By examining the resource request records, we find that there are two major causes of Same Content.

Version management of resources. In order to provide end users the up-to-date resources, some best practices of Web development suggest that developers attach random query strings to URLs. Therefore, every time the webpage with the resource's reference is visited, a new query string will be generated and the browser will treat the resource as a new one to download from the server. In other cases, some websites, such as Youku, use different directories to manage resource versions. Each time the website gets updated, a new directory with the new version number will be created. Since an update is not likely to change all the resource files, Same Content will happen if those unmodified resources are requested from the new directory.

Web hierarchy architecture. Figure 1 has shown the Web hierarchy architecture that there are middle-boxes to improve the Web performance such as CDN and reverse proxy. To leverage these middle-boxes, Web servers have to generate different URLs or attach hash code of route paths to resources. As a result, one resource could have different URLs when requested at different times or at different places, leading to Same Content.

5.3.2 Heuristic Expiration

We next investigate the Heuristic Expiration issue, which often happens when developers are unaware of the importance of cache and do not explicitly configure cache parameters. Heuristic Expiration is an important issue for the Random websites because their developers may be unskilled. However, Heuristic Expiration also takes the second place in the Top websites.

Table 6 shows the proportion of Heuristic Expiration resources as well as the average updating cycle (the interval between two updates). Totally, 6% and 33.7% of Top and Random resources are configured as Heuristic Expiration. For Top, HTML is the largest (37.4%). For Random, all proportions are above 20%, meaning that more than 1/5 of resources have not explicitly utilized the caching mechanism.

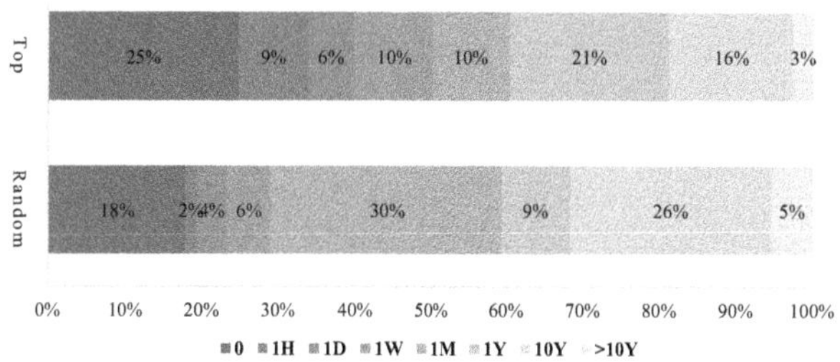

Figure 7. Expiration time distribution of Top and Random

Since different Web browsers have different algorithms to deal with Heuristic Expiration, we just consider the worst case in the previous analysis. Here we calculate the average updating cycle to study what is the proper expiration time for these resources. We can see that there is a big difference between Top and Random. Considering all the Heuristic Expiration resources, the cycle is 5.9 hours for Top while it is 107 hours for Random. This observation implies that resources configured as "Heuristic Expiration" can benefit a lot from caching if their expiration time is set to day-level. In contrast, the proper expiration time for Heuristic Expiration resources of Top is hour-level. Considering different resource types, JS has the longest updating cycle for both Top (7.2 hours) and Random (143 hours). HTML has the shortest cycle for Random (29 hours).

5.3.3 Conservative Expiration Time

Figure 7 shows the resource expiration time (indicated by Max-age primitive) distribution. 40% and 24% of the resources for Top and Random, respectively, are configured by less than one-day expiration time. This result implies that the Top websites are more conservative on expiration because their resources change more frequently than the Random websites. However, we find that as many as 89% and 86% resources with less than one-day expiration time have no updates for Top and Random, respectively. Therefore, the expiration time can be extended longer. However, longer expiration time may introduce the Miscached Resource problem. As a result, it is actually a tradeoff between website functionality and cache performance.

6. IMPLICATIONS

Table 7 summarizes the findings and implications of our measurement results. Overall, caching is helpful but it is a tradeoff between website functionality and cache performance when cache parameters are configured. To balance the two factors, we suggest using the HTML5 AppCache interface [6]. A manifest file can be attached to each webpage, specifying what to cache and what to load from the network. Resources in the cache list will always be loaded from the cache until the manifest file is updated.

7. RELATED WORK

With the popularity of mobile computing, research on Web has paced into mobile's era. Studies on mobile Web could roughly be categorized into two branches. One is to measure the performance of mobile Web, trying to understand the latency, data usage, and energy consumption of mobile Web. The other is to improve the performance with novel techniques. As a basic mechanism of Web, measurement and improvement of mobile Web cache performance have driven lots of attention. We next briefly discuss related research on general mobile Web performance and then discuss related research on mobile Web cache specifically.

Mobile Web Performance. Measurement studies have been conducted to understand mobile Web performance. Mobile HTTP Archive [7] records mobile Web performance information of

Table 7. Our major findings and implications of mobile Web cache performance

Findings	Implications
More than half of the total resource bytes and about 70% of the resource objects can be cached after 24 hours. Although 80% of the cacheable bytes are actually cached for Top, the percentage of cached objects is under 50%. For Random, both cached bytes and objects occupy not more than 50% of the cacheability.	Caching has substantial benefits for mobile Web browsing, especially for ordinary websites. But the cacheability has not been effectively utilized. Popular websites indeed make efforts on caching larger-size resources but do not consider small-size resources very well. Ordinary websites perform worse for both cacheable bytes and objects.
The cacheability varies for different types of resources, and the actual performance is also different. The results between Top and Random are not the same either.	Web developers should configure different caching policies for different types of resources based on the characteristics of websites. Developers from popular websites could consider more for caching JS, while developers from ordinary websites should check the cache configurations for all resources especially the images.
The Redundant Transfer problem is worse when a website is revisited after a shorter period. Some popular websites even have 100% Negative Miss Ratio.	Data traffic and energy of mobile Web browsing are wasted mostly from frequently visited websites. Popular websites should leverage new techniques to further reduce unnecessary network traffic.
NH of Top and Random share a similar proportion. HTML accounts for the largest NH. NH of CSS for Top is larger than for Random, while JS is on the contrary. NH of images is not 0.	Miscached Resource is a common problem for all the websites. Popular websites may have wrong layout and view while ordinary websites could suffer from wrong functionalities. Developers should avoid using the same URL for different images.
Same Content accounts for the main origins of NM. More than 20% of NM resources are resulted from Same Content for half of Top and 25% of Random. Same Content is caused by the version management and Web hierarchy architecture.	Current techniques to maintain website versions, such as random query strings, are not appropriate for mobile Web browsing. New techniques have to be adopted. Although the Web hierarchy architecture reduces the overall network traffic and releases server workload, it is harmful for user-centric mobile Web browsing. End-user based content distribution may help solve the problem.
6% and 33.7% of Top and Random resources are configured as Heuristic Expiration, but the average updating cycle is 5.9 hours and 107 hours for Top and Random, respectively.	It is better to set an explicit expiration time than using the Heuristic Expiration. Ordinary websites can set day-level expiration time to their resources while popular websites can set hour-level time.
40% and 24% of the resources for Top and Random are configured by less than one-day expiration time. But 89% and 86% of them have no updates for Top and Random, respectively.	The expiration time is conservatively configured. Developers can extend the expiration time for some resources that are not likely to change for a considerably long time. But longer expiration time could cause the Miscached Resource problem.

about 5000 mobile websites. But its recording period is 15 days, and is too coarse-grained to analyze the cache performance. Papapanagiotou et al. [14] compared smartphone and laptop Web traffic based on a three-week-long wireless communication trace collected in an enterprise environment. Thiagarajan et al. [19] measured the precise energy used by a mobile browser to render Web pages. Many techniques are proposed by researchers and employed by mobile developers to improve mobile Web performance. Jones et al. [12] studied how browser parallelization could help mobile browsers reduce latency and improve energy efficiency. PocketWeb [13] leverages prefetching techniques to load resources based on user behaviors with server support to reduce latency. Some latest commodity browsers such as Amazon Silk Browser [2], Google Chrome Beta [5], and OperaMini [8] are particularly designed for mobile browsing by leveraging server or cloud-based offloading [18]. New protocols, such as SPDY [10][22] and QUIC [4], are designed and deployed to optimize mobile Web performance from lower levels.

Mobile Web Cache. A lot of efforts have been done to study the performance of mobile Web cache. Wang et al. [24] examined three client-only solutions to accelerate mobile browser speed: caching, prefetching, and speculative loading, by using Web usage data collected from 24 iPhone users over one year. They found that caching has very limited effectiveness: 60% of the requested resources are either expired or not in the cache. Zhang et al. [25] performed a comprehensive measurement study on Web caching functionality of 1300 top ranked Android apps, not just Web browsers. Results revealed that imperfect web caching is a common and serious problem for Android apps generating Web traffic. They also implemented a system wide service called CacheKeeper to effectively reduce overhead caused by poor Web caching of mobile apps. Qian et al. [16] conducted a measurement study on Web caching in smartphones. By examining a one-day smartphone Web traffic dataset collected from a cellular carrier and a five-month Web access trace collected from 20 smartphone users, the study revealed that about 20% of the total Web traffic examined is redundant due to imperfect cache implementations. In their subsequent work [17], they studied caching efficiency for the most popular 500 websites. They found that caching is poorly utilized for many mobile sites. 26% of the top mobile sites mark their main HTML files as non-storable, leading to potential bandwidth waste. About 23% of objects in mobile sites are cacheable but have freshness lifetime of less than 1 hour. Our work differs in our methodology: we use a long-period sampling traces and determine the cache efficiency by resource evolution history. Recent work [23] examined how Web browsing can benefit from micro-cache that separately caches layout, code, and data at a fine granularity. It studied how and when these resources are updated and found that layout and code that block subsequent object loads are highly cacheable.

8. CONCLUSION

In this paper, we have presented a comprehensive measurement and analysis of mobile Web cache performance. We have proposed a proactive approach to crawling the resource update traces from two sets of websites periodically with a fine-grained time interval. We have built an analysis model to capture the relationship between cache behavior and resource updates. Based on the model, (1) we have examined the ideal cacheability and found that caching is substantially helpful for mobile Web browsing; (2) we have measured the actual performance and identified a big gap between ideality and reality; (3) we have investigated three main root causes – Same Content, Heuristic Expiration, and Conservative Expiration Time. We have provided recommendations for developers to improve mobile Web cache performance according to the implications of our findings.

9. ACKNOWLEDGMENTS

This work was supported by the National Basic Research Program (973) of China under Grant No. 2014CB347701, the Natural Science Foundation of China (Grant No. 61421091, 61370020, 61222203), and "Star-Track" Young Scholar Program of Microsoft Research Asia. Tao Xie's work was supported in part by NSF grants CNS-1434582, CNS-1439481, CCF-1349666, CCF-1409423, CCF-1434590, and CCF-1434596.

10. REFERENCES

[1] Alexa. http://www.alexa.com/

[2] Amazon Silk browser. http://aws.amazon.com/cn/documentation/silk/

[3] Charles Proxy. http://www.charlesproxy.com/

[4] Experimenting with QUIC. http://blog.chromium.org/2013/06/experimenting-with-quic.html.

[5] Google Chrome beta browser. https://www.google.com/chrome/browser/beta.html

[6] HTML5. http://www.w3.org/TR/html5/

[7] Mobile HTTP Archive. http://mobile.httparchive.org/

[8] Opera mini browser. http://www.opera.com/mobile/mini/iphone

[9] RFC 2616. http://www.w3.org/Protocols/rfc2616/rfc2616.txt

[10] SPDY Protocol - Draft 3. http://www.chromium.org/spdy/spdy-protocol/spdy-protocol-draft3

[11] J. Erman, A. Gerber, M. Hajiaghayi, D. Pei, S. Sen, and O. Spatscheck. To Cache or not to Cache: The 3G case. *IEEE Internet Computing*, vol. 15, pp. 27-34, 2011.

[12] C. G. Jones, R. Liu, L. Meyerovich, K. Asanovi, R. Bod, and K. Parallelizing the web browser. In *Proc. the 1st USENIX Conference on Hot Topics in Parallelism*, pp. 7-7, 2009.

[13] D. Lymberopoulos, O. Riva, K. Strauss, A. Mittal, and A. Ntoulas. PocketWeb: instant web browsing for mobile devices. In *Proc. the 17th International Conference on Architectural Support for Programming Languages and Operating Systems*, pp. 1-12, 2012.

[14] I. Papapanagiotou, E. Nahum and V. Pappas. Smartphones vs. laptops: comparing web browsing behavior and the implications for caching. *ACM SIGMETRICS Performance Evaluation Review*, vol. 40, pp. 423-424, 2012.

[15] F. Qian, J. Huang, J. Erman, Z. M. Mao, S. Sen, and O. Spatscheck. How to reduce smartphone traffic volume by 30%? In *Proc. Passive and Active Measurement Conference*, pp. 42-52, 2013.

[16] F. Qian, K. S. Quah, J. Huang, J. Erman, A. Gerber, Z. Mao, S. Sen, and O. Spatscheck. Web caching on smartphones: ideal vs. reality. In *Proc. the 10th International Conference on Mobile Systems, Applications, and Services*, pp. 127-140, 2012.

[17] F. Qian, S. Sen and O. Spatscheck. Characterizing resource usage for mobile web browsing. In *Proc. the 12th Annual International Conference on Mobile Systems, Applications, and Services*, pp. 218-231, 2014.

[18] A. Sivakumar, V. Gopalakrishnan, S. Lee, and S. Rao. Cloud is not a silver bullet: A case study of cloud-based mobile browsing. In *Proc. the 15th International Workshop on Mobile Computing Systems and Applications*, pp. 1-6, 2014.

[19] N. Thiagarajan, G. Aggarwal, A. Nicoara, D. Boneh, and J. P. Singh. Who killed my battery?: analyzing mobile browser energy consumption. In *Proc. the 21st International Conference on World Wide Web*, pp. 41-50, 2012.

[20] X. Wang, X. Liu, Y. Zhang, and G. Huang. Migration and execution of JavaScript applications between mobile devices and cloud. In *Proc. the 3rd Annual Conference on Systems, Programming, and Applications: Software for Humanity*, pp. 83-84, 2012.

[21] X. S. Wang, A. Balasubramanian, A. Krishnamurthy, and D. Wetherall. Demystifying page load performance with WProf. In *Proc. the 10th USENIX Conference on Networked Systems Design and Implementation*, pp. 473-486, 2013.

[22] X. S. Wang, A. Balasubramanian, A. Krishnamurthy, and D. Wetherall. How speedy is SPDY? In *Proc. the 11th USENIX Conference on Networked Systems Design and Implementation*, pp. 387-399, 2014.

[23] X. S. Wang, A. Krishnamurthy and D. Wetherall. How Much Can We Micro-Cache Web Pages? In *Proc. the 2014 Conference on Internet Measurement Conference*, pp. 249-256, 2014.

[24] Z. Wang, F. X. Lin, L. Zhong, and M. Chishtie. How far can client-only solutions go for mobile browser speed? In *Proc. the 21st International Conference on World Wide Web*, pp. 31-40, 2012.

[25] Y. Zhang, C. Tan and L. Qun. CacheKeeper: a system-wide web caching service for smartphones. In *Proc. the 2013 ACM International joint Conference on Pervasive and Ubiquitous Computing*, pp. 265-274, 2013.

[26] Y. Zhu and V.J. Reddi. WebCore: Architectural support for mobile Web browsing. In *Proc. the 2014 ACM/IEEE 41st International Symposium on Computer Architecture*, pp. 541-552, 2014.

SCULPT: A Schema Language for Tabular Data on the Web

Wim Martens
Universität Bayreuth

Frank Neven
Hasselt University and transnational University of Limburg

Stijn Vansummeren
Université Libre de Bruxelles

ABSTRACT

Inspired by the recent working effort towards a recommendation by the World Wide Web Consortium (W3C) for tabular data and metadata on the Web, we present in this paper a concept for a schema language for tabular web data called SCULPT. The language consists of rules constraining and defining the structure of regions in the table. These regions are defined through the novel formalism of region selection expressions. We present a formal model for SCULPT and obtain a linear time combined complexity evaluation algorithm. In addition, we consider weak and strong streaming evaluation for SCULPT and present a SCULPT fragment for each of these streaming variants. Finally, we discuss several extensions of SCULPT including alternative semantics, types, complex content, and explore region selection expressions as a basis for a transformation language.

Categories and Subject Descriptors

H.2.3 [**Information Systems**]: Languages—*Data description languages*

Keywords

Tabular data, comma separated values, metadata

1. INTRODUCTION

Despite the availability of numerous standardized formats for semi-structured and semantic web data such as XML, RDF, and JSON, a very large percentage of data and open data published on the web, remains tabular in nature.[1] Tabular data is most commonly published in the form of comma separated values (CSV) files because such files are open and therefore processable by numerous tools, and tailored for all sizes of files ranging from a number of KBs to several TBs. Despite these advantages, working with CSV files is often cumbersome because they are typically not accompanied by a *schema* that describes the file's structure (i.e., "the second column is of integer datatype", "columns are delimited by tabs", ...) and captures its intended meaning. Such a description is nevertheless vital for any user trying to interpret the file and execute queries or make changes to it. In other data models, the presence of a schema is also important for query optimization (required for scalable query execution if the file is large), as well as other static analysis tasks. Finally, we strongly believe that schemas are a prerequisite for unlocking huge amounts of tabular data to the Semantic Web. Indeed, unless we have a satisfactory way of describing the structure of tabular data we cannot specify how its content should be interpreted as RDF. Drawing parallels with relational databases, observe that R2RML mappings [7] (the W3C standard for mapping relational databases to RDF) inherently need to refer to the schema (structure) of the relational database in order to specify how database tuples can be represented as RDF.

In recognition of this problem, the *CSV on the Web* Working Group of the World Wide Web Consortium [34] argues for the introduction of a schema language for tabular data to ensure higher interoperability when working with datasets using the CSV or similar formats. In particular, their charter states [34]:

> *Whether converted to other formats or not, there is a need to describe the content of the CSV file: its structure, datatypes used in a specific column, language used for text fields, access rights, provenance, etc. This means that metadata should be available for the dataset, relying on standard vocabulary terms, and giving the necessary information for applications. The metadata can also be used for the conversion of the CSV content to other formats like RDF or JSON, it can enable automated loading of the data as objects, or it can provide additional information that search engines may use to gain a better understanding of the content of the data.*

In the present paper, we introduce SCULPT as a concept for such a schema language for tabular data.[2]

The critical reader may wonder whether designing such a schema language isn't trivial. After all, doesn't it suffice to

[1] Jeni Tennison, one of the two co-chairs of the W3C CSV on the Web working group claims that "over 90% of the data published on data.gov.uk is tabular data" [30].

[2] The name SCULPT for the language is in honour of Michelangelo, who allegedly said *"Every block of stone has a statue inside it and it is the task of the sculptor to discover it."* Readers who like acronyms can read SCULPT as **SC**hema for **U**n-**L**ocking and **P**rocessing **T**abular data.

WWW 2015, May 18–22, 2015, Florence, Italy.
ACM 978-1-4503-3469-3/15/05.
http://dx.doi.org/10.1145/2736277.2741142.

be able to specify, for each column, the column's name and the type of data allowed in its cells—similar to how relational database schemas are defined using the SQL data definition language? The answer is no. The reason is that there is a lot of variation in the tabular data available on the web and that examples abound of tabular data whose structure cannot be described by simple rules of the form "column x has datatype y". Figures 3, 5, and 7, for example, show some tabular data sets drawn from the Use Cases and Requirements document drafted by the W3C CSV on the Web working group [29]. Notice how, in contrast to "standard" CSV files, Figure 3 has a header consisting of multiple lines. This causes the data in the first column to be non-uniform. Further notice how the `provenance` data in the Figure 5 is spread among multiple columns. Finally, notice how the shape of the rows in Figure 7 depends on the label in the first column: `TITLE` rows have different structure than `AUTHOR` rows, which have a different structure than `ATOM` rows, and so on.

SCULPT schemas use the following idea to describe the structure of these tables. At their core, SCULPT schemas consist of rules of the form $\varphi \to \rho$. Here, φ selects a *region* in the input table (i.e., a subset of the table's cells) and ρ constrains the allowed structure and content of this region. A table is valid with respect to a SCULPT schema if, for each rule in the schema, the region selected by φ satisfies the content constraints specified by ρ. It is important to note that SCULPT's expressive power goes well beyond that of classical relational database schemas since SCULPT's region selectors are not limited to selecting columns. In particular, the language that we propose for selecting regions is capable of navigating through a table's cells bears much resemblance to the way XPath [3] navigates through the nodes of an XML tree. For tokenizing the content of single cells, we draw inspiration from XML Schema simple types [8, section 2.2]. Both features combined will allow us to express the use cases of the W3C CSV on the Web Working Group.

We note that the W3C is also working on a schema language for tabular data [24]. At the moment, however, that schema language focuses on orthogonal issues like describing, for instance, *datatypes* and *parsing cells*. Also, it only provides facilities for the selection of *columns*, and is hence not able to express the schema of the more advanced use cases. SCULPT, in contrast, draws inspiration from well-established theoretical tools from logic and formal languages, which adds to the robustness of our approach. Due to the above mentioned orthogonality we expect that it is not difficult to integrate ideas from this paper in the W3C proposal.

In summary, we make the following contributions.

1. We illustrate the power of SCULPT, and its suitability as a schema language for tabular data on the web, by expressing several use cases drafted by the W3C CSV on the Web working group [29]. (Section 2)
2. We provide a formal model for the core of SCULPT. A key contribution in this respect is the introduction of the region selection language. (Section 3)
3. We show that, despite its rather attractive expressiveness, tables can be efficiently validated w.r.t. SCULPT schemas. In particular, when the table is small enough to be materialized in main memory, we show that validation can be done in linear time combined complexity (Section 4.1). For scenarios where materialization in main memory is not possible, we consider the scenario of streaming (i.e., incremental) validation, for which formally introduce two versions: *weak streamability* and *strong streamability*. (Their differences are described in detail in Section 4.2.) We show in particular that the fragment of core-SCULPT where region selectors can only look "forward" and never "backward" in the CSV file is *weakly streamable*. If we further restrict region selectors to be both forward-looking and *guarded* (a notion formalized in Section 4.2) validation becomes *strongly streamable*. All of the W3C Working group use cases considered here can be expressed using forward and guarded region selectors, hence illustrating the practical usefulness of this fragment.
4. While our focus in this paper is on introducing SCULPT as a means for specifying the structure of CSV files and related formats, we strongly believe that region selector expressions are a fundamental component in developing other features mentioned in the charter of the W3C CSV on the Web Working Group, such as a CSV transformation language (for converting tabular data into other formats such as RDF or JSON), the specification of the language used for text fields; access rights; provenance; etc. While a full specification of these features is out of this paper's scope, we illustrate by means of example how SCULPT could be extended to incorporate them. (Section 5)

Note. Due to space restrictions, proofs of formal statements are only sketched. A full version containing all proofs is available on ArXiv [21].

Related Work. The present paper fits in the line of research, historically often published in the WWW conference, that aims to formalize and study the properties of various W3C working group drafts and standards (including XML Schema [4,5], SPARQL [2,18,23], and RDF [25,26]) with the aim of providing feedback and input to the working group's activities.

Given the numerous benefits of schemas for data processing, there is a large body of work on the development, expressiveness, and properties of schema languages for virtually all data models, including the relational data model, XML [4, 5, 11, 19, 20], and, RDF [25, 26]. SCULPT differs from the schema languages considered for XML and RDF in that it is specifically designed for tabular data, not tree-structured or graph-structured data. Nevertheless, the rule-based nature of SCULPT draws inspiration from our prior work on rule-based and pattern-based schema languages for XML [11, 19, 20].

As already mentioned, while traditional relational database schemas (formulated in e.g., the SQL data definition language) are specifically designed for tabular data, they are strictly less expressive than SCULPT schemas in the sense that relational schemas limit region selection expressions to those that select columns only. A similar remark holds for other recent proposals of CSV schema languages, including the CSV Schema language proposed by the UK National Archives [1], and Tabular Data Package [16]. The remark also applies to the part of Google's Dataset Publishing Language (DSPL) [12] describing the content of CSV files. In contrast, DSPL also has features to relate data from multiple CSV files, which SCULPT does not yet have.

The problem of streaming schema validation has been investigated in the XML context for DTDs and XML schemas [14, 20, 27, 28]. In this work, the focus is on finding algorithms that can validate an XML document in a single pass using constant memory or, if this is not possible, a memory that is bounded by the depth of the document. Our notion of streaming, in contrast, is one where we can use a memory that is not constant but at most logarithmic in the size of the table (for strong streaming), or at most linear in the number of columns and logarithmic in the number of rows (for weak streaming). This allows us to restrict memory when going from one row to the next and is essential to be able to navigate downwards in SCULPT region selection expressions.

While streaming validation is undoubtedly an important topic for all of the CSV schema languages mentioned above [1,12,16] (the National Archives Schema Language mentions it as an explicit design goal), no formal streaming validation algorithm has been proposed for them, to the best of our knowledge.

We briefly mention some major lines of research on tables on the web. One line of work considers HTML tables. Here, the focus is on finding (related) HTML tables (at a search engine scale) [6], extracting meaning of the tables based on its content (see, e.g. [33]), and extracting RDF from HTML tables [22]. Other work targets conversions from spreadsheets to RDF (e.g. [13]).

2. SCULPT BY EXAMPLE

In this section, we introduce SCULPT through a number of examples. The formal semantics of the examples is defined in Section 3. The syntax we use here is tuned for making the examples accessible to readers and is, of course, flexible.

SCULPT schemas operate on *tabular documents*, which are text files describing tabular data. SCULPT schemas consist of two parts (cf. Fig. 2). The first part, *parsing information*, defines the row and column delimiters and further describes how words should be tokenized. This allows to parse the text file and build a table-like structure consisting of rows and columns. In this section we allow some rows to have fewer columns than others but we require them to be aligned to the left. That is, non-empty rows always have a first column. The second part of the schema consists of *rules* that interpret the table defined by the first part as a rectangular grid and that enforce structure. In particular, rules are of the form $\varphi \rightarrow \rho$, where φ selects a *region* consisting of cells in the grid while ρ is a regular expression constraining the content of the selected region. We utilize a so-called *row-based* semantics: every row in the region selected by φ should be of a form allowed by ρ. We refer to φ as the *selector expression* and to ρ as the *content expression*.

Next, we illustrate the features of the language by means of examples. All examples are inspired by the use cases and requirements drafted by the CSV on the Web W3C working group [29].

EXAMPLE 2.1. Fig. 1 contains a slightly altered fragment (we use a comma as a column separator) of a CSV file mentioned in Use Case 3, *"Creation of consolidated global land surface temperature climate databank"* [29]. Its SCULPT schema, displayed as Fig. 2, starts by describing parsing information indicating that the column delimiter is a comma while the row delimiter is a newline. Lines starting with a %-sign are comments. Tokens are defined based on regular expressions (regex for short).[3] For instance, anything that

```
        ,  ARUA,  BOMBO, ENTEBBE AIR
 1935.04, -99.00, -99.00,       27.83
 1935.12, -99.00, -99.00,       25.72
 1935.21, -99.00, -99.00,       26.44
 1935.29, -99.00, -99.00,       25.72
 1935.37, -99.00, -99.00,       24.61
 1935.46, -99.00, -99.00,       24.33
 1935.54, -99.00, -99.00,       24.89
```

Figure 1: Example tabular data inspired by Use Case 3 in [29].

```
% Parsing information
%% Delimiters
Col Delim = ,
Row Delim = \n

%% Tokens
%% left: token name, right: regex
Timestamp = [0-9]{4}"."[0-9]{2}
Temperature = (-)?[0-9]{2}"."[0-9]{2}
ARUA = ARUA
BOMBO = BOMBO
ENTEBBE AIR = ENTEBBE AIR

% Rules
row(1) -> Empty, ARUA, BOMBO, ENTEBBE AIR
col(1) -> Empty | Timestamp
col(ARUA) -> Temperature
col(BOMBO) -> Temperature
col(ENTEBBE AIR) -> Temperature
```

Figure 2: Schema for tabular data of the type in Fig. 1.

matches the regex `[0-9]{4}"."[0-9]{2}` follows the format *four digits, dot, two digits*, and is interpreted by the token `Timestamp` in the rules of the schema (similar for `Temperature`). Notice that we keep the regexes short (and sometimes imprecise) for readability, but they can of course be made arbitrarily precise if desired.

All the XML Schema primitive types such as xs:integer, xs:string, xs:date, etc. are pre-defined as tokens in a SCULPT schema. There is also a special pre-defined token `Empty` to denote that a certain cell is empty.

Notice that the schema in Fig. 2 has three token definitions in which the regex defines only one character sequence (namely: `ARUA`, `BOMBO`, `ENTEBBE AIR`). In the sequel, we will omit such rules for reasons of parsimony. For the same reason, we omit the explicit definition of column and row delimiters when they are a comma and newline character, respectively.

The rule

`row(1) -> Empty, ARUA, BOMBO, ENTEBBE AIR`

selects all cells in the first row and requires that the first is empty, the second contains `ARUA`, the third `BOMBO`, and the fourth `ENTEBBE AIR`. Next, `col(1)` selects the region consisting of all cells in the first column. As SCULPT assumes a row-based semantics per default,[4] the rule

`col(1) -> Empty | Timestamp`

requires that every row in the selected region (notice that each such row consists of a single cell) is either empty (`Empty`) or contains data that matches the `Timestamp` token. The expression `col(ARUA)` selects all cells in the column below the

[3]For ease of exposition, we adopt the concise regex syntax popularized by scripting languages such as Perl, Python, and Ruby [10] in all of our examples.

[4]We discuss an extension in Section 5.

```
QS601EW
Economic activity
27/03/2011

         ,         , Count    , Count
         ,         , Person   , Person
         ,         , Activity, Activity
GeoID    , GeoArea, All      , Part-time
E92000001, England, 38881374, 27183134
W92000004, Wales  , 2245166 , 1476735
```

Figure 3: Fragment of a CSV-like-file, inspired by Use Case 2 in [29].

```
%% Tokens
%% left: token name, right: regex
name = QS[0-9]*EW
ctype = Economic Activity
geo_id = E[0-9]*

% Rules
row(1) -> name
row(2) -> ctype
row(3) -> Date
row(4) -> Empty
row(5) -> Empty, Empty, Count*
row(6) -> Empty, Empty, Person*
row(7) -> Empty, Empty, Activity*
row(8) -> GeoID, GeoArea, String*
col(GeoID) -> geo_id
col(GeoArea) -> String
down+(right+(GeoArea)) -> Number*
```

Figure 4: Schema for files of the type in Fig. 3.

cell containing `ARUA`. The rule

`col(ARUA) -> Temperature`

therefore requires that every row in this region matches the `Temperature` token. The two remaining rules are analogous. The fragment in Fig. 1 satisfies the schema of Fig. 2. ■

Before moving on to some more advanced examples, we discuss in more detail the semantics of selector and content expressions. Each cell in a table is identified by its *coordinate*, which is a pair (k, ℓ) where k indicates the row number ($k \geq 1$) and ℓ the column number ($\ell \geq 1$). We use the convention that the top left coordinate in tabular data bears the coordinate $(1, 1)$ — for *first row, first column*. In each rule $\varphi \to \rho$, the selector expression φ returns a *set* of coordinates (a region) and ρ is a regular expression defining the allowed structure of each row in the region selected by φ. It is important to note that in each such row only the cells which are selected by φ are considered. Another way to interpret the row-based semantics is that of a 'group by' on the selected region per row.

The last rule we discussed in Example 2.1 uses a symbolic coordinate `ARUA` in its selector expression. Its semantics is as follows: a token τ returns the set of all coordinates (k, ℓ) whose cell content matches τ. The operator `row` applied to a coordinate (k, ℓ) returns the set of coordinates $\{(k, \ell') \mid \ell' > \ell\}$. This corresponds to the row consisting of all elements to the right of (k, ℓ). Note that coordinate (k, ℓ) itself is not included. Applying `row` to a *set* S of coordinates amounts to taking the union of all `row`$((k, \ell))$ where $(k, \ell) \in S$. Similarly, the operator `col` applied to S returns the union of the regions $\{(k', \ell) \mid k' > k\}$ for each (k, ℓ) in S, corresponding to columns below elements in S. The selector expressions `row(1)` and `col(1)` that select the "first row" and "first column", respectively, use syntactic sugar to improve readability (see Remark 3.4).

The next example illustrates the use of slightly more complex expressions for navigation and content.

EXAMPLE 2.2. Fig. 3 displays a (slightly altered) fragment of a CSV-like-file inspired by Use Case 2 (*"Publication of National Statistics"*) in [29]. This fragment originates from the Office for National Statistics (UK) and refers to the dataset "QS601EW Economic activity" derived from the 2011 Census. The file starts with three lines of metadata, referring to the name of the file and the census date, continues with a blank line, before listing the actual data separated by commas. Notice that this file is, strictly speaking, not a comma-separated-value file because not all rows have an equal number of columns.[5] Indeed, the first four rows have only (at most) one column and the later rows have four columns. Fig. 4 depicts the SCULPT schema describing the structure of such tables.

The schema starts by describing parsing information, analogous to Example 2.1. The first four rules are very basic and are similar to those of Example 2.1. We first describe the fifth rule of the schema:

`row(5) -> Empty, Empty, Count*`

selects all cells in the fifth row, requiring the first two to be `Empty` and the remaining non-empty cells to contain `Count`. We note that the original data fragment from [29] contains 16 such columns.

The rule `col(GeoID) -> geo_id` selects all cells below cells containing the word `GeoID`. The content expression says that this column contains values that match the `geo_id` token. The last rule is the most interesting one:

`down+(right+(GeoArea)) -> Number*.`

This rule selects all cells appearing strictly downward and to the right of `GeoArea` and requires them to be of type `Number`. More precisely, `GeoArea` is a symbolic coordinate selecting all cells containing the word `GeoArea`. The navigational operators `right` and `down` select cells one step to the right and one step down, respectively, from a given coordinate. The operator `+` indicates an arbitrary strictly positive number of applications of the navigational operator to which it is applied. In particular, as on the table given in Fig. 3, `GeoArea` is the singleton cell with coordinate $(8, 2)$, `right(GeoArea)` returns $\{(8, 3)\}$, while `right+(GeoArea)` is the region $\{(8, \ell) \mid \ell > 2\}$. Likewise, `down(right+(GeoArea))` is the region $\{(9, \ell) \mid \ell > 2\}$ and, finally, `down+(right+(GeoArea))` is the region downward and to the right of the `GeoArea` coordinate, that is, $\{(k, \ell) \mid k > 8 \text{ and } \ell > 2\}$. ■

Example 2.2 uses more refined navigation than just selecting a row or a column. SCULPT has four navigational axes: `up`, `down`, `left`, `right` which navigate one cell upward, downward, leftward, or rightward. These axes can be applied to a set S of coordinates and add a vector v to it. More formally, an axis A, when applied to a set S of coordinates, returns $A(S) := \{c + v_A \mid c \in S\}$. Here,

- $v_A = (-1, 0)$ when $A =$ `up`,
- $v_A = (1, 0)$ when $A =$ `down`.

[5]Actually CSV does not have a standard, but the informative memo RFC4180 (http://tools.ietf.org/html/rfc4180) states rectangularity in paragraph 2.4.

```
subject  predicate      object   provenance
:e4      type           PER
:e4      mention        "Bart"   D00124 283-286
:e4      mention        "JoJo"   D00124 145-149 0.9
:e4      per:siblings   :e7      D00124 283-286 173-179 274-281
:e4      per:age        "10"     D00124 180-181 173-179 182-191 0.9
:e4      per:parent     :e9      D00124 180-181 381-380 399-406 D00101 220-225 230-233 201-210
```

Figure 5: Fragment of a CSV-like file, inspired by Use Case 13 in [29].

```
% Tokens
%% left: token name, right: regex
rdf-id      = [a-zA-Z0-9]*:[a-zA-Z0-9]*
rdf-lit     = "[a-zA-Z0-9]*"
prov-book   = D[0-9]{5}
prov-pos    = [0-9]{3}-[0-9]{3}
prov-node   = [0-9].[0.9]
word        = [a-z]*
entity-type = PER | ORG | GPE

% Rules
row(1) -> subject, predicate, object, provenance
col(subject)   -> rdf-id
col(predicate) -> word | rdf-id
col(object)    -> rdf-lit | rdf-id | entity-type
down+(right*(provenance))
        -> (prov-book, prov-pos*, prov-node?)*
```

Figure 6: Schema for files of the type in Fig. 5.

- $v_A = (0, 1)$ when $A =$ `right`, and
- $v_A = (0, -1)$ when $A =$ `left`.

Furthermore, there is also an axis `cell` that does not navigate away from the current cells, i.e., `cell`$(S) = S$. When applying an axis to a set of coordinates, we always return only the coordinates that are valid coordinates in the table. For example, `left({1,1})` returns the empty set because $(1, 0)$ is not a cell in the table.

While the just discussed features of SCULPT are sufficient to describe the structure of almost all CSV-like data on the Web Working group use cases [29], we extend in Section 3 SCULPT to include XPath-like navigation. These features will be useful for annotations and transformations, see Section 5. We now showcase SCULPT by illustrating it on the most challenging of the W3C use cases.

EXAMPLE 2.3. Fig. 5 contains a fragment of a CSV-like file, inspired by Use Case 13 in [29] (*"Representing Entities and Facts Extracted From Text"*). Fig. 6 depicts the SCULPT schema. Compared to the previous examples, the most interesting rule is

```
down+(right*(provenance))
        -> (prov-book, prov-pos*, prov-node?)*
```

which, since `provenance` only occurs in column 4, states that every row that starts with a coordinate of the form $(k, 4)$ with $k > 1$ should match `(prov-book, prov-pos*, prov-node?)*`. Notice that the empty row starting at $(2, 4)$ also matches this expression. Here, `right*` denotes an arbitrary number (including zero) of applications of the navigational operator `right`. ■

3. FORMAL MODEL

In this section, we present a formal model for the logical core of SCULPT. We refer to this core as core-SCULPT and discuss extensions in Section 5. We first define the data model.

Tables. For a number $n \in \mathbb{N}$, we denote the set $\{1, \ldots, n\}$ by $[n]$. By $\perp$ we denote a special distinguished null value. For any set $\mathcal{V}$, we denote the set $\mathcal{V} \cup \{\perp\}$ by $\mathcal{V}_\perp$. The W3C formalizes tabular documents through *tables*, which can be defined as follows.

DEFINITION 3.1 (CORE TABULAR DATA MODEL, [31]). Let $\mathcal{V}$ be a set. A *table* over $\mathcal{V}$ is an $n \times m$ matrix T (for some $n, m \in \mathbb{N}$) in which each cell carries a value from $\mathcal{V}_\perp$. We say that T has n *rows* and m *columns*. A *(table) coordinate* is an element of $[n] \times [m]$. A *cell* is determined by coordinate $(k, \ell) \in [n] \times [m]$ and its *content* is the value $T_{k,\ell} \in \mathcal{V}_\perp$ at the intersection of row k and column ℓ. We denote the set $[n] \times [m]$ of all *coordinates* of T by coords(T).

Tabular documents. Notice that tables are always rectangular[6] whereas, in Section 2, this was not the case for some of the use cases. We model this by padding shorter rows by $\perp$. More precisely, we see the correspondence between *tabular documents*, i.e., text files that describe tabular data (like CSV files), and tables as follows. Let Σ be a finite set of symbols and let D be a finite set of *delimiters*, disjoint from Σ. We assume that D contains two designated elements which we call *row delimiter* and *column delimiter*, which, as the name indicates, separate cells vertically or horizontally. (We discuss other delimiters in Section 5.) Therefore, a sequence of symbols in $(D \cup \Sigma)$ can be seen as a table over Σ^*: every row delimiter induces a new row in the table, every column delimiter a new column, and the sequences of Σ-symbols between delimiters define a cell's content. In the case that some rows have fewer columns than others, missing columns are expanded to the right and filled with $\perp$. Notice that, hence, we take a $\perp$-cell to be distinct from a cell that has empty content (i.e., a cell that contains the empty Σ-string). Conversely, a table over Σ^* can also be seen as a string over $(D \cup \Sigma)$ by concatenating all its cell values in top-down left-to-right order and inserting cell delimiters and row delimiters in the correct places; we do not insert column delimiters next to $\perp$-cells. As such, when we convert a tabular document into a table and back; we obtain the original tabular document.

We consider both representations in the remainder of the paper. In particular we view the table representation as a structure that allows efficient navigation in all directions and the string representation as structure for streaming validation.

Core-SCULPT schemas. Abstractly speaking, a core-SCULPT schema S is a tuple (D, Δ, Θ, R) where D is the finite set of

[6]Tables are required to be rectangular by Section 2.1 of [31]; as by paragraph 2.4 of the memo RFC4180 on CSV (http://tools.ietf.org/html/rfc4180).

delimiters; Δ is a finite set of tokens; Θ is a mapping that associates a regular expression over Σ to each token $\tau \in \Delta$; and R is a *tabular schema*, a set of rules that constrain the admissible table content (further defined below).

Checking whether a tabular document σ in $(D \cup \Sigma)^*$ satisfies S proceeds conceptually in three phases. In the first phase, the delimiters are used to parse σ into a table T^{raw} over Σ^*, as described above. In the second phase, the token definitions Θ are used to transform T^{raw} into a *tokenized* table T, which is a table where each cell contains a set of tokens (i.e., each cell contains a subset of Δ, namely those tokens that match the cell). Formally, T is the table of the same dimension as T^{raw} such that

$$T_{k,\ell} = \{\tau \in \Delta \mid T^{\text{raw}}_{k,\ell} \in \mathcal{L}(\Theta(\tau))\}.$$

Here $\mathcal{L}(\cdot)$ denotes the language of a regular expression. Finally, the rules in R check validity of the tokenized table T (and not of the raw table T^{raw}), as explained next.

Tabular schema. The *tabular schema* R describes the structure of the tokenized table. Intuitively, a tabular schema is a set of rules $s \to c$ in which s *selects* a region in the table and c describes what the *content* of the selected region should be. More formally, a *region* z of a table T is a subset of coords(T). A *region selection language* $\mathcal{S}$ is a set of expressions such that every $s \in \mathcal{S}$ defines a region in every table T. More precisely, $s[T]$ is always a (possibly empty) region of T. A *content language* $\mathcal{C}$ is a set of expressions such that every $c \in \mathcal{C}$ maps each region z of T to true or false. We denote by $T, z \models c$ that c maps z to true in T and say that z *satisfies* c in T.

Definition 3.2 (Tabular Schema). A *(tabular) schema* (over $\mathcal{S}$ and $\mathcal{C}$) is a finite set R of rules $s \to c$ for which $s \in \mathcal{S}$ and $c \in \mathcal{C}$. A table T *satisfies* R, denoted $T \models R$, when for every rule $s \to c \in R$ we have that $T, s[T] \models c$.

The above definition is very general as it allows arbitrary languages for selecting regions and defining content. We now propose concrete languages for these purposes.

Region selection expressions. Our region selection language is divided into two sorts of expressions: *coordinate expressions* (ranged over by φ, ψ) and *navigational expressions* (ranged over by α, β), defined by the following syntax:

$$\varphi, \psi := a \mid \mathsf{root} \mid \mathsf{true} \mid \varphi \vee \psi \mid \varphi \wedge \psi \mid \neg\varphi \mid \langle\alpha\rangle \mid \alpha(\varphi)$$
$$\alpha, \beta := \varepsilon \mid \mathsf{up} \mid \mathsf{down} \mid \mathsf{left} \mid \mathsf{right} \mid [\varphi] \mid (\alpha \cdot \beta) \mid (\alpha|\beta) \mid (\alpha^*)$$

Here, a ranges over tokens in Δ and root is a constant referring to coordinate $(1, 1)$. When evaluated over a table T over 2^{Δ}, a coordinate expression φ defines a region $[\![\varphi]\!]_T \subseteq \text{coords}(T)$, whereas a navigational expression α defines a function $[\![\alpha]\!] : 2^{\text{coords}(T)} \to 2^{\text{coords}(T)}$, as follows.

$$[\![a]\!]_T := \{(i, j) \in \text{coords}(T) \mid a \in T_{i,j}\}$$
$$[\![\mathsf{root}]\!]_T := \{(1, 1)\}$$
$$[\![\mathsf{true}]\!]_T := \text{coords}(T)$$
$$[\![(\varphi \vee \psi)]\!]_T := [\![\varphi]\!]_T \cup [\![\psi]\!]_T$$
$$[\![(\varphi \wedge \psi)]\!]_T := [\![\varphi]\!]_T \cap [\![\psi]\!]_T$$
$$[\![(\neg\varphi)]\!]_T := \text{coords}(T) \setminus [\![\varphi]\!]_T$$
$$[\![\langle\alpha\rangle]\!]_T := \{c \in \text{coords}(T) \mid [\![\alpha(\{c\})]\!]_T \neq \emptyset\}$$
$$[\![\alpha(\varphi)]\!]_T := [\![\alpha([\![\varphi]\!]_T)]\!]_T$$

Furthermore, for every $n \times m$ table T and every set of coordinates $C \subseteq \text{coords}(T)$,

$$[\![\varepsilon(C)]\!]_T := C$$
$$[\![\mathsf{up}(C)]\!]_T := \{(i-1, j) \mid (i, j) \in C, i > 1\}$$
$$[\![\mathsf{down}(C)]\!]_T := \{(i+1, j) \mid (i, j) \in C, i < n\}$$
$$[\![\mathsf{left}(C)]\!]_T := \{(i, j-1) \mid (i, j) \in C, j > 1\}$$
$$[\![\mathsf{right}(C)]\!]_T := \{(i, j+1) \mid (i, j) \in C, j < m\}$$
$$[\![[\varphi](C)]\!]_T := C \cap [\![\varphi]\!]_T$$
$$[\![(\alpha \cdot \beta)(C)]\!]_T := [\![\beta([\![\alpha(C)]\!]_T)]\!]_T$$
$$[\![(\alpha|\beta)(C)]\!]_T := [\![\alpha(C)]\!]_T \cup [\![\beta(C)]\!]_T$$
$$[\![(\alpha^*)(C)]\!]_T := \bigcup_{i \geq 0} [\![\alpha^i(C)]\!]_T$$

Here, $\alpha^i(C)$ abbreviates the i-fold composition $\alpha \cdots \alpha(C)$. We also use this abbreviation in the remainder. Notice that every coordinate (k, ℓ) of T can be expressed as $\mathsf{down}^{k-1} \cdot \mathsf{right}^{\ell-1}(\mathsf{root})$. For navigational expressions α, we abbreviate $\alpha \cdot \alpha^*$ by α^+ and $\alpha|\varepsilon$ by $\alpha?$. One can read $\alpha(\varphi)$ as "apply the regular expression α to φ". The definition of the semantics of $\alpha \cdot \beta$ conforms with this view.

Example 3.3. Region selection expressions navigate in tables, similar to how XPath expressions navigate on trees. For example, assuming dummy to be a token for `-99.00` in Figure 1, the expression

$$\mathsf{right}^+[\neg\langle\mathsf{down}^*[\mathsf{dummy}]\rangle](\mathsf{root})$$

selects top cells of columns (other than the first) that do not contain a dummy value anywhere. Starting from the root, it first navigates to the right and, from those cells, selects the cells c for which $\mathsf{down}^*[\mathsf{dummy}](c)$ is empty. In the excerpt of Figure 1, this expression hence selects the cell containing `ENTEBBE AIR`. Equivalently, one could also write

$$(\mathsf{right}^+(\mathsf{root}) \wedge \neg(\mathsf{up}^*(\mathsf{dummy})))$$

for the above expression. This expression selects cells right from the root that are not above a dummy-cell.

We present a second example. Assuming the token literal for cells with quotation marks (regex `\"[a-zA-Z0-9]\"`) in Figure 5, the expression

$$\mathsf{down}^+ \cdot [\mathsf{literal}] \cdot \mathsf{right}^+(\mathsf{object})$$

selects all provenance information for rows in which the `object` is between quotes, like `"Bart", "JoJo", and "10"`. Notice in particular that the semantics of the operator "[ ]" in navigational expressions is the same as filter-expressions in XPath. ■

Readers familiar with propositional dynamic logic (PDL for short) [9] will recognize that the above language is nothing more than propositional dynamic logic, tweaked to navigate in tables. As such, the language is also very close to some fragments of Graph XPath [17].

There are some differences between the syntax of core-Sculpt and the region selection expressions used in the examples of Section 2:

Remark 3.4. (i) As already observed, absolute coordinates in Section 2 are syntactic sugar for navigations that start at the root. For example, the coordinate $(2, 2)$ would be unfolded to $\mathsf{down} \cdot \mathsf{right}(\mathsf{root})$ in core-Sculpt.

(ii) The keywords `row` and `col` in Section 2 are syntactic sugar for right^+ and down^+ in core-Sculpt, respectively. So, `col((2,2))`, which denotes *the column below the cell* $(2, 2)$ in Section 2, is syntactic sugar for $\mathsf{down}^+(\mathsf{down} \cdot \mathsf{right}(\mathsf{root}))$.

(iii) The only exception to rule (ii) above are row and column expressions of the form $\mathsf{row}(k)$ and $\mathsf{col}(\ell)$. These abbreviate $\mathsf{right}^*(k,1)$ and $\mathsf{down}^*(1,\ell)$, respectively. (Where $(k,1)$ and $(1,\ell)$ need to be further unfolded themselves.)

As an example, the selection expression `row(1)` of Figure 6 can be written as $\mathsf{right}^*(\mathsf{root})$ or, equivalently, right^* and the expression `col(subject)` as down^+(`subject`).

(iv) It is also easy to add syntactic sugar in the form $\mathsf{rectangle}((k_1,\ell_1),(k_2,\ell_2))$ for selecting an area with (k_1,ℓ_1) and (k_2,ℓ_2) as upper left and lower right corner. ■

Content expressions. A *content expression* is simply a regular expression ρ over the set of tokens Δ. To define when a region in a tokenized table T is valid with respect to content expression ρ, let us first introduce the following order on coordinates. We say that coordinate (k,ℓ) precedes coordinate (k',ℓ') if we visit (k,ℓ) earlier than (k',ℓ') in a left-to-right top-down traversal of the cells of T, i.e., it precedes it in lexicographic order. Formally, $(k,\ell) < (k',\ell')$ if $k < k'$ or if $k = k'$ but $\ell < \ell'$.

Now, let T be a tokenized table, let z be a region of T, and let ρ be a content expression. Then (T,z) satisfies the content expression ρ *under the region-based semantics*, denoted $T,z \models_{\text{region}} \rho$ if there exist tokens $a_1,\ldots,a_n \in \Delta$ such that $a_1 \cdots a_n \in \mathcal{L}(\rho)$ and $a_i \in T_{c_i}$, where $c_1,\ldots,c_n$ is the enumeration in table order of all coordinates in z.

To define the row-based semantics we used in Section 2, we require the following notions. Let z be a region of T. We say that subregion $z' \subseteq z$ is a *row of* z if there exists some k such that $z' = \{(k,\ell) \mid (k,\ell) \in z\}$. Now, (T,z) satisfies the content expression ρ *under the row-based semantics*, denoted $T,z \models \rho$, if for every row z' of z, we have $T,z' \models_{\text{region}} \rho$.

REMARK 3.5. Recall that, for ease of exposition, we allowed tables to be non-rectangular in Section 2 whereas in our formal model, tables are always rectangular. In particular, shorter rows are padded with $\perp$ to obtain rectangularity. This implies that, some content expressions of Section 2 need to be adapted in our formal model. For example, the rule `row(1) -> name` of Figure 4 needs to be adapted to $\mathsf{row}(1) \to \texttt{name}, \perp, \perp, \perp$ to take the padding into account. ■

4. EFFICIENT VALIDATION

In this section we consider the *validation* (or *evaluation*) problem for tabular schemas. This problem asks, given a tokenized table or tabular document T and a tabular schema R, whether T satisfies R. We consider the problem in a *main-memory* and *streaming* variant. Intuitively, T is given as a table in the former and as a tabular document in the latter setting.

4.1 Validation in Linear Time

When T is given as a tokenized table, we can essentially assume that we can navigate from a cell (i,j) to any of its four neighbours $\mathsf{up}(\{(i,j)\})$, $\mathsf{down}(\{(i,j)\})$, $\mathsf{left}(\{(i,j)\})$, and $\mathsf{right}(\{(i,j)\})$ in constant time. Under these assumptions we show that T can be validated against a tabular schema in linear time combined complexity.[7] The proof strongly relies on the known linear time combined complexity of propositional dynamic logic.

[7]Combined complexity is a standard complexity measure introduced by Vardi; see [32].

THEOREM 4.1. *The evaluation problem for a tabular document T and a tabular schema R is in linear time combined complexity, that is, time $O(|T||R|)$.*

4.2 Streaming Validation

Even though Theorem 4.1 implies that SCULPT schemas can be efficiently validated, this only holds when the tabular document can be fully loaded in memory and multiple passes can be made through the document. However, when the input data is large it is sometimes desirable to have a *streaming validation algorithm* that makes only a single pass over the input tabular document and uses only limited memory. In this section we identify several fragments of core-SCULPT that admits such streaming validation algorithms.

Streaming model. Let us begin by defining when an algorithm validates in a streaming fashion. In this respect, we draw inspiration from the SAX Streaming API for XML: we can view a tokenized table T as a sequence of events generated by visiting the cells of T in table order. Here, whenever we visit a new cell, an event $\langle \mathsf{cell}\ \Gamma \rangle$ is emitted, with Γ the set of tokens in the visited cell. Whenever we move to a new row, an event of type $\langle \mathsf{new\ row} \rangle$ is emitted.

Note that the tokenized event stream can easily be generated "on the fly" when parsing a tabular document: we start reading the tabular document, one character at a time, until we reach a delimiter. All non-delimiter characters are used as input to, e.g., a finite state automaton that allows us to check which tokens match the current cell's content. When we reach a delimiter, a $\langle \mathsf{cell}\ \Gamma \rangle$ event is emitted with the corresponding set of matching tokens. If the delimiter is a row delimiter, then also a $\langle \mathsf{new\ row} \rangle$ is emitted. We repeat this until the end of the file.

EXAMPLE 4.2. Consider the tabular document from Figure 1 together with the corresponding SCULPT schema S in Figure 2. The tokenized table of this document according to S yields the event stream

$$\langle \mathsf{cell}\ \emptyset \rangle \langle \mathsf{cell}\ \{\texttt{ARUA}\} \rangle \langle \mathsf{cell}\ \{\texttt{BOMBO}\} \rangle \langle \mathsf{cell}\ \{\texttt{ENTEBBE AIR}\} \rangle$$
$$\langle \mathsf{new\ row} \rangle \langle \mathsf{cell}\ \{\texttt{Timestamp}\} \rangle \langle \mathsf{cell}\ \{\texttt{Temperature}\} \rangle$$
$$\langle \mathsf{cell}\ \{\texttt{Temperature}\} \rangle \langle \mathsf{cell}\ \{\texttt{Temperature}\} \rangle \langle \mathsf{new\ row} \rangle \ldots$$

DEFINITION 4.3 (STREAMABILITY). A tabular schema R is said to be *weakly streamable*, if there exists a Turing Machine M that

- can only read its input tape once, from left to right;
- for every tokenized table T, when started with the event stream of T on its input tape, accepts iff $T \models R$; and
- has an auxiliary work tape that can be used during processing, but it cannot use more than $O(m \log(n))$ of space on this work tape, where n is the total number of cells in T, and m the number of columns.

We say that R is *strongly streamable* if the Turing Machine M only requires $O(\log(n))$ space on its work tape.

Here, strong streamability corresponds to the commonly studied notions of streaming evaluation. We consider weak streamability to be very relevant as well because, based on the W3C use cases, tabular data often seems to be similar in spirit to relational tables and, in these cases, is very narrow and deep. In particular, $m = O(\log n)$ in these cases.

Weak streamability. To enable streaming validation, we restrict our attention to so-called *forward* coordinate and navigational expressions which are expressions where $\langle \alpha \rangle$ is not allowed, and we never look up or left. That is, a coordinate or navigational expression is *forward* if it is generated by the following syntax.

$$\varphi, \psi := a \mid \mathsf{root} \mid \mathsf{true} \mid \varphi \vee \psi \mid \varphi \wedge \psi \mid \neg\varphi \mid \alpha(\varphi)$$

$$\alpha, \beta := \varepsilon \mid \mathsf{down} \mid \mathsf{right} \mid [\varphi] \mid (\alpha \cdot \beta) \mid (\alpha + \beta) \mid (\alpha^*)$$

We do not consider the operator $\langle\alpha\rangle$ in the forward fragment because it can be seen as a backward operator: $\langle \mathsf{right} \cdot [a]\rangle$ is equivalent to $\mathsf{left}(a)$.

A core-SCULPT schema is *forward* if it mentions only forward coordinate expressions.

THEOREM 4.4. *Forward core-*SCULPT *is weakly streamable.*

PROOF SKETCH. Consider a rule $\varphi \to \rho$ with φ a forward coordinate expression and ρ a content expression. We can show that coordinate expressions φ can be evaluated in a streaming fashion by constructing a special kind of finite state automaton (called *coordinate automaton*) that allows us to decide, at each position in the event stream, if the currently visited cell is in $[\![\varphi]\!]_T$. Whenever we find that this is the case, we apply the current cell contents to ρ (which we also evaluate by means of a finite state automaton). Now observe that $T \models \varphi \to \rho$ iff (1) under the row based semantics, whenever we see $\langle \mathsf{new\ row}\rangle$, the automaton for ρ is in a final state and (2) under the region-based semantics, when we reach the end of the event stream, the automaton for ρ is in a final state. We then obtain weak streamability by showing that coordinate automata for φ can be simulated in space $O(m \log(n))$, whereas it is known that the finite state automaton for ρ can be simulated in constant space. □

Strong streamability. Forward core-SCULPT is unfortunately not strongly streamable: no schema with a rule that contains subexpressions of the form $\mathsf{col}(a)$ (which are prevalent in Section 2) can be strongly streamable. This can be seen using a simple argument from communication complexity. Indeed, assume that the first row has k cells, some of which have the token a and some of which do not. If we want to evaluate $\mathsf{col}(a)$ in a streaming fashion, we need to identify the cells in the second row that are in the same columns as the a-tokens in the first row. But, this is precisely the equality of two k-bit strings problem, which requires $\Omega(k)$ bits in deterministic communication complexity (Example 1.21 in [15]). These $\Omega(k)$ bits are what we need to store when going from the first to the second row. Since k can be $\Theta(n)$, this amount of space is more than we allow for strongly streamable tabular schemas, and hence no schema containing $\mathsf{col}(a)$ is strongly streamable.

The underlying reason why $\mathsf{col}(a)$ is not strongly streamable is because, in general, the token a can occur arbitrarily often. However, in all such cases in Section 2 and in the W3C use cases, the occurrences of a are very restricted. We could therefore obtain strong streamability for such expressions by adding constructs in the language that restrict how certain tokens can appear:

```
unique(a)          unique-per-row(a)
```

The former asserts that token a should occur only once in the whole table and the latter that a occurs at most once in each row. More formally, the former predicate holds in a table T if $[\![a]\!]_T$ contains at most one element and the latter holds in table T if $[\![a]\!]_T$ contains at most one element of the form (r, c) for each row number r. Notice that a strong streaming algorithm can easily check whether these predicates hold.

We use the above predicates to define two notions of *guardedness* for region selection expressions. Guarded formulas will be strongly streamable. We say that token a is *row-guarded* if `unique-per-row(a)` appears in the schema. If `unique(a)` appears in the schema it is, in addition, also *guarded*. The two notions of guardedness capture the following intuition: if φ is row-guarded, then $\mathsf{down}(\varphi)$ is strongly streamable and if it is guarded, then $\mathsf{down}^*(\varphi)$ is strongly streamable. The main idea is that, in both cases, the number of cells we need to remember when going from one row to the next does not depend on the width of the table. We now define (row)-guardedness inductively on the forward language:

- root and true are guarded and row-guarded;
- $\mathsf{right}^*(\varphi)$ is guarded and row-guarded for every φ that does not contain a navigational subexpression;
- if φ, ψ, $\alpha(\varphi)$, $\beta(\varphi)$ are guarded (resp., row-guarded), then
  - $\varphi \wedge \psi$, $\varphi \vee \psi$, $\varepsilon(\varphi)$, $\mathsf{down}(\varphi)$, $\mathsf{right}(\varphi)$,
  - $(\alpha \cdot \mathsf{down})(\varphi)$, $(\alpha \cdot \mathsf{right})(\varphi)$, and $(\alpha + \beta)(\varphi)$

  are guarded (resp., row-guarded);
- if φ and $\alpha(\psi)$ are guarded then $\mathsf{down}^*(\varphi)$ and $(\alpha \cdot \mathsf{down}^*)(\psi)$ are guarded; and
- if φ and $\alpha(\psi)$ are row-guarded then $\mathsf{right}^*(\varphi)$ and $(\alpha \cdot \mathsf{right}^*)(\psi)$ are guarded.

DEFINITION 4.5. A forward core-SCULPT schema is called *guarded*, if all region selection expressions that use the down-operator are row-guarded and all region selection expressions that use down^* are guarded.

Notice that guardedness of a SCULPT schema can be tested in linear time. Furthermore notice that every SCULPT schema in this paper becomes strongly streamable if we add the predicates `unique(a)` for tokens a that we use in expressions using col, down, or down^*.

THEOREM 4.6. *Guarded forward core-*SCULPT *is strongly streamable.*

5. SCULPT EXTENSIONS

Next, we describe a number of extensions to SCULPT. These include alternative grouping semantics, types, complex content cells, and a concept for a transformation language.

5.1 Region semantics

The examples in Section 2 all use a row-based semantics of SCULPT where the content expression is matched over every row in the selected region. That is, the cells in the selected region are 'grouped by' the row they occur in. There are of course other ways to group cells, by column, for instance, or by not grouping them at all. The latter case is already defined in Section 3 as *region-based semantics*. In SCULPT, we indicate rules using this semantics with a double arrow `=>` rather than a single arrow. Notice the difference between the rules `col(2) -> Null | Number` and `col(2) => (Null | Number)*`. Both require each cell in the second column to be empty or a number but express this differently. (The former way is closer to how one defines the schema of a table in SQL, which is why we chose it as a default.) Example 5.1 below describes a more realistic application of `=>`-rules. This example corresponds to use case 12 in [29], is called *"Chemical Structures"* and aims to interpret Protein Data Bank (PDB) files as tabular data. This particular use case is interesting because it illustrates that the view of W3C on tabular data is not restricted to traditional comma-separated values files. We note that Theorems 4.1, 4.4, and 4.6 still hold if SCULPT schemas contain both rules under row-based and region-based semantics.

EXAMPLE 5.1. Figure 7 displays a slightly shortened version of the PDB file mentioned in use case 12 in [29]. The corresponding SCULPT schema could contain the following rules:

```
row(1) -> HEADER, Type, Date, ID
col(1) => HEADER, TITLE*, dots, EXPDATA, AUTHOR*,
          dots, REMARK*, dots, SEQRES*, dots, ATOM*
```

The last rule employs the region semantics and specifies the order in which tokens in the first column should appear. ■

5.2 Token types

The PDB fragment in Figure 7 contains cells that have the same content but seem to have a different meaning. It can be convenient to differentiate between cells by using *token types*. In the following fragment, REMARK-Header is the topmost cell containing REMARK in Figure 7, REMARK-Comment is the one immediately below, and REMARK-Rest is the rest:

```
%% Token types
%% left: name of the token type
%% right: region selection expression for token type
REMARK-Header <= down*[dots]/down[REMARK]
REMARK-Comment <= down*[dots]/down[REMARK]/down
REMARK-Rest <=
  down*[dots]/down[REMARK]/down/(down[REMARK])*
```

Note that we abbreviated rules of the form α(root) by α. We denoted the concatenation operator of navigational expressions by "/". We can now use token types to write rules such as

```
row(REMARK-Header) -> ...
row(REMARK-Comment) -> ...
row(REMARK-Rest) -> ...
```

Token types do not add additional expressiveness to the language since one can simply replace REMARK-Header by down*[dots]/down[REMARK](root) in the rule. But the ability to use different names for fields with the same content may be useful for writing more readable schemas. In this case, the names suggest that the block of remarks is divided into a header, some comment, and the rest.

5.3 Transformations and Annotations

While it is beyond the scope of this document to develop a transformation language for tables, we argue that region selection expressions can be easily employed as basic building blocks for a transformation language aimed at transforming tables into a variety of formats like, for instance, RDF, JSON, or XML (one of the scopes expressed in [34]). Region selection expressions are then used to identify relevant parts of a table.

Basic Transformations. Consider Figure 1 (of Example 2.1) again, where we see that several columns have the value −99.00. Since winter does not get this extreme in Uganda, this value is simply a dummy which should not be considered when computing, e.g., the average temperature in Uganda in 1935. Instead, for the fragment of Figure 1, it would be desirable to only select the columns that do not contain −99.00. To do this, we can simply define a new token and a new token type for the region of the table we are interested in.

```
Useless-Temp = -99.00

%% Token type
Useful <= col(1) or
          (Temperature and not Useless-Temp) or
          (row(1) and not up*(Useless-Temp))
```

The region defined by Useful contains

```
         , ENTEBBE AIR
1935.04,        27.83
1935.12,        25.72
1935.21,        26.44
[...]
```

which could then be exported. Using simple for-loops we can iterate over rows, columns, or cells, and compute aggregates. For example,

```
Useful-values <= (Temperature and not Useless-Temp)

For each column c in Useful-values {
  print Average(c)
}
```

would output 25.65, the average of the values below ENTEBBE AIR in Figure 1. The region defined by Useful-values is a set of table cells, with coordinates. These coordinates can be used to handle information column-wise in the for-loop: It simply iterates over all column coordinates that are present in the region. Iteration over rows or single cells would work analogously.

Namespaces, Annotations and RDF. Assume that we want to say that certain cells in Figure 3 are geographical regions. To this end, the SCULPT schema could contain a definition of a default namespace:

```
namespace default =http://foo.org/nationalstats.csv
namespace x = [...]
```

Region selection expressions can then be used to specify which cells should be treated as objects in which namespace. For example, the code fragment

```
For each cell c in col(GeoArea) {
  c.namespace = default
}
```

could express that each cell below GeoArea is an entity in namespace http://foo.org/nationalstats.csv. So, the cell containing England represents the entity

http://foo.org/nationalstats.csv:England,

similar for the cell containing Wales, etc. (Here we assume that .namespace is a predefined operation on cells.)

We can also annotate cells with meta-information (as is currently being considered in Section 2.2 of [31]). The code fragment

```
For each cell c in col(GeoArea) {
  annotate c with "rdf:type dbpedia-owl:Place"
  annotate c with "owl:sameAs fbase:" + c.content
}
```

(assuming appropriate namespace definitions for rdf, owl, etc.) could express that each cell below GeoArea should be annotated with rdf:type dbpedia-owl:Place and, in addition, the England cell with owl:sameAs fbase:England, the

```
HEADER    EXTRACELLULAR MATRIX                     22-JAN-98   1A3I
TITLE     X-RAY CRYSTALLOGRAPHIC DETERMINATION OF A COLLAGEN-LIKE
TITLE    2 PEPTIDE WITH THE REPEATING SEQUENCE (PRO-PRO-GLY)
...
EXPDTA    X-RAY DIFFRACTION
AUTHOR    R.Z.KRAMER,L.VITAGLIANO,J.BELLA,R.BERISIO,L.MAZZARELLA,
AUTHOR   2 B.BRODSKY,A.ZAGARI,H.M.BERMAN
...
REMARK 350 BIOMOLECULE: 1
REMARK 350 APPLY THE FOLLOWING TO CHAINS: A, B, C
REMARK 350   BIOMT1   1  1.000000  0.000000  0.000000        0.00000
REMARK 350   BIOMT2   1  0.000000  1.000000  0.000000        0.00000
...
SEQRES   1 A    9  PRO PRO GLY PRO PRO GLY PRO PRO GLY
SEQRES   1 B    6  PRO PRO GLY PRO PRO GLY
SEQRES   1 C    6  PRO PRO GLY PRO PRO GLY
...
ATOM      1  N   PRO A   1       8.316  21.206  21.530  1.00 17.44           N
ATOM      2  CA  PRO A   1       7.608  20.729  20.336  1.00 17.44           C
ATOM      3  C   PRO A   1       8.487  20.707  19.092  1.00 17.44           C
ATOM      4  O   PRO A   1       9.466  21.457  19.005  1.00 17.44           O
ATOM      5  CB  PRO A   1       6.460  21.723  20.211  1.00 22.26           C
```

Figure 7: Fragment of a PDB file.

Wales cell with `owl:sameAs fbase:Wales`, etc. We assume that `annotate`, `with`, and `.content` are reserved words or operators in the language.

These ingredients also seem useful for exporting to RDF. We could write, e.g.,

```
print "@prefix : <http://foo.org/nationalstats.csv>"

For each cell c in col(GeoArea) {
 print ":"+c.content+"owl:sameAs fbase:"+c.content
}
```

to produce an RDF file that says that `:England` in the default namespace is the same as `fbase:England`. Looking at Figure 5, one can also imagine constructs like

```
RDF <= col(subject) or col(predicate) or col(object)

For each row r in RDF {
  print r.cells[1] +" "+ r.cells[2] +" "+ r.cells[3]
}
```

to facilitate the construction of RDF triples taking content from several cells.

5.4 Complex content

The CSV on the Web WG is considering allowing complex content (such as lists) in cells (Section 3.8 in [24]). SCULPT can be easily extended to reason about complex content. Our formal definition of tabular documents already considers (Section 3) a finite set of delimiters, which goes beyond the two delimiters (row- and column-) that we used until now.

In a spirit similar to region-based semantics, one can also imagine a subcell-based semantics, for example, a rule of the form

```
col(1) .> (String)*
```

could express that each cell in the first column contains a list of Strings. Notice the use of `.>` instead of `->` to denote that we specify the content of each individual cell in the region, instead of each row. The statement `List Delim = ;` in the beginning of the schema could say that the semicolon is the delimiter for lists within a cell.

6. CONCLUSIONS

We presented the schema language SCULPT for tabular data on the Web and showcased its flexibility and usability through a wide range of examples and use cases. While region selection expressions are at the very center of SCULPT, we think they can be more broadly applied. Region selection expressions can be used, for instance, as a cornerstone for annotation- and transformation languages for tabular data and thus for a principled approach for integrating such data into the Semantic Web. The whole approach of SCULPT is strongly rooted in theoretical foundations and, at the same time, in well established technology such as XPath. For these reasons, we expect the language to be very robust and, at the same time, highly accessible for users. The accessibility for users may greatly benefit from a XPath-like syntax for full-fledged region selection expressions, such as `right+::*[not(down*::dummy)]` for the first expression in Example 3.3. We leave the precise definition for such a syntax as future work. Two further prominent directions for future work are the following: (1) expand the usefulness of SCULPT by further exploring the extensions in Section 5; and, (2) study static analysis problems related to SCULPT and region selector expressions leveraging on the diverse box of tools from formal language theory and logic.

Acknowledgments

We are very grateful to Marcelo Arenas for bringing [31] to our attention.

7. REFERENCES

[1] R. W. Adam Retter, David Underdown. CSV schema 1.0: A language for defining and validating CSV data.

`http://digital-preservation.github.io/csv-schema/csv-schema-1.0.html`.

[2] M. Arenas, S. Conca, and J. Pérez. Counting beyond a yottabyte, or how SPARQL 1.1 property paths will prevent adoption of the standard. In *International World Wide Web Conference (WWW)*, pages 629–638, 2012.

[3] A. Berglund, S. Boag, D. Chamberlin, M. F. Fernández, M. Kay, J. Robie, and J. Siméon. XML Path Language (XPath) 2.0, 2007. W3C Recommendation, January 2007.

[4] G. J. Bex, W. Gelade, F. Neven, and S. Vansummeren. Learning deterministic regular expressions for the inference of schemas from XML data. In *International World Wide Web Conference (WWW)*, pages 825–834, 2008.

[5] G. J. Bex, W. Martens, F. Neven, and T. Schwentick. Expressiveness of XSDs: from practice to theory, there and back again. In *International World Wide Web Conference (WWW)*, pages 712–721, 2005.

[6] M. J. Cafarella, A. Y. Halevy, D. Z. Wang, E. Wu, and Y. Zhang. Webtables: exploring the power of tables on the web. *PVLDB*, 1(1):538–549, 2008.

[7] S. Das, S. Sundara, and R. Cyganiak. R2RML: RDB to RDF mapping language. W3C Recommendation, September 2012.

[8] D. Fallside and P. Walmsley. XML Schema Part 0: Primer (second edition). W3C Recommendation, October 2004.

[9] M. J. Fischer and R. E. Ladner. Propositional dynamic logic of regular programs. *J. Comput. Syst. Sci.*, 18(2):194–211, 1979.

[10] J. E. F. Friedl. *Mastering Regular Expressions.* O'Reilly Media, 3rd edition edition, 2006.

[11] W. Gelade and F. Neven. Succinctness of pattern-based schema languages for XML. *J. Comput. Syst. Sci.*, 77(3):505–519, 2011.

[12] Google. DSPL: Dataset publishing language. `https://developers.google.com/public-data/`. Last accessed 04/11/2014.

[13] L. Han, T. Finin, C. S. Parr, J. Sachs, and A. Joshi. RDF123: from spreadsheets to RDF. In *The Semantic Web - ISWC 2008*, volume 5318 of *LNCS*, pages 451–466. Springer, 2008.

[14] V. Kumar, P. Madhusudan, and M. Viswanathan. Visibly pushdown automata for streaming XML. In *International World Wide Web Conference (WWW)*, pages 1053–1062, 2007.

[15] E. Kushilevitz and N. Nisan. *Communication Complexity.* Cambridge University Press, 1997.

[16] O. K. F. Labs. Tabular data package. `http://dataprotocols.org/tabular-data-package/`. Version 1.0-beta-2. Last accessed 04/11/2014.

[17] L. Libkin, W. Martens, and D. Vrgoc. Querying graph databases with XPath. In *International Conference on Database Theory (ICDT)*, pages 129–140, 2013.

[18] K. Losemann and W. Martens. The complexity of evaluating path expressions in SPARQL. In *International Symposium on Principles of Database Systems (PODS)*, pages 101–112, 2012.

[19] W. Martens, F. Neven, M. Niewerth, and T. Schwentick. Developing and analyzing XSDs through BonXai. *PVLDB*, 5(12):1994–1997, 2012.

[20] W. Martens, F. Neven, T. Schwentick, and G. Bex. Expressiveness and complexity of XML Schema. *ACM Transactions on Database Systems*, 31(3):770–813, 2006.

[21] W. Martens, F. Neven, and S. Vansummeren. SCULPT: A schema language for tabular data on the web. http://arxiv.org/abs/1411.2351.

[22] V. Mulwad, T. Finin, and A. Joshi. Semantic message passing for generating linked data from tables. In *The Semantic Web (ISWC 2013)*, volume 8218 of *LNCS*, pages 363–378. Springer, 2013.

[23] J. Pérez, M. Arenas, and C. Gutierrez. Semantics and complexity of SPARQL. *ACM Transactions on Database Systems*, 34(3), 2009.

[24] R. Pollock and J. Tennison. Metadata vocabulary for tabular data. Technical report, World Wide Web Consortium (W3C), July 2014. www.w3.org/TR/2014/WD-tabular-metadata-20140710/.

[25] E. Prud'hommeaux, J. E. L. Gayo, and H. Solbrig. Shape expressions: An RDF validation and transformation language. In *International Conference on Semantic Systems*, 2014.

[26] A. G. Ryman, A. L. Hors, and S. Speicher. OSLC resource shape: A language for defining constraints on linked data. In *WWW Workshop on Linked Data on the Web*, 2013.

[27] L. Segoufin and C. Sirangelo. Constant-memory validation of streaming XML documents against DTDs. In *International Conference on Database Theory (ICDT)*, pages 299–313, 2007.

[28] L. Segoufin and V. Vianu. Validating streaming XML documents. In *International Symposium on Principles of Database Systems (PODS)*, pages 53–64, 2002.

[29] J. Tandy, D. Ceolin, and E. Stephan. CSV on the Web: Use cases and requirements. Technical report, World Wide Web Consortium (W3C), October 2014. `http://w3c.github.io/csvw/use-cases-and-requirements/`.

[30] J. Tennison. 2014: The year of CSV. `http://theodi.org/blog/2014-the-year-of-csv`. last accessed 04/11/2014.

[31] J. Tennison and G. Kellogg. Model for tabular data and metadata on the web. Technical report, World Wide Web Consortium (W3C), July 2014. `www.w3.org/TR/2014/WD-tabular-data-model-20140710/`.

[32] M. Y. Vardi. The complexity of relational query languages (extended abstract). In *ACM Symposium on Theory of Computing (STOC)*, pages 137–146, 1982.

[33] P. Venetis, A. Y. Halevy, J. Madhavan, M. Pasca, W. Shen, F. Wu, G. Miao, and C. Wu. Recovering semantics of tables on the web. *PVLDB*, 4(9):528–538, 2011.

[34] W3C. CSV on the web working group charter. http://www.w3.org/2013/05/lcsv-charter.html.

Author Index

www.ingramcontent.com/pod-product-compliance
Ingram Content Group UK Ltd.
Pitfield, Milton Keynes, MK11 3LW, UK
UKHW051420290926
15471UKWH00009B/1705

9 781450 338592